Gun Digest

1996/50th Annual Edition

EDITED BY KEN WARNER

DBI BOOKS, INC.

CONTENTS

FEATURES

Olympics 1996 by Gary L. Anderson
    It will be a different shooter's world in Atlanta this time 5

Fitz by Glen B. Ruh
    A man at ease in the world, with New Service Colts in his pants pockets 12

Switzerland's Feldschiessen by Stephen P. Halbrook
    It looks like a revolution in the streets, but it's just the Swiss shooters at play. 20

The Guns of Williamsburg by Edward R. Crews
    Politically correct or not, Colonial Williamsburg is still a gunny place 27

50 Years of Gun Digest by Gary M. Brown
    An independent view of a half-century history 33

Look What They Can Do To Your Shotgun Barrels! by Don Zutz
    Front, back or in the middle, they can change that tube for the better 81

After 50 Years, Still On Duty by Bob Bell
    A real soldier's pistol, five decades later 88

Schuetzen's Back For Sure by Dennis Bruns
    What goes around comes around in shooting—with Coors' help 92

In Search of Muzzle-Loading Excellence by Robert M. Kearns
    To hit big animals *hard*, even up close, isn't all that easy 97

Charles Newton's Leverbolt by Bruce M. Jennings, Jr.
    Another good idea gone sour in the Great Depression 102

World War II's Snipers and Sniper Rifles by Konrad F. Schreier, Jr.
    We had the rifles and the shooters, but—again—no real program 106

P.O. Ackley's Wildcats by Rob Lucas
    This grand old man's grand old wildcats are still in play 113

It's a 775 Rigby by Jim Dickson
    Big bore, heavy bullet, low velocity—still a killing prescription 136

The Whelen Models: Winchester's Ultimate Lever Guns by Gary M. Brown
    Everyone else listened to Townsend Whelen—why not Winchester? 140

The Guns of Summer by Pat DePasquale
    Ever think of fireworks as a mortar barrage? 145

Best Guns Are Made To Shoot by R.J. Robel
    You get what you pay for, even if you pay a lot 150

Collecting Gun Digest by Skip Criner
    Get all 50—it will only take a few years 160

AFTME Is 25 by C. Rodney James
    Taking bites out of crime in the lab 162

Krieghoff's Pre-War Autoloading Rifle by Don Zutz
    A gas-operated autoloader that died in World War II 166

The Big Little Mannlicher-Schoenauer by Don Henry
    The Mannlicher-Schoenauer is smaller than its myth, but just barely 170

The In-Line Muzzleloader In History by Doc Carlson
    The newest muzzleloader patterns are a lot older than you think 177

The Fabulous Martini by Ferdinand Hediger
    From Peabody to Martini to Hämmerli—the evolution of a classic 182

Custom Guns 221

Art of the Engraver 225

Thomas Horsley's Classic by David Baker
    Back when one man could do it, Horsley did it 229

The Leather Guns of the 17th Century by Gad Rausing
    When kings played at secret weapons, they tried wrapped cannon barrels 234

Shooting the French 35s by John Malloy
    Solving the ammo problem ain't easy, but it's fun 245

DEPARTMENTS

Expert Reports '96
- The Guns of Europe by Raymond Caranta 133
- Rifle Review by Layne Simpson 156
- Blackpowder Review by Doc Carlson 206
- Handguns Today: Autoloaders by J.B. Wood 209
- Handguns Today: Sixguns and Others by Hal Swiggett 213
- Shotgun Review by Don Zutz 218
- Handloading Update by Larry S. Sterett 241
- Scopes and Mounts by Bob Bell 251
- Ammunition, Ballistics and Components by Holt Bodinson . 254
- Ballistics Tables '96 260

One Good Gun
- My Little 284 Mauser by Bob Bell 126
- My First Model 70 by Mike Thomas 128
- My Diamondback Is a Jewel by John Haviland 129
- The Cadet and Me by John Malloy 131

Testfire
- American Arms' Escort by J.B. Wood 194
- Daisy's Pair of Fun Guns: PowerLine 400 & 2001 by J.I. Galan . 196
- AMT's DAO 45 by M.L. McPherson 199
- B-Square's Mounts by Paul Scarlata 200
- Kahr's K9 by J.B. Wood 202
- Intratec's CAT-9 by J.I. Galan 204

Shooter's Marketplace 266

CATALOG

GUNDEX® 302

Handguns
- Autoloaders 311
- Competition 341
- Double-Action Revolvers 351
- Single-Action Revolvers 362
- Miscellaneous 367

Rifles—Centerfire
- Autoloaders 371
- Lever & Slide Action 377
- Bolt Actions 381
- Single Shots 398
- Drillings, Combination Guns, Double Rifles 403

Rifles—Rimfire
- Autoloaders 405
- Lever & Slide Action 408
- Bolt Actions & Single Shots 409
- Competition Centerfires & Rimfires 415

Shotguns
- Autoloaders 422
- Slide Actions 427
- Over/Unders 432
- Side-by-Sides 443
- Bolt Actions & Single Shots 447
- Military & Police 452

Blackpowder Guns
- Single Shot Pistols 454
- Revolvers 457
- Muskets & Rifles 461
- Shotguns 476

Air Guns
- Handguns 478
- Long Guns 485

Warranty Service Center Directory 497

Metallic Sights 509
Chokes & Brakes 512
Scopes & Mounts 513
Scope Mounts 523
Spotting Scopes 527
Periodical Publications 529
Arms Library 531
Arms Associations 550

Directory of the Arms Trade
- Product Directory 553
- Manufacturers' Directory 570

ABOUT OUR COVERS

Over its fifty editions, Gun Digest has established a long-standing tradition of showcasing new, innovative or unusual firearms on its front covers. On our 50th Annual Edition, we are upholding one of those precepts by featuring Sturm, Ruger & Co.'s new Woodside over/under shotgun.

Gun Digest has recognized Ruger's innovative and forward-thinking firearm designs and manufacturing techniques by featuring their guns on Gun Digest covers many times over the years, as chronicled in this edition's special feature, "50 Years of Gun Digest."

The latest over/under shotgun from Ruger, the Woodside, is a radical design departure for an American maker. The most distinctive feature of the gun is its unique stock design, in which the Circassian walnut buttstock extends forward into the receiver as two side panels, almost like sideplates, and is inletted into graceful cutouts in the sides of the stainless steel frame. The gun retains its boxlock action, but the wood panels give it a very special look.

The Ruger Woodside has a newly patented cocking mechanism to make the gun easier and smoother to open. Like all Ruger shotguns, it features a high temperature silver-soldered barrel assembly. The barrels are of high strength, hammer-forged chrome molybdenum steel, are back-bored, and have stainless steel screw-in choke tubes.

Woodside guns are available with pistol grip or straight grip stocks, in 12- or 20-gauge, and can be ordered with hand-cut engraving typical of that shown on our cover gun.

Our back cover shows recent iterations of two well-respected Ruger rifle designs; both debuted on past Gun Digest covers. On the left is the M77EXP MKII Express Rifle, this one in 30-06 caliber.

On the Express Rifle, the barrel and sighting rib are machined from a single bar of steel, making the rib extremely strong and solid, while adding a custom-built feel and look. The integral rib has express sights, one stationary and one folding leaf drift-adjustable for windage. In addition, the receiver is machined for Ruger scope mounts and the gun comes with a set of 1-inch rings. The M77EXP MKII is built with a standard-length action, French walnut stock, three-postion safety, Mauser-type extractor, controlled feeding, steel grip cap, floorplate and trigger guard—all custom features at reasonable cost.

On the right is the Ruger No. 1A Light Sporter single shot rifle, one of the most handsome rifles on the market today.

The heart of this rifle is the massive receiver, a falling block design. The action readily accepts any type of factory cartridge—rimless, rimmed or belted magnum, and has a sliding shotgun-type safety that engages both sear and hammer.

The metal parts of the No. 1 rifle are polished and blued, the stock is of select American walnut with a satin finish, and the forend is of Alexander Henry style—fairly slim and with a groove just aft of the tip for a nice touch. The No. 1A Light Sporter comes with an adjustable folding-leaf rear sight set into a quarter rib and a dovetail-type gold bead front sight. The rib is machined to accept Ruger steel scope rings. This model is available in 243 Win., 270 Win., 7x57mm and 30-06.

We're proud to have these fine Ruger guns on our covers, and we think you'll agree it's fitting to have Sturm, Ruger & Co. with us once again. They're special guns for a special book.

Photos by John Hanusin.

GUN DIGEST STAFF

EDITOR-IN-CHIEF
Ken Warner

SENIOR STAFF EDITORS
Harold A. Murtz
Ray Ordorica

ASSOCIATE EDITOR
Robert S.L. Anderson

PRODUCTION MANAGER
John L. Duoba

EDITORIAL/PRODUCTION ASSOCIATES
Holly J. Porter
Jamie L. Puffpaff

EDITORIAL/PRODUCTION ASSISTANT
Laura M. Mielzynski

ASSISTANT TO THE EDITOR
Lilo Anderson

CONTRIBUTING EDITORS
Bob Bell
Holt Bodinson
Raymond Caranta
Doc Carlson
Layne Simpson
Larry S. Sterett
Hal Swiggett
J.B. Wood
Don Zutz

ELECTRONIC PUBLISHING MANAGER
Nancy J. Mellem

ELECTRONIC PUBLISHING ASSOCIATE
Larry Levine

GRAPHIC DESIGN
Jim Billy
John L. Duoba

MANAGING EDITOR
Pamela J. Johnson

PUBLISHER
Sheldon L. Factor

DBI BOOKS, INC.

PRESIDENT
Charles T. Hartigan

VICE PRESIDENT & PUBLISHER
Sheldon L. Factor

VICE PRESIDENT—SALES
John G. Strauss

VICE PRESIDENT/MANAGING EDITOR
Pamela J. Johnson

TREASURER
Frank R. Serpone

Copyright © MCMXCV by DBI Books, Inc., 4092 Commercial Ave., Northbrook, IL 60062. All rights reserved. Printed in the United States of America.

No part of this publication may be reproduced, stored in a retrieval system, or transmitted in any form or by any means, electronic, mechanical, photocopying, recording or otherwise, without the prior written permission of the publisher.

The views and opinions contained herein are those of the authors. The editors and publisher disclaim all responsibility for the accuracy or correctness of the authors' views.

Manuscripts, contributions and inquiries, including first class return postage, should be sent to the Gun Digest Editorial Offices, 4092 Commercial Ave., Northbrook, IL 60062. All materials received will receive reasonable care, but we will not be responsible for their safe return. Material accepted is subject to our requirements for editing and revisions. Author payment covers all rights and title to the accepted material, including photos, drawings and other illustrations. Payment is at our current rates.

CAUTION: Technical data presented here, particularly technical data on handloading and on firearms adjustment and alteration, inevitably reflects individual experience with particular equipment and components under specific circumstances the reader cannot duplicate exactly. Such data presentations therefore should be used for guidance only and with caution. DBI Books, Inc., accepts no responsibility for results obtained using this data.

Arms and Armour Press, London, G.B., exclusive licensees and distributor in Britain and Europe, India and Pakistan. Book Services International, Sandton, Transvaal, exclusive distributor in South Africa and Zimbabwe. Forrester Books N.Z. Limited, Auckland, exclusive distributor in New Zealand.

ISBN 0-87349-170-X

Library of Congress Catalog #44-32588

Special Report

The Olympic Running Target event is shot with air rifles on diminutive moving targets 10 meters away. This is the only Olympic event where telescopes are permitted.

by GARY L. ANDERSON

OLYMPICS 1996

Where shooting will be seen differently.

PEOPLE ALL OVER the world regard the Olympic Games as the world's greatest sports competition and an Olympic Gold Medal as the pinnacle of sports achievement. When the 1996 Summer Olympic Games open in Atlanta, Georgia, in July of 1996, 3.5 billion people, the most ever to witness a human event, will see the Olympic Opening Ceremonies in person or on television. The Olympics capture such universal interest because they bring the best athletes in the world's most popular sports from every country in the world together in one grand celebration of competition and friendship.

Shooting is an important, popular, respected Olympic sport. When the Olympic shooting events are staged in Atlanta, shooters will have an unprecedented opportunity to demonstrate how exciting and interesting it is.

Shooting's present position as a strong, highly regarded Olympic sport represents a tremendous turnaround from the situation it faced the last time the Olympic Games came to the United States, in 1984, at Los Angeles. Then there was doubt as to whether shooting would even remain in the Games. Shooting always had a strong international following among serious shooters, but it had almost no appeal to spectators and the media. Indeed, one 1984 gold medalist acknowledged that "watching shooting is like watching grass grow."

Spectators couldn't see shooters' shots hit their targets. The competition format made it impossible to know who was winning. Scoring the old paper targets was done in a back room, out of sight. Shooting's most dramatic moments were frequently at the main scoreboard when the final scores were posted long after the competition ended.

The shooting competitions in Atlanta will reveal just how far Olympic shooting has come. There are more great shooters from more countries than ever before. Paper targets have been replaced by electronic targets that score shots and display them instantly for shooters and spectators. The competition format now concludes each event with thrilling

An artist's rendition of the Wolf Creek Shooting Complex in July, 1996. Wolf Creek will have separate ranges for clay target (right), 25-meter pistol (left), airgun (center), and 50-meter rifle and pistol (top).

The interior of the Wolf Creek 50-meter range for all eleven Olympic rifle and pistol finals will look like this. It seats 2500 and is equipped with TV monitors and electronic scoreboards. Spectators can follow every final shot.

head-to-head, shot-by-shot finals that will be witnessed by thousands of spectators. All shooting finals will be telecast live to countries all over the world.

When the modern Olympic Games began 100 years ago in Athens, shooting already had international competitions and was readily accepted on the program. Since then, shooting has been in every Olympic Games except two, 1904 and 1928. Shooting is one of twenty-six different sports on the 1996 program.

The International Olympic Committee is the world governing body of an immense Olympic structure. The IOC currently recognizes 196 National Olympic Committees that will send 10,800 of their best athletes to the Games to compete in 271 events for 1879 medals. The athletes in Atlanta will be supported by 4500 team officials. Approximately 4000 paid staff and 40,000 volunteers are needed to conduct the sports competitions and other Olympic activities. More than 2,000,000 spectators will purchase over 11,000,000 tickets to see the competitions. An expected 5000 reporters, photographers and televi-

In rifle and pistol finals, the top eight shooters in the qualification shoot together, shot-by-shot, for ten shots to determine medal winners. It will be seen shot-by-shot as well.

sion crew members will report the Olympic stories.

Sports must enjoy worldwide popularity just to get into the Olympic program. There are active target shooting programs in more than 130 countries that belong to the world governing body of shooting, the International Shooting Union, so shooting easily meets that criterion. Eighty countries qualified shooters for the 1992 Olympics. Only track and field and swimming had more participating nations. Shooting, in fact, has ranked third in national participation in every Olympic Games since 1960.

The Atlanta Committee for the Olympic Games (ACOG) is planning, organizing and paying for the 1996 Games. ACOG's $1.6 billion budget comes primarily from major sponsors, the sale of television rights, ticket sales and Olympic memorabilia sales. ACOG is building over $500 million worth of new sports facilities to leave after the Games as a lasting legacy. The new Wolf Creek Shooting Complex that ACOG is building for the Olympic shooting competitions at an approximate cost of $15 million will be one of those permanent facilities.

Wolf Creek should become one of the finest shooting ranges in the world. Construction began in November, 1994. Completion is scheduled for late 1995. It is southwest of the center of the city, near Atlanta's Hartsfield Airport. Fulton County, Georgia, owns the land that already is the site of the Wolf Creek Skeet and Trap Club, one of the nation's largest and most active clay target facilities. ACOG will turn the new shooting ranges over to Fulton County for permanent operation after the Games.

Shooting has the unique honor of awarding the 1996 Games' first gold medal. The Olympic Opening Ceremony is on the evening of July 19, 1996. The next morning, at Wolf Creek, at precisely 11:30 a.m., the women's Air Rifle event will be the first competition to finish. That final and its award ceremony will be telecast live to a worldwide audience. Four hundred international journalists, photographers and TV commentators will be present to cover this extraordinary event. It probably will become the most-watched sport shooting event of all time.

All Olympic sports now have participation limits or "quotas" established by the IOC in an effort to control the size of the Games, but shooting was fortunate to be given one of the largest participation quotas. For 1996, shooting has a quota of 430 athletes, the fifth largest among all sports.

Shooting also has become a large sport in terms of the number of events. In Olympic circles, an event is a single competition for which gold, silver and bronze medals are awarded. In 1996, only four sports will have more events than the fifteen different clay target, pistol, rifle and Running Target events in shooting. The women's and men's Doubles Trap events that will be on the Olympic program for the first time in 1996 make shooting one of the few sports where the IOC agreed to allow new events. The addition of the Doubles Trap events, which bear a striking resemblance to ATA doubles, means women clay target shooters will have their own Olympic event for the first time in 1996.

Five of the fifteen Olympic shooting events on the 1996 program are rifle events. Five are pistol and four are shotgun events. One features moving targets shot with air rifles. Five events are for women; ten are for men.

Shooters unfamiliar with Olympic shooting events are usually dismayed by the difficult shooting positions, diminutive targets, demanding rules and specialized equipment when they try international-style shooting for the first time. They simply do not realize that Olympic events must be difficult to fulfill one of their primary purposes of determining the best athletes in the world.

Shooters active in the popular American trap and Skeet games are astonished when they see international clay targets for the first time. ATA trap targets that travel 50 yards are slow compared to international targets that fly 75 to 80 yards. American Skeet shooters call for targets with their shotguns on their shoulders, and targets are released instantly. International Skeet shooters start with the shotgun down at their hip and cannot mount their guns until the targets appear, which may be any time up to three seconds after the call.

Olympic rifle shooters do most of their shooting in the standing position at targets with 10-rings smaller than 1 minute of angle. The 10-ring on the target for high-power rifle, the most popular American rifle competition, is proportionally the same size as the 10, 9, 8 and part of the 7 rings on the Olympic rifle target. Olympic pistol shooters shoot only in the standing position, at equally difficult targets, holding the pistol with just one hand. All rifle and pistol events except Running Target require the use of more challenging metallic sights. Only the Running Target event permits a telescope, and it cannot exceed 4x.

Five of the ten rifle and pistol events are for airguns. The other five are for rimfire rifles and pistols. The 300-meter Free Rifle competition was a revered Olympic event until 1972, but too few countries are fortunate enough to have ranges for shooting centerfire guns. The Olympics stress air and rimfire shooting events simply because Olympic events must be available in the largest possible number of countries. That does not make them less challenging though. Airgun and rimfire targets are scaled to be even more difficult than big-bore targets.

The two dynamic new developments in Olympic shooting that have changed it the most are electronic targets and finals in every event. They transformed shooting from a closed sport, interesting only to insiders, into an open, exciting, public sport. The electronic targets that will be used in Atlanta provide instant, reliable results, more accurately scored than any human can score a shot hole on a paper target.

Not a single paper target will be used in the 1996 Olympics. Wolf Creek's electronic rifle and pistol targets will be provided by Olympic sponsor Swatch Swiss Timing and manufactured by the Swiss firm Sius AG. Sius targets have microphones mounted in the corners of the target frames. The microphones turn computer counters on and off when sound waves from the bullet passing through the target strike them. A microprocessor determines the precise bullet location on the target through triangulation. A computer then uses that information to project an image of the target, the shot hole location and score on a monitor near the shooter.

Shooters no longer need spotting scopes to see bullet holes, and they are never in doubt as to the value of a shot. Every new shot registers in a fraction of a second. The most recent shot shows as a large, bright circle, while previous shots remain on the

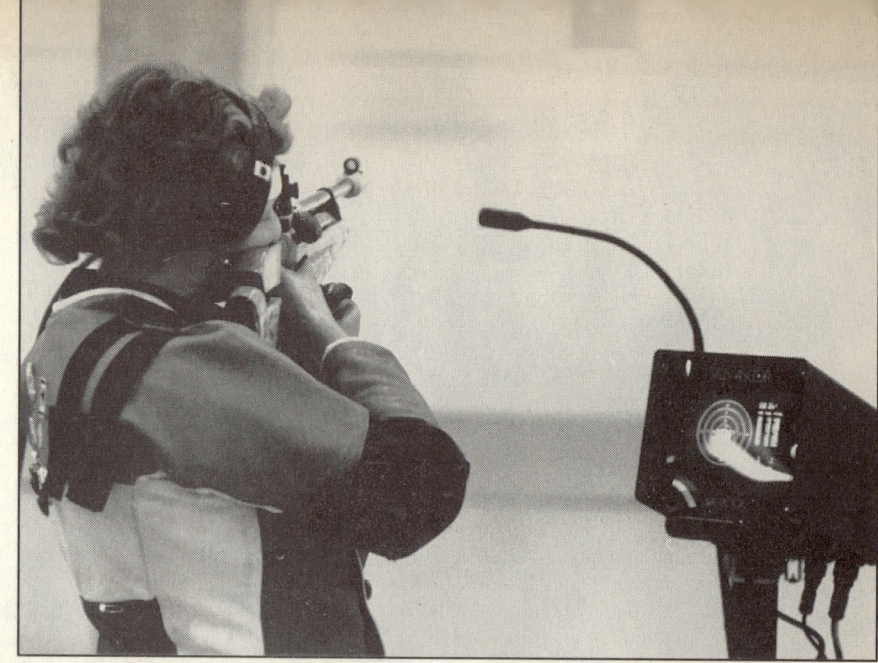

Rifle and pistol shooters will shoot only at electronic targets. Their shots are shown on monitors placed beside them.

screen as smaller "+" signs. All scores go to a master computer that drives electronic scoreboards and continually calculates cumulative total results.

At the Wolf Creek ranges, spectators can see how well shooters are doing by watching shooters' monitors and individual electronic scoreboards above each shooter. Current up-to-the-shot total scores for all shooters will scroll on large TV monitors or videoboards. During finals, large monitors in the spectator area will display the targets of all eight shooters. Additional monitors will portray video images of the shooters' faces.

In the days of paper targets, most people thought clay target contests and shooting games with knock-down targets like silhouette or biathlon were visually more interesting because spectators could see instant results. At the Atlanta Olympics, all shooting events will give spectators the same kind of instant, visual feedback.

Electronic targets make it possible for spectators to know how well shooters are doing, but it is the finals system that makes shooting so much more exciting. In the new competition format, each event has a "qualification round" and a "final round." All shooters shoot the qualification round over the traditional course of fire. At the end of the qualification round, the top eight rifle and pistol shooters or top six clay target shooters advance to the final round. In the final, rifle and pistol shooters shoot ten additional shots. Clay target shooters shoot one more series of twenty-five, forty or fifty shots, depending upon

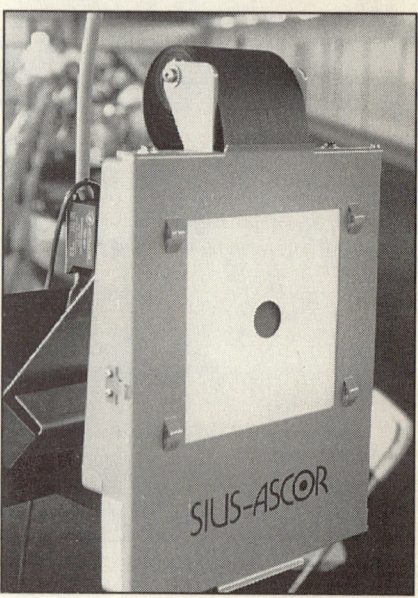

Electronic targets use microphones placed in the four corners of the target to sense the sound wave from bullets and give microprocessors information to calculate the exact location of each shot with a precision of one-tenth of a millimeter or greater.

the event. Finalists start the final with their qualification round scores. Their final score is the total of their scores in both rounds.

Slow-fire rifle and pistol event finals are conducted on a shot-by-shot basis. The range officer begins each shot with a countdown, "Attention, five, four, three, two, one, *start*." Each shooter must fire each final shot in a short time period, usually 75 seconds. After all eight shooters fire, the range officer announces scores for that shot. In the finals, it is critical to keep each shot as close as possible to the 10-ring center because each scoring ring is

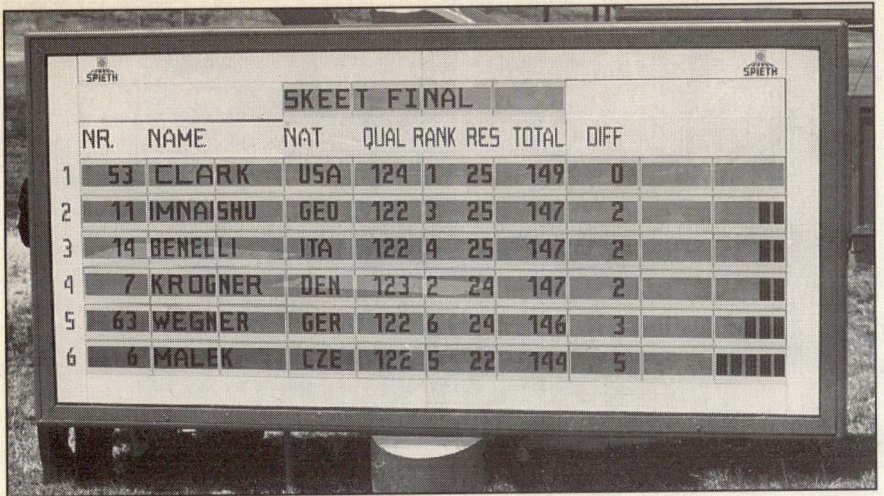

Spectators will follow shooter standings in the finals on electronic scoreboards that rerank shooters after each shot. The scoreboard here shows the final scores of the 1993 World Skeet Championship, won by Dean Clark of the U.S.A.

scored in tenths. Shooters who begin a final only separated by one or two points can change places in a hurry. That is because in finals a center 10 counts 10.8 or 10.9 points while a wide 9 counts only 9.0 or 9.1 points. As scores are announced, a master scoreboard is updated and shows any changes in places.

Clay target finals are a regular twenty-five, forty or fifty target series, but narrowing the field for the final ensures that the best six shooters finish the competition shooting together in the same squad. Clay target finals use "flash" targets containing fluorescent orange powder to make hits even more visible. Electronic scoreboards also will be used in Atlanta for the clay target events and finals.

Finals were first used at the 1988 Olympic Games, where several sportswriters praised the new system for making shooting "one of the most thrilling of all the Olympic sports to watch." Shooting experts always knew how exciting it is when shooters fight for every point in an important competition. The problem was shooting could not demonstrate that excitement to the public and media. Electronic targets and finals made it possible for everyone, even those unfamiliar with shooting, to become enthusiastic about these climaxes to the Olympic shooting events.

Finals place tremendous additional pressure on shooters, but spectators find that seeing the best shooters finish together, one shot at a time, and having instant scores from electronic targets make them absolutely sensational to watch. At the Barcelona Olympics, the cheering after finals shots was as emotional as it is in a football or basketball game between two great rivals.

With so many outstanding shooters in competition, Olympic finals always are close and hotly contested. Changes in the standings are the norm after almost every shot. In the men's Three-Position Rifle event in Barcelona, the leader changed eight times in ten final shots. In the men's Prone Rifle event, Eun Chul Lee of Korea moved from eighth place to first through ten final round shots.

Not only is Olympic shooting becoming a spectator-friendly sport, but in Atlanta, shooting expects some of its largest-ever spectator audiences. The Wolf Creek rifle and pistol finals pavilion will seat 2500 people. The grandstand behind the clay target finals field seats 5000. Prospects for selling that many tickets and more in Atlanta appear excellent. When the Olympic shooting events were in Los Angeles in 1984, the 5000 available daily tickets were sold out, and that was in the era of paper targets and no finals.

The changes in shooting are beginning to make Olympic shooting a great television sport. Most shooting finals in Barcelona were telecast live and were widely watched in Europe. Shooting received over eighteen hours of air time in Germany in 1992. In 1996, ACOG will produce live TV signals for all fifteen shooting finals. A key factor in setting up the 1996 shooting schedule was being able to show shooting finals live during the prime early evening hours in Europe.

Shooters who compete in Atlanta

How to Get Olympic Games Shooting Tickets

Shooting enthusiasts have an unprecedented opportunity to see their Olympic sport in action by attending 1996 Olympic Games shooting events in Atlanta. For people interested in attending Olympic shooting, here is some important information.

• There are eight days of shooting competition, beginning on Saturday, July 20, and ending on Sunday, July 27.
• All shooting events take place at the Wolf Creek Shooting Complex, southwest of Atlanta's Hartsfield Airport.
• Limited parking is available for spectators at the range.
• Daily shooting generally takes place between 9:00 a.m. and 3:00 p.m.
• There are two shooting finals each day, except July 22, which has one final.
• There are as many as three or four qualification round shooting events taking place on most days. Spectators can also watch training in other shooting events while at the ranges.
• Tickets cost $22 per day, but that entitles ticket holders to be at the range all day and to see all shooting activities taking place that day.
• To get Olympic shooting tickets, obtain an official ACOG Ticket Brochure and order tickets from it.
• ACOG ticket brochures and ticket order forms are available after May 1, 1995. The brochures are available in communities all over America or may be ordered from ACOG Ticket Services, P.O. Box 1996, Atlanta, GA 30301-1996.
• Shooting's daily ticket allocation is based on the capacity of range facilities, so to be sure of getting tickets, it is important to order them in advance.

Women have their own Olympic clay target event for the first time in 1996. The Double Trap event requires firing at two fast-moving trap targets thrown simultaneously. This shooter is Deena Julin, U.S.A., winner of four world championship sliver medals in Trap and Double Trap.

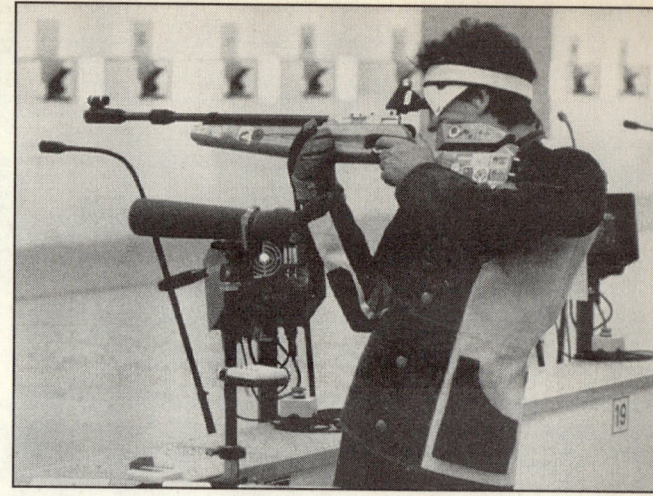

(Right) Men shoot "free rifles" equipped with adjustable hook buttplates and cheekpieces and thumbhole stocks in 50-meter rifle competition. Federal Gold Medal Match ammunition was used by U.S.A. shooters to win two medals in the 1992 Olympics.

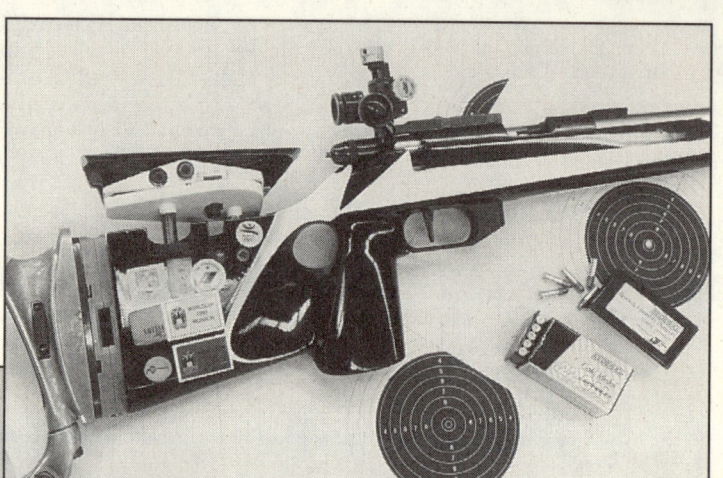

(Above) Air rifles preferred by top shooters have single-stroke cocking pneumatic systems and can shoot groups as small as one-third MOA at ten meters. Rifle shooters wear canvas or leather jackets and trousers to dampen muscle vibrations and heartbeats. The shooter is left-handed multiple-medalist Hans Riederer of Germany.

(Below) International Rapid-Fire shooters must hit a 100mm 10-ring at 25 meters shooting five shots on five targets in as little as four seconds. Low-velocity 22 Short cartridges minimize recoil.

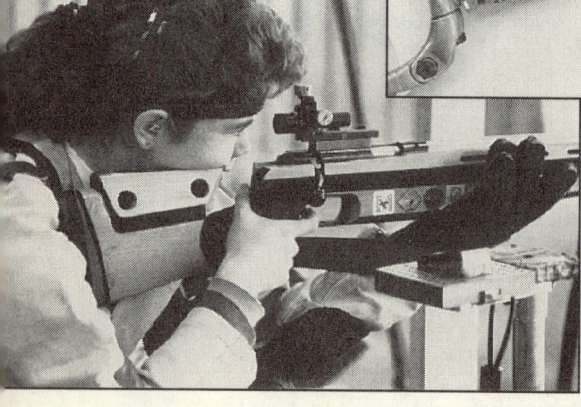

(Left) Women shoot "standard rifles" equipped with adjustable cheekpieces and buttplates in 50-meter rifle competition. This shooter is Ann-Marie Pfiffner, 1994 World Cup Final gold medalist.

will not be household names like Carl Lewis, Sergei Bubka or Shannon Miller, but they will work just as hard to get there. The superb shooting skills and incomprehensible emotional control that leading shooters like Lance Bade, Ann-Marie Pfiffner, Ralf Schumann, Kab Soon Yeo and others display took just as much intensive training and sacrifice to develop as the athletic skills of champions in any Olympic sport. Olympic contenders in shooting typically go through at least eight or ten years of development, shooting and dry-firing up to five or six hours a day, five or six days a week, all year long. Championship shooting form also requires superb coaching as well as lots of physical and mental training.

Most great shooters are products of comprehensive development programs supported by their National Olympic Committees or National Shooting Federations. These shooters must have financial and coaching assistance because few can afford the time or cost of so much training and competition. In the United States, the U.S. Olympic Committee, the U.S. Shooting Team Foundation and USA Shooting, the national governing body for Olympic shooting, provide development support. Most Olympic shooters are young, between twenty and thirty years of age, not because

Editor's Note

Gary Anderson, who prepared this report, is himself a two-time Olympic Gold winner. We have other shooters who have now won as many Golds, but Anderson, in the modern art of the rifle practiced by Americans, was the *first* to attain a winning world standard. Now, for 1996, he is helping us design a new world-class *presentation* of shooting events.

K.W.

OLYMPIC SHOOTING EVENTS

Event	Distance/Target	Qualification Round Course of Fire	Final Round Course of Fire	Firearm	Special Rules
Air Rifle, Men **Air Rifle**, Women	10m (33 feet)/ 1mm 10-ring	Men 60 shots Women 40 shots, all standing	10 shots, standing 75 sec. per shot	177-cal. single shot target; one-stroke pneumatic most popular. Max. wgt. 12 lbs.	Hip-rest standing position permitted.
Air Pistol, Men **Air Pistol**, Women	10m/ 11.5mm 10-ring	Men 60 shots Women 40 shots, all standing	10 shots, 75 sec. per shot	177-cal. single shot target; CO_2 or pneumatic; min. 500-gram trigger pull.	Pistol must be held with one extended arm only.
Running Target, Men	10m/ 5.5mm 10-ring	30 shots slow runs (5 sec.), 30 shots fast runs (2.5 sec.)	10 shots, fast runs	177-cal. single shot target air rifles with 4x scopes.	Target runs through 2m wide opening; rifle must remain at hip until target appears.
Free Rifle, Men 3 Positions	50m/ 12.4mm 10-ring	40 shots, prone 40 shots, standing 40 shots kneeling	10 shots, standing 75 sec. per shot	22 rimfire single shot bolt-action target rifles; max. wgt. 17.6 lbs.; metallic sights only.	Thumbhole stocks, hook buttplates and palm rests permitted.
Free Rifle, Men Prone	50m/ 12.4mm 10-ring	60 shots, prone	10 shots, prone 45 sec. per shot	22 rimfire single shot bolt-action target rifles; max. wgt. 17.6 lbs.; metallic sights only	Thumbhole stocks, hook buttplates and palm rests permitted.
Standard Rifle, Women 3 Positions	50m/ 12.4mm 10-ring	20 shots, prone 20 shots, standing 20 shots, kneeling	10 shots, standing 75 sec. per shot	22 rimfire single shot bolt-action target rifles; standard stocks; max. wgt. 12 lbs.; metallic sights only	Thumbhole stocks, hook buttplates and palm rests not permitted.
Free Pistol, Men	50m/ 50mm 10-ring	60 shots slow-fire; standing position; one arm extended	10 shots, 75 sec. per shot	22 rimfire single shot free pistols with falling blocks or bolt actions; wrap-around grips.	Trigger pull is unlimited; very light triggers common.
Rapid-Fire Pistol, Men	25m/ 100mm 10-ring	Series of 5 shots at 5 targets .75m apart. 4 series in 8 sec. ea. 4 series in 6 sec. ea. 4 series in 4 sec. ea.	Two 5-shot series in 4 sec. ea.	22 cal. rimfire semi-auto pistols; max. wgt. 1260 grams	22 Shorts permitted and universally used to reduce recoil; shooter starts series with pistol down at 45-degree angle.
Sport Pistol, Women	25m/ 50mm 10-ring for precision; 100mm 10-ring for duel	30 shots, precision; 5 shots in 6 min. 30 shots, duel; 3 sec. target exposure.	10 shots, precision 75 sec. per shot	22 rimfire semi-auto pistols or revolvers; max. wgt. 1400 grams; min. trigger pull 1000 grams	22 preferred for superior accuracy; shooters start each duel shot with pistol down at 45-degree angle.
Trap, Men	Single clay thrown from bunker 15m in front of shooters to dist. 70-75m	5 series of 25 over 2-day period	1 series of 25	12-ga. over/unders universally preferred; max. shot charge 24 grams (7/8-oz.)	Shooters may load and shoot 2 shots to break 1 target.
Double Trap, Men **Double Trap**, Women	Two clays thrown from bunker 15m in front of shooters to dist. 55m	Men/3 series, 25 doubles (50 shots); Women/3 series, 20 doubles (40 shots)	Men/1 series, 25 doubles; Women/1 series 20 doubles	12-ga. over/unders universally preferred; max. shot charge 24 grams (7/8-oz.)	Shooters load and shoot 2 shots at 2 different targets.
Skeet, Men	Single & double clay thrown from high & low Skeet houses for each 8 stations	5 series of 25 over 2-day period	1 series of 25	12-ga. over/unders universally preferred; max. shot charge 24 grams (7/8-oz.)	International Skeet sequence more difficult; includes doubles on station 4; target release has 0-3 sec. delay

youth is a prerequisite for shooting success, but because more young people have the time and family situations that allow them to train and compete so much.

Predicting who will win any of the forty-five shooting medals in Atlanta is perilous because there are so many great shooters from so many different countries. In 1992, medal winners came from eighteen different nations and four continents. Shooters from the Soviet Union dominated Olympic competition through the 1992 Games, but the breakup of the U.S.S.R. and catastrophic budget reductions in their sports programs will make the Atlanta competitions wide open. In 1996, strong teams are expected from Belarus, China, Czech Republic, Germany, Italy, Korea, Russia, Ukraine, U.S.A. and several other countries.

Olympic shooting has entered a new age. At the 1996 Olympic Games in Atlanta, a $15,000,000 range with high-tech electronics coupled with a new competition format will give shooting an unprecedented opportunity to show millions of people how big, popular, competitive and exciting it is. Shooting has again earned a significant position in the worldwide Olympic movement.

Before Elmer and Skeeter and Charlie and Bill and Jeff, there was...

FITZ

Fitz tunes Colt Government Models at Camp Perry.

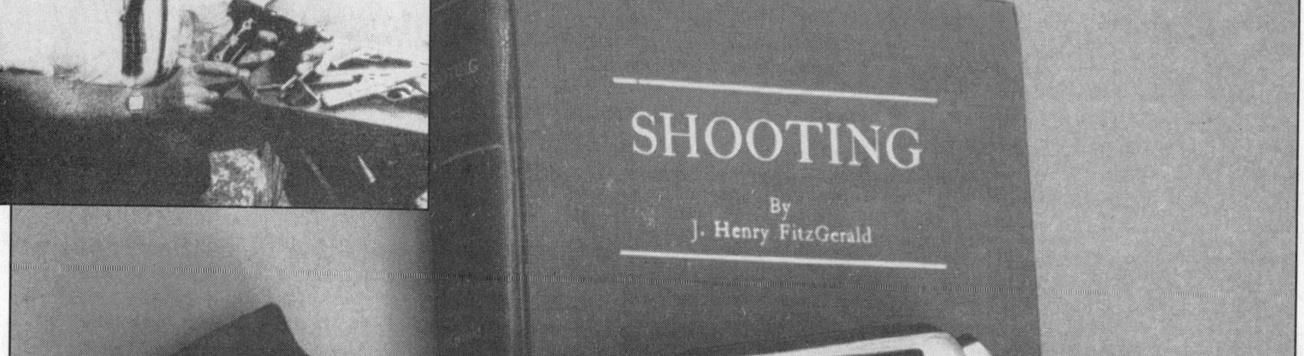

Engraved "From Fitz to Rex," this Fitz Special went through WWII with OSS Captain Rex Applegate. Blued, with ivory grips, the 45's brightly polished muzzle left "people looking down the receiving end...quite impressed" recalls Colonel Applegate. (Photo courtesy Rex Applegate)

by GLEN B. RUH

J. HENRY FITZGERALD was a man of many parts and, in many ways, a man ahead of his time. Gruff, opinionated and outspoken, he lived for shooting. He taught thousands of people to shoot and a lot of good shooters to shoot better. He outshot most of them, but he had no time for showoffs and phonies.

In the 1920s, shooters who went to the National Matches in Camp Perry, Ohio—The Big Camp, he called it—had no trouble locating Fitz. They just walked down Commercial Row, past the Shooter's Supply House run by the legendary P.J. O'Hare, and looked for a big black umbrella with "Colt" stenciled in blue and gold. Under the umbrella, they looked for a big 10-gallon Stetson. Under the Stetson sat Fitz, cigar clamped firmly between his jaws, dispensing firearms wisdom while poring over dismembered pistols.

He didn't go as a shooter; he was there on business. Fitz worked for Colt. His job was advising and encouraging shooters, repairing and tuning their pistols, and storing up enough gun lore to fill a book. In 1930 he did just that, putting on paper half a century of experience with the 1200 firearms he claimed to have owned and the many more he used during his career.

The book, simply titled *Shooting*, focused entirely on "the one hand gun" and how to use it. It was full of practical dope for police and bank guards—this was the era of Al Capone, Clyde Barrow, Bonnie Parker and the Karpis gang—as well as for the bullseye crowd and the recreational shooter. For a fellow who could afford a gun and ammunition in the depths of the Great Depression, Fitz's book distilled everything about pistols and revolvers and then some.

Not that Fitz didn't enjoy competitive shooting himself. He was shooting master at the Boston Rifle and Revolver Club, and he won blue ribbons and plenty of friends all around the country. He once pitted his 7½-inch Colt Officer's Model 38 against eleven men with hunting rifles at 200 yards. Thirty-four hits out of fifty on an 8-inch target let Fitz take the day.

Photographs of Fitz show a tall, well-built man, with baggy trousers hitched high, a heavy belt with flashy buckle, and the ever-present 10-gallon hat. He was an honorary New York state trooper, firearms inspector, handgun instructor, sporting goods salesman, adviser to banks and police departments, and expert firearms witness. For a quarter-century, he was head of testing for Colt's Patent Fire Arms Manufacturing Company in Hartford, Connecticut, where he evaluated, analyzed and improved the Colt product. But he was best known for his trademark six-shooters, the 45 New Service Fitz Specials.

Fitz went armed as a matter of course and figured that anyone else was entitled to do the same, as long as he knew how to handle a handgun. His opinions of sixty-five years past sound familiar:

> The remark is often heard, "Down with the 'Gun-Toter.' We should have a law to stop gun-toting." I wonder if the reader can recall an instance where a habitual 'Gun-Toter' (one who carries a revolver around in his pocket or traveling bag because of his love for firearms) ever got into any serious trouble with it...Personally I can see no reason why a respectable citizen should not be allowed to carry a revolver if he wishes.

To learn how to protect home and family, Fitz recommended the ordinary citizen join a shooting club.

> If the good citizens of our country knew how to handle firearms properly, crime would decrease by half. Our present firearm laws in many states so restrict the use of firearms that the honest, law-abiding citizen does not care to comply with the regulations and the red tape...yet how else can he protect his home? What greater assurance does a crook need than the fact that he knows not one house in fifty is protected? He carries a revolver to protect himself against the honest citizen and the police, and he will continue...regardless of any law that will ever be passed.

Fitz regularly trained police officers and bank guards, but he allowed that the private citizen was the best bulwark against lawlessness. He had no time for coddling criminals.

> How can we accomplish this unless we know how to shoot and have something to shoot with? A householder may have the courage to throw out his chest and walk downstairs to be killed by some cigarette-sucking, dope-crazed crook, and his friends will say "Wasn't John brave and doesn't he look natural." I call such a man the biggest kind of a damn fool who will walk toward a man with a revolver and his own hands empty. The householder has the advantage for he knows the lay of the house, position of light, stairs, etc., but the last ten or fifteen feet is best covered by a bullet if a crook cannot be taken alive.

Fitz encouraged women to shoot and expected them to match males with every caliber and kind of arm.

> Several years ago I visited the home of Major Harker in Baltimore and, of course, the first place we visited was the cellar range...Miss Mildred was just able to hold up a 22 Colt Police Positive Target Revolver, but she could hit the bull's eye and give her older sister a battle for first honors. That same little girl visited Camp Perry in 1929 and captured honors many of the older shooters would envy. She is without doubt the best shot with pistol, revolver, and rifle for her age in the United States.

The nearby photograph shows the poised young pistoleer, her lapels draped with medals; also shown, a less stylish Mrs. Gussie FitzGerald aims her 45 with steely determination.

Compared to today, gun fanciers in the 1920s saw little hands-on information about the firearms they used. *American Rifleman* and a few other journals dispensed useful data, but the public at large was poorly served. Custom gunsmithing was for the affluent few who could afford it and, by today's standards, was severely restrained. Aside from accessories like grip adapters and sight blades from Marble and Stoeger's, an aftermarket for shooters didn't exist. Fitz believed in letting the factories set up guns the right way and had little regard for amateur gunsmiths.

> Tools less experience mean nothing, and experience less tools means the same thing.

At a time when virtually everyone was a wheelgunner, Fitz thought highly of the new self-loading pistols. He advocated and promoted the Government Model in 45 ACP and later in 38 Super. There was little doubt in his mind that pistol matches were won with top-quality revolvers, but he thought that practice with the pistol taught the necessary disciplines of a good grip and a proper trigger squeeze.

Most American shooters got their first taste of shooting an auto pistol in World War I. As inherently dependable as the Model 1911 was, its reputation suffered in the hands of troops in the trenches, mainly through ignorance.

> I remember an instance in 1920 when a pistol was shown to me by a veteran of the World War and he told me that he had been over the top eight times and that he had never seen a 45 automatic that did not jam. I loaned him mine to try, and after seven shots he handed it back and told me the gun was like all the rest...the slide remained open after the last shot. When I told him it should do so in all well-behaved automatics, he told me he had never heard of such a thing.

Fitz knew the wartime product was really a dependable, accurate arm—all it needed was respectable treatment and a little help from a competent gunsmith. He recommended only a tuned trigger, properly adjusted sights and a good barrel. Fitz regularly took the standard 7-pound pull on a Government Model trigger down to 4 1/2 pounds for competition. He used a file, not a stone, and worked only on the hammer, never the sear. For the 1919 National Matches, Fitz brought to Camp Perry forty brand-new Colt Match barrels, the first of a breed.

In Fitz's day, shooters stood on their hind legs and shot one-handed. Photographs of military and police show the classic bullseye stance, gun arm rigid and weak hand on the hip or in the pocket. In 1920s-style National Matches, ammunition was furnished and adjustable sights were *verboten*. You learned to shoot where the factory ammo shot. Fitz advocated a 1/10-inch blade and liked the idea of opening up the rear notch for more light at the sides, tapered three degrees from the vertical to make the front blade look absolutely square. His method of sight adjustment employed a file; a little off the front blade or the rear notch. If the file didn't correct enough for windage, he could always turn the barrel in the frame. A sandblasted front blade or a swipe of his pal P.J. O'Hare's sight black could also improve things on a bright day.

Of all the marks Fitz left on the shooting world, the most enduring was the Fitz Special. His first experiments were with 38 Police Positive Specials, but the epitome of the breed were his pair of 2-inch-barreled New Service 45 Colts—the hammers bobbed, mainsprings lightened, butts rounded, ejector rods shortened, triggers straightened, and guards cut away at the front. Fitz toted these favorites in his trouser pockets for years, and he delighted in offhand demonstrations of their practicality.

> My own two pocket guns with short barrels are sufficiently powerful so that I feel at all times prepared for a hunting trip or constant protection whether home or traveling. They are accurate enough to place ten consecutive shots in an eight-inch black at twenty-five yards and would place ten said bullets in the ten ring at this distance if I could hold them.

As convinced as he was that Fitz Specials were right for Fitz, he cautioned others about doing the same thing. He explained the factory's reluctance to cut up perfectly good guns and the need to practice many hours with empty chambers before trying to duplicate his prowess with snub-nosed, big-bore custom guns.

Predictably, Fitz wouldn't hesitate to hunt with a handgun, although his writings are noticeably silent about the actual quarry that fell to the master.

> The proper placing of bullets is the answer to the full or empty game bag. I have derived more pleasure in hunting with revolvers and automatic pistols than I ever experienced when carrying a rifle and on stormy days the arms were dry when I arrived in camp.

He paid respects to his friend Elmer Keith, a younger man making a reputation out West using heavy handloads in big revolvers. Nonetheless, Fitz recommended staying with factory ammo. To Fitz, the 45 Colt was the hardest hitting round, preferably with blackpowder loads that pushed a 250-grain lead bullet at 910 fps with 460 pounds of striking energy; the factory smokeless load offered a mere 770 fps and 330 fpe. When the call came, however, Fitz took heavy handloads in stride. A shooting pal let Fitz try...

> ...some black powder cartridges, 45 Colt, a short time ago that registered five hundred twenty-five pounds striking force and made my favorite two-inch forty-five revolvers very nervous.

He ran a litany of ammo ballistics for the hunter's pistol, including the new 38 Super Auto. It topped the 45 ACP with a 130-grain bullet at 1146 fps, and Fitz urged the ammo companies to list a hollowpoint at 1200 fps or better, "now that a real pistol for this cartridge is on the market."

Comparing big-bore handgun loads for sporting use, he praises the 38-40 and 44-40, and curiously includes the 455 British. He reluctantly acknowledges the 44 Smith & Wesson Special favored by Keith—by Fitz's own admission it was equal to the big 45—but no double-action Colts came chambered for it. The 357 S&W Magnum was still some years in the future. Last but certainly not least, trappers and small game hunters should not forget the 22 Long Rifle, which "may be procured with a hollow point."

To prepare for taking the pistol or revolver into the field, he recommended the new-fangled running deer or running man targets like those installed at Camp Perry.

> Hunting is a matter of practice on moving objects. I feel that any if one, after a reasonable amount of preparation, should take his favorite side arm into the woods instead of a rifle, he would be pleased with the results...Two 45 caliber revolvers will make any bear wish he had lived a better life...

Acknowledging some limits to the game, however, Fitz added, "I never go after mountain goats."

The first few decades of this century were exciting times for rifle enthusiasts. Smokeless powder and jacketed bullets in small-bore rifles held many mysteries, and these years saw some of the most productive experimentation with cartridges and loads.

Pistols were different. Commercial ammunition makers dominated pistol ammunition, and relatively few handloaders tampered with their offerings. One reason was a dearth of available equipment, but an overriding factor had to be the inherent danger of high pressures in older guns designed for blackpowder. Consequently, there is little in Fitz's writing about handloads or wildcatting. He did, however, muse about one caliber in a way that suggests a yearning for working up some loads of his own.

I have always been a firm believer in the 41 caliber Colt cartridge and still am. With a bullet of approximately two hundred and fifteen grains in front of the correct charge of smokeless powder, a revolver built with barrel correctly fitting said bullet...what a prize that would be for hunting, protection, etc.

The problem, of course, was with his employer, which had produced nearly 20,000 Peacemakers and a lot of double actions in 41 Colt. In the 1890s, the ammunition makers improved the original loading by replacing the old blackpowder, outside-lubricated round with an inside-lubricated, smokeless version. The case diameter had to stay the same, but the new bullet was a few thousandths too small. The result: A bullet that failed to fill the rifling and wobbled down the barrel. Instead of altering bore diameter, Colt stuck by its specifications and the fine old round died the death of a thousand near-misses.

In a plea that presaged the 41 Remington Magnum three decades later, Fitz dreamed of the ideal revolver, the Colt Officer's Model on the 41 frame, in the ideal caliber.

(Above) Fitz's Specials: (top) a pair of 2-inch 45 New Service Colts the way Fitz liked them; (bottom) a pair of 38 Colt New Police revolvers done up the same way for light duty.

A crack exhibition shooter for Peters Cartridge Company, Captain A.H. Hardy (left) was a Camp Perry original, just like his pal Fitz.

Perhaps we should let the dead rest in peace, but I can look into the crystal ball and see the value of such an arm. Thousands of hunters, police officers, and gun lovers have discarded the larger caliber revolvers for the 38, sacrificing stopping power and possibly their lives because they did not wish to carry a few extra ounces of metal. I believe I would lay aside my constant companions, two 45 New Service 2-inch barrels, for a pair of the 2-inch 41 Specials.

Fitz was said to have trained more than 20,000 people to shoot in his lifetime, many at the Boston Rifle and Revolver Club. He was an official instructor for most state police in the northeastern U.S. and countless city police forces. He specialized in training bank guards, after convincing bank owners they needed more than safes and barred windows to keep Depression dollars inside. For small town police departments and banks, Fitz recommended a simple outdoor range and good reloading equipment—Ideal and Schmidts were the

The Weaver stance, forty years ahead of schedule. Cigar is optional.

albeit as an aid to the officer out of breath after running down his quarry.

...place the hand holding the revolver firmly in the palm of the other hand, the first finger just under the trigger guard and the thumb over the thumb of the hand holding the revolver. If inside of fifteen yards use double action; if at a longer range and time permits, cock the hammer and shoot single action. The left foot should be placed ahead of the right and slightly to the left or nearly the position of the feet for left-hand shooting. Very accurate shooting can be done in this manner....

The nearby photograph shows Fitz in a close approximation of the Weaver stance, cigar aimed unerringly downrange.

For the military and the few bold civilian users of the auto pistol, Fitz was firmly in the "cocked and locked"

Fitz's version of the gunfighter's crouch may be close to the way the old timers really did it.

favored brands—to ensure regular, inexpensive revolver practice. His permit to carry a handgun in Canada, where he worked with the Mounties as well as provincial forces, was the only one of its kind for a U.S. citizen.

As a police combat instructor, Fitz laid great stress on double-action shooting. He understood that most defensive police work is done inside 10 feet and that police have only a few seconds to get off the shot that can mean life or death. He also knew that many police officers had poor training and a woeful lack of familiarity with their weapons. Training sessions of unrealistic bullseye practice filled him with frustration, so he invented the Colt Silhouette Target. Used in both stationary and moving situations, it gave a dose of realism to regimented police training. He was an early advocate of the two-hand hold, school...the only way a self-loader could challenge a revolver on equal terms. He cautioned, however, that teaching large numbers of men how to safely carry and use the automatic was a daunting challenge. Fitz warned police officers about the fallacy of carrying any weapon merely for protection. They had to be ready to use it. His advice: Carry it where you can get it.

...very fast, between twenty-five and fifty one-hundredths of a second. In the crouch, revolver is pointed with the body movement at the hips...assuming a position that will tilt the thirty degree holster to a level position, bottom on a line with top. The shot is fired just after the revolver leaves the holster on the line it is drawn.

Despite a lengthy dissertation on gun leather, however, Fitz ultimately comes down in favor of carrying his pistols in his pockets. This was, of course, not an age of lightweight duds or jogging suits. Men on both sides of the law habitually wore heavy woolen trousers, vests, jackets and ties, plus overcoats and hats outdoors. It was not at all unreasonable to tote a heavy pistol in a pants or jacket pocket, especially if constructed and lined for the purpose.

...remember when you reach for a revolver something is started that must be finished with speed and accuracy, and it is better to never attempt to draw than to bungle it and lose your life. Do not attempt to draw for protection or to foil a hold-up man until you are possessed of four things—sand, a good revolver of 38 caliber or larger, a good holster, and the ability to draw and shoot fast and straight...Sand (others call it grit) may be acquired through the knowledge of firearms and confidence in your proficiency with them.

(Left) Fitz got into a lot of photos during his busy years at Camp Perry.

(Below) Gussie FitzGerald could stand up on her hind legs and shoot with the best.

Quick draw shooting is practical police shooting, the recognized system of protection used by proficient police officers...and it means just this: When occasion requires it, get your revolver quick and shoot quick and straight...without taking your eyes from the object you are to shoot at. Shoot double action if it is at short range and quick draw is not necessary at long range.

Although photographs show two-gun Fitz arched backwards with a pair of low-slung hip holsters tied down to his legs in the best William S. Hart tradition, he knew that low-slung holsters were unrealistic for most law enforcement work. Politely dismissing the traditional high-on-the-hip belt holster and various types of shoulder rigs, he perfected the cross-stomach draw, which he demonstrated with lightning speed. In a style out of favor by most pistoleros today, he coupled a circular hand motion with an exaggerated backward crouch, claiming to draw and fire...

Fitz's boyhood enthusiasm and curiosity for shooting knew no bounds. Born in New Hampshire in 1876, his introduction to the game was classic. He tells of sneaking his father's 22 Short revolver out of the Old Man's office and letting fly at a tin can on a stump.

As the gun was fired another boy jumped out of the bushes at one side of the stump, and the bullet had gone through his big toe instead of the can. While no monument was erected, the shot created more trouble...than the first shot in the Civil War. On arriving home, the culprit was disarmed and sent to bed.

In the best Tom Sawyer tradition, however, the young man proved his mettle and developed a deep concern for safety. While other boys squandered their time and money on bicycles and baseball, Fitz experimented with every gun on which he could get his hands. He forsook rifles for pistols at an early age and developed a passion for shooting them in pairs. With no opportunity for formal instruction, he taught himself the mysteries of disassembly and repair, reloading and ballistics. Lacking competition, he held matches with himself, pitting right hand against left.

When the time came to earn his fortune, Fitz set out for Boston, where he took a job as a salesman for Iver Johnson Sporting Goods. In 1918, he moved to Colt's in Hartford, serving ten years as a tester before assuming the post of head ballisician. In those days, before Ransom Rests and laser sighting, every revolver or pistol had to be fired and adjusted by hand. Fitz figured that by putting twelve to twenty-four shots though every arm that left the factory under his name, he fired between 1000 and 1200 shots a day for years, and between two and three million shots in a lifetime.

That kind of shooting builds nothing but confidence and a facility matched by very few. Fitz routinely did trick shots for visitors, such as aerial shooting, hitting cartridge cases and cutting playing cards edgewise. No one knew better than Fitz the importance of safety on and off the range, but he didn't escape his long years around firearms totally unscathed.

I was teaching a lady to shoot and one of my instructions was to lay down the revolver on the shelf every time she left the firing point. She asked me to change targets. I could not see the revolver and looked in her direction.

Fitz found this belly carry suited a *very* fast draw, but getting the other hand and arm out of the way was important.

The revolver was aimed at my hip and cocked, not intentionally but just through carelessness. I jumped backward just in time. The bullet went through coat and vest, flattened on my belt buckle, and out through the coat and vest on the other side.

At another time I was sitting at the range desk when one of the men at the firing point turned to tell me that he had a misfire. As he turned with the gun in his hand...the bullet put two holes in a new hat I was wearing. In addition to these close shaves I have had one bullet hole in each leg, part of a little finger shot away and one shot through my face; therefore, I shall continue to talk on safety.

As a self-taught ballistics expert, he learned the use of comparison microscopes, the distinctive characteristics of arms and ammunition, and the effects of bullets in flesh, which he simulated with pork rinds nailed to a plank. Those qualifications and his distinguished job with Colt's were enough for him to serve as an expert witness in more than 400 criminal cases, including the sensational Sacco-Vanzetti murder trial where he testified that a victim's wound was not from Sacco's pistol.

As if marksmanship was not enough, he enthusiastically gave instructions for subduing and disarming assailants unarmed. Maneuvers included the Throat Hold; Adams' Apple Blow; Arm Grip; Hip Lock; and Nose, Underarm and Hair Holds.

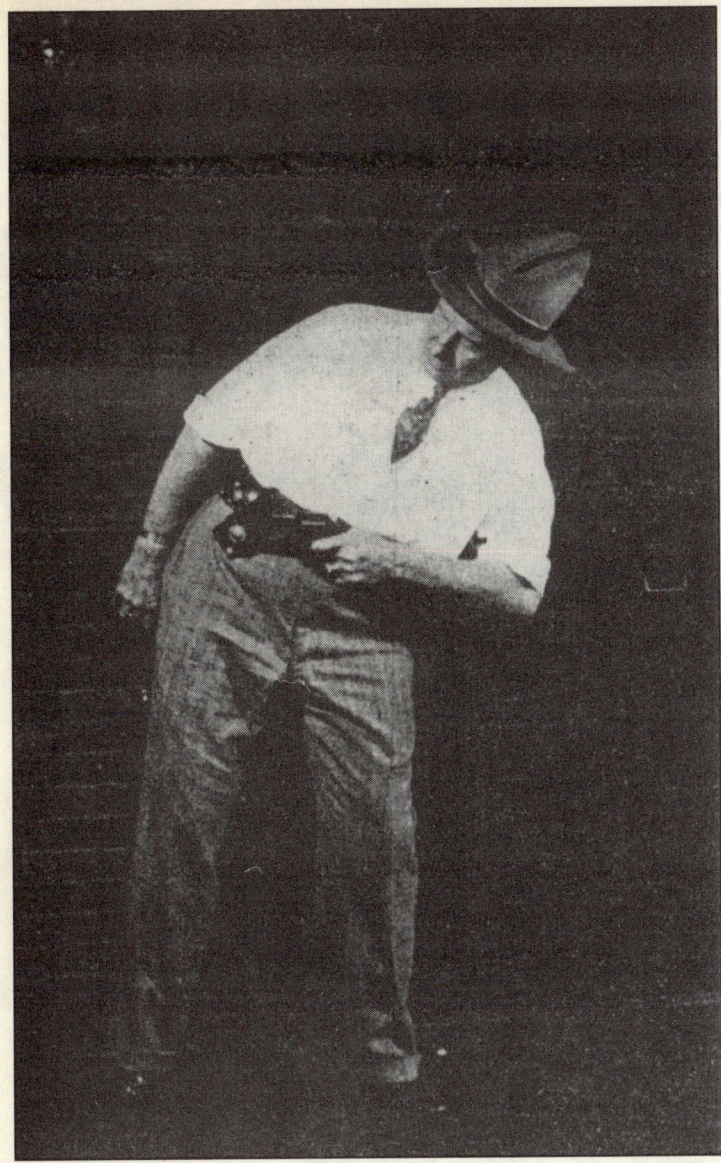

The short gun was twisted out and fired from right there, aimed as much with hips and belly as with hand or eye.

The Lip Hold is very effective on wild women and some little men and consists of catching the loose flesh of lower lip between first finger and thumb, pulling outward and twisting...Usually this hold is sufficient to lead a prisoner wherever necessary. It is usually as severe as the before-mentioned lady will care to endure and may be the means of cutting short a needless conversation.

He offered advice on coping with the luckless felon foolish enough to poke a pistol in his ribs. These stunts involved lightning moves and iron grips to immobilize cylinder or slide, followed by decisive blows with hand, foot or knee. Shooting from the running boards of moving cars, motorcycles and horses; night shooting; shooting on the run—all are discussed with intense vigor. Such cool bravado was guaranteed to thrill small boys and probably fueled Hollywood scriptwriters grinding out endless plots for Cagney, Raft and Bogart. One wonders what it did to the actuarial tables of law enforcement professionals.

Nonetheless, Fitz always had his priorities straight. He cautioned against damaging a revolver barrel by using it against an assailant, pointing out that hitting a crook with the right side of the cylinder might spring the crane out of alignment, ruining a perfectly good arm.

The proper way to use a revolver as a club is to strike from the right, bringing the left side of the cylinder against the head or other part of the anatomy; a needle and thread will repair all damage.

J. Henry FitzGerald died in June, 1945. He was mourned by his wife and fellow shooter, Gussie, as well as by the countless men and women he taught to shoot. He had worked and shot alongside some of the greatest names inside and outside the arms industry—riflemen like Morton Mumma and Julian Hatcher; trick shooters like A.H. Hardy and Ad Topperwein; and hundreds of other military men, police and bank officers, including Norman Schwarzkopf of the New Jersey State Police, investigator of the Lindbergh kidnapping. One tribute came from his pal H.L. Harker, Major, USAR, who officiated at the Camp Perry Pistol Range from 1918 to 1928:

...at night the Colt tent was usually packed to "busting" to accommodate those who wanted repairs and also with those who came to tell the latest jokes, good and otherwise...while Fitz was busy toiling...taking out the "creeps" and carefully placing them in a tin box to prevent them from getting in some other gun. With all the work he always found time to come in on the laugh of a good joke and offering one in his turn. Many of the old timers will recall these pleasant evenings.

Fitz is the outstanding figure of the hand-gun clan and being a practical shot in any position...he understands their very needs, and the boys come from far and near to bring him their ills, whether real or imagined...From the time he first opens his tool-kit until after the National Team Match, he is a man to be pitied and well deserves a reprieve to grow some new skin on his fingers that are about worn through.

●

Bibliographical note

Shooting was published in 1930 by the G.F. Book Company, Hartford, Connecticut. The haphazard editing and organization suggest an early form of self-publishing. I picked up my copy in a Connecticut second-hand store a few years ago, but it has recently been issued in facsimile by Wolfe Publishing Company, Prescott, AZ.

GBR

"It looks like a revolution."

The woman in the jeans jacket has *two* Sturmgewehr 90 5.6mm rifles—one on her right shoulder and one in her right hand. The other young people here at Salvenach only have one Sturmgewehr 90 each. By the year 2000, all adult Swiss males will have this rifle at home.

Switzerland's Feldschiessen

by STEPHEN P. HALBROOK

MACHIAVELLI WROTE some 450 years ago: "The Swiss are well armed and enjoy great freedom." The Italian noble had observed the well practiced exercises of the Swiss militia, which adopted the harquebus (a short matchlock shoulder arm) when most European armies were still using edged weapons—"they [the Swiss] are poor, yet anxious to defend their liberties against the ambition of the German princes..."

The Sturmgewehr, a modern assault rifle, has replaced the harquebus, but the Swiss are as determined as ever to defend their liberties. Recently, I had the great fortune not only to observe today's Swiss militia, but to participate with the entire armed Swiss populace in their greatest shooting festival—the *Feldschiessen*.

June 5, 1993, 9:10 a.m., Tram #8, Basel, Switzerland: A white-haired man who looks seventy gets aboard with his K31 bolt-action 7.5mm rifle with target sights and leather sight covers. It is not in a case, just strung over his shoulder. So now I know where to get off.

At the Allschwiler Weiher shooting range, in the midst of a quaint suburb of homes bordered by beautiful gardens and horse trails, are hundreds of people walking, riding bikes and getting out of cars—all with rifles and pistols strapped to their shoulders or belts. Women push baby strollers oblivious to the assault rifles and as if all of this is normal. I have to keep telling myself that it *is* normal *here*.

Today, I am the official guest of the Swiss Shooting Federation management, who are reviewing the *Feldschiessen*. This annual event takes place on a single weekend at shooting ranges in every nook and cranny of Switzerland. Every canton has several ranges available for every person to shoot with his or her rifle club. *Feldschiessen* is German for "field shooting"—*Tir en Campagne* in French—and is the sporting event which gets the widest participation in all of Switzerland.

While everyone may participate in the matches, it is also a good opportunity for the typical Swiss adult male who is a member of the militia to fulfill his yearly shooting qualification. The Feldschiessen competitor typically brings a 1931 bolt-action carbine or a federally issued rifle—a Model 1957 or 1990 assault rifle (i.e., selective fire, semi- or full-automatic)—and, using free (or government-subsidized) ammunition, shoots the standard 300-meter course. If the shooter is a militiaman fulfilling his obligatory qualification, he must shoot a minimum score.

I miss meeting my host, Rudolf Fritz, so I walk around the festival area behind the range. A white-haired man, Hans Grunder, speaks to me, and I respond with my best German. After a few minutes, the young president, Franco Cairoli, a dentist of the Stadtschützen Basel club, arrives. It is decided the club will sign me up to shoot and loan me a Sturmgewehr 57. I will shoot later, when the sun shines on the targets.

The Federation officials arrive, and we enjoy local white wine and lunch. A Basel politician, a social democrat, cannot believe I would say guns keep a country free from tyranny. We argue about the unarmed Jews in Nazi Europe. The funny thing is this: I only have words—in Switzerland there is an assault rifle in every house. It may not be polite to say that the armed Swiss people prevent a tyranny, but it is a fact. To paraphrase James Madison, the Swiss commonwealth is not afraid to trust the people with arms.

I shoot a 45, not the sufficient 58 to win the Swiss medal. I use the sling and a shooting jacket. My points keep getting better, then my shots all go low. My coach is excellent, but could we have been moving the sights down? The 7.5mm Sturmgewehr 57 shoots like it looks and weighs—a boat anchor. I'm later told you can use it to vault people over a wall, or as a hammer.

The Federation entourage then travels to the centuries-old town of Laufenburg, where I, of course, make known that I would like to shoot the pistol program. Local officials say it is impossible because "only Swiss" can shoot in the *Feldschiessen*. I get the decision reversed in about one minute.

The 50-meter pistol course is comprised of six shots, one minute each, with a look at the target after each shot. Then three shots in one minute, twice. Finally, six shots in one minute. Fun, but not IPSC. There is also a 25-meter course.

I shoot the pistol event with a SIG 210, shooting all within a small area of the silhouette target, most in an 8-inch circle with one 10X pin-

A self-portrait of the armed populace of Switzerland: This mural on the front of the Swiss Shooters Museum in Bern depicts armed citizens both in and out of uniforms. Switzerland has a well-regulated militia, not a standing army.

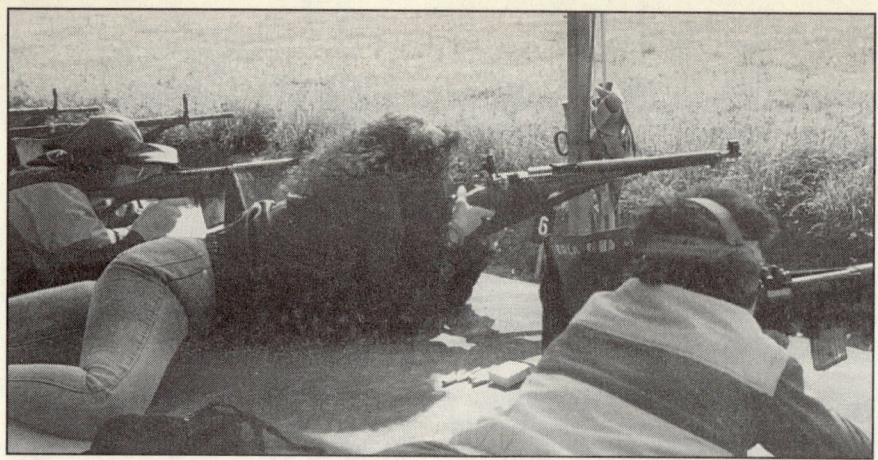

The Feldschiessen at Salvenach—a woman shoots the K31 bolt action; on her left is a Sturmgewehr 90, then two 57s.

(Right) Halbrook shot the 300-meter course at Basel with a Sturmgewehr 57, a selective-fire 7.5mm rifle kept at home by 70 percent of adult Swiss males.

A rifleman and his baby at the Fest tent in Alterswil—this shooting festival is a family event.

rization for the issuance of ammunition for shooting events throughout the year. In Switzerland, the government produces, subsidizes and dispenses ammunition to the shooting public. In 1992, the government provided 47,992,365 cartridges for rifles and 7,199,712 pistol cartridges for civilians to shoot.

I had met Col. Hurst a few days earlier at the military headquarters in Bern, the Swiss capital. As the colonel explained, all militiamen (i.e., most able-bodied males) in Switzerland are issued assault rifles or pistols to keep at home. The majority still have the 7.5mm 57, but thirty wheel. My score is 75, well over the minimum necessary to get the Swiss medal, which I wear with pride. In fact, after speeches by military and Federation leaders, who are dressed up and not shooters that day, one announces the American's score and all applaud me. Because of my excellent score, I am now called "a Swiss."

At dinner in the medieval town, the sports comes on TV, and we tell the waitress to turn it up. It's not soccer, it's the *Feldschiessen*, assault rifles and all.

The purpose of an assault rifle is to shoot as many 10Xs as possible within the short time allotted. Its purpose is not to shoot as many people as quickly as possible—unless they are armed invaders, perhaps Nazis. Hitler had a good reason for never trying to take Switzerland.

Sunday, June 7, 1993: Early morning at the train station in Fribourg. Today, I am the official guest of the Swiss military department, and I am met by Colonel Bernard Hurst, the person who heads all off-duty activities—shooting, military sports, NCO clubs. All clubs get his authopercent have the 5.6mm 90, which all will have by the year 2000. After a lifetime of service, by the way, you own your assault rifle or your pistol. Shooting is obligatory for all males aged twenty through forty-two, and is free thereafter. Those who fail to fire a minimum score in the federal obligatory program are required to undergo special training.

In 1992, a total of 547,504 Swiss (out of a 6.5 million population) participated in shooting the 300-meter rifle and 25- or 50-meter pistol courses. They included men who were required by the militia law to do so, as well as men, women and teens who participated voluntarily.

Today, Sunday, we are to visit the *Feldschiessen* at two of the seven ranges in the Fribourg canton—first at Salvenach, a French-speaking town, and then Alterswil, which is German-speaking.

As we arrive in Salvenach, it is clear from the flags and banners that shooting is the biggest sport in Switzerland, and the *Feldschiessen* is one of the most significant annual events for the public. The communities plan all year for this.

After being greeted at the range by local dignitaries, we review the target workings. While many ranges in Switzerland now have computer-scored targets, this massive range still relies on human scorers. Dozens of target boys stay in shelters until the shooting ends, then sprint to show the score for each target. Like everyone here, the boys are volunteers. Dressed in red, they swarm around each target like bees and wave signs to indicate points.

Scoring is controlled by an official score sheet, and you don't get your official score (and medal, if the gods were with you) for more than an hour later. That's partly on purpose to make you wait. But it's not "waiting"—you're having local beer and food with your family and friends in the Fest tent. Of course, the wife (or husband) and kids went with you to the range and cheered you there. Now is the real community manifestation in the tent—crowds talk and laugh, you hear shooting (it sounds like clapping at first), the band plays. There are dances on Friday, Saturday and Sunday night until 1:00 a.m.

These people are together and solid as a rock. Shooting is the great cement which brings the community together and unifies the people. Making you wait for your score is just one more way to encourage the armed populace to socialize and unify.

A lull in the shooting leads us to the shooting positions. Despite most shooters being guys, I had earlier seen females with Sturmgewehr 90 rifles on their shoulders—indeed, one young woman carried *two* assault rifles. Here, on a shooting position, is a middle-aged woman shooting a K31 bolt action, a very accurate 7.5mm rifle with more recoil than a semi-automatic. She is a crack shot.

The morning sun angles under the perhaps 100-meter-long roof over the shooting positions and hits the shooters' eyes, while the grayish green silhouette targets are in shadows. I will wait until afternoon to try my luck at another range.

Time for the Fest tent. Inside are hundreds of people and long rows of tables, each decorated with the colorful ancient banner of a shooting club which traces its origins for centuries. Bolt actions and assault rifles are casually leaned against the tables as women, men, children and babies all socialize and enjoy each other. We speak to scores of people. These assault rifle toters are the friendliest folks in the world.

Local shooters are still proud of their ancestors' victory at nearby Murten (Morat in French), which is celebrated on the label of a fine Vully Swiss wine which was, appropriately enough, served to us there at Salvenach. E.F. Friedli, secretary of the Lake County Rifle Association, explains the wine label: "The picture represents the battle of Murten (June 22, 1476), one of three encounters between the Swiss federal troops and the Duke of Burgundy (second battle in Grandson at the border of Lake Neuchâtel, third battle in Nancy, France). Historians agreed that the battle of Murten had an epoch-making importance for Europe." Yet another instance in which the armed Swiss people defeated an invading standing army.

Col. Hurst and I pass by bicyclers with assault rifles on their backs as we drive to Alterswil in the afternoon. There are 3000 shooters in Alterswil. In the Fest tent, it sounds like people clapping at a pep rally at first, but it's the shooting outside. Speeches and lively music fill the tent.

With the Alps in the background, cow bells, rifle fire and guitars blend simultaneously into a uniquely Swiss melody. Friendly conversation and lively toasting with good Swiss wine. What a wonderful country!

The community leaders are also the leaders of the shooting associations. The president of Fribourg, with whom we enjoyed lunch, is an official in the association. A town vice president I had the pleasure of meeting has been the head of his shooting club for more than twenty years.

Colonel Hurst and I speak to the officials in the Fest tent. I register to shoot the 300-meter rifle course. I will use the colonel's Sturmgewehr 90, which has a selector for one shot, three-shot burst and full-auto. We assemble by the Fest tent in a row by assigned position—I have number 1. There are seventy-two positions and targets, each in clumps of four.

An inspector looks at each gun—magazine out, safety on, chamber open—and down the barrel from the muzzle. With the 57, a white surface on the right shows the full-auto selector is not installed for full-auto fire.

The sun is hot. We are behind the group at the ammo depot, and they are behind the group at the firing line. At last we go to the next station, where 5.6mm ammunition is issued in plastic stripper clips and twenty-four rounds are put in the box magazine. We wait while the shooting group continues. All of the above is a kind of militia discipline. It enhances individual reflection on the coming event, and I work on my mindset as I gaze at the beautiful Alps in the background.

Finally we occupy the platform under the canopy and get into the prone position. We're on our stomach and elbows a long time. At last the command, *"Schuss."* I squeeze the trigger. Recoil of the gun is like that of the 5.56mm NATO—light. After three or four shots, my sights are set perfectly. Eyes are on me—the range commander mentioned the American—and I shoot my best.

I do not keep a good count, can't understand all the range commands, and from the more rapid fire I realize I must shoot three, not one, in one minute. My mind goes blank and I shoot three 4s (i.e. bullseyes) and a 3. I do it again! Then it's six shots in one minute. I'm used to the trigger pull now and have adjusted my shoulder to the short stock of the Sturmgewehr 90. This is exhilarating precision shooting—six shots, one minute each, with a break between each to adjust sights. There are three shots in one minute, then repeated, then six shots in one minute.

This is all at 300 meters against a target that's hard to see—a small gray area (the bullseye, worth four points), the green silhouette (three points for the head and torso), then a bland color background (two and one point circles)—a battlefield practice target.

We're done, and I wait to see if I made it. Suddenly I'm being congratulated by all. A perfect score, with eighteen shots and 4 being the highest per shot, is seventy-two. I scored fifty-nine, enough to win the Swiss medal. Later in the Fest tent, the medal is pinned to my shirt by a woman in traditional Alpine dress.

Do you know what a Swiss army knife is really for? Yes, the corkscrew is obvious and plays a significant part in Swiss life. Nor can the bottle opener be ignored on a continent where beer bottles are not all screw-off types. You might believe the most important function of the Swiss knife is to cut or perhaps to file nails. You are wrong.

The famous knife is built to adjust the sights on an assault rifle for 300-meter shooting. Remember that the
(text continues on page 26)

Early in the century, the Swiss Luger in 7.65mm was the military's choice. Ninety years later, some are still shot annually. (Photo courtesy Waffen Fabrik, Bern, Switzerland)

Now it's the Pistol 75, a 9mm double-action semi-auto recognizable, of course, as a SIG P220. (Photo courtesy Waffen Fabrik, Bern, Switzerland)

The Guns of Feldschiessen

The Pistol 49, also in 9mm, is still a big favorite—understandably—in the Swiss service. It is, of course, a SIG 210. (Photo courtesy Waffen Fabrik, Bern, Switzerland)

The KAR 31, a straight-pull high-capacity 7.5mm rifle that served for a quarter-century or more. Thousands of Swiss households still have them. (Photo courtesy Waffen Fabrik, Bern, Switzerland)

Here's the 7.5mm Sturmgewehr 57, a no-nonsense all-out military rifle. It's heavy, but no Swiss plans to travel far in a war. (Photo courtesy Waffen Fabrik, Bern, Switzerland)

For their own 5.6mm load, this is the Sturmgewehr 90, the one every Swiss male will have by the year 2000. It is a formidable weapon. (Photo courtesy Waffen Fabrik, Bern, Switzerland)

(text continued from page 23)
first stage is one shot per minute, plenty of time to adjust a sight. Yes, it's the wide screwdriver blade on the bottle opener. Every shooter on the firing line was adjusting sights with a red Swiss knife.

All good things must come to an end, and on Monday morning I find myself traveling across the country to catch my Swiss Air flight in Zurich. I had arrived there the weekend before and spent that Saturday night in Zurich's old city. There were hordes of people on the streets and in bars—those people know how to party—but I never saw one cop or one fight. The Swiss enjoy great freedom in regard to firearms ownership, yet have very little crime.

The music of rifles, guitars and cow bells fill the air. Just outside this Fest tent, with the Alps in the background, the writer won the Swiss medal with Colonel Hurst's Sturmgewehr 90.

During the following week, I lost count of the number of shooting ranges I saw from trains and cars, though I never saw a golf course. Ranges over corn fields, ranges in every community, even ranges up mountain sides with the clubhouses at the bottom and the targets 300 meters uphill.

In Bern, besides meeting with Colonel Hurst, I received an orientation session at the Swiss military library, thanks to Dr. Jürg Stüssi-Lauterburg (I noticed the late Dr. Ed Ezell signed the guest book before me). I admired the guns for sale at Gaston Poyet's Waffen store, whose owner is president of the Swiss Armorers Association and who answered all of my questions about the 5.6mm Swiss cartridge (5.56mm NATO is accurate in Swiss 5.6 barrels, but not vice versa).

The highlight of my visit to Bern was a tour of the Waffen Fabrik (Federal Arms Factory), hosted by Urs Stampfli and Andreas Wenger. The "WF" produces everything from the Sturmgewehr 90 rifles to 120mm cannon for defense of the country. The WF museum houses the most intriguing collection of Swiss small arms, from matchlock pistols to Swiss Lugers.

WF makes the slides and hammer-forged barrels for the Sphinx AT-2000 pistol family, the only Swiss-made semi-automatic 9mm pistol (the SIG/Sauer pistol, of course, is actually manufactured in Germany). The Sphinx frame, a CZ clone, and other parts are made at Porrentruy, near the French border. Thanks to the hospitality of Sphinx President Fernando Dal Zotto, I visited the Sphinx factory and fired their low-recoil 9mm as well as the new 380 pocket model.

Hammerli, at Lenzburg, also makes barrels for the Sturmgewehr 90, as does SIG at Rheinfall. At my visit there, Hammerli Managing Director Ferdinand Hediger tells me that Hammerli's barrels for the 90 are more accurate than those made by SIG or WF—I laugh, because SIG and WF officials told me the same about their barrels. Hammerli also makes Olympic-quality electronic air pistols and assembles military pistols. Neither "Ferdy" nor anyone else in Switzerland could explain why the military department still insists that issue pistols must have the old-style butt magazine latch instead of a button release.

Hanspeter Baumann, president of ProTell, the Swiss NRA, guided me on a tour of the Vieil-Armand battlefield in Alsace, just across the border into France. Countless French and German soldiers died there in 1914-18 to satisfy the pride of their generals, whose objectives were to extend their trenches a few yards on these strategically worthless mountains. The Swiss, of course, stayed out of both of the Big Ones in this century.

All of the above phenomena and impressions are related. Swiss factories produce enough rifles to arm every man in the country, as well as every woman who wants one, too. The Swiss people are thoroughly trained in marksmanship; many compete throughout the year, but all must shoot at least once, i.e., in the *Feldschiessen*. The armed populace, not a standing army, defends the country and guarantees domestic freedom. The neutral Swiss stay out of wars—they neither invade other countries nor does any aggressor dare invade them.

These Swiss facts were known two hundred years ago when America's Founding Fathers adopted the Constitution and its special amendment meant to promote a well-regulated militia to secure a free state. The Second Amendment right of the people of the United States to keep and bear arms was inspired in large part by the Swiss example. The American framers wanted to avoid standing armies, entangling foreign alliances, and the perpetual European wars stirred up by one tyranny after another. Somewhere along the way, America lost sight of this heritage. The Swiss haven't.

As we drove to Bern the morning after the *Feldschiessen* ended, I wondered how tourists—such as the Japanese, who are (as in tyrannies past) totally disarmed by their government—react when they see armed civilians all over the place. Colonel Hurst laughed and said, "They think it's a revolution."

It's revolutionary all right, in this world of despotism, aggression and domination, a world in which governments see subjects as fodder to disarm, enslave and kill. As they have for many centuries, the Swiss stand as a beacon to the world—armed, free and peaceful.

References
An attorney in Fairfax, Virginia, Dr. Halbrook is author of *That Every Man Be Armed: The Evolution of a Constitutional Right* (reprinted by Independent Institute 1994).

The Guns of Williamsburg

by EDWARD R. CREWS

All photos courtesy of Colonial Williamsburg Foundation, Williamsburg, Virginia

BENJAMIN CURLE, 8, didn't plan to join the militia this sunny, warm autumn morning on his family trip to Colonial Williamsburg.

This was supposed to be a day for wandering through the restored capital city of 18th-century Virginia, soaking up history by looking in shops, watching craftsmen make everything from harpsichords to horseshoes, and maybe riding in a carriage. It wasn't supposed to be a morning of flanking movements, military music and snarling sergeants, but that's the way it turned out.

When Benjamin and his parents walked down Duke of Gloucester Street and reached the Powder Magazine, the graceful brick armory, there stood an 18th-century recruiter, begging a crowd of 20th-century tourists to fight in the Revolutionary War.

"We need men! We need help," the soldier told the throng, "The Redcoats are threatening Virginia, and the Indians are raising a ruckus on the frontier. Come on! Sign up! The Commonwealth and the Congress need you, now!"

A rush to the colors ensued. And with visions of martial glory in his mind and the sound of fife and drums in his ears, young Benjamin enlisted. What the boy from rural

Colonial Williamsburg's musicians put a special feeling into the band's signature tune—"The World Turned Upside Down," played during the British surrender at Yorktown in 1781.

Goochland County, Virginia, had just gotten caught up in was one of the most popular and innovative programs Colonial Williamsburg has ever devised. It's a mini-boot camp that every year allows tens of thousands of people—all ages and both genders—to sample the tactics, drill and weapons that won American independence.

For example, before Benjamin finished his twenty-five-minute "hitch," he and the other twenty or so volunteers in his company would learn how to load and fire a musket (actually a stick), make some facing movements ("Your *other* left, recruit"), affix a bayonet to a gun, flank an enemy, and endure some mild-mannered military discipline. The costumed drill sergeant, in fact, threw two adults out of ranks for "sword fighting" with their stick muskets. All of this would be topped off with a short graduation parade behind a fifer and a drummer, and an inspiring speech by Patrick Henry.

"Men," the harried governor of Revolutionary War Virginia would say to the troops, "I'm proud of you. Virginia is in danger. It's up to you to uphold her honor. The safety of your homes, your wives and your children depends on your valor. I know you'll do the duty. I think that's all I have today; I'm late for a meeting at the Capitol. Sergeant, dismiss the men."

This notion of presenting history through first-person acting and visitor involvement is pervasive at Colonial Williamsburg. Today, tourists can participate in a wide range of 18th-century activities, including deciding a trial, arguing a political viewpoint, engaging in tavern gossip or even joining the militia. This represents a considerable departure for Williamsburg. For decades, this living history museum embraced a decidedly "hands-off" method of teaching people about our 1700s heritage. Visitors to the restored city simply watched the craftsmen ply their trades, listened to a mini-lecture at each shop or public building, and trooped to the next building where the process was repeated. It was educational, but not exactly engaging. This system began changing a few years ago when Williamsburg reconsidered how people really learn.

"You remember about twenty-five to thirty percent of what you hear. But forty-five to sixty percent of what you do is remembered," said Bill Rose, one of Colonial Williamsburg's full-time drill instructors. "What we're doing here is hands-on. People listen; people do. And it's clear they enjoy and learn."

Rose is right. Visitors do participate, and they do enjoy it. Spring or summer, anybody visiting the Powder Magazine will see a wide mix of people having fun playing Continental Army. According to Rose, the program is popular with all ages, but school children and veterans attending reunions at nearby convention centers seem to have the most fun. The children like the militia program's game aspect and catch on quickly. Given a little time, the drill instructors even can teach kids enough basics to pit school groups against one another in small mock battles that require rudimentary marching skills. Veterans, of course, quickly take to the drill and orders. Williamsburg interpreters say it's a little spooky to see how readily they fall into a military routine they never knew. One problem for the vets, said Rose, is that they never can get the facing movements quite right. Eighteenth-century drill was more flat-footed, emphasizing heels, not heels-and-toes, as does 20th-century American drill. Rose, himself a veteran,

A costumed interpreter teaches visitors the manual of arms for the flintlock musket. Soldiers in the 1700s drilled endlessly.

A drill instructor welcomes visitors to Williamsburg's training camp, an innovative program of drill, cannon firings and occasional small mock battles.

said it took him several years to unlearn what the Navy taught him at boot camp.

Anybody interested in Revolutionary America's military or its weapons will find today's Colonial Williamsburg a rich experience. Guns played an important and immediate role in this period. Hunting was commonplace, and militia members were all required to keep a weapon at home.

Somebody had to make and repair those guns. And, accordingly, the oldest and consistently most popular craft display related to weapons of the 1700s is the gunsmith's shop. Williamsburg's craftsmen still make pistols, fowling pieces and rifles using 18th-century techniques. Gunmaking

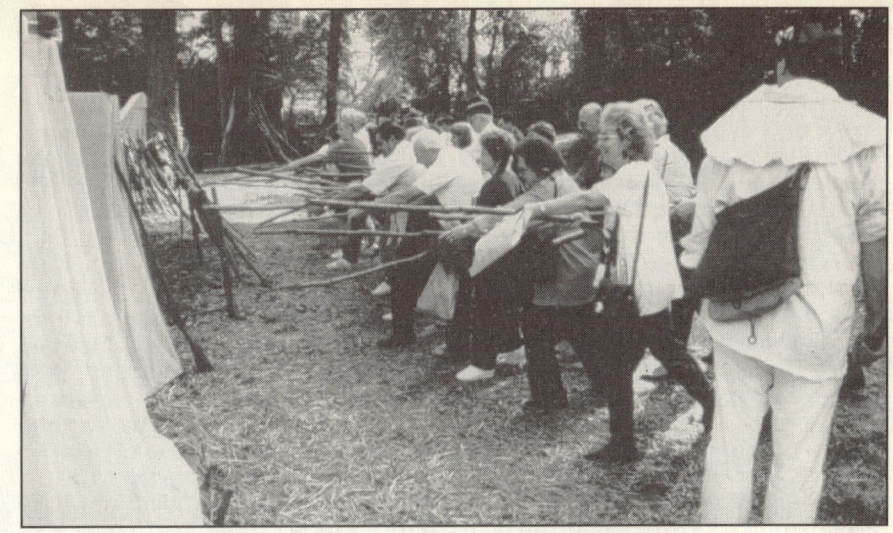

This is the summer military encampment, which recreates life in an American militia camp during the Revolutionary War, especially bayonet fighting.

(Left) Here, drill instructors teach new recruits the finer points of 18th-century bayonet fighting.

The professional parades in Williamsburg involve the interpreter staff and big crowds.

50th EDITION, 1996

isn't something that lends itself to the hands-on approach, but anybody with the interest can spend lots of time watching, talking and picking up pointers to build their own muzzle-loader back home. The subject of weapons making as artistry also is dealt with at DeWitt Wallace Decorative Arts Gallery, which features various displays showing how form and function met in the early American rifle.

Visitors more interested in rubbing elbows with soldiers of the Revolution get several opportunities during the year.

Over Labor Day weekend, for example, Colonial Williamsburg invites hundreds of Revolutionary War re-enactors to camp on Market Square in the restored area. There, they recreate the camp life of the period; show visitors their weapons, uniforms and other accoutrements; and participate in a huge Grand Muster.

Re-enactors also arrive around late June to recreate the brief British occupation of 1781. This activity recalls when the British troops stopped in Williamsburg on the way to nearby Yorktown. The re-enactors "occupy" the town, block roads with wagons, check passes for "townspeople" and arrest a few of them following carefully choreographed arguments.

A week or so later, a new batch of re-enactors arrive for the Continental liberation, which celebrates when the Americans passed through following the British.

In addition to these events, Williamsburg puts on a host of parades, reviews and tattoos throughout the year, featuring its own fife and drum band that puts a special verve into its signature tune, "The World Turned Upside Down," played during the British surrender at Yorktown.

The centerpiece of Williamsburg's military programs, of course, are the opportunities to sample 18th-century Army life. There are two. Besides the militia session at the Powder Magazine, the town runs a more elaborate session at a military encampment during the summer. This encampment takes longer than the other militia program and covers a lot more ground. It also gives the interpreters a chance to get into their roles as hardened drill instructors.

One day last summer, the Piacentini family (mom, Margaret; dad, Gary; Chris, 10; Brian, 7; and Michael, 5) of Richmond, Virginia, found themselves at the encampment, in the Army and listening to the harangue of a soldier dressed in a white linen colonial uniform.

"Well," the man told the forty-member company before him, "You're in the militia now, and we're going to make you into soldiers. If that can be done."

Then, he marched them off to camp where they were assigned tents, issued muskets, and taught the basics of loading a musket and firing in volleys. Williamsburg substitutes sticks for muskets, a technique borrowed from the supply-starved Continental Army.

Brian became flustered with the manual of arms and loading procedure. "At the rate you are going," his instructor told him, "All you're going to do is provide the British with a target to practice on."

Dad got some of this harassment, too: "If you're this slow on the battlefield, you won't need a musket. You can use a dagger because the Redcoats will be on top of you before you can fire a shot."

Having taught his recruits how to use a musket (more or less), the soldier had to teach them how to fire a cannon. In this case, Williamsburg uses a real cannon with a blank charge and a gun crew composed of tourists. Pre-firing instructions include a brief lesson on the use of artillery on the Revolutionary War battlefield and some blackpowder safety basics. Chris got picked for the cannon crew.

The cannon shooting marked the end of training, and the officers decided to give the Piacentini's and the other "recruits" a furlough.

"You're getting a couple of days off," their drill instructor said. "If you get into trouble, you'll have to stay here next time."

And then, with accompaniment provided by a drummer, he marched the whole company of tourists out of camp.

"It was entertaining, and I enjoyed it because the family enjoyed it," said Gary Piacentini, a tax attorney. "It was fun marching and pretending to be in the Army. But you know, that guy who was teaching us was tough. He never did tell us we were really great soldiers or that he enjoyed training us."

While Williamsburg wants people

In Williamsburg's gunsmith shop, modern-day craftsmen produce rifles, fowling pieces and pistols using 18th-century techniques and technology—and costumes.

to enjoy these programs, they also want them to learn. The drill instructor said his challenge is to impart at least three major lessons about the Revolution to visitors who join the militia:

First, the conflict was a global one of huge scope. The war lasted from 1775 to 1783. Not only did England send an army across the Atlantic Ocean to fight, but France entered the war in 1778. This pitted the two ancient antagonists against one another in North America, the Caribbean, Europe and the Far East. The war here raged along the East Coast and on the frontier. Before it was over, Americans would fight pitched European-style battles and conduct classic 18th-century sieges, as well as deliver as much partisan warfare as the British troops could possibly want.

Williamsburg employees drill in "civilian clothes" just as the militia did during the Revolutionary War, going through the firing drills used on the battlefields.

The British army understood this kind of warfare and built a military machine capable of fighting it. This gave them a huge advantage for most of the war. The Colonists, however, had neither standing army nor that many well-trained men. They also lacked the time and manpower to create a precision instrument once the war began.

"The Americans always were looking to get men on the field," Rose said. "As soon as the officers were confident that the men at least knew the basics, they generally put them on the field."

The results were not good. Half-trained soldiers typically could not best British regulars. America's salvation came from Baron Friedrich von Steuben, a Prussian army officer who was not a real baron. George Washington, however, didn't care about von Steuben's bogus title. Recognizing the Prussian's vast military knowledge and winning ways with the troops, Washington made him Inspector of Training.

It was a wise move because it is doubtful that the Colonists could have won the war without von Steuben's efforts at Valley Forge. There, he laid the foundation for a professional American Army. The Prussian officer realized immediately that the Americans simply did not have the time to build an army like the British. He also knew that they would have to fight this war using basically the same tactics, formations, weapons and methods as the British. Accordingly, he developed a streamlined drill system that bor-

The professional staffers get to shoot their muskets at drill—powder, no ball, of course.

Second, contrary to popular notions, Americans did not win the war by hiding in the bushes and sniping at the British. American battlefield victories, like Saratoga, came by fighting like Europeans. That style of warfare basically required large bodies of massed soldiers to march into battle. Then, these formations got as close as they could to the enemy and poured as many bullets into him as possible. Once the opposition took enough casualties, a bayonet charge either routed or crushed him.

This system only could work if soldiers knew a host of complex marching commands and responded to them instantly, regardless of the confusion of battle. The only way to instill the discipline and knowledge to do all that was through drill—hours and hours of it.

Tourists can take the place of this gun crew, learn the drill, and actually fire the gun.

Outside the Williamsburg Magazine, tourism as usual—elsewhere in the town, there's boot camp.

This view from the gunsmith's window shows a variety of pistols made in Colonial Williamsburg, where gunsmiths found a steady demand for their products and skills.

rowed from the existing French, British and American systems. His innovations included simplifying commands and reducing the motions required to load and maneuver. He cut the number of ranks for the basic battlefield formation to two from three. All this allowed the Americans to train men more rapidly than the British, which made a tremendous difference in getting soldiers into the field. He personally oversaw much of the Army's training, relying on a mix of patience, humor, discipline and a wide-ranging command of profanities in English, French and German. Von Steuben also put his ideas into a manual, "Regulations For the Order and Discipline of the Troops of the United States." This book was published in 1779, and it served the American Army for the next twenty-five years.

Third, the smoothbore musket, not the rifle, won the Revolution. European tactics relied on overwhelming firepower to smother, weaken and demoralize an enemy. British soldiers were masters of this. No British recruit could go into battle unless he could fire fifteen rounds in $3^{3}/_{4}$ minutes. Given 18th-century weapons technology, the only gun that allowed high rates of fire was the smoothbore muzzleloader. Rifles took too long to load and did not take a bayonet. The Americans formed rifle companies early in the war, but the experiment didn't work. The British simply accepted a few long-range casualties from these troops while they rushed their men to close range, where a high fire rate and the bayonet counted for more than accuracy. Riflemen were valuable on a skirmish line, along a flank and for long-range battlefield sniping, as more than one British officer learned to his dismay. But on a typical Revolutionary War battlefield, the smoothbore was king.

The basic British infantry weapon (often found in American hands through capture) was the Brown Bess, formally the Long Land Service musket. Placed into service about 1720, the musket was big and heavy. Like all military weapons of the period, the Brown Bess was a flintlock, depending on a piece of flint to strike an upright piece of metal to create a spark, which ultimately set off the main charge in the barrel. This gun fired a 753-caliber, 490-grain bullet from a 46-inch barrel using 124 grains of powder. The Brown Bess weighed about 11 pounds, and its effective range was about 200 yards.

Americans carried anything they could get. Some weapons were captured; some were made in the colonies; many were imported. Particularly popular in the Continental Army were the French service muskets. The French sent a variety of such weapons to America, but they were all generically known as Charlevilles, a name taken from a French arsenal. The typical French military musket was 69-caliber, fired a 450-grain bullet and weighed almost 10 pounds.

Colonial Williamsburg officials should be gratified to learn that these lessons do seem to get through to militia program participants.

"It's a great way for kids—for anybody—to learn history," said Margaret Piacentini, a history major who taught in elementary school before becoming a full-time homemaker. "My children remembered a lot more from taking on these roles as soldiers than they'd ever learn if somebody just told them about it."

Paula Curle, Benjamin's mother and a full-time elementary school teacher, agrees about the program's educational potential.

"I was impressed from the moment it started," she said. "The participation level was high from children and adults. When we were young and came to Williamsburg, all we did was look and listen. Today, they really draw people in."

The children did seem to learn a lot. If you ask Chris Piacentini, for example, how to load and fire an 18th-century cannon, he can answer in considerable detail. His brother Brian can explain linear tactics and the difficulties of staying in a straight line. And the two brothers give the experience rave reviews. Brian credits the military interpreter's enthusiasm and sense of humor for making the program a success. Chris simply gives it all the highest accolade a modern-day 10-year old can: "It was awesome." (The family did have one dissenting opinion. Brother Michael, 5, was a little less enchanted. "I didn't like it," he said, "because the guy kept yelling.")

When it comes to lessons learned, though, you'd have to go a long way to beat Benjamin Curle's key impression. It was an answer that would warm the heart of anybody who tried to teach Americans the basics of military life since 1776. "I learned to stand in formation," he said proudly, "and never goof off in the Army."

50 Years of Gun Digest

by Gary M. Brown

The author proudly furnishes a brief synopsis of every GUN DIGEST ever published from his own complete *Digest* set 1944, to date!

The GUN DIGEST 1944

The cover of the very first The GUN DIGEST (Edited by Charles Jacobs; Published by Milton Klein) features a lavishly engraved, inlaid, ventilated rib-equipped Ithaca Model 37 pump shotgun. This First Edition established the *Digest's* practice of featuring rare, unique, newly introduced, highly decorated, and/or desirable firearms on its covers. Contributing editors in 1944 include Jack O'Connor, "Choosing the Big Game Rifle"; and Major Chas. Askins, "Do's and Don'ts of Upland Game Shooting;" along with a supporting cast of lesser known scribes. This procedure is followed to this very day, combining the works of writers who are, literally, household names with the best efforts of the non-famous. A separate "Reference Price List" for cataloged firearms is inserted, but readers are admonished that the data is from 1940-1941 "last published" (pre-War) sources. There is no back cover illustration. No cover price is imprinted. The first edition was reprinted in 1963. The only difference between the original and the reprint was firearm prices in the catalog sections were included with the guns instead of on a separate "Reference Price List."

2nd Edition 1946

Essentially, a reprint of the First (1944) Edition, this initial Post WWII The GUN DIGEST rendition does have several noticeable differences. The front cover features the same deluxe Ithaca Model 37 used on the 1944 version; however, an ornate black border highlights the title and part of the shotgun. In a major and ironic twist Elmer Keith replaces Jack O'Connor on the topic of centerfire rifles under the heading: "The Proper Big Game Rifle." But, the photo atop the first page of the piece, remains the same as in the 1944 *Digest*. One of the hunters pictured is clearly Jack O'Connor, the other is not Elmer Keith. No firearms prices are given, and no price insert is contained in this scribe's copy. Once again, a back cover illustration is absent. No price is imprinted on the cover.

50 Years

1947 3rd Edition

There is a totally new illustration on the front cover of the 3rd Edition. The front cover shows a Belgian made 12-gauge Browning Over-Under Shotgun. This custom built gun it was noted "...is an outstanding example of the highest quality European engraving." For the first time, writers and contributing editors are credited for their articles in the Table of Contents. Walter Roper provides "Fun With a Handgun," while C.M. Palmer, Jr. chips-in with, "How to Shoot a Target Rifle." No prices are shown for guns featured in the catalog sections. There is a back-cover photo featuring: "A fine Belgian made, 12 gauge Browning Automatic Shotgun (Auto-5)." Back cover illustrations are included on *all* future GUN DIGESTS. No cover price is imprinted.

4th Edition 1949

This time its a gorgeous "Custom built, highly ornamented Winchester Model 70—one of the best high power rifles ever manufactured" on the front cover. Major Charles Askins returns to the *Digest* with "Handgun Facts," while C. M. Palmer, Jr. reprises his Target Rifle article from the Third Edition. Although prices are not yet given in the catalog sections, updates are provided for many guns as to when Post-War production resumed, or was expected to resume. The first "Index to Manufacturers" appears in this edition. The back cover features the same 12-gauge Auto-5 Belgian Browning shown on the 3rd Edition. Again, no cover price is imprinted.

1951 5th Edition

The first GUN DIGEST to be edited by John T. Amber. This edition was reprinted in 1977 and paired with the 1978 GUN DIGEST as a main selection for Outdoor Life Book Club. The front cover showcases a Smith & Wesson Pre-Model 27 ".357 Magnum" revolver with a 8¾" barrel (installed) plus a 4" spare. The piece is "profusely engraved and gold inlaid." For the first time prices are listed for virtually all guns (and accessories) shown in the catalog sections. More "name" gun writers of the period appear than in any previous *Digest*. Included are the likes of: Julian Hatcher, Jack O'Connor, Townsend Whelen, Phil Sharpe and Elmer Keith. But, lesser known names continue to make valuable contributions. The back cover shows a Colt Single Action Army revolver in 45 Colt with grade "C" engraving and "Eagle Head" carved ivory grips. It belonged to J.T.A. himself. Amber's services answering reader's questions on rifles, shotguns, or pistols "new or old" are offered for the price of return postage! Publisher is listed as: The Gun Digest Company, Chicago 6. The 1950 copyright is held by Klein's Sporting Goods. This is the first *Digest* with a price imprinted on its cover. The $2.00 tariff stays in effect until 1956!

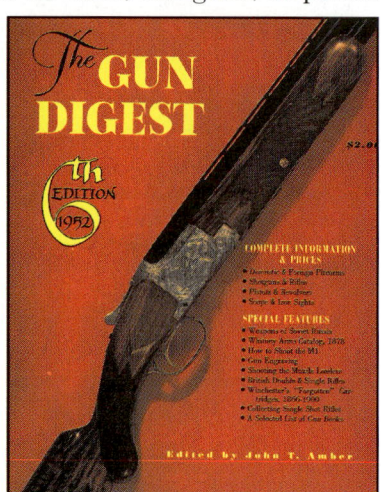

6th Edition 1952

The front cover spotlights "Browning's finest gun, the Superposed Grade V." On the inside front cover John T. Amber, clearly referring to Americans fighting in the Korean War (a.k.a. "police action"), opines as to whether upon returning home, their Second Amendment rights will remain intact. A topic still in question when "Gulf War" vets returned to the U.S. a few years ago! The cataloging of guns and accessories are still divided into separate "sections." Prices continue to be furnished. Warren Page joins as a contributing editor. Elmer Keith provides handgun data under the heading: "Sixguns"; soon to be the title of a Keith book. The Sixth Edition reprinted excerpts from the 1878 Whitney Arms Catalog (including a partial price list). Amber announces plans to publish a book of such old catalogs for about $7.50. Subsequent editions also occasionally contain reprints of this type. The back cover shows an engraved pair of S&W Combat Masterpieces in caliber 38 Special. Publisher and copyright holder is The Gun Digest Company.

1953 7th Edition

The 7th Edition cover is illuminated by a bright yellow background, quite a contrast from the dark reds and medium tans of prior volumes. The cover guns are a nickeled, European engraved S&W Pre-Model 27 "357 Magnum" and a blued Smith, five-shot, factory engraved "Chief's Special" (pre-Model 36) 38 Special. On page 13, the 1876 Remington Catalog is reproduced, including the stipulation on each page displaying firearms: Obsolete Arms—NOT FOR SALE. It appears some readers of the 1952 Sixth Edition had obviously attempted to buy arms, through GUN DIGEST, from the 1878 Whitney Arms Catalog reprint, excited by the prospect of the 1878 prices shown. The Seventh Edition is dedicated to the National Rifle Association—under the heading "Bulwark of a Free Citizenry." This is the first ever dedication. It seems fitting that the NRA was the first organization to be so honored! Catalog sections continue to be listed separately. The back cover shows: "A Midas Grade Browning Automatic Shotgun (Auto-5), gold inlaid and engraved."

8th Edition 1954

The 8th Edition returns to a somber black background which is, however, spectacularly highlighted by a full-color photo of the newly released Ruger Single-Six. This showpiece is described as being: ". . . in deluxe grade, gold and silver plated over Cole Agee's fine engraving." The 8th Edition is dedicated to Col. Townsend E. Whelen by J.T.A. Amber's true admiration of, and respect for, Whelen is clearly manifested in this dedication (which also contains a brief biography of Townsend). This is the first *Digest* dedicated to any one person. Warren Page and Jack O'Connor go head to head for the first time in the Rifle Section, a friendly competition that would continue for years through the pages of *Field & Stream* for the former and *Outdoor Life* for the latter. The back cover pictures a deluxe under-hammer "buggy rifle" from the 1840-1880 period shown against a bright yellow background.

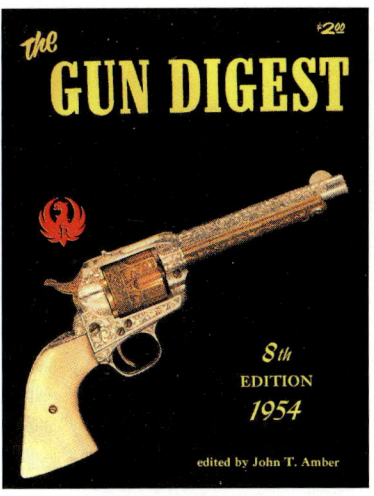

1955 9th Edition

Both front and back covers of the 9th edition display an artist's rendition (although the text claims the gun to be: " . . . engraved and prepared especially for GUN DIGEST by Alvin F. Herbert, Smith & Wesson engraver") of the new Smith & Wesson 9mm semi-automatic pistol. Smith collectors will recognize the piece as the single-action version of the gun. Designated the Model 44, in mid-1957, this particular variation was made in prototype form only. The double-action rendition (dubbed the Model 39, in 1957) went on to reasonable success, serving as the basis for many of Smith's current crop of centerfire semi-autos. There are articles by Hatcher, Keith and Page (who reviews the Winchester Model 50 semi-automatic shotgun, with its unique "independent chamber"), and others. The 1884 Kynoch Ammunition Catalog facsimile provides valuable insight as to available loads of that period.

50 Years

1956 10th Anniversary Edition

The "10th Anniversary 1956 De Luxe Edition" of the GUN DIGEST, was the most visually exciting, memorable and significant volume of this writer's youth. The front cover featured three views (including two "cutaways") of the brand new Ruger 357 Magnum Blackhawk single-action revolver. Provided inside, was a small sheet of gold "transfer-paper," allowing buyers of this book to personalize the depiction of the new Ruger with their initials, etc. Mine soon bore the G.M.B. logo! The edition is dedicated to The National Muzzle Loading Rifle Association. Products (guns, accessories, etc.) were, for the first time, grouped together toward the back of the book—although still separated by articles and/or reviews. In quite a departure from previous editions, the back cover of the 1956 *Digest* highlights the "Partial Contents" of the book. Under the names of the authors, a short blurb describes their articles. An inset pictures six of the then-available semi-automatic shotguns—referring the reader to a J.T.A. piece entitled "The Battle of the Automatics." The price increases to $2.50.

11th Edition 1957

The front and back covers of this edition show left- and right-side views of an exquisite wheellock pistol modestly described as the: "World's Most Valuable Firearm." Under the title "The Emperor's Pistol," the gun, and its history, are described in the lead article stretching from page two through page five. Both covers list partial contents by category: Exploded Drawings; Ballistic Tables; Original Technical Articles by America's Leading Experts, etc. Of great interest to African shooters (both then and now) is Richard Heck's "The 458 Winchester in Africa." The work reviews the early performance of the then-new Winchester Model 70 Super Grade African rifle in the revolutionary 458 Winchester Magnum cartridge. Also of intense interest are Col. Charlie Askins' "A Man's Sixgun;" and, in an incredible role reversal, Elmer Keith's, "Shotgun Choking." The catalog section moves completely to the rear. The price stays at $2.50.

1958 12th Edition

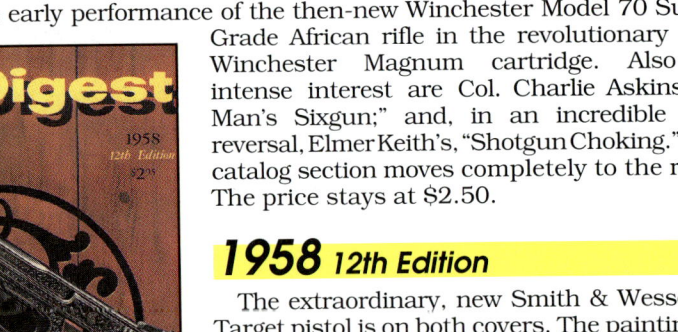

The extraordinary, new Smith & Wesson Model 41 22 rimfire semi-automatic Target pistol is on both covers. The painting, by James M. Triggs, depicts the 7 3/8" version of the 41, complete with muzzle compensator and with Class A (Full) engraving. Articles of note include: Elmer Keith's "The .44 Magnum" (Keith, the real "father" of the new round, sets the record straight on the cartridge itself, and its development); Jack O'Connor's "The Sheep Rifle"; and John T. Amber's "This Gun Collecting Game." James M. Triggs provides the exploded drawings. The catalog section is found in the rear. Price goes to $2.95—where it will stay through 1961—reflecting the low rate of inflation during this halcyon period.

13th Edition 1959

James M. Triggs' gorgeous painting of a Hammerli 22 Free pistol, set against a target range in the Alps is featured on both covers. The front cover is reduced and appears on the back cover in the upper right-hand portion. The balance of the back cover lists partial contents. Bill Toney's article "The Free Pistol," apropos of the cover, is the lead piece. Charlie Askins reviews the first of the 458 Winchester's spin-offs in "The 338 in Africa." Keith kicks in with "Handguns for Hunting," and, in "Ed McGivern—Fastest, Fanciest Sixgunner," Chad Wallin immortalizes America's greatest handgun trick-shot artist. James M. Triggs, again, provides the Exploded Drawings section. The catalog portion stays in the back.

1960 14th Edition

The blood red front and rear covers depict a superb James M. Triggs drawing of an elaborately adorned early Volcanic lever-action pistol. Although made by Smith & Wesson, Triggs includes a sketch of the Winchester galloping rider logo, illustrating the gun's link to the Model 1866. As in the previous edition, the cover art is "reduced" on the back cover, providing space for a partial table of contents. Townsend Whelen begins a two-part series on early U.S. Military rifles with "Days of the Krag." In "Ideal Military Rifle," Jac Weller reports on then state-of-the-art assault rifles, including the Belgian FN-FAL, the Spanish CETME (later to evolve into the German G-3); and America's then current darling, the recently adopted M14. In "Astra Automatics—Series 900," Larry S. Sterett details one of the "other" Broomhandle pistols. Once again, James M. Triggs pulls double-duty by providing extensive exploded drawings (including an insert that offers seven "bonus" guns). Catalog section, ballistics tables, etc., are found in the back.

15th Edition 1961

The semi-automatic rifle depicted on the front and back covers was a real "mystery gun." GUN DIGEST was sworn to secrecy by its maker, so the gun was shown in three superb paintings by James M. Triggs. Guesses as to its true identity ranged from the ridiculous (the "new" Winchester Model 100) to the sublime (a short-range "deer gun" in 44 Magnum). For once, the sublime won out. The little rifle was Sturm, Ruger's first long gun, indeed chambered for the 44 Magnum "revolver" round. The neat, trim gas-operated semi-automatic was fed from an internally housed, under-barrel, tubular magazine. For the next 25 years the gun remained a popular Ruger best seller. The back cover, in something of a departure, featured a different view of the 44 Magnum Carbine. The remaining two-thirds of the rear cover listed the contributing writers. Townsend Whelen completed his tribute to early U.S. military rifles with "Days of the Springfield." As an added bonus, the 32-page *Mauser 1893-95 Rifle Catalog* is reprinted at the very rear of the book. Various sources are cited for the Exploded Drawings section. The 1961 GUN DIGEST was nearly as significant to this writer as the 1956 edition. I was never able to shake the yen for a Deerstalker (the early name of the new gun, before a successful lawsuit by Ithaca, who found the moniker too close to the "Deer Slayer" version of their Model 37 pump shotgun) until I made one mine in the mid-1980s—just prior to its discontinuation in 1985!

1962 16th Edition

Pictured, again by James M. Triggs, on both covers of this edition was the remarkable new Smith & Wesson Model 53 22 Magnum centerfire revolver. The Model 53 was one of two basically unsuccessful U.S. factory attempts to adapt centerfire, small caliber rifle-type cartridges to production handguns. Intended primarily for the "varmint hunter" market, the Model 53, and its single shot competitor, the Ruger Hawkeye, were both dismal production failures. Today, naturally, both are highly prized collector's items due to their relative scarcity. Trigg's painting also illustrates the S&W's chamber inserts which allowed the owner to fire 22 rimfire ammo because of the gun's unique dual firing pins. The first *Gun Digest Treasury* (containing some of the best articles appearing in GUN DIGEST over the first 15 years) is offered for sale on page one. "Spencer's Great 7-Shooter," by Norman B. Wiltsey, details one of the few cartridge repeaters used during the American Civil War and includes a sketch of President Abraham Lincoln holding the rifle with a photo of the target actually shot by Lincoln with one of the guns. An extensive reprint of a *Civil War Gun Catalog* begins on page 161. Works by "household names" such as Kuhlhoff, Whelen, Page are included. Price increases to $3.95, and remains so through 1965. Catalog section is in the back.

50 Years

1963 17th Edition

The bright yellow covers of this edition highlight (in paintings probably done by James M. Triggs) the new SAKO Finnwolf "hammerless" lever-action rifle. The inside front cover features a eulogy of the late, great Townsend Whelen by Bradford Angier. John T. Amber himself, hardly a sentimentalist, perhaps best summed-up the feelings of virtually all gun enthusiasts upon establishing the Townsend Whelen Trophy not long before Whelen's death, with the following quotation: "I'm more grateful than I can say for the privilege of knowing this kind and generous man, so full of years and knowledge—he is, more than anyone I know, a gentleman in the very best sense of the word." In Parts I and II of "The Shot Shell Grows Up!," Warren Page discusses such modern advances as the pie-crimp, plastic hulls, and Winchester's Mark V shot-collar (predecessor of Remington's soon to be announced Power Piston one-piece collar/wad combination). "The 256 Magnum Finds a Home!," by Bob Wallack, previews the introduction of the Marlin Model 62. An extensive Exploded Views section is presented in "blue-print" style, without credits. The by-now familiar catalog section is in the back.

18th Edition 1964

The bright red front cover features two of the world's most significant early semi-automatic pistols. In the foreground is naturalized American citizen Hugo Borchardt's Model 1893 Borchardt pistol; in the background, Georg Luger's more successful, better-known adaptation of Borchardt's "toggle" action design, the 1900 American Eagle Luger. The James M. Triggs painting is duplicated several times in miniature on the back cover, with reviews of all articles in the book. "Handloads for the 256 Magnum" (primarily for rifles in that chambering), by E.M. Yard and C.H. Helbig, is the lead story. Jerry Rakusan (now Editor Emeritus of *Guns* Magazine) reviews a practical modification for the U.S. M-1 Carbine in "The 5.7 Johnson Spitfire." Sam B. Saxton chips-in with "The 7mm Magnum in Africa," which assesses the overall performance of the 1962-introduced Remington "Short" Magnum round. James Triggs once again receives credit for the Exploded Drawings section. The firearms pages of the *1908 Sears, Roebuck Catalog* are reprinted at the back of the book. This year catalog sections are separated by reviews.

1965 19th Edition

The front cover pictures an elaborately embellished French wheellock pistol. The back cover, in addition to brief reviews of articles contained within, offers a first look at a section of Ruger's new 10/22 detachable rotary magazine 22 LR semi-automatic rifle. In an article titled "M14, Hail and Farewell," John Lachuk details the passing of the short-lived M-14, and its replacement—the 223 (5.56x45mm) Colt/Fairchild/Stoner "Black Rifle." A fair comparison between Pre-'64 and Post-'64 Winchester Model 70 rifles is provided by Bob Hagel's, "Model 70 Winchesters." "Smith & Wesson Cartridge Pistols" are given an in-depth review by James E. Serven. An excellent study of all then-current U.S. bayonets is presented in Charles H. Yust Jr.'s, "United States Bayonets 1892-1958." So much additional data is included at the rear, the catalog section appears closer to the book's center.

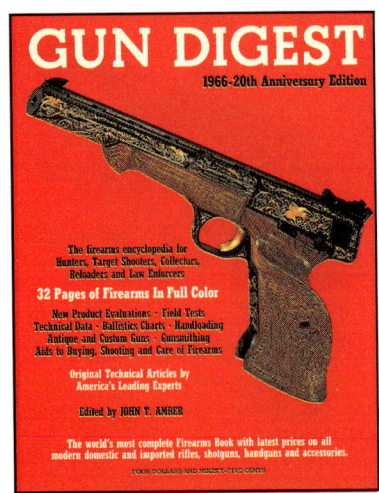

20th Edition 1966

The front cover of the 20th Anniversary Edition of GUN DIGEST pictures an engraved, gold inlaid Browning Medalist 22 rimfire semi-automatic pistol. The back cover displays several assorted arms including: Browning's new straight-pull T-Bolt 22 LR rifle; an engraved Ruger Standard 22 LR semi-automatic pistol; an unspecified S&W large ("N") frame engraved, inlaid revolver with elaborately carved Diamond target grips; a Midas Grade Browning Superposed shotgun; an embellished Winslow bolt-action rifle; and an engraved Marlin Model 39A 22 rimfire lever-action rifle. Some of these pieces, in addition to many other guns, are featured in a full color center section entitled: "The Wonderful World of Guns." James E. Serven provides a close-up of some of Winchester's most significant earlier rifles in "The Old Winchesters." A young fellow named Ken Warner covers "The Best Knives Made," before such items were dealt with in a separate publication. "The 41 Magnum" is reviewed by Dean Grennell. Another early gun catalog, this one from the Great Western Gun Works, is reproduced beginning on page 225. James M. Triggs gets credit for the Exploded Drawings. The catalog section appears further back and is not interrupted by reviews. Price increases to $4.95, and remains so through 1970.

1967 21st Edition

The front cover of this edition features a James M. Triggs rendition of two highly ornate Winchester lever-action rifles—a Model 1866 in caliber 44 Henry Flat and is an 1866-1966 Model 94 Centennial Commemorative in 30-30 Winchester. The back cover has two A.B. Frost game scenes, plus, a partial table of contents. Also mentioned are "Sixteen Magnificent Pages of Firearms in Full Color" found in the book's center section. Inside, Roger Barlow's lead story "Ruger's Reactionary Rifle," documents the introduction of Bill Ruger's newest pride and joy, the No. 1 single shot rifle. In "Guns of Viet Nam," Col. Jim Crossman reviews everything from the M14 to mortars to howitzers. Carrying on the 100th Anniversary of Winchester theme from the front cover, Pat Smith provides "Winchester Centennial." Ken Warner offers, "Is the GI Carbine Dead?"—a question often asked to this very day! For the first time no exploded drawings are included. Catalog is at the back.

22nd Edition 1968

The cover of the 22nd Anniversary *Digest* displays photographs of the receiver areas of three highly decorated Remington firearms on a red, white and blue shield, topped by a golden eagle. The golden eagle logo tops the back cover (also done in red, white and blue) along with partial contents and a more detailed description of the Remington front cover pieces. In "Browning vs. Winchester," Bill Resman compares the famed Belgian Browning Superposed and Winchester's then-new Model 101 Japanese-made over/under shotguns. "The Secret Pistol of World War I," by Wm. B. Edwards, details the famed Pedersen Device. More full-color gun photos appear in the center of the book. James M. Triggs does a two-page breakdown (including one exploded view) of the Savage Model 1910 Autoloading Pistol. Catalog and data sections are found in the back.

1969 23rd Edition

The front cover of the 23rd Anniversary GUN DIGEST pays homage to Bill Ruger's firearms genius, displaying partial views of a deluxe No. 1 single shot rifle and the brand new Model 77 bolt-action, repeating centerfire rifle. On the back cover are two fuller views of both guns. These illustrations appear to be actual photos. Each piece is reviewed in detail by John T. Amber, beginning on page 78, in "New Ruger Rifles." "Captain Samuel H. Walker," offered by James E. Serven, details the development of the famed Colt Walker percussion revolver, named after the Texas Ranger Captain. The 338 Winchester Magnum round is still being kicked around in Bob Hagel's, "The 338—What Does It Offer?" No inside color photos or exploded drawings appear.

50th EDITION, 1996 **39**

50 Years

1970 24th Edition

This edition's front cover is adorned by the receivers of a brace of decorated Marlin lever-action rifles, a centerfire Model 336 and a Model 39A 22 rimfire. Each of these Presentation Grade firearms wears the 1870-1970 Century Anniversary emblem. On the back cover is a full-length photograph of the Model 39A in Century Limited trim and an enlargement of the Marlin centennial medallion, along with a partial review of the book's contents. Pete Kuhlhoff expands on the Marlin 100th Anniversary theme in, "Marlin—A Century of Famous Firearms." Ruger's first centerfire, double-action revolver, a yet unnamed 357 Magnum, is reviewed by John T. Amber in, "Ruger's Double Action Revolver." The remarkable, caseless Daisy V/L rifle is brought to life by Maj. George C. Nonte, Jr. in, "Daisy V/L Rifles." And Dan Wesson revolvers are looked at in Mason Williams', "Dan Wesson Arms."

25th Edition 1971

The 1971 Silver Anniversary Deluxe Edition, fittingly has silver cover backgrounds. A huge 25th Anniversary logo appears on the lower right-hand corner of the front cover. Two Garcia-Beretta shotguns adorn the front, while two Sako bolt-action rifles grace the rear. The back cover also shows the 25th Anniversary logo, and a brief look at the book's contents. John T. Amber details the cover guns and others in "Garcia Guns." In "Firearms Advertising Envelopes," Robert F. Denny provides a glimpse in black-and-white of envelope advertising used years ago by the gun trade. James R. Olt reviews the handgunner's perennially favorite cartridge in, "The 38 Special." Unlike this 50th Anniversary GUN DIGEST, the 25th edition does not provide a special review of the publication's history. A number of exceptional full-page color photographs return to the center section. The 1970 copyright is held by Gun Digest Publishing Company. At this start of a new era, the price jumps $2.00 to $6.95, where it remains through 1973.

1972 26th Edition

The artistic talents of James M. Triggs return here with a rendition of the just reintroduced Sharps (Borchardt) single shot rifle. Against an aged wooden slat background, a buffalo sketch and the caption: "Old Reliable, The Return of the Sharps." The back cover is dominated by what appears to be photographs of Colt's Navy percussion revolvers commemorating Ulysses S. Grant. On the inside front cover, the 100th Anniversary of the National Rifle Association (1871-1971) is noted. At the top of the page three is pictured Ruger's newest single shot rifle, the No. 3. In "Age of the Autoloader," Tom Hayes traces that action type from inception, through the Remington gas-operated Model 742. George L. Wildgen offers "Guns of World War II," which includes true assault rifles, and Harry M. Campbell chips-in with "The Famed Luger," a basic review of the famous gun. There are 32 brilliant pages of Guns in Four-Color in the center. B.W. Brian bemoans the lack of new rounds for semi-automatic handguns in, "Wanted, a New Pistol Cartridge." The 1971 copyright is held by Digest Books, Inc.

27th Edition 1973

The front cover shows "a normal and cutaway" view of a short-barreled, bobbed hammer Ruger Speed Six revolver. The back cover displays Ruger's first percussion handgun, the 44-caliber Old Army revolver and a full-length shot of Ruger's recently introduced No. 3 single shot carbine. The editors mention the "great artistry" of James M. Triggs, who did both paintings and did the cutaway of the Speed Six without an actual cutaway revolver! Inside, Frank Barnes gives the current status of the 45-70 cartridge in "The .45-70—A Century Later." Jon R. Sundra provides "Great Guns: Winchester's Model 9422s." A true exploded drawing returns to GUN DIGEST in the form of a Lee-Enfield No. 4 Mark 1* rifle—rendered by Richard A. Hoffman. The drawing appears in Part Two of Larry Sterett's, "The Rifles of James Paris Lee." Part One of Sterett's work is found in the previous issue, dealing mostly with single shots. Many readers will find Part Two of greater interest since it concentrates primarily on Lee's repeating bolt-action designs. As usual, the catalog and data sections are found in the back.

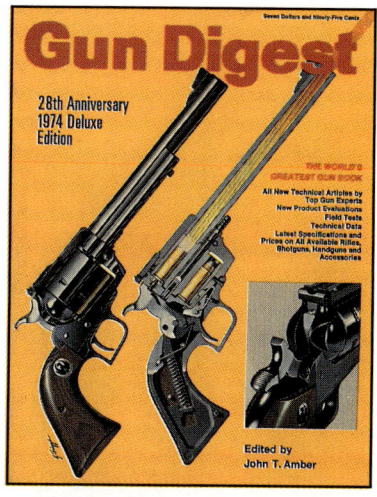

1974 28th Edition

The Ruger "New Model" Super Blackhawk 44 Magnum single-action revolver dominates the front cover of this issue. The three views illustrated by James M. Triggs show normal, cutaway, and action close-up shots. On the back cover, additional drawings by Triggs highlight the action of Ruger's revolutionary new Mini-14 223 semi-automatic rifle along with another variant of Ruger's rapidly expanding double-action revolver line, the stainless steel Security Six. Both inside front and rear covers, for the first time, offer photographs of additional firearms: the Colt-Sauer bolt-action rifle and the Colt Python revolver, respectively. Kam Nasser's lead story "The Model 70 Winchester 1936-1963," provides excellent data, for its time, on the "Pre-'64" Winchester Model-70s. Jack O'Connor offers, "Forty Years with the Little 7mm," the famed 7x57mm Mauser ex-military round. Despite his great love and admiration for the 270 Winchester cartridge, O'Connor, as much as anyone, helped to re-popularize the 7x57. In "Dream Gun or Zombie," H.V. Stent chips-in an excellent review of the 30-30 Winchester round, plus the lever-action Winchester Models 94 and 64 that fire it. Price goes to $7.95 and remains there through 1975.

29th Edition 1975

Covers of the 1975 GUN DIGEST "honor two of the world's best known and best loved gunmakers—Browning and Winchester." On the front are the actions of Winchester's Model 101 O/U and their new Super-X Model 1 gas-operated, semi-automatic shotguns. The back showcases the actions of Browning's recently announced B-78 Winchester High Wall look-alike rifle and their first gas-operated, semi-automatic shotgun, the ill-fated M-2000. "The man who did these brilliant drawings is the inimitable James M. Triggs" credits the source of the artwork. George Nonte offers, "Charter Arms Bulldog—the 44 Special Revived." Jim Horton provides, "The Ruger 220 Swift, an Instant Success." Roy F. Dunlap continues the "reborn classic cartridge" theme with "22 Hornet." Brief mention of proposed Ruger Over/Under shotguns is provided on page 137. Catalog is in the back.

1976 30th Edition

This *Digest* celebrates "John T. Amber's 25th Anniversary as Editor," and displays the action of an ornate Ruger No. 1 rifle featuring a bust of the likeness of John T. Amber, himself. The back cover shows normal and cutaway mid-section views of Ruger's M-77 bolt-action rifle in caliber 458 Winchester Magnum. The editors make note of James M. Triggs' artwork by stating: ". . . his superb portrayals of firearms need little introduction to our readers." In "The Shooting Editor," Jack O'Connor, with tongue-firmly-in-cheek, discloses "tricks of the trade" for aspiring gun writers. Donald M. Simmons, Jr. sheds light on S&W's relatively obscure early semi-automatic pistols in "Smith & Wesson 35 Auto Pistols—a History for Collectors." George C. Nonte reviews one of the first 45 ACP "mini-guns" in "Star's PD 45—a small potent package." In an interesting play on words, Don Lewis writes "The Plight of the Hornet," a story of the current status of the 22 Hornet round and its guns. Printed a year in advance, this 1976 edition makes little mention of America's 1776-1976 Bicentennial. Catalog and data sections are found in the rear. The 1975 copyright holder is DBI Books, Inc. The price increases to $8.95 where it will stay through 1978.

50 Years

1977 31st Edition

Identical photographs of two flintlock rifles and blackpowder accouterments, against a regal purple background, are found on both the front and back covers of this edition. On the inside front cover, John Madson acknowledges America's 200th birthday, under the lead "Observations on the Shooting Sports," with: "Hunting Beyond the Bicentennial." In "Ruger Rarities," Bill Bennington reviews such scarce oddities as the single shot Hawkeye 256 Winchester Magnum pistol, the Bearcat and Super Bearcat mini-revolvers, brass framed guns, etc. "Updating the 444 Marlin," by Don Zutz, traces the evolution of that round from its 240-grain "pistol bullet" beginnings, through the latest factory 265-grain "rifle bullet," plus several custom projectiles. And, Francis W. Gobel's "Elmer Keith—a Legend the World Over" honors America's greatest handgunner. Catalog is in the back.

32nd Edition 1978

Ruger's long awaited, long delayed Red Label 20-gauge Over/Under shotgun, shows up on this year's front cover. On the back is a customized Ruger Model 77, done expressly for John Amber. An obit for Warren Page appears on page 3. Warren was a boyhood favorite of this writer, and I followed many of his excellent writings in *Field & Stream* magazine for years. In "All Purpose Defense Gun: Colt 45 Auto or Charter 44 Bulldog?" Richard Allen opts for the smaller, lighter five-shot revolver. Bill Barlow Fors illuminates some of the earlier Smith & Wesson favorites in his "D.B. Wesson's Revolvers and Rivals," while John E. Ross' "The 220 Swift—Saint or Sinner?" debunks some of the "well known facts" concerning the world's fastest commercial round. Bob Steindler's, "The Wickliffe '76," documents that short-lived, dropping block single shot rifle. Catalog and data sections are found at the back.

1979 33rd Edition

Two impressive Browning-made guns grace the front and back covers. In celebration of Browning's 100th anniversary (1878-1978) they issued several "Centennial Commemoratives." The most exotic of these, the Over/Under Continental 30-06 centerfire rifle, dominates the front cover; another Centennial Commemorative, Browning's legendary P-35 "High-Power" 9x19mm pistol, wearing a bright chrome finish is on the back. For the second straight year an extremely sad obit appears, this one for Jack O'Connor. O'Connor greatly influenced the firearms knowledge of this scribe. Neither he nor Warren Page would ever be truely replaced! The full story of the Browning 100th Anniversary guns appears in "The Browning Centennials" by John T. Amber. The Ruger Model 77 gets its own separate review in Daniel Peterson's, "The Model 77 Ruger Rifle." Browning's new/old BPS pump shotgun is reviewed in Wallace Labisky's "Browning's New Pump Shotgun." Jon Sundra looks at a new source for factory loaded ammunition in, "Hornady's Frontier Ammo." Price increases to $9.95, the same as the 1980 edition.

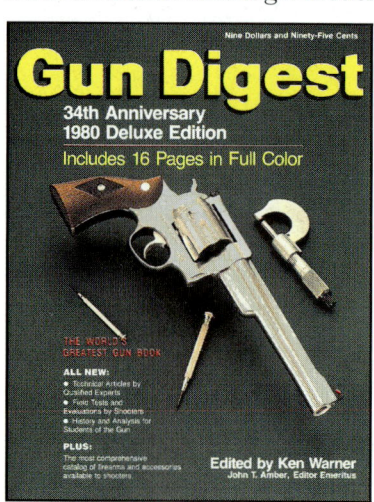

34th Edition 1980

Ken Warner's first GUN DIGEST features Ruger's then-new Redhawk 44 Magnum, stainless steel double-action revolver on its front cover. Ruger's Red Label 12-gauge Over/Under shotgun, with blued carbon steel receiver (one of only 500 produced before being recalled and replaced with a virtually identical gun whose receiver was fabricated of stainless steel), adorns the back. Warner, former editor of the *American Rifleman*, on the inside front cover, comments on the editorial change and Amber follows with his impressions. Obits for George

C. Nonte, Jr. and Daniel Baird Wesson appear on page 3. There are 16 pages of color paintings and photos as part of Ken Warner's excellent review of William B. Ruger, and his guns, in, "30 Years of Good Gun Designs." "The Winchester Model 94" is given yet another in-depth look by H.V. Stent. In "The 45-70—Born Again," Rick Hacker discusses the then-new Federal 300-grain JHP loading for that venerable shell (both Winchester and Remington would subsequently offer nearly identical rounds). Under the heading "The 45," Robert Skiles presents the history of the Model 1905 Colt 45 Automatic which preceded the far better known M-1911.

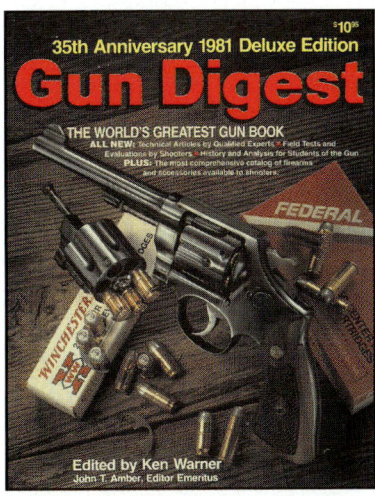

1981 35th Edition

The identical photographs on the front and back cover of this edition feature a "convertible" S&W Model 1917 45 ACP revolver. The gun has been fitted with a separate 45 "Long" Colt cylinder/crane/ejector rod assembly, which allows the piece to fire 45 ACP/45 Auto Rim rounds with one assembly, or the 45 "Long" Colt round using the other. Also shown are two then state-of-the-art, "high performance" cartridges for the gun—Winchester's 45 ACP 185-grain Silvertip JHP and Federal's 225-grain lead semi-wadcutter hollowpoint for the 45 Colt. John T. Amber gets credit at the bottom of both covers as "Editor Emeritus," with Ken Warner listed as Editor. Amber writes tales of his greatest gun collecting accomplishments in "My Triumphs in Gun Collecting." "The Afghan and His SMLE," by Jack Lott, traces both original and locally handmade SMLE 303 British-type rifles favored by Afghans fighting Soviet occupation. Robert A. Painter reviews the emerging Kimber line of longarms in "Kimber Model 82." And, Robert S.L. Anderson provides a look at the "obsolete" 32 WCF with "The 32-20 Never Say Die." Price increases to $10.95, initiating a $1.00 per year advance for most future issues.

36th Edition 1982

This time it's two of the latest Heckler & Koch firearms, on both the front and back covers. Within eight years the collapsible stocked 223 caliber HK M93A3 will be banned as an imported "assault rifle." The $1,000 John T. Amber Award for gun writing is announced, replacing the Townsend Whelen Award. Ken Warner expands on the Heckler & Koch theme with "HK: One Good Idea...Leads to Many Others." Ken details the "roller-delayed" blowback action of many of HK's weapons. In a piece titled "The Bren Ten: Intended to be Better," Jeff Cooper grudgingly concedes that the Czech CZ-75 is the best of the 9s. John Amber offers "Advices to Young Collectors." Price rises $1.00 to $11.95.

1983 37th Edition

Weaver's stainless steel handgun scope, rings and mount, perched atop an unspecified Smith & Wesson stainless steel revolver (likely, a Model 629 44 Magnum), adorn both covers of this issue. Unfortunately, Weaver, shortly thereafter, will go "belly-up" for good. The inside front cover is graced with Ruger's "Signature" stainless steel Standard semi-automatic 22 LR pistol, one of the final 5,000 of that model to be made, while the inside back cover displays one of Ruger's 12-gauge O/U Red Label shotguns. The winner of the first John T. Amber Literary Award with its $1,000 cash prize went to Stuart Otteson for his design story that appeared in the 1982 GUN DIGEST on the Remington 721-722 rifle. Lenard M. Brownell's obit appears on page 245. There are 24 full-color pages, located at the center of the book. Marshall R. Williams reviews the "The Maligned .410 Bore." In "Sixty Million Guns," L.R. "Bob" Wallack, Jr. documents some of America's best selling firearms models. Guns as diverse as Winchester's Model 94 lever-action rifle and Remington's Model 1100 semi-automatic shotgun are cited. New price is $12.95.

50 Years

1984 38th Edition

On the front cover are two handsome Weatherbys, a wooden-stocked Mark V bolt-action rifle and an Athena O/U shotgun. Two other Weatherby's are on the back cover—a composition-stocked Mark V and a semi-automatic shotgun. The Second Annual John T. Amber Literary Award for the best 1983 GUN DIGEST article is won by Arvid B. Pedersen for "How Choke Works." Eight pages of full-color are grouped together toward the front third of the book. L.R. "Bob" Wallack, Jr.'s obit is noted on page 3. In articles on the subject of "assault rifles," Ken Warner looks at "The Assault Rifle Syndrome." Next, Edward A. Matunas provides "Who Needs an Assault Rifle?" and Warner responds with "You Don't Need a Bass Boat Either." In "How to Collect Sporting Books," James Handcock cites the importance of such publications. The "One Good Gun" section is initiated (and will eventually become a "regular," yearly feature) with several good reviews of such classics as: the Remington 513-S; the Winchester Model 63; and, the Ruger Bearcat. Price is $13.95.

39th Edition 1985

Cutaways of three prominent Ruger firearms (the Red Label O/U shotgun; the just introduced Mark II 22 LR semi-automatic pistol; and the Redhawk Magnum double-action revolver), grace both covers of this edition. The inside front cover announces Edward A. Matunas as winner of the John T. Amber Award for his 1984 GUN DIGEST article "Rating Handgun Power." Fittingly, Elmer Keith's obituary takes up the entire inside back cover. Keith, like Page and O'Connor before him, had an immense, positive influence on this writer's gun knowledge. These three giants of the shooting/writing community have truly proven to be irreplaceable! Eight pages of full color appear near the book's center. In "Scopes and Mounts," Bob Bell cites Weaver's apparently permanent departure. Problems with the 357 "Maximum" cartridge are noted in several locations. In "Middle Ground Deer Rifles," Frances E. Sell discusses a number of "medium power" factory and wildcat rounds and the guns that fire them. D.A. Tomlinson provides a fascinating look at the famed Browning firearms legacy with "John M. Browning: The Man and His Patents." Unannounced in the book is the purchase of DBI Books, Inc. by President Charles T. Hartigan and Vice President John G. Strauss. Price is $14.95.

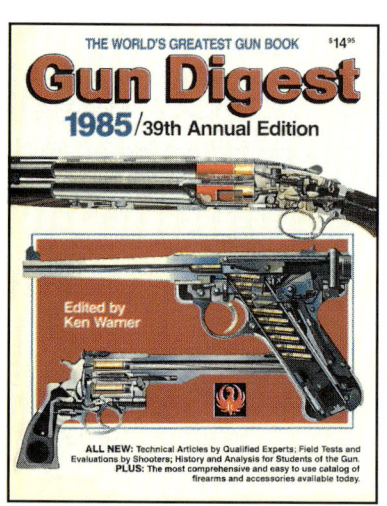

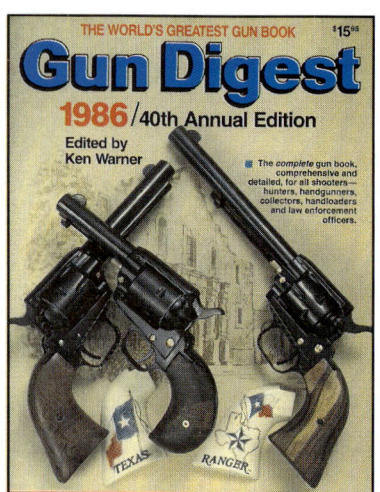

1986 40th Edition

FIE handguns on this front cover includes the neat little "birds-head" gripped, unfluted cylinder, Little Ranger single-action 22-caliber revolver actually designed—he says "styled"—by GUN DIGEST's Ken Warner. On the back cover are three of FIE's imported longarms. FIE, regrettably, went out of business not too many years after these photos were taken. D.A. Tomlinson was awarded the Fourth Annual John T. Amber Literary Award for his 1985 article "John M. Browning: The Man and His Patents." For the first time, full-color pages are scattered throughout the edition. C.E. Harris writes the definitive piece on the U.S. Military's M16A2 223 (5.56x45mm) rifle in "The M16A2: New Standard for Infantry Rifles." Sam Fadala pays homage to the Winchester Model 94 rifle and its 30 WCF cartridge, in "The Model 94 and the 30-30." There are some valuable excerpts from William S. Brophy's epic "The Springfield 1903 Rifles." The discontinuation of the Ruger 44 Magnum Carbine is noted by Layne Simpson as part of his "Rifle Review" and in a "One Good Gun" article, Bob Bell, with "A Good Gun Is a Good Gun," illuminates John Plowman's Remington Model 721 rifle. Price is $15.95.

1987 41st Edition

A prototype of Ruger's long anticipated, much delayed P-85 9mm (9x19mm) semi-automatic, against a "blueprint" background, makes this year's front cover. On the back cover is the "revolutionary in its own right" Ruger GP-100 revolver (a design that will eventually carry to most of Ruger's existing revolvers). There's a full "Testfire" review on the GP-100, where its "First-Born In The New Family" status is discussed. The inside front cover notes the passing of John T. Amber. Ken Warner provides a multi-page eulogy for J.T.A., beginning on page 33. The inside back cover announces C.E. Harris as the Fifth Annual John T. Amber Award winner for his 1986 GD article "The M16A2: New World Standard In Infantry Rifles." The death of James E. Serven is also noted on page 3. The gun writing world, unfortunately, continues to lose some of its best known names. Konrad F. Schreier, Jr.'s "Cal. 50 Super Snipers" reviews the controversial "shoulder-fired" weapons chambered for the 50 BMG (Browning Machine Gun) round. Included is the Barrett Light 50 semi-automatic, weighing-in at some 42 pounds. John Malloy's "Revolvers for the 45 ACP" provides an in-depth look at wheelguns that fire the automatic round. A "One Good Gun" offers two classic reviews: one, by Charlie Smith, entitled "Granny's Colt Is It for Me?" looks at the "snub-nosed" Colt Detective Special revolver in caliber 38 Special; the other, "Browning's T-Bolt I Like," by G.N. Ted Dentay, concerns Browning's "years ahead of its time" T-Bolt, straight-pull 22 LR bolt-action rifle. Price is 16.95.

42nd Edition 1988

Two custom handguns from FIE appear on this edition's covers. The front cover is graced by a deluxe engraved, and scrimshawed ivory stocked, TZ-75 double-action 9mm pistol. On the back appears an Hombre single-action revolver, with a beautiful color casehardened frame and scrimshawed ivory grips. It is hard to believe that a firm capable of such artistry would soon face its "swan song." This year's Sixth Annual John T. Amber Award goes to Wilfrid Ward for his 1987 GD article "The Essence of the Dueller." Inside is a veritable treasure chest of articles for the shooter, hunter, and collector. "My 50 Years With The Colt Woodsman," by Art Bevan, chronicles the history of, arguably, the world's "best trail gun ever built." Eric H. Archer's "Military Shotguns of World War II," provides a never-to-be-equaled look at those fascinating weapons. In "The Lever and Why It Lasted," Robert K. Sherwood describes the great popularity, past and present, of that action type. "Winchester Pump 22s," by William S. Snyder, will bring tears to the eyes of those over 40 years of age. And, "The 375 on Deer," by Paul A. Mathews, makes a case for the 375 H&H Magnum, as an acceptable deer rifle. For the first time in quite a while there is no "One Good Gun" segment. Price remains $16.95, the same as 1987.

1989 43rd Edition

In covers marking the 40th anniversary of Sturm, Ruger, the artistry of James M. Triggs returns. There are two Ruger wheelguns, a new variation of the GP-100 and the all-new, five-shot, SP-101 small-frame. On the back cover is the action portion of the newly updated MKII Model 77 bolt-action rifle, in caliber 223. Eric H. Archer is awarded the John T. Amber Literary Award for his 1988 GD article "Military Shotguns of World War II." The passing of Charles "Skeeter" Skelton is sadly noted on page 3, in the form of a request for financial assistance for his widow. John Malloy's "Early Rivals of the Model 1911 45 Automatic," spells-out the major early competitors of the Colt. Clay Harvey offers "Security Guns," a new review added to this edition. In "My Grandaddy's Shotgun," Charles E. Petty documents a classic Browning Superposed O/U, in 20 gauge. The returning "One Good Gun" section offers several excellent reviews. Price goes up to $17.95.

50 Years

1990 44th Edition

Assorted Browning replicas of classic Winchester firearms adorn both covers of this issue, including two Model 12 20-gauge shotguns (in standard Grade I, and highly decorated Grade V) on the front cover and two lever guns, a "plain-Jane" Model 71 and a deluxe/engraved Model 65 on the back. John Malloy wins the Eighth Annual John T. Amber Literary Award for his 1989 article "Early Rivals of the Model 1911 45 Automatic." Inside, Hoyt Bodinson debunks some of the legends and myths concerning pocket guns, with "The Truth about Derringers." "Colt's 1909 Military Revolver" traces the "stand-in" status of those pieces prior to the official adoption of the M1911 45 ACP semi-auto. Sam Fadala, in "The Takedown Rifle," also points out the portability of such guns. "One Good Gun's" sole entry is an excellent piece by Charlie Smith, entitled, "Second Chance Colt." Not about a "hideaway" gun at all, but the re-acquisition of a former possession! Price goes to $18.95.

45th Edition 1991

Sigarms (SIG-Sauer) semi-automatic pistols are featured on both front and back covers, each a high-capacity 9mm. There's a "full-size" P226 and a down-sized P228. The John T. Amber Literary Award goes to Charles Askins, Jr. for his 1990 GD article "My Old Man Was a Pistol." In "Straight-Pull Rifles: A Brief Overview," Finn Nielsen traces the history of that design. Included are such examples of the ilk as the Swiss Schmidt-Rubin, the Canadian Ross MKIII and America's own Lee-Navy 6mm. "The 44 Caliber Charter," by M.L. McPherson, reviews that fine, five-shot, wheelgun. John V. Miller, Jr.'s "The Mini-Thirty. . . Another 30-Caliber Success," explores Bill Ruger's latest variation of the Mini-14. "One Good Gun" provides C. Rodney James' "My 25 Years With a Winchester 52." After loosing both hands in his youth, James is still able to shoot a Model 52B target rifle—with excellent results. Price remains $18.95, the same as 1990.

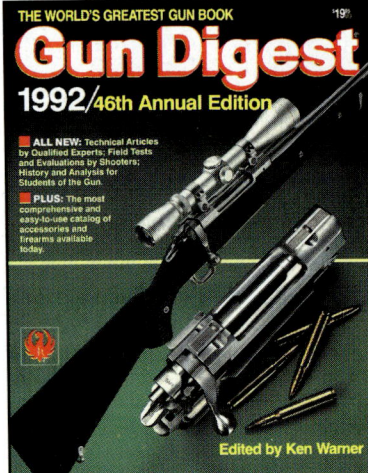

1992 46th Edition

Two versions of Ruger's Model 77 MKII rifles are shown on the front and back covers. Up front is a stainless steel M77 equipped with a black composition stock along with a blow-up of a stainless action. On the back is a wood-stocked left-hand Model 77 MKII in blued carbon steel and a close-up of its action. Wilfrid Ward wins his second John T. Amber Literary Award for "The Weapons of the Mail Coach." "The U.S.-Made Browning That Almost Was," by William G. Fohrman, documents the few TRW/U.S.-made BLR lever actions produced on these shores. In "Thompsons That Never Saw Battle," John Malloy outlines one of the more interesting guns ever to appear in GUN DIGEST, a Thompson submachine gun in caliber 30-06 Springfield! Ken Warner critiques one of the best known artistic contributors ever to grace the pages of the *Digest* in "The Remarkable Career of James M. Triggs." "One Good Gun" offers three selections. Price increases to $19.95.

47th Edition 1993

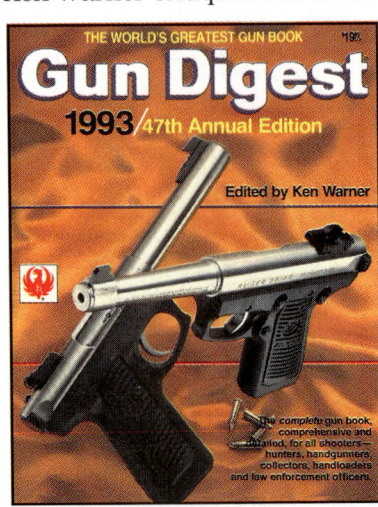

Ruger's injection-molded, Zytel nylon framed 22 semi-automatic is featured on both covers. The new 22/45 has a grip-frame comparable in size to the famed M1911(A1) 45 Automatic. This "best-of-both-worlds" handgun is designed to complement, not replace, other Ruger all-steel versions. For a second time, C.E. Harris wins the John T. Amber Award for his 1992 article "Getting the Best from Your 22 Rimfire." Ken Warner leads off this issue with an excellent suggestion to promote both game conservation and firearms proficiency in "A Modest Proposal." C.E. Harris provides current data on a sometimes overlooked, useful round in "About the 22 Short." David L. Ward makes a case for the often maligned U.S. M1 Carbine in "The 30 Carbine." Charlie Askins makes a "latter-day" appearance in his "Picking Safari Rifles." Three excellent pieces show up in the "One Good Gun" section. Price stays $19.95.

1994 48th Edition

Heckler & Koch's 40 S&W semi-automatic USP pistol is on both covers. H&K, noted as an innovator over its 40-year history, has designed the USP specifically for the American handgun market. Combining many modern technologies, the polymer-framed USP was created from the ground-up for the still-emerging 40 S&W cartridge. A round that gains popularity on an almost daily basis with both U.S. law-enforcement agencies, and U.S. shooters alike. The Twelfth Annual John T. Amber Award goes to John Malloy, his second, for "Blowback Nines." Inside, C.E. Harris makes a case for the 1959 rimfire phenomenon, the 22 Winchester Magnum Rimfire, in "Looking Again at the 22 WMR." It would be hard to dispute the basic premise set forth in the title of Jim Thompson's "The Most Important Rifle Ever Made," which refers to the Mauser Model 1898 bolt-action rifle. In "The Stinger Legacy," C. Rodney James gives credit to the CCI 22 rimfire round that initiated the "hyper-velocity" 22s. Don Zutz's "Shotguns of the Thirties" provides a glimpse of many of that era's classic scatterguns. "One Good Gun" swells to five excellent entries. There are twenty-eight pages of full color plus sixteen pages of full color from Mossberg in celebration of their 75th year. The price jumps to $21.95.

49th Edition 1995

The front and back covers feature differing views of several stainless steel over/under derringers by American Derringer Corporation. Jim Thompson is awarded the Thirteenth Annual John T. Amber Literary Award for his 1994 *GD* article "The Most Important Rifle Ever Made." Articles include a review of non-lever-action 30-30 deer hunting guns entitled "All Those Other 30-30s" by John Malloy. Highlighted are 30 WCF firearms ranging from a plethora of single shots (both old and new), to several bolt actions (including the Winchester Model 54, that firm's first strictly commercial centerfire rifle of this action type), to over/under combinations, to the Savage Model 170 pump (a modification of Savage-Stevens slide-action shotguns). Malloy also contributes "Early Auto Pistol Cartridges." Konrad F. Schreier, Jr. sums up the military usage of older U.S. submachine guns (and the recent adoption of the M-4 5.56x45mm Carbine) in "From Tommy Gun to Grease Gun." Schreier also provides "The 22 Rifles of World War II," recapping various U.S. smallbore rimfire "trainers." In "Elmer Keith—the Man and His Books," Gene Brown details the highly respected (and valuable) works written by, arguably, America's most famous firearms author. On a personal note, yours truly makes his initial GUN DIGEST appearance with "S&W's Massive M&P," the story of Smith & Wesson's Model 58 41 Magnum service revolver. Price remains $21.95.

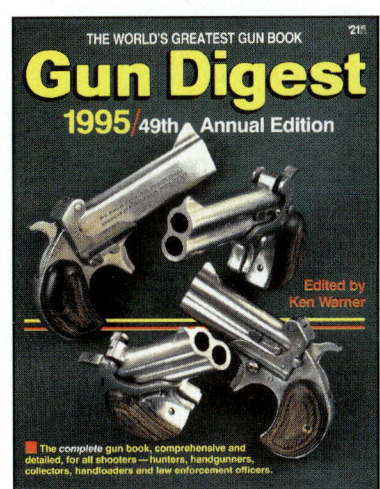

1996 50th Edition

Ruger's newest shotgun, the graceful Woodside, is on this milestone front cover, together with an embossed gold medallion reading "A Tradition of Editorial Excellence—50th Annual Edition." On the back are Ruger's Model 77 and Number One rifles in Safari Grade. John Malloy wins his third John T. Amber Literary Award for "All Those Other 30-30s" in the 49th Edition. On the inside is a cornucopia of classic *Digest* topics: "Olympic Shooting, 1996" by medalist Gary Anderson; "P.O. Ackley's Wildcats" surveyed by Rob Lucas; "Fitz" of Colt by Glen Ruh; and Jim Foral tells of Kentucky pistoleering pre-World War I. There's Schreier on "World War II Sniper Rifles;" Dickson on "Rigby's New 775"; Bruns on the modern Schuetzenfest; Hediger on Martini history; and Henry on the Mannlicher carbine. And even more, including this color review of all 50 covers.

From .416 to .22 LR
WE'VE GOT IT ALL!

- 26 Models
- 290 Variations
- 42 Calibers
- 3 Gauges
- 25 Barrel Lengths
- 19 Stock Variations
- 16 Grip Variations

Pictured at right is a modest sampling of the extensive firearms line manufactured by Sturm, Ruger & Company, Inc.

RUGER®
Arms Makers for Responsible Citizens

THE GUN DIGEST

1944 EDITION

Copyright 1944 by KLEIN'S SPORTING GOODS, 508 South Halsted Street, Chicago 7, Ill. Registered U. S. Pat. Off. All Rights Reserved. Reproduction or use, without express permission, of editorial or pictorial content, in any manner, is prohibited. Printed in U. S. A.

The listing in this book of standard guns and accessories is not, and should not be construed as, an offer to sell such or similar merchandise.

OUR SMALL ARMS AND THEIR MAKERS	4
CHOOSING THE BIG GAME RIFLE	15
HIGH POWER RIFLES	19
FIELD REPAIRS FOR THE BIG GAME HUNTER	23
SMALL GAME AND VARMINT HUNTING	26
.22 CALIBER RIFLES	30
SELECTING AND SHOOTING A TARGET RIFLE	45
MILITARY SMALL ARMS OF WORLD WAR II	55
MILITARY CARTRIDGE DEVELOPMENT	59
UPLAND GUNS AND LOADS	62
HOW TO CALL AND HUNT QUAIL WITHOUT A DOG	66
THE FOWLING PIECE	68
TIPS ON DECOYING	72
FLYWAYS OF NORTH AMERICA	77
SHOTGUNS FOR FIELD AND WATERFOWL SHOOTING	78
TRAP AND SKEET SHOOTING	94
SHOTGUNS—TRAP AND SKEET	98
GUNS WILL LAST A LIFETIME	104
DRESSING AND PREPARING GAME FOR THE TABLE	106
CHOOSING A HANDGUN AND LEARNING TO SHOOT IT	109
PISTOLS AND REVOLVERS	115
BALLISTIC TABLES FOR RIFLE AND REVOLVER AMMUNITION	128
RIFLE SIGHTING TABLES	135
SIGHTS, SCOPES, MOUNTS, BINOCULARS, SPECIAL CHOKES	138
GUN QUESTIONS AND ANSWERS	156

We commemorate the 50th Edition of GUN DIGEST by bringing you 32 pages of selected articles and catalog pages from the very first 1944 Edition of GUN DIGEST for your reading and perusing pleasure.

JACK O'CONNOR
really knows the subject about which he writes. Shot his first quail at 6 years of age, first deer at 12. Author of books and many magazine articles . . . Arms and Ammunition Editor of Outdoor Life.

Choosing the Big Game Rifle

IN A CERTAIN cemetery in British Columbia lie the remains of a hunter who took great pride in going after Canadian grizzly bears with a .22 High Power Savage using a 70-gr. bullet. It was his boast that he had killed 11 of the great predators with that little cartridge and that light bullet. The twelfth grizzly killed him. The .22 High Power isn't a bad woodchuck rifle, but by no means should it be used on grizzlies. Our Canadian hunter paid the price for using the wrong big game rifle, but it was rather a high one. This last year, another Canadian tackled a grizzly with a .30/30—admittedly a good rifle for whitetail deer. He shot the grizzly six times but didn't stop him. The grizzly mauled him and left him for dead. The last I heard he was in a hospital with two broken arms, a broken leg, and half his face gone. If those hunters had wisely chosen their rifles, both would be up and about today.

The whole subject of selecting a big game rifle is complicated by many factors—the skill of the hunter, the size and toughness of the game, the sort of country to be hunted. It is further complicated by the fact that every game animal on this continent has been killed very dead by practically every caliber of rifle. A friend of mine once shot a 1200-pound Alaskan brownie with a .22 long rifle. Another shot a 600-pound grizzly with a .22 Varminter and a 41-gr. bullet.

However, here's one rule the hunter should remember in

choosing his big game rifle: it should be adequately powerful for the largest game he is apt to encounter under the most unfavorable conditions.

A rifle which will kill a deer standing broadside at 50 yards, may only wound one shot in the rear and on the run. Another rifle which is perfectly adequate at 100 yards for use on bighorn sheep may make hitting at 300 impossible.

Most American big game hunting is deer hunting, since it is that fine game animal, the whitetail deer, which has kept big game hunting alive in most states. Consequently, about 75% of all "big game" rifles bought are for use on whitetail deer in the woods of Michigan, Wisconsin, Maine, New York, Pennsylvania and other deer states. The whitetail deer is not a large animal. The average buck the country over will weigh about 130 pounds dressed. Some will run much larger, others much smaller. Furthermore, the whitetail is not particularly tenacious of life. Shots at whitetails are usually short, at from 25 to 100 yards, and usually in heavy brush and timber. Usually the deer is on the move and it is difficult to place shots exactly, and often the bullet has to plow through brush and twigs before it connects.

Let us take a look at what the good whitetail rifle should be like. First, it should be fairly light and should be stocked so that it comes up as fast as a good shotgun. It should be fast to operate and the sights should be quick and sure to use, since the first shot may be a miss and is in the nature of a snap shot. Tens of thousands of bucks have been killed with rifles of the .30/30 class—the .25/35, the .32 Special, the .30 and .32 Remington rimless, the .33 Winchester and the .32/40 high speed, all with bullets weighing from 117 to 170 grains at velocities of around 2200 foot seconds. In the hands of cool, experienced hunters those rifles are perfectly adequate for whitetails, but I am inclined to believe that they are not quite good enough in the hands of the average hunter who goes out about one week a year and who does but little shooting.

Mr. Average Hunter needs either a heavier bullet of larger diameter or a bullet of higher velocity, which in either case gives greater shock power to kill or disable whitetails with the typical poorly placed shots—in the hams, in the guts, and so on. Certain rifles are stand-outs for whitetails, so good that it would be difficult to improve on them. One is the Savage Model 99 in .300 or .250/3000 caliber and in the excellently stocked EG, T, R, or R-S models. Those rifles come up quickly, operate fast, and pack a greater killing punch than those of the .30/30 class. The light, handy 99T (discontinued) equipped with a good hunting scope of about 2½-power or with a good peep sight is just about ideal for hunting whitetails under typical Middle Western or Eastern conditions. Above all, the whitetail hunter should avoid open sights, because when they are used on the quick shots and in the poor light of the fall woods, they almost always cause him to shoot high. It is simply too difficult to draw the bead down fine in that dim notch. Open sights are responsible for that ancient adage: "Always hold low, deer hunter!" With the scope or the peep, this does not hold true.

Other rifles made to order for deer hunting are the Remington pumps and autoloaders for the .35 Remington cartridge, which drives a 200-gr. bullet at 2200 foot seconds. That cartridge, with its big, round-nosed, heavy bullet will plow through a lot of brush and give a severe wound. The pump handles much like any pump-action shotgun and the automatic has much the same feel and balance as an automatic shotgun. Consequently, these rifles are excellent for the man who is mostly a shotgun user and only casually a deer hunter.

The .348 Winchester in the Model 71 is also a fine modern deer rifle with a most excellent modern stock. It packs lots of power, with a 150-gr. bullet at the high velocity of 2880 and a 200-gr. slug at 2520. Either bullet will kill deer almost instantly with almost any solid body hit, and the man who likes the lever action and wants plenty of power surely won't go wrong in selecting the .348.

Cartridges like the .35 Remington and the .348 for deer may sound a bit too powerful to some, but it is better to be overgunned than undergunned. With reasonably well-placed shots, rifles of the .30/30 class do very well for deer; but placing shots under deer hunting conditions is very difficult and the man getting a rifle will be wise to select one of those I have recommended. By no means should rifles of the .22 Hornet, .25/20, and .32/20 class be used. They will kill deer; but they will wound more than they kill and their use is criminal in that it wastes the game!

Conditions in the mountain and plains hunting of the West are very different from those of the East. Whereas a 100-yard shot in the East is a long one, it is an exceedingly short one under most Western hunting conditions. Mule deer, antelope, mountain sheep, Arizona and Mexican whitetail deer, and often elk are hunted in open country, across wide canyons, and on prairies where a shot at from 200 to 300 yards is about average and where much game is killed up to 400 yards by good riflemen with the proper equipment.

Such hunting calls for the utmost in accuracy and in long range killing power. Because of the superior ballistics of the cartridges made for them, good bolt-action rifles are in order and telescope sights are most satisfactory. The plains and mountain rifle will weigh somewhat more than the woods rifle and it will be slower to operate. It will be, however, more accurate; it will have a flatter trajectory, and it will carry more killing power at the longer ranges.

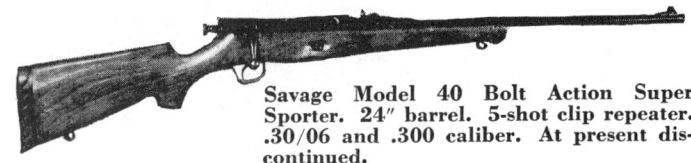

Savage Model 40 Bolt Action Super Sporter. 24″ barrel. 5-shot clip repeater. .30/06 and .300 caliber. At present discontinued.

A rifle for the mountains ought to have a velocity of at least 2700 foot seconds and ideally it should have 3,000 foot seconds or more, since high velocity means flat trajectory and good killing power at long range. The famous .30/06 is the most widely used mountain rifle. The factories all load a 150-grain bullet at a velocity of 2,960, a 180-grain at 2,720, and a 220-grain at 2410. In addition Remington loads a 110-grain bullet at about 3350; but this last loses its velocity so fast that it is not to be chosen for anything except varmints like woodchucks and coyotes. For deer, sheep, and antelope, the 150-gr. bullet has always struck me as being the best. All forms are good—the Western open point, the Winchester pointed expanding, the Remington bronze point. With the 150-gr., a .30/06 can be sighted in for 250 yards with a trajectory that will give hits with a dead-on hold anywhere up to around 300 yards.

For country where elk or big bear are apt to be encountered, the 180-gr. bullet in its various forms should be chosen, as that bullet does well on anything from deer to moose. The trajectory is not quite so flat as that of the 150-grain, and with it the rifle should be sighted in to strike the point of aim at 200 yards, or 3 inches high at 100.

One of the finest of all mountain cartridges is the .270 W.C.F., which has made a great name for itself in the past 20 years and which has killed all North American game, even large grizzlies. The load that made the reputation of the .270 is the 130-grain bullet at a velocity of 3,140, as loaded by all the major cartridge companies, by Winchester in pointed expanding form, by Western

Above is the author with a big Alberta grizzly bear which he shot with a .30-06, 200 gr. bullet. The great grizzly is one of the world's most dangerous game animals, hard to stop unless the bullet is well placed.

At left, a good mountain caribou shot by O'Connor in British Columbia. The animal was killed in its tracks with one shot, at long range, from a scope sighted .270 rifle.

in an open-point boattail, and by Remington in the Core-lokt. With either the 130-grain or the lighter, faster 100-grain bullet at the tremendous velocity of 3,540, a .270 can be sighted in to hit the point of aim at 300 yards and will give a practical point blank trajectory which will assure hits with a dead-on hold up to 350 yards, the flattest trajectory given by any commercial cartridge. The 100-grain bullet will kill mule and whitetail deer, sheep and antelope as if struck by bombs with almost any solid body hit; but the 130-grain kills just as well and should be used by preference, since its greater weight and sectional density gives better penetration on larger animals like moose, elk, and bear. Rifles in .30/06 and .270 caliber were available before the war from Winchester in the Model 70, from Remington in the Model 720, and from the firm of R. F. Sedgley of Philadelphia on remodeled Springfield actions with commercial barrels. In addition, many hundreds of custom rifles were made up on Springfield, Mauser, or Model 1917 actions by various custom makers. The .30/06 was available from Savage in the Model 40 (illustrated, page 16) and Model 45 (both discontinued) bolt action rifles, which are not of the Mauser type, and until a few years ago were made up in the lever-action Model 95 by Winchester.

The .300 H. and H. Magnum cartridge as adapted to the Model 70 Winchester is also a very fine mountain cartridge, particularly for the heavier game at the longer-ranges—moose, elk, and grizzly, which are often shot in big open basins near or above timberline. The .300 H. and H. really carries a lot of authority, since it uses a 180-grain bullet at 2930 foot seconds and a 220-grain at 2610. It is unnecessarily powerful for sheep and mule deer, but is an excellent killer on the larger game. For the man who does not mind the rather heavy recoil and wants more power than the .30/06 gives, here's the cartridge.

Another very good mountain cartridge is the 7 mm. as loaded in this country. Rifles are furnished by Winchester and by Sedgley as well as by custom makers. The 139-gr. bullet as loaded by Western to 2,900 gives a flat trajectory and good killing power, as does the 150-grain bullet loaded by Winchester to 2750. The 175-grain bullet at 2,460 will do just about anything that the 220-grain in the .30/06 will do and has killed plenty of elk, moose, and grizzlies.

Still other good mountain cartridges which do not have quite the range and power of the ones already mentioned are the .257 Roberts with the 100-grain bullet at 2,900 foot seconds or the 117-grain at 2630; the .30/40 Krag with the 180-grain at 2480, the 250/3000 with the 100-grain bullet at 2,810; the .300 Savage with the 150-grain bullet at 2,660 or the 180-grain at 2,380. The .348 with either the 150 or 200 grain bullet also does very well, although neither of those bullets is well shaped to retain velocity at long range.

By all means, the rifle for long range shooting should have a good hunting scope mounted as low as possible. The Model 30 (disc.) and 720 Remingtons and the U. S. 1917's and the

Mod. 70 Winchester lend themselves admirably to scope mounting. Mausers and Springfields can be adapted to scope mounting by an alteration of the bolt handle and safety. Most modern hunting scopes with long eye-relief, like the 330 Weaver, the Lyman Alaskan, or the Noske 2½-x can be mounted ahead of the safety of Springfields and Mausers so that only a bolt-alteration is necessary.

For all around use in forests as well as in mountains, a scope of about 2½ power is about right. For mountain use alone on a rifle with recoil no greater than that of a .30/06, a 4-x scope like the Weaver 440 or the German Zeiss Zeiliver is very satisfactory, since the greater magnification makes hits at long range somewhat easier. Good mounts are the Redfield, the Pachmayr, the Stith, or the Griffith and Howe.

The Model 99 Savages lend themselves to scope mounting because they have solid tops and eject to the side. Scopes are difficult to mount on top-ejecting Winchesters like the Mod. 71, but M. L. Stith makes an offset mount for the man who wants a Winchester lever action and also must have a scope.

It is not within the scope of this article to discuss varmint rifles for use on woodchucks, marmots, coyotes and such game (see "Small Game and Varmint Hunting" by C. S. Landis), but almost any of the rifles discussed here have the accuracy and the flatness of trajectory for this interesting form of shooting. Indeed, the .270 with the 100-grain bullet is just about the finest long-range varmint rifle made and the good .257 is just about on a par with it. The .30/06 with the 150 and the 110 grain bullets is also close to the top and one of the most widely used varmint rifles made.

As a matter of fact, these rifles are really all-around rifles and will kill deer like lightning. The .300 H. and H. Magnum cartridge was surely not designed with Pennsylvania whitetail deer in mind. The power is excessive for animals the size of deer and the recoil is rather severe. However, the man who hits a whitetail with a .300 Magnum slug is going to have himself a whitetail, whereas the man with the .30/30 may not. Anyone who wants an all-around rifle, one that may be used on deer in Pennsylvania, Texas, or Michigan, on elk and antelope in Wyoming, and on sheep, moose, and grizzlies in Canada should by all means select a rifle from the list above, preferably a bolt-action, scope-sighted rifle with a good shooting gunsling in .270, .30/06, 7 mm., or .300 caliber.

The man planning to hunt in the Canadian Rockies should carry a powerful rifle. Caribou are large animals. Moose are even larger. Grizzly bears are not only large but dangerous. The 7 mm. is about the smallest rifle that should be taken into the Rockies. The .30/06 and the .300 are excellent and the .270 does very well with well-placed shots.

For hunting large animals in thick timber, the most satisfactory cartridges are those which drive heavy bullets with good sectional density at velocities between 2,000 and 2,500 feet. Over much of their range moose are shot in very thick timber and so are elk. Grizzlies are sometimes encountered in the woods while the hunter is after moose. The typical shot under these conditions is at the rear end of a rapidly vanishing animal weighing close to a half ton, sometimes more, and the bullet has to drive clear through heavy muscles into the vitals.

For such work, the .348 Winchester with the 250 grain Silvertip bullet is excellent; so is the .30/06 with the 220-grain, the 7 mm. with the 175-grain, the .270 with the 150-grain soft point, the .35 Remington with the 200-grain. Rifles of the .30/30 class are by no means heavy enough and their use is to be discouraged since it results in many wounded animals escaping. Some of the older cartridges can hardly be improved upon. The old Model 95 Winchester chambered for either .35 W.C.F. cartridge with its 250-grain bullet at 2,160 or the .405 with its 300-grain bullet at 2,220 is just about what the doctor ordered for game under these conditions. Some of the older black-powder cartridges like the .45/70 with its 405-grain bullet at 1,310 are also very satisfactory, if used at short range.

So far I have not mentioned the real "power house" of American cartridges—the great .375 Magnum, for which the Model 70 Winchester rifle is chambered and for which custom gun makers like Neidner and Griffin and Howe have built rifles. This big rifle is one of the most useful cartridges in the world. It kicks like a mule but its accuracy is good and its power is surpassed only by the big British and European cartridges for heavy Magnum bolt-action and double rifles.

Actually, the .375 is a very good sheep rifle when it is used with the big 235-grain bullet at the high velocity of 2860 foot seconds, but with either the 270-grain bullet at 2720 or the 300-grain bullet at 2,540, the .375 is practically perfect life insurance against an indignant grizzly; it is also tops for one shot kills on moose, elk, or other large animals in timber. The British have long considered it the very finest all-around caliber in existence and use it on everything from sheep on the mountainous Indian frontier and large antelope in Africa to very dangerous African lions, buffalo and tigers.

Where the .375 really shines in North America is on our largest and most dangerous game animal, the Alaskan brown bear, the largest predator on earth and one that will often weigh 1,500 pounds or more. Brownies are shot in thick willows, along streams, and generally at close range. The man who hunts them should have a powerful rifle that will knock the big beasts down and keep them down, and the .375 seems to be the business! Anything lighter than the .30/06 with the 220 or 225-grain bullets should not be used on the big bears, and the .375 is undoubtedly better.

The man with a rifle especially selected for the game he is to hunt, under the conditions in which he is to hunt, has a definite advantage. To me it seems the height of foolishness for a man to spend several hundred dollars on a sheep hunt and carry an open sighted rifle with inadequate power and curved trajectory. It is downright reckless to tackle dangerous game like brown bears and grizzles with a rifle that packs insufficient power. After all, the cost of a rifle over the years is but a very small part of the cost of the various hunting trips on which it is to be taken, and the best rifle with the best ammunition is an investment in success.

Let me say, too, that the best rifle in the world will not assure success unless it is properly sighted in for the correct distance and unless the owner has learned to shoot it. A .270 sighted in for 50 yards, or not sighted in at all, in the hands of a poor shot won't get any antelope, and a bullet from a .375 Magnum in the guts of an Alaskan brown bear won't stop him as well as one from a .257 in the lungs. The proper rifle is important, surely, but the man behind the rifle is also important. Still, a good rifle, with the proper cartridge, with the proper sighting equipment and correctly sighted in, is a good part of the story, and if the man who owns it will only learn to shoot, he will usually come home with his game!

MARLIN LEVER ACTION HIGH POWER RIFLES

MODEL 36-A CARBINE.
(Top Illustration)

Modern successor to well-known, earlier lever action, high power repeating rifles made so long and well by the original Marlin company. Full magazine holds 7 cartridges, either .30-30 or .32 Special calibers. 20" round, tapered barrel of special smokeless, proof tested steel. Crowned muzzle, Ballard type rifling. Solid top receiver, side ejection, visible hammer. American walnut full pistol grip stock, semi-beavertail forearm. Unbreakable coiled main and trigger springs. Silver bead front, flat top Rocky Mountain rear sights. Drilled, tapped for tang peep sight. Length overall, 38". Wt. about 6½ lbs.

MODEL 36 SPORTING CARBINE.
(2nd Illustration)

Non-glare ramp front sight with silver bead, detachable hood. Two-thirds magazine holds 6 shots. Wt. about 6¼ lbs. Otherwise same as the 36 Carbine.

MODEL 36-A RIFLE.
(3rd Illustration)

24" barrel, non-glare ramp front sight with silver bead, detachable hood. 42" length; wt. about 6¼ lbs. Two-thirds magazine, 6-shots. Otherwise same as 36 Carbine.

MODEL 36-A DL.
(Bottom Illustration)

Same as Model 36-A but with hand-checkered grip and forearm, pistol grip cap, detachable swivels and 1" leather slip strap.

SAVAGE MODEL 99-EG SOLID FRAME, LEVER ACTION, HIGH POWER REPEATERS
(Top Illustration)

Introduced in 1899 in .303 Savage Cal. Action is the same today except for minor improvements. Has 24" tapered, medium weight round barrel. Proof tested. Matted trigger. Rotary box type magazine with numeral indicator. Capacity 5 cartridges plus one in chamber. Light weight, capped, full pistol grip stock and tapered fore-end of selected walnut. Rubbed oil finish, checkered grip and fore-end. Corrugated steel butt plate of shotgun design. Stock dimensions 13" x 1⅞" x 2⅝". Butt plate 1½" x 4⅞". Adjustable semi-buckhorn sporting rear sight and white metal bead front sight on raised ramp base. Case hardened lever. Polished breech bolt. Blued receiver. Receiver tang tapped and drilled for all standard aperture sights. Weight about 7¼ lbs. Calibers: .250/3000 for deer, mountain sheep and goat, etc.; .300 Savage for Alaskan Bear, moose, elk, etc.

SAVAGE MODEL 99-R
[Lower Illustration]

Same as Model 99-EG except larger stock. Dimensions 13½" x 1⅝" x 2⅞", butt plate 1⅜" x 5⅛". Also special large fore-end. Weight about 7½ lbs. Caliber: .300 Savage.

SAVAGE MODEL 99-RS

Same specifications as Model 99-R with following refinements: Redfield No. 70 windage and elevation adjustment rear peep sight and gold bead front sight; ⅞" leather sling strap with quick release swivels and screw studs.

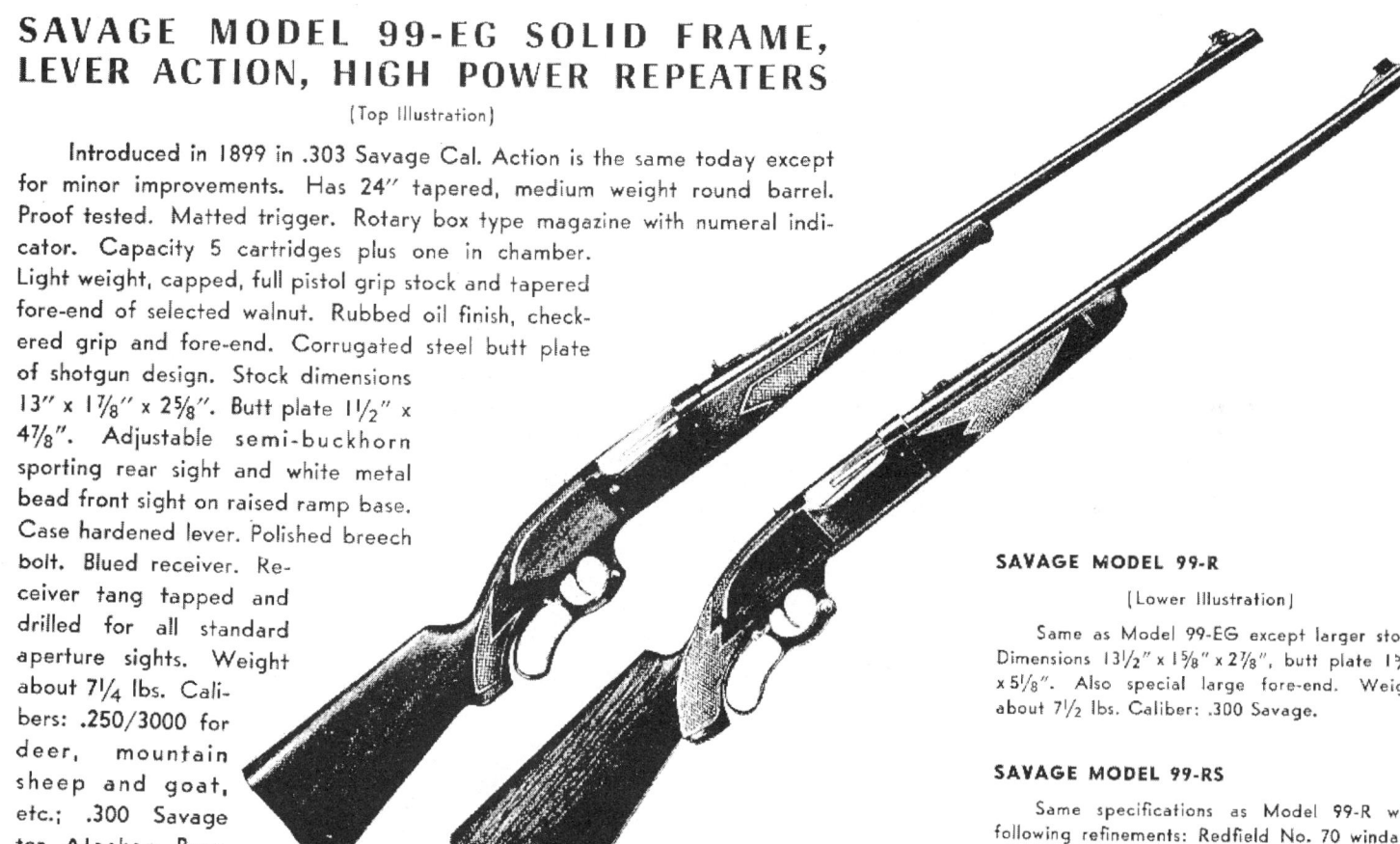

REMINGTON "WOODSMASTER" MODEL 81

The successor (in 1937) to the Model 8 designed by John M. Browning and one of the first successful Autoloaders on the market (1906). The only high power auto-loading rifle that locks the cartridge in the chamber until after the bullet has left the muzzle. No loss of power. Delivers full energy of the cartridge. Takedown. Hammerless. Solid breech. .300 Sav., .30, .32, or .35 Rem. caliber. Center fire and rimless. 22" barrel. Step adjustable rear sight. White metal bead front sight. Magazine holds five cartridges. Positive thumb operated safety. Sporting style stock of American walnut. Semi-beavertail fore-end. Half pistol grip. Shotgun style steel butt plate, checkered. Length over-all, 41½"; taken down, 23". Weight, about 8½ lbs.

REMINGTON "GAMEMASTER" MODEL 141

Only high power rifle manufactured with slide action. Suitable for all North American big game. Replaced the Remington Model 14 in 1937. Take-down. Hammerless. Solid breech. .30, .32, .35 Rem. caliber. Center fire and rimless. 24" barrel. Step adjustable rear sight. White metal bead front sight mounted on non-glare ramp. Magazine holds five cartridges with one in chamber. Cross bolt safety. Sporting stock, semi-beavertail fore-end. American walnut on standard grade rifle. Half pistol grip. Shotgun style steel butt plate, checkered. Length over-all, 42¾"; taken down, 29½". Weight, about 7¾ lbs. Standard grade, also Carbine (18½" barrel, .32 cal. only). Other grades with fancy stocks and engraving.

REMINGTON MODEL 720 BOLT ACTION

Round, tapered barrel of ordnance steel in 24", 22" or 20" lengths. Sporting stock of genuine American walnut. Properly shaped pistol grip. Long, full, well-rounded fore-end of semi-beavertail type. Fine checkering on grip and fore-end. Shotgun style steel butt plate, checkered. Swivel loops for ⅞" sling strap-loops easily removed, leaving wide screw eyes for quick release swivels. Rifle cocks on opening movement of bolt. Top of receiver matted. Short, single trigger pull—option of double military pull. Side-placed thumb operated safety. Magazine holds five cartridges. Detachable magazine bottom. Double locking lugs at front end of bolt, special bolt stop. For .30 Spfld. '06, .270 Win. or .257 Rem.—Roberts calibers, center fire. Solid frame. Introduced in 1941.

WINCHESTER MODEL 07 REPEATER

A 6-shot, self-loading repeater specially adapted to law enforcement service. Trigger lock. Walnut stock of semi-military style, steel butt plate, pistol grip. U-shaped walnut forearm. 20" round barrel. Either bead or blade front sights with open sporting rear. Former with 5-cartridge magazine. Blade front sight rifle has 10-shot magazine. Take-down only. Wt. approx. 7¾ lbs. Chambered only for .351 Win. Self-Loading center fire cartridges. In 1907, this automatic rifle was brought out as a more powerful version of the Model 1905, which in turn had been based on the Model 1903, the first really successful .22 automatic. In 1935, the gun was adapted to its present form.

SAVAGE MODEL 23-D BOLT ACTION

25" barrel. 6-shot; five in clip magazine plus one in chamber. Recessed bolt head. Convenient safety. Polished bolt. Weight about 6½ lbs. Recommended for those who wish to increase the range at which they can effectively hunt small game and vermin. The full pistol grip stock and forestock is of one-piece, genuine American walnut with fine cut checkering and rubbed oil finish. Dimensions 13½" x 1⅝" x 2¾". Corrugated steel butt plate of shotgun design. Fitted with ⅞" sling loops. Caliber: .22 Hornet. First made in 1923.

SAVAGE MODEL 23-C. Same as Model 23-D except 5 shot; four in magazine plus one in chamber. Caliber: .32/20.

Field Repairs for the Big Game Hunter

CLYDE BAKER

Through the courtesy of Sports Afield, this article, by an author considered to have written "the best material on gunsmithing ever to appear in the English language," is reprinted from the "Hunting Annual."

IN STARTING out, remember this: *you're going where things cannot be bought.* More, you're going where even personal service cannot be bought. If anything untoward happens to your outfit, you'll fix it yourself, or end the trip then and there. So it behooves you to take along a little something to work with.

For the average trip into big game country I would suggest the following, which I realize is more, by far, than the average trip requires; but I've had to take into consideration the possibility of boat repairs, boot repairs, AND gun repairs.

- 1 10-inch half round bastard file of best make.
- 4 6¼-inch die sinkers, needle files as follows: round, three-square, square, and equaling. See Figure 1.
- 1 good quality hatchet or hunter's belt axe.
- 1 small ball-peine hammer with nested screwdrivers in handle—from the "five and ten." They're all right, and very useful.
- 1 husky, "stubby" screwdriver—with blade ground to exact width and thickness to fit tang and guard screws on your rifle. Fig. 3.
- 1 or more smaller screwdrivers—best quality—to fit other screws on rifle. (An assortment of small screwdriver blades, with tangs filed 3-square for holding in chuck of pin-vise, will prove extremely useful—but you'll have to make them yourself. File them from round drill-rod, to shapes and sizes needed. Heat to cherry red and quench in water to harden. Polish, then draw temper in gas flame to purple color, and quench in linseed oil. "Y'got something there!")
- 1 assorted lot of drift punches, to fit all pins in sights or other gun parts. Fig. 3.
- 1 parallel-jaw hand-vise, and 1 pin-vise (preferably the larger type shown in Fig. 4, with a few heavy darning needles, small drills, etc., for use in pin-vise.)
- 1 pair 6-inch slip-joint pliers with wire cutting jaws. Fig. 5.
- 1 No. 29 Combination Pike India coarse-fine oilstone. Fig. 6.
- 1 ½-inch copper rod, 6 inches long, ground to blunt point. Fig. 7.
- 1 ½-pound spool acid-core wire solder.
- 1 ½-pound roll common iron stove-pipe wire.
- 1 ¼-pound roll No. 24 or No. 26 enameled copper radio coil wire, for fishing rod and other repairs.
- 1 square foot heavy calfskin (dry, not oil tanned) for boot repair.
- 1 4-oz. can cold patching rubber cement.
- 1 piece, ½ square foot semi-vulcanized tire patching rubber.
- 2 large tubes pyroxylin cement.
- 1 4-ounce can waterproof casein glue.
- 2 square feet heavy canvas, for canoe repairs.
- 1 small can best marine canoe glue.
- ½ dozen best rawhide boot laces, longest available.
-    Several long, narrow strips thin vellum rawhide, obtainable at artificial limb factories.

This all sounds like a lot of freight; actually, you can shove it all into a hunting coat pocket, or make it up into a compact bundle not more than a foot long by four or five inches in thickness.

SPARE PARTS for your guns will be dictated by the armament you carry. A spare extractor, and spare firing pin or striker for *any* type or make of arm, is always advisable; also spare screws for peep sights, as they do work out now and then. If your front sight is of the "quick change" variety, carry an extra one or two, and perhaps a spare elevation slide, complete, for your Lyman 48 or other receiver sight—they do get wrecked now and then!

Look this outfit over, study its possibilities, and take along what your conscience dictates . . . while praying that you'll never need it! But, if accidents should happen, proceed as follows:

FRONT SIGHT BEAD BROKEN OFF. Hold your piece of copper rod (Fig. 7) in a split sapling, heat it plenty hot in campfire; hold it against sight blade till it will melt off a drop of the acid-core wire solder which will stick to end of blade. With pocket knife and file, shape up the new "silver" bead as desired, and rub your thumb over it occasionally to keep it bright.

FRONT SIGHT LOOSENING IN BARREL SLOT. Remove sight, and with small hammer tap edges of barrel slot to make it tight. Drive in sight with copper rod; set smallest drift punch near each end and hit it a goodly wallop with hammer, to hold sight in place. Sight in by shooting at first opportunity.

RECEIVER SIGHT ELEVATION SLIDE DAMAGED. Replace with new one; if none available, curse, and take first train home. If attachment screws work loose, remove them one at a time, hold in pliers, heat nearly red hot, and replace quickly. If receiver sight is irreparably damaged, remove, and use folding leaf sight on barrel.

DAMAGED SCOPE, OR LOOSENED SCOPE MOUNT. Remove scope, and use receiver sight or folding leaf barrel sight. You can't hope to repair a scope or mount in the woods!

SHELL STUCK IN CHAMBER. Not likely to happen. If it should, pour in a bit of "Hoppe's" at breech. Let stand 10 minutes, then pour in some more from muzzle, and let stand 15 or 20 minutes. Insert one-piece steel cleaning rod from muzzle (you should never use any other kind, in the woods or anywhere else), and tap gently with hammer. If shell doesn't move, tap harder. If it still doesn't move, try the axe. If no success, remove barrel from stock, heat chamber portion over fire, and try again. Failing this, pack up, go home, and see your gunsmith.

RAG STUCK IN BARREL. I was once called in to diagnose a case of constipation in a pair of barrels belonging to a Browning Over and Under. It took but a moment to identify a severe case of acute ragitis, resulting from an over-zealous attempt to "protect" the bores by stuffing them with several yards of bed-sheet anointed with "3-in-1" or some equally volatile oil. I soaked the works with some penetrating oil for a day; then did a "high forceps" delivery with an old-fashioned muzzle-loading "worm" on a rod, yanking out the worst of the mess. The "oil" had evaporated in a few weeks, permitting the sheeting to absorb atmospheric moisture and rust tightly to barrel walls—and you've no idea what a splendid adhesive a good coat of ferric oxide is, when properly placed! The bore was left so badly pitted that only a

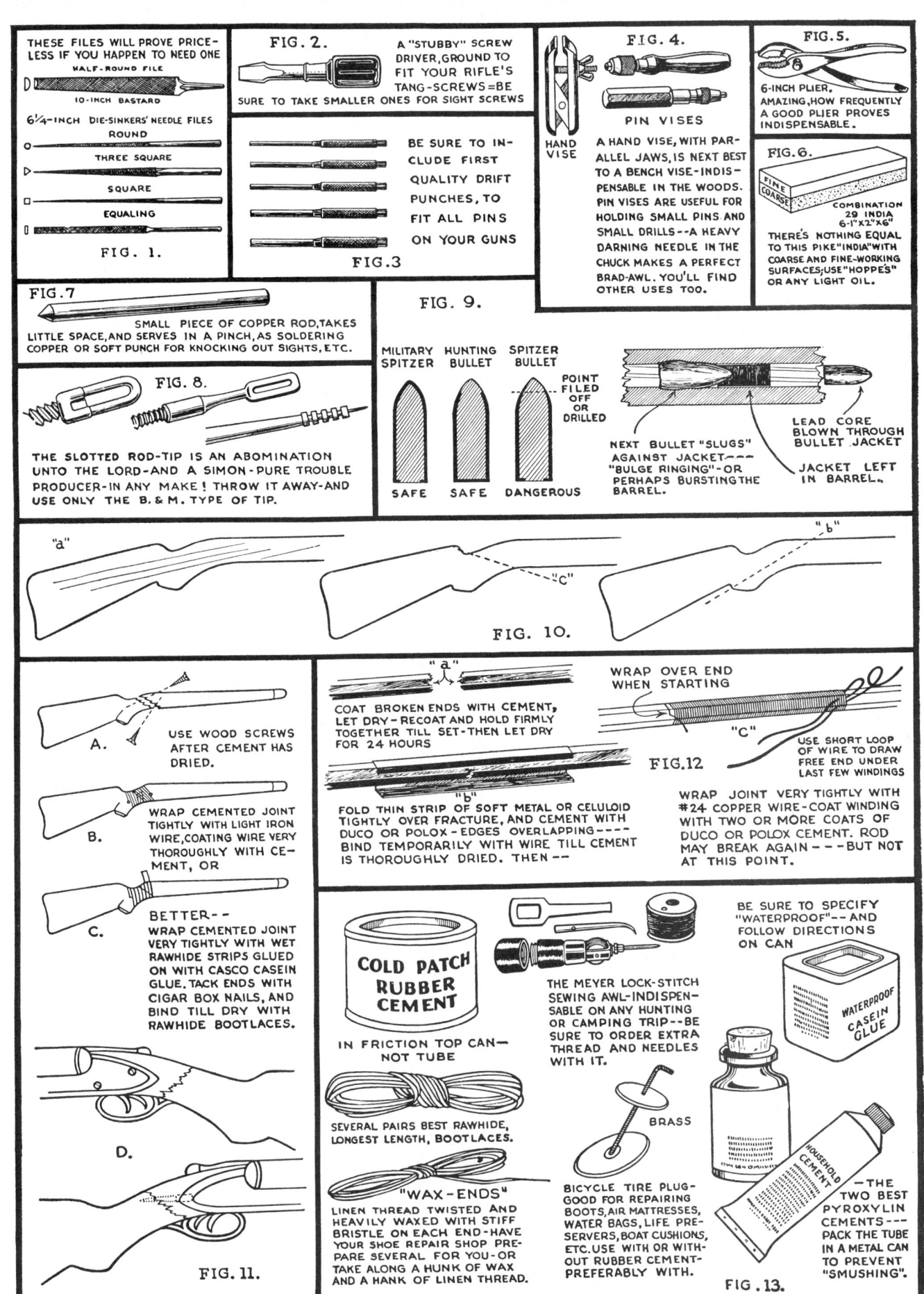

reboring job eventually left the barrels in a condition to be disposed of by the owner to an unsuspecting victim!

No self-respecting rag is likely to get bore-stuck, afield, or elsewhere; and if it does, it will most likely happen thisaway:

A long, gangling cleaning patch, threaded through a slotted tip, Fig. 8, pushed *part way* through a barrel, and then, a futile attempt to draw it back, doubling up and wedging said patch tighter than a Scottish banker during election year. If not that, then one of those bloomin', bloody English tips, where you wind the patch around 'em like a shroud, and hope for the best—but never get it.

However it occurs, first unscrew the main portion of rod from tip, and remove it, if possible. Then pour some Hoppe's No. 9, some Schaeller Ris-Lon, some C & J Motor Conditioner, or other highly penetrating oil, into the barrel *from both ends*. Let 'er soak, as long as you can stand the strain; then, insert your one-piece rod until it reaches obstruction; heat gently over fire, tapping rod at intervals, until everything starts moving along. When it does start, don't brag—just give thanks, and keep tapping.

"Slugged" Bullet Jacket in Barrel, Fig. 9. This will never happen unless you're fool enough to file or drill the points of military spitzer bullets, trying to make "dum-dums" out of them; if it does happen in this way, you'll get hurt, and deserve it. Spitzer point bullets have the jacket covering the point, but not the base; soft-point, open-point, or hollow-point bullets have the jacket covering the base *but not the point*. File or drill the points of the former, and you make, in effect, an open-end cylinder of the jacket, through which the lead core can, and most likely will, blow at the first shot, leaving said jacket somewhere in the bar'l! Usual result—next shot—bullet hits jacket—pressures build up—bar'l BLOWS UP—and your bloomin' head needs repairs . . . if you live through the ordeal. Generally, you don't.

Remedy: *NONE WHATEVER!*

Preventive: Keep your barrel always clean, bright, and free of rust and dirt, and never use your rifle for a walking-stick. Use all the cheap military ammunition, with spitzer bullets, you wish, *for practice only*; but in the hunting field, use ONLY the best hunting ammunition, with factory-made hunting bullets recommended by the manufacturers for the type of game you are seeking. Use only a steel cleaning rod (preferably a one-piece one) with a jagged tip with patch-retaining-pin, and square or round patches of the correct size for your bore; and NEVER start out, even for a few minutes, without first carefully inspecting the bore, to make SURE that all is clear, with no skeletons in the closet.

Broken Rifle Stock. If the wood has been properly selected, and the work properly done, the grain will run as shown in "a", Fig. 10, and your stock can't be broken by anything short of using it to drive fence posts with. But the exception proves the rule . . . and sometimes it will break—the long way of the grain—as in "b", Fig. 10, but, far more often, as in "c", Fig. 10.

If either of these breaks should occur, proceed as follows:

First, remove barrel and receiver, magazine and guard—in short, strip the stock. Remove any loose splinters—but save them, for the moment. Coat both broken surfaces with Polox or Duco Cement, rub in with finger tip, and let dry 30 minutes. Recoat with cement, and bring the broken parts accurately together, with firm, but not heavy pressure—just about what you can comfortably hold for 10 minutes or so with your fingers. *Heavy clamp pressure is useless, and defeats the purpose, of the pyroxylin cements.* Hold the parts gently, but steadily, and the cement, when set, will be stronger than the original wood. Let dry at least 12 hours . . . and 24 hours is better, no matter how firm the joint appears. (A-Fig. 11.)

After 12 hours, however, you may, if you wish, add two or three long brads, or slender wood screws, strategically placed. A typewriter ribbon box of assorted brads and wood screws, though not included in the "essentials" will never come amiss on a hunting trip. Better wrap the entire broken portion with a light iron stove-pipe wire (B, Fig. 11) fastening both ends with a small screw carefully sunk into the wood. Better still, wrap the broken grip (after glue is thoroughly dried) with thin strips of rawhide, well soaked and stretched in winding (C, Fig. 11). Fasten end with several small brads or 3/8" cigar-box nails after gluing it for a distance of at least three inches—then wind the whole assembly temporarily with rawhide boot laces until wrappings are dry and thoroughly shrunk,—then the laces may be removed and saved for other uses, of which you'll find many.

Casco Waterproof Casein Glue is excellent for cementing rawhide strips; and equally good for making the wood-joint if you don't want to pack two kinds of cement. The Casco, however, may be given a bit more pressure, by winding the joint immediately with light wire or heavy twine. If you use a wire winding over the cemented repair, it's a good idea to coat the wire thoroughly, two or three times, with the pyroxylin cement, forming the whole into a compact unit. Though looking like something the cat dragged in, it'll stay with you to the end of the trip—and then some!

If you use rawhide strips for wrapping, you can't go wrong by coating the whole business with Casco, or other good glue or cement, as you wrap it on. But at all events, be sure to glue or cement the last few inches of the wrapping, and fasten the end as before explained. There are many more artistic ways of repairing broken stocks, if a shop were available—but remember, we're now in the tall uncut, and must act accordingly!

D, Fig. 11, shows a method once used for permanently repairing a very bad break in a double sidelock shotgun stock, using a long brass screw set in through the action mortice, as shown, after cementing the break. A similar repair would, of course, be applicable to any double rifle, particularly if afterward wound with wire or rawhide as previously described. This same idea of screw location might, in some instances, be applied to a bolt action rifle stock, by introducing the screw through the magazine mortice.

Boat Repairs usually result from "snagging", and need only a neat patch with heavy canvas and marine canoe glue, used according to instructions on the can. A broken or smashed rib needing replacement can usually be fixed up from materials at hand, with Casco Waterproof Casein Glue as first choice for the woodwork.

When a canoe is an essential part of the equipment, a goodly handful of copper canoe nails would seem an essential part of the repair kit.

Boots, Shoes, Slings, Gun Cases, and other articles of leather and rubber, are best handled by means of patches attached by rubber cement. But remember, this will not hold well on the oil-soaked leather of hunting boots. Use the cement for temporary holding, but stitch it along the edges, either with an inexpensive sewing awl and a "wax-end" (which any shoe repair shop will prepare for you) or with a "lock-stitch sewing awl" which you may purchase complete from the mail order houses for less than a dollar. The latter is excellent for holding down a ripped sole, also.

Incidentally, the brass repair plugs, made for bicycle tires, with a thin brass outer nut screwing down tightly on the outside, are hard to beat on all rubber boots and waders, and just about the *only thing* that will get the job done on oiled leather boots. Two or three of these in the kit wouldn't take up any room, to speak of, and might save a lot of grief.

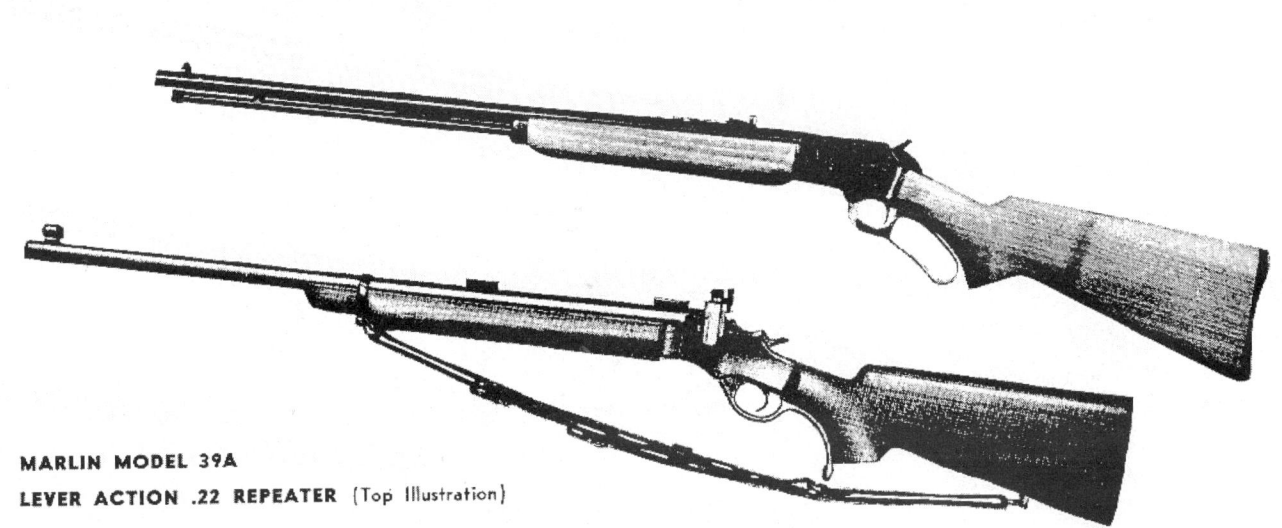

MARLIN MODEL 39A
LEVER ACTION .22 REPEATER (Top Illustration)

The modern version (about 1921) of the earlier, well-known Model 1897; the only lever action .22 caliber repeating rifle on the market. Take down style, exposing all working parts by the turning of a single hand screw. 24" semi-heavy, round-tapered, blued steel barrel with Ballard type rifling and crowned muzzle. The full magazine holds 25 Short, 20 Long or 18 Long Rifle cartridges, regular or high speed, without adjustment. Side ejection, visible hammer. Solid top, case-hardened receiver. Silver bead front sight, flat top Rocky Mountain rear sight, drilled and tapped for tang peep sight. Low sighting plane for telescope mounting. Full pistol grip, black walnut stock with semi-beavertail forearm; butt plate. Length overall, 41"; wt. about 6½ lbs.

STEVENS NO. 417 WALNUT HILL TARGET RIFLE. (Bottom Illustration)

Introduced in 1932. 28" heavy barrel, chambered for .22 Long Rifle, regular or high speed. Lever action. Stevens "Ideal" breech block. Short, fast hammer fall. Automatic ejector. American walnut, full pistol grip, target model, oil finished stock with high comb. Shotgun style butt, checkered steel butt plate. Broad fore-end. Fitted with military style 1¼" leather sling strap. Lyman No. 17A front sight. Telescope sight blocks. Weight about 10½ lbs. Length overall, 44". Loop style operating lever optional. Fitted with Lyman rear sights as follows: No. 417-0 with No. 52L sight. No. 417-1 with No. 48L sight. No. 417-2 with No. 144 sight. No. 417-3 without front or rear sights.

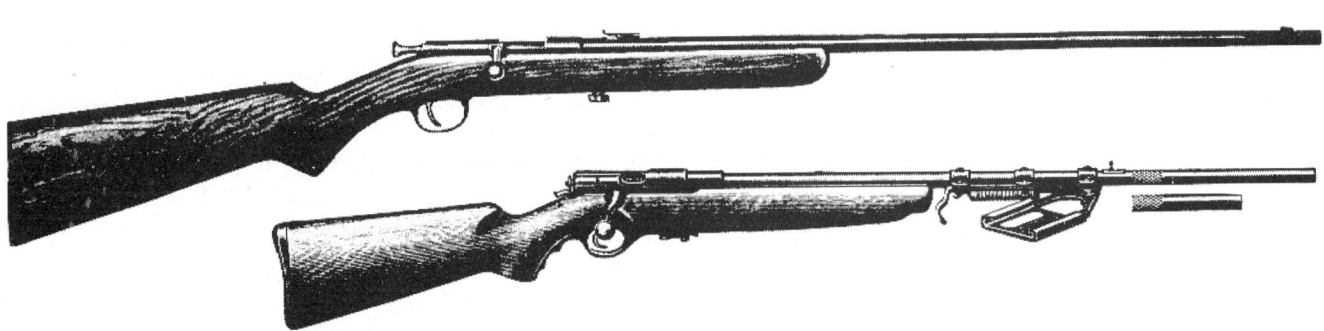

IVER JOHNSON MODEL 2-X SINGLE SHOT RIFLE. (Top Illustration)

Chambered for .22 regular and high velocity Long Rifle; also for .22 Long and Short. 24" round tapered barrel with Patridge type sights, the rear sight screw adjustable. Walnut stock with full pistol grip steel butt plate. Thumb screw take down. Bolt action, self cocking. Weight about 4 lbs., 6 oz. MODEL 2-XA, same as Model 2-X, but with ¾" leather sling strap with swivels and Lyman 55J receiver peep sight, and No. 3 ivory bead 1/16" front sight. MODEL X SINGLE SHOT .22 RIFLE. Has same self cocking safety feature of Model 2-X but has plain Patridge type sights. Takes .22 Long Rifle, Long and Short cartridges. MODEL X-A. With ¾" leather sling strap and swivels. Lyman 55J receiver peep sight, No. 3 ivory bead 1/16" front sight.

MOSSBERG MODEL 42TR TARGO SHOTGUN AND RIFLE. (Bottom Illustration)

Smooth bore, bolt action, 8-shot clip repeater using .22 Long Rifle shot shell. Walnut finish stock, pistol grip with finger grooves, molded butt plate. 8" Targo tube interchangeable with RA1 rifle adapter; silver bead, detachable hooded front and adjustable sporting rear sights for use with adapter. Length 43½"; weight about 5½ lbs.

MAJOR CHAS. ASKINS who wrote this keenly analytical article, needs no introduction as he is an institution in the shooting world. This veteran authority is now Acting Arms and Ammunition Editor of Sports Afield.

Upland Guns and Loads

IN THE selection of a shotgun for upland shooting, there are two standard types to be considered—the double gun and the repeater. All shooting men recognize the many improvements which have been made in the repeater, but, nevertheless, the preference of most gunners is for the dependable old double.

The beginner is invariably "taken over" by the additional magazine capacity of the repeater and regards it as a great benefit, yet actually the benefit is only accomplished in the hands of the expert shooter, and he is the one who needs it least in these days of short seasons and limited bags. The experienced shot who would empty his magazine at the first birds flushed, to secure his limit as quickly as possible, is ruining his own day's sport. But the man who hunts habitually for game in cover rarely has a chance to use to advantage more than two shots on a rise, and these two shots can be fired with far greater speed and smoothness, from a double gun, than from a repeater—for we continually find the double barrel noticeably smoother in operation and better in balance and appearance. The repeaters' most favorable factor is its single sighting plane, which undoubtedly promotes better accuracy.

Much could be written in regard to the double gun versus the repeater, but the discussion which follows will concern the most practical gun and proper loads to be used on upland game by the average shooter.

The 12-gauge is probably the most commonly used for every kind of game that falls to the shotgun. I personally do not believe that so large a bore is really needed in upland shooting, but this doesn't alter the fact that such gun is in use all over the world. Hence the necessity of giving the 12-bore honorable mention among the upland guns.

The English call our field gun a "game gun" as distinguished from a Duck or a Magnum shotgun. The standard weight of the so-called "game gun" is about 6½ pounds, and the standard load is $1\frac{1}{16}$ ounces in a 2½ inch case; they usually have 30-inch barrels. The velocity of the gun is low and the power moderate, the boring usually an improved cylinder or a straight cylinder, but the gun appears to be well adapted to driven game shooting. We have no such shooting in this country, the nearest approach to it being passing wildfowl—which is quite another thing.

The 12-gauge in upland shooting will be used mostly by the man who has but one gun, and a lot of us have just that for all kinds of wing-shooting. This gun will weigh between 7¼ and 8 pounds in double guns, and between 7¾ and 8 pounds in repeaters. Lighter guns are not to be had except built to order, or of foreign make. In case feather-weight arms are secured, the all-round feature will be done away with, and the guns are fit for nothing except quail and light shooting. In such arms, loads should be restricted to 3 drams and 1⅛ ounces of shot. Their weight, when last made by American manufacturers, was about 7 pounds.

In reality, for upland shooting there is nothing gained by reducing the shot charge below 1⅛ ounces, and, as compared with a 16 shooting the same shot charge, little is gained by shooting less than 1¼ ounces. A good 16 will shoot 1⅛ ounces of shot nearly as well as a 12. In the same way, a 20-bore handles an ounce of shot just about as well as any other gun, with a material reduction in weight of arm and less recoil.

In times past, some of us maintained that we were entitled to a lot of sporting credit for selecting a small bore instead of a 12. The guns are so nearly on an equality today, for upland shooting, that much of this feeling has disappeared. It is true that the 12, using 1¼ ounces of shot, can be given a little wider spread and still maintain the required density of pattern, as compared with any smaller bore. Thus a straight cylinder 12, 1¼ ounces, will throw as dense a pattern as an improved cylinder 16, or a quarter choked 20. However, a straight cylinder of any gauge is a poor tool, owing to its irregularity of performance. Besides, the added weight causes a loss of yardage, so many maintain. This being true, if the 6½-pound 16 gets its bird at 22 yards, and the 8-pound cylinder 12 at 25 yards, deadliness will be on the side of the 16.

So much for comparison, and we don't want to go on record as maintaining that the 12-bore is not as good upland gun as any of them. For no better or more killing gun is to be had, whether it weighs 7 pounds or 8 pounds, or anywhere between. No man is handicapped because he uses a 12 bore gun for quail shooting. Most of us can carry a 7½ pound gun in quail or snipe shooting without caring a tinker whether it weighs any less or not. Only the veteran shooter will feel the weight, for a 20-year old will handle a 9-pound gun just as fast as the man of 60 years will one of 6½ pounds. Hence, if I were giving advice here, that advice would be: young man, shoot a gun that is heavy enough to steady you; older man, shoot as light a gun as will do the work.

Where double guns are used for upland and duck shooting, many are ordered with two sets of barrels, full choked for the web-feet, open bored for quail and like birds. Other refinements can be added to the double gun: raised matter ribs, beaver-tail fore-ends, single trigger, ejector, Monte Carlo stock or cheek piece, soft rubber recoil pads, double shotgun sights, and about anything else a man thinks he wants. Barrels may have a raised rib or a solid flat rib, which in turn may be integral with the tube. Stocks can be had in various lengths and drops to order, though the pump gun man is quite apt to be content with that standard stock with which he learned to shoot. Weights are pretty apt to be standard in repeating shotguns, not varying more than a quarter of a pound. All pump and magazine guns will handle the most powerful 16-bore cartridges made, because these come in a standard length of case. Therefore, whether the gun is a Winchester, Ithaca, Marlin, Remington, Browning, Stevens or any other make, it will shoot the heavy, progressive powder ammunition. Weights of about 7 pounds are right, too, for the loads, whether in pump or double guns.

In maximum loads, 16-gauge, velocities are a trifle lower, about 25 feet lower than would be true of the same class of cartridge in 12-bore, but since the 12 is supposed to have from 7 to 10 yards the advantage of the 16, the latter really has the more energy per pellet up to the limits of its patterning range. That is, a single pellet from a 16-bore will do more execution at 50 yards than a similar pellet from a 12-gauge at 60 yards or even at 55 yards. The 16-bore then, and all smaller gauges, are really limited in range by patterns and not by velocities, or striking energy.

It is obvious that the beauty of the 12 lies in getting spread of pattern with density of pattern. The 12-bore can be opened to the limit, and will still account for the bird with great certainty. Nevertheless, I'd be inclined to consider all straight cylinder guns, whatever the gauge, as leaky tools, gas cylinders with poorly fitted pistons. Such guns simply waste power. They do not shoot a round or even pattern, but flare it, spreading it in great, useless branches that cannot be relied upon to either hit or miss. A straight cylinder gun is not a sporting weapon.

An improved cylinder 12, shooting into a 40 inch circle, or a little wider, at 40 yards, both barrels, is a good gun, not only on quail, snipe and grouse, but all kinds of game including ducks.

I know that the usual specifications are for a first barrel improved cylinder and second modified choke, and of course there is nothing wrong with that gun. Perhaps most men do their best shooting with that very arm, improved cylinder right and modified left, but it is hard for an individual to get away from conditions, as he finds them himself. In my own shooting, taking time enough with the first barrel but whipping in the second as quickly as I know how, I find that if I am to connect regularly with that second barrel it had better spread just as much as the first. But let every man measure his skill with his own yard-stick.

Gunmakers have not quite standardized their degree of choke. A cylinder by one maker may be found to be shooting just as close as an improved cylinder of another make. Then we have strong improved cylinders and light modified chokes, which may turn out to be the same thing. Additionally there may be ¾ choke, ½ choke and ¼ choke. Best thing to do is to tell the builder the pattern you want with some particular load and he will give you the pattern, or a little better one.

The old straight cylinder English game gun was supposed to spread over a 30-inch circle at 20 yards—I have never seen a gun that would do it, however. The widest spreading American shotgun that I have seen bored by a factory covered a 24-inch circle at 20 yards. It is a killing quail gun in a 12-bore. An ordinary improved cylinder, as it comes from the factory, will make an even spread over a 22-inch circle at 20 yards—this is a quail, snipe and grouse gun. The quarter choke will cover a 40-inch circle at 40 yards, and is a fine all-round gun for the novice or anybody else. A three-quarter choke is about as good constriction as can be had for big progressive powder loads or for trap-shooting, patterning a good 70%, without deforming many shot. The full-choke is not for the uplands—it has too much of a tendency to shoot to center, that is, within a 24-inch circle, rather than a 30-inch. I have never in my life seen a first-rate quail shot use a full-choked gun, though I have seen many who have tried to shoot with it.

The debate over the size of the load and the size of the shot to use in upland shooting never ends. I have been reading a book in which the author advises 5 drams of powder and 1 ounce of shot, No. 3, for duck shooting with a 10 bore. This load must have shot well in the writer's gun, but he deliberately advises it for everybody. He doesn't say what kind of a pattern he got, and probably didn't know, but such a load in the average gun should pretty well cover the side of a barn at 40 yards. Another is firm in the belief that No. 7 shot are the very best size for waterfowl, while someone else will be bold enough to tell us to use No. 2. I believe if we were restricted to one size of shot for upland shooting, that size would be 7½. Not being so restricted, we can use any size from No. 8 to No. 6, or larger if we feel like it—maybe on chickens. Recently I have been shooting doves with a full-choked Remington 12-gauge, using duck loads of 6 shot, and I couldn't see but the birds were killed just as cleanly and just as far as though the shot had been 8s. However, No. 8 shot will work well as anything I have ever used on snipe, No. 7½ on quail, No. 7 on grouse and No. 6 on prairie chickens. The man with a poor shooting gun may need to use smaller shot in order to secure density.

As to the size of load, the quantity of powder and shot, this should be governed largely by the weight of gun, which in turn governs the recoil. The load you use should be balanced with the weight of your gun. A heavy gun will handle loads without discomfort, but only light loads should be used in light guns. A recoil heavier than 30 pounds cannot be endured for any considerable length of time. Consequently these limits govern the load.

From my references I will not attempt to give a complete table, but will quote a few loads with the weight of gun which balances the load.

LOAD				SPEED of	
Powder (drams)	Shot (ounces)	Muzzle Velocity	Weight Gun	Recoil (Feet)	Pounds Recoil
3	1⅛	1,253	6¾	15.1	24
3¼	1⅛	1,371	7	16	27
3½	1⅛	1,487	7½	18.8	31.8
3	1¼	1,210	7	15	25.4
3¼	1¼	1,327	7½	15.9	29.6
3½	1¼	1,443	8½	15.7	31.8
3	1⅛	1,253	7¼	14.1	22.6

The last weight gun and load will prove very pleasant to shoot, and very effective on such birds as quail and snipe. The load could also be shot very nicely in a 7-pound gun, were a man willing to stop at that, but if he took a notion to shoot a heavier duck load of 3½ drams and 1¼ ounces in the little gun, the speed of recoil would amount to 18.5 feet, and pounds of recoil to 37.2.

For an upland gun, the man who shoots a double will ordinarily have one barrel a bit more choked than the other, and many who prefer a repeating shotgun will want it with two barrels. I do not like scatter loads in a full choke; they never pattern the same with two successive loads, and it is my observation that much crippling is done with them. Like the full cylinders, the scatter loads do not shoot a round or a good pattern in any respect.

A killing gun is an improved cylinder first barrel and a quarter choked second, for quail shooting, also ruffed grouse or woodcock. Snipe will bear a closer shooting gun, a modified choke doing the most execution in average hands. The full choke is useful in chicken shooting in cold weather, where the birds rise at a distance of 50 yards or more.

The repeating shotgun has been gaining in popularity the last few years. Where once all we ever saw was the standard double, we now have a fine assortment of pump repeaters and several automatics. The gunner who selects the repeating shotgun gains something in additional fire power, while at the same time he limits himself to a single boring. His gun can be bored full-choke and then it is pretty much a duck gun; or he can get a modified choke, which is neither duck gun nor upland weapon, or he can choose an improved cylinder and so possess a purely upland scatter gun. Despite the fact that the single tube on the repeater limits the shooter so far as the versatility of his gun is concerned, the bird gunners showed marked preference for this type of shotgun. It used to be that it was perfectly cricket to utilize the five or six shells which the repeater would hold in the magazine. In recent years the people who write the game laws put a taboo on the use of more than three shells in the pump gun. That is only one more cartridge than the double-barreled gun, but that extra round counts. Time and again I have snapped two quick shots after a booming Bob White and, missing with these openers, brought him down with the third and last shot.

Now the last disadvantage to the repeating shotgun has been pretty successfully overcome. That is the business of only one boring. There are three devices on the market at the present time, which make it possible to have any of the following patterns all out of one shotgun tube: cylinder, improved cylinder, quarter choke, modified choke, improved modified and full choke. The gadgets, which when screwed to the "business end" of the barrel, give all these different borings are: the Poly Choke, Cutts Compensator and the Weaver Choke. The Poly Choke, which is the handiest of the three variable choking devices, utilizes a collar which fits about a number of segments integral with the barrel muzzle. As the collar is rotated in one direction, the segments are squeezed together automatically, constricting the muzzle and thereby producing close shooting patterns; by twirling the adjusting ring in the opposite direction the gun is instantly made to shoot more openly. The Poly Choke is completely reliable and will produce the patterns and results claimed by the manufacturers. The Cutt's Compensator and Weaver Choke work upon a slightly different principle. The end of the barrel is threaded and to this threaded portion is screwed a ventilated cylinder about 3½ inches in length. To this ventilated part is screwed a choking cylinder, varying in length from about 1½ inches for the full cylinder tube, to around 6 inches for the full choke attachment. The ventilated portion of the gadget has a series of baffles built inside it and these divert the powder gases, thereby tending to reduce recoil. The Cutts Compensator and the Weaver Choke are thoroughly dependable, and will do everything claimed for them. It can be seen, however, that to change from, say, the improved cylinder tube to the modified tube, instead of simply reaching up to the muzzle and giving the adjusting collar a slight twist—as you do on the Poly Choke—you would have to carry the extra tube in your pocket, together with a wrench, to make the change.

The price of these variable choking devices is usually less than an extra barrel for the repeating gun. It is my belief that after the war, a good many of the makers of pump and auto-loading scatter guns will offer one, or all, of these very worth while muzzle attachments as standard equipment.

How to Call and Hunt Quail Without a Dog

"It's useless to go quail hunting without a good dog!" You've all heard this line. It means that the man who utters it has no confidence in his bird finding ability. No confidence in his shooting ability. No confidence in his gun or in HIMSELF. What a man!

I got over that idea when I was 11 years old. I *had* to learn to hunt and shoot quail without a dog, or not get any quail shooting. I've been hunting and shooting quail, wherever possible, practically all of my life. Mostly without a dog, almost always without a GOOD quail dog. And I hunt quail in preference to anything else that walks or flies.

Successful quail shooting without a dog depends upon these established conditions.

1. That there be at least SOME quail available to hunt.
2. That the shooter has a suitable field gun and shells.
3. That the gunner can and will walk for several hours, will thoroughly hunt what is obviously good quail cover, and at the times of day in which quail might logically be expected to be THERE.
4. That he can HIT quail on the wing, when they flush more or less unexpectedly.
5. That having raised a covey, or several birds, he will mark carefully his dead or crippled quail as well as carefully marking where the remainder of the covey alights.
6. That he will pace to where his down quail SHOULD lie, place his hat or a white handkerchief on top of a tall tuft of

grass, bush, or twig, to mark the presumed location of each down bird, then hunt until he finds them.

7. That having done this successfully, he will then give his other birds time to settle and run about a bit, after which he will attempt again to flush them, likely closing in from the OPPOSITE direction to do this.

8. Having scattered a covey, he will find himself a quiet spot, give the quail time to regain the reassembling idea and then proceed to call them until he has located the approximate position of practically every bird in the flock.

Having done this, anyone who can shoot at all should kill himself a nice mess of quail. Simply walk up the singles and drop them one at a time. Shooting singles in ordinary field cover, when you know about where they are, is a type of shooting at which any good shot should average better than 50% kills. Killing five or six straight is by no means uncommon. The writer has done so many a time. The hardest quail shooting without a dog is to kill a clean double out of the first covey rise.

Suppose, for example, you have walked into a wheat stubble and a good heavy covey has gotten up and roared buzzing down the field, you make one clean kill and wing the other. The remainder of the birds pitch across a fence into a corn field, which is in shock and with fine wiregrass six inches to a foot high in most of the corn rows. Brother, you have an almost perfect setting for good quail shooting for the rest of that day, particularly from 4 P. M. on until just before dark, when they will probably flush and fly out into an open stubble to roost.

What to do *now?* That's easy. You want to find both birds, don't you? Then, reload your gun immediately, and in *both* barrels. So many forget this, or reload only the one barrel.

If experienced, you have a mental picture of how FAR it was to the first quail which went down, about where it landed from the way it went down, whether it was a clean kill or only winged. And about how much farther on the second bird landed. And what it did then. PACE out to the spot where your FIRST bird should be. Look for feathers, and as soon as you find some, tie a white handkerchief over that spot, or hang up your hat, if you can risk it; then, if you can't find that bird, PACE out to the second one. It starts to flutter around and you grab it and wring the neck a bit. Stick it in your gunning coat pocket. Then walk back to the first bird. Where in H— is that white handkerchief? Lost it, didn't you? At last you find it—30 feet to one side and 10 feet beyond where you would have looked for the bird. Forget this location, go to that handkerchief and start looking ON the ground, carefully. Lay your dead bird down and look at it from all angles. Now start hunting again. Oh-ho! *There* it lies, dead as a stone, just 4 feet from where you put up the handkerchief. You see, it drifted a bit with the wind and drove along a few feet farther than you thought it might. They keep on moving while they fall through high grass. Only the ground stops them.

This last Thanksgiving I went back 6 times to finally find the clean killed bird of the first half of a double on the covey rise, and FOUND my bird. So can you, if you use patience. Not every time, but MOST times.

Now let's think about calling. All the books talk about the lovely notes the Bob White uses in his mating call—Bob—Bob *White!* Trouble with that idea is—Bob doesn't do his mating in November and he doesn't call "Bob White," either then or when he is giving his rallying call.

Sit down a while in high grass and cool your heels. Rest a bit. Then softly and then more loudly call, plaintively, "Whoi-Lee!" A moment later, "Whoi-Lee, Whoi-Lee, a Lee, a Lee." Yes, there is the answer. WHOI—A Lee. WHOI A Lee—on a rising note. The bird is a bit alarmed, a bit anxious. Also a bit out of patience. He wonders where the rest of the boys and girls are. He wonders where the old lady is. And he wonders just where HE is, in relation to everyone else.

Don't overdo the calling. Take it slow. Let HIM do the yelling. Let him do the running. Let him walk right up within 40 or 50 yards of you; if possible, let him come to about where you want him to come, and then—go out and flush him! Any quail—remember this—ANY quail which has called and has started to come to what he thinks is the remainder, or at least part, of the covey, will *flush* if you walk up on him. He will usually flush some place between a foot and 10 yards away from you. He may even flush BACK of you, if you are not very clever in locating exactly where his call came from. And he may run around you when you walk up. But on the average, by hunting around a little you are likely, by marking down mentally the approximate location of one bird after another, to flush one to eight or ten quail, either as singles, or in bunches of 2 to 5, to get up the whole covey. Shooting singles is really sport. You can usually concentrate on one bird without having to worry about a dog, about where your companion is parking his face at that instant, about whether this and that may happen! It is simply a case of one bird and you. Who is going to outwit the other, and then, can you kill your bird? In the woods, it will be hard shooting—if on old quail. In the open, it is fairly simple. In any place, it is up to you, and if you are a man—not a mouse—you can stand on your own feet, aim down the old gun rib and press her off!

You call ducks, don't you? You use decoys, don't you? You track rabbits. You depend upon a dog to find your game. You call moose when they are crazed with passion in rutting season. You trail deer through miles and miles of slashings and snow. All this is SPORT—so you say. You listen to gray squirrels barking, and then stalk them. You sit on a log and take in that Brrrrmmmmmm—Brmmmmmmm—of the ruffed grouse, then try to stalk him, through the sun-flecked forest. So why not pit YOUR wits against that smartest of all small game birds, Bob White Quail?

By C. S. LANDIS

BLACK DUCK

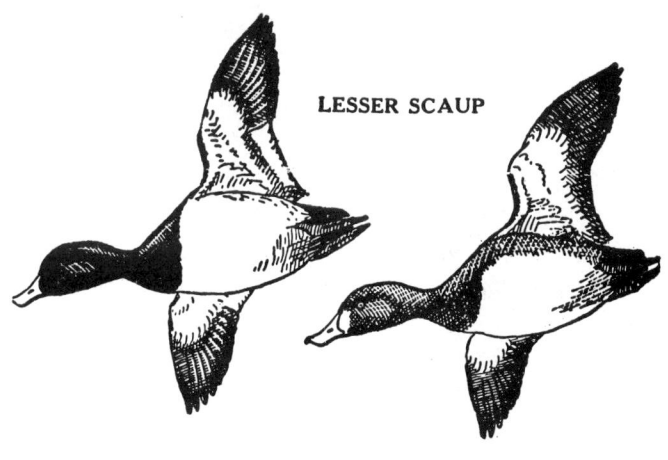
LESSER SCAUP

Tips on Decoying

Contributed by Ducks Unlimited, 342 Madison Ave., New York, from a regular column in the Ducks Unlimited Quarterly. Material by Rube Wood, Charles E. Wheeler, Jules P. Cuenin, Joel Barber was condensed into one fascinating article.

DECOYS have many angles, both of design and use. They are also a subject for much controversy. The round-bottomed model may serve the particular needs of inland gunners on more or less quiet waters. The flat-bottomed "stool" is largely preferred by the salt water wildfowler who has rough water to contend with. It seems to me that these angles and ideas should be exchanged, between East and West, North and South.

As everybody should know, decoys which flash in sunlight don't look like the real thing. But what is probably equally important is that you rarely see a half dozen ducks swimming in a straight line—as some novices string out their decoys on a single anchor line. From a distance, the wily mallard or sprig may not notice this unnatural alignment, but just outside fair gun range he does—and perhaps gets a single stray pellet which means another wasted bird.

Diving duck decoys often are set out by beginners at this intricate art of wildfowling who are gunning for marsh ducks. The fact that divers and surface feeders only occasionally fraternize—and rarely fly together—is unknown to the amateur. Here, again, lack of understanding of a fundamental contributes to needless wastage through long range shooting.

The most effective decoying is achieved by knowing where the birds have been "working." And that usually means where ducks have located a good supply of natural feed. Once they have become accustomed to fly to those spots from their rafting areas, it is often almost impossible to bring them to decoys rigged out in between.

These feeding places, in the case of marsh-feeding puddle ducks, often are small ponds remote from roads. Toting in a heavy sack of decoys would be a back-breaking job, but the few that can be taken along in hunting coat pockets are easily supplemented with no other tool than your own fowling piece.

The most seductive decoys are dead ducks—provided they are propped up in natural positions. Novices usually set them up carelessly in weird postures with reeds and then wonder why decoying flocks flare off. The usual method is to insert a pointed reed or stick under the head—leaving the neck stretched up as though the bird were strung on a gibbet.

Chary late season wildfowl who already have survived enough barrages to know decoys from the real thing are quick to spot unorthodox duck postures. Unless dead birds are properly set up, it would be far better to place them belly down, with head and necks hanging under water, in which position they give an excellent imitation of marsh ducks feeding on bottom plants.

The effectiveness of this arrangement will be appreciated by any gunner who has seen ducks pass up a setting of wooden blocks to alight directly alongside a bird just shot and floating off to leeward.

Stiff Wire Handy Item for Wildfowlers

One of the handiest items for gunners planning to use dead birds for decoys is stiff wire cut to suitable lengths—depending upon the depth of water and firmness of the bottom over which shot birds are to be propped up. The wire is pointed at one end for inserting under the breast skin. It is then passed on up through the neck to the head. With the head tilted down and the wire bent to give natural neck curvature the remaining wire is shoved into the pond bottom. This method provides the nearest thing available to a real, live decoy.

Van Campen Hielner describes a unique and actual "stool" for setting up decoys in his popular *A Book On Duck Shooting*. In gathering material for this book near Dantzig, on the Baltic, Hielner found wildfowlers employing long metal rods topped with small wooden ovals on which decoys were placed. These devices also served as perches to which live call ducks were tethered. It is from such devices that the term "stool," used with reference to decoys in sections of this country, may have been derived.

While dead birds make prime substitutes for wooden blocks, there are also rubber, canvas, papier mache and similar counterfeits of light weight which can be toted in to remote ponds. Profiles, of sheet metal or wood, offer still more relief from the back-breaking job. However, light cork and cedar blocks—even if only a half-dozen can be taken along, have few superiors. And in rigging only a few decoys, each one should be provided with individual anchor lines.

It's surprising what can be done with just a few singly-anchored decoys, properly spaced out—and spotted where there are indications that ducks have been feeding thereabouts. In the case of most ducks, this can usually be determined by pond-weeds that have been pulled up and washed ashore. On coastal bays, where divers have been feeding on small shellfish, a watch with field glasses will usually reveal whisps of birds sneaking into some favored spot. Toss over even a few decoys as near to the cafeteria as possible and you'll get ducks—while they will ignore the most elaborate setting anywhere else.

Of the various decoy outlines, probably none are more important than those seen from above. Even painting is of sec-

Female ... CANVASBACK ... Male

ondary importance, according to a unique study by C. W. B. Urmston, reported in the British Field.

"To get the best results from decoys, they should be made to offer the greatest attraction to ducks when seen from above. I have spent a good deal of time taking photographs of ducks from immediately overhead, and have even gone so far as to borrow an airplane and fly over different species sitting on the water. In all cases the same results and phenomena have been more and more vividly impressed on me," declares this English wildfowler.

"This data resolves itself into two main groups: that of color and shape. On the matter of coloration, it was most noticeable that the different species of ducks, when observed from overhead, instead of showing a difference of color showed a very definite body pattern. All color detail disappeared."

Body Shapes Identify Species from the Air

The inability to distinguish various species from the air by their coloration and the ease with which they could be told by the shape of their bodies was striking, the investigator found. It was so striking that after very little practice, even when flying over ducks at such a height that they were not alarmed by the roar of the plane's motor, the body pattern effect was so pronounced as to enable recognition of practically all more common waterfowl.

"The shape of different ducks when seen from above is very pronounced. For instance, mallard, pochard, tufted ducks and teal all have comparatively different shapes, and do not vary much in size or color. Although it is necessary to be much closer to ducks to notice the difference in shape, it does cause a sort of general effect even when seen from considerable height.

"What I am suggesting is that, in the construction of decoys, it is not the ordinary or already accepted ideas of construction that matter, but it is necessary to construct them to correspond with ducks as seen from above. This means that one should concentrate on coloring them, not in detail, but to get a bold general effect which, incidentally, is much easier to do," declares the British decoy authority.

Body Pattern Followed in Eastern Decoys

While inland and West Coast gunners specializing in decoying the finicky sprig and mallard prefer carefully painted decoys, the general effect idea of decoy painting long has been in use among greater scaup shooters in the northeast. These "stools" are painted flat black with white impressionistic dabs for wing patches and a smattering of white on the backs. No attention whatever is paid to more intimate details of plumage coloring—yet they bring in the birds.

The important factor in these northeastern "broadbill" decoys, however, is that they invariably have the squat, wide bodies so characteristic of the greater scaup while swimming or resting on the water. Similarly, the old-time canvasback decoy still in use on Chesapeake Bay has the familiar wide body of this diving species. And the most modern canvasback decoy, with carefully-painted plumage pattern, often is no more effective than the old square-shaped blocks first introduced on the Chesapeake's famed Susquehanna Flats in muzzle-loader days.

In the fall, young ducks are unsophisticated and once their brood or flock has been broken up by shooting, they become bewildered. For a while they will decoy readily to almost anything. Then, too, they are changing in plumage from the immature to the adult stage. During this period they are not too particular about how a bunch of decoys look.

But these birds soon become cagey or "educated" and if the gunner does not have good-looking decoys and doesn't set them out properly in the right place his sport will be rather mediocre.

I have rigged out in competition with a dozen other rigs and have seen birds start toward one outfit, swing away, turn and head toward another rig, rear up high and drift off to the leeward—then lead up to my setting and stick their feet out as gentle as kittens. The difference was not entirely because of better decoys. When the ducks act gentler and the nearer they come in, you can bet that you and your blind are OK and that your decoys look reassuring rather than like a lot of scare-crows.

I remember an instance when I was guest of a friend at Squibnocket on Martha's Vineyard off the southern coast of Massachusetts. The black duck shooting had been very good early in the season but for a couple of weeks the birds had been exceptionally timid. As we sat in the blind an occasional single or pair would lead up to within "a gunshot and a half" of our rig and then rear up, swing away and alight with a bunch gathered in the middle of the pond.

This was exasperating and my friend asked "What's wrong; did they see something?" To which I answered, "Yes, they saw that nondescript gang of 'stool.' No self-respecting black duck could be expected to associate with such an outfit."

My friend was naturally surprised at my brutal frankness, but he laughed it off and said that he didn't think decoys made much difference. When leaving for home I told my friend's caretaker that I would send down a dozen good decoys. I asked the caretaker to set them out by themselves, just a bit to one side of my friend's assortment.

Well, the caretaker did just what I told him. The result was that the ducks came up to the usual "gunshot and a half" and reared to go away. Then they would spot the small group of good decoys off to one side, swing and come in, on stiff wings, as gentle as chickens. That convinced my friend that there was a difference in decoys. He wrote me a very complimentary letter saying that my decoys had "sex appeal."

My experience has taught me that poor decoys are ineffective. They result in the gunner taking long shots and crippling a lot of birds. On the other hand, good decoys toll the birds within closer range, make them a slower, easier target, resulting in cleaner kills and practically eliminating crippled birds. That, it seems to me, is real conservation.

While I appreciate and like to use finely made "deacs," if I had a certain sum of money to spend on my blocks, I would look for quantity rather than quality except in a few instances, for I would want as many dummy ducks as I could get when gunning our larger waters.

Of course, if you are hunting mallards in potholes in tules or timber, a small set of the best possible imitation ducks you can get will bring in the singles, pairs and small flocks, but when you get out into larger bodies of water and you want action from the big flocks, then you should have as large a flock of decoys as you can get into your boat or a half-dozen boats, even if the blocks are not expertly made.

Some of the fastest shooting I have ever enjoyed was over "mud-lumps." Of course I didn't use just a few of these, but about 300, and I dressed each one with a white vest, consisting of a piece of white paper, and a gray back made of wet newspaper, for I wanted the pintails to come in, which they did in flocks of 50 to 100 or more. On that identical pond on the same day, I doubt if the big bunches would have "worked" to a mere handful of perfectly made decoys.

On another occasion, following a storm when there was supposed to be little chance of getting any shooting, we took out the two blinds, which are about 150 yards apart, all the decoys that could be loaded into four skiffs, which we dragged across the shallow pond. There were between 400 and 500 nondescript blocks of all shapes and sizes from flat pintails with backs less than an inch above the water, to overstuffed mallards that appeared like brant. The paint job on some of those decoys would make a live bird turn its head away in shame, but those big bands of pintails, which were not supposed to stop in that area during a storm, just pitched down from a height of a quarter of a mile and tried to alight.

Geese are supposed to be quite wary, and we are often told about the care with which one must set up his decoys, which must be so natural in appearance that they would actually honk if urged. Well, if you set up enough dummies, even though they are made of a double sheet of newspaper wadded into a lump with a twisted stump for a neck, not only the snow geese, but white fronts, Hutchin's and even honkers will come down.

Last fall, on the North Butte Gun Club in the Sacramento Valley, our decoys consisted of all the newspapers we could fold over grass clumps in a half-hour. We killed limits of "speckled beauties" in less than a half-hour, and the following morning, after the wind and rain had thoroughly "messed up" the set during the night, three flocks of geese, including one bunch of honkers, worked in to those bedraggled newspapers.

Buy the best made decoys you can afford, but if you can get only a few of the kind that are so natural you have to lock 'em up to prevent a cat from eating 'em, then select a cheaper grade in order to get a larger number, for in almost all instances, particularly on reasonably big bodies of water, the more decoys you have, the better are your chances of bringing ducks within positive killing range, which, for most of us, is under 40 yards rather than beyond that distance.

If my flock of cheaters fails to induce the birds to swing in properly, I don't condemn the shape or color of the blocks, but the manner in which I have set 'em out. If a couple of flocks head in and then swing off to the left to pass out of range, I take time out to shift my layout off to the right from 10 to 30 yards, so that if the birds decide to veer off, they'll pass within range. If the first few that come in pass too far to the right, I shift the decoys over to the left.

At times, especially late in the season, the birds are likely to be more wary than when they first arrive from the DU duck factories, and they will come up wind to within 40 to 50 yards of the decoys, then swing off or climb. Under such conditions, I have fooled 'em by moving my layout of dummies up wind behind the blind from 30 to 40 yards, which would bring the birds within easy killing distance by the time they became suspicious.

In choppy water I have found that setting out the decoys rather close together brought better results than scattering them widely, though in a calm, or a light wind, I believe a wide spread is more effective.

If all the blind debates on why particular bunches of ducks failed to come in to decoys were placed in the well-known end on end, the alibis probably would reach from Suisun marshes to the Susquehanna flats. Sometimes the birds will almost knock your hat off trying to "stool in." At other times an apparently perfect set won't bring 'em.

Decoying waterfowl is almost an art toward the end of gunning seasons when the webfeet become wary and "educated." These veterans of earlier barrages can usually be identified by the cautious way they circle and look a rig over before swinging in. Canny old diving ducks on larger waters usually keep wide of points and islands during late season flights. Experienced sprig, mallard and other shallow water feeders not only fly wide, but high over any possible hiding place for a gunner.

When decoys have to be set some distance from the line of flight due to lack of a nearer location for the blind, the problem of making a set that the birds can see is met with. There are several ways to solve this—provided the birds are in a decoying mood to begin with. One of the solutions is based on the fact, well known to old-time wildfowlers, that puddle ducks don't usually fraternize with divers, and *vice versa*.

To bring in wide-flying bluebills on big waters, a half dozen or so mallard, pintail or black duck decoys, anchored singly and well apart in a line running far off to the leeward of the main setting of bluebill decoys will sometimes work wonders. In the east, they call these out-of-gunshot decoys "tollers."

Birds flying well out over a lake or coastal bay often cannot see a setting of decoys placed close under shore. This is particularly true when the sun is low during early morning or late afternoon, if the birds are flying into the sun or if a high background casts a shadow over the decoys. But it is surprising how far off ducks can see just a few "tollers" placed well out on open water. They will pull in to investigate these, note that they are aliens, then spy the bigger concentration of their own kind inshore and come piling in.

Wood or Cork Blocks Serve as Tollers

Where mixed flights of both diving and shallow water feeders occur and shots at one or the other species might be missed because of birds lighting in to "tollers" of their own kind set out of shotgun range, various substitutes may be resorted to. Blocks of wood or cork, painted flat black or daubed up to faintly resemble a duck can be utilized. Even a string of watertight cans sometimes works.

One old-timer I know sets out a couple of wooden sea gulls. He claims that the presence of gulls gives ducks "confidence" as well as serving to attract the quackers. Another swears by a great blue heron which he whittled out as a "toller." The heron decoy is set up on a stick shoved down in shallow water well out from the blind. "As any duck hunter knows, a heron's a smart bird. He don't hang around where there's shootin'— an' the ducks seem to know it," this old-timer explained.

Wildfowlers "Down East" in Rhode Island and the Cape Cod section of Massachusetts now are seeing a new development of the "toller" idea. When rigged out for "broadbill" shooting from a coastal reef or point it was noted that black duck would occasionally drop in alongside the crude "toller" blocks anchored far out in deep water. The reason was puzzling until just recently when an enterprising Providence decoy maker began advertising "duck bags."

The decoy maker reasoned the puzzle out in this way: While no puddle duck feeds in deep water, nevertheless a roundish block of cork bears a striking resemblance to a duck feeding along with head and neck under water. And a few birds do drop in to such "tollers." Therefore, why wouldn't a more accurate imitation of a feeding puddle duck bring in more birds if used in shallow water where that species normally feeds? The idea was given a trial—and it worked.

Fathers are ever loath to let their sons learn the hard way. Profit by my experience is ever the theme of man-to-man talks from one generation to the next. Thus the following letter, written by a duck hunter and published by the Minnesota Conservation Department, seeks to take the place of an experience he had fondly hoped to share with his 17-year-old son:

"Dear Rog: I am sorry not to be around for ducks but we'll catch up. I want you to go, just as we planned.

"Be eternally careful about the gun; keep that barrel up and watch out if you happen to jab it into the ground. Don't load on the dock; unload before returning. Watch the safety. I always kept the barrel poked over the back end of the boat; watch to see it doesn't fall out when the boat tips.

How to Take Care of Gunning Equipment

"Keep that rubber raincoat right in the boat, but put the decoy sack over it to protect it from the sun, as sun is hard on rubber. Use the rubber-lined zipper bag for extra gloves, lunch, etc. (I wish you would send me a blow-by-blow description—it will be the next thing to being there myself.) Watch that old duckboat. It's tricky. When you reach over to pick up a duck, it might tip.

"When you load your boat at the dock, always get your hay—a small amount will do. Then put your decoys at one end of the boat, your gun and shells at the other where they'll be handy.

"Handling decoys requires care. Always handle them gently. They are very fragile and break easily. Never drop a sack of decoys or push them around roughly. Some hunters do that and lose much time with repairs. In putting decoys out, you have to be careful not to snarl the string.

"Setting decoys to pattern to make them seem more real is something you will learn, but remember never to set your decoys so that the ducks will have to swing over your blind to come in, into the wind, because then they detect you.

"One plan, if your reed blind will permit, is to set the decoys so that birds can swing across in front. For example, from the bog point we faced east, roughly. The day you were with me last year, the wind was from the north, as I remember it, so then the birds had to swing in from the south. But you will catch on to that quickly.

"Keep your blocks lifelike; half-tilted ones are bad; some overturned are not bad though, if they roll all the way. The idea is to keep them in rough water so that there is motion; however, I have seen them in dead calms and still fetch in the birds.

Always Sit Facing Your Decoys

"Fix your boat so that you face your decoys. Naturally there will be times when you have to shoot the other way or behind and you have to get on to twisting around in your boat. There's a knack to this as there is always danger of tipping. Keep the middle of your boat clear so you can maneuver; keep shells in one corner covered so they won't get splashed.

"Keep bright stuff covered, like white shell boxes, metal thermos bottles; even put hay over your gun barrel, just a bit, if the bright sun might make a shine and thus tip off your quarry. Blend into the blind—that's the idea. Don't move until it's time to shoot. It's always best to wait and be certain. A flock of wily mallards may circle many times. On location, of course, a fellow should never sit squarely down on his seat unless at lunch time.

"Never take a chance in the excitement of getting in a shot or chasing a cripple. Be sure not to shoot directly into the water, always at an angle when rounding up a crip. You will have a big advantage over the chap who smokes because smoke from a duck blind tips off those old mallards miles away.

"When it rains, stay out there and take it but keep your gun dry—especially the vital trigger mechanism and pump parts. If it gets wet, be sure to take it apart and dry it at night—better do it each night anyway as a gun always gets splashed.

"When you wound a bird and it drops some distance away, get your markings from the shore line, but remember that a winged bird may hit the water full of fight and may swim and dive far out of reach by the time you get to the spot where it dropped. You will learn by the way a bird falls how it is hit.

Obey the Rules of Wildfowling

"Always respect the 10 bird limit and watch the time. Never shoot before legal time or after. We were always careful and you know we always got our birds. Lots of yahoos will shoot up to half an hour before time and keep banging away afterwards but you be smart and play square with the law and gain accordingly.

"Take along a spare paddle if you can. I broke a paddle last year bucking a stiff wind and was lucky to have an old pole with me. Those poles are handy for getting into and out of a blind. Always be careful in working in and out of a blind not to knock down too many reeds.

"I only wish I could be hunting with you, as I had always fondly planned from the time you were a little shaver. But we'll catch up one of these days. Business at hand is get this war over quickly as possible and you know I'm glad and proud to have a part in it. Good luck.

With love,—POP."

A timely tip that will save the embarrassment of chasing a drifting decoy next fall is to check over anchor lines this summer. If the lines are attached to metal fasteners on the bottom of decoys, rust rots the lines during summer damp spells.

One of the most effective ways to eliminate rust-rotting of decoy anchor lines is to replace metal line fasteners with loops cut from rawhide or old leather shoe and boot tops. Strips of the leather one-half inch wide and four inches long are looped over and affixed to the decoy bottom with brass or galvanized screw. The leather also eliminates the chafing away of lines so common when decoys with metal line fasteners are used in rough water.

Before using binoculars, however, be sure that you are not in an area where they are banned by Coast Guard or military authorities.

Regardless of how few or how many decoys you use, and no matter how well they are made, you must hide and keep quiet in the blind, and that thing of remaining motionless in a blind seems to be more difficult to learn than to make or use decoys.

One of the favorite tricks to bring in distant birds when batteries were legal was to hoist a boot or swing a hat while lying in the flattened position required for this kind of wildfowling. Usually at least one bird in a flock would spot that distant movement, turn to give the strange object closer inspection and thus swing the whole flock in. The same trick sometimes will work today in blind shooting—but don't swing the chapeau more than once or twice unless you intend it as an au revoir.

Equally important in the ethics of real sportsmanship is bringing the birds in close enough for clean shooting. Cripples can be greatly reduced by waiting until the birds are over a previously established range marker—selected when the decoys are being set out. That marker may be a particular string of decoys.

Know Your Wildfowl

Through the courtesy of Ducks Unlimited, a non-profit organization devoted to wildfowl conservation, America's finest sporting ducks are presented on this and preceding pages. These drawings are the work of H. A. Hochbaum and were originally prepared for the Wisconsin Conservation Department.

Female . . . GOLDENEYE . . . Male

Male . . . GADWALL . . . Female

Female . . . SHOVELLER . . . Male

Female . . . PINTAIL . . . Male

Female . . . BALDPATE . . . Male

Female . . . BLUE-WINGED TEAL . . . Male

Female . . . MALLARD . . . Male

Males . . . BUFFLEHEAD . . . Female

Male . . . REDHEAD . . . Female

The GUN DIGEST 1944

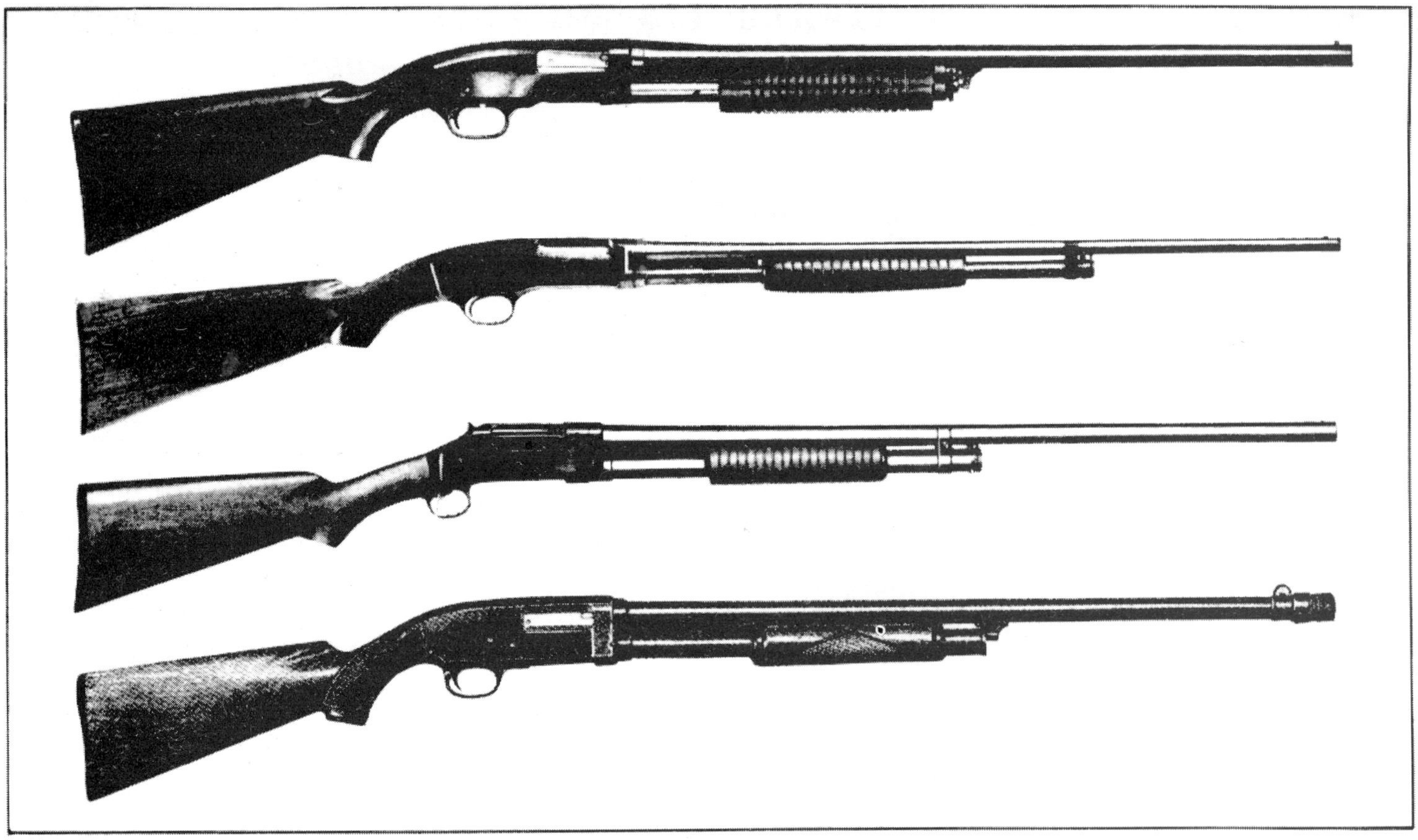

SLIDE ACTION SHOTGUNS

REMINGTON MODEL 31. (Top Illustration)

Improved model. Trigger has been moved back for more comfortable grip and better handling qualities; simple takedown with easy interchangeability of barrels; fast action with short fore-end stroke, side ejection. Cross bolt safety, top of receiver matted. Hammerless; solid breech. Chambered for 2¾" shells. 5-shot cap.; 3-shot plug furnished, or installed at factory if desired. The Model 31A "Standard" grade has walnut stock and fore-end, bakelite butt plate. Stock dimensions: 14" long, 2½" drop at heel, 1⅝" drop at comb. Half pistol grip. Weight: 12 ga., about 7½ lbs.; 16 ga., 6¾ lbs.; 20 ga. 6½ lbs. Full or modified chokes; cylinder or imp. cyl. in 26", 28", 30" or 32" lengths. Skeet choke in 26" only. Also comes with raised solid matted rib. Special long range choke, in 12 ga. 30" plain or solid rib barrels only. First manufactured in 1930.

REMINGTON MODEL 31R is the "Riot" grade with 20" plain cylinder barrel. Standard Model 31 with selected stocks and fancy engraving can be obtained in the following: Special grade, Tournament grade, Expert grade or Premier grade.

WINCHESTER MODEL 42. (2nd from Top)

A fast, small-bore, hammerless repeater chambered for 3" shells. This .410 bore will also handle standard 2½" loads. 26 or 28" Winchester proof steel barrel, full, modified or skeet chokes, or cyl. bore. Walnut pistol grip stock (straight grip optional) and standard slide handle. 5-shot magazine furnished with removable 3-shot plug. Takedown style. Dimensions: 13¾ x 1½ x 2¼"; weight approximately 5⅞ lbs. With plain or matted rib barrel.

WINCHESTER MODEL 97. (3rd from Top)

Smokeless powder was new when this model was first manufactured. With hammer at safety, half-cocked gun is locked against opening. 6-shot capacity; furnished with wooden magazine plug to reduce capacity to 3 shells. 12 gauge in 28, 30, and 32" barrel lengths, full choke. 26, 28, and 30" modified. 26" cyl. bore. In 16 gauge 26, 28, and 30" in full choke or modified; 26 or 28" cyl. bore. Walnut stock and slide handle, rounded comb. Chambered for 2¾" shells. Dimensions: 13⅞ x 1¾ x 2⅜". Weight of 12 gauge about 7¾ lbs.

The model 97 is also made as a guard and riot gun in 12 gauge only, 20" cyl. bore barrel. Pistol grip stock. 6-shot repeater. Chambered for 2¾" buckshot loads.

STEVENS NO. 620. (Bottom Illustration—No. 620-P)

Hammerless, side ejection, takedown repeater. Independent safety, visible locking bolt. Safety firing pin. Receiver drop forged, solid breech. American walnut stock with fluted comb and checkered, full capped pistol grip and hard composition butt plate. Length 13¾", drop at heel 2¾". Checkered slide handle. 5-shot magazine. Barrels bored as follows: 12 gauge, 28 and 30" full choke or modified; 26 and 28" cylinder. 16 gauge. 28" full, modified or cyl.; 26" cyl.; 20 gauge, 26 and 28" full, modified or cyl. Approximate weights: 12 ga., 7¾ lbs.; 16 ga., 7¼ lbs.; 20 ga., 6 lbs. Chambered for 2¾" shells. Also made with raised matted rib (No. 621).

No. 620-P is equipped with Aero-Dyne Super Poly choke built integral with barrel, 28 and 30" lengths in 12 gauge; 28" only in 16 and 20 gauge.

PARKER DOUBLE BARREL SHOTGUNS

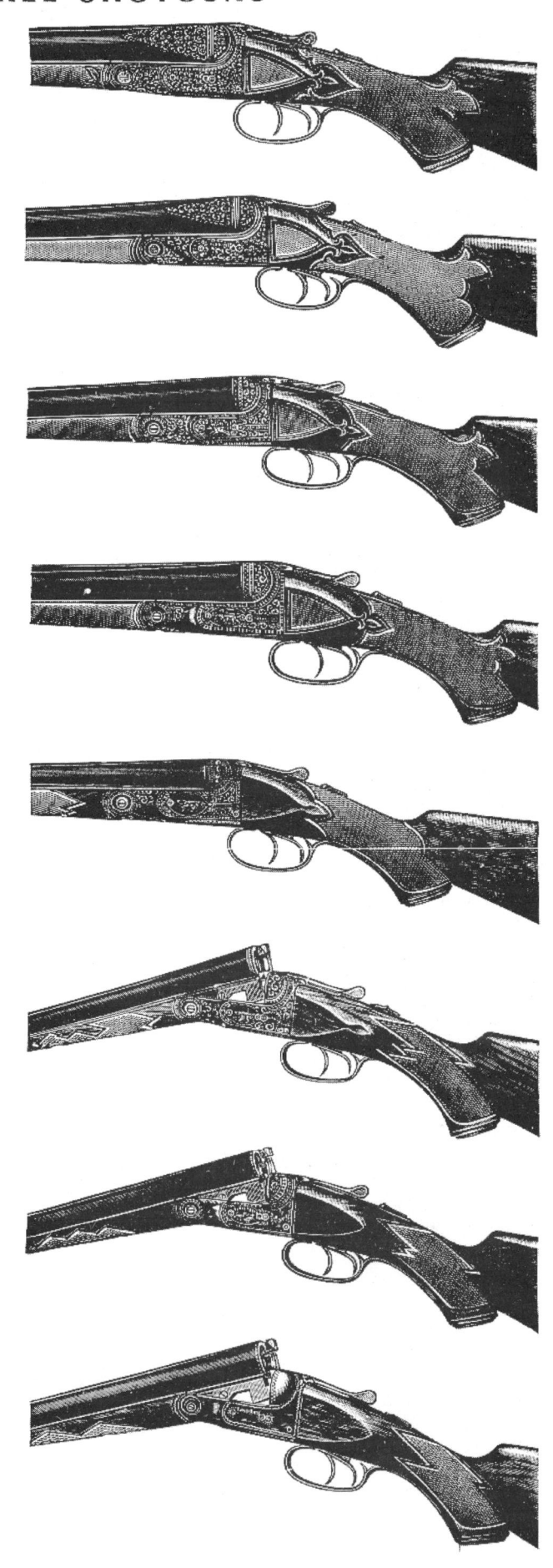

Among the very finest made. Furnished with any combination of borings desired. Unless otherwise specified, furnished with right modified, left full choke. 30" and 32" lengths in 10 gauge (3½" and 2⅞" chambers) and 12 gauge (3" chamber). Regular 12 gauge in 26, 28, 30 and 32". 16 and 20 gauge in 26, 28 and 30"; 28 gauge and .410 bore, 26 and 28". No extra charge for maximum long range 10 and 12 gauge. Stock dimensions to order; full, half or straight grip. Automatic ejectors; ivory sights if desired. Weights: 12 gauge, 6⅞-7¾ lbs.; 16 gauge, 6⅝-7⅜ lbs.; 20 gauge, 6⅛-6⅞ lbs.; 28 gauge, 5¾-6⅛ lbs.; .410 bore, 5⅝-6 lbs. Extra long range 10 gauge, 10½-11 lbs.; extra long range 12, 9-9½ lbs.

A.1. SPECIAL GRADE. (Top Illustration)
Finest specially selected curly walnut stock and fore-end; elaborate hand checkering. Stock includes Monte Carlo, cheek piece or cast off (in all grades except G.H.E. and V.H.E.). Rubber recoil pad or engraved skeleton steel butt plate. Extensively engraved; gold inlay if desired; gold plated triggers (front one hinged); solid gold name plate engraved with your name or monogram. With double triggers or with selective single trigger. Beavertail fore-end or raised ventilated rib furnished as "extras".

A.A.H.E. GRADE. (2nd from Top)
Beautiful, selected curly walnut stock and fore-end artistically checkered by hand. Solid gold name plate inlaid in grip or stock, engraved with your name or monogram. Scroll engraving, or combination of game scenes and scroll. Silver plated triggers (front one hinged). Recoil pad or engraved skeleton steel butt plate. With double triggers or selective single trigger. Beavertail fore-end and raised ventilated rib also obtainable.

A.H.E. GRADE. (3rd from Top)
Specially selected, high grade stock and fore-end of figured walnut, beautifully checkered. Solid gold name plate inlaid, engraved with name or monogram. Recoil pad or engraved skeleton steel butt plate. Tastefully applied engraving of English scroll, or game scenes and scroll. Nickel plated triggers (front one hinged). With double triggers or with selective single trigger. Beavertail fore-end and raised ventilated rib furnished at an additional charge.

B.H.E. GRADE. (4th from Top)
Stock and fore-end of high grade walnut with fine grain and beautiful figure. Handsomely checkered. Mounted with solid gold name plate. Recoil pad or engraved skeleton steel butt plate. Scroll engraving and life-like hunting scenes. Nickel plated triggers. With double triggers as standard; selective single trigger, beavertail fore-end, raised ventilated rib all considered as "extras".

C.H.E. GRADE. (5th from Top)
Selected, high grade walnut stock and forearm, handsomely checkered. Sterling silver name plate inlaid. Engraving is game scenes and scroll. Rubber recoil pad or skeleton steel butt plate. Nickel plated triggers. With double triggers or selective single trigger. Beavertail forearm and raised ventilated rib are each furnished at an additional charge.

D.H.E. GRADE. (3rd from Bottom)
Stock and forearm of fancy walnut, finely hand checkered. Sterling silver name plate inlaid. Rubber recoil pad or skeleton steel butt plate. Engraving is game scenes and scroll. Nickel plated triggers. With double triggers as standard. Selective single trigger, beavertail forearm, raised ventilated rib are all "extras".

G.H.E. GRADE. (2nd from Bottom)
Figured American walnut stock and fore-end. Nicely hand checkered. German silver name shield inlaid. Stocks made to order, lengths 13½ to 14½", drops from 2 to 3¼", without extra charge. Rubber butt plate. Game birds and scroll engraving. With double triggers or with selective single trigger. Beavertail forearm and raised ventilated rib are extra.

V.H.E. GRADE. (Bottom Illustration)
Stock and fore-end of selected American walnut, hand checkered. German silver name shield inlaid in stock. Stocks made to order without extra charge as in G.H.E. Grade. Rubber butt plate; line engraving. Furnished with double triggers as standard. Extras as on G.H.E. Grade.

MAURICE H. DECKER

For over 30 years Shooting Editor of Fur, Fish, Game Magazine; also Camping and Woodcraft Editor of Outdoor Life. Author of five books, and an untold number of magazine articles, on outdoor subjects. Take his advice to heart—and follow it well.

Guns Will Last a Lifetime

VERY FEW guns actually wear out. When any firearm needs repairs or replacements, the cause has usually been neglect or carelessness of the owner. All standard models of guns are built to last a lifetime or more. And to enjoy so much service, all the shooter has to do is supply a reasonable amount of care. Following is a digest of the simple attentions that will keep your gun accurate and working and looking like new for a great many years.

Most inaccurate guns have become that way from a lack of proper cleaning. Every firearm should be cleaned and then oiled or greased at certain intervals, no matter what type of ammunition it fires. The job is by no means a hard one. It takes only a few minutes of time and requires a small list of tools and supplies.

First, you must have a cleaning rod that fits the gun, neither too small nor too large, with a jagged tip on the end to hold cloth patches securely. You also need some type of cleaning brush or swab made of soft brass wire. Never use a steel brush. The cleaners that accompany some wooden shotgun rods are hard steel wire that quickly cuts the high polish of the bore. When you buy one of these outfits, throw that steel brush away.

You will need a bottle of some standard powder solvent, another of thin oil made for gun locks and working parts and some gun grease. This list will take care of ordinary cleaning problems. Use products made expressly for shooters, not auto greases or oil. Make (or buy) cloth patches from a strong absorbent cloth like cotton flannel. Don't use wornout material. It tears so easily the rod pushes on through, leaving the patch stuck in the bore.

It is best to clean your gun in the evening after each day's hunt, especially if it has been exposed to damp weather or snow. In emergencies, a gun can set a day or two after it has been fired without any real harm, but if at all possible, wipe out the bore and oil the outer metal surfaces the same day.

Here is a simple, easy and effective way to clean guns. First push a dry patch through the bore to remove loose particles of fouling. Then put some solvent on the soft metal brush or swab and scrub the bore from end to end, using at least a half dozen full length strokes. Clean gun barrels from the breach end whenever possible. When you must work from the muzzle, use what is known as a "muzzle protector" (small thimble of metal) to prevent cleaning rod wearing against the extreme ends of the lands.

Remove cleaner from the rod and put on a dry cloth patch. Scour the bore well and change patches until one comes out unsoiled. The barrel should now be clean and the next step is to protect it from rust or corrosion caused by moisture.

If the gun will be fired again within a week or two, an application of gun oil will be sufficient. Soak a clean patch with oil and push through the bore a couple of times. If the gun will be set away for several weeks, months or until next year, don't use oil. It may crawl away from parts of the bore's surface, leaving them exposed to rust. Use a soft, clinging grease made especially for guns. Such a product will protect stored guns for years.

Apply oil or grease to rifle barrels with cloth patches. For shotguns use the little wool swabs that accompany most cleaning rods. Keep these swabs saturated with grease and store them in empty tin typewriter ribbon boxes; then they're protected from dust and drying and are instantly available for use. Remember—if tools and supplies are handy and easy to use, you won't be tempted to postpone the job of cleaning your gun when you come in tired and hungry from a hunt.

In cleaning a revolver, there are several spots which need special attention. Clean the forward ends of the cylinder chambers well. Clean and apply oil around the end of the barrel that projects through the forward end of frame. Do the same to the end of the firing pin and to the recoil plate through which firing pin passes when it fires the primer.

The above program will protect gun bores from rust and the corrosion of modern powders and primers. If, sometime, you happen to shoot smokeless ammunition loaded twenty-five years or more ago, you may encounter trouble with metallic fouling and extra corrosion from very virulent powder. In this case, something extra is required. Use a liquid cleaner with ammonia base for the fouling. Several large rifle manufacturers make it. To neutralize corrosive fouling of old powders, apply boiling soapy water. It can't harm any barrel. Put muzzle end in the water and pump it up with a tight patch on end of cleaning rod. Then swab the bore dry and oil or grease as advised before.

Still another factor in gun depreciation, mostly in 22's and shotguns, must be considered and guarded against. This is "leading," the mark or plating left by lead bullets or shot pellets on the inside of the bore. Ungreased .22 bullets, soft drop shot and high velocity shot leads are the worst offenders in leading guns. Very thin coats or deposits of lead do no immediate harm but they should be removed before they get out of hand and before moisture or powder corrosion hides underneath and attacks the steel. Thick deposits of lead harm accuracy of rifles and patterns of shotguns. Because of these reasons and because thin deposits thicken fast due to the affinity of lead for itself, remove leading promptly.

A good soft brass wire or wire cloth brush will take it out. Moisten this tool with solvent and scrub the bore well. This operation has already been described. If you suspect lead, just prolong it a bit more. Lead mostly forms close to the breech end of a barrel. It will appear as little shiny streaks or lumps. This shiny appearance sometimes deceives the shotgun owner. Because the bore is bright, he assumes it is clean. After you have scrubbed the lead out (you can usually see little flakes of it on the cleaning tool) oil or grease the bore as usual.

Now give the outside of your gun some attention. Go over all the metal surfaces with an oiled rag. Be careful to get oil down in the slot of each screw head, in the matted ridges of ribs and every hard to reach corner or crack where moisture can lodge and start rust. A gun that has been rubbed down with oil many times can be carried all day in the rain without rusting. It's wise, also, to wipe off the gun with an oily rag after it has been only handled, since fingers leave invisible "prints" of moisture that can cause rust unless removed.

Each season, apply a few drops of non-gumming oil to the working parts of a gun. Don't put in too much. If you do, the gun may work stiff in cold weather. In sub-zero temperatures, oil congeals and jams the actions of repeaters. The remedy is not to use oil but to wash out the working parts with gasoline or hot water and dust them with powdered graphite after they've dried. Graphite lubricates without congealing and without catching dirt and dust.

The actions of automatic rifles and shotguns should be washed out with gasoline or boiling water every few years. Don't let either liquid contact the wood parts if possible. Boiling water won't rust gun actions, since the metal dries from the heat it absorbs. Then oil lightly with a long spout can to reach in back of the bolt. Or if gun will be carried in extreme cold, use graphite or some graphite preparation made expressly for shooters.

Care in the field will prolong both the life and good looks of your gun. Don't press barb wires down with it when you climb through a fence and don't use the muzzle to poke rabbits from grass hummocks. Wire scratches steel and wood. Poking a gun around the ground may force foreign material inside the bore. Remember that very slight obstructions in gun barrels, like wads of grass, snow, small sticks or rags, will burst or bulge them when they're fired. For this reason, never plug the end of a stored gun with rags to keep out dust. You might forget to remove that rag before you shoot. The barrels of new guns, and those stored for long periods of time, are usually coated heavily with grease. Remove most of this before you fire a load.

Watch your shotgun ammunition and don't get different sizes of shells mixed. Serious accidents have occurred when a hunter hurriedly put a 20 gauge shell in his 12 gauge gun. That shell was small enough to slip into the barrel out of sight. When the gun didn't fire, the hunter thought he had forgotten to reload. So he put a 12 gauge shell in on top of the 20, pulled the trigger, and blew his gun apart.

Every gun needs a case. Dents and scratches in barrels and stocks are largely caused by guns knocking together in a car, boat or wagon, or by falling down in a closet at home. Guns can be banged up more in transportation to the shooting cover than when carried through it. A case will prevent these accidents, protect the gun from rain and snow and keep dirt out of its breech action. Arctic hunters, for example, often keep their rifles in cases until just a few minutes before they are needed.

Watch the small adjusting screws on rear sights and keep them tight. If they loosen, they let the alignment slip or may possibly fall out and be lost.

When a firearm needs serious repairs, it should be sent promptly to a gunsmith. Repairing guns is a skilled profession and success is attained only after considerable training and experience. There are, however, a few simple repairs the sportsman can make at home. For instance, he can restore the blued finish of a barrel or any smaller part when it becomes worn. Use the bluing kits sold by gun dealers. They are complete and contain easy to follow directions. The important part is absolute cleanliness. The metal must be completely free of oil and grease and never touched by the hands during the process.

Varnished gun stocks and forearms, the sort most guns carry, wear poorly. When they are scratched or dulled, remove the old varnish with paint remover, smooth the wood with very fine garnet paper and apply a number of coats of boiled linseed or tung oil. This gives what is known as an "oiled" finish, which is both durable and good looking. One pint of either oil will finish a couple of stocks. Heat it, mix in two ounces of rosin and stir until rosin is dissolved. Apply this warm with a rag, let stock stand twenty minutes, then rub it off with paper towels. Polish briskly with a cloth. After twenty-four hours, sand surface lightly with fine garnet paper and apply more oil. From five to ten applications are usually needed before the outer pores of the wood are filled and highly polished. When an oiled stock becomes dirty and dull, simply smooth with garnet paper and apply another coat of oil.

Steam will remove shallow dents in stock or forearm. Lay a wet pad on the dent and press with a hot iron. The steam expands the fibers and straightens them up level with the surface.

When tip or bead breaks from a front sight, put on a drop of solder and file it into the proper shape. When working with gun sights, remember that you move the rear sight the way you want to change the bullet impact, and move the front sight the opposite way you want to move the bullet. For example, raising the rear sight and lowering the front one, makes the gun shoot higher.

Don't ever forget that as long as you take care of your gun, your gun will take care of you.

SMITH & WESSON REVOLVERS

S & W .38 TERRIER

2" Barrel
Round Butt

FINE LIGHT-WEIGHT UNDERCOVER GUN

Caliber: .38 S & W. Number of Shots: 5. Barrel: 2 inches. Length: 6¼ inches. Weight: 17 ounces. Sights: Fixed, 1/10-inch service type front; square notch rear. Stocks: Checkered Circassian walnut with S & W Monograms, or hard rubber. Finish: S & W Blue or Nickel.

AMMUNITION
.38 S & W
.38 S & W Super Police
.38 Colt New Police

S & W .38 SAFETY HAMMERLESS

PERFECT FOR PERSONAL PROTECTION AND HOME DEFENSE

Caliber: .38 S & W. Number of Shots: 5. Barrel: 2 inches. Length: 6¼ inches. Weight: 17 ounces. Sights: Fixed-blade front, U-notch rear. Specially designed for smooth drawing. Stocks: Checkered Circassian walnut or hard rubber with S & W Monograms. Finish: S & W Blue or Nickel.

AMMUNITION
.38 S & W
.38 S & W Super Police
.38 Colt New Police

.32 HAND EJECTOR
SMALL AND LIGHT—A BEAUTIFUL HANDLING GUN

Caliber: .32 S & W Long. Number of Shots: 6. Barrel: 3¼, 4¼ or 6 inches. Length: With 4¼-inch barrel, 8¼ inches. Weight: With 4¼-inch barrel, 18½ ounces. Sights: Fixed, 1/10-inch service type front; square notch rear. Stocks: Checkered Circassian walnut or hard rubber with S & W Monograms. Finish: S & W Blue or Nickel.

AMMUNITION
.32 S & W
.32 S & W Long
.32 S & W Mid-Range
.32 Colt New Police

THE SMITH & WESSON REGULATION POLICE MODELS
Designed to Meet the Specifications of One of America's Greatest Police Departments

Caliber: .32 S & W Long. Number of Shots: 6. Barrel: 3¼, 4¼ or 6 inches. Length: With 4¼-inch barrel, 8½ inches. Weight: With 4¼-inch barrel, 19 ounces. Sights: Fixed, 1/10-inch service type front, square notch rear. Stocks: Checkered Circassian walnut with S & W Monograms. Finish: S & W Blue or Nickel.

AMMUNITION
.32 S & W
.32 S & W Long
.32 S & W Mid-Range
.32 Colt New Police

Caliber: .38 S & W. Number of Shots: 5. Barrel: 4 inches. Length: 8¼ inches. Weight: 18 ounces. Sights: Fixed, 1/10-inch service type front; square notch rear. Stocks: Checkered Circassian walnut with S & W Monograms. Finish: S & W Blue or Nickel.

AMMUNITION
.38 S & W
.38 S & W Super Police
.38 Colt New Police

WESSON GRIP ADAPTER

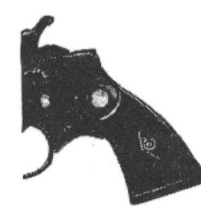

The Adapter is of simple construction; two plates, two screws, and a rubber filler block. The installation takes but a moment and requires no change or alteration of the gun. Two sizes: (1) for .38 M & P, K-22 and K-32. (2) for .38/44, .44, .45 and ".357" Magnum.

S & W "HUMPBACK" HAMMER

Affords a constant or increasing leverage as the spring tension increases and the power of the thumb lessens. Renders cocking far easier than the conventional hammer. Supplied on the larger models on request at no extra charge. Installed on used arms by the Factory.

COLT BANKERS' SPECIAL REVOLVER

CALIBERS: .22 Long Rifle and .38 Police Positive (New Police)

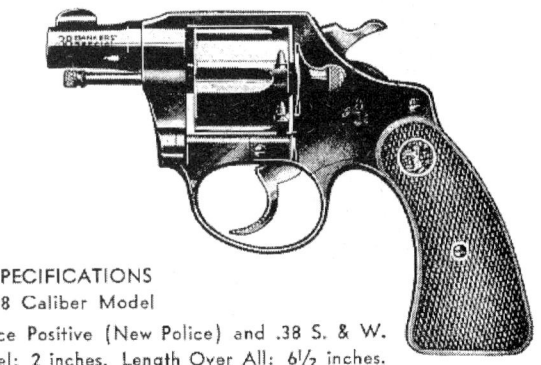

The .38 caliber Colt Bankers' Special Model is a great favorite for use by bank messengers, tellers, guards and plain clothes men. It is compact, absolutely dependable and powerful. Easily carried and concealed in pocket or shoulder holster. The .22 Caliber Model uses the regular or high speed .22 Long Rifle cartridges—including the hard-hitting, hollow point. It is in great demand as an arm to be carried at all times, ready for any emergency. Except for caliber and weight, both guns are identical. Both models have Colt Positive Safety Lock.

SPECIFICATIONS
.22 Caliber Model

Ammunition: .22 Long Rifle cartridges, Regular or High Speed, including Hollow Point. Length of Barrel: 2 inches. Length Over All: 6½ inches. Sights: Fixed type, stippled. Cylinder: Embedded Head Type. Stocks: Rounded, checked walnut. Weight: 23 ounces. Finish: Blued or Nickel. Top of frame matted to prevent light reflection. Trigger and Hammer Spur: Checked.

SPECIFICATIONS
.38 Caliber Model

Ammunition: .38 Police Positive (New Police) and .38 S. & W. cartridges. Length of Barrel: 2 inches. Length Over All: 6½ inches. Sights: Fixed type, stippled. Weight: 19 ounces. Stocks: Rounded, checked walnut. Finish: Blued or Nickel. Top of frame matted to prevent light reflection. Trigger and Hammer Spur: Checked.

COLT SINGLE ACTION ARMY REVOLVER

CALIBERS:
.32-20 (.32 Winchester)
.38 Special
.357 Magnum
.38-40 (.38 Winchester)
.44 Special
.44-40 (.44 Winchester)
.45 Colt

This is the Colt that played so famous a part in the winning of the West and is still extremely popular in many sections of the country. Its dependability and ruggedness have earned the confidence of shooters for over sixty years. It is popularly known as the Colt "Frontier Model," or Colt "Six Shooter." The shape and size of the grip adapt this model to the largest and brawniest hands. Single action with rod ejection.

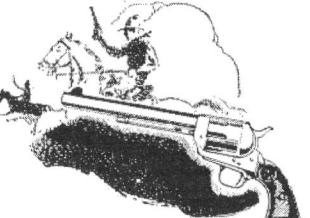

SPECIFICATIONS

Ammunition: .32-20 (.32 Winchester). .38 Short Colt; .38 Long Colt; .38 Colt Special; .38 S. & W. Special (full and mid-range loads); .38 Colt Special High Speed; .38 S. & W. Special High Speed and .38-44 S. & W. Special cartridges in .38 caliber model. .357 Magnum. .38-40 (.38 Winchester). .44 Special. .44-40 (.44 Winchester). .45 Colt.

Lengths of Barrel: 4¾, 5½, 7½ inches. Length Over All: With 4¾ inch barrel, 10¼ inches. Weight: .45 Caliber, with 4¾ inch barrel, 36 ounces. Sights: Fixed type. Hammer Spur: Checked. Stocks: Checked black rubber. Finish: Blued, with case hardened frame, or Nickel.

COLT DETECTIVE SPECIAL REVOLVER

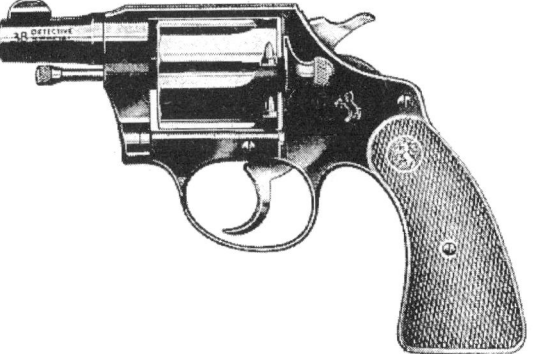

CALIBER: .38 Special

The Detective Special is exactly the same as the Police Positive Special Revolver, except that it has been furnished with the short 2-inch barrel. This model is designed especially for pocket use, and has been adopted by large police departments for use by detectives, special investigators and plain clothes men. It handles the same ammunition as the Official Police Model, making it the most powerful arm of its size and weight available. Unusually accurate at short range, and absolutely reliable. Equipped with Colt Positive Safety Lock. Weighs only 21 ounces.

SPECIFICATIONS

Ammunition: .38 Short Colt; .38 Long Colt; .38 Colt Special; .38 S. & W. Special (full and mid-range loads); .38 Colt Special High Speed; .38 S. & W. Special High Speed and .38-44 S. & W. Special cartridges. Length of Barrel: 2 inches. Length Over All: 6¾ inches.

Weight: 21 ounces. Sights: Fixed type, stippled. Trigger and Hammer Spur: Checked. Stocks: Rounded, checked Walnut. Finish: Blued or Nickel. Top of frame matted to prevent light reflection.

COLT WOODSMAN AUTOMATIC PISTOL

The Colt Woodsman Model is a most popular .22 Caliber automatic pistol. Thousands of shooters have found it ideal for all around shooting — and for target shooting. Graceful in appearance and beautifully finished. It is furnished with an unusually comfortable grip that fits the hand snugly and securely. Checked walnut stocks make slipping impossible. Fast and certain action — a trigger pull that is smooth and crisp. Ten shot magazine, and slide lock safety. Target sights, either Bead or Patridge.

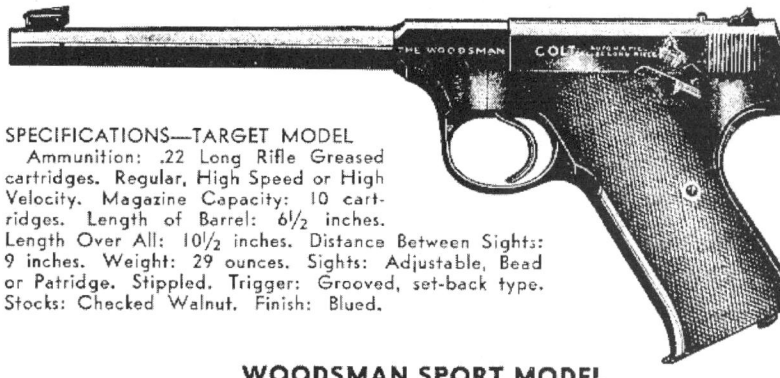

SPECIFICATIONS—TARGET MODEL
Ammunition: .22 Long Rifle Greased cartridges. Regular, High Speed or High Velocity. Magazine Capacity: 10 cartridges. Length of Barrel: 6½ inches. Length Over All: 10½ inches. Distance Between Sights: 9 inches. Weight: 29 ounces. Sights: Adjustable, Bead or Patridge. Stippled. Trigger: Grooved, set-back type. Stocks: Checked Walnut. Finish: Blued.

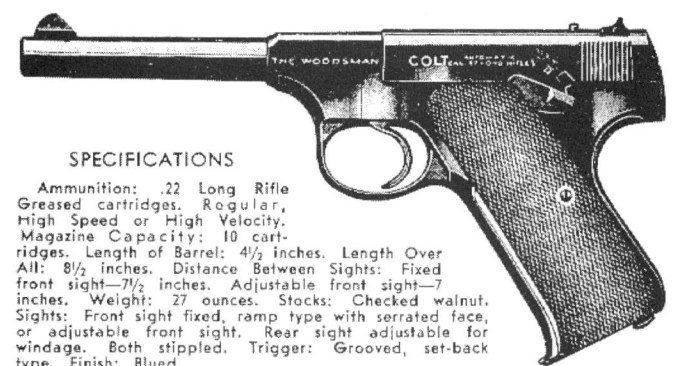

SPECIFICATIONS
Ammunition: .22 Long Rifle Greased cartridges. Regular, High Speed or High Velocity. Magazine Capacity: 10 cartridges. Length of Barrel: 4½ inches. Length Over All: 8½ inches. Distance Between Sights: Fixed front sight—7½ inches. Adjustable front sight—7 inches. Weight: 27 ounces. Stocks: Checked walnut. Sights: Front sight fixed, ramp type with serrated face, or adjustable front sight. Rear sight adjustable for windage. Both stippled. Trigger: Grooved, set-back type. Finish: Blued.

WOODSMAN SPORT MODEL

The Woodsman Sport Model is exactly the same as the standard model described above, except for length of barrel. Ramp type front sight is sturdy and rugged, built to stand up under hard service and abuse. Adjustable type front sight is same as on target model. Rear sight is adjustable for windage. This model was produced for use in the woods and on the trail, where compactness is essential. Unusually accurate and a thoroughbred Colt in every way. Uses either Regular or High Speed cartridges, including hollow point type. Ten shot magazine.

MATCH TARGET WOODSMAN

The New Colt Match Target Woodsman has what every target shooter desires . . . extreme accuracy. It has been designed to provide target shooters with the finest .22 caliber arm that could be built . . . with extra weight, extra steadiness and extra smooth action. The Match Target Model is seven ounces heavier than the standard Woodsman Target Model . . . with the weight so expertly distributed that it seems to weigh no more than the lighter model. The action is hand honed to a glassy smoothness, and the new style trigger and improved trigger mechanism provide a short, clean pull without backlash or excess travel. Has fixed front sight and improved Stevens two-way adjustable rear sight. The new style rear sight is equipped with binding spring, and gives "click" adjustment operation. Note the extra long hand-fitted stocks, comfortable for the largest hand.

Heavy Tapered Barrel

CALIBER: .22 Long Rifle

SPECIFICATIONS
Ammunition: .22 Long Rifle Greased cartridges, Regular, High Speed or High Velocity. Magazine Capacity: 10 cartridges. Action: Hand finished. Velvet-smooth. Barrel: Of special weighted design. Slightly tapered, with flat sides. Length of Barrel: 6½ inches. Length Over All: 11 inches. Distance Between Sights: 9¼ inches. Weight: 36 ounces. Sights: Front sight fixed. Rear sight adjustable, with adjustments for both elevation and windage. Trigger: Grooved. Of special design, with excess travel and backlash removed. Stocks: Checked Walnut. Specially designed to cover front strap and extend below bottom strap. Finish: Blued. Top of barrel, receiver and slide stippled. Rear of slide and receiver also stippled.

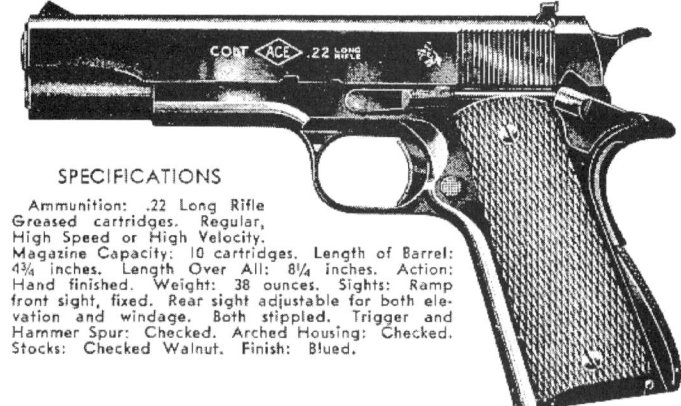

SPECIFICATIONS
Ammunition: .22 Long Rifle Greased cartridges. Regular, High Speed or High Velocity. Magazine Capacity: 10 cartridges. Length of Barrel: 4¾ inches. Length Over All: 8¼ inches. Action: Hand finished. Weight: 38 ounces. Sights: Ramp front sight, fixed. Rear sight adjustable for both elevation and windage. Both stippled. Trigger and Hammer Spur: Checked. Arched Housing: Checked. Stocks: Checked Walnut. Finish: Blued.

COLT TARGET ACE AUTOMATIC PISTOL

The ACE is designed especially for shooters of the Government Model and Super .38 Automatic Pistols—and has also been in demand by shooters for all around service. Built on the same frame as the Government Model and has the same safety features. Special super-precisioned barrel and hand finished target action. Exceptionally smooth operation and unusually accurate. Rear sight is of target design with adjustments for both elevation and windage. Allows economical target practice for military men, using .22 caliber ammunition in an arm of the same design as the regular military model. For Regular and High Speed Greased cartridges.

SERVICE MODEL ACE AUTOMATIC. Similar to the regular Ace, plus the Floating Chamber. Caliber .22 Long Rifle, 5" barrel, 8½" over all length, 42 oz. in weight. For economical practice with an arm that allows shooter to later change to heavier caliber without additional recoil being noticeable.

Ballistic Tables for Rifle and Revolver Ammunition

The following tables represent standard velocity, energy and trajectory figures as adopted by the Sporting Arms and Ammunition Manufacturers' Institute and are generally representative of all similar ammunition of factory loading. Reprinted from the Winchester Ammunition Guide through the cooperation of the Winchester Repeating Arms Co., Division of Western Cartridge Co.

Pistol and Revolver Ballistics of Winchester Center Fire Cartridges

All these Cartridges are Staynless (Smokeless powder) except those marked Black powder

Symbol	Primer No.	CARTRIDGE	BULLET Type	Wt.-Grs.	MUZZLE VELOCITY Feet Per Second	MUZZLE ENERGY Foot Lbs.	PENETRATION 7/8" Soft Pine Boards at 15 ft.	BARREL LENGTH Inches
K2541T	108	.25 Auto Colt (6.35 m/m)	F.P.	50	820	75	3	2
K3272T	108	.32 S. & W. Staynless	Lead	85	720	98	3	3
K3278T	108	.32 S. & W. Long, Staynless	Lead	98	820	146	4	4¼
K7631T	108	7.63 m/m Mauser (.30 Mauser)	F.P.	86	1,420	385	11	5½
K7653T	108	7.65 m/m Luger (.30 Luger)	F.P.	93	1,250	323	11	4½
K7654T	108	7.65 m/m Luger (.30 Luger)	H.S.P.	93	1,250	323	11	4½
K3256T	108	.32 Short Colt	Lead	80	800	114	3	4
K3254T	108	.32 Long Colt	Lead	82	800	117	3	4
K3241T	108	.32 Automatic Colt (7.65 m/m)	F.P.	74	980	158	5	4
K3289T	108	.32 S. & W. Long, Sharp Corner Match	Lead	98	770	129	....	6
K3208T	112	.32 Winchester Staynless	Lead	100	1,030	235	6	6
K3249T	108	.32 Colt New Police	Lead	98	795	138	3	4
K3570T	111	Super Speed S. & W. .357 Magnum	Lead	158	1,510	800	12.5	8¾
K9001T	108	9 m/m Luger	F.P.	125	1,150	367	10	4
K9002T	108	9 m/m Luger	H.S.P.	125	1,150	367	10	4
K3849T	108	.38 Colt New Police	Lead	150	695	161	4	4
K3856T	108	.38 Short Colt	Lead	130	770	171	4	6
K3872T	108	.38 S. & W. Staynless	Lead	145	745	179	4	4
K3867T	108	.38 S. & W.	Lead	200	630	176	5	4
K3862T	111	Super Speed .38 Special	Lead	158	1,115	436	7.5	5
K3863T	111	Super Speed .38 Special, lead bearing	Metal Point	158	1,115	436	10	5
K3898T	111	Super Speed .38 Special, metal piercing	Metal Piercing	150	1,175	460	11	5
K3859T	108	.38 Colt Special	Lead	158	870	266	6.5	6
K3884T	108	.38 S. & W. Special, Staynless	Lead	158	870	266	7	6
K3866T	108	.38 S. & W. Special Match	Lead	158	870	266	7	6
K3885T	108	.38 S. & W. Special, lead bearing	M.P.	158	870	266	8	6
K3868T	108	.38 S. & W. Special	Lead	200	745	247	7.5	6
K3877T	108	.38 S. & W. Special, Mid Range Sharp Corner	Lead	148	770	195	..	6
K3897T	108	.38 S. & W. Special, Full Charge, Sharp Corner	Lead	148	870	249	..	6
K3844T	112	.38 Automatic Colt	F.P.	130	1,070	331	9	4½
K3841T	112	Super Speed .38 Automatic Colt	F.P.	130	1,300	488	10	5
K3840T	112	Super Speed .38 Automatic Colt	H.S.P.	130	1,300	488	10	5
K3854T	108	.38 Long Colt	Lead	150	785	205	6	6
K3851T	108	.380 Automatic Colt	F.P.	95	970	199	5.5	3¾
K4154T	103	.41 Long Colt	Lead	196	745	242	5	6
K4474T	111	.44 S. & W. Russian	Lead	246	770	324	4	6½
K4484T	111	.44 S. & W. Special	Lead	246	770	324	7.5	6½
K4544T	111	.45 Colt	Lead	255	870	429	6	5½
K4556T	111	.45 Automatic Colt	F.P.	230	860	378	6	5
K4553T	111	.45 Auto Rim	Lead	230	820	343	6	5½
K4554T	111	.45 Auto Rim	F.P.	230	820	343	6	5½
K4555T	111	.45 Auto Colt Match	F.P.	230	750	287	..	5

S.P. = Soft Point   H.P. = Hollow Point   F.P. = Full Patch   P.E. = Pointed Expanding   H.C.P. = Hollow Copper Point

Revolver Ballistics of Winchester Rim Fire Cartridges

When Fired in Revolver with 6-inch Barrel. All these Cartridges are Winchester Staynless (Smokeless powder)

CARTRIDGE	BULLET WT.	MUZ. VEL.	MUZ. ENERGY	CARTRIDGE	BULLET WT.	MUZ. VEL.	MUZ. ENERGY
Super Speed .22 Short	29	1,035	69	Leader .22 Long Rifle	40	980	85
Leader .22 Short	29	925	55	Super Speed .22 W.R.F.	45	1,170	137
Super Speed .22 Long	29	1,125	81	.22 W.R.F. Staynless	45	985	97
Leader .22 Long	29	930	56	.41 Short Staynless	130	520	78
Super Speed .22 Long Rifle	40	1,160	120				

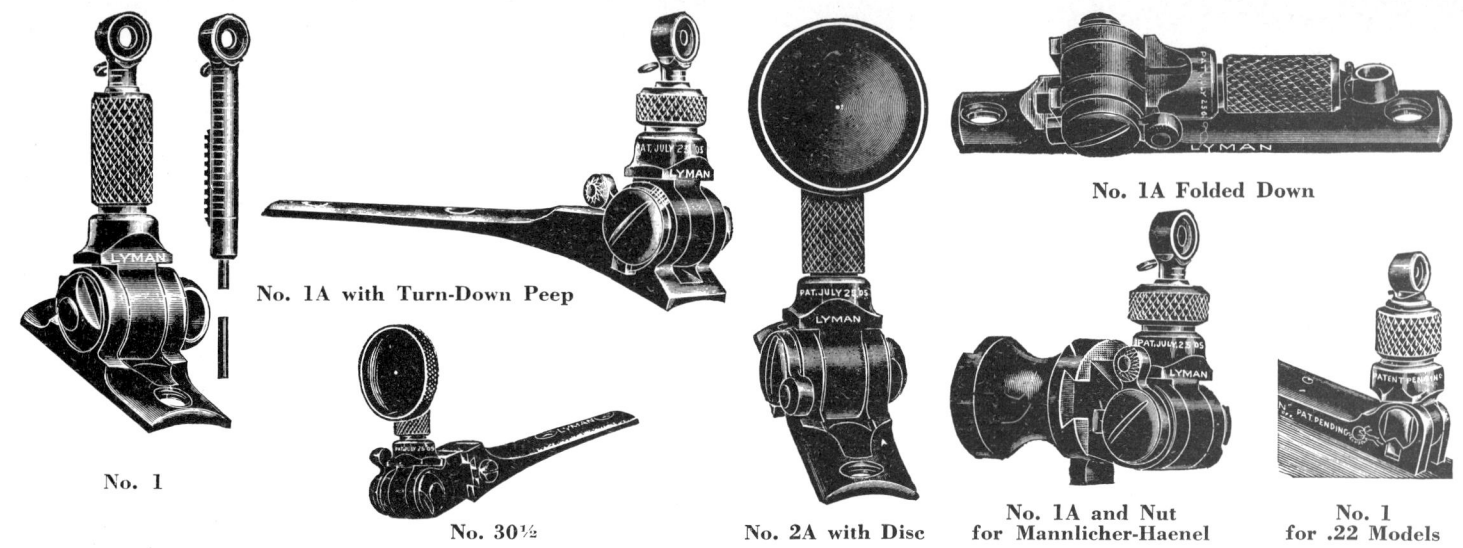

No. 1A with Turn-Down Peep
No. 1
No. 30½
No. 2A with Disc
No. 1A Folded Down
No. 1A and Nut for Mannlicher-Haenel
No. 1 for .22 Models

Lyman Sights

THE rear aperture sight, surprisingly enough, was first used by the ancient Romans on their cross bows. But with the first firearms, sights of any kind were more or less superfluous; guns were pointed rather than aimed. With improvements in barrels and the introduction of rifling came either the resurrection or re-discovery of the rear aperture sight. In the last century, some crude attempts were made at an elevating rear aperture sight, usually consisting merely of screws flattened on the end with a small hole drilled in this flat portion; elevation was obtained by turning this screw in the stock, one-half revolution giving an elevation equal to one-half the pitch of the thread. Later, sights were manufactured with a base which screwed to the tang and to which perpendicular slides were attached on which the aperture rode; it was not positive in adjustment and was no great improvement.

This was the condition of the rear aperture sight up to the latter 1860's and early '70's when the old, long barreled rifles were being replaced with the shorter ones. This entailed a reduction of the sight radius; i.e., the distance between the front and rear sights, which did not tend to increase accuracy of aim, for it is well known that decreasing the sight radius increases the error of holding a proportionate amount. Accordingly, several inventive hunters set to work to discover some way of increasing the sight radius. The crotch sight was eliminated because it was found impossible to use much nearer than 12 or 14" from the eye. Several more or less successful rear aperture sights were made, but it remained for William Lyman to develop and perfect the Tang Rear Sight which, in all its essential details, remains the standard today.

With the introduction of repeating rifles, and in particular the Winchester 95 on which it was found impractical to mount a tang sight, Mr. Lyman brought out the No. 21 sight, the first practical receiver sight ever placed on the market. Other receiver sights for various models of rifles soon followed. Refer to the Lyman Chart for the complete line.

How to Aim with Lyman Sights

The aperture rear sights are so designed that the *point of strongest light* is in the center of the aperture and the eye will automatically draw the front sight to this point, thus centering the sights without conscious effort; the shooter can *disregard the rear sight—merely look through it.*

Lyman Hunting Peep Sights have only a slight rim around the aperture; this should appear as a blur so that no portion of the field of view is hidden; the center of this blur is still the point of strongest light, and there the eye will bring the front sight if attention is focused on the front sight and object. Practice at throwing up the rifle quickly and aiming at distant objects is necessary to become proficient with this method of sighting, but more inaccuracy is caused by trying to focus the front sight in the center of the rear aperture than in letting the rear sight blur and paying attention to the front sight and object to be hit.

In target shooting, a large disc is recommended which definitely cuts off the light from around the aperture. The point of strongest light is still in the center and the eye will automatically function as it does in the hunting sights. This simplification of the aiming process makes much quicker shooting possible, because the front sight is more easily and accurately placed on the object to be fired at, while eye strain is greatly lessened, if not entirely eliminated.

Applying and Using Lyman Tang Rear Sights

A set of mounting screws is furnished with every sight. After screwing the base to the tang, turn the sight up so that the spring in the joint holds it in position for shooting; on some rifles, the sight should fold down forward instead of backward when not in use.

If the tang is not true and allows the sight to lean to one side, put a strip of thick paper under that side of the base. The rear open sight should be removed from the barrel, for it stands directly in the way of a large part of the view; it can be replaced by the Lyman No. 6 Folding Leaf Sight or the slot can be filled with a Lyman No. 12 Blank.

Sight the rifle at a target by adjusting front sight sideways, rear sight by its elevation. The desired results may also be obtained by loosening the mounting screws of the rear sight and inserting under one side of the sight a paper shim of the proper thickness; placed under the right side it will throw the aperture to the left and change the grouping of shots on the target proportionately to the left; to change to the right, insert shim under left side of sight base.

The graduations on the stems of the tang sight are .05" apart; they indicate arbitrary adjustments, but are a valuable aid in determining definite adjustments for the shooter's particular gun. If shooting low, raise the stem by turning knurled sleeve clockwise; if too high, lower stem by turning counter clockwise.

REFERENCE PRICE LIST
For Readers of "The GUN DIGEST"

The following approximate prices, quoted solely as a guide for readers of "The GUN DIGEST" in determining relative values, represent 1940 and 1941 (last published) approximate list prices of then current models.

The listing in "The GUN DIGEST" of standard guns and accessories is not, and should not be construed as, an offer to sell such or similar merchandise. **Do not order merchandise from this Price List or from "The GUN DIGEST".**

For a list of available guns, accessories and other "hard-to-get" items, send 25¢ in coin or War Stamps (refunded with first order) for Klein's Guaranteed Bargain Catalog.

KLEIN'S SPORTING GOODS   508 South Halsted St., Chicago 7, Illinois.

HIGH POWER RIFLES

Page		Approx. Price
19	Winchester Model 70 Standard Grade	$78
	With Lyman No. 48WJS Receiver Sight	93
	With Lyman No. 57W Receiver Sight	85
	Winchester Model 70 National Match	121
	Winchester Model 70 Target	132
	Winchester Model 70 Bull Gun	143
	Winchester Model 70 Super Grade	108
	With Lyman 48WJS Receiver Sight	128
20	Winchester Model 71	75
	Without checkering, grip cap, sling and swivels	65
	Winchester Model 64	61
	With Lyman No. 56 Receiver Sight	71
	Winchester Model 64 Deer Rifle	75
	.219 Winchester Zipper Model 64	67
	With 22H Sporting Rear Sight	63
	Winchester Model 65	51
	.218 Bee Model 65	57
	With Open Sporting Rear Sight	51
	Winchester Model 94 Carbine	41
21	Remington "Woodmaster" Model 81	88
	Special Grade	99
	Peerless Grade	203
	Expert Grade	284
	Premier Grade	364
	Remington "Gamemaster" Model 141	70
	Special Grade	81
	Peerless Grade	184
	Premier Grade	350
	Remington Model 720, with Open Sights	78
	With Redfield No. 70RST	86
	With Marble-Goss Receiver Sight	89
	With Lyman No. 48 Receiver Sight	93
	Winchester Model 07, 5-shot magazine	88
	With 10-shot magazine	90
	Savage Model 23-D and 23-C	42
22	Marlin Model 36-A Carbine	38
	Marlin Model 36 Sporting Carbine	38
	Marlin Model 36-A Rifle	42
	Marlin Model 36-A DL	53
	Savage Model 99-EG	62
	Savage Model 99-R	70
	Savage Model 99-RS	84

.22 CALIBER RIFLES

Page		Approx. Price
30	Winchester Model 52 Standard Target (flat top)	
	Without sights	57
	Win. 93B front, 82A rear sights	64
	Lyman 17A front, 82A rear sights	67
	Lyman 17A, Marble-Goss 52 ext. receiver	76
	Lyman 17 SN, Vaver W52 L.T. ext. receiver	80
	Model 52 Standard Target (round top receiver)	
	Lyman 17A front, 57F receiver sights	68
	Or with 48F receiver sight	76
	Or with Lyman 52F extension receiver	78
	With Win. 93B front, Lyman 48F receiver	73
	Model 52 Heavy Barrel Match (flat top)	
	Without sights	66
	Lyman 77 or Redfield 66 front only	71
	Lyman 77, Marble-Goss 52 M.S. ext.	87
	Vaver 36 F.S. with 35E barrel band front, Vaver 35 Mielt Ext. receiver	97
	Model 52 Heavy Barrel Match (round top)	
	Lyman 77 front, 4B FH receiver sights	87
	Lyman 77 front and 52 FH ext. receiver	89
	Vaver W11AT front, Vaver 5237 ext. rec.	94
	Model 52 Bull Gun (without sights)	78
	Model 52 Sporting Rifle (without sights)	91
	Redfield full gold bead, Lyman 57 FH	101
	Or with Lyman 48F receiver sight	109
31	Winchester Model 75 Target (without sights)	33
	Win. 99A front, 84A ext. rear peep	39
	With Winchester 8X telescope sight	46
	Lyman 77 front, 58E receiver sights	48
	Vaver 1175 front, 3875 receiver	49
	Redfield 63 front, 75 HW receiver	49
	Winchester Model 75 Sporting Rifle	34
	With Lyman 57E receiver sight	41
	Winchester Model 72	18
	With 97B front and 80A peep rear	19
	Winchester Model 72 Gallery	18
32	Winchester Model 67	7

Page		Approx. Price
32	Model 67 Miniature Target Boring	$11.50
	Model 67 Junior	7
	Winchester Model 68	8
	Winchester Model 69	14
	Winchester Model 69 Target	17
	Winchester Model 69 Match Rifle	24
33	Marlin Model 80-DL	14
	Marlin Model 80-C	12
	Marlin Model 80-CSB	15
	Marlin Model 81-DL	17
	Marlin Model 81-C	16
	Marlin Model 100	7
	Marlin Model 100-SB	9.50
	Marlin Model 101-DL	9
	Marlin Model 101	7
35	Remington "Rangemaster" Model 37 (without sights)	69
	With Redfield globe front sight	72
	With Redfield globe front, Rem. receiver	88
	Redfield globe front, Marble-Goss rec.	88
	Redfield globe, Wittek Vaver receiver	92
	Remington "Matchmaster" Model 513 Target	39
	Without sights	33
	Remington Model 513 S Sporter	34
	With Remington receiver peep sight	36
	Remington "Sportmaster" Model 512	18
	512 P Grade	19
	512 SB Grade	18
	Remington "Scoremaster" Model 511	14
	511 P Grade	14.50
	Remington "Targetmaster" Model 510	7
	510 P Grade	8
	510 SB Grade	7
36	Savage Model 23AA Sporter	32
	Savage Model 19 Target	38
	Without sights	32
	Model 19M Heavy Barrel Target	48
	Model 19H	38
	Savage Model 5	17.50
	Model 5-S	18
	Savage Model 4	13
	Model 4-S	14
	Savage Model 3	7
	Model 3-S	8
37	Mossberg Model 46M	19.50
	Mossberg Model 46B	17
	Mossberg Model 42M	17
	Mossberg Model 44B (for .22 L.R. only)	18
	Mossberg Model 26B (for all .22 cartridges)	7
38	Springfield No. 86	15
	No. 086	16
	Springfield No. 84	12
	No. 084	12.50
	Springfield No. 15	6
	Stevens No. 26 Crack Shot	7
39	Stevens No. 416-2 Target	39
	Without sights	33
	Stevens No. 66	16
	No. 066	17
	Stevens No. 56	12.50
	No. 056	13.50
	Stevens No. 53	7
	No. 053	8
40	Marlin Model 39A	36
	Stevens No. 417 Walnut Hill Target	
	No. 417-0	72.50
	No. 417-1	71
	No. 417-2	63
	No. 417-3	56
	With extra-heavy, 29" barrel, add	40
	Iver Johnson Model 2-X	6
	Model 2-XA	11
	Model X	5
	Model X-A	10
	Mossberg Model 42TR (with trap)	19
	Without trap	13
41	Remington "Fieldmaster" Model 121	32.50
	Peerless Grade, $99; Expert Grade	143.50
	Remington Model 121 SB Standard	35
	Savage Model 29	31
	Winchester Model 61	32.50
	With 24" octagon barrel for .22 Short, L.R. or W.R.F. individually	34
	Model 61 Miniature Target	37
	Winchester Model 62	24

Page		Approx. Price
43	Winchester Model 74	$22
	With elevating peep sight	23
	Winchester Model 63	40
	Remington Model 550	24
	Model 550P	25
	Remington "Speedmaster" Model 241	40
	Special Grade, $51; Peerless, $107; Expert, $151; Premier Grade	182
	Savage Model 7	19
	Model 7-S	20
	Savage Model 6 and 602	21
	Model 6-S	22
	Stevens Model 76	21
	Model 076	21.50
	Stevens Model 57	18
	Model 057	19
44	Marlin Model A-DL	18
	Marlin A-1 C	17
	Mossberg Model 51M	22.50
	Springfield No. 87	20
	Model 087	20.50
	Springfield No. 85	17
	Model 085	18

SHOTGUNS

Page		Approx. Price
78	Remington Model 11 with plain barrel	68
	With raised solid matted rib	78
	Raised ventilated rib	85
	Special Grade, $74; Tournament Grade	183
	Expert Grade, $264; Premier Grade	344
	Special Long Range Choke, extra	5
	Built-in Poly Choke, extra	11
	Cutts Compensator, extra	22.50
	Model 11R, Riot Grade	68
	Remington "Sportsman" (same as Model 11)	
	Savage Model 720	61
	Model 720 with Poly Choke	72
	Model 720 with Cutts Comp	83
	Winchester Model 40	68
	Model 40 Skeet, with Cutts Comp	99
79	Browning Utility Field Gun	82
	Browning Grade I	69
	Browning Special, with raised matted rib	78
	With ventilated rib	86
	Ithaca Model 37R	66
	Ithaca Model 37 Featherlight	57
80	Winchester Model 12 Standard Grade	57
	With solid raised matted rib	66
	With ventilated rib	103
	Model 12 Heavy Duck Gun	63
	With matted rib	73
	Model 12 Pigeon Grade	200
81	Remington Model 31	57
	With raised solid matted rib	67
	Special Long Range Choke, extra	5
	Model 31R, Riot Grade	57
	Special Grade, $68; Tournament Grade	170
	Expert Grade, $253; Premier Grade	336
	Winchester Model 42	46.50
	With matted rib	56
	Winchester Model 97 (Standard and Riot)	45
	Stevens No. 620	48
	No. 621 with matted rib	52
	No. 620-P with Poly Choke	54
82	Ithaca Field Grade Double	60
	Extras: Automatic ejector, $17; selective single trigger, $25; beavertail forearm, $15; ventilated rib	20
	Magnum 12 and 10 gauges, extra	16
	Ithaca No. 2 Grade (extras same as Field Grade)	75
	Ithaca No. 4 Ejector Grade	146
	With selective single trigger, beavertail forearm, ventilated rib	218
	Ithaca No. 5 Ejector Grade	255
	Ventilated rib, extra	30
	Ithaca No. 7 Ejector Grade	468
	Ithaca $1000 Grade Double	1060
83	L. C. Smith Field Grade	64
	Extras: Automatic ejectors, $17; non-selective one-trigger, $16; selective trigger, $25; beavertail forearm	19
	L. C. Smith Ideal Grade (extras same as Field Grade)	85
	Specialty Grade, with automatic ejectors	150
	Selective trigger, extra	32
	Beavertail forearm, extra	25
	Crown Grade, with automatic ejectors	315
	Selective trigger, extra	33
	Beavertail forearm, extra	36
	Monogram Grade	640
	Beavertail forearm, extra	63
	DeLuxe Grade	1458
	Wild Fowl Gun, available in any Grade; extra	7
84	Parker V.H.E. Grade	140
	Extras: Selective single trigger, $29; beavertail forearm, $15; vent. rib	28
	G.H.E. Grade (extras same as V.H.E.)	160
	D.H.E. Grade	197
	Extras: Selective single trigger, $32; beavertail forearm, $19; vent. rib	30
	C.H.E. Grade	293
	Extras: Selective single trigger, $32; beavertail forearm, $25; vent. rib	35
	B.H.E. Grade	393.50
	Extras same as C.H.E. except beavertail forearm	29

Page		Approx. Price
84	A.H.E. Grade	$535
	Extras same as C.H.E. except beavertail forearm	31
	A.A.H.E. Grade	757
	With selective single trigger	799
	Beavertail forearm, $38; vent. rib	46
	A.I. Special Grade	898
	With selective single trigger	950
	Beavertail forearm, vent. rib, each	46
85	Fox Model B	34
	Fox Sterlingworth Grade	65
	Sterlingworth Ejector Grade	83
	Sterlingworth DeLuxe Grade	70
	Sterlingworth DeLuxe Ejector Grade	87
	Selective single trigger, extra	28
	Beavertail forearm, extra	14
	Fox AE Grade	104
	Extras: Beavertail forearm, $18; vent. rib, $45; selective single trigger	28
	Fox CE Grade	171
	Beavertail forearm, $26; other extras same as AE Grade.	
	Fox SP Grade	86
	SPE Grade	104
86	Winchester Model 24	38
	Winchester Model 21 Standard Grade	
	Double trigger, plain extractors	94
	Double trigger, selective ejectors	111
	Single trigger, plain extractors	111
	Single trigger, selective ejector	128
	Ventilated rib, extra	40
	Winchester Model 21 Duck Gun	144
	Ventilated rib, extra	40
	Winchester Model 21 Custom Built	
	Field guns, from $144 to	177
	Skeet and Trap guns	181
	Duck gun	184
87	Lefever Nitro Special	39
	With single trigger	44
	Western Arms Long Range Double	27
	With single trigger	31
	Hunter Special	45
	The Fulton	39
	With recoil pad and two ivory sights	41
	Iver Johnson Double Barrel	35
	With selective automatic ejector	42
88	Stevens No. 530M	29
	Stevens No. 530	31
	With non-selective single trigger	34.50
	Springfield No. 311	29
	Springfield No. 5151	30
	No. 5151-ST	34
89	Marlin Model 90	52
	Model 90 ST	57
	Stevens No. 22-410	20
	Remington Model 32A Standard	154
	With raised solid matted rib	164
	Tournament Grade, $337; Expert Grade	398
	Premier Grade	501
	Stevens No. 240	20
	Savage Models 420 and 430, from $47 to	65
90	Stevens No. 107	13
	Springfield No. 94	11
	No. 94-P	17
	Savage Model 220	14
	With Poly Choke	20
	Savage Model 219	19
	Savage Utility Gun	25
91	Winchester Model 37	12
	H & R Bay State No. 9	12
	H & R Standard Model 48	13
	Iver Johnson Matted Top Rib	12.50
	Iver Johnson Champion	9
92	H & R Game Gun	20
	Stevens No. 59	18
	Stevens No. 58	15
	Mossberg Model 85D	17
	Mossberg Model 83D	15
	Stevens No. 258	17
	Springfield No. 39	17
	Springfield No. 38	14
	Springfield No. 238	16
99	Parker Single Barrels; S.C. Grade	227
	S.B. Grade, $293; S.A. Grade, $453; S.A.A. Grade, $652; S.A.I Grade	768
	Parker Double Barrels; V.H.E. Grade	217
	G.H.E., $238; D.H.E., $278; C.H.E., $385; B.H.E., $490; A.H.E., $634; A.A.H.E., $883; A.I Special Grade	1043
	Ithaca Single Barrels; No. 4 Ejector Grade	159
	No. 5 Ejector, $202; No. 7 Ejector, $382 and $1000 Grade.	
	L. C. Smith Single Barrels; Olympic Grade	100
	Specialty Grade, $155; Crown, $288; Monogram, $476; DeLuxe	1190
	L. C. Smith Doubles; Ideal Grade	185
	Specialty, $247; Crown, $423; Monogram, $749; DeLuxe	1577
	Winchester Model 21	142
	With ventilated rib	182
	Iver Johnson Supertrap	53
	Iver Johnson Special Trap	20
	Lefever Model 3	47.50
100	Remington Model 32TC	$189
	Remington Model 31TC Target Grade	111
	Special Long Range Choke, extra	5
	Model 31 Trap Special	80
	Winchester Model 12	80.50
	With Ventilated rib	117
	Ladies' and Juniors' Model 12	83
	Trap Heavy Duck Gun	87
	Ithaca Model 37T	100
101	Parker Double Barrel Skeet; V.H.E. Grade	184
	G.H.E., $204; D.H.E., $248; C.H.E., $350; B.H.E., $455; A.H.E., $598; A.A.H.E., $837; A.I Special Grade	977
	Ithaca Skeet; Field Grade, $118; No. 2	133
	Ventilated rib, extra	20
	No. 4, $190; No. 5, $258; No. 7, $438, $1000 Grade	1056
	Ventilated rib, extra	30
101	L. C. Smith Double Barrel Skeet Special	127
	Specialty Skeet, $215; Crown Skeet	388
	Monogram Skeet, $707; DeLuxe Skeet	1534
	Winchester Model 21 Skeet	142
	With ventilated rib	182
	Iver Johnson Skeet-er	55
	With selective automatic ejector	65
103	Browning Automatic Skeet	112
	With beavertail forearm	121
	Ithaca Model 37S Repeater	77
	Winchester Model 12 (plain barrel)	68
	With matted rib barrel	77
	With ventilated rib barrel	114
	With Cutts Comp. on plain barrel	90
	Winchester Model 42 (plain barrel)	53
	With matted rib barrel	63
	Remington "Sportsman" (plain barrel)	77
	With raised solid rib	87
	With raised ventilated rib	94
	Remington Model 31 (plain barrel)	68
	With raised solid rib	77
	With raised ventilated rib	92.50
	Remington Model 32 (plain barrels)	157
	With raised solid rib	167
	With raised ventilated rib	182
	Stevens No. 620-CS	85
	Savage Model 720-C	90

ACCESSORIES

Page		Approx. Price
138	Lyman No. 12 Blank	.50
139	Lyman Disc	.50
	Lyman No. 1 and No. 2 Tang Rear Sights, each	4
	No. 1A and No. 2A Tang Rear Sights, each	4.50
	Tang Rear Sight No. 29½, $6; No. 30½	6.50
140	Nos. 48S, 48K, each	11
	Nos. 48C, 48WJS, 48RS, 48M, 48F, 48FH, each	11.50
	Nos. 48J, 48JH, each	13
	No. 55 Receiver Sight	2
	No. 56 Micrometer Receiver Sight	7
	No. 58 Micrometer Target Sight	7
	No. 57 Receiver Sight	6
	No. 35 Receiver Sight (without disc)	10
141	Nos. 3, 28, 20 Jack, 31, 37 and 39, each	1
	No. 4 Hunting Sight	1.50
	Ivory Bead Carbine Front Sights, each	1
	Ivory Tipped Caterpillar No. 23	2
	No. 17A Globe Target	2.50
	No. 77 Detachable Target	4
	No. 5 and No. 5B, each	5
	Ramp Style Front Sight Holder	4
	No. 6 Folding Leaf Sight	2
	Nos. 10 and 11 (with reamer), each	1
	No. 10D (with tap and wrench)	1
144	Marble-Goss Receiver Tang Sight	12
	For M1, M2 Springfields, Rem. Model 34, Winchester Single Shots and B.S.A.	13.50
	Extra Bases	2.50
	Discs	.75
	Series 750 Marble-Goss Receiver Sight	7.50
	No. 70R Receiver Sight	12
	Extended Receiver Sight No. 30	9
	Super Springfield Sight No. 7	9
	Flexible Rear Sight	4
	Extra discs, 50c; Nos. 1 and 2	.25
	Special Rear Sight	4
	Simplex Rear Sight	2
	Receiver Sight	6.50
	No. 95 Adjustable Leaf Sight	1.25
145	Sporting Leaf Sights	1.50
	For Remington Models 8 and 81	2
	Standard or Improved Bead Front Sights	1
	Reversible or Sheard "Gold" Sights	1.50
	Carbine and Special Sights	1
	V-M Front Sight	1.50
	Ivory Front and Rear Shotgun Sights (for double barrel guns, with reamer)	1
	Bi-Color front, ivory rear	1
	Ivory or Bi-Color (for single barrel guns, with tap and wrench)	1
	Redfield No. 100, from $10.50 to	12
	Redfield No. 90, from $8 to	9.50
	No. 70 Micrometer Receiver Sight	6.50
	No. 75 Extension	7.50
	Olympic Micrometer Receiver Sight	12.50
	With master sighting disc	14.50
	No. 102 Hunting Receiver Sight	4.50
	For .22's, with two adjustments	4
	For .22's, with windage only	2.50
146	Redfield Sporting Rear Sights	$ 1.75
	Adjustable Folding Leaf Sights	1.50
	Olympic Detachable Target Front Sight	6.50
	Globe Front Sight	2.50
	Detachable Globe	4
	Ramp Front Sight (without hood)	5.50
	With hood	6.50
	Protected Gold Face Patridge Sight	1.50
	Full Gold Bead Sight	1.50
	Ivory and Gold Tip Sights	1
	Full Block Sight	2
	Pistol and Revolver (Ivory and Gold Tip)	1
	Protected Gold Face Patridge	1.50
149	Combination Target and Spotting Scope	85
	¾" Target Scope (clock mounts)	45
	With plain mounts	38
	High power eyepiece, extra	9
150	1⅛" Target Scope (click mounts)	60
	With plain mounts	53
	Small Game Scope (click mounts)	38
	With plain mounts	30
	10", 12" or 14" lengths, extra	4
	Model A Target Scope	85
	Model B Target Scope	65
	Model C Target or Varmint Scope	50
	No. 15 Telescope Attachment	22
	For Jr. Targetspot, Fecker Scopes	27
	No. 12 and No. 9 Telescope Attachment, each	18
	No. 200 Telescope Attachment	16
	No. 850 Telescope Attachment	10
	Above models without dust caps, $2 less	
	Model T Mounts	16.50
	Model H Mounts	15
	No. RF1 Range Finder	11
	No. 5M4 Internal Adjustment Scope	8
	No. 8M4	8
	No. 9R Side Mounting Scope	9
	No. 7M4 Top Mounting Scope	9
	No. 7R Scope	10
	Redfield Senior Mount 20 to	25
	Junior Mount, for Weaver Scopes	8
	For other scopes	10
	Stith "Install-It-Yourself" Mount	12
	For Savage Model 23 and Weaver 29S combination	10
	Stith Streamline Mounts (factory installed)	16.50
	Griffin & Howe Standard Mount	23
	Double Lever Mount	28
	Double Lever with micrometer wind gauge	30
	For 26 mm scopes or larger	33
	Double Lever for Lyman Alaskan	25
	Double Screw-locking for Weaver scopes	15
	Fitting mounts to rifle, extra	5
151	Lyman Super-Targetspot	75
	In 20 power	80
	Lyman Targetspot	60
	Lyman Junior Targetspot	45
	438 Field Scope (with regular mount)	18
	With Micrometer Mount	25
	"Known Ranger"	1.50
	Alaskan All-Weather Hunting Scope	50
	With Griffin & Howe Mount	75
	With Redfield Jr. Mount	60
152	Weaver Model 440, with T Mount	37.50
	With B Mount	42
	Weaver Model 330, with T Mount	32
	With B Mount	36
	Weaver Model 29S, with T Mount	14
	With B Mount	19
	Weaver Model 329, with T Mount	5.50
	With B Mount	10
	Weaver Model 333, with T Mount	9
	With B Mount	14
	Weaver Model 355, with T Mount	10.50
	With B Mount	15
	Weaver Model 1X, with T Mount	19.50
	With B Mount	22.50
153	Mossberg Model A "Spotshot"	23.50
	Model A "Spotshot" Stand	8
	B & L 65 mm Spotting Scope	78
	B & L 80 mm Team Captain (21X)	275
	Extra eyepieces	7.50
	B & L NRA (with 19.5X eyepiece)	55
	12.8 or 26X eyepieces, each	6
	36.5X eyepiece	7.50
	B & L 45 mm Draw Tube Scope	30
	Wollensak Vari-Power Spotting Scope	30.50
	With Case only	21
	Telescope Clamp, extra	13
	Tripod and Case only	10
	Fecker No. 1 (2⅛") Scope	62.50
	Fecker No. 1 Special Scope (2 eyepieces)	100
	Fecker No. 2 Scope	56
	Extra eyepieces for all models	7.50
154	B & L Binoculars, Center Focusing $72 to	93.50
	Individual Focusing $66 to	88.50
	Zephyr-Light Binoculars $80 to	101.50
	Companion and Balar, each	19.50
	Ray Ban Shooting Glasses	13
	Wollensak Vari-Power Telescope $15 to	26.50
	Standard Telescope $11 to	58.50
	Explorer Telescope	5
	Pockescope Sr.	3
	Wollensak 8X Prism Binoculars	62.50
	Rambler	15
155	Poly Choke, installed	15
	Cutts Comp. ($3.50 extra for fitting)	18.50
	Additional Tubes, each	3
	Weaver Choke ($2.50 extra for attaching)	10
	Extra Chokes, each	1.50

SMITH & WESSON THE FIRST NAME IN .357 MAGNUM® JUST GOT SMALLER!

NEW MODEL 640

One of the most popular small frame revolvers ever, is now available in .357 Magnum®. The 5-shot Smith & Wesson Centennial® Model 640 has been re-engineered to accommodate the original Magnum round introduced by Smith & Wesson 60 years ago. Weighing in at 25 ounces and measuring only 6 ¾ inches in length the Model 640 will become the small revolver of choice.

The new Model 640 features a full lug barrel and pinned black ramp front sight for sure sight alignment.

This American made stainless steel revolver features a fully concealed hammer, a 2 ⅛ inch barrel, fixed notch rear sight and pinned black ramp front sight for improved sight alignment. A longer extractor rod makes it easier to extract

Smith & Wesson offers powerful 357 Magnum® performance in the small Model 640 Centennial.

both .357 Magnum® and .38 Special® cases. The smooth trigger pull and comfortable Uncle Mike's Boot Grip give the shooter positive control of this powerful package.

The Model 640 comes with a Lifetime Service Policy and a Worldwide Warranty Repair Network, just part of the SMITH & WESSON ADVANTAGE™.

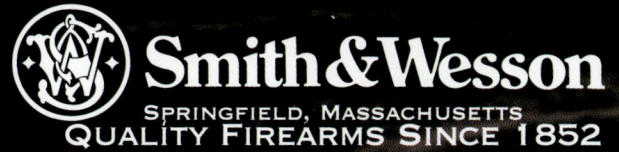

Smith & Wesson
SPRINGFIELD, MASSACHUSETTS
QUALITY FIREARMS SINCE 1852

For more information and the name of a Stocking Dealer near you

Compare the outstanding balance of the
32" CONQUISTA™

...with other premier quality over and unders in 28" and 30"

A new action with extraordinary fast locktime. Trigger can be instantly adjusted in 2.5mm increments for precise pull length. Broad, double ventilated matted rib sighting plane. Exact wood to metal fit. Carefully selected, pleasing American Walnut with outstanding 20 line cut checkering. And, each Conquista is individually hand balanced for perfect pointability whether you choose the 28", 30" or 32" barrel. 5 Contre choke tubes supplied.

From MAROCCHI • One of Italy's most outstanding gun makers with a legend of fine family craftsmanship.

From Precision Sales International, exclusive importers of fine products from the world's best gun makers. Send for full line catalog and information, or write: P.O. BOX 1776, WESTFIELD, MA 01086 • (413) 562-5055
THROUGH BETTER DEALERS EVERYWHERE

▲ For complete information on the **Conquista, Conquista Left** and **Lady Sport** by **Marocchi**, please refer to the **GUNDEX®** section of Gun Digest.

For complete information on the incomparable line of **Anschütz** rifles and pistols, please refer to the **GUNDEX®** section of Gun Digest. ▼

What is missing in most .22 rifles?

...the incredible accuracy of an Anschutz.

ANSCHÜTZ
SINCE 1856

- SPORTER RIFLES
- SILHOUETTE RIFLES
- MATCH RIFLES
- EXEMPLAR PISTOLS
- AIR RIFLES
- ACHIEVER RIFLES

From Precision Sales International, exclusive importers of fine products from the world's best gun makers. Send $2.00 for full line catalog and information, or write: P.O. BOX 1776, WESTFIELD, MA 01086 • (413) 562-5055
THROUGH BETTER DEALERS EVERYWHERE

US SHOOTING TEAM OFFICIAL SUPPLIER

"America's Defender"... for things worth protecting.

AMERICA'S DEFENDER
Beretta M9/92F
U.S. Armed Forces
The 1ST Decade
1985-1995

In the long, colorful history of handguns, nothing equals the record of the Beretta 92FS. Since 1985, "America's Defender" has been the official sidearm of the U.S. Military. It's an honor that was won the hard way; by defeating all comers in the toughest series of handgun trials ever conducted.

During the past decade, the Beretta M9/92FS has proved its worth in the thick of U.S. military action; in operations such as Just Cause, Urgent Fury, Desert Storm, Restore Hope and Uphold Democracy to name a few. The Beretta 9mm 92 series and the .40 caliber 96 series have also been named official sidearm of thousands of law enforcement agencies in the U.S. and in over 50 countries throughout the world.

For personal protection, these same superbly balanced, ergonomically engineered Berettas provide the ultimate in quality, reliability, accuracy and firepower. So if you're considering a handgun to protect home, family or business, make "America's Defender" your defender. There's a Beretta designed for your exact needs waiting at your Beretta dealer.
Beretta U.S.A. Corp., 17601 Beretta Drive, Accokeek, Maryland 20607, (301) 283-2191.

Beretta U.S.A.

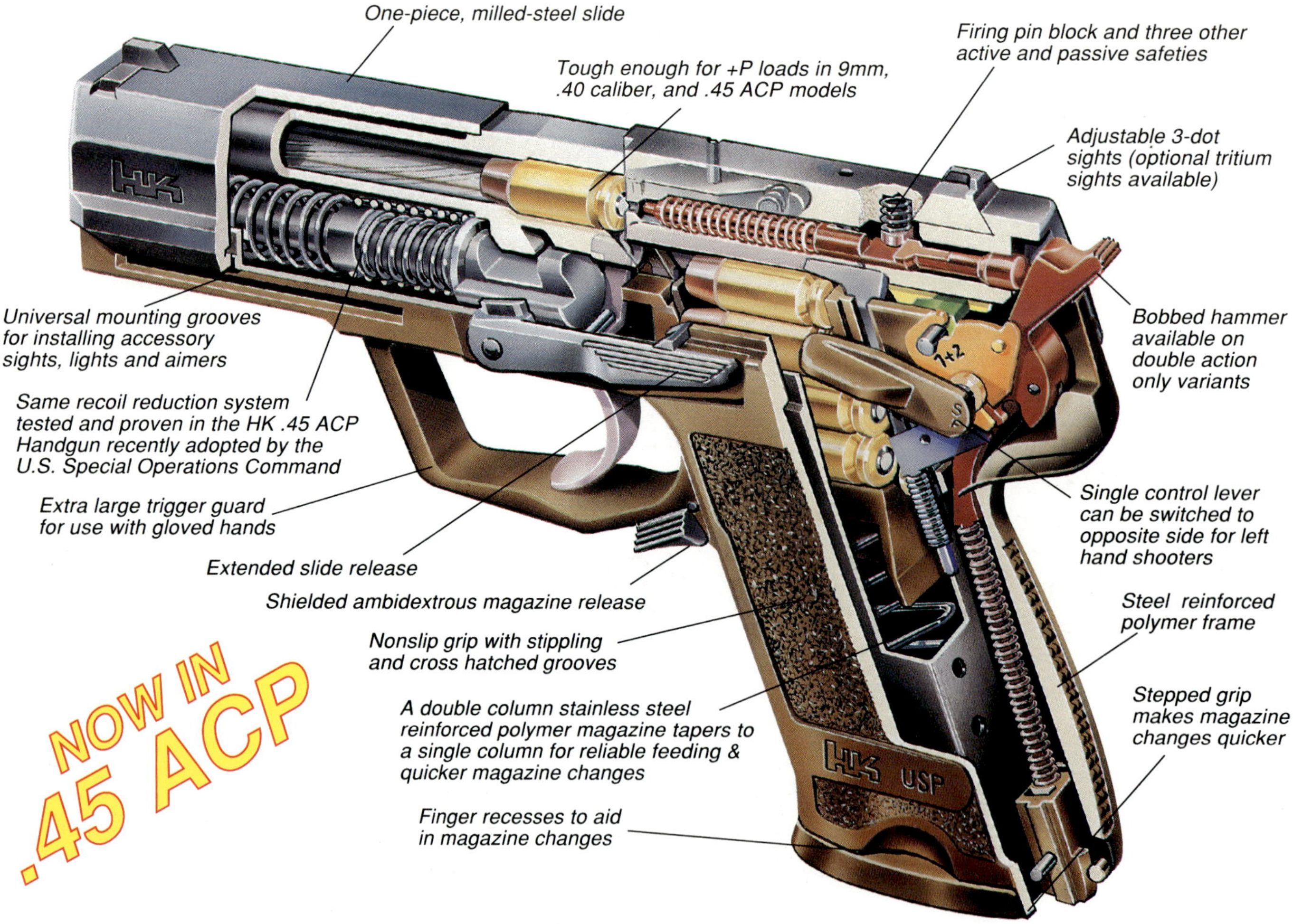

One-piece, milled-steel slide

Tough enough for +P loads in 9mm, .40 caliber, and .45 ACP models

Firing pin block and three other active and passive safeties

Adjustable 3-dot sights (optional tritium sights available)

Bobbed hammer available on double action only variants

Universal mounting grooves for installing accessory sights, lights and aimers

Same recoil reduction system tested and proven in the HK .45 ACP Handgun recently adopted by the U.S. Special Operations Command

Extra large trigger guard for use with gloved hands

Extended slide release

Shielded ambidextrous magazine release

Nonslip grip with stippling and cross hatched grooves

A double column stainless steel reinforced polymer magazine tapers to a single column for reliable feeding & quicker magazine changes

Finger recesses to aid in magazine changes

Single control lever can be switched to opposite side for left hand shooters

Steel reinforced polymer frame

Stepped grip makes magazine changes quicker

NOW IN .45 ACP

Form follows function.

In 1993, Heckler & Koch introduced a revolutionary new pistol — the USP. The HK USP (Universal Self-loading Pistol) represents the epitome of a modern pistol, designed especially for you, the American shooter. Each USP variant gives you a distinct choice. Choice of fire modes. Choice of controls. Choice of conditions of carry. Choice of calibers (.40 S&W, 9mm and now .45 ACP).

Special features favored by law enforcement, military, and civilian shooters provided the design criteria for the USP. Its controls are uniquely American — influenced by such famous pistols as the Government Model 1911. And like the Model 1911, the USP can be safely carried "cocked and locked".

The control lever, a combination safety and decocking lever, is frame mounted and quickly accessible, unlike the slide mounted safeties common on many other pistols.

A special "HE" (Hostile Environment) finish protects metal parts of the USP from the worst types of corrosion and wear, including prolonged exposure to salt water.

Another unique feature of the HK USP is its patented mechanical recoil reduction system incorporated into the recoil and buffer spring assembly located below the barrel. This recoil reduction system was tested and proven in the HK .45 ACP Handgun recently designed for the U.S. Special Operations Command (SOCOM). Using the same system as the USP, the "SOCOM pistol" fired more than 30,000 +P cartridges without damage to any major components.

At Heckler & Koch, form follows function. All HK pistols are designed and manufactured to meet the operational requirements of the most demanding users. And they're covered by a lifetime warranty.

In a world of compromise, some don't.

USP
Handgun innovation for the next century.

For more information and the location of your nearest Authorized Dealer, contact:
Heckler & Koch, Inc.
21480 Pacific Boulevard
Sterling, Virginia 20166 USA
Telephone (703) 450-1900

For your 22–minute USP video tape, call 1-800-262-2079. $6.95 shipping & handling, please have VISA or Mastercard ready.

LOOK WHAT THEY CAN DO TO YOUR SHOTGUN BARRELS!

by DON ZUTZ

DID THE ANCIENT Romans have a way with words or what? *Nihil novus sub sole,* they used to say, meaning that there's nothing really new under the sun. And despite all the changes that seem to be taking place in and on shotgun barrels currently available to the shooter, the Latin expression prevails.

The typical shotgunner is picking up a lot of new terms—over-boring, back-boring, lengthening forcing cones, porting, rifling, threading for screw-in chokes, fitting the larger gauges for full-length small-bore in-serts, and cutting parabolic (curved) choke tapers—but the concepts themselves aren't all that recent. We've known about them for a long time. It's only now that typical shooters have begun to accept them, and technological advances have made them readily available.

Over-Boring

Today we also call it "back-boring," a term devised by Seattle barrelsmith Stan Baker, who thought that skeptical shooters would react unfavorably to anything with the "over-" prefix. In reality, however, the two terms mean the very same thing: A shotgun barrel bored larger than the industry or traditional standard.

And what, pray tell, is the standard? How were they arrived at for each respective gauge? In fact, to begin with, where does the term "gauge" come from?

This all started centuries ago before gunmakers had precise measuring instruments with which to detect the interior diameter of a smoothbore barrel. A method using lead balls was devised to check bore diameters and to build a semblance of uniformity into the business. The bores were gauged by the diameters of lead balls which counted a certain number to the pound. If a bore were cut to match the diameter of a lead ball which scaled 1 ounce, for instance, it was called a 16-bore because there were sixteen such balls per pound. If another barrel were cut larger so that lead balls fitting its diameter scaled ten to the pound, it was then a 10-bore. And so it went.

Originally, the sizes were referred to as "bores," but gradually the term "gauge" slipped in because the lead balls then performed the same job as the modern machinist's GO/NO-GO gauges.

When precise measuring equipment became available, the lead balls were dropped and the gunmakers set up dimensional bases for the respective bore sizes that had been developed during the lead-ball era. Those standard bore diameters, in inches, were:

Bore Size	Dia. (ins.)
4-gauge	0.935
8-gauge	0.835
10-gauge	0.775
12-gauge	0.729
14-gauge	0.693
16-gauge	0.662
20-gauge	0.615
24-gauge	0.580
28-gauge	0.550
32-gauge	0.501

The 410 is *not* considered a gauge. Its designation stems from its basic bore diameter, as it actually evolved from 44-caliber rifle cartridges. If it were converted to a gauge, it would be a 67-gauge, as it takes that many lead balls of .410-inch diameter to make a pound. Some sources mistakenly call the 410 a 36-gauge for reasons unknown to this writer, although a guess would assume that they merely came to that faulty judgment by placing it after the 32-gauge.

Despite the above standards, gunmakers throughout the world have varied their basic bore diameters variously. Many European gunmakers have used smaller diameters, especially in 12-gauge where diameters of .722- to .725-inch are common. Remington has long opted for a .727-inch 12-gauge bore. Indeed, anyone with an inquisitive mind and an interior bore micrometer can find myriad variations; however, we must quickly point out that most of them weren't radical departures from the standards until our current move to over-boring came along.

It is a moot question as to when over-boring was first used. In an 1882 book, *The Modern Sportsman's Gun & Rifle, Vol. One,* a Britisher named J.H. Walsh, who used the pseudonym "Stonehenge," was already writing about what he called "relieved" bores. Major Sir Charles Burrard, whose three-volume work, *The Modern Shotgun,* is rated an all-time classic in shotgun and shotgunning theory, also said a widening of the bore was employed shortly after the break-action breechloaders came into vogue. Wrote Burrard: "...with the universal adoption of the breech-loader, guns became to be bored as true cylinders from end to end, although this method was modified to one in which the front portion was of slightly greater diameter than the rear part...This widening of the bore...tended to greater regularity of pattern..."

In the United States, the first commercial attempts at over-boring came in the 1930s when the advent of progressive-burning powders permitted successively heavier shot charges than those formerly matched to the old standard bore diameters. The first of these may well have

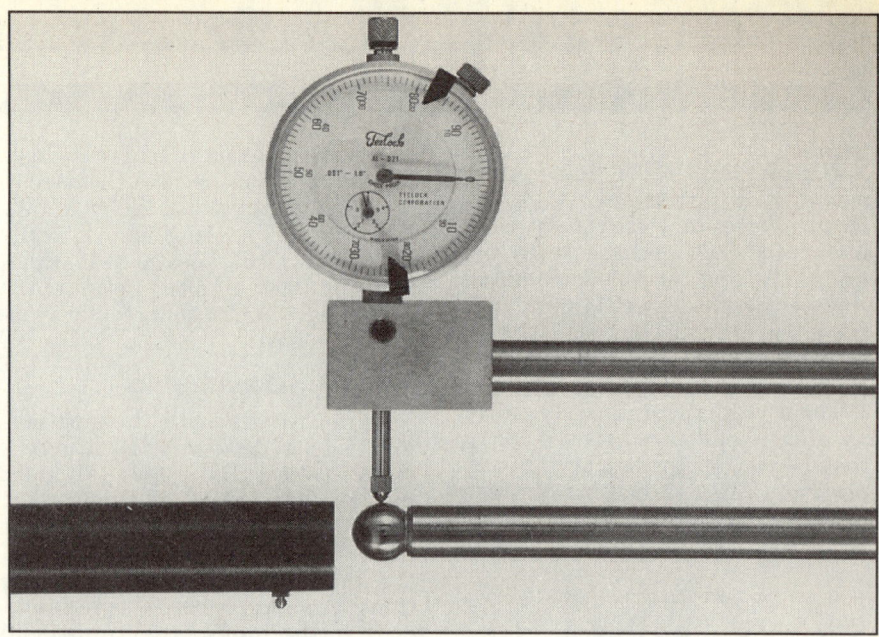

The Clymer barrel wall thickness gauge helps gunsmiths check for safety when over-boring and installing choke tube systems.

The 12-gauge main bore was long standardized at .729-inch; today, the 12 is commonly over-bored to .740-inch.

Many new shotguns of target and field grade are being designed with lengthened forcing cones and over-bored barrels. This is the Remington 90-T trap single in development.

been the A.H. Fox Gun Co., which, under the leadership of barrel specialist Burt Becker, came up with an over-bored double for the then-new, 12-gauge, 3-inch magnum load. This found publicity in the hands of Nash Buckingham, a leading outdoor scribe of the period; and in due course, A.H. Fox marketed a so-called "Super Fox," alias the H Grade, with similarly over-bored barrels. The Super Fox is a desirable collector's item today as it represents the cutting edge of scattergun technology for the 1930s.

About this same time, Remington made over-bored waterfowl barrels for the 12-gauge Models 11 and 31. These were chambered for the standard-length loads, of course, since neither gun was made in magnum persuasion. It was thought over-boring was an advantage for the then-also-new, high-velocity, 1 1/4-ounce duck loads.

These over-bores of the 1930s did not catch on. Perhaps the public was not ready for the concept. More important, however, was the matter of wads. The old card/filler stack was still in use then, and they didn't produce optimum gas seals in over-bored tubes. Today's plastic obturators are considerably more efficient in spacious bores. Suffice it to say that World War II wiped out the first attempts to popularize over-bored barrels, and the practice did not slip back into vogue until the 1970s when a scattering of trap shooters accepted it.

Exemplified by the decisions of Ruger and Browning to market over-bored 20-gauges in 1994, it would seem that back-boring is here to stay. It might help relieve some of the friction built up by steel shot loads.

Forcing Cone Lengths

Forcing cones show up as a dark ring between the chamber and main bore of a shotgun. They are conical in shape, and their purpose is to funnel the shot/wad ejecta from the larger chamber into the smaller main bore. This all sounds simple enough until one realizes that the shape of a forcing cone can impact recoil and pattern by the way it handles the charge. A short, abrupt forcing cone can actually act as a minor impediment to a smooth, transitional flow, thereby increasing recoil and causing pellet deformation.

For reasons never given, some gunmakers cut their forcing cones quite short. The Belgian-made Browning Superposed was such a piece, and it gained a reputation as a severe "kicker" among trap and Skeet shooters. I once had a Browning that beat me up quite badly, and the late Ralph T. Walker, who wrote DBI's *Shotgun Gunsmithing*, lengthened the cone to a full 2 inches; thereafter, the gun not only shot comfortably, but its patterns picked up significantly. Francis E. Sell also wrote about the advantages of lengthened cones in various GUN DIGEST features in past decades.

The lengthened forcing cone isn't a new development, either. Greener's monumental *The Gun And Its Development*, which was first published in 1881, said, "The proper shape for the chamber where it unites with the base of the barrel is a not too abrupt cone...Sometimes it is required to

The Ljutic trap gun, one of the first highly refined and hand-tuned American trap singles, had improved barrel dimensions.

have the cone longer," depending upon the charge. The smoother and easier the flow from chamber to bore, then the lower will be the recoil and the greater will be the patterning potential.

The forcing cone's hindrance of ejecta flow was noted before the 1880s, and some gunmakers attempted to negate it by making what was called a "chamberless gun." This is somewhat of a misnomer, because there was a definite chamber; however, the remainder of the bore was held to basically chamber dimensions so that the ejecta could flow without bumping through an inclined cone. The chamberless shotgun eliminated pellet deformation at the cone and apparently lowered recoil. But it required a very thin-walled case so that the wads would seal the main bore and minimize gas leakage as the ejecta exited the case mouth. These hulls were brass for strength, despite thinness. Obviously, the chamberless concept did not prevail, either.

But the lengthened forcing cone concept has arrived with gusto. They are regularly being cut into existing barrels via a T-handle wrench and reamers, and many gunmakers are now including them as part of the factory package. There is no such thing as a standard here; each gunmaker or barrelsmith goes according to his own experience, but a 5/8-inch cone is about minimal these days with 1 to 1 1/2 inches tending to be adequate for most loads. Longer cones of 2 inches or so seem advantageous with long, heavy, magnum charges. Like the over-bore, the long cone is here to stay.

Porting

The vented muzzle device for stabilizing small arms traces well back to Col. Cutts and his bulbous Compensator on the Thompson submachine gun. One look at a rack of Skeet guns in the 1930s and '40s found Model 12s and Model 31s with the vertically vented Cutts "corn cob" muzzle attachment. Known as "muzzle bandages," these devices fell from favor in the 1960s.

The current popularity of barrel porting began with Larry Kelly and his Mag-na-port operation which, using electrical discharge machining (EDM), vents the barrel tops of hard-kicking handguns like the 44 Magnum. This was subsequently carried into shotgun porting, and the scattergun phase of the business is now known as Pro-port. Others have since followed Kelly's lead, employing either drilled holes or another EDM pattern.

The reason for porting isn't purely recoil reduction. It's intended to reduce muzzle jump by invoking the action-reaction principle: The upward-spurting powder gases apply a downward pressure on the barrel, thus tending to offset the upward muzzle flip normally generated by recoil. The main skeptics are those who have never used a ported shotgun, as most designs do damp muzzle jump. In this writer's opinion, those barrels with the longer rows of ports work best, and the Pro-port feature was improved by the introduction of the "pigeon porting" design, which extends the upper line of ports rearward for added hold-down energy.

Porting wasn't intended to put a massive dent in recoil, although it can lessen it a bit by sending a certain amount of gas at an angle to the gun rather than straight back into the shooter. This might take out 10 to 20 percent of the recoil, depending upon the exact amount of gases emitted. For sheer recoil reduction, vertical cuts as used in the Perazzi Skeet guns seem to function well, as the powder gases can push against the flat surface of the vents' leading edge and give a forward impetus to the muzzle.

Screw-in Chokes

The main difference between the Roper chokes of 1866 and those of today is that the Ropers screwed onto the exterior of the muzzle, while today's models fit counter-bored interior niches. Otherwise, they're the same in principle—easy in and out for versatility.

But, alas, the modern choke tube scene is a can of worms! Not only do interior configurations and dimensions vary from maker to maker, but we now have tubes for (a) lead shot

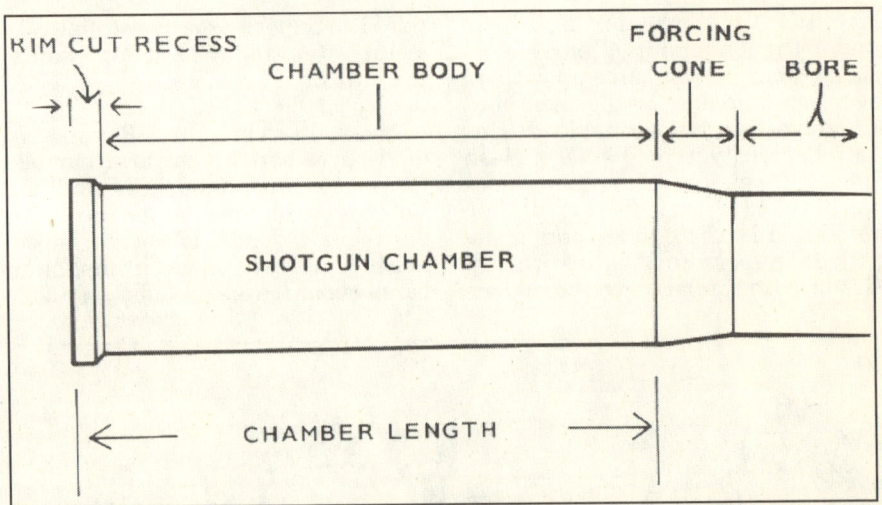

A shotgun barrel's interior dimensions seem simple enough—until actual performance is evaluated. Now we seem to believe alterations, normally to larger dimensions, work better. So did a lot of earlier folks, but their progress was impeded by ineffective wads.

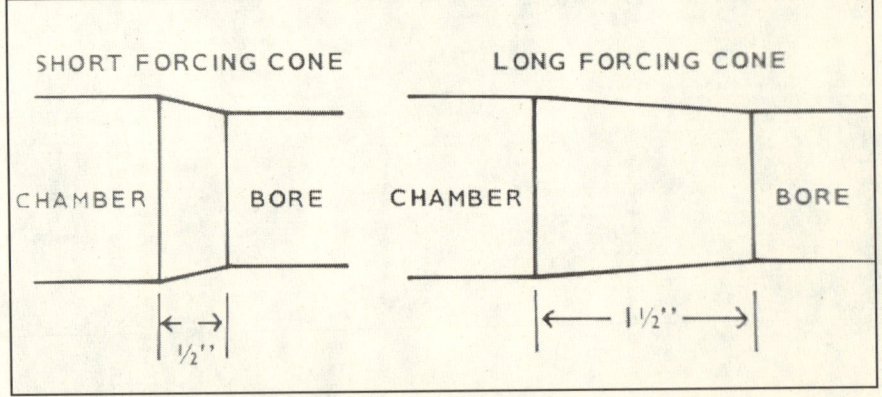

Short forcing cones are supposed to funnel shot and wads into the main bore; however, they actually act like minor obstructions. The long forcing cone permits a smoother chamber-to-bore transition for shot charges and relieves recoil severity.

only, (b) steel shot only, (c) steel and/or lead, and (d) standard bores and over-bores. Toss in the rifled tubes, as well as extra-long Full-choke turkey tubes, and we've got quite a mess. While each tube can't be discussed in its entirety here, the individual shooter is cautioned against taking too much for granted. Try to learn as much as possible about the tubes you'll use or buy.

Interior dimensions are a major point. In general, choke tubes have been altered to the side of loose dimensions. The exact reason for this isn't known, although an educated guess would be that the industry fears barrel bulging with bulky steel shot such as BBBs, Ts and Fs. This may be a sound precaution, but when a casual hunter uses lead shot with such lightly constricted chokes, he'll get weak patterns. A plastic shotcup won't compensate for 0.015- to 0.020-inch of reduced constriction! One cannot assume that all factory-supplied chokes are alike or even that they follow traditional constrictions! For best results, it's best to have a machinist or gunsmith measure them.

The advent of the short-barreled turkey gun, followed by the introduction of extra-length turkey choke tubes, is really quite humorous. First the short-barreled gun is boomed for manipulation in the blind, then the industry comes along with choke tubes that extend beyond the muzzle to lengthen it. The extended turkey tubes are designed to lengthen the taper for a gradual compression of the lead shot charge, and it's wrong to use steel shot in them.

Other extended choke tubes are made specially for steel shot. Their purpose is to take the point of maximum choke constriction away from the barrel wall, thus relieving the basic barrel of the stresses of steel shot passage. Mossberg was probably the first to make these.

Choke Configurations

Most shotgunners think of choke in terms of a conical configuration, meaning a straightline taper. However, another term is popping up more frequently, the "parabolic" choke. Simply stated, a parabolic choke is one with a curved configuration. In practice, the parabolic curve seems to do a better job of easing the shot charge into the choke's point of maximum constriction for fewer deformed pellets and a smoother flow. This helps to reduce the number of fliers and sweetens the pattern. While the theory of the parabolic was known long ago, it is mainly now that the application is coming on line, thanks to computerized machining.

Most chokes which retain a conical configuration also have a parallel section between their point of maximum constriction and the muzzle. The old rule of thumb, dating from the 19th century and reflected in Major

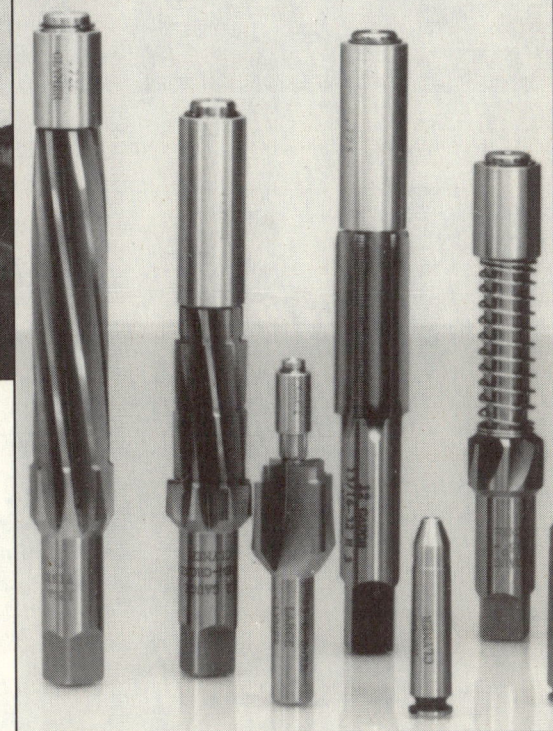

(Below) These pilot-equipped Clymer reamers are used for altering the interiors of shotgun barrels.

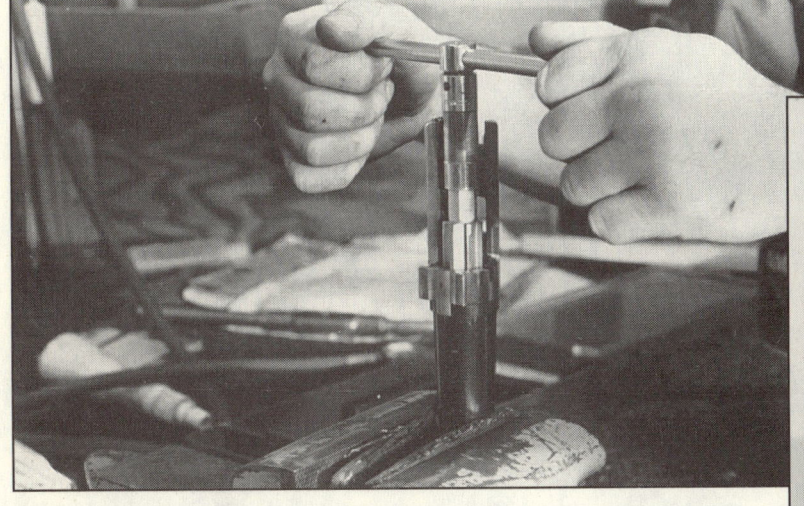

Most gunsmiths use the T-handle wrench to cut long forcing cones. This is an old Ralph Walker photo.

The Ljutic employs a Roper-type screw-*on* choke tube body with screw-in tubes.

America is a nation of choke tube changers. Cliff Moller, vice president of Briley, shows a rack of the many, many tubes made by his company in Houston, Texas.

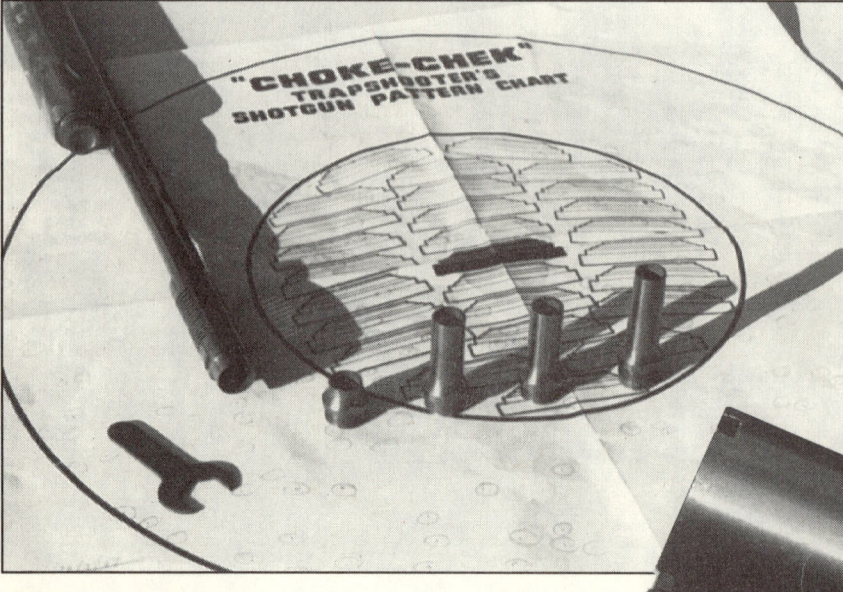

The Cutts Compensator was an early variation of the old Roper choke system, utilizing screw-in choke tubes in a ventilated body.

To get optimum pattern density for turkey loads, extra-length Full-choke tubes were developed with gradual tapers to handle massive magnum charges. These extend an inch or more from the original muzzle and do, indeed, deliver.

Sir Charles Burrard's three-volume work, *The Modern Shotgun*, states that, "...the greater the constriction, the longer both the Parallel and the Cone." The parallel section seems to stabilize the shot charge prior to exit.

A number of aftermarket suppliers turn out choke tubes with parallels and/or parabolic tapers. These are almost too numerous to mention. I have recently been patterning with parabolics turned out by Pete Elsen, Inc., and they do a splendid job of providing outer ring density in 30-inch patterns. Many of these choke suppliers offer their tubes in five-point (.005-inch) increments to give the shooter a precise choice of constrictions.

Rifling

Rifled shotgun barrels were deemed a novelty when Hastings began advertising them more than a decade ago. Made by Verney-Carron of France, a firm that had a splendid reputation for barrel making in Europe and was one of the first to employ hammer-forging for shotgun barrels, these rifled barrels improved slug accuracy, especially when the sabot slugs were used.

Historically, however, rifling had been put into shotgun barrels long before. During the heyday of the British Empire, some famous English gunmakers turned out a so-called "Paradox" gun, which was a side-by-side with at least one barrel given shallow rifling near its muzzle to help stabilize a lead projectile not unlike our current Foster-type shotgun slugs. This gave military officers and government officials a versatile sporting piece to carry to their far-flung outposts. The rifled barrel would pattern akin to a Cylinder bore with fine shot for small game, yet deliver a heavy wallop with the Paradox slugs. Burrard, in *The Modern Shotgun*, mentions full-length "invisible" (shallow) rifling in some such pieces, so the concept is at least a century old.

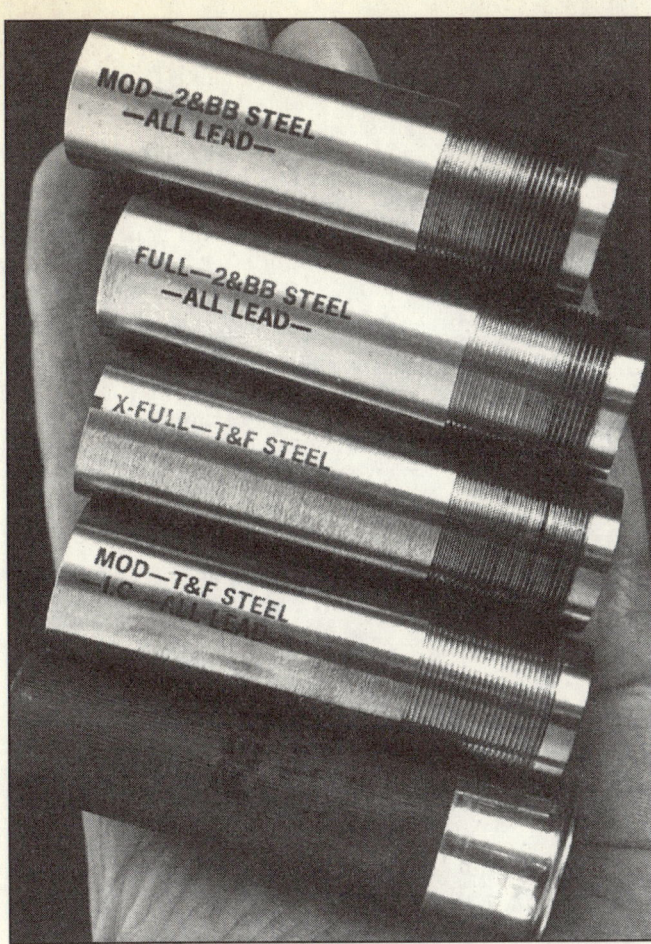

Steel shot has opened the proverbial can of worms in choke tube manufacturing. Read choke tube markings carefully to understand how each should be used.

Rifled choke tubes are now common for slugs, and Briley makes a straight-groove, Ultra-Full turkey tube, but the concept isn't exactly new.

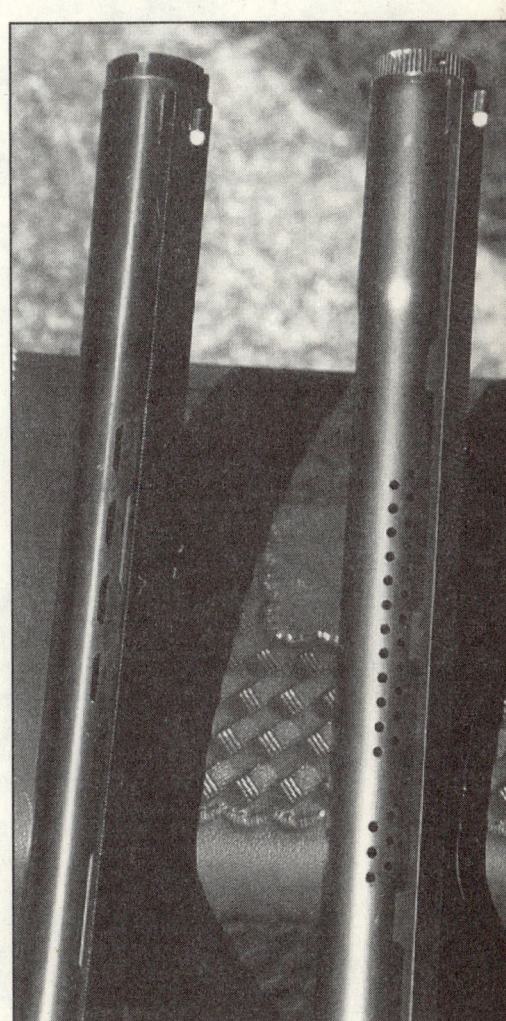

Various barrel portings work against muzzle jump to keep the gun hanging for quick second shots: (from left) a Lazer porting job and a salt-and-pepper by Stan Baker.

For optimum accuracy, shotgun barrel rifling should match the kind of slug being used. Lead Foster slugs do better with a slow twist, such as 1:38 inches, while the sabot-type slugs are better with a faster pitch of 1:27 or 1:28 inches. The twists of 1:34 and 1:35 inches are compromise twists which, in my experience, don't do well with the lead Foster slugs beyond 60 to 75 yards. On the other hand, some sabots like the Winchester and Remington Copper Solid will often group tightly from the compromise pitches.

It is indeed a question as to whether a shotgun barrel with spiraling rifling is still a shotgun. It's more like a rifle based on gauge rather than caliber.

This isn't to say that shotguns aren't rifled for use with fine shot. But it isn't a spiral rifling. It's a straight-groove rifling. Why? One of the first explanations was to eliminate pattern-spoiling wad spin. The straight-groove rifling stabilizes the wad, and the ejecta emerges without "English."

But the capable hands at Briley recently developed an Ultra-Full-choke turkey tube with straight-groove rifling, and they have another reason beyond thwarting wad spin—reduced pellet deformation. The Briley turkey tube tightens to a radical .665-inch (12-bore), and that would tend to make lead shot swage down to flow through, resulting in pellet deformation. The Briley way of thinking, however, is that the grooves between rifling lands provide relief to minimize pellet compression while still bunching up the charge.

I find it difficult to argue with the Briley concept. In a Beretta A-303, I get 90-percent patterns at 30 yards using Winchester's 1⅝-ounce, 12-gauge short magnum with copper-plated No. 5 lead shot. The turkey I took with it never quivered. That's the reason for all these barrel modifications, isn't it? We want good clean hits. Actually we're only now putting into practice some of the scattergun theories we've known for ages. It's about time.

I'VE NEVER BEEN much of a handgunner, and my 45 ACP ain't much of a gun when compared to what's available nowadays. To look at, that is. Like me, all it does is shoot. Nothing fancy, but every time I squeeze trigger, it goes bang. That has been important a few times.

I got it back in the spring of '45, somewhere in northern Germany. It's an Ithaca-built Model 1911A1, No. 1230844. The war was still on—the big one.

Guess I got it sort of indirectly. Nineteen-year-old corporals aren't often issued 45s, or sidearms of any kind, but many of us sort of acquired pistols along the way. We liked the idea of having one as a backup if we ever needed it. I got mine in a swap—for a P-38 that I'd taken from a Kraut who "didn't need it anymore," as we used to say. That's a Walther P-38, not a Lockheed Lightning, which I never saw in Europe.

Lots of guys wanted German stuff, which was understandable in the case of good 98 Mausers, Sauer drillings, and Zeiss scopes, say, but I never really understood what anyone wanted with a Luger or Walther when the shooting was serious. Of course, anything was better than nothing. One friend thought a 32 was OK. But anyhow, this Air Corps guy I met somewhere learned I had a P-38, and he wanted it something awful. He started by offering me fifty bucks, which was sorta standard in those days, and when I refused, he worked his way up to $100, which was a lot. "What in blazes do you want?" he then demanded when I shook my head.

I knew what I didn't want—a pistol chambered for the 9mm cartridge. That's what the Walther handled, of course, but I'd seen all of that I wanted to. Let me give you an example: One time some infantrymen were running across a field to-

After 50 Years...
STILL ON DUTY

by BOB BELL

Bell's Old Faithful always shoots. The M1911A1 is Ithaca-built.

This is that young man who swapped a P-38 for a 45. Bell used his rifle a lot in Europe.

Bob Wise did the shooting with the as-issued 1911A1. Poor sights and a gritty trigger, but the results were plenty good.

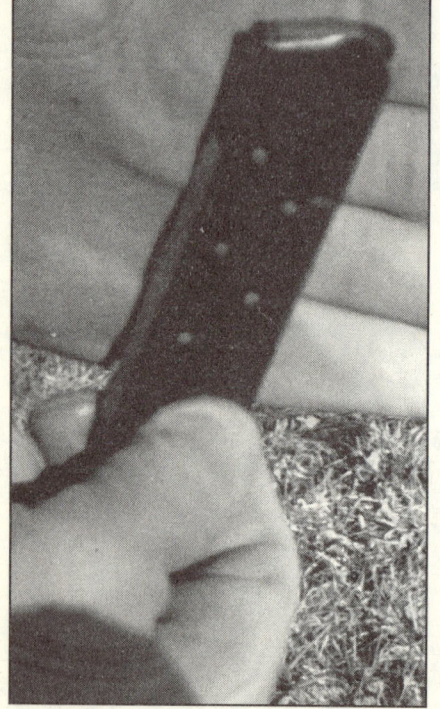

The 45 clip was loaded with GI ammo during WWII, stayed that way for almost half a century, then worked great.

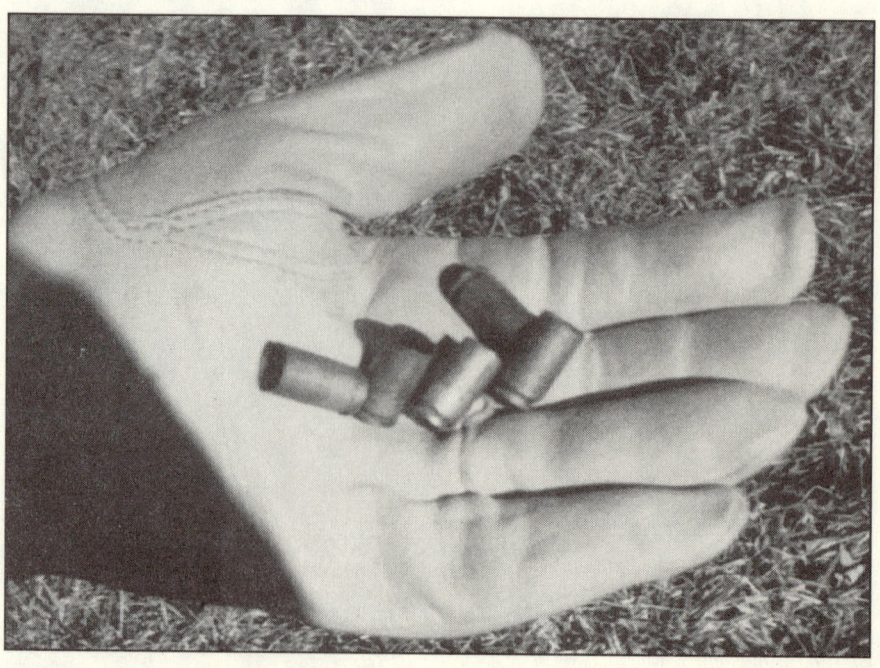

Five of the seven empties—all they could find in the grass—after firing. Headstamp was ECS43.

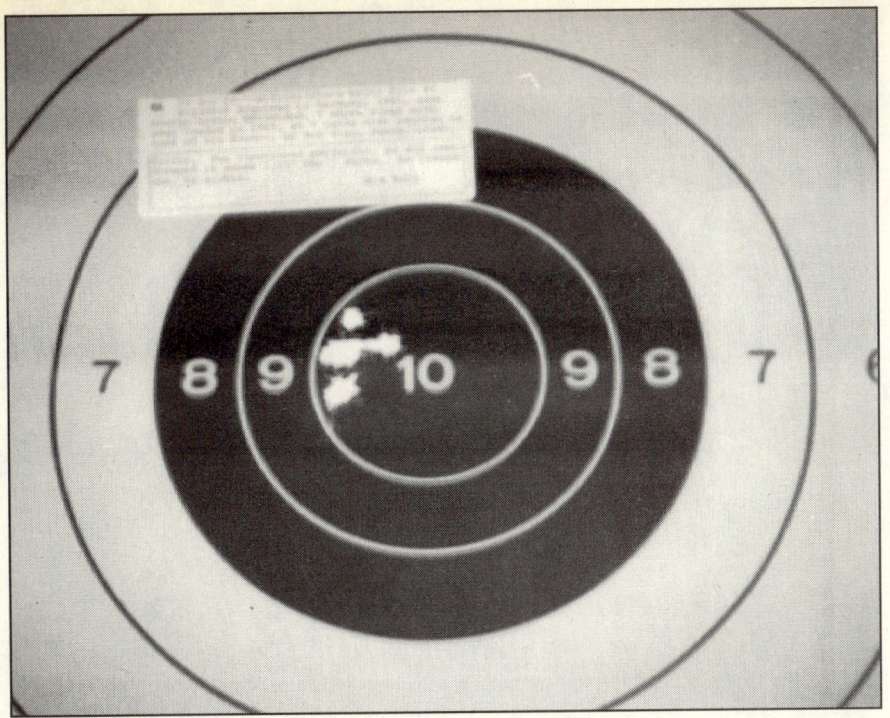

That fifty-year-old ammo, fired from 7 yards, put its seven shots in 1.37 inches, almost on point of aim. The magazine spring didn't take a set in a half-century.

ward an open woods concealing some Krauts. At short range, one German opened up with a Schmeisser. He hit a GI right up the middle with a good burst—six shots, we learned later—from crotch to shoulder. Fatal, sure as blazes. But not quick enough. The American killed the German with his M1 before he fell over.

I've always felt vaguely sorry for that Kraut. He did everything he—or his weapon—could do, but it wasn't enough. I can't imagine anyone being hit like that with a Thompson and doing anything except fall over.

So I've never really been enamored of the 9mm. Sure, I know their bullets have been improved an awful lot over the years, but one reason they could be improved is because they had so far to go. And I know the 9mm's high velocity compared with a 45 makes hitting at near-rifle range easier, but a handgun is of most use across a room. If you have to use one at a hundred yards against a rifleman, you're in bad shape.

Anyway, when the Air Corps guy repeated his question, "What do you want for that Walther?" I had an answer.

"I want your 45," I said.

That silenced him for a moment. Then he spluttered. He cussed and griped, and maybe even moaned a bit, but in the end, he took off his holstered 45 and gave it to me as I handed over the P-38.

I still have the 45. As issued. It's a clunker, really. An Ithaca-built model with a gritty trigger pull, non-adjustable sights and cheesy homemade walnut grips, replacements for the plastic ones, one of which broke when I dropped it. I used to occasionally think about having it tuned up by some good gunsmith, but when I checked years ago, I learned that sometimes they make tolerances so tight the gun doesn't always function.

That's something I won't stand for. In a match, there are often alibis when guns hang up, but in a situation when you really need a 45—never. So this one is untouched. It's nothing to brag about so far as shooting goes—about 5- or 6-inch groups at 25 yards off sandbags with GI ammo—but it always shoots. And a 6-inch group on a man's chest is gonna do the job, believe me.

I've kept it within hand's reach for many years now and fortunately haven't had to use it. When my wife was working as a drug counselor in one of the most dangerous cities in the country, I had it on the car seat, fully cocked and chamber loaded, every time I went to pick her up at 11 p.m. Never had to use it, but it was nice to know it was there.

When I got this gun in '45, two magazines came with it. As it happened—I didn't plan it that way—through the decades I did all my shooting with the same magazine. The other one was loaded in 1945 in Germany and has laid on one shelf or another ever since—within a couple of months of a half century at this writing.

As it happens, the 1996 GUN DIGEST is the 50th edition. So it went through my mind, "Now is the time to shoot that old clipfull. See how it does. If it works at all, how the magazine spring has held up, how the gun and ammo do. No fancy tests, just everyday use."

The only trouble was I've had some medical problems during the last year and I didn't think I was in good enough shape to hold as well as I wanted to. But this was solvable. I just called a longtime friend, Bob Wise, who shoots handguns better than I ever did, and he was eager to take over the chore.

So on 29 December 1994, a clear, sunny but chilly day here in Pennsylvania, we went out to his family's farm and set up a target at seven yards. No, that's not long range, but it's about the maximum when you have trouble that a handgun might solve.

He put a sandbag on the hood of his Bronco, then inserted the clip of ammo—seven rounds—that I'd loaded in '45. It seemed to be a significant moment, somehow, but we didn't know of anything special to do, so he simply rested on the bag with a two-hand hold, aimed carefully and squeezed.

I didn't even remember anything about the ammo that was in the clip. It turned out that the cartridges had been headstamped ECS43. We found five of the seven ejected cases in the grass. Every cartridge fired perfectly; every hit was practically on point of aim; the gun and magazine functioned. That crazy magazine spring had been fully compressed for half a century, but it shoved every cartridge up as well as a brand-new one could. And the seven-shot group measured 1.37 inches, on centers.

So my old battle baby did just what it was designed to do, even after fifty years. That says something about the people who built guns and ammo back then and helps explain why I think the 45 is the greatest combat pistol ever made.

We brought it home, field-stripped, thoroughly cleaned and reloaded it. And we began waiting for the next fifty years to pass.

BACK IN 1980, I heard Adolph Coors Company of Golden, Colorado, was interested in sponsoring some sort of blackpowder match. Two years later, this information took on a more substantial form as Coors staged their 1982 National Schuetzen Match. Every year since then, this match has been a little bigger and a little better, until now it has become the Coors International Schuetzenfest with regional matches held throughout the United States, one regional match in Canada, and the possibility of additional matches in other countries as well. The Coors Schuetzenfests have become a centerpiece of revived interest in turn-of-the-century rifle competition with single shot rifles and lead bullets.

Early on, German and Swiss immigrants began to hold shooting competitions of the type they had known in the old country. These rifle events were called, from the German language, *schuetzen* matches. If prizes were awarded and associated festivities were held, the event was called a *schuetzenfest*. Most early schuetzen matches were shot off-hand with iron sights and there were few limits on rifles. If a competitor thought some feature might improve shooting, it was added. With several hundred years of experimentation behind them, the Germanic rifles were highly developed for

clubs allowed for benchrest competition with heavy rifles which were just as specialized and cumbersome in their own ways as the original German schuetzen rifles.

When the National Rifle Association of America was formed in 1871, it adopted rules limiting competition

Eventually, they formed the North American Schuetzen Bund. The period from 1880 through 1915 was the heyday of schuetzen competition, with a national match held every two years and numerous regional matches drawing hundreds of shooters, competing for thousands of dol-

Schuetzen's Back ...For Sure

by DENNIS BRUNS

shooting targets off-hand, but too cumbersome for hunting or military use. From about 1845 to 1915, schuetzen clubs were formed throughout the United States wherever there were groups of Swiss or German immigrants.

Prior to the existence of a national shooting organization, local clubs were free to exercise their own ideas as to what rifles and targets should be used. The more Americanized clubs, following English tradition, tended to limit competition to light hunting-type rifles, although some

to light sporting-type rifles weighing less than 10 pounds, with a 3-pound trigger pull and iron sights. Thus, shooting competition was generally divided into two classes with some events limited to the NRA match rifle, while others allowed the heavier, more highly developed schuetzen rifles.

The schuetzen clubs began banding together in the late 1860s to hold larger regional competitions.

lars in merchandise and prize money. The bigger schuetzenfests often lasted for several days and included parades, dancing and entertainment for the whole family, plus beer and German- or Swiss-style food. Non-Germans joined in the fun, and until about 1895, most large matches offered separate events for NRA-type match rifles and schuetzen rifles.

The North American Schuetzen Bund was reorganized as the Central Sharpshooters Union in 1896, the name change reflecting a merg-

Firing the scope benchrest event shot with old-timey rifles—at the 1991 Coors Schuetzenfest.

ing of the two styles of shooting. Thereafter, the Germanic schuetzen rifles tended to dominate off-hand competition. The addition of benchrest matches to schuetzen competition was an American innovation, and this, in turn, led to the use of telescopic sights in the search for greater accuracy. The old-world schuetzen men stuck with off-hand competition and iron sights.

The anti-German sentiment generated by World War I pretty much brought an end to the Germanic schuetzenfests, although competition with the old-style target rifles continued intermittently in various clubs to the present day.

In the old days, there was always a strong association between schuetzen matches and beer, and the Adolph Coors Brewery was one of the businesses contributing trophies to rifle matches in Colorado. Thus, when that same Adolph Coors Company decided to sponsor a schuetzen match in 1982, they were simply renewing an old association.

At present, the standard Coors Schuetzen Match consists of four events: benchrest and off-hand with iron sights, and with any sights (which usually means scopes.) A competitor may shoot any or all of the four events as he chooses. These events are twenty-shot matches at regionals and fifty-shot matches at the International Schuetzenfest. In addition, there is usually a one-shot King Match (off-hand, any sight, shot closest to center wins), and there may be some fun matches if time permits. All these matches are fired at 200 yards on the old German 25-ring target, which consists of a 1½-inch diameter center worth twenty-five points surrounded by ¾-inch-wide rings of decreasing value.

Competitors are limited to traditional-style, single shot actions (no

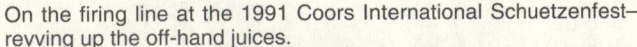

On the firing line at the 1991 Coors International Schuetzenfest— revving up the off-hand juices.

A Schoyen Ballard target rifle of the 1880s, built to conform to the rules of the National Rifle Association.

bolt-action rifles allowed) firing plain-base lead bullets (no gas checks or jacketed bullets allowed). Time limits are generous by modern standards, normally twenty-five to thirty minutes for each ten record shots. Unlimited sighter shots are allowed on a practice target except for the King Match. More recently, Coors has started including some matches for 22-caliber rifles at 100 and 200 yards, and there are special celebrity, media, women and youth matches.

The generous time limits are necessary because few competitors use loaded cartridges. Most schuetzen riflemen breech-seat bullets into the rifling for greater accuracy. The cast bullet is placed in a special breech seating tool, which uses some form of mechanical advantage to force the bullet into the rifling to a point where the base of the bullet is about $1/16$-inch ahead of the mouth of the cartridge case. The same cartridge case is often used for all shooting, reprimed and recharged, then inserted into the chamber of the rifle behind the bullet. This is probably the most accurate way to shoot a lead bullet. Competitors using fixed ammunition never have been quite able to match the top shooters using breech-seated bullets.

To be competitive in the Coors Schuetzen matches, a shooter needs a rifle and ammunition capable of minute-of-angle accuracy, and a 2-inch group at 200 yards isn't likely to win much except on a windy day. Several years ago, I saw a competitor using fixed ammunition, with paper-patched bullets, put five shots into a 1-inch group at 200 yards during a fun match at the Coors nationals. Now this is good cast-bullet shooting by any standards, but as I remember, this individual had to settle for a fifth-place medal in the match, having been beaten by a group of $6/10$-inch and three other groups running $8/10$- to $9/10$-inch, fired with breech-seated bullets. One of the fun matches held during the 1991 Coors International Schuet-

Classic iron sight off-hand stance at the 1985 Coors Schuetzenfest.

There's lots of hoopla, but they shoot awfully well, too. This is a 200-yard target that drops just one point.

A small sample of some of the merchandise and trophies handed out during the Schuetzenfest.

A Schoyen Ballard schuetzen rifle of the 1890s, reworked in more recent times with a modern scope added.

In the new look, competitors on the firing line at the 1993 Coors International Schuetzenfest exhibit some new silhouettes, but 19th-century shooters would feel at home.

(Left) A Ballard rifle with pump-action breech seater in place, levering the bullet into the rifling.

(Above) This tool hooks onto the receiver ring to force-seat the bullet into the rifling. Its mechanical advantage is 10 to 1.

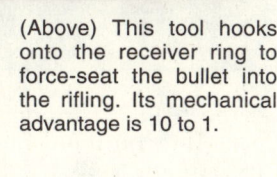

These are 32-caliber schuetzen bullets. The modern pointed bullet hopes to cure the blunt Pope-style bullet's wind behavior. The middle bullet is, of course, a compromise.

zenfest required shooting five shots for group on each of four targets, best group to count. A highly variable wind was blowing and some of my bullets were drifting 4 inches or more, even though I waited out the worst gusts. In spite of the wind, the winner of the match shot a group measuring .675-inch, and the next eight finishers *all* made groups measuring less than 1 inch at 200 yards.

Although breech-seating bullets into the rifling produces gilt-edge accuracy, the system does seem to limit shooters to velocities around 1350 feet per second. Most schuetzen competitors use bullets cast of traditional tin-lead alloy. Drive such bullets much faster than 1350 fps and they lose accuracy. Make the bullets of harder alloy to hold accuracy at higher velocities and they become too hard for the breech-seating tool to force into the rifling. Lead bullets at 1350 fps are very sensitive to wind drift. Thus, the modern schuetzen competitor is working with a rifle capable of minute-of-angle accuracy, using loads that will drift 2 to 4 inches for every 5 miles per hour of wind. Clearly, a shooter's ability to accurately judge the effects of wind is critical to making a good score.

Experienced schuetzen competitors like to put out wind flags to aid them in spotting changes in wind direction and velocity. Since everyone seems to have a different idea as to what makes a good wind indicator, the first 100 yards of a schuetzen range often tends to resemble a flower garden because of the number and variety of different colored wind flags and mechanical wind indicators placed there by competitors. The wind drift problem has also led to some changes in bullet design during the twelve years the Coors matches have been held. In the early matches, most competitors used blunt-nosed bullets copied from designs of the last century. Now, most competitors are using more sharply pointed bullets, hoping to minimize velocity loss and reduce wind drift.

The cartridge most popular with competitors at the Coors Schuetzenfest is the old 32-40 Winchester or close copies thereof. A few competitors are using cases such as the 357 Magnum and 357 Maximum necked down to 32-caliber. There are a growing number of 30-caliber fans, and a few of the more rabid experimenters are trying 7mm, 25-caliber, and even 22-caliber cartridges. At the other extreme, several shooters have made good scores with the old 38-55 and with 35-caliber cartridges based on modified 30-30 brass, but these larger calibers are not much in favor due to their heavier recoil. The story is pretty much the same with the various 40-caliber cartridges—too much recoil for shooting a 50- or 100-shot match at 200 yards.

Modern large-capacity bottleneck cartridges such as the 308 or 30-06 often appear in the hands of beginners, but seldom make high scores. The old 45-70 is another cartridge often used by beginners. I have done some pretty good shooting using my New Model 1875 Sharps long-range rifle and blackpowder silhouette loads in local schuetzen matches, but the noise and recoil are a bit much over a

DeHaas-Miller or Meacham-Hoch actions. The graceful old-style schuetzen rifle with 30- to 32-inch octagon barrel, deep perch-belly stock with high cheekpiece, and small tapered forend has fallen from favor. Today, most modern schuetzen competitors prefer to use a shorter, larger diameter, round barrel of 24 to 28 inches, with a wide, heavy, beavertail forend and modern pistol grip stock.

The firing line at one of the Coors schuetzen matches offers an enjoyable show for the spectator interested in single shot rifles. In spite of the trend toward rifles of modern design, there are still a few of the old schuetzen rifles in use and more rifles of traditional design, built on old actions. An observer can stand back of the firing line and watch these rifles in action. If he has a spotting scope, he can move up and down the firing line, looking at targets to see how well, or poorly, some interesting old rifle is shooting.

the Coors International Schuetzenfest about two weeks before the match was to be held. A substitute match was arranged on one week's notice at the Prairie Dog Range near Porcupine, South Dakota, so people who had made arrangements to attend the Coors match, often as far as a year in advance, would have something to attend. Since then, county officials have forced Coors and the Golden Gun Club to tear down about half of the range which they had specifically built up for the Coors International Schuetzenfest, making a return to the Golden range highly unlikely.

The 1993 Coors International Schuetzenfest was held at the NRA Whittington Center Range near Raton, New Mexico. The makeshift range was somewhat crowded, but competitors were satisfied and the local authorities were friendlier. The mayor of Raton actually came out to the range and made a welcoming

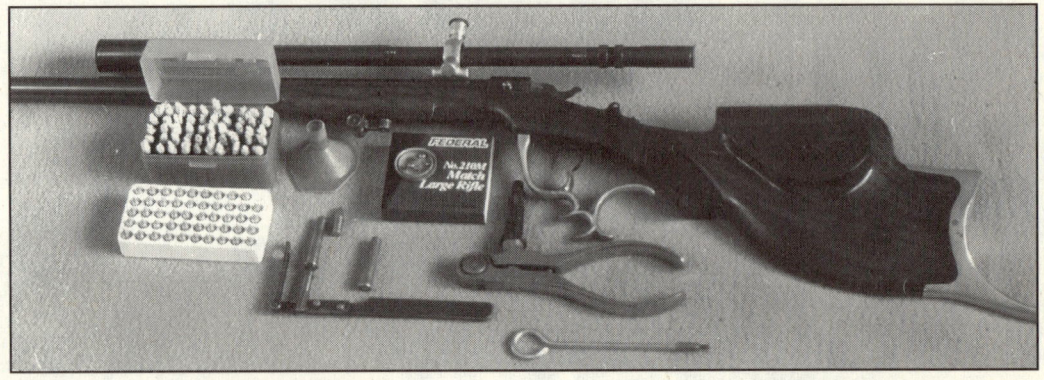

The author's Schoyen Ballard schuetzen rifle with the equipment needed to fire it. There's a breech seater, an Ideal tool, primer pocket cleaner, box of primers, box of bullets, cartridge case, powder funnel, and box of weighed powder charges.

50- or 100-shot match. Virtually all Coors competitors use smokeless powder, #4227 (Hogdon or DuPont), H-110 (Hogdon), and Reloder 7 (Hercules) being among the most popular because they work well through a powder measure.

At the first Coors Schuetzenfest in 1982, most shooters used original rifles—veterans of the old schuetzen matches. Rifles that had been rebarreled or built on new actions were looked upon as curiosities. This situation changed quickly. Original schuetzen rifles in good enough condition to be competitive are too expensive for most shooters, and even old junk rifles from which actions can be salvaged to build a new rifle are becoming expensive. Furthermore, the slow lock time of the old exposed hammer single shot rifles is too much of a handicap, given the high level of today's competition. The trend now is toward the faster hammerless designs such as the

From 1982 through 1991, the Coors International Schuetzenfest was held on the Golden Gun Club range just north of Golden, Colorado. Since interested shooters were not always able to come to Colorado, Coors started a program of Regional Schuetzenfests at different locations around the U.S. and Canada. The 1994 Regional Schuetzenfests were planned for Tacoma, Washington; Modesto, California; San Diego, California; Phoenix, Arizona; Midland, Texas; Tulsa, Oklahoma; Albuquerque, New Mexico; Grand Junction, Colorado; Porcupine, South Dakota; Eau Claire, Wisconsin; Midvale, Ohio; Wapwallopen, Pennsylvania; Asheville, North Carolina; and Edmonton, Alberta, Canada.

Unfortunately in 1992, one of the neighbors complained to county authorities about the Golden range. The local authorities went along with the complaint, forcing cancellation of

speech, then stayed around to watch the match. A new seventy-five-point schuetzen range has been built at the NRA Whittington Center, and the 1994 Coors International Schuetzenfest was held there. Hopefully, this most challenging style of shooting competition will continue on into the next century. ●

Editor's Note

Coors is now reducing their role in the management of the Coors Schuetzenfests. Persons wishing for further information on the Coors Schuetzenfest can write to the International Single Shot Association, 2138 Sunstone Drive, Fort Collins, Colorado, 80525.

In Search Of MUZZLE-LOADING EXCELLENCE

by ROBERT M. KEARNS

THE LIGHT WAS slipping fast from the icy gray sky. As the smell of burned powder gradually faded from my nostrils, I became increasingly aware of the numbing cold creeping down the back of my neck. I prayed for another ten minutes of shooting light as I frantically fumbled to reload my old smoker.

The frost came through the seat of my pants like cruel medical tongs, but I dared not rise lest I spook the spike bull. Cold and exhausted, I desperately tried to sort out another load and ram it home. I wasn't even certain if the little bull I had just shot at carried my ball. Only minutes before, the spike and a cow had drifted out of the doghair aspen 200 yards below me. They might have escaped detection had the cow not chirped at her escort.

The cover was sparse, and I had needed to gain at least 100 yards before I could even try a shot. The steep wall of the draw was mostly grass covered with a foot of late December snow. The angle allowed me to sit, lift my heels and scoot like a schoolboy.

Every time the feeding elk lowered their heads, I was able to slide a few yards closer. When the cover gave out, I reckoned I was within the sure-kill range of 100 yards. Having implicit faith in my rifle and a solid rest from which to shoot, I set the trigger on my Hawken and applied about one pound of pressure, releasing its 170-grain ball, fueled with 100 grains of blackpowder.

At the shot, both elk nonchalantly turned complete circles looking for the source of the noise. As I strained with my 9x35s to find any telltale

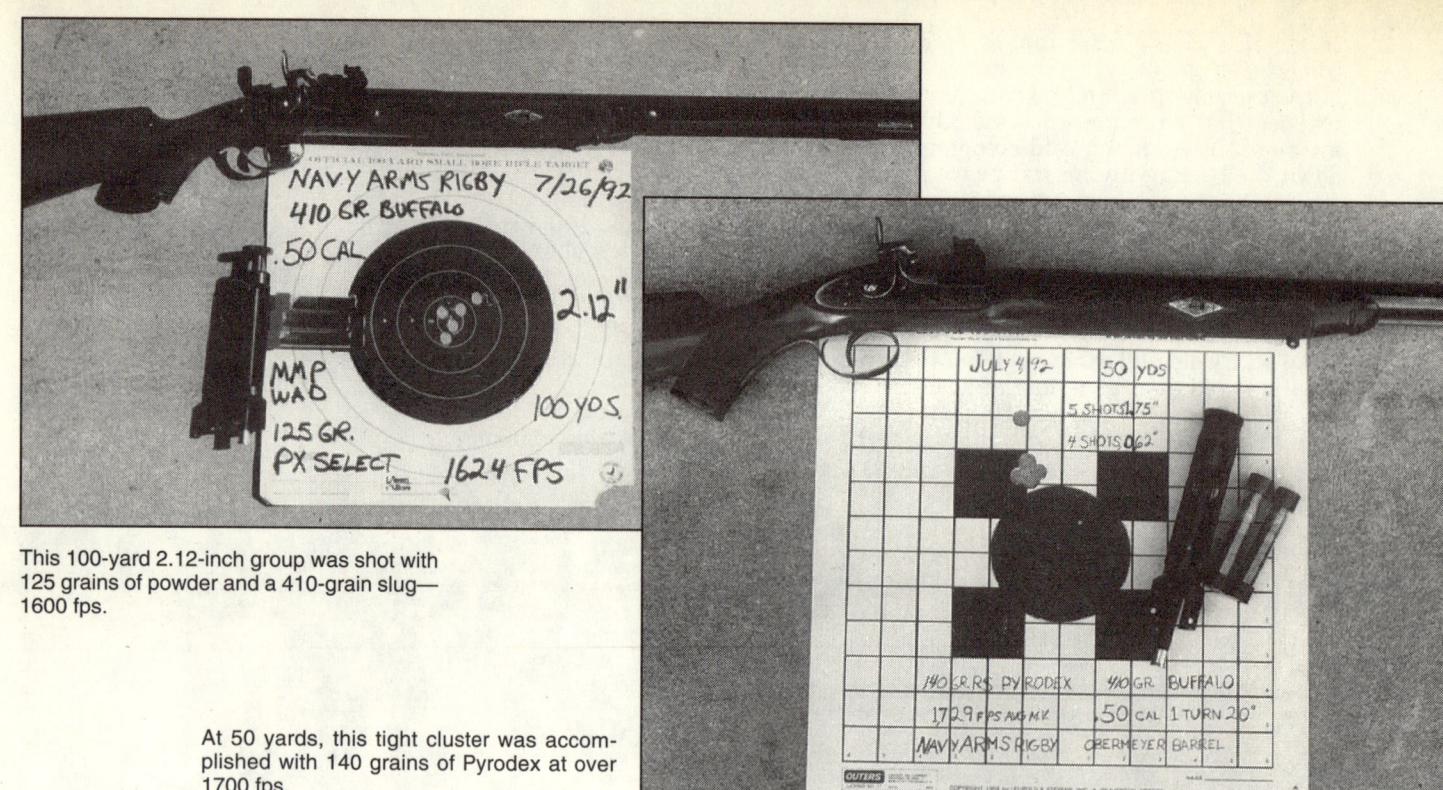

This 100-yard 2.12-inch group was shot with 125 grains of powder and a 410-grain slug—1600 fps.

At 50 yards, this tight cluster was accomplished with 140 grains of Pyrodex at over 1700 fps.

sign of a hit, the quarry slowly melted back into the doghair thicket.

I was bewildered. I didn't see how I could have possibly missed, but the elk showed no sign whatever of being hit. Approaching his track, I found neither blood nor hair. I had followed the trail for only a minute or two when the young bull exploded 10 yards in front of me. The gold bead found his shoulder, and the elk disappeared in a dark cloud of thick clinging smoke.

Did I get him this time? I assumed I had because all was silent, and I knew I would hear him crashing through the thicket if he were not down. Eternity passed before the smoke finally cleared. I took another step and his head popped up; the elk and I stared at each other. My smoke-pole was empty again as darkness clawed the edges of the miserable canyon.

Editor's Note:

Bob Kearns is unusual—he's an entrepreneur who writes well and the story is interesting. And there's a lot to learn in it because Kearns explains the physical bases for his designs. This ain't your average plug.

KW

My patches, balls and gear were strewn out on a log as I scrambled to recharge. The whole time I was reloading, the elk would lift his head and stare back at me while I klutzed around.

Finally recharged, I again set the trigger and planned to send the elk to his final resting place when he lifted his head again. A minute passed with no movement, and I figured he had died. I took another step, and the elk thrashed violently. As I raised the rifle, my cold rubbery finger unleashed the hair trigger, and old smokey discharged impotently into the impending blackness.

I was in a terrible predicament. The hill was so steep that every time the elk so much as wiggled an ear, he slid another 10 yards deeper into the hellhole I had to carry him out of. Cussing all through the loading procedure, I dumped some powder down the bore followed by an unpatched ball and let him have it. It was time for a smoke.

Back at my warm camp at midnight, I contemplated the events of the day. I was disturbed about my poor performance and my rifle's poor performance. Obviously, everything I had read was not exactly true.

A 50-caliber round ball was definitely not 100-yard elk medicine, it now seemed. The first ball had bounced off the shoulder blade creating no damage to speak of, just a little hole about 2 inches deep. The second shot administered at only 10 yards did break his shoulder high up, and the damage to his spine anchored him to the ground till I was able to give him the coup de grace.

That night, I vowed to have a bigger gun and figure out a better way to load it before next season. In the two years that followed, I made that vow three times over. I had been getting an elk every year, but I was not satisfied with the performance of my rifles or their projectiles. Neither was I happy with the loading devices I tried. What follows is the story of my search for the muzzle-loading excellence I finally found.

I became a regular collector of cavern-bored percussion guns. I couldn't find a gun that would shoot a heavy bullet at high velocity to my satisfaction. I wanted 2 MOA with at least a ton of energy at 100 yards.

I had shot a lot of muzzleloaders. Most were accurate with round balls. A few were reasonably accurate with bullets, if the powder charge was quite light. None shot acceptably as powder charges approached the 100-grain mark.

A metallurgist explained part of the accuracy problem. Aside from needing a rapid rate of twist to stabilize heavy slugs, the bullet itself is the problem. Assuming you can load

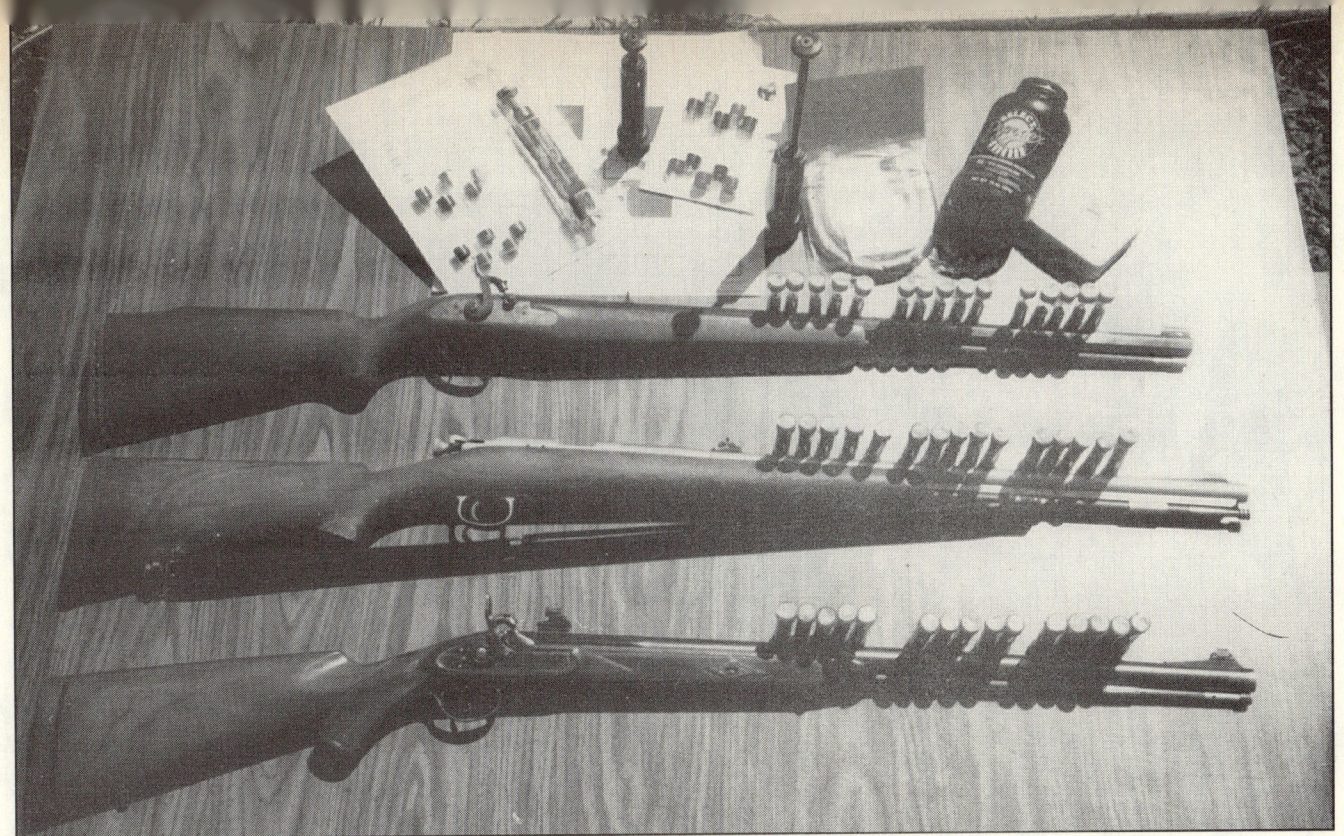

The complications of testfiring muzzleloaders are only slightly tamed by using pre-measured loads.

an over-bore size projectile without somehow hammering it out of shape, you still must be able to send it downrange with repeatability.

When you put a heavy charge behind a pure lead bullet, the explosion itself deforms the slug. If the deformity is severe, the potential for accuracy is ruined. I have actually blown the skirts off of hollow-base conicals. If the projectile is cast from a harder alloy, the projectile is nearly impossible to load and suffers flame cutting and erosion from the hot gases. I was told by many experts that the high velocity and accuracy I wanted to achieve was impossible. Well, I enjoy doing the impossible, even though it is not always easy.

The Hodgdon loading manual showed the 500 B.P. Express brass cartridge stoked with 142 grains of blackpowder sent a 440-grain lead bullet out the muzzle at 1775 fps. That's over 3000 foot pounds of muzzle energy—a blackpowder elk load supreme.

It seemed to me if that kind of performance was possible with a straight-walled cartridge, I could get close with a frontloader. Not wanting to bear the expense of a custom rifle on an experiment, I decided to piece a gun together utilizing off-the-shelf parts everywhere I could. I knew I was going to have to rebarrel a rifle to take this tremendous load, and also to get the twist I needed.

I found Boots Obermeyer of Obermeyer Rifled Barrels building superb quality barrels for single shot sniper rifles in 50 BMG. I ordered Obermeyer's best-grade chromemoly blank, 1 turn in 20 inches. It is bored .500-inch and grooved .511-inch.

Next, I had to choose a rifle to hang this barrel on. The Navy Arms Rigby Target Rifle looked real good to me, very elegant. It required some major modification. The rifle had no provision to carry a ramrod, but its stock had relatively little drop compared to other sidelocks, and the comb was generous. I knew there was not much point having a super-accurate elk gun if some fancy curved brass buttplate and razor-like comb were going to cause a bad flinch.

The UPS man finally showed up with my stuff, and I got the project under way. The breech plug from the Rigby barrel was pulled and installed in my new blank. The blank was then machined to the same dimensions as the original barrel, but shortened to 26 inches.

I milled a groove in the barrel channel of the stock to accept a ramrod and replaced the escutcheon lug with a sort of recoil lug drilled to accept the ramrod. A Decelerator pad was added to tame recoil and also to alter the angle of pitch.

The quality lock's single trigger let off cleanly at 3 pounds. Williams peep rear sight and a Remington front sight were installed. Finally, I had what I perceived to be the ultimate elk getter.

This rifle was gorgeous—brown steel, case-hardened lock and furniture, and a nice walnut stock fully checkered on the grip and forend. Man, it was sleek and sexy. Weighing exactly 7 pounds, the point of balance is perfect for long hours of carry. Neither muzzle heavy, nor muzzle light, it fairly leaped to my shoulder and aimed itself.

Initial results at the range, however, were discouraging. No matter what bullets I tried, accuracy was not what I expected. Groups would start out small, and as the load increased to over 100 grains of powder, they would open up to 6 or 8 inches at 100 yards.

My new rifle shot 240- and 260-grain jacketed bullets at over 1700 fps, using MMP sabots, and the groups were under 2 inches—super deer slayers, but I wanted more energy. For awhile, I thought the experts were right. To get a truly powerful load and small groups seemed hopeless. I looked in the Yellow Pages for witch doctors, but I could not find a good medicine man.

Kearns developed his Black Belt bullets to make his ideas work. The flat base is for sabot loading.

Kearns claims his plastic Insta-Loads will stay dry in a glass of water.

In desperation, I trudged back to the range to try one last experiment. And this final try provided the solution to my dilemma. Cutting the fins off the MMP sabots and using them as a wad, I was able to print tight groups with heavy lead bullets. Eureka!

The load I settled on for hunting groups less than 2 inches with iron sights. It consisted of 140 grains of Pyrodex, followed by a finless 50-caliber sabot, and topped with a 410-grain Buffalo Bullet. Muzzle velocity is 1750 fps (according to my PACT Chronograph), with 2790 foot pounds of muzzle energy.

At 100 yards, I could reach out and touch an elk with a little more than 1500 foot pounds. Sighted 1.5 inches high at 50 yards, it's dead on at 100 yards, and that's elk medicine! *Under no circumstances is this data to be used where manufacturers' recommended maximum loads will be exceeded.*

With all this established, I then began to spend lots of time trimming the MMP sabots with a razor, getting them just right. Another drawback was the chore of having to engrave the bullet to the rifling at the muzzle. I thought there had to be a better way.

I knew ease of loading and good accuracy were possible with loose fitting bullets. However, I did not relish the thought of a loose fitting slug working its way off the charge and creating dangerous pressures.

Risking some borrowed money, I had Del Ramsey at MMP build me a mould to make plastic gas checks. The gas checks are a trifle over-bore. What I now call a Power Check has a $3/16$-inch hole in the center.

Doc Blackmon at Bullet Swaging Supply, in West Monroe, Louisiana, made me some fine bullet swaging dies. I ordered them .001-inch under bore size. He also built them to swage a little nub in the center of the bullet base so the gas check and bullet press together for handling. They fly apart when shot.

This secret of melding fine accuracy and killing power is really simple: The little wad seals the base of the bullet from the cutting torch effect of gas blow-by and acts as a cushion for the soft lead base. This allows you to burn enough powder to achieve superior velocity. Being under-sized, the bullets wind up seating easily on the charge. They are also in perfect condition when they get there because there is no need to force or pound on them. The projectile stays put due to the friction fit of the wad.

Shoot undeformed bullets out of a fast-twist premium barrel at high speed and you have what it takes to put big, tough game down awfully close to where you hit it.

Does it really work? I have shot two elk with this rifle. The first was a smallish cow at 65 yards. It suffered two broken shoulders and was dead when I got there. The second was a spike bull, front-on at about 100 yards. My 410-grain slug penetrated the brisket, knocked off a heart string, and is still out there somewhere in the gut pile on the mountainside. I can't wait to test this rig on a big bull.

Then I remembered my vow to have an easier way to load and designed a tool called the Mag-Charger. This tool uses an adjustable false muzzle and a cartridge. The cartridges are loaded acrylic tubes that contain the charge and the bullet or patched ball. The cartridge ends are sealed with frangi-

 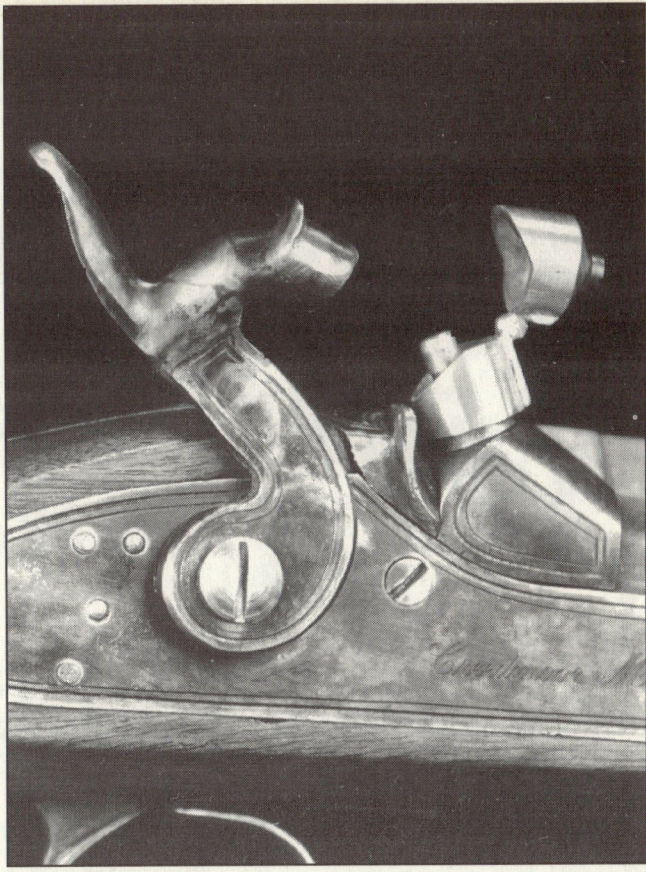

This prototype Cap-Locker keeps the hammer off the cap and keeps wet out of the works.

Just cock the hammer and the Cap-Locker opens for business—it's spring-loaded.

ble waterproof membrane after loading.

To reload, you simply place the tool over the muzzle and snap a cartridge into its loading port. Slap the starting rod and the entire load is short-started. Finish by seating normally with the ramrod. Total time: about ten seconds.

There was one last bugaboo encountered far too often in the late muzzle-loading elk season here in Idaho. That is the tendency for caps to get wet from rain or snow. I sure hate getting a click when I want a bang.

This appeared to be the toughest problem I had to tackle. The challenge nagged me for two years, but finally the light went on. I machined a race into my nipple and built a steel frame and spring-loaded hinge that clips on the nipple. To this frame I riveted a brass cap on one leg of the hinge. A gasket was also installed.

Operation of the Cap-Locker is automatic. The spring-loaded cover is closed over the cap and the hammer then lowered. The hammer's weight on the gasketted cover forms a water-resistant seal. A measure of safety is also gained because the hammer cannot contact the percussion cap. When you cock the hammer to shoot, the cover flies open like a hunter-model pocket watch, exposing the cap to the hammer blow.

At last, I feel I have outsmarted the old-time rifles. If I ever learn how to outsmart the big bull elk, I will need a new hobby.

There is a good selection of rifles on the market these days that will shoot as good as my sweetheart. Most of them are in-line-type guns. I don't see anything wrong with being able to walk into the gun store and buy a good shooter. On the other hand, refurnishing and rebarreling a rifle to your exact specification makes a lot of sense, especially if you want or, for legal reasons, need a sidelock.

An investment of $400-$600, not counting the original cost of the gun to remodel, will get you the best shooting rifle in your neck of the woods. If that sounds expensive, add up what you would have in a centerfire for the same species. With an old smoker, you only have one shot. Isn't it logical to invest a few extra dollars to ensure that shot goes where you want it and does a lot of damage when it gets there?

Hunting with your own creation can add an extra dimension of pleasure to your trips, not to mention all the fun showing off at the range. Remember, though, even with optimum performance, front-loading is still a short-range affair. Velocity and energy fall off so fast that it makes killing at more than 100 yards very iffy and wounding very probable.

For most of us, long-range hits are much easier to make when we are talking than when we are shooting. All those impressive ballistics I have spouted off here are for the purpose of killing game at the most modest of ranges. Please remember that. I didn't do this to be hearing about incidents like the two I recounted at the beginning of this story, with the only difference being another 50 yards or so.

Hunters go to Africa every day with rifles so potent that mine seems merely suitable for camp vermin or signaling trackers. Still, I never read about anyone shooting Cape buffalo at long range.

The longer we have sportsmen, the longer we will have sport.

An American Classic That Never
CHARLES NEWTON'S

MY ADMIRATION FOR Charles Newton began about forty years ago when I first became interested in high-velocity rifles. His name would show up in print from time to time, and I was fascinated with his cartridges. Then came The Day in 1952 when I saw—and bought—my first Newton Arms Co. rifle. It was a 256 in good condition, and with it I got two boxes of Western cartridges—and the fifteenth edition of the Newton Arms Co. catalog.

After devouring the catalog, I was hopelessly hooked. I read everything I could find on Newton in the current magazines. I acquired other Newton rifles, as well as other catalogs, including a LeverBolt catalog.

Newton did most of his experimental work with single shot rifles, but was especially fond of lever actions. He wrote several magazine articles on their superiority over the bolt action for speed of reloading. He also liked straight-pull rifles and did some experimenting with the 236 Lee Navy. He also liked that feature of the Ross, but did not care for the internal lock-up on the Model 1910. His objection to the bolt action was what he felt were two unnecessary motions required in reloading. The lever action and the straight-pull

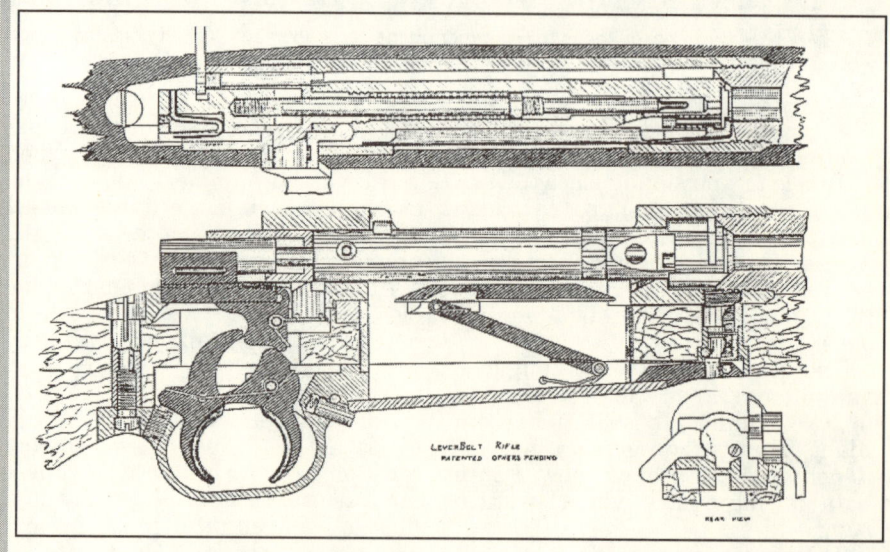

This drawing may have been done by Newton himself. It is an ingenious improvement, seeming to solve a lot of straight-pull problems at once.

required only two motions, while the bolt action needed four.

When Newton prepared to make his first rifles, he found the lever action strong enough, but too springy to handle his high-intensity cartridges. He liked the Savage Model 99, but it would not accept the long 30-06-length Newton cartridges. Those, however, are different stories for another time.

After the demise of his early companies, Newton's inventive genius was not laid to rest. About 1929, he built the LeverBolt rifle. He wrote Frank Kenna of Marlin Firearms Co. proposing that Marlin build the rifle and Newton would sell it. They would split the profits 50-50. According to the LeverBolt brochure, Marlin gave this proposal a long, hard look, then required that Newton get

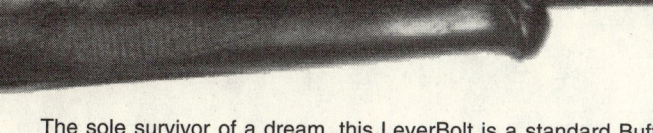

The sole survivor of a dream, this LeverBolt is a standard Buffalo Newton with a new bolt and lug seats.

Had a Chance LEVERBOLT

by BRUCE M. JENNINGS, JR.

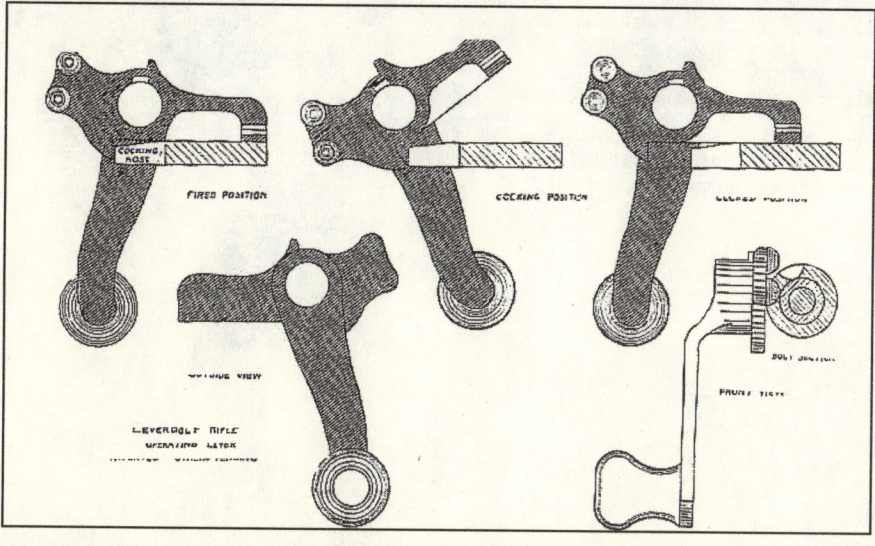

The lever itself is the key to the invention—almost all the change is in the bolt. It could be made today.

orders for 500 rifles in advance to show that the venture would be practical.

Newton printed a descriptive catalog, along with order blanks and a "Special Notice" explaining that orders for 500 rifles with a down payment of $25 each would be necessary in order for Marlin to begin manufacture of the gun. Evidently he did not get the orders, as production never began. This could be blamed in part on the timing—early in the Great Depression.

Still, the LeverBolt catalog held my interest for decades. I knew there *must* have been a prototype rifle. About 1972, I thought I had located it. A friend in Washington said he had heard of such a rifle in the Northwest. When he checked it out, however, he found a Mauser converted to straight-pull by a local gunsmith.

In early 1988, when I heard the LeverBolt had been located, I was delighted, but skeptical. I called the owner, and to my surprise he said, "Yes, I have it."

Then came the persuasion that was necessary to convince him the only proper place for this critter was in my Newton collection. I sat quiet for a while, dreaming of acquiring that "only one." Then came the happy day when I got the letter saying, "I'll sell it to you."

When the rifle arrived, I found it was *exactly* like the illustration in the catalog. There has been much speculation about which rifle might have been used as a basis for a LeverBolt, but it proved to be simple. The rifle is a plain Buffalo Newton 30 USG (30-06) that Newton modified. Other than changing the front receiver ring to accept solid front bolt lugs and the removal of some wood and metal at the right side of the rear receiver ring, where the lever moves, only the bolt was changed.

The bolt lugs on this prototype are solid, like Springfield or Mauser lugs. I am sure this was a change for convenience, not a technical requirement. The bolt closes with a 90-degree

It wasn't very far from the trigger to the lever handle, and then it was just pull-push for the next shot.

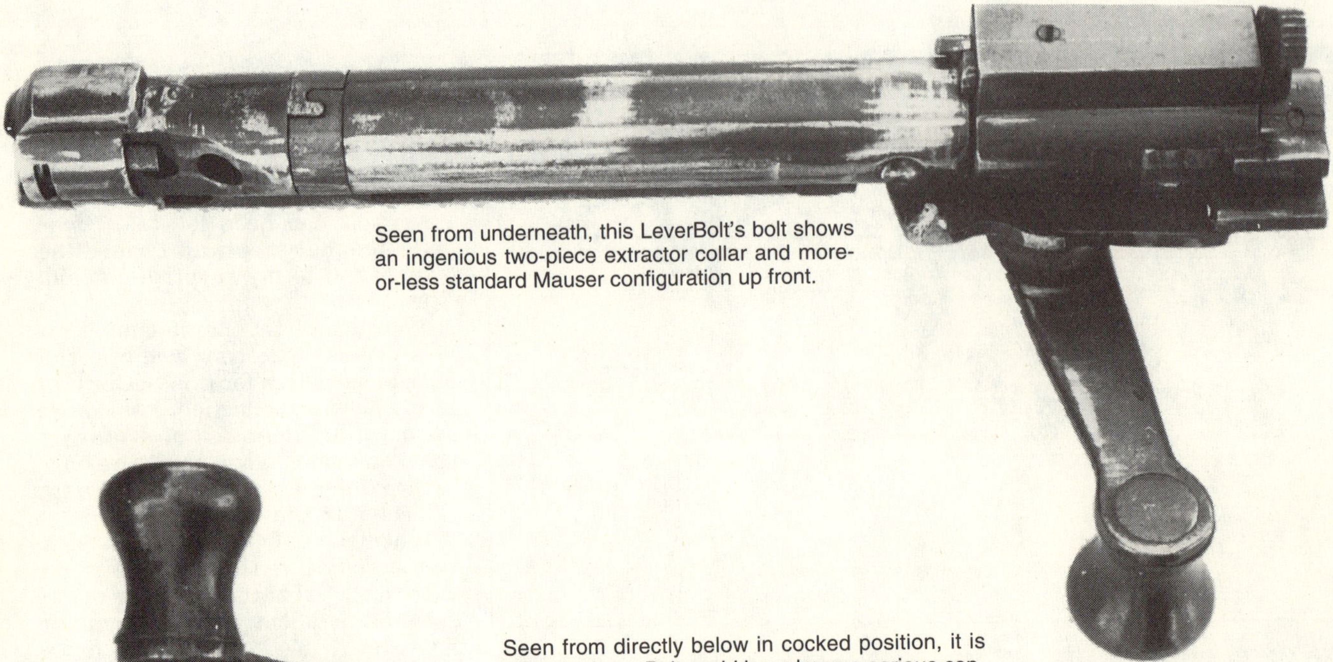

Seen from underneath, this LeverBolt's bolt shows an ingenious two-piece extractor collar and more-or-less standard Mauser configuration up front.

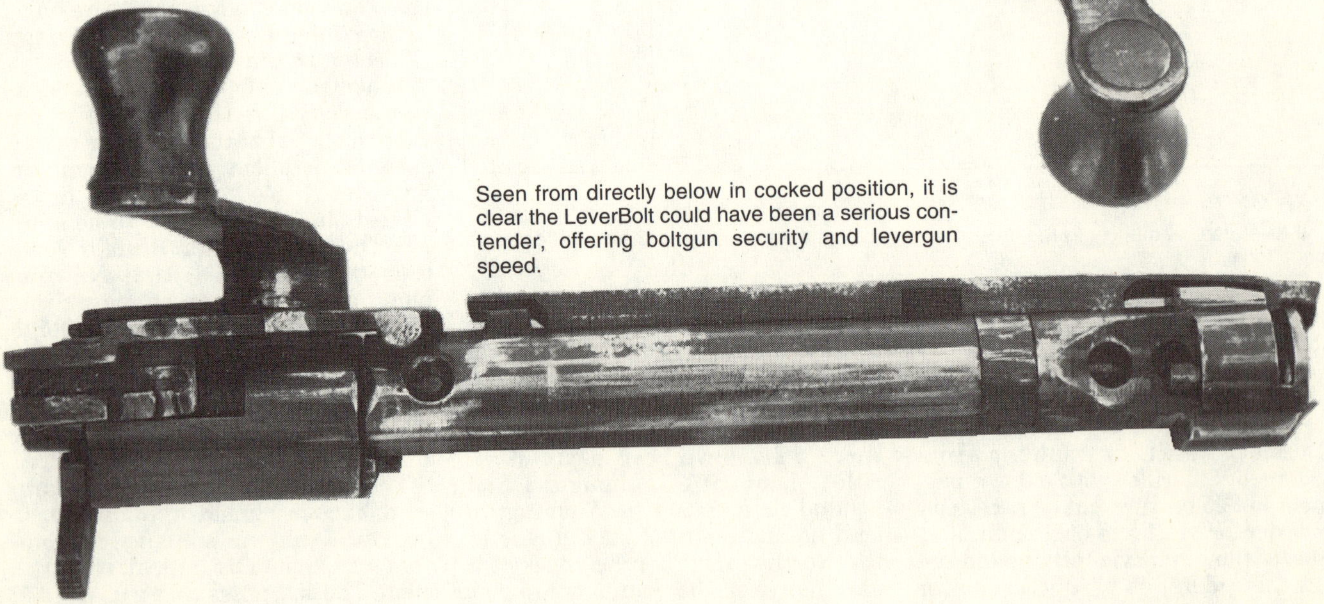

Seen from directly below in cocked position, it is clear the LeverBolt could have been a serious contender, offering boltgun security and levergun speed.

turn to the left, and that would require interrupted-thread Newton lugs to be "left-hand." The extractor is a shortened Buffalo Newton extractor, attached to the bolt with an unusual two-piece extractor collar.

The bolt lever is fashioned after the Lee, except that it closes about 20 degrees in front of vertical. On the upper front extension of the bolt lever are two hardened hemispheres that match two recesses in the bolt body. As the bolt lever is pulled to the rear, there is a gear action that rotates the bolt 90 degrees to the right to open it. As the bolt lever is pulled back, the firing pin is cocked with no noticeable effort. In the opened position, the bolt lever is about 15 degrees back of vertical for a movement of about 35 degrees from closed to open.

This long letter from one great to another is very enlightening, and very sad. Newton is obviously at the last throw of the dice, and the Depression was really tough on gamblers.

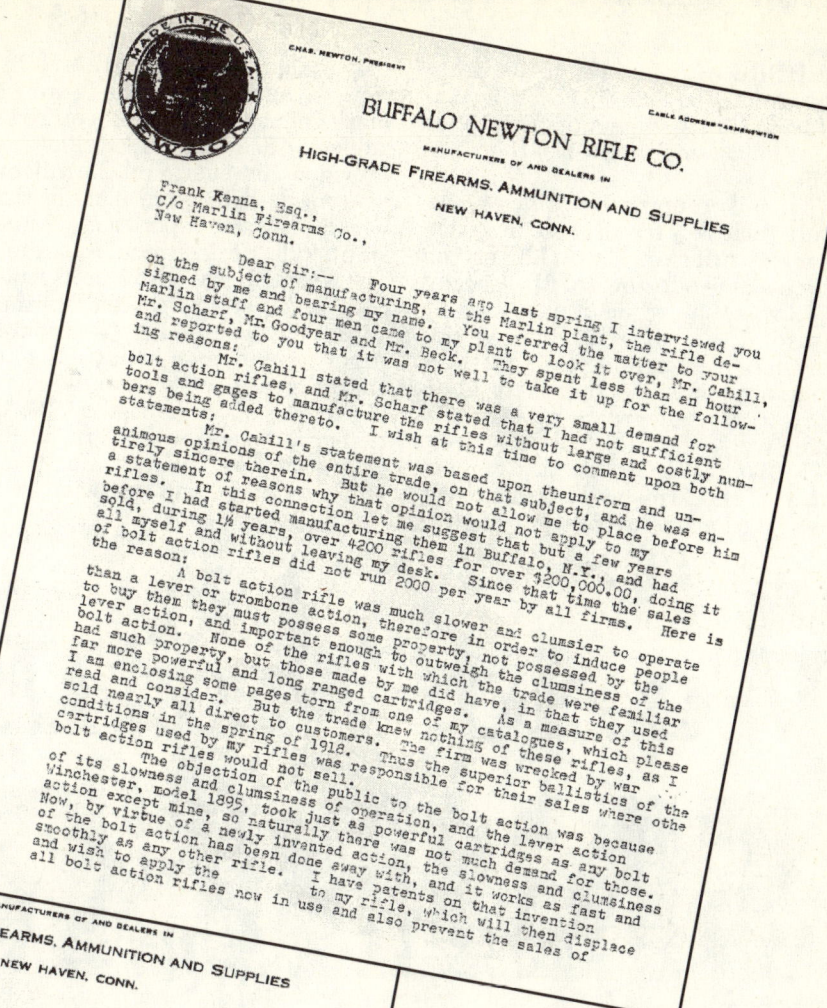

The safety is a three-position affair that locks the bolt or allows it to be opened while on safe. The single safety lug and ejector are the same as on the Buffalo Newton. The bolt lugs do not contain the split left lug for the ejector slot. The firing pin will not fire the cartridge unless the bolt is fully closed. The cocking piece is sealed and the firing pin is locked forward upon firing, thus preventing pierced primers and escaping gas blowback.

The principle involved is rather simple, once after it is seen. It could be applied to nearly any bolt-action rifle. I am sure the trigger mechanism and other parts could be refined, but as a whole this critter really works great! It is a nice, smooth rifle for an inventor's prototype, with no apparent safety faults.

It never worked commercially, but with this effort, Newton accomplished his dream of an action with the speed of the lever action and the stability of the bolt action. Hence the name: LeverBolt.

50th EDITION, 1996 105

THERE ARE MANY stories about the various exploits of U.S. Army and Marine Corps snipers of World War II. A surprising number of them are true.

This is remarkable since there were relatively few of these precision combat riflemen. The U.S. armed forces' attitude toward the special skill was that, while unquestionably a useful combat skill, sniping was nowhere near as important as others ranging from leadership to the ability to carry out orders quickly and effectively.

In World War II, the basic requirement of the Army and Marine Corps was for as many "average" riflemen as they could train, and there was little time available for the extensive marksmanship training required by snipers. Adequate sniper rifles were provided, however, and the riflemen who used them were usually those who had shown superior marksmanship skills during regular training. This situation had been true as long as there had been soldiers and Marines.

In the Revolutionary War, skilled American riflemen took their toll of the enemy. In the Civil War, Col. Hiram Berdan organized a U.S. Volunteer Regiment, the "Corps of Rifle Sharpshooters," whose marksmanship was feared and respected by the enemy.

In the 1898 Spanish-American War, U.S. Army sharpshooters did some very effective sniping. They did it with the Army-issue 30-caliber Krag rifle or, in a few cases, with civilian target rifles firing the standard Krag ammunition. By this time, Army rifle marksmanship training had been much improved, but there was no such thing as special sniper training.

When the Army adopted the caliber 30 Rifle Model of 1903, the 30-06 Springfield, it proved to be very accurate, and the "Telescopic Musket Sight Model of 1908" was developed for "sharpshooting" with it. Although this sight was later improved and

World War II's
SNIPERS AND

by KONRAD F. SCHREIER, JR.

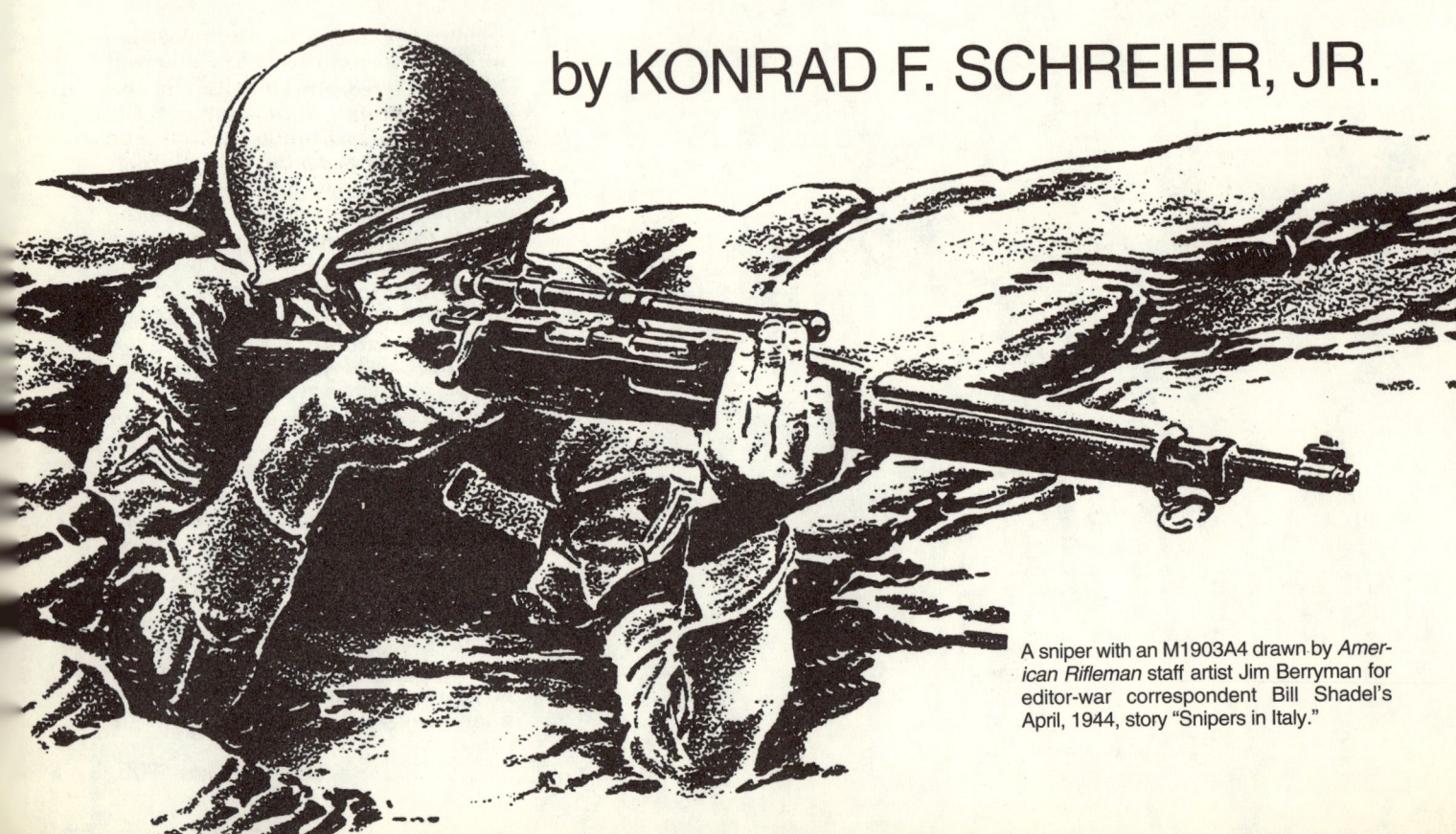

A sniper with an M1903A4 drawn by *American Rifleman* staff artist Jim Berryman for editor-war correspondent Bill Shadel's April, 1944, story "Snipers in Italy."

then re-issued as the Model of 1913, it was a primitive periscopic rifle design. It did, however, improve the ability of sharpshooters to hit targets at longer ranges than with the rifle's regular iron sights.

U.S. Army General Orders 23 of 1909 authorized the issue of two Model of 1903 rifles with telescopic musket sights per infantry company, and this order remained in effect through World War II! These rifles were to be issued to soldiers who made the highest scores in training exercises, but no special training regulations for their use were ever published. Unit commanders could decline the issue of these scoped concealment. Although they were used, telescopic sights were not required for that.

During World War I, the Army found the two-man sniper team was the most effective. While one man did the shooting, the other was the observer who located targets. Both had to be proficient marksmen since they traded roles. Sniper teams were also expected to observe enemy activities. This was the beginning of the scout-sniper teams much used in World War II and since.

During World War I, troop dissatisfaction with the old Model of 1908 and Model of 1913 scope sights caused the Army to procure some

19. Snipers a. Purpose and use. Snipers are expert riflemen stationed in the forward areas of a defensive position for the purpose of firing on enemy soldiers who expose themselves. Specifically, their duties are: (1) to fire on enemy scouts or patrols who attempt to approach or observe the positions; (2) to protect observers and sentinels by firing at hostile snipers who are firing at them; (3) in case of attack by the enemy; (a) to fire on the leaders of the attack, thus compelling deployment at long range and possibly delaying it; (b) to fire on individuals who are especially active in filtering to the front, and also upon machine

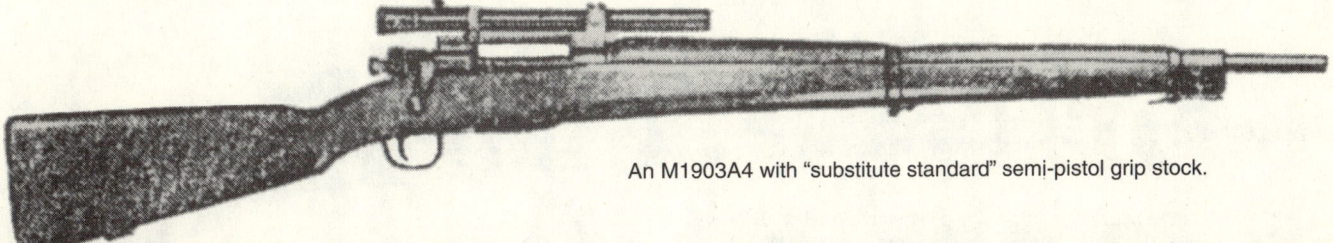

An M1903A4 with "substitute standard" semi-pistol grip stock.

SNIPER RIFLES

rifles if they felt their unit's assignment would not require them, and this also held true through World War II!

Records indicate that by the end of World War I, at least 1550 Model of 1908 and 5041 Model of 1913 Telescopic Musket sights had been procured. They saw service with U.S. Army units in France in World War I. Unfortunately, their vulnerability to the dirt and moisture conditions of World War I trench warfare severely limited their combat use.

The Army adopted the term "sniping" from the British in World War I, and it was a very important element of the trench warfare tactics of that war. However, in actual World War I combat, most sniping was done by the units' most proficient riflemen using standard-issue iron-sighted rifles. The ranges were short, less than a dozen yards to no more than a couple hundred yards. A sniper had to be an expert marksman who could make the best use of camouflage, cover and 5000 commercial Winchester A5 scopes to replace them. These were also 6x and mounted on '03 Springfields with standard commercial mounts. The Winchester A5 remained in the inventory until early World War II, but it never satisfactorily met the military requirement for resistance to moisture and dirt.

In the early 1920s, Army Ordnance did some experimenting with sniper sights. While none was adopted, the work led the way to the development of much improved commercial telescopic sights.

Improved commercial scopes led to long-range target shooting with military-caliber rifles. All through the 1920s and 1930s, long-range matches were popular among both civilian and military riflemen, and they were a major event at the Camp Perry National Matches and at many other rifle events.

Although the armed forces had no standard sniper rifle at the time, the following training regulations for snipers were published in 1940:

gunners. In the attack, when the platoon halts for any purpose, as for example to reorganize following a successful assault, snipers are placed in favorable locations to the front and flanks in order to prevent hostile reconnaissance and delay counterattacks. When a force withdraws from a battle front snipers are usually left in position in order to keep back hostile scouts or patrols. Snipers operate in pairs when sufficient men are available, and scouts are habitually employed and trained for this duty.

b. The sniper's post; location; concealment. (1) Sniper's posts or nests are generally located in the same terrain as advanced observation points. In fact sniping and observation posts are sometimes combined, and snipers always observe and report what they see. Usually, the observation posts proper occupy the highest ground favorable for observation, while the sniper's posts are on somewhat lower ground, more favorable for fire. Sniper's posts are,

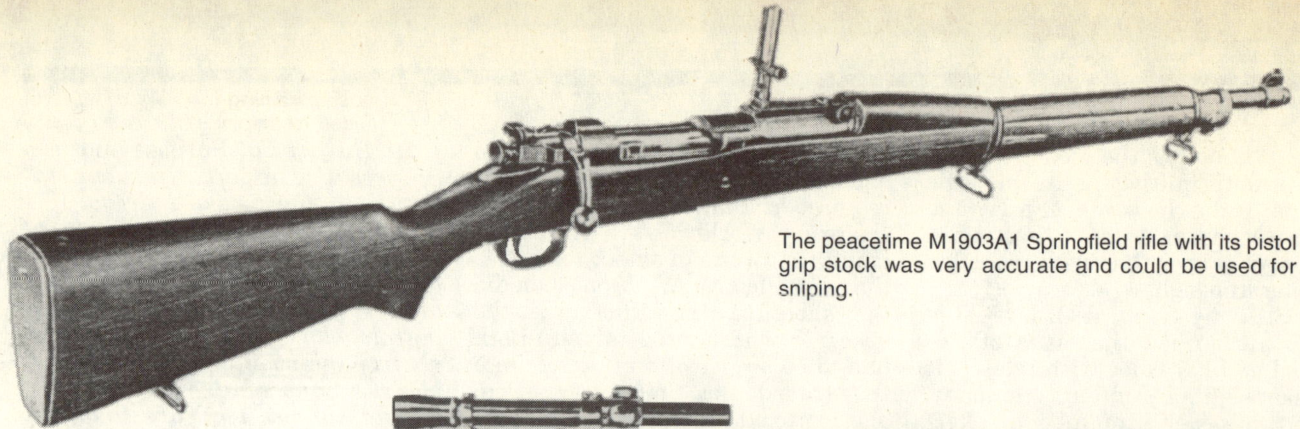

The peacetime M1903A1 Springfield rifle with its pistol grip stock was very accurate and could be used for sniping.

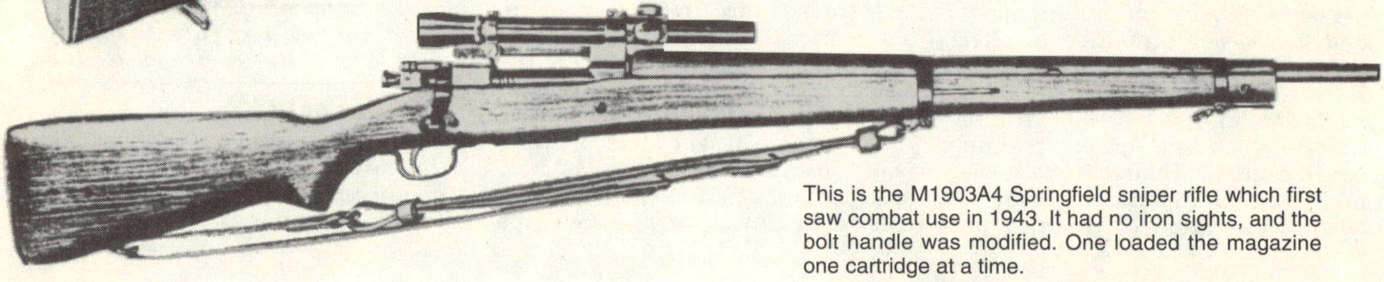

This is the M1903A4 Springfield sniper rifle which first saw combat use in 1943. It had no iron sights, and the bolt handle was modified. One loaded the magazine one cartridge at a time.

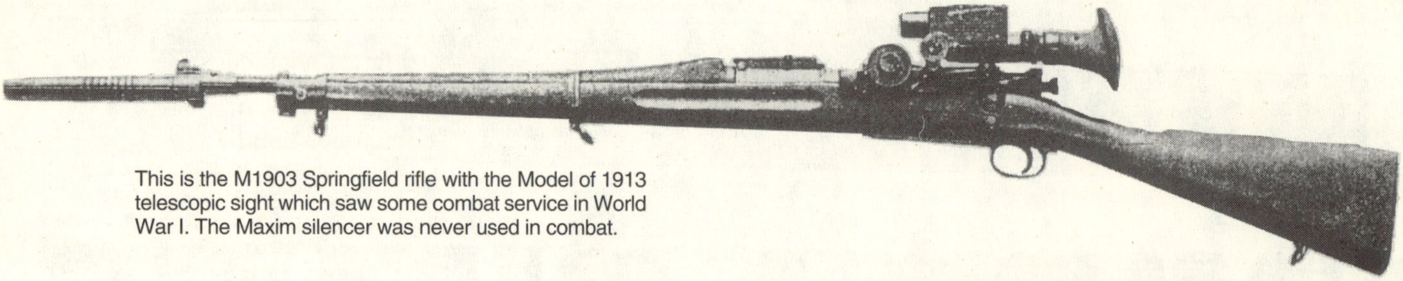

This is the M1903 Springfield rifle with the Model of 1913 telescopic sight which saw some combat service in World War I. The Maxim silencer was never used in combat.

in general, similar to small observation posts.

(2) Temporary posts may be located in trees (preferably trees with plenty of foliage), behind rocks, stumps, hedges or bushes, or in shell holes. More permanent posts are dug into the ground, camouflaged, and provided with overhead cover.

(3) When a sniper's post is manned by a single individual, he performs the duties of both observer and sniper. When there are two men, one acts as observer and the other as sniper.

c. Organizing the sector. As soon as the post is occupied the scouts proceed to organize their sector.

d. Duties of the rifleman. The scout acting as sniper must be able to fire quickly and accurately on moving or still targets. As the sniper fires, the observer watches the effect. Long-range sniping may be carried on with rifles equipped with telescopic sights.

20. Platoon Scouts. *Each rifle squad includes two men designated as scouts. These men should be good rifle shots, especially trained in the use of cover and concealment, in movements, and in the methods taught in this chapter. At least one, and preferably both, should be*

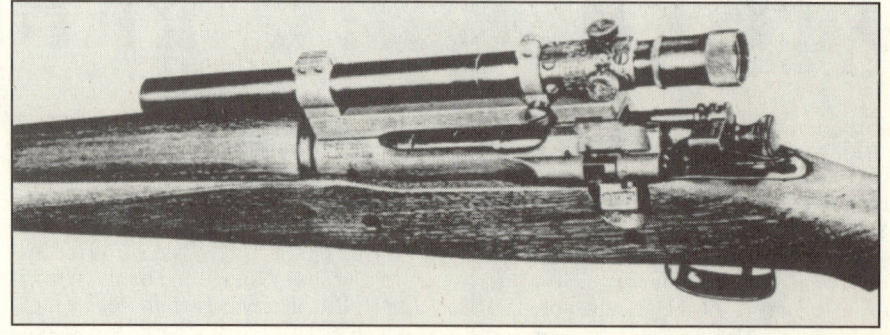

This is the Weaver 330C mounted on the M1903A4—a sniper mainstay in service.

equipped with compasses. Both are equipped with tracer ammunition for designating targets.

While this training regulation mentions the use of rifles with telescopic sights, it was basically intended for sniping with standard iron-sighted guns. However, at the time, the Army often issued the most accurate available issue rifle to riflemen designated as scout-snipers. These could be peacetime '03 Springfields in the "National Match target grade" or the beautifully made M1903A1 Springfield which had a special pistol grip stock and alloy steel action. These were standard issue with iron sights, but capable of superior accuracy.

World War II regulations recognized that the maximum range at which any rifleman could expect to hit a man-size target with any '03 Springfield rifle was about 600 yards. They also recognized that the longer the range, the harder it was to find a man-size target, let alone hit it. In combat, it was found the longest range at which a rifleman could find and hit man-size targets regularly was 300 to 400 yards. This would become a principal reason the U.S.

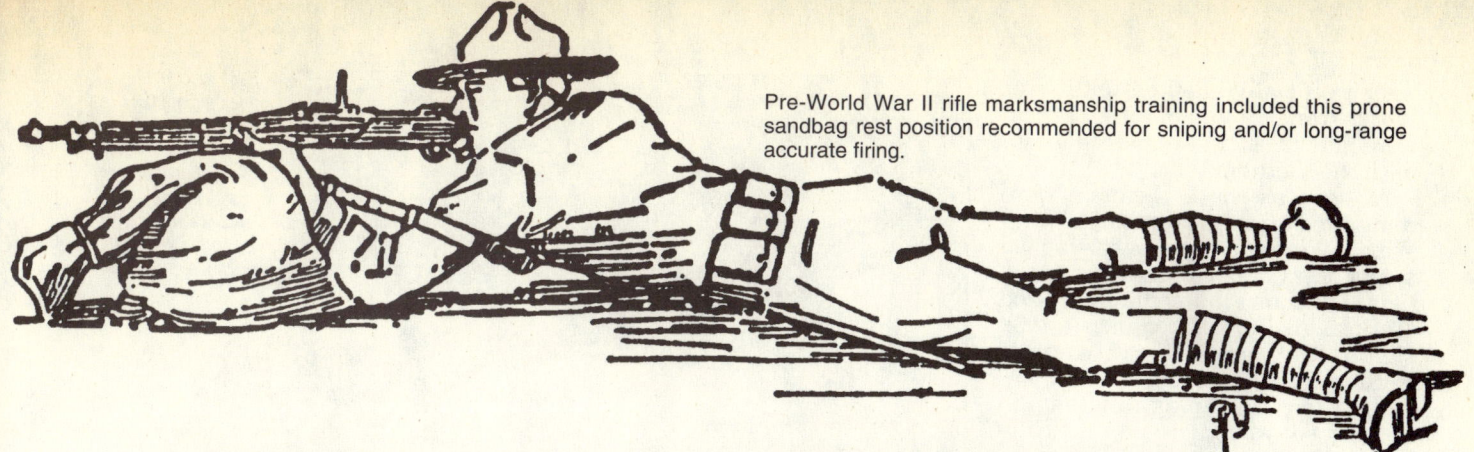

Pre-World War II rifle marksmanship training included this prone sandbag rest position recommended for sniping and/or long-range accurate firing.

This 1943 ad shows a Winchester Model 70 target rifle with a high-power telescopic sight. Many such became sniper rifles used in combat.

This Weaver ad featuring their telescopic sight for the M1903A4 Springfield sniper rifle appeared in 1943 magazines.

armed forces adopted scoped sniper rifles in World War II.

Another problem that combat riflemen had was estimating the range to a man-sized target so they could set their iron sights for maximum accuracy at ranges past a couple of hundred yards. Training targets were shot at known ranges, but combat riflemen had to estimate the distance by eye, with no instruments or rangefinders to help them.

World War II riflemen received training in range estimation by eye. The scout-snipers had to be experts at this task, and some received considerable training.

There was no standard-issue telescopic-sighted sniper rifle in the U.S. armed forces when we entered World War II. During the 1930s, practically every Army and Marine Corps regular, reserve or National Guard unit had a rifle team. These teams regularly had scope-sighted '03 Springfields privately purchased for use in matches, and these often went into combat with the units and riflemen who had them.

The most popular of these were match-grade '03s with commercial 6x to 8x sights in commercial mounts. These found limited combat use throughout World War II, though they were never officially adopted.

Another popular prewar rifle, particularly in the U.S. Marine Corps, was the Winchester Model 70 30-06 target rifle. Most such had sights in the 6x to 8x range, though some had 10x or even more powerful. This was a superb outfit for long ranges. It

50th EDITION, 1996 **109**

wasn't officially adopted until after World War II, and a number of them were purchased and remained in use until the Vietnam War!

As soon as the U.S. forces were committed to ground combat in World War II, urgent requests for scoped sniper rifles were submitted from the field. Ordnance immediately tested '03 Springfields with commercial 2.5x sights. The reason the 2.5x types were selected for testing is they seemed best for the sniping ranges up to 600 or so yards, which tactically proved best in combat.

By the fall of 1942, Ordnance selected peacetime Springfield '03s or '03A1s with a 2.2x Weaver sight in Redfield Junior mounts. The rifle had its regular iron sights removed and the bolt handle bent to clear the scope. While a few of these were assembled and issued, it was impossible to locate enough selected '03s to build enough sniper rifles to meet the ever-increasing requirement.

Ordnance turned to Remington, who was manufacturing the '03A3 Springfield, and had them equip it with the same Weaver 330 telescopic sight in Redfield Junior mounts, with the bolt handle bent to clear the scope. The Springfield's regular iron sights were omitted, and either a full- or semi-pistol grip stock was used. The Army adopted this as the Cal. 30 Rifle M1903A4 (Sniper's); the scope was designated the Telescopic Rifle Sight M73 in December, 1942, and it was immediately put in production. The model was first issued to troops in early 1943.

Some 30,000 '03A4 Springfield sniper rifles were built during World War II. They have been frequently criticized by many people. The rough wartime finish and stamped metal parts did not satisfy many riflemen who expected a sniper rifle to have the precision finish and look of a commercial long-range target rifle, but the gun's performance in combat was satisfactory.

U.S. Army records show that the '03A4 Springfield performed as well or better than any other World War II military-issue sniper rifle. An "as issued" '03A4 with its telescopic sight properly zeroed was deadly accurate at ranges out to at least 400 yards. When given a gunsmith-style, target-shooter's fine-tuning, it could shoot very well out to 600 yards and farther, and many gunsmiths who had joined the Army Ordnance Department worked them over. There are records of '03A4 sniper Springfields making effective shots at ranges as long as 1000 yards. This, however,

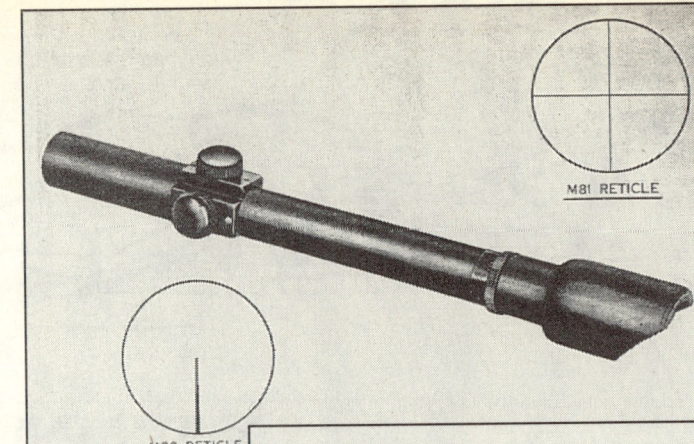

M81 and M82 2.2x sights for the Garand M-1C and M-1D sniper rifles. The M84 with a different reticle was adopted too late to see combat.

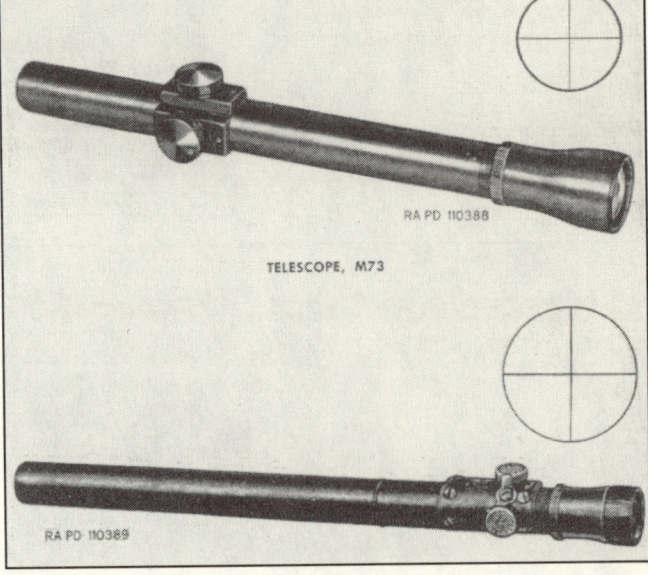

At top is the Lyman Alaskan 2.2x designated the M73; the bottom is the Weaver 330C 2.2x designated the M73B1. The Weaver was the model most commonly issued with the M1903A4 Springfield sniper rifle.

required perfect light and weather conditions.

The '03A4 Springfield remained sniper standard in the U.S. armed forces until the change to 7.62mm NATO-caliber rifles in the late 1950s. They remained in "war reserve" until some were used in the Vietnam War, and there may still be some stored.

At the time the '03A4 sniper Springfield was being developed, the Army Ground Forces Command issued a request for a study of a sniper rifle based on the M-1 Garand. A series of experimental prototypes were built and tested in 1943, but the availability and combat performance of the '03A4 Springfield made this a low-priority project for Ordnance.

This testing did establish several characteristics an M-1 sniper rifle would need to have. One was that the telescopic sight would have to be offset to the left so the Garand's regular iron sights could be used, and so it could be clip-loaded in the usual manner. To do this, a buttstock cheekrest would be required.

The Army adopted two M-1 Garand sniper rifles in mid-1944. The experimental M-1E7 version was adopted as the Cal. 30 Rifle M-1C (Sniper's) and went into production at Springfield Armory. It used a Griffin & Howe commercial scope mount on the left side of the rifle's receiver, which would suit any of the several models of standard 2.5x scopes then available.

The M-1C Sniper Garand was the model which first reached troops in World War II. They were some of the best M-1 Garands that Springfield Armory produced and were carefully selected for the modification. Unfortunately, they lacked the accuracy beyond 500 yards that snipers wanted. Garand accuracy was adversely affected by its muzzle-mounted gas cylinder and its multi-piece stock. Some 8000 M-1C Garand sniper rifles had been built by the end of World War II.

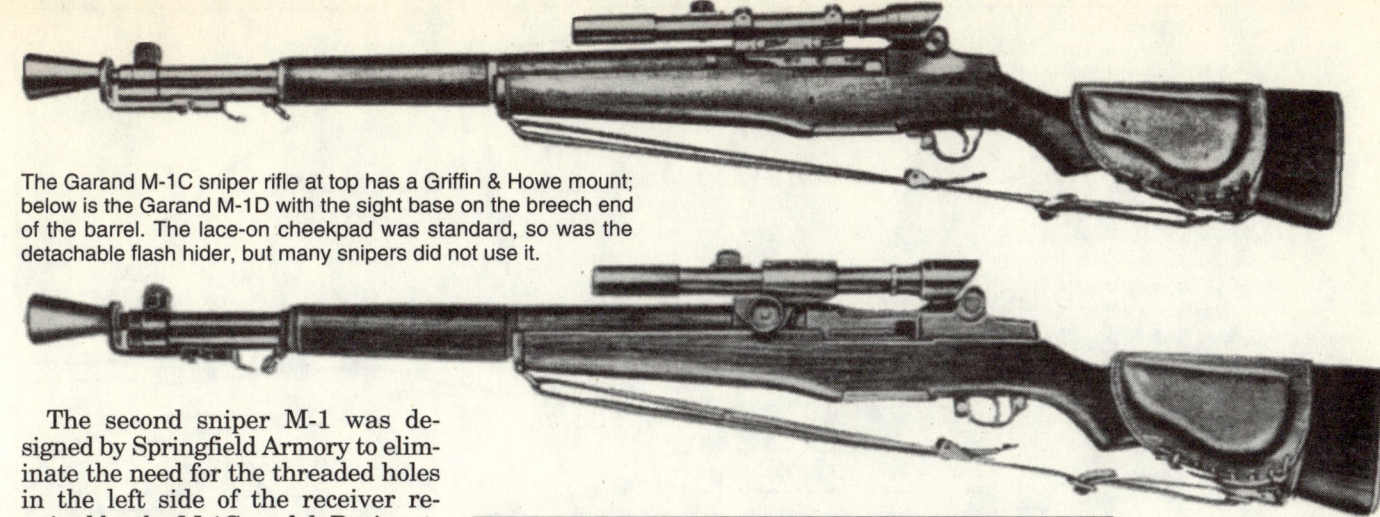

The Garand M-1C sniper rifle at top has a Griffin & Howe mount; below is the Garand M-1D with the sight base on the breech end of the barrel. The lace-on cheekpad was standard, so was the detachable flash hider, but many snipers did not use it.

The second sniper M-1 was designed by Springfield Armory to eliminate the need for the threaded holes in the left side of the receiver required by the M-1C model. Designated the Cal. 30 Rifle M-1D (Sniper's), its scope mount attached to the left side of the breech end of the rifle's barrel. A number of M-1D Garand sniper rifles were issued to troops and used in combat in the last months of World War II.

By the end of the war, the U.S. Army had adopted five sniper rifle scopes which could be used interchangeably on any sniper rifle. The M73 was the original model, and it was used on most of the '03A4 Springfields. The M73B1, a commercial 2.2x Lyman Alaskan, was adopted as an alternate standard for the M73, but it saw little combat use.

The M81, M82 and M84 scopes were all special models designed to have better resistance to dirt and moisture. The Army described them as 2.5x scopes, but they were all actually 2.2x. During World War II, these sights were mostly assembled on the M-1C and M-1D Garand sniper rifles, and they, along with the M73 and M73B1 scopes, remained in use long after the end of the war.

No matter what kind of sniper rifle a World War II GI or Marine had, he always had problems finding accurate ammunition for it. Many trained with the superbly accurate match target ammunition the Army Ordnance Department had been providing since 1908. However, under wartime or combat conditions, there was no way the Service of Supply could distribute this special ammunition to combat troops with any assurance it would reach the snipers who could use it. The quanities of 30-caliber rifle ammunition in the supply lines were just too vast. Even so, some units departing for combat from the United States did manage to take supplies of this special target-grade ammunition along for their snipers.

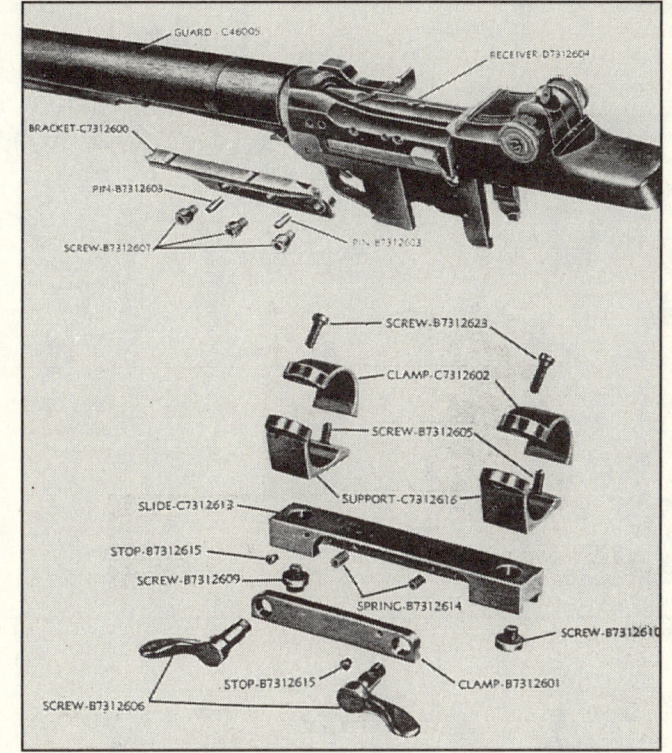

The Griffin & Howe side mount for the M-1C was pretty complex.

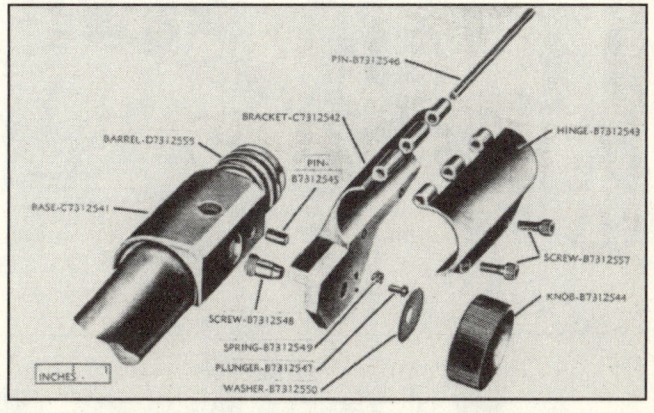

Springfield Armory's mount for the M-1D was hardly simpler.

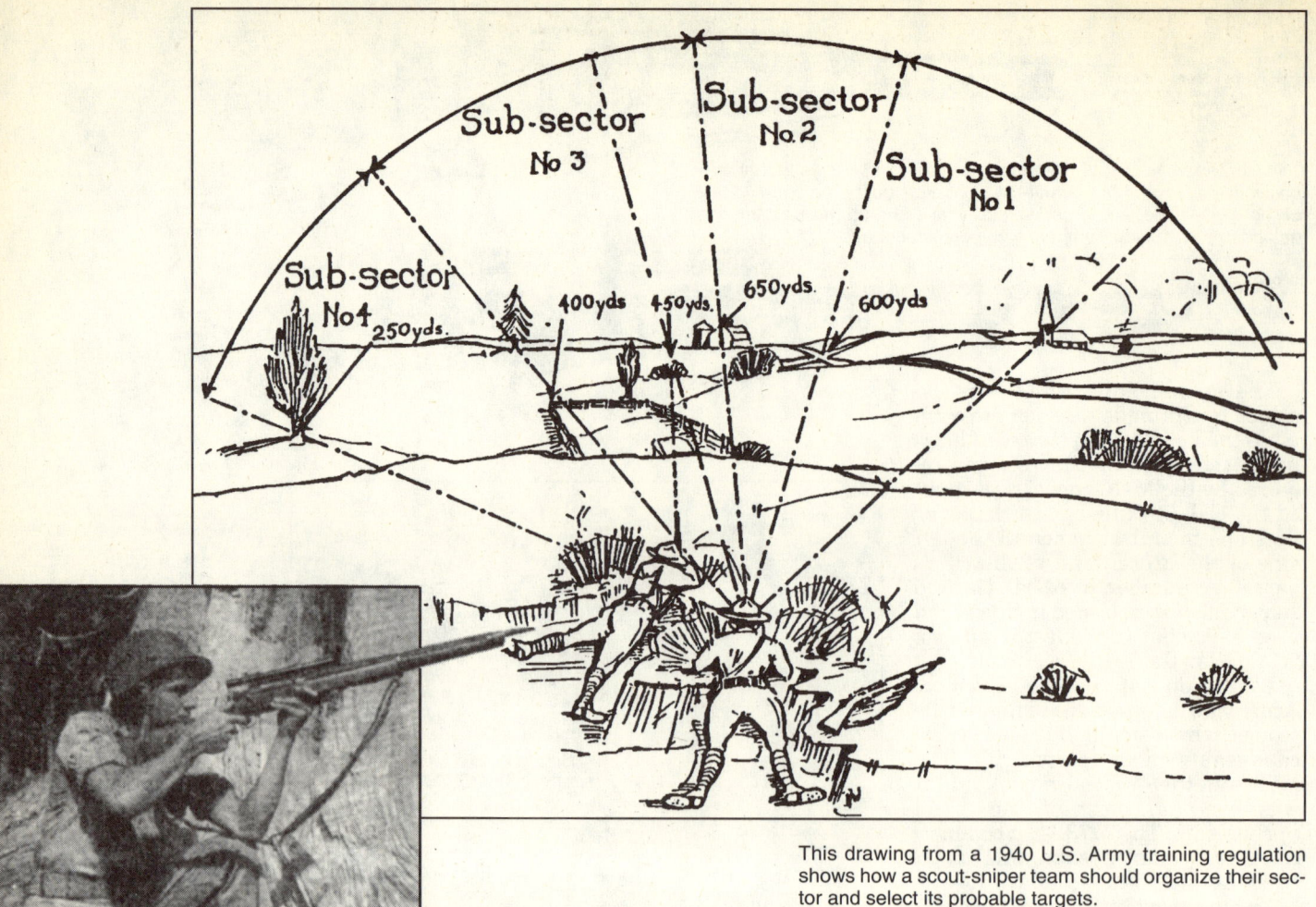

This drawing from a 1940 U.S. Army training regulation shows how a scout-sniper team should organize their sector and select its probable targets.

A Marine Corps sniper in the Pacific with an M1903A4 Springfield. (U.S. Marine Corps photo)

This drawing from a pre-World War II training regulation shows how to set up a training range for eye range estimation. Their use declined when replacement training had to be accelerated, but they always existed at World War II training facilities.

Another way World War II Army and Marine Corps snipers found the accurate ammunition they wanted sounds impractical, but it was done. The huge amount of ammo was made in batches known as "lots," some of which had superior accuracy to others. In fact, some of the match target ammunition the Ordnance Department provided was simply the result of careful selection of the most accurate production lots.

Snipers could, and did, testfire ammunition from the many lots available in their supplies to find the one which had the best accuracy. Then they would draw a supply of that lot to meet their needs. This was another unauthorized but effective procedure.

After World War II, the effectiveness of Army and Marine Corps snipers was well recognized, but ignored. An unsigned article in the February-March issue of *Army Ordnance* magazine was titled: "Sniping—A Neglected Art." Snipers were among the most resourceful, determined soldiers in the U.S. armed forces, but they seldom received recognition. However, they did get the rifles they needed.

The Future Of Firearms

What makes the new Colt® .38 SF-VI™ different from any other .38 on the market?

.38 SF-VI

George Vezina, Head of Colt Security, predicts superior shootability will make the SF-VI the new .38 standard. It gives shooters a new concept in .38's, whether used for personal protection or as a law enforcement officer's back-up.

Internal design and shootability. That's what. With revolutionary new bolt design and lock works, new firing pin placement, and new energy-transfer safety system, the SF-VI has a light, smooth trigger pull that surprised even the Colt® engineers. That enhances the accuracy of the familiar snub-nose profile, which features a new stainless finish. It's quality that competitive models cannot duplicate. Quality that makes it a Colt.

Get your FREE Colt Firearms and Wearables Catalogs at your Colt Dealer today. Or call 1-800-962-COLT

QUALITY MAKES IT A COLT.™

Warning: Never chamber a round until you are ready to shoot. Read and follow manual accompanying each firearm. Free manuals available on request. © 1995

Come Hail or High Water...

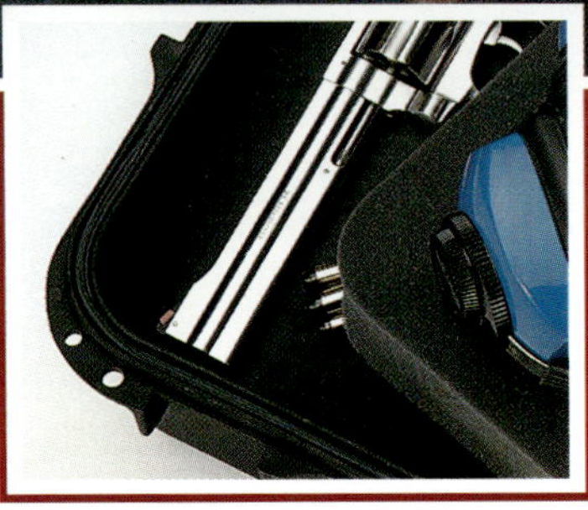

Dust, Water & Air tight O-Ring Seal

You've trusted Gun Guard for years for reliable case protection, but now's the time to step up to the ultimate case Gun Guard has to offer. Ruggedly attractive and guaranteed forever, the All-Weather Double Rifle meets the demands of the experienced hunter under the most extreme conditions.

Designed with features like: the exclusive **six-latch system** for protection and strength, **high density foam** perfect for customizing and the unique **O-Ring Seal** that makes the case water tight, air tight and dustproof.

When it comes to extremes, the Gun Guard All-Weather is the best protection you can buy.

Available in Double Scoped Rifle, Large and Extra-Large Pistol/Accessory Cases.

DOSKOCIL®

A Strong Case for Quality
P.O. Box 1246, Arlington, Texas 76004-1246

Natural Pointers.

Bred over generations.

Sculpted in form, flawless in function.

Like a polished gun dog, our Model 11-87™ Premier™ autoloader has a natural instinct for upland hunting. You could say it was bred for the task, coming as it does from a long line of field-proven autoloaders. But this one is fitted with our exclusive light contour barrel, which makes it a half-pound lighter in weight—and a whole lot faster on point. It's superbly balanced, so it goes to your shoulder like it belongs there, then swings with remarkable ease. And late in the day, you'll feel the difference that half-pound makes, because this classic shotgun won't wear you out carrying what you don't need. It's available with 26", 28" or 30" barrel, each with Rem™ Chokes. The Remington® 11-87 Premier. It's pure pointer.

Remington® COUNTRY

A Safety Reminder: Always keep the muzzle pointed in a safe direction.

Remington is a trademark registered in the U.S. Patent & Trademark Office by Remington Arms Company, Inc. Model 11-87, Premier and Rem are trademarks of Remington Arms Company, Inc., Wilmington, DE 19805. © 1995 Remington Arms Company, Inc. All rights reserved.

CONTENDER® Versatility...

All It Takes Is A Screwdriver.

For over 25 years, the Contender pistol has led the field of "hunting handguns." Its MOA accuracy has made it the top choice among serious handgun hunters as well as those who "bust steel." Many shooters will even tell you that the Contender will outshoot some of the rifles they own.

The Contender could stand alone with just these credentials, but there's more to a Contender than its accuracy. Contender barrels are interchangeable...in seconds. Remove the forend, punch out the pivot pin and you're now ready to install a new barrel.

We've got plenty of barrels to choose from: blued or stainless steel; 10", 14" and 16 1/4" and, they are all interchangeable. Calibers? We've chambered the Contender for 18 cartridges including the .410 bore shotshell; proven deer cartridges like .30/30 Win., .35 Rem., 7-30 Waters and the potent .375 Win. Even the awesome 45/70 Gov't. For varmints, you can't go wrong with a .17 Rem, .223 Rem or the venerable .22 Hornet.

T/C's Contender; the beauty of it is that you only need one gun, after that it's all a matter of barrels... and a screwdriver.

Check one out at your dealers. You'll see why it's America's #1 hunting handgun.

Robert C. Dillon with his #1 SCI Handgun mountain goat. Robert shot the Colorado goat with a 14" Contender Hunter chambered in .375 Win. at 110 yds; elevation 13,000 ft.

Write for our free catalog.

THOMPSON/CENTER ARMS COMPANY, INC.
P.O. BOX 5002, DEPT. GD96
FARMINGTON ROAD
ROCHESTER, NEW HAMPSHIRE 03867

by ROB LUCAS

P.O. Ackley wrote three volumes of solid stuff for shooters between 1959 and 1966.

P.O. ACKLEY'S WILDCATS

"SO DID YOU and Mr. Ackley ever solve your respective historical mysteries?" hunting partner Bob Sturgis asked, chomping on crisply burnt bacon.

It was after the New Year. I'd been holed up with the Ackley research, so it had been awhile since we chased pheasants. I had called Bob and set up an early breakfast and some bird shooting—to come up for air.

Sturgis knows about historical whodunnits. Among his distant cousins is 2nd Lt. James Garland Sturgis, one of Custer's doomed officers on the afternoon of June 25, 1876. At least every generation somebody comes up with a new and revised explanation of how the promising lieutenant and the infamous colonel met their ends at the Little Bighorn, including which Sioux chief actually overwhelmed Custer on the knoll. Bob Sturgis thinks the descendants of either Gall or Crazy Horse can count coup for Custer; I served in Vietnam with a Cheyenne PFC whose great-grandfather fought at Greasy Grass, so I heard a different demise for Yellow Hair. We regularly chew on the Custer mystery.

"Nope. Mr. Ackley and I both failed, you might say. Ackley didn't reproduce a detonation in his lab, and I can't put Ackley up on a pedestal, not yet."

P.O. Ackley was the foremost cartridge wildcatter and experimenter of his time, and maybe of *all* time. He was a rifle builder, barrel maker, general gunsmith, licensed firearms importer, a magna cum laude graduate and college professor of metallurgy, author of books, and magazine columnist, all of which gave him a pretty broad approach to his craft. You should also know that P.O. Ackley broke both his legs in a stockcar crash in 1948, so he liked a little excitement, too. In *Handbook for Reloaders and Shooters Volumes I & II* by P.O.

50th EDITION, 1996 113

The 219 Zipper on the right is Improved. The new shoulder is a stretch.

Ackley's friend, Jack O'Connor, got a detonation shooting handloads in a 270 Winchester; a "report like that of a cannon," smoke coming from the action, a cracked locking lug, and a case stuck so hard in the chamber the barrel had to be unscrewed. When O'Connor pulled the bullets from the remaining handloads, he found one case half-full. At the time he was using two cranks of a powder measure to throw one 60-grain charge of 4831, a dubious practice but not considered dangerous.

O'Connor wrote it up in *Outdoor Life*, warning against the use of reduced loads of slow-burning powder. The NRA staff at the *American Rifleman* ran some tests and concluded that "detonations" didn't just happen and that O'Connor—not by name, of course—was nuts. Ackley jumped into this frying pan by providing the feisty O'Connor with a format to

degree shoulder later in the review of Ackley's rimless wildcats. Meanwhile, an old issue resurfaced: P.O. Ackley and the "fireform improved" wildcat cartridge, loosely known as the "Ackley Improved" today, hit the gunsmithing scene at about the same time, the late 1930s. But did Parker Otto Ackley or someone else invent "Ackley Improved"? Of Ackley's sixty-two wildcat rifle cartridges, forty-two are variously "improved" and nineteen of those are "fireform improved," or we could say "true improved," including the five that are still on the RCBS Top 15 list of most popular rifle wildcat reloading dies. The term "improved," though he didn't care for it, became a P.O. Ackley legacy, but did he pioneer or merely popularize this clever piece of gunsmithing?

Elmer Keith did not think Ackley had much to do with the first fire-

Ackley, we see that in any area of gunsmithing unknown, Ackley simply set up an experiment, usually involving blowing up a rifle or two, until he figured things out. There was one experiment he didn't finish, though.

The reason we quit hearing spooky stories of hunting rifles wrecked by practice loads of slow-burning powder is that word finally got around: Don't take a chance, don't use reduced loads of slow powders. But it crossed my mind that maybe P.O. solved this mystery as he all but guaranteed we would in his chapter called "Reduced Loads" in the 1962 edition of *Handbook Vol I*.

Rumors of erratic pressure caused by reduced loads of slow-burning powder trace back to the 1940s, but handloading became popular in the '50s, which is when the "detonation phenomenon" was quite the fiery controversy. While gunwriters got angry fan mail, gunsmith Ackley got parcel post packages containing mangled rifle parts at his Colorado shop, as often as not "overbore" calibers like the 25-06 Remington and the 25-06 Ackley Improved.

Among the fascinating theories circulating was this one: Under some unknown circumstance, a half-charge plug of slow-burning powder was blown forward by the primer spark into the shoulder/neck area where it wedged, smoldering, until it detonated just like a bomb. Still sounds plausible, doesn't it?

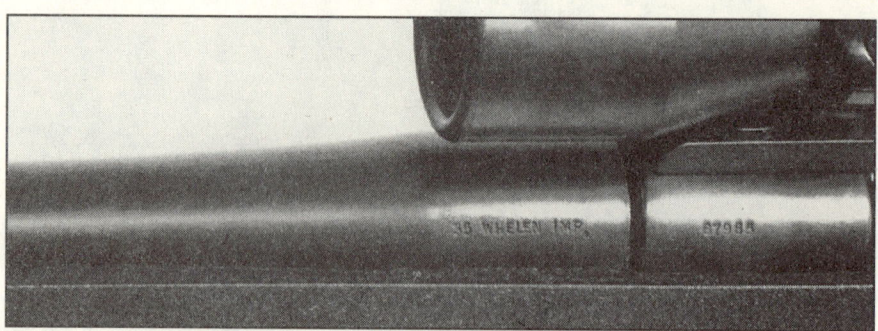

When it says "IMP" on a barrel, it means "Improved"—often "Ackley Improved."

rebut the NRA in *Handbook Vol. I*, and he finished off O'Connor's remarks with a short, resolute statement that "in the not too distant future" he would prove the detonation theory in his lab.

To find out if he ever did, I spoke to Mike Bellm, the man who bought Ackley's barrel making business when he retired for the last time. With obvious pride in his voice, Mike said no, P.O. never did blow up a gun under laboratory conditions, but he never quit trying. It was a mystery the grand old guy took with him to the hereafter in 1989. End of story.

My historical mystery had to do with the early part of Ackley's wildcat career. I was hoping to contribute a significant Ackley connection to the year 1945-46 for the 50th Anniversary Edition of GUN DIGEST. No problem—a half-century ago, P.O. Ackley used his trademark 40-degree shoulder for the first time with the 30-06 Springfield Ackley Improved. We'll look into the controversial Improved '06 and the 40-

form wildcat. In 1979, Elmer all but swallowed his cigar when I asked him this question: "Maybe I should go all the way and build the Ackley Improved version?"

I'd been reading Elmer Keith for twenty years, but only recently had gotten into Ackley. Meeting Keith in person a second time, we talked about a pair of great old wildcats from the 30-06 case, the 35 Whelen and Keith's own 333 OKH, and he advised going with the Whelen because of better bullet selection. But with a raised eyebrow and a finger pointed my way like the barrel of a 44 Magnum, Keith answered my question this way, as I recall:

"Charles Newton invented the improved wildcat before 1920; it was the blown-out old 256 Newton. Charlie O'Neil fooled with the Improved '06 case before we brought out the 333 after the war. But Charlie Newton beat Charlie O'Neil an' everybody else, including Ackley, by twenty years!"

It wasn't the answer I expected,

but it was definite. Of course, Keith's opinion of Ackley was tainted; the two men disliked each other, although I didn't know it at the time. It was another ten years before I learned of the "Keith-Ackley Battles" of World War II, when the two diametrically opposed experts built Springfield rifles together at the Ogden Utah Depot. Now there's a subject for the historian!

I built that 35 Whelen Ackley Improved rifle, and I was carrying it in 1986 when I heard a "hometown favorite" version of the birth of the fireform wildcat. I ran into a mule deer hunter from the state of Oklahoma, home of famed gunsmith Art Mashburn. This gentleman showed me a pre-'64 Winchester 70 rifle in 300 Mashburn Magnum through which he said he'd fired 5000 rounds. He made custom 300 Mashburn ammo by fireforming 300 Weatherby factories. I was impressed, considering I was still making 35 Whelen Improved cases the old fashioned way by necking up and reforming 30-06 brass. According to this source, Art Mashburn invented the fireform improved wildcat in 1937, the year Winchester introduced the Model 70 rifle and factory-loaded 300 H&H ammo. Mashburn fireformed the 300 H&H to his trademark 30-degree shoulder, and it

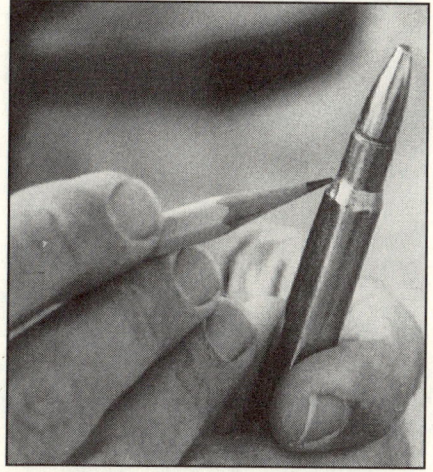

This is the place where the 30-06 case should headspace in an Improved chamber, after creating a shiny ring.

was no coincidence that eight years later Roy Weatherby brought out his 300 Weatherby with the same chamber dimensions, but with his "venturied" shoulder.

A man who knows the history of wildcat cartridges as well as anyone living is writer Ken Waters. Waters is on record crediting Lysle Kilbourne with the first fireform improved wildcat cartridge, the K-Hornet. Waters wrote this in the 1992 *Wildcat Cartridges Vol. I*, describing Kilbourne's design goal when, in 1939 or '40, he fired factory Hornets in his K-Hornet chamber:

> ...the Kilbourne concept involves far more than just a simple expansion of a case to fit a chamber of the same shape...in a Kilbourne chamber...firing expands the case to a different shape. Never before, to the best of my recollection, had anyone come up with such a simple method of forming wildcat cases while retaining the undeniable asset of being able to fire factory cartridges in the same chamber, safely. That was Kilbourne's irrefutable contribution...

In giving New York gunsmith Kilbourne "irrefutable" credit for the fireform wildcat, Waters also gives us a concise description of what the fireform improved idea was all about. The wildcatter, instead of creating a brand-new cartridge from scratch, simply reamed a standard chamber to less taper and a sharper shoulder while staying within headspace tolerance, and then fired factory cartridges to make wildcat brass. A sensational idea. The result was a more powerful wildcat chamber that would still handle factory ammo. With his convincing salute to Kilbourne, Ken Waters seems to slam the door shut; P.O. Ackley was not the originator of the fireform idea.

Waters is exactly right about one thing: The first fireform improved wildcat was a rimmed 22 centerfire. In the 1930s, wildcatting was really wild, and the rimmed case was known to be safer and stronger than the rimless case. Art Mashburn's belted 300 Magnum probably isn't the original fireform cartridge, but his rimmed 218 Mashburn Bee is in the running, as is the rimmed 218 Gipson Bee, the Kilbourne K-Hornet, Ackley's 219 Improved Zipper, Donaldson's 219 Wasp, the 22 Lindahl Chucker, two or three "improved" 22 Savage High-Powers, and who knows how many other rimmed 22 wildcats.

When you really dig for the origin of "fireform improved," you run smack into the concurrent development of "modern and efficient," i.e., less body taper and a sharper shoulder angle combined with shorter case length, which opens the door for everybody from Charles Newton and A.O. Wiedner to Harvey Donaldson and Hervey Lovell. It was all happening in the '20s and '30s; most of the experimenters were New Yorkers who either knew each other or worked together; they were all working on some form of high-velocity 22 centerfire; and there was only a handful of basic brass usable for starting points. For his part, P.O. Ackley never claimed bragging rights for the fireform improved, while others did, like New York wildcatter Harvey Donaldson.

Donaldson began looking for an accurate 22 centerfire in the mid-'30s, starting from the stout, rimmed 22 Niedner Magnum case, which was the 25-35 Winchester necked down. Unable to get it exactly right, he switched back and forth between the Niedner case, the 25-35, the rimless 25 Remington case, and the 1937 219 Zipper case, which P.O. Ackley wildcatted at about the same time.

Donaldson was a sociable sort of 'smith. He knew everybody in the business, and his experiments were well documented. In 1935, Donaldson's friend, M.S. Risley, designed a new chambering reamer for the wildcat 22-3000 Lovell which sharpened the shoulder from 5 to 15 degrees. The "improved" 22-3000 cartridge became known as the R2 Lovell, or simply the R2, and stepped up the velocity of a 45-grain bullet to 3200 fps from a case not much bigger than the 22 Hornet. Donaldson eventually formed a partnership with New Yorker Vernor Gipson, and they settled on the 219 Wasp from a necked-down 25-35 case with .015-inch body taper and a 30-degree shoulder angle. After this, Donaldson promptly claimed credit for inventing both the "Modern and Efficient" cartridge and the so-called "Improved" cartridge, because he gave Risley the idea how to change the shoulder angle of the 22-3000 Lovell to add case volume. What a guy.

And so, summing up my progress in establishing P.O. Ackley as first with the fireform improved, I told Bob Sturgis: "Crediting P.O. Ackley or any other famous gunsmith with the invention of the improved wildcat is like crediting one or another Sioux chief at the Battle of the Little Bighorn with knocking off Custer; it was a long time ago and there were a lotta guys in the area."

P.O. Ackley's first wildcat cartridge was the rimmed 219 Zipper Improved of 1938, the Winchester factory Zipper blown out with a 28-degree shoulder. It was a winner, but as with the 219 Wasp, it wasn't just right on the first go-round and there were three versions. The wide Zipper rim, pinched between the breechblock and barrel, was a headspace safety valve to rookie wildcatter Ackley, holding the case snug as the firing pin struck the primer and gas expanded in all directions blowing out the case with it. From the photograph that shows a factory Zipper beside Ackley's Improved version, you can see that it was indeed quite a stretch. In fact, Zipper brass made after WWII couldn't cut it; they split their shoulders on fireforming. Ackley recommended using cut-down, necked-down 30-30 brass instead to make his good wildcat cartridge, but a gain of 300 fps with a 45-grain bullet to nearly 220 Swift velocity was well worth the trouble to varmint shooters.

In addition to its positive headspacing, the rimmed case had another magical property: the rim was a positive reinforcement of the primer pocket area which acted to decrease pocket expansion and therefore prevent gas leakage into the breech. This premise was one that Ackley later challenged in the *Handbook Vol. I* chapter called "Rimmed vs. Rimless." By comparing four hot-loaded 25 Krag rimmed wildcats against his own 25-06 Improved and 257 Roberts Improved rimless wildcats, plus the factory 257 Weatherby belted magnum, Ackley showed that the rimless case, no matter what the breeching system, held pressure in the primer pocket area as well as the rimmed case. Even so, and long after Ackley switched the focus of his wildcat work to rimless cases and the modern bolt-action guns that fired them, he never lost his fondness for lever action rifles and for rimmed cases. The Ackley recipe for efficiency—his combination of body taper, shoulder angle, neck length, and the ratio between case and bore capacities—applied to any factory-made case whether it headspaced on a belt or a shoulder or an old-fashioned rim.

Ackley built a pair of 17-caliber rimmed wildcats and another 17 on the rimless 222 Remington, which we'll look at with his rimless cartridges. The 17 Ackley Bee is the old 218 Winchester Bee with a sharper 30-degree shoulder and .009-inch body taper, necked down to 17-caliber. Ackley recommended simply pouring powder into the case until it was full, scraping the mouth level, and then cramming in a 20- to 25-grain bullet for an accurate, almost recoiless varmint cartridge usable out to 200 yards or so. The 17 Ackley Hornet is the famous Hornet case given the 30-degree shoulder and about .011-inch of taper.

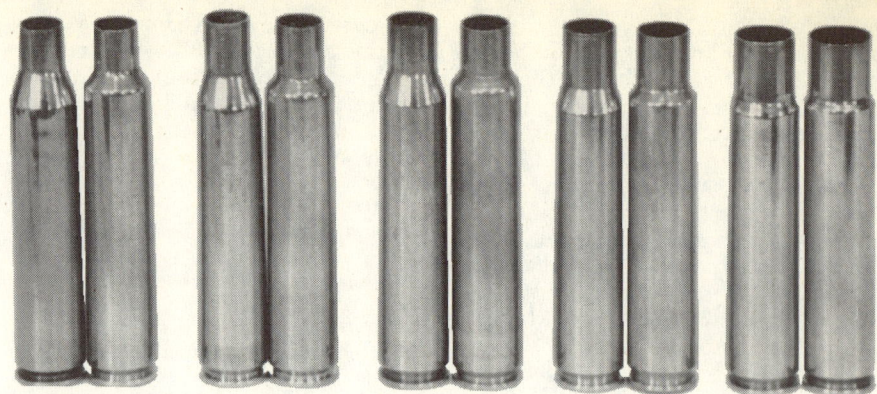

These five factory cases—25-06, 270, 280, 30-06 and 35 Whelen—are paired with their improved versions here.

Ackley's rimmed 22 wildcats in the order they appear in *Handbook Vol. I* are the 22 Improved Jet based on the 357 Magnum case; the final version of his original 219 Ackley Improved Zipper; the 22-30/30 Ackley Improved on the 30-30 case; the semi-rimmed 220 Swift Ackley Improved from the factory Swift discussed later with the rimless 22s; the 22 Savage High-Power Improved from Charles Newton's 1912 original; and the 228 Krag Ackley from the 30-40 Krag case.

Rimmed 22-caliber wildcats look like antiques now, but not so long ago there was a market and a demand for Ackley's designs. The Improved Zipper, the Improved 22-30/30, the Improved Savage High-Power, and the 228 Krag were all matched for use in the most popular rifles of the day. His 22-30/30 with 40-degree shoulder and .017-inch taper designed for the Winchester '94 pushed a 45-grain bullet more than 4000 fps, which made some people very nervous. But, post-WWII, Ackley simply saw the 22-30/30 as the successor to the Improved Zipper and a step up.

In the 1962 *Handbook Vol. I*, Ackley describes an experiment on the subject of chamber pressure and the strength of the Winchester Model 94 rifle. After rebarreling a "junk pile" Model 94 to 30-30 Ackley Improved, he fired a series of factory cases while incrementally unscrewing the barrel and lengthening the firing pin so it could hit the primer. His point: The Improved case with less body taper tightly gripped chamber walls and thereby transferred less pressure in the form of thrust back to the bolt. And the Model 94 was stronger than the experts gave it credit. The icing on this experimental cake came when he fired factory 30-30s in the Improved 94 with its locking lug removed—no support but the finger lever—with the result that there was no special result but excessive primer protrusion.

For Model 94 users in states where the 22 was banned on big game, Ackley offered a 6mm/30-30 that equaled the performance of the 243 Winchester, a 90-grain bullet at 3300 fps. There were two versions of the Ackley 6mm Krag Improved, the short one with a 25-degree shoulder and the full-length, blown-out version with 40-degree shoulder, both for single shot rifles.

Among Ackley's 25-caliber rimmed wildcats is one of his best, developed from the feeble old 25-35 Winchester. The 25-35 Ackley Improved for lever-action rifles came along about 1950, and it jumped the velocity of 100-grain bullets in a 25-35 Model 94 by a whopping 600 fps. Originally, the 25-35 Ackley Improved was a straight fireform wildcat—buy a box of factory 25-35s and fire them in the wildcat chamber, then commence handloading. But post-WWII 25-35 brass, like post-war Zipper brass, was too thin for this treatment, and Ackley again recommended using 30-30 Winchester brass instead. The 25-35 Improved became a "pure" wildcat instead of a fireform improved, and this partly explains why this great cartridge lost popularity. In an Ackley 25-35 Savage 99 or Winchester 94, 100-grain bullets could safely leave the muzzle at 3000 fps. Designer Ackley went to great lengths to explain that this was largely due to the effect of the straight-sided case "taking the load," flattening against the chamber walls and reducing thrust to the bolt. There was more to the improved wildcat than just velocity.

There are a pair of Ackley wildcats from history's first modern wildcat, the 25 Krag. The 25 Short Krag Improved has a case length of 2.14 inches and 28-degree shoulder, while the 25 Krag Improved is the full-length 2.31-inch case, 40-degree shoulder and only .010-inch of taper. These, depending on your terminology, could be either the 6mm Krag necked up or the re-shaped 30-40 necked down. Ackley's full-sized 25 Krag was too hot for Krag rifles—100-grain bullets at 3400 fps—and was intended for P-14 Enfields and single shots.

P.O. Ackley's excellent 30-30 Improved makes anybody's list of all-time best wildcats. It hoists 30-30 Winchester velocity in a lever-action rifle up to nearly 308 Winchester performance from a modern bolt-action or semi-automatic. Ackley's 30-30 illustrates the improved concept perfectly: 40-degree shoulder, .017-inch body taper, and still a good length of neck. Ackley lists loads in *Handbook Vol. I* showing 2700 fps with a 150 round-nose. Being a lever-action guy myself, I'd prefer something like the 170-grain RN Corelokt at 2500 fps. Now that's an improvement over the factory's 2200 fps.

Ackley wrote that his rimmed 30-40 Krag Improved was among his very best wildcats, but in its cartridge description he points out that it was not popular due to the lack of suitable actions. And we can see why. How'd you like to try for 2900 fps with a 180-grain bullet in a Krag rifle? Ackley says it's possible with a 30-40 Improved, but best in a Hi-Wall or P-14 Enfield.

I can find no Ackley wildcats based on the 45-70 case, so that brings us to his work with our largest rimmed case, the 348 Winchester. Ackley necked the 348 both up and down, gave it the 40-degree shoulder, and one or two of his 348s deserve special note. If I ever build an American double rifle on a 12-gauge shotgun frame, the cartridge will be the rimmed 30-348 Ackley Improved, and if you've never seen a 30-348 Ackley Improved cartridge, you've missed a corker.

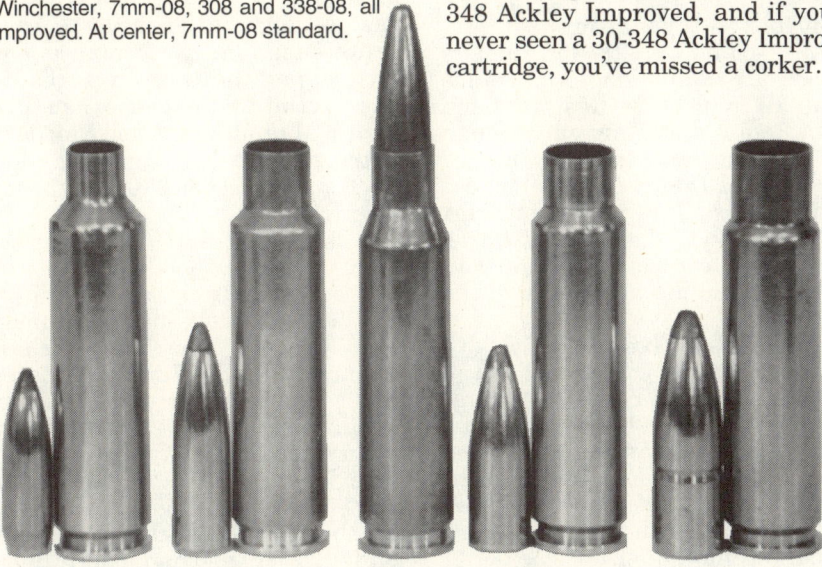

Here's the 308 family, all with the 40-degree Ackley shoulder: (from left) 243 Winchester, 7mm-08, 308 and 338-08, all improved. At center, 7mm-08 standard.

Imagine the squat, sloping 348 case blown out to minimum taper with a 40-degree shoulder, making the shoulder look as wide as the rim. This is an impressive wildcat, and like most of Ackley's work on the 348 case, it was a personal request from *Guns & Ammo* writer Bob Hutton for the Winchester Model 71 rifle. With its minimum-taper case helping to reduce thrust to the Model 71's rear-lug locking mechanism, a 170-grain bullet from a 30-348 could safely beat a 180-grain bullet from a 30-06, going about 2800. I've read that 2900 fps is no problem in modern guns.

And there's the original 348 Ackley Improved, the 35-348, 40-348 and 450-348, all of them with the 40-degree Ackley shoulder and minimum taper. Have a peek at what's possible with the 450-348, which is the same cartridge as the 450 Alaskan, with numbers that look like those from the 458 Winchester Magnum: Ahead of 68 grains of IMR-4064, Ackley shows a 500-grain bullet for the 450-348 Improved traveling 2040 fps!

Initially, the big English belted case, a new frontier to explore, intrigued P.O. Ackley. When 375 H&H brass became available on the West Coast in early 1939, and some of his customers wanted "magnum" performance in a standard length action, Ackley got very busy. Though it was barely a year since the Improved Zipper put him in the wildcat business to stay, he designed the 30 Short Ackley Magnum No. 1—the 375 case shortened to 2.45-inch and necked down with 28-degree shoulder. It failed, dead and buried shortly after WWII, but better Ackley magnums later followed, and by the 1950s, his customers had three distinct families of magnums to choose from with two shoulder angles and three case lengths.

The belted case taught P.O. the law of diminishing return with respect to maximum case capacity: With any magnum there was a point, based on the ratio of case capacity to bore capacity, when adding more powder to gain velocity meant giving up everything else—case life, barrel life and cartridge efficiency. Ackley labeled most belted magnums, factory or wildcat, his designs or someone else's, "overbore" or "badly overbore." He tried to build belted magnums that made sense and which filled a market need, cartridges of better design and better efficiency than those from the factories. In his 1966 *Handbook Vol. II*, a time when every American arms company was cranking out belted magnums of good, bad and ugly design, some of his most interesting and unrestrained rhetoric shows up. But, as always, Ackley let the customer make the decision.

Ackley's smallest belted cartridge is a 22, but is neither based on a belted case nor qualifies as a magnum. It was a customer special request known as the 228 Belted Express; the shortened 30-06 case with a belt swaged around its head. It took three separate swaging steps to build up a belt on an '06 case, but with characteristic enthusiasm Ackley started with one and ended up with a whole family of these hybrid magnums, including 224 Ackley Belted Express, the 228, 6mm, 243, and 25 Belted Express. The 228 Belted Express became the best known and was meant to duplicate

These are the four steps to 35 Whelen Improved: the 30-06 case, the 40-caliber cylinder, the sized case, the fireformed case.

the old 1938 228 Ackley Magnum for shooters who, in Ackley's words "feel the belt affords a better headspace and produces a stronger case." In the '50s, this crowd was persecuted but persistent, big game hunters who preferred very small, very fast bullets. And they were right fussy about their cases.

Of his two belted wildcats in 244-caliber, Ackley praised one and condemned the other. One had "the ideal maximum capacity" for the 6mm, and the other was "over capacity and in no way compares to the 243 Winchester and the 244 Remington." The 6mm Belted Express, or 228 Express necked up, is "one of the finest of all 6mm wildcats," while the 6mm Ackley Magnum from the shortened 300 Winchester Magnum case was a waste of time and gunpowder. In describing another "overbore" 6mm, the original 244 Holland & Holland Magnum, Ackley tells his readers about a load of slow-burning 50 BMG machinegun powder reduced just 15 percent in a 244 H&H which completely disintegrated a rifle, a reminder that "detonations" were especially likely in the big belted cases.

The belted magnums we think of today as "standard length"—the 300 Winchester, 264, 338 and 7mm Remington Magnum—Ackley thought of as "short," because they came from the 2.85-inch 375 H&H case shortened to about 2.50-inch to work through a 30-06-sized action. Calling them "short" was accurate, but bad market strategy—nobody wanted a magnum that's "short" because magnums were supposed to be "big." Even the stubby Remington 350 Magnum which Ackley thoroughly despised was never called "short" by Remington. Ackley's short magnums were right for the time, about 1940 into the 1970s, and were the forerunners of today's medium-length magnums from 264 Winchester Magnum and 7mm Remington Magnum through 458 Winchester Magnum. Ackley started with the 28-degree shoulder in 1939 and stayed with it in his short No. 1s and No. 2s, figuring that 28 degrees was sharp enough up front with the belt handling headspace at the rear.

The smallest "Short Belted" Ackley magnum was his 30 Short No. 1 necked down to 25-caliber, 28-degree shoulder, .024-inch body taper and a case length of 2.45-inch, and called the 25 Ackley Magnum. Or it could be the 300 H&H case shortened and necked down. He didn't like this one much, but he thought it was better than most because it held a little less powder and thus had a better ratio of powder capacity to bore size. (Question: Does a cut-down 257 Weatherby in a lever-action BLR sound intriguing to anyone?)

Next is a very interesting Ackley magnum—the 6.5mm—which isn't listed in *Handbook Vol. I or II*, but is mentioned with other wildcat 6.5 magnums. Ackley was blunt about this one—not recommended, badly overbore. As you know, the 264 Winchester Magnum is a 6.5mm magnum, actually a 256-caliber. Of all factory belted magnums introduced over the years, the 264 Winchester held a special place in Ackley's heart—it was inexcusable. Ackley figured the 264 was way overbore, for starters, and had a neck that was obviously too short. On top of that, Winchester had to counteract bad case design with a sneaky double-diameter bullet that was supposed to hold down initial thrust pressures so this lousy cartridge could reach its published velocity numbers, which it didn't do in any case.

Ackley thought his 6.5 magnum would have been a better deal for both Winchester and the shooting public *if* a 256-caliber magnum was needed in the first place. You won't see the Ackley 6.5 magnum in his books, but have a look at his nicely proportioned 270 Magnum and you see the design.

The 270 Ackley is one of the original Short No. 1s, and it needs 10 more grains of IMR-4350 to move a 130-grain bullet 140 fps faster than the standard 270 Winchester. Though Ackley did like his 270 magnum design, it is an example of the "diminished return" characteristic he was so quick to point out: If one wants magnum performance one must to pay the price in increased blast, recoil and expense. The 270 Ackley Magnum is a good modern cartridge and holds up well compared to the bigger 270 Weatherby Magnum.

Necking the 270 Ackley up to 7mm, or the 30 Short down, gets us to a word P.O. was damned stingy with in describing any belted magnum—flexible. The 7mm Ackley Magnum, like the 7mm Weatherby that came before it and the 7mm Remington that followed, can do lots of things with different bullet weights. Case length of the Ackley Seven Mag is the same 2.45-inch, while the Weatherby is 2.54-inch and Remington is 2.50-inch. The modern Remington Magnum gets 3020 fps with a 175-grain bullet, while the older and slightly shorter Ackley version shows 2950 fps with the 175-grain weight. A 160-grain bullet chronographs 3150 fps in the Remington and 3125 in the Ackley, so we perceive that these are virtually the same cartridge, but the Ackley wildcat is obsolete. P.O. Ackley, the barrelmaker, found that pushing Seven Mag bullets any faster shortened barrel life dramatically.

When you hit 30-caliber-and-up in the Ackley belted magnums, you find three different wildcats of the same bore size and a bunch of confusion. There are the Short No. 1s, the Short No. 2s, and the full-sized Improved Magnums. The differences can be explained by going back to Ackley's first belted wildcat in 1939.

The 30 Short Magnum No. 1 was Ackley's third career wildcat design and his first from a belted case. It had the 28-degree shoulder, .024-inch taper, and a case length of 2.45

inches, compared to the 12-degree shoulder and nearly .07-inch taper and 2.85-inch length of the "new" 375 H&H which all the fuss was about. The 30 Ackley Short No. 1 gave 3000 fps with a 180-grain bullet, a tad more than the older, bigger 300 H&H, but a bit less than the modern 300 Winchester Magnum. This was a good wildcat, but it's long obsolete.

All the Short No. 1s with the 2.45-inch case length are obsolete, and the reason is a matter of history rather than performance. A rifle chambered for the 30-06 Springfield could not be rechambered to 30 Ackley Short No. 1 without setting the barrel back a thread; a 30-06 cartridge could not accidentally be fired in a 30 Short rifle. I don't know if Ackley designed the 30 Short No. 1 with this in mind, but it's why he designed the Short No. 2s, which have a case length of 2.53 inches, almost as long as the Weatherby. A 30-06 chamber can become a 30 Short No. 2 by opening the bolt face and reaming to the magnum specs.

The 30 Short Magnum No. 2 came along in 1946 and was one of Ackley's first wildcats following his Ogden, Utah, Army Depot experience. He recognized his earlier mistake and fixed it, while keeping the 28-degree shoulder and trimming body taper to .020-inch. Ackley shows, in the *Handbook*, a 180-grain bullet from the 30 Short No. 2 Magnum leaving the barrel 10 fps faster than from a Short No. 1 with the same load of 67 grains of 4350. We can think of the No. 1 and No. 2 Short Magnums as nearly identical except for case length.

The 333-caliber bullets were popular for a time, and Ackley chambered his No. 2 Short to take 33-caliber bullets. The big difference between 30 and 33 calibers was bullet weight— up to 220 grains in 30-caliber, but all the way to 300 grains in 33. The most popular 33-caliber was 333 OKH, the 30-06 necked up. Ackley liked 333 OKH just fine and said it made an efficient big game cartridge, except for the difficulty in getting 33-caliber bullets. Ackley's 333 No. 2 pushed a 275-grain bullet to 2478 fps using 66 grains of IMR-4831, while the 333 OKH took 57 grains of the same 4831 to reach 2314.

The 333 Ackley Improved Magnum isn't pictured in the *Handbook* either—a 300 Improved was substituted. But for big bore enthusiasts, this 33-caliber magnum compares to the wildcat 338-375 H&H, which is a slam-dunk long-range big game cartridge. Here again, Ackley shows his occasional lack of patience for the big bores, saying that his 333 is "concocted by necking up any of the big cases" and that it should be "relatively satisfactory," emphasis on the word relative.

Moving to 35-caliber in the belted magnums, Ackley thought two of his own were pretty good ones—the 35 Ackley Magnum No. 2, made by necking up the 30 No. 2 Short, and the impressive 35 Improved Ackley Magnum from a full-blown 375 H&H necked down. Ackley described the 35 No. 2 as maximum bore capacity for the 35-caliber, powerful enough to dispatch anything that walks or crawls, while feeding nicely through a standard-length action. The 35 Ackley Improved Magnum requires a Model 70 or FN magnum-length action, Magnum Mauser or Brevex. If a magnum action were the shooter's preference, then the 35 Ackley, Mashburn, Apex, or Norma super-magnums could all outperform the parent 375 H&H with 300-grain bullets by as much as 200 fps.

Ackley could not resist improving the old 375 H&H, as did most of his contemporaries. He found the old British standby overrated and unchanged since the time of his own birth. The 375 Ackley Improved resembles the extinct 375 Weatherby, but with a sharper shoulder angle. Ackley recommended his 375 over the competition with customary reservation, saying that if so much power were really needed then his design at least had a decent neck, minimum taper to cut down bolt thrust, and relative bore efficiency. The big news with the Ackley 375 was that it was a true fireform improved, and cases could be made by simply firing factory 375 H&Hs in the improved chamber. This one shoved a 300-grain bullet out the muzzle at 2750 fps, but at the expense of a 10-grain increase in the powder charge.

Finally, despite his preference for "smaller and more efficient," Ackley took a couple of shots at the super-magnum market. I think he had some fun with his 450 and 475 Ackley Magnums because the English counterparts with their long sloping shoulders, steep body tapers and cigar lengths represented antiquity. A full year before the 458 Winchester came out, Ackley necked his 375 Ackley Improved to 45-caliber and then all the way up to 475. The 450 Ackley Magnum has a tiny little shoulder, more of a bump, and the 475 Ackley is a virtual cylinder. You would think Ackley shortened his 450 or 475 Magnums to work through a standard-length action, but he didn't. I don't think he was much interested.

"There are few so-called English elephant guns which approach it in power," he wrote of his 450.

We have reached the last and most important group of Ackley wildcat cartridges, the rimless wildcats. These are the Ackley designs that survived, the wildcat kittens from his 1938 rimless 228 Express Magnum. It is time to hear from the man himself, P.O. Ackley's stated purpose from *Handbook Vol. 1* for "improving" a factory or original cartridge. It reads as follows, and note the restraint in the language.

> ...to increase the capacity of any given cartridge through the process of fire-forming, and to perhaps change its shape to what would be considered a more efficient one.

Ackley "standardized" the wildcat cartridge, which sounds odd but is accurate, and the four ingredients in the standard Ackley recipe are:

1. Minimum body taper. To Ackley, a case with too much taper was a "self-actuating wedge" that backed itself out of the chamber during combustion. For the rimless case, Ackley preferred a taper of .0075-inch per case inch. An improved rimless case with a length of 2 inches got a taper of .015-inch. The improved straight case stretched less, lasted longer and provided a better gas seal than a tapered case. Most importantly, a brass case with minimum taper gripped chamber walls tighter, which meant less thrust transmitted rearward to the locking mechanism. And a straight-walled case ejected easier than a tapered case.

Ackley tried some interesting and semi-dangerous experiments to prove his point about the benefits of minimum body taper in a rifle cartridge. Starting with that most popular of the old-fashioned tapered cases, Charles Newton's 250-3000 Savage, and a Savage 99 rifle, Ackley loaded it hot and fired it until a case backed up so hard against the bolt that the action froze. Then, after improving the chamber to give .015-inch taper, he fired the same overload in this 99 rifle and the case ejected like butter. Not finished yet, Ackley worked up more loads until pressure caused a primer to fall out of the action, a load way too hot for regular use. But when he cranked the lever, the case ejected as easily as a plinking load.

2. A sharp shoulder angle—40 degrees being best for a rimless case. A sharp shoulder angle aided in the perfect headspacing of the rimless case and better defined the distance between the bolt face and the contact point on the chamber shoulder. The sharp shoulder increased case life by restricting brass flow in the shoulder area; a sharp shoulder confined burning gas longer within the case during initial thrust and thus helped complete powder combustion.

Interestingly, Ackley started his career in Charles Newton's footsteps; the first three Ackley wildcat designs had the 28-degree Newton shoulder—the rimmed 219 Improved Zipper, the belted 30 Short No. 1 Magnum, and the rimless 228 Ackley Magnum from the 7x57 case. Newton's shoulder angle impressed the young Ackley because, most important to the young barrelmaker who held Harry M. Pope in high esteem, it meant better barrel life and long case life. If Harry Pope could resize one brass case 30,000 times, then Parker Ackley should be able to design a sharp-shouldered chamber that would give 100 firing/reloading cycles. In the 1930s, a 28-degree shoulder was radical, but P.O. Ackley was just getting started.

Before enlisting for service in World War II, Ackley opened the 30-06 Springfield's 17-degree shoulder to 28 degrees, but he did not like the result. Returning home after the war, he moved his gun shop around a couple times before settling in Trinidad, Colorado, and it was 1945 before he could get around to fixing what was wrong with his wildcat '06—there was not much performance gain over the standard '06. The 28-degree angle did not raise the shoulder height enough on the '06 case to make more powder space unless neck length was sacrificed, which he would not do. I've heard that Ackley tried Kilbourne's 35-degree shoulder, but I can't find evidence of it, and in any event he settled on 40 degrees as proper for the '06 Improved. The 40-degree shoulder worked so well in every way that Ackley adopted it for all rimless cases, including the five Ackley designs on the current RCBS most popular list.

3. A good length of neck. No short necks for P.O. Ackley, unless a customer or a factory case left him no choice. He felt that a short neck was indefensible: It put the bullet too deep in the powder space, made resizing unnecessarily difficult because bullets sometimes pushed right through, and decreased bullet pull at the critical moment of ignition. And a short neck just looked like hell, too.

4. A correct case and bore capacity ratio—with a goal of near maximum, but not over maximum. The hole in the barrel through which the bullet was being pushed could handle only so much gas volume in a relatively short period of time, and for each bore size there was an ideal maximum which could be equated in grains of powder. Because few factory cartridges have the perfect "load density," this is the tricky ingredient in the Ackley wildcat recipe, and the least understood. It means, as Ackley tried to explain, when you reload your first improved wildcat case, you can expect bullet velocity to go down before it goes up.

By "improving" a rifle chamber, reaming out body taper and sharpening the shoulder angle, Ackley got a better and more efficient case as well as one that held more powder—10 percent more in some old rimless designs. But when a factory cartridge is fired in an Improved chamber, velocity went down because the bigger chamber lowered loading density, or foot/seconds of velocity per grain of powder. Therefore, to realize the full wildcat wallop of a fireform cartridge, one must top off with more powder, *use* the powder space gained by improving—use all of it, or nearly all. And then, quite often but not always, you achieve both maximum velocity and the ideal ratio of case capacity to bore capacity.

In my own thinking, my experience reloading for three Ackley Improved wildcats plus the new Ruger No. 1 in 30-06 Improved, there is a sort of "take-over point" with the fireform wildcat. It's the point where, using a particular powder in improved cases, I work reloads up to maximum level in a standard case with that same powder, and I find that chronographed velocities are always lower. Sometimes a couple hundred feet per second under factory numbers. There I stop and sort things out, compare accuracy, set velocity goals, look for pressure signs, etc. Then working up again toward the actual maximum powder capacity of the improved case, chronographing as I go, it happens, velocity goes over the top into wildcat country and I'm getting 200, 300, and even 400 fps above factory numbers.

As an example, my Savage 99 in 250 Ackley Improved is a pre-war gun with the brass cartridge counter and push safety on the bottom of the action, so I settle for modest velocity gains compared to what's possible. The barrel is a 20-inch heavy taper, about the same as the cut-down factory barrel it replaced, and it likes 100-grain Noslers at 2950 fps. There's a chart for five different loads with 100-grain Noslers chronographed in my rifle with both the old barrel and new Harry McGowan Improved barrel, and you can see the Ackley Improved recipe at work:

THE ACKLEY 250 DIFFERENCE

Load (Grs./Type)	Standard 250 Sav. Velocity (fps)	250 Sav. Ackley Imp. Velocity (fps)
FL Remington 100 CL	2708	2624
35.5/IMR-4064	2727	2640
36.5/IMR-4064	2819	2738
37.2/IMR-4064	2900	2878
38.0/IMR-4064		2950

BEFORE & AFTER IMPROVING: INSTRUMENTAL VELOCITY COMPARISON OF FACTORY 30-06 AMMO

Bullet (Wgt.Grs.)	Fact. Vel. (fps)	Ruger 30-06 Chamber (fps)	Improved 30-06 Chamber (fps)
150	2910	2937	2902
180	2700	2736	2669

Oehler 33 chronograph with 10-foot screen spacing

It takes 36.5 grains in the Improved chamber to get the same velocity as 35.5 grains in the factory chamber. But once past the "take-over point," more powder in the Improved really increases velocity. Ackley recommended 40 grains of 4064 to reach 3271 fps in his tests. You can see more examples in the charts on 30-06 handloads and 250 Savage Improved, 257 Roberts Improved, 35 Whelen Improved factory loads.

There were a few rimless wildcat 17s before Remington brought out their 17 Remington based on the 223

Duane Wiebe inspects a new 30-06 Improved chamber. This is how they all do it.

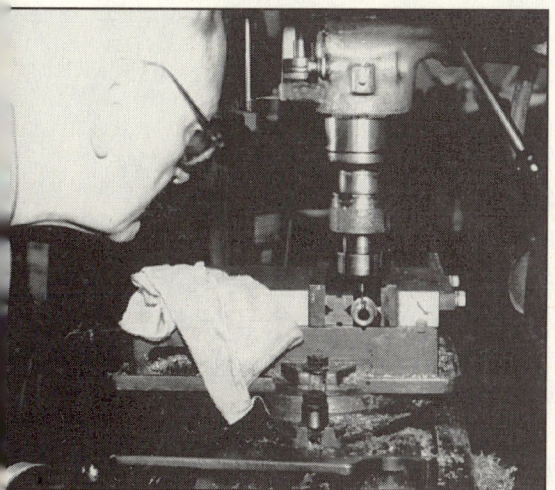
If you have to set a wildcat barrel back, you have to deepen the extractor cut.

case in 1971. Ackley's experiments with the 17 go back to 1944 and the rimmed 17 Ackley Bee, but his rimless 17 appeared when Remington announced the 222 Remington Magnum in 1958. Ackley was too late with the 17 Ackley Magnum to make the 1959 *Handbook Vol. I*, but it shows up in the 1962 *Volume II*. The factory 17 Remington load shows a 25-grain bullet at 4020, and the Ackley wildcat gives a 25-grain bullet from 3650 to 4187, so they are about identical. It's curious that, while most rimless 17 wildcats were based on their 222 Remington case, Remington picked the 223 case to standardize the 17. The 223 has the same case capacity as the 222 Remington Magnum which was Ackley's choice a dozen years earlier.

The list of Ackley wildcat 22s on rimless cases is surprisingly short. They are the customer-requested 222 Remington Magnum Improved; the 22-250 Improved which is a fine cartridge, but not for the usual reasons; the semi-rimmed 220 Swift Improved; and three versions of the original 228

Ackley Magnum, two short ones from the 7x57 case and the longer, most popular 228 from the 30-06 case. The Ackley 22-250 and 220 Swift wildcats are "mechanical" improvements, as Ackley termed them, designed less to goose up velocities than to improve case life by better case design. The 22-250 is on the RCBS list of most popular, so it must work.

A very interesting wildcat is the 230 Ackley. When the 228 Ackley Mag-

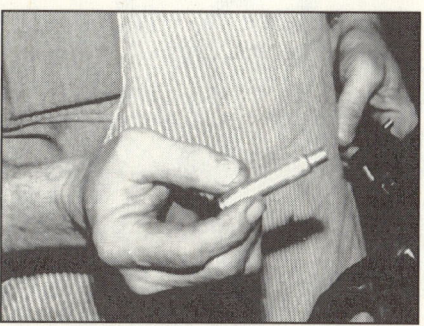
When the first fired case looks like this, the job is OK.

num with its true 228-inch diameter bullets was outlawed for use on large game in some states, Ackley responded with this 230-caliber wildcat. It is the 30-06 case shortened and necked to 23-caliber with a 28-degree shoulder. Ackley designed it in 1957 to move a 23-caliber, 70-grain bullet at nearly 3500 fps, which compares to the 243 Winchester. The issue here became whether or not light bullets held up at high impact speeds on big game, and it is still in question. Ackley maintained throughout his career that a properly constructed small bullet at high velocity was the killing equal of the slower big bullet.

In 244-caliber, we find an Ackley

fireform wildcat design that P.O. himself disliked, the 243 Winchester Ackley Improved. It was a customer request of straight fireform variety. I can picture Ackley staring at the short-necked factory 243 and shaking his head, wondering what he could do with it to make it look decent while admitting that it was already a pretty efficient cartridge. He reamed out more taper, sharpened the shoulder to 40 degrees, but he couldn't do a thing with that neck. Velocity with the 243 and 243 Improved are about the same, a small gain, but Ackley's wildcat looks more "crisp" and gives better case life in bolt guns.

Ackley gave the 26-degree-shouldered 244 Remington exactly the same treatment because his customers wanted a fireform 6mm. It worked out that a 244 Ackley Improved gives the 105-grain bullet about the same velocity as the standard 244 gives the 100 with better case life, not a bad trade. Order RCBS 6mm Remington Ackley Improved 40-degree dies if you want to reload for this wildcat.

Stepping up to 25-caliber, we have two of Ackley's all-time greats, the 250 Savage Improved and the 257 Roberts Improved. And we have a third which Mike Bellm remembers Ackley describing as "just a damned abortion," the 25-06 Ackley Improved. Ackley's favorite rifle cartridge was the 250-3000 Savage fireformed to a 40-degree shoulder and .016-inch body taper. Again, checking with Mike, whose Bellm Contender Barrels is the successor to "Barrels by Ackley," the reason is simple: The 250 Improved shows one of the highest velocity increases over the factory numbers while proving to be *the* ideal case capacity for the 25-bore. The 250

The all-time Ackley favorite—the Savage Improved. It will hold 47.4 grains of IMR-4350.

Improved steps up the performance of Newton's old-time cartridge almost to 25-06 Remington levels in a bolt action, and to 257 Roberts level in the lever-action 99. In any kind of rifle, the old 250 Savage has a reputation for accuracy, and the accuracy is the same or better in an Ackley Improved chamber.

I read somewhere that RCBS' most popular set of custom reloading dies, in a rifle caliber, are in 257 Roberts Ackley Improved. That seemed unlikely because Ackley designed this fireform wildcat in 1950, so I called Jeanne Reilly at RCBS and she sent me the list. The 257 Ackley Improved is not number one, it's number two on the Top 15 custom die chart. One of many wildcat 257s from the 7x57 case, Ackley blew out the standard Roberts 20-degree shoulder to 40 degrees and reduced body taper to .017-inch for a net case capacity gain of five full grains of slow-burning powder—not quite 10 percent. My FN-actioned 257 Ackley Improved gives velocities with 100- and 120-grain bullets that make me wonder why some factory doesn't figure a way to standardize this fine wildcat.

I was cautious at first about using data from Ackley's thirty-five-year-old reloading books, but not anymore. Ackley said a charge of 47 grains of IMR-4350 starts a 125-grain bullet at 2970 fps in an Improved Roberts, and it does start a 120 Nosler that fast. My accuracy load with the 120 Nosler is 45.5/4350 for 2903 fps, and this past deer season I put five of them into a sight-in group of 2x3 inches at 300 yards. No wonder this wildcat is still popular.

Why did Ackley dislike his 25-06 Improved? Remember the detonation mystery that he never solved? He assumed that guys who couldn't understand how to fireform cases were the same guys who were blowing up 25-caliber wildcats. Ackley wrote that it was flat dangerous to fireform the 25-06 Improved with reduced loads, and that it wasn't a flexible hunting caliber at reduced velocities anyway. Ackley's 25-06 Improved originated from the necked-down and fireformed '06 case, but of course now you can fireform factory 25-06s in an Improved chamber. Ackley recommended the 25-06 Improved for those who wanted "the highest velocity possible from the .25

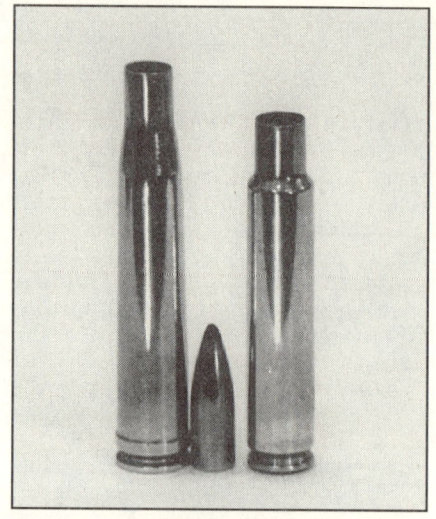

These are the 300 H&H and the 30-06 Improved, once called the "poor man's magnum."

bore regardless of other considerations."

Here, on the subject of fireforming cases, is what the most prolific wildcatter of all time had to say: Use a good stiff load with a medium or heavy bullet, and save the "cream of wheat" routine for breakfast. Or language to that effect. So you get one less shot in the life of a brass case, but you get headspace exactly right and avoid a bad accident for a dumb reason, like trying to save money. Mike Beeks of Grayback Wildcats, formerly called Buzztail Brass, makes preformed Ackley Improved cases, the perfect compromise. Buy pre-formed cases from Mike, size them in your wildcat dies, and shoot targets or game right now. Mike's wildcat case business is 90 percent Ackley designs, and he has some modern applications of the Ackley 40-degree shoulder recipe that Ackley didn't cook!

There is only one rimless 256-caliber Ackley wildcat. It's based on the '06 case and called the 256-06 Ackley Improved. Ackley suggested that while his wildcat might have a better shape, the standard 6.5-06 wildcat had maximum case capacity for the 256-bore and was more efficient.

In 270-caliber rimless, there are two Improved designs, one P.O. liked and the other he wouldn't recommend. He thought the 270-257 Roberts Ackley Improved should be a great big game cartridge and compared it to the still-born 270 Savage round. Ackley saw the 257 Roberts case as the perfect volume for the 270-bore, and 130-grain bullets from a 270-257 Improved could be loaded to equal the standard 270 Winchester, making a very efficient wildcat. But the 270 Winchester Ackley Improved was a different story altogether, another customer request that resulted in a wildcat inferior to the standard cartridge. P.O. wrote that the standard 270 was already "over-bore," so a 40-degree shoulder with minimum taper couldn't offer much improvement, if any.

The 7x57 Ackley Improved Mauser is in the same class as his 250 Savage and 30-30 Winchester—it is a great cartridge with a significant performance gain over the original factory round. Ackley rated the 7x57 Improved more useful than any Seven Mag for the "average shooter." With a 40-degree Ackley shoulder and .015-inch taper, a modern 7x57 Improved Mauser sneaks up close to 280 Remington and 7mm Remington Magnum performance—3100 fps with 140-grain bullets.

And what about a 7mm-06 Ackley Improved or 280 Remington Ackley Improved as an "all-around" big game cartridge? They are the same cartridge, with the latter being a tiny bit longer starting from the 280 Remington case: 40-degree Ackley shoulder, .015-inch taper, 5 percent more powder space than the standard 7mm-'06 or 280 Remington. While the 7mm STW is *the* hottest Seven Mag on the market and is currently RCBS' "Most Popular Wildcat," ask yourself if 3500 fps (sometimes) with a 140-grain bullet in a necked-down 8mm Remington belted case is all that much better than 3300 fps from the '06-sized 280 Remington Improved? A cartridge similar to the 7mm STW was available in 1950, the 7mm Mashburn Magnum Long from the full-length 300 H&H case, but Ackley essentially trashed it as inferior to any of the shorter 7mm magnums. The 280 Ackley Improved is now number ten on RCBS' current list of most popular wildcat dies sold, and it will climb that chart because I intend to have one!

Quick, how many rimless 30-caliber factory cartridges are there? Answer, only six if you count the comatose 30 Remington. At some point in his career, Ackley gave the 7.62 NATO/308 Winchester the improved treatment, but he ignored the 30 Carbine and 300 Savage, and there was no 307 Winchester until just before he retired. The Ackley gold in 30-caliber rimless is found in the 30-06 Springfield.

Starting in 1945, the 30-06 Ackley Improved has had more bad press than all the other sixty-one Ackley wildcats combined, with detractors usually trying to prove that the Improved '06 wasn't even as good as the standard model. Ackley, somewhat chagrined by the controversy, patiently explained that writers who did not understand the Improved idea always show his '06 Improved with loads that made it look bad, or from rifles with 22-inch barrels.

I've read one or two articles knocking the '06 Improved; there's one in *Wildcats Volume II,* and I'd rate the weird-looking test gun itself a wildcat. I agree with Ackley. Let's say it again: Open up a brass case for more powder space and load density goes down, and velocity goes down with the same powder charge. Ackley thought he explained all this rather well, but some guys never got the message.

Ackley had a great respect for the standard 30-06 cartridge and preferred it over the 270, a surprise coming from the consummate small bore advocate. P.O. argued that "real world" 30-06 ballistics were better than 270 ballistics, and he offered this opinion in the "which is better: the 270 or 30-06?" debate that's seventy-five years old and still going strong:

> It will be seen that the 30-06 is a lot more gun over the average hunting ranges than the 270 is with equal weight bullets. Of course, the 270 150-grain factory load may be flatter at ranges out beyond 1000 or 1500 yards than the 30-06 150-grain factory load, but very few shooters are able to hit a flock of circus tents at these ranges without first sighting in. Within game ranges the 150-grain 30-06 bullet is quite noticeably flatter and has more oomph when it arrives.

The 30-06 Ackley Improved adds 100-150 fps to the best handloads in an '06 rifle and is at its best with 180-grain bullets. At 2900-3000 fps, a 180-grain spitzer from an '06 Improved is on the heels of the 300 H&H and 300 Winchester. Look at Ackley's 30-06 Improved and note the length of neck. Ackley could have gone the route of wildcatter Rocky Gibbs whose 30-caliber wildcat from the '06 case has a neck as short as that of the 243 Winchester, but a long body for greater powder capacity. The 30 Gibbs Improved will outshoot the 30-06 Ackley Improved by a couple fps. Ackley stuck to the principle that a long neck resists bullet pull without a crimp and is practical in ammunition used in hunting rifles, holding the bullet firmly through action cycling and recoil. The one thing P.O. Ackley was not was a target shooter. So, like it or not, he got exactly what he wanted with his 30-06 Improved and happy 50th anniversary to it. The 30-06 Ackley Improved is currently number twelve on the RCBS chart.

In his 8mm-06 Improved, Ackley saw a standard-sized wildcat equal to the performance of the 300 Winchester or H&H magnums, and he wasn't far wrong. Again, he suggested a 5 percent increase over maximum 8mm-06 loads, meaning a 200-grain 323-caliber could be started above 2800 fps, which is also what's possible with 200-grain bullets in his 30-06 Improved.

And finally, Ackley's biggest rimless improved wildcats were the 35 Whelen Improved and 375 Whelen Improved. He necked the Improved '06 up to 35-caliber to make 35 Whelen cases, and then necked the 35 Improved up again to get 375 Improved, both with 40-degree shoulder. He recommended both. My Mauser-action 35 Improved will almost beat factory 338 Winchester Magnum velocity with 200-grain bullets. Since Remington picked up the wildcat 35 Whelen as a factory cartridge, I just buy these and shoot them in my rifle, just like the Oklahoma hunter with his 300 Mashburn.

Besides the four basic ingredients in the Ackley Improved recipe, the matter of correct headspace for the rimless case in an improved chamber was of paramount importance to P.O., and to owners of custom rifles in wildcat calibers. Ackley went so far as to suggest that custom riflemakers really ought to provide a set of custom dies with every rifle, with the sizing die locked down tight.

P.O. ACKLEY FIREFORM IMPROVED WILDCATS FROM CURRENT FACTORY CARTRIDGES

Cartridge	Performance Gain over Factory	Ackley Comment
222 Rem. Mag. Ack. Imp.	About 5% more powder capacity	More useful if necked up to 6mm
219 Ack. Imp. Zipper	350 fps above top 45-gr. factory Zipper load	Recommended, but use 30-30 brass post-WWII
22 Swift Imp.	Better extraction, case life	Mechanical advantage with velocity equal to Swift
22-250 Ack. Imp.	50 to 100 fps, case life	Use Swift data and buy RCBS dies with 40° shoulder
22 Sav. H.P. Imp.	300-400 fps with 70-gr. 228-cal. bullets	One of best 22s with heavy bullets
243 Ack. Imp.	Extraction, case life	Mechanical advantage; originally a customer request
244 Rem. Ack. Imp.	Very little gain in any bullet weight	Auth. note: use RCBS 6mm Ack. Imp. 40 in 6mm rifles
25-35 Ack. Imp.	500-600 fps with 100-gr. bullets	Recommended, use 30-30 brass post-WWII
250 Sav. Ack. Imp.	300-400 fps with 100-gr. bullets	Recommended, Ackley's all-time favorite
257 Robts. Ack. Imp.	300 fps with 100- or 120-gr. bullets	Recommended, Ackley's "all-around" cartridge
25-06 Rem. Ack. Imp.	About 200 fps with 100-gr. bullets	Not recommended, despite customer success. "Overbore"
270 Win. Ack. Imp.	Little or none with more powder	Not recommended, factory 270 is better
7x57mm Ack. Imp.	300-350 fps with 140-gr. and 200-250 fps with 175	Recommended, more useful to avg. shooter than 7 mags
280 Rem. Ack. Imp.	250 fps with 140-gr. bullets	Recommended, 7 mag veloc. in '06 case
30-30 Win. Ack. Imp.	250-300 fps with 150-gr. bullets	Recommended, excellent for lever guns
30-06 Spfld. Ack. Imp.	100-150 fps in any bullet weight	Recommended, equal to 300 H&H
30-40 Krag Ack. Imp.	500 fps with both 150s and 180s	Good, but not many rifles can use. Hot
348 Win. Ack. Imp.	200-250 fps above 348 factory load	Recommended, better case life, less thrust
35 Whelen Ack. Imp.	5% powder capacity, 100-150 fps in 200s, 225s, 250s	Recommended, flexible big game cartridge

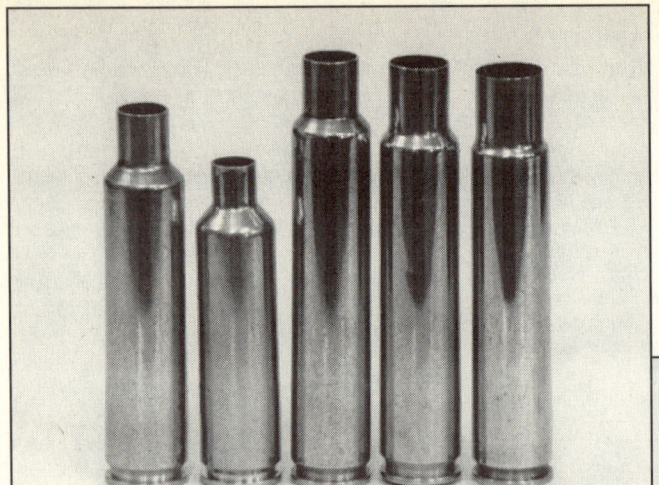

These five Ackley's are on RCBS' "most popular dies" list—257 Roberts, 22-250, 280, 30-06 and 35 Whelen, all Improved.

Writer Lucas got good enough to chronograph without sights.

If, in improving a chamber, the interior length from bolt face to chamber shoulder contact point was cut too long, the fireform process became dangerous, to include protruding primers, stretched cases, and even complete head separations. Gunsmithing the improved chamber had to be done right with no shortcuts, and it wasn't good enough just to wiggle a 30-06 Improved chambering reamer inside an '06 chamber to "clean it up." In Ackley's view, the barrel had to be set back the distance of one thread.

To take you through P.O. Ackley's prescribed method of gunsmithing the improved chamber, I chose the 30-06 Springfield and a Ruger No. 1 rifle. I'm lucky enough to live within a few miles of where two of the best gunsmiths in America do business, and for allotting me after-hours time during their busy season I owe a debt to Gander Mountain's director of gunsmithing, Jim Tertin, and to Duane Wiebe who agreed to cut my improved chamber as I shot pictures and pestered him with questions.

My Ruger No. 1 was brand new; other than 100 or so factory and handloaded rounds fired over the chronograph screens there wasn't a scratch on it. Surrendering the soft case to Duane, I noted the time, 4:40 p.m., grabbed my camera gear, and followed him back into the Gander Mountain gunsmith shop in Wilmot, Wisconsin. The rifle was snugged into an oversized Wilton vise where its headspace was checked with standard "go" and "no go" gauges. This Ruger chamber closed normally behind the 1.940-inch "go," but refused to close behind the 1.946-inch "no go." (I forgot to write down if Duane was using the old standard or new standard 30-06 gauges so I'm using the old standards.) There was just .006-inch between minimum and maximum headspace.

Off with the stock, action parts on the bench, and out came the Ruger barrel using the biggest crescent wrench I have ever seen.

"Sixteen threads per inch, so .0625-inch comes off," Duane informed me, carrying the barrel across to the Clausing Mark II machine. The lathe, turning against the stationary cutter, made a sort of rubbing sound as it scraped .0625-inch from the rear end of the barrel, one full barrel turn. Looking through the camera lens I thought I saw a wisp of smoke among the sprigs of silvery metal that peeled off.

"Well, there goes the factory warranty," I said to nobody.

The rear end of the barrel complete, checked and re-checked, Duane took the same .0625-inch of metal from the barrel shoulder and then used a Bridgeport milling machine to deepen the Ruger's extractor slot the same .0625-inch. From there it was back to the vise for some very careful licks with a pair of sharp files before Duane rotated the action back onto the barrel to check rib alignment and extractor function. Perfect so far. Then the barrel was chucked back into the Mark II machine for the big step—a JGS 30-06 Ackley Improved chambering reamer was fitted into a floating bit and carefully guided into the turning Ruger chamber to open it to Ackley Improved dimensions. Using a small flashlight and the 1.940 "go" gauge to make depth checks, Duane's goal was to cut the Improved chamber exactly .004-inch short, as P.O. Ackley advised. The reamer widened the Ruger's chamber shoulder from .440- to .455-inch to give fireformed 30-06 cartridges a shoulder angle of 40-degrees and a body taper of .015-inch. In what seemed like no time at all, Duane switched off the lathe.

There were two tests to verify correct rechambering to Ackley Improved. First, the chamber being .004-inch shorter in headspace dimension, or approximately 1.936, the Ruger's breechblock should now *not* close on the "go" gauge. Second, with the breech locked behind it, a standard 30-06 cartridge should make contact in the Improved chamber at the junction of neck and shoulder in order to fireform perfectly without case head stretching. I watched Duane thumb the "go" gauge home and try to close the action; the polished breechblock

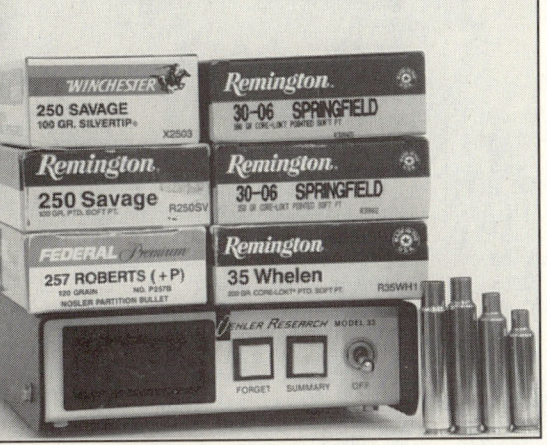

These four Ackley Improved wildcats were chronographed for this article with an Oehler 33—35 Whelen, 30-06, 257 Roberts and 250 Savage.

came within three whiskers of closing, but positively would not close. Then I tried a Frontier 180-grain softpoint factory cartridge in the chamber, and the Ruger's lever gave me a light "feel fit" locking up. Perfect Improved headspace. Duane poked the muzzle into the Snail machine and fired the barreled-action hand-held, and pausing for a picture, then presented me with a sharp-shouldered, fireformed 30-06 Improved case. Now that was something. The time was 7:17 p.m.

The complete job, made longer because of the necessity of removing the No. 1's tight-fitting rib, took 2½ hours with no shortcuts, and the gunsmithing charge was $92. Was it worth the money? What can I say? The work is great; the results show it. Duane advises me that a competent, careful gunsmith can do the same work, but in less time, for the average bolt action. Yes, it was worth the money—have a look at the handload chart for the Ruger No. 1 30-06 Improved.

Stopping well short of the maximums in *Handbook For Shooters And Reloaders*, my 30-06 reloads with 150-grain bullets in the improved chamber chronograph 3066 fps, as compared to max handload velocity of 2978 fps and Remington factory 2938 fps in the standard chamber for the same rifle. With 180-grain bullets, I get 2903 fps easily from the Improved '06, or nearly 200 fps above the performance of factory ammunition, and these numbers make my Ruger the long-range energy and trajectory twin of the 300 H&H.

The Ackley recipe works, but some day it will be obsolete and forgotten. What, fifty years from now for the 100th Anniversary of GUN DIGEST, will be written about Parker O. Ackley and his place in the "Wildcatter's Hall of Fame?" Did he invent the fireform improved wildcat? Will they think the Ackley wildcats was a football team? Was Ackley a great gunsmith with an intuitive knack for problem solving, or was he a me-too businessman copying the techniques of others because they paid the freight? Maybe P.O. Ackley was just like that other famous colonel, Harlan Sanders of "Kentucky Fried" fame; Col. Sanders didn't invent chickens, but he sure had the recipe for cooking 'em!

Here's what I think, and the answer's been in front of my face the whole time.

Ackley sold the family potato farm in 1936 to buy a one-man gunsmith business in the one-horse town of Roseburg, Oregon. But he was very much in tune with the New York action in his chosen profession, especially Risley's work with the R2 chambering reamer. How so, way out on the Coast? That farm Ackley sold was in New York State; at the outset of his career, P.O. Ackley moved *away* from the wildcat capital of the United States. Out of sight, out of mind.

And, unlike Harvey Donaldson, Ackley didn't specialize. He reacted to 1938 market conditions with three different wildcat cartridges in rimmed, belted and rimless cases, all in less than two years, instead of spending his time trying to figure out why one cartridge punched .01-inch smaller groups than another one on a paper target. P.O. was definitely more enterprising than inventive, and he loses points with the purists.

Re-reading Ken Waters on Lysle Kilbourne I see "...irrefutable..." in the same paragraph with "...to the best of my recollection...?" Now that's interesting. Re-reading *Handbook Vol. I*, keeping in mind Ackley's reputation for modesty and honest reporting (when was the last time anybody referred to a wildcatter in any field as "honest?"), I see Ackley describing his Improved Zipper as "...Originally it was simply a fireforming proposition..." I think he did pull the trigger on the first fireform improved cartridge.

It's that post-War Winchester Zipper brass again, the stuff that split instead of stretch in an Ackley Improved chamber. After the war, Ackley had to recommend using homemade 30-30 brass to make his Improved Zipper, and that's what history remembers: Like the 25-35 Ackley Improved, the Improved Zipper became a "pure" wildcat. But before the war, in 1938 and a full year before the K-Hornet, P.O. did to factory Zipper brass what M.S. Risley did to the wildcat 22-3000 Lovell brass; he reamed a chamber, and with that fat Zipper rim snug between the breech and barrel, he pulled the trigger to find out what the heck would happen. Another 300 fps is what happened, and he fireformed Zipper cases this way until the war production put an end to barrel blanks for wildcatters and brass cartridges for civilians.

There, it's settled. Lots of guys, including M.S. Risley, may have "improved" some wildcat before Ackley came along, but P.O. was first to "fireform improve" a standard cartridge.

Oh, I almost forgot. Chief Crazy Horse went into the Battle of the Little Bighorn unarmed, no rifle. While he was off picking daisies, Cheyenne Chief Two Moons was zeroing in on Custer's command position on the knoll. Two Moons retrieved a battlefield Model '73 rifle with a broken buttstock and rode to within 20 feet of the Colonel and hip-shot him from horseback. I heard that story at least a dozen times, no, fifty times. And every time I heard it...it improved. ●

One Good Gun

by BOB BELL

My Little 284 Mauser

IT STARTED WITH a barrel. My wife and I were on vacation at Cape Hatteras many years ago, and on the way home, we stopped to see the widow of Phil Sharpe at "That Place," between Emmittsburg, Maryland, and Fairfield, Pennsylvania. Phil and I had been friends from just after the war until his death in the early '60s, and we visited Mrs. Sharpe occasionally, when we were in the area.

Anyway, when wandering through his old range house, I happened to see four or five barrels standing in a corner. All were chambered for the 7x61 cartridge and threaded for the Schultz & Larsen action, except one unthreaded 25-caliber barrel. I didn't know what I might do with them, but ended up buying them all. Most everything else of his—guns, loading tools, etc.—had already been sold.

I didn't need another 7x61. I'd had one built in the early '50s, when Phil and Dick Hart finalized the design. But I did not see any sense in letting those barrels go to waste.

Eventually, I concluded the most sensible thing to do was cut off the threads and rechamber for the 284 Winchester, a short wide case which would clean up what was left of the 7x61 chamber. Al Wardrop threaded it to fit an Argentine Mauser action, chambered it, and cut the length to 21 inches. It was heavy sporter weight, and I considered turning it down but didn't as it was already blued and I didn't want to re-do that. Twist was 1:12.

I installed a Buehler Lo-Swing safety, Mashburn adjustable trigger, and Redfield one-piece scope mount base. Then it went to Earl Hock, a friend who occasionally made stocks, with a fancy walnut blank I'd got from D.W. Thomas, over in Jersey, when I'd been writing an article about his business for *Guns Magazine*. A few months later, the Mannlicher-style stock was done, glassed all the way to prevent that full-length forend from warping—a job it has done very well for decades.

I don't remember which scope I put on first. Over the years, it has worn many—Weaver V4.5, Lyman All-American 3x, Weaver K4 and others. At present, an old Lyman Alaskan 2½x is aboard. Doesn't matter. All worked.

So did all loads that I tried, and I used many bullet weights, from Hornady's 139-grain to the 175-grain Speer, and the same weight Nosler Partition. All were handloads, worked up to maximums. Not a single factory load was ever fired through it. Not that I have anything against factory loads; they always worked fine when I used 'em. I just prefer to load my own. In this case, cartridges considerably longer than Win-

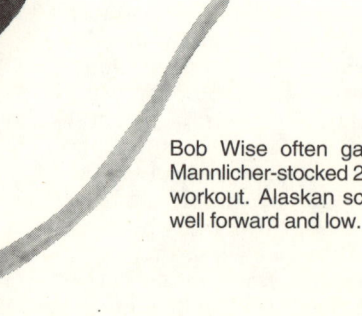

Bob Wise often gave my little Mannlicher-stocked 284 Mauser a workout. Alaskan scope mounts well forward and low.

Pennsylvania whitetail country can be wide open, but not very often. You need a gun that gets on target easily, like my 284 does.

Earl Hock made the comb on my 284 so high it just clears the cocking piece—the way I like 'em. That's a Buehler safety, and there's a Mashburn adjustable trigger, too.

Even with a magic rifle, I take a rest alongside a tree any time I can get one. That's a Weaver V4.5.

chester's are possible. There's lots of powder room, and I use it.

As it's turned out, this little 284 Mauser is close to perfect in its results. It's given me a clean kill on every deer I ever pointed it at. I've used it only for deer, but of the two dozen or so taken with it, only two required more than one shot, and in those cases the first bullet blew up before it got to the animal, once on an ice-coated limb, the other on plain brush. I've never had that good a kill ratio with any other rifle I own, and the odds are that I won't. Not that no other cartridge is as good as the 284, but I don't expect to be so lucky indefinitely. That has something to do with it, of course.

Consider one deer: It was angling downhill on a sidehill, not moving fast, and I was sitting alongside a small tree, leaning, with my elbows hooked over knees when I shot. The Lee Dot was low behind the near shoulder when the gun went off, and the small buck just sagged down as it managed a few steps, then collapsed, some 85 yards away. I didn't think anything of it until I went over. There wasn't a mark on that critter except a 2-inch groove, half the bullet diameter deep, in the extreme bottom of the ribcage, just behind the right front leg. There was no way I could imagine that could be a fatal hit, but it was. I'd come within less than a quarter-inch of missing that whole animal, yet there he lay, deader than dead.

I got the whitetails that were initially missed through luck, too. One was easy. I was out at dawn on a day when most hunters had enough sense to stay home. Everything was coated with thick ice. It was slippery as hell, and limbs breaking under the added weight fell often. Well, one time each, but a lot of them. Sitting under a thick evergreen, I happened to spot a deer in the creekbottom maybe 75 yards below me. I could just make out its outline. It was unaware of me.

I put the crosswires of the little Lyman 3x All-American I was using then on the shoulder area and squeezed. The 160-grain Speer never got there. There was an explosion of ice, yards my side of the animal. But he wasn't frightened—I guess he had become used to the falling limbs—and he took a few slow steps and stood there still, broadside, now fully exposed. He never moved another step after I fired my second shot.

The other one, an eight-point, was standing in a thick clump when I first fired. The bullet never got through, and the buck ran off before I could reload. This made me cuss because I felt my streak was broken. Then the same critter came back my way when he was shot at twice by another hunter. As he stood above me behind a small oak, just his head and neck projecting, my 139-grain Hornady centered what I could see for an instant kill.

So a good helping of luck figured in both those chances, I'm the first to admit, but I figure it's due to the good vibes this little 284 gives off.

Maybe my first kill with it indicated what kind of rifle this was going to be. I was up in Perry County, alone as usual, sitting on a downed tree and debating with myself whether it was time for an apple yet, when a small buck materialized. Only the head/neck area was visible about 90 yards away. But the dot stayed plastered on it when the trigger broke and sent a 140-grain Nosler on its way.

I worked the bolt automatically, and as I did the cocking piece didn't catch; there was no resistance when the bolt closed. So I was sitting there with an empty gun. (It turned out the inletting for the trigger wasn't quite full enough and wet weather had swollen the wood a bit and bound the trigger. I later scraped it out and had no trouble that way on any other hunt.)

It didn't matter. As it turned out, I didn't need a second shot. The first one had centered the deer's neck, leaving a fist-size exit hole and giving an instant kill.

So everything considered, maybe we should conclude that it's better to be lucky than good. Also, maybe luck just comes when you've got a good gun. ●

50th EDITION, 1996 **127**

One Good Gun

by MIKE THOMAS

My First Model 70

LATE SUMMER, 1964, was quite memorable indeed for one fifteen-year-old soon-to-be gun enthusiast.

Shortly before school started that year, I carefully selected and purchased my first centerfire rifle, a pre-War Model 70 Winchester chambered in 30-06. The time was right to have a "real" rifle; my Winchester 74 had become woefully inadequate.

At the time, $72 seemed a tremendous sum, but here was quite a rifle, too. The walnut stock had figure and a few hunting scratches. The exterior was in good shape; the bore did have some pitting, but I wanted *this* rifle.

I don't really know whether it was a good buy at the time or not. Though I had read, researched and studied about all I could find on rifles, the moment caught me unprepared to make a truly objective decision. My father was with me and had a practical knowledge of firearms himself, yet he did not try to influence me as to my selection—I liked that.

As it turned out, I don't recall the pitted bore being a problem. Santa Claus brought some R.F. Wells handloading equipment that year, and I was really in business. I shot 110- and 220-grain bullets. I suppose I tried some weights in between as well. Over time, handloading quickly became a fascinating hobby in itself.

I soon decided a flatter-shooting caliber might prove advantageous and a telescopic sight would be necessary as well. In the spring of 1965, the late E.L. Brown, a gunsmith in rural southeastern Oklahoma, rebarreled the M70 action with a varmint-weight 26-inch Douglas barrel in the then-wildcat 25-06. He floated that barrel in the original stock. After drilling and tapping the action, Brown mounted a 4x Bushnell scope affixed with Weaver rings and bases.

I purchased 100 G.I. 30-06 cases from the gunsmith and necked them down to 25-caliber using his loading press. For loading data, he suggested using Sierra 87- or 100-grain spitzer bullets over healthy charges of Hodgdon's economical H-4831 powder. As I remember, the 100-grain bullet and the recommended dosage of H-4831 was about all that was used in this rifle for quite a few years. It proved to be so accurate from the very beginning that no load development was necessary. Somewhat hot by today's standards, it always appeared to be a perfectly safe load in my rifle.

I have used my Winchester Model 70 for whitetail deer hunting for a number of years. A little heavy, it steadied for a shot more easily than today's ultra-extra-light mountain carbines with barrels slightly larger in diameter than cleaning rods. After successfully harvesting several deer, I began using the 117-grain Sierra boattail bullet. Also a very accurate bullet, it is to this day the only one I use in any 25-06 rifle. Originally, I had hoped the additional weight and decreased velocity of this bullet would leave less bloodshot meat on a deer carcass. Actually, I don't believe there was a significant difference. A minor point, I suppose, but then perhaps the 25-06 is simply too much gun for our small Texas whitetail deer anyway.

The gunsmith emphasized the fact that the 26-inch barrel would give added velocity. Few of us had chronographs in the '60s, so we relied on the figures published in loading manuals. When I finally purchased a chronograph a decade or so ago, I found that I could safely achieve a muzzle velocity of 3100 feet per second with the 117-grain Sierra boattail. Most factory-built 25-06 rifles today come with 24-inch barrels; muzzle velocities suffer accordingly.

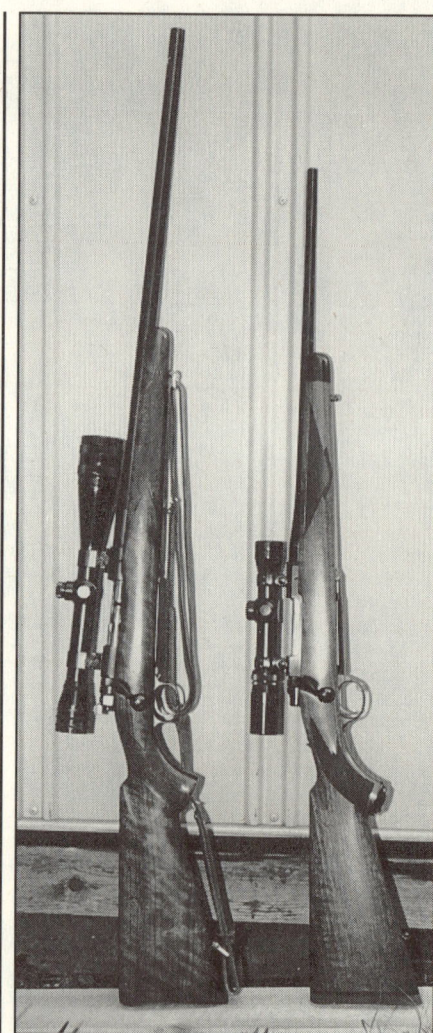

My 1942-vintage Model 70, with its heavy 26-inch barrel and large Redfield 8x silhouette scope, looks and is a few pounds heavier than my Ruger M77 UltraLight with its thin 20-inch barrel and Burris Mini scope. But I don't care.

The Model 70 has had other scopes on it at various times. Not long after the original 4x Bushnell was mounted, I tried one of the Bushnell Booster attachments. This device looked like a miniature scope, and it screwed into the objective lens of the 4x. The device was rated at 2.5x which effectively gave me a 10x scope. The Booster sold for around $15 in the mid-'60s. It was a "poor man's variable," so to speak, and it worked quite well except for one big drawback. The scope's zero was affected in a major way. If the Booster was used, the scope had to be re-zeroed with the device attached. The same held true for when the Booster was removed. I still have that gadget somewhere.

I enjoy hunting, but I enjoy shooting small groups better, and I can do that year 'round. This is where I have derived most of my pleasure from the Model 70. I regret not having kept records and now have no idea how many rounds have been fired in the rifle. Furthermore, twenty-five or thirty years ago, not many shooters had heard about the removal of copper fouling from bores, potential bore damage from the improper use of cleaning rods, etc. This makes me wonder if some of our present-day concerns along these lines may be unfounded, or at least exaggerated, as the bore of my rifle appears unharmed. Still, there must be some wear in the bore or the chamber throat or both that's just not visible to my untrained eyes.

In 1972, I bought a box of Remington 25-06 ammunition to find out how it would function in the wildcat chamber. The ammo chambered and fired properly, and there appeared to be no headspacing problem or high pressure signs. Apparently, 25-06 wildcat chambers, or at least some of them, must have been pretty much standardized by the 1960s. I would still exercise caution when dealing with any 25-06 rifle that was built prior to 1969 when the round was legitimized by Remington, but mine works.

I have used several other rifles over the years since I bought the Model 70. Some were just as accurate; a select few even more accurate. Most did not shoot nearly as well.

I have not hunted with the old gun or even fired it in some time now. The bore looks in excellent shape; there is a slight ring around the bolt's firing pin hole, no doubt due to so much firing. It's still safe to fire, and the action is as tight as ever.

As I write this, I begin to wonder why I have not been using it. Coincidentally, today's date is November 4th; Texas' deer season opens tomorrow. I do have a couple of boxes of ammo... •

One Good Gun

by JOHN HAVILAND

My Diamondback Is a Jewel

IVER HENRIKSON took one look at the 22 revolver in my hand and said, "I know what you're going to ask, and the answer is, 'No I can't fix the trigger pull. The metal's no good on those South American guns.'"

That dashed the hopes I had for the imported 22 revolver I had just bought. The gun fit my hand well, and the adjustable sight let me sight-in for a variety of 22 ammunition. But the heavy and rough trigger pull was like yanking the lever on a tire jack. So about all the gun was good for was propping open the back door on warm summer evenings.

That was back in 1977. I had just graduated from college to make room for someone else and didn't have a whole lot of money stashed away in the bank. That didn't stop me from cruising the gun stores in hopes of finding a better-grade 22 handgun.

Beneath the glass counters at the stores rested all sorts of High Standard, Ruger, Smith & Wesson and other quality brand handguns. I eliminated the autoloading pistols right off the bat. Although many will argue the point, I felt they were not as safe as a revolver with a swing-out cylinder. I kind of liked the Ruger Single-Six. My brother owned one, and it shot well, and by the way it was built, it would last forever. Yet I didn't like poking the empties out of the Ruger one at a time.

I really liked the Smith & Wesson 22 revolvers. My imported gun was a replica of the S&W Model 63 22/32 kit gun. The kit gun, however, had a much smoother and lighter single- and double-action trigger

Thousands of rounds, hundreds of miles, and scores of grouse and rabbits later, the Diamondback 22 is still ready to go.

pull. Its big brother, the Model 17 K-22, really caught my eye.

"Lot of guys buy those K-22s," said the store clerk.

That was the problem. My friend, Bob, owned a K-22. He had been bragging to me for years about what a great gun it was and what a great shot he was with it. If I bought one, then Bob would have some basis for thinking he knew it all and I would never hear the end of it.

I checked one last store that Saturday. At the far end of the case sat a Colt Diamondback.

"Don't get many of these in," said the clerk as he handed me the revolver.

With a steep price tag of $175, I almost remarked he probably never moved many out the door, either. But I immediately liked the Diamondback more than the other 22s. The action was smooth, and the gun was solid. The cylinder swung out from the frame with a touch of the release. The full-length ejector housing under the barrel gave the pistol a balance toward the muzzle and, with the ventilated rib, provided a rakish look that set it—and its big brother, the Python—apart from other handguns. Pythons were all the rage back then.

I had to have that Diamondback. I handed it back to the clerk and told him I'd be back.

"It'll be right here waiting for

you," the clerk replied. He lovingly wiped off the gun with a cloth and put it back under glass.

The following week I connived about how to buy the Diamondback. The next Saturday I walked back into the store with my imported 22. "How much trade will you give me on this for the 22 Diamondback?" I asked.

The clerk said he would allow $75, which was $15 more than I had paid for it. I said that sounded good and wrote a check for the balance.

I immediately drove out to the shooting range. I sighted-in the Colt at 25 yards. The adjustable rear sight had arrows indicating the direction the sight screws should be turned to adjust bullet impact—a classy touch.

I don't remember the size of the groups I shot that day. I do remember that I spun pop cans around time after time out to 40 yards.

I walked over to Iver Henriksen's basement shop that evening to garner his approval of my new Colt. Iver was working on a rifle stock for a country-western star. A neat pile of walnut shavings was the only thing out of place in his tidy shop.

"I see you bought the 4-inch," he said. "You'll like that for packing in the hills for grouse."

For a small man, Iver had huge hands, and they almost hid the pistol as he examined it. His hands must have grown so large from his decades as a butcher, and then as a rifle maker for everyone from local guys at the sawmill to famous entertainers and gun writers.

Every time I went to the range, I packed the Colt along. If I do say so myself, I got pretty good plinking cans with it.

The following September, I packed the Colt on my belt on hikes into the mountains to listen for bugling elk. Spruce grouse perched along the creeks in the high country. Blue grouse fed on grasshoppers in the grassy openings on the ridge spines.

One hot afternoon, I stopped for a nap next to a spring. A cool breeze flowed through the forest, and in a minute I was asleep. I awoke to the rustling of pine needles. A covey of spruce grouse had come to water. I rolled over on my stomach and, with the Diamondback, shot three of the five birds.

A prime target is the tree-sitting or trail-ambushed grouse, now done in with hollowpoints for the quick quietus.

Another time, I was walking down a ridge toward the road when I flushed a covey of blue grouse. The grouse perched above in the Douglas fir trees and gawked down at me. I leaned against the trunk of a fir and shot one bird through the side. It jumped out of the tree at the shot, flying on set wings for a short distance then falling out of the air. I tried to hit the next bird in the head. The bullets clipped branches all around the grouse's head, but never raised a feather. I could not hit that bobbing head, only about the size of a quarter.

Actually, a 22 handgun shooting solidpoint Long Rifle bullets is marginally effective on big blue grouse. A long time ago, I switched to shooting hollowpoints or Stingers in my Diamondback, and the grouse flop over, beat their wings, then die.

Over the years, I have carried my Diamondback hundreds of miles and shot thousands of rounds through it. I have shot around fifty grouse with it, piles of ground squirrels in hay fields and a landfill full of cans. Not once has it ever jammed nor failed to fire.

The only modification I have made to the gun is to replace the factory grips with Pachmayr Presentation grips. The factory grips were way too thick at the butt. The rubber Pachmayrs are slimmer and fit my small hand better.

I used to carry the pistol in an open-topped leather holster. Slapping branches and the general dings that come with carrying a gun, though, wore at the pistol's finish. Now I carry the gun in a Hunter flap-top holster, which completely protects the gun.

Because I used the Diamondback mostly in the field, I never shot it much at paper targets. Last summer, I decided to see how well it actually shot. I borrowed a Smith & Wesson Model Kit Gun and a Ruger Mark II Target Auto to compare.

I shot all three pistols with CCI Mini Mag hollowpoint and Stinger Long Rifle ammunition. From a solid rest, the Ruger put five shots as tight as .5-inch with Stingers to as large as 1.75 inches with Mini Mags at 25 yards. The Kit Gun shot from 2.1 inches with Stingers to 1.8 inches with Mini Mags. The Diamondback shot Stingers into 1 inch and Mini Mags 1.5 inches.

That's more than adequate for all three.

Off-hand, the Ruger and Colt were easy to hit with because their weight balanced well in my hand. The light S&W waved around. The Ruger, though, is much too heavy to freight around all day on a belt. The Diamondback is heavy enough to hold steady yet light enough not to be a burden.

Around 1986, Colt discontinued the Diamondback. The shooting press howled in indignation, and Colt brought the Diamondback back into production for awhile. But not enough shooters bought the pistol, and Colt dropped it for good. The fact few shooters bought the Diamondback is no wonder. The 1986 retail price had climbed to $429.95 for a blued 4-inch model.

The abandonment of the Diamondback bothered me at the time. What if I needed a replacement part? But then I got to thinking. After thousands of rounds, the pistol was as tight as the day it was made. I would be fortunate to shoot enough shells through the Diamondback to wear it out. The Diamondback may be gone from the display cases, but I have mine. •

One Good Gun

by JOHN MALLOY

The Cadet and Me

EVERY ONCE IN a while, a group of not particularly good features somehow combine to make a pretty good gun. I have one of those guns—an Iver Johnson Cadet, Model 55-SA, a simple solid-frame 22-caliber revolver.

Its mechanical heritage dates back to before 1900, the year the Iver Johnson Arms and Cycle Works introduced their new line of improved solid-frame revolvers. Variations of this design remained in production until after World War II. In the mid-1950s, the frame was enlarged, and the Model 55 series was born. Then about 1961, a loading gate was added. This same basic frame was used for several different models, with the Model 55-SA Cadet being the low-priced, bottom-of-the-line offering. Calibers were 22, 32 and 38. The 22-caliber versions were probably the most popular, though. The little eight-shot 22 stayed in the line until all the Iver Johnson revolvers were discontinued. This took place when the company moved its plant to a new city at the end of the 1970s.

I got my Cadet in 1968, before the Gun Control Act of 1968 had actually gone into effect. I was living in Southern Louisiana at the time and had become interested in running a weekend trapline for some of the area's prolific aquatic furbearers. I already had a couple of 22 revolvers, but I didn't really want to carry a good one or a large one while I was sloshing through the brackish marshes. What I needed was a small, cheap 22—a clunker—one I wouldn't have to care much about.

At a gun show, there was the little Iver Johnson on a table. I wasn't particularly impressed with it, but the price was low, and I certainly wouldn't mind exposing it to the elements.

When I got it home, I carefully looked it over. It was a strange conglomeration of features.

The barrel, cylinder and trigger guard were blued. The frame had a non-glare, phosphate-type finish. The hammer and trigger were color case-hardened. Actually not bad looking.

With its 2½-inch barrel, it measured about 4 inches high and 6¾ inches long, just ¼-inch or so longer than a Smith & Wesson Chief's Special Airweight. It was rather heavy, weighing slightly over a pound and a half, a full 10 ounces heavier than the Airweight, and just a few ounces lighter than a Colt Commander 45.

The frame was solid. You unloaded it by pushing a release button that allowed the axis pin to be pulled forward and out so you could remove the cylinder. The pin was the right size to poke the empties, one at a time, out of the eight chambers.

Well, it wasn't actually quite that straightforward. The cylinder was the exclusive Iver Johnson "flash control" cylinder, with a rim or lip that extended forward. Its purpose was to divert any gas leakage from the barrel/cylinder junction to the front, instead of to the side. This seemed a strange feature for a cylinder that had to be removed regularly. A notch had been designed into the flash shield, and that notch had to be aligned with the rear portion of the barrel, or else the cylinder would not come out.

Following the style of target revolvers of decades past, the Cadet had a widened target-style hammer spur and a grooved trigger. These features seemed a bit out of place on a short-barrel inexpensive plinker such as this. However, except for the fact that the oversized hammer made the gun a bit less compact, they didn't really hurt anything. The hammer did not rebound or retract after firing, but could be thumbed back to a half-cock notch.

When loaded, the hammer could be carried in this half-cock position or, preferably, down on an empty chamber. In all positions except full-cock, the large hammer was high enough to completely block the rear sight notch. Double-action shooting using the sights was definitely not an option.

The rear sight was a simple notch, not just at the end of the frame, but cut as a continuous groove for the entire length of the frame. The front sight was a rounded blade mounted atop the barrel.

My revolver was the variant made after 1961, and a loading gate was provided on the right. The cylinder did not have to be removed for loading; just open the gate, load the cartridges, and close the gate. Standard procedure for those familiar with a Colt Single Action Army revolver. Unlike the Colt, however, no spring was included on the loading gate; friction held it closed. If the pivot screw was tight, the gate stayed closed. If the screw was loose, the gate flopped open.

The grips were simple smooth plastic panels on the sides of the grip frame. A single screw went in through the left grip, through an opening in the frame to reach

Many different guns, like this 03A3, have gone into the woods. The little Iver Johnson also went along, most of the time, tucked under the writer's belt.

the right grip, then screwed into, would you believe, the plastic of the right grip! No grip bushing for *this* Iver Johnson.

On the first trip to the range, late in 1968, I took it along as an afterthought. While there, I just sprinkled a few cylinders, single action, at a 25-yard target. I didn't get particularly impressive results, but I intended to use it only for point-blank shooting, anyway.

A few months later, in early 1969, I tried it at what seemed to be a more realistic range—30 feet. From a rest, the little revolver indicated it might shoot better than I had anticipated. It shot slightly low and to the right, but those 10-yard groups ran about 1½ inches. Plenty good enough to dispatch animals at short ranges.

I bought a cheap inside-the-pants holster, and the little Iver Johnson regularly went riding along with me on outdoor excursions. Thinking back on it, I can't ever remember using it for its intended purpose of dispatching trapped furbearers. I didn't want to put unnecessary holes in the skins and got pretty good at making trap sets that killed the critters outright. Those not killed outright were dispatched in other ways.

Nutria, the big aquatic furbearers originally brought in from South America to provide pen-raised fur, had been released into the coastal marshes when the 1946 hurricane destroyed their pens. They were overrunning some areas of Southern Louisiana and damaging the sugar cane crops. Trapping was encouraged, but fur prices were not high. I doubt if I ever made more than gas money from selling my furs, but I had fun and learned a lot about the real ecology of the area.

Although the Iver Johnson wasn't actually used on the trapline the way I'd planned, I carried it a lot and shot it a lot. I had learned how far off to hold, and had fun plinking with it while in the outdoors.

In July, 1970, I participated in a pistol match in the New Orleans area. The match was not long, and it was a nice day. A number of us decided to stay and practice a bit, by running an additional "300." It would be thirty shots total, ten shots at each stage of slow, timed and rapid fire.

The little Iver Johnson was in the car, so on an impulse I decided to use it, instead of one of my target pistols.

By then, I knew how far off to

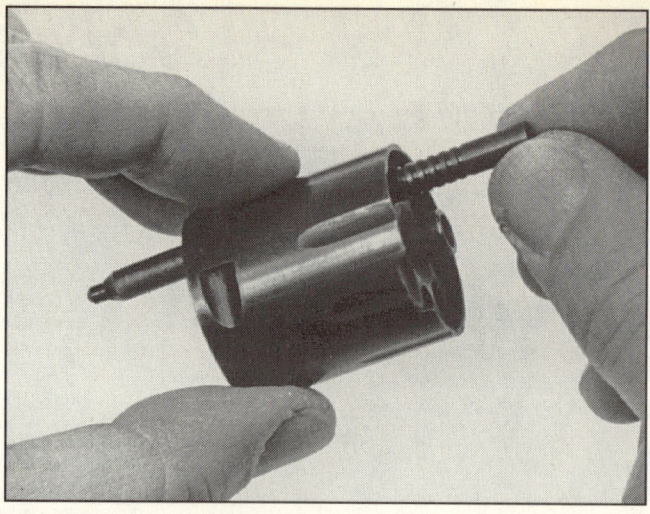

The axis pin for the cylinder is just the right size to push empty cases from the chambers, so it also serves as an ejector rod.

hold. The gun turned in slow, timed and rapid scores of 46, 76 and 58, for an aggregate of 180 out of a possible 300 points. Not great, but much better than any of the shooters there (including me) expected.

Still, nothing spectacular. Nobody else felt moved to acquire one like it to use for target shooting.

The following year, in the spring of 1971, the Iver Johnson also missed its chance to do something heroic. By then, it was going along with me pretty regularly. On a visit to Texas, a friend and I were going out to test a new 22 rifle. The Iver Johnson was inside my belt.

We had not gotten to where we were going and had not even loaded the guns. I was just walking across a pasture when events took a sudden turn.

I felt a hard blow on the back of my right calf, as if I had been hit by a baseball bat, but bats generally don't have red-hot icepicks in them. My mind sorted through the possibilities, then screamed, "Rattlesnake!"

I turned, and sure enough, there it was, about 6 feet of Texas diamondback. I must admit that my first estimate was more like 20 feet. Looking back, though, it is hard to remember my exact thoughts. Certainly, revenge was present. Also, my background thought was that proper treatment might require positive identification of the snake. Whatever the reason, I wanted that snake dead!

I pulled out the Iver Johnson and a box of ammunition. Spilling most of the cartridges onto the ground, I fumbled a few through the loading gate and into the chambers, turned the cylinder and got off one shot as the rattler disappeared under a clump of brush.

There was little to be gained by reaching in after it, it seemed. So, revenge against the snake was canceled. We made a quick trip to the nearest hospital.

I spent nine days in the hospital. Antivenin was not used, perhaps because I had not had the foresight to bring in the snake for positive identification. If only the Iver Johnson had been loaded! I did get to know the emergency room doctor, a hunter and shooter himself. We still exchange Christmas cards.

As the years went by, I did a lot of small game hunting and target shooting with 22 pistols. I always seemed to use something else. However, when I didn't really plan to do any serious pistol shooting, the Iver Johnson went along, just in case.

The years continued to go by, as they tend to do, and in the summer of 1986, I was living in Texas. I went to the range in Houston to practice for a pistol match. The Iver Johnson was in the car, so I took it out and shot it a bit.

Suddenly, I was disgusted with myself. I realized that I had owned the little revolver for eighteen years, and it still shot low and to the right. The next weekend, I went back to the range with an assortment of files and plenty of ammunition.

When I left, for the first time in its life, the Iver Johnson shot to point of aim at 25 yards.

It took just a short while to become accustomed to not having to hold off. Why hadn't I done it before? I now liked the little gun even better.

By 1991, I had moved to Florida. That year, however, I returned to Texas for the NRA Annual Meetings in San Antonio. A former neighbor then lived in the country not far from San Antonio, and we planned to attend the meetings together. To kill some time before we left, he suggested we do some plinking. The only 22 I had in the car was the Iver Johnson.

The revolver seemed to recognize its natural habitat—a private dumping area loaded with plenty of plinking targets. It rose to the occasion. Although my friend was using his Ruger bull-barrel Mark I target pistol, the Iver Johnson matched him shot for shot on those informal targets.

It is hard to realize that I have had that revolver for almost three decades. It (at last) shoots to point of impact at 25 yards. At that range, it will group its eight shots into a circle smaller than the 5½-inch black bullseye of a standard 25-yard pistol target.

Of course, it doesn't really shoot well enough for competition, but I think it is plenty good enough for small game and pests at short ranges. However, I really can't prove it. I don't remember ever killing any game with it and, of course, have no recollection of its ever dispatching a furbearer. It certainly wasn't ready to do the job when I wanted to kill that snake.

Yet, somehow, over almost three decades, it has become something of a constant companion to me in the outdoors. Although I fumble sometimes, I've become used to having to align the notch of the flash control rim in order to remove the cylinder. I am also used to not being able to see the sights unless the hammer is cocked. The wide spur digs into my side a bit when the little gun is carried at my belt, but it actually does aid in cocking the hammer. Hardly without a conscious thought, the Iver Johnson often winds up in my pack or on my belt.

I look at it now as a nice little gun. It is still a hodge-podge of features that are not all particularly good, and it hasn't done any of the things I expected of it. But I've had a lot of fun with it, and it has inadvertently become part of my life's history, and I'm glad I have it.

●

by RAYMOND CARANTA

THE GUNS OF EUROPE

GUNS FOR SMALL BIRDS

larded in brochettes. It was not uncommon, forty years ago, in remote areas of the Alps, in Corsica, or Algeria to kill 100 to 200 thrushes in a single day with small 9mm, 410, 32- or 24-gauge singles, shot from blinds, or on the wing with 28- or 20-gauge doubles.

Wingshooting with these nice shotguns was a very difficult proposition. Thrushes often have unpredictable trajectories, and the shooting must be extremely fast. A hunter who got two hits out of three shots on the wing all day long with a 28- or 20-gauge was a good man, indeed.

Those who shot from blinds favored small bolt-action, folding or trapdoor guns, but many old percussion single or double muzzleloaders of 28-, 24- or, even 16-gauge, loaded with blackpowder, finished their careers as bird guns, because of the trifling cost of ammunition—the cap, a few grains of blackpowder, a piece of yesterday's paper and a fraction of an ounce of shot. After World War II, many people were eating meat only once a week and mod-

In Southern Europe now, in spite of multiple laws protecting many species, birds are becoming less abundant, but not because of hunters. The decline is in relation to the more general treatment of crops with chemical products during the last thirty years. Moreover, in France, for instance, the number of hunters has decreased from about three million to two million, during the same period.

And, of course, our whole situation is very different. Fewer people earn their livings in rural activity, and young city women, once they have found good jobs, are less and less determined to found a family, not to speak of plucking hundreds of small birds brought home by a husband on Sunday evening.

The range for such bird shooting was usually 10 to 20 yards from a blind and never exceeded 30 yards on the wing.

For blind shooting, the smallest caliber commonly used was the 9mm Flobert rimfire, loaded with #10, 11 or 12 shot. When

Charming little pen-and-inks like these were scattered all through 1900-1930 European catalogs.

IN ENGLISH SPEAKING countries and, more generally, in the modern civilized world, hunting birds smaller than thrush is condemned by ethics, if not by law. Likewise, live pigeon shooting has practically disappeared as a barbarous custom. It was highly popular in the most sophisticated places, such as Monte Carlo, at the turn of the century.

Pigeon shooting was mostly an amusement for wealthy people, but small bird hunting was practiced in all classes of society around the Mediterranean basin. It was traditional, a direct prolongation of glue or net capture during medieval times when small birds were on the menu often.

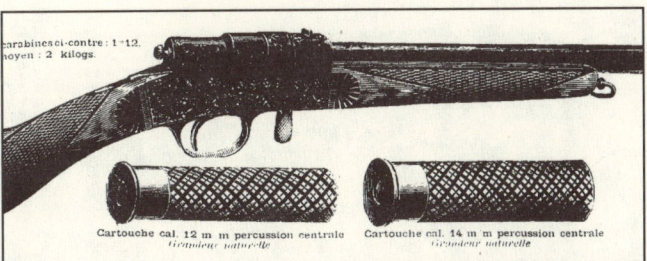

Here's the classic single shot bolt-action garden bird gun and its loads.

Those bird hunters were either plain country people who did it because it made a cheap meal for the family or gourmets who were eating them by the dozen as we now do oysters, ern guns were quite rare—most had been seized by the Germans during the Occupation—and both the birds and these old muzzleloaders had the merit of availability.

this writer started hunting in 1949, the simple load (.14-ounce) was already obsolete, and the double load (.28-ounce) was standard. The practical range was 10 yards, and most guns were either bolt-action or trapdoor single shots.

The 9mm centerfire was obsolete in the early Fifties, used only in old secondhand bolt-action clunkers. The standard load was .16-ounce of small shot for a shell length of 1.7-inch.

Contrary to the modern American 410 magnum 3-inch load with .75-ounce of shot, the standard European 12mm was only 2 inches long and loaded with .23-ounce of shot—#8, 9, 10, 11 or 12. The practical range was

50th EDITION, 1996 **133**

also about 10 yards on the birds; guns were similar to the 9mms, but bigger.

The 32-gauge had a 2½-inch shell and a load of .43-ounce of #8, 9, 10, 11 or 12 shot, so its practical range could exceed 15 yards. This caliber was also mostly available in single shot bolt-action or trapdoor guns.

The 28-gauge is a genuine 14mm bore (in spite of the name, the 32-gauge is only 12.75mm—.50-inch), and with the then-standard 2½-inch (65mm) shell, the load was .57-ounce of #6, 8, 9, 10, 11 or 12 shot. The 28-gauge was often supplanted by the 24-gauge, after having been quite popular, mostly in aristocratic circles from the turn of the century up to the Great War. It has regained a certain popularity during these last twenty years, thanks to American shotguns imported in Europe. It could be used up to 25 yards for bird shooting, in elegant side-by-sides with narrow actions.

The 24-gauge, with its .578-inch bore and a .73-ounce load of #4, 6, 8, 9, 10, 11 or 12 shot for the standard 2½-inch shell, covered the range up to 30 yards and was more than a bird gun. Still popular, the 24-gauge is also good for partridge or the rabbit in brush country. It was mostly available as a swinging-barrel single shot, like the Manufrance "Simplex."

The 20-gauge is now the smallest multi-purpose caliber on the international market. Forty years ago, in Europe, loaded with .80-ounce of any size shot in its 2½-inch shell (or .90-ounce in the then-new 2¾-inch shell), it was the typical lady's or youngster's caliber and was chambered both in side-by-sides and over/unders, which began to be fashionable.

For metric calibers in the European bird guns (i.e., 9mm, 12mm and 14mm), the most widespread system was the bolt action. In 14mm, an additional bolt was sometimes added behind the operating lever. The old Warnant trapdoor action was also commonly available, usually in a hammerless version. It was more expensive and, when worn, more liable to spit through the bolt joint.

With the exception of custom guns, the smallest gauge available with single shot swinging barrels was the 32 (or 14mm),

The French Gaucher "Simplarm" single, available in 12mm, 14mm and 410, a direct development of the Manufrance "Simplex."

The Italian Beretta folding single-barrel shotgun, available in all calibers, from 12mm to 9mm, is very popular around the Mediterranean basin.

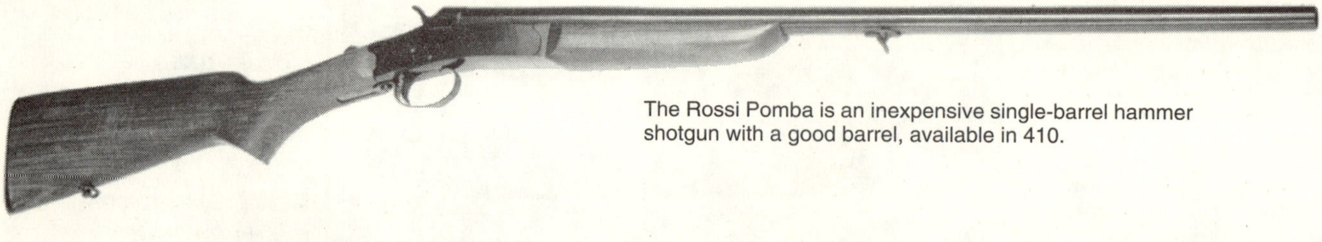

The Rossi Pomba is an inexpensive single-barrel hammer shotgun with a good barrel, available in 410.

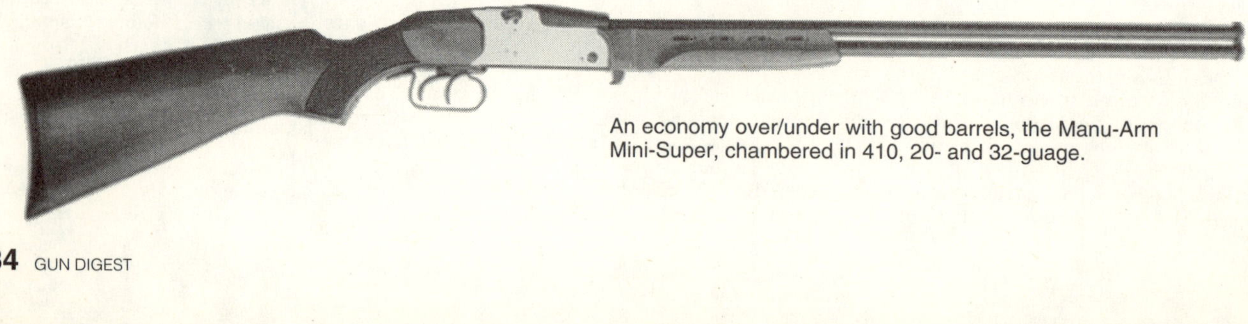

An economy over/under with good barrels, the Manu-Arm Mini-Super, chambered in 410, 20- and 32-guage.

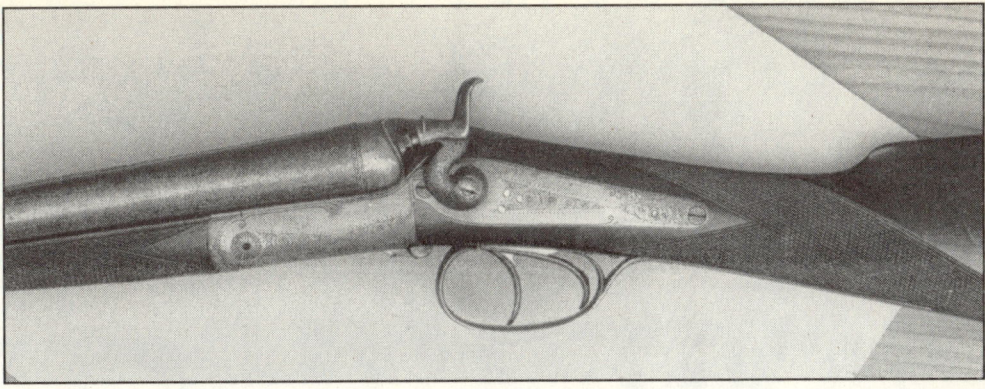

The clean-lined 28 that Bugatti used had back-action locks, side-lever, and was built for very light loads.

then very popular in Europe. Now, Gaucher, in Saint-Etienne, is making a "Simplarm" single chambered in 12mm (the 410 with 2-inch shell), 410 (the 410, with 3-inch shell) and 32-gauge (14mm), which is very similar to the original Manufrance "Simplex" which disappeared with the company in 1984. Several swinging-barrel singles are now available from Italy and Brazil in these calibers, as well. There are also modern over/unders made by Manu-Arm and Sidna, in Saint-Etienne, for the same purpose.

The 28-gauge is more aristocratic than ever and definitely dedicated to fine custom side-by-sides or over/unders. The 24-gauge, however, is seriously suffering from the 410 magnum competition. Many old Manufrance "Simplex" are still around among farmers in the countryside. Of course, the 20-gauge with 3-inch chambering is more popular than ever as a multi-purpose light gun.

Dove shooting is traditional in the southwest of France, in the Basque country. They shoot from miradors—blinds on the ridges. During the last twenty years, there has been a strong opposition to this activity from both the Brussels European Commission and private associations, but the Basque hunters with their elected representatives are holding tight, and the conflict is not close to an end. Guns for this shooting are conventional side-by-sides, mostly in 12-gauge.

Small bird shooting is barely hanging on and will probably be a mere folkloric matter by the end of the next century. Bird guns, however, will remain in the collections of our grandsons. They will be vestiges of a past when people were still living traditionally in a natural environment.

This was Ettore Bugatti's 28-bore small bird gun, now owned by the writer.

From this sketch, one is led to believe garden parties included shooting small bores.

This muzzleloader, signed at Aix-en-Provence, the writer's home, saw bird gun service post-World War II.

It's a 775 Rigby

The 10-bore rifle is alive and well in London.

◆ ◆

by JIM DICKSON

John Farmer (left) and Chris Collins with John's second buffalo. The 1880 Rigby 10-bore leaning against the buffalo had proven itself once more.

THERE IS GOOD news for American Cape buffalo hunters. Rigby has made a pair of modern 10-bore rifles especially designed for Cape buffalo. Named the 775 Rigby, the gun fires a 900-grain steel-tipped, hardened lead slug at 1500 fps for 149.4 of John Taylor's Knock Down Values. The 600 Nitro Express provides 150.4 Knock Down Value. The 775, however, doesn't kick like the 600. Its felt recoil is no more than a 416 Rigby.

Men who can't fire more than two shots comfortably from a 10-pound 458 can comfortably fire twenty with a 12¼-pound 775 Rigby. The recoil seems no more than a heavy waterfowl load in a 12-bore. The 775's weight and low-pressure cartridge moving a large diameter bullet at moderate velocity combine to produce a stopping rifle that is a pussycat to shoot.

Writers are always declaring deer and antelope calibers like the 375 H&H Magnum to be all-around rifles for Africa, despite the fact that Kenya banned the use of that cartridge on dangerous game, because of the numerous failures back in the days when you could still hunt Kenya. For some reason beyond my comprehension, said writers dismiss anything with a hint of recoil from contention. As a 3-inch 577 devotee, I think they are crazy, but there is no problem because now we have a gun with genuine one-shot stopping power and low recoil. The 775 was designed to be the only gun needed for a rancher in remote parts of Africa. To this end, it can be furnished with a set of 26-inch rifle barrels and a set of 32-inch 10-gauge magnum shotgun barrels. The 775 slug at 1500 fps does not ruin meat on smaller game and shoots flat enough out to 150 yards.

With the first rifle produced, both barrels' bullet holes touch at 50 yards; at 150 yards, they will stay on a 5-inch target. You don't need any more accuracy or range for African big game. Actual measurement, as opposed to estimates, quickly prove that almost all game is actually shot inside 150 yards.

The first pair of guns was made with a standard bead front sight, a fixed shallow V rear sight for 50 yards, and folding sights for 100 and 150 yards. The 100-yard sight has proved superfluous as there is too little drop to warrant the use of it. The 50-yard and the 150-yard sights are the only ones needed.

The 775 Rigby, being built to measure, is perfectly fitted to its user so that it can be fired accurately by instinct shooting like a shotgun in an emergency. There are times when there is simply no time for even a flash sight picture—despite all the drivel written about sights—times when you can only point and pull the trigger. A fitted gunstock and a lively, responsive double can make the difference between life and death in that situation. That instantly available extra shot is worth more than a twenty-round magazine in a bolt action when the beast is only 5 feet away.

In the old days, men often hunted dangerous game without another gun to back them up. It is easy to see how the double rifle became the favorite dangerous game gun. When it is your life on the line and you have only your own gun to depend on, it had better be a double or the first time you need a gunsmith may well be the last.

The history of the 775 Rigby began when John Farmer, noted Lloyds of

London broker of Thurgood, Farmer and Hackett, got the 10-bore bug and began downing pheasants with a Holland & Holland 10-bore shotgun. This led to reloading because only #3 shot was available in factory shells, and you want #5 and #6 shot for pheasants.

One gun led to another, actually two more—a magnificent pair of 1880 Rigby 10-bore double rifles originally built for the well-known British big game hunters, the James brothers, who hunted in Sudan in the 1880s. One of them was killed by an elephant and the other gave up hunting, so the guns were little used and in fine condition.

The guns came with two bullet moulds. One cast a 1150-grain solid propelled at 900 fps by 5 drams of blackpowder, and the other made a 1350-grain exploding shell containing 40 grains of antimony sulphite and potassium chlorate in equal parts at 750 fps. The 50-50 mixture of antimony sulphite and potassium chlorate was the standard Victorian exploding shell compound, and it received widespread acclaim in its day. Even today, John Farmer's experiments with it have found it to live up to its reputation.

Farmer knew that he could raise the velocity without raising the pressure by using smokeless powder instead of blackpowder, and that the lighter weight of the smokeless powder charge would give much less recoil than blackpowder would. So, working with the Birmingham proof house, two loads were developed. A 1350-grain solid with a steel core was propelled at 950 fps with 42 grains of Blue Dot, and an 875-grain slug was driven to 1350 fps with 52.5 grains of Blue Dot and 6 grains of blackpowder for ignition over a standard primer. Magnum primers later solved the ignition problems and the blackpowder was eliminated. Remington plastic 10-gauge cases were cut down to $2^{5}/_{8}$ inches, and the slugs were seated on a shot cup wad with the shot cup cut off.

Having gotten in this deep, there was no turning back, so Farmer went on safari to shoot Cape buffalo with his 10-bore rifle and 875-grain loads. The old gun won over guide Tony Henley of Safari South when its heavy slugs demolished a termite hill in a most spectacular manner. Now the problem was to find a good trophy buffalo. The selection process was decided for them when such a buffalo decided to hunt them.

Farmer was riding unarmed on the roof of the Land Rover trying to spot game in thick brush. From 25 yards away, a buffalo charged and gored the Land Rover, bending the chassis. The horn went through the side of the Rover to give Mrs. Farmer a good start.

"Shoot him," yelled the guide, and the 10-bore was snatched from the rack and passed up to Farmer.

The right barrel went in at a 40-degree angle between the shoulders, ending up unmarked on the underskin between the two hind legs. The animal had his adrenaline up and was determined to live up to the reputation of charging Cape buffalo, so he ran 25 yards away and faced the vehicle to charge again. As he lowered his head, the left barrel's slug hit him in the eye and dashed out his brains as it exited, resulting in a total shutdown of all charging buffalo systems. Only now could they examine it for trophy

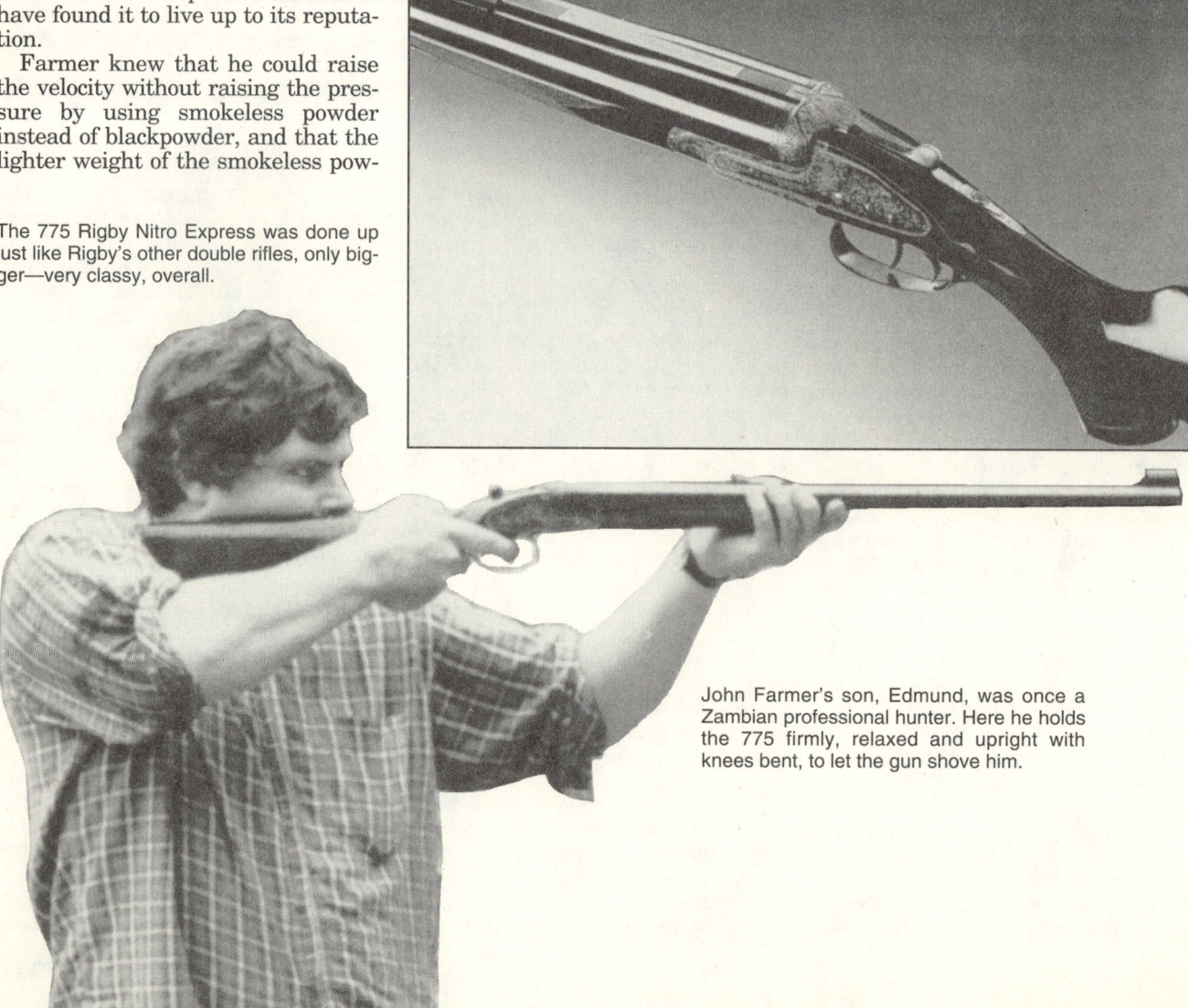

The 775 Rigby Nitro Express was done up just like Rigby's other double rifles, only bigger—very classy, overall.

John Farmer's son, Edmund, was once a Zambian professional hunter. Here he holds the 775 firmly, relaxed and upright with knees bent, to let the gun shove him.

size. Amazingly, it was a fine animal, instead of one of the smaller ones they had been seeing. It would be the ninth day and many buffalo later before they saw another good one.

This next buffalo proved to be another good example of the need for a powerful stopping rifle. Farmer had been following this one for hours, and when he finally got a shot at it, he hit it too far back. The buffalo ran from left to right at 65 yards, and the second barrel also struck too far back. Had he been using a little 375 Magnum, he would be facing the prospect of tracking a wounded buffalo in thick brush, a thrill-a-minute pastime, with an impressive record of wins for the buffalo's side.

However, using a 10-bore rifle resulted in the buffalo lying down and dying, instead of charging from ambush. A neck shot failed when the slug deflected off the edge of the vertebrae, and the second barrel was fired into the center back where it also deflected off the vertebrae, going into the heart-lung area and finishing him off.

Happy with his 1880 10-bore, John Farmer returned to England where he talked his friend, Paul Roberts, owner of John Rigby & Co., into building him a pair of modern 10-bore rifles out of a pair of Rigby action forgings originally earmarked to be 470 fixed-crosspin sidelocks. For the modern gun, there was new ammunition—a 900-grain, steel-cored, hard-lead conical slug driven at 1500 fps by 60 grains of Blue Dot powder. Solid brass $2^{7}/_{8}$-inch cases were made with recessed heads so that the slug seats on the shoulder. The powder charge is kept in position by an $1/_{8}$-inch plastic obturator made in Italy. There is airspace between the obturator and the bullet.

The old blackpowder 10-bores had a twist of 1:70 inches, but this was too slow for accuracy at 1500 fps, so Josef Hambrusch in Austria made the new barrels with 1:41 inches. The groove diameter is .774-inch, and the land diameter is .764-inch. An extra set of 32-inch 10-gauge magnum shotgun barrels turned the 10-bore rifle into a true all-around African gun system.

Africa was explored early by 10-bore users such as Sir Samuel Baker. It is fitting that Rigby has brought the old workhorse back. It still has much to offer.

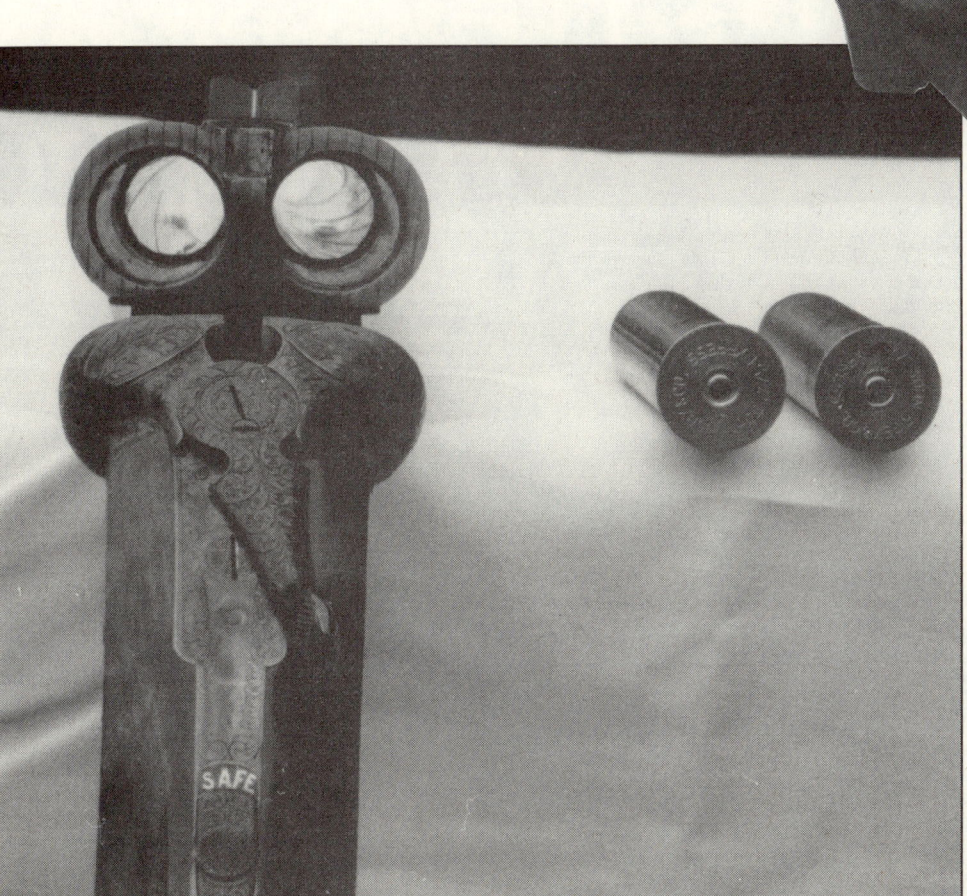

The 775 Rigby double has a certain no-nonsense hefty look to it—graceful, but not very dainty.

Now it's brass $2^{7}/_{8}$-inch cases and a 900-grain bullet at 1500 fps for controllable recoil and a quick second shot.

by GARY M. BROWN

(Top) Early Model 65 rifle in 32-20, fitted with a 22-inch barrel and the Whelen-designed "NRA" stock with slim forearm. The later M65 218 Bee had a 24-inch tube. (Above) First-year Model 64 219 Zipper has the Whelen buttstock and slim forearm. The 219 Zipper was Winchester's attempt to offer 220 Swift performance in their lever actions.

The Whelen Models:
Winchester's Ultimate

(Below) Circa-1950, this Model 64 Standard Rifle in 30-30 Winchester displays the Whelen buttstock and the later wider forearm. (Bottom) This Model 71 348 Winchester Special (i.e. *deluxe*) rifle is barrel-dated 1954—making it among the last of its type to be produced. It displays both the checkered Whelen stock and checkered semi-beavertail forearm, along with quick-detachable swivels.

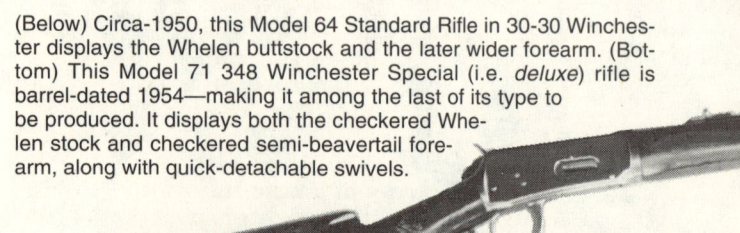

TOWNSEND WHELEN didn't actually redesign Winchester's basic rifles himself, but his NRA stock was incorporated on Winchester's Model 64, Model 65 and Model 71 lever actions—the ultimate developments of John M. Browning's M1894, M1892 and M1886.

During his middle years with the National Rifle Association, Whelen was involved in improving and updating the stocks and forends of commercial sporting rifles, especially the lever actions. Such stocks would come to be known as NRA and/or Whelen designs. The first appearance of the Whelen stock redesign on a Winchester-made firearm was likely the Model 54 bolt-action rifle. Introduced in 1925, the 54 was Winchester's first totally commercial centerfire bolt action,

Whelen portrait by Graves Gladney.

Lever Guns

offered in 30-06 and the radically new 270 Winchester. The initial Model 54 design had a relatively low comb along with a shallow, sloping pistol grip, an extremely narrow wrist, and a thin shotgun butt. The slim forend was combined with a schnabel tip, and while both were aesthetically pleasing, neither provided much gripping area.

The 1931 Winchester catalog features side-by-side illustrations of the Standard Model 54 Rifle and the Model 54 Bolt Action Rifle—N.R.A. Type. The new stock had a longer, more forward raking, thick-wristed pistol grip; a higher comb; a decidedly taller, wider shotgun butt; and a fuller, deeper forend without the schnabel tip. This NRA version had improved shooting control, and it was fitted with a Lyman 48W rear aperture receiver sight.

None of the Whelen-influenced lever actions appear in the 1931 catalog, although the straight-stocked Model 53 and Model 55 lever actions are shown.

Throughout his writing career, Whelen emphasized the importance of a rifle's stock in achieving accuracy. In an article appearing in the 1951 GUN DIGEST, Whelen said, "...the stock should fit its owner perfectly. It should contribute to a very steady hold in all firing positions. Particularly when the cheek is snuggled comfortably against the side of the comb of the butt-stock, the pupil of the eye should come precisely in the line of aim..." Improvements Whelen made on the NRA stock, later adapted to Winchesters, helped guarantee positive results.

The earliest mention of an NRA stock installed on a rifle of any type appears to be the Springfield M1922 22 LR Target Rifle. Thereafter, stocks of that type came to be designated as the Model 1922 Pistol Grip Stock. The NRA stock design seems to appear next on the NRA Sporter, a sporterized Model 1903 Springfield rifle, sold through the Director of Civilian Marksmanship (DCM) to members of the National Rifle Association, beginning about 1924. These super accurate "star-gauged" barreled rifles were available until around 1932.

In his book, published in 1970, *The Hunting Rifle*, Jack O'Connor, an admirer of Townsend Whelen, has this to say about those inexpensive NRA sporters: "...a big hearted Uncle Sam sold to members of the N.R.A. a Springfield sporter with a star-gauged barrel, an oversize sporting stock, and a Lyman 48 receiver sight for as little as $40. This no doubt gladdened the hearts of Savage, Winchester, and Remington, who had to make 30-06 rifles, cut the jobber and dealer in for a modest bit of gravy, advertise, pay taxes, and yet try to set aside a few dimes for the stockholders."

In the same book, O'Connor says this about the post-World War I popularity of commercial turnbolt rifles: "The stocks on these rifles were not so hot. They were low of comb, had excessive heel drop, rather skimpy forends, and air-rifle-size buttplates."

O'Connor provides us with our first definite tie-in between Townsend Whelen and the Winchester/NRA/Whelen stock design: "Gun writers led by Townsend Whelen needled the gun manufacturers until they put more seemly stocks on their muskets. The NRA MODEL Winchester Model 70 and the Remington Model 30-S had rather satisfactory stocks of classic inspiration...stocks became straighter, pistol grips better designed, and fore-ends fuller."

Whelen had also been a part of the developmental process that resulted in the Type C or M1903A1 Springfield rifle and stock, officially approved sometime during 1928. William S. Brophy's *The Springfield 1903 Rifles* shows a sketch of Townsend Whelen's suggested design for a pistol grip stock with a unique squared-off toe, flattened over its final 2 inches, thus permitting the stock to be easily reduced in length (by sawing) for shorter military personnel. That version was never adopted, but Whelen clearly had a hand in the Type C design.

In Whelen's classic piece "Days of

the Springfield" in the 1961 GUN DIGEST, a pistol grip-fitted, M1903A1 Type C-stocked Springfield rifle appears in the middle of the first page. The Type C was the most advanced, controllable stock ever produced for the 1903 Springfields, and it was the stock Whelen had assisted in designing!

So what about the lever-action guns? In O'Connor's *Complete Book Of Rifles and Shotguns*, he says: "Stocks for the older lever-action sporting rifles had combs that were too thin and too low, stocks that were too short, forends that had to be held like a pickle fork."

In Roger C. Rule's *The Rifleman's Rifle*, a treatise on the pre-'64 Model 70 rifle, appears the following on the NRA Standard (Model 54) Rifle: "Introduced in 1931...Its distinguishing feature was a new stock especially designed to conform with the recommendations of the National Rifle Association"

There was the following footnote: "Appointed by Gen. M.A. Reckford, NRA executive vice president, a committee consisting of *Col. Townsend Whelen* and Mr. Laurence J. Hathaway conferred with Winchester engineers in designing the NRA stock."

Rule continues: "This stock, logically, became known as 'the NRA stock' and its design remained unchanged long into the succeeding Model 70 line."

Since Rule was privy not only to all written Winchester records, but also conducted extensive interviews with living former Winchester employees as well, there is little doubt this is the very same committee that worked with Winchester to redesign the stocks for the soon-to-be-announced Model 64, Model 65 and Model 71, the ultimate lever actions.

The 1933 Winchester catalog contains the first mention of the extensive availability of NRA stocks on lever-action rifles. The Model 54 bolt gun is pictured, now offered only with: "One-piece walnut stock of improved N.R.A. type..." Both Model 64 and Model 65 Winchester lever actions also appear, in both descriptions and illustrations, equipped with the improved NRA-type walnut stock. The Model 1886 is still listed, offered with a straight stock in Extra Lightweight, Takedown Style only, in one caliber—33 WCF.

In 1936, the Model 71, the ultimate update of the Model 1886, joined the Model 64 and Model 65. Fitted, initially, with 24- or 20-inch barrel, the M71 had the high-combed pistol-grip NRA/Whelen stocks. The Model 71 was apparently always equipped with the broadened forend later furnished on the Models 64 and 65 as well.

At first, the Model 64 came with either 20- or 24-inch barrel (neither the Model 64 nor the Model 71 were catalogued with short barrels after 1947) and was eventually chambered for four cartridges: 219 Zipper, 25-35, 30-30 and 32 Winchester Special. Its two-thirds magazine held five rounds, giving it a total capacity of six shots with a shell in the chamber.

The Model 65's three standard chamberings were 25-20 WCF, 32-20 WCF and 218 Bee. Its button-shaped half-magazine held seven standard rounds; six of the 218 Bee. The M65's two barrel lengths were 22 inches in 25-20 and 32-20; 24 inches in 218 Bee.

The Model 71's one standard caliber was 348 Winchester. The magazine of the 71 held four rounds, exactly the same as that of the discontinued Extra Lightweight Model 1886.

Both the Model 64 and the 71 were available as Deluxe versions. The Model 64 Deer Rifle came in 30-30 and 32 Winchester Special only, with a checkered, capped pistol grip; checkered semi-beavertail forend; quick-detachable Super Grade swivels; and a sling. The Model 71 Special was of almost identical (albeit heavier) configuration.

The three new cartridges of the ultimate lever-action rifles were the 218 Bee, the 219 Zipper and, of course, the 348 Winchester in the Model 71. Each of these hot, high-velocity chamberings was chosen for a very specific reason. Although the Model 54 bolt-action rifle provided

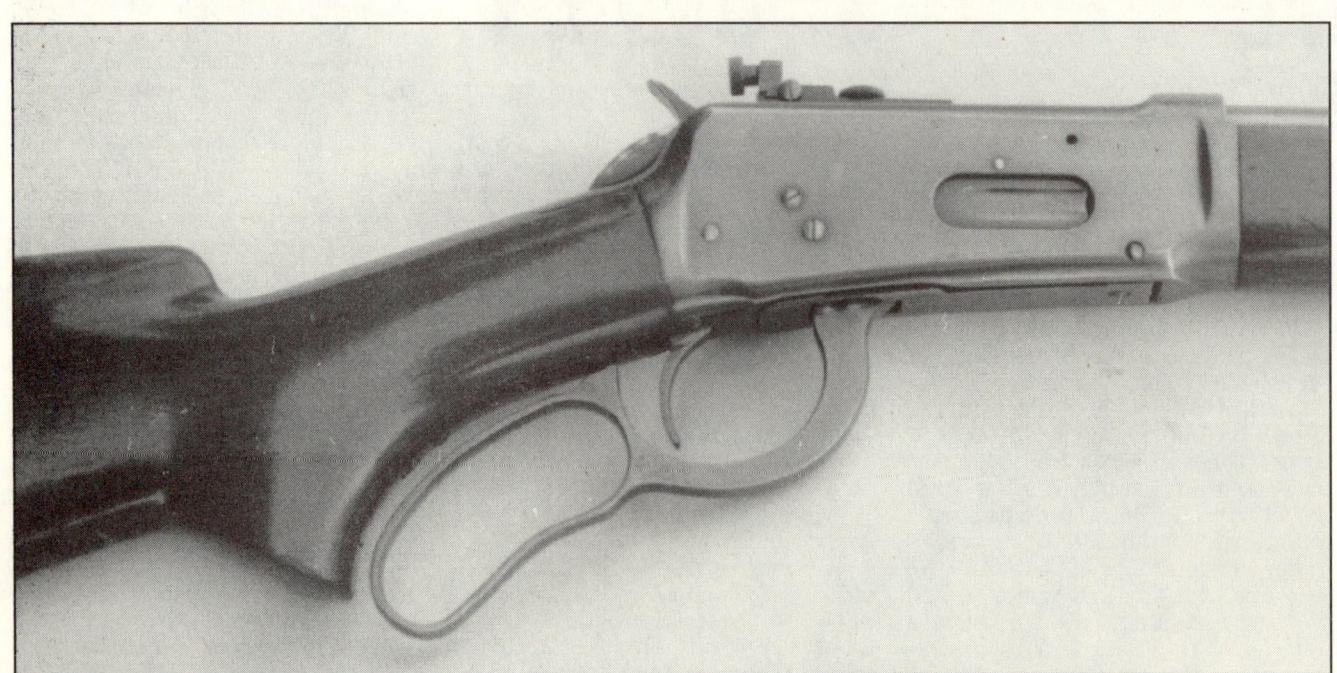

The #98A "bolt peep" rear sight was featured on some Winchester Model 71 348 and Model 64 219 Zipper (pictured) rifles. The nearly identical #98C version was fitted to many Model 65s in 218 Bee.

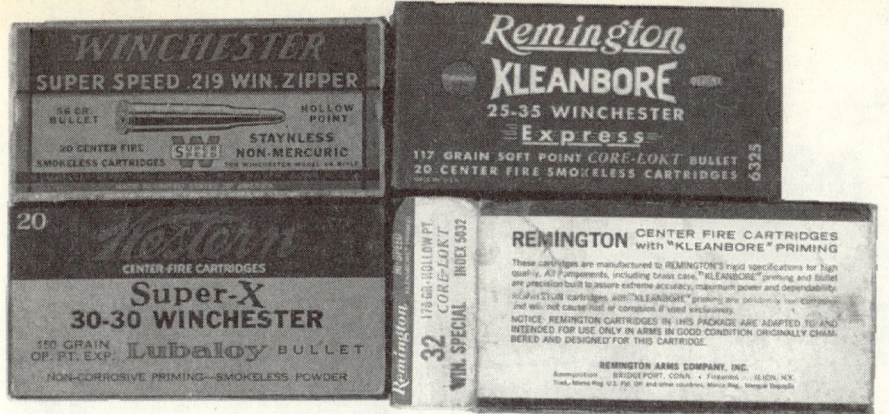

The four standard production calibers of the Winchester Model 64: 219 Zipper, 30-30, 25-35 and 32 Winchester Special. Introduced in 1938, the 219 Zipper was, the author believes, a Whelen-inspired cartridge.

(Above) The Winchester Model 65's three standard production chamberings: 218 Bee, 25-20 and 32-20. When it debuted in 1939, the 218 Bee was designed to duplicate (or better) 22 Hornet bolt-action performance.

(Left) The four 348 bullet weights: Winchester 150-grain softpoint, Peters 210-grain belted (virtually unheard of), Western/Super-X 200-grain Silvertip (the only current factory offering) and Western/Super-X 250-grain Silvertip.

such advanced rounds as the 22 Hornet, 220 Swift and 30-06 Springfield, Winchester had literally built its reputation on lever-action guns. Despite the popularity of turnbolt actions, due to their almost exclusive usage as the combat rifles of World War I, Winchester's retail customers were still predominantly buyers of lever-action guns. It was quite logical to attempt to perpetuate the design by offering rounds for lever-action guns similar to those offered in bolt-action rifles.

Again, we can clearly see the hand of Townsend Whelen in at least two of the three ultimate lever-action rounds. The 22 Hornet was developed and perfected by Whelen, Wotkyns and others at the U.S. Springfield Armory in the late 1920s. Somewhat tame by today's standards, the Hornet at 2400 fps (later 2650 fps) was the first high-velocity varmints-only centerfire round offered on these shores.

The later 218 Bee was definitely intended to duplicate (or better) 22 Hornet energy and velocity figures in a lever-action arm. The earlier 219 Zipper, especially in its rare, early 46-grain configuration at 3390 fps, was an obvious attempt to provide near 220 Swift velocity in the lever-action Model 64.

The 46-grain load must have proven to be ballistically unsatisfactory and extremely unpopular, as this writer has amassed over ten boxes of 56-grain factory cartridges for his Model 64 Zipper, but has been unable to find even a single round loaded with the lighter projectile. Whelen's (and others') experiments with various high-velocity cartridge designs both at the Frankford Arsenal and at the U.S. Springfield Armory likely inspired not only the 219 Zipper, but the 1935 introduction of the 220 Swift as well.

The 348 Winchester does not appear to have a direct Whelen connection. In its heavier 200- and 250-grain loadings, the 348 was designed to replace the 405 WCF round. The goal of the 150-grain version of that cartridge was to duplicate the "paper" ballistics of the 150-grain 30-06 load.

The 1938 *Winchester Sales Manual*, issued by the company to all of its sales representatives, has this to say regarding the 150-grain 348 loading: "As has been previously mentioned, the 86 was our strongest and smoothest lever action and this mechanism was taken as a basis to handle the new cartridge. The advent of new powders, new priming mixtures, and better ballistic data has enabled us to produce a lever gun handling a cartridge with 150 gr. bullet at 2880 feet per second... (which is) directly comparable to the .30 Govt. '06 cartridge with 150 gr. bullet having a velocity of 2960 feet per second..."

However, the stubby 348 150-grain bullet possessed terrible sectional density and soon developed a reputation for not only rapidly shedding its energy, but of being very unstable in flight. Due to the flat- or round-nosed bullets that tubular magazines require, poor long-range ballistic performance applied not only to the 150-grain version of the 348, but also to the 218 Bee and the 219 Zipper.

Edwin Pugsley, in an addendum penned at the back of Harold F. Williamson's *Winchester: The Gun That Won The West*, seems to give credit for the theory behind these three rounds to a German ballistician named Hermann Gerlich. Townsend Whelen possessed both the historical

Only accurate rifles, Whelen said, are interesting, and he did his best for Winchester lever actions.

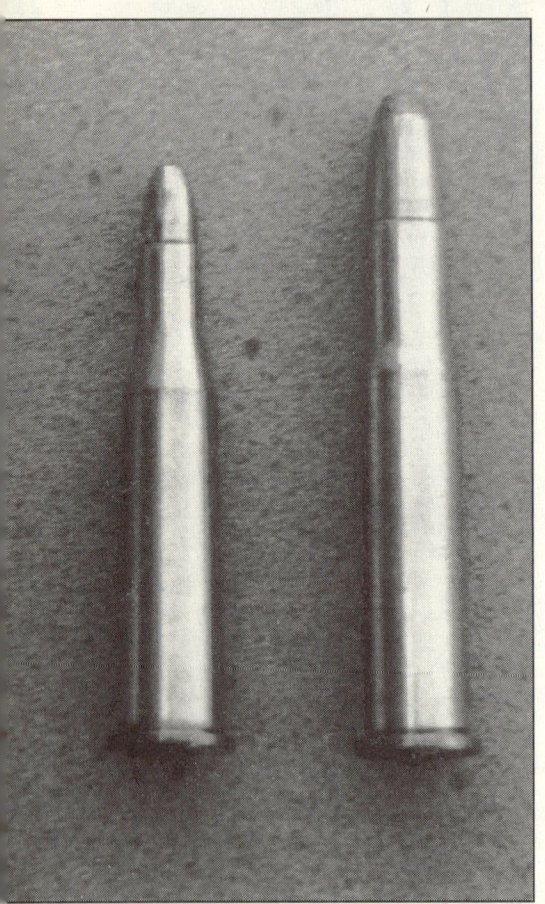

The 219 Zipper and the 30-30 were the cartridges that lasted in the Model 64 series.

background and technical credibility required for the development of such cartridges—and he was there.

Although the hot rounds of the Models 64, 65 or 71 never actually succeeded in truly duplicating bolt-action performance, they were close enough to satisfy many lever-action fans.

None of the ultimate lever actions were particularly successful in terms of overall sales. Least popular was the Model 65. There were just over 1500 sold in 25-20; just under 1300 in 32-20 (making the Model 65 32-20 pictured in this piece one of the scarcest Winchester lever guns ever produced); the balance of the 5704 total production was chambered in 218 Bee (first offered in 1939).

Model 65s in 218 Bee were often fitted with a #98C Bolt Peep rear sight. The #98C is virtually identical to the #98A pictured in this article on the Model 64 in 219 Zipper (the #98A was also fitted to some Model 71s). Such sights were thought to provide the inherent accuracy of rear aperture "peep" sights while affording "maximum sighting radius." Unfortunately, each time the bolt was cycled, the sight could change (if only slightly) its point of zero.

Model 65s were offered from 1933 until 1947. The Model 71 was far more successful, with a total production of 47,254 between 1936 and 1957. The Model 64 was, definitely, in terms of numbers sold, the most successful of the ultimate lever-action variations. A total of 66,783 of all versions of the Model 64 were sold between 1933 and 1957.

Fewer than 1000 were made in 219 Zipper. The Zipper was offered as a prototype in 1937 and was added as a regular production item in 1938. With a serial number of 1,139,292, the Model 64 219 Zipper shown in this article may well be one of the rare 1937 guns.

Townsend Whelen was certainly not the first to propose or design a pistol grip stock for Winchester lever-action rifles. As an example, a deluxe, special-order Model 1894 is pictured on page 22 of the 1951 (5th) GUN DIGEST. The early pistol grip stock shown on this gun displays a shallow, elongated grip curvature; a very low comb; and a narrow shotgun butt. Each of these features are far cries from the NRA/Whelen versions. It is definite that Whelen was surely among the first to combine the improved NRA stock design with the traditional exposed-hammer, under-barrel tubular magazine lever-action rifle. The Models 64, 65 and 71 were thus, in this sense, Townsend Whelen Winchesters.

●

U.S. Repeating Arms Co.
The Adventure Continues

The King of Rifles is Now the Boss!

Model 70 Classic Sporter with BOSS®

No rifle has a reputation like the Winchester Model 70®. Now it can be yours with the optional, patented BOSS™ accuracy device. It's the only way to make one of the world's most accurate rifle designs even more accurate. • BOSS stands for Ballistic Optimizing Shooting System. This breakthrough in technology allows you to actually control barrel vibrations. Instead of tuning or selecting ammunition which is partial to your rifle's barrel vibrations, you tune your barrel to the ammunition. It's an idea so important, some have compared it to the invention of rifling. Three-shot groups well under one inch at 100 yards are commonplace. • The integral muzzle brake offers significant recoil reduction — up to 40% with some calibers. • All this can be yours on new Model 70 Classics with Pre-'64® type action.

> Warning: The BOSS includes a recoil reducing muzzle brake which provides substantial increased noise/muzzle blast. Always wear hearing protection to prevent hearing loss or damage.

WINCHESTER
Rifles and Shotguns
LICENSEE

For more information write for our free catalog: U.S. Repeating Arms Co., Dept. A71, 275 Winchester Avenue, Morgan, Utah 84050-9333.
Winchester, Pre-'64, The Rifleman's Rifle and Model 70 are registered trademarks of the Olin Corporation.

LEARN SAFE HANDLING AND PROVIDE SECURE STORAGE

GUN SAFETY TIPS

- Firearms should be stored unloaded and secured in a locked storage case or cabinet inaccessible to children and untrained adults
- Store ammunition away from firearms
- transport firearms in a locked case in accordance with applicable laws

NEW COLORS!

Firearms Safety Depends on You

Homak manufactures a complete line of home security cabinets, safes and carrying cases.

Homak HOME SECURITY

HOMAK MANUFACTURING CO., INC.
5151 W. 73rd ST., Bedford Park, IL 60638
1-800-874-6625

MADE In U.S.A.

Own an Original.

Hi-Power Standard in 9mm or 40 S&W

Hi-Power Mark III in 9mm or 40 S&W

Hi-Power Silver Chrome in 9mm or 40 S&W

Today's Hi-Power has all the features that made it legendary: machined steel frame, crisp trigger pull, and extraordinary reliability. (Shown disassembled)

Browning Hi-Power.

"The greatest pistol ever!" A lot of people think so. When the first Hi-Power prototype was built in 1923 it was the best, and it has been the world leader ever since. And for good reason.

The original tilt barrel design delivers levels of accuracy and reliable extraction that defy improvement. Dozens have copied it. Even today, you'll see the "Browning tilt barrel" design praised in magazine articles describing the competitions' "new" pistol designs.

The Hi-Power's crisp, single action trigger pull is something today's double actions can only aspire to — and it's a big reason the Hi-Power is standard equipment for many of the world's SWAT and anti-terrorist teams. Having a trigger "like a Browning" is the highest compliment other pistols can hope for.

When pistol shooters compare overall dimensions of other brands, they'll likely say "not quite as trim as a Browning."

Of course, this is the 90s, and a good portion of a pistol can be made out of space-age materials. But when your life is on the line, "machined from solid steel" sounds much more reassuring.

And when you see how easily the Hi-Power design adapts to the modern 40 S&W cartridge you get an idea how much ahead of its time the Hi-Power really was, 72 years ago.

The Hi-Power came from the mind of a genius — John M. Browning — and it remains as near to perfection as any pistol ever will. It *is* the Best. It *is* the Original.

Visit your Browning dealer for a free 1995 Hunting & Shooting catalog.
For $3.00 we'll send you a catalog by priority mail.
Call 1-800-333-3504 to order by credit card, or send payment to Browning, Dept. M34, One Browning Place, Morgan, Utah 84050-9326.
If you have questions on Browning products call 1-800-333-3288.

THE BEST THERE IS.

THE SIG SAUER P 226...
Full-Time Safety, Impressive Firepower

Firepower? When your situation demands maximum firepower, the Sig Sauer P 226 will always deliver. Developed specifically for today's law enforcement officer, the Sig Sauer P 226 can deliver 16, 9mm rounds (21 optional) rapid-fire at outstanding accuracy. Adjustable high-contrast sights provide easy target acquisition even when visibility is diminished.

Safe...Always! The unique multiple internal safety and decocking feature make the P 226 the safest gun you can carry under *any* conditions. The loaded and decocked weapon puts the hammer in register with the safety intercept notch, so firing is possible only when the trigger is pulled.

Leather goods courtesy of Don Hume, Inc.

It is the perfect transitional weapon from revolver to semi-automatic. Now being carried by many elite law enforcement agencies in the U.S. and Europe, it has proven itself to be the most efficient, safe and reliable handgun in the world.

Contact us today for the name of your nearest Sigarms dealer. He's anxious to show you the safest ...and most effective gun you can carry.

SIGARMS

SIGARMS, Inc.,
Industrial Drive,
Exeter, NH 03833

THE SIG SAUER P 226...YOUR TACTICAL EDGE!

THE GUNS OF SUMMER

by PAT DePASQUALE

I HAVE WONDERFUL memories of summer celebrations back in the '50s. The best times were Fourth of July barbecues with too many hamburgers and too much soda and loud, loud fireworks after dark. I remember being very small and sitting next to my parents on bench seats at the high school stadium watching a very good professional fireworks show shot from one end zone. My attention was on the shooting area and the reports of the big guns as they sent their loads up. There was smoke and fire on the ground. Orange muzzle flashes picked out dark figures moving around mysterious cylindrical objects.

They were very obviously not watching the show, nor were their movements coordinated with the ground blasts of the lifting charges or the aerial detonations that flattened the skin against my cheekbones. I was too young to figure out they were lighting timed fuses and proceeding to the next chore while the fuse burned unattended, so their movements made no sense to me.

My mother, when asked who they were, replied that they were fireworks men. I said it would be fun to do that. She said they were crazy and no one in their right mind would go near them. It didn't seem right to me we should be so happily enjoying the work of disreputable lunatics, and I suspected she was overstating the situation.

Jump forward about thirty years. I am standing in a vacant lot with my good friend, Tony Gentile, as he waves a railroad flare over his head to let the crowd of 10,000 know the Independence Day fireworks show we had just set off is over. Our hands are black with soot. Our faces are dirty. Our shirts have many small cinder holes burned in them. The ovation we receive is so unexpected in its length and intensity we feel giddy, maybe a little the way, say, Frank Sinatra would feel on a good night before a good audience. The whole experience does seem kind of crazy, and maybe my mother was right, after all.

My purpose in writing this article is not to tell you why I've worked as a technician at twenty or so fireworks shows (I like anything that shoots), or how this happened (my hunting partner Tony is a licensed pyrotechnician and veteran of hundreds of commercial performances), but to tell you about the biggest, loudest, smokiest guns ever seen outside the military, and how they are used. Pyrotechnic mortars and their shells have elements of muzzle-loading cannon, matchlock muskets and paper cartridges, all things with which shooters are familiar.

The history of pyrotechnics is part of the legendary past of shooting in general. The earliest military use of gunpowder in China was not to injure or kill, but to terrify enemy troops by sound, smoke and flame. The image of battle-hardened Asian troops being routed by a barrage of whizbangs brings to mind the Viking settlement at Vinland being attacked by a still unidentified Native American group called *Skrellings* in the Norse sagas. These locals let loose a pole tipped with what scholar Samuel Eliot Morrison, in his two-volume history *The European Discovery of America*, surmised was an inflated moose bladder, rather like a kid's balloon blown up and let loose to zip around the room. He called it "...a primitive weapon of Skrelling ballistics."

Testimony of the day said it flew over the heads of the men and made a frightening noise when it fell. This terrified the Vikings. Morrison notes that Eric the Red's bastard daughter Freydis ran out undaunted "...bared her breasts, slapped them with a sword, and screamed like a hellcat." This terrified the Skrellings.

I don't quite know what to make of this sequence of events. In any case, projectile applications of powder intended to wound or kill came later.

In China, rockets were popular; these were carried back to the Middle East by Arab traders who called them Chinese arrows. Back in prehistory, before the invention of attorneys, much pyrotechnic display was accomplished with the use of rockets. Rockets can produce all the effects of unpowered projectiles and quite a few others besides, but no one is ever certain that after launch a rocket will not capriciously buzz the crowd of

An 8-inch chrysanthemum from China showing the spherical shell with fuse and appended lifting charge.

spectators, or worse, ground itself in the midst of same.

The Pentagon's fascination with guided missiles is no doubt based on dubious experience with the unguided variety. Even the big boosters of the 1960s race to the moon went awry too frequently. The more humble engineers of night sky color do not try to fight the caprice inherent in rocket effects. The way one puts on an aerial display these days is with mortars, hundreds of them. The thing about mortar shells is that, once launched from their smoothbore tubes, they will not vary a jot from their parabolic trajectory, leaving aside the effects of wind or the unlikely circumstance of colliding with a bird. The ejecta simply go where the gun is pointed, which is a claim no rocketeer can ever make with certainty.

Pyrotechnic shells are cylinders or spheres that contain the aerial effect; appended to the bottom is a paper extension holding the lifting charge into which the fuse is inserted. They are similar in form to the paper cartridges issued to riflemen during the Civil War, except the place of the lead Minie ball is held by a cardboard and paper ball or tube, and a fuse goes into the blackpowder charge. Such shells range in size from 3 inches in diameter up to 10, 12, or even more if the customer can afford it and is willing to pay for them. A 12-inch spherical shell has approximately 70 percent more internal volume than a 10-inch shell, since volume goes up as the cube of linear dimension; so also does weight. Material, labor, and cost all go up directly as volume and weight; in addition, bigger shells are just plain harder to make than smaller ones.

The shells are a loose fit in a bore of the appropriate size, because they must drop into the tubes under the influence of gravity alone. There must be sufficient excess clearance to pass fouling or charred paper bits left from the previous shot. A time fuse of appropriate length extends from the lift into the body of the shell, ensuring a delay of several seconds after ignition before the start of the aerial effect.

That effect often includes a charge of flash powder to produce the characteristic white light followed by a thunderous detonation. Flash powder is more powerful than black, giving a brighter, hotter flame with enhanced report. It seems to me to deliver more energy quicker than its darker counterpart. Other effects have a blackpowder bursting charge surrounded by a shell of chemical balls, each of which will be thrown out radially from the center. These burn brightly with a color dependent on their elemental composition. The commonly

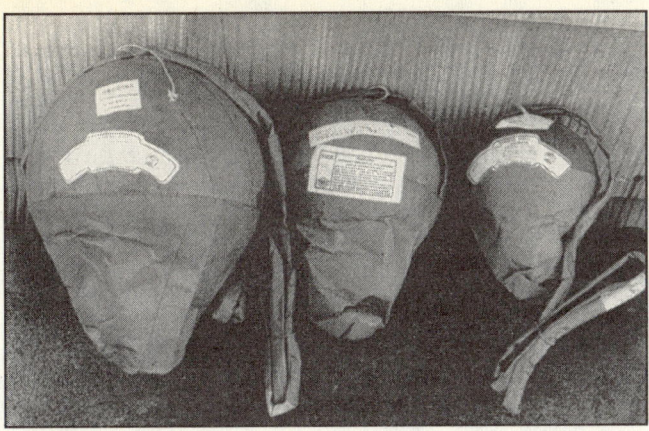
One each of 4-, 5- and 8-inch spherical shells—no metal in them—for lofting by mortar tubes.

A volley of forty 3-inch and five 5-inch guns loaded for a show. Only five out of six 3-inch guns have shells in them.

seen chrysanthemum shells are made after this pattern.

Cylindrical shells frequently have several effects stacked one above the other, linked by timed fuses. These produce a sequence of effects as the shells fall toward earth. Each individual effect is called a "break," and shells are characterized as, say, three-break or five-break shells, as appropriate. A three-break shell might include a shower of red stars at the peak of trajectory, followed by a shower of green stars after a one-second interval, and finally after another pause by a bright white flash and sharp report. This latter effect, a very loud detonation accompanied by a strobe-like intense flash, is the product of a shell called a maroon. All the various effects have linguistically interesting foreign names, but they are too boring to list.

The design and construction of these festive projectiles never includes any metal, and only occasionally soft wooden plugs. Kraft paper, glue and string, along with a little cardboard, are the basic structural ingredients in pretty much every case. This sort of design precludes the formation of metal fragments either in the air, where the shell bursts by design, or on the ground, where a shell occasionally bursts by accident.

Often, fireworks people call lengths of fuse used for various purposes "match," a usage that can certainly be traced back to the early days of firearms in Europe, the time of hand-cannon and matchlocks. The fuse is sometimes handmade using blackpowder, string and heavy paper.

The lifting charge corresponds to the load of Red Dot in your 12-gauge Skeet loads or the Bullseye in a loaded pistol cartridge. It is always blackpowder, of a particularly coarse granulation not available at your local buckskinner mart, and is always measured in ounces rather than drams or grains. The large bores of the guns and low sectional densities of the shells demand a lot of powder to get the payload high enough to detonate without danger to the technicians below. The lift can be lit electrically or by hand-lighting conventional fuses with flares or propane torches. Many old-time shooters used cigars as a source of ignition, but that is considered a backward and unsophisticated practice in the enlightened present.

The guns themselves are various as to size and construction, although pretty uniform as to length, which is generally between about 18 and 48 inches, with length proportional to bore. I have, however, seen long 3- and 4-inch guns, while my friend,

These are 4-inch cardboard guns; behind them is a line of racks trenched and ready for loading a 200-gun finale.

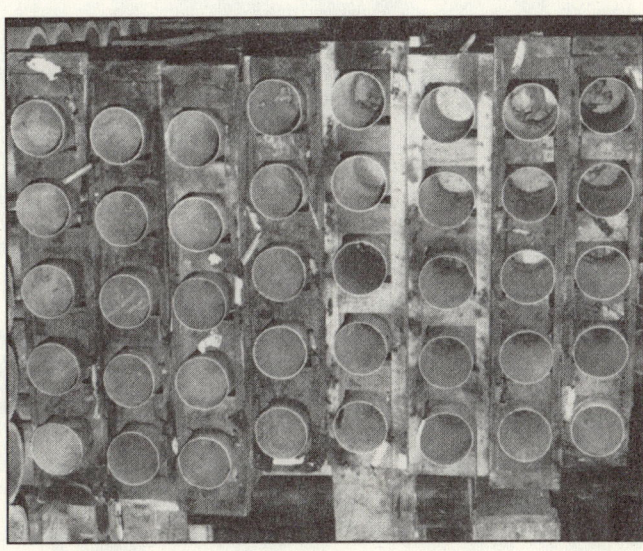
Finale racks of 3-inch sheet steel tubes—fired from dug-in positions.

Tony, has used a short 10-incher. He remembers the roar of the lifting charge from this piece of ordnance with more respect than affection. You could reasonably expect the concussion from a short smoothbore tube nearly a foot in diameter and only a foot and a half long to be memorable, to say the least.

These cylinders are always smoothbores and generally have a breech plug affixed in a manner appropriate to the expected stress. A small bore might have a wooden plug affixed by nails or screws, while a 10-inch steel gun will be pretty certainly equipped with a welded breech plate. The breech is always supported by earth from below, so it is not easy to blow one out.

One of the most interesting aspects of these mortars is the variety of materials from which they are constructed. Some of the tubes I have seen were made up of spirally wrapped cardboard—for all the world like the toilet paper tubes of the gods. Others were heavy-duty PVC tubing, while yet more cylinders were thin steel sheets folded and riveted. The riveted seams of these were designed-in weak points; in the event of failure, the barrel would tear open at the lap joint rather than bursting with the accompaniment of metal fragments.

Some of the largest guns are seamless steel tubes, while others, thought by some to be the best, are non-corroding seamless aluminum. Cast iron tubing is never used since it is brittle and will crack and shatter, producing unwelcome flying fragments. The guns used for the heavier shells are often buried about half their length in the ground and angled into the prevailing breeze. This keeps them firmly in place for sequential loading and firing, absolutely prevents falling over at the critical moment, and helps to contain and more harmlessly dissipate energy in the event of a burst breech.

The effect of pointing the guns into the wind is to let the moving air carry the shells back over the firing area. It is obviously better to have the aerial detonations occur above that cleared space. The dug-in portions of the set-up require a lot of dull pick and shovel labor, although frequently a backhoe is used to minimize wear and tear to our backs.

Several years ago at a local firefighters' charity carnival, we were digging in a show by hand on the bank of a pond, across the water from the midway. A man walking the perimeter stopped near us, watching, and we answered his questions regarding our occupation. In a clear voice having a pronounced British accent, he told us he was a veteran of the Royal Artillery, a survivor of the Dunkirk evacuation, and was much accustomed to the entrenching we were doing. He told us that in his service such trenches were called ground work. He hopped into the ditch and grabbed a shovel, which he plied with the vigor of youth for about five minutes. Then he put down his tool, announced that he now remembered vividly what "bloody hard work" it was, and continued his stroll around the water.

Such digging is not necessary with groups of smaller tubes. They are often firmly nailed up in wooden racks and braced to stakes driven into the ground. At an amusement park on a lake, there is an off-shore barge having semi-permanent mortar emplacements in the form of gravel-filled boxes with tubes in place and wooden rain covers to keep things dry. This is serviced by a rowboat and serves for a weekly display through the season.

Il Sparatore (The Shooter) himself, Anthony Gentile, holding a cluster of 3-inch finale shells and one 8-incher.

A racked volley of 6-inchers, foil-topped against the damp.

An 8- and a 10-inch steel tube, buried and pointed and ready to load.

For the finale of a show, lines of racks, commonly five or six tubes to a rack, are fastened together back to back. Thus, a 200-gun finale may consist of an array five guns wide and forty guns long, all fused in sequence and lit at a single point at one end. Finale racks are loaded before the show begins, but the big guns are often reloaded several times during the presentation. The ammunition for these biggies is held in a covered magazine and handed out to the loaders by a person whose responsibilities include safeguarding the materials in his charge from exposure to any airborne debris.

As mortar barrel material, cardboard, PVC and aluminum share the desirable quality of corrosion resistance. The hefty charges of coarse blackpowder leave more residue than you would believe, and the wildly hygroscopic nature of this soot causes a coating of a substance not unlike badly used motor oil covering the inside of the barrels from breech to muzzle. The steel tubes rust quickly; the fact that fireworks are usually shot during the hot muggies does not help. It is not uncommon for dry stiff fuses to become limp, and sometimes unreliable, on a scorching humid Fourth of July day.

The water-absorbing properties of the propellant create other obstacles to success. Coastal towns like to have their heavenly extravaganzas shot from the ocean beach. There really isn't anything more pleasant than setting off a show from the seaside. It's easy to angle the guns to send their projectiles out over the water. Digging into the sandy beach is a snap. Also, there is plenty of clear viewing room for the crowd, no potentially entangling trees or wires overhead, and often an appreciative flotilla of pleasure boats offshore tooting horns and sirens after especially nice bursts. Unless, of course, the evening fog rolls in and turns the blackpowder in the fuses to licorice Jello. If that does not shut down the act, sending up a test shot will often do it; the fog will eat the most carefully crafted effect, and only a thin flash like heat lightning will reach watching eyes on the ground. Inland show contracts usually provide for a rain date. Seaside towns call for fog dates as well.

My friend Tony likes to call on "Sant' Amedio, il patrone di terra moto" (Holy Amedio, the patron saint of earthquakes) to give his displays the right tone. That is not in any way to disparage the good offices of Saint Barbara, the patron of pyrotechnicians and cannoneers. We need all the help we can get. But safety is never taken for granted, as the consequences of inattention are more horrific than even the consequences of conventional firearms accidents.

Tony and I have between us twenty fingers, four eyes, and four ears that work just fine. That is the result of healthy respect for the medium of fireworks. The shells are pretty heavy, and I guesstimate velocity at 300 feet per second. This feels like a conservative estimate, but I hate to be melodramatic. At that speed, a 1-pound projectile (many shells are heavier, some are lighter, and if one hits you, the difference is academic) has about the same kinetic energy as a 30-30, along with around seven times the momentum.

The probability of death, dismemberment or massive head wound upon impact is high. Shattering injuries ("He broke every bone in his hand") are not exaggerations. The least harmful error (usually) is to load a shell into a gun one size too big. The shot is then a very loose fit in the bore, with the result of greatly diminished pressure from the lift due to gas blow-by. The final result is poor muzzle velocity and a low detonation, too close to the shooters. This is unnerving, but in most cases no damage is done.

Technicians wear eye and ear protection while working. They *never* look into a gun to see why a fuse is hanging fire. During a show, they *never* put any portion of their body, not a fingernail, over the muzzle of a gun whether it is loaded or not. At the end of a show, the guns are pushed or tipped over, away from the clean-up crew, and shaken out to find duds and smoldering material before the loose and racked tubes are cleaned and stowed on trucks for use another day. The sense of this is so common that it need not be elaborated. After all, pyrotechnics is a dangerous business. People get hurt through carelessness, or oversight, or sometimes without doing anything wrong at all.

The fabrication of pyrotechnic devices is an activity so arcane and arbitrary and definite in its consequences that to undertake it except under the tutelage of an experienced commercial master is, well, what can one say? There is no information in this article about size of charge, or wall thickness of tubes, or grade of materials used to make tubes. It is one of my personal inviolate policies, with all due respect to Dr. Kevorkian, never to help a person kill him/herself.

●

by R.J. ROBEL

Best Guns Are

WE HAD JUST scattered a covey while hunting in southeastern Kansas, and my English pointer had a single bobwhite nailed in a ragweed patch. Gun ready, I stepped in and flushed the bird. It flew low and banked sharply as the gunstock came to my shoulder. The right barrel of the little double spoke when it swung through the fast moving bird. My pointer seemed to be smiling as she retrieved the dead quail. Excellent dog work, an exceptional game bird, and a clean kill with a quality gun. A truly gratifying experience.

Factory records reveal that work began on this gun in 1890, and it was probably completed in 1891. I obtained it in 1967—secondhand, of course—from an elderly individual in Forfar, Scotland. It is a Royal-grade 16-bore double-barreled Holland & Holland with fluid steel barrels. It weighs only 6 pounds and is perfectly balanced. The checkering was smooth in places when I purchased the gun, indicating that it had been used over the years, but close examination of the interior and exterior indicated no traces of pitting. The gun was still well within proof, and the bores of the barrels were not marked. The gun had been used, but not abused.

I took the gun to Holland & Holland in London to have the stock refurbished and fitted to me. I also had them open the Full-choked barrels to quarter (Improved Cylinder)

Robel shooting prairie chickens in Kansas with his 12-bore Holland & Holland Royal.

almost glows when a drop of linseed oil is rubbed into it after a day in the field. The sidelocks have an antique appearance that highlights the delicate scroll engraving done by an artisan more than 100 years ago. Those early gunmakers combined the natural qualities of dense walnut with superb metalworking to create a functional firearm of lasting beauty. I relish hunting with this high quality gun because it is a work of art and is an absolute delight to carry and shoot.

"What a beautiful piece of craftsmanship," the admirer comments as he closely examines the deep acanthus leaf engraving on the sidelock of one of my English shotguns. He almost drools as he hefts the gun and pushes the top lever to the right. The tight action opens effortlessly, revealing an unblemished receiver face, crisply cut chambers in chopper lump barrels, and precisely fitted ejectors. Closing the action, the barrels squish back into place.

"It's a beautiful gun," he says, "however, I would rather own a gun that I can use in the field."

"But I do use it in the field," I quickly retort.

"You do?" he responds in amazement. "Why, I would never dare hunt with a gun like that. You must take it out only in good weather."

Such is what I normally encounter when a friend examines any of my best English doubles. A hunting partner of mine owns several shotguns, ranging in quality from an old Franchi semi-auto to a beautiful Skeet-grade Winchester Model 21 left to him by his father. He hunts with the old battered Franchi because he does not want to expose the Model 21 to inclement weather.

That same individual drives a Lincoln Continental. Does he drive that car only in good weather? No, he takes pride in the fact that the heavy car handles well on snow-covered roads and goes through mud like a four-wheel-drive pickup. Admittedly he runs the vehicle through a car wash afterward to remove road grime and mud, and sweeps out the interior quite often. He drives his Lincoln in all kinds of weather, takes good care of it, and doesn't bat an eye.

Why he doesn't take the same approach to his guns has always puzzled me. He believes that using the Model 21 in the field will damage it and reduce its value. He won't even consider using that gun to hunt bobwhites on a sunny day because the stock might get scratched or dented in the process. It's not that he can't shoot well with the gun. He's just afraid to take it out of the house on a hunting trip.

I find that truly a shame. With the exception of some commemorative pieces, guns are built to be used. High-quality guns that are used and not abused will bring pleasure to their owners for many decades. Given proper care, it is almost impossible to wear out a high-quality shotgun while hunting game birds in North America.

Acquiring high-quality guns can be very expensive and even become rather addictive. One must not get carried away. I always ask myself if I can really afford it, and how and when I will put the gun to use before seriously considering buying one. Now we all know it is easy to rationalize buying another gun, but with high-quality guns, you must act within some constraints.

Made To Shoot

and half (Modified) chokes. The chambers were 2½ inches, and I did not have them lengthened to accommodate 2¾-inch shells because I did not want to subject the gun to re-proofing. Obtaining 2½-inch shells in the United States is no big problem, and the 1-ounce loads currently available are excellent for upland gamebirds.

This little 16-bore has become my favorite ruffed grouse and quail gun. The stock is a rich, dark brown that

My teaching salary never permitted me the luxury of ordering a new best gun built to my specifications. Rather, I scrimped and niggardly squirreled away a few dollars each month for several years as I diligently monitored the used-gun market and longingly ogled pictures of fine English guns wherever I found them. It was a long six to eight years between my first deep cravings for a best gun and finally owning one.

That first London-made best gun was a Holland & Holland 12-bore double made in 1900. That gun cost

The Lang & Hussey guns drop doves in style and do so every year.

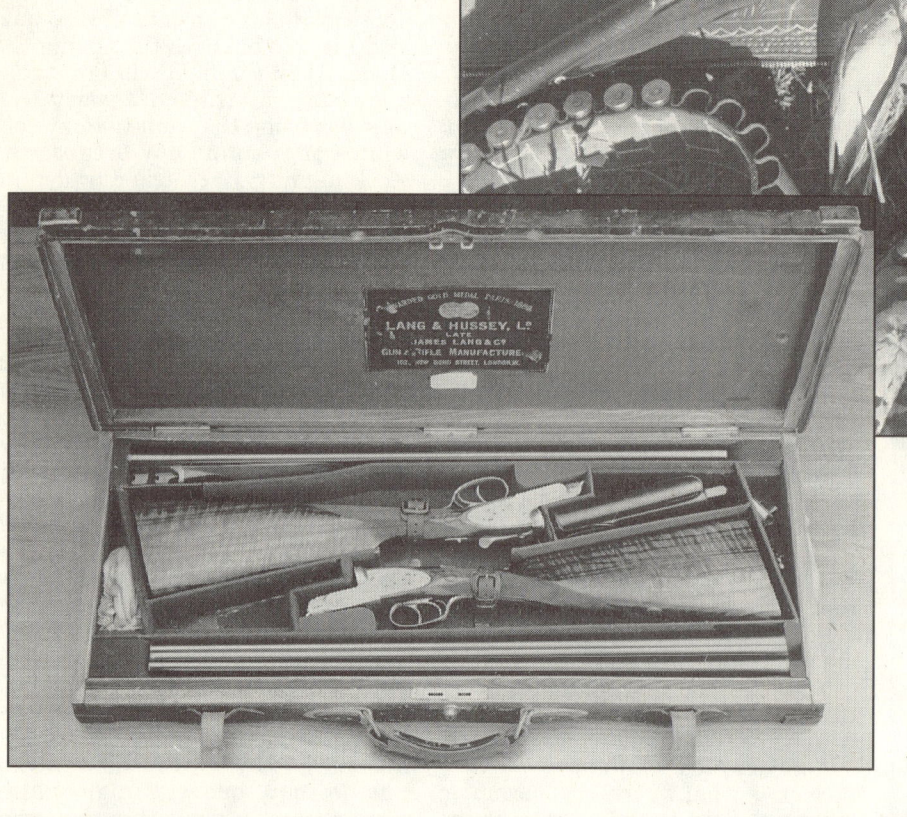

Robel's Lang & Hussey 16s, nicely cased for travel. (Jon Blumb photo)

me less than $500 in the early 1960s, but is worth many times that amount now. The gun had recently been fitted with new 27-inch barrels by the maker. The 2$3/4$-inch chambers with Modified and Full borings suited it ideally for pheasant and prairie chicken hunting in the Midwest, so I bought it. For the first few years, I used that 12-bore exclusively for pheasants and prairie chickens, then I expanded its use to waterfowl, until steel shot restrictions came into being.

My first double weighs 6 pounds, 4 ounces and throws beautiful patterns with 1$1/8$-ounce loads of #6 or #7$1/2$ shot. When I return to a motel after a day of hunting with it, the day is relived as the barrels are caressed with a lightly oiled rag. It's been at least twenty years since I made a right and left on a flock of greater prairie chickens flying into a feed field in the Flint Hills of Kansas, but I still can vividly recall the event.

Eight of us were situated around a 40-acre field of winter wheat, adjacent to a harvested grain sorghum field. We have gathered there for the opening of the prairie chicken season for the past thirty years. Our chicken hunts have become an annual social event, a time to visit and exchange stories. On that day, a distant flock of prairie chickens swung north of our field and disappeared from sight, probably heading to a field of cut soybeans a couple of miles away.

Impatiently, I turned on my swivel seat, searching the horizon for birds approaching. The 12-bore Holland & Holland lay across my lap. It's a Royal model with detachable sidelocks. The surfaces of the sidelocks are fully covered with deep scroll engraving. The French walnut stock is streaked with black grain that gives it a marble-like appearance. The butt has a hide-covered recoil pad, much more aesthetically pleasing than modern rubber pads. A gun of this quality brings visual pleasure like a treasured painting by one of the masters of the middle ages.

My reverie over the shotgun was interrupted when I glanced up to see a large flock—twenty-five to thirty—of prairie chickens strung out across the rosy dawn sky. They were flying over the prairie straight toward our field. Strong fliers, prairie chickens often will travel a mile or more to feed each morning and evening.

Closer they came, and I began to flex my cold fingers. Like a squadron of low-flying World War II bombers, they came to 300 yards, 200 yards, and 100 yards. Excitement peaked and my heart almost exploded when the birds were 60 yards out. I positioned my feet and stood up, the 12-bore brought to my shoulder.

The birds began to veer, but the barrels swung through the lead bird and it crumpled in the shot string of #7$1/2$s. Swinging through a second bird, I pressed the rear trigger and that one dropped from the flock.

That series of events still is etched in my mind. I often visualize the blissfully quiet sunrise and the flock of prairie grouse approaching over the tallgrass prairie as I handle that 12-bore Holland & Holland. If only the craftsmen who worked on that gun at the turn of the century could appreciate the pleasure it is delivering to its owner, some ninety years later.

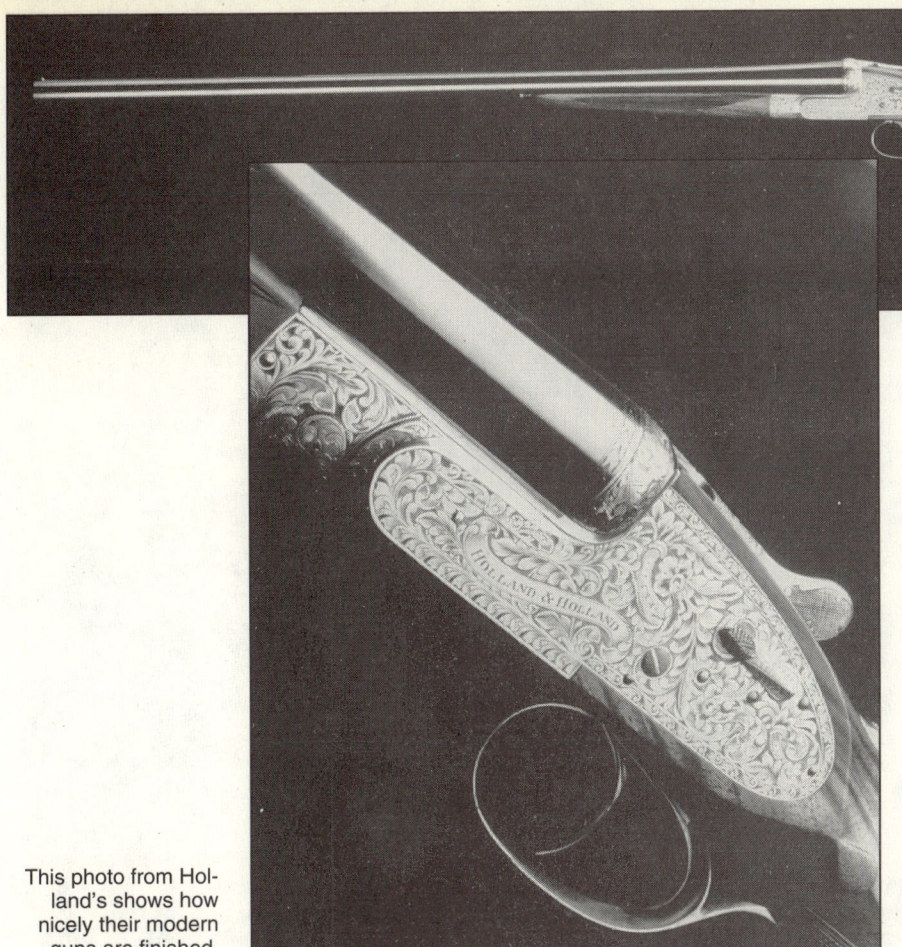

The Holland & Holland Royal gun demonstrates in every line its right to be called a best gun.

This photo from Holland's shows how nicely their modern guns are finished.

Each of my English shotguns has a folio of similar pleasant memories associated with them. Pity the shooter who has a gun with no memories. Quality begets quality, and quality guns will often elevate mundane experiences into cherished ones that will remain with you for many years.

Shooting driven grouse in Scotland generally requires a pair of shotguns. It is a superlative experience known as the "Sport of Kings" because it was cherished and practiced by British monarchs on their well-managed moors during the late 1800s. Gunmakers of England and Scotland quickened the emergence of such driven grouse shooting with the development of reliable and well-balanced, breech-loading, double-barreled, ejector shotguns.

The beauty of best guns blends naturally with the magnificent Scottish scenery, with the light purple of bell heather, and with the dark purple of ling heather. I believe driven grouse shooting provides the most exciting and difficult bird shooting in the world. Quality sport demands quality equipment, so best guns are the norm in the butts of the grouse moors of Scotland and northern England.

I was privileged to be invited to shoot driven grouse in the Highlands of Scotland when I lived there in the mid-'60s. I used my prized Holland & Holland gun and thoroughly enjoyed the challenging sport. However, I felt out of place as I was the only shooter in the party not using a pair of guns. That memorable experience stimulated my interest in pairs of best guns, just in case I might be invited to shoot driven birds again in the future. Thus began a year-long search for an affordable pair, secondhand.

I found several pairs of 12-bore Purdeys, Bosses, and Hollands, but they were all priced far beyond my means. However, I was determined to acquire London-made best guns, narrow selection or not.

After a year of visiting gun shops in many small towns in northern Scotland, I located a marvelous pair of 16-bore best London guns almost by accident in a tiny fishing tackle shop in Dornoch, Scotland, a little village eight or so miles north of Inverness. A highly respected shooter had died earlier in the year, and his widow had brought them in to be sold on consignment. They were Lang & Hussey Imperial Ejector guns in immaculate condition, nestled snugly in a felt-lined,

Anice Robel waits out the mourning doves, her Joseph Lang 16-bore lightly poised.

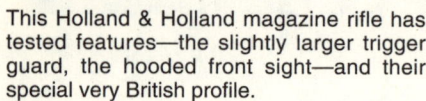

This Holland & Holland magazine rifle has tested features—the slightly larger trigger guard, the hooded front sight—and their special very British profile.

Robel's 244 Holland & Holland Magnum put this Scottish stag down with no fuss—the right tool for the job.

leather-covered oak case. The 12-bore is much preferred in Great Britain, so these 16-bores were not attracting much attention.

I made a ridiculously modest offer for the guns, and much to my surprise, the widow accepted the offer. After having the guns restocked in London to my specific measurements, I still had less than $1000 invested in them. Today the value of that pair of guns exceeds what I would expect to pay for a moderately priced pickup.

Those Lang & Husseys are a fleet pair of guns that add immeasurably to my shooting enjoyment. With 1-ounce loads, they seem equal to 12-bore guns. Actually, I think I shoot more effectively with these than several of my 12-bore doubles because their more compact actions and slimmer barrels just suit me a shade better, and they are now my favorite dove guns in this country. My only problem is deciding which to take to the dove field, Number 1 or Number 2. Even pondering that choice adds to the pleasure.

My wife shares my infatuation with quality guns and relishes using hers when she shoots an occasional round of Sporting Clays or pursues mourning doves with me. Her favorite is also a 16-bore, a best-quality Joseph Lang & Son sidelock ejector double. The gun was built in 1923. Its receiver is trimmer than today's 20-bore Purdey gun, and it weighs a mere 5 pounds, 13 ounces, balanced like a precision gyroscope. Other shooters openly admire that Lang shotgun whenever she uses it.

Two years ago, when we were going through British Customs at London's Heathrow Airport, the Customs official, instead of matching the serial number of the gun with that on her Visitor's Shot Gun Permit, asked if she would assemble the gun so he could handle it. She proudly complied and made the day for that beleaguered civil servant. She glowed as he marveled at the quality workmanship of her favorite prize.

Because of the Lang's light weight, Anice normally shoots $15/16$-ounce loads, but grabs the full-ounce loads when we head for the prairie chicken field. She handles that little double with confidence and lovingly whips a lightly oiled rag over it at the end of a hunting day.

Anice is a therapeutic dietitian and a professional sensory analyst. She relates quality shooting to a gratifying dining experience, i.e., her gun enhances the enjoyment of a shooting experience like a 1966 Chateau Lafite Rothchild Bordeaux red wine accentuates the flavor of a chateaubriand meal.

Best quality is not restricted to shotguns. Just as using high-quality shotguns while shooting game birds increases the enjoyment of that sport, pursuing big game with a first quality rifle contributes immeasurably to a first-rate experience as well. The expansive deer forests of Scotland were developed by the royalty in the late 19th century in the rich Edwardian tradition for their own sporting pleasure and the entertainment of their peers. For me, stalking stags in the craggy Grampian Mountains of Scotland is much more emotionally captivating with a proper stalking rifle than with one of lesser quality. A stalking rifle by a best gunmaker is designed for that specific purpose. The rifle needs to deliver pinpoint accuracy, be able to withstand the harsh weather normally encountered on the Scottish moor, as well as being well-balanced, comfortable to shoot, totally reliable, and pleasing in design.

My two Royal De Luxe rifles by Holland & Holland meet those requirements. Both were built in the late 1950s on commercial Mauser actions and have slimly tapered barrels skillfully inletted into beautiful walnut stocks, sensitive but dependable crisp triggers, elegant scroll engraving flowing across the receivers and floorplates, and Zeiss telescopes that are second to none. These guns provide me a more than comfortable feeling up on the moor.

Stag stalking in the mid-1800s was challenging—it is still today, and superbly enjoyable with a first-quality rifle. One of mine is chambered for the 244 H&H Magnum, a proprietary deer stalking cartridge of the Holland & Holland firm, and the other for the 270 Winchester. Which to use is a question I face each year when I plan a week of stalking in the Highlands.

In 1847, H.M. Queen Victoria entitled the 77,500-acre Mar deer forest to the Duke of Fife and H.R.H.

On the Scottish moorland—the Holland & Holland magazine rifle is chambered for the 244 H&H Magnum cartridge—one shoots from the place and at the animal the guide selects.

Princess Louise, daughter of King Edward VII. I stalked stags on that Scottish estate in 1991 with the 244. The estate's Head Keeper and I had glassed more than fifty mature stags that day before we located one that was shootable. He was a huge beast past breeding prime, but controlled a harem of eighteen hinds. Roaring incessantly, the old boy kept younger stags at bay while his ladies fed leisurely on the lush green heather. Crawling across the treeless moor, we approached undetected and slithered on our bellies through wet heather to within 160 yards of the deer.

I quietly removed the Holland & Holland from its canvas case as the stag repelled the challenge of an immature beast. Resting the slim forend of the rifle on my shoulder bag, the crosshairs of the 1.5-6x Zeiss scope settled just behind the stag's muscular shoulder. The rifle barked and the 100-grain bullet sped unerringly at over 3400 fps to its target. The stag dropped instantly.

"A marvelous killing machine" is how the Head Keeper described the rifle as I ejected the spent cartridge, closed the bolt on an empty chamber, and slid the rifle back into its protective case.

I smiled and nodded my head in agreement.

Do not be nervous about using your best gun in the field, but do be cautious and considerate of its special needs. You would take more care handling and using a Stradivarius than an old fiddle costing $15. Likewise, more care should be taken with a best gun than an old and undistinguished single shot shotgun. Obviously, you do not toss your best gun unprotected into the trunk of your car or suspend it on a gun rack across the rear window of your pickup.

The barrels of best guns are thin and cannot withstand impacts as the barrels of a Winchester Model 12 duck gun can, so treat a high-quality gun with respect. Even a light blow by a sharp object can dent the thin tubes of a best gun and result in a costly repair bill or serious damage to the barrels if not attended to quickly. Always have the gun in a good lined case when transporting it in a vehicle. When I travel long distances, my best guns are protected in the traditional leather-and-oak cases provided by the maker. After I arrive at the hunting location, my guns are carried about in stiff leather cases lined with sheepskin.

If you are staying in a motel, never leave your good guns in the trunk of your car overnight. Take that prized possession inside and make sure the room is secured when you are not inside yourself. It may ease your mind to insure your gun against theft with a short-term floater policy unless it is already covered in some other way.

Check that your hunting jacket does not have metal fasteners to mar the stock of your gun when you are shooting. For instance, the rims of cartridges in exposed shell loops can act like chainsaws on walnut stocks of high quality guns. Carry your spare cartridges in your pants pockets or in a cartridge belt underneath your jacket.

If you go on an extended trip, include gun cleaning equipment in your duffle. I normally don't clean the inside of the barrels of my guns each night unless wet conditions are encountered. However, I remove the barrels from the action and wipe all of the exposed areas of the action and barrels with an oily cloth after a day in the field. Ocassionally, a drop or two of linseed oil placed in the palm of the hand and rubbed into the stock keeps the wood in good condition.

If you have hunted all day in the rain, let your gun dry before you apply oil to it. I simply spread some newspapers on a bed, remove the forend from the barrels and the barrels from the action, wipe the pieces with absorbent paper, and lay them on the newspapers while we have dinner. After dinner, the dry gun parts are lightly oiled and reassembled. Only on rare occasions do I remove the sidelocks from my guns. If they are correctly inletted into the stock by the gunmaker, they will let very little water into the action. A drenching rain is a different matter, and if that occurs, removing the sidelocks is necessary to dry them. Let the locks dry at room temperature and don't oil them too heavily before inserting them back into the sides of the gun.

High-grade guns, I believe, are made to be used, not confined to a dark closet or hidden in a locked cabinet for their life. The dedicated gunmakers who craft the English best guns do so with the intent that the guns will be reliable and serve their owners for decades. I believe it is the owner's responsibility to let the guns prove themselves in the field, to permit the guns to perform their tasks with distinction, and to display the unique craftsmanship that has changed little over the past 100 years. Anybody who owns an English best gun and does not use it regularly is abrogating a personal responsibility and should be horsewhipped. I work hard to keep my English best guns contented. All owners should.

by LAYNE SIMPSON

RIFLE REVIEW

THINGS COST A bit more today than they did 50 issues ago, back when the first issue of GUN DIGEST was published. I don't have that premier issue, but the original owner of the "2nd Annual Edition" in my collection bought it at Sears, Roebuck and Company for $1.25. At least that's what its faded price tag reads. One thing's for sure: I'd like to hop aboard a time machine with my pockets full of today's greenbacks, travel back to those innocent times and buy up every Model 70, every Model 71, every Model 52 Sporter, every Parker and every Winchester 21 pictured on its pages. What would I steal those guns for at back-then prices? I'm not sure because, you see, very few of the guns in the second edition of GUN DIGEST were priced. The reason for that is none were actually available. It was too soon after World War II for firearms manufacturers to even begin to catch up with the demand for sporting firearms. GUN DIGEST number two was nothing more than a wish book full of things that had been and might someday be again. Not so for the fat 50th edition of the same book you now hold in your hands. If you've got the money, you can buy each and every new rifle I'm here to tell you about and more. The good old days actually weren't there and then; they are here and now.

Arnold Arms

Arnold Arms builds super-accurate rifles for big game hunt-

The author and the new American-made stainless steel Weatherby Mark V dropped this Alaska caribou with one shot.

Made by Saco Defense Industries, of Saco, Maine, the new Weatherby Stainless is the first Mark V to be manufactured in the U.S. in thirty-five years.

ing, varminting, target shooting and law enforcement. They are built around the Remington 700, Winchester 70 and Arnold Apollo actions, either right- or left-hand. Most wear Pacific Research synthetic stocks and Hart, Lilja or Krieger barrels.

The Apollo receiver is precision machined from a block of 15-5PH VAR stainless steel, and the bolt, with its integral handle, starts out as a block of E-4340. During machining, the receiver is drilled, reamed and honed, and its locking lug seats are cut and finished by the EDM process rather than by the more common broaching. Chamberings include all the standard options plus the Weatherby-like 257, 300 and 338 Arnold Magnums.

A-Square

Nothing new at A-Square except 338-06 and 358 Shooting Times Alaskan chamberings for Hannibal and Hamilcar rifles, and loaded ammo for both. The latest word I get is A-Square's 338-06 ammo with its 210-grain Nosler Partition produces 2750 fps, while the 358 STA goes 3100 and 3000 fps, respectively, with its 225- and 250-grain Partition loadings.

Briley

Jess Briley makes screw-in chokes and full-length, small-gauge insert tubes of such quality that his name has become a household word to shotgunners around the world. Not quite as widely known is the fact that Jess and crew also spend a lot of their time building custom rifles. In addition to heavy-barrel Ruger 10/22s, they're building super-accurate varmint and big game rifles around the Winchester 70 and Remington 700 actions.

There's a really interesting scope mounting option: Send your rifle and the scope you want mounted and they will dovetail its receiver and make a set of rings that position the scope as low as its objective diameter will allow. Factory rings don't always allow that flexibility because "low" rings are sometimes too low while, at the same time, "medium" rings are a tad too high. Briley's system also eliminates the separate mounting base thereby decreasing gun weight by an ounce or two. More important, inaccessible screws that can vibrate loose are eliminated.

Browning

Biggest rifle news from Browning for '95 is a Low Wall version of its Model 1885 High Wall single shot. The new offspring is 2½ pounds lighter, considerably trimmer and available in 22 Hornet, 223 and 243. Its octagon barrel is 24 inches long, and its buttstock has a nicely curved wrist. What a nice little pronghorn rifle it would be in 243 (and even more so in 257 Roberts, one might observe).

Jim Clark

Jim Clark has long been known among bullseye shooters as the fellow who makes the old Colt 1911 autoloading pistol consistently shoot five 45-caliber bullets inside 3 inches at 50 yards, and he is no slouch when it comes to making rifles perform. His accuracy conversion of Ruger's 10/22 autoloader has made lots of plinkers, small game hunters and competitors in the annual Chevy Truck Team Challenge so happy, they've bought over 2000 of them during the past two years.

Clark recently showed me several half-inch groups he had fired with a Ruger Model 77/22 in 22 Hornet that had averaged 2 to 4 inches with its factory barrel. I could hardly wait to get home so I could send mine to him for the same treatment. The only thing he had done to the rifle was install a new heavy barrel with what he described as a chamber reamed the way it is supposed to be.

Colt

Colt's AR-15 is now available in five basic Match Target configurations. The main difference between the Competition HBAR (heavy barrel) and the Competition HBAR II is a 20-inch barrel on the former and a 16.1-inch barrel on the latter. Both are in 223, as are variants called Match Target and just plain Match Target HBAR. The Lightweight is available only with a 16-inch barrel in 223, 9x19mm and 7.62x39mm. All Colt rifles come with two magazines with five-round limiters, target-style sling and cleaning kit.

Cooper Arms

If I were to put together a short list of those who build the most handsome rifles in the world, Cooper Arms would definitely be on it. Workmanship is as close to perfection as human hands are likely ever to go, and they are using some of the most gorgeous wood I have ever seen. A former Kimber employee, Dan Cooper, started his company by building high-grade 22 rimfire sporters, but his family of rifles has grown to include many variations and calibers. The original Model 36 in 22 LR is still there, but now has plenty of company. There's the Model 40 in 22 Hornet, 22 K-Hornet, 22 CCM, 17 CCM and 17 Ackley Hornet; the Model 38 in those chamberings plus the 218 Bee and 17 Bee; the Model 21 Varmint Extreme in 221 Fireball, 222, 223, 17 Remington, 17 Mach IV and 22 PPC; and the Model 22 Pro Varmint Extreme in 22-250, 243, 308, 7mm-08, 220 Swift, 25-06 and 6mm PPC. Then we have the Model 36 BR-50 in 22 LR; the Model 21 Benchrest in 223 and 22 PPC; and the Model 22 Benchrest in 243, 6mm PPC and 308—all with heavy stainless steel barrels and synthetic stocks.

The many custom options offered on the wood-stocked models include skeleton butt-plate and grip cap, inletted Model 70 Super Grade-style sling swivel studs, checkered bolt knob, quarter-rib with express sights, barrel band-style hooded front sight, and several grades of American and French walnut.

H&R 1871/NEF

There are a couple of new rifle offerings from the dual-named Massachusetts company, both single shots, of course.

In the H&R line, they've updated their ULTRA rifles with laminated-wood Monte Carlo stock and forend with hand checkering, which is practical for a varmint gun. It also looks good. Back in the line is the 223 Remington chambering with a bull barrel. Calibers added to the big game hunting rifles are 25-06 and 308. The latter rifles have cinammon-colored laminated wood, which is attractive; the former have lighter, natural birch. Inside the stocks of both guns rests a high-polished blue barrel and frame.

On the New England Firearms front, the handy Survivor is now available in 45 Colt/410-bore chambering. Barrel length is 22 inches; it's reamed for the 3-inch 410 shell and comes with a choke tube. Stock is a black polymer, modified thumbhole design with storage for extra ammo in the butt and forend. It's available in matte black or electroless nickel.

Hendricks Gun Works

Mark Hendricks' specialty, besides bolt-action big-bore rifles up through 505 Gibbs, is an altogether affordable outfit called the Guide's Rifle. Built around the Interarms Mark X action, it wears a synthetic stock and Shilen barrel, and is available in a variety of chamberings including 338 Winchester Magnum, 358 Shooting Times Alaskan and 375 H&H Magnum.

Ithaca Gun

I recently examined a prototype of an interesting single shot rifle slated for possible introduction by the Ithaca Aquisition Corp (IAC). Called the Model 89, it had a falling block action and Shilen barrel resting in, interesting enough, a one-piece walnut stock. IAC officials say its price should be somewhere in the neighborhood of $700, and caliber options will include 243, 30-06, 7mm Remington Magnum and 375 H&H Magnum. It is an interesting rifle, one that just might make it to production.

Jarrett Rifles, Inc.

Kenny Jarrett is the only gunsmith I'm aware of who will build a custom big game or varmint rifle, accuracy tune it so it will average less than 1/2-MOA before it is shipped, and guarantee the customer it will shoot that accurately. In the unlikely event that the customer is unable to shoot half-inch groups with the rifle, he has the option of returning it for a full refund. As has long been said, you can't beat that with the biggest of sticks.

Jarrett says one reason he is able to guarantee such accuracy is due to the fact that he makes his own barrels. At first they were made exclusively for his own rifles, but he now sells the barrels alone for installation by others. As this is written, available calibers range from 224 to 375, and several rifling twist rates are offered in each. Like Jarrett rifles, Jarrett barrels ain't exactly cheap, but they're the same as most everything else in life: You get exactly what you pay for.

Magnum Research

Magnum Research, Inc., is now the importer of BRNO rifles, except they now go by the name of Ceska Zbrojovka or CZ for short. Made in the Czech Republic, the rugged, no-frills, no-nonsense centerfires have an integral scope mounting base on the receiver and Mauser-style claw extractor. They are available in most standard chamberings, ranging from the 22 Hornet to the 7x57mm Mauser to the 458 Winchester Magnum. There is also the little ZKM452 rifle in 22 LR or 22 WMR. I am particularly fond of the ZKK602 with its dropped magazine, express sights, pure classic styling and 375 H&H chambering. Another Magnum Research import is the BRNO ZKM611, an autoloader in 22 WMR.

MRI is also in the semi-custom rifle business. The action of its new Mountain Eagle is made by Sako and is similar to the one you see on Sako rifles, except its receiver is drilled and tapped for scope mounting rather than having the integral mounting base. The rifle wears a 24-inch Krieger barrel and Bell & Carlson synthetic stock, and is available in 270, 280, 30-06 and three belted magnums—7mm Remington, 300 Winchester and 338 Winchester. The one I shot, a 280, showed its preference for Norma MRP and the Speer 130-grain spitzer boat-tail by averaging 1.27 inches. Second choice at 1.39 inches was the Nosler 140-grain Ballistic Tip seated atop the same powder.

Marlin

In commemoration of its 125th birthday, Marlin is dressing up 2500 of its Model 1895 lever-action rifles with half-round/half-octagon barrel, half magazine, engraved receiver with French gray finish, semi-fancy American walnut stock with cut checkering and curved steel buttplate. To avoid any confusion, I'll mention that, like all current-production Marlin "Model 1895" rifles, this one is actually built around the Model 336 action. For those of us who still appreciate the 45-70 cartridge, this is a must-have addition to the rifle battery.

Also new in the Marlin camp are stainless steel and synthetic 22 rimfire autoloaders called Model 995SS and Model 70PSS Papoose, and the same song in a bolt action called Model 882SS. I like the new Papoose variant. Its price is right, it won't rust or rot, it is accurate enough for its intended purpose—rugged as a tire tool, reliable with good ammo, easy-toting light, floats like Ivory soap when stowed in its padded carrying case—and on top of all that it's a Marlin. What more could one possibly ask of a 22 rimfire priced at less than a thousand bucks?

McBros

Founded in 1992 by brothers Rock and Kelly McMillan, McBros offers custom rifles built around various turn-bolt actions. The typical Hunter Model is on a Remington 700, Winchester 70 or Sako action, available in about any chambering you can think of, including the 7mm STW and 300 Imperial. Chambered only for 50 BMG, the Boomer is on a custom action available in four versions: Single Shot Sporter, Repeater Sporter, Light Benchrest and

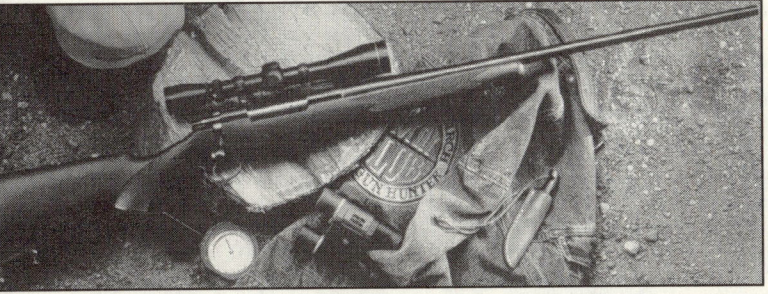

The Mountain Eagle from Magnum Research has Krieger barrel, Bell & Carlson stock and action by Sako. Available in 280 Remington like this one, as well as a number of other calibers.

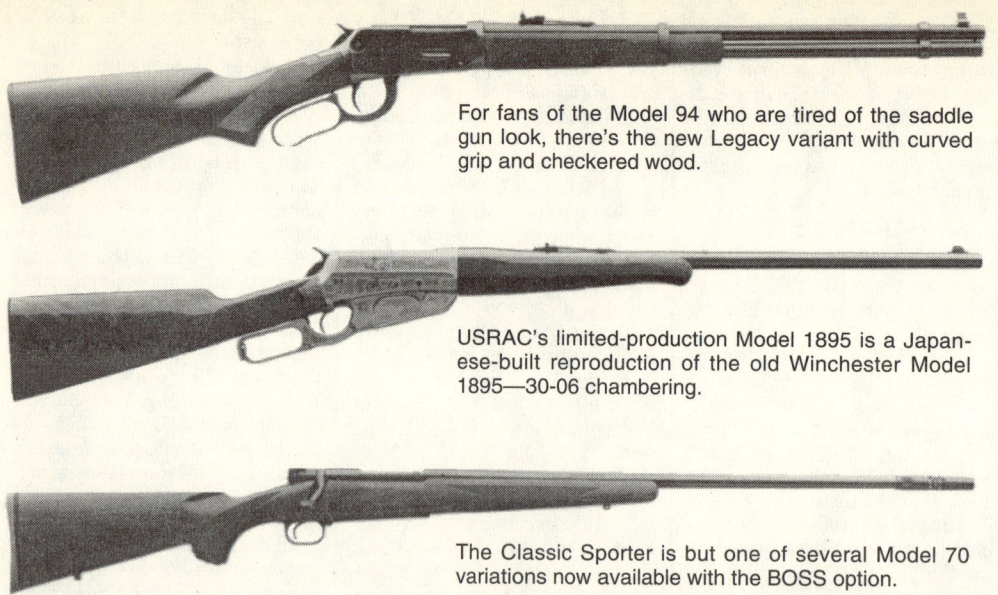

For fans of the Model 94 who are tired of the saddle gun look, there's the new Legacy variant with curved grip and checkered wood.

USRAC's limited-production Model 1895 is a Japanese-built reproduction of the old Winchester Model 1895—30-06 chambering.

The Classic Sporter is but one of several Model 70 variations now available with the BOSS option.

Remington's Model 700 BDL/SS/DM shown here has a detachable magazine, as do the Model 700 Mountain Rifle/DM and the Model 700BDL/DM.

With its medium-heavy barrel and target-style laminated wood stock, the Savage Model 112BVSS Long Range Rifle is just the ticket for deer hunters who sit a lot and walk very little.

Heavy Benchrest. As might be expected, all McBros custom rifles wear the fine McMillan fiberglass stock.

Remington

I have never been sold on the idea of a detachable magazine on a big game rifle simply because of the possibility of the two going their separate ways while I'm on a hunt. I'll have to admit, though, the design of the quick-detach magazine Remington now offers on its Models 700 BDL, 700 BDLSS and 700 Mountain Rifle is the best I have seen. Since recessed, dual-opposed buttons have to be pressed to release the magazine, it is not likely to be accidentally released as the rifle rubs against the side of a pack frame or gets bumped against something in the field. And yet, removing the magazine is a one-handed operation.

Other news from the boys in green includes out with the old walnut stock and in with a new laminated wood stock for the heavy-barrel Model 700 Varmint Special. Calibers are 222, 223, 22-250, 243 and 308. The Limited Edition Model 700 Classic is in 300 Winchester Magnum for 1995, and let's not overlook the new limited-edition reproduction of the 1816 flintlock, the first Remington rifle ever built. It has a 39-inch, 50-caliber barrel, is built by an outside vendor, and its price tag uses up most of a $2000 bill.

Rifles, Inc.

I would never have thought it possible to build a big game rifle around the Remington 700 action that weighs less than 5 pounds until I held one in my hands that was built by Lex Webernick of Cedar City, Utah. Chambered to 7mm STW, the rifle I examined was stocked in fiberglass and had a 26-inch barrel replete with muzzle-brake. Lex starts the program by fitting a relatively thin match-grade barrel to a Model 700 action that has what he considers unnecessary weight removed by various lightening cuts. Examples are a bolt handle that ends up as hollow rather than solid and a deeply fluted bolt body. He then fits the barreled action to an 11-ounce fiberglass stock, absolutely the lightest I have ever held in my hand. What he ends up with is a man-sized rifle with a full-length barrel at a remarkable 4³/₄ pounds. The stock and recoil pad are made in his shop.

Ruger

I received one of the first heavy barrel Model 77/22 rifles in 22 WMR built by Ruger, and it has been great fun to use on prairie dog shoots. Any time I decide to take a break from the muzzle-blast churned up by various centerfires, I reach for the little 22 WMR and start working on pasture poodles inside 150 yards or so of its muzzle. Now the same basic rifle is available in 22 Long Rifle (M77/22VBZ) and 22 Hornet (MK77/22VH). Like my old M77/22VMB, both have a laminated wood stock and a stainless steel barreled action.

I have not shot the new heavy barrel Hornet, but have worked rather extensively with a standard version. With eleven handloads and four factory loads, it averaged from 1.78 to 4.48 inches for five-shot groups at 100 yards. Its best accuracy was with Winchester's 45-grain softnose factory load (1.88 inches), 9.5 grains of H-110 with the Sierra 50-grain Blitz (1.78 inches) and the Speer 50-grain TNT (1.83 inches), and 10.2 grains of the same powder with the Nosler 40-grain Ballistic Tip (1.92 inches). In case you're wondering why the Ruger will stabilize 50-grain spitzers, it has a 1:14-inch twist rather than the slower 1:16 twist which has long been common for rifles in 22 Hornet.

Savage

The old reliable Savage 110 family keeps on growing like weeds. New on the scene is the Model 112BVSS Long Range, which will be appreciated by hunters who sit in a tower blind while awaiting the arrival of that big buck on yon side of a vast soybean field or down at the far end of a Texas sendero. In other words, this one is for hunters who sit a lot and walk very little. It has a laminated wood stock shaped for shooting over sandbags; weighs around 9 pounds empty; has a medium-heavy and fluted stainless steel barrel; and is available in 25-06, 7mm Remington Magnum and 300 Winchester Magnum. It is also available as the Model 112FVSS with a synthetic stock.

The new Model 116US Ultra Stainless is rated at just over 7 pounds and combines a stainless steel barreled action with an extremely handsome walnut stock. The 270 and 30-06 have 22-inch barrels, while those on the 7mm Remington Magnum and 300 Winchester Magnum measure 2 inches longer. Nice rifle.

The 300 Winchester Magnum chambering is now available in the Model 112BTS Competition, and you can now buy the Model 110P Tactical in that caliber, as well as 7mm Remington Magnum and 25-06.

USRAC

Lots of good news from U.S.

Repeating Arms, the company that has managed to keep Winchester firearms alive and well. For starters, since USRAC and Browning are owned by a French government-owned company called GIAT (Groupement Industriel des Armements Terrestres), it comes as no surprise to see the Browning-introduced BOSS (Ballistic Optimizing Shooting System) now available on the Winchester Model 70.

I shot five handloads and five factory loads in one of the first BOSS-equipped Model 70 Classic Sporters built. With handloads, the rifle averaged 1.49 inches with the BOSS removed and 1.61 inches with it installed and dialed to its factory-recommended sweet spot. The most accurate load was 60.0 grains of Winchester's new WMR powder behind the Sierra 130-grain flatbase for 1.18 inches with the BOSS removed and 1.41 inches with it installed. Yep, when digesting handloads, the rifle was more accurate without its BOSS. Factory loads were a different story and averaged 1.95 inches without the BOSS and 1.55 inches with it. The most accurate factory recipes with the BOSS installed was Winchester's Supreme loadings of the 140-grain Silvertip and 140-grain Fail Safe at respective averages of 1.10 and 1.14 inches.

That particular Classic Sporter may be a lucky rifle for me. A few weeks after wringing it out at the range, I took a very impressive 29-inch mule deer while hunting with outfitter Ron Dube out of Cody, Wyoming. A single round of the equally new 140-grain Fail Safe ammo did it.

Also new from USRAC for '95 is "375 H&H Magnum" roll-marked on the barrel of the Model 70 Classic Stainless. With its powerful new chambering, stainless steel barreled action, synthetic stock and Mauser-style extractor, this one is likely to become popular among brown bear guides in Alaska or, for that matter, any place where both game and weather can turn downright nasty. And while I'm on the subject, more Model 70 variations are now available with the pre-'64-style claw extractor. On average, they cost about $21 more than Model 70s with the post-'64 push-feed extractor.

The Model 94 Trapper is now available in 357 Magnum, and for those who are tired of Model 94s with that saddle gun look, the new Legacy variation has a curved grip. Available only in 30-30, its plain, blade-style front sight is dovetailed to the barrel in lieu of ramped and hooded. Also in the lever-action department, USRAC has introduced a Japanese-built reproduction of the Model 1895 Winchester. Basically the same rifle once offered by Browning, it is available in 30-06, and planned production is said to be limited to 8000 units, half in Grade I and the rest in High Grade with fancy checkered wood and receiver engraving quite similar to Winchester's old No. 3 pattern. Such a pity that USRAC didn't do this one up right by offering a Teddy Roosevelt Special in 405 Winchester. My second choice would have been the 35 Winchester. Last but not least in lever guns, the new Model 9422 High Grade with its engraved receiver and fancy wood is, without doubt, one of the most handsome standard-production Winchesters USRAC has ever built.

USRAC's custom shop crew also has a few new goodies for 1995 rifle shoppers. The Model 70 Ultimate Classic has high-grade American walnut with cut checkering; special serial numbers; pre-'64 Super Grade-style sling swivels; hinged floorplate or detachable magazine; round, half-round/half-octagon, or full taper octagon barrel contour options; and hard case. Caliber options range from 243 Winchester to 7mm STW to 338 Winchester Magnum. Due to the fact that orders for the super-accurate Sporting Sharpshooter in 7mm STW have exceeded the custom shop crew's ability to produce them, all other calibers have been dropped from that particular rifle. On the other hand, the 300 Petersen has been added to the list of options for the Model 70 Custom Express.

Weatherby

Back in the early 1940s, Roy Weatherby built custom rifles around several turn-bolt actions, but beginning around 1948, most were on the FN Mauser action. Exceptions were the Schultz & Larson action of rifles in 378 Weatherby Magnum and left-hand rifles built on the Mathieu action. The Mark V action was introduced in 1958, and the first 5000 or so rifles on that action were also built in the United States. J.P. Sauer began producing Mark V rifles in 1959, and that arrangement lasted until the early 1970s when Howa Machinery Co., Ltd., won the contract. Howa built the last rifles for Weatherby in October of 1994.

I said all that to say that Mark V production has come full circle as the rifle is once again being built in America. The manufacturer is Saco (pronounced "Sock-O") Defense Industries, of Saco, Maine. First off the line is the new Mark V Stainless, Weatherby's first rifle with a stainless steel barreled action. I shot one of the first built, a 300 Weatherby; its worst 100-yard average was 1.29 inches with Norma MRP and the Speer 180-grain spitzer, and its best was 1.11 inches with H-1000 and Nosler's 180-grain Ballistic Tip. The latter recipe averaged 2.98 inches for three, five-shot groups at 300 meters. A week or so later, I bagged a nice caribou in Alaska with that rifle and that load. So I say, "Welcome home, Mark V."

With its handsome walnut stock and stainless steel action, the Savage Model 116 Ultra Stainless combines the old with the new.

The Remington 1816 commemorative flintlock has a fancy curly maple stock, Ketland-style lock, deep-cut rifling with a 1:66-inch twist and 50-caliber 39-inch octagon barrel.

Fit a laminated wood stock to the old Remington Model 700 Varmint and you've got the new Model 700 Varmint LS in 222, 223, 22-250, 243 and 308.

H&R 1871's updated Ultra Varmint rifle looks good scoped. It's stocked in laminated wood and can be had in 223.

by SKIP CRINER

Collecting Gun Digest

It could take years to get 'em all

THE 1957 GUN DIGEST represented a goal achieved for me. I now had a complete collection of GUN DIGEST, from 1944 thru 1995. My search for the 49 Holy Grails had taken slightly over four years, at a cost of about $500 for the books themselves. I spent a few hundred more going to gun shows, book stores, and in long distance calls.

In the 1984 GUN DIGEST, the article "How To Collect Sporting Books," written by James Handcock, says "A complete set of GUN DIGEST isn't easy to get, but it's a valuable year-to-year post-World War II history."

It struck me that a complete set of Digests was going to be much harder to acquire with each passing year. And that the information contained in the earlier editions would become a great reference source.

Plus, articles by Col. Whelen, Jack O'Connor, and all the other "kings" of the shooting world would become treasures in their own right. I was hooked, and I felt the timing was very good. I still feel this way.

Actually, my interest in GUN DIGEST goes back to 1982. I had made the mistake of opening a letter from Uncle Sam, informing me that my presence at Camp Gurnsey, Wyoming, was needed for two weeks. As luck would have it, someone felt the best place for a captain in the Inactive Reserve was far away from everyone who knew what they were doing. I became a range officer.

This was the one—the one he was looking for—the last one. He paid $10 straight off.

To while away the hours, I had checked out the 1981 Digest. By the end of two weeks I had read virtually every article in it. I was impressed with the technical data, most of which I didn't understand, but also the recreational articles. It was just an interesting and enjoyable book.

Over the years I found a few Digests in used book stores and at garage sales. Then the night in 1991 and James Handcock's article triggered a course of action that I, for one, am very pleased with.

The Lady claims I'm a pack rat; I prefer to think of myself as a collector. As we finished off the basement, I happened to end up with a small room of my own.

This room now contains most of my toys. A few guns, some reloading equipment and supplies, hundreds of golf balls, books on hunting, fishing, dogs and shooting. There are also two calendars with scantily clad young women on them, who appear to be blessed.

Anyone contemplating collecting anything has to understand some of the basics.

The condition of anything greatly determines its value. I'm still surprised at prices quoted for books that are in terrible shape. Condition is fairly subjective. Avoid books with covers or pages missing. Also, books that have obviously been abused, or that the kids may have used for a coloring book. In my collection, the 1990 edition has the cover creased in two places and I consider this my worst book. The rest are either good or better.

Quantity is another of the basics. If 50,000 items were made, they will be more valuable than a similar product that may have been made in the millions.

I also discovered very early on that calling a bookstore, or a book dealer, is probably the most expensive way to go, and flea markets, swap meets, and garage sales are the cheapest.

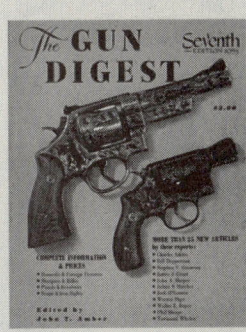

(Above) The author got these three for $165 cash.

(Right) The dealer asked $250 for these six books. The author swapped him a 22 instead.

My best deal just happened to come via a garage sale at which I bought the 1981, '82, and '83 GUN DIGEST for two bucks each. I already had the 1981 edition, but mine was missing the first six pages, so this gave me a chance to "upgrade" the collection.

Used bookstores that don't specialize and gun shows provided most of my books. Gun shows were far and away the best place to find those editions I didn't have. I found that tables where the individuals did not "target" books offered their GUN DIGESTS at much more reasonable prices than those tables that dealt solely in books. Oftentimes, these tables would yield one or two books in the $5 to $7 range.

In my experience, if I were buying more than one book, a package deal was much better than the individual price. I paid $165 for the first three editions (1944, 1946, and 1947) at a gun show in Salt Lake City. If I had paid the individual asking price it would have cost $215. Another package deal I'm proud of involved the transfer of a fine little Voere semi-automatic 22 rifle for the 1949, '51, '52, '53, '54, '55 and '56 editions. I had a total of $125 invested in the Voere, and the dealer wanted $250 for his books.

The last day of a gun show was a better day to buy than the first. Also, if you are buying, dress casually or down. If you're selling, wear your best clothes. The Voere trade actually took two days to work out and happened on the last day of the gun show, with me pointing out how much easier the Voere would be to pack, sell or trade.

Know the market. Call around or write to get a clear picture of the going rate on the books you are looking for. If you are buying books through the mail, make sure there is a review period. It's also wise to discuss the possibility of negotiating the price after you've had a chance to judge the condition of the books for yourself. Don't be shy about pointing out the flaws of a book, or for that matter offering less. The only time I did not do this was with the 1957 edition. The old boy asked $10 for it and I just couldn't bring myself to dicker, simply because it meant too much to me.

I also suggest that you try to establish a working relationship with a local book dealer. Let them know what you are interested in and draw on their experience. It's also nice to ask their permission to use them as a reference when dealing with other book dealers who are out of the area.

When traveling, take time to visit the local bookstores, flea markets and swap meets.

It's a great feeling when you are holding that last book that completes your collection. It's also nice to know that you've done it in such a way that The Lady is still talking to you and the kids have shoes.

Finally, if you've used your head more than your billfold, you should be able to see a return on your investment. (If you choose to do so.) Store your books in a cool, dry place, away from mice and water. Then after the hunting season is over and the guns have been cleaned and put away, take a book down, find a place in front of the fire, and share the evening with one of the kings. Even two, if you're not sleepy.

AFTE IS 25

by C. RODNEY JAMES

As GUN DIGEST celebrates its fiftieth anniversary, another important organization celebrates its twenty-fifth. The Association of Firearm and Tool Mark Examiners grew out of the work of such pioneers as Calvin Goddard, Julian Hatcher and the Gunther brothers in the 1920s and '30s, and has now been with us a quarter-century. Firearms examiners, AFTE notwithstanding, unfortunately get short shrift in the media. "Send that gun down to Ballistics" is the classic throwaway line in hundreds of movie and TV cop epics. "Ballistics," of course, has to do with the properties of a bullet in flight and has little to do with firearms investigation—the process of identifying crime weapons and matching fired bullets and cartridge cases to specific guns—generally carried out by what is more correctly a "crime lab."

Firearms examiners are some of the best friends law-abiding shooters and gun owners have. Through their training, research and acquired knowledge, they stand—often alone—to give voice to otherwise mute evidence by which the guilty are punished and the innocent freed. Many of these technicians came to their vocation through an interest in guns and shooting as a hobby and later as a business.

After World War II, violent crime grew in America, much of it committed with guns. The groundwork for firearms investigation had been laid in the 1930s, but its practical application on a day-to-day basis was much slower in coming. It has to be said that there were charlatans and that incompetence plagued the field of firearms examination from its inception, together with charges from naysayers who would discount the entire

DrugFire is in the first wave of computer ammunition comparison systems, taking much of the drudgery out of comparison work.

field. With the increase in crime and the evolution of criminal science, the need became ever greater for standards of objectivity, as well as the training and testing of potential firearms examiners.

During the 1960s, informal gatherings of firearms examiners at meetings of the American Academy of Forensic Sciences began a sharing of information previously not possible. In looking back to that time, Walter Howe wrote in his message to the twenty-fifth anniversary meeting: "Most of the participants in those *ad hoc* hotel room sessions were members of the American Academy of Forensic Sciences and, as such, received the *AAFS Journal*. The quarterly journal was (and still is today) a scholarly publication. But because the AAFS serves so many forensic disciplines, the pages allotted to firearm and tool mark subjects, while informative, were few—very few. Another reason for the dearth of relevant articles was that many crime lab operations of thirty years ago were more internally contained—indeed, in some cases almost secret. The idea of an operations level examiner revealing the nitty-gritty aspects of his department's techniques, protocols and problems was discouraged by some old-line section chiefs and lab directors."

Still, out of those hotel room meetings evolved a conviction there was a real need for an organization devoted to firearm and tool mark information with its own publication. On a miserably cold February 26, 1969, thirty-four representatives from major state, federal and municipal police agencies, the NRA and the firearms industry gathered in the headquarters of the Chicago Police Department to form AFTE. The organization now has over 700 members in the U.S. and thirty-six other countries. AFTE has published two editions of a glossary of firearm and tool mark terms and 100 issues of its quarterly journal devoted to the technical aspects of firearms crime and its detection.

One hot topic at that first meeting was whether the newly enacted Gun Control Act of 1968 would have a significant effect on reducing gun crime. Howe's original assessment that "the Act was really quite toothless" and unlikely to reduce gun crime significantly has been borne out. Howe has seen nothing to convince him that current efforts at gun control will put firearms examiners out of business.

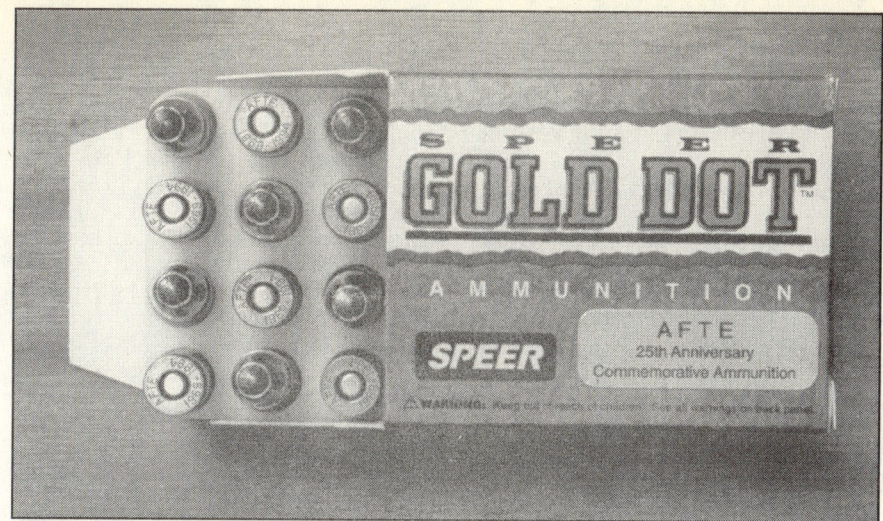

CCI-Speer commemorated the anniversary with a special headstamp—everybody got a box. It says "AFTE 1969-1994."

Richard Graham showed metal detectors which can indicate the type of metal they are picking up.

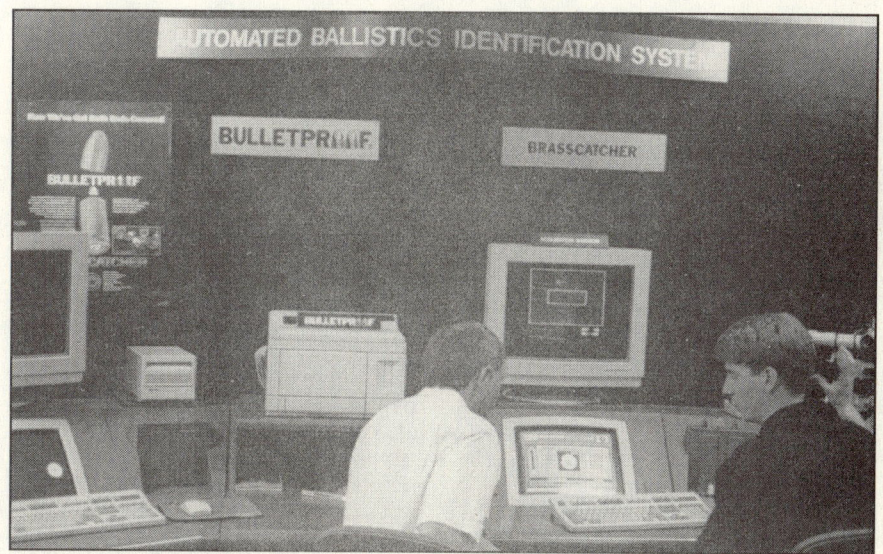

Bulletproof and Brasscatcher are not for reloaders—they're programs to check crime evidence nationwide and all at once.

In many discussions I have had with AFTE members, none expressed support for the belief that gun control is a solution to the violence problem. What I heard was plenty of enthusiasm for catching criminals and applying the new technology to that end.

The six-day Twenty-Fifth Anniversary meeting in Indianapolis in 1994 was hosted by James Hamby, Director of the Indianapolis-Marion County Crime Laboratory. It was a far cry from any sort of sit-in-a-three-piece-suit-till-your-butt-gets-numb experience. Dress was casual; lunches and dinners, except for the banquet, were outdoors.

For those not interested in a golf tournament, the Indianapolis Police Department opened their range for an opportunity to fire a variety of firearms most examiners rarely get to handle, including the Heckler & Koch MP5 submachine gun, a Thompson M1921, a Sten, an M-16, a 308 FN-FAL, a German MG 42 and two tables loaded with assorted foreign and domestic handguns.

The importance of such an organization and the need for it was brought home in presentations over the whole week. The basics of firearms investigation were established by the mid-1930s, true enough, but the application of these techniques has just been revolutionized by computer and video technology. New products in the firearm and ammunition fields threaten to swamp investigators with a mind-boggling array of new headstamps, cartridges and firearms. Increases in gun crime require police to do more with fewer resources at a faster pace.

The most exciting breakthroughs in the field are the new computer programs to make bullet and cartridge case comparisons. Ron Stafford and Bob Sibert of the FBI demonstrated "DrugFire," and later Joe Mason and Mark Potter of Forensic Technology did a presentation of "Bulletproof" and "Brasscatcher"—the first technological wave to break through manual bullet and case examination with a comparison microscope, the method used for the past seventy years.

While the final determination of the match of an evidence cartridge or bullet to a test bullet or case is still done through a comparison microscope, the computer can take an

The author discovered that hitting things with a Thompson was not as easy as the movies would have you believe.

image of a crime bullet and in a matter of seconds sort through a vast number of *potential* matches. Thus can be determined "class characteristics" of land and groove width, rifling pitch, and firing pin size and shape, which eliminates most of the contenders when it comes to determining the make and type of weapon that actually produced the crime bullet or case.

On a more specific basis, in ongoing investigations, images of crime bullets and cartridges from as yet unrecovered weapons can be scanned and matched with a high degree of reliability to new bullets and cartridges as they come in. Even better, independent systems are now in the initial stages of forming computer links over the country for comparisons by departments in different states. With the alarming rise in serial killings, the new system allows instant access by an investigator in one laboratory to the image files of all others on the network. An image of a crime bullet or cartridge from California will soon be instantly available for comparison in New York. The most immediate success of the system, currently available in six states and the District of Columbia, is in making what examiners call "cold hits."

With the ability to do a fast scan of bullets and cartridges, *all* guns found in the possession of suspects involved in *any* crime are now given a testfire and the ammunition components are scanned for a possible match to crimes under investigation. A rapidly growing number of criminals are being caught in this net of "cold hits," where there was no belief or evidence that a suspect in one crime might be involved in another.

As an adjunct to the bullet and cartridge programs at AFTE, the BATF offered a program, on CD-ROM, of computer images of firearms from its collection, providing visualizations of weapons that examiners in small labs may never have heard of, but may someday be searching for. Alex Jason demonstrated how another aspect of computer technology—computer animation—is now becoming a useful tool in creating moving images of reenactments of crimes based on witness testimony.

Ammunition expert George Kass brought books, samples and indispensable knowledge.

Dr. Martin Fackler, Chairman of the International Wound Ballistics Assoc., thumped the medical establishment on gun deaths.

The nitty-gritty of firearm and tool mark work is still at the core of most investigative work and was represented by two presentations on garbage bag identification. Sergeant Todd Reynolds and Michelle Navrotski focused on the use of garbage bags to keep inconvenient body parts from soiling automobiles in the process of disposal. The bags can be matched to others on the same roll through dye patterns and separation marks (tool mark examination) to the undoubted amazement of several convicted murderers.

Luke Haag discussed the effects of the fire-lapping process, described in a recent *Guns & Ammo* article to improve the accuracy of rough barrels, on barrel characteristics—it changes them. But alert investigators can detect abrasive residue in a lapped barrel and still find the occasional matching characteristic.

Accidental long-range shootings are becoming more of a problem as population density increases and were the subject of a program plus an in-depth trajectory workshop that went through the step-by-step process of tracing a bullet back to its firing point. Lasers and soft "bendee" mannequins through which metal rods, simulating the path of a bullet, can be inserted are two of the latest tools used in the craft of trajectory calculation.

Other niche presentations revealed the latest in metal detection, X-ray bullet detection, matching bullets from consecutively made barrels (it can be done), firearm safety designs, lead deposits in clothing, and the mechanics of pen and cigarette lighter guns. There was a new wrinkle in enhancing bullet and cartridge surfaces with magnesium smoke and using mirrors to reverse images for physical matching. P.A. Zigler of the RCMP called his program "smoke and mirrors." Homemade lead shot was traced to a game poacher through its chemical content and form. Marks on bullet cores were matched to those in separated jackets, aiding in determining the numbers of shots and guns involved in a crime. The type of gun used in a murder can be deduced by the muzzle print it leaves on clothing in a contact shot. We even learned that it was possible to get matchable marks from a hole in a plastic truck bed made by a bullet that passed through it.

The constant need for updating the knowledge of ammunition was the contribution of George Kass. His Forensic Ammunition Service provides samples of about everything that goes bang to police investigators who need test ammunition. Kass gave a product review called simply "What's New."

The politics of firearms work received some attention from several angles, befitting the world of political correctness in which we now live. Attorney David Hennessy spoke of the "expert" witness and of the need for good communication between the firearms examiner and the lawyer in a court of law; of the tactics lawyers can use against the examiner; and of the need for clear terminology and consistent testimony. Gene Wolberg spoke of Bull-istics, a call to arms for firearms examiners against media and politically motivated organizations attempting to define national firearms policy and set agendas and priorities for future legislation. Wolberg called for an activist movement to rebut and expose politically motivated "dispensers of illusionary firearms obfuscation, before many of these falsehoods become established fact in case law and in the legislature."

Some polite sparks flew in an exchange between Dr. Stephen Hargarten, representing the public health sector of the government, and Dr. Martin Fackler, president of the International Wound Ballistics Association. Hargarten spoke about firearms deaths as a "public health problem" citing the "tragedy" of 38,000 gun deaths annually as a problem that should be met with a concerted effort of all those concerned with firearms. Hargarten went on to describe the problem in terms of a communicable disease model wherein there is a host (people) and an agent (guns) and an environment (America). His solution was the production of "safer" guns, and to this end used as an analogy the automobile industry and the drive by Ralph Nader and others which resulted in seat belts, air bags and better engineering in automobiles.

Fackler challenged Hargarten to admit that the NRA safety program *had* produced measurable improvements in reducing accidental shootings among children without safety engineering of firearms and gun bans, and Hargarten did. He grilled Hargarten on the 38,000 "tragic deaths," pointing out that if one subtracted felons killed legitimately by police, by citizens shooting in self-defense, drug-related and similar murders of felons by one another, and suicides by elderly white males, this "national tragedy" of 38,000 drops to 3500 to 3800 "truly lamentable deaths" and hardly a national crisis, Fackler believed.

Most sobering was Luke Haag's presentation "First Stones." It is rare to see an organization deal in self-criticism. The talk was preceded by video tapes of court testimony by firearm and tool mark "experts" making statements and claims in courts of law that produced audible gasps and sighs from the audience. Haag's point was that no one is immune from identifying with a cause or position held by one's employer, and that influence can run the gamut from overlooking evidence running counter to an employer's position to functioning as a technician, doing the bidding of an employer. In closing, he recalled principles set forth some sixty years ago by Julian Hatcher who demanded *absolute* honesty and integrity in firearms examination.

Said Haag: "The evidence we examine is not the state's, the plaintiff's or the defendant's, nor is it ours. It is evidence we hold in trust until the court decides to accept or reject it. We do not work for the government, the police, or for any of the attorneys involved. Your credibility and ultimate survival as a true forensic scientist mandates that you work for yourself even though payment for your efforts always originates from some outside source."

It seemed, on balance, perfectly clear to this reporter there were sound reasons why AFTE had reached twenty-five years of age. It also seemed those same factors would see it reach fifty.

by DON ZUTZ

In 1939, there was a gas-operated sporter:

KRIEGHOFF'S PRE-WAR AUTOLOADING RIFLE

WHEN THE LIGHTS went out all over Europe for 1939-1945, the darkness blotted out the first major step toward gas-operated semi-automatic centerfire sporting rifles. The historic piece was made by Krieghoff, then of Suhl, and was virtually unknown then and since. Its only appearance in the U.S. was in 1939 when it was advertised full length in *The Shooter's Bible*, as published by Stoeger, the New York City gun house which had exclusive rights to the gun. The published price was $500, and, obviously, it didn't sell—$500 was a considerable sum in a nation whose economy was slowly struggling back from the Great Depression.

Known as the Krieghoff High Powered Autoloading Rifle, it was billed as "The only high power gas-operated autoloading rifle for caliber .30-06 or any other rimless cartridge." Perhaps that was overstating the case a bit, since the Browning military BAR and the M-1 Garand were already in various stages of development or manufacture. Insofar as sporting rifles went, however, one couldn't argue with Stoeger's advertising. True, there had been an attempt to build an American semi-auto gas-gun back in 1906, the Standard Rifle, but it had malfunctioned on the mild cartridges for which it was chambered (the Remington rimless line) and had failed long before. As a gas-operated sporting arm, the Krieghoff was well out front.

I have never seen a Krieghoff High Powered Autoloading Rifle as illustrated in *The Shooter's Bible*, but I have seen and handled one made in Mannlicher style for the 8x57mmR. As the nearby photos show, this one was embellished in artistic fashion with contrasting walnut and engravings in the deep relief style so famous in Eastern Europe.

The artistry speaks for itself. What isn't so apparent is the mechanical ingenuity that went into the gun. For example, a glance at its loading/ejection port shows 30-06

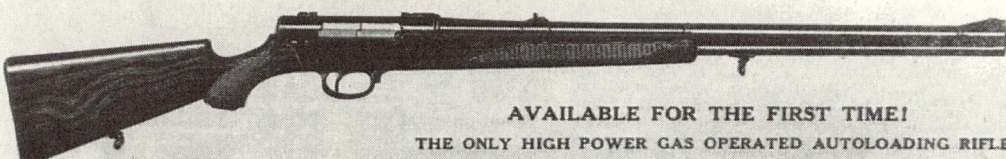

The only pre-war evidence of the Krieghoff's existence was this 1939 advertisement with a listed price of $500. In 1939, that was quite a sum!

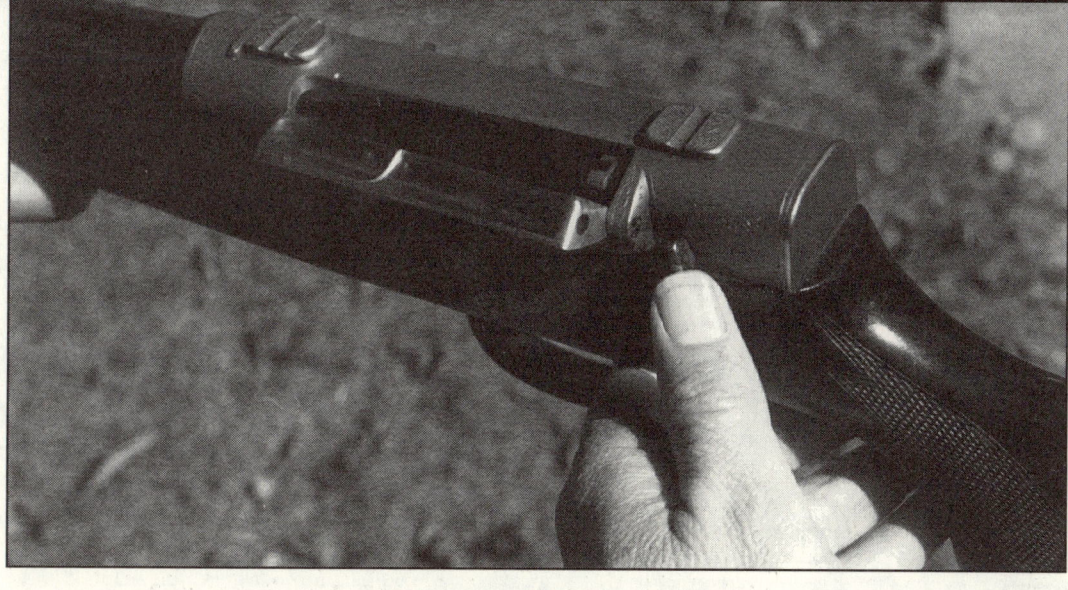

The Krieghoff High Powered Autoloading Rifle's magazine was placed on the left side of the receiver, the cartridges being pushed down after a pivoted cover swings open.

length, but if one allows his eyes to slide backward on the gun, he quickly sees that there is no room for a full-length bolt's rearward travel. Where does the bolt go?

It is a two-part, telescoping design. The rear half of the bolt is merely a shield employed to close the port. It slips over the front half of the bolt assembly as the action bars ram the front half backward. Thus, the bolt doesn't need as much rearward room as it does on, say, the Remington Model 7400 or the Browning sporting BAR.

The telescoping bolt was really nothing completely new in 1939. As early as 1911, Stevens made a 3-inch-chambered 20-gauge pump gun that used a similar, although not identical, method of sealing the port with a two-part mechanism.

The bolting system of the Krieghoff is unique. There are no front rotating lugs or locking blocks. The bolt is secured from below and behind by a sizable steel block that is operated by the travels of the action bar.

A careful look at the Krieghoff uncovers no magazine. The trigger is placed well forward under the receiver, taking up the area where a box magazine would be set. And the gas chamber and action bar occupy the space where a tubular magazine would run. Thus, a new area had to be found for the cartridges. This turned out to be a port on the upper left side of the receiver. The magazine was covered by a thumb-operated lever and required careful hand fitting.

The surplus powder gases vented through a hole under the muzzle. Gases to function the action were bled off near the muzzle, necessitating a long action rod. The rod was supported by a barrel band that also served as a base for the rear open sight as well as being a hanger for a segment of the Mannlicher-type forend.

Access to the Krieghoff's receiver was simple. The entire right side was a big, detachable sideplate. The opening lever is found directly behind the

50th EDITION, 1996 167

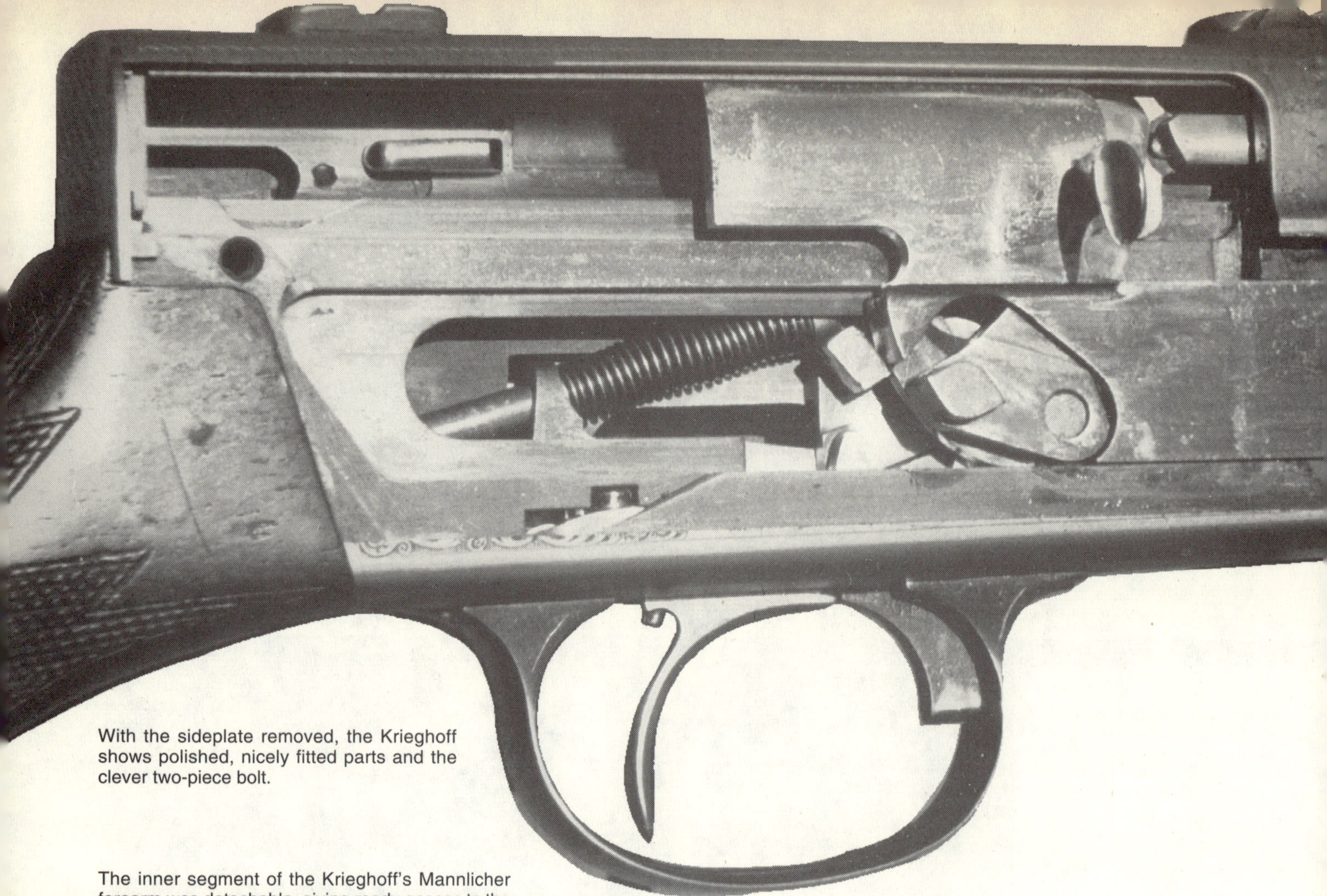

With the sideplate removed, the Krieghoff shows polished, nicely fitted parts and the clever two-piece bolt.

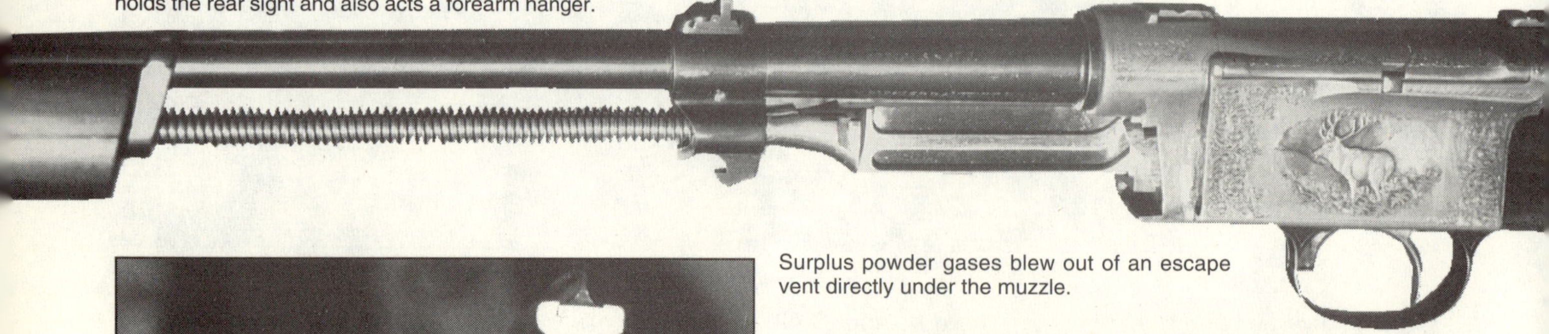

The inner segment of the Krieghoff's Mannlicher forearm was detachable, giving ready access to the action rod. Note that the hanger supporting the rod holds the rear sight and also acts a forearm hanger.

Surplus powder gases blew out of an escape vent directly under the muzzle.

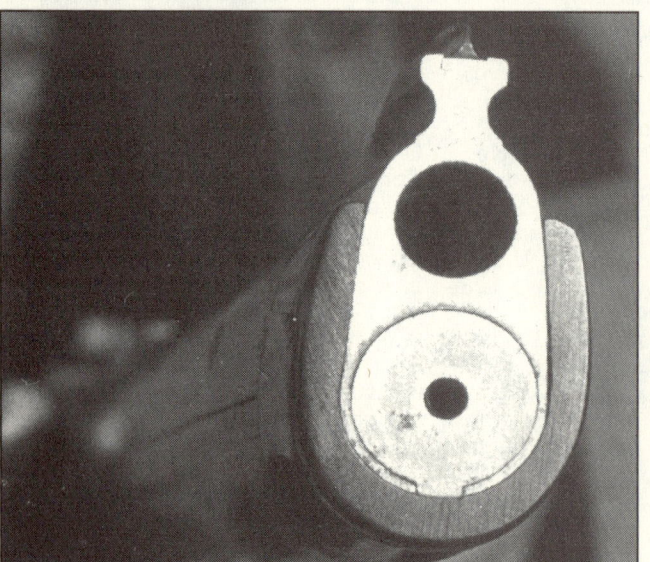

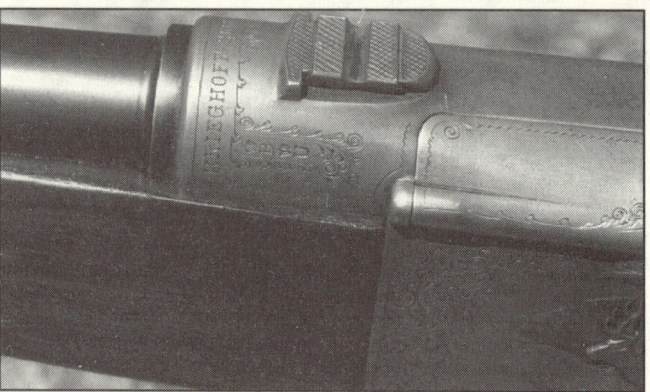

The maker's name was rolled into the leading edge of the receiver. Minor border scroll traced the gun's profile.

(Above) The left side of the receiver showed this stag in Germanic deep relief and somewhat better than average engraving.

The earlier American-devised Standard Rifle failed miserably because it was limited to low-pressure cartridges and jammed with them.

lower rear corner of the ejection port, looking exactly like the screw-type detaching lever on a Holland & Holland sideplated double shotgun or rifle. To complete the fit, the sideplate is beveled on the leading edge to enter a matching bevel worked into the receiver. Thus, the gun can be readily stripped for cleaning or gunsmithing, something which has always been the forte of all sideplated pieces.

The receiver is a satiny gray such as that found on the early Merkels, a finish that was quite common on pre-WWII guns of Eastern Europe. The scroll is bold, albeit geometric, and ranges over the receiver. The maker's name appears just ahead of the forward scope mount. Proof marks dot the area just behind the Krieghoff name.

The game scenes are done in Germanic deep relief for a three-dimensional effect. The right side has a bear on a mountainside; the left shows an elk on a woodland meadow. If the basic Krieghoff High Powered Autoloading Rifle cost $500, one is inclined to ponder the value of this one-of-a-kind gem, then and now!

I was not able to shoot the gun because of a local shortage of 8x57R cartridges. However, the owner has taken some deer with it on hunts in the upper Midwest.

The stock and forend are of French walnut with some contrast. It had apparently been fitted carefully during assembly, then given a traditional hand-rubbed oil finish. The checkering was done to a point pattern, but mistakes were readily apparent. I will never understand why Europeans will make exceptional sporting arms, then cobble them up with, at best, mediocre checkering. Apparently checkering is not a prideful profession in gunmaking, the task being done as a mere necessity to promote improved gripping. Whatever. If it takes machines to perfect checkering, then I am in favor of machines. There is little sense in paying thousands of dollars for a checkering mess.

Regardless of the mediocre checkering, though, the gun is a remarkable item, a true collector's gem. It is not only a period piece and an artistic exercise. This Krieghoff High Powered Autoloading Rifle illustrates gunmaking ingenuity and progress prior to the time when the 30-caliber M-1 Garand seemed to prove (for most Americans, anyway) the feasibility of reliable, gas-operated rifles.

by DON L. HENRY

THE BIG LITTLE MANNLICHER-SCHOENAUER

A RIFLE OF unique design and a cartridge for it appeared in 1900. From Africa to the Arctic, it excelled in extremes. Halcyon days are described in turn-of-the-century literature testifying that the petite Mannlicher-Schoenauer was popular with professionals for hunting the world's biggest game. Many of those fantastic books are in reprint because they are classic; sad to relate, the same cannot be said of the Mannlicher-Schoenauer.

Functional design, ballistic performance, reliability and handling qualities endeared the Mannlicher-Schoenauer to Walter D.M. Bell, a Scot. After a stint in the Boer War (1899-1902), Bell returned to the Karamojo district of Uganda-Kenya to hunt elephants for ivory. Bell took more pachyderms with smallbore rifles than any man before him. He favored a reliable bolt action of short throw and said that his only close call in Africa resulted from a rifle with too much bolt travel.

Bell took tuskers with a 256 Mannlicher (6.5x54mm), which pushed a 160-grain bullet at about 2300 fps. "I once had a carbine Mannlicher-Schoenauer with a 20-inch barrel down to $5\frac{1}{2}$ pounds with a hollowed-out stock that was simply lightning on elephant. I only once failed to kill the animal I fired at with the .256 and that was due to a misfire because of a faulty round."

Vilhajalmur Stefannson outfitted his expedition in 1906 with Model 1903 Mannlichers. During twelve Arctic winters, they served him on the ice in taking fox, seal and polar bear.

Like Bell, Stefansson's only trouble with Mannlichers was ammunition. In *The Friendly Arctic,* he reports:

> Just at this time I suffered a slight injury through an accident with defective ammunition. On my expedition of 1908-12 I used the Austrian 6.5mm Mannlicher-Schoenauer rifle and found it most satisfactory. The advertised muzzle velocity was 2560 feet. For the present expedition I was using the Mannlicher-Schoenauer as remodeled by Gibbs of Bristol, said to have a muzzle velocity of 3160 feet, attained through a considerable increase of the powder charge. I found the Gibbs modification excellent, if the blame for the sort of accident which happened to me September 22nd is put upon the ammunition rather than the rifle.
>
> This day I was sealing and had already killed and secured six seals. When the seventh appeared in the water a hundred yards away I fired but never knew whether I hit him, for as I fired I saw a flash of light and for several days thereafter saw very little more with my right eye. The shell had cracked from the primer out to the edge and about a quarter of an inch up the side. It seems unbelievable in examining the Mannlicher-Schoenauer that powder could come back through the bolt, but it did. The black spots made by it were on my nose and cheek and forehead. They were so conspicuous and hurt so much that I can only explain the slight injury to the eye itself by supposing that it was partly closed and protected. It was about a week before the inflammation disappeared.

Harold Noice of Kansas City hunted with Stefansson:

> Finally, the bear reached a spot nearly opposite us. Stealthily he raised his massive forepaws upon the ice. Then quickly but without a sound, he lifted himself out of the water and in an instant this ferocious beast with its wicked pig-like eyes and yellow-fanged snarling muzzle, was nearly on top of us. Stefansson and I were crouched down behind the sled about three yards apart with only our heads showing. The bear was headed directly for Stefansson, giving me a quartering view. He was coming so fast that he had covered more than half the distance to us when I fired. At the report of my rifle the bear rolled over, turning a somersault towards us before he stopped, for he was going so fast. Stefansson told me to fire again, for our now frantically barking dogs were in danger should the wounded bear turn towards where they were tied. I pulled the trigger, but it would not budge—my gun was jammed. The Commander then used his Mannlicher-Schoenauer and finished the job.[1]

Alexander Lake, in *Killers in Africa,* states:

> At least ten of Africa's best-known big-game hunters, however, preferred a .256 for all game. Those hunters are Buxton, Hodson, Littledale, Loder, Lyell, Millias, Selous, Stigand, Sheldon, and Vanderbyl. W.D.M. Bell, professional elephant hunter, usually used either a .275 (7x57) or a .256 (6.5x54) for bagging big tuskers. Personally, I prefer a military Lee-Enfield .303. If deprived of my .303 I'd be perfectly happy with a 6.5 Mannlicher-Schoenauer and a 160-grain bullet....[2]

Ernest Hemingway immortalized the M1903 Mannlicher in *The Short Happy Life of Francis Macomber.* Whether a Mannlicher was present during the actual event which he fictionalized is uncertain, though not unlikely. Hemingway used a Mannlicher carbine afield and often posed with one; and Bror von Blixen, a Hemingway acquaintance and the white hunter often alleged involved with the affair portrayed in *Macomber,* also favored and was photographed with a 6.5 Mannlicher.

Walter Winans, Colonel Richard Meinertzhagen, Roy Chapman Andrews, Major Powell-Cotton, Blaney Percival, Sir Alfred Pease, Major H.C. Maydon, Percy Madiera, John McCutcheon, Norman "Mannlicher" Smith, Count Vasco da Gamma, and Edison Marshall staked their lives on the Mannlicher's reliability.

The 1910 catalog of Abercrombie & Fitch proclaimed: "This rifle is without question the most accurate and dependable arm for long range shooting and all-around use ever made, and we recommend and guarantee it as such without reserve." Many hunters, whose lives and larder depended daily on their choice of firearm, seconded that judgment.

In June of 1950, big-bore advocate Elmer Keith praised the diminutive 6.5 Mannlicher-Schoenauer carbine and cartridge in *American Rifleman.* He pronounced it "...capable in a pinch of killing all species of North American game." Keith reported "excellent penetration and good uniform wound channel" with the 160-grain softpoint bullet on mule deer, mountain goats, sheep, black bear and bull elk.

William B. Ruger wrote:

> ...The early literature of African exploration and hunting—books

---

[1]Stefansson, Vilhajamur. *Hunters of the Great North.* New York: Harcourt, Brace & Co., 1922.

[2]Lake, Alexander. *Killers in Africa.* Garden City: Doubleday, 1953.

50th EDITION, 1996 **171**

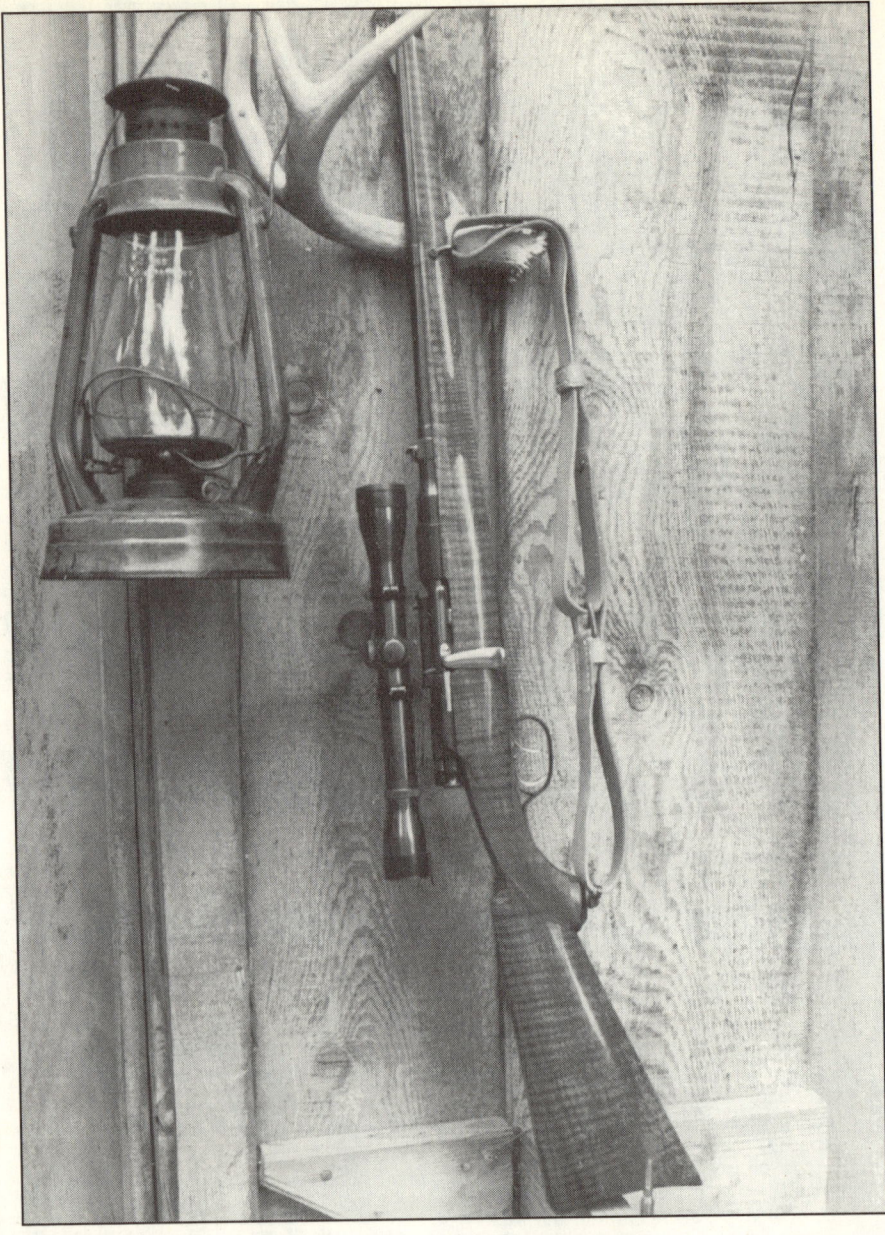

The classic M1903 M-S hangs handy beside the author's cabin door. The rear sling swivel has been relocated to the grip, and it is fitted with a Weaver 4x in Jaeger side-mount.

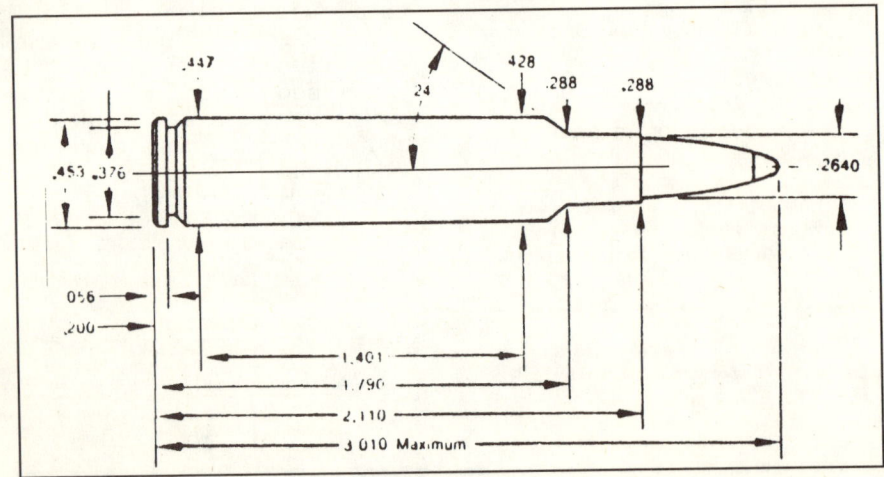

Dimensions of the 6.5x54mm M-S cartridge—right down the middle of the current range of centerfire sporting rifle cartridges. It succeeds in moderation.

which were published around the turn of the century, often illustrated the Mannlicher-Schoenauer as the rifle used in the taking of all kinds of plains game...and they were all universally praised by their owners as handy light rifles with outstanding ballistics....[W]henever I had the opportunity to examine a Mannlicher-Schoenauer, I was fascinated by the smoothness of the action and the fine finish on all the working parts.... [W]hen I acquired an early post-war Mannlicher in 1952, I found it to be exceptionally accurate. In many informal and impromptu shooting contests, the Mannlicher won begrudging praise from some friends like Jack O'Connor, Warren Page, and others who were enamored of their custom built Mauser-type sporters. I didn't stop using the Mannlicher until our Company had gotten into production on the M77, in which I incorporated all the characteristics that my own experience told me would make the ideal rifle.... [O]ur International models have many of the best features of the Mannlicher-Schoenauer, and we certainly acknowledge a debt of gratitude to those old Austrian designers.[3]

Two cartridges are called the 256 Mannlicher. The 6.5x53R (*Rand* for rimmed) fit Models 1891, 1892, 1893 and 1895 turn-bolt straight magazine Mannlichers. Jeffrey, Gibbs and the Steyr factory turned out sporting models based on these Dutch and Romanian actions.

Mannlichers made entirely in Austria were subject to English reproof and were conspicuously marked "Not English Make." Brits do not consistently designate caliber by bore or groove. Metric designations are no more predictable. Rim thickness is included in metric nomenclature or not. With the 256 Mannlicher, however, length measurement does not include the rim. If it did, the round would be a 6.5x54R, as one English ammo manufacturer marked them; nevertheless, it is the 6.5x53R measured to the rim.

English proof law required desig-

[3]Ruger, William B. Unpublished correspondence. October, 1994.

nation of caliber. British-proofed rifles for the 6.5x53R were marked ".256 Mannlicher," those for the 6.5x54 were proof-marked ".256 MAN/SCH." Because case capacities were the same and ballistics were as identical as could be, and since "Two-fifty-six Mannlicher-Schoenauer" seemed a superfluous mouthful, the practical hunter and raconteur called them both "256 Mannlicher." Colloquial short-speak lacked the specificity scholars of later times wish for. No animal knew the difference and the man buying cartridges likely just said "rimmed" or "rimless."

Whatever it is called, both shoot a .264-inch bullet.

Patent drawings of the Model 1900 show it in military configuration. Though military sales models were produced, the Model 1900 was first successfully marketed as sporting rifles and carbines. This fact alone distinguishes the Mannlicher-Schoenauer from all other bolt-action rifles of the period.

Greece equipped her armies with the M1903 M-S rifle and carbine, both in military configuration with full stock and bayonet lug. Modification of rear sight graduations, grasping grooves in the forend, and handguard length define the M03/14. The M15, rarely encountered, had front sight ears similar to the U.S. 1917 Enfield added. The "System 1930" was the last Greek variant and is so marked on the left receiver wall. This M-S is not to be confused with the 1924 FN Mauser in 7.92 which was called "Model 30." Greek military Mannlichers, many of which have been sporterized, some exquisitely so, are distinguished from commercial sporters by absence of the bolt holddown spring. Military Mannlicher-Schoenauers had a round bolt knob.

The combinations of options, to meet every conceivable taste and expectation, are listed in the *1935 Steyr Catalogue*. Besides the requirements for special applications, a great variety of configurations and embellishments was demanded by sportsmen who wouldn't think of ordering a rifle exactly like someone else's.

Österreichische Waffenfabrik Gesellschaft Steyr, the Mannlicher factory in Steyr, Austria, was not inclined to introduce changes to the action mechanism. The qualities which commended M1903 Mannlicher-Schoenauers to the world's hunters remained essentially unchanged from the beginning of production in 1900 to the discontinuance in 1945, and account for near-fanatic loyalty among those who carried the arm afield or who acquired examples merely to grace their gun cabinets.

How much Mannlicher contributed to the design of the M1900 is debatable. Clearly, it is a logical evolution from his prolific work. Ludwig Olson, noted American authority on Germanic arms, states:

> There is evidence that Steyr used his name for the rifle as an honorary gesture...The bolt and receiver of the Mannlicher-Schoenauer owe their heritage chiefly to the German Commission Rifle 88, developed by The Rifle Testing Commission at Spandau Arsenal. Louis Schlegelmilch, a member of the Commission, used several features of the Mauser Rifle 71/84 in designing the bolt and receiver of the Rifle 88.[4]

Ferdinand Ritter von Mannlicher was born in Mainz, Germany, in 1848. Before his death in 1904, he had completed more than 150 working firearms designs, a record of prolific ingenuity which has not yet been approached. The Model 1903 was the final work within his lifetime to bear his name. The 6.5x54 M-S is the only cartridge that was chambered continuously through production of the Model 1900.

In the Schoenauer magazine, cartridges are held by a rotor which aligns them with the bolt and chamber. The claw extractor on the non-rotating bolt head, while not of Mauser length or style, provides the often extolled "controlled feed" from the moment the round is picked up from the magazine until it is ejected. Model '03 Mannlicher magazines are quickly reloaded with a five-round clip charger. Opening the bolt and pressing the release button delivers

This takedown rifle, with folding adjustable tang diopter, was purchased from Steyr in 1937 and cased by James Purdey & Sons. John Rigby and Company subsequently bought it for resale to a client who preferred Mannlichers. It appears unfired.

---

[4] Olson, Ludwig. Unpublished correspondence. December, 1988.

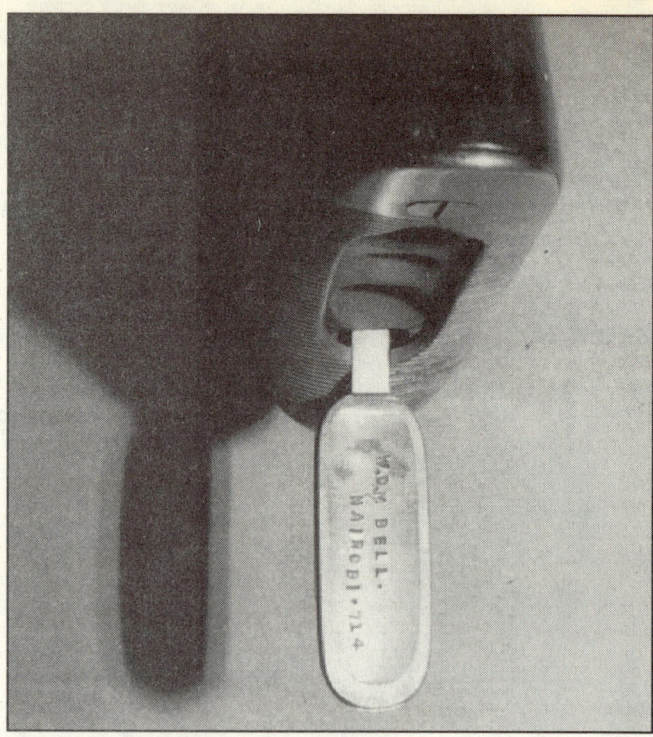

W.D.M. Bell's early round-knob 6.5 Mannlicher-Schoenauer carbine is now owned by Mike Hill, who carries on the tradition by hunting with it.

Bell identified his 6.5 carbine on the butt trap. When telephones came to Nairobi his phone number was 714.

the magazine's contents back into the palm of the hand; a function fast and precise when compared to a hinged floorplate system. Unlike the hinged floorplates common on high-grade Mauser sporters, the Schoenauer system cannot drop its contents at an inopportune moment.

Models 1900 and 1903 were factory chambered exclusively for the 6.5x54mm M-S cartridge. The M1905 was chambered for the 9x56mm M-S, the M1908 fired the 8x56mm M-S, and the M1910 was bored for the 9.5x57mm cartridge, also known variously as the 9.5x56, 9.5x56.7 and 375 Nitro Express Rimless to the Brits. The M1924 was lengthened to accommodate several cartridges, including the U.S. 30-06.

The manufacture of sporting rifles was curtailed in 1939. Some were assembled from parts on hand, and among these were presentation pieces. There are two M1903 M-S carbines in the U.S. which were purportedly liberated from Hermann Goering's collection. Both were made at Steyr in the 1937-38 period. Another M1903 Nazi "presentation piece" was awarded, according to its brass plate, to a minor official for exemplary service in recovering scrap metal. Mannlichers of the Nazi occupation are identified by the legend "Made in Germany," in English, on the receiver ring and, except for the supposed Goering pieces, by a lower quality of finish.

Besides the fact that no pre-war Mannlicher had a swept-back bolt handle and that pre-war models were slow-rust blued, the significant mechanical distinction between the pre-1924 and post-war models is the construction of the Schoenauer magazine. The star rotor separating each cartridge and which prevents bullet battering required extensive machine work on the pre-war models and is a major reason those rifles are difficult to convert to other chamberings. The cartridge rim and bullet ogive rode in a milled recess, and the floorplate was machined to be non-directional (two release holes) in the early magazines.

Post-1924 magazines incorporate a carrier ring eliminating the fore and aft raceways, and simplifying manu-

CHARACTERISTICS OF MANNLICHER-SCHOENAUER
MODELS CHAMBERED FOR 6.5X54MM M-S

Model	Bolt	Safety	Action size	Stock type
Pre-War—1900-1939 (1945)				
1900: 6.5x54 M-S	butterknife, round	wing	very small	carbine, rifle & takedown, w/ butt-trap
1903: 6.5x54 M-S	butterknife, straight	wing	small	carbine, rifle & takedown, w/butt-trap
Post-War—1950-1971				
1950: 6.5x54	flat-top butterknife, straight	wing & side	standard (M1924)	GK rifle & carbine w/plain butt
1950 Improved: 6.5x54	low butterknife, straight	wing & side	standard (M1924)	GK rifle & carbine w/plain butt
1952: 6.5x54	low butterknife, swept back	wing & side	standard (M1924)	GK rifle & carbine w/plain butt
1952 Improved: 6.5x54	low butterknife, swept back	wing & side	standard (M1924)	GK rifle & carbine w/plain butt

Beginning in 1952, stocks employed thicker wood, shadow-line cheekpiece, more checkering, oil finish, and 1-inch swivels. Clip guides were removed and the receiver cut for a side mount. These "improvements" continued in the models MC and MCA through end of production.

facture of the star rotor. The carrier ring added to magazine girth. This "improvement" made it 90-percent easier and *still* extremely difficult to convert the M-S to a different cartridge.

Mannlichers made in early 1950 were structurally identical to the M1924. Soon, a rounded and checkered thumb safety appeared on M1950 cocking pieces. Early single-trigger versions had an integral milled guard bow similar to Greek military models. The "Improved 1950" dispensed with safety checkering and the solid guard, and the rifle had a wider forend and ebony wood tip. Beginning in 1951, both rifle and carbine receivers incorporated a flat for side scope mounting, and the bolt was made closer to the stock to clear a scope. The addition of the scope base plate to the "Improved 1950" required extra wood on the port side. A shotgun-type side safety was added, and the stock cut accordingly.

The M1952 bolt handle was swept back toward the trigger, 1-inch swivels replaced the early 3/4-inch and later 7/8-inch styles, and the stock was again widened to cover thicker sideplate scope mounts like the Griffin & Howe and Pachmayr Lo-Swing. Clip loading ears were eliminated on the M1952, and the bolt thrust was lowered again, permitting still lower scope mounting which was demanded by Americans who did not practice the English and European style of "heads-up" shooting. By 1952, the rifle's ebony forend tip was black plastic.

Some rifles arrived from Steyr stamped "Model 1950." Later shipments bore "Model 1952" to identify the Stoeger-requested design changes. Mannlicher-Schoenauers from this period are encountered which are identical except for the marking "Model 1950" or "Model 1952." Year of manufacture is shown by two digits on the left receiver wall and barrel, so much of the guessing is eliminated.

Stoeger did not change the nomenclature of the M1961 MCA when a tang safety replaced the side safety in mid-1963. In 1964, the receiver ring was drilled and tapped for Redfield scope mounts. Owners wanting to scope the M-S should note that the factory-drilled mounting holes on the left rear split-bridge are of metric thread to fit the original Steyr swing mount. The factory tapped holes on receiver rings of arms intended for the U.S. market are of English thread size. Redfield supplied screws for both with their mounts. Buyers of used M-Ss should confirm that the rear screw holes have not been forced or stripped by incorrect threads.

Some of these differences marked model changes and some did not. Even so, actions manufactured from 1900 through discontinuation are so similar that all are readily identifiable as the classic Mannlicher-Schoenauer.

The Steyr archive, the entire production record of one of the world's largest arms factories, was displaced during the Soviet occupation following World War II. In a letter dated January 19, 1983, the Steyr factory estimated production of Mannlicher-Schoenauer firearms: "Between 1903 and 1971 we produced about 185,000 Original Mannlicher-Schoenauer. More exact figures can't be ascertained because during the war our drawings (records) were lost. Only from 1950 (do) we have exact drawings. These notes say that we produced between 1950 and 1971, 61,120 Original Mannlicher-Schoenauer."

In 1987, the Steyr factory answered an inquiry by stating that more information exists in the Mannlicher Collectors Association's Archive than in Austria. (A sample of *The Mannlicher Collector* journal and membership prospectus is available postpaid for $3; see "Arms Associations.") Data on serial number ranges from Mannlicher Collector Association members worldwide shows that pre-war models had separate serial number ranges. At least 25,000 sporting M1903s were produced.

Factory production seldom reached two digits a day because each M-S required extensive hand labor. Orders for options made many into semi-custom rifles.

Mannlichers are encountered marked by other makers, including Holland & Holland, James Purdey, Cogswell & Harrison, J. Manton, Gibbs, Westley Richards, Alexander Henry, W.J. Jeffrey, and Alexander Martin, all of whom offered their own versions of the Mannlicher-Schoenauer, some with Steyr barrels and others with barrels of their own manufacture. Safari outfitters such as Cearns of India and Charles Heyer of

A picture from *Hunters of the Great North* shows Stefansson "bringing home a seal" with full-stock M-S carbine slung horizontally.

Nairobi ordered Mannlichers to their specifications with their names roll-stamped on the barrels.

Steyr sold directly to gunmakers while John Rigby held the sole English distributorship for Mauser actions which precluded factory-direct purchase of Mausers. Rigby's monopoly on Mausers makes one Model

Guide Chuck Kinkaid with bear hunter L. T. "Tom" Foster, who finds the high cheekpiece of the Model 1956 MC Mannlicher-Schoenauer suited to his shooting style. "You can't outrun them without legs," Tom observed, "so I just hold my ground and drop 'em with my Mannlicher."

Don Henry hunts thick creek bottoms with a 20-inch-barreled Mannlicher-Schoenauer carbine because it is light to carry, fast to fire, and he finds pleasure in a good tool. His standard pre-war 6.5 carbine had a 17.7-inch barrel.

1903 takedown rifle particularly interesting. It was purchased from Steyr in 1937 and cased by James Purdey & Sons. John Rigby and Company subsequently bought it for resale to a client who preferred Mannlichers, as letters from both companies testify. It appears still unfired. The serial number is in the high 24,000 range.

Takedown Mannlichers are variant options available during pre-war production. Each model could be ordered with the take-apart feature for ease of transport. An example of British notions is the Holland & Holland takedown system. In the H&H approach, the barrel and forend were separated from the receiver by threads which were locked in place by the front action screw. These have been encountered both with full and with interrupted threads. The two pieces of different length were usually stored in a fitted case.

The Steyr system permitted the barreled action to be lifted from the stock, retaining the barrel-to-receiver fit which contributes to accuracy. The metal and stock were usually of identical length. A takedown half-stock style fits a 28-inch package with room to spare.

Unlike British makers, Steyr offered no "Best" grade firearms. Regardless of the degree of checkering, carving, engraving or precious metal inlay, the fit and function did not vary. Because Steyr's arms embellishment was a cottage industry, it is not quite correct to call fancy Mannlichers "factory original." Even though Stoeger and Steyr listed engraving options, the work was done "out of house." The owner of a basic model need not worry that the more affluent possessed a functionally superior Mannlicher.

When Steyr-Daimler-Puch A.G. announced new sporting arms designs in the mid-1960s, aficionados of the Mannlicher-Schoenauer were assured that production of the classic would continue. Subsequent correspondence from Steyr refers to a "tragedy" in the factory section dedicated to the Mannlicher-Schoenauer. Presumably, this was a fire. Whatever happened, the old tooling was damaged beyond repair. Delivery slowed in 1968. Components on hand were assembled until, in 1971, the last action was used. Along with the year-long, 2000-mile, one hunter, ton-and-a-half-of-ivory foot safari, gone was the little rifle that did big things.

If You Can't Decide Among All These Finishes, Try This Handy Decision-Making Device.

The point is this: the semi-automatic Desert Eagle Pistol is available in a wide variety of beautiful finishes. And no matter which finish you choose, the Desert Eagle gives you the unparalleled stopping power that has made this gun famous.

In .357, .44 or .50 Magnum, the Desert Eagle packs awesome firepower while being comfortable to shoot and easy to control.

Ask your dealer about the Desert Eagle Pistol, its many finishes and other options, and the informative (and fun) Magnum Research video.

You can order the new, 20-minute video directly from Magnum Research for $15.00 (plus $2.00 postage and handling).

The Desert Eagle Pistol. Smart looking, smart shooting.

Invented, patented and marketed by

Magnum Research, Inc.

7110 University Avenue N.E. • Minneapolis, Minnesota 55432
(612) 574-1868 • 1-800-772-6168

CAN A HANDGUN LIVE FOREVER?

You can bury Glock in sand. Submerge it in water. It'll still come out firing.

A pistol is a tool, pure and simple. And people don't buy pistols to pamper them.

That's why the durability of Glock firearms takes on a special significance. And the reasons for that durability take on a special importance in deciding whether Glock is the pistol to buy.

There are very few parts in a Glock. So it follows, fewer parts wear out or break. About those parts that do exist: the polymer frame is durable, lightweight and helps reduce recoil. It can't corrode. Sweat and salt water have no effect whatsoever.

The steel slide on a Glock is Tenifer treated. It can't rust. The barrel features hammer-forged rifling. This provides you with smoother surfaces. And that gives you far better accuracy, increased projectile velocity and added strength. It is all but impossible to blow that barrel up.

And any Glock pistol can be broken down, cleaned and reassembled quickly with one simple tool.

All this engineering and craftsmanship work together to assure Glock owners that their Glocks will perform at precisely the moment they need them. Even if it's the kind of moment that seems to last forever.

This Glock 17 has fired more than 347,000 rounds.

You'll find hammer-forged rifling in the barrel. You get better accuracy, higher velocity and added strength.

This is the complete Glock armorer's kit. It's all you need to break down and reassemble any Glock pistol.

The Tenifer finish on the steel slide is virtually as hard and strong as a diamond.

GLOCK PERFECTION

©1995 Glock, Inc. PRINTED IN THE USA

After the military's 3000 round torture test,

only the Mossberg 590 survived.

The Mossberg Model 590 took everything that the U.S. Military could throw at it.

When the military buys shotguns, they don't go to the local gun store and buy off the rack. They select production samples from the manufacturer, then do everything they can to break them or wear them out. They freeze, bake and drop the guns, then they punish them with 3000 rounds of hard-hitting 00 buck shot. The test to meet milspec Mil-S-3443E requirements has chewed up and spit out every shotgun tested except the Mossberg 590. And they continue to perform this test on every lot of Model 590s we deliver.

We build every Mossberg 590 to exceed military requirements, even yours.

Why should you accept anything less than mil-spec toughness in the defense shotgun you rely on? With the Mossberg 590 you don't have to. You get the same features because you get a shotgun made to the same specs. Dual action bars, 9-shot capacity and tough synthetic stock. You can choose blued finish, corrosion fighting Marinecote™ or Parkerized finish.

You get one important feature that the U.S. Military doesn't get, a Ten-Year Limited Warranty.

In addition to proven mil-spec toughness, every shotgun we build is backed by Mossberg's Ten-Year Limited Warranty. Military tests prove that you can spend more, but you can't buy a better defense shotgun. Nobody tests shotguns harder than the U.S. Military and nobody backs their pump guns better than Mossberg.

The Mossberg Model 590

Mossberg Shooting Systems™ are always in season.
O.F. Mossberg & Sons, Inc. • 7 Grasso Avenue • P.O. Box 497 • North Haven, CT 06473-9844

© 1995, O.F. Mossberg & Sons, Inc.

Safety and safe firearms handling is everyone's responsibility.

"Simmons Whitetail Classic is earning the reputation for being brighter and working harder than most of the more expensive scopes. Feature for feature, they perform as good as or better than a lot of scopes that cost twice as much. In fact, most of the hunters that I have talked to, who own Whitetails, swear they shame the "big buck" scopes."

LARRY WEISHUHN — Professional Wildlife Biologist & outdoor writer. Known as "Mr. Whitetail".

Everyday we hear comments like Larry's, and we sure do appreciate them. Our goal has always been to produce the brightest scopes possible at affordable prices.

A good example of Whitetail brightness is our 50MM model. It gives you a sharper image in low light situations because of its extra-large, camera-quality objective lens, and it has multi-coated optics like all of our Whitetail Classics®. Each model is waterproof, fog and shockproof.

They are all beautifully styled and feature a handsome Whitetail medallion on the saddle. Eight models come in Simmons exclusive BlackGranite® finish. It's rugged, non-glare, and good looking.

We make eleven Whitetail models in all, so that you can get the scope that best matches your rifle and your type of hunting.

We also make two compact wide-angle Whitetail Binoculars (8x25 and 10x25) that match our BlackGranite scopes. They are rubber-covered, have camera-quality BAK4 multi-coated optics and a Whitetail medallion on the bridge. There's no better binocular choice when size and weight matters.

Simmons also makes other popular scopes like the 44 MAG® and ProHunter® series. So when you're looking for a great "low-light" scope, be sure to look at Simmons. Riflescope Headquarters.

Simmons Outdoor Corporation 201 Plantation Oak Drive, Thomasville, Georgia 31792.

"If you can find a scope this bright for less money, jump on it."

SIMMONS
Riflescope Headquarters™

The In-Line MUZZLE-LOADER In HISTORY

by DOC CARLSON

The Paczelt single-barrel flint in-line in the Tower of London Collection. (Photo credit: The Board of Trustees of the Royal Armouries)

In November, 1957, Clark Frazier cradled his winning in-line rifle on the cover of *Muzzle Blasts*.

IN THE LATE 1800s, the muzzle-loading firearm went out of general use and was replaced, as every schoolboy knows, by the "modern" breechloader. The new guns, while not necessarily more powerful, were more efficient and, with the brass cartridge, certainly faster to load.

The key word in the opening line is "general." Muzzleloaders remained in use among those who couldn't afford anything else, were more comfortable with the familiar muzzleloader or simply preferred the old guns for traditional and historical reasons. In many backwoods areas, the muzzleloader continued to hold a place of honor among hunters and target shooters.

In the late 1920s and early 1930s, there was renewed interest in shooting the old frontloaders. The new group was relatively small, but dedicated. They would get together, locally, for target shoots and rifle frolics. The guns used by the majority then were original firearms that had been handed down for generations or found gathering dust in some attic. The few newly made guns in use were, without exception, handmade replicas of the traditional guns that

50th EDITION, 1996 **177**

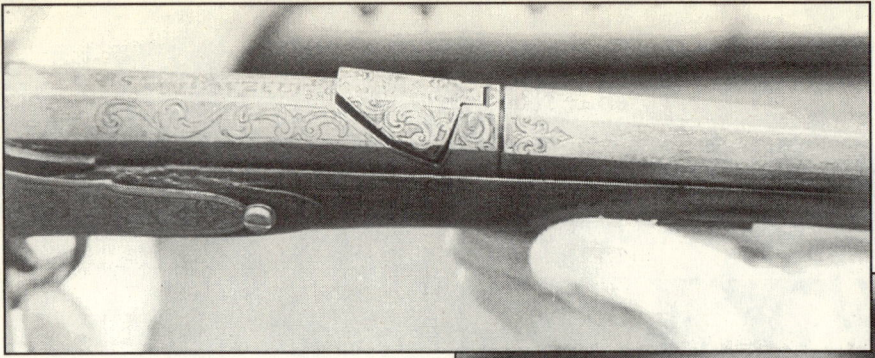

The Paczelt in-line flintlock did not expose much of the lockwork to the elements. The trapdoor you see is the frizzen.

The flint in the Paczelt went straight ahead, driven by a coil spring, to strike the frizzen and pop it up. That's the touchhole you see.

everyone else was shooting. A few craftsmen had kept alive the old skills attendant to gunmaking as it was done in the early days of Colonial America.

After World War II, with the return of thousands of GIs and a newfound prosperity, hobbies began to occupy important places in American life. And muzzle-loading was one of those hobbies. By the 1950s, Dixie Gun Works and a few others had begun to import new guns and gun parts for this market. With the approach of the Civil War Centennial, even more guns were imported by newly minted companies, such as Navy Arms Company and their reproduction of a Colt Navy percussion revolver. This was no flood of firearms, but the imports helped to foster interest in shooting and hunting with guns the founders of this country used. All the new muzzleloaders were either direct copies of traditional guns or reasonable facsimiles.

During and after the Civil War Centennial, from 1961 to 1965, interest remained high. Clubs were formed all over the country bringing together like-minded individuals who enjoyed competing with and studying antique muzzle-loading firearms. There were still a limited number of reproduction firearms available, and many shooters were building their own guns out of parts available from several mail-order suppliers.

Then, in the early 1970s, something remarkable happened. A small and relatively unknown company up in Rochester, New Hampshire, brought out a mass-produced, reasonably priced muzzleloader. While the form of the new rifle followed the traditional rifles, it was designed to be produced on automated machinery, taking advantage of the most modern manufacturing processes—including investment casting. The Hawken rifle made by Thompson/Center Arms Co. had arrived.

Deeply involved in the muzzle-loading sport by that time, I remember very well the hue and cry that immediately went up from the shooters of traditional guns. Cries of, "This will ruin the sport" and "It's a sacrilege and an insult to the old guns" were heard throughout the land. The main fear was that this would get many who were not sufficiently history-oriented into the muzzle-loading sport, and it would then deteriorate into something the present shooters would not recognize or be happy with. In other words, the new Hawken would somehow affect the "purity" of the sport. A similar feeling was engendered in the archery people by the introduction of the compound bow, as I recall.

What actually happened was that the Thompson/Center Hawken triggered a remarkable growth of the sport which led to the vast interest in shooting and hunting with muzzle-loaders today. Far from being detrimental, it was a tremendous shot in the arm for muzzle-loading.

We are now seeing a similar revolution in the eyes of some. Brought on primarily by the intense interest in hunting with muzzle-loading arms, there has come on the market a new, non-traditional-looking type of rifle. They are called, collectively, "in-lines." Their actions provide a striker or hammer that hits the percussion cap along a horizontal line similar to firing pin travel in a modern bolt-action rifle. Stock styling is also like the bolt-action big game rifle. And the same hue and cry has again been heard through the land. The fear is, once more, that the in-lines, being a modern invention, will somehow spoil the purity of muzzle-loading hunting.

How new and radical are these in-line guns? Are they a modern invention? Does the lack of a sidelock and external hammer render them non-traditional and unclean? Are they more powerful and more accurate than the traditional-looking gun?

If we look back at relatively recent history, in-line target rifles were in use at the National Muzzle Loading Rifle Association Championships in

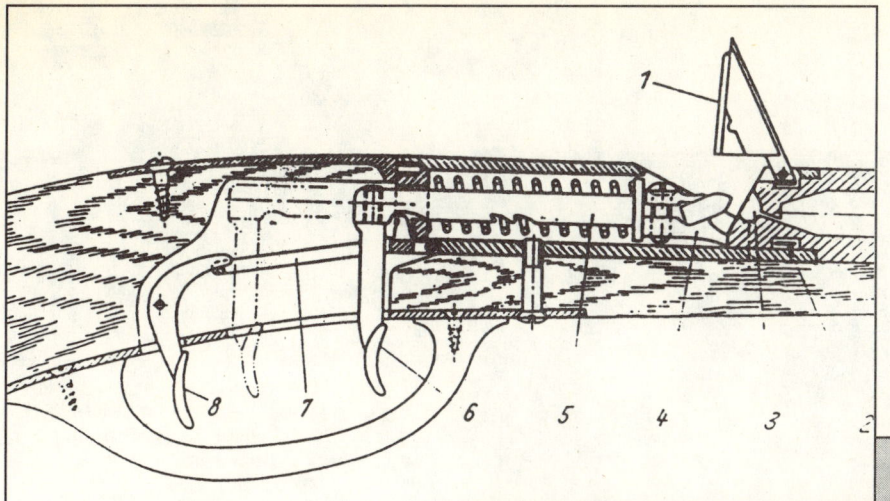

Except for the ingenious flintlock system, this schematic of a Paczelt could be used to build a modern percussion in-line rifle.

The Paczelt is plainly marked No. 11, which seems to take it out of the one-of-a-kind category.

Friendship, Indiana, in the 1950s. This was before the introduction of most of the reproduction *traditional* guns of today. A 1957 cover photograph on the NMLRA's magazine *Muzzle Blasts* shows one of these rifles in the hands of one of the top shooters, Clark Frazier. So this "new" action type is certainly not an invention of the 1990s.

In 1814, an English (and French) gunsmith named Jean Samuel Pauly obtained a patent for an "apparatus for discharging firearms by means of compressed air." This in-vention used a horizontally acting striker assembly that, when released under spring tension, compressed a small volume of air with such rapidity that it generated enough heat to ignite gunpowder, thereby firing a gun. Now, think about that. In 1814, someone had figured out not only how to build an in-line type of action but understood the principles of the diesel engine!

Remember that, historically, gunsmiths were the mechanics of society at the time. It was these craftsmen who developed many of the mechanical contrivances. In fact, the vast majority of the machinery developed for manufacturing in general, and mass production in particular, was developed by the gunmaking industry, especially in America.

On the other hand, it was the medical profession that did most of the innovation and development in the chemical field. It was a doctor who invented the percussion cap at about the same time that Pauly patented his "diesel" firing gun. It would be a very short step from Pauly's original patent to its use to fire a percussion cap.

The horizontal shaft or striker principle was not new even in Pauly's time. The crossbow uses a similar action, if you look at the arrow or bolt. No, the principle was well understood.

The Tower of London collections in England contain many odd-ball firearms inventions. There are many in-line types of firearms dating from the percussion era. Given my previous statement that the gunsmiths were the mechanical inventors, it's not surprising that there are so many in-line variations exhibited in the Tower collections. The vast number of such firearms becomes mind-numbing after a while. Also, among the many very early firearms inventions are several repeating firearms, both revolving and magazine types, to prove that there is little that one can think of with which some gunsmith hasn't already toyed.

The in-line star of the Tower collections is, however, not a percussion or diesel in-line. It's a little earlier than that. It's a flintlock with an in-line action very similar to the percussion hunting rifles being made today.

The firearm is a well-made, top-quality gun that was fabricated for someone of means. It shows many years of mishandling, but the quality and beauty of line show through its age. It is a sporting arm with a 33$^1/_2$-inch smoothbored barrel, 57-caliber. The lock mechanism is contained in an octagonal housing that is a continuation of the breech and is the same size as the barrel. The jaws of the cock are fitted to the end of a rod operated by a coil mainspring. The rod is connected to a cocking lever in front of the trigger in the trigger guard. The frizzen or battery is formed by a wedge-shaped section of the housing which fits flush with the outer surfaces when closed. When the lock is fired, the jaws push forward under spring tension and the flint strikes the sloped surface of the frizzen. The frizzen is pivoted upward exposing the pan, which is fitted into the rear of the breech and contains the touchhole.

The gun, which is of fowler design, is half-stocked with brass furniture. The wood on either side of the lock housing is reinforced with brass sideplates which are nicely engraved with a boar and stag hunt, respectively. The brass trigger guard is engraved with a floral design.

The gun was made by a Bohemian

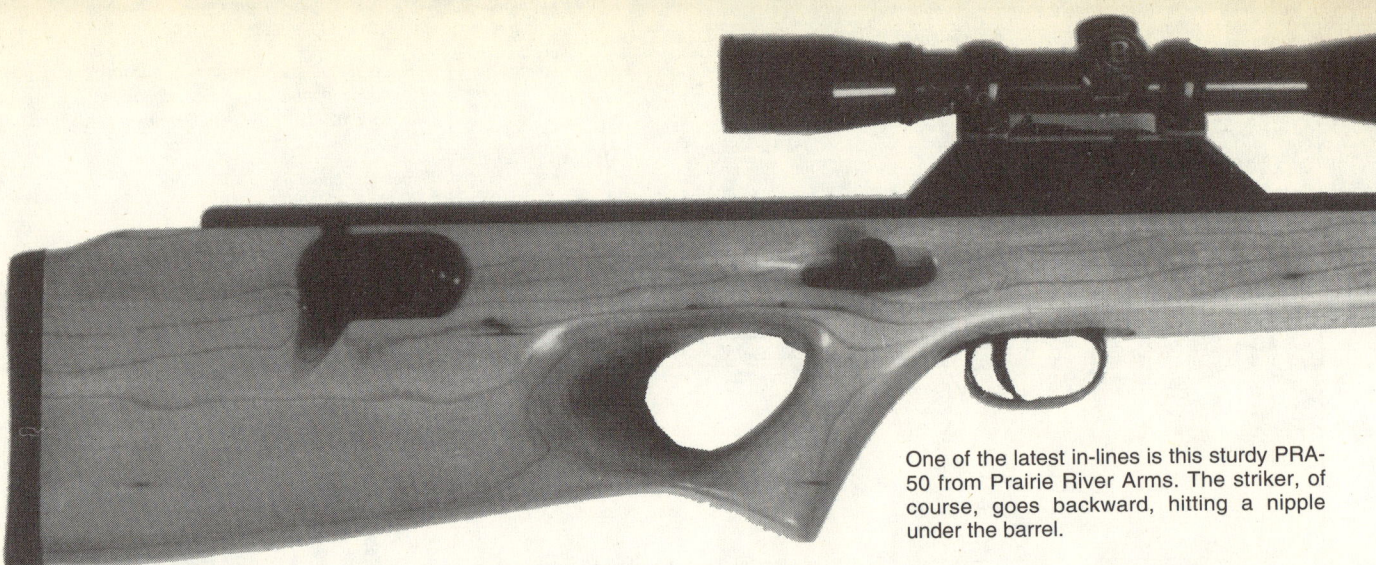

One of the latest in-lines is this sturdy PRA-50 from Prairie River Arms. The striker, of course, goes backward, hitting a nipple under the barrel.

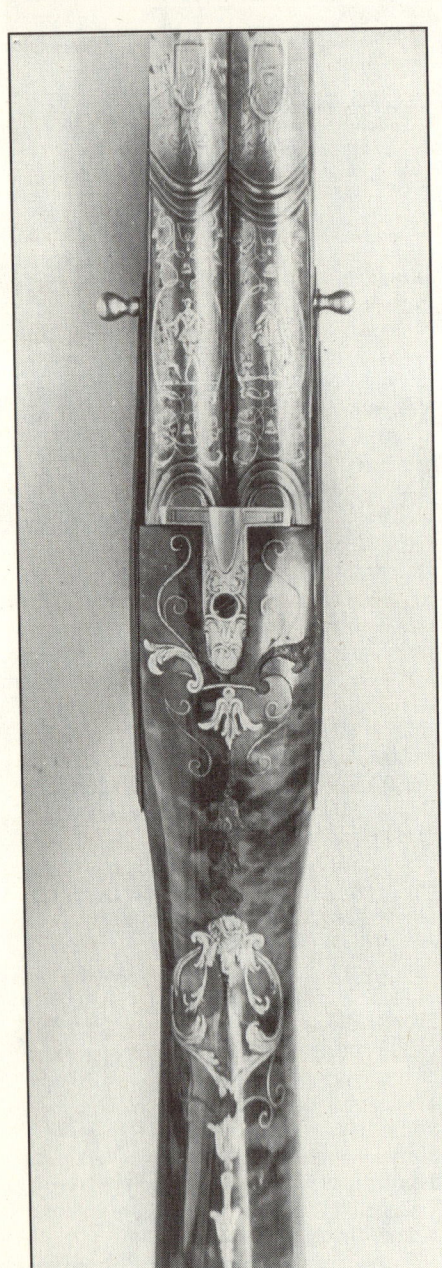

gunmaker named Stanislas Paczelt and is dated 1738! Early enough for you? It gets better. Let me quote from the Tower of London folks: "This form of lock construction is associated with the maker Stanislas Paczelt, whose name appears on the majority of the weapons of this type which have been preserved. It is improbable, however, that he is the inventor, since weapons of a very similar design by other makers and of earlier dating are known."

So, this is obviously not a rare, unheard of and one-of-a-kind gun. They *were* probably uncommon. There are also earlier specimens known. It does seem that these guns appeared sometime around 1730 and were, I would imagine, expensive.

The other example of such guns that I have found is in the German National Museum in Munich. This gun is a double-barrel side-by-side. The barrels are approximately 35 inches long, 57-caliber and smoothbored. This gun differs from the previous one in that the lock mechanism uses small knobs on each side to hand-cock the locks. The internal mechanism is nearly identical to the Tower of London gun, and the use of the cocking knobs was necessary with the side-by-side action. Two triggers and two cocking triggers would have been a bit much to include in the trigger guard. The locks are tripped by individual triggers, similar to double barrel guns of all periods.

The Munich gun, unlike the Tower of London one, is in almost unfired condition. The stock is beautifully veneered with tortoise shell and has extensive silver inlay work. The metalwork is heavily engraved and inlaid also. Obviously, this gun was also built for a very well-to-do

The flint-fired in-line double in Munich's Bayerishces Nationalmuseum is in nearly as-new (and deluxe) condition. (Photo: Bayerisches Nationalmuseum)

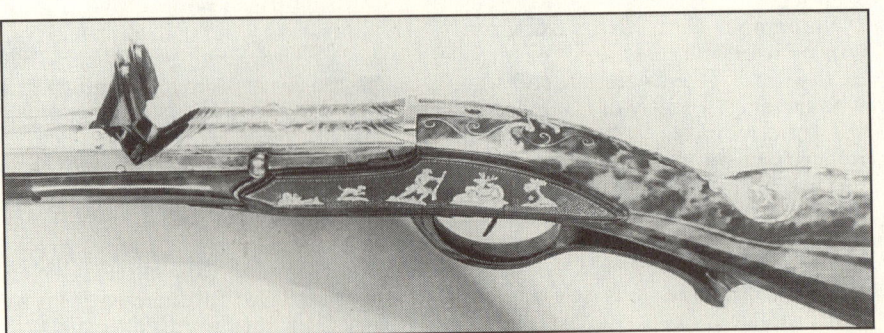

Shown here with the frizzens popped up, the flintlock in-line double in Munich blazed a sleek trail not many followed.

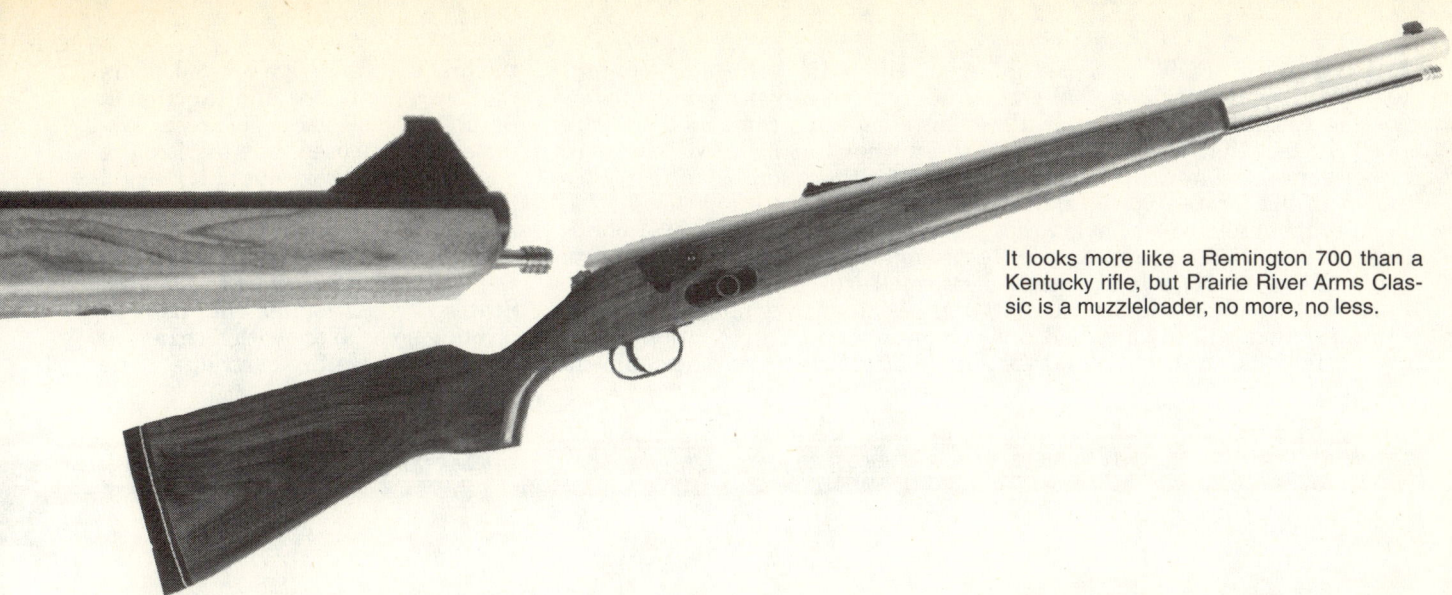

It looks more like a Remington 700 than a Kentucky rifle, but Prairie River Arms Classic is a muzzleloader, no more, no less.

person. The gun is German and dated about 1740. It is unsigned, leading me to believe that the maker was probably someone other than Stanislas Paczelt.

Of particular interest to students of the in-line action is the fact that both guns utilize almost the exact action design and components used in the modern in-lines. While these are flintlock in ignition, the action is the same. They both utilize coil springs, which according to many, were not invented until the early days of the industrial age. It shows the importance of doing your research before making any sweeping historical statements.

While the in-line flintlock was certainly well ahead of its time and very ingenious, it obviously didn't catch on and become the common arm of the 18th century. A couple of reasons for this are apparent. First, this type of firearm was, no doubt, expensive, probably well beyond the reach of any but the most wealthy. Second, and probably more important, the flash and gas coming back through the touchhole and spraying into the action would have made the cleaning of it a real chore, probably entailing total disassembly of the action. Too, this same gas and fire would have been blown backward toward the shooter's face. While it would have been partially deflected by the design, I suspect there would still be a problem, as anyone who has fired flintlocks to any extent will testify.

So, the in-line concept is old, much older than the percussion cap, in fact. Are these much maligned in-lines more powerful or able to shoot farther than their more traditional brothers? The answer to that is a resounding no. Study after study, done by everyone from the manufacturers to game departments to myself show that it makes little difference how the fire is lit. The ballistics of muzzle-loading firearms are determined by the inside of the barrel, the projectile and the load. By inside of the barrel, I mean the caliber and rifling twist. Faster twist rifling, in the 1:22 to 1:30-inch range, stabilizes longer, slug-type projectiles better, and the bullet-shaped missiles will carry further than a round ball of the same caliber, given the same velocity at launch. Barrel length, of course, has some bearing on muzzle velocity, but less than you might think.

So, it makes little difference whether the gun is a percussion in-line or a traditional, carved Kentucky rifle. If both have the same internal barrel characteristics, they will both shoot the same, or at least very close to it. There is nothing in the shape or design of either that will add or subtract from bullet performance.

While you may not like the looks of the modern in-line-type hunting rifles, and they may not be your idea of what shooting frontloaders is all about, they certainly can't be dismissed because they are more accurate, more powerful, longer ranging or not historically correct. The in-line design of today is much older than the traditional side hammer percussion lock found on many traditional hunting and target guns. It predates the percussion form of ignition by over a half-century, and even predates the appearance of the typically American Kentucky long rifle in the later part of the 18th century, although not by much.

Live and let live—I suspect that in a few years the current in-line crisis will be looked back upon much as the Thompson/Center Hawken crisis is today. Time has shown that one was a tempest in a teapot and was actually healthy for muzzle-loading as a sport. Probably we'll eventually accept the in-line in the same way. ●

The T/C Fire Hawk has everything—short 24-inch barrel, Rynite or wood stock, stainless steel construction—for the modern muzzle-loading hunter.

THIS IS AN EFFORT to trace the extraordinary history of one of the most successful target rifles of all time. The fact that, apart from true connoisseurs, the Martini is hardly known in the United States shows that a prophet often does not get the deserved attention and appreciation in his native country. It also gives proof that a really sound design and a fine product will always find an appropriate use and clientele. As you will notice, the story unfolds mainly from a Swiss point of view. This should not come as a surprise; the author has been working with Hämmerli for more than thirty-five years.

The story starts back in America. Around the middle of the last century, small arms development was leaping ahead in big jumps. With the invention and introduction of the metallic cartridge, it was possible for the first time to design breechloaders that were both safe and functional. An unbelievable variety of breech systems was proposed. In America, the Secession War broke out in 1861, and this undoubtedly speeded up things even more.

Henry O. Peabody, born in Boston, was granted a patent of the United States in 1862 for his rifle using a pivoting breechblock with an external hammer for rimfire cartridges. The

The Fabulous MARTINI

by FERDINAND HEDIGER

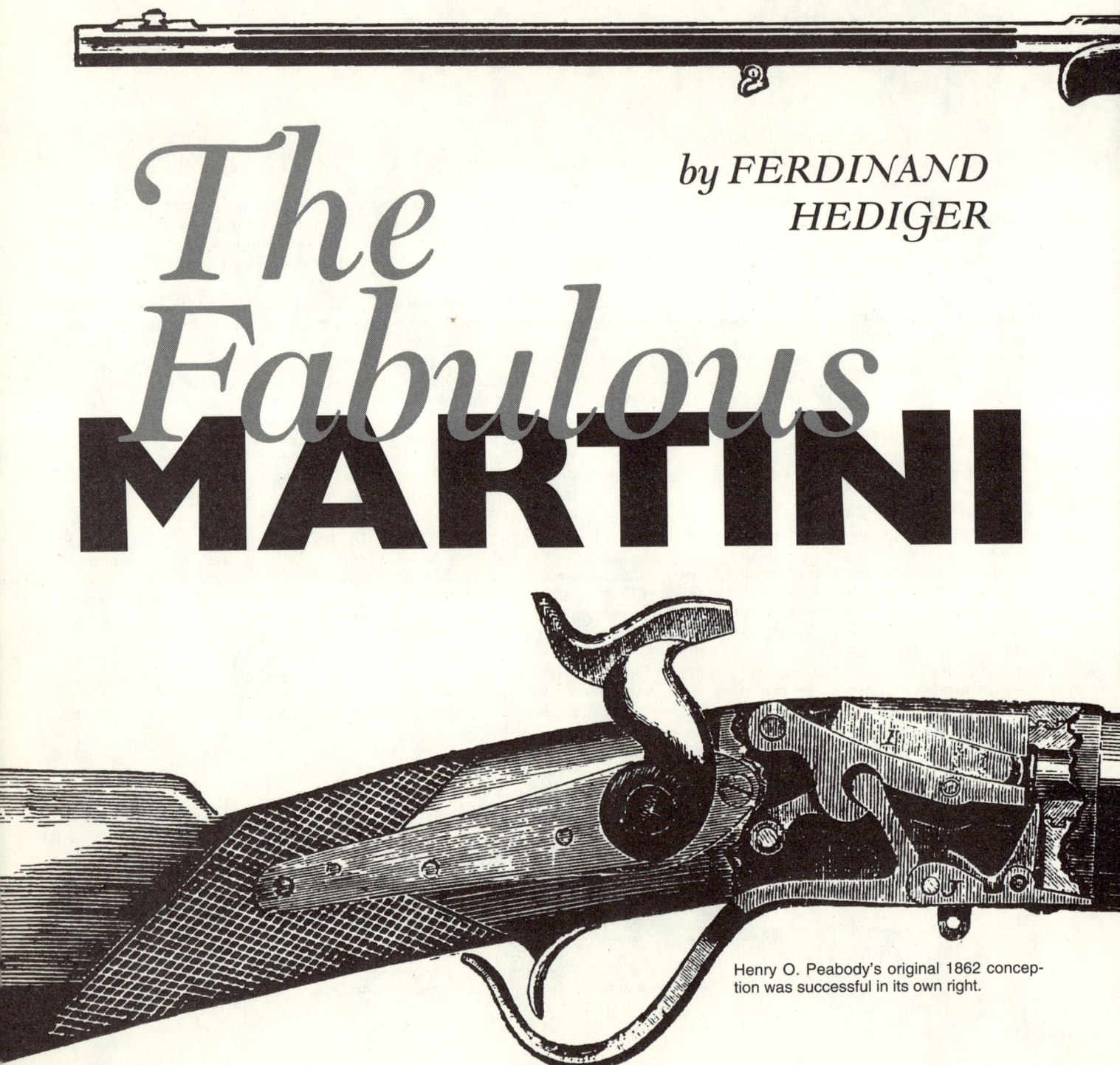

Henry O. Peabody's original 1862 conception was successful in its own right.

new rifle, still in the large 55-caliber, was very well received and was already used by certain troops of the Union. When the long and bloody war finally came to an end in 1865, the government of the United States invited all known inventors and producers of military rifles to submit their products for extensive tests and evaluations.

Peabody did, of course, participate, but there were not fewer than sixty-four competitors also trying to win laurels and orders. The new rifles were first subjected to a true horror test. For a full ten-day period, all the rifles were left in the open and got a daily shower of water. Then the maltreated and fairly rusty contenders had to prove to be ready to shoot without any cleaning beforehand. There remained only nine!

Nine little rifles now were buried in the snow and left there for another few days. After uncovering and thawing them out in a hot oven, they were expected to shoot, again without any preliminary cleaning. There remained only four.

The accuracy and durability tests followed. Considerably overloaded cartridges were fired resulting in extremely high pressures, and finally there remained only one rifle which had endured all tests, the Peabody. The evaluation commission strongly

Von Martini's invention, based on Peabody's, went on for over a century.

Friedrich von Martini was an entirely successful businessman/inventor in several fields.

recommended the Peabody for procurement. In view of the availability of huge quantities of muzzle-loading rifles, the more economical solution of a breech-loading conversion as proposed by Berdan was chosen. The Springfield Trapdoor modification for centerfire cartridges was ordered and adopted.

The successful tests convinced Providence Tool Co. in Rhode Island to take up production of the Peabody rifle. Only a few orders were placed by the U.S. Government and the Connecticut State Militia, but the new rifle found considerable interest abroad. Canada placed an order for 3000 rifles; Romania bought 25,000; France, where the Chassepot needle-fire rifle introduced in 1866 had rapidly become obsolete, ordered 39,000 Peabody rifles.

In Switzerland, where the old muzzle-loading muskets and rifles were hastily converted into breech-loaders, making use of the Milbank-Amsler conversion, there also was an urgent need for a more up-to-date rifle. The government therefore ordered 15,000 Peabody guns to bridge the gap until a new home-bred rifle would be adopted. Instead of caliber 45 or 50, the Swiss got their Peabody rifles in caliber 10.4mm (41), the new cartridge adopted for the converted muzzleloaders. This cartridge, with a copper case and rimfire ignition, used a round-nose lead bullet of 300 grains, a development of the Henry rimfire cartridge, and was considered to be very accurate. It is interesting in passing to note that a centerfire ordnance cartridge would not be introduced in Switzerland for twenty years. The Peabody rifle was adopted in many other countries. Large contracts were filled for the governments of Turkey, Mexico, Cuba, Denmark and Serbia. Nearly 700,000 rifles are reported to have been sold to Europe.

ing various kinds of special machinery used in the textile industry and for book binding, Friedrich von Martini worked on various other projects as well.

Based on the Peabody rifle, already hailed as one of the best of the new generation of breechloaders, he created the Martini action. His patent was granted in 1867, the same year the Swiss Confederation put the 15,000 Peabody rifles into service. Martini had done away with the external hammer and replaced it with an internal firing pin and cocking device. The short striker travel made a powerful coil spring necessary and was responsible for the comparatively heavy trigger pull. There is no denying the Peabody action was the basis of Martini's invention, but the improvement was considerable and

but remained the Swiss military cartridge until 1890.

The new rifle was, naturally, also chambered for the 41-caliber cartridge. Compared with the Milbank-Amsler conversion, it offered substantial advantages, especially its high accuracy. Modern military rifles were developing at high speed; in fact, spilling over in some places. In 1868, only a year after Martini obtained the patent, Friedrich Vetterli, technical director of the Small Arms Division of SIG (Swiss Industrial Company) in Neuhausen, submitted a repeating military rifle. This ultra-modern rifle, its magazine developed from the American Henry rifle, held twelve 41 Rimfire rounds in its magazine. After extensive and highly successful tests, the Swiss Federal Council decided to procure a

Johann Ulrich Hämmerli, founder of Hämmerli, created a world-class enterprise going strong today.

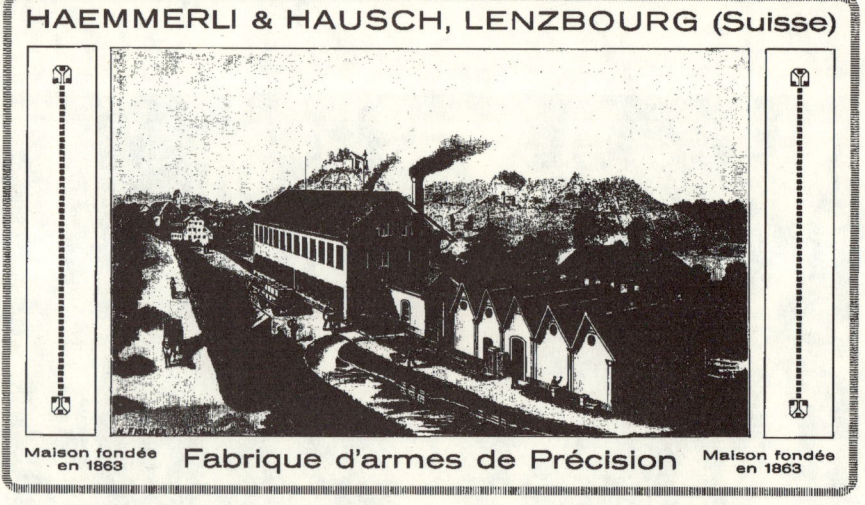

Hämmerli & Hausch Target Arms Factory, Lenzburg, Switzerland, around 1900 after twenty years of firearms production at this site.

The name Martini has an Italian ring, and for most people it will mean a well-known cocktail. Yet the family originated in Bavaria. Friedrich von Martini was born in 1833 in Herkulesbad in Imperial Austria-Hungary. As a young trained engineer, he worked in several European countries before settling down in Switzerland. He worked for the reputable company of Sulzer. Then he went to a newly founded machine factory which, after a short while, he took over together with the works foreman Heinrich Tanner. These two capable men developed the small enterprise into a well-respected industrial company.

Apart from inventing and produc-

had long-lasting effects. Friedrich Ritter von Martini became a Swiss citizen of Frauenfeld in 1869 and dropped the "Ritter."

As breech-loading rifles were increasingly adopted in armed forces around the world, the Swiss Federal Council decided in 1867 to have the various muzzle-loading rifles converted using the Milbank-Amsler breech-loading system. The locked-flap action patented by the American Milbank was improved by the Swiss professor Amsler. For the majority of the converted rifles, the new 41-caliber ordnance cartridge was used. (A smaller number used a 71-caliber cartridge.) The 41 Rimfire cartridge was subject to various improvements,

first batch of 31,000 Vetterli rifles. The Swiss army thus was the first in Europe to obtain a repeating rifle. Small wonder the Martini, in spite of its merits, had no chance from the beginning to be adopted in Switzerland as a military arm. In the fields of target shooting and hunting, it would, however, have a very long and admirably successful career.

In Great Britain, the supremacy of the Prussian needle-fire breech-loading rifles in the Danish war of 1864 had considerably stirred the minds of the responsible army commanders. As in other countries, making further use of the available muzzle-loading arms was of great importance. The Snider conversion, with a "flap action" for the centerfire cartridge in the original caliber of 577, was adopted in 1867. This gave the procurement commission the necessary time to have the many new models of breech-loading rifles tested and carefully evaluated. The breech actions and the various calibers and barrels were tested separately.

In 1869, the commission recommended the adoption of a rifle consisting of the action proposed by Friedrich von Martini, Switzerland, and the barrel in calibre 450 (with seven grooves) of the Edinburgh gun maker Alexander Henry. Next year, a small pre-series of 22 rifles was submitted for further tests. These proved most satisfactory, and in April, 1871, the Henry-Martini (also Martini-Henry) rifle was adopted. In addition to the rifle with a barrel length of 33 rifle was produced in very large quantities and remained the military rifle of Great Britain until 1891. As these rifles were very sturdy and simple, they remained in service with police, guard and local security troops in many parts of the world for many more years.

Around the middle of the 19th century, Swiss marksmen regularly participated in shooting contests in the neighboring countries. In return, they invited foreigners to take part in competitions in Switzerland. On the occasion of the important *Bundesschiessen* 1868 in Vienna, Swiss sharpshooter Master Sgt. Brechbühl gave proof of the excellent accuracy of the new Peabody rifle and the 10.4mm ammunition. Three years later, a very large delegation of about 3000 Swiss pilgrimaged to Lyon and sands of Martini-Henry rifles made his name famous. He now concentrated on further development of the embroidering and bookbinding machines and started studies on the internal combustion engine. Probably around the early 1880s, the rights to produce Martini actions, and the remaining stocks, tools and fixtures, were sold to Hämmerli & Hausch, a company founded in 1863 in Lenzburg. Regretably, there are only a few documents left of the activities of Martini & Tanner in Frauenfeld and Hämmerli & Hausch in Lenzburg. Therefore we have to rely on speculation and verbal information passed from one generation to the next. Hämmerli & Hausch had a new factory built in 1883 which matches nicely with an assumption that the start of production of Marti-

Hämmerli's Lenzburg shop around 1900.

This space was where they finished rifles in Lenzburg.

inches, a carbine with a shorter 22-inch barrel for a slightly weaker cartridge was produced.

There is no doubt Great Britain had chosen one of the very best single shot rifles of the world. Tradition had won over in competition with the very latest developments. Apart from the British Empire, the Martini-Henry rifle was also adopted by Romania, Portugal, Turkey and China. In addition to the excellent accuracy, the main advantages mentioned were "fast and simple handling with only three loading movements, a rugged construction of the action with only very rare needs for repair, and an extractor of the fired case that would hardly ever fail." The Martini-Henry Macon in France. Some of them certainly had their new Martini rifles with them. Friendly relations were further enhanced by participating in the shooting contests in Stuttgart 1871, Vienna 1880, Munich 1881, Leipzig 1884, Frankfurt 1887 and Paris 1889. The British Martini-Henry was used in substantial numbers and with good success in the shooting competition at Wimbledon in 1875. It was then the trusted rifle in many important shooting events all over the world.

Friedrich von Martini's licensing agreement in Great Britain for his action was certainly quite rewarding. His design had won in a very tough competition, and hundreds of thou- ni target rifles in Lenzburg was in 1883.

However, what we know for sure is that Martini target rifles began to spread rapidly in Switzerland and abroad among marksmen as so-called "private" rifles to differentiate them from the military rifle for which separate competitions were held. As these Martini rifles often had to be used in the kneeling position in accordance with the rules, many of them had stocks with very pronounced drop. Sometimes, therefore, they were called Martini "kneeling rifles."

In 1889, together with the new ordnance rifle with the first Schmidt-Rubin straight-pull action, the modern 7.5x53mm cartridge with smokeless

(Above) This is the shipment to the U.S. that resulted in U.S. wins.

The Henry-Martini rifle, adopted by the British Government in 1871, was a stout and simple breechloader.

powder and centerfire ignition was adopted. Immediately, new Martini rifles were chambered for this markedly more accurate cartridge. As it was of the rimless variety, the extractor had to be modified.

Many Swiss gunsmiths were regular customers of Hämmerli & Hausch for Martini actions, target barrels, set-triggers, sights and buttplates. With these components, they would make complete rifles. Very often such were engraved with the name and address of the gunsmith even if the majority of steel parts had been purchased. Most Martini target rifles were neither blued nor browned, but rather left in the white. This tradition was followed into the 1920s. According to an old master gunsmith, the reason for this unusual finish was the fact that marksmen used to maintain their private rifles very carefully. Any antirust protection would have thrown a bad light on the owner as being careless. Hämmerli & Hausch also produced complete Martini target rifles sold on the home market and exported into a number of countries. Surprisingly, some even made it to Argentina, where a Swiss national handled the sales.

It is generally agreed that the first International 300-Meter Match took place in 1897 in Lyon, France. The Shooting Association of Lyon was celebrating its twenty-fifth anniversary; by inviting marksmen from friendly nations, they gave the event an international touch. Well-known Dutch

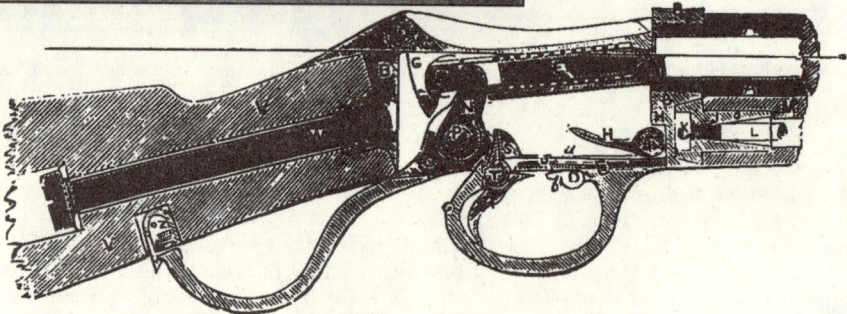

The Martini-Henry Breech-loader and its Parts.

Barrel.
Body.
Block.
Block axis-pin.
Striker.
Main-spring.
Stop-nut.
Extractor.
Extractor axis-pin.
J Rod and fore-end holder.
K Rod and fore-end holder screw.
L Ramrod.
M Stock, fore-end.
N Tumbler.
O Lever.
P Lever and tumbler axis-pin.
Q Trigger-plate and guard.
R Trigger.
S Tumbler-rest.
T Trigger and rest axis-pin.
U Trigger and rest-spring.
V Stock-butt.
W Stock-bolt washer.
Z Lever catch-bolt spring and
a Locking-bolt.   [pin.
b Thumb-piece.

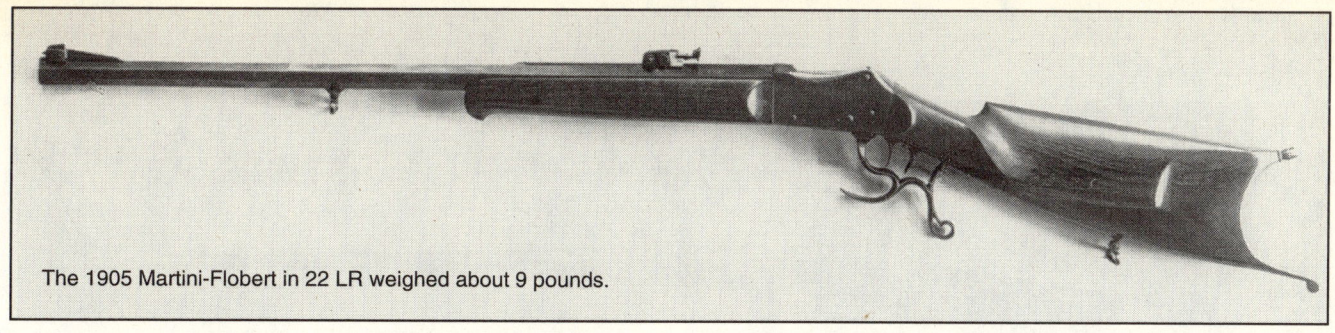
The 1905 Martini-Flobert in 22 LR weighed about 9 pounds.

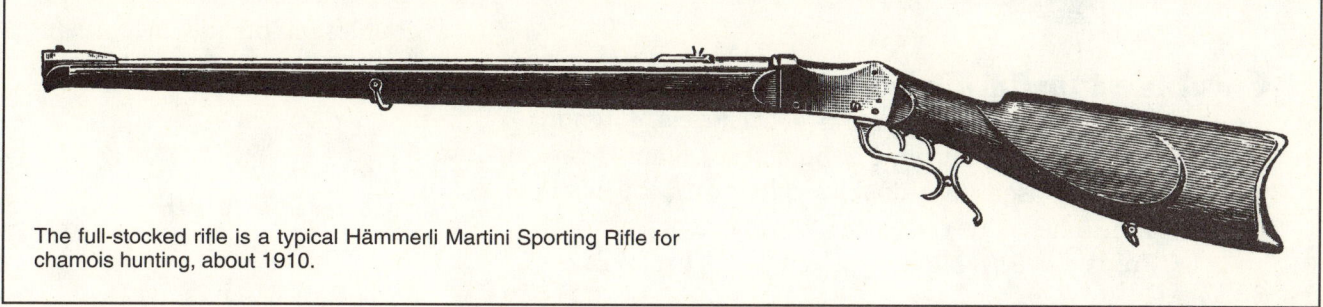
The full-stocked rifle is a typical Hämmerli Martini Sporting Rifle for chamois hunting, about 1910.

shooter Henri Sillens, who was also invited, proposed to add a 120-round three-position match to the traditional competitions. His idea was very well received, and thus the very first International 300-meter Match was born. The target had a diameter of 1 meter with five rings and a black centre of 60 centimeters. Marksmen were allowed to use their private rifles—so-called free rifles—with ammunition of their choice. Slings, palm rests and aperture sights, however, were not allowed. These rules corresponded with the Swiss prescriptions, and the Martini target rifles were, of course, eminently suitable. The shooting positions—prone, kneeling and standing—were also exactly stipulated. A team consisted of five marksmen. Apart from the shooting associations of France, Belgium, the Netherlands, Italy, Denmark, Sweden, Norway and Austria, the Swiss also received an invitation. As the assembly of delegates was planned for April only, Switzerland could not nominate an official team.

Nevertheless, Switzerland was represented in this first match. A team was formed in the French-speaking part of the country. They took up the challenge with their Martini target rifles shooting the Swiss 7.5mm cartridge made in a special competition version for the event. This team from western Switzerland scored 2310 points and won the competition. Norway, the runner-up team, was sixty-two points behind. Frank Jullien, from Geneva, won the individual three-position contest with a score of

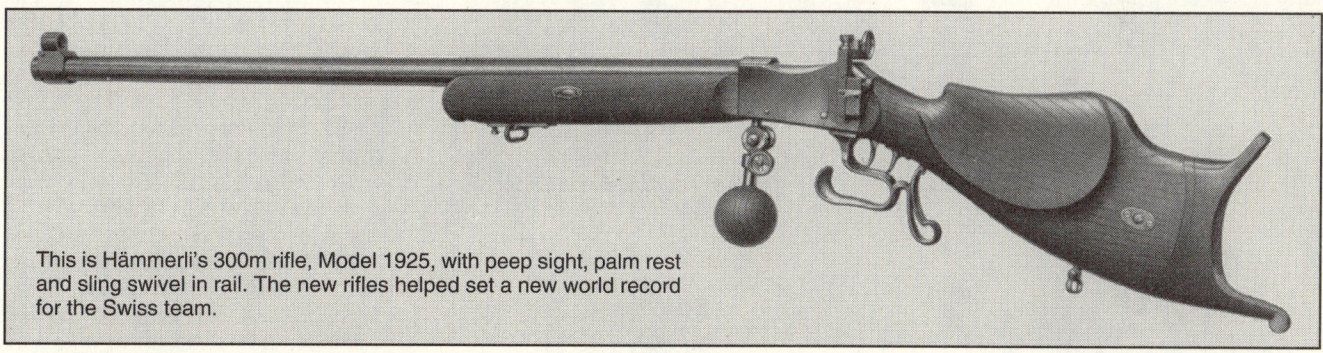
This is Hämmerli's 300m rifle, Model 1925, with peep sight, palm rest and sling swivel in rail. The new rifles helped set a new world record for the Swiss team.

This is the Model 1931 Free Rifle with heavy round barrel and the buttplate in standing/kneeling position. Caliber is 7.5x55mm.

Armes de précision en tous calibres
Nº 7 A

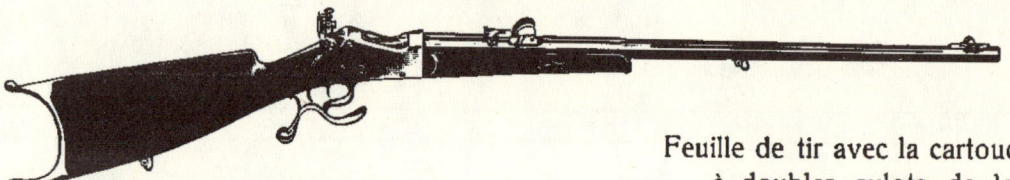

Carabine Martini-Flobert Canon cannelé, guidon à support, double détente à 4 balanciers, lorgnon américain, bois quadrillé et pommeau; tirant la cartouche Bosquette à doubles culots 6 m/m ou n'importe une autre cartouche Winchester.
Poids 5—5½ kilos   **Frs. 178.—**

Nous établissons aussi toutes nos armes d'après dessin.
Garantie pour solidité et parfaite précision.

Feuille de tir avec la cartouche 6 m/m à doubles culots de la Société Française des Munitions à Paris.

5 coups à 12 mètres.

10 coups à 12 mètres.

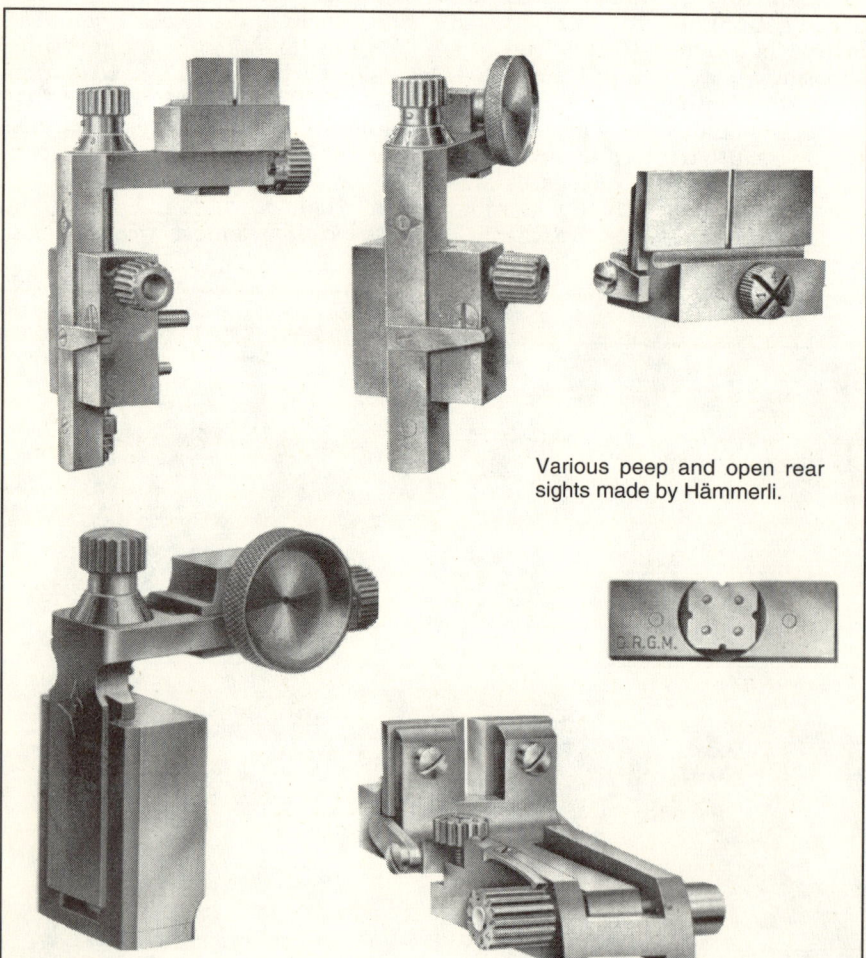

Various peep and open rear sights made by Hämmerli.

(Above) The Model 7A small-bore Hämmerli Martini—1900-1914—was the export model. Note the 50-foot groups.

501 points. This, then, was the basis for many future wins for the Swiss team and the Martini target rifle.

A year later, in 1898, the International Match took place in Turin, Italy. For various reasons, only three national teams participated. The Swiss suffered a defeat, being beaten by the French and Italian teams. This second match, however, is important for two reasons. The target now was changed and held ten rings. A young Swiss marksman named Konrad Stäheli won his very first gold medal in this match, which indeed was a forerunner of the World Championship shoot. Stäheli, then thirty-two years old and living in the eastern part of Switzerland, scored 322 points in the kneeling position. He was to become one of the most successful marksman with rifle and pistol ever.

It was Konrad Stäheli who took the poor performance of the Swiss team to heart. He started a systematic practice for target shooters and launched the idea of selection competitions to nominate the Swiss team in the future. He was supported by many of his friends, and their combined efforts for improved practice and preparations were to show very encouraging results just one year lat-

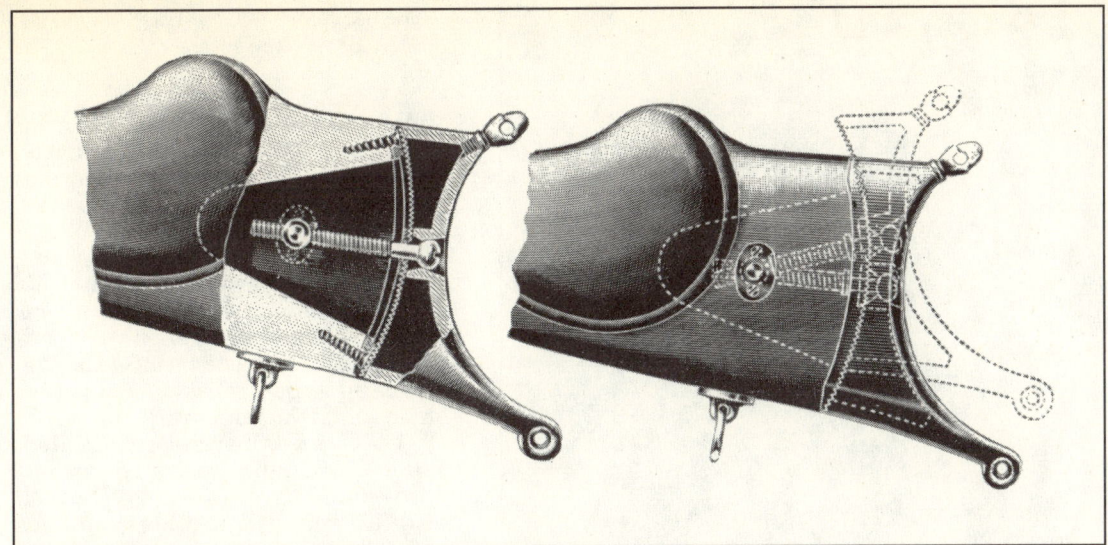

About 1920, Hämmerli's adjustable buttplate looked like this. Over the years there have been several such systems.

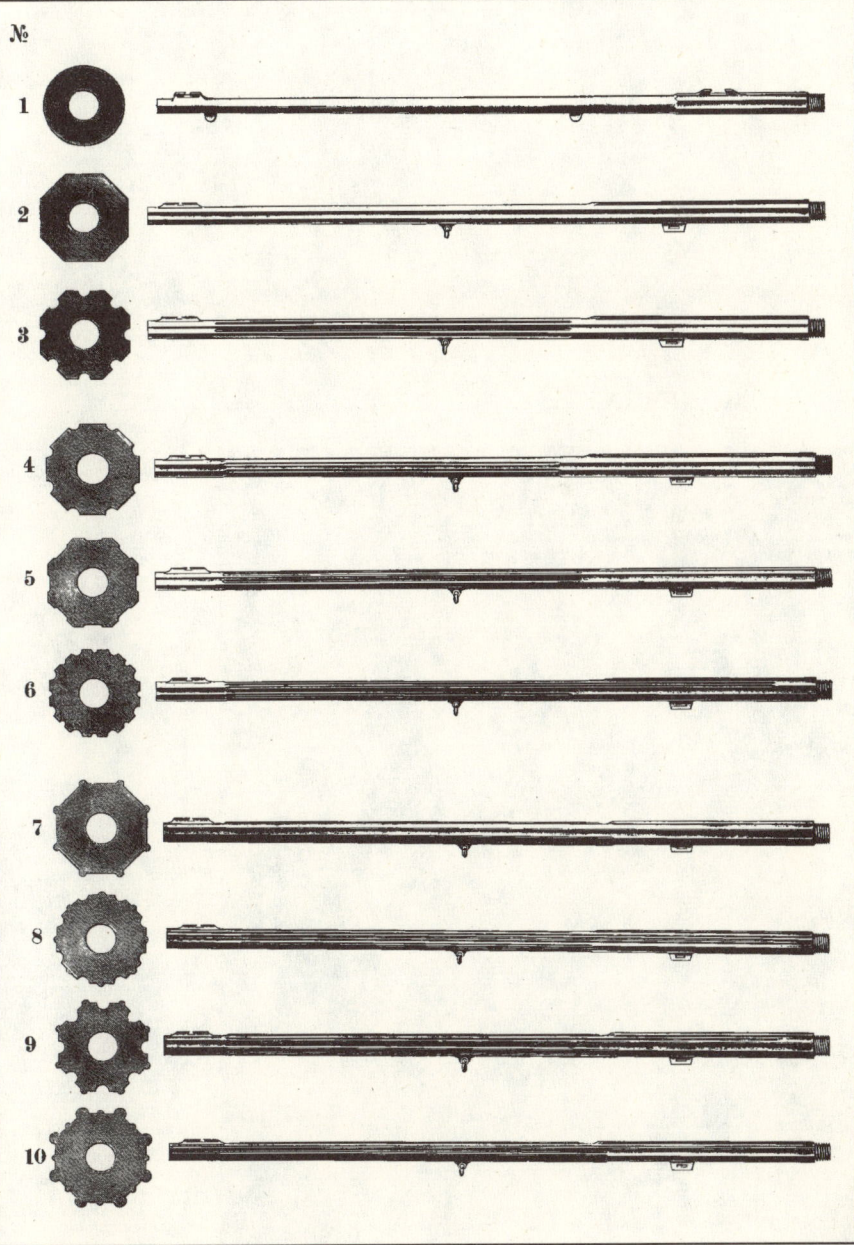

(Below) There have been at least these ten barrel styles for Hämmerli Martini rifles.

er. The Swiss team won the International Match of 1899 in Loosduinen, Holland, with a score of 4528 points. The French team was second with 4404 points.

In 1901, the International 300-Meter Match was held for the first time in Switzerland. With national teams from the Netherlands, Belgium, France, Italy, Austria, Germany and Switzerland, the event in Lucerne had a fine participation. As usual, the invitations were a matter of personal friendship and agreement between the associations. In 1907, the International Shooting Union (UIT) was founded in Zurich on occasion of that year's International Match. This match was organized concurrently with the Swiss Federal Shooting Competition where 591 clubs with about 18,000 marksmen participated. By the end of 1907, the UIT had ten national associations as members.

Up until 1914, the International 300-Meter Matches (now 300-Meter World Championships) were organized every year. Apart from the exception in 1893, the Swiss team proved to be unbeatable in seventeen championships. Very often their members claimed gold medals for the individual champions in all three positions as well. This unbroken record of wins in international 300-meter shooting had several reasons. In Switzerland, the marksmen could shoot regularly on hundreds of ranges scattered all over the country. Due to the militia system of the Swiss army with compulsory annual shooting for all soldiers who keep their military rifle at home, every village and town had and still has to provide adequate shooting ranges. Obviously, there always was a good selection of talented and success-

In 1900 in Paris, this team—Kellenberger, Stäheli, Roderer—won several golds.

ful marksmen. In many regional, cantonal and federal shooting contests, they would gain much experience in competitive shooting. The repeated wins of International and World Championships motivated the young marksmen. Konrad Stäheli and his friends nominated year after year strong teams hungry to prove superiority. Last, but by no means least, the Swiss had their reliable, high-performance Martini target rifles.

The Swiss ordnance cartridge Mod. 90 (7.5x53mm) was a great improvement over the old Vetterli rimfire round, but other countries also had introduced and adopted modern infantry cartridges before the turn of the century. At the match in Rome in 1902, the Swiss had to admit the superiority of the Italian Carcano cartridge in caliber 6.5x 51mm over their own ammuni-

Konrad Stäheli put Swiss marksmanship on its track to glory by personal example and sound management.

In 1930, Karl Zimmermann was world champion, here shooting a very fancy Hämmerli Martini.

tion. Not only was it less susceptible to wind drift, but it was also more accurate. As a result, some marksmen had their privately owned Martini target rifles rebarreled for the Italian 6.5mm or for the Norwegian Krag-Jorgensen (6.5x55mm) cartridge. Only in 1910 when the Swiss Military Department handed out preproduction lots of the new Swiss ordnance round Mod. 11 to the top marksmen on the team did they return to home-bred cartridges. This GP 11 (7.5x55mm) cartridge with full metal jacket, spitzer boattail bullet offered excellent accuracy and remained one of the best cartridges for 300-meter competition shooting into present times.

The rules for the 300-meter target rifles in the International Matches were similar to regulations in Switzerland for the privately owned target rifles. In the first sales catalogs of Hämmerli & Hausch, Lenzburg, dating from around 1910, Martini target rifles were offered in various versions.

The simplest and cheapest Model No. 1 had an octagonal barrel and three-lever set-trigger. The open rear sight was adjustable for windage and elevation, and its position could be freely adjusted forward and back by the shooter as it was fixed on a dovetailed barrel rib. The rifle weight was 5 to 5.5 kg, and the price Sfr. 140 (about U.S. $32). For comparison, the Swiss ordnance rifle Mod. 1889/96 sold for Sfr. 112. Model No. 2 differed mainly in having a fluted barrel and a more elaborate trigger guard. It sold for Sfr. 145. For an extra Sfr. 5 it was also available with a more sensitive set-trigger.

Model No. 3 was offered for export markets. It was very similar to No. 2, but had an adjustable palm rest and an "American-type" aperture rear sight, neither allowed in the International or Swiss matches. Furthermore, the fine four-lever set-trigger was fitted, and the stock as well as forend were hand checkered. Price: Sfr. 178.

For all three models, the precision barrel was made of Böhler special barrel steel. All prices were quoted for rifles chambered in 7.5mm Swiss. On request, they could be had for 6.5mm Dutch Mannlicher or 6.5mm Norwegian Krag-Jorgensen at extra cost. A test group of fourteen rounds at a distance of 125 meters was pictured in the catalog. The dispersion was a bit over 6 inches at 300 meters.

Stocks for the three models were made of walnut. They were fitted with a fixed buttplate, but the drop could be individually ordered. Extremely sophisticated (and wealthy) customers could also order a special stock developed by Hämmerli allowing an adjustable drop at an extra cost. Also on special request, fully fluted and channeled barrels, rear sights with adjustable notch-width and special front sights were available.

From the turn of the century, Hämmerli offered small-bore, so-called Martini-Flobert target rifles. They looked very much the same as the big-bore versions except had a somewhat lighter stock. They were chambered either for the 6mm rimfire cartridge of the French Société Française de Munitions (SFM) for shooting at 20 meters or for the American Winchester 22 Long Rifle cartridge for 50 or 100 meters. Instead of the double-tongue set-trigger, some had direct or double-pull triggers. The weight of these rifles was 3.5 to 5.5 kg depending on the model, and the prices ranged from Sfr. 95 to Sfr. 178.

Finally, there were the Hämmerli-Martini hunting rifles, Model 4A and 4B, with thinner round barrels and full-length stocks. Their weight was about 3.5 kg. These compact rifles, which nevertheless had barrels of 70 cm (27.5 inches) length, were especially preferred for hunting in the mountains. They were made in all current hunting calibers. Such a Hämmerli-Martini hunting rifle cost Sfr. 140.

In America, the Peabody-Martini was launched around 1872 and marketed as "What Cheer Mid Range" or "Long Range" and as "Creedmoor models." They were chambered for the special "What Cheer" target ammunition in calibers 44-95-550 and 40-70-380. These finely made rifles were not expensive and very popular.

The British service Martini-Henry was used very successfully in many competitions from the year of its adoption in 1871. In Army competitions, it was replaced by the Lee-Enfield repeater with the new and more accurate 303 cartridge. For civilian shooters, Greener, Westley-Richards and others offered Martini target rifles in caliber 22 Long Rifle and 300 Sherwood. These were sold in considerable quantities and were used throughout Great Britain in shooting clubs. For hunting, repeaters and double rifles in the heavy calibers were preferred. Only for small-bore rifles was the Martini action sometimes used.

Other European marksmen quickly noticed the potential of the Martini action for target shooting. In the fat 1910 catalog of H. Burgsmüller & Söhne, the largest gun dealer of Germany, as they proudly marked on the cover where several Martini target rifles made by Kessler and Stahl were shown, such rifles were chambered for the German 8.15x46 1/2mm Schützen cartridge. The standard model with Swiss stock, open iron sights and double-tongue set-trigger cost 78 Marks. The deluxe model with Tyrolean stock, aperture rear sight, engraving and carving on the stock cost up to 300 marks, made to order only. There also was an indoor model for the miniature 4mm cartridge.

After World War I, Martini target rifles in caliber 22 and various centerfire cartridges were again offered. Apart from the British and German companies mentioned, there were other manufacturers such as BSA, Birmingham, Vickers and the famous Belgian Francotte factory in Liege. There were not many true alternatives to the Martini target rifles. The most important in Europe was perhaps the Aydt falling block action made by Büchel in Suhl. It was quite popular in Germany. In many countries, more or less modified army rifles were used for the shooting competitions at distances of 100 meters to 1000 yards.

In 1920, the International Shooting Union was revitalized. At the assembly of the delegates in Paris, the Americans proposed to allow the use of any kind of rear sight as well as the match sling. Without giving it too much thought and without properly fathoming the consequences, the Swiss also approved this modification of rules.

The next 300-Meter World Championship took place in 1921 in Lyon, France. The American team, equipped with modified Springfield rifles with aperture rear sight, annulus front sight, double match sling and excellent ammunition, won its first team gold medal. The winning team consisted of Stokes (who also won the individual three-position gold medal), Osburn, Fisher, Christian and Rotrock. The score of 5015 points was 10 points below the Swiss winning score at the event of 1914 in Viborg, Denmark, and even 157 points below the record score of 1912 in Biarritz, but the Swiss team now was only runner-up. The Swiss were still shooting their Martini target rifles with open sights and without the match sling.

In January, 1922, the Swiss Match Shooting Association was founded. The World Championship held in Milan, Italy, saw another team win for the Americans. This time the Swiss team lost only 12 points on the winning score, and Swiss top marksman Karl Zimmermann won the gold medals for individuals in prone and standing position. The American Stokes again won gold in the individual three-position. One year later, the International 300-Meter Match was at Camp Perry, U.S.A. Because not one single European team could afford the costly trip, the Americans were the only marksmen on the shooting line, and with 5501 points they set a new record. In 1924, the World Championship took place in Reims, and there were fourteen teams participating. The Swiss improved their team score by 70 points, but the American team won gold for the fourth time in a row. One of the most successful American rifle marksmen, Fisher, won the individual three-position gold medal.

As the next championship was to be held in St. Gall, Switzerland, in 1925, the Swiss had to make a special effort. They started early with serious practice, set up very demanding rules for the selection and took great care to have the best possible rifles and ammunition available. In the meantime, Swiss marksmen also had learned how to handle aperture rear sights and match slings, but compared to the American rifles and the specially manufactured 30-06 match ammunition, their material was just not good enough. Something had to be done. The Swiss steelworks of von Roll supplied a lot of sixty especially selected steel bars to Hämmerli, Lenzburg, where the most-accurate-yet match barrels for the Martini rifles were produced. The Swiss Federal Ammunition factory improved the accuracy of the Model 11 ammunition by manufacturing a few lots of special match target rounds with the tightest tolerances.

The heavy Martini Free Rifle, which Hämmerli added to their production line in view of the World Championships, had a newly designed stock with a very pronounced cheekrest, thumbrest and adjustable hook buttplate. The combined trigger guard/loading lever had a very elaborate shape and served as a handrest and finger support. On the forend, a sling swivel rail was bedded in the lower surface. The palm rest had two joints and set-screws to allow any individually chosen position. Instead of the open sight, a new fine click-adjustable peep rear sight was mounted on the left side of the Martini receiver. The hooded front sight was of the annular type. The double-latch set-trigger was of the four-lever type and could be adjusted to an extremely low trigger pull weight.

The Swiss team, consisting of crack marksmen Hartmann, Lienhard, Pelli, Reich and Zimmermann, was really very well equipped. By setting a new world record with 5386 points—which meant an improvement of 85 points—they beat the strong American team. After four years, the trophy was returned to Switzerland. Hartmann was world champion in three-position, standing and kneeling position, and Lienhard won the gold medal in prone position. This fabulous new record and success in the most important competition had many reasons, not least of which was the excellent new Martini rifles made in Lenzburg.

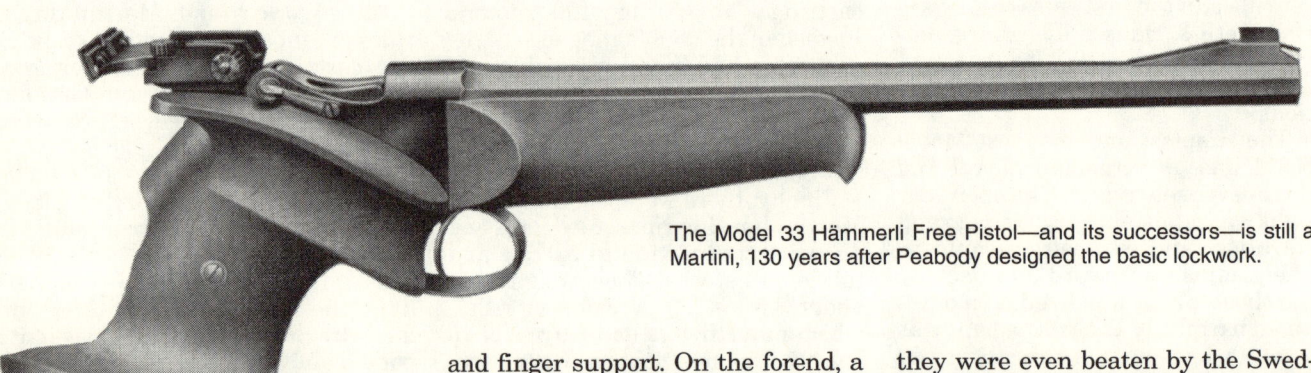

The Model 33 Hämmerli Free Pistol—and its successors—is still a Martini, 130 years after Peabody designed the basic lockwork.

The Swiss team, sometimes with Kuchen and Tellenbach as new members, won the next three World Championships. Little wonder the American marksmen and their officials and coaches began to seriously reconsider their equipment. The heavy, modified Springfield rifles were excellent for prone shooting, but they definitely were not the very best choice for the demanding standing and kneeling position. Compared to the new Hämmerli-Martini Free Rifles, they were handicapped by their unfavorable balance, their markedly slower lock time and by their lack of the fine set-trigger.

In spite of the fact that the American team had further improved rifles for the 1927 event with set-triggers, new 28-inch match barrels and improved lock time, they did not have a chance against the Swiss; worse, they were even beaten by the Swedish team. After this defeat, the officers of the U.S. team decided to order a number of the Martini Free Rifles so successfully used by the Swiss. Rudolf Hämmerli, Lenzburg, Switzerland, received the order for ten complete rifles and thirty sets of Martini actions and stocks. Apart from the chambering, which was for the 30-06 Springfield match cartridge, the rifles were identical in every respect with those of the world champions. The Martini actions and stocks were complemented with American barrels and sights, and the complete rifles were then offered to civilian marksmen.

In 1928, the Americans came with their Hämmerli rifles to the World Championship in Loosduinen, Netherlands. With a fine score of 5339 points, the team promptly set a new American record. But the Swiss were very strong, beating their own world record by another 5 points, winning gold medals and the trophy with a score of 5391 points. One year later, the Americans improved their score to a great 5397 points. The Swiss, however, countered the challenge with a fantastic score of 5442 points, soundly beating their previous world record by 51 points. Hartmann and Zimmermann set a new double world record mark in the individual score with 1114 points.

At the World Championship of 1930 in Antwerp, Belgium, at long last came the hour for the American team. After six years of continuous effort, they finally beat the Swiss by 34 points with an excellent score of 5441. Seitzinger (also winning gold in the kneeling position), Sharp, Renshaw, Fisher and Dr. Swanson formed the U.S. team. After this sweet success, the American team did not further participate in World Championships until after the end of World War II.

One year later, the Swiss team again set a new world record with a score of 5482 points in Lemberg, Poland. From 1931 onward, the World Championship was held only every two years. In 1933, the Swiss with their Martini rifles again won the event in Granada, Spain.

In America, the Martini rifles had been completed. The NRA offered them at the rather stiff price of $231.46. This was a lot of money, and it therefore is little wonder that, apart from the forty Martini Free Rifles, only a very few more found their way across the Atlantic. It is surprising that such a fine rifle, which had roots in America and which helped the U.S. team toward its great triumph by winning the World Championship, found only very little acceptance in its birth country. Perhaps there were too many fine rifles made by American manufacturers.

The American Maitland Steward wrote in his excellent article on Martini rifles in the April, 1962, issue of *Guns & Ammo*: "There are many reasons to place the Martini among the top in Rifledom's Hall of Fame. It was the official military arm of many nations. It was one of the best and strongest single shot breechloaders, and because of its extremely fast lock time, it outlasted all of the single shots. If the Swiss Martini wasn't the world's greatest target rifle, it was certainly the toughest rifle in the world to beat. It was supreme in world competition for over 40 years. During that time it won a total of 24 out of 31 World Championships."

For the World Championships of 1935, once again the choice fell on Rome. Whereas the individual double world record of 1114 points of Hartmann and Zimmermann was not in danger, the Finnish team was very strong and the scores of the members well balanced. With a new team world record of 5488 points, the Finns won the famous Argentine challenge trophy and gold medals for the first time. The silver trophy, weighing some 60 pounds, was offered by the Argentine Shooting Federation in 1903. Ever since, it was awarded to the winning team in the 300-Meter Rifle World Championships until the next event. Its value was estimated at over $8000 in the 1930s. Silver medals were won by the team of Estonia in 1935, and the Swiss had to content themselves with the bronze medals.

This was the turning point because for the first time the so-called Finnish Free Rifles—with turn-bolt action, straight stock and thumbhole—in the hands of highly motivated and well-trained marksmen had proven their supremacy over the Martini rifles. Especially in prone position, the new design offered definite advantages. Two years later, the Estonians won the competition in Helsinki, Finland, by setting yet another new world record of 5526 points. The Finnish team was runner-up and the Swiss, in spite of a good score of 5481, came third.

The highly successful career of the Martini target rifle for 300-meter competitions had finally come to an end. Part of the Swiss team was already shooting the new "Federal Free Rifle," which was making use of the straight-pull Schmidt-Rubin action of the Model 31 Swiss army rifle. It was developed by the Swiss Federal Arms Factory at Bern and, of course, had a straight thumbhole stock. Some still kept their Martini rifles, and Hämmerli tried with a new model, the "Trecento" with a side-lever action, to combine the virtues of the Martini with the advantages of a modern stock. Only very few were made, but they could not turn the tide. In 1939, the World Championships came to Switzerland, held in Lucerne. The scores, in general, were lower. Estonia won gold again with 5433 points. The silver and bronze medals were awarded, just as two years past, to the marksmen of Finland and Switzerland.

The Swiss team climbed again to the top of the winning platform in the first World Championship after World War II in Stockholm in 1947. The team, however, used the Free Rifles with straight-pull action, and the events of the next years therefore are another story.

Hämmerli, as well as various other manufacturers, made small-bore target rifles in (22 Long Rifle) from the turn of the century. International competitions for 50-meter rifles started only in the 1920s and did not reach nearly the same popularity and prestige as the "true" 300-meter three-position event until well after the war. Martini 22 rifles did not dominate these competitions in the same way as in the full-bore championships. It is therefore rather amazing that a 22-caliber Martini target rifle, the BSA International, was still offered into the 1970s. In Great Britain, and especially in the special 50-meter prone competitions also called the English match abroad, these sturdy and accurate rifles were well liked and most successful.

Before the 300-meter Martini rifles became collector's items, they could be bought cheaply in Switzerland, and consequently a great many were disassembled to use the actions as base for modern sporting rifles. Especially for hunting deer, chamois and, when permitted, ibex in the alpine regions of Switzerland, the Martini-Stutzer with full-length stock was and still is the preferred rifle of many hunters. Not only will it handle modern hunting rounds, provided the action is of the tough forged variety (better abstain from using old versions, some of which were cast and will not take the pressure of high-speed cartridges), but it is still one of the quietest actions to cock and provides a fairly short and light single shot rifle with useful barrel length.

This article on the history of the Martini would be incomplete without at least mentioning the fact that miniaturized and modified Martini actions have been for decades, and still are, used for all the Hämmerli Free Pistols as well as for most of their Russian competitors. A more in-depth description of this branch of development would, however, crack the frame of this article. Therefore, a marking of some of the greatest success has to suffice. In the Olympic Games of 1984 in Los Angeles, all three medal winners shot Hämmerlis; the World Champion in 1990 in Moscow and many others used Hämmerli Free Pistols with Martini actions. Most certainly a founded proof of the decisive advantages the Martini action and design have to offer.

●

American Arms' Escort

TESTFIRE

The total width of the Escort at the grips is 13/16-inch.

Really clean, the Escort's only fire control device is its DAO trigger.

THERE HAVE BEEN, in the recent past, 380 ACP pistols as *small* as this one, but never one this *slim*. Its width is just 13/16-inch, and there are no projections of any sort. The only control that protrudes, very slightly, is the low-profile magazine release button.

No manual safety is provided, and none is needed. The firing system is, to use the new acronym, DAO. For the benefit of those who joined us recently, that's Double Action Only. A full long pull of the trigger is necessary to cock and release the internal pivoting hammer.

Actually, the trigger pull is not all that long. There is about 1/8-inch take-up, and the trigger movement to firing is just 3/8-inch more. The pull is medium-stiff, but easy and quick. The trigger is wide and smooth, with no grooves, and it has good ergonomic shape and rounded edges. The measurement from trigger center to backstrap is 2½ inches.

Except for the magazine and sights, the material throughout is stainless steel with a satin finish. The grips are semi-soft polymer. Everything is nicely fitted. The only negative point I could find was at the lower rear edges of the grip frame, where a few strokes with a fine Grobet file were necessary for comfort.

The Escort sits well in the hand, and the grip frame has a

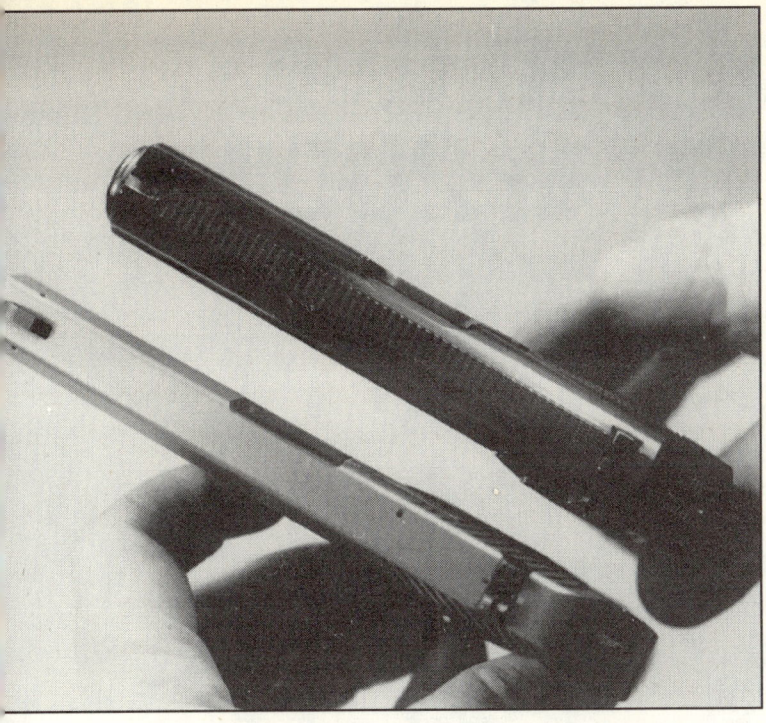
This is the Escort alongside a Walther PPK/S, which looks fat.

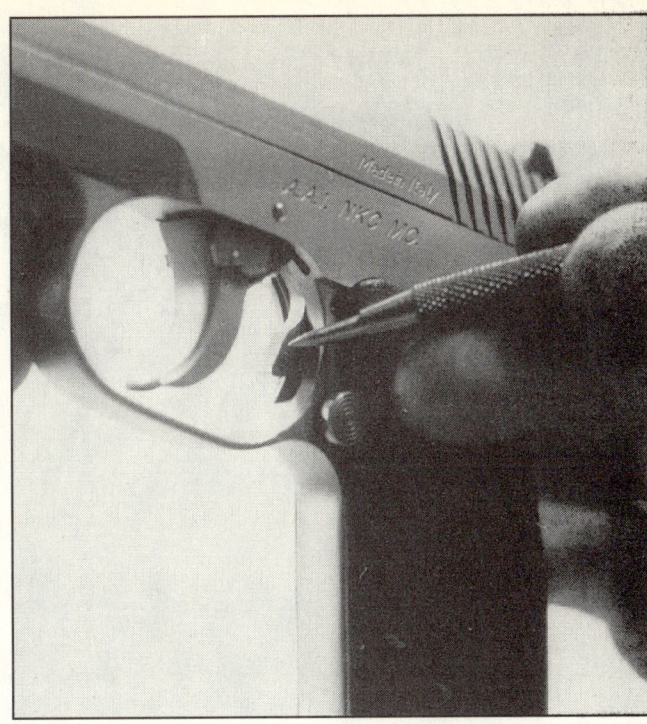
Depress this lever behind the trigger for takedown.

deep and high incurve at its upper rear. This is always a good thing, as it puts the axis of the bore close to the top of the hand. The pistol weighs just 19 ounces, and I expected more felt recoil than it gave. The fine design of the grip frame seems to tame the kick.

I tried it at the range with full-jacket and hollowpoint loads by Winchester, and there were no problems with either load.

The blued-steel fixed sights are excellent—a square post and square notch. The DAO trigger system precluded any serious target work, but keeping all shots in the black of a standard target at 50 feet was easy.

The rear sight is dovetail-mounted, and the front sight is cross-pinned to the slide. The extractor has a red dot on top, visible when the chamber is loaded, and the cammed-out front can be felt in the dark. The blued steel magazine is particularly well-made, and the capacity is seven rounds.

The takedown system is rather unique. With the magazine removed, you depress the serrated lever behind the trigger, inside the guard, and run the slide and barrel assembly off toward the front. The captive recoil spring unit is lifted out of the slide, and the barrel comes out toward the front. The whole thing takes about four seconds.

Putting it back together, the hammer and ejector are folded over forward as the slide is moved back. Keeping the takedown lever depressed, the slide and barrel assembly are then snapped into place. The slide is cycled to be sure the lever pops back out, and that's it. It's a neat system.

The recoil spring unit has two springs on the guide, the shorter and stronger inner one acting as a buffer to cushion the slide impact. The full-length slide rails are entirely inside the frame. The pistol is very "closed," with few openings that will admit dirt or clothing lint. In general appearance, the adjective that comes to mind is "sleek."

And it certainly is flat. This is going to be a superb pistol for personal protection or for law enforcement backup. Its slimness and relatively short trigger reach will be perfect for small hands, but it is also comfortable in my medium-sized grip.

The Sites firm of Italy originally designed this pistol, in slightly larger form, to be a full 9x19mm gun. For several reasons that project didn't work out. So, they reduced the size further and made a marvelous little 380 Auto. And thanks to American Arms, it is now made here in the U.S., and we can get it.

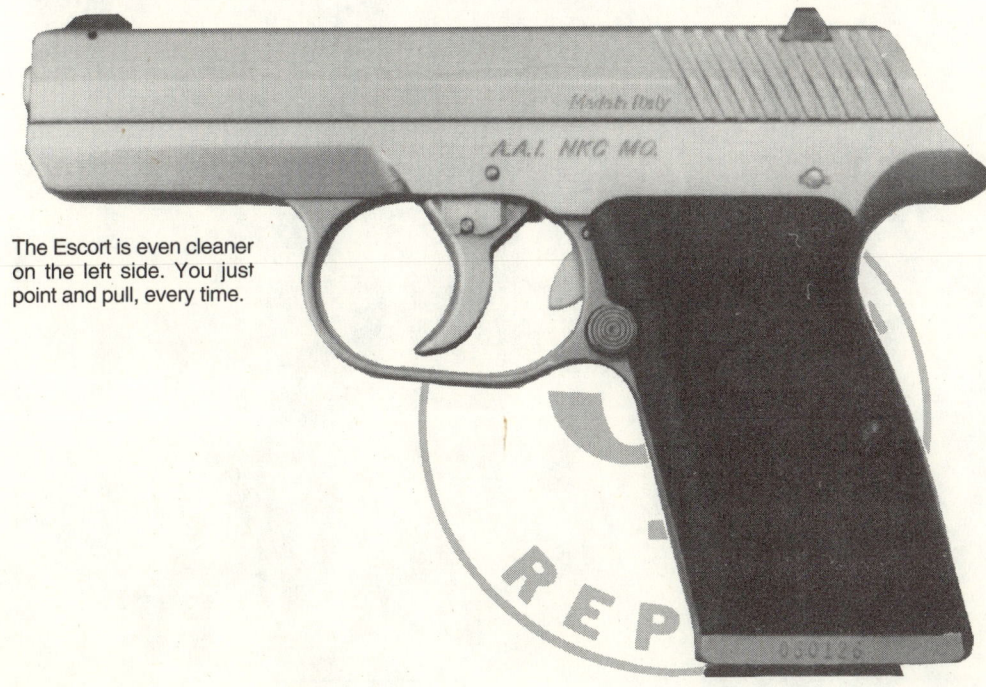
The Escort is even cleaner on the left side. You just point and pull, every time.

J.B. Wood

Daisy's Pair of Fun Guns: PowerLine 400 & 2001

TESTFIRE

Look-alike to the Desert Eagle, Daisy's PowerLine 400 holds twenty BBs and has a recoiling slide.

DAISY HAS BEEN right on the mark for quite a few years with its ever-growing line of CO_2-powered pellet and BB guns. Some of their models are in the "spittin' image" category, just about exact look-alikes of highly popular powder burners, especially in the area of handguns.

The two we're looking at here were first displayed at the 1994 SHOT Show, but weren't available then. In fact, the PowerLine 2001 rifle got to market in early 1995. The PowerLine 400 pistol reached store shelves a couple of months earlier and almost instantly became a real hit with a wide variety of recreational shooters.

The PowerLine 400 is really made in Japan and is an eye-popping replica of the ponderous Desert Eagle self-shucker, a veritable hand cannon that

The Daisy 400 houses a 12-gram CO_2 cylinder in the grip and keeps twenty rounds in a group like this at 25 feet.

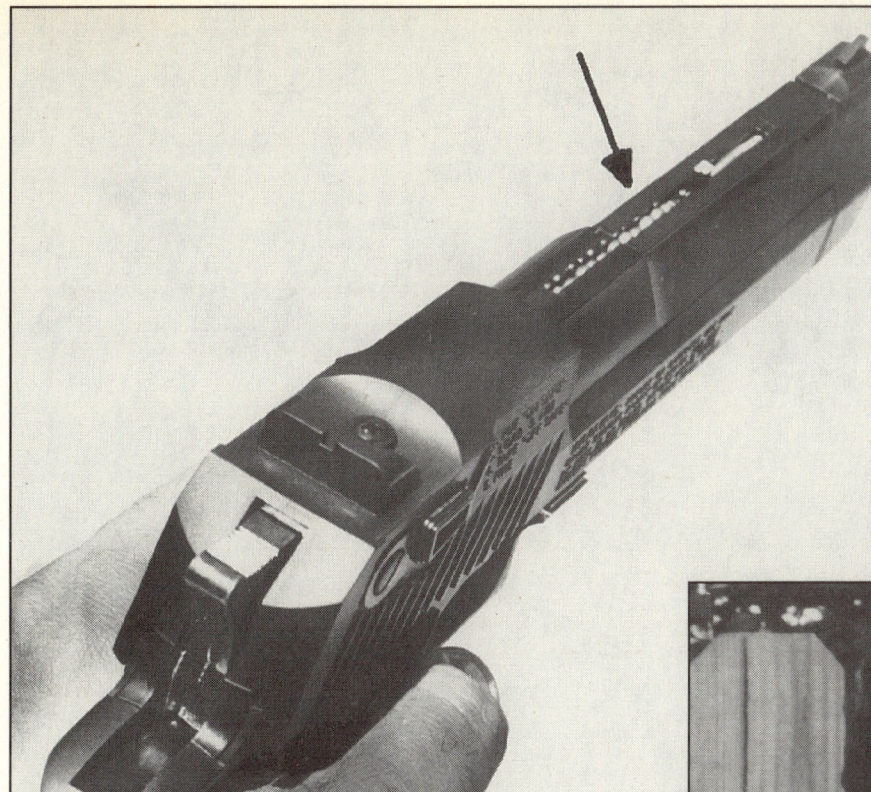

A removable forced-feed BB magazine fits horizontally atop the barrel.

Protective eyewear is a must when shooting BBs, especially at close targets.

has become extremely popular with fans of big-bore handguns. The Daisy 400 is just as large as its powder-burning counterpart, but it tips the scales at just 1.4 pounds. Overall length is 10 3/4 inches.

The matte black finish mimics the real thing, but the sights are simple and non-adjustable—a blade up front and a good-sized square notch at the rear. That's no problem, because this pistol shoots BBs from a smoothbore brass barrel. Even with the fixed sights, BB ammo and smooth tube, the 400's accuracy is better than ho-hum. There is an incredibly realistic semi-auto blowback action. The slide of the 400 cycles with each shot, just like the real Desert Eagle. The "kick," of course, is nowhere near as fearsome as that of the real thing, but there is still plenty there.

Interestingly, the use of a reciprocating slide in a CO_2 pistol is not new at all. In the late 1960s, Crosman's Model 451, a highly realistic-looking copy of the 45 Auto Government Model, cycled the "slide." Sadly, the old and rather complex gun consumed a lot of CO_2. Barely twelve to eighteen shots used up the gas.

Daisy got the system down pat in the Model 400. In most of my tests, I got close to 100 shots before the 12-gram CO_2 cartridge needed replacing. That's four full magazines, which carry up to twenty BBs and fit horizontally atop the barrel shroud. The CO_2 cylinder is housed in the grip.

The 400 is a single-action semi-auto. Once the gun is pressurized with CO_2 and the loaded magazine is in place, the hammer must be manually cocked in order to fire the first shot. Thereafter, the slide will take care of recocking the hammer after each shot. The hammer can be manually lowered—carefully, of course—just like in many powder-burning semi-autos. Incidentally, the trigger pull is realistically short as well and required about 5 1/2 pounds of pressure in the test gun. There is also a manual rotary trigger block safety located on the right side above the trigger area. A bright red dot is clearly visible when this safety is in the "off" position. The letters F and S are also in relief on their respective ends of the safety-lever travel.

The Model 400 is no slouch when it comes to velocity and produces about 420 fps. That's decidedly on the peppy side for a BB pistol and entirely adequate for all sorts of limited-area plinking. Accuracy, as mentioned earlier, was surprising, grouping an entire magazine (twenty BBs) into a 1 1/2-inch circle from 25 feet away, firing from a two-handed combat stance at a fairly rapid cadence. The Daisy PowerLine 400 pistol is a huge load of fun, and its retail price, which hovers around the $50 mark, is quite affordable.

Let's switch gears now and take a look at the PowerLine 2001 rifle. Here we have what can only be described as a revolutionary development in the field of CO_2-powered pellet rifles. Daisy, incidentally, has had an enviable track record in the area of pellet rifles during more than two decades, but nothing comes even close to this new model.

In a nutshell, the PowerLine 2001 is a 177-caliber pellet repeater that can sure give you a lot of shooting fun almost anywhere. The key to this amazing new rifle is a slick 35-shot helical pellet magazine developed for Daisy by none other than Calico, the same folks that gave us those 50- and 100-shot 22 rimfire and 9mm semi-auto pistols and rifles that also employ helical magazines.

The 2001 is not, however, a semi-auto. It is an elegantly styled bolt-action repeater that'll keep on spitting out 177-caliber diabolo pellets just as fast as the shooter can operate the bolt.

The patented Mag-Clip can be quickly and easily loaded. In fact, for those who plan on doing a lot of shooting, it would be advisable to purchase several

50th EDITION, 1996 **197**

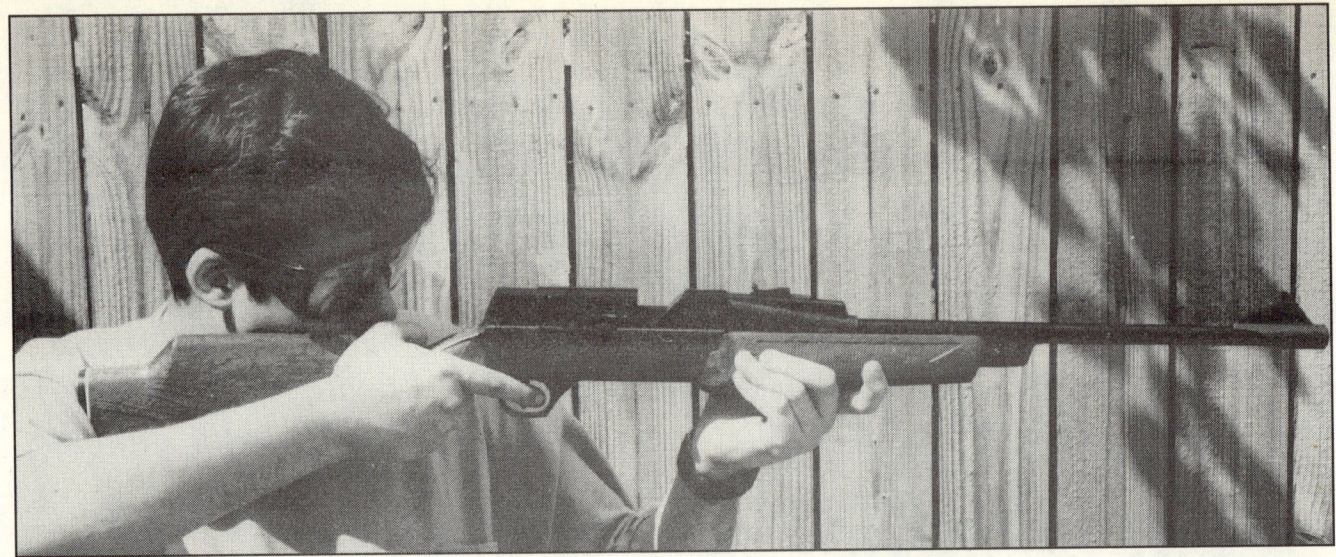

The Daisy PowerLine 2001 introduces a new concept in the field of CO_2-powered pellet rifles.

The thirty-five pellet magazine is housed at the rear of the receiver and is easily removed for loading. The rifle action functions with a straight-pull bolt.

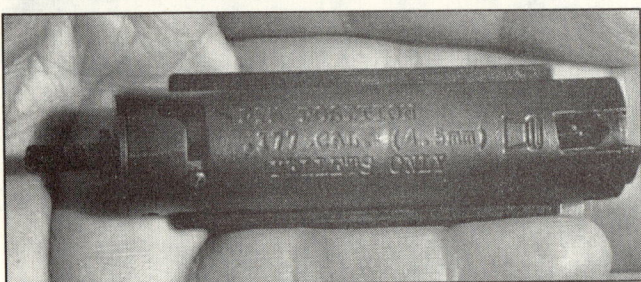

The removable Mag-Clip has a patented helical design and can load up the thirty-five 177-caliber pellets.

The Daisy 2001 has the looks of an elegant centerfire hunting rifle, with a Monte Carlo-style, moulded woodgrain buttstock with checkering in the pistol grip area. The moulded forend also has lots of checkering. The open rear sight is fully adjustable, while up front there is a blade mounted atop a rakish ramp that's part of a muzzle sleeve. The receiver also has grooves to allow the installation of a scope.

Overall, the 2001 measures 38 1/4 inches and tips the scales at around 3 1/2 pounds. Its rifled steel barrel is 19.9 inches long. As for safety mechanisms, the 2001 is state-of-the-art for its genre. There is a manual cross-bolt trigger block safety button. When it's in the *off* position (pushed all the way in from the right), a clearly visible red band is exposed to warn the shooter. In addition, the bolt must be fully closed or the rifle will not fire.

Tests with two sample 2001s revealed little difference in their respective capabilities. They both operated flawlessly, feeding Daisy Quick Silver match-style pellets without a hiccup. Using the open sights, both delivered respectable accuracy at 10 meters, grouping well within 1 inch from a benchrest. Their respective triggers were entirely acceptable for sporting rifles of this type. However, the 2001 is neither a match rifle nor meant to be shot from a benchrest, so I quickly put the guns to more mundane (and pleasurable) uses, such as plinking. That's where the 2001 truly excels.

extra Mag-Clips and load them all beforehand. That way, all one has to do is simply remove the empty mag and snap in a loaded one—which takes about five seconds—and you're back in business.

Interestingly, the 2001 also gives the shooter the option of manual loading, one pellet at a time, through the open view/loading port. The magazine must, however, be empty in order to prevent a double-feed. The Mag-Clip fits neatly in the rear of the receiver, and all one has to do to reach it is snap off the end receiver cap.

Each 12-gram CO_2 cylinder gives enough juice for quite a bit of shooting before it needs replacement, producing an average muzzle velocity of up to 630 fps with a fresh cylinder. Keep in mind, though, that ambient temperature has a decided effect on the number of shots obtained from each cylinder. Fast shooting, likewise, tends to lower the number of shots.

J.I. Galan

AMT's DAO 45

TESTFIRE TESTFIRE TESTFIRE

AMT'S 45 DAO is a highly specialized semi-automatic handgun, chambered for the 45 Automatic cartridge, holding five rounds in its magazine and functioning double-action only (DAO). There are no manipulated safety devices. There is a striker block, which positively prevents the striker from hitting a primer until the slide is fully locked and the trigger pulled. Sights are rudimentary—only a full-length groove in the top of the slide.

Physical dimensions are as follows: length, 6 inches; height, $4^{1}/_{8}$ inches; width, $1^{1}/_{16}$ inches; weight, 23 ounces. Minor disassembly for cleaning is straightforward. Anyone familiar with Browning-designed pistols will have no trouble here.

The 45 DAO fires from a modified Browning-style locked breech designed to place full mainspring pressure directly against the actuating pin. The mainspring is also fully contained by a guide rod. There is no separate barrel bushing, and both barrel and slide are robust in design and weight.

Grip panels are made of a durable matte black plastic with an effective checkering pattern for grip control. All steel surfaces are matte or brushed to minimize glare and reflections.

That about describes the physical characteristics of this gun. What about handling?

Several hundred rounds through the 45 DAO provided, on average, recoil very similar to my Lightweight Commander. So the 45 DAO's relatively light weight doesn't equate to killer recoil.

However, don't get me wrong. The 45 DAO does kick, and with heavier loads—especially with 230-grain bullets—it kicks very hard. The uninitiated might find it beyond manageable. If you want this caliber of protection, you are going to have to live with a bit of recoil.

Considering its designed purpose and the limitations of the so-called sights and the necessarily heavy trigger pull, I was amazed at my shooting. With careful aiming and trigger manipulation, I had no problem hitting pop cans at about twenty yards.

A more realistic test was to simply pick out an appropriately sized target at close range. Where a handy dirt cutbank provided ample aiming points, this was easy to do. I tested myself and the gun by pulling it from a back pocket, pointing over the top of the slide—not really using the sights but pointing like one does a shotgun—and squeezing off six "aimed" shots as fast as possible. I had no trouble hitting the sweet spot with any shot thus fired at ten feet or so, and I could do this all in well under two seconds.

In my opinion, there is no point whatsoever in testing the 45 DAO or any other of its ilk on paper targets: These guns are designed and intended for use in encounters of the worst kind where split-second decisions at very close range can mean survival. Inherent accuracy is not primary.

Another surprise was the AMT's functioning. In direct violation of the included instructions, which specify only hardball factory ammunition, my wife and I and a friend all tried the gun with a plethora of factory ammunition and handloads ranging from very light target to very stout handloads, with bullets ranging through swaged lead round-nose, cast truncated cone, cast modified semi-wadcutter, cast round-nose, light and heavy JHP and FMJ. My wife fired the gun one-handed using her weak-side hand with the lightest loads I had available, a 155-grain SWC generating less than 800 fps. The 45 DAO cycled correctly under those circumstances—very light load and very light grip—so I figure any full-house factory load will cycle the action properly under any realistic shooting situation.

Obviously, a 3-inch barrel will develop less velocity than a typical Model 1911-style pistol with a 5-inch tube, which explains the hardball edict. How much of a reduction in velocity? Limited testing indicates that with 230-grain loads, using relatively fast-burning powders, about 125 fps; with 185-grain bullets, using relatively slow-burning powders, about 175 fps. For "designed to expand" bullets, velocity is particularly important, and the 3-inch barrel simply may not provide that in all instances.

Yes, for purposes of evaluation testing, I tried dozens of haphazard handloads through my 45 DAO, firing hundreds of rounds and having not one failure. However, if I load this gun for its intended purpose, I shall either use best factory loads or I shall produce a few hundred very careful handloads and ensure they cycle and fire flawlessly every time. To do less would be foolish.

There are no protruding buttons, knobs, handles, projections on the 45 DAO to catch on anything. The tough checkered plastic grip panels work well, and the slide serrations are deep and sharp edged enough to facilitate first round chambering. And the gun is 100-percent ambidextrous in form and function. The magazine release is in a logical place for a gun of this type—bottom rear center of the grip—and there's no magazine safety or slide lock to muddle matters. The extractor and ejector are massive and well designed. The AMT 45 DAO works simply and it simply works.

I would like to see a heavier hammer and a lighter hammer spring so trigger pull could be reduced below the 12-pound factory level. However, the liability varmint bites us on that one. And the grip screws work loose. Those are my only complaints.

M.L. McPherson

B-Square's Mounts

The M1903A3, as-issued and uncut, accommodates a high-mounted scope in B-Square mounts.

I'M OFTEN ASKED by fellow shooters why I bother to shoot "...that old military surplus junk." Aside from historical and aesthetic reasons, the main reason I end up shooting them is that it's *fun*. And inexpensive fun to boot.

A fine shooting Swedish Mauser, Finnish Moisin or Lee-Enfield can be had for well under $150, and military surplus ball ammunition is also cheap. Most of it is Berdan primed and can't be reloaded, and some of it has corrosive primers, but at low prices, it's well worth cleaning the bore.

Most of the complaints I hear about shooting these classic rifles are related to the sights. With few exceptions, military rifles made before the 1930s had rear sights whose minimum adjustment was 300 to 400 meters, the "battle sight" setting. The best solution is to mount a scope on the rifle.

The B-Square company manufactures an extensive line of telescopic and optical sight mounts for the classic military rifles. Most attach without the necessity of drilling and tapping holes or modifying the gun in any way. The B-Square catalog lists mounts for the following classic bolt-action military rifles: M1917/P14 Enfields (this one *does* require one hole to be drilled and tapped); German Kar 98k Mauser; Swedish M96 and M38 Mausers; Spanish M93 Mauser; M91 and M91-30 Moisin-Nagant; M44/Type 53 Moisin-Nagant carbines; No. 1, 4 and 5 Lee-Enfields; and the M1903/03A3 Springfield.

I am a big fan of both the Swedish Mauser and Finnish Moisin-Nagant, so these were first on my want list, and I also ordered a mount for one of my M1903 Springfields. The mounts are made from beaded and hard-anodized alloy. The workmanship was excellent, and each mount came with a set of 1-inch scope rings. The mounts for the M96 and Moisin are designed to accept any standard dovetail-type rings, while the M1903 must use the special rings supplied with it. Each mount came with the proper sized Allen wrenches needed for installation and adjustment.

The rifles on which I mounted the scopes are all rebuilt. My M1903 was made at Springfield Arsenal around 1940. It had been re-Parkerized before I purchased it, and I replaced a rather ratty stock with new wood. The bore is clean, but has seen quite a bit of use. My Swedish Mauser was made at the Carl Gustaf arsenal in 1905, then completely rebuilt by the Swedish army sometime after 1941. It sports a brand-new barrel (with threaded muzzle), stock and bolt. M96s were equipped with a straight bolt handle, but this one has a bent handle. The M1891 Moisin-Nagant is an ex-Finnish rifle rebuilt at the VKT arsenal in 1942, although the Russian-made receiver is dated 1897. It is in excellent condition with a new barrel, stock and sights.

Attaching the mounts required no more tools than a few screwdrivers, punches, a small hammer and the Allen wrenches previously mentioned. I installed the M96 mount first, as it seemed the easiest and required nothing to be removed from the

Shooting was easier than with irons. The Mosin-Nagant set up with an Extended Eye Relief scope mounted in the rear sight.

rifle. It attaches to the M96's rear sight leaf. First you place a flat nut plate under the leaf, put the mount on top of the leaf and secure it in place with two mounting screws into the nut plate. Finally, two adjusting screws are turned in, one bearing on the front of the sight leaf and the other on the rifle's barrel in front of the sight base. These securely position the scope mount and prevent any movement, and can also be used to make elevation adjustments if necessary. They are both secured by lock screws located on the ends of the mount. It was a quick operation, taking about ten minutes. I mounted a Tasco 3x20 LER scope that I borrowed from my friend Pat Linthicum. He gave it to me equipped with a set of Tasco rings which perfectly fit the B-Square mount.

The M1903 was a bit more complicated. First you remove the magazine cutoff pin and lever. Then, place the small ball bearing supplied over the ejector pin hole, insert the bracket into the cutout for the magazine cutoff and replace the cutoff pin. Both of the set-screws on the top of the bracket are then tightened. This securely locks the bracket to the rifle's receiver. The sight base can then be attached to the bracket by means of the plastic-headed knob. The sight base has two adjusting screws on top for manipulating elevation, if necessary. The special rings are then placed on the scope and over the base to match up with the two mounting holes. Shims are provided that can be placed between the rings and the base to adjust windage. I mounted a Tasco 3-9x32 scope. The mount allows you to remove the scope without altering zero simply by unscrewing the plastic-headed knob. The only disadvantage to this mount is that, with the

The Swede 6.5x55 looks rather natty with its up-front scope in B-Square mounts. It shot well, too.

M1903's straight comb stock, the scope is mounted quite high.

The Moisin-Nagant mount also went on very quickly. To begin, drive out the rear sight pin with a small punch and remove the leaf spring. The B-Square base is then placed between the sight ears and secured by two screws that go through the original pin holes in the sight ears. Adjusting screws on the front and rear of the base allow you to tighten it in place and adjust for elevation if needed. Like the M96 mount, setscrews are located on either end of the mount.

I fired all three rifles from an improvised rolled blanket rest at 100 yards. To give my shoulder a break, I fired the soft-recoiling 6.5x55 Mauser first. I have fired this gun extensively with open sights and surplus ammunition, and while it has always been a very accurate rifle, with the lowest sight setting of 300 meters it tends to print about 9.5 inches high. It has the usual two-stage military trigger, but the let-off is very crisp. First, I used some of my handloads to get the rig zeroed in, and then I proceeded to test three different commercial loads.

This was my first experience with an LER scope on a rifle, so it took a bit of getting used to, but once I found out where to position my face on the stock, it proved to be very easy to shoot. The M96 Mauser and 6.5x55 cartridge lived up to their reputations, and all of my groups were dead on to point of aim. I had little reason to complain about the results:

Federal Premium	1 1/2 inches
Remington	1 5/8 inches
PMC	1 3/4 inches

The M1903 Springfield was next. It proved the most difficult to shoot due to the high position of the scope. To zero, I used some Dutch 30 M2 surplus ball ammo. After the light-kicking M96, the Springfield was quite a change. A lace-on cheekpiece would have been a most welcome accessory.

The groups were not the best of the day, but more than acceptable, and it was nice to again have them impacting exactly at the point of aim because this M1903 shoots about 11 inches high with its open U-notch battle sight. The results were as follows:

Hansen	1 3/4 inches
Remington	1 3/4 inches
PMC	2 1/2 inches

I then removed the Tasco LER scope from the M96 and mounted it on my Finnish Moisin-Nagant. This was the heaviest of the three rifles, and while the 7.62x54R generates as much recoil as the 30-06, the Moisin's weight made it an easier rifle to shoot than the Springfield. The lowest sight setting on this rifle is 200 meters, and it tends to print about 7 inches high with most loads I've shot through it. The 7.62x54R ammo was some Chinese surplus ball and some Century Arms 180-grain soft-nosed loads that were made in Yugoslavia.

In spite of having the heaviest trigger of the three, the Moisin performed quite well as the following groups showed, all printing to point of aim:

Century Arms	1 7/8 inches
ChiCom surplus	2 7/8 inches

I was suitably impressed with both the performance of my rifles and the B-Square scope mounts. Being able to shoot these rifles and not have to worry about holding low to get them on the target was a very rewarding experience. I was also pleased to see that they were capable of performing as well as modern sporting rifles with the right load.

The next time some shooting snob denigrates my classic military "junk," I'm going to unlimber one of these scoped rifles and take him and his modern rifle to task.

Paul Scarlata

THE TEST AMMO

Rifle	Ammunition
6.5x55 Swedish Mauser	Remington 140-grain PSP bullet
	Federal Premium 140-grain Nosler Partition
	PMC 139-grain PSP
30-06 Springfield	Hansen 150-grain Posi-Feed PSP
	Remington 150-grain Core-Lokt
	PMC 150-grain PSP
7.62x54R Russian	Century Arms 180-grain softpoint
	1963 Chinese surplus 149-grain FMJ

Kahr's K9

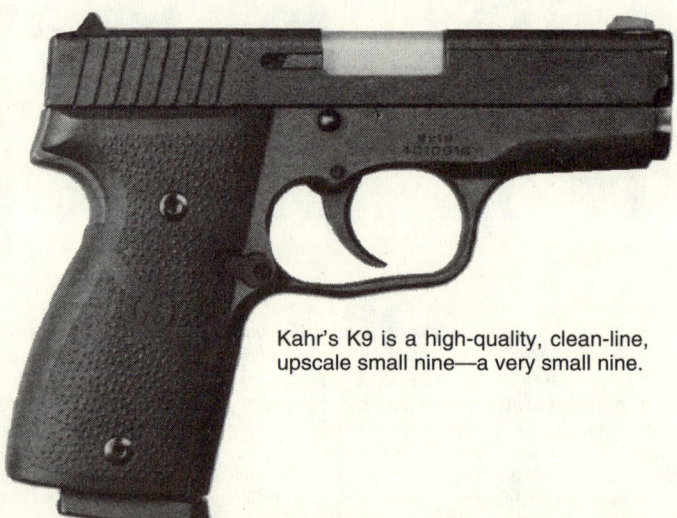

Kahr's K9 is a high-quality, clean-line, upscale small nine—a very small nine.

AMONG THE NEW small nines, there is one that stands out because it is smaller, flatter, and all-steel. The Kahr K9 is a striker-fired true hammerless, but it has a pivoting trigger. Its straight-line magazine holds seven rounds of 9x19mm. The only external controls are the slide latch and the magazine release.

Designed by Justin Moon, and made in Worcester, Massachusetts, the K9 has been referred to as "380-sized," and it is. Actually, there are a few 380 pistols that are slightly larger. The Kahr is 6 inches long and just under 4 1/2 inches in height.

The grip frame is particularly well designed. The incurve at upper rear is high, bringing the axis of the bore nearer to the top of the hand. The lower back of the grip has a nice outcurve, and the result is natural pointing. What appears to be a one-piece rubber grip is actually separate panels, meeting precisely to form the backstrap.

The Kahr weighs only 24 ounces, and I expected the felt recoil to be sharp. It wasn't. I have fired 380s that had heavier felt recoil. There are two reasons for this relatively light kick: the ergonomic shape of the grip frame and the good locking system.

The K9 uses the classic falling-barrel arrangement, but with two modern touches. The enlarged rectangular chamber section of the barrel locks into the large ejection port, and the

The slide locks open after the last shot. Slide latch, magazine release and trigger are the only controls.

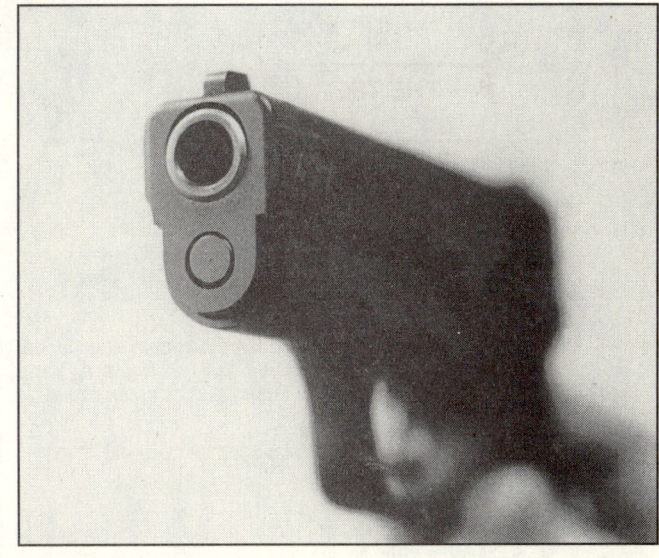

The muzzle area is very clean and flat—no protrusions.

On the left side, there's a slide latch and a magazine release—that's it.

barrel movement is controlled by a bent-oblong enclosed track in the underlug of the barrel. This smooth system spreads out the recoil felt by the hand.

The recoil spring is, necessarily, rather stiff. To those who may have difficulty in pulling the slide back, a word of advice: Don't try. Instead, grip the slide serrations firmly and push the frame toward the front using the stronger hand. I have used this method for many years on all auto pistols.

I tried the Kahr at the range with hollowpoint loads by Black Hills and Winchester, and with full jackets by Federal. It ate all of them without a hitch. Fired from a casual rest at 50 feet, it kept all shots in the black of a standard target. One group measured 4 inches. The polygonal-rifled barrel was easy to clean.

The firing system of the K9 is nicely engineered. A drawbar from the trigger turns a two-lobed lever over rearward. As the primary lobe cocks the striker, the secondary lobe comes up to depress the striker block, leaving the striker free for full travel to fire the cartridge. This system is unique, and patents have been applied for.

The K9 lockwork gives a double-action pull listed at 7 pounds, but it seems less. This is probably because of the shortness of the pull, as well as the smooth surface and good shape of the trigger. There is about $1/4$-inch of easy take-up, and then the trigger movement to let-off is only about $3/8$-inch. It's very quick.

The sights are just right—low profile, but with enough protrusion for easy eye pick-up. The picture is square post and square notch. There is a white vertical bar below the rear notch, and a white dot in the angled rear face of the front blade.

The rear sight is laterally adjustable by loosening an Allen screw in the notch and moving the sight in its dovetail. The front sight, also dovetail-mounted, appears to be movable, but it isn't. It is held at center by a spring and plunger accessible from inside the slide.

There are only three non-steel parts on the K9: the rubber grips, the polymer magazine floorplate, and the aluminum magazine follower. On the follower, at the point contacted by the slide latch, there is a steel bearing pin. Except for the automatic internal striker block, there is no safety, and none is needed. Just as with revolvers: If you pull the trigger, expect it to fire.

From the center of the trigger to the backstrap, the distance is only $2 3/8$ inches. With the easy slack taken up, this measurement is $1/4$-inch less. Smaller hands will find the Kahr to be very comfortable. The K9 is going to be perfect for ladies, for personal defense for anyone, and for a backup piece for law enforcement. It's a high-quality pistol; I like it.

J.B. Wood

Intratec's CAT-9

TESTFIRE TESTFIRE TESTFIRE

The CAT-9 has a well-shaped, comfortable grip, which it needs because this is not a big gun.

The CAT-9 from Intratec is flat, devoid of protrusions, and weighs 18 ounces empty.

INTRATEC DECIDED some time back to produce a new semi-auto pistol that would be state-of-the-art, destined to be their main offering once the TEC-9 and TEC-22 autoloaders went the way of dinosaurs, along with a slice of our cherished Second Amendment. In late 1994, they produced the CATegory 9—or CAT-9, for short.

Intratec calls this new handgun "...a radically new type of semi-automatic pistol, designed to offer a compact, lightweight, self-defense weapon." There is, however, much more.

If the novel but short-lived Israeli-made Sirkis pistol of the early 1980s comes to mind, it's because the CAT-9 is also the brainchild of Nehemiah Sirkis.

The CAT-9 is state-of-the-art from a design standpoint, but eminently practical as well, totally in line with the marketing and political climates of the 1990s. The pistol's frame is made of an extremely strong nylon-related polymer, through a process called Metal Moulding Manufacturing, "MIM" for short. Slide rails are stainless steel, injection-moulded in place. The resulting receiver is dimensionally exact and clean, and tremendously strong. The latter point is very important, because the CAT-9 employs a simple blowback action, something definitely rare in a pistol—particularly a *compact* pistol—that fires the 9mm Parabellum cartridge.

Overall, this pistol measures just 5 3/4 inches long by 4 1/4 inches high, and weighs just 18 ounces empty. For all its compactness, though, the CAT-9 still manages to incorporate a 3-inch barrel. The barrel, slide, breechblock and recoil spring assembly are all made of high-tensile, heat-treated steel.

The pistol has three main subassemblies: the slide/barrel group, the frame and the seven-round magazine. The latter is made of stamped steel with a synthetic finger rest for a base. The slide/barrel group consists of the chunky, squarish chrome-moly steel slide containing the breechblock, barrel and recoil spring assembly. The recoil spring is captive to the spring guide. The breechblock contains the striker firing mechanism and extractor.

The CAT-9 striker system is really a modified version of that employed in the massive Heckler & Koch VP-70Z pistol. Pulling the trigger cocks the striker and then releases it to act upon the firing pin. The trigger bar doubles as a firing pin block, securing the striker so that, even if the gun is dropped, it will not go off accidentally. The frame assembly houses the trigger mechanism, magazine catch and ejector. The trigger blade itself is quite beefy and made of fortified Delrin.

The CAT-9's frame and slide assemblies are pinned together at the center of the frame, just above the trigger. This pin engages the massive lug beneath the breech, while the breechblock has a top lug that fits into a mating hole atop the slide. During the firing sequence, the breechblock and slide recoil as a single unit; the barrel remains stationary.

The CAT-9 is double-action-only (DAO). The fairly long, straight-back trigger pull needed for every shot ensures the same kind of operational safety found on the majority of current DAO semi-autos and revolvers. The CAT-9 tested had a trigger

The compact CAT-9 almost disappears when a big man holds it two-handed.

The CAT-9 field-strips easily for cleaning, revealing relatively large simple parts.

pull that broke right at the 13-pound mark. Besides the somewhat long and heavy pull, there was a marked hesitation just before the point at which the striker let go, ensuring even further that firing this pistol requires a deliberate action on the part of the user. The CAT-9 has no external safeties to play with or forget about. The pistol's lines are extremely smooth and clean all over, with absolutely nothing that would cause the gun to snag on clothing or other concealment if it needs to be pulled real fast.

The CAT-9's profile is so clean, in fact, it doesn't have regular sights. There's a shallow longitudinal groove atop the square slide. Designed as a compact, low-key, yet potent defensive piece for "up-close-and-deadly" encounters, traditional sights were thought superfluous.

During tests with the CAT-9, I quickly realized that I could do very well off-hand, even in rapid fire, out to roughly 30 feet. Point shooters might find the CAT-9 much to their liking. Ergonomically, the gun scores high. Its grip is .95-inch thick and shaped in such a manner that it can fit a wide range of hands. This is important, because the CAT-9's recoil is fairly stout, although manageable.

Recoil is the reason Intratec recommends no +P 9mm ammo be used in this gun. I fully agree. I did fire some +P fodder, and the recoil could be regarded as excessive for the average user.

To soften the pounding on the straight blowback action, the CAT-9 has a synthetic buffer ring around the barrel. Several extra buffer rings are included with each pistol.

My tests were carried out with a variety of defensive loads such as Federal Hydra-Shok (both 124 and 147 grains), as well as Winchester Silvertip—two highly popular 9mm cartridges—plus a few others. In all instances, the CAT-9 produced the required combat accuracy by grouping most shots, off-hand and in rapid fire, well within the "kill zone" of standard training silhouettes at up to 10 yards.

Out of 350 rounds fired, only one failure to fire occurred, due to what appeared to be a "hard" primer. Intratec, again, warns in the manual against this possibility and recommends that only brand-name, new factory ammo be used in the CAT-9. Tests also showed that the magazine falls clear of the gun instantly when the release button, located on the left side of the grip, is pushed all the way in. The slide does not lock open after the last round, but there are rather large and easy-to-grip grooves that allow quick and positive racking for that first round.

With its unmistakable "Glock-ish" looks, clever design, hard-wearing matte-black finish and uncomplicated DAO system, the Intratec CAT-9 is certain to do well. It's a quality semi-auto at an affordable price that is just as concealable as the average five-shot J-frame revolver. •

J.I. Galan

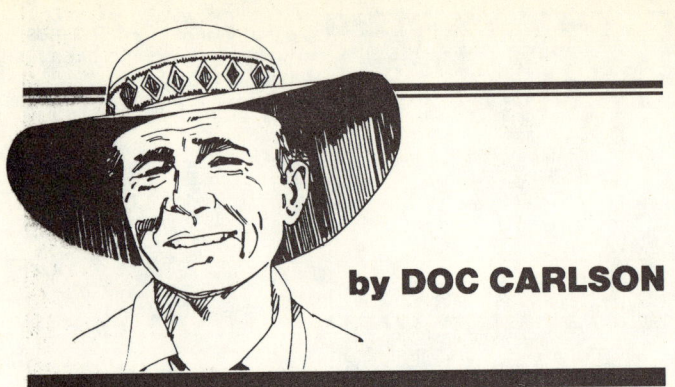

by DOC CARLSON

BLACKPOWDER REVIEW

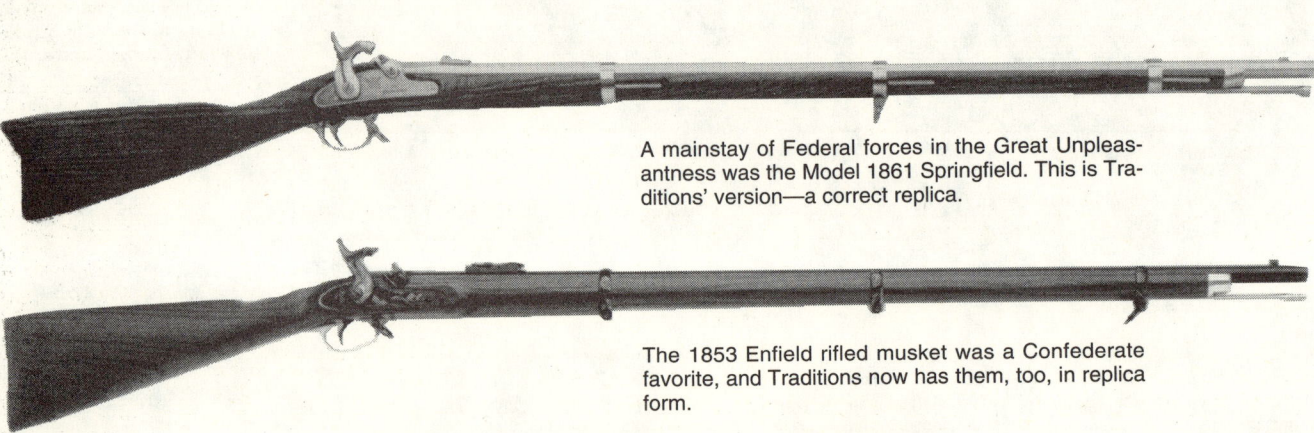

A mainstay of Federal forces in the Great Unpleasantness was the Model 1861 Springfield. This is Traditions' version—a correct replica.

The 1853 Enfield rifled musket was a Confederate favorite, and Traditions now has them, too, in replica form.

Prairie River Arms' bullpup hunting rifle makes a standard in-line look old-timey, but they say it shoots fine.

FIFTY YEARS AGO, something happened that would have a profound effect upon the American firearms industry and the way that Americans viewed firearms: Thousands of World War II veterans came home. They brought with them a knowledge of firearms and entered a time when folks had money and a newfound abundance of leisure time in which to spend some of it. There was time and money for hobbies and recreation. Hunting, target shooting, collecting, reloading and other firearms pursuits were in vogue. Guns, primarily considered tools before the war, now became sources of spare-time pleasure.

A natural outgrowth of this firearms interest was the popularity of collecting. Suddenly, the old Colts and Winchesters, along with Grandpa's old muzzleloader, were now interesting from a historical perspective, rather than as the obsolete tools of a bygone era. Fostered by a typically American curiosity toward the workings of things mechanical, shooting antique guns became a legitimate hobby.

And here we are in 1995. Over those fifty years there have been literally millions of examples of thousands of products on the market targeting (pun intended) the American shooter and collector. A few of this year's crop are here:

Connecticut Valley Arms has an accessory to delight blackpowder shooters who dislike the cleaning process. Called the Barrel Blaster, it's an electric pump that circulates cleaning solution through the barrel without taking it out of the stock. The company says it takes five minutes to clean the average rifle. The unit runs on 110-volt household current or, with an adapter, on 12-volt automotive current. It should make that messy job a little easier.

CVA also has a series of very reasonably priced rifles with a traditional side hammer, half-stock design, but utilizing modern synthetics for the stock. The result is a rugged, accurate rifle that is priced at $99.95—a price not often seen these days. Called the Bobcats, these rifles sure are worth a look.

Remington Arms Co. will be manufacturing a replica of a flintlock rifle made by Eliphalet Remington in 1816. The gun will be a limited-edition model on a build-to-order basis only through 1995. There will be a 39-inch browned barrel, 1:66-inch twist, in 50-caliber, stocked in curly maple.

The most sweeping design change recently is the in-line action. It burst on the scene a few years ago with the introduction of the Knight line of rifles. Lately, there have been many variations, and 1995 will be no exception.

Thompson/Center, the company that brought out their Hawken Rifle in 1970 and started the reproduction revolution, has a new model of their successful in-line called the Firehawk. In either American black walnut or synthetic Rynite stock, the Firehawk is a streamlined Thunderhawk, more sculptured in the grip area, with a typical Monte Carlo cheekpiece. Its weight is 7 pounds, the barrel length 24 inches, so it's a trim, quick rifle for the hunter. Rifling twist is 1:38 inches for use with slugs.

The T/C folks brought out the Scout rifle a year or so ago, with a center-hung hammer and the lines of a Model 94 Winchester. The original had a 21-inch barrel. This year there is a 24-inch barrel, part octagon, stepping down to round as it leaves the forend—a nice touch.

T/C was the first major manufacturer to embrace natural lubricants for bullet, patch and bore lubrication. They have since been followed by darn near everybody. Natural, tallow-like lubes, like our forefathers used, make cleaning easier, allowing more shots between wipings.

The only thing I have not liked is that most of the natural lubes have oil of wintergreen added to them which makes them smell like liniment. I guess this has little effect on game animals. I always figured the deer thought anyone who smelled like that was so arthritic they were little threat in the woods. Anyway, T/C has given their 1000 Plus Natural Lube a pine scent. I still would prefer no scent at all, but pine is infinitely preferable to wintergreen.

Hornady Manufacturing does have a natural lube with no scent. It comes in a 4-ounce tube and is used as a patch lube, bullet lube or to grease the bore of the rifle after cleaning. When added to Hornady's complete line of swaged round balls, their good Great Plains bullets, and the plastic sabot bullets, it would seem that Hornady can supply the projectile needs of the muzzleloader—whatever they might be.

Buffalo Bullets, one of the original slug manufacturers, continues to improve their line.

A relative newcomer among the non-traditional, in-line-type gunmakers is **White Shooting Systems**. They market an in-line-action firearm that we have reported upon here previously. New for White this year is a two-hand pistol called the Javelina. It will be available in 45- and 50-caliber. The pistol comes with a sling that is used for both carrying and as a stabilizer for the gun while shooting. It is a handy little outfit and shoots with velocities, energies and accuracy that almost duplicate rifles. Where legal, it should be popular with hunters.

White has a line of bullets tailored to use in their guns. The bullets and the White firearms together are called the White System. The bullets are designed to be slightly undersize for ease of loading and upset on firing to give a good bore seal. Accuracy is very good with these bullets, and they also perform quite well in guns other than the White in-lines.

Along with the Javelina pistol, there is to be a more traditional White hunting rifle called the Green River. These guns will be side-hammer percussion rifles in English hunting rifle style, half-stocked and pistol-gripped. Unlike the traditional English rifle, they have composite stocks, finished in a crotch walnut pattern that looks more like wood than the real thing. I'm really looking forward to getting a chance to shoot this one. It will be available in 41-, 45- and 50-caliber.

Modern Muzzle Loading, Inc., has an interesting accessory—a sub-caliber insert to allow the rifle to be shot using 22 LR rimfire ammunition. This will encourage off-season practice and plinking with the same rifle used in the muzzle-loading seasons. As Tony Knight, the inventor, says, "Where else can you get a 22 rifle that has a Timney trigger, match chamber, and match-grade accuracy for this kind of money?"

Probably the most unconventional of the new firearms this year is the **Prairie River Arms** offering. They have come to market with a bullpup that puts the action of the rifle back in the thumbhole stock under the cheek of the shooter. The entire striker system is enclosed in the buttstock area, and the access hole in the right side of the stock is covered by a pivoting door to totally seal up the system. The bullpup design has been around, off and on. It remains to be seen if it catches on with muzzle-loader shooters.

Among the more traditional firearms that are available to hunters and target shooters are several new reproductions on the market this year. The shooter of traditional guns certainly shouldn't feel left out of the new-product parade.

Traditions, Inc., has stepped into the reenacting and skirmishing activities with the introduction of two War of Northern Aggression muskets. The first is a very nice copy of the 1853 three-band Enfield rifle musket with walnut stock; color case-hardened lock; and solid brass buttplate, trigger guard and nose cap. The round, blued 58-caliber barrel is 39 inches long, rifled 1:48 inches. A steel ramrod, sling swivels, single trigger and military sights, as original, complete the make-up of this gun.

Traditions' other offering is an authentic reproduction of the 1861 U.S. Springfield, the mainstay of the Federal forces during the first half of the Southern Rebellion. The musket has walnut stock with a steel nose cap and a 40-inch round barrel with three bands of steel. Caliber is, of course, 58 with rifling of 1:66 inches. The lock is correctly marked with the Federal eagle and U.S. Springfield 1861. Buttplate, trigger guard, ramrod and sling hardware are also steel and finished, as were the originals, "in the white."

A few years back, the **Colt Firearms Co.** continued the production of the Colt cap-and-ball revolvers of the 1800s. The project was dropped for various reasons, much to the dismay of many blackpowder shooters. Now, they're back.

Called the Signature Series, the 1847 Walker, 1849 Pocket, 1851 Navy, 1860 Army, 1862

Dixie's Sharps in 45-70 and 40-65 is aimed at the blackpowder silhouette game—it ought to hit it.

There's a new lube claimed to keep fouling softer than previous slug lubes. There has been a real problem with slugs from the beginning. Loading becomes difficult, if not impossible, after two or three shots. This new bullet coating addresses that problem; we can all hope.

Buffalo now has a very short slug-type bullet for muzzleloaders. It's only slightly longer than a conventional round ball. The intent is to offer a projectile that delivers more energy than a round ball, is easier to load than a sabot, and gives higher velocity than a standard conical bullet. Sort of a half ball/half conical. It gives good accuracy in both fast and slow twist barrels with much less recoil than the heavier conical bullets.

One other muzzle-loading projectile deserves a look, I think. **Black Belt Bullets** is making a soft lead swaged bullet fitted with a plastic skirt to seal the bore and ride the rifling. Accuracy is very good, and the soft lead bullet expands well. They are available in several weights and in 50- and 54-caliber. The skirt allows the use of a slightly undersize bullet that makes loading easier.

The knurled Ball-Et from Buffalo Bullet Co. has more energy than a ball, higher velocity than a slug.

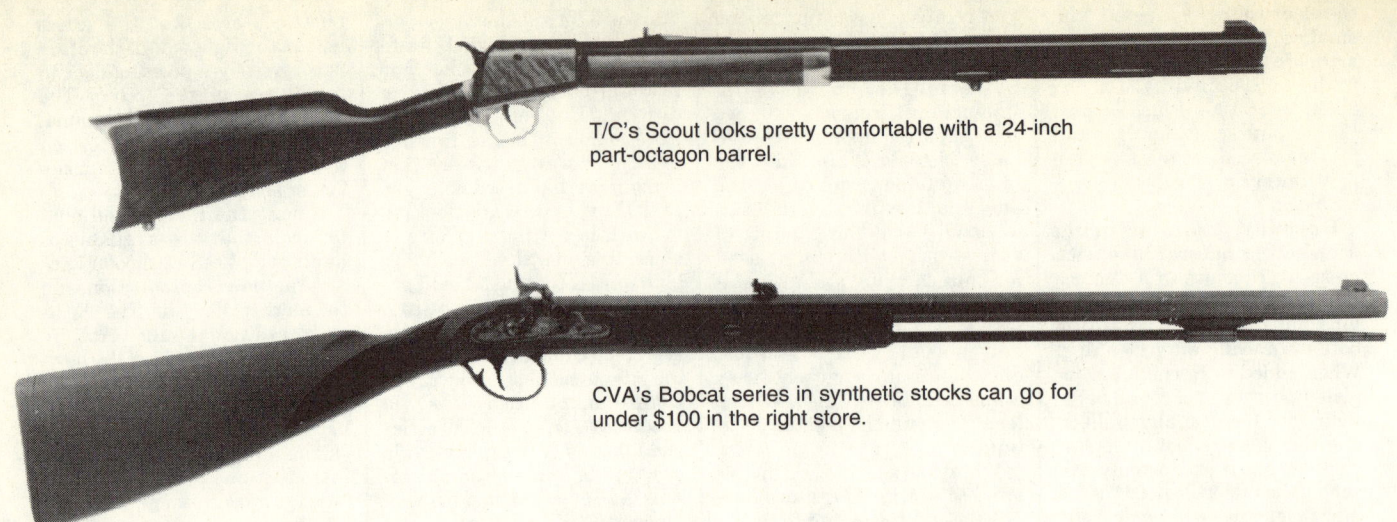

T/C's Scout looks pretty comfortable with a 24-inch part-octagon barrel.

CVA's Bobcat series in synthetic stocks can go for under $100 in the right store.

Trapper, and 3rd Model Dragoon will be remanufactured with authentic Colt markings and continuation of the original serial numbers, as before. There will be a few "enhanced" models with gold inlays and such. The blue on all guns will be the typical Colt charcoal blue that is so distinctive with color case-hardened finish where appropriate. These guns are not reproductions or facsimiles, but are, in fact, the continuation of the original Colt blackpowder models, as before.

New to the series will be the 1861 Colt Civil War Musket. It will come in a wooden case and is a faithful continuation of the production of the original gun. The bright-finished lockplate is marked "1861 US Colt's Pt F A Mfg Co, Hartford Ct," as before. The stock is one piece, oil-finished walnut with all the steel metalwork being finished bright. I think we'll all look forward to seeing these guns at dealers around the country.

U.S. Patent Firearm Co. is also reproducing the line of old Colt percussion revolvers using the Colt charcoal blue and color case-hardening on the frames. These guns are made in the United States and follow the originals very closely. This company is just getting started, and the product appears to be of very high quality.

CVA's electric pump system cleans, they say, an average dirty rifle in five minutes.

Of special interest to the blackpowder cartridge shooter will be the news that **Dixie Gun Works** is bringing in some good quality reproductions of the 1874 Sharps Buffalo Rifle. These Italian-made copies will be available in a lightweight version with a straight grip buttstock and light, tapered, octagon 30-inch barrel, finished in a matte blue, and a model set up for silhouette shooting with heavy, octagon 30-inch barrel and shotgun-type butt with pistol grip. The grip area and steel buttplate are both nicely checkered on the Silhouette model. The lightweight model will be available in 45-70 only, while the Silhouette will be made in both 45-70 with a 1:18-inch twist and 40-65 in a 1:16-inch twist. The 40-65 caliber is becoming very popular with the metal-animal shooters, so this Italian-Dixie effort should be well received.

Both models have double-set triggers and color case-hardened receivers. There are four holes in the tangs, two tapped 10x28 and two with metric threads for the attachment of whatever tang sight suits your fancy. The lightweight gun weighs in at 10 pounds, 3 ounces; the Silhouette at 10 pounds, 6 ounces—well below the 12-pound, 2-ounce limit for blackpowder cartridge silhouette shooting. Both guns also fit the requirements for stock configuration for those matches.

Lyman has added a new bullet, intended for the silhouette game, to their list of moulds. This 45-caliber bullet, #457658, is a 480-grain spire-point design, which should give it good downrange ballistics. It appears to have well-designed grease grooves to carry plenty of lube, a must in the blackpowder games.

We also have a new blackpowder substitute in the marketplace. Called Black Canyon Powder, it is manufactured by **Legend Products Corp.** and is now available. The new powder contains no sulfur and generates very little fouling or corrosive elements in the bore. It is usable in all muzzle-loading firearms including flintlocks, which is nice, as well as cartridge applications. Black Canyon must be well compressed for consistent velocities and pressures. Time will tell how well it will be accepted by blackpowder shooters and hunters, but it would appear to have real promise. The stuff can be shipped via UPS with the same restrictions as smokeless powders, which is a real plus. Storage requirements are also the same as for smokeless. This certainly helps the availability of propellants for the blackpowder sport. •

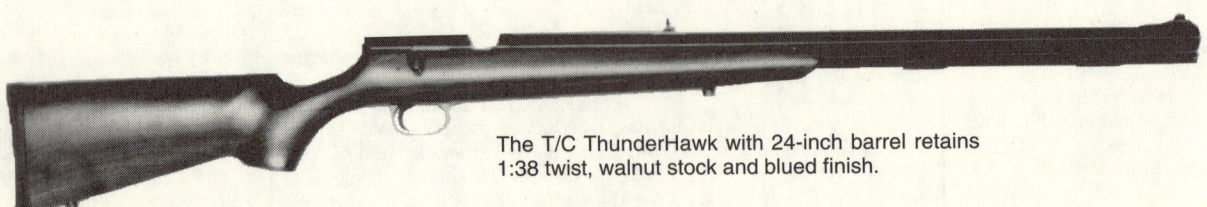

The T/C ThunderHawk with 24-inch barrel retains 1:38 twist, walnut stock and blued finish.

CUT YOUR COST IN HALF.

Why would anybody mount only half a scope? Probably because that's all they could afford.

On the other hand, you could take the same amount of money and buy a Weaver®.

Not only do you get a complete scope, you get one that's equal in quality to any high-priced brand.

But don't take our word for it, do your own comparison – look through a Weaver. The multi-coated, precision ground lenses reduce glare and offer unbeatable light transmission for clear, crisp images from dawn to dusk.

Zeroing-in is easy and repeatable with our precise 1/4-minute adjustments.

How about fogging and moisture? It's common on those pricey two-piece scopes. But not with Weaver. The nitrogen filled, one-piece tube has no joints, so moisture stays out, and lenses remain locked in alignment – defying recoils from the ugliest magnums.

And all scopes, from the K2.5 up to the V16, are protected by Weaver's exclusive limited lifetime warranty.

So buy a Weaver and cut your cost, without sacrificing quality.

And if you act now, you can really clean up; because we're giving away a compact field gun cleaning kit with every scope purchase. See your local Weaver dealer for details.

NOT YOUR SCOPE.

WEAVER

TO DO IT RIGHT.

Sporting Equipment Division, Blount Inc., P.O. Box 856, Dept. **BUG**, Lewiston, ID 83501. Phone: (800) 627-3640.

Convenient, Reliable, Effective!

♠ *Five-Shot, Stainless Steel Construction*

♠ *Life-Time Warranty*

♠ *Call or Write to receive your Free NAA Catalog featuring our complete line of Firearms and Accessories*

North American Arms, Inc.
2150 South 950 East
Provo, Utah 84606
1-(800)-821-5783

Rest Assured.
You've finally got what you need.

Hoppe's new one-hand-opening knife and our new 14-in-one screwdriver set are masterpieces of form and function. Neither achievement was single-handed, however. Renowned knife designer Blackie Collins worked with us to create both of these precision multipurpose instruments. **Shooter's Knife for Bench and Field** So durable, light and versatile, there is no other knife like this compact four-ounce classic. **Opens and Closes with Just One Hand.** Unique SwingLock design locks the blade solidly for safety. **Drop-Point Blade** gives you maximum control for field dressing and general use. High carbon stainless, heat treated to a Rockwell C 57-58. Excellent edge holding and resistance to breakage and corrosion. **Allen Wrenches and Screwdrivers** fit most scope rings, adjustable sights and take-down bows. **Military-Grade Polymer Handle.** Moisture proof. Withstands extreme temperatures and rugged use. **Shooter's Screwdriver Set** At the shooting bench or the workbench, your fine firearms deserve precision tools you can use with confidence.

Black Cordura™ Sheath with slip-on/slip-off clip holds tight to your belt while you move and work.

At last you've got them -- all in one neat package. **14 Bits Most Widely Used for Firearms.** Two Phillips heads, seven slotted heads and five Allen wrenches. **Unique Five Chamber Design** for easy bit selection. Clear markings on each bit and on the handle ribs mean no more dump and search. Rotate the end cap and pick just what you need. **Built to Last a Lifetime.** Bits and shaft are premium grade S2 steel, machined to stringent tolerances for a snug, no-slip fit. **Special Spanner handle** for maximum torque made from the same grade material as the main handle.

HOPPE'S 9

THE GUN CARE PEOPLE.

A Division of Penguin Industries Inc. Airport Industrial Mall Coatesville, PA 19320

FAIL SAFE TECHNOLOGY

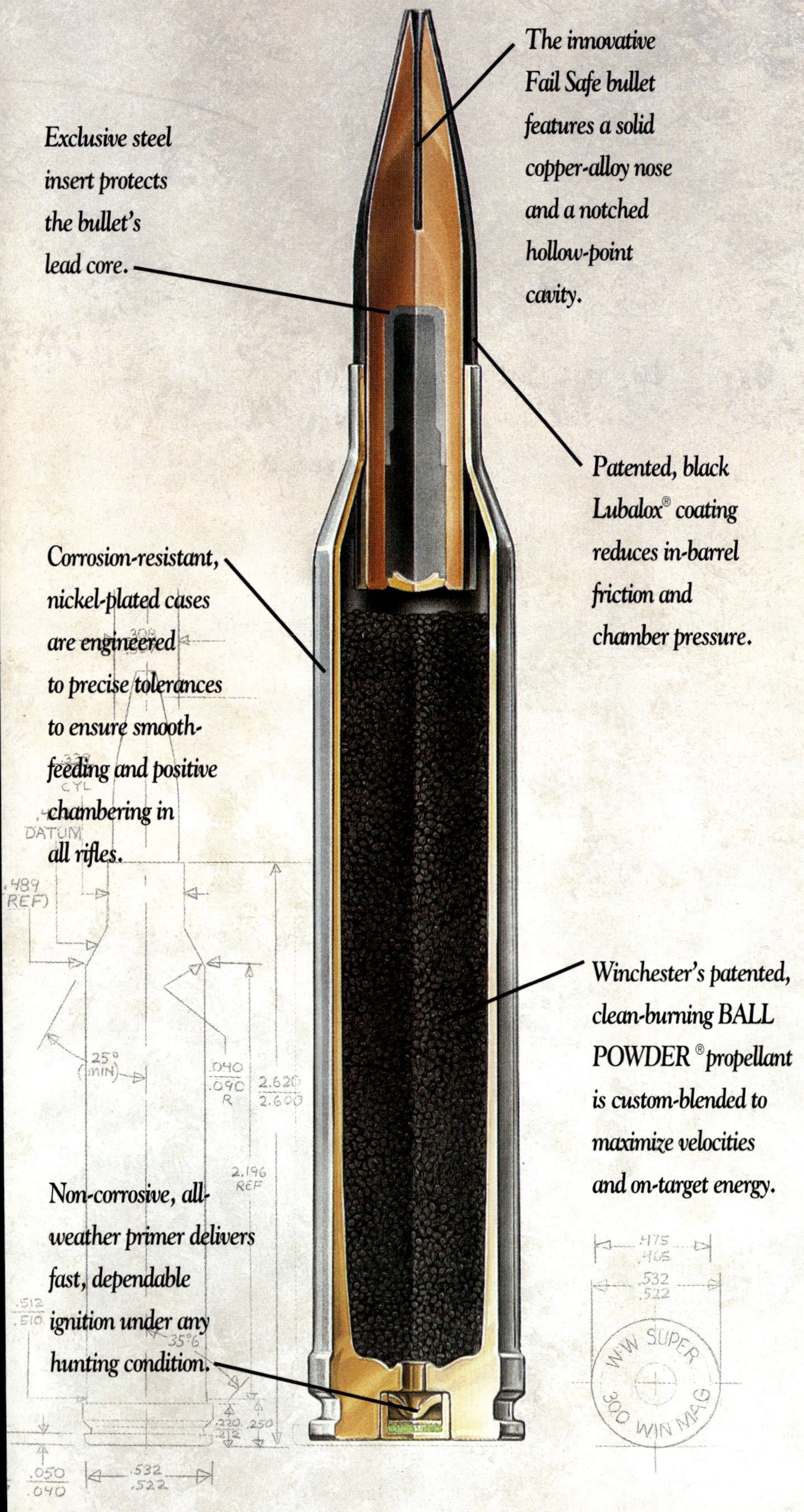

Exclusive steel insert protects the bullet's lead core.

The innovative Fail Safe bullet features a solid copper-alloy nose and a notched hollow-point cavity.

Patented, black Lubalox® coating reduces in-barrel friction and chamber pressure.

Corrosion-resistant, nickel-plated cases are engineered to precise tolerances to ensure smooth-feeding and positive chambering in all rifles.

Winchester's patented, clean-burning BALL POWDER® propellant is custom-blended to maximize velocities and on-target energy.

Non-corrosive, all-weather primer delivers fast, dependable ignition under any hunting condition.

© 1995 Winchester/Olin Corporation, East Alton, Illinois 62024

WINCHESTER AMMUNITION

What America Shoots™

Supreme® Fail Safe® Centerfire Rifle Ammunition.

Load up with the ultimate performer–Winchester's Supreme **Fail Safe** Centerfire Rifle ammunition.

Fail Safe features:
• Technology So Innovative It's Covered By 6 Active and Pending Patents.
• Dramatic Expansion and Upset Performance
• Friction-Reducing Black Lubalox® Coating
• Virtual 100% Weight Retention
• Smooth-Feeding, Corrosion-Resistant Nickel-Plated Shellcase
• Exclusive Steel Insert Protects The Bullet's Lead Core

Available in:
270 Winchester 140 gr. FS
7mm Rem. Magnum 160 gr. FS
308 Winchester 180 gr. FS
30-06 Springfield 180 gr. FS
300 Winchester Magnum 180 gr. FS
338 Winchester Magnum 230 gr. FS

New Fail Safe Cartridge Offerings:
280 Rem. 160 gr., 308 Winchester 150 gr., 30-06 Springfield 165 gr.

Winchester's Supreme Fail Safe Centerfire Rifle Ammunition: Revolutionary, patented design giving you the ultimate in superior performance. Stop by your Winchester Ammunition Dealer - today!

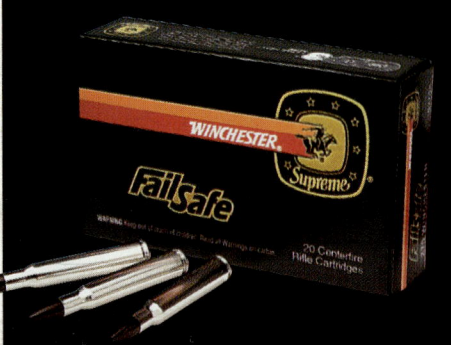

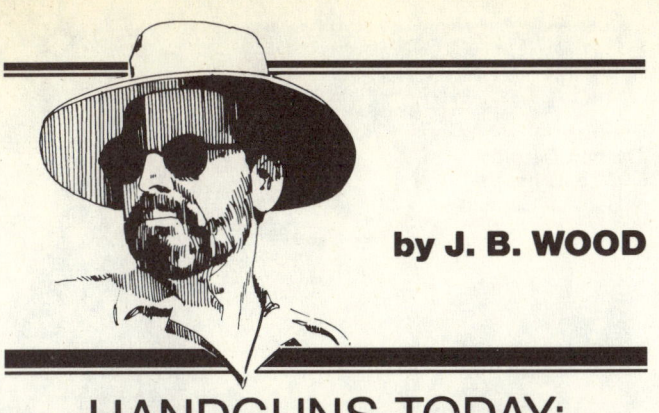

by J. B. WOOD

HANDGUNS TODAY:

AUTOLOADERS

As YOU MAY have noticed by now, this is the 50th annual edition of GUN DIGEST. Time flies when you're having fun, eh? I've seen this grand old book grow from a half-inch thickness to its present magnificent proportions. This edition also marks a smaller anniversary—I've been writing this section for fifteen years.

In the future, those who study auto pistols may call this the year of the small nines. Most of the larger pistols are now being chambered for 40 S&W and 45 Auto, and there seems to be a trend toward making very small guns in full 9x19mm caliber. From a size standpoint, some of these qualify as pocket pistols.

One was announced here last year, the **Kahr K9**. Since then, I have fired the little K9 quite a lot. It is of all-steel construction, double-action-only, and with the chamber loaded it holds eight rounds. The DA trigger pull is quick and easy, and the felt recoil is relatively light. The workmanship is excellent; it's a very nice 380-sized gun.

George Kellgren was designing and making polymer-frame pistols long before there was a Glock. His new firm, **Kel-Tec CNC, Inc.**, has a new 9mm DA-only pistol called the P-11. It weighs just 14 ounces, and the fully loaded capacity is eleven rounds. A unique expansion-type hammer spring gives a smooth trigger pull. The grip frame is polymer, and the firing system parts are of high-grade steel.

Other small nines abound. **AMT** plans to offer their DAO Back Up in 9x19mm and in other chamberings. The AT-9 is finally coming from **Accu-Tek**, and it will also be made in 40 S&W and 45 ACP. **European American Armory** (E.A.A.) has the lightweight Astra A-75 in both chamberings. **Intratec** already had the DAO Category 9 and is now planning to offer it in 40 S&W, 45 Auto, and 380 Auto.

Interarms has the DA Ultrastar in 9mm with a polymer frame at 26 ounces, and their Firestar Plus is now offered in 40 S&W and 45 Auto. **MKS Supply** offers the Hi-Point 9mm Compact in alloy or polymer frame, reliable and very inexpensive. **Heritage Mfg.** is considering the DuPlessis small 9mm from South Africa, a neat DAO with a polymer frame. This is the one Smith & Wesson looked at before they produced the Sigma.

As the 9mm Parabellums have gotten smaller, the 380 pistols have begun to shrink proportionately. A case in point is the elegant little Escort, designed by **Sites** in Italy, and made in the U.S. by **American Arms**. An all-stainless DAO, its full width is $13/16$-inch. It has a seven-round magazine and soft polymer grips, and weighs only 19 ounces. The magazine release is low-profile, and the takedown latch is inside the guard, behind the trigger. A very neat design.

Among the 380 pistols is one that I frequently carry, the fine CZ 83. Made before the ridiculous ten-round limit, it has a thirteen-shot magazine. It also has a silky-smooth DA trigger pull, and ambidextrous safety and magazine release. The entire CZ line, including the renowned CZ 75 and CZ 85 pistols,

Kel-Tec's P-11 is DA-only, holds eleven rounds, and weighs 14 ounces empty.

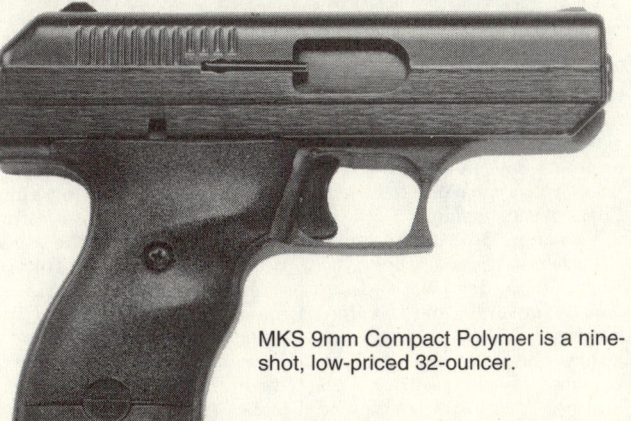

MKS 9mm Compact Polymer is a nine-shot, low-priced 32-ouncer.

is now imported by **Magnum Research**.

Smith and Wesson's 380 Sigma is a reality on magazines covers at this writing. It's a six-shot ergonomic delight at 14 ounces, empty. The **Glock** 380 is on the market in Europe; there are, they say, "no plans" for U.S. availability. Time will tell, if no one else.

Moving into the full-sized pistols, we come to the **Beretta**

Model 8000 and Model 8040 Cougar in 9x19mm and 40 S&W, respectively. A break from tradition in both appearance and mechanism, the Cougar has a rotating barrel locking system. When I said "full-sized" above, I meant the frame. The Cougar is actually a "compact," 7 inches long overall.

The Model 909 has a curved backstrap and a straight-line nine-round magazine. The Model 910 has a straight backstrap and a double-row ten-round magazine.

The lovely 9mm Luger in stainless steel is now from **Stoeger**, and, thanks to an old trademark registry, they can

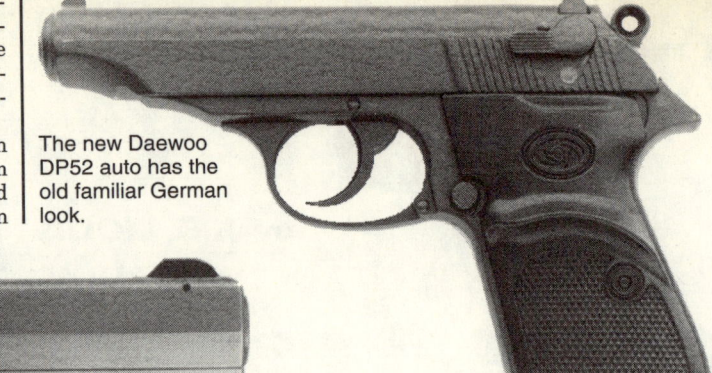
The new Daewoo DP52 auto has the old familiar German look.

The elegant little Escort from American Arms is just 13/16-inch at its widest point.

rear sight that some importers have added.

The magazine capacity restrictions that are bothering the makers of double-row 9mms have caused many to look again at the 45-caliber. The theory seems to be that if you can't make as many holes, make bigger ones. **Taurus** has the PT945, with selective DA/SA action and an eight-round magazine, and it weighs only 29 ounces. Nice.

There is a new double-action

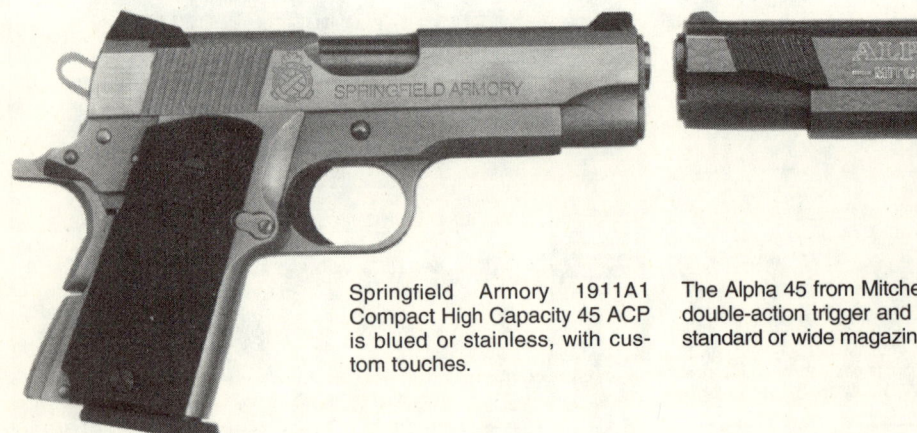
Springfield Armory 1911A1 Compact High Capacity 45 ACP is blued or stainless, with custom touches.

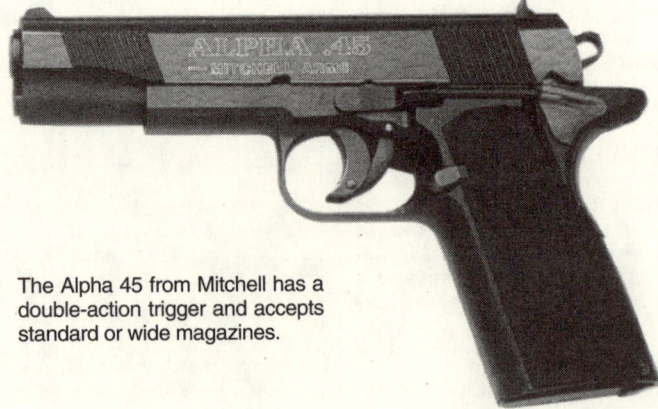
The Alpha 45 from Mitchell has a double-action trigger and accepts standard or wide magazines.

The news from the other big names is mostly that pistols announced last year are finally becoming available. The **SIG/Sauer** P229 in 357 SIG is here, as is the **Heckler & Koch** USP. The KP94 and KP94L (the L is for the factory-installed laser) are now coming through from **Ruger**, and **Browning** now has the Hi-Power in 40 S&W.

In addition to the Sigma in 9mm and 40 S&W, **Smith & Wesson** has two new moderately priced guns in 9x19mm.

call it a Luger. I have fired one of these extensively, and it works fine. The workmanship is also excellent. With most of the old originals now in the collector-price category, it's nice to have a Luger to shoot again.

Two of my favorite 9mm pistols are now in good supply: the Bersa Thunder Nine from **Eagle Imports**, and the Bernardelli P.One from **Armsport**. The Bersa has all of the features of the Walther P88 and more, and at a fraction of the price. The Bernardelli is of

machined steel in the old European way, with no shortcuts. Both of these pistols are of outstanding quality, and both are moderately priced.

Two other interesting nines: **K-Sports Imports,** of Pomona, California, has the Model 213B, essentially a Tokarev with the wrap-around grip and manual safety of the rare Tokagypt. **Sentinel Arms** of Detroit has a 9x18mm Makarov from Bulgaria that appears to be the basic military-style gun, without the adjustable

45 Auto with several interesting features, the Alpha 45 from **Mitchell Arms**. It has a module-style trigger system, allowing easy change between SA-only, DA-only, and regular DA/SA operation. Another unique feature is its acceptance of either standard GM-pattern magazines or wide-bodied double-row types.

Mil-Spec Industries, of Great Neck, New York, has a new 45 or 9mm pistol of general GM-1911 design, but with a combination stainless steel

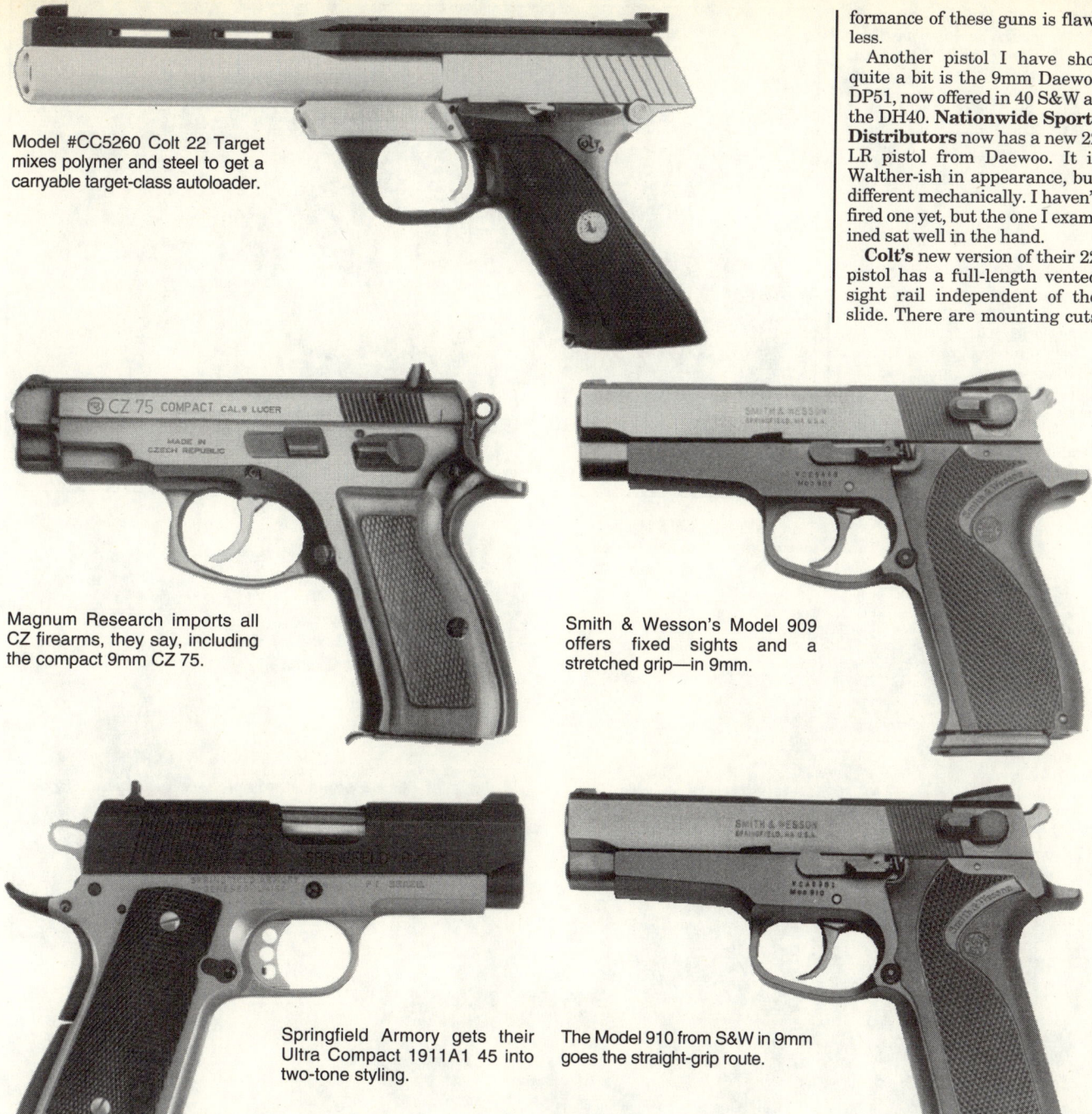

Model #CC5260 Colt 22 Target mixes polymer and steel to get a carryable target-class autoloader.

Magnum Research imports all CZ firearms, they say, including the compact 9mm CZ 75.

Smith & Wesson's Model 909 offers fixed sights and a stretched grip—in 9mm.

Springfield Armory gets their Ultra Compact 1911A1 45 into two-tone styling.

The Model 910 from S&W in 9mm goes the straight-grip route.

formance of these guns is flawless.

Another pistol I have shot quite a bit is the 9mm Daewoo DP51, now offered in 40 S&W as the DH40. **Nationwide Sports Distributors** now has a new 22 LR pistol from Daewoo. It is Walther-ish in appearance, but different mechanically. I haven't fired one yet, but the one I examined sat well in the hand.

Colt's new version of their 22 pistol has a full-length vented sight rail independent of the slide. There are mounting cuts and polymer grip frame. It is the BUL M-5, made in Israel, and offered in Standard and Commander sizes. In the U.S. and Canada, the magazines will be of ten-round capacity. Elsewhere, it will be thirteen and eighteen rounds, respectively.

Brolin Arms, of Pomona, California, has the P45—a standard GM-pattern gun with a conical barrel lock-up. It is offered in many styles, with options that include factory compensators and compact versions. The guns that I examined at the SHOT Show were very nicely made. Also seen was the Bald Eagle from **STI International,** of Austin, Texas, with many custom features and options, in 45 Auto and 40 S&W. As with most custom guns, it was pricey, but well done.

Springfield, Inc., has two new small 45 pistols—the Ultra-Compact and the Compact High Capacity. The Ultra has a seven-round magazine, weighs 31 ounces, and has a 3½-inch barrel. A ported version is also offered. The Compact High Capacity holds ten-plus-one. The barrel is 4 inches, and a Novak rear sight is available as an option.

J&S Worldwide is the new owner of **Coonan Arms,** and all of their precisely made 357 Magnum pistols are still available, including the neat Cadet compact version. A new full-sized gun is also offered, with many custom features and options. After many rounds fired through a Coonan, I can say that the per- for optical sights, and the trigger pull and travel are factory adjusted. The new 22 Target version is equipped with a 6-inch bull barrel.

Desert Industries is alive and well, and their pretty little 22 LR Double Deuce is now being produced in good quantity. All in stainless steel, it is very small, with a selective DA/SA trigger and a hammer-block safety. This gun is beautifully made. A version in 25 Auto will be along soon.

Phoenix Arms is still making the old, reliable Raven 25 Auto, but the real news is their 2-in-1 Conversion Kit for the fine little HP22 pistol in 22 LR. It consists of an extended barrel, 5 inches long, and a ten-round magazine with a generous finger extension. The barrel change is easily made and turns a protection piece into a casual target pistol. The rear sight of the HP22 is adjustable.

Shooting Systems Group, of Fenton, Missouri, has a new line of holsters called the Contour Series with a polymer belt panel, and holsters of quilted ballistic nylon. A patented feature provides adjustable gun-retaining tension. There are four styles, three with keeper-straps and one without. The small-of-the-back version is particularly well-engineered. •

Beretta deservedly brags of its big-ticket M9 sales to lots of agencies.

Yes, it's a Beretta—the 9mm/40 S&W Cougar with a different locking set-up.

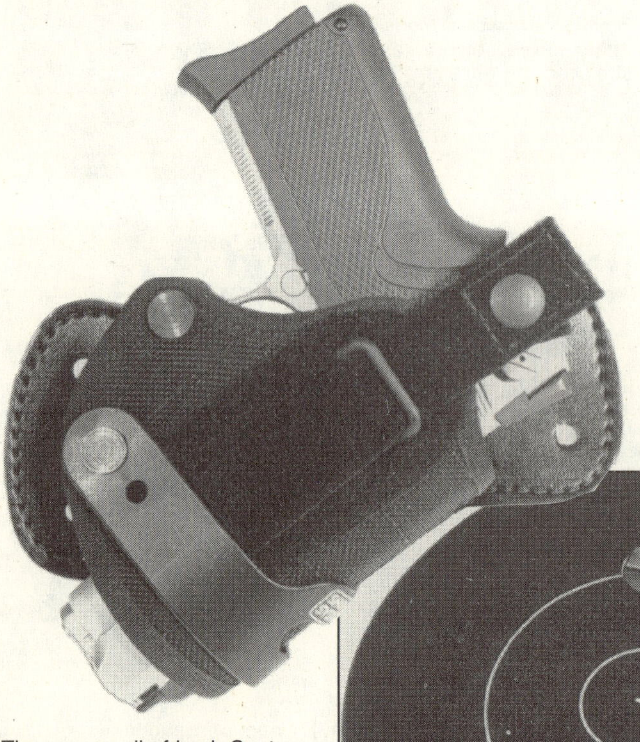

The new small-of-back Contour Series holster from Shooting Systems is well-engineered.

The "2-in-1" conversion kit from Phoenix Arms turns the HP22 into a casual target pistol.

by HAL SWIGGETT

HANDGUNS TODAY:

SIXGUNS AND OTHERS

REMINGTON HAS SEEN fit to abandon their XP-100 bolt-action pistols. There are others: Bill Wiseman builds fine bolt pistols on Sako actions. Melvin Forbes builds fine bolt pistols on his own Ultra Light action. Thompson/Center pistols are known all over the world. Al Straitiff's Competitor is off and running a winning race. Jim Rock's RPM XL pistols are ranked highly among silhouette shooters, as are the M.O.A. pistols built by Richard Mertz. And there is a new bolt-action caseless pistol on the horizon built in Austria and manufactured by Voere.

As for single shot details:

Bill Wiseman builds bolt-action pistols on Sako actions in most any caliber, barrel length and stock configuration you might dream up. They don't ship when the order is received; each is built to order.

Melvin Forbes at Ultra Light designed his own action, and every pistol turned out is built to fit the order. I was privileged to take on West Virginia groundhogs with one of his 223s several years ago. A landowner was visibly impressed watching, with binoculars, those critters go over backwards. He had never seen it before because he was doing the shooting.

Thompson/Center pistols are known worldwide and are used on targets, silhouettes, small game and big game. This writer put his tag on the state of Maine's new Handgun Record bull moose with a T/C Super 14 (with Muzzle Tamer) 45-70 topped with their 2.5x scope. The ammunition? Randy Garrett's great 415-grain super-hardcast. It did a perfect job—acknowledged by several lookers-on at more than 180 yards. T/C offers a lengthy list of chamberings for the Contender, with *all* barrels interchangeable on that single frame.

Competitor, by Al Straitiff, is truly off and running. Harrington & Richardson is handling their marketing, which means the Competitor is already known worldwide. This is the cannon-breeched single shot that cocks as it ejects and is barely 2 inches longer than its barrel. A second safety, a tiny device in the trigger, depresses as the trigger is pulled. Very efficient/effective. And yes, a very lengthy list of chamberings is offered, all to be used on that one frame.

RPM XL pistols by Jim Rock

This moose scored $157\tfrac{5}{8}$ to become #1 in the state of Maine Handgun Record book.

are updated, improved, single shots originally known as Merrill. The safety is novel in that it is under the thumb and must be depressed as the pistol is fired. Jim has added several features, including an enlarged underlug, opening lever, positive extraction and a hammer that moves only $\tfrac{1}{4}$-inch. Barrels are interchangeable on that one frame.

M.O.A. Maximum is a falling block single shot pistol by Richard Mertz and is offered in more chamberings than could possibly be listed here. M.O.A.s have won many silhouette titles and are used by more than a few hunters.

Magnum Research's Lone Eagle is a cannon-breeched single shot with interchangeable barreled actions chambered for thirteen or fourteen cartridges. A cocking lever on its left side readies it for firing.

Wichita Master Pistol, a three-shot repeater, offers both left- or right-hand action and is chambered for a half-dozen cartridges. This one also has a distinguished silhouette record.

Voere from Austria has a bolt-action repeater brought to the U.S. of A. by Jim Morey's JägerSport, Ltd. This is a caseless cartridge pistol offered with a choice of two stock/grip styles and, at least for the moment, two chamberings: 5.56 and 6mm. I have not had the opportunity to shoot caseless ammunition in this particular format, but did take a blackbuck antelope in its initial rifle configuration and see no reason why it won't do as well in a pistol barrel/stock. Ignition is by camera battery,

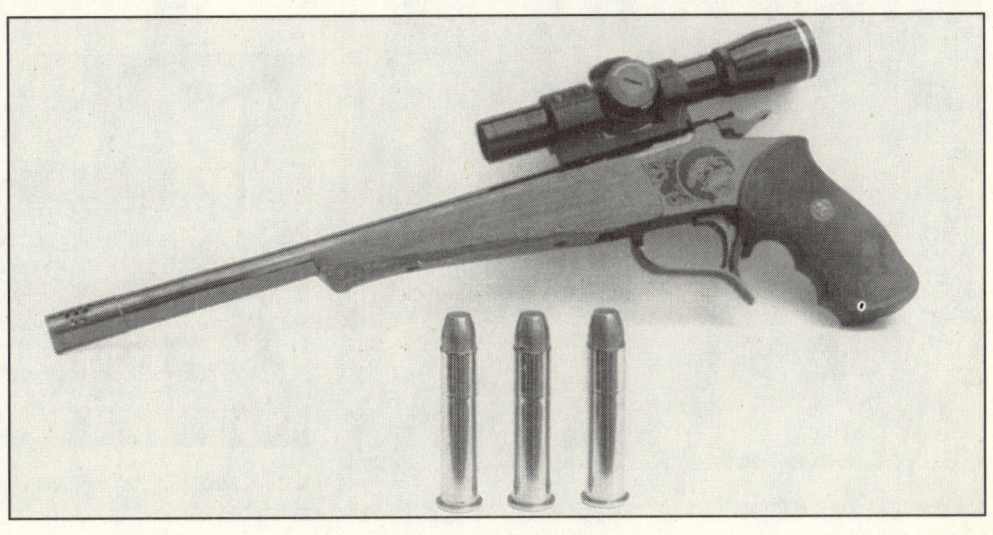

The Thompson/Center 14-inch "Hunter" 45-70 pistol Hal used for his Maine #1 handgun moose.

50th EDITION, 1996 213

Herb Bobchin with Voere's new "caseless cartridge" bolt-action pistol, 5.56 and 6mm.

Jim Rock with one of his newest model RPM "XL" pistols.

Bill Wiseman with one of his custom bolt-action pistols built on Sako actions.

and there are no empty cases to pick up—only a wisp of smoke from the ejection port. Velocities are comparable to regulation 5.56 and 6mm ammo. This one you *will* have to see in action to believe.

Charter Arms

There is now a new compact double action, the Model M-P 352, a five-shot, 2.2-inch, 19-ounce, blue only, 357 Magnum. It looks, and feels, like all earlier Charter Arms five-guns. One of their 44 Specials has been a constant companion for many years, and there's a Charter 22 scoped so long ago it would now be shaving if it were human. It has put a lot of cottontails and squirrels on our table. Its scope is a long obsolete Hutson 1x. So the 357 is joining good company.

Cimarron

There's to be a Doc Holliday Commemorative Limited Edition Thunderer—3½-inch, nickel-plated, with micarta grip. Its backstrap is engraved with "Doc Holliday" and the series number up to 500. It's part of a set which includes a shoulder holster with boot knife scabbard and boot knife, all numbered to match the revolver.

The Storekeeper has 3½ inches of barrel with ejector rod housing, standard walnut grip offered smooth or checkered, and choice of blue or charcoal blue finish. Thunderer Sheriff Model offers 3- or 4-inch barrel without ejector rod.

Schofields are also offered, along with Model P single actions featuring the old model pinched frame, 100 percent parts interchangeable with original Colts. Cimarron is alive and well 70 or so miles north by west of this typewriter.

Colt

The new owners and new business outlook are off and running. There's a new small-frame six-shot, matte stainless steel, 38 Special with a 2-inch barrel. The 38 SF-VI has fixed sights—ramp front—and weighs 21 ounces. Grip is black composition. Other 38s include the 2-inch Detective Special, a 4-inch Police Positive and a Custom Shop Detective Special.

Colt's Python, introduced in 1955, is offered in three barrel

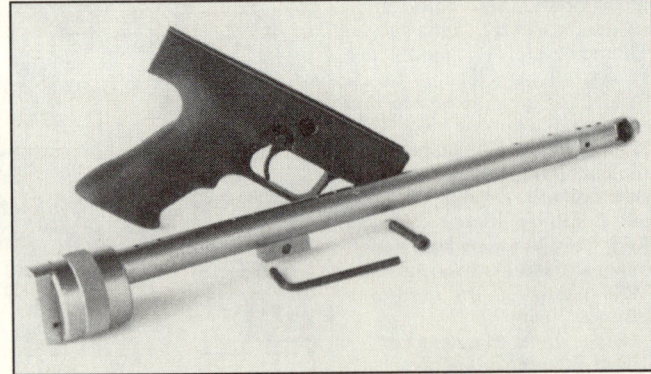

Magnum Research Lone Eagle is an interchangeable barreled-action design.

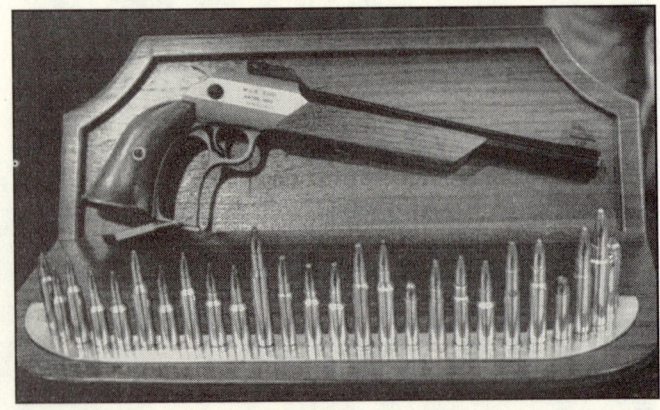

M.O.A. Maximum falling block pistols are still front-runners in silhouette shooting.

lengths; their Cobra, first issued in 1951, grew into King Cobra, currently cataloged in 4- and 6-inch versions in stainless steel, 357 Magnum. And the Anaconda, 4-, 6-, and 8-inch versions in stainless steel with one model, of all things, camouflaged.

Davis

These derringers are known worldwide and are now offered in 22 WMR and 9mm. These are Standard D-Series and Long-Bore and Big-Bore, chambered for 22 LR, 25 Auto, 32 Auto, 32 H&R Mag and 38 Special, plus the two new ones.

H&R 1871

Harrington & Richardson dates back to 1871, the reason for their new name. Production was continuous through 1986,

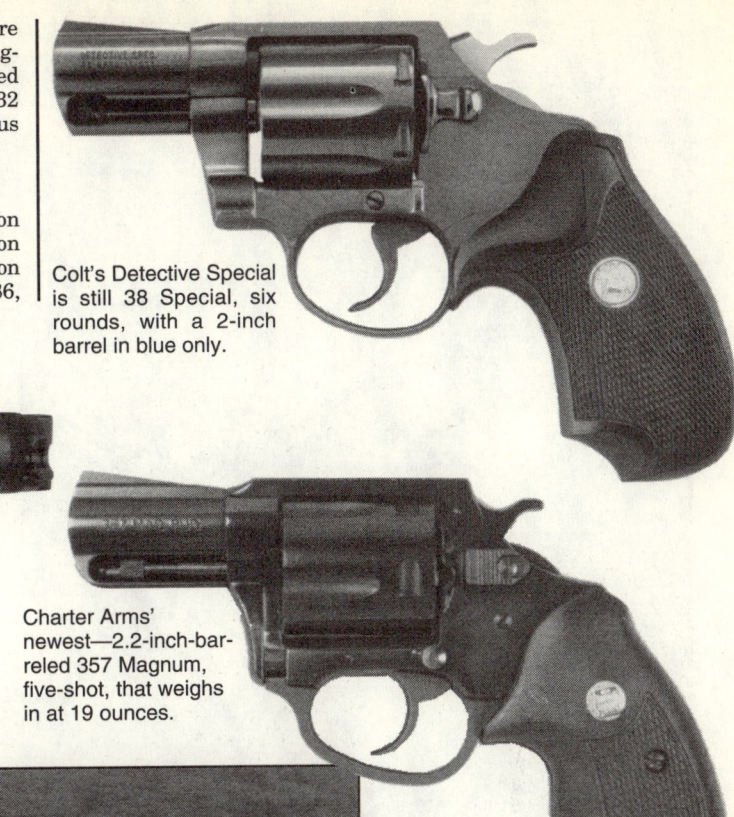

Colt's Detective Special is still 38 Special, six rounds, with a 2-inch barrel in blue only.

Competitor pistols are now marketed by H&R 1871. This one is chambered 284 Winchester, wearing a muzzlebrake and a Leupold scope.

Charter Arms' newest—2.2-inch-barreled 357 Magnum, five-shot, that weighs in at 19 ounces.

then after a five-year interlude, production was again started under the new name, H&R 1871. Their Sportsman 999 was first as it is part of the H&R legacy dating back to the original patents of 1871. New for 1995 are two 22 models: 939 Premier, a target-grade double-action nine-shot with a swing-out cylinder and fully adjustable sights. Barrel length is 6 inches with transfer bar safety and walnut-stained hardwood grips. Model 949 is a Western-styled nine-shot with fixed sights and with 5½- or 7½-inch barrel. This one also features authentic case-colored backstrap and grip frame.

Heritage

American-made single-action 22 rimfire revolvers in four versions: 9-, 6½-, 4¾- and 3-inch barrels. The 3-incher is bird's-head-gripped; the others are conventional. Sights are fixed on all Heritage Rough Rider SAs; all are six-shooters. Interchangeable 22 WMR cylinders are available. This company also offers double-action revolvers in 22 LR or WMR, 9mm and 38 Special. Barrel lengths are 2 or 4 inches. Sights fixed. Finishes are nickel-

Hal took this West Virginia groundhog with one of Melvin Forbes "Ultra Light" 223 bolt-action pistols.

Tom Conrad, Taurus executive, shows their newest seven-shot, 6½-inch barrel, double-action revolver.

Yes—seven in the cylinder.

plate or blue. There's a transfer bar system in all Heritage revolvers.

Mitchell Arms

Don Mitchell has added a pair of double actions to his catalog: Guardian II in 38 Special and Titan II in 357 Magnum. Guardian II is offered in 3-, 4- or 6-inch, blue, and with choice of Target or Combat grip. There is also a Guardian III with adjustable sights. Titan II is 357 Magnum, 2- or 4-inch blue, and 2-, 4- or 6-inch stainless. Titan III is as above but with adjustable sights. Trigger pull, double action, is set at 12 pounds, and single action at 3 pounds.

Ruger

Nothing new at this point other than information. Their high- ly touted and very fine little New Bearcat, introduced in 1993 with a transfer bar and pair of cylinders, is/was out. Take that as typed. Could be only 500 were made/released. A thing of beauty to be sure. If any reader has an extra pair of grips for that first Bearcat, a note to me would be appreciated. I have one, bought used, and with not very well-made "custom" handles. Originals were much better.

Smith & Wesson

The Model 686 PowerPort is aptly described as "Perfect for Competitors and Hunters." It is 357 Magnum, 6-inch full lug barrel featuring an integral compensator with the frame drilled and tapped for scope mounting. Sights are black

Smith & Wesson's Performance Center 357 Magnum K-Comp with 3-inch barrel on the L-frame, ported and round butt combat-style rubber grip.

H&R's Top-Break Model 999 Sportsman is nine-shot, with adjustable sights and automatic shell ejection—as nearly always.

Heritage bird's-head-grip single action is available in 3¾- or 4¾-inch versions, 100 percent made in U.S.A.

Newest from Interarms—2½-inch, stainless steel, ported, 357 Magnum six-shot. Also available are 4- and 6-inch versions.

pinned blade front and adjustable black blade rear. Grips are Hogue premium synthetic. Stainless steel with satin finish. S&W's Performance Center is also offering a 3-inch L-frame 357 Magnum K-Comp with matte black finish, described as a utilitarian carry gun. Sounds good to me.

SSK

J.D. Jones and his SSK Industries comes up with all sorts of innovations, inventions and things new on a regular basis. One of the newest: Super accurate 22 barrels for T/C Contender pistols. Not wedded to standard procedure, J.D. dives in and, more often than not, comes up with great results. He put two and two together and came up with a changed twist, tighter bore and groove diameters, and his own chamber. It is outshooting everything so far put against it, J.D. says, including match-grade pistols.

Taurus

Billed as the world's smallest 357 Magnum by Tom Conrad, the new five-shot Taurus revolver wears a 2 1/4-inch barrel and is available in both blue or stainless steel with fixed sights. There's another "new" Taurus—hold on tight—a seven-shot DA 357 in blue or stainless steel. This one has adjustable sights, integral compensator and, on the 6 1/2-inch, a vent rib, and to repeat—it's a *seven*-shooter.

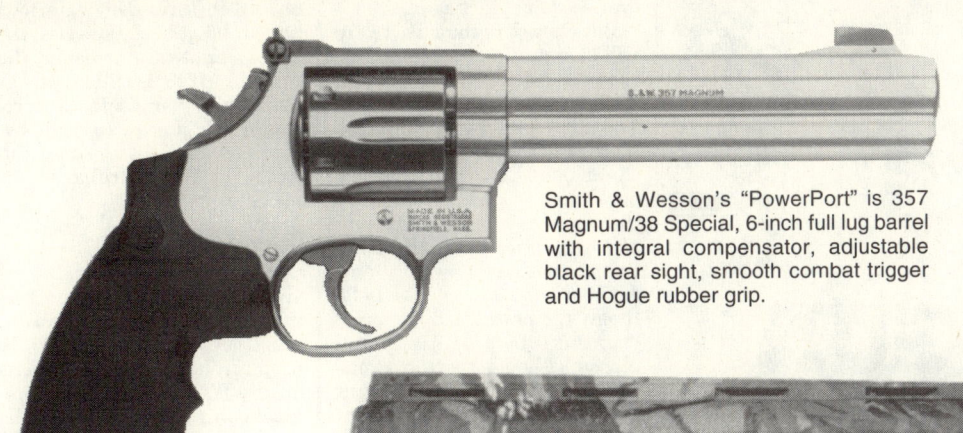

Smith & Wesson's "PowerPort" is 357 Magnum/38 Special, 6-inch full lug barrel with integral compensator, adjustable black rear sight, smooth combat trigger and Hogue rubber grip.

Lay this one down in the woods and it just might be hard to find—Colt's newest finish for the great Anaconda 44.

Texas Longhorn Arms

Newest from Bill Grover is the North Paw, a right-hand (or conventional) single action. It's a stainless steel SA Army 45 Colt six-shot with a 4 3/4-inch barrel. There is also a Target Model stainless steel 7 1/2-inch in the works to be called the King James Version. Jezebel *is* out in 22 Long Rifle; the WMR version will follow in a year.

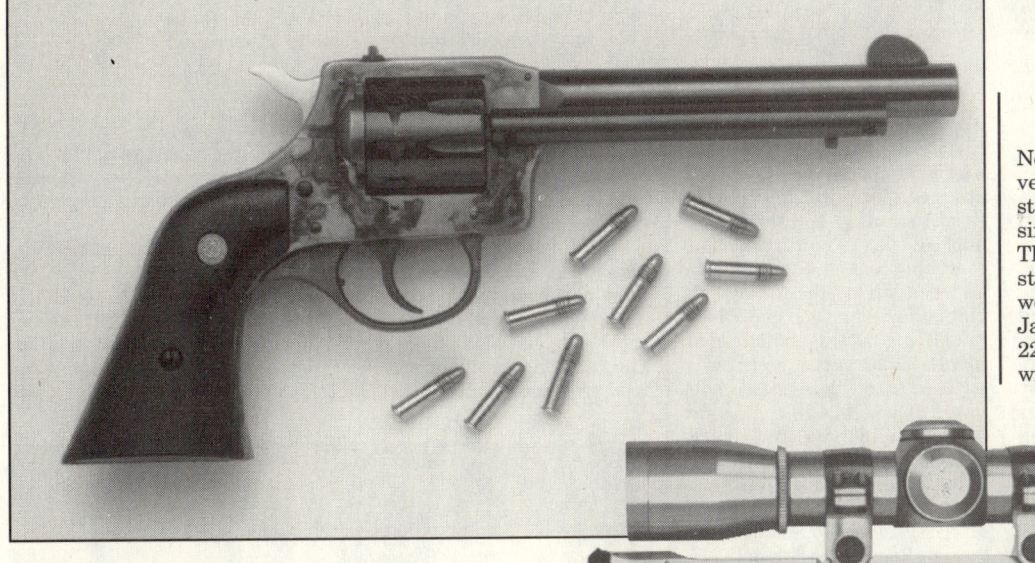

Harrington & Richardson's Model 949 Classic Western 22 revolver is offered with 5 1/2- or 7-inch barrel, holds nine.

Ruger's New Model 44 Magnum Super Blackhawk Hunter arrives ready to go except for the addition of your choice of scope. My preference is 2x or, at the most, 2.5x.

by DON ZUTZ

SHOTGUN REVIEW

Merkel 28-gauge side-by-sides will be available in 1995, thanks to GSI, Inc. This is a Model 478, and it'll spin on a dime to catch ruffed grouse and woodcock.

MOST OUTDOORISH writers would open retrospective narratives with flowery adjectives describing a waterfowling scene at dawn or an upland panorama under an autumn sun. This one begins in the shade of a dying maple tree standing alone on a high flat above a rendering plant. Even in those days, a rendering plant had little left after its day's business, but there were smelly sweepings to scatter atop the hill within shotgun range of the drooping maple. These remains generated an almighty stench, and it was terrible (nay, virtually unbearable) when the breeze wafted it toward the shade of the ol' maple.

It was there I stood to await the starlings which thought the daily dumpings were elegant cuisine. I was in my earliest teens. The gun was a Stevens 410-bore bolt action. And the year was 1945.

I cut my wingshooting teeth on those starlings, but on many occasions the results were meager. Then one day I happened to find an ugly starling sitting atop the tree as I approached. I took aim and fired. Nothing. I cranked the bolt and let drive again. The starling looked down with sheer disdain, then flew off. Not believing myself capable of missing a sitting starling at about 20-25 yards, I threw a pattern into the nearest snow bank. It was horrible. Big, fat people could have done cartwheels in that pattern without being plinked by a pellet!

And so it was I quickly found after-school jobs to finance a 20-gauge Remington Model 31L that held much better patterns than the rinky-dink 410. My interest in shotguns, wingshooting, and pattern performance had been piqued, and the interest has lasted for a half-century. That's more than I can say for a lot of other things.

The rendering plant is long gone, and the high flat now is home to a Honda agency. A four-lane bypass bisects the place. A credit union office stands where my pellets, as well as more than a few starlings, fell, and there's a new shopping mall mighty close. The starlings still flit around, and I sometimes wonder what would happen if somebody were to start rattlin' a 20-gauge pumpgun at them now. Likewise, I wonder where a youngster might learn to swing a shotgun on so many obliging live targets as I did those fifty ever-so-short years ago...

But enough of that. There are still shotguns and shotgunning, however restricted they may be in this modern, progressive era. The story line for 1995 is that there are very few new concepts. Gunmakers have such extensive backlogs of orders from 1994 that they have focused on supplying existing demand rather than creating a whole new demand that they can't satisfy. If only the newest guns interest you, this'll be a relatively dull season, although there are some exceptions. But if you thought that the last few years brought on some solid models, you'll finally be able to buy them as production catches up with promises...

American Arms

If you're interested in entry-level pricing on doubles, both side-by-side and over/under, this is the company to explore. American Arms, Inc., isn't doing anything new or novel for 1995, but the company is holding on with break-actions of modest cost. The Silver Series of O/Us is still good value, especially for the bird hunter, and the Gentry and Brittany horizontal doubles are about as economical as you'll find these days.

There are also specialty magnum models at American Arms, Inc., including 3½-inch-chambered 10- and 12-gauges in O/U or SxS in turkey or waterfowl barrel lengths. Likewise, the world's lightest autoloader, the Franchi AL/48, is still around at about 5¼ pounds in 20-bore. And if a higher-priced side-by-side is your dish, American Arms, Inc., has Grulla No. 2s made to order.

Browning

If any gunmaker has aggressively attacked the shotgun market this year, it is Browning. Gone is the basic BT-99. In its place is a trio of variations on the BT-99 theme, the foremost being a BT-100 with bells and whistles that include a drop-out trigger group, lofted rib, and adjustable comb. There is also a thumbhole version of the BT-100 which, Browning hopes, will effectively counter recoil by positioning the shooter's trigger hand to absorb the blow.

Gone, too, is the fast-selling B325 Sporting Clays gun. We now have the B425, which is said to be closer to the features desired by the successful British and European competitors. This involves a trim forend to

Robin Sharpless, VP of H&R, 1871, likes the groups his company's bull-barreled ULTRA Slug Gun dishes out at 100 yards.

put the hand close to the bores for accurate pointing via hand-to-eye coordination, plus a new engraving pattern. There also is a back-bored 20-gauge B425 and a noteworthy women's model known as the WSSF (Women's Sport Shooting Federation) Sporting Clays shotgun. It is scaled for lady shooters, finished in (get this) teal, and also sports the WSSF official logo.

The Browning GTI is now known as the Ultra Sporter. It is alone among Browning sporters with ventilated side rails which, the company says, reduce swing resistance and speed barrel cooling. Frankly, I like the feature for an entirely different reason: It sheds some barrel weight to leave the gun a bit more responsive. I am left in a puzzlement regarding the Ultra Sporter, since those I've handled bear schnabel-tipped forends while those in the catalog have round-tipped forearms.

For those who like 'em on the gaudy side (and there are lots of Americans who do), Browning is turning out a Golden Clays grade for every target model. This has a rainbow of gold images arching upward on each receiver panel as either a duck or a quail is progressively transformed into a clay saucer.

Otherwise, the bolt-actioned Browning announced here last year is now in the catalog as a combination short-barreled turkey gun and/or deer slug gun with an extra-length rifled tube screwed in. And, hopefully, the Gold Hunter semi-autos will begin showing up on dealer shelves.

Beretta U.S.A.

The target-grade Beretta A-390s, which first appeared with semi-humpbacked receivers, will be offered with rounded receivers in 1995. These guns also have a step-up rib, and as a new feature they'll have ported barrels to reduce muzzle jump. The Model 682 trap combos and Sporting guns will also come with ported barrels. There will also be extended Mobilchoke tubes with a 1-inch knurled section for shooters who like longer choke tapers and a gripping circumference.

Colt

Colt is hardly the name you'd expect in a shotgun review nowadays, but the over/under market is still bubbling, and Colt, fresh out of bankruptcy, is entering it on the high end. The new Colt stackbarrel bears English proofmarks and is known by the name of Armsmear. To a pair of weary ol' eyes, the barreled action looks a lot like those being used widely in Italy; there is the seashell receiver configuration and side lug bolting. Gold and scroll cover this Colt, and the wood is definitely top shelf. A basic boxlock gun, it holds lavishly engraved false sideplates. I have no idea what its handling qualities are, as the only one I saw at the 1995 SHOT Show was entombed in a glass cage, and the personnel knew virtually nothing of it.

Hanus Bird Guns

Just as this review was being completed, word arrived that the Bill Hanus Bird Guns will again be available. The supply of these pieces was cut off abruptly a couple seasons back because of problems at Ugartechea of Eibar, Spain. The Hanus guns are designed for fast handling and accurate pointing, and they are made in the oft-neglected gauges of 16 and 28. A Skeet #1 and #2 choke tandem has been an usual offering. We await further developments.

Harrington & Richardson

Although these guys only make single shot break actions, they always seem to

The Bill Hanus Bird Gun is scheduled to return for '95, giving the upland hunter a spirited double at tolerable prices. That's a 16-bore Hanus the writer's holding while he attends to business.

come up with something novel, yet useful. This year it's a bull-barreled slug gun with amazing accuracy performances. The H&R is listed as the Model S82-980 ULTRA Slug Hunter, and it's a 12-gauge built on the massive 10-gauge barreled action. This leaves a lot of steel in the barrel to stiffen it and counter the whip and vibrations of firing. Its 1:35-inch twist is a compromise twist to handle both sabots and Foster slugs. Like a heavy-barreled varmint rifle, the ULTRA pumps out small groups at 100 yards while also offsetting recoil. You might not want to carry it all day, but if you sit on a stump or a tree stand, it'll provide a positive "hang" for hits to the vital areas.

Heckler & Koch

The ingenious Benelli autoloaders imported by H&K are being taken to new heights by the inclusion of an Executive series. This is a special-order situation, the guns being made in Executive Types I, II and III with varying amounts of receiver engraving and gold inlay. There is also a limited series of 20-gauge Benelli Elite grades, and in the basic Montefeltro 20-bore we'll be able to order a 24-inch upland barrel.

Kolar

Skeet shooters have long known Kolar of Racine, Wisconsin, as a supplier of small-bore inserts for O/Us. But behind the scenes a quality target-grade O/U has been a-building. About ten of these are now out in the hands of foremost competitors, and production is expected to improve during the year. This O/U is compact, tightly fitted, and the recoil level is quite low. This one should be a major winner in all clay target games when it gets going.

Krieghoff

Of all the over/unders on target ranges, the Krieghoff K-80 has some of the best dynamics. Hardly a cheapie, the K-80s have superb barrel responsiveness and all the features that an advanced shotgunner would want.

A new semi-light barrel assembly graces the 1995 guns as a noteworthy option, especially for American-style Sporting Clays which is a close-range game. The semi-light barrels weigh 5 ounces less than the standards, are choked IC & IC, come only in 30-inch length, but are lively and spirited for fast action and small "windows."

Laurona

The Laurona O/U has tried to penetrate the American scene for years, but has come up short. It's a sturdy gun and, interestingly, has a twin single-trigger lock in its Model X Game styling. The front trigger first taps off the lower barrel, then the top; the rear trigger launches the upper barrel on first pull, then empties the lower chamber. It's the quickest barrel selection device around.

Marlin

The Marlin Model 512 Slugmaster has come along to be a serviceable and accurate deer gun, and the 36-inch Model 55 Goose Gun is still with us and is not a bad selection with steel shot for optimum velocity.

Marocchi

Marocchi O/Us are being handled by Precision Sales International, Inc., under the name of Conquista. These are still the only target grades built to accommodate a left-handed shooter, thanks to a reversed opening lever and southpaw stock. The Conquista is also being made in a new woman's model which is sized for the female figure.

Merkel

Distributed stateside by GSI, Inc., of Alabama, the Merkel guns are being refined to Western tastes. For 1995, there is a 28-gauge side-by-side, and a Model 200SC O/U Sporting Clays model has been prototyped. Merkel O/Us have always had exceptional pointing qualities for the field, and that should carry through in Sporting.

Mossberg/Maverick

Mossberg keeps changing the trappings of its basic Model 500 pump. This year it's a 20-gauge M500 Trophy Slugster with rifled barrel, cheekpad for scope use, and mounts. They've also hacked the barrel of the Mossberg M9200 semi-auto to make it a defensive piece labeled the "Persuader."

Over at closely connected Maverick, there's a new bolt-actioned 12-gauge with 25-inch barrel bedded in a black synthetic stock. The bore is smooth, the chambering is for standard and 3-inch loads, and the choke is a fixed Modified. Interesting how bolt actions are coming into play again, isn't it?

Remington

Remington is bringing back one of the best-pointing repeaters ever made—the Model 1100. This one's called the M1100 "Synthetic," and it has positive checkering in the black synthetic stock/forend assemblies plus a black matte finish and recoil pad. To be made in both 20- and 12-gauge, these 1100s will have Rem-Choke barrels and standard-length chambers. The price will be below that of the 11-87.

Otherwise, there's a new defensive version of the M870 Express with 21-inch barrel and black synthetic stuff, and the Peerless with 30-inch barrels should begin showing up soon.

Ruger

Ruger is showing a bar-in-wood Red Label for 1995. It's a copy of some gunmaking done overseas in past decades when the extended stock jaws were thought to contribute leverage to the cocking move on horizontal doubles with the Birmingham system. On the Ruger, it's mainly cosmetic. Called the Woodside, it sports Circassian walnut and a higher price tag than regular Red Labels.

SKB

SKB is changing numbers. Hope things will soon settle down. Gone are the 685 and 885. In their stead will be the 505, 585, and 785. The 505 is a blued-receiver field gun at promotional pricing. The 585 is a step up with silver-gray receiver and better wood, while the 785 is top-of-the-line with a new step-up ventilated rib, chromed chamber and bores, and lengthened forcing cones. Both the 585 and 785 have overbored barrels.

New in the SKB line is a Waterfowl model with bead-blasted barreled action, nitrided receiver, chromed bore and oil-finished wood. Obviously, it's steel-shot compatible.

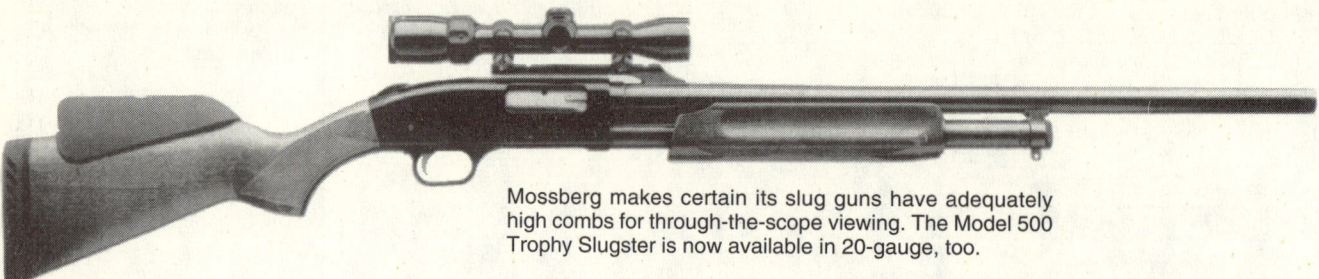

Mossberg makes certain its slug guns have adequately high combs for through-the-scope viewing. The Model 500 Trophy Slugster is now available in 20-gauge, too.

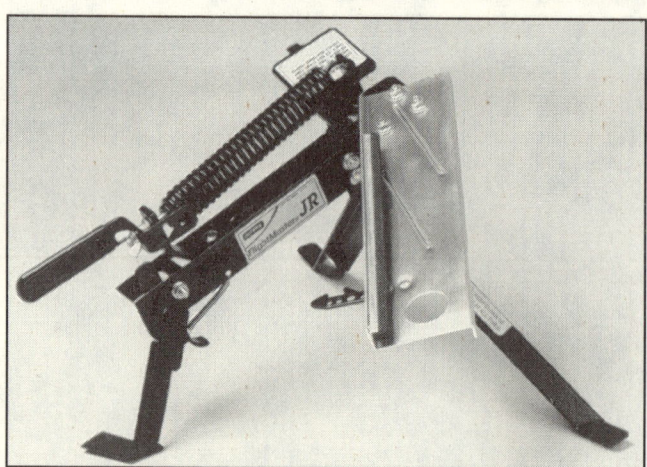

For under $40, the no-stake FlightMaster Jr. from Outers puts you into personal clay practice.

Finally, SKB has a new 585 with shortened stock in both 12- and 20-gauge for milady and youngsters.

Turkish Guns

Last year, the Turkish Firearms Corp. brought the HHF line of Turkish-made doubles to these shores. The guns have substantial workmanship and, apparently, excellent materials. American hunters haven't cozied up to them yet, but might be missing a good bet.

Also getting in on the ground floor of Turkish gun importing is a new company, Tristar Sporting Arms, Ltd., of North Kansas City, Missouri. Headed up by George Woford, formerly a vice president at American Arms, and Marty Fajen, formerly of the Fajen stockmaking concern, Tristar will have O/Us, SxSs, and a semi-auto. One immediate goal is designing guns for the female shooter.

Weatherby

Some beautiful bird guns rest in the Weatherby line of over/unders. The Athena remains an eye-catcher, and the Grade II and III Orions can be equally attractive. Moreover, the Weatherbys also have excellent pointing qualities. The Classic variants show European styling with trim forends and semi-pistol grips. The 20-gauges score heavily on upland game, while the Orion Sporting Clays guns handle well from the low-gun starting position.

Winchester

After a couple years of waiting, the Model 1001 flopped because of deficiencies in barrel strength and material. It is no more, all the M1001s having been recalled and replaced by Browning Citoris.

For its new 1995 guns, Winchester relied on camouflage artists rather than gun designers. There's a stumpy Deer Gun duo, one with a rifled bore and the other with a smooth one, which carries Winchester's fresh Advantage Camo pattern. And, as usual, Winchester has turned out a new paint job on the M1300 turkey gun, this camo being termed All-Purpose Camo. Finally, there's a Model 1300 Black Shadow field gun which is basic black. I wonder if a kid standing in the shade would have gotten more starlings fifty years ago if he'd had a black gun rather than one with real walnut and nicely blued metal. Naw...

●

CUSTOM GUNS

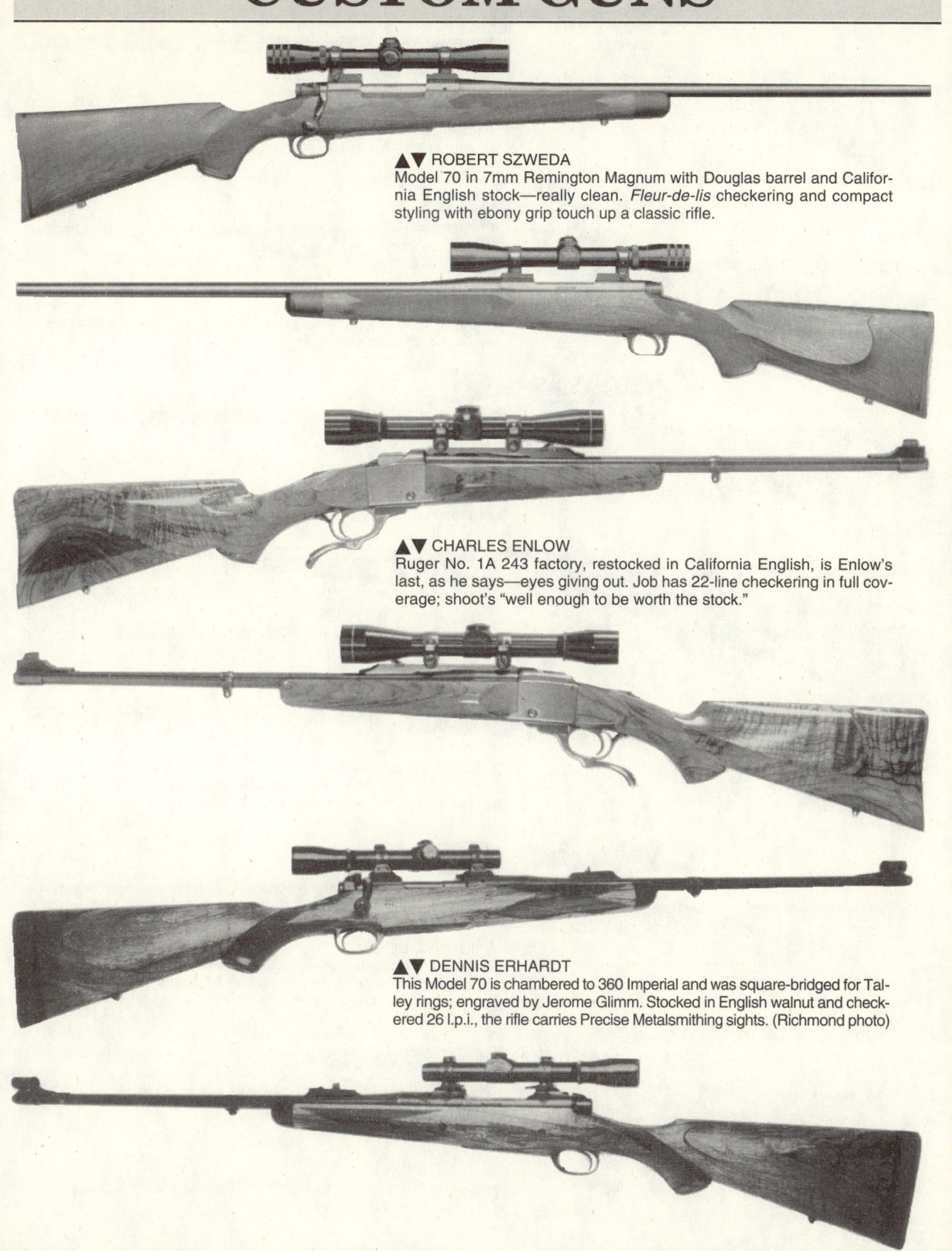

▲▼ ROBERT SZWEDA
Model 70 in 7mm Remington Magnum with Douglas barrel and California English stock—really clean. *Fleur-de-lis* checkering and compact styling with ebony grip touch up a classic rifle.

▲▼ CHARLES ENLOW
Ruger No. 1A 243 factory, restocked in California English, is Enlow's last, as he says—eyes giving out. Job has 22-line checkering in full coverage; shoot's "well enough to be worth the stock."

▲▼ DENNIS ERHARDT
This Model 70 is chambered to 360 Imperial and was square-bridged for Talley rings; engraved by Jerome Glimm. Stocked in English walnut and checkered 26 l.p.i., the rifle carries Precise Metalsmithing sights. (Richmond photo)

▲ **DUANE WIEBE**
Takedown/switch barrel in 338 Winchester Magnum and 416 Taylor on Mauser 98—full thread system, one forend.

▲ **DALE TUTTLE**
Ruger 77 in 257 Roberts, all in maple with rosewood tip and cleanly lined out in modern classic style.

▲ **FRED F. WELLS**
Laminated-stock heavy barrel shooter for a lefty—those lines are hard to miss.

▲ **STEVEN DODD HUGHES**
Transformed Marlin Model 39A, engraved by Michael Dubber, in the grand 19th-century deluxe style. (Hughes photo)

▲ **STEPHEN L. BILLEB**
A-grade Fox waterfowl gun restocked in English walnut, re-colored by Mazur and Huff engraved. Left 30-inch Full and Full.

▲ **JOHN M. BOLTIN**
Model 70 Winchester now has Douglas featherweight barrel—work by Talley, McFarland, Blackburn and Billingsley. Stock is New Zealand walnut. (Carter photo)

▲ **BILL McGUIRE**
Ruger No. 1 factory restocked in extraordinary American black walnut—full checkering fore-and-aft.

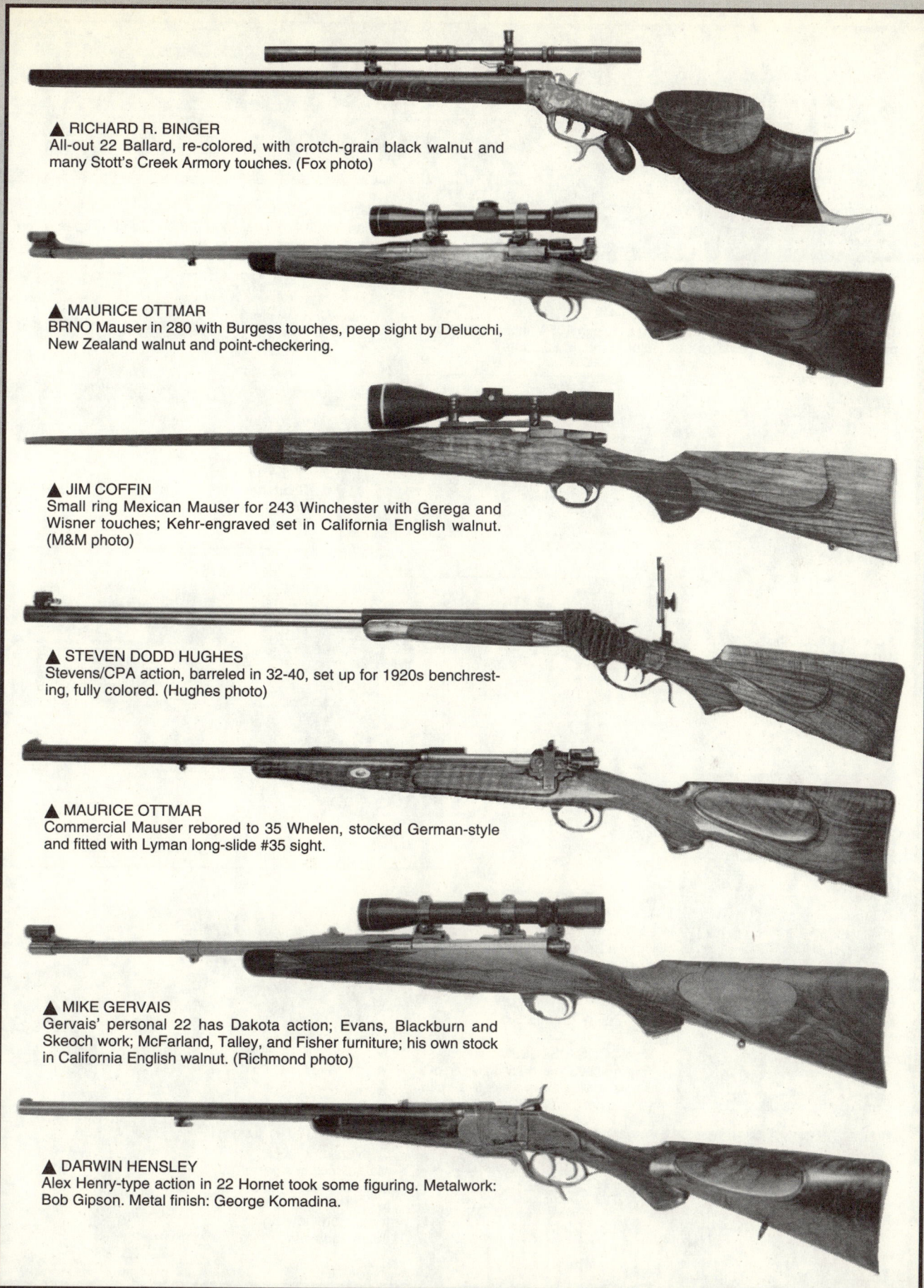

▲ **RICHARD R. BINGER**
All-out 22 Ballard, re-colored, with crotch-grain black walnut and many Stott's Creek Armory touches. (Fox photo)

▲ **MAURICE OTTMAR**
BRNO Mauser in 280 with Burgess touches, peep sight by Delucchi, New Zealand walnut and point-checkering.

▲ **JIM COFFIN**
Small ring Mexican Mauser for 243 Winchester with Gerega and Wisner touches; Kehr-engraved set in California English walnut. (M&M photo)

▲ **STEVEN DODD HUGHES**
Stevens/CPA action, barreled in 32-40, set up for 1920s benchresting, fully colored. (Hughes photo)

▲ **MAURICE OTTMAR**
Commercial Mauser rebored to 35 Whelen, stocked German-style and fitted with Lyman long-slide #35 sight.

▲ **MIKE GERVAIS**
Gervais' personal 22 has Dakota action; Evans, Blackburn and Skeoch work; McFarland, Talley, and Fisher furniture; his own stock in California English walnut. (Richmond photo)

▲ **DARWIN HENSLEY**
Alex Henry-type action in 22 Hornet took some figuring. Metalwork: Bob Gipson. Metal finish: George Komadina.

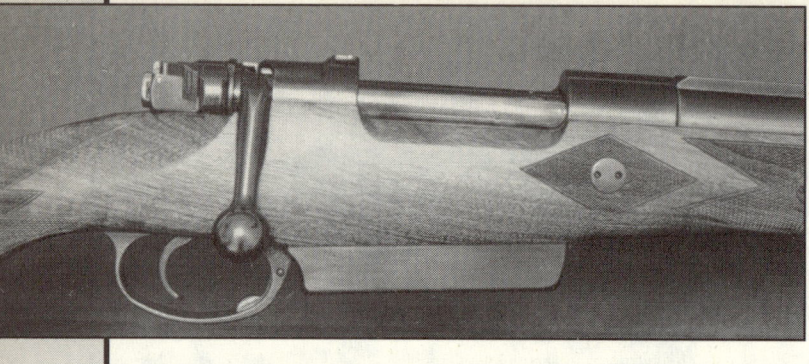

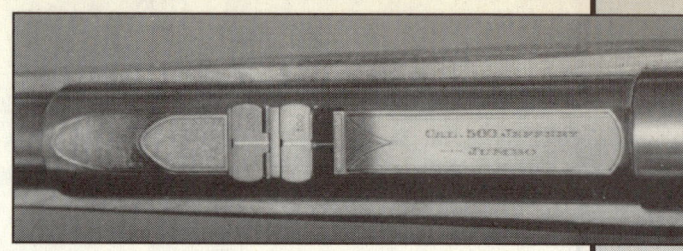

▼▲▼ HARRY BAELDER
German smith furnishes 500 Jeffery Jumbo repeater on standard 98 action with a lot of very nice touches.

▼ AMERICAN CUSTOM GUNMAKERS GUILD
This is ACGG #11, the American Double Rifle in 405 Winchester. Work by Anthony Fleming, Paul Dressel, Ralph Bone. (Bilal photo)

▼ GARY GOUDY
Shortened '03 Springfield from Stephen Heilmann in 6mm PPC has all the bells and whistles set in place.

▶ EVOLUTION GUN WORKS
Not quite all-out, this 1911 Auto is still a carry gun by EGW standards. There are at least twelve major changes shown here.

◀ WOODS PISTOLSMITHING
Elegant fit and finish of a Brown hammer and grip safety, Wilson thumb safety and Pachmayr thumb guard.

▼ WOODS PISTOLSMITHING
This is what a "melted" installation of a Bo-Mar BMCS sight looks like—plus some other touches clearly in view.

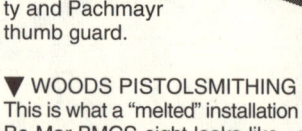

▲ BROKEN GUN RANCH
Conversion of a Ruger Mark II includes barrel sculpture and weight, M1911 magazine release, trigger job, new sights, safety, grips and more.

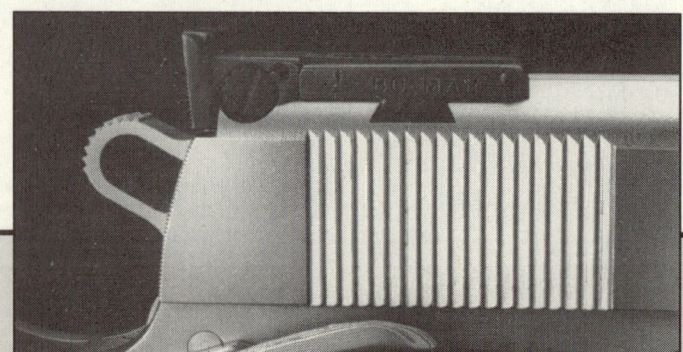

ART OF THE ENGRAVER

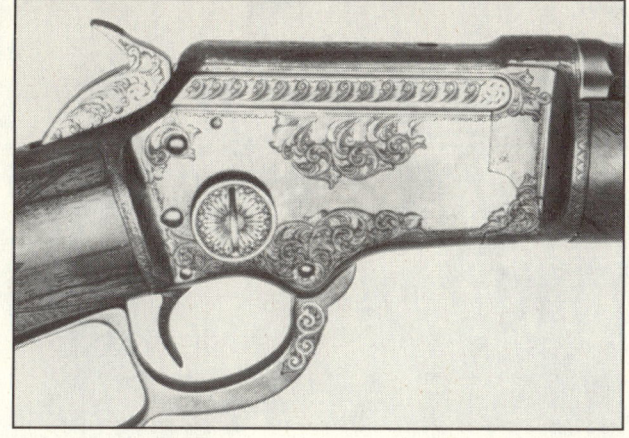

▲ MICHAEL DUBBER

▲ DAVE VORHES

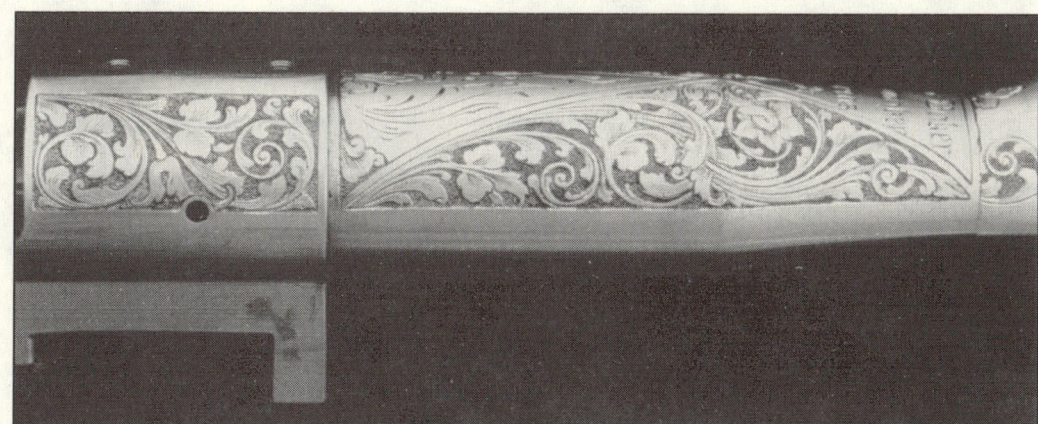

◄ TERRY THEIS

► BARRY LEE HANDS

◄► SAM WELCH

▲▶ CLAUS WILLIG

◀▶ SCOTT PILKINGTON

▲ ROBERT D. SWARTLEY   ▲ ROBERT D. SWARTLEY

▶ ED DELORGE

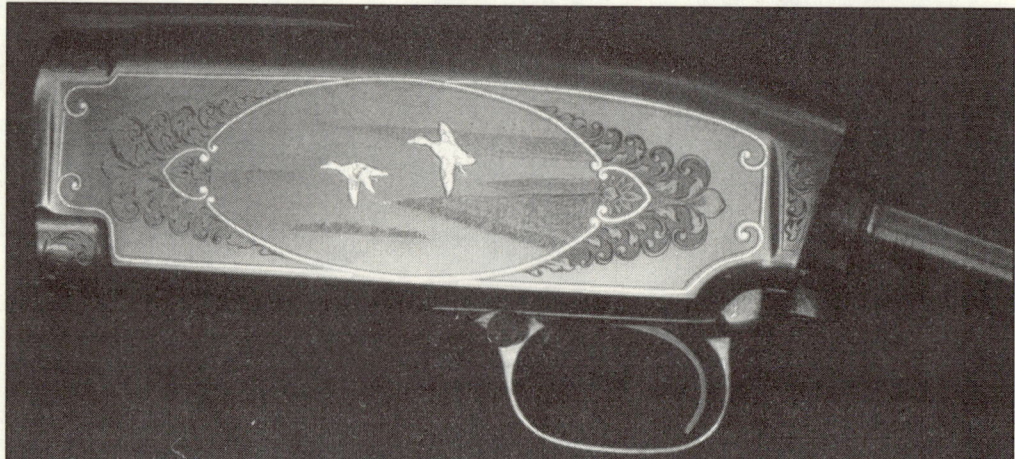

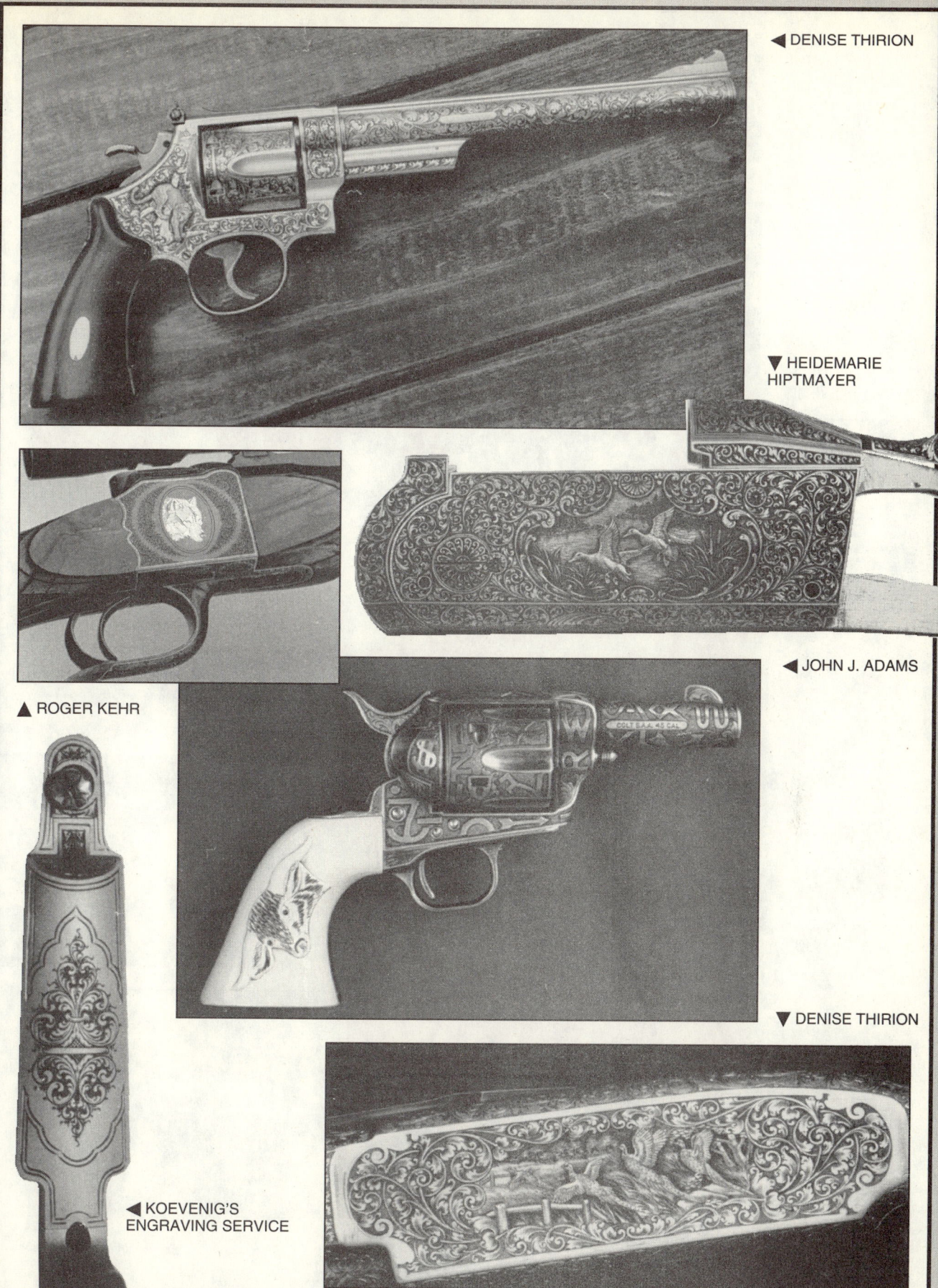

◀ DENISE THIRION

▼ HEIDEMARIE HIPTMAYER

◀ JOHN J. ADAMS

▲ ROGER KEHR

▼ DENISE THIRION

◀ KOEVENIG'S ENGRAVING SERVICE

50th EDITION, 1996 **227**

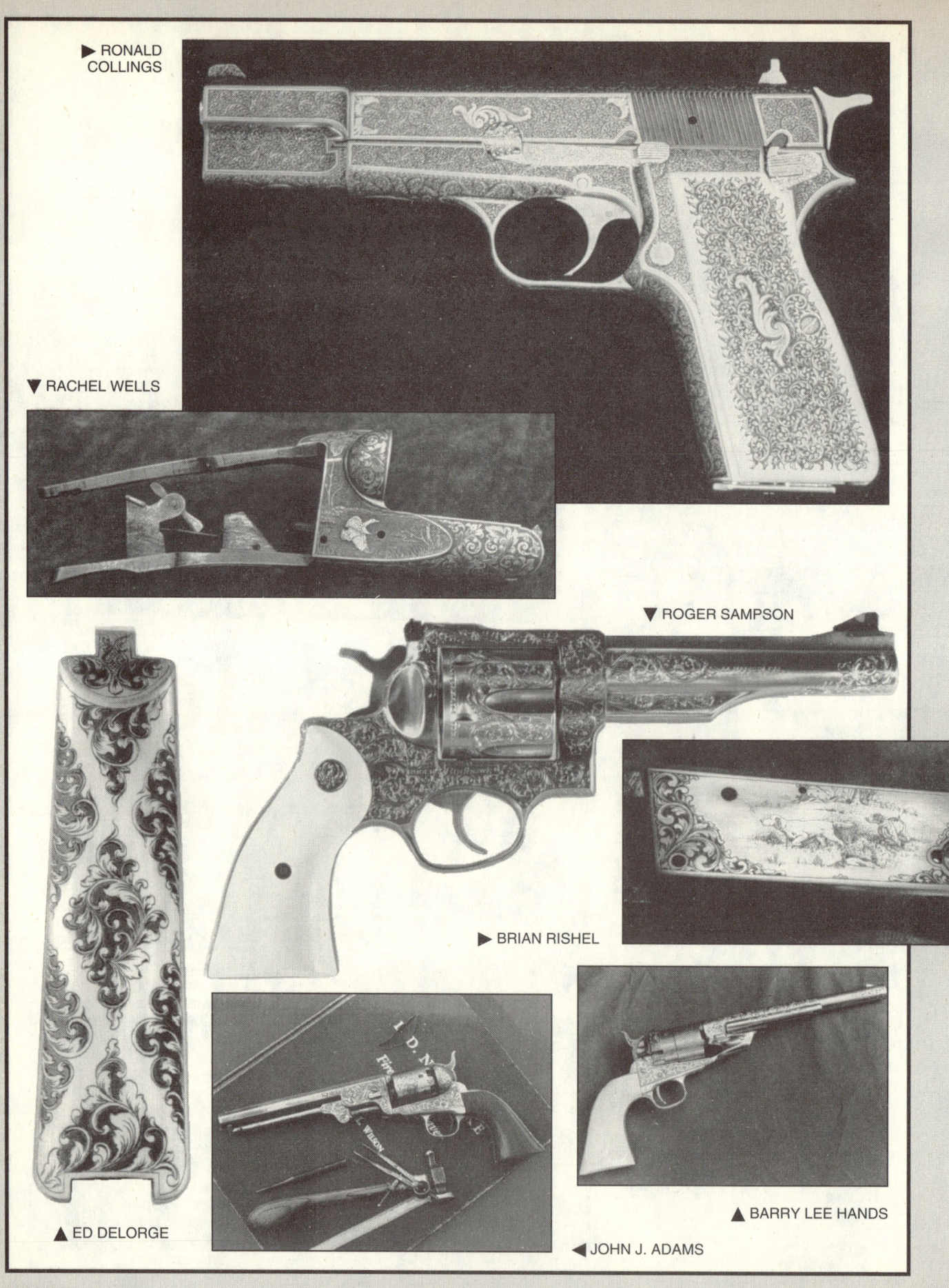

This 12-bore pinfire shotgun No. 1221 was sold in 1863 to F.W. Tetley, Esq. (Sotheby's photo)

From pinfire hammer gun to hammerless centerfire, this was...

Thomas Horsley's CLASSIC

by DAVID BAKER

In CONNECTION with practically every brand name you care to think of, be it airplane, gun or a motor car, there is one model that instantly springs to mind whenever its maker's name is mentioned. In England, say "Bentley" and a "Straight Eight" immediately flashes to mind; likewise "Hawker" conjures up a "Battle of Britain Hurricane." Somehow these classic models embody for us the essence of their name, and anything else that the firm made, even if in greater numbers, is less important than this standard bearer.

So it is with the gunmakers Thomas Horsley & Son of York. Their classic action was the one which used the pull-back top-lever, patent number 2410 of 1863. With this they saw their very best period, in all senses of the term. Their guns were distinctive, their craftsmanship of the finest, and their clientele a roll of peers, officers, clergy and gentlemen that reads like "Who Was Who in Yorkshire."

Drawn in the patent is a sectionalized gun in which the top slide is linked to a vertical lever pivoted at its bottom just outside the underside of the gun. This vertical lever fits through a slot cut in the rear of a round sectional sliding bolt so that, as the thumb slide is pulled back, the bolt is drawn back. As it does so, it compresses a coil spring, mounted around a shank cut in the bolt against the rear of the bolt slot. A point in passing concerning this patent is that the patentee was Thomas Jr., son of the founder of the firm, and one of the witnesses to it was his mother Elizabeth, who had presumably gone down to London with young Thomas to register his patent. The other witness was a clerk with a London address.

Considering as we are an expensive luxury item, it was a very successful design. From the surviving Horsley records, it is possible to identify 760 or so such guns built over a twenty-eight-year period. The bulk of

Thomas Horsley, Jr., as a young man, with his trail yet to blaze.

Thomas Horsley, Jr., in later life, with many classic guns sold. Pictured in his workshop at 10 Coney Street, York.

these were from 1863 to about 1875, but with late stragglers right on until the 1890s. The first 200-odd were built to fire the pinfire cartridge, but in 1867 there was an almost complete switch to the use of the centerfire, with only a very small smattering built for pinfire diehards thereafter. Most interesting of all is the note of one gun built to fire both pin- and centerfire cartridges—No. 1645 of 1868 for "The Hon. Massey."

Over the years, there appeared subtle variants in the style of the classic Horsley game guns. For in-

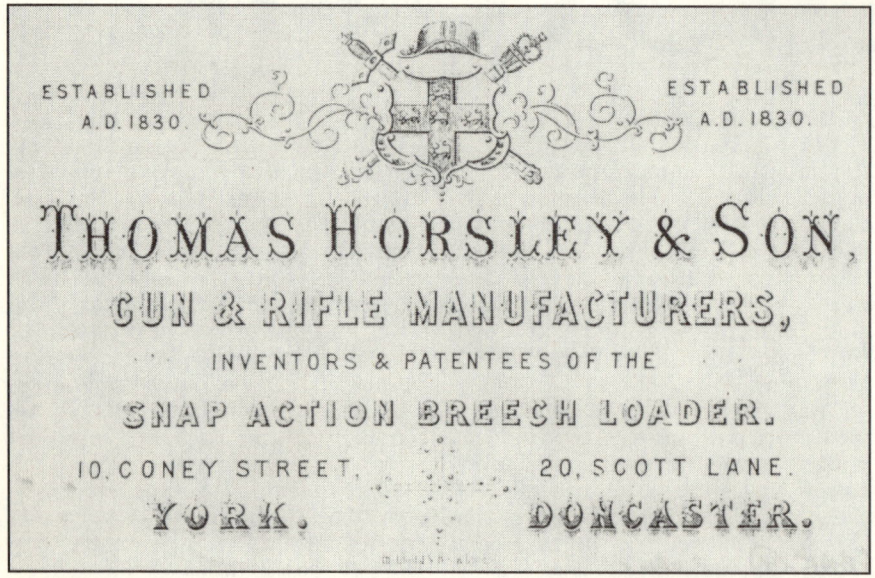

As was normal, Horsley's label made the most of the firm's inventions.

stance, the thumb lever tends to become more upstanding at its rear to afford a user's thumb a better grip. Such changes do not exactly follow the serial numbers, so it is that the gun I am using to illustrate the early style is in fact serial number 1805, something like 200 serial numbers on from the earliest examples.

This gun was the first Horsley I ever saw and the one that must take the blame for my long running project researching this maker. The very first time I saw it, it was in use, despite its ruinous, neglected condition, firing the inevitable nitro cartridges in the trusting hands of a fellow village lad. He had found it hidden behind the meal bins in a barn on the farm where he was working.

To return to my theme; a large proportion of these guns use anoth-

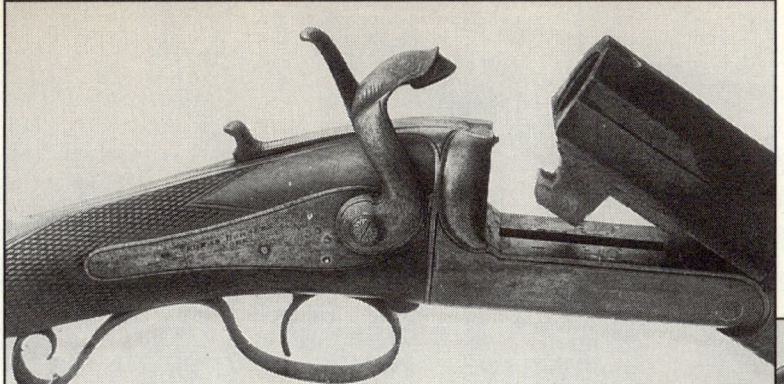

The No. 1603 4-bore pinfire, sold in 1867 to Edward York, has the typical snap action.

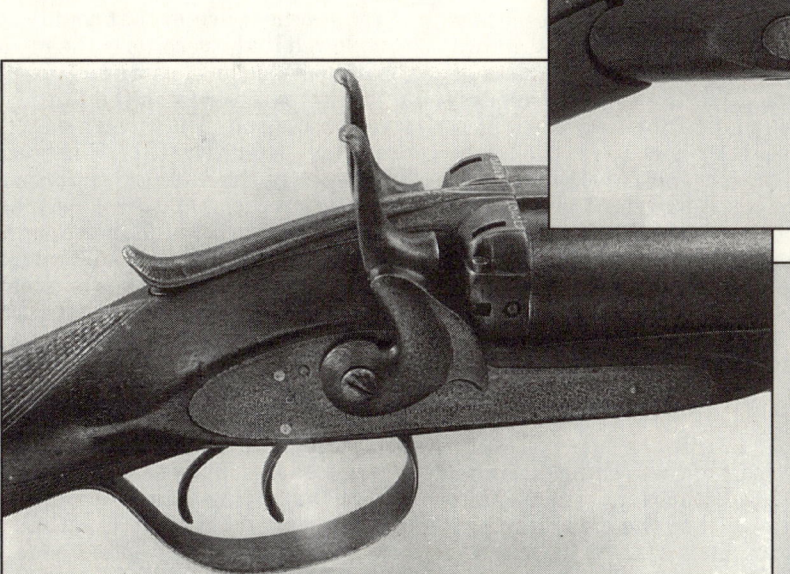

Rifle No. 1772 in 450-caliber was sold in 1868 to I.C. Lister-Kay Esq.

Gun No. 1805, a 12-bore, was sold in 1805 to R.S. Bagges. This top-lever is almost exactly like the patent drawings. The gun is the first Horsley owned by the author.

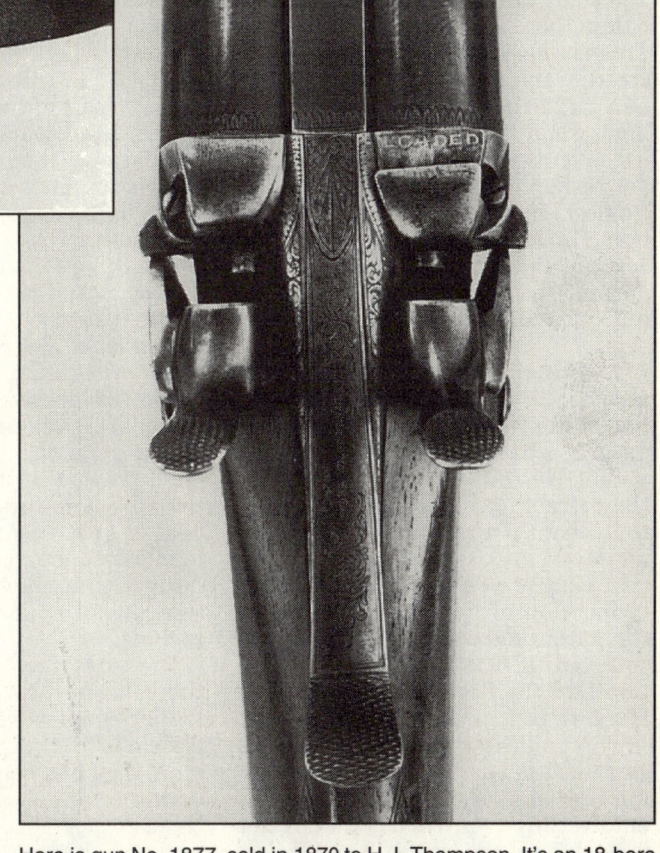

Here is gun No. 1877, sold in 1870 to H.J. Thompson. It's an 18-bore centerfire with back-action locks, retracting firing pins and "Loaded" indicators.

er Horsley patent, No. 1138 of 1867, concerned with retracting firing pins. The idea was to have two levers that lie horizontally in the standing breech hung at about their centers on vertical pivots. The outside ends of these levers project beyond the standing breech and are thus able to be pushed forward by the characteristic cams formed on the breasts of the hammers. The internal ends of the horizontal levers are slotted onto the firing pins so that, as the outside end is forced forward, the firing pin is retracted. In later examples, that is to say on guns with a serial number of about 1900-odd and over, this pattern changes subtly and is neatened by making the retracting levers pro-

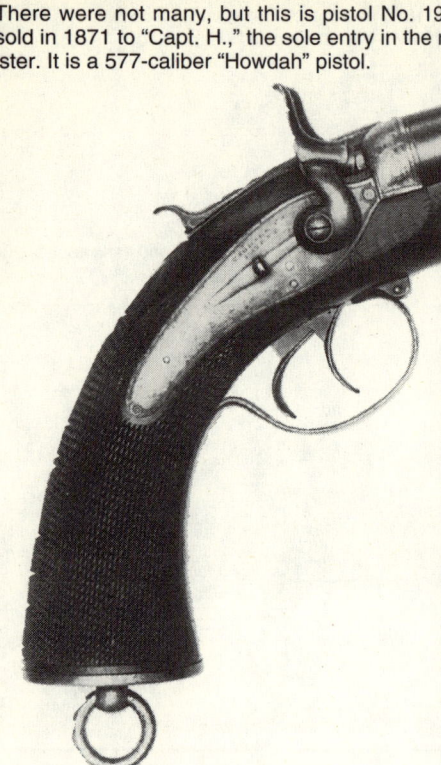

There were not many, but this is pistol No. 1943, sold in 1871 to "Capt. H.," the sole entry in the register. It is a 577-caliber "Howdah" pistol.

trude from the undersides of the standing breech.

It could be said with fair truth that patent No. 710 of 1868 represents Thomas Horsley's conversion to the creed of the centerfire cartridge, for included in it is a tool that is the best known and most used of all the Horsley inventions—the twin pillar capper/recapper which is still made in England by Lightwoods of Birmingham. In fact, Thomas Horsley had several other loading tools of his own design, but this tempting alley we must leave unexplored for the present.

The final and least common feature of the classic guns is the addition of the Horsley "loaded indicator" patent which is also part of the patent No. 710. Unfortunately, like the retracting firing pin, the use of this idea is not recorded in the Horsley records, but my own notes suggest that it was only a fairly small proportion of guns made between the patent date and 1874 that were so fitted. It was thus the last addition and the first deletion from the Horsley gun.

This indicator works by having a shutter fitted on the top of the standing breech so that, when the gun is empty, the forward end of the shutter is flush with the breech face. However, when a cartridge, loaded or fired incidentally, is in the breech, it pushes back a stud, something like a second off-center firing pin. This in turn pushes back a vertical lever in the standing breech on the top of which is fitted the shutter. The shutter moves to the rear to reveal the word "Loaded" inlaid in gold on the standing breech.

The use of this device necessitated filing up the top of the standing breech as a simple curve, and it is an interesting feature of contemporary Horsleys that do not have this indicator that they too have the same shaped breech—not, I believe, simply because it's a standard action, but rather to preserve the "house style." However, with the abandonment of the loaded indicator, we see the reversion to "ball" fences in the early 1870s. As that decade wore on, the increasing use of the rebound lock made the retracting firing pin idea also redundant, and it too was deleted.

The result of these changes is that we have the somewhat curious state of affairs in that the early and late models resemble each other, and it is in the mid-range where we find the variants.

Speaking of variants on the basic design as applied to game guns, one of the least-used ideas is the back-action lock. The records reveal only three of these, a single and a pair, made respectively in 1870 and 1872. This is somewhat strange because the back action was a standard pattern of the time and was used by some makers of the very best of guns. So there are muzzleloaders converted to the Horsley design that use these locks, but they do not appear in the surviving records.

However, if we look at other uses of the basic pull-back top-lever action, we find there were three pistols made with it. Of the two of these that I have seen, they had back-action locks, and both were large-caliber "Howdah" or "Man-stoppers" and looked like abbreviated shotguns. Also looking like shotguns are a few medium-caliber double rifles.

To return to the shotgun theme, another source of variants are the calibers made. Once again, the records are not utterly reliable, for some 14-bores are noted, but other calibers which are known have not been found recorded. Of those that I know at the moment, there are two 4-bores, a few 8s, more 10s, the overwhelming majority are 12-bore, 14-bores possibly equal 8-bores in number, but strangely to us nothing smaller is seen.

Yet another variant that could not be followed in the records is the modification of the basic patent No. 2410 to marry its top-lever to the Purdey-style double bolt. The latter's patent protection expired in 1877. The basic leverwork of the Horsley action remained, but the snap spring became a flat spring fitted round the triggers that is pressed down by a shoulder on the vertical lever. It is a great pity from our point of view that such modifications were not recorded in the maker's records. The probable reason was that they were not considered sufficiently important. So while the discovery of these records was an enormous research coup, I am still gathering details of Horsley guns to expand the picture that I have. Certainly, the greatest oddity that I have been told of is a side-lever-actioned gun that had a dummy top slide as per patent No. 2410, but no mention of this in the records, alas!

At this distance in time, it is very difficult to be precise as to why a style of gun action was abandoned. However, the fact remains that as the 1870s wore on, fewer Horsleys were made with the pull-back top-lever and more and more used the push-down side-lever, which is a puzzling path because we know that the top-lever, albeit a turning top-lever, was to become the normal shotgun action. A possible answer is that when the top slide lever was combined with the Purdey double bolt, it became that much stiffer to work. Certainly, the side-lever is very pleasant to use; a Horsley so equipped has been one of my favorite guns for the last ten years.

For whatever reason, side-lever and later turning top-lever guns, referred to as "Lat. Top Lever," take

Sold in 1872 to Sherwin Smith, gun No. 2025 is a 12-bore centerfire with levers to retract firing pins set almost vertically.

This is gun No. 1887, the second of a pair sold in 1870 to Cookson Esq. They were 12-bore centerfires with firing pins retracted by horizontal levers.

are probably customer preferences, which explanation I am sure also applies to the very few pull-back top-lever hammerless guns made, for what would be more natural than to wish to retain a tried and trusted feature on an otherwise strange new gun?

Despite these stragglers, eventually the style ceased to be made, the last one in 1896. Patent No. 2410 has become part of history and another facet of the richness of the British shotgun heritage. •

over in the Horsley records. But the pull-back lever remained in limited use for as long as Horsleys made good quality hammer guns. The reasons that lie behind these later produced models we can, in many cases, only surmise, but with a little detective work some can be explained as being made to match other, much earlier guns to form pairs. The rest

Quite rare, gun No. 2451 is a 20-bore shotgun—sold in 1877 to Colonel Wombwell.

This hammerless ejector 12-bore gun No. 3195, the second of a pair, was sold in 1890 to Ralph Creyke. It has the pull-back lever—very sleek.

THE LEATHER GUNS OF THE 17TH CENTURY

We shall never know who "invented" gunpowder, nor who first conceived the idea of using that mixture of potassium nitrate, charcoal and sulphur to shoot projectiles. In the very early 14th century, Berthold Schwarz, a German friar more known by his monastic name Bertholdus Niger, seems to have known of it, and by the middle of the 14th century, firearms are often mentioned in the texts.

By the 15th century, guns, both cannon and hand-arms, had been developed to the point where they could actually influence the outcome of battles. The Hussite wars in Bohemia provided the definite breakthrough. The powder used was of very uneven quality, a simple mixture of finely ground potassium nitrate, sulphur and charcoal. These earliest guns were usually fairly light, breech-loading iron pieces, welded together from a number of iron rods arranged longitudinally and reinforced by iron hoops shrunk on to the barrels, much as a wooden barrel consists of staves held together by bands. Their rate of fire was high, but their range was limited and their accuracy was poor. The balls were of stone, a material with low density, thus comparatively light, and very expensive to manufacture. Such guns were of little use in siege warfare.

Very soon thereafter, the technology acquired when casting church bells was applied to the manufacture of bronze guns. Bronze has a much higher tensile strength than welded iron, and since the barrels were cast in one piece with the breech, such guns could fire heavy cast iron balls with much heavier charges than could the iron guns. Being muzzleloaders, their rate of fire was very much lower than that of the iron breechloaders. When these new bronze barrels were also bored, accuracy was improved dramatically.

Bronze guns were to dominate artillery for some time, until complemented and, later, supplanted by cast iron pieces. Cast iron guns were very much cheaper, but the barrel walls were necessarily thicker, so iron guns were heavy. Continental iron ore usually contained phosphorus, which made the iron brittle, whereas Swedish ores lacked phosphorus. This made Swedish iron much more difficult to cast, but such guns were much less prone to burst than those of Continental manufacture, and Swedish guns soon took a very appreciable piece of the international gun market. At a time when Spain, Portugal, France, Holland, England, Denmark-Norway and Sweden were all building men-of-war in great numbers, and when every merchantman had to carry a gun for self-defense against pirates and privateers, this market was large indeed!

Cast iron guns were widely used in the 16th century. In his *Carta Marina*, printed in Venice in 1539, Olaus Magnus shows a Swedish field battery in action against Russian troops on the ice of the Baltic. The guns are large muzzleloaders, their barrels colored the same blue as the cavalrymens armor, quite different from the golden yellow of the trumpeters brass instrument. These guns had no trunnions, each barrel being inletted in a wooden stock which formed the body and tail of the carriage. By the middle of the 16th century, trunnions had been introduced, the barrels being mounted in carriages of essentially the same type as those used all through the 17th century.

Bronze guns could still be made very much lighter than iron guns of equal strength. Since field artillery had to be mobile in order to be able to follow the army on the march, most field guns were cast of bronze until well into the 18th century, despite the high cost. All through the 15th and 16th centuries, master founders served the princes and cities of Europe, often changing masters for pecuniary gain, but seldom revealing the real or imagined advantages of their proprietary casting methods. They also served their masters as artillery officers, even laying and firing their pieces in battle.

The great disadvantage of the cast guns, be they of bronze or of iron, was their weight. Charles VIII of France mounted his guns on wheeled, horsedrawn carriages; Bartolomeo Colleoni, who died in 1475 and whose equestrian statue is familiar to every tourist in Italy, used his guns in support of his infantry on the battlefield. In his day, trunnions were introduced in Italy whereby the barrel was affixed to the carriage and it could be tipped to increase or decrease its elevation. However, the guns remained extremely heavy. It was difficult enough to bring such guns onto the battlefield or into the siegeworks, and it usually proved impossible to move them during the battle, so there could simply be no question of artillery tactics. It should be remembered that even in Continental Europe, the roads of the time were hardly worth the name. When battle proved imminent, the commander of the artillery would

with his gunfounders (1564-1567), King Erik attempted to establish the standards for his artillery:

The guns were cast individually by different masters, so Erik's standards are approximate only. Guns were still as heavy as ever, and their size and calibers still varied widely in 1600. In his early years, Gustavus Adolphus (1611-1632) brought order into this chaos, standardizing the guns of the Swedish artillery. This made the ammunition supply somewhat easier to master. His standard guns were named for the weight of the appropriate round shot of iron, in Swedish "markpund" (of 340 grams). Swedish guns consequently had some-

sures. The "ordinary" guns of the day used powder charges equal to half the weight of the iron ball, whereas the new regimental guns of bronze used charges one-third of the weight of the ball. They could thus be cast very light. By limiting the size of these guns to three-pounders, which could be moved by teams of four horses, Gustavus created the first true field artillery. He introduced a new type of harness by which the field guns could,

by GAD RAUSING

have to move his guns into position before the first shot was fired or the first infantry made its charge, hoping that he would have chosen a position from which his guns would be able to dominate the battlefield.

Most of the tacticians of the time realized that, to dominate Europe, the problem of weight would need to be solved to create a truly mobile field artillery. Thus, all through the 16th century, gunfounders tried to reduce the weight of their guns, though without noticeable success. Swedish master founder Gillius Packett promised his king to cast guns weighing three quarters of conventional ones of the same caliber, but disappointed King Erik XIV (1561-1568), who reproached him that "your words comfort us, but not your work." By a series of contracts

what smaller bores than their French or English counterparts.

All through the Thirty Years War (1618-1648), the standard guns were all much shorter and had thinner walls than corresponding guns in the Imperial army, and were consequently much lighter.

In order to increase the firepower of his infantry, Gustavus introduced an entirely new concept: light field artillery—guns capable of following the infantry in the vicissitudes of battle. The initiators were the two colonels von Sigroth, Hans Henrik and his son, David Fredrik, who realized that such guns, which would usually shoot canister or grape, did not need a range much greater than that of the ordinary musket of the time and could consequently use quite light powder charges generating fairly low pres-

when necessary, be pulled by horses or by their own crews muzzle forward, ready to fire. The guns thus did not have to be unlimbered and turned, and could open fire within a few seconds of the order being given. Although the carriages of most of these guns were of the conventional type, some of the very lightest were fitted with turntables so they could be aimed without the entire carriage having to be realigned. The great victories in the Polish war and in the Thirty Years War were won by such guns.

Gustavus also introduced pre-measured powder loads for all six-pound and heavier guns. Complete cartridges were used in the three-pounders, containing both powder and shot, usually grape, the former in a turned wooden cup rather like a modern over-powder wad turned back to front. The powder charge, in its cup, and the shot were cased in canvas, the case being closed over the open end of the powder cup. The grape shot were held firmly together by a twine net which afforded dimensional stability. The whole cartridge thus had a slightly smaller diameter than the bore of the gun, and could be loaded as a unit.

When the gun was to be loaded, the bore was first rapidly swabbed with water, so as to extinguish any embers remaining after the previous shot. The whole cartridge was then pushed into the barrel, powder end first, and set with the ramrod. The canvas case and the wooden cup were pierced with the touchhole prick, and either a powder-filled goose quill was inserted into the touchhole and pushed down until in contact with the powder charge, or the touchhole was filled to the brim with loose powder from the

his regimental pieces, and all the best brains of the time devoted their energy to solving this seemingly insoluble problem. The obvious solution was to use ultra-light barrels, but such were extremely difficult to cast, and being apt to burst, they would be very dangerous, splinters flying like shrapnel. The solution was to wrap the light barrel with a covering which would contain the splinters, acting like a blasting mat.

It seems the idea of reinforcing a very light metal barrel with an outer layer of leather or other organic material was first conceived by Philip Ebernard and Alexander Bierbrauer of Zürich, sometime in the early 1620s. The time seems to have been ripe for the idea, since contemporary writers ascribed the invention variously to the Swiss, the Dutch and the Swedes. The question was how to produce the ultra-light barrels to form the cores of such reinforced guns.

desmuseum in Zürich, two in the Musée d'Artillerie in Paris and one in the Heeresmuseum in Vienna. There were five in the Zeughaus in Berlin and one in Copenhagen. One leather gun is preserved in the Army Museum in Munich and one in the Nürnberg Museum. There was, or is, also a leather gun in the armoury of the knights of St. John, in Malta. The guns in Zürich are known to be of Swiss origin and so, probably, are the others.

Austrian colonel Melchior Wurmprandt visited Zürich in 1622. Even though Ebernard and Bierbrauer later accused him of stealing their "secret," he was most likely innocent, since the two Swiss inventors were not employed by the City Council until January 9, 1623, with a yearly payment of 25 Guldens, a sum which was to remain unchanged until 1627. This suggests that they did not complete their first gun until sometime

KING ERIK'S GUNS

Gun	Bore (mm)	Wgt. (kg)	Bore Lgth. (calibers)	Ball Wgt. (kg)
Cannon (helkartog)	186	4100	26	17.00
3/4 cannon	170	3300	29	12.75
Demi-cannon (halvkartog)	149	2200	28	8.50
Culverin (fältslanga)	118	1650	41	4.25
3/4 Culverin	107	960	37	8.75
1/2 Culverin (halvslanga)	75	500	49	1.30
Double falcon (dubbelfalkonett)	65	350	45	0.85
Falcon (falkonett)	52	170	44	0.25

SWEDISH GUNS OF THE THIRTY YEARS WAR

Gun	Bore (mm)	Wgt. (kg)	Bore Lgth. (calibers)	Ball Wgt. (kg)*
48-pounder	192	1260-3675	18	20
24-pounder, light	152	855	16	10
24-pounder, heavy	152	2700	24	10
12-pounder, light	122	580	17.5	5
12-pounder, heavy	122	1800	25	5
6-pounder	96	400-950	22-24	2.5
3-pounder	76	380-410	22-25	1.25
3-pounder regimental gun	76	90-125	17	1.25

*Approximate

gun captain's flask. If the supply of cartridges had been exhausted, the gun could be loaded with loose powder, wads, and grape or ball.

The gun captain laid the gun, which was fired by the constable, everybody standing well clear of the recoil. After the shot, everybody joined in manhandling the gun back into position and the whole operation was repeated.

Altogether, this meant that the "regimental pieces" could, and did, fire very rapidly indeed—up to four rounds a minute at a time when musketeers could fire but one volley per minute. In 1623, the entire artillery of the army was organized as an independent branch of the service, the "artillery company," which was expanded into an artillery regiment in 1629.

Realizing what the combination of firepower and movement meant, the king wanted guns even lighter than

Experimental light guns of the 17th century were of two entirely different types—those made in much the same way as were musket barrels and those cast, as were ordinary pieces of ordnance. For a long time, smoothbore handgun and musket barrels had been made by forming a rectangular piece of sheet iron into a cylinder around a steel mandrel, hammer-welding the longitudinal seam and finally boring the inside smooth. In much the same way, Ebernard and Bierbrauer, as well as several other designers of ultra-light guns, rolled a sheet of bronze around a steel mandrel. Bronze doesn't lend itself to welding, so they soldered the longitudinal seams of their barrels. Such soldered joints lacked the strength of welded ones, and such bronze barrels never stood up to field use.

Five such pieces have been preserved in the Schweizerisches Lan-

in the winter of 1622-23.

Be that as it may, Wurmprandt realized that soldered barrels were not strong enough and that another solution to the problem must be found. He designed an entirely new type of barrel, one where the core was cast, as were those of conventional guns at the time, but with very thin walls, consequently making them very light. These barrels were reamed or bored, as were those of conventional guns.

Obviously, such ultra-light barrels could be used with light loads only, and even so, there was always a risk of their bursting with dire consequences for the crew. Wurmprandt accepted the risk of the bursting, but at least he did something to protect the gun crews. Although none of Wurmprandt's guns have survived, it seems they were cast with integral breeches and integral trunnions, and he dispensed with longitudinal iron rods, simply wrapping his barrels with hemp rope and covering the whole contraption with leather. This wrapping and leather layer did not contribute markedly to the strength of the barrel, but it did prevent fragments from flying in all directions should the barrel burst.

As to the weight of such guns: In 1628, five metal barrels with their trunnions for three-pounder leather guns weighed 2 *skeppund*, 5 *lispund*, 5 *marker*, i.e. 307.9 kilos, thus averaging 61.58 kilos each. In the same year, six three-pounders weighed 3 *skeppund*, 8 *lispund*, 7 *marker*, i.e. 465.08 kilos, for an average of 75.13 kilos each.

The leather guns mostly fired grape. Evidently, they used the same ammunition and charges as the regimental bronze three-pounders. Powder and grape were combined in cartridges, several of which have survived. Although leather guns could be brought into position very rapidly and could fire rapidly, they heated up very fast and were thus good for no more than a few rounds before they had to be allowed to cool. They were of little value in normal battle, where sustained fire was usually necessary.

By 1625, the Russian War had been successfully concluded. Sweden was still at war with Poland, but had not yet become involved against the Empire in the Thirty Years War. Wurmprandt was thus no renegade when he entered the Swedish service in 1625, to test his first "leather guns" at Stockholm on July 15 and 20 of that year. These were six-pounders, firing balls of cast iron. In 1626, some three-pounders were tested (as were some "light copper muskets"), and on March 12, 1627, the king ordered such guns to be produced. By the end of September, the first guns were delivered, to be immediately shipped to a field unit on active service in the German theater of war.

In November, 1627, King Gustavus ordered 100 leather guns of Wurmprandt's type to be manufactured at Stockholm and at Arboga. The barrels were cast by Metardus Gessus in Stockholm; the rope was manufactured by Michael Ropemaker; Arendt Papermaker delivered the material for the powder cartridges. Captain Evert von Hoelle was responsible for the manufacture of the ammunition. On May 16, 1629, the last delivery of twenty-six three-pounders was sent to the war in Germany.

Later, Wurmprandt turned his inventive genius to casting iron guns. Such had been manufactured in Sweden at least since the 1530s, but evidently Wurmprandt improved them vastly. By the turn of the year 1631-1632, he went on active service in Germany, only to become a prisoner in the battle of Kerchersberg, on June 18, 1636. Nothing is known about his fate.

How did the leather guns perform in battle? By the end of September, 1627, the first shipment of leather guns, under Wurmprandt's own command, arrived at Elbing, a battery of two six-pounders and four three-pounders. At Braunsberg, he joined a unit under Didrik von Falkenberg, who wrote that the "new guns could easily be carried between two horsemen, and could fire several rounds before having to be cleaned." On October 1, the Swedes laid siege to the fortress of Wormditt, the leather guns opening fire two days later, but the three-pounders and six-pounders could make little impression on the walls, which had to be mined. The mine was blown on October 8, and the fortress taken. Polish Colonel Sliatkowski and his men were accorded full military honors and permitted to march off.

Quite clearly, these light guns could make little impression on modern fortifications, but neither were they intended for such use.

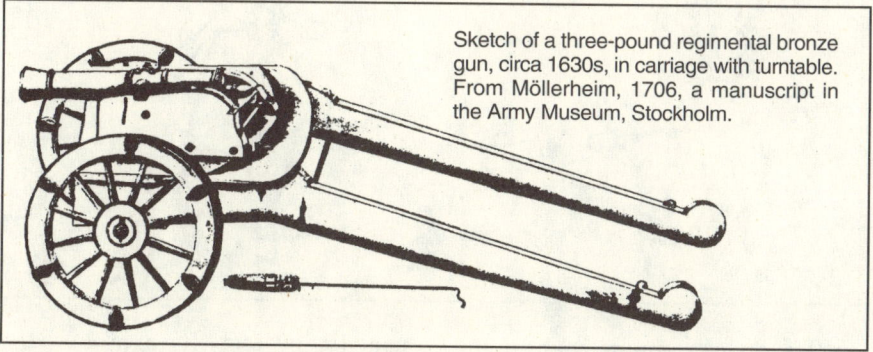

Three ways they moved the gun toward the enemy: (1) Using "attack beams:" The gun can be fired immediately. (2) Action horses: These have to be moved away before the gun can be fired, which required about 30 seconds. (3) Traction tackle: The men throw themselves to either side. The gun can be fired within a few seconds.

Sketch of a three-pound regimental bronze gun, circa 1630s, in carriage with turntable. From Möllerheim, 1706, a manuscript in the Army Museum, Stockholm.

They were to prove their value in the following year at Weichselmünde. The river was blockaded by a number of Polish ships, an obstacle to the use of the harbor and river which had to be neutralized. On the night of June 25, the king led Colonel Alexander von Essens' regiment, reinforced with eight leather guns and a screen of eight squadrons of cavalry, through a forest which the Poles believed to be an absolute obstacle to artillery. The troops reached their goal without having been discovered. At dawn, the guns opened on the Polish ships which were anchored close to the shore, the surprise being complete. The ship *Tiger* blew up with all hands, and the *St. George* was sunk, though the *David* was saved, a sudden shower extinguishing the fire aboard caused by the gunfire. A Swedish corporal with his men swam out to another ship, capturing it in spite of the crew's desperate resistance. These must have been very small ships. It should be remembered that "ships of the line" were developed somewhat later, and the warships of the 1620s were very small and lightly built.[1] Such light field pieces would have made little impression on the men-of-war of the 1640s, but they were lethal to the small, light ships of the 1620s.

The English newspaper, *The Continuation of our weekly Newes*, August 7, 1628, writes:

> His Majestie (Gustavus Adolphus) hath beene lately in open field in Battaile (with Englands order of St. George about his necke) against the Poll in Prussia, and the Poll hath taken the retreat...They are now more afraid of Sweden than ever they were before, in respect of a new Ordnance of Leather Cannon...and they doe him as good and better service than his Copper Cannon: for as fast as the souidiers are able to march, the Cannon is conveyed as quickly along with them, having but one horse to draw the biggest of them, and three or foure men can carry the biggest of them on their shoulders over any straight place or narrow bridge whatsoever, so that the Polls are not aware ere the Cannon play upon them, for it will shoot with as great force as any other: which makes the Polonians say, his Majestie useth Devilrie: but that is all untrue: for I myselfe haue heard those Cannons several times shott with as great force as any other...

The secret of the leather guns was soon out. In June, 1629, the Poles wiped out a Swedish unit at Honigfelde, between Marienwerder and Marienburg in Prussia, capturing ten leather guns. The victor, General von Arnim (does the name sound familiar?), immediately sent them to the Imperial commander in chief, Wallenstein. However, after 1629 we hear no more of the leather guns, the whole of the infantry now being equipped with the new light bronze "regimental" three-pounders.

In the meantime, Robert Scott and Ludvig Ripp had designed leather guns that were tested in Stockholm in 1628. They were not produced in quantity and were apparently never issued. Even though Wurmprandt's guns proved their worth in the field, today the only surviving Swedish leather gun is one of Ripp's, which was transferred in 1858 to the Royal Armoury from the old private armoury at Tidö castle, which belonged to a descendant of Gustavus' prime minister, Axel Oxenstierna. The barrel of this gun is of very thin cast iron with a thin coating of cop-

Operating a muzzle-loading cannon involved a virtual dance of sponging, charging and tamping, as seen here.

per to protect it against rust. (According to the records, Wurmprandt used bronze for his barrels.) The rear end of the barrel is reinforced by a sleeve of metal, in front of which the barrel is tightly wrapped with steel wire. In much the same way, the barrels of the heavy naval guns of World War I were reinforced with a wrapping of steel wire, over which the outercase of the barrel was shrunk.

---

[1] In 1630, the English navy listed fourteen ships of 100-500 tonnes, out of a total of thirty-eight, the Dutch 113 out of 125, Denmark-Norway twenty-one out of forty-two, and Sweden twelve out of thirty-one. (Glete 1993.) The Polish ships at Weichselmünde were probably of this size.

The trunnions are attached to an iron ring surrounding the barrel (whereas the trunnions of Wurmprandt's guns were probably integral with the barrel). This iron ring also serves as attachment for eight flat steel laths, four reaching to the muzzle and four to the breech of the gun, behind which they cross. These laths are supported against the iron barrel by a series of wooden laths. The whole of the barrel is then tightly

The ball was loaded on a tamped wad. The cartridge primed, the gun laid—all out in the open on a battlefield— and only then fired. Any speed gain was vital.

wrapped with rope. The entire barrel is then covered with a double layer of thick linen, which is then encased in thick leather. The gun now weighs 49.3 kilos, or considerably less than Wurmprandt's barrels, whose bronze cores alone averaged 60-75 kilos.

In 1621, Ripp was a lieutenant serving with Baner's company of Mansfelt's regiment; in 1625-26, he served at the royal court; and on May 27, 1628, he commanded Wurmprandt's guns in the field. In 1629, he commanded all the Swedish artillery in Prussia. We do not know how or when he died.

During 1624-1625, Robert Scott was a company commander in Jacob Spens' regiment of the Swedish army. He designed a leather gun, tested in Stockholm on January 2, 1628, but it was not accepted into the service. In July of that year, Scott sold his gun to Denmark and joined the Danish service, rising to the rank of general. After one year, he returned to England, where he died in 1631, to be buried in Lambeth Church in London.

In 1656, George Schreiber, chief gunner to the Prince of Brieg, published his *Büchsenmeister-Discours*, in which he described a Swedish leather gun as follows: "...a leather gun of the same type (as one illustrated) was sent from Sweden in to Prussia in 1627. The core of the barrel is of copper, wrapped with flax from the breech to the dolphins, which was then impregnated with glue. On this lay a series of iron plates, held together with iron rings which had been fitted when hot. To these is attached an iron breech, in which is also the touch-hole. Outside this, the whole barrel is wrapped with hemp ropes one finger thick, coated with animal glue. The whole is then coated with plaster of Paris and, outside this, with thin leather. Outside this are three iron rings, one at the breach, one at the dolphins, holding the trunnions, and one at the muzzle. Five strong men can carry such a piece, which throws five pounds of iron." Since the barrel had a separate breech, it was evidently a soldered one, probably one of Ripp's or Scott's guns.

Schreiber described a second gun as follows: "...which was invented by a clergyman in Antorff (Antwerp) in 1630. Such guns would do excellent service at sea...Its barrel is 24 calibres long, and shoots one pound of iron." (Assuming the pound to be a Swedish one, of about 360 grams, the ball would have had a diameter of about 22.6mm. Assuming a clearance of 0.5mm, the bore would have been about 23.6mm in diameter and about 57cm long, the whole barrel consequently somewhat longer.) "The interior is lined with copper as thick as a shilling-piece. From breech to mouth it is covered with iron plates, which are held together by 6 iron rings. The whole barrel is then wrapped with ropes of hemp or of flax, drenched in glue." The text of the accompanying drawing states that the barrel was made of copper and iron plates wrapped with hemp ropes. This seems to mean that the barrel core was actually a copper plate, bent to cylindrical shape and soldered together.

A gun corresponding to this description, even though somewhat bigger, is kept in the Royal Armoury at Copenhagen. This piece, which was acquired from Hamburg in 1856, has a bore of 65mm and a total length of slightly more than one meter. The barrel itself consists of a welded copper tube, 2mm thick, onto which are shrunk iron rings. The breech is of iron. The whole piece is wrapped with ropes and cased in leather.

Colonel Ulrich v. Cranach, whose work *Rare und Kunstreiche Fried- und Krieges-Inventiones* was published posthumously in 1672, states that he depicts a "kind of light regimental cannon...iron rings must be shrunk on the thin barrel of copper which is then wrapped with ropes and provided with a leather outer casing to look good." Evidently he did not trust the leather guns, since he also describes a light bronze gun of the same dimensions, stating that its "bore should be 17 calibres long, the wall thickness at the touch-hole half a calibre, at the front of the chamber one quarter of a calibre and at the mouth one eighth of a calibre. It must be cast of the very best bronze."

Saxon artillery Lieutenant Johann Siegmund Buchner's book, *Theoria et praxis artilleriae* (Nürnberg 1682), also describes very light guns with wrapped barrels: "...even though these are called leather guns, they still are not of leather but are called thus since they are covered with leather. Such guns have long been known, the first having been brought from Sweden to Prussia in 1627. Any expert may judge for himself what use they are."

He goes on to describe a copper barrel with iron rings shrunk on to it, with a breech and a touchhole plug of bronze or iron. The whole is wrapped with hemp ropes, impregnated with putty and then finally covered with leather.

"Such guns may be fired with powder loads equal to no more than one quarter or, at most, one third of the weight of an iron shot, but never with iron shot, only with grape." Apparently the good lieutenant could not imagine leather guns firing iron shot sinking men of war!

We meet the leather guns for the last time in Captain Michael Mieth's *Artillerae recentior Praxis*, published at Frankfurt in 1684. Mieth was to fall at the defense of Vienna against the Turks later in the same year. "The leather guns were made famous by the Swedes, who used them in the Thirty Years' War. And this for two reasons: first of all they do not cost much, and can be manufactured rapidly. And secondly, they can be brought up fast on the battlefield, both matters of extreme importance to the Swedes, because of their rapid marches. But even the Swedes soon abandoned them, since they would burst after a few rounds. A good field gun must stand a lot...A gun which can fire but ten rounds is not worth its price. This is why I have not described their manufacture."

Contemporary opinion varied. Wurmprandt's guns could follow the infantry anywhere, could be brought into position very rapidly, and it is also probable that such light guns could be rapidly brought back into firing position after recoiling. They could keep up a high rate of fire for a short period of time, and they were cheap. But they could fire light loads only, they heated rapidly, becoming dangerous to load after comparatively few rounds, and could fire no more than about ten rounds before overheating, so their service life was short. Such weapons seem admirably suited for sudden-fire attacks, but very much less so for use in ordinary battles, where very many rounds would have to be fired in a short time.

One can but admire the devotion to duty, and the foolhardiness, of the men who served these "leather guns." They explored a technology which was centuries ahead of its time, one which could not be realized until steel barrels could be wrapped with high-tensile steel wire over which could be shrunk a steel sleeve. Thus were the naval guns built for the ships of the First and Second World Wars. Because of their inherent weaknesses, and in spite of their occasionally impressive performances, leather guns were soon replaced by ultra-light bronze guns. ●

Bibliography:

Åberg, A. and Göransson, G. *Karoliner*. Höganäs: 1984.

Buchner, J.S. *Theorla et Praxis Artilleriae*. Nürnberg: 1682.

v. Cranach, U. *Rare und Kunstreiche Fried- und Krieges-lnventiones*. 1672.

Erben, W. & John, W. *Katalog des K. und K.* Heeresmuseum, Wien. Wien: 1903.

Erben, W. *Die "goldenen Kanonan" von 1640 und 1643*. Zertschrift f. Historische Waffenkunde, V.

Gessler, E.A. *Die sogenannte Lederkanonen aus dem Zeughasbestand der Stadt Zuerich*. Anzeiger fuer Schweizerische Altertumskunde. Zuerich: 1924.

Glete, J. *Navies and Nations*. Acta Universitatis Stockholmiensis, 48:1. Stocholm: 1993.

Gohlke, W. *Geschichte der gesamten Feuerwaffen bis 1850*. Leipzig: 1911.

Hammarskioeld, Ludvig. *Gustav II Adolfs artilleri*. Artilleri Tidskrift: 1937.

Hammarskioeld, Ludvig. *Artilleriöverstarna von Siegroth*. Personhistorisk Tidskrift: 1935.

Laking, G. *A Catalogue of the Armour and Arms in the Armoury of the Knights of St. John of Jerusalem, now in the Palace, Valetta, Malta*. London: 1902.

Mieth, M. *Artilleriae recentior Praxis*. Frankfurt: 1684.

Rathgen, B. *Das Geschuetz im Mittelalter*. Berlin: 1928.

Robert, L. *Le Musée Artillerie en 1889*. Catalogue par L. Robert. Paris: 1890.

Schreiber, G. *Buechsenmeister-Diskurs*. Brieg: 1656.

Spak, F.A. *Artilleriets uppkornst och utveckling i Europa*. Stockholm: 1881.

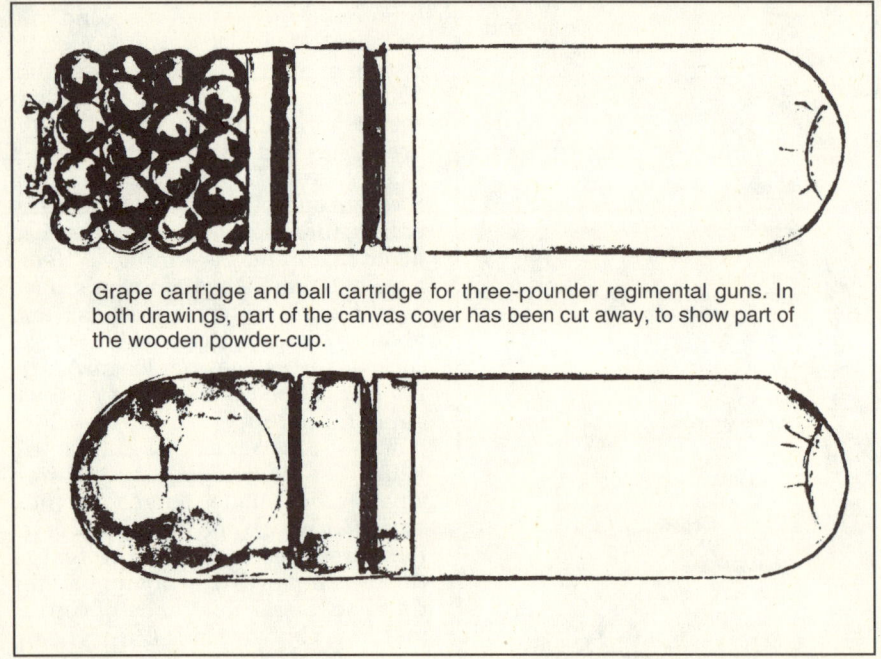

Grape cartridge and ball cartridge for three-pounder regimental guns. In both drawings, part of the canvas cover has been cut away, to show part of the wooden powder-cup.

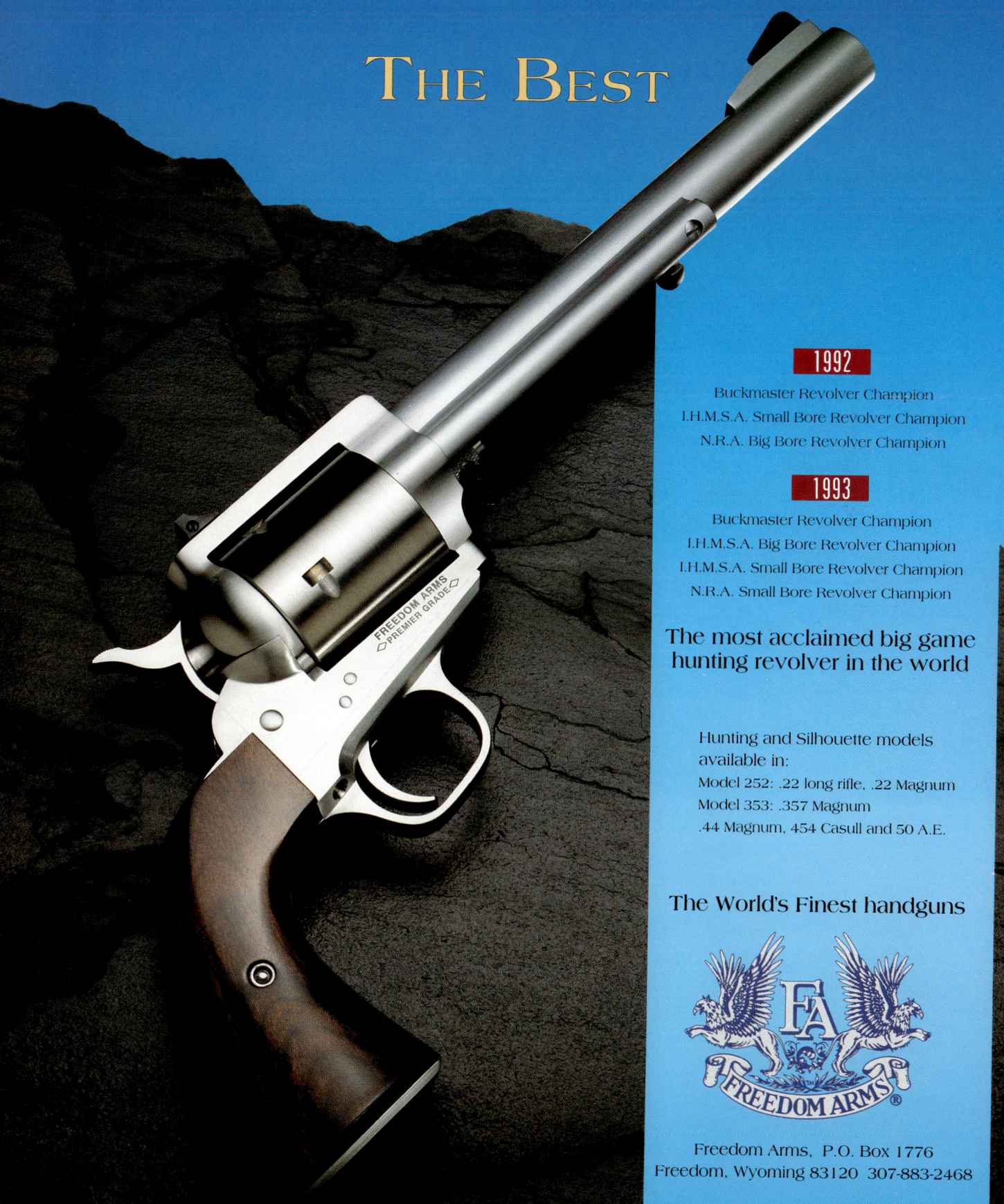

DEMAND
"The Difference"®
55-09778
THE
D
DIFFERENCE SM
Lifetime
Replacement Coverage!
Ask your dealer for details!
"The Difference"® is not a manufacturer's warranty.

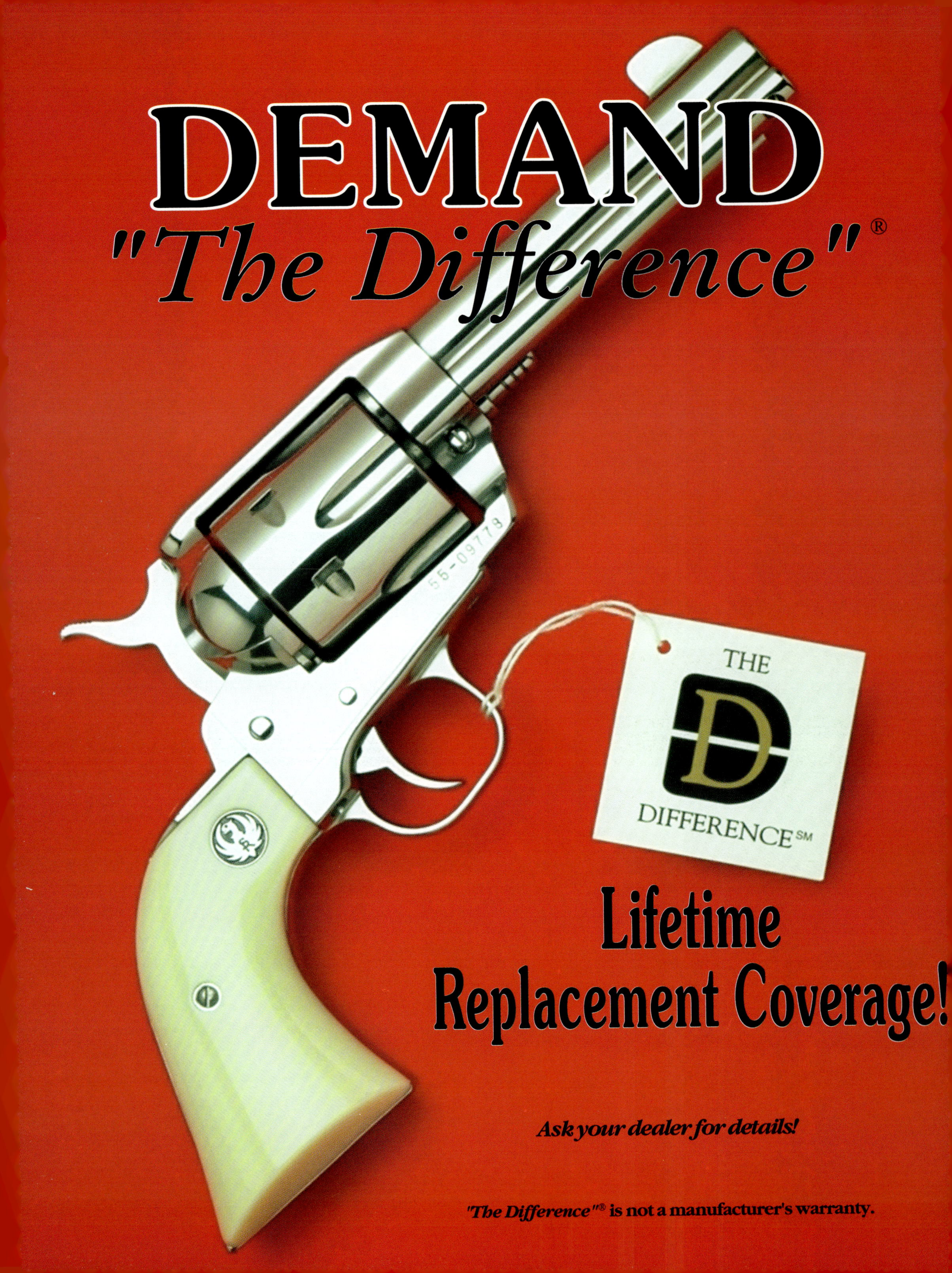

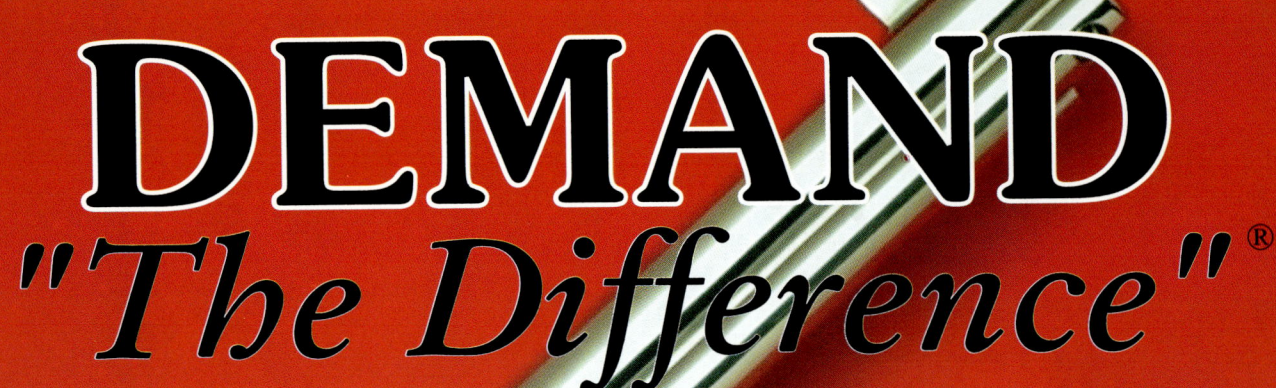

Load 8 Shotshells in Under 4 Seconds.

TECLoader®

12 Gauge SHOTGUN SPEEDLOADER

FOR THE FOLLOWING SHOTGUNS:

MAKE:	MODEL:
BENELLI	SUPER 90
BERETTA	1200 FP
ITHACA	37
ITHACA	87
MOSSBERG	500
MOSSBERG	590
REMINGTON	870
REMINGTON	1100
REMINGTON	11-87
WINCHESTER	120
WINCHESTER	140
WINCHESTER	1200
WINCHESTER	1300

Complete System Includes:
(2) Speedloader Tubes & Handles, Custom Nylon Holster, Bracket, Hardware, and Complete Instructions.
NO GUNSMITHING REQUIRED.

Note: The SL-12 Shotgun Speedloader may not work with some shotguns or shotgun accessories, such as guns equipped with a long forearm which covers the receiver in the rearward position, and some with side mounted scope mounts.

U.S.A. MAGAZINES, INC.

P.O. Box 39115 • Downey, CA 90239 • FAX: 310-903-7857

800-USA-2577

SEND $5.00 FOR CATALOG & VIDEO ONLY.
Patented.   Made in U.S.A.

U.S.A. MAGAZINES INC.

SL-12

Suggested Retail
$59.95
Includes Video

THE SEMI-AUTO CROSMAN 1077 REPEATAIR® RIFLE

HOT

We Keep Hearing The Same Thing From People Who Shoot The New 1077 RepeatAir® Rifle.

Fun. Exciting. Unique. Unbelievable. Just a few of the words to describe the new Crosman 1077 RepeatAir® - the first truly reliable semi-automatic air rifle. It features our patented, 12-shot removable clip to deliver real semi-automatic action. Fires as fast as you can pull the trigger.

Classic design, durable synthetic stock, rifled steel barrel, and fully adjustable rear sights. CO_2 powered for velocity up to 625 fps.

Express yourself with the fun and excitement of the semi-automatic 1077 RepeatAir. We'll be listening.

Crosman AirGuns
#1 IN AMERICAN AIR POWER!

Rts. 5 & 20 Dept. • E. Bloomfield, NY 14443 • (716) 657-6161 • Fax: (716) 657-5405

HANDLOADING UPDATE

by LARRY S. STERETT

WHEN THE FIRST GUN DIGEST, containing 164 pages, was advertised by Klein's Sporting Goods for $1, postpaid, in March 1944, the U.S. was still at war; D-Day was three months away. Most manufacturers of handloading equipment were producing such equipment for military use—yes, Virginia, the military and other governmental agencies apparently did handload, particularly in laboratories and for some recreational use—or were engaged in the manufacture of other vital equipment. All such supplies available to civilians were quickly snapped up, but by trading, sharing, and resorting to home manufacture of loading tools and some components, handloaders managed to survive.

The equipment available bore names not always familiar to today's shooters, such as the case trimmer, cut-off tool, and primer pocket reamer by the G.T. Smiley Co., or the Model 28 Straight-line tool and powder measure by Belding & Mull. Bullet moulds and the Model "C" press by the Modern-Bond Corporation were popular, as were the No. 5 Powder Measure, Lyman Tru-Line Loading Press, No. 45 Lubricator and Sizer, and the Ideal No. 310 Tool by the Lyman Gun Sight Company. G.R. Sharp produced the Essanee Bullet Sizer & Lubricator, and the Cameron Mfg. Corporation had taken over manufacture of the excellent Jorden Multiple Reloading Press. Advertised as the No. 1 reloading press, if you could find one available, was the "C" by Pacific Gun Sight, a firm that also manufactured a reloading scale and a powder measure. Other such tools included the Potter Duplex, Schmitt Model 24, Star Progressive Loading Machine, the Presco Automatic Reloader, and the Meepos.

Some components were available, but the classified sections in the *American Rifleman* and the big three sporting magazines were full of "wanted" or "for sale or trade" ads listing components. Fred Huntington of RCBS fame had just come out with a kit for making jacketed bullets using fired 22 rimfire cases, and the Alcan Paper Co. (later Alcan, Inc.) was advertising 12-gauge over-powder wads for $1 per thousand, with 5/16-inch felt filler wads costing $3.50 per thousand. Winchester 209 primers could sometimes be purchased at $6.75 per thousand, and lead shot in sizes #1-12 cost $4.50 per 25 pounds. DuPont powders, when available, cost $1.60 per pound, with the Hercules brand going for about $2 per pound.

Handloading data back then was definitely not as available as it is today. The "big" book was *Complete Guide to Handloading* by Phil Sharpe, but it didn't contain actual loads. Other goodies were the *Handloader's Manual* by Naramore, *Sixgun Cartridges & Loads* by Elmer Keith, *Modern Shotguns & Loads* by Major Askins, and a small book with the title *The ABC of Reloading* by F.C. Ness. Known as "Technical Bulletin No. 106," and published by the National Rifle Association for 25 cents, 106 covered the essentials, but contained no actual loads. The best sources for loading data were the *American Rifleman*, which usually had at least one article with specific loads for a particular cartridge each month, in addition to the *Belding & Mull Handbook* and the *Ideal Handbook*. Today, of course, many of the components listed, such as Western Tool & Copper bullets; FA70 primers; No. 6 Pistol Powder; IMR No. 1147, No. 15½, No. 17½, No. 1185, Pyro D.G., and Bulk Shotgun powders, to mention only a few, are not available, having been gone for decades.

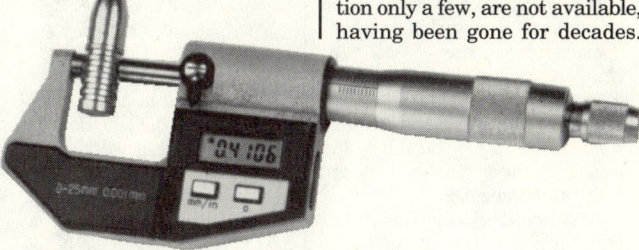

This is the Lyman electronic digital micrometer. It converts from inches to millimeters.

The Hanned Line dies make cutting bullet tips simple and safe—you insert the whole cartridge.

Handloading when the first GUN DIGEST was introduced was not easy, but it was fun.

Handloaders loading steel shot today may find a small booklet, "Modern Shotshells Illustrated, Pattern Percentage Guidebook" by **Hayes and Carpenteri**, helpful. It provides such information as the number of pellets per weighed charge for most shot sizes, for both lead and steel shot.

Handloaders can never have enough information on hand, and one of the best books available for metallic cartridge dimensions is *Designing and Forming Custom Cartridges*,

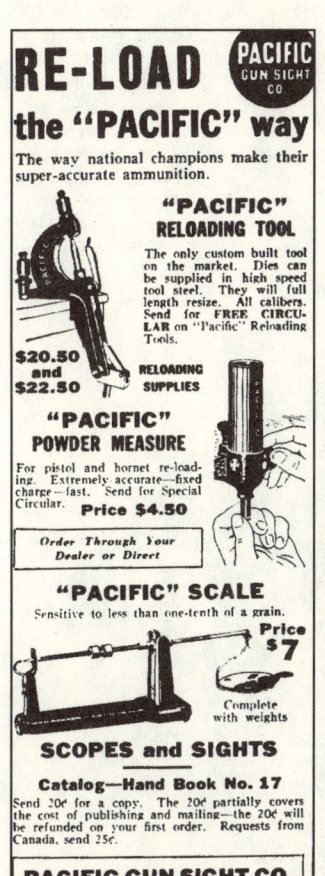

Pacific tools were popular back when GUN DIGEST came into being. The prices are from the 1940s.

50th EDITION, 1996 **241**

published by **The International Cartridge Archives**. Available direct or through dealers such as Gander Mountain, this hardcover volume contains 608 pages with over 900 dimensioned drawings of factory and wildcat cartridges, American and foreign, military and sporting, all drawn to the same format and enlarged 50 percent. The drawings range from the 14 Walker Hornet to the 12.7x64mm HK, and include original designer's drawings.

Spolar Enterprises has a number of innovative accessories to aid handloaders using Ponsness/Warren reloaders. The biggie is the Power Load, a foot-operated hydraulic attachment that leaves both hands free to feed shells and wads. With a shell in the right hand, wad in the left, and a foot on the pedal, a loaded shell can be produced every three seconds.

Another device is the Super Die Lube Kit that attaches to the loader and is long enough to lubricate the dies all the way down to the sizing ring, helping to prevent plastic buildup in the dies.

Every so often a loaded shell will mushroom, and removing it can be a problem, unless a Spolar Jam-Fixer is handy. Available in four gauges, as is the Super Crimp Set, the Jam-Fixer enables the jammed shell to be removed without being cut or spilling the shot charge.

Forster Products' case trimmer, with neck reamer, outside neck turner and hollow pointer, has been a mainstay of many handloaders for years, but Forster also has other excellent handloading items and gunsmithing tools. A couple of the newest products are the E-Z out expander on Bench Rest sizing dies and the Ultra bullet seater dies. (Ultra Upgrade Kits are available to fit older Bench Rest seater dies.) Currently, Forster Bench Rest dies are available to fit fifty-three different cartridges, ranging from the 17 Remington to the 340 Weatherby Magnum, and including the 7mm STW. Dies for seven of the Weatherby calibers are available, as are dies for a few wildcat cartridges.

The late Joyce Hornady was producing jacketed bullets for his own use about the time the first GUN DIGEST appeared. Now run by Steve Hornady, **Hornady Manufacturing** has become one of the largest manufacturers of handloading equipment in the world. Last year, Hornady introduced the Chronomax chronograph, a new case tumbler, and a host of other goodies. This year it's a new shotshell loader, the APEX 3.0 in Standard and Auto versions. Featuring a new priming system, new shell retainer system, new shot/powder drop system, and available in 12- or 20-gauge, the APEX 3.0 is the Hornady ultimate.

Also new are custom-grade New Dimension dies in both rifle and handgun calibers. They have all-steel construction and a brighter finish, and are available for twenty-six different cartridges, additional calibers to follow. Even the die box is new, with plenty of room to add shellholders and up to four dies, plus an extra seating stem.

Neil Jones is a name well known to benchrest shooters and handloaders interested in accuracy. The Jones products are custom designs and include a Micro powder measure; Micro adjustable neck sizing and bullet seating dies, both hand and press types; a decapping tool; and an arbor press. There are also special forming dies, with bushings that permit sizing a case such as the 308 down to 22 or smaller; the bushings are the same size externally, with a 30-degree interior shoulder, and are available down to 14-caliber.

Lee Precision, Inc., has been responsible for getting many handloaders started, providing quality tools at reasonable prices. They have a new Anniversary Reloading Kit for just under a C-note. It includes a Challenger press, Perfect powder measure, safety scale, powder funnel, sizing lube, case mouth chamfer tool, primer pocket cleaner, Lee Auto-Primer with shellholders suitable for over 115 different cartridges, instructions and loading data. There's also a new Deluxe Pistol Reloading Kit, for a bit more; this kit includes a Turret Press, Auto-Disk Powder Measure, along with most of the items in the Anniversary Kit. Loading dies are separate. Other kits are available for under $35.

New Lyman Auto-Scale dispenses the exact amount of powder at the push of a button—you can quickly weigh every charge.

The RCBS Powder Pro Scale provides digital readouts to 1500 grains, and other bells and whistles.

In addition to die sets for metallic cartridges and loading presses, Lee Precision has bullet moulds available in sizes from 30- to 58-caliber, in handgun and rifle designs. Lube and sizing kits are available, and there are five electric furnaces to make casting easier.

Lee Precision hasn't forgotten shotshell handloaders. The Load-All II is available in 12-, 16- or 20-gauge, for under $50, complete with a Safety Charge Bar and twenty-four shot and powder bushings. Conversion kits are available to change gauges, if desired, as are updating kits for older Load-All presses. For trap and Skeet shooters, there's the Lee Load-Fast in 12-gauge. It automatically indexes to every station, and powder and shot bushings are easily changed without having to empty the hoppers. It costs a bit more, but it also requires fewer manual operations.

Lyman Products has a number of new products for handloaders, ranging from the electronic AutoScale to the T-Mag II reloading press. If the new AutoScale has a familiar appearance, it should. It was manufactured by AMT for several years and is available in 110- or 220-volt versions. It features a solid-state electronic light-emitting diode and photo transistor sensors. With the scale set to the desired weight, powder is dispensed through two trickle tubes at up to 10 grains per second, slowing to achieve the final precise balance. It's fast and accurate.

The new T-Mag II press has a flat machined base for solid bench mounting, a new turret system that permits quick removal of the head without tools, and right- or left-hand operation. It's not the old Hollywood, but it's getting close.

Lyman has a number of new moulds. In addition to four Devastator big mouth hollow-point designs in 9mm, 10mm 44 and 45, there's a new 45-70 Schmittzer #2640658 mould that casts a beautifully pointed, 480-grain bullet with a high ballistic coefficient, making it suitable for long-range silhouette shooting. For shotgunners, the new #2654112 mould casts a 12-gauge hollow-base, hourglass-shaped sabot slug that should be a real winner. Designed to fit standard Winchester wads, the loaded slug does not require roll crimping, but can be star crimped in regular reloaders.

Both of these are single-cavity moulds.

A lot of handloaders started their shotshell loading careers using one of the **Mayville Engineering Company** single-stage reloaders. Thus, the firm can advertise MEC as being the "World's No. 1 Shotshell Reloader" with good reason.

There are currently three single-stage tools, the 600 Jr. Mark 5, Sizemaster, and Steelmaster; two progressive mod-

Fourth edition of the Lyman *Shotshell Handbook* has data on the newest components, including steel shot and shotgun slugs.

els, the 650 and 8567 Grabber; and two automatics, 9000 G and 9000 H, both of which feature automatic indexing and shell ejection. The Steelmaster is designed for loading 12- or 10-gauge shells, including 3½-inch, with steel shot, while the other reloaders are available in 12-, 16-, 20-, and 28-gauge, plus 410-bore versions. Brand new is a MEC "Short Kit" to permit any 600 Jr., Sizemaster or Steelmaster reloader that has been set up to load 3½- or 3-inch shells to load shells of a shorter length. This could save the cost of buying a separate loader.

Designed especially for shotshell reloading is the new MEC 1000 scale. Many powder scales weigh up to 505 grains, or about that weight; this new scale will weigh up to 1005 grains, using a supplied counterweight. Constructed of high-impact Styrene, with dual agate bearings, the scale has a larger damper for fast zeroing and a smooth leveling wheel.

Reloading Specialties, Inc., has components for handloading steel, including Super Sam steel shot in sizes from #7 to TTT, plus the second edition of their *Steel Shotshell Reloading Handbook* and universal patterning targets.

Ballistic Engineering & Software, Inc., presents a choice of IBM-compatible 3½- or 5¼-inch disks with over 3000 different loads for shotshells, ranging from the 410-bore to the 10-gauge. There's even one for steel shot, plus a club version. At least 512K RAM is required, with 640K recommended, and the loads are listed by shell brand and type, and usage with the powder, primers, wads,

velocity, and pressure provided. Different powder, wad and primer combinations can provide the same approximate velocity, but at different pressure.

At one time, handloaders used all sorts of rigged materials and coffee-can gadgets to keep their brass cases polished, but no more. The number of case polishing devices on the market seems unlimited. **VibraShine** has three such, the VS-30, VS-20 and VS-10, with capacities from 1½ gallons down to three pints. The first two are vortex designs, while the third is a vibrating model. **Berry's Manufacturing**, the firm that produces plated pistol bullets for handloading, has a new case polisher. Similar to some of the other vortex models currently available, its capacity is sufficient to meet the needs of most handloaders.

Every dedicated handloader needs a chronograph. Yours truly's first was a T-333, which used silver-coated screens that required replacing after each shot. It was bulky and not exactly cheap, but it was "state-of-the-art," so to speak, for that time. Earlier models included the Hollywood, Owen and one or two others. Today, the top of the line is one of the excellent **Oehler** models, such as the Model 35P, with or without printer. At double the price is the Model 35BNC which has a built-in printer and Proof Channel, but requires different screens.

Oehler also has one of the best IBM-compatible ballistics programs on the market. Termed the *Ballistic Explorer*, the current Version 4.0 program is available on 3½- or 5¼-inch disks and uses DOS 2.0, or higher, and needs 432K of RAM. It has easy to use graph controls, both ammo and bullet library displays, and works with ranges out to 2500 yards and velocities up to 6000 feet per second.

Chronotech Ltd. has a handy model that can be placed on a camera tripod, a table or some other suitable surface. It's battery-operated, and the latest version has a micro-processor chip that provides accuracy of 99.5 percent from 75 to 9999 feet per second. Firing must be done from at least five feet away, and the display screen registers the reading of one shot until the next shot is fired or the unit is turned off. An added plus is a five-year warranty against defects in electronic circuitry.

Shooting Chrony, Inc., has a new Gamma-Chrony chrono-

Handloaders using Ponsness/Warren reloaders will find the Spolar Enterprises accessories handy: (left to right) the Jam-Fixer, Super Die Lube Kit, and the Super Crimp Set.

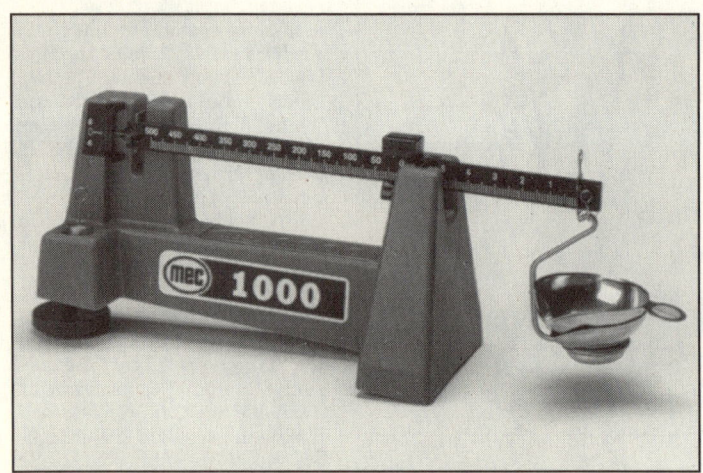

The new MEC 1000 scale will weigh up to 1005 grains. It has dual agate bearings, a leveling wheel and a damper for fast zeroing.

graph that includes memory for 1000 shots, with an optional capability of 4000- or 8000-shot memory, remote control, IBM/PC interface and a download ballistics program that will display graphic trajectory curves and a lot more—all for less than $200. Chrony also has the F-1 and F-2 chronographs for under $100. Both are compact and measure velocities from 70 to 5000 feet per second with a 0.5 percent accuracy. The F-2 has memory for twenty-nine numbered shots; measures in English or metric units; will retrieve individual shot data; and shows low, high, and average velocity and standard deviation.

It's difficult to determine which firm—Hornady, RCBS, or Redding—manufactures the most reloading dies, but **Redding** does manufacture both two- and three-dies sets in four different series for 194 different cartridges, and that doesn't include whether it full-length sizes or neck-sizes, or whether it is a standard or a deluxe set, or whether it is titanium carbide. In addition, there are other choices, such as the new Straight Line benchrest competition bullet seating die, a new carbide size button kit, custom dies, form and trim dies, profile crimp dies and taper crimp dies. Redding has four new Magnum mould blocks to cast some heavy 40- and 45-caliber bullets for blackpowder shooters. The new moulds (#640, #740, #645 and #745) will cast bullets weighing about 370 and 410 grains, and 480 and 525 grains, respectively.

Newcomers might want to consider the new **Boss** Pro-Pak, which contains nearly everything needed to get started but the components. Included in the Pro-Pak are a Boss reloading press, Model #2 powder and bullet scale, powder trickler, a set of Series A dies, case lube kit, Model #18 Case Preparation Kit, powder funnel, deburring tool, and a copy of Volume 26 of the *Hodgdon Loading Data Manual*.

Hercules, Inc., has a new brochure, "New Sporting Clays and Other Target Loads," that provides handloading data for Hercules powders and the new Federal 209A primer for shotshells. It lists a number of new $7/8$- and 1-ounce loads at three different velocity levels, in addition to regular $1^1/8$-ounce loads, including new heavy handicap loads.

If a handloader has been in the game long, he or she is bound to have made a few mistakes that required pulling some bullets. **Quinetics**, the firm that introduced the Kinetic Bullet Puller back in 1952, has a new "Ultimate Model" with a quick-twist chuck assembly. After the bullet has been pulled, the cap is twisted a quarter-turn, the cap end of the puller tapped lightly on the bottom of a receptacle, and the case, powder and bullet drop out; no more pulling or shaking.

MTM Molded Products has a couple of new items for handloaders. One is a pistol rest to use while trying out the handloads. The padded Y-fork locks in any of twenty different positions and can be used to support the forearm of a rifle. The second item is the Handloaders Log, a looseleaf binder that contains 150 specialized sheets with space for recording detailed data on pet loads, ammunition performance, shotshell loading data, firearms inventory and other bits of useful information.

RCBS has a new digital Powder Pro scale that provides LCD readout up to 1500 grains with 0.1-grain accuracy. It operates on a choice of 110 or 220 volts, and has a recessed platform suitable for a powder trickler.

Another useful item is the *Byte the Bullet* PC ballistic program. This program allows the viewer to compare up to eight loads at once, display nine different trajectory plots, and access information for over 500 bullets, and most powders and primers, in an instant.

Handloaders using FMJ surplus bullets for loading plinking ammunition, or regular surplus ammunition, might want to check out the **Hanned Line** Convert-a-Dies. Two $7/8$x14 threaded, hardened-steel dies permit the tips to be cut off 7.62x39, 5.56, 308, etc., bullets using a fine-tooth hacksaw, similar to cutting necks off cartridge cases. The dies are designed so only a small amount is removed. A smaller, hand-held die, the 22 SGB, is available to make 22 rimfire cartridges more efficient. ●

SHOOTING THE FRENCH 35s

by JOHN MALLOY

THE FRENCH 1935 pistols first came to the attention of American shooters during the 1960s. Sold as surplus by the French, large quantities of the pistols and their peculiar 7.65 MAS French Long cartridge were imported into this country.

Americans bought them at low prices and shot them for a while, until the supply of ammunition was gone. Discovering that no other cartridge would work, and that the pistols could not be realistically converted to any other caliber, their owners simply put them away.

There has been limited interest in World War II French pistols, but for most Americans, the French pistols had their brief moment of interest and were forgotten.

Perhaps they deserve better. These little automatics are interesting both historically and mechanically.

Until World War I, France (like Great Britain) had been devoted to the revolver as a military sidearm. Caught short at the start of hostilities, the French had ordered large

The 1935-A encorporates a packaged firing system, a captive mainspring, and an elegant and comfortable grip.

The 1935-S was designed to speed and simplify production, but lost a little something in the process.

quantities of simple 32 ACP blowback semi-automatics from Spain.

By the end of the war, the "automatic" pistol was well-known to the French military, and a project was begun to find a replacement for their aging 1873 and 1892 revolvers.

The cartridge chosen is of special interest. The 7.65mm MAS is essentially identical to the U.S. Army's special cartridge for World War I's secret Pedersen device. One story to explain this similarity is that, shortly after the war, John M. Browning demonstrated to the French a light automatic rifle chambered for the Pedersen

50th EDITION, 1996 245

cartridge. If it's true, the French were impressed by the cartridge, but not by the rifle.

The Pedersen cartridge originally was made with an 85-grain bullet. A small quantity was made with 90-grain bullets in 1919, after the war. This later round with its longer bullet was the one that won the hearts of the French military, and development of the new French sidearm centered on this unlikely cartridge.

The pistol project was not of high priority, and a final design was not adopted until 1935. Known as the Modele 1935-A, the gun was based on the work of Charles G. Petter of Societe Alsacienne de Constructions Mecaniques (SACM). Petter's design is a modification of the Colt-Browning short-recoil system introduced by the 1911 Colt.

The 1935-A was, in many respects, a very good pistol. It was well made of good materials, performed reliably and had a well-designed, comfortable grip.

Innovations in mechanical design were several: The mainspring was held captive on a shaft, with spring and shaft removed as a unit during disassembly. Such packaging of components was highlighted by the firing mechanism, in which the hammer, mainspring, sear and ejector could be removed as a unit. This unitized firing mechanism was Petter's primary design contribution.

The final pistol weighed about 26½ ounces. Barrel length, measured from the muzzle to the breech face, was 4⅜ inches. Overall length was about 7¾ inches.

The pistol had barely gotten into production by 1938 when German actions made it apparent that war was coming. To speed production, the Manufacture d'Armes de St. Etienne (MAS) redesigned the pistol with an eye toward easier manufacture. The basic features of removable recoil spring and firing mechanism packages remained. However, the locking mechanism was simplified—the entire chamber portion of the barrel served as a single lug which locked into the recess of the ejection port. Other mechanical changes were made, and the nicely shaped grip of the original pistol was straightened.

The new pistol was designated Modele 1935-S.

The barrel length was reduced slightly to 4¼ inches, with a corresponding decrease in overall length to about 7⅜ inches. Weight, probably due to less detailed machining,

The 30 Pedersen cartridge (left) was the secret round of WWI. This specimen has the 80-grain bullet and was made by Remington in 1918. The 1940 7.65mm Long French military round was shot in pistols and SMGs.

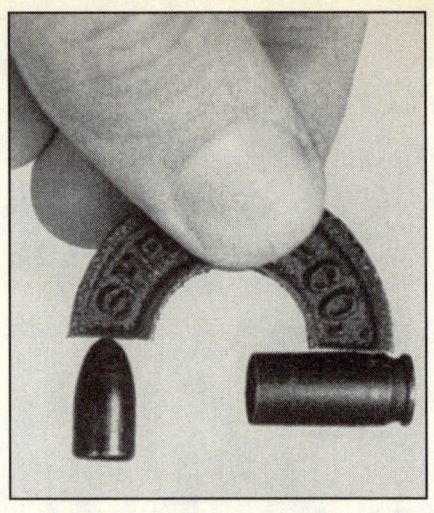

Most French military ammunition encountered has steel cases and steel-jacketed bullets. Even if available in quantity, these components offer little help to the handloader.

increased slightly to about 27½ ounces.

Magazine capacity was retained at eight rounds, but the design of the magazine was changed and 1935-A and 1935-S magazines will not interchange. Actually, no parts interchange between the two variants. Even the grip screws, though of the same thread, are of slightly different design.

The 1935-A was made at SACM. The simplified 1935-S was produced at SACM and three other locations: Manufacture d'Armes de Tulle (MAT), Manufactures d'Armes de Chatellerault (MAC) and Societe d'Applications Generales Electriques et Mecaniques (SAGEM).

The trigger action of the pistols came in for some criticism. Although the linkage is different for the two pistols, both have an unusual pivot placement that makes the trigger move down almost as much as it moves back. However, for any use except precision target shooting, the shooter soon becomes used to the unusual movement.

Some criticism was made of the black enamel finish, but for a military weapon such a finish is practical. During WWII, the British got excellent performance with similarly painted firearms.

More to the point was criticism of the cartridge. The 7.65mm MAS propelled a bullet of 85 grains at a velocity of about 1100 fps. The resulting energy of about 230 foot pounds was an improvement over the 32 ACP, but was poor by any military standard.

An interesting point of both pistols is the safety. It is simply a rocker that moves through an arc of 90 degrees. A flat surface allows the hammer to reach the pin in firing position, while a curved portion shields the firing pin at the "safe" position, preventing the hammer from contacting it.

When engaged, the safety-lever protrudes in a way that could interfere with holster use. This has led to some discussion as to the proper use of the safety. The 1935-A's floating firing pin allows a hammer-down carry; the 1935-S has a rebounding hammer. Both pistols are safe enough at rest, and the act of cocking the hammer is at least as easy as thumbing off the safety-lever.

It would seem that the safety is not designed to be left on with the hammer cocked. It does, however, serve a useful function of limiting the chances of accidental discharge when closing the slide or lowering the hammer on a loaded chamber.

Unusual or controversial features notwithstanding, production had barely gotten off to a start when it was interrupted in June, 1940, by the German invasion. During the long occupation, the Germans may have continued production of the 1935-A, as specimens exist with German acceptance marks. Just as likely, pistols already in use by the French may have been stamped. Apparently, no 1935-S pistols have been observed with such markings. Whatever the status of wartime pistol production, manufacture of the 7.65 MAS ammunition was continued through the occupation years.

After the war, the French resumed production of both pistols, and the cartridge remained standard for French pistols and submachine guns through 1949. Large quantities of the guns and ammunition were used in French action in Indo-China (Vietnam).

In 1950, the 9mm Parabellum cartridge was adopted, and with it the Modele 1950 pistol in that caliber. The new pistol was essentially an enlarged 1935-S with the better grip shape of the 1935-A. After a decade or so, the older pistols were declared surplus.

When the 7.65mm MAS pistols arrived on these shores, they sold for about $25 for the 1935-S and, surprisingly, only $23 for the more intricately machined 1935-A. Creative advertising described them as, "chambered for the most powerful straight cased .32 cartridge ever made," and listed the surplus ammunition as "32 Long Magnum."

American shooters must have wondered about the concept behind these pistols. To those familiar with a 45, they must have appeared as hybrids between conventional full-size military pistols and pocket pistols.

Still, although not particularly powerful, they were fun to shoot. Fairly light and compact, they could dispatch a rabbit or a tin can. People plinked with them until the surplus ammunition ran out.

I suspect that many an owner, realizing he had an orphan, simply saved the last few cartridges just in case, put the pistol in a drawer, and never shot it again.

The man with an interest in shooting these pistols faces a formidable task in obtaining ammunition. Remaining military rounds are now collector's items, and at any rate may be unreliable. As for making cases, even the late George C. Nonte, Jr., dean of cartridge conversions, was forced to conclude that "there is no case suitable for reforming to this caliber."

Still, these pistols will not be used on a regular basis, so a large supply of dependable ammunition is not really necessary. For those who just want the feel of shooting them with a few rounds now and then, such activity is still possible.

I first became interested in making ammunition in this caliber in 1968, when the supplies of once-common surplus began to disappear. French pistols were recently again offered for sale, so my experiences may be of some interest.

Reloading military cases turned out to be a dead end. The cases are Berdan-primed, and almost all are made of steel. Indeed, the .309-inch military bullets are steel-jacketed. As components for reloading, the military rounds were a washout.

From all reports, original Pedersen cases will work fine. They fit perfectly, are Boxer-primed, and are the cases actually used by Nonte for his testing. Unfortunately for the handloader, they are very rare—much more so than French military rounds—and are strictly in the realm of the collector.

Among available cases, an obvious choice for consideration was the slightly shorter 32 ACP. The question immediately arose: Could the 32 ACP round be used at all, even as an underpowered one for single loading? The answer came out a resounding yes—and no.

Realizing that the machining of individual pistols may vary, in general, it may be said that the 1935-A will and the 1935-S won't handle the 32 ACP loading. The narrower magazine and smaller breechface cut of the 1935-S just will not accommodate the semi-rimmed 32 case. The 1935-A pistols, on the other hand, will generally feed a cartridge out of the magazine, with the rim slipping under the extractor. The extractor will then hold the short case against the firing pin blow. This is not very satisfactory from the standpoint of expected extractor life, and the lower power

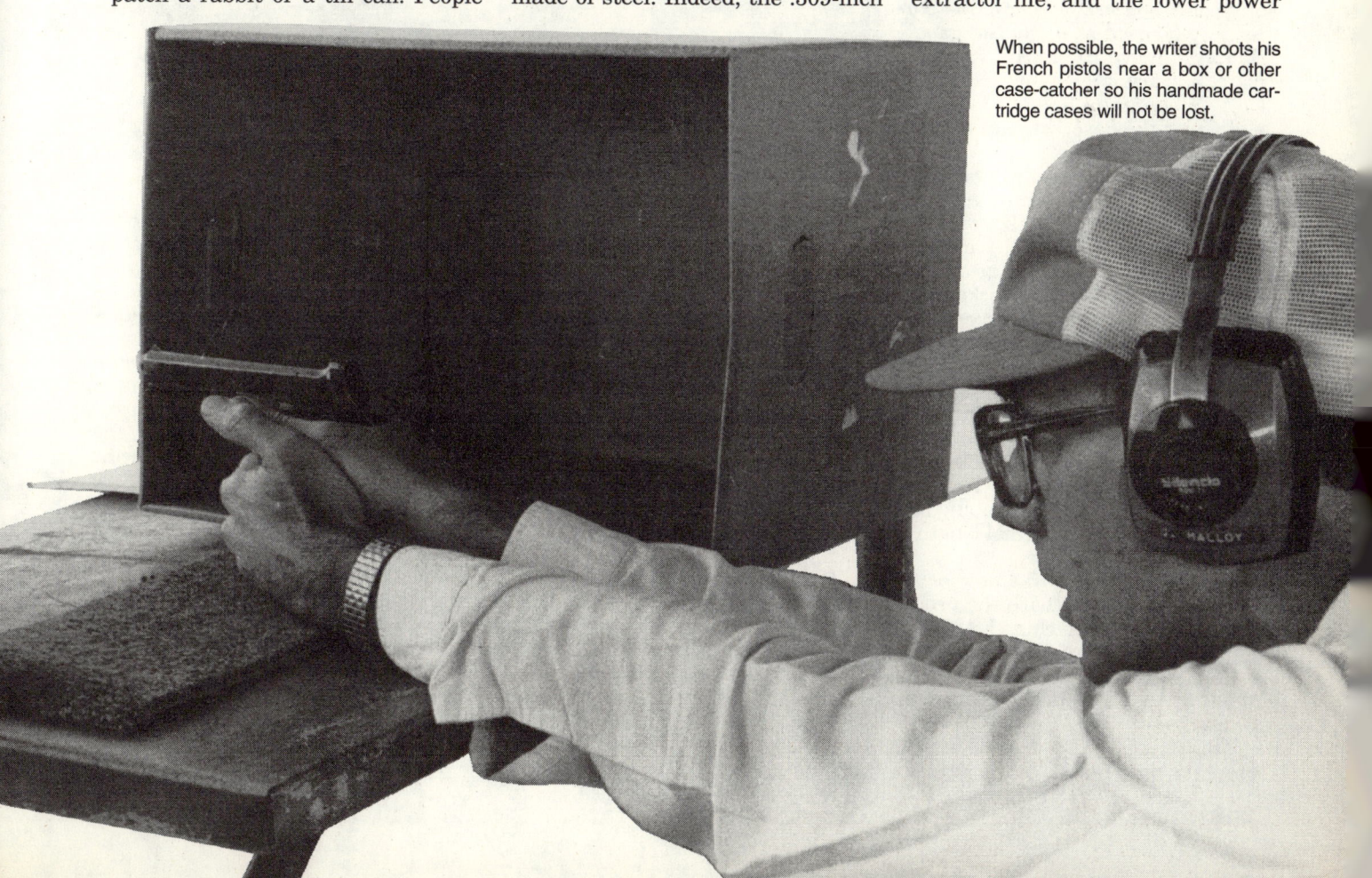

When possible, the writer shoots his French pistols near a box or other case-catcher so his handmade cartridge cases will not be lost.

level generally will not cycle the action enough to eject the case. It is better than not being able to shoot at all, but even this option is not available with the 1935-S.

At the time the pistols were common, military surplus 30-caliber M-1 Carbine ammunition was also commonly available. The cases were the right caliber, but were much too long and way too large at the rear.

Sectioning some cases showed me, however, that the large diameter at the rear represented rearward thickening of the brass. If a 30 Carbine case could be turned to a uniform external dimension of .337-inch, it could be shortened and used as a basis for making the French cases. The strong 30 Carbine case can accommodate this reduction in rear diameter.

"Turned" implies lathe work, but it is possible to perform this operation in the average home workshop. A 30-caliber jacketed bullet can be inserted into a case, allowing it to be chucked in a 3/8-inch electric drill without collapsing. While the case is spinning, filing with a fine mill file will accomplish the necessary reduction. A micrometer should be used to check the diameter.

However, as the case is truly cylindrical, it will measure the same at any point, so the chamber of the barrel may be used as a "No-Go" gauge. Simply remove the barrel from the pistol and try it over the base of the case. When the chamber will just slide over the case, you are close to the final dimension.

The extractor groove will be made shallow by this procedure. And the rim left is thicker top-to-bottom than that of the original French cartridge. Both these situations may be corrected by spinning the still-chucked case again and using a three-cornered file to simultaneously deepen the groove and thin the rim from the front. Lacking a French cartridge as a standard, the slide of the pistol may be used as a gauge. If the case will slide easily under the extractor into the breech-face recess, it will serve. The case may be shortened with a tubing cutter, then trimmed to a final length of .780-inch.

Several cautions: Use new or resized cases to start with the proper dimensions. Never thin the rim by removing metal from the rear—this would make the primer pocket too shallow, with a resulting protruding primer.

This method can provide usable cases for the French pistols. Remem-

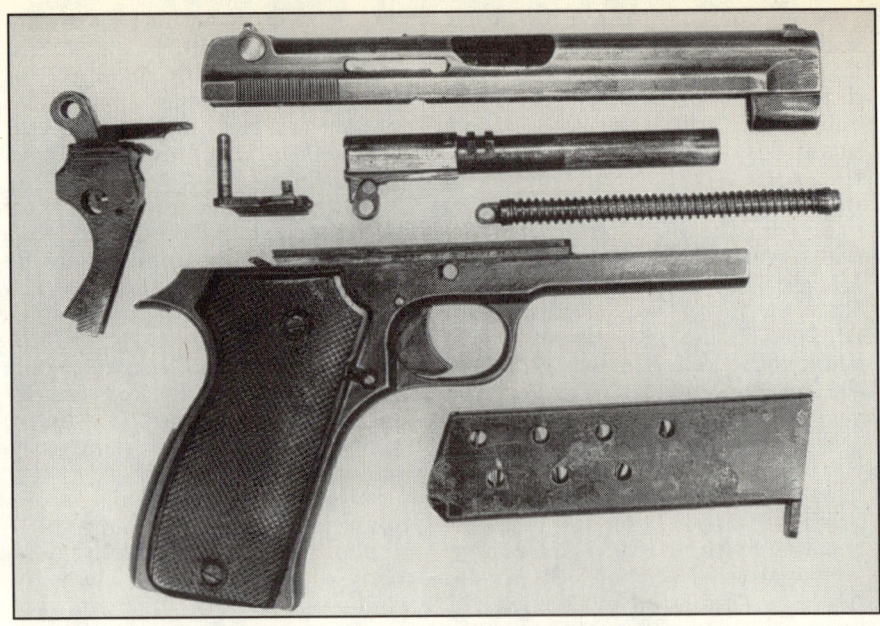

The 1935-A (above), disassembled, shows the basic Colt/Browning design with the addition of a packaged firing mechanism and captive mainspring. The similarity to (and the difference from) the 1935-S (facing page) is clear. Strangely, there is no interchangeability whatsoever.

(Below) The 7.65mm Long case will handle a variety of bullets up to about 100 grains. Bullets and loaded rounds: (from left) cast 74-grain bullet from Lee 311-74-2R mould; Winchester 93-grain 30 Luger bullet; Speer Plinker, 100 grains; 100-grain cast bullet made by shortening Lyman 311410 by one band.

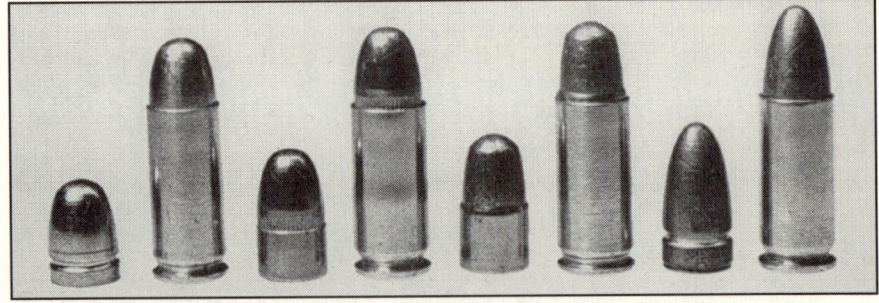

ber, though, that considerable pressures are involved. For safety, great care should be exercised at each step.

When the supply of surplus 30 Carbine ammunition was used up, these cases became less plentiful. So it became worthwhile to look at other options.

And there—lo and behold—was the 32 Smith & Wesson Long! The case is longer than the French case and is approximately the same outside diameter. It needs only removal of the rim, an improved extractor groove and trimming to make a usable case.

The same method used to modify the 30 Carbine cases works for the 32 S&W Long. Slip in a 30-caliber bullet to prevent crushing, chuck into a drill, and file the spinning case to shape.

Note, though, that the S&W cartridge is customarily loaded with lead bullets of .312- or .313-inch diameter. With the same outside case dimension as the French round, the case walls may be somewhat thinner. To use jacketed bullets (generally available only in .308-inch diameter), make sure your dies will size the case adequately to hold them.

Here, a brief digression: The same method of modifying the case can, of course, be used with 32 ACP cases. Such modification would allow the short case to feed under the extractor of both the 1935-A and 1935-S pistols. They would then be held in position to fire. Because of stress on the extractor, this cannot really be recommended.

However, author/gunsmith J.B. Wood has used a chamber insert ring in a 1935-A to allow the 32 ACP to headspace on the case mouth for single shots. A similar method might be employed with modified cases to permit semi-automatic functioning with the short rounds.

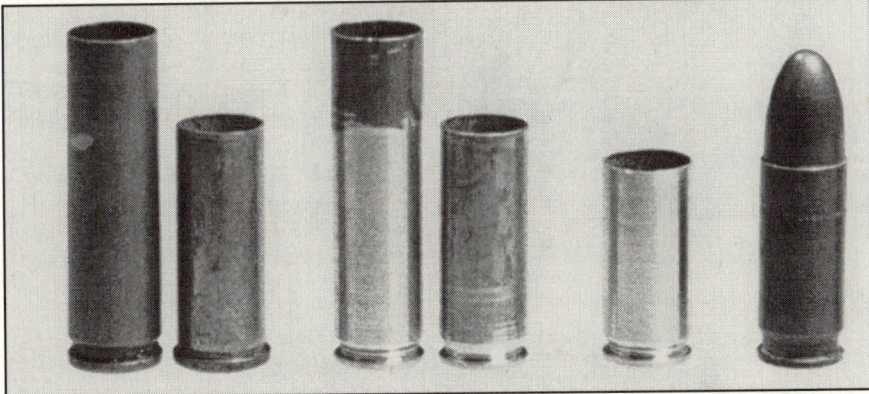

Making 7.65mm Long cases: (from left) unaltered 30 Carbine and 32 S&W Long cases; same cases "in progress;" trimmed, finished case; military round for comparison.

Cartridges loaded with these bullets fed and functioned perfectly. Accuracy was not bad, but was not consistent. The lack of consistency may be due to the short bearing surface relative to length, or possible base irregularities caused by the shortening process.

At any rate, I still load them. They do well enough for casual shooting, and I like the way they look. No one on the range mistakes them for 32 ACP rounds!

Bullseye is the powder most often recommended for this round and has given me good results. Charges of 2.3 to 2.5 grains, depending on bullet weight (lighter charges with heavier bullets), have worked well.

Be aware, though, that recoil spring rates and smoothness of operation may vary from pistol to pistol. I have seen 32 ACP loads eject from one pistol, while military ammunition might not cycle reliably through another.

It might be wise to start out with a 32 ACP load and work up from there. The pistol will not be a first-choice defense or hunting arm, but once reliable functioning is achieved, do you really need more power?

Reloading die designs and dimensions vary somewhat among manufacturers, so, if possible, try out several before you select those to be used for the 7.65mm MAS. I use 32 Smith & Wesson Long dies for sizing and seating. For neck expansion, the .313-inch plug is replaced by one of .308-inch for jacketed bullets. Cast bullets go in at .311-inch. The 32 ACP dies reportedly work well, but I have not used them.

For a shellholder, 32 ACP seems the best choice. Again, one company's tools may be "tighter" than other's, so try them out first if you can.

French military ammunition has produced groups of 3 to 5 inches for me. This shooting was done with steel-case surplus at 25 yards, using a casual two-handed rest position. Not Camp Perry material, but the French apparently felt it to be adequate for military use. Under similar conditions, all my handloads have produced groups within this general range, with some very much better. The exception is the less-consistent loading using cut-down #311410 bullets, which may shoot better or worse groups.

The 7.65mm MAS is actually an easy round to load. The straight case can use a variety of cast and jacketed bullets, and needs only readily available loading tools. The problem, of course, is the supply of cases. It is discouraging to spend considerable time

Still, just a little more effort will produce a full-length case, and the pistol need not be modified. The long case allows use of a variety of bullets up to about 100 grains.

Any jacketed bullet suitable for 32 ACP (71 grains), 30 Mauser (86 grains), or 30 Luger (93 grains) will work. These bullets are generally .308-inch diameter, slightly undersize for the pistols' .310-inch bores, but I have gotten very good accuracy with them.

The half-jacket Speer "Plinker" (.308-inch, 100 grains) feeds reliably and gives good accuracy. Any round-nose cast bullets designed for the 32 ACP or the 32 revolver rounds, sized to .310- or .311-inch, may be used.

Because of the lower cost, most of my shooting has been done with cast-bullet loads. The grease grooves of such bullets must be inside the case, thus giving an overall cartridge length of less than the military round. My initial concern about the feeding of these shorter rounds was not justified, as they fed and functioned flawlessly.

Still, they didn't look much different than 32 ACP cartridges, and shooting a 32 auto doesn't get much respect on the range. I attempted to develop a cast-bullet load that would approximate the length of the military load.

I had noticed that cast rifle bullets from the Lyman #311410 mould (although somewhat more pointed) were similar in general nose shape to the military bullet. That bullet is much too long and heavy, so I shortened some by the length of one band. This was accomplished by simply placing a sharp knife in the lower grease groove and rolling the bullet back and forth. The resulting projectiles weighed about 100 grains and could be loaded to the 1.2-inch length of the military round.

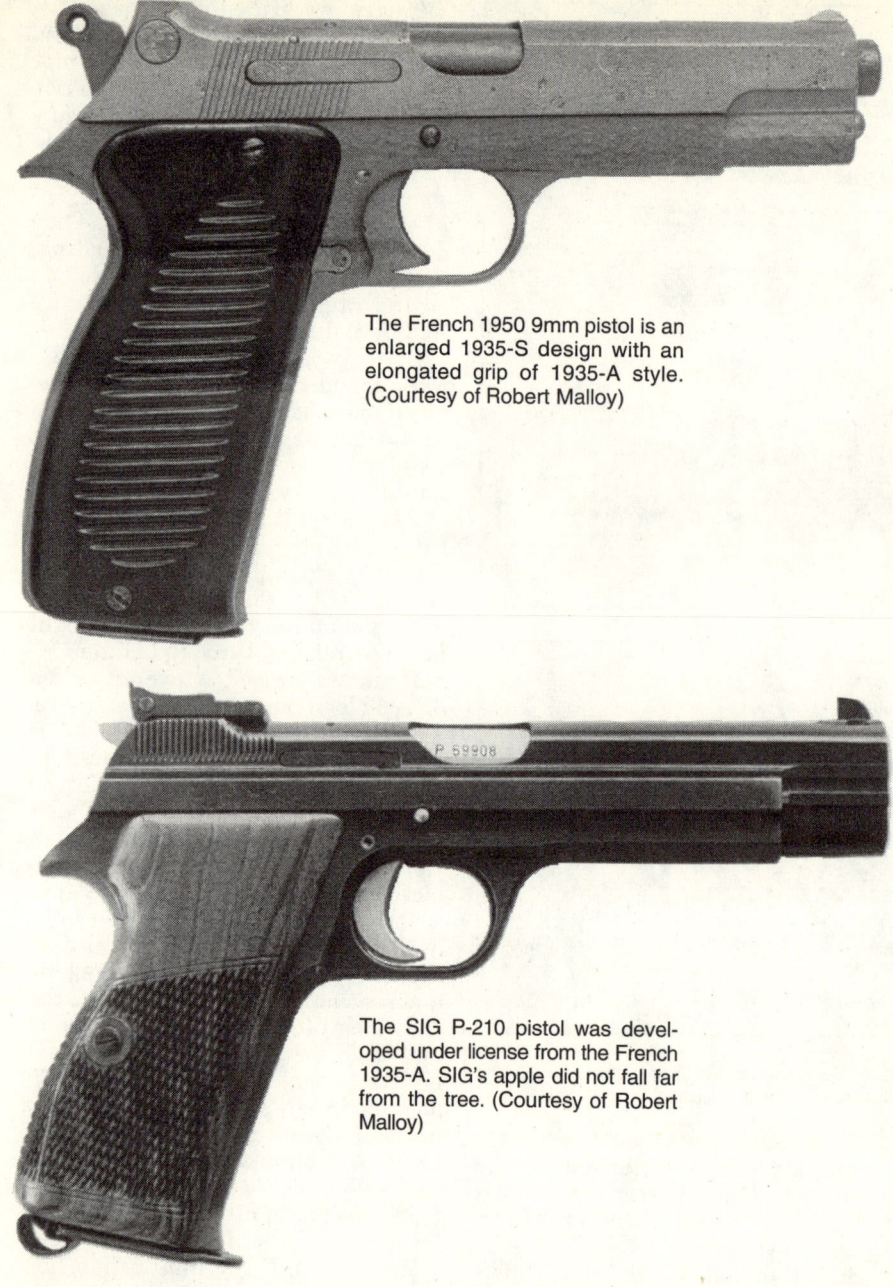

The French 1950 9mm pistol is an enlarged 1935-S design with an elongated grip of 1935-A style. (Courtesy of Robert Malloy)

The SIG P-210 pistol was developed under license from the French 1935-A. SIG's apple did not fall far from the tree. (Courtesy of Robert Malloy)

hand-making a case, only to have it bound into the bushes on the first firing. When possible, I catch those precious empties in a cardboard box.

Is it worth all the trouble? Well, that depends...

If you are deciding what to shoot in the next Regional 2700, forget the French pistols. However, just a few rounds will allow a shooter to try out a pistol that would otherwise be only a paperweight. They are fun to shoot, as well as being interesting both historically and mechanically.

True, they played no great historical role. Only a small number had been made prior to the German occupation in 1940. The Germans had little interest in them. If any occupation production took place, it apparently was only of the 1935-A and then only in small quantities. Later sent to Vietnam, the pistols did not particularly distinguish themselves.

Mechanically, they fared better. The "packaged" firing mechanism was an innovation. The 1935-A was licensed to Schweizerische Industrie Gesallschaft (SIG) and became the starting point for development of the SIG P-210 pistol. The 1935-S introduced the concept that the ejection port could serve as part of the locking system, mating with a single barrel lug over the chamber. This simplified system has become almost universal for recently introduced pistols.

This, then, is the story of the French 7.65mm MAS pistols, of which only two types were ever made. In spite of their lack of success, they contributed design features to other pistols that were successes. And as shooters, they are handicapped by an orphan cartridge. Still, it is possible for the careful and determined handloader to produce ammunition and to enjoy shooting the French 32s.

References

Barnes, Frank C. *Cartridges of the World.* Northfield, IL: DBI Books, Inc., 4th ed., pp. 166, 192.

Earl, Robert. "Reloading 7.65mm Long." *American Rifleman*, Vol. 133, No. 1 (Jan., 1985), p. 64.

Ezel, Edward C. *Small Arms of the World.* 11th ed. Harrisburg, PA: Stackpole Books, 1977, pp. 266-7.

Ezel, Edward C. *Handguns of the World.* Harrisburg, PA: Stackpole Books, 1981, pp. 451-459.

Hogg, Ian V. *Encyclopedia of Infantry Weapons of World War II.* New York: Crowell, 1977, p. 33.

Hogg, Ian V. and John Weeks. *Pistols of the World.* Northfield, IL: DBI Books, Inc., 1982, pp. 109-10.

Nonte, George C., Jr. *Home Guide to Cartridge Conversions.* Harrisburg, PA: Stackpole Books, 1967, p. 369.

Nonte, George C., Jr. *Handloading for Handgunners.* Northfield, IL: DBI Books, Inc., 1978, pp. 248-9, 265.

Nonte, George C., Jr. *Pistol Guide.* S. Hackensack, NJ: Stoeger, 1980, pp. 261, 271.

Smith, W.H.B., and Joseph E. Smith. *Book of Pistols and Revolvers.* Harrisburg, PA: Stackpole Books, 1968, pp. 194, 626-8.

Smith, W.H.B. and Joseph E. Smith. *Small Arms of the World.* Harrisburg, PA: Stackpole Books, 1969, pp. 355-7.

Suydam, Charles R. *U.S. Cartridges and Their Handguns.* N. Hollywood, CA: Beinfeld, 1977, pp. 252-3.

Wilson, R.K., and I.V. Hogg. *Textbook of Automatic Pistols.* Harrisburg, PA: Stackpole Books, 1975, p. 340.

Wood, J.B. *Troubleshooting Your Handgun.* Northfield, IL: DBI Books, Inc., 1978, pp. 48-51.

Wood, J.B. "Shooting the Obsolete Handguns," *Guns Illustrated.* Northfield, IL: DBI Books, Inc., 1981, 14th ed., pp. 87-93.

by BOB BELL

SCOPES AND MOUNTS

THIS IS THE 50th edition of GUN DIGEST, and that says something about the importance of guns in this country. Most publications, let alone gun books, don't survive nearly that long.

Such occasions are a reason for looking backward to see where we've come from. And since a lot of my writing for GUN DIGEST has related to scopes, they're what I looked at. In the first edition, a man named Milton M. Idzal had an article called "Scope Dope," which shows that the basic laws of optics haven't changed. I don't expect they ever will.

A recent edition listed some three dozen scope companies and more than 550 individual scopes, plus more mounts than I felt like counting. Things weren't always that way. That first edition listed four Fecker scopes, four more by Litschert, and another four by Mossberg. Lyman had five, including the legendary Super-Targetspot for competition and the Alaskan for hunting, and Weaver had seven, including the 440, the 330 (which was used as a sniper scope in WWII) and the 29S, which happens to have been my first scope. That's twenty-four scopes from five companies.

Quite a difference in a half-century, but that's to be expected. You might even say it's the American way. When something good comes along, a lot of people get on it and do a lot of thinking about it, and a lot of improvements result. So we, the shooters in this case, benefit. Truth is, we never had it so good, and this year past was no different—lots of things to talk about. Here, in random order, it is:

Sightron is the name of a new scope company based near Miami, and their scope line is called SII. Initial offerings for rifle include a 3-9x, 4x, 6x and 8x, all with 42mm objectives. Built on 1-inch one-piece tubes with black satin finish, all have multi-coated lenses, an extended eye relief of almost 4 inches for added safety, Plex reticle, and 1/4-MOA ExacTrack adjustments.

For handgunners, there are two conventional-style models in 1x and 2x, having eye reliefs of 9-24 inches. In electronic red dot models, Sightron has the S33, with 3-, 5- or 10-MOA dot, and the S33-3D which gives the option of selecting dot sizes. Both are built on 33mm tubes, are less than 6 inches long, and weigh about an ounce per inch.

Simmons believes their Aetec 2.8-10x44mm aspherical-lens scope is a breakthrough—crisp right to the edge of the picture.

Sightron president Scott Helmer says they're aiming at Leupold-quality scopes, and prices are in that ballpark.

Redfield has introduced a 3-10x50 Widefield to their Illuminator line, a series well known for the way they supply bright images under dark conditions. In the Golden Five Star line, shooters can now get a 6x40; a 4-12x40 with adjustable objective, Accu-Trac and target knobs; and a 6-18x40 with the Accu-Trac unit. This allows the shooter to estimate his target range and compensate for bullet drop while aiming dead-on, if you're new to the shooting game.

In the Tracker line, an 8x40 is new and should prove to be useful for big game at long range, such as pronghorns. I've used this power for years on these critters with good luck. A 6x40 Five Star will give similar results and be usable in open woods, too.

Leupold has added a 6.5-20x50 to their Vari-X III line, redesigning the optical system to accommodate the 50mm objective unit while adding only 1/3-inch to the length and 2 1/2 ounces to the weight, all of which should make long-range varmint shooters happy. For big game hunters, the 1.75-6x has been stretched 3/4-inch to accommodate magnum-length actions. Shrewd idea, seems to us. Like all Vari-X IIIs, this one also has Multicoat 4 lens treatment. Clicks on the adjustments can be heard as well as felt.

S&K also makes mounts, the "world's strongest," they claim, and they come in the Insta-Mount version for countless military rifles and SKulptured versions for commercial jobs. Or custom rifles. Tell 'em what you need.

Nikon spokesmen say this company has combined all of its technology into a single line of scopes, each model being the best they can make it. There's no denying that's pretty good, for Nikons rank with the best in America. Currently, they have models ranging from a 1.5-4.5x20 to a 6.5-20x44, which oughta mean anyone can find what he needs. Almost all are variables—which suggests how far this style has advanced in a few decades.

That big variable, incidentally, has an adjustable objective to eliminate parallax, target-type turrets, a sunshade and fine crosswire reticle with 1/8-MOA clicks. Maybe it deserves mention that a friend of mine, who hunts all over the world, replaced all of his other scopes with Nikons.

From JENA rifle scopes come in straight powers from 4x to 6x and 8x, with objectives from 36mm to 56mm, and variables from 1.5-6x42 to 4-16x56. All of their models are normally built on hardened aluminum tubes, but some models are available with steel construction for five percent extra. That can be significant when you realize that From JENA's most expensive model costs $1490.

Zeiss scopes in their Z-series (which includes the 6x42, 8x56, 1.25-4x24, 1.5-6x42, 2.5-10x48 and 3-12x56) now can be had with a Bullet Drop Compensator. The special ring utilized in the BDC can be installed on new scopes, upon request, at the factory, or the Carl Zeiss Optical Riflescopes Service Center in Petersburg, Virginia, can quickly retrofit a customer's current scope. Zeiss can even retrofit the old ZA-series scopes.

Weaver scopes were reintroduced in 1987 by Blount, after a hiatus of some time—most of them. Missing were the T-models, and many shooters asked about them. That's understandable, for in addition to fine optics they had wonderfully consistent adjustments called Micro-Tracs. Bearing points on the inside tube were tiny carbide spheres which contacted hardened surfaces. Well, the T-Series is back for '95, in 10x, 16x, 24x and 36x, and according to Guy Neill, technical services coordinator, the Micro-Trac mechanism features those tiny carbide spheres again. I had to ask specifically—the latest catalog fails to mention that fact.

The Ts have tall, modified target knobs with screw-on covers; the two lower powers have 1/4-MOA adjustment, the higher powers 1/8-minute. As-

Swarovski has just announced three new fixed-power scopes in their Professional Hunter (PH) Series to go with the variable powers introduced last year. The 6x42 is built on an inch tube, while the 8x50 and 8x56 are on 30mm. For best solidity, the objective and ocular bells, middle tube, and turret housing are all machined from solid bar stock, either in steel or aluminum alloy. The internal optical system uses coil-spring suspension to ensure accuracy and reticle adjustment.

Another more-than-interesting announcement is the LRS or Laser Ranging Scope, due out in late '95. This model combines the qualities of the 3-12x50 with

three grades—Huntur, Gunnur and Custom.

Pentax has added three scopes to their extensive offerings this year, a 4-16x Lightseeker and two shotgun models. The former is only a whisper over 15 inches long, so can be used on a big game rifle, if desired. The power spread makes it useful in the woods or when watching the widest beanfield. The so-called Shotgun Scopes have objectives that are enlarged only minutely over the 1-inch diameter tubes, have heavy Deepwoods plex reticles and unusually long eye relief, so should serve perfectly on slug guns, muzzleloaders, or

Aetec scope because it features an aspherical lens. Most positive lenses can be thought of as a slice taken off a sphere (thus a spherical lens). Aspherical obviously means it's not part of a true sphere. The difference in the curve of the lens surface is too small to be seen with the naked eye, but it's there, and it's important because it has a positive effect on the image by lessening inherent aberrations. It especially gives a flatter image at the outer edge of a wide-angle system, according to Byron Saper, who was important in creating the scope that uses it.

The aspherical lens has been around for many years. It has been used in some high-grade cameras and a few binoculars, but was not suitable for rifle scopes because of their recoil.

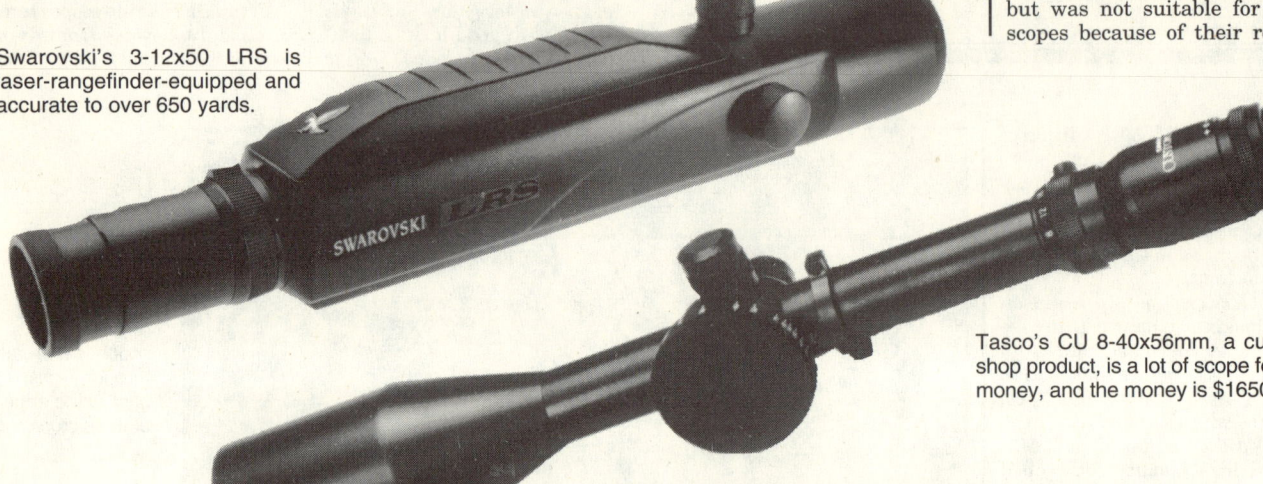

Swarovski's 3-12x50 LRS is laser-rangefinder-equipped and accurate to over 650 yards.

Tasco's CU 8-40x56mm, a custom shop product, is a lot of scope for the money, and the money is $1650.

suming the new models are equals of the originals, which seems likely, repeatability will be great.

Fine crosswire or small dot reticle is available, 1/8-MOA in 36x, 1 1/4 in 10x usually. The AO unit eliminates parallax from 42 1/2 feet to infinity. Eye relief is just over 3 inches.

A new line is the Qwik-Point electronic red dot for rifles, shotguns or pistols. They come in three tube diameters. One 30mm sight has a 4-MOA dot; the other has a 12-MOA dot for action shooting. A 33mm tube has instant selection of three dot sizes—4-, 8- and 12-MOA. A 45mm model gives a choice of dot size. It has an integral rail-type mounting bracket, whereas the more slender models use Weaver QD rings. All objectives are secured with lock rings, not glue as in some.

the latest in Swarovski's laser-rangefinding technology. The LRS has an accurate laser range of more than 650 yards (up to 1100 in ideal conditions). It weighs just under 2 1/2 pounds and uses four AAA batteries. Obviously an answer for sheep or pronghorn hunters or shoot-'em-in-the-next-county woodchuckers—if money is no problem, like $4439.

Conetrol makes their sleek mount for so many rifle/scope combinations it would be impossible to list them, but one new one that deserves mention is a base that replaces the factory rib on a Ruger No. 1. It gives more latitude in the fore-and-aft placement of the scope, something that can give trouble with short-tubed variables and compacts. The Conetrol base positions the rear scope ring back over the action. Made in all

for dangerous game. The Zero-X model has no magnification, while the Zero-X/V goes from unit power, which is what the unaided eye sees, to 4x. Pentax offers three pistol scopes, too—a straight 2x, 1 1/2-4x and 2 1/2-7x, as well as a whole raft of rifle models.

Schmidt & Bender scopes, which have been recognized as among the world's best for years, don't have a lot of new models this year, but have some announcements: Reticle No. 9 (a small circle superimposed over the crosshair intersection, with three posts) is now available in all S&B scopes; the 1 1/4-4x20, 1 1/2-6x42, 3-12x42, 3-12x50, and 2 1/2-10x56 are now made with hardened aluminum tubes; the 3-12x42 aluminum version is new and supersedes the older 4-12x42; all 42, 50 and 56mm scopes are now threaded inside to accept screw-in sunshades.

Simmons has a bunch of new items this year, but the most interesting is the new

Simmons has apparently solved this problem. Now the aspherical lens has been incorporated into the optical system of the Aetec scope, located within the one-inch part of the tube.

The Aetec is a 2.8-10x model with 44mm objective. Field is 44 feet at bottom power, 14 at top. Eye relief is up to 5 inches (another advantage of the system) and adjustments are 1/4-MOA clicks. Lenses are multicoated, of course. The Aetec is available now.

Aimpoint is well known for its red dot sights for use on rifles and handguns (Models 3000, 5000 and 5000-2x). There is also a variation for archers called the Aimpoint Bow Sight. Dunno if we can mention that in a gun book, but there's a lot of overlap in shooters. The Bow Sight is a non-magnifying optical device that requires no focusing or centering of the dot in the field. It mounts on most compound bows and comes complete with a cam-operated mounting system.

Thompson/Center now has an extensive line of scopes, the Hunter series, for use on muzzle-loading rifles, which of course they also offer in abundance. The scopes range from a small 1x red dot model on a 30mm tube, which has infinite eye relief, to a 6-18x variable. We dunno why any hunter would need that much magnification on a muzzleloader, but it's available if you do. Most normal powers can be had too. A standard duplex reticle is offered, plus a Pro-Diamond design which has four heavy posts contacting a center diamond which subtends 15 inches at 40 yards. The diamond overlays fine crosshairs which can be used when there's plenty of time for precise aiming. T/C's Recoil Proof models are still available for pistols, and there's a new line of Weaver-style scope bases and rings, plus assorted styles to fit scopes on ML rifles and Contender pistols and carbines.

U.S. Optics Technologies has taken a completely different approach to scopes. Their basic model is the SN-8. It's 5 3/8 inches long without any objective and comes with an integral mount. Four objectives are offered—4x, 10x, 20x and 40x—and can be interchanged by the user. Fixed-power eyepieces can be calibrated with 2-, 3-, or 4-inch eye relief, and 4:1 variable-power zoom eyepieces are to be offered, as well as night vision eyepieces. Reticles, too, are interchangeable, in over 200 patterns. Or you can design your own at additional charge, if you're that hard to satisfy.

This unit has a different than normal look to it—more military—and it's expensive. The SN-8 body only (no objective) currently lists at $595, to which you add $295 for the 4x objective (35mm), to $1295 for the 40x (88mm), and $185 for the reticle, if standard.

The SN-8 is made in the U.S., including lenses, which are of high density recompressed optical glass, multicoated. It is claimed to have the best resolution of any scope made—over 100 line pairs per millimeter throughout the field. I couldn't say; I've never used one. But ain't today's high tech wonderful?

Bausch & Lomb is continuing to concentrate on their Elite Series 4000 models this year. A matte finish is now offered on the 6-24x40, for those like me who do not like shiny finishes. The adjustable-objective units on the Elites (Series 3000 as well as 4000), incidentally, have a spring behind the lenses to cushion impact and force proper lens alignment. Reticles are attached with screws, a metal ring and sealant, which contrasts with the sealant-only method in some makes.

Speaking of reticles, B&L now has a custom reticle program for adjustable-objective Elites only. These are 1/4- or 1/2-MOA dots in the 6-24x40 and 4-12x40, 1/8 in the 36x40. They can be retrofitted.

Bushnell now offers a 4-12x40 AO matte finish, a 3-9x40 with Circle-X reticle and the same size Light Sight reticle in their Trophy line. The Circle-X has four heavy posts projecting inward from the cardinal compass points to meet a circle which is divided by fine crosshairs. Fine for either fast or precise aim.

Kahles has three new variables this year, according to Swarovski Optik, who announces them as additions to the Value Class Optics line. They are produced in Austria by Kahles, GmbH, and like the Swarovski premium PH models, the Kahles scopes offer the optical clarity and brightness available from a 30mm tube using large diameter lenses throughout. The new models are a 1 1/2-6x42, 2.2-9x42 and 3-12x56. They're multicoated, of course, waterproof and shockproof.

I've been using an 8x56 Kahles for many years on my old 7x61 S&H, and the optics are unbelievable. What can be seen at long range in almost nonexistent light is...well, unbelievable. This scope is big and, with its steel tube, heavy, but when it's time to sit and look rather than walk, it's really something. If the new models are somewhere in the same class, they'll do the job.

Tasco has a bunch of new items this year, some intended for riflemen who do their sniping at the longest ranges, others for shotgunners and handgunners. And even some for "normal" hunters. From their custom shop come the CU 8-40x56 with either 30-30 or glass-etched reticle, the latter with 1/8-inch dot, parallax adjustment from 100 meters to infinity and, most interesting, a large parallax wheel on the left side, amidships, which adjusts the innards for fine tuning for distance. Power is 8-40x, price is $1650—and ain't that something when you consider what Tasco scopes sold for back in the '50s?

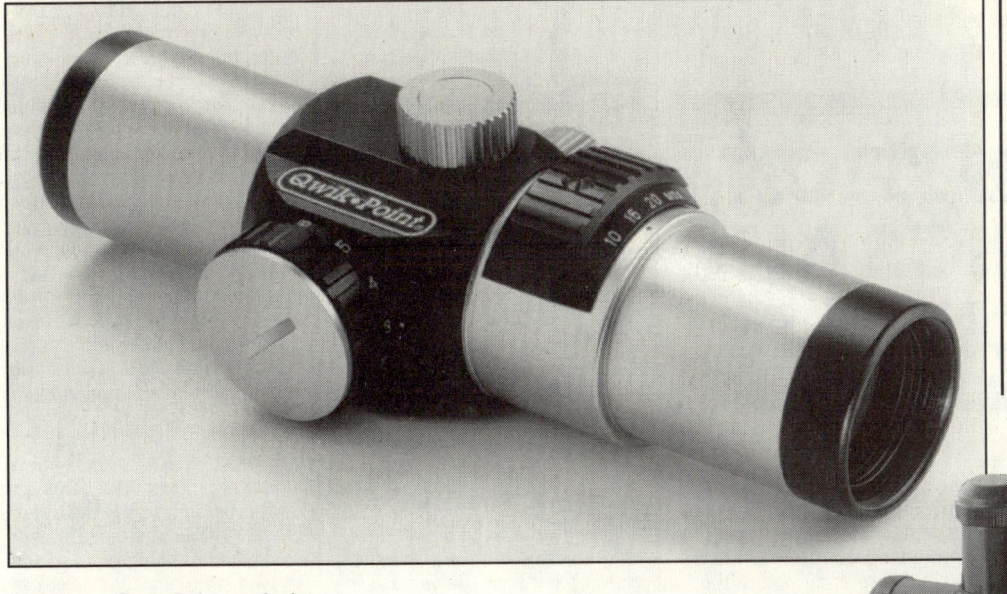

Weaver's Qwik-Point red dot scopes cover the size range—45mm, 33mm, 30mm—with a lot of features. This is the 1x33mm variable.

The Weaver Ts are back and with the same internal systems.

by **HOLT BODINSON**

AMMUNITION, BALLISTICS AND COMPONENTS

THE RECENT "primer and components" scare and the resulting hoarding that took place brings back memories.

Fifty years ago, WWII was just winding down. There were those who had done enough shooting to last them a lifetime; those who had been awakened to the fascination of firearms, courtesy of Uncle Sam; and those who had left their guns behind in the closet and could not wait to return to the simple pleasures of hunting and target shooting.

What they found was a civilian ammunition and components larder fairly empty. Wars are hard on shooting supplies, and WWII was especially hard. The production of powder, bullets and brass was entirely co-opted by the military, so ads of the day in the *American Rifleman* carried headlines like: "Sorry, fellows, Uncle Sam's orders come first."

The positive side of this frustrating story is that inventive individuals like Fred Huntington and Vernon Speer began supplying .224-inch bullets by ironing out and forming spent 22 rimfire brass. Their gifts to the beleaguered shooters of the day have become the handloading powerhouses of today's RCBS and Speer. Vernon's brother Dick began what was to become the CCI domain of primers, brass and a complete loaded-cartridge line. Small manufacturers like Sisk in Texas and ABC (the Arizona Bullet Company) began producing some exceptional bullets in quantity. Bruce Hodgdon later entered the civilian component market after acquiring boxcars of surplus powder and bringing us market memories like H-4831 at less than one dollar a pound.

Then finally we began to receive the "peace dividend"—lots of surplus military ammunition and great ammo, powder, brass and bullet components from the office of the Director of Civilian Marksmanship.

Today, we can be thankful that the ammunition and components production and supply system is so broadly based and diverse. Indeed, when you realize that a modern handloader may be loading Finnish powder in Israeli cases, primed with German caps, behind Australian bullets, you can have 1946; 1996 looks good to me.

A-Square

A-Square's line of proprietary cartridges now includes the 300 Petersen, for which it claims a muzzle velocity of 3500 fps with a 180-grain bullet. Both the Winchester Custom Shop and A-Square are offering rifles for this new hotshot of the Super 30s. In the mid-field is the introduction of the 358 STA (Shooting Times Alaskan—essentially an 8mm Remington case necked up to 35-caliber) rated at 2850 fps with a 275-grain bullet. And for the masochists among us, A-Square has created the 577 Tyrannosaur that launches a 750-grain bullet at 2400 fps. As their catalog puts it: "The recoil is heavy, but the stopping power is unmatched!"

Accurate Arms

Having acquired the Scot Powder Company, Accurate Arms has introduced three new shotgun powders: Steel Scot—a single-base, cut-flake propellant designed specifically for steel shot loads; Solo 1250—a broad spectrum shotshell powder with field and target applications from 12 to 28 gauges; 4100—a fine-grained ball powder developed for 410 loadings. Also new is a line of lower cost but high performance powders being offered under the "Golden Eagle" label. First in this new line is Golden Eagle MagR—an extruded single-base magnum rifle powder with applications from the 220 Swift to the 460 Weatherby. And finally, Accurate has returned 5744 to production. This double-based extruded powder has proved ideal for cast bullets and low-recoiling reduced loads.

AFSCO Ammunition

Tony Sailer, who heads the C-H reloading die and tool firm, currently offers the most complete line of custom loaded ammunition for foreign and obsolete that I know of—cartridges like the 405 Winchester, the 450/360 Purdey and the 8x58R Sauer. Put those oletimers back to work.

American Ammunition

Alpha Delayed Expansion is the designation given American Ammunition's new jacketed hollowpoint bullet loaded in 45 ACP, 40 S&W and 9mm nickel-plated cases packed in air-tight cans that look like ring-opened cat food containers. Fired into 20-percent ballistic gelatin, the new bullet doesn't begin to expand until it has zipped through 6 inches of medium. American is also now loading a completely copper-coated lead bullet throughout its handgun cartridge line to reduce lead contamination in indoor ranges.

Arco Powder

New for this year is an improved non-corrosive, non-fouling, ascorbic acid-based substitute for blackpowder labeled "Black Mag." We haven't seen any of the improved lots yet, but if it is as good as its hype and some NASA analyses indicate, it should prove to be quite popular. The earlier lot produced wide velocity variations and had a limited shelf life. This powder must be highly compressed with a stout range rod when loading, which limits its application somewhat to the target range.

Ballistic Products, Inc.

If you reload shotgun shells, you need Ballistic Products' mail-order catalog. Here, assembled in fifty-six pages, is every wad, shot and slug type; specialty loading tool; and customized BPI loading manual imaginable

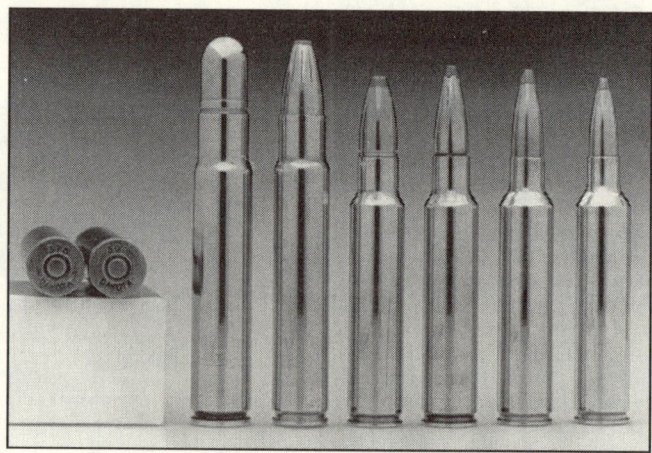

Dakota's beltless magnums in 450, 416, 375, 330, 300 and 7mm—all big guys.

for the shotshell loader. BPI also features a complete line of G/BP European wads that provide the reloader with an endless variety of options to tailor loads to specific targets, conditions and chokes. BPI even stocks Fiocchi non-lethal defensive ammunition featuring rubber buckshot and slugs as well as cubical plastic shot!

Barnes

The Barnes line of X-Bullets and solids continues to expand. New for this year are 150- and 165-grain flatpoints for the venerable 30-30 and a 225-grain flat-nose X-Bullet for the 348 Winchester. And new shapes are being added. The 185- and 210-grain 338 X-Bullets now sport boattails. Several popular X-Bullets will be offered with a secant ogive and a boattail. I have handled the 150-grain 30-caliber secant-ogive bullet and it's a beauty—less bearing surface, reduced fouling and a higher ballistic coefficient. Also new are 45- and 50-caliber sabot-encased X-Bullets labeled Expander-MZ for muzzleloaders. Barnes claims superior accuracy, expansion at velocities as low as 1000 fps and total weight retention. A new Barnes reloading manual will be out in August, 1995.

Berger Bullets

Benchrest champion Walt Berger is now supplying his quality bullets at very competitive prices. New for this year are very low drag (VLD) bullets: a 17-caliber 35-grain; 70-, 75- and 80-grain 224s; and a 180-grain 7mm. Also new is a 40-grain 224-caliber varmint bullet designated MEF (maximum expansion factor).

Bertram Bullet Company

Bertram of Australia continues to expand its line of obsolete brass. New this year are 50-70; 45-110; 32 WSL; 280 flanged; 360 No. 2; 375 rimless 2¼-inch; 500/450 No. 2; 450 No. 2 3¼-inch; 475 No. 2 3½-inch; 461 Gibbs No. 2; 500 Jeffery; 505 Gibbs; 585 Nyati 3-inch basic; 10.3x60R; 10.75x68; 11.15x58R Werndl; 11.7x51 Danish; and 12.7x44.

Big Bore Bullets of Alaska

Here's a specialty outfit that can provide bonded-core 375-caliber bullets in any weight from 180 to 350 grains, and 458 bullets in weights from 200 to 500 grains. The nose forms offered include lead tip, open tip or hollowpoint.

Bismuth Cartridge Company

Approved by the U.S. Fish and Wildlife Service for the 1994-1995 waterfowl season, bismuth is the only heavy metal (it lies next to lead in the periodic table of elements) proven to be non-toxic and non-carcinogenic. In fact, bismuth is the active ingredient in Pepto Bismol. Ballistically superior to steel shot because of its weight, bismuth shot is now available from the Bismuth Cartridge Co. as a reloading component, and as loaded field and target shells, in shot sizes from BB through #9. We're going to hear a lot more about the bismuth alternative to lead and steel in the months ahead. The company is also an agent for the Kent Cartridge Company of England that offers shotgun ammunition using biodegradable wads and also sells biodegradable clay pigeons.

Black Canyon Powder

Black Canyon Powder manufactured by Legend Products in Las Vegas is intended to be an alternative to blackpowder on a weight for weight basis. It is clean burning. Like the Arco product it requires an unusually high degree of compression for ignition uniformity. The difference between light compression and heavy compression of the powder charge is a variance in muzzle velocity by as much as 300 fps.

Brenneke

Brenneke is returning to the American shores with a more aggressive marketing program for its factory-loaded Brenneke shotgun slugs in two velocities and in 12, 16, and 20 gauges. The 12-gauge 1⅛-ounce high-velocity load is listed at 1510 fps and the low recoil 1-ounce load at 1150 fps; eleven different slug loads altogether for 1995.

BRP Bullets

Cast with a virgin linotype alloy measuring 20 or more on the Brinell hardness scale, BRP bullets are making a name for themselves at magnum velocities. The line of available handgun and rifle bullets continues to expand with the addition of heavyweights like their 305-grain 45-caliber and 290-grain 44-caliber handgun bullets.

Buffalo Arms Company

Here's a mail-order company that specializes in hard-to-find components for obsolete American and foreign calibers including such Civil War cartridges as the Burnside, Smith, Gallagher and Maynard. They also offer a full line of paper-patched bullet supplies.

Bull-X Incorporated

This high-quality mail-order supplier of cast bullets offers new for this year a 98-grain double-ended wadcutter for the 32 S&W; a 95-grain round-nose for the 380 ACP; a 93-grain round-nose for the 9x18 Makarov; a 180-grain SWC for the 40 S&W; and a 140-grain SWC for the 38 Super. Bull-X also has developed a computer program called "Load FAX" covering 1300 lead bullet loads for fifteen of the most popular handgun cartridges.

Cor-Bon

Cor-Bon keeps pushing the envelope on high-performance ammunition. Two new exclusives being offered by the firm this year are 135-grain JHP loads for the 40 S&W and 10mm, and loaded ammunition featuring Swift's new bonded-core A-frame handgun bullets—240- and 300-grain loads for the 44 Magnum, and 265- and 300-grain loads for the 45 Colt. Cor-Bon continues to offer a line of superior rifle ammunition under the CHAA label. The company has just relocated to expanded facilities in South Dakota.

Dakota Arms

Dakota now offers a full line of proprietary beltless magnum cartridges based on an "improved" 404 Jeffery case. Loaded with premium hunting bullets by Barnes, Nosler and Swift, the Dakota cartridge family currently consists of the 7mm, 300, 330, 375, 416 and 450 Dakota. Beltless magnums are coming on strong as witnessed by the Dakota, Imperial and A-Square lines.

Eley

Manufacturing twenty-one different 22 rimfire loads includ-

Bull-X's new 32-caliber wadcutter; 95-grain 380 ACP; and 93-grain Makarov.

ing their match-winning Tenex, Eley's entire shotgun shell line will be offered on a mail-order basis by the Old Western Scrounger. What's unique? How about 2-inch 12-gauge and 410 loads or Eley buckshot loads for less than $10 a box!

Elkhorn Bullets

Elkhorn is one of the newer, small premium bullet makers. It offers a line of bonded-core, copper-tubing jacketed bullets in two jacket thicknesses and some very heavyweight numbers like their 240-grain 30-caliber, and even bonded-core flat-nose bullets for the 348 Winchester.

Federal

Federal is becoming a major innovator in high-performance ammunition and is offering forty-one new loads in 1995. If you had trouble finding Nosler Ballistic Tips on the shelf of your dealer recently, it may be because Federal has introduced Ballistic Tips across its entire rifle ammunition line. Another bullet that Federal has integrated into their rifle line is the Trophy Bonded Bear Claw—a truly premium big game bullet. Among other things, Federal now offers this bullet in the 270, 7mm and 300 Weatherby calibers as well as the 416 Rigby and 470 Nitro Express. Added to their premium pistol offerings is the new 357 SIG cartridge loaded with a hot-performing 125-grain jacketed hollowpoint. In the shotgun shell line, Federal has almost doubled its steel shot loads (now *headstamped* as steel shot loads to reassure those doubting wardens) and has introduced a variety of new 1-ounce 12-gauge target loads. Even the 22 rimfire magnum line was upgraded this year with the addition of a 30-grain copper-plated hollowpoint.

Garrett Cartridges, Inc.

For shooters wishing to try a heavy 44 Magnum hunting load, Garrett's super-hard-cast 310-grain SWC ammunition clocking 1320 fps from a 7½-inch revolver is ideal. It is field proven to be among the best 44 Magnum loads ever assembled. Garrett has now taken the concept over to the 45-70, in which he loads a hard-cast 415-grain gas-checked bullet generating 1730 fps from a 22-inch barrel.

George & Roy's

For handloaders who wish to seal their primers for additional protection, George & Roy's is marketing a little blue bottle of primer sealant that does just that.

Glaser Safety Slug, Inc.

With the recent flap about the Rhino bullet, Glaser simply continues to make a good product better. It is now offered in the original Blue version that contains compressed #12 shot as well as a newer Silver version containing #6 shot. The Silver version offers approximately 50 percent more penetration than the original bullet before fragmenting. Available in all popular handgun calibers, the Blue variety is also offered in 223, 7.62x39, 308 and 30-06.

GOEX

As the major supplier of blackpowder to the U.S. market, GOEX now carries a "Cartridge" powder in its line. Users report that it burns much cleaner than the standard powders. Upon examination, it does show a brighter, cleaner granule surface and is worth trying in your favorite blackpowder arm.

Gramps Antique Cartridges

Well-known gunsmith and supplier, Ellwood Epps, of Ontario, has started this new business to sell collector cartridges and hard-to-find reloading supplies. One of his more interesting lines is a variety of "everlasting" style cases turned in England from bar stock brass in calibers like 577 Snider, 50-110 Winchester, 500 BP 3-inch, and 10.4x38 Swiss Vetterli. Send for his lists.

Grayback Wildcat Brass

If wildcats are your bag, Grayback Brass offers an incredibly complete line of pre-formed cases. It includes all of the Ackley and Gibbs Improved calibers and just about everything else between the 17 Mach IV and the 375-06 Ackley Improved.

Hansen Cartridge Company

Purveyor of military and commercial sporting ammunition marketed under their brand label, Hansen recently added the 50 Action Express cartridge to its line.

Hercules

The big news from Hercules is that they were acquired by Alliant Techsystems as part of the sale of the Hercules Aerospace Company. Alliant is the leading supplier of munitions to the Department of Defense. We'll keep our fingers crossed that Alliant maintains the leadership we have become accustomed to from the Hercules Commercial Smokeless Powder Group. New this year is an expanded reloading guide providing additional coverage of loads for Federal's 209A shotshell primer; the 284 Winchester; 38-40; the heavy bullet loads for many handgun calibers; as well as new data for Winchester Fail Safe rifle bullets. Packaging will be improved this year. Gone are the paper canisters. Plastic is in. We may also see a new high-performance pistol powder and a cleaner burning shotgun powder introduced soon.

Hodgdon Powder Company

Building on the success of their recently introduced short-grained H-4831SC, Hodgdon has just released its newest rifle powder called "Varget." Varget has a burning speed approximating that of IMR-4064, is very temperature tolerant and also offers those short grains. In calibers like the 308, it develops excellent velocities with moderate pressures and seems to be inherently accurate. Varget loads from 222 to the 375 H&H are contained in Hodgdon's latest basic reloaders manual.

Hornady

Hornady's development of the light magnum load for cartridges like the 308 and 30-06 turned everyone's head last year. It wasn't surprising that the company decided this year to extend the concept, and here are more light magnums with their published velocities: 303 British, 150-grain SP, 2830 fps; 257 Roberts, 117-grain BTSP, 2940 fps; 243 Winchester, 100-grain SP, 3100 fps; 7x57, 139-grain BTSP, 2830 fps; 7mm-08, 139-grain BTSP, 3000 fps. Hornady has also introduced a Very Low Drag 162-grain 7mm match bullet; a 115-grain 9mm Vector (tracer) bullet; and a load data program for the home computer named Reloader for Windows.

Imperial

The Imperial Cartridge Company of Canada has recently located some production facilities in the U.S. It continues with its lines of Imperial and Canuck shotshells, rimfire, rifle and handgun ammunition, and recently added its line of proprietary magnum rifle cartridges based on an improved 404 Jeffery case. The Imperial Magnum 7mm, 311, 338 and 360 rifle cartridges have been excellent performers; however, the company, like others, is having difficulty obtaining brass drawn to its

(Above and below) KLA Enterprises' stackable multi-projectile 50-grain 38-caliber bullets and the loaded case.

New Speer 308 200-grain and 311 200-grain Grand Slams; 429 270-grain Gold Dot; and 416 350-grain Mag-Tip—heavy-duty projectiles.

Speer Gold Dot 40 S&W 165-grain; CCI Blazer 40 S&W 165-grain; Gold Dot 380 Auto 90-grain.

specifications. Many reloaders now simply resize RWS 404 brass and fire-form them in the Imperial chamber.

KLA Enterprises

Loading two or three light bullets stacked in 357 and 38 Special cases is not a unique idea, but KLA has come up with a new twist. The company offers jacketed 50-grain stackable bullet units as prefragmented shot or with solid lead cores. Eight-inch patterns at 25 yards are possible.

Lapua Ammunition

Lapua of Finland has always been regarded as a precision ammunition company. Its match bullets and match rimfires have captured a number of world titles, while the development of its 338 Lapua Magnum for hunting and sniping caught many asleep at the switch. The company has had a difficult time becoming established in the U.S., but with its new importer, Keng's Firearms Specialty, Inc., it can hope for change.

Lightfield Ammunition Corp.

Lightfield has introduced a 1 1/4-ounce hollowpoint 12-gauge sabot-carried shotgun slug for rifled barrels. The slug is keyed into the sabot to resist the torque of the rifling, and it shows excellent accuracy and impressive expansion. It is offered as a loaded 2 3/4-inch round. Lightfield is recommended and marketed by the Slug Group that markets the Tar-Hunt bolt-action rifled slug gun, and that's a pretty good endorsement.

Lyman

Lyman's big release for the year was an expanded and upgraded *Pistol and Revolver Reloading Handbook*. The new edition adds some of the current popular cartridges like the 40 S&W, 9mm Makarov, 9x21, 9x25 Dillon, 454 Casull, 445 Super Magnum and 50 Action Express. The single shot pistol section expands the list of favorites as well. Excellent editorial content plus the inclusion of many new handgun powders makes this latest edition a "must have" on the reloading bench. Lyman continues to add new moulds for a variety of cast bullet making.

M&D Munitions

Picking up on environmental concerns about indoor lead exposure, M&D has developed a totally lead-free ammunition line consisting of a copper-plated lead bullet and a lead-free primer. It is offered as loaded ammunition or components.

Mi-Te Bullets

Adding 0.5 percent silver to their casting alloy, Mi-Te offers a full range of precision cast handgun and rifle bullets with a Brinell rating of 16. This unique casting alloy is also marketed by the firm under the name of "Acculoy," and the price doesn't seem bad.

Montana Precision Swaging

For the big-bore blackpowder cartridge shooter, this outfit offers an impressive assortment of swaged, straight-sided and tapered paper-patch bullets in calibers 38 through 50, as well as a complete line of big-bore rifle cast bullets.

National Bullet Company

National offers a diversified list of handgun and rifle bullets that can be ordered as cast or copper-plated. Growing in shooter popularity are their 200-grain 357; 300-grain 44; and 300-grain 45-caliber bullets.

Naval Ordnance Works

Need some 900-grain 600 Nitro solids or softpoints? Or any Lyman cast bullet you can imagine? Naval Ordnance probably has them. This is a unique jacketed and cast bullet emporium, and it is well worth asking for their current listing.

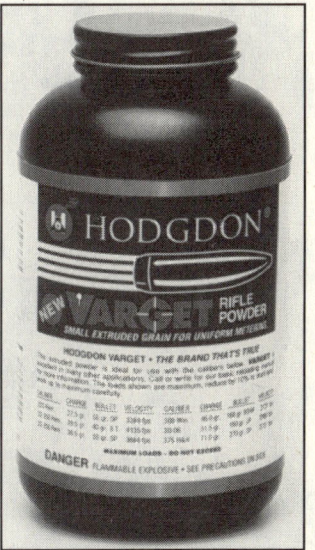

Hodgdon's Varget rifle powder for 223 to 375 cartridges.

Norma

Norma is back, we hope. The Paul Company is this year's big importer of the full line of Norma powders, bullets and brass. The new Norma catalog contains a wealth of information about the terminal ballistics of popular cartridges with numerous colored photographs of ballistic gelatin and actual field results on game animals. New this year are a 139-grain softpoint loading for the 6.5x54 Mannlicher; a 470 Nitro; 45 ACP match brass; and powder cans that contain 454 grams (one pound) rather than 500 grams of powder, thereby reducing Norma per-can powder prices 10 percent.

Northern Precision

Northern Precision has taken the 416, 44 and 458 calibers to new heights of flexibility and performance. Want to hunt varmints with your 416? Then

50th EDITION, 1996 **257**

here is the place to buy 198-grain thin jacketed softpoints. Deer? Again, they offer 275- to 350-grain thin jacketed whitetail bullets. Bonded-core big game bullets? Or 429 or 458 cast bullets with a copper scraping disk on the base? You need this catalog. Very original concepts in bullet design and not expensive.

The Old Western Scrounger

Dangerous Dave and Mean Mark preside over this den of the most exotic assemblage of ammunition and components known. Their $3 catalog is worth twice the price. No serious reloader can afford to be without it. If you can't find it here, you can't find it.

Paragon

Need the 223 Malaysian? 308 Portuguese? German 303 Non-Corrosive? If you need quantities of surplus military ammunition, Paragon is the place to shop.

PMC

The 30-30 just took on a new look when loaded with the Starfire 150-grain solid copper hollowpoint bullet. Also added to PMC's Eldorado cartridge line are the 380 Starfire; 155-grain Starfire and 155-grain truncated hollowpoint loadings for the 40 S&W; and X-Bullets for the 338 Winchester Magnum and 375 H&H Magnum.

Polywad

Polywad produces the highly successful "Spred-R" wad, as well as 12-gauge ammunition in #6-#9 shot that incorporates this unique spreader design. The Spred-R wad available in 10/12, 16, and 20/28 gauge sizes consists of a thin polywad with a post extending from it. Just before applying a crimp, the wad is inserted post-down into the top of the shot column and then crimped normally. Under field and competitive conditions, the Spred-R design opens the pattern at least one degree of choke in most guns and produces very uniform patterns. It's doubly useful in steel shot loads which tend to have heavy core densities.

Precision Reloading, Inc.

This is a very diversified supplier of components and is particularly strong in the shotshell arena. Excellent catalog, and when I needed a quantity of a specific shotgun primer recently, this company really came through.

Remington

The old company seems to be doing well under its new owners. New for this year are Swift bonded-core A-Frame bullets in the 30-06 (180-grain) and 270 (140-grain); Golden Saber JHP loads for the 9mm and 380; "Leadless" handgun ammunition featuring lead-free primers and "Lead-Lokt" bullets that encapsulate the lead core; a competition-designed Handicap trap load labeled "Premier Nitro 27"; light recoiling $2^3/_4$-dram 12-gauge target loads; a 20-gauge Sporting Clays load featuring a $2^1/_2$-dram, $7/_8$-ounce of #8s; Premier $2^1/_2$-inch 410 target loads with #$8^1/_2$ and #9 shot; a heavy $3^1/_4$-dram $1^1/_4$-ounce 12-gauge field load; and expanded offerings under the UMC economy label.

Sellier & Bellot U.S.A.

Sellier & Bellot rifle, shotgun and handgun ammunition shows excellent quality, and the S&B line offers a great variety of metric calibers including the 8x57J (0.318-inch bullet) loading that has been dropped by RWS and Norma. Sellier & Bellot has targeted a number of large distributors in the U.S. this year, so you will be seeing more of its product in distribution.

Shotgun Bullets Mfg.

This firm offers an excellent selection of hollowpoint and flat-point 12-gauge shotgun slugs in 380, 435 and 500 grains designed to be loaded in normal shotcups that perform like sabots. The handloading guidelines that accompany their shotgun slugs are very well done indeed.

Sierra

It's catch-up time at Sierra. The only new products this year are two instructional videos—*Introduction to Rifle Reloading* by David Tubb and *Introduction to Handgun Reloading* by Doug Koenig. Both

Hercules 1995 Reloader's Guide is bigger, this year.

This 12th Edition runs 720 pages, which is what it takes these days.

Winchester's 40-grain hollowpoint Power-Point load is aimed at better small game results.

Speer/CCI

Speer's newly released Edition #12 rifle and pistol reloading manual was widely anticipated, and the wait was definitely worthwhile. It is an impressive work of 720 pages that offers data for as many as fifteen powders (many new ones) for some cartridges. Since Edition #11, Speer has introduced fifty-four new rifle and handgun bullets. This new volume covers them all.

This year, Speer has added four new component bullets: 308 200-grain and 311 200-grain Grand Slams; a 416 350-grain Mag-Tip; and a 429 270-grain Gold Dot softpoint. Also new in the Gold Dot ammunition line are 165-grain 40 S&W and 90-grain 380 Auto offerings. CCI has added a totally metal jacketed 165-grain 40 S&W cartridge to its Blazer line which provides a virtually lead-free practice load with the ballistics of the Speer Gold Dot defense load, as well as the 357 SIG cartridge loaded with a 125-grain Gold Dot bullet. Responding to "slam-fire" problems experienced when using normal sensitivity primers in semi-automatic military firearms, CCI has just introduced small (No. 41) and large (No. 34) rifle size primers made to mil-spec sensitivity standards established to minimize the possibility of slam-fires.

Swift Bullets

New for this year is a line of bonded A-frame handgun bullets in 41, 44, and 45 calibers for handguns as well as a 6.5mm rifle bullet.

are recommended even for veteran handloaders.

Supreme 380s in their twenty-round black box.

Trophy Bonded Bullets

The complete Trophy Bonded line is being redesigned this year to provide a better ballistic coefficient for each bullet. There's also a new jacket material to reduce metallic fouling. The new bullet to be introduced will be a 458-caliber 350-grain spitzer designed for 458 Winchester Magnum velocities.

VihtaVuori Oy

If you missed the first (and highly entertaining) edition of VihtaVuori's reloading manual, edition two should be available by the time you read this. Excellent data on the world's most popular sporting cartridges—even the intriguing 7x33 Sako and 338 Lapua Magnum. The "high energy" powders, specifically N-500 for rifle and single shot pistol cartridges, that add velocity without exceeding industry pressure standards should come along this year.

Vulpes Ventures, Inc.

A custom ammunition manufacturer, Vulpes offers premium bullets in most standard rifle cartridges and some of the harder to get calibers like 7mm S&H and the 450 Ackley.

Winchester

Winchester has added two new double-based Ball powders to its reloading line this year—Winchester Magnum Rifle (WMR) that has a burning rate slower than 4831 and is designed for the largest of the popular magnum cartridges; and Winchester Action Pistol (WAP) powder with a burning rate between WW-231 and WW-296. Also added to their expanding component line for reloaders are two new 30-caliber Fail Safe bullets in 150- and 165-grain weights, and an economical 12-gauge target shotshell wad designed around $1^1/_8$-ounce loads carrying the name Western Target Wad. Winchester expanded its Supreme Fail Safe rifle ammunition line with the addition of a 160-grain loading at 2840 fps in the 280 Remington; its Supreme handgun ammunition line with a 95-grain SXT bullet in the 380 Auto at 955 fps. Also coming along are a lead-free 230-grain 45 Auto Super-X cartridge; a 1-ounce 12-gauge AA target load; a high-performance 22 rimfire hollowpoint labeled the Power-Point; and a half-ounce loading of hard #$8^1/_2$ shot in the AA $2^1/_2$-inch 410 as well as a $^3/_4$-ounce AA 28-gauge loading of hard #8 shot.

Zero Ammunition and Bullet Co.

This section had to end with a "Z" and here it is. Zero sells new and remanufactured handgun ammunition. Their mail-order catalog lists lot prices of 25,000 units or more.

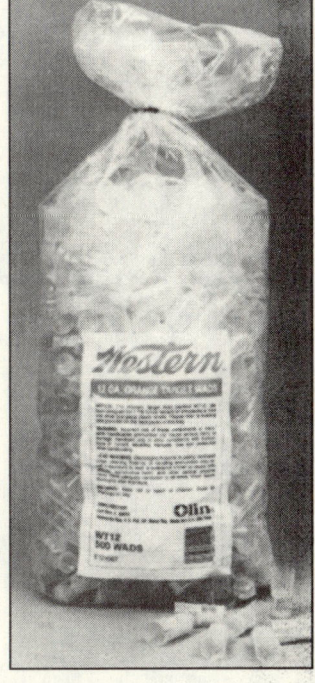

Orange target wads packaged practically.

AVERAGE CENTERFIRE RIFLE CARTRIDGE BALLISTICS AND PRICES

Caliber	Bullet weight grains	VELOCITY (fps)					ENERGY (ft. lbs.)					TRAJ. (in.)				Approx. Price per box
		Muzzle	100 yds.	200 yds.	300 yds.	400 yds.	Muzzle	100 yds.	200 yds.	300 yds.	400 yds.	100 yds.	200 yds.	300 yds.	400 yds.	
17																
17 Remington	25	4040	3284	2644	2086	1606	906	599	388	242	143	+2.0	+1.7	-4.0	-17.0	$17
22																
221 Fireball	50	2800	2137	1580	1180	988	870	507	277	155	109	0.0	-7.0	-28.0	NA	$14
22 Hornet	45	2690	2042	1502	1128	948	723	417	225	127	90	0.0	-7.7	-31.0	NA	$27**
218 Bee	46	2760	2102	1550	1155	961	788	451	245	136	94	0.0	-7.2	-29.0	NA	$46**
222 Remington	50	3140	2602	2123	1700	1350	1094	752	500	321	202	+2.0	-0.4	-11.0	-33.0	$11
222 Remington	55	3020	2562	2147	1773	1451	1114	801	563	384	257	+2.0	-0.4	-11.0	-33.0	$12
22 PPC	52	3400	2930	2510	2130	NA	1335	990	730	525	NA	+2.0	1.4	-5.0	NA	NA
223 Remington	40	3650	3010	2450	1950	1530	1185	805	535	340	265	+2.0	+1.0	-6.0	-22.0	$14
223 Remington	52/53	3330	2882	2477	2106	1770	1305	978	722	522	369	+2.0	+0.6	-6.5	-21.5	$14
223 Remington	55	3240	2748	2305	1906	1556	1282	922	649	444	296	+2.0	-0.2	-9.0	-27.0	$12
223 Remington	60	3100	2712	2355	2026	1726	1280	979	739	547	397	+2.0	+0.2	-8.0	-24.7	$16
223 Remington	64	3020	2621	2256	1920	1619	1296	977	723	524	373	+2.0	-0.2	-9.3	-23.0	$14
223 Remington	69	3000	2720	2460	2210	1980	1380	1135	925	750	600	+2.0	+0.8	-5.8	-17.5	$15
222 Rem. Mag.	55	3240	2748	2305	1906	1556	1282	922	649	444	296	+2.0	-0.2	-9.0	-27.0	$14
225 Winchester	55	3570	3066	2616	2208	1838	1556	1148	836	595	412	+2.0	+1.0	-5.0	-20.0	$19
224 Wea. Mag.	55	3650	3192	2780	2403	2057	1627	1244	943	705	516	+2.0	+1.2	-4.0	-17.0	$32
22-250 Rem.	40	4000	3320	2720	2200	1740	1420	980	660	430	265	+2.0	+1.8	-3.0	-16.0	$14
22-250 Rem.	52/55	3680	3137	2656	2222	1832	1654	1201	861	603	410	+2.0	+1.3	-4.0	-17.0	$13
22-250 Rem.	60	3600	3195	2826	2485	2169	1727	1360	1064	823	627	+2.0	+2.0	-2.4	-12.3	$19
220 Swift	50	3780	3158	2617	2135	1710	1586	1107	760	506	325	+2.0	+1.4	-4.4	-17.9	$20
220 Swift	55	3650	3194	2772	2384	2035	1627	1246	939	694	506	+2.0	+2.0	-2.6	-13.4	$19
220 Swift	60	3600	3199	2824	2475	2156	1727	1364	1063	816	619	+2.0	+1.6	-4.1	-13.1	$19
22 Savage H.P	71	2790	2340	1930	1570	1280	1225	860	585	390	190	+2.0	-1.0	-10.4	-35.7	NA
6mm (24)																
6mm BR Rem.	100	2550	2310	2083	1870	1671	1444	1185	963	776	620	+2.5	-0.6	-11.8	NA	$22
6mm PPC	70	3140	2750	2400	2070	NA	1535	1175	895	665	NA	+2.0	+1.4	-5.0	NA	NA
243 Winchester	60	3600	3110	2660	2260	1890	1725	1285	945	680	475	+2.0	+1.8	-3.3	-15.5	$17
243 Winchester	75/80	3350	2955	2593	2259	1951	1993	1551	1194	906	676	+2.0	+0.9	-5.0	-19.0	$16
243 Winchester	85	3320	3070	2830	2600	2380	2080	1770	1510	1280	1070	+2.0	+1.2	-4.0	-14.0	$18
243 Winchester*	100	2960	2697	2449	2215	1993	1945	1615	1332	1089	882	+2.5	+1.2	-6.0	-20.0	$16
243 Winchester	105	2920	2689	2470	2261	2062	1988	1686	1422	1192	992	+2.5	+1.6	-5.0	-18.4	$21
243 Light Mag.	100	3100	2839	2592	2358	2138	2133	1790	1491	1235	1014	+1.5	0.0	-6.8	-19.8	NA
6mm Remington	80	3470	3064	2694	2352	2036	2139	1667	1289	982	736	+2.0	+1.1	-5.0	-17.0	$16
6mm Remington*	100	3100	2829	2573	2332	2104	2133	1777	1470	1207	983	+2.5	+1.6	-5.0	-17.0	$16
6mm Remington	105	3060	2822	2596	2381	2177	2105	1788	1512	1270	1059	+2.5	+1.1	-3.3	-15.0	$21
240 Wea. Mag.	87	3500	3202	2924	2663	2416	2366	1980	1651	1370	1127	+2.0	+2.0	-2.0	-12.0	$32
240 Wea. Mag.*	100	3395	3106	2835	2581	2339	2559	2142	1785	1478	1215	+2.5	+2.8	-2.0	-11.0	$43
25																
25-20 Win.	86	1460	1194	1030	931	858	407	272	203	165	141	0.0	-23.5	NA	NA	$32**
25-35 Win.	117	2230	1866	1545	1282	1097	1292	904	620	427	313	+2.5	-4.2	-26.0	NA	$24
250 Savage	100	2820	2504	2210	1936	1684	1765	1392	1084	832	630	+2.5	+0.4	-9.0	-28.0	$17
257 Roberts	100	2980	2661	2363	2085	1827	1972	1572	1240	965	741	+2.5	-0.8	-5.2	-21.6	$20
257 Roberts+P	117	2780	2411	2071	1761	1488	2009	1511	1115	806	576	+2.5	-0.2	-10.2	-32.6	$18
257 Roberts+P*	120	2780	2560	2360	2160	1970	2060	1750	1480	1240	1030	+2.5	+1.2	-6.4	-23.6	$22
257 Roberts	122	2600	2331	2078	1842	1625	1831	1472	1169	919	715	+2.5	0.0	-10.6	-31.4	$21
257 Light Mag.	117	2940	2694	2460	2240	2031	2245	1885	1572	1303	1071	+1.7	0.0	-7.6	-21.8	NA
25-06 Rem.	87	3440	2995	2591	2222	1884	2286	1733	1297	954	686	+2.0	+1.1	-2.5	-14.4	$17
25-06 Rem.	90	3440	3043	2680	2344	2034	2364	1850	1435	1098	827	+2.0	+1.8	-3.3	-15.6	$17
25-06 Rem.	100	3230	2893	2580	2287	2014	2316	1858	1478	1161	901	+2.0	+0.8	-5.7	-18.9	$17
25-06 Rem.	117	2990	2770	2570	2370	2190	2320	2000	1715	1465	1246	+2.5	+1.0	-7.9	-26.6	$19
25-06 Rem.*	120	2990	2730	2484	2252	2032	2382	1985	1644	1351	1100	+2.5	+1.2	-5.3	-19.6	$17
25-06 Rem.	122	2930	2706	2492	2289	2095	2325	1983	1683	1419	1189	+2.5	+1.8	-4.5	-17.5	$23
257 Wea. Mag.	87	3825	3456	3118	2805	2513	2826	2308	1870	1520	1220	+2.0	+2.7	-0.3	-7.6	$32
257 Wea. Mag.	100	3555	3237	2941	2665	2404	2806	2326	1920	1576	1283	+2.5	+3.2	0.0	-8.0	$32
6.5																
6.5x50mm Jap.	139	2360	2160	1970	1790	1620	1720	1440	1195	985	810	+2.5	-1.0	-13.5	NA	NA
6.5x50mm Jap.	156	2070	1830	1610	1430	1260	1475	1155	900	695	550	+2.5	-4.0	-23.8	NA	NA
6.5x52mm Car.	139	2580	2360	2160	1970	1790	2045	1725	1440	1195	985	+2.5	0.0	-9.9	-29.0	NA
6.5x52mm Car.	156	2430	2170	1930	1700	1500	2045	1630	1285	1005	780	+2.5	-1.0	-13.9	NA	NA
6.5x55mm Swe.	140	2550	NA	NA	NA	NA	2020	NA	NA	NA	NA	NA	NA	NA	NA	$18
6.5x55mm Swe.*	139/140	2850	2640	2440	2250	2070	2525	2170	1855	1575	1330	+2.5	+1.6	-5.4	-18.9	$18
6.5x55mm Swe.	156	2650	2370	2110	1870	1650	2425	1950	1550	1215	945	+2.5	0.0	-10.3	-30.6	NA
6.5 Rem. Mag.	120	3210	2905	2621	2353	2102	2745	2248	1830	1475	1177	+2.5	+1.7	-4.1	-16.3	Disc.
264 Win. Mag.	140	3030	2782	2548	2326	2114	2854	2406	2018	1682	1389	+2.5	+1.4	-5.1	-18.0	$24
27																
270 Winchester	100	3430	3021	2649	2305	1988	2612	2027	1557	1179	877	+2.0	+1.0	-4.9	-17.5	$17
270 Winchester	130	3060	2776	2510	2259	2022	2702	2225	1818	1472	1180	+2.5	+1.4	-5.3	-18.2	$17

CAUTION: PRICES SHOWN ARE SUPPLIED BY THE MANUFACTURER OR IMPORTER. CHECK YOUR LOCAL GUNSHOP.

AVERAGE CENTERFIRE RIFLE CARTRIDGE BALLISTICS AND PRICES (cont.)

Caliber	Bullet weight grains	VELOCITY (fps) Muzzle	100 yds.	200 yds.	300 yds.	400 yds.	ENERGY (ft. lbs.) Muzzle	100 yds.	200 yds.	300 yds.	400 yds.	TRAJ. (in.) 100 yds.	200 yds.	300 yds.	400 yds.	Approx. Price per box
27 (cont.)																
270 Winchester	135	3000	2780	2570	2369	2178	2697	2315	1979	1682	1421	+2.5	+1.4	-6.0	-17.6	$23
270 Winchester*	140	2940	2700	2480	2260	2060	2685	2270	1905	1590	1315	+2.5	+1.8	-4.6	-17.9	$20
270 Winchester*	150	2850	2585	2336	2100	1879	2705	2226	1817	1468	1175	+2.5	+1.2	-6.5	-22.0	$17
270 Wea. Mag.	100	3760	3380	3033	2712	2412	3139	2537	2042	1633	1292	+2.0	+2.4	-1.2	-10.1	$32
270 Wea. Mag.	130	3375	3119	2878	2649	2432	3287	2808	2390	2026	1707	+2.5	+2.9	-0.9	-9.9	$32
270 Wea. Mag.*	150	3245	3036	2837	2647	2465	3507	3070	2681	2334	2023	+2.5	+2.6	-1.8	-11.4	$47
7mm																
7mm BR	140	2215	2012	1821	1643	1481	1525	1259	1031	839	681	+2.0	-3.7	-20.0	NA	$23
7mm Mauser*	139/140	2660	2435	2221	2018	1827	2199	1843	1533	1266	1037	+2.5	0.0	-9.6	-27.7	$17
7mm Mauser	145	2690	2442	2206	1985	1777	2334	1920	1568	1268	1017	+2.5	+0.1	-9.6	-28.3	$18
7mm Mauser	154	2690	2490	2300	2120	1940	2475	2120	1810	1530	1285	+2.5	+0.8	-7.5	-23.5	$17
7mm Mauser	175	2440	2137	1857	1603	1382	2313	1774	1340	998	742	+2.5	-1.7	-16.1	NA	$17
7mm Light Mag.	139	2830	2620	2450	2250	2070	2475	2135	1835	1565	1330	+1.8	0.0	-7.6	-22.1	NA
7x30 Waters	120	2700	2300	1930	1600	1330	1940	1405	990	685	470	+2.5	-0.2	-12.3	NA	$18
7mm-08 Rem.	120	3000	2725	2467	2223	1992	2398	1979	1621	1316	1058	+2.0	0.0	-7.6	-22.3	$18
7mm-08 Rem.*	140	2860	2625	2402	2189	1988	2542	2142	1793	1490	1228	+2.5	+0.8	-6.9	-21.9	$18
7mm-08 Rem.	154	2715	2510	2315	2128	1950	2520	2155	1832	1548	1300	+2.5	+1.0	-7.0	-22.7	$23
7mm-08 Light Mag.	139	3000	2790	2590	2399	2216	2777	2403	2071	1776	1515	+1.5	0.0	-6.7	-19.4	NA
7x64mm Bren.	140	Not Yet Announced														$17
7x64mm Bren.	154	2820	2610	2420	2230	2050	2720	2335	1995	1695	1430	+2.5	+1.4	-5.7	-19.9	NA
7x64mm Bren.*	160	2850	2669	2495	2327	2166	2885	2530	2211	1924	1667	+2.5	+1.6	-4.8	-17.8	$24
7x64mm Bren.	175	Not yet announced														$17
284 Winchester	150	2860	2595	2344	2108	1886	2724	2243	1830	1480	1185	+2.5	+0.8	-7.3	-23.2	$24
280 Remington	120	3150	2866	2599	2348	2110	2643	2188	1800	1468	1186	+2.0	+0.6	-6.0	-17.9	$17
280 Remington	140	3000	2758	2528	2309	2102	2797	2363	1986	1657	1373	+2.5	+1.4	-5.2	-18.3	$17
280 Remington*	150	2890	2624	2373	2135	1912	2781	2293	1875	1518	1217	+2.5	+0.8	-7.1	-22.6	$17
280 Remington	160	2840	2637	2442	2556	2078	2866	2471	2120	1809	1535	+2.5	+0.8	-6.7	-21.0	$20
280 Remington	165	2820	2510	2220	1950	1701	2913	2308	1805	1393	1060	+2.5	+0.4	-8.8	-26.5	$17
7x61mm S&H Sup.	154	3060	2720	2400	2100	1820	3200	2520	1965	1505	1135	+2.5	+1.8	-5.0	-19.8	NA
7mm Dakota	160	3200	3001	2811	2630	2455	3637	3200	2808	2456	2140	+2.1	+1.9	-2.8	-12.5	NA
7mm Rem. Mag.*	139/140	3150	2930	2710	2510	2320	3085	2660	2290	1960	1670	+2.5	+2.4	-2.4	-12.7	$21
7mm Rem. Mag.	150/154	3110	2830	2085	2320	2085	3221	2667	2196	1792	1448	+2.5	+1.6	-4.6	-16.5	$21
7mm Rem. Mag.*	160/162	2950	2730	2520	2320	2120	3090	2650	2250	1910	1600	+2.5	+1.8	-4.4	-17.8	$34
7mm Rem. Mag.	165	2900	2699	2507	2324	2147	3081	2669	2303	1978	1689	+2.5	+1.2	-5.9	-19.0	$28
7mm Rem. Mag.	175	2860	2645	2440	2244	2057	3178	2718	2313	1956	1644	+2.5	+1.0	-6.5	-20.7	$21
7mm Wea. Mag.	140	3225	2970	2729	2501	2283	3233	2741	2315	1943	1621	+2.5	+2.0	-3.2	-14.0	$35
7mm Wea. Mag.	154	3260	3023	2799	2586	2382	3539	3044	2609	2227	1890	+2.5	+2.8	-1.5	-10.8	$32
7mm Wea. Mag.*	160	3200	3004	2816	2637	2464	3637	3205	2817	2469	2156	+2.5	+2.7	-1.5	-10.6	$47
7mm Wea. Mag.	165	2950	2747	2553	2367	2189	3188	2765	2388	2053	1756	+2.5	+1.8	-4.2	-16.4	$43
7mm Wea. Mag.	175	2910	2693	2486	2288	2098	3293	2818	2401	2033	1711	+2.5	+1.2	-5.9	-19.4	$35
30																
30 Carbine	110	1990	1567	1236	1035	923	977	600	373	262	208	0.0	-13.5	NA	NA	$28**
303 Savage	190	1890	1612	1327	1183	1055	1507	1096	794	591	469	+2.5	-7.6	NA	NA	$24
30 Remington	170	2120	1822	1555	1328	1153	1696	1253	913	666	502	+2.5	-4.7	-26.3	NA	$20
30-30 Win.	55	3400	2693	2085	1570	1187	1412	886	521	301	172	+2.0	0.0	-10.2	-35.0	$18
30-30 Win.	125	2570	2090	1660	1320	1080	1830	1210	770	480	320	+2.0	-2.6	-19.9	NA	$13
30-30 Win.	150	2390	1973	1605	1303	1095	1902	1296	858	565	399	+2.5	-3.2	-22.5	NA	$13
30-30 Win.	160	2300	1997	1719	1473	1268	1879	1416	1050	771	571	+2.5	-2.9	-20.2	NA	$18
30-30 Win.*	170	2200	1895	1619	1381	1191	1827	1355	989	720	535	+2.5	-5.8	-23.6	NA	$13
300 Savage	150	2630	2354	2094	1853	1631	2303	1845	1462	1143	886	+2.5	-0.4	-10.1	-30.7	$17
300 Savage	180	2350	2137	1935	1754	1570	2207	1825	1496	1217	985	+2.5	-1.6	-15.2	NA	$17
30-40 Krag	180	2430	2213	2007	1813	1632	2360	1957	1610	1314	1064	+2.5	-1.4	-13.8	NA	$18
7.65x53mm Arg.	180	2590	2390	2200	2010	1830	2685	2280	1925	1615	1345	+2.5	0.0	-27.6	NA	NA
307 Winchester	150	2760	2321	1924	1575	1289	2530	1795	1233	826	554	+2.5	-1.5	-13.6	NA	Disc.
307 Winchester	180	2510	2179	1874	1599	1362	2519	1898	1404	1022	742	+2.5	-1.6	-15.6	NA	$20
7.5x55 Swiss	180	2650	2450	2250	2060	1880	2805	2390	2020	1700	1415	+2.5	+0.6	-8.1	-24.9	NA
308 Winchester	55	3770	3215	2726	2286	1888	1735	1262	907	638	435	+2.0	+1.4	-3.8	-15.8	$22
308 Winchester	150	2820	2533	2263	2009	1774	2648	2137	1705	1344	1048	+2.5	+0.4	-8.5	-26.1	$17
308 Winchester	165	2700	2440	2194	1963	1748	2670	2180	1763	1411	1199	+2.5	0.0	-9.7	-28.5	$20
308 Winchester	168	2680	2493	2314	2143	1979	2678	2318	1998	1713	1460	+2.5	0.0	-8.9	-25.3	$18
308 Winchester	178	2620	2415	2220	2034	1857	2713	2306	1948	1635	1363	+2.5	0.0	-9.6	-27.6	$23
308 Winchester*	180	2620	2393	2178	1974	1782	2743	2288	1896	1557	1269	+2.5	-0.2	-10.2	-28.5	$17
308 Light Mag.*	150	2980	2703	2442	2195	1964	2959	2433	1986	1606	1285	+1.6	0.0	-7.5	-22.2	NA
308 Light Mag.	165	2870	2658	2456	2263	2078	3019	2589	2211	1877	1583	+1.7	0.0	-7.5	-21.8	NA
30-06 Spfd.	55	4080	3485	2965	2502	2083	2033	1483	1074	764	530	+2.0	+1.9	-2.1	-11.7	$22
30-06 Spfd.	125	3140	2780	2447	2138	1853	2736	2145	1662	1279	953	+2.0	+1.0	-6.2	-21.0	$17
30-06 Spfd.	150	2910	2617	2342	2083	1853	2820	2281	1827	1445	1135	+2.5	+0.8	-7.2	-23.4	$17
30-06 Spfd.	152	2910	2654	2413	2184	1968	2858	2378	1965	1610	1307	+2.5	+1.0	-6.6	-21.3	$23
30-06 Spfd.*	165	2800	2534	2283	2047	1825	2872	2352	1909	1534	1220	+2.5	+0.4	-8.4	-25.5	$17
30-06 Spfd.	168	2710	2522	2346	2169	2003	2739	2372	2045	1754	1497	+2.5	+0.4	-8.0	-23.5	$18

CAUTION: PRICES SHOWN ARE SUPPLIED BY THE MANUFACTURER OR IMPORTER. CHECK YOUR LOCAL GUNSHOP.

50th EDITION, 1996

AVERAGE CENTERFIRE RIFLE CARTRIDGE BALLISTICS AND PRICES (cont.)

Caliber	Bullet weight grains	VELOCITY (fps) Muzzle	100 yds.	200 yds.	300 yds.	400 yds.	ENERGY (ft. lbs.) Muzzle	100 yds.	200 yds.	300 yds.	400 yds.	TRAJ. (in.) 100 yds.	200 yds.	300 yds.	400 yds.	Approx. Price per box
30-06 Spfd.	178	2720	2511	2311	2121	1939	2924	2491	2111	1777	1486	+2.5	+0.4	-8.2	-24.6	$23
30-06 Spfd.*	180	2700	2469	2250	2042	1846	2913	2436	2023	1666	1362	+2.5	0.0	-9.3	-27.0	$17
30-06 Spfd.	220	2410	2130	1870	1632	1422	2837	2216	1708	1301	988	+2.5	-1.7	-16.0	NA	$17
30-06 Light Mag.	150	3100	2815	2548	2295	2058	3200	2639	2161	1755	1410	+1.4	0.0	-6.8	-20.3	NA
30-06 Light Mag.	180	2880	2676	2480	2293	2114	3316	2862	2459	2102	1786	+1.7	0.0	-7.3	-21.3	NA
308 Norma Mag.	180	3020	2820	2630	2440	2270	3645	3175	2755	2385	2050	+2.5	+2.0	-3.5	-14.8	NA
300 Dakota	200	3000	2824	2656	2493	2336	3996	3542	3131	2760	2423	+2.2	+1.5	-4.0	-15.2	NA
300 H&H Magnum*	180	2880	2640	2412	2196	1990	3315	2785	2325	1927	1583	+2.5	+0.8	-6.8	-21.7	$24
300 H&H Magnum	220	2550	2267	2002	1757	NA	3167	2510	1958	1508	NA	+2.5	-0.4	-12.0	NA	NA
300 Peterson	180	3500	3319	3145	2978	2817	4896	4401	3953	3544	3172	+2.3	+2.9	0.0	-6.8	NA
300 Win. Mag.	150	3290	2951	2636	2342	2068	3605	2900	2314	1827	1424	+2.5	+1.9	-3.8	-15.8	$22
300 Win. Mag.	165	3100	2877	2665	2462	2269	3522	3033	2603	2221	1897	+2.5	+2.4	-3.0	-16.9	$24
300 Win. Mag.	178	2980	2769	2568	2375	2191	3509	3030	2606	2230	1897	+2.5	+1.4	-5.0	-17.6	$29
300 Win. Mag.*	180	2960	2745	2540	2344	2157	3501	3011	2578	2196	1859	+2.5	+1.2	-5.5	-18.5	$22
300 Win. Mag.	190	2885	2691	2506	2327	2156	3511	3055	2648	2285	1961	+2.5	+1.2	-5.7	-19.0	$26
300 Win. Mag.*	200	2825	2595	2376	2167	1970	3545	2991	2508	2086	1742	+2.5	+1.6	-4.7	-17.2	$36
300 Win. Mag.	220	2680	2448	2228	2020	1823	3508	2927	2424	1993	1623	+2.5	0.0	-9.5	-27.5	$23
300 Wea. Mag.	110	3900	3441	3038	2652	2305	3714	2891	2239	1717	1297	+2.0	+2.6	-0.6	-8.7	$32
300 Wea. Mag.	150	3600	3307	3033	2776	2533	4316	3642	3064	2566	2137	+2.5	+3.2	0.0	-8.1	$32
300 Wea. Mag.	165	3450	3210	3000	2792	2593	4360	3796	3297	2855	2464	+2.5	+3.2	0.0	-7.8	NA
300 Wea. Mag.	178	3120	2902	2695	2497	2308	3847	3329	2870	2464	2104	+2.5	-1.7	-3.6	-14.7	$43
300 Wea. Mag.*	180	3120	2866	2667	2400	2184	3890	3284	2758	2301	1905	+2.5	+1.7	-3.8	-15.0	$35
300 Wea. Mag.	190	3030	2830	2638	2455	2279	3873	3378	2936	2542	2190	+2.5	+1.6	-4.3	-16.0	$38
300 Wea. Mag.	220	2850	2541	2283	1984	1736	3967	3155	2480	1922	1471	+2.5	+0.4	-8.5	-26.4	$35
32-20 Win.	100	1210	1021	913	834	769	325	231	185	154	131	0.0	-32.3	NA	NA	$23**
303 British	150	2685	2441	2210	1992	1787	2401	1984	1627	1321	1064	+2.5	+0.6	-8.4	-26.2	$18
303 British	180	2460	2124	1817	1542	1311	2418	1803	1319	950	687	+2.5	-1.8	-16.8	NA	$18
303 Light Mag.	150	2830	2570	2325	2094	1884	2667	2199	1800	1461	1185	+2.0	0.0	-8.4	-24.6	NA
7.62x39mm Rus.	123/125	2300	2030	1780	1550	1350	1445	1125	860	655	500	+2.5	-2.0	-17.5	NA	$13
7.62x54mm Rus.	146	2950	2730	2520	2320	NA	2820	2415	2055	1740	NA	+2.5	+2.0	-4.4	-17.7	NA
7.62x54mm Rus.	180	2580	2370	2180	2000	1820	2650	2250	1900	1590	1100	+2.5	0.0	-9.8	-28.5	NA
7.7x58mm Jap.	180	2500	2300	2100	1920	1750	2490	2105	1770	1475	1225	+2.5	0.0	-10.4	-30.2	NA
8x57mm JS Mau.	165	2850	2520	2210	1930	1670	2965	2330	1795	1360	1015	+2.5	+1.0	-7.7	NA	NA
32 Win. Special	170	2250	1921	1626	1372	1175	1911	1393	998	710	521	+2.5	-3.5	-22.9	NA	$14
8mm Mauser	170	2360	1969	1622	1333	1123	2102	1464	993	671	476	+2.5	-3.1	-22.2	NA	$18
8mm Rem. Mag.	185	3080	2761	2464	2186	1927	3896	3131	2494	1963	1525	+2.5	+1.4	-5.5	-19.7	$30
8mm Rem. Mag.	220	2830	2581	2346	2123	1913	3912	3254	2688	2201	1787	+2.5	+0.6	-7.6	-23.5	Disc.
330 Dakota	250	2900	2719	2545	2378	2217	4668	4103	3595	3138	2727	+2.3	+1.3	-5.0	-17.5	NA
338 Lapua	250	2963	2795	2640	2493	NA	4842	4341	3881	3458	NA	+1.9	0.0	-7.9	NA	NA
338 Win. Mag.	200	2960	2658	2375	2110	1862	3890	3137	2505	1977	1539	+2.5	+1.0	-6.7	-22.3	$27
338 Win. Mag.*	210	2830	2590	2370	2150	1940	3735	3130	2610	2155	1760	+2.5	+1.4	-6.0	-20.9	$33
338 Win. Mag.*	225	2785	2517	2266	2029	1808	3871	3165	2565	2057	1633	+2.5	+0.4	-8.5	-25.9	$27
338 Win. Mag.	230	2780	2573	2375	2186	2005	3948	3382	2881	2441	2054	+2.5	+1.2	-6.3	-21.0	$40
338 Win. Mag.*	250	2660	2456	2261	2075	1898	3927	3348	2837	2389	1999	+2.5	+0.2	-9.0	-27.0	$27
340 Wea. Mag.*	210	3250	2991	2746	2515	2295	4924	4170	3516	2948	2455	+2.5	1.9	-1.8	-11.8	$56
340 Wea. Mag.*	250	3000	2806	2621	2443	2272	4995	4371	3812	3311	2864	+2.5	+2.0	-3.5	-14.8	$56
338 A-Square	250	3120	2799	2500	2220	1958	5403	4348	3469	2736	2128	+2.5	+2.7	-1.5	-10.5	NA
348 Winchester	200	2520	2215	1931	1672	1443	2820	2178	1656	1241	925	+2.5	-1.4	-14.7	NA	$42
357 Magnum	158	1830	1427	1138	980	883	1175	715	454	337	274	0.0	-16.2	-33.1	NA	$25**
35 Remington	150	2300	1874	1506	1218	1039	1762	1169	755	494	359	+2.5	-4.1	-26.3	NA	$16
35 Remington	200	2080	1698	1376	1140	1001	1921	1280	841	577	445	+2.5	-6.3	-17.1	-33.6	$16
356 Winchester	200	2460	2114	1797	1517	1284	2688	1985	1434	1022	732	+2.5	-1.8	-17.1	NA	$31
356 Winchester	250	2160	1911	1682	1476	1299	2591	2028	1571	1210	937	+2.5	-3.7	-22.2	NA	$31
358 Winchester	200	2490	2171	1876	1619	1379	2753	2093	1563	1151	844	+2.5	-1.6	-15.6	NA	$31
358 STA	275	2850	2562	2292	2039	NA	4958	4009	3208	2539	NA	+1.9	0.0	-8.6	NA	NA
350 Rem. Mag.	200	2710	2410	2130	1870	1631	3261	2579	2014	1553	1181	+2.5	-0.2	-10.0	-30.1	$33
35 Whelen	200	2675	2378	2100	1842	1606	3177	2510	1958	1506	1145	+2.5	-0.2	-10.3	-31.1	$20
35 Whelen	250	2400	2197	2005	1823	1652	3197	2680	2230	1844	1515	+2.5	-1.2	-13.7	NA	$20
358 Norma Mag.	250	2800	2510	2230	1970	1730	4350	3480	2750	2145	1655	+2.5	+1.0	-7.6	-25.2	NA
9.3x57mm Mau.	286	2070	1810	1590	1390	1110	2710	2090	1600	1220	955	+2.5	-2.6	-22.5	NA	NA
9.3 x 62mm Mau.	286	2360	2089	1844	1623	NA	3538	2771	2157	1670	1260	+2.5	-1.6	-21.0	NA	NA
9.3 x 64mm	286	2700	2505	2318	2139	1968	4629	3984	3411	2906	2460	+2.5	+2.7	-4.5	-19.2	NA
9.3 x 74Rmm	286	2360	2089	1844	1623	NA	3538	2771	2157	1670	NA	+2.5	-2.0	-11.0	NA	NA
38-55 Win.	255	1320	1190	1091	1018	963	987	802	674	587	525	0.0	-23.4	NA	NA	$25
375 Winchester	200	2200	1841	1526	1268	1089	2150	1506	1034	714	527	+2.5	-4.0	-26.2	NA	$27
375 Winchester	250	1900	1647	1424	1239	1103	2005	1506	1126	852	676	+2.5	-6.9	-33.3	NA	$27
375 Dakota	300	2600	2316	2051	1804	1579	4502	3573	2800	2167	1661	+2.4	0.0	-11.0	-32.7	NA
375 N.E. 2½"	270	2000	1740	1507	1310	NA	2398	1815	1362	1026	NA	+2.5	-6.0	-30.0	NA	NA

CAUTION: PRICES SHOWN ARE SUPPLIED BY THE MANUFACTURER OR IMPORTER. CHECK YOUR LOCAL GUNSHOP.

AVERAGE CENTERFIRE RIFLE CARTRIDGE BALLISTICS AND PRICES (cont.)

Caliber	Bullet weight grains	VELOCITY (fps)					ENERGY (ft. lbs.)					TRAJ. (in.)				Approx. Price per box
		Muzzle	100 yds.	200 yds.	300 yds.	400 yds.	Muzzle	100 yds.	200 yds.	300 yds.	400 yds.	100 yds.	200 yds.	300 yds.	400 yds.	
375 (cont.)																
375 Flanged	300	2450	2150	1886	1640	NA	3998	3102	2369	1790	NA	+2.5	-2.4	-17.0	NA	NA
375 H&H Magnum	250	2670	2450	2240	2040	1850	3955	3335	2790	2315	1905	+2.5	-0.4	-10.2	-28.4	NA
375 H&H Magnum	270	2690	2420	2166	1928	1707	4337	3510	2812	2228	1747	+2.5	0.0	-10.0	-29.4	$28
375 H&H Magnum*	300	2530	2245	1979	1733	1512	4263	3357	2608	2001	1523	+2.5	-1.0	-10.5	-33.6	$28
375 Wea. Mag.	300	2700	2420	2157	1911	1685	4856	3901	3100	2432	1891	+2.5	-0.4	-10.7	-	NA
378 Wea. Mag.	270	3180	2976	2781	2594	2415	6062	5308	4635	4034	3495	+2.5	+2.6	-1.8	-11.3	$71
378 Wea. Mag.	300	2929	2576	2252	1952	1680	5698	4419	3379	2538	1881	+2.5	+1.2	-7.0	-24.5	$77
375 A-Square	300	2920	2626	2351	2093	1850	5679	4594	3681	2917	2281	+2.5	+1.4	-6.0	-21.0	NA
38-40 Win.	180	1160	999	901	827	764	538	399	324	273	233	0.0	-33.9	NA	NA	$42**
40																
450/400-3"	400	2150	1932	1730	1545	1379	4105	3316	2659	2119	1689	+2.5	-4.0	-9.5	-30.3	NA
416 Dakota	400	2450	2294	2143	1998	1859	5330	4671	4077	3544	3068	+2.5	-0.2	-10.5	-29.4	NA
41																
416 Taylor	400	2350	2117	1896	1693	NA	4905	3980	3194	2547	NA	+2.5	-1.2	-15.0	NA	NA
416 Hoffman	400	2380	2145	1923	1718	1529	5031	4087	3285	2620	2077	+2.5	-1.0	-14.1	NA	NA
416 Rigby	350	2600	2449	2303	2162	2026	5253	4661	4122	3632	3189	+2.5	-1.8	-10.2	-26.0	NA
416 Rigby	400	2370	2210	2050	1900	NA	4990	4315	3720	3185	NA	+2.5	-0.7	-12.1	NA	NA
416 Rigby	410	2370	2110	1870	1640	NA	5115	4050	3165	2455	NA	+2.5	-2.4	-17.3	NA	$110
416 Rem. Mag.*	350	2520	2270	2034	1814	1611	4935	4004	3216	2557	2017	+2.5	-0.8	-12.6	-35.0	$82
416 Rem. Mag.*	400	2400	2175	1962	1763	1579	5115	4201	3419	2760	2214	+2.5	-1.2	-14.6	NA	$80
416 Wea. Mag.*	400	2700	2397	2115	1852	1613	6474	5104	3971	3047	2310	+2.5	0.0	-10.1	-30.4	$96
404 Jeffrey	400	2150	1924	1716	1525	NA	4105	3289	2614	2064	NA	+2.5	-4.0	-22.1	NA	NA
425																
425 Express	400	2400	2160	1934	1725	NA	5115	4145	3322	2641	NA	+2.5	-1.0	-14.0	NA	NA
44-40 Win.	200	1190	1006	900	822	756	629	449	360	300	254	0.0	-33.3	NA	NA	$36**
44																
44 Rem. Mag.	210	1920	1477	1155	982	880	1719	1017	622	450	361	0.0	-17.6	NA	NA	$14
44 Rem. Mag.	240	1760	1380	1114	970	878	1650	1015	661	501	411	0.0	-17.6	NA	NA	$13
444 Marlin	240	2350	1815	1377	1087	941	2942	1753	1001	630	472	+2.5	-15.1	-31.0	NA	$22
444 Marlin	265	2120	1733	1405	1160	1012	2644	1768	1162	791	603	+2.5	-6.0	-32.2	NA	Disc.
45																
45-70 Govt.	300	1810	1497	1244	1073	969	2182	1492	1031	767	625	0.0	-14.8	NA	NA	$21
45-70 Govt.	405	1330	1168	1055	977	918	1590	1227	1001	858	758	0.0	-24.6	NA	NA	$21
458 Win. Magnum	350	2470	1990	1570	1250	1060	4740	3065	1915	1205	870	+2.5	-2.5	-21.6	NA	$43
458 Win. Magnum	400	2380	2170	1960	1770	NA	5030	4165	3415	2785	NA	+2.5	-0.4	-13.4	NA	$73
458 Win. Magnum	465	2220	1999	1791	1601	NA	5088	4127	3312	2646	NA	+2.5	-2.0	-17.7	NA	NA
458 Win. Magnum	500	2040	1823	1623	1442	1237	4620	3689	2924	2308	1839	+2.5	-3.5	-22.0	NA	$61
458 Win. Magnum	510	2040	1770	1527	1319	1157	4712	3547	2640	1970	1516	+2.5	-4.1	-25.0	NA	$41
450 Dakota	500	2450	2235	2030	1838	1658	6663	5544	4576	3748	3051	+2.5	-0.6	-12.0	-33.8	NA
450 N.E.-3¼"	465	2190	1970	1765	1577	NA	4952	4009	3216	2567	NA	+2.5	-3.0	-20.0	NA	NA
450 N.E.-3¼"	500	2150	1920	1708	1514	NA	5132	4093	3238	2544	NA	+2.5	-4.0	-22.9	NA	NA
450 No. 2	465	2190	1970	1765	1577	NA	4952	4009	3216	2567	NA	+2.5	-3.0	-20.0	NA	NA
450 No. 2	500	2150	1920	1708	1514	NA	5132	4093	3238	2544	NA	+2.5	-4.0	-22.9	NA	NA
458 Lott	465	2380	2150	1932	1730	NA	5848	4773	3855	3091	NA	+2.5	-1.0	-14.0	NA	NA
458 Lott	500	2300	2062	1838	1633	NA	5873	4719	3748	2960	NA	+2.5	-1.6	-16.4	NA	NA
450 Ackley Mag.	465	2400	2169	1950	1747	NA	5947	4857	3927	3150	NA	+2.5	-1.0	-13.7	NA	NA
450 Ackley Mag.	500	2320	2081	1855	1649	NA	5975	4085	3820	3018	NA	+2.5	-1.2	-15.0	NA	NA
460 Short A-Sq.	500	2420	2175	1943	1729	NA	6501	5250	4193	3319	NA	+2.5	-0.8	-12.8	NA	NA
460 Wea. Mag.	500	2700	2404	2128	1869	1635	8092	6416	5026	3878	2969	+2.5	+0.6	-8.9	-28.0	$72
475																
500/465 N.E.	480	2150	1917	1703	1507	NA	4926	3917	3089	2419	NA	+2.5	-4.0	-22.2	-	NA
470 Rigby	500	2150	1940	1740	1560	NA	5130	4170	3360	2695	NA	+2.5	-2.8	-19.4	NA	NA
470 Nitro Ex.	480	2190	1954	1735	1536	NA	5111	4070	3210	2515	NA	+2.5	-3.5	-20.8	NA	NA
470 Nitro Ex.	500	2150	1890	1650	1440	1270	5130	3965	3040	2310	1790	+2.5	-4.3	-24.0	NA	$177
475 No. 2	500	2200	1955	1728	1522	NA	5375	4243	3316	2573	NA	+2.5	-3.2	-20.9	NA	NA
50 58																
505 Gibbs	525	2300	2063	1840	1637	NA	6166	4922	3948	3122	NA	+2.5	-3.0	-18.0	NA	NA
500 N.E.-3"	570	2150	1928	1722	1533	NA	5850	4703	3752	2975	NA	+2.5	-3.7	-22.0	NA	NA
500 N.E.-3"	600	2150	1927	1721	1531	NA	6158	4947	3944	3124	NA	+2.5	-4.0	-22.0	NA	NA
495 A-Square	570	2350	2117	1896	1693	NA	5850	4703	3752	2975	NA	+2.5	-1.0	-14.5	NA	NA
495 A-Square	600	2280	2050	1833	1635	NA	6925	5598	4478	3562	NA	+2.5	-2.0	-17.0	NA	NA
500 A-Square	600	2380	2144	1922	1766	NA	7546	6126	4920	3922	NA	+2.5	-3.0	-17.0	-30.3	NA
500 A-Square	707	2250	2040	1841	1567	NA	7947	6530	5318	4311	NA	+2.5	-2.0	-17.0	NA	NA
577 Nitro Ex.	750	2050	1793	1562	1360	NA	6990	5356	4065	3079	NA	+2.5	-5.0	-26.0	NA	NA
577 Tyrannosaur	750	2400	2141	1898	1675	NA	9591	7633	5996	4671	NA	+3.0	0.0	-12.9	NA	NA
600-700																
600 N.E.	900	1950	1680	1452	NA	NA	7596	5634	4212	NA	NA	+5.6	0.0	NA	NA	NA
700 N.E.	1200	1900	1676	1472	NA	NA	9618	7480	5774	NA	NA	+5.7	0.0	NA	NA	NA

Notes: NA in vel. or eng. column = This data not available from manufacturer. NA in trajectory column = Bullet has fallen more than 3 feet below line of sight and further hold-over is not practical. Wea. Mag. = Weatherby Magnum. Spfd. = Springfield. A-Sq. = A-Square. N.E.= Nitro Express. Many manufacturer's do not supply suggested retail prices. Others did not get their pricing to us before press time. All pricing can vary dependent on the exact brand and style of ammo selected and/or the retail outlet from which you make your purchase. Pricing has been rounded to the nearest dollar and represent our best estimate of average pricing. An * after the bullet weight means these loads are available with Nosler Partition or Swift A-Frame bullets. Listed pricing may or may not reflect this bullet type. ** = these are packed 50 to box, all others are 20 to box.

CAUTION: PRICES SHOWN ARE SUPPLIED BY THE MANUFACTURER OR IMPORTER. CHECK YOUR LOCAL GUNSHOP.

CENTERFIRE HANDGUN CARTRIDGES—BALLISTICS AND PRICES

Caliber	Bullet Wgt. Grs.	Velocity (fps) MV	Velocity 50 yds.	Velocity 100 yds.	Energy (ft. lbs.) ME	Energy 50 yds.	Energy 100 yds.	Mid-Range Traj. (in.) 50 yds.	Mid-Range Traj. 100 yds.	Bbl. Lgth. (in.)	Est. Price /box
221 Rem. Fireball	50	2650	2380	2130	780	630	505	0.2	0.8	10.5"	$15
25 Automatic	35	900	813	742	63	51	43	NA	NA	2"	$18
25 Automatic	45	815	730	655	65	55	40	1.8	7.7	2"	$21
25 Automatic	50	760	705	660	65	55	50	2.0	8.7	2"	$17
7.5mm Swiss	107	1010	NA	NA	240	NA	NA	NA	NA	NA	NEW
7.62mm Tokarev	87	1390	NA	NA	365	NA	NA	0.6	NA	4.5"	NA
7.62mm Nagant	97	1080	NA	NA	350	NA	NA	NA	NA	NA	NEW
7.63mm Mauser	88	1440	NA	NA	405	NA	NA	NA	NA	NA	NEW
30 Luger	93†	1220	1110	1040	305	255	225	0.9	3.5	4.5"	$34
30 Carbine	110	1790	1600	1430	785	625	500	0.4	1.7	10"	$28
32 S&W	88	680	645	610	90	80	75	2.5	10.5	3"	$17
32 S&W Long	98	705	670	635	115	100	90	2.3	10.5	4"	$17
32 Short Colt	80	745	665	590	100	80	60	2.2	9.9	4"	$19
32 H&R Magnum	85	1100	1020	930	230	195	165	1.0	4.3	4.5"	$21
32 H&R Magnum	95	1030	940	900	225	190	170	1.1	4.7	4.5"	$19
32 Automatic	60	970	895	835	125	105	95	1.3	5.4	4"	$22
32 Automatic	71	905	855	810	130	115	95	1.4	5.8	4"	$19
8mm Lebel Pistol	111	850	NA	NA	180	NA	NA	NA	NA	NA	NEW
8mm Steyr	113	1080	NA	NA	290	NA	NA	NA	NA	NA	NEW
8mm Gasser	126	850	NA	NA	200	NA	NA	NA	NA	NA	NEW
380 Automatic	85/88	990	920	870	190	165	145	1.2	5.1	4"	$20
380 Automatic	90	1000	890	800	200	160	130	1.2	5.5	3.75"	$10
380 Automatic	95/100	955	865	785	190	160	130	1.4	5.9	4"	$20
38 Super Auto +P	115	1300	1145	1040	430	335	275	0.7	3.3	5"	$26
38 Super Auto +P	125/130	1215	1100	1015	425	350	300	0.8	3.6	5"	$26
38 Super Auto +P	147	1100	1050	1000	395	355	325	0.9	4.0	5"	NA
9x18mm Makarov	95	1000	NA	NA	NA	NA	NA	NA	NA	NA	NEW
9x18mm Ultra	100	1050	NA	NA	240	NA	NA	NA	NA	NA	NEW
9x23mm Largo	124	1190	1055	966	390	306	257	0.7	3.7	4"	NA
9mm Steyr	115	1180	NA	NA	350	NA	NA	NA	NA	NA	NEW
9mm Luger	88	1500	1190	1010	440	275	200	0.6	3.1	4"	$24
9mm Luger	90	1360	1112	978	370	247	191	NA	NA	4"	$26
9mm Luger	95	1300	1140	1010	350	275	215	0.8	3.4	4"	NA
9mm Luger	115	1155	1045	970	340	280	240	0.9	3.9	4"	$21
9mm Luger	123/125	1110	1030	970	340	290	260	1.0	4.0	4"	$23
9mm Luger	140	935	890	850	270	245	225	1.3	5.5	4"	$23
9mm Luger	147	990	940	900	320	290	265	1.1	4.9	4"	$26
9mm Luger +P	115	1250	1113	1019	399	316	265	0.8	3.5	4"	$27
9mm Federal	115	1280	1130	1040	420	330	280	0.7	3.3	4"V	$24
9mm Luger Vector	115	1155	1047	971	341	280	241	NA	NA	4"	NA
9mm Luger +P	124	1180	1089	1021	384	327	287	0.8	3.8	4"	NA
38 S&W	146	685	650	620	150	135	125	2.4	10.0	4"	$19
38 Short Colt	125	730	685	645	150	130	115	2.2	9.4	6"	$19
38 Special	110	945	895	850	220	195	175	1.3	5.4	4"V	$23
38 Special	130	775	745	710	175	160	120	1.9	7.9	4"V	$22
38 (Multi-Ball)	140	830	730	505	215	130	80	2.0	10.6	4"V	$10**
38 Special	148	710	635	565	165	130	105	2.4	10.6	4"V	$17
38 Special	158	755	725	690	200	185	170	2.0	8.3	4"V	$18
38 Special +P	95	1175	1045	960	290	230	195	0.9	3.9	4"V	$23
38 Special +P	110	995	925	870	240	210	185	1.2	5.1	4"V	$23
38 Special +P	125	975	929	885	264	238	218	1	5.2	4"	NA
38 Special +P	125	945	900	860	250	225	205	1.3	5.4	4"V	$23
38 Special +P	129	945	910	870	255	235	215	1.3	5.3	4"V	$11
38 Special +P	147/150(c)	884	NA	NA	264	NA	NA	NA	NA	4"V	$27
38 Special +P	158	890	855	825	280	255	240	1.4	6.0	4"V	$20
357 SIG	125	1350	1190	1080	510	395	325	0.7	3.1	4"	NA
356 TSW	147	1220	1120	1040	485	410	355	0.8	3.5	5"	NA
357 Magnum	110	1295	1095	975	410	290	230	0.8	3.5	4"V	$25
357 (Med. Vel.)	125	1220	1075	985	415	315	270	0.8	3.7	4"V	$25
357 Magnum	125	1450	1240	1090	585	425	330	0.6	2.8	4"V	$25
357 (Multi-Ball)	140	1155	830	665	420	215	135	1.2	6.4	4"V	$11**
357 Magnum	140	1360	1195	1075	575	445	360	0.7	3.0	4"V	$25
357 Magnum	145	1290	1155	1060	535	430	360	0.8	3.5	4"V	$26
357 Magnum	150/158	1235	1105	1015	535	430	360	0.8	3.5	4"V	$25
357 Magnum	165	1290	1189	1108	610	518	450	0.7	3.1	8 3/8"	NA
357 Magnum	180	1145	1055	985	525	445	390	0.9	3.9	4"V	$25
357 Rem. Maximum	158	1825	1590	1380	1170	885	670	0.4	1.7	10.5"	$14**
40 S&W	155	1140	1026	958	447	362	309	0.9	4.1	4"	$14***
40 S&W	165	1150	NA	NA	485	NA	NA	NA	NA	4"	$18***
40 S&W	180	985	936	893	388	350	319	1.4	5.0	4"	$14***
40 S&W	180	1015	960	914	412	368	334	1.3	4.5	4"	NA
10mm Automatic	155	1125	1046	986	436	377	335	0.9	3.9	5"	$26
10mm Automatic	170	1340	1165	1145	680	510	415	0.7	3.2	5"	$31
10mm Automatic	175	1290	1140	1035	650	505	420	0.7	3.3	5.5"	$11**
10mm Auto.(FBI)	180	950	905	865	361	327	299	1.5	5.4	4"	$16**
10mm Automatic	180	1030	970	920	425	375	340	1.1	4.7	5"	$16**
10mm Auto H.V.	180†	1240	1124	1037	618	504	430	0.8	3.4	5"	$27
10mm Automatic	200	1160	1070	1010	495	510	430	0.9	3.8	5"	$14**
10.4mm Italian	177	950	NA	NA	360	NA	NA	NA	NA	NA	NEW
41 Action Exp.	180	1000	947	903	400	359	326	0.5	4.2	5"	$13**
41 Rem. Magnum	170	1420	1165	1015	760	515	390	0.7	3.2	4"V	$33
41 Rem. Magnum	175	1250	1120	1030	605	490	410	0.8	3.4	4"V	$14**
41 (Med. Vel.)	210	965	900	840	435	375	330	1.3	5.4	4"V	$30
41 Rem. Magnum	210	1300	1160	1060	790	630	535	0.7	3.2	4"V	$33
44 S&W Russian	247	780	NA	NA	335	NA	NA	NA	NA	NA	NA
44 S&W Special	180	980	NA	NA	383	NA	NA	NA	NA	6.5"	NA
44 S&W Special	180	1000	935	882	400	350	311	NA	NA	7.5"V	NA
44 S&W Special	200†	875	825	780	340	302	270	1.2	6.0	6"	$13**
44 S&W Special	200	1035	940	865	475	390	335	1.1	4.9	6.5"	$13**
44 S&W Special	240/246	755	725	695	310	285	265	2.0	8.3	6.5"	$26
44 Rem. Magnum	180	1610	1365	1175	1035	745	550	0.5	2.3	4"V	$18***
44 Rem. Magnum	200	1400	1192	1053	870	630	492	0.6	NA	6.5"	$20
44 Rem. Magnum	210	1495	1310	1165	1040	805	635	0.6	2.5	6.5"	$18***
44 (Med. Vel.)	240	1000	945	900	535	475	435	1.1	4.8	6.5"	$17
44 R.M.(Jacketed)	240	1180	1080	1010	740	625	545	0.9	3.7	4"V	$18***
44 R.M. (Lead)	240	1350	1185	1070	970	750	610	0.7	3.1	4"V	$29
44 Rem. Magnum	250	1180	1100	1040	775	670	600	0.8	3.6	6.5"V	$21
44 Rem. Magnum	275	1235	1142	1070	931	797	699	0.8	3.3	6.5"	NA
44 Rem. Magnum	300	1200	1100	1026	959	806	702	NA	NA	7.5"	$17
450 Short Colt	226	830	NA	NA	350	NA	NA	NA	NA	NA	NEW
45 Automatic	185	1000	940	890	410	360	325	1.1	4.9	5"	$28
45 Auto. (Match)	185	770	705	650	245	204	175	2.0	8.7	5"	$28
45 Auto. (Match)	200	940	890	840	392	352	312	2.0	8.6	5"	$20
45 Automatic	200	975	917	860	421	372	328	1.4	5.0	5"	$18
45 Automatic	230	830	800	675	355	325	300	1.6	6.8	5"	$27
45 Automatic	230	880	846	816	396	366	340	1.5	6.1	5"	NA
45 Automatic +P	185	1140	1040	970	535	445	385	0.9	4.0	5"	$31
45 Automatic +P	200	1055	982	925	494	428	380	NA	NA	5"	NA
45 Win. Magnum	230	1400	1230	1105	1000	775	635	0.6	2.8	5"	$14**
45 Win. Magnum	260	1250	1137	1053	902	746	640	0.8	3.3	5"	$16**
455 Webley MKII	262	850	NA	NA	420	NA	NA	NA	NA	NA	NA
45 Colt	200	1000	938	889	444	391	351	1.3	4.8	5.5"	$21
45 Colt	225	960	890	830	460	395	345	1.3	5.5	5.5"	$22
45 Colt	250/255	860	820	780	410	375	340	1.6	6.6	5.5"	$27
50 Action Exp.	325	1400	1209	1075	1414	1055	835	0.2	2.3	6"	$24**

Notes: Blanks are available in 32 S&W, 38 S&W, and 38 Special. V after barrel length indicates test barrel was vented to produce ballistics similar to a revolver with a normal barrel-to-cylinder gap. Ammo prices are per 50 rounds except when marked with an ** which signifies a 20 round box; *** signifies a 25-round box. Not all loads are available from all ammo manufacturers. Listed loads are those made by Remington, Winchester, Federal, and others. DISC. is a discontinued load. Prices are rounded to nearest whole dollar and will vary with brand and retail outlet. †= new bullet weight this year; "c" indicates a change in data.

RIMFIRE AMMUNITION—BALLISTICS AND PRICES

Cartridge type	Bullet Wt. Grs.	Velocity (fps) 22 1/2" Barrel Muzzle	Velocity 22 1/2" 50 Yds.	Velocity 22 1/2" 100 Yds.	Energy (ft. lbs.) 22 1/2" Barrel Muzzle	Energy 22 1/2" 50 Yds.	Energy 22 1/2" 100 Yds.	Velocity (fps) 6" Barrel Muzzle	Velocity 6" 50 Yds.	Energy (ft. lbs) 6" Barrel Muzzle	Energy 6" 50 Yds.	Approx. Price Per Box 50 Rds.	Approx. Price Per Box 100 Rds.
22 Short Blank	—				Not applicable							$4	NA
22 CB Short	30	725	667	610	34	29	24	706	—	32	—	$2	NA
22 Short Match	29	830	752	695	44	36	31	786	—	39	—	—	NA
22 Short Std. Vel.	29	1045	—	810	70	—	42	865	—	48	—	Discontinued	
22 Short High Vel.	29	1095	—	903	77	—	53	—	—	—	—	$2	NA
22 Short H.V. H.P.	27	1120	—	904	75	—	49	—	—	—	—	—	NA
22 CB Long	30	725	667	610	34	29	24	706	—	32	—	$2	NA
22 Long Std. Vel.	29	1180	1038	946	90	69	58	1031	—	68	—	—	—
22 Long High Vel.	29	1240	—	962	99	—	60	—	—	—	—	$2	NA
22 L.R. Sub Sonic	38/40	1070	970	890	100	80	70	940	—	—	—	$2	NA
22 L.R. Std. Vel.	40	1138	1047	975	116	97	84	1027	925	93	76	$2	NA
22 L.R. High Vel.	40	1255	1110	1017	140	109	92	1060	—	100	—	$2	NA
22 L.R. H.V. Sil.	42	1220	—	1003	139	—	94	1025	—	98	—	$2	NA
22 L.R. H.V. H.P.	36/38	1280	1126	1010	131	101	82	1089	—	95	—	$2	NA
22 L.R. Shot	#11 or #12	1047	—	—	—	—	—	950	—	—	—	$5	NA
22 L.R. Hyper Vel	36	1410	1187	1056	159	113	89	—	—	—	—	$2	NA
22 L.R. Hyper H.P	32/33/34	1500	1240	1075	165	110	85	—	—	—	—	$2	NA
22 WRF	45	1320	—	1055	175	—	111	—	—	—	—	NA	$5
22 Win. Mag.	30	2200	1750	1373	322	203	127	1610	—	—	—	—	NA
22 Win. Mag.	40	1910	1490	1326	324	197	156	1428	—	181	—	$6	NA
22 Win. Mag.	50	1650	—	1280	300	180	—	—	—	—	—	NA	NA
22 Win. Mag. Shot	#11	1126	—	—	—	—	—	—	—	—	—	NA	NA

Note: The actual ballistics obtained with your firearm can vary considerably from the advertised ballistics. Also ballistics can vary from lot to lot with the same brand and type load. Prices can vary with manufacturer and retail outlet. NA in the price column indicates this size packaging currently unavailable.

SHOTSHELL LOADS AND PRICES

Dram Equivalent	Shot Ozs.	Load Style	Shot Sizes	Brands	Avg.Nom. Price /box	Velocity (fps)
10 Gauge 3½" Magnum						
4½	2¼	premium	BB, 2, 4, 6	Win., Fed., Rem.	$33	1205
4¼	2	high velocity	BB, 2, 4	Rem.	$22	1210
4½	2¼	duplex	4x6	Rem.	$14*	1205
Max	18 pellets	premium	00 buck	Fed., Win.	$7**	1100
4¼	1¾	steel	TT, T, BBB, BB, 1, 2, 3	Win., Rem.	$27	1260
Mag	1⅝	steel	T, BBB	Win.	$27	1285
4⅝	1⅝	steel	F, T, BBB	Fed.	$26	1350
Max	1⅜	Steel	BBB, BB	Fed.	NA	1425
Max	1¾	slug, rifled	slug	Fed.	NA	1280
12 Gauge 3½" Magnum						
Max	2¼	premium	4, 6	Fed., Rem., Win.	$13*	1150
Max	18 pellets	premium	00 buck	Fed., Win.	$7**	1100
4⅛	1 9/16	steel	TT, F, T, BBB, BB, 1, 2	Rem., Win., Fed.	$22	1335
Max	1⅜	steel	BBB, BB	Fed.	NA	1450
12 Gauge 3" Magnum						
4	2	premium	BB, 2, 4, 5, 6	Win., Fed., Rem.	$9*	1175
4	2	duplex	4x6	Rem.	$10	1175
4	1⅞	premium	BB, 2, 4, 6	Win., Fed., Rem.	$19	1210
4	1⅞	duplex	4x6	Rem.	$9*	1210
4	1⅝	premium	2, 4, 5, 6	Win., Fed., Rem.	$18	1290
4	24 pellets	buffered	1 buck	Win., Fed., Rem.	$5**	1040
4	15 pellets	buffered	00 buck	Win., Fed., Rem.	$6**	1210
4	10 pellets	buffered	000 buck	Win., Fed., Rem.	$6**	1225
4	41 pellets	buffered	4 buck	Win., Fed., Rem.	$6**	1210
Max	1¼	slug, rifled	slug	Fed.	NA	1600
Max	1 3/16	saboted slug	copper slug	Rem.	NA	1500
Max	1	slug, rifled	slug, magnum	Win., Rem.	$5**	1760
Max	1	saboted slug	slug	Win., Fed.	$10**	1550
3⅝	1⅜	steel	TT, F, T, BBB, BB, 1, 2, 3, 4	Win., Fed., Rem.	$19	1275
Max	1⅛	steel	BBB, BB	Fed.	NA	1450
4	1¼	steel	TT, F, T, BBB, BB, 1, 2, 3, 4, 6	Win., Fed., Rem.	$18	1375
12 gauge 2¾"						
Max	1⅝	magnum	4, 5, 6	Win., Fed.	$8*	1250
3¾	1½	magnum	BB, 2, 4, 5, 6	Win., Fed., Rem.	$16	1260
3¾	1½	duplex	BBx4, 2x4, 2x6, 4x6	Rem.	$9*	1260
3¾	1¼	high velocity	BB, 2, 4, 5, 6, 7½, 8, 9	Win., Fed., Rem.	$13	1330
3½	1¼	mid velocity	7, 8, 9	Win.	Disc.	1275
3¼	1¼	standard velocity	6, 7½, 8, 9	Win., Fed., Rem.	$11	1220
3¼	1⅛	standard velocity	4, 6, 7½, 8, 9	Win., Fed., Rem.	$9	1255
3¼	1	standard velocity	6, 7½, 8	Rem., Fed.	$6	1290
3¼	1¼	target	7½, 8, 9	Win., Fed., Rem.	$10	1220
3	1⅛	duplex target	7½x8	Rem.	NA	1200
3	1⅛	target	7½, 8, 9, 7½x8	Win., Fed., Rem.	$7	1200
3	1⅛	duplex clays	7½x8½	Rem.	NA	1200
2¾	1⅛	target	7½, 8, 8½, 9, 7½x8	Win., Fed., Rem.	$7	1145
2¾	1⅛	duplex target	7½x8	Rem.	NA	1145
2¼	1⅛	target	7½, 8, 8½, 9	Rem., Fed.	$7	1080
3¼	28grams(1oz)	target	7½, 8, 9	Win., Fed., Rem.	$8	1290
3	1	target	7½, 8, 9	Win.	NA	1235
2¾	1	target	7½, 8, 8½, 9	Fed., Rem.	NA	1180
3¼	24grams	target	7½, 8, 9	Fed., Win.	NA	1325
3¾	8 pellets	buffered	000 buck	Win., Fed., Rem.	$4**	1325
4	12 pellets	premium	00 buck	Win., Fed., Rem.	$5**	1290
3¾	9 pellets	buffered	00 buck	Win., Fed., Rem.	$19	1325
3¾	12 pellets	buffered	0 buck	Win., Fed., Rem.	$4**	1275
4	20 pellets	buffered	1 buck	Win., Fed., Rem.	$4**	1075
3¾	16 pellets	buffered	1 buck	Win., Fed., Rem.	$4**	1250
4	34 pellets	premium	4 buck	Fed., Rem.	$5**	1250
3¾	27 pellets	buffered	4 buck	Win., Fed., Rem.	$4**	1325
Max	1	saboted slug	slug	Win., Fed., Rem.	$10**	1450
Max	1¼	slug, rifled	slug	Fed.	NA	1520
Max	1	slug, rifled	slug, magnum	Rem.	$5**	1680
Max	1	slug, rifled	slug	Win., Fed., Rem.	$4**	1610
3	1⅛	steel target	6½, 7	Rem.	NA	1200
2¾	1⅛	steel target	7, 8	Rem.	NA	1145
3	1#	steel	7	Win.	$11	1235
3½	1¼	steel	T, BBB, BB, 1, 2, 3, 4, 5, 6	Win., Fed., Rem.	$18	1275
3¾	1⅛	steel	BB, 1, 2, 3, 4, 5, 6	Win., Fed., Rem.	$16	1365
3¾	1	steel	2, 3, 4, 5, 6	Win., Fed., Rem.	$13	1390
16 Gauge 2¾"						
3¼	1¼	magnum	2, 4, 6	Fed., Rem.	$16	1260
3¼	1⅛	high velocity	4, 6, 7½	Win., Fed., Rem.	$12	1295
2¾	1⅛	standard velocity	6, 7½, 8	Fed., Rem.	$9	1185
Max	15/16	steel	2, 4	Fed., Rem.	NA	1300
Max	⅞	steel	2, 4	Win.	$16	1300
3	12 pellets	buffered	1 buck	Win., Fed., Rem.	$4**	1225
Max	⅘	slug, rifled	slug	Win., Fed., Rem.	$4**	1570
20 Gauge 3" Magnum						
3	1¼	premium	2, 4, 6, 7½	Win., Fed., Rem.	$15	1185
Max	18 pellets	buck shot	2 buck	Fed.	NA	1200
Max	24 pellets	buffered	3 buck	Win.	$5**	1150
2¾	20 pellets	buck	3 buck	Rem.	$4**	1200
3¼	1	steel	1, 2, 3, 4, 5, 6	Win., Fed., Rem.	$15	1330
Mag.	⅝	saboted slug	275 gr.	Fed.	NA	1450
20 Gauge 2¾"						
2¾	1⅛	magnum	4, 6, 7½	Win., Fed., Rem.	$14	1175
2¾	1	high velocity	4, 5, 6, 7½, 8, 9	Win., Fed., Rem.	$12	1220
2½	1	standard velocity	6, 7½, 8	Win., Rem., Fed.	$6	1165
2½	⅞	clays	8	Rem.	NA	1200
2½	⅞	promotional	6, 7½, 8	Win., Rem.	$6	1210
2½	1#	target	8, 9	Win., Rem.	$8	1165
2½	⅞	target	8, 9	Win., Fed., Rem.	$8	1200
Max	20 pellets	buffered	3 buck	Win., Fed.	$4	1200
Max	⅝	slug, saboted	slug	Win.	$9**	1400
2¾	⅝	slug, rifled	slug	Rem.	$4**	1580
Max	¾	saboted slug	copper slug	Rem.	NA	1450
Max	¾	slug, rifled	slug	Win., Fed., Rem.	$4**	1570
Max	¾	steel	2, 3, 4, 6	Win., Fed., Rem.	$14	1425
28 Gauge 2¾"						
2	1	high velocity	6, 7½, 8	Win.	$12	1125
2¼	¾	high velocity	6, 7½, 8	Win., Fed., Rem.	$11	1295
2	¾	target	8, 9	Win., Fed., Rem.	$9	1200
410 Bore 3"						
Max	11/16	high velocity	4, 5, 6, 7½, 8, 9	Win., Fed., Rem.	$10	1135
410 Bore 2½"						
Max	½	high velocity	4, 6, 7½	Win., Fed., Rem.	$9	1245
Max	⅕	slug, rifled	slug	Win., Fed., Rem.	$4**	1815
1½	½	target	8½, 9	Win., Fed., Rem.	$8	1200

NOTES: * = 10 rounds per box. ** = 5 rounds per box. Pricing variations and number of rounds per box can occur with type and brand of ammunition. Listed pricing is the average nominal cost for load style and box quantity shown. Not every brand is available in all shot size variations. Some manufacturers do not provide suggested list prices. All prices rounded to nearest whole dollar. The price you pay will vary dependent upon outlet of purchase. # = new load spec this year; "C" indicates a change in data.

CAUTION: PRICES SHOWN ARE SUPPLIED BY THE MANUFACTURER OR IMPORTER. CHECK YOUR LOCAL GUNSHOP.

Shooter's Marketplace

ADJUSTABLE DISC APERTURE

Hunters in the field are constantly faced with continually changing light conditions. A receiver sight with a fixed aperture is adequate for only one light condition.

The Merit Hunting Disc aperture is instantly adjustable from .025- to .155-inch in diameter, allowing a clear sight picture to be maintained under changing light conditions.

The aperture leaves are supported to withstand recoil from heavy calibers, and the shank is tapered to provide solid lockup of the disc to your receiver sight.

Contact Merit Corporation for a free copy of their brochure describing this and other sighting aids for shooters.

MERIT CORPORATION

SELF-ADHESIVE RECOIL PAD

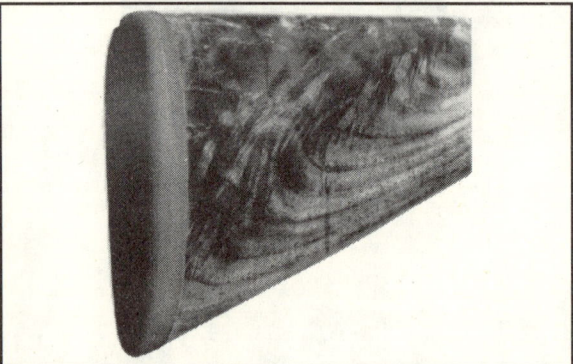

Add-A-Pad, for rifles or shotguns, can be installed in minutes by simply pressing a pad on the end of the butt, trimming it with a sharp knife and then sanding it to the exact shape of the stock.

Add-A-Pad is made from a shock-absorbent blended neoprene with a specially formulated adhesive backing.

The package includes two 1/4" and one 1/2" pads, allowing the use of any one pad or a combination of pads to build a recoil pad up to 1" thick. The result is an economical pad which looks professionally installed.

Add-A-Pad costs $10.95 and comes with complete installation instructions. Call or write Palsa Outdoor Products for more information.

PALSA OUTDOOR PRODUCTS

SHOOTING GLASSES APERTURE

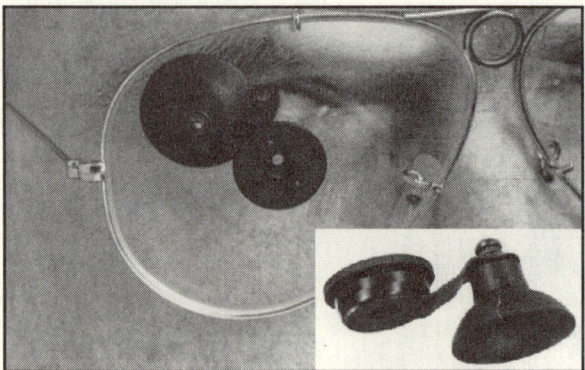

Pistol shooters are able to see their sights and target clearly with the Merit Optical Attachment and its instantly adjustable diameter aperture.

An aperture (pinhole) increases the eyes' depth of field (range of focus) dramatically.

The Merit Optical Attachment is instantly adjustable from .022- to .156-inch in diameter to accommodate different light conditions. Thus the sights and target remain in clear focus.

Additionally, using an aperture improves a shooter's concentration by helping maintain a consistent head position. This device works equally well with bifocals, trifocals and plain-lensed shooting glasses.

Contact Merit Corporation for a free brochure.

MERIT CORPORATION

See manufacturers' addresses on page 299.

Shooter's Marketplace

COMPACT PISTOL REST

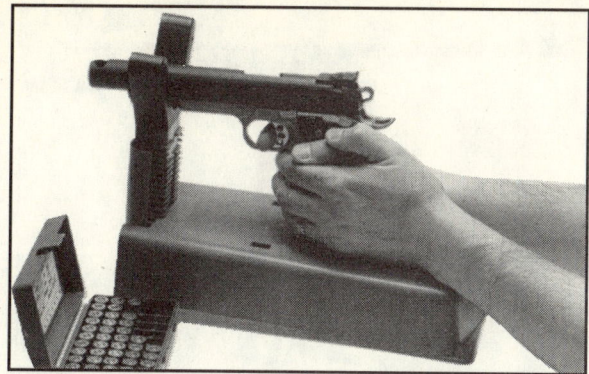

The PR-30 from MTM® Case-Gard is a fully adjustable, all-plastic pistol rest versatile enough to accommodate small and large handguns from derringers to 14" Contenders.

The base of the rest is 6" x 11" and stands 2.5" high. It locks into the fork at 20 different positions, allowing it to be lowered or raised for a variety of handgun sizes.

The rubber padded fork protects handgun barrels from marring during use. When not in use, the fork clips into the bottom of the base for compact storage.

Made of tough polypropylene, this lightweight, red pistol rest can also be used as a front rifle rest. For more information, contact MTM.

MTM MOLDED PRODUCTS CO., INC.

NEW SEE-THROUGH SCOPE MOUNT

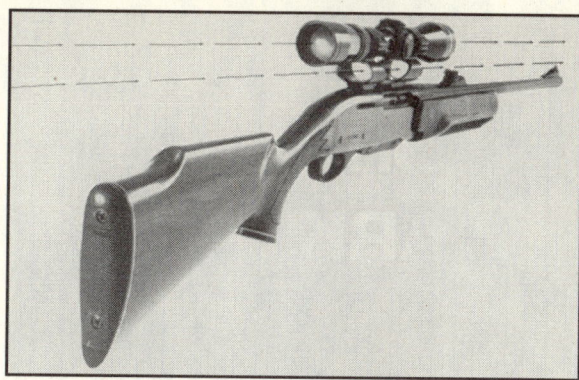

The Ironsighter Company introduced the patented Ironsighter® "See-Thru" scope mount line in 1967. Today, the Ironsighter two-way sighting option is accepted as standard. The new Wide Ironsighters are their very latest development. The new 700 series Ironsighters are now available for most centerfire, rimfire and muzzle-loading rifles as well as many handguns and shotguns.

Ironsighter offers a superior aluminum alloy which is stronger than the materials found in similar products. When combined with solid engineering designs, added metal thickness in high-stress areas, and precision-machined contact surfaces, Ironsighter mounts will withstand the heaviest types of use.

IRONSIGHTER CO.

FREE CATALOG OFFER

The MTM® Case-Gard catalog offers products for pistol and rifle enthusiasts, reloaders, shotgunners, small-bore shooters, law enforcement officers, benchresters and bowhunters.

This year's catalog features the PR-30, a fully adjustable, compact, all-plastic pistol benchrest that can be used to sight-in handguns as small as a derringer or as large as a T/C Contender. Also featured is MTM's HL-95 handloader's log which contains more than 150 pages for detailed data recording with special areas devoted to benchrest shooters and firearms inventory.

MTM Case-Gard, a leading manufacturer of ammo boxes, also offers a variety of other items for the hunter, competition shooter and camper.

Write MTM for a free catalog.

MTM MOLDED PRODUCTS CO., INC.

NEW BLACKPOWDER SCOPE MOUNT

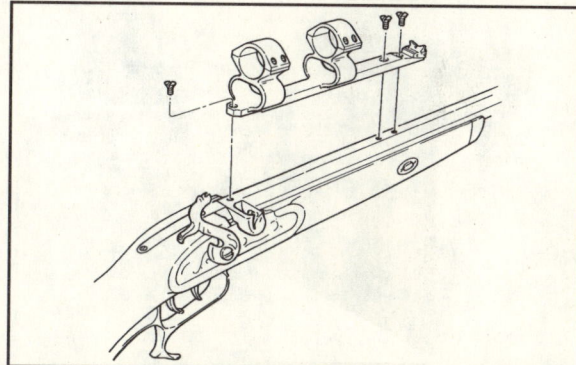

Recent innovations from the Ironsighter company include the new Ironsighter® 365, 375 and 385 Black Powder Scope Mounts for popular 1991 and later Thompson/Center rifles.

This unique product design, which attaches to factory-drilled holes on the barrel, offers an adjustable rear sight, see-through scope rings and mounting base which are precision-machined from a single piece of high-strength alloy. The result is a product designed for stability and durability. As the lead product in the recently expanding line of Ironsighter no-gunsmithing blackpowder scope mounts, each of these new Ironsighters provides superior strength and mounting stability.

Write for a catalog and serial number list of drilled and tapped T/C barrels.

IRONSIGHTER CO.

See manufacturers' addresses on page 299.

Shooter's Marketplace

SHOTGUN SADDLE MOUNTS

B-Square Shotgun Saddle Mounts are now available for most popular 12-gauge guns. These newly designed mounts straddle the receiver and fit the top of the gun tightly. All mounts have a standard dovetail base and "see-thru" design, allowing for continued use of the gun's sight. Standard dovetail rings can be used.

B-Square shotgun mounts do not require gunsmithing, have a blued finish and attach to the gun's side with included hardware. Saddle mounts are available for Remington 870/1100; Mossberg 500, 5500 and 835; Winchester 1400/1300/1200; Ithaca 37/87; and Browning A-5 shotguns.

The mounts retail for $49.95 at your local dealer, or call B-Square toll-free. A catalog featuring the complete line of B-Square products is available upon request.

B-SQUARE COMPANY, INC.

NEW BIPOD MODELS

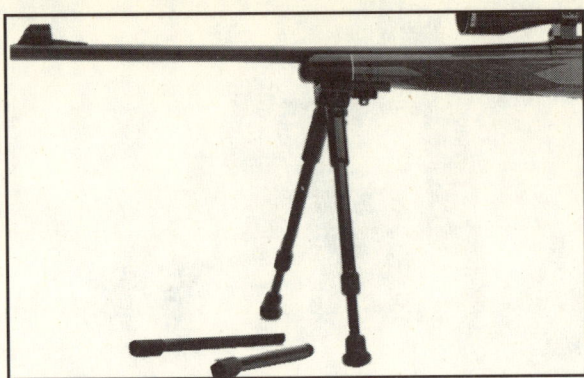

B-Square bipods are offered in several models.

The Rigid Bipod provides strong support and is available with swivel stud "Sporter" or barrel clamp "Service" attachment.

The Tilt Bipod offers rigid support and cants from side to side for fine tuning aim. Tilt Bipods are also available with swivel stud or barrel clamp attachment.

The Roto-Tilt provides that same support and side-to-side canting, but also swivels in a 30-degree angle, enabling shooters to follow perfectly aimed shots. It is available with swivel stud or barrel clamp attachment.

All B-Square bipods are available in blue or stainless finish and feature an Unlimited Leg Extension System with 7" leg extenders, sold separately.

B-SQUARE COMPANY, INC.

COMPETITION GEAR

B-Square has a shooting accessory line for competitive shooters.

Mounting systems are currently available for CZ 75/Tanfoglio and Colt/Para Ordnance 1911 handguns. The mounts attach to tapped holes on the side of the gun. All standard optical sight and dovetail rings can be used. Drill jigs for each model can be purchased to ensure perfect installation of the sight mount.

Slide pulls and magazine bumpers for race guns are also available from B-Square.

Competition mounts retail for $99.50 at your local dealer, or call B-Square toll-free. A catalog featuring the complete line of their products is available for $2.00.

B-SQUARE COMPANY, INC.

CHOKE TUBE SPEED WRENCH

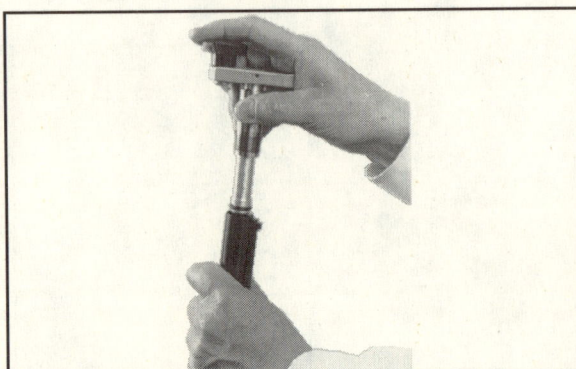

The Texas Twister© Choke Tube Speed Wrench from B-Square is currently available for most 12-gauge shotguns.

The wrench inserts into the choke tube so it can be cranked out of the bore and has a bore guide to prevent crooked starts and damaged threads. The T-handle is designed to break stubborn tubes loose so they can be cranked out quickly and easily.

Texas Twister wrenches are available for Briley, Beretta, Browning, Mossberg, Weatherby, Remington, Ruger, SKB and Winchester 12-gauge shotguns.

Retail price is $24.95 at your local dealer, or call B-Square toll-free. A catalog featuring the complete line of B-Square products is available upon request.

B-SQUARE COMPANY, INC.

See manufacturers' addresses on page 299.

Shooter's Marketplace

GUNSMITHING SCREWDRIVER

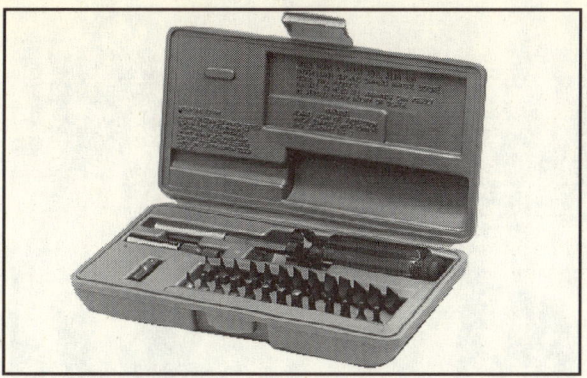

B-Square offers a new addition to their long line of gunsmithing tools for the professional and hobbyist—the Gunsmith Screwdriver.

The Gunsmith Screwdriver features hardened, gunsmith ground bits for work on the firearms of such manufacturers as Smith & Wesson, Colt, Ruger, Remington, Browning and many others.

The ergonomically designed handle provides non-slip gripping for 'smithing work and doubles as a convenient storage area for the screwdriver bits. The tool comes complete in an attractive B-Square storage box.

See your local dealer or call toll-free, write or fax B-Square for a catalog of their entire line of quality gunsmithing tools.

B-SQUARE COMPANY, INC.

NO-GUNSMITHING SCOPE MOUNTS

B-Square offers a complete line of scope mounts for pistols, revolvers, shotguns, sporting rifles and military rifles. Installation of any B-Square scope mount is simple and requires no gunsmithing.

Most mounts feature a "see-thru" standard dovetail base which accepts all standard dovetail (Weaver) rings. Scope mounts are available in blued and stainless finish and come with socket head screws.

New mounts are always being developed at B-Square. For additional information, ask your dealer or call B-Square toll-free. A 32-page catalog featuring the complete line of products is available for $2.00.

B-SQUARE COMPANY, INC.

COMPACT MINI LASERS

The Compact Mini Laser from B-Square is only 1.1"x1.1"x.6" and delivers 5mW of power (Class IIIa) while operating on common A76 size batteries (lithium or alkaline). Visibility with the Mini Laser is 1.0" at 25 yards.

The laser makes use of an omnidirectional screw-type aiming method with windage and elevation adjustments and has an "Aim-Lock" feature. Moisture-proof and shock-resistant, it comes with a lifetime warranty.

Mounting systems are available for long guns and handguns. Their vertical T-slot design makes them quick-detachable and ensures no change in zero.

For more information or a catalog, see your local dealer or call B-Square toll-free.

B-SQUARE COMPANY, INC.

GUNSMITH TOOLS

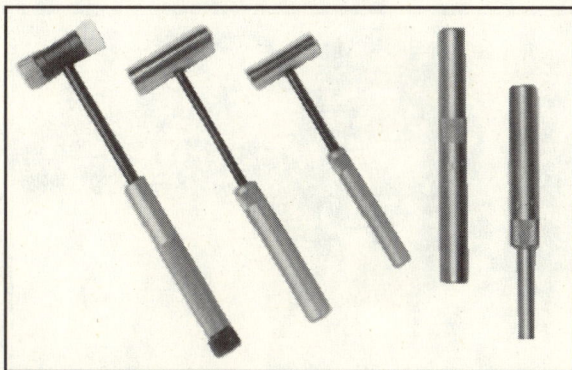

B-Square brass hammers and punches are known for their design and quality.

For the professional and hobby gunsmith, solid brass-headed hammers are perfect for dent removal and setting work in machine vises.

They provide the right sensitivity and feel for gunsmithing and other delicate jobs. Hammers are available in three weights: 2.5 ounces, 5 ounces and 10 ounces.

B-Square solid brass drifts are used for driving out gunsights and large pins without damage. The set of two knurled $1/4$" diameter and $3/8$" diameter punches retails for $9.95 at your local dealer.

Call B-Square toll-free for a catalog featuring their complete line of tools and accessories.

B-SQUARE COMPANY, INC.

See manufacturers' addresses on page 299.

Shooter's Marketplace

NEW PORTABLE KNIFE SHARPENER

The Diamond Mini-Sharp™ knife sharpener is now available from Diamond Machining Technology (DMT). With its 70mm (2¾″) monocrystalline diamond sharpening surface, which bears the familiar DMT polka dot pattern, this highly portable tool rapidly restores knife blades to razor edge sharpness. The Mini-Sharp can be used dry or with a few drops of water for lubrication.

Weighing just over 1-ounce, the Mini-Sharp is about the size of a shotgun shell and can be attached to accessory loops and zipper pulls, carried loose or used as a key chain. The handle folds for protected storage.

Retailing for around $10.00, the Mini-Sharp will maximize the performance of quality edge cutlery, broadheads and even fish hooks. Contact DMT for a full-line catalog of their U.S.-made precision products.

DIAMOND MACHINING TECHNOLOGY, INC.

RANGE-FINDING SCOPE

Shepherd Scope offers a German-design Speed Focus eyepiece that provides razor sharp images with a twist of the rear ring.

The eyepiece remains rock solid throughout focusing and zooming.

Also available is an adjustable objective lens housing which will accept Shepherd Scope's sunshade. The scopes have a scratch-resistant 340 hard matte finish.

All scopes have Shepherd's patented dual reticle system that provides one-shot zeroing, instant range finding, bullet drop and constant visual verification of the original zero.

Call, write or fax Shepherd Scope direct for a free brochure.

SHEPHERD SCOPE LTD.

CUSTOM RESTORATION/CASE COLORING

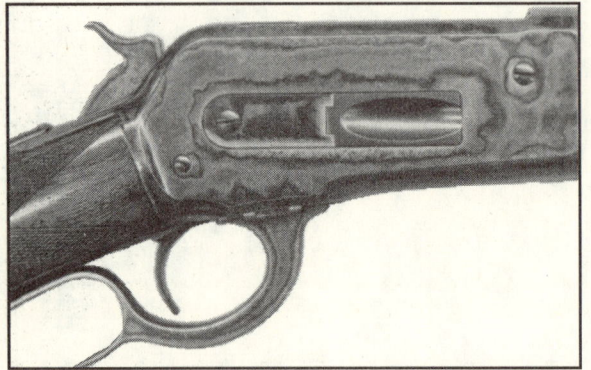

Doug Turnbull Restoration continues to offer bone charcoal color case work plus nitre and charcoal bluing. Turnbull will match the original case colors produced by Winchester, Colt, Marlin, Parker, L.C. Smith, Ansley Fox and other noted manufacturers, without reassembly problems. Also available is charcoal blue, known as Carbona or machine blue, a prewar finish used by most makers. In addition, Turnbull now offers new Winchester 94, 94-22, Ruger SA and Browning Citori guns, all case-colored using Turnbull's traditional process. Turnbull offers production work with single run control. He will restore partially or completely. Pre-polished parts can also be sent in for finish work. Send your gun to Turnbull for complete metal and wood preparation and finish.

DOUG TURNBULL RESTORATION

CUSTOM GUN RAFFLE

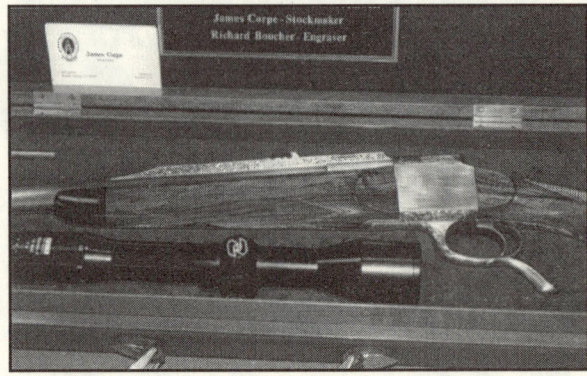

This January at the annual American Custom Gunmakers (ACGG) & Firearms Engravers Guild joint exhibition, the ACGG will raffle off a rifle commemorating the late John T. Amber. A connoisseur of fine custom guns and a supporter of the custom gun industry, Amber was Editor-in-Chief of GUN DIGEST from 1950 to 1978. The 1996 Amber commemorative is based on a Hagn action in 8x68S and scoped with a Zeiss 1.5x6. Metalwork by Mark Cromwell, Mark Silver and Joe Bautz; stock work by James Corpe; and engraving by Richard Boucher. It comes complete with turn-screws, oil bottle and patch box by John Hackley in a case crafted by Marvin Huey. For raffle ticket information or ACGG Directory of Services, contact the Executive Director or any member of the ACGG. Three thousand tickets at $20.00 each are available.

AMERICAN CUSTOM GUNMAKERS GUILD

See manufacturers' addresses on page 299.

Shooter's Marketplace

CUSTOM REPAIR AND PARTS

High Standard offers full custom repair and tuning of all High Standard target pistols, including HD and Slant Grip models as well as all military models. All repair work is performed at their factory in Houston, Texas, and usually takes about a week.

Repair services offered range from welding or replacing cracked frames on Old Connecticut pistols to refinishing, replacing parts and customizing a pistol for competitive matches.

Replacement parts and 22 Short Conversion Kits are now available from High Standard authorized dealers or directly from their national parts distributor, G.W. Elliott, Inc. in East Hartford, Connecticut.

For more information, see your local authorized retailer or call High Standard direct.

HIGH STANDARD MANUFACTURING COMPANY, INC.

TOURNAMENT SERIES PISTOL

The Supermatic Tournament® Series from High Standard is an excellent choice for entry into serious bullseye target competition.

One of the most successful production models ever manufactured by High Standard, the 22-caliber Supermatic features the same micro-adjustable rear sight as the more expensive models, but with the sight attached directly to the slide.

The Supermatic is available in three barrel lengths, $4^{1}/_{2}''$, $5^{1}/_{2}''$ and $6^{3}/_{4}''$, has a non-adjustable trigger and comes in Parkerized blue finish. Retail price for the Supermatic is $395.00, an excellent value for beginning shooters.

For more information, see your local authorized retailer or call High Standard direct.

HIGH STANDARD MANUFACTURING COMPANY, INC.

POPULAR TARGET PISTOLS

The Supermatic Trophy® and Citation® Series pistols manufactured by High Standard are their most popular target guns.

The Trophy Series pistol with all-American craftsmanship features a high-polish finish and gold-plated components. It has a fully adjustable sight, securely mounted to a bracket on the frame. For customizing, the Trophy is available in two barrel lengths and with barrel weights and a detachable muzzlebrake.

The Citation Series pistol is similar in function and finish to the Trophy except for the trigger pull, and the nickel accents which complete the classic look of this target pistol. The Citation is also available with 10" barrel. The suggested retail price of these pistols, depending on the model, ranges from $425 to $536.

HIGH STANDARD MANUFACTURING COMPANY, INC.

ACCURATE TARGET PISTOL

The Victor™ from High Standard is among the finest target pistols currently available.

The Victor comes with a barrel-mounted sighting system for shot-to-shot accuracy and is available with an aluminum rib or a new scope mount rib without sights for mounting your preferred optics.

The trigger is adjustable for weight and travel, and the rear sight is micro-click adjustable for windage and elevation. Various custom options are available, including a steel rib, barrel weights and a 22 Short Conversion Kit.

The suggested retail price of the Victor is $532.

For more information, see your local authorized retailer or call High Standard direct.

HIGH STANDARD MANUFACTURING COMPANY, INC.

See manufacturers' addresses on page 299.

Shooter's Marketplace

LINSEED RUBBING OIL

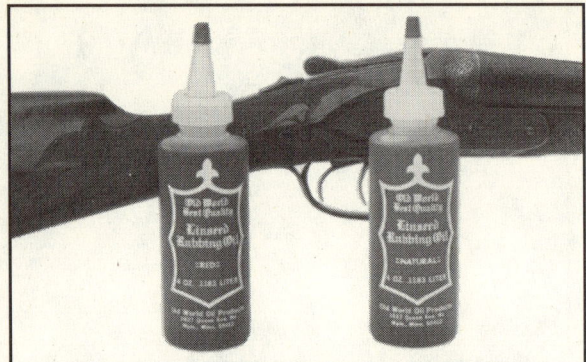

Old World Oil Products has been offering best-quality linseed oil for over a decade. Long recognized as *the* professional gun stock finish, linseed oil brings out the full character and quality of a walnut gun stock.

This linseed oil is available in red or amber shades and is perfect for the expert refinishing of old gun lumber or the complete and total enhancement of a brand new gun stock.

This product is also ideal for maintaining original, oil-finished stocks.

Each bottle of linseed oil comes complete with instructions. Simply send $8.00 for a 4-oz. bottle of red or amber Old World Linseed Oil. Catalogs are not available.

OLD WORLD OIL PRODUCTS

COMPUTER BALLISTICS PROGRAM

The Modern Ballistics Program from FlashTek evaluates data quickly, easily and accurately. Shooters can look at drop, muzzle velocity and muzzle energy at various shooting distances; view the effects ballistic coefficents have on point-blank target size or time of flight; generate tables and plots showing the effects of changing the zero range on point-blank size; and plot the effects of muzzle velocity on windage and time of flight. The program will also generate tables to show the effects of sighting-in at sea level using one type of ammo and shooting different ammo in the same gun in the mountains. Hundreds of popular bullets are included. Shooters can build databases of guns, ammo and shooting conditions to suit individual needs.

FLASHTEK, INC.

GUN PARTS CATALOG

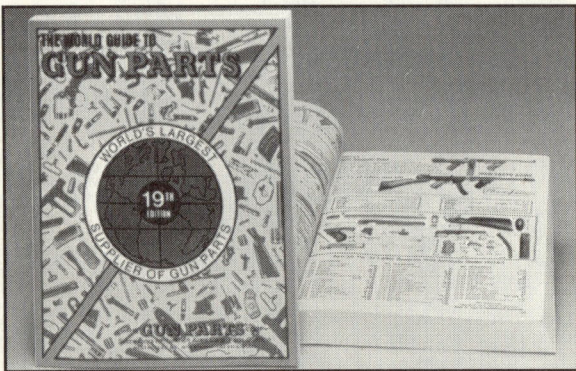

The Gun Parts Corp. is one of the world's largest suppliers of gun parts, and this year introduces its newly updated 19th Edition Catalog—a standard reference for gunsmiths, shooters, collectors and for military organizations worldwide.

Its 700-plus pages contain complete listings and prices for more than 450 million gun parts currently in stock.

Machinegun, military, U.S., foreign, commercial and antique gun parts are included, as well as hundreds of schematic drawings.

To order, U.S. customers send $7.95; foreign surface mail orders $13.00; airmail delivery $25.00.

THE GUN PARTS CORP.

SELF-ADHESIVE TARGETS

N.B.B., Inc. offers a wide variety of Post-it® Targets for the competitive shooter or plinker as well as shotgun hunter wanting to pattern his shotgun.

Their 28-page four-color wholesale catalog contains a broad selection of self-adhesive and removable targets that will stick to any dry, clean surface such as cardboard or even other targets. All targets come with either two or four stripes of Post-it glue.

In all, 28 types of targets are offered to include: 4″ and 8″ bullseyes; professional sight-in targets; police silhouettes; gangsters with replaceable kill zones; bar room and alley scenes with stick-on bottles, cans and rats; and turkey and duck shotgun patterning targets.

For more information, contact N.B.B. Dealer inquiries welcome.

N.B.B., INC.

SHOOTER'S MARKETPLACE

NEW ULTRA LASER SIGHTS

Quarton USA is now offering the Beamshot™ 1000S and 1000U laser sights. The 650nm 1000 Super is five times brighter than standard Beamshot Lasersights; the 635nm 1000 Ultra is ten times brighter for long-range visibility range of 800 yards. Both laser sights are powered by a single 3-volt lithium battery, providing up to 20 hours of continuous usage.

Made of aircraft-grade 6061 aluminum, both lasersights have a window lens, are available in black or silver, have windage and elevation adjustments and come with mounts for rifle, pistol, revolver, shotgun or crossbow. The 1000S and 1000U are easily holstered and come with a 1-year warranty. Longer cable switches are available. Call, write or fax Quarton USA for a free copy of their brochure.

QUARTON USA, LTD. CO.

NEW BORE SIGHTING KIT

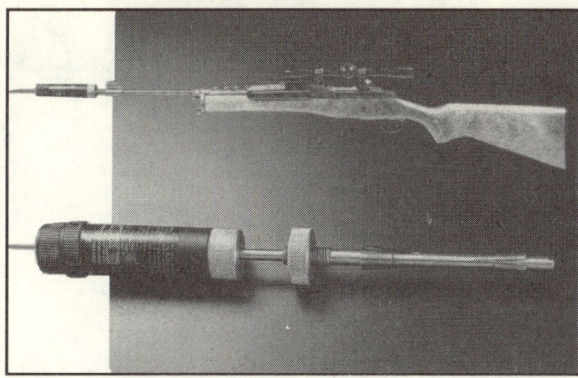

A new high-tech Laser Bore Sighting Kit is now available from Quarton USA, manufacturers of the Beamshot™ line of laser sights.

The kit consists of three parts, available either in kit form or sold separately. The three parts are the Arbor #1, for .22″ through .264″ diameter bullets; the Arbor #2, for .264″ through .308″ diameter bullets; and the bore sight laser.

This Laser Bore Sighting Kit provides an easy, inexpensive way to bore sight a rifle before taking it to the range. Sighting-in before you get to the range saves both time and ammunition.

For more information about any of their products or for a free copy of their brochure, contact Quarton USA.

QUARTON USA, LTD. CO.

NEW LONG-RANGE LASER SIGHT

The Beamshot™ 1000 from Quarton USA is a long-range laser sight precision-engineered for acute accuracy and performance plus rugged durability. Constructed of aircraft-grade 6061 aluminum, the Beamshot's pin-point laser sight is activated by an adjustable pressure switch mounted on the handgrip. With a single 3-volt lithium battery providing up to 20 hours of continuous use, the super lightweight 1000 has 670nm wave length, windage and elevation adjustments and range to 300 yards. It is easily holstered, is available in black or silver and comes with a 1-year warranty. The Beamshot 1000 comes standard with one mount. Easily interchangeable, extra mounts may be purchased to fit most any pistol, revolver, rifle, shotgun, crossbow or compound bow. Call, write or fax Quarton USA for a free copy of their brochure.

QUARTON USA, LTD. CO.

NEW MINIATURE LASER SIGHT

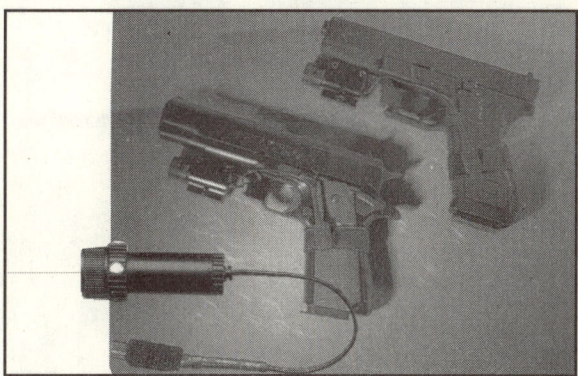

Quarton USA introduces the newest member of its Beamshot™ laser sight family. The Beamshot 3000S represents a high-quality laser sight in a more convenient, miniature model. The ultra lightweight 3000S adds only 2 ounces of total weight to any large or small gun and is powered with three SR44 silver oxide watch batteries to allow for a minimum of four hours of continuous usage. Constructed from aircraft-grade aluminum, the 3000S is adjustable for windage and elevation and has a range to 500 yards. Complete with black finish and window lens, the 3000S fits existing Beamshot mounts and is easily holstered. This Beamshot laser sight comes with a 1-year limited warranty. Contact Quarton USA for a free copy of their brochure.

QUARTON USA, LTD. CO.

See manufacturers' addresses on page 299.

Shooter's Marketplace

NYLON COATED GUN CLEANING RODS

J. Dewey cleaning rods have been used by the U.S. Olympic shooting team and the benchrest community for over 20 years. These one-piece, spring-tempered, steel-base rods will not gall delicate rifling or damage the muzzle area of front-cleaned firearms. The nylon coating eliminates the problem of abrasives adhering to the rod during the cleaning operation. Each rod comes with a hard non-breakable plastic handle supported by ball-bearings, top and bottom, for ease of cleaning.

The brass cleaning jags are designed to pierce the center of the cleaning patch or wrap around the knurled end to keep the patch centered in the bore.

Coated rods are available from 17-caliber to shotgun bore size in several lengths to meet the needs of any shooter. Write for more information.

J. DEWEY MFG. CO., INC.

NEW MUZZLE-LOADING RIFLE

Prairie River Arms offers a unique bullpup-style, thumbhole-stock blackpowder rifle.

With an overall length of only 32", the Bullpup features a full-length 28" barrel. Locating the barrel directly over the stock gives the rifle excellent balance and optimum control, and the shallow 1:28" twist rifling contributes to its fine accuracy. The patented ignition system is housed entirely within the gun stock, protecting the shooter from cap fragmentation by deflecting debris down and away from the face. Available in 50- and 54-caliber, the rifle features two built-in safeties, one takedown screw and only two moving parts. The scope is optional. To receive a free catalog and price list, call or write to Prairie River and mention *Shooter's Marketplace*.

PRAIRIE RIVER ARMS LIMITED

ADJUSTABLE BORE SAVER ROD GUIDES

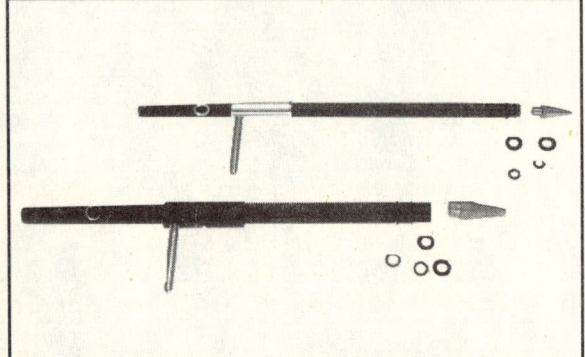

The Dewey Bore Saver cleaning rod guide replaces the bolt in your action while cleaning. The cleaning rod enters the bore straight, without harming the chamber or throat. Made from anodized aluminum in six bore sizes, the Delrin rod guide collar with threaded brass adjustment pin allows for quick adjustment to any bolt length. Chamber-sealing O-rings prohibit solvents from entering the action, trigger and magazine areas. On some rifles, the bolt stop will retain the rod guide by using the groove on the guide collar.

The guide can be used with all cleaning rods; all models fit .695- to .700-inch bolt diameter rifles. All guides allow brush clearance through tube I.D. and come with spare O-rings and O-ring assembly tool. Weatherby models available. Write for information.

J. DEWEY MFG. CO., INC.

STRESS RELIEF BARREL TEMPERING

Cryo-Accurizing, a Division of 300° Below, Inc., offers deep Cryogenic tempering for barrel stress relief.

The key to the increased accuracy long sought after by precision shooters and hunters alike is a reduction in residual stresses on the barrel. Often uneven and random, such stresses are inevitable in any given piece of steel. As a barrel heats, it warps off-axis.

Deep Cryogenic tempering is an effective method to help counteract the effects of barrel stress, providing both stress relief and dimensional stabilization. The results—improved accuracy and longer barrel life.

Other advantages of this unique tempering process are significant increases in abrasive wear resistance and durability.

For more information, call or write Cryo-Accurizing.

CRYO-ACCURIZING, DIV. OF 300° BELOW, INC.

See manufacturers' addresses on page 299.

SHOOTER'S MARKETPLACE

HOME-DEFENSE LASER SIGHT

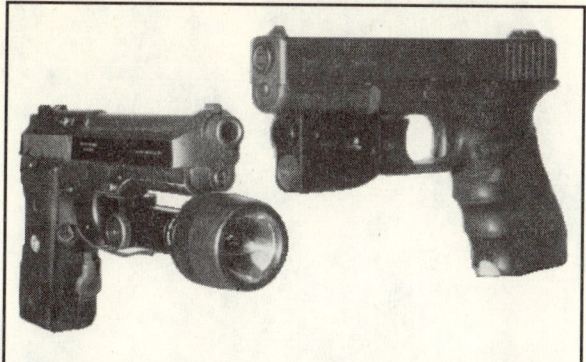

Laser Devices has recently introduced its latest interchangeable laser and flashlight combination. Simply install their Universal Laser Mount onto your pistol. This dove-tailed trigger guard mount adapts to both the UL laser system or TLS-4P flashlight. The flashlight is quick-detachable, has a long-life Xenon bulb with high brightness and provides 2.5 hours of continuous battery life. Mounting the UL laser system requires no modifications to the pistol and its external windage and elevation adjustments make it easy to adjust. The laser can be turned on or off with a conveniently located toggle switch. This laser/flashlight combination is available at a special price when purchased together. For an instruction video and/or catalog, contact Laser Devices and mention *Shooter's Marketplace*.

LASER DEVICES, INC.

PREMIUM BULLET MOULDS

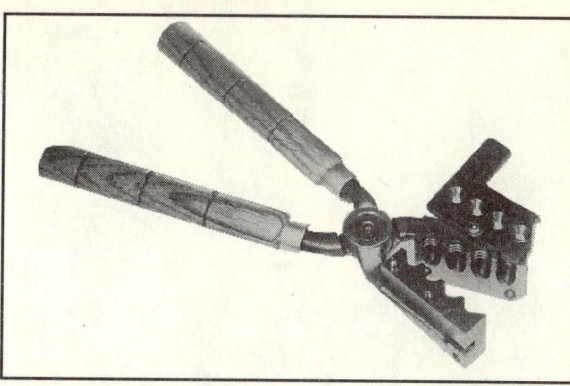

SAECO has long been regarded as one of the premier names in production bullet moulds by knowledgeable casters.

Several years ago, Redding Reloading purchased the remains of the old SAECO Reloading Company and is now producing the SAECO bullet mould line.

Redding has been constantly refining and adding to the lineup of sizes and styles to choose from and offers two-cavity and four-cavity blocks as standard items. Single-, three-, six- and eight-cavity moulds are also available on special order.

When you write or call Redding Reloading for a free catalog of SAECO products, be sure to mention you read about the SAECO lineup in *Shooter's Marketplace*.

REDDING RELOADING EQUIPMENT

AMBIDEXTROUS HANDGUN LASER

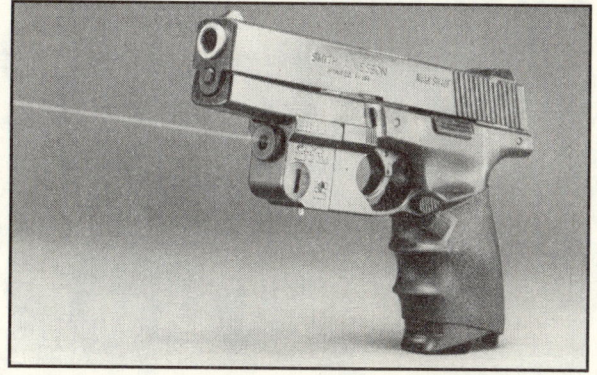

The BA-1 laser sight's ergonomic design allows it to perform flawlessly with the movements of the handgunner. Upgraded, sophisticated and easy to install, the BA-1 has been computer-designed to fit each handgun without any modification, while still remaining field-strippable. The ambidextrous bottom toggle switch allows turning the unit on and off while leaving a finger on the trigger. An optional slip-on Hogue grip with a pressure-sensitive switch is also available. The BA-1 is a true 5mW output and available with daytime laser diode. Laser Devices also offers leather duty holsters at a special price when laser and holster are purchased together. For an instruction video and/or catalog, contact Laser Devices and mention *Shooter's Marketplace*.

LASER DEVICES, INC.

SPECIALTY RELOADING DIES

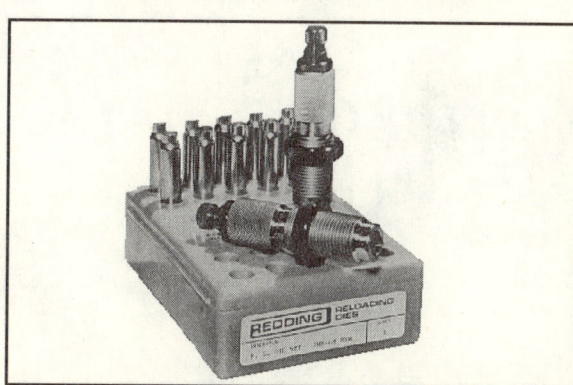

Redding Reloading has built a reputation equal to the quality of the reloading gear they produce, and they continue to expand their line of reloading dies that are available from stock.

The latest catalog from Redding lists dies for over 400 different calibers and a whole host of special-purpose dies. There are neck-sizing dies, benchrest competition dies, special-purpose crimping dies, trim dies, custom-made dies and a section on case forming that lists what is needed to form one caliber from another.

If you have something you've always wanted to shoot, or if you're contemplating building up a wildcat, contact Redding Reloading and they'll be happy to supply the dies.

REDDING RELOADING EQUIPMENT

See manufacturers' addresses on page 299.

Shooter's Marketplace

NEW WATERPROOFING PRODUCTS

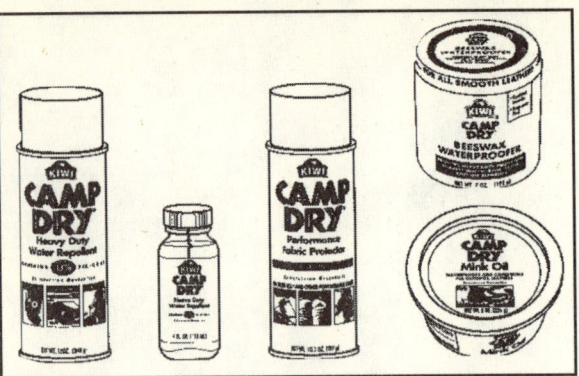

The Kiwi Camp Dry offers a wide range of outdoor care products for waterproofing boots, apparel and accessories.

Their line includes Heavy Duty Water Repellent with silicone in liquid or aerosol spray for waterproofing tents, backpacks, heavy-duty boots and hunting apparel. New this year is Performance Fabric Protector, an aerosol spray to protect all fabrics, including nylon, canvas and Gore-Tex® from water, dirt and oily stains. Mink Oil and Beeswax Waterproofer, two traditional waterproofing products, soften and extend the life of all leathers while they protect. The Kiwi Camp Dry line is used by outdoor enthusiasts to reliably protect their gear from the elements. All products are unconditionally guaranteed and available in sporting goods and outdoor specialty stores.

KIWI BRANDS INC.

CASE GAUGE

The NECO Concentricity, Wall Thickness and Runout Gauge™ identifies and measures the imperfections in brass cartridge cases, case head squareness, bullets and loaded ammunition. It verifies possible accuracy problems caused by imperfections in rifle chambers, sizing and bullet seating dies and/or reloading techniques. Handmade to precision tolerances from solid stainless steel and hard-anodized aluminum, it is equipped with a Gem Model 222 all-angle dial indicator, two removable guides for bullet tips, two step cones for empty cases, a chord anvil for case wall thickness measurements and an instruction manual. Standard model handles 22 to 45-70 cartridge cases (17-caliber and 50 BMG models also available) and retails for $137.15 plus shipping.

NECO/NOSTALGIA ENTERPRISES COMPANY

NEW SHOTSHELL HANDBOOK

The 4th Edition of Lyman's respected *Shotshell Handbook* is one of the most comprehensive shotshell manuals available on the market and is one of the first to offer a complete reloading data section for steel shot.

Covering all gauges from 410-bore to 10-gauge, including the new 12-gauge 3½", the *Shotshell Handbook* includes data for all the newest components—Remington RTL, Activ and Fiocchi cases; Winchester, Hodgdon, Accurate and Vihtavuori powders; and Federal 209A primers.

In addition to data sections on shotgun slugs, steel shot target and hunting loads, the handbook also features articles written by well known shotgunners.

The suggested retail price for the handbook is $24.95.

LYMAN PRODUCTS CORPORATION

AUTHENTIC BROWNING REPRODUCTION

An authentic reproduction of the Baby Browning is being produced by Precision Small Arms under exclusive worldwide license from Fabrique National of Herstal, Belgium, the parent company of Browning.

The seven-shot, single-action, semi-automatic 25-caliber pistol is manufactured entirely in the United States and sold under the Browning label throughout Europe, Asia and North America as the PSP-25.

The PSP-25 is machined entirely from stainless steel. It is accurate, highly concealable and comes in either a deep blue or polished stainless steel finish.

For more information, contact Precision Small Arms.

PRECISION SMALL ARMS

Shooter's Marketplace

10/22 TARGET HAMMER

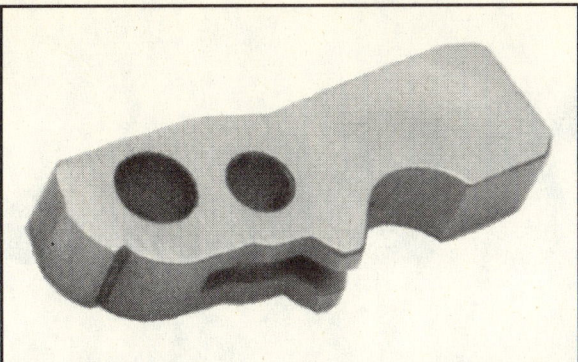

This new target hammer with replacement hammer spring from Volquartsen Custom is designed to give the stock Ruger 10/22 a superb "trigger job" by simply installing it in place of the factory hammer. No stoning or fitting is required to the sear or springs.

This hammer may appear similar to the production hammer, but is geometrically advanced in the sear engagement area. The hammers are heat-treated to achieve 60-61 Rc, then sapphire-honed for ultra smooth RMS. Trigger pull is reduced to $1\frac{1}{3}$ pounds to $1\frac{3}{4}$ pounds, depending on the gun.

The target hammer sells for $33.00 plus $4.00 shipping and handling, satisfaction guaranteed. To receive a catalog, send $4.00; mention *Shooter's Marketplace* and that catalog is yours for just $3.00.

VOLQUARTSEN CUSTOM LTD.

MATCH PISTOL BARRELS

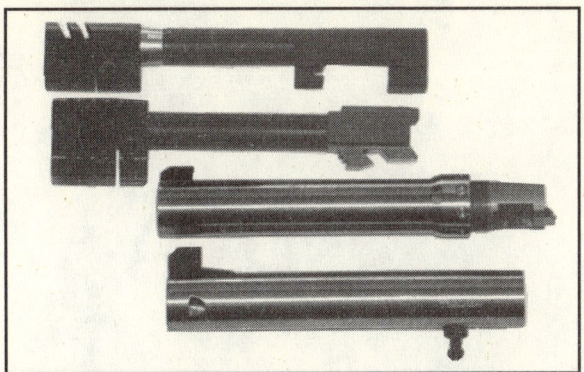

Volquartsen offers stainless steel match barrels for High Standard, Glock, Beretta and Taurus pistols. Teflon coating available. High Standard 5.5" or 6" barrels feature a match chamber and target crown, front sight and locking pin, and come drilled and tapped for a Volquartsen scope mount. Glock 17 9mm barrels require no fitting on most slides and frames and are offered with optional compensator. Beretta and Taurus match barrels are 5.1" in length and have a match chamber and target crown. Beretta & Taurus Accurizing System with accurizing bushing and compensator also available. High Standard, $135.00; Glock 17, $210.00; Beretta and Taurus, $210.00; Beretta & Taurus Accurizing System, $295.00. Send $4.00 for a catalog or mention *Shooter's Marketplace* and receive the catalog for $3.00.

VOLQUARTSEN CUSTOM LTD.

NEW RUGER MATCH BARREL

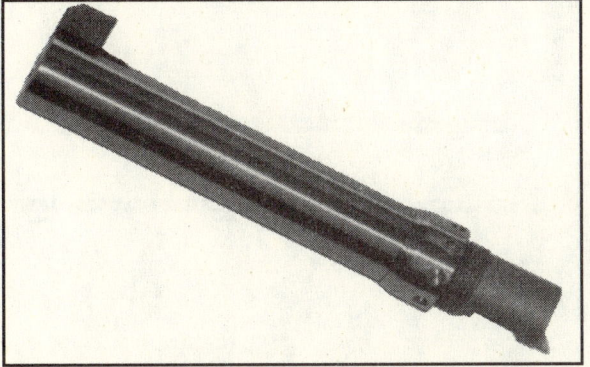

Now available from Volquartsen Custom is a 6" stainless steel match barrel for the Ruger MKI and MKII pistols. Requiring no lathe or mill work to install, the barrel comes complete with two wrenches, one to remove the existing factory barrel and one to install the new barrel. Features include a match bore and match chamber, machined front sight and complete installation instructions. Installation time is approximately 15 minutes. Future plans include offering 8" and 10" lengths as well as barrel sets complete with walnut case. Retail price is $275.00 plus $4.00 shipping and handling, satisfaction guaranteed.

For a complete catalog, send $4.00; mention *Shooter's Marketplace* and receive the catalog for $3.00.

VOLQUARTSEN CUSTOM LTD.

10/22 BULL BARREL STOCK

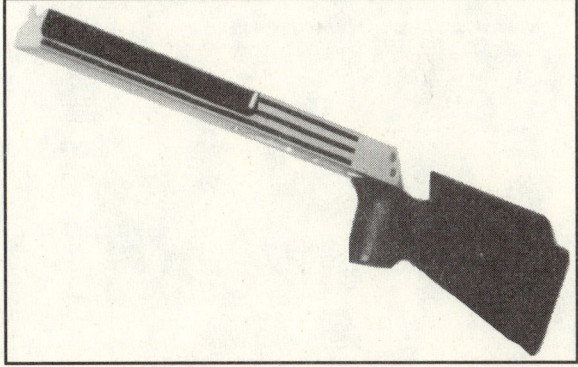

Volquartsen Custom introduces the ultimate in a 10/22 stock for the bull barrel. Their new VX-2500 stock is machined from a solid block of aircraft aluminum and mated with a dense fiberglass grip, cheekpiece and bedding block to provide the most rigid, most exact stock Volquartsen has ever designed. The unique, tapered spring bedding block for the barrel is in perfect alignment with the receiver, a must for optimum accuracy, and provides the most rigid barrel support that can be achieved with this rifle design.

The VX-2500 retails for $395.00 plus $4.00 shipping and handling, and is available in black, blue, green or red.

For a complete catalog, send $4.00; mention *Shooter's Marketplace* and receive the catalog for $3.00.

VOLQUARTSEN CUSTOM LTD.

See manufacturers' addresses on page 299.

Shooter's Marketplace

GUNSMITHING LATHE

Blue Ridge Machinery and Jet Equipment & Tools have teamed up to offer the gunsmith a lathe for handgun, shotgun and rifle 'smithing.

The Jet 1336 lathe comes standard with cabinet floor stand, three- and four-jaw chuck, faceplate, steady rest, four-way toolpost, thread dial, change gear for metric threading, centers and wrenches. The 36" span between centers will accommodate the longest barrels. The hole through the headstock is a large 1½".

Suggested list price for the 1336 is $4,550, but gunsmiths should contact Blue Ridge for information on promotions and free shipping. Complete satisfaction is guaranteed. Call their toll-free number for more information or to receive a free full-line catalog.

BLUE RIDGE MACHINERY & TOOLS, INC.

MULTI-SECTION DEFENSE BULLETS

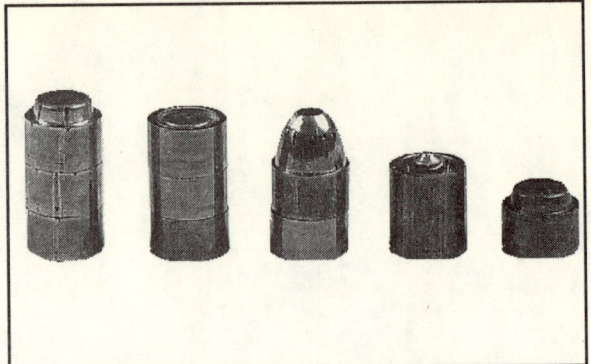

KLA offers unique 50-grain pre-fragmented Safeguard Tri-Pro slugs for 357 Magnum, 38 Special or 9mm handgun cartridges. Three stackable slugs can be loaded into a 357 case; two in 38 Special or 9mm. This three-in-one concept delivers multiple hits to the target with a single pull of the trigger. When fired, the bullet sections travel to the target as a tightly clustered group, striking within an average pattern of 8 inches at 25 yards. The tight pattern increases the chances for a hit on the target while the light weight of individual sections reduces the hazard of over penetration and ricochet. Tri-Pros are sold in stackable sections; individual slugs can be loaded to velocities in excess of 2100 fps if desired.

For a brochure and a sample, send $1.00 to KLA.

KLA ENTERPRISES

TOP-QUALITY BULLET LUBE

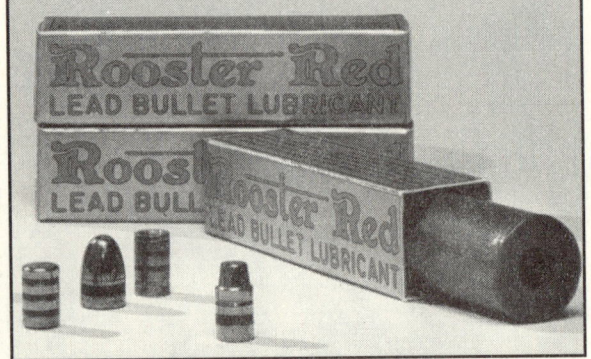

Rooster Laboratories offers consistently high performance, professional high-melt cannelure bullet lubricants in a choice of two hardnesses. Both are available in 2"x 6" sticks for the commercial reloader, and 1"x 4" hollow and solid sticks.

With a 230°F melting point, both are ideal for indoor and outdoor shooting. Both bond securely to the bullet, remaining intact during shipping.

Zambini is a hard, tough lubricant designed primarily for pistols. HVR is softer, but still firm. Designed primarily for high-velocity rifles, HVR is easier to apply, and also excellent for pistols. Application requires the lubesizer be heated.

Prices: 2"x 6" sticks $4.00; 1"x 4" sticks $135.00 per 100. Contact Rooster for more information.

ROOSTER LABORATORIES

TARGET SCOPES

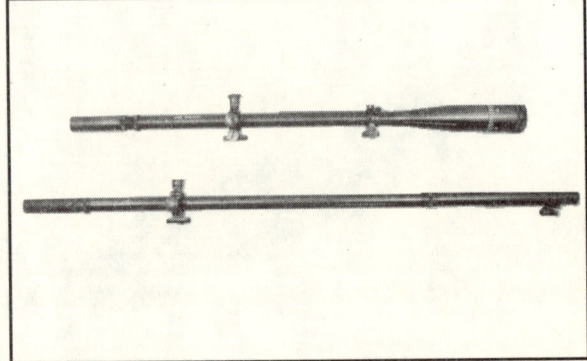

Parsons Optical offers two high-grade target scopes—the Lyman Super Targetspot and the Parsons Long Scope. Manufactured completely in the U.S., both scopes are all blued steel and use the finest of coated optics.

The Super Targetspot is made using original Lyman blueprints and in all the original powers. It comes with steel mounts, lens caps, rubber eye cup and three-point suspension rear mount with ¼-micrometer click adjustments. The Long Scope, designed by Gil Parsons, uses turn-of-the-century specifications, but with modern improvements. Available in 6x only and in lengths beginning at 28", it comes with blued steel mounts and four-point suspension rear mount with micrometer click adjustments. Accessories for both scopes are available. Parsons also operates a full-service repair shop.

PARSONS OPTICAL MFG. CO.

See manufacturers' addresses on page 299.

Shooter's Marketplace

RUGER BARRELS AND ACCESSORIES

Barrels and accessories for Ruger 10/22® and 77/22® rifles are available from B. Perazone Gunsmith.

The barrels are manufactured by Wilson Arms, utilizing ultra-modern CNC technology, to internal tolerances of less than .0002″. Match-quality Ruger bull barrels are .920″ in diameter and button-rifled, air-gauged and lead-lapped. The 10/22 barrels come in either 18″ or 22″ lengths; 77/22 barrels in 22″. Both come with Wilson Semi-Auto Match chamber. Blued 4140 steel barrels retail for $109.00; 416 stainless, $129.00. Add $6.00 for shipping and handling. Also available from Perazone are synthetic stocks, triggers, sears, target hammers, scope mounts, accessories and a variety of gunsmithing services. A complete catalog is $3.00 or free with order. Dealer inquiries welcome; send FFL.

B. PERAZONE GUNSMITH

SHOOTER'S EAR MUFF

Silencio's CDS-80 Magnum Deluxe ear muff provides the competition shooter or plinker with quality hearing protection.

Each pair of muffs was designed with comfort, style, protection and affordability in mind. The CDS-80 features a padded, non-absorbent head cushion plus liquid-filled ear cushions, which provide an excellent seal for prescription glasses wearers and are extremely comfortable. Also featured are side-bar adjusters and rotating ear cups. The muffs are available in black, white or blue.

Silencio's CDS-80 noise reduction rating is one of the highest in the industry.

For information on all Silencio products check with your local gun dealer or contact Silencio direct.

SILENCIO/SAFETY DIRECT

MAUSER SPORTER BARRELS & ACCESSORIES

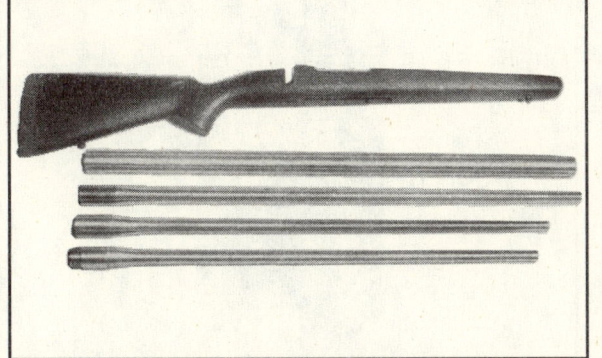

B. Perazone Gunsmith offers threaded and chambered barrels for the Mauser 98 and 93 through 96 rifles. Manufactured by Wilson Arms on state-of-the-art CNC machinery, barrels come in 4140 steel or 416 stainless steel in sporter and varmint contours. Air-gauged, lead-lapped, crowned and button-rifled, these match-quality barrels have .010″ deep chambers, 320 finish, internal tolerances to .0002″ and come in 24″ to 26″ lengths. Most calibers available from 22-250 through 458 Win. Mag. Sporter in 4140 steel from $89.00; varmint, $99.00. Sporter in stainless from $129; varmint, $139.00. Add $6.00 for shipping and handling. Garand barrels, many accessories and a variety of gunsmithing services also available. A complete catalog is $3.00 or free with order. Dealer inquiries invited; send FFL.

B. PERAZONE GUNSMITH

NEW SHOTGUN CLEANING SYSTEM

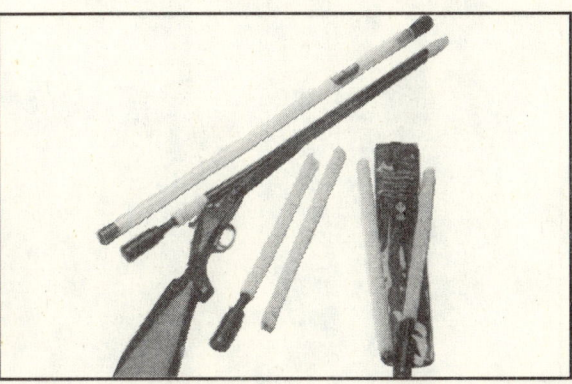

Silencio offers their Tico Tool Shotgun Cleaner System for cleaning and oiling your smoothbore thoroughly in about 30 seconds.

The Tico Tool is a one-piece, or two-piece takedown, cleaning bar with oiling bob attachment. The washable bar is run down the barrel for the cleaning and polishing operation, and then, with the oiling bob attached, a final stroke down the barrel prepares your shotgun for storage.

The standard one-piece model is available for 12-, 16-, 20-, 28-gauge and .410 bore; the two-piece takedown model is offered for 12-, 16- and 20-gauge.

For information on all Silencio products currently available, visit your local gun store or call, write or fax Silencio directly.

SILENCIO/SAFETY DIRECT

See manufacturers' addresses on page 299.

Shooter's Marketplace

SHOTGUN GHOST-RING SIGHTS

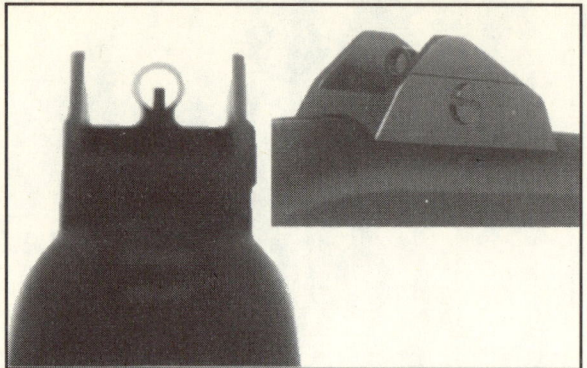

Miniature Machine Corp. (MMC) offers their Ghost Ring shotgun sight for the buckshot/slug shotgunner. Machined from 4140 steel and heat-treated to 40 RC, the Ghost Ring has 30 MOA of adjustment in elevation and windage with 3 MOA detent stops (20-inch barrel). Elevation is adjusted by turning an eccentric with the rim of a shotshell, allowing easy and quick point of impact adjustments for the transition between buckshot and slug loads. For windage adjustments the aperature slides in a dovetail with recoil-proof detents.

This sight is compatible with many types of front sights though fastest sight acquisition is achieved when used in conjunction with MMC's serrated ramp front sight. Ghost-Ring sights come with a lifetime warranty on materials and workmanship.

MINIATURE MACHINE CORP.

MUZZLE-LOADING PRODUCTS

White Shooting Systems is a leading manufacturer of muzzle-loading firearms, bullets and accessories. They offer the revolutionary White Muzzleloading System in their traditional Green River Series and modern straight-line W, G and SG Series muzzle-loading rifles as well as in their G Series pistol and BG Series shotguns. The White System is recognized as one of the most advanced forms of muzzle-loading technology available today. White Rifles are used by professional hunters throughout the world and are acclaimed for their accuracy, dependability, safety and power. White also offers a complete line of innovative bullets, sights, scope mounts and muzzle-loading/hunting accessories. For more information contact White Shooting Systems direct.

WHITE SHOOTING SYSTEMS, INC.

FULLY ADJUSTABLE PISTOL SIGHTS

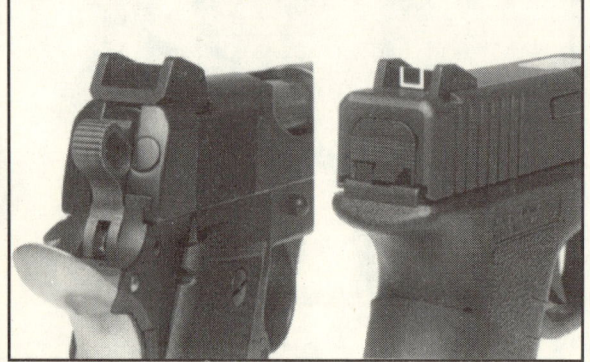

From Miniature Machine Corp. (MMC) comes new low-profile, snag-free, fully adjustable pistol sights designed for Glocks, Colt 1911s, H&K USPs and others. Machined from 4140 steel and heat-treated to 40 RC, these sights provide a target quality sight picture. Elevation adjustments are made with a 0.035" Allen wrench that moves an eccentric through 22 detent stop positions, making the rear sight compatible with other vendors' front sights. Windage adjustment is made by drifting the sight in its dovetail. Available with tritium, white dots or white outline, or all black. The tritium option is exclusively the P-T Night Sight line with three dot, single bar dot and double bar dot configurations. Tritium color choices include green, orange and yellow with others available by the end of the year.

MINIATURE MACHINE CORP.

GUN SAFES AND CABINETS

American Security Products Co. (AMSEC) has been manufacturing and marketing burglar-proof safes for the security industry since 1948. They have a complete line of safes and cabinets for gun enthusiasts.

Standard features on all AMSEC gun safes include a recessed door, a minimum of ten 1" diameter locking bolts, reinforced door jambs, independent relocking devices to protect the lock from a drill attack and Sargent and Greenleaf key-locking dials.

Safe capacities range from 8 to 60 guns; fireliners are available on all 60" and 72" high safes.

AMSEC gun safes have passed UL burglary testing procedures for drill, punch and pry attacks. AMSEC has four warehouse locations. For more information or a free brochure, contact AMSEC.

AMERICAN SECURITY PRODUCTS CO.

See manufacturers' addresses on page 299.

Shooter's Marketplace

ACCESSORY/SERVICE BROCHURE

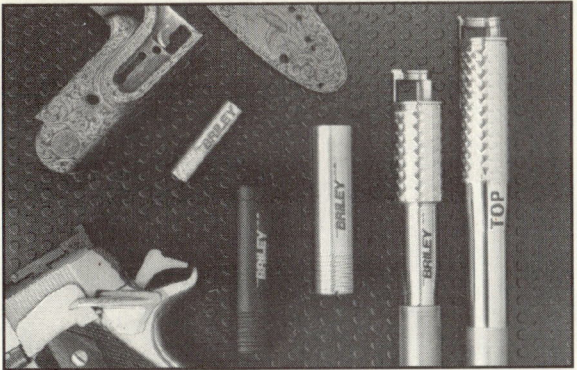

This Houston-based firm is well-known for providing precision products to the avid shotgunner. The Briley tradition of attention to detail and complete customer satisfaction keeps the hunter and competition shooter happy.

Their brochure describes Briley's line of shotgun and now pistol and revolver services. Briley has added a new division for the discerning handgun enthusiast.

Everything from screw-in chokes to competition Skeet tubes to pistol and revolver customizing and accessories is available. Briley offers an extensive line of products and services for the shotgunner and handgunner.

Write or call toll-free for a free brochure.

BRILEY MFG., INC.

DROP-IN CONVERSION TUBES

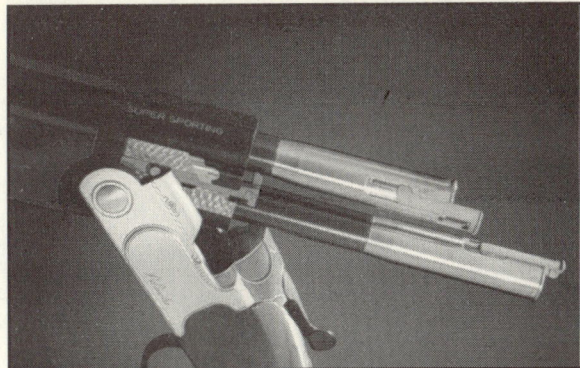

The Companion from Briley Mfg. is a 28-gauge drop-in tube insert set designed to fit all 12-gauge double-barrel shotguns.

Each tube set comes in a vinyl slip cover containing full instructions, two Briley screw-in chokes, a wrench, and a power knock-out tool for insertion and removal. No additional tools and no alterations to the shotgun are necessary. You simply insert the tubes and shoot.

Additional screw-in chokes for the tube set are available and include: Cylinder, Skeet, Improved Cylinder, Light Modified, Modified, Improved Modified, Light Full, Full and Extra Full. Briley also manufactures .410-bore and 20-gauge inserts on a fitted basis. See your local dealer or call Briley toll-free for more information. Mention *Shooter's Marketplace*.

BRILEY MFG., INC.

PISTOL CUSTOMIZING/ACCESSORIES

Briley Mfg. has a new fully specialized Pistol Division. For the dedicated handgun enthusiast, Briley offers some of the finest modifications, customizing, repair parts and accessories currently available.

Compensators, extended slide releases, thumb guards, squared trigger guards and more are just some of the services currently available from the new division.

The Pistol Division is currently manufacturing custom slides, barrels, custom titanium compensators and other unique accessories for the discerning handgun shooter and competitor.

Briley also offers complete, conventional repair services for all makes of handguns.

BRILEY MFG., INC.

SCREW-IN CHOKES

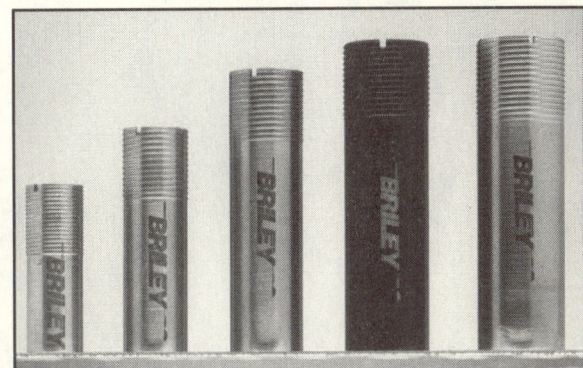

Briley screw-in chokes produce reliable, uniform patterns. This system allows the shooter the complete choke control necessary to utilize the full spectrum of ammunition available to today's shotgunner.

There are new innovations in chokes, as well. The unique "Comp-Choke" gives the shooter not only reliable patterns, but aids in second-shot recovery time by porting gases upward at the muzzle.

Total steel shot compatibility is also available with the screw-in choke system. Even the largest shot sizes are usable through their steel shot chokes. Briley also offers exclusive choke designs and constrictions for turkey hunters.

Write or call toll-free for a free brochure.

BRILEY MFG., INC.

See manufacturers' addresses on page 299.

SHOOTER'S MARKETPLACE

REFLECTIVE MARKERS

Birchwood Casey Reflective Trail Markers are designed for fast, easy navigation in complete darkness and unfamiliar places. They are equally useful for the hunter and outdoorsmen of all types.

Trail Markers are visible from all directions. Their permanent, adhesive backing and wrap-around design allow use in a variety of terrain and regions. They can be wrapped around small twigs, branches and underbrush, or attached directly to trees, large branches and rocks. By holding a flashlight at eye level, Trail Markers will reflect an easy-to-follow path as far as the light will carry.

Each pack of Trail Markers contains 96 markers—48-$\frac{1}{2}$"x2" strips and 48-$\frac{1}{2}$"x$\frac{1}{2}$" squares.

For a free catalog, see your dealer or write to Birchwood Casey directly.

BIRCHWOOD CASEY

NEW SHOOTERS AND COLLECTORS CATALOG

Galazan's first direct-order catalog *Galazan Things For Fine Guns...and More* offers shooters and collectors of fine guns a large selection of hard-to-find firearms products. The catalog features recoil pads and buttplates, leather gun cases and shooting accessories, shooting bags, gunmaker trade labels, shotgun tools and gauges, gunstock wood, gun parts, published materials and gift items from the "Golden Age" of gunning.

A major buyer in the field of fine firearms and manufacturer of fine gun products for the past 15 years, Galazan also serves as the factory parts and repair center for the Winchester Model 21.

To purchase this new catalog send $5.00 or order direct by phone. Major credit cards accepted.

GALAZAN

REPLICA FIREARMS

Navy Arms Company, well-known in the industry for their blackpowder replica firearms, also offers a variety of cartridge reproductions to the collector and shooter. The newest addition to the Navy Arms product line is the 1875 Schofield, a replica of the S&W top-break revolver carried by Jesse James and Gen. George Armstrong Custer.

Their full-color catalog is packed with arms, accoutrements and accessories. Weapons represented range from replicas from the Revolutionary War period to reproductions from the Old West.

Mention *Shooter's Marketplace* and you'll receive their $2.00 catalog for only $1.00. Dealers send a copy of your F.F.L. for a free catalog and inclusion on Navy Arms' dealer special/military surplus mailing list.

NAVY ARMS COMPANY

FULLY-ADJUSTABLE TRIGGERS

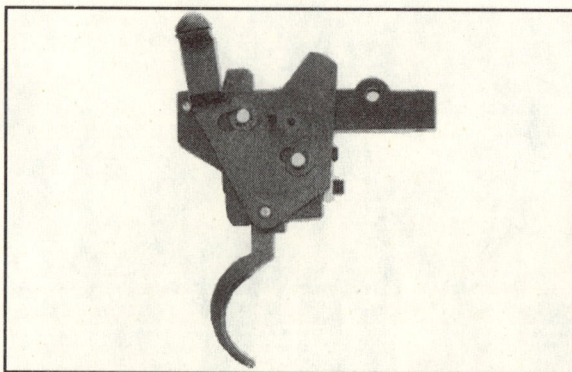

Precision-machined, Timney triggers give the feel of a much lighter trigger pull for consistent, above-average shooting.

The Timney Trigger is fully adjustable for a pull weight between 2 and 4 pounds on most models; for creep, with the sear engagement visible through a sight window in the housing; and overtravel. Available for most modern bolt-action rifles including Remington, Winchester, Weatherby, Sako, Ruger and most Mausers. All triggers are tested in rifle actions before shipment to ensure your trigger will work as intended in your rifle. Timney prides itself on the precision machining and workmanship that goes into each trigger and guarantees satisfaction.

For a free brochure, call, write or fax Timney Mfg.

TIMNEY MFG., INC.

See manufacturers' addresses on page 299.

Shooter's Marketplace

SHOOTERS' NEWSPAPER

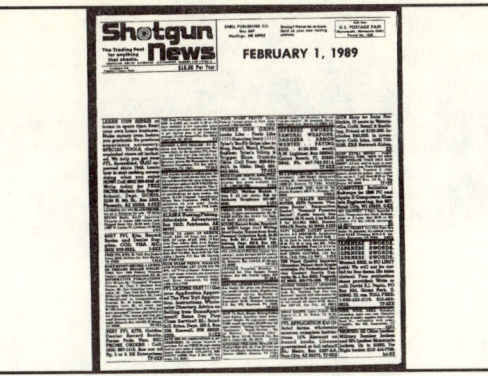

Established in 1946, *The Shotgun News* is a leader in its field.

It offers some of the finest gun buys in the United States. More than 160,000 people read, enjoy and profit from this newspaper, which is published three times a month.

The Shotgun News has helped thousands of gun enthusiasts locate firearms, both modern and antique—rifles, pistols, shotguns, scopes, etc...all at money-saving prices.

The money saved on the purchase of any of the 10,000 plus listings could more than pay for the $22.00 (36-issue) annual subscription cost.

As it says on the cover, it's "the trading post for anything that shoots."

THE SHOTGUN NEWS

SEE-THRU SCOPE MOUNTS

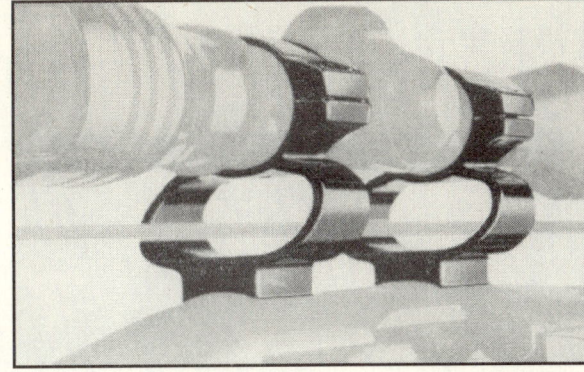

Kwik-Site See-Thru Scope Mounts are among the finest mounts on the market.

With their forward look, they are lowest to the receiver and have the largest viewing area of any see-thru scope mount made today. Popular in dense brush and forest their low profile and wide "see-thru" design gives hunters the immediate option of using iron sights or scope.

Made of high strength bright black anodized aluminum alloy, Kwik-Site mounts install in minutes using supplied allen wrench and screws.

Kwik-Site mounts are available for all popular centerfire rifles, shotguns, muzzleloaders and 22 rimfire rifles.

Write for more information.

KWIK-SITE CO.

BULLET SEATING DEPTH SYSTEM

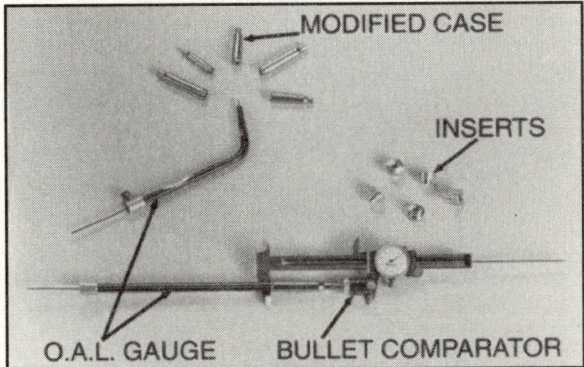

Small changes in the clearance between the bullet and the rifling can make a dramatic difference in accuracy. By fine-tuning the bullet seating depth of handloads, you can often cut group size in half. Stoney Point offers a versatile and affordable two-gauge system which precisely regulates the clearance between the bullet and rifling. Using any bullet of choice and the O.A.L. Gauge, you can, in about one minute, produce an accurate model of your chamber. Then, caliper measurement from case base to ogive determines the precise seating depth needed for the bullet to contact the rifling. This gauge system makes it easy to set your seating die for the exact bullet jump you desire. Modified Cases are available to fit any chamber size, including wildcats. Dealer program available.

STONEY POINT PRODUCTS, INC.

SCOPE MOUNTS

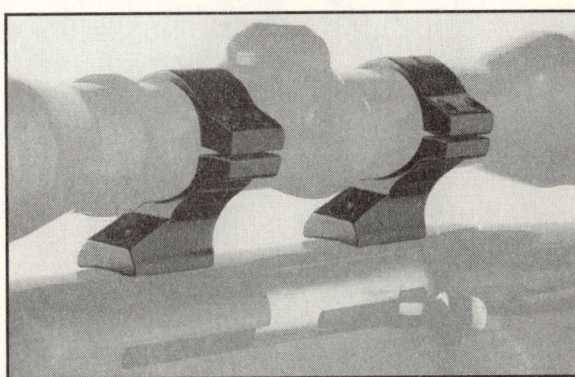

Bench Rest Kwik-Mounts are another great innovation from Kwik-Site Co.

They are ideal for the hunter who is looking for strong, rigid low mounts for use in open country.

This rugged, lightweight aluminum mount features an integral one-piece base and ring. Installation time is cut in half compared to most popular makes. It uses existing factory holes in the gun's receiver and comes with precision machined allen head screws and wrench. With its bright finish and good looks, it complements the finest scopes and rifles.

Kwik-Site Bench Rest Mounts are available for all popular rifles.

Write for more information.

KWIK-SITE CO.

See manufacturers' addresses on page 299.

Shooter's Marketplace

22 RIMFIRE ACCURACY GAUGE

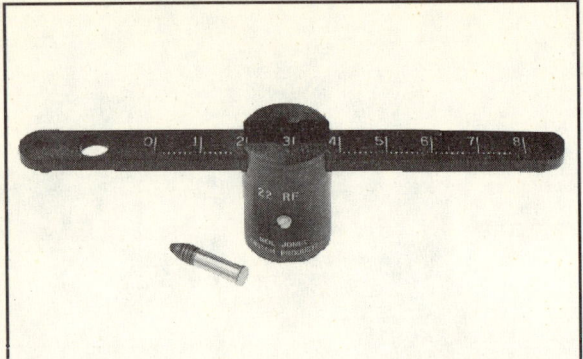

The 22 Rimfire Accuracy Gauge from Neil Jones Custom Products measures the thickness of the cartridge rim and enables ammunition to be sorted for consistent headspacing. The use of this gauge helps eliminate flyers, which results in smaller groups.

The rimfire gauge has been used for 15 years by thousands of satisfied customers. It is 100% safe, with nothing to wear out or break. It is easily modified for use with 22 Rimfire Magnum ammunition.

Shooter's Marketplace readers can send for a free catalog of prices and information on this and other Neil Jones accuracy products for shooters and handloaders.

NEIL JONES CUSTOM PRODUCTS

FIELD-RELIABLE RIFLESCOPES

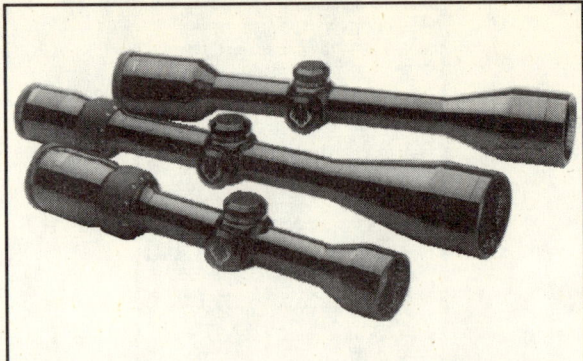

Bushnell® Trophy® riflescopes have proven reliable in the field and have features usually found only in higher-priced scopes.

With amber-coated optics to increase brightness and contrast in shade and low light conditions, the wide-angle view and sure-grip power change ring make finding and tracking game easier.

Fogproof and waterproof, Trophy scopes have fast-focus eyepieces and fingertip adjustable windage and elevation knobs.

In addition to fixed and variable models, the Trophy Series includes 2x and 2-6x handscopes with long eye relief of 9" to 26". The new Circle-X reticle is available on the 3-9x 40mm and the 1.75-4x Turkey and Brush scopes. For more information, call or write Bushnell.

BUSHNELL SPORTS OPTICS WORLDWIDE

DUTY AND COMPETITION GEAR CATALOG

Safariland Ltd. has published their 1995 Product Guide. The new catalog contains 79 pages of full-color graphics displaying their innovative, state-of-the-art law enforcement and competition gear. In addition to law enforcement duty holsters, belts and accessories, the catalog features concealment holsters and magazine carriers, tactical holsters and shoulder holsters.

Included is a Competition Products section devoted to Team Safariland filled with the latest holsters and accessories for IPSC, USPSA, PPC and Stock competitions, many of which were used to win most major USPSA/IPSC events including the U.S. Nationals and World Shoot. Write, call or fax Safariland for more information and a free copy of their catalog.

SAFARILAND LTD., INC.

MULTI-COATED RIFLESCOPES

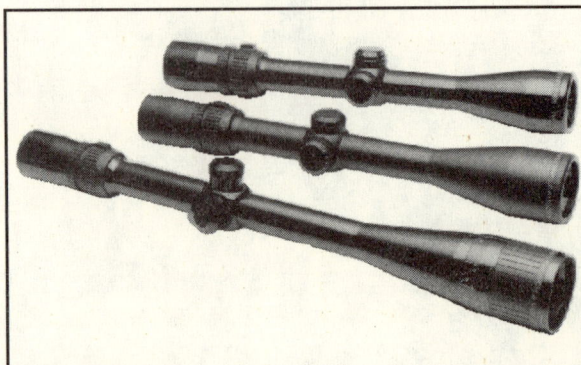

Bausch & Lomb® Elite™ riflescopes from Bushnell utilize the finest in optical glass and extra lenses for a sharp, bright sight picture. Multi-coating on air-to-glass surfaces increases light transmission for maximum brightness. Built to perform perfectly even after taking 10,000 375-caliber H&H Magnum rounds, Elite scopes are constructed of aircraft-grade aluminum. The single-piece aluminum tube is sealed and nitrogen-purged for fogproof and waterproof performance. The aim point is controlled by windage and elevation adjustments on the erector assembly. Adjustable objective features a high-strength steel spring which is held in place by an exclusive spring clip housing welded to the scope body to secure lens position. For more information, call or write Bushnell.

BUSHNELL SPORTS OPTICS WORLDWIDE

Shooter's Marketplace

CHOKE TUBE INSTALLATION

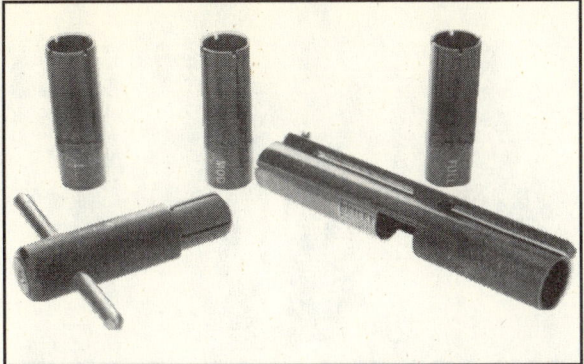

Everything from close-flushing woodcock to high-flying geese can be hunted with a single gun when shooters use the Briley Screw-In Choke System.

If outstanding patterns with target loads, turkey loads, steel or buckshot are important, there is a Briley System for the job. Briley tubes can be installed in nearly any shotgun of any gauge, including most single-barrel guns, plus thin-walled over/unders and side-by-sides.

Hastings is the master distributor and installer of Briley Chokes. They have perfected installation to ensure correct point of impact (tubes are concentric with the bore and fit to exacting tolerances).

Call for complete information.

HASTINGS BARRELS

NEW ADJUSTABLE TRIGGER

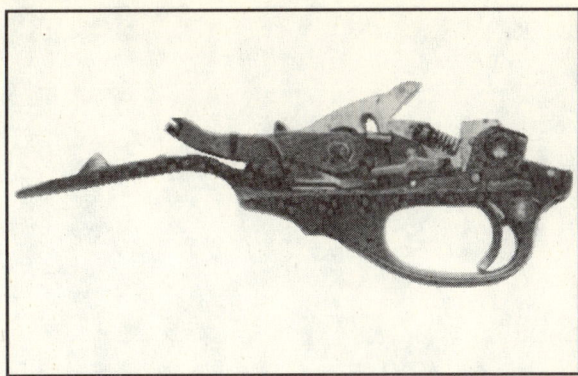

The trigger control needs of the wingshooter versus those of the big game rifled slug hunter are quite different. Wingshooters pull their triggers for best performance; big game hunters squeeze off their shots. The big game hunter who uses a multi-purpose shotgun with interchangeable barrels must contend with a trigger designed for the wingshooter and that often means excessive pull weight, trigger creep and overtravel.

Hastings Barrels announces their new fully adjustable shotgun triggers. The triggers feature drop-in interchangeability and are designed to fit all Remington Model 870, 1100 and 11-87 shotguns in both 12 and 20 gauge.

For Hastings' fully adjustable triggers, contact your local gun dealer or contact Hastings direct.

HASTINGS BARRELS

RIFLED SLUG BARREL

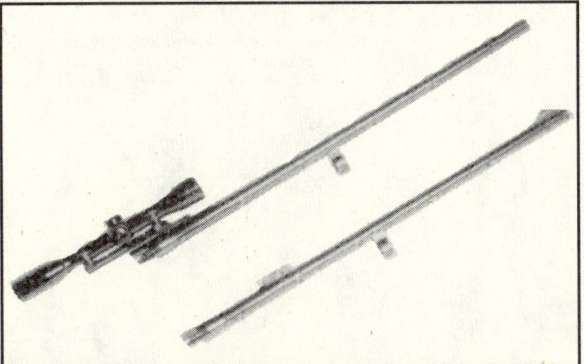

The Hastings Paradox Rifled Slug Barrel puts rifle-like accuracy within the reach and budget of every shotgun hunter. The rifled bore has a 1:34 twist for increased slug stability and superb accuracy. These are the only rifled slug barrels sold as exact replacement barrels for most popular single-barrel 12-gauge shotguns (no fitting required).

Barrels are offered in 20″ and 24″ lengths and are equipped with rifle sights or extended scope mounts. The popular Cantilever Scope Mount barrel has an extended mount to allow the use of a standard eye relief scope. All barrels have a high-polish blued finish and are proof-tested and serial-numbered.

Paradox barrels are available from select gunshops or directly from Hastings. Call for more information.

HASTINGS BARRELS

HIGH-IMPACT GUN CASE

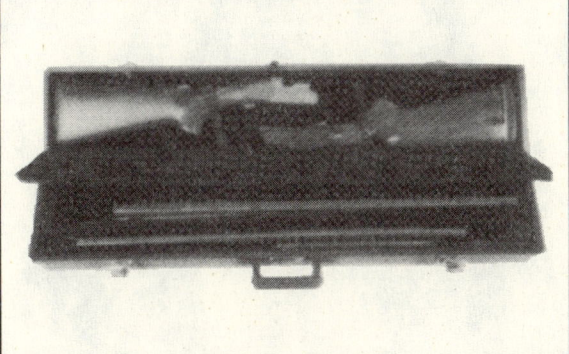

All-America shooting champion John Hall designed the Hastings/John Hall™ line of gun cases. Made of ultra-high-impact polycarbonate for extra strength and rigidity, these cases are among the toughest, most durable available.

Three models are offered, all in black. The Universal™ model gives the maximum in protection with minimum size. Compact, easy to carry and weighing just 8 pounds, it holds two receivers and three sets of barrels. The Auto model holds two automatic or pump shotguns, and the Four Barrel case holds one receiver and four sets of barrels. They are used by traveling hunters as well as competitive trap, Skeet and live pigeon shooting champions.

Available from fine gunshops or direct from Hastings.

HASTINGS BARRELS

See manufacturers' addresses on page 299.

Shooter's Marketplace

QUALITY CUSTOM BULLETS

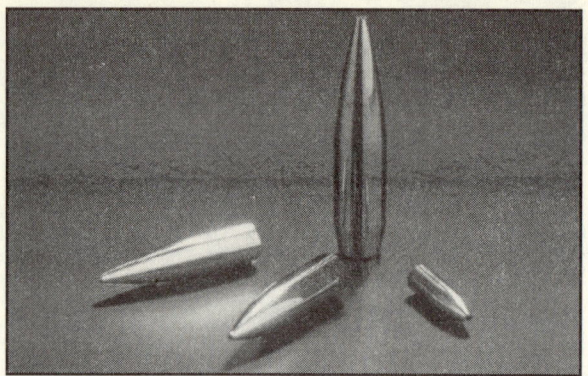

Shot after shot, competition and varmint shooters can count on the precision and accuracy of Berger bullets—match-quality bullets at competitive prices. Bullets in calibers 172, 224, 243, 257, 7mm and 308 in a wide range of weights in flat base, boattail and VLD are currently available.

In the custom bullet business for over 40 years, Berger makes bullets known around the world for their high-performance standards, standards which include using the J-4 bullet jacket exclusively. The J-4 is recognized industry-wide for its consistent uniformity and concentricity.

Berger, though a large-volume custom bullet company, operates under the close guidance and supervision of Walt Berger, its founder. Write for a free brochure.

BERGER BULLETS, LTD.

PROGRESSIVE SHOTSHELL RELOADER

The L-S-1000, a fully progressive shotshell reloader, is available from Ponsness/Warren. The L-S-1000 will load lead, steel or bismuth shot progressively. It is equipped with a patented Uni-Drop shot drop system which allows the use of all sizes and types of shot.

All shells are automatically full-length resized and deprimed with the Auto-Size and De-Primer system. Shells drop out of the shellholders when complete. Each shell is precrimped and final crimped with the Tru-Crimp system.

The L-S-1000 is available in 10-gauge $3\frac{1}{2}''$; 12-gauge $2\frac{3}{4}''$ and 3''; and 20-gauge $2\frac{3}{4}''$ and 3''. Also available is a 12-gauge $3\frac{1}{2}''$ conversion kit. For more information contact your nearest Ponsness/Warren dealer or call the company direct.

PONSNESS/WARREN

QUALITY GUNSTOCK BLANKS

Cali'co Hardwoods has been cutting superior-quality shotgun and rifle blanks for more than 31 years. Cali'co supplies blanks to many of the major manufacturers—Browning, Weatherby, Ruger, Holland & Holland, to name a few—as well as custom gunsmiths the world over.

Profiled rifle blanks are available, ready for inletting and sanding. Cali'co sells superior California hardwoods in Claro walnut, French walnut, Bastogne, maple and myrtle.

Cali'co offers good, serviceable blanks and some of the finest exhibition blanks available. Satisfaction guaranteed.

Color catalog, retail and dealer price list (FFL required) free upon request.

CALI'CO HARDWOODS, INC.

BORE BRUSHES

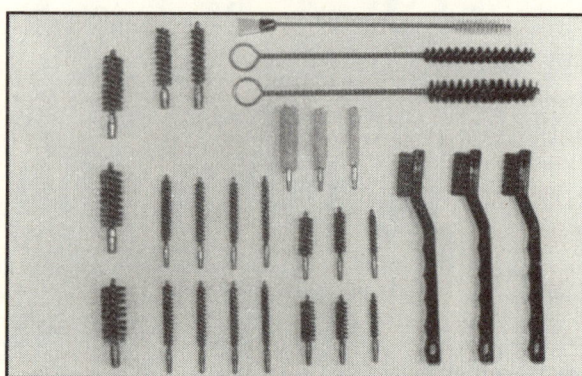

Faith Associates specializes in wholesale gun cleaning brushes and shooting accessories. Brushes ranging from 22-caliber through 10-gauge are available with bronze or stainless steel bristles; cotton swabs are also available. Brush stems are threaded in the standard $8/32''$ for pistol and rifle calibers, and $5/16$-27'' for shotgun gauges.

Faith Associates also handles a variety of shooter accessories such as ear protection, shooting glasses, drift pin punches, and bore inspection lights and much more. In addition they offer the excellent line of Tetra gun lubricants. Quantity discount pricing is available on all items.

For a copy of their current brochure, call or write the manufacturer. Mention *Shooter's Marketplace* and they'll send one free of charge.

FAITH ASSOCIATES, INC.

SHOOTER'S MARKETPLACE

14X BORESCOPE

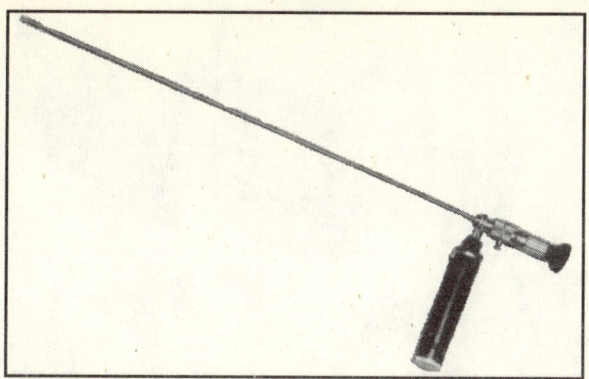

Bald Eagle has introduced a new borescope with 14x magnification. The 360° panoramic view permits the user to see the entire inside of the bore at one time. When a glitch is found in the barrel, the eyepiece can be slid forward and the problem area viewed in the 90° mode. The depth of field is almost unlimited and it's 3 to 5 times clearer than fiber optics. In fact, the clarity is such that the user can actually distinguish the difference between a shadow and a stain.

These instruments were manufactured in Germany for the military to enable them to check aircraft gatling gun barrels. They are not surplus and are of current production having a full warranty. The borescopes are 5mm in diameter and 19.5 inches long and are sold exclusively by Bald Eagle.

BALD EAGLE PRECISION MACHINE CO.

RIMFIRE CARTRIDGE GAGE

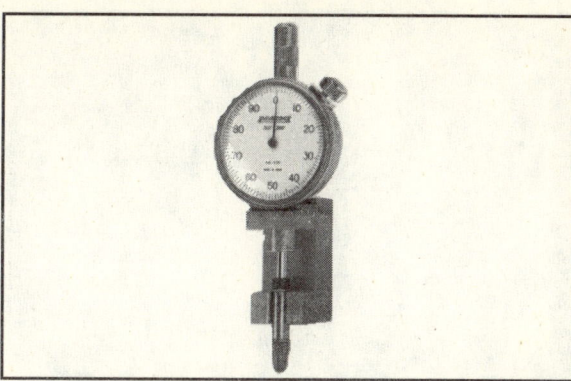

The Rimfire Cartridge Gage from Bald Eagle Precision Machine Co. can improve overall group size by up to 25% by sorting rimfire ammo into uniform rim-thickness lots.

The more consistent the rim thickness, the more consistent the ignition of the primer and powder charge, and the firing pin travel remains uniform from shot-to-shot.

The Cartridge Gage is a snap to use—grab a box or two of rimfire ammo and start sorting. It is ideal for BR-50 benchrest competitors and serious small game hunters.

Normally $80.00, mention *Shooter's Marketplace* and it's only $74.95. Write Bald Eagle for a free brochure.

BALD EAGLE PRECISION MACHINE CO.

PRECISION RIFLE REST

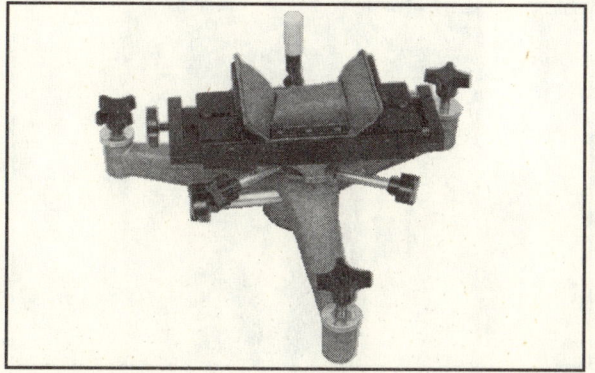

Bald Eagle Precision Machine Co. offers a rifle rest perfect for the serious benchrester or the dedicated varminter.

The rest is constructed of aircraft-quality aluminum and weighs 7 pounds, 12 ounces. It's finished with three coats of Imron Clear. Height adjustments are made with a rack and pinion and a mariner wheel. A fourth leg allows lateral movement on the bench.

Bald Eagle offers approximately 56 rest models to choose from, including windage adjustments, right or left hand, cast aluminum or cast iron. The Standard Rest with rifle stop and bag is pictured above.

Prices: $99.95 to $260.00. For more information or a free brochure, contact Bald Eagle.

BALD EAGLE PRECISION MACHINE CO.

RE-ENERGIZING SERRATED KNIVES

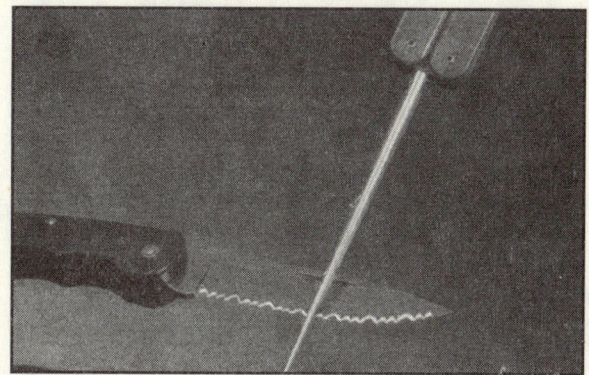

Diamond Machining Technology (DMT) offers a pocket Serrated Knife Sharpener that quickly restores the edges of serrated knives and other cutting tools. The sharpener is a 4-inch cone that tapers in diameter from $1/16$- to $1/4$-inch, the most common serration sizes found on cutting tools.

The knife sharpener is coated with micronized diamond crystals in coarse or fine grit. The diamond abrasive quickly sharpens one serration at a time, restoring knives and tools to peak efficiency.

The sharpener is part of DMT's Diafold™ line of sharpening tools. Diafold sharpeners are housed in a plastic case that unfolds into a convenient handle.

Contact DMT for a full-line catalog of precision Diamond products, all made in the United States.

DIAMOND MACHINING TECHNOLOGY, INC.

See manufacturers' addresses on page 299.

Shooter's Marketplace

COMPLETE GUNSMITHING SERVICES

Walker Arms Co., Inc., one of the nation's oldest firearms service centers, provides factory authorized warranty service and general repair for many of the world's best known manufacturers—Bersa, Browning, Colt, Gamo Airguns, Lakefield, Llama, Mossberg, Remington, Smith & Wesson, Stoeger, Thompson/Center, Weatherby, Winchester and others.

Walker Arms also provides warranty firearm service for major U.S. retailers, and is a major parts distributor. The almost 100 years combined experience of their professional gunsmiths is available to assist customers with any gunsmithing need. Services include screw-in choke systems, barrel, sight and action work, metal and wood refinishing, custom-made guns, antique gun restoration, appraisals and others.

WALKER ARMS CO., INC.

MULTI-CALIBER ADAPTERS

MCA Sports offers adapters and conversion devices for all types of firearms, including inserts for break-open shotguns and chamber adapters for rifles and pistols.

These inserts/adapters add versatility to any firearm. Big-bore shooters can practice on urban indoor ranges or take small game using the same rifle they used for big game hunting. For survival purposes, these adapters are unequaled, allowing a single rifle or pistol to fire a variety of ammunition. Wildcat and odd calibers are their specialty.

Write for prices; hundreds of combinations available. Offered in blue or stainless steel. Send self-addressed, stamped envelope (52¢ postage) to MCA Sports for information.

MCA SPORTS

SAFARI SLING

Boonie Packer's Safari Sling attaches easily to both 1" and 1¼" swivels interchangeably and allows rifles and shotguns to be carried upright in front of or at the side of the body. The patented design allows hunters to quickly bring their guns up and aim because there is nothing to undo or release.

The sling, which has been adopted by the U.S. military, stays securely on the shoulder and allows hunters' hands to be free, which reduces fatigue and permits them to perform other tasks, such as use binoculars. The sling also works well with backpacks.

The 2"-wide carrying strap is available in Black, Woodland Camo, Realtree™ Camo and Blaze Orange. Write or call for free literature.

BOONIE PACKER PRODUCTS

NEW CHRONOGRAPHS

Shooting Chrony has introduced a new family of chronographs—the Alpha-, Beta-, Delta- and Gamma-Chrony. Each model is an upgraded, more sophisticated version of the previous model. These chronographs accurately measure the speed of ammo from 30 to 5,000 fps, within 0.5% and feature 32-, 60- or 1,000-shot memory. With all-metal construction for durability, the chronographs are a light 2.3 pounds and fold into a compact 4½"x 2¼"x 7½" size for storage. All are available with a variety of optional accessories, including an Indoor Shooting Light Fixture, Lexan shields, IBM PC interface, carrying cases, ballistic programs, remote controls and come with a two-year warranty. Starting from $74.95, Shooting Chronys are a must for shooters, reloaders and bowhunters.

SHOOTING CHRONY, INC.

See manufacturers' addresses on page 299.

Shooter's Marketplace

RUGER 10/22® TARGET BARRELS

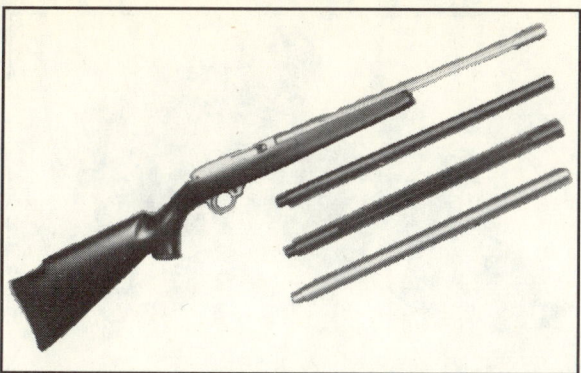

Butler Creek is marketing a high-quality series of 22 Long Rifle target replacement barrels for factory Ruger 10/22® rifles.

The new barrels are fully machined and contoured to ensure correct barrel-to-receiver fit. Available in blued and stainless steel, fluted and non-fluted, all barrels are 20" long with .920" diameter and feature six-groove button rifling and a recessed target crown for accuracy.

Fluted barrels have six heat-dissipating, precision-machined grooves starting 4" from the receiver and ending 2" from the muzzle.

A new Ruger 10/22 Heavy Barrel Synthetic Replacement Stock is also available, an ideal stock for .920" diameter target barrels.

BUTLER CREEK CORPORATION

CUSTOM SCOPES

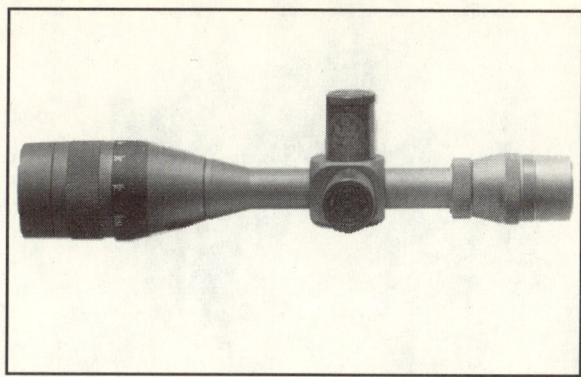

U.S. Optics offers ultra-high resolution, long-range fixed and variable sighting systems made to your specifications. Choose from aluminum or steel alloy tubes, 30mm to 50mm in diameter; MOA up to 300 MOA; objectives from 58mm to 82mm; windage and elevation clicks from .100 to 1.00 M.O.A. per click; fixed powers from 10x to 40x; and variable powers from 1-4x to 8-40x. Shooters can design a scope to best suit their needs. U.S. Optics offers high-resolution, 40 to 60 D.L.P./mm, or ultra-high resolution, 50 to 100 D.L.P./mm, lens systems and over 200 chromed, etched and cut glass reticle patterns from which to choose. Thick, modular housings mean strength and variety of optic design. All lenses, tubes, reticles and assembly work is completed in their U.S.-based factory.

U.S. OPTICS TECHNOLOGIES, INC.

9MM/40 S&W MAGAZINE LOADER

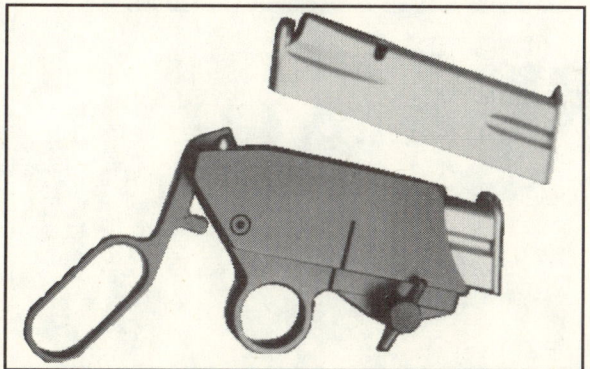

Butler Creek introduces their new Lever Loader™ to efficiently load 9mm and 40 Smith & Wesson magazines.

The Lever Loader is a two-stage loading device that not only depresses the magazine follower, but draws the bullet completely into the back of the magazine.

Operated just like the old lever-action saddle guns, you just insert the magazine, raise the lever and drop the bullets into the slot. The lever holds the spring down and pulls each round all the way into the magazine.

Fast and easy, the magazine retainer adjusts for normal single stack and staggered magazines.

The Lever Loader retails for $16.95. For more information, call or write Butler Creek.

BUTLER CREEK CORPORATION

NEW SCOPE RINGS

With Lever Lok® Rings from U.S. Optics, shooters can remove the scope from their long-range or precision rifle without disturbing the zero.

Lever Lok Rings stay on the rifle. The top half of each ring opens for scope removal, while the bottom half remains in perfect alignment, lateral position and tilt, similar to precision V-blocks.

Originally designed for military use, Lever Lok Rings are currently being sold commercially to police departments and foreign agencies.

The rings are made in 1", 30mm, 35mm, 40mm and 50mm sizes and fit standard Picatinney and Weaver rails. Retail price starts at $175.00.

For more information, call or write U.S. Optics and mention *Shooter's Marketplace*.

U.S. OPTICS TECHNOLOGIES, INC.

See manufacturers' addresses on page 299.

Shooter's Marketplace

PROTECTIVE METAL CASES

A complete line of protective metal transport/shipping cases are available through ICC (Impact Case Company) and KK International. Both lines are products of Knouff & Knouff, Inc. In addition to the flat case design, Knouff & Knouff offers three-piece and trunk-style cases as standard. Customized cases are manufactured by KK Air International, cases built to meet each customer's design and size requirements. KK Air can build one case or large quantities of cases. All cases offer uncompromised quality and strength and are designed for the serious sportsman who must subject his equipment to third-party handling and where often the success of a trip depends upon the equipment arriving intact. Write or call Knouff & Knouff, Inc. for more information, detail sheets and pricing.

KNOUFF & KNOUFF, INC.

LASER/ELECTRONIC SIGHT MOUNTS

Aimtech offers a full line of unique scope, electronic sight and laser mounting systems. Right-side auto-pistol mounts, saddle shotgun mounts, double decker bow mounts, see-through solid rifle and muzzleloader mounts, as well as their patented revolver and Glock mount, were all designed with the convenience of the shooter in mind.

Highest-quality computer-aided design/manufacture and modern heat-treated alloy combine to make them among the best looking, best feeling mounts in the industry.

Aimtech products are available through all major distributors and quality gun dealers.

Write or call the manufacturer for more information or a free catalog.

AIMTECH MOUNT SYSTEMS

FULL LINE OF CLAY TARGETS

For over 100 years White Flyer has manufactured a line of targets for the clay bird shooting sports. Three plants across the country produce a complete line-up that meets the specifications of all clay target shooting organizations including trap, Skeet, Sporting Clays and International (trap, Skeet & Bunker). The targets are available in a variety of colors and color combinations to match almost any background or lighting condition. Also available are high visibility "Flash" targets suitable for special shoot-offs, demo shoots etc. White Flyer's Sporting Clay offerings include Pheasant, Rabbit, Midi, Mini and Battue targets. Dealers and clubs can call White Flyer's toll-free number for the name of their local distributor or the special 602 number for export operations.

WHITE FLYER

RIFLE REST

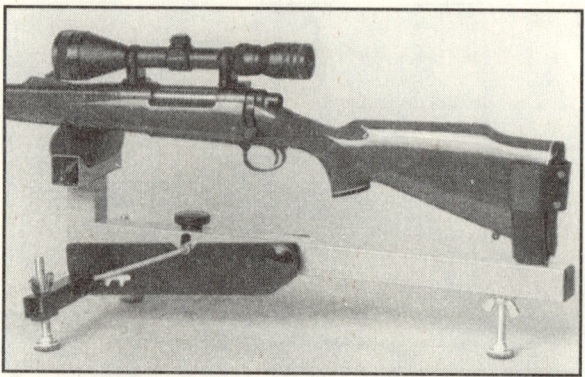

The Bench Master rifle rest from Desert Mountain Mfg. offers precision line-up and recoil reduction for load testing, varmint shooting or just sighting-in.

It features three course positions totaling 5½" with 1½" fine adjustment in each position, plus leveling and shoulder height adjustments for maximum control and comfort.

Because of its unique design, the Bench Master can easily double as a rifle vise for scope mounting, bore sighting, cleaning and more.

The Bench Master comes with a Lifetime Warranty and a list price of $119.95.

Contact your local dealer, or call or write Desert Mountain Mfg. for additional information or a free brochure.

DESERT MOUNTAIN MFG.

Shooter's Marketplace

WESTERN-STYLE TARGET REVOLVER

The new Model 939 Premier™ 22-caliber revolver from H&R mates all the features of a target revolver to a western-style grip frame profile. A double action with 9-shot, swing-out cylinder, the Premier features a heavy target-grade 6" barrel with barrel rib and fully-adjustable sights. A deeply recessed barrel crown protects the rifling. The 939 Premier reliably uses 22 Short, Long and Long Rifle cartridges.

The western-style walnut-stained hardwood grip, long favored for its pointability and comfort, accents the high polish and traditional deep blue of the gun. In keeping with H&R tradition, the Premier is equipped with the patented transfer bar safety system and is American-made using only high-quality ferrous metals. For more information, call or write H&R 1871.

H&R 1871, INC.

SPECIALTY 12-GA. SLUG GUN

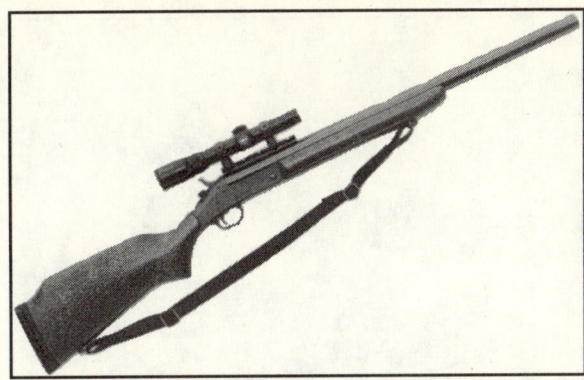

The unique 12-ga. SB2-980 Ultra Slug Hunter from H&R 1871 features a heavy target-style rifled barrel for a level of long-range accuracy previously found only in high-priced custom slug shotguns.

Built on a 10-ga. action, it uses a 10-ga. barrel blank under-bored to 12-ga. and rifled with a 1:35" twist to give it the extra weight and strength necessary to moderate the recoil generated by high-velocity slug loads. The 980 features factory-mounted Weaver-style scope base, walnut-stained American hardwood Monte Carlo stock and forend, ventilated recoil pad, sling swivels, black nylon sling, matte black receiver and low-luster blued barrel. The American-made 980 with patented transfer bar safety system sells for a suggested retail price of $224.95. For information call or write H&R.

H&R 1871, INC.

NEW SINGLE SHOT BIG GAME RIFLE

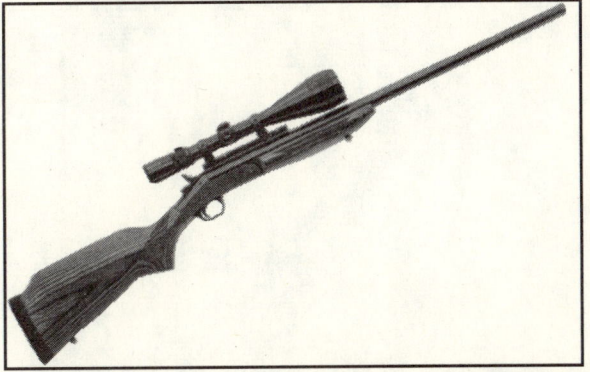

H&R 1871 has expanded their single shot Ultra rifle line with the introduction of two big game hunting rifles in 25-06 Remington and 308 Winchester.

Made to the same standards of quality and accuracy as H&R's Varmint Ultras, these newest members of the Ultra line feature heat-treated investment-cast steel frames, high polish blue actions and barrels, Monte Carlo stocks, scope rails, sling swivel studs and premium recoil pads. The big game rifles will showcase rich cinnamon color wood stocks and forends with a dark brown laminate stripe and are precisely carved, hand sanded, carefully finished and hand checkered. Like all H&R 1871 rifles, the new American-made Ultra big game rifles have the patented transfer bar safety system. For more information, see your dealer or write H&R directly.

H&R 1871, INC.

NEW SURVIVAL SHOTGUN

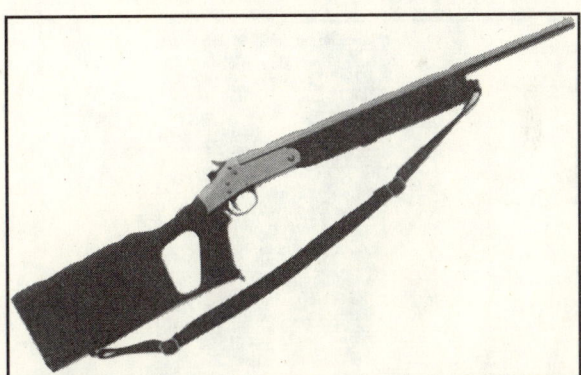

A new short-barreled 45 Colt/410 survival gun has been announced by New England Firearms. The Survivor™ features the NEF single shot action with transfer bar safety and a fully rifled 22" single barrel to handle both 3" 410 shotshells and 45 Colt revolver cartridges. The barrel's unique removable choke tube stabilizes the wad and shot charge down bore. The high-impact polymer stock with modified thumbhole design sports a full pistol grip for a secure hold. A removable buttplate accesses a storage compartment in the stock with additional storage contained in the full beaver-tail forend. Available in matte black or electroless nickel finish for extra durability. For more information, call or write New England Firearms.

NEW ENGLAND FIREARMS

See manufacturers' addresses on page 299.

SHOOTER'S MARKETPLACE

GATLING GUN BUILDER'S PACKAGE

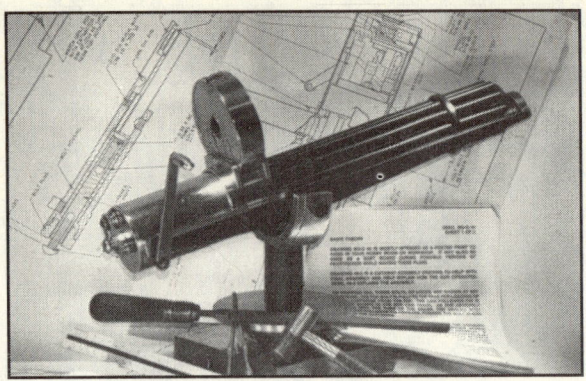

Complete plans for the 22-caliber Long Rifle Gatling are now available and have been fully adapted to incorporate obtainable materials and makeable parts. No castings are required.

The to-scale blueprints are fully dimensioned and toleranced. A 40-page instruction booklet lists materials and explains each part and how it is made.

The package includes drawings and instructions for making rifled barrels, wooden spoked wheels and all internal parts. The finished piece has 10 rifled barrels and is 3 feet long by 2 feet high.

Plans for the gun and carriage are $58.46; priority postage within the U.S. included. Overseas air add $14.00. Materials kits also available. Only check or money order accepted. Include a self-addressed card.

R.G.-G., INC.

ASPHERICAL BINOCULARS

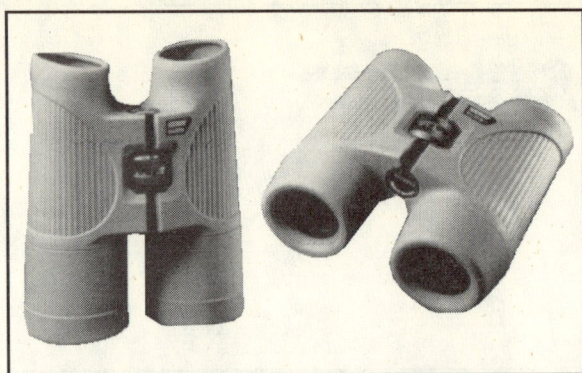

Docter® Optic introduces two new aspherical-lense binoculars—the 10x40 B/GA and the 8x32 B/GA.

Aspherical lenses provide six image-correction parameters to deliver sharper, more brilliant, true-to-life imaging. All glass-to-air surfaces have a special multi-level phase correction coating matched to the eye's twilight vision for optimized color fidelity and light transmission. Resilient rubber armoring makes them shock absorbent, slip-proof and dirt resistant on the outside while the completely sealed interior of the die-cast aluminum body makes them impervious to dust and climatic conditions. The intricate roof-prism construction allows for a compact, ergonomic design. Manufactured to high German optical standards, the 10x40 and 8x32 B/GA are backed by a 30-year warranty.

DOCTER OPTIC TECHNOLOGIES, INC.

CLASSIC GUN SAFES

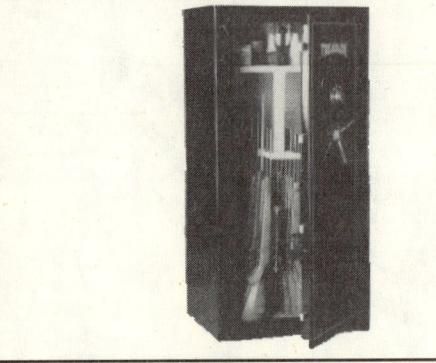

A classic series of gun safes is available from Treadlok for the safe and secure storage of your firearms.

All Treadlok safes feature the Posilok locking system, one of the finest in the industry. Posilok secures the safe door with large rectangular bolts and is backed up by a floating, drill-resistant, hard-plate, remote relocking device and industry standard S&G lock.

Treadlok safes come in three sizes with the capacity to hold up to fifty guns and are offered in four designer colors with brass hardware and accents. All have an attractive high gloss finish.

Write or call Treadlok for additional information. Be sure to mention *Shooter's Marketplace*.

TREADLOK GUN SAFE, INC.

QUICK-CHANGE MUZZLE BRAKE

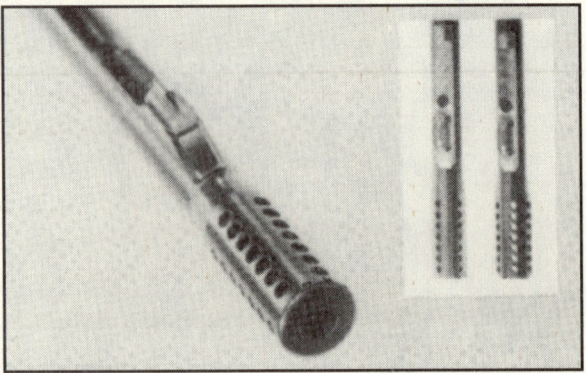

The Hastings Quick-Change Muzzle Brake is right at home on the range or in the woods.

The HQC tames recoil and muzzle jump by deflecting expanding gases perpendicular to the bore. This reduces the pounding taken during extended shooting sessions and helps eliminate flinching.

All effective muzzlebrakes do increase noise for the shooter (this is not a problem on the range when ear protection is worn, but can be a problem when hunting). The HQC is unique in that a quick rotation of the outer sleeve seals the gas ports deactivating the brake and returns noise levels to normal.

Hastings installs the HQC on most centerfire rifles. It's available in stainless steel or blued finish. Contact Hastings for complete details.

HASTINGS BARRELS

See manufacturers' addresses on page 299.

Shooter's Marketplace

CLAY TARGET TRAPS

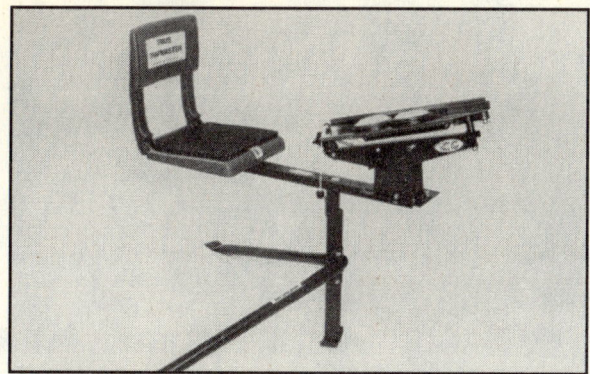

A company who has set the standard for the industry for 40 years, Trius offers low-cost, easy-cocking mechanical clay target traps with lay-on loading. Singles, doubles and piggy-back doubles make it possible to put up to four birds in the air at one time.

For the casual shooter, Trius offers three models: the Birdshooter—quality at an affordable price, now with a high-angle retainer; the Model 92 Trius Trap—their best selling trap with high-angle clip and can thrower; and the Trapmaster—with sit-down comfort and pivoting action.

For Sporting Clays/Hunter Clays, Trius offers five trap models to throw all types of Sporting Clay targets including rabbits.

A free catalog is available.

TRIUS PRODUCTS, INC.

PERSONAL DEFENSE AMMUNITION

Glaser Safety Slug's state-of-the-art, professional-grade personal defense ammunition is offered in two bullet styles: Blue uses a #12 compressed shot core for maximum ricochet protection; and Silver uses a #6 compressed shot core for maximum penetration.

The Glaser Safety Slug manufacturing process results in outstanding accuracy with documented groups of less than 1" at 100 yards. This is one reason Glaser has been a top choice of professional and private law enforcement agencies worldwide for more than sixteen years.

Currently available in every caliber from 25 ACP through 30-06, plus 40 S&W, 10mm, 223 and 7.62x39.

Write Glaser Safety Slug for a free brochure.

GLASER SAFETY SLUG, INC.

RELOADING/SHOOTING SUPPLY CATALOG

Midway Arms' 64-page monthly catalog contains one of the world's largest selections of reloading and shooting products.

The catalog features products from nearly every manufacturer of reloading equipment and shooting accessories. There are over 7,000 items offered for reloaders of every level.

Experienced shooters as well as beginners will find everything they need to perfect their reloading skills. Handloaders will find an extensive selection of bulk-packed bullets and brass at attractive prices.

Midway's staff has been providing fast, friendly service since 1977. For convenience, free shipping to the first 48 states is provided. Call or write for a free three-month catalog subscription.

MIDWAY ARMS, INC.

STOCK KIT AND BIPOD

Glaser's MG-42 Stock Kit transforms your Ruger 10/22™ into a 2/3-scale semi-auto replica of the WWII MG-42 machine gun. The lightweight MG-42 stock fully encloses the 10/22 receiver and barrel to give the appearance and feel of the original machine gun. Ventilation slots in the barrel shroud provide barrel cooling just like the original, and front and rear sights come with adjustments for both windage and elevation. Fully assembled, the replica weighs no more than the original 10/22, maintains excellent balance and has the feel and appearance of a totally new gun. For authenticity, a Featherweight Bipod can be added to enhance prone and bench shooting accuracy. No alterations to the 10/22 are required and the old stock can be replaced in minutes. For a free brochure, contact Glaser Safety Slug.

GLASER SAFETY SLUG, INC.

See manufacturers' addresses on page 299.

Shooter's Marketplace

RIFLE AND SHOTGUN IRON SIGHTS

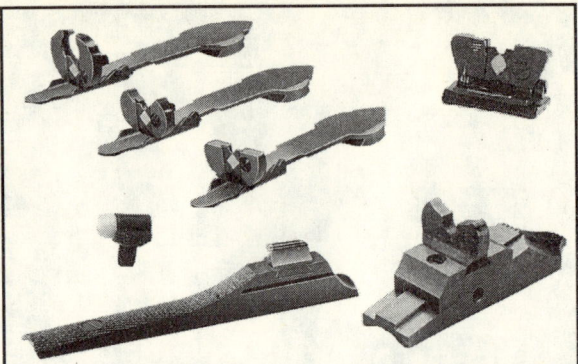

Continuing its 100-year tradition of quality and precision, Marble Arms offers a complete selection of iron sights for rifles and shotguns. Machined from solid steel and blued to match the finest firearms, Marble sights include the exclusive Flat Top Folding Leaf Sight with elevation and windage adjustments. This feature allows sight centering with a screwdriver instead of brass block and hammer, resulting in faster sighting-in and no off-center profile. Marble Arms also offers a complete selection of sporting rear sights, a universal rear sight with five base sizes and three upright styles, and traditional front ramps and bases. For double- and single-barrel shotguns, Marble manufactures many styles and colors of Marble and Poly-Choke® front and rear shotgun sights.

MARBLE ARMS CORP.

NEW AMMUNITION SERVICE

New England Ammunition Co. offers a comprehensive selection of Hansen Cartridge Co. ammunition which is well-known as a quality alternative to high-priced ammunition.

Their constantly updated supply of high-quality surplus ammunition fits the needs of avid American target shooters, plinkers, hunters and reloaders. It's all newly manufactured, brass cased, non-corrosive, Boxer-primed and fully reloadable.

New England Ammunition Co. offers many unique and specialty calibers from the SS109/5.56 through the 50 Browning Super Match as well as a large selection of hollowpoint, softpoint and FMJ handgun and rifle cartridges. Write New England Ammunition Co. for pricing information and ordering instructions.

NEW ENGLAND AMMUNITION CO.

SKS ACCESSORIES

GUNS, a division of D.C. Engineering, Inc., offers a full line of accessories for the SKS rifle. Blue steel magazines, scopes and mounts, rings, muzzlebrakes, competition trigger groups, ventilated handguards, bipods, buttpads, peep sight systems, five-round plugs, tools and gunstocks are some of the accessories available from this Detroit-based firm.

Many of their innovative accessories are patented designs and all are built with quality and function in mind. Twenty years of manufacturing experience combined with new and improved computer-aided design and manufacturing techniques ensure exact tolerances of all their products.

To order, call their toll-free line; for inquiries or catalog call GUNS direct.

GUNS, DIV. OF D.C. ENGINEERING, INC.

SIZING AND FORMING LUBE

Imperial Sizing Wax from E-Z-Way Systems was developed in the early 1970s to allow simple, easy and effective reloading and reforming.

A blend of two waxes and two oils, a thin film of high-lubricity Imperial applied to the outside of a rifle case with your fingertips will ensure smooth loading tool operation with no stuck or dented cases. The lube can be removed simply with a paper towel.

Because it is used sparingly, it is very economical—one tin will size several thousand cases. It is available in 1- and 2-ounce tins with suggested retail prices of $3.75 and $6.00, respectively.

See your local dealer or write directly to E-Z-Way Systems for more information.

E-Z-WAY SYSTEMS

See manufacturers' addresses on page 299.

SHOOTER'S MARKETPLACE

NEW FIELD RIFLE

The newest offering from Eagle Arms is their Predator rifle, made specifically for varmint and predator hunting.

Its unusually stiff 1¼" diameter barrel is 18" in length, making it convenient for field use.

The Predator is equipped with the Eagle International-style upper receiver bearing an integral Weaver-style cross-section mount and their National Match trigger. The cylindrical handguard allows the barrel to float freely for best accuracy.

Also available is the Eagle Eye Match Rifle, which has the same features as the Predator, but comes with 24" long barrel. Williams rear and Anschutz front sight assemblies are available upon request. Write for more information.

EAGLE ARMS INCORPORATED

LIFETIME WARRANTY

Eagle Arms has significantly improved the terms of its warranty. Under the new limited Lifetime Warranty, each Eagle Arms rifle, delivered from the factory after November 30, 1994, is warranted to be free of defects in either material or workmanship for the life of the original owner. Terms of the Lifetime Warranty are similar to those of the previous one-year policy and follow industry standards. Normal wear and damage due to accident, negligence, misuse, unauthorized repair or alteration and the use of handloaded ammunition are not covered. This warranty reflects Eagle Arm's confidence in the quality and reliability of its M15 series rifles. Like the military M16 family from which they were derived, M15s have proven robust and problem-free. Write for more information.

EAGLE ARMS INCORPORATED

PREMIER TARGET RIFLE

The Action Master M15A3 is Eagle Arm's premier target-grade rifle.

Specifically intended for IPSC and other action matches, this rifle features a free-floating 20" premium stainless steel barrel with 1 in 9" twist and an overall length of 40½". The barrel bears an improved recoil check for quick recovery from recoil. Weight of the M15A3 Action Master is at 8 pounds, 4 ounces.

The Action Master is equipped with the Eagle one-piece international-style upper receiver for scope mounting, solid aluminuim handguard tube, and National Match Trigger.

For more information, call or write Eagle Arms and mention *Shooter's Marketplace*.

EAGLE ARMS INCORPORATED

REESTABLISHED FIREARMS LINE

ArmaLite, Inc. has been reestablished. Eagle Arms Incorporated has purchased the ArmaLite trademark and certain other assets, and has reestablished the ArmaLite line of firearms. The combined company bears the ArmaLite name, with Eagle Arms as a Division of ArmaLite.

The ArmaLite line includes the M15A2 223-caliber rifle, the fixed-stock M4C Carbine and the M15A2 National Match Rifle, scheduled for release in August of 1995. In addition, ArmaLite is seriously considering the reintroduction of the 223-caliber AR-180 and the 308-caliber AR-10.

The Eagle Arms Division will continue to offer the Action Master, Spirit, Eagle Eye, Predator and Golden Eagle rifles. Write for more information.

ARMALITE, INC.

See manufacturers' addresses on page 299.

Shooter's Marketplace

SHOOTING GLASSES

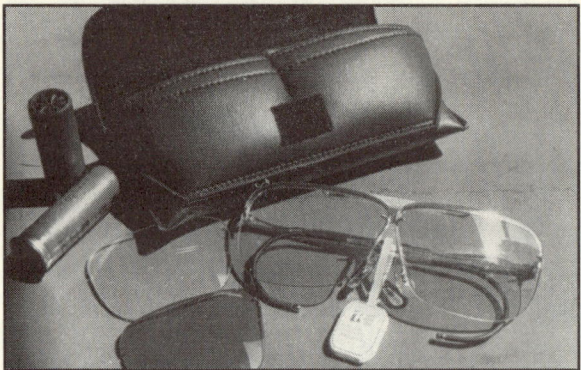

New Randolph Ranger shooting glasses combine safety, comfort, visual acuity and flexibility. The standard shatter-proof interchangeable polycarbonate lenses are designed to withstand multiple 12-gauge shotgun blasts from 12 meters and offer 100% UV ray lens protection. Choose any three of the ten lens colors offered: clear, yellow, canary, orange, sunset, vermilion, purple, brown, bronze, or gray. Ranger shooting glasses now come in three sizes—small, medium and large—and in two finishes—23k gold-plate or matte black finish. The Ranger can be purchased with the three-lens system or as Rx frame only for prescription wearers. For more information, write, call or fax Randolph Engineering, or see your local gun dealer or sporting goods store.

RANDOLPH ENGINEERING, INC.

FOLDING BIPODS

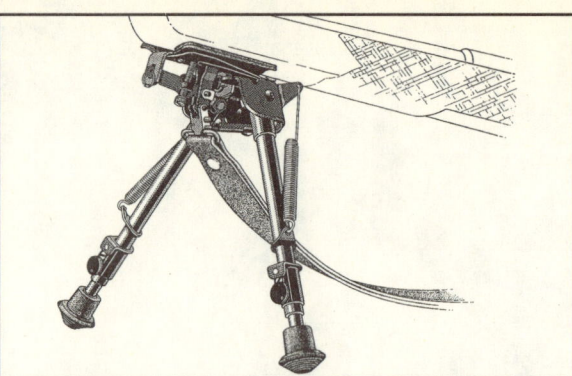

Harris Bipods clamp securely to most stud-equipped bolt-action rifles and are quick-detachable. With adapters, they will fit some other guns. On all models except the Model LM, folding legs have completely adjustable spring-return extensions. The sling swivel attaches to the clamp. This time-proven design is manufactured with heat-treated steel and hard alloys and has a black anodized finish.

Series S Bipods rotate 45° for instant leveling on uneven ground. Hinged base has tension adjustment and buffer springs to eliminate tremor or looseness in crotch area of bipod. They are otherwise similar to non-rotating Series 1A2.

Eleven models are available from Harris Engineering; literature is free.

HARRIS ENGINEERING, INC.

CUSTOM 1911 PISTOLS AND PARTS

Les Baer manufactures top-quality 1911-style custom pistols and offers a complete line of precision-machined custom 1911 parts and accessories.

More than 20 high-performance pistol models are available for defense, law enforcement and competition use. Each pistol is custom-built and hand-fitted on Baer's American-made, National Match forged frames, slides and barrels by Baer custom gunsmiths. Match-grade accuracy is guaranteed. Baer also offers standard and reduced "Commanche" sizes, stainless steel and aluminum models, and some high-capacity 1911s.

Their exclusive forged steel, stainless steel and aluminum frames and slides in standard and reduced sizes, and Baer National Match barrels are also available as separate components.

LES BAER CUSTOM, INC.

NEW SHOTGUN SLING SYSTEM

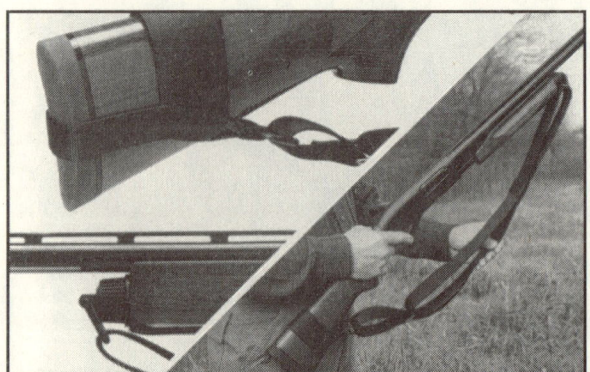

The Total Shotgun Sling from The Outdoor Connection is a complete, fully assembled sling system for 12-gauge Remington shotguns, Models 870, 1100 and 11-87. The system includes a unique magazine tube cap, called the Total Cap, a reliable buttstock attaching device and the $1\frac{1}{4}$"-wide Super Sling-2. The Total Cap is designed to fit all models of 12-gauge Remington shotguns and is installed by simply removing and replacing the original tube cap by hand; no tools are required.

The Total Sling System can be installed or removed in less than 1-minute and requires no drilling, screws, tools or alterations to the shotgun. It is a safe, secure, easily manageable system for the serious hunter and shooter.

THE OUTDOOR CONNECTION, INC.

See manufacturers' addresses on page 299.

Shooter's Marketplace

NEW 65MM SPOTTING SCOPE

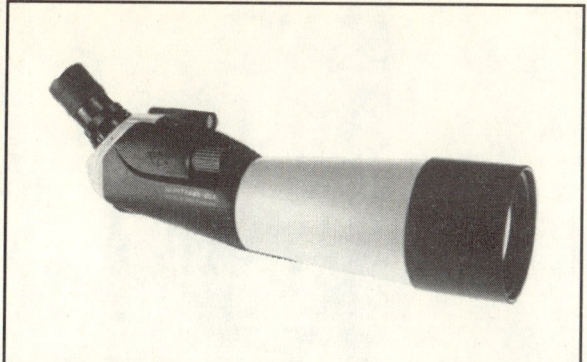

The Model 850U Nighthawk 65mm spotting scope is among the world's most compact, lightweight scopes. Manufactured of modern materials, including polycarbon, aluminum, zamex and rubber, it offers the same optics as the 80mm but a different objective lens. Features include a focal length of 386mm, a retractable hood to protect the objective lens, a rubber-armored main body housing and a 1.8x optical finder. Available as accessories are interchangeable eyepieces (20x, 25x, 40x, 60x), a zoom lens from 22-60x, an ingenious carrying case that can be left on the scope while viewing and telephotographic equipment. All optics are multi-coated and eyepieces have a bayonet-type mounting for quick lens attachment. Also offered as a straight viewing scope (Model 850). Both come attractively gift-boxed.

SWIFT INSTRUMENTS, INC.

NEW 80MM SPOTTING SCOPE

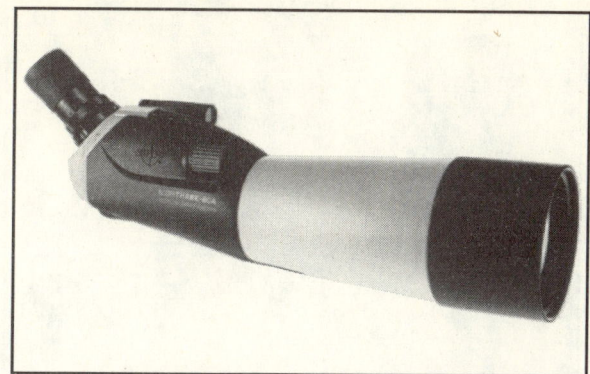

The Model 849U Nighthawk from Swift Instruments is geared for the hunter and nature photographer. Measuring 350mm in length without the eyepiece, this compact, lightweight spotting scope is virtually free from chromatic aberration or distortion and offers excellent depth of field and resolving power. The rubber-armored main body housing features a 1.8x optical finder and a retractable hood to protect the objective lens from direct exposure to sunlight and dew. Accessories include interchangeable eyepieces, 25x, 31x, 50x, 75x; a zoom eyepiece, 28-75x; a soft carrying case; and telephotographic equipment. All optics are multi-coated and eyepieces feature a bayonet-type mounting for quick lens attachment. Also available as a straight viewing scope (Model 849). Both come attractively gift-boxed.

SWIFT INSTRUMENTS, INC.

WIDE-FIELD RIFLESCOPE

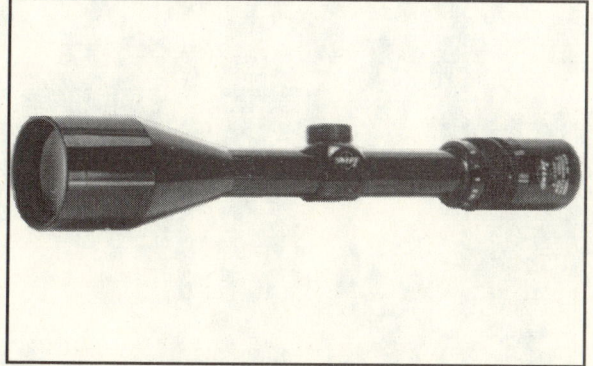

The 649 Swift from Swift Instruments is a wide-field, multi-coated riflescope with a maximum effective objective lens diameter of 50mm.

The large objective lens on this scope makes it especially effective in poor light conditions. However, its 4-12x range also makes it useful under most hunting conditions.

The 649 is hard-anodized, fog- and waterproof, and is equipped with a self-centering quadraplex reticle.

Two finishes are available—regular (649) and matte (649M).

Shock tested by Swift, the 649 comes gift-boxed. For more information on this and other available products, write Swift Instruments.

SWIFT INSTRUMENTS, INC.

COMPACT RIFLESCOPE

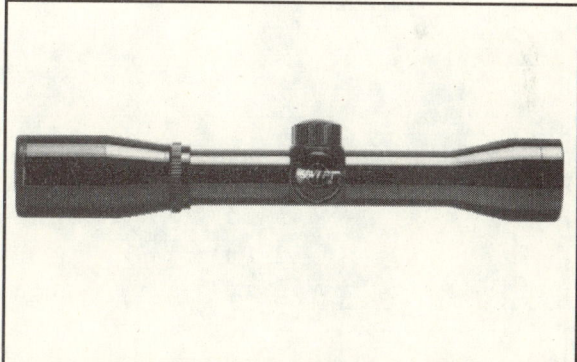

The 668 riflescope from Swift Instruments is a compact, general-purpose scope designed especially for 22-caliber rifles.

It has a 1-inch diameter tube, is 10 inches long and weighs just 8.9 ounces.

This 4x32mm lightweight scope has all the features of a full-sized Swift scope: it is fog-proof, waterproof and multi-coated.

The 668 is equipped with a self-centering Quadraplex reticle and is matte-finished.

The field of view of the 668 is 25 feet at 100 yards. It has an eye relief of 4 inches and a relative brightness reading of 64.

It is available from Swift Instruments attractively gift-boxed.

SWIFT INSTRUMENTS, INC.

See manufacturers' addresses on page 299.

Shooter's Marketplace

NEW SCOPE MOUNT

S&K Manufacturing Co. offers their new scope mount with SKulptured Base and Smooth Kontoured Rings for most factory drilled and tapped rifles.

Available in stainless steel, matte or polished blued finish, the mounts feature front and rear base windage adjustments and ring interchangeability. In addition there are no projections, bulges, lobes or joints and no ring halves to join together with fragile caps.

Made from steel, the base weighs approximately 1 ounce, the rings 1/2-ounce each. They are not interchangeable with any other brands.

S&K carries a complete inventory for all popular rifles. The mounts come with a lifetime guarantee. For a current catalog, send $1.00 to S&K Manufacturing Co.

S&K MANUFACTURING CO.

FIREARM SAFES

Liberty Safes offers 18 different models of UL certified safes in many sizes and colors for fire and burglary protection. Four series of safes are available.

The Presidential Series features quad-wall fire protection, a 1″ thick door with gear drive and security clutch, 1/4″ body and 24K gold package and weighs 1120 to 1700 pounds. The Washington Series weighs from 700 to 1350 pounds and features double-wall fire protection, a 3/8″ or optional 1/2″ thick door and 3/16″ body. The Lincoln Series with 10-gauge body and 1/4″ thick door weighs 420 to 900 pounds and has a gloss exterior with polished brass accents. Weighing from 310 to 570 pounds, the Franklin Series features a 3/16″ thick door, 1/8″ body and charcoal gray enamel finish. For more information, call Liberty's toll-free number.

LIBERTY SAFES

RIFLE/SHOTGUN SIGHT-IN VISE

Ideal for any caliber firearm, the Sight-Vise SSV-2 from Lohman Manufacturing is a precision instrument that makes accurate rifle sighting and shotgun patterning easy. The Sight-Vise features adjustable dual clamps to hold the gun stock firmly, regardless of size or shape, and padded jaws to prevent stock marring. An adjustable rear post and wide stable base combine to reduce recoil and provide a solid rest for accurate, precise shotgun patterning or rifle sighting. For extra support and stability, lead shot can be added to the compartment in the base. The American-made SSV-2 also serves to secure guns for scope mounting, cleaning or repair work.

Contact Lohman for more information.

LOHMAN MANUFACTURING CO., INC.

GUN REPAIR SCHOOL

Modern Gun Repair School has taught gun repair the home-study way to more than 45,000 students since 1946. All courses are nationally accredited and approved for Veterans Training.

Courses include all lessons (including how to get your FFL), a custom tool kit, Powley Calculator and Powley Computer, a copy of GUN DIGEST, the Gun Parts Catalog and Brownell's Catalog, a mainspring vise, school binders, a pull and drop gauge and trigger pull gauge, two parchment diplomas ready for framing and free consultation service, plus much more.

You can enjoy your career; start your own business and make money in your spare time. No experience is needed. Write or call for free information; there is no obligation and no salesman will call.

MODERN GUN REPAIR SCHOOL

See manufacturers' addresses on page 299.

SHOOTER'S MARKETPLACE MANUFACTURERS' ADDRESSES

AIMTECH MOUNT SYSTEMS (Pg. 290)
Attn: Dept. SM'96
P.O. Box 223
Thomasville, GA 31792
Phone: 912-226-4313
Fax: 912-227-0222

AMERICAN CUSTOM GUNMAKERS GUILD (A.C.G.G.) (Pg. 270)
Attn: Dept. SM'96
P.O. Box 812
Burlington, IA 52601-0812
Phone/Fax: 319-752-6114

AMERICAN SECURITY PRODUCTS CO. (AMSEC) (Pg. 280)
Attn: Dept. SM'96
11925 Pacific Avenue
Fontana, CA 92337

ARMALITE, INC. (Pg. 295)
Attn: Dept. SM'96
P.O. Box 486
Coal Valley, IL 61240
Phone: 309-799-5767
Fax: 309-799-5150

LES BAER CUSTOM, INC. (Pg. 296)
Attn: Dept. SM'96
29601 34th Ave.
Hillsdale, IL 61257
Phone: 309-658-2716
Fax: 309-658-2610

BALD EAGLE PRECISION MACHINE CO. (Pg. 287)
Attn: Dept. SM'96
101 Allison Street
Lock Haven, PA 17745
Phone: 717-748-6772
Fax: 717-748-4443

BERGER BULLETS, LTD. (Pg. 286)
Attn: Dept. SM'96
5342 W. Camelback Rd., Suite 500
Glendale, AZ 85301
Phone: 602-842-4001
Fax: 602-934-9083

BIRCHWOOD CASEY (Pg. 282)
Attn: Dept. SM'96
7900 Fuller Road
Eden Prairie, MN 55344
Phone: 800-328-6156
Fax: 612-937-7979

BLUE RIDGE MACHINERY & TOOLS, INC. (Pg. 278)
Attn: Dept. GD'96
P.O. Box 536
Hurricane, WV 25526
Phone: 800-872-6500
Fax: 304-562-5311

BOONIE PACKER PRODUCTS (Pg. 288)
Attn: Dept. SM'96
P.O. Box 12204
Salem, OR 97309
Phone: 800-477-3244
Fax: 503-581-3191

BRILEY MFG., INC. (Pg. 281)
Attn: Dept. SM'96
1230 Lumpkin
Houston, TX 77043
Phone: 800-331-5718 or 713-932-6995
Fax: 713-932-1043

B-SQUARE COMPANY, INC. (Pgs. 268, 269)
Attn: Dept. SM'96
P.O. Box 11281
Fort Worth, TX 76110
Phone: 800-433-2909 or 817-923-0964
Fax: 817-926-7012

BUSHNELL SPORTS OPTICS WORLDWIDE (Pg. 284)
Attn: Dept. SM'96
9200 Cody
Overland Park, KS 66214
Phone: 800-423-3537
Fax: 913-752-3489

BUTLER CREEK CORPORATION. (Pg. 289)
Attn: Dept. SM'96
290 Arden Drive
Belgrade, MT 59714
Phone: 800-423-8327 or 406-388-1356
Fax: 406-388-7204

CALI'CO HARDWOODS, INC. (Pg. 286)
Attn: Dept. SM'96
1648 Airport Boulevard
Windsor, CA 95492
Phone: 707-546-4045
Fax: 707-546-4027

CRYO-ACCURIZING, DIV. OF 300° BELOW, INC. (Pg. 274)
Attn: Dept. SM'96
1160 South Monroe
Decatur, IL 62521
Phone: 217-423-3070
Fax: 217-423-2756

DESERT MOUNTAIN MFG. (Pg. 290)
Attn: Dept. SM'96
P.O. Box 2767
Columbia Falls, MT 59912
Phone: 800-477-0762 or 406-892-7772
Fax: 406-892-7772

J. DEWEY MFG. CO., INC. (Pg. 274)
Attn: Dept. SM'96
P.O. Box 2014
Southbury, CT 06488
Phone: 203-264-3064

DIAMOND MACHINING TECHNOLOGY, INC. (DMT) (Pg. 270, 287)
Attn: Dept. SM'96
85 Hayes Memorial Drive
Marlborough, MA 01752-1892
Phone: 508-481-5944
Fax: 508-485-3924

DOCTER OPTIC TECHNOLOGIES, INC. (Pg. 292)
Attn: Dept. SM'96
4685 Boulder Hwy., Suite A
Las Vegas, NV 89121
Phone: 800-290-3634
Fax: 702-898-3737

EAGLE ARMS, INCORPORATED (Pg. 295)
Attn: Dept. SM'96
P.O. Box 457, 128 East 23rd Avenue
Coal Valley, IL 61240
Phone: 800-336-0184
Fax: 309-799-5150

E-Z-WAY SYSTEMS (Pg. 294)
Attn: Dept. SM'96
P.O. Box 4310-0700
Newark, OH 43058
Phone: 614-345-6645 or 800-848-2072
Fax: 614-345-6600

FAITH ASSOCIATES, INC. (Pg. 286)
Attn: Dept. SM'96
1139 South Greenville Hwy.
Hendersonville, NC 28739
Phone: 704-692-1916
Fax: 704-697-6827

FLASHTEK, INC. (Pg. 272)
Attn: Dept. SM'96
714 Indian Hills Dr.
Moscow, ID 83843
Phone: 208-882-6893
Fax: 208-882-7275

GALAZAN (Pg. 282)
Attn: Dept. SM'96
P.O. Box 1692
New Britain, CT 06051-1692
Phone: 203-225-6581
Fax: 203-832-8707

GLASER SAFETY SLUG, INC. (Pg. 293)
Attn: Dept. SM'96
P.O. Box 8223
Foster City, CA 94404-8223
Phone: 800-221-3489
Fax: 415-345-8217

THE GUN PARTS CORP. (Pg. 272)
Attn: Dept. SM'96
226 Williams Lane
West Hurley, NY 12491
Phone: 914-679-2417
Fax: 914-679-5849

GUNS, DIV. OF D.C. ENGINEERING, INC. (Pg. 294)
Attn: Dept. SM'96
8633 Southfield Fwy.
Detroit, MI 48228
Phone: 313-271-7111 or 800-886-7623 Orders Only
Fax: 313-271-7112

HARRIS ENGINEERING, INC. (Pg. 296)
Attn: Dept. SM'96
Route 1
Barlow, KY 42024
Phone: 502-334-3633
Fax: 502-334-3000

HASTINGS BARRELS (Pg. 285, 292)
Attn: Dept. SM'96
P.O. Box 224
Clay Center, KS 67432
Phone: 913-632-3169
Fax: 913-632-6554

HIGH STANDARD MANUFACTURING COMPANY (Pg. 271)
Attn: Dept. SM'96
264 Whitney St.
Hartford, CT 06105
Phone: 203-586-8220
Fax: 203-231-0411

H&R 1871, INC. (Pg. 291)
Attn: Dept. SM'96
60 Industrial Rowe
Gardner, MA 01440
Phone: 508-632-9393
Fax: 508-632-2300

IRONSIGHTER CO. (Pg. 267)
Attn: Dept. SM'96
P.O. Box 85070
Westland, MI 48185
Phone: 313-326-8731
Fax: 313-326-3378

NEIL JONES CUSTOM PRODUCTS (Pg. 284)
Attn: Dept. SM'96
RD 1, Box 483-A
Saegertown, PA 16433
Phone: 814-763-2769
Fax: 814-763-4228

KIWI BRANDS, INC. (Pg. 276)
Attn: Dept. SM'96
447 Old Swede Road
Douglassville, PA 19518
Phone: 800-BUY-KIWI
Fax: 610-385-6177

KLA ENTERPRISES (Pg. 278)
Attn: Dept. SM'96
P.O. Box 2028
Eaton Park, FL 33840
Phone: 813-682-2829

KNOUFF & KNOUFF, INC. (Pg. 290)
Attn: Dept. SM'96
P.O. Box 9912
Spokane, WA 99209
Phone: 800-262-3322
Fax: 509-326-5436

KWIK-SITE CO. (Pg. 283)
Attn: Dept. SM'96
5555 Treadwell Ave.
Wayne, MI 48184
Phone: 313-326-1500
Fax: 313-326-4120

LASER DEVICES, INC. (Pg. 275)
Attn: Dept. SM'96
2 Harris Court, A-4
Monterey, CA 93940
Phone: 800-235-2162
Fax: 408-373-0903

LIBERTY SAFES *(Pg. 298)*
Attn: Dept. SM'96
1060 N. Spring Creek Place
Springville, UT 84663
Phone: 800-247-5625 or 801-489-8550
Fax: 801-489-6409

LOHMAN MANUFACTURING CO., INC. *(Pg. 298)*
Attn: Dept. SM'96
4500 Doniphan Drive
Neosho, MO 64850
Phone: 417-451-4438
Fax: 417-451-2576

LYMAN PRODUCTS CORPORATION *(Pg. 276)*
Attn: Dept. 874
475 Smith Street
Middletown, CT 06457
Phone: 800-225-9626
Fax: 203-349-3586

MARBLE ARMS CORP. *(Pg. 294)*
Attn: Dept. SM'96
P.O. Box 111
Gladstone, MI 49837
Phone: 906-428-3710
Fax: 906-428-3711

MCA SPORTS *(Pg. 288)*
Attn: Dept. SM'96
P.O. Box 8868
Palm Springs, CA 92263
Phone/Fax: 619-770-2005

MERIT CORPORATION *(Pg. 266)*
Attn: Dept. SM'96
P.O. Box 9044
Schenectady, NY 12309
Phone: 518-346-1420

MIDWAY ARMS, INC. *(Pg. 293)*
Attn: Dept. SM'96
P.O. Box 1483
Columbia, MO 65205
Phone: 800-243-3220
Fax: 314-446-1018

MINIATURE MACHINE CORP. (MMC) *(Pg. 280)*
Attn: Dept. SM'96
606 Grace Avenue
Ft. Worth, TX 76111
Phone: 817-831-0837
Fax: 817-831-1439

MODERN GUN REPAIR SCHOOL *(Pg. 298)*
Attn: Dept. GSX'96
2538 N. 8th Street, P.O. Box 5338
Phoenix, AZ 85010
Phone: 602-990-8346

MTM MOLDED PRODUCTS CO., INC. *(Pg. 267)*
Attn: Dept. SM'96
P.O. Box 14117
Dayton, OH 45414

NAVY ARMS COMPANY *(Pg. 282)*
Attn: Dept. SM'96
689 Bergen Blvd
Ridgefield, NJ 07657
Phone: 201-945-2500
Fax: 201-945-6859

N.B.B. INC. *(Pg. 272)*
Attn: Dept. SM'96
P.O. Box 738
Sterling, MA 01564
Phone: 800-942-9444
Fax: 508-422-3302

NECO/NOSTALGIA ENTERPRISES COMPANY *(Pg. 276)*
Attn: Dept. SM'96
P.O. Box 427
Lafayette, CA 94549
Phone: 510-450-0420
Fax: 510-450-0421

NEW ENGLAND AMMUNITION CO. *(Pg. 294)*
Attn: Dept. SM'96
1771 Post Road East, Suite 223
Westport, CT 06880
Phone: 203-254-8048

NEW ENGLAND FIREARMS *(Pg. 291)*
Attn: Dept. SM'96
60 Industrial Rowe
Gardner, MA 01440
Phone: 508-632-9393
Fax: 508-632-2300

OLD WORLD OIL PRODUCTS *(Pg. 272)*
Attn: Dept. SM'96
3827 Queen Avenue, North
Minneapolis, MN 55412
Phone: 612-522-5037

THE OUTDOOR CONNECTION, INC. *(Pg. 296)*
Attn: Dept. SM'96
201 Cotton Drive, P.O. Box 7751
Waco, TX 76714-7751
Phone: 817-772-5575 or 800-533-6076
Fax: 817-776-3553

PALSA OUTDOOR PRODUCTS *(Pg. 266)*
Attn: Dept. SM'96
P.O. Box 81336
Lincoln, NE 68501-1336
Phone: 800-456-9281
Fax: 402-488-2321

PARSONS OPTICAL MFG. CO. *(Pg. 278)*
Attn: Dept. SM'96
P.O. Box 192
Ross, OH 45061
Phone: 513-867-0820
Fax: 513-867-8380

B. PERAZONE GUNSMITH *(Pg. 279)*
Attn: Dept. SM'96
P.O. Box 275, Cold Spring Road
Roxbury, NY 12474
Phone: 607-326-4088
Fax: 607-326-3140

PONSNESS/WARREN *(Pg. 286)*
Attn: Dept. SM'96
P.O. Box 8
Rathdrum, ID 83858
Phone: 208-687-2231
Fax: 208-687-2233

PRAIRIE RIVER ARMS LIMITED *(Pg. 274)*
Attn: Dept. SM'96
1220 N. Sixth Street
Princeton, IL 61356
Phone: 815-875-1616
Fax: 815-875-1402

PRECISION SMALL ARMS *(Pg. 276)*
Attn: Dept. SM'96
155 Carlton Road
Charlottesville, VA 22902
Phone: 804-293-6124
Fax: 804-295-0780

QUARTON USA, LTD. CO. *(Pg. 273)*
Attn: Dept. SM'96
7042 Alamo Downs Pkwy., Suite 250
San Antonio, TX 78238-4518
Phone: 800-520-8435 or 210-520-8430
Fax: 210-520-8433

RANDOLPH ENGINEERING, INC. *(Pg. 296)*
Attn: Dept. SM'96
26 Thomas Patten Drive
Randolph, MA 02368
Phone: 800-541-1405
Fax: 617-986-0337

REDDING RELOADING EQUIPMENT *(Pg. 275)*
Attn: Dept. SM'96
1096 Starr Road
Cortland, NY 13045
Phone: 607-753-3331
Fax: 607-756-8445

R.G.-G., INC. *(Pg. 292)*
Attn: Dept. SM'96
P.O. Box 1261
Conifer, CO 80433-1261

ROOSTER LABORATORIES *(Pg. 278)*
Attn: Dept. SM'96
P.O. Box 412514
Kansas City, MO 64141
Phone: 816-474-1622
Fax: 816-474-1307

SAFARILAND LTD., INC. *(Pg. 284)*
Attn: Dept. SM'96
3120 E. Mission Blvd.
Ontario, Calif. 91761
Phone: 909-923-7300
Fax: 909-923-7400

SHEPHERD SCOPE LTD. *(Pg. 270)*
Attn: Dept. SM'96
P.O. Box 189
Waterloo, NE 68069
Phone: 402-779-2424
Fax: 402-779-4010

SHOOTING CHRONY, INC. *(Pg. 288)*
Attn: Dept. SM'96
3269 Niagara Falls Blvd.
N. Tonawanda, NY 14120
Phone: 905-276-6292
Fax: 905-276-6295

THE SHOTGUN NEWS *(Pg. 283)*
Attn: Dept. SM'96
P.O. Box 669
Hastings, NE 68902
Phone: 402-463-4589
Fax: 402-463-3893

SILENCIO/SAFETY DIRECT *(Pg. 279)*
Attn: Dept. SM'96
56 Coney Island Drive, Bldg. 22
Sparks, NV 89431
Phone: 800-648-1812
Fax: 702-359-1074

S&K MANUFACTURING CO. *(Pg. 298)*
Attn: Dept. SM'96
P.O. Box 247
Pittsfield, PA 16340
Phone/Fax: 814-563-7808

STONEY POINT PRODUCTS, INC. *(Pg. 283)*
Attn: Dept. SM'96
P.O. Box 5
Courtland, MN 56021-0005
Phone: 507-354-3360
Fax: 507-354-7236

SWIFT INSTRUMENTS, INC. *(Pg. 297)*
Attn: Dept. SM'96
952 Dorchester Avenue
Boston, MA 02125
Phone: 800-446-1116
Fax: 617-436-3232

TIMNEY MFG., INC. *(Pg. 282)*
Attn: Dept. SM'96
3939 North 31st Avenue
Phoenix, AZ 85017
Phone: 602-274-2999
Fax: 602-241-0361

TREADLOK GUN SAFE, INC. *(Pg. 292)*
Attn: Dept. SM'96
1764 Granby St., N.E.
Roanoke, VA 24012
Phone: 800-729-8732
Fax: 703-982-1059

TRIUS PRODUCTS, INC. *(Pg. 293)*
Attn: Dept. SM'96
P.O. Box 25
Cleves, OH 45002
Phone: 513-941-5682
Fax: 513-941-7970

DOUG TURNBULL RESTORATION *(Pg. 270)*
Attn: Dept. SM'96
P.O. Box 471
Bloomfield, NY 14469
Phone: 716-657-6338

U.S. OPTICS TECHNOLOGIES, INC. *(Pg. 289)*
Attn: Dept. SM'96
5900 Dale St.
Buena Park, CA 90621
Phone: 714-994-4901
Fax: 714-994-4904

VOLQUARTSEN CUSTOM LTD. *(Pg. 277)*
Attn: Dept. SM'96
P.O. Box 271
Carroll, IA 51401
Phone: 712-792-4238
Fax: 712-792-2542

WALKER ARMS CO., INC. *(Pg. 288)*
Attn: Dept. SM'96
499 County Road 820
Selma, AL 36701
Phone: 334-872-6231

WHITE FLYER TARGETS *(Pg. 290)*
Attn: Dept. SM'96
124 River Rd.
Middlesex, NJ 08846
Phone: 800-647-2898 or 417-673-5551
Phone (Export): 602-972-7528
Fax: 602-530-3360

WHITE SHOOTING SYSTEMS, INC. *(Pg. 280)*
Attn: Dept. SM'96
25 E. Hwy. 40 (330-12)
Roosevelt, UT 84066
Phone: 800-213-1315
Fax: 801-722-3054

1996 GUN DIGEST Complete Compact CATALOG

GUNDEX® 302-310	Shotguns—Bolt Actions & Single Shots . .447-451
	Shotguns—Military & Police 452-454
Autoloading Handguns 311-341	Blackpowder Single Shot Pistols 454-457
Competition Handguns 341-351	Blackpowder Revolvers 457-461
Double-Action Revolvers 351-362	Blackpowder Muskets & Rifles 461-476
Single-Action Revolvers 362-367	Blackpowder Shotguns 476-478
Miscellaneous Handguns 367-371	Air Guns—Handguns 478-484
Centerfire Rifles—Autoloaders 371-376	Air Guns—Long Guns 485-496
Centerfire Rifles—Lever & Slide 377-381	
Centerfire Rifles—Bolt Action 381-398	Warranty Service Center Directory 497
Centerfire Rifles—Single Shot 398-402	
Drillings, Combination Guns, Double	Metallic Sights 509
Rifles 403-404	Chokes & Brakes 512
Rimfire Rifles—Autoloaders 405-408	Scopes & Mounts 513
Rimfire Rifles—Lever & Slide 408-409	Scope Mounts 523
Rimfire Rifles—Bolt Actions & Single	Spotting Scopes 527
Shots 409-415	Periodical Publications 529
Competition Rifles—Centerfire &	Arms Library 531
Rimfire 415-422	Arms Associations 550
Shotguns—Autoloaders 422-426	
Shotguns—Slide Actions 427-431	**Directory of the Arms Trade**
Shotguns—Over/Unders 432-442	Product Directory 553
Shotguns—Side By Sides 443-447	Manufacturers' Directory 570

GUNDEX®

A

A-Square Caesar Bolt-Action Rifle, 382
A-Square Hamilcar Bolt-Action Rifle, 382
A-Square Hannibal Bolt-Action Rifle, 382
A. Zoli Rifle-Shotgun O/U Combo, 404
A.H. Fox CE Grade Side-by-Side Shotgun, 445
A.H. Fox DE Grade Side-by-Side Shotgun, 445
A.H. Fox Exhibition Grade Shotgun, 445
A.H. Fox FE Grade Side-by-Side Shotgun, 445
A.H. Fox Side-by-Side Shotgun, 445
A.H. Fox XE Grade Side-by-Side Shotgun, 445
AAO Model 2000 50-Caliber Bolt-Action Rifle, 381
Accu-Tek AT-9SS Auto Pistol, 311
Accu-Tek AT-32SS Auto Pistol, 311
Accu-Tek AT-32SSB Auto Pistol, 311
Accu-Tek AT-40SS Auto Pistol, 311
Accu-Tek AT-45SS Auto Pistol, 311
Accu-Tek AT-380SS Auto Pistol, 311
Accu-Tek AT-380SSB Auto Pistol, 311
Accu-Tek HC-380SS Auto Pistol, 311
Airrow Model A6 Air Pistol, 478
Airrow Model A-8SRB Stealth Air Gun, 485
Airrow Model A-8S1P Stealth Air Gun, 485
Alpine Bolt-Action Rifle, 381
American Arms Brittany Shotgun, 443
American Arms Buckhorn Single-Action Revolver, 362
American Arms CX-22 DA Auto Pistol, 311
American Arms Escort Auto Pistol, 311
American Arms Gentry Double Shotgun, 443
American Arms Grulla #2 Double Shotgun, 443
American Arms P-98 Auto Pistol, 312
American Arms PK22 DA Auto Pistol, 312
American Arms PX-22 Auto Pistol, 312
American Arms Regulator DLX Single Action Revolver, 362
American Arms Regulator Single-Action Revolvers, 362
American Arms Silver I Over/Under Shotgun, 431
American Arms Silver II Lite Over/Under Shotgun, 432
American Arms Silver II Over/Under Shotgun, 432
American Arms Silver Sporting Over/Under Shotgun, 432
American Arms TS/SS 12 Double Shotgun, 443
American Arms TS/OU 12 Shotgun, 432
American Arms WS/OU 12 Shotgun, 432
American Arms WT/OU 10 Over/Under Shotgun, 432
American Arms/Franchi Black Magic 48/AL Auto Shotgun, 422
American Derringer DA 38 Model, 368
American Derringer Lady Derringer, 368
American Derringer Model 1, 367
American Derringer Model 4, 368
American Derringer Model 4 Alaskan Survival Model, 368
American Derringer Model 6, 368
American Derringer Model 7 Ultra Lightweight, 368
American Derringer Model 10 Lightweight, 368
American Derringer Texas Commemorative, 368
AMT 45 ACP Hardballer Auto Pistol, 313
AMT 45 ACP Hardballer Government Model Auto Pistol, 313
AMT 45 ACP Hardballer Long Slide Auto Pistol, 313
AMT Automag II Auto Pistol, 312
AMT Automag III Auto Pistol, 312
AMT Automag IV Auto Pistol, 312
AMT Automag V Auto Pistol, 312
AMT Backup II DAO Auto Pistol, 313
AMT Backup II Auto Pistol, 313
AMT Magnum Hunter Auto Rifle, 405
Anschutz 54.18MS/Fortner Silhouette Rifle, 417
Anschutz 54.18MS REP Deluxe Silhouette Rifle, 416
Anschutz 54.18MS REP Standard Silhouette Rifle, 416
Anschutz 54.18MS Silhouette Rifle, 416
Anschutz 54.18MSL Silhouette Rifle, 416
Anschutz 64-MS Left Silhouette Rifle, 416
Anschutz 64-MS Silhouette Rifle, 416
Anschutz 525 Deluxe Auto Rifle, 405
Anschutz 1416D Classic Rifle, 410
Anschutz 1416D Custom Rifle, 410
Anschutz 1418D Mannlicher Rifle, 410
Anschutz 1516D Classic Rifle, 410
Anschutz 1516D Custom Rifle, 410
Anschutz 1518D Mannlicher Rifle, 410
Anschutz 1700D Bavarian Bolt-Action Rifle, 382
Anschutz 1700D Custom Bolt-Action Rifles, 382, 410
Anschutz 1700 FWT Bolt-Action Rifle, 410
Anschutz 1700D Bavarian Bolt-Action Rifle, 409
Anschutz 1700D Graphite Custom Rifle, 410
Anschutz 1700D Graphite Hornet Bolt-Action Rifle, 382
Anschutz 1733D Mannlicher Bolt-Action Rifle, 382
Anschutz 1808D RT Super Running Target Rifle, 416
Anschutz 1827B Biathlon Rifle, 416
Anschutz 1827BT Fortner Biathlon Rifle, 416
Anschutz 1903 Match Rifle, 416
Anschutz 1907 ISU Standard Match Rifle, 417
Anschutz 1907-L ISU Standard Match Rifle, 417
Anschutz 1910 Super Match Rifle, 417
Anschutz 1911 Prone Match Rifle, 416
Anschutz 1913 Super Match Rifle, 416
Anschutz 2002 Match Air Rifle, 485
Anschutz 2002D-RT Running Target Air Rifle, 485
Anschutz Achiever Bolt-Action Rifle, 409
Anschutz Achiever ST-Super Target Rifle, 416
Anschutz BR-50 Benchrest Rifle, 415
Anschutz Exemplar Bolt-Action Pistol, 368
Anschutz Super Match Model 2013 Rifle, 417
Anschutz Super Match Model 2007 ISU Standard Rifle, 417
Argentine Hi-Power 9mm Auto Pistol, 313
Argentine Hi-Power Detective Model Auto Pistol, 313
Arietta Model 557 Double Shotgun, 443
Arietta Model 570 Double Shotgun, 443
Arietta Model 578 Double Shotgun, 443
Arietta Model 600 Imperial Double Shotgun, 443
Arietta Model 601 Imperial Tiro Double Shotgun, 443
Arietta Model 801 Double Shotgun, 443
Arietta Model 802 Double Shotgun, 443
Arietta Model 803 Double Shotgun, 443
Arietta Model 871 Double Shotgun, 443
Arietta Model 872 Double Shotgun, 443
Arietta Model 873 Double Shotgun, 443
Arietta Model 874 Double Shotgun, 443
Arietta Model 875 Double Shotgun, 443
Arietta Sidelock Double Shotguns, 443
Arizaga Model 31 Double Shotgun, 443
Armoury R140 Hawken Rifle, 461
Armscor Model 14D Deluxe Bolt-Action Rifle, 410
Armscor Model 14P Bolt-Action Rifle, 410
Armscor Model 20C Auto Rifle, 405
Armscor Model 20P Auto Rifle, 405
Armscor Model 50S Auto Rifle, 405
Armscor Model 1500 Rifle, 410
Armscor Model 1600 Auto Rifle, 405
Armscor Model 1600R Auto Rifle, 405
Armscor Model 2000SC Auto Rifle, 405
Armscor Model AK22 Auto Rifle, 405
Armsport 1050 Series Double Shotguns, 443
Armsport 1863 Sharps Carbine, 461
Armsport 1863 Sharps Rifle, 461
Armsport 1866 Sharps Single-Shot Carbine, 398
Armsport 1866 Sharps Single-Shot Rifle, 398
Armsport 2700 O/U Goose Gun, 432
Armsport 2700 Series Over/Under Shotguns, 432
Armsport M2705 Over/Under Shotgun, 432
Armsport M2730 Over/Under Shotgun, 432
Armsport M2731 Over/Under Shotgun, 432
Armsport M2733 Over/Under Shotgun, 432
Armsport M2735 Over/Under Shotgun, 432
Armsport M2741 Over/Under Shotgun, 432
Armsport M2742 Sporting Clays Over/Under Shotgun, 432
Armsport M2744 Sporting Clays Over/Under Shotgun, 432
Armsport M2750 Sporting Clays Over/Under Shotgun, 432
Armsport M2751 Sporting Clays Over/Under Shotgun, 432
Armsport Single Barrel Shotgun, 447
Army 1851 Percussion Revolver, 457
Army 1860 Percussion Revolver, 457
ARS/Farco CO_2 Air Shotgun, 485
ARS/Farco CO_2 Stainless Steel Air Rifle, 485
ARS/Farco FP Survival Air Rifle, 486
ARS Hunting Master AR6 Air Rifle, 485
ARS/King Hunting Master 900 Air Rifle, 486
ARS/King Hunting Master Air Rifle, 486
ARS/Magnum 6 Air Rifle, 486
ARS/QB77 Deluxe Air Rifle, 486
Astra A-70 Auto Pistol, 313
Astra A-75 Decocker Auto Pistol, 313
Astra A-100 Auto Pistol, 313
Auto-Ordnance 27 A-1 Thompson Rifle, 371
Auto-Ordnance 45 ACP General Model Auto Pistol, 314
Auto-Ordnance 1911A1 Competition Model Auto Pistol, 314, 341
Auto-Ordnance 1911A1 Auto Pistol, 314
Auto-Ordnance 1927A-1C Lightweight Thompson Rifle, 371
Auto-Ordnance Thompson M1 Rifle, 371
Auto-Ordnance ZG-51 Pit Bull Auto Pistol, 314
AyA Boxlock Shotguns, 444
AyA Model 1 Double Shotgun, 444
AyA Model 2 Double Shotgun, 444
AyA Model 4 Deluxe Double Shotgun, 444
AyA Model 4 Double Shotgun, 444
AyA Model 53 Double Shotgun, 444
AyA Model 56 Double Shotgun, 444
AyA Model 931 Double Shotgun, 444
AyA Model XXV Sidelock Double Shotgun, 444
AyA Model XXV Shotgun, 444
AyA Sidelock Double Shotguns, 444

B

Baby Bretton Model Fairplay Over/Under Shotgun, 432
Baby Bretton Over/Under Shotgun, 432
Baby Bretton Sprint Deluxe Over/Under Shotgun, 432
Baby Bretton Sprint Standard Over/Under Shotgun, 432
Baby Dragoon 1848 Revolvers, 458
Baby Dragoon 1848 Wells Fargo Revolvers, 458
Baby Dragoon 1849 Pocket Revolvers, 458
Baby Eagle Auto Pistol, 314
Baer 1911 Bullseye Wadcutter Pistol, 342
Baer 1911 Concept I Auto Pistol, 314
Baer 1911 Concept II Auto Pistol, 314
Baer 1911 Concept III Auto Pistol, 315
Baer 1911 Concept IV Auto Pistol, 315
Baer 1911 Concept V Auto Pistol, 315
Baer 1911 Concept VI Auto Pistol, 315
Baer 1911 Concept VII Auto Pistol, 315
Baer 1911 Concept VIII Auto Pistol, 315
Baer 1911 Concept IX Auto Pistol, 315
Baer 1911 Concept X Auto Pistol, 315
Baer 1911 Custom Carry Auto Pistol, 315
Baer 1911 National Match Hardball Pistol, 342
Baer 1911 Premier II Auto Pistol, 314
Baer 1911 Prowler III Auto Pistol, 314
Baer 1911 Target Master Pistol, 342
Baer 1911 Ultimate Master Combat Pistol, 342
Baer 1911 Ultimate Master "Steel Special" Pistol, 342
Baikal IJ-18 Single Barrel Shotgun, 447
Baikal IJ-18EM Shotgun, 447
Baikal IJ-18M Shotgun, 447
Baikal IJ-27 EIC Over/Under Shotgun, 433
Baikal IJ-27 Over/Under Shotgun, 433
Baikal IJ-27EM Over/Under Shotgun, 433
Baikal IJ-27M Over/Under Shotgun, 433
Baikal IJ-43 Double Shotgun, 444
Baikal IJ-43EM Double Shotgun, 444
Baikal IJ-43M Double Shotgun, 444
Baikal IJ-70 DA Auto Pistol, 315
Baikal IJ-70 HC Auto Pistol, 315
Baikal TOZ-34P Over-Under Shotgun, 433
Barrett Model 82A-1 Semi-Automatic Rifle, 372
Barrett Model 95 Bolt-Action Rifle, 383
Beeman Carbine Model C1, 486
Beeman Crow Magnum Air Rifle, 486
Beeman Kodiak Air Rifle, 487
Beeman Mako Air Rifle, 486
Beeman P1 Magnum Air Pistol, 479
Beeman P2 Match Air Pistol, 479
Beeman R1 Air Rifle, 488
Beeman R1 Carbine, 488
Beeman R1 Laser Air Rifle, 488
Beeman R7 Air Rifle, 488
Beeman R8 Air Rifle, 488
Beeman R9 Air Rifle, 488
Beeman R10 Deluxe Air Rifle, 488
Beeman R10 Standard Air Rifle, 488
Beeman R11 Air Rifle, 488
Beeman RX-1 Gas-Spring Magnum Air Rifle, 488
Beeman S1 Magnum Air Rifle, 489
Beeman Super 7 Air Rifle, 489
Beeman Super 12 Air Rifle, 489
Beeman/Feinwerkbau 65 MKII Air Pistol, 479
Beeman/Feinwerkbau 102 Air Pistol, 479
Beeman/Feinwerkbau 300-S Mini-Match Air Rifle, 487
Beeman/Feinwerkbau 300-S Series Match Air Rifle, 487
Beeman/Feinwerkbau C20 CO_2 Pistol, 479
Beeman/Feinwerkbau C25 CO_2 Pistol, 479
Beeman/Feinwerkbau C25 Mini CO_2 Pistol, 479
Beeman/Feinwerkbau C55 CO_2 Rapid Fire Pistol, 480
Beeman/Feinwerkbau C60 CO_2 Rifle, 487
Beeman/Feinwerkbau C60 CO_2 Running Target Rifle, 487
Beeman/Feinwerkbau C62 CO_2 Rifle, 487
Beeman/Feinwerkbau Mini C60 CO_2 Rifle, 487
Beeman/Feinwerkbau Model 601 Running Target Air Rifle, 487
Beeman/Feinwerkbau Model 602 Air Rifle, 487
Beeman/Feinwerkbau P30 Match Pistol, 479
Beeman/HW30 Air Rifle, 487
Beeman/HW70A Air Pistol, 479
Beeman/HW 97 Air Rifle, 487
Beeman/Webley Eclipse Air Rifle, 489
Beeman/Webley Hurricane Air Pistol, 480
Beeman/Webley Nemesis Air Pistol, 480
Beeman/Webley Tempest Air Pistol, 480
Beeman/Webley Vulcan III Air Rifle, 489
Benelli Black Eagle Competition Auto Shotgun, 423
Benelli Black Eagle Competition Limited Edition Auto Shotgun, 423
Benelli Executive Series Type I Shotgun, 423
Benelli Executive Series Type II Shotgun, 423
Benelli Executive Series Type III Shotgun, 423
Benelli M1 Sporting Special Auto Shotgun, 423
Benelli M1 Super 90 Defense Shotgun, 452
Benelli M1 Super 90 Field Auto Shotgun, 423
Benelli M1 Super 90 Shotgun, 452

Benelli M1 Super 90 Tactical Shotgun, 452
Benelli M3 Super 90 Pump/Auto Shotgun, 452
Benelli Montefeltro Super 90 20-Gauge Shotgun, 423
Benelli Montefeltro Super 90 Auto Shotgun, 423
Benelli Montefeltro Super 90 Limited Edition Shotgun, 423
Benelli MP 95E Match Pistol, 342
Benelli MP 90S Match Pistol, 342
Benelli Super Black Eagle Auto Shotgun, 423
Benelli Super Black Eagle Auto Slug Gun, 423
Benjamin Sheridan CO_2 Air Rifles, 489
Benjamin Sheridan CO_2 Pellet Pistols, 480
Benjamin Sheridan CO_2 E17 Pellet Pistol, 480
Benjamin Sheridan CO_2 E20 Pellet Pistol, 480
Benjamin Sheridan CO_2 E22 Pellet Pistol, 480
Benjamin Sheridan CO_2 EB17 Pellet Pistol, 480
Benjamin Sheridan CO_2 EB20 Pellet Pistol, 480
Benjamin Sheridan CO_2 EB22 Pellet Pistol, 480
Benjamin Sheridan Pneumatic H17 Pellet Pistol, 480
Benjamin Sheridan Pneumatic H20 Pellet Pistol, 480
Benjamin Sheridan Pneumatic H22 Pellet Pistol, 480
Benjamin Sheridan Pneumatic HB17 Pellet Pistol, 480
Benjamin Sheridan Pneumatic HB20 Pellet Pistol, 480
Benjamin Sheridan Pneumatic HB22 Pellet Pistol, 480
Benjamin Sheridan Model 392 Pneumatic Air Rifle, 489
Benjamin Sheridan Model 397 Pneumatic Air Rifle, 489
Benjamin Sheridan Model 397C Pneumatic Carbine, 490
Benjamin Sheridan Model F9 Air Rifle, 489
Benjamin Sheridan Model FB9 Air Rifle, 489
Benjamin Sheridan Model G392 Pneumatic Air Rifle, 489
Benjamin Sheridan Model G397 Pneumatic Air Rifle, 489
Benjamin Sheridan Model GS392 Air Rifle, 489
Benjamin Sheridan Model GS397 Air Rifle, 489
Benjamin Sheridan Model S392 Pneumatic Air Rifle, 489
Benjamin Sheridan Model S397 Pneumatic Air Rifle, 489
Benjamin Sheridan Pneumatic (Pump-Up) Air Rifles, 489
Benjamin Sheridan Pneumatic Pellet Pistols, 480
Benton & Brown Bolt-Action Rifle, 383
Beretta 390 Gold Mallard Auto Shotgun, 424
Beretta 390 Silver Mallard Auto Shotgun, 424
Beretta 390 Slug Auto Shotgun, 424
Beretta 390 Sport Skeet Auto Shotgun, 424
Beretta 390 Sport Sporting Auto Shotgun, 424
Beretta 390 Sport Trap Auto Shotgun, 424
Beretta 390 Super Skeet Auto Shotgun, 424
Beretta 390 Super Trap Auto Shotgun, 424
Beretta 390 Waterfowl/Turkey Auto Shotgun, 424
Beretta 682 Skeet Over/Under Shotgun, 433
Beretta 682 Sporting Over/Under Shotgun, 434
Beretta 682 Super Skeet Over/Under Shotgun, 433
Beretta 682 Super Sporting Over/Under Shotgun, 434
Beretta 682 Super Trap Over/Under Shotgun, 433
Beretta 682 Trap Combo Over/Under Shotguns, 433
Beretta 682 Trap Mono Shotgun, 433
Beretta 682 Trap Over/Under Shotgun, 433
Beretta 682 Trap Top Single Shotgun, 433
Beretta 686 Continental Course Sporting Over/Under Shotgun, 434
Beretta 686 Essential O/U Shotgun, 433
Beretta 686 Onyx Over/Under Shotgun, 434
Beretta 686 Onyx Sporting Over/Under Shotgun, 434
Beretta 686 Silver Perdiz Over/Under Shotgun Set, 434
Beretta 686 Silver Perdiz Skeet Over/Under Shotgun, 433
Beretta 686 Silver Perdiz Sporting Combo Over/Under Shotgun, 434
Beretta 686 Ultralight Onyx Over/Under Shotgun, 433
Beretta 686 Silver Perdiz Sporting Over/Under Shotgun, 433
Beretta 686EL Gold Perdiz Over/Under Shotgun, 434
Beretta 687 Diamond Pigeon EELL Sporter Over/Under Shotgun, 434
Beretta 687 Silver Perdiz Sporting Over/Under Shotgun, 434
Beretta 687 Silver Pigeon Sporting Combo Over/Under Shotgun, 434
Beretta 687EELL Diamond Pigeon Combo Over/Under Shotgun, 434
Beretta 687EELL Diamond Pigeon Over/Under Shotgun, 434
Beretta 687EELL Diamond Pigeon Skeet Over/Under Shotgun, 433
Beretta 687EELL Diamond Pigeon Trap Over/Under Shotgun, 433
Beretta 687EL Gold Pigeon Over/Under Shotgun, 434
Beretta 687EL Gold Pigeon Sporting Over/Under Shotgun, 434
Beretta 687EL Pigeon Sporting Over/Under Shotgun, 434
Beretta 687L Silver Perdiz Over/Under Shotgun, 434
Beretta A-303 Auto Shotgun, 423
Beretta A-303 Sporting Clays Auto Shotgun, 423
Beretta A-303 Upland Model Auto Shotgun, 423
Beretta A-303 Youth Gun Auto Shotgun, 423
Beretta ASE 90 Gold Sporting Clay Shotgun, 434
Beretta ASE 90 Sporting Clays Over/Under Shotgun, 433
Beretta Express SSO O/U Double Rifle, 403
Beretta Express SSO6 Double Rifle, 403
Beretta Express SSO6 Gold Double Rifle, 403
Beretta Model 21 Bobcat Auto Pistol, 316
Beretta Model 80 Cheetah Series DA Auto Pistols, 315
Beretta Model 84 Cheetah Auto Pistol, 315
Beretta Model 85 Cheetah Auto Pistol, 315
Beretta Model 86 Cheetah Auto Pistol, 315
Beretta Model 87 Cheetah Auto Pistol, 315
Beretta Model 89 Wood Sport Gold Standard Pistol, 343
Beretta Model 92 Brigadier Auto Pistol, 316
Beretta Model 92FS Centurion Auto Pistol, 316
Beretta Model 92FS Auto Pistol, 316
Beretta Model 92D Centurion Auto Pistol, 316
Beretta Model 92D Auto Pistol, 316
Beretta Model 92F Stainless Auto Pistol, 316
Beretta Model 92F-EL Stainless Auto Pistol, 316
Beretta Model 96 Brigadier Auto Pistol, 316
Beretta Model 96 Centurion Auto Pistol, 316
Beretta Model 96 Auto Pistol, 316
Beretta Model 96D Centurion Auto Pistol, 316
Beretta Model 96D Auto Pistol, 316
Beretta Model 452 Sidelock Shotgun, 444
Beretta Model 452EELL Sidelock Shotgun, 403, 444
Beretta Model 455 SxS Express Rifle, 403
Beretta Model 455EELL SxS Express Rifle, 403
Beretta Model 950BS Jetfire Auto Pistol, 316
Beretta Model 1201FP Auto Shotgun, 452
Beretta Model 8000 Cougar Auto Pistol, 317
Beretta Model 8040 Cougar Auto Pistol, 317
Beretta Model SO5 Over/Under Shotgun, 434
Beretta Model SO5 Skeet Over/Under Shotgun, 434
Beretta Model SO5 Sporting Over/Under Shotgun, 434
Beretta Model SO5 Trap Over/Under Shotgun, 434
Beretta Model SO6 EELL Field Over/Under Shotgun, 434
Beretta Model SO6 Skeet Over/Under Shotgun, 434
Beretta Model SO6 Sporting Over/Under Shotgun, 434
Beretta Model SO6 Trap Over/Under Shotgun, 434
Beretta Model SO9 Over/Under Shotgun, 434
Beretta Onyx Sporting Over/Under Shotgun, 433
Beretta Over/Under Field Shotguns, 434
Beretta Pintail Auto Shotgun, 424
Beretta Series 682 Competition Over/Unders, 433
Beretta Sporting Clays Shotguns, 434
Bernardelli Hemingway Lightweight Double Shotguns, 444
Bernardelli Model 69 Target Pistol, 343
Bernardelli Model 115 Over/Under Shotgun, 434
Bernardelli Model 115 S Over/Under Shotgun, 434
Bernardelli Model 115 S Trap/Skeet Over/Under Shotguns, 434
Bernardelli Model 192 MS Sporting Clays Over/Under Shotgun, 434
Bernardelli Model 192 MS-MC Over/Under Shotgun, 434
Bernardelli Model 192 Waterfowler Over/Under Shotgun, 434
Bernardelli Model 220 MS Over/Under Shotgun, 434
Bernardelli Model 220 Over/Under Shotgun, 434
Bernardelli Model AMR Auto Pistol, 317
Bernardelli Model USA Auto Pistol, 317
Bernardelli P018 Compact DA Auto Pistol, 317
Bernardelli P018 DA Auto Pistol, 317
Bernardelli P. One Customized VB Auto Pistol, 317
Bernardelli P. One DA Auto Pistol, 317
Bernardelli P. One Practical VB Auto Pistol, 317
Bernardelli Roma 3 Double Shotgun, 444
Bernardelli Roma 4 Double Shotgun, 444
Bernardelli Roma 6 Double Shotgun, 444
Bernardelli Roma 7M Double Shotgun, 444
Bernardelli Roma 8M Double Shotgun, 444
Bernardelli Roma 9M Double Shotgun, 444
Bernardelli Roma Las Palomas Double Shotgun, 444
Bernardelli Series Roma Shotguns, 444
Bernardelli F.S. Model Uberto Double Shotguns, 444
Bernardelli Series S. Uberto Double Shotguns, 444
Bersa Series 95 Auto Pistol, 318
Bersa Thunder 9 Auto Pistol, 318
Bersa Thunder 22 Auto Pistol, 317
Bersa Thunder 380 Auto Pistol, 317
Bersa Thunder 380 Plus Auto Pistol, 317
BF Single Shot Pistol, 342
Black Watch Scotch Pistol, 454
Blaser R93 Bolt-Action Rifle, 383
Blaser R93 Safari Bolt-Action Rifle, 383
Bostonian Percussion Rifle, 461
BRNO Tau-7 CO_2 Match Pistol, 480
BRNO Tau-200 Air Rifle, 490
BRNO CZ 537 Sporter Bolt-Action Rifle, 383
BRNO CZ 550 Bolt-Action Rifle, 383
BRNO ZKB 527 Fox Bolt-Action Rifle, 383
BRNO ZKK 600 Bolt-Action Rifle, 383
BRNO ZKK 601 Bolt-Action Rifle, 383
BRNO ZKK 602 Bolt-Action Rifle, 383
BRNO ZKM-452 Deluxe Bolt-Action Rifle, 410
BRNO ZKM 611 Auto Rifle, 405
Brown Model One Single Shot Rifle, 398
Browning 425 Golden Clays Sporting Clays, 436
Browning 425 Grade I Sporting Clays, 436
Browning 425 Sporting Clays, 436
Browning 425 WSSF Shotgun, 436
Browning A-Bolt 22 Bolt-Action Rifle, 411
Browning A-Bolt Gold Medallion Bolt-Action Rifle, 411
Browning A-Bolt Hunter Shotgun, 447
Browning A-Bolt Shotgun, 447
Browning A-Bolt Stalker Shotgun, 447
Browning A-Bolt II Composite Stalker Bolt-Action Rifle, 384
Browning A-Bolt II Gold Medallion Bolt-Action Rifle, 384
Browning A-Bolt II Left-Hand Bolt-Action Rifle, 384
Browning A-Bolt II Micro Medallion Bolt-Action Rifle, 384
Browning A-Bolt II Bolt-Action Rifle, 384
Browning A-Bolt II Short Action Bolt-Action Rifle, 384
Browning A-Bolt II Stainless Stalker Bolt-Action Rifle, 384
Browning A-Bolt II Varmint Bolt-Action Rifle, 384
Browning Auto-5 Light 12 Auto Shotgun, 424
Browning Auto-5 Light 20 Auto Shotgun, 424
Browning Auto-5 Magnum 12 Auto Shotgun, 424
Browning Auto-5 Magnum 20 Auto Shotgun, 424
Browning Auto-5 Stalker Auto Shotgun, 424
Browning Auto-22 Grade VI Rifle, 405
Browning Auto-22 Rifle, 405
Browning BAR Mark II Safari Magnum Rifle, 372
Browning BAR Mark II Safari Semi-Auto Rifle, 372
Browning BDA-380 DA Auto Pistol, 319
Browning BDM DA Auto Pistol, 318
Browning BL-22 Grade I Lever-Action Rifle, 408
Browning BL-22 Grade II Lever-Action Rifle, 408
Browning BL-22 Lever-Action Rifle, 408
Browning BPS 10-Gauge Waterfowl Model Shotgun, 427
Browning BPS Buck Special Pump Shotgun, 427
Browning BPS Game Gun Deer Special Pump Shotgun, 427
Browning BPS Game Gun Turkey Special Pump Shotgun, 427
Browning BPS Hunting Pump Shotgun, 427
Browning BPS Ladies and Youth Model Pump Shotgun, 427
Browning BPS Pigeon Grade Pump Shotgun, 427
Browning BPS Pump Shotguns, 427
Browning BPS Stalker Pump Shotgun, 427
Browning BPS Upland Special Pump Shotgun, 427
Browning BPS Waterfowl Pump Shotgun, 427
Browning BT-99 Max Grade I Shotgun, 448
Browning BT-99 Max Shotgun, 448
Browning BT-99 Max Stainless Shotgun, 448
Browning BT-100 Trap Grade I Shotgun, 448
Browning BT-100 Trap Shotgun, 448
Browning BT-100 Trap Stainless Shotgun, 448
Browning Buck Mark Field 5.5 Pistol, 343
Browning Buck Mark Auto Pistol, 319
Browning Buck Mark Plus Auto Pistol, 319
Browning Buck Mark Silhouette, 343
Browning Buck Mark Target 5.5 Pistol, 343
Browning Buck Mark Unlimited Match Pistol, 343
Browning Buck Mark Varmint Auto Pistol, 319
Browning Citori Grade I Hunting Over/Under Shotgun, 435
Browning Citori Grade I Lightning Over/Under Shotgun, 435
Browning Citori Grade III Hunting Over/Under Shotgun, 435
Browning Citori Grade III Lightning Over/Under Shotgun, 435
Browning Citori Grade VI Hunting Over/Under Shotgun, 435
Browning Citori Grade VI Lightning Over/Under Shotgun, 435
Browning Citori Gran Lightning, 435
Browning Citori O/U Special Skeet, 435
Browning Citori O/U Special Skeet Four Barrel Skeet Set, 435
Browning Citori O/U Special Skeet Golden Clays Shotgun, 435
Browning Citori O/U Special Skeet Golden Clays Shotgun Set, 435
Browning Citori O/U Special Skeet Grade I Shotgun, 435
Browning Citori O/U Special Skeet Grade III Shotgun, 435
Browning Citori O/U Special Trap Grade I Model, 435
Browning Citori O/U Special Trap Grade III Model, 435
Browning Citori Special Trap Golden Clays, 435
Browning Citori Special Trap Models, 435
Browning Citori Ultra Sporter, 435
Browning Citori Ultra Sporter Golden Clays, 435
Browning Euro-Bolt II Bolt-Action Rifle, 384
Browning Gold 10 Auto Shotgun, 425
Browning Gold 10 Stalker Auto Shotgun, 425
Browning Gold Auto Shotgun, 424
Browning Hi-Power 9mm Auto Pistol, 318
Browning Hi-Power 9mm Mark III Auto Pistol, 318
Browning Hi-Power 40 S&W Mark III Auto Pistol, 318
Browning Hi-Power Capitan Auto Pistol, 318
Browning Hi-Power HP-Practical Auto Pistol, 318
Browning Lightning Sporting Golden Clays Over/Under Shotgun, 435
Browning Lightning Sporting Clays Over/Under Shotgun, 435
Browning Micro Buck Mark Auto Pistol, 319
Browning Micro Buck Mark Plus Auto Pistol, 319
Browning Micro Citori Lightning, 435
Browning Micro Recoilless Trap Shotgun, 448
Browning Model 81 BLR Lever-Action Rifle, 377
Browning Model 81 Long Action BLR Rifle, 377
Browning Model 1885 Low Wall Single Shot Rifle, 398
Browning Model 1885 High Wall Single Shot Rifle, 398
Browning Recoilless Trap Shotgun, 448
Browning Special Sporting Golden Clays Over/Under Shotgun, 435
Browning Special Sporting Clays Over/Under Shotgun, 435
Browning Superlight Citori Grade I Upland Special Over/Under Shotgun, 435
Browning Superlight Citori Grade I Over/Under Shotgun, 435
Browning Superlight Citori Grade III Over/Under Shotgun, 435
Browning Superlight Citori Grade VI Over/Under Shotgun, 435
Browning Superlight Citori Over/Under Shotgun, 435

GUNDEX

Bryco Model 38 Auto Pistol, 319
Bryco Model 48 Auto Pistol, 319
Bryco Model 59 Auto Pistol, 319

C

C.S. Richmond 1863 Musket, 471
Cabanas Espronceda IV Bolt-Action Rifle, 411
Cabanas Leyre Bolt-Action Rifle, 411
Cabanas Leyre Mini 82 Youth Bolt-Action Rifle, 411
Cabanas Leyre Model R83 Bolt-Action Rifle, 411
Cabanas Leyre Pony Youth Bolt-Action Rifle, 411
Cabanas Master Bolt-Action Rifle, 411
Cabanas Master Varmint Model Bolt-Action Rifle, 411
Cabanas Taser Rifle, 411
Cabela's 1858 Henry Replica, 377
Cabela's 1866 Winchester Replica, 377
Cabela's 1873 Winchester Replica, 377
Cabela's Blackpowder Shotguns, 477
Cabela's Blue Ridge Flintlock Rifle, 462
Cabela's Blue Ridge Percussion Rifle, 462
Cabela's Cattleman's Carbine, 377
Cabela's Paterson Revolver, 458
Cabela's Red River Rifle, 462
Cabela's Rolling Block Muzzleloader Carbine, 462
Cabela's Rolling Block Muzzleloader, 462
Cabela's Sharps Sporting Single Shot Rifle, 399, 462
Cabela's Sporterized Hawken Hunter Carbine, 462
Cabela's Sporterized Hawken Hunter Rifle, 462
Cabela's Traditional Hawken Flintlock Rifle, 462
Cabela's Traditional Hawken Percussion Rifle, 462
Calico Liberty 50 Carbine, 372
Calico Liberty 100 Carbine, 372
Calico M-110 Auto Pistol, 319
Century Centurion 14 Sporter Bolt-Action Rifle, 385
Century Centurion Over/Under Shotgun, 436
Century Custom Sporting Bolt-Action Rifle, 385
Century Deluxe Custom Sporter Bolt-Action Rifle, 385
Century Enfield Sporter #4 Bolt-Action Rifle, 385
Century FEG P9R Auto Pistol, 320
Century FEG P9RK Auto Pistol, 320
Century Gun Distributors Model 100 Single Action Revolver, 363
Century International FAL Sporter Rifle, 372
Century International M-14 Semi-Auto Rifle, 372
Century Swedish Sporter #38 Bolt-Action Rifle, 385
Century International Tiger Dragunov Rifle, 372
Charles Daly Deluxe Over/Under Shotgun, 436
Charles Daly Field Grade O/U Shotgun, 436
Charles Daly Sporting Clays O/U Shotgun, 436
Charleville Flintlock Pistol, 454
Charter Bulldog Pug Revolver, 351
Charter Lady On Duty Revolver, 351
Charter Magnum Pug Revolver, 351
Charter Off-Duty Revolver, 351
Charter Police Undercover Revolver, 351
Chipmunk Deluxe Single Shot Rifle, 411
Chipmunk Single Shot Rifle, 411
Churchill Turkey Auto Shotgun, 425
Churchill Windsor IV Over/Under Shotgun, 436
Churchill Windsor Sporting Clays Over/Under Shotgun, 436
Cimarron 1860 Henry Replica, 377
Cimarron 1866 Winchester Replica Carbine, 377
Cimarron 1866 Winchester Replica Rifle, 377
Cimarron 1873 30" Express Rifle, 377
Cimarron 1873 Frontier Six Shooter Single Action Revolver, 363
Cimarron 1873 Peacemaker Repro Revolver, 363
Cimarron 1873 Saddle Ring Carbine, 377
Cimarron 1873 Short Rifle, 377
Cimarron 1873 Single Action Army Single Action Revolver, 363
Cimarron 1873 Sporting Rifle, 377
Cimarron Artillery Model Single Action Revolver, 363
Cimarron New Thunderer Revolver, 363
Cimarron U.S. Cavalry Model Single Action Revolver, 363
Colt 38 SF-VI Revolver, 352
Colt 1847 Walker Percussion Revolver, 458
Colt 1849 Pocket Dragoon Revolver, 458
Colt 1851 Navy Percussion Revolver, 458
Colt 1860 Army Percussion Revolver, 458
Colt 1860 "Cavalry Model" Percussion Revolver, 458
Colt 1861 Navy Percussion Revolver, 458
Colt 1862 Pocket Police "Trapper Model" Revolver, 458
Colt Anaconda Revolver, 351
Colt Army Police Percussion Revolver, 457
Colt Armsmear Over/Under Shotgun, 436
Colt Combat Commander Auto Pistol, 320
Colt Combat Elite MK IV/Series 80 Auto Pistol, 320
Colt Delta Elite 10mm Auto Pistol, 320
Colt Gold Cup National Match MK IV/Series 80 Delta Gold Cup Auto Pistol, 343
Colt Detective Special Revolver, 352
Colt Double Eagle Combat Commander Auto Pistol, 320
Colt Double Eagle MK II/Series 90 Auto Pistol, 320
Colt Double Eagle Officer's ACP Auto Pistol, 320
Colt Gold Cup National Match MK IV/Series 80 Auto Pistol, 343
Colt Government Model 380 Auto Pistol, 321

Colt Government Model MK IV/Series 80 Auto Pistol, 320
Colt King Cobra Revolver, 352
Colt Lightweight Commander MK IV/Series 80 Auto Pistol, 320
Colt Match Target Competition HBAR Rifle, 417
Colt Match Target Competition HBAR II Rifle, 417
Colt Match Target Competition HBAR Model R6700 Rifle, 417
Colt Match Target HBAR Rifle, 417
Colt Match Target Lightweight Rifle, 373
Colt Match Target Model Rifle, 417
Colt Model 1861 Musket, 462
Colt Model 1991 A1 Commander Auto Pistol, 321
Colt Model 1991 A1 Compact Auto Pistol, 321
Colt Model 1991 A1 Auto Pistol, 321
Colt Mustang 380 Auto Pistol, 321
Colt Mustang Plus II Auto Pistol, 321
Colt Mustang Pocketlite Auto Pistol, 321
Colt Officer's ACP MK IV/Series 80 Auto Pistol, 321
Colt Pocketlite 380 Auto Pistol, 321
Colt Police Positive Revolver, 352
Colt Python Revolver, 352
Colt Single Action Army Revolver, 363
Colt Third Model Dragoon, 458
Colt's 22 Automatic Pistol, 320
Colt's 22 Target Auto Pistol, 320
Competitor Single Shot Pistol, 343
Connecticut Valley Classics Classic Field Waterfowler O/U Shotgun, 436
Connecticut Valley Classics Classic Sporter O/U Shotgun, 436
Connecticut Valley Classics Classic Sporter Stainless O/U Shotgun, 436
Cook & Brother Confederate Carbine, 462
Cook & Brother Confederate Rifle, 462
Coonan 357 Magnum Auto Pistol, 321
Coonan 357 Magnum Classic Auto Pistol, 321
Coonan Compact Cadet 357 Magnum Auto Pistol, 321
Cooper Arms Model 21 Varmint Extreme Bolt-Action Rifle, 385
Cooper Arms Model 21 Varmint Extreme Bolt-Action Rifle Benchrest Model, 385
Cooper Arms Model 22 Pro Varmint Extreme Bolt-Action Rifle, 385
Cooper Arms Model 22 Pro-Varmint Extreme Bolt-Action Rifle Benchrest Model, 385
Cooper Arms Model 22 Pro-Varmint Extreme Bolt-Action Rifle Black Jack Model, 385
Cooper Arms Model 36 Classic Sporter Rifle, 411
Cooper Arms Model 36 Featherweight Rifle, 411
Cooper Arms Model 40 Centerfire Sporter Bolt-Action Rifle, 385
Cooper Arms Model BR-50 Rifle, 417
Crosman Auto Air II Air Pistol, 481
Crosman Model 66 Powermaster Air Rifle, 490
Crosman Model 66RT Powermaster Air Rifle, 490
Crosman Model 357 Air Pistol, 481
Crosman Model 664SB Powermaster Air Rifle, 490
Crosman Model 664X Powermaster Air Rifle, 490
Crosman Model 760 Pumpmaster Air Rifle, 491
Crosman Model 760SB Pumpmaster Air Rifle, 491
Crosman Model 781 Single Pump Air Rifle, 490
Crosman Model 782 Black Diamond Air Rifle, 490
Crosman Model 788 BB Scout Rifle, 490
Crosman Model 795 Spring Master Rifle, 490
Crosman Model 1008 Repeat Air Pistol, 481
Crosman Model 1008SB Repeat Air Pistol, 481
Crosman Model 1077 Constantair Rifle, 490
Crosman Model 1077 Repeatair Rifle, 491
Crosman Model 1322 Air Pistol, 481
Crosman Model 1357 Air Pistol, 481
Crosman Model 1377 Air Pistol, 481
Crosman Model 1389 Backpacker Rifle, 491
Crosman Model 2100 Classic Air Rifle, 491
Crosman Model 2100SB Classic Air Rifle, 491
Crosman Model 2200 Magnum Air Rifle, 491
Crosman Model SSP 250 Pistol, 481
Crucelegui Hermanos Model 150 Double Shotgun, 445
Cumberland Mountain Blackpowder Rifle, 462
Cumberland Mountain Plateau Single Shot Rifle, 399
CVA Apollo Classic Rifle, 462
CVA Apollo Comet Rifle, 462
CVA Apollo Shadow Rifle, 462
CVA Bison Revolver, 460
CVA Bobcat Hunter Rifle, 463
CVA Bobcat Rifle, 463
CVA Classic Turkey Double Shotgun, 476
CVA Colt Sheriff's Model Revolver, 458
CVA Express Rifle, 463
CVA Frontier Hunter Carbine, 463
CVA Grey Wolf Rifle, 464
CVA Hawken Pistol, 454
CVA Hawken Flintlock Rifle, 463
CVA Hawken Percussion Rifle, 463
CVA Kentucky Percussion Rifle, 463
CVA Lynx Rifle, 463
CVA Plainshunter Rifle, 463
CVA Plainsman Rifle, 463

CVA Pocket Revolver, 459
CVA Silver Wolf Rifle, 464
CVA St. Louis Hawken Classic Rifle, 463
CVA St. Louis Hawken Rifle, 463
CVA Timber Wolf Rifle, 464
CVA Trapper Percussion Shotgun, 477
CVA Varmint Rifle, 464
CVA Vest Pocket Derringer, 455
CVA Wolf Series Rifles, 464
CZ 75 Compact Auto Pistol, 322
CZ 75 Auto Pistol, 322
CZ 75 Semi-Compact Auto Pistol, 322
CZ 83 DA Auto Pistol, 322
CZ 85 Auto Pistol, 322
CZ 85 Combat Auto Pistol, 322
CZ 98 Hunter Classic Bolt-Action Rifle, 386

D

Daewoo DH40 Fastfire Auto Pistol, 322
Daewoo DH380 Auto Pistol, 323
Daewoo DP51 Fastfire Auto Pistol, 322
Daewoo DP51C Auto Pistol, 322
Daewoo DP51S Auto Pistol, 322
Daewoo DP52 Auto Pistol, 323
Daewoo DR200 Varmint Rifle, 373
Daisy 1938 Red Ryder Classic Air Rifle, 492
Daisy Model 91 Match Pistol, 481
Daisy Model 225 American Legend Air Rifle, 492
Daisy Model 288 Air Pistol, 481
Daisy Model 500 Raven Air Pistol, 482
Daisy Model 840 Air Rifle, 492
Daisy Model 990 Dual-Power Air Rifle, 493
Daisy Model 1894 BB Rifle, 492
Daisy/Power Line 44 Revolver, 482
Daisy/Power Line 45 Air Pistol, 482
Daisy/Power Line 93 Air Pistol, 482
Daisy/Power Line 400 BB Pistol, 482
Daisy/Power Line 645 Air Pistol, 482
Daisy/Power Line 693 Air Pistol, 482
Daisy/Power Line 717 Pellet Pistol, 482
Daisy/Power Line 747 Pellet Pistol, 482
Daisy/Power Line 753 Target Air Rifle, 492
Daisy/Power Line 853 Air Rifle, 492
Daisy/Power Line 856 Pump-Up Air Gun, 492
Daisy/Power Line 880 Pump-Up Air Gun, 492
Daisy/Power Line 920 Air Rifle, 493
Daisy/Power Line 922 Air Rifle, 493
Daisy/Power Line 970 Air Rifle, 493
Daisy/Power Line 1140 Pellet Rifle, 483
Daisy/Power Line 1150 Pellet Rifle, 493
Daisy/Power Line 1170 Pellet Rifle, 493
Daisy/Power Line 1700 Air Pistol, 483
Daisy/Power Line 2001 Air Rifle, 493
Daisy/Power Line 2002 Pellet Rifle, 493
Daisy/Power Line CO_2 1200 Pistol, 483
Daisy/Power Line Eagle 7856 Pump-Up Air Gun, 493
Daisy/Power Line Match 777 Pellet Pistol, 482
Daisy/Youth Line 95 Air Rifle, 491
Daisy/Youth Line 105 Air Rifle, 491
Daisy/Youth Line 111 Air Rifle, 491
Dakota 22 Sporter Bolt-Action Rifle, 411
Dakota 76 Classic Bolt-Action Rifle, 386
Dakota 76 Safari Bolt-Action Rifle, 386
Dakota 76 Short Action Bolt-Action Rifles, 386
Dakota 76 Short Classic Short Action Rifle, 386
Dakota 76 Varmint Bolt-Action Rifle, 386
Dakota 416 Rigby African Bolt-Action Rifle, 386
Dakota Single Shot Rifle, 399
Davis Derringers, 368
Davis D-Series Derringers, 368
Davis Long-Bore Big-Bore Derringer, 368
Davis Long-Bore Derringers, 368
Davis P-32 Auto Pistol, 323
Davis P-380 Auto Pistol, 323
Desert Eagle Magnum Auto Pistol, 323
Desert Industries Double Deuce Auto Pistol, 323
Desert Industries G-90 Single Shot Rifle, 399
Desert Industries Two Bit Special Auto Pistol, 323
Desert Industries War Eagle Auto Pistol, 323
Dixie 1863 Springfield Musket, 465
Dixie 1874 Sharps Blackpowder Silhouette Single Shot Rifle, 399
Dixie 1874 Sharps Lightweight Hunter/Target Single Shot Rifle, 399
Dixie Deerslayer Rifle, 464
Dixie Delux Cub Rifle, 464
Dixie English Matchlock Musket, 464
Dixie Engraved 1873 Rifle, 378
Dixie Inline Carbine, 464
Dixie Magnum Percussion Shotgun, 477
Dixie Pennsylvania Pistol, 455
Dixie Screw Barrel Pistol, 455
Dixie Sharps New Model 1859 Military Rifle, 464
Dixie Tennessee Mountain Flintlock Rifle, 465
Dixie Tennessee Mountain Percussion Rifle, 465
Dixie Tennessee Mountain Squirrel Rifle, 465
Dixie Third Model Dragoon Revolver, 459
Dixie U.S. Model 1816 Flintlock Musket, 465

GUNDEX

Dixie U.S. Model 1861 Springfield Rifle, 465
Dixie Wyatt Earp Revolver, 459
D-Max Sidewinder Revolver, 363

E

E.A.A. Big Bore Bounty Hunter Revolvers, 364
E.A.A. European Ladies Model Auto Pistol, 324
E.A.A. European Model Auto Pistol, 323
E.A.A./HW 660 Match Rifle, 417
E.A.A./Sabatti Model 1822 Auto Rifle, 406
E.A.A./Sabatti Model 1822 Heavy Auto Rifle, 406
E.A.A./Sabatti Model 1822 Sporter Auto Rifle, 406
E.A.A./Sabatti Model 1822 Thumbhole Auto Heavy Rifle, 406
E.A.A. Standard Grade Revolvers, 352
E.A.A./Weihrauch HW 60 Target Rifle, 418
E.A.A. Windicator Target Grade Revolvers, 344
E.A.A. Witness DA Auto Pistol, 324
E.A.A. Witness Gold Team Auto Pistol, 344
E.A.A. Witness Silver Team Auto Pistol, 344
Eagle Arms Eagle Spirit, 373
Eagle Arms M15A2 Golden Eagle Rifle, 418
Eagle Arms M15A2 Post-Ban Heavy Barrel Rifle, 373
Eagle Arms M15A3 Action Master Auto Rifle, 373
Eagle Arms M15A3 Eagle Eye Rifle, 373
Eagle Arms M15A3 Post-Ban Predator Rifle, 373
Eagle Arms M15A3 S.P.R. Rifle, 373
Eagle Arms M4A1C Carbine, 373
Eagle Arms M4C Carbine, 373
EMF 1860 Henry Rifle, 378
EMF 1863 Sharps Military Carbine, 465
EMF 1866 Yellowboy Lever Action Carbine, 378
EMF 1866 Yellowboy Lever Action Rifle, 378
EMF 1894 Target Bisley Single Action Revolver, 364
EMF Dakota 1875 Outlaw Revolver, 364
EMF Dakota 1890 Police Revolver, 364
EMF Dakota New Model Single-Action Revolvers, 364
EMF Dakota Single Action Pinkerton Revolver, 364
EMF Hartford Single Action Artillery Revolver, 364
EMF Hartford Single Action Cavalry Revolver, 364
EMF Hartford Single Action Revolvers, 364
EMF Model 73 Lever-Action Carbine, 378
EMF Model 73 Lever-Action Rifle, 378
EMF Sharps Military Carbine, 465
EMF Sharps Single Shot Carbine, 399
EMF Sharps Single Shot Rifle, 399
Erma EM1 Carbine, 406
Erma ER Match Revolver, 344
Erma ER-777 Sporting Revolver, 352
Erma ESP 85A Match Pistol, 344
Erma ESP Junior Match Pistol, 344
Erma KGP 68 Auto Pistol, 324
Euroarms 1861 Springfield Rifle, 465
Euroarms Buffalo Carbine, 465
Euroarms Volunteer Target Rifle, 465

F

Famas Semi-Auto Air Rifle, 493
FAS 601 Match Pistol, 344
FAS 603 Match Pistol, 344
FAS 607 Match Pistol, 344
Feather AT-9 Semi-Auto Carbine, 374
Feather AT-22 Semi-Auto Carbine, 406
Feather Guardian Angel Pistol, 369
Feather Model F2 Semi-Auto Carbine, 406
Feather Model F9 Semi-Auto Carbine, 374
Federal Engineering XC222 Auto Carbine, 406
FEG B9R Auto Pistol, 324
FEG FP9 Auto Pistol, 324
FEG GKK-40C DA Auto Pistol, 324
FEG GKK-45C DA Auto Pistol, 324
FEG P9R Auto Pistol, 325
FEG PJK-9HP Auto Pistol, 324
FEG SMC-22 DA Auto Pistol, 324
FEG SMC-380 Auto Pistol, 325
FEG SMC-918 Auto Pistol, 325
Finnish Lion Standard Target Rifle, 418
Auguste Francotte Bolt-Action Rifles, 386
Auguste Francotte Boxlock Double Rifle, 403
Auguste Francotte Boxlock Mountain Rifle, 403
Auguste Francotte Boxlock Shotgun, 445
Auguste Francotte Sidelock Double Rifles, 403
Auguste Francotte Sidelock Mountain Rifle, 403
Auguste Francotte Sidelock Shotgun, 445
Freedom Arms Casull 44 Mag Revolver, 364
Freedom Arms Casull Model 252 Silhouette Revolver, 345
Freedom Arms Casull Model 252 Varmint Revolver, 345
Freedom Arms Casull Model 353 Revolver, 364
Freedom Arms Model 555 Revolver, 364
Freedom Arms Premier 454 Casull Revolver, 364
French-Style Dueling Pistol, 455

G

Garbi Model 100 Double Shotgun, 445
Garbi Model 101 Side-by-Side Shotgun, 445
Garbi Model 103A Side-by-Side Shotgun, 445
Garbi Model 103B Side-by-Side Shotgun, 445
Garbi Model 200 Side-by-Side, 445
GAT Air Pistol, 483
GAT Air Rifle, 493
Gaucher GN1 Silhouette Pistol, 369
Gaucher GP Silhouette Pistol, 345, 369
Glock 17 Auto Pistol, 325
Glock 17L Auto Pistol, 325
Glock 17L Competition Auto Pistol, 345
Glock 19 Auto Pistol, 325
Glock 20 10mm Auto Pistol, 325
Glock 21 Auto Pistol, 325
Glock 22 Auto Pistol, 325
Glock 23 Auto Pistol, 325
Glock 24 Competition Model Auto Pistol, 345
Gonic GA-87 M/L Rifle, 465
Gonic GA-93 Magnum M/L Rifle, 466
Grendel P-12 Auto Pistol, 325
Griswold & Gunnison Percussion Revolver, 459

H

Hammerli 480 Competition Air Pistol, 483
Hammerli Model 160 Free Pistol, 345
Hammerli Model 162 Free Pistol, 345
Hammerli Model 208s Pistol, 345
Hammerli Model 280 Target Pistol, 345
Hammerli Model 450 Match Air Rifle, 494
Harper's Ferry 1806 Pistol, 455
Harper's Ferry 1803 Flintlock Rifle, 466
Harrington & Richardson 939 Premier Revovler, 353
Harrington & Richardson 949 Western Revolver, 353
Harrington & Richardson N.W.T.F Turkey Mag Shotgun, 448
Harrington & Richardson N.W.T.F Youth Turkey Shotgun, 448
Harrington & Richardson Rocky Mountain Elk Foundation Commemorative Single Shot Rifle, 399
Harrington & Richardson Sportsman 999 Revolver, 353
Harrington & Richardson Tamer Shotgun, 449
Harrington & Richardson Topper Classic Youth Shotgun, 448
Harrington & Richardson Topper Deluxe Model 098 Shotgun, 448
Harrington & Richardson Topper Deluxe Rifled Slug Gun, 449
Harrington & Richardson Topper Junior 098 Shotgun, 448
Harrington & Richardson Topper Model 098 Shotgun, 448
Harrington & Richardson SB2-980 Ultra Slug, 448
Harrington & Richardson Ultra Hunter Single Shot Rifle, 399
Harrington & Richardson Ultra Varmint Single Shot Rifle, 399
Harris-McMillan Antietam Sharps Single Shot Rifle, 400
Harris-McMillan Classic Stainless Sporter Bolt-Action Rifle, 418
Harris-McMillan Combo M-87 50-Caliber Single Shot Rifle, 418
Harris-McMillan Combo/Repeater M-87 Rifle, 418
Harris-McMillan Long Range Rifle, 418
Harris-McMillan M-86 Sniper Rifle, 418
Harris-McMillan M-86 Takedown Model, 418
Harris-McMillan M-87R Repeater Rifle, 418
Harris-McMillan M-89 Sniper Rifle, 418
Harris-McMillan M-92 50 Caliber Bullpup Rifle, 418
Harris-McMillan M-93SN 50 Caliber Rifle, 418
Harris-McMillan National Match Rifle, 418
Harris-McMillan Signature Alaskan Bolt-Action Rifle, 387
Harris-McMillan Signature Classic Sporter Bolt-Action Rifle, 386
Harris-McMillan Signaure Jr. Long Range Pistol, 346
Harris-McMillan Signature Super Varminter Bolt-Action Rifle, 386
Harris-McMillan Signature Titanium Mountain Bolt-Action Rifle, 386
Harris-McMillan Talon Safari Magnum, 387
Harris-McMillan Talon Safari Bolt-Action Rifle, 387
Harris-McMillan Talon Safari Super Magnum, 387
Harris-McMillan Talon Sporter Bolt-Action Rifle, 387
Harris-McMillan Wolverine Combat Auto Pistol, 346
Harris-McMillan Wolverine Competition Match Pistol, 346
Harris-McMillan Wolverine Pistol, 346
Hartford Percussion Revolver, 457
Hatfield Mountain Rifle, 466
Hatfield Squirrel Rifle, 466
Hatfield Uplander Grade I Shotgun, 436, 445
Hatfield Uplander Grade II Shotgun, 445
Hatfield Uplander Over/Under Shotgun, 436
Hawken Rifle, 466
Heckler & Koch P7M8 Auto Pistol, 326
Heckler & Koch PSG-1 Marksman Rifle, 419
Heckler & Koch USP 45 Auto Pistol, 326
Heckler & Koch USP Auto Pistol, 326
Heritage Rough Rider Revolver, 364
Heritage Sentry Double-Action Revolvers, 353
HHF Model 101 B 12 AT-DT Trap Over/Under, 437
HHF Model 101 B 12 ST Trap Over/Under, 437
HHF Model 103 B 12 ST Over/Under, 437
HHF Model 103 C 12 ST Over/Under, 437
HHF Model 103 D 12 ST Over/Under, 437
HHF Model 103 F 12 ST Over/Under, 437
HHF Model 104 A 12 ST Over/Under, 437
HHF Model 200 A 12 ST Side-By-Side, 446
HHF Model 202 A 12 ST Side-By-Side, 446
Hi-Point Firearms JS-9mm Compact Auto Pistol, 326
Hi-Point Firearms JS-9mm Auto Pistol, 326
Hi-Point Firearms JS-40 S&W Auto Pistol, 326
Hi-Point Firearms JS-45 Caliber Auto Pistol, 326
High Standard 10X Model Target Pistol, 346
High Standard Olympic ISU Pistol, 346
High Standard Olympic Military Target Pistol, 346
High Standard Supermatic Citation Pistol, 346
High Standard Supermatic Tournament Pistol, 346
High Standard Supermatic Trophy Pistol, 346
High Standard Victor Target Pistol, 346
HJS Antigua Derringer, 369
HJS Frontier Four Derringer, 369
HJS Lone Star Derringer, 369
Howa Lightning Bolt-Action Rifle, 387
Hungarian T-58 Auto Pistol, 326

I

IBUS M17S 223 Bullpup Rifle, 374
Intratec Category 9 Auto Pistol, 327
Intratec Protec-22 Auto Pistol, 326
Intratec Protec-25 Auto Pistol, 326
Intratec TEC-DC9 Auto Pistol, 327
Intratec TEC-DC9K Auto Pistol, 327
Intratec TEC-DC9M Auto Pistol, 327
Intratec TEC-DC9MK Auto Pistol, 327
Intratec TEC-DC9MS Auto Pistol, 327
Intratec TEC-DC9S Auto Pistol, 327
Intratec TEK-22T Auto Pistol, 327
Intratec TEK-22TK Auto Pistol, 327
Ithaca Deerslayer II Rifled Pump Shotgun, 427
Ithaca Model 87 Deerslayer Pump Shotgun, 427
Ithaca Model 87 Deluxe Pump Shotgun, 427
Ithaca Model 87 English Pump Shotgun, 427
Ithaca Model 87 Hand Grip Shotgun, 452
Ithaca Model 87 M&P Shotgun, 452
Ithaca Model 87 Supreme Pump Shotgun, 427
Ithaca Model 87 Turkey Pump Shotgun, 427
Ithaca-Navy Hawken Rifle, 466

J

J.P. Murray 1862-1864 Cavalry Carbine, 469
Jennings J-22 Auto Pistol, 327
Jennings J-25 Auto Pistol, 327
Judge Single Shot Pistol, 370

K

Kahr K9 DA Auto Pistol, 327
Kareen Mark II Barak 9mm Auto Pistol, 327
Kareen MK II Auto Pistol, 327
Kel-Tec P-11 Auto Pistol, 328
Kemen KM-4 Extra Gold Over/Under Shotgun, 437
Kemen KM-4 Extra Luxe-A Over/Under Shotgun, 437
Kemen KM-4 Extra Luxe-B Over/Under Shotgun, 437
Kemen KM-4 Luxe-A Over/Under Shotgun, 437
Kemen KM-4 Luxe-B Over/Under Shotgun, 437
Kemen KM-4 Standard Over/Under Shotgun, 437
Kemen KM-4 Super Luxe Over/Under Shotgun, 437
Kemen Over/Under Shotguns, 437
Kentuckian Flintlock Carbine, 467
Kentuckian Flintlock Rifle, 467
Kentuckian Percussion Carbine, 467
Kentuckian Percussion Rifle, 467
Kentucky Flintlock Pistol, 455
Kentucky Flintlock Rifle, 466
Kentucky Percussion Pistol, 455
Kentucky Percussion Rifle, 466
Kimber Classic 45 Custom Auto Pistol, 328
Kimber Classic 45 Gold Match Auto Pistol, 328
Kimber Classic 45 Royal Auto Pistol, 328
Kimber Model 82C Classic Bolt-Action Rifle, 412
Kimber Model 82C Custom Match Bolt-Action Rifle, 412
Kimber Model 82C Custom Shop SuperAmerica Bolt-Action Rifle, 412
Kimber Model 82C SuperAmerica Bolt-Action Rifle, 412
Kimber Model 82C SuperClassic Bolt-Action Rifle, 412
Kimber Model 82C Varmint Bolt-Action Rifle, 412
Knight BK-92 Black Knight Rifle, 467
Knight Hawkeye Pistol, 455
Knight LK-93 Wolverine Rifle, 467
Knight MK-85 Grand American Rifle, 467
Knight MK-85 Hunter Rifle, 467
Knight MK-85 Knight Hawk Rifle, 467
Knight MK-85 Predator Rifle, 467
Knight MK-85 Stalker Rifle, 467
Knight MK-95 Magnum Elite Rifle, 467
Kodiak MK. III Double Rifle, 467
Krico Model 260 Auto Rifle, 406
Krico Model 300 Bolt-Action Rifles, 412
Krico Model 360 S2 Biathlon Rifle, 420
Krico Model 360S Biathlon Rifle, 419
Krico Model 400 Match Rifle, 419
Krico Model 500 Kricotronic Match Rifle, 419
Krico Model 600 Bolt-Action Rifle, 387
Krico Model 600 Match Rifle, 419
Krico Model 600 Sniper Rifle, 419
Krico Model 700 Bolt-Action Rifles, 387
Krico Model 700 Deluxe Bolt-Action Rifle, 387
Krico Model 700 Deluxe S Bolt-Action Rifle, 387
Krico Model 700 Stutzen Bolt-Action Rifle, 387

Krieghoff K-80 Combo Trap Over/Under Shotgun, 437
Krieghoff K-80 Four-Barrel Skeet Set Shotgun, 437
Krieghoff K-80 International Skeet Over/Under Shotgun, 437
Krieghoff K-80 O/U Trap Shotgun, 437
Krieghoff K-80 Single Barrel Trap Gun, 449
Krieghoff K-80 Skeet Lightweight Shotgun, 437
Krieghoff K-80 Skeet Shotgun, 437
Krieghoff K-80 Skeet Special Shotgun, 437
Krieghoff K-80 Skeet Two-Barrel Set Shotgun, 437
Krieghoff K-80 Sporting Clays O/U Shotgun, 438
Krieghoff K-80 Trap Full Unsingle Shotgun, 449
Krieghoff K-80 Trap Top Single Combo Shotgun, 449
Krieghoff K-80 Unsingle Trap Shotgun, 437
Krieghoff K-80/RT Shotguns, 437
Krieghoff KS-5 Special Shotgun, 449
Krieghoff KS-5 Trap Gun, 449

L

L.A.R. Grizzly 44 Mag Mark IV Auto Pistol, 328
L.A.R. Grizzly 50 Big Boar Bolt-Action Rifle, 388
L.A.R. Grizzly 50 Mark V Auto Pistol, 328
L.A.R. Grizzly Win Mag 8" Auto Pistol, 328
L.A.R. Grizzly Win Mag 10" Auto Pistol, 328
L.A.R. Grizzly Win Mag MK I Auto Pistol, 328
Lakefield Arms Mark I Bolt-Action Rifle, 412
Lakefield Arms Mark II Bolt-Action Rifle, 412
Lakefield Arms Mark II-Y Youth Bolt-Action Rifle, 412
Lakefield Arms Mark IY Youth Bolt-Action Rifle, 412
Lakefield Arms Model 64B Auto Rifle, 406
Lakefield Arms Model 90B Target Rifle, 419
Lakefield Arms Model 91T Target Rifle, 419
Lakefield Arms Model 91-TR Target Rifle, 419
Lakefield Arms Model 92S Silhouette Rifle, 419
Lakefield Arms Model 93M Bolt-Action Rifle, 412
Lanber 82 Over/Under Shotgun, 438
Lanber 87 Deluxe Over/Under Shotgun, 438
Lanber 87 Sporting Clays Over/Under Shotgun, 438
Laseraim Arms Series I Auto Pistol, 329
Laseraim Arms Series II Auto Pistol, 329
Laseraim Arms Series III Auto Pistol, 329
Laurona Model 83 MG Over/Under Shotgun, 438
Laurona Model 84 S Super Trap Over/Under Shotgun, 438
Laurona Model 85 MS Super Pigeon Over/Under Shotgun, 438
Laurona Model 85 MS Super Trap Over/Under Shotgun, 438
Laurona Model 85 S Super Skeet Over/Under Shotgun, 438
Laurona Model 85 Super Game Over/Under Shotgun, 438
Laurona Silhouette 300 Sporting Clays Over/Under Shotgun, 438
Laurona Silhouette 300 Trap Over/Under Shotgun, 438
Laurona Silhouette Ultra-Magnum Over/Under Shotgun, 438
Laurona Super Model Over/Unders, 438
LeMat Army Model Revolver, 459
LeMat Cavalry Model Revolver, 459
LeMat Revolver, 459
LePage Percussion Dueling Pistol, 456
Ljutic LM-6 Deluxe O/U Shotgun, 438
Ljutic LM-6 O/U Combo Shotgun, 438
Ljutic LTX Super Deluxe Mono Gun, 449
Ljutic Mono Gun Single Barrel Shotgun, 449
Ljutic Recoilless Space Gun Shotgun, 449
Llama IX-C Large Frame Auto Pistol, 329
Llama IX-O Compact Frame Auto Pistol, 329
Llama Max-I Auto Pistol, 329
Llama Max-I Compact Model Auto Pistol, 329
Llama Max-I Government Model Auto Pistol, 329
Llama III-A Small Frame Auto Pistol, 329
London Armory 2-Band 1858 Enfield, 468
London Armory 3-Band 1853 Enfield, 468
London Armory 1861 Enfield Musketoon, 467
Lorcin L 9mm Auto Pistol, 330
Lorcin L-22 Auto Pistol, 329
Lorcin L-25 Auto Pistol, 330
Lorcin LT-25 Auto Pistol, 330
Lorcin L-32 Auto Pistol, 330
Lorcin L-380 Auto Pistol, 330
Lyman Deerstalker Custom Carbine, 468
Lyman Deerstalker Flintlock Rifle, 468
Lyman Deerstalker Percussion Rifle, 468
Lyman Deerstalker Rifle, 468
Lyman Great Plains Flintlock Rifle, 468
Lyman Great Plains Percussion Rifle, 468
Lyman Plains Pistol, 456
Lyman Trade Flintlock Rifle, 468
Lyman Trade Percussion Rifle, 468

M

Magnum Research Lone Eagle Single Shot Pistol, 369
Magtech Model 122.2R Bolt-Action Rifle, 413
Magtech Model 122.2S Bolt-Action Rifle, 413
Magtech Model 122.2T Bolt-Action Rifle, 413
Magtech Model 586.2-VR Pump Shotgun, 428
Magtech MT 586P Pump Shotgun, 452
Mandall/Cabanas Pistol, 369
Manurhin MR 73 Sport Revovler, 353
Marksman 28 International Air Rifle, 494
Marksman 40 International Air Rifle, 494
Marksman 45 Air Rifle, 494

Marksman 55 Air Rifle, 494
Marksman 60 Air Rifle, 494
Marksman 61 Carbine, 494
Marksman 70T Air Rifle, 494
Marksman 1010 Repeater Air Pistol, 483
Marksman 1010X Repeater Air Pistol, 483
Marksman 1015 Special Edition Air Pistol, 483
Marksman 1710 Plainsman Air Rifle, 495
Marksman 1740 Air Rifle, 494
Marksman 1750 BB Biathlon Repeater Rifle, 494
Marksman 1780 Air Rifle, 494
Marksman 1790 Biathlon Trainer Air Rifle, 495
Marksman 1792 Competition Trainer Air Rifle, 495
Marlin Model 9 Camp Carbine, 374
Marlin Model 15YN "Little Buckaroo" Rifle, 413
Marlin Model 25MN Bolt-Action Rifle, 413
Marlin Model 25N Bolt-Action Repeater, 413
Marlin Model 30AS Lever-Action Carbine, 378
Marlin Model 39AS Golden Lever-Action Rifle, 408
Marlin Model 39TDS Carbine, 409
Marlin Model 45 Carbine, 374
Marlin Model 55 Goose Gun Bolt-Action Shotgun, 449
Marlin Model 60 Self-Loading Rifle, 406
Marlin Model 60SS Self-Loading Rifle, 406
Marlin Model 70HC Auto Rifle, 407
Marlin Model 70PSS Rifle, 407
Marlin Model 336CS Lever-Action Carbine, 378
Marlin Model 444SS Lever-Action Sporter Rifle, 378
Marlin Model 512 Slugmaster Shotgun, 450
Marlin Model 880 Bolt-Action Rifle, 413
Marlin Model 880SS Stainless Bolt-Action Rifle, 413
Marlin Model 881 Bolt-Action Rifle, 413
Marlin Model 882 Bolt-Action Rifle, 413
Marlin Model 882SS Bolt-Action Rifle, 413
Marlin Model 882L Bolt-Action Rifle, 413
Marlin Model 883 Bolt-Action Rifle, 413
Marlin Model 883SS Bolt-Action Rifle, 413
Marlin Model 922 Magnum Self-Loading Rifle, 407
Marlin Model 995SS Self-Loading Rifle, 407
Marlin Model 1894S Lever-Action Carbine, 378
Marlin Model 1894CS Lever-Action Carbine, 378
Marlin Model 1895CLTD Rifle, 379
Marlin Model 1895SS Lever-Action Rifle, 378
Marlin Model 2000 Target Rifle, 420
Marocchi Conquista Skeet Grade I Over/Under Shotgun, 439
Marocchi Conquista Skeet Grade II Over/Under Shotgun, 439
Marocchi Conquista Skeet Grade III Over/Under Shotgun, 439
Marocchi Conquista Sporting Clays Grade I O/U Shotgun, 438
Marocchi Conquista Sporting Clays Grade II O/U Shotgun, 438
Marocchi Conquista Sporting Clays Grade III O/U Shotgun, 438
Marocchi Conquista Trap Grade I Over/Under Shotgun, 439
Marocchi Conquista Trap Grade II Over/Under Shotgun, 439
Marocchi Conquista Trap Grade III Over/Under Shotgun, 439
Marocchi Lady Sport Grade I O/U Shotgun, 439
Marocchi Lady Sport Grade II O/U Shotgun, 439
Marocchi Lady Sport Grade III O/U Shotgun, 439
Marocchi Lady Sport Left-Hand O/U Shotgun, 439
Maverick Model 88 Pump Security Shotgun, 453
Maverick Model 88 Pump Shotgun, 428
Maverick Model 91 Accu-Mag Pump Shotgun, 428
Maverick Model 95 Bolt-Action Shotgun, 450
Maximum Single Shot Pistol, 369
Merkel Drillings, 404
Merkel Model 8 Side-by-Side Shotgun, 446
Merkel Model 47E Side-by-Side Shotgun, 446
Merkel Model 47S Side-by-Side Shotgun, 446
Merkel Model 90K Drilling, 404
Merkel Model 90S Drilling, 404
Merkel Model 95K Drilling, 404
Merkel Model 95S Drilling, 404
Merkel Model 122 Side-by-Side Shotgun, 446
Merkel Model 140-1 Boxlock Double Rifle, 403
Merkel Model 140-1.1 Boxlock Double Rifle, 403
Merkel Model 147 Side-by-Side Shotgun, 446
Merkel Model 147E Side-by-Side Shotgun, 446
Merkel Model 147S Side-by-Side Shotgun, 446
Merkel Model 150-1 Boxlock Double Rifle, 403
Merkel Model 150-1.1 Boxlock Double Rifle, 403
Merkel Model 160 SxS Double Rifle, 403
Merkel Model 200E O/U Shotgun, 439
Merkel Model 200E Skeet Over/Under Shotgun, 439
Merkel Model 200E Trap Over/Under Shotgun, 439
Merkel Model 200ET Over/Under Shotgun, 439
Merkel Model 200 SC Sporting Clays O/U, 439
Merkel Model 201E O/U Shotgun, 439
Merkel Model 201ES Over/Under Shotgun, 439
Merkel Model 201ET Over/Under Shotgun, 439
Merkel Model 202E O/U Shotgun, 439
Merkel Model 203E O/U Shotgun, 439
Merkel Model 203ES Over/Under Shotgun, 439
Merkel Model 203ET Over/Under Shotgun, 439
Merkel Model 210E Over/Under Combination Gun, 403
Merkel Model 211E Over/Under Combination Gun, 403
Merkel Model 213E Over/Under Combination Gun, 403

Merkel Model 221E Over/Under Double Rifle, 403
Merkel Model 223E Over/Under Double Rifle, 403
Merkel Model 247S Side-by-Side Shotgun, 446
Merkel Model 303E O/U Shotgun, 439
Merkel Model 313E Over/Under Combination Gun, 403
Merkel Model 323E Over/Under Double Rifle, 403
Merkel Model 347S Side-by-Side Shotgun, 446
Merkel Model 447S Side-by-Side Shotgun, 446
Merkel Over/Under Combination Guns, 403
Merkel Over/Under Double Rifles, 403
Mississippi Model 1841 Percussion Rifle, 476
Mitchell 45 Gold Series Auto Pistol, 330
Mitchell Arms Alpha Auto Pistol, 331
Mitchell Arms American Eagle Auto Pistol, 330
Mitchell Arms Citation II Pistol, 347
Mitchell Arms Guardian II Revolver, 353
Mitchell Arms Guardian III Revolver, 353
Mitchell Arms Olympic II I.S.U. Auto Pistol, 347
Mitchell Arms Sharpshooter II Pistol, 347
Mitchell Arms Sport-King II Auto Pistol, 330
Mitchell Arms Titan II Revolver, 354
Mitchell Arms Titan III Revolver, 354
Mitchell Arms Trophy II Pistol, 347
Mitchell Arms Victor II Auto Pistol, 347
Mitchell High Standard 20/22 Rifle, 407
Mitchell High Standard 20/22 Special Rifle, 407
Mitchell High Standard 20/22D Rifle, 407
Mitchell High Standard Bolt-Action Rifles, 414
Mitchell High Standard Model 9301 Bolt-Action Rifle, 414
Mitchell High Standard Model 9302 Bolt-Action Rifle, 414
Mitchell High Standard Model 9303 Bolt-Action Rifle, 414
Mitchell High Standard Model 9304 Bolt-Action Rifle, 414
Mitchell High Standard Model 9305 Bolt-Action Rifle, 414
Mitchell High Standard Pump Shotguns, 428
Mitchell High Standard Model 9104 Pump Shotgun, 428
Mitchell High Standard Model 9104-CT Pump Shotgun, 428
Mitchell High Standard Model 9105 Pump Shotgun, 428
Mitchell High Standard Model 9108-B Pump Shotgun, 428
Mitchell High Standard Model 9108-BL Pump Shotgun, 428
Mitchell High Standard Model 9108-CT Pump Shotgun, 428
Mitchell High Standard Model 9108-HG-B Pump Shotgun, 428
Mitchell High Standard Model 9108-HG-BL Pump Shotgun, 428
Mitchell High Standard Model 9109 Pump Shotgun, 428
Mitchell High Standard Model 9111-B Pump Shotgun, 428
Mitchell High Standard Model 9111-BL Pump Shotgun, 428
Mitchell High Standard Model 9111-CT Pump Shotgun, 428
Mitchell High Standard Model 9113-B Pump Shotgun, 428
Mitchell High Standard Model 9114-PG Pump Shotgun, 428
Mitchell High Standard Model 9115 Pump Shotgun, 428
Mitchell High Standard Model 9115-CT Pump Shotgun, 428
Mitchell High Standard Model 9115-HG Pump Shotgun, 428
Mitchell Wide-Body Gold Series Auto Pistol, 330
Model 1885 High Wall Single Shot Rifle, 400
Morini 162E Match Air Pistol, 483
Morini Model 84E Free Pistol, 347
Mossberg Model 500 Bantam Pump Shotgun, 428
Mossberg Model 500 Camo Pump Shotgun, 428
Mossberg Model 500 Cruiser Security Shotgun, 453
Mossberg Model 500 Ghost-Ring Shotgun, 453
Mossberg Model 500 Mariner Pump Shotgun, 453
Mossberg Model 500 Muzzloader Combo Pump Shotgun, 428
Mossberg Model 500 Persuader Security Shotgun, 453
Mossberg Model 500 Sporting Pump Shotgun, 428
Mossberg Model 500 Trophy Slugster Pump Shotgun, 429
Mossberg Model 500 Turkey Pump Shotgun, 428
Mossberg Model 590 Ghost-Ring Shotgun, 453
Mossberg Model 590 Mariner Pump Shotgun, 453
Mossberg Model 590 Shotgun, 453
Mossberg Model 835 Crown Grade Ulti-Mag Pump Shotgun, 429
Mossberg Model 835 American Field Grade Pump Shotgun, 429
Mossberg Model 835 Trophy Slugster Pump Shotgun, 429
Mossberg Model 9200 Camo Auto Shotgun, 425
Mossberg Model 9200 Camo Turkey Auto Shotgun, 425
Mossberg Model 9200 Crown Grade Auto Shotgun, 425
Mossberg Model 9200 N.W.T.F. Edition Auto Shotgun, 425
Mossberg Model 9200 Trophy Auto Shotgun, 425
Mossberg Model 9200 Turkey Auto Shotgun, 425
Mossberg Model 9200 USST Auto Shotgun, 425
Mossberg Model HS410 Shotgun, 453
Mountain Eagle Auto Pistol, 331
Mountain Eagle Compact Auto Pistol, 331
Mountain Eagle Standard Auto Pistol, 331
Mountain Eagle Target Edition Auto Pistol, 331
Mowrey 1 N 30 Conical Rifle, 468
Mowrey Percussion Shotgun, 477
Mowrey Plains Rifle, 468
Mowrey Rocky Mountain Hunter Plains Rifle, 468
Mowrey Silhouette Rifle, 468
Mowrey Squirrel Rifle, 468

N

Navy 1861 Percussion Revolver, 457
Navy Arms 1777 Charleville Musket, 469

GUNDEX

Navy Arms 1816 M.T. Wickham Musket, 469
Navy Arms 1862 C.S. Richmond Rifle, 469
Navy Arms 1863 Sharps Cavalry Carbine, 469
Navy Arms 1863 Springfield Rifle, 469
Navy Arms 1866 Yellowboy Carbine, 379
Navy Arms 1866 Yellowboy Rifle, 379
Navy Arms 1873 Single Action Revolver, 365
Navy Arms 1873 Sporting Rifle, 379
Navy Arms 1873 U.S. Artillery Model Revolver, 365
Navy Arms 1873 U.S. Cavalry Model Revolver, 365
Navy Arms 1873 Winchester-Style Carbine, 379
Navy Arms 1873 Winchester-Style Rifle, 379
Navy Arms 1874 Sharps Cavalry Single Shot Carbine, 400
Navy Arms 1874 Sharps Infantry Single Shot Rifle, 400
Navy Arms 1874 Sharps Sniper Single Shot Rifle, 400
Navy Arms 1875 Schofield Revolver, 365
Navy Arms 1875 Schofield U.S. Cavalry Model Single Action Revolver, 365
Navy Arms 1875 Schofield Wells Fargo Single Action Revolver, 365
Navy Arms #2 Creedmoor Single Shot Rifle, 400
Navy Arms Berdan 1859 Sharps Infantry Rifle, 469
Navy Arms Berdan 1859 Sharps Rifle, 469
Navy Arms Deluxe 1858 Remington-Style Revolver, 459
Navy Arms Fowler Shotgun, 477
Navy Arms Henry Carbine, 379
Navy Arms Henry Trapper, 379
Navy Arms Iron Frame Henry, 379
Navy Arms LePage Dueling Pistol, 456
Navy Arms LePage Flintlock Dueling Pistol, 456
Navy Arms LePage Percussion Dueling Pistol, 456
Navy Arms Military Henry Rifle, 379
Navy Arms Mortimer Flintlock Rifle, 469
Navy Arms Mortimer Flintlock Shotgun, 477
Navy Arms Mortimer Match Rifle, 469
Navy Arms Pennsylvania Flintlock Long Rifle, 470
Navy Arms Pennsylvania Percussion Long Rifle, 470
Navy Arms Rolling Block Buffalo Single Shot Rifle, 400
Navy Arms Smith Artillery Carbine, 470
Navy Arms Smith Cavalry Carbine, 470
Navy Arms Steel Shot Magnum Shotgun, 477
Navy Arms T&T Percussion Shotgun, 478
Navy Arms Tryon Creedmoor Target Model Rifle, 475
Navy Arms TU-33/40 Rimfire Carbine, 414
Navy Arms TU-KKW Training Rifle, 414
Navy Model 1851 Percussion Revolver, 459
Navy Model Confederate Navy Model 1851 Revolver, 459
Navy Model Hartford Model 1851 Revolver, 459
New Advantage Arms Derringer, 370
New England Firearms Handi-Rifle, 400
New England Firearms Lady Ultra Revolver, 354
New England Firearms N.W.T.F. Shotgun, 450
New England Firearms Standard Pardner Shotgun, 450
New England Firearms Standard Revolvers, 354
New England Firearms Survivor Shotgun, 451
New England Firearms Tracker II Slug Gun, 450
New England Firearms Tracker Slug Gun, 450
New England Firearms Turkey and Goose Gun, 450
New England Firearms Turkey Special Shotgun, 450
New England Firearms Ultra Mag Revolver, 354
New England Firearms Ultra Revolver, 354
New England Firearms Youth Pardner Shotgun, 450
New Model 1858 Army Percussion Revolver, 460
New Model 1858 Buffalo Model Percussion Revolver, 460
New Model 1858 Hartford Model Percussion Revolver, 460
New Model 1858 Stainless Steel Model Percussion Revolver, 460
New Model 1858 Target Model Percussion Revolver, 460
Norinco JW-15 Bolt-Action Rifle, 414
Norinco JW-27 Bolt-Action Rifle, 414
Norinco MAK 90 Semi-Auto Rifle, 374
Norinco Model 22 ATD Rifle, 407
North American Black Widow Revolver, 365
North American Mini-Master Revolver, 365
North American Mini-Revolvers, 365

O

Olympic Arms PCR-1 Rifle, 374
Olympic Arms PCR-2 Rifle, 374
Olympic Arms PCR-3 Rifle, 374
Olympic Arms PCR-4 Rifle, 374
Olympic Arms PCR-5 Rifle, 375
Olympic Arms PCR-6 Rifle, 375
Olympic Arms PCR-9 Rifle, 375
Olympic Arms PCR-15 Carbine, 375
Olympic Arms PCR-40 Carbine, 375
Olympic Arms PCR-45 Carbine, 375
Olympic Arms PCR Series Carbines, 375

P

Para-Ordnance P12.45E Auto Pistol, 331
Para-Ordnance P12.45R Auto Pistol, 331
Para-Ordnance P13.45R Auto Pistol, 331
Para-Ordnance P14.45E Auto Pistol, 331
Para-Ordnance P14.45R Auto Pistol, 331
Para-Ordnance P16.40E Auto Pistol, 331
Para-Ordnance P-Series Auto Pistols, 331
Pardini GP Rapid Fire Match Pistol, 347
Pardini K50 Free Pistol, 347
Pardini K58 Match Air Pistol, 484
Pardini K60 Match Air Pistol, 484
Pardini GP Schuman, 347
Pardini HP Target Pistol, 347
Pardini SP Target Pistol, 347
Parker Reproductions A-1 Special Side-by-Side Shotgun, 446
Parker Reproductions A-1 Special Side-by-Side Two Barrel Set, 446
Parker Reproductions D Grade Side-by-Side Shotgun, 446
Parker Reproductions Side-by-Side Shotgun, 446
Parker-Hale Volunteer Rifle, 470
Parker-Hale Whitworth Military Target Rifle, 470
Pedersoli Mang Target Pistol, 347
Pennsylvania Full-Stock Flintlock Rifle, 470
Pennsylvania Full-Stock Percussion Rifle, 470
Perazzi Mirage Special Four-Gauge Skeet O/U Shotgun, 439
Perazzi Mirage Special Skeet Over/Under Shotgun, 440
Perazzi Mirage Special Sporting Over/Under Shotgun, 439
Perazzi MX7 Over/Under Shotgun, 440
Perazzi MX8 Special Combo Shotgun, 439
Perazzi MX8 Special Single Shotgun, 439
Perazzi MX8/20 Over/Under Shotgun, 440
Perazzi MX8 Special Skeet Over/Under, 439
Perazzi MX8 Special Trap Over/Under, 439
Perazzi MX9 Over/Under Shotgun, 440
Perazzi MX10 Over/Under Shotgun, 440
Perazzi MX12 Hunting Over/Under Shotgun, 440
Perazzi MX12C Over/Under Shotgun, 440
Perazzi MX20 Hunting Over/Under Shotgun, 440
Perazzi MX20C Over/Under Shotgun, 440
Perazzi MX28 Game Over/Under Shotgun, 440
Perazzi MX410 Game Over/Under Shotgun, 440
Perazzi Sporting Classic Over/Under Shotgun, 439
Perazzi TM1 Special Single Trap Shotgun, 451
Perazzi TMX Special Single Shotgun, 451
Phoenix Arms HP22 Auto Pistol, 331
Phoenix Arms HP25 Auto Pistol, 331
Phoenix Arms Model Raven Auto Pistol, 331
Piotti Boss Over/Under Shotgun, 440
Piotti King Extra Side-by-Side Shotgun, 446
Piotti King No. 1 Side-by-Side Shotgun, 446
Piotti Lunik Side-by-Side Shotgun, 446
Piotti Piuma Side-by-Side Shotgun, 446
Pocket Police 1862 Percussion Revolver, 460
Pocket Police Hartford Model Revolver, 460
Prairie River Arms PRA 50/54 Rifle, 470
Prairie River Arms PRA Classic Rifle, 470
PSP-25 Auto Pistol, 331

Q

Quality Parts/Bushmaster XM-15 E-2 Carbine Dissipator, 375
Quality Parts Shorty XM-15 E-2 Carbine, 375
Quality Parts/Bushmaster V Match Rifle, 420
Quality Parts/Bushmaster XM-15-E2 Target Model Rifle, 420
Queen Anne Flintlock Pistol, 456

R

Record Jumbo Deluxe Air Pistol, 484
Remington 11-87 Premier Cantilever Deer Barrel Auto Shotgun, 425
Remington 11-87 Premier Auto Shotgun, 425
Remington 11-87 Premier Skeet Auto Shotgun, 425
Remington 11-87 Premier Trap Auto Shotgun, 425
Remington 11-87 Special Purpose Magnum Auto Shotgun, 426
Remington 11-87 Special Purpose Magnum-Turkey Auto Shotgun, 426
Remington 11-87 Special Purpose Synthetic Camo Auto Shotgun, 426
Remington 11-87 Sporting Clays Auto Shotgun, 425
Remington 11-87 SPS Cantilever Auto Shotgun, 426
Remington 11-87 SPS-Deer Auto Shotgun, 426
Remington 11-87 SPS-T Camo Auto Shotgun, 426
Remington 40-XB KS Target Rifle, 420
Remington 40-XB Rangemaster Target Centerfire Rifle, 420
Remington 40-XBBR KS Rifle, 420
Remington 40-XC KS National Match Course Rifle, 421
Remington 40-XR KS Rimfire Position Rifle, 420
Remington 40-XR Rimfire Custom Sporter, 414
Remington 90-T Super Single Shotgun, 451
Remington 541-T Bolt-Action Rifle, 414
Remington 541-T HB Bolt-Action Rifle, 414
Remington 552 BDL Speedmaster Rifle, 407
Remington 572 BDL Fieldmaster Pump Rifle, 409
Remington 581-S Sportsman Rifle, 414
Remington 700 ADL Bolt-Action Rifle, 388
Remington 700 APR African Plains Bolt-Action Rifle, 389
Remington 700 AWR Alaskan Wilderness Bolt-Action Rifle, 388
Remington 700 BDL Bolt-Action Rifle, 388
Remington 700 BDL DM Bolt-Action Rifle, 389
Remington 700 BDL Left-Hand Bolt-Action Rifle, 387
Remington 700 BDL SS Bolt-Action Rifle, 389
Remington 700 BDL SS DM Bolt-Action Rifle, 389
Remington 700 Classic Bolt-Action Rifle, 389
Remington 700 Custom KS Mountain Bolt-Action Rifle, 389
Remington 700 MTN DM Bolt-Action Rifle, 389
Remington 700 Safari Bolt-Action Rifle, 389
Remington 700 Safari Custom KS Bolt-Action Rifle, 389
Remington 700 Sendero Bolt-Action Rifle, 388
Remington 700 Varmint Synthetic Bolt-Action Rifle, 388
Remington 700 VLS Varmint Laminated Stock Bolt-Action Rifles, 388
Remington 700 VS SF Bolt-Action Rifle, 388
Remington 870 Express HD Pump Shotgun, 430
Remington 870 Express Pump Shotgun, 429
Remington 870 Express Synthetic Pump Shotgun, 430
Remington 870 Express Turkey Pump Shotgun, 429
Remington 870 Express Youth Deer Gun, 429
Remington 870 Express Youth Pump Shotgun, 429
Remington 870 High Grades, 430
Remington 870D High Grade Pump Shotgun, 430
Remington 870F High Grade Pump Shotgun, 430
Remington 870 Marine Magnum Pump Shotgun, 429
Remington 870 Special Field Pump Shotgun, 430
Remington 870 Special Purpose Synthetic Camo Shotgun, 430
Remington 870 SPS Cantilever Pump Shotgun, 430
Remington 870 SPS-Deer Pump Shotgun, 430
Remington 870 SPS-T Camo Pump Shotgun, 430
Remington 870 SPS-T Special Purpose Magnum Pump Shotgun, 430
Remington 870 Wingmaster Pump Shotgun, 429
Remington 870 Wingmaster Small Gauges, 430
Remington 870P Police Shotgun, 453
Remington 1100 20-Gauge Deer Gun, 426
Remington 1100 Cantilever 20-Gauge Deer Auto Shotgun, 426
Remington 1100 LT-20 Auto Shotgun, 426
Remington 1100 LT-20 Youth Auto Shotgun, 426
Remington 1100 Special Field Auto Shotgun, 426
Remington 1816 Commemorative Flintlock Rifle, 470
Remington 7600 Slide-Action Carbine, 379
Remington 7600 Slide-Action Rifle, 379
Remington Model 522 Viper Autoloading Rifle, 408
Remington Model 7400 Auto Carbine, 375
Remington Model 7400 Auto Rifle, 375
Remington Model Seven Bolt-Action Rifle, 390
Remington Model Seven Custom KS Bolt-Action Rifle, 390
Remington Model Seven Custom MS Bolt-Action Rifle, 390
Remington Model Seven SS Bolt-Action Rifle, 390
Remington Model Seven Youth Bolt-Action Rifle, 390
Remington Peerless Over/Under Shotgun, 440
Remington SP-10 Magnum Auto Shotgun, 426
Remington SP-10 Magnum-Camo Auto Shotgun, 426
Rizzini Boxlock Side-by-Side Shotgun, 447
Rizzini Sidelock Side-by-Side Shotgun, 447
Rocky Mountain Arms Patriot Auto Pistol, 332
Rogers & Spencer Percussion Revolver, 460
Rogers & Spencer Target Percussion Revolver, 460
Rossi Lady Rossi Revolver, 354
Rossi M92 SRC Saddle-Ring Carbine, 380
Rossi M92 SRS Short Carbine, 380
Rossi Model 62 SA Pump Rifle, 409
Rossi Model 62 SAC Carbine, 409
Rossi Model 65 Saddle-Ring Carbine, 380
Rossi Model 68 Revolver, 354
Rossi Model 68/2 Revolver, 354
Rossi Model 88 Stainless Revolver, 354
Rossi Model 515 Revolver, 354
Rossi Model 518 Revolver, 354
Rossi Model 720 Revolver, 355
Rossi Model 720C Revolver, 355
Rossi Model 851 Revolver, 355
Rossi Model 971 Comp Revolver, 355
Rossi Model 971 Revolver, 355
RPM XL Hunter Model Single Shot Pistol, 370
RPM XL Silhouette Model Single Shot Pistol, 370
RPM XL Single Shot Pistol, 370
Ruger 10/22 Autoloading Carbine, 408
Ruger 10/22 Deluxe Sporter, 408
Ruger 10/22 DSP Deluxe Sporter, 408
Ruger 10/22 International Carbine, 408
Ruger 10/22RBI International Carbine, 408
Ruger 20-Gauge Sporting Clays O/U Shotgun, 440
Ruger Mark II 22/45 Auto Pistol, 333
Ruger Mark II 22/45 KP4 Auto Pistol, 333
Ruger Mark II 22/45 KP512 Auto Pistol, 333
Ruger Mark II 22/45 P512 Auto Pistol, 333
Ruger 77/22 Hornet Bolt-Action Rifle, 390
Ruger 77/22 Rimfire Bolt-Action Rifle, 415
Ruger Bisley Single-Action Revolver, 365
Ruger Bisley Small Frame Revolver, 366
Ruger Blackhawk Revolver, 365
Ruger Blackhawk BN31 Revolver, 365
Ruger Blackhawk BN34 Revolver, 365
Ruger Blackhawk BN34X Revolver, 365
Ruger Blackhawk BN36 Revolver, 365
Ruger Blackhawk BN36X Revolver, 365
Ruger Blackhawk BN41 Revolver, 365
Ruger Blackhawk BN42 Revolver, 365
Ruger Blackhawk BN45 Revolver, 365
Ruger Blackhawk GKBN36 Revolver, 365
Ruger Blackhawk GKBN44 Revolver, 365

50th EDITION, 1996

GUNDEX

Ruger Blackhawk GKBN45 Revolver, 365
Ruger Blackhawk GKBN34 Revolver, 365
Ruger Blackhawk KBN34 Revolver, 321
Ruger Blackhawk KBN36 Revolver, 321
Ruger English Field Over/Under Shotgun, 440
Ruger GP-100 Revolvers, 355
Ruger GP-141 Revolver, 355
Ruger GP-160 Revolver, 355
Ruger GP-161 Revolver, 355
Ruger GPF-331 Revolver, 355
Ruger GPF-340 Revolver, 355
Ruger GPF-341 Revolver, 355
Ruger GPF-831 Revolver, 355
Ruger GPF-840 Revolver, 355
Ruger GPF-841 Revolver, 355
Ruger K10/22RB Autoloading Carbine, 408
Ruger K10/22RBI International Carbine, 408
Ruger K77/22 Varmint Rifle, 415
Ruger K77/22VH Varmint Bolt-Action Rifle, 390
Ruger K-Mini-14/5R Ranch Rifle, 375
Ruger K-Mini-14/5 Autoloading Rifle, 375
Ruger KGP-141 Revolver, 355
Ruger KGP-160 Revolver, 355
Ruger KGP-161 Revolver, 355
Ruger KGPF-330 Revolver, 355
Ruger KGPF-331 Revolver, 355
Ruger KGPF-340 Revolver, 355
Ruger KGPF-341 Revolver, 355
Ruger KGPF-830 Revolver, 355
Ruger KGPF-831 Revolver, 355
Ruger KGPF-840 Revolver, 355
Ruger KGPF-841 Revolver, 355
Ruger KP89 Auto Pistol, 332
Ruger KP89D Decocker Auto Pistol, 332
Ruger KP90 Auto Pistol, 332
Ruger KP93 Auto Pistol, 332
Ruger KP93DAO Auto Pistol, 332
Ruger KP94 Auto Pistol, 333
Ruger KP94D Auto Pistol, 333
Ruger KP94DAO Auto Pistol, 333
Ruger KP944 Auto Pistol, 333
Ruger KP944DAO Auto Pistol, 333
Ruger M77 Mark II All-Weather Stainless Bolt-Action Rifle, 391
Ruger M77 Mark II Express Bolt-Action Rifle, 391
Ruger M77 Mark II Magnum Bolt-Action Rifle, 390
Ruger M77 Mark II Bolt-Action Rifle, 390
Ruger M77RL Ultra Light Bolt-Action Rifle, 391
Ruger M77RSI International Bolt-Action Carbine, 390
Ruger M77VT Target Bolt-Action Rifle, 391
Ruger Mark II Bull Barrel Pistol, 347
Ruger Mark II Government Target Model Pistol, 348
Ruger Mark II KMK4 Standard Auto Pistol, 333
Ruger Mark II KMK6 Standard Auto Pistol, 333
Ruger Mark II KMK-10 Bull Barrel Pistol, 347
Ruger Mark II KMK-512 Bull Barrel Pistol, 347
Ruger Mark II KMK-514 Target Model Auto Pistol, 347
Ruger Mark II KMK-678 Target Model Auto Pistol, 347
Ruger Mark II KMK-678G Government Target Model Pistol, 348
Ruger Mark II KMK-678GC Government Competition Model 22 Pistol, 348
Ruger Mark II KM77MKIILSP All Weather Bolt-Action Rifle, 391
Ruger Mark II KM77MKIIRP All Weather Bolt-Action Rifle, 391
Ruger Mark II KM77MKIIVT Target Rifle, 391
Ruger Mark II M77EXPMKII Express Bolt-Action Rifle, 391
Ruger Mark II MK4 Standard Auto Pistol, 333
Ruger Mark II MK6 Standard Auto Pistol, 333
Ruger Mark II MK-10 Bull Barrel Pistol, 347
Ruger Mark II MK-512 Bull Barrel Pistol, 347
Ruger Mark II MK-514 Target Model Auto Pistol, 347
Ruger Mark II MK-678 Target Model Auto Pistol, 347
Ruger Mark II MK-678G Government Target Model Auto Pistol, 348
Ruger Mark II Standard Auto Pistol, 333
Ruger Mark II Target Model Auto Pistol, 347
Ruger Mini Thirty Rifle, 375
Ruger Mini-14/5 Autoloading Rifle, 375
Ruger Mini-14/5R Ranch Rifle, 375
Ruger New Super Bearcat KSBC4 Single-Action Revolver, 366
Ruger New Super Bearcat SBC4 Single-Action Revolver, 366
Ruger New Super Bearcat Single-Action Revolver, 366
Ruger No. 1 RSI International Single Shot Rifle, 401
Ruger No. 1A Light Sporter Single Shot Rifle, 401
Ruger No. 1B Single Shot Rifle, 401
Ruger No. 1H Tropical Single Shot Rifle, 401
Ruger No. 1S Medium Sporter Single Shot Rifle, 401
Ruger No. 1V Special Varminter Single Shot Rifle, 401
Ruger Old Army Percussion Revolver, 460
Ruger P89 Double Action Only Auto Pistol, 332
Ruger P89 Auto Pistol, 332
Ruger P89D Decocker Auto Pistol, 332
Ruger P90 Decocker Auto Pistol, 332
Ruger P90 Auto Pistol, 332
Ruger P93 Compact Auto Pistol, 332
Ruger P94L Auto Pistol, 332

Ruger Red Label Over/Under Shotgun, 440
Ruger Redhawk Revolver, 356
Ruger SP101 Double Action Only Revolver, 355
Ruger SP101 Revolvers, 355
Ruger SP101 KSP-221 Revolver, 355
Ruger SP101 KSP-240 Revolver, 355
Ruger SP101 KSP-241 Revolver, 355
Ruger SP101 KSP-321 Revolver, 355
Ruger SP101 KSP-321XL Double Action Only Revolver, 355
Ruger SP101 KSP-331 Revolver, 355
Ruger SP101 KSP-821 Revolver, 355
Ruger SP101 KSP-821L Double Action Only Revolver, 355
Ruger SP101 KSP-831 Revolver, 355
Ruger SP101 KSP-921 Revolver, 355
Ruger SP101 KSP-3231 Revolver, 355
Ruger Sporting Clays O/U Shotgun, 440
Ruger SSM Single-Six Revolver, 366
Ruger Stainless Government Competition Model 22 Pistol, 348
Ruger Super Blackhawk Revolver, 366
Ruger Super Redhawk KSRH-7 Revolver, 356
Ruger Super Redhawk KSRH-9 Revolver, 356
Ruger Super Redhawk Revolver, 356
Ruger Super Single-Six Convertible Revolver, 366
Ruger Vaquero BNV44 Single-Action Revolver, 366
Ruger Vaquero BNV45 Single-Action Revolver, 366
Ruger Vaquero BNV445 Single-Action Revolver, 366
Ruger Vaquero KBNV44 Single-Action Revolver, 366
Ruger Vaquero KBNV45 Single-Action Revolver, 366
Ruger Vaquero KBNV455 Single-Action Revolver, 366
Ruger Vaquero Single-Action Revolver, 366
Ruger Woodside Over/Under Shotgun, 441
RWS Model CA 100 Air Rifle, 495
RWS TX 200 Magnum Air Rifle, 496
RWS/Diana Model 5G Air Pistol, 484
RWS/Diana Model 6G Air Pistol, 484
RWS/Diana Model 6M Match Air Pistol, 484
RWS/Diana Model 24 Air Rifle, 495
RWS/Diana Model 24C Carbine, 495
RWS/Diana Model 34 Air Rifle, 495
RWS/Diana Model 34BC Air Rifle, 495
RWS/Diana Model 34N Air Rifle, 495
RWS/Diana Model 36 Air Rifle, 495
RWS/Diana Model 36 Carbine, 495
RWS/Diana Model 45 Air Rifle, 495
RWS/Diana Model 48 Air Rifle, 495
RWS/Diana Model 48B Air Rifle, 495
RWS/Diana Model 52 Air Rifle, 495
RWS/Diana Model 54 Air King Rifle, 495
RWS/Diana Model 100 Match Air Rifle, 496

S

SA-85M Semi-Auto Rifle, 376
Sako Classic Bolt-Action Rifle, 392
Sako Fiberclass Sporter Bolt-Action Rifle, 392
Sako Finnfire Bolt-Action Rifle, 415
Sako Hunter Left-Hand Bolt-Action Rifle, 392
Sako Hunter Bolt-Action Rifle, 391
Sako Laminated Bolt-Action Rifle, 391
Sako Lightweight Deluxe Bolt-Action Rifle, 392
Sako Mannlicher-Style Bolt-Action Carbine, 391
Sako Safari Grade Bolt-Action Rifle, 391
Sako Super Deluxe Sporter Bolt-Action Rifle, 392
Sako TRG-21 Bolt-Action Rifle, 421
Sako TRG-S Bolt-Action Rifle, 392
Sako Varmint Heavy Barrel Bolt-Action Rifle, 391
Sauer 90 Bolt-Action Rifle, 393
Sauer 90 Safari Model Bolt-Action Rifle, 393
Sauer 202 TR Target Rifle, 421
Sauer Drilling, 404
Sauer Model 202 Alaska Bolt-Action Rifle, 392
Sauer Model 202 Bolt-Action Rifle, 392
Sauer Model 202 Hunter-Match Bolt-Action Rifle, 392
Sauer Model 202 Super Grade Magnum Bolt-Action Rifle, 392
Sauer Model 202 Super Grade Standard Bolt-Action Rifle, 392
Savage 24F Predator O/U Combination Gun, 404
Savage Model 110CY Ladies/Youth Bolt-Action Rifle, 393
Savage Model 110FP Tactical Bolt-Action Rifle, 393
Savage Model 110GCXP3 Package Gun, 393
Savage Model 110GXP3 Package Gun, 393
Savage Model 111F Classic Hunter Bolt-Action Rifle, 393
Savage Model 111FC Classic Hunter Bolt-Action Rifle, 393
Savage Model 111FNS Classic Hunter Bolt-Action Rifle, 393
Savage Model 111FCXP3 Package Gun, 393
Savage Model 111FXP3 Package Gun, 393
Savage Model 111G Classic Hunter Bolt-Action Rifle, 393
Savage Model 111GC Classic Hunter Bolt-Action Rifle, 393
Savage Model 111GNS Classic Hunter Bolt-Action Rifle, 393
Savage Model 112BT Competition Grade Bolt-Action Rifle, 421
Savage Model 112BVSS Varmint Bolt-Action Rifle, 393
Savage Model 112BVSS-S Varmint Bolt-Action Rifle, 393
Savage Model 112FV Varmint Bolt-Action Rifle, 393
Savage Model 112FVSS Varmint Bolt-Action Rifle, 393
Savage Model 112FVSS-S Varmint Bolt-Action Rifle, 393

Savage Model 114CU Classic Ultra Bolt-Action Rifle, 394
Savage Model 116FCS Weather Warrior Bolt-Action Rifle, 394
Savage Model 116FCSAK Weather Warrior Bolt-Action Rifle, 394
Savage Model 116FSAK Weather Warrior Bolt-Action Rifle, 394
Savage Model 116FSK Weather Warrior Bolt-Action Rifle, 394
Savage Model 116FSS Weather Warrior Bolt-Action Rifle, 394
Savage Model 116SE Safari Express Bolt-Action Rifle, 394
Savage Model 116US Ultra Stainless Bolt-Action Rifle, 394
Schuetzen Gun Works Enforcer Carrycomp II Pistol, 333
Schuetzen Pistol Works Big Deuce Auto Pistol, 333
Schuetzen Pistol Works Crest Series Auto Pistol, 333
Schuetzen Pistol Works Enforcer Auto Pistol, 333
Schuetzen Pistol Works Griffon Pistol, 333
Schuetzen Pistol Works Matchmaster Carrycomp I, 348
Schuetzen Pistol Works Matchmaster Pistol, 348
Second Model Brown Bess Carbine, 471
Second Model Brown Bess Musket, 471
Seecamp LWS 32 Auto Pistol, 334
Sharps 1874 Old Reliable Single Shot Rifle, 402
C. Sharps Arms 1875 Business Single Shot Rifle, 401
C. Sharps Arms 1875 Single Shot Carbine, 401
C. Sharps Arms 1875 Classic Sharps Single Shot Rifle, 401
C. Sharps Arms 1875 Saddle Single Shot Rifle, 401
C. Sharps Arms 1875 Sporting Single Shot Rifle, 401
C. Sharps Arms New Model 1874 Old Reliable Single Shot Rifle, 401
C. Sharps Arms New Model 1875 Target & Long Range Single Shot Rifle, 401
C. Sharps Arms New Model 1875 Single Shot Rifle, 401
Sheridan Blue Streak CB9 Pneumatic Air Rifle, 496
Sheridan Pneumatic (Pump-Up) Air Rifles, 496
Sheridan Silver Streak C9 Pneumatic Air Rifle, 496
Sheriff Model 1851 Percussion Revolver, 460
Shiloh Sharps 1874 Business Rifle, 402
Shiloh Sharps 1874 Hartford Model Single Shot Rifle, 402
Shiloh Sharps 1874 Long Range Express Single Shot Rifle, 402
Shiloh Sharps 1874 Montana Roughrider Single Shot Rifle, 402
Shiloh Sharps 1874 Saddle Single Shot Rifle, 402
Shiloh Sharps 1874 Sporting Single Shot Rifle No. 1, 402
Shiloh Sharps 1874 Sporting Single Shot Rifle No. 3, 402
SIG P-210-2 Auto Pistol, 334
SIG P-210-2 Service Auto Pistol, 334
SIG P-210-6 Auto Pistol, 334
SIG P-210-5 Target Auto Pistol, 334
SIG Sauer P220 "American" Auto Pistol, 334
SIG Sauer P225 DA Auto Pistol, 334
SIG Sauer P226 DA Auto Pistol, 334
SIG Sauer P228 DA Auto Pistol, 334
SIG Sauer P229 DA Auto Pistol, 334
SIG Sauer P230 DA Auto Pistol, 334
SIG Sauer P230SL DA Auto Pistol, 334
Silma Model 70 Over/Under Shotgun, 441
SKB Model 585 Field Over/Under Shotgun, 441
SKB Model 585 Over/Under Shotgun, 441
SKB Model 585 Skeet Over/Under Shotgun, 441
SKB Model 585 Skeet Set Over/Under Shotgun, 441
SKB Model 585 Sporting Clays Over/Under Shotgun, 441
SKB Model 585 Trap Over/Under Shotgun, 441
SKB Model 585 Two-Barrel Field Set Over/Under Shotgun, 441
SKB Model 585 Two-Barrel Trap Combo Over/Under Shotgun, 441
SKB Model 585 Youth Model Shotgun, 441
SKB Model 585 Waterfowler Shotgun, 441
SKB Model 785 Field Set Over/Under Shotgun, 441
SKB Model 785 Field Over/Under Shotgun, 441
SKB Model 785 Over/Under Shotgun, 441
SKB Model 785 Sporting Clays Over/Under Shotgun, 441
SKB Model 785 Sporting Clays Set Over/Under Shotgun, 441
SKB Model 785 Skeet Three-Barrel Set Over/Under Shotgun, 441
SKB Model 785 Skeet Over/Under Shotgun, 441
SKB Model 785 Trap Combo Over/Under Shotgun, 441
SKB Model 785 Trap Over/Under Shotgun, 441
Smith & Wesson Model 10 38 M&P Heavy Barrel Revolver, 356
Smith & Wesson Model 10 M&P Revolver, 356
Smith & Wesson Model 13 H.B. M&P Revolver, 356
Smith & Wesson Model 14 Full Lug Revolver, 356
Smith & Wesson Model 15 Combat Masterpiece Revolver, 356
Smith & Wesson Model 19 Combat Magnum Revolver, 356
Smith & Wesson Model 29 Revolver, 357
Smith & Wesson Model 36 Chiefs Special Revolver, 357
Smith & Wesson Model 36LS LadySmith Revolver, 357
Smith & Wesson Model 37 Airweight Revolver, 357
Smith & Wesson Model 38 Bodyguard Revolver, 357
Smith & Wesson Model 41 Target Pistol, 348
Smith & Wesson Model 49 Bodyguard Revolver, 357
Smith & Wesson Model 60 3" Full Lug Revolver, 357

Smith & Wesson Model 60 Chiefs Special Stainless Revolver, 357
Smith & Wesson Model 60LS LadySmith Revolver, 357
Smith & Wesson Model 63 Kit Gun Revolver, 358
Smith & Wesson Model 64 Stainless M&P Revolver, 358
Smith & Wesson Model 65 H.B. M&P Revolver, 356
Smith & Wesson Model 65LS LadySmith Revolver, 358
Smith & Wesson Model 66 Stainless Combat Magnum Revolver, 358
Smith & Wesson Model 67 Combat Masterpeice Revolver, 358
Smith & Wesson Model 411 DA Auto Pistol, 335
Smith & Wesson Model 422 Auto Pistol, 335
Smith & Wesson Model 442 Centen. Airweight Revolver, 359
Smith & Wesson Model 586 Distinguished Combat Magnum Revolver, 358
Smith & Wesson Model 617 Full Lug Revolver, 358
Smith & Wesson Model 622 Auto Pistol, 335
Smith & Wesson Model 625 Revolver, 358
Smith & Wesson Model 629 Classic DX Revolver, 357
Smith & Wesson Model 629 Classic Revolver, 357
Smith & Wesson Model 629 Revolver, 357
Smith & Wesson Model 640 Centennial Revolver, 359
Smith & Wesson Model 649 Bodyguard Revolver, 357
Smith & Wesson Model 651 Revolver, 359
Smith & Wesson Model 657 Revolver, 359
Smith & Wesson Model 686 Distinguished Combat Magnum Revolver, 358
Smith & Wesson Model 909 DA Auto Pistol, 335
Smith & Wesson Model 910 DA Auto Pistol, 335
Smith & Wesson Model 940 Centennial Revolver, 359
Smith & Wesson Model 2206 Auto Pistol, 335
Smith & Wesson Model 2206 Target Auto Pistol, 335
Smith & Wesson Model 2213 Auto Pistol, 335
Smith & Wesson Model 2214 Sportsman Auto Pistol, 335
Smith & Wesson Model 3913 LadySmith Auto Pistol, 335
Smith & Wesson Model 3913 Double Action Auto Pistol, 335
Smith & Wesson Model 3914 Double Action Auto Pistol, 335
Smith & Wesson Model 3953 DA Auto Pistol, 335
Smith & Wesson Model 4006 DA Auto Pistol, 336
Smith & Wesson Model 4013 Auto Pistol, 336
Smith & Wesson Model 4046 DA Auto Pistol, 336
Smith & Wesson Model 4053 Auto Pistol, 336
Smith & Wesson Model 4500 Series Auto Pistols, 336
Smith & Wesson Model 4506 Auto Pistol, 336
Smith & Wesson Model 4516 Auto Pistol, 336
Smith & Wesson Model 4566 Auto Pistol, 336
Smith & Wesson Model 4586 Auto Pistol, 336
Smith & Wesson Model 5900 Series Auto Pistols, 336
Smith & Wesson Model 5903 Auto Pistol, 336
Smith & Wesson Model 5904 Auto Pistol, 336
Smith & Wesson Model 5906 Auto Pistol, 336
Smith & Wesson Model 5946 Auto Pistol, 336
Smith & Wesson Model 6904 Double Action Auto Pistol, 336
Smith & Wesson Model 6906 Double Action Auto Pistol, 336
Smith & Wesson Model 6946 Double Action Auto Pistol, 336
Smith & Wesson Model Sigma Series Auto Pistols, 336
Smith & Wesson Model SW9F Auto Pistol, 336
Smith & Wesson Model SW40F Auto Pistol, 336
Smith & Wesson Sigma 380 Auto Pistol, 336
Smith & Wesson Sigma Compact SW9C Auto Pistol, 336
Smith & Wesson Sigma Compact SW40 Auto Pistol, 336
Snake Charmer II Shotgun, 451
Snake Charmer New Generation, 451
Sphinx AT-380 Auto Pistol, 337
Sphinx AT-2000C Competitor Pistol, 348
Sphinx AT-2000CS Competitor Pistol, 348
Sphinx AT-2000GM Grand Master Pistol, 348
Sphinx AT-2000GMS Grand Master Pistol, 348
Sphinx AT-2000H Auto Pistol, 337
Sphinx AT-2000P Auto Pistol, 337
Sphinx AT-2000PS Auto Pistol, 337
Sphinx AT-2000S Double Action Auto Pistol, 337
Spiller & Burr Percussion Revolver, 460
Springfield Inc. 1911A1 Bullseye Wadcutter Pistol, 349
Springfield Inc. 1911A1 Champion Auto Pistol, 338
Springfield Inc. 1911A1 Champion Comp Auto Pistol, 338
Springfield Inc. 1911A1 Champion Mil-Spec Auto Pistol, 338
Springfield Inc. 1911A1 Compact Auto Pistol, 338
Springfield Inc. 1911A1 Compact Lightweight Auto Pistol, 338
Springfield Inc. 1911A1 Compact Mil-Spec Auto Pistol, 338
Springfield Inc. 1911A1 Custom Carry Auto Pistol, 337
Springfield Inc. 1911A1 Factory Comp Auto Pistol, 337
Springfield Inc. 1911A1 High Capacity 45 ACP Factory Auto Pistol, 338
Springfield Inc. 1911A1 High Capacity Auto Pistol, 338
Springfield Inc. 1911A1 High Capacity Comp. Auto Pistol, 338
Springfield Inc. 1911A1 High Capacity Comp. Lightweight Auto Pistol, 338
Springfield Inc. 1911A1 High Capacity Compact Auto Pistol, 338
Springfield Inc. 1911A1 Lightweight Auto Pistol, 337
Springfield Inc. 1911A1 Mil-Spec Auto Pistol, 337
Springfield Inc. 1911A1 N.M. Hardball Pistol, 349
Springfield Inc. 1911A1 Auto Pistol, 337
Springfield Inc. 1911A1 Product Improved Defender Auto Pistol, 338

Springfield Inc. 1911A1 Trophy Match Pistol, 349
Springfield Inc. Basic Competiton Pistol, 349
Springfield Inc. Champion MD-1 Auto Pistol, 338
Springfield Inc. Competiton Pistol, 349
Springfield Inc. Distinguished Pistol, 349
Springfield Inc. Distinguished Limited Pistol, 349
Springfield Inc. Expert Pistol, 349
Springfield Inc. M1A-A1 Bush Rifle, 376
Springfield Inc. M-1A National Match Rifle, 376
Springfield Inc. M-1A Rifle, 376
Springfield Inc. M-1A Super Match Rifle, 376, 421
Springfield Inc. M1A/M-21 Tactical Model Rifle, 421
Springfield Inc. M6 Scout Rifle, 404
Springfield Inc. M6 Scout Shotgun, 404
Springfield Inc. N.R.A. PPC Auto Pistol, 337
Springfield Inc. SAR-8 Sporter Rifle, 376
Springfield Inc. SAR-4800 Rifle, 376
Springfield Inc. Trophy Master Expert Pistol, 349
Springfield Inc. V10 Ultra Compact Auto Pistol, 338
Springfield Inc. V10 Ultra Compact MD-1 Lightweight Auto Pistol, 338
Star Firestar M45 Auto Pistol, 338
Star Firestar Auto Pistol, 338
Star Firestar Plus Auto Pistol, 339
Star Ultrastar Double Action Auto Pistol, 339
Steyr CO_2 Match 91 Air Rifle, 496
Steyr CO_2 Match 91 Running Target Air Rifle, 496
Steyr CO_2 Match LP1 Pistol, 484
Steyr CO_2 Match LP1C Pistol, 484
Steyr LP5 Match Air Pistol, 484
Steyr LP5C Match Air Pistol, 484
Steyr-Mannlicher Luxus Model L Bolt-Action, 395
Steyr-Mannlicher Luxus Model M Bolt-Action, 395
Steyr-Mannlicher Luxus Model S Bolt-Action, 395
Steyr-Mannlicher Match SPG-CISM Rifle, 422
Steyr-Mannlicher Match SPG-T Rifle, 422
Steyr-Mannlicher Match SPG-UIT Rifle, 422
Steyr-Mannlicher MIII Professional Bolt-Action Rifle, 394
Steyr-Mannlicher Sporter Models L Bolt-Action Rifle, 394
Steyr-Mannlicher Sporter Models M Bolt-Action Rifle, 394
Steyr-Mannlicher Sporter Models S Bolt-Action Rifle, 394
Steyr-Mannlicher Sporter Models SL Bolt-Action Rifle, 394
Steyr-Mannlicher Sporter Models S/T Bolt-Action Rifle, 394
Steyr-Mannlicher SSG P-I Rifle, 421
Steyr-Mannlicher SSG PII Rifle, 421
Steyr-Mannlicher SSG P-IV Rifle, 421
Stoeger American Eagle Luger Auto Pistol, 339
Stoeger American Eagle Navy Model 6", 339
Stoeger/IGA Condor I Over/Under Shotgun, 442
Stoeger/IGA Condor II Over/Under Shotgun, 442
Stoeger/IGA Condor Supreme Over/Under Shotgun, 442
Stoeger/IGA Reuna Single Barrel Shotgun, 451
Stoeger/IGA Reuna Youth Model Shotgun, 451
Stoeger/IGA Uplander Coach Gun Side-by-Side Shotgun, 447
Stoeger/IGA Uplander Side-by-Side Shotgun, 447
Stoner SR-25 Lightweight Match, 422
Stoner SR-25 Match Rifle, 422
Stoner SR-25 Carbine, 376
Stoner SR-25 Sporter Rifle, 376
Stone Mountain 1853 Enfield Musket, 471
Stone Mountain Silver Eagle Hunter Rifle, 471
Stone Mountain Silver Eagle Rifle, 471
Sundance BOA Auto Pistol, 339
Sundance Model A-25 Auto Pistol, 339
Sundance Point Blank O/U Derringer, 370
Survival Arms AR-7 Explorer Rifle, 408
Survival Arms AR-7 Sporter Rifle, 408
Survival Arms AR-7 Wildcat Rifle, 408

T

Tactical Response TR-870 Border Patrol Model Shotgun, 454
Tactical Response TR-870 FBI Model Shotgun, 454
Tactical Response TR-870 K-9 Model Shotgun, 454
Tactical Response TR-870 Louis Awerbuck Model, 454
Tactical Response TR-870 Military Model Shotgun, 454
Tactical Response TR-870 Patrol Model Shotgun, 454
Tactical Response TR-870 Practical Turkey Model, 454
Tactical Response TR-870 Shotgun, 454
Tactical Response TR-870 Urban Sniper Shotgun, 454
Tanner 50 Meter Free Rifle, 422
Tanner 300 Meter Free Rifle, 422
Tanner Standard UIT Rifle, 4220
Tar-Hunt Matchless Model, 451
Tar-Hunt Peerless Model, 451
Tar-Hunt RSG-12 Professional Rifled Slug Gun, 451
Tar-Hunt Turkey Model, 451
Taurus Model 44 Revolver, 359
Taurus Model 65 Revolver, 359
Taurus Model 66 Revolver, 359
Taurus Model 80 Standard Revolver, 359
Taurus Model 82 Heavy Barrel Revolver, 360
Taurus Model 83 Revolver, 360
Taurus Model 85 Revolver, 360
Taurus Model 85CH Revolver, 360
Taurus Model 94 Revolver, 360
Taurus Model 96 Revolver, 360
Taurus Model 431 Revolver, 360

Taurus Model 441 Revolver, 360
Taurus Model 605 Revolver, 360
Taurus Model 607 Revolver, 361
Taurus Model 669 Revolver, 361
Taurus Model 689 Revolver, 361
Taurus Model 941 Revolver, 361
Taurus PT 22 Auto Pistol, 339
Taurus PT 25 Auto Pistol, 339
Taurus PT 58 Auto Pistol, 339
Taurus PT 92AF Pistol, 340
Taurus PT 92AFC Compact Pistol, 340
Taurus PT 99AF Auto Pistol, 340
Taurus PT 100 Auto Pistol, 340
Taurus PT 101 Auto Pistol, 340
Taurus PT 908 Auto Pistol, 340
Taurus PT 945 Auto Pistol, 340
Texas Armory Defender Derringer, 370
Texas Longhorn "The Jezebel" Pistol, 370
Texas Longhorn Arms Cased Set, 367
Texas Longhorn Arms Grover's Improved No. Five Revolver, 366
Texas Longhorn Arms Right-Hand Single-Action Revolver, 366
Texas Longhorn Arms Sesquicentennial Model Revolver, 366
Texas Longhorn Arms Texas Border Special, 367
Texas Longhorn Arms West Texas Flat Top Target, 367
Texas Paterson 1836 Revolver, 461
Thompson/Center Big Boar Rifle, 471
Thompson/Center Contender Carbine Youth Model, 402
Thompson/Center Contender Single Shot Carbine, 402
Thompson/Center Contender Hunter Package, 371
Thompson/Center Contender, 370
Thompson/Center Fire Hawk Rifle, 471
Thompson/Center Grey Hawk Percussion Rifle, 471
Thompson/Center Hawken Custom Rifle, 472
Thompson/Center Hawken Flintlock Rifle, 472
Thompson/Center Hawken Percussion Rifle, 472
Thompson/Center New Englander Rifle, 472
Thompson/Center New Englander Shotgun, 478
Thompson/Center Pennsylvania Hunter Flintlock Carbine, 472
Thompson/Center Pennsylvania Hunter Percussion Carbine, 472
Thompson/Center Pennsylvania Hunter Flintlock Rifle, 472
Thompson/Center Pennsylvania Hunter Percussion Rifle, 472
Thompson/Center Renegade Hunter Rifle, 472
Thompson/Center Renegade Flintlock Rifle, 472
Thompson/Center Renegade Percussion Rifle, 472
Thompson/Center Scout Pistol, 456
Thompson/Center Scout Carbine, 472
Thompson/Center Scout Rifle, 472
Thompson/Center Stainless Contender Single Shot Carbine, 402
Thompson/Center Stainless Contender, 370
Thompson/Center Stainless Super 14 Contender, 371
Thompson/Center Stainless Super 16 Contender, 371
Thompson/Center Super 14 Contender, 349
Thompson/Center Super 16 Contender, 349
Thompson/Center Thunderhawk Carbine, 472
Thompson/Center White Mountain Flintlock Carbine, 473
Thompson/Center White Mountain Percussion Carbine, 473
Tikka Model 512S Combination Gun, 404
Tikka Model 512S Double Rifle, 404
Tikka Model 512S Field Grade Over/Under, 442
Tikka Model 512S Premier Grade Over/Under, 442
Tikka Model 512S Sporting Clays Over/Under, 442
Traditions 1853 Three-Band Enfield, 475
Traditions 1861 U.S. Springfield Rifle, 475
Traditions Buckskinner Flintlock Carbine, 473
Traditions Buckskinner Percussion Carbine, 473
Traditions Buckskinner Pistol, 456
Traditions Creedmore Match Rifle, 473
Traditions Deerhunter Flintlock Rifle, 473
Traditions Deerhunter Percussion Rifle, 473
Traditions Frontier Scout Rifle, 473
Traditions Fowler Shotgun, 478
Traditions Hawken Match Rifle, 474
Traditions Hawken Woodsman Rifle, 474
Traditions Henry Match Rifle, 473
Traditions In-Line Buckhunter Series Rifles, 474
Traditions Kentucky Pistol, 457
Traditions Kentucky Rifle, 474
Traditions Pennsylvania Flintlock Rifle, 474
Traditions Pennsylvania Percussion Rifle, 474
Traditions Pioneer Flintlock Carbine, 474
Traditions Pioneer Percussion Rifle, 474
Traditions Pioneer Pistol, 457
Traditions Tennessee Flintlock Rifle, 474
Traditions Tennessee Percussion Rifle, 474
Traditions Flintlock Trapper Pistol, 457
Traditions Percussion Trapper Pistol, 457
Traditions Trapper Pistol, 457
Traditions Whitetail Flintlock Rifles, 474
Traditions Whitetail Percussion Rifles, 474
Traditions William Parker Pistol, 457
Tryon Trailblazer Rifle, 475

GUNDEX

U

Uberti 1st Model Dragoon Revolver, 461
Uberti 2nd Model Dragoon Revolver, 461
Uberti 3rd Model Dragoon Revolver, 461
Uberti 1861 Navy Percussion Revolver, 458
Uberti 1862 Pocket Navy Percussion Revolver, 461
Uberti 1866 Sporting Rifle, 380
Uberti 1866 Yellowboy Carbine, 380
Uberti 1873 Buckhorn Single-Action Revolver, 367
Uberti 1873 Carbine, 380
Uberti 1873 Cattleman Single-Action Revolvers, 367
Uberti 1873 Sporting Rifle, 380
Uberti 1875 SA Army Outlaw Revolver, 367
Uberti 1890 Army Outlaw Revolver, 367
Uberti Civilian Revolver, 461
Uberti Henry Carbine, 380
Uberti Henry Rifle, 380
Uberti Henry Trapper, 380
Uberti Military Model Revolver, 461
Uberti Rolling Block Baby Carbine, 402
Uberti Rolling Block Target Pistol, 371
Uberti Santa Fe Hawken Rifle, 475
UFA Grand Teton Rifle, 475
UFA Teton Blackstone Rifle, 475
UFA Teton Rifle, 475
Ugartechea 10-Gauge Magnum Shotgun, 447
Ultra Light Arms Model 20 REB Hunter's Pistol, 371
Ultra Light Arms Model 20 RF Bolt-Action Rifle, 415
Ultra Light Arms Model 20 Bolt-Action Rifle, 395
Ultra Light Arms Model 24 Bolt-Action Rifle, 395
Ultra Light Arms Model 28 Bolt-Action Rifle, 395
Ultra Light Arms Model 40 Bolt-Action Rifle, 395
Ultra Light Arms Model 90 Muzzleloader, 475
Unique D.E.S. 32U Target Pistol, 349
Unique D.E.S. 69U Target Pistol, 350

V

Voere VEC-91 Lightning Bolt-Action Rifle, 395
Voere VEC-91BR Caseless Bolt-Action Rifle, 395
Voere VEC-91HB Varmint Special Caseless Bolt-Action Rifle, 395
Voere VEC-91SS Caseless Bolt-Action Rifle, 395
Voere VEC-95CG Single Shot Pistol, 371
Voere VEC-RG Repeater Pistol, 371

W

Walker 1847 Percussion Revolver, 461
Walther CPM-1 CO_2 Match Pistol, 484
Walther GSP Match Pistol, 350
Walther GSP-C Match Pistol, 350
Walther P-5 Compact Auto Pistol, 340
Walther P-5 Auto Pistol, 340
Walther P-38 Auto Pistol, 340
Walther PP Auto Pistol, 341
Walther PPK American Auto Pistol, 341
Walther PPK/S American Auto Pistol, 341
Walther TPH Auto Pistol, 341
Weatherby Athena Grade IV O/U Shotguns, 442
Weatherby Athena Grade V Classic Field O/U Shotgun, 442
Weatherby Euromark Bolt-Action Rifle, 396
Weatherby Lazermark V Bolt-Action Rifle, 396
Weatherby Mark V Crown Custom Bolt-Action Rifles, 396
Weatherby Mark V Custom Bolt-Action Rifles, 396
Weatherby Mark V Deluxe Bolt-Action Rifles, 396
Weatherby Mark V Eurosport Bolt-Action Rifle, 396
Weatherby Mark V Safari Grade Custom Bolt-Action Rifles, 396
Weatherby Mark V Sporter Bolt-Action Rifle, 396
Weatherby Mark V Stainless Bolt-Action Rifle, 396
Weatherby Mark V Synthetic Bolt-Action Rifle, 396
Weatherby Orion I Field O/U Shotgun, 442
Weatherby Orion II Classic Field Over/Under, 442
Weatherby Orion II Classic Sporting Clays Over/Under, 442
Weatherby Orion II Sporting Clays Over/Under, 442
Weatherby Orion III Classic Field Over/Under, 442
Weatherby Orion III Field O/U Shotgun, 442
Weatherby Orion O/U Shotguns, 442
Wesson Firearms 45 Pin Gun, 350
Wesson Firearms Hunter Series Revolvers, 362
Wesson Firearms Model 8 Revolver, 362
Wesson Firearms Model 9 Revolver, 362
Wesson Firearms Model 14 Revolver, 362
Wesson Firearms Model 15 Gold Series Revolver, 362
Wesson Firearms Model 15 Revolver, 362
Wesson Firearms Model 22 Revolver, 362
Wesson Firearms Model 22 Silhouette Revolver, 350
Wesson Firearms Model 32M Revolver, 362
Wesson Firearms Model 40 Silhouette Revolver, 350
Wesson Firearms Model 41V Revolver, 362
Wesson Firearms Model 44V Revolver, 362
Wesson Firearms Model 45V Revolver, 362
Wesson Firearms Model 322/7322 Target Revolver, 350
Wesson Firearms Model 445 Supermag Revolver, 350
Wesson Firearms Model 738P Revolver, 361
Wesson Firearms Model FB14-2 Revolver, 361
Wesson Firearms Model FB15 Revolver, 361
Wesson Firearms Model FB15-3 Revolver, 361
Wesson Firearms Model FB714-2 Revolver, 361
Wesson Firearms Model FB715 Revolver, 361
Wesson Firearms Model FB44 Revolver, 361
Wesson Firearms Model FB44-4 Revolver, 361
Wesson Firearms Model FB44-5 Revolver, 361
Wesson Firearms Model FB44-6 Revolver, 361
Wesson Firearms Model FB44-8 Revolver, 361
Wesson Firearms Model FB744 Revolver, 361
Wesson Firearms Model FB744-4 Revolver, 361
Wesson Firearms Model FB744-5 Revolver, 361
Wesson Firearms Model FB744-6 Revolver, 361
Wesson Firearms Model FB744-8 Revolver, 361
Wesson & Harrington Buffalo Classic Rifle, 402
Whiscombe JW50 Air Rifle, 496
Whiscombe JW60 Air Rifle, 496
Whiscombe JW70 Air Rifle, 496
Whiscombe JW75 Air Rifle, 496
Whiscombe JW75 High Power Air Rifle, 496
White Shooting Systems Bison Blackpowder Rifle, 476
White Shooting Systems Javelina Pistol, 457
White Shooting Systems Sporting Rifle, 476
White Shooting Systems Super 91 Blackpowder Rifle, 476
White Shooting Systems Super Safari Rifle, 476
White Shooting Systems Tominator Shotgun, 478
White Shooting Systems White Lightning Rifle, 476
White Shooting Systems White Thunder Shotgun, 478
White Shooting Systems Whitetail Rifle, 476
Wichita Classic Bolt-Action Rifle, 397
Wichita Classic Silhouette Pistol, 350
Wichita Silhouette Pistol, 351
Wichita Silhouette Rifle, 422
Wichita Varmint Bolt-Action Rifle, 397
Wildey Auto Pistol, 341
Wilkinson "Linda" Auto Pistol, 341
Wilkinson "Sherry" Auto Pistol, 341
Wilkinson Terry Carbine, 376
Winchester 8-Shot Pistol Grip Defender, 454
Winchester 8-Shot Pistol Grip Pump Security Shotguns, 454
Winchester Model 12 Pump Shotgun, 431
Winchester Model 70 Classic SM Bolt-Action Rifle, 397
Winchester Model 70 Classic Sporter Bolt-Action Rifle, 397
Winchester Model 70 Classic Stainless Bolt-Action Rifle, 397
Winchester Model 70 Classic Super Express Magnum Bolt-Action Rifle, 398
Winchester Model 70 Classic Super Grade Bolt-Action Rifle, 397
Winchester Model 70 Featherweight Classic Bolt-Action Rifle, 397
Winchester Model 70 Lightweight Bolt-Action Rifle, 398
Winchester Model 70 Synthetic Heavy Varmint Bolt-Action Rifle, 397
Winchester Model 94 Big Bore Side Eject Lever-Action Rifle, 381
Winchester Model 94 Legacy, 380
Winchester Model 94 Limited Edition Grade I, 381
Winchester Model 94 Limited Edition High Grade Rifle, 381
Winchester Model 94 Ranger Side Eject Lever-Action Rifle, 380
Winchester Model 94 Side Eject Lever-Action Rifle, 380
Winchester Model 94 Trapper Side Eject, 380
Winchester Model 94 Wrangler Side Eject Lever-Action Rifle, 381
Winchester Model 1300 Advantage Camo Deer Pump Shotgun, 431
Winchester Model 1300 Black Shadow Deer Pump Shotgun, 431
Winchester Model 1300 Black Shadow Field Pump Shotgun, 430
Winchester Model 1300 Black Shadow Turkey Pump Shotgun, 431
Winchester Model 1300 Defender Field Combo Shotgun, 454
Winchester Model 1300 Defender Pump Gun, 454
Winchester Model 1300 Ladies/Youth Pump Shotgun, 430
Winchester Model 1300 Ranger Deer Combo Shotgun, 431
Winchester Model 1300 Ranger Pump Gun Combo & Deer Gun, 431
Winchester Model 1300 Ranger Pump Shotgun, 431
Winchester Model 1300 Ranger Rifled Deer Combo Shotgun, 431
Winchester Model 1300 Realtree Turkey Pump Shotgun, 431
Winchester Model 1300 Slug Hunter Deer Pump Shotgun, 431
Winchester Model 1300 Stainless Marine Pump Gun, 454
Winchester Model 1300 Walnut Pump Shotgun, 430
Winchester Model 1895 High Grade Rifle, 381
Winchester Model 1895 Lever-Action Rifle, 381
Winchester Model 9422 High Grade Lever-Action Rifle, 409
Winchester Model 9422 Lever-Action Rifle, 409
Winchester Model 9422 Magnum Lever-Action Rifle, 409
Winchester Ranger Ladies/Youth Rifle, 398
Winchester Ranger Bolt-Action Rifle, 398

Z

Zouave Percussion Rifle, 476

HANDGUNS—AUTOLOADERS, SERVICE & SPORT

Includes models suitable for several forms of competition and other sporting purposes.

ACCU-TEK MODEL AT-9SS AUTO PISTOL
Caliber: 9mm Para., 8-shot magazine.
Barrel: 3.2".
Weight: 28 oz. **Length:** 6.25" overall.
Stocks: Black checkered nylon.
Sights: Blade front, rear adjustable for windage; three-dot system.
Features: Stainless steel construction. Double action only. Firing pin block with no external safeties. Lifetime warranty. Introduced 1992. Made in U.S. by Accu-Tek.
Price: Satin stainless $317.00

Acc-Tek AT-9SS

Accu-Tek AT-40SS Auto Pistol
Same as the Model AT-9 except chambered for 40 S&W, 7-shot magaszine. Introduced 1992.
Price: Stainless $317.00

Accu-Tek AT-45SS Auto Pistol
Same as the Model AT-9SS except chambered for 45 ACP, 6-shot magazine. Introduced 1995. Made in U.S. by Accu-Tek.
Price: Stainless steel $327.00

ACCU-TEK MODEL HC-380SS AUTO PISTOL
Caliber: 380 ACP, 10-shot magazine.
Barrel: 2.75".
Weight: 28 oz. **Length:** 6" overall.
Stocks: Checkered black composition.
Sights: Blade front, rear adjustable for windage.
Features: External hammer; manual thumb safety with firing pin and trigger disconnect; bottom magazine release. Stainless finish. Introduced 1993. Made in U.S. by Accu-Tek.
Price: Satin stainless $243.00
Price: Black finish over stainless $248.00

Accu-Tek HC-380SS

ACCU-TEK MODEL AT-380SS AUTO PISTOL
Caliber: 380 ACP, 5-shot magazine.
Barrel: 2.75".
Weight: 20 oz. **Length:** 5.6" overall.
Stocks: Grooved black composition.
Sights: Blade front, rear adjustable for windage.
Features: Stainless steel frame and slide. External hammer; manual thumb safety; firing pin block, trigger disconnect. Lifetime warranty. Introduced 1991. Made in U.S. by Accu-Tek.
Price: Satin stainless $191.00
Price: Black finish over steel (AT-380B) $196.00

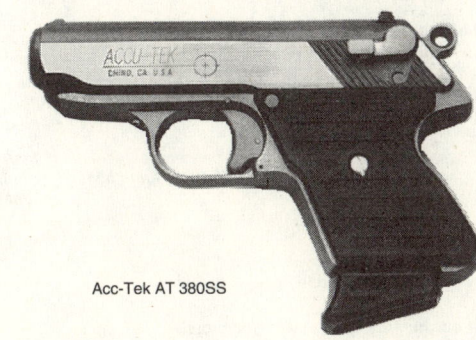
Acc-Tek AT 380SS

American Arms Escort

Accu-Tek Model AT-32SS Auto Pistol
Same as the AT-380SS except chambered for 32 ACP. Introduced 1991.
Price: Satin stainless $185.00
Price: Black finish over steel (AT-32B) $190.00

AMERICAN ARMS MODEL CX-22 DA AUTO PISTOL
Caliber: 22 LR, 8-shot magazine.
Barrel: $3^{1}/_{3}$".
Weight: 22 oz. **Length:** $6^{1}/_{3}$" overall.
Stocks: Checkered black polymer.
Sights: Blade front, rear adjustable for windage.
Features: Double action with manual hammer-block safety, firing pin safety. Alloy frame. Has external appearance of Walther PPK. Blue/black finish. Introduced 1990. Made in U.S. by American Arms, Inc.
Price: $213.00

AMERICAN ARMS ESCORT AUTO PISTOL
Caliber: 380 ACP, 7-shot magazine.
Barrel: $3^{3}/_{8}$".
Weight: 19 oz. **Length:** $6^{1}/_{8}$" overall.
Stocks: Soft polymer.
Sights: Blade front, rear adjustable for windage.
Features: Double-action-only trigger; stainless steel construction; chamber loaded indicator. Introduced 1995. From American Arms, Inc.
Price: $312.00

HANDGUNS—AUTOLOADERS, SERVICE & SPORT

AMERICAN ARMS MODEL PK22 DA AUTO PISTOL
Caliber: 22 LR, 8-shot magazine.
Barrel: 3.3".
Weight: 22 oz. **Length:** 6.3" overall.
Stocks: Checkered plastic.
Sights: Fixed.
Features: Double action. Polished blue finish. Slide-mounted safety. Made in the U.S. by American Arms, Inc.
Price: $213.00

AMERICAN ARMS MODEL P-98 AUTO PISTOL
Caliber: 22 LR, 8-shot magazine.
Barrel: 5".
Weight: 25 oz. **Length:** 8 1/8" overall.
Stocks: Grooved black polymer.
Sights: Blade front, rear adjustable for windage.
Features: Double action with hammer-block safety, magazine disconnect safety. Alloy frame. Has external appearance of the Walther P-38 pistol. Introduced 1989. Made in U.S. by American Arms, Inc.
Price: $229.00

AMERICAN ARMS MODEL PX-22 AUTO PISTOL
Caliber: 22 LR, 7-shot magazine.
Barrel: 2.85".
Weight: 15 oz. **Length:** 5.39" overall.
Stocks: Black checkered plastic.
Sights: Fixed.
Features: Double action; 7-shot magazine. Polished blue finish. Introduced 1989. Made in U.S. From American Arms, Inc.
Price: $206.00

AMT AUTOMAG II AUTO PISTOL
Caliber: 22 WMR, 9-shot magazine (7-shot with 3 3/8" barrel).
Barrel: 3 3/8", 4 1/2", 6".
Weight: About 23 oz. **Length:** 9 3/8" overall.
Stocks: Grooved carbon fiber.
Sights: Blade front, adjustable rear.
Features: Made of stainless steel. Gas-assisted action. Exposed hammer. Slide flats have brushed finish, rest is sandblast. Squared trigger guard. Introduced 1986. From AMT.
Price: $405.95

AMT AUTOMAG III PISTOL
Caliber: 30 Carbine, 8-shot magazine.
Barrel: 6 3/8".
Weight: 43 oz. **Length:** 10 1/2" overall.
Stocks: Carbon fiber.
Sights: Blade front, adjustable rear.
Features: Stainless steel construction. Hammer-drop safety. Slide flats have brushed finish, rest is sandblasted. Introduced 1989. From AMT.
Price: $469.79

AMT AUTOMAG IV PISTOL
Caliber: 45 Winchester Magnum, 6-shot magazine.
Barrel: 6.5".
Weight: 46 oz. **Length:** 10.5" overall with 6.5" barrel.
Stocks: Carbon fiber.
Sights: Blade front, adjustable rear.
Features: Made of stainless steel with brushed finish. Introduced 1990. Made in U.S. by AMT.
Price: $699.99
Price: Automag V (50 A.E.) $899.99

American Arms PK22

American Arms P-98

American Arms PX-22

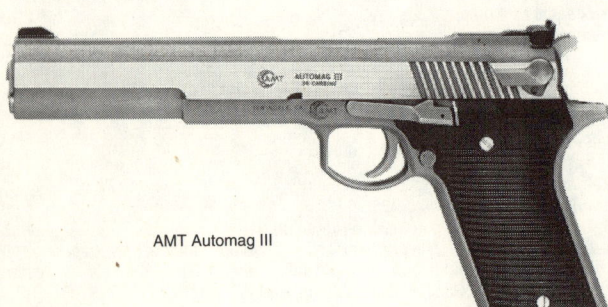
AMT Automag III

AMT Automag II

HANDGUNS—AUTOLOADERS, SERVICE & SPORT

AMT 45 ACP Backup

AMT BACKUP II AUTO PISTOL
Caliber: 380 ACP, 5-shot magazine.
Barrel: 2½".
Weight: 18 oz. **Length:** 5" overall.
Stocks: Carbon fiber.
Sights: Fixed, open, recessed.
Features: Concealed hammer, blowback operation; manual and grip safeties. All stainless steel construction. Smallest domestically-produced pistol in 380. From AMT.
Price: $309.99

AMT 45 ACP HARDBALLER
Caliber: 45 ACP.
Barrel: 5".
Weight: 39 oz. **Length:** 8½" overall.
Stocks: Wrap-around rubber.
Sights: Adjustable.
Features: Extended combat safety, serrated matte slide rib, loaded chamber indicator, long grip safety, beveled magazine well, adjustable target trigger. All stainless steel. From AMT.
Price: $549.95
Price: Government model (as above except no rib, fixed sights) $489.99

ARGENTINE HI-POWER 9MM AUTO PISTOL
Caliber: 9mm Para., 10-shot magazine.
Barrel: 4²¹⁄₃₂".
Weight: 32 oz. **Length:** 7¾" overall.
Stocks: Checkered walnut.
Sights: Blade front, adjustable rear.
Features: Produced in Argentina under F.N. Browning license. Introduced 1990. Imported by Century International Arms, Inc.
Price: About $299.95

Argentine Hi-Power Detective Model
Similar to the standard model except has 3.8" barrel, 6.9" overall length and weighs 33 oz. Grips are finger-groove, checkered soft rubber. Matte black finish. Introduced 1994. Imported by Century International Arms, Inc.
Price: About $310.00

ASTRA A-70 AUTO PISTOL
Caliber: 9mm Para., 8-shot; 40 S&W, 7-shot magazine.
Barrel: 3.5".
Weight: 29.3 oz. **Length:** 6.5" overall.
Stocks: Checkered black plastic.
Sights: Blade front, rear adjustable for windage.
Features: All steel frame and slide. Checkered grip straps and trigger guard. Nickel or blue finish. Introduced 1992. Imported from Spain by European American Armory.
Price: Blue, 9mm Para. $360.00
Price: Blue, 40 S&W $360.00
Price: Nickel, 9mm Para. $385.00
Price: Nickel, 40 S&W $385.00
Price: Stainless steel, 9mm $450.00
Price: Stainless steel, 40 S&W $450.00

Astra A-75 Decocker Auto Pistol
Same as the A-70 except has ambidextrous decocker system, different trigger, contoured pebble-grain grips. Introduced 1993. Imported from Spain by European American Armory.
Price: Blue, 9mm or 40 S&W $415.00
Price: Nickel, 9mm or 40 S&W $440.00
Price: Blue, 45 ACP $445.00
Price: Nickel, 45 ACP $460.00
Price: Stainless steel, 9mm, 40 S&W $495.00
Price: Stainless steel, 45 ACP $525.00
Price: Featherweight (23.5 oz.), 9mm, blue $440.00

ASTRA A-100 AUTO PISTOL
Caliber: 9mm Para., 10-shot; 40 S&W, 10-shot; 45 ACP, 9-shot magazine.
Barrel: 3.9".
Weight: 29 oz. **Length:** 7.1" overall.
Stocks: Checkered black plastic.
Sights: Blade front, interchangeable rear blades for elevation, screw adjustable for windage.
Features: Double action. Decocking lever permits lowering hammer onto locked firing pin. Automatic firing pin block. Side button magazine release. Introduced 1993. Imported from Spain by European American Armory.
Price: Blue, 9mm, 40 S&W, 45 ACP $450.00
Price: As above, nickel $475.00

AMT Backup Double Action Only Pistol
Similar to the standard Backup except has double-action-only mechanism, enlarged trigger guard, slide is rounded ar rear. Has 5-shot magazine. Introduced 1992. From AMT.
Price: $329.99
Price: 9mm Para., 38 Super, 40 S&W, 45 ACP $449.99

AMT 45 ACP HARDBALLER LONG SLIDE
Caliber: 45 ACP.
Barrel: 7". **Length:** 10½" overall.
Stocks: Wrap-around rubber.
Sights: Fully adjustable rear sight.
Features: Slide and barrel are 2" longer than the standard 45, giving less recoil, added velocity, longer sight radius. Has extended combat safety, serrated matte rib, loaded chamber indicator, wide adjustable trigger. From AMT.
Price: $595.99

Argentine Hi-Power

Astra A-75

Astra A-100

CAUTION: PRICES SHOWN ARE SUPPLIED BY THE MANUFACTURER OR IMPORTER. CHECK YOUR LOCAL GUNSHOP.

HANDGUNS—AUTOLOADERS, SERVICE & SPORT

AUTO-ORDNANCE 1911A1 AUTOMATIC PISTOL
Caliber: 9mm Para., 38 Super, 9-shot; 10mm, 45 ACP, 7-shot magazine.
Barrel: 5".
Weight: 39 oz. **Length:** 8½" overall.
Stocks: Checkered plastic with medallion.
Sights: Blade front, rear adjustable for windage.
Features: Same specs as 1911A1 military guns—parts interchangeable. Frame and slide blued; each radius has non-glare finish. Made in U.S. by Auto-Ordnance Corp.
Price: 45 ACP, blue $388.95
Price: 45 ACP, Parkerized $379.25
Price: 45 ACP, satin nickel $405.00
Price: 9mm, 38 Super $415.00
Price: 10mm (has three-dot combat sights, rubber wrap-around grips) ..$420.95
Price: 45 ACP General Model (Commander style) $427.95
Price: Duo Tone (nickel frame, blue slide, three-dot sight system, textured black wrap-around grips) $405.00

Auto-Ordnance ZG-51 Pit Bull Auto
Same as the 1911A1 except has 3½" barrel, weighs 36 oz. and has an overall length of 7¼". Available in 45 ACP only; 7-shot magazine. Introduced 1989.
Price: $420.95

BABY EAGLE AUTO PISTOL
Caliber: 9mm Para., 40 S&W, 41 A.E.
Barrel: 4.37".
Weight: 35 oz. **Length:** 8.14" overall.
Stocks: High-impact black polymer.
Sights: Combat.
Features: Double-action mechanism; polygonal rifling; ambidextrous safety. Model 9mm F has frame-mounted safety on left side of pistol; Model 9mm FS has frame-mounted safety and 3.62" barrel. Introduced 1992. Imported by Magnum Research.
Price: 40 S&W, 41 A.E., 9mm (9mm F, 9mm FS), black finish $569.00
Price: Conversion kit, 9mm Para. to 41 A.E. $239.00
Price: 9mm FS, chrome finish $659.00
Price: 9mm FSS, matte black finish, frame-mounted safety, short grip, short barrel $569.00
Price: As above, chrome finish $659.00

Auto-Ordnance 1911A1

Auto-Ordnance 1911A1 Competition Model
Similar to the standard Model 19911A1 except has barrel compensator. Commander hammer, flat mainspring housing, three-dot sight system, low-profile magazine funnel, Hi-Ride beavertail grip safety, full-length recoil spring guide system, black-textured rubber, wrap-around grips, and extended slide stop, safety and magazine catch. Introduced 1994. Made in U.S. by Auto-Ordnance Corp.
Price: $615.00

Baby Eagle FS

Les Baer Premier II

Baer 1911 Prowler III Auto Pistol
Same as the Premier II except also has tapered cone stub weight and reverse recoil plug. Made in U.S. by Les Baer Custom, Inc.
Price: Standard size, blued $1,795.00
Price: Standard size, stainless $1,895.00
Price: Commanche size, blued $1,795.00
Price: Commanche size, stainless $1,895.00

BAER 1911 CONCEPT I AUTO PISTOL
Caliber: 45 ACP, 7-shot magazine.
Barrel: 5".
Weight: 37 oz. **Length:** 8.5" overall.
Stocks: Checkered rosewood.
Sights: Baer dovetail front, Bo-Mar deluxe low-mount rear with hidden leaf.
Features: Baer forged steel frame, slide and barrel with Baer stainless bushing; slide fitted to frame; double serrated slide; Baer beavertail grip safety, checkered slide stop, tuned extractor, extended ejector, deluxe hammer and sear, match disconnector; lowered and flared ejection port; fitted recoil link; polished feed ramp, throated barrel; Baer fitted speed trigger, flat serrated mainspring housing. Blue finish. Made in U.S. by Les Baer Custom, Inc.
Price: $1,279.00
Price: Concept II (with Novak fixed rear sight) $1,249.00

CONSULT SHOOTER'S MARKETPLACE Page 266, This Issue

BAER 1911 PREMIER II AUTO PISTOL
Caliber: 45 ACP, 7- or 10-shot magazine.
Barrel: 5".
Weight: 37 oz. **Length:** 8.5" overall.
Stocks: Checkered rosewood, double diamond pattern.
Sights: Baer dovetailed front, low-mount Bo-Mar rear with hidden leaf.
Features: Baer NM forged steel frame and barrel with stainless bushing; slide fitted to frame; double serrated slide; lowered, flared ejection port; tuned, polished extractor; Baer extended ejector, checkered slide stop, aluminum speed trigger with 4-lb. pull, deluxe Commander hammer and sear, beavertail grip safety with pad, beveled magazine well, extended ambidextrous safety; flat mainspring housing; polished feed ramp and throated barrel; 30 lpi checkered front strap. Made in U.S. by Les Baer Custom, Inc.
Price: Blued $1,428.00
Price: Stainless $1,528.00

HANDGUNS—AUTOLOADERS, SERVICE & SPORT

Baer Custom Carry

Baer Concept IV

Baer 1911 Concept IX Auto Pistol
Same as the Commanche Concept VII except has Baer lightweight forged aluminum frame, blued steel slide, Novak rear sight. Chambered for 45 ACP, 7-shot magazine. Made in U.S. by Les Baer Custom, Inc.
Price: $1,439.00
Price: Concept X (as above with stainless slide) $1,489.00

BAIKAL IJ-70 DA AUTO PISTOL
Caliber: 9x18mm Makarov, 8-shot magazine.
Barrel: 4".
Weight: 25 oz. **Length:** 6.25" overall.
Stocks: Checkered composition.
Sights: Blade front, rear adjustable for windage and elevation.
Features: Double action; all-steel construction; frame-mounted safety with decocker. Comes with two magazines, cleaning rod, universal tool. Introduced 1994. Imported from Russia by Century International Arms, K.B.I., Inc.
Price: 9x18mm, blue $199.00
Price: IJ-70HC, 9x18, 10-shot magazine, from K.B.I. $239.00
Price: As above, 380 ACP (K.B.I.) $249.00

BERETTA MODEL 80 CHEETAH SERIES DA PISTOLS
Caliber: 380 ACP, 10-shot magazine (M84); 8-shot (M85); 22 LR, 7-shot (M87), 22 LR, 8-shot (M89).
Barrel: 3.82".
Weight: About 23 oz. (M84/85); 20.8 oz. (M87). **Length:** 6.8" overall.
Stocks: Glossy black plastic (wood optional at extra cost).
Sights: Fixed front, drift-adjustable rear.
Features: Double action, quick takedown, convenient magazine release. Introduced 1977. Imported from Italy by Beretta U.S.A.
Price: Model 84 Cheetah, plastic grips $529.00
Price: Model 84 Cheetah, wood grips $557.00
Price: Model 84 Cheetah, wood grips, nickel finish $600.00
Price: Model 85 Cheetah, plastic grips, 8-shot $486.00
Price: Model 85 Cheetah, wood grips, 8-shot $514.00
Price: Model 85 Cheetah, wood grips, nickel, 8-shot $551.00
Price: Model 87 Cheetah wood, 22 LR, 7-shot $493.00

Beretta Model 86 Cheetah
Similar to the 380-caliber Model 85 except has tip-up barrel for first-round loading. Barrel length is 4.33", overall length of 7.33". Has 8-shot magazine, walnut or plastic grips. Introduced 1989.
Price: $514.00

BAER 1911 CUSTOM CARRY AUTO PISTOL
Caliber: 45 ACP, 7- or 10-shot magazine.
Barrel: 5".
Weight: 37 oz. **Length:** 8.5" overall.
Stocks: Checkered walnut.
Sights: Baer improved ramp-style dovetailed front, Novak low-mount rear.
Features: Baer forged NM frame, slide and barrel with stainless bushing; fitted slide to frame; double serrated slide (full-size only); Baer speed trigger with 4-lb. pull; Baer deluxe hammer and sear, tactical-style extended ambidextrous safety, beveled magazine well; polished feed ramp and throated barrel; tuned extractor; Baer extended ejector, checkered slide stop; lowered and flared ejection port, full-length recoil guide rod; recoil buff. Made in U.S. by Les Baer Custom, Inc.
Price: Standard size, blued $1,265.00
Price: Standard size, stainless $1,365.00
Price: Commanche size, blued $1,265.00
Price: Commanche size, stainless $1,375.00
Price: Commanche size, aluminum frame, blued slide $1,375.00
Price: Commanche size, aluminum frame, stainless slide $1,420.00

Baer 1911 Concept III Auto Pistol
Same as the Concept I except has forged stainless frame with blued steel slide, Bo-Mar rear sight, 30 lpi checkering on front strap. Made in U.S. by Les Baer Custom, Inc.
Price: $1,499.00
Price: Concept IV (with Novak rear sight) $1,479.00
Price: Concept V (all stainless, Bo-Mar sight, checkered front strap) .. $1,559.00
Price: Concept VI (stainless, Novak sight, checkered front strap) $1,529.00

Baer 1911 Concept VII Auto Pistol
Same as the Concept I except reduced Commanche size with 4.25" barrel, weighs 27.5 oz., 7.75" overall. Blue finish, checkered front strap. Made in U.S. by Les Baer Custom, Inc.
Price: $1,439.00
Price: Concept VIII (stainless frame and slide, Novak rear sight) $1,529.00

Biakal IJ-70

Consult our Directory pages for the location of firms mentioned.

Beretta 84 Cheetah

CAUTION: PRICES SHOWN ARE SUPPLIED BY THE MANUFACTURER OR IMPORTER. CHECK YOUR LOCAL GUNSHOP.

HANDGUNS—AUTOLOADERS, SERVICE & SPORT

BERETTA MODEL 92FS PISTOL
Caliber: 9mm Para., 10-shot magazine.
Barrel: 4.9".
Weight: 34 oz. **Length:** 8.5" overall.
Stocks: Checkered black plastic; wood optional at extra cost.
Sights: Blade front, rear adjustable for windage. Tritium night sights available.
Features: Double action. Extractor acts as chamber loaded indicator, squared trigger guard, grooved front- and backstraps, inertia firing pin. Matte finish. Introduced 1977. Made in U.S. and imported from Italy by Beretta U.S.A.
Price: With plastic grips $626.00
Price: With wood grips $647.00
Price: Tritium night sights, add $90.00

Beretta Model 92F Stainless Pistol
Same as the Model 92FS except has stainless steel barrel and slide, and frame of aluminum-zirconium alloy. Has three-dot sight system. Introduced 1992.
Price: $757.00
Price: Model 92F-EL Stainless (gold trim, engraved barrel, slide, frame, gold-finished safety-levers, trigger, magazine release, grip screws) $1,240.00
Price: For Trijicon sights, add $90.00

Beretta Model 96 Auto Pistol
Same as the Model 92F except chambered for 40 S&W. Ambidextrous safety mechanism with passive firing pin catch, slide safety/decocking lever, trigger bar disconnect. Has 10-shot magazine. Available with Trijicon or three-dot sights. Introduced 1992.
Price: Model 96, plastic grips $643.00
Price: Model 96D, double action only, three-dot sights $607.00
Price: For Trijicon sights, add $90.00

Beretta Models 92FS/96 Centurion Pistols
Identical to the Model 92FS and 96F except uses shorter slide and barrel (4.3"). Trijicon or three-dot sight systems. Plastic or wood grips. Available in 9mm or 40 S&W. Also available in D Models (double action only). Introduced 1992.
Price: Model 92FS Centurion, three-dot sights, plastic grips $626.00
Price: Model 92FS Centurion, wood grips $647.00
Price: Model 96 Centurion, three-dot sights, plastic grips $643.00
Price: Model 92D Centurion $586.00
Price: Model 96D Centurion $607.00
Price: For Trijicon sights, add $90.00

Beretta Model 92FS

Beretta Model 92D Pistol
Same as the Model 92FS except double action only and has bobbed hammer, no external safety. Introduced 1992.
Price: With plastic grips, three-dot sights $586.00
Price: As above with Trijicon sights $676.00

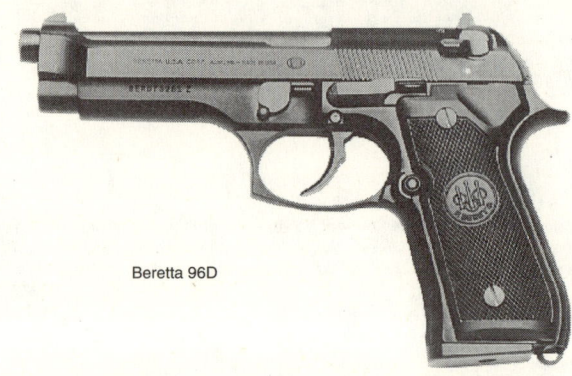

Beretta 96D

Beretta Model 92/96 Brigadier Auto Pistol
Similar to the Beretta Model 92/96 series except has removable front sight and reconfigured high slide wall profile to reduce felt recoil. Has 10-shot magazine, three-dot sight system, 4.9" barrel, weighs 35.3 oz. Matte black Bruniton finish. Introduced 1995. From Beretta U.S.A.
Price: Model 92 Brigadier (9mm) .... NA
Price: Model 96 Brigadier (40 S&W) .... NA

Beretta 950BS Jetfire

Beretta Model 92/96 Brigadier

BERETTA MODEL 950BS JETFIRE AUTO PISTOL
Caliber: 25 ACP, 8-shot.
Barrel: 2.5".
Weight: 9.9 oz. **Length:** 4.5" overall.
Stocks: Checkered black plastic or walnut.
Sights: Fixed.
Features: Single action, thumb safety; tip-up barrel for direct loading/unloading, cleaning. From Beretta U.S.A.
Price: Jetfire wood, blue $187.00
Price: Jetfire wood, nickel $221.00
Price: Jetfire wood, engraved $267.00
Price: Jetfire plastic, matte blue $159.00

Beretta Model 21 Bobcat Pistol
Similar to the Model 950 BS. Chambered for 22 LR or 25 ACP. Both double action. Has 2.5" barrel, 4.9" overall length; 7-round magazine on 22 cal.; available in nickel, matte, engraved or blue finish. Plastic or walnut grips. Introduced in 1985.
Price: Bobcat, 22-cal. $244.00
Price: Bobcat, nickel, 22-cal. $254.00
Price: Bobcat, 25-cal. $244.00
Price: Bobcat, nickel, 25-cal. $254.00
Price: Bobcat wood, engraved, 22 or 25 .... $294.00
Price: Bobcat plastic matte, 22 or 25 .... $194.00

HANDGUNS—AUTOLOADERS, SERVICE & SPORT

BERETTA MODEL 8000/8040 COUGAR PISTOL
Caliber: 9mm Para., 10-shot, 40 S&W, 10-shot magazine.
Barrel: 3.5".
Weight: 33.5 oz. **Length:** 7" overall.
Stocks: Textured composition.
Sights: Blade front, rear drift adjustable for windage.
Features: Slide-mounted safety; exposed hammer. Matte black Bruniton finish. Announced 1994. Imported from Italy by Beretta U.S.A.
Price: $636.00
Price: D models $611.00

BERNARDELLI P018 DA AUTO PISTOL
Caliber: 9mm Para., 10-shot magazine.
Barrel: 4.8".
Weight: 34.2 oz. **Length:** 8.23" overall.
Stocks: Checkered plastic; walnut optional.
Sights: Blade front, rear adjustable for windage and elevation; low profile, three-dot system.
Features: Manual thumb half-cock, magazine and auto-locking firing pin safeties. Thumb safety decocks hammer. Reversible magazine release. Imported from Italy by Armsport.
Price: Blue $505.00
Price: Chrome $568.00

Bernardelli P018 Compact DA Auto Pistol
Similar to the P018 except has 4" barrel, 7.44" overall length, 10-shot magazine. Weighs 31.7 oz. Imported from Italy by Armsport.
Price: Blue $552.00
Price: Chrome $600.00

BERNARDELLI MODEL USA AUTO PISTOL
Caliber: 22 LR, 10-shot, 380 ACP, 7-shot magazine.
Barrel: 3.5".
Weight: 26.5 oz. **Length:** 6.5" overall.
Stocks: Checkered plastic with thumbrest.
Sights: Ramp front, white outline rear adjustable for windage and elevation.
Features: Hammer-block slide safety; loaded chamber indicator; dual recoil buffer springs; serrated trigger; inertia-type firing pin. Imported from Italy by Armsport.
Price: Blue, either caliber $387.00
Price: Chrome, either caliber $412.00
Price: Model AMR (6" barrel, target sights) $440.00

BERNARDELLI P. ONE DA AUTO PISTOL
Caliber: 9mm Para., 16-shot, 40 S&W, 10-shot magazine.
Barrel: 4.8".
Weight: 34 oz. **Length:** 8.35" overall.
Stocks: Checkered black plastic.
Sights: Blade front, rear adjustable for windage and elevation; three dot system.
Features: Forged steel frame and slide; full-length slide rails; reversible magazine release; thumb safety/decocker; squared trigger guard. Introduced 1994. Imported from Italy by Armsport.
Price: 9mm Para., blue/black $530.00
Price: 9mm Para., chrome $580.00
Price: 40 S&W, blue/black $530.00
Price: 40 S&W, chrome $580.00

Bernardelli P. One Practical VB Pistol
Similar to the P. One except chambered for 9x21mm, two- or four-port compensator, straight trigger, micro-adjustable rear sight. Introduced 1994. Imported from Italy by Armsport.
Price: Blue/black, two-port compensator $1,425.00
Price: As above, four-port compensator $1,475.00
Price: Chrome, two-port compensator $1,498.00
Price: As above, four-port compensator $1,540.00
Price: Customized VB, four-plus-two-port compensator $2,150.00
Price: As above, chrome $2,200.0

BERSA THUNDER 380 AUTO PISTOLS
Caliber: 380 ACP, 7-shot (Thunder 380), 10-shot magazine (Thunder 380 Plus).
Barrel: 3.5".
Weight: 25.75 oz. **Length:** 6.6" overall.
Stocks: Black rubber.
Sights: Blade front, notch rear adjustable for windage; three-dot system.
Features: Double action; firing pin and magazine safeties. Available in blue or nickel. Introduced 1995. Distributed by Eagle Imports, Inc.
Price: Thunder 380, 7-shot, deep blue finish $308.95
Price: As above, satin nickel $341.95
Price: As above, Duo-Tone finish $324.95
Price: Thunder 380 Plus, 10-shot, matte blue ... $367.95
Price: As above, satin nickel $408.00
Price: As above, Duo-Tone finish $384.95

Beretta M8000/8040 Cougar

Bernadelli PO18

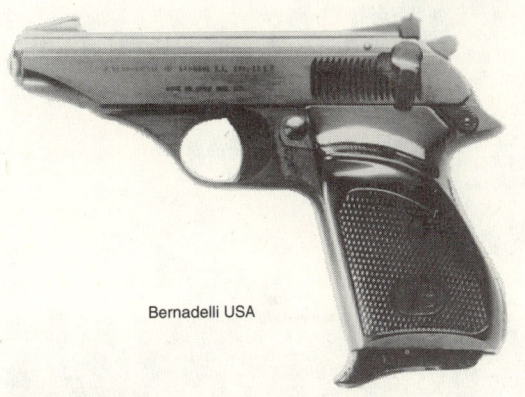
Bernadelli USA

Bersa Thunder 380

BERSA THUNDER 22 AUTO PISTOL
Caliber: 22 LR, 10-shot magazine.
Barrel: 3.5".
Weight: 24.2 oz. **Length:** 6.6" overall.
Stocks: Black polymer.
Sights: Blade front, notch rear adjustable for windage; three-dot system.
Features: Double action; firing pin and magazine safeties. Available in blue or nickel. Introduced 1995. Distributed by Eagle Imports, Inc.
Price: Blue $308.95
Price: Nickel $341.95

CAUTION: PRICES SHOWN ARE SUPPLIED BY THE MANUFACTURER OR IMPORTER. CHECK YOUR LOCAL GUNSHOP.

HANDGUNS—AUTOLOADERS, SERVICE & SPORT

BERSA SERIES 95 AUTO PISTOL
Caliber: 380 ACP, 7-shot magazine.
Barrel: 3.5".
Weight: 22 oz. **Length:** 6.6" overall.
Stocks: Wraparound textured rubber.
Sights: Blade front, rear adjustable for windage; three-dot system.
Features: Double action; firing pin and magazine safeties; combat-style trigger guard. Matte blue or satin nickel. Introduced 1992. Distributed by Eagle Imports, Inc.
Price: Matte blue $274.95
Price: Satin nickel $291.95

BERSA THUNDER 9 AUTO PISTOL
Caliber: 9mm Para., 10-shot magazine.
Barrel: 4".
Weight: 30 oz. **Length:** 7 3/8" overall.
Stocks: Checkered black polymer.
Sights: Blade front, rear adjustable for windage and elevation; three-dot system.
Features: Double action. Ambidextrous safety, decocking levers and slide release; internal automatic firing pin safety; reversible extended magazine release; adjustable trigger stop; alloy frame. Link-free locked breech design. Matte blue finish. Introduced 1993. Imported from Argentina by Eagle Imports, Inc.
Price: Matte finish $474.95
Price: Satin nickel $524.95
Price Duo-Tone finish $491.95

Bersa Series 95

Bersa Thunder 9

Browning BDM

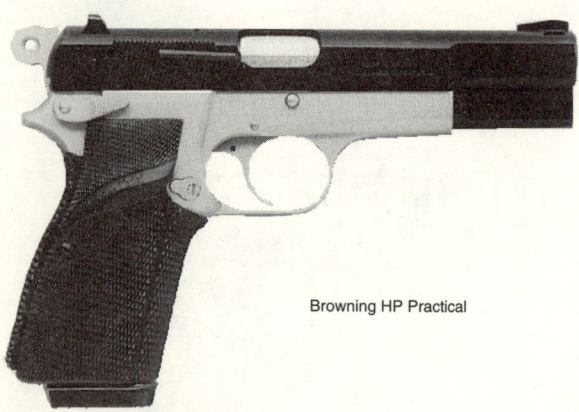
Browning HP Practical

Browning 40 S&W Hi-Power Mark III Pistol
Similar to the standard Hi-Power except chambered for 40 S&W, 10-shot magazine, weighs 35 oz., and has 4 3/4" barrel. Comes with matte blue finish, low profile front sight blade, drift-adjustable rear sight, ambidextrous safety, moulded polyamide grips with thumb rest. Introduced 1993. Imported from Belgium by Browning.
Price: Mark III $524.95

Browning Capitan Hi-Power Pistol
Similar to the standard Hi-Power except has adjustable tangent rear sight authentic to the early-production model. Also has Commander-style hammer. Checkered walnut grips, polished blue finish. Reintroduced 1993. Imported from Belgium by Browning.
Price: 9mm only $659.95

BROWNING BDM DA AUTO PISTOL
Caliber: 9mm Para., 10-shot magazine.
Barrel: 4.73".
Weight: 31 oz. **Length:** 7.85" overall.
Stocks: Moulded black composition; checkered, with thumbrest on both sides.
Sights: Low profile removable blade front, rear screw adjustable for windage.
Features: Mode selector allows switching from DA pistol to "revolver" mode via a switch on the slide. Decocking lever/safety on the frame. Two redundant, passive, internal safety systems. All steel frame; matte black finish. Introduced 1991. Made in the U.S. From Browning.
Price: $594.95

BROWNING HI-POWER 9mm AUTOMATIC PISTOL
Caliber: 9mm Para., 40 S&W, 10-shot magazine.
Barrel: 4 21/32".
Weight: 32 oz. **Length:** 7 3/4" overall.
Stocks: Walnut, hand checkered, or black Polyamide.
Sights: 1/8" blade front; rear screw-adjustable for windage and elevation. Also available with fixed rear (drift-adjustable for windage).
Features: External hammer with half-cock and thumb safeties. A blow on the hammer cannot discharge a cartridge; cannot be fired with magazine removed. Fixed rear sight model available. Ambidextrous safety available only with matte finish, moulded grips. Imported from Belgium by Browning.
Price: Fixed sight model, walnut grips $556.95
Price: 9mm with rear sight adj. for w. and e., walnut grips $605.95
Price: Mark III, standard matte black finish, fixed sight, moulded grips, ambidextrous safety $524.95
Price: Silver chrome, adjustable sight, Pachmayr grips $619.95

Browning Hi-Power HP-Practical Pistol
Similar to the standard Hi-Power except has silver-chromed frame with blued slide, wrap-around Pachmayr rubber grips, round-style serrated hammer and removable front sight, fixed rear (drift-adjustable for windage). Available in 9mm Para. or 40 S&W. Introduced 1991.
Price: $599.95
Price: With fully adjustable rear sight $649.95

HANDGUNS—AUTOLOADERS, SERVICE & SPORT

Browning BDA 380

Browning Micro Buck Mark Standard

Browning Buck Mark Varmint

BRYCO MODEL 48 AUTO PISTOLS
Caliber: 22 LR, 32 ACP, 380 ACP, 6-shot magazine.
Barrel: 4".
Weight: 19 oz. **Length:** 6.7" overall.
Stocks: Polished resin-impregnated wood.
Sights: Fixed.
Features: Safety locks sear and slide. Choice of satin nickel, bright chrome or black Teflon finishes. Announced 1988. From Jennings Firearms.
Price: 22 LR, 32 ACP, about $139.00
Price: 380 ACP, about $139.00

BRYCO MODEL 59 AUTO PISTOL
Caliber: 9mm Para., 10-shot magazine.
Barrel: 4".
Weight: 33 oz. **Length:** 6.5" overall.
Stocks: Black composition.
Sights: Blade front, fixed rear.
Features: Striker-fired action; manual thumb safety; polished blue finish. Comes with two magazines. Introduced 1994. From Jennings Firearms.
Price: About $169.00
Price: Model 58 (5.5" overall length, 30 oz.) $169.00

CALICO M-110 AUTO PISTOL
Caliber: 22 LR. 100-shot magazine.
Barrel: 6".
Weight: 3.7 lbs. (loaded). **Length:** 17.9" overall.
Stocks: Moulded composition.
Sights: Adjustable post front, notch rear.
Features: Aluminum alloy frame; flash suppressor; pistol grip compartment; ambidextrous safety. Uses same helical-feed magazine as M-100 Carbine. Introduced 1986. Made in U.S. From Calico.
Price: $359.00

BROWNING BDA-380 DA AUTO PISTOL
Caliber: 380 ACP, 10-shot magazine.
Barrel: 3 13/16".
Weight: 23 oz. **Length:** 6 3/4" overall.
Stocks: Smooth walnut with inset Browning medallion.
Sights: Blade front, rear drift-adjustable for windage.
Features: Combination safety and de-cocking lever will automatically lower a cocked hammer to half-cock and can be operated by right- or left-hand shooters. Inertia firing pin. Introduced 1978. Imported from Italy by Browning.
Price: Blue $614.95
Price: Nickel $646.95

BROWNING BUCK MARK 22 PISTOL
Caliber: 22 LR, 10-shot magazine.
Barrel: 5 1/2".
Weight: 32 oz. **Length:** 9 1/2" overall.
Stocks: Black moulded composite with skip-line checkering.
Sights: Ramp front, Browning Pro Target rear adjustable for windage and elevation.
Features: All steel, matte blue finish or nickel, gold-colored trigger. Buck Mark Plus has laminated wood grips. Made in U.S. Introduced 1985. From Browning.
Price: Buck Mark, blue $249.95
Price: Buck Mark, nickel finish with contoured rubber stocks $292.95
Price: Buck Mark Plus $304.95

Browning Micro Buck Mark
Same as the standard Buck Mark and Buck Mark Plus except has 4" barrel. Available in blue or nickel. Has 16-click Pro Target rear sight. Introduced 1992.
Price: Blue $249.95
Price: Nickel $292.95
Price: Micro Buck Mark Plus $304.95

Browning Buck Mark Varmint
Same as the Buck Mark except has 9 7/8" heavy barrel with .900" diameter and full-length scope base (no open sights); walnut grips with optional forend, or finger-groove walnut. Overall length is 14", weight is 48 oz. Introduced 1987.
Price: $379.95

BRYCO MODEL 38 AUTO PISTOLS
Caliber: 22 LR, 32 ACP, 380 ACP, 6-shot magazine.
Barrel: 2.8".
Weight: 15 oz. **Length:** 5.3" overall.
Stocks: Polished resin-impregnated wood.
Sights: Fixed.
Features: Safety locks sear and slide. Choice of satin nickel, bright chrome or black Teflon finishes. Introduced 1988. From Jennings Firearms.
Price: 22 LR, 32 ACP, about $109.95
Price: 380 ACP, about $129.95

Bryco Model 48

Calico M-110

CAUTION: PRICES SHOWN ARE SUPPLIED BY THE MANUFACTURER OR IMPORTER. CHECK YOUR LOCAL GUNSHOP.

HANDGUNS—AUTOLOADERS, SERVICE & SPORT

CENTURY FEG P9R PISTOL
Caliber: 9mm Para., 10-shot magazine.
Barrel: 4.6".
Weight: 35 oz. **Length:** 8" overall.
Stocks: Checkered walnut.
Sights: Blade front, rear drift adjustable for windage.
Features: Double action with hammer-drop safety. Polished blue finish. Comes with spare magazine. Imported from Hungary by Century International Arms.
Price: About $263.00
Price: Chrome finish, about $375.00

COLT'S 22 AUTOMATIC PISTOL
Caliber: 22 LR, 10-shot magazine.
Barrel: 4.5".
Weight: 33 oz. **Length:** 8.62" overall.
Stocks: Textured black polymer.
Sights: Blade front, rear drift adjustable for windage.
Features: Stainless steel construction; ventilated barrel rib; single action mechanism; cocked striker indicator; push-button safety. Introduced 1994. Made in U.S. by Colt.
Price: $248.00

Colt's 22 Target Pistol
Similar to the Colt 22 pistol except has 6" bull barrel, full-length sighting rib with lightening cuts and mounting rail for optical sights; fully adjustable rear sight; removable sights; two-point factory adjusted trigger travel. Stainless steel frame. Introduced 1995. Made in U.S. by Colt's.
Price: .... NA

COLT COMBAT COMMANDER AUTO PISTOL
Caliber: 38 Super, 9-shot; 45 ACP, 8-shot.
Barrel: 4 1/4".
Weight: 36 oz. **Length:** 7 3/4" overall.
Stocks: Checkered rubber composite.
Sights: Fixed, glare-proofed blade front, square notch rear; three-dot system.
Features: Long trigger; arched housing; grip and thumb safeties.
Price: 45, blue $735.00
Price: 45, stainless $789.00
Price: 38 Super, stainless $789.00

COLT DOUBLE EAGLE MKII/SERIES 90 DA PISTOL
Caliber: 45 ACP, 8-shot magazine.
Barrel: 4 1/2", 5".
Weight: 39 ozs. **Length:** 8 1/2" overall.
Stocks: Black checkered Xenoy thermoplastic.
Sights: Blade front, rear adjustable for windage. High profile three-dot system. Colt Accro adjustable sight optional.
Features: Made of stainless steel with matte finish. Checkered and curved extended trigger guard, wide steel trigger; decocking lever on left side; traditional magazine release; grooved frontstrap; bevelled magazine well; extended grip guard; rounded, serrated combat-style hammer. Announced 1989.
Price: $727.00
Price: Combat Comm., 45, 4 1/2" bbl. $727.00

COLT GOVERNMENT MODEL MK IV/SERIES 80
Caliber: 38 Super, 9-shot; 45 ACP, 8-shot magazine.
Barrel: 5".
Weight: 38 oz. **Length:** 8 1/2" overall.
Stocks: Black composite.
Sights: Ramp front, fixed square notch rear; three-dot system.
Features: Grip and thumb safeties and internal firing pin safety, long trigger.
Price: 45 ACP, blue $735.00
Price: 45 ACP, stainless $789.00
Price: 45 ACP, bright stainless $863.00
Price: 38 Super, blue $735.00
Price: 38 Super, stainless $789.00
Price: 38 Super, bright stainless $863.00

Colt 10mm Delta Elite
Similar to the Government Model except chambered for 10mm auto cartridge. Has three-dot high profile front and rear combat sights, checkered rubber composite stocks, internal firing pin safety, and new recoil spring/buffer system. Introduced 1987.
Price: Blue $807.00
Price: Stainless $860.00

Century FEG P9RK Auto Pistol
Similar to the P9R except has 4.12" barrel, 7.5" overall length and weighs 33.6 oz. Checkered walnut grips, fixed sights, 10-shot magazine. Introduced 1994. Imported from Hungary by Century International Arms, Inc.
Price: About $290.00

Colt 22 Target

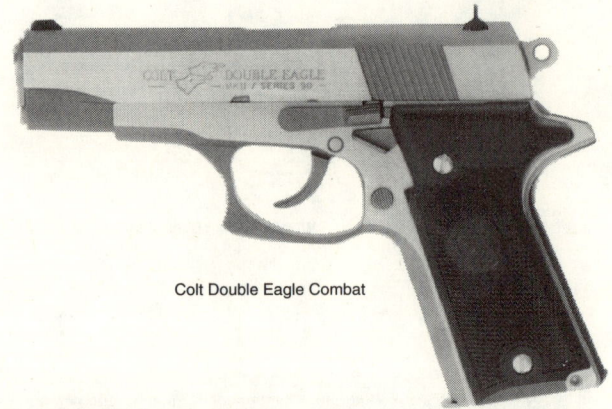
Colt Double Eagle Combat

Colt Lightweight Commander MK IV/Series 80
Same as Commander except high strength aluminum alloy frame, checkered rubber composite stocks, weight 27 1/2 oz. 45 ACP only.
Price: Blue $735.00

Consult our Directory pages for the location of firms mentioned.

Colt Double Eagle Officer's ACP
Similar to the regular Double Eagle except 45 ACP only, 3 1/2" barrel, 35 oz., 7 1/4" overall length. Has 5 1/4" sight radius. Introduced 1991.
Price: $727.00

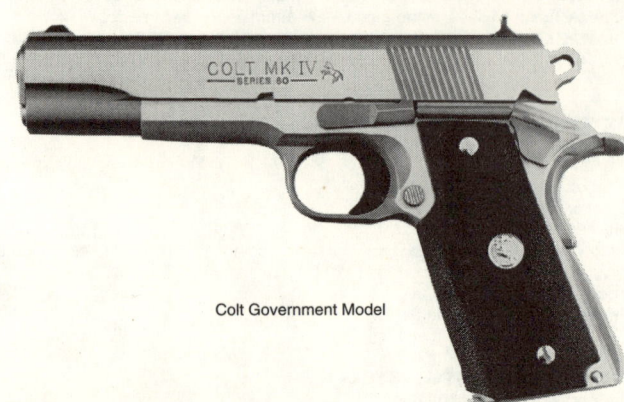
Colt Government Model

Colt Combat Elite MK IV/Series 80
Similar to the Government Model except has stainless frame with ordnance steel slide and internal parts. High profile front, rear sights with three-dot system, extended grip safety, beveled magazine well, checkerred rubber composite stocks. Introduced 1986.
Price: 45 ACP, STS/B $895.00
Price: 38 Super, STS/B $895.00

HANDGUNS—AUTOLOADERS, SERVICE & SPORT

COLT MODEL 1991 A1 AUTO PISTOL
Caliber: 45 ACP, 7-shot magazine.
Barrel: 5".
Weight: 38 oz. **Length:** 8.5" overall.
Stocks: Checkered black composition.
Sights: Ramped blade front, fixed square notch rear, high profile.
Features: Parkerized finish. Continuation of serial number range used on original G.I. 1911-A1 guns. Comes with one magazine and moulded carrying case. Introduced 1991.
Price: $538.00

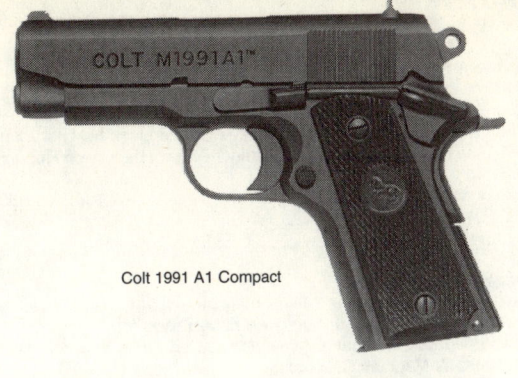

Colt 1991 A1 Compact

Colt Model 1991 A1 Compact Auto Pistol
Similar to the Model 1991 A1 except has 3½" barrel. Overall length is 7", and gun is ⅜" shorter in height. Comes with one 6-shot magazine, moulded case. Introduced 1993.
Price: $538.00

Colt Model 1991 A1 Commander Auto Pistol
Similar to the Model 1991 A1 except has 4¼" barrel. Parkerized finish. 7-shot magazine. Comes in moulded case. Introduced 1993.
Price: $538.00

COLT GOVERNMENT MODEL 380
Caliber: 380 ACP, 7-shot magazine.
Barrel: 3¼".
Weight: 21¾ oz. **Length:** 6" overall.
Stocks: Checkered composition.
Sights: Ramp front, square notch rear, fixed.
Features: Scaled-down version of the 1911A1 Colt G.M. Has thumb and internal firing pin safeties. Introduced 1983.
Price: Blue $462.00
Price: Stainless $493.00
Price: Pocketlite 380, blue $462.00

Colt Government Model 380

Colt Mustang 380, Mustang Pocketlite
Similar to the standard 380 Government Model. Mustang has steel frame (18.5 oz.), Pocketlite has aluminum alloy (12.5 oz.). Both are ½" shorter than 380 G.M., have 2¾" barrel. Introduced 1987.
Price: Mustang 380, blue $462.00
Price: As above, stainless $493.00
Price: Mustang Pocketlite, blue $462.00
Price: Mustang Pocketlite STS/N $493.00

Colt Mustang Plus II
Similar to the 380 Government Model except has the shorter barrel and slide of the Mustang. Introduced 1988.
Price: Blue $462.00
Price: Stainless $493.00

COLT OFFICER'S ACP MK IV/SERIES 80
Caliber: 45 ACP, 6-shot magazine.
Barrel: 3½".
Weight: 34 oz. (steel frame); 24 oz. (alloy frame). **Length:** 7¼" overall.
Stocks: Checkered rubber composite.
Sights: Ramp blade front with white dot, square notch rear with two white dots.
Features: Trigger safety lock (thumb safety), grip safety, firing pin safety; long trigger; flat mainspring housing. Also available with lightweight alloy frame and in stainless steel. Introduced 1985.
Price: Blue $735.00
Price: L.W., blue finish $789.00
Price: Stainless $735.00
Price: Bright stainless $863.00

Colt Mustang 380

COONAN 357 MAGNUM PISTOL
Caliber: 357 Mag., 7-shot magazine.
Barrel: 5".
Weight: 42 oz. **Length:** 8.3" overall.
Stocks: Smooth walnut.
Sights: Interchangeable ramp front, rear adjustable for windage.
Features: Stainless and alloy steel construction. Unique barrel hood improves accuracy and reliability. Linkless barrel. Many parts interchange with Colt autos. Has grip, hammer, half-cock safeties, extended slide latch. Made in U.S. by Coonan Arms, Inc.
Price: 5" barrel $720.00
Price: 6" barrel $755.00
Price: With 6" compensated barrel $999.00
Price: Classic model (Teflon black two-tone or Kal-Gard finish, 8-shot magazine, fully adjustable rear sight, integral compensated barrel) $1,400.00

Coonan Compact Cadet 357 Magnum Pistol
Similar to the 357 Magnum full-size gun except has 3.9" barrel, shorter frame, 6-shot magazine. Weight is 39 oz., overall length 7.8". Linkless bull barrel, full-length recoil spring guide rod, extended slide latch. Introduced 1993. Made in U.S. by Coonan Arms, Inc.
Price: $841.00

Coonan 357 Magnum Classic

CAUTION: PRICES SHOWN ARE SUPPLIED BY THE MANUFACTURER OR IMPORTER. CHECK YOUR LOCAL GUNSHOP.

HANDGUNS—AUTOLOADERS, SERVICE & SPORT

CZ 75 AUTO PISTOL
Caliber: 9mm Para., 40 S&W, 10-shot magazine.
Barrel: 4.7".
Weight: 34.3 oz. **Length:** 8.1" overall.
Stocks: High impact checkered plastic.
Sights: Square post front, rear adjustable for windage; three-dot system.
Features: Single action/double action design; choice of black polymer, matte or high-polish blue finishes. All-steel frame. Imported from the Czech Republic by Magnum Research.
Price: Black polymer finish $539.00
Price: Nickel $569.00

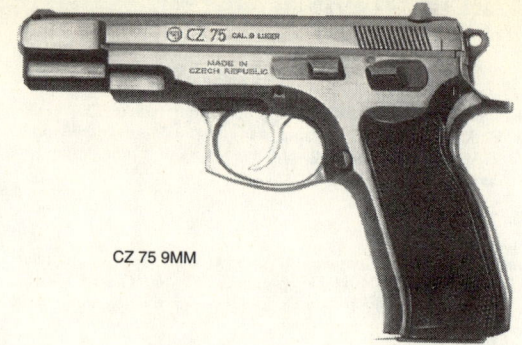
CZ 75 9MM

CZ 75 Compact Auto Pistol
Similar to the CZ 75 except has 10-shot magazine, 3.9" barrel and weighs 32 oz. Has removable front sight, non-glare ribbed slide top. Trigger guard is squared and serrated; combat hammer. Introduced 1993. Imported from the Czech Republic by Magnum Research.
Price: Black polymer finish $539.00

CZ 75 Semi-Compact Auto Pistol
Uses the shorter slide and barrel of the CZ 75 Compact with the full-size frame of the standard CZ 75. Has 10-shot magazine; 9mm Para. only. Introduced 1994. Imported from the Czech Republic by Magnum Research.
Price: Black polymer finish $519.00
Price: Matte blue finish $539.00
Price: High-polish blue finish $559.00

CZ 85 Auto Pistol
Same gun as the CZ 75 except has ambidextrous slide release and safety-levers; non-glare, ribbed slide top; squared, serrated trigger guard; trigger stop to prevent overtravel. Introduced 1986. Imported from the Czech Republic by Magnum Research.
Price: Black polymer finish $549.00

CZ 85 Combat Auto Pistol
Same as the CZ 85 except has walnut grips, round combat hammer, fully adjustable rear sight, extended magazine release. Trigger parts coated with friction-free beryllium copper. Introduced 1992. Imported from the Czech Republic by Magnum Research.
Price: Black polymer finish $649.00

CZ 83 DOUBLE-ACTION PISTOL
Caliber: 32, 380 ACP, 10-shot magazine.
Barrel: 3.8".
Weight: 26.2 oz. **Length:** 6.8" overall.
Stocks: High impact checkered plastic.
Sights: Removable square post front, rear adjustable for windage; three-dot system.
Features: Single action/double action; ambidextrous magazine release and safety. Blue finish; non-glare ribbed slide top. Imported from the Czech Republic by Magnum Research.
Price: $409.00

CZ 83 380

DAEWOO DP51 FASTFIRE AUTO PISTOL
Caliber: 9mm Para., 10-shot magazine.
Barrel: 4.1".
Weight: 28.2 oz. **Length:** 7.5" overall.
Stocks: Checkered composition.
Sights: 1/8" blade front, square notch rear drift adjustable for windage. Three dot system.
Features: Patented Fastfire mechanism. Ambidextrous manual safety and magazine catch, automatic firing pin block. No magazine safety. Alloy frame, squared trigger guard. Matte black finish. Introduced 1991. Imported from Korea by Kimber of America, distributed by Nationwide Sports Dist.
Price: DP51 .... $400.00
Price: DH40 (40 S&W) $450.00

Daewoo DP51 Fastfire

> Consult our Directory pages for the location of firms mentioned.

Daewoo DP51C Compact

Daewoo DP51C, DP51S Auto Pistols
Same as the DP51 except DP51C has 3.6" barrel, 1/4-inch shorter grip frame, flat mainspring housing, and is 2 oz. lighter. Model DP51S has 3.6" barrel, same grip as standard DP51, weighs 27 oz. Introduced 1995. Imported from Korea by Kimber of America, Inc., distributed by Nationwide Sports Dist.
Price: DP51C $445.00
Price: DP51S $420.00

HANDGUNS—AUTOLOADERS, SERVICE & SPORT

DAEWOO DP52, DH380 AUTO PISTOLS
Caliber: 22 LR, 10-shot magazine.
Barrel: 3.8".
Weight: 23 oz. **Length:** 6.7" overall.
Stocks: Checkered black composition with thumbrest.
Sights: 1/8" blade front, rear drift adjustable for windage; three-dot system.
Features: All-steel construction with polished blue finish. Dual safety system with hammer block. Introduced 1994. Imported from Korea by Kimber of America, distributed by Nationwide Sports Distributors.
Price: $380.00
Price: DH380 (as above except 380 ACP, 8-shot magazine) $410.00

DAVIS P-32 AUTO PISTOL
Caliber: 32 ACP, 6-shot magazine.
Barrel: 2.8".
Weight: 22 oz. **Length:** 5.4" overall.
Stocks: Laminated wood.
Sights: Fixed.
Features: Choice of black Teflon or chrome finish. Announced 1986. Made in U.S. by Davis Industries.
Price: $87.50

DAVIS P-380 AUTO PISTOL
Caliber: 32 ACP, 6-shot, 380 ACP, 5-shot magazine.
Barrel: 2.8".
Weight: 22 oz. **Length:** 5.4" overall.
Stocks: Black composition.
Sights: Fixed.
Features: Choice of chrome or black Teflon finish. Introduced 1991. Made in U.S. by Davis Industries.
Price: $98.00

Daewoo DP52

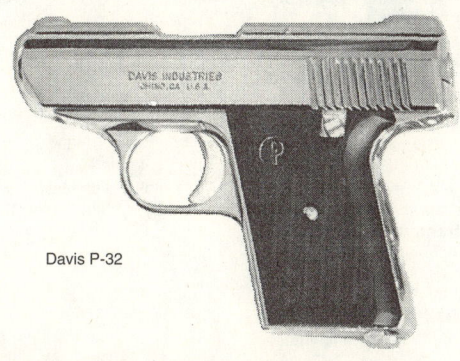

Davis P-32

Desert Eagle Magnum

DESERT EAGLE MAGNUM PISTOL
Caliber: 357 Mag., 9-shot; 41 Mag., 44 Mag., 8-shot; 50 Magnum, 7-shot.
Barrel: 6", 10", 14" interchangeable.
Weight: 357 Mag.—62 oz.; 41 Mag., 44 Mag.—69 oz.; 50 Mag.—72 oz.
Length: 10 1/4" overall (6" bbl.).
Stocks: Wraparound plastic.
Sights: Blade on ramp front, combat-style rear. Adjustable available.
Features: Rotating three-lug bolt; ambidextrous safety; combat-style trigger guard; adjustable trigger optional. Military epoxy finish. Satin, bright nickel, hard chrome, polished and blued finishes available. Imported from Israel by Magnum Research, Inc.
Price: 357, 6" bbl., standard pistol $789.00
Price: As above, stainless steel frame $839.00
Price: 41 Mag., 6", standard pistol $899.00
Price: 41 Mag., stainless steel frame $949.00
Price: 44 Mag., 6", standard pistol $899.00
Price: As above, stainless steel frame $949.00
Price: 50 Magnum, 6" bbl., standard pistol $1,249.00

Desert Industries War Eagle

DESERT INDUSTRIES WAR EAGLE PISTOL
Caliber: 380 ACP, 8- or 10-shot; 9mm Para., 14-shot; 10mm, 10-shot; 40 S&W, 10-shot; 45 ACP, 10-shot.
Barrel: 4".
Weight: 35.5 oz. **Length:** 7.5" overall.
Stocks: Rosewood.
Sights: Fixed.
Features: Double action; matte-finished stainless steel; slide mounted ambidextrous safety. Announced 1986. From Desert Industries, Inc.
Price: $795.00
Price: 380 ACP $725.00

DESERT INDUSTRIES DOUBLE DEUCE, TWO BIT SPECIAL PISTOLS
Caliber: 22 LR, 6-shot; 25 ACP, 5-shot.
Barrel: 2 1/2".
Weight: 15 oz. **Length:** 5 1/2" overall.
Stocks: Rosewood.
Sights: Special order.
Features: Double action; stainless steel construction with matte finish; ambidextrous slide-mounted safety. From Desert Industries, Inc.
Price: 22 ....$399.95
Price: 25 (Two-Bit Special) $399.95

Desert Industries Double Deuce

HANDGUNS—AUTOLOADERS, SERVICE & SPORT

E.A.A. WITNESS DA AUTO PISTOL
Caliber: 9mm Para., 10-shot magazine; 38 Super, 40 S&W, 10-shot magazine; 45 ACP, 10-shot magazine.
Barrel: 4.50".
Weight: 35.33 oz. **Length:** 8.10" overall.
Stocks: Checkered rubber.
Sights: Undercut blade front, open rear adjustable for windage.
Features: Double-action trigger system; round trigger guard; frame-mounted safety. Introduced 1991. Imported from Italy by European American Armory.
Price: 9mm, blue $399.00
Price: 9mm, satin chrome $425.00
Price: 9mm Compact, blue, 10-shot $399.00
Price: As above, chrome $425.00
Price: 40 S&W, blue $425.00
Price: As above, chrome $450.00
Price: 40 S&W Compact, 8-shot, blue $425.00
Price: As above, chrome $450.00
Price: 45 ACP, blue $525.00
Price: As above, chrome $550.00
Price: 45 ACP Compact, 8-shot, blue $525.00
Price: As above, chrome $550.00
Price: 9mm/40 S&W Combo, blue, compact or full size $595.00
Price: 9mm or 40 S&W Carry Comp, blue $550.00

ERMA KGP68 AUTO PISTOL
Caliber: 32 ACP, 6-shot, 380 ACP, 5-shot.
Barrel: 4".
Weight: 22 1/2 oz. **Length:** 7 3/8" overall.
Stocks: Checkered plastic.
Sights: Fixed.
Features: Toggle action similar to original "Luger" pistol. Action stays open after last shot. Has magazine and sear disconnect safety systems. Imported from Germany by Mandall Shooting Supplies.
Price: $795.00

FEG B9R AUTO PISTOL
Caliber: 380 ACP, 10-shot magazine.
Barrel: 4".
Weight: 25 oz. **Length:** 7" overall.
Stocks: Hand-checkered walnut.
Sights: Blade front, drift-adjustable rear.
Features: Hammer-drop safety; grooved backstrap; squared trigger guard. Comes with spare magazine. Introduced 1993. Imported from Hungary by Century International Arms.
Price: About $312.00

FEG GKK-45C DA AUTO PISTOL
Caliber: 45 ACP, 8-shot magazine.
Barrel: 4 1/8".
Weight: 36 oz. **Length:** 7 3/4" overall.
Stocks: Hand-checkered walnut.
Sights: Blade front, rear adjustable for windage; three-dot system.
Features: Combat-type trigger guard. Polished blue finish. Comes with two magazines, cleaning rod. Introduced 1995. Imported from Hungary by K.B.I., Inc.
Price: Blue $399.00
Price: GKK-40C (40 S&W, 9-shot magazine) $399.00

FEG PJK-9HP AUTO PISTOL
Caliber: 9mm Para., 10-shot magazine.
Barrel: 4.75".
Weight: 32 oz. **Length:** 8" overall.
Stocks: Hand-checkered walnut.
Sights: Blade front, rear adjustable for windage; three dot system.
Features: Single action; polished blue or hard chrome finish; rounded combat-style serrated hammer. Comes with two magazines and cleaning rod. Imported from Hungary by K.B.I., Inc.
Price: Blue $349.00
Price: Hard chrome $429.00

FEG SMC-22 DA AUTO PISTOL
Caliber: 22 LR, 8-shot magazine.
Barrel: 3.5".
Weight: 18.5 oz. **Length:** 6.12" overall.
Stocks: Checkered composition with thumbrest.
Sights: Blade front, rear adjustable for windage.
Features: Patterned after the PPK pistol. Alloy frame, steel slide; blue finish. Comes with two magazines, cleaning rod. Introduced 1994. Imported from Hungary by K.B.I., Inc.
Price: $279.00

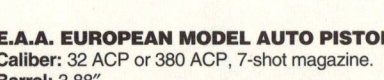

E.A.A. Witness

E.A.A. EUROPEAN MODEL AUTO PISTOLS
Caliber: 32 ACP or 380 ACP, 7-shot magazine.
Barrel: 3.88".
Weight: 26 oz. **Length:** 7 3/8" overall.
Stocks: European hardwood.
Sights: Fixed blade front, rear drift-adjustable for windage.
Features: Chrome or blue finish; magazine, thumb and firing pin safeties; external hammer; safety-lever takedown. Imported from Italy by European American Armory.
Price: Blue $160.00
Price: Chrome $175.00
Price: Ladies Model $225.00

FEG FP9 AUTO PISTOL
Caliber: 9mm Para., 10-shot magazine.
Barrel: 5".
Weight: 35 oz. **Length:** 7.8" overall.
Stocks: Checkered walnut.
Sights: Blade front, windage-adjustable rear.
Features: Full-length ventilated rib. Polished blue finish. Comes with extra magazine. Introduced 1993. Imported from Hungary by Century International Arms.
Price: About $269.00

FEG GKK-45

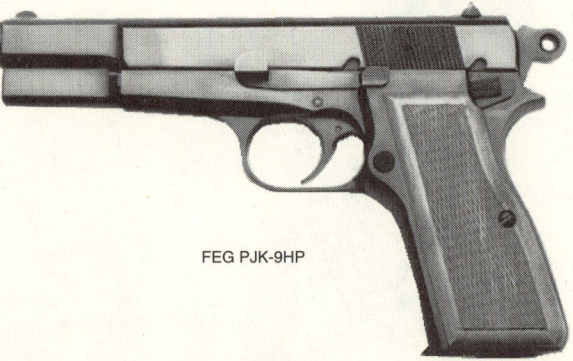

FEG PJK-9HP

HANDGUNS—AUTOLOADERS, SERVICE & SPORT

FEG P9R AUTO PISTOL
Caliber: 9mm Para., 10-shot magazine.
Barrel: 4.6".
Weight: 35 oz. **Length:** 7.9" overall.
Stocks: Checkered walnut.
Sights: Blade front, rear adjustable for windage.
Features: Double-action mechanism; slide-mounted safety. All-Steel construction with polished blue finish. Comes with extra magazine. Introduced 1993. Imported from Hungary by Century International Arms.
Price: About $262.00

FEG P9R

CONSULT Shooter's Marketplace Page 266, This Issue

FEG SMC-380 AUTO PISTOL
Caliber: 380 ACP, 6-shot magazine.
Barrel: 3.5".
Weight: 18.5 oz. **Length:** 6.1" overall.
Stocks: Checkered composition with thumbrest.
Sights: Blade front, rear adjustable for windage.
Features: Patterned after the PPK pistol. Alloy frame, steel slide; double action. Blue finish. Comes with two magazines, cleaning rod. Imported from Hungary by K.B.I.
Price: $279.00

FEG SMC-918 Auto Pistol
Same as the SMC-380 except chambered for 9x18 Makarov. Alloy frame, steel slide, blue finish. Comes with two magazines, cleaning rod. Introduced 1995. Imported from Hungary by K.B.I., Inc.
Price: $279.00

GLOCK 17 AUTO PISTOL
Caliber: 9mm Para., 10-shot magazine.
Barrel: 4.49".
Weight: 21.9 oz. (without magazine). **Length:** 7.28" overall.
Stocks: Black polymer.
Sights: Dot on front blade, white outline rear adjustable for windage.
Features: Polymer frame, steel slide; double-action trigger with "Safe Action" system; mechanical firing pin safety, drop safety; simple takedown without tools; locked breech, recoil operated action. Adopted by Austrian armed forces 1983. NATO approved 1984. Imported from Austria by Glock, Inc.
Price: With extra magazine, magazine loader, cleaning kit $608.95
Price: Model 17L (6" barrel) $806.67

Glock 19

Glock 19 Auto Pistol
Similar to the Glock 17 except has a 4" barrel, giving an overall length of 6.85" and weight of 20.99 oz. Magazine capacity is 10 rounds. Fixed or adjustable rear sight. Introduced 1988.
Price: $608.95

Glock 20 10mm Auto Pistol
Similar to the Glock Model 17 except chambered for 10mm Automatic cartridge. Barrel length is 4.60", overall length is 7.59", and weight is 26.3 oz. (without magazine). Magazine capacity is 10 rounds. Fixed or adjustable rear sight. Comes with an extra magazine, magazine loader, cleaning rod and brush. Introduced 1990. Imported from Austria by Glock, Inc.
Price: $670.41

Glock 21

Glock 21 Auto Pistol
Similar to the Glock 17 except chambered for 45 ACP, 10-shot magazine. Overall length is 7.59", weight is 25.2 oz. (without magazine). Fixed or adjustable rear sight. Introduced 1991.
Price: $670.41

Glock 22 Auto Pistol
Similar to the Glock 17 except chambered for 40 S&W, 10-shot magazine. Overall length is 7.28", weight is 22.3 oz. (without magazine). Fixed or adjustable rear sight. Introduced 1990.
Price: $670.41

GRENDEL P-12 AUTO PISTOL
Caliber: 380 ACP, 10-shot magazine.
Barrel: 3".
Weight: 13 oz. **Length:** 5.3" overall.
Stocks: Checkered DuPont ST-800 polymer.
Sights: Fixed.
Features: Double action only with inertia safety hammer system. All steel frame; grip forms magazine well and trigger guard. Introduced 1992. Made in U.S. by Grendel, Inc.
Price: Blue $175.00
Price: Electroless nickel $195.00

Glock 23 Auto Pistol
Similar to the Glock 19 except chambered for 40 S&W, 10-shot magazine. Overall length is 6.85", weight is 20.6 oz. (without magazine). Fixed or adjustable rear sight. Introduced 1990.
Price: $608.95

CAUTION: PRICES SHOWN ARE SUPPLIED BY THE MANUFACTURER OR IMPORTER. CHECK YOUR LOCAL GUNSHOP.

HANDGUNS—AUTOLOADERS, SERVICE & SPORT

HECKLER & KOCH USP AUTO PISTOL
Caliber: 9mm Para., 10-shot magazine, 40 S&W, 10-shot magazine.
Barrel: 4.25".
Weight: 28 oz. (USP40). **Length:** 6.9" overall.
Stocks: Non-slip stippled black polymer.
Sights: Blade front, rear adjustable for windage.
Features: New HK design with polymer frame, modified Browning action with recoil reduction system, single control lever. Special "hostile environment" finish on all metal parts. Available in SA/DA, DAO, left- and right-hand versions. Introduced 1993. Imported from Germany by Heckler & Koch, Inc.
Price: Right-hand $636.00
Price: Left-hand $656.00

HECKLER & KOCH P7M8 AUTO PISTOL
Caliber: 9mm Para., 8-shot magazine.
Barrel: 4.13".
Weight: 29 oz. **Length:** 6.73" overall.
Stocks: Stippled black plastic.
Sights: Blade front, adjustable rear; three dot system.
Features: Unique "squeeze cocker" in frontstrap cocks the action. Gas-retarded action. Squared combat-type trigger guard. Blue finish. Compact size. Imported from Germany by Heckler & Koch, Inc.
Price: P7M8, blued $1,141.00

Heckler & Koch USP

Heckler & Koch USP 45 Auto Pistol
Similar to the 9mm and 40 S&W USP except chambered for 45 ACP, 10-shot magazine. Has 4.13" barrel, overall length of 7.87" and weighs 30.4 oz. Has adjustable three-dot sight system. Available in SA/DA, DAO, left- and right-hand versions. Introduced 1995. Imported from Germany by Heckler & Koch, Inc.
Price: Right-hand $696.00
Price: Left-hand $716.00

HI-POINT FIREARMS JS-9MM AUTO PISTOL
Caliber: 9mm Para., 9-shot magazine.
Barrel: 4.5".
Weight: 41 oz. **Length:** 7.72" overall.
Stocks: Textured acetal plastic.
Sights: Fixed, low profile.
Features: Single-action design. Scratch-resistant, non-glare blue finish. Introduced 1990. From MKS Supply, Inc.
Price: Matte black $139.95

HI-POINT FIREARMS MODEL JS-9MM COMPACT PISTOL
Caliber: 380 ACP, 9mm Para., 8-shot magazine.
Barrel: 3.5".
Weight: 35 oz. **Length:** 6.7" overall.
Stocks: Textured acetal plastic.
Sights: Combat-style fixed three-dot system; low profile.
Features: Single-action design; frame-mounted magazine release. Scratch-resistant matte finish. Introduced 1993. From MKS Supply, Inc.
Price: $124.95
Price: With polymer frame (32 oz.), non-slip grips $132.95
Price: 380 ACP $79.95

Hi-Point JS-9MM Compact

HI-POINT FIREARMS JS-40 S&W AUTO
Caliber: 40 S&W, 8-shot magazine.
Barrel: 4.5".
Weight: 42 oz. **Length:** 7.72" overall.
Stocks: Checkered acetal resin.
Sights: Fixed; low profile.
Features: Internal drop-safe mechansim; all aluminum frame. Introduced 1991. From MKS Supply, Inc.
Price: Matte black $148.95

HI-POINT FIREARMS JS-45 CALIBER PISTOL
Caliber: 45 ACP, 7-shot magazine.
Barrel: 4.5".
Weight: 44 oz. **Length:** 7.95" overall.
Stocks: Checkered acetal resin.
Sights: Fixed; low profile.
Features: Internal drop-safe mechanism; all aluminum frame. Introduced 1991. From MKS Supply, Inc.
Price: Matte black $148.95

HUNGARIAN T-58 AUTO PISTOL
Caliber: 7.62mm and 9mm Para., 8-shot magazine.
Barrel: 4.5".
Weight: 31 oz. **Length:** 7.68" overall.
Stocks: Grooved composition.
Sights: Blade front, rear adjustable for windage.
Features: Comes with both barrels and magazines. Thumb safety locks hammer. Blue finish. Imported by Century International Arms.
Price: About $187.00

Hi-Point JS-40

INTRATEC PROTEC-22, 25 AUTO PISTOLS
Caliber: 22 LR, 10-shot; 25 ACP, 8-shot magazine.
Barrel: 2 1/2".
Weight: 14 oz. **Length:** 5" overall.
Stocks: Wraparound composition in gray, black or driftwood color.
Sights: Fixed.
Features: Double-action only trigger mechanism. Choice of black, satin or TEC-KOTE finish. Announced 1991. Made in U.S. by Intratec.
Price: 22 or 25, black finish $102.00
Price: 22 or 25, satin or TEC-KOTE finish $107.95

HANDGUNS—AUTOLOADERS, SERVICE & SPORT

Intratec Category 9

INTRATEC CATEGORY 9 AUTO PISTOL
Caliber: 9mm Para., 7-shot magazine.
Barrel: 3".
Weight: 21 oz. **Length:** 5.5" overall.
Stocks: Textured black polymer.
Sights: Fixed channel.
Features: Black polymer frame. Announced 1993. Made in U.S. by Intratec.
Price: About $225.00

INTRATEC TEC-DC9 AUTO PISTOL
Caliber: 9mm Para., 10-shot magazine.
Barrel: 5".
Weight: 50 oz. **Length:** 12 1/2" overall.
Stock: Moulded composition.
Sights: Fixed.
Features: Semi-auto, fires from closed bolt; firing pin block safety; matte blue finish. Made in U.S. by Intratec.
Price: $269.00
Price: TEC-DC9S (as above, except stainless) $362.00
Price: TEC-DC9K (finished with TEC-KOTE) $297.00

Intratec TEC-DC9M Auto Pistol
Similar to the TEC-DC9 except smaller. Has 3" barrel, weighs 44 oz.; 20-shot magazine. Made in U.S. by Intratec.
Price: $245.00
Price: TEC-DC9MS (as above, stainless) $339.00
Price: TEC-DC9MK (finished with TEC-KOTE) $277.00

INTRATEC TEC-22T AUTO PISTOL
Caliber: 22 LR, 10-shot magazine.
Barrel: 4".
Weight: 30 oz. **Length:** 11 3/16" overall.
Stocks: Moulded composition.
Sights: Protected post front, front and rear adjustable for windage and elevation.
Features: Ambidextrous cocking knobs and safety. Matte black finish. Accepts any 10/22-type magazine. Introduced 1988. Made in U.S. by Intratec.
Price: $161.00
Price: TEC-22TK (as above, TEC-KOTE finish) $183.50

JENNINGS J-22, J-25 AUTO PISTOLS
Caliber: 22 LR, 25 ACP, 6-shot magazine.
Barrel: 2 1/2".
Weight: 13 oz. (J-22). **Length:** 4 15/16" overall (J-22).
Stocks: Walnut on chrome or nickel models; grooved black Cycolac or resin-impregnated wood on Teflon model.
Sights: Fixed.
Features: Choice of bright chrome, satin nickel or black Teflon finish. Introduced 1981. From Jennings Firearms.
Price: J-22, about $79.95
Price: J-25, about $79.95

Jenning J-25

Kahr K9

CONSULT
Shooter's Marketplace
Page 266, This Issue

KAHR K9 DA AUTO PISTOL
Caliber: 9mm Para., 7-shot magazine.
Barrel: 3.5".
Weight: 25 oz. **Length:** 6" overall.
Stocks: Wrap-around textured soft polymer.
Sights: Blade front, rear drift adjustable for windage; bar-dot combat style.
Features: Trigger-cocking double-action mechanism with passive firing pin block. Made of 4140 ordnance steel with matte black finish. Introduced 1994. Made in U.S. by Kahr Arms.
Price: $595.00

Kareen MK II

KAREEN MK II AUTO PISTOL
Caliber: 9mm Para., 10-shot magazine.
Barrel: 4.75".
Weight: 32 oz. **Length:** 8" overall.
Stocks: Textured composition.
Sights: Blade front, rear adjustable for windage.
Features: Single-action mechanism; external hammer safety; magazine safety; combat trigger guard. Blue finish standard, optional two-tone or matte black. Optional Meprolight sights, improved rubberized grips. Introduced 1969. Imported from Israel by J.O. Arms & Ammunition.
Price: . . . .$425.00 to $575.00
Price: Barak 9mm (3.25" barrel, 28 oz., 6.5" overall length) . .$425.00 to $575.00

CAUTION: PRICES SHOWN ARE SUPPLIED BY THE MANUFACTURER OR IMPORTER. CHECK YOUR LOCAL GUNSHOP.

HANDGUNS—AUTOLOADERS, SERVICE & SPORT

KEL-TEC P-11 AUTO PISTOL
Caliber: 9mm Para., 10-shot magazine.
Barrel: 3.1".
Weight: 14 oz. Length: 5.6" overall.
Stocks: Checkered black polymer.
Sights: Blade front, rear adjustable for windage.
Features: Ordnance steel slide, aluminum frame. Double-action-only trigger mechanism. Introduced 1995. Made in U.S. by Kel-Tec CNC Industries, Inc.
Price: Blue $300.00
Price: Electroless nickel $330.00
Price: Gray finish $310.00

Kel-Tec P-11

Kimber Classic 45 Custom

KIMBER CLASSIC 45 CUSTOM AUTO PISTOL
Caliber: 45 ACP, 8-shot magazine.
Barrel: 5".
Weight: 38 oz. Length: 8.5" overall.
Stocks: Checkered hard synthetic.
Sights: McCormick dovetailed front, low combat rear.
Features: Uses Chip McCormick Corp. forged frame and slide, match barrel, extended combat thumb safety, high beavertail grip safety, skeletonized lightweight composite trigger, skeletonized Commander-type hammer, elongated Commander ejector, and 8-shot magazine. Bead-blasted black oxide finish; flat mainspring housing; short guide rod; lowered and flared ejection port; serrated front and rear of slide; relief cut under trigger guard; Wolff spring set; beveled magazine well. Introduced 1995. Made in U.S. by Kimber of America, Inc.
Price: Custom $575.00
Price: Custom Stainless $650.00

Kimber Classic 45 Royal Auto Pistol
Same as the Custom model except has checkered diamond-pattern walnut grips, long guide rod, polished blue finish, and comes with two 8-shot magazines. Introduced 1995. Made in U.S. by Kimber of America, Inc.
Price: $715.00

Kimber Classic 45 Gold Match Auto Pistol
Same as the Custom Royal except also has Bo-Mar BMCS low-mount adjustable rear sight, fancy walnut grips, tighter tolerances. Comes with one 10-shot and one 8-shot magazine, factory proof target. Introduced 1995. Made in U.S. by Kimber of America, Inc.
Price: $925.00

Kimber Classic 45 Gold Match

L.A.R. GRIZZLY WIN MAG MK I PISTOL
Caliber: 357 Mag., 357/45, 10mm, 44 Mag., 45 Win. Mag., 45 ACP, 7-shot magazine.
Barrel: 5.4", 6.5".
Weight: 51 oz. Length: 10 1/2" overall.
Stocks: Checkered rubber, non-slip combat-type.
Sights: Ramped blade front, fully adjustable rear.
Features: Uses basic Browning/Colt 1911A1 design; interchangeable calibers; beveled magazine well; combat-type flat, checkered rubber mainspring housing; lowered and back-chamfered ejection port; polished feed ramp; throated barrel; solid barrel bushings. Available in satin hard chrome, matte blue, Parkerized finishes. Introduced 1983. From L.A.R. Mfg., Inc.
Price: 45 Win. Mag. $920.00
Price: 357 Mag. $933.00
Price: Conversion units (357 Mag.) $228.00
Price: As above, 45 ACP, 10mm, 45 Win. Mag., 357/45 Win. Mag. $214.00

L.A.R. Grizzly Win Mag 8" & 10"
Similar to the standard Grizzly Win Mag except has lengthened slide and either 8" or 10" barrel. Available in 45 Win. Mag., 45 ACP, 357/45 Grizzly Win. Mag., 10mm or 357 Magnum. Introduced 1987.
Price: 8", 45 ACP, 45 Win. Mag., 357/45 Grizzly Win. Mag. $1,313.00
Price: As above, 10" $1,375.00
Price: 8", 357 Magnum $1,337.50
Price: As above, 10" $1,400.00

L.A.R. Girzzly MK I

L.A.R. Grizzly 50 Mark V Pistol
Similar to the Grizzly Win Mag Mark I except chambered for 50 Action Express with 6-shot magazine. Weight, empty, is 56 oz., overall length 10 5/8". Choice of 5.4" or 6.5" barrel. Has same features as Mark I, IV pistols. Introduced 1993. From L.A.R. Mfg., Inc.
Price: $1,060.00

L.A.R. Grizzly 44 Mag MK IV
Similar to the Win. Mag. Mk I except chambered for 44 Magnum, has beavertail grip safety. Matte blue finish only. Has 5.4" or 6.5" barrel. Introduced 1991. From L.A.R. Mfg., Inc.
Price: $933.00

HANDGUNS—AUTOLOADERS, SERVICE & SPORT

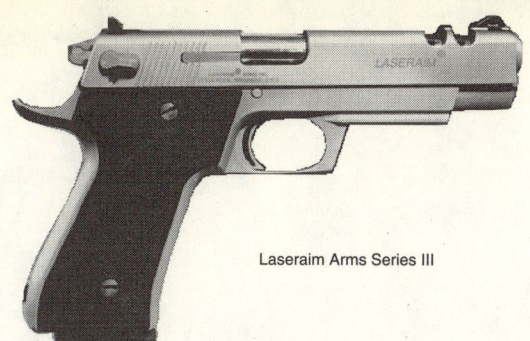

Laseraim Arms Series III

Laseraim Arms Series III Auto Pistol
Similar to the Series II except has 5" barrel only, with dual-port compensator; weighs 43 oz.; overall length is 7 5/8". Choice of fixed or adjustable rear sight. Introduced 1994. Made in U.S. by Emerging Technologies, Inc.
Price: Fixed sight $533.95
Price: Adjustable sight $559.95
Price: Fixed sight Dream Team Laseraim laser sight $629.95

LLAMA MAX-I AUTO PISTOLS
Caliber: 9mm Para., 9-shot, 45 ACP, 7-shot.
Barrel: 4 1/4" (Compact); 5 1/8" (Government).
Weight: 34 oz. (Compact); 36 oz. (Government). **Length:** 7 3/8" overall (Compact).
Stocks: Black rubber.
Sights: Blade front, rear adjustable for windage; three-dot system.
Features: Single-action trigger; skeletonized combat-style hammer; steel frame; extended manual and grip safeties. Introduced 1995. Imported from Spain by SGS Importers, International.
Price: 9mm, 9-shot, Government model $349.95
Price: As above, Compact model $349.95
Price: 45 ACP, 7-shot, Government model $349.95
Price: As above, Duo-Tone finish $366.95
Price: As above, Compact model $349.95

LLAMA IX-O COMPACT FRAME AUTO PISTOL
Caliber: 45 ACP, 10-shot.
Barrel: 4 1/4".
Weight: 39 oz.
Stocks: Black rubber.
Sights: Blade front, rear adjustable for windage; three-dot system.
Features: Scaled-down version of the Large Frame gun. Locked breech mechanism; manual and grip safeties. Introduced 1995. Imported from Spain by SGS Importers Int'l., Inc.
Price: Matte finish $399.95

LLAMA IX-C LARGE FRAME AUTO PISTOL
Caliber: 45 ACP, 10-shot.
Barrel: 5 1/8".
Weight: 41 oz. **Length:** 8 1/2" overall.
Stocks: Black rubber.
Sights: Blade front, rear adjustable for windage; three-dot system.
Features: Grip and manual safeties, ventilated rib. Imported from Spain by SGS Importers Int'l., Inc.
Price: Matte finish $399.95

LLAMA III-A SMALL FRAME AUTO PISTOL
Caliber: 380 ACP.
Barrel: 3 11/16".
Weight: 23 oz. **Length:** 6 1/2" overall.
Stocks: Checkered polymer, thumbrest.
Sights: Fixed front, adjustable notch rear.
Features: Ventilated rib, manual and grip safeties. Imported from Spain by SGS Importers International, Inc.
Price: Blue $258.95
Price: Satin Chrome $291.95

LORCIN L-22 AUTO PISTOL
Caliber: 22 LR, 9-shot magazine.
Barrel: 2.5".
Weight: 16 oz. **Length:** 5.25" overall.
Stocks: Black combat, or pink or pearl.
Sights: Fixed three-dot system.
Features: Available in chrome or black Teflon finish. Introduced 1989. From Lorcin Engineering.
Price: About $89.00

Laseraim Arms Series I Auto Pistol
Caliber: 10mm Auto, 8-shot, 45 ACP, 7-shot magazine.
Barrel: 6", with compensator.
Weight: 46 oz. **Length:** 9.75" overall.
Stocks: Pebble-grained black composite.
Sights: Blade front, fully adjustable rear.
Features: Single action; barrel compensator; stainless steel construction; ambidextrous safety-levers; extended slide release; matte black Teflon finish; integral mount for laser sight. Introduced 1993. Made in U.S. by Emerging Technologies, Inc.
Price: Standard, fixed sight $552.95
Price: Standard, Compact (4 3/8" barrel), fixed sight $552.95
Price: Adjustable sight $579.95
Price: Standard, fixed sight, Auto Illusion red dot sight system ... $649.95
Price: Standard, fixed sight, Laseraim Laser with Hotdot $694.95

Laseraim Arms Series II Auto Pistol
Similar to the Series I except without compensator, has matte stainless finish. Standard Series II has 5" barrel, weighs 43 oz., Compact has 3 3/8" barrel, weighs 37 oz. Blade front sight, rear adjustable for windage or fixed. Introduced 1993. Made in U.S. by Emerging Technologies, Inc.
Price: Standard or Compact (3 3/8" barrel), fixed sight $399.95
Price: Adjustable sight, 5" only $429.95
Price: Standard, fixed sight, Auto Illustion red dot sight $499.95
Price: Standard, fixed sight, Laseraim Laser $499.95

Llama Max-I

Llama Large Frame

Llama Small Frame

CAUTION: PRICES SHOWN ARE SUPPLIED BY THE MANUFACTURER OR IMPORTER. CHECK YOUR LOCAL GUNSHOP.

HANDGUNS—AUTOLOADERS, SERVICE & SPORT

LORCIN L9MM AUTO PISTOL
Caliber: 9mm Para., 10-shot magazine.
Barrel: 4.5".
Weight: 31 oz. **Length:** 7.5" overall.
Stocks: Grooved black composition.
Sights: Fixed; three-dot system.
Features: Matte black finish; hooked trigger guard; grip safety. Introduced 1994. Made in U.S. by Lorcin Engineering.
Price: $159.00

LORCIN L-25, LT-25 AUTO PISTOLS
Caliber: 25 ACP, 7-shot magazine.
Barrel: 2.4".
Weight: 14.5 oz. **Length:** 4.8" overall.
Stocks: Smooth composition.
Sights: Fixed.
Features: Available in choice of finishes: chrome, black Teflon or camouflage. Introduced 1989. From Lorcin Engineering.
Price: L-25 .... $69.00
Price: LT-25 .... $79.00

LORCIN L-32, L-380 AUTO PISTOLS
Caliber: 32 ACP, 380 ACP, 7-shot magazine.
Barrel: 3.5".
Weight: 27 oz. **Length:** 6.6" overall.
Stocks: Grooved composition.
Sights: Fixed.
Features: Black Teflon or chrome finish with black grips. Introduced 1992. From Lorcin Engineering.
Price: L-32 32 ACP $89.00
Price: L-380 380 ACP $100.00

MITCHELL ARMS SPORT-KING II AUTO PISTOL
Caliber: 22 LR, 10-shot magazine.
Barrel: 4.5", 6.75".
Weight: 39 oz. (4.5" barrel). **Length:** 9" overall (4.5" barrel).
Stocks: Checkered black plastic.
Sights: Blade front, rear adjustable for windage.
Features: Military grip; standard trigger; push-button barrel takedown. Stainless steel or blue. Introduced 1992. From Mitchell Arms, Inc.
Price: $325.00

MITCHELL 45 GOLD SERIES
Caliber: 45 ACP, 8- or 10-shot magazine.
Barrel: 5".
Weight: 39 oz. **Length:** 8.75" overall.
Stocks: Smooth American walnut or checkered black rubber.
Sights: Interchangeable blade front, drift adjustable combat rear or fully adjustable rear.
Features: Royal blue or stainless steel. Also available with 10-shot skirted magazine. Bull barrel/slide lockup (no bushing design); full-length guide rod; extended ambidextrous safety; adjustable trigger; beveled magazine well; interchangeable front sight. Introduced 1994. Made in U.S. From Mitchell Arms, Inc.
Price: Blue, drift adjustable sight $535.00
Price: As above, stainless $565.00
Price: Blue, fully adjustable sight $575.00
Price: As above, stainless $599.00

Lorcin L9MM

Lorcin L-25

Mitchell Sport King II

Mitchell 45 Gold Series

Mitchell Wide-Body Gold Series
Similar to the Gold Series except comes only with 10-shot magazine (accepts 8- and 13-shot magazines). Blue or stainless steel. Introduced 1994. Made in U.S. From Mitchell Arms, Inc.
Price: Blue, fixed combat sights, black rubber stocks $685.00
Price: As above, stainless $710.00
Price: Blue, adjustable sight, changeable front sight blade, smooth walnut stocks $750.00
Price: As above, stainless $750.00

MITCHELL ARMS AMERICAN EAGLE AUTO
Caliber: 9mm Para., 7-shot magazine.
Barrel: 4".
Weight: 29.6 oz. **Length:** 9.6" overall.
Stocks: Checkered walnut.
Sights: Blade front, fixed rear.
Features: Recreation of the American Eagle Parabellum pistol in stainless steel. Chamber loaded indicator. Made in U.S. From Mitchell Arms, Inc.
Price: $695.00

Mitchell American Eagle

HANDGUNS—AUTOLOADERS, SERVICE & SPORT

MITCHELL ARMS ALPHA AUTO PISTOL
Caliber: 45 ACP, 8- and 10-shot magazine.
Barrel: 5".
Weight: 41 oz. **Length:** 8.5" overall.
Stocks: Smooth polymer.
Sights: Interchangeable blade front, fully adjustable rear or drift adjustable rear.
Features: Interchangeable trigger modules permit double-action-only, single-action-only or SA/DA fire. Accepts any single-column, 8-shot 1911-style magazine. Frame-mounted decocker/safety; extended ambidextrous safety; extended slide latch; serrated combat hammer; beveled magazine well; heavy bull barrel (no bushing design); extended slide underlug; full-length recoil spring guide system. Introduced 1995. Made in U.S. From Mitchell Arms, Inc.
Price: Blue, fixed sight $689.00
Price: Blue, adjustable sight $725.00
Price: Stainless, fixed sight $725.00
Price: Stainless, adjustable sight $749.00

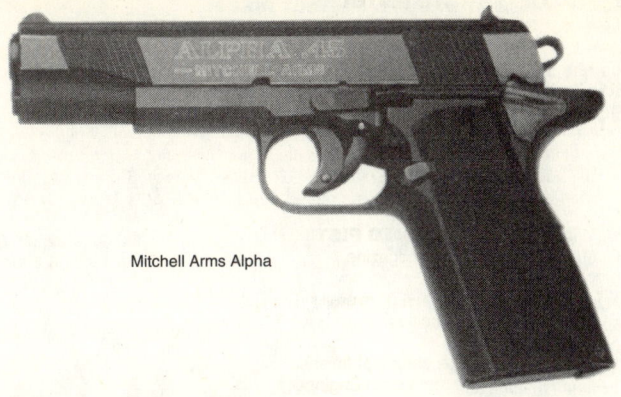
Mitchell Arms Alpha

Mountain Eagle Target

MOUNTAIN EAGLE AUTO PISTOL
Caliber: 22 LR, 10-shot magazine.
Barrel: 6.5", 8".
Weight: 21 oz., 23 oz. **Length:** 10.6" overall (with 6.5" barrel).
Stocks: One-piece impact-resistant polymer in "conventional contour"; checkered panels.
Sights: Serrated ramp front with interchangeable blades, rear adjustable for windage and elevation; interchangeable blades.
Features: Injection moulded grip frame, alloy receiver; hybrid composite barrel replicates shape of the Desert Eagle pistol. Flat, smooth trigger. Introduced 1992. From Magnum Research.
Price: Mountain Eagle Compact $199.00
Price: Mountain Eagle Standard $239.00
Price: Mountain Eagle Target Edition (8" barrel) $279.00

PARA-ORDNANCE P-SERIES AUTO PISTOLS
Caliber: 40 S&W, 45 ACP, 10-shot magazine.
Barrel: 5".
Weight: 28 oz. (alloy frame). **Length:** 8.5" overall.
Stocks: Textured composition.
Sights: Blade front, rear adjustable for windage. High visibility three-dot system.
Features: Available with alloy, steel or stainless steel frame with black finish (silver or stainless gun). Steel and stainless steel frame guns weigh 38 oz. (P14.45), 35 oz. (P13.45), 33 oz. (P12.45). Grooved match trigger, rounded combat-style hammer. Beveled magazine well. Manual thumb, grip and firing pin lock safeties. Solid barrel bushing. Introduced 1990. Made in Canada by Para-Ordnance.
Price: P14.45E (steel frame) $745.00
Price: P14.45R (alloy frame) $700.00
Price: P12.45R 3 1/2" bbl., 24 oz., alloy) $700.00
Price: P13.45R 4 1/4" barrel, 28 oz., alloy) $700.00
Price: P12.45E (steel frame) $745.00
Price: P16.40E (steel frame) $745.00

Para-Ordnance P16.40

PHOENIX ARMS MODEL RAVEN AUTO PISTOL
Caliber: 25 ACP, 6-shot magazine.
Barrel: 2 7/16".
Weight: 15 oz. **Length:** 4 3/4" overall.
Stocks: Ivory-colored or black slotted plastic.
Sights: Ramped front, fixed rear.
Features: Available in blue, nickel or chrome finish. Made in U.S. Available from Phoenix Arms.
Price: $69.95

PHOENIX ARMS HP22, HP25 AUTO PISTOLS
Caliber: 22 LR, 10-shot (HP22), 25 ACP, 10-shot (HP25).
Barrel: 3".
Weight: 20 oz. **Length:** 5 1/2" overall.
Stocks: Checkered composition.
Sights: Blade front, adjustable rear.
Features: Single action, exposed hammer; manual hold-open; button magazine release. Available in satin nickel, polished blue finish. Introduced 1993. Made in U.S. by Phoenix Arms.
Price: $99.95

PSP-25 AUTO PISTOL
Caliber: 25 ACP, 6-shot magazine.
Barrel: 2 1/8".
Weight: 9.5 oz. **Length:** 4 1/8" overall.
Stocks: Checkered black plastic.
Sights: Fixed.
Features: All steel construction with polished finish. Introduced 1990. Made in the U.S. by PSP.
Price: Blue $249.00
Price: Hard chrome $299.00

Phoenix Arms Raven

Phoenix Arms HP22

CAUTION: PRICES SHOWN ARE SUPPLIED BY THE MANUFACTURER OR IMPORTER. CHECK YOUR LOCAL GUNSHOP.

HANDGUNS—AUTOLOADERS, SERVICE & SPORT

ROCKY MOUNTAIN ARMS PATRIOT PISTOL
Caliber: 223, 10-shot magazine.
Barrel: 7", with muzzle brake.
Weight: 5 lbs. **Length:** 20.5" overall.
Stocks: Black composition.
Sights: None furnished.
Features: Milled upper receiver with enhanced Weaver base; milled lower receiver from billet plate; machined aluminum National Match handguard. Finished in DuPont Teflon-S matte black or NATO green. Comes with black nylon case, one magazine. Introduced 1993. From Rocky Mountain Arms, Inc.
Price: With A-2 handle top ....$2,500.00 to $2,800.00
Price: Flat top model ....$3,000.00 to $3,500.00

RUGER P89 AUTOMATIC PISTOL
Caliber: 9mm Para., 10-shot magazine.
Barrel: 4.50".
Weight: 32 oz. **Length:** 7.84" overall.
Stocks: Grooved black Xenoy composition.
Sights: Square post front, square notch rear adjustable for windage, both with white dot inserts.
Features: Double action with ambidextrous slide-mounted safety-levers. Slide is 4140 chrome moly steel or 400-series stainless steel, frame is a lightweight aluminum alloy. Ambidextrous magazine release. Blue or stainless steel. Introduced 1986; stainless introduced 1990.
Price: P89, blue, with extra magazine and magazine loading tool, plastic case $410.00
Price: KP89, stainless, with extra magazine and magazine loading tool, plastic case $452.00

Ruger P89D Decocker Automatic Pistol
Similar to the standard P89 except has ambidextrous decocking levers in place of the regular slide-mounted safety. The decocking levers move the firing pin inside the slide where the hammer can not reach it, while simultaneously blocking the firing pin from forward movement—allows shooter to decock a cocked pistol without manipulating the trigger. Conventional thumb decocking procedures are therefore unnecessary. Blue or stainless steel. Introduced 1990.
Price: P89D, blue with extra magazine and loader, plastic case $410.00
Price: KP89D, stainless, with extra magazine, plastic case $452.00

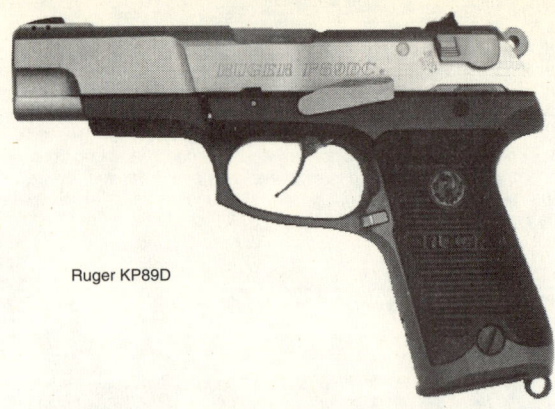
Ruger KP89D

Ruger P89 Double-Action Only Automatic Pistol
Same as the KP89 except operates only in the double-action mode. Has a spurless hammer, gripping grooves on each side of the rear of the slide; no external safety or decocking lever. An internal safety prevents forward movement of the firing pin unless the trigger is pulled. Available in 9mm Para., stainless steel only. Introduced 1991.
Price: With lockable case, extra magazine, magazine loading tool $452.00

Ruger KP93D

Consult our Directory pages for the location of firms mentioned.

Ruger P93 Compact Automatic Pistol
Has 3.9" barrel, 7.3" overall length, and weighs 31 oz. The forward third of the slide is tapered and polished to the muzzle. Front of the slide is crowned with a convex curve. Slide has seven finger grooves. Trigger guard bow is higher for better grip. Square post front sight, square notch rear drift adjustable for windage, both with white dot inserts. Slide is 400-series stainless steel, lightweight alloy frame. Available as decocker-only or double action-only. Introduced 1993.
Price: KP93DAO (double action only), KP93 (decocker) $520.00

RUGER P90 AUTOMATIC PISTOL
Caliber: 45 ACP, 7-shot magazine.
Barrel: 4.50".
Weight: 33.5 oz. **Length:** 7.87" overall.
Stocks: Grooved black Xenoy composition.
Sights: Square post front, square notch rear adjustable for windage, both with white dot inserts.
Features: Double action with ambidextrous slide-mounted safety-levers which move the firing pin inside the slide where the hammer can not reach it, while simultaneously blocking the firing pin from forward movement. Stainless steel only. Introduced 1991.
Price: KP90 with lockable case, extra magazine $488.65

Ruger KP90

Ruger P90 Decocker Automatic Pistol
Similar to the P90 except has a manual decocking system. The ambidextrous decocking levers move the firing pin inside the slide where the hammer can not reach it, while simultaneously blocking the firing pin from forward movement—allows shooter to decock a cocked pistol without manipulating the trigger. Available only in stainless steel. Overall length 7.87", weight 34 oz. Introduced 1991.
Price: P90D with lockable case, extra magazine, and magazine loading tool $488.65

Ruger P94L Automatic Pistol
Same as the KP94 except mounts a laser sight in a housing cast integrally with the frame. Allen-head screws control windage and elevation adjustments. Announced 1994. Made in U.S. by Sturm, Ruger & Co.
Price: For law enforcement only ....NA

HANDGUNS—AUTOLOADERS, SERVICE & SPORT

Ruger KP94 Automatic Pistol
Sized midway between the full-size P-Series and the compact P93. Has 4.25" barrel, 7.5" overall length and weighs about 33 oz. KP94 is manual safety model; KP94DAO is double-action-only (both 9mm Para., 10-shot magazine); KP94D is decocker-only in 40 S&W with 10-shot magazine. Slide gripping grooves roll over top of slide. KP94 has ambidextrous safety-levers; KP94DAO has no external safety, full-cock hammer position or decocking lever; KP94D has ambidextrous decocking levers. Matte finish stainless slide, barrel, alloy frame. Introduced 1994. Made in U.S. by Sturm, Ruger & Co.
Price: KP94 (9mm), KP944 (40 S&W) $520.00
Price: KP94DAO (9mm), KP944DAO (40 S&W) $520.00
Price: KP94D (40 S&W) $520.00

Ruger KP94

RUGER MARK II STANDARD AUTO PISTOL
Caliber: 22 LR, 10-shot magazine.
Barrel: 4 3/4" or 6".
Weight: 25 oz. (4 3/4" bbl.). **Length:** 8 5/16" (4 3/4" bbl.).
Stocks: Checkered plastic.
Sights: Fixed, wide blade front, square notch rear adjustable for windage.
Features: Updated design of the original Standard Auto. Has new bolt hold-open latch. 10-shot magazine, magazine catch, safety, trigger and new receiver contours. Introduced 1982.
Price: Blued (MK 4, MK 6) $252.00
Price: In stainless steel (KMK 4, KMK 6) $330.25

Ruger 22/45 Mark II Pistol
Similar to the other 22 Mark II autos except has grip frame of Zytel that matchs the angle and magazine latch of the Model 1911 45 ACP pistol. Available in 4 3/4" standard and 5 1/2" bull barrel. Introduced 1992.
Price: KP4 (4 3/4" barrel) $280.00
Price: KP512 (5 1/2" bull barrel) $330.00
Price: P512 (5 1/2" bull barrel, all blue) $237.50

Ruger P512 22/45

SCHUETZEN PISTOL WORKS CREST SERIES PISTOLS
Caliber: 45 ACP, 7-shot magazine (standard), 6-shot (4-Star).
Barrel: 5" (standard), 4.5" (4-Star); 416 stainless steel.
Weight: 39 oz. (standard), 35.7 oz. (4-Star). **Length:** 8.5" overall (standard).
Stocks: Checkered walnut.
Sights: Ramped blade front, LPA adjustable rear.
Features: Right- or left-hand models available. Long aluminum trigger, full-length recoil spring guide; throated, polished, tuned. Satin stainless steel. Introduced 1993. Made in U.S. by Olympic Arms, Inc.
Price: Right-hand, standard $815.00
Price: Left-hand, standard $1,165.00
Price: Right-hand, 4-Star $875.00
Price: Left-hand, 4-Star $1,135.00

Schuetzen Big Deuce

SCHUETZEN PISTOL WORKS BIG DEUCE PISTOL
Caliber: 45 ACP, 7-shot magazine.
Barrel: 6"; 416 stainless steel.
Weight: 40.3 oz. **Length:** 9.5" overall.
Stocks: Smooth walnut.
Sights: Ramped blade front, LPA adjustable rear.
Features: Beavertail grip safety; extended thumb safety and slide release; Commander-style hammer. Throated, polished and tuned. Parkerized matte black slide with satin stainless steel frame. Introduced 1995. Made in U.S. by Olympic Arms, Inc.
Price: $1,035.00

SCHUETZEN PISTOL WORKS GRIFFON PISTOL
Caliber: 45 ACP, 10-shot magazine.
Barrel: 5"; 416 stainless steel.
Weight: NA. **Length:** 8.5" overall.
Stocks: Smooth walnut.
Sights: Ramped blade front, LPA adjustable rear.
Features: 10+1 1911 enhanced 45. Beavertail grip safety; long aluminum trigger; full-length recoil spring guide; Commander-style hammer. Throated, polished and tuned. Grip size comparable to standard 1911. Satin stainless steel finish. Announced 1995. Made in U.S. by Olympic Arms, Inc.
Price: .... NA

SCHUETZEN PISTOL WORKS ENFORCER PISTOL
Caliber: 45 ACP, 6-shot magazine.
Barrel: 3.8"; stainless.
Weight: 36 oz. **Length:** 7.3" overall.
Stocks: Smooth walnut with etched black widow spider logo.
Sights: Ramped blade front, LPA adjustable rear.
Features: Extended safety, extended slide release; Commander-style hammer; beavertail grip safety; throated, polished, tuned. Parkerized matte black or satin stainless steel finishes. Made in U.S. by Olympic Arms
Price: $825.00

Schuetzen Gun Works Enforcer Carrycomp II Pistol
Similar to the Enforcer except has Wil Schueman-designed hybrid compensator system. Introduced 1993. Made in U.S. by Olympic Arms, Inc.
Price: $1,425.00

Schuetzen Enforcer

HANDGUNS—AUTOLOADERS, SERVICE & SPORT

SEECAMP LWS 32 STAINLESS DA AUTO
Caliber: 32 ACP Win. Silvertip, 6-shot magazine.
Barrel: 2", integral with frame.
Weight: 10.5 oz. **Length:** 4 1/8" overall.
Stocks: Glass-filled nylon.
Sights: Smooth, no-snag, contoured slide and barrel top.
Features: Aircraft quality 17-4 PH stainless steel. Inertia-operated firing pin. Hammer fired double-action only. Hammer automatically follows slide down to safety rest position after each shot—no manual safety needed. Magazine safety disconnector. Polished stainless. Introduced 1985. From L.W. Seecamp.
Price: $375.00

SIG P-210-6 AUTO PISTOL
Caliber: 9mm Para., 8-shot magazine.
Barrel: 4 3/4".
Weight: 36.2 oz. **Length:** 8 1/2" overall.
Stocks: Checkered black plastic; walnut optional.
Sights: Blade front, micro. adjustable rear for windage and elevation.
Features: Adjustable trigger stop; target trigger; ribbed frontstrap; sandblasted finish. Conversion unit for 22 LR consists of barrel, recoil spring, slide and magazine. Imported from Switzerland by Mandall Shooting Supplies.
Price: P-210-6 ....$3,700.00
Price: P-210-5 Target $3,700.00

SIG SAUER P220 "AMERICAN" AUTO PISTOL
Caliber: 38 Super, 45 ACP, (9-shot in 38 Super, 7 in 45).
Barrel: 4 3/8".
Weight: 28 1/4 oz. (9mm). **Length:** 7 3/4" overall.
Stocks: Checkered black plastic.
Sights: Blade front, drift adjustable rear for windage.
Features: Double action. De-cocking lever permits lowering hammer onto locked firing pin. Squared combat-type trigger guard. Slide stays open after last shot. Imported from Germany by SIGARMS, Inc.
Price: "American," blue (side-button magazine release, 45 ACP only) ...$805.00
Price: 45 ACP, blue, Siglite night sights $905.00
Price: K-Kote finish $850.00
Price: K-Kote, Siglite night sights $950.00

SIG Sauer P226 DA Auto Pistol
Similar to the P220 pistol except has 4.4" barrel, and weighs 26 1/2 oz. 9mm only. Imported from Germany by SIGARMS, Inc.
Price: Blue $825.00
Price: With Siglite night sights $930.00
Price: Blue, double-action only $825.00
Price: Blue, double-action only, Siglite night sights $930.00
Price: K-Kote finish $875.00
Price: K-Kote, Siglite night sights $975.00
Price: K-Kote, double-action only $875.00
Price: K-Kote, double-action only, Siglite night sights $975.00

SIG Sauer P228 DA Auto Pistol
Similar to the P226 except has 3.86" barrel, with 7.08" overall length and 3.35" height. Chambered for 9mm Para. only, 10-shot magazine. Weight is 29.1 oz. with empty magazine. Introduced 1989. Imported from Germany by SIGARMS, Inc.
Price: Blue $825.00
Price: Blue, with Siglite night sights $930.00
Price: Blue, double-action only $825.00
Price: Blue, double-action only, Siglite night sights $930.00
Price: K-Kote finish $875.00
Price: K-Kote, Siglite night sights $975.00
Price: K-Kote, double-action only $875.00
Price: K-Kote, double-action only, Siglite night sights $975.00

SIG Sauer P229 DA Auto Pistol
Similar to the P228 except chambered for 9mm Para., 40 S&W, 357 SIG. Has 3.86" barrel, 7.08" overall length and 3.35" height. Weight is 30.5 oz. Introduced 1991. Frame made in Germany, stainless steel slide assembly made in U.S.; pistol assembled in U.S. From SIGARMS, Inc.
Price: Blue $875.00
Price: Blue, double-action only $875.00
Price: With Siglite night sights $975.00

SIG SAUER P230 DA AUTO PISTOL
Caliber: 380 ACP, 7-shot.
Barrel: 3 3/4".
Weight: 16 oz. **Length:** 6 1/2" overall.
Stocks: Checkered black plastic.
Sights: Blade front, rear adjustable for windage.
Features: Double action. Same basic action design as P220. Blowback operation, stationary barrel. Introduced 1977. Imported from Germany by SIGARMS, Inc.
Price: Blue $510.00
Price: In stainless steel (P230 SL) $595.00

SIG P-210-2 AUTO PISTOL
Caliber: 7.65mm or 9mm Para., 8-shot magazine.
Barrel: 4 3/4".
Weight: 31 3/4 oz. (9mm). **Length:** 8 1/2" overall.
Stocks: Checkered black composition.
Sights: Blade front, rear adjustable for windage.
Features: Lanyard loop; matte finish. Conversion unit for 22 LR available. Imported from Switzerland by Mandall Shooting Supplies.
Price: P-210-2 Service Pistol $3,500.00

SIG Sauer P220 American

SIG SAUER P225 DA AUTO PISTOL
Caliber: 9mm Para., 8-shot magazine.
Barrel: 3.8".
Weight: 26 oz. **Length:** 7 3/32" overall.
Stocks: Checkered black plastic.
Sights: Blade front, rear adjustable for windage. Optional Siglite night sights.
Features: Double action. De-cocking lever permits lowering hammer onto locked firing pin. Square combat-type trigger guard. Shortened, lightened version of P220. Imported from Germany by SIGARMS, Inc.
Price: Blue, SA/DA or DAO $780.00
Price: With Siglite night sights, blue, SA/DA or DAO ...$880.00
Price: K-Kote finish $850.00
Price: K-Kote with Siglite night sights $950.00

SIG Sauer P228

SIG Sauer P230

HANDGUNS—AUTOLOADERS, SERVICE & SPORT

SMITH & WESSON MODEL 422, 622 AUTO
Caliber: 22 LR, 10-shot magazine.
Barrel: 4½", 6".
Weight: 22 oz. (4½" bbl.). **Length:** 7½" overall (4½" bbl.).
Stocks: Checkered simulated woodgrain polymer.
Sights: Field—serrated ramp front, fixed rear; Target— serrated ramp front, adjustable rear.
Features: Aluminum frame, steel slide, brushed stainless steel or blue finish; internal hammer. Introduced 1987. Model 2206 introduced 1990.
Price: Blue, 4½", 6", fixed sight $235.00
Price: As above, adjustable sight $290.00
Price: Stainless (Model 622), 4½", 6", fixed sight $284.00
Price: As above, adjustable sight $337.00

Smith & Wesson Model 422

Smith & Wesson Model 2214 Sportsman Auto
Similar to the Model 422 except has 3" barrel, 8-shot magazine; dovetail Patridge front sight with white dot, fixed rear with two white dots; matte blue finish, black composition grips with checkered panels. Overall length 6⅛", weight 18 oz. Introduced 1990.
Price: $269.00
Price: Model 2213 (stainless steel) $314.00

Smith & Wesson Model 2206 Auto
Similar to the Model 422/622 except made entirely of stainless steel with non-reflective finish. Weight is 35 oz. with 4½" barrel, 39 oz. with 6" barrel. Introduced 1990.
Price: With fixed sight $327.00
Price: With adjustable sight $385.00

Smith & Wesson Model 2214

Smith & Wesson Model 2206 Target Auto
Same as the Model 2206 except 6" barrel only; Millett Series 100 fully adjustable sight system; Patridge front sight; smooth contoured Herrett walnut target grips with thumbrest; serrated trigger with adjustable stop. Frame is bead-blasted along sighting plane, drilled and tapped for optics mount. Introduced 1994. Made in U.S. by Smith & Wesson.
Price: $433.00

SMITH & WESSON MODEL 909, 910 DA AUTO PISTOLS
Caliber: 9mm Para., 10-shot magazine.
Barrel: 4".
Weight: 28 oz. **Length:** 7⅜" overall.
Stocks: One-piece Xenoy, wraparound with straight backstrap.
Sights: Post front with white dot, fixed two-dot rear.
Features: Alloy frame, blue carbon steel slide. Slide-mounted decocking lever. Introduced 1995.
Price: Model 910 ....$467.00
Price: Model 909 (9-shot magazine, curved backstrap, 27 oz.) $443.00

Smith & Wesson Model 910

Smith & Wesson Model 411 DA Auto Pistol
Same as the Model 910 except chambered for 40 S&W, 10-shot magazine. Alloy frame, blue carbon steel slide. Introduced 1994. Made in U.S. by Smith & Wesson.
Price: $525.00

SMITH & WESSON MODEL 3913/3914 DOUBLE ACTIONS
Caliber: 9mm Para., 8-shot magazine.
Barrel: 3½".
Weight: 26 oz. **Length:** 6¹³⁄₁₆" overall.
Stocks: One-piece Delrin wraparound, textured surface.
Sights: Post front with white dot, Novak LoMount Carry with two dots, adjustable for windage.
Features: Aluminum alloy frame, stainless slide (M3913) or blue steel slide (M3914). Bobbed hammer with no half-cock notch; smooth .304" trigger with rounded edges. Straight backstrap. Extra magazine included. Introduced 1989.
Price: Model 3913 ....$622.00
Price: Model 3914 ....$562.00

Smith & Wesson 3913 LadySmith

Smith & Wesson Model 3913 LadySmith Auto
Similar to the standard Model 3913/3914 except has frame that is upswept at the front, rounded trigger guard. Comes in frosted stainless steel with matching gray grips. Grips are ergonomically correct for a woman's hand. Novak LoMount Carry rear sight adjustable for windage, smooth edges for snag resistance. Extra magazine included. Introduced 1990.
Price: $640.00

Smith & Wesson Model 3953DA Pistol
Same as the Models 3913/3914 except double-action only. Model 3953 has stainless slide with alloy frame. Overall length 7"; weight 25.5 oz. Extra magazine included. Introduced 1990.
Price: $622.00

HANDGUNS—AUTOLOADERS, SERVICE & SPORT

SMITH & WESSON MODEL 4013, 4053 AUTOS
Caliber: 40 S&W, 8-shot magazine.
Barrel: 3 1/2".
Weight: 26 oz. **Length:** 7" overall.
Stocks: One-piece Xenoy wraparound with straight backstrap.
Sights: Post front with white dot, fixed Novak LoMount Carry rear with two white dots.
Features: Model 4013 is traditional double action; Model 4053 is double-action only; stainless slide on alloy frame. Introduced 1991.
Price: Model 4013 ....$722.00
Price: Model 4053 ....$722.00

SMITH & WESSON MODEL 4006 DA AUTO
Caliber: 40 S&W, 10-shot magazine.
Barrel: 4".
Weight: 38.5 oz. **Length:** 7 7/8" overall.
Stocks: Xenoy wraparound with checkered panels.
Sights: Replaceable post front with white dot, Novak LoMount Carry fixed rear with two white dots, or micro. click adjustable rear with two white dots.
Features: Stainless steel construction with non-reflective finish. Straight backstrap. Extra magazine included. Introduced 1990.
Price: With adjustable sights $775.00
Price: With fixed sight $745.00
Price: With fixed night sights $855.00

SMITH & WESSON MODEL 4500 SERIES AUTOS
Caliber: 45 ACP, 7-shot (M4516), 8-shot magazine for M4506, 4566/4586.
Barrel: 3 3/4" (M4516), 5" (M4506).
Weight: 41 oz. (4506). **Length:** 7 1/8" overall (4516).
Stocks: Xenoy one-piece wraparound, arched or straight backstrap on M4506, straight only on M4516.
Sights: Post front with white dot, adjustable or fixed Novak LoMount Carry on M4506.
Features: M4506 has serrated hammer spur. Extra magazine included. Contact Smith & Wesson for complete data. Introduced 1989.
Price: Model 4506, fixed sight $774.00
Price: Model 4506, adjustable sight $806.00
Price: Model 4516, fixed sight $774.00
Price: Model 4566 (stainless, 4 1/4", traditional DA, ambidextrous safety, fixed sight) $774.00
Price: Model 4586 (stainless, 4 1/4", DA only) $774.00

SMITH & WESSON MODEL 5900 SERIES AUTO PISTOLS
Caliber: 9mm Para., 10-shot magazine.
Barrel: 4".
Weight: 28 1/2 to 37 1/2 oz. (fixed sight); 38 oz. (adj. sight). **Length:** 7 1/2" overall.
Stocks: Xenoy wraparound with curved backstrap.
Sights: Post front with white dot, fixed or fully adjustable with two white dots.
Features: All stainless, stainless and alloy or carbon steel and alloy construction. Smooth .304" trigger, .260" serrated hammer. Extra magazine included. Introduced 1989.
Price: Model 5903 (stainless, alloy frame, traditional DA, fixed sight, ambidextrous safety) $690.00
Price: Model 5904 (blue, alloy frame, traditional DA, adjustable sight, ambidextrous safety) $642.00
Price: Model 5906 (stainless, traditional DA, adjustable sight, ambidextrous safety) $742.00
Price: As above, fixed sight $707.00
Price: With fixed night sights $817.00
Price: Model 5946 (as above, stainless frame and slide) $707.00

Smith & Wesson Model 6904/6906 Double-Action Autos
Similar to the Models 5904/5906 except with 3 1/2" barrel, 10-shot magazine, fixed rear sight, .260" bobbed hammer. Extra magazine included. Introduced 1989.
Price: Model 6904, blue $614.00
Price: Model 6906, stainless $677.00
Price: Model 6906 with fixed night sights $788.00
Price: Model 6946 (stainless, DA only, fixed sights) $677.00

SMITH & WESSON SIGMA SW380 AUTO
Caliber: 380 ACP, 6-shot magazine.
Barrel: 3".
Weight: 14 oz. **Length:** 5.8" overall.
Stocks: Integral.
Sights: Fixed groove in the slide.
Features: Polymer frame; double-action-only trigger mechanism; grooved/serrated front and rear straps; two passive safeties. Introduced 1995. Made in U.S. by Smith & Wesson.
Price: $300.00

Smith & Wesson Model 4053

Smith & Wesson Model 4046 DA Pistol
Similar to the Model 4006 except is double-action only. Has a semi-bobbed hammer, smooth trigger, 4" barrel; Novak LoMount Carry rear sight, post front with white dot. Overall length is 7 1/2", weight 28 oz. Extra magazine included. Introduced 1991.
Price: $745.00
Price: With fixed night sights $855.00

Smith & Wesson Sigma SW380

Smith & Wesson Sigma

SMITH & WESSON SIGMA SERIES PISTOLS
Caliber: 9mm Para., 40 S&W, 10-shot magazine.
Barrel: 4.5".
Weight: 26 oz. **Length:** 7.4" overall.
Stocks: Integral.
Sights: White dot front, fixed rear; three-dot system. Tritium night sights available.
Features: Ergonomic polymer frame; low barrel centerline; internal striker firing system; corrosion-resistant slide; Teflon-filled, electroless-nickel coated magazine. Introduced 1994. Made in U.S. by Smith & Wesson.
Price: Model SW9F (9mm Para.) $593.00
Price: Model SW40F (40 S&W) $593.00
Price: Model Compact, SW9C, SW 40C (4" bbl., 24.4 oz.) $593.00
Price: With fixed tritium night sights $697.00

HANDGUNS—AUTOLOADERS, SERVICE & SPORT

SPHINX AT-380 AUTO PISTOL
Caliber: 380 ACP, 10-shot magazine.
Barrel: 3.27".
Weight: 25 oz. **Length:** 6.03" overall.
Stocks: Checkered plastic.
Sights: Fixed.
Features: Double-action-only mechanism, Chamber loaded indicator; ambidextrous magazine release and slide latch. Blued slide, bright Palladium frame, or bright Palladium overall. Introduced 1993. Imported from Switzerland by Sphinx USA, Inc.
Price: Two-tone $575.00

Sphinx AT-380M

SPHINX AT-2000S DOUBLE-ACTION PISTOL
Caliber: 9mm Para., 9x21mm, 40 S&W, 10-shot magazine.
Barrel: 4.53".
Weight: 36.3 oz. **Length:** 8.03" overall.
Stocks: Checkered neoprene.
Sights: Fixed, three-dot system.
Features: Double-action mechanism changeable to double-action-only. Stainless frame, blued slide. Ambidextrous safety, magazine release, slide latch. Introduced 1993. Imported from Switzerland by Sphinx USA, Inc.
Price: 9mm, two-tone $1,183.00
Price: 9mm, Palladium finish $1,273.00
Price: 40 S&W, two-tone $1,207.00
Price: 40 S&W, Palladium finish $1,297.00

Sphinx AT-2000P, AT-2000PS Auto Pistols
Same as the AT-2000S except AT-2000P has shortened frame, 3.74" barrel, 7.25" overall length, and weighs 34 oz. Model AT-2000PS has full-size frame. Both have stainless frame with blued slide or bright Palladium finish. Introduced 1993. Imported from Switzerland by Sphinx USA, Inc.
Price: 9mm, two-tone $1,056.00
Price: 9mm, Palladium finish $1,146.00
Price: 40 S&W, two-tone $1,079.00
Price: 40 S&W, Palladium finish $1,169.00

Sphinx AT-2000P

Sphinx AT-2000H Auto Pistol
Similar to the AT-2000P except has shorter slide with 3.54" barrel, shorter frame, 10-shot magazine, with 7" overall length. Weight is 32.2 oz. Stainless frame with blued slide, or overall bright Palladium finish. Introduced 1993. Imported from Switzerland by Sphinx USA, Inc.
Price: 9mm, two-tone $1,056.00
Price: 9mm, Palladium finish $1,146.00
Price: 40 S&W, two-tone $1,079.00
Price: 40 S&W, Palladium $1,169.00

SPRINGFIELD INC. 1911A1 AUTO PISTOL
Caliber: 9mm Para., 9-shot; 38 Super, 9-shot; 45 ACP, 8-shot.
Barrel: 5".
Weight: 35.6 oz. **Length:** 8 5/8" overall.
Stocks: Checkered plastic.
Sights: Fixed three-dot system.
Features: Beveled magazine well. All forged parts, including frame, barrel, slide. All new production. Introduced 1990. From Springfield Inc.
Price: Basic, 45 ACP, Parkerized $459.00
Price: Standard, 45 ACP, blued $515.00
Price: Basic, 45 ACP, stainless $555.00
Price: Mil-spec (Parkerized), 38 Super $515.00
Price: Lightweight (28.6 oz., matte finish) $515.00
Price: Standard, 9mm, 38 Super, blued $545.00
Price: Standard, 9mm, stainless steel $570.00
Price: Factory Comp, 45 ACP $915.00
Price: As above, 38 Super $949.00

Springfield Standard

Springfield Inc. 1911A1 Custom Carry Gun
Similar to the standard 1911A1 except has fixed three-dot low profile sights, Videki speed trigger, match barrel and bushing; extended thumb safety, beavertail grip safety; beveled, polished magazine well, polished feed ramp and throated barrel; match Commander hammer and sear, tuned extractor; lowered and flared ejection port; recoil buffer system, full-length spring guide rod; walnut grips. Comes with two magazines with slam pads, plastic carrying case. Available in all popular calibers. Introduced 1992. From Springfield Inc.
Price: $1,388.00

Springfield Inc. N.R.A. PPC Pistol
Specifically designed to comply with NRA rules for PPC competition. Has custom slide-to-frame fit; polished feed ramp; throated barrel; total internal honing; tuned extractor; recoil buffer system; fully checkered walnut grips; two fitted magazines; factory test target; custom carrying case. Introduced 1995. From Springfield Inc.
Price: $1,632.00

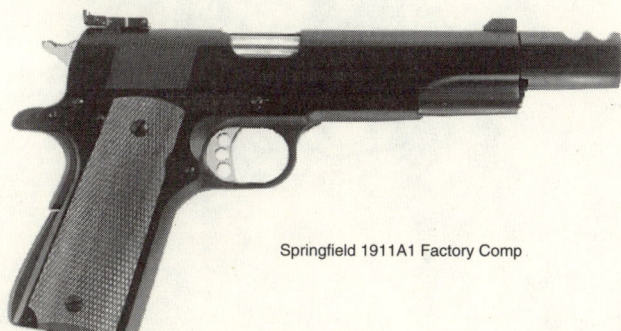
Springfield 1911A1 Factory Comp

Springfield Inc. 1911A1 Factory Comp
Similar to the standard 1911A1 except comes with bushing-type dual-port compensator, adjustable rear sight, extended thumb safety, Videki speed trigger, and beveled magazine well. Checkered walnut grips standard. Available in 38 Super or 45 ACP, blue only. Introduced 1992.
Price: 38 Super $1,074.00
Price: 45 ACP $1,049.00

CAUTION: PRICES SHOWN ARE SUPPLIED BY THE MANUFACTURER OR IMPORTER. CHECK YOUR LOCAL GUNSHOP.

HANDGUNS—AUTOLOADERS, SERVICE & SPORT

Springfield Champion Comp

Springfield V10 Ultra Compact

Springfield High Capacity Factory Comp

Springfield Inc. 1911A1 Champion Pistol
Similar to the standard 1911A1 except slide is 4.25". Has low-profile three-dot sight system. Comes with skeletonized hammer and walnut stocks. Available in 45 ACP only; blue or stainless. Introduced 1989.
- **Price:** Blue $525.00
- **Price:** Stainless $565.00
- **Price:** Blue, comp $840.00
- **Price:** Mil-Spec $459.00
- **Price:** Champion Comp (single-port compensator) $840.00

Springfield Inc. Champion MD-1 Auto Pistol
Similar to the 1911A1 Champion except chambered for 380 ACP, 7-shot magazine. Weighs 30 oz., has 3 1/2" barrel, 7 1/8" overall. Three-dot "hi-viz" sights. Blued or Parkerized. Introduced 1995. From Springfield, Inc.
- **Price:** Parkerized $424.00
- **Price:** Blued $429.00

Springfield Inc. Product Improved 1911A1 Defender Pistol
Similar to the 1911A1 Champion except has tapered cone dual-port compensator system, rubberized grips. Has reverse recoil plug, full-length recoil spring guide, serrated frontstrap, extended thumb safety, skeletonized hammer with modified grip safety to match and a Videki speed trigger. Bi-Tone finish. Introduced 1991.
- **Price:** 45 ACP $958.00

Springfield Inc. 1911A1 Compact Pistol
Similar to the Champion model except has a shortened slide with 4.025" barrel, 7.75" overall length. Magazine capacity is 7 shots. Has Commander hammer, checkered walnut grips. Available in 45 ACP only. Introduced 1989.
- **Price:** Blued $525.00
- **Price:** Stainless $565.00
- **Price:** Compact Lightweight $525.00
- **Price:** Mil-Spec $459.00

Springfield Inc. V10 Ultra Compact Pistol
Similar to the 1911A1 Compact except has recoil reducing compensator built into the barrel and slide. Beavertail grip safety, beveled magazine well, "hi-viz" combat sights, Videcki speed trigger, flared ejection port, stainless steel frame, blued slide, match grade barrel, walnut grips. Introduced 1995. From Springfield, Inc.
- **Price:** 45 ACP $637.00
- **Price:** Ultra Compact (no compensator), 45 ACP $549.00
- **Price:** Ultra Compact MD-1 Lightweight, (380 ACP, matte finish) $449.00

Springfield Inc. 1911A1 High Capacity Pistol
Similar to the Standard 1911A1 except available in 45 ACP and 9mm with 10-shot magazine (45 ACP). Has Commander-style hammer, walnut grips, ambidextrous thumb safety, beveled magazine well, plastic carrying case. Introduced 1993. From Springfield, Inc.
- **Price:** 45 ACP $622.00
- **Price:** 9mm $638.00
- **Price:** 45 ACP Factory Comp $964.00
- **Price:** 45 ACP Comp Lightweight, matte finish $840.00
- **Price:** 45 ACP Compact, blued $609.00
- **Price:** As above, stainless steel $648.00

STAR FIRESTAR AUTO PISTOL
Caliber: 9mm Para., 7-shot; 40 S&W, 6-shot.
Barrel: 3.39".
Weight: 30.35 oz. **Length:** 6.5" overall.
Stocks: Checkered rubber.
Sights: Blade front, fully adjustable rear; three-dot system.
Features: Low-profile, combat-style sights; ambidextrous safety. Available in blue or weather-resistant Starvel finish. Introduced 1990. Imported from Spain by Interarms.
- **Price:** Blue, 9mm $469.00
- **Price:** Starvel finish 9mm $496.00
- **Price:** Blue, 40 S&W $486.00
- **Price:** Starvel finish, 40 S&W $513.00

Star Firestar M45 Auto Pistol
Similar to the standard Firestar except chambered for 45 ACP with 6-shot magazine. Has 3.6" barrel, weighs 35 oz., 6.85" overall length. Reverse-taper Acculine barrel. Introduced 1992. Imported from Spain by Interarms.
- **Price:** Blue $516.00
- **Price:** Starvel finish $543.00

Star Firestar

338 THE GUN DIGEST   **CAUTION:** PRICES SHOWN ARE SUPPLIED BY THE MANUFACTURER OR IMPORTER. CHECK YOUR LOCAL GUNSHOP.

HANDGUNS—AUTOLOADERS, SERVICE & SPORT

Star Firestar Plus

Star Firestar Plus Auto Pistol
Same as the standard Firestar except has 10-shot magazine in 9mm. Also available in 40 S&W and 45 ACP. Introduced 1994. Imported from Spain by Interarms.

Price: Blue, 9mm	$507.00
Price: Starvel, 9mm	$533.00
Price: Blue, 40 S&W	$527.00
Price: Starvel, 40 S&W	$554.00
Price: Blue, 45 ACP	$554.00
Price: Starvel, 45 ACP	$580.00

STAR ULTRASTAR DOUBLE-ACTION PISTOL
Caliber: 9mm Para., 9-shot magazine.
Barrel: 3.57".
Weight: 26 oz. **Length:** 7" overall.
Stocks: Checkered black polymer.
Sights: Blade front, rear adjustable for windage; three-dot system.
Features: Polymer frame with inside steel slide rails; ambidextrous two-position safety (Safe and Decock). Introduced 1994. Imported from Spain by Interarms.
Price: $547.00

Consult our Directory pages for the location of firms mentioned.

Stoeger American Eagle Luger

Star Ultrastar

STOEGER AMERICAN EAGLE LUGER
Caliber: 9mm Para., 7-shot magazine.
Barrel: 4", 6".
Weight: 32 oz. **Length:** 9.6" overall.
Stocks: Checkered walnut.
Sights: Blade front, fixed rear.
Features: Recreation of the American Eagle Luger pistol in stainless steel. Chamber loaded indicator. Introduced 1994. From Stoeger Industries.
Price: $695.00
Price: Navy Model, 6" barrel $695.00

SUNDANCE BOA AUTO PISTOL
Caliber: 25 ACP, 7-shot magazine.
Barrel: 2 1/2".
Weight: 16 oz. **Length:** 4 7/8".
Stocks: Grooved ABS or smooth simulated pearl; optional pink.
Sights: Fixed.
Features: Patented grip safety, manual rotary safety; button magazine release; lifetime warranty. Bright chrome or black Teflon finish. Introduced 1991. Made in the U.S. by Sundance Industries, Inc.
Price: $95.00

Sundance BOA

Taurus PT 25

SUNDANCE MODEL A-25 AUTO PISTOL
Caliber: 25 ACP, 7-shot magazine.
Barrel: 2.5".
Weight: 16 oz. **Length:** 4 7/8" overall.
Stocks: Grooved black ABS or simulated smooth pearl; optional pink.
Sights: Fixed.
Features: Manual rotary safety; button magazine release. Bright chrome or black Teflon finish. Introduced 1989. Made in U.S. by Sundance Industries, Inc.
Price: $79.95

TAURUS MODEL PT 22/PT 25 AUTO PISTOLS
Caliber: 22 LR, 9-shot (PT 22); 25 ACP, 8-shot (PT 25).
Barrel: 2.75".
Weight: 12.3 oz. **Length:** 5.25" overall.
Stocks: Smooth Brazilian hardwood.
Sights: Blade front, fixed rear.
Features: Double action. Tip-up barrel for loading, cleaning. Blue or stainless. Introduced 1992. Made in U.S. by Taurus International.
Price: 22 LR or 25 ACP $193.00
Price: Stainless $201.00

TAURUS MODEL PT58 AUTO PISTOL
Caliber: 380 ACP, 10-shot magazine.
Barrel: 4.01".
Weight: 30 oz. **Length:** 7.2" overall.
Stocks: Brazilian hardwood.
Sights: Integral blade on slide front, notch rear adjustable for windage. Three-dot system.
Features: Double action with exposed hammer; inertia firing pin. Introduced 1988. Imported by Taurus International.
Price: Blue $462.00
Price: Stainless steel $526.00

HANDGUNS—AUTOLOADERS, SERVICE & SPORT

TAURUS MODEL PT 92AF AUTO PISTOL
Caliber: 9mm Para., 10-shot magazine.
Barrel: 4.92".
Weight: 34 oz. **Length:** 8.54" overall.
Stocks: Brazilian hardwood.
Sights: Fixed notch rear. Three-dot sight system.
Features: Double action, exposed hammer, chamber loaded indicator. Inertia firing pin. Imported by Taurus International.
Price: Blue $511.00
Price: Blue, Deluxe Shooter's Pak (extra magazine, case) $542.00
Price: Stainless steel $582.00
Price: Stainless, Deluxe Shooter's Pak (extra magazine, case) $610.00

Taurus PT 92AFC Compact Pistol
Similar to the PT-92 except has 4.25" barrel, 10-shot magazine, weighs 31 oz. and is 7.5" overall. Available in stainless steel, blue or satin nickel. Introduced 1991. Imported by Taurus International.
Price: Blue $511.00
Price: Stainless steel $582.00

TAURUS PT 100 AUTO PISTOL
Caliber: 40 S&W, 10-shot magazine.
Barrel: 5".
Weight: 34 oz.
Stocks: Smooth Brazilian hardwood.
Sights: Fixed front, drift-adjustable rear. Three-dot combat.
Features: Double action, exposed hammer. Ambidextrous hammer-drop safety; inertia firing pin; chamber loaded indicator. Introduced 1991. Imported by Taurus International.
Price: Blue $522.00
Price: Blue, Deluxe Shooter's Pak (extra magazine, case) $551.00
Price: Stainless $592.00
Price: Stainless, Deluxe Shooter's Pak (extra magazine, case) $622.00

Taurus PT 101 Auto Pistol
Same as the PT 100 except has micro-click rear sight adjustable for windage and elevation, three-dot combat-style. Introduced 1991.
Price: Blue $564.00
Price: Blue, Deluxe Shooter's Pak (extra magazine, case) $594.00
Price: Stainless $644.00
Price: Stainless, Deluxe Shooter's Pak (extra magazine, case) $673.00

TAURUS MODEL PT-908 AUTO PISTOL
Caliber: 9mm Para., 8-shot magazine.
Barrel: 3.8".
Weight: 30 oz. **Length:** 7.05" overall.
Stocks: Checkered black composition.
Sights: Drift-adjustable front and rear; three-dot combat.
Features: Double action, exposed hammer; manual ambidextrous hammer-drop; inertia firing pin; chamber loaded indicator. Introduced 1993. Imported by Taurus International.
Price: Blue $511.00
Price: Stainless steel $582.00

TAURUS PT-945 AUTO PISTOL
Caliber: 45 ACP, 8-shot magazine.
Barrel: 4.25".
Weight: 29.5 oz. **Length:** 7.48" overall.
Stocks: Santoprene II.
Sights: Drift-adjustable front and rear; three-dot system.
Features: Double-action mechanism. Has manual ambidextrous hammer drop safety, intercept notch, firing pin block, chamber loaded indicator, last-shot hold-open. Introduced 1995. Imported by Taurus International.
Price: Blue $570.00
Price: Stainless $646.00

WALTHER P-38 AUTO PISTOL
Caliber: 9mm Para., 8-shot.
Barrel: 4 15/16".
Weight: 28 oz. **Length:** 8 1/2" overall.
Stocks: Checkered plastic.
Sights: Fixed.
Features: Double action; safety blocks firing pin and drops hammer. Matte finish standard, polished blue, engraving and/or plating available. Imported from Germany by Interarms.
Price: $824.00
Price: Engraved models .... On Request

Taurus PT 92

Taurus PT 99AF Auto Pistol
Similar to the PT-92 except has fully adjustable rear sight, smooth Brazilian walnut stocks and is available in stainless steel, polished blue or satin nickel. Introduced 1983.
Price: Blue $554.00
Price: Blue, Deluxe Shooter's Pak (extra magazine, case) $584.00
Price: Stainless steel $605.00
Price: Stainless, Deluxe Shooter's Pak (extra magazine, case) $659.00

Taurus PT 101

Taurus PT 945

Walther P-38

Walther P-5 Auto Pistol
Latest Walther design that uses the basic P-38 double-action mechanism. Caliber 9mm Para., barrel length 3 1/2"; weight 28 oz., overall length 7".
Price: $1,096.00
Price: P-5 Compact $1,096.00

HANDGUNS—AUTOLOADERS, SERVICE & SPORT

WALTHER PP AUTO PISTOL
Caliber: 32 ACP, 380 ACP, 7-shot magazine.
Barrel: 3.86".
Weight: 23 1/2 oz. **Length:** 6.7" overall.
Stocks: Checkered plastic.
Sights: Fixed, white markings.
Features: Double action; manual safety blocks firing pin and drops hammer; chamber loaded indicator on 32 and 380; extra finger rest magazine provided. Imported from Germany by Interarms.
Price: 32 .... $1,206.00
Price: 380 .... $1,206.00
Price: Engraved models .... On Request

Walther PPK/S American

Walther PPK/S American Auto Pistol
Similar to Walther PP except made entirely in the United States. Has 3.27" barrel with 6.1" length overall. Introduced 1980.
Price: 380 ACP only, blue $651.00
Price: As above, stainless $651.00

Walther PPK American Auto Pistol
Similar to Walther PPK/S except weighs 21 oz., has 6-shot capacity. Made in the U.S. Introduced 1986.
Price: Stainless, 380 ACP only $651.00
Price: Blue, 380 ACP only $651.00

WALTHER MODEL TPH AUTO PISTOL
Caliber: 22 LR, 25 ACP, 6-shot magazine.
Barrel: 2 1/4".
Weight: 14 oz. **Length:** 5 3/8" overall.
Stocks: Checkered black composition.
Sights: Blade front, rear drift-adjustable for windage.
Features: Made of stainless steel. Scaled-down version of the Walther PP/PPK series. Made in U.S. Introduced 1987. From Interarms.
Price: Blue or stainless steel, 22 or 25 .... $486.00

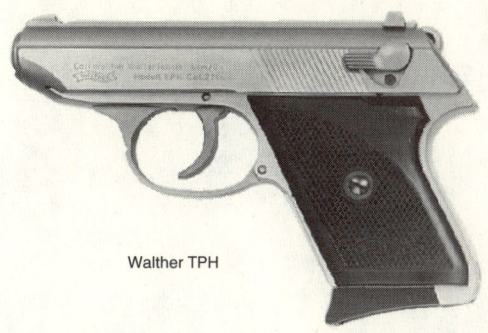

Walther TPH

WILKINSON "SHERRY" AUTO PISTOL
Caliber: 22 LR, 8-shot magazine.
Barrel: 2 1/8".
Weight: 9 1/4 oz. **Length:** 4 3/8" overall.
Stocks: Checkered black plastic.
Sights: Fixed, groove.
Features: Cross-bolt safety locks the sear into the hammer. Available in all blue finish or blue slide and trigger with gold frame. Introduced 1985.
Price: $195.00

WILDEY AUTOMATIC PISTOL
Caliber: 10mm Wildey Mag., 11mm Wildey Mag., 30 Wildey Mag., 357 Peterbuilt, 45 Win. Mag., 475 Wildey Mag., 7-shot magazine.
Barrel: 5", 6", 7", 8", 10", 12", 14" (45 Win. Mag.); 8", 10", 12", 14" (all other cals.). Interchangeable.
Weight: 64 oz. (5" barrel). **Length:** 11" overall (7" barrel).
Stocks: Hardwood.
Sights: Ramp front (interchangeable blades optional), fully adjustable rear. Scope base available.
Features: Gas-operated action. Made of stainless steel. Has three-lug rotary bolt. Double or single action. Polished and matte finish. Made in U.S. by Wildey, Inc.
Price: .... $1,175.00 to $1,495.00

WILKINSON "LINDA" AUTO PISTOL
Caliber: 9mm Para.
Barrel: 8 5/16".
Weight: 4 lbs., 13 oz. **Length:** 12 1/4" overall.
Stocks: Checkered black plastic pistol grip, walnut forend.
Sights: Protected blade front, aperture rear.
Features: Fires from closed bolt. Semi-auto only. Straight blowback action. Cross-bolt safety. Removable barrel. From Wilkinson Arms.
Price: $533.33

Wilkinson Sherry

HANDGUNS—COMPETITION HANDGUNS
Includes models suitable for several forms of competition and other sporting purposes.

AUTO-ORDNANCE 1911A1 COMPETITION MODEL
Caliber: 45 ACP.
Barrel: 5".
Weight: NA. **Length:** NA.
Stocks: Black textured rubber wrap-around.
Sights: Blade front, rear adjustable for windage; three-dot system.
Features: Machined compensator, combat Commander hammer; flat mainspring housing; low profile magazine funnel; metal form magazine bumper; high-ride beavertail grip safety; full-length recoil spring guide system; extended slide stop, safety and magazine catch; Videcki adjustable speed trigger; extended combat ejector. Introduced 1994. Made in U.S. by Auto-Ordnance Corp.
Price: $615.00

Auto-Ordnance Competition Model

CAUTION: PRICES SHOWN ARE SUPPLIED BY THE MANUFACTURER OR IMPORTER. CHECK YOUR LOCAL GUNSHOP.

HANDGUNS—COMPETITION HANDGUNS

Baer 1911 Ultimate Master

Baer 1911 Bullseye Wadcutter

Baer 1911 Target Master Pistol
Similar to the National Match Hardball except available in 45 ACP and other calibers, has Baer post-style dovetail front sight, flat serrated mainspring housing, standard trigger. Made in U.S. by Les Baer Custom, Inc.
Price: $1,233.00

Benelli MP95E

BF SINGLE SHOT PISTOL
Caliber: 22 LR, 357 Mag., 44 Mag., 7-30 Waters, 30-30 Win., 375 Win., 45-70; custom chamberings from 17 Rem. through 45-cal.
Barrel: 10", 10.75", 12", 15+".
Weight: 52 oz. **Length:** NA.
Stocks: Custom Herrett finger-groove grip and forend.
Sights: Undercut Patridge front, 1/2-MOA match-quality fully adjustable RPM Iron Sight rear; barrel or receiver mounting. Drilled and tapped for scope mounting.
Features: Rigid barrel/receiver; falling block action with short lock time; automatic ejection; air-gauged match barrels by Wilson or Douglas; matte black oxide finish standard, electroless nickel optional. Barrel has 11-degree recessed target crown. Introduced 1988. Made in U.S. by E.A. Brown Mfg.
Price: 10", no sights $499.95
Price: 10", RPM sights $564.95
Price: 10.75", no sights $529.95
Price: 10.75", RPM sights $594.95
Price: 12", no sights $562.95
Price: 12", RPM sights $643.75
Price: 15", no sights $592.95
Price: 15", RPM sights $675.00
Price: 10.75" Ultimate Silhouette (heavy barrel, special forend, RPM rear sight with hooded front, gold-plated trigger) $687.95

BAER 1911 ULTIMATE MASTER COMBAT PISTOL
Caliber: 45 ACP (others available), 10-shot magazine.
Barrel: 5"; Baer NM.
Weight: 37 oz. **Length:** 8.5" overall.
Stocks: Checkered rosewood.
Sights: Baer dovetail front, low-mount Bo-Mar rear with hidden leaf.
Features: Full-house competition gun. Baer forged NM blued steel frame and double serrated slide; Baer triple port, tapered cone compensator; fitted slide to frame; lowered, flared ejection port; Baer reverse recoil plug; full-length guide rod; recoil buff; beveled magazine well; Baer Commander hammer, sear; Baer extended ambidextrous safety, extended ejector, checkered slide stop, beavertail grip safety with pad, extended magazine release button; Baer speed trigger. Made in U.S. by Les Baer Custom, Inc.
Price: Compensated, open sights $1,996.00
Price: Uncompensated "Limited" Model $1,843.00
Price: Compensated, with Baer optics mount $2,360.00

Baer 1911 Ultimate Master "Steel Special" Pistol
Similar to the Ultimate Master except chambered for 38 Super with supported chamber (other calibers avaiaoble), lighter slide, bushing-type compensator; two-piece guide rod. Designed for maximum 150 power factor. Comes without sights—scope and mount only. Hard chrome finish. Made in U.S. by Les Baer Custom, Inc.
Price: $2,570.00

Baer 1911 Bullseye Wadcutter Pistol
Similar to the National Match Hardball except designed for wadcutter loads only. Has polished feed ramp and barrel throat; Bo-Mar rib on slide; full-length recoil rod; Baer speed trigger with 3½-lb. pull; Baer deluxe hammer and sear; Baer beavertail grip safety with pad; flat mainspring housing checkered 20 lpi. Blue finish; checkered walnut grips. Made in U.S. by Les Baer Custom, Inc.
Price: $1,347.00

BAER 1911 NATIONAL MATCH HARDBALL PISTOL
Caliber: 45 ACP, 7-shot magazine.
Barrel: 5".
Weight: 37 oz. **Length:** 8.5" overall.
Stocks: Checkered walnut.
Sights: Baer dovetail front with undercut post, low-mount Bo-Mar rear with hidden leaf.
Features: Baer NM forged steel frame, double serrated slide and barrel with stainless bushing; slide fitted to frame; Baer match trigger with 4-lb. pull; polished feed ramp, throated barrel; checkered front strap, arched mainspring housing; Baer beveled magazine well; lowered, flared ejection port; tuned extractor; Baer extended ejector, checkered slide stop; recoil buff. Made in U.S. by Les Baer Custom, Inc.
Price: $1,130.00

BENELLI MP95E MATCH PISTOL
Caliber: 22 LR, 10-shot magazine, or 32 S&W WC, 10-shot magazine.
Barrel: 4.33".
Weight: 38.8 oz. **Length:** 11.81" overall.
Stocks: Checkered walnut match type; anatomically shaped.
Sights: Match type. Blade front, click-adjustable rear for windage and elevation.
Features: Removable, adjustable trigger. Special internal weight box on sub-frame below barrel. Cut for scope rails. Introduced 1993. Imported from Italy by European American Armory.
Price: Blue $550.00
Price: Chrome $625.00
Price: MP90S (competition version of MP95E), 22 LR $1,295.00
Price: As above, 32 S&W $1,495.00

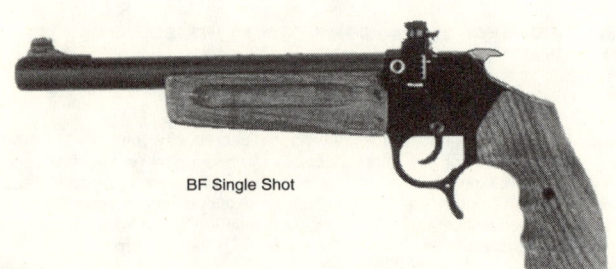

BF Single Shot

HANDGUNS—COMPETITION HANDGUNS

BERNARDELLI MODEL 69 TARGET PISTOL
Caliber: 22 LR, 10-shot magazine.
Barrel: 5.9".
Weight: 38 oz. **Length:** 9" overall.
Stocks: Wrap-around, hand-checkered walnut with thumbrest.
Sights: Fully adjustable and interchangeable target type.
Features: Conforms to U.I.T. regulations. Has 7.1" sight radius, .27" wide grooved trigger. Manual thumb safety and magazine safety. Introduced 1987. Imported from Italy by Armsport.
Price: $612.00

BERETTA MODEL 89 WOOD SPORT GOLD STANDARD PISTOL
Caliber: 22 LR, 8-shot magazine.
Barrel: 6"
Weight: 41 oz. **Length:** 9.5" overall.
Stocks: Target-type walnut with thumbrest.
Sights: Interchangeable blade front, fully adjustable rear.
Features: Single-action target pistol. Matte blue finish. Imported from Italy by Beretta U.S.A.
Price: $736.00

BROWNING BUCK MARK SILHOUETTE
Caliber: 22 LR, 10-shot magazine.
Barrel: 9 7/8".
Weight: 53 oz. **Length:** 14" overall.
Stocks: Smooth walnut stocks and forend, or finger-groove walnut.
Sights: Post-type hooded front adjustable for blade width and height; Pro Target rear fully adjustable for windage and elevation.
Features: Heavy barrel with .900" diameter; 12 1/2" sight radius. Special sighting plane forms scope base. Introduced 1987. Made in U.S. From Browning.
Price: $421.95

Browning Buck Mark Unlimited Match
Same as the Buck Mark Silhouette except has 14" heavy barrel. Conforms to IHMSA 15" maximum sight radius rule. Introduced 1991.
Price: $519.95

Browning Buck Mark Target 5.5
Same as the Buck Mark Silhouette except has a 5 1/2" barrel with .900" diameter. Has hooded sights mounted on a scope base that accepts an optical or reflex sight. Rear sight is a Browning fully adjustable Pro Target, front sight is an adjustable post that customizes to different widths, and can be adjusted for height. Contoured walnut grips with thumbrest, or finger-groove walnut. Matte blue finish. Overall length is 9 5/8", weight is 35 1/2 oz. Has 10-shot magazine. Introduced 1990. From Browning.
Price: $399.95
Price: Target 5.5 Gold (as above with gold anodized frame and top rib) $449.95
Price: Target 5.5 Nickel (as above with nickel frame and top rib) $449.95

COLT GOLD CUP NATIONAL MATCH MK IV/SERIES 80
Caliber: 45 ACP, 8-shot magazine.
Barrel: 5", with new design bushing.
Weight: 39 oz. **Length:** 8 1/2".
Stocks: Checkered rubber composite with silver-plated medallion.
Sights: Patridge-style front, Colt-Elliason rear adjustable for windage and elevation, sight radius 6 3/4".
Features: Arched or flat housing; wide, grooved trigger with adjustable stop; ribbed-top slide, hand fitted, with improved ejection port.
Price: Blue $937.00
Price: Stainless $1,003.00
Price: Bright stainless $1,073.00
Price: Delta Gold Cup (10mm, stainless) $1,027.00

Beretta Model 89

Browning Buck Mark Target 5.5

Browning Buck Mark Field 5.5
Same as the Target 5.5 except has hoodless ramp-style front sight and low profile rear sight. Matte blue finish, contoured or finger-groove walnut stocks. Introduced 1991.
Price: $399.95

Consult our Directory pages for the location of firms mentioned.

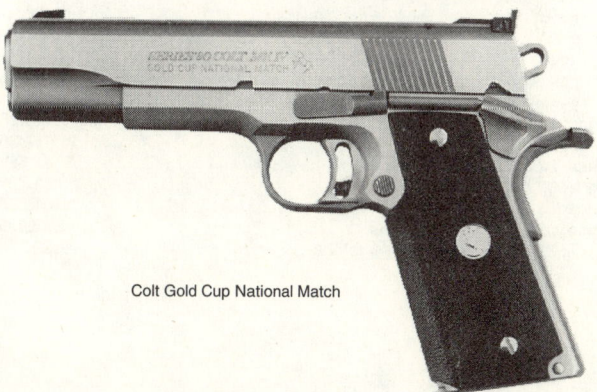
Colt Gold Cup National Match

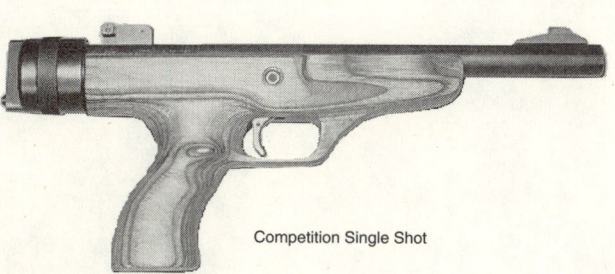
Competition Single Shot

COMPETITOR SINGLE SHOT PISTOL
Caliber: 22 LR through 50 Action Express, including belted magnums.
Barrel: 14" standard; 10.5" silhouette; 16" optional.
Weight: About 59 oz. (14" bbl.). **Length:** 15.12" overall.
Stocks: Ambidextrous; synthetic (standard) or laminated or natural wood.
x**Sights:** Ramp front, adjustable rear.
Features: Rotary canon-type action cocks on opening; cammed ejector; interchangeable barrels, ejectors. Adjustable single stage trigger, sliding thumb safety and trigger safety. Matte blue finish. Introduced 1988. From Competitor Corp., Inc.
Price: 14", standard calibers, synthetic grip $379.90
Price: Extra barrels, from $132.95

HANDGUNS—COMPETITION HANDGUNS

E.A.A. WITNESS GOLD TEAM AUTO
Caliber: 9mm Para., 9x21, 38 Super, 40 S&W, 45 ACP.
Barrel: 5.1".
Weight: 41.6 oz. **Length:** 9.6" overall.
Stocks: Checkered walnut, competition style.
Sights: Square post front, fully adjustable rear.
Features: Triple-chamber cone compensator; competition SA trigger; extended safety and magazine release; competition hammer; beveled magazine well; beavertail grip. Hand-fitted major components. Hard chrome finish. Match-grade barrel. From E.A.A. Custom Shop. Introduced 1992. From European American Armory.
Price: $2,195.00

E.A.A. Witness Gold Team

E.A.A. Witness Silver Team Auto
Similar to the Wittness Gold Team except has double-chamber compensator, oval magazine release, black rubber grips, double-dip blue finish. Comes with Super Sight and drilled and tapped for scope mount. Built for the intermediate competition shooter. Introduced 1992. From European American Armory Custom Shop.
Price: 9mm Para., 9x21, 38 Super, 40 S&W, 45 ACP $975.00

E.A.A. WINDICATOR TARGET GRADE REVOLVERS
Caliber: 22 LR, 8-shot, 38 Special, 357 Mag., 6-shot.
Barrel: 6".
Weight: 50.2 oz. **Length:** 11.8" overall.
Stocks: Walnut, competition style.
Sights: Blade front with three interchangeable blades, fully adjustable rear.
Features: Adjustable trigger with trigger stop and trigger shoe; frame drilled and tapped for scope mount; target hammer. Comes with barrel weights, plastic carrying box. Introduced 1991. Imported from Germany by European American Armory.
Price: $299.00

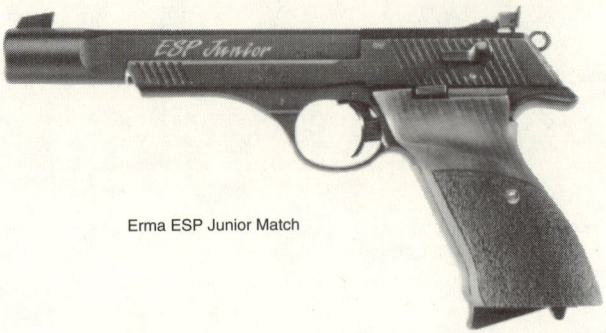

Erma ESP Junior Match

ERMA ER MATCH REVOLVER
Caliber: 32 S&W Long, 6-shot.
Barrel: 6".
Weight: 47.3 oz. **Length:** 11.2" overall.
Stocks: Stippled walnut, adjustable match-type.
Sights: Blade front, micrometer rear adjustable for windage and elevation.
Features: Polished blue finish. Introduced 1989. Imported from Germany by Precision Sales International.
Price: 32 S&W Long $1,248.00

ERMA ESP 85A MATCH PISTOL
Caliber: 22 LR, 6-shot; 32 S&W, 6-shot magazine.
Barrel: 6".
Weight: 39 oz. **Length:** 10" overall.
Stocks: Match-type of stippled walnut; adjustable.
Sights: Interchangeable blade front, micrometer adjustable rear with interchangeable leaf.
Features: Five-way adjustable trigger; exposed hammer and separate firing pin block allow unlimited dry firing practice. Blue or matte chrome; right- or left-hand. Introduced 1989. Imported from Germany by Precision Sales International.
Price: 22 LR $1,695.00
Price: 22 LR, left-hand $1,735.00
Price: 22 LR, matte chrome $1,890.00
Price: 32 S&W $1,790.00
Price: 32 S&W, left-hand $1,830.00
Price: 32 S&W, matte chrome $2,095.00
Price: 32 S&W, matte chrome, left-hand $2,135.00

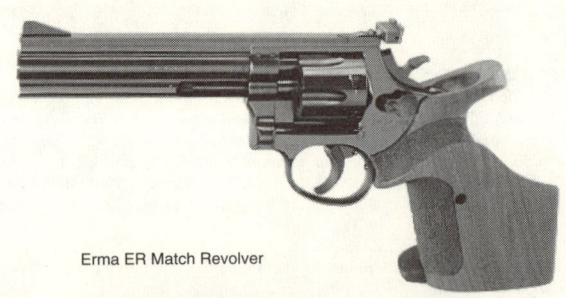

Erma ER Match Revolver

Erma ESP Junior Match Pistol
Similar to the ESP 85A Match except chambered only for 22 LR, blue finish only. Stippled non-adjustable walnut match grips (adjustable grips optional). Introduced 1995. Imported from Germany by Precision Sales International.
Price: $1,295.00

FAS 607 MATCH PISTOL
Caliber: 22 LR, 5-shot.
Barrel: 5.6".
Weight: 37 oz. **Length:** 11" overall.
Stocks: Walnut wraparound; sizes small, medium or large, or adjustable.
Sights: Match. Blade front, open notch rear fully adjustable for windage and elevation. Sight radius is 8.66".
Features: Line of sight is only 11/32" above centerline of bore; magazine is inserted from top; adjustable and removable trigger mechanism; single lever takedown. Full 5-year warranty. Imported from Italy by Nygord Precision Products.
Price: $1,175.00
Price: Model 603 (32 S&W) $1,175.00

FAS 601 Match Pistol
Similar to Model 607 except has different match stocks with adjustable palm shelf, 22 Short only for rapid fire shooting; weighs 40 oz., 5.6" bbl.; has gas ports through top of barrel and slide to reduce recoil; slightly different trigger and sear mechanisms. Imported from Italy by Nygord Precision Products.
Price: $1,250.00

FAS 607 Match

HANDGUNS—COMPETITION HANDGUNS

FREEDOM ARMS CASULL MODEL 252 SILHOUETTE
Caliber: 22 LR, 5-shot cylinder.
Barrel: 9.95".
Weight: 63 oz. **Length:** NA
Stocks: Black micarta, western style.
Sights: 1/8" Patridge front, Iron Sight Gun Works silhouette rear, click adjustable for windage and elevation.
Features: Stainless steel. Built on the 454 Casull frame. Two-point firing pin, lightened hammer for fast lock time. Trigger pull is 3 to 5 lbs. with pre-set overtravel screw. Introduced 1991. From Freedom Arms.
Price: Silhouette Class $1,432.00
Price: Extra fitted 22 WMR cylinder $247.00

Freedom Arms Casull Model 252 Varmint
Similar to the Silhouette Class revolver except has 7.5" barrel, weighs 59 oz., has black and green laminated hardwood grips, and comes with brass bead front sight, express shallow V rear sight with windage and elevation adjustments. Introduced 1991. From Freedom Arms.
Price: Varmint Class $1,384.00
Price: Extra fitted 22 WMR cylinder $247.00

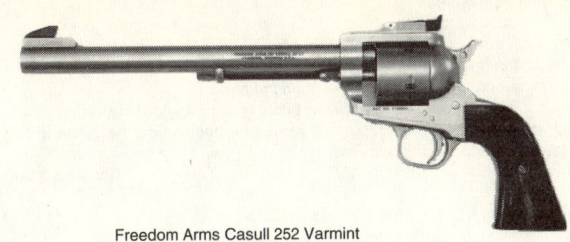
Freedom Arms Casull 252 Varmint

GLOCK 17L COMPETITION AUTO
Caliber: 9mm Para., 10-shot magazine.
Barrel: 6.02".
Weight: 23.3 oz. **Length:** 8.85" overall.
Stocks: Black polymer.
Sights: Blade front with white dot, fixed or adjustable rear.
Features: Polymer frame, steel slide; double-action trigger with "Safe Action" system; mechanical firing pin safety, drop safety; simple takedown without tools; locked breech, recoil operated action. Introduced 1989. Imported from Austria by Glock, Inc.
Price: $806.67

GLOCK 24 COMPETITION MODEL PISTOL
Caliber: 40 S&W, 10-shot magazine.
Barrel: 6.02".
Weight: 29.5 oz. **Length:** 8.85" overall.
Stocks: Black polymer.
Sights: Blade front with dot, white outline rear adjustable for windage.
Features: Long-slide competition model available as compensated or non-compensated gun. Factory-installed competition trigger; drop-free magazine. Introduced 1994. Imported from Austria by Glock, Inc.
Price: $806.67

GAUCHER GP SILHOUETTE PISTOL
Caliber: 22 LR, single shot.
Barrel: 10".
Weight: 42.3 oz. **Length:** 15.5" overall.
Stocks: Stained hardwood.
Sights: Hooded post on ramp front, open rear adjustable for windage and elevation.
Features: Matte chrome barrel, blued bolt and sights. Other barrel lengths available on special order. Introduced 1991. Imported by Mandall Shooting Supplies.
Price: $425.00

Glock 24 Competition

HAMMERLI MODEL 160/162 FREE PISTOLS
Caliber: 22 LR, single shot.
Barrel: 11.30".
Weight: 46.94 oz. **Length:** 17.52" overall.
Stocks: Walnut; full match style with adjustable palm shelf. Stippled surfaces.
Sights: Changeable blade front, open, fully adjustable match rear.
Features: Model 160 has mechanical set trigger; Model 162 has electronic trigger; both fully adjustable with provisions for dry firing. Introduced 1993. Imported from Switzerland by Hammerli Pistols USA.
Price: Model 160, about $2,034.00
Price: Model 162, about $2,189.00

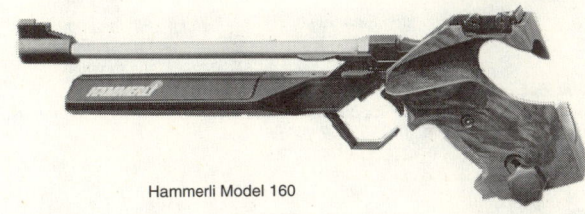
Hammerli Model 160

HAMMERLI MODEL 208s PISTOL
Caliber: 22 LR, 8-shot magazine.
Barrel: 5.9".
Weight: 37.5 oz. **Length:** 10" overall.
Stocks: Walnut, target-type with thumbrest.
Sights: Blade front, open fully adjustable rear.
Features: Adjustable trigger, including length; interchangeable rear sight elements. Imported from Switzerland by Hammerli Pistols USA, Mandall Shooting Supplies.
Price: About $1,768.00

Hammerli Model 208s

HAMMERLI MODEL 280 TARGET PISTOL
Caliber: 22 LR, 6-shot; 32 S&W Long WC, 5-shot.
Barrel: 4.5".
Weight: 39.1 oz. (32). **Length:** 11.8" overall.
Stocks: Walnut match-type with stippling, adjustable palm shelf.
Sights: Match sights, micrometer adjustable; interchangeable elements.
Features: Has carbon-reinforced synthetic frame and bolt/barrel housing. Trigger is adjustable for pull weight, take-up weight, let-off, and length, and is interchangeable. Interchangeable metal or carbon fiber counterweights. Sight radius of 8.8". Comes with barrel weights, spare magazine, loading tool, cleaning rods. Introduced 1990. Imported from Switzerland by Hammerli Pistols USA and Mandall Shooting Supplies.
Price: 22-cal., about $1,558.00
Price: 32-cal., about $1,747.00

Hammerli Model 280

CAUTION: PRICES SHOWN ARE SUPPLIED BY THE MANUFACTURER OR IMPORTER. CHECK YOUR LOCAL GUNSHOP.

HANDGUNS—COMPETITION HANDGUNS

HARRIS-McMILLAN SIGNATURE JR. LONG RANGE PISTOL
Caliber: Any suitable caliber.
Barrel: To customer specs.
Weight: 5 lbs.
Stock: McMillan fiberglass.
Sights: None furnished; comes with scope rings.
Features: Right- or left-hand McMillan benchrest action of titanium or stainless steel; single shot or repeater. Comes with bipod. Introduced 1992. Made in U.S. by Harris-McMillan Gunworks, Inc.
Price: $2,400.00

HIGH STANDARD OLYMPIC ISU PISTOL
Caliber: 22 Short, 5-shot magazine.
Barrel: 6.75"; tapered with integral stabilizer; push-button takedown.
Weight: 45 oz. **Length:** 10.75" overall.
Stocks: Checkered walnut.
Sights: Undercut ramp front, micro-click rear adjustable for windage and elevation.
Features: Adjustable trigger and sear; stippled front grip and backstrap. Comes with weights and brackets. Reintroduced 1994. From High Standard Mfg. Co., Inc.
Price: $625.00

High Standard Olympic Military Target Pistol
Same as the Olympic ISU model except has 5.50" bull barrel with removable stabilizer. High strength aluminum slide, carbon steel frame. Barrel weights and brackets included. Adjustable trigger and sear. Overall blue finish. Reintroduced 1994. From High Standard Mfg. Co., Inc.
Price: $504.00

HIGH STANDARD SUPERMATIC TOURNAMENT PISTOL
Caliber: 22 LR, 10-shot magazine.
Barrel: 4.5", 5.5"; push-button takedown.
Weight: 43 oz. **Length:** 8.5" overall.
Stocks: Black rubber; ambidextrous.
Sights: Undercut ramp front, micro-click rear adjustable for windage and elevation.
Features: Slide-mounted rear sight; 5.5" barrel drilled and tapped for scope mount. Blue finish. Reintroduced 1994. From High Standard Mfg. Co., Inc.
Price: $425.00

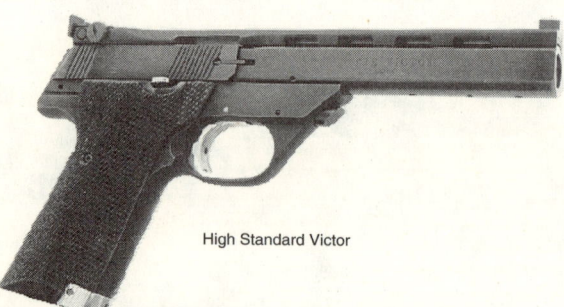

High Standard Victor

HIGH STANDARD 10X MODEL TARGET PISTOL
Caliber: 22 LR, 10-shot magazine.
Barrel: 5.5"; push-button takedown.
Weight: 44 oz. **Length:** 9.5" overall.
Stocks: Checkered black epoxied walnut; ambidextrous.
Sights: Undercut ramp front, micro-click rear adjustable for windage and elevation.
Features: Hand built with select parts. Adjustable trigger and sear; Parkerized finish; stippled front grip and backstrap. Barrel weights optional. Comes with test target, extended warranty. Reintroduced 1994. From High Standard Mfg. Co., Inc.
Price: $790.00

HIGH STANDARD SUPERMATIC TROPHY PISTOL
Caliber: 22 LR, 10-shot magazine.
Barrel: 5.5" or 7.25"; push-button takedown; drilled and tapped for scope mount.
Weight: 44 oz. **Length:** 9.5" overall.
Stocks: Checkered walnut with thumbrest.
Sights: Undercut ramp front, micro-click rear adjustable for windage and elevation.
Features: Removable muzzle stabilizer; gold-plated trigger, slide lock, safety-lever and magazine release; stippled front grip and backstrap; adjustable trigger and sear. Barrel weights optional. A 22 Short version is available. Reintroduced 1994. From High Standard Mfg. Co., Inc.
Price: $536.00

HARRIS-McMILLAN WOLVERINE AUTO PISTOL
Caliber: 9mm Para., 10mm Auto, 38 Wadcutter, 38 Super, 45 Italian, 45 ACP.
Barrel: 6".
Weight: 45 oz. **Length:** 9.5" overall.
Stocks: Pachmayr rubber.
Sights: Blade front, fully adjustable rear; low profile.
Features: Integral compensator; round burr-style hammer; extended grip safety; checkered backstrap; skeletonized aluminum match trigger. Many finish options. Announced 1992. Made in U.S. by Harris-McMillan Gunworks, Inc.
Price: Combat or Competition Match $1,700.00

High Standard Olympic ISU

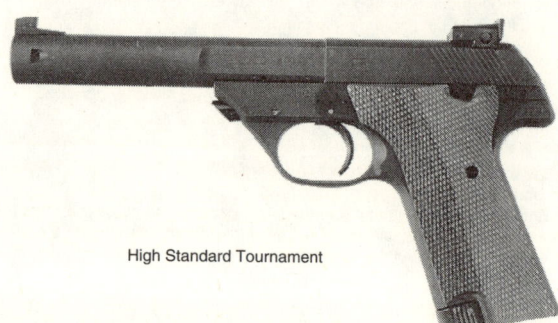

High Standard Tournament

HIGH STANDARD VICTOR TARGET PISTOL
Caliber: 22 LR, 10-shot magazine.
Barrel: 4.5" or 5.5"; push-button takedown.
Weight: 46 oz. **Length:** 9.5" overall.
Stocks: Checkered walnut with thumbrest.
Sights: Undercut ramp front, micro-click rear adjustable for windage and elevation.
Features: Full-length aluminum vent rib (steel optional). Gold-plated trigger, slide lock, safety-lever and magazine release; stippled front grip and backstrap; adjustable trigger and sear. Comes with barrel weight. Blue or Parkerized finish. Reintroduced 1994. From High Standard Mfg. Co., Inc.
Price: $532.00

High Standard Supermatic Trophy

High Standard Supermatic Citation Pistol
Same as the Supermatic Trophy except has nickel-plated trigger, slide lock, safety lever, magazine release, and has slightly heavier trigger pull. Has stippled front-grip and backstrap, checkered walnut thumbrest grips, adjustable trigger and sear. Blue finish. Conversion unit for 22 Short available. Reintroduced 1994. From High Standard Mfg. Co., Inc.
Price: $425.00

HANDGUNS—COMPETITION HANDGUNS

MITCHELL ARMS SHARPSHOOTER II PISTOL
Caliber: 22 LR, 10-shot magazine.
Barrel: 5.5" bull.
Weight: 45 oz. **Length:** 10.25" overall.
Stocks: Checkered walnut.
Sights: Ramp front, slide-mounted square notch rear adjustable for windage and elevation.
Features: Military grip. Slide lock; smooth grip straps; push-button takedown; drilled and tapped for barrel weights. Introduced 1992. From Mitchell Arms, Inc.
Price: Stainless steel, blue or combo $395.00

MITCHELL ARMS TROPHY II PISTOL
Caliber: 22 LR, 10-shot magazine.
Barrel: 5.5" bull, 7.25" fluted.
Weight: 44.5 oz. **Length:** 9.75" overall (5.5" barrel).
Stocks: Checkered walnut with thumbrest.
Sights: Undercut ramp front, click-adjsutable frame-mounted rear.
Features: Grip duplicates feel of military 45; positive action magazine latch; front and rear straps stippled. Trigger adjustable for pull, over-travel; gold-filled roll marks, gold-plated trigger, safety, magazine release; push-button barrel takedown. Introduced 1992. From Mitchell Arms, Inc.
Price: Stainless steel or blue $498.00

MITCHELL ARMS OLYMPIC II I.S.U. AUTO PISTOL
Caliber: 22 Short, 22 LR, 10-shot magazine.
Barrel: 6.75" round tapered, with stabilizer.
Weight: 40 oz. **Length:** 11.25" overall.
Stocks: Checkered walnut with thumbrest.
Sights: Undercut ramp front, frame-mounted click adjustable square notch rear.
Features: Integral stabilizer with two removable weights. Trigger adjustable for pull and over-travel; blue finish or stainless or combo; stippled front and backstraps; push-button barrel takedown. Announced 1992. From Mitchell Arms.
Price: $599.00

MITCHELL VICTOR II AUTO PISTOL
Caliber: 22 LR, 10-shot magazine.
Barrel: 4.5" vent rib, 5.5" vent, dovetail or Weaver ribs.
Weight: 44 oz. **Length:** 9.75" overall.
Stocks: Military-type checkered walnut with thumbrest.
Sights: Blade front, fully adjustable rear mounted on rib.
Features: Push-button takedown for barrel interchangeability. Bright stainless steel combo or royal blue finish. Introduced 1994. Made in U.S. From Mitchell Arms.
Price: Vent rib, 4.5" barrel $595.00
Price: Dovetail rib, 5.5" barrel $650.00
Price: Weaver rib, 5.5" barrel $675.00
Price: Dual color $675.00

MORINI MODEL 84E FREE PISTOL
Caliber: 22 LR, single shot.
Barrel: 11.4".
Weight: 43.7 oz. **Length:** 19.4" overall.
Stocks: Adjustable match type with stippled surfaces.
Sights: Interchangeable blade front, match-type fully adjustable rear.
Features: Fully adjustable electronic trigger. Introduced 1995. Imported from Switzerland by Nygord Precision Products.
Price: $1,495.00

PARDINI MODEL SP, HP TARGET PISTOLS
Caliber: 22 LR, 32 S&W, 5-shot magazine.
Barrel: 4.7".
Weight: 38.9 oz. **Length:** 11.6" overall.
Stocks: Adjustable; stippled walnut; match type.
Sights: Interchangeable blade front, interchangeable, fully adjustable rear.
Features: Fully adjustable match trigger. Introduced 1995. Imported from Italy by Nygord Precision Products.
Price: Model SP (22 LR) $950.00
Price: Model HP (32 S&W) $1,095.00

RUGER MARK II TARGET MODEL AUTO PISTOL
Caliber: 22 LR, 10-shot magazine.
Barrel: 5 1/2", 6 7/8".
Weight: 42 oz. **Length:** 11 1/8" overall.
Stocks: Checkered hard plastic.
Sights: .125" blade front, micro-click rear, adjustable for windage and elevation. Sight radius 9 3/8".
Features: Introduced 1982.
Price: Blued (MK-514, MK-678) $310.50
Price: Stainless (KMK-514, KMK-678) $389.00

Mitchell Sharpshooter II

Mitchell Arms Citation II Pistol
Same as the Trophy II except has nickel-plated trigger, safety and magazine release, and has silver-filled roll marks. Available in satin finish stainless steel or blue. Introduced 1992. From Mitchell Arms, Inc.
Price: $489.00

Mitchell Olympic II I.S.U.

Mitchell Victor II

PARDINI GP RAPID FIRE MATCH PISTOL
Caliber: 22 Short, 5-shot magazine.
Barrel: 4.6".
Weight: 43.3 oz. **Length:** 11.6" overall.
Stocks: Wrap-around stippled walnut.
Sights: Interchangeable post front, fully adjustable match rear.
Features: Model GP Schuman has extended rear sight for longer sight radius. Introduced 1995. Imported from Italy by Nygord Precision Products.
Price: Model GP $995.00
Price: Model GP Schuman $1,395.00

PARDINI K50 FREE PISTOL
Caliber: 22 LR, single shot.
Barrel: 9.8".
Weight: 34.6 oz. **Length:** 18.7" overall.
Stocks: Wrap-around walnut; adjustable match type.
Sights: Interchangeable post front, fully adjustable match open rear.
Features: Removable, adjustable match trigger. Barrel weights mount above the barrel. Introduced 1995. Imported from Italy by Nygord Precision Products.
Price: $995.00

Ruger Mark II Bull Barrel
Same gun as the Target Model except has 5 1/2" or 10" heavy barrel (10" meets all IHMSA regulations). Weight with 5 1/2" barrel is 42 oz., with 10" barrel, 51 oz.
Price: Blued (MK-512) $310.50
Price: Blued (MK-10) $294.50
Price: Stainless (KMK-10) $373.00
Price: Stainless (KMK-512) $389.00

HANDGUNS—COMPETITION HANDGUNS

Ruger Government Target

Ruger Mark II Government Target Model
Same gun as the Mark II Target Model except has 6 7/8" barrel, higher sights and is roll marked "Government Target Model" on the right side of the receiver below the rear sight. Identical in all aspects to the military model used for training U.S. armed forces except for markings. Comes with factory test target. Introduced 1987.
Price: Blued (MK-678G) $356.50
Price: Stainless (KMK-678G) $427.25

Ruger Stainless Government Competition Model 22 Pistol
Similar to the Mark II Government Target Model stainless pistol except has 6 7/8" slab-sided barrel; the receiver top is drilled and tapped for a Ruger scope base adaptor of blued, chrome moly steel; comes with Ruger 1" stainless scope rings with integral bases for mounting a variety of optical sights; has checkered laminated grip panels with right-hand thumbrest. Has blued open sights with 9 1/4" radius. Overall length is 11 1/8", weight 45 oz. Introduced 1991.
Price: KMK-678GC $441.00

SCHUETZEN PISTOL WORKS MATCHMASTER PISTOL
Caliber: 45 ACP, 7-shot magazine.
Barrel: 5", 6"; stainless steel.
Weight: 38 oz. **Length:** 8.5" overall.
Stocks: Smooth walnut with etched scorpion logo.
Sights: Ramped blade front, LPA adjustable rear.
Features: Beavertail grip safety, extended safety, extended slide release, Commander-style hammer; throated, polished, tuned. Finishes: Parkerized matte black, or satin stainless steel. Made in U.S. by Olympic Arms, Inc.
Price: $770.00

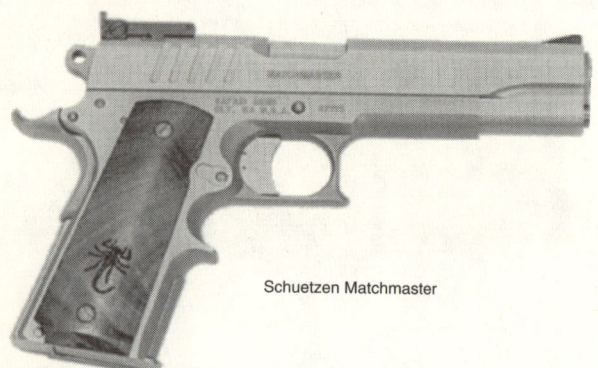

Schuetzen Matchmaster

Schuetzen Pistol Works Matchmaster Carrycomp I
Similar to the Matchmaster except has Wil Schueman-designed hybrid compensator system. Introduced 1993. Made in U.S. by Olympic Arms, Inc.
Price: $1,275.00

SMITH & WESSON MODEL 41 TARGET
Caliber: 22 LR, 10-shot clip.
Barrel: 5 1/2", 7".
Weight: 44 oz. (5 1/2" barrel). **Length:** 9" overall (5 1/2" barrel).
Stocks: Checkered walnut with modified thumbrest, usable with either hand.
Sights: 1/8" Patridge on ramp base; micro-click rear adjustable for windage and elevation.
Features: 3/8" wide, grooved trigger; adjustable trigger stop.
Price: S&W Bright Blue, either barrel $753.00

Sphinx AT-2000c Competitor

Smith & Wesson Model 41

SPHINX AT-2000C COMPETITOR PISTOL
Caliber: 9mm Para., 9x21mm, 40 S&W, 10-shot.
Barrel: 5.31".
Weight: 40.56 oz. **Length:** 9.84" overall.
Stocks: Checkered neoprene.
Sights: Fully adjustable Bo-Mar or Tasco Pro-Point dot sight in Sphinx mount.
Features: Extended magazine release. Competition slide with dual-port compensated barrel. Two-tone finish only. Introduced 1993. Imported from Switzerland by Sphinx U.S.A., Inc.
Price: With Bo-Mar sights (AT-2000CS) $1,902.00
Price: With Tasco Pro-Point and mount $2,189.00

Sphinx AT-2000GM Grand Master Pistol
Similar to the AT-2000C except has single-action-only trigger mechanism, squared trigger guard, extended beavertail grip, safety and magazine release; notched competition slide for easier cocking. Two-tone finish only. Has dual-port compensated barrel. Available with fully adjustable Bo-Mar sights or Tasco Pro-Point and Sphinx mount. Introduced 1993. Imported from Switzerland by Sphinx U.S.A., Inc.
Price: With Bo-Mar sights (AT-2000GMS) $2,894.00
Price: With Tasco Pro-Point and mount (AT-2000GM) ...$2,972.00

Sphinx AT-2000 GM Grand Master

HANDGUNS—COMPETITION HANDGUNS

SPRINGFIELD INC. 1911A1 BULLSEYE WADCUTTER PISTOL
Caliber: 45 ACP.
Barrel: 5".
Weight: 45 oz. **Length:** 8.59" overall (5" barrel).
Stocks: Checkered walnut.
Sights: Bo-Mar rib with undercut blade front, fully adjustable rear.
Features: Built for wadcutter loads only. Has full-length recoil spring guide rod, fitted Videki speed trigger with 3.5-lb. pull; match Commander hammer and sear; beavertail grip safety; lowered and flared ejection port; tuned extractor; fitted slide to frame; recoil buffer system; beveled and polished magazine well; checkered front strap and steel mainspring housing (flat housing standard); polished and throated National Match barrel and bushing. Comes with two magazines with slam pads, plastic carrying case, test target. Introduced 1992. From Springfield Inc.
Price: $1,665.00

Springfield 1911A1 Trophy Match

Springfield Inc. Expert Pistol
Similar to the 1911A1 Trophy Master Competition Pistol except has triple-chamber tapered cone compensator on match barrel with dovetailed front sight; lowered and flared ejection port; fully tuned for reliability. Comes with two magazines, plastic carrying case. Introduced 1992. From Springfield Inc.
Price: 45 ACP, Duotone finish $1,915.00
Price: Trophy Master Expert Ltd. $1,804.00

> Consult our Directory pages for the location of firms mentioned.

Springfield Inc. Basic Competition Pistol
Has low-mounted Bo-Mar adjustable rear sight, undercut blade front; match throated barrel and bushing; polished feed ramp; lowered and flared ejection port; fitted Videki speed trigger with tuned 3.5-lb. pull; fitted slide to frame; recoil buffer system; Pachmayr mainspring housing; Pachmayr grips. Comes with two magazines with slam pads, plastic carrying case. Introduced 1992. From Springfield Inc.
Price: 45 ACP, blue, 5" only $1,439.00

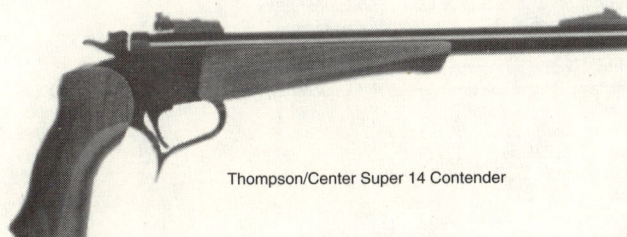
Thompson/Center Super 14 Contender

UNIQUE D.E.S. 32U TARGET PISTOL
Caliber: 32 S&W Long wadcutter.
Barrel: 5.9".
Weight: 40.2 oz.
Stocks: Anatomically shaped, adjustable stippled French walnut.
Sights: Blade front, micrometer click rear.
Features: Trigger adjustable for weight and position; dry firing mechanism; slide stop catch. Optional sleeve weights. Introduced 1990. Imported from France by Nygord Precision Products.
Price: Right-hand, about $1,350.00
Price: Left-hand, about $1,380.00

Springfield Inc. Competition Pistol
Similar to the 1911A1 Entry Level Wadcutter Pistol except has brazed, serrated improved ramp front sight; extended ambidextrous thumb safety; match Commander hammer and sear; serrated rear slide; Pachmay flat mainspring housing; extended magazine release; beavertail grip safety; full-length recoil spring guide; Pachmayr wrap-around grips. Comes with two magazines with slam pads, plastic carrying case. Introduced 1992. From Springfield Inc.
Price: 45 ACP, blue $1,598.00

Springfield Inc. 1911A1 N.M. Hardball Pistol
Has Bo-Mar adjustable rear sight with undercut front blade; fitted match Videki trigger with 4-lb. pull; fitted slide to frame; throated National Match barrel and bushing, polished feed ramp; recoil buffer system; tuned extractor; Herrett walnut grips. Comes with two magazines, plastic carrying case, test target. Introduced 1992. From Springfield Inc.
Price: 45 ACP, blue $1,485.00

Springfield Inc. 1911A1 Trophy Match Pistol
Similar to the 1911A1 except factory accurized, has 4- to 5½-lb. trigger pull, click adjustable rear sight, match-grade barrel and bushing. Comes with checkered walnut grips. Introduced 1994. From Springfield, Inc.
Price: Blue $919.00
Price: Stainless steel $951.00

Springfield Inc. Distinguished Pistol
Has all the features of the 1911A1 Trophy Master Expert except is full-house pistol with Bo-Mar low-mounted adjustable rear sight; full-length recoil spring guide rod and recoil spring retainer; beveled and polished magazine well; walnut grips. Hard chrome finish. Comes with two magazines with slam pads, plastic carrying case. From Springfield Inc.
Price: 45 ACP $2,717.00
Price: Distinguished Limited $2,606.00

THOMPSON/CENTER SUPER 14 CONTENDER
Caliber: 22 LR, 222 Rem., 223 Rem., 7mm TCU, 7-30 Waters, 30-30 Win., 35 Rem., 357 Rem. Maximum, 44 Mag., 10mm Auto, 445 Super Mag., single shot.
Barrel: 14".
Weight: 45 oz. **Length:** 17¼" overall.
Stocks: T/C "Competitor Grip" (walnut and rubber).
Sights: Fully adjustable target-type.
Features: Break-open action with auto safety. Interchangeable barrels for both rimfire and centerfire calibers. Introduced 1978.
Price: Blued $460.00
Price: Stainless steel $490.00
Price: Extra barrels, blued $217.50
Price: Extra barrels, stainless steel $232.50

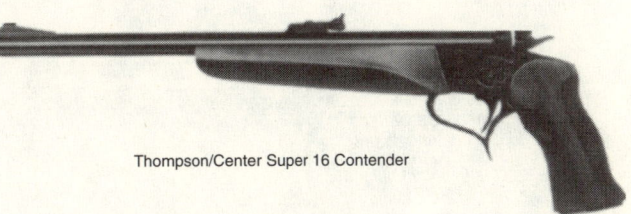
Thompson/Center Super 16 Contender

Thompson/Center Super 16 Contender
Same as the T/C Super 14 Contender except has 16¼" barrel. Rear sight can be mounted at mid-barrel position (10¾" radius) or moved to the rear (using scope mount position) for 14¾" radius. Overall length is 20¼". Comes with T/C Competitor Grip of walnut and rubber. Available in 22 LR, 22 WMR, 223 Rem., 7-30 Waters, 30-30 Win., 35 Rem., 44 Mag., 45-70 Gov't. Also available with 16" vent rib barrel with internal choke, caliber 45 Colt/410 shotshell.
Price: Blue $465.00
Price: Stainless steel $495.00
Price: 45-70 Gov't., blue $470.00
Price: As above, stainless steel $515.00
Price: Super 16 Vent Rib, 45-70, blued $495.00
Price: As above, stainless steel $525.00
Price: Extra 16" barrel, blued $222.50
Price: As above, stainless steel $237.50
Price: Extra 45-70 barrel, blued $227.50
Price: As above, stainless steel $257.50
Price: Extra Super 16 vent rib barrel, blue $252.50
Price: As above, stainless steel $257.50

HANDGUNS—COMPETITION HANDGUNS

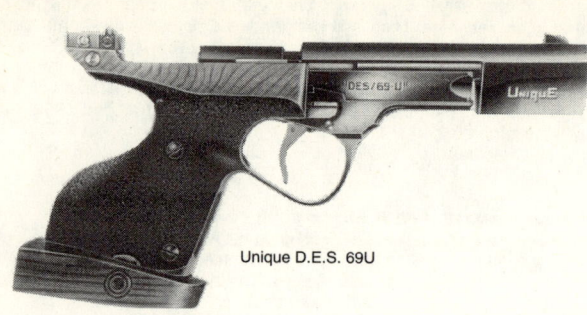

Unique D.E.S. 69U

WESSON FIREARMS MODEL 40 SILHOUETTE
Caliber: 357 Maximum, 6-shot.
Barrel: 4", 6", 8", 10".
Weight: 64 oz. (8" bbl.). **Length:** 14.3" overall (8" bbl.).
Stocks: Smooth walnut, target-style.
Sights: 1/8" serrated front, fully adjustable rear.
Features: Meets criteria for IHMSA competition with 8" slotted barrel. Blue or stainless steel. Made in U.S. by Wesson Firearms Co., Inc.
Price: Blue, 4"...$502.00
Price: Blue, 6"...$544.00
Price: Blue, 8"...$567.00
Price: Blue, 10"...$597.00
Price: Stainless, 4"...$567.00
Price: Stainless, 6"...$610.00
Price: Stainless, 8" slotted..................................$645.00
Price: Stainless, 10"...$671.00

Wesson Firearms Model 445 Supermag Revolver
Similar size and weight as the Model 40 revolvers. Chambered for the 445 Supermag cartridge, a longer version of the 44 Magnum. Barrel lengths of 4", 6", 8", 10". Contact maker for complete price list. Introduced 1989. From Wesson Firearms Co., Inc.
Price: 4", vent heavy, blue....................................$542.00
Price: As above, stainless.....................................$621.00
Price: 8", vent heavy, blue....................................$597.00
Price: As above, stainless.....................................$665.00
Price: 10", vent heavy, blue..................................$619.00
Price: As above, stainless.....................................$687.00
Price: 8", vent slotted, blue..................................$577.00
Price: As above, stainless.....................................$636.00
Price: 10", vent slotted, blue................................$601.00
Price: As above, stainless.....................................$661.00

Wesson Firearms 45 Pin Gun

WESSON FIREARMS MODEL 22 SILHOUETTE REVOLVER
Caliber: 22 LR, 6-shot.
Barrel: 10", regular vent or vent heavy.
Weight: 53 oz.
Stocks: Combat style.
Sights: Patridge-style front, .080" narrow notch rear.
Features: Single action only. Available in blue or stainless. Introduced 1989. From Wesson Firearms Co., Inc.
Price: Blue, regular vent......................................$474.00
Price: Blue, vent heavy..$492.00
Price: Stainless, regular vent................................$504.00
Price: Stainless, vent heavy..................................$532.00

UNIQUE D.E.S. 69U TARGET PISTOL
Caliber: 22 LR, 5-shot magazine.
Barrel: 5.91".
Weight: 35.3 oz. **Length:** 10.5" overall.
Stocks: French walnut target-style with thumbrest and adjustable shelf; hand-checkered panels.
Sights: Ramp front, micro. adj. rear mounted on frame; 8.66" sight radius.
Features: Meets U.I.T. standards. Comes with 260-gram barrel weight; 100, 150, 350-gram weights available. Fully adjustable match trigger; dry-firing safety device. Imported from France by Nygord Precision Products.
Price: Right-hand, about.....................................$1,250.00
Price: Left-hand, about.......................................$1,290.00

WALTHER GSP MATCH PISTOL
Caliber: 22 LR, 32 S&W Long (GSP-C), 5-shot magazine.
Barrel: 4.22".
Weight: 44.8 oz. (22 LR), 49.4 oz. (32). **Length:** 11.8" overall.
Stocks: Walnut.
Sights: Post front, match rear adjustable for windage and elevation.
Features: Available with either 2.2 lb. (1000 gm) or 3 lb. (1360 gm) trigger. Spare magazine, barrel weight, tools supplied. Imported from Germany by Nygord Precision Products.
Price: GSP, with case...$1,495.00
Price: GSP-C, with case......................................$1,595.00

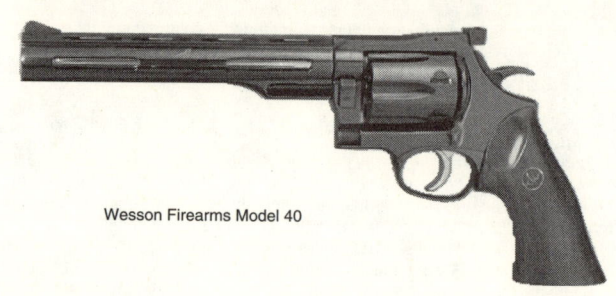

Wesson Firearms Model 40

WESSON FIREARMS 45 PIN GUN
Caliber: 45 ACP, 6-shot.
Barrel: 5" with 1:14" twist; Taylor two-stage forcing cone; compensated shroud.
Weight: 54 oz. **Length:** 12.5" overall.
Stocks: Finger-groove Hogue Monogrip.
Sights: Pin front, fully adjustable rear. Has 8.375" sight radius.
Features: Based on 44 Magnum frame. Polished blue or brushed stainless steel. Uses half-moon clips with 45 ACP, or 45 Auto Rim ammunition. Introduced 1994. Made in U.S. by Wesson Firearms Co., Inc.
Price: Blue, regular vent......................................$654.00
Price: Blue, vent heavy..$663.00
Price: Stainless, regular vent................................$713.00
Price: Stainless vent heavy..................................$762.00

WESSON FIREARMS MODEL 322/7322 TARGET REVOLVER
Caliber: 32-20, 6-shot.
Barrel: 2.5", 4", 6", 8", standard, vent, vent heavy.
Weight: 43 oz. (6" VH). **Length:** 11.25" overall.
Stocks: Checkered walnut.
Sights: Red ramp interchangeable front, fully adjustable rear.
Features: Brigh blue or stainless. Introduced 1991. From Wesson Firearms Co., Inc.
Price: 6", blue..$377.00
Price: 6", stainless...$419.00
Price: 8", vent, blue...$429.00
Price: 8", stainless...$472.00
Price: 6", vent heavy, blue...................................$437.00
Price: 6", vent heavy, stainless..............................$480.00
Price: 8", vent heavy, blue...................................$449.00
Price: 8", vent heavy, stainless..............................$501.00

WICHITA CLASSIC SILHOUETTE PISTOL
Caliber: All standard calibers with maximum overall length of 2.800".
Barrel: 11 1/4".
Weight: 3 lbs. 15 oz.
Stocks: AAA American walnut with oil finish, checkered grip.
Sights: Hooded post front, open adjustable rear.
Features: Three locking lug bolt, three gas ports; completely adjustable Wichita trigger. Introduced 1981. From Wichita Arms.
Price:...$3,450.00

HANDGUNS—COMPETITION HANDGUNS

WICHITA SILHOUETTE PISTOL
Caliber: 308 Win. F.L., 7mm IHMSA, 7mm-308.
Barrel: 14 15/16".
Weight: 4 1/2 lbs. **Length:** 21 3/8" overall.
Stock: American walnut with oil finish. Glass bedded.
Sights: Wichita Multi-Range sight system.
Features: Comes with left-hand action with right-hand grip. Round receiver and barrel. Fluted bolt, flat bolt handle. Wichita adjustable trigger. Introduced 1979. From Wichita Arms.
Price: Center grip stock $1,350.00
Price: As above except with Rear Position Stock and target-type Lightpull trigger $1,350.00

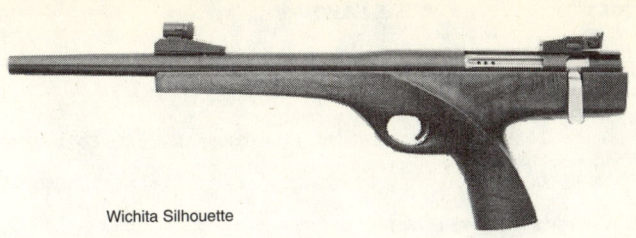
Wichita Silhouette

HANDGUNS—DOUBLE-ACTION REVOLVERS, SERVICE & SPORT

Includes models suitable for hunting and competitive courses for fire, both police and international.

CHARTER BULLDOG PUG REVOLVER
Caliber: 44 Spec., 5-shot.
Barrel: 2 1/2".
Weight: 19 1/2 oz. **Length:** 7" overall.
Stocks: Checkered walnut Bulldog.
Sights: Ramp-style front, fixed rear.
Features: Blue or stainless steel construction. Fully shrouded barrel. Available with Pocket Hammer. Reintroduced 1993. Made in U.S. by Charco, Inc.
Price: Blue $267.60
Price: Nickel $289.51

Charter Bulldog Pug

CHARTER OFF-DUTY REVOLVER
Caliber: 22 LR, 22 WMR, 6-shot, 38 Spec., 5-shot.
Barrel: 2".
Weight: 17 oz. (38 Spec.). **Length:** 6 1/4" overall.
Stocks: Checkered walnut or rubber combat.
Sights: Ramp-style front, fixed rear.
Features: Available in blue, stainless or electroless nickel. Fully shrouded barrel. Introduced 1993. Made in U.S. by Charco, Inc.
Price: Blue, 22 or 38 Spec. $200.48
Price: Electroless nickel, 22 or 38 Spec. $239.68
Price: Blue, DA only $207.98
Price: Electroless nickel, DA only $247.18

Charter Lady On Duty Revolver
Similar to the Off-Duty except has rosewood-color checkered plastic grips and comes in a lockable plastic case and nightglow trigger lock. Choice of spur, pocket or double-action hammer. Introduced 1995. Made in U.S. by Charco, Inc.
Price: 38 Spec., 5 shot, blue or nickel $219.28
Price: 32 S&W, 6 shot, blue or nickel $219.28

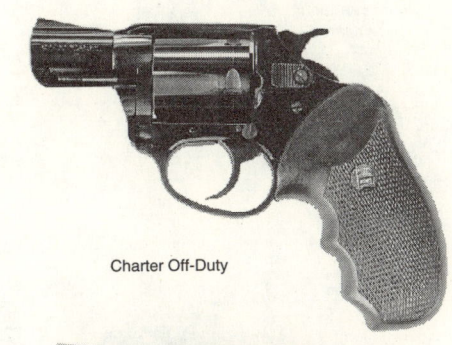
Charter Off-Duty

Charter Magnum Pug Revolver
Similar to the Off-Duty except chambered for 357 Mag., has 2.2" barrel, Bulldog or neoprene combat grips. Weighs 18 oz. Blue finish only. Pocket or spur hammer. Introduced 1995. Made in U.S. by Charco, Inc.
Price: $273.50

CHARTER POLICE UNDERCOVER REVOLVER
Caliber: 32 H&R Mag., 38 Spec., 6-shot.
Barrel: 2.2".
Weight: 16 oz. (38 Spec.). **Length:** 6 1/4" overall.
Stocks: Checkered walnut.
Sights: Ramp-style front, fixed rear.
Features: Blue or stainless steel. Fully shrouded barrel. Reintroduced 1993. Made in U.S. by Charco, Inc.
Price: Blue $237.75
Price: Electroless nickel $252.00

Charter Magnum Pug

COLT ANACONDA REVOLVER
Caliber: 44 Rem. Magnum, 45 Colt, 6-shot.
Barrel: 4", 6", 8".
Weight: 53 oz. (6" barrel). **Length:** 11 5/8" overall.
Stocks: TP combat style with finger grooves.
Sights: Red insert front, adjustable white outline rear.
Features: Stainless steel; full-length ejector rod housing; ventilated barrel rib; offset bolt notches in cylinder; wide spur hammer. Introduced 1990.
Price: $612.00
Price: 45 Colt, 6", 8" barrel only $612.00

Colt Anaconda

HANDGUNS—DOUBLE ACTION REVOLVERS, SERVICE & SPORT

COLT DETECTIVE SPECIAL REVOLVER
Caliber: 38 Special, 6-shot.
Barrel: 2".
Weight: 22 oz. **Length:** 6⅝" overall.
Stocks: Black composition.
Sights: Fixed. Ramp front, square notch rear.
Features: Glare-proof sights, grooved trigger, shrouded ejector rod. Colt blue finish. Reintroduced 1993.
Price: $400.00

Colt Police Positive Revolver
Similar to the Detective Special except has 4" barrel. Blue finish, fixed sight, black composition grips. Introduced 1995. From Colt's Mfg.
Price: $400.00

COLT 38 SF-VI REVOLVER
Caliber: 38 Special, 6-shot.
Barrel: 2".
Weight: 21 oz. **Length:** 7" overall.
Stocks: Checkered black composition.
Sights: Ramp front, fixed rear.
Features: Has new lockwork. Made of stainless steel. Introduced 1995. From Colt's Mfg.
Price: .... NA

COLT KING COBRA REVOLVER
Caliber: 357 Magnum, 6-shot.
Barrel: 4", 6".
Weight: 42 oz. (4" bbl.). **Length:** 9" overall (4" bbl.).
Stocks: TP combat style.
Sights: Red insert ramp front, adjustable white outline rear.
Features: Full-length contoured ejector rod housing, barrel rib. Introduced 1986.
Price: Stainless $455.00

COLT PYTHON REVOLVER
Caliber: 357 Magnum (handles all 38 Spec.), 6-shot.
Barrel: 4", 6" or 8", with ventilated rib.
Weight: 38 oz. (4" bbl.). **Length:** 9¼" (4" bbl.).
Stocks: Hogue Monogrip (4"), TP combat style (6", 8").
Sights: ⅛" ramp front, adjustable notch rear.
Features: Ventilated rib; grooved, crisp trigger; swing-out cylinder; target hammer.
Price: Royal blue, 4", 6", 8" $815.00
Price: Stainless, 4", 6", 8" $904.00
Price: Bright stainless, 4", 6", 8" $935.00

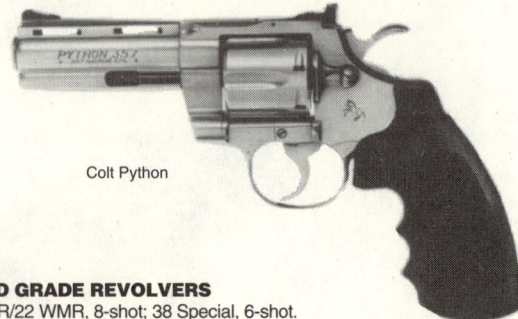
Colt Python

E.A.A. STANDARD GRADE REVOLVERS
Caliber: 22 LR, 22 LR/22 WMR, 8-shot; 38 Special, 6-shot.
Barrel: 4", 6" (22 rimfire); 2", 4" (38 Special).
Weight: 38 oz. (22 rimfire, 4"). **Length:** 8.8" overall (4" bbl.).
Stocks: Rubber with finger grooves.
Sights: Blade front, fixed or adjustable on rimfires; fixed only on 32, 38.
Features: Swing-out cylinder; hammer block safety; blue finish. Introduced 1991. Imported from Germany by European American Armory.
Price: 38 Special 2" $180.00
Price: 38 Special, 4" $199.00
Price: 22 LR, 6" $199.00
Price: 22 LR/22 WMR combo, 4" $200.00
Price: As above, 6" $200.00

ERMA ER-777 SPORTING REVOLVER
Caliber: 357 Mag., 6-shot.
Barrel: 5½".
Weight: 43.3 oz. **Length:** 9½" overall (4" barrel).
Stocks: Stippled walnut service-type.
Sights: Interchangeable blade front, micro-adjustable rear for windage and elevation.
Features: Polished blue finish. Adjustable trigger. Imported from Germany by Precision Sales Int'l. Introduced 1988.
Price: $1,019.00

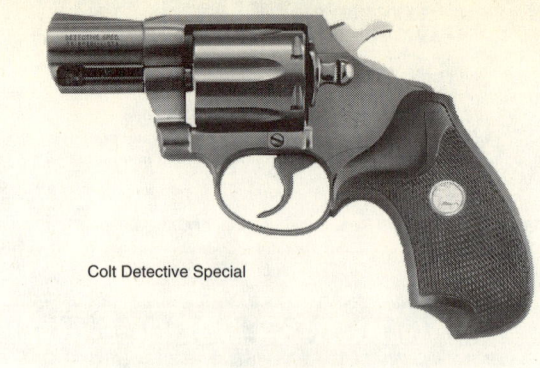
Colt Detective Special

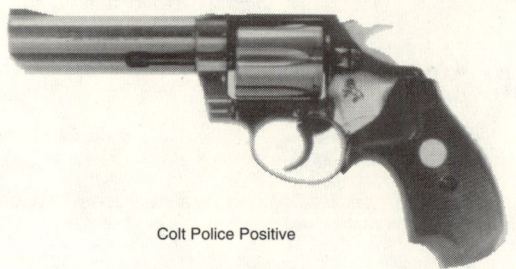
Colt Police Positive

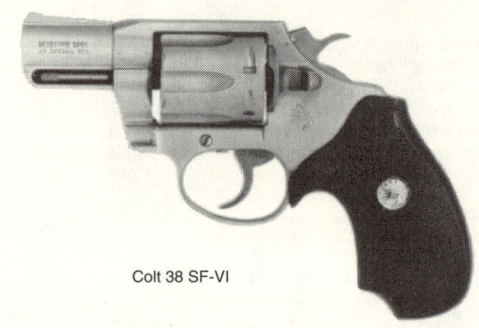
Colt 38 SF-VI

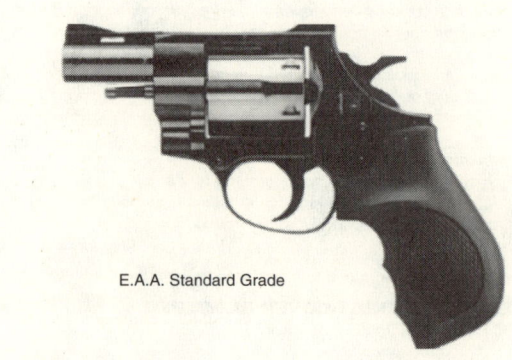
E.A.A. Standard Grade

Erma ER-777

HANDGUNS—DOUBLE ACTION REVOLVERS, SERVICE & SPORT

HARRINGTON & RICHARDSON 939 PREMIER REVOLVER
Caliber: 22 LR, 9-shot cylinder.
Barrel: 6" heavy.
Weight: 36 oz. **Length:** NA.
Stocks: Walnut-finished hardwood.
Sights: Blade front, fully adjustable rear.
Features: Swing-out cylinder with plunger-type ejection; solid barrel rib; high-polish blue finish; double-action mechanism; Western-style grip. Introduced 1995. Made in U.S. by H&R 1871, Inc.
Price: $184.95

Harrington & Richardson 939

HARRINGTON & RICHARDSON SPORTSMAN 999 REVOLVER
Caliber: 22 Short, Long, Long Rifle, 9-shot.
Barrel: 4", 6".
Weight: 30 oz. (4" barrel). **Length:** 8.5" overall.
Stocks: Walnut-finished hardwood.
Sights: Blade front adjustable for elevation, rear adjustable for windage.
Features: Top-break loading; polished blue finish; automatic shell ejection. Reintroduced 1992. From Harrington & Richardson.
Price: $279.95

Harrington & Richardson Sportsman 999

Harrington & Richardson 949

HARRINGTON & RICHARDSON 949 WESTERN REVOLVER
Caliber: 22 LR, 9-shot cylinder.
Barrel: 5 1/2", 7 1/2".
Weight: 36 oz. **Length:** NA.
Stocks: Walnut-stained hardwood.
Sights: Blade front, adjustable rear.
Features: Color case-hardened frame and backstrap, traditional loading gate and ejector rod. Introduced 1994. Made in U.S. by Harrington & Richardson.
Price: About $184.95

Heritage Sentry

HERITAGE SENTRY DOUBLE-ACTION REVOLVERS
Caliber: 22 LR, 8-shot, 22 WMR, 9mm Para., 38 Spec., 6-shot.
Barrel: 2", 4".
Weight: 23 oz. (2" barrel). **Length:** 6 1/4" overall (2" barrel).
Stocks: Magnum-style round butt; checkered plastic.
Sights: Ramp front, fixed rear.
Features: Pill-pin-type ejection; serrated hammer and trigger. Polished blue or nickel finish. Introduced 1993. Made in U.S. by Heritage Mfg., Inc.
Price: .... $124.95 to $134.95

MANURHIN MR 73 SPORT REVOLVER
Caliber: 357 Magnum, 6-shot cylinder.
Barrel: 6".
Weight: 37 oz. **Length:** 11.1" overall.
Stocks: Checkered walnut.
Sights: Blade front, fully adjustable rear.
Features: Double action with adjustable trigger. High-polish blue finish, straw-colored hammer and trigger. Comes with extra sight. Introduced 1984. Imported from France by Century International Arms.
Price: About $1,500.00

Manurhin MR73 Sport Revolver

Consult our Directory pages for the location of firms mentioned.

MITCHELL ARMS GUARDIAN II, III REVOLVERS
Caliber: 38 Spec., 6-shot.
Barrel: 3", 4" (Guardian II); 3", 4", 6" (Guardian III).
Weight: 32 oz. (3" barrel). **Length:** 8 1/2" overall (3" barrel).
Stocks: Combat, target; checkered black rubber, walnut.
Sights: Blade on ramp front, fixed rear (Guardian II); adjustable rear on Guardian III.
Features: Target hammer; shrouded ejector rod; smooth trigger. Blue only. Introduced 1995. Made in U.S. From Mitchell Arms, Inc.
Price: Guardian II, fixed sight $275.00
Price: Guardian III, adjustable sight $305.00

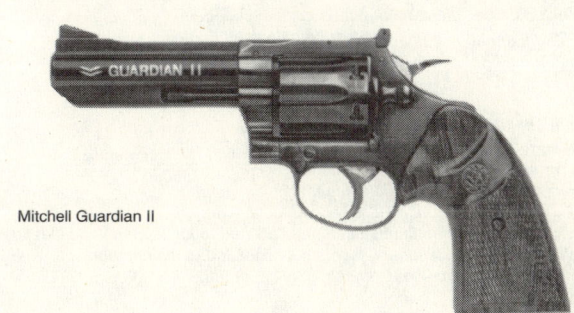
Mitchell Guardian II

CAUTION: PRICES SHOWN ARE SUPPLIED BY THE MANUFACTURER OR IMPORTER. CHECK YOUR LOCAL GUNSHOP.

HANDGUNS—DOUBLE ACTION REVOLVERS, SERVICE & SPORT

MITCHELL ARMS TITAN II, III REVOLVERS
Caliber: 357 Magnum, 6-shot.
Barrel: 2", 4", 6".
Weight: 38 oz. (2" barrel). **Length:** 7 3/4" overall (2" barrel).
Stocks: Pachmayr black rubber; combat or target.
Sights: Blade front, fixed rear (Titan II); adjustable rear (Titan III).
Features: Blue or stainless steel; crane-mounted cylinder release; shrouded ejector rod. Introduced 1995. Made in U.S. From Mitchell Arms, Inc.
Price: Titan II, blue or stainless, fixed sight $339.00
Price: Titan III, blue or stainless, adjustable sight $429.00

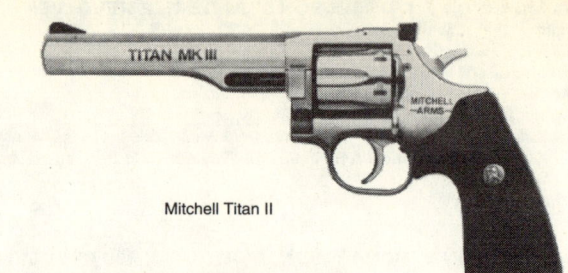
Mitchell Titan II

NEW ENGLAND FIREARMS LADY ULTRA REVOLVER
Caliber: 32 H&R Mag., 5-shot.
Barrel: 3".
Weight: 31 oz. **Length:** 7.25" overall.
Stocks: Walnut-finished hardwood with NEF medallion.
Sights: Blade front, fully adjustable rear.
Features: Swing-out cylinder; polished blue finish. Comes with lockable storage case. Introduced 1992. From New England Firearms Co.
Price: $165.95

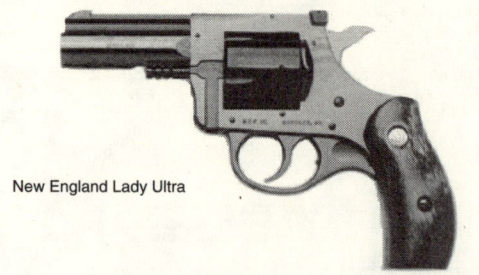
New England Lady Ultra

NEW ENGLAND FIREARMS ULTRA REVOLVER
Caliber: 22 LR, 9-shot; 22 WMR, 6-shot.
Barrel: 4", 6".
Weight: 36 oz. **Length:** 10 5/8" overall (6" barrel).
Stocks: Walnut-finished hardwood with NEF medallion.
Sights: Blade front, fully adjustable rear.
Features: Blue finish. Bull-style barrel with recessed muzzle, high "Lustre" blue/black finish. Introduced 1989. From New England Firearms.
Price: $165.95
Price: Ultra Mag 22 WMR $165.95

NEW ENGLAND FIREARMS STANDARD REVOLVERS
Caliber: 22 LR, 9-shot; 32 H&R Mag., 5-shot.
Barrel: 2 1/2", 4".
Weight: 26 oz. (22 LR, 2 1/2"). **Length:** 8 1/2" overall (4" bbl.).
Stocks: Walnut-finished American hardwood with NEF medallion.
Sights: Fixed.
Features: Choice of blue or nickel finish. Introduced 1988. From New England Firearms Co.
Price: 22 LR, 32 H&R Mag., blue $129.95
Price: 22 LR, 2 1/2", 4", nickel, 32 H&R Mag. 2 1/2" nickel $139.95

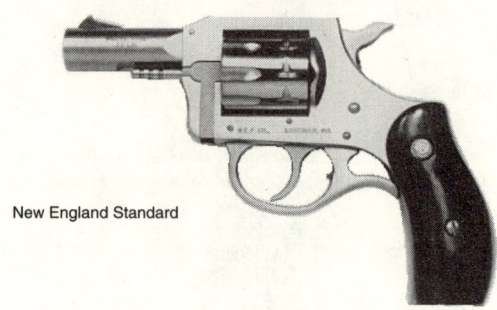
New England Standard

ROSSI LADY ROSSI REVOLVER
Caliber: 38 Spec., 5-shot.
Barrel: 2", 3".
Weight: 21 oz. **Length:** 6.5" overall (2" barrel).
Stocks: Smooth rosewood.
Sights: Fixed.
Features: High-polish stainless steel with "Lady Rossi" engraved on frame. Comes with velvet carry bag. Introduced 1995. Imported from Brazil by Interarms.
Price: $312.00

Rossi Lady Rossi

ROSSI MODEL 68 REVOLVER
Caliber: 38 Spec.
Barrel: 2", 3".
Weight: 22 oz.
Stocks: Checkered wood and rubber.
Sights: Ramp front, low profile adjustable rear.
Features: All-steel frame, thumb latch operated swing-out cylinder. Introduced 1978. Imported from Brazil by Interarms.
Price: 38, blue, 3", wood or rubber grips $234.00
Price: M68/2 (2" barrel), wood or rubber grips $246.00
Price: 3", nickel $238.00

ROSSI MODEL 88 STAINLESS REVOLVER
Caliber: 38 Spec., 5-shot.
Barrel: 2², 3².
Weight: 22 oz. **Length:** 7.5² overall.
Stocks: Checkered wood, service-style, and rubber.
Sights: Ramp front, square notch rear drift adjustable for windage.
Features: All metal parts except springs are of 440 stainless steel; matte finish; small frame for concealability. Introduced 1983. Imported from Brazil by Interarms.
Price: 3² barrel, wood or rubber grips $265.00
Price: 2² barrel, wood or rubber grips $281.00

ROSSI MODEL 515, 518 REVOLVERS
Caliber: 22 LR (Model 518), 22 WMR (Model 515), 6-shot.
Barrel: 4".
Weight: 30 oz. **Length:** 9" overall.
Stocks: Checkered wood and finger-groove wrap-around rubber.
Sights: Blade front with red insert, rear adjustable for windage and elevation.
Features: Small frame; stainless steel construction; solid integral barrel rib. Introduced 1994. Imported from Brazil by Interarms.
Price: Model 518, 22 LR $281.00
Price: Model 515, 22 WMR $296.00

Rossi Model 518

HANDGUNS—DOUBLE ACTION REVOLVERS, SERVICE & SPORT

ROSSI MODEL 720 REVOLVER
Caliber: 44 Special, 5-shot.
Barrel: 3″.
Weight: 27.5 oz. **Length:** 8″ overall.
Stocks: Checkered rubber, combat style.
Sights: Red insert front on ramp, fully adjustable rear.
Features: All stainless steel construction; solid barrel rib; full ejector rod shroud. Introduced 1992. Imported from Brazil by Interarms.
Price: $320.00
Price: Model 720C, spurless hammer, DA only $320.00

ROSSI MODEL 851 REVOLVER
Caliber: 38 Special, 6-shot.
Barrel: 3″ or 4″.
Weight: 27.5 oz. (3″ bbl.). **Length:** 8″ overall (3″ bbl.).
Stocks: Checkered Brazilian hardwood.
Sights: Blade front with red insert, rear adjustable for windage.
Features: Medium-size frame; stainless steel construction; ventilated barrel rib. Introduced 1991. Imported from Brazil by Interarms.
Price: $281.00

Rossi Model 720C

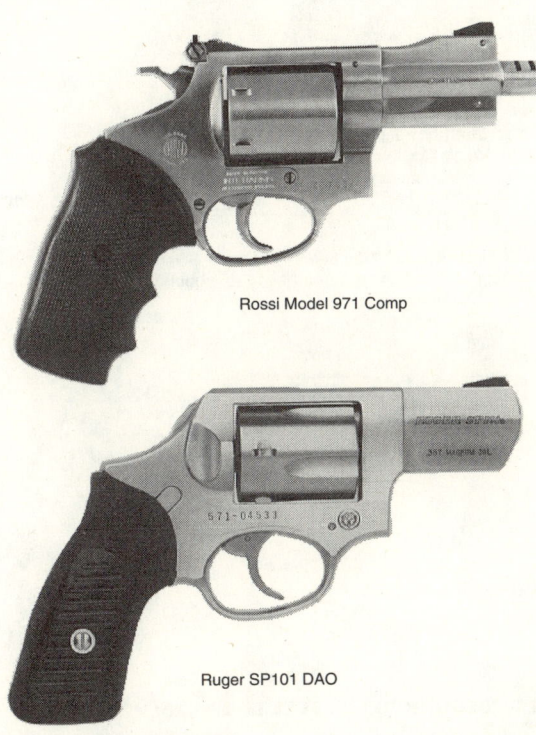
Rossi Model 971 Comp

Ruger SP101 DAO

ROSSI MODEL 971 REVOLVER
Caliber: 357 Mag., 6-shot.
Barrel: 2 1/2″, 4″, 6″, heavy.
Weight: 36 oz. **Length:** 9″ overall.
Stocks: Checkered Brazilian hardwood. Stainless models have checkered, contoured rubber.
Sights: Blade front, fully adjustable rear.
Features: Full-length ejector rod shroud; matted sight rib; target-type trigger, wide checkered hammer spur. Introduced 1988. Imported from Brazil by Interarms.
Price: 4″, stainless $320.00
Price: 6″, stainless $320.00
Price: 4″, blue $281.00
Price: 2 1/2″, stainless $320.00

Rossi Model 971 Comp Gun
Same as the Model 971 stainless except has 3 1/4″ barrel with integral compensator. Overall length is 9″, weight 32 oz. Has red insert front sight, fully adjustable rear. Checkered, contoured rubber grips. Introduced 1993. Imported from Brazil by Interarms.
Price: $320.00

RUGER SP101 REVOLVERS
Caliber: 22 LR, 32 H&R Mag., 6-shot, 9mm Para., 38 Special +P, 357 Mag., 5-shot.
Barrel: 2 1/4″, 3 1/16″, 4″.
Weight: 2 1/4″—25 oz.; 3 1/16″—27 oz.
Sights: Adjustable on 22, 32, fixed on others.
Stocks: Ruger Santoprene Cushioned Grip with Xenoy inserts.
Features: Incorporates improvements and features found in the GP-100 revolvers into a compact, small frame, double-action revolver. Full-length ejector shroud. Stainless steel only. Available with high-polish finish. Introduced 1988.
Price: KSP-821 (2 1/2″, 38 Spec.) $428.00
Price: KSP-831 (3 1/16″, 38 Spec.) $428.00
Price: KSP-221 (2 1/4″, 22 LR) $428.00
Price: KSP-240 (4″, 22 LR) $428.00
Price: KSP-241 (4″ heavy bbl., 22 LR) $428.00
Price: KSP-3231 (3 1/16″, 32 H&R) $428.00
Price: KSP-921 (2 1/4″, 9mm Para.) $428.00
Price: KSP-931 (3 1/16″, 9mm Para.) $428.00
Price: KSP-321 (2 1/4″, 357 Mag.) $428.00
Price: KSP-331 (3 1/16″, 357 Mag.) $428.00

Ruger SP101 Double-Action-Only Revolver
Similar to the standard SP101 except is double action only with no single-action sear notch. Has spurless hammer for snag-free handling, floating firing pin and Ruger's patented transfer bar safety system. Available with 2 1/4″ barrel in 38 Special +P and 357 Magnum only. Weight is 25 1/2 oz., overall length 7.06″. Natural brushed satin or high-polish stainless steel. Introduced 1993.
Price: KSP821L (38 Spec.), KSP321XL (357 Mag.) $428.00

RUGER GP-100 REVOLVERS
Caliber: 38 Special, 357 Magnum, 6-shot.
Barrel: 3″, 3″ heavy, 4″, 4″ heavy, 6″, 6″ heavy.
Weight: 3″ barrel—35 oz., 3″ heavy barrel—36 oz., 4″ barrel—37 oz., 4″ heavy barrel—38 oz.
Sights: Fixed; adjustable on 4″ heavy, 6″, 6″ heavy barrels.
Stocks: Ruger Santoprene Cushioned Grip with Goncalo Alves inserts.
Features: Uses action and frame incorporating improvements and features of both the Security-Six and Redhawk revolvers. Full length and short ejector shroud. Satin blue and stainless steel. Available in high-gloss stainless steel finish. Introduced 1988.
Price: GP-141 (357, 4″ heavy, adj. sights, blue) $425.00
Price: GP-160 (357, 6″, adj. sights, blue) $425.00
Price: GP-161 (357, 6″ heavy, adj. sights, blue) $425.00
Price: GPF-331 (357, 3″ heavy), GPF-831 (38 Spec.) $408.00
Price: GPF-340 (357, 4″), GPF-840 (38 Spec.) $408.00
Price: GPF-341 (357, 4″ heavy), GPF-841 (38 Spec.) $408.00
Price: KGP-141 (357, 4″ heavy, adj. sights, stainless) $459.00
Price: KGP-160 (357, 6″, adj. sights, stainless) $459.00
Price: KGP-161 (357, 6″ heavy, adj. sights, stainless) $459.00
Price: KGPF-330 (357, 3″, stainless), KGPF-830 (38 Spec.) $442.00
Price: KGPF-331 (357, 3″ heavy, stainless), KGPF-831 (38 Spec.) .$442.00
Price: KGPF-340 (357, 4″, stainless), KGPF-840 (38 Spec.) $442.00
Price: KGPF-341 (357, 4″ heavy, stainless), KGPF-841 (38 Spec.) .$442.00

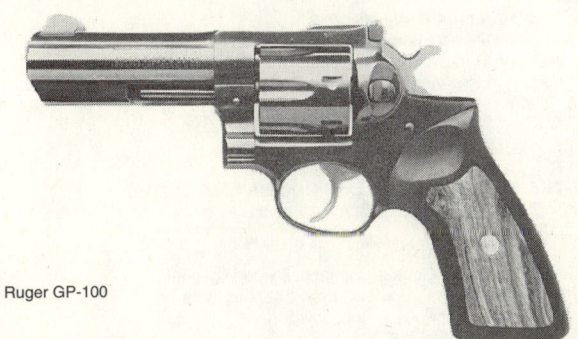
Ruger GP-100

CAUTION: PRICES SHOWN ARE SUPPLIED BY THE MANUFACTURER OR IMPORTER. CHECK YOUR LOCAL GUNSHOP.

HANDGUNS—DOUBLE ACTION REVOLVERS, SERVICE & SPORT

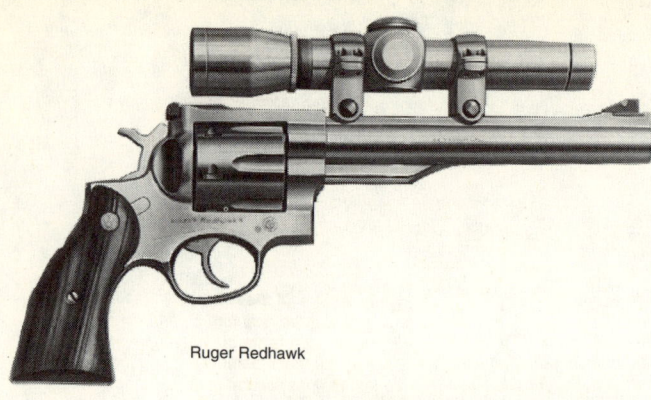

Ruger Redhawk

RUGER REDHAWK
Caliber: 44 Rem. Mag., 6-shot.
Barrel: 5½", 7½".
Weight: About 54 oz. (7½" bbl.). **Length:** 13" overall (7½" barrel).
Stocks: Square butt Goncalo Alves.
Sights: Interchangeable Patridge-type front, rear adjustable for windage and elevation.
Features: Stainless steel, brushed satin finish, or blued ordnance steel. Has a 9½" sight radius. Introduced 1979.
Price: Blued, 44 Mag., 5½", 7½" $475.00
Price: Blued, 44 Mag., 7½", with scope mount, rings $512.00
Price: Stainless, 44 Mag., 5½", 7½" $532.00
Price: Stainless, 44 Mag., 7½", with scope mount, rings $574.00

Ruger Super Redhawk Revolver
Similar to the standard Redhawk except has a heavy extended frame with the Ruger Integral Scope Mounting System on the wide topstrap. The wide hammer spur has been lowered for better scope clearance. Incorporates the mechanical design features and improvements of the GP-100. Choice of 7½" or 9½" barrel, both with ramp front sight base with Redhawk-style Interchangeable Insert sight blades, adjustable rear sight. Comes with Ruger "Cushioned Grip" panels of Santoprene with Goncalo Alves wood panels. Satin or high-polished stainless steel. Introduced 1987.
Price: KSRH-7 (7½"), KSRH-9 (9½") $574.00

Smith & Weson Model 10

SMITH & WESSON MODEL 10 M&P REVOLVER
Caliber: 38 Special, 6-shot.
Barrel: 2", 4".
Weight: 30 oz. **Length:** 9 5/16" overall.
Stocks: Uncle Mike's Combat soft rubber; square butt. Wood optional.
Sights: Fixed, ramp front, square notch rear.
Price: Blue $383.00

Smith & Wesson Model 10 38 M&P Heavy Barrel
Same as regular M&P except has heavy 4² ribbed barrel with square butt grips. Weighs 33½ oz.
Price: Blue $390.00

SMITH & WESSON MODEL 13 H.B. M&P
Caliber: 357 and 38 Special, 6-shot.
Barrel: 3" or 4".
Weight: 34 oz. **Length:** 9 5/16" overall (4" bbl.).
Stocks: Uncle Mike's Combat soft rubber; wood optional.
Sights: 1/8" serrated ramp front, fixed square notch rear.
Features: Heavy barrel, K-frame, square butt (4"), round butt (3").
Price: Blue $394.00
Price: Model 65, as above in stainless steel $427.00

Smith & Wesson Model 65

Smith & Wesson Model 14

SMITH & WESSON MODEL 14 FULL LUG REVOLVER
Caliber: 38 Special, 6-shot.
Barrel: 6", full lug.
Weight: 47 oz. **Length:** 11 1/8" overall.
Stocks: Hogue soft rubber; wood optional.
Sights: Pinned Patridge front, adjustable micrometer click rear.
Features: Has .500" target hammer, .312" smooth combat trigger. Polished blue finish. Reintroduced 1991. Limited production.
Price: $465.00

SMITH & WESSON MODEL 15 COMBAT MASTERPIECE
Caliber: 38 Special, 6-shot.
Barrel: 4².
Weight: 32 oz. **Length:** 9 5/16² (4² bbl.).
Stocks: Uncle Mike's Combat soft rubber; wood optional.
Sights: Front, Baughman Quick Draw on ramp, micro-click rear adjustable for windage and elevation.
Price: Blued $419.00

SMITH & WESSON MODEL 19 COMBAT MAGNUM
Caliber: 357 Magnum and 38 Special, 6-shot.
Barrel: 2½", 4", 6".
Weight: 36 oz. **Length:** 9 9/16" (4" bbl.).
Stocks: Uncle Mike's Combat soft rubber; wood optional.
Sights: Serrated ramp front 2½" or 4" bbl., red ramp on 4", 6" bbl., micro-click rear adjustable for windage and elevation.
Price: S&W Bright Blue, adj. sights ....$416.00 to $430.00

Smith & Wesson Model 19

HANDGUNS—DOUBLE ACTION REVOLVERS, SERVICE & SPORT

Smith & Wesson Model 629

Smith & Wesson Model 629 Classic Revolver
Similar to the standard Model 629 except has full-lug 5", 6½" or 8⅜" barrel; chamfered front of cylinder; interchangable red ramp front sight with adjustable white outline rear; Hogue grips with S&W monogram; the frame is drilled and tapped for scope mounting. Factory accurizing and endurance packages. Overall length with 5" barrel is 10½"; weight is 51 oz. Introduced 1990.
Price: Model 629 Classic (stainless), 5", 6½" $629.00
Price: As above, 8⅜" $650.00

Smith & Wesson Model 37

Smith & Wesson Model 60LS

Smith & Wesson Model 60 3" Full-Lug Revolver
Similar to the Model 60 Chief's Special except has 3" full-lug barrel, adjustable micrometer click black blade rear sight; rubber Uncle Mike's Custom Grade Boot Grip. Overall length 7½"; weight 24½ oz. Introduced 1991.
Price: $458.00

Smith & Wesson Model 649

SMITH & WESSON MODEL 29, 629 REVOLVERS
Caliber: 44 Magnum, 6-shot.
Barrel: 6", 8⅜" (Model 29); 4", 6", 8⅜" (Model 629).
Weight: 47 oz. (6" bbl.). **Length:** 11⅜" overall (6" bbl.).
Stocks: Soft rubber; wood optional.
Sights: ⅛" red ramp front, micro-click rear, adjustable for windage and elevation.
Price: S&W Bright Blue, 6" $554.00
Price: S&W Bright Blue, 8⅜" $566.00
Price: Model 629 (stainless steel), 4" $587.00
Price: Model 629, 6" $592.00
Price: Model 629, 8⅜" barrel $606.00

Smith & Wesson Model 629 Classic DX Revolver
Similar to the Classic Hunters except offered only with 6½" or 8⅜" full-lug barrel; comes with five front sights: 50-yard red ramp; 50-yard black Patridge; 100-yard black Patridge with gold bead; 50-yard black ramp; and 50-yard black Patridge with white dot. Comes with Hogue combat-style round butt grip. Introduced 1991.
Price: Model 629 Classic DX, 6½" $811.00
Price: As above, 8⅜" $838.00

SMITH & WESSON MODEL 36, 37 CHIEFS SPECIAL & AIRWEIGHT
Caliber: 38 Special, 5-shot.
Barrel: 2".
Weight: 19½ oz. (2" bbl.); 13½ oz. (Airweight). **Length:** 6½" (2" bbl. and round butt).
Stocks: Round butt soft rubber; wood optional.
Sights: Fixed, serrated ramp front, square notch rear.
Price: Blue, standard Model 36 .... $377.00
Price: Blue, Airweight Model 37, 2" only $412.00
Price: As above, nickel, 2" only $428.00

Smith & Wesson Model 36LS, 60LS LadySmith
Similar to the standard Model 36. Available with 2" barrel. Comes with smooth, contoured rosewood grips with the S&W monogram. Has a speedloader cutout. Comes in a fitted carry/storage case. Introduced 1989.
Price: Model 36LS $408.00
Price: Model 60LS (as above except in stainless) $461.00

Smith & Weson Model 60 3"

Smith & Wesson Model 60 Chiefs Special Stainless
Same as Model 36 except all stainless construction, 2" bbl. and round butt only.
Price: Stainless steel $431.00

SMITH & WESSON MODEL 38 BODYGUARD
Caliber: 38 Special, 5-shot.
Barrel: 2".
Weight: 14½ oz. **Length:** 6 5/16" overall.
Stocks: Soft rubber; wood optional.
Sights: Fixed serrated ramp front, square notch rear.
Features: Alloy frame; internal hammer.
Price: Blue $444.00
Price: Nickel $460.00

Smith & Wesson Model 49, 649 Bodyguard Revolvers
Same as Model 38 except steel construction, weight 20½ oz.
Price: Blued, Model 49 .... $409.00
Price: Stainless, Model 649 .... $469.00

CAUTION: PRICES SHOWN ARE SUPPLIED BY THE MANUFACTURER OR IMPORTER. CHECK YOUR LOCAL GUNSHOP.

HANDGUNS—DOUBLE ACTION REVOLVERS, SERVICE & SPORT

Smith & Wesson Model 63

SMITH & WESSON MODEL 63 KIT GUN
Caliber: 22 LR, 6-shot.
Barrel: 2", 4".
Weight: 24 oz. (4" bbl.). **Length:** 8 3/8" (4" bbl. and round butt).
Stocks: Round butt soft rubber; wood optional.
Sights: Red ramp front, micro-click rear adjustable for windage and elevation.
Features: Stainless steel construction.
Price: 2" $458.00
Price: 4" $462.00

SMITH & WESSON MODEL 64 STAINLESS M&P
Caliber: 38 Special, 6-shot.
Barrel: 2", 3", 4".
Weight: 34 oz. **Length:** 9 5/16" overall.
Stocks: Soft rubber; wood optional.
Sights: Fixed, 1/8" serrated ramp front, square notch rear.
Features: Satin finished stainless steel, square butt.
Price: 2" $415.00
Price: 3", 4" $423.00

SMITH & WESSON MODEL 65LS LADYSMITH
Caliber: 357 Magnum, 6-shot.
Barrel: 3".
Weight: 31 oz. **Length:** 7.94" overall.
Stocks: Rosewood, round butt.
Sights: Serrated ramp front, fixed notch rear.
Features: Stainless steel with frosted finish. Smooth combat trigger, service hammer, shrouded ejector rod. Comes with soft case. Introduced 1992.
Price: $461.00

SMITH & WESSON MODEL 66 STAINLESS COMBAT MAGNUM
Caliber: 357 Magnum and 38 Special, 6-shot.
Barrel: 2 1/2", 4", 6".
Weight: 36 oz. (4" barrel). **Length:** 9 9/16" overall.
Stocks: Soft rubber; wood optional.
Sights: Red ramp front, micro-click rear adjustable for windage and elevation.
Features: Satin finish stainless steel.
Price: 2 1/2" $466.00
Price: 4", 6" $471.00

Smith & Wesson Model 65LS

SMITH & WESSON MODEL 67 COMBAT MASTERPIECE
Caliber: 38 Special, 6-shot.
Barrel: 4".
Weight: 32 oz. **Length:** 9<+>5/16" overall.
Stocks: Soft rubber; wood optional.
Sights: Red ramp front, micro-click rear adjustable for windage and elevation.
Features: Stainless steel with satin finish. Smooth combat trigger, semi-target hammer. Introduced 1994.
Price: $467.00

Smith & Wesson Model 686

SMITH & WESSON MODEL 586, 686 DISTINGUISHED COMBAT MAGNUMS
Caliber: 357 Magnum.
Barrel: 4", 6", full shroud.
Weight: 46 oz. (6"), 41 oz. (4").
Stocks: Soft rubber; wood optional.
Sights: Baughman red ramp front, four-position click-adjustable front, S&W micrometer click rear. Drilled and tapped for scope mount.
Features: Uses new L-frame, but takes all K-frame grips. Full-length ejector rod shroud. Smooth combat-type trigger, semi-target type hammer. Trigger stop on 6" models. Also available in stainless as Model 686. Introduced 1981.
Price: Model 586, blue, 4", from $461.00
Price: Model 586, blue, 6" $466.00
Price: Model 686, 6", ported barrel $528.00
Price: Model 686, 8 3/8" $515.00
Price: Model 686, 2 1/2" $481.00

SMITH & WESSON MODEL 617 FULL LUG REVOLVER
Caliber: 22 LR, 6-shot.
Barrel: 4", 6", 8 3/8".
Weight: 42 oz. (4" barrel). **Length:** NA.
Stocks: Soft rubber; wood optional.
Sights: Patridge front, adjustable rear. Drilled and tapped for scope mount.
Features: Stainless steel with satin finish; 4" has .312" smooth trigger, .375" semi-target hammer; 6" has either .312" combat or .400" serrated trigger, .375" semi-target or .500" target hammer; 8 3/8" with .400" serrated trigger, .500" target hammer. Introduced 1990.
Price: 4" $460.00
Price: 6", target hammer, combat trigger $490.00
Price: 8 3/8" $501.00

SMITH & WESSON MODEL 625 REVOLVER
Caliber: 45 ACP, 6-shot.
Barrel: 5".
Weight: 46 oz. **Length:** 11.375" overall.
Stocks: Soft rubber; wood optional.
Sights: Patridge front on ramp, S&W micrometer click rear adjustable for windage and elevation.
Features: Stainless steel construction with .400" semi-target hammer, .312" smooth combat trigger; full lug barrel. Introduced 1989.
Price: $597.00

Smith & Wesson Model 625

HANDGUNS—DOUBLE ACTION REVOLVERS, SERVICE & SPORT

Smith & Wesson Model 640

Smith & Wesson Model 442

SMITH & WESSON MODEL 651 REVOLVER
Caliber: 22 WMR, 6-shot cylinder.
Barrel: 4".
Weight: 24 1/2 oz. **Length:** 8 11/16" overall.
Stocks: Soft rubber; wood optional.
Sights: Red ramp front, adjustable micrometer click rear.
Features: Stainless steel construction with semi-target hammer, smooth combat trigger. Reintroduced 1991. Limited production.
Price: $460.00

Smith & Wesson Model 657

TAURUS MODEL 66 REVOLVER
Caliber: 357 Magnum, 6-shot.
Barrel: 2.5", 4", 6".
Weight: 35 oz.(4" barrel).
Stocks: Checkered Brazilian hardwood.
Sights: Serrated ramp front, micro-click rear adjustable for windage and elevation. Red ramp front with white outline rear on stainlees models only.
Features: Wide target-type hammer spur, floating firing pin, heavy barrel with shrouded ejector rod. Introduced 1978. Imported by Taurus International.
Price: Blue, 2.5", 4", 6" $329.00
Price: Stainless, 2.5", 4", 6" $405.00

Taurus Model 65 Revolver
Same as the Model 66 except has fixed rear sight and ramp front. Available with 2.5" or 4" barrel only, round butt grip. Imported by Taurus International.
Price: Blue, 2.5", 4" $299.00
Price: Stainless, 2.5", 4" $369.00

TAURUS MODEL 80 STANDARD REVOLVER
Caliber: 38 Spec., 6-shot.
Barrel: 3" or 4".
Weight: 30 oz. (4" bbl.). **Length:** 9 1/4" overall (4" bbl.).
Stocks: Checkered Brazilian hardwood.
Sights: Serrated ramp front, square notch rear.
Features: Imported by Taurus International.
Price: Blue $260.00
Price: Stainless $308.00

SMITH & WESSON MODEL 640 CENTENNIAL
Caliber: 357/38 Special, 5-shot.
Barrel: 2 1/8".
Weight: 25 oz. **Length:** 6 3/4" overall.
Stocks: Uncle Mike's Boot Grip.
Sights: Serrated ramp front, fixed notch rear.
Features: Stainless steel version of the original Model 40 but without the grip safety. Fully concealed hammer, snag-proof smooth edges. Introduced 1995 in 357 Magnum.
Price: $469.00
Price: Model 940 (9mm Para.) $474.00

Smith & Wesson Model 442 Centennial Airweight
Similar to the Model 640 Centennial except has alloy frame giving weight of 15.8 oz. Chambered for 38 Special, 2" carbon steel barrel; carbon steel cylinder; concealed hammer; Uncle Mike's Custom Grade Santoprene grips. Fixed square notch rear sight, serrated ramp front. Introduced 1993.
Price: Blue $427.00
Price: Nickel $442.00

Smith & Wesson Model 651

SMITH & WESSON MODEL 657 REVOLVER
Caliber: 41 Magnum, 6-shot.
Barrel: 6".
Weight: 48 oz. **Length:** 11 3/8" overall.
Stocks: Soft rubber; wood optional.
Sights: Pinned 1/8" red ramp front, micro-click rear adjustable for windage and elevation.
Features: Stainless steel construction.
Price: $528.00

TAURUS MODEL 44 REVOLVER
Caliber: 44 Magnum, 6-shot.
Barrel: 4", 6 1/2", 8 3/8".
Weight: 44 3/4 oz. (4" barrel). **Length:** NA.
Stocks: Checkered Brazilian hardwood.
Sights: Serrated ramp front, micro-click rear adjustable for windage and elevation.
Features: Heavy solid rib on 4", vent rib on 6 1/2", 8 3/8". Compensated barrel. Blued model has color case-hardened hammer and trigger. Introduced 1994. Imported by Taurus International.
Price: Blue, 4" $439.00
Price: Blue, 6 1/2", 8 3/8" $457.00
Price: Stainless, 4" $499.00
Price: Stainless, 6 1/2", 8 3/8" $520.00

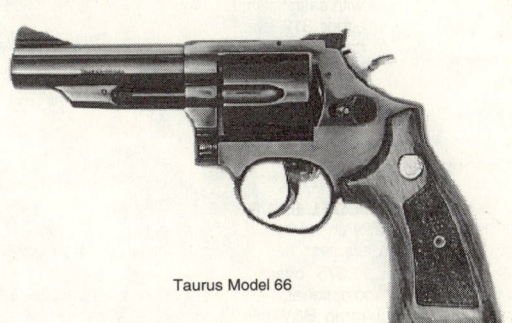
Taurus Model 66

CAUTION: PRICES SHOWN ARE SUPPLIED BY THE MANUFACTURER OR IMPORTER. CHECK YOUR LOCAL GUNSHOP.

HANDGUNS—DOUBLE ACTION REVOLVERS, SERVICE & SPORT

TAURUS MODEL 82 HEAVY BARREL REVOLVER
Caliber: 38 Spec., 6-shot.
Barrel: 3" or 4", heavy.
Weight: 34 oz. (4" bbl.). **Length:** 9 1/4" overall (4" bbl.).
Stocks: Checkered Brazilian hardwood.
Sights: Serrated ramp front, square notch rear.
Features: Imported by Taurus International.
Price: Blue $260.00
Price: Stainless $308.00

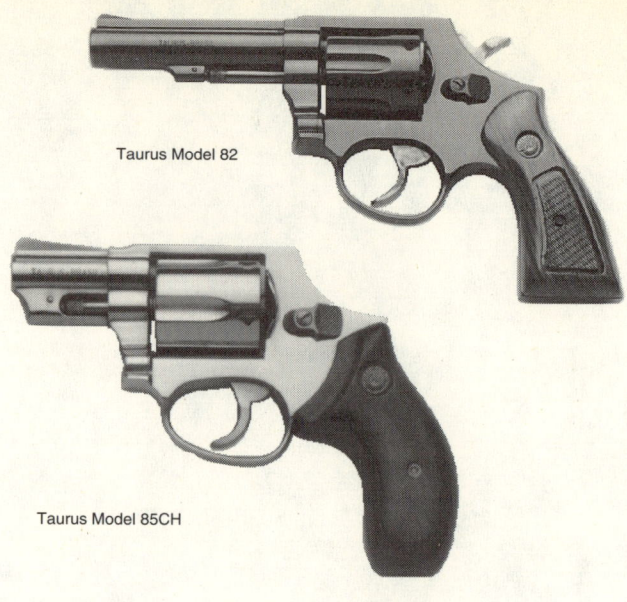

Taurus Model 82

TAURUS MODEL 83 REVOLVER
Caliber: 38 Spec., 6-shot.
Barrel: 4" only, heavy.
Weight: 34 oz.
Stocks: Oversize checkered Brazilian hardwood.
Sights: Ramp front, micro-click rear adjustable for windage and elevation.
Features: Blue or nickel finish. Introduced 1977. Imported by Taurus International.
Price: Blue $274.00
Price: Stainless $319.00

TAURUS MODEL 85 REVOLVER
Caliber: 38 Spec., 5-shot.
Barrel: 2", 3".
Weight: 21 oz.
Stocks: Checkered Brazilian hardwood.
Sights: Ramp front, square notch rear.
Features: Blue, satin nickel finish or stainless steel. Introduced 1980. Imported by Taurus International.
Price: Blue, 2", 3" $284.00
Price: Stainless steel $343.00

Taurus Model 85CH

Taurus Model 85CH Revolver
Same as the Model 85 except has 2" barrel only and concealed hammer. Smooth Brazilian hardwood stocks. Introduced 1991. Imported by Taurus International.
Price: Blue $284.00
Price: Stainless $343.00

TAURUS MODEL 94 REVOLVER
Caliber: 22 LR, 9-shot cylinder.
Barrel: 3", 4".
Weight: 25 oz.
Stocks: Checkered Brazilian hardwood.
Sights: Serrated ramp front, click-adjustable rear for windage and elevation.
Features: Floating firing pin, color case-hardened hammer and trigger. Introduced 1989. Imported by Taurus International.
Price: Blue $303.00
Price: Stainless $350.00

Taurus Model 96

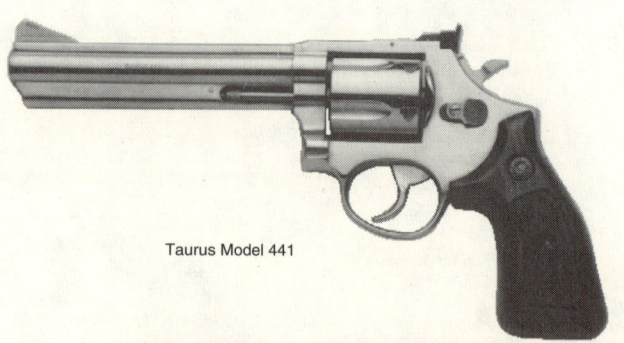

TAURUS MODEL 96 REVOLVER
Caliber: 22 LR, 6-shot.
Barrel: 6".
Weight: 34 oz. **Length:** NA.
Stocks: Checkered Brazilian hardwood.
Sights: Patridge-type front, micrometer click rear adjustable for windage and elevation.
Features: Heavy solid barrel rib; target hammer; adjustable target trigger. Blue only. Imported by Taurus International.
Price: $370.00

Taurus Model 441

TAURUS MODEL 441/431 REVOLVERS
Caliber: 44 Special, 5-shot.
Barrel: 3", 4", 6".
Weight: 40.4 oz. (6" barrel). **Length:** NA.
Stocks: Checkered Brazilian hardwood.
Sights: Serrated ramp front, micrometer click rear adjustable for windage and elevation.
Features: Heavy barrel with solid rib and full-length ejector shroud. Introduced 1992. Imported by Taurus International.
Price: Blue, 3", 4", 6" $307.00
Price: Stainless, 3", 4", 6" $386.00
Price: Model 431 (fixed sights), blue $295.00
Price: Model 431 (fixed sights), stainless $362.00

CONSULT Shooter's Marketplace Page 266, This Issue

TAURUS MODEL 605 REVOLVER
Caliber: 357 Mag., 5-shot.
Barrel: 2 1/4".
Weight: 24.5 oz. **Length:** NA.
Stocks: Finger-groove Santoprene I.
Sights: Serrated ramp front, fixed notch rear.
Features: Heavy, solid rib barrel; floating firing pin. Blue or stainless. Introduced 1995. Imported by Taurus International.
Price: Blue $305.00
Price: Stainless $369.00

HANDGUNS—DOUBLE ACTION REVOLVERS, SERVICE & SPORT

TAURUS MODEL 607 REVOLVER
Caliber: 357 Mag., 7-shot.
Barrel: 4", 6 1/2".
Weight: 44 oz. **Length:** NA.
Stocks: Santoprene I with finger grooves.
Sights: Serrated ramp front, fully adjustable rear.
Features: Ventilated rib with built-in compensator on 6 1/2" barrel. Available in blue or stainless. Introduced 1995. Imported by Taurus international.
Price: Blue, 4" $439.00
Price: Blue, 6 1/2" $457.00
Price: Stainless, 4" $499.00
Price: Stainless, 6 1/2" $520.00

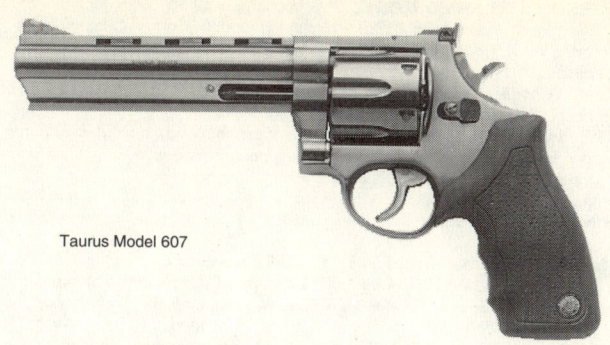
Taurus Model 607

TAURUS MODEL 669 REVOLVER
Caliber: 357 Mag., 6-shot.
Barrel: 4", 6".
Weight: 37 oz., (4" bbl.).
Stocks: Checkered Brazilian hardwood.
Sights: Serrated ramp front, micro-click rear adjustable for windage and elevation.
Features: Wide target-type hammer, floating firing pin, full-length barrel shroud. Introduced 1988. Imported by Taurus International.
Price: Blue, 4", 6" $338.00
Price: Blue, 4", 6" compensated $357.00
Price: Stainless, 4", 6" $414.00
Price: Stainless, 4", 6" compensated $434.00

Taurus Model 689 Revolver
Same as the Model 669 except has full-length ventilated barrel rib. Available in blue or stainless steel. Introduced 1990. From Taurus International.
Price: Blue, 4" or 6" $352.00
Price: Stainless, 4" or 6" $428.00

Taurus Model 669

TAURUS MODEL 941 REVOLVER
Caliber: 22 WMR, 8-shot.
Barrel: 3", 4".
Weight: 27.5 oz. (4" barrel). **Length:** NA.
Stocks: Checkered Brazilian hardwood.
Sights: Serrated ramp front, rear adjustable for windage and elevation.
Features: Solid rib heavy barrel with full-length ejector rod shroud. Blue or stainless steel. Introduced 1992. Imported by Taurus International.
Price: Blue $326.00
Price: Stainless $378.00

WESSON FIREARMS FB15, FB715 REVOLVERS
Caliber: 357 Magnum, 6-shot.
Barrel: 2 1/2", 4" (Service models), 3", 4", 5", 6" (target models).
Weight: 40 oz. (4" barrel). **Length:** 9 3/4" overall (4" barrel).
Stocks: Service style or Hogue rubber.
Sights: Blade front, adjustable rear (Target); fixed rear on Service.
Features: Fixed barrels, but other features same as other Wesson revolvers. Service models in brushed stainless, satin blue, Target in brushed stainless or polished blue. Introduced 1993. Made in U.S. by Wesson Firearms Co., Inc.
Price: FB14-2 (Service, 2 1/2", blue) $289.00
Price: As above, 4" $296.00
Price: FB714-2 (Service, 2 1/2", stainless) $313.00
Price: As above, 4" $319.00
Price: FB15-3 (Target, 3", blue) $322.00
Price: As above, 5" $331.00
Price: FB715 (Target, 4", stainless) $354.00
Price: As above, 6" $370.00

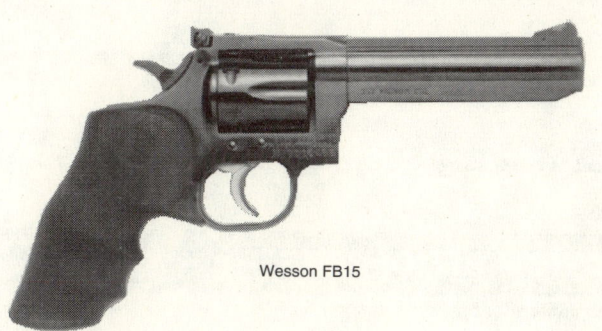
Wesson FB15

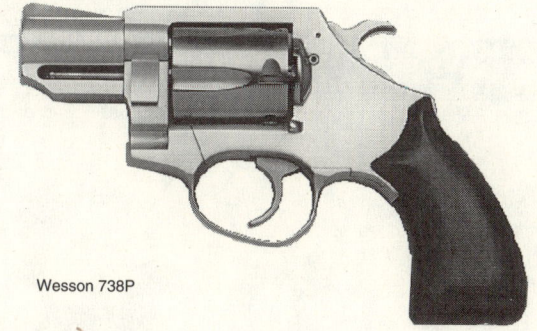
Wesson 738P

WESSON FIREARMS FB44, FB744 REVOLVERS
Caliber: 44 Magnum, 6-shot.
Barrel: 4", 5", 6", 8".
Weight: 50 oz. (4" barrel). **Length:** 9 3/4" overall (4" barrel).
Stocks: Hogue finger-groove rubber.
Sights: Interchangeable blade front, fully adjustable rear.
Features: Fixed, non-vented heavy barrel shrouds, but other features same as other Wesson revolvers. Brushed stainless or polished blue finish. Introduced 1994. Made in U.S. by Wesson Firearms Co., Inc.
Price: FB44-4 (4", blue) $447.00
Price: As above, stainless (FB744-4) $493.00
Price: FB44-5 (5", blue) $450.00
Price: As above, stainless (FB744-5) $496.00
Price: FB44-6 (6", blue) $454.00
Price: As above, stainless (FB744-6) $500.00
Price: FB44-8 (8", blue) $462.00
Price: As above, stainless (FB744-8) $508.00

WESSON FIREARMS MODEL 738P REVOLVER
Caliber: 38 Special +P, 5-shot.
Barrel: 2".
Weight: 24.6 oz. **Length:** 6.5" overall.
Stocks: Pauferro wood or rubber.
Sights: Blade front, fixed notch rear.
Features: Designed for +P ammunition. Stainless steel construction. Introduced 1992. Made in U.S. by Wesson Firearms Co., Inc.
Price: $340.00

HANDGUNS—DOUBLE ACTION REVOLVERS, SERVICE & SPORT

WESSON FIREARMS MODEL 8 & MODEL 14
Caliber: 38 Special (Model 8); 357 (Model 14), both 6-shot.
Barrel: 2½", 4", 6"; interchangeable.
Weight: 30 oz. (2½"). **Length:** 9¼" overall (4" bbl.).
Stocks: Checkered, interchangeable.
Sights: 1/8" serrated front, fixed rear.
Features: Interchangeable barrels and grips; smooth, wide trigger; wide hammer spur with short double-action travel. Available in stainless or Brite blue. Contact Wesson Firearms for complete price list.
Price: Model 8-2, 2½", blue $274.00
Price: As above except in stainless $319.00

Wesson Firearms Model 9, 15 & 32M Revolvers
Same as Models 8 and 14 except they have adjustable sight. Model 9 chambered for 38 Special, Model 15 for 357 Magnum. Model 32M is chambered for 32 H&R Mag. Same specs and prices as for Model 15 guns. Available in blue or stainless. Contact Wesson Firearms for complete price list.
Price: Model 9-2 or 15-2, 2½", blue $346.00
Price: As above except in stainless $376.00

WESSON FIREARMS MODEL 22 REVOLVER
Caliber: 22 LR, 22 WMR, 6-shot.
Barrel: 2½", 4", 6", 8"; interchangeable.
Weight: 36 oz. (2½"), 44 oz. (6"). **Length:** 9¼" overall (4" barrel).
Stocks: Checkered; undercover, service or over-size target.
Sights: 1/8" serrated, interchangeable front, white outline rear adjustable for windage and elevation.
Features: Built on the same frame as the Wesson 357; smooth, wide trigger with over-travel adjustment, wide spur hammer, with short double-action travel. Available in Brite blue or stainless steel. Contact Wesson Firearms for complete price list.
Price: 2½" bbl., blue $357.00
Price: As above, stainless $400.00
Price: With 4", vent. rib, blue $392.00
Price: As above, stainless $432.00
Price: Blue Pistol Pac, 22 LR $653.00

WESSON FIREARMS MODEL 41V, 44V, 45V REVOLVERS
Caliber: 41 Mag., 44 Mag., 45 Colt, 6-shot.
Barrel: 4", 6", 8", 10"; interchangeable.
Weight: 48 oz. (4"). **Length:** 12" overall (6" bbl.).
Stocks: Smooth.
Sights: 1/8" serrated front, white outline rear adjustable for windage and elevation.
Features: Available in blue or stainless steel. Smooth, wide trigger with adjustable over-travel; wide hammer spur. Available in Pistol Pac set also. Contact Wesson Firearms for complete price list.
Price: 41 Mag., 4", vent $447.00
Price: As above except in stainless $524.00
Price: 44 Mag., 4", blue $447.00
Price: As above except in stainless $524.00
Price: 45 Colt, 4", vent $447.00
Price: As above except in stainless $524.00

Wesson Model 32M

Wesson Firearms Model 15 Gold Series
Similar to the Model 15 except has smoother action to reduce DA pull to 8-10 lbs.; comes with either 6" or 8" vent heavy slotted barrel shroud with bright blue barrel. Shroud is stamped "Gold Series" with the Wesson signature engraved and gold filled. Hammer and trigger are polished bright; rosewood grips. New sights with orange dot Patridge front, white triangle on rear blade. Introduced 1989.
Price: 6" ....NA
Price: 8" ....NA

Consult our Directory pages for the location of firms mentioned.

WESSON FIREARMS HUNTER SERIES REVOLVERS
Caliber: 357 Supermag, 41 Mag., 44 Mag., 445 Supermag, 6-shot.
Barrel: 6", 7½", depending upon model.
Weight: About 64 oz. **Length:** 14" overall.
Stocks: Hogue finger-groove rubber, wood presentation.
Sights: Blade front, dovetailed Iron Sight Gunworks rear.
Features: Fixed barrel revolvers. Barrels have 1:18.75" twist, Alan Taylor two-stage forcing cone; non-fluted cylinder; bright blue or satin stainless. Introduced 1994. Made in U.S. by Wesson Firearms Co., Inc.
Price: Open Hunter (open sights, 7½" barrel), blue $805.00
Price: As above, stainless $849.00
Price: Compensated Open Hunter (6" compensated barrel, 7" shroud), blue $837.00
Price: As above, stainless $881.00
Price: Scoped Hunter (7½" barrel, no sights, comes with scope rings on shroud), blue $838.00
Price: As above, stainless $881.00
Price: Compensated Scoped Hunter (6" barrel, 7" shroud, scope rings on shroud), blue $871.00
Price: As above, stainless $914.00

HANDGUNS—SINGLE-ACTION REVOLVERS

Both classic six-shooters and modern adaptations for hunting and sport.

American Arms Regulator

AMERICAN ARMS REGULATOR SINGLE ACTIONS
Caliber: 357 Mag. 44-40, 45 Colt.
Barrel: 4¾", 5½", 7½".
Weight: 32 oz. (4¾" barrel) **Length:** 8 1/6" overall (4¾" barrel).
Stocks: Smooth walnut.
Sights: Blade front, groove rear.
Features: Blued barrel and cylinder, brass trigger guard and backstrap. Introduced 1992. Imported from Italy by American Arms, Inc.
Price: Regulator, single cylinder $328.00
Price: Regulator, dual cylinder (44-40/44 Spec. or 45 Colt/45 ACP) $374.00
Price: Regulator DLX (all steel) $374.00

American Arms Buckhorn Single Action
Similar to the Regulator single action except chambered for 44 Magnum. Available with 4¾", 6" or 7½" barrel. Overall length 11¾", weight is 44 oz. with 6" barrel. Introduced 1993. Imported from Italy by American Arms, Inc.
Price: $359.00

HANDGUNS—SINGLE ACTION REVOLVERS

CENTURY GUN DIST. MODEL 100 SINGLE ACTION
Caliber: 30-30, 375 Win., 444 Marlin, 45-70, 50-70.
Barrel: 6½" (standard), 8", 10", 12".
Weight: 6 lbs. (loaded). **Length:** 15" overall (8" bbl.).
Stocks: Smooth walnut.
Sights: Ramp front, Millett adjustable square notch rear.
Features: Highly polished high tensile strength manganese bronze frame, blue cylinder and barrel; coil spring trigger mechanism. Calibers other than 45-70 start at $2,000.00. Contact maker for full price information. Introduced 1975. Made in U.S. From Century Gun Dist., Inc.
Price: 6½" barrel, 45-70 ....$1,250.00

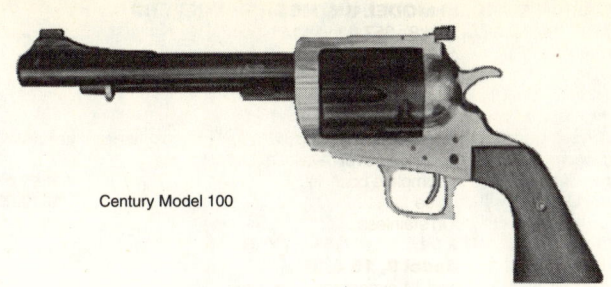
Century Model 100

CIMARRON U.S. CAVALRY MODEL SINGLE ACTION
Caliber: 45 Colt
Barrel: 7½".
Weight: 42 oz. **Length:** 13½" overall.
Stocks: Walnut.
Sights: Fixed.
Features: Has "A.P. Casey" markings; "U.S." plus patent dates on frame, serial number on backstrap, trigger guard, frame and cylinder, "APC" cartouche on left grip; color case-hardened frame and hammer, rest charcoal blue. Exact copy of the original. Imported by Cimarron Arms.
Price: $459.00

Consult our Directory pages for the location of firms mentioned.

Cimarron Artillery Model Single Action
Similar to the U.S. Cavalry model except has 5½" barrel, weighs 39 oz., and is 11½" overall. U.S. markings and cartouche, case-hardened frame and hammer; 45 Colt only.
Price: $459.00

CIMARRON 1873 PEACEMAKER REPRO
Caliber: 38 WCF, 357 Mag., 44 WCF, 44 Spec., 45 Colt.
Barrel: 4¾", 5½", 7½".
Weight: 39 oz. **Length:** 10" overall (4" barrel).
Stocks: Walnut.
Sights: Blade front, fixed or adjustable rear.
Features: Uses "old model" blackpowder frame with "Bullseye" ejector or New Model frame. Imported by Cimarron Arms.
Price: Peacemaker Reproduction, 4¾" barrel $429.95
Price: Frontier Six Shooter, 5½" barrel $429.95
Price: Single Action Army, 7½" barrel $429.95

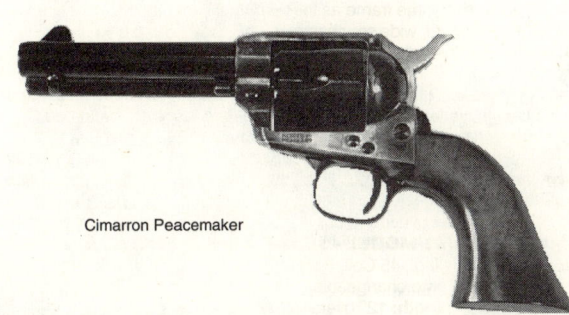
Cimarron Peacemaker

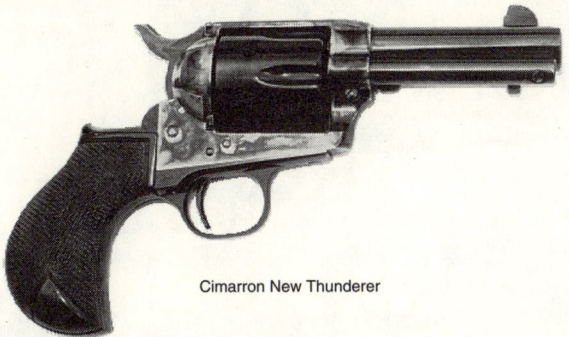
Cimarron New Thunderer

CIMARRON NEW THUNDERER REVOLVER
Caliber: 357 Mag., 44 WCF, 44 Spec., 45 Colt, 6-shot.
Barrel: 3½", 4¾", with ejector.
Weight: 38 oz. (3½" barrel). **Length:** NA.
Stocks: Hand-checkered walnut.
Sights: Blade front, notch rear.
Features: Thunderer grip; color case-hardened frame with balance blued, or nickel finish. Introduced 1993. Imported by Cimarron Arms.
Price: Color case-hardened $439.95
Price: Nickeled $559.95

COLT SINGLE ACTION ARMY REVOLVER
Caliber: 44-40, 45 Colt, 6-shot.
Barrel: 4¾", 5½", 7½".
Weight: 40 oz. (4¾" barrel). **Length:** 10¼" overall (4¾" barrel).
Stocks: Black Eagle composite.
Sights: Blade front, notch rear.
Features: Available in full nickel finish with nickel grip medallions, or Royal Blue with color case-hardened frame, gold grip medallions. Reintroduced 1992.
Price: $1,213.00

Colt Single Action Army

D-Max Sidewinder

D-MAX SIDEWINDER REVOLVER
Caliber: 45 Colt/410 shotshell, 6-shot.
Barrel: 6.5" or 7.5".
Weight: 57 oz. (6.5"). **Length:** 14.1" (6.5" barrel).
Stocks: Hogue black rubber with finger grooves.
Sights: Blade on ramp front, fully adjustable rear.
Features: Stainless steel construction. Has removable choke for firing shotshells. Grooved, wide-spur hammer; transfer bar ignition; satin stainless finish. Introduced 1992. Made in U.S. by D-Max, Inc.
Price: $750.00

CAUTION: PRICES SHOWN ARE SUPPLIED BY THE MANUFACTURER OR IMPORTER. CHECK YOUR LOCAL GUNSHOP.

HANDGUNS—SINGLE-ACTION REVOLVERS

E.A.A. BIG BORE BOUNTY HUNTER SA REVOLVERS
Caliber: 357 Mag., 44 Mag., 45 Colt, 6-shot.
Barrel: 4 1/2", 7 1/2".
Weight: 2.5 lbs. **Length:** 11" overall (4 5/8" barrel).
Stocks: Smooth walnut.
Sights: Blade front, grooved topstrap rear.
Features: Transfer bar safety; three position hammer; hammer forged barrel. Introduced 1992. Imported by European American Armory.
Price: Blue $299.00
Price: Color case-hardened frame $310.00

EMF DAKOTA 1875 OUTLAW REVOLVER
Caliber: 357, 44-40, 45 Colt.
Barrel: 7 1/2".
Weight: 46 oz. **Length:** 13 1/2" overall.
Stocks: Smooth walnut.
Sights: Blade front, fixed groove rear.
Features: Authentic copy of 1875 Remington with firing pin in hammer; color case-hardened frame, blue cylinder, barrel, steel backstrap and brass trigger guard. Also available in nickel, factory engraved. Imported by E.M.F.
Price: All calibers $465.00
Price: Nickel $550.00
Price: Engraved $600.00
Price: Engraved Nickel $710.00

EMF HARTFORD SINGLE-ACTION REVOLVERS
Caliber: 22 LR, 357 Mag., 32-20, 38-40, 44-40, 44 Spec., 45 Colt.
Barrel: 4 3/4", 5 1/2", 7 1/2".
Weight: 45 oz. **Length:** 13" overall (7 1/2" barrel).
Stocks: Smooth walnut.
Sights: Blade front, fixed rear.
Features: Identical to the origianl Colts with inspector cartouche on left grip, original patent dates and U.S. markings. All major parts serial numbered using original Colt-style lettering, numbering. Bullseye ejector head and color case-hardening on frame and hammer. Introduced 1990. From E.M.F.
Price: $600.00
Price: Cavalry or Artillery $655.00
Price: Nickel plated $725.00
Price: Engraved, nickel plated $840.00
Price: Pinkerton (bird's-head grip), 45 Colt, 4" barrel $680.00

EMF 1894 Target Bisley Revolver
Similar to the Hartford single-action revolver except has special grip frame and trigger guard, wide spur hammer; available in 45 Colt only, 5 1/2" or 7 1/2" barrel. Introduced 1995. Imported by EMF.
Price: Blue $680.00
Price: Nickel $805.00

FREEDOM ARMS PREMIER 454 CASULL
Caliber: 454 Casull with 45 Colt, 45 ACP, 45 Win. Mag. optional cylinders, 5-shot.
Barrel: 4 3/4", 6", 7 1/2", 10".
Weight: 50 oz. **Length:** 14" overall (7 1/2" bbl.).
Stocks: Impregnated hardwood.
Sights: Blade front, notch or adjustable rear.
Features: All stainless steel construction; sliding bar safety system. Lifetime warranty. Made in U.S. by Freedom Arms, Inc.
Price: Field Grade (matte finish, Pachmayr grips), adjustable sights, 4 3/4", 6", 7 1/2", 10" $1,263.00
Price: Field Grade, fixed sights, all barrel lengths $1,171.00
Price: Field Grade, 44 Rem. Mag., adjustable sights, all lengths $1,216.00
Price: Premier Grade 454 (brush finish, impregnated hardwood grips) adjustable sights, 4 3/4", 6", 7 1/2", 10" $1,612.00
Price: Premier Grade, fixed sights, all barrel lengths $1,507.00
Price: Premier Grade, 44 Rem. Mag., adjustable sights, all lengths ... $1,564.00
Price: Fitted 45 ACP, 45 Colt or 45 Win. Mag cylinder, add $247.00

Freedom Arms Casull 44 Mag and Model 353 Revolvers
Similar to the Premier 454 Casull except chambered for 357 Magnum with 5-shot cylinder; 4 3/4", 6", 7 1/2" or 9" barrel. Weighs 59 oz. with 7 1/2" barrel. Standard model has adjustable sights, matte finish, Pachmayr grips, 7 1/2" or 9" barrel; Silhouette has 9" barrel, Patridge front sight, Iron Sight Gun Works Silhouette adjustable rear, Pachmayr grips, trigger over-travel adjustment screw. All stainless steel. Introduced 1992.
Price: Field Grade $1,216.00
Price: Premier Grade (brushed finish, impregnated hardwood grips, Premier Grade sights) $1,564.00
Price: Silhouette (9", 357 Mag., 10", 44 Mag.) $1,304.35

Freedom Arms Model 555 Revolver
Same as the 454 Casull except chambered for the 50 A.E. (Action Express) cartridge. Offered in Premier and Field Grades with adjustable sights, 4 3/4", 6", 7 1/2" or 10" barrel. Introduced 1994. Made in U.S. by Freedom Arms, Inc.
Price: Premier Grade $1,612.00
Price: Field Grade $1,263.00

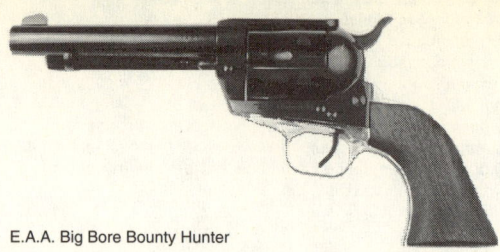

E.A.A. Big Bore Bounty Hunter

EMF Dakota 1890 Police Revolver
Similar to the 1875 Outlaw except has 5 1/2" barrel, weighs 40 oz., with 12 1/2" overall length. Has lanyard ring in butt. No web under barrel. Calibers 357, 44-40, 45 Colt. Imported by E.M.F.
Price: All calibers $470.00
Price: Nickel $560.00
Price: Engraved $620.00
Price: Engraved nickel $725.00

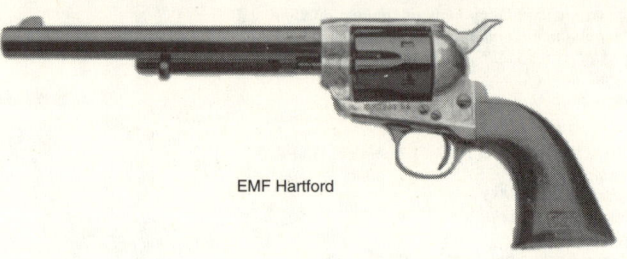

EMF Hartford

EMF Dakota New Model Single-Action Revolvers
Similar to the standard Dakota except has color case-hardened forged steel frame, black nickel backstrap and trigger guard. Calibers 357 Mag., 44-40, 45 Colt only.
Price: $460.00
Price: Nickel $585.00

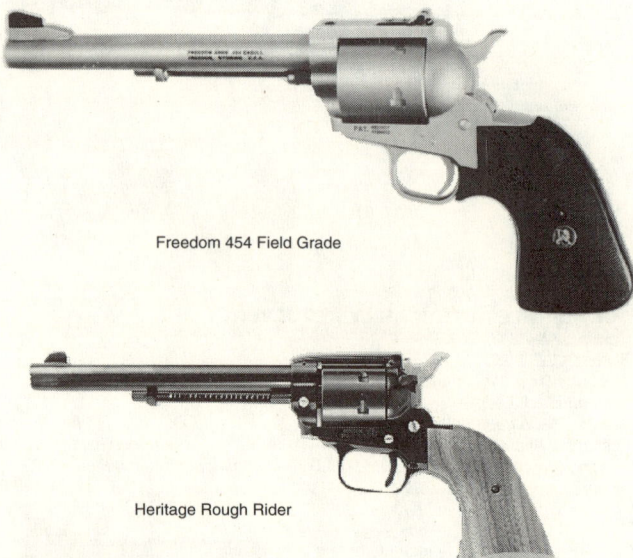

Freedom 454 Field Grade

Heritage Rough Rider

HERITAGE ROUGH RIDER REVOLVER
Caliber: 22 LR, 22 LR/22 WMR combo, 6-shot.
Barrel: 4 3/4", 6 1/2", 9".
Weight: 31 to 38 oz. **Length:** NA
Stocks: Goncolo Alves.
Sights: Blade front, fixed rear.
Features: Hammer block safety. High polish blue or nickel finish. Introduced 1993. Made in U.S. by Heritage Mfg., Inc.
Price: .... $104.95 to $134.95
Price: 2", 3", 4", birdshead grip .... $104.95 to $149.95

HANDGUNS—SINGLE-ACTION REVOLVERS

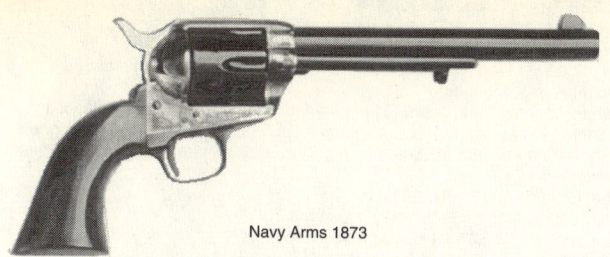

Navy Arms 1873

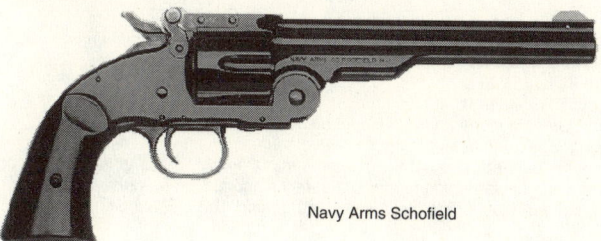

Navy Arms Schofield

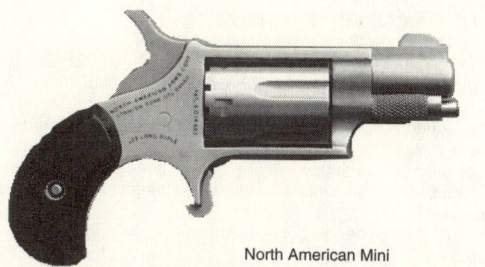

North American Mini

North American Mini-Master

Ruger Blackhawk

NAVY ARMS 1873 SINGLE-ACTION REVOLVER
Caliber: 44-40, 45 Colt, 6-shot cylinder.
Barrel: 3", 4 3/4", 5 1/2", 7 1/2".
Weight: 36 oz. **Length:** 10 3/4" overall (5 1/2" barrel).
Stocks: Smooth walnut.
Sights: Blade front, groove in topstrap rear.
Features: Blue with color case-hardened frame, or nickel. Introduced 1991. Imported by Navy Arms.
Price: Blue $390.00
Price: Nickel $455.00
Price: Economy model with brass backstrap and trigger guard $345.00
Price: 1873 U.S. Cavalry Model (7 1/2", 45 Colt, arsenal markings) $480.00
Price: 1895 U.S. Artillery Model (as above, 5 1/2" barrel) $480.00

NAVY ARMS 1875 SCHOFIELD REVOLVER
Caliber: 44-40, 45 Colt, 6-shot cylinder.
Barrel: 5", 7".
Weight: 39 oz. **Length:** 10 3/4" overall (5" barrel).
Stocks: Smooth walnut.
Sights: Blade front, notch rear.
Features: Replica of Smith & Wesson Model 3 Schofield. Single-action, top-break with automatic ejection. Polished blue finish. Introduced 1994. Imported by Navy Arms.
Price: Wells Fargo (5" barrel, Wells Fargo markings) $795.00
Price: U.S. Cavalry model (7" barrel, military markings) $795.00

NORTH AMERICAN MINI-REVOLVERS
Caliber: 22 Short, 22 LR, 22 WMR, 5-shot.
Barrel: 1 1/8", 1 5/8".
Weight: 4 to 6.6 oz. **Length:** 3 5/8" to 6 1/8" overall.
Stocks: Laminated wood.
Sights: Blade front, notch fixed rear.
Features: All stainless steel construction. Polished satin and matte finish. Engraved models available. From North American Arms.
Price: 22 Short, 22 LR, 1 1/8" bbl. $157.00
Price: 22 LR, 1 5/8" bbl. $157.00
Price: 22 WMR, 1 5/8" bbl. $178.00
Price: 22 WMR, 1 1/8" or 1 5/8" bbl. with extra 22 LR cylinder $210.00

NORTH AMERICAN MINI-MASTER
Caliber: 22 LR, 22 WMR, 5-shot cylinder.
Barrel: 4".
Weight: 10.7 oz. **Length:** 7.75" overall.
Stocks: Checkered hard black rubber.
Sights: Blade front, white outline rear adjustable for elevation, or fixed.
Features: Heavy vent barrel; full-size grips. Non-fluted cylinder. Introduced 1989.
Price: Adjustable sight, 22 WMR or 22 LR $279.00
Price: As above with extra WMR/LR cylinder $317.00
Price: Fixed sight, 22 WMR or 22 LR $264.00
Price: As above with extra WMR/LR cylinder $302.00

North American Black Widow Revolver
Similar to the Mini-Master except has 2" Heavy Vent barrel. Built on the 22 WMR frame. Non-fluted cylinder, black rubber grips. Available with either Millett Low Profile fixed sights or Millett sight adjustable for elevation only. Overall length 5 7/8", weight 8.8 oz. From North American Arms.
Price: Adjustable sight, 22 LR or 22 WMR $249.00
Price: As above with extra WMR/LR cylinder $285.00
Price: Fixed sight, 22 LR or 22 WMR $235.00
Price: As above with extra WMR/LR cylinder $270.00

RUGER BLACKHAWK REVOLVER
Caliber: 30 Carbine, 357 Mag./38 Spec., 41 Mag., 45 Colt, 6-shot.
Barrel: 4 5/8" or 6 1/2", either caliber; 7 1/2" (30 Carbine, 45 Colt only).
Weight: 42 oz. (6 1/2" bbl.). **Length:** 12 1/4" overall (6 1/2" bbl.).
Stocks: American walnut.
Sights: 1/8" ramp front, micro-click rear adjustable for windage and elevation.
Features: Ruger transfer bar safety system, independent firing pin, hardened chrome moly steel frame, music wire springs throughout.
Price: Blue, 30 Carbine (7 1/2" bbl.), BN31 .... $345.00
Price: Blue, 357 Mag. (4 5/8", 6 1/2"), BN34, BN36 .... $345.00
Price: Blue, 357/9mm Convertible (4 5/8", 6 1/2"), BN34X, BN36X ... $365.00
Price: Blue, 41 Mag., 45 Colt (4 5/8", 6 1/2"), BN41, BN42, BN45 ... $345.00
Price: Stainless, 357 Mag. (4 5/8", 6 1/2"), KBN34, KBN36 .... $428.00
Price: High-gloss stainless, 357 Mag. (4 5/8", 6 1/2"), GKBN34, GKBN36 . $428.00
Price: High-gloss stainless, 45 Colt (4 5/8", 7 1/2"), GKBN44, GKBN45 ... $428.00

Ruger Bisley Single-Action Revolver
Similar to standard Blackhawk except the hammer is lower with a smoothly curved, deeply checkered wide spur. The trigger is strongly curved with a wide smooth surface. Longer grip frame has a hand-filling shape. Adjustable rear sight, ramp-style front. Has an unfluted cylinder and roll engraving, adjustable sights. Chambered for 357, 41, 44 Mags. and 45 Colt; 7 1/2" barrel; overall length of 13". Introduced 1985.
Price: $415.00

CAUTION: PRICES SHOWN ARE SUPPLIED BY THE MANUFACTURER OR IMPORTER. CHECK YOUR LOCAL GUNSHOP.

HANDGUNS—SINGLE-ACTION REVOLVERS

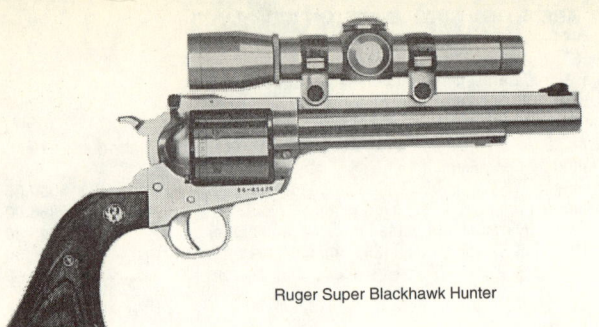

Ruger Super Blackhawk Hunter

Ruger Bisley

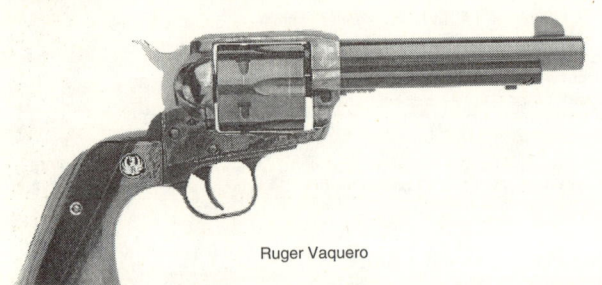

Ruger Vaquero

RUGER VAQUERO SINGLE-ACTION REVOLVER
Caliber: 44-40, 44 Magnum, 45 Colt, 6-shot.
Barrel: 4⅝", 5½", 7½".
Weight: 41 oz. **Length:** 13⅜" overall (7½" barrel).
Stocks: Smooth rosewood with Ruger medallion.
Sights: Blade front, fixed notch rear.
Features: Uses Ruger's patented transfer bar safety system and loading gate interlock with classic styling. Blued model has color case-hardened finish on the frame, the rest polished and blued. Stainless model has high-gloss polish. Introduced 1993. From Sturm, Ruger & Co.
Price: BNV44 (4⅝"), BNV445 (5½"), BNV45 (7½"), blue $419.00
Price: KBNV44 (4⅝"), KBNV455 (5½"), KBNV45 (7½"), stainless $419.00

TEXAS LONGHORN ARMS GROVER'S IMPROVED NO. FIVE
Caliber: 44 Magnum, 6-shot.
Barrel: 5½".
Weight: 44 oz. **Length:** NA.
Stocks: Fancy AAA walnut.
Sights: Square blade front on ramp, fully adjustable rear.
Features: Music wire coil spring action with double locking bolt; polished blue finish. Handmade in limited 1,200-gun production. Grip contour, straps, over-sized base pin, lever latch and lockwork identical copies of Elmer Keith design. Lifetime warranty to original owner. Introduced 1988.
Price: $1,195.00

TEXAS LONGHORN ARMS RIGHT-HAND SINGLE ACTION
Caliber: All centerfire pistol calibers.
Barrel: 4¾".
Weight: NA. **Length:** NA.
Stocks: One-piece fancy walnut, or any fancy AAA wood.
Sights: Blade front, grooved topstrap rear.
Features: Loading gate and ejector housing on left side of gun. Cylinder rotates to the left. All steel construction; color case-hardened frame; high polish blue; music wire coil springs. Lifetime guarantee to original owner. Introduced 1984. From Texas Longhorn Arms.
Price: South Texas Army Limited Edition—handmade, only 1,000 to be produced; "One of One Thousand" engraved on barrel $1,595.00

RUGER SUPER BLACKHAWK
Caliber: 44 Magnum, 6-shot. Also fires 44 Spec.
Barrel: 4⅝", 5½", 7½", 10½".
Weight: 48 oz. (7½" bbl.), 51 oz. (10½" bbl.). **Length:** 13⅜" overall (7½" bbl.).
Stocks: American walnut.
Sights: ⅛" ramp front, micro-click rear adjustable for windage and elevation.
Features: Ruger transfer bar safety system, non-fluted cylinder, steel grip and cylinder frame, square back trigger guard, wide serrated trigger and wide spur hammer.
Price: Blue (S45N, S47N, S411N) $398.00
Price: Stainless (KS45N, KS47N, KS411N) $435.00
Price: Stainless KS47NH Hunter with scope rings, 7½" $498.00
Price: High-gloss stainless (4⅝", 5½", 7½"), GKS458N, GKS45N, GKS47N $435.00

RUGER NEW SUPER BEARCAT SINGLE ACTION
Caliber: 22 LR/22 WMR, 6-shot.
Barrel: 4".
Weight: 23 oz. **Length:** 8⅞" overall.
Stocks: Smooth rosewood with Ruger medallion.
Sights: Blade front, fixed notch rear.
Features: Reintroduction of the Ruger Super Bearcat with slightly lengthened frame, Ruger patented transfer bar safety system. Comes with two cylinders. Available in blue or stainless steel. Introduced 1993. From Sturm, Ruger & Co.
Price: SBC4, blue $298.00
Price: KSBC4, stainless $325.00

RUGER SUPER SINGLE-SIX CONVERTIBLE
Caliber: 22 LR, 6-shot; 22 WMR in extra cylinder.
Barrel: 4⅝", 5½", 6½", or 9½" (6-groove).
Weight: 34½ oz. (6½" bbl.). **Length:** 11 13/16" overall (6½" bbl.).
Stocks: Smooth American walnut.
Sights: Improved Patridge front on ramp, fully adjustable rear protected by integral frame ribs; or fixed sight.
Features: Ruger transfer bar safety system, gate-controlled loading, hardened chrome moly steel frame, wide trigger, music wire springs throughout, independent firing pin.
Price: 4⅝", 5½", 6½", 9½" barrel, blue, fixed or adjustable sight (5½", 6½") $298.00
Price: 5½", 6½" bbl. only, high-gloss stainless steel, fixed or adjustable sight $378.00

Ruger SSM Single-Six Revolver
Similar to the Super Single-Six revolver except chambered for 32 H&R Magnum (also handles 32 S&W and 32 S&W Long). Weight is about 34 oz. with 6½" barrel. Barrel lengths: 4⅝", 5½", 6½", 9½". Introduced 1985.
Price: $298.00

Ruger Bisley Small Frame Revolver
Similar to the Single-Six except frame is styled after the classic Bisley "flat-top." Most mechanical parts are unchanged. Hammer is lower and smoothly curved with a deeply checkered spur. Trigger is strongly curved with a wide smooth surface. Longer grip frame designed with a hand-filling shape, and the trigger guard is a large oval. Adjustable dovetail rear sight; front sight base accepts interchangeable square blades of various heights and styles. Has an unfluted cylinder and roll engraving. Weight about 41 oz. Chambered for 22 LR and 32 H&R Mag., 6½" barrel only. Introduced 1985.
Price: $345.00

Texas Longhorn Grover's No. Five

Texas Longhorn Arms Sesquicentennial Model Revolver
Similar to the South Texas Army Model except has ¾-coverage Nimschke-style engraving, antique golden nickel plate finish, one-piece elephant ivory grips. Comes with handmade solid walnut presentation case, factory letter to owner. Limited edition of 150 units. Introduced 1986.
Price: $2,500.00

366 THE GUN DIGEST — CAUTION: PRICES SHOWN ARE SUPPLIED BY THE MANUFACTURER OR IMPORTER. CHECK YOUR LOCAL GUNSHOP.

HANDGUNS—SINGLE-ACTION REVOLVERS

Texas Longhorn Arms Texas Border Special
Similar to the South Texas Army Limited Edition except has 3½" barrel, bird's-head style grip. Same special features. Introduced 1984.
Price: $1,595.00

Texas Longhorn Arms West Texas Flat Top Target
Similar to the South Texas Army Limited Edition except choice of barrel length from 7½" through 15"; flat-top style frame; ⅛" contoured ramp front sight, old model steel micro-click rear adjustable for windage and elevation. Same special features. Introduced 1984.
Price: $1,595.00

Uberti 1873 Buckhorn Single Action
A slightly larger version of the Cattleman revolver. Available in 44 Magnum or 44 Magnum/44-40 convertible, otherwise has same specs.
Price: Steel backstrap, trigger guard, fixed sights $410.00
Price: Convertible (two cylinders) $460.00

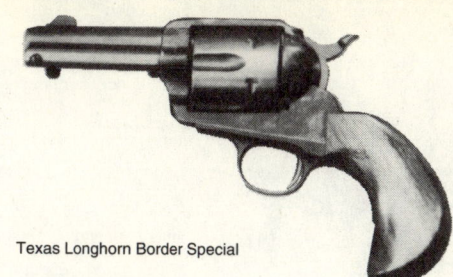
Texas Longhorn Border Special

Texas Longhorn Arms Cased Set
Set contains one each of the Texas Longhorn Right-Hand Single Actions, all in the same caliber, same serial numbers (100, 200, 300, 400, 500, 600, 700, 800, 900). Ten sets to be made (#1000 donated to NRA museum). Comes in hand-tooled leather case. All other specs same as Limited Edition guns. Introduced 1984.
Price: $5,750.00
Price: With ¾-coverage "C-style" engraving $7,650.00

UBERTI 1873 CATTLEMAN SINGLE ACTIONS
Caliber: 22 LR/22 WMR, 38 Spec., 357 Mag., 44 Spec., 44-40, 45 Colt/45 ACP, 6-shot.
Barrel: 4¾", 5½", 7½"; 44-40, 45 Colt also with 3", 4".
Weight: 38 oz. (5½" bbl.). **Length:** 10¾" overall (5½" bbl.).
Stocks: One-piece smooth walnut.
Sights: Blade front, groove rear; fully adjustable rear available.
Features: Steel or brass backstrap, trigger guard; color case-hardened frame, blued barrel, cylinder. Imported from Italy by Uberti USA.
Price: Steel backstrap, trigger guard, fixed sights $410.00
Price: Brass backstrap, trigger guard, fixed sights $365.00

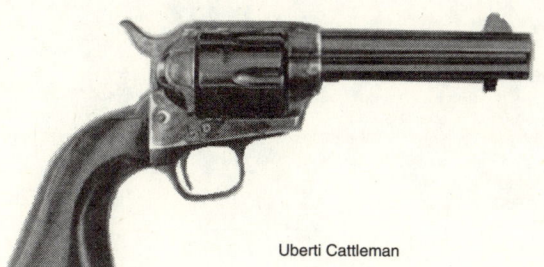
Uberti Cattleman

UBERTI 1875 SA ARMY OUTLAW REVOLVER
Caliber: 357 Mag., 44-40, 45 Colt, 45 Colt/45 ACP convertible, 6-shot.
Barrel: 5½", 7½".
Weight: 44 oz. **Length:** 13¾" overall.
Stocks: Smooth walnut.
Sights: Blade front, notch rear.
Features: Replica of the 1875 Remington S.A. Army revolver. Brass trigger guard, color case-hardened frame, rest blued. Imported by Uberti USA.
Price: $405.00
Price: 45 Colt/45 ACP convertible $450.00

UBERTI 1890 ARMY OUTLAW REVOLVER
Caliber: 357 Mag., 44-40, 45 Colt, 45 Colt/45 ACP convertible, 6-shot.
Barrel: 5½", 7½".
Weight: 37 oz. **Length:** 12½" overall.
Stocks: American walnut.
Sights: Blade front, groove rear.
Features: Replica of the 1890 Remington single action. Brass trigger guard, rest is blued. Imported by Uberti USA.
Price: $410.00
Price: 45 Colt/45 ACP convertible $415.00

Uberti 1875 Army

HANDGUNS—MISCELLANEOUS
Specially adapted single-shot and multi-barrel arms.

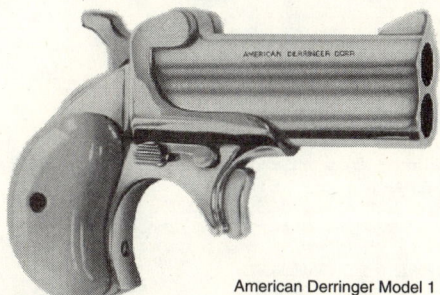
American Derringer Model 1

AMERICAN DERRINGER MODEL 1
Caliber: 22 LR, 22 WMR, 30 Carbine, 30 Luger, 30-30 Win., 32 H&R Mag., 32-20, 380 ACP, 38 Super, 38 Spec., 38 Spec. shotshell, 38 Spec. +P, 9mm Para., 357 Mag., 357 Mag./45/410, 357 Maximum, 10mm, 40 S&W, 41 Mag., 38-40, 44-40 Win., 44 Spec., 44 Mag., 45 Colt, 45 Win. Mag., 45 ACP, 45 Colt/410, 45-70 single shot.
Barrel: 3".
Weight: 15½ oz. (38 Spec.). **Length:** 4.82" overall.
Stocks: Rosewood, Zebra wood.
Sights: Blade front.
Features: Made of stainless steel with high-polish or satin finish. Two-shot capacity. Manual hammer block safety. Introduced 1980. Available in almost any pistol caliber. Contact the factory for complete list of available calibers and prices. From American Derringer Corp.
Price: 22 LR $245.00
Price: 38 Spec. $245.00
Price: 357 Maximum $265.00
Price: 357 Mag. $257.00
Price: 9mm, 380, ...$245.00
Price: 40 S&W $257.00
Price: 44 Spec., ...$320.00
Price: 44-40 Win., 45 Colt $320.00
Price: 30-30, 41, 44 Mags., 45 Win. Mag. ....$375.00 to $385.00
Price: 45-70, single shot $312.00
Price: 45 Colt, 410, 2½" $320.00
Price: 45 ACP, 10mm Auto $257.00

CAUTION: PRICES SHOWN ARE SUPPLIED BY THE MANUFACTURER OR IMPORTER. CHECK YOUR LOCAL GUNSHOP.

HANDGUNS—MISCELLANEOUS

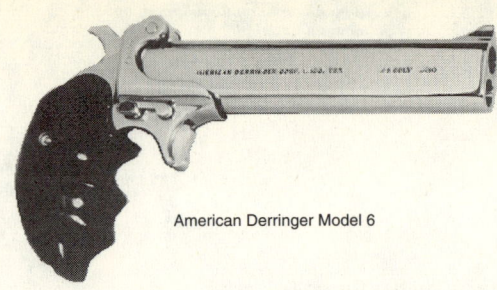
American Derringer Model 6

American Derringer Model 4
Similar to the Model 1 except has 4.1" barrel, overall length of 6", and weighs 16½ oz.; chambered for 357 Mag., 357 Maximum, 45-70, 3" 410-bore shotshells or 45 Colt or 44 Magnum. Made of stainless steel. Manual hammer block safety. Introduced 1985.
Price: 3" 410/45 Colt $352.00
Price: 3" 410/45 Colt or 45-70 (Alaskan Survival model) $387.50
Price: 44 Magnum with oversize grips $422.00
Price: Alaskan Survival model (45-70 upper, 410 or 45 Colt lower) $387.50

American Derringer Model 10 Lightweight
Similar to the Model 1 except frame is of aluminum, giving weight of 10 oz. Stainless barrels. Available in 38 Spec., 45 Colt or 45 ACP only. Matte gray finish. Introduced 1989.
Price: 45 Colt $320.00
Price: 45 ACP $257.00
Price: 38 Spec. $240.00

AMERICAN DERRINGER DA 38 MODEL
Caliber: 9mm Para., 38 Spec., 357 Mag., 40 S&W.
Barrel: 3".
Weight: 14.5 oz. **Length:** 4.8" overall.
Stocks: Rosewood, walnut or other hardwoods.
Sights: Fixed.
Features: Double-action only; two-shots. Manual safety. Made of satin-finished stainless steel and aluminum. Introduced 1989. From American Derringer Corp.
Price: 38 Spec. $300.00
Price: 9mm Para. $325.00
Price: 357 Mag., 40 S&W $350.00

ANSCHUTZ EXEMPLAR BOLT-ACTION PISTOL
Caliber: 22 LR, 5-shot; 22 Hornet, 5-shot.
Barrel: 10", 14".
Weight: 3½ lbs. **Length:** 17" overall.
Stock: European walnut with stippled grip and forend.
Sights: Hooded front on ramp, open notch rear adjustable for windage and elevation.
Features: Uses Match 64 action with left-hand bolt; Anschutz #5091 two-stage trigger set at 9.85 oz. Receiver grooved for scope mounting; open sights easily removed. The 22 Hornet version uses Match 54 action with left-hand bolt, Anschutz #5099 two-stage trigger set at 19.6 oz. Introduced 1987. Imported from Germany by Precision Sales International.
Price: 22 LR $558.00
Price: 22 LR, left-hand $558.00
Price: 22 LR, 14" barrel $562.00
Price: 22 Hornet (no sights, 10" bbl.) $995.00

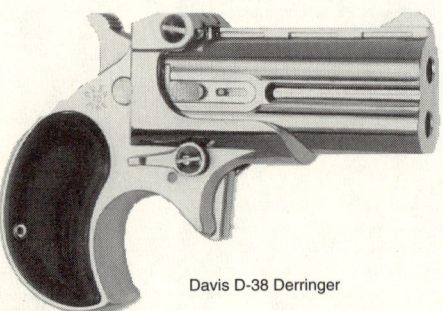
Davis D-38 Derringer

American Derringer Model 6
Similar to the Model 1 except has 6" barrels chambered for 3" 410 shotshells or 22 WMR, 357 Mag., 45 ACP, 45 Colt; rosewood stocks; 8.2" o.a.l. and weighs 21 oz. Shoots either round for each barrel. Manual hammer block safety. Introduced 1986.
Price: 22 WMR $300.00
Price: 357 Mag. $310.00
Price: 45 Colt/410 .... $362.50
Price: 45 ACP $345.00

American Derringer Model 7 Ultra Lightweight
Similar to Model 1 except made of high strength aircraft aluminum. Weighs 7½ oz., 4.82" o.a.l., rosewood stocks. Available in 22 LR, 22 WMR, 32 H&R Mag., 380 ACP, 38 Spec., 44 Spec. Introduced 1986.
Price: 22 LR, WMR $240.00
Price: 38 Spec. $240.00
Price: 380 ACP $240.00
Price: 32 H&R Mag. $240.00
Price: 44 Spec. $500.00

American Derringer Lady Derringer
Same as the Model 1 except has tuned action, is fitted with scrimshawed synthetic ivory grips; chambered for 32 H&R Mag. and 38 Spec.; 357 Mag., 45 Colt. Deluxe Grade is highly polished; Deluxe Engraved is engraved in a pattern similar to that used on 1880s derringers. All come in a French fitted jewelry box. Introduced 1991.
Price: 32 H&R Mag. $255.00
Price: 357 Mag. $275.00
Price: 38 Spec. $235.00
Price: 45 Colt $320.00

American Derringer Texas Commemorative
A Model 1 Derringer with solid brass frame, stainless steel barrel and rosewood grips. Available in 38 Speical, 44-40 Win., or 45 Colt. Introduced 1987.
Price: 38 Spec. $225.00
Price: 44-40 or 45 Colt $320.00

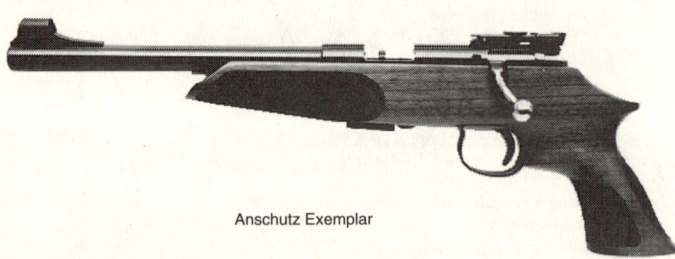
Anschutz Exemplar

DAVIS DERRINGERS
Caliber: 22 LR, 22 WMR, 25 ACP, 32 ACP.
Barrel: 2.4".
Weight: 9.5 oz. **Length:** 4" overall.
Stocks: Laminated wood.
Sights: Blade front, fixed notch rear.
Features: Choice of black Teflon or chrome finish; spur trigger. Introduced 1986. Made in U.S. by Davis Industries.
Price: $75.00

DAVIS LONG-BORE DERRINGERS
Caliber: 22 WMR, 32 H&R Mag., 38 Spec., 9mm Para.
Barrel: 3.5".
Weight: 16 oz. **Length:** 5.4" overall.
Stocks: Textured black synthetic.
Sights: Fixed.
Features: Chrome or black teflon finish. Larger than Davis D-Series models. Introduced 1995. Made in U.S. by Davis Industries.
Price: $104.00
Price: Big-Bore models (same calibers, ¾" shorter barrels) $98.00

DAVIS D-SERIES DERRINGERS
Caliber: 22 WMR, 32 H&R, 38 Special.
Barrel: 2.75".
Weight: 11.5 oz. **Length:** 4.65" overall.
Stocks: Textured black synthetic.
Sights: Blade front, fixed notch rear.
Features: Alloy frame, steel-lined barrels, steel breech block. Plunger-type safety with integral hammer block. Chrome or black Teflon finish. Introduced 1992. Made in U.S. by Davis Industries.
Price: $98.00

HANDGUNS—MISCELLANEOUS

Gaucher GN1 Silhouette

HJS Antigua Derringer
Same as the Frontier Four except blued barrel, brass frame, brass pivot pins. Brown plastic grips. Introduced 1994. Made in U.S. by HJS Arms, Inc.
Price: $180.00

HJS LONE STAR DERRINGER
Caliber: 380 ACP.
Barrel: 2".
Weight: 6 oz. **Length:** $3^{15}/_{16}$" overall.
Stocks: Brown plastic.
Sights: Groove.
Features: Stainless steel Construction. Beryllium copper firing pin. Button-rifled barrel. Introduced 1993. Made in U.S. by HJS Arms, Inc.
Price: $185.00

GAUCHER GN1 SILHOUETTE PISTOL
Caliber: 22 LR, single shot.
Barrel: 10".
Weight: 2.4 lbs. **Length:** 15.5" overall.
Stock: European hardwood.
Sights: Blade front, open adjustable rear.
Features: Bolt action, adjustable trigger. Introduced 1990. Imported from France by Mandall Shooting Supplies.
Price: About $525.00
Price: Model GP Silhouette $425.00

MAGNUM RESEARCH LONE EAGLE SINGLE SHOT PISTOL
Caliber: 22 Hornet, 223, 22-250, 243, 7mm BR, 7mm-08, 30-30, 308, 30-06, 357 Max., 35 Rem., 358 Win., 44 Mag., 444 Marlin.
Barrel: 14", interchangable.
Weight: 4lbs, 3 oz. to 4 lbs, 7 oz. **Length:** 15" overall.
Stocks: Composition, with thumbrest.
Sights: None furnished; drilled and tapped for scope mounting and open sights. Open sights optional.
Features: Cannon-type rotating breech with spring-activated ejector. Ordnance steel with matte blue finish. Cross-bolt safety. External cocking lever on left side of gun. Introduced 1991. Available from Magnum Research, Inc.
Price: Complete pistol $344.00
Price: Barreled action only $254.00
Price: Scope base $14.00
Price: Adjustable open sights $35.00

CONSULT **Shooter's Marketplace** Page 266, This Issue

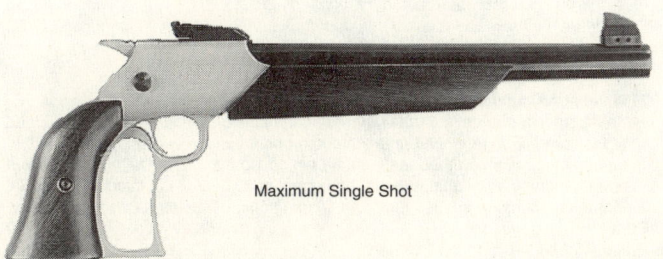
Maximum Single Shot

FEATHER GUARDIAN ANGEL PISTOL
Caliber: 22 LR/22 WMR.
Barrel: 2".
Weight: 12 oz. **Length:** 5" overall.
Stocks: Black composition.
Sights: Fixed.
Features: Uses a pre-loaded two-shot drop-in "magazine." Stainless steel construction; matte finish. From Feather Industries. Introduced 1988.
Price: $119.95

HJS FRONTIER FOUR DERRINGER
Caliber: 22 LR.
Barrel: 2".
Weight: $5^1/_2$ oz. **Length:** $3^{15}/_{16}$" overall.
Stocks: Brown plastic.
Sights: None.
Features: Four barrels fire with rotating firing pin. Stainless steel construction. Introduced 1993. Made in U.S. by HJS Arms, Inc.
Price: $165.00

HJS Frontier Four

Magnum Research Lone Eagle

MANDALL/CABANAS PISTOL
Caliber: 177, pellet or round ball; single shot.
Barrel: 9".
Weight: 51 oz. **Length:** 19" overall.
Stock: Smooth wood with thumbrest.
Sights: Blade front on ramp, open adjustable rear.
Features: Fires round ball or pellets with 22 blank cartridge. Automatic safety; muzzlebrake. Imported from Mexico by Mandall Shooting Supplies.
Price: $139.95

MAXIMUM SINGLE SHOT PISTOL
Caliber: 22 LR, 22 Hornet, 22 BR, 22 PPC, 223 Rem., 22-250, 6mm BR, 6mm PPC, 243, 250 Savage, 6.5mm-35M, 270 MAX, 270 Win., 7mm TCU, 7mm BR, 7mm-35, 7mm INT-R, 7mm-08, 7mm Rocket, 7mm Super Mag., 30 Herrett, 30 Carbine, 30-30, 308 Win., 30x39, 32-20, 357 Mag., 357 Maximum, 358 Win., 44 Mag., 454 Casull.
Barrel: $8^3/_4$", $10^1/_2$", 14".
Weight: 61 oz. ($10^1/_2$" bbl.); 78 oz. (14" bbl.). **Length:** 15", $18^1/_2$" overall (with $10^1/_2$" and 14" bbl., respectively).
Stocks: Smooth walnut stocks and forend.
Sights: Ramp front, fully adjustable open rear.
Features: Falling block action; drilled and tapped for M.O.A. scope mounts; integral grip frame/receiver; adjustable trigger; Douglas barrel (interchangeable). Introduced 1983. Made in U.S. by M.O.A. Corp.
Price: Stainless receiver, blue barrel $653.00
Price: Stainless receiver, stainless barrel $711.00
Price: Extra blued barrel $180.00
Price: Extra stainless barrel $244.00
Price: Scope mount $52.00

CAUTION: PRICES SHOWN ARE SUPPLIED BY THE MANUFACTURER OR IMPORTER. CHECK YOUR LOCAL GUNSHOP.

HANDGUNS—MISCELLANEOUS

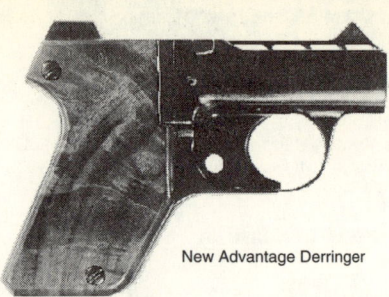
New Advantage Derringer

RPM XL SINGLE SHOT PISTOL
Caliber: 22 LR through 45-70.
Barrel: 8", 10 3/4", 12", 14".
Weight: About 60 oz. **Length:** NA.
Stocks: Smooth Goncalo Alves with thumb and heel rests.
Sights: Hooded front with interchangeable post, or Patridge; ISGW rear adjustable for windage and elevation.
Features: Barrel drilled and tapped for scope mount. Visible cocking indicator. Spring-loaded barrel lock, positive hammer-block safety. Trigger adjustable for weight of pull and over-travel. Contact maker for complete price list. Made in U.S. by RPM.
Price: Hunter model (stainless frame, 5/16" underlug, latch lever and positive extractor) $1,195.00
Price: Silhouette model (chrome-moly frame, blue or hard chrome finish) $857.50
Price: Extra barrel, 8" through 10 3/4" $287.50
Price: Muzzle brake $100.00

SUNDANCE POINT BLANK O/U DERRINGER
Caliber: 22 LR, 2-shot.
Barrel: 3".
Weight: 8 oz. **Length:** 4.6" overall.
Stocks: Grooved composition.
Sights: Blade front, fixed notch rear.
Features: Double-action trigger, push-bar safety, automatic chamber selection. Fully enclosed hammer. Matte black finish. Introduced 1994. Made in U.S. by Sundance Industries.
Price: $99.00

TEXAS ARMORY DEFENDER DERRINGER
Caliber: 9mm Para., 357 Mag., 44 Mag., 45 ACP, 45 Colt/410.
Barrel: 3".
Weight: 21 oz. **Length:** 5" overall.
Stocks: Smooth wood.
Sights: Blade front, fixed rear.
Features: Interchangeable barrels; retracting firing pins; rebounding hammer; cross-bolt safety; removable trigger guard; automatic extractor. Blasted finish stainless steel. Introduced 1993. Made in U.S. by Texas Armory.
Price: $310.00
Price: Extra barrel $100.00

TEXAS LONGHORN "THE JEZEBEL" PISTOL
Caliber: 22 Short, Long, Long Rifle, single shot.
Barrel: 6".
Weight: 15 oz. **Length:** 8" overall.
Stocks: One-piece fancy walnut grip (right- or left-hand), walnut forend.
Sights: Bead front, fixed rear.
Features: Handmade gun. Top-break action; all stainless steel; automatic hammer block safety; music wire coil springs. Barrel is half-round, half-octagon. Announced 1986. From Texas Longhorn Arms.
Price: About $250.00

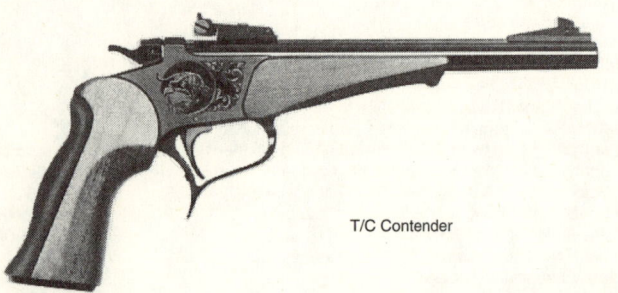
T/C Contender

NEW ADVANTAGE ARMS DERRINGER
Caliber: 22 LR, 22 WMR, 4-shot.
Barrel: 2 1/2".
Weight: 15 oz. **Length:** 4 1/2" overall.
Stocks: Smooth walnut.
Sights: Fixed.
Features: Double-action mechanism, four barrels, revolving hammer with four firing pins. Rebounding hammer. Blue or stainless. Reintroduced 1989. From New Advantage Arms Corp.
Price: 22 LR, 22 WMR, blue, about $249.99
Price: As above, stainless, about $249.99

RPM XL Pistol

Texas Armory Defender

THE JUDGE SINGLE SHOT PISTOL
Caliber: 22 Hornet, 22 K-Hornet, 218 Bee, 7-30 Waters, 30-30.
Barrel: 10" or 16.2".
Weight: NA. **Length:** NA.
Stocks: Walnut.
Sights: Bead on ramp front, open adjustable rear.
Features: Break-open design; made of 17-4 stainless steel. Also available as a kit. Introduced 1995. Made in U.S. by Cumberland Mountain Arms.
Price: .... NA

THOMPSON/CENTER CONTENDER
Caliber: 7mm TCU, 30-30 Win., 22 LR, 22 WMR, 22 Hornet, 223 Rem., 270 Ren, 7-30 Waters, 32-20 Win., 357 Mag., 357 Rem. Max., 44 Mag., 10mm Auto, 445 Super Mag., 45/410, single shot.
Barrel: 10", tapered octagon, bull barrel and vent. rib.
Weight: 43 oz. (10" bbl.). **Length:** 13 1/4" (10" bbl.).
Stocks: T/C "Competitor Grip." Right or left hand.
Sights: Under-cut blade ramp front, rear adjustable for windage and elevation.
Features: Break-open action with automatic safety. Single-action only. Interchangeable bbls., both caliber (rim & centerfire), and length. Drilled and tapped for scope. Engraved frame. See T/C catalog for exact barrel/caliber availability.
Price: Blued (rimfire cals.) $450.00
Price: Blued (centerfire cals.) $450.00
Price: Extra bbls. (standard octagon) $207.50
Price: 45/410, internal choke bbl. $227.50

Thompson/Center Stainless Contender
Same as the standard Contender except made of stainless steel with blued sights, black Rynite forend and ambidextrous finger-groove grip with a built-in rubber recoil cushion that has a sealed-in air pocket. Receiver has a different cougar etching. Available with 10" bull barrel in 22 LR, 22 LR Match, 22 Hornet, 223 Rem., 30-30 Win., 357 Mag., 44 Mag., 45 Colt/410. Introduced 1993.
Price: $480.00
Price: 45 Colt/410 .... $485.00
Price: With 22 LR match chamber $490.00

HANDGUNS—MISCELLANEOUS

T/C Stainless Super 14

UBERTI ROLLING BLOCK TARGET PISTOL
Caliber: 22 LR, 22 WMR, 22 Hornet, 357 Mag., 45 Colt, single shot.
Barrel: 9 7/8", half-round, half-octagon.
Weight: 44 oz. **Length:** 14" overall.
Stocks: Walnut grip and forend.
Sights: Blade front, fully adjustable rear.
Features: Replica of the 1871 rolling block target pistol. Brass trigger guard, color case-hardened frame, blue barrel. Imported by Uberti USA.
Price: $380.00

ULTRA LIGHT ARMS MODEL 20 REB HUNTER'S PISTOL
Caliber: 22-250 thru 308 Win. standard. Most silhouette calibers and others on request. 5-shot magazine.
Barrel: 14", Douglas No. 3.
Weight: 4 lbs.
Stock: Composite Kevlar, graphite reinforced. Du Pont Imron paint in green, brown, black and camo.
Sights: None furnished. Scope mount included.
Features: Timney adjustable trigger; two-position, three-function safety; benchrest quality action; matte or bright stock and metal finish; right- or left-hand action. Shipped in hard case. Introduced 1987. From Ultra Light Arms.
Price: $1,600.00

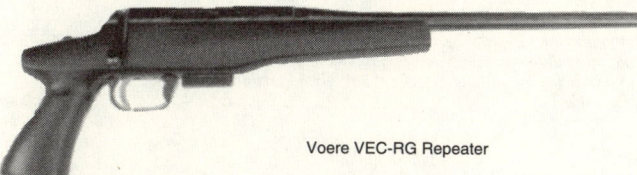

Voere VEC-RG Repeater

VOERE VEC-95CG SINGLE SHOT PISTOL
Caliber: 5.56mm, 6mm UCC caseless, single shot.
Barrel: 12", 14".
Weight: 3 lbs. **Length:** NA.
Stock: Black synthetic; center grip.
Sights: None furnished.
Features: Fires caseless ammunition via electronic ignition; two batteries in the grip last about 500 shots. Bolt action has two forward locking lugs. Tang safety. Drilled and tapped for scope mounting. Introduced 1995. Imported from Austria by JagerSport, Ltd.
Price: $1,495.00

Thompson/Center Stainless Super 14, Super 16 Contender
Same as the standard Super 14 and Super 16 except they are made of stainless steel with blued sights. Both models have black Rynite forend and finger-groove, ambidextrous grip with a built-in rubber recoil cushion that has a sealed-in air pocket. Receiver has a different cougar etching. Available in 22 LR, 22 LR Match, 22 Hornet, 223 Rem., 30-30 Win., 35 Rem. (Super 14), 45-70 (Super 16 only), 45 Colt/410. Introduced 1993.
Price: 14" bull barrel $490.00
Price: 16 1/4" bull barrel $495.00
Price: 45 Colt/410, 14" $520.00
Price: 45 Colt/410, 16" $525.00

Thompson/Center Contender Hunter Package
Package contains the Contender pistol in 223, 7-30 Waters, 30-30, 375 Win., 357 Rem. Maximum, 35 Rem., 44 Mag. or 45-70 with 14" with T/C's Muzzle Tamer, a 2.5x Recoil Proof Long Eye Relief scope with lighted reticle, q.d. sling swivels with a nylon carrying sling. Comes with a suede leather case with foam padding and fleece lining. Introduced 1990. From Thompson/Center Arms.
Price: 14" barrel $765.00

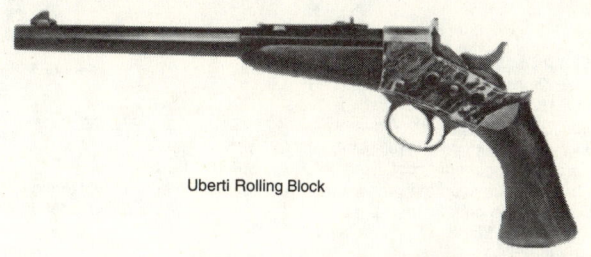

Uberti Rolling Block

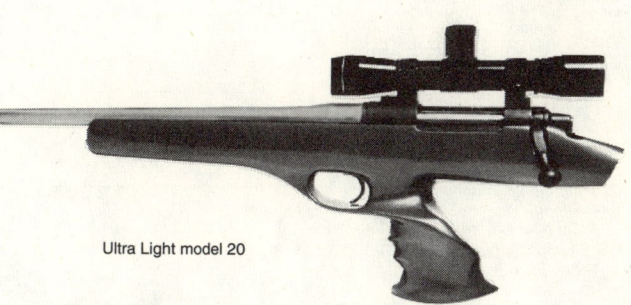

Ultra Light model 20

Consult our Directory pages for the location of firms mentioned.

Voere VEC-RG Repeater pistol
Similar to the VEC-95CG except has rear grip stock and detachable 5-shot magazine. Available with 12" or 14" barrel. Introduced 1995. Imported from Austria by JagerSport, Ltd.
Price: $1,495.00

CENTERFIRE RIFLES—AUTOLOADERS

Both classic arms and recent designs in American-style repeaters for sport and field shooting.

Thompson M1

Auto-Ordnance Thompson M1
Similar to the Model 27 A-1 except is in the M-1 configuration with side cocking knob, horizontal forend, smooth unfinned barrel, sling swivels on butt and forend. Matte black finish. Introduced 1985.
Price: $772.50

AUTO-ORDNANCE 27 A-1 THOMPSON
Caliber: 45 ACP, 30-shot magazine.
Barrel: 16".
Weight: 11 1/2 lbs. **Length:** About 42" overall (Deluxe).
Stock: Walnut stock and vertical forend.
Sights: Blade front, open rear adjustable for windage.
Features: Recreation of Thompson Model 1927. Semi-auto only. Deluxe model has finned barrel, adjustable rear sight and compensator; Standard model has plain barrel and military sight. From Auto-Ordnance Corp.
Price: Deluxe $795.00
Price: 1927A1C Lightweight model $767.00

CENTERFIRE RIFLES—AUTOLOADERS

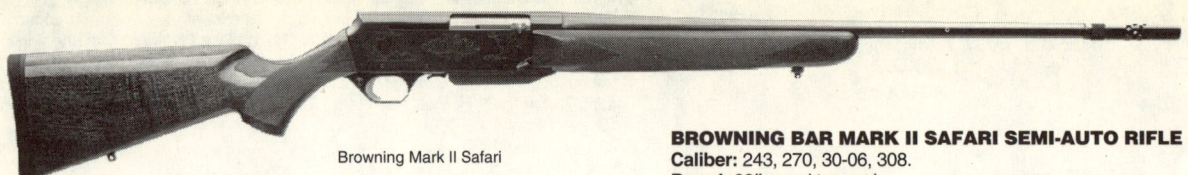
Browning Mark II Safari

BROWNING BAR MARK II SAFARI SEMI-AUTO RIFLE
Caliber: 243, 270, 30-06, 308.
Barrel: 22" round tapered.
Weight: 7 3/8 lbs. **Length:** 43" overall.
Stock: French walnut p.g. stock and forend, hand checkered.
Sights: Gold bead on hooded ramp front, click adjustable rear, or no sights.
Features: Has new bolt release lever; removable trigger assembly with larger trigger guard; redesigned gas and buffer systems. Detachable 4-round box magazine. Scroll-engraved receiver is tapped for scope mounting. BOSS barrel vibration modulator and muzzle brake system available only on models without sights. Mark II Safari introduced 1993. Imported from Belgium by Browning.
Price: Safari, with sights $694.95
Price: Safari, no sights $679.95
Price: Safari, no sights, BOSS $772.95

Browning BAR Mark II Safari Magnum Rifle
Same as the standard caliber model, except weighs 8 3/8 lbs., 45" overall, 24" bbl., 3-round mag. Cals. 7mm Mag., 300 Win. Mag., 338 Win. Mag. BOSS barrel vibration modulator and muzzle brake system available only on models without sights. Introduced 1993.
Price: Safari, with sights $744.95
Price: Safari, no sights $729.95
Price: Safari, no sights, BOSS $822.95

CALICO LIBERTY 50, 100 CARBINES
Caliber: 9mm Para.
Barrel: 16.1".
Weight: 7 lbs. **Length:** 34.5" overall.
Stock: Glass-filled, impact resistant polymer,
Sights: Adjustable front post, fixed notch and aperture flip rear.
Features: Helical feed magazine; ambidextrous, rotating sear/striker block safety; static cocking handle; retarded blowback action; aluminum alloy receiver. Introduced 1995. Made in U.S. by Calico.
Price: Liberty 50 .... $503.00
Price: Liberty 100 .... $517.00

Calico Liberty 50

BARRETT MODEL 82A-1 SEMI-AUTOMATIC RIFLE
Caliber: 50 BMG, 10-shot detachable box magazine.
Barrel: 29".
Weight: 28.5 lbs. **Length:** 57" overall.
Stock: Composition with Sorbothane recoil pad.
Sights: Scope optional.
Features: Semi-automatic, recoil operated with recoiling barrel. Three-lug locking bolt; muzzlebrake. Self-leveling bipod. Fires same 50-cal. ammunition as the M2HB machinegun. Introduced 1985. From Barrett Firearms.
Price: From $6,750.00

Consult our Directory pages for the location of firms mentioned.

Century FAL Sporter

CENTURY INTERNATIONAL FAL SPORTER RIFLE
Caliber: 308 Win.
Barrel: 20.75".
Weight: 9 lbs., 13 oz. **Length:** 41.125" overall.
Stock: Bell & Carlson thumbhole sporter.
Sights: Protected post front, adjustable aperture rear.
Features: Matte blue finish; rubber butt pad. From Century International Arms.
Price: About $625.00

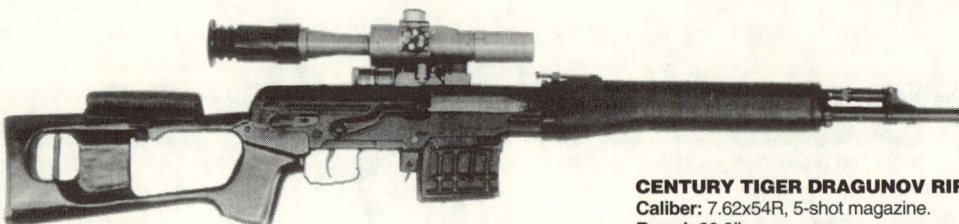
Century Tiger Dragunov

CENTURY TIGER DRAGUNOV RIFLE
Caliber: 7.62x54R, 5-shot magazine.
Barrel: 20.8".
Weight: 8.5 lbs. **Length:** 42.9" overall.
Stock: Thumbhole design of laminated European hardwood, black composition forend.
Sights: Blade front, open rear adjustable for elevation; comes with 4x rangefinding scope with sunshade, lighted reticle.
Features: Shortened version of Russian SVD sniper rifle. New manufacture. Blued metal. Quick-detachable scope mount. Comes with sling, cleaning kit, gas regulator tool, case. Imported from Russia by Century International Arms.
Price: About $1,350.00

CENTURY INTERNATIONAL M-14 SEMI-AUTO RIFLE
Caliber: 308 Win., 10-shot magazine.
Barrel: 22".
Weight: 8.25 lbs. **Length:** 40.8" overall.
Stock: Walnut with rubber recoil pad.
Sights: Protected blade front, fully adjustable aperture rear.
Features: Gas-operated; forged receiver; Parkerized finish. Imported from China by Century International Arms.
Price: About $468.95

CENTERFIRE RIFLES—AUTOLOADERS

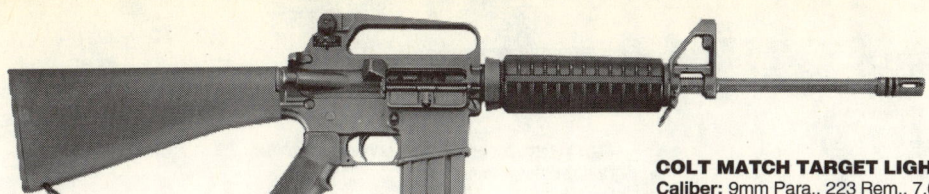

Colt Match Target Lightweight

COLT MATCH TARGET LIGHTWEIGHT RIFLE
Caliber: 9mm Para., 223 Rem., 7.62x39mm, 5-shot magazine.
Barrel: 16".
Weight: 6.7 lbs. (223); 7.1 lbs. (9mm Para.). **Length:** 34.5" overall extended.
Stock: Composition stock, grip, forend.
Sights: Post front, rear adjustable for windage and elevation.
Features: 5-round detachable box magazine, flash suppressor, sling swivels. Forward bolt assist included. Introduced 1991.
Price: $987.00
Price: 7.62x39mm $987.00

Daewoo DR200 Varmint

DAEWOO DR200 VARMINT RIFLE
Caliber: 223 Rem. 6-shot magazine.
Barrel: 18.3".
Weight: 9 lbs. **Length:** 39.2" overall.
Stock: Synthetic thumbhole style with rubber buttpad.
Sights: Post front in ring, aperture rear adjustable for windage and elevation.
Features: Forged aluminum receiver; bolt, bolt carrier, firing pin, piston and recoil spring contained in one assembly. Rotating bolt locking. Uses AR-15 magazines. Introduced 1995. Imported from Korea by Kimber of America, Inc.; distributed by Nationwide Sports Dist.
Price: About $750.00

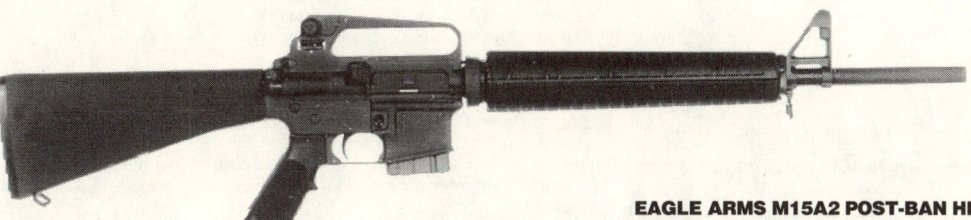

Eagle Arms M15A2

EAGLE ARMS M15A2 POST-BAN HEAVY BARREL RIFLE
Caliber: 223 Rem., 10-shot magazine.
Barrel: 20", premium, heavy; 1:9" twist.
Weight: 8 lbs., 2 oz. **Length:** $38\frac{3}{8}$" overall.
Stock: Black composition; weighted.
Sights: Elevation-adjustable front, E-2-style NM rear with 1/2-MOA adjustments, NM aperture.
Features: Upper and lower receivers have push-type pivot pin for easy takedown. Receivers hard coat anodized. A2-style forward assist mechanism. Integral raised M-16A2-type fence around magazine release button. Introduced 1995. Made in U.S. by Eagle Arms, Inc.
Price: $895.00

Eagle Arms M4C Carbine
Collapsible carbine-type buttstock, 16" heavy carbine barrel. Has M15A2-style upper receiver; full front sight housing; M177-type flash supressor. Weighs about 7 lbs., 3 oz. Introduced 1989. Made in U.S. by Eagle Arms, Inc.
Price: $1,525.00
Price: M4A1C (as above except one-piece international-style upper receiver for scope mounting) $1,525.00

Eagle Arms M15A3 Action Master Auto Rifle
One-piece international-style upper receiver for scope mounting, no front sight; solid aluminum handguard tube; free-floating 20" premium heavy barrel; muzzle compensator; NM trigger group. Weighs about 8 lbs., 4 oz. Introduced 1991. Made in U.S. by Eagle Arms, Inc.
Price: $1,475.00
Price: Eagle Spirit (as above except 16" premium air-gauged barrel, weighs 8 lbs.) $1,475.00

Eagle Arms M15A3 Eagle Eye Rifle
Has 24", $1\frac{1}{4}$" diameter, free-floating, stainless steel bull barrel with 1:8" twist. One-piece international-style upper receiver for scope mounting; solid aluminum tube; NM trigger. Weighs 13 lbs., $42\frac{1}{2}$" overall. Introduced 1994. Made in U.S. by Eagle Arms, Inc.
Price: $1,495.00

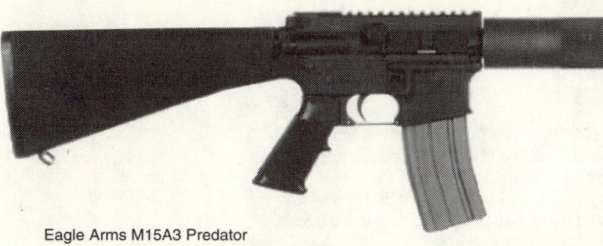

Eagle Arms M15A3 Predator

EAGLE ARMS M15A3 POST-BAN PREDATOR RIFLE
Caliber: 223, 10-shot magazine.
Barrel: 18"; $1\frac{1}{4}$" diameter; stainless; 1:8" twist.
Weight: 9 lbs., 4 oz. **Length:** $34\frac{3}{8}$" overall.
Stock: Black composition.
Sights: None furnished; optional.
Features: One-piece international-style upper receiver; NM trigger; free-floating barrel. Receiver hard-coat anodized. Integral raised M16A2-type fence around magazine release button; A2-style forward assist. Introduced 1995. Made in U.S. by Eagle Arms, Inc.
Price: $1,350.00
Price: M15A3 S.P.R. (18" barrel, 1:9" twist, front sight housing) $1,475.00

CENTERFIRE RIFLES—AUTOLOADERS

Feather Model F9

FEATHER AT-9 SEMI-AUTO CARBINE
Caliber: 9mm Para.
Barrel: 17".
Weight: 5 lbs. **Length:** 35" overall (stock extended); 26½" (closed).
Stock: Telescoping wire, composition pistol grip.
Sights: Hooded post front, adjustable aperture rear.
Features: Semi-auto only. Matte black finish. From Feather Industries. Announced 1988.
Price: $499.95
Price: Model F9 (fixed stock) $534.95

IBUS M17S 223 BULLPUP RIFLE
Caliber: 223, 10-shot magazine.
Barrel: 21.5".
Weight: 8.2 lbs. **Length:** 30" overall.
Stock: Zytel glass-filled nylon.
Sights: None furnished. Comes with scope mount for Weaver-type rings.
Features: Gas-operated, short-stroke piston system. Ambidextrous magazine release. Introduced 1993. Made in U.S. by Quality Parts Co./Bushmaster Firearms.
Price: $975.00

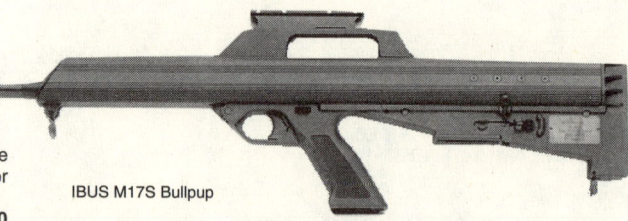

IBUS M17S Bullpup

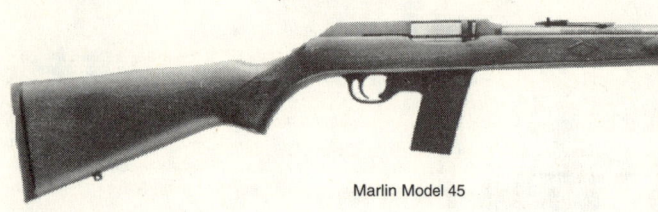

Marlin Model 45

Marlin Model 45 Carbine
Similar to the Model 9 except chambered for 45 ACP, 7-shot magazine. Introduced 1986.
Price: $404.20

MARLIN MODEL 9 CAMP CARBINE
Caliber: 9mm Para., 10-shot magazine.
Barrel: 16½", Micro-Groove® rifling.
Weight: 6¾ lbs. **Length:** 35½" overall.
Stock: Press-checkered walnut-finished Maine birch; rubber buttpad; Mar-Shield® finish; swivel studs.
Sights: Ramp front with orange post, cutaway Wide-Scan™ hood, adjustable open rear.
Features: Manual bolt hold-open; Garand-type safety, magazine safety; loaded chamber indicator; receiver drilled, tapped for scope mounting. Introduced 1985.
Price: $404.20

Olympic PCR-1

NORINCO MAK 90 SEMI-AUTO RIFLE
Caliber: 7.62x39, 223, 5-shot magazine.
Barrel: 16.25".
Weight: 8 lbs., 3 oz. **Length:** 35.5" overall.
Stock: Walnut-finished thumbhole with recoil pad.
Sights: Adjustable post front, open adjustable rear.
Features: Chrome-lined barrel; forged receiver; black oxide finish. Comes with extra magazine, oil bottle, cleaning kit, sling. Imported from China by Century International Arms.
Price: About $312.00

OLYMPIC ARMS PCR-1 RIFLE
Caliber: 223, 10-shot magazine.
Barrel: 20"; 416 stainless steel.
Weight: 10 lbs., 3 oz. **Length:** 38.25" overall.
Stock: A2 stowaway grip and trapdoor butt.
Sights: None supplied; flat-top upper receiver, cut-down front sight base.
Features: Based on the AR-15 rifle. Broach-cut, free-floating barrel with 1:8.5" or 1:10" twist. No bayonet lug. Crowned barrel; fluting available. Introduced 1994. Made in U.S. by Olympic Arms, Inc.
Price: $1,100.00

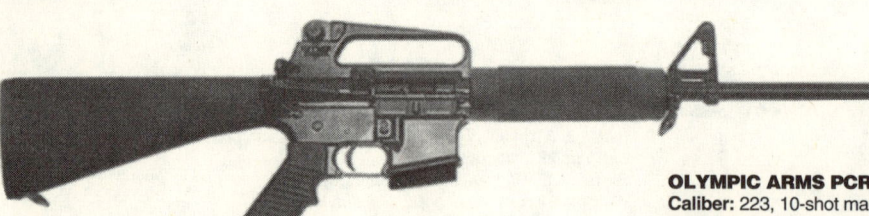

Olympic PCR-2

Olympic Arms PCR-2, PCR-3 Rifles
Similar to the PCR-1 except has 16" barrel, weighs 8 lbs., 2 oz.; has post front sight, fully adjustable aperture rear. Model PCR-3 has flat-top upper receiver, cut-down front sight base. Introduced 1994. Made in U.S. by Olympic Arms, Inc.
Price: $1,050.00

OLYMPIC ARMS PCR-4 RIFLE
Caliber: 223, 10-shot magazine.
Barrel: 20".
Weight: 8 lbs., 5 oz. **Length:** 38.25" overall.
Stock: A2 stowaway grip, trapdoor buttstock.
Sights: Post front, A1 rear adjustable for windage.
Features: Based on the AR-15 rifle. Barrel is button rifled with 1:7", 1:9", 1:12" or 1:14" twist. No bayonet lug. Introduced 1994. Made in U.S. by Olympic Arms, Inc.
Price: $793.00

CENTERFIRE RIFLES—AUTOLOADERS

Olympic PCR-5

OLYMPIC ARMS PCR SERIES CARBINES
Caliber: 223, 9mm Para., 45 ACP, 10mm, 40 S&W, 7.62x39mm, 10-shot.
Barrel: 16".
Weight: 7 lbs. **Length:** 34" overall (stock extended).
Stock: Telescoping butt.
Sights: Post front adjustable for elevation, rear adjustable for windage.
Features: Based on the AR-15 rifle. Has A2 Stowaway pistol grip and stock. Introduced 1982. Made in U.S. by Olympic Arms, Inc.
Price: PCR-15, 223 caliber $650.00
Price: PCR-9, 9mm Para. $700.00
Price: PCR-45, 45 ACP $730.00
Price: PCR-40, 40 S&W $780.00
Price: 7.62x39mm $700.00

OLYMPIC ARMS PCR-5, PCR-6 RIFLES
Caliber: 9mm Para., 40 S&W, 45 ACP, 223, 7.62x39mm (PCR-6), 10-shot magazine.
Barrel: 16".
Weight: 7 lbs. **Length:** 34.75" overall.
Stock: A2 stowaway grip, trapdoor buttstock.
Sights: Post front, A1 rear adjustable for windage.
Features: Based on the CAR-15. No bayonet lug. Introduced 1994. Made in U.S. by Olympic Arms, Inc.
Price: 9mm Para., 40 S&W, 45 ACP $790.00
Price: 223 Rem. $760.00
Price: 7.62x39mm (PCR-6) $837.00

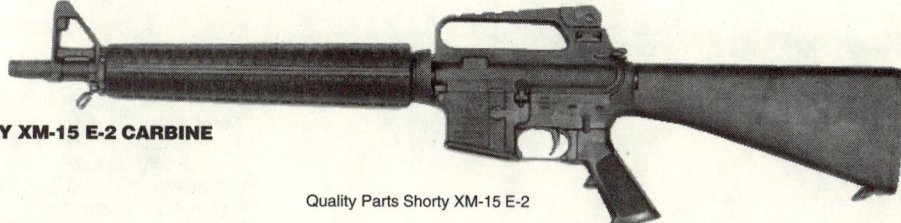
Quality Parts Shorty XM-15 E-2

QUALITY PARTS/BUSHMASTER SHORTY XM-15 E-2 CARBINE
Caliber: 223, 10-shot magazine.
Barrel: 16".
Weight: 7.2 lbs. **Length:** 34.5" overall.
Stock: Fixed black composition.
Sights: Adjustable post front, adjustable aperture rear.
Features: Patterned after Colt M-16A2. Chrome-lined barrel with manganese phosphate finish. "Shorty" handguards. Has E-2 lower receiver with push-pin. From Quality Parts Co./Bushmaster Firearms.
Price: $850.00
Price: XM-15 E-2 Carbine Dissipator (comes with "Dissipator" handguard and fixed stock) $895.00

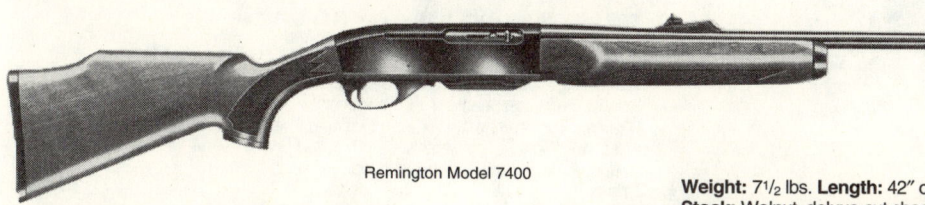
Remington Model 7400

REMINGTON MODEL 7400 AUTO RIFLE
Caliber: 243 Win., 270 Win., 280 Rem., 308 Win., 30-06, 35 Whelan, 4-shot magazine.
Barrel: 22" round tapered.
Weight: 7 1/2 lbs. **Length:** 42" overall.
Stock: Walnut, deluxe cut checkered p.g. and forend. Satin or high-gloss finish.
Sights: Gold bead front sight on ramp; step rear sight with windage adjustable.
Features: Redesigned and improved version of the Model 742. Positive cross-bolt safety. Receiver tapped for scope mount. Comes with green Remington hard case. Introduced 1981.
Price: About $547.00
Price: Carbine (18 1/2" bbl., 30-06 only) $547.00

Ruger Mini-14/5R

Ruger Mini Thirty Rifle
Similar to the Mini-14 Ranch Rifle except modified to chamber the 7.62x39 Russian service round. Weight is about 7 lbs., 3 oz. Has 6-groove barrel with 1-10" twist, Ruger Integral Scope Mount bases and folding peep rear sight. Detachable 5-shot staggered box magazine. Blued finish. Introduced 1987.
Price: Blue $556.00
Price: Stainless $609.00

RUGER MINI-14/5 AUTOLOADING RIFLE
Caliber: 223 Rem., 5-shot detachable box magazine.
Barrel: 18 1/2". Rifling twist 1:9".
Weight: 6.4 lbs. **Length:** 37 1/4" overall.
Stock: American hardwood, steel reinforced.
Sights: Ramp front, fully adjustable rear.
Features: Fixed piston gas-operated, positive primary extraction. New buffer system, redesigned ejector system. Ruger S100RH scope rings included. 20-, 30-shot magazine available to police departments and government agencies only.
Price: Mini-14/5R, Ranch Rifle, blued, scope rings $556.00
Price: K-Mini-14/5R, Ranch Rifle, stainless, scope rings $609.00
Price: Mini-14/5, blued, no scope rings $516.00
Price: K-Mini-14/5, stainless, no scope rings $569.00

CAUTION: PRICES SHOWN ARE SUPPLIED BY THE MANUFACTURER OR IMPORTER. CHECK YOUR LOCAL GUNSHOP.

CENTERFIRE RIFLES—AUTOLOADERS

Springfield M-1A

SA-85M SEMI-AUTO RIFLE
Caliber: 7.62x39mm, 6-shot magazine.
Barrel: 16.3".
Weight: 7.6 lbs. **Length:** 34.7" overall.
Stock: European hardwood; thumbhole design.
Sights: Post front, open adjustable rear.
Features: BATF-approved version of the Kalashnikov rifle. Gas operated. Black phosphate finish. Comes with one magazine, cleaning rod, cleaning/tool kit. Introduced 1995. Imported from Hungary by K.B.I., Inc.
Price: $599.00

SPRINGFIELD INC. M-1A RIFLE
Caliber: 7.62mm NATO (308), 5-, 10- or 20-shot box magazine.
Barrel: 25 1/16" with flash suppressor, 22" without suppressor.
Weight: 8 3/4 lbs. **Length:** 44 1/4" overall.
Stock: American walnut with walnut-colored heat-resistant fiberglass handguard. Matching walnut handguard available. Also available with fiberglass stock.
Sights: Military, square blade front, full click-adjustable aperture rear.
Features: Commercial equivalent of the U.S. M-14 service rifle with no provision for automatic firing. From Springfield Inc.
Price: Standard M-1A rifle, about $1,329.00
Price: National Match, about $1,670.00
Price: Super Match (heavy premium barrel), about $1,980.00
Price: M1A-A1 Bush Rifle, walnut stock, about $1,359.00

Springfield SAR-4800

SPRINGFIELD INC. SAR-4800 RIFLE
Caliber: 5.56, 7.62 NATO (308 Win.), 10-shot magazine.
Barrel: 21".
Weight: 9.5 lbs. **Length:** 43.3" overall.
Stock: Fiberglass forend, wood thumbhole butt.
Sights: Protected post front, adjustable peep rear.
Features: New production. Reintroduced 1995. From Springfield, Inc.
Price: $1,199.00

Springfield SAR-8

SPRINGFIELD INC. SAR-8 SPORTER RIFLE
Caliber: 308 Win., 10-shot magazine.
Barrel: 18".
Weight: 8.7 lbs. **Length:** 40.3" overall.
Stock: Black composition, thumbhole style.
Sights: Protected post front, rotary-style adjustable rear.
Features: Delayed roller-lock action; fluted chamber; matte black finish. Reintroduced 1995. From Springfield, Inc.
Price: $1,175.00

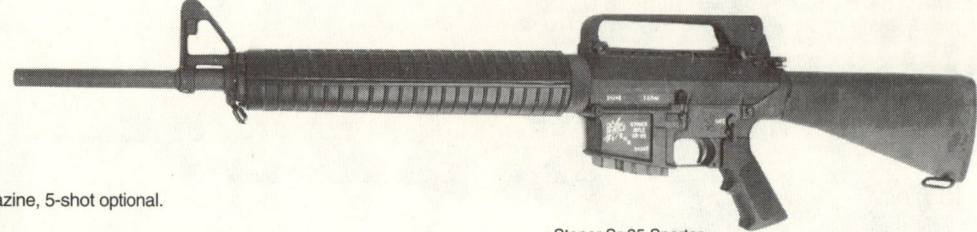
Stoner Sr-25 Sporter

STONER SR-25 SPORTER RIFLE
Caliber: 7.62 NATO, 10-shot steel magazine, 5-shot optional.
Barrel: 20".
Weight: 8.75 lbs. **Length:** 40" overall.
Stock: Black synthetic AR-15A2 design, AR-15A2-type synthetic round forend.
Sights: AR-15A2-style front adjustable for elevation, detachable rear is adjustable for windage.
Features: AR-15 trigger; AR-15-style seven-lug rotating bolt. Upper and lower receivers made of lightweight aircraft aluminum alloy. Quick-detachable carrying handle/rear sight assembly. Two-stage target trigger, shell deflector, bore guide, scope rings optional. Introduced 1993. Made in U.S. by Knight's Mfg. Co.
Price: $2,995.00

Stoner SR-25 Carbine
Similar to the SR-25 Sporter except has 16" light/hunting contour barrel, weighs 7.75 lbs., 36" overall. No sights furnished; has integral Weaver-style rail. Scope rings, iron sights optional. Introduced 1995. Made in U.S. by Knight's Mfg. Co.
Price: $2,995.00

WILKINSON TERRY CARBINE
Caliber: 9mm Para., 31-shot magazine.
Barrel: 16 3/16".
Weight: 6 lbs. 3 oz. **Length:** 30" overall.
Stock: Maple stock and forend.
Sights: Protected post front, aperture rear.
Features: Semi-automatic blowback action fires from a closed breech. Bolt-type safety and magazine catch. Ejection port has automatic trap door. Receiver equipped with dovetail for scope mounting. Made in U.S. From Wilkinson Arms.
Price: $636.29

CENTERFIRE RIFLES—LEVER & SLIDE

Both classic arms and recent designs in American-style repeaters for sport and field shooting.

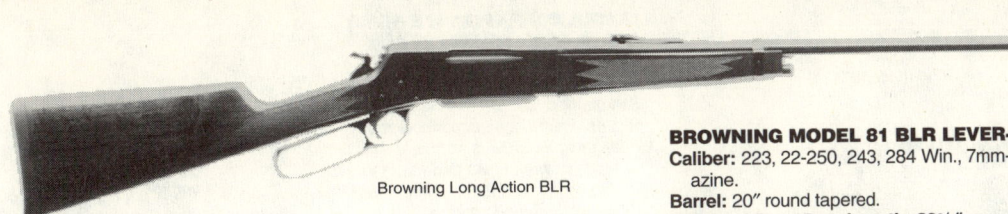

Browning Long Action BLR

Browning Model 81 Long Action BLR
Similar to the standard Model 81 BLR except has long acton to accept 30-06, 270 and 7mm Rem. Mag. Barrel lengths are 22" for 30-06 and 270, 24" for 7mm Rem. Mag. Has six-lug rotary bolt; bolt and receiver are full-length fluted. Fold-down hammer at half-cock. Weight about 8½ lbs., overall length 42½" (22" barrel). Introduced 1991.
Price: $579.95

CABELA'S CATTLEMAN'S CARBINE
Caliber: 44-40, 6-shot.
Barrel: 18".
Weight: 4 lbs. **Length:** 34" overall.
Stock: European walnut.
Sights: Blade front, notch rear.
Features: Revolving carbine. Color case-hardened frame, rest blued. Introduced 1994. Imported by Cabela's.
Price: $299.95

CABELA'S 1866 WINCHESTER REPLICA
Caliber: 44-40, 13-shot.
Barrel: 24¼".
Weight: 9 lbs. **Length:** 43" overall.
Stock: European walnut.
Sights: Bead front, open adjustable rear.
Features: Solid brass receiver, buttplate, forend cap. Octagonal barrel. Faithful to the original Winchester '66 rifle. Introduced 1994. Imported by Cabela's.
Price: $499.95

CIMARRON 1860 HENRY REPLICA
Caliber: 44 WCF, 13-shot magazine.
Barrel: 24¼" (rifle), 22" (carbine).
Weight: 9½ lbs. **Length:** 43" overall (rifle).
Stock: European walnut.
Sights: Bead front, open adjustable rear.
Features: Brass receiver amd buttplate. Uses original Henry loading system. Faithful to the original rifle. Introduced 1991. Imported by Cimarron Arms.
Price: $799.95

BROWNING MODEL 81 BLR LEVER-ACTION RIFLE
Caliber: 223, 22-250, 243, 284 Win., 7mm-08, 308 Win., 4-shot detachable magazine.
Barrel: 20" round tapered.
Weight: 6 lbs., 15 oz. **Length:** 39¾" overall.
Stock: Walnut. Checkered straight grip and forend, high-gloss finish.
Sights: Gold bead on hooded ramp front; low profile square notch adj. rear.
Features: Wide, grooved trigger; half-cock hammer safety; fold-down hammer. Receiver tapped for scope mount. Recoil pad installed. Imported from Japan by Browning.
Price: With sights $549.95

CABELA'S 1858 HENRY REPLICA
Caliber: 44-40, 13-shot magazine.
Barrel: 24¼".
Weight: 9.5 lbs. **Length:** 43" overall.
Stock: European walnut.
Sights: Bead front, open adjustable rear.
Features: Brass receiver and buttplate. Uses original Henry loading system. Faithful to the original rifle. Introduced 1994. Imported by Cabela's.
Price: $649.95

CABELA'S 1873 WINCHESTER REPLICA
Caliber: 44-40, 45 Colt, 13-shot.
Barrel: 24¼", 30".
Weight: 8.5 lbs. **Length:** 43¼" overall.
Stock: European walnut.
Sights: Bead front, open adjustable rear; globe front, tang rear.
Features: Color case-hardened steel receiver. Faithful to the original Model 1873 rifle. Introduced 1994. Imported by Cabela's.
Price: With tang sight, globe front $639.95
Price: Sporting model, 30" barrel, 44-40, 45 Colt $599.95
Price: With half-round/half-octagon barrel, half magazine $639.95

CIMARRON 1866 WINCHESTER REPLICAS
Caliber: 22 LR, 22 WMR, 38 Spec., 44 WCF.
Barrel: 24¼" (rifle), 19" (carbine).
Weight: 9 lbs. **Length:** 43" overall (rifle).
Stock: European walnut.
Sights: Bead front, open adjustable rear.
Features: Solid brass receiver, buttplate, forend cap. Octagonal barrel. Faithful to the original Winchester '66 rifle. Introduced 1991. Imported by Cimarron Arms.
Price: Rifle $689.95
Price: Carbine $679.95

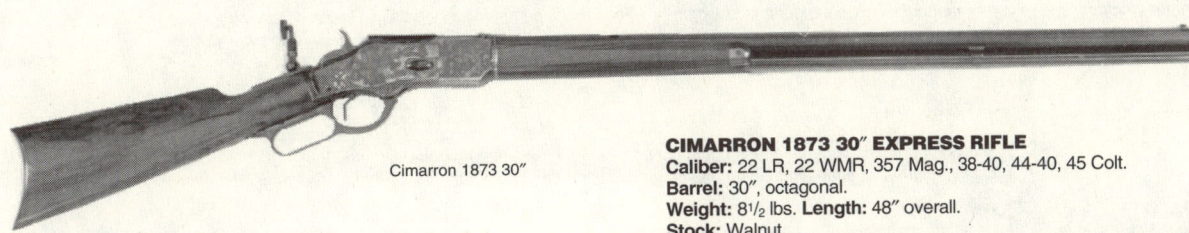

Cimarron 1873 30"

CIMARRON 1873 SHORT RIFLE
Caliber: 22 LR, 22 WMR, 357 Magnum, 44-40, 45 Colt.
Barrel: 20" tapered octagon.
Weight: 7.5 lbs. **Length:** 39" overall.
Stock: Walnut.
Sights: Bead front, adjustable semi-buckhorn rear.
Features: Has half "button" magazine. Original-type markings, including caliber, on barrel and elevator and "Kings" patent. From Cimarron Arms.
Price: $799.95

CIMARRON 1873 30" EXPRESS RIFLE
Caliber: 22 LR, 22 WMR, 357 Mag., 38-40, 44-40, 45 Colt.
Barrel: 30", octagonal.
Weight: 8½ lbs. **Length:** 48" overall.
Stock: Walnut.
Sights: Blade front, semi-buckhorn ramp rear. Tang sight optional.
Features: Color case-hardened frame; choice of modern blue-black or charcoal blue for other parts. Barrel marked "Kings improvement." From Cimarron Arms.
Price: $819.95

Cimarron 1873 Sporting Rifle
Similar to the 1873 Express except has 24" barrel with half-magazine.
Price: $799.95
Price: 1873 Saddle Ring Carbine, 19" barrel $799.95

CAUTION: PRICES SHOWN ARE SUPPLIED BY THE MANUFACTURER OR IMPORTER. CHECK YOUR LOCAL GUNSHOP.

CENTERFIRE RIFLES—LEVER & SLIDE

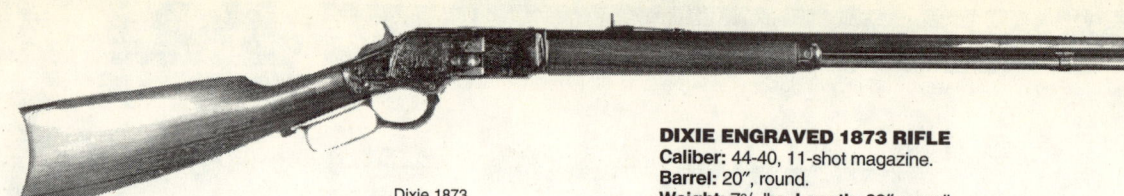
Dixie 1873

E.M.F. 1866 YELLOWBOY LEVER ACTIONS
Caliber: 38 Spec., 44-40.
Barrel: 19" (carbine), 24" (rifle).
Weight: 9 lbs. **Length:** 43" overall (rifle).
Stock: European walnut.
Sights: Bead front, open adjustable rear.
Features: Solid brass frame, blued barrel, lever, hammer, buttplate. Imported from Italy by E.M.F.
Price: Rifle $848.00
Price: Carbine $825.00

E.M.F. 1860 HENRY RIFLE
Caliber: 44-40 or 44 rimfire.
Barrel: 24.25".
Weight: About 9 lbs. **Length:** About 43.75" overall.
Stock: Oil-stained American walnut.
Sights: Blade front, rear adjustable for elevation.
Features: Reproduction of the original Henry rifle with brass frame and buttplate, rest blued. From E.M.F.
Price: Standard $1,100.00

DIXIE ENGRAVED 1873 RIFLE
Caliber: 44-40, 11-shot magazine.
Barrel: 20", round.
Weight: 7¾ lbs. **Length:** 39" overall.
Stock: Walnut.
Sights: Blade front, adjustable rear.
Features: Engraved and case-hardened frame. Duplicate of Winchester 1873. Made in Italy. From Dixie Gun Works.
Price: $1,250.00
Price: Plain, blued carbine $895.00

> Consult our Directory pages for the location of firms mentioned.

E.M.F. MODEL 73 LEVER-ACTION RIFLE
Caliber: 357 Mag., 44-40, 45 Colt.
Barrel: 24".
Weight: 8 lbs. **Length:** 43¼" overall.
Stock: European walnut.
Sights: Bead front, rear adjustable for windage and elevation.
Features: Color case-hardened frame (blue on carbine). Imported by E.M.F.
Price: Rifle $1,050.00
Price: Carbine, 19" barrel $1,020.00

Marlin Model 336CS

Marlin Model 30AS Lever-Action Carbine
Same as the Marlin 336CS except has press-checkered, walnut-finished Maine birch pistol grip stock, 30-30 only, 6-shot. Hammer-block safety. Adjustable rear sight, brass bead front.
Price: $366.60

MARLIN MODEL 444SS LEVER-ACTION SPORTER
Caliber: 444 Marlin, 5-shot tubular magazine.
Barrel: 22" Micro-Groove®.
Weight: 7½ lbs. **Length:** 40½" overall.
Stock: Checkered American black walnut, capped p.g. with white line spacers, rubber rifle buttpad. Mar-Shield® finish; swivel studs.
Sights: Hooded ramp front, folding semi-buckhorn rear adjustable for windage and elevation.
Features: Hammer-block safety. Receiver tapped for scope mount; offset hammer spur.
Price: $507.40

MARLIN MODEL 336CS LEVER-ACTION CARBINE
Caliber: 30-30 or 35 Rem., 6-shot tubular magazine.
Barrel: 20" Micro-Groove®.
Weight: 7 lbs. **Length:** 38½" overall.
Stock: Checkered American black walnut, capped p.g. with white line spacers. Mar-Shield® finish; rubber buttpad; swivel studs.
Sights: Ramp front with Wide-Scan™ hood, semi-buckhorn folding rear adjust-able for windage and elevation.
Features: Hammer-block safety. Receiver tapped for scope mount, offset hammer spur; top of receiver sand blasted to prevent glare.
Price: $430.55

MARLIN MODEL 1894S LEVER-ACTION CARBINE
Caliber: 44 Special/44 Magnum, 10-shot tubular magazine.
Barrel: 20" Micro-Groove®.
Weight: 6 lbs. **Length:** 37½" overall.
Stock: Checkered American black walnut, straight grip and forend. Mar-Shield® finish. Rubber rifle buttpad; swivel studs.
Sights: Wide-Scan™ hooded ramp front, semi-buckhorn folding rear adjustable for windage and elevation.
Features: Hammer-block safety. Receiver tapped for scope mount, offset hammer spur, solid top receiver sand blasted to prevent glare.
Price: $454.80

Marlin Model 1894CS

Marlin Model 1894CS Carbine
Similar to the standard Model 1894S except chambered for 38 Special/357 Magnum with full-length 9-shot magazine, 18½" barrel, hammer-block safety, brass bead front sight. Introduced 1983.
Price: $454.80

MARLIN MODEL 1895SS LEVER-ACTION RIFLE
Caliber: 45-70, 4-shot tubular magazine.
Barrel: 22" round.
Weight: 7½ lbs. **Length:** 40½" overall.
Stock: Checkered American black walnut, full pistol grip. Mar-Shield® finish; rubber buttpad; q.d. swivel studs.
Sights: Bead front with Wide-Scan™ hood, semi-buckhorn folding rear adjustable for windage and elevation.
Features: Hammer-block safety. Solid receiver tapped for scope mounts or receiver sights; offset hammer spur.
Price: $507.40

CENTERFIRE RIFLES—LEVER & SLIDE

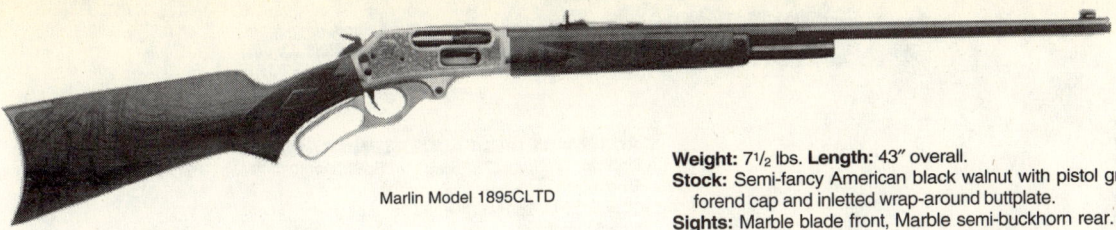

Marlin Model 1895CLTD

MARLIN MODEL 1895CLTD RIFLE
Caliber: 45-70, 4-shot tubular magazine.
Barrel: 24", half-round/half-octagon with Micro-Groove® rifling.
Weight: 7½ lbs. **Length:** 43" overall.
Stock: Semi-fancy American black walnut with pistol grip, cut checkering, steel forend cap and inletted wrap-around buttplate.
Sights: Marble blade front, Marble semi-buckhorn rear. Solid-top receiver drilled and tapped for scope mount or receiver sight.
Features: Commemorates 100th anniversary of the Marlin 1895, 125th anniversary of Marlin. Receiver has French gray finish and is etched with the centennial dates. Introduced 1995. Made in U.S. by Marlin Firearms Co.
Price: $1,103.85

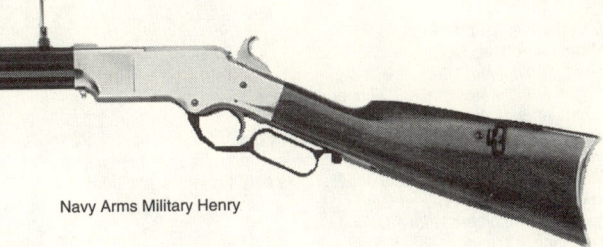

Navy Arms Military Henry

NAVY ARMS MILITARY HENRY RIFLE
Caliber: 44-40, 12-shot magazine.
Barrel: 24¼".
Weight: 9 lbs., 4 oz.
Stock: European walnut.
Sights: Blade front, adjustable ladder-type rear.
Features: Brass frame, buttplate, rest blued. Recreation of the model used by cavalry units in the Civil War. Has full-length magazine tube, sling swivels; no forend. Introduced 1991. Imported from Italy by Navy Arms.
Price: $880.00

Navy Arms Henry Carbine
Similar to the Military Henry rifle except has 22" barrel, weighs 8 lbs., 12 oz., is 41" overall; no sling swivels. Caliber 44-40. Introduced 1992. Imported from Italy by Navy Arms.
Price: $860.00

Navy Arms Henry Trapper
Similar to the Military Henry Rifle except has 16½" barrel, weighs 7½ lbs. Brass frame and buttplate, rest blued. Introduced 1991. Imported from Italy by Navy Arms.
Price: $860.00

Navy Arms Iron Frame Henry
Similar to the Military Henry Rifle except receiver is blued or color case-hardened steel. Introduced 1991. Imported by Navy Arms.
Price: $895.00

Navy Arms 1873 Sporting Rifle
Similar to the 1873 Winchester-Style rifle except has checkered pistol grip stock, 30" octagonal barrel (24" available). Introduced 1992. Imported by Navy Arms.
Price: 30" barrel $900.00
Price: 24" barrel $870.00

NAVY ARMS 1866 YELLOWBOY RIFLE
Caliber: 44-40, 12-shot magazine.
Barrel: 24", full octagon.
Weight: 8½ lbs. **Length:** 42½" overall.
Stock: European walnut.
Sights: Blade front, adjustable ladder-type rear.
Features: Brass frame, forend tip, buttplate, blued barrel, lever, hammer. Introduced 1991. Imported from Italy by Navy Arms.
Price: $675.00
Price: Carbine, 19" barrel $670.00

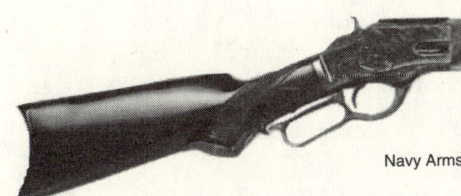

Navy Arms 1873

NAVY ARMS 1873 WINCHESTER-STYLE RIFLE
Caliber: 44-40, 45 Colt, 12-shot magazine.
Barrel: 24".
Weight: 8¼ lbs. **Length:** 43" overall.
Stock: European walnut.
Sights: Blade front, buckhorn rear.
Features: Color case-hardened frame, rest blued. Full-octagon barrel. Introduced 1991. Imported by Navy Arms.
Price: $790.00
Price: Carbine, 19" barrel $780.00

Remington 7600 Rifle

REMINGTON 7600 SLIDE ACTION
Caliber: 243, 270, 280, 30-06, 308, 35 Whelen.
Barrel: 22" round tapered.
Weight: 7½ lbs. **Length:** 42" overall.
Stock: Cut-checkered walnut p.g. and forend, Monte Carlo with full cheekpiece. Satin or high-gloss finish.
Sights: Gold bead front sight on matted ramp, open step adjustable sporting rear.
Features: Redesigned and improved version of the Model 760. Detachable 4-shot clip. Cross-bolt safety. Receiver tapped for scope mount. Also available in high grade versions. Comes with green Remington hard case. Introduced 1981.
Price: About $513.00
Price: Carbine (18½" bbl., 30-06 only) $513.00

CAUTION: PRICES SHOWN ARE SUPPLIED BY THE MANUFACTURER OR IMPORTER. CHECK YOUR LOCAL GUNSHOP.

CENTERFIRE RIFLES—LEVER & SLIDE

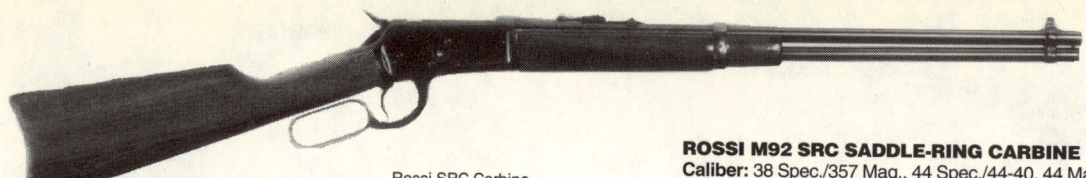

Rossi SRC Carbine

Rossi M92 SRS Short Carbine
Similar to the standard M92 except has 16" barrel, overall length of 33", in 38/357 only. Puma medallion on side of receiver. Introduced 1986.
Price: $347.00

UBERTI HENRY RIFLE
Caliber: 44-40, 45 Colt.
Barrel: 18 1/2", 22 1/4", 24 1/4", half-octagon.
Weight: 9.2 lbs. **Length:** 43 3/4" overall.
Stock: American walnut.
Sights: Blade front, rear adjustable for elevation.
Features: Frame, elevator, magazine follower, buttplate are brass, balance blue (also available in polished steel). Imported by Uberti USA.
Price: $895.00
Price: Henry Carbine (22 1/4" bbl.) $900.00
Price: Henry Trapper (16", 18" bbl.) $900.00

ROSSI M92 SRC SADDLE-RING CARBINE
Caliber: 38 Spec./357 Mag., 44 Spec./44-40, 44 Mag., 45 Colt, 10-shot magazine.
Barrel: 20".
Weight: 5 3/4 lbs. **Length:** 37" overall.
Stock: Walnut.
Sights: Blade front, buckhorn rear.
Features: Recreation of the famous lever-action carbine. Handles 38 and 357 interchangeably. Has high-relief puma medallion inlaid in the receiver. Introduced 1978. Imported by Interarms.
Price: $347.00
Price: 44 Spec./44 Mag. (Model 65) $364.00

UBERTI 1866 SPORTING RIFLE
Caliber: 22 LR, 22 WMR, 38 Spec., 44-40, 45 Colt.
Barrel: 24 1/4", octagonal.
Weight: 8.1 lbs. **Length:** 43 1/4" overall.
Stock: Walnut.
Sights: Blade front adjustable for windage, rear adjustable for elevation.
Features: Frame, buttplate, forend cap of polished brass, balance charcoal blued. Imported by Uberti USA.
Price: $780.00
Price: Yellowboy Carbine (19" round bbl.) $720.00

UBERTI 1873 SPORTING RIFLE
Caliber: 22 LR, 22 WMR, 38 Spec., 357 Mag., 44-40, 45 Colt.
Barrel: 24 1/4" half-octagon, 24 1/4", 30", octagonal.
Weight: 8.1 lbs. **Length:** 43 1/4" overall.
Stock: Walnut.
Sights: Blade front adjustable for windage, open rear adjustable for elevation.
Features: Color case-hardened frame, blued barrel, hammer, lever, buttplate, brass elevator. Also available with pistol grip stock ($100.00 extra). Imported from Italy by Uberti USA.
Price: $900.00
Price: 1873 Carbine (19" round barrel) $890.00

CONSULT **Shooter's Marketplace** Page 266, This Issue

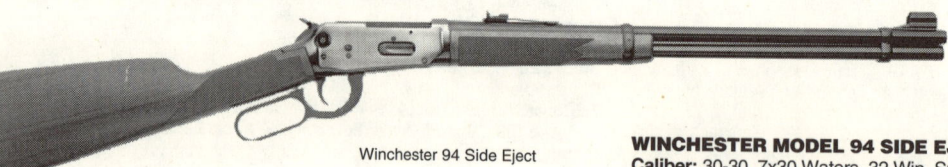

Winchester 94 Side Eject

WINCHESTER MODEL 94 SIDE EJECT LEVER-ACTION RIFLE
Caliber: 30-30, 7x30 Waters, 32 Win. Spec., 6-shot tubular magazine.
Barrel: 20".
Weight: 6 1/2 lbs. **Length:** 37 3/4" overall.
Stock: Straight grip walnut stock and forend.
Sights: Hooded blade front, semi-buckhorn rear. Drilled and tapped for scope mount. Post front sight on Trapper model.
Features: Solid frame, forged steel receiver; side ejection, exposed rebounding hammer with automatic trigger-activated transfer bar. Specially inscribed with "1894-1994" on the receiver. Introduced 1984.
Price: Checkered walnut $381.00
Price: No checkering, walnut $352.00
Price: With WinTuff laminated hardwood stock, 30-30 only ... $393.00

Winchester 94 Legacy

Winchester Model 94 Legacy
Similar to the Model 94 Side Eject except has half pistol grip walnut stock, checkered grip and forend. Chambered only for 30-30. Introduced 1995. Made in U.S. by U.S. Repeating Arms Co., Inc.
Price: $381.00

Winchester Model 94 Ranger Side Eject Lever-Action Rifle
Same as Model 94 Side Eject except has 5-shot magazine, American hardwood stock and forend, post front sight. Specially inscribed with "1894-1994" on the receiver. Introduced 1985.
Price: $311.00
Price: With 4x32 Bushnell scope, mounts $366.00

Winchester Model 94 Trapper Side Eject
Same as the Model 94 except has 16" barrel, 5-shot magazine in 30-30, 9-shot in 357 Mag., 44 Magnum/44 Special, 45 Colt. Has stainless steel claw extractor, saddle ring, hammer spur extension, walnut wood. Specially inscribed with "1894-1994" on the receiver.
Price: 30-30 .... $352.00
Price: 357 Mag., 44 Mag./44 Spec., 45 Colt $372.00

CENTERFIRE RIFLES—LEVER & SLIDE

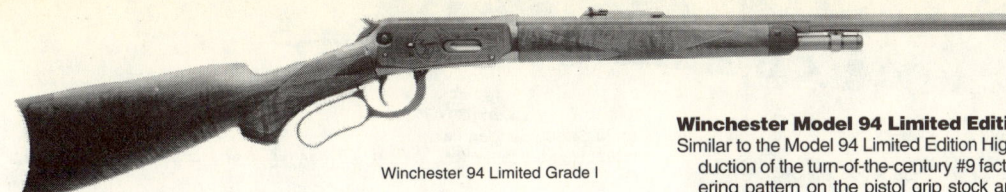

Winchester 94 Limited Grade I

Winchester Model 94 Limited Edition High Grade Rifle
Similar to the Model 94 Custom Limited Edition except has blued receiver with gold inlays and #6-style engraving pattern showing a gold deer on the right, gold mountain sheep on the left. Has the replica Lyman No. 2 tang sight, spade-pattern checkering on pistol grip stock. Only 3,000 of this grade produced. Introduced 1994. From U.S. Repeating Arms Co., Inc.
Price: $1,272.00

Winchester Model 94 Wrangler Side Eject
Same as the Model 94 except has 16" barrel and large loop lever for large and/or gloved hands. Has 9-shot capacity (5-shot for 30-30), stainless steel claw extractor. Available in 30-30, 44 Magnum/44 Special. Specially inscribed with "1894-1994" on the receiver. Reintroduced 1992.
Price: 30-30 ....$372.00
Price: 44 Magnum/44 Special $393.00

Winchester Model 94 Limited Edition Grade I
Similar to the Model 94 Limited Edition High Grade rifle except uses a close reproduction of the turn-of-the-century #9 factory engraving, diamond-style "H" checkering pattern on the pistol grip stock and forend. Engraving on receiver sides shows whitetail deer profiles. Top tang drilled and tapped for a tang sight. Has half-round/half-octagon barrel with half-magazine tube. Introduced 1994. From U.S. Repeating Arms Co., Inc.
Price: $811.00

WINCHESTER MODEL 94 BIG BORE SIDE EJECT
Caliber: 307 Win., 356 Win., 6-shot magazine.
Barrel: 20".
Weight: 7 lbs. **Length:** 38 5/8" overall.
Stock: American walnut. Satin finish.
Sights: Hooded ramp front, semi-buckhorn rear adjustable for windage and elevation.
Features: All external metal parts have Winchester's deep blue finish. Rifling twist 1:12". Rubber recoil pad fitted to buttstock. Specially inscribed with "1894-1994" on the receiver. Introduced 1983. From U.S. Repeating Arms Co.
Price: $393.00

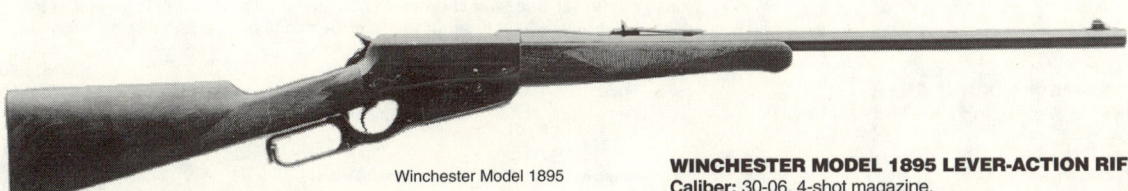

Winchester Model 1895

Winchester Model 1895 High Grade Rifle
Same as the Grade I except has silvered receiver with extensive engraving: right side shows two scenes portraying large big horn sheep; left side has bull elk and cow elk. Gold borders accent the scenes. Magazine and cocking lever also engraved. Has classic Winchester H-style checkering pattern on fancy grade American walnut. Only 4000 rifles made. Introduced 1995. From U.S. Repeating Arms Co., Inc.
Price: $1,360.00

WINCHESTER MODEL 1895 LEVER-ACTION RIFLE
Caliber: 30-06, 4-shot magazine.
Barrel: 24", round.
Weight: 8 lbs. **Length:** 42" overall.
Stock: American walnut.
Sights: Gold bead front, buckhorn rear adjustable for elevation.
Features: Recreation of the original Model 1895. Polished blue finish with Nimschke-style scroll engraving on receiver. Scalloped receiver, two-piece cocking lever, schnabel forend, straight-grip stock. Introduced 1995. Only 4000 rifles made. From U.S. Repeating Arms Co., Inc.
Price: Grade I $853.00

CENTERFIRE RIFLES—BOLT ACTION

Includes models for a wide variety of sporting and competitive purposes and uses.

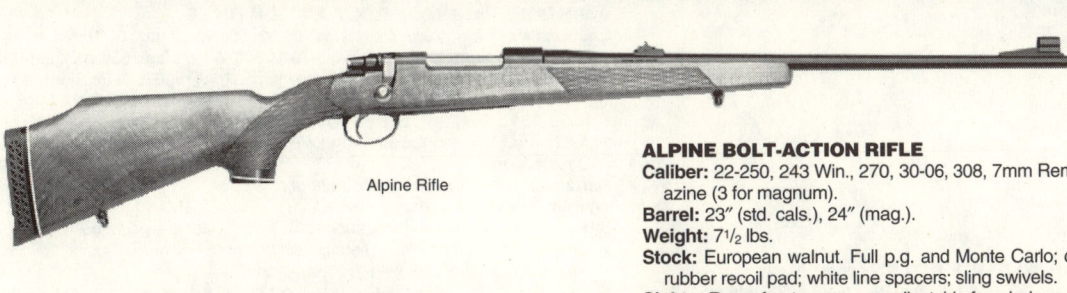

Alpine Rifle

ALPINE BOLT-ACTION RIFLE
Caliber: 22-250, 243 Win., 270, 30-06, 308, 7mm Rem. Mag., 8mm, 5-shot magazine (3 for magnum).
Barrel: 23" (std. cals.), 24" (mag.).
Weight: 7 1/2 lbs.
Stock: European walnut. Full p.g. and Monte Carlo; checkered p.g. and forend; rubber recoil pad; white line spacers; sling swivels.
Sights: Ramp front, open rear adjustable for windage and elevation.
Features: Made by Firearms Co. Ltd. in England. Imported by Mandall Shooting Supplies.
Price: Custom Grade $395.00
Price: Supreme Grade $425.00

AAO MODEL 2000 50-CALIBER RIFLE
Caliber: 50 BMG, 5-shot magazine.
Barrel: 30"; 1:15" twist; muzzle brake.
Weight: 24 lbs. **Length:** NA.
Stock: Cast alloy with gray anodized finish, Kick-Ease recoil pad.
Sights: None furnished. Drilled and tapped for scope base.
Features: Controlled feeding via rotating enclosed claw extractor; 90-degree bolt rotation; cone bolt face and barrel; trigger-mounted safety blocks sear; fully adjustable, detachable tripod. Introduced 1994. From American Arms & Ordnance.
Price: $4,000.00

CONSULT **Shooter's Marketplace** Page 266, This Issue

CAUTION: PRICES SHOWN ARE SUPPLIED BY THE MANUFACTURER OR IMPORTER. CHECK YOUR LOCAL GUNSHOP.

CENTERFIRE RIFLES—BOLT ACTION

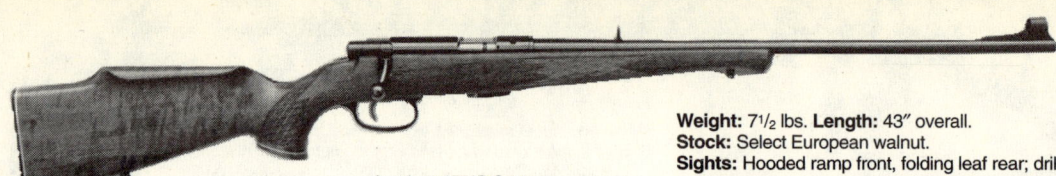

Anschutz 1700D Custom

ANSCHUTZ 1700D CUSTOM RIFLES
Caliber: 22 Hornet, 5-shot clip; 222 Rem., 3-shot clip.
Barrel: 24".
Weight: 7 1/2 lbs. **Length:** 43" overall.
Stock: Select European walnut.
Sights: Hooded ramp front, folding leaf rear; drilled and tapped for scope mounting.
Features: Adjustable single stage trigger. Stock has roll-over Monte Carlo cheekpiece, slim forend with schnabel tip, Wundhammer palm swell on grip, rosewood grip cap with white diamond insert. Skip-line checkering on grip and forend. Introduced 1988. Imported from Germany by Precision Sales International.
Price: $1,534.00
Price: Meistergrade (select stock, gold engraved trigger guard) $1,733.00

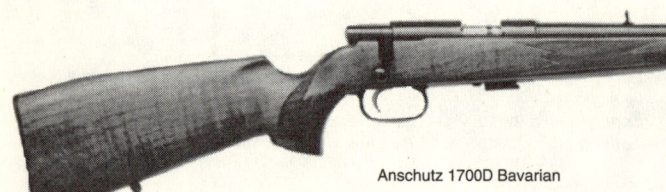

Anschutz 1700D Bavarian

ANSCHUTZ 1700D BAVARIAN BOLT-ACTION RIFLE
Caliber: 22 Hornet, 222 Rem., detachable clip.
Barrel: 24".
Weight: 7 1/2 lbs. **Length:** 43" overall.
Stock: European walnut with Bavarian cheek rest. Checkered pistol grip and forend.
Sights: Hooded ramp front, folding leaf rear. Drilled and tapped for scope mounting.
Features: Uses the improved 1700 Match 54 action with adjustable trigger. Introduced 1988. Imported from Germany by Precision Sales International.
Price: $1,534.00
Price: Meistergrade (select stock, gold engraved trigger guard) $1,733.00

ANSCHUTZ 1700D GRAPHITE HORNET RIFLE
Caliber: 22 Hornet, 5-shot clip.
Barrel: 22"
Weight: 7.5 lbs. **Length:** 41" overall.
Stock: Graphite-reinforced fiberglass.
Sights: None furnished; receiver grooved, drilled and tapped for scope mounting.
Features: Built on Anschutz sporter action and bedded in a McMillan graphite-reinforced, roll-over cheekpiece stock. Fitted with Anschutz logo sling and quick-release swivels. Introduced 1995. Imported from Germany by Precision Sales International.
Price: $1,478.00

Anschutz 1733D Mannlicher Rifle
Similar to the 1700D Bavarian except chambered only for 22 Hornet and has Mannlicher stock. Uses improved Match 54 action with #5096 single-stage trigger with 2.6 lb. adjustable pull weight. Has 19.75" barrel, overall length of 39". Comes with sling swivels, Lyman folding rear sight and hooded ramp front, 5-shot magazine. Introduced 1993. Imported from Germany by Precision Sales International.
Price: $1,657.00

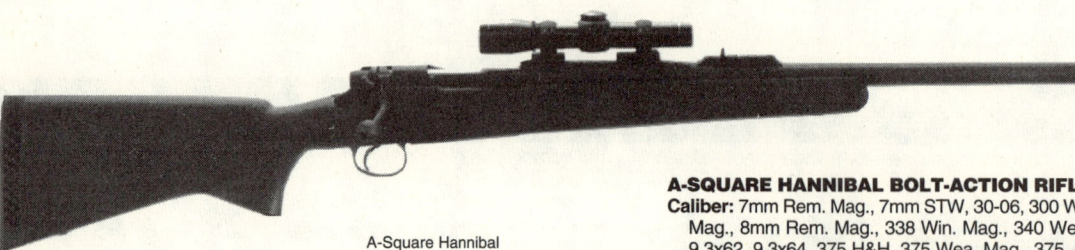

A-Square Hannibal

A-SQUARE HANNIBAL BOLT-ACTION RIFLE
Caliber: 7mm Rem. Mag., 7mm STW, 30-06, 300 Win. Mag., 300 H&H, 300 Wea. Mag., 8mm Rem. Mag., 338 Win. Mag., 340 Wea. Mag., 338 A-Square Mag., 9.3x62, 9.3x64, 375 H&H, 375 Wea. Mag., 375 JRS, 375 A-Square Mag., 378 Wea. Mag., 416 Taylor, 416 Rem. Mag., 416 Hoffman, 416 Rigby, 416 Wea. Mag., 404 Jeffery, 425 Express, 458 Win. Mag., 458 Lott, 450 Ackley, 460 Short A-Square Mag., 460 Wea. Mag., 470 Capstick, 495 A-Square Mag., 500 A-Square Mag.
Barrel: 20" to 26" (no-cost customer option).
Weight: 9 to 11 3/4 lbs.
Stock: Claro walnut with hand-rubbed oil finish; classic style with A-Square Coil-Chek® features for reduced recoil; flush detachable swivels. Customer choice of length of pull. Available with synthetic stock.
Sights: Choice of three-leaf express, forward or normal-mount scope, or combination (at extra cost).
Features: Matte non-reflective blue, double cross-bolts, steel and fiberglass reinforcement of wood from tang to forend tip; Mauser-style claw extractor; expanded magazine capacity; two-position safety; three-way target trigger. Right-hand only. Introduced 1983. Made in U.S. by A-Square Co., Inc.
Price: Walnut stock $2,995.00
Price: Synthetic stock $3,345.00

A-SQUARE CAESAR BOLT-ACTION RIFLE
Caliber: 7mm Rem. Mag., 7mm STW, 30-06, 300 Win. Mag., 300 H&H, 300 Wea. Mag., 8mm Rem. Mag., 338 Win. Mag., 340 Wea. Mag., 338 A-Square, 9.3x62, 9.3x64, 375 Wea. Mag., 375 H&H, 375 JRS, 375 A-Square, 416 Hoffman, 416 Rem. Mag., 416 Taylor, 404 Jeffery, 425 Express, 458 Win. Mag., 458 Lott, 450 Ackley, 460 Short A-Square, 470 Capstick, 495 A-Square.
Barrel: 20" to 26" (no-cost customer option).
Weight: 8 1/2 to 11 lbs.
Stock: Claro walnut with hand-rubbed oil finish; classic style with A-Square Coil-Chek® features for reduced recoil; flush detachable swivels. Customer choice of length of pull.
Sights: Choice of three-leaf express, forward or normal-mount scope, or combination (at extra cost).
Features: Matte non-reflective blue, double cross-bolts, steel and fiberglass reinforcement of wood from tang to forend tip; three-position positive safety; three-way adjustable trigger; expanded magazine capacity. Right- or left-hand. Introduced 1984. Made in U.S. by A-Square Co., Inc.
Price: Walnut stock $2,995.00
Price: Synthetic stock $3,345.00

A-Square Hamilcar Bolt-Action Rifle
Similar to the A-Square Hannibal rifle except chambered for 25-06, 6.5x55, 270 Win., 7x57, 280 Rem., 30-06, 338-06, 9.3x62, 257 Wea. Mag., 264 Win. Mag., 270 Wea. Mag., 7mm Rem. Mag., 7mm Wea. Mag., 7mm STW, 300 Win. Mag., 300 Wea. Mag. Weighs 8-8 1/2 lbs. Introduced 1994. From A-Square Co., Inc.
Price: $2,995.00

CENTERFIRE RIFLES—BOLT ACTION

BARRETT MODEL 95 BOLT-ACTION RIFLE
Caliber: 50 BMG, 5-shot magazine.
Barrel: 29".
Weight: 22 lbs. **Length:** 45" overall.
Stock: Sorbothane recoil pad.
Sights: Scope optional.
Features: Updated version of the Model 90. Bolt-action, bullpup design. Disassembles without tools; extendable bipod legs; match-grade barrel; high efficiency muzzlebrake. Introduced 1995. From Barrett Firearms Mfg., Inc.
Price: From $4,650.00

BENTON & BROWN BOLT-ACTION RIFLE
Caliber: 243, 6mm Rem., 25-06, 270, 280 Rem., 308, 30-06 (standard calibers); 257 Wea. Mag., 264 Win. Mag., 7mm Rem. Mag., 300 Wea. Mag., 300 Win. Mag., 338 Win. Mag., 340 Wea. Mag., 375 H&H (magnum calibers).
Barrel: 22" (standard calibers), 24" (magnum calibers).
Weight: 8 1/2 lbs. (standard). **Length:** 41" overall (22" barrel).
Stock: Two-piece design of fancy walnut or fiberglass, oil finish; 20 lpi borderless checkering.
Sights: Optional. Factory-fitted low profile, one-piece steel.
Features: Short-throw bolt action with 60° bolt throw. Takedown design, interchangeable barrels and bolt assemblies. Left-hand models available. Safety locks firing pin and bolt. Introduced 1995. Made in U.S. by Benton & Brown Firearms, Inc.
Price: Right- or left-hand, standard or magnum calibers $2,075.00
Price: Fiberglass stock model $1,875.00
Price: Interchangeable barrels $450.00
Price: Interchangeable bolt assemblies $400.00

Blaser R93

BLASER R93 BOLT-ACTION RIFLE
Caliber: 222, 243, 6.5x55, 270, 7x57, 308, 30-06, 7mm Rem. Mag., 300 Win. Mag., 300 Wea. Mag., 338 Win. Mag., 375 H&H, 416 Rem. Mag., 3-shot magazine.
Barrel: 22" (standard calibers), 24" (magnum calibers).
Weight: 6.5 to 7.5 lbs. **Length:** 40" overall (22" barrel).
Stock: Two-piece European walnut.
Sights: Blade front on ramp, open rear, or no sights.
Features: Straight-pull bolt action with thumb-activated safety slide/cocking mechanism. Interchangeable barrels and bolt heads. Introduced 1994. Imported from Germany by Autumn Sales, Inc.
Price: Standard $2,800.00
Price: Deluxe (better wood, engraving) $3,100.00
Price: Super Deluxe (best wood, gold animal inlays) $3,500.00
Price: Safari, standard grade, 375 H&H, 416 Rem. Mag. $3,300.00
Price: Safari Deluxe $3,600.00
Price: Safari Super Deluxe $4,000.00

BRNO CZ 550 BOLT-ACTION RIFLE
Caliber: 243, 308 (4-shot detachable magazine), 7x57, 270, 30-06, 7mm Rem. Mag., 300 Win. Mag. (5-shot internal magazine).
Barrel: 23.6".
Weight: 7.2 lbs. **Length:** 44.7" overall.
Stock: Walnut with high comb; checkered grip and forend.
Sights: None furnished; drilled and tapped for Remington 700-style bases.
Features: Polished blue finish. Introduced 1995. Imported from the Czech Republic by Magnum Research.
Price: $649.00

BRNO CZ537 Sporter

Barrel: 23.6".
Weight: 7 lbs., 9 oz. **Length:** 44.7" overall.
Stock: Checkered walnut.
Sights: Hooded ramp front, adjustable folding leaf rear.
Features: Improved standard size Mauser-style action with non-rotating claw extractor; externally adjustable trigger, American-style safety; streamlined bolt shroud with cocking indicator. Introduced 1992. Imported from the Czech Republic by Magnum Research.
Price: $649.00
Price: Full stock, 308, 30-06 ....$709.00

BRNO CZ537 SPORTER BOLT-ACTION RIFLE
Caliber: 270, 30-06 (internal 5-shot magazine), 243, 308 (detachable 5-shot magazine).

BRNO ZKB 527 Fox

BRNO ZKB 527 FOX BOLT-ACTION RIFLE
Caliber: 22 Hornet, 222 Rem., 223 Rem., detachable 5-shot magazine.
Barrel: 23 1/2"; standard or heavy barrel.
Weight: 6 lbs., 1 oz. **Length:** 42 1/2" overall.
Stock: European walnut with Monte Carlo.
Sights: Hooded front, open adjustable rear.
Features: Improved mini-Mauser action with non-rotating claw extractor; grooved receiver. Imported from the Czech Republic by Magnum Research.
Price: $629.00

BRNO ZKK 602

BRNO ZKK 600, 601, 602 BOLT-ACTION RIFLES
Caliber: 7x57, 30-06, 270 (M600); 243, 308 (M601); 375 H&H, 458 Win. Mag. (M602), 5-shot magazine.

Barrel: 23 1/2" (M600, 601); 25" (M602).
Weight: 7 lbs., 3 oz. to 9 lbs., 9 oz. **Length:** 43" overall (M601).
Stock: Classic-style checkered walnut.
Sights: Hooded ramp front, open folding leaf adjustable rear.
Features: Improved Mauser action with controlled feed, claw extractor; safety blocks trigger and locks bolt; sling swivels. Imported from the Czech Republic by Magnum Research.
Price: Model 600, 601 ....$589.00
Price: Model 602 ....$799.00

CAUTION: PRICES SHOWN ARE SUPPLIED BY THE MANUFACTURER OR IMPORTER. CHECK YOUR LOCAL GUNSHOP.

CENTERFIRE RIFLES—BOLT ACTION

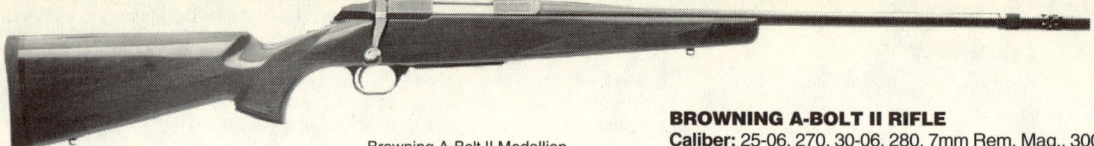
Browning A-Bolt II Medallion

BROWNING A-BOLT II RIFLE
Caliber: 25-06, 270, 30-06, 280, 7mm Rem. Mag., 300 Win. Mag., 338 Win. Mag., 375 H&H Mag.
Barrel: 22" medium sporter weight with recessed muzzle; 26" on mag. cals.
Weight: 6½ to 7½ lbs. **Length:** 44¾" overall (magnum and standard); 41¾" (short action).
Stock: Classic style American walnut; recoil pad standard on magnum calibers.
Features: Short-throw (60°) fluted bolt, three locking lugs, plunger-type ejector; adjustable trigger is grooved and gold-plated. Hinged floorplate, detachable box magazine (4 rounds std. cals., 3 for magnums). Slide tang safety. Medallion has glossy stock finish, rosewood grip and forend caps, high polish blue. BOSS barrel vibration modulator and muzzle brake system not available in 375 H&H. Introduced 1985. Imported from Japan by Browning.
Price: Medallion, no sights $672.95
Price: Hunter, no sights $576.95
Price: Hunter, with sights $649.95
Price: Medallion, 375 H&H Mag., with sights $779.95
Price: For BOSS (except 375 H&H), add $93.00

Browning A-Bolt II Stainless Stalker
Similar to the Hunter model A-Bolt except receiver and barrel are made of stainless steel; the rest of the exposed metal surfaces are finished with a durable matte silver-gray. Graphite-fiberglass composite textured stock. No sights are furnished. Available in 223, 22-250, 243, 308, 7mm-08, 270, 30-06, 7mm Rem. Mag., 375 H&H. BOSS barrel vibration modulator and muzzle brake system not available in 375 H&H. Introduced 1987.
Price: $749.95
Price: With BOSS $842.95
Price: Left-hand, no sights $772.95
Price: With BOSS $865.95
Price: 375 H&H, with sights $852.95
Price: 375 H&H, left-hand, with sights $879.95

Browning A-Bolt II Short Action
Similar to the standard A-Bolt except has short action for 223, 22-250, 243, 257 Roberts, 7mm-08, 284 Win., 308 chamberings. Available in Hunter or Medallion grades. Weighs 6½ lbs. Other specs essentially the same. BOSS barrel vibration modulator and muzzle brake system optional. Introduced 1985.
Price: Medallion, no sights $672.95
Price: Hunter, no sights $576.95
Price: Hunter, with sights $649.95
Price: Composite, no sights $594.95
Price: For BOSS, add $93.00

Browning A-Bolt II Composite Stalker
Similar to the A-Bolt II Hunter except has black graphite-fiberglass stock with textured finish. Matte blue finish on all exposed metal surfaces. Available in 223, 22-250, 243, 7mm-08, 308, 30-06, 270, 280, 25-06, 7mm Rem. Mag., 300 Win. Mag., 338 Win. Mag. BOSS barrel vibration modulator and muzzle brake system offered in all calibers. Introduced 1994.
Price: No sights $594.95
Price: No sights, BOSS $687.95

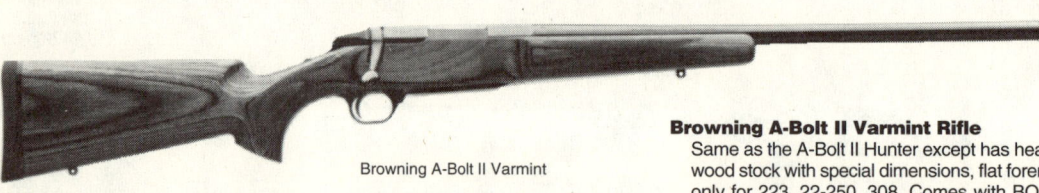
Browning A-Bolt II Varmint

Browning A-Bolt II Varmint Rifle
Same as the A-Bolt II Hunter except has heavy varmint/target barrel, laminated wood stock with special dimensions, flat forend and palm swell grip. Chambered only for 223, 22-250, 308. Comes with BOSS barrel vibration modulator and muzzle brake system. Introduced 1994.
Price: With BOSS, gloss or matte finish $894.95

Browning A-Bolt II Gold Medallion
Similar to the standard A-Bolt except has select walnut stock with brass spacers between rubber recoil pad and between the rosewood grip cap and forend tip; gold-filled barrel inscription; palm-swell pistol grip, Monte Carlo comb, 22 lpi checkering with double borders; engraved receiver flats. In 270, 30-06, 7mm Rem. Mag. only. Introduced 1988.
Price: $904.95
Price: For BOSS, add $93.00

Browning A-Bolt II Left Hand
Same as the Medallion model A-Bolt except has left-hand action and is available only in 270, 30-06, 7mm Rem. Mag., 375 H&H. BOSS barrel vibration modulator and muzzle brake system not available in 375 H&H. Introduced 1987.
Price: $699.95
Price: With BOSS $792.95
Price: 375 H&H, with sights $806.95

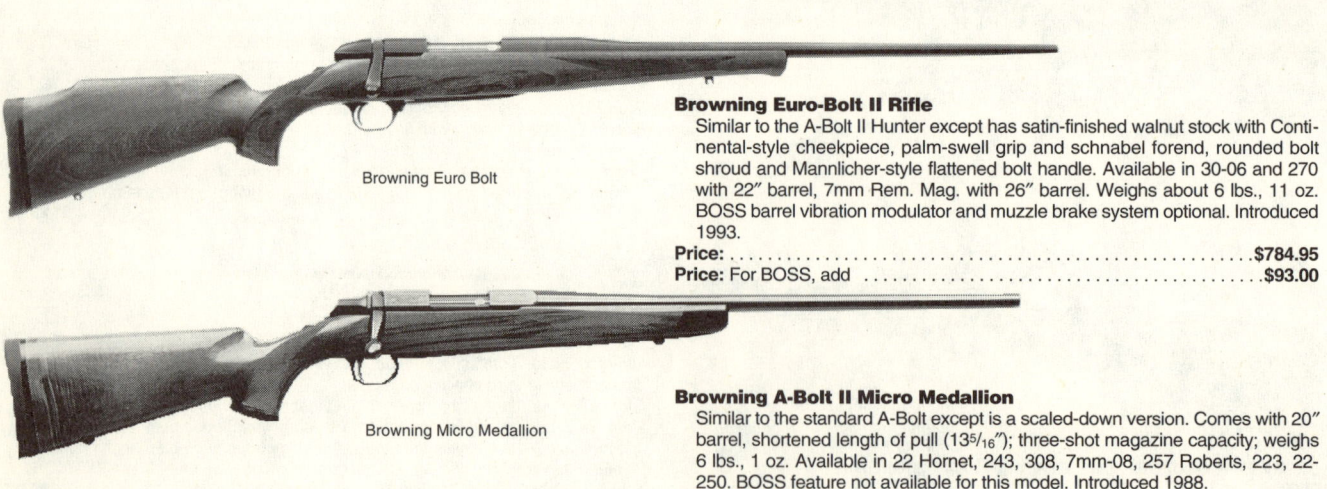
Browning Euro Bolt

Browning Micro Medallion

Browning Euro-Bolt II Rifle
Similar to the A-Bolt II Hunter except has satin-finished walnut stock with Continental-style cheekpiece, palm-swell grip and schnabel forend, rounded bolt shroud and Mannlicher-style flattened bolt handle. Available in 30-06 and 270 with 22" barrel, 7mm Rem. Mag. with 26" barrel. Weighs about 6 lbs., 11 oz. BOSS barrel vibration modulator and muzzle brake system optional. Introduced 1993.
Price: $784.95
Price: For BOSS, add $93.00

Browning A-Bolt II Micro Medallion
Similar to the standard A-Bolt except is a scaled-down version. Comes with 20" barrel, shortened length of pull (13 5/16"); three-shot magazine capacity; weighs 6 lbs., 1 oz. Available in 22 Hornet, 243, 308, 7mm-08, 257 Roberts, 223, 22-250. BOSS feature not available for this model. Introduced 1988.
Price: No sights $672.95

CENTERFIRE RIFLES—BOLT ACTION

Century Custom Sporting Rifle

CENTURY CUSTOM SPORTING RIFLE
Caliber: 308, 7.62x39mm.
Barrel: 22".
Weight: 6.7 lbs. **Length:** 43.75".
Stock: Walnut-finished hardwood.
Sights: None furnished; comes with two-piece Weaver-type base.
Features: Uses small ring Model 98 action; low-swing safety; blue finish. Introduced 1994. From Century International Arms.
Price: About $275.00

CENTURY DELUXE CUSTOM SPORTER
Caliber: 243, 270, 308, 30-06.
Barrel: 24".
Weight: NA. **Length:** 44" overall.
Stock: Black synthetic.
Sights: None furnished. Scope base installed.
Features: Mauser 98 action; bent bolt handle for scope use; low-swing safety; matte black finish; blind magazine. Introduced 1992. From Century International Arms.
Price: About $288.00

CENTURY SWEDISH SPORTER #38
Caliber: 6.5x55 Swede, 5-shot magazine.
Barrel: 24".
Weight: NA. **Length:** 44.1" overall.
Stock: Walnut-finished European hardwood with checkered p.g. and forend; Monte Carlo comb.
Sights: Blade front, adjustable rear.
Features: Uses M38 Swedish Mauser action; comes with Holden Ironsighter see-through scope mount. Introduced 1987. From Century International Arms.
Price: About $237.50

CENTURY ENFIELD SPORTER #4
Caliber: 303 British, 10-shot magazine.
Barrel: 25.2".
Weight: 8 lbs., 5 oz. **Length:** 44.5" overall.
Stock: Beechwood with checkered p.g. and forend, Monte Carlo comb.
Sights: Blade front, adjustable aperture rear.
Features: Uses Lee-Enfield action; blue finish. Trigger pinned to receiver. Introduced 1987. From Century International Arms.
Price: About $156.00

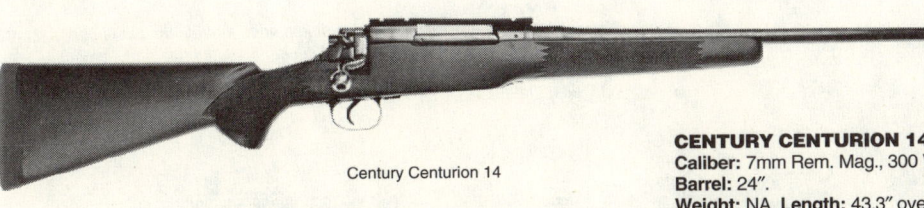

Century Centurion 14

CENTURY CENTURION 14 SPORTER
Caliber: 7mm Rem. Mag., 300 Win. Mag., 5-shot magazine.
Barrel: 24".
Weight: NA. **Length:** 43.3" overall.
Stock: Walnut-finished European hardwood. Checkered p.g. and forend. Monte Carlo comb.
Sights: None furnished.
Features: Uses modified Pattern 14 Enfield action. Drilled and tapped; scope base mounted. Blue finish. From Century International Arms.
Price: About $275.00

Consult our Directory pages for the location of firms mentioned.

Cooper Pro Varmint Extreme

COOPER ARMS MODEL 22 PRO VARMINT EXTREME
Caliber: 22-250, 220 Swift, 243, 25-06, 6mm PPC, 308, single shot.
Barrel: 26"; stainless steel match grade, straight taper; free-floated.
Weight: NA. **Length:** NA.
Stock: AAA Claro walnut, oil finish, 22 lpi wrap-around borderless ribbon checkering, beaded cheekpiece, steel grip cap, flared varminter forend, Pachmayr pad.
Sights: None furnished; drilled and tapped for scope mounting.
Features: Uses a three front locking lug system. Available with sterling silver inlaid medallion, skeleton grip cap, and French walnut. Introduced 1995. Made in U.S. by Cooper Arms.
Price: $1,595.00
Price: Benchrest model $1,695.00
Price: Black Jack model (McMillan synthetic stock) $1,395.00

COOPER ARMS MODEL 40 CENTERFIRE SPORTER
Caliber: 17 CCM, 17 Ackley Hornet, 22 CCM, 22 Hornet, 22 K-Hornet, 5-shot magazine.
Barrel: 23".
Weight: 7 lbs. **Length:** 42 1/2" overall.
Stock: AAA Claro walnut with 22 lpi borderless wrap-around ribbon checkering, oil finish, steel grip cap, Pachmayr pad.
Sights: None furnished.
Features: Action has three mid-bolt locking lugs, 45-degree bolt rotation; fully adjustable trigger; swivel studs. Pachmayr butt pad. Introduced 1994. Made in U.S. by Cooper Arms.
Price: Classic $1,495.00
Price: Custom Classic (AAA Claro walnut, Monte Carlo beaded cheekpiece, oil finish) $1,695.00
Price: Classic Varminter (AAA Claro walnut, wrap-around ribbon checkering, beaded cheekpiece, steel grip cap, flared varminter forend, Pachmayr pad) $1,695.00

COOPER ARMS MODEL 21 VARMINT EXTREME RIFLE
Caliber: 17 Rem., 17 Mach IV, 221 Fireball, 222, 222 Rem. Mag., 223, 22 PPC, 6x47, single shot.
Barrel: 23.75"; stainless steel, with competition step crown; free-floated.
Weight: NA. **Length:** NA.
Stock: AAA Claro walnut with flared oval forend, ambidextrous palm swell, 22 lpi checkering, oil finish, Pachmayr buttpad.
Sights: None furnished; drilled and tapped for scope mounting.
Features: Action has three mid-bolt locking lugs; adjustable trigger; glass bedded; swivel studs. Introduced 1994. Made in U.S. by Cooper Arms.
Price: $1,495.00
Price: Benchrest with Jewell trigger $1,695.00

CENTERFIRE RIFLES—BOLT ACTION

CZ 98 HUNTER CLASSIC RIFLE
Caliber: 243, 6.5x55, 270, 7x57, 7x64, 308, 30-06, 7.92x57, 7mm Rem. Mag., 300 Win. Mag.
Barrel: 24".
Weight: 7.69 lbs. **Length:** 45" overall.
Stock: Walnut or synthetic.
Sights: Optional; has integral Weaver-type base.
Features: Controlled round feeding, fixed ejector; hinged floorplate; adjustable trigger; swivel studs. Introduced 1995. Imported from the Czech Republic by Springfield, Inc.
Price: Walnut stock $449.00
Price: Synthetic stock $411.00

Dakota 76 Classic

Dakota 76 Short Action Rifles
A scaled-down version of the standard Model 76. Standard chamberings are 22-250, 243, 6mm Rem., 250-3000, 7mm-08, 308, others on special order. Short Classic Grade has 21" barrel; Alpine Grade is lighter (6½ lbs.), has a blind magazine and slimmer stock. Introduced 1989.
Price: Short Classic $2,300.00

DAKOTA 76 CLASSIC BOLT-ACTION RIFLE
Caliber: 257 Roberts, 270, 280, 30-06, 7mm Rem. Mag., 338 Win. Mag., 300 Win. Mag., 375 H&H, 458 Win. Mag.
Barrel: 23".
Weight: 7½ lbs. **Length:** 43½" overall.
Stock: Medium fancy grade walnut in classic style. Checkered p.g. and forend; solid buttpad.
Sights: None furnished; drilled and tapped for scope mounts.
Features: Has many features of the original Model 70 Winchester. One-piece rail trigger guard assembly; steel grip cap. Model 70-style trigger. Many options available. Left-hand rifle available at same price. Introduced 1988. From Dakota Arms, Inc.
Price: $2,500.00

Dakota 76 Varmint

Dakota 76 Varmint Rifle
Similar to the Dakota 76 except is a single shot with heavy barrel contour and special stock dimensions for varmint shooting. Chambered for 17 Rem., 22 BR, 222 Rem., 22-250, 220 Swift, 223, 6mm BR, 6mm PPC. Introduced 1994. Made in U.S. by Dakota Arms, Inc.
Price: $2,300.00

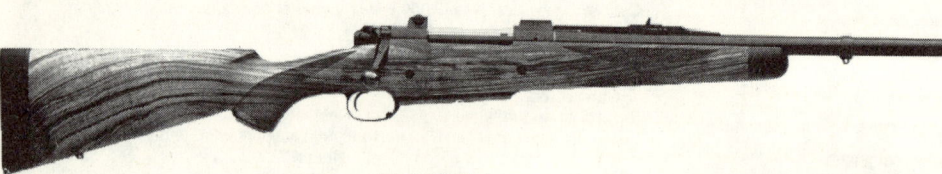

Dakota 416 Rigby

Dakota 416 Rigby African
Similar to the 76 Safari except chambered for 404 Jeffery, 416 Rigby, 416 Dakota, 450 Dakota, 4-round magazine, select wood, two stock cross-bolts. Has 24" barrel, weight of 9-10 lbs. Ramp front sight, standing leaf rear. Introduced 1989.
Price: $3,750.00

HARRIS-McMILLAN SIGNATURE CLASSIC SPORTER
Caliber: 22-250, 243, 6mm Rem., 7mm-08, 284, 308 (short action); 25-06, 270, 280 Rem., 30-06, 7mm Rem. Mag., 300 Win. Mag., 300 Wea. (long action); 338 Win. Mag., 340 Wea., 375 H&H (magnum action).
Barrel: 22", 24", 26".
Weight: 7 lbs. (short action).
Stock: McMillan fiberglass in green, beige, brown or black. Recoil pad and 1" swivels installed. Length of pull up to 14¼".
Sights: None furnished. Comes with 1" rings and bases.
Features: Uses McMillan right- or left-hand action with matte black finish. Trigger pull set at 3 lbs. Four-round magazine for standard calibers; three for magnums. Aluminum floorplate. Fibergrain and wood stocks optional. Introduced 1987. From McMillan Gunworks, Inc.
Price: $2,400.00

Harris-McMillan Signature Titanium Mountain Rifle
Similar to the Classic Sporter except action made of titanium alloy, barrel of chromemoly steel. Stock is of graphite reinforced fiberglass. Weight is 5½ lbs. Chambered for 270, 280 Rem., 30-06, 7mm Rem. Mag., 300 Win. Mag. Fibergrain stock optional. Introduced 1989.
Price: $3,000.00

DAKOTA 76 SAFARI BOLT-ACTION RIFLE
Caliber: 270 Win., 7x57, 280, 30-06, 7mm Dakota, 7mm Rem. Mag., 300 Dakota, 300 Win. Mag., 330 Dakota, 338 Win. Mag., 375 Dakota, 458 Win. Mag., 300 H&H, 375 H&H, 416 Rem.
Barrel: 23".
Weight: 8½ lbs. **Length:** 43½" overall.
Stock: XXX fancy walnut with ebony forend tip; point-pattern with wraparound forend checkering.
Sights: Ramp front, standing leaf rear.
Features: Has many features of the original Model 70 Winchester. Barrel band front swivel, inletted rear. Cheekpiece with shadow line. Steel grip cap. Introduced 1988. From Dakota Arms, Inc.
Price: Wood stock $3,300.00

AUGUSTE FRANCOTTE BOLT-ACTION RIFLES
Caliber: 243, 270, 7x64, 30-06, 308, 300 Win. Mag., 338, 7mm Rem. Mag., 375 H&H, 458 Win. Mag.; others on request.
Barrel: 23½" to 26½".
Weight: 8 to 10 lbs.
Stock: Fancy European walnut. To customer specs.
Sights: To customer specs.
Features: Basically a custom gun, Francotte offers many options. Imported from Belgium by Armes de Chasse.
Price: From about (no engraving) ....$10,600.00 to $14,800.00

Harris-McMillan Signature Super Varminter
Similar to the Classic Sporter except has heavy contoured barrel, adjustable trigger, field bipod and special hand-bedded fiberglass stock (Fibergrain optional). Chambered for 223, 22-250, 220 Swift, 243, 6mm Rem., 25-06, 7mm-08, 7mm BR, 308, 350 Rem. Mag. Comes with 1" rings and bases. Introduced 1989.
Price: $2,400.00

CENTERFIRE RIFLES—BOLT ACTION

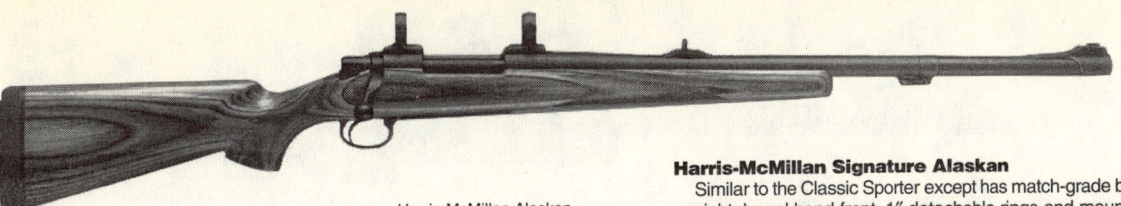

Harris-McMillan Alaskan

Harris-McMillan Signature Alaskan
Similar to the Classic Sporter except has match-grade barrel with single leaf rear sight, barrel band front, 1" detachable rings and mounts, steel floorplate, electroless nickel finish. Has wood Monte Carlo stock with cheekpiece, palm-swell grip, solid buttpad. Chambered for 270, 280 Rem., 30-06, 7mm Rem. Mag., 300 Win. Mag., 300 Wea., 358 Win., 340 Wea., 375 H&H. Introduced 1989.
Price: $3,300.00

Harris-McMillan Classic Stainless

Harris-McMillan Classic Stainless Sporter
Similar to the Classic Sporter except barrel and action made of stainless steel. Same calibers, in addition to 416 Rem. Mag. Comes with fiberglass stock, right- or left-hand action in natural stainless, glass bead or black chrome sulfide finishes. Introduced 1990. From McMillan Gunworks, Inc.
Price: $2,500.00

HARRIS-McMILLAN TALON SPORTER RIFLE
Caliber: 22-250, 243, 6mm Rem., 6mm BR, 7mm BR, 7mm-08, 25-06, 270, 280 Rem., 284, 308, 30-06, 350 Rem. Mag. (Long Action); 7mm Rem. Mag., 7mm STW, 300 Win. Mag., 300 Wea. Mag., 300 H&H, 338 Win. Mag., 340 Wea. Mag., 375 H&H, 416 Rem. Mag.
Barrel: 24" (standard).
Weight: About 7 1/2 lbs. **Length:** NA.
Stock: Choice of walnut or McMillan fiberglass.
Sights: None furnished; comes with rings and bases. Open sights optional.
Features: Uses pre-'64 Model 70-type action with cone breech, controlled feed, claw extractor and three-position safety. Barrel and action are of stainless steel; chromemoly optional. Introduced 1991. From McMillan Gunworks, Inc.
Price: $2,600.00

HARRIS-McMILLAN TALON SAFARI RIFLE
Caliber: 300 Win. Mag., 300 Wea. Mag., 300 Phoenix, 338 Win. Mag., 30/378, 338 Lapua, 300 H&H, 340 Wea. Mag., 375 H&H, 404 Jeffery, 416 Rem. Mag., 458 Win. Mag. (Safari Magnum); 378 Wea. Mag., 416 Rigby, 416 Wea. Mag., 460 Wea. Mag. (Safari Super Magnum).
Barrel: 24".
Weight: About 9-10 lbs. **Length:** 43" overall.
Stock: McMillan fiberglass Safari.
Sights: Barrel band front ramp, multi-leaf express rear.
Features: Uses McMillan Safari action. Has q.d. 1" scope mounts, positive locking steel floorplate, barrel band sling swivel. Match-grade barrel. Matte black finish standard. Introduced 1989. From Harris-McMillan Gunworks, Inc.
Price: Talon Safari Magnum $3,600.00
Price: Talon Safari Super Magnum $4,200.00

Howa Lightning

HOWA LIGHTNING BOLT-ACTION RIFLE
Caliber: 223, 22-250, 243, 270, 308, 30-06, 7mm Rem. Mag., 300 Win. Mag., 338 Win. Mag.
Barrel: 22", 24" magnum calibers.
Weight: 7 1/2 lbs. **Length:** 42" overall (22" barrel).
Stock: Black Bell & Carlson Carbelite composite with Monte Carlo comb; checkered grip and forend.
Sights: None furnished. Drilled and tapped for scope mounting.
Features: Sliding thumb safety; hinged floorplate; polished blue/black finish. Introduced 1993. From Interarms.
Price: Standard calibers $469.00
Price: Magnum calibers $486.00

KRICO MODEL 600 BOLT-ACTION RIFLE
Caliber: 222, 223, 22-250, 243, 308, 5.6x50 Mag., 4-shot magazine.
Barrel: 23.6".
Weight: 7.9 lbs. **Length:** 43.7" overall.
Stock: European walnut with Monte Carlo comb.
Sights: None furnished; drilled and tapped for scope mounting.
Features: Rubber recoil pad, sling swivels, checkered grip and forend. Polished blue finish. Imported from Germany by Mandall Shooting Supplies.
Price: $1,295.00

Krico Model 700

KRICO MODEL 700 BOLT-ACTION RIFLES
Caliber: 17 Rem., 222, 222 Rem. Mag., 223, 5.6x50 Mag., 243, 308, 5.6x57 RWS, 22-250, 6.5x55, 6.5x57, 7x57, 270, 7x64, 30-06, 9.3x62, 6.5x68, 7mm Rem. Mag., 300 Win. Mag., 8x68S, 7.5 Swiss, 9.3x64, 6x62 Freres.
Barrel: 23.6" (std. cals.); 25.5" (mag. cals.).
Weight: 7 lbs. **Length:** 43.3" overall (23.6" bbl.).
Stock: European walnut, Bavarian cheekpiece.
Sights: Blade on ramp front, open adjustable rear.
Features: Removable box magazine; sliding safety. Drilled and tapped for scope mounting. Imported from Germany by Mandall Shooting Supplies.
Price: Model 700 .... $995.00
Price: Model 700 Deluxe S $1,495.00
Price: Model 700 Deluxe $1,025.00
Price: Model 700 Stutzen (full stock) $1,249.00

CENTERFIRE RIFLES—BOLT ACTION

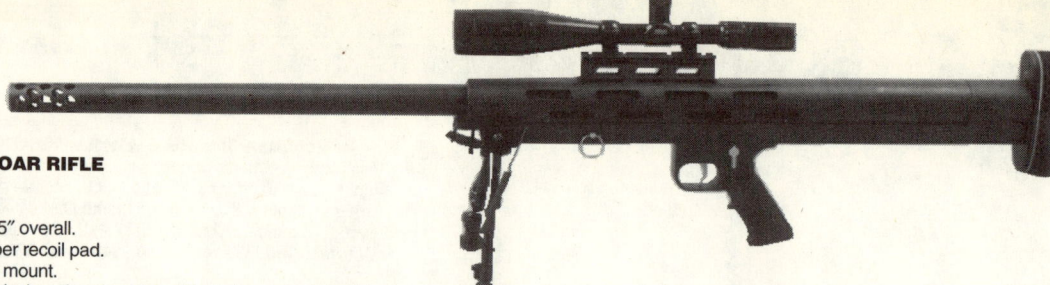

L.A.R. Grizzly 50

L.A.R. GRIZZLY 50 BIG BOAR RIFLE
Caliber: 50 BMG, single shot.
Barrel: 36″.
Weight: 28.4 lbs. **Length:** 45.5″ overall.
Stock: Integral. Ventilated rubber recoil pad.
Sights: None furnished; scope mount.
Features: Bolt-action bullpup design; thumb safety. All-steel construction. Introduced 1994. Made in U.S. by L.A.R. Mfg., Inc.
Price: $2,400.00

REMINGTON 700 ADL BOLT-ACTION RIFLE
Caliber: 243, 270, 308, 30-06 and 7mm Rem. Mag.
Barrel: 22″ or 24″ round tapered.
Weight: 7 lbs. **Length:** 41½″ to 43½″ overall.
Stock: Walnut. Satin-finished p.g. stock with fine-line cut checkering, Monte Carlo.
Sights: Gold bead ramp front; removable, step-adj. rear with windage screw.
Features: Side safety, receiver tapped for scope mounts.
Price: About $452.00
Price: 7mm Rem. Mag., about $479.00

Remington 700 BDL Bolt-Action Rifle
Same as the 700 ADL except chambered for 222, 223 (short action, 24″ barrel), 22-250, 25-06, 6mm Rem. (short action, 22″ barrel), 243, 270, 7mm-08, 280, 300 Savage, 30-06, 308; skip-line checkering; black forend tip and grip cap with white line spacers. Matted receiver top, quick-release floorplate. Hooded ramp front sight; q.d. swivels.
Price: About $549.00
Also available in 17 Rem., 7mm Rem. Mag., 300 Win. Mag. (long action, 24″ barrel), 338 Win. Mag., 35 Whelen (long action, 22″ barrel). Overall length 44½″, weight about 7½ lbs.
Price: About $576.00
Price: Custom Grade, about $2,387.00

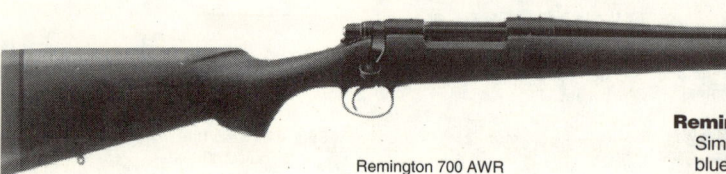

Remington 700 AWR

Remington 700 AWR Alaskan Wilderness Rifle
Similar to the Model 700 BDL except has stainless barreled action with satin blue finish; special 24″ Custom Shop barrel profile; matte gray stock of fiberglass and graphite, reinforced with DuPont Kevlar, straight comb with raised cheekpiece, magnum-grade black rubber recoil pad. Chambered for 7mm Rem. Mag., 300 Win. Mag., 300 Wea. Mag., 338 Win. Mag., 375 H&H. Introduced 1994.
Price: $1,256.00

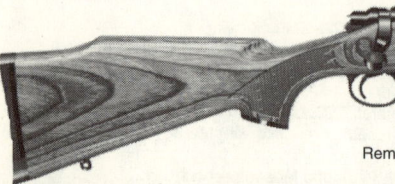

Remington 700 BDL VLS

Remington 700 VLS VArmint Laminated Stock
Similar to the 700 BDL except has 26″ heavy barrel without sights, brown laminated stock with forend tip, grip cap, rubber buttpad. Available in 222 Rem., 223 Rem., 22-250, 243, 308. Polished blue finish. Introduced 1995.
Price: $585.00

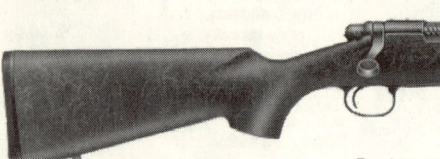

Remington 700 Varmint Synthetic

Remington 700 Varmint Synthetic Rifle
Similar to the 700 BDL Varmint Special except has composite stock reinforced with DuPont Kevlar, fiberglass and graphite. Has aluminum bedding block that runs the full length of the receiver. Free-floating 26″ barrel. Metal has black matte finish; stock has textured black and gray finish and swivel studs. Available in 220 Swift, 223, 22-250, 308. Introduced 1992.
Price: $665.00

Remington 700 VS SF Rifle
Similar to the Model 700 Varmint Synthetic except has satin-finish stainless barreled action with 26″ fluted barrel, spherical concave muzzle crown. Chambered for 223, 220 Swift, 22-250, 308. Introduced 1994.
Price: $798.00

Remington 700 Sendero

Remington 700 Sendero Rifle
Similar to the Model 700 Varmint Synthetic except has long action for magnum calibers. Has 26″ heavy varmint barrel with spherical concave crown. Chambered for 25-06, 270, 7mm Rem. Mag., 300 Win. Mag. Introduced 1994.
Price: 25-06, 270 .... $665.00
Price: 7mm Rem. Mag., 300 Win. Mag. $692.00

CENTERFIRE RIFLES—BOLT ACTION

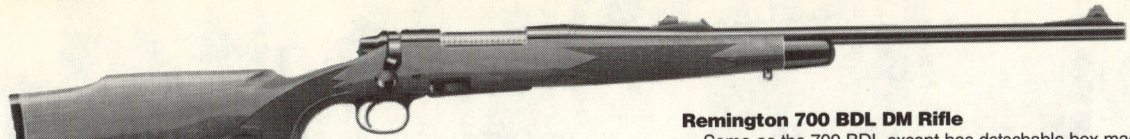
Remington 700 BDL DM

Remington 700 APR African Plains Rifle
Similar to the Model 700 BDL except has magnum receiver and specially contoured 26" Custom Shop barrel with satin finish, laminated wood stock with raised cheekpiece, satin finish, black buttpad, 20 lpi cut checkering. Chambered for 7mm Rem. Mag., 300 Win. Mag., 300 Wea. Mag., 338 Win. Mag., 375 H&H. Introduced 1994.
Price: $1,466.00

Remington 700 Custom KS Mountain Rifle
Similar to the 700 "Mountain Rifle" except custom finished with Kevlar reinforced resin synthetic stock. Available in both left- and right-hand versions. Chambered for 270 Win., 280 Rem., 30-06, 7mm Rem. Mag., 300 Win. Mag., 300 Wea. Mag., 35 Whelen, 338 Win. Mag., 8mm Rem. Mag., 375 H&H, all with 24" barrel only. Weight is 6 lbs., 6 oz. Introduced 1986.
Price: Right-hand $1,037.00
Price: Left-hand $1,101.00
Price: Stainless $1,182.00

Remington 700 BDL DM Rifle
Same as the 700 BDL except has detachable box magazine (4-shot, standard calibers, 3-shot for magnums). Has glossy stock finish, open sights, recoil pad, sling swivels. Right-hand action calibers: 6mm, 243, 25-06, 270, 280, 7mm-08, 30-06, 308, 7mm Rem. Mag., 300 Win. Mag., 338 Win. Mag.; left-hand calibers: 243, 270, 7mm-08, 30-06, 7mm Rem. Mag., 300 Win. Mag. Introduced 1995.
Price: Right-hand, standard calibers $603.00
Price: Left-hand, standard calibers $629.00
Price: Right-hand, magnum calibers $629.00
Price: Left-hand, magnum calibers $656.00

Remington 700 BDL Left Hand
Same as 700 BDL except mirror-image left-hand action, stock. Available in 22-250, 243, 308, 270, 30-06 only.
Price: About $576.00
Price: 7mm Rem. Mag., 338 Win. Mag., about $603.00

Remington 700 Safari
Similar to the BDL except custom finished and tuned. In 8mm Rem. Mag., 375 H&H, 416 Rem. Mag. or 458 Win. Magnum calibers only with heavy barrel. Hand checkered, oil-finished stock in classic or Monte Carlo style with recoil pad installed. Delivery time is about 5 months.
Price: About $1,041.00
Price: Classic stock, left-hand $1,105.00
Price: Safari Custom KS (Kevlar stock), right-hand $1,198.00
Price: As above, left-hand $1,264.00

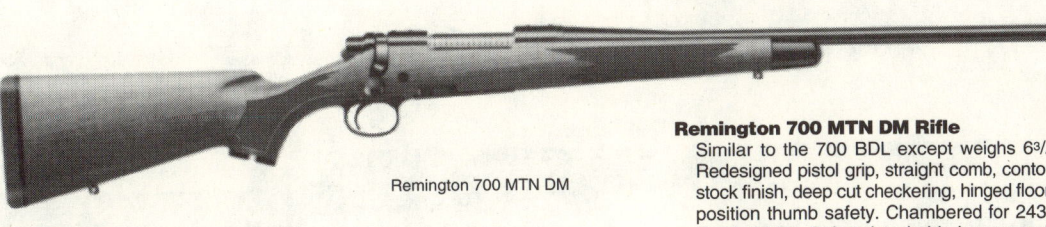
Remington 700 MTN DM

Remington 700 MTN DM Rifle
Similar to the 700 BDL except weighs 6¾ lbs., has a 22" tapered barrel. Redesigned pistol grip, straight comb, contoured cheekpiece, hand-rubbed oil stock finish, deep cut checkering, hinged floorplate and magazine follower, two-position thumb safety. Chambered for 243, 270 Win., 7mm-08, 25-06, 280 Rem., 30-06, 4-shot detachable box magazine. Overall length is 42½". Introduced 1986.
Price: About $603.00

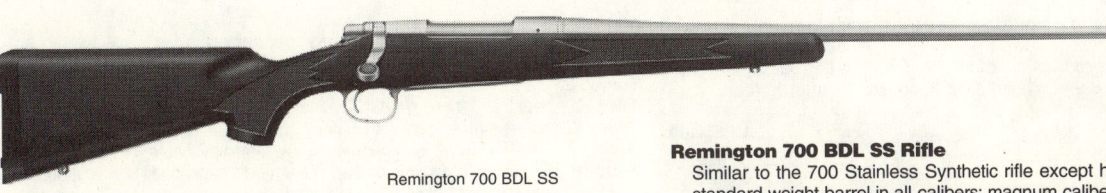
Remington 700 BDL SS

REMINGTON 700 CLASSIC RIFLE
Caliber: 300 Win. Mag.
Barrel: 24".
Weight: About 7¾ lbs. **Length:** 44½" overall.
Stock: American walnut, 20 lpi checkering on p.g. and forend. Classic styling. Satin finish.
Sights: None furnished. Receiver drilled and tapped for scope mounting.
Features: A "classic" version of the M700 ADL with straight comb stock. Fitted with rubber recoil pad. Sling swivel studs installed. Hinged floorplate. Limited production in 1995 only.
Price: About $576.00

Remington 700 BDL SS Rifle
Similar to the 700 Stainless Synthetic rifle except has hinged floorplate, 24" standard weight barrel in all calibers; magnum calibers have magnum-contour barrel. No sights supplied, but comes drilled and tapped. Has corrosion-resistant follower and fire control, stainless BDL-style barreled action with fine matte finish. Synthetic stock has straight comb and cheekpiece, textured finish, positive checkering, plated swivel studs. Short action calibers—223, 243, 6mm Rem., 7mm-08 Rem., 308; standard long action—25-06, 270, 280 Rem., 30-06; magnums—7mm Rem. Mag., 7mm Wea. Mag., 300 Win. Mag., 300 Wea. Mag., 338 Win. Mag. Weighs 6¾-7 lbs. Introduced 1993.
Price: Standard calibers, about $603.00
Price: Magnum calibers, about $629.00

Remington 700 BDL SS DM

Remington 700 BDL SS DM Rifle
Same as the 700 BDL SS except has detachable box magazine. Barrel, receiver and bolt made of #416 stainless steel; black synthetic stock. Available in 6mm, 243, 25-06, 270, 280, 7mm-08, 7mm Rem. Mag., 300 Win. Mag., 300 Wea. Mag. Introduced 1995.
Price: Standard calibers $656.00
Price: Magnum calibers $682.00

CAUTION: PRICES SHOWN ARE SUPPLIED BY THE MANUFACTURER OR IMPORTER. CHECK YOUR LOCAL GUNSHOP.

CENTERFIRE RIFLES—BOLT ACTION

Remington Model Seven

REMINGTON MODEL SEVEN BOLT-ACTION RIFLE
Caliber: 17 Rem., 223 Rem. (5-shot); 243, 6mm Rem., 7mm-08, 6mm, 308 (4-shot).
Barrel: 18 1/2".
Weight: 6 1/4 lbs. **Length:** 37 1/2" overall.
Stock: Walnut, with modified schnabel forend. Cut checkering.
Sights: Ramp front, adjustable open rear.
Features: Short-action design; silent side safety; free-floated barrel except for single pressure point at forend tip. Introduced 1983.
Price: About $549.00
Price: 17 Rem., about $576.00

Remington Model Seven Youth Rifle
Similar to the Model Seven except has hardwood stock with 12 3/16" length of pull and chambered for 6mm Rem., 243, 7mm-08. Introduced 1993.
Price: About $452.00

Remington Model Seven Custom MS Rifle
Similar to the Model Seven except has full-length Mannlicher-style stock of laminated wood with straight comb, solid black recoil pad, black steel forend tip, cut checkering, gloss finish. Barrel length 20", weight 6 3/4 lbs. Availabloe in 222 Rem., 223, 22-250, 243, 6mm Rem., 7mm-08 Rem., 308, 350 Rem. Mag. Calibers 250 Savage, 257 Roberts, 35 Rem. available on special order. Polished blue finish. Introduced 1993. From Remington Custom Shop.
Price: About $1,041.00

Remington Model Seven Custom KS
Similar to the standard Model Seven except has custom finished stock of lightweight Kevlar aramid fiber and chambered for 223 Rem., 7mm-08, 308, 35 Rem. and 350 Rem. Mag. Barrel length is 20", weight 5 3/4 lbs. Comes with iron sights and is drilled and tapped for scope mounting. Special order through Remington Custom Shop. Introduced 1987.
Price: $1,037.00

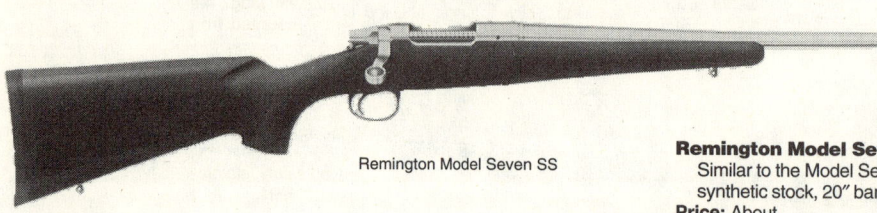
Remington Model Seven SS

Remington Model Seven SS
Similar to the Model Seven except has stainless steel barreled action and black synthetic stock, 20" barrel. Chambered for 243, 7mm-08, 308. Introduced 1994.
Price: About $603.00

RUGER M77 MARK II MAGNUM RIFLE
Caliber: 375 H&H, 404 Jeffery, 4-shot magazine; 416 Rigby, 3-shot magazine.
Barrel: 26", with integral steel rib; hammer forged.
Weight: 9.25 lbs. (375, 404); 10.25 lbs. (416, 458). **Length:** 40.5" overall.
Stock: Circassian walnut with hand-cut checkering, swivel studs, steel grip cap, rubber butt pad.
Sights: Ramp front, three leaf express on serrated integral steel rib. Rib also serves as base for front scope ring.
Features: Uses an enlarged Mark II action with three-position safety, stainless bolt, steel trigger guard and hinged steel floorplate. Controlled feed. Introduced 1989.
Price: M77MKIIRSM $1,550.00

Ruger 77/22 Hornet

RUGER 77/22 HORNET BOLT-ACTION RIFLE
Caliber: 22 Hornet, 6-shot rotary magazine.
Barrel: 20".
Weight: About 6 lbs. **Length:** 39 3/4" overall.
Stock: Checkered American walnut, black rubber buttpad.
Sights: Brass bead front, open adjustable rear; also available without sights.
Features: Same basic features as the rimfire model except has slightly lengthened receiver. Uses Ruger rotary magazine. Three-position safety. Comes with 1" Ruger scope rings. Introduced 1994.
Price: 77/22RH (rings only) $452.00
Price: 77/22RSH (with sights) $469.00
Price: K77/22VH Varmint, laminated stock $525.00

RUGER M77 MARK II RIFLE
Caliber: 223, 243, 6mm Rem., 257 Roberts, 25-06, 6.5x55 Swedish, 270, 280 Rem., 308, 30-06, 7mm Rem. Mag., 300 Win. Mag., 338 Win. Mag., 4-shot magazine.
Barrel: 20", 22"; 24" (magnums).
Weight: About 7 lbs. **Length:** 39 3/4" overall.
Stock: Hand-checkered American walnut; swivel studs, rubber butt pad.
Sights: None furnished. Receiver has Ruger integral scope mount base, comes with Ruger 1" rings. Some models have iron sights.
Features: Short action with new trigger and three-position safety. New trigger guard with redesigned floorplate latch. Left-hand model available. Introduced 1989.
Price: M77MKIIR (no sights) $574.00
Price: M77MKIIRS (open sights) $635.00
Price: M77MKIILR (left-hand, 270, 30-06, 7mm Rem. Mag., 300 Win. Mag.) $574.00

CONSULT **Shooter's Marketplace** Page 266, This Issue

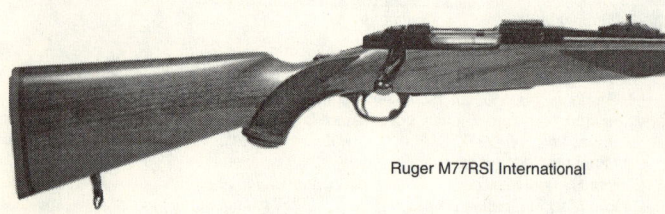
Ruger M77RSI International

Ruger M77RSI International Carbine
Same as the standard Model 77 except has 18 1/2" barrel, full-length International-style stock, with steel forend cap, loop-type steel sling swivels. Integral-base receiver, open sights, Ruger 1" steel rings. Improved front sight. Available in 243, 270, 308, 30-06. Weighs 7 lbs. Length overall is 38 3/8".
Price: M77MKIIRSI $642.00

CENTERFIRE RIFLES—BOLT ACTION

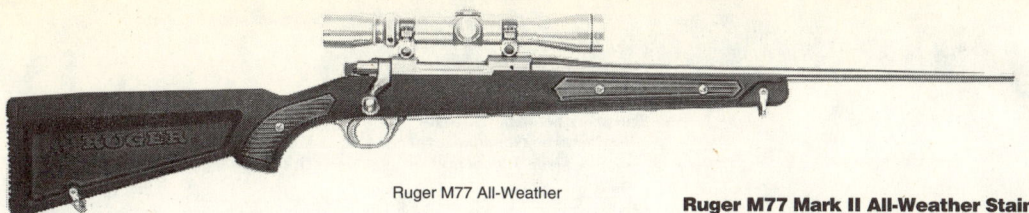

Ruger M77 All-Weather

Ruger M77RL Ultra Light
Similar to the standard M77 except weighs only 6 lbs., chambered for 223, 243, 308, 270, 30-06, 257; barrel tapped for target scope blocks; has 20" Ultra Light barrel. Overall length 40". Ruger's steel 1" scope rings supplied. Introduced 1983.
Price: M77MKIIRL $610.00

Ruger M77 Mark II All-Weather Stainless Rifle
Similar to the wood-stock M77 Mark II except all metal parts are of stainless steel, and has an injection-moulded, glass-fiber-reinforced Du Pont Zytel stock. Chambered for 223, 243, 270, 308, 30-06, 7mm Rem. Mag., 300 Win. Mag., 338 Win. Mag. Has the fixed-blade-type ejector, three-position safety, and new trigger guard with patented floorplate latch. Comes with integral Scope Base Receiver and 1" Ruger scope rings, built-in sling swivel loops. Introduced 1990.
Price: KM77MKIIRP $574.00
Price: KM77MKIILSP, open sights $635.00

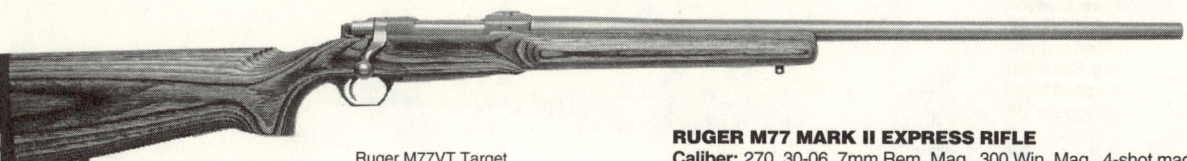

Ruger M77VT Target

RUGER M77VT TARGET RIFLE
Caliber: 22 PPC, 22-250, 220 Swift, 223, 243, 6mm PPC, 25-06, 308.
Barrel: 26" heavy stainless steel with target gray finish.
Weight: Approx. 9.25 lbs. **Length:** Approx. 44" overall.
Stock: Laminated American hardwood with beavertail forend, steel swivel studs; no checkering or grip cap.
Sights: Integral scope mount bases in receiver.
Features: Ruger diagonal bedding system. Ruger steel 1" scope rings supplied. Fully adjustable trigger. Steel floorplate and trigger guard. New version introduced 1992.
Price: KM77MKIIVT $684.00

RUGER M77 MARK II EXPRESS RIFLE
Caliber: 270, 30-06, 7mm Rem. Mag., 300 Win. Mag., 4-shot magazine.
Barrel: 22", with integral steel rib; barrel-mounted front swivel stud; hammer forged.
Weight: 7.5 lbs. **Length:** 42.125" overall.
Stock: Hand-checkered medium quality French walnut with steel grip cap, black rubber butt pad, swivel studs.
Sights: Ramp front, open rear adjustable for windage and elevation mounted on rib.
Features: Mark II action with three-position safety, stainless steel bolt, steel trigger guard, hinged steel floorplate. Introduced 1991.
Price: M77EXPMKII $1,550.00

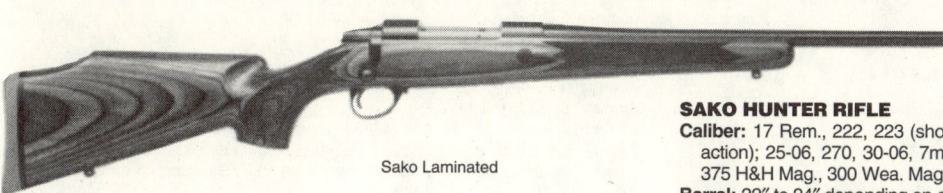

Sako Laminated

Sako Laminated Rifle
Same gun as the Sako Hunter except has laminated stock with dull finish. Chambered for same calibers. Also available in left-hand version. Introduced 1987.
Price: Medium action $1,200.00
Price: Long action, from $1,255.00
Price: Magnum cals., from $1,275.00
Price: 375 H&H, 416 Rem. Mag., from $1,295.00

SAKO HUNTER RIFLE
Caliber: 17 Rem., 222, 223 (short action); 22-250, 243, 7mm-08, 308 (medium action); 25-06, 270, 30-06, 7mm Rem. Mag., 300 Win. Mag., 338 Win. Mag., 375 H&H Mag., 300 Wea. Mag., 416 Rem. Mag. (long action).
Barrel: 22" to 24" depending on caliber.
Weight: 5 3/4 lbs. (short); 6 1/4 lbs. (med.); 7 1/4 lbs. (long).
Stock: Hand-checkered European walnut.
Sights: None furnished.
Features: Adj. trigger, hinged floorplate. Imported from Finland by Stoeger.
Price: 17 Rem., 222, 223 .... $1,030.00
Price: 22-250, 243, 308, 7mm-08 .... $1,030.00
Price: Long action cals. (except magnums) $1,066.00
Price: Magnum cals. $1,080.00
Price: 375 H&H, 416 Rem. Mag., from $1,095.00
Price: 300 Wea. $1,095.00

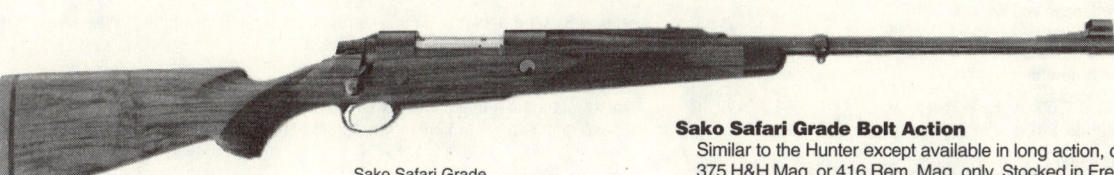

Sako Safari Grade

Sako Mannlicher-Style Carbine
Same as the Hunter except has full "Mannlicher" style stock, 18 1/2" barrel, weighs 7 1/2 lbs., chambered for 243, 25-06, 270, 308 and 30-06, 7mm Rem. Mag., 300 Win. Mag., 338 Win. Mag., 375 H&H. Introduced 1977. From Stoeger.
Price: 243, 308 .... $1,245.00
Price: 270, 30-06 .... $1,285.00
Price: 338 Win. Mag., 375 H&H $1,300.00
Price: 375 H&H $1,320.00

Sako Safari Grade Bolt Action
Similar to the Hunter except available in long action, calibers 338 Win. Mag. or 375 H&H Mag. or 416 Rem. Mag. only. Stocked in French walnut, checkered 20 lpi, solid rubber buttpad; grip cap and forend tip; quarter-rib "express" rear sight, hooded ramp front. Front sling swivel band-mounted on barrel.
Price: $2,715.00

Sako Varmint Heavy Barrel
Same as std. Super Sporter except has beavertail forend; available in 17 Rem., 222, 223 (short action), 22 PPC, 6mm PPC (single shot), 22-250, 243, 308, 7mm-08 (medium action). Weight from 8 1/4 to 8 1/2 lbs., 5-shot magazine capacity.
Price: 17 Rem., 222, 223 (short action) $1,215.00
Price: 22-250, 243, 308 (medium action) $1,215.00
Price: 22 PPC, 6mm PPC (single shot) $1,440.00

CAUTION: PRICES SHOWN ARE SUPPLIED BY THE MANUFACTURER OR IMPORTER. CHECK YOUR LOCAL GUNSHOP.

CENTERFIRE RIFLES—BOLT ACTION

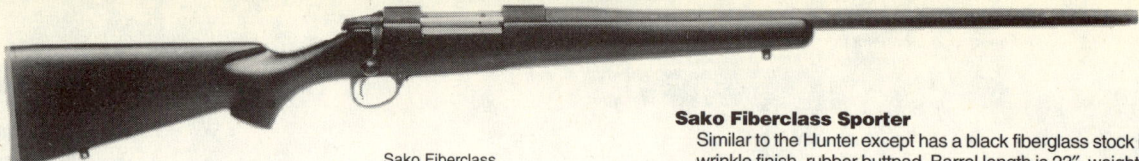
Sako Fiberclass

Sako Super Deluxe Sporter
Similar to Hunter except has select European walnut with high-gloss finish and deep-cut oak leaf carving. Metal has super high polish, deep blue finish. Special order only.
Price: $3,030.00

Sako Hunter Left-Hand Rifle
Same gun as the Sako Hunter except has left-hand action, stock with dull finish. Available in medium, long and magnum actions. Introduced 1987.
Price: Standard calibers, 22-250 to 7mm-08 .... $1,110.00
Price: Magnum calibers $1,160.00
Price: 375 H&H, 416 Rem. Mag. $1,175.00
Price: Long action, 25-06, 270, 280, 30-06 .... $1,145.00

Sako Fiberclass Sporter
Similar to the Hunter except has a black fiberglass stock in the classic style, with wrinkle finish, rubber buttpad. Barrel length is 23", weight 7 lbs., 2 oz. Introduced 1985.
Price: 25-06, 270, 280 Rem., 30-06 .... $1,360.00
Price: 7mm Rem. Mag., 300 Win. Mag., 338 Win. Mag. .. $1,375.00
Price: 375 H&H, 416 Rem. Mag. $1,395.00

Sako Classic Bolt Action
Similar to the Hunter except has classic-style stock with straight comb. Has 21³⁄₄" barrel, weighs 6 lbs. Matte finish wood. Introduced 1993. Imported from Finland by Stoeger.
Price: 243 .... $1,030.00
Price: 270, 30-06 .... $1,060.00
Price: 7mm Rem. Mag. $1,080.00

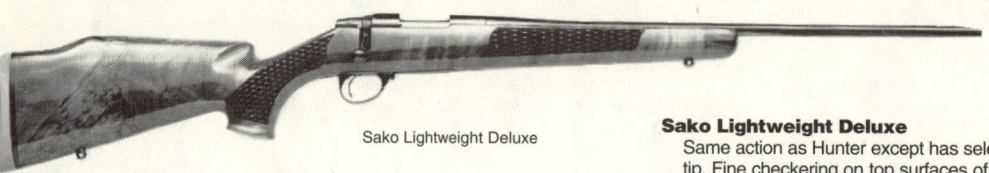
Sako Lightweight Deluxe

Sako Lightweight Deluxe
Same action as Hunter except has select wood, rosewood p.g. cap and forend tip. Fine checkering on top surfaces of integral dovetail bases, bolt sleeve, bolt handle root and bolt knob. Vent. recoil pad, skip-line checkering, mirror finish bluing.
Price: 17 Rem., 222, 223, 22-250, 243, 308, 7mm-08 .. $1,445.00
Price: 25-06, 270, 280 Rem., 30-06 .... $1,480.00
Price: 7mm Rem. Mag., 300 Win. Mag., 338 Win. Mag. .. $1,485.00
Price: 300 Wea., 375 H&H, 416 Rem. Mag. $1,515.00

Sako TRG-S

SAKO TRG-S BOLT-ACTION RIFLE
Caliber: 243, 7mm-08, 270, 30-06, 7mm Rem. Mag., 300 Win. Mag., 338 Win. Mag., 375 H&H, 416 Rem. Mag., 5-shot magazine (4-shot for 375 H&H).
Barrel: 22", 24" (magnum calibers).
Weight: 7.75 lbs. **Length:** 45.5" overall.
Stock: Reinforced polyurethane with Monte Carlo comb.
Sights: None furnished.
Features: Resistance-free bolt with 60-degree lift. Recoil pad adjustable for length. Free-floating barrel, detachable magazine, fully adjustable trigger. Matte blue metal. Introduced 1993. Imported from Finland by Stoeger.
Price: 243, 7mm-08, 270, 30-06 .... $775.00
Price: Magnum calibers $815.00

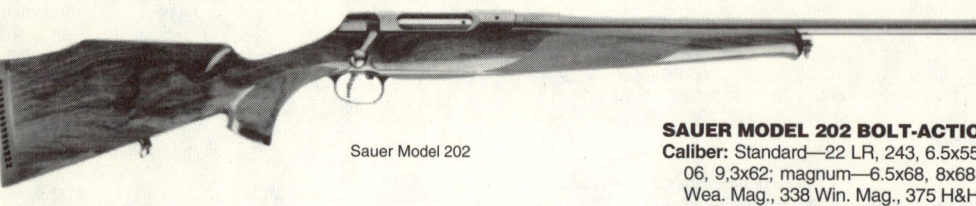
Sauer Model 202

Sauer Model 202 Alaska Bolt-Action Rifle
Similar to the standard Model 202 except chambered for 300 Wea. Mag. or 300 Win. Mag. only, with 26" barrel; laminated brown stock; metal coated with "Ilaflon" for protection. Accepts any Model 202 magnum barrel. Weighs 8.4 lbs. Introduced 1994. Imported from Germany by Paul Co.
Price: $1,335.00

Sauer Model 202 Hunter-Match Rifle
Similar to the standard Model 202 except has 26" or 28.5" match-grade heavy barrel, chambered for 6.5x55 or 308 Win. French walnut, two-piece stock has a wide, flat target-type forend, target-type alloy rail for swivels or bipod; butt has Monte Carlo comb. Drilled and tapped for scope mounting. Accepts standard-caliber Model 202 interchangeable barrels, including 22 LR conversion unit. Weighs 10.1 lbs. Matte black metal finish. Introduced 1994. Imported from Germany by Paul Co.
Price: $1,495.00

SAUER MODEL 202 BOLT-ACTION RIFLE
Caliber: Standard—22 LR, 243, 6.5x55, 6.5x57, 25-06, 270, 280, 7x64, 308, 30-06, 9.3x62; magnum—6.5x68, 8x68S, 7mm Rem. Mag., 300 Win. Mag., 300 Wea. Mag., 338 Win. Mag., 375 H&H.
Barrel: 24" (standard calibers), 26" (magnum calibers).
Weight: 7.5 lbs. (steel), 6.5 lbs. (alloy). **Length:** NA.
Stock: Standard—fancy Claro walnut, two-piece, with Monte Carlo comb, palm swell grip, semi-schnabel forend tip; Super Grade has extra-fancy Claro walnut with rosewood grip cap, forend tip, high-gloss epoxy finish. French walnut Eurostock available (oil finish).
Sights: Optional; drilled and tapped for scope mounting.
Features: Modular receiver accepts interchangeable barrels. Steel or alloy receiver; right- or left-hand bolt; tang safety; fully adjustable trigger; cocking indicator; detachable magazine. Introduced 1994. Imported from Germany by Paul Co.
Price: Standard $899.00
Price: Magnum $949.00
Price: Super Grade Standard $1,025.00
Price: Super Grade Magnum $1,060.00
Price: 375 H&H Magnum $1,075.00
Price: 375 H&H Magnum Super Grade $1,185.00
Price: Extra barrel, standard calibers $240.00
Price: Extra barrel, magnum calibers $250.00
Price: 22 LR conversion unit $585.00

CENTERFIRE RIFLES—BOLT ACTION

SAUER 90 BOLT-ACTION RIFLE
Caliber: Standard—222, 22-250, 243, 25-06, 6.5x55, 6.5x57, 270, 7x64, 308, 30-06, 9.3x62, 4-shot magazine; magnum—6.5x68, 7mm Rem. Mag., 300 Win. Mag., 300 Wea. Mag., 8x68S, 338 Win. Mag., 375 H&H, 458 Win. Mag., 3-shot magazine.
Barrel: 21" (Stutzen), 24" (standard calibers), 26" (magnum calibers).
Weight: 7.25 lbs. (standard and Stutzen). **Length:** 44" overall (24" barrel).
Stock: Monte Carlo style with sculptured cheekpiece, Wundhammar palm swell, hand-checkered grip and forend, rosewood grip cap and forend tip. Lux is French walnut with hand-rubbed oil finish, Supreme is fancy Claro walnut with high-gloss epoxy finish.
Sights: None furnished; drilled and tapped for scope mounting. Safari model has iron sights.
Features: Bolt has rear-cam activated locking lugs, 65-degree lift; fully adjustable gold-plated trigger; chamber loaded and cocking indicators; tang safety; push-button bolt release; hammer-forged barrel; detachable box magazine. Introduced 1986. Imported from Germany by Paul Co.
Price: Lux, Supreme or Stutzen $1,495.00
Price: With Grade I engraving $2,495.00
Price: With Grade II engraving $3,095.00
Price: With Grade III engraving $3,495.00
Price: With Grade IV engraving $3,995.00
Price: Safari model, 458 Win. Mag. $1,995.00

SAVAGE MODEL 110FP TACTICAL RIFLE
Caliber: 223, 308, 300 Win. Mag., 7mm Rem. Mag., 25-06, 4-shot magazine.
Barrel: 24", heavy; recessed target muzzle.
Weight: 8 1/2 lbs. **Length:** 45.5" overall.
Stock: Black graphite/fiberglass composition; positive checkering.
Sights: None furnished. Receiver drilled and tapped for scope mounting.
Features: Black matte finish on all metal parts. Double swivel studs on the forend for sling and/or bipod mount. Introduced 1990. From Savage Arms.
Price: $425.00

SAVAGE MODEL 110GXP3, 110GCXP3 PACKAGE GUNS
Caliber: 223, 22-250, 243, 250 Savage, 25-06, 270, 300 Sav., 30-06, 308, 7mm Rem. Mag., 7mm-08, 300 Win. Mag. (Model 110GXP3); 270, 30-06, 7mm Rem. Mag., 300 Win. Mag. (Model 110GCXP3).
Barrel: 22" (standard calibers), 24" (magnum calibers).
Weight: 7.25-7.5 lbs. **Length:** 43.5" overall (22" barrel).
Stock: Monte Carlo-style hardwood with walnut finish, rubber buttpad, swivel studs.
Sights: None furnished.
Features: Model 110GXP3 has fixed, top-loading magazine, Model 110GCXP3 has detachable box magazine. Rifles come with a factory-mounted and bore-sighted 3-9x32 scope, rings and bases, quick-detachable swivels, sling. Left-hand models available in all calibers. Introduced 1991 (GXP3); 1994 (GCXP3). Made in U.S. by Savage Arms, Inc.
Price: Model 110GXP3, right- or left-hand $418.00
Price: Model 110GCXP3, right- or left-hand $480.00

Savage Model 111FCXP3

Savage Model 111FXP3, 111FCXP3 Package Guns
Similar to the Model 110 Series Package Guns except with lightweight, black graphite/fiberglass composite stock with non-glare finish, positive checkering. Same calibers as Model 110 rifles, plus 338 Win. Mag. Model 111FXP3 has fixed top-loading magazine; Model 111FCXP3 has detachable box. Both come with mounted 3-9x32 scope, quick-detachable swivels, sling. Introduced 1994. Made in U.S. by Savage Arms, Inc.
Price: Model 111FXP3, right- or left-hand $447.00
Price: Model 111FCXP3, right- or left-hand $488.00

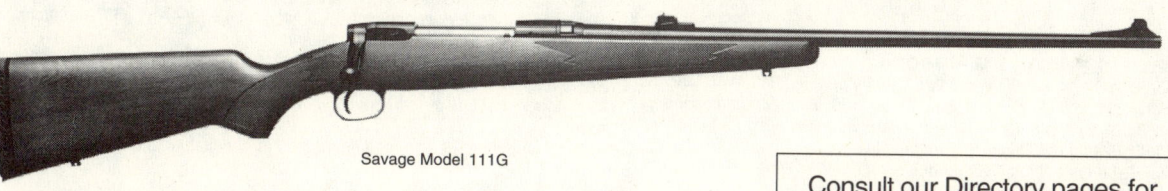
Savage Model 111G

Consult our Directory pages for the location of firms mentioned.

SAVAGE MODEL 110CY LADIES/YOUTH RIFLE
Caliber: 223, 243, 270, 300 Sav., 308, 5-shot magazine.
Barrel: 22".
Weight: About 6.5 lbs. **Length:** 42.5" overall.
Stock: Walnut-stained hardwood with high comb, cut checkering.
Sights: Ramp front, fully adjustable rear.
Features: Length of pull is 12.5", with red rubber buttpad. Drilled and tapped for scope mounting. Uses standard Model 110 barreled action. Introduced 1991. Made in U.S. by Savage Arms, Inc.
Price: $362.00

SAVAGE MODEL 112 VARMINT RIFLES
Caliber: 220 Swift (single shot), 22-250, 223, 5-shot magazine.
Barrel: 26" heavy.
Weight: 8.8 lbs. **Length:** 47.5" overall.
Stock: Black graphite/fiberglass filled composite with positive checkering.
Sights: None furnished; drilled and tapped for scope mounting.
Features: Blued barrel with recessed target-style muzzle. Double front swivel studs for attaching bipod. Introduced 1991. Made in U.S. by Savage Arms, Inc.
Price: Model 112FV $400.00
Price: Model 112FVSS (cals. 223, 22-250, 25-06, 7mm Rem. Mag., 300 Win. Mag., stainless barrel, bolt handle, trigger guard) $500.00
Price: Model 112FVSS-S (as above, single shot) $500.00
Price: Model 112BVSS (heavy-prone laminated stock with high comb, Wundhammer swell, fluted stainless barrel, bolt handle, trigger guard) $525.00
Price: Model 112BVSS-S (as above, single shot) $525.00

SAVAGE MODEL 111 CLASSIC HUNTER RIFLES
Caliber: 223, 22-250, 243, 250 Sav., 25-06, 270, 300 Sav., 30-06, 308, 7mm Rem. Mag., 7mm-08, 300 Win. Mag., 338 Win. Mag. (Models 111G, GL, GNS, F, FL, FNS); 270, 30-06, 7mm Rem. Mag., 300 Win. Mag. (Models 111GC, GLC, FC, FLC).
Barrel: 22", 24" (magnum calibers).
Weight: 6.3 to 7 lbs. **Length:** 43.5" overall (22" barrel).
Stock: Walnut-finished hardwood (M111G, GC); graphite/fiberglass filled composite.
Sights: Ramp front, open fully adjustable rear; drilled and tapped for scope mounting.
Features: Three-position top tang safety, double front locking lugs, free-floated button-rifled barrel. Comes with trigger lock, target, ear puffs. Introduced 1994. Made in U.S. by Savage Arms, Inc.
Price: Model 111FC (detachable magazine, composite stock, right- or left-hand) $418.00
Price: Model 111F (top-loading magazine, composite stock, right- or left-hand) $376.00
Price: Model 111FNS (as above, no sights, right-hand only) $372.00
Price: Model 111G (wood stock, top-loading magazine, right- or left-hand) $362.00
Price: Model 111GC (as above, detachable magazine) $407.00
Price: Model 111GNS (wood stock, top-loading magzine, no sights, right-hand only) $353.00

CAUTION: PRICES SHOWN ARE SUPPLIED BY THE MANUFACTURER OR IMPORTER. CHECK YOUR LOCAL GUNSHOP.

CENTERFIRE RIFLES—BOLT ACTION

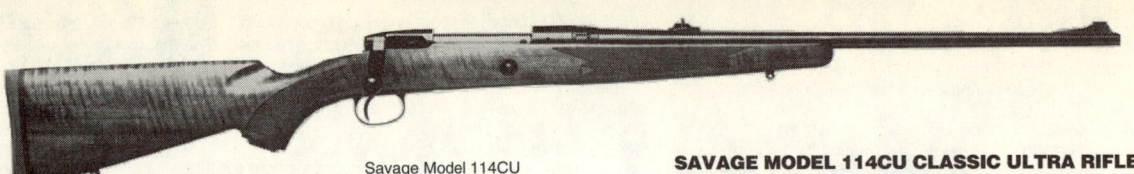
Savage Model 114CU

SAVAGE MODEL 114CU CLASSIC ULTRA RIFLE
Caliber: 270, 30-06, 7mm Rem. Mag., 300 Win. Mag.
Barrel: 22", 24" (magnum calibers).
Weight: 7.1 lbs. **Length:** 43.5" overall (22" barrel).
Stock: Select grade walnut with oil finish; red rubber buttpad.
Sights: Ramp front, open fully adjustable rear; drilled and tapped for scope mounting.
Features: Barrel, receiver and bolt handle have high-lustre blue finish, bolt body has laser-etched Savage logo. Detachable box magazine. Introduced 1991. Made in U.S. by Savage Arms, Inc.
Price: $525.00

Savage Model 116SE

SAVAGE MODEL 116SE SAFARI EXPRESS RIFLE
Caliber: 300 Win. Mag., 338 Win. Mag., 425 Express, 458 Win. Mag.
Barrel: 24".
Weight: 8.5 lbs. **Length:** 45.5" overall.
Stock: Classic-style select walnut with ebony forend tip, deluxe cut checkering. Two cross bolts; internally vented recoil pad.
Sights: Bead on ramp front, three-leaf express rear.
Features: Controlled-round feed design; adjustable muzzle brake; one-piece barrel band stud. Satin-finished stainless steel barreled action. Introduced 1994. Made in U.S. by Savage Arms, Inc.
Price: $900.00

Savage Model 116US Ultra Stainless Rifle
Similar to the Model 116SE except chambered for 270, 30-06, 7mm Rem. Mag., 300 Win. Mag.; stock has high-gloss finish; no open sights. Stainless steel barreled action with satin finish. Introduced 1995. Made in U.S. by Savage Arms, Inc.
Price: $700.00

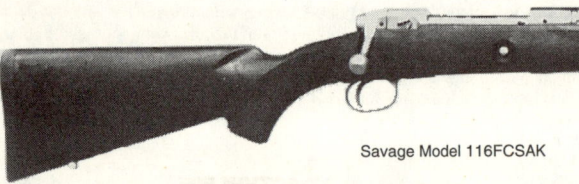
Savage Model 116FCSAK

SAVAGE MODEL 116 WEATHER WARRIORS
Caliber: 223, 243, 270, 30-06, 7mm Rem. Mag., 300 Win. Mag., 338 Win. Mag. (Model 116FSS); 270, 30-06, 7mm Rem. Mag., 300 Win. Mag. (Models 116FCSAK, 116FCS); 270, 30-06, 7mm Rem. Mag., 300 Win. Mag., 338 Win. Mag. (Models 116FSAK, 116FSK).
Barrel: 22", 24" for 7mm Rem. Mag., 300 Win. Mag., 338 Win. Mag. (M116FSS only).
Weight: 6.25 to 6.5 lbs. **Length:** 43.5" overall (22" barrel).
Stock: Graphite/fiberglass filled composite.
Sights: None furnished; drilled and tapped for scope mounting.
Features: Stainless steel with matte finish; free-floated barrel; quick-detachable swivel studs; laser-etched bolt; scope bases and rings. Left-hand models available in all models, calibers at same price. Models 116FCS, 116FSS introduced 1991; Model 116FSK introduced 1993; Model 116FCSAK, 116FSAK introduced 1994. Made in U.S. by Savage Arms, Inc.
Price: Model 116FSS (top-loading magazine) $489.00
Price: Model 116FCS (detachable box magazine) $552.00
Price: Model 116FCSAK (as above with Savage Adjustable Muzzle Brake system) $644.00
Price: Model 116FSAK (top-loading magazine, Savage Adjustable Muzzle Brake system) $581.00
Price: Model 116FSK Kodiak (as above with 22" Shock-Suppressor barrel) $552.00

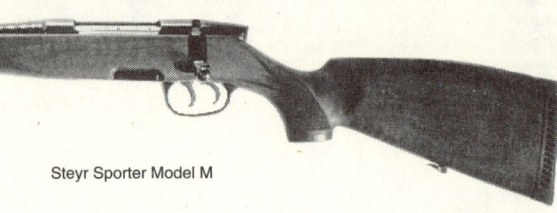
Steyr Sporter Model M

STEYR-MANNLICHER SPORTER MODELS SL, L, M, S, S/T
Caliber: 222 Rem., 222 Rem. Mag., 223 Rem., 5.6x50 Mag. (Model SL); 5.6x57, 243, 308 (Model L); 6.5x57, 270, 7x64, 30-06, 9.3x62, 7.5 Swiss, 7x57, 8x57 JS (Model M); 6.5x68, 7mm Rem. Mag., 300 Win. Mag., 8x68S, 9.3x64, 375 H&H, 458 Win. Mag. (Model S).
Barrel: 20" (full-stock), 23.6" (half-stock), 26" (magnums).
Weight: 6.8 to 7.5 lbs. **Length:** 39" (full-stock), 43" (half-stock).
Stock: Hand-checkered European walnut. Full Mannlicher or standard half-stock with Monte Carlo comb and rubber recoil pad.
Sights: Ramp front, open adjustable rear.
Features: Choice of single- or double-set triggers. Detachable 5-shot rotary magazine. Drilled and tapped for scope mounting. Model M actions available in left-hand models; S (magnum) actions available in half-stock only. Imported by GSI, Inc.
Price: Models SL, L, M, half-stock $2,023.00
Price: As above, full-stock, 20" barrel $2,179.00
Price: Models SL, L Varmint, 26" heavy barrel $2,179.00
Price: Model M left-hand, half-stock (270, 30-06, 7x64) $2,179.00
Price: As above, full-stock (270, 7x57, 7x64, 30-06) $2,335.00
Price: Model S Magnum $2,179.00
Price: Model S/T, 26" heavy barrel (375 H&H, 9.3x64, 458 Win. Mag.) $2,335.00

Steyr-Mannlicher MIII Professional Rifle
Similar to the Sporter series except has black ABS Cycolac half-stock, 23.6" barrel, no sights. Available in 270, 30-06, 7x64, Single trigger or optional double-set. Weighs about 7 lbs., 5 oz. Introduced 1994. Imported by GSI, Inc.
Price: $995.00
Price: With stipple-checkered walnut stock $1,125.00

394 THE GUN DIGEST

CENTERFIRE RIFLES—BOLT ACTION

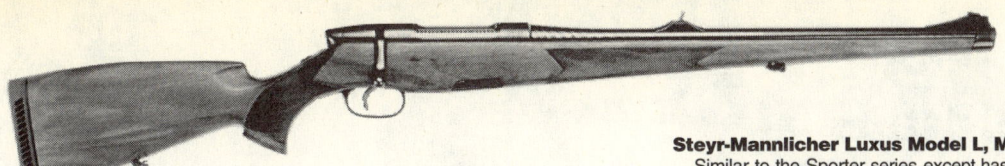

Steyr Luxus

Steyr-Mannlicher Luxus Model L, M, S
Similar to the Sporter series except has single set trigger, detachable steel 3-shot, in-line magazine, rear tang slide safety. Calibers: 5.6x57, 243, 308 (Model L); 6.5x57, 270, 7x64, 30-06, 9.3x62, 7.5 Swiss (Model M); 6.5x68, 7mm Rem. Mag., 300 Win. Mag., 8x68S (Model S). S (magnum) calibers available in half-stock only. Imported by GSI, Inc.
Price: Model L, M, half-stock $2,648.00
Price: As above, full-stock $2,804.00
Price: Model S (magnum) $2,804.00

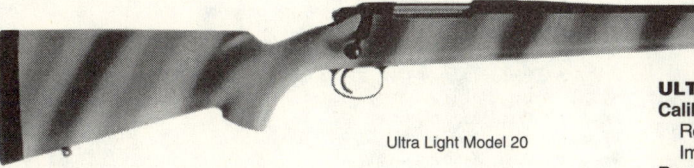

Ultra Light Model 20

ULTRA LIGHT ARMS MODEL 20 RIFLE
Caliber: 17 Rem., 22 Hornet, 222 Rem., 223 Rem. (Model 20S); 22-250, 6mm Rem., 243, 257 Roberts, 7x57, 7x57 Ackley, 7mm-08, 284 Win., 308 Savage. Improved and other calibers on request.
Barrel: 22" Douglas Premium No. 1 contour.
Weight: 4$\frac{1}{2}$ lbs. **Length:** 41$\frac{1}{2}$" overall.
Stock: Composite Kevlar, graphite reinforced. Du Pont imron paint colors—green, black, brown and camo options. Choice of length of pull.
Sights: None furnished. Scope mount included.
Features: Timney adjustable trigger; two-position three-function safety. Benchrest quality action. Matte or bright stock and metal finish. 3" magazine length. Shipped in a hard case. From Ultra Light Arms, Inc.
Price: Right-hand $2,400.00
Price: Model 20 Left Hand (left-hand action and stock) $2,500.00
Price: Model 24 (25-06, 270, 280 Rem., 30-06, 3$\frac{3}{8}$" magazine length) $2,500.00
Price: Model 24 Left Hand (left-hand action and stock) $2,600.00

Ultra Light Arms Model 28, Model 40 Rifles
Similar to the Model 20 except in 264, 7mm Rem. Mag., 300 Win. Mag., 338 Win. Mag. (Model 28), 300 Wea. Mag., 416 Rigby (Model 40). Both use 24" Douglas Premium No. 2 contour barrel. Weight 5$\frac{1}{2}$ lbs., 45" overall length. KDF or ULA recoil arrestor built in. Any custom feature available on any ULA product can be incorporated.
Price: Right-hand, Model 28 or 40 .... $2,900.00
Price: Left-hand, Model 28 or 40 .... $3,000.00

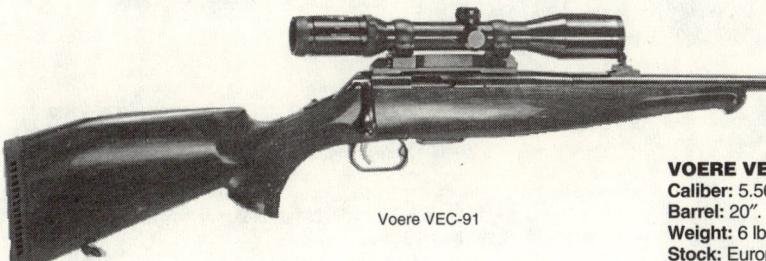

Voere VEC-91

VOERE VEC-91 LIGHTNING BOLT-ACTION RIFLE
Caliber: 5.56 UCC (223-cal.), 6mm UCC caseless, 5-shot magazine.
Barrel: 20".
Weight: 6 lbs. **Length:** 39" overall.
Stock: European walnut with cheekpiece, checkered grip and schnabel forend.
Sights: Blade on ramp front, open adjustable rear.
Features: Fires caseless ammunition via electric ignition; two batteries housed in the pistol grip last for about 5000 shots. Trigger is adjustable from 5 oz. to 7 lbs. Bolt action has twin forward locking lugs. Top tang safety. Drilled and tapped for scope mounting. Ammunition available from importer. Introduced 1991. Imported from Austria by JagerSport, Ltd.
Price: About $1,995.00

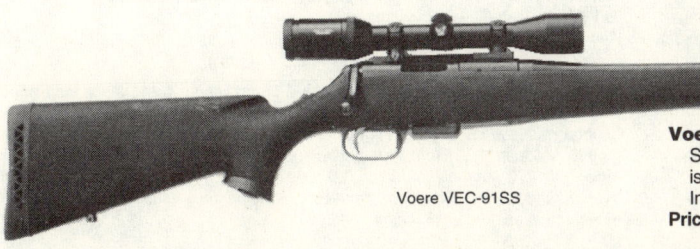

Voere VEC-91SS

Voere VEC-91SS Caseless Rifle
Similar to the VEC-91 except has synthetic stock with straight comb, matte-finished metal. Drilled and tapped for scope mounting. No open sights furnished. Introduced 1995. Imported from Austria by JagerSport, Ltd.
Price: 5.56mm UCC or 6mm UCC $1,495.00

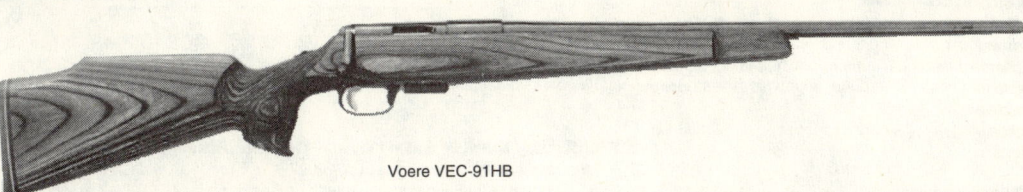

Voere VEC-91HB

Voere VEC-91BR Caseless Rifle
Similar to the VEC-91 except has heavy 20" barrel, synthetic benchrest stock, and is a single shot. Drilled and tapped for scope mounting. Introduced 1995. Imported from Austria by JagerSport, Ltd.
Price: $1,995.00

Voere VEC-91HB Varmint Special Caseless Rifle
Similar to the VEC-91 except has 22" heavy sporter barrel, black synthetic or laminated wood stock. Drilled and tapped for scope mounts. Introduced 1995. Imported from Austria by JagerSport, Ltd.
Price: $1,695.00

CAUTION: PRICES SHOWN ARE SUPPLIED BY THE MANUFACTURER OR IMPORTER. CHECK YOUR LOCAL GUNSHOP.

CENTERFIRE RIFLES—BOLT ACTION

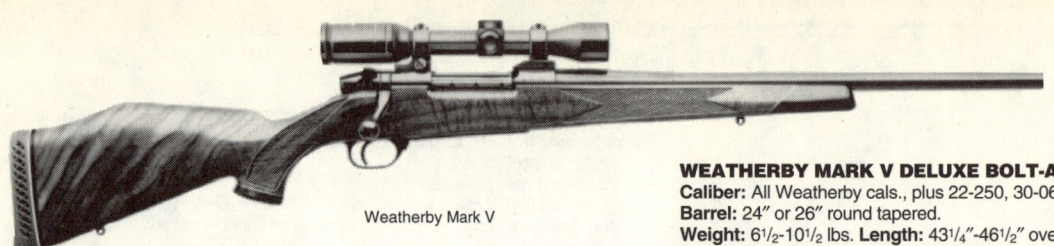

Weatherby Mark V

Weatherby Mark V Stainless Rifle
Similar to the Mark V except made of 400-series stainless steel. Has lightweight injection-moulded synthetic stock with raised Monte Carlo comb, checkered grip and forend, custom floorplate release. Right-hand only. Introduced 1995. Made in U.S. From Weatherby.
Price: 257, 270, 7mm, 300, 340 Wea. Mags. $960.00
Price: 7mm Rem. Mag., 300, 338 Win. Mags., 24" barrel $925.00
Price: 375 H&H, 24" barrel $1,094.00

Weatherby Lazermark V Rifle
Same as standard Mark V except stock has extensive laser carving under cheekpiece on butt, p.g. and forend. Introduced 1981.
Price: 240, 257, 270, 7mm Wea. Mag., 300, 340, right-hand, 26" $1,453.00
Price: 378 Wea. Mag., right-hand, 26" $1,532.00
Price: 416 Wea. Mag., right-hand, 26" $1,580.00
Price: 460 Wea. Mag., right-hand, 26" $1,958.00
Price: 300 Wea. Mag., left-hand, 26" $1,453.00

Weatherby Mark V Deluxe Bolt-Action Rifle
Caliber: All Weatherby cals., plus 22-250, 30-06, 460 Wea. Mag.
Barrel: 24" or 26" round tapered.
Weight: 6$\frac{1}{2}$-10$\frac{1}{2}$ lbs. **Length:** 43$\frac{1}{4}$"-46$\frac{1}{2}$" overall.
Stock: Walnut, Monte Carlo with cheekpiece, high luster finish, checkered p.g. and forend, recoil pad.
Sights: Optional (extra).
Features: Cocking indicator, adjustable trigger, hinged floorplate, thumb safety, quick detachable sling swivels.
Price: 22-250, 26" $1,297.00
Price: 30-06, 270 Wea. Mag., right-hand, left-hand available, 24" . . .$1,343.00 to $1,415.00
Price: 240, 257, 270, 7mm Wea. Mag., right-hand, 26" $1,343.00
Price: 300 Wea. Mag., left-hand available, 340 Wea. Mag., right-hand, 26" $1,343.00
Price: 378 Wea. Mag., right-hand, 26" $1,415.00
Price: 416 Wea. Mag., right-hand, 26" $1,459.00
Price: 460 Wea. Mag., right-hand, 26" $1,799.00

Weatherby Mark V Crown Custom Rifles
Uses hand-honed, engraved Mark V barreled action with fully-checkered bolt knob, damascened bolt and follower. Floorplate is engraved "Weatherby Custom." Super fancy walnut stock with inlays and stock carving. Gold monogram with name or initials. Right-hand only. Available in 257, 270, 7mm, 300 Wea. Mag. Introduced 1989.
Price: ....NA

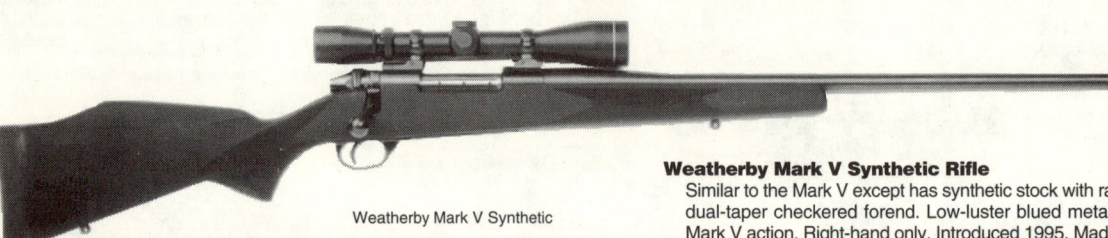

Weatherby Mark V Synthetic

Weatherby Mark V Synthetic Rifle
Similar to the Mark V except has synthetic stock with raised Monte Carlo comb, dual-taper checkered forend. Low-luster blued metal. Weighs 7$\frac{1}{2}$ lbs. Uses Mark V action. Right-hand only. Introduced 1995. Made in U.S. From Weatherby.
Price: 257, 270, 7mm, 300, 340 Wea. Mags., 26" barrel $727.00
Price: 7mm Rem. Mag., 300, 338 Win. Mags., 24" barrel $695.00
Price: 375 H&H, 24" barrel $827.00

Weatherby Mark V Eurosport Rifle
Similar to the Mark V except has raised-comb Monte Carlo stock with hand-rubbed satin oil finish, low-luster blue metal. No grip cap or forend tip. Right-hand only. Introduced 1995. Made in U.S. From Weatherby.
Price: 257, 270, 7mm, 300, 340 Wea. Mags., 26" barrel $878.00
Price: 7mm Rem. Mag., 300, 338 Win. Mags., 24" barrel $825.00
Price: 375 H&H, 24" barrel $937.00

Weatherby Euromark

Weatherby Euromark Rifle
Similar to the Mark V except has raised-comb Monte Carlo stock with hand-rubbed oil finish, fine-line hand-cut checkering, ebony grip and forend tips. All metal has low-luster blue. Right-hand only. Uses Mark V action. Introduced 1995. Made in U.S. From Weatherby.
Price: 257, 270, 7mm Wea. Mags., 26" barrel $1,245.00
Price: 300, 340 Wea. Mags, 26" barrel $1,318.00
Price: 416 Wea. Mag., 26" barrel $1,866.00

> Consult our Directory pages for the location of firms mentioned.

Weatherby Mark V Custom Bolt-Action Rifle
Similar to the Mark V Deluxe except has super-fancy walnut stock with buttstock inlay, two forend inlays, gold monogram inlay engraved with name or initials, and stock carving with stained background. Fully checkered bolt knob, damascened bolt and follower, hand-honed action, floorplate engraved "Weatherby Custom."
Price: 240, 257, 270, 7mm, 300 Wea. Mags., right-hand, 26" $3,553.00

Weatherby Mark V Sporter Rifle
Same as the Mark V Deluxe without the embellishments. Metal has low-luster blue, Stock is Claro walnut with high-gloss epoxy finish, Monte Carlo comb, recoil pad. Introduced 1993.
Price: 257, 270, 7mm, 300, 340 Wea. Mags., right-hand, 26" $878.00
Price: 375 H&H, right-hand, 24" $937.00
Price: 7mm Rem. Mag., 300 Win. Mag., 338 Win. Mag., 24", right-hand .$825.00

Weatherby Mark V Safari Grade Custom Rifles
Uses the Mark V barreled action. Stock is of European walnut with satin oil finish, rounded ebony tip and cap, black presentation recoil pad, no white spacers, and pattern #16 fine-line checkering. Matte finish bluing, floorplate is engraved "Weatherby Safari Grade"; 24" barrel. Standard rear stock swivel, barrel band front swivel. Has quarter-rib rear sight with a stationary leaf and one folding shallow V leaf. Front sight is a hooded ramp with brass bead. Right- or left-hand. Allow 8-10 months delivery. Introduced 1985.
Price: ....NA

CENTERFIRE RIFLES—BOLT ACTION

WICHITA CLASSIC RIFLE
Caliber: 17-222, 17-222 Mag., 222 Rem., 222 Rem. Mag., 223 Rem., 6x47; other calibers on special order.
Barrel: 21 1/8".
Weight: 8 lbs. **Length:** 41" overall.
Stock: AAA Fancy American walnut. Hand-rubbed and checkered (20 lpi). Hand-inletted, glass bedded, steel grip cap. Pachmayr rubber recoil pad.
Sights: None. Drilled and tapped for scope mounting.
Features: Available as single shot only. Octagonal barrel and Wichita action, right- or left-hand. Checkered bolt handle. Bolt is hand-fitted, lapped and jeweled. Adjustable trigger is set at 2 lbs. Side thumb safety. Firing pin fall is 3/16". Non-glare blue finish. From Wichita Arms.
Price: Single shot $3,495.00

WICHITA VARMINT RIFLE
Caliber: 222 Rem., 222 Rem. Mag., 223 Rem., 22 PPC, 6mm PPC, 22-250, 243, 6mm Rem., 308 Win.; other calibers on special order.
Barrel: 20 1/8".
Weight: 9 lbs. **Length:** 40 1/8" overall.
Stock: AAA Fancy American walnut. Hand-rubbed finish, hand checkered, 20 lpi pattern. Hand-inletted, glass bedded, steel grip cap. Pachmayr rubber recoil pad.
Sights: None. Drilled and tapped for scope mounts.
Features: Right- or left-hand Wichita action with three locking lugs. Available as a single shot only. Checkered bolt handle. Bolt is hand fitted, lapped and jeweled. Side thumb safety. Firing pin fall is 3/16". Non-glare blue finish. From Wichita Arms.
Price: Single shot $2,695.00

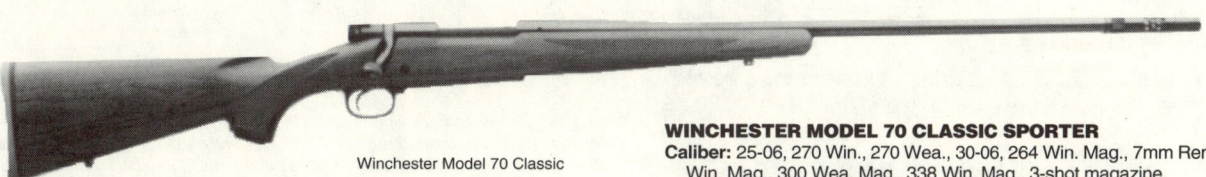
Winchester Model 70 Classic

Winchester Model 70 Classic SM
Same as the Model 70 Sporter except has pre-64 controlled feed action, black composite, graphite-impregnated stock and matte-finished metal. Available in 270, 30-06, 7mm Rem. Mag., 300 Win. Mag., 338 Win. Mag., 375 H&H. Weighs about 7.8 lbs. BOSS barrel vibration modulator and muzzle brake system optional. Introduced 1994.
Price: $602.00
Price: 375 H&H, with sights $653.00
Price: With BOSS (270, 30-06, 7mm Rem. Mag., 300 Win. Mag., 338 Win. Mag.) $699.00

WINCHESTER MODEL 70 CLASSIC SPORTER
Caliber: 25-06, 270 Win., 270 Wea., 30-06, 264 Win. Mag., 7mm Rem. Mag., 300 Win. Mag., 300 Wea. Mag., 338 Win. Mag., 3-shot magazine.
Barrel: 24", 26" for magnums.
Weight: 7 3/4 lbs. **Length:** 44 3/4" overall.
Stock: American walnut with cut checkering and satin finish. Classic style with straight comb.
Sights: Optional hooded ramp front, adjustable folding leaf rear. Drilled and tapped for scope mounting.
Features: Uses pre-64-type action with controlled round feeding. Three-position safety, stainless steel magazine follower; rubber buttpad; epoxy bedded receiver recoil lug. BOSS barrel vibration modulator and muzzle brake system optional. From U.S. Repeating Arms Co.
Price: With sights $632.00
Price: Without sights $595.00
Price: With BOSS (25-06, 264 Win. Mag., 270 Win., 30-06, 7mm Rem. Mag., 300 Win. Mag., 338 Win. Mag.) $692.00

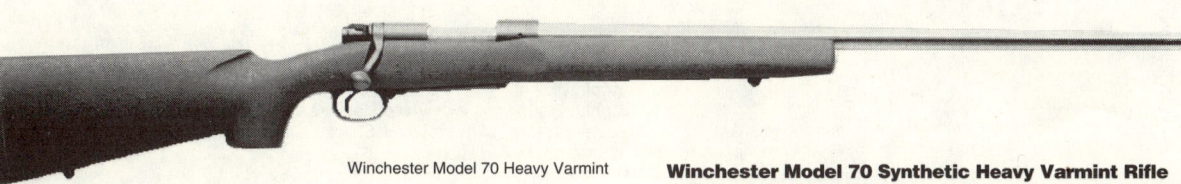
Winchester Model 70 Heavy Varmint

Winchester Model 70 Synthetic Heavy Varmint Rifle
Similar to the Model 70 Varmint except has fiberglass/graphite stock, 26" heavy stainless steel barrel, blued receiver. Weighs about 10 3/4 lbs. Available in 220 Swift, 223, 22-250, 243, 308. Uses full-length Pillar Plus Accu Block bedding system. Introduced 1993.
Price: $742.00

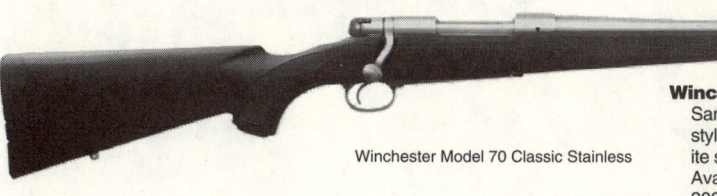
Winchester Model 70 Classic Stainless

Winchester Model 70 Classic Stainless Rifle
Same as the Model 70 Sporter except has stainless steel barrel and pre-64-style action with controlled round feeding and matte gray finish, black composite stock impregnated with fiberglass and graphite, contoured rubber recoil pad. Available in 22-250, 243, 308, 270, 30-06, 7mm Rem. Mag., 300 Win. Mag., 300 Wea. Mag., 338 Win. Mag., 375 H&H Mag. (24" barrel), 3- or 5-shot magazine. Weighs 6.75 lbs. BOSS barrel vibration modulator and muzzle brake system optional. Introduced 1994.
Price: Without sights $653.00
Price: 375 H&H Mag., with sights $703.00
Price: With BOSS (all except 300 Wea. Mag., 375 H&H Mag.) $750.00

Winchester Model 70 Featherweight Classic

Winchester Model 70 Featherweight Classic
Same as the Model 70 Classic except has claw controlled-round feeding system; action is bedded in a standard-grade walnut stock. Available in 223, 22-250, 243, 308, 7mm-08. Drilled and tapped for scope mounts. Weighs 7.25 lbs. Introduced 1992.
Price: $602.00

WINCHESTER MODEL 70 CLASSIC SUPER GRADE
Caliber: 270, 30-06, 5-shot magazine; 7mm Rem. Mag., 300 Win. Mag., 338 Win. Mag., 3-shot magazine.
Barrel: 24".
Weight: About 7 3/4 lbs. **Length:** 44 1/2" overall.
Stock: Walnut with straight comb, sculptured cheekpiece, wraparound cut checkering, tapered forend, solid rubber buttpad.
Sights: None furnished; comes with scope bases and rings.
Features: Controlled round feeding with stainless steel claw extractor, bolt guide rail, three-position safety; all steel bottom metal, hinged floorplate, stainless magazine follower. BOSS barrel vibration modulator and muzzle brake system optional. Introduced 1994. From U.S. Repeating Arms Co.
Price: $816.00
Price: With BOSS system $912.00

CAUTION: PRICES SHOWN ARE SUPPLIED BY THE MANUFACTURER OR IMPORTER. CHECK YOUR LOCAL GUNSHOP.

CENTERFIRE RIFLES—BOLT ACTION

Winchester Model 70 Lightweight

Winchester Ranger Rifle
Similar to Model 70 Lightweight except chambered only for 223, 243, 270, 30-06, with 22" barrel. American hardwood stock, no checkering, composition buttplate. Metal has matte blue finish. Introduced 1985.
Price: $468.00
Price: Ranger Ladies/Youth, 243, 308 only, scaled-down stock $468.00

WINCHESTER MODEL 70 CLASSIC SUPER EXPRESS MAGNUM
Caliber: 375 H&H Mag., 416 Rem. Mag., 458 Win. Mag., 3-shot magazine.
Barrel: 24" (375); 22" (458).
Weight: 8½ lbs.
Stock: American walnut with Monte Carlo cheekpiece. Wraparound checkering and finish.

WINCHESTER MODEL 70 LIGHTWEIGHT RIFLE
Caliber: 270, 280, 30-06 (standard action); 22-250, 223, 243, 308 (short action), both 5-shot magazine, except 6-shot in 223.
Barrel: 22".
Weight: 6¼ lbs. **Length:** 40½" overall (std.), 40" (short).
Stock: American walnut with satin finish, deep-cut checkering.
Sights: None furnished. Drilled and tapped for scope mounting.
Features: Three position safety; stainless steel magazine follower; hinged floorplate; sling swivel studs. Introduced 1984.
Price: Walnut $513.00

Sights: Hooded ramp front, open rear.
Features: Controlled round feeding. Two steel cross bolts in stock for added strength. Front sling swivel stud mounted on barrel. Contoured rubber buttpad. From U.S. Repeating Arms Co.
Price: $840.00

CENTERFIRE RIFLES—SINGLE SHOT
Classic and modern designs for sporting and competitive use.

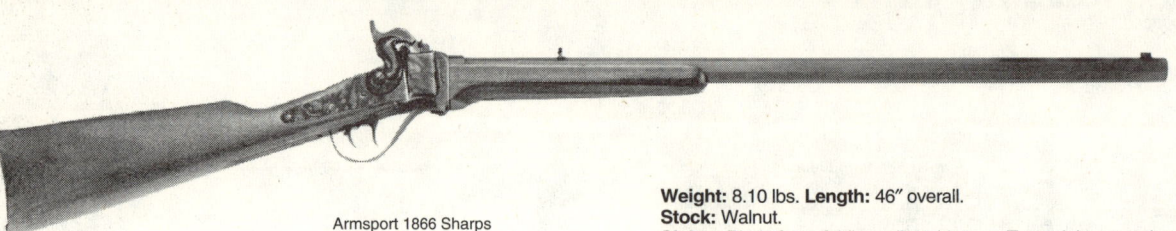
Armsport 1866 Sharps

ARMSPORT 1866 SHARPS RIFLE, CARBINE
Caliber: 45-70.
Barrel: 28", round or octagonal.
Weight: 8.10 lbs. **Length:** 46" overall.
Stock: Walnut.
Sights: Blade front, folding adjustable rear. Tang sight set optionally available.
Features: Replica of the 1866 Sharps. Color case-hardened frame, rest blued. Imported by Armsport.
Price: $860.00
Price: With octagonal barrel $880.00
Price: Carbine, 22" round barrel $830.00

BROWN MODEL ONE SINGLE SHOT RIFLE
Caliber: 22 LR, 357 Mag., 44 Mag., 7-30 Waters, 30-30 Win., 375 Win., 45-70; custom chamberings from 17 Rem. through 45-caliber available.
Barrel: 22" or custom, bull or tapered.
Weight: 6 lbs. **Length:** NA.
Stock: Smooth walnut; custom takedown design by Woodsmith. Palm swell for right- or left-hand; rubber butt pad.
Sights: Optional. Drilled and tapped for scope mounting.
Features: Rigid barrel/receiver; falling block action with short lock time, automatic case ejection; air-gauged barrels by Wilson and Douglas. Muzzle has 11-

Brown Model One

degree target crown. Matte black oxide finish standard, polished and electroless nickel optional. Introduced 1988. Made in U.S. by E.A. Brown Mfg.
Price: $750.00

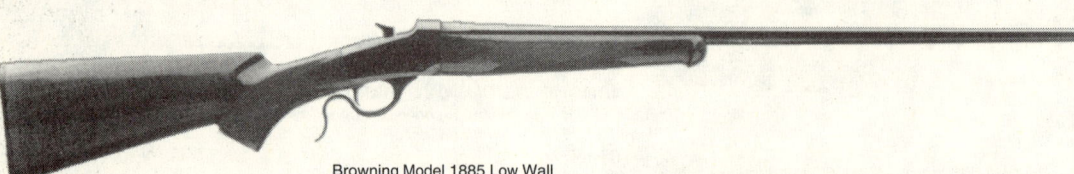
Browning Model 1885 Low Wall

Browning Model 1885 Low Wall Rifle
Similar to the Model 1885 High Wall except has trimmer receiver, thinner 24" octagonal barrel. Forend is mounted to the receiver. Adjustable trigger. Walnut pistol grip stock, trim schnabel forend with high-gloss finish. Available in 22 Hornet, 223 Rem., 243 Win. Overall length 39½", weight 6 lbs., 4 oz. Rifling twist rates: 1:16" (22 Hornet); 1:12" (223); 1:10" (243). Polished blue finish. Introduced 1995. Imported from Japan by Browning.
Price: $894.95

BROWNING MODEL 1885 HIGH WALL SINGLE SHOT RIFLE
Caliber: 22-250, 30-06, 270, 7mm Rem. Mag., 45-70.
Barrel: 28".
Weight: About 8½ lbs. **Length:** 43½" overall.
Stock: Walnut with straight grip, schnabel forend.
Sights: None furnished; drilled and tapped for scope mounting.
Features: Replica of J.M. Browning's high-wall falling block rifle. Octagon barrel with recessed muzzle. Imported from Japan by Browning. Introduced 1985.
Price: $894.95

CENTERFIRE RIFLES—SINGLE SHOT

Cumberland Mountain Plateau

CABELA'S SHARPS SPORTING RIFLE
Caliber: 45-70.
Barrel: 32"; tapered octagon.
Weight: 9 lbs. **Length:** 47 1/4" overall.
Stock: Checkered walnut.
Sights: Blade front, open adjustable rear.
Features: Color case-hardened receiver and hammer, rest blued. Introduced 1995. Imported by Cabela's.
Price: $749.95

CUMBERLAND MOUNTAIN PLATEAU RIFLE
Caliber: 40-65, 45-70.
Barrel: Up to 32"; round.
Weight: About 10 1/2 lbs. (32" barrel). **Length:** 48" overall (32" barrel).
Stock: American walnut.
Sights: Marble's bead front, Marble's open rear.
Features: Falling block action with underlever. Blued barrel and receiver. Stock has lacquer finish, crescent buttplate. Introduced 1995. Made in U.S. by Cumberland Mountain Arms, Inc.
Price: $1,085.00

Dakota Single Shot

DESERT INDUSTRIES G-90 SINGLE SHOT RIFLE
Caliber: 22-250, 220 Swift, 223, 6mm, 243, 25-06, 257 Roberts, 270 Win., 270 Wea. Mag., 280, 7x57, 7mm Rem. Mag., 30-06, 300 Win. Mag., 300 Wea. Mag., 338 Win. Mag., 375 H&H, 45-70, 458 Win. Mag.
Barrel: 20", 22", 24", 26"; light, medium, heavy.
Weight: About 7.5 lbs.
Stock: Walnut.
Sights: None furnished. Drilled and tapped for scope mounting.
Features: Cylindrical falling block action. All steel construction. Blue finish. Announced 1990. From Desert Industries, Inc.
Price: $795.00

DAKOTA SINGLE SHOT RIFLE
Caliber: Most rimmed and rimless commercial calibers.
Barrel: 23".
Weight: 6 lbs. **Length:** 39 1/2" overall.
Stock: Medium fancy grade walnut in classic style. Checkered grip and forend.
Sights: None furnished. Drilled and tapped for scope mounting.
Features: Falling block action with under-lever. Top tang safety. Removable trigger plate for conversion to single set trigger. Introduced 1990. Made in U.S. by Dakota Arms.
Price: $2,500.00
Price: Barreled action $1,850.00
Price: Action only $1,500.00

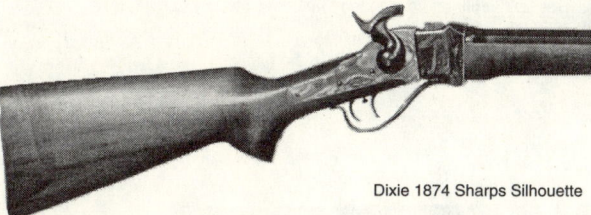
Dixie 1874 Sharps Silhouette

Dixie 1874 Sharps Lightweight Hunter/Target Rifle
Same as the Dixie 1874 Sharps Blackpowder Silhouette model except has a straight-grip buttstock with military-style buttplate. Based on the 1874 military model. Introduced 1995. Imported from Italy by Dixie Gun Works.
Price: $895.00

DIXIE 1874 SHARPS BLACKPOWDER SILHOUETTE RIFLE
Caliber: 45-70.
Barrel: 30"; tapered octagon; blued; 1:18" twist.
Weight: 10 lbs., 3 0z. **Length:** 47 1/2" overall.
Stock: Oiled walnut.
Sights: Blade front, ladder-type hunting rear.
Features: Replica of the Sharps #1 Sporter. Shotgun-style butt with checkered metal buttplate; color case-hardened receiver, hammer, lever and buttplate. Tang is drilled and tapped for tang sight. Double-set triggers. Meets standards for NRA blackpowder cartridge matches. Introduced 1995. Imported from Italy by Dixie Gun Works.
Price: $895.00

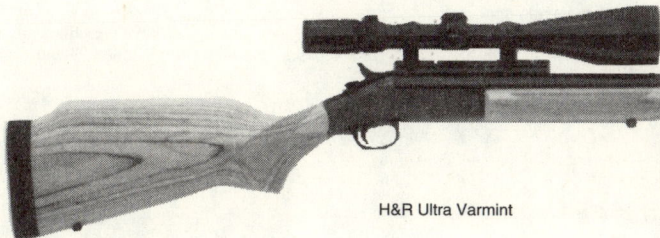
H&R Ultra Varmint

E.M.F. SHARPS RIFLE
Caliber: 45-70.
Barrel: 28", octagon.
Weight: 10 3/4 lbs. **Length:** NA.
Stock: Oiled walnut.
Sights: Blade front, flip-up open rear.
Features: Replica of the 1874 Sharps Sporting rifle. Color case-hardened lock; double-set trigger; blue finish. Imported by E.M.F.
Price: $950.00
Price: With browned finish $1,000.00
Price: Carbine (round 22" barrel, barrel band) $860.00

HARRINGTON & RICHARDSON ULTRA VARMINT RIFLE
Caliber: 223.
Barrel: 22", heavy.
Weight: About 7.5 lbs. **Length:** NA.
Stock: Hand-checkered laminated birch with Monte Carlo comb.
Sights: None furnished. Drilled and tapped for scope mounting.
Features: Break-open action with side-lever release, positive ejection. Comes with scope mount. Blued receiver and barrel. Swivel studs. Introduced 1993. From H&R 1971, Inc.
Price: $249.95

Harrington & Richardson Ultra Hunter Rifle
Similar to the Ultra Varmint rifle except chambered for 25-06 with 26" barrel, or 308 Win. with 22" barrel. Stock and forend are of cinnamon-colored laminate; hand-checkered grip and forend. Introduced 1995. Made in U.S. by H&R 1871, Inc.
Price: $249.95
Price: Rocky Mountain Elk Foundation Commemorative (280 Rem., 26" barrel) $259.95

CAUTION: PRICES SHOWN ARE SUPPLIED BY THE MANUFACTURER OR IMPORTER. CHECK YOUR LOCAL GUNSHOP.

CENTERFIRE RIFLES—SINGLE SHOT

Harris-McMillan Antietam Sharps

HARRIS-McMILLAN ANTIETAM SHARPS RIFLE
Caliber: 40-65, 45-75.
Barrel: 30", 32", octagon or round, hand-lapped stainless or chrome moly.
Weight: 11.25 lbs. **Length:** 47" overall.
Stock: Choice of straight grip, pistol grip or Creedmoor with schnabel forend; pewter tip optional. Standard wood is A Fancy; higher grades available.
Sights: Montana Vintage Arms #111 Low Profile Spirit Level front, #108 mid-range tang rear with windage adjustments.
Features: Recreation of the 1874 Sharps sidehammer. Action is color case-hardened, barrel satin black. Chrome moly barrel optionally blued. Optional sights include #112 Spirit Level Globe front with windage, #107 Long Range rear with windage. Introduced 1994. Made in U.S. by McMillan Gunworks.
Price: $2,000.00

MODEL 1885 HIGH WALL RIFLE
Caliber: 30-40 Krag, 32-40, 38-55, 40-65 WCF, 45-70.
Barrel: 26" (30-40), 28" all others. Douglas Premium #3 tapered octagon.
Weight: NA. **Length:** NA.
Stock: Premium American black walnut.
Sights: Marble's standard ivory bead front, #66 long blade top rear with reversible notch and elevator.
Features: Recreation of early octagon top, thick-wall High Wall with Coil spring action. Tand drilled, tapped for High Wall tand sight. Receiver, lever, hammer and breechblock color case-hardened. Introduced 1991. Avaiable from Montana Armory, Inc.
Price: $1,095.00

> Consult our Directory pages for the location of firms mentioned.

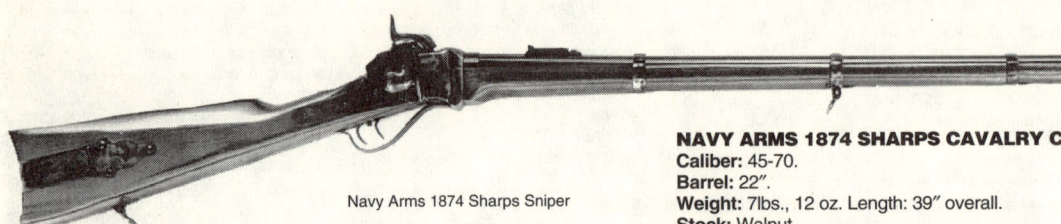
Navy Arms 1874 Sharps Sniper

NAVY ARMS 1874 SHARPS CAVALRY CARBINE
Caliber: 45-70.
Barrel: 22".
Weight: 7lbs., 12 oz. **Length:** 39" overall.
Stock: Walnut.
Sights: Blade front, military ladder-type rear.
Features: Replica of the 1874 Sharps miltary carbine. Color case-hardened receiver and furniture. Introduced 1991. Imported by Navy Arms.
Price $875.00

NAVY ARMS 1874 SHARPS SNIPER RIFLE
Similar to the Navy Arms Sharps Carbine except has 30" barrel, double-set triggers; weighs 8 lbs., 8 oz., overall length 46¾". Introduced 1984. Imported by Navy Arms.
Price: $1,055.00
Price: 1874 Sharps Infantry Rifle (three-band) $990.00

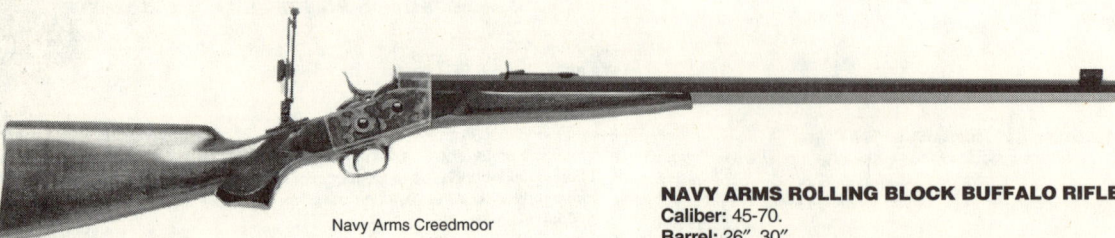
Navy Arms Creedmoor

NAVY ARMS ROLLING BLOCK BUFFALO RIFLE
Caliber: 45-70.
Barrel: 26", 30".
Stocks: Walnut.
Sights: Blade front, adjustable rear.
Features: Reproduction of classic rolling block action. Available with full-octagon or half-octagon-half-round barrel. Color case-hardened action. From Navy Arms.
Price: $620.00

Navy Arms #2 Creedmoor Rifle
Similar to the Navy Arms Buffalo Rifle except has 30" tapered octagon barrel, checkered full-pistol grip stock, blade front sight, open adjustable rear sight and Creedmoor tang sight. Introduced 1991. Imported by Navy Arms.
Price: $845.00

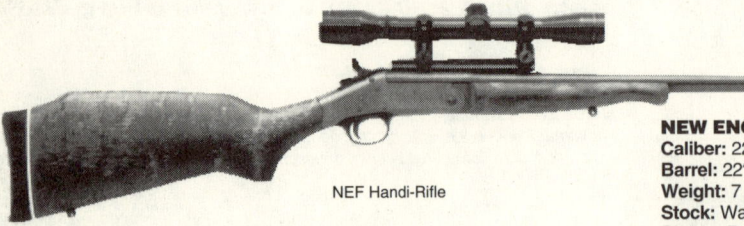
NEF Handi-Rifle

NEW ENGLAND FIREARMS HANDI-RIFLE
Caliber: 22 Hornet, 223, 243, 30-30, 270, 30-06, 45-70.
Barrel: 22".
Weight: 7 lbs.
Stock: Walnut-finished hardwood; black rubber recoil pad.
Sights: Ramp front, folding rear (22 Hornet, 30-30, 45-70). Drilled and tapped for scope mount; 223, 243, 270, 30-06 have no open sights, come with scope mounts.
Features: Break-open action with side-lever release. The 223, 243, 270 and 30-06 have recoil pad and Monte Carlo stock for shooting with scope. Swivel studs on all models. Blue finish. Introduced 1989. From New England Firearms.
Price: 223, standard barrel $199.95
Price: 22 Hornet, 223 (bull barrel),243, 270, 30-06, 30-30, 45-70 .... $204.95

CENTERFIRE RIFLES—SINGLE SHOT

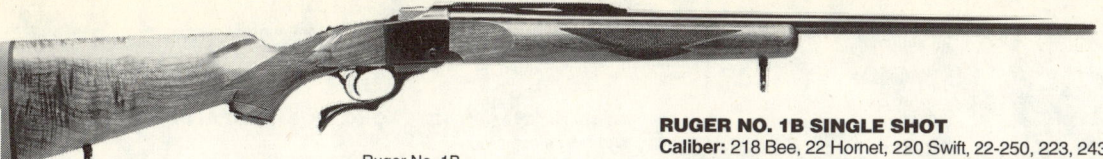
Ruger No. 1B

RUGER NO. 1B SINGLE SHOT
Caliber: 218 Bee, 22 Hornet, 220 Swift, 22-250, 223, 243, 6mm Rem., 25-06, 257 Roberts, 270, 280, 30-06, 7mm Rem. Mag., 300 Win. Mag., 338 Win. Mag., 270 Wea., 300 Wea.
Barrel: 26" round tapered with quarter-rib; with Ruger 1" rings.
Weight: 8 lbs. **Length:** 43 3/8" overall.
Stock: Walnut, two-piece, checkered p.g. and semi-beavertail forend.
Sights: None, 1" scope rings supplied for integral mounts.
Features: Under-lever, hammerless falling block design has auto ejector, top tang safety.
Price: $665.00
Price: Barreled action $450.00

Ruger No. 1S Medium Sporter
Similar to the No. 1B Standard Rifle except has Alexander Henry-style forend, adjustable folding leaf rear sight on quarter-rib, ramp front sight base and dovetail-type gold bead front sight. Calibers 218 Bee, 7mm Rem. Mag., 338 Win. Mag., 300 Win. Mag. with 26" barrel, 45-70 with 22" barrel. Weight about 7 1/2 lbs. In 45-70.
Price: No. 1S $665.00
Price: Barreled action $440.00

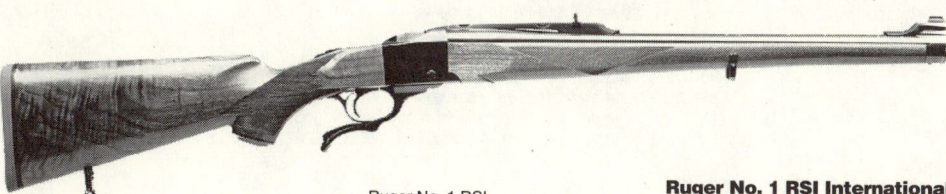
Ruger No. 1 RSI

Ruger No. 1 RSI International
Similar to the No. 1B Standard Rifle except has lightweight 20" barrel, full-length International-style forend with loop sling swivel, adjustable folding leaf rear sight on quarter-rib, ramp front with gold bead. Calibers 243, 30-06, 270 and 7x57. Weight is about 7 1/4 lbs.
Price: No. 1 RSI $668.00
Price: Barreled action $450.00

Ruger No. 1A Light Sporter
Similar to the No. 1B Standard Rifle except has lightweight 22" barrel, Alexander Henry-style forend, adjustable folding leaf rear sight on quarter-rib, dovetailed ramp front with gold bead. Calibers 243, 30-06, 270 and 7x57. Weight about 7 1/4 lbs.
Price: No. 1A $665.00
Price: Barreled action $450.00

Ruger No. 1V Special Varminter
Similar to the No. 1B Standard Rifle except has 24" heavy barrel. Semi-beavertail forend, barrel tapped for target scope block, with 1" Ruger scope rings. Calibers 22 PPC, 22-250, 220 Swift, 223, 6mm PPC, 25-06. Weight about 9 lbs.
Price: No. 1V $665.00
Price: Barreled action $440.00

Ruger No. 1H Tropical Rifle
Similar to the No. 1B Standard Rifle except has Alexander Henry forend, adjustable folding leaf rear sight on quarter-rib, ramp front with dovetail gold bead, 24" heavy barrel. Calibers 375 H&H, 404 Jeffery, 416 Rem. Mag. (weight about 8 1/4 lbs.), 416 Rigby, and 458 Win. Mag. (weight about 9 lbs.).
Price: No. 1H $665.00
Price: Barreled action $440.00

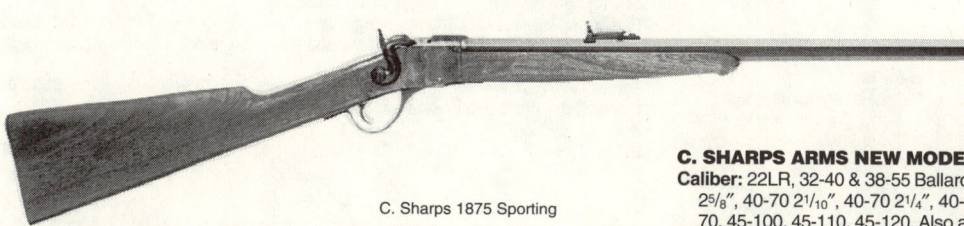
C. Sharps 1875 Sporting

C. SHARPS ARMS NEW MODEL 1875 RIFLE
Caliber: 22LR, 32-40 & 38-55 Ballard, 38-56 WCF, 40-65 WCF, 40-90 3 1/4", 40-90 2 5/8", 40-70 2 1/10", 40-70 2 1/4", 40-70 2 1/2", 40-50 1 11/16", 40-50 1 7/8", 45-90, 45-70, 45-100, 45-110, 45-120. Also available on special order only in 50-70, 50-90, 50-140.
Barrel: 24", 26", 30" (standard); 32", 34" optional.
Weight: 8-12 lbs.
Stocks: Walnut, straight grip, shotgun butt with checkered steel buttplate.
Sights: Silver blade front, Rocky Mountain buckhorn rear.
Features: Recreation of the 1875 Sharps rifle. Production guns will have case colored receiver. Available in Custom Sporting and Target versions upon request. Announced 1986. From C. Sharps Arms Co. and Montana Armory, Inc.
Price: 1875 Carbine (24" tapered round bbl.) $725.00
Price: 1875 Saddle Rifle (26" tapered oct. bbl.) $825.00
Price: 1875 Sporting Rifle (30" tapered oct. bbl.) $850.00
Price: 1875 Business Rifle (28" tapered round bbl.) $775.00

C. Sharps Arms 1875 Classic Sharps
Similar to the New Model 1875 Sporting Rifle except has 26", 28" or 30" full octagon barrel, crescent buttplate with toe plate, Hartford-style forend with cast German silver nose cap. Blade front sight, Rocky Mountain buckhorn rear. Weight is 10 lbs. Introduced 1987. From C. Sharps Arms Co. and Montana Armory, Inc.
Price: $1,075.00

C. SHARPS ARMS NEW MODEL 1874 OLD RELIABLE
Caliber: 40-50, 40-70, 40-90, 45-70, 45-90, 45-100, 45-110, 45-120, 50-70, 50-90, 50-140.
Barrel: 26", 28", 30" tapered octagon.
Weight: About 10 lbs. **Length:** NA.
Stock: American black walnut; shotgun butt with checkered steel buttplate; straight grip, heavy forend with schnabel tip.
Sights: Blade front, buckhorn rear. Drilled and tapped for tang sight.
Features: Recreation of the Model 1874 Old Reliable Sharps Sporting Rifle. Double set triggers. Reintroduced 1991. Made in U.S. by C. Sharps Arms. Available from Montana Armory, Inc.
Price: $995.00

C. Sharps Arms New Model 1875 Target & Long Range
Similar to the New Model 1875 except available in all listed calibers except 22 LR; 34" tapered octagon barrel; globe with post front sight, Long Range Vernier tang sight with windage adjustments. Pistol grip stock with cheek rest; checkered steel buttplate. Introduced 1991. From C. Sharps Arms Co. and Montana Armory, Inc.
Price: $1,165.00

CAUTION: PRICES SHOWN ARE SUPPLIED BY THE MANUFACTURER OR IMPORTER. CHECK YOUR LOCAL GUNSHOP.

CENTERFIRE RIFLES—SINGLE SHOT

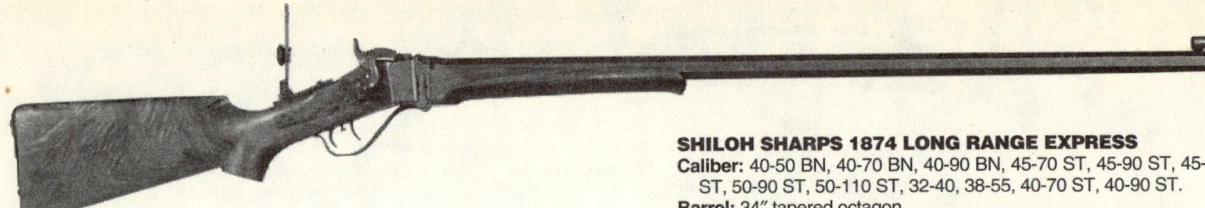

Shiloh Long Range Express

SHARPS 1874 OLD RELIABLE
Caliber: 45-70.
Barrel: 28″, octagonal.
Weight: 9 1/4 lbs. Length: 46″ overall.
Stock: Checkered walnut.
Sights: Blade front, adjustable rear.
Features: Double set triggers on rifle. Color case-hardened receiver and butt-plate, blued barrel. Imported from Italy by E.M.F.
Price: Rifle or carbine $950.00
Price: Military rifle, carbine $860.00
Price: Sporting rifle $860.00

Shiloh Sharps 1874 Montana Roughrider
Similar to the No. 1 Sporting Rifle except available with half-octagon or full-octagon barrel in 24″, 26″, 28″, 30″, 34″ lengths; standard supreme or semi-fancy wood, shotgun, pistol grip or military-style butt. Weight about 8 1/2 lbs. Calibers 30-40, 30-30, 40-50x1 11/16″ BN, 40-70x2 1/10″ BN, 45-70x2 1/10″ ST. Globe front and tang sight optional.
Price: Standard supreme $904.00
Price: Semi-fancy $988.00

SHILOH SHARPS 1874 LONG RANGE EXPRESS
Caliber: 40-50 BN, 40-70 BN, 40-90 BN, 45-70 ST, 45-90 ST, 45-110 ST, 50-70 ST, 50-90 ST, 50-110 ST, 32-40, 38-55, 40-70 ST, 40-90 ST.
Barrel: 34″ tapered octagon.
Weight: 10 1/2 lbs. Length: 51″ overall.
Stock: Oil-finished semi-fancy walnut with pistol grip, shotgun-style butt, traditional cheek rest, schnabel forend.
Sights: Globe front, sporting tang rear.
Features: Recreation of the Model 1874 Sharps rifle. Double set triggers. Made in U.S. by Shiloh Rifle Mfg. Co.
Price: $1,134.00
Price: Sporting Rifle No. 1 (similar to above except with 30″ bbl., blade front, buckhorn rear sight) $1,108.00
Price: Sporting Rifle No. 3 (similar to No. 1 except straight-grip stock, standard wood) $1,004.00
Price: 1874 Hartford model $1,174.00

Shiloh Sharps 1874 Business Rifle
Similar to No. 3 Rifle except has 28″ heavy round barrel, military-style buttstock and steel buttplate. Weight about 9 1/2 lbs. Calibers 40-50 BN, 40-70 BN, 40-90 BN, 45-70 ST, 45-90 ST, 50-70 ST, 50-100 ST, 32-40, 38-55, 40-70 ST, 40-90 ST.
Price: $1,010.00
Price: 1874 Saddle Rifle (similar to Carbine except has 26″ octagon barrel, semi-fancy shotgun butt) $1,062.00

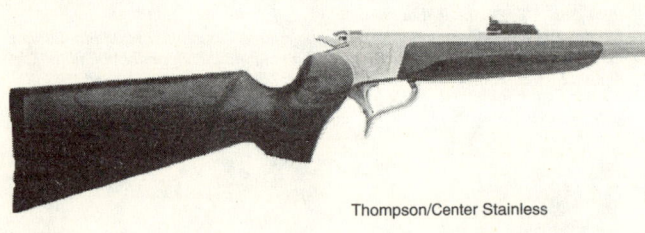

Thompson/Center Stainless

Thompson/Center Stainless Contender Carbine
Same as the blued Contender Carbine except made of stainless steel with blued sights. Available with walnut or Rynite stock and forend. Chambered for 22 LR, 22 Hornet, 223 Rem., 7-30 Waters, 30-30 Win., 410-bore. Youth model has walnut buttstock with 12″ pull length. Introduced 1993.
Price: Rynite stock, forend $495.00

Thompson/Center Contender Carbine Youth Model
Same as the standard Contender Carbine except has 16 1/4″ barrel, shorter buttstock with 12″ length of pull. Comes with fully adjustable open sights. Overall length is 29″, weight about 4 lbs., 9 oz. Available in 22 LR, 22 WMR, 223 Rem., 7x30 Waters, 30-30, 35 Rem., 44 Mag. Also available with 16 1/4″, rifled vent. rib barrel chambered for 45/410.
Price: $465.00
Price: Extra barrels $222.50
Price: Extra 45/410 barrel $252.50
Price: Extra 45-70 barrel $227.50

WESSON & HARRINGTON BUFFALO CLASSIC RIFLE
Caliber: 45-70.
Barrel: 32″ heavy.
Weight: 9 lbs. Length: 52″ overall.
Stock: American black walnut.
Sights: None furnished; drilled and tapped for peep sight; barrel dovetailed for front sight.
Features: Color case-hardened Handi-Rifle action with exposed hammer; color case-hardened crescent buttplate; 19th century checkering pattern. Introduced 1995. Made in U.S. by H&R 1871, Inc.
Price: About $349.95

THOMPSON/CENTER CONTENDER CARBINE
Caliber: 22 LR, 22 Hornet, 223 Rem., 7mm T.C.U., 7x30 Waters, 30-30 Win., 357 Rem. Maximum, 35 Rem., 44 Mag., 410, single shot.
Barrel: 21″.
Weight: 5 lbs., 2 oz. Length: 35″ overall.
Stock: Checkered American walnut with rubber buttpad. Also with Rynite stock and forend.
Sights: Blade front, open adjustable rear.
Features: Uses the T/C Contender action. Eleven interchangeable barrels available, all with sights, drilled and tapped for scope mounting. Introduced 1985. Offered as a complete Carbine only.
Price: Rifle calibers $500.00
Price: Extra barrels, rifle calibers, each $227.50
Price: 410 shotgun $520.00
Price: Extra 410 barrel $252.00

CONSULT Shooter's Marketplace Page 266, This Issue

UBERTI ROLLING BLOCK BABY CARBINE
Caliber: 22 LR, 22 WMR, 22 Hornet, 357 Mag., single shot.
Barrel: 22″.
Weight: 4.8 lbs. Length: 35 1/2″ overall.
Stock: Walnut stock and forend.
Sights: Blade front, fully adjustable open rear.
Features: Resembles Remington New Model No. 4 carbine. Brass trigger guard and buttplate; color case-hardened frame, blued barrel. Imported by Uberti USA.
Price: $460.00

DRILLINGS, COMBINATION GUNS, DOUBLE RIFLES

Designs for sporting and utility purposes worldwide.

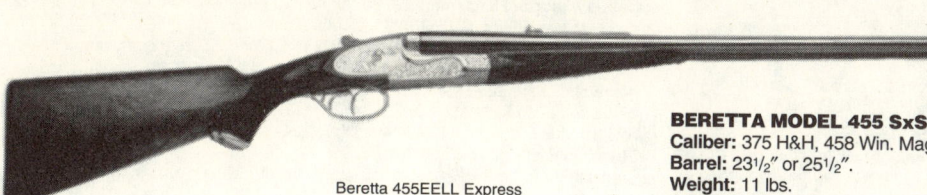

Beretta 455EELL Express

BERETTA EXPRESS SSO O/U DOUBLE RIFLES
Caliber: 375 H&H, 458 Win. Mag., 9.3x74R.
Barrel: 25.5".
Weight: 11 lbs.
Stock: European walnut with hand-checkered grip and forend.
Sights: Blade front on ramp, open V-notch rear.
Features: Sidelock action with color case-hardened receiver (gold inlays on SSO6 Gold). Ejectors, double triggers, recoil pad. Introduced 1990. Imported from Italy by Beretta U.S.A.
Price: SSO6 .... $21,000.00
Price: SSO6 Gold $23,500.00

AUGUSTE FRANCOTTE BOXLOCK MOUNTAIN RIFLE
Caliber: 5.6x57R, 5.6x65R, 6.5x57R, 7x57R, 7x65R.
Barrel: 24.5".
Weight: NA. **Length:** NA.
Stock: Deluxe walnut to customer specifications.
Sights: Ramp front, quarter-rib fixed rear.
Features: Anson & Deeley boxlock action; many options available. Made to customer specifications. Imported from Belgium by Armes de Chasse.
Price: From about (no engraving) $15,000.00

AUGUSTE FRANCOTTE BOXLOCK DOUBLE RIFLE
Caliber: 243, 270, 30-06, 7x64, 7x65R, 8x57JRS, 9.3x74R, 375 H&H, 470 N.E.; other calibers on request.
Barrel: 23.5" to 26".
Weight: NA. **Length:** NA.
Stock: Deluxe European walnut to customer specs; pistol grip or straight grip with Francotte cheekpiece; checkered butt; oil finish.
Sights: Bead front on long ramp, quarter-rib with fixed V rear.
Features: Side-by-side barrels; Anson & Deeley boxlock action with double triggers (front hinged), manual safety, floating firing pins and gas vent safety screws. Splinter or beavertail forend. English scroll engraving; coin finish or color case-hardening. Many options available. Made to customer specs. Imported from Belgium by Armes de Chasse.
Price: From about (no engraving) $16,500.00

MERKEL MODEL 160 SIDE-BY-SIDE DOUBLE RIFLE
Caliber: 22 Hornet, 5.6x50R Mag., 5.6x52R, 222 Rem., 243 Win., 6.5x55, 6.5x57R, 7x57R, 7x65R, 308, 30-06, 8x57JRS, 9.3x74R, 375 H&H.
Barrel: 25.6".
Weight: About 7.7 lbs, depending upon caliber. **Length:** NA.
Stock: Oil-finished walnut with pistol grip, cheekpiece.
Sights: Blade front on ramp, fixed rear.
Features: Sidelock action. Double barrel locking lug with Greener cross-bolt; fine engraved hunting scenes on sideplates; Holland & Holland ejectors; double triggers. Imported from Germany by GSI.
Price: From $10,995.00

Merkel Boxlock Double Rifles
Similar to the Model 160 double rifle except with Anson & Deely boxlock action with cocking indicators, double triggers, engraved color case-hardened receiver. Introduced 1995. Imported from Germany by GSI.
Price: Model 140-1 .... $4,995.00
Price: Model 140-1.1 (engraved silver-gray receiver) $5,595.00
Price: Model 150-1 (false sideplates, silver-gray receiver, Arabesque engraving) $5,995.00
Price: Model 150-1.1 (as above with English Arabesque engraving) ... $6,995.00

BERETTA MODEL 455 SxS EXPRESS RIFLE
Caliber: 375 H&H, 458 Win. Mag., 470 NE, 500 NE 3", 416 Rigby.
Barrel: 23 1/2" or 25 1/2".
Weight: 11 lbs.
Stock: European walnut with hand-checkered grip and forend.
Sights: Blade front, folding leaf V-notch rear.
Features: Sidelock action with easily removable sideplates; color case-hardened finish (455), custom big game or floral motif engraving (455EELL). Double triggers, recoil pad. Introduced 1990. Imported from Italy by Beretta U.S.A.
Price: Model 455 .... $36,000.00
Price: Model 455EELL $47,000.00

AUGUSTE FRANCOTTE SIDELOCK MOUNTAIN RIFLE
Caliber: Rimmed calibers from 5mm to 9mm.
Barrel: 23" to 26"; chopper lump.
Weight: NA. **Length:** NA.
Stock: Deluxe walnut to customer specifications.
Sights: Ramp front, quarter-rib fixed rear.
Features: True Holland & Holland system; many options available. Made to customer specifications. Imported from Belgium by Armes de Chasse.
Price: From about (no engraving) $28,000.00

AUGUSTE FRANCOTTE SIDELOCK DOUBLE RIFLES
Caliber: 243, 7x64, 7x65R, 8x57JRS, 270, 30-06, 9.3x74R, 375 H&H, 470 N.E.; others on request.
Barrel: 23 1/2" to 26".
Weight: 7.61 lbs. (medium calibers), 11.1 lbs. (mag. calibers).
Stock: Fancy European walnut; dimensions to customer specs. Straight or pistol grip style. Checkered butt, oil finish.
Sights: Bead on ramp front, leaf rear on quarter-rib; to customer specs.
Features: Custom made to customer's specs. Special extractor for rimless cartridges; back-action sidelocks; double trigger with hinged front trigger. Automatic or free safety. Wide range of options available. Imported from Belgium by Armes de Chasse.
Price: From about (no engraving) .... $30,000.00 to $36,000

MERKEL OVER/UNDER COMBINATION GUNS
Caliber/Gauge: 12, 16, 20 (2 3/4" chamber) over 22 Hornet, 5.6x50R, 5.6x52R, 222 Rem., 243 Win., 6.5x55, 6.5x57R, 7x57R, 7x65R, 308 Win., 30-06, 8x57JRS, 9.3x74R, 375 H&H.
Barrel: 25.6".
Weight: About 7.6 lbs. **Length:** NA.
Stock: Oil-finished walnut; pistol grip, cheekpiece.
Sights: Bead front, fixed rear.
Features: Kersten double cross-bolt lock; scroll-engraved, color case-hardened receiver; Blitz action; double triggers. Imported from Germany by GSI.
Price: Model 210E $6,195.00
Price: Model 211E (silver-grayed receivcer, fine hunting scene engraving) $6,995.00
Price: Model 213E (sidelock action, English-style, large scroll Arabesque engraving) $13,595.00
Price: Model 313E (as above, medium-scroll engraving) ... $20,695.00

MERKEL OVER/UNDER DOUBLE RIFLES
Caliber: 22 Hornet, 5.6x50R Mag., 5.6x52R, 222 Rem., 243 Win., 6.5x55, 6.5x57R, 7x57R, 7x65R, 308, 30-06, 8x57JRS, 9.3x74R.
Barrel: 25.6".
Weight: About 7.7 lbs, depending upon caliber. **Length:** NA.
Stock: Oil-finished walnut with pistol grip, cheekpiece.
Sights: Blade front, fixed rear.
Features: Kersten double cross-bolt lock; scroll-engraved, case-hardened receiver; Blitz action with double triggers. Imported from Germany by GSI.
Price: Model 221 E (silver-grayed receiver finish, hunting scene engraving) $9,995.00
Price: Model 223E (sidelock action, English-style large-scroll Arabesque engraving) $16,295.00
Price: Model 323E (as above with medium-scroll engraving) $24,595.00

DRILLINGS, COMBINATION GUNS, DOUBLE RIFLES

Savage 24F Predator

MERKEL DRILLINGS
Caliber/Gauge: 12, 20, 3" chambers, 16, 2 3/4" chambers; 22 Hornet, 5.6x50R Mag., 5.6x52R, 222 Rem., 243 Win., 6.5x55, 6.5x57R, 7x57R, 7x65R, 308, 30-06, 8x57JRS, 9.3x74R, 375 H&H.
Barrel: 25.6".
Weight: 7.9 to 8.4 lbs. depending upon caliber. **Length:** NA.
Stock: Oil-finished walnut with pistol grip; cheekpiece on 12-, 16-gauge.
Sights: Blade front, fixed rear.
Features: Double barrel locking lug with Greener cross-bolt; scroll-engraved, case-hardened receiver; automatic trigger safety; Blitz action; double triggers. Imported from Germany by GSI.
Price: Model 90S (selective sear safety) $5,995.00
Price: Model 90K (manually cocked rifle system) $6,495.00
Price: Model 95S (selective sear safety) $7,195.00
Price: Model 95K (manually cocked rifle system) $7,695.00

> Consult our Directory pages for the location of firms mentioned.

SAVAGE 24F PREDATOR O/U COMBINATION GUN
Caliber/Gauge: 22 Hornet, 223, 30-30 over 12 (24F-12) or 22 LR, 22 Hornet, 223, 30-30 over 20-ga. (24F-20); 3" chambers.
Action: Takedown, low rebounding visible hammer. Single trigger, barrel selector spur on hammer.
Barrel: 24" separated barrels; 12-ga. has Full, Mod., Imp. Cyl. choke tubes, 20-ga. has fixed Mod. choke.
Weight: 8 lbs. **Length:** 40 1/2" overall.
Stock: Black Rynite composition.
Sights: Ramp front, rear open adjustable for elevation. Grooved for tip-off scope mount.
Features: Removable butt cap for storage and accessories. Introduced 1989.
Price: 24F-12 ....$400.00
Price: 24F-20 ....$400.00

SAUER DRILLING
Caliber/Gauge: 12, 2 3/4" chambers/243, 6.5x57R, 7x57R, 7x65R, 30-06, 9.3x74R; 16, 2 3/4" chambers/6.5x57R, 7x57R, 7x65R, 30-06.
Barrel: 25".
Weight: 7.5 lbs. **Length:** 46" overall.
Stock: Fancy French walnut with checkered grip and forend, hog-back comb, sculptured cheekpiece, hand-rubbed oil finish.
Sights: Bead front, automatic pop-up rifle rear.
Features: Greener boxlock cross-bolt action with double underlugs, Greener side safety; separate rifle cartridge extractor. Side-by-side shotgun barrels over rifle barrel. Nitride-coated, hand-engraved receiver available with English Arabesque or relief game animal scene engraving. Lux has profuse relief-engraved game scenes, extra-fancy stump wood. Imported from Germany by Paul Co.
Price: Standard $4,600.00
Price: Lux $6,100.00

Springfield M6 Scout

SPRINGFIELD INC. M6 SCOUT RIFLE/SHOTGUN
Caliber/Gauge: 22 LR or 22 Hornet over 410-bore.
Barrel: 18.25".
Weight: 4 lbs. **Length:** 32" overall.
Stock: Folding detachable with storage for 15 22 LR, four 410 shells.
Sights: Blade front, military aperture for 22; V-notch for 410.
Features: All-metal construction. Designed for quick disassembly and minimum maintenance. Folds for compact storage. Introduced 1982; reintroduced 1995. Imported from the Czech Republic by Springfield, Inc.
Price: $155.00

Price: Stainless steel $185.00

TIKKA MODEL 512S DOUBLE RIFLE
Caliber: 9.3x74R.
Barrel: 24".
Weight: 8 5/8 lbs.
Stock: American walnut with Monte Carlo style.
Sights: Ramp front, adjustable open rear.
Features: Barrel selector mounted in trigger. Cocking indicators in tang. Recoil pad. Valmet scope mounts available. Introduced 1980. Imported from Italy by Stoeger.
Price: With ejectors $1,525.00

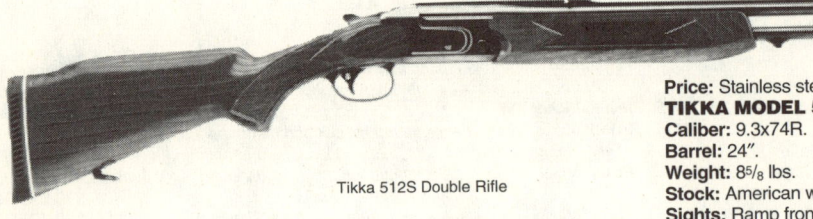

Tikka 512S Double Rifle

TIKKA MODEL 512S COMBINATION GUN
Caliber/Gauge: 12 over 222, 308.
Barrel: 24" (Imp. Mod.).
Weight: 7 5/8 lbs.
Stock: American walnut, with recoil pad. Monte Carlo style. Standard measurements 14"x1 3/5"x2"x2 3/5".
Sights: Blade front, flip-up-type open rear.
Features: Barrel selector on trigger. Hand-checkered stock and forend. Barrels are screw-adjustable to change bullet point of impact. Barrels are interchangeable. Introduced 1980. Imported from Italy by Stoeger.
Price: $1,350.00
Price: Extra barrels, from $725.00

A. ZOLI RIFLE-SHOTGUN O/U COMBO
Caliber/Gauge: 12-ga. over 222, 308 or 30-06.
Barrel: Combo—24"; shotgun—28" (Mod. & Full).
Weight: About 8 lbs. **Length:** 41" overall (24" bbl.).
Stock: European walnut.
Sights: Blade front, flip-up rear.
Features: Available with German claw scope mounts on rifle/shotgun barrels. Comes with set of 12/12 (Mod. & Full) barrels. Imported from Italy by Mandall Shooting Supplies.
Price: With two barrel sets $1,895.00

RIMFIRE RIFLES—AUTOLOADERS

Designs for hunting, utility and sporting purposes, including training for competition.

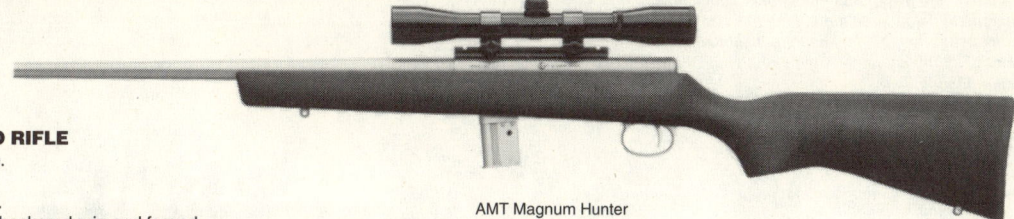

AMT MAGNUM HUNTER AUTO RIFLE
Caliber: 22 WMR, 10-shot magazine.
Barrel: 20".
Weight: 6 lbs. **Length:** 40 1/2" overall.
Stock: Black fiberglass-filled nylon; checkered grip and forend.
Sights: None furnished; drilled and tapped for Weaver mount.
Features: Stainless steel construction. Free-floating target-weight barrel. Introduced 1995. Made in U.S. by AMT.
Price: $459.99

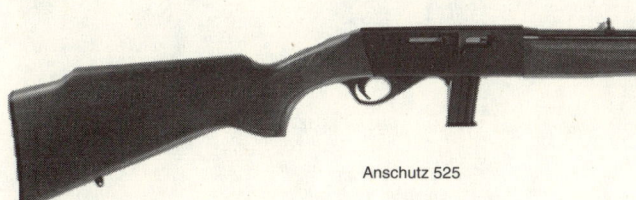

Anschutz 525

ANSCHUTZ 525 DELUXE AUTO
Caliber: 22 LR, 10-shot clip.
Barrel: 24".
Weight: 6 1/2 lbs. **Length:** 43" overall.
Stock: European hardwood; checkered pistol grip, Monte Carlo comb, beavertail forend.
Sights: Hooded ramp front, folding leaf rear.
Features: Rotary safety, empty shell deflector, single stage trigger. Receiver grooved for scope mounting. Introduced 1982. Imported from Germany by Precision Sales International.
Price: $547.00

Armscor Model 2000SC

ARMSCOR MODEL AK22 AUTO RIFLE
Caliber: 22 LR, 15- and 30-shot magazine.
Barrel: 18.5".
Weight: 7 lbs. **Length:** 36" overall.
Stock: Plain mahogany.
Sights: Post front, open rear adjustable for windage and elevation.
Features: Resembles the AK-47. Matte black finish. Introduced 1987. Imported from the Philippines by Ruko Products.
Price: About $269.00
Price: With folding steel stock, about $299.00

ARMSCOR MODEL 1600 AUTO RIFLE
Caliber: 22 LR, 15-shot magazine.
Barrel: 19.5".
Weight: 6 lbs. **Length:** 38" overall.
Stock: Mahogany.
Sights: Post front, aperture rear.
Features: Resembles Colt AR-15. Matte black finish. Introduced 1987. Imported from the Philippines by Ruko Products.
Price: About $199.00
Price: M1600R (as above except has retractable buttstock, ventilated forend), about $199.00

ARMSCOR MODEL 20P AUTO RIFLE
Caliber: 22 LR, 15-shot magazine.
Barrel: 21".
Weight: 6.5 lbs. **Length:** 39.75" overall.
Stock: Walnut-finished mahogany.
Sights: Hooded front, rear adjustable for elevation.
Features: Receiver grooved for scope mounting. Blued finish. Introduced 1990. Imported from the Philippines by Ruko Products.
Price: About $129.00
Price: With checkered stock $159.00
Price: Model 20C (carbine-style stock, steel barrel band, buttplate) $149.00
Price: Model 2000SC (as above except has checkered stock, fully adjustable sight, rubber buttpad, forend tip), about ....NA
Price: Model 50S (similar to Model 20P except has ventilated barrel shroud, and 30-shot magazine) $209.00

BRNO ZKM 611 AUTO RIFLE
Caliber: 22 WMR, 6-shot magazine.
Barrel: 20".
Weight: 6 lbs., 2 oz. **Length:** 37" overall.
Stock: Walnut; checkered grip and forend.
Sights: Blade front, open rear.
Features: Removable box magazine; polished blue finish; grooved receiver for scope mounting; sling swivels; thumbscrew takedown. Introduced 1995. Imported from the Czech Republic by Magnum Research.
Price: $569.00

Browning Auto-22

Browning Auto-22 Grade VI
Same as the Grade I Auto-22 except available with either grayed or blued receiver with extensive engraving with gold-plated animals: right side pictures a fox and squirrel in a woodland scene; left side shows a beagle chasing a rabbit. On top is a portrait of the beagle. Stock and forend are of high-grade walnut with a double-bordered cut checkering design. Introduced 1987.
Price: Grade VI, blue or gray receiver $780.00

BROWNING AUTO-22 RIFLE
Caliber: 22 LR, 11-shot.
Barrel: 19 1/4".
Weight: 4 3/4 lbs. **Length:** 37" overall.
Stock: Checkered select walnut with p.g. and semi-beavertail forend.
Sights: Gold bead front, folding leaf rear.
Features: Engraved receiver with polished blue finish; cross-bolt safety; tubular magazine in buttstock; easy takedown for carrying or storage. Imported from Japan by Browning.
Price: Grade I $379.95

CAUTION: PRICES SHOWN ARE SUPPLIED BY THE MANUFACTURER OR IMPORTER. CHECK YOUR LOCAL GUNSHOP.

RIMFIRE RIFLES—AUTOLOADERS

E.A.A./SABATTI MODEL 1822 AUTO RIFLE
Caliber: 22 LR, 10-shot magazine.
Barrel: 18½" round tapered; bull barrel on Heavy and Thumbhole Heavy models.
Weight: 5¼ lbs. (Sporter). **Length:** 37" overall.
Stock: Stained hardwood; Thumbhole model has one-piece stock.
Sights: Bead front, folding leaf rear adjustable for elevation on Sporter model. Heavy and Thumbhole models only dovetailed for scope mount.
Features: Cross-bolt safety. Blue finish. Lifetime warranty. Introduced 1993. Imported from Italy by European American Armory.
Price: Sporter $190.00
Price: Heavy $205.00
Price: Thumbhole Heavy $350.00

ERMA EM1 CARBINE
Caliber: 22 LR, 10-shot magazine.
Barrel: 18".
Weight: 5.6 lbs. **Length:** 35.5" overall.
Stock: Polished beech or oiled walnut.
Sights: Blade front, fully adjustable aperture rear.
Features: Blowback action. Receiver grooved for scope mounting. Imported from Germany by Mandall Shooting Supplies.
Price: $499.95

Federal XC222

FEDERAL ENGINEERING XC222 AUTO CARBINE
Caliber: 22 LR, 30-shot magazine.
Barrel: 16.5" (with flash hider).
Weight: 7.25 lbs. **Length:** 34.5" overall.
Stock: Quick-detachable tube steel.
Sights: Hooded post front, Williams adjustable rear; sight bridge grooved for scope mounting.
Features: Quick takedown; all-steel heli-arc welded construction; internal parts industrial hard chromed. Made in U.S. by Federal Engineering Corp.
Price: Includes receiver cap, sling, swivels $459.00

FEATHER AT-22 SEMI-AUTO CARBINE
Caliber: 22 LR, 20-shot magazine.
Barrel: 17".
Weight: 3.25 lbs. **Length:** 35" overall (stock extended).
Stock: Telescoping wire; composition pistol grip.
Sights: Protected post front, adjustable aperture rear.
Features: Removable barrel. Length when folded is 26". Matte black finish. From Feather Industries. Introduced 1986.
Price: $249.95
Price: Model F2 (fixed stock) $279.95

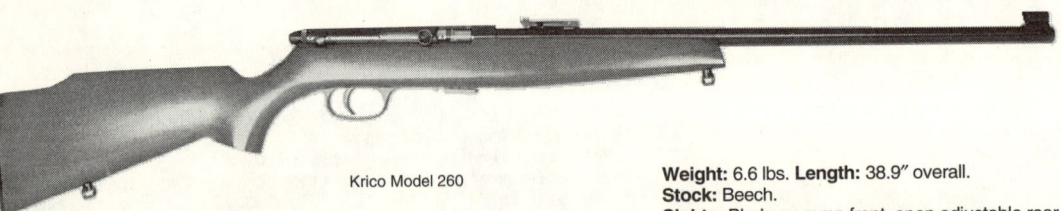
Krico Model 260

KRICO MODEL 260 AUTO RIFLE
Caliber: 22 LR, 5-shot magazine.
Barrel: 19.6".
Weight: 6.6 lbs. **Length:** 38.9" overall.
Stock: Beech.
Sights: Blade on ramp front, open adjustable rear.
Features: Receiver grooved for scope mounting. Sliding safety. Imported from Germany by Mandall Shooting Supplies.
Price: $700.00

Lakefield Arms Model 64B

LAKEFIELD ARMS MODEL 64B AUTO RIFLE
Caliber: 22 LR, 10-shot magazine.
Barrel: 20".
Weight: 5½ lbs. **Length:** 40" overall.
Stock: Walnut-finished hardwood with Monte Carlo-type comb, checkered grip and forend.
Sights: Bead front, open adjustable rear. Receiver grooved for scope mounting.
Features: Thumb-operated rotating safety. Blue finish. Side ejection, bolt hold-open device. Introduced 1990. Made in Canada by Lakefield Arms Ltd.
Price: About $142.95

Marlin Model 60

Marlin Model 60SS Self-Loading Rifle
Same as the Model 60 except breech bolt, barrel and outer magazine tube are made of stainless steel; most other parts are either nickel-plated or coated to match the stainless finish. Monte Carlo stock is of black/gray Main birch laminate, and has nickel-plated swivel studs, rubber butt pad. Introduced 1993.
Price: $237.10

MARLIN MODEL 60 SELF-LOADING RIFLE
Caliber: 22 LR, 14-shot tubular magazine.
Barrel: 22" round tapered.
Weight: About 5½ lbs. **Length:** 40½" overall.
Stock: Press-checkered, walnut-finished Maine birch with Monte Carlo, full pistol grip; Mar-Shield® finish.
Sights: Ramp front, open adjustable rear.
Features: Matted receiver is grooved for scope mount. Manual bolt hold-open; automatic last-shot bolt hold-open.
Price: $158.40

RIMFIRE RIFLES—AUTOLOADERS

Marlin Model 70 HC

MARLIN MODEL 70 HC AUTO
Caliber: 22 LR, 7-shot clip magazine.
Barrel: 18" (16-groove rifling).
Weight: 5 lbs. **Length:** 36¾" overall.
Stock: Press-checkered, walnut-finished Maine birch with Monte Carlo, full p.g. Mar-Shield® finish.
Sights: Ramp front, adjustable open rear. Receiver grooved for scope mount.
Features: Receiver top has serrated, non-glare finish; cross-bolt safety; manual bolt hold-open. Comes with two magazines.
Price: $167.35

Marlin Model 70PSS

Marlin Model 70PSS Rifle
Similar to the Model 70 HC except is a takedown model with easily removable barrel—no tools needed. Has stainless steel 16¼" Micro-Groove® barrel, stainless steel bolt; black, fiberglass-filled synthetic stock with abbreviated forend, nickel-plated swivel studs, moulded-in checkering; nickel-plated 7-shot magazine; ramp front, adjustable open rear sights, cross-bolt safety. Takedown feature allows removal of barrel without tools. Overall length is 35¼", weight is 3¼ lbs. Receiver grooved for scope mounting. Comes with zippered case. Introduced 1986.
Price: $224.95

Marlin Model 922

MARLIN MODEL 995SS SELF-LOADING RIFLE
Caliber: 22 LR, 7-shot clip magazine.
Barrel: 18" Micro-Groove®; stainless steel.
Weight: 5 lbs. **Length:** 36¾" overall.
Stock: Black fiberglass-filled synthetic with nickel-plated swivel studs, moulded-in checkering.
Sights: Ramp front with orange post and cut-away Wide-Scan® hood; screw-adjustable open rear.
Features: Stainless steel breechbolt and barrel. Receiver grooved for scope mount; bolt hold-open device; cross-bolt safety. Introduced 1979.
Price: $230.65

MARLIN MODEL 922 MAGNUM SELF-LOADING RIFLE
Caliber: 22 WMR, 7-shot magazine.
Barrel: 20.5".
Weight: 6.5 lbs. **Length:** 39.75" overall.
Stock: Checkered American black walnut with Monte Carlo comb, swivel studs, rubber buttpad.
Sights: Ramp front with bead and removable Wide-Scan® hood, adjustable folding semi-buckhorn rear.
Features: Action based on the centerfire Model 9 Carbine. Receiver drilled and tapped for scope mounting. Automatic last-shot bolt holdopen; magazine safety. Introduced 1993.
Price: $391.20

Mitchell High STandard 20/22

MITCHELL HIGH STANDARD 20/22 RIFLES
Caliber: 22 LR, 10-shot magazine.
Barrel: 20.5".
Weight: 6.25 lbs. **Length:** 37.5" overall.
Stock: American walnut.
Sights: Blade on ramp front, open adjustable rear.
Features: Polished blue finish; barrel band on forend. Comes with two 10-shot magazines. Introduced 1994. Imported from Philippines by Mitchell Arms.
Price: $179.00
Price: Model 20/22D (fancy walnut stock with checkering, rosewood grip and forend caps) $199.95
Price: Model 20/22 Special (same as 20/22 Deluxe except has heavy barrel) $139.95

Norinco Model 22 ATD

REMINGTON 552 BDL SPEEDMASTER RIFLE
Caliber: 22 S (20), L (17) or LR (15) tubular mag.
Barrel: 21" round tapered.
Weight: About 5¾ lbs. **Length:** 40" overall.
Stock: Walnut. Checkered grip and forend.
Sights: Bead front, step open rear adjustable for windage and elevation.
Features: Positive cross-bolt safety, receiver grooved for tip-off mount.
Price: About $319.00

NORINCO MODEL 22 ATD RIFLE
Caliber: 22 LR, 11-shot magazine.
Barrel: 19.4".
Weight: 4.6 lbs. **Length:** 36.6" overall.
Stock: Checkered hardwood.
Sights: Blade front, open adjustable rear.
Features: Browning-design takedown action for storage, transport. Cross-bolt safety. Tube magazine loads through buttplate. Blue finish with engraved receiver. Introduced 1987. Imported from China by Interarms.
Price: $166.00

CAUTION: PRICES SHOWN ARE SUPPLIED BY THE MANUFACTURER OR IMPORTER. CHECK YOUR LOCAL GUNSHOP.

RIMFIRE RIFLES—AUTOLOADERS

Remington 522 Viper

REMINGTON MODEL 522 VIPER AUTOLOADING RIFLE
Caliber: 22 LR, 10-shot magazine.
Barrel: 20".
Weight: 4-5/8 lbs. **Length:** 40" overall.
Stock: Black synthetic with positive checkering, beavertail forend.
Sights: Bead on ramp front, fully adjustable open rear. Integral grooved rail for scope mounting.
Features: Synthetic stock and receiver with overall matte black finish. Has magazine safety, cocking indicator; manual and last-shot hold-open; trigger mechanism has primary and secondary sears; integral ejection port shield. Introduced 1993.
Price: $165.00

Ruger 10/22 International

Ruger 10/22 International Carbine
Similar to the Ruger 10/22 Carbine except has full-length International stock of American hardwood, checkered grip and forend; comes with rubber buttpad, sling swivels. Reintroduced 1994.
Price: Blue (10/22RBI) $262.00
Price: Stainless (K10/22RBI) $282.00

Ruger 10/22 Deluxe Sporter
Same as 10/22 Carbine except walnut stock with hand checkered pistol grip and forend; straight buttplate, no barrel band, has sling swivels.
Price: Model 10/22 DSP $274.00

RUGER 10/22 AUTOLOADING CARBINE
Caliber: 22 LR, 10-shot rotary magazine.
Barrel: 18-1/2" round tapered.
Weight: 5 lbs. **Length:** 37-1/4" overall.
Stock: American hardwood with p.g. and bbl. band.
Sights: Brass bead front, folding leaf rear adjustable for elevation.
Features: Detachable rotary magazine fits flush into stock, cross-bolt safety, receiver tapped and grooved for scope blocks or tip-off mount. Scope base adaptor furnished with each rifle.
Price: Model 10/22 RB (blue) $207.00
Price: Model K10/22RB (bright finish stainless barrel) $248.00

SURVIVAL ARMS AR-7 EXPLORER RIFLE
Caliber: 22 LR, 8-shot magazine.
Barrel: 16".
Weight: 2.5 lbs. **Length:** 34.5" overall; 16.5" stowed.
Stock: Moulded Cycolac; snap-on rubber butt cap.
Sights: Square blade front, aperture rear adjustable for elevation.
Features: Takedown design stores barrel and action in hollow stock. Light enough to float. Black, Silvertone or camouflage finish. Reintroduced 1992. From Survival Arms, Inc.
Price: Silver or camo $150.00
Price: Sporter (black finish with telescoping stock, 25-shot magazine) ...$200.00
Price: Wildcat (black finish with wood stock) $150.00

Consult our Directory pages for the location of firms mentioned.

RIMFIRE RIFLES—LEVER & SLIDE ACTION
Classic and modern models for sport and utility, including training.

Browning BL-22

Marlin Model 39AS

BROWNING BL-22 LEVER-ACTION RIFLE
Caliber: 22 S (22), L (17) or LR (15), tubular magazine.
Barrel: 20" round tapered.
Weight: 5 lbs. **Length:** 36-3/4" overall.
Stock: Walnut, two-piece straight grip Western style.
Sights: Bead post front, folding-leaf rear.
Features: Short throw lever, half-cock safety, receiver grooved for tip-off scope mounts. Imported from Japan by Browning.
Price: Grade I $329.95
Price: Grade II (engraved receiver, checkered grip and forend) $376.95

MARLIN MODEL 39AS GOLDEN LEVER-ACTION RIFLE
Caliber: 22 S (26), L (21), LR (19), tubular magazine.
Barrel: 24" Micro-Groove®.
Weight: 6-1/2 lbs. **Length:** 40" overall.
Stock: Checkered American black walnut with white line spacers at p.g. cap and buttplate; Mar-Shield® finish. Swivel studs; rubber buttpad.
Sights: Bead ramp front with detachable Wide-Scan™ hood, folding rear semi-buckhorn adjustable for windage and elevation.
Features: Hammer-block safety; rebounding hammer. Takedown action, receiver tapped for scope mount (supplied), offset hammer spur; gold-plated steel trigger.
Price: $431.85

RIMFIRE RIFLES—LEVER & SLIDE ACTION

MARLIN 39TDS CARBINE
Caliber: 22 S (16), 22 L (12), 22 LR (11).
Barrel: 16½" Micro-Groove®.
Weight: 5¼ lbs. **Length:** 32⅝" overall.
Stock: Checkered American black walnut with straight grip; short forend with blued tip. Mar-Shield® finish.
Sights: Ramp front with Wide-Scan™ hood, adjustable semi-buckhorn folding rear.
Features: Takedown style, comes with carrying case. Hammer-block safety, rebounding hammer; blued metal, gold-plated steel trigger. Intorduced 1988.
Price: With case $443.15

REMINGTON 572 BDL FIELDMASTER PUMP RIFLE
Caliber: 22 S (20), L (17) or LR (14), tubular magazine.
Barrel: 21" round tapered.
Weight: 5½ lbs. **Length:** 42" overall.
Stock: Walnut with checkered p.g. and slide handle.
Sights: Blade ramp front; sliding ramp rear adjustable for windage and elevation.
Features: Cross-bolt safety; removing inner magazine tube converts rifle to single shot; receiver grooved for tip-off scope mount.
Price: About $332.00

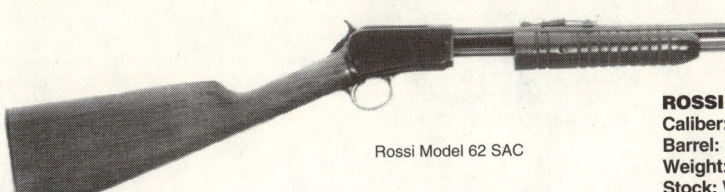

Rossi Model 62 SAC

Rossi Model 62 SAC Carbine
Same as standard model except 22 LR only, has 16¼" barrel. Magazine holds slightly fewer cartridges.
Price: Blue $226.00
Price: Nickel $243.00

ROSSI MODEL 62 SA PUMP RIFLE
Caliber: 22 LR, 22 WMR.
Barrel: 23", round or octagonal.
Weight: 5¾ lbs. **Length:** 39¼" overall.
Stock: Walnut, straight grip, grooved forend.
Sights: Fixed front, adjustable rear.
Features: Capacity 20 Short, 16 Long or 14 Long Rifle. Quick takedown. Imported from Brazil by Interarms.
Price: Blue $226.00
Price: Nickel $243.00
Price: Blue, with octagonal barrel $251.00
Price: 22 WMR, as Model 59 .... $276.00

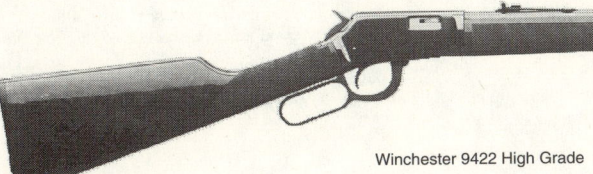

Winchester 9422 High Grade

Winchester Model 9422 High Grade Rifle
Same as the standard Model 9422 except has high grade walnut with gloss finish, blued and engraved receiver with a coonhound on the right side, a racoon profile on the left, both framed with detailed Nimschke-style scrollwork. Chambered only for 22 LR. Introduced 1995. From U.S. Repeating Arms Co., Inc.
Price: $475.00

WINCHESTER MODEL 9422 LEVER-ACTION RIFLE
Caliber: 22 S (21), L (17), LR (15), tubular magazine.
Barrel: 20½".
Weight: 6¼ lbs. **Length:** 37⅛" overall.
Stock: American walnut, two-piece, straight grip (no p.g.).
Sights: Hooded ramp front, adjustable semi-buckhorn rear.
Features: Side ejection, receiver grooved for scope mounting, takedown action. From U.S. Repeating Arms Co.
Price: Walnut $395.00
Price: With WinTuff laminated stock $395.00

Winchester Model 9422 Magnum Lever-Action Rifle
Same as the 9422 except chambered for 22 WMR cartridge, has 11-round mag. capacity.
Price: Walnut $412.00
Price: With WinCam green stock $412.00
Price: With WinTuff brown laminated stock $412.00

RIMFIRE RIFLES—BOLT ACTIONS & SINGLE SHOTS
Includes models for a variety of sports, utility and competitive shooting.

Anschutz Achiever

ANSCHUTZ 1700D BAVARIAN BOLT-ACTION RIFLE
Caliber: 22 LR, 5-shot clip.
Barrel: 24".
Weight: 7¼ lbs. **Length:** 43" overall.
Stock: European walnut with Bavarian cheek rest. Checkered pistol grip and forend.
Sights: Hooded ramp front, folding leaf rear; drilled and tapped for scope mounting.
Features: Uses the Improved 1700 Match 54 action with adjustable #5096 trigger. Introduced in 1988. Imported from Germany by Precision Sales International.
Price: 22 LR $1,364.00
Price: Custom 1700D Meistergrade (select walnut, gold engraved trigger guard) $1,563.00

ANSCHUTZ ACHIEVER BOLT-ACTION RIFLE
Caliber: 22 LR, 5-shot clip, single shot adaptor.
Barrel: 19½".
Weight: 5 lbs. **Length:** 35½" to 36⅔" overall.
Stock: Walnut-finished hardwood with adjustable buttplate, vented forend, stippled pistol grip. Length of pull adjustable from 11⅞" to 13".
Sights: Hooded front, open rear adjustable for windage and elevation.
Features: Uses Mark 2000-type action with adjustable two-stage trigger. Receiver grooved for scope mounting. Designed for training in junior rifle clubs and for starting young shooters. Introduced 1987. Imported from Germany by Precision Sales International.
Price: $399.00
Price: Sight Set #1 .... $74.75

CAUTION: PRICES SHOWN ARE SUPPLIED BY THE MANUFACTURER OR IMPORTER. CHECK YOUR LOCAL GUNSHOP.

RIMFIRE RIFLES—BOLT ACTIONS & SINGLE SHOTS

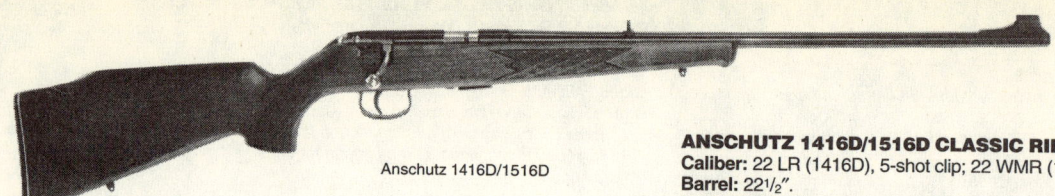

Anschutz 1416D/1516D

Anschutz 1416D/1516D Custom Rifles
Similar to the Classic models except have European walnut stocks with roll-over Monte Carlo cheekpiece, slim forend with schnabel tip, fine cut checkering on grip and forend. Introduced 1988. Imported from Germany by Precision Sales International.
Price: 1416D (22 LR) $785.00
Price: 1516D (22 WMR) $799.00

Anschutz 1418D/1518D Mannlicher Rifles
Similar to the 1416D/1516D rifles except have full-length Mannlicher-style stocks, shorter 19 3/8" barrels. Weigh 5 1/2 lbs. Stock has mahogany schnabel tip. Model 1418D chambered for 22 LR, 1518D for 22 WMR. Imported from Germany by Precision Sales International.
Price: 1418D $1,159.00
Price: 1518D $1,170.00

> Consult our Directory pages for the location of firms mentioned.

Anschutz 1700 FWT Bolt-Action Rifle
Similar to the Anschutz 1700D Custom except has McMillan fiberglass stock with Monte Carlo, roll-over cheekpiece, Wundhammer swell, and checkering. Comes without sights but the receiver is drilled and tapped for scope mounting. Has 22" barrel, single stage #5096 trigger. Weighs 6.25 lbs. Introduced 1989. Imported from Germany by Precision Sales International.
Price: With gray fiberglass stock $1,230.00
Price: As above, with Fibergrain stock $1,460.00

ANSCHUTZ 1416D/1516D CLASSIC RIFLES
Caliber: 22 LR (1416D), 5-shot clip; 22 WMR (1516D), 4-shot clip.
Barrel: 22 1/2".
Weight: 6 lbs. **Length:** 41" overall.
Stock: European walnut; classic style with straight comb, checkered pistol grip and forend.
Sights: Hooded ramp front, folding leaf rear.
Features: Uses Match 64 action. Adjustable single stage trigger. Receiver grooved for scope mounting. Imported from Germany by Precision Sales International.
Price: 1416D, 22 LR $785.00
Price: 1516D, 22 WMR $799.00
Price: 1416D Classic left-hand $785.00

ANSCHUTZ 1700D CUSTOM RIFLE
Caliber: 22 LR, 5-shot clip.
Barrel: 24 1/4.
Weight: 7 3/8 lbs. **Length:** 42 1/2" overall.
Stock: Select European walnut.
Sights: Hooded ramp front, folding leaf rear; drilled and tapped for scope mounting.
Features: Match 54 action with adjustable single-stage trigger; roll-over Monte Carlo cheekpiece, slim forend with schnabel tip, Wundhammer palm swell on pistol grip, rosewood grip cap with white diamond insert; skip-line checkering on grip and forend. Introduced 1988. Imported from Germany by Precision Sales International.
Price: $1,364.00
Price: Meistergrade (select wood, gold engraved trigger guard) $1,563.00

Anschutz 1700D Graphite Custom Rifle
Similar to the Model 1700D FWT except has McMillan graphite reinforced stock with Monte Carlo roll-over cheekpiece. No sights furnished, but drilled and tapped for scope mounting. Comes with Anschutz logo sling, quick-detachable swivels. Introduced 1991.
Price: $1,299.00

Armscor Model 14D

Armscor Model 1500 Rifle
Similar to the Model 14P except chambered for 22 WMR. Has 21.5" barrel, double lug bolt, checkered stock, weighs 6.5 lbs. Introduced 1987.
Price: About $199.00

ARMSCOR MODEL 14P BOLT-ACTION RIFLE
Caliber: 22 LR, 10-shot magazine.
Barrel: 23".
Weight: 7 lbs. **Length:** 41.5" overall.
Stock: Walnut-finished mahogany.
Sights: Bead front, rear adjustable for elevation.
Features: Receiver grooved for scope mounting. Blued finish. Introduced 1987. Imported from the Philippines by Ruko Products.
Price: About $129.00
Price: Model 14D Deluxe (checkered stock) $149.00

BRNO ZKM 452 Deluxe

BRNO ZKM-452 DELUXE BOLT-ACTION RIFLE
Caliber: 22 LR, 22 WMR, detachable 6- or 10-shot magazine.
Barrel: 23.6".
Weight: 6.9 lbs. **Length:** 43.5" overall.
Stock: Checkered walnut.
Sights: Hooded bead front, open rear adjustable for windage and elevation.
Features: Dual claw extractors, safety locks firing pin. Blue finish; grooved receiver; oiled stock; sling swivels. Introduced 1992. Imported from the Czech Republic by Magnum Research.
Price: 22 LR, standard $299.00
Price: 22 LR, Lux $329.00
Price: 22 WMR, 6-shot, standard $379.00
Price: 22 WMR, 10-shot, Lux $399.00

RIMFIRE RIFLES—BOLT ACTIONS & SINGLE SHOTS

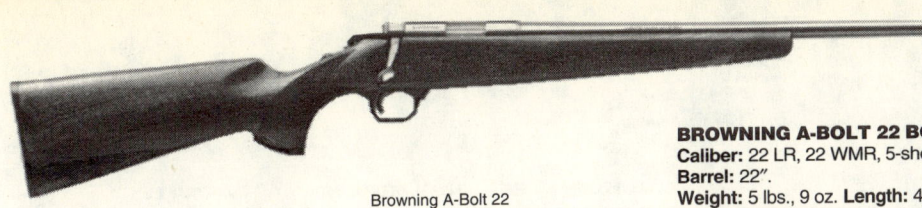
Browning A-Bolt 22

BROWNING A-BOLT 22 BOLT-ACTION RIFLE
Caliber: 22 LR, 22 WMR, 5-shot magazines standard.
Barrel: 22".
Weight: 5 lbs., 9 oz. **Length:** 40 1/4" overall.
Stock: Walnut with cut checkering, rosewood grip cap and forend tip.
Sights: Offered with or without open sights. Open sight model has ramp front and adjustable folding leaf rear.
Features: Short 60-degree bolt throw. Top tang safety. Grooved for 22 scope mount. Drilled and tapped for full-size scope mounts. Detachable magazines. Gold-colored trigger preset at about 4 lbs. Imported from Japan by Browning. Introduced 1986.
Price: A-Bolt 22, no sights $404.95
Price: A-Bolt 22, with open sights $417.95
Price: A-Bolt 22 WMR, no sights $469.95
Price: As above, with sights $479.95

Browning A-Bolt Gold Medallion
Similar to the standard A-Bolt except stock is of high-grade walnut with brass spacers between stock and rubber recoil pad and between the rosewood grip cap and forend. Medallion-style engraving covers the receiver flats, and the words "Gold Medallion" are engraved and gold filled on the right side of the barrel. High gloss stock finish. Introduced 1988.
Price: No sights $539.95

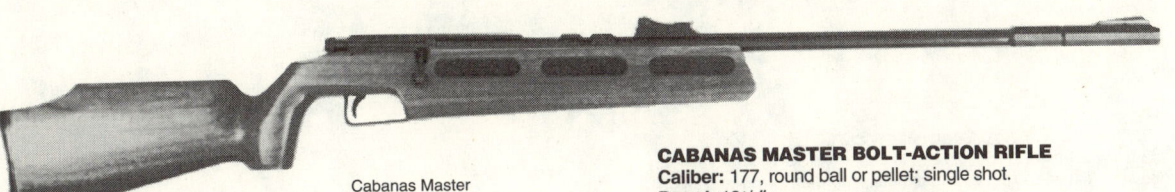
Cabanas Master

CABANAS MASTER BOLT-ACTION RIFLE
Caliber: 177, round ball or pellet; single shot.
Barrel: 19 1/2".
Weight: 8 lbs. **Length:** 45 1/2" overall.
Stocks: Walnut target-type with Monte Carlo.
Sights: Blade front, fully adjustable rear.
Features: Fires round ball or pellet with 22-cal. blank cartridge. Bolt action. Imported from Mexico by Mandall Shooting Supplies. Introduced 1984.
Price: $189.95
Price: Varmint model (has 21 1/2" barrel, 4 1/2 lbs., 41" o.a.l., varmint-type stock) $119.95

Cabanas Espronceda IV Bolt-Action Rifle
Similar to the Leyre model except has full sporter stock, 18 3/4" barrel, 40" overall length, weighs 5 1/2 lbs.
Price: $134.95

Cabanas Leyre Bolt-Action Rifle
Similar to Master model except 44" overall, has sport/target stock.
Price: $149.95
Price: Model R83 (17" barrel, hardwood stock, 40" o.a.l.) $79.95
Price: Mini 82 Youth (16 1/2" barrel, 33" o.a.l., 3 1/2 lbs.) $69.95
Price: Pony Youth (16" barrel, 34" o.a.l., 3.2 lbs.) $69.95

CABANAS TASER RIFLE
Caliber: 177.
Barrel: 19".
Weight: 6 lbs., 12 oz. **Length:** 42" overall.
Stock: Target-type thumbhole.
Sights: Blade front, open fully adjustable rear.
Features: Fires round ball or pellets with 22 blank cartridge. Imported from Mexico by Mandall Shooting Supplies.
Price: $159.95

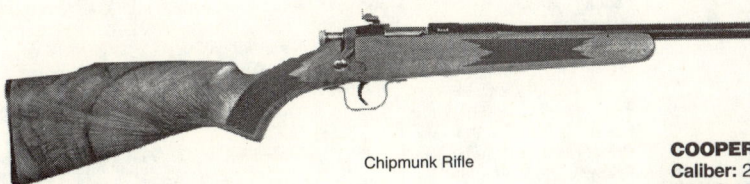
Chipmunk Rifle

COOPER ARMS MODEL 36 CLASSIC SPORTER RIFLE
Caliber: 22 LR, 5-shot magazine.
Barrel: 22 3/4".
Weight: 7 lbs. **Length:** 42 1/2" overall.
Stock: AAA Claro walnut with 22 lpi checkering, oil finish.
Sights: None furnished.
Features: Action has three mid-bolt locking lugs, 45-degree bolt rotation; fully adjustable single stage match trigger; swivel studs. Pachmayr butt pad. Introduced 1991. Made in U.S. by Cooper Arms.
Price: Standard $1,495.00
Price: Custom Classic (AAA Claro walnut, Monte Carlo beaded cheekpiece, oil finish) $1,695.00
Price: Model 36 Featherweight (custom stock shape, black textured finish, 6.5 lbs.) $1,595.00

CHIPMUNK SINGLE SHOT RIFLE
Caliber: 22, S, L, LR, single shot.
Barrel: 16 1/8".
Weight: About 2 1/2 lbs. **Length:** 30" overall.
Stocks: American walnut, or camouflage.
Sights: Post on ramp front, peep rear adjustable for windage and elevation.
Features: Drilled and tapped for scope mounting using special Chipmunk base ($9.95). Made in U.S. Introduced 1982. From Oregon Arms.
Price: Standard $174.95
Price: Deluxe (better wood, checkering) $225.00

Dakota 22 Sporter

Weight: About 6.5 lbs. **Length:** 42 1/2" overall.
Stock: Claro or English walnut in classic design; 13.6" length of pull. Point panel hand checkering. Swivel studs. Black buttpad.
Sights: None furnished.
Features: Combines features of Winchester 52 and Dakota 76 rifles. Full-sized receiver; rear locking lug and bolt machined from bar stock. Trigger and striker-blocking safety; Model 70-style trigger. Introduced 1992. From Dakota Arms, Inc.
Price: $1,500.00

DAKOTA 22 SPORTER BOLT-ACTION RIFLE
Caliber: 22 LR, 5-shot magazine.
Barrel: 22" Premium.

CAUTION: PRICES SHOWN ARE SUPPLIED BY THE MANUFACTURER OR IMPORTER. CHECK YOUR LOCAL GUNSHOP.

50th EDITION, 1996 **411**

RIMFIRE RIFLES—BOLT ACTIONS & SINGLE SHOTS

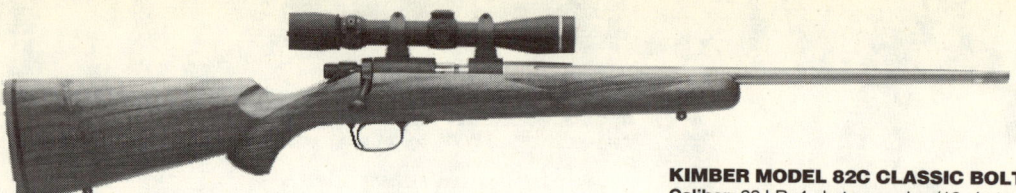

Kimber Model 82C

Kimber Model 82C SuperAmerica Bolt-Action Rifle
Similar to the Model 82C except has AAA fancy grade Claro walnut with beaded cheekpiece, ebony forend cap; hand-checkered 22 lpi patterns with wrap-around coverage; black rubber buttpad. Reintroduced 1994. Made in U.S. by Kimber of America, Inc.
Price: $1,175.00

KIMBER MODEL 82C CLASSIC BOLT-ACTION RIFLE
Caliber: 22 LR, 4-shot magazine (10-shot available).
Barrel: 21"; premium air-gauged.
Weight: 6.5 lbs. **Length:** 40.5" overall.
Stock: Classic style of Claro walnut; 13.5" length of pull; hand-checkered; red rubber buttpad; polished steel grip cap.
Sights: None furnished; drilled and tapped for Warne scope mounts (optionally available from factory).
Features: Action uses aluminum pillar bedding for consistent accuracy; single-set trigger with 2.5-lb. pull is fully adjustable. Reintroduced 1994. Made in U.S. by Kimber of America, Inc.
Price: Right- or left-hand $785.00

Kimber Model 82C SuperAmerica

Kimber Model 82C Custom Shop SuperAmerica
Similar to standard SuperAmerica except has Neidner-style buttplate. Available options include: steel skeleton grip cap and buttplate; quarter-rib and open express sights; jewelled bolt; checkered bolt knob; special length of pull; rust blue finish. Reintroduced 1994. Made in U.S. by Kimber of America, Inc.
Price: Basic Custom Shop SuperAmerica $1,250.00

Kimber Model 82C Custom Match Bolt-Action Rifle
Same as the Model 82C Classic except has high grade stock of French walnut with black ebony forend tip, full coverage 22 lpi borderless checkering, steel Neidner (uncheckered) buttplate, and satin rust blue finish. Reintroduced 1995. Made in U.S. by Kimber of America, Inc.
Price: $1,850.00

Kimber Model 82C Varmint Bolt-Action Rifle
Similar to the Model 82C Classic except has a slightly larger forend to accommodate the medium/heavy barrel profile. Has fluted, stainless steel match-grade barrel. Weighs about 7 1/2 lbs. Introduced 1995. Made in U.S. by Kimber of America, Inc.
Price: $885.00

Kimber Model 82C SuperClassic Bolt-Action Rifle
Same as the Model 82C Classic except has AAA Claro walnut stock with black rubber buttpad, as used on the SuperAmerica. Introduced 1995. Made in U.S. by Kimber of America, Inc.
Price: $1,090.00

> Consult our Directory pages for the location of firms mentioned.

KRICO MODEL 300 BOLT-ACTION RIFLES
Caliber: 22 LR, 22 WMR, 22 Hornet.
Barrel: 19.6" (22 RF), 23.6" (Hornet).
Weight: 6.3 lbs. **Length:** 38.5" overall (22 RF).
Stock: Walnut-stained beech.
Sights: Blade on ramp front, open adjustable rear.
Features: Double triggers, sliding safety. Checkered grip and forend. Imported from Germany by Mandall Shooting Supplies.
Price: Model 300 Standard $700.00
Price: Model 300 Deluxe $795.00
Price: Model 300 Stutzen (walnut full-length stock) $825.00
Price: Model 300 SA (walnut Monte Carlo stock) $750.00

LAKEFIELD ARMS MARK I BOLT-ACTION RIFLE
Caliber: 22 LR, single shot.
Barrel: 20 1/2".
Weight: 5 1/2 lbs. **Length:** 39 1/2" overall.
Stock: Walnut-finished hardwood with Monte Carlo-type comb, checkered grip and forend.
Sights: Bead front, open adjustable rear. Receiver grooved for scope mounting.
Features: Thumb-operated rotating safety. Blue finish. Rifled or smooth bore. Introduced 1990. Made in Canada by Lakefield Arms Ltd.
Price: Mark I, rifled or smooth bore $134.95
Price: Mark I left-hand $148.95
Price: Mark IY (Youth), 19" barrel, 37" overall, 5 lbs. $134.95
Price: Mark IY left-hand $148.95
Price: Mark I left-hand, smooth bore $148.95
Price: Mark IY left-hand, smooth bore $148.95

Lakefield Model 93M

LAKEFIELD ARMS MODEL 93M BOLT-ACTION RIFLE
Caliber: 22 WMR, 5-shot magazine.
Barrel: 20.75".
Weight: 5.75 lbs. **Length:** 39.5" overall.
Stock: Walnut-finished hardwood with Monte Carlo-type comb, checkered grip and forend.
Sights: Bead front, adjustable open rear. Receiver grooved for scope mount.
Features: Thumb-operated rotary safety. Blue finish. Introduced 1994. Made in Canada by Lakefield Arms Ltd.
Price: About $167.95

LAKEFIELD ARMS MARK II BOLT-ACTION RIFLE
Caliber: 22 LR, 10-shot magazine.
Barrel: 20 1/2".
Weight: 5 1/2 lbs. **Length:** 39 1/2" overall.
Stock: Walnut-finished hardwood with Monte Carlo-type comb, checkered grip and forend.
Sights: Bead front, open adjustable rear. Receiver grooved for scope mounting.
Features: Thumb-operated rotating safety. Blue finish. Introduced 1990. Made in Canada by Lakefield Arms Ltd.
Price: About $139.95
Price: Mark II-Y (youth), 19" barrel, 37" overall, 5 lbs. $139.95
Price: Mark II left-hand $154.95
Price: Mark II-Y (youth) left-hand $154.95

RIMFIRE RIFLES—BOLT ACTIONS & SINGLE SHOTS

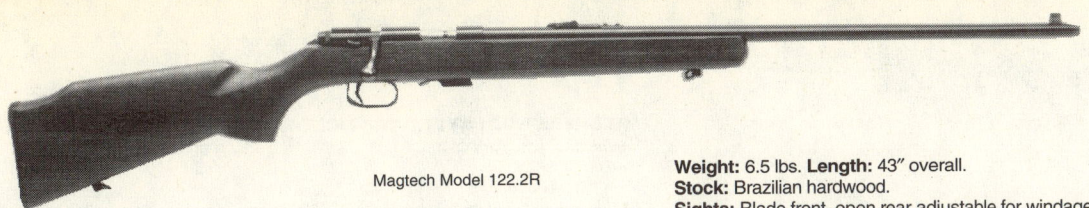
Magtech Model 122.2R

MAGTECH MODEL 122.2 BOLT-ACTION RIFLES
Caliber: 22 S, L, LR, 6- and 10-shot magazines.
Barrel: 24" (six-groove).
Weight: 6.5 lbs. **Length:** 43" overall.
Stock: Brazilian hardwood.
Sights: Blade front, open rear adjustable for windage and elevation.
Features: Sliding safety; double extractors; receiver grooved for scope mount. Introduced 1994. Imported from Brazil by Magtech Recreational Products, Inc.
Price: Model 122.2S (no sights) $139.95
Price: Model 122.2R (open sights) $149.95
Price: Model 122.2T (ramp front, micro-type open rear) $169.95

Marlin Model 15YN

MARLIN MODEL 15YN "LITTLE BUCKAROO"
Caliber: 22 S, L, LR, single shot.
Barrel: 16 1/4" Micro-Groove®.
Weight: 4 1/4 lbs. **Length:** 33 1/4" overall.
Stock: One-piece walnut-finished, press-checkered Maine birch with Monte Carlo; Mar-Shield® finish.
Sights: Ramp front, adjustable open rear.
Features: Beginner's rifle with thumb safety, easy-load feed throat, red cocking indicator. Receiver grooved for scope mounting. Introduced 1989.
Price: $162.80

Marlin Model 880

MARLIN MODEL 880 BOLT-ACTION RIFLE
Caliber: 22 LR; 7-shot clip magazine.
Barrel: 22" Micro-Groove®.
Weight: 5 1/2 lbs. **Length:** 41".
Stock: Checkered Monte Carlo American black walnut with checkered p.g. and forend. Rubber buttpad, swivel studs. Mar-Shield® finish.
Sights: Wide-Scan™ ramp front, folding semi-buckhorn rear adjustable for windage and elevation.
Features: Receiver grooved for scope mount. Introduced 1989.
Price: $233.25

Marlin Model 25MN Bolt-Action Rifle
Similar to the Model 25N except chambered for 22 WMR. Has 7-shot clip magazine, 22" Micro-Groove® barrel, checkered walnut-finished Maine birch stock. Introduced 1989.
Price: $192.40

Marlin Model 882 Bolt-Action Rifle
Same as the Marlin 880 except 22 WMR cal. only with 7-shot clip magazine; weight about 6 lbs. Comes with swivel studs.
Price: $257.20
Price: Model 882L (laminated hardwood stock) $272.70

Marlin Model 25N Bolt-Action Repeater
Similar to Marlin 880, except walnut-finished p.g. stock, adjustable open rear sight, ramp front.
Price: $168.25

Marlin Model 880SS Stainless Steel Bolt-Action Rifle
Same as the Model 880 except barrel, receiver, front breech bolt, striker knob, trigger stud, cartridge lifter stud and outer magazine tube are made of stainless steel. Most other parts are nickel-plated to match the stainless finish. Has black fiberglass-filled AKZO synthetic stock with moulded-in checkering, stainless steel swivel studs. Introduced 1994. Made in U.S. by Marlin Firearms Co.
Price: $249.20

Marlin Model 881 Bolt-Action Rifle
Same as the Marlin 880 except tubular magazine, holds 17 Long Rifle, 19 Long, 25 Short cartridges. Weighs 6 lbs.
Price: $242.95

Marlin Model 883SS Bolt-Action Rifle
Same as the Model 883 except front breech bolt, striker knob, trigger stud, cartridge lifter stud and outer magazine tube are of stainless steel; other parts are nickel-plated. Has two-tone brown laminated Monte Carlo stock with swivel studs, rubber butt pad. Introduced 1993.
Price: $283.85

Marlin Model 883 Bolt-Action Rifle
Same as Marlin 882 except tubular magazine holds 12 rounds of 22 WMR ammunition.
Price: $266.60

Marlin Model 882 SS

Marlin Model 882SS Bolt-Action Rifle
Same as the Marlin Model 882 except has stainless steel front breech bolt, barrel, receiver and bolt knob. All other parts are either stainless steel or nickel-plated. Has black Monte Carlo stock of fiberglass-filled polycarbonate with moulded-in checkering, nickel-plated swivel studs. Introduced 1995. Made in U.S. by Marlin Firearms Co.
Price: $274.95

CAUTION: PRICES SHOWN ARE SUPPLIED BY THE MANUFACTURER OR IMPORTER. CHECK YOUR LOCAL GUNSHOP.

RIMFIRE RIFLES—BOLT ACTIONS & SINGLE SHOTS

Mitchell High Standard 9302

MITCHELL HIGH STANDARD BOLT-ACTION RIFLES
Caliber: 22 LR, 10-shot magazine; 22 WMR, 5-shot magazine.
Barrel: 22.5".
Weight: About 6.5 lbs. **Length:** 40.75" overall.
Stock: American walnut (Models 9301, 9302 have rosewood grip and forend caps, checkering).
Sights: Bead on ramp front, open adjustable rear.
Features: Polished blue finish. Introduced 1994. Imported from the Philippines by Mitchell Arms.
Price: Model 9301 (22 LR, checkering, rosewood caps) $312.50
Price: Model 9302 (as above, 22 WMR) $325.00
Price: Model 9303 (22 LR, no checkering or rosewood caps) $275.00
Price: Model 9304 (as above, 22 WMR) $289.00
Price: Model 9305 (22 LR, heavy barrel) $199.00

NAVY ARMS TU-KKW TRAINING RIFLE
Caliber: 22 LR, 5-shot detachable magazine.
Barrel: 26".
Weight: 8 lbs. **Length:** 44" overall.
Stock: 98k-style walnut-stained hardwood.
Sights: Blade front, open rear adjustable for elevation; military style.
Features: Replica of the German WWII training rifle. Polished blue metal. Bayonet lug, cleaning rod, takedown disk in butt. Introduced 1991. Imported by Navy Arms.
Price: $210.00

Navy Arms TU-33/40 Carbine
Similar to the TU-KKW Training Rifle except has 20.75" barrel, weighs 6.5 lbs., 38" overall. Based on Mauser G.33/40 mountain carbine. Comes with bayonet lug, sling, cleaning rod. Introduced 1992. Imported by Navy Arms.
Price: $210.00

Norinco JW-27

NORINCO JW-15 BOLT-ACTION RIFLE
Caliber: 22 LR, 5-shot detachable magazine.
Barrel: 24".
Weight: 5 lbs., 12 oz. **Length:** 41 3/4" overall.
Stock: Walnut-stained hardwood.
Sights: Hooded blade front, open rear drift adjustable for windage.
Features: Polished blue finish; sling swivels; wing-type safety. Introduced 1991. Imported by Interarms, Navy Arms.
Price: About ....$100.00 to $118.00

NORINCO JW-27 BOLT-ACTION RIFLE
Caliber: 22 LR, 5-shot magazine.
Barrel: 22.75".
Weight: 5 lbs., 14 oz. **Length:** 41.75" overall.
Stock: Walnut-finished hardwood with checkered grip and forend.
Sights: Dovetailed bead on blade front, fully adjustable rear.
Features: Receiver grooved for scope mounting. Blued finish. Introduced 1992. Imported from China by Century International Arms.
Price: About $106.95

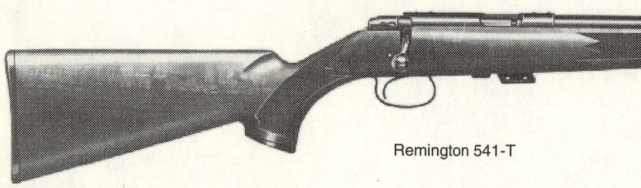

Remington 541-T

REMINGTON 541-T
Caliber: 22 S, L, LR, 5-shot clip.
Barrel: 24".
Weight: 5 7/8 lbs. **Length:** 42 1/2" overall.
Stock: Walnut, cut-checkered p.g. and forend. Satin finish.
Sights: None. Drilled and tapped for scope mounts.
Features: Clip repeater. Thumb safety. Reintroduced 1986.
Price: About $425.00

REMINGTON 40-XR RIMFIRE CUSTOM SPORTER
Caliber: 22 LR.
Barrel: 24".
Weight: 10 lbs. **Length:** 42 1/2" overall.
Stock: Full-sized walnut, checkered p.g. and forend.
Sights: None furnished; drilled and tapped for scope mounting.
Features: Custom Shop gun. Duplicates Model 700 centerfire rifle.
Price: Grade I $2,387.00

Remington 541-T HB Bolt-Action Rifle
Similar to the 541-T except has a heavy target-type barrel without sights. Receiver is drilled and tapped for scope mounting. American walnut stock with straight comb, satin finish, cut checkering, black checkered buttplate, black grip cap and forend tip. Weight is about 6 1/2 lbs. Introduced 1993.
Price: $452.00

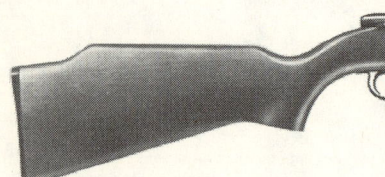

Remington 581-S

REMINGTON 581-S SPORTSMAN RIFLE
Caliber: 22 S, L or LR, 5-shot clip magazine.
Barrel: 24" round.
Weight: 4 3/4 lbs. **Length:** 42 3/8" overall.
Stock: Walnut-finished hardwood, Monte Carlo with p.g.
Sights: Bead post front, screw adjustable open rear.
Features: Sliding side safety, wide trigger, receiver grooved for tip-off scope mounts. Comes with single shot adaptor. Reintroduced 1986.
Price: About $225.00

RIMFIRE RIFLES—BOLT ACTIONS & SINGLE SHOTS

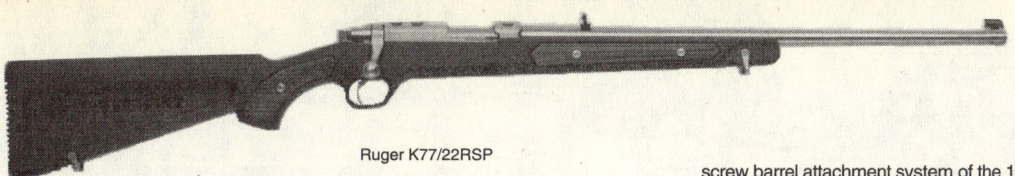

Ruger K77/22RSP

RUGER 77/22 RIMFIRE BOLT-ACTION RIFLE
Caliber: 22 LR, 10-shot rotary magazine; 22 WMR, 9-shot rotary magazine.
Barrel: 20".
Weight: About 5 3/4 lbs. **Length:** 39 3/4" overall.
Stock: Checkered American walnut or injection-moulded fiberglass-reinforced Du Pont Zytel with Xenoy inserts in forend and grip, stainless sling swivels.
Sights: Brass bead front, adjustable folding leaf rear or plain barrel with 1" Ruger rings.
Features: Mauser-type action uses Ruger's 10-shot rotary magazine. Three-position safety, simplified bolt stop, patented bolt locking system. Uses the dual-screw barrel attachment system of the 10/22 rifle. Integral scope mounting system with 1" Ruger rings. Blued model introduced in 1983. Stainless steel model and blued model with the synthetic stock introduced in 1989.

Price: 77/22R (no sights, rings, walnut stock) $431.00
Price: 77/22RS (open sights, rings, walnut stock) $458.00
Price: K77/22RP (stainless, no sights, rings, synthetic stock) $431.00
Price: K77/22RSP (stainless, open sights, rings, synthetic stock) $458.00
Price: 77/22RM (22 WMR, blue, walnut stock) $431.00
Price: K77/22RSMP (22 WMR, stainless, open sights, rings, synthetic stock) $458.00
Price: K77/22RMP (22 WMR, stainless, synthetic stock) $431.00
Price: 77/22RSM (22 WMR, blue, open sights, rings, walnut stock) $458.00

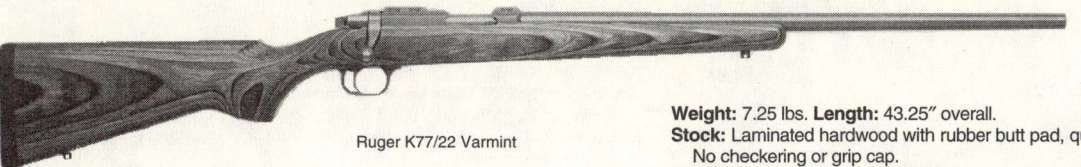

Ruger K77/22 Varmint

RUGER K77/22 VARMINT RIFLE
Caliber: 22 LR, 10-shot, 22 WMR, 9-shot detachable rotary magazine.
Barrel: 24", heavy.
Weight: 7.25 lbs. **Length:** 43.25" overall.
Stock: Laminated hardwood with rubber butt pad, quick-detachable swivel studs. No checkering or grip cap.
Sights: None furnished. Comes with Ruger 1" scope rings.
Features: Made of stainless steel with target gray finish. Three-position safety, dual extractors. Stock has wide, flat forend. Introduced 1993.
Price: K77/22VBZ, 22 LR $499.00
Price: K77/22VMB, 22 WMR $499.00

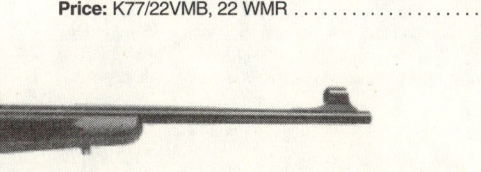

Sako Finnfire

SAKO FINNFIRE BOLT-ACTION RIFLE
Caliber: 22 LR, 5-shot magazine.
Barrel: 22".
Weight: 5.25 lbs. **Length:** 40" overall.
Stock: European walnut with checkered grip and forend.
Sights: Hooded blade front, open adjustable rear.
Features: Adjustable single-stage trigger; has 50-degree bolt lift. Introduced 1994. Imported from Finland by Stoeger Industries.
Price: $685.00

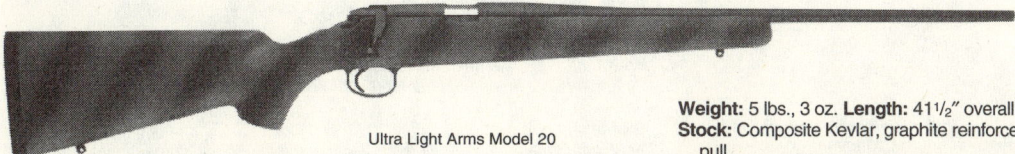

Ultra Light Arms Model 20

ULTRA LIGHT ARMS MODEL 20 RF BOLT-ACTION RIFLE
Caliber: 22 LR, single shot or 5-shot repeater.
Barrel: 22" Douglas Premium, #1 contour.
Weight: 5 lbs., 3 oz. **Length:** 41 1/2" overall.
Stock: Composite Kevlar, graphite reinforced. Du Pont Imron paint; 13 1/2" length of pull.
Sights: None furnished. Drilled and tapped for scope mounting.
Features: Available as either single shot or repeater with 5-shot removable magazine. Comes with scope mounts. Introduced 1993. Made in U.S. by Ultra Light Arms, Inc.
Price: $800.00

COMPETITION RIFLES—CENTERFIRE & RIMFIRE

Includes models for classic American and ISU target competition and other sporting and competitive shooting.

Anschutz BR-50

ANSCHUTZ BR-50 BENCHREST RIFLE
Caliber: 22 LR, single shot.
Barrel: 19.75" (without 11-oz. muzzle weight).
Weight: About 11 lbs. **Length:** 37.75" to 42.5" overall.
Stock: Benchrest style of European hardwood with stippled grip. Cheekpiece vertically adjustable to 1". Stock length adjustable via spacers and buttplate. Finished with glossy blue-black paint.
Sights: None furnished. Receiver grooved for mounts, barrel drilled and tapped for target mounts.
Features: Uses the Anschutz 2013 target action, #5018 two-stage adjustable target trigger factory set at 3.9 oz. Introduced 1994. Imported from Germany by Precision Sales International.
Price: $3,312.00

COMPETITION RIFLES—CENTERFIRE & RIMFIRE

Anschutz Achiever ST Super

ANSCHUTZ 64-MS, 64-MS LEFT SILHOUETTE RIFLE
Caliber: 22 LR, single shot.
Barrel: 21½", medium heavy; 7/8" diameter.
Weight: 8 lbs. **Length:** 39.5" overall.
Stock: Walnut-finished hardwood, silhouette-type.
Sights: None furnished. Receiver drilled and tapped for scope mounting.
Features: Uses Match 64 action. Designed for metallic silhouette competition. Stock has stippled checkering, contoured thumb groove with Wundhammer swell. Two-stage #5091 trigger. Slide safety locks sear and bolt. Introduced 1980. Imported from Germany by Precision Sales International.
Price: 64-MS $987.00
Price: 64-MS Left $1,087.00

ANSCHUTZ 1827B BIATHLON RIFLE
Caliber: 22 LR, 5-shot magazine.
Barrel: 21½".
Weight: 8½ lbs. with sights. **Length:** 42½" overall.
Stock: European walnut with cheekpiece, stippled pistol grip and forend.
Sights: Globe front specially designed for Biathlon shooting, micrometer rear with hinged snow cap.
Features: Uses Super Match 54 action and nine-way adjustable trigger; adjustable wooden buttplate, Biathlon butthook, adjustable hand-stop rail. **Special Order Only.** Introduced 1982. Imported from Germany by Precision Sales International.
Price: Right-hand $2,457.00

ANSCHUTZ 1911 PRONE MATCH RIFLE
Caliber: 22 LR, single shot.
Barrel: 27¼".
Weight: 11 lbs. **Length:** 46" overall.
Stock: Walnut-finished European hardwood; American prone style with Monte Carlo, cast-off cheekpiece, checkered p.g., beavertail forend with swivel rail and adjustable swivel, adjustable rubber buttplate.
Sights: None furnished. Receiver grooved for Anschutz sights (extra). Scope blocks.
Features: Two-stage #5018 trigger adjustable from 2.1 to 8.6 oz. Extremely fast lock time. Imported from Germany by Precision Sales International.
Price: Right-hand, no sights $2,325.00

Anschutz 1913 Super Match Rifle
Same as the Model 1911 except European walnut International-type stock with adjustable cheekpiece, adjustable aluminum hook buttplate, adjustable hand stop, weight 15.5 lbs., 46" overall. Imported from Germany by Precision Sales International.
Price: Right-hand, no sights $3,422.00
Price: M1913 left-hand $3,592.00

ANSCHUTZ ACHIEVER ST SUPER TARGET RIFLE
Caliber: 22 LR, single shot.
Barrel: 22", .75" diameter.
Weight: About 6.5 lbs. **Length:** 38.75" to 39.75" overall.
Stock: Walnut-finished European hardwood with hand-stippled panels on grip and forend; 13.5" accessory rail on forend.
Sights: Optional. Anschutz #1 or #2 Sight Set. Receiver grooved for scope mounting.
Features: Designed for the advanced junior shooter with adjustable length of pull from 13.25" to 14.25" via removable butt spacers. Two-stage #5066 adjustable trigger factory set at 2.6 lbs. Introduced 1994. Imported from Germany by Precision Sales International.
Price: $485.00
Price: Sight Set #1 .... $74.75
Price: Sight Set #2 .... $276.75

Anschutz 1827BT Fortner Biathlon Rifle
Similar to the Anschutz 1827B Biathlon rifle except uses Anschutz/Fortner system straight-pull bolt action. Introduced 1982. Imported from Germany by Precision Sales International.
Price: Right-hand $3,722.00
Price: Left-hand $4,168.00

> Consult our Directory pages for the location of firms mentioned.

ANSCHUTZ 1808D RT SUPER RUNNING TARGET RIFLE
Caliber: 22 LR, single shot.
Barrel: 32½".
Weight: 9.4 lbs. **Length:** 50.5" overall.
Stock: European walnut. Heavy beavertail forend; adjustable cheekpiece and buttplate. Stippled grip and forend.
Sights: None furnished. Grooved for scope mounting.
Features: Designed for Running Target competition. Nine-way adjustable single-stage trigger, slide safety. Introduced 1991. Imported from Germany by Precision Sales International.
Price: Right-hand $1,963.00

ANSCHUTZ 1903 MATCH RIFLE
Caliber: 22 LR, single shot.
Barrel: 25", .75" diameter.
Weight: 8.6 lbs. **Length:** 43.75" overall.
Stock: Walnut-finished hardwood with adjustable cheekpiece; stippled grip and forend.
Sights: None furnished.
Features: Uses Anschutz Match 64 action and #5098 two-stage trigger. A medium weight rifle for intermediate and advanced Junior Match competition. Introduced 1987. Imported from Germany by Precision Sales International.
Price: Right-hand $1,163.00
Price: Left-hand $1,221.00
Price: #6823 sight set $339.75

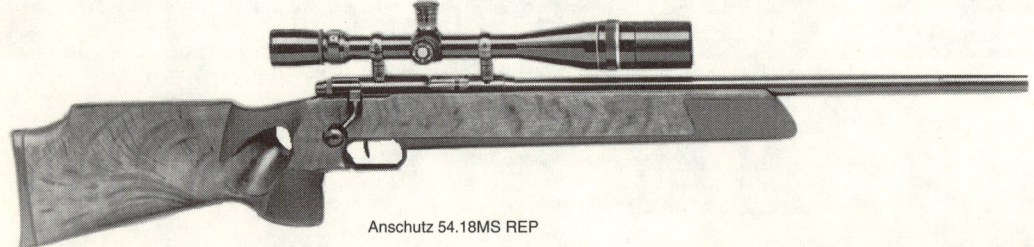

Anschutz 54.18MS REP

Anschutz 54.18MS Silhouette Rifle
Same basic features as Anschutz 1913 Super Match but with special metallic silhouette European hardwood stock and two-stage trigger. Has 22" barrel; receiver drilled and tapped.
Price: $1,579.00
Price: 54.18MSL (true left-hand version of above) $1,675.00

Anschutz 54.18MS REP Deluxe Silhouette Rifle
Same basic action and trigger specifications as the Anschutz 1913 Super Match but with removable 5-shot clip magazine, 22" barrel extendable to 30" using optional extension and weight set. Receiver drilled and tapped for scope mounting. Silhouette stock with thumbhole grip is of fiberglass with walnut wood Fibergrain finish. Introduced 1990. Imported from Germany by Precision Sales International.
Price: 54.18MS REP Deluxe $2,450.00
Price: 54.18MS Standard with fiberglass stock $2,066.00

COMPETITION RIFLES—CENTERFIRE & RIMFIRE

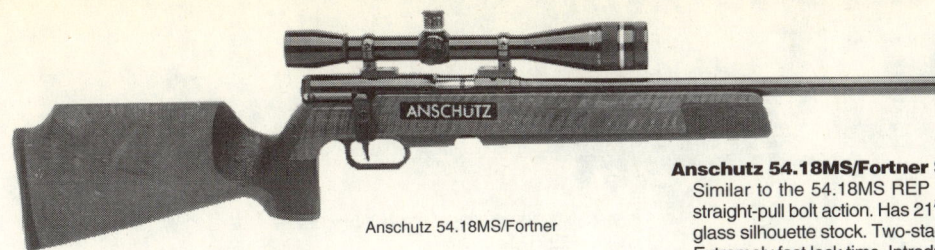

Anschutz 54.18MS/Fortner

Anschutz 1907 ISU Standard Match Rifle
Same action as Model 1913 but with 7/8" diameter 26" barrel. Length is 44.5" overall, weight 10 lbs. Choice of stock configurations. Vented forend. Designed for prone and position shooting ISU requirements; suitable for NRA matches. Imported from Germany by Precision Sales International.
Price: Right-hand, no sights, European hardwood stock $1,983.00
Price: With laminated hardwood stock $2,139.00
Price: Right-hand, no sights, walnut stock $2,060.00
Price: M1907-L (true left-hand action and stock) $2,164.00

Anschutz 54.18MS/Fortner Silhouette Rifle
Similar to the 54.18MS REP Deluxe except uses Anschutz/Fortner system straight-pull bolt action. Has 21", .75"-diameter barrel, McMillan Fibergrain fiberglass silhouette stock. Two-stage #5020 trigger adjustable from 3.5 oz. to 2 lbs. Extremely fast lock time. Introduced 1995. Imported from Germany by Precision Sales International.
Price: Right-hand $3,855.00
Price: Left-hand $4,168.00

Anschutz 1910 Super Match Rifle
Similar to the Super Match 1913 rifle except has a stock of European hardwood with tapered forend and deep receiver area. Hand and palm rests not included. Uses Match 54 action. Adjustable hook buttplate and cheekpiece. Sights not included. Introduced 1982. Imported from Germany by Precision Sales International.
Price: Right-hand $2,967.00
Price: Left-hand $3,116.00

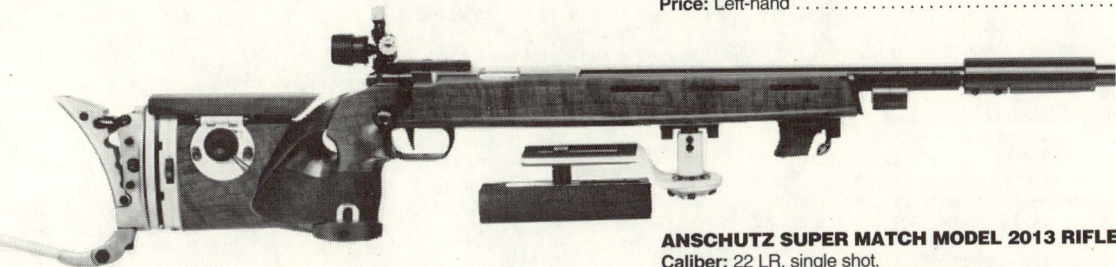

Anschutz 2013

Anschutz Super Match Model 2007 ISU Standard Rifle
Similar to the Model 2013 except has ISU Standard design. European walnut or blonde hardwood stock. Sights optional. Introduced 1992. Imported from Germany by Precision Sales International.
Price: Right-hand $2,961.00
Price: Left-hand $3,025.00

ANSCHUTZ SUPER MATCH MODEL 2013 RIFLE
Caliber: 22 LR, single shot.
Barrel: 19.75" (26" with tube installed).
Weight: 15.5 lbs. **Length:** 43" to 45.5" overall.
Stock: European walnut; target adjustable.
Sights: Optional. Uses #7020/20 sight set.
Features: Improved Super Match 54 action, #5018 trigger give fastest consistent lock time for a production target rifle. Barrel is micro-honed; trigger has nine points of adjustment, two stages. Slide safety. Comes with test target. Introduced 1992. Imported from Germany by Precision Sales International.
Price: Right-hand $4,067.00
Price: Left-hand $4,270.00

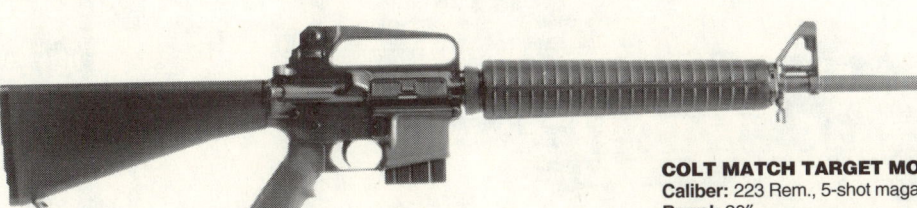

Colt Match Target HBAR

Colt Match Target HBAR Rifle
Similar to the Target Model except has heavy barrel, 800-meter rear sight adjustable for windage and elevation. Introduced 1991.
Price: $1,067.00

Colt Match Target Competition HBAR II Rifle
Similar to the Match Target Competition HBAR except has 16.1" barrel, weighs 7.1 lbs., overall length 34.5"; 1:9" twist barrel. Introduced 1995.
Price: $1,044.00

E.A.A./HW 660 MATCH RIFLE
Caliber: 22 LR.
Barrel: 26".
Weight: 10.7 lbs. **Length:** 45.3" overall.
Stock: Match-type walnut with adjustable cheekpiece and buttplate.
Sights: Globe front, match aperture rear.
Features: Adjustable match trigger; stippled p.g. and forend; forend accessory rail. Introduced 1988. Imported from Germany by European American Armory.
Price: About $795.00

COLT MATCH TARGET MODEL RIFLE
Caliber: 223 Rem., 5-shot magazine.
Barrel: 20".
Weight: 7.5 lbs. **Length:** 39" overall.
Stock: Composition stock, grip, forend.
Sights: Post front, aperture rear adjustable for windage and elevation.
Features: Five-round detachable box magazine, standard-weight barrel, sling swivels. Has forward bolt assist. Military matte black finish. Model introduced 1991.
Price: $1,019.00

Colt Match Target Competition HBAR Rifle
Similar to the Sporter Target except has flat-top receiver with integral Weaver-type base for scope mounting. Counter-bored muzzle, 1:9" rifling twist. Introduced 1991.
Price: Model R6700 .... $1,073.00

COOPER ARMS MODEL BR-50
Caliber: 22 LR, single shot.
Barrel: 22"; .860" straight.
Weight: 6.8 lbs. **Length:** 40.5" overall.
Stock: McMillan Benchrest.
Sights: None furnished.
Features: Action has three mid-bolt locking lugs; fully adjustable match grade trigger; stainless barrel. Introduced 1994. Made in U.S. by Cooper Arms.
Price: $1,595.00

COMPETITION RIFLES—CENTERFIRE & RIMFIRE

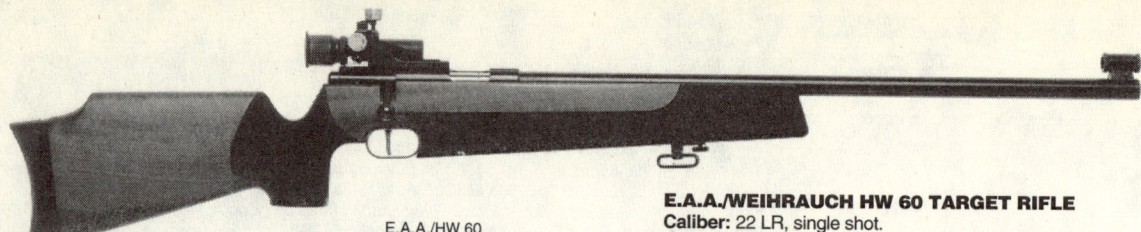

E.A.A./HW 60

E.A.A./WEIHRAUCH HW 60 TARGET RIFLE
Caliber: 22 LR, single shot.
Barrel: 26.8".
Weight: 10.8 lbs. **Length:** 45.7" overall.
Stock: Walnut with adjustable buttplate. Stippled p.g. and forend. Rail with adjustable swivel.
Sights: Hooded ramp front, match-type aperture rear.
Features: Adjustable match trigger with push-button safety. Left-hand version also available. Introduced 1981. Imported from Germany by European American Armory.
Price: Right-hand $695.00
Price: Left-hand $875.00

EAGLE ARMS M15A2 GOLDEN EAGLE RIFLE
Caliber: 223 Rem.
Barrel: 20" extra-heavy NM; 1:8" twist.
Weight: 9 lbs., 10 oz. **Length:** 39 5/8" overall.
Stock: Black composition; weighted.
Sights: Elevation-adjustable NM extra-fine front with set screw, E2-style NM rear with 1/2-min. adjustments for windage and elevation; NM aperture.
Features: Upper and lower receivers have push-type pivot pin for easy takedown. Receivers hard coat anodized. Fence-type magazine release. Introduced 1989. Made in U.S. by Eagle Arms, Inc.
Price: $1,600.00

FINNISH LION STANDARD TARGET RIFLE
Caliber: 22 LR, single shot.
Barrel: 27 5/8".
Weight: 10 1/2 lbs. **Length:** 44 9/16" overall.
Stock: French walnut, target style.
Sights: Globe front, International micrometer rear.
Features: Optional accessories: palm rest, hook buttplate, forend stop and swivel assembly, buttplate extension, five front sight aperture inserts, three rear sight apertures, Allen wrench. Adjustable trigger. Imported from Finland by Mandall Shooting Supplies.
Price: Without sights $695.00
Price: Sight set $195.00

HARRIS-McMILLAN NATIONAL MATCH RIFLE
Caliber: 7mm-08, 308, 5-shot magazine.
Barrel: 24", stainless steel.
Weight: About 11 lbs. (std. bbl.). **Length:** 43" overall.
Stock: Modified ISU fiberglass with adjustable buttplate.
Sights: Barrel band and Tompkins front; no rear sight furnished.
Features: McMillan repeating action with clip slot, Canjar trigger. Match-grade barrel. Available in right-hand only. Fibergrain stock, sight installation, special machining and triggers optional. Introduced 1989. From Harris-McMillan Gunworks, Inc.
Price: $2,600.00

HARRIS-McMILLAN COMBO M-87 SERIES 50-CALIBER RIFLES
Caliber: 50 BMG, single shot.
Barrel: 29", with muzzlebrake.
Weight: About 21 1/2 lbs. **Length:** 53" overall.
Stock: McMillan fiberglass.
Sights: None furnished.
Features: Right-handed McMillan stainless steel receiver, chromemoly barrel with 1:15 twist. Introduced 1987. From Harris-McMillan Gunworks, Inc.
Price: $3,735.00
Price: M87R 5-shot repeater $4,000.00
Price: M-87 (5-shot repeater) "Combo" $4,300.00
Price: M-92 Bullpup (shortened M-87 single shot with bullpup stock) ..$4,000.00
Price: M-93SN (10-shot repeater with folding stock, detachable magazine) $4,300.00

HARRIS-McMILLAN M-89 SNIPER RIFLE
Caliber: 308 Win., 5-shot magazine.
Barrel: 28" (with suppressor).
Weight: 15 lbs., 4 oz.
Stock: McMillan fiberglass; adjustable for length; recoil pad.
Sights: None furnished. Drilled and tapped for scope mounting.
Features: Uses McMillan repeating action. Comes with bipod. Introduced 1990. From Harris-McMillan Gunworks, Inc.
Price: Standard (non-suppressed) $2,700.00

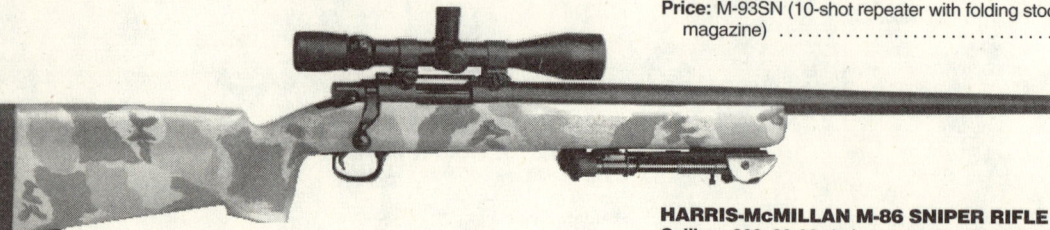

Harris-McMillan M-86

HARRIS-McMILLAN M-86 SNIPER RIFLE
Caliber: 308, 30-06, 4-shot magazine; 300 Win. Mag., 3-shot magazine.
Barrel: 24", McMillan match-grade in heavy contour.
Weight: 11 1/4 lbs. (308), 11 1/2 lbs. (30-06, 300). **Length:** 43 1/2" overall.
Stock: Specially designed McHale fiberglass stock with textured grip and forend, recoil pad.
Sights: None furnished.
Features: Uses McMillan repeating action. Comes with bipod. Matte black finish. Sling swivels. Introduced 1989. From Harris-McMillan Gunworks, Inc.
Price: $2,300.00
Price: Takedown model $2,500.00

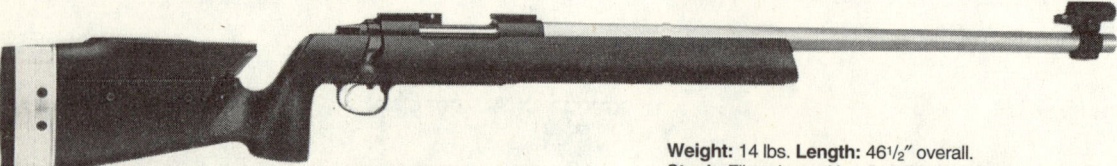

Harris-McMillan Long Range

HARRIS-McMILLAN LONG RANGE RIFLE
Caliber: 300 Win. Mag., 7mm Rem. Mag., 300 Phoenix, 338 Lapua, single shot.
Barrel: 26", stainless steel, match-grade.
Weight: 14 lbs. **Length:** 46 1/2" overall.
Stock: Fiberglass with adjustable buttplate and cheekpiece. Adjustable for length of pull, drop, cant and cast-off.
Sights: Barrel band and Tompkins front; no rear sight furnished.
Features: Uses McMillan solid bottom single shot action and Canjar trigger. Barrel twist 1:12". Introduced 1989. From Harris-McMillan Gunworks, Inc.
Price: $2,600.00

COMPETITION RIFLES—CENTERFIRE & RIMFIRE

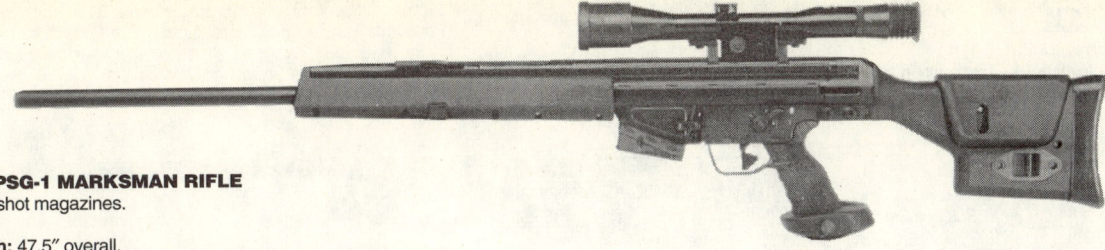
Heckler & Koch PSG-1

HECKLER & KOCH PSG-1 MARKSMAN RIFLE
Caliber: 308, 5- and 20-shot magazines.
Barrel: 25.6", heavy.
Weight: 17.8 lbs. **Length:** 47.5" overall.
Stock: Matte black high impact plastic, adjustable for length, pivoting butt cap, vertically-adjustable cheekpiece; target-type pistol grip with adjustable palm shelf.
Sights: Hendsoldt 6x42 scope.
Features: Uses HK-91 action with low-noise bolt closing device, special Marksman trigger group; special forend with T-way rail for sling swivel or tripod. Gun comes in special foam-fitted metal transport case with tripod, two 20-shot and two 5-shot magazines, tripod. Imported from Germany by Heckler & Koch, Inc. Introduced 1986.
Price: $10,093.00

Krico Model 360S Biathlon

KRICO MODEL 400 MATCH RIFLE
Caliber: 22 LR, 22 Hornet, 5-shot magazine.
Barrel: 23.2" (22 LR), 23.6" (22 Hornet).
Weight: 8.8 lbs. **Length:** 42.1" overall (22 RF).
Stock: European walnut, match type.
Sights: None furnished; receiver grooved for scope mounting.
Features: Heavy match barrel. Double-set or match trigger. Imported from Germany by Mandall Shooting Supplies.
Price: $950.00

KRICO MODEL 600 SNIPER RIFLE
Caliber: 222, 223, 22-250, 243, 308, 4-shot magazine.
Barrel: 23.6".
Weight: 9.2 lbs. **Length:** 45.2" overall.
Stock: European walnut with adjustable rubber buttplate.
Sights: None supplied; drilled and tapped for scope mounting.
Features: Match barrel with flash hider; large bolt knob; wide trigger shoe. Parkerized finish. Imported from Germany by Mandall Shooting Supplies.
Price: $2,645.00

KRICO MODEL 360S BIATHLON RIFLE
Caliber: 22 LR, 5-shot magazine.
Barrel: 21.25".
Weight: 9.26 lbs. **Length:** 40.55" overall.
Stock: Walnut with high comb, adjustable buttplate.
Sights: Globe front, fully adjustable Diana 82 match peep rear.
Features: Straight-pull action with 17.6-oz. match trigger. Comes with five magazines (four stored in stock recess), muzzle/sight snow cap. Introduced 1991. Imported from Germany by Mandall Shooting Supplies.
Price: $1,695.00

KRICO MODEL 500 KRICOTRONIC MATCH RIFLE
Caliber: 22 LR, single shot.
Barrel: 23.6".
Weight: 9.4 lbs. **Length:** 42.1" overall.
Stock: European walnut, match type with adjustable butt.
Sights: Globe front, match micrometer aperture rear.
Features: Electronic ignition system for fastest possible lock time. Completely adjustable trigger. Barrel has tapered bore. Imported from Germany by Mandall Shooting Supplies.
Price: $3,950.00

KRICO MODEL 600 MATCH RIFLE
Caliber: 222, 223, 22-250, 243, 308, 5.6x50 Mag., 4-shot magazine.
Barrel: 23.6".
Weight: 8.8 lbs. **Length:** 43.3" overall.
Stock: Match stock of European walnut with cheekpiece.
Sights: None furnished; drilled and tapped for scope mounting.
Features: Match stock with vents in forend for cooling, rubber recoil pad, sling swivels. Imported from Germany by Mandall Shooting Supplies.
Price: $1,250.00

Lakefield Model 92S

Lakefield Arms Model 92S Silhouette Rifle
Similar to the Model 90B except has high-comb target-type stock of walnut-finished hardwood, one 5-shot magazine. Comes without sights, but receiver is drilled and tapped for scope base. Weight about 8 lbs. Introduced 1992. Made in Canada by Lakefield Arms.
Price: $387.95
Price: left-hand $424.95

LAKEFIELD ARMS MODEL 91T TARGET RIFLE
Caliber: 22 LR, single shot.
Barrel: 25".
Weight: 8 lbs. **Length:** 43 5/8" overall.
Stock: Target-type, walnut-finished hardwood.
Sights: Target front with inserts, peep rear with 1/4-minute click adjustments.

LAKEFIELD ARMS MODEL 90B TARGET RIFLE
Caliber: 22 LR, 5-shot magazine.
Barrel: 21".
Weight: 8 1/4 lbs. **Length:** 39 5/8" overall.
Stock: Natural finish hardwood with clip holder, carrying and shooting rails, butt hook, hand stop.
Sights: Target front with inserts, peep rear with 1/4-minute click adjustments.
Features: Biathlon-style rifle with snow cap muzzle protector. Comes with five magazines. Introduced 1991. Made in Canada by Lakefield Arms.
Price: About $569.95
Price: left-hand, about $624.95

Features: Comes with shooting rail and hand stop. Also available as 5-shot repeater as Model 91-TR. Introduced 1991. Made in Canada by Lakefield Arms.
Price: Model 91T $454.95
Price: Model 91T left-hand $499.95
Price: Model 91-TR (repeater) $484.95
Price: Model 91-TR left-hand $529.95

COMPETITION RIFLES—CENTERFIRE & RIMFIRE

KRICO MODEL 360 S2 BIATHLON RIFLE
Caliber: 22 LR, 5-shot magazine.
Barrel: 21.25".
Weight: 9 lbs., 15 oz. **Length:** 40.55" overall.
Stock: Biathlon design of black epoxy-finished walnut with pistol grip.
Sights: Globe front, fully adjustable Diana 82 match peep rear.
Features: Pistol-grip-activated action. Comes with five magazines (four stored in stock recess), muzzle/sight snow cap. Introduced 1991. Imported from Germany by Mandall Shooting Supplies.
Price: $1,595.00

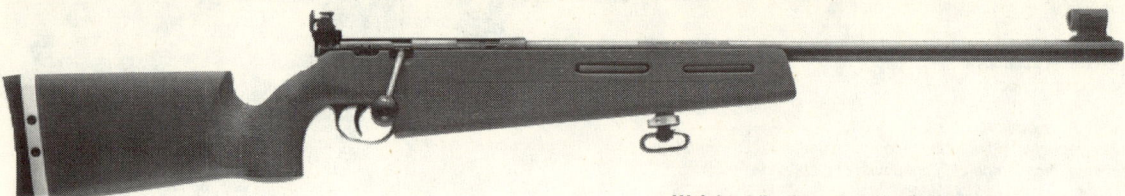
Marlin Model 2000

MARLIN MODEL 2000 TARGET RIFLE
Caliber: 22 LR, single shot.
Barrel: 22" heavy, Micro-Groove® rifling, match chamber, recessed muzzle.
Weight: 8 lbs. **Length:** 41" overall.
Stock: High-comb fiberglass/Kevlar with stipple finish grip and forend.
Sights: Hooded front with seven aperture inserts, fully adjustable target rear peep.
Features: Stock finished with royal blue enamel. Buttplate adjustable for length of pull, height and angle. Aluminum forend rail with stop and quick-detachable swivel. Two-stage target trigger; red cocking indicator. Five-shot adaptor kit available. Introduced 1991. From Marlin.
Price: $602.30

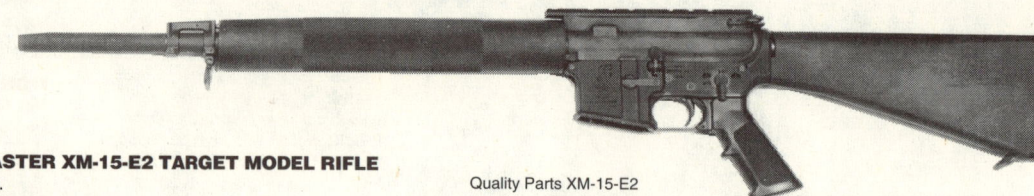
Quality Parts XM-15-E2

QUALITY PARTS/BUSHMASTER XM-15-E2 TARGET MODEL RIFLE
Caliber: 223, 10-shot magazine.
Barrel: 20", 24", 26"; 1:7" or 1:9" twist; heavy.
Weight: 8.3 lbs. **Length:** 38" overall (20" barrel).
Stock: Black composition.
Sights: Adjustable post front, adjustable aperture rear.
Features: Patterned after Colt M-16A2. Chrome-lined barrel with manganese phosphate exterior. Has E-2 lower receiver with push-pin. From Quality Parts Co./Bushmaster Firearms Co.
Price: 20" match heavy barrel $895.00
Price: 24" match heavy barrel $905.00
Price: 26" match heavy barrel $915.00

QUALITY PARTS/BUSHMASTER V MATCH RIFLE
Caliber: 223, 10-shot magazine.
Barrel: 20", 24", 26"; 1:9" twist.
Weight: 8.2 lbs. **Length:** 38.25" overall (20" barrel).
Stock: Black composition.
Sights: None furnished; comes with scope mount base installed.
Features: Hand-built match gun. E2 lower reveiver with push-pin-style takedown. Barrel is .950" outside diameter with counter-bored crown: integral flash suppressor; upper receiver has brass deflector; free-floating steel handguard accepts laser sight, flashlight, bipod. From Quality Parts Co./Bushmaster Firearms Co.
Price: From $1,200.00

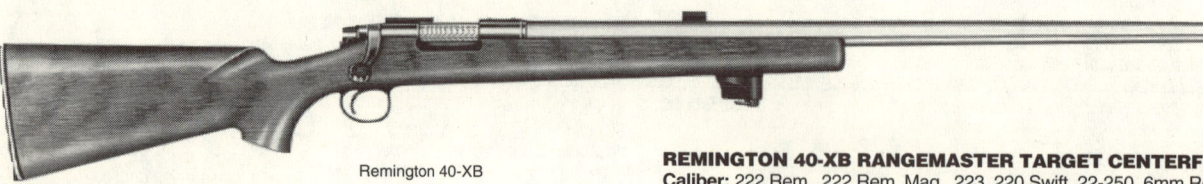
Remington 40-XB

REMINGTON 40-XBBR KS
Caliber: 22 BR Rem., 222 Rem., 222 Rem. Mag., 223, 6mmx47, 6mm BR Rem., 7.62 NATO (308 Win.).
Barrel: 20" (light varmint class), 24" (heavy varmint class).
Weight: 7 1/4 lbs. (light varmint class); 12 lbs. (heavy varmint class).
Length: 38" (20" bbl.), 42" (24" bbl.).
Stock: Kevlar.
Sights: None. Supplied with scope blocks.
Features: Unblued stainless steel barrel, trigger adjustable from 1 1/2 lbs. to 3 1/2 lbs. Special 2-oz. trigger at extra cost. Scope and mounts extra.
Price: With Kevlar stock $1,413.00
Price: Extra for 2-oz. trigger, about $160.00

REMINGTON 40-XB RANGEMASTER TARGET CENTERFIRE
Caliber: 222 Rem., 222 Rem. Mag., 223, 220 Swift, 22-250, 6mm Rem., 243, 25-06, 7mm BR Rem., 7mm Rem. Mag., 30-338 (30-7mm Rem. Mag.), 300 Win. Mag., 7.62 NATO (308 Win.), 30-06, single shot.
Barrel: 27 1/4".
Weight: 11 1/4 lbs. **Length:** 47" overall.
Stock: American walnut or Kevlar with high comb and beavertail forend stop. Rubber non-slip buttplate.
Sights: None. Scope blocks installed.
Features: Adjustable trigger. Stainless barrel and action. Receiver drilled and tapped for sights.
Price: Standard single shot, stainless steel barrel, about $1,269.00
Price: Repeater model $1,365.00
Price: Model 40-XB KS $1,432.00
Price: Repeater model (KS) $1,526.00
Price: Extra for 2-oz. trigger $160.00

Remington 40-XR KS

REMINGTON 40-XR KS RIMFIRE POSITION RIFLE
Caliber: 22 LR, single shot.
Barrel: 24", heavy target.
Weight: 10 lbs. **Length:** 43" overall.
Stock: Kevlar. Position-style with front swivel block on forend guide rail.
Sights: Drilled and tapped. Furnished with scope blocks.
Features: Meets all ISU specifications. Deep forend, buttplate vertically adjust~able, wide adjustable trigger.
Price: About $1,360.00

COMPETITION RIFLES—CENTERFIRE & RIMFIRE

REMINGTON 40-XC KS NATIONAL MATCH COURSE RIFLE
Caliber: 7.62 NATO, 5-shot.
Barrel: 24", stainless steel.
Weight: 11 lbs. without sights. **Length:** 43½" overall.
Stock: Kevlar, position-style, with palm swell, handstop.
Sights: None furnished.
Features: Designed to meet the needs of competitive shooters firing the national match courses. Position-style stock, top loading clip slot magazine, anti-bind bolt and receiver, stainless steel barrel and action. Meets all ISU Army Rifle specifications. Adjustable buttplate, adjustable trigger.
Price: About $1,413.00

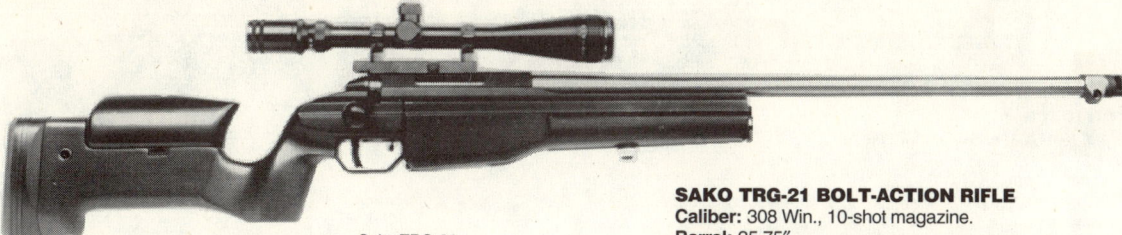

Sako TRG-21

SAKO TRG-21 BOLT-ACTION RIFLE
Caliber: 308 Win., 10-shot magazine.
Barrel: 25.75".
Weight: 10.5 lbs. **Length:** 46.5" overall.
Stock: Reinforced polyurethane with fully adjustable cheekpiece and buttplate.
Sights: None furnished. Optional quick-detachable, one-piece scope mount base, 1" or 30mm rings.
Features: Resistance-free bolt, free-floating heavy stainless barrel, 60-degree bolt lift. Two-stage trigger is adjustable for length, pull, horizontal or vertical pitch. Introduced 1993. Imported from Finland by Stoeger.
Price: $4,185.00

SAUER 202 TR TARGET RIFLE
Caliber: 6.5x55mm, 308 Win., 5-shot magazine.
Barrel: 26" or 28.5", heavy match target.
Weight: 12.1 lbs. **Length:** 44.5" overall.
Stock: One-piece true target type of laminated beechwood/epoxy; adjustable buttplate and cheekpiece.
Sights: Globe front, Sauer-Busk 200-600m diopter rear. Drilled and tapped for scope mounting.
Features: Interchangeable free-floating, hammer-forged barrel; two-stage adjustable trigger; vertical slide safety; 3 millisecond lock time; rail for swivel, bipod; right- or left-hand; Converts to 22 rimfire. Introduced 1994. Imported from Germany by Paul Co.
Price: $1,900.00
Price: Spare Match-Target barrel $425.00

SAVAGE MODEL 112BT COMPETITION GRADE RIFLE
Caliber: 223, 308, 5-shot magazine, 300 Win. Mag., single shot.
Barrel: 26", heavy contour stainless with black finish; 1:9" twist (223), 1:10" (308).
Weight: 10.8 lbs. **Length:** 47.5" overall.
Stock: Laminated wood with straight comb, adjustable cheek rest, Wundhammer palm swell, ventilated forend. Recoil pad is adjustable for length of pull.
Sights: None furnished; drilled and tapped for scope mounting and aperture target-style sights. Recessed target-style muzzle has .812" diameter section for universal target sight base.
Features: Matte black alloy receiver. Bolt has black titanium nitride coating, large handle ball. Has alloy accessory rail on forend. Comes with safety gun lock, target and ear puffs. Introduced 1994. Made in U.S. by Savage Arms, Inc.
Price: $1,000.00
Price: 300 Win. Mag. (single shot) $1,000.00

Springfield M1A/M-21

Springfield Inc. M1A/M-21 Tactical Model Rifle
Similar to the M1A Super Match except has Douglas Premium match barrel and special sniper stock with adjustable cheekpiece. Weighs 11.2 lbs. From Springfield, Inc.
Price: $2,125.00

SPRINGFIELD INC. M1A SUPER MATCH
Caliber: 243, 7mm-08, 308 Win.
Barrel: 22", heavy Douglas Premium or National Match.
Weight: About 10 lbs. **Length:** 44.31" overall.
Stock: Heavy walnut competition stock with longer pistol grip, contoured area behind the rear sight, thicker butt and forend, glass bedded.
Sights: National Match front and rear.
Features: Has figure-eight-style operating rod guide. Introduced 1987. From Springfield, Inc.
Price: About $1,980.00

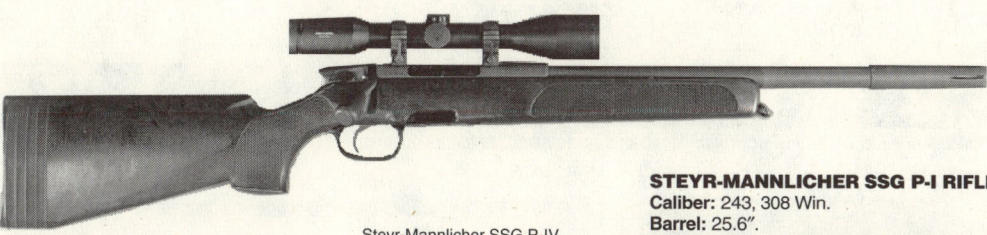

Steyr-Mannlicher SSG P-IV

Steyr-Mannlicher SSG P-IV Rifle
Similar to the SSG P-I except has 16.75" heavy barrel with flash hider. Available in 308 only. ABS Cycolac synthetic stock in green or black. Introduced 1992. Imported from Austria by GSI, Inc.
Price: $2,660.00

STEYR-MANNLICHER SSG P-I RIFLE
Caliber: 243, 308 Win.
Barrel: 25.6".
Weight: 8.6 lbs. **Length:** 44.5" overall.
Stock: ABS Cycolac synthetic half-stock. Removable spacers in butt adjusts length of pull from 12¾" to 14".
Sights: Hooded blade front, folding leaf rear.
Features: Parkerized finish. Choice of interchangeable single- or double-set triggers. Detachable 5-shot rotary magazine (10-shot optional). Receiver grooved for Steyr and Bock Quick Detach mounts. Imported from Austria by GSI, Inc.
Price: Synthetic half-stock $1,995.00
Price: SSG-PII (as above except has large bolt knob, heavy bbl., no sights, forend rail) $1,995.00

CAUTION: PRICES SHOWN ARE SUPPLIED BY THE MANUFACTURER OR IMPORTER. CHECK YOUR LOCAL GUNSHOP.

COMPETITION RIFLES—CENTERFIRE & RIMFIRE

STEYR-MANNLICHER MATCH SPG-UIT RIFLE
Caliber: 308 Win.
Barrel: 25.5".
Weight: 10 lbs. **Length:** 44" overall.
Stock: Laminated and ventilated. Special UIT Match design.
Sights: Steyr globe front, Steyr peep rear.
Features: Double-pull trigger adjustable for let-off point, slack, weight of first-stage pull, release force and length; buttplate adjustable for height and length. Meets UIT specifications. Introduced 1992. Imported from Austria by GSI, Inc.
Price: $3,995.00
Price: SPG-CISM $4,295.00
Price: SPG-T $3,695.00

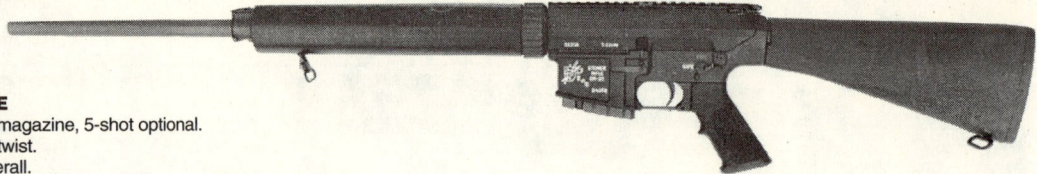

STONER SR-25 MATCH RIFLE
Caliber: 7.62 NATO, 10-shot steel magazine, 5-shot optional.
Barrel: 24" heavy match; 1:11.25" twist.
Weight: 10.75 lbs. **Length:** 44" overall.
Stock: Black synthetic AR-15A2 design. Full floating forend of Mil-spec synthetic attaches to upper receiver at a single point.
Sights: None furnished. Has integral Weaver-style rail. Rings and iron sights optional.
Features: Improved AR-15 trigger; AR-15-style seven-lug rotating bolt. Gas block rail mounts detachable front sight. Introduced 1993. Made in U.S. by Knight's Mfg. Co.

Stoner SR-25 Match

Price: $2,995.00
Price: SR-25 Lightweight Match (20" medium match target contour barrel, 9.5 lbs., 40" overall) $2,995.00

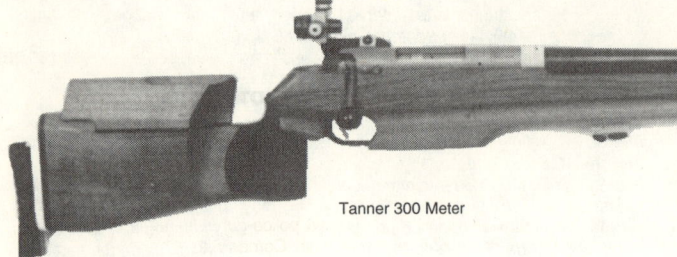

Tanner 300 Meter

TANNER 300 METER FREE RIFLE
Caliber: 308 Win., 7.5 Swiss, single shot.
Barrel: 27.58".
Weight: 15 lbs. **Length:** 45.3" overall.
Stock: Seasoned walnut, thumbhole style, with accessory rail, palm rest, adjustable hook butt.
Sights: Globe front with interchangeable inserts, Tanner-design micrometer-diopter rear with adjustable aperture.
Features: Three-lug revolving-lock bolt design; adjustable set trigger; short firing pin travel; supplied with 300-meter test target. Imported from Switzerland by Mandall Shooting Supplies. Introduced 1984.
Price: About $4,900.00

TANNER 50 METER FREE RIFLE
Caliber: 22 LR, single shot.
Barrel: 27.7".
Weight: 13.9 lbs. **Length:** 44.4" overall.
Stock: Seasoned walnut with palm rest, accessory rail, adjustable hook buttplate.
Sights: Globe front with interchangeable inserts, Tanner micrometer-diopter rear with adjustable aperture.
Features: Bolt action with externally adjustable set trigger. Supplied with 50-meter test target. Imported from Switzerland by Mandall Shooting Supplies. Introduced 1984.
Price: About $3,900.00

TANNER STANDARD UIT RIFLE
Caliber: 308, 7.5mm Swiss, 10-shot.
Barrel: 25.9".
Weight: 10.5 lbs. **Length:** 40.6" overall.
Stock: Match style of seasoned nutwood with accessory rail; coarsely stippled pistol grip; high cheekpiece; vented forend.
Sights: Globe front with interchangeable inserts, Tanner micrometer-diopter rear with adjustable aperture.
Features: Two locking lug revolving bolt encloses case head. Trigger adjustable from 1/2 to 6 1/2 lbs.; match trigger optional. Comes with 300-meter test target. Imported from Switzerland by Mandall Shooting Supplies. Introduced 1984.
Price: About $4,700.00

CONSULT **SHOOTER'S MARKETPLACE** Page 266, This Issue

WICHITA SILHOUETTE RIFLE
Caliber: All standard calibers with maximum overall cartridge length of 2.800".
Barrel: 24" free-floated Matchgrade.
Weight: About 9 lbs.
Stock: Metallic gray fiberthane with ventilated rubber recoil pad.
Sights: None furnished. Drilled and tapped for scope mounts.
Features: Legal for all NRA competitions. Single shot action. Fluted bolt, 2-oz. Canjar trigger; glass-bedded stock. Introduced 1983. From Wichita Arms.
Price: $2,275.00
Price: Left-hand $2,400.00

SHOTGUNS—AUTOLOADERS

Includes a wide variety of sporting guns and guns suitable for various competitions.

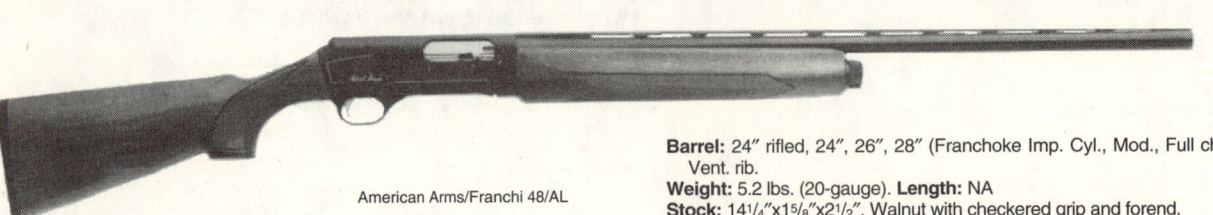

American Arms/Franchi 48/AL

AMERICAN ARMS/FRANCHI BLACK MAGIC 48/AL
Gauge: 12 or 20, 2 3/4" chamber.
Barrel: 24" rifled, 24", 26", 28" (Franchoke Imp. Cyl., Mod., Full choke tubes). Vent. rib.
Weight: 5.2 lbs. (20-gauge). **Length:** NA
Stock: 14 1/4"x1 5/8"x2 1/2". Walnut with checkered grip and forend.
Features: Recoil-operated action. Chrome-lined bore; cross-bolt safety. Imported from Italy by American Arms, Inc.
Price: $625.00

SHOTGUNS—AUTOLOADERS

Benelli Super Black Eagle

BENELLI SUPER BLACK EAGLE SHOTGUN
Gauge: 12, 3 1/2" chamber.
Barrel: 24", 26", 28" (Imp. Cyl., Mod., Imp. Mod., Full choke tubes).
Weight: 7 lbs., 5 oz. **Length:** 49 5/8" overall (28" barrel).
Stock: European walnut with satin finish, or polymer. Adjustable for drop.
Sights: Bead front.
Features: Uses Montefeltro inertia recoil bolt system. Fires all 12-gauge shells from 2 3/4" to 3 1/2" magnums. Introduced 1991. Imported from Italy by Heckler & Koch, Inc.
Price: With 28" barrel $1,144.00
Price: With 24", 26" barrel, polymer stock $1,129.00

Benelli Super Black Eagle Slug Gun
Similar to the Benelli Super Black Eagle except has 24" E.R. Shaw Custom rifled barrel with 3" chamber, and comes with scope mount base. Uses the Montefeltro inertia recoil bolt system. Matte-finish receiver. Weight is 7.5 lbs., overall length 45.5". Wood or polymer stocks available. Introduced 1992. Imported from Italy by Heckler & Koch, Inc.
Price: $1,171.00
Price: With polymer stock $1,171.00

Benelli M1 Super 90 Field

BENELLI M1 SUPER 90 FIELD AUTO SHOTGUN
Gauge: 12, 3" chamber.
Barrel: 21", 24", 26", 28" (choke tubes).
Weight: 7 lbs., 4 oz.
Stock: High impact polymer; wood on 26", 28".
Sights: Metal bead front.
Features: Sporting version of the military & police gun. Uses the rotating Montefeltro bolt system. Ventilated rib; blue finish. Comes with set of five choke tubes. Imported from Italy by Heckler & Koch, Inc.
Price: $848.00
Price: Wood stock version $863.00

Benelli Montefeltro Super 90 Shotgun
Similar to the M1 Super 90 except has checkered walnut stock with high-gloss finish. Uses the Montefeltro rotating bolt system with a simple inertia recoil design. Full, Imp. Mod, Mod., Imp. Cyl. choke tubes. Weight is 7-7 1/2 lbs. Finish is matte black. Introduced 1987.
Price: 21", 24", 26", 28" $868.00
Price: Left-hand, 26", 28" $887.00
Price: 20-ga., Montefeltro Super 90, 26", 5 3/4 lbs. $868.00

BENELLI M1 SPORTING SPECIAL AUTO SHOTGUN
Gauge: 12, 3" chamber.
Barrel: 18.5" (Imp. Cyl. Mod., Full choke tubes).
Weight: 6 lbs., 8 oz. **Length:** 39.75" overall.
Stock: Sporting-style polymer with drop adjustment.
Sights: Ghost ring.
Features: Uses Montefeltro inertia recoil bolt system. Matte-finish receiver. Introduced 1993. Imported from Italy by Heckler & Koch, Inc.
Price: $868.00

Benelli Montefeltro Super 90 20-Gauge Shotgun
Similar to the 12-gauge Montefeltro Super 90 except chambered for 3" 20-gauge, 24" or 26" barrel (choke tubes), weighs 5 lbs., 12 oz. Has drop-adjustable walnut stock with gloss finish, blued receiver. Overall length 47.5". Introduced 1993. Imported from Italy by Heckler & Koch, Inc.
Price: $868.00
Price: Limited Edition (26" barrel, special nickel-plated and engraved receiver inlaid with gold) $2,000.00

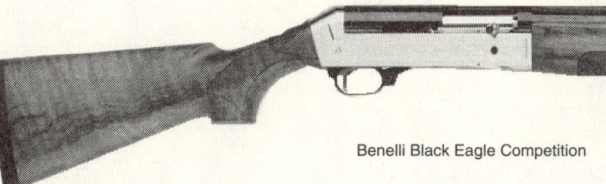

Benelli Black Eagle Competition

BENELLI BLACK EAGLE COMPETITION AUTO SHOTGUN
Gauge: 12, 3" chamber.
Barrel: 26", 28" (Full, Mod., Imp. Cyl., Imp. Mod., Skeet choke tubes). Mid-bead sight.
Weight: 7.1 to 7.6 lbs. **Length:** 49 5/8" overall (26" barrel).
Stock: European walnut with high-gloss finish. Special competition stock comes with drop adjustment kit.
Features: Uses the Montefeltro rotating bolt inertia recoil operating system with a two-piece steel/aluminum etched receiver (bright on lower, blue upper). Drop adjustment kit allows the stock to be custom fitted without modifying the stock. Black lower receiver finish, blued upper. Introduced 1989. Imported from Italy by Heckler & Koch, Inc.
Price: $1,156.00
Price: Limited Edition model (gold inlays, high grade wood, special serial numbers) $2,000.00

Benelli Executive Series Shotguns
Similar to the Black Eagle except has grayed steel lower receiver, hand-engraved and gold inlaid (Type III), and has highest grade of walnut stock with drop adjustment kit. Barrel lengths of 21", 24", 26", 28"; 3" chamber. **Special order only.** Introduced 1995. Imported from Italy by Heckler & Koch Inc.
Price: Type I (about two-thirds engraving coverage) $4,375.00
Price: Type II (full coverage engraving) $5,010.00
Price: Type III (full coverage, gold inlays) $5,800.00

BERETTA A-303 AUTO SHOTGUN
Gauge: 12, 20, 2 3/4" or 3" chamber.
Barrel: 24", 26", 28", 30", Mobilchoke choke tubes.
Weight: About 6 1/2 lbs., 20-gauge; about 7 1/2 lbs., 12-gauge.
Stock: American walnut; hand-checkered grip and forend.
Features: Gas-operated action, alloy receiver, magazine cut-off, push-button safety. Mobilchoke models come with three interchangeable flush-mounted screw-in choke tubes. Imported from Italy by Beretta U.S.A. Introduced 1983.
Price: Mobilchoke, 20-ga. $757.00
Price: 20-ga., Skeet $736.00
Price: A-303 Youth Gun, 20-ga., 3" chamber, 24" barrel $736.00
Price: A-303 Sporting Clays with Mobilchoke, 20 gauge $779.00

Consult our Directory pages for the location of firms mentioned.

Beretta A-303 Upland Model
Similar to the field A-303 except has straight English-style stock, 26" vent. rib barrel with Mobilchoke choke tubes, 3" chamber. Introduced 1989.
Price: $736.00

SHOTGUNS—AUTOLOADERS

Beretta 390 Super Trap

Beretta 390 Super Trap, Super Skeet Shotguns
Similar to the 390 Field except have adjustable-comb stocks that allow height adjustments via interchangeable comb inserts. Rounded recoil pad system allows adjustments for length of pull. Wide ventilated rib with orange front sight. Factory ported barrels in 28" (fixed Skeet), 30", 32" Trap (Mobilchoke tubes). Weight 7 lbs., 10 oz. In 12-gauge only, with 3" chamber. Introduced 1993. Imported from Italy by Beretta U.S.A.

Price: 390 Super Trap $1,256.00
Price: 390 Super Skeet $1,203.00

BERETTA 390 SILVER MALLARD AUTO SHOTGUN
Gauge: 12, 3" chamber.
Barrel: 24", 26", 28", 30", Mobilchoke choke tubes.
Weight: About 7 lbs.
Stock: Select walnut. Adjustable drop and cast.
Features: Gas-operated action with self-compensating valve allows shooting all loads without adjustment. Alloy receiver, reversible safety; chrome-plated bore; floating vent. rib. Matte-finish models for turkey/waterfowl and Deluxe with gold, engraving also available. Slug model available. Introduced 1992. Imported from Italy by Beretta U.S.A.

Price: $779.00
Price: Waterfowl/Turkey (matte finish) $779.00
Price: Gold Mallard $936.00
Price: Slug model $779.00

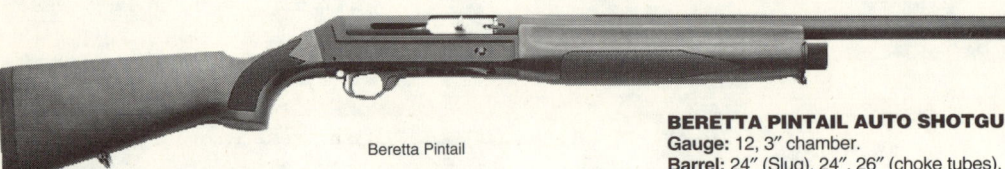

Beretta Pintail

Beretta 390 Sport Trap/Skeet/ Sporting Shotguns
Similar to the 390 Silver Mallard except has lower-contour, rounded receiver. Available with ported barrel. Trap has 30", 32" barrel (Full, Imp. Mod., Mod. choke tubes); Skeet has 26", 28" barrel (fixed Skeet); Sporting has 28", 30" (Full, Mod., Imp. Cyl., Skeet tubes). Introduced 1995. Imported from Italy by Beretta U.S.A.

Price: 390 Sport Trap $821.00
Price: As above, fixed Full choke $807.00
Price: 390 Sport Skeet $779.00
Price: 390 Sport Sporting $807.00
Price: Ported barrel, above models, add about $100.00

BERETTA PINTAIL AUTO SHOTGUN
Gauge: 12, 3" chamber.
Barrel: 24" (Slug), 24", 26" (choke tubes).
Weight: 7 lbs.
Stock: Checkered walnut.
Features: Montefeltro-type short recoil action. Matte finish on wood and metal. Slug version has rifle sights and rifled choke tube. Comes with sling swivels. Introduced 1993. Imported from Italy by Beretta U.S.A.

Price: $700.00

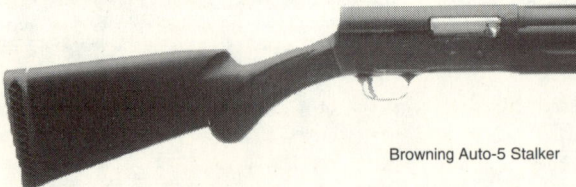

Browning Auto-5 Stalker

Browning Auto-5 Stalker
Similar to the Auto-5 Light and Magnum models except has matte blue metal finish and black graphite-fiberglass stock and forend. Stock is scratch and impact resistant and has checkered panels. Light Stalker has 2 3/4" chamber, 26" or 28" vent. rib barrel with Invector choke tubes, weighs 8 lbs., 1 oz. (26"). Magnum Stalker has 3" chamber, 28" or 30" back-bored vent. rib barrel with Invector choke tubes, weighs 8 lbs., 11 oz. (28"). Introduced 1992.

Price: Light Stalker $799.95
Price: Magnum Stalker $824.95

Browning Auto-5 Magnum 12
Same as standard Auto-5 except chambered for 3" magnum shells (also handles 2 3/4" magnum and 2 3/4" HV loads). 28" Mod., Full; 30" and 32" (Full) bbls. Back-bored barrel comes with Invector choke tubes. 14"x1 5/8"x2 1/2" stock. Recoil pad. Wgt. 8 3/4 lbs.

Price: With back-bored barrel, Invector Plus $824.95
Price: Extra Invector Plus barrel $292.95

BROWNING AUTO-5 LIGHT 12 AND 20
Gauge: 12, 20, 5-shot; 3-shot plug furnished; 2 3/4" or 3" chamber.
Action: Recoil operated autoloader; takedown.
Barrel: 26", 28", 30" Invector (choke tube) barrel; also available with Light 20-ga. 28" (Mod.) or 26" (Imp. Cyl.) barrel.
Weight: 12-, 16-ga. 7 1/4 lbs.; 20-ga. 6 3/8 lbs.
Stock: French walnut, hand checkered half-p.g. and forend. 14 1/4"x1 5/8"x2 1/2".
Features: Receiver hand engraved with scroll designs and border. Double extractors, extra bbls. Interchangeable without factory fitting; mag. cut-off; cross-bolt safety. All models except Buck Special and game guns have back-bored barrels with Invector Plus choke tubes. Imported from Japan by Browning.

Price: Light 12, 20, vent. rib., Invector Plus $799.95
Price: Extra Invector barrel $292.95
Price: Light 12 Buck Special $789.95
Price: 12, 12 magnum barrel $292.95
Price: Light 12, Hunting, Invector Plus $799.95
Price: Buck Special barrel $282.95

Browning Auto-5 Magnum 20
Same as Magnum 12 except 20-gauge, 26" or 28" barrel with Invector Plus choke tubes with back-bored barrels. With ventilated rib, 7 1/2 lbs.

Price: Invector Plus $824.95
Price: Extra Invector barrel $292.95

Browning Gold Auto

BROWNING GOLD AUTO SHOTGUN
Gauge: 12, 20, 3" chamber.
Barrel: 12-ga.—26", 28", 30", Invector Plus choke tubes; 20-ga.—26", 30", Invector choke tubes.
Weight: 7 lbs., 9 oz. (12-ga.), 6 lbs., 12 oz. (20-ga.) **Length:** 46 1/4" overall (20-ga., 26" barrel).
Stock: 14"x1 1/2"x2 1/3"; select walnut with gloss finish; palm swell grip.
Features: Self-regulating, self-cleaning gas system shoots all loads; lightweight receiver with special non-glare deep black finish; large reversible safety button; large rounded trigger guard, gold trigger. The 20-gauge has slightly smaller dimensions; 12-gauge have back-bored barrels, Invector Plus tube system. Introduced 1994. Imported by Browning.

Price: 12- or 20-gauge $699.95
Price: Extra barrels $259.95

424 THE GUN DIGEST   CAUTION: PRICES SHOWN ARE SUPPLIED BY THE MANUFACTURER OR IMPORTER. CHECK YOUR LOCAL GUNSHOP.

SHOTGUNS—AUTOLOADERS

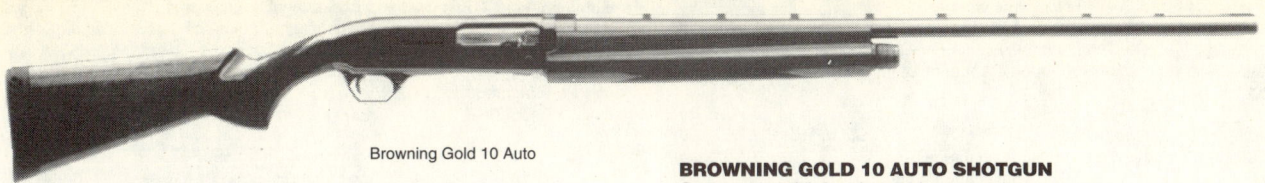

Browning Gold 10 Auto

Browning Gold 10 Stalker Auto Shotgun
Same as the standard Gold 10 except has non-glare metal finish and black graphite-fiberglass composite stock with dull finish and checkering. Introduced 1993. Imported by Browning.
Price: $959.95
Price: Extra barrel $249.95

CHURCHILL TURKEY AUTOMATIC SHOTGUN
Gauge: 12, 3" chamber, 5-shot magazine.
Barrel: 25" (Mod., Full, Extra Full choke tubes).
Weight: 7 lbs. **Length:** NA.

BROWNING GOLD 10 AUTO SHOTGUN
Gauge: 10, 3½" chamber, 5-shot magazine.
Barrel: 26", 28", 30" (Imp. Cyl., Mod., Full standard Invector).
Weight: 10 lbs, 7 oz. (28" barrel).
Stock: 14³⁄₈"x1½"x2³⁄₈". Select walnut with gloss finish, cut checkering, recoil pad.
Features: Short-stroke, gas-operated action, cross-bolt safety. Forged steel receiver with polished blue finish. Introduced 1993. Imported by Browning.
Price: $959.95
Price: Extra barrel $249.95

Stock: Walnut with satin finish, hand checkering.
Features: Gas-operated action, magazine cut-off, non-glare metal finish. Gold-colored trigger. Introduced 1990. Imported by Ellett Bros.
Price: $569.95

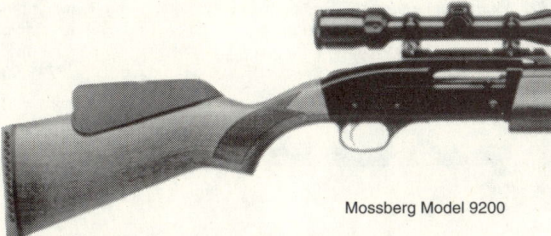

Mossberg Model 9200

Mossberg Model 9200 USST Autoloading Shotgun
Same as the Model 9200 Crown Grade except has "United States Shooting Team" custom engraved receiver. Comes with 26" vent rib barrel with Accu-Choke tubes (including Skeet), cut-checkered walnut-finish stock and forend. Introduced 1993.
Price: $478.00

MOSSBERG MODEL 9200 CROWN GRADE AUTO SHOTGUN
Gauge: 12, 3" chamber.
Barrel: 24" (rifled bore), 24", 28" (Accu-Choke tubes); vent. rib.
Weight: About 7.5 lbs. **Length:** 48" overall (28" bbl.).
Stock: Walnut with high-gloss finish, cut checkering.
Features: Shoots all 2¾" or 3" loads without adjustment. Alloy receiver, ambidextrous top safety. Introduced 1992.
Price: 28", vent rib $478.00
Price: Turkey, 24" vent rib $478.00
Price: Trophy, 24" with scope base, rifled bore, Dual-Comb stock $500.00
Price: 24", rifle sights, rifled bore $478.00

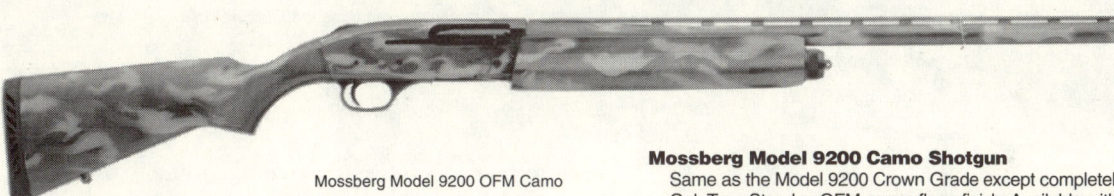

Mossberg Model 9200 OFM Camo

Mossberg Model 9200 NWTF Edition
Same as the Model 9200 Crown Grade except has black matte receiver etched on both sides with turkey scenes; rest of gun has Realtree camo finish. Introduced 1994. From Mossberg.
Price: $562.00

Mossberg Model 9200 Camo Shotgun
Same as the Model 9200 Crown Grade except completely covered with Mossy Oak Tree Stand or OFM camouflage finish. Available with 24" barrel with Accu-Choke tubes. Has synthetic stock and forend. Introduced 1993.
Price: Turkey, 24" vent rib, Mossy Oak finish $562.00
Price: 28" vent rib, Accu-Chokes, OFM camo finish $463.00

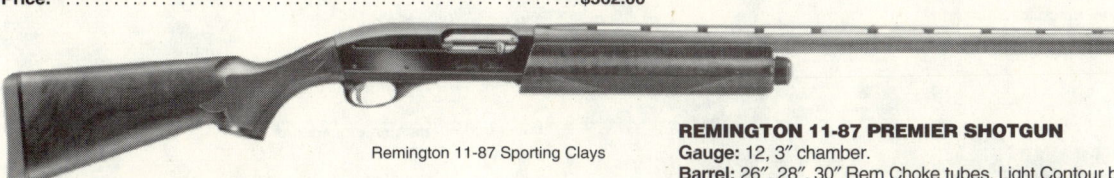

Remington 11-87 Sporting Clays

REMINGTON 11-87 SPORTING CLAYS
Gauge: 12, 2¾" chamber
Barrel: 26", 28", vent. rib, Rem Choke (Skeet, Imp. Cyl., Mod., Full); Light Contour barrel. Medium height rib.
Weight: 7.5 lbs. **Length:** 46.5" overall (26" barrel).
Stock: 14³⁄₁₆"x1½"x2¼". Walnut, with cut checkering; sporting clays butt pad.
Features: Top of receiver, barrel and rib have matte finish; shortened magazine tube and forend; lengthened forcing cone; ivory bead front sight; competition trigger. Special no-wrench choke tubes marked on the outside. Comes in two-barrel fitted hard case. Introduced 1992.
Price: $725.00

Remington 11-87 Premier Skeet
Similar to 11-87 Premier except Skeet dimension stock with cut checkering, satin finish, two-piece buttplate; 26" barrel with Skeet or Rem Chokes (Skeet, Imp. Skeet). Gas system set for 2¾" shells only. Introduced 1987.
Price: $700.00

REMINGTON 11-87 PREMIER SHOTGUN
Gauge: 12, 3" chamber.
Barrel: 26", 28", 30" Rem Choke tubes. Light Contour barrel.
Weight: About 8¼ lbs. **Length:** 46" overall (26" bbl.).
Stock: Walnut with satin or high-gloss finish; cut checkering; solid brown buttpad; no white spacers.
Sights: Bradley-type white-faced front, metal bead middle.
Features: Pressure compensating gas system allows shooting 2¾" or 3" loads interchangeably with no adjustments. Stainless magazine tube; redesigned feed latch, barrel support ring on operating bars; pinned forend. Introduced 1987.
Price: $644.00
Price: Left-hand $692.00
Price: Premier Cantilever Deer Barrel, sling, swivels, Monte Carlo stock .$706.00

Remington 11-87 Premier Trap
Similar to 11-87 Premier except trap dimension stock with straight or Monte Carlo combs; select walnut with satin finish and Tournament-grade cut checkering; 30" barrel with Rem Chokes (Trap Full, Trap Extra Full, Trap Super Full). Gas system set for 2¾" shells only. Introduced 1987.
Price: With Monte Carlo stock $725.00

CAUTION: PRICES SHOWN ARE SUPPLIED BY THE MANUFACTURER OR IMPORTER. CHECK YOUR LOCAL GUNSHOP.

SHOTGUNS—AUTOLOADERS

Remington 11-87 Special Purpose Magnum
Similar to the 11-87 Premier except has dull stock finish, Parkerized exposed metal surfaces. Bolt and carrier have dull blackened coloring. Comes with 26" or 28" barrel with Rem Chokes, padded Cordura nylon sling and q.d. swivels. Introduced 1987.
Price: $625.00
Price: With synthetic stock and forend (SPS) $625.00
Price: Magnum-Turkey with synthetic stock (SPS-T) $639.00

Remington 11-87 Special Purpose Synthetic Camo
Similar to the 11-87 Special Purpose Magnum except has synthetic stock and all metal (except bolt and trigger guard) and stock covered with Mossy Oak Bottomland camo finish. In 12-gauge only, 26", Rem Choke. Comes with camo sling, swivels. Introduced 1992.
Price: $705.00

Remington 11-87 SPS-Deer Shotgun
Similar to the 11-87 Special Purpose Camo except has fully-rifled 21" barrel with rifle sights, black non-reflective, synthetic stock and forend, black carrying sling. Introduced 1993.
Price: $647.00

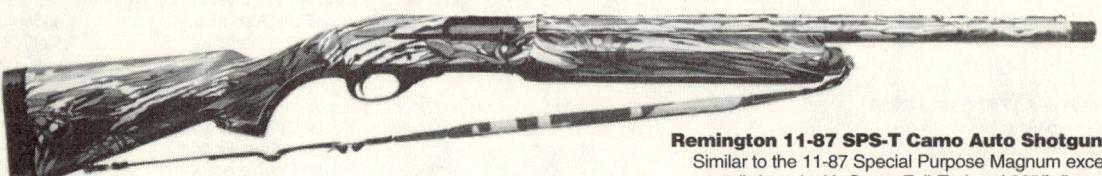
Remington 11-87 SPS-T Camo

Remington 11-87 SPS-T Camo Auto Shotgun
Similar to the 11-87 Special Purpose Magnum except with synthetic stock, 21" vent rib barrel with Super-Full Turkey (.665" diameter with knurled extension) and Imp. Cyl. Rem Choke tubes. Completely covered with Mossy Oak Green Leaf camouflage. Bolt body, trigger guard and recoil pad are non-reflective black. Introduced 1993.
Price: $718.00

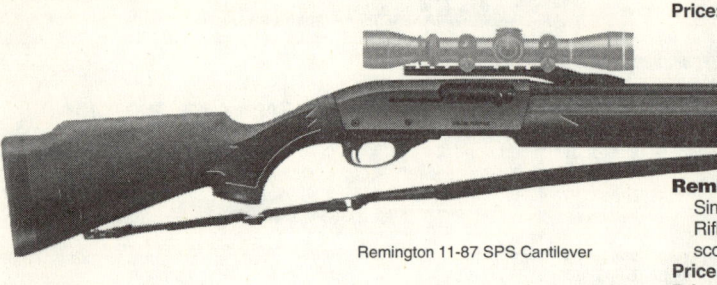
Remington 11-87 SPS Cantilever

Remington 11-87 SPS Cantilever Shotgun
Similar to the 11-87 SPS except has smoothbore barrel with Imp. Cyl. and 3½" Rifled Rem Choke tubes; synthetic stock with Monte Carlo comb; cantilever scope mount deer barrel. Comes with sling and swivels. Introduced 1994.
Price: $706.00
Price: With Rem Chokes $665.00

Remington SP-10 Magnum-Camo

Remington SP-10 Magnum-Camo Auto Shotgun
Similar to the SP-10 Magnum except buttstock, forend, receiver, barrel and magazine cap are covered with Mossy Oak Bottomland camo finish; bolt body and trigger guard have matte black finish. Comes with Extra-Full Turkey Rem Choke tube, 23" vent rib barrel with mid-rib bead and Bradley-style front sight, swivel studs and quick-detachable swivels, and a non-slip Cordura carrying sling in the same camo pattern. Introduced 1993.
Price: $1,078.00

REMINGTON SP-10 MAGNUM AUTO SHOTGUN
Gauge: 10, 3½" chamber, 3-shot magazine.
Barrel: 26", 30" (Full and Mod. Rem Chokes).
Weight: 11 to 11¼ lbs. **Length:** 47½" overall (26" barrel).
Stock: Walnut with satin finish. Checkered grip and forend.
Sights: Metal bead front.
Features: Stainless steel gas system with moving cylinder; 3/8" ventilated rib. Receiver and barrel have matte finish. Brown recoil pad. Comes with padded Cordura nylon sling. Introduced 1989.
Price: $993.00

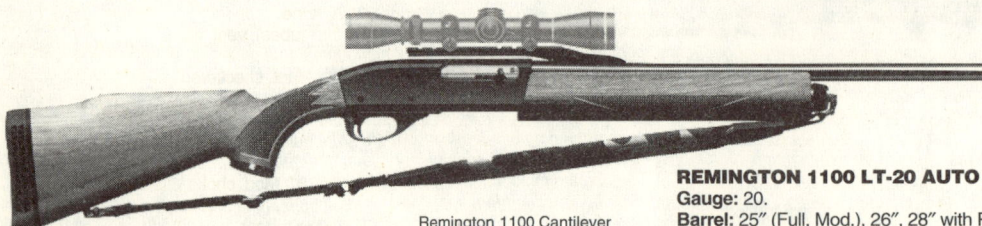
Remington 1100 Cantilever

Remington 1100 Cantilever 20-Gauge Deer
Similar to the 1100 LT-20 except comes with cantilever scope mount, fully rifled 21" slug barrel. Walnut stock and forend. Comes with sling and swivels. Introduced 1994.
Price: $682.00

Remington 1100 Special Field
Similar to Standard Model 1100 except 12- and 20-ga. only, comes with 23" Rem Choke barrel. LT-20 version 6½ lbs.; has straight-grip stock, shorter forend, both with cut checkering. Comes with vent. rib only; matte finish receiver without engraving. Introduced 1983.
Price: 12- and 20-ga., 23" Rem Choke, about $605.00

REMINGTON 1100 LT-20 AUTO
Gauge: 20.
Barrel: 25" (Full, Mod.), 26", 28" with Rem Chokes.
Weight: 7½ lbs.
Stock: 14"x1½"x2½". American walnut, checkered p.g. and forend.
Features: Quickly interchangeable barrels. Matted receiver top with scroll work on both sides of receiver. Cross-bolt safety.
Price: With Rem Chokes, 20-ga. about $605.00
Price: Youth Gun LT-20 (21" Rem Choke) $605.00
Price: 20-ga., 3" magnum $605.00

Remington 1100 20-Gauge Deer Gun
Same as 1100 except 20-ga. only, 21" barrel (Imp. Cyl.), rifle sights adjustable for windage and elevation; recoil pad with white spacer. Weight 7¼ lbs.
Price: About $565.00

SHOTGUNS—SLIDE ACTIONS

Includes a wide variety of sporting guns and guns suitable for competitive shooting.

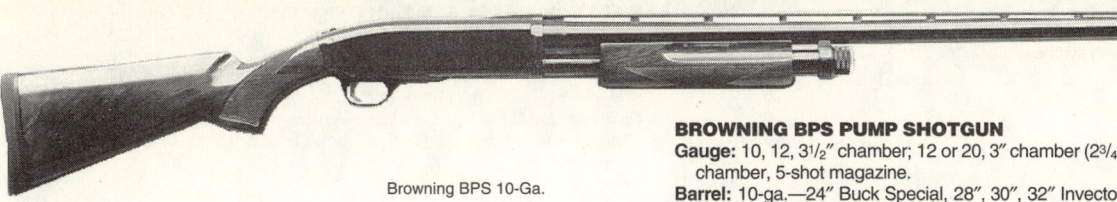

Browning BPS 10-Ga.

Browning BPS Game Gun Turkey Special
Similar to the standard BPS except has satin-finished walnut stock and dull-finished barrel and receiver. Receiver is drilled and tapped for scope mounting. Rifle-style stock dimensions and swivel studs. Has Extra-Full Turkey choke tube. Introduced 1992.
Price: $544.95

Browning BPS Pigeon Grade Pump Shotgun
Same as the standard BPS except has select high grade walnut stock and forend, and gold-trimmed receiver. Available in 12-gauge only with 26" or 28" vent. rib barrels. Introduced 1992.
Price: $679.95
Price: 10-gauge Waterfowl Model $819.95

BROWNING BPS PUMP SHOTGUN
Gauge: 10, 12, 3½" chamber; 12 or 20, 3" chamber (2¾" in target guns), 28, 2¾" chamber, 5-shot magazine.
Barrel: 10-ga.—24" Buck Special, 28", 30", 32" Invector; 12-, 20- ga.—22", 24", 26", 28", 30", 32" (Imp. Cyl., Mod. or Full). Also available with Invector choke tubes, 12- or 20-ga.; Upland Special has 22" barrel with Invector tubes. BPS 3" and 3½" have back-bored barrel.
Weight: 7 lbs. 8 oz. (28" barrel). **Length:** 48¾" overall (28" barrel).
Stock: 14¼"x1½"x2½". Select walnut, semi-beavertail forend, full p.g. stock.
Features: All 12-gauge 3" guns except Buck Special and game guns have back-bored barrels with Invector Plus choke tubes. Bottom feeding and ejection, receiver top safety, high post vent. rib. Double action bars eliminate binding. Vent. rib barrels only. All 12- and 20-gauge guns with 3" chamber available with fully engraved receiver flats at no extra cost. Each gsuge has its own unique game scene. Introduced 1977. Imported from Japan by Browning.
Price: 10-ga., Hunting, Invector $639.95
Price: 12-ga., 3½" Mag., Hunting, Invector Plus $639.95
Price: 12-, 20-ga., Hunting, Invector Plus $509.95
Price: 12-, 20-ga., Upland Special, Invector Plus $509.95
Price: 10-ga. Buck Special $644.95
Price: 12-ga. Buck Special $494.95
Price: 28-ga., Hunting, Invector $509.95

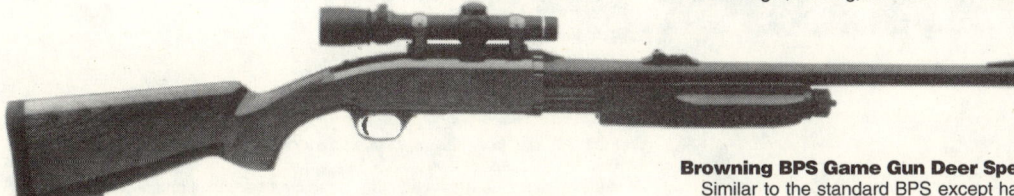

Browning BPS Game Deer

Browning BPS Stalker Pump Shotgun
Same gun as the standard BPS except all exposed metal parts have a matte blued finish and the stock has a durable black finish with a black recoil pad. Available in 10-ga. (3½") and 12-ga. with 3" or 3½" chamber, 22", 28", 30" barrel with Invector choke system. Introduced 1987.
Price: 12-ga., 3" chamber, Invector Plus $509.95
Price: 10-, 12-ga., 3½" chamber $639.95

Browning BPS Game Gun Deer Special
Similar to the standard BPS except has newly designed receiver/magazine tube/barrel mounting system to eliminate play, heavy 20.5" barrel with rifle-type sights with adjustable rear, solid receiver scope mount, "rifle" stock dimensions for scope or open sights, sling swivel studs. Gloss or matte finished wood with checkering, polished blue metal. Introduced 1992.
Price: $574.95

Browning BPS Pump Shotgun Ladies and Youth Model
Same as BPS Upland Special except 20-ga. only, 22" Invector barrel, stock has pistol grip with recoil pad. Length of pull is 13¼". Introduced 1986.
Price: $509.95

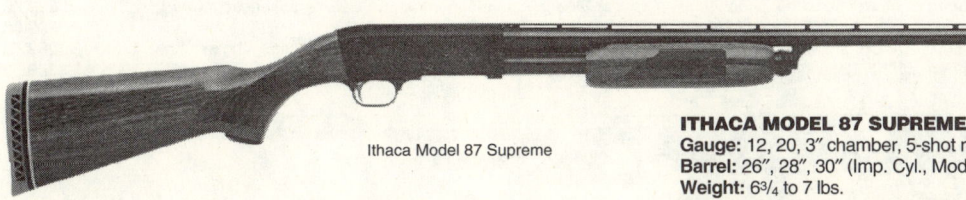

Ithaca Model 87 Supreme

Ithaca Deerslayer II Rifled Shotgun
Similar to the Deerslayer except has rifled 25" barrel and checkered American walnut stock and forend with high-gloss finish and Monte Carlo comb. Solid frame construction. Introduced 1988.
Price: 12 or 20 ....$566.50

ITHACA MODEL 87 DEERSLAYER SHOTGUN
Gauge: 12, 20, 3" chamber.
Barrel: 20", 25" (Special Bore), or rifled bore.
Weight: 6 to 6¾ lbs.
Stock: 14"x1½"x2¼". American walnut. Checkered p.g. and slide handle.
Sights: Raybar blade front on ramp, rear adjustable for windage and elevation, and grooved for scope mounting.
Features: Bored for slug shooting. Bottom ejection, cross-bolt safety. Reintroduced 1988. From Ithaca Acquisition Corp.
Price: $464.75
Price: Deluxe $498.25
Price: Field Deerslayer, Basic $424.50
Price: Smooth Bore Basic $424.50
Price: Smooth Bore Deluxe $464.75

ITHACA MODEL 87 SUPREME PUMP SHOTGUN
Gauge: 12, 20, 3" chamber, 5-shot magazine.
Barrel: 26", 28", 30" (Imp. Cyl., Mod., Full tubes); vent. rib.
Weight: 6¾ to 7 lbs.
Stock: 14"x1½"x2¼". Full fancy-grade walnut, checkered p.g. and slide handle.
Sights: Raybar front.
Features: Bottom ejection, cross-bolt safety. Polished and blued engraved receiver. Reintroduced 1988. From Ithaca Acquisition Corp.
Price: $808.50
Price: M87 green or brown Camo Vent. (28", Mod. choke tube, camouflage finish) $542.00
Price: M87 English (20-ga., 24", 26", choke tubes) $545.50

Ithaca Model 87 Deluxe Pump Shotgun
Similar to the Model 87 Supreme Vent. Rib except comes with three choke tubes in 26", 28", 30". Standard-grade walnut.
Price: $533.25

Ithaca Model 87 Turkey Gun
Similar to the Model 87 Supreme except comes with 22" or 24" (fixed Full or Full choke tube) barrel, either Camoseal camouflage or matte blue finish, oiled wood, blued trigger.
Price: With fixed choke, blue $465.75
Price: With choke tube, blue $508.25
Price: With fixed choke, green camo $508.25
Price: With choke tube, green camo $550.75

SHOTGUNS—SLIDE ACTIONS

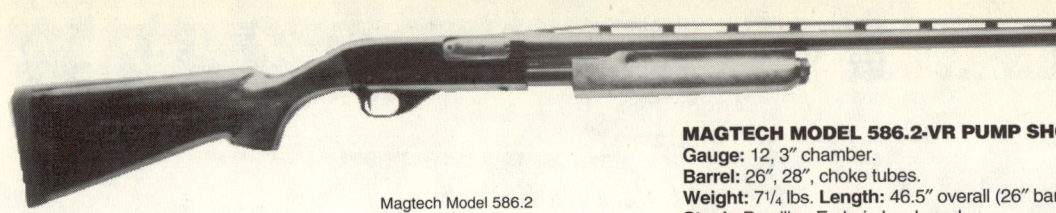

Magtech Model 586.2

MAGTECH MODEL 586.2-VR PUMP SHOTGUN
Gauge: 12, 3" chamber.
Barrel: 26", 28", choke tubes.
Weight: 7¼ lbs. **Length:** 46.5" overall (26" barrel).
Stock: Brazilian Embuia hardwood.
Features: Double action slide bars. Ventilated rib with bead front sight. Polished blue finish. Introduced 1995. Imported from Brazil by Magtech Recreational Products.
Price: About $255.00

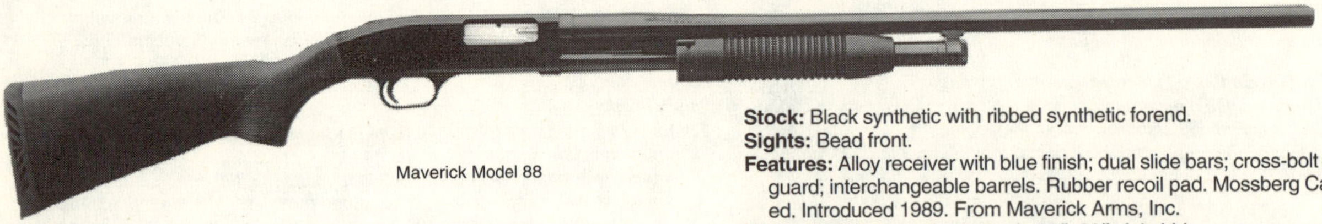

Maverick Model 88

MAVERICK MODEL 88 PUMP SHOTGUN
Gauge: 12, 3" chamber.
Barrel: 18½" (Cyl.), 28" (Mod.), plain or vent. rib; 30" (Full), plain or vent. rib.
Weight: 7¼ lbs. **Length:** 48" overall with 28" bbl.
Stock: Black synthetic with ribbed synthetic forend.
Sights: Bead front.
Features: Alloy receiver with blue finish; dual slide bars; cross-bolt safety in trigger guard; interchangeable barrels. Rubber recoil pad. Mossberg Cablelock included. Introduced 1989. From Maverick Arms, Inc.
Price: Model 88, synthetic stock, 28", 30" plain bbl. $230.00
Price: Model 88, synthetic stock, 28", 30" vent. rib $241.00
Price: Model 88, synthetic stock, 24" with rifle sights $247.00
Price: Model 88, synthetic stock, Combo 18½", 28" plain bbl. $275.00
Price: Model 88, synthetic stock, Combo 18½" (plain), 28" (vent. rib) . . . $284.00
Price: Model 88, synthetic stock, 28" vent. rib, ACCU-TUBE set $293.00

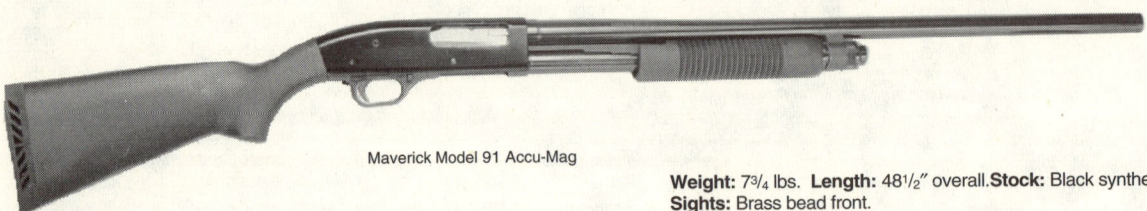

Maverick Model 91 Accu-Mag

MAVERICK MODEL 91 ACCU-MAG PUMP SHOTGUN
Gauge: 12, 3½" chamber.
Barrel: 28" (ACCU-MAG Mod. tube); vent. rib.
Weight: 7¾ lbs. **Length:** 48½" overall. **Stock:** Black synthetic.
Sights: Brass bead front.
Features: Dual slide bars; cross-bolt safety; rubber recoil pad. Accessories interchangeable with Mossberg Model 835. Cablelock included. Introduced 1993. From Mossberg.
Price: $271.00

MITCHELL HIGH STANDARD PUMP SHOTGUNS
Gauge: 12, 2¾" chamber.
Barrel: 18½", 20" (Imp. Cyl., Mod., Full choke tubes or fixed Cyl.).
Weight: 7½ lbs.
Stock: Walnut-finished hardwood.
Features: Fixed barrel with steel receiver, polished blue finish. Introduced 1994. Imported from the Philippines by Mitchell Arms.
Price: Model 9104, 6-shot, 20", wood stock, bead sight, fixed choke $279.00
Price: Model 9105, as above with rifle sights $299.00
Price: Model 9108-B, 9108-BL, 8-shot, bead sight, black or brown stock . $279.00
Price: Model 9108-HG-B, 9108-HG-BL, as above with handgrip $299.00
Price: Model 9109, 8-shot, 20", rifle sights $299.00
Price: Model 9111-B, 9111-BL, 7-shot, 18½", bead sight, black or brown handgrip $299.00
Price: Model 9113-B, 7-shot, 18½", rifle sights, brown stock $299.00
Price: Model 9114-PG, 7-shot, 18½", pistol grip $349.00
Price: Model 9115, 9115-HG, as above with SAS stock, handgrip $349.00
Price: Model 9104-CT, 6-shot, 20", bead sight, choke tubes $299.00
Price: Model 9108-CT, as above, 8-shot $299.00
Price: Model 9111-CT, 7-shot, 18½", bead sight, choke tubes $299.00
Price: Model 9115-CT, as above with SAS stock $369.00

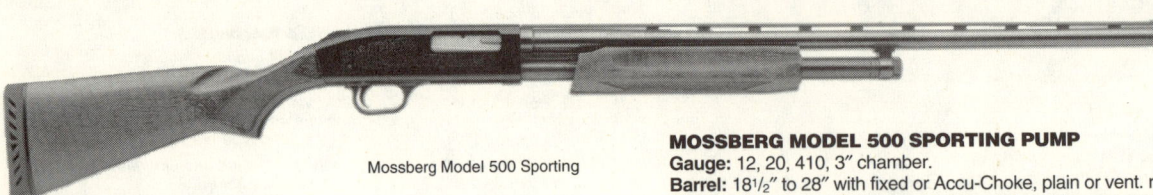

Mossberg Model 500 Sporting

Mossberg Model 500 Bantam Pump
Same as the Model 500 Sporting Pump except 20-gauge only, 22" vent. rib Accu-Choke barrel with Mod. choke tube; has 1" shorter stock, reduced length from pistol grip to trigger, reduced forend reach. Introduced 1992.
Price: $281.00

Mossberg Turkey Model 500 Pump
Same as the Model 500 Sporting Pump except has overall OFM camo finish, Ghost-Ring sights, Accu-Choke barrel with Imp. Cyl., Mod., Full, Extra-Full lead shot choke tubes, 24" barrel, swivel studs, camo sling. Introduced 1992.
Price: $384.00

Mossberg Model 500 Muzzleloader Combo
Same as the Model 500 Sporting Pump except comes with 24" rifled bore, rifle-sighted Slugster barrel and 24" fully rifled 50-caliber muzzle-loading barrel and ramrod. Uses #209 standard primer. Introduced 1992.
Price: $457.00

MOSSBERG MODEL 500 SPORTING PUMP
Gauge: 12, 20, 410, 3" chamber.
Barrel: 18½" to 28" with fixed or Accu-Choke, plain or vent. rib.
Weight: 6¼ lbs. (410), 7¼ lbs. (12). **Length:** 48" overall (28" barrel).
Stock: 14"x1½"x2½". Walnut-stained hardwood. Cut-checkered grip and forend.
Sights: White bead front, brass mid-bead.
Features: Ambidextrous thumb safety, twin extractors, disconnecting safety, dual action bars. Quiet Carry forend. Mossberg Cablelock included. From Mossberg.
Price: From about $281.00
Price: Sporting Combos (field barrel and Slugster barrel), from $312.00

Mossberg Model 500 Camo Pump
Same as the Model 500 Sporting Pump except 12-gauge only and entire gun is covered with special camouflage finish. Receiver drilled and tapped for scope mounting. Comes with q.d. swivel studs, swivels, camouflage sling, Mossberg Cablelock.
Price: From about $296.00
Price: Camo Combo (as above with extra Slugster barrel), from about . . $415.00

SHOTGUNS—SLIDE ACTIONS

Mossberg Model 500 Trophy Slugster

MOSSBERG MODEL 500 TROPHY SLUGSTER
Gauge: 12, 3" chamber.
Barrel: 24", rifled bore. Integral scope mount.
Weight: 7¼ lbs. **Length:** 44" overall.
Stock: 14" pull, 1⅜" drop at heel. Walnut; Dual Comb design for proper eye positioning with or without scoped barrels. Recoil pad and swivel studs.
Features: Ambidextrous thumb safety, twin extractors, dual slide bars. Comes with scope mount. Mossberg Cablelock included. Introduced 1988.
Price: Rifled bore, with scope mount $354.00
Price: Cyl. bore, rifle sights $288.00
Price: Rifled bore, rifle sights $326.00
Price: With Marinecoat finish $415.00

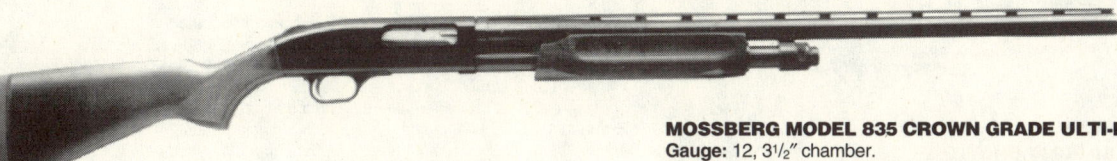

Mossberg Model 835 Crown Grade

MOSSBERG MODEL 835 CROWN GRADE ULTI-MAG PUMP
Gauge: 12, 3½" chamber.
Barrel: 24" rifled bore, 24", 28", Accu-Mag with four choke tubes for steel or lead shot.
Weight: 7¾ lbs. **Length:** 48½" overall.
Stock: 14"x1½"x2½". Dual Comb. Cut-checkered walnut or camo synthetic; both have recoil pad.
Sights: White bead front, brass mid-bead.
Features: Shoots 2¾", 3" or 3½" shells. Backbored barrel to reduce recoil, improve patterns. Ambidextrous thumb safety, twin extractors, dual slide bars. Mossberg Cablelock included. Introduced 1988.
Price: 28" vent rib, Dual-Comb stock $412.00
Price: As above, standard stock $404.00
Price: 24" Trophy Slugster, rifled bore, scope base, Dual-Comb stock ..$434.00
Price: Combo, 24" rifled bore, rifle sights, 28" vent rib, Accu-Mag choke tubes, Dual-Comb stock $476.00
Price: Combo, 24" Trophy Slugster rifled bore, 28" vent rib, Accu-Mag choke tubes, Dual-Comb stock $487.00
Price: Realtree or Mossy Oak Camo Turkey, 24" vent rib, Accu-Mag Extra-Full tube, synthetic stock $482.00
Price: Realtree Camo, 28" vent rib, Accu-Mag tubes, synthetic stock ...$482.00
Price: Realtree Camo Combo, 24" rifled bore, rifle sights, 24" vent rib, Accu-Mag choke tubes, synthetic stock, hard case $590.00
Price: OFM Camo, 28" vent rib, Accu-Mag tubes, synthetic stock $441.00
Price: OFM Camo Combo, 24" rifled bore, rifle sights, 28" vent rib, Accu-Mag tubes, synthetic stock $515.00

CONSULT Shooter's MARKETPLACE Page 266, This Issue

Mossberg American Field Model 835 Pump Shotgun
Same as the Model 835 Crown Grade except has walnut-stained hardwood stock and comes only with Modified choke tube, 28" barrel. Introduced 1992.
Price: $310.00

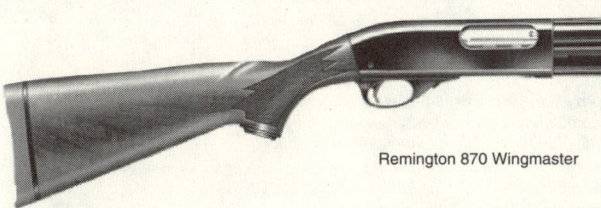

Remington 870 Wingmaster

Remington 870 Express
Similar to the 870 Wingmaster except has a walnut-toned hardwood stock with solid, black recoil pad and pressed checkering on grip and forend. Outside metal surfaces have a black oxide finish. Comes with 26" or 28" vent. rib barrel with a Mod. Rem Choke tube. Introduced 1987.
Price: 12 or 20 ....$292.00
Price: Express Combo (with extra 20" Deer barrel), 12 or 20 ....$395.00
Price: Express 20-ga., 28" with Mod. Rem Choke tubes $292.00

Remington 870 Express Rifle-Sighted Deer Gun
Same as the Model 870 Express except comes with 20" barrel with fixed Imp. Cyl. choke, open iron sights, Monte Carlo stock. Introduced 1991.
Price: $287.00
Price: With fully rifled barrel $325.00

Remington 870 Express Turkey
Same as the Model 870 Express except comes with 3" chamber, 21" vent. rib turkey barrel and Extra-Full Rem Choke Turkey tube; 12-ga. only. Introduced 1991.
Price: $305.00

REMINGTON 870 WINGMASTER
Gauge: 12, 3" chamber.
Barrel: 26", 28", 30" (Rem Chokes). Light Contour barrel.
Weight: 7¼ lbs. **Length:** 46½" overall (26" bbl.).
Stock: 14"x2½"x1". American walnut with satin or high-gloss finish, cut-checkered p.g. and forend. Rubber buttpad.
Sights: Ivory bead front, metal mid-bead.
Features: Double action bars; cross-bolt safety; blue finish. Available in right- or left-hand style. Introduced 1986.
Price: $479.00
Price: LW-20 20-ga., vent. rib, 26", 28" (Rem Choke) $473.00
Price: Fully rifled Cantilever, 20" $556.00
Price: As above, 20-ga. $556.00

Remington 870 Marine Magnum
Similar to the 870 Wingmaster except all metal is plated with electroless nickel and has black synthetic stock and forend. Has 18" plain barrel (Cyl.), bead front sight, 7-shot magazine. Introduced 1992.
Price: $489.00

Remington Model 870 Express Youth Gun
Same as the Model 870 Express except comes with 12½" length of pull, 21" barrel with Mod. Rem Choke tube. Hardwood stock with low-luster finish. Introduced 1991.
Price: 20-ga. Express Youth (1" shorter stock) $292.00
Price: 20-ga. Express Youth Deer (rifle sights, fully rifled barrel) $325.00

CAUTION: PRICES SHOWN ARE SUPPLIED BY THE MANUFACTURER OR IMPORTER. CHECK YOUR LOCAL GUN SHOP.

SHOTGUNS—SLIDE ACTIONS

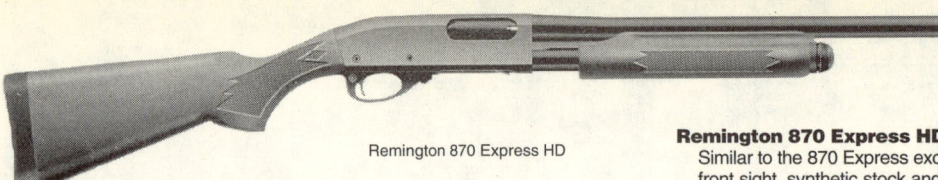

Remington 870 Express HD

Remington 870 Express HD
Similar to the 870 Express except in 12-gauge only, 18″ (Cyl.) barrel with bead front sight, synthetic stock and forend with non-reflective black finish and positive checkering. Introduced 1995.
Price: $292.00

Remington 870 Express Synthetic
Similar to the 870 Express with 26″, 28″ barrel except has synthetic stock and forend. Introduced 1994.
Price: $299.00

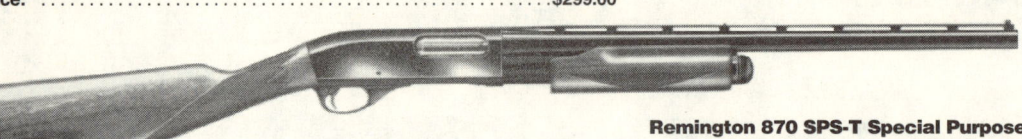

Remington 870 Special Field

Remington 870 SPS-T Special Purpose Magnum
Similar to the Model 870 except chambered only for 12-ga., 3″ shells, 26″ or 28″ Rem Choke barrel. All exposed metal surfaces are finished in dull, non-reflective black. Black synthetic stock and forend. Comes with padded Cordura 2″ wide sling, quick-detachable swivels. Chrome-lined bores. Dark recoil pad. Introduced 1985.
Price: $399.00

Remington 870 Special Field
Similar to the standard Model 870 except comes with 23″ barrel only, 3″ chamber, choked Imp. Cyl., Mod., Full and Rem Choke; 12-ga. weighs 6 3/4 lbs., LW-20 weighs 6 lbs.; has straight-grip stock, shorter forend, both with cut checkering. Vent. rib barrel only. Introduced 1984.
Price: 12- or 20-ga., Rem Choke, about $473.00

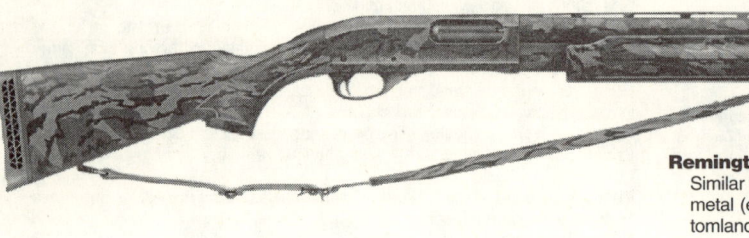

Remington 870 SPS Camo

Remington 870 Special Purpose Synthetic Camo
Similar to the 870 Special Purpose Magnum except has synthetic stock and all metal (except bolt and trigger guard) and stock covered with Mossy Oak Bottomland camo finish, In 12-gauge only, 26″ vent. rib, Rem Choke. Comes with camo sling, swivels. Introduced 1992.
Price: $465.00

Remington 870 SPS-Deer Shotgun
Has fully-rifled 20″ barrel with rifle sights, black non-reflective, synthetic stock and forend, black carrying sling. Introduced 1993.
Price: $407.00

Remington 870 SPS Cantilever Shotgun
Similar to the 870 SPS-Deer except has smoothbore barrel with Imp. Cyl. and 3 1/2″ Rifled Rem Choke tubes; synthetic stock with Monte Carlo comb; cantilever scope mount deer barrel. Comes with sling and swivels. Introduced 1994.
Price: $425.00
Price: With fully rifled barrel $467.00

Remington 870 SPS-T Camo Pump Shotgun
Similar to the 870 Special Purpose Magnum except with synthetic stock, 21″ vent rib barrel with Super-Full Turkey (.665″ diameter with knurled extension) and Imp. Cyl. Rem Choke tubes. Completely covered with Mossy Oak Green Leaf camouflage. Bolt body, trigger guard and recoil pad are non-reflective black. Introduced 1993.
Price: $479.00

Remington 870 High Grades
Same as 870 except better walnut, hand checkering. Engraved receiver and barrel. Vent. rib. Stock dimensions to order.
Price: 870D, about $2,610.00
Price: 870F, about $5,377.00
Price: 870F with gold inlay, about $8,062.00

Remington 870 Wingmaster Small Gauges
Same as the standard Model 870 Wingmaster except chambered for 20-ga. (2 3/4″ and 3″), 28-ga., and 410-bore. The 20-ga. available with 26″, 28″ vent. rib barrel with Rem Choke tubes, high-gloss or satin wood finish; 28 and 410 available with 25″ Full or Mod. fixed choke, satin finish only.
Price: 20-ga. $473.00

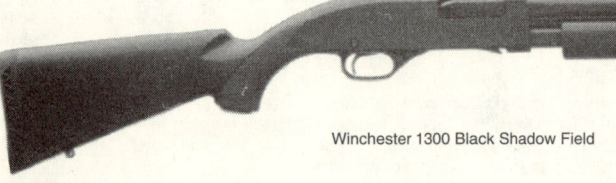

Winchester 1300 Black Shadow Field

WINCHESTER MODEL 1300 WALNUT PUMP
Gauge: 12 and 20, 3″ chamber, 5-shot capacity.
Barrel: 26″, 28″, vent. rib, with Full, Mod., Imp. Cyl. Winchoke tubes.
Weight: 6 3/8 lbs. **Length:** 42 5/8″ overall.
Stock: American walnut, with deep cut checkering on pistol grip, traditional ribbed forend; high luster finish.
Sights: Metal bead front.
Features: Twin action slide bars; front-locking rotary bolt; roll-engraved receiver; blued, highly polished metal; cross-bolt safety with red indicator. Introduced 1984. From U.S. Repeating Arms Co., Inc.
Price: $340.00
Price: Model 1300 Ladies/Youth, 20-ga., 22″ vent. rib $309.00

Winchester Model 1300 Black Shadow Field Gun
Similar to the Model 1300 Walnut except has black composite stock and forend, matte black finish. Have vent rib 26″ or 28″ barrel, 3″ chamber, comes with Mod. Winchoke tube. Introduced 1995. From U.S. Repeating Arms Co.
Price: $296.00

SHOTGUNS—SLIDE ACTIONS

Winchester 1300 Realtree Turkey

Winchester Model 1300 Black Shadow Deer Gun
Similar to the Model 1300 Black Shadow Turkey Gun except has ramp-type front sight, fully adjustable rear, drilled and tapped for scope mounting. Black composite stock and forend, matte black metal. Smoothbore 22″ barrel with one Imp. Cyl. WinChoke tube; 12-gauge only, 3″ chamber. Weighs 7 1/4 lbs. Introduced 1994. From U.S. Repeating Arms Co., Inc.
Price: $296.00

> Consult our Directory pages for the location of firms mentioned.

Winchester Model 1300 Realtree® Turkey Gun
Similar to the standard Model 1300 except has synthetic Realtree® camo stock and forend, matte finished barrel and receiver, 22″ barrel with Extra Full, Full and Mod. WinChoke tubes. Drilled and tapped for scope mounting. Comes with padded, adjustable sling. In 12-gauge only, 3″ chamber; weight about 7 lbs. Introduced 1994. From U.S. Repeating Arms Co., Inc.
Price: $370.00
Price: With full coverage All-Purpose Realtree® camo $432.00

Winchester Model 1300 Black Shadow Turkey Gun
Similar to the Model 1300 Realtree® Turkey except synthetic stock and forend are matte black, and all metal surfaces finished matte black. Drilled and tapped for scope mounting. In 12-gauge only, 3″ chamber, 22″ vent. rib barrel; comes with one Full WinChoke tube. Introduced 1994. From U.S. Repeating Arms Co., Inc.
Price: $296.00

Winchester 1300 Advantage

Winchester 1300 Slug Hunter Deer

Winchester 1300 Ranger

Winchester Model 1300 Advantage Camo Deer Gun
Similar to the Model 1300 Black Shadow Deer Gun except has full coverage Advantage camouflage. Has 22″ rifled or smoothbore barrel, padded camouflage sling, swivels and swivel posts, rifle sights. Receiver drilled and tapped for scope mounting. Introduced 1995. From U.S. Repeating Arms Co.
Price: Rifled bore $432.00
Price: Smoothbore $410.00

Winchester Model 1300 Slug Hunter Deer Gun
Same as the Model 1300 except has rifled 22″ barrel, walnut stock, rifle-type sights. Introduced 1990.
Price: Walnut stock $404.00

WINCHESTER MODEL 1300 RANGER PUMP GUN
Gauge: 12 or 20, 3″ chamber, 5-shot magazine.
Barrel: 26″, 28″ vent. rib with Full, Mod., Imp. Cyl. Winchoke tubes.
Weight: 7 to 7 1/4 lbs.
Length: 48 5/8″ to 50 5/8″ overall.
Stock: Walnut-finished hardwood with ribbed forend.
Sights: Metal bead front.
Features: Cross-bolt safety, black rubber recoil pad, twin action slide bars, front-locking rotating bolt. From U.S. Repeating Arms Co., Inc.
Price: Vent. rib barrel, Winchoke $309.00

Winchester Model 1300 Ranger Pump Gun Combo & Deer Gun
Similar to the standard Ranger except comes with two barrels: 22″ (Cyl.) deer barrel with rifle-type sights and an interchangeable 28″ vent. rib Winchoke barrel with Full, Mod. and Imp. Cyl. choke tubes. Drilled and tapped; comes with rings and bases. Available in 12- and 20-gauge 3″ only, with recoil pad. Introduced 1983.
Price: Deer Combo with two barrels $379.00
Price: 12-ga., 22″ rifled barrel $343.00
Price: 12-ga., 22″ (Imp. Cyl., rifled sabot tubes) $404.00
Price: Combo 12-ga. with 18″ (Cyl.) and 28″ (Mod. tube) ...$393.00
Price: Rifled Deer Combo (22″ rifled and 28″ vent. rib barrels, 12 or 20-ga.) $404.00

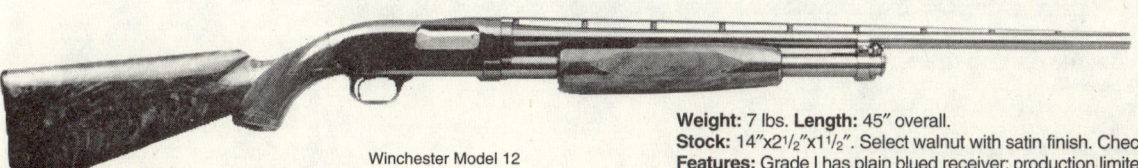
Winchester Model 12

WINCHESTER MODEL 12 PUMP SHOTGUN
Gauge: 20, 2 3/4″ chamber, 5-shot magazine.
Barrel: 26″ (Imp. Cyl.). Vent. rib.
Weight: 7 lbs. **Length:** 45″ overall.
Stock: 14″x2 1/2″x1 1/2″. Select walnut with satin finish. Checkered grip and forend.
Features: Grade I has plain blued receiver; production limited to 4000 guns. Grade IV receiver has engraved game scenes and gold highlights identical to traditional Grade IV, and is limited to 1000 guns. Introduced 1993. From U.S. Repeating Arms Co.
Price: Grade I $879.00
Price: Grade IV $1,431.00

CAUTION: PRICES SHOWN ARE SUPPLIED BY THE MANUFACTURER OR IMPORTER. CHECK YOUR LOCAL GUN SHOP.

SHOTGUNS—OVER/UNDERS

Includes a variety of game guns and guns for competitive shooting.

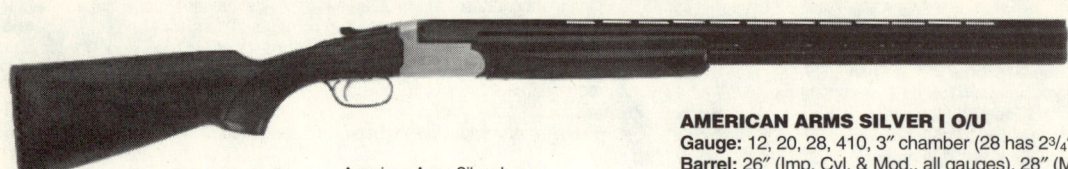
American Arms Silver I

AMERICAN ARMS SILVER I O/U
Gauge: 12, 20, 28, 410, 3" chamber (28 has 2 3/4").
Barrel: 26" (Imp. Cyl. & Mod., all gauges), 28" (Mod. & Full, 12, 20).
Weight: About 6 3/4 lbs.
Stock: 14 1/8"x1 3/8"x2 3/8". Checkered walnut.
Sights: Metal bead front.
Features: Boxlock action with scroll engraving, silver finish. Single selective trigger, extractors. Chrome-lined barrels. Manual safety. Rubber recoil pad. Introduced 1987. Imported from Italy by American Arms, Inc.
Price: 12- or 20-gauge $593.00
Price: 28 or 410 ....$658.00

American Arms Silver II Lite
Similar to the Silver II except weighs 6 lbs., 4 oz. (12-gauge), 5 lbs., 12 oz. (20-gauge), 6 lbs. (28-gauge). Single selective trigger, automatic selective ejectors. Franchoke tubes on 12- and 20-gauge. Vent. rib, engraved frame with antique silver finish. Introduced 1994. Imported by American Arms, Inc.
Price: 12-, 20-ga., 3" chambers, 26" $984.00

AMERICAN ARMS SILVER SPORTING O/U
Gauge: 12, 2 3/4" chambers.
Barrel: 28", 30" (Skeet, Imp. Cyl., Mod., Full choke tubes).
Weight: 7 3/8 lbs. **Length:** 45 1/2" overall.
Stock: 14 3/8"x1 1/2"x2 3/8". Figured walnut, cut checkering; Sporting Clays quick-mount buttpad.
Sights: Target bead front.
Features: Boxlock action with single selective mechanical trigger, automatic selective ejectors; special broadway channeled rib; vented barrel rib; chrome bores. Chrome-nickel finish on frame, with engraving. Introduced 1990. Imported from Italy by American Arms, Inc.
Price: $937.00

American Arms Silver II Shotgun
Similar to the Silver I except 26" barrel (Imp. Cyl., Mod., Full choke tubes, 12- and 20-ga.), 28" (Imp. Cyl., Mod., Full choke tubes, 12-ga. only), 26" (Imp. Cyl. & Mod. fixed chokes, 28 and 410), 26" two-barrel set (Imp. Cyl. & Mod., fixed, 28 and 410); automatic selective ejectors. Weight is about 6 lbs., 15 oz. (12-ga., 26").
Price: $748.00
Price: 28, 410 ....$765.00

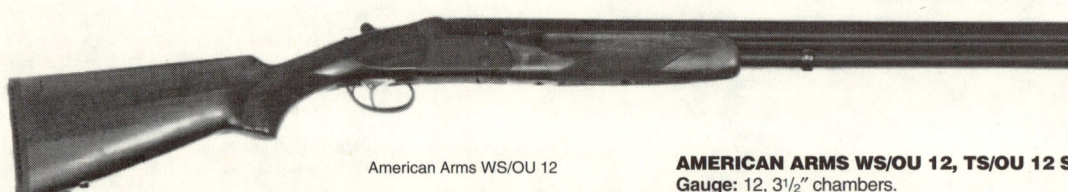
American Arms WS/OU 12

American Arms WT/OU 10 Shotgun
Similar to the WS/OU 12 except chambered for 10-gauge 3 1/2" shell, 26" (Full & Full, choke tubes) barrel. Single selective trigger, extractors. Non-reflective finish on wood and metal. Imported by American Arms, Inc.
Price: $1,029.00

AMERICAN ARMS WS/OU 12, TS/OU 12 SHOTGUNS
Gauge: 12, 3 1/2" chambers.
Barrel: WS/OU—28" (Imp. Cyl., Mod., Full choke tubes); TS/OU—24" (Imp. Cyl., Mod., Full choke tubes).
Weight: 6 lbs., 15 oz. **Length:** 46" overall.
Stock: 14 1/8"x1 1/8"x2 3/8". European walnut with cut checkering, black vented recoil pad, matte finish.
Features: Boxlock action with single selective trigger, automatic selective ejectors; chrome bores. Matte metal finish. Imported by American Arms, Inc.
Price: $765.00

ARMSPORT 2700 SERIES O/U
Gauge: 10, 12, 20, 28, 410.
Barrel: 26" (Imp. Cyl. & Mod.); 28" (Mod. & Full); vent. rib.
Weight: 8 lbs.
Stock: European walnut, hand-checkered p.g. and forend.
Features: Single selective trigger, automatic ejectors, engraved receiver. Imported by Armsport. Contact Armsport for complete list of models.
Price: M2733/2735 (Boss-type action, 12, 20, extractors) $790.00
Price: M2741 (as above with ejectors) $825.00
Price: M2730/2731 (as above with single trigger, screw-in chokes) ...$975.00
Price: M2705 (410 bore, 26" Imp. & Mod., double triggers) $785.00
Price: M2742 Sporting Clays (12-ga., 28", choke tubes) $930.00
Price: M2744 Sporting Clays (20-ga., 26", choke tubes) $930.00
Price: M2750 Sporting Clays (12-ga., 28", choke tubes, sideplates) ..$1,050.00
Price: M2751 Sporting Clays (20-ga., 26", choke tubes, sideplates) ..$1,050.00

ARMSPORT 2700 O/U GOOSE GUN
Gauge: 10, 3 1/2" chambers.
Barrel: 28" (Full & Imp. Mod.), 32" (Full & Full).
Weight: About 9.8 lbs.
Stock: European walnut.
Features: Boss-type action; double triggers; extractors. Introduced 1986. Imported from Italy by Armsport.
Price: Fixed chokes $1,190.00
Price: With choke tubes $1,299.00

Baby Bretton

BABY BRETTON OVER/UNDER SHOTGUN
Gauge: 12 or 20, 2 3/4" chambers.
Barrel: 27 1/2" (Cyl., Imp. Cyl., Mod., Full choke tubes).
Weight: About 5 lbs.
Stock: Walnut, checkered pistol grip and forend, oil finish.
Features: Receiver slides open on two guide rods, is locked by a large thumb lever on the right side. Extractors only. Light alloy barrels. Imported from France by Mandall Shooting Supplies.
Price: Sprint Standard $895.00
Price: Sprint Deluxe $975.00
Price: Model Fairplay $1,025.00

SHOTGUNS—OVER/UNDERS

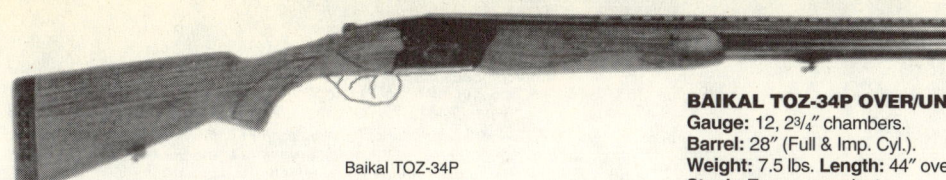
Baikal TOZ-34P

BAIKAL IJ-27 OVER/UNDER SHOTGUN
Gauge: 12, 2¾" chambers.
Barrel: 28" (Mod. & Full).
Weight: 7 lbs.
Stock: Checkered walnut.
Features: Double triggers; extractors; blued receiver with engraving. Reintroduced 1994. Imported from Russia by K.B.I., Inc.
Price: $299.00
Price: IJ-27 EIC (single trigger, automatic ejectors) $339.00

> Consult our Directory pages for the location of firms mentioned.

BAIKAL TOZ-34P OVER/UNDER SHOTGUN
Gauge: 12, 2¾" chambers.
Barrel: 28" (Full & Imp. Cyl.).
Weight: 7.5 lbs. **Length:** 44" overall.
Stock: European walnut.
Features: Engraved, blued receiver; cocking indicator; double triggers. Ventilated rib, ventilated rubber buttpad. Imported from Russia by Century International Arms.
Price: About $405.00
Price: With ejectors, about $475.00

BAIKAL IJ-27M OVER-UNDER SHOTGUN
Gauge: 12, 2¾" chambers.
Barrel: 28.5" (Mod. & Full).
Weight: 7.5 lbs. **Length:** 44.5" overall.
Stock: European hardwood.
Features: Engraved boxlock action with double triggers, extractors; chrome-lined barrels; sling swivels. Imported from Russia by Century International Arms.
Price: About $340.00
Price: IJ-27EM (selective automatic ejectors), about $365.00

Beretta Model 686 Essential

BERETTA ASE 90 SPORTING CLAYS O/U SHOTGUN
Gauge: 12, 2¾" chambers.
Barrel: 28" (Sporting Clays), 30" (Sporting Clays), Mobilchoke choke tubes.
Weight: About 8 lbs., 6 oz.
Stock: High grade walnut.
Features: Has drop-out trigger assembly, wide ventilated top and side ribs, hard-chrome bores. Comes with hard case. Introduced 1992. Imported from Italy by Beretta U.S.A.
Price: Sporting Clays $8,387.00

BERETTA MODEL 686 ESSENTIAL O/U
Gauge: 12, 3" chambers.
Barrel: 26", 28", Mobilchoke tubes (Imp. Cyl., Mod., Full).
Weight: 6.7 lbs. **Length:** 45.7" overall (28" barrels).
Stock: 14.5"x2.2"x1.4". American walnut; radiused black buttplate.
Features: Matte finish on receiver and barrels; hard-chrome bores; low-profile receiver with dual conical locking lugs; single selective trigger, ejectors. Introduced 1994. Imported from Italy by Beretta U.S.A.
Price: $1,186.00

Beretta 682 Competition

BERETTA SERIES 682 COMPETITION OVER/UNDERS
Gauge: 12, 2¾" chambers.
Barrel: Skeet—26" and 28"; trap—30" and 32", Imp. Mod. & Full and Mobilchoke; trap mono shotguns—32" and 34" Mobilchoke; trap top single guns—32" and 34" Full and Mobilchoke; trap combo sets—from 30" O/U, to 32" O/U, 34" top single.
Stock: Close-grained walnut, hand checkered.
Sights: White Bradley bead front sight and center bead.
Features: Trap Monte Carlo stock has deluxe trap recoil pad. Various grades available; contact Beretta U.S.A. for details. Imported from Italy by Beretta U.S.A.
Price: 682 Skeet $2,597.00
Price: 682 Trap $2,650.00
Price: 682 Trap Mono shotguns $3,606.00
Price: 682 Trap Top Single shotguns $2,734.00
Price: 682 Trap Combo sets ....$3,440.00 to $3,606.00
Price: 686 Silver Perdiz Skeet (28") $1,434.00
Price: 687 EELL Diamond Pigeon Trap $4,749.00
Price: 687 EELL Diamond Pigeon Skeet (4-bbl. set) $8,284.00
Price: 682 Super Skeet (adjustable comb and butt pads, bbl. porting) .$3,006.00
Price: 682 Super Trap (adjustable comb and butt pad, barrel porting) ....$2,907.00 to $3,983.00

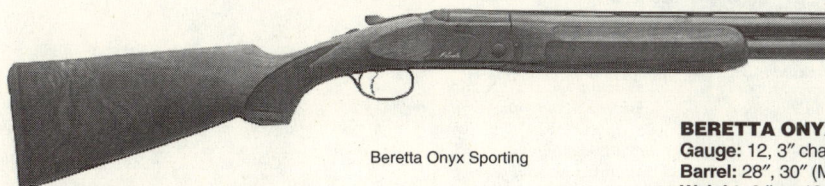
Beretta Onyx Sporting

BERETTA MODEL 686 ULTRALIGHT ONYX O/U
Gauge: 12, 2¾" chambers.
Barrel: 26", 28", Mobilchoke choke tubes.
Weight: About 5 lbs., 13 oz.
Stock: Select American walnut with checkered grip and forend.
Features: Low-profile aluminum alloy receiver with titanium breech face insert. Matte black receiver finish with gold P. Beretta signature inlay. Single selective trigger; automatic safety. Introduced 1992. Imported from Italy by Beretta U.S.A.
Price: $1,574.00

BERETTA ONYX SPORTING O/U SHOTGUN
Gauge: 12, 3" chambers.
Barrel: 28", 30" (Mobilchoke tubes).
Weight: 6 lbs., 13 oz.
Stock: Checkered American walnut.
Features: Intended for the beginning sporting clays shooter. Has wide, vented 12.5mm target rib, radiused recoil pad. Matte black finish on receiver and barrels. Introduced 1993. Imported from Italy by Beretta U.S.A.
Price: $1,399.00
Price: 686 Silver Perdiz Sporting (as above except coin silver receiver with scroll engraving; 12- or 20-ga.) $1,427.00

CAUTION: PRICES SHOWN ARE SUPPLIED BY THE MANUFACTURER OR IMPORTER. CHECK YOUR LOCAL GUN SHOP.

SHOTGUNS—OVER/UNDERS

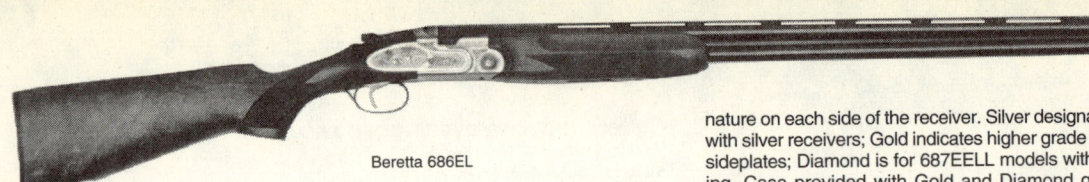
Beretta 686EL

BERETTA OVER/UNDER FIELD SHOTGUNS
Gauge: 12, 20, 28, and 410 bore, 2 3/4", 3" and 3 1/2" chambers.
Barrel: 26" and 28" (Mobilchoke tubes).
Stock: Close-grained walnut.
Features: Highly-figured, American walnut stocks and forends, and a unique, weather-resistant finish on barrels. The 686 Onyx bears a gold P. Beretta signature on each side of the receiver. Silver designates standard 686, 687 models with silver receivers; Gold indicates higher grade 686EL, 687EL models with full sideplates; Diamond is for 687EELL models with highest grade wood, engraving. Case provided with Gold and Diamond grades. Silver Gold, Diamond grades introduced 1994. Imported from Italy by Beretta U.S.A.

Price: 686 Onyx $1,399.00
Price: Silver Perdiz 686 two bbl. set $2,149.00
Price: 686 Silver Perdiz $1,427.00
Price: 686EL Gold Perdiz (engraved sideplates, hard case) $2,226.00
Price: 687L Silver Perdiz $1,927.00
Price: 687EL Gold Pigeon (gold inlays, sideplates) ...... $3,276.00 to $3,423.00
Price: 687EL Gold Pigeon, 410, 26", 28-ga., 28" $3,423.00
Price: 687EELL Diamond Pigeon (engraved sideplates) .. $4,764.00 to $5,287.00
Price: 687EELL Diamond Pigeon, 28-ga., 28" $4,764.00
Price: 687EELL Diamond Pigeon Combo, 20- and 28-ga., 26" $5,287.00

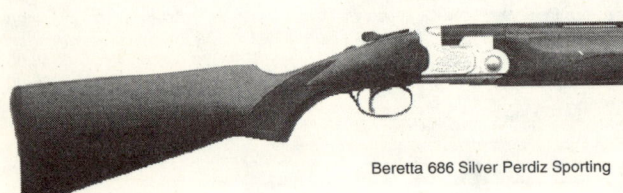
Beretta 686 Silver Perdiz Sporting

Beretta 682 Super Sporting O/U
Similar to the 682 Sporting except has stock with adjustable comb that allows height adjustments via interchangeable inserts. Accessory recoil pad system and adjustable trigger allow length of pull changes. Factory ported barrels, raised tapered top rib with mid-rib bead, bright orange front sight. Available in 12-gauge only, 2 3/4" chambers, 28" 30", Mobilchoke tubes. Introduced 1993. Imported from Italy by Beretta U.S.A.
Price: $3,017.00

Beretta 687EL Gold Pigeon Sporting O/U
Similar to the 687 Silver Pigeon Sporting except has sideplates with gold inlay game scene, vent side and top ribs, bright orange front sight. Stock and forend are of high grade walnut with fine-line checkering. Available in 12-gauge only with 28" or 30" barrels and Mobilchoke tubes. Weight is 6 lbs., 13 oz. Introduced 1993. Imported from Italy by Beretta U.A.S.
Price: $3,320.00

BERETTA SPORTING CLAYS SHOTGUNS
Gauge: 12 and 20, 2 3/4" chambers.
Barrel: 28", 30", Mobilchoke.
Stock: Close-grained walnut.
Features: Equipped with Beretta Mobilchoke flush-mounted screw-in choke tube system. Dual-purpose O/U for hunting and Sporting Clays. 12- or 20-gauge, 28", 30" Mobilchoke tubes (four, Skeet, Imp. Cyl., Mod., Full). Wide 12.5mm top rib with 2.5mm center groove; 686 Onyx models have matte black receiver, 686 Silver Perdiz has silver receiver with scroll engraving, 687 Silver Pigeon Sporting has silver receiver, highly figured walnut, 687 EL Pigeon Sporting has game scene engraving with gold inlaid animals on full sideplate. Introduced 1994. Imported from Italy by Beretta U.S.A.

Price: 682 Sporting, 30" (with case) $2,915.00
Price: 682 Super Sporting, 28", 30", ported, adj. l.o.p. $3,017.00
Price: 686 Onyx Sporting $1,427.00
Price: 686 Continental Course Sporting, 2 3/4" chambers, 28", 30" ... $2,796.00
Price: 686 Silver Perdiz Sporting $1,471.00
Price: 686 Silver Perdiz Sporting Combo, 28" and 30" $2,687.00
Price: 687 Silver Perdiz Sporting $2,354.00
Price: 687 Silver Pigeon Sporting (20 gauge) $2,354.00
Price: 687 Diamond Pigeon EELL Sporter (hand engraved sideplates, deluxe wood) $4,850.00
Price: 687 Silver Pigeon Sporting Combo, 28" and 30" $3,516.00
Price: 687EL Pigeon Sporting $3,320.00
Price: ASE 90 Gold Sporting Clay $8,387.00

BERETTA MODEL SO5, SO6, SO9 SHOTGUNS
Gauge: 12, 2 3/4" chambers.
Barrel: To customer specs.
Stock: To customer specs.
Features: SO5—Trap, Skeet and Sporting Clays models SO5; SO6—SO6 and SO6 EELL are field models. SO6 has a case-hardened or silver receiver with contour hand engraving. SO6 EELL has hand-engraved receiver in a fine floral or "fine English" pattern or game scene, with bas-relief chisel work and gold inlays. SO6 and SO6 EELL are available with sidelocks removable by hand. Imported from Italy by Beretta U.S.A.

Price: SO5 Trap, Skeet, Sporting $13,000.00
Price: SO6 Trap, Skeet, Sporting $17,500.00
Price: SO6 EELL Field, custom specs $28,000.00
Price: SO9 (12, 20, 28, 410, 26", 28", 30", any choke) $31,000.00

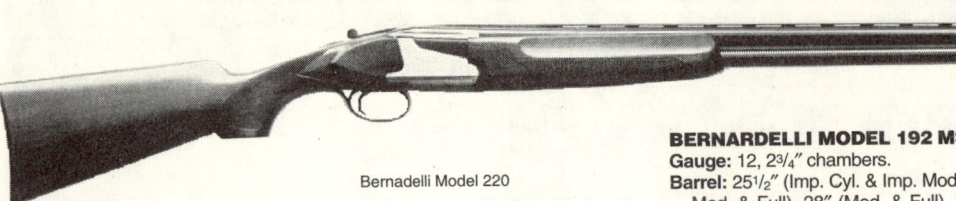
Bernardelli Model 220

Bernardelli Model 115 Over/Under Shotgun
Similar to the Model 192 except designed for competition shooting with thicker barrel walls, specially designed stock with anatomical grip. Leather-faced recoil pad and schnabel forend on Sporting Clays and Skeet guns. Concave top rib, ventilated middle rib. Imported from Italy by Armsport.
Price: Model 115 S (inclined-plane locking, ejectors, selective or non-selective trigger, Multichoke standard on Sporting Clays) $2,895.00
Price: Model 115 S Trap/Skeet $2,799.00

BERNARDELLI MODEL 192 MS-MC O/U SHOTGUN
Gauge: 12, 2 3/4" chambers.
Barrel: 25 1/2" (Imp. Cyl. & Imp. Mod., Cyl. & Mod.), 26 3/4" (Imp. Cyl. & Imp. Mod., Mod. & Full), 28" (Mod. & Full), 29 1/2" (Imp. & Imp. Full); or with Multichoke tubes.
Weight: About 7 lbs.
Stock: 14"x1 3/8"x2 3/8". Hand-checkered European walnut. English or pistol grip style.
Features: Boxlock action; single selective trigger. Silvered, engraved action. Imported from Italy by Armsport.
Price: With Multichokes $1,340.00
Price: Model 192 Waterfowler (3 1/2" chambers, three Multichoke tubes) $1,460.00
Price: Model 192 MS (Sporting Clays, non-selective or selective trigger) $2,140.00
Price: Model 220 MS (similar to M192 except 20-ga., different frame) . $1,490.00
Price: Model 220 (20-ga., 3" chambers) $1,420.00

SHOTGUNS—OVER/UNDERS

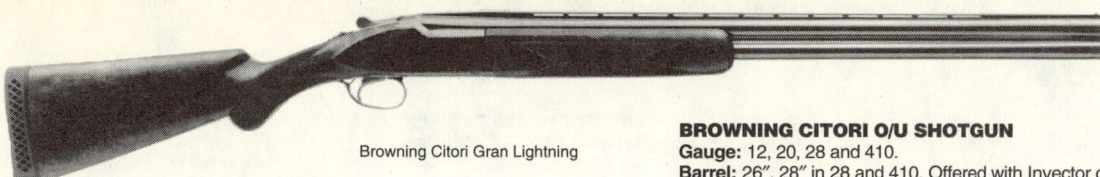
Browning Citori Gran Lightning

Browning Citori Special Trap Models
Similar to standard Citori except 12 gauge only; 30", 32" ported or non-ported (Invector Plus); Monte Carlo cheek piece (14 3/8"x1 3/8"x1 3/8"x2"); fitted with trap-style recoil pad; high post target rib, ventilated side ribs.
Price: Grade I, Invector Plus, ported bbls. $1,510.00
Price: Grade III, Invector Plus Ported $2,075.00
Price: Golden Clays $3,085.00
Price: Adjustable comb stock, add $200.00

BROWNING CITORI O/U SHOTGUN
Gauge: 12, 20, 28 and 410.
Barrel: 26", 28" in 28 and 410. Offered with Invector choke tubes. All 12- and 20-gauge models have back-bored barrels and Invector Plus choke system.
Weight: 6 lbs., 8 oz. (26" 410) to 7 lbs., 13 oz. (30" 12-ga.).
Length: 43" overall (26" bbl.).
Stock: Dense walnut, hand checkered, full p.g., beavertail forend. Field-type recoil pad on 12-ga. field guns and trap and Skeet models.
Sights: Medium raised beads, German nickel silver.
Features: Barrel selector integral with safety, automatic ejectors, three-piece takedown. Imported from Japan by Browning. Contact Browning for complete list of models and prices.
Price: Grade I, Hunting, Invector, 12 and 20 . . . . $1,270.00
Price: Grade III, Hunting, Invector, 12 and 20 . . . . $1,875.00
Price: Grade VI, Hunting, Invector, 12 and 20 . . . . $2,715.00
Price: Grade I, Lightning, 28 and 410, Invector $1,350.00
Price: Grade III, Lightning, 28 and 410, Invector $2,135.00
Price: Grade VI, 28 and 410 Lightning, Invector $2,995.00
Price: Grade I, Lightning, Invector Plus, 12, 20 . . . . $1,310.00
Price: Grade I, Hunting, 28", 30" only, 3 1/2", Invector Plus $1,350.00
Price: Grade III, Lightning, Invector, 12, 20 . . . . $1,910.00
Price: Grade VI, Lightning, Invector, 12, 20 . . . . $2,780.00
Price: Gran Lightning, 26", 28", Invector, 12 ,20 . . . . $1,780.00
Price: Gran Lightning, 28, 410 . . . . $1,875.00

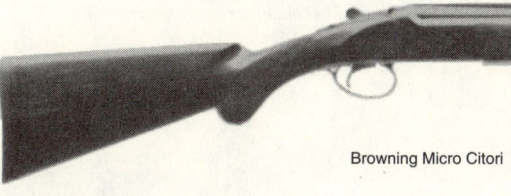
Browning Micro Citori

Browning Micro Citori Lightning
Similar to the Citori 20-ga. Lightning except scaled down for smaller shooter. Comes with 24" Invector Plus back-bored barrels, 13 3/4" length of pull. Weighs about 6 lbs., 3 oz. Introduced 1991.
Price: Grade I $1,360.00

Browning Superlight Citori Over/Under
Similar to the standard Citori except available in 12, 20 with 24", 26" or 28" Invector barrels, 28 or 410 with 26" barrels choked Imp. Cyl. & Mod. or 28" choked Mod. & Full. Has straight grip stock, schnabel forend tip. Superlight 12 weighs 6 lbs. 9 oz. (26" barrels); Superlight 20, 5 lbs., 12 oz. (26" barrels). Introduced 1982.
Price: Grade I only, 28 or 410, Invector $1,370.00
Price: Grade III, Invector, 12 or 20 . . . . $1,910.00
Price: Grade III, 28 or 410, Invector $2,135.00
Price: Grade VI, Invector, 12 or 20 . . . . $2,780.00
Price: Grade VI, 28 or 410, Invector $2,995.00
Price: Grade I Invector, 12 or 20 . . . . $1,320.00
Price: Grade I Invector, Upland Special (24" bbls.), 12 or 20 . . . . $1,320.00

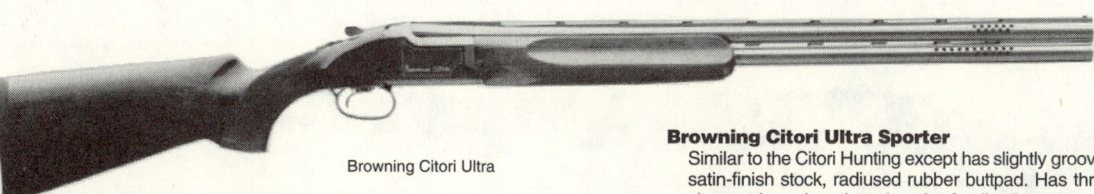
Browning Citori Ultra

Browning Special Sporting Clays
Similar to the Citori Ultra Sporter except has full pistol grip stock with palm swell, gloss finish, 28", 30" or 32" barrels with back-bored Invector Plus chokes (ported or non-ported); high post tapered rib. Also available as 28" and 30" two-barrel set. Introduced 1989.
Price: With ported barrels $1,490.00
Price: As above, adjustable comb $1,690.00
Price: Golden Clays $3,050.00
Price: Adjustable comb stock, add $200.00

Browning Lightning Sporting Clays
Similar to the Citori Lightning with rounded pistol grip and classic forend. Has high post tapered rib or lower hunting-style rib with 30" back-bored Invector Plus barrels, ported or non-ported, 3" chambers. Gloss stock finish, radiused recoil pad. Has "Lightning Sporting Clays Edition" engraved and gold filled on receiver. Introduced 1989.
Price: Low-rib, ported $1,425.00
Price: High-rib, ported $1,490.00
Price: Golden Clays, low rib, ported $2,945.00
Price: Golden Clays, high rib, ported $3,050.00
Price: Adjustable comb stock, all models, add $200.00

Browning Citori Ultra Sporter
Similar to the Citori Hunting except has slightly grooved, semi-beavertail forend, satin-finish stock, radiused rubber buttpad. Has three interchangeable trigger shoes, trigger has three length of pull adjustments. Ventilated rib tapers from 13mm to 10mm, 28" or 30" barrels (ported or non-ported) with Invector Plus choke tubes. Ventilated side ribs. Introduced 1989.
Price: With ported barrels $1,640.00
Price: Golden Clays $3,050.00

Browning Citori O/U Special Skeet
Similar to standard Citori except 26", 28" barrels, ventilated side ribs, Invector choke tubes; stock dimensions of 14 3/8"x1 1/2"x2", fitted with Skeet-style recoil pad; conventional target rib and high post target rib.
Price: Grade I Invector, 12-, 20-ga., Invector Plus (high post rib) $1,510.00
Price: Grade I, 28 and 410 (high post rib) $1,475.00
Price: Grade III, 28, 410 (high post rib) $2,080.00
Price: Four barrel Skeet set—12, 20, 28, 410 barrels, with case, Grade I $4,450.00
Price: Grade III, four-barrel set (high post rib) $5,450.00
Price: Grade I, three-barrel set $3,100.00
Price: Grade III, three-barrel set $3,900.00
Price: Golden Clays, three-barrel set $5,100.00
Price: Golden Clays $3,085.00
Price: Golden Clays, four-barrel set $6,750.00
Price: Grade III, 12-ga. Invector Plus $2,075.00
Price: Adjustable comb stock, add $200.00

CAUTION: PRICES SHOWN ARE SUPPLIED BY THE MANUFACTURER OR IMPORTER. CHECK YOUR LOCAL GUN SHOP.

SHOTGUNS—OVER/UNDERS

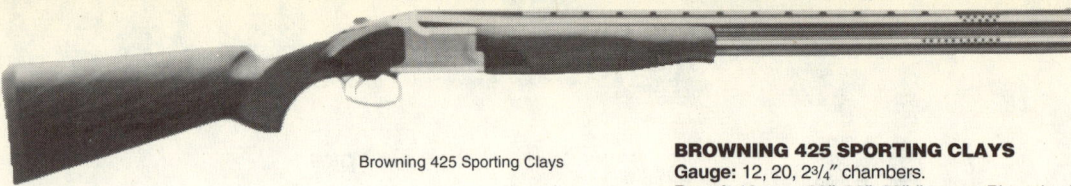

Browning 425 Sporting Clays

Browning 425 WSSF Shotgun
Similar to the 425 Sporting Clays except in 12-gauge only, has stock dimensions specifically tailored to women shooters ($14^{1}/_{4}"x1^{1}/_{2}"x1^{1}/_{2}"$); top lever and takedown lever are easier to operate. Stock and forend have teal-colored finish with WSSF logo. Introduced 1995. Imported by Browning.
Price: $1,690.00

CHURCHILL WINDSOR IV OVER/UNDER SHOTGUN
Gauge: 12, 20, 3" chambers.
Barrel: 12 ga.—26", 28"; 20 ga.—26"; choke tubes.
Weight: About 7.5 lbs.
Stock: Walnut; rubber recoil pad.
Features: Automatic ejectors, single selective trigger; ventilated top and side ribs; silvered receiver. Introduced 1995. Imported by Ellett Bros.
Price: $932.00

COLT ARMSMEAR OVER/UNDER SHOTGUN
Gauge: 12 $2^{3}/_{4}"$ chambers.
Barrel: 28", 30", choke tubes.
Weight: 7.5 lbs. **Length:** NA.
Stock: European walnut, deluxe and exhibition grades.

BROWNING 425 SPORTING CLAYS
Gauge: 12, 20, $2^{3}/_{4}"$ chambers.
Barrel: 12-ga.—28", 30", 32" (Invector Plus tubes), back-bored; 20-ga.—28", 30" (Invector Plus tubes).
Weight: 7 lbs., 13 oz. (12-ga., 28").
Stock: $14^{13}/_{16}"$ ($+/-^{1}/_{8}"$)x$1^{7}/_{16}"$x$2^{3}/_{16}"$ (12-ga.). Select walnut with gloss finish, cut checkering, schnabel forend.
Features: Grayed receiver with engraving, blued barrels. Barrels are ported on 12-gauge guns. Has low 10mm wide vent rib. Comes with three interchangeable trigger shoes to adjust length of pull. Introduced in U.S. 1993. Imported by Browning.
Price: Grade I, 12-, 20-ga., Invector Plus $1,690.00
Price: Golden Clays, 12-, 20-ga., Invector Plus $3,150.00
Price: Adjustable comb stock, add $200.00

Churchill Windsor Sporting Clays Over/Under
Similar to the Windsor IV except 12-gauge only, with 28" or 30" barrels (choke tubes); barrels are ported, back-bored and have lengthened forcing cones; tapered ventilated rib, ventilated side rib; Sporting-style forend with finger grooves; select walnut stock with palm swell grip. Introduced 1995. Imported by Ellett Bros.
Price: $1,125.00

Features: Automatic ejectors, selective single trigger; semi-beavertail forend. Removable trigger group. Engraved frame with gold inlaid birds on sides, gold Colt stallion on underside. Introduced 1995. Imported by Colt's Mfg.
Price: 28", heavily engraved, deluxe grade wood .... NA
Price: 30", lightly engraved, exhibition grade wood .... NA

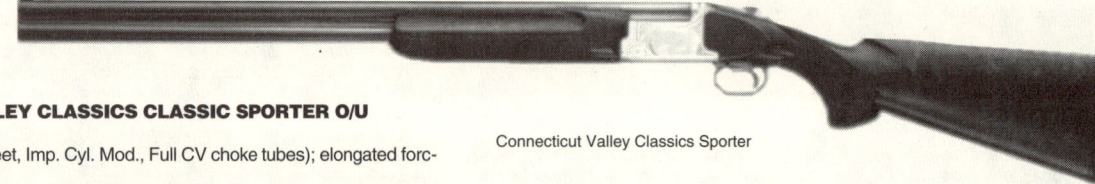

Connecticut Valley Classics Sporter

CONNECTICUT VALLEY CLASSICS CLASSIC SPORTER O/U
Gauge: 12, 3" chambers.
Barrel: 28", 30", 32" (Skeet, Imp. Cyl. Mod., Full CV choke tubes); elongated forcing cones.
Weight: $7^{3}/_{4}$ lbs. **Length:** $44^{7}/_{8}"$ overall (28" barrels).
Stock: $14^{1}/_{2}"x1^{1}/_{2}"x2^{1}/_{8}"$. American black walnut with hand-checkered grip and forend.
Features: Receiver duplicates Classic Doubles M101 specifications. Stainless receiver with fine engraving. Chrome-lined bores and chambers suitable for steel shot. Optionally available are CV Plus ($2^{3}/_{8}"$ tubes) choke tubes. Introduced 1993. Made in U.S. by Connecticut Valley Classics.
Price: Classic Sporter Stainless $2,995.00

Connecticut Valley Classics Classic Field Waterfowler
Similar to the Classic Sporter except with 30" barrel only, blued, non-reflective overall finish. Interchangeable CV choke tube system includes Skeet, Imp. Cyl., Mod. Full tubes. Introduced 1995. Made in U.S. by Connecticut Valley Classics.
Price: $2,495.00

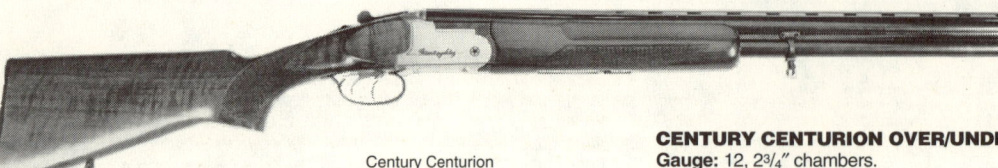

Century Centurion

CHARLES DALY FIELD GRADE O/U
Gauge: 12 or 20, 3" chambers.
Barrel: 12- and 20- ga.—26" (Imp. Cyl. & Mod.), 12-ga.—28" (Mod. & Full).
Weight: 6 lbs., 15 oz. (12-ga.); 6 lbs., 10 oz. (20-ga.). **Length:** $43^{1}/_{2}"$ overall (26".).
Stock: $14^{1}/_{8}"x1^{3}/_{8}"x2^{3}/_{8}"$. Walnut with cut-checkered grip and forend. Black, vent. rubber recoil pad. Semi-gloss finish.
Features: Boxlock action with manual safety; extractors; single selective trigger. Color case-hardened receiver with engraving. Introduced 1989. Imported from Europe by Outdoor Sports Headquarters.
Price: $545.00
Price: Sporting Clays model (12-ga., 28", 30", choke tubes) $895.00

Charles Daly Deluxe Over/Under
Similar to the Field Grade except available in 12 and 20 gauge, has automatic selective ejectors, antique silver finish on frame, and has choke tubes for Imp. Cyl., Mod. and Full. Introduced 1989.
Price: $770.00

CENTURY CENTURION OVER/UNDER SHOTGUN
Gauge: 12, $2^{3}/_{4}"$ chambers.
Barrel: 28" (Mod. & Full).
Weight: 7.3 lbs. **Length:** 44.5" overall.
Stock: European walnut.
Features: Double triggers; extractors. Polished blue finish. Introduced 1993. Imported by Century International Arms.
Price: About $380.00

HATFIELD UPLANDER OVER/UNDER SHOTGUN
Gauge: 20, 28, 3" chambers.
Barrel: 26" (Imp. Cyl. & Mod.).
Weight: 5 lbs., 4 oz.
Stock: Straight English grip of special select XXX fancy walnut; hand-checkered grip and forend; hand-rubbed oil finish.
Features: Boxlock action with single selective trigger; half-coverage hand engraving; French gray finish. Comes with English-style oxblood leather luggage case with billiard felt interior. Special engraving, stock dimensions, metal finish available. Introduced 1994. From Hatfield Gun Co.
Price: Grade I $3,749.00

SHOTGUNS—OVER/UNDERS

HHF Model 103 C 12 ST

HHF MODEL 103 F 12 ST OVER/UNDER
Gauge: 12, 20, 3″ chambers.
Barrel: 28″, choke tubes or fixed chokes.
Weight: About 7 1/2 lbs.
Stock: Circassian walnut.
Features: Boxlock action with dummy sideplates. Single selective trigger; manual safety; extractors. Can be ordered with many custom options. Has 100 percent engraving coverage, inlaid animals on blackened sideplates. Introduced 1995. Imported from Turkey by Turkish Firearms Corp.
Price: With extractors $1,120.00
Price: With automatic ejectors $1,750.00
Price: Model 103 C 12 ST (black receiver, 50 percent engraving coverage, extractors) $1,050.00
Price: As above, ejectors $1,680.00
Price: Model 103 D 12 ST (standard boxlock with 80 percent engraving coverage, extractors) $1,050.00
Price: As above, ejectors $1,680.00
Price: Model 103 B 12 ST (double triggers, extractors, 80 percent engraving coverage, fixed chokes) $995.00
Price: As above, 28, 410 . . . .$1,550.00
Price: With choke tubes, extractors (12, 20) $1,050.00

HHF MODEL 104 A 12 ST OVER/UNDER
Gauge: 12, 3″ chambers.
Barrel: 28″, fixed chokes or choke tubes.
Weight: About 7 1/2 lbs.
Stock: Circassian walnut, field dimensions.
Features: Boxlock action with manual safety, extractors, double triggers. Silvered, engraved receiver. Has 15 percent engraving coverage. Introduced 1995. Imported from Turkey by Turkish Firearms Corp.
Price: Fixed chokes, extractors $925.00
Price: As above, 28, 410 . . . .$1,295.00
Price: Choke tubes, ejectors (12, 20) $925.00

HHF MODEL 101 B 12 ST TRAP O/U
Gauge: 12, 3″ chambers.
Barrel: 30″, fixed chokes or choke tubes; 16mm rib.
Weight: About 8 lbs.
Stock: Circassian walnut to trap dimensions; Monte Carlo comb, palm swell grip, recoil pad.
Features: Single selective trigger; manual safety; automatic ejectors or extractors. Many custom features available. Silvered frame with 50 percent envgraving coverage. Introduced 1995. Imported from Turkey by Turkish Firearms Corp.
Price: With extractors $1,050.00
Price: With ejectors $1,680.00
Price: Model 101 B 12 AT-DT (trap combo, 32″ barrels) $2,295.00

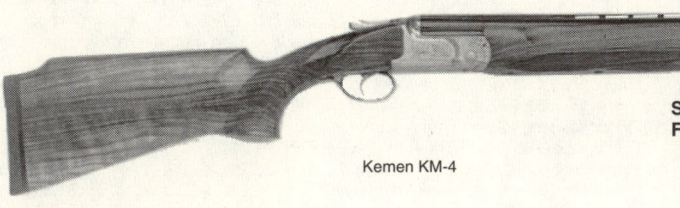
Kemen KM-4

KEMEN OVER/UNDER SHOTGUNS
Gauge: 12, 2 3/4″ or 3″ chambers.
Barrel: 27 5/8″ (Hunting, Pigeon, Sporting Clays, Skeet), 30″, 32″ (Sporting Clays, Trap).
Weight: 7.25 to 8.5 lbs.
Stock: Dimensions to customer specs. High grade walnut.
Features: Drop-out trigger assembly; ventilated flat or step top rib, ventilated, solid or no side ribs. Low-profile receiver with black finish on Standard model, antique silver on sideplate models and all engraved, gold inlaid models. Barrels, forend, trigger parts interchangeable with Perazzi. Comes with hard case, accessory tools, spares. Introduced 1989. Imported from Spain by USA Sporting Clays.
Price: KM-4 Standard $6,179.00
Price: KM-4 Luxe-A (engraved scroll), Luxe-B (game scenes) $10,644.00
Price: KM-4 Super Luxe (engraved game scene) $12,064.00
Price: KM-4 Extra Luxe-A (scroll engraved sideplates) $13,960.00
Price: KM-4 Extra Luxe-B (game scene sideplates) $16,030.00
Price: KM-4 Extra Gold (inlays, game scene) $19,607.00

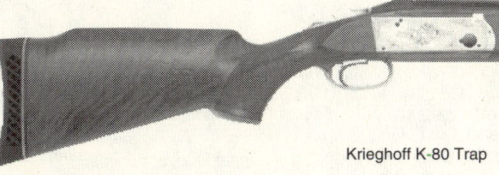
Krieghoff K-80 Trap

KRIEGHOFF K-80 SKEET SHOTGUN
Gauge: 12, 2 3/4″ chambers.
Barrel: 28″ (Skeet & Skeet, optional Tula or choke tubes).
Weight: About 7 3/4 lbs.
Stock: American Skeet or straight Skeet stocks, with palm-swell grips. Walnut.
Features: Satin gray receiver finish. Selective mechanical trigger adjustable for position. Choice of ventilated 8mm parallel flat rib or ventilated 8-12mm tapered flat rib. Introduced 1980. Imported from Germany by Krieghoff International, Inc.
Price: Standard, Skeet chokes $6,650.00
Price: As above, Tula chokes $7,450.00
Price: Lightweight model (weighs 7 lbs.), Standard $6,650.00
Price: Two-Barrel Set (tube concept), 12-ga., Standard $11,305.00
Price: Skeet Special (28″, tapered flat rib, Skeet & Skeet choke tubes) $7,300.00

Krieghoff K-80 Four-Barrel Skeet Set
Similar to the Standard Skeet except comes with barrels for 12, 20, 28, 410. Comes with fitted aluminum case.
Price: Standard grade $15,950.00

KRIEGHOFF K-80 O/U TRAP SHOTGUN
Gauge: 12, 2 3/4″ chambers.
Barrel: 30″, 32″ (Imp. Mod. & Full or choke tubes).
Weight: About 8 1/2 lbs.
Stock: Four stock dimensions or adjustable stock available; all have palm-swell grips. Checkered European walnut.
Features: Satin nickel receiver. Selective mechanical trigger, adjustable for position. Ventilated step rib. Introduced 1980. Imported from Germany by Krieghoff International, Inc.
Price: K-80 O/U (30″, 32″, Imp. Mod. & Full), from $7,100.00
Price: K-80 Unsingle (32″, 34″, Full), Standard, from $7,650.00
Price: K-80 Combo (two-barrel set), Standard, from $9,970.00

Krieghoff K-80 International Skeet
Similar to the Standard Skeet except has 1/2″ ventilated Broadway-style rib, special Tula chokes with gas release holes at muzzle. International Skeet stock. Comes in fitted aluminum case.
Price: Standard grade $7,450.00

Krieghoff K-80/RT Shotguns
Same as the standard K-80 shotguns except has a removable internally selective trigger mechanism. Can be considered an option on all K-80 guns of any configuration. Introduced 1990.
Price: RT (removable trigger) option on K-80 guns, add $1,000.00
Price: Extra pull trigger mechanisms $1,275.00

SHOTGUNS—OVER/UNDERS

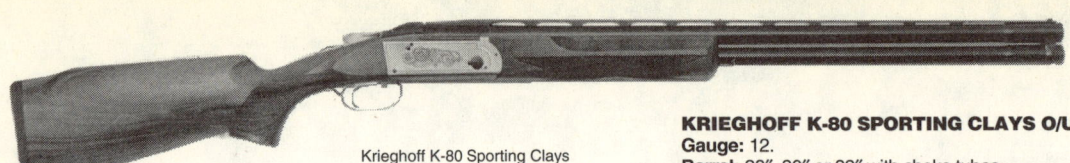

Krieghoff K-80 Sporting Clays

KRIEGHOFF K-80 SPORTING CLAYS O/U
Gauge: 12.
Barrel: 28", 30" or 32" with choke tubes.
Weight: About 8 lbs.
Stock: #3 Sporting stock designed for gun-down shooting.
Features: Choice of standard or lightweight receiver with satin nickel finish and classic scroll engraving. Selective mechanical trigger adjustable for position. Choice of tapered flat or 8mm parallel flat barrel rib. Free-floating barrels. Aluminum case. Imported from Germany by Krieghoff International, Inc.
Price: Standard grade with five choke tubes $7,850.00

LANBER 82 OVER/UNDER SHOTGUN
Gauge: 12, 20, 3" chamber.
Barrel: 26" (Imp. Cyl. & Mod.), 28" (Mod. & Full).
Weight: About 7 lbs., 2 oz.
Stock: 14 3/8"x1 1/2"x2 1/2". European walnut.
Features: Double triggers; silvered, engraved receiver. Introduced 1994. Imported from Spain by Eagle Imports, Inc.
Price: $584.95

Lanber 87 Deluxe Over/Under Shotgun
Similar to the Lanber 82 except comes with Lanberchoke choke tubes, single selective trigger, better wood. Introduced 1994. Imported from Spain by Eagle Imports, Inc.
Price: $914.95
Price: Sporting Clays (12-ga., 28", 2 3/4" chambers) $964.95

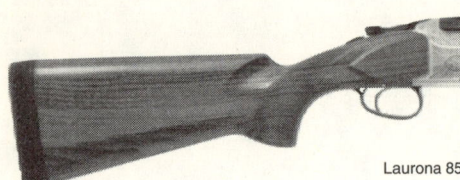

Laurona 85 MS Super Pigeon

LAURONA SUPER MODEL OVER/UNDERS
Gauge: 12, 20, 2 3/4" or 3" chambers.
Barrel: 26", 28" (Multichoke), 29" (Multichokes and Full).
Weight: About 7 lbs.
Stock: European walnut. Dimensions may vary according to model. Full pistol grip.
Features: Boxlock action, silvered with engraving. Automatic selective ejectors; choke tubes available on most models; single selective or twin single triggers; clack chrome barrels. Has 5-year warranty, including metal finish. Imported from Spain by Galaxy Imports.
Price: Model 83 MG, 12- or 20-ga. $1,215.00
Price: Model 84S Super Trap (fixed chokes) $1,340.00
Price: Model 85 Super Game, 12- or 20-ga. $1,215.00
Price: Model 85 MS Super Trap (Full/Multichoke) $1,390.00
Price: Model 85 MS Super Pigeon $1,370.00
Price: Model 85 S Super Skeet, 12-ga. $1,300.00

LAURONA SILHOUETTE 300 SPORTING CLAYS
Gauge: 12, 2 3/4" or 3" chambers.
Barrel: 28", 29" (Multichoke tubes, flush-type or knurled).
Weight: 7 lbs., 12 oz.
Stock: 14 3/8"x1 3/8"x2 1/2". European walnut with full pistol grip, beavertail forend. Rubber buttpad.
Features: Selective single trigger, automatic selective ejectors. Introduced 1988. Imported from Spain by Galaxy Imports.
Price: $1,250.00
Price: Silhouette Ultra-Magnum, 3 1/2" chambers $1,265.00

Laurona Silhouette 300 Trap
Same gun as the Silhouette 300 Sporting Clays except has 29" barrels, trap stock dimensions of 14 3/8"x1 7/16"x1 5/8", weighs 7 lbs., 15 oz. Available with flush or knurled Multichokes.
Price: $1,310.00

Ljutic LM-6 Deluxe

LJUTIC LM-6 DELUXE O/U SHOTGUN
Gauge: 12.
Barrel: 28" to 34", choked to customer specs for live birds, trap, International Trap.
Weight: To customer specs.
Stock: To customer specs. Oil finish, hand checkered.
Features: Custom-made gun. Hollow-milled rib, pull or release trigger, pushbutton opener in front of trigger guard. From Ljutic Industries.
Price: Super Deluxe LM-6 O/U $19,995.00
Price: Over/under Combo (interchangeable single barrel, two trigger guards, one for single trigger, one for doubles) $26,995.00
Price: Extra over/under barrel sets, 29"-32" $5,995.00

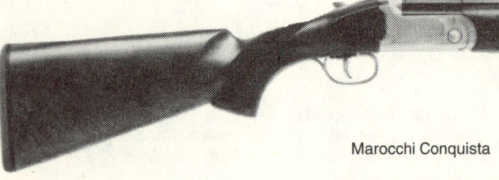

Marocchi Conquista

MAROCCHI CONQUISTA SPORTING CLAYS O/U SHOTGUNS
Gauge: 12, 2 3/4" chambers.
Barrel: 28", 30", 32" (Contrechoke tubes); 10mm concave vent. rib.
Weight: About 8 lbs.
Stock: 14 1/2"-14 7/8"x2 3/16"x1 7/16"; American walnut with checkered grip and forend; Sporting Clays butt pad.
Sights: 16mm luminescent front.
Features: Has lower monoblock and frame profile. Fast lock time. Ergonomically-shaped trigger is adjustable for pull length and weight. Automatic selective ejectors. Coin-finished receiver, blued barrels. Comes with five choke tubes, hard case, stock wrench. Also available as true left-hand model—opening lever operates from left to right; stock has left-hand cast. Introduced 1994. Imported from Italy by Precision Sales International.
Price: Grade I, right-hand $1,895.00
Price: Grade I, left-hand $1,945.00
Price: Grade II, right-hand $2,285.00
Price: Grade II, left-hand $2,335.00
Price: Grade III, right-hand, from $3,250.00
Price: Grade III, left-hand, from $3,350.00

SHOTGUNS—OVER/UNDERS

Marocchi Conquista Trap Over/Under Shotgun
Similar to the Conquista Sporting Clays model except has 30" or 32" barrels choked Full & Full, stock dimensions of 14½"-14⅞"x1¹¹⁄₁₆"x1⁹⁄₃₂"; weighs about 8¼ lbs. Introduced 1994. Imported from Italy by Precision Sales International.
Price: Grade I, right-hand $1,895.00
Price: Grade II, right-hand $2,285.00
Price: Grade III, right-hand, from $3,250.00

Marocchi Conquista Skeet Over/Under Shotgun
Similar to the Conquista Sporting Clays except has 28" (Skeet & Skeet) barrels, stock dimensions of 14⅜"-14¾"x2³⁄₁₆"x1½". Weighs about 7¾ lbs. Introduced 1994. Imported from Italy by Precision Sales International.
Price: Grade I, right-hand $1,895.00
Price: Grade II, right-hand $2,285.00
Price: Grade III, right-hand, from $3,250.00

Marocchi Lady Sport O/U Shotgun
Ergonomically designed specifically for women shooters. Similar to the Conquista Sporting Clays model except has 28" or 30" barrels with five Contrechoke tubes, stock dimensions of 13⅞"-14¼"x1¹¹⁄₃₂"x2⁹⁄₃₂"; weighs about 7½ lbs. Also available as left-hand model—opening lever operates from left to right; stock has left-hand cast. Also available with colored graphics finish on frame and opening lever. Introduced 1995. Imported from Italy by Precision Sales International.
Price: Grade I, right-hand $1,945.00
Price: Grade II, right-hand $2,335.00
Price: Grade III, right-hand, from $3,350.00
Price: Left-hand, add (all grades) $50.00
Price: Colored graphics frame (Grade I only), add $50.00

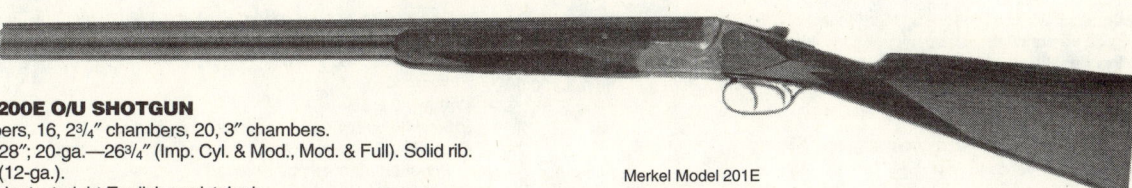
Merkel Model 201E

MERKEL MODEL 200E O/U SHOTGUN
Gauge: 12, 3" chambers, 16, 2¾" chambers, 20, 3" chambers.
Barrel: 12-, 16-ga.—28"; 20-ga.—26¾" (Imp. Cyl. & Mod., Mod. & Full). Solid rib.
Weight: About 7 lbs. (12-ga.).
Stock: Oil-finished walnut; straight English or pistol grip.
Features: Scroll engraved, color case-hardened receiver. Single selective or double triggers; ejectors. Imported from Germany by GSI.
Price: Model 200E $3,395.00
Price: Model 201E (as above except silver-grayed receiver with engraved hunting scenes, also 28-ga.) $4,895.00
Price: Model 202E (as above except has false sideplates, fine hunting scenes with Arabesque engraving) $8,895.00

> Consult our Directory pages for the location of firms mentioned.

Merkel Model 200E Skeet, Trap Over/Unders
Similar to the Model 200E except in 12-gauge only with 2¾" chambers, tapered ventilated rib, competition stock with full pistol grip, half-coverage Arabesque engraving on silver-grayed receiver. Single selective trigger only. Model 200ES has 26¾" (Skeet & Skeet) barrels; Model 200ET has 30" (Full & Full) barrles. Imported from Germany by GSI.
Price: Model 200ET $4,895.00
Price: Model 201ES (full-coverage engraving) $7,495.00
Price: Model 201ET (full-coverage engraving) $7,495.00
Price: Model 203ES (sidelock action, Skeet) $12,950.00
Price: Model 203ET (sidelock action, Trap) $12,950.00

Merkel Model 203E, 303E Over/Under Shotguns
Similar to the Model 200E except with Holland & Holland-style sidelocks, both quick-detachable: Model 203E with cranked screw, 303E with integral retracting hook. Model 203E has coil spring ejectors; 303E H&H ejectors. Both have silver-grayed receiver with English-style Arabesque engraving—large scrolls on 203E, medium on 303E. Imported from Germany by GSI.
Price: Model 203E $10,695.00
Price: Model 303E $19,950.00

Merkel Model 200 SC Sporting Clays O/U
Similar to the Model 200E except has 30" barrels with lengthened forcing cones, five Briley choke tubes. Kersten double cross-bolt lock, color case-hardened receiver, Blitz action; single selective trigger adjustable for length of pull. Select grade stock with competition recoil pad; tapered vent. rib. Comes with fitted luggage case. Introduced 1995. Imported from Germany by GSI.
Price: $7,495.00
Price: With fixed Imp. Cyl. and light Mod. chokes $6,995.00

Perazzi Mirage Sporting

PERAZZI MIRAGE SPECIAL SPORTING O/U
Gauge: 12, 2¾" chambers.
Barrel: 28⅜" (Imp. Mod. & Extra Full), 29½" (choke tubes).
Weight: 7 lbs., 12 oz.
Stock: Special specifications.
Features: Has single selective trigger; flat ⁷⁄₁₆"x⁵⁄₁₆" vent. rib. Many options available. Imported from Italy by Perazzi U.S.A., Inc.
Price: $8,890.00

Perazzi Mirage Special Four-Gauge Skeet
Similar to the Mirage Sporting model except has Skeet dimensions, interchangeable, adjustable four-position trigger assembly. Comes with four barrel sets in 12, 20, 28, 410, flat ⁵⁄₁₆"x⁵⁄₁₆" rib.
Price: From $18,820.00

Perazzi Sporting Classic

PERAZZI MX8/MX8 SPECIAL TRAP, SKEET
Gauge: 12, 2¾" chambers.
Barrel: Trap—29½" (Imp. Mod. & Extra Full), 31½" (Full & Extra Full). Choke tubes optional. Skeet—27⅝" (Skeet & Skeet).
Weight: About 8½ lbs. (Trap); 7 lbs., 15 oz. (Skeet).
Stock: Interchangeable and custom made to customer specs.
Features: Has detachable and interchangeable trigger group with flat V springs. Flat ⁷⁄₁₆" ventilated rib. Many options available. Imported from Italy by Perazzi U.S.A., Inc.
Price: From $7,850.00
Price: MX8 Special (adj. four-position trigger), from $8,320.00
Price: MX8 Special Single (32" or 34" single barrel, step rib), from $8,000.00
Price: MX8 Special Combo (o/u and single barrel sets), from $10,950.00

Perazzi Sporting Classic O/U
Same as the Mirage Special Sporting except is deluxe version with select wood and engraving, Available with flush mount choke tubes, 29.5" barrels. Introduced 1993.
Price: From $9,900.00

CAUTION: PRICES SHOWN ARE SUPPLIED BY THE MANUFACTURER OR IMPORTER. CHECK YOUR LOCAL GUN SHOP.

SHOTGUNS—OVER/UNDERS

Perazzi MX8/20 Over/Under Shotgun
Similar to the MX8 except has smaller frame and has a removable trigger mechanism. Available in trap, Skeet, sporting or game models with fixed chokes or choke tubes. Stock is made to customer specifications. Introduced 1993.
Price: From $7,850.00

Perazzi Mirage Special Skeet Over/Under
Similar to the MX8 Skeet except has adjustable four-position trigger, Skeet stock dimensions.
Price: From $8,320.00

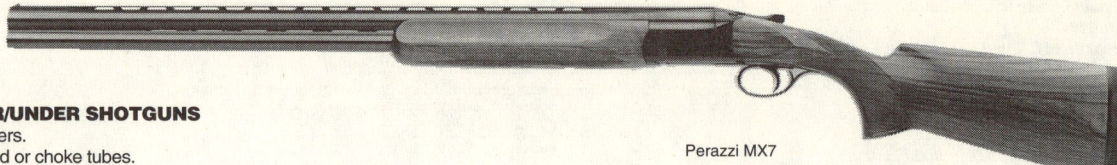
Perazzi MX7

PERAZZI MX7 OVER/UNDER SHOTGUNS
Gauge: 12, 2 3/4" chambers.
Barrel: 29.5", 31.5", fixed or choke tubes.
Weight: NA.
Stock: To customer specifications.
Features: Has fixed coil spring trigger mechanism; selective firing order. Available in combo or over/under configurations. Introduced 1992. Imported from Italy by Perazzi U.S.A.
Price: From $6,100.00

PERAZZI MX12 HUNTING OVER/UNDER
Gauge: 12, 2 3/4" chambers.
Barrel: 26", 27 5/8", 28 3/8", 29 1/2" (Mod. & Full); choke tubes available in 27 5/8", 29 1/2" only (MX12C).
Weight: 7 lbs., 4 oz.
Stock: To customer specs; Interchangeable.
Features: Single selective trigger; coil springs used in action; schnabel forend tip. Imported from Italy by Perazzi U.S.A., Inc.
Price: From $7,850.00
Price: MX12C (with choke tubes), from $8,420.00

PERAZZI MX9 OVER/UNDER SHOTGUNS
Gauge: 12, 2 3/4" chambers.
Barrel: 29.5", 31.5" (choke tubes).
Weight: NA.
Stock: Walnut; cheekpiece adjustable for elevation and cast.
Features: Comes with six pattern adjustment rib inserts. Vent side rib. Externally selective trigger. Available in single barrel, combo, over/under trap, Skeet, pigeon and sporting models. Introduced 1993. Imported from Italy by Perazzi U.S.A.
Price: From $9,900.00
Price: MX10 (fixed chokes, different rib), from $10,300.00

Perazzi MX20 Hunting Over/Under
Similar to the MX12 except 20-ga. frame size. Available in 20, 28, 410 with 2 3/4" or 3" chambers. 26" standard, and choked Mod. & Full. Weight is 6 lbs., 6 oz.
Price: From $7,850.00
Price: MX20C (as above, 20-ga. only, choke tubes), from $8,420.00

PERAZZI MX28, MX410 GAME O/U SHOTGUNS
Gauge: 28, 2 3/4" chambers, 410, 3" chambers.
Barrel: 26" (Imp. Cyl. & Full).
Weight: NA.
Stock: To customer specifications.
Features: Made on scaled-down frames proportioned to the gauge. Introduced 1993. Imported from Italy by Perazzi U.S.A.
Price: From $15,100.00

PIOTTI BOSS OVER/UNDER SHOTGUN
Gauge: 12, 20.
Barrel: 26" to 32", chokes as specified.
Weight: 6.5 to 8 lbs.
Stock: Dimensions to customer specs. Best quality figured walnut.
Features: Essentially a custom-made gun with many options. Introduced 1993. Imported from Italy by Wm. Larkin Moore.
Price: From $33,000.00

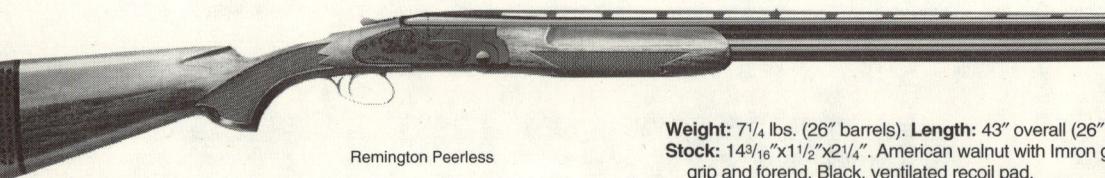
Remington Peerless

REMINGTON PEERLESS OVER/UNDER SHOTGUN
Gauge: 12, 3" chambers.
Barrel: 26", 28", 30" (Imp. Cyl., Mod., Full Rem Chokes).
Weight: 7 1/4 lbs. (26" barrels). Length: 43" overall (26" barrels).
Stock: 14 3/16"x1 1/2"x2 1/4". American walnut with Imron gloss finish, cut-checkered grip and forend. Black, ventilated recoil pad.
Features: Boxlock action with removable sideplates. Gold-plated, single selective trigger, automatic safety, automatic ejectors. Fast lock time. Mid-rib bead, Bradley-type front. Polished blue finish with light scrollwork on sideplates, Remington logo on bottom of receiver. Introduced 1993.
Price: $1,225.00

Ruger English Field

RUGER RED LABEL O/U SHOTGUN
Gauge: 12 and 20, 3" chambers.
Barrel: 26", 28" (Skeet, Imp. Cyl., Full, Extra-Full, Mod. screw-in choke tubes). Proved for steel shot.
Weight: About 7 lbs. (20-ga.); 7 1/2 lbs. (12-ga.). Length: 43" overall (26" barrels).
Stock: 14"x1 1/2"x2 1/2". Straight grain American walnut. Checkered pistol grip and forend, rubber butt pad.
Features: Choice of blue or stainless receiver. Single selective mechanical trigger, selective automatic ejectors; serrated free-floating vent. rib. Comes with two Skeet, one Imp. Cyl., one Mod., one Full choke tube and wrench; Extra-Full tube available at extra cost. Made in U.S. by Sturm, Ruger & Co.
Price: Red Label with pistol grip stock $1,215.00
Price: English Field with straight-grip stock $1,215.00

Ruger 20-Gauge Sporting Clays O/U Shotgun
Similar to the 12-gauge Sporting Clays except chambered for 3" 20-gauge shells; 30" barrels back-bored to .631"-.635". No barrel side spacers. Comes with four special longer, 2", interchangeable, screw-in choke tubes: two Skeet, one Mod., one Imp. Cyl.; Full and Extra-Full tubes available. Introduced 1994.
Price: $1,349.00

Ruger Sporting Clays O/U Shotgun
Similar to the Red Label except 12-gauge only, 30" barrels back-bored to .744" diameter with stainless steel choke tubes. Weight is 7.75 lbs., overall length 47". Stock dimensions of 14 1/8"x1 1/2"x2 1/2". Free-floating serrated vent. rib with brass front and mid-rib beads. No barrel side spacers. Comes with two Skeet, one Imp. Cyl., one Mod. choke tubes. Full and Extra-Full available at extra cost. Introduced 1992.
Price: $1,349.00

SHOTGUNS—OVER/UNDERS

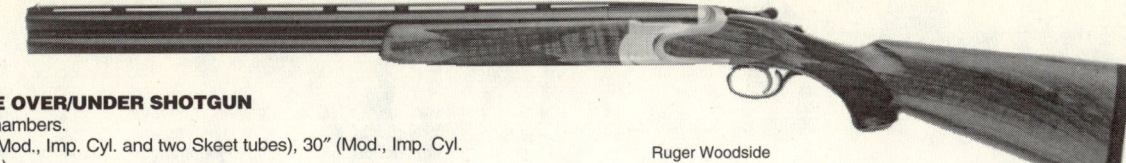
Ruger Woodside

RUGER WOODSIDE OVER/UNDER SHOTGUN
Gauge: 12 or 20, 3" chambers.
Barrel: 26", 28" (Full, Mod., Imp. Cyl. and two Skeet tubes), 30" (Mod., Imp. Cyl. and two Skeet tubes).
Weight: 7 1/2 to 8 lbs.
Stock: 14 1/8"x1 1/2"x2 1/2". Select Circassian walnut; pistol grip or straight English grip.
Features: Has a newly patented Ruger cocking mechanism for easier, smoother opening. Buttstock extends forward into action as two side panels. Single selective mechanical trigger, selective automatic ejectors; serrated free-floating rib; back-bored barrels with stainless steel choke tubes. Blued barrels, stainless steel receiver. Engraved action available. Introduced 1995. Made in U.S. by Sturm, Ruger & Co.
Price: $1,675.00

> Consult our Directory pages for the location of firms mentioned.

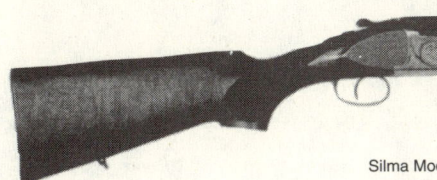
Silma Model 70

SILMA MODEL 70 OVER/UNDER SHOTGUN
Gauge: 12, 3" chambers.
Barrel: 27.5" (Mod. & Imp. Cyl.).
Weight: 6.8 lbs. **Length:** 44.75" overall.
Stock: European walnut.
Features: Engraved, blued boxlock action with single trigger; sling swivels. Introduced 1995. Imported from Italy by Century International Arms.
Price: About $540.00

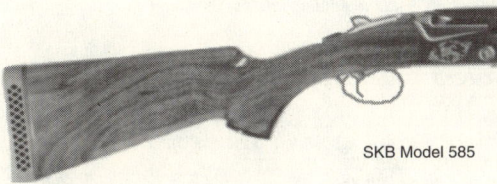
SKB Model 585

SKB MODEL 585 OVER/UNDER SHOTGUN
Gauge: 12 and 20, 3"; 28, 2 3/4"; 410, 3".
Barrel: 12-ga.—26", 28", 30", 32", 34" (Inter-Choke tube); 20-ga.—26", 28" (Inter-Choke tube); 28—26", 28" (Inter-Choke tube); 410—26", 28" (Imp. Cyl. & Mod., Mod. & Full). Ventilated side ribs.
Weight: 6.6 to 8.5 lbs. **Length:** 43" to 51 3/8" overall.
Stock: 14 1/8"x1 1/2"x2 3/16". Hand checkered walnut with high-gloss finish. Target stocks available in standard and Monte Carlo.
Sights: Metal bead front (field), target style on Skeet, trap, Sporting Clays.
Features: Boxlock action; silver nitride finish with Field or Target pattern engraving; manual safety, automatic ejectors, single selective trigger. All 12-gauge barrels are back-bored, have lengthened forcing cones and longer choke tube system. Sporting Clays models in 12-gauge with 28" or 30" barrels available with optional 3/8" step-up target-style rib, matte finish, nickel center bead, white front bead. Introduced 1992. Imported from Japan by G.U., Inc.

SKB Model 585 Waterfowler Shotgun
Similar to the Model 585 Field except 12-gauge only, 28" or 30" barrels with Imp. Cyl., Skeet 1, Mod. Inter-Choke tubes. Bead-blasted receiver with silver nitride finish; bead-blasted, blued barrels. Oil-finished stock and forend. Introduced 1995. Imported from Japan by G.U., Inc.
Price: $1,329.00

SKB Model 585 Youth Model Shotgun
Similar to the Field Model 585 except has 13 1/2" length of pull. Available in 12-gauge with 26" or 28", or 20-gauge with 26" barrels. The 12-gauge has .755" bores, lengthened forcing cones and competition series choke tubes. Introduced 1994. Imported from Japan by G.U., Inc.
Price: $1,179.00

Price: Field $1,179.00
Price: Two-barrel Field Set, 12 & 20 . . . . $1,929.00
Price: Two-barrel Field Set, 20 & 28 or 28 & 410) $1,989.00
Price: Trap, Skeet $1,279.00
Price: Two-barrel trap combo $1,929.00
Price: Sporting Clays model . . . . $1,329.00-$1,379.00
Price: Skeet Set (20, 28, 410) $2,999.00

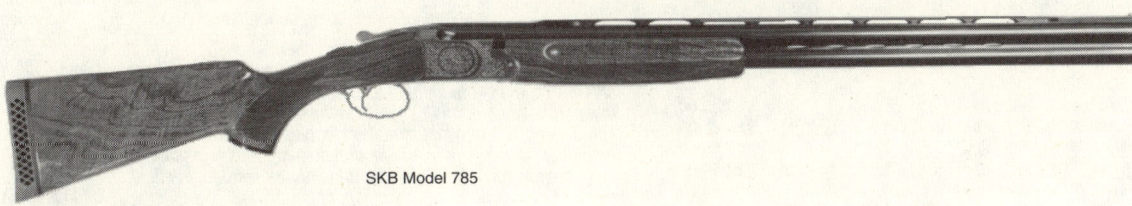
SKB Model 785

SKB MODEL 785 OVER/UNDER SHOTGUN
Gauge: 12, 20, 3"; 28, 2 3/4"; 410, 3".
Barrel: 26", 28", 30", 32" (Inter-Choke tubes).
Weight: 6 lbs., 10 oz. to 8 lbs.
Stock: 14 1/8"x1 1/2"x2 3/16" (Field). Hand-checkered American black walnut with high-gloss finish; semi-beavertail forend. Target stocks available in standard or Monte Carlo styles.
Sights: Metal bead front (Field), target style on Skeet, trap, Sporting Clays models.
Features: Boxlock action with Greener-style cross bolt; single selective chrome-plated trigger, chrome-plated selective ejectors; manual safety. Chrome-plated, over-size, back-bored barrels with lengthened forcing cones. Introduced 1995. Imported from Japan by G.U. Inc.

Price: Field, 12 or 20 . . . . $1,899.00
Price: Field, 28 or 410 . . . . $1,949.00
Price: Field set, 12 and 20 . . . . $2,749.00
Price: Field set, 20 and 28 or 28 and 410 . . . . $2,819.00
Price: Sporting Clays, 12 or 20 . . . . $2,029.00
Price: Sporting Clays, 28 . . . . $2,079.00
Price: Sporting Clays set, 12 and 20 . . . . $2,889.00
Price: Skeet, 12 or 20 . . . . $1,949.00
Price: Skeet, 28 or 410 . . . . $1,999.00
Price: Skeet, three-barrel set, 20, 28, 410 . . . . $3,929.00
Price: Trap, standard or Monte Carlo $1,949.00
Price: Trap combo, standard or Monte Carlo $2,719.00

CAUTION: PRICES SHOWN ARE SUPPLIED BY THE MANUFACTURER OR IMPORTER. CHECK YOUR LOCAL GUN SHOP.

SHOTGUNS—OVER/UNDERS

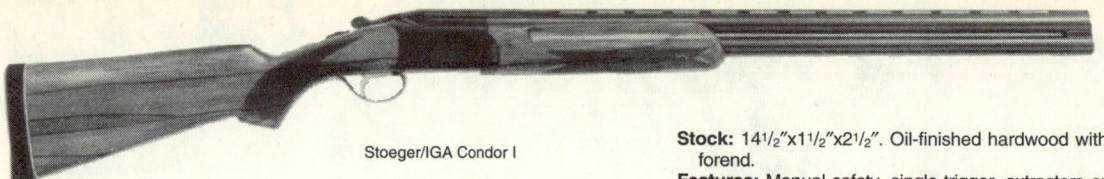

Stoeger/IGA Condor I

STOEGER/IGA CONDOR I OVER/UNDER SHOTGUN
Gauge: 12, 20, 3" chambers.
Barrel: 26" (Imp. Cyl. & Mod. choke tubes), 28" (Mod. & Full choke tubes).
Weight: 6¾ to 7 lbs.
Stock: 14½"x1½"x2½". Oil-finished hardwood with checkered pistol grip and forend.
Features: Manual safety, single trigger, extractors only, ventilated top rib. Introduced 1983. Imported from Brazil by Stoeger Industries.
Price: With choke tubes $500.00
Price: Condor II (sames as Condor I except has double triggers, moulded buttplate) $375.00
Price: Condor Supreme (same as Condor I with single trigger, choke tubes, but with auto. ejectors), 12- or 20-ga., 26", 28" $689.00

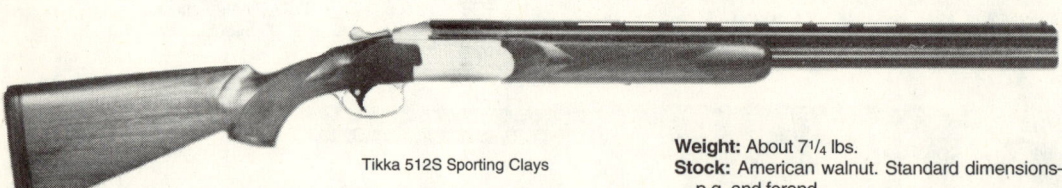

Tikka 512S Sporting Clays

TIKKA MODEL 512S FIELD GRADE OVER/UNDER
Gauge: 12, 20, 3" chambers.
Barrel: 26", 28", with stainless steel screw-in chokes (Imp. Cyl, Mod., Imp. Mod., Full); 20-ga., 28" only.
Weight: About 7¼ lbs.
Stock: American walnut. Standard dimensions—13⁹⁄₁₀"x1½"x2²⁄₅". Checkered p.g. and forend.
Features: Free interchangeability of barrels, stocks and forends into double rifle model, combination gun, etc. Barrel selector in trigger; auto. top tang safety; barrel cocking indicators. Introduced 1980. Imported from Italy by Stoeger.
Price: Model 512S (ejectors), Field Grade $1,275.00
Price: Model 512S Premium Grade $1,275.00
Price: Model 512S Sporting Clays, 12-ga., 28", choke tubes $1,315.00

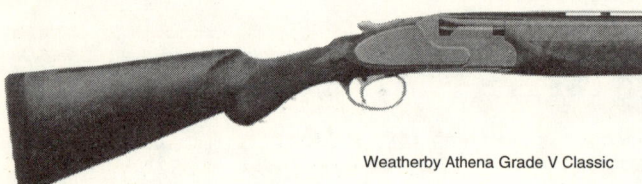

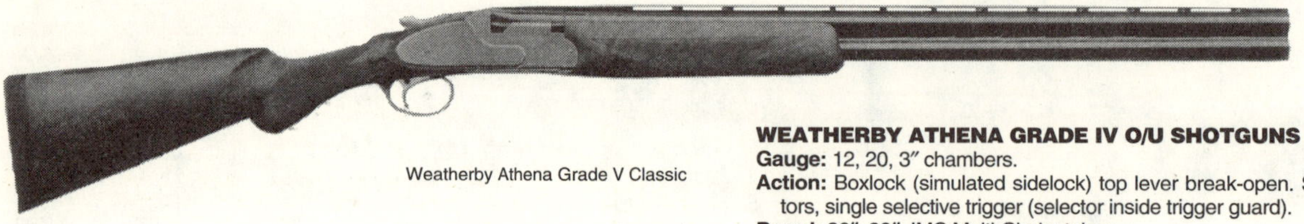

Weatherby Athena Grade V Classic

WEATHERBY ATHENA GRADE IV O/U SHOTGUNS
Gauge: 12, 20, 3" chambers.
Action: Boxlock (simulated sidelock) top lever break-open. Selective auto ejectors, single selective trigger (selector inside trigger guard).
Barrel: 26", 28", IMC Multi-Choke tubes.
Weight: 12-ga., 7⅜ lbs.; 20-ga. 6⅞ lbs.
Stock: American walnut, checkered p.g. and forend (14¼"x1½"x2½").
Features: Mechanically operated trigger. Top tang safety, Greener cross bolt, fully engraved receiver, recoil pad installed. IMC models furnished with three interchangeable flush-fitting choke tubes. Introduced 1982. Imported from Japan by Weatherby.
Price: 12-ga., IMC, 26", 28" $2,200.00
Price: 20-ga., IMC, 26", 28" $2,200.00

Weatherby Athena Grade V Classic Field O/U
Similar to the Athena Grade IV except has rounded pistol grip, slender forend, oil-finished Claro walnut stock with fine-line checkering, Old English recoil pad. Sideplate receiver has rose and scroll engraving. Available in 12-gauge, 26", 28", 30", 20-gauge, 26", 28", all with 3" chambers. Introduced 1993.
Price: $2,527.00

WEATHERBY ORION O/U SHOTGUNS
Gauge: 12, 20, 3" chambers.
Barrel: 12-gauge—26", 28", 30"; 20-gauge— 26", 30"; IMC Multi-Choke tubes.
Weight: 6½ to 9 lbs.
Stock: American walnut, checkered grip and forend. Rubber recoil pad. Dimensions for Field and Skeet models, 14¼"x1½"x2½".
Features: Selective automatic ejectors, single selective mechanical trigger. Top tang safety, Greener cross bolt. Orion I has plain blued receiver, no engraving; Orion III has silver-gray receiver with engraving. Imported from Japan by Weatherby.
Price: Orion I, Field, 12, IMC, 26", 28", 30" $1,225.00
Price: Orion I, Field, 20, IMC, 26", 28" $1,225.00
Price: Orion III, Field, 12, IMC, 26", 28", 30" $1,545.00
Price: Orion III, Field, 20, IMC, 26", 28" $1,545.00

Weatherby Orion II, III Classic Field O/Us
Similar to the Orion II, Orion III except with rounded pistol grip, slender forend, high gloss Claro walnut stock with fine-line checkering, Old English recoil pad. Sideplate receiver has rose and scroll engraving. Available in 12-gauge, 26", 28", 30" (IMC tubes), 20-gauge, 26", 28" (IMC tubes), 28-gauge, 26" (IMC tubes), 3" chambers. Introduced 1993.
Price: Orion II Classic Field $1,395.00
Price: Orion III Classic Field (12 and 20 only) $1,545.00

Weatherby Orion II Sporting Clays O/U
Similar to the Orion II Field except in 12-gauge only with 2¾" chambers, 28", 30" barrels with Imp. Cyl., Mod., Full chokes. High-gloss stock finish. Stock dimensions are 14¼"x1½"x2¼"; weight 7.5 to 8 lbs. Matte finish, competition center vent. rib, mid-barrel and enlarged front beads. Rounded recoil pad. Receiver finished in silver nitride with acid-etched, gold-plate clay pigeon monogram. Barrels have lengthened forcing cones. Introduced 1992.
Price: $1,395.00

Weatherby Orion Grade II Classic Sporting

Weatherby Orion II Classic Sporting Clays O/U
Similar to the Orion II Sporting Clays except has rounded pistol grip, slender forend, high-gloss wood finish. Silver-gray nitride receiver has scroll engraving with clay pigeon monogram in gold-plate overlay. Stepped Broadway-style competition vent rib, vent side rib. Available in 12-gauge, 28", 30" with choke tubes. Introduced 1993.
Price: $1,395.00

SHOTGUNS—SIDE BY SIDES

Variety of models for utility and sporting use, including some competitive shooting.

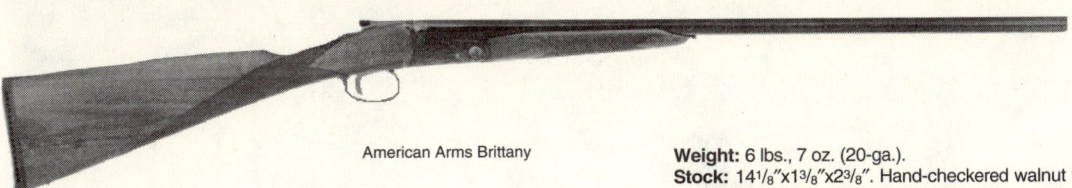

American Arms Brittany

AMERICAN ARMS BRITTANY SHOTGUN
Gauge: 12, 20, 3" chambers.
Barrel: 12-ga.—27"; 20-ga.—25" (Imp. Cyl., Mod., Full choke tubes).
Weight: 6 lbs., 7 oz. (20-ga.).
Stock: 14 1/8"x1 3/8"x2 3/8". Hand-checkered walnut with oil finish, straight English-style with semi-beavertail forend.
Features: Boxlock action with case-color finish, engraving; single selective trigger, automatic selective ejectors; rubber recoil pad. Introduced 1989. Imported from Spain by American Arms, Inc.
Price: $875.00

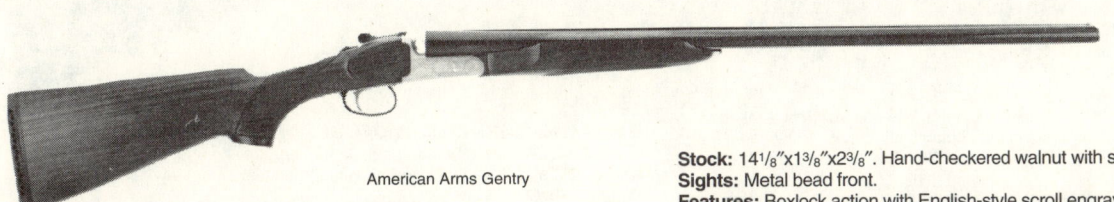

American Arms Gentry

AMERICAN ARMS GENTRY DOUBLE SHOTGUN
Gauge: 12, 20, 28, 410, 3" chambers.
Barrel: 26" (Imp. Cyl. & Mod., all gauges), 28" (Mod., & Full, 12 and 20 gauges).
Weight: 6 1/4 to 6 3/4 lbs.
Stock: 14 1/8"x1 3/8"x2 3/8". Hand-checkered walnut with semi-gloss finish.
Sights: Metal bead front.
Features: Boxlock action with English-style scroll engraving, color case-hardened finish. Double triggers, extractors. Independent floating firing pins. Manual safety. Five-year warranty. Introduced 1987. Imported from Spain by American Arms, Inc.
Price: 12 or 20 ....$734.00
Price: 28 or 410 ....$765.00

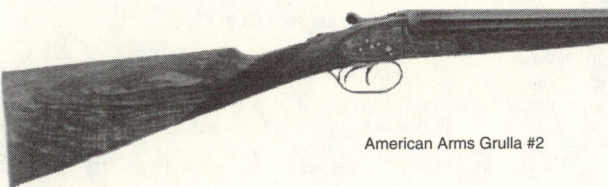

American Arms Grulla #2

AMERICAN ARMS GRULLA #2 DOUBLE SHOTGUN
Gauge: 12, 20, 28, 410.
Barrel: 12-ga.—28" (Mod. & Full); 26" (Imp. Cyl. & Mod.), all gauges.
Weight: 5 lbs., 13 oz. to 6 lbs., 4 oz.
Stock: Select walnut with straight English grip, splinter forend; hand-rubbed oil finish; checkered grip, forend, butt.
Features: True sidelock action with double triggers, detachable locks, automatic selective ejectors, cocking indicators, gas escape valves. Color case-hard~ened receiver with scroll engraving. English-style concave rib. Introduced 1989. Imported from Spain by American Arms, Inc.
Price: 12, 20, 28, 410 ....Special order only
Price: Two-barrel sets ....Special order only

AMERICAN ARMS TS/SS 12 DOUBLE
Gauge: 12, 3 1/2" chambers.
Barrel: 26", choke tubes; solid raised rib.
Weight: 7 lbs., 6 oz.
Stock: Walnut; cut-checked grip and forend.
Features: Non-reflective metal and wood finishes; boxlock action; single trigger; extractors. Imported by American Arms, Inc.
Price: $765.00

ARMSPORT 1050 SERIES DOUBLE SHOTGUNS
Gauge: 12, 20, 410, 28, 3" chambers.
Barrel: 12-ga.—28" (Mod. & Full); 20-ga.—26" (Imp. & Mod.); 410—26" (Full & Full); 28-ga.—26" (Mod. & Full).
Weight: About 6 3/4 lbs.
Stock: European walnut.
Features: Chrome-lined barrels. Boxlock action with engraving. Imported from Italy by Armsport.
Price: 12, 20 ....$785.00
Price: 28, 410 ....$860.00

ARRIETA SIDELOCK DOUBLE SHOTGUNS
Gauge: 12, 16, 20, 28, 410.
Barrel: Length and chokes to customer specs.
Weight: To customer specs.
Stock: 14 1/2"x1 1/2"x2 1/2" (standard dimensions), or to customer specs. Straight English with checkered butt (standard), or pistol grip. Select European walnut with oil finish.
Features: Essentially a custom gun with myriad options. Holland & Holland-pattern hand-detachable sidelocks, selective automatic ejectors, double triggers (hinged front) standard. Some have self-opening action. Finish and engraving to customer specs. Imported from Spain by Wingshooting Adventures.
Price: Model 557, auto ejectors, from $2,750.00
Price: Model 570, auto ejectors, from $3,380.00
Price: Model 578, auto ejectors, from $3,740.00
Price: Model 600 Imperial, self-opening, from $4,990.00
Price: Model 601 Imperial Tiro, self-opening, from $5,750.00
Price: Model 801, from $7,950.00
Price: Model 802, from $7,950.00
Price: Model 803, from $5,850.00
Price: Model 871, auto ejectors, from $4,290.00
Price: Model 872, self-opening, from $9,790.00
Price: Model 873, self-opening, from $6,850.00
Price: Model 874, self-opening, from $7,950.00
Price: Model 875, self-opening, from $12,950.00

CONSULT **Shooter's Marketplace** Page 266, This Issue

ARIZAGA MODEL 31 DOUBLE SHOTGUN
Gauge: 12, 16, 20, 28, 410.
Barrel: 26", 28" (standard chokes).
Weight: 6 lbs., 9 oz. **Length:** 45" overall.
Stock: Straight English style or pistol grip.
Features: Boxlock action with double triggers; blued, engraved receiver. Imported by Mandall Shooting Supplies.
Price: $550.00

CAUTION: PRICES SHOWN ARE SUPPLIED BY THE MANUFACTURER OR IMPORTER. CHECK YOUR LOCAL GUN SHOP.

SHOTGUNS—SIDE BY SIDES

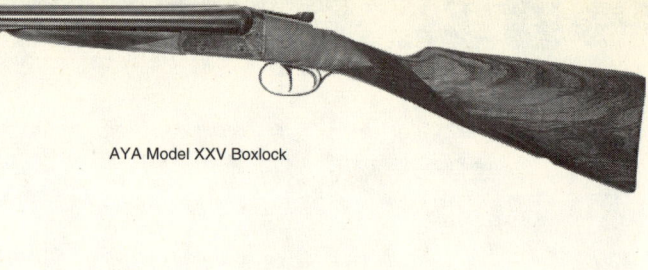

AYA Model XXV Boxlock

AYA BOXLOCK SHOTGUNS
Gauge: 12, 16, 20, 28, 410.
Barrel: 26", 27", 28", depending upon gauge.
Weight: 5 to 7 lbs.
Stock: European walnut.
Features: Anson & Deeley system with double locking lugs; chopper lump barrels; bushed firing pins; automatic safety and ejectors; articulated front trigger. Imported by Armes de Chasse.
Price: Model 931, self-opening, from $14,500.00
Price: Model XXV, 12 or 20 . . . . $3,000.00
Price: Model 4 Deluxe, 12, 16, 20, 28, 410 . . . . $3,000.00
Price: Model 4, 12, 16, 20, 28, 410 . . . . $1,700.00

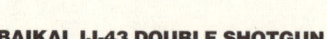

AYA Model No. 2 Sidelock

AYA SIDELOCK DOUBLE SHOTGUNS
Gauge: 12, 16, 20, 28, 410.
Barrel: 26", 27", 28", 29", depending upon gauge.
Weight: NA.
Stock: Figured European walnut; cut checkering; oil finish.
Features: Sidelock actions with double triggers (articulated front), automatic safety, automatic ejectors, cocking indicators, bushed firing pins, replaceable hinge pins, chopper lump barrels. Many options available. Imported by Armes de Chasse.
Price: Model 1, 12 or 20, exhibition-quality wood $6,600.00
Price: Model 2, 12, 16, 20, 28, 410 . . . . $3,200.00
Price: Model 53, 12, 16, 20 . . . . $5,000.00
Price: Model 56, 12 only $8,000.00
Price: Model XXV, 12 or 20, Churchill-type rib $4,000.00

BAIKAL IJ-43M DOUBLE SHOTGUN
Gauge: 12, 2 3/4" chambers.
Barrel: 28.5" (Mod. & Full).
Weight: NA. **Length:** 44.5" overall.
Stock: European hardwood.
Features: Blued boxlock action with double triggers, extractors, automatic safety; sling swivels. Chrome-lined bores. Imported from Russia by Century International Arms.
Price: About $255.00
Price: IJ-43EM (automatic ejectors), about $270.00

BAIKAL IJ-43 DOUBLE SHOTGUN
Gauge: 12, 2 3/4" chambers.
Barrel: 20" (Cyl. & Cyl.), 28" (Mod. & Full).
Weight: About 6.75 lbs.
Stock: Checkered walnut.
Features: Double triggers; extractors; blued, engraved receiver. Reintroduced 1994. Imported from Russia by K.B.I., Inc.
Price: $249.00

BERETTA MODEL 452 SIDELOCK SHOTGUN
Gauge: 12, 2 3/4" or 3" chambers.
Barrel: 26", 28", 30", choked to customer specs.
Weight: 6 lbs., 13 oz.
Stock: Dimensions to customer specs. Highly figured walnut; Model 452 EELL has walnut briar.
Features: Full sidelock action with English-type double bolting; automatic selective ejectors, manual safety; double triggers, single or single non-selective trigger on request. Essentially custom made to specifications. Model 452 is coin finished without engraving; 452 EELL is fully engraved. Imported from Italy by Beretta U.S.A.
Price: 452 . . . . $22,500.00
Price: 452 EELL $31,000.00

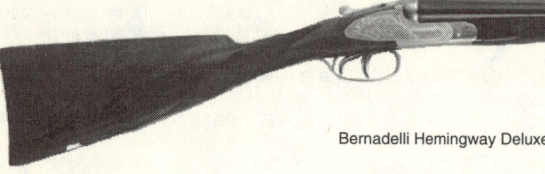

Bernadelli Hemingway Deluxe

BERNARDELLI HEMINGWAY LIGHTWEIGHT DOUBLES
Gauge: 12, 20, 2 3/4" or 3", 16, 2 3/4" chambers.
Barrel: 23 1/2" to 28" (Cyl. & Imp. Cyl. to Mod. & Full).
Weight: 6 1/4 lbs.
Stock: Straight English grip of checkered European walnut.
Features: Silvered and engraved boxlock action. Folding front trigger on double-trigger models. Ejectors. Imported from Italy by Armsport.
Price: 12 or 20 . . . . $1,750.00
Price: With single trigger $1,800.00
Price: Deluxe, double trigger $1,900.00
Price: As above, single trigger $2,000.00

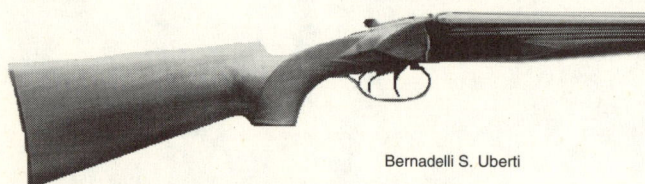

Bernadelli S. Uberti

BERNARDELLI SERIES S. UBERTO DOUBLES
Gauge: 12, 20, 28, 2 3/4" or 3" chambers.
Barrel: 25 5/8", 26 3/4", 28", 29 1/2" (Mod. & Full).
Weight: 6 to 6 1/2 lbs.
Stock: 14 3/16"x2 3/8"x1 9/16" standard dimensions. Select walnut with hand checkering.
Features: Anson & Deeley boxlock action with Purdey locks, choice of extractors or ejectors. Custom options available. Imported from Italy by Armsport.
Price: With ejectors $1,555.00
Price: With extractors $1,435.00
Price: F.S. model, ejectors $1,750.00

Bernardelli Series Roma Shotguns
Similar to the Series S. Uberto models except with dummy sideplates to simulate sidelock action. In 12-, 16-, 20-, 28-gauge, 25 1/2", 26 3/4", 28", 29" barrels. Straight English or pistol grip stock. Chrome-lined barrels, boxlock action, double triggers, ejectors, automatic safety. Checkered butt. Special choke combinations, barrel lengths available. Imported from Italy by Armsport.
Price: Roma 3, extractors, about $1,470.00
Price: Roma 4, about $1,800.00
Price: Roma 6, about $1,970.00
Price: Roma 7M, ejectors, about $2,750.00
Price: Roma 8M, ejectors, about $3,250.00
Price: Roma 9M, ejectors, about $3,850.00
Price: Las Palomas, 12, 20, about $3,350.00

SHOTGUNS—SIDE BY SIDES

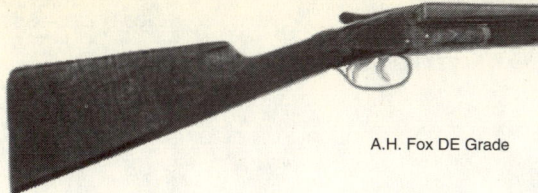

A.H. Fox DE Grade

Consult our Directory pages for the location of firms mentioned.

A.H. FOX SIDE-BY-SIDE SHOTGUNS
Gauge: 20, 2¾" chambers.
Barrel: Length and chokes to customer specifications. Rust-blued Chromox or Krupp steel.
Weight: 5½ to 7 lbs.
Stock: Dimensions to customer specifications. Hand-checkered Turkish Circassian walnut with hand-rubbed oil finish. Straight, semi- or full pistol grip; splinter, schnabel or beavertail forend; traditional pad, hard rubber buttplate or skeleton butt.
Features: Boxlock action with automatic ejectors; double or Fox single selective trigger. Scalloped, rebated and color case-hardened receiver; hand finished and hand-engraved. Grades differ in engraving, inlays, grade of wood, amount of hand finishing. Introduced 1993. Made in U.S. by Connecticut Shotgun Mfg.
Price: CE Grade $7,200.00
Price: XE Grade $8,500.00
Price: DE Grade $12,500.00
Price: FE Grade $17,500.00
Price: Exhibition Grade $25,000.000

AUGUSTE FRANCOTTE BOXLOCK SHOTGUN
Gauge: 12, 16, 20, 28 and 410-bore, 2¾" or 3" chambers.
Barrel: 26" to 29", chokes to customer specs.
Weight: NA. **Length:** NA.
Stock: Deluxe European walnut to customer specs. Straight or pistol grip; checkered butt; oil finish; splinter or beavertail forend.
Sights: Bead front.
Features: Anson & Deeley boxlock action with double locks, double triggers (front hinged), manual or automatic safety, Holland & Holland ejectors. English scroll engraving, coin finish or color case-hardening. Custom made to customer's specs. Many options available. Imported from Belgium by Armes de Chasse.
Price: From about (no engraving) $16,500.00

AUGUSTE FRANCOTTE SIDELOCK SHOTGUN
Gauge: 12, 16, 20, 28 and 410-bore, 2¾" or 3" chambers.
Barrel: 26" to 29", chokes to customer specs.
Weight: NA. **Length:** NA.
Stock: Deluxe European walnut to customer specs. Straight or pistol grip; checkered butt; oil finish; splinter or beavertail forend.
Sights: Bead front.
Features: True Holland & Holland sidelock action with double locks, double triggers (front hinged), manual or automatic safety, Holland & Holland ejectors. English scroll engraving, coin finish or color case-hardening. Many options available. Imported from Belgium by Armes de Chasse.
Price: From about (no engraving) .... $20,000.00 to $25,000.00

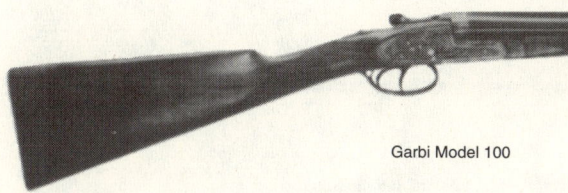

Garbi Model 100

Garbi Model 101 Side-by-Side
Similar to the Garbi Model 100 except is hand engraved with scroll engraving, select walnut stock. Better overall quality than the Model 100. Imported from Spain by Wm. Larkin Moore.
Price: From $5,250.00

Garbi Model 103A, B Side-by-Side
Similar to the Garbi Model 100 except has Purdey-type fine scroll and rosette engraving. Better overall quality than the Model 101. Model 103B has nickel-chrome steel barrels, H&H-type easy opening mechanism; other mechanical details remain the same. Imported from Spain by Wm. Larkin Moore.
Price: Model 103A, from $6,550.00
Price: Model 103B, from $9,200.00

GARBI MODEL 100 DOUBLE
Gauge: 12, 16, 20, 28.
Barrel: 26", 28", choked to customer specs.
Weight: 5½ to 7½ lbs.
Stock: 14½"x2¼"x1½". European walnut. Straight grip, checkered butt, classic forend.
Features: Sidelock action, automatic ejectors, double triggers standard. Color case-hardened action, coin finish optional. Single trigger; beavertail forend, etc. optional. Five other models are available. Imported from Spain by Wm. Larkin Moore.
Price: From $4,100.00

Garbi Model 200 Side-by-Side
Similar to the Garbi Model 100 except has heavy-duty locks, magnum proofed. Very fine Continental-style floral and scroll engraving, well figured walnut stock. Other mechanical features remain the same. Imported from Spain by Wm. Larkin Moore.
Price: $8,800.00

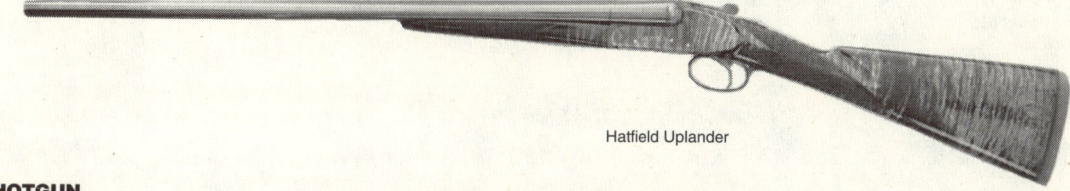

Hatfield Uplander

HATFIELD UPLANDER SHOTGUN
Gauge: 20, 3" chambers.
Barrel: 26" (Imp. Cyl. & Mod.).
Weight: 5¾ lbs.
Stock: Straight English style, special select XXX fancy maple. Hand-rubbed oil finish. Splinter forend.
Features: Double locking under-lug boxlock action; color case-hardened frame; single non-selective trigger. Grades differ in engraving, finish, gold work. Introduced 1988. From Hatfield.
Price: Grade I $2,249.00
Price: Grade II $2,995.00

CRUCELEGUI HERMANOS MODEL 150 DOUBLE
Gauge: 12, 16 or 20, 2¾" chambers.
Action: Greener triple cross bolt.
Barrel: 20", 26", 28", 30", 32" (Cyl. & Cyl., Full & Full, Mod. & Full, Mod. & Imp. Cyl., Imp. Cyl. & Full, Mod. & Mod.).
Weight: 5 to 7¼ lbs.
Stock: Hand-checkered walnut, beavertail forend.
Features: Double triggers; color case-hardened receiver; sling swivels; chrome-lined bores. Imported from Spain by Mandall Shooting Supplies.
Price: $450.00

SHOTGUNS—SIDE BY SIDES

HHF MODEL 200 A 12 ST SIDE-BY-SIDE
Gauge: 12, 3" chambers.
Barrel: 28", fixed chokes or choke tubes.
Weight: About 7½ lbs.
Stock: Circassian walnut, field dimensions.
Features: Boxlock action with single selective trigger, extractors, manual safety. Silvered receiver with 15 percent engraving coverage. Many options available. Introduced 1995. Imported from Turkey by Turkish Firearms Corp.
Price: Fixed chokes, extractors $1,050.00
Price: As above, 28, 410 .... $1,495.00
Price: Choke tubes, extractors $1,050.00
Price: Model 202 A 12 ST (double triggers, 30 percent engraving coverage $1,025.00
Price: As above, 28, 410 .... $1,495.00
Price: With extractors, choke tubes, 12, 20 .... $1,025.00

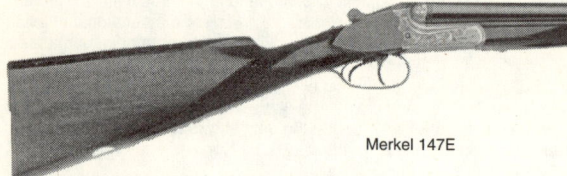
Merkel 147E

Merkel Model 47S, 147S Side-by-Sides
Similar to the Model 122 except with Holland & Holland-style sidelock action with cocking indicators, ejectors. Silver-grayed receiver and sideplates have Arabesque engraving, engraved border and screws (Model 47S), or fine hunting scene engraving (Model 147S). Imported from Germany by GSI.
Price: Model 47S $4,495.00
Price: Model 147S $5,595.00
Price: Model 247S (English-style engraving, large scrolls) $6,895.00
Price: Model 347S (English-style engraving, medium scrolls) ... $7,895.00
Price: Model 447S (English-style engraving, small scrolls) $8,995.00

MERKEL MODEL 8, 47E SIDE-BY-SIDE SHOTGUNS
Gauge: 12, 3" chambers, 16, 2¾" chambers, 20, 3" chambers.
Barrel: 12-, 16-ga.—28"; 20-ga.—26¾" (Imp. Cyl. & Mod., Mod. & Full).
Weight: About 6¾ lbs. (12-ga.).
Stock: Oil-finished walnut; straight English or pistol grip.
Features: Anson & Deeley-type boxlock action with single selective or double triggers, automatic safety, cocking indicators. Color case-hardened receiver with standard Arabesque engraving. Imported from Germany by GSI.
Price: Model 8 (extractors only) $1,395.00
Price: Model 47E (H&H ejectors) $1,795.00
Price: Model 147 (extractors, silver-grayed receiver with hunting scenes) $1,895.00
Price: Model 147E (as above with ejectors) $2,295.00
Price: Model 122 (as above with false sideplates, fine engraving) .. $3,795.00

PARKER REPRODUCTIONS SIDE-BY-SIDE SHOTGUN
Gauge: 12, 16/20 combo, 20, 28, 2¾" and 3" chambers.
Barrel: 26" (Skeet 1 & 2, Imp. Cyl. & Mod.), 28" (Mod. & Full, 2¾" and 3", 12, 20, 28; Skeet 1 & 2, Imp. Cyl. & Mod., Mod. & Full 16-ga. only).
Weight: 6¾ lbs. (12-ga.)
Stock: Checkered (26 lpi) AAA fancy California English or Claro walnut, skeleton steel and checkered butt. Straight or pistol grip, splinter or beavertail forend.
Features: Exact reproduction of the original Parker—parts interchange. Double or single selective trigger, selective ejectors, hard-chromed bores, designed for steel shot. One, two or three (16-20, 20) barrel sets available. Hand-engraved snap caps included. Introduced 1984. Made by Winchester. Imported from Japan by Parker Division, Reagent Chemical.
Price: D Grade, one-barrel set $3,370.00
Price: Two-barrel set, same gauge $4,200.00
Price: Two-barrel set, 16/20 .... $4,870.00
Price: Three-barrel set, 16/20/20 .... $5,630.00
Price: A-1 Special two-barrel set $11,200.00
Price: A-1 Special three-barrel set $13,200.00

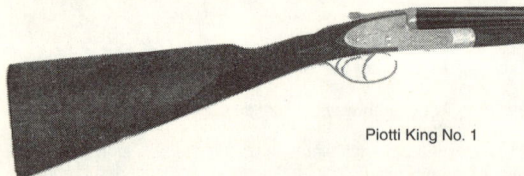
Piotti King No. 1

Piotti Lunik Side-by-Side
Similar to the Piotti King No. 1 except better overall quality. Has Renaissance-style large scroll engraving in relief, gold crown in top lever, gold name and gold crest in forend. Best quality Holland & Holland-pattern sidelock ejector double with chopper lump (demi-bloc) barrels. Other mechanical specifications remain the same. Imported from Italy by Wm. Larkin Moore.
Price: From $20,000.00

Piotti King Extra Side-by-Side
Similar to the Piotti King No. 1 except highest quality wood and metal work. Choice of either bulino game scene engraving or game scene engraving with gold inlays. Engraved and signed by a master engraver. Exhibition grade wood. Other mechanical specifications remain the same. Imported from Italy by Wm. Larkin Moore.
Price: From $22,500.00

PIOTTI KING NO. 1 SIDE-BY-SIDE
Gauge: 12, 16, 20, 28, 410.
Barrel: 25" to 30" (12-ga.), 25" to 28" (16, 20, 28, 410). To customer specs. Chokes as specified.
Weight: 6½ lbs. to 8 lbs. (12-ga. to customer specs.).
Stock: Dimensions to customer specs. Finely figured walnut; straight grip with checkered butt with classic splinter forend and hand-rubbed oil finish standard. Pistol grip, beavertail forend, satin luster finish optional.
Features: Holland & Holland pattern sidelock action, automatic ejectors. Double trigger with front trigger hinged standard; non-selective single trigger optional. Coin finish standard; color case-hardened optional. Top rib; level, file-cut standard; concave, ventilated optional. Very fine, full coverage scroll engraving with small floral bouquets, gold crown in top lever, name in gold, and gold crest in forend. Imported from Italy by Wm. Larkin Moore.
Price: From $18,600.00

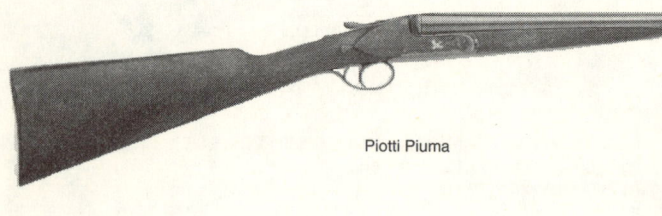
Piotti Piuma

PIOTTI PIUMA SIDE-BY-SIDE
Gauge: 12, 16, 20, 28, 410.
Barrel: 25" to 30" (12-ga.), 25" to 28" (16, 20, 28, 410).
Weight: 5½ to 6¼ lbs. (20-ga.).
Stock: Dimensions to customer specs. Straight grip stock with walnut checkered butt, classic splinter forend, hand-rubbed oil finish are standard; pistol grip, beavertail forend, satin luster finish optional.
Features: Anson & Deeley boxlock ejector double with chopper lump barrels. Level, file-cut rib, light scroll and rosette engraving, scalloped frame. Double triggers with hinged front standard, single non-selective optional. Coin finish standard, color case-hardened optional. Imported from Italy by Wm. Larkin Moore.
Price: From $10,800.00

SHOTGUNS—SIDE BY SIDES

RIZZINI BOXLOCK SIDE-BY-SIDE
Gauge: 12, 16, 20, 28, 410.
Barrel: 25" to 30" (12-, 16-, 20-ga.), 25" to 28" (28, 410).
Weight: 5½ to 6¼ lbs. (20-ga.).
Stock: Dimensions to customer specs. Straight grip stock with checkered butt, classic splinter forend, hand-rubbed oil finish are standard; pistol grip, beavertail forend; satin luster finish optional.
Features: Anson & Deeley boxlock ejector double with chopper lump barrels. Level, file-cut rib, scalloped frame. Double triggers with hinged front optional, single non-selective standard. Coin finish standard. Imported from Italy by Wm. Larkin Moore.
Price: 12-, 20-ga., from $25,000.00
Price: 28, 410 bore, from $28,000.00

RIZZINI SIDELOCK SIDE-BY-SIDE
Gauge: 12, 16, 20, 28, 410.
Barrel: 25" to 30" (12-, 16-, 20-ga.), 25" to 28" (28, 410). To customer specs. Chokes as specified.
Weight: 6½ lbs. to 8 lbs. (12-ga. to customer specs).
Stock: Dimensions to customer specs. Finely figured walnut; straight grip with checkered butt with classic splinter forend and hand-rubbed oil finish standard. Pistol grip, beavertail forend, satin luster finish optional.
Features: Holland & Holland pattern sidelock action, auto ejectors. Double triggers with front trigger hinged optional; non-selective single trigger standard. Coin finish standard. Top rib level, file cut standard; concave optional. Imported from Italy by Wm. Larkin Moore.
Price: 12-, 20-ga., from $41,000.00
Price: 28, 410 bore, from $46,000.00

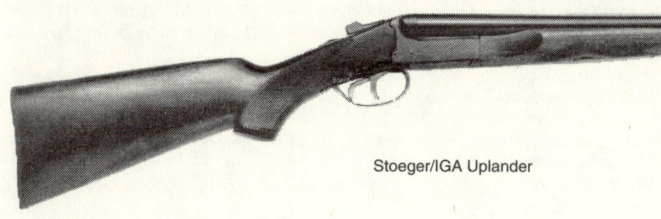
Stoeger/IGA Uplander

STOEGER/IGA UPLANDER SIDE-BY-SIDE SHOTGUN
Gauge: 12, 20, 28, 2¾" chambers; 410, 3" chambers.
Barrel: 26" (Full & Full, 410 only, Imp. Cyl. & Mod.), 28" (Mod. & Full).
Weight: 6¾ to 7 lbs.
Stock: 14½"x1½"x2½". Oil-finished hardwood. Checkered pistol grip and forend.
Features: Automatic safety, extractors only, solid matted barrel rib. Double triggers only. Introduced 1983. Imported from Brazil by Stoeger Industries.
Price: $398.00
Price: With choke tubes $442.00
Price: Coach Gun, 12, 20, 410, 20" bbls. $382.00

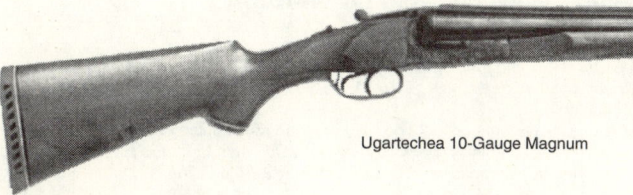
Ugartechea 10-Gauge Magnum

UGARTECHEA 10-GAUGE MAGNUM SHOTGUN
Gauge: 10, 3½" chambers.
Action: Boxlock.
Barrel: 32" (Full).
Weight: 11 lbs.
Stock: 14½"x1½"x2⅝". European walnut, checkered at pistol grip and forend.
Features: Double triggers; color case-hardened action, rest blued. Front and center metal beads on matted rib; ventilated rubber recoil pad. Forend release has positive Purdey-type mechanism. Imported from Spain by Mandall Shooting Supplies.
Price: $699.50

SHOTGUNS—BOLT ACTIONS & SINGLE SHOTS

Variety of designs for utility and sporting purposes, as well as for competitive shooting.

ARMSPORT SINGLE BARREL SHOTGUN
Gauge: 20, 3" chamber.
Barrel: 26" (Mod.).
Weight: About 6½ lbs.
Stock: Hardwood with oil finish.
Features: Chrome-lined barrel, manual safety, cocking indicator. opening lever behind trigger guard. Imported by Armsport.
Price: $100.00

BAIKAL IJ-18 SINGLE BARREL SHOTGUN
Gauge: 12, 3" chamber.
Barrel: 28.5".
Weight: 6 lbs. **Length:** 44.5" overall.
Stock: European hardwood.
Features: Chrome-lined bore; extractor; cocking indicator; cross-bolt safety. Imported from Russia by Century International Arms.
Price: About $95.00
Price: IJ-18EM (automatic ejector), about $108.00

BAIKAL IJ-18M SHOTGUN
Gauge: 12, 16, 2¾", 20, 410, 3" chamber.
Barrel: 12, 20-ga.—26" (Imp. Cyl.), 410 (Full); 12, 20-ga.—28" (Full, Mod.).
Weight: 5.5 to 6 lbs.
Stock: Stained hardwood.
Features: External hammer with cocking indicator; trigger block safety; engraved, blued receiver. Re-introduced 1994. Imported from Russia by K.B.I., Inc.
Price: $69.00

> Consult our Directory pages for the location of firms mentioned.

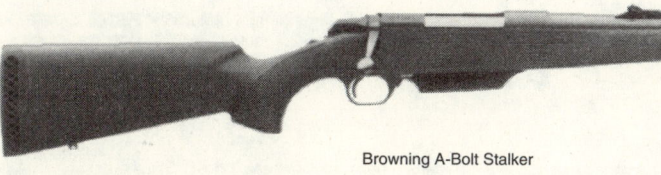
Browning A-Bolt Stalker

BROWNING A-BOLT SHOTGUN
Gauge: 12, 3" chamber, 2-shot detachable magazine.
Barrel: 22" (fully rifled), 23" (5" Invector choke tube).
Weight: 7 lbs., 2 oz. **Length:** 44¾" overall.
Stock: 14"x⅝"x1½". Walnut with satin finish on Hunter; black graphite fiberglass composite. Swivel studs.
Sights: Blade front with red insert, open adjustable rear. Drilled and tapped for scope mounting.
Features: Uses same bolt system as A-Bolt rifle with 60° bolt throw; front-locking bolt with claw extractor; hinged floorplate. Matte finish on barrel and receiver. Introduced 1995. Imported by Browning.
Price: Hunter, rifled barrel $839.95
Price: Stalker, rifled barrel $759.95
Price: Hunter, Invector barrel $789.95
Price: Stalker, Invector barrel $709.95

CAUTION: PRICES SHOWN ARE SUPPLIED BY THE MANUFACTURER OR IMPORTER. CHECK YOUR LOCAL GUN SHOP.

SHOTGUNS—BOLT ACTIONS & SINGLE SHOTS

Browning BT-100 Trap

BROWNING BT-100 TRAP SHOTGUN
Gauge: 12, 2¾" chamber.
Barrel: 32", 34" (Invector Plus); back-bored; also with fixed Full choke.
Weight: 8 lbs., 9 oz. **Length:** 48½" overall (32" barrel).
Stock: 14⅜"x1⁹⁄₁₆"x17⁄162½"x2" (Monte Carlo); 14⅜"x1¾"x1¼"x2⅛" (thumbhole). Walnut with high gloss finish; cut checkering. Wedge-shaped forend with finger groove.
Features: Available in stainless steel or blue. Has drop-out trigger adjustable for weight of pull from 3½ to 5½ lbs., and for three length postions; Ejector-Selector allows ejection or extraction of shells. Available with adjustable comb stock and thumbhole style. Introduced 1995. Imported from Japan by Browning.
Price: Grade I, blue, Monte Carlo, Invector Plus $1,900.00
Price: As above, fixed Full choke $1,855.00
Price: Stainless steel, Monte Carlo, Invector Plus $2,300.00
Price: As above, fixed Full choke $2,255.00
Price: Thunbhole stock, blue, stainless, Invector Plus .... NA
Price: Adjustable comb stock, add $200.00
Price: Replacement trigger assembly $500.00

BROWNING BT-99 MAX SHOTGUN
Gauge: 12, 2¾" chamber.
Barrel: 32" or 34" with ¹¹⁄₃₂" wide high post floating vent. rib. Comes with Invector Plus choke tubes; .745" overbore.
Weight: 8 lbs., 10 oz. (32" bbl.).
Stock: Walnut; hand-checkered, full pistol grip, full finger groove forend; recoil pad. Trap dimensions with M.C. 14⅜"x1⁹⁄₁₆"x1⁷⁄₁₆"x2".
Sights: Ivory front and middle beads.
Features: Gold-plated trigger with 3½-lb. pull, deluxe trap-style recoil pad, automatic ejector, no safety. Available with either Monte Carlo or standard stock. Imported from Japan by Browning.
Price: Grade I Invector, Plus Ported barrels $1,495.95
Price: Stainless, ported $1,895.95

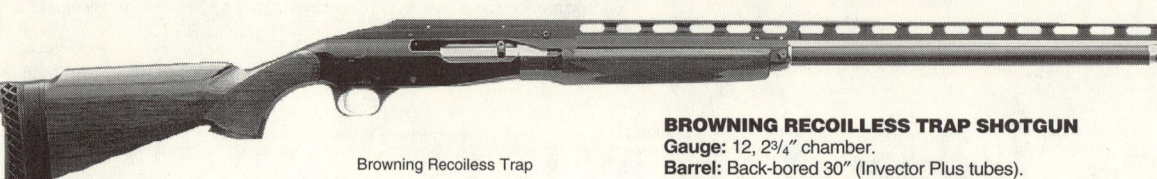

Browning Recoiless Trap

BROWNING RECOILLESS TRAP SHOTGUN
Gauge: 12, 2¾" chamber.
Barrel: Back-bored 30" (Invector Plus tubes).
Weight: 9 lbs., 1 oz. **Length:** 51⅝" overall.
Stock: 14"-14¾"x1⅜"-1¾"x1⅛"-1¾". Select walnut with high gloss finish, cut checkering.
Features: Eliminates up to 72 percent of recoil. Mass of the inner mechansim (barrel, receiver and inner bolt) is driven forward when trigger is pulled, cancelling most recoil. Forend is used to cock action when the action is forward. Ventilated rib adjusts to move point of impact; drop at comb and length of pull adjustable. Introduced 1993. Imported by Browning.
Price: $1,900.00

Browning Micro Recoilless Trap Shotgun
Same as the standard Recoilless Trap except has 27" barrel, weighs 8 lbs., 10 oz., and stock length of pull adjustable from 13" to 13¾", Overall length 47⅝". Introduced 1993. Imported by Browning.
Price: $1,900.00

H&R Bull Barrel Slug Gun

HARRINGTON & RICHARDSON SB2-980 ULTRA SLUG
Gauge: 12, 3" chamber.
Barrel: 24", fully rifled.
Weight: 9 lbs. **Length:** NA.
Stock: Walnut-stained hardwood.
Sights: None furnished; comes with scope mount.
Features: Uses the H&R 10-gauge action with heavy-wall barrel. Monte Carlo stock has sling swivels; comes with black nylon sling. Introduced 1995. Made in U.S. by H&R 1871, Inc.
Price: $209.95

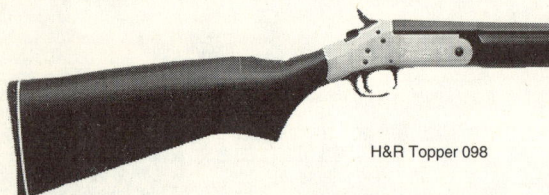

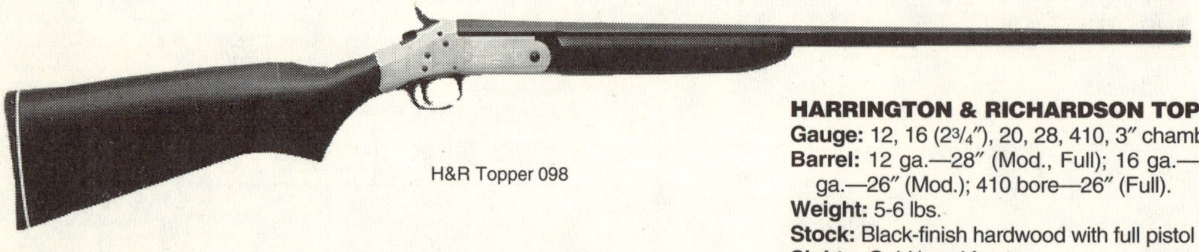

H&R Topper 098

HARRINGTON & RICHARDSON TOPPER MODEL 098
Gauge: 12, 16 (2¾"), 20, 28, 410, 3" chamber.
Barrel: 12 ga.—28" (Mod., Full); 16 ga.— 28" (Mod.); 20 ga.—26" (Mod.); 28 ga.—26" (Mod.); 410 bore—26" (Full).
Weight: 5-6 lbs.
Stock: Black-finish hardwood with full pistol grip; semi-beavertail forend.
Sights: Gold bead front.
Features: Break-open action with side-lever release, automatic ejector. Satin nickel frame, blued barrel. Reintroduced 1992. From H&R 1871, Inc.
Price: $109.95
Price: Topper Junior 098 (as above except 22" barrel, 20-ga. (Mod.), 410-bore (Full), 12½" length of pull) $114.95

Harrington & Richardson Topper Deluxe Model 098
Similar to the standard Topper 098 except 12-gauge only with 3½" chamber, 28" barrel with choke tube (comes with Mod. tube, others optional). Satin nickel frame, blued barrel, black-finished wood. Introduced 1992. From H&R 1871, Inc.
Price: $129.95

Harrington & Richardson N.W.T.F Turkey Mag
Similar to the Topper 098 except covered with Mossy Oak camouflage. Chambered for 12-gauge 3½" chamber, 24" barrel (comes with Turkey Full choke tube, others available); weighs 6 lbs., overall length 40". Comes with Mossy Oak sling, swivels, studs. Introduced 1992. From H&R 1871, Inc.
Price: $179.95
Price: N.W.T.F. Youth Turkey (3" 20-ga., 22", Full choke, recoil pad) ... $159.95

Harrington & Richardson Topper Classic Youth Shotgun
Similar to the Topper Junior 098 except available in 20-gauge (3", Mod.), 410-bore (Full) with 3" chamber; 28-gauge, 2¾" chamber (Mod.); all have 22" barrel. Stock is American black walnut with cut-checkered pistol grip and forend. Ventilated rubber recoil pad with white line spacers. Blued barrel, blued frame. Introduced 1992. From H&R 1871, Inc.
Price: $139.95

SHOTGUNS—BOLT ACTIONS & SINGLE SHOTS

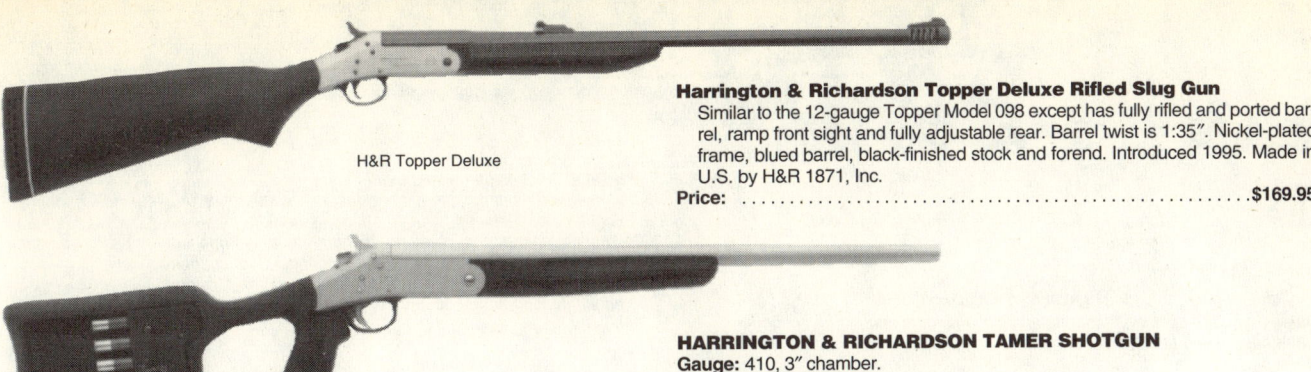

H&R Topper Deluxe

Harrington & Richardson Topper Deluxe Rifled Slug Gun
Similar to the 12-gauge Topper Model 098 except has fully rifled and ported barrel, ramp front sight and fully adjustable rear. Barrel twist is 1:35". Nickel-plated frame, blued barrel, black-finished stock and forend. Introduced 1995. Made in U.S. by H&R 1871, Inc.
Price: $169.95

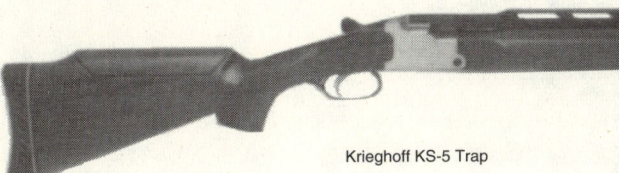

H&R Tamer

HARRINGTON & RICHARDSON TAMER SHOTGUN
Gauge: 410, 3" chamber.
Barrel: 19 1/2" (Full).
Weight: 5-6 lbs. **Length:** 33" overall.
Stock: Thumbhole grip of high density black polymer.
Features: Uses H&R Topper action with matte electroless nickel finish. Stock holds four spare shotshells. Introduced 1994. From H&R 1871, Inc.
Price: $124.95

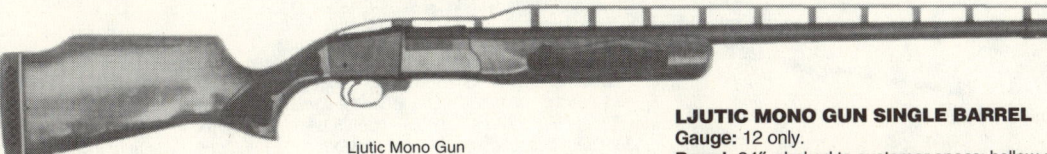

Krieghoff KS-5 Trap

KRIEGHOFF KS-5 TRAP GUN
Gauge: 12, 2 3/4" chamber.
Barrel: 32", 34"; Full choke or choke tubes.
Weight: About 8 1/2 lbs.
Stock: Choice of high Monte Carlo (1 1/2"), low Monte Carlo (1 3/8") or factory adjustable stock. European walnut.
Features: Ventilated tapered step rib. Adjustable trigger or optional release trigger. Satin gray electroless nickel receiver. Comes with fitted aluminum case. Introduced 1988. Imported from Germany by Krieghoff International, Inc.
Price: Fixed choke, cased $3,575.00
Price: With choke tubes $3,975.00

Krieghoff KS-5 Special
Same as the KS-5 except the barrel has a fully adjustable rib and adjustable stock. Rib allows shooter to adjust point of impact from 50%/50% to nearly 90%/10%. Introduced 1990.
Price: $4,480.00

KRIEGHOFF K-80 SINGLE BARREL TRAP GUN
Gauge: 12, 2 3/4" chamber.
Barrel: 32" or 34" Unsingle; 34" Top Single. Fixed Full or choke tubes.
Weight: About 8 3/4 lbs.
Stock: Four stock dimensions or adjustable stock available. All hand-checkered European walnut.
Features: Satin nickel finish with K-80 logo. Selective mechanical trigger adjustable for finger position. Tapered step vent. rib. Adjustable point of impact on Unsingle.
Price: Standard grade full Unsingle $7,595.00
Price: Standard grade full Top Single combo (special order), from ... $9,595.00
Price: RT (removable trigger) option, add $1,000.00

Ljutic Mono Gun

LJUTIC MONO GUN SINGLE BARREL
Gauge: 12 only.
Barrel: 34", choked to customer specs; hollow-milled rib, 35 1/2" sight plane.
Weight: Approx. 9 lbs.
Stock: To customer specs. Oil finish, hand checkered.
Features: Totally custom made. Pull or release trigger; removable trigger guard contains trigger and hammer mechanism; Ljutic pushbutton opener on front of trigger guard. From Ljutic Industries.
Price: With standard, medium or Olympic rib, custom 32"-34" bbls. ... $4,595.00
Price: As above with screw-in choke barrel $4,795.00

Ljutic LTX Super Deluxe Mono Gun
Super Deluxe version of the standard Mono Gun with high quality wood, extra-fancy checkering pattern in 24 lpi, double recessed choking. Available in two weights: 8 1/4 lbs. or 8 3/4 lbs. Extra light 33" barrel; medium-height rib. Introduced 1984. From Ljutic Industries.
Price: $5,799.00
Price: With three screw-in choke tubes $5,995.00

LJUTIC RECOILLESS SPACE GUN SHOTGUN
Gauge: 12 only, 2 3/4" chamber.
Barrel: 30" (Full). Screw-in or fixed-choke barrel.
Weight: 8 1/2 lbs.
Stock: 14 1/2" to 15" pull length; universal comb; medium or large p.g.
Sights: Vent. rib.
Features: Pull trigger standard, release trigger available; anti-recoil mechanism. Revolutionary design. Introduced 1981. From Ljutic Industries.
Price: From $5,995.00

Marlin Model 55

MARLIN MODEL 55 GOOSE GUN BOLT ACTION
Gauge: 12 only, 2 3/4" or 3" chamber.
Action: Bolt action, thumb safety, detachable two-shot clip. Red cocking indicator.
Barrel: 36" (Full).
Weight: 8 lbs. **Length:** 56 3/4" overall.
Stock: Walnut-finished hardwood, p.g., ventilated recoil pad. Swivel studs, MarShield® finish.
Features: Brass bead front sight, U-groove rear sight.
Price: $298.60

SHOTGUNS—BOLT ACTIONS & SINGLE SHOTS

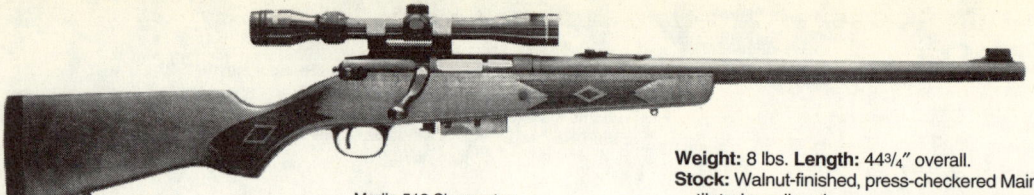
Marlin 512 Slugmaster

MARLIN MODEL 512 SLUGMASTER SHOTGUN
Gauge: 12, 3" chamber; 2-shot detachable box magazine.
Barrel: 21", rifled (1:28" twist).
Weight: 8 lbs. **Length:** 44¾" overall.
Stock: Walnut-finished, press-checkered Maine birch with Mar-Shield® finish, ventilated recoil pad.
Sights: Ramp front with brass bead and removable Wide-Scan™ hood, adjustable folding semi-buckhorn rear. Drilled and tapped for scope mounting.
Features: Uses Model 55 action with thumb safety. Designed for shooting saboted slugs. Comes with special Weaver scope mount. Introduced 1994. Made in U.S. by Marlin Firearms Co.
Price: $353.35

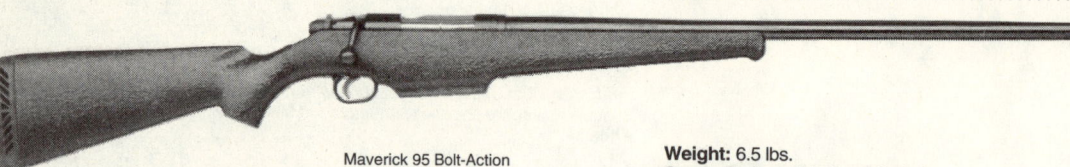
Maverick 95 Bolt-Action

MAVERICK MODEL 95 BOLT-ACTION SHOTGUN
Gauge: 12, 3" chamber, 2-shot magazine.
Barrel: 25" (Mod.).
Weight: 6.5 lbs.
Stock: Textured black synthetic.
Sights: Bead front.
Features: Full-length stock with integral magazine; ambidextrous rotating safety; twin extractors; rubber recoil pad. Blue finish. Introduced 1995. From Maverick Arms.
Price: $176.00

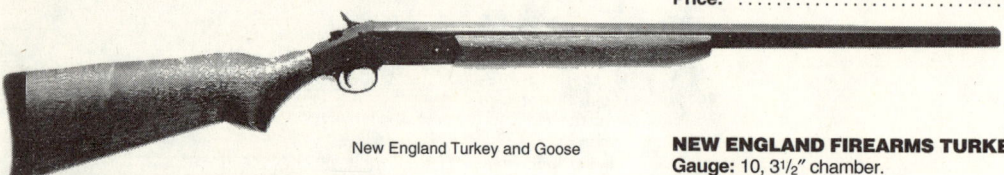
New England Turkey and Goose

New England Firearms Turkey Special
Similar to the Turkey and Goose gun except 12-gauge, 3" chamber, 24" (fixed Full Turkey choke). Full coverage Realtree camouflage. Weighs 5-6 lbs, overall length 40". Stock has modified pistol grip, recoil pad, swivel studs. Introduced 1994. From New England Firearms.
Price: About $115.00

NEW ENGLAND FIREARMS TURKEY AND GOOSE GUN
Gauge: 10, 3½" chamber.
Barrel: 28" (Full).
Weight: 9.5 lbs. **Length:** 44" overall.
Stock: American hardwood with walnut, or matte camo finish; ventilated rubber recoil pad.
Sights: Bead front.
Features: Break-open action with side-lever release; ejector. Matte finish on metal. Introduced 1992. From New England Firearms.
Price: Walnut-finish wood $159.95
Price: Camo finish, sling and swivels $169.95

New England Firearms N.W.T.F.

New England Firearms N.W.T.F. Shotgun
Similar to the Turkey/Goose Gun except completely covered with Mossy Oak camouflage finish; 24" barrel with interchangeable choke tubes (comes with Turkey Full, others optional); comes with Mossy Oak sling. Drilled and tapped for long eye relief scope mount. Introduced 1992. From New England Firearms.
Price: $229.95
Price: 20-ga., 24" (Mod.), Mossy Oak camo $149.95

NEW ENGLAND FIREARMS STANDARD PARDNER
Gauge: 12, 20, 410, 3" chamber; 16, 28, 2¾" chamber.
Barrel: 12-ga.—28" (Full, Mod.), 32" (Full); 16-ga.—28" (Full), 32" (Full); 20-ga.—26" (Full, Mod.); 28-ga.—26" (Mod.); 410-bore—26" (Full).
Weight: 5-6 lbs. **Length:** 43" overall (28" barrel).
Stock: Walnut-finished hardwood with full pistol grip.
Sights: Bead front.
Features: Transfer bar ignition; break-open action with side-lever release. Introduced 1987. From New England Firearms.
Price: $99.95
Price: Youth model (20-, 28-ga., 410, 22" barrel, recoil pad) $109.95
Price: 12-ga., 32" (Full) $104.95
Price: 16-ga., 32" (Full) $104.95

CONSULT **Shooter's Marketplace** Page 266, This Issue

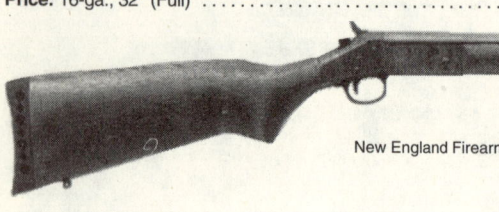
New England Firearms Tracker

NEW ENGLAND FIREARMS TRACKER SLUG GUN
Gauge: 12, 20, 3" chamber.
Barrel: 24" (Cyl.).
Weight: 6 lbs. **Length:** 40" overall.
Stock: Walnut-finished hardwood with full pistol grip, recoil pad.
Sights: Blade front, fully adjustable rifle-type rear.
Features: Break-open action with side-lever release; blued barrel, color case-hardened frame. Introduced 1992. From New England Firearms.
Price: Tracker $124.95
Price: Tracker II (as above except fully rifled bore) $129.95

SHOTGUNS—BOLT ACTIONS & SINGLE SHOTS

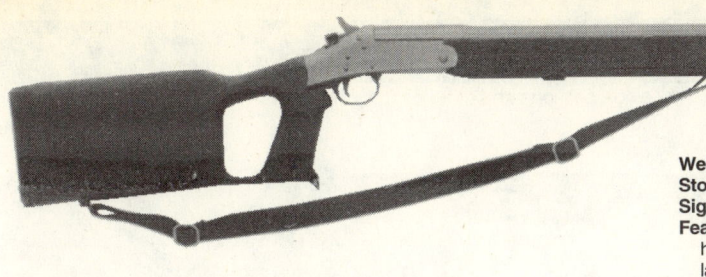

New England Firearms Survivor

NEW ENGLAND FIREARMS SURVIVOR
Gauge: 12, 20, 410/45 Colt, 3" chamber.
Barrel: 22" (Mod.); 20" (410/45 Colt, rifled barrel, choke tube).
Weight: 6 lbs. **Length:** 36" overall.
Stock: Black polymer with thumbhole/pistol grip, sling swivels; beavertail forend.
Sights: Bead front.
Features: Buttplate removes to expose storage for extra ammunition; forend also holds extra ammunition. Black or nickel finish. Introduced 1993. From New England Firearms.
Price: Black $129.95
Price: Nickel $145.95
Price: 410/45 Colt, black $145.95
Price: 410/45 Colt, nickel $164.95

Perazzi TM1 Special

PERAZZI TM1 SPECIAL SINGLE TRAP
Gauge: 12, 2 3/4" chambers.
Barrel: 32" or 34" (Extra Full).
Weight: 8 lbs., 6 oz.
Stock: To customer specs; interchangeable.
Features: Tapered and stepped high rib; adjustable four-position trigger. Also available with choke tubes. Imported from Italy by Perazzi U.S.A., Inc.
Price: From $6,150.00
Price: TMX Special Single (as above except special high rib), from ... $6,400.00

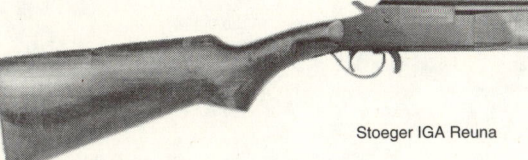

Remington 90-T Super Single Trap

REMINGTON 90-T SUPER SINGLE SHOTGUN
Gauge: 12, 2 3/4" chamber.
Barrel: 30", 32", 34"; fixed choke or Rem Choke tubes; ported or non-ported. Medium-high tapered, ventilated rib; white Bradley-type front bead, stainless center bead.
Weight: About 8 3/4 lbs.
Stock: 14 3/8" x 1 3/8" (or 1 1/2" or 1 1/4") x 1 1/2". Choice of drops at comb, pull length available plus or minus 1". Figured American walnut with low-luster finish, checkered 18 lpi; black vented rubber recoil pad. Cavity in forend and buttstock for added weight.
Features: Barrel is over-bored with elongated forcing cones. Removable sideplates can be ordered with engraving; drop-out trigger assembly. Metal has non-glare matte finish. Available with extra barrels in different lengths, chokes, extra trigger assemblies and sideplates, porting, stocks. Introduced 1990. From Remington.
Price: Depending on options $3,199.00
Price: With high post adjustable rib $3,992.00

Stoeger IGA Reuna

STOEGER/IGA REUNA SINGLE BARREL SHOTGUN
Gauge: 12, 2 3/4" chamber; 20, 410, 3" chamber.
Barrel: 12-ga.—26" (Imp. Cyl.), 28" (Full); 20-ga.—26" (Full); 410 bore—26" (Full).
Weight: 5 1/4 lbs.
Stock: 14" x 1 1/2" x 2 1/2". Brazilian hardwood.
Sights: Metal bead front.
Features: Exposed hammer with half-cock safety; extractor; blue finish. Introduced 1987. Imported from Brazil by Stoeger Industries.
Price: $120.00
Price: 12-, 20-ga., Full choke tube $142.00
Price: Youth model (20-ga., 410, 22" Full) $132.00

SNAKE CHARMER II SHOTGUN
Gauge: 410, 3" chamber.
Barrel: 18 1/4".
Weight: About 3 1/2 lbs. **Length:** 28 5/8" overall.
Stock: ABS grade impact resistant plastic.
Features: Thumbhole-type stock holds four extra rounds. Stainless steel barrel and frame. Reintroduced 1989. From Sporting Arms Mfg., Inc.
Price: $149.00
Price: New Generation Snake Charmer (as above except with black carbon steel bbl.) $139.00

Tar-Hunt Bolt Action

TAR-HUNT RSG-12 PROFESSIONAL RIFLED SLUG GUN
Gauge: 12, 20, 2 3/4" chamber.
Barrel: 21 1/2"; fully rifled, with muzzle brake.
Weight: 7 3/4 lbs. **Length:** 41 1/2" overall.
Stock: Matte black McMillan fiberglass with Pachmayr Decelerator pad.
Sights: None furnished; comes with Weaver-style bases and Burris Zee steel rings.
Features: Uses new rifle-style action with two locking lugs; two-position safety; single-stage, adjustable rifle trigger; muzzle brake. Many options available. Right- and left-hand models at same prices. Introduced 1991. Made in U.S. by Tar-Hunt Custom Rifles, Inc.
Price: Professional model, right- or left hand $1,395.00
Price: Turkey model (smoothbore, black McMillan fiberglass stock, Remington Rem-Choke thread system), right- or left hand $1,439.00
Price: Matchless model (400-grit gloss metal finish, McMillan Fibergrain or camouflage stock), right- or left-hand $1,783.50
Price: Peerless model (NP-3 nickel/teflon metal finish, McMillan Fibergrain fiberglass stock), right- or left-hand $1,973.25

CAUTION: PRICES SHOWN ARE SUPPLIED BY THE MANUFACTURER OR IMPORTER. CHECK YOUR LOCAL GUN SHOP.

SHOTGUNS—MILITARY & POLICE

Designs for utility, suitable for and adaptable to competitions and other sporting purposes.

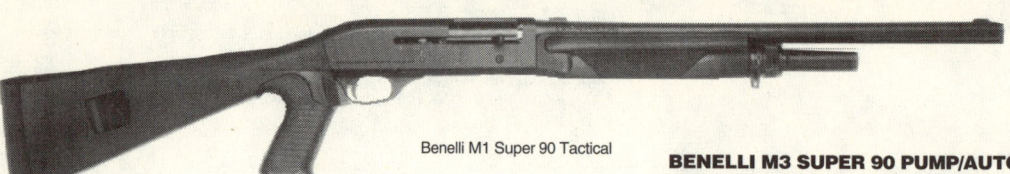

Benelli M1 Super 90 Tactical

Benelli M1 Super 90 Tactical Shotgun
Similar to the M1 Super 90 except has 18.5" barrel with Imp. Cyl., Mod., Full choke tubes, rifle sights of Ghost Ring system (tritium night sights optional), 5-shot magazine. In 12-gauge (3" chamber) only, matte-finish receiver. Overall length 39.75". Introduced 1993. Imported from Italy by Heckler & Koch, Inc.
Price: With rifle sights, standard stock $825.00
Price: As above, pistol grip stock $858.00
Price: With Ghost Rifle sights, standard stock $865.00
Price: As above, pistol grip stock $898.00

Benelli M1 Super 90
Similar to the M3 Super 90 except is semi-automatic only, has overall length of 39$3/4$" and weighs 6.5 lbs. Introduced 1986.
Price: Slug Gun with standard stock $785.00
Price: With pistol grip stock (Defense) $816.00
Price: With ghost ring sight system (standard stock) $825.00
Price: With ghost ring sight system, pistol grip stock (Defense) ..$855.00

BENELLI M3 SUPER 90 PUMP/AUTO SHOTGUN
Gauge: 12, 3" chamber, 7-shot magazine.
Barrel: 19$3/4$" (Cyl.).
Weight: 7 lbs., 8 oz. **Length:** 41" overall.
Stock: High-impact polymer with sling loop in side of butt; rubberized pistol grip on stock.
Sights: Post front, buckhorn rear adjustable for windage. Ghost ring system available.
Features: Combination pump/auto action. Alloy receiver with inertia recoil rotating locking lug bolt; matte finish; automatic shell release lever. Introduced 1989. Imported by Heckler & Koch, Inc.
Price: With standard stock $975.00
Price: With Ghost Ring sight system, standard stock $1,042.00

Benelli M1 Super 90 Defense Shotgun
Similar to the M1 Super 90 except has 18.5" barrel, rifle sights or Ghost Ring system (tritium night sights optional), 3-shot magazine with 2-shot extension. In 12-gauge (3" chamber) only, matte finish receiver. Overall length 39$3/4$". Introduced 1993. Imported from Italy by Heckler & Koch, Inc.
Price: With rifle sights, pistol grip stock $816.00
Price: With Ghost Ring sights, pistol grip stock $855.00

Beretta Model 1201FP3

BERETTA MODEL 1201FP3 AUTO SHOTGUN
Gauge: 12, 3" chamber.
Barrel: 20" (Cyl.).
Weight: 7.3 lbs. **Length:** NA
Stock: Special strengthened technopolymer, matte black finish.
Stock: Fixed rifle type.
Features: Has 6-shot magazine. Introduced 1988. Imported from Italy by Beretta U.S.A.
Price: $683.00

ITHACA MODEL 87 M&P DSPS SHOTGUNS
Gauge: 12, 3" chamber, 5- or 8-shot magazine.
Barrel: 18$1/2$", 20" (Cyl.).
Weight: 7 lbs.
Stock: Walnut.
Sights: Bead front on 5-shot, rifle sights on 8-shot.
Features: Parkerized finish; bottom ejection; cross-bolt safety. Reintroduced 1988. From Ithaca Acquisition Corp.
Price: M&P, 5-shot $428.75
Price: DSPS, 8-shot $428.75
Price: DSPS, 5-shot, rifled $462.75
Price: DSPS, rifled, 20", 25" $583.25

> Consult our Directory pages for the location of firms mentioned.

Ithaca Model 87 Hand Grip Shotgun
Similar to the Model 87 M&P except has black polymer pistol grip and slide handle. In 12- or 20-gauge, 18$1/2$" barrel (Cyl.), 5-shot magazine. Reintroduced 1988.
Price: $430.50

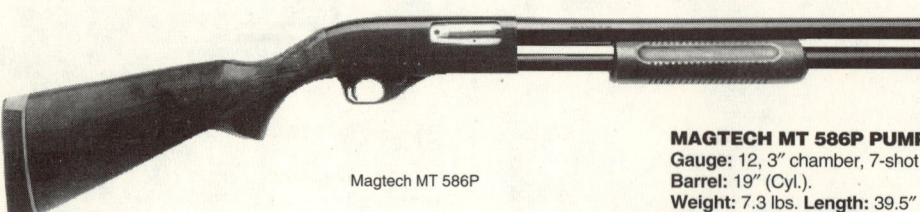

Magtech MT 586P

MAGTECH MT 586P PUMP SHOTGUN
Gauge: 12, 3" chamber, 7-shot magazine (8-shot with 2$3/4$" shells).
Barrel: 19" (Cyl.).
Weight: 7.3 lbs. **Length:** 39.5" overall.
Stock: Brazilian hardwood.
Sights: Bead front.
Features: Dual action slide bars, cross-bolt safety. Blue finish. Introduced 1991. Imported from Brazil by Magtech Recreational Products.
Price: About $219.00

SHOTGUNS—MILITARY & POLICE

Maverick Model 88

MAVERICK MODEL 88 PUMP SECURITY SHOTGUN
Gauge: 12, 3" chamber.
Barrel: 18 1/2", 20" (Cyl.).
Weight: 6.8 lbs. (full stock); 5.8 lbs. (pistol grip model). **Length:** 40" overall (full stock).
Stock: Synthetic full stock or pistol grip only.
Sights: Brass bead front.
Features: Dual action slide bars; cross-bolt safety; optional heat shield. Accessories interchangeable with Mossberg Model 500. Cablelock included. Introduced 1993. From Maverick Arms, Inc.
Price: 6-shot, full stock $230.00
Price: 8-shot, full stock $246.00
Price: 8-shot, full stock with pistol grip kit $260.00
Price: 8-shot pistol grip model $246.00
Price: 8-shot, pistol grip, heat shield $260.00

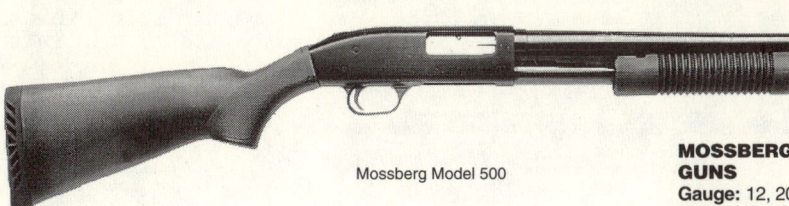

Mossberg Model 500

Mossberg Model 500, 590 Mariner Pump
Similar to the Model 500 or 590 Security except all metal parts finished with Marinecote metal finish to resist rust and corrosion. Synthetic field stock; pistol grip kit included. Mossberg Cablelock included.
Price: 6-shot, 18 1/2" barrel $403.00
Price: As above with Ghost-Ring sights $459.00
Price: 9-shot, 20" barrel $415.00
Price: As above with Ghost-Ring sights $471.00

MOSSBERG MODEL 500 PERSUADER/CRUISER SECURITY SHOTGUNS
Gauge: 12, 20, 410, 3" chamber.
Barrel: 18 1/2", 20" (Cyl.).
Weight: 7 lbs.
Stock: Walnut-finished hardwood or synthetic field.
Sights: Metal bead front.
Features: Available in 6- or 8-shot models. Top-mounted safety, double action slide bars, swivel studs, rubber recoil pad. Blue, Parkerized, Marinecote finishes. Mossberg Cablelock included. From Mossberg.
Price: 12- or 20-ga., 18 1/2", blue, wood or synthetic stock, 6-shot $281.00
Price: As above, Parkerized finish, synthetic stock, 6-shot $315.00
Price: Cruiser, 12- or 20-ga., 18 1/2", blue, pistol grip, heat shield $272.00
Price: As above, 410-bore $279.00
Price: 12-ga., 8-shot, blue, wood or synthetic stock $281.00
Price: As above with rifle sights $304.00
Price: 6- or 8-shot with Accu-Choke barrel $281.00

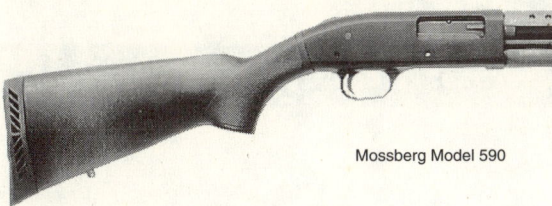

Mossberg Model 590

MOSSBERG MODEL 590 SHOTGUN
Gauge: 12, 3" chamber.
Barrel: 20" (Cyl.).
Weight: 7 1/4 lbs.
Stock: Synthetic field or Speedfeed.
Sights: Metal bead front.
Features: Top-mounted safety, double slide action bars. Comes with heat shield, bayonet lug, swivel studs, rubber recoil pad. Blue, Parkerized or Marinecote finish. Mossberg Cablelock included. From Mossberg.
Price: Blue, synthetic stock $329.00
Price: Parkerized, synthetic stock $379.00
Price: Blue, Speedfeed stock $362.00
Price: Parkerized, Speedfeed stock $412.00

Mossberg Model 500, 590 Ghost-Ring Shotguns
Similar to the Model 500 Security except has adjustable blade front, adjustable Ghost-Ring rear sight with protective "ears." Model 500 has 18.5" (Cyl.) barrel, 6-shot capacity; Model 590 has 20" (Cyl.) barrel, 9-shot capacity. Both have synthetic field stock. Mossberg Cablelock included. Introduced 1990. From Mossberg.
Price: Model 500, blue $331.00
Price: As above, Parkerized $384.00
Price: Model 590, blue $379.00
Price: As above, Parkerized $432.00
Price: Parkerized, Speedfeed stock $465.00
Price: Parkerized, synthetic stock, Accu-Choke barrel $454.00

Mossberg Model HS410 Shotgun
Similar to the Model 500 Security pump except chambered for 410 with 3" chamber; has pistol grip forend, thick recoil pad, muzzle brake and has special spreader choke on the 18.5" barrel. Overall length is 37.5", weight is 6.25 lbs. Blue finish; synthetic field stock. Mossberg Cablelock and video included. Introduced 1990.
Price: HS 410 .... $293.00

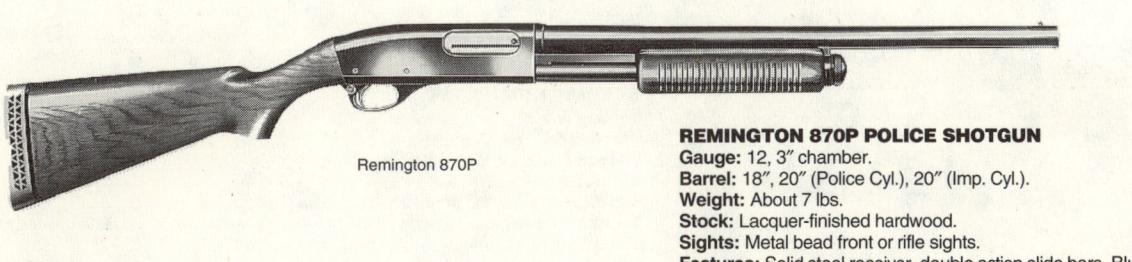

Remington 870P

REMINGTON 870P POLICE SHOTGUN
Gauge: 12, 3" chamber.
Barrel: 18", 20" (Police Cyl.), 20" (Imp. Cyl.).
Weight: About 7 lbs.
Stock: Lacquer-finished hardwood.
Sights: Metal bead front or rifle sights.
Features: Solid steel receiver, double action slide bars. Blued or Parkerized finish.
Price: 18" or 20", bead sight, about $399.00
Price: As above, Parkerized $412.00

CAUTION: PRICES SHOWN ARE SUPPLIED BY THE MANUFACTURER OR IMPORTER. CHECK YOUR LOCAL GUN SHOP.

SHOTGUNS—MILITARY & POLICE

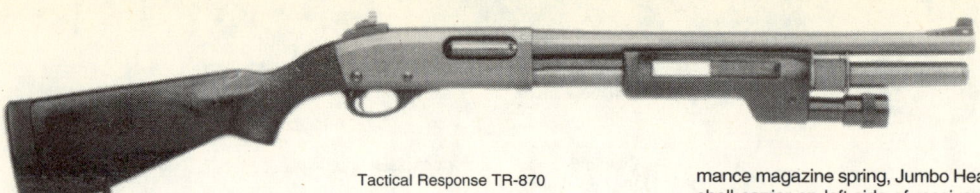
Tactical Response TR-870

TACTICAL RESPONSE TR-870 SHOTGUN
Gauge: 12, 3″ chamber, 7-shot magazine.
Barrel: 18″ (Cyl.).
Weight: 9 lbs. **Length:** 38″ overall.
Stock: Fiberglass-filled polypropolene with non-snag recoil absorbing butt pad. Nylon tactical forend houses flashlight.
Sights: Trak-Lock ghost ring sight system. Front sight has tritium insert.
Features: Highly modified Remington 870P with Parkerized finish. Comes with nylon three-way adjustable sling, high visibility non-binding follower, high performance magazine spring, Jumbo Head safety, and Side Saddle extended 6-shot shell carrier on left side of receiver. Introduced 1991. From Scattergun Technologies, Inc.
Price: Standard model $775.00
Price: FBI model, 5-shot $740.00
Price: Patrol model, 5-shot, no Side Saddle $545.00
Price: Border Patrol model, 7-shot, standard forend $575.00
Price: Military model, 7-shot, bayonet lug $670.00
Price: K-9 model, 7-shot (Rem. 11-87 action) $825.00
Price: Urban Sniper, 7-shot, rifled bbl., Burris Scout scope, Rem. 11-87 action $1,060.00
Price: Louis Awerbuck model $675.00
Price: Practical Turkey model $665.00

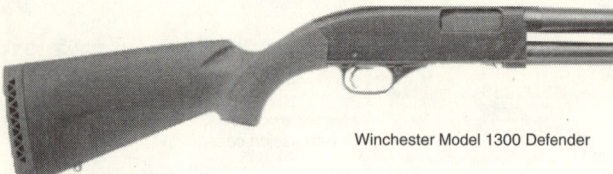
Winchester Model 1300 Defender

Winchester 8-Shot Pistol Grip Pump Security Shotguns
Same as regular Defender Pump but with pistol grip and forend of high-impact resistant ABS plastic with non-glare black finish. Introduced 1984.
Price: Pistol Grip Defender $290.00

Winchester Model 1300 Stainless Marine Pump Gun
Same as the Defender except has bright chrome finish, stainless steel barrel, rifle-type sights only. Phosphate coated receiver for corrosion resistance. Pistol grip optional.
Price: $460.00

WINCHESTER MODEL 1300 DEFENDER PUMP GUN
Gauge: 12, 20, 3″ chamber, 5- or 8-shot capacity.
Barrel: 18″ (Cyl.).
Weight: 6 3/4 lbs. **Length:** 38 5/8″ overall.
Stock: Walnut-finished hardwood stock and ribbed forend, or synthetic; or pistol grip.
Sights: Metal bead front.
Features: Cross-bolt safety, front-locking rotary bolt, twin action slide bars. Black rubber buttpad. From U.S. Repeating Arms Co.
Price: 8-shot, wood or synthetic stock $290.00
Price: 5-shot, wood stock $290.00
Price: Defender Field Combo with pistol grip $393.00

BLACKPOWDER SINGLE SHOT PISTOLS—FLINT & PERCUSSION

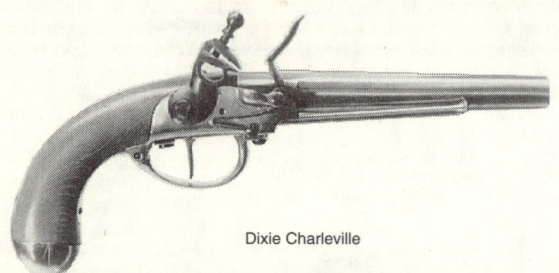
Dixie Charleville

BLACK WATCH SCOTCH PISTOL
Caliber: 577 (.500″ round ball).
Barrel: 7″, smoothbore.
Weight: 1 1/2 lbs. **Length:** 12″ overall.
Stock: Brass.
Sights: None.
Features: Faithful reproduction of this military flintlock. From Dixie Gun Works.
Price: $175.00

CHARLEVILLE FLINTLOCK PISTOL
Caliber: 69 (.680″ round ball).
Barrel: 7 1/2″.
Weight: 48 oz. **Length:** 13 1/2″ overall.
Stock: Walnut.
Sights: None.
Features: Brass frame, polished steel barrel, iron belt hook, brass buttcap and backstrap. Replica of original 1777 pistol. Imported by Dixie Gun Works.
Price: $195.00

CONSULT Shooter's Marketplace Page 266, This Issue

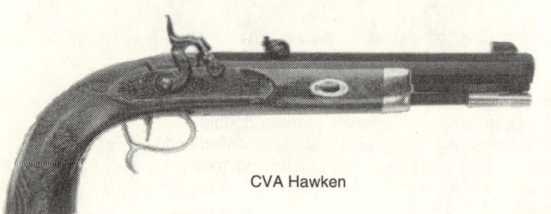
CVA Hawken

CVA HAWKEN PISTOL
Caliber: 50.
Barrel: 9 3/4″; 15/16″ flats.
Weight: 50 oz. **Length:** 16 1/2″ overall.
Stock: Select hardwood.
Sights: Beaded blade front, fully adjustable open rear.
Features: Color case-hardened lock, polished brass wedge plate, nose cap, ramrod thimble, trigger guard, grip cap. Imported by CVA.
Price: $139.95
Price: Kit $119.95
Price: With laminated stock $159.95

BLACKPOWDER SINGLE SHOT PISTOLS—FLINT & PERCUSSION

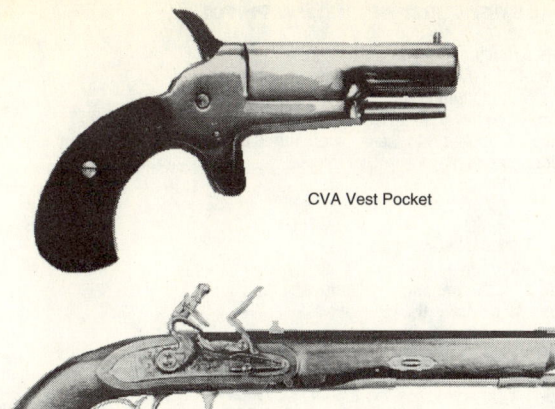

CVA Vest Pocket

CVA VEST POCKET DERRINGER
Caliber: 31.
Barrel: 2 1/2", brass.
Weight: 16 oz.
Stock: Two-piece walnut.
Features: All brass frame and barrel. A muzzle-loading version of the Colt No. 3 derringer. Imported by CVA.
Price: Finished $84.95

DIXIE PENNSYLVANIA PISTOL
Caliber: 44 (.430" round ball).
Barrel: 10" (7/8" octagon).
Weight: 2 1/2 lbs.
Stock: Walnut-stained hardwood.
Sights: Blade front, open rear drift-adjustable for windage; brass.
Features: Available in flint only. Brass trigger guard, thimbles, nosecap, wedgeplates; high-luster blue barrel. Imported from Italy by Dixie Gun Works.
Price: Finished $149.95
Price: Kit $119.95

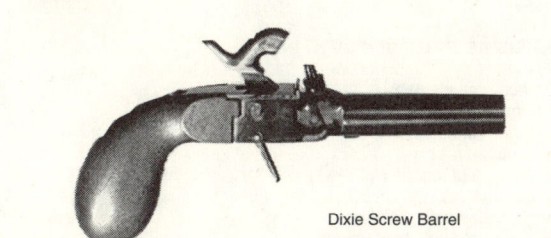

Dixie Pennsylvania

DIXIE SCREW BARREL PISTOL
Caliber: .445".
Barrel: 2 1/2".
Weight: 8 oz. **Length:** 6 1/2" overall.
Stock: Walnut.
Features: Trigger folds down when hammer is cocked. Close copy of the originals once made in Belgium. Uses No. 11 percussion caps. From Dixie Gun Works.
Price: $89.00
Price: Kit $74.95

Dixie Screw Barrel

FRENCH-STYLE DUELING PISTOL
Caliber: 44.
Barrel: 10".
Weight: 35 oz. **Length:** 15 3/4" overall.
Stock: Carved walnut.
Sights: Fixed.
Features: Comes with velvet-lined case and accessories. Imported by Mandall Shooting Supplies.
Price: $295.00

HARPER'S FERRY 1806 PISTOL
Caliber: 58 (.570" round ball).
Barrel: 10".
Weight: 40 oz. **Length:** 16" overall.
Stock: Walnut.
Sights: Fixed.
Features: Case-hardened lock, brass-mounted browned barrel. Replica of the first U.S. Gov't.-made flintlock pistol. Imported by Navy Arms, Dixie Gun Works.
Price: ....$249.95 to $405.00
Price: Kit (Dixie) $199.95
Price: Cased set (Navy Arms) $335.00

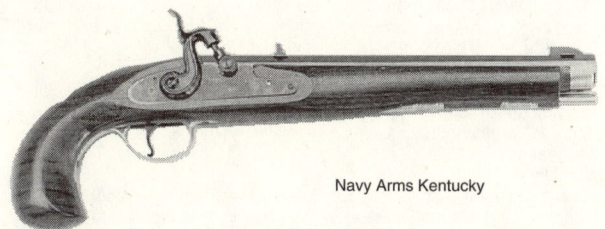

Dixie Harper's Ferry

KENTUCKY FLINTLOCK PISTOL
Caliber: 44, 45.
Barrel: 10 1/8".
Weight: 32 oz. **Length:** 15 1/2" overall.
Stock: Walnut.
Sights: Fixed.
Features: Specifications, including caliber, weight and length may vary with importer. Case-hardened lock, blued barrel; available also as brass barrel flint Model 1821. Imported by Navy Arms (44 only), The Armoury.
Price: ....$145.00 to $225.00
Price: In kit form, from ....$90.00 to $112.00
Price: Single cased set (Navy Arms) $325.00
Price: Double cased set (Navy Arms) $550.00

Navy Arms Kentucky

Kentucky Percussion Pistol
Similar to flint version but percussion lock. Imported by The Armoury, Navy Arms, CVA (50-cal.).
Price: ....$129.95 to $250.00
Price: Steel barrel (Armoury) $179.00
Price: Single cased set (Navy Arms) $310.00
Price: Double cased set (Navy Arms) $525.00

Knight Hawkeye

KNIGHT HAWKEYE PISTOL
Caliber: 50.
Barrel: 12", 1:20" twist.
Weight: 3 1/4 lbs. **Length:** 20" overall.
Stock: Black composite, autumn brown or shadow black laminate.
Sights: Bead front on ramp, open fully adjustable rear.
Features: In-line ignitiion design; patented double safety system; removeable breech plug; fully adjustable trigger; receiver drilled and tapped for scope mounting. Made in U.S. by Modern Muzzle Loading, Inc.
Price: Blued $374.95
Price: Stainless $424.50

CAUTION: PRICES SHOWN ARE SUPPLIED BY THE MANUFACTURER OR IMPORTER. CHECK YOUR LOCAL GUN SHOP.

BLACKPOWDER SINGLE SHOT PISTOLS—FLINT & PERCUSSION

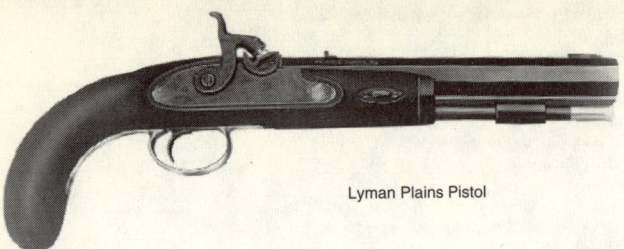

Lyman Plains Pistol

LE PAGE PERCUSSION DUELING PISTOL
Caliber: 45.
Barrel: 10", rifled.
Weight: 40 oz. **Length:** 16" overall.
Stock: Walnut, fluted butt.
Sights: Blade front, notch rear.
Features: Double-set triggers. Blued barrel; trigger guard and buttcap are polished silver. Imported by Dixie Gun Works.
Price: $259.95

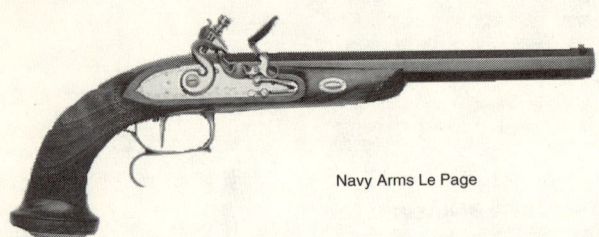

Navy Arms Le Page

LYMAN PLAINS PISTOL
Caliber: 50 or 54.
Barrel: 8", 1:30 twist, both calibers.
Weight: 50 oz. **Length:** 15" overall.
Stock: Walnut half-stock.
Sights: Blade front, square notch rear adjustable for windage.
Features: Polished brass trigger guard and ramrod tip, color case-hardened coil spring lock, spring-loaded trigger, stainless steel nipple, blackened iron furniture. Hooked patent breech, detachable belt hook. Introduced 1981. From Lyman Products.
Price: Finished $224.95
Price: Kit $179.95

Consult our Directory pages for the location of firms mentioned.

NAVY ARMS LE PAGE DUELING PISTOL
Caliber: 44.
Barrel: 9", octagon, rifled.
Weight: 34 oz. **Length:** 15" overall.
Stock: European walnut.
Sights: Adjustable rear.
Features: Single-set trigger. Polished metal finish. From Navy Arms.
Price: Percussion $500.00
Price: Single cased set, percussion $775.00
Price: Double cased set, percussion $1,300.00
Price: Flintlock, rifled $625.00
Price: Flintlock, smoothbore (45-cal.) $625.00
Price: Flintlock, single cased set $900.00
Price: Flintlock, double cased set $1,575.00

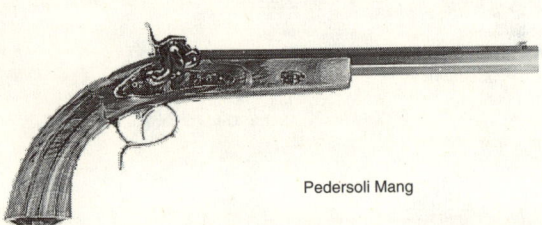

Pedersoli Mang

PEDERSOLI MANG TARGET PISTOL
Caliber: 38.
Barrel: 10.5", octagonal; 1:15" twist.
Weight: 2.5 lbs. **Length:** 17.25" overall.
Stock: Walnut with fluted grip.
Sights: Blade front, open rear adjustable for windage.
Features: Browned barrel, polished breech plug, rest color case-hardened. Imported from Italy by Dixie Gun Works.
Price: $749.00

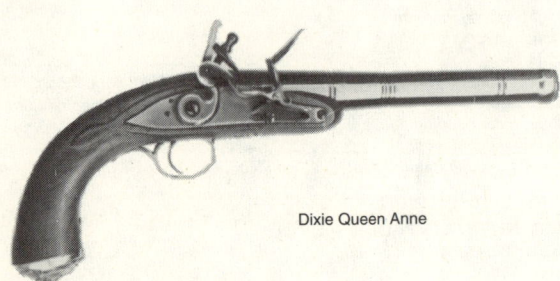

Dixie Queen Anne

QUEEN ANNE FLINTLOCK PISTOL
Caliber: 50 (.490" round ball).
Barrel: 7 1/2", smoothbore.
Stock: Walnut.
Sights: None.
Features: Browned steel barrel, fluted brass trigger guard, brass mask on butt. Lockplate left in the white. Made by Pedersoli in Italy. Introduced 1983. Imported by Dixie Gun Works.
Price: $189.95
Price: Kit $138.50

THOMPSON/CENTER SCOUT PISTOL
Caliber: 45, 50 and 54.
Barrel: 12", interchangeable.
Weight: 4 lbs., 6 oz. **Length:** NA.
Stocks: American black walnut stocks and forend.
Sights: Blade on ramp front, fully adjustable Patridge rear.
Features: Patented in-line ignition system with special vented breech plug. Patented trigger mechanism consists of only two moving parts. Interchangeable barrels. Wide grooved hammer. Brass trigger guard assembly. Introduced 1990. From Thompson/Center.
Price: 45-, 50- or 54-cal. $340.00
Price: Extra barrel, 45-, 50- or 54-cal. $145.00

TRADITIONS BUCKSKINNER PISTOL
Caliber: 50.
Barrel: 10" octagonal, 15/16" flats.
Weight: 40 oz. **Length:** 15" overall.
Stocks: Stained beech or laminated wood.
Sights: Blade front, rear adjustable for windage.
Features: Percussion ignition. Blackened furniture. Imported by Traditions.
Price: Beech stocks $165.00
Price: Laminated stocks $181.50

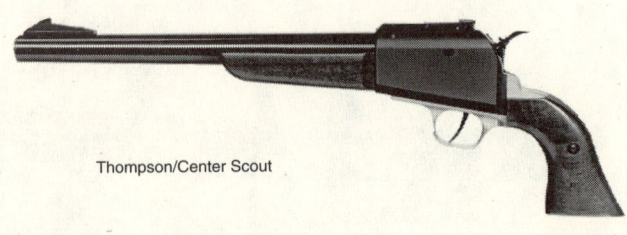

Thompson/Center Scout

BLACKPOWDER SINGLE SHOT PISTOLS—FLINT & PERCUSSION

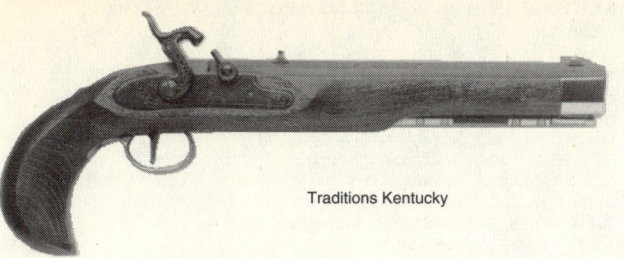

Traditions Kentucky

TRADITIONS KENTUCKY PISTOL
Caliber: 50.
Barrel: 9 3/4"; octagon with 7/8" flats; 1:20" twist.
Weight: 40 oz. **Length:** 15 1/2" overall.
Stock: Stained beech.
Sights: Blade front, drift-adjustable rear.
Features: Birds-head grip; brass thimbles; color case-hardened lock. Percussion only. Introduced 1995. From Traditions.
Price: Finished $142.00
Price: Kit $106.50

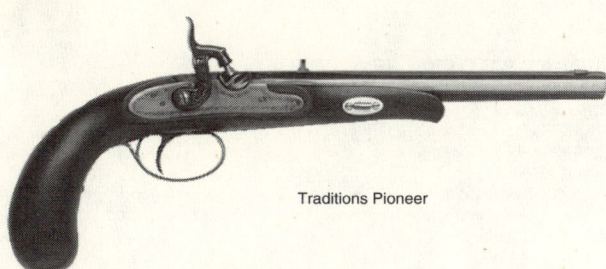

Traditions Pioneer

TRADITIONS PIONEER PISTOL
Caliber: 45.
Barrel: 9 5/8", 13/16" flats.
Weight: 31 oz. **Length:** 15" overall.
Stock: Beech.
Sights: Blade front, fixed rear.
Features: V-type mainspring; 1:16" twist. Single trigger. German silver furniture, blackened hardware. From Traditions.
Price: $160.00
Price: Kit $126.50

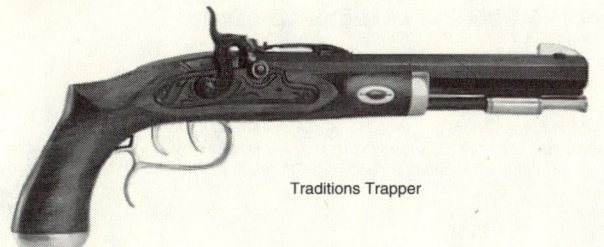

Traditions Trapper

TRADITIONS TRAPPER PISTOL
Caliber: 50.
Barrel: 9 3/4", 7/8" flats.
Weight: 2 3/4 lbs. **Length:** 16" overall.
Stock: Beech.
Sights: Blade front, adjustable rear.
Features: Double-set triggers; brass buttcap, trigger guard, wedge plate, forend tip, thimble. From Traditions.
Price: Percussion $178.00
Price: Flintlock $198.00
Price: Kit $139.00

TRADITIONS WILLIAM PARKER PISTOL
Caliber: 50.
Barrel: 10 3/8", 15/16" flats; polished steel.
Weight: 40 oz. **Length:** 17 1/2" overall.
Stock: Walnut with checkered grip.
Sights: Brass blade front, fixed rear.
Features: Replica dueling pistol with 1:20" twist, hooked breech. Brass wedge plate, trigger guard, cap guard; separate ramrod. Double-set triggers. Polished steel barrel, lock. Imported by Traditions.
Price: $274.00

WHITE SHOOTING SYSTEMS JAVELINA PISTOL
Caliber: 45, 50.
Barrel: 14".
Weight: 5.2 lbs. **Length:** 22" overall.
Stock: Black composite; two-hand style.
Sights: Blade or bead front, fully adjustable rear.
Features: Has stainless steel action with InstaFire ignition system; match-grade trigger. Drilled and tapped for scope mounting. Announced 1995. From White Shooting Systems, Inc.
Price: $449.00

BLACKPOWDER REVOLVERS

ARMY 1860 PERCUSSION REVOLVER
Caliber: 44, 6-shot.
Barrel: 8".
Weight: 40 oz. **Length:** 13 5/8" overall.
Stocks: Walnut.
Sights: Fixed.
Features: Engraved Navy scene on cylinder; brass trigger guard; case-hardened frame, loading lever and hammer. Some importers supply pistol cut for detachable shoulder stock, have accessory stock available. Imported by American Arms, Cabela's (1860 Lawman), E.M.F., Navy Arms, The Armoury, Cimarron, Dixie Gun Works (half-fluted cylinder, not roll engraved), Euroarms of America (brass or steel model), Armsport, Traditions (brass or steel), Uberti USA.
Price: About .... $92.95 to $300.00
Price: Hartford model, steel frame, German silver trim, cartouches (E.M.F.) $215.00
Price: Single cased set (Navy Arms) $300.00
Price: Double cased set (Navy Arms) $490.00
Price: 1861 Navy: Same as Army except 36-cal., 7 1/2" bbl., wgt. 41 oz., cut for shoulder stock; round cylinder (fluted avail.), from CVA (brass frame, 44-cal.) .... $99.95 to $249.00
Price: Steel frame kit (E.M.F., Navy, Euroarms) .... $125.00 to $216.25
Price: Colt Army Police, fluted cyl., 5 1/2", 36-cal. (Cabela's) $124.95

American Arms 1860 Army

ARMY 1851 PERCUSSION REVOLVER
Caliber: 44, 6-shot.
Barrel: 7 1/2".
Weight: 45 oz. **Length:** 13" overall.
Stocks: Walnut finish.
Sights: Fixed.
Features: 44-caliber version of the 1851 Navy. Imported by The Armoury, Armsport.
Price: $129.00

CAUTION: PRICES SHOWN ARE SUPPLIED BY THE MANUFACTURER OR IMPORTER. CHECK YOUR LOCAL GUN SHOP.

BLACKPOWDER REVOLVERS

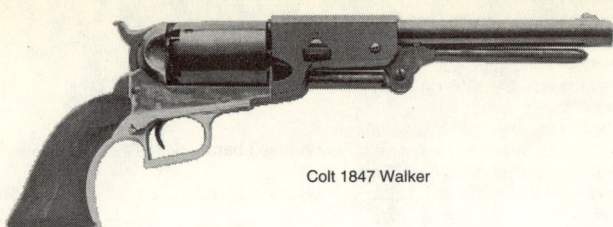
Colt 1847 Walker

COLT 1847 WALKER PERCUSSION REVOLVER
Caliber: 44.
Barrel: 9", 7 groove, right-hand twist.
Weight: 73 oz.
Stocks: One-piece walnut.
Sights: German silver front sight, hammer notch rear.
Features: Made in U.S. Faithful reproduction of the original gun, including markings. Color case-hardened frame, hammer, loading lever and plunger. Blue steel backstrap, brass square-back trigger guard. Blue barrel, cylinder, trigger and wedge. From Colt Blackpowder Arms Co.
Price: $442.50

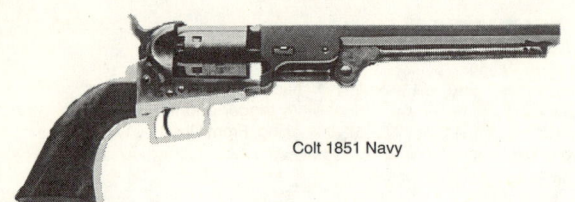
Colt 1851 Navy

Uberti 1861 Navy Percussion Revolver
Similar to 1851 Navy except has round 7 1/2" barrel, rounded trigger guard, German silver blade front sight, "creeping" loading lever. Available with fluted or round cylinder. Imported by Uberti USA.
Price: Steel backstrap, trigger guard, cut for stock $300.00

CVA Colt Sheriff's Model
Similar to the Uberti 1861 Navy except has 5 1/2" barrel, brass or steel frame, semi-fluted cylinder. In 36-caliber only.
Price: Brass frame, finished $149.95
Price: Brass frame (Armsport) $155.00
Price: Steel frame (Armsport) $193.00

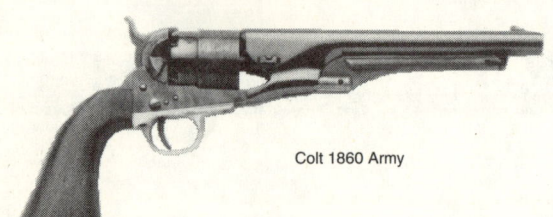
Colt 1860 Army

Colt 1860 "Cavalry Model" Percussion Revolver
Similar to the 1860 Army except has fluted cylinder. Color case-hardened frame, hammer, loading lever and plunger; blued barrel, backstrap and cylinder, brass trigger guard. Has four-screw frame cut for optional shoulder stock. From Colt Blackpowder Arms Co.
Price: $465.00

COLT THIRD MODEL DRAGOON
Caliber: 44.
Barrel: 7 1/2".
Weight: 66 oz. **Length:** 13 3/4" overall.
Stocks: One-piece walnut.
Sights: Blade front, hammer notch rear.
Features: Color case-hardened frame, hammer, lever and plunger; round trigger guard; flat mainspring; hammer roller; rectangular bolt cuts. From Colt Blackpowder Arms Co.
Price: Three-screw frame with brass grip straps $487.50
Price: Four-screw frame with blued steel grip straps, shoulder stock cuts, dovetailed folding leaf rear sight $502.50

BABY DRAGOON 1848, 1849 POCKET, WELLS FARGO
Caliber: 31.
Barrel: 3", 4", 5", 6"; seven-groove, RH twist.
Weight: About 21 oz.
Stock: Varnished walnut.
Sights: Brass pin front, hammer notch rear.
Features: No loading lever on Baby Dragoon or Wells Fargo models. Unfluted cylinder with stagecoach holdup scene; cupped cylinder pin; no grease grooves; one safety pin on cylinder and slot in face; straight (flat) mainspring. From Armsport, Dixie Gun Works, Uberti USA, Cabela's, Stone Mountain Arms.
Price: 6" barrel, with loading lever (Dixie Gun Works) $254.00
Price: 4" (Cabela's, Uberti USA) $169.95

CABELA'S PATERSON REVOLVER
Caliber: 36, 5-shot cylinder.
Barrel: 7 1/2".
Weight: 24 oz. **Length:** 11 1/2" overall.
Stocks: One-piece walnut.
Sights: Fixed.
Features: Recreation of the 1836 gun. Color case-hardened frame, steel backstrap; roll-engraved cylinder scene. Imported by Cabela's.
Price: $229.95

COLT 1849 POCKET DRAGOON REVOLVER
Caliber: 31.
Barrel: 4".
Weight: 24 oz. **Length:** 9 1/2" overall.
Stocks: One-piece walnut.
Sights: Fixed. Brass pin front, hammer notch rear.
Features: Color case-hardened frame. No loading lever. Unfluted cylinder with engraved scene. Exact reproduction of original. From Colt Blackpowder Arms Co.
Price: $390.00

COLT 1851 NAVY PERCUSSION REVOLVER
Caliber: 36.
Barrel: 7 1/2", octagonal, 7 groove left-hand twist.
Weight: 40 1/2 oz.
Stocks: One-piece oiled American walnut.
Sights: Brass pin front, hammer notch rear.
Features: Faithful reproduction of the original gun. Color case-hardened frame, loading lever, plunger, hammer and latch. Blue cylinder, trigger, barrel, screws, wedge. Silver-plated brass backstrap and square-back trigger guard. From Colt Blackpowder Arms Co.
Price: $427.50

COLT 1860 ARMY PERCUSSION REVOLVER
Caliber: 44.
Barrel: 8", 7 groove, left-hand twist.
Weight: 42 oz.
Stocks: One-piece walnut.
Sights: German silver front sight, hammer notch rear.
Features: Steel backstrap cut for shoulder stock; brass trigger guard. Cylinder has Navy scene. Color case-hardened frame, hammer, loading lever. Reproduction of original gun with all original markings. From Colt Blackpowder Arms Co.
Price: $427.50

COLT 1861 NAVY PERCUSSION REVOLVER
Caliber: 36.
Barrel: 7 1/2".
Weight: 42 oz. **Length:** 13 1/8" overall.
Stocks: One-piece walnut.
Sights: Blade front, hammer notch rear.
Features: Color case-hardened frame, loading lever, plunger; blued barrel, backstrap, trigger guard; roll-engraved cylinder and barrel. From Colt Blackpowder Arms Co.
Price: $465.00

COLT 1862 POCKET POLICE "TRAPPER MODEL" REVOLVER
Caliber: 36.
Barrel: 3 1/2".
Weight: 20 oz. **Length:** 8 1/2" overall.
Stocks: One-piece walnut.
Sights: Blade front, hammer notch rear.
Features: Has separate 4 5/8" brass ramrod. Color case-hardened frame and hammer; silver-plated backstrap and trigger guard; blued semi-fluted cylinder, blued barrel. From Colt Blackpowder Arms Co.
Price: $442.50

BLACKPOWDER REVOLVERS

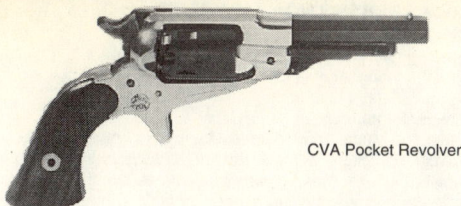
CVA Pocket Revolver

CVA POCKET REVOLVER
Caliber: 31, 5-shot.
Barrel: 4", octagonal.
Weight: 15 oz. **Length:** 7½" overall.
Stocks: Two-piece walnut.
Sights: Post front, grooved topstrap rear.
Features: Spur trigger, brass frame with blued barrel and cylinder. Introduced 1984. Imported by CVA.
Price: Finished $139.95

DIXIE THIRD MODEL DRAGOON
Caliber: 44 (.454" round ball).
Barrel: 7⅜".
Weight: 4 lbs., 2½ oz.
Stocks: One-piece walnut.
Sights: Brass pin front, hammer notch rear, or adjustable folding leaf rear.
Features: Cylinder engraved with Indian fight scene. This is the only Dragoon replica with folding leaf sight. Brass backstrap and trigger guard; color case-hardened steel frame, blue-black barrel. Imported by Dixie Gun Works.
Price: $199.95

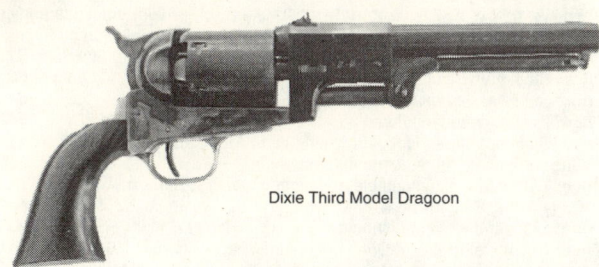
Dixie Third Model Dragoon

DIXIE WYATT EARP REVOLVER
Caliber: 44.
Barrel: 12" octagon.
Weight: 46 oz. **Length:** 18" overall.
Stocks: Two-piece walnut.
Sights: Fixed.
Features: Highly polished brass frame, backstrap and trigger guard; blued barrel and cylinder; case-hardened hammer, trigger and loading lever. Navy-size shoulder stock ($45) will fit with minor fitting. From Dixie Gun Works.
Price: $130.00

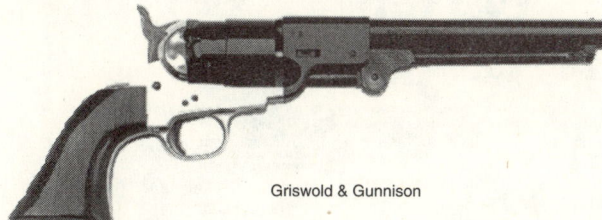
Griswold & Gunnison

GRISWOLD & GUNNISON PERCUSSION REVOLVER
Caliber: 36 or 44, 6-shot.
Barrel: 7½".
Weight: 44 oz. (36-cal.). **Length:** 13" overall.
Stocks: Walnut.
Sights: Fixed.
Features: Replica of famous Confederate pistol. Brass frame, backstrap and trigger guard; case-hardened loading lever; rebated cylinder (44-cal. only). Rounded Dragoon-type barrel. Imported by Navy Arms as Reb Model 1860.
Price: $115.00
Price: Kit $90.00
Price: Single cased set $235.00
Price: Double cased set $365.00

LE MAT REVOLVER
Caliber: 44/65.
Barrel: 6¾" (revolver); 4⅞" (single shot).
Weight: 3 lbs., 7 oz.
Stocks: Hand-checkered walnut.
Sights: Post front, hammer notch rear.
Features: Exact reproduction with all-steel construction; 44-cal. 9-shot cylinder, 65-cal. single barrel; color case-hardened hammer with selector; spur trigger guard; ring at butt; lever-type barrel release. From Navy Arms.
Price: Cavalry model (lanyard ring, spur trigger guard) $595.00
Price: Army model (round trigger guard, pin-type barrel release) $595.00
Price: Naval-style (thumb selector on hammer) $595.00
Price: Engraved 18th Georgia cased set $795.00
Price: Engraved Beauregard cased set $1,000.00

Le Mat Revolver

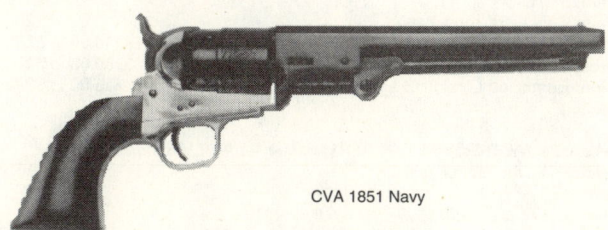
CVA 1851 Navy

NAVY MODEL 1851 PERCUSSION REVOLVER
Caliber: 36, 44, 6-shot.
Barrel: 7½".
Weight: 44 oz. **Length:** 13" overall.
Stocks: Walnut finish.
Sights: Post front, hammer notch rear.
Features: Brass backstrap and trigger guard; some have 1st Model squareback trigger guard, engraved cylinder with navy battle scene; case-hardened frame, hammer, loading lever. Imported by American Arms, The Armoury, Cabela's, Navy Arms, E.M.F., Dixie Gun Works, Euroarms of America, Armsport, CVA (36-cal. only), Traditions (44 only), Uberti USA, Stone Mountain Arms.
Price: Brass frame ....$99.95 to $280.00
Price: Steel frame ....$130.00 to $285.00
Price: Kit form ....$110.00 to $123.95
Price: Engraved model (Dixie Gun Works) $139.75
Price: Single cased set, steel frame (Navy Arms) $280.00
Price: Double cased set, steel frame (Navy Arms) $455.00
Price: Confederate Navy (Cabela's) $69.95
Price: Hartford model, steel frame, German silver trim, cartouche (E.M.F.) $190.00

CONSULT Shooter's Marketplace Page 266, This Issue

NAVY ARMS DELUXE 1858 REMINGTON-STYLE REVOLVER
Caliber: 44.
Barrel: 8".
Weight: 2 lbs., 13 oz.
Stocks: Smooth walnut.
Sights: Dovetailed blade front.
Features: First exact reproduction—correct in size and weight to the original, with progressive rifling; highly polished with blue finish, silver-plated trigger guard. From Navy Arms.
Price: Deluxe model $415.00

CAUTION: PRICES SHOWN ARE SUPPLIED BY THE MANUFACTURER OR IMPORTER. CHECK YOUR LOCAL GUN SHOP.

BLACKPOWDER REVOLVERS

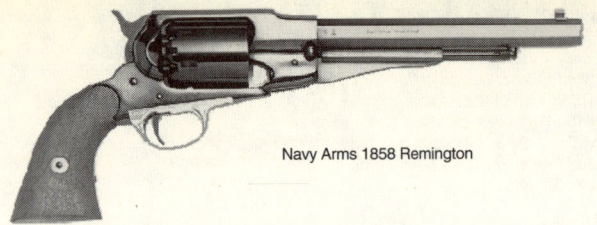
Navy Arms 1858 Remington

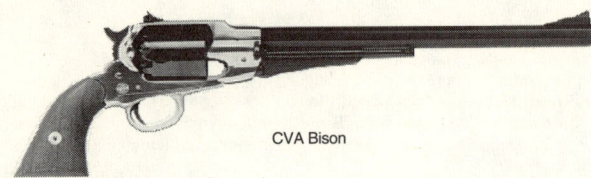
CVA Bison

NEW MODEL 1858 ARMY PERCUSSION REVOLVER
Caliber: 36 or 44, 6-shot.
Barrel: 6½" or 8".
Weight: 38 oz. **Length:** 13½" overall.
Stocks: Walnut.
Sights: Blade front, groove-in-frame rear.
Features: Replica of Remington Model 1858. Also available from some importers as Army Model Belt Revolver in 36-cal., a shortened and lightened version of the 44. Target Model (Uberti USA, Navy Arms) has fully adjustable target rear sight, target front, 36 or 44. Imported by American Arms, Cabela's, Cimarron, CVA (as 1858 Army, steel or brass frame, 44 only), Dixie Gun Works, Navy Arms, The Armoury, E.M.F., Euroarms of America (engraved, stainless and plain), Armsport, Traditions (44 only), Uberti USA, Stone Mountain Arms.
Price: Steel frame, about .... $99.95 to $280.00
Price: Steel frame kit (Euroarms, Navy Arms) .... $115.95 to $242.00
Price: Single cased set (Navy Arms) $290.00
Price: Double cased set (Navy Arms) $480.00
Price: Stainless steel Model 1858 (American Arms, Euroarms, Uberti USA, Cabela's, Navy Arms, Armsport, Traditions) .... $169.95 to $380.00
Price: Target Model, adjustable rear sight (Cabela's, Euroarms, Uberti USA, Navy Arms, Stone Mountain Arms) .... $95.95 to $399.00
Price: Brass frame (CVA, Cabela's, Traditions, Navy Arms) ... $79.95 to $212.95
Price: As above, kit (CVA, Dixie Gun Works, Navy Arms) ... $145.00 to $188.95
Price: Buffalo model, 44-cal. (Cabela's) $129.95
Price: Hartford model, steel frame, German silver trim, cartouche (E.M.F.) $215.00

CVA Bison Revolver
Similar to the CVA 1858 except has 10¼" octagonal barrel, 44-caliber, brass frame, two-piece walnut grips, adjustable target rear sight.
Price: Finished $187.95
Price: From Armsport $222.00

POCKET POLICE 1862 PERCUSSION REVOLVER
Caliber: 36, 5-shot.
Barrel: 4½", 5½", 6½", 7½".
Weight: 26 oz. **Length:** 12" overall (6½" bbl.).
Stocks: Walnut.
Sights: Fixed.
Features: Round tapered barrel; half-fluted and rebated cylinder; case-hardened frame, loading lever and hammer; silver or brass trigger guard and backstrap. Imported by CVA (7½" only), Navy Arms (5½" only), Uberti USA (5½", 6½" only).
Price: About .... $139.95 to $310.00
Price: Single cased set with accessories (Navy Arms) $365.00
Price: Hartford model, steel frame, German silver trim, cartouche (E.M.F.) $215.00

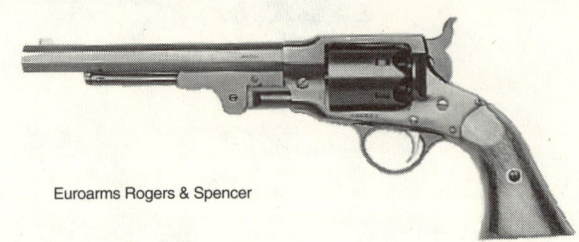
Euroarms Rogers & Spencer

ROGERS & SPENCER PERCUSSION REVOLVER
Caliber: 44.
Barrel: 7½".
Weight: 47 oz. **Length:** 13¾" overall.
Stocks: Walnut.
Sights: Cone front, integral groove in frame for rear.
Features: Accurate reproduction of a Civil War design. Solid frame; extra large nipple cut-out on rear of cylinder; loading lever and cylinder easily removed for cleaning. From Euroarms of America (standard blue, engraved, burnished, target models), Navy Arms, Stone Mountain Arms.
Price: .... $160.00 to $289.00
Price: Nickel-plated $215.00
Price: Engraved (Euroarms) $287.00
Price: Kit version .... $245.00 to $252.00
Price: Target version (Euroarms, Navy Arms) .... $239.00 to $270.00
Price: Burnished London Gray (Euroarms, Navy Arms) ..... $245.00 to $270.00

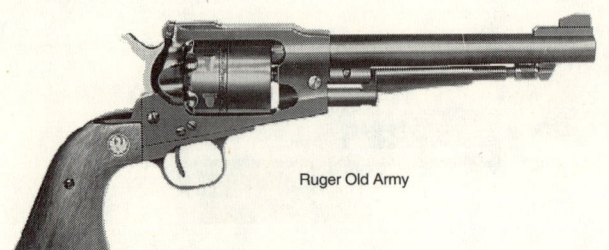
Ruger Old Army

RUGER OLD ARMY PERCUSSION REVOLVER
Caliber: 45, 6-shot. Uses .457" dia. lead bullets.
Barrel: 7½" (6-groove, 16" twist).
Weight: 46 oz. **Length:** 13¾" overall.
Stocks: Smooth walnut.
Sights: Ramp front, rear adjustable for windage and elevation; or fixed (groove).
Features: Stainless steel; standard size nipples, chrome-moly steel cylinder and frame, same lockwork as in original Super Blackhawk. Also available in stainless steel. Made in USA. From Sturm, Ruger & Co.
Price: Stainless steel (Model KBP-7) $450.00
Price: Blued steel (Model BP-7) $398.00
Price: Stainless steel, fixed sight (KBP-7F) $450.00
Price: Blued steel, fixed sight (BP-7F) $398.00

SHERIFF MODEL 1851 PERCUSSION REVOLVER
Caliber: 36, 44, 6-shot.
Barrel: 5".
Weight: 40 oz. **Length:** 10½" overall.
Stocks: Walnut.
Sights: Fixed.
Features: Brass backstrap and trigger guard; engraved navy scene; case-hardened frame, hammer, loading lever. Imported by E.M.F., Stone Mountain Arms (5½" barrel).
Price: Steel frame (E.M.F.) $172.00
Price: Brass frame (E.M.F.) $140.00
Price: Steel frame (Stone Mountain Arms) $159.95

SPILLER & BURR REVOLVER
Caliber: 36 (.375" round ball).
Barrel: 7", octagon.
Weight: 2½ lbs. **Length:** 12½" overall.
Stocks: Two-piece walnut.
Sights: Fixed.
Features: Reproduction of the C.S.A. revolver. Brass frame and trigger guard. Also available as a kit. From Cabela's, Dixie Gun Works, Navy Arms.
Price: .... $89.95 to $199.00
Price: Kit form $95.00
Price: Single cased set (Navy Arms) $270.00
Price: Double cased set (Navy Arms) $430.00

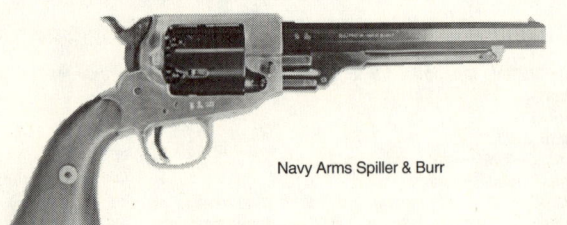
Navy Arms Spiller & Burr

CAUTION: PRICES SHOWN ARE SUPPLIED BY THE MANUFACTURER OR IMPORTER. CHECK YOUR LOCAL GUN SHOP.

BLACKPOWDER REVOLVERS

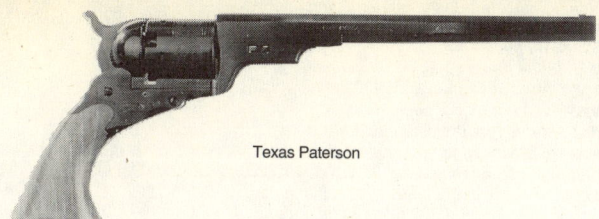

Texas Paterson

TEXAS PATERSON 1836 REVOLVER
Caliber: 36 (.375" round ball).
Barrel: 7 1/2".
Weight: 42 oz.
Stocks: One-piece walnut.
Sights: Fixed.
Features: Copy of Sam Colt's first commercially-made revolving pistol. Has no loading lever but comes with loading tool. From Dixie Gun Works, Navy Arms, Uberti USA.
Price: About ....$325.00 to $395.00
Price: With loading lever (Uberti USA) $450.00
Price: Engraved (Navy Arms) $465.00

UBERTI 1862 POCKET NAVY PERCUSSION REVOLVER
Caliber: 36, 5-shot.
Barrel: 5 1/2", 6 1/2", octagonal, 7-groove, LH twist.
Weight: 27 oz. (5 1/2" barrel). **Length:** 10 1/2" overall (5 1/2" bbl.).
Stocks: One-piece varnished walnut.
Sights: Brass pin front, hammer notch rear.
Features: Rebated cylinder, hinged loading lever, brass or silver-plated backstrap and trigger guard, color-cased frame, hammer, loading lever, plunger and latch, rest blued. Has original-type markings. From Uberti USA.
Price: With brass backstrap, trigger guard $310.00

Uberti 1862 Pocket

UBERTI 1st MODEL DRAGOON
Caliber: 44.
Barrel: 7 1/2", part round, part octagon.
Weight: 64 oz.
Stocks: One-piece walnut.
Sights: German silver blade front, hammer notch rear.
Features: First model has oval bolt cuts in cylinder, square-back flared trigger guard, V-type mainspring, short trigger. Ranger and Indian scene roll-engraved on cylinder. Color case-hardened frame, loading lever, plunger and hammer; blue barrel, cylinder, trigger and wedge. Available with old-time charcoal blue or standard blue-black finish. Polished brass backstrap and trigger guard. From Uberti USA.
Price: $325.00

Uberti 2nd Model Dragoon Revolver
Similar to the 1st Model except distinguished by rectangular bolt cuts in the cylinder.
Price: $325.00

Uberti 3rd Model Dragoon Revolver
Similar to the 2nd Model except for oval trigger guard, long trigger, modifications to the loading lever and latch. Imported by Uberti USA.
Price: Military model (frame cut for shoulder stock, steel backstrap) $330.00
Price: Civilian (brass backstrap, trigger guard) $325.00

WALKER 1847 PERCUSSION REVOLVER
Caliber: 44, 6-shot.
Barrel: 9".
Weight: 84 oz. **Length:** 15 1/2" overall.
Stocks: Walnut.
Sights: Fixed.
Features: Case-hardened frame, loading lever and hammer; iron backstrap; brass trigger guard; engraved cylinder. Imported by American Arms, Cabela's, CVA, Navy Arms, Dixie Gun Works, Uberti USA, E.M.F., Cimarron, Traditions.
Price: About ....$225.00 to $360.00
Price: Single cased set (Navy Arms) $405.00
Price: Deluxe Walker with French fitted case (Navy Arms) $505.00
Price: Hartford model, steel frame, German silver trim, cartouche (E.M.F.) $295.00

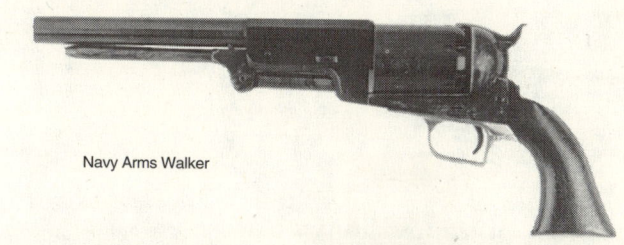

Navy Arms Walker

BLACKPOWDER MUSKETS & RIFLES

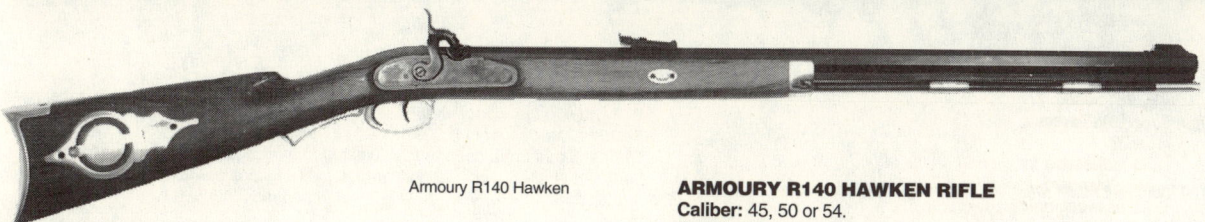

Armoury R140 Hawken

ARMOURY R140 HAWKEN RIFLE
Caliber: 45, 50 or 54.
Barrel: 29".
Weight: 8 3/4 to 9 lbs. **Length:** 45 3/4" overall.
Stock: Walnut, with cheekpiece.
Sights: Dovetail front, fully adjustable rear.
Features: Octagon barrel, removable breech plug; double set triggers; blued barrel, brass stock fittings, color case-hardened percussion lock. From Armsport, The Armoury.
Price: ....$225.00 to $245.00

ARMSPORT 1863 SHARPS RIFLE, CARBINE
Caliber: 45, 54.
Barrel: 28", round.
Weight: 8.4 lbs. **Length:** 46" overall.
Stock: Walnut.
Sights: Blade front, folding adjustable rear. Tang sight set optionally available.
Features: Replica of the 1863 Sharps. Color case-hardened frame, rest blued. Imported by Armsport.
Price: $740.00
Price: Carbine, 54 caliber, 22" barrel $640.00

BOSTONIAN PERCUSSION RIFLE
Caliber: 45.
Barrel: 30", octagonal
Weight: 7 1/4 lbs. **Length:** 46" overall.
Stock: Walnut.
Sights: Blade front, fixed notch rear.
Features: Color case-hardened lock, brass trigger guard, buttplate, patchbox. Imported from Italy by E.M.F.
Price: $285.00

CAUTION: PRICES SHOWN ARE SUPPLIED BY THE MANUFACTURER OR IMPORTER. CHECK YOUR LOCAL GUN SHOP.

BLACKPOWDER MUSKETS & RIFLES

CABELA'S BLUE RIDGE RIFLE
Caliber: 32, 36, 45, 50, 54.
Barrel: 39", octagonal.
Weight: About 7 3/4 lbs. **Length:** 55" overall.
Stock: American black walnut.
Sights: Blade front, rear drift adjustable for windage.
Features: Color case-hardened lockplate and cock/hammer, brass trigger guard and buttplate, double set, double-phased triggers. From Cabela's.
Price: Percussion $299.95
Price: Flintlock $319.95
Price: Percussion carbine (28" barrel) $259.95

CABELA'S ROLLING BLOCK MUZZLELOADER
Caliber: 50, 54.
Barrel: 26 1/2" octagonal; 1:32" (50), 1:48" (54) twist.
Weight: About 9 1/4 lbs. **Length:** 43 1/2" overall.
Stock: American walnut, rubber butt pad.
Sights: Blade front, adjustable buckhorn rear.
Features: Uses in-line ignition system, Brass trigger guard, color case-hardened hammer, block and buttplate; black-finished, engraved receiver; easily removable screw-in breech plug; black ramrod and thimble. From Cabela's.
Price: $289.95

Cabela's Rolling Block Muzzleloader Carbine
Similar to the rifle version except has 22 1/4" barrel, weighs 8 1/4 lbs. Has bead on ramp front sight, modern fully adjustable rear. From Cabela's.
Price: $269.95

COLT MODEL 1861 MUSKET
Caliber: 58.
Barrel: 40".
Weight: 9 lbs., 3 oz. **Length:** 56" overall.
Stock: Oil-finished walnut.
Sights: Blade front, adjustable folding leaf rear.
Features: Made to original specifications and has authentic Civil War Colt markings. Bright-finished metal, blued nipple and rear sight. Bayonet and accessories available. From Colt Blackpowder Arms Co.
Price: $615.00

Cook & Brother

COOK & BROTHER CONFEDERATE CARBINE
Caliber: 58.
Barrel: 24".

Cumberland Mountain

CUMBERLAND MOUNTAIN BLACKPOWDER RIFLE
Caliber: 50.
Barrel: 26", round.

CVA Apollo Classic

CVA Apollo Comet Rifle
Similar to the Apollo Shadow except stainless steel barrel and action, synthetic stock with matte black finish. Available in 50-caliber only. Introduced 1995. From CVA.
Price: $259.95

CABELA'S RED RIVER RIFLE
Caliber: 45, 50, 54, 58.
Barrel: NA.
Weight: About 7 lbs. **Length:** 45" overall.
Stock: Walnut-stained hardwood.
Sights: Blade front, adjustable buckhorn rear.
Features: Brass trigger guard, forend cap, thimbles; color case-hardened lock and hammer; rubber recoil pad. Introduced 1995. Imported by Cabela's.
Price: $119.95

CABELA'S SHARPS SPORTING RIFLE
Caliber: 45, 54.
Barrel: 31", octagonal.
Weight: About 10 lbs. **Length:** 49" overall.
Stock: American walnut with checkered grip and forend.
Sights: Blade front, ladder-type adjustable rear.
Features: Color case-hardened lock and buttplate. Adjustable double set, double-phased triggers. From Cabela's.
Price: $649.00

CABELA'S TRADITIONAL HAWKEN
Caliber: 45, 50, 54, 58.
Barrel: 29".
Weight: About 9 lbs.
Stock: Walnut.
Sights: Blade front, open adjustable rear.
Features: Flintlock or percussion. Adjustable double-set triggers. Polished brass furniture, color case-hardened lock. Imported by Cabela's.
Price: Percussion, right-hand $159.95
Price: Percussion, left-hand $169.95
Price: Flintlock, right-hand $184.95

Cabela's Sporterized Hawken Hunter Rifle
Similar to the Traditional Hawken's except has more modern stock style with rubber recoil pad, blued furniture, sling swivels. Percussion only, in 45-, 50-, 54- or 58-caliber.
Price: Carbine or rifle, right-hand $179.95
Price: Carbine or rifle, left-hand $189.95

Weight: 7 1/2 lbs. **Length:** 40 1/2" overall.
Stock: Select walnut.
Features: Recreation of the 1861 New Orleans-made artillery carbine. Color case-hardened lock, browned barrel. Buttplate, trigger guard, barrel bands, sling swivels and nose cap of polished brass. From Euroarms of America.
Price: $440.00
Price: Cook & Brother rifle (33" barrel) $470.00

Weight: 9 1/2 lbs. **Length:** 43" overall.
Stock: American walnut.
Sights: Bead front, open rear adjustable for windage.
Features: Falling block action fires shotshell primer. Blued receiver and barrel. Introduced 1993. Made in U.S. by Cumberland Mountain Arms, Inc.
Price: $931.50

CVA APOLLO SHADOW, CLASSIC RIFLES
Caliber: 50, 54.
Barrel: 24"; round with octagon integral receiver; 1:32" twist.
Weight: 9 lbs. **Length:** 42" overall.
Stock: Hardwood with black textured DuraGrip finish (Shadow); brown laminate with swivel studs (Classic); pistol grip, solid rubber buttpad.
Sights: Blade on ramp front, fully adjustable rear; drilled and tapped for scope mounting.
Features: In-line ignition, modern-style trigger with automatic safety; oversize trigger guard; synthetic ramrod. From CVA.
Price: Shadow $219.95
Price: Classic $259.95

462 THE GUN DIGEST   CAUTION: PRICES SHOWN ARE SUPPLIED BY THE MANUFACTURER OR IMPORTER. CHECK YOUR LOCAL GUN SHOP.

BLACKPOWDER MUSKETS & RIFLES

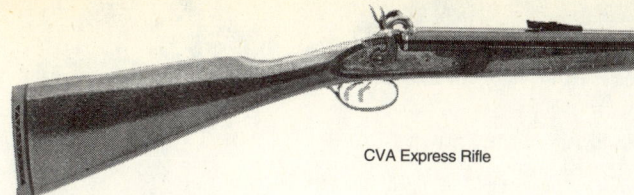

CVA Express Rifle

CVA BOBCAT RIFLE
Caliber: 50 and 54.
Barrel: 26"; 1:48" twist.
Weight: 6½ lbs. **Length:** 40" overall.
Stock: Dura-Grip synthetic.
Sights: Blade front, open rear.
Features: Oversize trigger guard; wood ramrod; matte black finish. Introduced 1995. From CVA.
Price: $99.95

CVA EXPRESS RIFLE
Caliber: 50.
Barrel: 28", round; 1:48" twist.
Weight: 10 lbs.
Stock: Select hardwood; ventilated rubber recoil pad.
Sights: Bead and blade front, adjustable rear.
Features: Double rifle with twin percussion locks and triggers, adjustable barrels. Button breech. Introduced 1989. From CVA.
Price: Finished $429.95

CVA Bobcat Hunter
Similar to the Bobcat except has black synthetic stock with checkered wrist and forend, drilled and tapped for scope mounting, engraved, blued lockplate and offset hammer, and has sporter adjustable rear sight. Available in 50- and 54-caliber. Introduced 1995. From CVA.
Price: $149.95

CVA St. Louis Hawken

CVA FRONTIER HUNTER CARBINE
Caliber: 50, 54.
Barrel: 24"; 15/16" flats; 1:32" twist.
Weight: 6¾ lbs. **Length:** 40" overall.
Stock: Laminated hardwood.
Sights: Bead front, Patridge-style click-adjustable rear.
Features: Offset hammer; black-chromed furniture; solid buttpad; barrel drilled and tapped for scope mounting. From CVA.
Price: $219.95

CVA HAWKEN RIFLE
Caliber: 50, 54.
Barrel: 28", octagon; 15/16" across flats; 1:48" twist.
Weight: 8 lbs. **Length:** 44" overall.
Stock: Select hardwood.
Sights: Beaded blade front, fully adjustable open rear.
Features: Fully adjustable double-set triggers; synthetic ramrod (kits have wood); brass patch box, wedge plates, nosecap, thimbles, trigger guard and buttplate; blued barrel; color case-hard~ened, engraved lockplate. V-type mainspring. Button breech. Introduced 1981. From CVA.
Price: St. Louis Hawken, finished (50-, 54-cal.) $209.95
Price: As above, combo kit (50-, 54-cal. bbls.) $229.95
Price: Left-hand, percussion $234.95
Price: Flintlock, 50-cal. only $234.95
Price: Flintlock, left-hand $249.95
Price: Percussion kit (50-cal., blued, wood ramrod) $169.95
Price: St. Louis Hawken Classic (laminated stock) $249.95

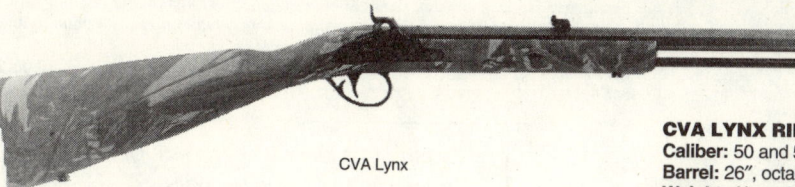

CVA Lynx

CVA KENTUCKY RIFLE
Caliber: 50.
Barrel: 33½", rifled, octagon; 7/8" flats.
Weight: 7½ lbs. **Length:** 48" overall.
Stock: Select hardwood.
Sights: Brass Kentucky blade-type front, fixed open rear.
Features: Available in percussion only. Color case-hardened lockplate. Stainless steel nipple included. From CVA.
Price: Percussion $279.95
Price: Percussion kit $189.95

CVA LYNX RIFLE
Caliber: 50 and 54.
Barrel: 26", octagonal; 15/16" flats; 1:48" twist.
Weight: About 6½ lbs. **Length:** 40" overall.
Stock: Dura-Grip synthetic.
Sights: Beaded blade front, rear adjustable for windage.
Features: Oversize trigger guard; color case-hardened lock, blued barrel, Realtree All Purpose® camo stock. Drilled and tapped for scope mounting. Synthetic ramrod. Introduced 1995. From CVA.
Price: $179.95

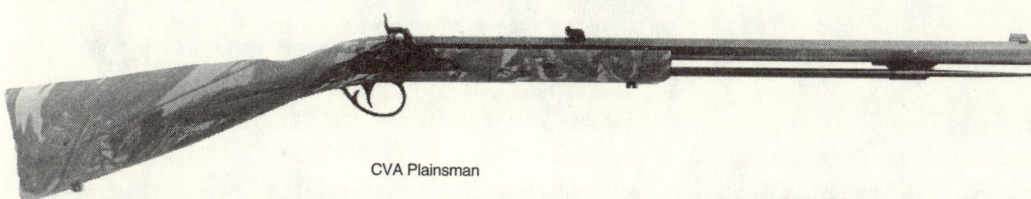

CVA Plainsman

CVA PLAINSHUNTER RIFLE
Caliber: 50.
Barrel: 26", octagonal; 15/16" flats; 1:48" twist.
Weight: About 6½ lbs. **Length:** 40" overall.
Stock: Select hardwood.
Sights: Brass blade front, semi-buckhorn rear.
Features: Brass nosecap, thimbles, wedge plates; wood ramrod. Introduced 1995. From CVA.
Price: $174.95

CVA PLAINSMAN RIFLE
Caliber: 50.
Barrel: 26", octagonal; 15/16" flats; 1:48" twist.
Weight: 6½ lbs. **Length:** 40" overall.
Stock: Stained hardwood.
Sights: Brass blade front, fixed rear.
Features: Oversize trigger guard; color case-hardened lock; wood ramrod; matte finish. Introduced 1995. From CVA.
Price: $159.95

CAUTION: PRICES SHOWN ARE SUPPLIED BY THE MANUFACTURER OR IMPORTER. CHECK YOUR LOCAL GUN SHOP.

BLACKPOWDER MUSKETS & RIFLES

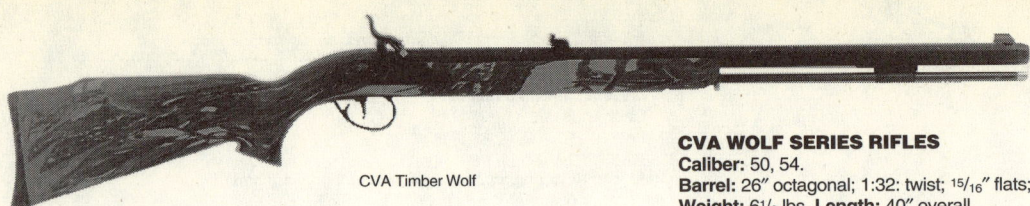
CVA Timber Wolf

CVA VARMINT RIFLE
Caliber: 32.
Barrel: 24" octagonal; 7/8" flats; 1:48" rifling.
Weight: 6 3/4 lbs. **Length:** 40" overall.
Stock: Select hardwood.
Sights: Blade front, Patridge-style click adjustable rear.
Features: Brass trigger guard, nose cap, wedge plate, thimble and buttplate. Drilled and tapped for scope mounting. Color case-hardened lock. Single trigger. Aluminum ramrod. Imported by CVA.
Price: $219.95

CVA WOLF SERIES RIFLES
Caliber: 50, 54.
Barrel: 26" octagonal; 1:32: twist; 15/16" flats; blue finish.
Weight: 6 1/2 lbs. **Length:** 40" overall.
Stock: Tuff-Lite polymer—gray finish, solid buttplate (Grey Wolf); Realtree All Purpose® camo finish, solid buttplate (Timber Wolf); checkered grip.
Sights: Blade front on ramp, fully adjustable open rear; drilled and tapped for scope mounting.
Features: Oversize trigger guard; synthetic ramrod; offset hammer. From CVA.
Price: Grey Wolf $199.95
Price: Timber Wolf (50-cal. only) $229.95

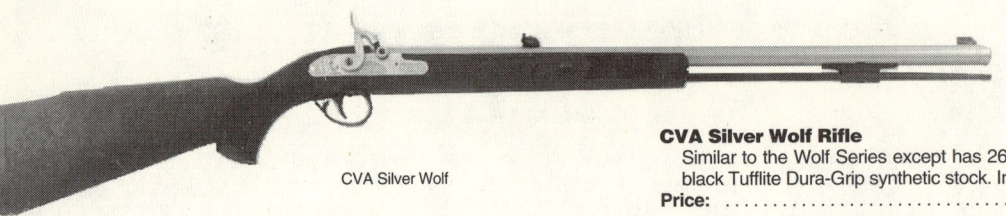
CVA Silver Wolf

CVA Silver Wolf Rifle
Similar to the Wolf Series except has 26" stainless steel barrel, nickeled lock, black Tufflite Dura-Grip synthetic stock. Introduced 1995. From CVA.
Price: $229.95

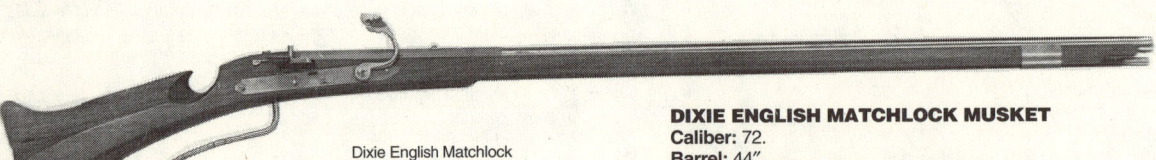
Dixie English Matchlock

DIXIE ENGLISH MATCHLOCK MUSKET
Caliber: 72.
Barrel: 44".
Weight: 8 lbs. **Length:** 57.75" overall.
Stock: Walnut with satin oil finish.
Sights: Blade front, open rear adjustable for windage.
Features: Replica of circa 1600-1680 English matchlock. Getz barrel with 11" octagonal area at rear, rest is round with cannon-type muzzle. All steel finished in the white. Imported by Dixie Gun Works.
Price: $895.00

DIXIE DELUX CUB RIFLE
Caliber: 40.
Barrel: 28".
Weight: 6 1/2 lbs.
Stock: Walnut.
Sights: Fixed.
Features: Short rifle for small game and beginning shooters. Brass patchbox and furniture. Flint or percussion. From Dixie Gun Works.
Price: Finished $335.00
Price: Kit $259.00
Price: Deerslayer (50-caliber) $350.00

> Consult our Directory pages for the location of firms mentioned.

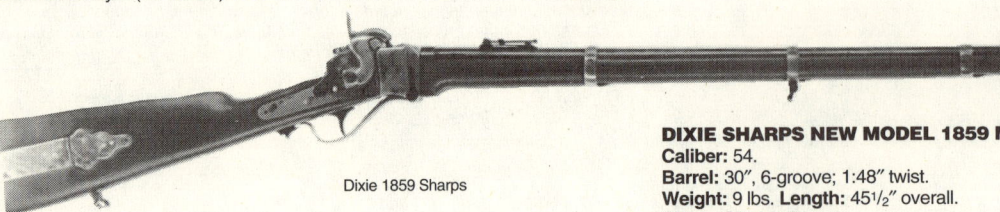
Dixie 1859 Sharps

DIXIE SHARPS NEW MODEL 1859 MILITARY RIFLE
Caliber: 54.
Barrel: 30", 6-groove; 1:48" twist.
Weight: 9 lbs. **Length:** 45 1/2" overall.
Stock: Oiled walnut.
Sights: Blade front, ladder-style rear.
Features: Blued barrel, color case-hardened barrel bands, receiver, hammer, nose cap, lever, patchbox cover and buttplate. Introduced 1995. Imported from Italy by Dixie Gun Works.
Price: $895.00

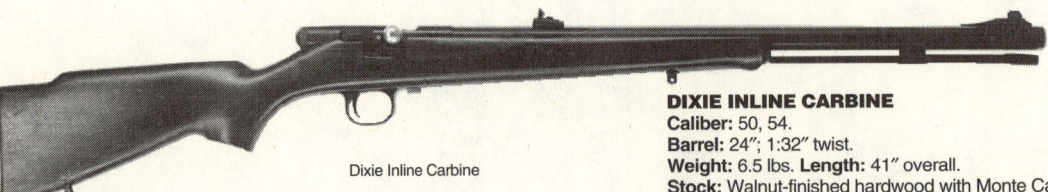
Dixie Inline Carbine

DIXIE INLINE CARBINE
Caliber: 50, 54.
Barrel: 24"; 1:32" twist.
Weight: 6.5 lbs. **Length:** 41" overall.
Stock: Walnut-finished hardwood with Monte Carlo comb.
Sights: Ramp front with red insert, open fully adjustable rear.
Features: Sliding "bolt" fully encloses cap and nipple. Fully adjustable trigger, automatic safety. Aluminum ramrod. Imported from Italy by Dixie Gun Works.
Price: $349.95

BLACKPOWDER MUSKETS & RIFLES

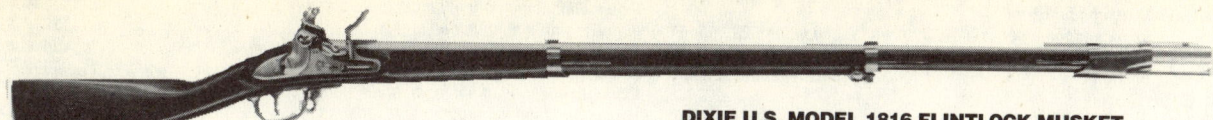

Dixie Model 1816

DIXIE TENNESSEE MOUNTAIN RIFLE
Caliber: 32 or 50.
Barrel: 41 1/2", 6-groove rifling, brown finish. **Length:** 56" overall.
Stock: Walnut, oil finish; Kentucky-style.
Sights: Silver blade front, open buckhorn rear.
Features: Recreation of the original mountain rifles. Early Schultz lock, interchangeable flint or percussion with vent plug or drum and nipple. Tumbler has fly. Double-set triggers. All metal parts browned. From Dixie Gun Works.
Price: Flint or percussion, finished rifle, 50-cal. $575.00
Price: Kit, 50-cal. $495.00
Price: Left-hand model, flint or percussion $575.00
Price: Left-hand kit, flint or perc., 50-cal. $495.00
Price: Squirrel Rifle (as above except in 32-cal. with 13/16" barrel flats), flint or percussion $575.00
Price: Kit, 32-cal., flint or percussion $495.00

DIXIE 1863 SPRINGFIELD MUSKET
Caliber: 58 (.570" patched ball or .575" Minie).
Barrel: 50", rifled.
Stocks: Walnut stained.
Sights: Blade front, adjustable ladder-type rear.
Features: Bright-finish lock, barrel, furniture. Reproduction of the last of the regulation muzzleloaders. Imported from Japan by Dixie Gun Works.
Price: Finished $595.00
Price: Kit $525.00

DIXIE U.S. MODEL 1816 FLINTLOCK MUSKET
Caliber: 69.
Barrel: 42", smoothbore.
Weight: 9.75 lbs. **Length:** 56.5" overall.
Stock: Walnut with oil finish.
Sights: Blade front.
Features: All metal finished "National Armory Bright"; three barrel bands with springs; steel ramrod with buttom-shaped head. Imported by Dixie Gun Works.
Price: $725.00

DIXIE U.S. MODEL 1861 SPRINGFIELD
Caliber: 58.
Barrel: 40".
Weight: About 8 lbs. **Length:** 55 13/16" overall.
Stock: Oil-finished walnut.
Sights: Blade front, step adjustable rear.
Features: Exact recreation of original rifle. Sling swivels attached to trigger guard bow and middle barrel band. Lockplate marked "1861" with eagle motif and "U.S. Springfield" in front of hammer; "U.S." stamped on top of buttplate. From Dixie Gun Works.
Price: $550.00
Price: From Stone Mountain Arms $599.00
Price: Kit $472.00

E.M.F. 1863 SHARPS MILITARY CARBINE
Caliber: 54.
Barrel: 22", round.
Weight: 8 lbs. **Length:** 39" overall.
Stock: Oiled walnut.
Sights: Blade front, military ladder-type rear.
Features: Color case-hardened lock, rest blued. Imported by E.M.F.
Price: $860.00

Euroarms Volunteer

EUROARMS BUFFALO CARBINE
Caliber: 58.
Barrel: 26", round.
Weight: 7 3/4 lbs. **Length:** 42" overall.
Stock: Walnut.
Sights: Blade front, open adjustable rear.
Features: Shoots .575" round ball. Color case-hardened lock, blue hammer, barrel, trigger; brass furniture. Brass patchbox. Imported by Euroarms of America.
Price: $440.00

EUROARMS VOLUNTEER TARGET RIFLE
Caliber: .451.
Barrel: 33" (two-band), 36" (three-band).
Weight: 11 lbs. (two-band). **Length:** 48.75" overall (two-band).
Stock: European walnut with checkered wrist and forend.
Sights: Hooded bead front, adjustable rear with interchangeable leaves.
Features: Alexander Henry-type rifling with 1:20" twist. Color case-hardened hammer and lockplate, brass trigger guard and nose cap, rest blued. Imported by Euroarms of America.
Price: Two-band $720.00
Price: Three-band $773.00

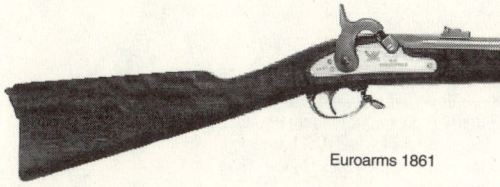

Euroarms 1861

EUROARMS 1861 SPRINGFIELD RIFLE
Caliber: 58.
Barrel: 40".
Weight: About 10 lbs. **Length:** 55.5" overall.
Stock: European walnut.
Sights: Blade front, three-leaf military rear.
Features: Reproduction of the original three-band rifle. Lockplate marked "1861" with eagle and "U.S. Springfield." Metal left in the white. Imported by Euroarms of America.
Price: $564.00

Gonic GA-87

GONIC GA-87 M/L RIFLE
Caliber: 30, 38, 44, 45, 50, 54, 20-ga.
Barrel: 26".
Weight: 6 to 6 1/2 lbs. **Length:** 43" overall (Carbine).
Stock: American walnut with checkered grip and forend, or laminated stock.
Sights: Optional bead front, open or peep rear adjustable for windage and elevation; drilled and tapped for scope bases (included).
Features: Closed-breech action with straight-line ignition. Modern trigger mechanism with ambidextrous safety. Satin blue finish on metal, satin stock finish. Introduced 1989. From Gonic Arms, Inc.
Price: Standard rifle, no sights $569.40
Price: As above, with sights, from $616.20
Price: Laminated stock, no sights $618.80
Price: Laminated stock, open sights $665.60
Price: Walnut stock, peep sight $621.40
Price: Laminated stock, peep sight $669.50

CAUTION: PRICES SHOWN ARE SUPPLIED BY THE MANUFACTURER OR IMPORTER. CHECK YOUR LOCAL GUN SHOP.

BLACKPOWDER MUSKETS & RIFLES

Gonic GA-93 Magnum M/L Rifle
Similar to the GA-87 except has open bolt mechanism, single safety, 22" barrel and comes only in 50-caliber. Stock is black wrinkle-finish wood or gray or brown, standard or thumbhole laminate. **Partial listing shown.** Introduced 1993. From Gonic Arms, Inc.
Price: Black stock, blue, no sights $460.20
Price: As above, stainless $542.10
Price: Laminated stock, blue, no sights $525.20
Price: As above, stainless $621.40
Price: Black, thumbhole stock, blue, no sights $656.50
Price: As above, stainless $656.50
Price: Black stock, blue, open sights $498.39
Price: As above, stainless $578.99
Price: Laminated stock, blue, open sights $562.09
Price: As above, stainless $658.29
Price: Thumbhole stock, blue, open sights $692.09
Price: As above, stainless $692.09

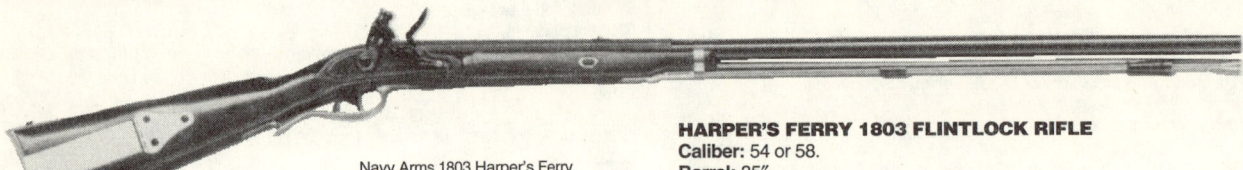
Navy Arms 1803 Harper's Ferry

HARPER'S FERRY 1803 FLINTLOCK RIFLE
Caliber: 54 or 58.
Barrel: 35".
Weight: 9 lbs. **Length:** 59 1/2" overall.
Stock: Walnut with cheekpiece.
Sights: Brass blade front, fixed steel rear.
Features: Brass trigger guard, sideplate, buttplate; steel patch box. Imported by Euroarms of America, Navy Arms (54-cal. only), Cabela's, Stone Mountain Arms.
Price: .... $495.95 to $729.00
Price: 54-cal. (Navy Arms) $615.00

HATFIELD MOUNTAIN RIFLE
Caliber: 50, 54.
Barrel: 32".
Weight: 8 lbs. **Length:** 49" overall.
Stock: Select American fancy maple. Half-stock with nose cap.
Sights: Silver blade front on brass base, fixed buckhorn rear.
Features: Traditional leaf spring and fly lock with extra-wide tumbler of 4140 steel. Slow rust brown metal finish. Double-set triggers. From Hatfield Gun Co.
Price: $950.00

Hatfield Squirrel Rifle

HATFIELD SQUIRREL RIFLE
Caliber: 36, 45, 50.
Barrel: 39 1/2", octagon, 32" on half-stock.
Weight: 7 1/2 lbs. (32-cal.).
Stock: American fancy maple.
Sights: Silver blade front, buckhorn rear.
Features: Recreation of the traditional squirrel rifle. Available in flint or percussion with brass trigger guard and buttplate. From Hatfield Rifle Works. Introduced 1983.
Price: Full stock, percussion, Grade II $819.00
Price: As above, flintlock $819.00
Price: As above, Grade III, flint or percussion $969.00

HAWKEN RIFLE
Caliber: 45, 50, 54 or 58.
Barrel: 28", blued, 6-groove rifling.
Weight: 8 3/4 lbs. **Length:** 44" overall.
Stock: Walnut with cheekpiece.
Sights: Blade front, fully adjustable rear.
Features: Coil mainspring, double-set triggers, polished brass furniture. From Armsport, Navy Arms, E.M.F.
Price: .... $220.00 to $345.00

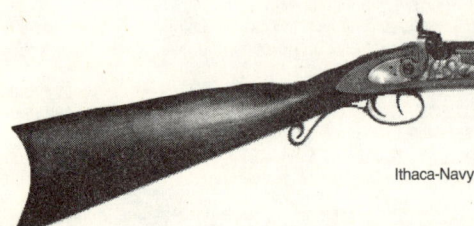
Ithaca-Navy Hawken

ITHACA-NAVY HAWKEN RIFLE
Caliber: 50.
Barrel: 32" octagonal, 1" dia.
Weight: About 9 lbs.
Stocks: Walnut.
Sights: Blade front, rear adjustable for windage.
Features: Hooked breech, 1 7/8" throw percussion lock. Attached twin thimbles and under-rib. German silver barrel key inlays, Hawken-style toe and buttplates, lock bolt inlays, barrel wedges, entry thimble, trigger guard, ramrod and cleaning jag, nipple and nipple wrench. Introduced 1977. From Navy Arms.
Price: Complete, percussion $400.00
Price: Kit, percussion $360.00

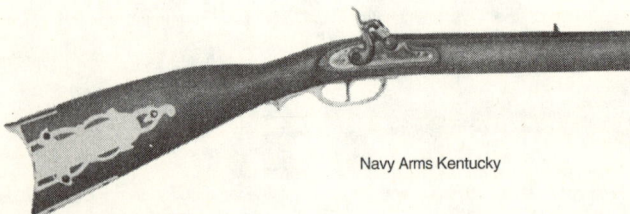
Navy Arms Kentucky

Kentucky Percussion Rifle
Similar to flintlock except percussion lock. Finish and features vary with importer. Imported by Navy Arms, The Armoury, CVA.
Price: About $259.95
Price: 45- or 50-cal. (Navy Arms) $375.00
Price: Kit, 50-cal. (CVA) $189.95

KENTUCKY FLINTLOCK RIFLE
Caliber: 44, 45, or 50.
Barrel: 35".
Weight: 7 lbs. **Length:** 50" overall.
Stock: Walnut stained, brass fittings.
Sights: Fixed.
Features: Available in carbine model also, 28" bbl. Some variations in detail, finish. Kits also available from some importers. Imported by Navy Arms, The Armoury.
Price: About .... $217.95 to $345.00
Price: Flintlock, 45 or 50-cal. (Navy Arms) $390.00

BLACKPOWDER MUSKETS & RIFLES

KENTUCKIAN RIFLE & CARBINE
Caliber: 44.
Barrel: 35" (Rifle), 27 1/2" (Carbine).
Weight: 7 lbs. (Rifle), 5 1/2 lbs. (Carbine). Length: 51" overall (Rifle), 43" (Carbine).
Stock: Walnut stain.
Sights: Brass blade front, steel V-ramp rear.
Features: Octagon barrel, case-hardened and engraved lockplates. Brass furniture. Imported by Dixie Gun Works.
Price: Rifle or carbine, flint, about $269.95
Price: As above, percussion, about $259.95

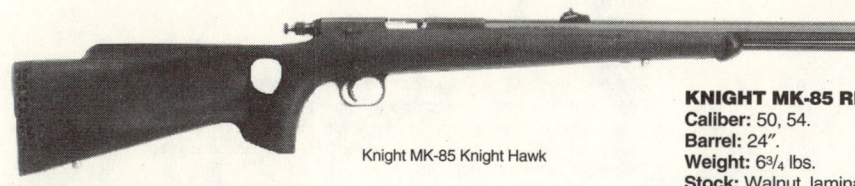
Knight MK-85 Knight Hawk

Knight MK-85 Grand American Rifle
Similar to the MK-85 Hunter except comes with Shadow Black or Shadow Brown thumbhole stock. Hand-selected barrel and components. Comes with test target, hard gun case. Blue finish.
Price: $995.00
Price: As above except in stainless steel $1,095.00

KNIGHT MK-85 RIFLE
Caliber: 50, 54.
Barrel: 24".
Weight: 6 3/4 lbs.
Stock: Walnut, laminated or composition.
Sights: Hooded blade front on ramp, open adjustable rear.
Features: Patented double safety; Sure-Fire in-line percussion ignition; Timney Featherweight adjustable trigger; aluminum ramrod; receiver drilled and tapped for scope bases. Made in U.S. by Modern Muzzleloading, Inc.
Price: Hunter, walnut stock $559.95
Price: Stalker, laminated or composition stock $669.95
Price: Predator (stainless steel), laminated or composition stock $739.95
Price: Knight Hawk, blued, composition thumbhole stock $759.95
Price: As above, stainless steel $849.95

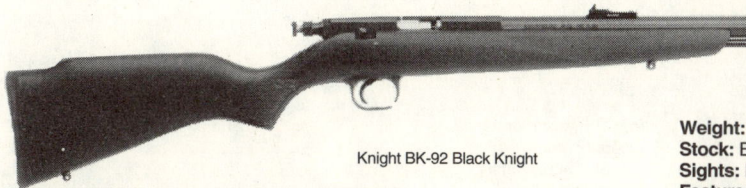
Knight BK-92 Black Knight

KNIGHT BK-92 BLACK KNIGHT RIFLE
Caliber: 50, 54.
Barrel: 24", blued.

Weight: 6 1/2 lbs.
Stock: Black composition.
Sights: Blade front on ramp, open adjustable rear.
Features: Patented double safety system; removeable breech plug for cleaning; adjustable Accu-Lite trigger; Green Mountain barrel; receiver drilled and tapped for scope bases. Made in U.S. by Modern Muzzleloading, Inc.
Price: With composition stock $479.95

Knight MK-95 Magnum

KNIGHT MK-95 MAGNUM ELITE RIFLE
Caliber: 50, 54.
Barrel: 24", stainless.

Weight: 6 3/4 lbs.
Stock: Composition; black or Realtree All-Purpose camouflage.
Sights: Hooded blade front on ramp, open adjustable rear.
Features: Enclosed Posi-Fire ignition system uses large rifle primers; Timney Featherweight adjustable trigger; Green Mountain barrel; receiver drilled and tapped for scope bases. Made in U.S. by Modern Muzzleloading, Inc.
Price: Black composition stock $749.95
Price: Realtree camouflage composition stock $799.95

KNIGHT LK-93 WOLVERINE RIFLE
Caliber: 50.
Barrel: 22", blued.
Weight: 6 lbs.
Stock: Black Fiber-Lite synthetic.
Sights: Blade front on ramp, open adjustable rear.
Features: Patented double safety system; removeable breech plug; Sure-Fire in-line percussion ignition system. Made in U.S. by Modern Muzzleloading, Inc.
Price: $269.95
Price: LK-93 Stainless $369.95

KODIAK MK. III DOUBLE RIFLE
Caliber: 54x54, 58x58, 50x50.
Barrel: 28", 5-groove, 1:48 twist.
Weight: 9 1/2 lbs. Length: 43 1/4" overall.
Stock: Czechoslovakian walnut, hand-checkered.
Sights: Adjustable bead front, adjustable open rear.
Features: Hooked breech allows interchangeability of barrels. Comes with sling, swivels, bullet mould and bullet starter. Engraved lockplates, top tang and trigger guard. Locks and top tang polished, rest browned. Introduced 1976. Imported from Italy by Navy Arms.
Price: 50-, 54-, 58-cal. SxS $775.00

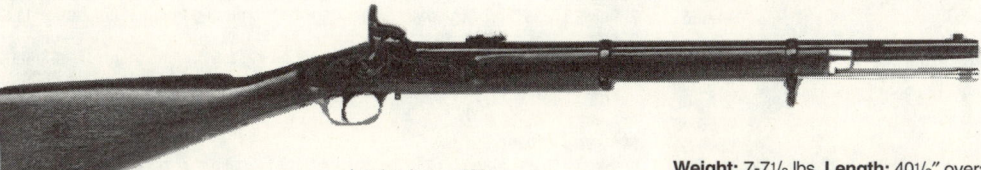
London Armory 1861

LONDON ARMORY 1861 ENFIELD MUSKETOON
Caliber: 58, Minie ball.
Barrel: 24", round.

Weight: 7-7 1/2 lbs. Length: 40 1/2" overall.
Stock: Walnut, with sling swivels.
Sights: Blade front, graduated military-leaf rear.
Features: Brass trigger guard, nose cap, buttplate; blued barrel, bands, lockplate, swivels. Imported by Euroarms of America, Navy Arms.
Price: ....$300.00 to $427.00
Price: Kit ....$365.00 to $373.00

CAUTION: PRICES SHOWN ARE SUPPLIED BY THE MANUFACTURER OR IMPORTER. CHECK YOUR LOCAL GUN SHOP.

BLACKPOWDER MUSKETS & RIFLES

LONDON ARMORY 3-BAND 1853 ENFIELD
Caliber: 58 (.577" Minie, .575" round ball, .580" maxi ball).
Barrel: 39".
Weight: 9 1/2 lbs. **Length:** 54" overall.
Stock: European walnut.
Sights: Inverted "V" front, traditional Enfield folding ladder rear.
Features: Recreation of the famed London Armory Company Pattern 1853 Enfield Musket. One-piece walnut stock, brass buttplate, trigger guard and nose cap. Lockplate marked "London Armoury Co." and with a British crown. Blued Baddeley barrel bands. From Dixie Gun Works, Euroarms of America, Navy Arms.
Price: About . . . . $350.00 to $484.00
Price: Assembled kit (Dixie, Euroarms of America) . . . . $425.00 to $431.00

LONDON ARMORY 2-BAND 1858 ENFIELD
Caliber: .577" Minie, .575" round ball.
Barrel: 33".
Weight: 10 lbs. **Length:** 49" overall.
Stock: Walnut.
Sights: Folding leaf rear adjustable for elevation.
Features: Blued barrel, color case-hardened lock and hammer, polished brass buttplate, trigger guard, nosecap. From Navy Arms, Euroarms of America, Dixie Gun Works.
Price: . . . . $385.00 to $531.00

LYMAN DEERSTALKER RIFLE
Caliber: 50, 54.
Barrel: 24", octagonal; 1:48 rifling.
Weight: 7 1/2 lbs.
Stock: Walnut with black rubber buttpad.
Sights: Lyman #37MA beaded front, fully adjustable fold-down Lyman #16A rear.
Features: Stock has less drop for quick sighting. All metal parts are blackened, with color case-hardened lock; single trigger. Comes with sling and swivels. Available in flint or percussion. Introduced 1990. From Lyman.
Price: 50- or 54-cal., percussion $299.95
Price: 50- or 54-cal., flintlock $319.95
Price: 50- or 54-cal., percussion, left-hand $299.95
Price: 50-cal., flintlock, left-hand $319.95

Lyman Deerstalker Custom Carbine
Similar to the Deerstalker rifle except in 50-caliber only with 21" stepped octagon barrel; 1:24 twist for optimum performance with conical projectiles. Comes with Lyman 37MA front sight, Lyman 16A folding rear. Weighs 6 3/4 lbs., measures 38 1/2" overall. Percussion or flintlock. Comes with Delrin ramrod, modern sling and swivels. Introduced 1991.
Price: Percussion $309.95
Price: Percussion, left-hand $309.95

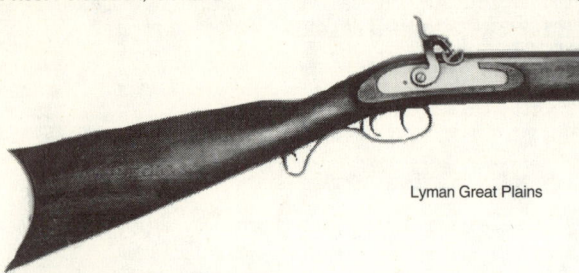
Lyman Great Plains

LYMAN GREAT PLAINS RIFLE
Caliber: 50- or 54-cal.
Barrel: 32", 1:66 twist.
Weight: 9 lbs.
Stock: Walnut.
Sights: Steel blade front, buckhorn rear adjustable for windage and elevation and fixed notch primitive sight included.
Features: Blued steel furniture. Stainless steel nipple. Coil spring lock, Hawken-style trigger guard and double-set triggers. Round thimbles recessed and sweated into rib. Steel wedge plates and toe plate. Introduced 1979. From Lyman.
Price: Percussion $416.95
Price: Flintlock $445.95
Price: Percussion kit $329.95
Price: Flintlock kit $359.95
Price: Left-hand percussion $416.95
Price: Left-hand flintlock $445.95

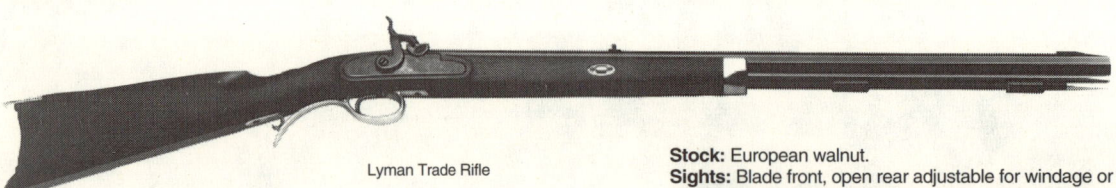
Lyman Trade Rifle

LYMAN TRADE RIFLE
Caliber: 50 or 54.
Barrel: 28" octagon, 1:48 twist.
Weight: 8 3/4 lbs. **Length:** 45" overall.
Stock: European walnut.
Sights: Blade front, open rear adjustable for windage or optional fixed sights.
Features: Fast twist rifling for conical bullets. Polished brass furniture with blue steel parts, stainless steel nipple. Hook breech, single trigger, coil spring percussion lock. Steel barrel rib and ramrod ferrules. Introduced 1980. From Lyman.
Price: Percussion $299.95
Price: Flintlock $319.95

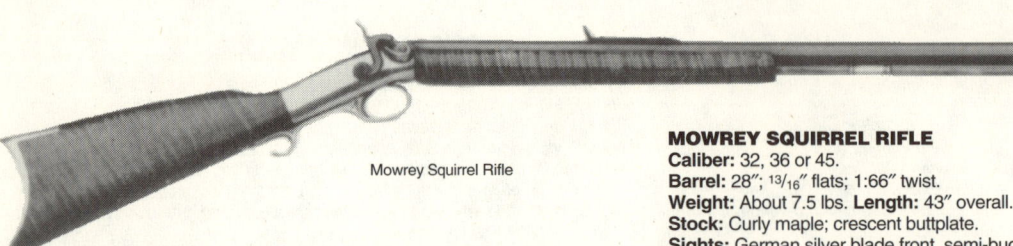
Mowrey Squirrel Rifle

MOWREY SQUIRREL RIFLE
Caliber: 32, 36 or 45.
Barrel: 28"; 13/16" flats; 1:66" twist.
Weight: About 7.5 lbs. **Length:** 43" overall.
Stock: Curly maple; crescent buttplate.
Sights: German silver blade front, semi-buckhorn rear.
Features: Brass or steel boxlock action; cut-rifled barrel. Steel rifles have browned finish, brass have browned barrel. Adjustable sear and trigger pull. Made in U.S. by Mowrey Gun Works.
Price: Brass or steel $350.00
Price: Kit $300.00

Mowrey Silhouette Rifle
Similar to the Squirrel Rifle except in 40-caliber with 32" barrel. Available in brass or steel frame.
Price: Brass frame $350.00
Price: Steel frame $350.00
Price: Kit, brass or steel $300.00

Mowrey 1 N 30 Conical Rifle
Similar to the Squirrel Rifle except in steel frame only, 45-, 50- or 54-caliber. Has special 1:24" twist barrel for conical- and sabot-style bullets. The 50 and 54-caliber barrels have 1" flats.
Price: $350.00
Price: Kit $300.00

Mowrey Plains Rifle
Similar to the Squirrel Rifle except in 50- or 54-caliber with 32" barrel. Available in brass or steel frame.
Price: Brass frame $350.00
Price: Steel frame $350.00
Price: Rocky Mountain Hunter (as above except 28" bbl.), brass $350.00
Price: As above, steel frame $350.00
Price: All above in kit form $300.00

BLACKPOWDER MUSKETS & RIFLES

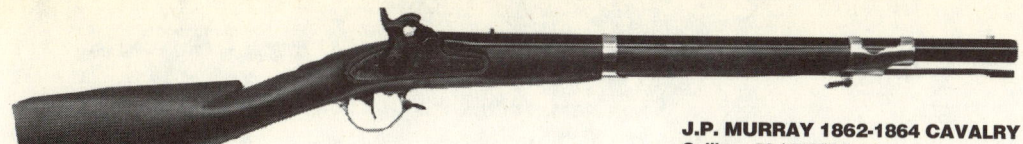
Navy Arms J.P. Murray

NAVY ARMS 1777 CHARLEVILLE MUSKET
Caliber: 69.
Barrel: 44 5/8".
Weight: 10 lbs., 4 oz. **Length:** 59 3/4" overall.
Stock: Walnut.
Sights: Brass blade front.
Features: Exact copy of the musket used in the French Revolution. All steel is polished, in the white. Brass flashpan. Introduced 1991. Imported by Navy Arms.
Price: $765.00
Price: 1816 M.T. Wickham Musket $765.00

J.P. MURRAY 1862-1864 CAVALRY CARBINE
Caliber: 58 (.577" Minie).
Barrel: 23".
Weight: 7 lbs., 9 oz. **Length:** 39" overall.
Stock: Walnut.
Sights: Blade front, rear drift adjustable for windage.
Features: Browned barrel, color case-hardened lock, blued swivel and band springs, polished brass buttplate, trigger guard, barrel bands. From Navy Arms, Euroarms of America.
Price: ....$405.00 to $440.00

Navy Arms Berdan

NAVY ARMS 1863 SHARPS CAVALRY CARBINE
Caliber: 54.
Barrel: 22".
Weight: 7 3/4 lbs. **Length:** 39" overall.
Stock: Walnut.
Sights: Blade front, military ladder-type rear.
Features: Color case-hardened action, blued barrel. Has saddle ring. Introduced 1991. Imported from Navy Arms.
Price: $835.00

NAVY ARMS BERDAN 1859 SHARPS RIFLE
Caliber: 54.
Barrel: 30".
Weight: 8 lbs., 8 oz. **Length:** 46 3/4" overall.
Stock: Walnut.
Sights: Blade front, folding military ladder-type rear.
Features: Replica of the Union sniper rifle used by Berdan's 1st and 2nd Sharpshooter regiments. Color case-hardened receiver, patch box, furniture. Double-set triggers. Imported by Navy Arms.
Price: $1,020.00
Price: 1859 Sharps Infantry Rifle (three-band) $890.00

NAVY ARMS 1863 C.S. RICHMOND RIFLE
Caliber: 58.
Barrel: 40".
Weight: 10 lbs. **Length:** NA.
Stock: Walnut.
Sights: Blade front, adjustable rear.
Features: Copy of the three-band rifle musket made at Richmond Armory for the Confederacy. All steel polished bright. Imported by Navy Arms.
Price: $550.00

Consult our Directory pages for the location of firms mentioned.

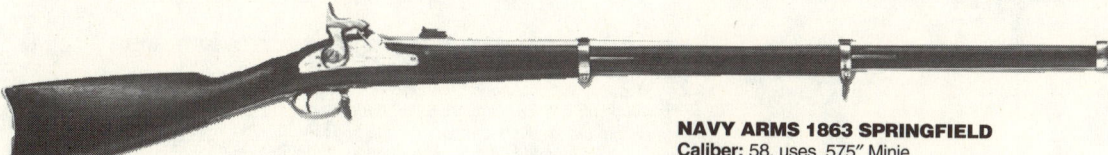
Navy Arms 1863

NAVY ARMS 1863 SPRINGFIELD
Caliber: 58, uses .575" Minie.
Barrel: 40", rifled.
Weight: 9 1/2 lbs. **Length:** 56" overall.
Stock: Walnut.
Sights: Open rear adjustable for elevation.
Features: Full-size three-band musket. Polished bright metal, including lock. From Navy Arms.
Price: Finished rifle $550.00
Price: Kit $450.00

Navy Arms Mortimer Match

NAVY ARMS MORTIMER FLINTLOCK RIFLE
Caliber: 54.
Barrel: 36".
Weight: 9 lbs. **Length:** 52 1/4" overall.
Stock: Checkered walnut.
Sights: Bead front, rear adjustable for windage.
Features: Waterproof pan, roller frizzen; sling swivels; browned barrel; external safety. Introduced 1991. Imported by Navy Arms.
Price: $725.00
Price: Mortimer Match Rifle (hooded globe front sight, fully adjustable target aperture rear, color case-hardened lock) $875.00

CAUTION: PRICES SHOWN ARE SUPPLIED BY THE MANUFACTURER OR IMPORTER. CHECK YOUR LOCAL GUN SHOP.

BLACKPOWDER MUSKETS & RIFLES

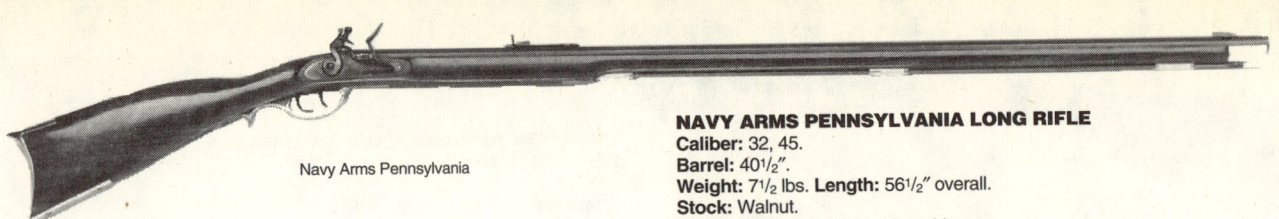

Navy Arms Pennsylvania

NAVY ARMS PENNSYLVANIA LONG RIFLE
Caliber: 32, 45.
Barrel: 40 1/2".
Weight: 7 1/2 lbs. **Length:** 56 1/2" overall.
Stock: Walnut.
Sights: Blade front, fully adjustable rear.
Features: Browned barrel, brass furniture, polished lock with double-set triggers. Introduced 1991. Imported by Navy Arms.
Price: Percussion $425.00
Price: Flintlock $410.00

Navy Arms Smith Carbine

NAVY ARMS SMITH CARBINE
Caliber: 50.
Barrel: 21 1/2".
Weight: 7 3/4 lbs. **Length:** 39" overall.
Stock: American walnut.
Sights: Brass blade front, folding ladder-type rear.
Features: Replica of the breech-loading Civil War carbine. Color case-hardened receiver, rest blued. Cavalry model has saddle ring and bar, Artillery model has sling swivels. Introduced 1991. Imported by Navy Arms.
Price: Cavalry model $600.00
Price: Artillery model $600.00

PRAIRIE RIVER ARMS PRA CLASSIC RIFLE
Caliber: 50, 54.
Barrel: 26"; 1:28" twist.
Weight: 7 lbs., 12 oz. **Length:** 40 1/2" overall.
Stock: Hardwood or black all-weather finish.
Sights: Blade front, open adjustable rear.
Features: Patented internal percussion ignition system. Introduced 1995. Made in U.S. by Prairie River Arms, Ltd.
Price: 4140 alloy barrel, hardwood stock $375.00
Price: As above, stainless barrel $425.00
Price: 4140 alloy barrel, black all-weather stock $390.00
Price: As above, stainless barrel $440.00

Prairie River Arms PRA 50/54 Rifle
Similar to the PRA Classic except has thumbhole bullpup stock, 28" barrel with 1:28" twist, weighs 7 1/2 lbs. Overall length 31 1/2". Introduced 1995. Made in U.S. by Prairie River Arms, Ltd.
Price: 4140 alloy barrel $495.00
Price: Stainless barrel $575.00

PENNSYLVANIA FULL-STOCK RIFLE
Caliber: 45 or 50.
Barrel: 32" rifled, 15/16" dia.
Weight: 8 1/2 lbs.
Stock: Walnut.
Sights: Fixed.
Features: Available in flint or percussion. Blued lock and barrel, brass furniture. Offered complete or in kit form. From The Armoury.
Price: Flint $250.00
Price: Percussion $225.00

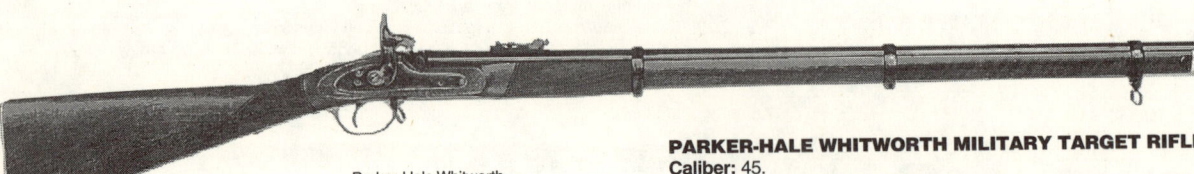

Parker-Hale Whitworth

PARKER-HALE WHITWORTH MILITARY TARGET RIFLE
Caliber: 45.
Barrel: 36".
Weight: 9 1/4 lbs. **Length:** 52 1/2" overall.
Stock: Walnut. Checkered at wrist and forend.
Sights: Hooded post front, open step-adjustable rear.
Features: Faithful reproduction of the Whitworth rifle, only bored for 45-cal. Trigger has a detented lock, capable of being adjusted very finely without risk of the sear nose catching on the half-cock bent and damaging both parts. Introduced 1978. Distributed by Navy Arms.
Price: $815.00

PARKER-HALE VOLUNTEER RIFLE
Caliber: .451".
Barrel: 32".
Weight: 9 1/2 lbs. **Length:** 49" overall.
Stock: Walnut, checkered wrist and forend.
Sights: Globe front, adjustable ladder-type rear.
Features: Recreation of the type of gun issued to volunteer regiments during the 1860s. Rigby-pattern rifling, patent breech, detented lock. Stock is glass bedded for accuracy. Distributed by Navy Arms.
Price: $750.00

Remington 1816

REMINGTON 1816 COMMEMORATIVE FLINTLOCK RIFLE
Caliber: 50.
Barrel: 39", octagonal; 1:66" twist.
Weight: 8 lbs. **Length:** 56" overall.
Stock: Extra fancy curly maple.
Sights: Blade front, open V-leaf rear.
Features: Authentic replica of New York state rifles produced in the early 1800s using Remington barrels. Has Ketland-style lock; slow rust browned barrel; six hand-engraved brass escutcheons; set trigger; polished brass trigger guard, engraved patch box, buttplate, toe and nose caps. Comes with certificate of authenticity. Limited production in 1995 only. From Remington Arms Co.
Price: $1,899.00

BLACKPOWDER MUSKETS & RIFLES

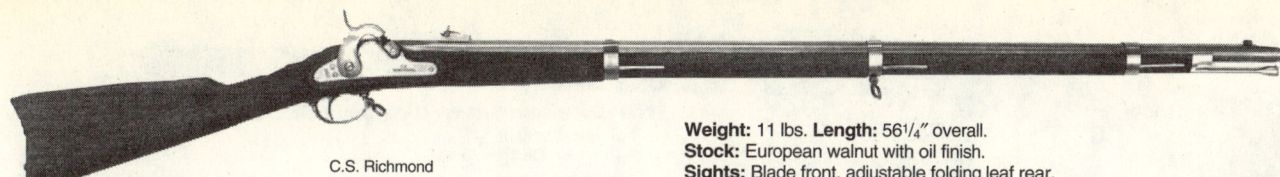

C.S. Richmond

C.S. RICHMOND 1863 MUSKET
Caliber: 58.
Barrel: 40".
Weight: 11 lbs. **Length:** 56 1/4" overall.
Stock: European walnut with oil finish.
Sights: Blade front, adjustable folding leaf rear.
Features: Reproduction of the three-band Civil War musket. Sling swivels attached to trigger guard and middle barrel band. Lock plate marked "1863" and "C.S. Richmond." All metal left in the white. Brass buttplate and forend cap. Imported by Euroarms of America.
Price: $564.00

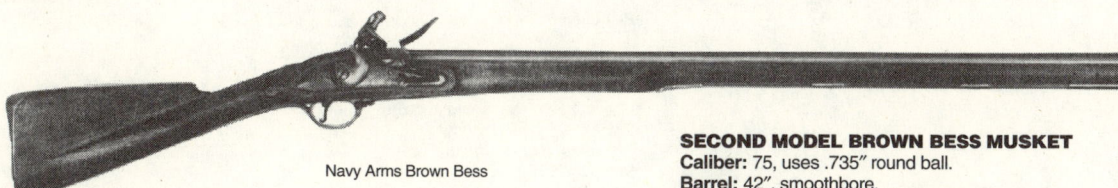

Navy Arms Brown Bess

SECOND MODEL BROWN BESS MUSKET
Caliber: 75, uses .735" round ball.
Barrel: 42", smoothbore.
Weight: 9 1/2 lbs. **Length:** 59" overall.
Stock: Walnut (Navy); walnut-stained hardwood (Dixie).
Sights: Fixed.
Features: Polished barrel and lock with brass trigger guard and buttplate. Bayonet and scabbard available. From Navy Arms, Dixie Gun Works, Cabela's.
Price: Finished ....$475.00 to $850.00
Price: Kit (Dixie Gun Works, Navy Arms) ....$510.00 to $595.00
Price: Carbine (Navy Arms) $705.00

STONE MOUNTAIN SILVER EAGLE RIFLE
Caliber: 50.
Barrel: 26", octagonal; 15/16" flats; 1:48" twist.
Weight: About 6 1/2 lbs. **Length:** 40" overall.
Stock: Dura-Grip synthetic; checkered grip and forend.
Sights: Blade front, fixed rear.
Features: Weatherguard nickel finish on metal; oversize trigger guard. Introduced 1995. From Stone Mountain Arms.
Price: $139.95
Price: Silver Eagle Hunter (adjustable sight, drilled and tapped for scope mount, swivel studs, synthetic ramrod) $159.95

STONE MOUNTAIN 1853 ENFIELD MUSKET
Caliber: 58.
Barrel: 39".
Weight: About 9 lbs. **Length:** 54" overall.
Stock: Walnut.
Sights: Inverted V front, rear step adjustable for elevation.
Features: Three-band musket. Barrel, tang, breech plug are blued, color case-hardened lock, brass nose cap, trigger guard and buttplate. From Stone Mountain Arms.
Price: $550.00

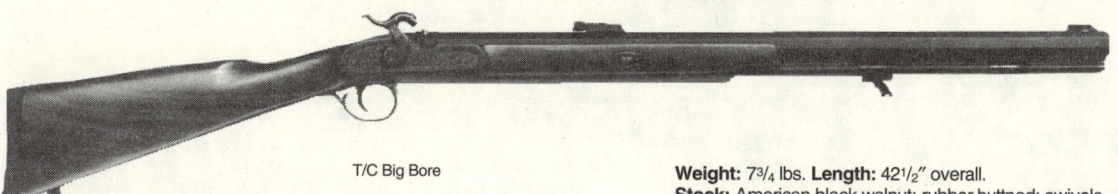

T/C Big Bore

THOMPSON/CENTER BIG BOAR RIFLE
Caliber: 58.
Barrel: 26" octagon; 1:48 twist.
Weight: 7 3/4 lbs. **Length:** 42 1/2" overall.
Stock: American black walnut; rubber buttpad; swivels.
Sights: Bead front, fullt adjustable open rear.
Features: Percussion lock; single trigger with wide bow trigger guard. Comes with soft leather sling. Introduced 1991. From Thompson/Center.
Price: $355.00

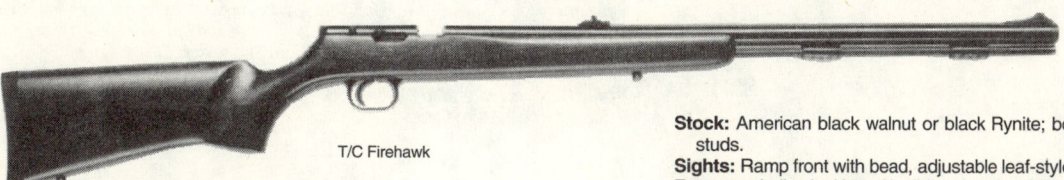

T/C Firehawk

THOMPSON/CENTER FIRE HAWK RIFLE
Caliber: 50 and 54.
Barrel: 24"; 1:38" twist.
Weight: 7 lbs. **Length:** 41 3/4" overall.
Stock: American black walnut or black Rynite; both with cheekpiece and swivel studs.
Sights: Ramp front with bead, adjustable leaf-style rear.
Features: In-line ignition with sliding thumb safety; free-floated barrel; exposed nipple; adjustable trigger. Available in blue or stainless. Comes with Weaver-style scope mount bases. Introduced 1995. Made in U.S. by Thompson/Center Arms.
Price: Blue, walnut stock $350.00
Price: Stainless, walnut stock $385.00
Price: Stainless, Rynite stock $370.00

T/C Grey Hawk

THOMPSON/CENTER GREY HAWK PERCUSSION RIFLE
Caliber: 50, 54.
Barrel: 24"; 1:48" twist.
Weight: 7 lbs. **Length:** 41" overall.
Stock: Black Rynite with rubber recoil pad.
Sights: Bead front, fully adjustable open hunting rear.
Features: Stainless steel barrel, lock, hammer, trigger guard, thimbles; blued sights. Percussion only. Introduced 1993. From Thompson/Center Arms.
Price: $330.00

CAUTION: PRICES SHOWN ARE SUPPLIED BY THE MANUFACTURER OR IMPORTER. CHECK YOUR LOCAL GUN SHOP.

BLACKPOWDER MUSKETS & RIFLES

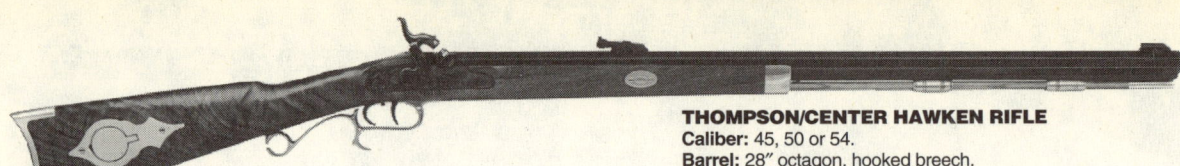

T/C Hawken

Thompson/Center Hawken Custom Rifle
Same as the standard Hawken except has select grade American walnut stock; barrel and all hardware polished to a high luster and deeply blued. Does not have patch box in stock. From Thompson/Center Arms.
Price: $495.00

THOMPSON/CENTER NEW ENGLANDER RIFLE
Caliber: 50, 54.
Barrel: 28", round.
Weight: 7 lbs., 15 oz.
Stock: American walnut or Rynite.
Sights: Open, adjustable.

THOMPSON/CENTER PENNSYLVANIA HUNTER RIFLE
Caliber: 50.
Barrel: 31", half-octagon, half-round.
Weight: About 7 1/2 lbs. Length: 48" overall.
Stock: Black walnut.
Sights: Open, adjustable.
Features: Rifled 1:66 for round ball shooting. Available in flintlock or percussion. From Thompson/Center.
Price: Percussion $350.00
Price: Flintlock $365.00

Thompson/Center Renegade Hunter
Similar to standard Renegade except has single trigger in a large-bow shotgun-style trigger guard, no brass trim. Available in 50- or 54-caliber. Color case-hardened lock, rest blued. Introduced 1987. From Thompson/Center.
Price: $335.00

THOMPSON/CENTER HAWKEN RIFLE
Caliber: 45, 50 or 54.
Barrel: 28" octagon, hooked breech.
Stock: American walnut.
Sights: Blade front, rear adjustable for windage and elevation.
Features: Solid brass furniture, double-set triggers, button rifled barrel, coil-type mainspring. From Thompson/Center.
Price: Percussion model (45-, 50- or 54-cal.) $405.00
Price: Flintlock model (50-cal.) $415.00
Price: Percussion kit $300.00
Price: Flintlock kit $320.00

Features: Color case-hardened percussion lock with engraving, rest blued. Also accepts 12-ga. shotgun barrel. Introduced 1987. From Thompson/Center.
Price: Right-hand model $295.00
Price: As above, Rynite stock $280.00
Price: Left-hand model $315.00
Price: Accessory 12-ga. barrel, right-hand $165.00

Thompson/Center Pennsylvania Hunter Carbine
Similar to the Pennsylvania Hunter except has 21" barrel, weighs 6.5 lbs., and has an overall length of 38". Designed for shooting patched round balls. Available in percussion or flintlock styles. Introduced 1992. From Thompson/Center.
Price: Percussion $340.00
Price: Flintlock $355.00

THOMPSON/CENTER RENEGADE RIFLE
Caliber: 50 and 54.
Barrel: 26", 1" across the flats.
Weight: 8 lbs.
Stock: American walnut.
Sights: Open hunting (Patridge) style, fully adjustable for windage and elevation.
Features: Coil spring lock, double-set triggers, blued steel trim. From Thompson/Center.
Price: Percussion model $360.00
Price: Flintlock model, 50-cal. only $370.00
Price: Percussion kit $260.00
Price: Left-hand percussion, 50- or 54-cal. $370.00

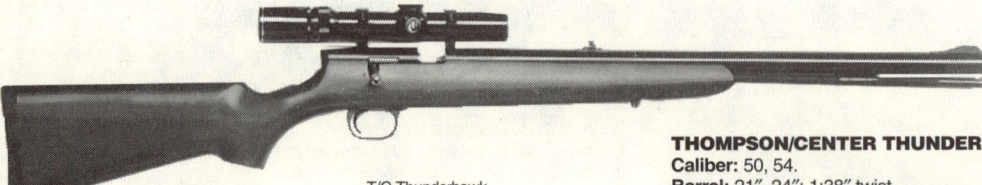

T/C Thunderhawk

THOMPSON/CENTER THUNDERHAWK CARBINE
Caliber: 50, 54.
Barrel: 21", 24"; 1:38" twist.
Weight: 6.75 lbs. Length: 38.75" overall.
Stock: American walnut or black Rynite with rubber recoil pad.
Sights: Bead on ramp front, adjustable leaf rear.
Features: Uses modern in-line ignition system, adjustable trigger. Knurled striker handle indicators for Safe and Fire. Black wood ramrod, Drilled and tapped for T/C scope mounts. Introduced 1993. From Thompson/Center Arms.
Price: Blue with walnut stock $310.00
Price: Stainless steel with Rynite stock $330.00
Price: Blue with Rynite stock $290.00

T/C Scout Rifle

Thompson/Center Scout Rifle
Similar to the Scout Carbine except has 24" part octagon, part round barrel (round only on Rynite-stocked model), solid brass forend cap on walnut-stocked gun. Barrel twist is 1:38". Available in 50- and 54-caliber. Introduced 1995. Made in U.S. by Thompson/Center Arms.
Price: With walnut stock $425.00
Price: With Rynite stock $340.00

THOMPSON/CENTER SCOUT CARBINE
Caliber: 50 and 54.
Barrel: 21", interchangeable, 1:38" twist.
Weight: 7 lbs., 4 oz. Length: 38 5/8" overall.
Stocks: American black walnut stock and forend.
Sights: Bead front, adjustable semi-buckhorn rear.
Features: Patented in-line ignition system with special vented breech plug. Patented trigger mechanism consists of only two moving parts. Interchangeable barrels. Wide grooved hammer. Brass trigger guard assembly, brass barrel band and buttplate. Ramrod has blued hardware. Comes with q.d. swivels and suede leather carrying sling. Drilled and tapped for standard scope mounts. Introduced 1990. From Thompson/Center.
Price: 50- or 54-cal. $425.00
Price: With black Rynite stock $340.00
Price: Extra barrel, 50- or 54-cal. $165.00

BLACKPOWDER MUSKETS & RIFLES

T/C White Mountain

THOMPSON/CENTER WHITE MOUNTAIN CARBINE
Caliber: 50, 54.
Barrel: 21", half-octagon, half-round.
Weight: 6½ lbs. **Length:** 38" overall.
Stock: American black walnut.
Sights: Open hunting (Patridge) style, fully adjustable rear.
Features: Percussion or flintlock. Single trigger, large trigger guard; rubber buttpad; rear q.d. swivel, front swivel mounted on thimble; comes with sling. Introduced 1989. From Thompson/Center.
Price: Percussion $350.00

Traditions Buckskinner

TRADITIONS BUCKSKINNER CARBINE
Caliber: 50 or 54.
Barrel: 21", 15/16" flats, half octagon, half round; 1:20", 1:48" or 1:66" twist.
Weight: 6 lbs. **Length:** 36¼" overall.
Stock: Beech or black laminated.
Sights: Beaded blade front, hunting-style open rear click adjustable for windage and elevation.
Features: Uses V-type mainspring, single trigger. Non-glare hardware. From Traditions.
Price: Flintlock $274.00
Price: Flintlock, laminated stock $331.00
Price: Percussion, 50 or 54 .... $250.00
Price: Percussion, laminated stock, 50 or 54 .... $315.00
Price: Percussion, left-hand $265.00

Traditions Creedmore Match

Traditions Henry Match Rifle
Similar to the Creedmore Match except has full-octagon barrel, target trigger, metal ramrod with jag, sling swivels. Weighs 11 lbs., 2 oz. Introduced 1995. From Traditions.
Price: $1,325.00

TRADITIONS CREEDMORE MATCH RIFLE
Caliber: .451".
Barrel: 32", octagon to round; 1:20" twist.
Weight: 8 lbs., 8 oz. **Length:** 50" overall.
Stock: Walnut.
Sights: Tunnel front, diopter rear.
Features: Stock has cheekpiece and fine-line checkering at wrist and forend; hooked breech; color case-hardened lock. Comes with range tool kit. Introduced 1995. From Traditions.
Price: $1,150.00

Traditions Deerhunter

Consult our Directory pages for the location of firms mentioned.

TRADITIONS DEERHUNTER RIFLE SERIES
Caliber: 50 or 54.
Barrel: 24", octagonal, 15/16" flats; 1:48" or 1:66" twist.
Weight: 5 lbs., 14 oz. **Length:** 39¼" overall.
Stock: Stained beech with rubber buttpad, sling swivels.
Sights: Blade front, rear adjustable for windage.
Features: Flint or percussion with color case-hardened lock. Hooked breech, oversized trigger guard, blackened furniture, PVC ramrod. Imported by Traditions, Inc.
Price: Percussion, 50 or 54, 1:48" twist $173.00
Price: Flintlock, 50-caliber only, 1:66" twist $190.00
Price: Percussion kit, 50 or 54 .... $152.75

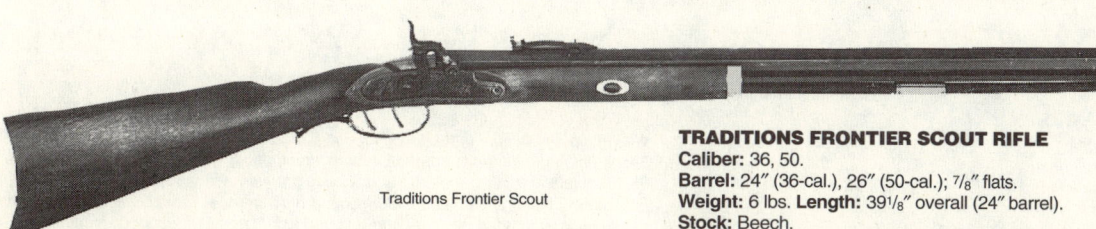

Traditions Frontier Scout

TRADITIONS FRONTIER SCOUT RIFLE
Caliber: 36, 50.
Barrel: 24" (36-cal.), 26" (50-cal.); 7/8" flats.
Weight: 6 lbs. **Length:** 39⅛" overall (24" barrel).
Stock: Beech.
Sights: Blade Front, primitive-style adjustable rear.
Features: Scaled-down version of the Frontier rifle for smaller shooters. Percussion only. Color case-hardened lock plate. From Traditions.
Price: $215.00

CAUTION: PRICES SHOWN ARE SUPPLIED BY THE MANUFACTURER OR IMPORTER. CHECK YOUR LOCAL GUN SHOP.

BLACKPOWDER MUSKETS & RIFLES

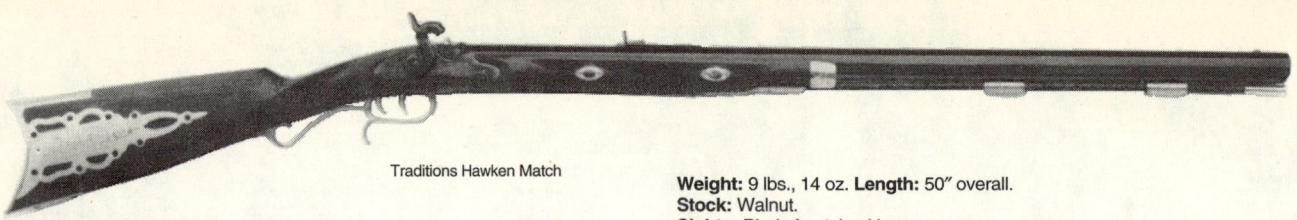

Traditions Hawken Match

TRADITIONS HAWKEN MATCH RIFLE
Caliber: .451".
Barrel: 32", octagonal; 1:20" twist.
Weight: 9 lbs., 14 oz. **Length:** 50" overall.
Stock: Walnut.
Sights: Blade front, buckhorn rear.
Features: Checkered wrist and forend; engraved brass patchbox and furniture; double-set trigger. Introduced 1995. From Traditions.
Price: $607.00

Traditions Buckhunter

TRADITIONS IN-LINE BUCKHUNTER SERIES RIFLES
Caliber: 50, 54.
Barrel: 24", round; 1:32" (50), 1:48" (54) twist.
Weight: 7 lbs., 6 oz. to 8 lbs., 1 oz. **Length:** 41" overall.
Stock: Beech, epoxy coated beech, laminated or fiberglass thumbhole; rubber recoil pad.
Sights: Beaded blade front, click adjustable rear. Drilled and tapped for scope mounting.
Features: Three-postion safety; removable breech plug; PVC ramrod; sling swivels. Eighteen models available with blackened furniture, blued, C-nickel barrels, thumbhole stock. Introduced 1995. From Traditions.
Price: ....$222.00 to $364.00

TRADITIONS HAWKEN WOODSMAN RIFLE
Caliber: 50 and 54.
Barrel: 28"; $15/16$" flats.
Weight: 7 lbs. **Length:** 45.75" overall.
Stock: Walnut-stained hardwood.
Sights: Beaded blade front, hunting-style open rear adjustable for windage and elevation.
Features: Percussion only. Brass patchbox and furniture. Double triggers. From Traditions.
Price: 50 or 54 ....$240.00
Price: 50-cal., left-hand $256.00

TRADITIONS PENNSYLVANIA RIFLE
Caliber: 50.
Barrel: $40 1/4$", $7/8$" flats; 1:66" twist.
Weight: 9 lbs. **Length:** $57 1/2$" overall.
Stock: Walnut.
Sights: Blade front, adjustable rear.
Features: Brass patchbox and ornamentation. Double-set triggers. From Traditions.
Price: Flintlock $497.00
Price: Percussion $490.00

TRADITIONS KENTUCKY RIFLE
Caliber: 50.
Barrel: $33 1/2$"; $7/8$" flats; 1:66" twist.
Weight: 7 lbs., 8 oz. **Length:** 48" overall.
Stock: Beech; inletted toe plate.
Sights: Blade front, fixed rear.
Features: Full-length, two-piece stock; brass furniture; color case-hardened lock. Introduced 1995. From Traditions.
Price: Finished $240.00
Price: Kit $198.00

TRADITIONS PIONEER RIFLE/CARBINE
Caliber: 50, 54.
Barrel: 24" (carbine), 28" (rifle); $15/16$" flats.
Weight: 7 lbs. **Length:** 44" overall.
Stock: Beech with pistol grip, recoil pad.
Sights: German silver blade front, buckhorn rear with elevation ramp.
Features: V-type mainspring, adjustable single trigger; blackened furniture; color case-hardened lock; large trigger guard. From Traditions.
Price: Percussion only, rifle $208.00
Price: Carbine. 24" barrel, 50-cal. only $208.00

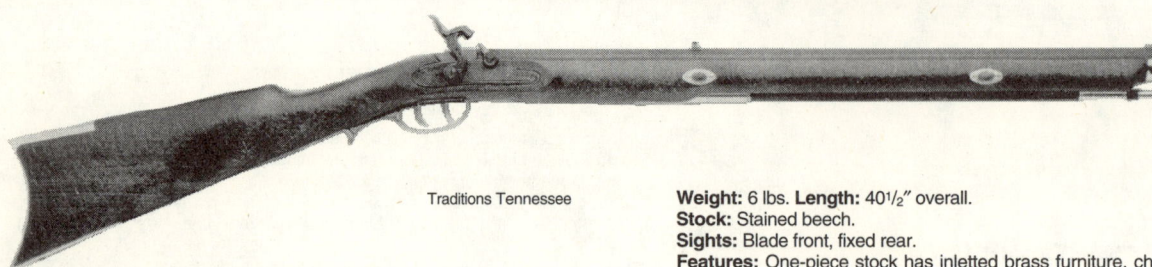

Traditions Tennessee

TRADITIONS TENNESSEE RIFLE
Caliber: 50.
Barrel: 24", octagon with $15/16$" flats; 1:32" twist.
Weight: 6 lbs. **Length:** $40 1/2$" overall.
Stock: Stained beech.
Sights: Blade front, fixed rear.
Features: One-piece stock has inletted brass furniture, cheekpiece; double-set trigger; V-type mainspring. Flint or percussion. Introduced 1995. From Traditions.
Price: Percussion $298.00
Price: Flintlock $314.00

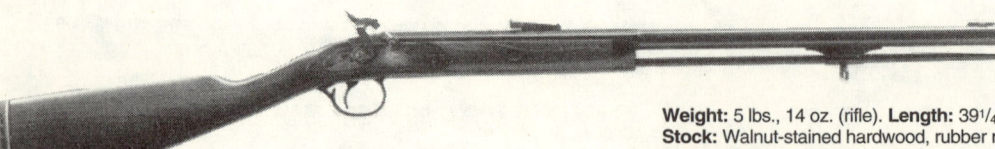

Traditions Whitetail

TRADITIONS WHITETAIL SERIES RIFLES
Caliber: 50, 54 (percussion only).
Barrel: 24" octagon to round, $15/16$" flats.
Weight: 5 lbs., 14 oz. (rifle). **Length:** $39 1/4$" overall (rifle).
Stock: Walnut-stained hardwood, rubber recoil pad; or synthetic.
Sights: Beaded blade front with flourescent dot, fully adjustable hunting-style rear.
Features: Flint or percussion. Color case-hardened, engraved lock with V-type mainspring, offset hammer. Barrel drilled and tapped for scope mounting (percussion only). Oversized trigger guard, sling swivels, blackened furniture, inletted wedge plates. Imported by Traditions.
Price: Flintlock, wood stock, rifle $256.00
Price: Percussion, wood stock, 50 or 54 ....$240.00

BLACKPOWDER MUSKETS & RIFLES

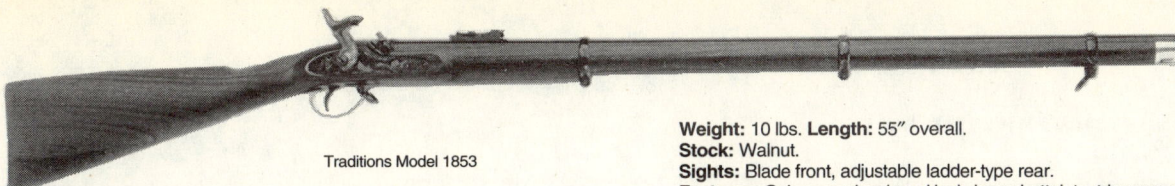
Traditions Model 1853

TRADITIONS 1853 THREE-BAND ENFIELD
Caliber: 58.
Barrel: 39"; 1:48" twist.
Weight: 10 lbs. **Length:** 55" overall.
Stock: Walnut.
Sights: Blade front, adjustable ladder-type rear.
Features: Color case-hardened lock; brass buttplate, trigger guard, nose cap. Has V-type mainspring; steel ramrod; sling swivels. Introduced 1995. From Traditions.
Price: $580.00

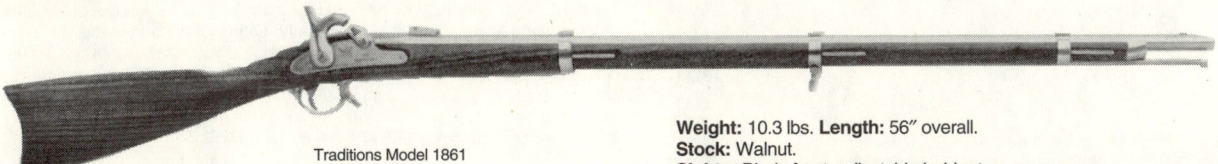
Traditions Model 1861

TRADITIONS 1861 U.S. SPRINGFIELD RIFLE
Caliber: 50.
Barrel: 40"; 1:66" twist.
Weight: 10.3 lbs. **Length:** 56" overall.
Stock: Walnut.
Sights: Blade front, adjustable ladder-type rear.
Features: Full-length stock with white steel barrel, buttplate, ramrod, trigger guard, barrel bands, swivels, lockplate. Introduced 1995. From Traditions.
Price: $630.00

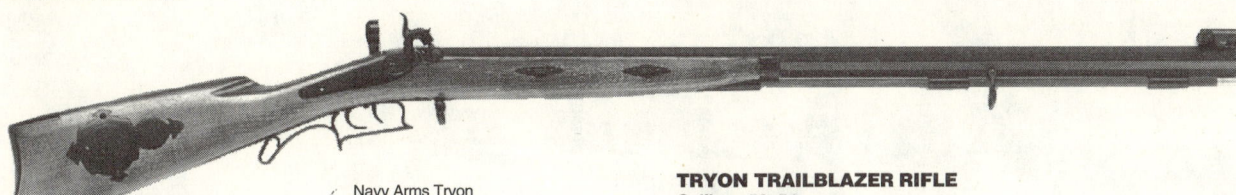
Navy Arms Tryon

Navy Arms Tryon Creedmoor Target Model
Similar to the standard Tryon rifle except 45-caliber only, 33" octagon barrel, globe front sight with inserts, fully adjustable match rear. Has double-set triggers, sling swivels. Imported by Navy Arms.
Price: $740.00

TRYON TRAILBLAZER RIFLE
Caliber: 50, 54.
Barrel: 28", 30".
Weight: 9 lbs. **Length:** 48" overall.
Stock: European walnut with cheekpiece.
Sights: Blade front, semi-buckhorn rear.
Features: Reproduction of a rifle made by George Tryon about 1820. Double-set triggers, back action lock, hooked breech with long tang. From Armsport.
Price: About $825.00

UBERTI SANTA FE HAWKEN RIFLE
Caliber: 50 or 54.
Barrel: 32", octagonal.
Weight: 9.8 lbs. **Length:** 50" overall.
Stock: Walnut, with beavertail cheekpiece.
Sights: German silver blade front, buckhorn rear.
Features: Browned finish, color case-hardened lock, double triggers, German silver ferrule, wedge plates. Imported by Uberti USA.
Price: $495.00

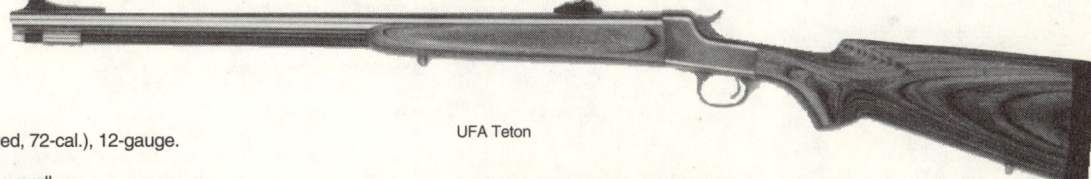
UFA Teton

UFA TETON RIFLE
Caliber: 45, 50, 12-bore (rifled, 72-cal.), 12-gauge.
Barrel: 26".
Weight: 8 lbs. **Length:** 42" overall.
Stock: Black or brown laminated wood; 1" recoil pad.
Sights: Marble's bead front, Marble's fully adjustable rear.
Features: Removable, interchangeable barrel; removable one-piece breech plug/nipple, hammer/trigger assembly; hammer blow-back block; glass-bedded stock and forend. Introduced 1994. Made in U.S. by UFA, Inc.
Price: Stainless or blued $834.00
Price: With premium walnut or maple $984.00
Price: Extra barrels $165.00

UFA Teton Blackstone Rifle
Similar to the Teton model except in 50-caliber only, 26" barrel with shallow groove 1:26" rifling. Available only in stainless steel with matte finish. Has hardwood stock with black epoxy coating, 1" recoil pad. Weighs 7 1/2 lbs., overall length 42". Introduced 1994. Made in U.S. by UFA, Inc.
Price: $534.00

UFA Grand Teton Rifle
Similar to the Teton model except has 30" tapered octagon barrel in 45- or 50-caliber only. Available in blue or stainless steel with brushed or matte finish, brown or black laminated wood stock and forend. Weighs 9 lbs., overall length 46". Introduced 1994. Made in U.S. by UFA, Inc.
Price: $995.00
Price: With premium walnut or maple $1,145.00

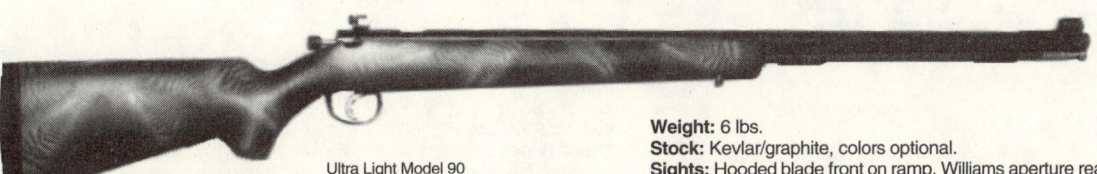
Ultra Light Model 90

ULTRA LIGHT ARMS MODEL 90 MUZZLELOADER
Caliber: 45, 50.
Barrel: 28", button rifled; 1:48 twist.
Weight: 6 lbs.
Stock: Kevlar/graphite, colors optional.
Sights: Hooded blade front on ramp, Williams aperture rear adjustable for windage and elevation.
Features: In-line ignition system with top loading port. Timney trigger; integral side safety. Comes with recoil pad, sling swivels and hard case. Introduced 1990. Made in U.S. by Ultra Light Arms.
Price: $950.00

CAUTION: PRICES SHOWN ARE SUPPLIED BY THE MANUFACTURER OR IMPORTER. CHECK YOUR LOCAL GUN SHOP.

BLACKPOWDER MUSKETS & RIFLES

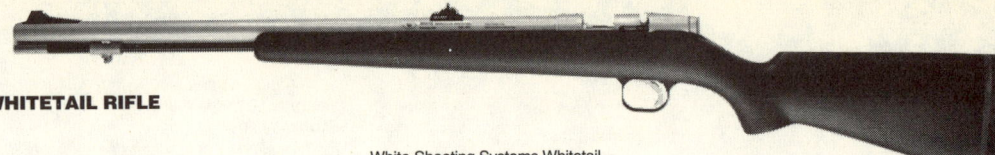

White Shooting Systems Whitetail

WHITE SHOOTING SYSTEMS WHITETAIL RIFLE
Caliber: 41, 45 or 50.
Barrel: 22".
Weight: 6.5 lbs. **Length:** 39.5" overall.
Stock: Black composite; classic style; recoil pad, swivel studs.
Sights: Bead front on ramp, fully adjustable open rear.
Features: Insta-Fire straight-line ignition; action and trigger safeties; adjustable trigger; stainless steel. Introduced 1992. Made in U.S. by White Shooting Systems, Inc.
Price: Blue, composite stock $399.00
Price: Stainless, composite stock $499.00
Price: Stainless, laminate stock $549.00

White Shooting Systems White Lightning Rifle
Similar to the Whitetail stainless rifle except uses smaller action with cocking lever and secondary safety on right side, primary safety on the left. Available only in 50-caliber with 22" barrel. Weighs 6.4 lbs., 40" overall. Has black hardwood stock. Announced 1995. From White Shooting Systems, Inc.
Price: ....NA

White Shooting Systems Bison Blackpowder Rifle
Similar to the blued Whitetail model except in 50-caliber (1:24" twist) or 54-caliber (1:28" twist) with 22" ball barrel. Uses Insta-Fire in-line percussion system, double safety. Adjustable sight, black-finished hardwood stock, matte blue metal finish, Delron ramrod, swivel studs. Drilled and tapped for scope mounting. Weighs 7 1/4 lbs. Introduced 1993. From White Shooting Systems, Inc.
Price: $349.00

WHITE SHOOTING SYSTEMS SPORTING RIFLE
Caliber: 41, 45, 50.
Barrel: 26".
Weight: 8 3/4 lbs. **Length:** NA.
Stock: Figured crotchwood fiber composite.
Sights: Bead front on ramp, fully adjustable open rear.
Features: Traditional sidelock action; Delron ramrod; swivel studs; matte blue finish. Introduced 1994. From White Shooting Systems, Inc.
Price: $799.00

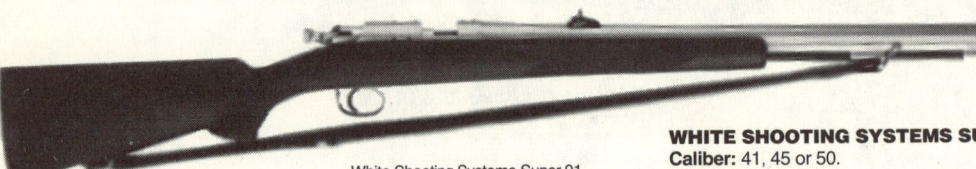

White Shooting Systems Super 91

WHITE SHOOTING SYSTEMS SUPER 91 BLACKPOWDER RIFLE
Caliber: 41, 45 or 50.
Barrel: 26".
Weight: 7 1/2 lbs. **Length:** 43.5" overall.
Stock: Black laminate or black composite; recoil pad, swivel studs.
Sights: Bead front on ramp, fully adjustable open rear.
Features: Insta-Fire straight-line ignition system; all stainless steel construction; side-swing safety; fully adjustable trigger; full barrel under-rib with two ramrod thimbles. Introduced 1991. Made in U.S. by White Shooting Systems, Inc.
Price: Blue $599.00
Price: Stainless $699.00
Price: Stainless, laminate stock $749.00

White Shooting Systems Super Safari Rifle
Same as the stainless Super 91 except has Mannlicher-style stock of black composite. Introduced 1993. From White Shooting Systems, Inc.
Price: $799.00

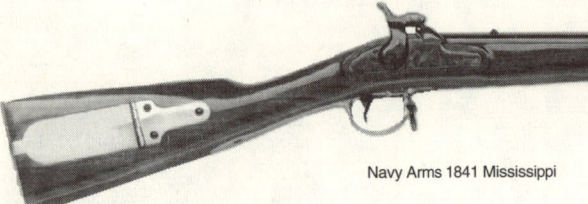

Navy Arms 1841 Mississippi

Mississippi 1841 Percussion Rifle
Similar to Zouave rifle but patterned after U.S. Model 1841. Imported by Dixie Gun Works, Euroarms of America, Navy Arms, Stone Mountain Arms.
Price: ....$430.00 to $487.00

ZOUAVE PERCUSSION RIFLE
Caliber: 58, 59.
Barrel: 32 1/2".
Weight: 9 1/2 lbs. **Length:** 48 1/2" overall.
Stock: Walnut finish, brass patchbox and buttplate.
Sights: Fixed front, rear adjustable for elevation.
Features: Color case-hardened lockplate, blued barrel. From Navy Arms, Dixie Gun Works, Euroarms of America (M1863), E.M.F., Cabela's.
Price: About ....$325.00 to $460.00
Price: Kit (Euroarms 58-cal. only) $331.00

BLACKPOWDER SHOTGUNS

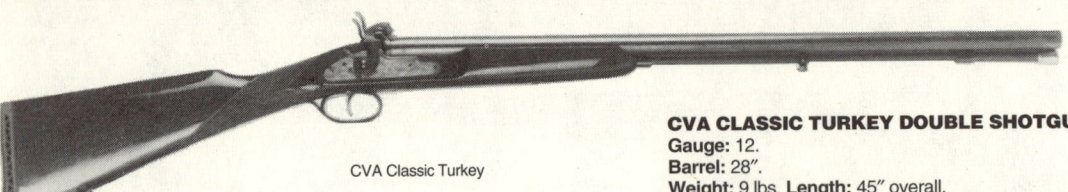

CVA Classic Turkey

CVA CLASSIC TURKEY DOUBLE SHOTGUN
Gauge: 12.
Barrel: 28".
Weight: 9 lbs. **Length:** 45" overall.
Stock: European walnut; classic English style with checkered straight grip, wrap-around forend with bottom screw attachment.
Sights: Bead front.
Features: Hinged double triggers; color case-hardened and engraved lockplates, trigger guard and tang. Polymer-coated fiberglass ramrod. Rubber recoil pad. Not suitable for steel shot. Introduced 1990. Imported by CVA.
Price: $429.95

BLACKPOWDER SHOTGUNS

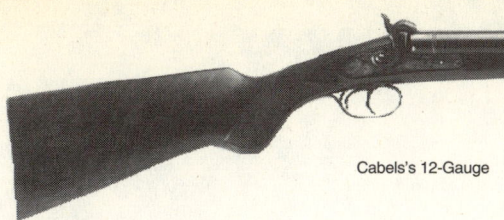
Cabela's 12-Gauge

CABELA'S BLACKPOWDER SHOTGUNS
Gauge: 10, 12, 20.
Barrel: 28 1/2" (10-, 12-ga.), Imp. Cyl., Mod., Full choke tubes; 27 1/2" (20-ga.), Imp. Cyl., Mod. choke tubes.
Weight: 6 1/2 to 7 lbs. **Length:** 45" overall (28 1/2" barrel).
Stock: American walnut with checkered grip; 12- and 20-gauge have straight stock, 10-gauge has pistol grip.
Features: Blued barrels, engraved, color case-hardened locks and hammers, brass ramrod tip. From Cabela's.
Price: 10-gauge $379.95
Price: 12-gauge $359.95
Price: 20-gauge $329.95

CVA TRAPPER PERCUSSION
Gauge: 12.
Barrel: 28".
Weight: 6 lbs.
Length: 46" overall.
Stock: English-style checkered straight grip of walnut-finished hardwood.
Sights: Brass bead front.
Features: Single blued barrel; color case-hardened lockplate and hammer; screw adjustable sear engagements, V-type mainspring; brass wedge plates; color case-hardened and engraved trigger guard and tang. From CVA.
Price: Finished $239.95

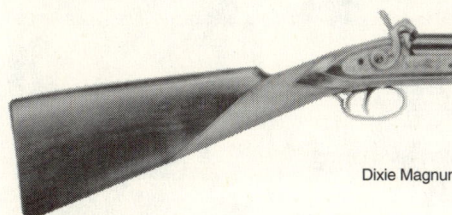
Dixie Magnum

Weight: 6 1/4 lbs. **Length:** 45" overall.
Stock: Hand-checkered walnut, 14" pull.
Features: Double triggers; light hand engraving; case-hardened locks in 12-gauge, polished steel in 10-gauge; sling swivels. From Dixie Gun Works.
Price: Upland $495.00
Price: 12-ga. kit $375.00
Price: 20-ga. $495.00
Price: 10-ga. $495.00
Price: 10-ga. kit $375.00

DIXIE MAGNUM PERCUSSION SHOTGUN
Gauge: 10, 12, 20.
Barrel: 30" (Imp. Cyl. & Mod.) in 10-gauge; 28" in 12-gauge.

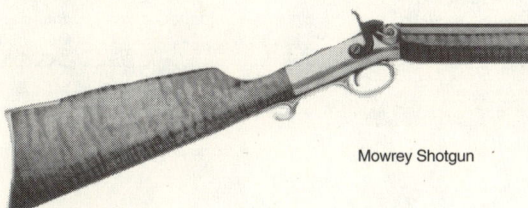
Mowrey Shotgun

Weight: About 8 lbs. **Length:** 48" overall (32" barrel).
Stock: Curly maple.
Sights: Bead front.
Features: Brass or steel frame; shotgun butt. Made in U.S. by Mowrey Gun Works.
Price: Finished $350.00
Price: Kit $300.00

MOWREY SHOTGUN
Gauge: 12, 28.
Barrel: 28" (28-gauge, Cyl.); 32" (12-gauge, Cyl.); octagonal.

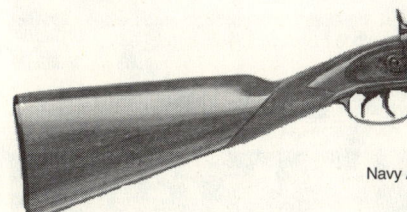
Navy Arms Fowler

NAVY ARMS FOWLER SHOTGUN
Gauge: 12.
Barrel: 28".
Weight: 7 lbs., 12 oz. **Length:** 45" overall.
Stock: Walnut-stained hardwood.
Features: Color case-hardened lockplates and hammers; checkered stock. Imported by Navy Arms.
Price: Fowler model, 12-ga. only $340.00

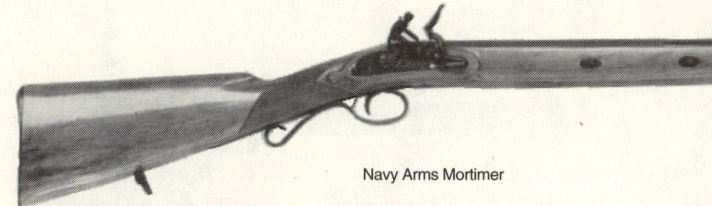
Navy Arms Mortimer

NAVY ARMS STEEL SHOT MAGNUM SHOTGUN
Gauge: 10.
Barrel: 28" (Cyl. & Cyl.).
Weight: 7 lbs., 9 oz. **Length:** 45 1/2" overall.
Stock: Walnut, with cheekpiece.
Features: Designed specifically for steel shot. Engraved, polished locks; sling swivels; blued barrels. Introduced 1991. Imported by Navy Arms.
Price: $560.00

NAVY ARMS MORTIMER FLINTLOCK SHOTGUN
Gauge: 12.
Barrel: 36".
Weight: 7 lbs. **Length:** 53" overall.
Stock: Walnut, with cheekpiece.
Features: Waterproof pan, roller frizzen, external safety. Color case-hardened lock, rest blued. Introduced 1991. Imported by Navy Arms.
Price: $700.00

CAUTION: PRICES SHOWN ARE SUPPLIED BY THE MANUFACTURER OR IMPORTER. CHECK YOUR LOCAL GUN SHOP.

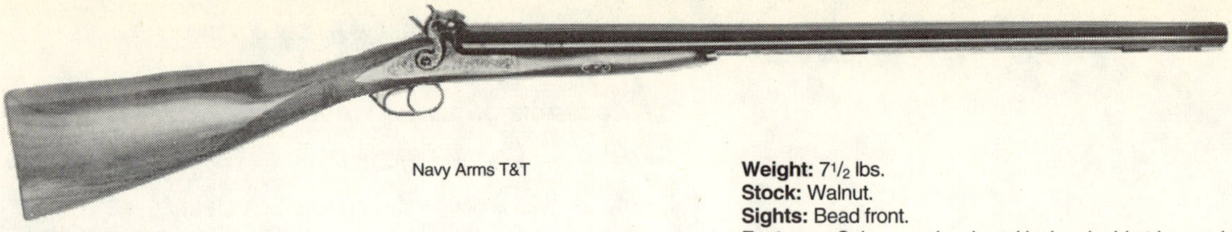

BLACKPOWDER SHOTGUNS

Navy Arms T&T

NAVY ARMS T&T SHOTGUN
Gauge: 12.
Barrel: 28" (Full & Full).
Weight: 7½ lbs.
Stock: Walnut.
Sights: Bead front.
Features: Color case-hardened locks, double triggers, blued steel furniture. From Navy Arms.
Price: $540.00

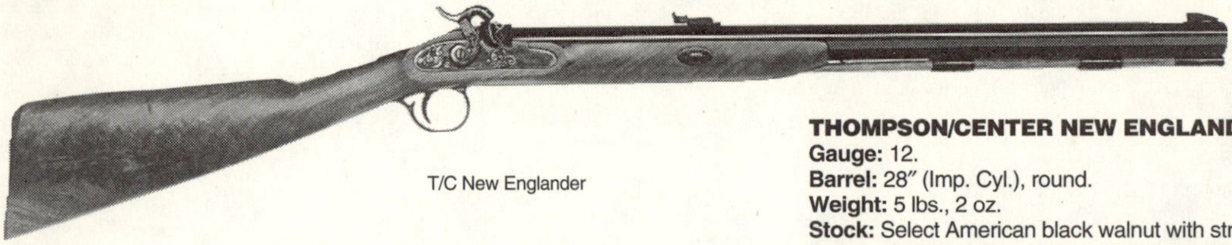

T/C New Englander

THOMPSON/CENTER NEW ENGLANDER SHOTGUN
Gauge: 12.
Barrel: 28" (Imp. Cyl.), round.
Weight: 5 lbs., 2 oz.
Stock: Select American black walnut with straight grip.
Features: Percussion lock is color case-hardened, rest blued. Also accepts 26" round 50- and 54-cal. rifle barrel. Introduced 1986. From Thompson/Center.
Price: Right-hand $315.00
Price: Accessory rifle barrel, right-hand, 50 or 54 ....$165.00

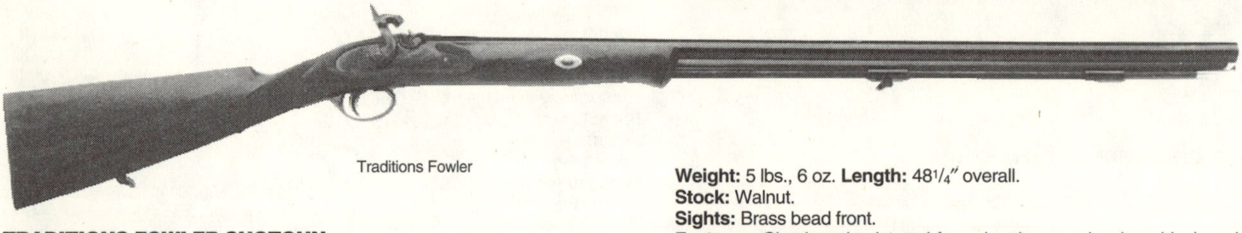

Traditions Fowler

TRADITIONS FOWLER SHOTGUN
Gauge: 12.
Barrel: 32", octagon to round.
Weight: 5 lbs., 6 oz. **Length:** 48¼" overall.
Stock: Walnut.
Sights: Brass bead front.
Features: Checkered wrist and forend; color-case-hardened lock and buttplate; hooked breech. Introduced 1995. From Traditions.
Price: $430.00

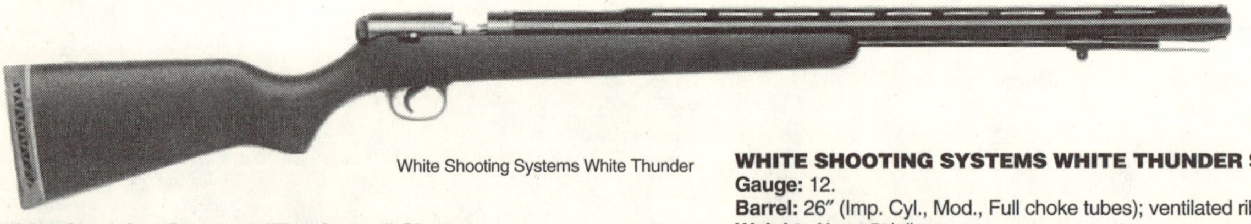

White Shooting Systems White Thunder

WHITE SHOOTING SYSTEMS WHITE THUNDER SHOTGUN
Gauge: 12.
Barrel: 26" (Imp. Cyl., Mod., Full choke tubes); ventilated rib.
Weight: About 5¾ lbs.
Stock: Black hardwood.
Features: InstaFire in-line ignition; double safeties; match-grade trigger; Delron ramrod. Introduced 1995. From White Shooting Systems, Inc.
Price: $599.00

White Shooting Systems "Tominator" Shotgun
Similar to the White Thunder except has Imp. Cyl., Mod., Full and Super Full Turkey choke tubes; black laminate stock. Introduced 1995. From White Shooting Systems, Inc.
Price: $699.00

AIRGUNS—HANDGUNS

AIRROW MODEL A6 AIR PISTOL
Caliber: #2512 10.75" arrow.
Barrel: 10.75".
Weight: 1.75 lbs. **Length:** 16.5" overall.
Power: CO$_2$ or compressed air.
Stocks: Checkered composition.
Sights: Bead front, fully adjustable Williams rear.
Features: Velocity to 375 fps. Pneumatic air trigger. Floating barrel. All aircraft aluminum and stainless steel construction; Mil-spec materials and finishes. Announced 1993. From Swivel Machine Works, Inc.
Price: About $597.00

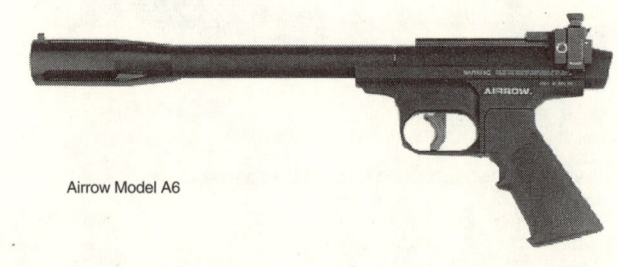

Airrow Model A6

Consult our Directory pages for the location of firms mentioned.

AIRGUNS—HANDGUNS

BEEMAN P1 MAGNUM AIR PISTOL
Caliber: 177, 5mm, single shot.
Barrel: 8.4".
Weight: 2.5 lbs. **Length:** 11" overall.
Power: Top lever cocking; spring-piston.
Stocks: Checkered walnut.
Sights: Blade front, square notch rear with click micrometer adjustments for windage and elevation. Grooved for scope mounting.
Features: Dual power for 177 and 20-cal.: low setting gives 350-400 fps; high setting 500-600 fps. Rearward expanding mainspring simulates firearm recoil. All Colt 45 auto grips fit gun. Dry-firing feature for practice. Optional wooden shoulder stock. Introduced 1985. Imported by Beeman.
Price: 177, 5mm $395.00

Beeman P1

Beeman P2 Match Air Pistol
Similar to the Beeman P1 Magnum except shoots only 177 pellets; completely recoilless single-stroke pnuematic action. Weighs 2.2 lbs. Choice of thumbrest match grips or standard style. Introduced 1990.
Price: 177, 5mm, standard grip $435.00
Price: 177, match grip $465.00

BEEMAN/FEINWERKBAU C20 CO₂ PISTOL
Caliber: 177, single shot.
Barrel: 10.1"; 12-groove rifling.
Weight: 2.5 lbs. **Length:** 16" overall.
Power: Special CO₂ cylinder.
Stock: Stippled walnut with adjustable palm shelf.
Sights: Blade front, open rear adjustable for windage and elevation. Notch size adjustable for width. Interchangeable front blades.
Features: Fully adjustable trigger; can be set for dry firing. Separate gas chamber for uniform power. Cylinders interchangeable even when full. Short-barrel model also available. Introduced 1988. Imported by Beeman.
Price: Right-hand, regular or Mini $1,160.00
Price: Left-hand $1,225.00

BEEMAN/FEINWERKBAU 65 MKII AIR PISTOL
Caliber: 177, single shot.
Barrel: 6.1", removable bbl. wgt. available.
Weight: 42 oz. **Length:** 13.3" overall.
Power: Spring, sidelever cocking.
Stocks: Walnut, stippled thumbrest; adjustable or fixed.
Sights: Front, interchangeable post element system, open rear, click adjustable for windage and elevation and for sighting notch width. Scope mount available.
Features: New shorter barrel for better balance and control. Cocking effort 9 lbs. Two-stage trigger, four adjustments. Quiet firing, 525 fps. Programs instantly for recoil or recoilless operation. Permanently lubricated. Steel piston ring. Imported by Beeman.
Price: Right-hand $1,140.00
Price: Left-hand $1,185.00

BEEMAN/FEINWERKBAU C25 CO₂ PISTOL
Caliber: 177, single shot.
Barrel: 10.1"; 12-groove rifling.
Weight: 2.5 lbs. **Length:** 16.5" overall.
Power: Vertical interchangeable CO₂ bottles.
Stocks: Stippled walnut with adjustable palm shelf.
Sights: Blade front, rear micrometer adjustable. Notch size adjustable for width; interchangeable front blades.
Features: Fully adjustable trigger; can be set for dry firing. Has special vertical CO₂ cylinder and weight rail for balance. Short-barrel model (C25 Mini) also available. Introduced 1992. Imported by Beeman.
Price: Right-hand $1,325.00
Price: Left-hand $1,375.00
Price: C25 Mini $1,325.00

BEEMAN/FEINWERKBAU 102 PISTOL
Caliber: 177, single shot.
Barrel: 10.1"; 12-groove rifling.
Weight: 2.5 lbs. **Length:** 16.5" overall.
Power: Single-stroke pneumatic, underlever cocking.
Stocks: Stippled walnut with adjustable palm shelf.
Sights: Blade front, open rear adjustable for windage and elevation. Notch size adjustable for width. Interchangeable front blades.
Features: Velocity 460 fps. Fully adjustable trigger. Cocking effort 12 lbs. Introduced 1988. Imported by Beeman.
Price: Right-hand $1,410.00
Price: Left-hand $1,460.00

BEEMAN/FWB P30 MATCH AIR PISTOL
Caliber: 177, single shot.
Barrel: 10⁵/₁₆", with muzzle brake.
Weight: 2.4 lbs. **Length:** 16.5" overall.
Power: Pre-charged pneumatic.
Stocks: Stippled walnut; adjustable match type.
Sights: Undercut blade front, fully adjustable match rear.
Features: Velocity to 525 fps; up to 200 shots per CO₂ cartridge. Fully adjustable trigger; built-in muzzle brake. Introduced 1995. Imported from Germany by Beeman.
Price: Right-hand $1,410.00
Price: Left-hand $1,460.00

Beeman/Feinwekbau 102

Beeman/FWB P30

BEEMAN HW70A AIR PISTOL
Caliber: 177, single shot.
Barrel: 6¼", rifled.
Weight: 38 oz. **Length:** 12¾" overall.
Power: Spring, barrel cocking.
Stocks: Plastic, with thumbrest.
Sights: Hooded post front, square notch rear adjustable for windage and elevation. Comes with scope base.
Features: Adjustable trigger, 24-lb. cocking effort, 410 fps MV; automatic barrel safety. Imported by Beeman.
Price: $205.00

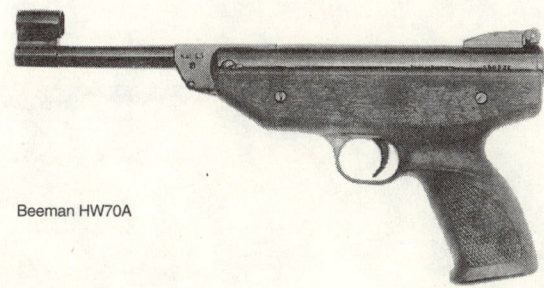
Beeman HW70A

CAUTION: PRICES SHOWN ARE SUPPLIED BY THE MANUFACTURER OR IMPORTER. CHECK YOUR LOCAL GUN SHOP.

AIRGUNS—HANDGUNS

Beeman/FWB C55

BEEMAN/WEBLEY NEMESIS AIR PISTOL
Caliber: 177, single shot.
Barrel: 7".
Weight: 2.2 lbs. **Length:** 9.8" overall.
Power: Single-stroke pneumatic.
Stocks: Checkered black composition.
Sights: Blade on ramp front, fully adjustable rear. Integral scope rail.
Features: Velocity to 400 fps. Adjustable two-stage trigger, manual safety. Recoilless action. Introduced 1995. Imported from England by Beeman.
Price: $180.00

BEEMAN/WEBLEY TEMPEST AIR PISTOL
Caliber: 177, 22, single shot.
Barrel: 6 7/8".
Weight: 32 oz. **Length:** 8.9" overall.
Power: Spring-piston, break barrel.
Stocks: Checkered black plastic with thumbrest.
Sights: Blade front, adjustable rear.
Features: Velocity to 500 fps (177), 400 fps (22). Aluminum frame; black epoxy finish; manual safety. Imported from England by Beeman.
Price: $190.00

Beeman/Webley Hurricane Air Pistol
Similar to the Tempest except has extended frame in the rear for a click-adjustable rear sight; hooded front sight; comes with scope mount. Imported from England by Beeman.
Price: $215.00

Benjamin Sheridan Pneumatic

Benjamin Sheridan CO2

BRNO TAU-7

BEEMAN/FWB C55 CO2 RAPID FIRE PISTOL
Caliber: 177, single shot or 5-shot magazines.
Barrel: 7.3".
Weight: 2.5 lbs. **Length:** 15" overall.
Power: Special CO2 cylinder.
Stocks: Anatomical, adjustable.
Sights: Interchangeable front, fully adjustable open micro-click rear with adjustable notch size.
Features: Velocity 510 fps. Has 11.75" sight radius. Built-in muzzle brake. Introduced 1993. Imported by Beeman Precision Airguns.
Price: Right-hand $1,630.00
Price: Left-hand $1,700.00

Beeman/Webley Nemesis

Beeman/Webley Tempest

BENJAMIN SHERIDAN PNEUMATIC PELLET PISTOLS
Caliber: 177, 20, 22, single shot.
Barrel: 9 3/8", rifled brass.
Weight: 38 oz. **Length:** 13 1/8" overall.
Power: Underlever pnuematic, hand pumped.
Stocks: Walnut stocks and pump handle.
Sights: High ramp front, fully adjustable notch rear.
Features: Velocity to 525 fps (variable). Bolt action with cross-bolt safety. Choice of black or nickel finish. Made in U.S. by Benjamin Sheridan Co.
Price: Black finish, HB17 (177), HB20 (20), HB22 (22), about $106.00
Price: Nickel finish, H17 (177), H20 (20), H22 (22), about $112.75

BENJAMIN SHERIDAN CO2 PELLET PISTOLS
Caliber: 177, 20, 22, single shot.
Barrel: 6 3/8", rifled brass.
Weight: 29 oz. **Length:** 9.8" overall.
Power: 12-gram CO2 cylinder.
Stocks: Walnut.
Sights: High ramp front, fully adjustable notch rear.
Features: Velocity to 500 fps. Turn-bolt action with cross-bolt safety. Gives about 40 shots per CO2 cylinder. Black or nickel finish. Made in U.S. by Benjamin Sheridan Co.
Price: Black finish, EB17 (177), EB20 (20), EB22 (22), about $97.25
Price: Nickel finish, E17 (177), E20 (20), E22 (22), about $110.50

BRNO TAU-7 CO2 MATCH PISTOL
Caliber: 177.
Barrel: 10.24".
Weight: 37 oz. **Length:** 15.75" overall.
Power: 12.5-gram CO2 cartridge.
Stocks: Stippled hardwood with adjustable palm rest.
Sights: Blade front, open fully adjustable rear.
Features: Comes with extra seals and counterweight. Blue finish. Imported by Century International Arms, Great Lakes Airguns.
Price: About $326.50

AIRGUNS—HANDGUNS

Crosman Auto Air II

Crosman Model 1008

Crosman Model 1322

Crosman SSP 250

CROSMAN AUTO AIR II PISTOL
Caliber: BB, 17-shot magazine, 177 pellet, single shot.
Barrel: $8^{5}/_{8}$" steel, smoothbore.
Weight: 13 oz. **Length:** $10^{3}/_{4}$" overall.
Power: CO_2 Powerlet.
Stocks: Grooved plastic.
Sights: Blade front, adjustable rear; highlighted system.
Features: Velocity to 480 fps (BBs), 430 fps (pellets). Semi-automatic action with BBs, single shot with pellets. Silvered finish. Introduced 1991. From Crosman.
Price: About $29.00

CROSMAN MODEL 357 AIR PISTOL
Caliber: 177, 6- and 10-shot pellet clips.
Barrel: 4" (Model 357-4), 6" (Model 357-6), rifled steel; 8" (Model 357-8), rifled brass.
Weight: 32 oz. (6"). **Length:** $11^{3}/_{8}$" overall (357-6).
Power: CO_2 Powerlet.
Stocks: Checkered wood-grain plastic.
Sights: Ramp front, fully adjustable rear.
Features: Average 430 fps (Model 357-6). Break-open barrel for easy loading. Single or double action. Vent. rib barrel. Wide, smooth trigger. Two cylinders come with each gun. Model 357-8 has matte gray finish, black grips. From Crosman.
Price: 4" or 6", about $46.50
Price: 8", about $53.25
Price: Model 1357 (same gun as above, except shoots BBs, has 6-shot clip), about $46.50

CROSMAN MODEL 1008 REPEAT AIR
Caliber: 177, 8-shot pellet clip
Barrel: 4.25", rifled steel.
Weight: 17 oz. **Length:** 8.625" overall.
Power: CO_2 Powerlet.
Stocks: Checkered plastic.
Sights: Post front, adjustable rear.
Features: Velocity about 430 fps. Break-open barrel for easy loading; single or double semi-automatic action; two 8-shot clips included. Optional carrying case available. Introduced 1992. From Crosman.
Price: About $45.00
Price: With case, about $55.00
Price: Model 1008SB (silver and black finish), about $47.00

CROSMAN MODEL 1322, 1377 AIR PISTOLS
Caliber: 177 (M1377), 22 (M1322), single shot.
Barrel: 8", rifled steel.
Weight: 39 oz. **Length:** $13^{5}/_{8}$".
Power: Hand pumped.
Sights: Blade front, rear adjustable for windage and elevation.
Features: Moulded plastic grip, hand size pump forearm. Cross-bolt safety. Model 1377 also shoots BBs. From Crosman.
Price: About $53.00

CROSMAN MODEL SSP 250 PISTOL
Caliber: 177, 20, 22, single shot.
Barrel: $9^{7}/_{8}$", rifled steel.
Weight: 3 lbs., 1 oz. **Length:** 14" overall.
Power: CO_2 Powerlet.
Stocks: Composition; black, with checkering.
Sights: Hooded front, fully adjustable rear.
Features: Velocity about 560 fps. Interchangeable accessory barrels. Two-stage trigger. High/low power settings. From Crosman.
Price: About $52.00

DAISY MODEL 91 MATCH PISTOL
Caliber: 177, single shot.
Barrel: 10.25", rifled steel.
Weight: 2.5 lbs. **Length:** 16.5" overall.
Power: CO_2, 12-gram cylinder.
Stocks: Stippled hardwood; anatomically shaped and adjustable.
Sights: Blade and ramp front, changeable-width rear notch with full micrometer adjustments.
Features: Velocity to 476 fps. Gives 55 shots per cylinder. Fully adjustable trigger. Imported by Daisy Mfg. Co.
Price: About $670.00

DAISY MODEL 288 AIR PISTOL
Caliber: 177 pellets, 24-shot.
Barrel: Smoothbore steel.
Weight: .8 lb. **Length:** 12.1" overall.
Power: Single stroke spring-air.
Stocks: Moulded resin with checkering and thumbrest.
Sights: Blade and ramp front, open fixed rear.
Features: Velocity to 215 fps. Cross-bolt trigger block safety. Black finish. From Daisy Mfg. Co.
Price: About $26.00

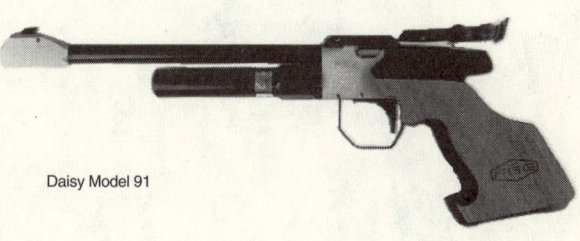
Daisy Model 91

CAUTION: PRICES SHOWN ARE SUPPLIED BY THE MANUFACTURER OR IMPORTER. CHECK YOUR LOCAL GUN SHOP.

AIRGUNS—HANDGUNS

Daisy Model 500

DAISY MODEL 500 RAVEN AIR PISTOL
Caliber: 177 pellets, single shot.
Barrel: Rifled steel.
Weight: 36 oz. **Length:** 8.5" overall.
Power: CO_2.
Stocks: Moulded plastic with checkering.
Sights: Blade front, fixed rear.
Features: Velocity up to 500 fps. Hammer-block safety. Resembles semi-auto centerfire pistol. Barrel tips up for loading. Introduced 1993. From Daisy Mfg. Co.
Price: About $65.00

Daisy/Power Line 717

DAISY/POWER LINE 717 PELLET PISTOL
Caliber: 177, single shot.
Barrel: 9.61".
Weight: 2.8 lbs. **Length:** 13 1/2" overall.
Stocks: Moulded wood-grain plastic, with thumbrest.
Sights: Blade and ramp front, micro-adjustable notch rear.
Features: Single pump pneumatic pistol. Rifled steel barrel. Cross-bolt trigger block. Muzzle velocity 385 fps. From Daisy Mfg. Co. Introduced 1979.
Price: About $80.00

Daisy/Power Line 747 Pistol
Similar to the 717 pistol except has a 12-groove rifled steel barrel by Lothar Walther, and adjustable trigger pull weight. Velocity of 360 fps. Manual cross-bolt safety.
Price: About $160.00

DAISY/POWER LINE 44 REVOLVER
Caliber: 177 pellets, 6-shot.
Barrel: 6", rifled steel; interchangeable 4" and 8".
Weight: 2.7 lbs.
Power: CO_2.
Stocks: Moulded plastic with checkering.
Sights: Blade on ramp front, fully adjustable notch rear.
Features: Velocity up to 400 fps. Replica of 44 Magnum revolver. Has swingout cylinder and interchangeable barrels. Introduced 1987. From Daisy Mfg. Co.
Price: $70.00

DAISY/POWER LINE 45 AIR PISTOL
Caliber: 177, 13-shot clip.
Barrel: 5", rifled steel.
Weight: 1.25 lbs. **Length:** 8.5" overall.
Power: CO_2.
Stocks: Checkered plastic.
Sights: Fixed.
Features: Velocity 400 fps. Semi-automatic repeater with double-action trigger. Manually operated lever-type trigger block safety; magazine safety. Introduced 1990. From Daisy Mfg. Co.
Price: About $80.00
Price: Model 645 (nickel-chrome plated), about $85.00

DAISY/POWER LINE 93 PISTOL
Caliber: 177, BB, 15-shot clip.
Barrel: 5", steel.
Weight: 17 oz. **Length:** NA.
Power: CO_2.
Stocks: Checkered plastic.
Sights: Fixed.
Features: Velocity to 400 fps. Semi-automatic repeater. Manual lever-type trigger-block safety. Introduced 1991. From Daisy Mfg. Co.
Price: About $80.00
Price: Model 693 (nickel-chrome plated), about $85.00

DAISY/POWERLINE 400 BB PISTOL
Caliber: BB, 20-shot magazine.
Barrel: Smoothbore steel.
Weight: 1.4 lbs. **Length:** 10.7" overall.
Power: 12-gram CO_2.
Stocks: Moulded black checkered plastic.
Sights: Blade front, fixed open rear.
Features: Velocity to 420 fps. Blowback slide cycles automatically on firing. Rotary trigger block safety. Introduced 1994. From Daisy Mfg. Co.
Price: About $83.00

DAISY/POWER LINE MATCH 777 PELLET PISTOL
Caliber: 177, single shot.
Barrel: 9.61" rifled steel by Lothar Walther.
Weight: 32 oz. **Length:** 13 1/2" overall.
Power: Sidelever, single-pump pneumatic.
Stocks: Smooth hardwood, fully contoured with palm and thumbrest.
Sights: Blade and ramp front, match-grade open rear with adjustable width notch, micro. click adjustments.
Features: Adjustable trigger; manual cross-bolt safety. MV of 385 fps. Comes with cleaning kit, adjustment tool and pellets. From Daisy Mfg. Co.
Price: About $335.00

Daisy/Power Line 45

Daisy/Power Line 93

Daisy/Power Line 400

AIRGUNS—HANDGUNS

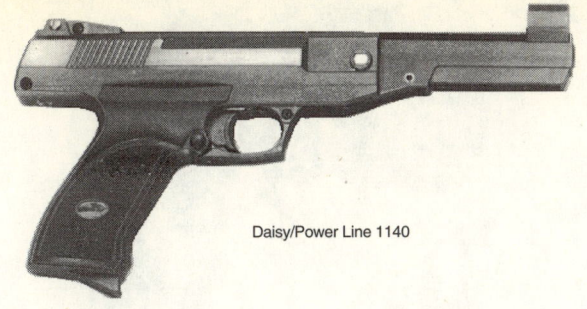
Daisy/Power Line 1140

Daisy/Power Line 1200

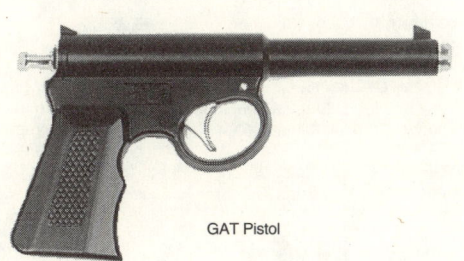
GAT Pistol

DAISY/POWER LINE 1140 PELLET PISTOL
Caliber: 177, single shot.
Barrel: Rifled steel.
Weight: 1.3 lbs. **Length:** 11.7″ overall.
Power: Single-stroke barrel cocking.
Stocks: Checkered resin.
Sights: Hooded post front, open adjustable rear.
Features: Velocity to 325 fps. Made of black lightweight engineering resin. Introduced 1995. From Daisy.
Price: About $45.50

DAISY/POWER LINE CO_2 1200 PISTOL
Caliber: BB, 177.
Barrel: 10 1/2″, smooth.
Weight: 1.6 lbs. **Length:** 11.1″ overall.
Power: Daisy CO_2 cylinder.
Stocks: Contoured, checkered moulded wood-grain plastic.
Sights: Blade ramp front, fully adjustable square notch rear.
Features: 60-shot BB reservoir, gravity feed. Cross-bolt safety. Velocity of 420-450 fps for more than 100 shots. From Daisy Mfg. Co.
Price: About $37.50

DAISY/POWERLINE 1700 AIR PISTOL
Caliber: 177 BB, 60-shot magazine.
Barrel: Smoothbore steel.
Weight: 1.4 lbs. **Length:** 11.2″ overall.
Power: CO_2.
Stocks: Moulded checkered plastic.
Sights: Blade front, adjustable rear.
Features: Velocity to 420 fps. Cross-bolt trigger block safety; matte finish. Has 3/8″ dovetail mount for scope or point sight. Introduced 1994. From Daisy Mfg. Co.
Price: About $40.00

"GAT" AIR PISTOL
Caliber: 177, single shot.
Barrel: 7 1/2″ cocked, 9 1/2″ extended.
Weight: 22 oz.
Power: Spring-piston.
Stocks: Cast checkered metal.
Sights: Fixed.
Features: Shoots pellets, corks or darts. Matte black finish. Imported from England by Stone Enterprises, Inc.
Price: $21.95

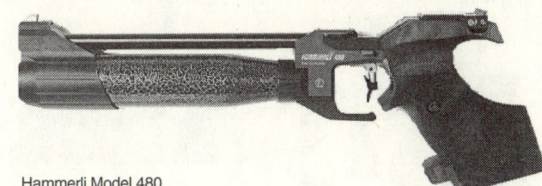
Hammerli Model 480

HAMMERLI 480 COMPETITION AIR PISTOL
Caliber: 177, single shot.
Barrel: 9.8″.
Weight: 37 oz. **Length:** 16.5″ overall.
Power: Air or CO_2.
Stocks: Walnut with 7-degree rake adjustment. Stippled grip area.
Sights: Undercut blade front, fully adjustable open match rear.
Features: Under-barrel cannister charges with air or CO_2 for power supply; gives 320 shots per filling. Trigger adjustable for position. Introduced 1994. Imported from Switzerland by Hammerli Pistols USA.
Price: $1,353.00

MARKSMAN 1010 REPEATER PISTOL
Caliber: 177, 18-shot repeater.
Barrel: 2 1/2″, smoothbore.
Weight: 24 oz. **Length:** 8 1/4″ overall.
Power: Spring.
Features: Velocity to 200 fps. Thumb safety. Black finish. Uses BBs, darts or pellets. Repeats with BBs only. From Marksman Products.
Price: Matte black finish $25.50
Price: Model 1010X (as above except nickel-plated) $33.50

MARKSMAN 1015 SPECIAL EDITION AIR PISTOL
Caliber: 177, 24-shot repeater.
Barrel: 3.8″, rifled.
Weight: 22 oz. **Length:** 10.3″ overall.
Power: Spring-air.
Stocks: Checkered brown composition.
Sights: Fixed.
Features: Velocity about 230 fps. Skeletonized trigger, extended barrel with "ported compensator." Shoots BBs, pellets, darts or bolts. From Marksman Products.
Price: $31.75

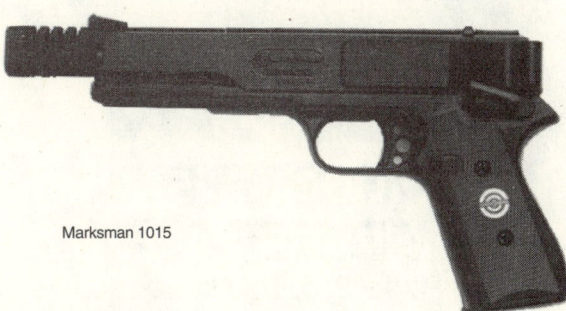
Marksman 1015

MORINI 162E MATCH AIR PISTOL
Caliber: 177, single shot.
Barrel: 9.4″.
Weight: 32 oz. **Length:** 16.1″ overall.
Power: Pre-charged CO_2.
Stocks: Adjustable match type.
Sights: Interchangeable blade front, fully adjustable match-type rear.
Features: Power mechanism shuts down when pressure drops to a pre-set level. Adjustable electronic trigger. Introduced 1995. Imported from Switzerland by Nygord Precision Products.
Price: $950.00

AIRGUNS—HANDGUNS

PARDINI K58 MATCH AIR PISTOL
Caliber: 177, single shot.
Barrel: 9.0".
Weight: 37.7 oz. **Length:** 15.5" overall.
Power: Pre-charged compressed air; single-stroke cocking.
Stocks: Adjustable match type; stippled walnut.
Sights: Interchangeable post front, fully adjustable match rear.
Features: Fully adjustable trigger. Introduced 1995. Imported from Italy by Nygord Precision Products.
Price: $650.00
Price: K60 model (CO_2) $650.00

RECORD JUMBO DELUXE AIR PISTOL
Caliber: 177, single shot.
Barrel: 6", rifled.
Weight: 1.9 lbs. **Length:** 7.25" overall.
Power: Spring-air, lateral cocking lever.
Stocks: Smooth walnut.
Sights: Blade front, fully adjustable open rear.
Features: Velocity to 322 fps. Thumb safety. Grip magazine compartment for extra pellet storage. Introduced 1983. Imported from Germany by Great Lakes Airguns.
Price: $113.50

Record Jumbo

RWS/DIANA MODEL 5G AIR PISTOL
Caliber: 177, single shot.
Barrel: 7".
Weight: 2 3/4 lbs. **Length:** 16" overall.
Power: Spring-air, barrel cocking.
Stocks: Plastic, thumbrest design.
Sights: Tunnel front, micro-click open rear.
Features: Velocity of 410 fps. Two-stage trigger with automatic safety. Imported from Germany by Dynamit Nobel-RWS, Inc.
Price: $225.00

RWS/Diana Model 5G

RWS/Diana Model 6G Air Pistols
Similar to the Model 6M except does not have the movable barrel shroud. Has click micrometer rear sight, two-stage adjustable trigger, interchangeable tunnel front sight. Available in right- or left-hand models.
Price: Right-hand $395.00
Price: Left-hand $425.00

RWS/DIANA MODEL 6M MATCH AIR PISTOL
Caliber: 177, single shot.
Barrel: 7".
Weight: 3 lbs. **Length:** 16" overall.
Power: Spring-air, barrel cocking.
Stocks: Walnut-finished hardwood with thumbrest.
Sights: Adjustable front, micro. click open rear.
Features: Velocity of 410 fps. Recoilless double piston system, movable barrel shroud to protect from sight during cocking. Imported from Germany by Dynamit Nobel-RWS, Inc.
Price: Right-hand $525.00
Price: Left-hand $560.00

STEYR CO_2 MATCH LP1 PISTOL
Caliber: 177, single shot.
Barrel: 9".
Weight: 38.7 oz. **Length:** 15.3" overall.
Power: Pre-compressed CO_2 cylinders.
Stocks: Fully adjustable Morini match with palm shelf; stippled walnut.
Sights: Interchangeable blade in 4mm, 4.5mm or 5mm widths, fully adjustable open rear with interchangeable 3.5mm or 4mm leaves.
Features: Velocity about 500 fps. Adjustable trigger, adjustable sight radius from 12.4" to 13.2". Imported from Austria by Nygord Precision Products.
Price: About $1,095.00
Price: LP1C (compensated) $1,150.00

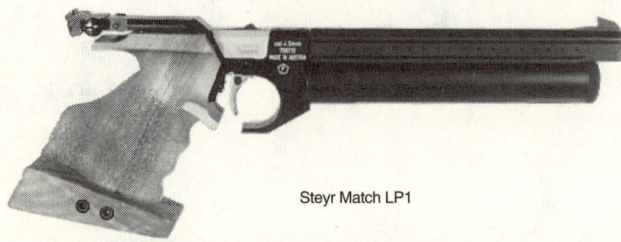

Steyr Match LP1

STEYR LP 5C MATCH AIR PISTOL
Caliber: 177, 5-shot magazine.
Barrel: NA.
Weight: 40.7 oz. **Length:** 15.2" overall.
Power: Pre-charged air cylinder.
Stocks: Adjustable match type.
Sights: Interchangeable blade front, fully adjustable match rear.
Features: Adjustable sight radius; fully adjustable trigger. Has barrel compensator. Introduced 1995. Imported from Austria by Nygord Precision Products.
Price: $1,325.00

CONSULT
Shooter's Marketplace
Page 266, This Issue

STEYR LP5 MATCH PISTOL
Caliber: 177, 5-shot magazine.
Barrel: NA.
Weight: 40.2 oz. **Length:** 13.39" overall.
Power: Pre-compressed CO_2 cylinders.
Stocks: Adjustable Morini match with palm shelf; stippled walnut.
Sights: Movable 2.5mm blade front; 2-3mm interchangeable in .2mm increments; fully adjustable open match rear.
Features: Velocity about 500 fps. Fully adjustable trigger; has dry-fire feature. Barrel and grip weights available. Introduced 1993. Imported from Austria by Nygord Precision Products.
Price: About $1,250.00

WALTHER CPM-1 CO_2
Caliber: 177, single shot.
Barrel: 8.66".
Weight: NA. **Length:** 15.1" overall.
Power: CO_2.
Stocks: Orthopaedic target type.
Sights: Undercut blade front, open match rear fully adjustable for windage and elevation.
Features: Adjustable velocity; matte finish. Introduced 1995. Imported from Germany by Nygord Precision Products.
Price: $950.00

AIRGUNS—LONG GUNS

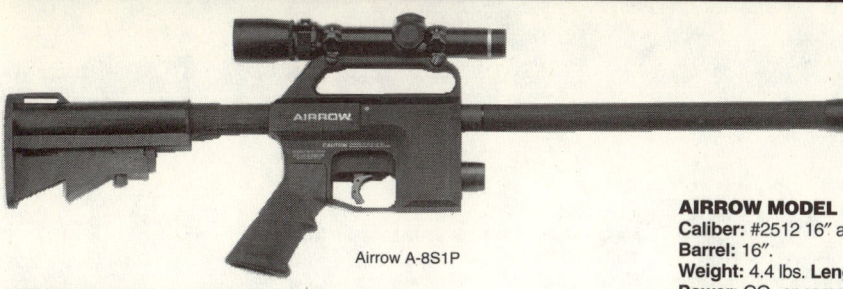
Airrow A-8S1P

AIRROW MODEL A-8SRB STEALTH AIR GUN
Caliber: 177, 22, 25, 38, 9-shot.
Barrel: 19.7"; rifled.
Weight: 6 lbs. **Length:** 34" overall.
Power: CO_2 or compressed air; variable power.
Stock: Telescoping CAR-15-type.
Sights: 3.5-10x A.O. variable power scope.
Features: Velocity 1100 fps in all calibers. Pneumatic air trigger. All aircraft aluminum and stainless steel construction. Mil-spec materials and finishes. Introduced 1992. From Swivel Machine Works, Inc.
Price: About $2,599.00

AIRROW MODEL A-8S1P STEALTH AIR GUN
Caliber: #2512 16" arrow.
Barrel: 16".
Weight: 4.4 lbs. **Length:** 30.1" overall.
Power: CO_2 or compressed air; variable power.
Stock: Telescoping CAR-15-type.
Sights: 1.5-5x variable power scope.
Features: Velocity to 650 fps with 260-grain arrow. Pneumatic air trigger. All aircraft aluminum and stainless steel construction. Mil-spec materials and finishes. Waterproof case. Introduced 1991. From Swivel Machine Works, Inc.
Price: About $1,899.00

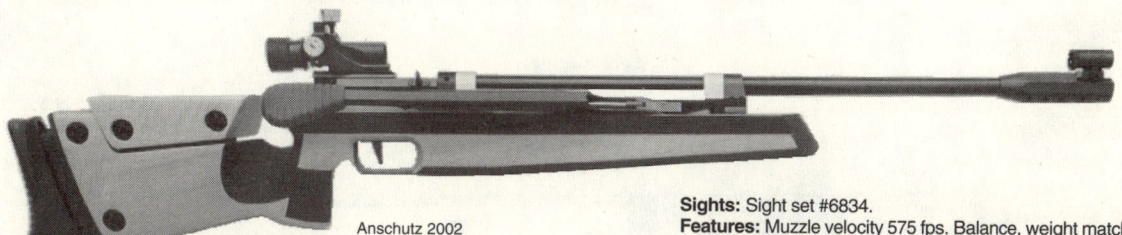
Anschutz 2002

ANSCHUTZ 2002 MATCH AIR RIFLE
Caliber: 177, single shot.
Barrel: 26".
Weight: 10½ lbs. **Length:** 44.5" overall.
Stock: European walnut, blonde hardwood or colored laminated hardwood; stippled grip and forend.
Sights: Sight set #6834.
Features: Muzzle velocity 575 fps. Balance, weight match the 1907 ISU smallbore rifle. Uses #5021 match trigger. Recoil and vibration free. Fully adjustable cheekpiece and buttplate; accessory rail under forend. Introduced 1988. Imported from Germany by Precision Sales International.
Price: Right-hand, blonde hardwood stock $2,043.00
Price: Left-hand, blonde hardwood stock $2,120.00
Price: Right-hand, walnut stock $2,108.00
Price: Right-hand, color laminated stock $2,160.00
Price: Left-hand, color laminated stock $2,243.00
Price: Model 2002D-RT Running Target, right-hand, no sights $2,130.00

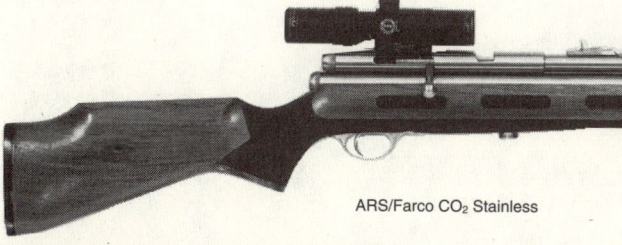
ARS/Farco CO₂ Stainless

ARS/Farco CO₂ Stainless Steel Air Rifle
Similar to the ARS/Farco CO₂ shotgun except in 22- or 25-caliber with 21½" barrel; weighs 6¾ lbs, 42½" overall; Philippine hardwood stock with stippled grip and forend; blade front sight, adjustable rear, grooved for scope mount. Uses 10-oz. refillable CO_2 cylinder. Made of stainless steel. Imported from the Philippines by Air Rifle Specialists.
Price: Including CO_2 cylinder $395.00

ARS/FARCO CO₂ AIR SHOTGUN
Caliber: 51 (28-gauge).
Barrel: 30".
Weight: 7 lbs. **Length:** 48½" overall.
Power: 10-oz. refillable CO_2 tank.
Stock: Hardwood.
Sights: Blade front, fixed rear.
Features: Gives over 100 ft. lbs. energy for taking small game. Imported from the Philippines by Air Rifle Specialists.
Price: $395.00

ARS Hunting Master AR6

ARS HUNTING MASTER AR6 AIR RIFLE
Caliber: 22, 6-shot repeater.
Barrel: 25½".
Weight: 7 lbs. **Length:** 41¼" overall.
Power: Pre-compressed air from 3000 psi diving tank.
Stock: Indonesian walnut with checkered grip; rubber buttpad.
Sights: Blade front, adjustable peep rear.
Features: Velocity over 1000 fps with 32-grain pellet. Receiver grooved for scope mounting. Has 6-shot rotary magazine. Imported by Air Rifle Specialists.
Price: $550.00

CAUTION: PRICES SHOWN ARE SUPPLIED BY THE MANUFACTURER OR IMPORTER. CHECK YOUR LOCAL GUN SHOP.

AIRGUNS—LONG GUNS

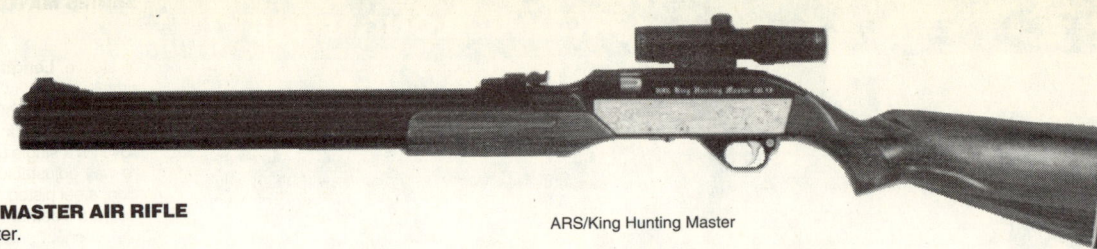

ARS/King Hunting Master

ARS/KING HUNTING MASTER AIR RIFLE
Caliber: 22, 5-shot repeater.
Barrel: 22 3/4".
Weight: 7 3/4 lbs. **Length:** 42" overall.
Power: Pre-compressed air from 3000 psi diving tank.
Stock: Indonesian walnut with checkered grip and forend; rubber buttpad.
Sights: Blade front, fully adjustable open rear. Receiver grooved for scope mounting.
Features: Velocity over 1000 fps with 32-grain pellet. High and low power switch for hunting or target velocities. Side lever cocks action and inserts pellet. Rotary magazine. Imported from Korea by Air rifle Specialists.
Price: $550.00
Price: Hunting Master 900 (9mm, limited production) $1,000.00

ARS/FARCO FP SURVIVAL AIR RIFLE
Caliber: 22, 25, single shot.
Barrel: 22 3/4".
Weight: 5 3/4 lbs. **Length:** 42 3/4" overall.
Power: Multi-pump foot pump.
Stock: Philippine hardwood.
Sights: Blade front, fixed rear.
Features: Velocity to 850 fps (22 or 25). Receiver grooved for scope mounting. Imported from the Philippines by Air Rifle Specialists.
Price: $295.00

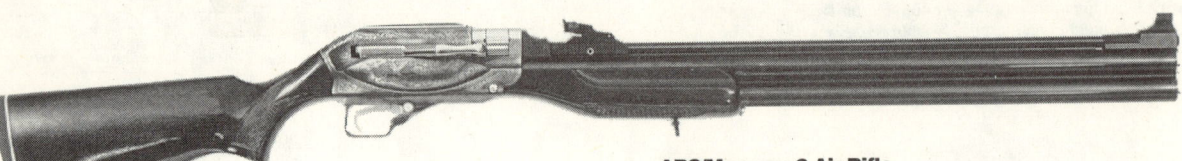

ARS/Magnum 6

ARS/Magnum 6 Air Rifle
Similar to the King Hunting Master except is 6-shot repeater with 23 3/4" barrel, weighs 8 1/4 lbs. Stock is walnut-stained hardwood with checkered grip and forend; rubber buttpad. Velocity of 1000+ fps with 32-grain pellet. Imported from Korea by Air Rifle Specialists.
Price: $500.00

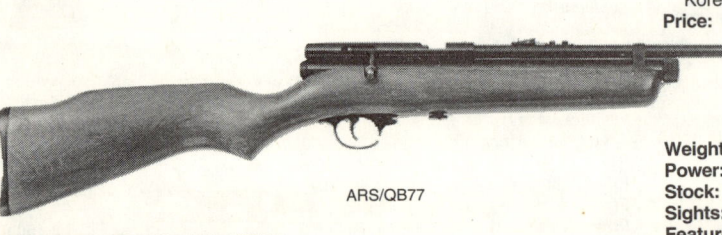

ARS/QB77

ARS/QB77 DELUXE AIR RIFLE
Caliber: 177, 22, single shot.
Barrel: 21 1/2".
Weight: 5 1/2 lbs. **Length:** 40" overall.
Power: Two 12-oz. CO_2 cylinders.
Stock: Walnut-stained hardwood.
Sights: Blade front, adjustable rear.
Features: Velocity to 625 fps (22), 725 fps (177). Receiver grooved for scope mounting. Comes with bulk-fill valve. Imported by Air Rifle Specialists.
Price: $199.00

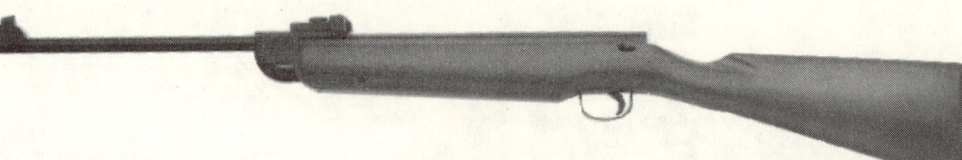

Beeman Carbine C1

BEEMAN CARBINE MODEL C1
Caliber: 177, single shot.
Barrel: 14", 12-groove rifling.
Weight: 6 1/4 lbs. **Length:** 38" overall.
Power: Spring-piston, barrel cocking.
Stock: Walnut-stained beechwood with rubber buttpad.
Sights: Blade front, rear click-adjustable for windage and elevation.
Features: Velocity 830 fps. Adjustable trigger. Receiver grooved for scope mounting. Imported by Beeman.
Price: $290.00

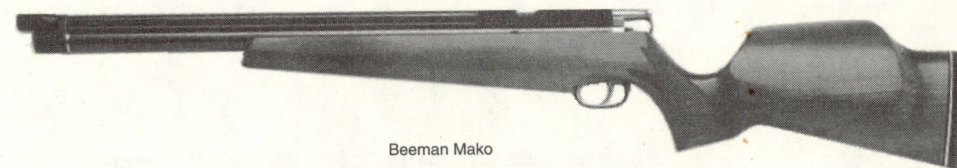

Beeman Mako

BEEMAN MAKO AIR RIFLE
Caliber: 177, single shot.
Barrel: 20", with compensator.
Weight: 7.3 lbs. **Length:** 38.5" overall.
Power: Pre-charged pneumatic.
Stock: Stained beech; Monte Carlo cheekpiece; checkered grip.
Sights: None furnished.
Features: Velocity to 930 fps. Gives over 50 shots per charge. Manual safety; brass trigger blade; vented rubber butt pad. Requires scuba tank for air. Introduced 1994. Imported from England by Beeman.
Price: $775.00

BEEMAN CROW MAGNUM AIR RIFLE
Caliber: 20, 25, single shot.
Barrel: 16"; 10-groove rifling.
Weight: 8.5 lbs. **Length:** 46" overall.
Power: Gas-spring; adjustable power to 32 foot pounds muzzle energy. Barrel-cocking.
Stock: Classic-style hardwood; hand checkered.
Sights: For scope use only; built-in base and 1" rings included.
Features: Adjustable two-stage trigger. Automatic safety. Also available in 22-caliber on special order. Introduced 1992. Imported by Beeman.
Price: $1,195.00

AIRGUNS—LONG GUNS

BEEMAN KODIAK AIR RIFLE
Caliber: 25, single shot.
Barrel: 17.6".
Weight: 9 lbs. **Length:** 45.6" overall.
Power: Spring-piston, barrel cocking.
Stock: Stained hardwood.
Sights: Blade front, open fully adjustable rear.
Features: Velocity to 820 fps. Up to 30 foot pounds muzzle energy. Introduced 1993. Imported by Beeman.
Price: $580.00

BEEMAN/FEINWERKBAU 300-S MINI-MATCH
Caliber: 177, single shot.
Barrel: 17 1/8".
Weight: 8.8 lbs. **Length:** 40" overall.
Power: Spring-piston, single stroke sidelever cocking.
Stock: Walnut. Stippled grip, adjustable buttplate. Scaled-down for youthful or slightly built shooters.

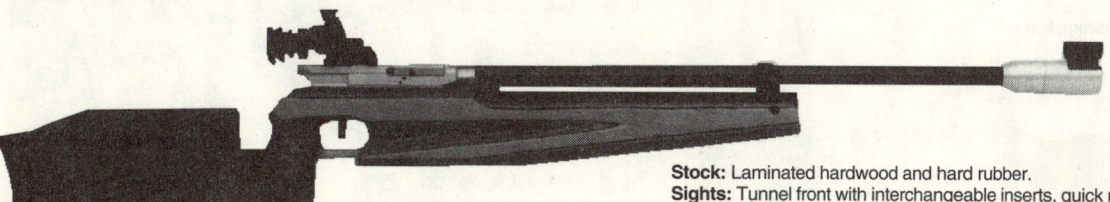
Beeman/FWB C60

BEEMAN/FEINWERKBAU C60, C62 CO$_2$ RIFLES
Caliber: 177.
Barrel: 16.9". With barrel sleeve, 25.4".
Weight: 10 lbs. **Length:** 42.6" overall.

BEEMAN/FEINWERKBAU 300-S SERIES MATCH RIFLE
Caliber: 177, single shot.
Barrel: 19.9", fixed solid with receiver.
Weight: Approx. 10 lbs. with optional bbl. sleeve. **Length:** 42.8" overall.
Power: Spring-piston, single stroke sidelever.
Stock: Match model—walnut, deep forend, adjustable buttplate.
Sights: Globe front with interchangeable inserts. Click micro. adjustable match aperture rear. Front and rear sights move as a single unit.
Features: Recoilless, vibration free. Five-way adjustable match trigger. Grooved for scope mounts. Permanent lubrication, steel piston ring. Cocking effort 9 lbs. Optional 10-oz. barrel sleeve. Available from Beeman.
Price: Right-hand $1,245.00
Price: Left-hand $1,350.00

Sights: Globe front with interchangeable inserts, micro. adjustable rear. Front and rear sights move as a single unit.
Features: Recoilless, vibration free. Grooved for scope mounts. Steel piston ring. Cocking effort about 9 1/2 lbs. Barrel sleeve optional. Left-hand model available. Introduced 1978. Imported by Beeman.
Price: Right-hand $1,245.00
Price: Left-hand $1,350.00

Stock: Laminated hardwood and hard rubber.
Sights: Tunnel front with interchangeable inserts, quick release micro. click match aperture rear.
Features: Similar features, performance as Beeman/FWB 601. Virtually no cocking effort. Right- or left-hand. Running target version available. Introduced 1987. Imported from Germany by Beeman.
Price: Right-hand, C62 ....$1,675.00
Price: Left-hand, C62 ....$1,825.00
Price: Running Target, right-hand, C60 ....$1,575.00
Price: Running Target, left-hand, C60 ....$1,725.00
Price: Mini C60, right-hand, C60 ....$1,575.00

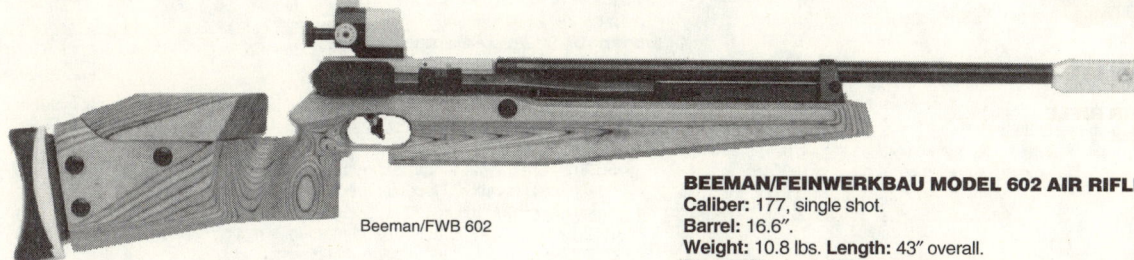
Beeman/FWB 602

Beeman/Feinwerkbau 601 Running Target
Similar to the standard Model 601. Has 16.9" barrel (33.7" with barrel sleeve); special match trigger, short loading gate which allows scope mounting. No sights—built for scope use only. Introduced 1987.
Price: Right-hand $1,650.00

BEEMAN/FEINWERKBAU MODEL 602 AIR RIFLE
Caliber: 177, single shot.
Barrel: 16.6".
Weight: 10.8 lbs. **Length:** 43" overall.
Power: Single stroke pneumatic.
Stock: Special laminated hardwoods and hard rubber for stability.
Sights: Tunnel front with interchangeable inserts, click micrometer match aperture rear.
Features: Recoilless action; double supported barrel; special, short rifled area frees pellet from barrel faster so shooter's motion has minimum effect on accuracy. Fully adjustable match trigger. Trigger and sights blocked when loading latch is open. Imported by Beeman.
Price: Right-hand $1,800.00
Price: Left-hand $1,960.00

Beeman/HW 97

BEEMAN/HW 97 AIR RIFLE
Caliber: 177, 20, single shot.
Barrel: 17.75".
Weight: 9.2 lbs. **Length:** 44.1" overall.
Power: Spring-piston, underlever cocking.
Stock: Walnut-stained beech; rubber buttpad.
Sights: None. Receiver grooved for scope mounting.
Features: Velocity 830 fps (177). Fixed barrel with fully opening, direct loading breech. Adjustable trigger. Introduced 1994. Imported by Beeman Precision Airguns.
Price: Right-hand only $535.00

BEEMAN/HW30 AIR RIFLE
Caliber: 177, 22, single shot.
Barrel: 17" (177), 16.9" (20); 12-groove rifling.
Weight: 5.5 lbs.
Power: Spring-piston; single-stroke barrel cocking.
Stock: Walnut-finished hardwood.
Sights: Blade front, adjustable rear.
Features: Velocity about 660 fps (177). Double-jointed cocking lever. Cast trigger guard. Synthetic non-drying breech and piston seals. Introduced 1990. Imported by Beeman.
Price: 177 ....$215.00

CAUTION: PRICES SHOWN ARE SUPPLIED BY THE MANUFACTURER OR IMPORTER. CHECK YOUR LOCAL GUN SHOP.

AIRGUNS—LONG GUNS

BEEMAN R1 AIR RIFLE
Caliber: 177, 20 or 22, single shot.
Barrel: 19.6", 12-groove rifling.
Weight: 8.5 lbs. **Length:** 45.2" overall.
Power: Spring-piston, barrel cocking.
Stock: Walnut-stained beech; cut-checkered pistol grip; Monte Carlo comb and cheekpiece; rubber buttpad.
Sights: Tunnel front with interchangeable inserts, open rear click-adjustable for windage and elevation. Grooved for scope mounting.
Features: Velocity of 940-1000 fps (177), 860 fps (20), 800 fps (22). Non-drying nylon piston and breech seals. Adjustable metal trigger. Milled steel safety. Right- or left-hand stock. Available with adjustable cheekpiece and buttplate at extra cost. Custom and Super Laser versions available. Imported by Beeman.
Price: Right-hand, 177, 20, 22 .... $495.00
Price: Left-hand, 177, 20, 22 .... $550.00

BEEMAN R1 CARBINE
Caliber: 177, 20, 22, 25, single shot.
Barrel: 16.1".
Weight: 8.6 lbs. **Length:** 41.7" overall.
Power: Spring-piston, barrel cocking.
Stock: Stained beech; Monte Carlo comb and checkpiece; cut checkered pistol grip; rubber buttpad.
Sights: Tunnel front with interchangeable inserts, open adjustable rear; receiver grooved for scope mounting.
Features: Velocity up to 1000 fps (177). Non-drying nylon piston and breech seals. Adjustable metal trigger. Machined steel receiver end cap and safety. Right- or left-hand stock. Imported by Beeman.
Price: 177, 20, 22, 25, right-hand $495.00
Price: As above, left-hand $550.00

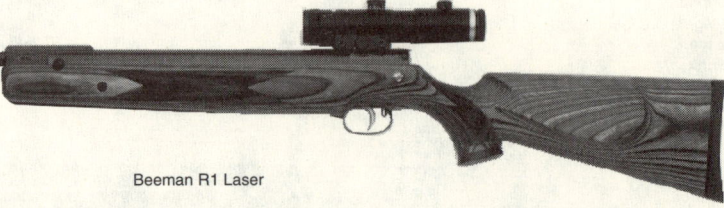
Beeman R1 Laser

BEEMAN R1 LASER AIR RIFLE
Caliber: 177, 20, 22, 25, single shot.
Barrel: 16.1" or 19.6".
Weight: 8.4 lbs. **Length:** 41.7" overall (16.1" barrel).
Power: Spring-piston, barrel cocking.
Stock: Laminated wood with Monte Carlo comb and cheekpiece; checkered p.g. and forend; rubber buttpad.
Sights: Tunnel front with interchangeable inserts, open adjustable rear.
Features: Velocity up to 1150 fps (177). Special powerplant components. Built from the Beeman R1 rifle by Beeman.
Price: 177, 20, 22, 25 .... $975.00

Beeman R7 Air Rifle
Similar to the R8 model except has lighter ambidextrous stock, match-grade trigger block; velocity of 680-700 fps; barrel length 17"; weight 5.8 lbs. Milled steel safety. Imported by Beeman.
Price: 177 .... $310.00

BEEMAN R8 AIR RIFLE
Caliber: 177, single shot.
Barrel: 18.3".
Weight: 7.2 lbs. **Length:** 43.1" overall.
Power: Spring-piston, barrel cocking.
Stock: Walnut with Monte Carlo cheekpiece; checkered pistol grip.
Sights: Globe front, fully adjustable rear; interchangeable inserts.
Features: Velocity of 735 fps. Similar to the R1. Nylon piston and breech seals. Adjustable match-grade, two-stage, grooved metal trigger. Milled steel safety. Rubber buttpad. Imported by Beeman.
Price: $375.00

BEEMAN R9 AIR RIFLE
Caliber: 177, single shot.
Barrel: 16".
Weight: 7.3 lbs. **Length:** 42 3/4" overall.
Power: Spring-piston, barrel cocking.
Stock: Stained beech.
Sights: Post front, click adjustable rear.
Features: Velocity to 1025 fps. Automatic safety; adjustable trigger pull; receiver grooved for scope mounting. Has nylon piston seals. Introduced 1995. Imported by Beeman.
Price: $325.00

BEEMAN R10 AIR RIFLES
Caliber: 177, 20, single shot.
Barrel: 16.1"; 12-groove rifling.
Weight: 7.9 lbs. **Length:** 46" overall.
Power: Spring-piston, barrel cocking.
Stock: Standard—walnut-finished hardwood with Monte Carlo comb, rubber buttplate; Deluxe has white spacers at grip cap, buttplate, checkered grip, cheekpiece, rubber buttplate.
Sights: Tunnel front with interchangeable inserts, open rear click adjustable for windage and elevation. Receiver grooved for scope mounting.
Features: Over 1000 fps in 177-cal. only; 26-lb. cocking effort; milled steel safety and body tube. Right- and left-hand models. Similar in appearance to the Beeman R8. Introduced 1986. Imported by Beeman.
Price: 177 or 20, Standard $400.00
Price: 177 or 20, Deluxe, right-hand $460.00
Price: 177 or 20, Deluxe, left-hand $500.00

Beeman R11

BEEMAN R11 AIR RIFLE
Caliber: 177, single shot.
Barrel: 19.6".
Weight: 8.8 lbs. **Length:** 47" overall.
Power: Spring-piston, barrel cocking.
Stock: Walnut-stained beech; adjustable buttplate and cheekpiece.
Sights: None furnished. Has dovetail for scope mounting.
Features: Velocity 910-940 fps. All-steel barrel sleeve. Imported by Beeman.
Price: $500.00

BEEMAN RX-1 GAS-SPRING MAGNUM AIR RIFLE
Caliber: 177, 20, 22, 25, single shot.
Barrel: 19.6"; 12-groove rifling.
Weight: 8.8 lbs.
Power: Gas-spring piston air; single stroke barrel cocking.
Stock: Walnut-finished hardwood, hand checkered, with cheekpiece. Adjustable cheekpiece and buttplate.
Sights: Tunnel front, click-adjustable rear.
Features: Velocity adjustable to about 1200 fps. Uses special sealed chamber of air as a mainspring. Gas-spring cannot take a set. Introduced 1990. Imported by Beeman.
Price: 177 or 22, regular, right-hand $550.00
Price: 20 or 25, regular, right hand $550.00
Price: 177, 20, 22, 25, left-hand $600.00

CONSULT **SHOOTER'S MARKETPLACE** Page 266, This Issue

AIRGUNS—LONG GUNS

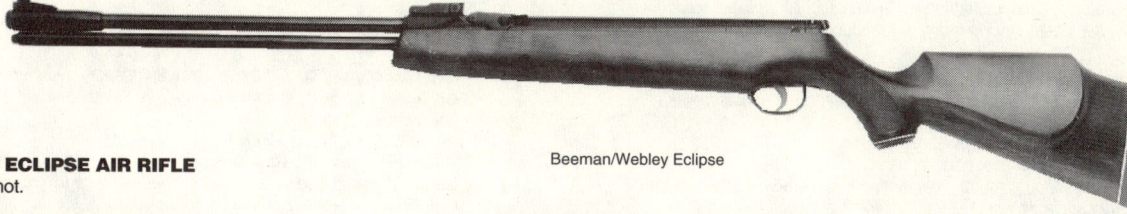
Beeman S1

BEEMAN S1 MAGNUM AIR RIFLE
Caliber: 177, single shot.
Barrel: 19″.
Weight: 7.1 lbs. **Length:** 45.5″ overall.
Power: Spring-piston, barrel cocking.
Stock: Stained beech with Monte Carlo cheekpiece; checkered grip.
Sights: Hooded post front, fully adjustable micrometer click rear.
Features: Velocity to 900 fps. Automatic safety; receiver grooved for scope mounting; two-stage adjustable trigger; curved rubber buttpad. Introduced 1995. Imported by Beeman.
Price: $199.00

Beeman Super 12 Air Rifle
Similar to the Super 7 except is 25-caliber, weighs 7.8 lbs., has 12-shot rotary magazine. Velocity to 850 fps. Pre-charged pneumatic system with adjustable power settings gives 30-70 shots per 400cc air bottle. Requires scuba tank for air. Introduced 1995. Imported by Beeman.
Price: $1,675.00

BEEMAN SUPER 7 AIR RIFLE
Caliber: 22, 7-shot repeater.
Barrel: 19″; 12-groove rifling.
Weight: 7.2 lbs. **Length:** 41″ overall.
Power: Pre-charged pneumatic, external air reservoir.
Stock: Walnut; high cheekpiece; rubber buttpad.
Sights: None furnished; drilled and tapped; 1″ ring scope mounts included.
Features: Two-stage adjustable trigger; 7-shot rotary magazine. Receiver of anodized aircraft aluminum. All working parts either hardened or stainless steel. Imported by Beeman.
Price: $1,575.00

Beeman/Webley Eclipse

BEEMAN/WEBLEY ECLIPSE AIR RIFLE
Caliber: 177, single shot.
Barrel: 18″.
Weight: 7.9 lbs. **Length:** 44″ overall.
Power: Spring-piston, underlever cocking.
Stock: Stained beech with Monte Carlo cheekpiece; checkered grip.
Sights: Blade on ramp front, open fully adjustable rear.
Features: Velocity to 950 fps. Has "power intensification" modifications. Flip-up breech system for easy loading; automatic safety. Imported from England by Beeman.
Price: $510.00

Beeman/Webley Vulcan III

BEEMAN/WEBLEY VULCAN III AIR RIFLE
Caliber: 177, single shot.
Barrel: 17.5″.
Weight: 7.9 lbs. **Length:** 44″ overall.
Power: Spring-piston, barrel cocking.
Stock: Stained beech with Monte Carlo cheekpiece.
Sights: Hooded post front, fully adjustable open rear.
Features: Velocity to 830 fps. Manual safety; adjustable single-stage trigger. Introduced 1995. Imported from England by Beeman.
Price: $290.00

Benjamin Sheridan CO_2

BENJAMIN SHERIDAN CO_2 AIR RIFLES
Caliber: 177, 20 or 22, single shot.
Barrel: $19^{3/8}$″, rifled brass.
Weight: 5 lbs. **Length:** $36^{1/2}$″ overall.
Power: 12-gram CO_2 cylinder.
Stock: American walnut with buttplate.
Sights: High ramp front, fully adjustable notch rear.
Features: Velocity to 680 fps (177). Bolt action with ambidextrous push-pull safety. Gives about 40 shots per cylinder. Black or nickel finish. Introduced 1991. Made in the U.S. by Benjamin Sheridan Co.
Price: Black finish, Model G397 (177), Model G392 (22), about $115.25
Price: Nickel finish, Model GS397 (177), Model GS392 (22), about $122.00
Price: Black finish, Model FB9 (20), about $124.50
Price: Nickel finish, Model F9 (20), about $131.95

Benjamin Sheridan Pneumatic

BENJAMIN SHERIDAN PNEUMATIC (PUMP-UP) AIR RIFLES
Caliber: 177 or 22, single shot.
Barrel: $19^{3/8}$″, rifled brass.
Weight: $5^{1/2}$ lbs. **Length:** $36^{1/4}$″ overall.
Power: Underlever pneumatic, hand pumped.
Stock: American walnut stock and forend.
Sights: High ramp front, fully adjustable notch rear.
Features: Variable velocity to 800 fps. Bolt action with ambidextrous push-pull safety. Black or nickel finish. Introduced 1991. Made in the U.S. by Benjamin Sheridan Co.
Price: Black finish, Model 397 (177), Model 392 (22), about $126.50
Price: Nickel finish, Model S397 (177), Model S392 (22), about $135.25

CAUTION: PRICES SHOWN ARE SUPPLIED BY THE MANUFACTURER OR IMPORTER. CHECK YOUR LOCAL GUN SHOP.

AIRGUNS—LONG GUNS

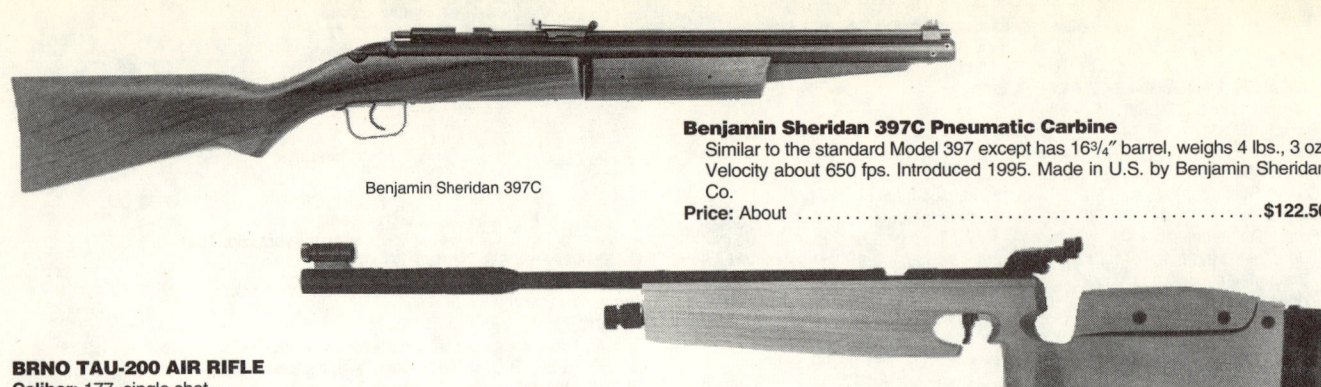

Benjamin Sheridan 397C

Benjamin Sheridan 397C Pneumatic Carbine
Similar to the standard Model 397 except has 16¾" barrel, weighs 4 lbs., 3 oz. Velocity about 650 fps. Introduced 1995. Made in U.S. by Benjamin Sheridan Co.
Price: About $122.50

BRNO TAU-200

BRNO TAU-200 AIR RIFLE
Caliber: 177, single shot
Barrel: 19", rifled.
Weight: 8 lbs. **Length:** 42" overall.
Power: 6-oz. CO_2 cartridge.
Stock: Wood match style with adjustable comb and buttplate.
Sights: Globe front with interchangeable inserts, fully adjustable open rear.
Features: Adjustable trigger. Comes with sling, extra seals, CO_2 cartridges, large CO_2 bottle, counterweight. Introduced 1993. Imported by Century International Arms, Great Lakes Airguns..
Price: About $423.25
Price: Junior Match (synthetic stock, 7 lbs.) $259.95

CROSMAN MODEL 66 POWERMASTER
Caliber: 177 (single shot pellet) or BB, 200-shot reservoir.
Barrel: 20", rifled steel.
Weight: 3 lbs. **Length:** 38½" overall.
Power: Pneumatic; hand pumped.
Stock: Wood-grained ABS plastic; checkered p.g. and forend.
Sights: Ramp front, fully adjustable open rear.
Features: Velocity about 645 fps. Bolt action, cross-bolt safety. Introduced 1983. From Crosman.
Price: About $44.00
Price: Model 66RT (as above with Realtree camo finish), about $50.00
Price: Model 664X (as above, with 4x scope) $55.00
Price: Model 664SB (as above with silver and black finish), about ... $57.00

CROSMAN MODEL 781 SINGLE PUMP
Caliber: 177 pellets (5-shot pellet clip) or BB (195-shot BB reservoir).
Barrel: 19½"; steel.
Weight: 2 lbs., 14 oz. **Length:** 35.8" overall.
Power: Pneumatic, single pump.
Stock: Wood-grained ABS plastic; checkered pistol grip and forend.
Sights: Blade front, open adjustable rear.
Features: Velocity of 405 fps (pellets). Uses only one pump. Hidden BB reservoir holds 195 shots; pellets loaded via 5-shot clip. Introduced 1984. From Crosman.
Price: About $35.75

CROSMAN MODEL 782 BLACK DIAMOND AIR RIFLE
Caliber: 177 pellets (5-shot clip) or BB (195-shot reservoir).
Barrel: 18", rifled steel.
Weight: 3 lbs.
Power: CO_2 Powerlet.
Stock: Wood-grained ABS plastic; checkered grip and forend.
Sights: Blade front, open adjustable rear.
Features: Velocity up to 595 fps (pellets), 650 fps (BB). Black finish with white diamonds. Introduced 1990. From Crosman.
Price: About $42.75

CROSMAN MODEL 788 BB SCOUT RIFLE
Caliber: BB only, 20-shot magazine.
Barrel: 14", steel.
Weight: 2 lbs. 7 oz. **Length:** 31½" overall.
Power: Pneumatic; hand pumped.
Stock: Wood-grained ABS plastic, checkered p.g. and forend.
Sights: Blade front, open adjustable rear.
Features: Variable pump power—three pumps give MV of 330 fps, six pumps 437 fps, 10 pumps 465 fps (BBs, average). Steel barrel, cross-bolt safety. Introduced 1978. From Crosman.
Price: About $25.00

Crosman Model 795

CROSMAN MODEL 795 SPRING MASTER RIFLE
Caliber: 177, single shot.
Barrel: NA.
Weight: 4 lbs., 8 oz. **Length:** NA.
Power: Spring-piston.
Stock: NA.
Sights: Hooded front, fully adjustable rear.
Features: Velocity about 550 fps. Introduced 1995. From Crosman.
Price: About $101.25

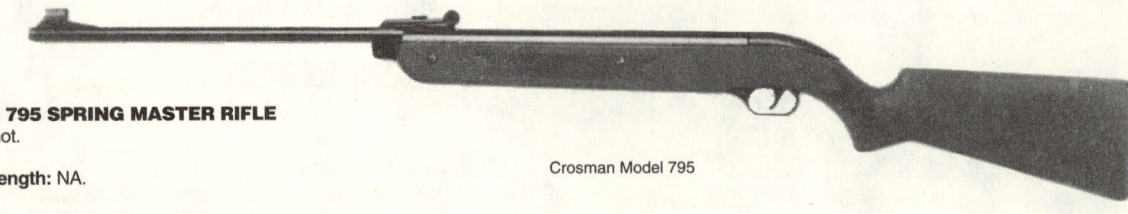

Crosman Model 1077 Constantair

CROSMAN MODEL 1077 CONSTANTAIR RIFLE
Caliber: 177, 12-shot clip.
Barrel: 20.3", rifled steel.
Weight: 5 lbs., 4 oz. **Length:** NA.
Power: 7-oz. refillable CO_2 tank.
Stock: NA.
Sights: Blade front, fully adjustable rear.
Features: Velocity about 590 fps. True semi-automatic action. Introduced 1995. From Crosman.
Price: About $175.50

AIRGUNS—LONG GUNS

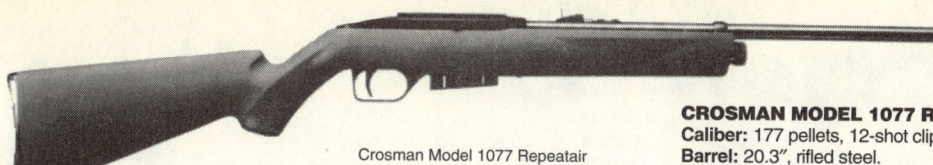
Crosman Model 1077 Repeatair

CROSMAN MODEL 1077 REPEATAIR RIFLE
Caliber: 177 pellets, 12-shot clip
Barrel: 20.3″, rifled steel.
Weight: 3 lbs, 11 oz. **Length:** 38.8″ overall.
Power: CO_2 Powerlet.
Stock: Textured synthetic.
Sights: Blade front, fully adjustable rear.
Features: Velocity 590 fps. Removable 12-shot clip. True semi-automatic action. Introduced 1993. From Crosman.
Price: About $62.75

CROSMAN MODEL 1389 BACKPACKER RIFLE
Caliber: 177, single shot.
Barrel: 14″, rifled steel.
Weight: 3 lbs. 3 oz. **Length:** 31″ overall.
Power: Hand pumped, pneumatic.
Stock: Composition, skeletal type.
Sights: Blade front, rear adjustable for windage and elevation.
Features: Velocity to 560 fps. Detachable stock. Receiver grooved for scope mounting. Metal parts blued. From Crosman.
Price: About $54.75

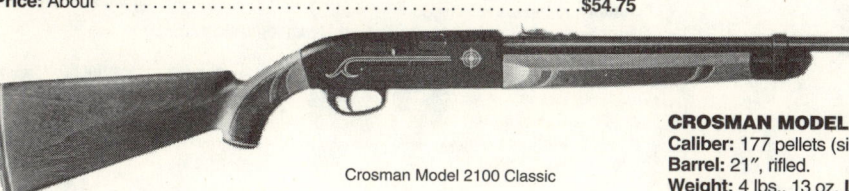
Crosman Model 2100 Classic

CROSMAN MODEL 2100 CLASSIC AIR RIFLE
Caliber: 177 pellets (single shot), or BB (200-shot BB reservoir).
Barrel: 21″, rifled.
Weight: 4 lbs., 13 oz. **Length:** 39¾″ overall.
Power: Pump-up, pneumatic.
Stock: Wood-grained checkered ABS plastic.
Features: Three pumps give about 450 fps, 10 pumps about 755 fps (BBs). Cross-bolt safety; concealed reservoir holds over 200 BBs. From Crosman.
Price: About $58.50
Price: Model 2100SB (silver and black finish), about $60.25

Crosman Model 2200 Magnum

CROSMAN MODEL 2200 MAGNUM AIR RIFLE
Caliber: 22, single shot.
Barrel: 19″, rifled steel.
Weight: 4 lbs., 12 oz. **Length:** 39″ overall.
Stock: Full-size, wood-grained ABS plastic with checkered grip and forend.
Sights: Ramp front, open step-adjustable rear.
Features: Variable pump power—three pumps give 395 fps, six pumps 530 fps, 10 pumps 595 fps (average). Full-size adult air rifle. Has white line spacers at pistol grip and buttplate. Introduced 1978. From Crosman.
Price: About $58.50

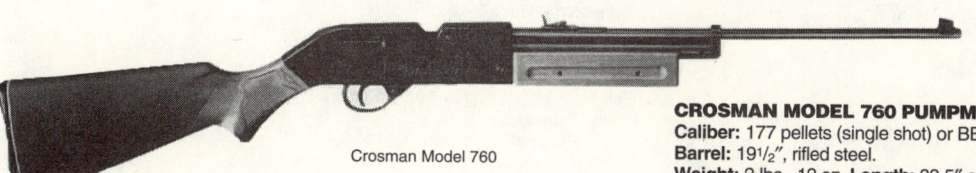
Crosman Model 760

CROSMAN MODEL 760 PUMPMASTER
Caliber: 177 pellets (single shot) or BB (200-shot reservoir).
Barrel: 19½″, rifled steel.
Weight: 2 lbs., 12 oz. **Length:** 33.5″ overall.
Power: Pneumatic, hand pumped.
Stock: Walnut-finished ABS plastic stock and forend
Features: Velocity to 590 fps (BBs, 10 pumps). Short stroke, power determined by number of strokes. Post front sight and adjustable rear sight. Cross-bolt safety. Introduced 1966. From Crosman.
Price: About $32.00
Price: Model 760SB (silver and black finish), about $45.25

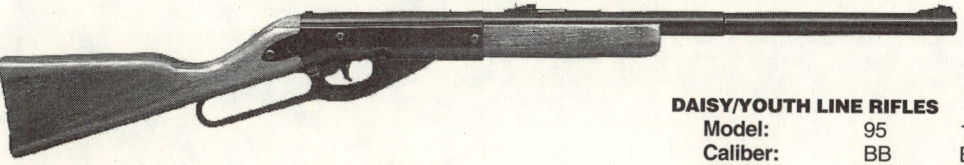
Daisy Model 95

DAISY/YOUTH LINE RIFLES

Model:	95	111	105
Caliber:	BB	BB	BB
Barrel:	18″	18″	13½″
Length:	35.2″	34.3″	29.8″
Power:	Spring	Spring	Spring
Capacity:	700	650	400
Price: About	$45.00	$35.00	$29.00

Features: Model 95 stock and forend are wood; 105 and 111 have plastic stocks. From Daisy Mfg. Co.

AIRGUNS—LONG GUNS

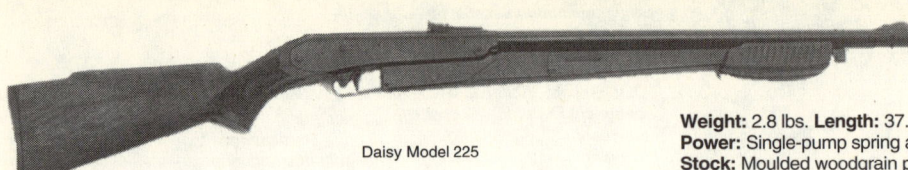
Daisy Model 225

DAISY MODEL 225 AMERICAN LEGEND
Caliber: 177 BB, 650-shot magazine.
Barrel: Smoothbore steel.
Weight: 2.8 lbs. **Length:** 37.2" overall.
Power: Single-pump spring air.
Stock: Moulded woodgrain plastic.
Sights: Blade and ramp front, adjustable open rear,
Features: Velocity to 330 fps. Grooved pump handle; Monte Carlo-style stock with cheekpiece and checkered grip. Cross-bolt trigger block safety. Introduced 1994. From Daisy.
Price: About $50.00

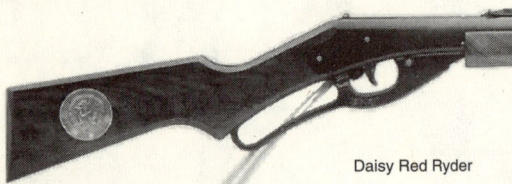
Daisy Red Ryder

DAISY 1938 RED RYDER CLASSIC
Caliber: BB, 650-shot repeating action.
Barrel: Smoothbore steel with shroud.
Weight: 2.2 lbs. **Length:** 35.4" overall.
Stock: Walnut stock burned with Red Ryder lariat signature.
Sights: Post front, adjustable V-slot rear.
Features: Walnut forend. Saddle ring with leather thong. Lever cocking. Gravity feed. Controlled velocity. One of Daisy's most popular guns. From Daisy Mfg. Co.
Price: About $45.00

DAISY/POWER LINE 753 TARGET RIFLE
Caliber: 177, single shot.
Barrel: 20.9", Lothar Walther.
Weight: 6.4 lbs. **Length:** 39.75" overall.
Power: Recoilless pneumatic, single pump.
Stock: Walnut with adjustable cheekpiece and buttplate.
Sights: Globe front with interchangeable inserts, diopter rear with micro. click adjustments.
Features: Includes front sight reticle assortment, web shooting sling. From Daisy Mfg. Co.
Price: About $412.00

Daisy Model 840

DAISY MODEL 840
Caliber: 177 pellet single shot; or BB 350-shot.
Barrel: 19", smoothbore, steel.
Weight: 2.7 lbs. **Length:** 36.8" overall.
Power: Pneumatic, single pump.
Stock: Moulded wood-grain stock and forend.
Sights: Ramp front, open, adjustable rear.
Features: Muzzle velocity 335 fps (BB), 300 fps (pellet). Steel buttplate; straight pull bolt action; cross-bolt safety. Forend forms pump lever. Introduced 1978. From Daisy Mfg. Co.
Price: About $40.00

Daisy Model 1894

DAISY MODEL 1894 BB RIFLE
Caliber: BB, 40-shot magazine.
Barrel: 17.5". Round shroud.
Weight: 2.2 lbs. **Length:** 39.5" overall.
Power: Spring-air.
Stock: Moulded woodgrain plastic.
Sights: Blade on ramp front, adjustable open rear.
Features: Velocity 300 fps. Side loading port; sliding sear-block safety; die-cast receiver. Made in U.S. From Daisy Mfg. Co.
Price: $42.00

DAISY/POWER LINE 853
Caliber: 177 pellets.
Barrel: 20.9"; 12-groove rifling, high-grade solid steel by Lothar Walther™, precision crowned; bore size for precision match pellets.
Weight: 5.08 lbs. **Length:** 38.9" overall.
Power: Single-pump pneumatic.
Stock: Full-length, select American hardwood, stained and finished; black buttplate with white spacers.
Sights: Globe front with four aperture inserts; precision micrometer adjustable rear peep sight mounted on a standard 3/8" dovetail receiver mount.
Features: Single shot. From Daisy Mfg. Co.
Price: About $245.00

DAISY/POWER LINE 856 PUMP-UP AIRGUN
Caliber: 177 pellets (single shot) or BB (100-shot reservoir).
Barrel: Rifled steel with shroud.
Weight: 2.7 lbs. **Length:** 37.4" overall.
Power: Pneumatic pump-up.
Stock: Moulded wood-grain with Monte Carlo cheekpiece.

DAISY/POWER LINE 880 PUMP-UP AIRGUN
Caliber: 177 pellets, BB.
Barrel: Rifled steel with shroud.
Weight: 4.5 lbs. **Length:** 37 3/4" overall.
Power: Pneumatic pump-up.
Stock: Wood-grain moulded plastic with Monte Carlo cheekpiece.
Sights: Ramp front, open rear adjustable for elevation.
Features: Crafted by Daisy. Variable power (velocity and range) increase with pump strokes. 10 strokes for maximum power. 100-shot BB magazine. Cross-bolt trigger safety. Positive cocking valve. From Daisy Mfg. Co.
Price: About $60.00

Sights: Ramp and blade front, open rear adjustable for elevation.
Features: Velocity from 315 fps (two pumps) to 650 fps (10 pumps). Shoots BBs or pellets. Heavy die-cast metal receiver. Cross-bolt trigger-block safety. Introduced 1984. From Daisy Mfg. Co.
Price: About $45.00

AIRGUNS—LONG GUNS

DAISY MODEL 990 DUAL-POWER AIR RIFLE
Caliber: 177 pellets (single shot) or BB (100-shot magazine).
Barrel: Rifled steel.
Weight: 4.1 lbs. **Length:** 37.4″ overall.
Power: Pneumatic pump-up and 12-gram CO_2.
Stock: Moulded woodgrain.
Sights: Ramp and blade front, adjustable open rear.
Features: Velocity to 650 fps (BB), 630 fps (pellet). Choice of pump or CO_2 power. Shoots BBs or pellets. Heavy die-cast receiver dovetailed for scope mount. Cross-bolt trigger block safety. Introduced 1993. From Daisy Mfg. Co.
Price: About $70.00

DAISY/POWER LINE 922
Caliber: 22, 5-shot clip.
Barrel: Rifled steel with shroud.
Weight: 4.5 lbs. **Length:** 37 3/4″ overall.
Stock: Moulded wood-grained plastic with checkered p.g. and forend, Monte Carlo cheekpiece.
Sights: Ramp front, fully adjustable open rear.
Features: Muzzle velocity from 270 fps (two pumps) to 530 fps (10 pumps). Straight-pull bolt action. Separate buttplate and grip cap with white spacers. Introduced 1978. From Daisy Mfg. Co.
Price: About $85.00
Price: Models 970/920 (same as Model 922 except with hardwood stock and forend), about $120.00

Daisy/Power Line 1150

DAISY/POWER LINE 1150 PELLET RIFLE
Caliber: 177, single shot.
Barrel: Rifled steel.
Weight: NA. **Length:** 37″ overall.
Power: Spring-air, barrel cocking.
Stock: Black moulded plastic.
Sights: Blade on ramp front, micrometer adjustable open rear.
Features: Velocity to 600 fps. Introduced 1995. From Daisy Mfg. Co.
Price: About $90.00

DAISY/POWER LINE 1170 PELLET RIFLE
Caliber: 177, single shot.
Barrel: Rifled steel.
Weight: 5.5 lbs. **Length:** 42.5″ overall.
Power: Spring-air, barrel cocking.
Stock: Hardwood.
Sights: Hooded post front, micrometer adjustable open rear.
Features: Velocity to 800 fps. Monte Carlo comb. Introduced 1995. From Daisy Mfg. Co.
Price: About $162.00

> Consult our Directory pages for the location of firms mentioned.

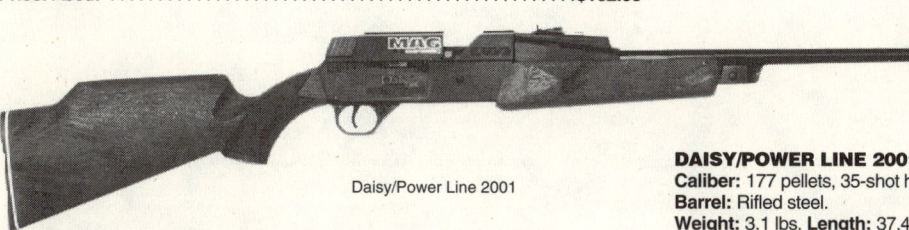
Daisy/Power Line 2001

DAISY/POWER LINE 2001 AIR RIFLE
Caliber: 177 pellets, 35-shot helical magazine.
Barrel: Rifled steel.
Weight: 3.1 lbs. **Length:** 37.4″ overall.
Power: CO_2.
Stock: Moulded woodgrain with Monte Carlo comb.
Sights: Ramp and blade front, fully adjustable open rear.
Features: Velocity to 625 fps. Bolt-action repeater with cross-bolt trigger block safety; checkered grip and forend; white buttplate spacer. Introduced 1994. From Daisy Mfg. Co.
Price: About $75.00

DAISY/POWER LINE 2002 PELLET RIFLE
Caliber: 177, 35-shot magazine.
Barrel: Rifled steel.
Weight: 3.6 lbs. **Length:** 37.5″ overall.
Power: 12-gram CO_2.
Stock: Moulded polymer.
Sights: Ramped blade front, open fully adjustable rear.
Features: Velocity to 630 fps. Continuous-feed helical design Mag Clip. Cross-bolt trigger block safety. Introduced 1995. From Daisy Mfg. Co.
Price: About $82.50

DAISY/POWER LINE EAGLE 7856 PUMP-UP AIRGUN
Caliber: 177 (pellets), BB, 100-shot BB magazine.
Barrel: Rifled steel with shroud.
Weight: 2 3/4 lbs. **Length:** 37.4″ overall.
Power: Pneumatic pump-up.
Stock: Moulded wood-grain plastic.
Sights: Ramp and blade front, open rear adjustable for elevation.
Features: Velocity from 315 fps (two pumps) to 650 fps (10 pumps). Finger grooved forend. Cross-bolt trigger-block safety. Introduced 1985. From Daisy Mfg. Co.
Price: With 4x scope, about $60.00

FAMAS SEMI-AUTO AIR RIFLE
Caliber: 177, 10-shot magazine.
Barrel: 19.2″.
Weight: About 8 lbs. **Length:** 29.8″ overall.
Power: 12-gram CO_2.
Stock: Synthetic bullpup design.
Sights: Adjustable front, aperture rear.
Features: Velocity of 425 fps. Duplicates size, weight and feel of the centerfire MAS French military rifle in caliber 223. Introduced 1988. Imported from France by Century International Arms.
Price: About $275.00

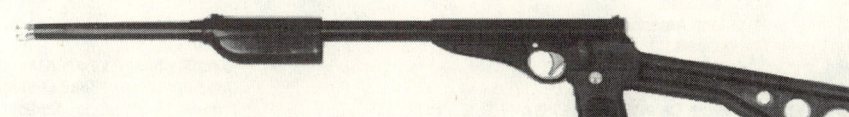
GAT Air Rifle

"GAT" AIR RIFLE
Caliber: 177, single shot.
Barrel: 17 1/4″ cocked, 23 1/4″ extended.
Weight: 3 lbs.
Power: Spring-piston.
Stock: Composition.
Sights: Fixed.
Features: Velocity about 450 fps. Shoots pellets, darts, corks. Imported from England by Stone Enterprises, Inc.
Price: $34.95

CAUTION: PRICES SHOWN ARE SUPPLIED BY THE MANUFACTURER OR IMPORTER. CHECK YOUR LOCAL GUN SHOP.

AIRGUNS—LONG GUNS

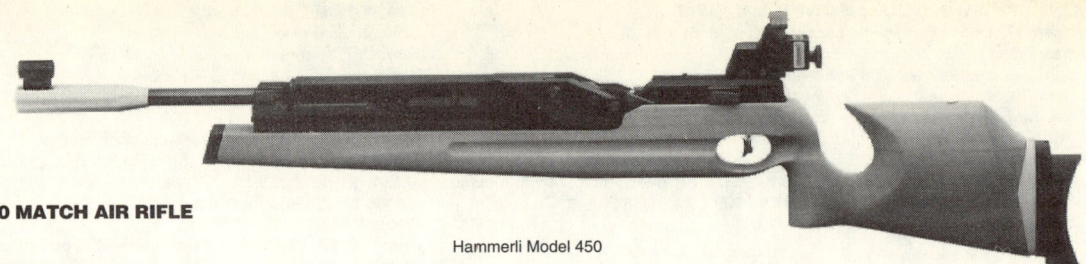
Hammerli Model 450

HAMMERLI MODEL 450 MATCH AIR RIFLE
Caliber: 177, single shot.
Barrel: 19.5".
Weight: 9.8 lbs. **Length:** 43.3" overall.
Power: Pneumatic.
Stock: Match style with stippled grip, rubber buttpad. Beach or walnut.
Sights: Match tunnel front, Hammerli diopter rear.
Features: Velocity about 560 fps. Removeable sights; forend sling rail; adjustable trigger; adjustable comb. Introduced 1994. Imported from Switzerland by Hammerli USA.
Price: Beech stock $1,353.00
Price: Walnut stock $1,393.00

MARKSMAN 28 INTERNATIONAL AIR RIFLE
Caliber: 177, single shot.
Barrel: 17".
Weight: 5 3/4 lbs.
Power: Spring-air, barrel cocking.
Stock: Hardwood.
Sights: Hooded front, adjustable rear.
Features: Velocity of 580-620 fps. Introduced 1989. Imported from Germany by Marksman Products.
Price: $220.00

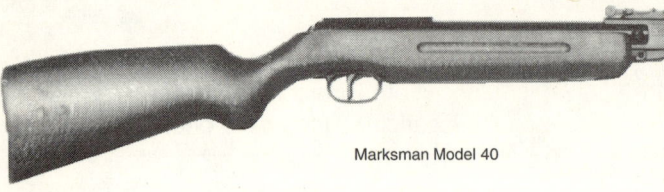
Marksman Model 40

MARKSMAN 40 INTERNATIONAL AIR RIFLE
Caliber: 177, single shot.
Barrel: 18 3/8".
Weight: 7 1/3 lbs.
Power: Spring-air, barrel cocking.
Stock: Hardwood.
Sights: Hooded front, adjustable rear.
Features: Velocity of 700-720 fps. Introduced 1989. Imported from Germany by Marksman Products.
Price: $245.00

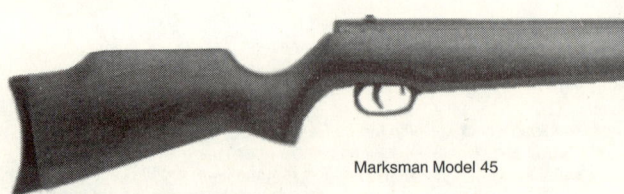
Marksman Model 45

MARKSMAN MODEL 45 AIR RIFLE
Caliber: 177, single shot.
Barrel: 19.1".
Weight: 7.3 lbs. **Length:** 46.75" overall.
Power: Spring-air, barrel cocking.
Stock: Stained hardwood with Monte Carlo cheekpiece, butt pad.
Sights: Hooded front, fully adjustable micrometer rear.
Features: Velocity 900-930 fps. Adjustable trigger; automatic safety. Introduced 1993. Imported from Spain by Marksman Products.
Price: $189.00

MARKSMAN MODEL 60 AIR RIFLE
Caliber: 177, single shot.
Barrel: 18.5", rifled.
Weight: 8.9 lbs. **Length:** 44.75" overall.
Power: Spring-piston, underlever cocking.
Stock: Walnut-stained beech with Monte Carlo comb, hand-checkered pistol grip, rubber butt pad.
Sights: Blade front, open, micro. adjustable rear.
Features: Velocity of 810-840 fps. Automatic button safety on rear of receiver. Receiver grooved for scope mounting. Fully adjustable Rekord trigger. Introduced 1990. Imported from Germany by Marksman Products.
Price: $485.00
Price: Model 61 Carbine $485.00

MARKSMAN 70T AIR RIFLE
Caliber: 177, single shot.
Barrel: 19.75".
Weight: 8 lbs. **Length:** 45.5" overall.
Power: Spring-air, barrel cocking.
Stock: Stained hardwood with Monte Carlo cheekpiece, rubber buttpad, cut checkered p.g.
Sights: Hooded front, open fully adjustable rear.
Features: Velocity of 910-940 fps; adjustable Rekord trigger. Introduced 1988. Imported from Germany by Marksman Products.
Price: 177 ....$350.00

Marksman 55 Air Rifle
Similar to the Model 70T except has uncheckered hardwood stock, no cheekpiece, plastic buttplate. Adjustable Rekord trigger. Overall length is 45.25", weight is 7 1/2 lbs. Available in 177-caliber only.
Price: $295.00

MARKSMAN 1750 BB BIATHLON REPEATER RIFLE
Caliber: BB, 18-shot magazine.
Barrel: 15", smoothbore.
Weight: 4.7 lbs.
Power: Spring-piston, barrel cocking.
Stock: Moulded composition.
Sights: Tunnel front, open adjustable rear.
Features: Velocity of 450 fps. Automatic safety. Positive Feed System loads a BB each time gun is cocked. Introduced 1990. From Marksman Products.
Price: $57.00

MARKSMAN 1740 AIR RIFLE
Caliber: 177 or 18-shot BB repeater.
Barrel: 15 1/2", smoothbore.
Weight: 5 lbs., 1 oz. **Length:** 36 1/2" overall.
Power: Spring, barrel cocking.
Stock: Moulded high-impact ABS plastic.
Sights: Ramp front, open rear adjustable for elevation.
Features: Velocity about 450 fps. Automatic safety; fixed front, adjustable rear sight; positive feed BB magazine; shoots 177-cal. BBs, pellets and darts. From Marksman Products.
Price: $50.00
Price: Model 1780 (deluxe sights, rifled barrel, shoots only pellets) $66.00

AIRGUNS—LONG GUNS

Marksman 1710

MARKSMAN 1710 PLAINSMAN AIR RIFLE
Caliber: BB, 20-shot repeater.
Barrel: Smoothbore steel with shroud.
Weight: 2.25 lbs. Length: 34" overall.
Power: Spring-air.
Stock: Stained hardwood.
Sights: Blade on ramp front, adjustable V-slot rear.
Features: Velocity about 275 fps. Positive feed; automatic safety. Introduced 1994. Made in U.S. From Marksman Products.
Price: $36.00

Marksman 1790

MARKSMAN 1790 BIATHLON TRAINER
Caliber: 177, single shot.
Barrel: 15", rifled.
Weight: 4.7 lbs.
Power: Spring-air, barrel cocking.
Stock: Synthetic.
Sights: Hooded front, match-style diopter rear.
Features: Velocity of 450 fps. Endorsed by the U.S. Shooting Team. Introduced 1989. From Marksman Products.
Price: $69.00

MARKSMAN 1792 COMPETITION TRAINER AIR RIFLE
Caliber: 177, single shot.
Barrel: 15", rifled.
Weight: 4.7 lbs.
Power: Spring-air, barrel cocking.
Stock: Synthetic.
Sights: Hooded front, match-style diopter rear.
Features: Velocity about 450 fps. Automatic safety. Introduced 1993. More economical version of the 1790 Biathlon Trainer. Made in U.S. From Marksman Products.
Price: $60.00

RWS MODEL CA 100 AIR RIFLE
Caliber: 177, single shot.
Barrel: 22".
Weight: 11.4 lbs. Length: 44" overall.
Power: Compressed air; interchangeable cylinders.
Stock: Laminated hardwood with adjustable cheekpiece and buttplate.
Sights: Optional.
Features: Gives 250 shots per full charge. Double-sided power regulator. Introduced 1995. Imported from England by Dynamit Nobel-RWS, Inc.
Price: $2,100.00

RWS/DIANA MODEL 24 AIR RIFLE
Caliber: 177, 22, single shot.
Barrel: 17", rifled.
Weight: 6 lbs. Length: 42" overall.
Power: Spring-air, barrel cocking.
Stock: Beech.
Sights: Hooded front, adjustable rear.
Features: Velocity of 700 fps (177). Easy cocking effort; blue finish. Imported from Germany by Dynamit Nobel-RWS, Inc.
Price: $215.00
Price: Model 24C $215.00

RWS/Diana Model 34 Air Rifle
Similar to the Model 24 except has 19" barrel, weighs 7.5 lbs. Gives velocity of 1000 fps (177), 800 fps (22). Adjustable trigger, synthetic seals. Comes with scope rail.
Price: 177 or 22 .... $265.00
Price: Model 34N (nickel-plated metal, black epoxy-coated wood stock) . $265.00
Price: Model 34BC (matte black metal, black stock, 4x32 scope, mounts) $445.00

RWS/DIANA MODEL 36 AIR RIFLE
Caliber: 177, 22, single shot.
Barrel: 19", rifled.
Weight: 8 lbs. Length: 45" overall.
Power: Spring-air, barrel cocking.
Stock: Beech.
Sights: Hooded front (interchangeable inserts avail.), adjustable rear.
Features: Velocity of 1000 fps (177-cal.). Comes with scope mount; two-stage adjustable trigger. Imported from Germnay by Dynamit Nobel-RWS, Inc.
Price: $380.00
Price: Model 36 Carbine (same as Model 36 except has 15" barrel) $380.00

RWS/DIANA MODEL 45 AIR RIFLE
Caliber: 177, single shot.
Weight: 7 3/4 lbs. Length: 46" overall.
Power: Spring-air, barrel cocking.
Stock: Walnut-finished hardwood with rubber recoil pad.
Sights: Globe front with interchangeable inserts, micro. click open rear with four-way blade.
Features: Velocity of 820 fps. Dovetail base for either micrometer peep sight or scope mounting. Automatic safety. Imported from Germany by Dynamit Nobel-RWS, Inc.
Price: $300.00

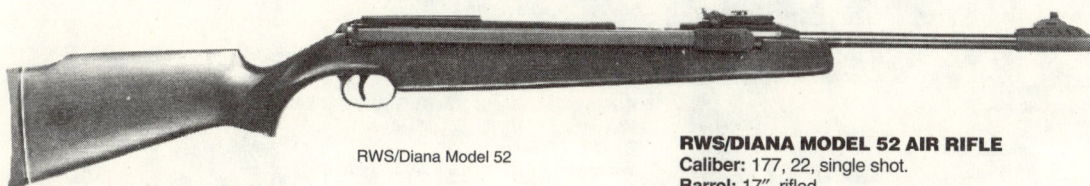
RWS/Diana Model 52

RWS/DIANA MODEL 52 AIR RIFLE
Caliber: 177, 22, single shot.
Barrel: 17", rifled.
Weight: 8 1/2 lbs. Length: 43" overall.
Power: Spring-air, sidelever cocking.
Stock: Beech, with Monte Carlo, cheekpiece, checkered grip and forend.
Sights: Ramp front, adjustable rear.
Features: Velocity of 1100 fps (177). Blue finish. Solid rubber buttpad. Imported from Germany by Dynamit Nobel-RWS, Inc.
Price: $495.00
Price: Model 52 Deluxe (select walnut stock, rosewood grip and forend caps, palm swell grip) $725.00
Price: Model 48B (as above except matte black metal, black stock) $495.00
Price: Model 48 (same as Model 52 except no Monte Carlo, cheekpiece or checkering) $440.00

RWS/DIANA MODEL 54 AIR KING RIFLE
Caliber: 177, 22, single shot.
Barrel: 17".
Weight: 9 lbs. Length: 43" overall.
Power: Spring-air, sidelever cocking.
Stock: Walnut with Monte Carlo cheekpiece, checkered grip and forend.
Sights: Ramp front, fully adjustable rear.
Features: Velocity to 1000 fps (177), 900 fps (22). Totally recoilless system; floating action absorbs recoil. Imported from Germany by Dynamit Nobel-RWS, Inc.
Price: $680.00

CAUTION: PRICES SHOWN ARE SUPPLIED BY THE MANUFACTURER OR IMPORTER. CHECK YOUR LOCAL GUN SHOP.

AIRGUNS—LONG GUNS

RWS/Diana Model 100

RWS/DIANA MODEL 100 MATCH AIR RIFLE
Caliber: 177, single shot.
Barrel: 19".
Weight: 11 lbs. **Length:** 43" overall.
Power: Spring-air, sidelever cocking.
Stock: Walnut.
Sights: Tunnel front, fully adjustable match rear.
Features: Velocity of 580 fps. Single-stroke cocking; cheekpiece adjustable for height and length; recoilless operation. Cocking lever secured against rebound. Introduced 1990. Imported from Germany by Dynamit Nobel-RWS, Inc.
Price: Right-hand only $1,500.00

RWS TX200 MAGNUM AIR RIFLE
Caliber: 177, 22, single shot.
Barrel: 14 3/4"; 12-groove Walther with choke.
Weight: 8 1/2 lbs. **Length:** 42" overall.
Power: Spring-air, underlever cocking.
Stock: Beech or walnut (177 only) with Monte Carlo cheekpiece; checkered grip and forend; rubber recoil pad.
Sights: None furnished; scope rail.
Features: Adjustable two-stage match trigger; automatic safety; floating piston. Made by Air Arms. Introduced 1995. Imported from England by Dynamit Nobel-RWS, Inc.
Price: $530.00

SHERIDAN PNEUMATIC (PUMP-UP) AIR RIFLES
Caliber: 20 (5mm), single shot.
Barrel: 19 3/8", rifled brass.
Weight: 6 lbs. **Length:** 36 1/2" overall.
Power: Underlever pneumatic, hand pumped.
Stock: Walnut with buttplate and sculpted forend.
Sights: High ramp front, fully adjustable notch rear.
Features: Variable velocity to 675 fps. Bolt action with ambidextrous push-pull safety. Blue finish (Blue Streak) or nickel finish (Silver Streak). Introduced 1991. Made in the U.S. by Benjamin Sheridan Co.
Price: Blue Streak, Model CB9, about $141.25
Price: Silver streak, Model C9, about $150.00

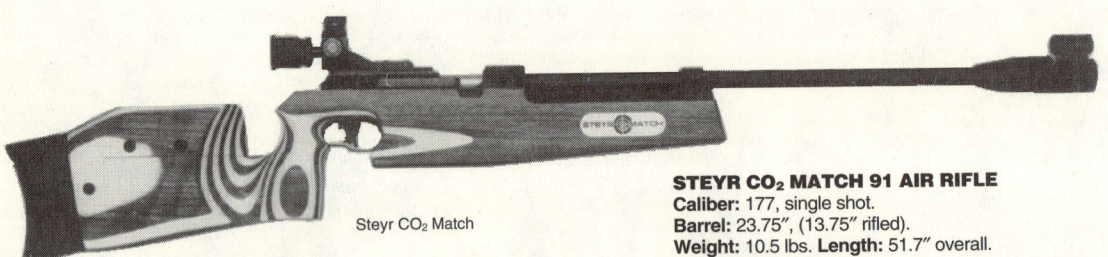
Steyr CO_2 Match

STEYR CO_2 MATCH 91 AIR RIFLE
Caliber: 177, single shot.
Barrel: 23.75", (13.75" rifled).
Weight: 10.5 lbs. **Length:** 51.7" overall.
Power: CO_2.
Stock: Match. Laminated wood. Adjustable buttplate and cheekpiece.
Sights: None furnished; comes with scope mount.
Features: Velocity 577 fps. CO_2 cylinders are refillable; about 320 shots per cylinder. Designed for 10-meter shooting. Introduced 1990. Imported from Austria by Nygord Precision Products.
Price: About $1,350.00
Price: Left-hand, about $1,400.00
Price: Running Target Rifle, right-hand, about $1,450.00
Price: As above, left-hand, about $1,425.00

Whiscombe JW70 FB

WHISCOMBE JW SERIES AIR RIFLES
Caliber: 177, 20, 22, 25, single shot.
Barrel: 15", Lothar Walther.
Weight: 9 lbs., 8 oz. **Length:** 39" overall.
Power: Spring-piston, multi-stroke; underlever cocking.
Stock: Walnut with adjustable buttplate.
Sights: None furnished; grooved scope rail.
Features: Velocity 660-890 fps (22-caliber, fixed barrel) depending upon model. Interchangeable barrels on JW60, JW75; automatic safety; muzzle weight; semi-floating action; twin opposed pistons with counter-wound springs; adjustable trigger. Introduced 1995. Imported from England by Pelaire Products.
Price: JW50, fixed barrel only $1,440.00
Price: JW60 ....$1,492.00
Price: JW70, fixed barrel only $1,550.00
Price: JW75 ....$1,575.00
Price: JW75 High Power $1,599.00

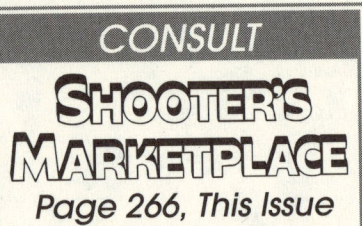
CONSULT SHOOTER'S MARKETPLACE Page 266, This Issue

WARRANTY SERVICE CENTER DIRECTORY

A

A&M Sales, 23 W. North Ave., Northlake, IL 60264/708-562-8190
A-Square Co., Inc., One Industrial Park, Bedford, KY 40006-9667/502-255-7456; FAX: 502-255-7657
Accu-Tek, 4525 Carter Ct., Chino, CA 91710/909-627-2404; FAX: 909-627-7817
Accuracy Gun Shop, 1240 Hunt Ave., Columbus, GA 31907/706-561-6386
Accuracy Gun Shop, Inc., 5903 Boulder Highway, Las Vegas, NV 89122/702-458-3330
Ace Custom 45's, 1880½ Upper Turtle Creek Rd., Kerrville, TX 78028/210-257-4290; FAX: 210-257-5724
Adventure A.G.R., 2991 St. Jude, Waterford, MI 48329/810-673-3090
Ahlman's Custom Gun Shop, Inc., 9525 West 230th St., Morristown, MN 55052/507-685-4244
Aimpoint, Inc., 580 Herndon Parkway, Suite 500, Herndon, VA 22070/703-471-6828; FAX: 703-689-0575
Aimtech Mount Systems, P.O. Box 223, 101 Inwood Acres, Thomasville, GA 31799/912-226-4313; FAX: 912-227-0222
Air Arms, Hailsham Industrial Park, Diplocks Way, Hailsham, E. Sussex, BN27 3JF ENGLAND/011-0323-845853 (U.S. importers—Air Werks International; World Class Airguns)
Air Gun Shop, The, 2312 Elizabeth St., Billings, MT 59102/406-656-2983
Air Guns Unlimited, 15866 Main St., La Puente, CA 91744/818-333-4991
Air Rifle Specialists, 311 East Water St., Elmira, NY 14901/607-734-7340; FAX: 607-733-3261
Air Venture, 9752 E. Flower St., Bellflower, CA 90706/310-867-6355
Air Werks International, 403 W. 24th St., Norfolk, VA 23517-1204/800-247-9375
Airgun Repair Centre, 3227 Garden Meadows, Lawrenceburg, IN 47025/812-637-1463; FAX: 812-637-1463
Airguns International, 3451 G Airway Dr, Santa Rosa, CA 95403/707-578-7900; FAX: 707-578-0951
Airrow (See Swivel Machine Works, Inc.)
Alessandri and Son, Lou, 24 French St., Rehoboth, MA 02769/508-252-3436, 800-248-5652; FAX: 508-252-3436
Alexander, Gunsmith, W.R., 1406 Capitol Circle N.E. #D, Tallahassee, FL 32308/904-656-6176
All Game Sport Center, 6076 Guinea Pike, Milford, OH 45150/513-575-0134
Allison & Carey Gun Works, 17311 S.E. Stark, Portland, OR 97233/503-256-5166
Alpine Arms Corp., 6716 Fort Hamilton Pkwy., Brooklyn, NY 11219/718-833-2228
American Arms & Ordnance, Inc., P.O. Box 2691, 1303 S. College Ave., Bryan, TX 77805/409-822-4983
American Arms, Inc., 715 Armour Rd., N. Kansas City, MO 64116/816-474-3161; FAX: 816-474-1225
American Derringer Corp., 127 N. Lacy Dr., Waco, TX 76705/800-642-7817, 817-799-9111; FAX: 817-799-7935
Ammo Load, Inc., 1560 E. Edinger, Suite G, Santa Ana, CA 92705/714-558-8858; FAX: 714-569-0319
AMT, 6226 Santos Diaz St., Irwindale, CA 91702/818-334-6629; FAX: 818-969-5247
Anderson Manufacturing Co., Inc., P.O. Box 2640, 2741 N. Crosby Rd., Oak Harbor, WA 98277/360-675-7300; FAX: 360-675-3939
Anderson, Inc., Andy, 2125 NW Expressway, Oklahoma City, OK 73112/405-842-3305
Anschutz GmbH, Postfach 1128, D-89001 Ulm, Donau, GERMANY (U.S. importer—PSI, Inc.)
Answer Products Co., 1519 Westbury Drive, Davison, MI 48423/810-653-2911
Argonaut Gun Shop, 607 McHenry Ave., Modesto, CA 95350/209-522-5876
Arizaga (See U.S. importer—Mandall Shooting Supplies, Inc.)
Armadillo Air Gun Repair, 5892 Hampshire Rd., Corpus Christi, TX 78408/512-289-5458
Armas Azor, J.A. (See U.S. importer—Armes de Chasse)
Armes de Chasse, P.O. Box 827, Chadds Ford, PA 19317/610-388-1146; FAX: 610-388-1147
Armi Sport (See U.S. importers—Cape Outfitters; Taylor's & Co., Inc.)
Armoury, Inc., The, Rt. 202, Box 2340, New Preston, CT 06777/203-868-0001
Armscorp USA, Inc., 4424 John Ave., Baltimore, MD 21227/410-247-6200; FAX: 410-247-6205
Armsport, Inc., 3950 NW 49th St., Miami, FL 33142/305-635-7850; FAX: 305-633-2877
Armurier De L'Outaouais, 28 Rue Bourque, Hull, Quebec, CANADA J8Y 1X1/819-777-9824
Arrieta, S.L., Morkaiko, 5, Elgoibar, E-20870, SPAIN/(43) 74 31 50; FAX: (43) 74 31 54 (U.S. importers—Hi-Grade Imports; Jansma, Jack J.; New England Arms Co.; The Orvis Co., Inc.; Quality Arms, Inc.)
Astra Sport, S.A., Apartado 3, 48300 Guernica, Espagne, SPAIN/34-4-6250100; FAX: 34-4-6255186 (U.S. importer—E.A.A. Corp.)
ATIS Armi S.A.S., via Gussalli 24, Zona Industriale-Loc. Fornaci, 25020 Brescia, ITALY
Atlantic Guns, Inc., 944 Bonifant St., Silver Spring, MD 20910/301-585-4448/301-279-7983
Atlas Gun Repair, 4908 E. Judge Perez Dr., Violet, LA 70092/504-277-4229
Auto Electric & Parts, Inc., 24 W. Baltimore Ave., Media, PA 19063/215-565-2432
Auto-Ordnance Corp., Williams Lane, West Hurley, NY 12491/914-679-4190; FAX: 914-679-2698
Autumn Sales, Inc. (Blaser), 1320 Lake St., Fort Worth, TX 76103/817-335-1634; FAX: 817-338-0119
AWC Systems Technology, P.O. Box 41938, Phoenix, AZ 85080-1938/602-780-1050
AYA (See U.S. importer—Armes de Chasse)

B

B&B Supply Co., 4501 Minnehaha Ave., Minneapolis, MN 55406/612-724-5230
B&T, 1777 Central Ave., Albany, NY 12205/518-869-7934
B&W Gunsmithing, 505 Main Ave. N.W., Cullman, AL 35055/205-737-9595
B-Square Company, Inc., P.O. Box 11281, 2708 St. Louis Ave., Ft. Worth, TX 76110/817-923-0964, 800-433-2909; FAX: 817-926-7012
Bachelder Custom Arms, 1229 Michigan N.E., Grand Rapids, MI 49503/616-459-3636
Badger Gun & Ammo, Inc., 2339 S. 43rd St., West, Milwaukee, WI 53219/414-383-0855
Badger's Shooters Supply, Inc., 202 N. Harding, Owen, WI 54460/715-229-2101; FAX: 715-229-2332
Baer Custom, Inc., Les, 29601 34th Ave., Hillsdale, IL 61257/309-658-2716; FAX: 309-658-2610
Baikal (See U.S. importers—Air Werks International; K.B.I., Inc.)
Bain & Davis, Inc., 307 E. Valley Blvd., San Gabriel, CA 91776-3522/818-573-4241, 213-283-7449
Baity's Custom Gunworks, 2623 Boone Trail, N. Wilkesboro, NC 28659/919-667-8785
Baltimore Gunsmiths, 218 South Broadway, Baltimore, MD 21231/410-276-6908
Barrett Firearms Manufacturer, Inc., P.O. Box 1077, Murfreesboro, TN 37133/615-896-2938; FAX: 615-896-7215
Bausch & Lomb Sports Optics Div., 9200 Cody, Overland Park, KS 66214/913-752-3400, 800-423-3537; FAX: 913-752-3550

Bausch & Lomb, Inc., 42 East Ave., Rochester, NY 14603/913-752-3433, 800-828-5423; FAX: 913-752-3489
Beard's Sport Shop, 811 Broadway, Cape Girardeau, MO 63701/314-334-2266
Beauchamp & Son, Inc., 160 Rossiter Rd., Richmond, MA 01254/413-698-3822; FAX: 413-698-3866
Bedlan's Sporting Goods, Inc., 1318 E. Street, P.O. Box 244, Fairbury, NE 68352/402-729-6112
Beeman Precision Airguns, 5454 Argosy Dr., Huntington Beach, CA 92649/714-890-4800; FAX: 714-890-4808
Bell's Legendary Country Wear, 22 Circle Dr., Bellmore, NY 11710/516-679-1158
Belleplain Supply, Inc., Box 346, Handsmill Rd., Belleplain, NJ 08270/609-861-2345
Bellrose & Son, L.E., 21 Forge Pond Rd., Granby, MA 01033-0184/413-467-3637
Ben's Gun Shop, 1151 S. Cedar Ridge, Duncanville, TX 75137/214-780-1807
Benelli Armi, S.p.A., Via della Stazione, 61029 Urbino, ITALY/39-722-328633; FAX: 39-722-327427 (U.S. importers—E.A.A. Corp.; Heckler & Koch, Inc.; Sile Distributors)
Benjamin (See page 503)
Benson Gun Shop, 35 Middle Country Rd., Coram L.I., NY 11727/516-736-0065
Benton & Brown Firearms, Inc., 311 W. First, P.O. Box 326, Delhi, LA 71232-0326/318-878-2499; FAX: 817-284-9300
Beretta Firearms, Pietro, 25063 Gardone V.T., ITALY (U.S. importer—Beretta U.S.A. Corp.)
Beretta U.S.A. Corp., 17601 Beretta Drive, Accokeek, MD 20607/301-283-2191; FAX: 301-283-0435
Beretta, Dr. Franco, via Rossa, 4, Concesio (BC), Italy I-25062/030-2751955; FAX: 030-218-0414 (U.S. importer—Nevada Cartridge Co.)
Bernardelli Vincenzo S.p.A., 125 Via Matteotti, P.O. Box 74, Gardone V.T., Brescia ITALY, 25063/39-30-8912851-2-3; FAX: 39-30-8910249 (U.S. importer—Armsport, Inc.)
Bertuzzi (See U.S. importers—Cape Outfitters; Moore & Co., Wm. Larkin; New England Arms Co.)
Bickford's Gun Repair, 426 N. Main St., Joplin, MO 64801/417-781-6440
Billings Gunsmiths, Inc., 1940 Grand Ave., Billings, MT 59102/406-652-3104
Blaser Jagdwaffen GmbH, D-88316 Isny Im Allgau, GERMANY (U.S. importer—Autumn Sales, Inc.)
Blount, Inc., Sporting Equipment Div., 2299 Snake River Ave., P.O. Box 856, Lewiston, ID 83501/800-627-3640, 208-746-2351; FAX: 208-746-2915
Blue Ridge Outdoor Sports, Inc., 2314 Spartansburg Hwy., E. Flat Rock, NC 28726/704-697-3006
Bob's Crosman Repair, 2510 E. Henry Ave., Cudahy, WI 53110/414-769-8256
Bob's Gun & Tackle Shop, (Blaustein & Reich, Inc.), 746 Granby St., Norfolk, VA 23510/804-627-8311/804-622-9786
Boggus Gun Shop, 1402 W. Hopkins St., San Marcos, TX 78666/512-392-3513
Bohemia Arms Co., 17101 Los Modelos, Fountain Valley, CA 92708/619-442-7005; FAX: 619-442-7005
Bolsa Gunsmithing, 7404 Bolsa Ave., Westminster, CA 92683/714-894-9100
Boracci, E. John, Village Sport Center, 38-10 Merrick Rd., Seaford L.I., NY 11783/516-785-7110
Borden's Accuracy, RD 1, Box 250BC, Springville, PA 18844/717-965-2505; FAX: 717-965-2328
Borgheresi, Enrique, 106 E. Tallalah, P.O. Box 8063, Greenville, SC 29604/803-271-2664
Bosis (See U.S. importer—New England Arms Co.)
Boudreaux, Gunsmith, Preston, 412 W. School St., Lake Charles, LA 70605/318-478-0640
Bradys Sportsmans Surplus, P.O. Box 4166, Missoula, MT 59806/406-721-5500; FAX: 406-721-5581
Braverman Corp., R.J., 88 Parade Rd., Meridith, NH 03293/800-736-4867
Brenneke KG, Wilhelm, Ilmenauweg 2, 30851 Langenhagen, GERMANY/0511/97262-0; FAX: 0511/97262-62 (U.S. importer—Dynamit Nobel-RWS, Inc.)
Brenner Sport Shop, Charlie, 344 St. George Ave., Rahway, NJ 07065/908-382-4066
Bretton, 19, rue Victor Grignard, F-42026 St.-Etienne (Cedex 1) FRANCE/77-93-54-69; FAX: 77-93-57-98 (U.S. importer—Mandall Shooting Supplies, Inc.)
Bridge Sportsmen's Center, 1319 Spring St., Paso Robles, CA 93446/805-238-4407
BRNO (See U.S. importers—Bohemia Arms Co.)
Broadway Arms, 4116 E. Broadway, N. Little Rock, AR 72117/501-945-9348
Brock's Gunsmithing, Inc., North 2104 Division St., Spokane, WA 99207/509-328-9788
Brolin Arms, 2755 Thompson Creek Rd., Pomona, CA 91767/909-392-2345; FAX: 909-392-2354
Brown Co., E. Arthur, 3404 Pawnee Dr., Alexandria, MN 56308/612-762-8847
Brown, Don, Gunsmith, 1085 Tunnel Rd., Ashville, NC 28805/704-298-4867
Browning (See page 503)
Browning Arms Co. (Parts & Service), 3005 Arnold Tenbrook Rd., Arnold, MO 63010-9406/314-287-6800; FAX: 314-287-9751
Bryan & Associates, 201 S. Gosset, Anderson, SC 29623/803-261-6810
Bryco Arms (See U.S. distributor—Jennings Firearms, Inc.)
BSA Guns Ltd., Armoury Rd. Small Heath, Birmingham, ENGLAND B11 2PX/011-021-772-8543; FAX: 011-021-773-0845 (U.S. importer—John Groenewold)
Buffalo Arms, 123 S. Third, Suite 6, Sandpoint, ID 83864/208-263-6953; FAX: 208-265-2096
Buffalo Gun Center, Inc., 3385 Harlem Rd., Buffalo, NY 14225/716-835-1546
Bullseye Gun Works, 7949 E. Frontage Rd., Overland Park, KS 66204/913-648-4867
Burby, Inc. Guns & Gunsmithing, Rt. 7 South RR #3, Box 345, Middlebury, VT 05753/802-388-7365
Burgins Gun Shop, RD #1 Box 66, Mericksville Rd., Sidney Center, NY 13839/607-829-8668
Burris Co., Inc., P.O. Box 1747, 331 E. 8th St., Greeley, CO 80631/303-356-1670; FAX: 303-356-8702
Burton Hardware, 200 N. Huntington, Sulphur, LA 70663/318-527-8651
Bushmaster Firearms (See Quality Parts Co./Bushmaster Firearms)
Bushnell (See Bausch & Lomb)

C

C-H Tool & Die Corp. (See 4-D Custom Die Co.)
Cabanas (See U.S. importer—Mandall Shooting Supplies, Inc.)
Cabela's, 812 13th Ave., Sidney, NE 69160/308-254-6644; FAX: 308-254-6669
Cal's Customs, 110 E. Hawthorne, Fallbrook, CA 92028/619-728-5230
Calico Light Weapon Systems, 405 E. 19th St., Bakersfield, CA 93305/805-323-1327; FAX: 805-323-7844
Camdex, Inc., 2330 Alger, Troy, MI 48083/810-528-2300; FAX: 810-528-0989
Cape Outfitters, 599 County Rd. 206, Cape Girardeau, MO 63701/314-335-4103; FAX: 314-335-1555
Capitol Sports & Western Wear, 1092 Helena Ave., Helena, MT 59601/406-443-2978

50th EDITION, 1996 **497**

WARRANTY SERVICE CENTER DIRECTORY

Carl's Gun Shop, 100 N. Main, El Dorado Springs, MO 64744/417-876-4168
Carpenter's Gun Works, RD 1 Box 43D, Newton Rd., Proctorsville, VT 05153/802-226-7690
Carroll's Gun Shop, Inc., 1610 N. Alabama Rd., Wharton, TX 77488/409-532-3175
Carter's Country, 8925 Katy Freeway, Houston, TX 77024/713-461-1844
Casey's Gun Shop, 59 Des E Rables, P.O. Box 100, Rogersville, New Brunswick E0A 2T0 CANADA/506-775-6822
Catfish Guns, 900 Jeffco-Executive Park, Imperial, MO 63052/314-464-1217
CBC, Avenida Humberto de Campos, 3220, 09400-000 Ribeirao Pires-SP-BRAZIL/55-11-742-7500; FAX: 55-11-459-7385 (U.S. importer—MAGTECH Recreational Products, Inc.)
Central Ohio Police Supply, c/o Wammes Guns, 225 South Main St., Bellefontaine, OH 43311
Century Gun Dist., Inc., 1467 Jason Rd., Greenfield, IN 46140/317-462-4524
Century International Arms, Inc., P.O. Box 714, St. Albans, VT 05478-0714/802-527-1252; FAX: 802-527-0470
Cervera, Albert J., Rt. 1 Box 808, Hanover, VA 23069/804-994-5783
CHAA, Ltd., P.O. Box 565, Howell, MI 48844/800-677-8737; FAX: 313-894-6930
Chapuis Armes, 21 La Gravoux, BP15, 42380 St. Bonnet-le-Chateau, FRANCE/(33)77.50.06.96 (U.S. importer—Chapuis USA)
Chapuis USA, 416 Business Park, Bedford, KY 40006
CHARCO, 26 Beaver St., Ansonia, CT 06401/203-735-4686; 203-735-6569
Charlie's Sporting Goods, Inc., 7401-H Menaul Blvd. N.E., Albuquerque, NM 87110/505-884-4545
Charlton Co., Ltd., M.D., Box 153, Brentwood Bay, B.C., CANADA V0S 1A0/604-652-5266
Charter Arms (See CHARCO)
Cherry Corners, Inc., 11136 Congress Rd., P.O. Box 38, Lodi, OH 44254/216-948-1238
Chet Paulson Outfitters, 1901 South 72nd St., Suite A-14, Tacoma, WA 98408/206-475-8831
Christopher Firearms Co., E., Inc., Route 128 & Ferry St., Miamitown, OH 45041/513-353-1321
Chuck's Gun Shop, P.O. Box 597, Waldo, FL 32694/904-468-2264
Chung, Gunsmith, Mel, 8 Ing Rd., P.O. Box 1008, Kaunakakai, HI 96748/808-553-5888
Churchill (See U.S. importer—Ellett Bros.)
Cimarron Arms, P.O. Box 906, Fredericksburg, TX 78624-0906/210-997-9090; FAX: 210-997-0802
Clark's Custom Guns, Inc., P.O. Box 530, 11462 Keatchie Rd., Keithville, LA 71047/318-925-0836; FAX: 318-925-9425
Colabaugh Gunsmith, Inc., Craig, R:D. 4, Box 4168 Gumm St., Stroudsburg, PA 18360/717-992-4499
Coleman, Inc., Ron, 1600 North I-35 #106, Carrollton, TX 75006/214-245-3030
Coliseum Gun Traders, Ltd., 1180 Hempstead Turnpike, Uniondale, NY 11553/516-481-3593
Colonial Repair, P.O. Box 372, Hyde Park, MA 02136-9998/617-469-4951
Colt Blackpowder Arms Co., 5 Centre Market Place, New York, NY 10013/212-925-2159; FAX: 212-966-4986
Colt's Mfg. Co., Inc., P.O. Box 1868, Hartford, CT 06144-1868/800-962-COLT, 203-236-6311; FAX: 203-244-1449
Competitor Corp., Inc., P.O. Box 244, 293 Townsend Rd., West Groton, MA 01472/508-448-3521; FAX: 508-448-6691
Connecticut Shotgun Mfg. Co., P.O. Box 1692, 35 Woodland St., New Britain, CT 06051-1692/203-225-6581; FAX: 203-832-8707
Connecticut Valley Arms Co. (See CVA)
Connecticut Valley Classics, P.O. Box 2068, 12 Taylor Lane, Westport, CT 06880/203-435-4600; FAX: 203-256-1180
Coonan Arms, 1465 Selby Ave., St. Paul, MN 55104/612-641-1263; FAX: 612-641-1173
Cooper Arms, P.O. Box 114, Stevensville, MT 59870/406-777-5534; FAX: 406-777-5228
Corbin, Inc., 600 Industrial Circle, P.O. Box 2659, White City, OR 97503/503-826-5211; FAX: 503-826-8669
Cosmi Americo & Figlio s.n.c., Via Flaminia 307, Ancona, ITALY I-60020/071-888208; FAX: 071-887008 (U.S. importer—New England Arms Co.)
Creekside Gun Shop, Inc., East Main St., Holcomb, NY 14469/716-657-6131; FAX: 716-657-7900
Crosman (See page 503)
Crosman Airguns, Rts. 5 and 20, E. Bloomfield, NY 14443/716-657-6161; FAX: 716-657-5405
Crucelegui Hermanos (See U.S. importer—Mandall Shooting Supplies, Inc.)
Cumberland Arms, Rt. I, Box 1150 Shafer Rd., Blantons Chapel, Manchester, TN 37355/800-797-8414
Cumberland Knife & Gun Works, 5661 Bragg Blvd., Fayetteville, NC 28303/919-867-0009
Custom Firearms Shop, The, 1133 Indiana Ave., Sheboygan, WI 53081/414-457-3320
Custom Gun Service, 1104 Upas Ave., McAllen, TX 78501/210-686-4670
Custom Gun Shop, 12505 97th St., Edmonton, Alberta, CANADA T5G 1Z8/403-477-3737
Custom Gun Works, 4952 Johnston St., Lafayette, LA 70503/318-984-0721
CVA, 5988 Peachtree Corners East, Norcross, GA 30071/800-251-9412; FAX: 404-242-8546
Cylinder & Slide, Inc., William R. Laughridge, 245 E. 4th St., Fremont, NE 68025/402-721-4277; FAX: 402-721-0263
CZ (See U.S. importer—Magnum Research, Inc.)

D

D&D Sporting Goods, 108 E. Main, Tishomingo, OK 73460/405-371-3571
D&J Bullet Co., 426 Ferry St., Russel, KY 41169/606-836-2663
D&J Coleman Service, 4811 Guadalupe Ave., Hobbs, NM 88240/505-392-5318
D&L Gunsmithing/Guns & Ammo, 3615 Summer Ave., Memphis, TN 38122/901-327-4384
D&L Shooting Supplies, 2663 W. Shore Rd., Warwick, RI 02886/401-738-1889
D-Max, Inc., RR1, Box 473, Bagley, MN 56621/218-785-2278
Daenzer, Charles E., 142 Jefferson Ave., Otisville, MI 48463/810-631-2415
Daewoo Precision Industries Ltd., 34-3 Yeoeuido-Dong, Yeongdeungoo-GU, 15th, Fl./Seoul, KOREA (U.S. importer—Nationwide Sports Distributors)
Daisy Mfg. Co., P.O. Box 220, Rogers, AR 72757/501-636-1200; FAX: 501-636-1601
Dakota (See U.S. importer—EMF Co., Inc.)
Dakota Arms, Inc., HC 55, Box 326, Sturgis, SD 57785/605-347-4686; FAX: 605-347-4459
Dale's Guns & Archery Center, 3915 Eighteenth Ave., S.W. Rte. 8, Rochester, MN 55902/507-289-8308
Damiano's Field & Stream, 172 N. Highland Ave., Ossining, NY 10562/914-941-6005
Danny's Gun Repair, Inc., 811 East Market St., Louisville, KY 40206/502-583-7100
Darnall's Gun Works, RR #3, Box 274, Bloomington, IL 61704/309-379-4331
Daryl's Gun Shop, Inc., R.R. #2 Highway 30 West, Box 145, State Center, IA 50247/515-483-2656
Dave's Airgun Service, 1525 E. LaVieve Ln., Tempe, AZ 85284/602-491-8304
Davidson's of Canada, 584 Neal Dr., Box 479, Peterborough, Ontario, CANADA K9J 6Z6/705-742-5405; 800-461-7663
Davis Industries, 15150 Sierra Bonita Ln., Chino, CA 91710/909-597-4726; FAX: 909-393-9771
Dayton Traister, 4778 N. Monkey Hill Rd., P.O. Box 593, Oak Harbor, WA 98277/206-679-4657; FAX:206-675-1114
Delhi Small Arms, 22B Argyle Ave., Delhi, Ontario, CANADA N4B 1J3/519-582-0522
Delisle Thompson Sporting Goods, Ltd., 1814A Loren Ave., Saskatoon, Saskatchewan, CANADA S7H 1Y4/306-653-2171
Denver Instrument Co., 6542 Fig St., Arvada, CO 80004/800-321-1135, 303-431-7255; FAX: 303-423-4831
Desert Industries, Inc., P.O. Box 93443, Las Vegas, NV 89193-3443/702-597-1066; FAX: 702-871-9452
Diana (See U.S. importer—Dynamit Nobel-RWS, Inc.)
Dillon Precision Products, Inc., 8009 East Dillon's Way, Scottsdale, AZ 85260/602-948-8009, 800-762-3845; FAX: 602-998-2786
Dixie Gun Works, Inc., Hwy. 51 South, Union City, TN 38261/901-885-0561, order 800-238-6785; FAX: 901-885-0440
Dollar Drugs, Inc., 15A West 3rd, Lee's Summit, MO 64063/816-524-7600
Don & Tim's Gun Shop, 3724 Northwest Loop 410 and Fredricksburg, San Antonio, TX 78229/512-736-0263
Don's Sport Shop, Inc., 7803 E. McDowell Rd., Scottsdale, AZ 85257/602-945-4051
Dorn's Outdoor Center, 4388 Mercer University Drive, Macon, GA 31206/912-471-0304
Douglas Sporting Goods, 138 Brick Street, Princeton, WV 24740/304-425-8144
Down Under Gunsmiths, 318 Driveway, Fairbanks, AK 99701/907-456-8500
Dubbs, Gunsmith, Dale R., 32616 U.S. Hwy. 90, Seminole, AL 36574/205-946-3245
Duncan Gun Shop, Inc., 414 Second St., North Wilksboro, NC 28659/919-838-4851
Duncan's Gunworks, Inc., 1619 Grand Ave., San Marcos, CA 92069/619-727-0515
Dynamit Nobel-RWS, Inc., 81 Ruckman Rd., Closter, NJ 07624/201-767-7971; FAX: 201-767-1589

E

E&L Mfg., Inc., 4177 Riddle by Pass Rd., Riddle, OR 97469/503-874-2137; FAX: 503-874-3107
E.A.A. Corp., P.O. Box 1299, Sharpes, FL 32959/407-639-4842, 800-536-4442; FAX: 407-639-7006
Eagle Arms, Inc., 128 E. 23rd Ave., Coal Valley, IL 61240/309-799-5619, 800-336-0184; FAX: 309-799-5150
Ed's Gun & Tackle Shop, Inc., Suite 90, 2727 Canton Rd. (Hwy. 5), Marietta, GA 30066/404-425-8461
Elbe Arms Co., Inc., 610 East 27th St., Cheyenne, WY 82001/307-634-5731
Ellett Bros., P.O. Box 128, 267 Columbia Ave., Columbia, SC 29036/803-345-3751, 800-845-3711; FAX: 803-345-1820
Emerging Technologies, Inc., 721 Main St., Little Rock, AR 72201/501-375-2227; FAX: 501-372-1445
EMF Co., Inc., 1900 E. Warner Ave. Suite 1-D, Santa Ana, CA 92705/714-261-6611; FAX: 714-756-0133
Enstad & Douglas, 211 Hedges, Oregon City, OR 97045/503-655-3751
Epps, Ellwood, RR 3, Hwy. 11 North, Orillia, Ontario CANADA L3V 6H3/705-689-5333
Erma Werke GmbH, Johan Ziegler St., 13/15/FeldiglSt., D-8060 Dachau, GERMANY (U.S. importers—Mandall Shooting Supplies, Inc.; PSI, Inc.)
Ernie's Gun Shop, Ltd., 1031 Marion St., Winnipeg, Manitoba, CANADA R2J 0L1/204-233-1928
Essex Arms, P.O. Box 345, Island Pond, VT 05846/802-723-4313
Euroarms of America, Inc., 208 E. Piccadilly St., Winchester, VA 22601/703-662-1863; FAX: 703-662-4464
Europtik Ltd., P.O. Box 319, Dunmore, PA 18512/717-347-6049; FAX: 717-969-4330
Eversull, Ken, #1 Tracemont, Boyce, LA 71409/318-793-8728
Ewell Cross Gun Shop, Inc., 8240 Interstate 30W, Ft. Worth, TX 76108/817-246-4622
Eyster Heritage Gunsmiths, Inc., Ken, 6441 Bishop Rd., Centerburg, OH 43011/614-625-6131

F

F&D Guns, 5140 Westwood Drive, St. Charles, MO 63304/314-441-5897
Fabarm S.p.A., Via Averolda 31, 25039 Travagliato, Brescia, ITALY/030-6863629; FAX: 030-6863684 (U.S. importer—Ithaca Acquisition Corp.)
Famas (See U.S. importer—Century International Arms, Inc.)
FAS, Via E. Fermi, 8, 20019 Settimo Milanese, Milano, ITALY/02-3285846; FAX: 02-33500196 (U.S. importer—Nygord Precision Products)
Fausti Cav. Stefano & Figlie snc, Via Martiri Dell Indipendenza, 70, Marcheno, ITALY 25060 (U.S. importer—American Arms, Inc.)
Feather Industries, Inc., 37600 Liberty Dr., Trinidad, CO 81082/719-846-2699; FAX: 719-846-2644
Federal Engineering Corp., 1090 Bryn Mawr, Bensenville, IL 60106/708-860-1938; FAX: 708-860-2085
Federal Firearms Co., Inc., 5035 Thom's Run Rd., Oakdale, PA 15071/412-221-0300
FEG, Budapest, Soroksariut 158, H-1095 HUNGARY (U.S. importers—Century International Arms, Inc.; K.B.I., Inc.)
Feinwerkbau Westinger & Altenburger GmbH (See FWB)
Felton, James, Custom Gunsmith, 1033 Elizabeth St., Eugene, OR 97402/503-689-1687
FERLIB, Via Costa 46, 25063 Gardone V.T. (Brescia) ITALY/30 89 12 586; FAX: 30 89 12 586 (U.S. importers—Wm. Larkin Moore & Co.; New England Arms Co., Pachmayr Co.)
Fiocchi Munizioni s.p.a. (See U.S. importer—Fiocchi of America)
Fiocchi of America, Inc., 5030 Fremont Rd., Ozark, MO 65721/417-725-4118, 800-721-2666; FAX: 417-725-1039
Firearms Co. Ltd./Alpine (See U.S. importer—Mandall Shooting Supplies, Inc.)
Firearms Repair & Refinish Shoppe, 639 Hoods Mill Rd., Woodbine, MD 21797/410-795-5859
Firearms Service Center, 2140 Old Shepherdsville Rd., Louisville, KY 40218/502-458-1148
Fix Gunshop, Inc., Michael D., 334 Mt. Penn Rd., Reading, PA 19607/215-775-2067
FN Herstal, Voie de Liege 33, Herstal 4040, BELGIUM/(32)41.40.82.83; FAX: (32)41.40.86.79
Foothills Shooting Center, 7860 W. Jewell Ave., Lakewood, CO 80226/303-985-4417
Forgett Jr., Valmore J., 689 Bergen Blvd., Ridgefield, NJ 07657/201-945-2500; FAX: 201-945-6859
Forster Products, 82 E. Lanark Ave., Lanark, IL 61046/815-493-6360; FAX: 815-493-2371
Four Seasons, 76 R Winn St., Woburn, MA 01801/617-932-3133/3255
4-D Custom Die Co., 711 N. Sandusky St., P.O. Box 889, Mt. Vernon, OH 43050-0889/614-397-7214; FAX: 614-397-6600
Fox & Company, 2211 Dutch Valley Rd., Knoxville, TN 37918/615-687-7411
Franchi S.p.A., Luigi, Via del Serpente, 12, 25020 Fornaci, ITALY (U.S. importer—American Arms, Inc.)
Francotte & Cie S.A., Auguste, rue du Trois Juin 109, 4400 Herstal-Liege, BELGIUM/41-48.13.18; FAX: 41-48.11.79 (U.S. importer—Armes de Chasse)
Franklin Sports, Inc., 3941 Atlanta Hwy., Bogart, GA 30622/706-543-7803
Freedom Arms, Inc., P.O. Box 1776, Freedom, WY 83120/307-883-2468, 800-833-4432 (orders only); FAX: 307-883-2005
Freer's Gun Shop, Building B-1, 8928 Spring Branch Dr., Houston, TX 77080/713-467-3016
Fremont Tool Works, 1214 Prairie, Ford, KS 67842/316-369-2327
Friedman's Army Surplus, 2617 Nolenville Rd., Nashville, TN 37211/615-244-1653
Frontiersman's Sports, 6925 Wayzata Blvd., Minneapolis, MN 55426/612-544-3775
FWB, Neckarstrasse 43, 78727 Oberndorf a. N., GERMANY/07423-814-0; FAX: 07423-814-89 (U.S. importer—Beeman Precision Airguns, Inc.)

G

G.H. Outdoor Sports, 520 W. "B" St., McCook, NE 69001/308-345-1250
G.I. Loan Shop, 1004 W. Second St., Grand Island, NE 68801/308-382-9573
G.U. Inc., 4325 S. 120th St., Omaha, NE 68137/402-330-4492; FAX: 402-330-8029
Galaxy Imports Ltd., Inc., P.O. Box 3361, Victoria, TX 77903/512-573-4867; FAX: 512-576-9622
Galazan, Div. of Connecticut Shotgun Mfg. Co., P.O. Box 622, 35 Woodland St., New Britain, CT

WARRANTY SERVICE CENTER DIRECTORY

06051-0622/203-225-6581; FAX: 203-832-8707
Gamba, USA, P.O. Box 60452, Colorado Springs, CO 80960/719-578-1145; FAX: 719-444-0731
Gamba-Societa Armi Bresciane Srl., Renato, Via Artigiani, 93, 25063 Gardone Val Trompia (BS), ITALY/30-8911640, 30-8911648 (U.S. importers—Cape Outfitters; Giacomo Sporting, Inc.; New England Arms Co.)
Gamo (See U.S. importers—Daisy Mfg. Co.; Dynamit Nobel-RWS, Inc.)
Gander Mountain, Inc., P.O. Box 128, Hwy. W, Wilmot, WI 53192/414-862-2331
Gander Mt. Inc., 1307 Miller Trunk Highway, Duluth, MN 55811/218-726-1100
Garbi, Armas Urki, 12-14, 20.600 Eibar (Guipuzcoa) SPAIN/43-11 38 73 (U.S. importer—Moore & Co., Wm. Larkin)
Garfield Gunsmithing, 237 Wessington Ave., Garfield, NJ 07026/201-478-0171
Garrett Gunsmiths, Inc., Peter, 838 Monmouth St., Newport, KY 41071-1821/606-261-1855
Gart Brothers Sporting Goods, 1000 Broadway, Denver, CO 80203/303-861-1122
Gary's Gun Shop, 905 W. 41st St., Sioux Falls, SD 57104/605-332-6119
Gene's Gunsmithing, Box 34 GRP 326 R.R. 3, Selkirk, Manitoba, CANADA R1A 2A8/204-757-4413
Genecco Gun Works, K., 10512 Lower Sacramento Rd., Stockton, CA 95210/209-951-0706
Gentry Custom Gunmaker, David, 314 N. Hoffman, Belgrade, MT 59714/406-388-4867
GFR Corp., P.O. Box 430, Andover, NH 03216/603-735-5300
Giacomo Sporting, Inc., Delta Plaza, Rt. 26N, Rome, NY 13440
Gibbs Rifle Co., Inc., Cannon Hill Industrial Park, Rt. 2, Box 214 Hoffman, Rd./Martinsburg, WV 25401/304-274-0458; FAX: 304-274-0078
Gilbert Equipment Co., Inc., 960 Downtowner Rd., Mobile, AL 36609/205-344-3322
Girard, Florent, Gunsmith, 598 Verreault, Chicoutimi, Quebec, CANADA G7H 2B8/418-696-3329
Glades Gunworks, 4360 Corporate Square, Naples, FL 33942/813-643-2922
Glenn's Reel & Rod Repair, 2210 E. 9th St., Des Moines, IA 50316/515-262-2990
Glock GmbH, P.O. Box 50, A-2232 Deutsch Wagram, AUSTRIA (U.S. importer—Glock, Inc.)
Glock, Inc., 6000 Highlands Parkway, Smyrna, GA 30082/404-432-1202: FAX: 404-433-8719
Gonic Arms, Inc., 134 Flagg Rd., Gonic, NH 03839/603-332-8456, 603-332-8457
Gonzalez Guns, Ramon B., P.O. Box 370, Monticello, NY 12701/914-794-4515
Gordon's Wigwam, 501 S. St. Francis, Wichita, KS 67202/316-264-5891
Gorenflo Gunsmithing, 1821 State St., Erie, PA 16501/814-452-4855
Great Lakes Airguns, 6175 S. Park Ave., Hamburg, NY 14075/716-648-6666; FAX: 716-648-5279
Green Acres Sporting Goods, Inc., 8774 Normandy Blvd., Jacksonville, FL 32221/904-786-5166
Greene's Gun Shop, 4778 Monkey Hill Rd., Oak Harbor, WA 98277/206-675-3421
Greenwood Precision, P.O. Box 468, Nixa, MO 65714-0468/417-725-2330
Grenada Gun Works, 942 Lakeview Drive, Grenada, MS 38901/601-226-9272
Grice Gun Shop, Inc., 216 Reed St., P.O. 1028, Clearfield, PA 16830/814-765-9273
Griffiths & Sons, E.J., 1014 N. McCullough St., Lima OH 45801/419-228-2141
Groenwold, John, P.O. Box 830, Mundelein, IL 60060-0830/708-566-2365
Grulla Armes, Apartado 453, Avda Otaloa, 12, Eiber, SPAIN (U.S. importer—American Arms, Inc.)
Grundman's, Inc., 75 Wildwood Ave., Rio Dell, CA 95562/707-764-5744
GSI, Inc., 108 Morrow Ave., P.O. Box 129, Trussville, AL 35173/205-655-8299; FAX: 205-655-7078
Gun & Tackle Store, The, 6041 Forrest Ln., Dallas, TX 75230/214-239-8181
Gun Ace Gunsmithing, 3975 West I-40 North, Hurricane, UT 84737/801-635-5212
Gun Center, The, 5831 Buckeystown Pike, Frederick, MD 21701/301-694-6887
Gun City USA, Inc., 573 Murfreesboro Rd., Nashville, TN 37210/615-256-6127
Gun City, 212 W. Main Ave., Bismarck, ND 58501/701-223-2304
Gun Corral, Inc., 2827 East College Ave., Decatur, GA 30030/404-299-0288
Gun Doc, Inc., 5405 N.W. 82nd Ave., Miami, FL 33166/305-477-2777
Gun Exchange, Inc., 5317 W. 65th St., Little Rock, AR 72209/501-562-4668
Gun Hospital, The, 45 Vineyard Ave., E. Providence, RI 02914/401-438-3495
Gun Rack, Inc., The, 213 Richland Ave., Aiken, SC 29801/803-648-7100
Gun Room, The, 201 Clark St., Chapin, SC 29036/803-345-2199
Gun Shop, The, 5550 S. 900 East, Salt Lake City, UT 84117/801-263-3633
Gun World, 392 Fifth Street, Elko, NV 89801/702-738-2666
Gunshop, Inc., The, 44633 N. Sierra Hwy., Lancaster CA 93534/805-942-8377
Gunsite Training Center, P.O. Box 700, Paulden, AZ 86334/602-636-4565; FAX: 602-636-1236
Gunsmith Co., The, 3435 S. State St., Salt Lake City, UT 84115/801-467-8244; FAX: 801-467-8256
Gunsmith, Inc., The, 1410 Sunset Blvd., West Columbia, SC 29169/803-791-0250
Gunsmithing Ltd., 57 Unquowa Rd., Fairfield, CT 06430/203-254-0436
Gunsmithing Specialties Co., 110 North Washington St., Papillion, NE 68046/402-339-1222

H

H&B Service, Inc., 7150 S. Platte Canyon Road, Littleton, CO 80123/970-979-5447
H&R 1871, Inc., 60 Industrial Rowe, Gardner, MA 01440/508-632-9393; FAX: 508-632-2300
H-S Precision, Inc., 1301 Turbine Dr., Rapid City, SD 57701/605-341-3006; FAX: 605-342-8964
Hämmerli Ltd., Seonerstrasse 37, CH-5600 Lenzburg, SWITZERLAND/064-50 11 44; FAX: 064-51 38 27 (U.S. importer—Hammerli USA)
Hagstrom, E.G., 2008 Janis Dr., Memphis, TN 38116/901-398-5333
Hal's Gun Supply, 320 Second Avenue SE, Cullman, AL 35055/205-734-7546
Hammerli USA, 19296 Oak Grove Circle, Groveland, CA 95321/209-962-5311; FAX: 209-962-5931
Hampel's, Inc., 710 Randolph, Traverse City, MI 49684/616-946-5485
Harris-McMillan Gunworks, 302 W. Melinda Lane, Phoenix, AZ 85027/602-582-9627; FAX: 602-582-5178
Harry's Army & Navy Store, 691 NJSH Rt. 130, Yardville, NJ 08691/609-585-5450
Hart & Son, Inc., Robert W., 401 Montgomery St., Nescopeck, PA 18635/717-752-3655, 800-368-3656; FAX: 717-752-1088
Hart's Gun Supply, Ed, U.S. Route 415, Bath, NY 14810/607-776-4228
Hatfield Gun Co., Inc., 224 N. 4th St., St. Joseph, MO 64501/816-279-8688; FAX: 816-279-2716
Hawken Shop, The (See Dayton Traister)
Heckler & Koch GmbH, Postfach 1329, D-7238 Oberndorf, Neckar, GERMANY (U.S. importer—Heckler & Koch, Inc.)
Heckler & Koch, Inc., 21480 Pacific Blvd., Sterling, VA 20166-8903/703-450-1900; FAX: 703-450-8160
Heckman Arms Company, 1736 Skyline Dr., Richmond Heights, OH 44143/216-289-9182
Helwan (See U.S. importer—Interarms)
Hemlock Gun Shop, Box 149, Rt. 590 & Crane Rd., Lakeville, PA 18438/717-226-9410
Henry's Airguns, 1204 W. Locust, Belvidere, IL 61008/815-547-5091
Herold's Gun Shoppe, 1498 E. Main Street, Box 350, Waynesboro, PA 17268/717-762-4010
Heym GmbH & Co. KG, Friedrich Wilh, Coburger Str.8, D-97702 Muennerstadt, GERMANY
Hi-Grade Imports, 8655 Monterey Rd., Gilroy, CA 95021/408-842-9301; FAX: 408-842-2374
Hi-Point Firearms, 5990 Philadelphia Dr., Dayton, OH 45415/513-275-4991; FAX: 513-275-4991
High Standard Mfg. Co., Inc., 264 Whitney St., Hartford, CT 06105-2270/203-586-8220; FAX: 203-231-0411
Hill Top Gunsmithing, Rt. 3, Box 85, Canton, NY 13617/315-386-4875
Hill's Hardware & Sporting Goods, 1234 S. Second St., Union City, TN 38261/901-885-1510
Hill's, Inc., 1720 Capital Blvd., Raleigh, NC 27604/919-833-4884
HJS Arms, Inc., P.O. Box 3711, Brownsville, TX 78523-3711/800-453-2767, 210-542-2767
Hobbs Bicycle & Gun Sales, 406 E. Broadway, Hobbs, NM 88240/505-393-9815
Hodson & Son Pell Gun Repair, 4500 S. 100 E., Anderson, IN 46013/317-643-2055
Hoffman's Gun Center, Inc., 2208 Berlin Turnpike, Newington, CT 06111/203-666-8827
Hollywood Engineering, 10642 Arminta St., Sun Valley, CA 91352/818-842-8376
Holston Ent., Inc., P.O. Box 493, Piney Flats, TN 37686
Horchler's Gun Shop, 100 Ratlum Rd. RFD, Collinsville, CT 06022/203-379-1977
Hornady Mfg. Co., P.O. Box 1848, Grand Island, NE 68802/800-338-3220, 308-382-1390; FAX: 308-382-5761
Houma Gun Works, 1520 Grand Caillou Rd., Houma, LA 70363/504-872-2782
Howa Machinery, Ltd., Sukaguchi, Shinkawa-cho, Nishikasugai-gun, Aichi 452, JAPAN (U.S. importer—Interarms)
Huntington Die Specialties, 601 Oro Dam Blvd., Oroville, CA 95965/916-534-1210; FAX: 916-534-1212
Hutch's, 50 E. Main St., Lehi, UT 84043/801-768-3461
Hutchinson's Gun Repair, 507 Clifton St., Pineville, LA 71360/318-640-4315

I

IAI, 6226 Santos Diaz St., Irwindale, CA 91702/818-334-1200
IGA (See U.S. importer—Stoeger Industries)
Imbert & Smithers, Inc., 1144 El Camino Real, San Carlos, CA 94070/415-593-4207
IMI, P.O. Box 1044, Ramat Hasharon 47100, ISRAEL/972-3-5485222 (U.S. importer—Magnum Research, Inc.)
Interarms, 10 Prince St., Alexandria, VA 22314/703-548-1400; FAX: 703-549-7826
Intermountain Arms & Tackle, Inc., 105 E. Idaho St., Meridian, ID 83642/208-888-4911; FAX: 208-888-4381
Intermountain Arms & Tackle, Inc., 1375 E. Fairfield Ave., Meridian, ID 83642/208-888-4911; FAX: 208-888-4381
Intratec, 12405 SW 130th St., Miami, FL 33186/305-232-1821; FAX: 305-253-7207
Island Pond Gunshop, P.O. Box 428 Cross St., Island Pond, VT 05846/802-723-4546
Ithaca Aquisition Corp., Ithaca Gun, 891 Route 34B, King Ferry, NY 13081/315-364-7171; FAX: 315-364-5134

J

J&G Gunsmithing, 625 Vernon St., Roseville, CA 95678/916-782-7075
J&T Services, 12½ Woodlawn Ave., Bradford, PA 16701/814-368-3034
J.O. Arms Inc., 5709 Hartsdale, Houston, TX 77036/713-789-0745; FAX: 713-789-7513
Jack First, 1201 Turbine Drive, Rapid City, SD 57701/605-343-9544
Jack's Lock & Gun Shop, 32 4th St., Fond Du Lac, WI 54935/414-922-4420
Jackalope Gun Shop, 1048 S. 5th St., Douglas, WY 82633/307-358-3441
Jackson, Inc., Bill, 9501 U.S. 19 N., Pinellas Park, FL 34666/813-576-4169
Jacobsen's Gun Center, 612 Broadway St., Story City, IA 50248/515-733-2995
Jaeger, Inc., Paul/Dunn's, P.O. Box 449, 1 Madison Ave., Grand Junction, TN 38039/901-764-6909; FAX: 901-764-6503
JagerSport, Ltd., One Wholesale Way, Cranston, RI 02920/800-962-4867, 401-944-9682; FAX: 401-946-2587
Jansma, Jack J., 4320 Kalamazoo Ave., Grand Rapids, MI 49508/616-455-7810; FAX: 616-455-5212
Jay's Sports, Inc., North 88 West 15263 Main St., Menomonee Falls, WI 53051/414-251-0550
Jennings Firearms, Inc., 17692 Cowan, Irvine, CA 92714/714-252-7621; FAX: 714-252-7626
Jensen's Custom Ammunition, 5146 E. Pima, Tucson, AZ 85712/602-325-3346; FAX: 602-322-5704
Jerry's Gun Shop, P.O. Box 88, 100 Main St., Glenarm, IL 62536/217-483-4606
Jim's Gun & Service Center, 514 Tenth Ave. S.E., Aberdeen, SD 57401/605-225-9111
Jim's Trading Post, #10 Southwest Plaza, Pine Bluff, AR 71603/501-534-8591
Joe's Gun Shop, 4430 14th St., Dorr, MI 49323/616-877-4615
Joe's Gun Shop, 5215 W. Edgemont Ave., Phoenix, AZ 85035/602-233-0694
John Q's Quality Gunsmithing, 5165 Auburn Blvd., Sacramento, CA 95841/916-344-7669
Johnson Service, Inc., W., 3654 N. Adrian Rd., Adrian, MI 49221/517-265-2545
Jones, J.D. (See SSK Industries)
Jordan Gun Shop, 28 Magnolia Dr., Tifton, GA 31794/912-382-4251
JSL (Hereford) Ltd., 35 Church St., Hereford HR1 2LR ENGLAND/0432-355416; FAX: 0432-355242 (U.S. importer—Specialty Shooters Supply, Inc.)

K

K&M Industries, Inc., Box 66, 510 S. Main, Troy, ID 83871/208-835-2281; FAX: 208-835-5211
K.B.I., Inc., P.O. Box 5440, Harrisburg, PA 17110-0440/717-540-8518; FAX: 717-540-8567
Kahles U.S.A., P.O. Box 81071, Warwick, RI 02888/800-752-4537: FAX: 401-946-2587
Kahnke Gunworks, 206 West 11th St., Redwood Falls, MN 56283/507-637-2901
Kahr Arms, P.O. Box 220, 630 Route 303, Blauvelt, NY 10913/914-353-5996; FAX: 914-353-7833
Karrer's Gunatorium, 5323 N. Argonne Rd., Spokane, WA 99212/509-924-3030
Kassnar (See U.S. importer—K.B.I., Inc.)
Keidel's Gunsmithing Service, 927 Jefferson Ave., Washington, PA 15301/412-222-6379
Kel-Tec CNC Industries, Inc., P.O. Box 3427, Cocoa, FL 32924/407-631-0068; FAX: 407-631-1169
Kelbly, Inc., 7222 Dalton Fox Lake Rd., North Lawrence, OH 44666/216-683-4674; FAX: 216-683-7349
Keller's Co., Inc., 511 Spielman Hwy., Rt. 4, Burlington, CT 06013/203-583-2220
Keng's Firearms Specialty, Inc., 875 Wharton Dr. SW, Atlanta, GA 30336/404-691-7611; FAX: 404-505-8445
Kesselring Gun Shop, 400 Hwy. 99 North, Burlington, WA 98233/206-724-3113; FAX: 206-724-7003
Kesselring Gun Shop, 400 Pacific Hwy. 99 North, Burlington, WA 98233/206-724-3113; FAX: 206-724-7003
Kick's Sport Center, 300 Goodge St., Claxton, GA 30417/912-739-1734
Kielon, Gunsmith, Dave, 57 Kittleberger Park, Webster, NY 14580/716-872-2256
Kimber of America, Inc., 9039 SE Jannsen Rd., Clackamas, OR 97015/503-656-1704, 800-880-2418; FAX: 503-656-5357
Kimel Industries, 3800 Old Monroe Rd., P.O. Box 335, Matthews, NC 28105/800-438-9288; FAX: 704-821-6339
King's Gun Shop, Inc., 32301 Walter's Hwy., Franklin, VA 23851/804-562-4725
Kingyon, Paul L., 607 N. 5th St., Burlington, IA 52601/319-752-4465
Kirkpatrick, Gunsmith, Larry, 707 79th St., Lubbock, TX 79404/806-745-5308
Knight's Mfg. Co., 7750 9th St. SW, Vero Beach, FL 32968/407-562-5697; FAX: 407-569-2955
Kopp, Prof. Gunsmith, Terry K., 1301 Franklin, Lexington, MO 64067/816-259-2636
Korth, Robert-Bosch-Str. 4, P.O. Box 1320, 23909 Ratzeburg, GERMANY/0451-4991497; FAX: 0451-4993230 (U.S. importers—Interarms; Mandall Shooting Supplies, Inc.)
Kotila Gun Shop, 726 County Rd. 3SW, Cokato, MN 55321/612-286-5636
Kowa Optimed, Inc., 20001 S. Vermont Ave., Torrance, CA 90502/310-327-1913; FAX: 310-327-4177

WARRANTY SERVICE CENTER DIRECTORY

Krebs Gunsmithing, 7417 N. Milwaukee Ave., Niles, IL 60714/708-647-6994
Krico/Kriegeskorte GmbH, A., Nurnbergerstrasse 6, D-90602 Pyrbaum GERMANY/0911-796092; FAX: 0911-796074 (U.S. importer—Mandall Shooting Supplies, Inc.)
Krieghoff Gun Co., H., Boschstrasse 22, D-89079 Ulm, GERMANY/731-401820; FAX: 731-4018270 (U.S. importer—Krieghoff International, Inc.)
Krieghoff International, Inc., 7528 Easton Rd., Ottsville, PA 18942/610-847-5173; FAX: 610-847-8691
KSN Industries, Ltd. (See U.S. importer—J.O. Arms Inc.)

L

L&S Technologies, Inc. (See Aimtech Mount Systems)
L'Armurier Alain Bouchard, Inc., 420 Route 143, Ulverton, Quebec CANADA J0B 2J0/819-826-6611
L.A.R. Mfg., Inc., 4133 W. Farm Rd., West Jordan, UT 84088/801-280-3505; FAX: 801-280-1972
Labs Air Gun Shop, 2307 N. 62nd St., Omaha, NE 68104/402-553-0990
LaFrance Specialties, P.O. Box 178211, San Diego, CA 92177-8211/619-293-3373
Laib's Gunsmithing, North Hwy. 23, R.R. 1, Spicer, MN 56288/612-796-2686
Lakefield Arms Ltd., 248 Water St., P.O. Box 129, Lakefield, Ont. K0L 2H0, CANADA/705-652-6735, 705-652-8000; FAX: 705-652-8431
Lapua Ltd., P.O. Box 5, Lapua, FINLAND SF-62101/64-310111; FAX: 64-4388951 (U.S. importers—Champion's Choice; Keng's Firearms Specialty, Inc.
Laser Devices, Inc., 2 Harris Ct. A-4, Monterey, CA 93940/408-373-0701; FAX: 408-373-0903
Laseraim, Inc. (See Emerging Technologies, Inc.)
Laurona Armas Eiber, S.A.L., Avenida de Otaola 25, P.O. Box 260, 20600 Eibar, SPAIN/34-43-700600; FAX: 34-43-700616 (U.S. importers—Continental Imports & Distribution; Galaxy Imports Ltd., Inc.)
Lawson's Custom Firearms, Inc., Art, 313 S. Magnolia Ave., Ocala, FL 32671/904-629-7793
Lebeau-Courally, Rue St. Gilles, 386, 4000 Liege, BELGIUM/041 52 48 43; FAX: 041 52 20 08 (U.S. importer—New England Arms Co.
Lee Precision, Inc., 4275 Hwy. U, Hartford, WI 53027/414-673-3075
LeFever & Sons, Inc., Frank, 6234 Stokes-Lee Center Rd., Lee Center, NY 13363/315-337-6722
Leica USA, Inc., 156 Ludlow Ave., Northvale, NJ 07647/201-767-7500; FAX: 201-767-8666
Leo's Custom Stocks, 1767 Washington Ave., Library, PA 15129/412-835-4126
Les Gun & Pawn Shop, 1423 New Boston Rd., Texarkana, TX 75501/903-793-2201
Leupold & Stevens, Inc., P.O. Box 688, Beaverton, OR 97075/503-646-9171; FAX: 503-526-1455
Levan's Sporting Goods, 433 N. Ninth St., Lebanon, PA 17042/717-273-3148
Lew's Mountaineer Gunsmithing, Route 2, Box 330A, Charleston, WV 25314/304-344-3745
Lewis Arms, 1575 Hooksett Rd., Hooksett, NH 03106/603-485-7334
Llama Gabilondo Y Cia, Apartado 290, E-01080, Victoria, SPAIN (U.S. importer—SGS Importers International, Inc.)
Lock Stock & Barrel, 115 SW H St., Grants Pass, OR 97526/503-474-0775
Loftin & Taylor, 2619 N. Main St., Jacksonville, FL 32206/904-353-9634
Log Cabin Sport Shop, 8010 Lafayette Rd., Lodi, OH 44254/216-948-1082
Lolo Sporting Goods, 1026 Main St., Lewiston, ID 83501/208-743-1031
Lone Star Guns, Inc., 2452 Avenue K, Plano, TX 75074/214-424-4501; 800-874-7923
Long Beach Uniform Co., Inc., 2789 Long Beach Blvd., Long Beach, CA 90806/310-424-0220
Longacres, Inc., 358 Chestnut St., Abilene, TN 79602/915-672-9521
Longs Gunsmithing Ltd., W.R., P.O. Box 876, 2 Coverdale St., Cobourg, Ontario CANADA K9A 4H1/416-372-5955
Lorcin Engineering Co., Inc., 10427 San Sevaine Way, Ste. A, Mira Loma, CA 91752/909-360-1406; FAX: 909-360-0623
Lounsbury Sporting Goods, Bob, 104 North St., Middletown, NY 10940/914-343-1808
Lusignant, Armurier, A. Richard, 15820 St. Michel, St. Hyacinthe, Quebec, CANADA, J2T 3R7/514-773-7997
Lutter, Robert E., 3547 Auer Dr., Ft. Wayne, IN 46835/219-485-8319
Lyman Products Corp., Rt. 147, Middlefield, CT 06455/203-349-3421, 800-22-LYMAN; FAX: 203-349-3586

M

M.O.A. Corp., 2451 Old Camden Pike, Eaton, OH 45320/513-456-3669
Mac-1 Distributors, 13974 Van Ness Ave., Gardena, CA 90249/310-327-3582
Magasin Latulippe, Inc., 637 West St. Vallier, P.O. Box 395, Quebec City, Quebec, CANADA G1K 6W8/418-529-0024; FAX: 418-529-6381
Magma Engineering Co., P.O. Box 161, 20955 E. Ocotillo Rd., Queen Creek, AZ 85242/602-987-9008; FAX: 602-987-0148
Magnum Gun Service, 357 Welsh Track Rd., Newark, DE 19702/302-454-0141
Magnum Research, Inc., 7110 University Ave. NE, Minneapolis, MN 55432/612-574-1868; FAX: 612-574-0109
MAGTECH Recreational Products, Inc., 4737 College Park, Ste. 101, San Antonio, TX 78249/210-493-4427; FAX: 210-493-9534
Mandall Shooting Supplies, Inc., 3616 N. Scottsdale Rd., Scottsdale, AZ 85252/602-945-2553; FAX: 602-949-0734
Marksman Products, 5482 Argosy Dr., Huntington Beach, CA 92649/714-898-7535, 800-822-8005; FAX: 714-372-3041
Marlin Firearms Co., 100 Kenna Dr., New Haven, CT 06473/203-239-5621; FAX: 203-234-7991
Marocchi F.lli S.p.A., Via Galileo Galilei, I-25068 Zanano di Sarezzo, ITALY (U.S. importers—PSI, Inc.; Sile Distributors)
Martin Gun Shop, Henry, 206 Kay Lane, Shreveport, LA 71115/318-797-1119
Martin's Gun Shop, 3600 Laurel Ave., Natchez, MS 39120/601-442-0784
Mashburn Arms Co., Inc., 1218 North Pennsylvania Ave., Oklahoma City, OK 73107/405-236-5151
Mason, Guns & Ammo Co., Tom, 68 Lake Avenue, Danbury, CT 06810/203-778-6421
Master Gunsmiths, Inc., 12621 Tyconderoga, Houston, TX 77044/713-459-1631
Matt's 10X Gunsmithing, Inc., 5906 Castle Rd., Duluth, MN 55803/218-721-4210
Mauser Werke Oberndorf Waffensysteme GmbH, Postfach 1349, 78722 Oberndorf/N. GERMANY (U.S. importer—Gibbs Rifle Co., Inc.)
Maverick Arms, Inc., 7 Grasso Ave., P.O. Box 497, North Haven, CT 06473/203-230-5300; FAX: 203-230-5420
May & Company, Inc., P.O. Box 1111, 838 W. Capitol St., Jackson, MS 39203/601-354-5781
McBride's Guns, Inc., 2915 San Gabriel, Austin, TX 78705/512-472-3532
McBros Rifle Co., P.O. Box 86549, Phoenix, AZ 85080/602-780-2115; FAX: 602-581-3825
McCann's Machine & Gun Shop, P.O. Box 641, Spanaway, WA 98387/206-537-6919; FAX: 206-537-6993
McClelland Gun Shop, 1533 Centerville Rd., Dallas, TX 75228-2597/214-321-0231
McDaniel Co., Inc., B., 8880 Pontiac Tr., P.O. Box 119, South Lyon, MI 48178/313-437-8989
McGuns, W.H., N. 22nd Ave. at Osborn St., Humboldt, TN 38343/901-784-5742
McMillan Rifle Barrels, P.O. Box 3427, Bryan, TX 77805/409-690-3456; FAX: 409-690-0156
MCS, Inc., 34 Delmar Dr., Brookfield, CT 06804/203-775-1013; FAX: 203-775-9462
MEC, Inc., 715 South St., Mayville, WI 53050/414-387-4500; FAX: 414-387-5802
MEC-Gar S.R.L., Via Madonnina 64, Gardone V.T., Brescia, ITALY 25063/39-30-8912687; FAX: 39-30-8910065 (U.S. importer—MEC-Gar U.S.A., Inc.)
MEC-Gar U.S.A., Inc., Box 112, 500B Monroe Turnpike, Monroe, CT 06468/203-635-8662; FAX: 203-635-8662
Merkel Freres, Strasse 7 October, 10, Suhl, GERMANY (U.S. importer—GSI, Inc.)
Metro Rod & Reel, 236 S.E. Grand Ave., Portland, OR 97214/503-232-3193
Meydag, Peter, 12114 East 16th, Tulsa, OK 74128/918-437-1928
Miclean, Bill, 499 Theta Ct., San Jose, CA 95123/408-224-1445
Midwestern Shooters Supply, Inc., 150 Main St., Lomira, WI 53048/414-269-4995
Mike's Crosman Service, 5995 Renwood Dr., Winston-Salem, NC 27106/910-922-1031
Mill Creek Sport Center, 8180 Main St., Dexter, MI 48104/313-426-3445
Miller Arms, Inc., P.O. Box 260 Purl St., St. Onge, SD 57779/605-642-5160; FAX: 605-642-5160
Miller's Sport Shop, 2 Summit View Dr., Mountaintop, PA 18707/717-474-6931
Millers Gun Shop, 915 23rd St., Gulfport, MS 39501/601-684-1765
Milliken's Gun Shop, Rt. 2, Box 167, Elm Grove, WV 26003/304-242-0827
Mines Gun Shack, Rt. 4 Box 4623, Tullahoma, TN 37388/615-455-1414
Mirador Optical Corp., P.O. Box 11614, Marina Del Rey, CA 90295-7614/310-821-5587; FAX: 310-305-0386
Miroku, B.C./Daly, Charles (See U.S. importer—Bell's Legendary Country Wear; U.S. distributor—Outdoor Sports Headquarters, Inc.)
Mitchell Arms, Inc., 3400-I W. MacArthur Blvd., Santa Ana, CA 92704/714-957-5711; FAX: 714-957-5732
MKS Supply, Inc., 174 S. Mulberry St., Mansfield, OH 44902/419-522-8330; FAX: 513-522-8330
Mo's Competitor Supplies (See MCS, Inc.)
Moates Sport Shop, Bob, 10418 Hull St. Rd., Midlothian, VA 23112/804-276-2293
Modern Guncraft, 148 N. Branford Rd., Wallingford, CT 06492/203-265-1015
Modern MuzzleLoading, Inc., 234 Airport Rd., P.O. Box 130, Centerville, IA 52544/515-856-2626; FAX: 515-856-2628
Moneymaker Guncraft Corp., 1420 Military Ave., Omaha, NE 68131/402-556-0226
Montana Armory, Inc., 100 Centennial Dr., Big Timber, MT 59011/406-932-4353
Montana Gun Works, 3017 10th Ave. S., Great Falls, MT 59405/406-761-4346
Moore & Co., Wm. Larkin, 31360 Via Colinas, Suite 109, Westlake Village, CA 91361/818-889-1986
Moreau, Gunsmith, Pete, 1807 S. Erie, Bay City, MI 48706/517-893-7106
Morini (See U.S. importers—Mandall Shooting Shpplies, Inc.; Nygord Precision Products)
Morrison Gun Shop, Middle Rd., Bradford, ME 04410/207-327-1116
Mossberg (See page 503)
Mowrey Gun Works, P.O. Box 246, Waldron, IN 46182/317-525-6181; FAX: 317-525-6181
Mueschke Manufacturing Co., 1003 Columbia St., Houston, TX 77008/713-869-7073
Mulvey's Marine & Sport Shop, 994 E. Broadway, Monticello, NY 12701/914-794-2000

N

N.A. Guns, Inc., 10220 Florida Blvd., Baton Rouge, LA 70815/504-272-3620
Nagel Gun Shop, Inc., 6201 San Pedro Ave., San Antonio, TX 78216/210-342-5420; 210-342-9893
Nationwide Sports Distributors, Inc., 70 James Way, Southampton, PA 18966/215-322-2050, 800-355-3006; FAX: 702-358-2093
Navy Arms Co., 689 Bergen Blvd., Ridgefield, NJ 07657/201-945-2500; FAX: 201-945-6859
NCP Products, Inc., 721 Maryland Ave. SW, Canton, OH 44710
Nelson's Engine Shop, 620 State St., Cedar Falls, IA 50613/319-266-4497
Nesika Bay Precision, 22239 Big Valley Rd., Poulsbo, WA 98370/206-697-3830
Nevada Air Guns, 3297 "J" Las Vegas Blvd. N., Las Vegas, NV 89115/702-643-8532
Nevada Cartridge Co., 44 Montgomery St., Suite 500, San Francisco, CA 94104/415-925-9394; FAX: 415-925-9396
New Advantage Arms Corp., 2843 N. Alvernon Way, Tucson, AZ 85712/602-881-7444; FAX: 602-323-0949
New England Arms Co., Box 278, Lawrence Lane, Kittery Point, ME 03905/207-439-0593; FAX: 207-439-6726
New England Firearms, 60 Industrial Rowe, Gardner, MA 01440/508-632-9393; FAX: 508-632-2300
Newby, Stewart, Gunsmith, Main & Cross Streets, Newburgh, Ontario CANADA K0K 2S0/613-378-6613
Nicholson's Gunsmithing, 35 Hull St., Shelton, CT 06484/203-924-5635
Nikon, Inc., 1300 Walt Whitman Rd., Melville, NY 11747/516-547-8623; FAX: 516-547-0309
Noreen, Peter H., 5075 Buena Vista Dr., Belgrade, MT 59714/406-586-7383
Norinco, 7A, Yun Tan N Beijing, CHINA (U.S. importers—Century International Arms, Inc.; Interarms)
Norma Precision AB (See U.S. importers—Dynamit Nobel-RWS Inc.; Paul Co. Inc., The)
Norman Custom Gunstocks, Jim, 14281 Cane Rd., Valley Center, CA 92082/619-749-6252
Norrell Arms, John, 2608 Grist Mill Rd., Little Rock, AR 72207/501-225-7864
North American Arms, Inc., 2150 South 950 East, Provo, UT 84606-6285/800-821-5783, 801-374-9990; FAX: 801-374-9998
Northern Precision Airguns, 1161 Grove St., Tawas City, MI 48763/517-362-6949
Northern Virginia Gun Works, Inc., 7518-K Fullerton Road, Springfield, VA 22153/703-644-6504
Northland Sport Center, 1 Mile W. on U.S. Rt. 2, Bagley, MN 56621/218-694-2464
Northwest Arms Service, 720 S. Second St., Atwood, KS 67730/913-626-3700
Nu-Line Guns, Inc., 1053 Caulks Hill Rd., Harvester, MO 63304/314-441-4500; FAX: 314-447-5018
Nusbaum Enterprises, Inc., 1364 Ridgewood Dr., Mobile, AL 36608/205-344-1079
Nygord Precision Products, P.O. Box 8394, La Crescenta, CA 91224/818-352-3027; FAX: 818-352-3378

O

Old Dominion Engravers, 100 Progress Drive, Lynchburg, VA 24502/804-237-4450
Old Western Scrounger, Inc., 12924 Hwy. A-l2, Montague, CA 96064/916-459-5445; FAX: 916-459-3944
Olympic Arms, 620-626 Old Pacific Hwy. SE, Olympic, WA 98503/360-456-3471; FAX: 360-491-3447
On Target Gunshop, Inc., 6984 West Main St., Kalamazoo, MI 49009/616-375-4570
Oregon Arms, Inc., 790 Stevens St., Medford, OR 97504-6746/503-560-4040
Orvis Co., The, Rt. 7, Manchester, VT 05254/802-362-3622 ext. 283; FAX: 802-362-3525
Oshman's Sporting Goods, Inc., 975 Gessner, Houston, TX 77024/713-467-1155
Ott's Gun Service, Rt. 2, Box 169A, Atmore, AL 36502/205-862-2588
Outdoor America Store, 1925 N. MacArthur Blvd., Oklahoma City, OK 73127/405-789-0051
Outdoorsman Sporting Goods Co., The, 1707 Radner Ct., Geneva, IL 60134/708-232-9518
Outdoorsman, The, Village West Shopping Center, Fargo, ND 58103/701-282-0131
Outpost, The, 2451 E. Maple Rapids Rd., Eureka, MI 48833/517-224-9562
Ozark Shooters, Inc., P.O. Box 6518, Branson, MO 65616/417-587-3093

P

Pace Marketing, Inc., P.O. Box 2039, Stuart, FL 34995/407-223-2189; FAX: 407-286-9547
Pachmayr, Ltd., 1875 S. Mountain Ave., Monrovia, CA 91016/818-357-7771, 800-423-9704; FAX: 818-358-7251
Pacific International Service Co., Mountain Way, P.O. Box 3, Janesville, CA 96114/916-253-2218

WARRANTY SERVICE CENTER DIRECTORY

Paducah Shooters Supply, Inc., 3919 Cairo St., Paducah, KY 42001/502-443-3758
Para-Ordnance Mfg., Inc., 3411 McNicoll Ave., Unit 14, Scarborough, Ont. M1V 2V6, CANADA/416-297-7855; FAX: 416-297-1289 (U.S. importer—Para-Ordnance, Inc.)
Para-Ordnance, Inc., 1919 NE 45th St., Ft. Lauderdale, FL 33308
Pardini Armi Srl, Via Italica 154, 55043 Lido Di Camaiore Lu, ITALY/584-90121; FAX: 584-90122 (U.S. importers—MCS, Inc.; Nygord Precision Products)
Pasadena Gun Center, 206 E. Shaw, Pasadena, TX 77506/713-472-0417; FAX: 713-472-1322
Paul Co., The, 27385 Pressonville Rd., Wellsville, KS 66092/913-883-4444; FAX: 913-883-2525
Pedersoli Davide & C., Via Artigiani 57, Gardone V.T., Brescia, ITALY 25063/030-8912402; FAX: 030-8911019 (U.S. importers—Beauchamp & Son, Inc.; Cabela's; Cape Outfitters; Dixie Gun Works; EMF Co., Inc.; Navy Arms Co.; Taylor's & Co., Inc.)
Pederson Co., C.R., 2717 S. Pere Marquette, Ludington, MI 49431/616-843-2061
Pekin Gun & Sporting Goods, 1304 Derby St., Pekin, IL 61554/309-347-6060
Pentax Corp., 35 Inverness Dr. E., Englewood, CO 80112/303-799-8000; FAX: 303-790-1131
Perazzi m.a.p. S.P.A., Via Fontanelle 1/3, 1-25080 Botticino Mattina, ITALY (U.S. importer—Perazzi USA, Inc.)
Perazzi USA, Inc., 1207 S. Shamrock Ave., Monrovia, CA 91016/818-303-0068; FAX: 818-303-2081
Peregrine Sporting Arms, Inc., 14155 Brighton Rd., Brighton, CO 80601/303-654-0850
Perry's Gunshop, P.O. Box 10, 21 E. Third St., Wendell, NC 27591/919-365-4200
Pete's Gun Shop, 31 Columbia St., Adams, MA 01220/413-743-0780
Peters Stahl GmbH, Stettiner Strasse 42, D-33106 Paderborn, GERMANY/05251-750025; FAX: 05251-75611 (U.S. importers—Harris-McMillan Gunworks; Olympic Arms)
Phillips, D.J., Gunsmith, Rt. 1, N31-W22087 Shady Ln., Pewaukee, WI 53072/414-691-2165
Phoenix Armoury, Inc., 248 Miami Ave., Norristown, PA 19403/215-539-0733
Phoenix Arms, 1420 S. Archibald Ave., Ontario, CA 91761/909-947-4843; FAX: 909-947-6798
PHOXX Shooters Supply, 5807 Watt Ave., N. Highlands, CA 95660/800-280-8668
Pietta (See U.S. importers—Navy Arms Co.; Taylor's & Co., Inc.)
Pintos Gun Shop, 827 N. Central #102, Kent, WA 98032/206-859-6333
Pioneer Arms Co., 355 Lawrence Rd., Broomall, PA 19008/215-356-5203
Piotti (See U.S. importer—Moore & Co., Wm. Larkin)
Plaza Gunworks, Inc., 983 Gasden Highway, Birmingham, AL 35235/205-836-6206
Ponsness/Warren, P.O. Box 8, Rathdrum, ID 83858/208-687-2231; FAX: 208-687-2233
Poor Borch's, Inc., 1204 E. College Dr., Marshall, MN 56258/507-532-4880
Potter Gunsmithing, 13960 Boxhorn Dr., Muskego, WI 53150/414-425-4830
Powell & Son (Gunmakers) Ltd., William, 35-37 Carrs Lane, Birmingham B4 7SX ENGLAND/21-643-0689; FAX: 21-631-3504 (U.S. importer—The William Powell Agency)
Powell Agency, William, The, 22 Circle Dr., Bellmore, NY 11710/516-679-1158
Prairie River Arms, 1220 N. Sixth St., Princeton, IL 61356/815-875-1616; FAX: 815-875-1402
Precision Airgun Sales, Inc., 5139 Warrensville Center Rd., Maple Hts., OH 44137-1906/216-587-5005
Precision Arms & Gunsmithing Ltd., Hwy. 27 & King Road Box 809, Nobleton, Ontario, CANADA L0G 1N0/416-859-0965
Precision Gun Works, 4717 State Rd. 44, Oshkosh, WI 54904/414-233-2274
Precision Gunsmithing, 2723 W. 6th St., Amarillo, TX 79106/806-376-7223
Precision Pellet, 1016 Erwin Dr., Joppa, MD 21085/410-679-8179
Precision Reloading, Inc., P.O. Box 122, Stafford Springs, CT 06076/203-684-7979; FAX: 203-684-6788
Precision Sales International, Inc., P.O. Box 1776, Westfield, MA 01086/413-562-5055; FAX: 413-562-5056
Precision Small Arms, 155 Carlton Rd., Charlottesville, VA 22902/804-293-6124; FAX: 804-295-0780
Precision Sport Optics, 15571 Producer Lane, Unit G, Huntington Beach, CA 92649/714-891-1309; FAX: 714-892-6920
Preuss Gun Shop, 4545 E. Shepherd, Clovis, CA 93612/209-299-6248
Professional Armaments, Inc., 3695 South Redwood Rd., West Valley City, UT 84119/801-975-7422

Q

Quad City Gun Repair, 220 N. Second St., Eldridge, IA 52748/319-285-4153
Quality Arms, Inc., Box 19477, Dept. GD, Houston, TX 77224/713-870-8377; FAX: 713-870-8524
Quality Firearms of Idaho, Inc., 114 13th Ave. S., Nampa, ID 83651/208-466-1631
Quality Parts Co./Bushmaster Firearms, 999 Roosevelt Trail, Bldg. 3, Windham, ME 04062/800-998-7928, 207-892-2005; FAX: 207-892-8068

R

R&R Shooters Supply, W6553 North Rd., Mauston, WI 53948/608-847-4562
R.D.P. Tool Co., Inc., 49162 McCoy Ave., East Liverpool, OH 43920/216-385-5129
R.L. "Skeet" Hill Gun Shop, 209½ Raymond Street, P.O. Box 457, Verona, MS 38879/601-566-8353
Rajo Corporation, 2106 W. Franklin St., Evansville, IN 47712/812-422-6945
Ralph's Gun Shop, 200 Fourth St., South, Niverville, Manitoba, CANADA R0A 1E0/204-338-4581
Ram-Line, Inc., 545 Thirty-One Rd., Grand Junction, CO 81504/303-434-4500; FAX: 303-434-4004
Randy's Gun Repair, P.O. Box 106, 231 Hierlihy High, Tabustinac, N.B. CANADA E0C 2A0/506-779-4768
Ranging, Inc., Routes 5 & 20, East Bloomfield, NY 14443/716-657-6161; FAX: 716-657-5405
Rapids Gun Shop, 7811 Buffalo Ave., Niagara Falls, NY 14304/716-283-7873
Ravell Ltd., 289 Diputacion St., 08009, Barcelona SPAIN
Ray's Gunsmith Shop, 3199 Elm Ave., Grand Junction, CO 81504/970-434-6162
Ray's Liquor and Sporting Goods, 1956 Solano St., Box 677, Corning, CA 96021/916-824-5625
Ray's Rod & Reel Service, 414 Pattie St., Wichita, KS 67211/316-267-9462
Ray's Sport Shop, Inc., 559 Route 22, North Plainfield, NJ 07060/908-561-4400
Ray's Sporting Goods, 730 Singleton Blvd., Dallas, TX 75212/214-747-7916
RCBS, Div. of Blount, Inc., 605 Oro Dam Blvd., Oroville, CA 95965/800-533-5000, 916-533-5191; FAX: 916-533-1647
Red's Gunsmithing, P.O. Box 1251, Chickaloon, AK 99674/907-745-4500
Redding Reloading Equipment, 1089 Starr Rd., Cortland, NY 13045/607-753-3331; FAX: 607-756-8445
Redfield, Inc., 5800 E. Jewell Ave., Denver, CO 80227/303-757-6411; FAX: 303-756-2338
Reliable Gun & Tackle, Ltd., 3227 Fraser St., Vancouver, British Columbia CANADA V5V 4B8/604-874-4710
Reloading Center, 515 W. Main St., Burley, ID 83318/208-678-5053
Remington (See page 503)
Reynold's Gun Shop, Inc., 3502A S. Broadway, Tyler, TX 75702/903-592-1531
Reynolds Gun Shop, 314 N. Western Ave., Peoria, IL 61606/309-674-5790
Richland Gun Shop, 207 Park St., Box 645, Richland, PA 17087/717-866-4246
Richmond Gun Shop, 517 E. Main St., Richmond, VA 23219/804-644-7207
Rigby & Co., John, 66 Great Suffolk St., London SE1 OBU, ENGLAND
River Bend Sport Shop, 230 Grand Seasons Dr., Waupaca, WI 54981/715-258-3583
Rizzini, Battista, Via 2 Giugno, 7/7Bis-25060 Marcheno (Brescia), ITALY (U.S. importers—Alessandri & Son, Lou; New England Arms Co.)
Rizzini, F.LLI (See U.S. importers—Moore & Co. Wm. Larkin; New England Arms Co.)
Robinson's Sporting Goods, Ltd., 1307 Broad St., Victoria, British Columbia CANADA V8W 2A8/604-385-3429
Rocking S Gun Shop, 316 VC Ranches, Hwy. 287, P.O. Box 1469, Ennis, MT 59729/406-682-5229
Rocky Mountain Arms, Inc., 600 S. Sunset, Unit C, Longmont, CO 80501/303-768-8522; FAX: 303-678-8766
Ron's Gun Repair, 1212 Benson Road, Sioux Falls, SD 57104/605-338-7398
Rossi S.A., Amadeo, Rua: Amadeo Rossi, 143, Sao Leopoldo, RS, BRAZIL 93030-220/051-592-5566 (U.S. importer—Interarms)
Ruko Products, Inc., 2245 Kenmore Ave., No. 102, Buffalo, NY 14207/716-874-2707; FAX: 905-826-1353
Rusk Gun Shop, Inc., 6904 Watts Rd., Madison, WI 53719/608-274-8740
Russell's Sporting Goods, 8228 Macleod Trail SE, Calgary, Alberta, CANADA T2M 2B8/403-276-9222
Rutko Corp. d/b/a Stonewall Range, 100 Ken-Mar Dr., Broadview Heights, OH 44147/216-526-0029
RWS (See U.S. importer—Dynamit Nobel-RWS, Inc.)

S

S.E.M. Gun Works, 3204 White Horse Rd., Greenville, SC 29611/803-295-2948
S.K. Guns, Inc., 302 25th St. South, Suite A, Fargo, ND 58103/701-293-4867; FAX: 701-232-0001
Sabatti S.R.L., via Alessandro Volta 90, 25063 Gardone V.T., Brescia, ITALY/030-8912207-831312; FAX: 030-8912059 (U.S. importer—E.A.A. Corp.)
Safari Arms/SWG (See Olympic Arms)
Sako Ltd., P.O. Box 149, SF-11101, Riihimaki, FINLAND (U.S. importer—Stoeger Industries)
Sams Gunsmithing, David, 225 Front St., Lititz, PA 17543/717-626-0021
San Marco (See U.S. importers—Cape Outfitters; EMF Co., Inc.)
Sanders Custom Gun Service, 2358 Tyler Ln., Louisville, KY 40205/502-454-3338
Sanders Custom Gun Shop, P.O. Box 5967, 2031 Bloomingdale Ave., Augusta, GA 30906/706-798-5220
Sanders Gun Shop, 3001 Fifth St., P.O. Box 4181, Meridian, MS 39301/601-485-5301
Saskatoon Gunsmith Shoppe, Ltd., 2310 Avenue C North, Saskatoon, Saskachewan, CANADA S7L 5X5/306-244-2023
Sauer (See U.S. importer—Paul Co., The)
Savage Arms, Inc., 100 Springdale Rd., Westfield, MA 01085/413-568-7001; FAX: 413-562-7764
Saville Iron Co. (See Greenwood Precision)
Scalzo's Sporting Goods, 1520 Farm to Market Road, Endwell, NY 13760/607-746-7586
Scattergun Technologies, Inc., 518 3rd Ave. S., Nashville, TN 37202/615-254-1441; FAX: 615-254-1449
Scharch Mfg., Inc., 10325 Co. Rd. 120, Unit C, Salida, CO 81201/719-539-7242; FAX: 719-539-3021
Schmidt & Bender, Inc., Brook Rd., P.O. Box 134, Meriden, NH 03770/603-469-3565, 800-468-3450; FAX: 603-469-3471
Schultheis Sporting Goods, 8 Main St., Arkport, NY 14807/607-295-7485
Sea Gull Marina, 1400 Lake, Two Rivers, WI 54241/414-794-7533
Seecamp Co., Inc., L.W., P.O. Box 255, New Haven, CT 06502/203-877-3429
Selin Gunsmith, Ltd., Del, 2803 23rd Street, Vernon, British Columbia, CANADA V1T 4Z5/604-545-6413
SGS Importers International, Inc., 1750 Brielle Ave., Unit B1, Wanamassa, NJ 07712/908-493-0302; FAX: 908-493-0301
Shaler Eagle, 102 Arrow Wood, Jonesbrough, TN 37659/615-753-7620
Shamburg's Wholesale Spt. Gds., 403 Frisco Ave., Clinton, OK 73601/405-323-0209
Shapel's Gun Shop, 1708 N. Liberty, Boise, ID 83704/208-375-6159
Sharp (See U.S. importer—Great Lakes Airguns)
Sharps Arms Co., Inc., C. (See Montana Armory, Inc.)
Shepherd Scope Ltd., Box 189, Waterloo, NE 68069/402-779-2424; FAX: 402-779-4010
Sheridan USA, Inc., Austin, P.O. Box 577, 36 Haddam Quarter Rd., Durham, CT 06422/203-349-1772; FAX: 203-349-1771
Shiloh Rifle Mfg., 201 Centennial Dr., Big Timber, MT 59011/406-932-4454; FAX: 406-932-5627
Shockley, Harold, 2204 E. Farmington Road, Hanna City, IL 61536/309-565-4524
Shooters Supply, 1120 Tieton Dr., Yakima, WA 98902/509-482-1181; FAX: 509-575-0315
Shooting Gallery, The, 249 Seneca, Weirton, WV 26062/304-723-3298
Siegle's Gunshop, Inc., 508 W. MacArthur Blvd., Oakland, CA 94609/415-655-8789
Sievert's Guns 4107 W. Northern, Pueblo, CO 81005/719-564-0035
SIG, CH-8212 Neuhausen, SWITZERLAND (U.S. importer—Mandall Shooting Supplies, Inc.)
SIG-Sauer (See U.S. importer—Sigarms, Inc.)
Sigarms, Inc., Corporate Park, Exeter, NH 03833/603-772-2302; FAX: 603-772-9082
Sile Distributors, Inc., 7 Centre Market Pl., New York, NY 10013/212-925-4111; FAX: 212-925-3149
Sillman, Hal, Associated Services, 1514 NE 205 Terrace, Miami, FL 33179/305-651-4450
Simmons Enterprises, Ernie, 709 East Elizabethtown Rd., Manheim, PA 17545/717-664-4040
Simmons Gun Repair, 700 S. Rodgers Rd., Olathe, KS 66062/913-782-3131
Simmons Outdoor Corp., 2120 Killearney Way, Tallahassee, FL 32308-3402/904-878-5100; FAX: 904-878-0300
Sipes Gun Shop, 7415 Asher Ave., Little Rock, AR 72204/501-565-8480
SKB Arms Co., C.P.O. Box 1401, Tokyo, JAPAN (U.S. importer—G.U., Inc.)
Skeet's Gun Shop, Rt. 3, Box 235, Tahlequah, OK 74464/918-456-4749
Skip's Gunshop, 3 Pleasant St., Bristol, NH 03222/603-744-3100
Smith & Smith Gun Shop, Inc., 2589 Oscar Johnson Drive, North Charleston, SC 29405/803-744-2024
Smith & Wesson (See page 503)
Smith's Lawn & Marine Svc., 9100 Main St., Clarence, NY 14031/716-633-7868
Societa Armi Bresciane Srl. (See U.S. importer—Gamba, USA)
Sodak Sport & Bait, 850 South Hwy 281, Aberdeen, SD 57401/605-225-2737
Solvay Home & Outdoor Center, 102 First St., Solvay, NY 13209/315-468-6285
Southland Gun Works, Inc., 1134 Hartsville Rd., Darlington, SC 29532/803-393-6291
Southwest Airguns, 3311 Ryan St., Lake Charles, LA 70601/318-474-6038
Southwest Shooters Supply, Inc., 1940 Linwood Blvd., Oklahoma City, OK 73106/405-235-4476; FAX: 405-235-7022
Specialty Shooters Supply, Inc., 3325 Griffin Rd., Suite 9mm, Fort Lauderdale, FL 33317
Speer Products, Div. of Blount, Inc., P.O. Box 856, Lewiston, ID 83501/208-746-2351; FAX: 208-746-2915
Sporting Arms Mfg., Inc., 801 Hall Ave., Littlefield, TX 79339/806-385-5665; FAX: 806-385-3394
Sports Mart, The, 828 Ford St., Ogdensburg, NY 13669/315-393-2865
Sports Shop, The, 8055 Airline Highway, Baton Rouge, LA 70815/504-927-2600
Sports World, Inc., 5800 S. Lewis Ave., Suite 154, Tulsa, OK 74105/918-742-4027
Sports World, Route 52, Liberty, NY 12754/914-292-3077
Sportsman's Center, U.S. Hwy. 130, Box 731, Bordentown, NJ 08505/609-298-5300
Sportsman's Depot, 644 Miami St., Urban, OH 43078/513-653-4429
Sportsman's Haven, 14695 E. Pike Rd., Cambridge, OH 43725/614-432-7243
Sportsman's Paradise Gunsmith, 640 Main St., Pineville, LA 71360/318-443-6041

WARRANTY SERVICE CENTER DIRECTORY

Sportsman's Shop, 101 W. Main St., New Holland, PA 17557/717-354-4311
Sportsmen's Exchange & Western Gun Traders, Inc., 560 South C St., Oxnard, CA 93030/805-483-1917
Sportsmen's Repair Ctr., Inc., 106 S. High St., Box 134, Columbus Groves, OH 45830/419-659-5818
Spradlin's, 113 Arthur St., Pueblo, CO 81004/719-543-9462
Springfield, Inc., 420 W. Main St., Geneseo, IL 61254/309-944-5631; FAX: 309-944-3676
SSK Industries, 721 Woodvue Lane, Wintersville, OH 43952/614-264-0176; FAX: 614-264-2257
Stalwart Corporation, P.O. Box 357, Pocatello, ID 83204/208-232-7899; FAX: 208-232-0815
Stan's Gun Repair, RR #2 Box 48, Westbrook, MN 56183-9521/507-274-5649
Star Bonifacio Echeverria S.A., Torrekva 3, Eibar, SPAIN 20600/43-107340; FAX: 43-101524 (U.S. importer—Interarms)
Star Machine Works, 418 10th Ave., San Diego, CA 92101/619-232-3216
Starnes, Ken, 32900 SW Laurelview Rd., Hillsboro, OR 97123/503-628-0705
Steyr Mannlicher AG, Mannlicherstrasse 1, P.O.B. 1000, A-4400 Steyr, AUSTRIA/0043-7252-896-0; FAX: 0043-7252-68621 (U.S. importer—GSI, Inc.)
Stocker's Shop, 5199 Mahoning Ave., Warren, OH 44483/216-847-9579
Stoeger (See page 503)
Stoeger Industries, 5 Mansard Ct., Wayne, NJ 07470/201-872-9500, 800-631-0722; FAX: 201-872-0722
Sundance Industries, Inc., 25163 W. Avenue Stanford, Valencia, CA 91355/805-257-4807
Surplus Center, 515 S.E. Spruce Street, Roseburg, OR 97470/503-672-4312
Survival Arms, Inc., 4500 Pine Cone Place, Cocoa, FL 32922/407-633-4880; FAX: 407-633-4975
Swarovski Optik North America Ltd., One Wholesale Way, Cranston, RI 02920/401-942-3380, 800-426-3089; FAX: 401-946-2587
Swift Instruments, Inc., 952 Dorchester Ave., Boston, MA 02125/617-436-2960; FAX: 617-436-3232
Swivel Machine Works, Inc., 167 Cherry St., Suite 286, Milford, CT 06460/203-926-1840; FAX: 203-874-9212

T

T.J.'s Firing Line Gunsmith, 692-A Peoria Street, Aurora, CO 80011/303-363-1911
Tanfoglio S.r.l., Fratelli, via Valtrompia 39, 41, 25068 Gardone V.T., Brescia, ITALY/30-8910361; FAX: 30-8910183 (U.S. importer—E.A.A. Corp.)
Tank's Rifle Shop, P.O. Box 474, Fremont, NE 68025/402-727-1317; FAX: 402-721-2573
Tanner (See U.S. importer—Mandall Shooting Supplies, Inc.)
Tapco, Inc., 3615 Kennesaw N. Ind. Pkwy, Kennesaw, GA 30144/800554-1445; FAX: 404-425-1510
Tar-Hunt Custom Rifles, Inc., RR3, P.O. Box 572, Bloomsburg, PA 17815-9351/717-784-6368; FAX: 717-784-6368
Tasco Sales, Inc., 7600 NW 26th St., Miami, FL 33156/305-591-3670; FAX: 305-592-5895
Taurus Firearms, Inc., 16175 NW 49th Ave., Miami, FL 33014/305-624-1115; FAX: 305-623-7506
Taurus International Firearms (See U.S. importer—Taurus Firearms, Inc.)
Taylor & Vadney, Inc., 303 Central Ave., Albany, NY 12206/518-472-9183
Taylor's & Co., Inc., 304 Lenoir Dr., Winchester, VA 22603/703-722-2017; FAX: 703-722-2018
Taylor's Sporting Goods, Gene, 445 W. Gunnison Ave., Grand Junction, CO 81505/303-242-8165
Ted's Gun & Reel Repair, 311 Natchitoches St. Box 1635, W. Monroe, LA 71291/318-323-0661
Ten Ring Service, 2227 West Lou Dr., Jacksonville, FL 32216/904-724-7419
Texas Armory, P.O. Box 154906, Waco, TX 76715/817-867-6972
Texas Longhorn Arms, Inc., 5959 W. Loop South, Suite 424, Bellaire, TX 77401/713-341-0775; FAX: 713-660-0493
Theoben Engineering, Stephenson Road, St. Ives, Huntingdon, Cambs., PE17 4WJ ENGLAND/011-0480-461718
Thompson's Gunshop, Inc., 10254 84th St., Alto, MI 49302/616-891-0440
Thompson/Center (See page 503)
300 Gunsmith Service Inc., at Cherry Creek Park Shooting Center, 12500 E. Bellview Ave., Englewood, CO 80111/303-690-3300
Thunder Mountain Arms, P.O. Box 593, Oak Harbor, WA 98277/206-679-4657; FAX: 206-675-1114
Tikka (See U.S. importer—Stoeger Industries)
Time Precision, Inc., 640 Federal Rd., Brookfield, CT 06804/203-775-8343
TOZ (See Nygord Precision Products)
Traders, The, 885 E. 14th St., San Leandro, CA 94577/510-569-0555
Trading Post, The, 412 Erie St. S., Massillon, OH 44646/216-833-7761
Traditions, Inc., P.O. Box 235, Deep River, CT 06417/203-526-9555; FAX: 203-526-4564
Trester, Inc., Verne, 3604 West 16th St., Indianapolis, IN 46222/317-638-6921
Trijicon, Inc., 49385 Shafer Ave., P.O. Box 6029, Wixom, MI 48393-6029/810-960-7700; FAX: 810-960-7725

U

U.S. General Technologies, Inc., 145 Mitchell Ave., South San Francisco, CA 94080/415-634-8440; FAX: 415-634-8452
Uberti USA, Inc., 362 Limerock Rd., P.O. Box 509, Lakeville, CT 06039/203-435-8068; FAX: 203-435-8146
Uberti, Aldo, Casella Postale 43, I-25063 Gardone V.T., ITALY (U.S. importers—American Arms, Inc.; Cape Outfitters; Cimarron Arms; Dixie Gun Works; EMF Co., Inc.; Forgett Jr., Valmore J.; Navy Arms Co; Taylor's & Co., Inc.; Uberti USA, Inc.)
Ugartechea S.A., Ignacio, Chonta 26, Eibar, SPAIN 20600/43-121257; FAX: 43-121669 (U.S. importer—Mandall Shooting Supplies, Inc.)
Ultimate Accuracy, 121 John Shelton Rd., Jacksonville, AR 72076/501-985-2530
Ultra Light Arms, Inc., P.O. Box 1270, 214 Price St., Granville, WV 26505/304-599-5687; FAX: 304-599-5687
Ultralux (See U.S. importer—Keng's Firearms Specialty, Inc.)
Unertl Optical Co., Inc., John, 308 Clay Ave., P.O. Box 818, Mars, PA 16046-0818/412-625-3810
Unique Sporting Goods, 1538 Columbia St., Lorreto, PA 15940/814-674-8889
Unique/M.A.P.F., 10, Les Allees, 64700 Hendaye, FRANCE 64700/33-59 20 71 93 (U.S. importer—Nygord Precision Products)
Upper Missouri Trading Co., 304 Harold St., Crofton, NE 68730/402-388-4844
Upton's Gun Shop, 810 Croghan St., Fremont, OH 43420/419-332-1326

V

Valley Gun Shop, 7719 Harford Rd., Baltimore, MD 21234/410-668-2171
Valley Gunsmithing, John A. Foster, 619 Second St., Webster City, IA 50595/515-832-5102
Valor Corp., 5555 NW 36th Ave., Miami, FL 33142/305-633-0127; FAX: 305-634-4536
Van's Gunsmith Service, Rt. 69A, Parish, NY 13131/315-625-7251
VanBurnes Gun Shop, 2706 Sylvania Ave., Toledo, OH 43613/419-475-9526
Voere-KGH m.b.H., P.O. Box 416, A-6333 Kufstein, Tirol, AUSTRIA/0043-5372-62547; FAX: 0043-5372-65752 (U.S. importers—JagerSport, Ltd.)
Volquartsen Custom Ltd., RR 1, Box 33A, P.O. Box 271, Carroll, IA 51401/712-792-4238; FAX: 712-792-2542

W

Walker Arms Co., Inc., 499 County Rd. 820, Selma, AL 36701/334-872-6231
Wallace & Cockrell Gunsmiths, Inc., 8240 I-30 West, Fort Worth, TX 76108/817-246-4622
Wallace Gatlin Gun Repair, 140 Gatlin Rd., Oxford, AL 36203/205-831-6993
Walther GmbH, Carl, B.P. 4325, D-89033 Ulm, GERMANY (U.S. importer—Interarms)
Warren's Sports Hdqts., 240 W. Main St., Washington, NC 27889/919-946-0960
Way It Was Sporting, The, 620 Chestnut Street, Moorestown, NJ 08057/609-231-0111
Weapon Works, The, 7017 N. 19th Ave., Phoenix, AZ 85021/602-995-3010
Weatherby (See page 503)
Weaver Scope Repair Service, 1121 Larry Mahan Dr., Suite B, El Paso, TX 79925/915-593-1005
Webley and Scott Ltd., Frankley Industrial Park, Tay Rd., Rubery, Rednal, Birmingham B45 0PA, ENGLAND/011-021-453-1864; FAX: 021-457-7846 (U.S. importer—Beeman Precision Airguns, Inc.)
Weihrauch KG, Hermann, Industriestrasse 11, 8744 Mellrichstadt, GERMANY/09776-497-498 (U.S. importers—Beeman Precision Airguns; E.A.A. Corp.)
Welsh, Bud, 80 New Road, E. Amherst, NY 14051/716-688-6344
Wessel Ring Service, 4000 E. 9-Mile Rd., Warren, MI 48091/313-756-2660
Wessinger Custom Guns & Engraving, 268 Limestone Rd., Chapin, SC 29036/803-345-5677
Wesson Firearms Co., Inc., Maple Tree Industrial Center, Rt. 20, Wilbraham, Rd./Palmer, MA 01069
West Gate Gunsports, Inc., 10116 175th Street, Edmonton, Alberta, CANADA T5S 1A1/403-489-9633
West Luther Gun Repair, R.R. #1, Conn, Ontario, CANADA N0G 1N0/519-848-6260
Westley Richards & Co., 40 Grange Rd., Birmingham, ENGLAND B29 6AR/010-214722953 (U.S. importer—Cape Outfitters)
Wheeler Gun Shop, C., 1908 George Washington Way Bldg. F, Richland, WA 99352/509-946-4634
White Dog Gunsmithing, 62 Central Ave., Ilion, NY 13357/315-894-6211
White Shooting Systems, Inc., 25 E. Hwy. 40, Box 330-12, Roosevelt, UT 84066/801-722-3085; FAX: 801-722-3054
Wholesale Sports, 12505 97 St., Edmonton, Alberta, CANADA T5G 1Z8/403-426-4417; 403-477-3737
Wichita Arms, Inc., 923 E. Gilbert, P.O. Box 11371, Wichita, KS 67211/316-265-0661; FAX: 316-265-0760
Wichita Guncraft, Inc., 4607 Barnett Rd., Wichita Falls, TX 76310/817-692-5622
Wild West Guns, Inc., 7521 Old Seward Highway #A, Anchorage, Alaska 99518/907-344-4500; FAX: 907-344-4005
Wildey, Inc., P.O. Box 475, Brookfield, CT 06804/203-355-9000; FAX: 203-354-7759
Wilkinson Arms, 26884 Pearl Rd., Parma, ID 83660/208-722-6771; FAX: 208-722-5197
Will's Gun Shop, 5603 N. Hubbard Lake Rd., Spruce, MI 48762/517-727-2500
Willborn Outdoors & Feed, 505 Main Avenue N.W., Cullman, AL 35055/205-737-9595
William's Gun Shop, Ben, 1151 S. Cedar Ridge, Duncanville, TX 75137/214-780-1807
Williams Gun Sight & Outfitters, 7389 Lapeer Rd., Rt. #1, Davison, MI 48423/313-653-2131, 800-530-9028; FAX: 313-658-2140
Williams Gunsmithing, 4985 Cole Rd., Saginaw, MI 48601/517-777-1240
Williamson Precision Gunsmithing, 117 W. Pipeline, Hurst, TX 76053/817-285-0064; FAX: 817-285-0064
Winchester (See page 503)
Windsor Gun Shop, 8410 Southeastern Ave., Indianapolis, IN 46239/317-862-2512
Wiseman and Co., Bill, P.O. Box 3427, Bryan, TX 77805/409-690-3456; FAX: 409-690-0156
Wisner's Gun Shop, Inc., 287 NW Chehalis Ave., Chehalis, WA 98532/206-748-8942; FAX: 206-748-7011
Wolf Custom Gunsmithing, Gregory, c/o Albright's Gun Shop, 36 E. Dover St., Easton, MD 21601/410-820-8811
Wolfer Brothers, Inc., 1701 Durham, Houston, TX 77007/713-869-7640
Woodman's Sporting Goods, 223 Main Street, Norway, ME 04268/207-743-6602
World Class Airguns, 2736 Morningstar Dr., Indianapolis, IN 46229/317-897-5548
Wortner Gun Works, Ltd., 433 Queen St., Chatham, Ont., CANADA N7M 5K5/519-352-0924
Wright's Hardwood Gunstock Blanks, 8540 SE Kane Rd., Gresham, OR 97080/503-666-1705
Wyoming Armory, Inc., Box 28, Farson, WY 82932/307-273-5556

Y

Ye Olde Blk Powder Shop, 994 W. Midland Rd., Auburn, MI 48611/517-662-2271; FAX: 512-662-2666

Z

Zabala Hermanos S.A., P.O. Box 97, Eibar, SPAIN 20600/43-768085, 43-768076; FAX: 43-768201 (U.S. importer—American Arms, Inc.)
Zanes Gun Rack, 4167 N. High St., Columbus, OH 43214/614-263-0369
Zanoletti, Pietro, Via Monte Gugielpo, 4, I-25063 Gardone V.T., ITALY (U.S. importer—Mandall Shooting Supplies, Inc.)
Zeiss Optical, Carl, 1015 Commerce St., Petersburg, VA 23803/804-861-0033; FAX: 804-733-4024

Warranty Service Centers

■BE=Benjamin ■BR=Browning ■CR=Crosman ■MO=Mossberg ■RE=Remington ■ST=Stoeger ■SW=Smith & Wesson ■TC=Thompson/Center ■WN=Winchester ■WE=Weatherby

SERVICE CENTER	CITY	BE	BR	CR	MO	RE	ST	SW	TC	WN	WE
ALABAMA											
B&W Gunsmithing	Cullman					●					
Dubbs, Gunsmith, Dale R.	Seminole					●					
Hal's Gun Supply	Cullman	●									
Nusbaum Enterprises, Inc.	Mobile				●	●					
Ott's Gun Service	Atmore	●				●					
Plaza Gunworks, Inc.	Birmingham					●			●		
Walker Arms Co., Inc.	Selma		●		●	●		●	●	●	
Wallace Gatlin Gun	Oxford					●				●	
Willborn Outdoors & Feed	Cullman										
ALASKA											
Down Under Gunsmiths	Fairbanks	●	●								●
Red's Gunsmithing	Chickaloon				●	●					
Wild West Guns, Inc.	Anchorage								●	●	
ARIZONA											
Dave's Airgun Service	Tempe	●									
Don's Sport Shop, Inc.	Scottsdale		●	●		●					
Jensen's Custom Ammunition	Tucson		●			●			●	●	
Joe's Gun Shop	Phoenix			●							
Weapon Works, The	Phoenix										
ARKANSAS											
Broadway Arms	North Little Rock					●				●	
Gun Exchange, Inc.	Little Rock				●	●		●			
Jim's Trading Post	Pine Bluff	●									
Sipes Gun Shop	Little Rock	●									
CALIFORNIA											
Air Guns Unlimited	La Puente	●									
Air Venture Air Guns	Bellflower	●	●								
Airguns International	Santa Rosa	●	●								
Argonaut Gun Shop	Modesto										
Bain & Davis	San Gabriel				●	●					
Beeman Precision Arms, Inc.	Santa Rosa	●									
Bolsa Gunsmithing	Westminster		●		●	●					
Bridge Sportsman's Ctr.	Paso Robles					●					
Cal's Customs	Fallbrook					●					

SERVICE CENTER	CITY	BE	BR	CR	MO	RE	ST	SW	TC	WN	WE
Duncan's Gunworks	San Marcos										●
Grundman's	Rio Dell					●					
Gunshop, Inc., The	Lancaster		●		●	●				●	●
Huntington Sportsman's Store	Oroville		●		●	●				●	
Imbert & Smithers, Inc.	San Carlos		●			●				●	
J&G Gunsmithing	Roseville					●					
John Q's Quality Gunsmithing	Sacramento							●			
Long Beach Uniform Co., Inc.	Long Beach	●									
Mac-1	Gardena	●									
Miclean, Bill	San Jose	●									
Pacific International Service Co.	Janesville		●		●	●		●	●		
PHOXX Shooters Supply	N. Highlands		●								
Preuss Gun Shop	Clovis										
Ray's Liquor and Sporting Goods	Corning					●					
Siegle's Gunshop, Inc.	Oakland										
Sportsman's Exchange, Inc.	Oxnard					●					
Traders, The	San Leandro										
COLORADO											
Foothills Shooting Ctr.	Lakewood					●					
Gart Brothers Sporting Goods	Denver		●		●	●				●	
H&B Service, Inc.	Littleton		●		●						
Ray's Gunsmith Shop	Grand Junction										
Sievert's Guns	Pueblo										
Spradlin's	Pueblo					●				●	
Taylor's Sporting Goods, Gene	Grand Junction					●				●	
300 Gunsmith Service (Wichita Guncraft)	Englewood					●			●	●	●
T.J.'s Firing Line Gunsmith	Aurora										
CONNECTICUT											
Gunsmithing Limited	Fairfield		●			●				●	
Hoffman's Gun Center, Inc.	Newington					●					
Horchler's Gun Shop	Collinsville					●					
Keller's Co., Inc.	Burlington										
Mason, Gun & Ammo Co., Tom	Danbury							●			
Modern Guncraft	Wallingford		●		●	●				●	
Nicholson's Gunsmithing	Shelton					●					
DELAWARE											
Magnum Gun Service	Newark					●					

See page 497 for Service Center addresses.

Warranty Service Centers (cont.)

■BE=Benjamin ■BR=Browning ■CR=Crosman ■MO=Mossberg ■RE=Remington ■ST=Stoeger ■SW=Smith & Wesson ■TC=Thompson/Center ■WN=Winchester ■WE=Weatherby

SERVICE CENTER	CITY	BE	BR	CR	MO	RE	ST	SW	TC	WN	WE
FLORIDA											
Air Gun Rifle Repair	Sebring			●							
Alexander, Gunsmith, W.R.	Tallahassee										
Glades Gunworks	Naples										
Green Acres Sporting Goods, Inc.	Jacksonville		●		●	●	●	●			
Gun Doc, Inc.	Miami		●			●					
Jackson, Inc., Bill	Pinellas Park			●							
Lawsons Custom Firearms, Inc., Art	Ocala				●	●				●	
Loftin & Taylor	Jacksonville					●					
Sillman, Hal, Associated Services	Miami	●		●							
Ten Ring Service	Jacksonville							●			
GEORGIA											
Accuracy Gun Shop	Columbus		●		●	●				●	
Dorn's Outdoor Center	Macon		●		●	●				●	
Ed's Gun & Tackle Shop, Inc.	Marietta		●	●		●		●			
Franklin Sports, Inc.	Bogart		●			●					
Gun Corral, Inc.	Decatur		●								
Jordan Gun & Pawn Shop	Tifton					●					
Kick's Sport Center	Claxton					●					
Sanders Custom Gun Shop	Augusta									●	
HAWAII											
Chung, Gunsmith, Mel	Kaunakakai		●		●	●				●	
IDAHO											
Intermountain Arms & Tackle, Inc.	Meridian		●		●	●				●	●
Lolo Sporting Goods	Lewiston		●			●				●	
Quality Firearms	Nampa					●				●	
Reloading Center	Burley					●					
Shapel's Gun Shop	Boise										
ILLINOIS											
A&M Sales	North Lake	●				●					
Darnall's Gun Works	Bloomington	●				●				●	
Groenwald, John	Mundelein			●							
Henny's Airguns	Belvidere			●							
Jerry's Gunshop	Glenarm									●	
Krebs Gunsmithing	Niles					●					
Outdoorsman Sporting Goods Co.	Geneva	●									
Pekin Gun & Sporting Goods	Pekin			●							
Reynolds Gun Shop	Peoria			●							
Shockley, Harold	Hanna City			●							
INDIANA											
Airgun Centre, Ltd.	Lawrenceburg			●							
Hodson & Son Pell Gun Repair	Anderson	●		●							

SERVICE CENTER	CITY	BE	BR	CR	MO	RE	ST	SW	TC	WN	WE
Lutter, Robert E.	Ft. Wayne		●			●					
Rajo Corporation	Evansville		●			●					
Trester, Inc.	Indianapolis				●						
Windsor Gun Shop	Indianapolis			●	●						
IOWA											
Daryl's Gun Shop, Inc.	State Center					●					
Glenn's Reel & Rod Repair	Des Moines		●			●					
Jacobson's Gun Center	Story City				●						●
Nelson's Engine Shop	Cedar Falls					●					
Quad City Gun Repair	Eldridge				●	●					
Valley Gunsmithing, John A. Foster	Webster City									●	
KANSAS											
Bullseye Gun Works	Overland Park					●					
Gordon's Wigwam	Wichita		●								
Northwest Arms Service	Atwood					●					
Ray's Rod & Reel Service	Wichita		●			●					
Simmons Gun Repair	Olathe								●		
KENTUCKY											
D&J Bullet Co.	Russel					●					
Danny's Gun Repair, Inc.	Louisville					●		●			
Firearms Service Center	Louisville					●					
Garrett Gunsmiths, Inc.	Newport					●				●	
Paducah Shooters Supply, Inc.	Paducah				●						
LOUISIANA											
Atlas Gun Repair	Violet		●			●					
Boudreaux, Gunsmith	Lake Charles					●					
Burton Hardware	Sulphur					●					
Clark's Custom Guns, Inc.	Keithville							●			
Custom Gun Works	Lafayette					●					
Eversull, Ken	Boyce		●			●					
Houma Gun Works	Houma		●								
Hutchinson's Gun Repair	Pineville					●					
Martin Gun Shop	Shreveport					●					
N.A. Guns, Inc.	Baton Rouge					●					
Southwest Airguns	Lake Charles	●									
Sports Shop, The	Baton Rouge		●			●					
Sportsman's Paradise Gunsmith	Pineville					●				●	
Ted's Gun & Reel Repair	W. Monroe					●					
MAINE											
Brunswick Gun Shop	Brunswick					●		●		●	●
Morrison Gun Shop	Bradford									●	
Woodman's Sporting Goods	Norway					●					

See page 497 for Service Center addresses.

Warranty Service Centers (cont.)

■BE=Benjamin ■BR=Browning ■CR=Crosman ■MO=Mossberg ■RE=Remington ■ST=Stoeger ■SW=Smith & Wesson ■TC=Thompson/Center ■WN=Winchester ■WE=Weatherby

SERVICE CENTER	CITY	BE	BR	CR	MO	RE	ST	SW	TC	WN	WE
MARYLAND											
Atlantic Guns, Inc.	Silver Spring										
Baltimore Gunsmiths	Baltimore				•	•					
Firearms Repair & Refinish Shoppe	Woodbine				•						•
Gun Center, The	Frederick			•							
Precision Pellet	Joppa	•		•							
Valley Gun Shop	Baltimore				•	•				•	
Wolf Custom Gunsmithing, Gregory, c/o Albright's Gun Shop	Easton		•			•					
MASSACHUSETTS											
Bellrose & Son, L.E.	Granby			•							
Four Seasons	Woburn				•	•					
Pete's Gun Shop	Adams				•						
MICHIGAN											
Adventure A.G.R.	Waterford										•
Bachelder Custom Arms	Grand Rapids			•		•		•		•	
Daenzer, Charles E.	Otisville	•									
Hampel's, Inc.	Traverse City									•	
Joe's Gun Shop	Dorr			•							
Johnson Service, Inc., W.	Adrian					•					
McDaniel Co., Inc., B.	South Lyon		•			•					
Mill Creek Sport Center	Dexter		•			•					
Moreau. Gunsmith, Pete	Bay City	•									
Northern Precision Airguns	Tawas City				•						
On Target Gunshop, Inc.	Kalamazoo				•	•				•	
Outpost, The	Eureka		•								
Pederson Co., C.R.	Ludington										
Thompson's Gunshop, Inc.	Alto										
Wessel Gun Service	Warren		•		•	•					
Williams Gun Sight & Outfitters	Davison		•		•	•			•		
Williams Gunsmithing	Saginaw					•					
Will's Gun Shop	Spruce								•		
Ye Olde Blk Powder Shop	Auburn										
MINNESOTA											
Ahlman's Custom Gun Shop, Inc.	Morristown		•		•	•		•		•	
B&B Supply Co.	Minneapolis	•									
Dale's Gunshop	Rochester										
Gander Mt., Inc.	Duluth				•						
Frontiersman's Sports	Minneapolis		•		•	•					
Kotila Gun Shop	Cokato				•						
Laib's Gunsmithing	Spicer					•					
Matt's 10X Gunsmithing, Inc.	Duluth					•					
Northland Sport Center	Bagley					•				•	

SERVICE CENTER	CITY	BE	BR	CR	MO	RE	ST	SW	TC	WN	WE
Poor Borch's, Inc.	Marshall					•					
Stan's Gun Repair	Westbrook					•				•	
MISSISSIPPI											
Grenada Gun Works	Grenada				•						
Martins Gun Shop	Natchez				•	•					
May & Company, Inc.	Jackson			•							
Millers Gun Shop	Gulfport								•		
Saffle Repair Service	Jackson										
R.L. "Skeet" Hill Gun Shop	Verona		•								
MISSOURI											
Beard's Sport Shop	Cape Girardeau			•		•					
Bickford's Gun Repair	Joplin				•	•				•	
Carl's Gun Shop	El Dorado Springs					•					
Catfish Guns	Imperial							•			
Dollar Drugs, Inc.	Lee's Summit		•								
F&D Guns	St. Charles										
Kopp, Prof. Gunsmith, Terry K.	Lexington			•		•		•			
Nu-Line Guns, Inc.	Harvester				•	•		•		•	
Ozark Shooters, Inc.	Branson										
MONTANA											
Air Gun Shop, The	Billings										
Billings Gunsmiths	Billings					•				•	
Brady's Sportsmans Surplus	Missoula				•						
Capitol Sports & Western Wear	Helena					•		•		•	
Montana Gun Works	Great Falls					•					
Rocking S Gunshop	Ennis										
NEBRASKA											
Bedlan's Sporting Goods, Inc.	Fairbury		•								
Cylinder & Slide, Inc.	Fremont										
G.H. Outdoor Sports	McCook										
G.I. Loan Shop	Grand Island		•			•				•	
Gunsmithing Specialties, Co.	Papillion					•					
Labs Air Gun Shop	Omaha	•									
Moneymaker Gun Craft, Inc.	Omaha				•	•					
Upper Missouri Trading Co., Inc.	Crofton										
NEVADA											
Accuracy Gun Shop, Inc.	Las Vegas										
Gun World	Elko				•	•					
Nevada Air Guns	Las Vegas	•									
NEW HAMPSHIRE											
Lewis Arms	Hooksett		•		•	•				•	
Skip's Gunshop	Bristol										

See page 497 for Service Center addresses.

Warranty Service Centers (cont.)

■BE=Benjamin ■BR=Browning ■CR=Crosman ■MO=Mossberg ■RE=Remington ■ST=Stoeger ■SW=Smith & Wesson ■TC=Thompson/Center ■WN=Winchester ■WE=Weatherby

SERVICE CENTER	CITY	BE	BR	CR	MO	RE	ST	SW	TC	WN	WE
NEW JERSEY											
Belleplain Supply, Inc.	Belleplain		●								
Brenner Sport Shop, Charlie	Rahway	●		●							
Garfield Gunsmithing	Garfield		●			●					
Harry's Army & Navy Store	Robbinsville		●	●							
Ray's Sport Shop, Inc.	North Plainfield		●			●		●			
Sportsman's Center	Bordentown				●	●					
The Way It Was Sporting	Moorestown		●			●					
NEW MEXICO											
Charlie's Sporting Goods, Inc.	Albuquerque			●		●		●			●
D&J Coleman Service	Hobbs			●							
Hobbs Bicycle & Gun Sales	Hobbs										
NEW YORK											
Alpine Arms Corp.	Brooklyn							●			
B&T, Inc.	Albany		●								
Benson Gun Shop	Coram L.I.	●		●							
Boracci, E. John, Village Sport Ctr.	Seaford L.I.	●		●							
Buffalo Gun Center, Inc.	Buffalo					●					
Burgins Gun Shop	Sidney Center				●	●					
Coliseum Gun Traders, Ltd.	Uniondale				●	●					
Creekside Gun Shop	Holcomb		●								●
Damiano's Field & Stream	Ossining			●		●					
Hart's Gun Supply, Ed	Bath					●					
Hill Top Gunsmithing	Canton			●							
Kielon, Gunsmith, Dave	Webster		●								
LeFever & Sons, Inc., Frank	Lee Center								●		
Lounsbury Sporting Goods, Bob	Middletown			●							
Mulvey's Marine & Sport Shop	Monticello			●							
Rapids Gun Shop	Niagara Falls			●							
Scalzo's Sporting Goods	Endwell										
Schultheis Sporting Goods	Arkport					●					
Smith's Lawn & Marine Svc.	Clarence			●							
Solvay Home & Outdoor Center	Solvay										●
Sports Mart, The	Ogdensburg			●	●						
Sports World	Liberty	●		●							
Taylor & Vadney, Inc.	Albany										
Van's Gunsmith Service	Parish					●		●			
White Dog Gunsmithing	Ilion					●		●			
NORTH CAROLINA											
Baity's Custom Gunworks	North Wilksboro				●	●					
Blue Ridge Outdoor Sports, Inc.	E. Flat Rock		●								
Brown, Don, Gunsmith	Ashville			●							
Cumberland Knife & Gun Works	Fayetteville							●			●

SERVICE CENTER	CITY	BE	BR	CR	MO	RE	ST	SW	TC	WN	WE
Duncan Gun Shop, Inc.	North Wilksboro										
Hill's, Inc.	Raleigh		●			●					
Mike's Crosman Service	Winston-Salem			●							
Perry's Gunshop	Wendell					●					
Warren's Sports Hdqts.	Washington					●					
NORTH DAKOTA											
Gun City, Inc.	Bismarck		●								
Outdoorsman, The	Fargo		●	●							
S.K. Guns, Inc.	Fargo					●					●
OHIO											
All Game Sport Center	Milford		●			●					
Central Ohio Police Supply, c/o Wammes Guns	Bellefontaine			●							
Cherry Corners, Inc.	Lodi										
Eyster Heritage Gunsmiths, Ken	Centerburg		●							●	
Griffiths & Sons, E.J.	Lima				●						
Heckman Arms Company	Richmond Heights									●	
Log Cabin Sport Shop	Lodi										
Precision Airgun Sales	Maple Heights	●									
Rutko Corp. (Stonewall Range)	Broadview Heights							●			
Sportsman's Depot	Urban		●								
Sportsman's Haven	Cambridge					●		●		●	
Sportsmen's Repair Ctr., Inc.	Columbus Groves			●		●					
Stocker's Shop	Warren			●							
Trading Post, The	Massillon		●	●							
Upton's Gun Shop	Fremont			●							
VanBurne's Gun Shop	Toledo			●							
Zanes Gun Rack	Columbus										
OKLAHOMA											
Anderson, Andy	Oklahoma City		●								
D&D Sporting Goods	Tishomingo					●					
Mashburn Arms Co., Inc.	Oklahoma City					●					
Meydag, Peter	Tulsa										
Outdoor America Store	Oklahoma City					●					
Shamburg's Wholesale Spt. Gds.	Clinton		●								
Skeet's Gun Shop	Tahlequah					●					
Southwest Shooters Supply, Inc.	Oklahoma City					●		●	●	●	
Sports World, Inc.	Tulsa									●	
OREGON											
Allison & Carey Gun Works	Portland		●			●		●			
Enstad & Douglas	Oregon City								●		
Felton, James	Eugene										

See page 497 for Service Center addresses.

Warranty Service Centers (cont.)

■BE=Benjamin ■BR=Browning ■CR=Crosman ■MO=Mossberg ■RE=Remington ■ST=Stoeger ■SW=Smith & Wesson ■TC=Thompson/Center ■WN=Winchester ■WE=Weatherby

SERVICE CENTER	CITY	BE	BR	CR	MO	RE	ST	SW	TC	WN	WE
Lock Stock & Barrel	Grants Pass										
Metro Rod & Reel	Portland	•									
Starnes, Gunmaker, Ken	Hillsboro									•	
Surplus Center	Roseburg				•	•					
PENNSYLVANIA											
Auto Electric & Parts, Inc.	Media			•							
Colabaugh Gunsmith., Inc., Craig	Stroudsburg					•					
Federal Firearms Co., Inc.	Oakdale				•	•					
Fix Gunshop, Inc., Michael D.	Reading					•					
Gorenflo Gunsmithing	Erie			•		•					
Grice Gun Shop, Inc.	Clearfield									•	
Hart & Son, Robert W.	Nescopeck							•			
Hemlock Gun Shop	Lakeville					•					
Herold's Gun Shoppe	Waynesboro		•								
J&T Services	Bradford					•					
Keidel's Gunsmithing Service	Washington		•		•	•					
Leo's Custom Stocks	Library									•	
Levan's Sporting Goods	Lebanon			•		•					
Miller's Sport Shop	Mountaintop				•	•					
Phoenix Armoury, Inc.	Norristown				•						
Richland Gun Shop	Richland					•					
Sams Gunsmithing, David	Lititz					•					
Sportsman's Shop	New Holland		•		•	•					
Unique Sporting Goods	Lorreto										
RHODE ISLAND											
D&L Shooting Supplies	Warwick					•					
Gun Hospital, The	E. Providence									•	
SOUTH CAROLINA											
Borgheresi, Enrique	Greenville					•					
Bryan & Associates	Anderson			•							
Gun Rack, Inc., The	Aiken				•						
Gun Room, The	Chapin									•	
Gunsmith, Inc., The	West Columbia	•									
S.E.M. Gun Works	Greenville										
Smith & Smith Gun Shop, Inc.	North Charleston		•								
Southland Gun Works, Inc.	Darlington					•					
SOUTH DAKOTA											
Gary's Gun Shop	Sioux Falls					•					
Jack First	Rapid City				•						
Jim's Gun & Service Center	Aberdeen				•	•				•	
Ron's Gun Repair	Sioux Falls				•	•				•	
Sodak Sport & Bait	Aberdeen				•	•				—	

SERVICE CENTER	CITY	BE	BR	CR	MO	RE	ST	SW	TC	WN	WE
TENNESSEE											
D&L Gunsmithing/Guns & Ammo	Memphis		•		•	•				•	
Fox & Company	Knoxville		•	•	•	•					
Friedman's Army Surplus	Nashville										
Gun City USA, Inc.	Nashville		•		•	•		•	•	•	
Hagstrom, E.G.	Memphis		•		•	•		•	•	•	
Hill's Hardware & Sporting Goods	Union City					•					
McGuns, W.H.	Humboldt		•		•	•					•
Mines Gun Shack	Tullahoma					•					
Shaler Eagle	Jonesbrough										
TEXAS											
Armadillo Air Gun Repair	Corpus Christi					•					
Ben's Gun Shop	Duncanville			•		•					
Boggus Gun Shop	San Marcos										
Carroll's Gun Shop, Inc.	Wharton		•			•					
Carter's Country	Houston		•			•					
Coleman, Inc., Ron	Carrollton					•					
Custom Gun Service	McAllen										
Don & Tim's Gun Shop	San Antonio		•			•					
Ewell Cross Gun Shop, Inc.	Ft. Worth				•	•					
Freer's Gun Shop	Houston		•			•					
Gun & Tackle Store, The	Dallas		•			•					
Kirkpatrick, Gunsmith, Larry	Lubbock					•					
Les Gun & Pawn Shop	Texarkana					•					
Lone Star Guns, Inc.	Plano				•	•				•	
Longacre's, Inc.	Abilene		•		•	•					
Master Gunsmiths, Inc.	Houston		•		•	•		•		•	
McBride's Guns, Inc.	Austin		•		•	•		•		•	
McClelland Gun Shop	Dallas		•		•	•		•		•	
Mueschke Manufacturing Co.	Houston		•	•	•	•				—	
Nagel Gun Shop, Inc.	San Antonio		•		•	•		•			
Oshman's Sporting Goods, Inc.	Houston				•	•					
Pasadena Gun Center	Pasadena								•		
Precision Gunsmithing	Amarillo				•	•					
Ray's Sporting Goods	Dallas		•		•	•				•	
Reynold's Gun Shop, Inc.	Tyler					•					
Wallace & Cockrell, Gunsmiths, Inc.	Fort Worth					•					
Wichita Guncraft, Inc.	Wichita Falls								•		
Williamson Precision	Hurst					•					
Wolfer Brothers, Inc.	Houston										
UTAH											
Gun Ace Gunsmithing	Hurricane					•					
Gun Shop, The	Salt Lake City		•								

See page 497 for Service Center addresses.

Warranty Service Centers (cont.)

■BE=Benjamin ■BR=Browning ■CR=Crosman ■MO=Mossberg ■RE=Remington ■ST=Stoeger ■SW=Smith & Wesson ■TC=Thompson/Center ■WN=Winchester ■WE=Weatherby

SERVICE CENTER	CITY	BE	BR	CR	MO	RE	ST	SW	TC	WN	WE
Gunsmith Co., The	Salt Lake City					●			●		
Hutch's	Lehi			●	●						
Professional Armaments, Inc.	West Valley City				●	●					
VERMONT											
Burby, Inc. Guns & Gunsmithing	Middlebury					●					
Carpenter's Gun Works	Proctorsville								●		
Island Pond Gunshop	Island Pond					●				●	
VIRGINIA											
Bob's Gun & Tackle Shop, (Blaustein & Reich, Inc.)	Norfolk		●		●	●				●	
Cervera, Albert J.	Hanover		●								
King's Gun Shop, Inc.	Franklin		●								
Moates Sport Shop, Bob	Midlothian		●								
Northern Virginia Gun Works, Inc.	Springfield				●	●			●		
Old Dominion Engraver, Inc.	Lynchburg					●					
Richmond Gun Shop	Richmond				●	●				●	
WASHINGTON											
Brock's Gunsmithing, Inc.	Spokane				●	●				●	●
Chet Paulson Outfitters	Tacoma		●			●				●	
Greene's Gun Shop	Oak Harbor					●					
Karrer's Gunatorium	Spokane					●					
Kesselring Gun Shop	Burlington		●								
Pintos Gun Shop	Kent	●									
Shooters Supply	Yakima								●		
Wisner's Gun Shop, Inc.	Chehalis		●		●	●			●	●	
Wheeler Gun Shop, C.	Richland				●	●				●	●
WEST VIRGINIA											
Douglas Sporting Goods	Princeton					●					
Lew's Mountaineer Gunsmithing	Charleston				●	●					
Milliken's Gun Shop	Elm Grove									●	
Shooting Gallery, The	Weirton		●								
WISCONSIN											
Badger Gun & Ammo, Inc.	Milwaukee				●	●					
Badger's Shooters Supply, Inc.	Owen				●	●					
Bob's Crosman Repair	Cudahy			●							
Custom Firearms Shop, The	Sheboygan		●								
Gander Mountain, Inc.	Wilmot		●			●			●	●	
Jack's Lock & Gun Shop	Fond Du Lac										●
Jay's Sports, Inc.	Menomonee Falls		●								
Midwestern Shooters Supply, Inc.	Lomira		●			●				●	
Phillips, D.J. Gunsmith	Pewaukee					●					

SERVICE CENTER	CITY	BE	BR	CR	MO	RE	ST	SW	TC	WN	WE
Potter Gunsmithing	Muskego					●					
Precision Gun Works	Oshkosh					●					
River Bend Sport Shop	Waupaca				●						
R&R Shooters Supply	Mauston	●									
Rusk Gun Shop, Inc.	Madison					●					●
Sea Gull Marina	Two Rivers		●							●	
WYOMING											
Elbe Arms Co., Inc.	Cheyenne					●					
Jackalope Gun Shop	Douglas				●						
CANADA											
Armurier De L'Outaouais	Hull, PQ				●	●				●	
Casey's Gun Shop	Rogersville, NB		●			●				●	
Delisle Thompson Sport Goods	Brentwood Bay, BC					●					
Chariton Co., Ltd., M.D.	Orillia, ON		●								
Custom Gun Shop	Edmonton, AB				●	●				●	
Davidson's of Canada	Peterborough, ON					●				●	
Delhi Small Arms	Delhi, ON								●	●	
Epps, Ellwood	Saskatoon, SK					●					
Ernie's Gun Shop, Ltd.	Winnipeg, MB							●	●		
Gene's Gunsmithing	Selkirk, MB							●			
Girard, Florent, Gunsmith	Chicoutimi, PQ					●				●	
L'Armurier Alain Bouchard, Inc.	Ulverton, PQ		●		●	●				●	
Longs Gunsmithing Ltd., W.R.	Coburg, ON		●			●				●	
Lusignant Armurier, A. Richard	St. Hyacinthe, PQ					●					
Magasin Latulippe, Inc.	Quebec City, PQ		●			●					
Newby, Stewart, Gunsmith	New Burgh, ON					●					
Precision Arms & Gunsmithing Ltd.	Nobleton, ON				●	●					
Ralph's Gun Shop	Niverville, MB					●					
Randy's Gun Repair	Tabustinac, NB					●					
Reliable Gun & Tackle, Ltd.	Vancouver, BC									●	
Robinson's Sporting Goods, Ltd.	Victoria, BC									●	
Russell's Sporting Goods	Calgary, AB									●	
Saskatoon Gunsmith Shoppe, Ltd.	Saskatoon, SK				●	●					
Selin Gunsmith, Ltd. Del	Vernon, BC				●	●					
West Gate Gunsports, Inc.	Edmonton, AB										●
West Luther Gun Repair	Conn, ON					●					
Wholesale Sports	Edmonton, AB									●	
Wortner Gun Works, Ltd.	Chatham, ON				●					●	

See page 497 for Service Center addresses.

METALLIC SIGHTS

Sporting Leaf and Open Sights

ERA EXPRESS SIGHTS A wide variety of open sights and bases for custom installation. Partial listing shown. From New England Custom Gun Service.
Price: One-leaf express $66.00
Price: Two-leaf express $71.50
Price: Three-leaf express $77.00
Price: Bases for above $27.50
Price: Standing rear sight, straight $13.20
Price: Base for above $16.50

ERA PROFESSIONAL EXPRESS SIGHTS Standing or folding leaf sights are securely locked to the base with the ERA Magnum Clamp, but can be loosened for sighting in. Base can be attached with two socket-head cap screws or soldered. Finished and blued. Barrel diameters from .600" to .930".
Price: Standing leaf $49.00
Price: One-leaf express $87.00
Price: Two-leaf express $92.00
Price: Three-leaf express $99.00

ERA MASTERPIECE REAR SIGHT Adjustable for windage and elevation, and adjusted and locked with a small screwdriver. Comes with 8-36 socket-head cap screw and wrench. Barrel diameters from .600" to .930".
Price: $75.00

LYMAN No. 16 Middle sight for barrel dovetail slot mounting. Folds flat when scope or peep sight is used. Sight notch plate adjustable for elevation. White triangle for quick aiming. 3 heights: A—.400" to .500", B—.345" to .445", C—.500" to .600".
Price: $13.95

MARBLE FALSE BASE #76, #77, #78 New screw-on base for most rifles replaces factory base. $3/8$" dovetail slot permits installation of any folding rear sight. Can be had in sweat-on models also.
Price: $7.95

MARBLE CONTOUR RAMP #14R For late model Rem. 725, 740, 760, 742 rear sight mounting. $9/16$" between mounting screws. Accepts all sporting rear sights.
Price: $10.55

MARBLE FOLDING LEAF Flat-top or semi-buckhorn style. Folds down when scope or peep sights are used. Reversible plate gives choice of "U" or "V" notch. Adjustable for elevation.
Price: $14.60
Price: Also available with both windage and elevation adjustment $16.70

MARBLE SPORTING REAR With white enamel diamond, gives choice of two "U" and two "V" notches or different sizes. Adjustment in height by means of double step elevator and sliding notch piece. For all rifles; screw or dovetail installation.
Price: .... $13.75-$15.75

MARBLE #20 UNIVERSAL New screw or sweat-on base. Both have .100" elevation adjustment. In five base sizes. Three styles of U-notch, square notch, peep. Adjustable for windage and elevation.
Price: Screw-on $22.55
Price: Sweat-on $20.70

MILLETT RIFLE SIGHT Open, fully adjustable rear sight fits standard $3/8$" dovetail cut in barrel. Choice of white outline or target rear blades, .360". Front with white or orange bar, .343", .400", .430", .460", .500", .540".
Price: Rear sight $55.60
Price: Front sight $12.34

MILLETT SCOPE-SITE Open, adjustable or fixed rear sights dovetails into a base integral with the top scope-mounting ring. Blaze orange front ramp sight is integral with the front ring half. Rear sights have white outline aperture. Provides fast, short-radius, Patridge-type open sights on the top of the scope. Can be used with all Millett rings, Weaver-style bases, Ruger 77 (also fits Redhawk), Ruger Ranch Rifle, No. 1, No. 3, Rem. 870, 1100; Burris, Leupold and Redfield bases.
Price: Scope-Site top only, windage only $31.15
Price: As above, fully adjustable $66.10
Price: Scope-Site Hi-Turret, fully adjustable, low, medium, high $66.10

WICHITA MULTI RANGE SIGHT SYSTEM Designed for silhouette shooting. System allows you to adjust the rear sight to four repeatable range settings, once it is pre-set. Sight clicks to any of the settings by turning a serrated wheel. Front sight is adjustable for weather and light conditions with one adjustment. Specify gun when ordering.
Price: Rear sight $99.50
Price: Front sight $74.85

WILLIAMS DOVETAIL OPEN SIGHT (WDOS) Open rear sight with windage and elevation adjustment. Furnished with "U" notch or choice of blades. Slips into dovetail and locks with gib lock. Heights from .281" to .531".
Price: With blade $15.40
Price: Less Blade $9.63

WILLIAMS GUIDE OPEN SIGHT (WGOS) Open rear sight with windage and elevation adjustment. Bases to fit most military and commercial barrels. Choice of square "U" or "V" notch blade, $3/16$", $1/4$", $5/16$", or $3/8$" high.
Price: Less blade $15.40
Price: Extra blades, each $6.00

WILLIAMS WGOS OCTAGON Open rear sight for 1" octagon barrels. Installs with two 6-48 screws and uses same hole spacing as most T/C muzzleloading rifles. Four heights, choice of square, U, V, B blade.
Price: $20.55

WILLIAMS WSKS, WAK47 Replaces original military-type rear sight. Adjustable for windage and elevation. No drilling or tapping. Peep aperture or open. For SKS carbines, AK-47.
Price: Aperture $23.00
Price: Open $20.50

WILLIAMS WM-96 Fits Mauser 96-type military rifles, replaces original rear sight with open blade or aperture. Fully adjustable for windage and elevation. No drilling; tapping.
Price: Aperture $23.00
Price: Open $20.50

Micrometer Receiver Sights

BEEMAN/FEINWERKBAU 5454 MATCH APERTURE SIGHT Small size, new-design sight uses constant-pressure flat springs to eliminate point of impact shifts.
Price: $299.00

BEEMAN SPORT APERTURE SIGHT Positive click micrometer adjustments. Standard units with flush surface screwdriver adjustments. Deluxe version has target knobs. For air rifles with grooved receivers.
Price: Standard $36.50
Price: Deluxe $47.00

EAW RECEIVER SIGHT A fully adjustable aperture sight that locks securely into the EAW quick-detachable scope mount rear base. Imported by New England Custom Gun Service.
Price: $125.00

LYMAN NO. 2 TANG SIGHT Designed for the Winchester Model 94. Has high index marks on aperture post; comes with both .093" quick sighting aperture, .040" large disk aperture, and replacement mounting screws.
Price: $75.00
Price: For Marlin lever actions $79.95

LYMAN No. 57 $1/4$-minute clicks. Stayset knobs. Quick release slide, adjustable zero scales. Made for almost all modern rifles.
Price: $68.00
Price: No. 57SME, 57SMET (for White Systems Model 91 and Whitetail rifles) $68.00

LYMAN No. 66 Fits close to the rear of flat-sided receivers, furnished with Stayset knobs. Quick release slide, $1/4$-min. adjustments. For most lever or slide action or flat-sided automatic rifles.
Price: $68.00
Price: No. 66MK (for all current versions of the Knight MK-85 in-line rifle with flat-sided receiver) $68.00

LYMAN No. 66U Light weight, designed for most modern shotguns with a flat-sided, round-top receiver. $1/4$-minute clicks. Requires drilling, tapping. Not for Browning A-5, Rem. M11.
Price: $68.00

LYMAN 90MJT RECEIVER SIGHT Mounts on standard Lyman and Williams FP bases. Has $1/4$-minute audible micrometer click adjustments, target knobs with direction indicators. Adjustable zero scales, quick release slide. Large $7/8$" diameter aperture disk.
Price: $79.95

MILLETT RIFLE SIGHTS Fully adjustable, heat-treated nickel steel peep aperture receiver sight for the AR-15A-1 and Mini-14. Has fine windage and elevation adjustments; replaces original.
Price: Rear sight, Mini-14 .... $54.00
Price: Front sight, Mini-14 .... $18.75
Price: Rear sight, AR-15A-1 .... $51.45
Price: Serrated ramp front sight, AR-15A-1 .... $12.25

WILLIAMS FP Internal click adjustments. Positive locks. For virtually all rifles, T/C Contender, Heckler & Koch HK-91, Ruger Mini-14, plus Win., Rem. and Ithaca shotguns.
Price: From $57.06
Price: With Target Knobs $67.77
Price: With Square Notched Blade $60.00
Price: With Target Knobs & Square Notched Blade $70.80
Price: FP-GR (for dovetail-grooved receivers, 22s and air guns) $57.06
Price: FP-94BBSE (for Win. 94 Big Bore A.E.; uses top rear scope mount holes) $57.06

WILLIAMS TARGET FP Similar to the FP series but developed for most bolt-action rimfire rifles. Target FP High adjustable from 1.250" to 1.750" above cen-

METALLIC SIGHTS

terline of bore; Target FP Low adjustable from .750" to 1.250". Attaching bases for Rem. 540X, 541-S, 580, 581, 582 (#540); Rem. 510, 511, 512, 513-T, 521-T (#510); Win. 75 (#75); Savage/Anschutz 64 and Mark 12 (#64). Some rifles require drilling, tapping.
Price: High or Low $77.15
Price: Base only $12.98
Price: FP-T/C Scout rifle, from $57.06
Price: FP-94BBSE (for Win. 94 Big Bore A.E.; uses top rear scope mount holes) $57.06
WILLIAMS 5-D SIGHT Low cost sight for shotguns, 22s and the more popular big game rifles. Adjustment for windage and elevation. Fits most guns without drilling and tapping. Also for British SMLE, Winchester M94 Side Eject.
Price: From $30.85
Price: With Shotgun Aperture $30.85
WILLIAMS GUIDE (WGRS) Receiver sight for 30 M1 Carbine, M1903A3 Springfield, Savage 24s, Savage-Anschutz and Weatherby XXII. Utilizes military dovetail; no drilling. Double-dovetail windage adjustment, sliding dovetail adjustment for elevation.
Price: $30.85
Price: WGRS-CVA (for rifles with octagon barrels, receivers) $30.85

FRONT SIGHTS

ERA FRONT SIGHTS European-type front sights inserted from the front. Various heights available. From New England Custom Gun Service.
Price: 1/16" silver bead $11.55
Price: 3/32" silver bead $15.95
Sourdough bead $14.30
Price: Tritium night sight $39.60
Price: Folding night sight with ivory bead $39.60
LYMAN HUNTING SIGHTS Made with gold or white beads 1/16" to 3/32" wide and in varying heights for most military and commercial rifles. Dovetail bases.
Price: $10.50
MARBLE STANDARD Ivory, red, or gold bead. For all American-made rifles, 1/16" wide bead with semi-flat face which does not reflect light. Specify type of rifle when ordering.
Price: $8.75
MARBLE CONTOURED Has 3/8" dovetail base, .090" deep, is 5/8" long. Uses standard 1/16" or 3/32" bead, ivory, red, or gold. Specify rifle type.
Price: $10.15
POLY-CHOKE Rifle front sights available in six heights and two widths. Model A designed to be inserted into the barrel dovetail; Model B is for use with standard .350" ramp; both have standard 3/8" dovetails. Gold or ivory 7/16" bead. From Marble Arms.
Price: $6.65
WILLIAMS RISER BLOCKS For adding .250" height to front sights when using a receiver sight. Two widths available: .250" for Williams Streamlined Ramp or .340" on all standard ramps having this base width. Uses standard 3/8" dovetail.
Price: $5.30

Globe Target Front Sights

LYMAN 20 MJT TARGET FRONT Has 7/8" diameter, one-piece steel globe with 3/8" dovetail base. Height is .700" from bottom of dovetail to center of aperture; height on 20 LJT is .750". Comes with seven Anschutz-size steel inserts—two posts and five apertures .126" through .177".
Price: 20 MJT or 20 LJT $36.00
LYMAN No. 17A TARGET Includes seven interchangeable inserts: four apertures, one transparent amber and two posts .50" and .100" in width.
Price: $29.95
Price: Insert set $10.50
LYMAN No. 93 MATCH Has 7/8" diameter, fits any rifle with a standard dovetail mounting block. Comes with seven target inserts and accepts most Anschutz accessories. Hooked locking bolt and nut allows quick removal, installation. Base available in .860" (European) and .562" (American) hole spacing.
Price: $48.00
WILLIAMS TARGET GLOBE FRONT Adapts to many rifles. Mounts to the base with a knurled locking screw. Height is .545" from center, not including base. Comes with inserts.
Price: $30.85
Price: Dovetail base (low) .220" $17.00
Price: Dovetail base (high) .465" $17.00
Price: Screw-on base, .300" height, .300" radius $15.45
Price: Screw-on base, .450" height, .350" radius $15.45
Price: Screw-on base, .215" height, .400" radius $15.45

Ramp Sights

ERA MASTERPIECE Banded ramps; 21 sizes; hand-detachable beads and hood; beads inserted from the front. Various heights available. From New England Custom Gun Service.
Price: Banded ramp $53.90
Price: Hood $10.45
Price: 1/16" silver bead $11.55
Price: 3/32" silver bead $15.95
Price: Sourdough bead $14.30
Price: Tritium night sight $39.60
Price: Folding night sight with ivory bead $39.60
LYMAN SCREW-ON RAMP Used with 8-40 screws but may also be brazed on. Heights from .10" to .350". Ramp without sight.
Price: $15.95

MARBLE FRONT RAMPS Available in either screw-on or sweat-on style, five heights: 3/16", 5/16", 3/8", 7/16", 9/16". Standard 3/8" dovetail slot.
Price: $16.80
Price: Hoods for above ramps $3.70
WILLIAMS SHORTY RAMP Companion to "Streamlined" ramp, about 1/2" shorter. Screw-on or sweat-on. It is furnished in 1/8", 3/16", 9/32", and 3/8" heights without hood only. Also for shotguns.
Price: $13.34
Price: With dovetail lock $15.91
WILLIAMS STREAMLINED RAMP Available in screw-on or sweat-on models. Furnished in 9/16", 7/16", 3/8", 5/16", 3/16" heights.
Price: $16.00
Price: Sight hood $3.75
WILLIAMS STREAMLINED FRONT SIGHTS Narrow (.250" width) for Williams Streamlined ramps and others with 1/4" top width; medium (.340" width) for all standard factory ramps. Available with white, gold or flourescent beads, 1/16" or 3/32".
Price: .... $8.50 to $8.81

Handgun Sights

BO-MAR DELUXE BMCS Gives 3/8" windage and elevation adjustment at 50 yards on Colt Gov't 45; sight radius under 7". For GM and Commander models only. Uses existing dovetail slot. Has shield-type rear blade.
Price: $65.95
Price: BMCS-2 (for GM and 9mm) $65.95
Price: Flat bottom $65.95
Price: BMGC (for Colt Gold Cup), angled serrated blade, rear $65.95
Price: BMGC front sight $12.00
Price: BMCZ-75 (for CZ-75, TZ-75, P-9 and most clones. Works with factory front $65.95
BO-MAR FRONT SIGHTS Dovetail style for S&W 4506, 4516, 1076; undercut style (.250", .280", 5/16" high); Fast Draw style (.210", .250", .230" high).
Price $12.00
BO-MAR BMU XP-100/T/C CONTENDER No gunsmithing required; has .080" notch.
Price: $77.00
BO-MAR BMML For muzzleloaders; has .062" notch, flat bottom.
Price: $65.95
Price: With 3/8" dovetail $65.95
BO-MAR RUGER "P" ADJUSTABLE SIGHT Replaces factory front and rear sights.
Price: Rear sight $65.95
Price: Front sight $12.00
BO-MAR BMR Fully adjustable rear sight for Ruger MKI, MKII Bull barrel autos.
Price: Rear $65.95
Price: Undercut front sight $12.00
BO-MAR BMSW SMITH & WESSON SIGHTS Replace the S&W Novak-style fixed sights. A .385" high front sight and minor machining required. For models 4506, 4516, 1076; all 9mms with 5 3/4" and 6 3/16" radius.
Price: $65.95
Price: .385" front sight $12.00
Price: BM-645 rear sight (for S&W 645, 745), uses factory front $65.95
Price: BMSW-52 rear sight (for Model 52), fits factory dovetail, uses factory front . $65.95
BO-MAR LOW PROFILE RIB & ACCURACY TUNER Streamlined rib with front and rear sights; 7 1/8" sight radius. Brings sight line closer to the bore than standard or extended sight and ramp. Weight 5 oz. Made for Colt Gov't 45, Super 38, and Gold Cup 45 and 38.
Price: $123.00
BO-MAR COMBAT RIB For S&W Model 19 revolver with 4" barrel. Sight radius 5 3/4", weight 5 1/2 oz.
Price: $110.00
BO-MAR HUNTER REAR SIGHT Replacement rear sight in two models—S&W K and L frames use 2 3/4" Bo-Mar base with 7/16" overhang, has two screw holes; S&W N frame has 3" base, three screw holes. A .200" taller front blade is required.
Price: $79.00
BO-MAR WINGED RIB For S&W 4" and 6" length barrels—K-38, M10, HB 14 and 19. Weight for the 6" model is about 7 1/4 oz.
Price: $123.00
BO-MAR COVER-UP RIB Adjustable rear sight, winged front guards. Fits right over revolver's original front sight. For S&W 4" M-10HB, M-13, M-58, M-64 & 65, Ruger 4" models SDA-34, SDA-84, SS-34, SS-84, GF-34, GF-84.
Price: $117.00
C-MORE SIGHTS Replacement front sight blades offered in two types and five styles. Made of Du Pont Acetal, they come in a set of five high-contrast colors: blue, green, pink, red and yellow. Easy to install. Patridge style for Colt Python (all barrels), Ruger Super Blackhawk (7 1/2"), Ruger Blackhawk (4 5/8"); ramp style for Python (all barrels), Blackhawk (4 5/8"), Super Blackhawk (7 1/2" and 10 1/2"). From C-More Systems.
Price: Per set $19.95
MMC COMBAT FIXED REAR SIGHT (Colt 1911-Type Pistols) This veteran MMC sight is well known to those who prefer a true combat sight for "carry" guns. Steel construction for long service. Choose from a wide variety of front sights.
Price: Combat Fixed Rear, plain $18.45
Price: As above, white outline $23.65
Price: Combat Front Sight for above, six styles, from $5.15
MMC M/85 ADJUSTABLE REAR SIGHT Designed to be compatible with the

Ruger P-85 front sight. Fully adjustable for windage and elevation.
Price: M/85 Adjustable Rear Sight, plain **$52.45**
Price: As above, white outline **$57.70**
MMC STANDARD ADJUSTABLE REAR SIGHT Available for Colt 1911 type, Ruger Standard Auto, and now for S&W 469, and 659 pistols. No front sight change is necessary, as this sight will work with the original factory front sight.
Price: Standard Adjustable Rear Sight, plain leaf **$46.05**
Price: Standard Adjustable Rear Sight, white outline **$51.15**
MMC MINI-SIGHT Miniature size for carrying, fully adjustable, for maximum accuracy with your pocket auto. MMC's Mini-Sight will work with the factory front sight. No machining is necessary; easy installation. Available for Walther PP, PPK, and PPK/S pistols. Will also fit fixed sight Browning Hi-Power (P-35).
Price: Mini-Sight, plain **$58.45**
Price: Mini-Sight, white bar **$63.45**
MEPROLIGHT TRITIUM NIGHT SIGHTS Replacement sight assemblies for use in low-light conditions. Available for rifles, shotguns, handguns and bows. **TRU-DOT** models carry a 12-year warranty on the useable illumination, while non-TRU-DOT have a 5-year warranty. Contact Hesco, Inc. for complete details.
Price: Shotgun bead sight **$22.95**
Price: AR-15/M-16 front sight only **$34.95**
Price: AR-15/M-16 sight sets, Rem. rifle sights **$89.95**
Price: TRU-DOT fixed sight sets **$94.95**
Price: TRU-DOT adjustable sight sets, pistols **$139.95**
Price: TRU-DOT adjustable sights for Python, King Cobra, Taurus 669, Ruger GP-100 . . . .**$124.95**
Price: H&K MP5, SR9 front sight only **$49.95**
Price: H&K MP5, SR9 sight sets **$94.95**
MILLETT 3-DOT SYSTEM SIGHTS The 3-Dot System sights use a single white dot on the front blade and two dots flanking the rear notch. Fronts available in Dual-Crimp and Wide Stake-On styles, as well as special applications. Adjustable rear sight available for most popular auto pistols and revolvers.
Price: Front, from **$16.00**
Price: Adjustable rear . . . .**$55.60 to $56.80**
MILLETT REVOLVER FRONT SIGHTS All-steel replacement front sights with either white or orange bar. Easy to install. For Ruger GP-100, Redhawk, Security-Six, Police-Six, Speed-Six, Colt Trooper, Diamondback, King Cobra, Peacemaker, Python, Dan Wesson 22 and 15-2.
Price: . . . .**$13.60 to $16.00**
MILLETT DUAL-CRIMP FRONT SIGHT Replacement front sight for automatic pistols. Dual-Crimp uses an all-steel two-point hollow rivet system. Available in eight heights and four styles. Has a skirted base that covers the front sight pad. Easily installed with the Millett Installation Tool Set. Available in Blaze Orange Bar, White Bar, Serrated Ramp, Plain Post.
Price: **$16.00**
MILLETT STAKE-ON FRONT SIGHT Replacement front sight for automatic pistols. Stake-On sights have skirted base that covers the front sight pad. Easily installed with the Millet Installation Tool Set. Available in seven heights and four styles—Blaze Orange Bar, White Bar, Serrated Ramp, Plain Post.
Price: **$16.00**
OMEGA OUTLINE SIGHT BLADES Replacement rear sight blades for Colt and Ruger single action guns and the Interarms Virginian Dragoon. Standard Outline available in gold or white notch outline on blue metal. From Omega Sales, Inc.
Price: **$8.95**
OMEGA MAVERICK SIGHT BLADES Replacement "peep-sight" blades for Colt, Ruger SAs, Virginian Dragoon. Three models available—No. 1, Plain; No. 2, Single Bar; No. 3, Double Bar Rangefinder. From Omega Sales, Inc.
Price: Each **$6.95**
P-T TRITIUM NIGHT SIGHTS Self-luminous tritium sights for most popular handguns, Colt AR-15, H&K rifles and shotguns. Replacement handgun sight sets available in 3-Dot style (green/green, green/yellow, green/orange) with bold outlines around inserts; Bar-Dot available in green/green with or without white outline rear sight. Functional life exceeds 15 years. From Innovative Weaponry, Inc.
Price: Handgun sight sets **$99.95**
Price: Rifle sight sets **$99.95**
Price: Rifle, front only **$49.95**
Price: Shotgun, front only **$49.95**
TRIJICON NIGHT SIGHTS Three-dot night sight system uses tritium inserts in the front and rear sights. Tritium "lamps" are mounted in silicone rubber inside a metal cylinder. A polished crystal sapphire provides protection and clarity. Inlaid white outlines provide 3-dot aiming in daylight also. Available for most popular handguns with fixed or adjustable sights. From Trijicon, Inc.
Price: . . . .**$19.95 to $175.00**
THOMPSON/CENTER SILHOUETTE SIGHTS Replacement front and rear sights for the T/C Contender. Front sight has three interchangeable blades. Rear sight has three notch widths. Rear sight can be used with existing soldered front sights.
Price: Front sight **$34.10**
Price: Rear sight **$88.00**
WICHITA SERIES 70/80 SIGHT Provides click windage and elevation adjustments with precise repeatability of settings. Sight blade is grooved and angled back at the top to reduce glare. Available in Low Mount Combat or Low Mount Target styles for Colt 45s and their copies, S&W 645, Hi-Power, CZ 75 and others.
Price: Rear sight, target or combat **$71.45**
Price: Front sight, Patridge or ramp **$12.00**
WICHITA GRAND MASTER DELUXE RIBS Ventilated rib has wings machined into it for better sight acquisition and is relieved for Mag-Na-Porting. Milled to accept Weaver see-thru-style rings. Made of stainless or blued steel; front and rear sights blued. Has Wichita Multi-Range rear sight system, adjustable front sight. Made for revolvers with 6″ barrel.
Price: Model 301S, 301B (adj. sight K frames with custom bbl. of 1″ to 1.032″ dia. L and N frame with 1.062″ to 1.100″ dia. bbl.) **$160.00**
Price: Model 303S, 303B (adj. sight K, L, N frames with factory barrel) . .**$160.00**

Shotgun Sights

ACCURA-SITE For shooting shotgun slugs. Three models to fit most shotguns—"A" for vent. rib barrels, "B" for solid ribs, "C" for plain barrels. Rear sight has windage and elevation provisions. Easily removed and replaced. Includes front and rear sights. From All's, The Jim Tembeils Co.
Price: . . . .**$27.95 to $34.95**
FIRE FLY EM-109 SL SHOTGUN SIGHT Made of aircraft-grade aluminum, this 1/4-oz. "channel" sight has a thick, sturdy hollowed post between the side rails to give a Patridge sight picture. All shooting is done with both eyes open, allowing the shooter to concentrate on the target, not the sights. The hole in the sight post gives reduced-light shooting capability and allows for fast, precise aiming. For sport or combat shooting. Model EM-109 fits all vent. rib and double barrel shotguns and muzzleloaders with octagon barrel. Model MOC-110 fits all plain barrel shotguns without screw-in chokes. From JAS, Inc.
Price: **$35.00**
LYMAN Three sights of over-sized ivory beads. No. 10 Front (press fit) for double barrel or ribbed single barrel guns...**$5.00**; No. 10D Front (screw fit) for non-ribbed single barrel guns (comes with wrench)...**$6.50**; No. 11 Middle (press fit) for double and ribbed single barrel guns...**$5.30**.
MMC M&P COMBAT SHOTGUN SIGHT SET A durable, protected ghost ring aperture, combat sight made of steel. Fully adjustable for windage and elevation.
Price: M&P Sight Set (front and rear) **$73.45**
Price: As above, installed **$83.95**
MARBLE SHOTGUN BEAD SIGHTS No. 214—Ivory front bead, 11/64″, tapered shank...**$4.40**; No. 223—Ivory rear bead, .080″, tapered shank...**$4.40**; No. 217—Ivory front bead, 11/64″, threaded shank...**$4.40**; No. 223-T—Ivory rear bead, .080″, threaded shank...**$5.95**. Reamers, taps and wrenches available from Marble Arms.
MILLETT SHURSHOT SHOTGUN SIGHT A sight system for shotguns with ventilated rib. Rear sight attaches to the rib, front sight replaces the front bead. Front has an orange face, rear has two orange bars. For 870, 1100 or other models.
Price: Rear **$13.15**
Price: Adjustable rear **$22.00**
Price: Front **$9.15**
POLY-CHOKE Replacement front shotgun sights in four styles—Xpert, Poly Bead, Xpert Mid Rib sights, and Bev-L-Block. Xpert Front available in 3x56, 6x48 thread, 3/32″ or 5/32″ shank length, gold, ivory...**$4.70**; or Sun Spot orange bead...**$5.00**; Poly Bead is standard replacement 1/8″ bead, 6x48...**$2.85**; Xpert Mid Rib in tapered carrier (ivory only) **$4.15**, or 3x56 threaded shank (gold only)...**$2.85**; Hi and Lo Blok sights with 6x48 thread, gold or ivory...**$4.70** or Sun Spot Orange...**$5.00**. From Marble Arms.
SLUG SIGHTS Made of non-marring black nylon, front and rear sights stretch over and lock onto the barrel. Sights are low profile with blaze orange front blade. Adjustable for windage and elevation. For plain-barrel (non-ribbed) guns in 12-, 16- and 20-gauge, and for shotguns with 5/16″ and 3/8″ ventilated ribs. From Innovision Ent.
Price: **$11.95**
WILLIAMS GUIDE BEAD SIGHT Fits all shotguns, 1/8″ ivory, red or gold bead. Screws into existing sight hole. Various thread sizes and shank lengths.
Price: **$4.63**
WILLIAMS SLUGGER SIGHTS Removable aluminum sights attach to the shotgun rib. High profile front, fully adjustable rear. Fits 1/4″, 5/16″ or 3/8″ (special) ribs.
Price: **$34.95**

Sight Attachments

MERIT IRIS SHUTTER DISC Eleven clicks give 12 different apertures. No. 3 Disc and Master, primarily target types, 0.22″ to .125″; No. 4, 1/2″ dia. hunting type, .025″ to .155″. Available for all popular sights. The Master Deluxe, with flexible rubber light shield, is particularly adapted to extension, scope height, and tang sights. All Merit Deluxe models have internal click springs; are hand fitted to minimum tolerance.
Price: Master Deluxe **$63.00**
Price: No. 3 Disc **$52.00**
Price: No. 4 Hunting Disc **$45.00**
MERIT LENS DISC Similar to Merit Iris Shutter (Model 3 or Master) but incorporates provision for mounting prescription lens integrally. Lens may be obtained locally from your optician. Sight disc is 7/16″ wide (Model 3), or 3/4″ wide (Master). Model 3 Target.
Price: **$65.00**
Price: Master Deluxe **$75.00**
MERIT OPTICAL ATTACHMENT For revolver and pistol shooters, instantly attached by rubber suction cup to regular or shooting glasses. Any aperture .020″ to .156″.
Price: Deluxe (swings aside) **$63.00**
WILLIAMS APERTURES Standard thread, fits most sights. Regular series 3/8″ to 1/2″ O.D., .050″ to .125″ hole. "Twilight" series has white reflector ring.
Price: Regular series **$4.82**
Price: Twilight series **$6.59**
Price: Wide open 5/16″ aperture for shotguns fits 5-D or Foolproof sights (specify model) **$8.52**

CHOKES & BRAKES

Briley Screw-In Chokes
Installation of these choke tubes requires that all traces of the original choking be removed, the barrel threaded internally with square threads and then the tubes are custom fitted to the specific barrel diameter. The tubes are thin and, therefore, made of stainless steel. Cost of installation for single-barrel guns (pumps, autos), lead shot, 12-gauge, **$129.00**, 20-gauge **$139.00**; steel shot **$159.00** and **$169.00**, all with three chokes; un-single target guns run **$190.00**; over/unders and side-by-sides, lead shot, 12-gauge, **$349.00**, 20-gauge **$369.00**; steel shot **$449.00** and **$469.00**, all with five chokes. For 10-gauge auto or pump with two steel shot chokes, **$149.00**; over/unders, side-by-sides with three steel shot chokes, **$329.00**. For 16-gauge auto or pump, three lead shot chokes, **$239.00**; over/unders, side-by-sides with five lead shot chokes, **$429.00**. The 28 and 410-bore run **$159.00** for autos and pumps with three lead shot chokes, **$429.00** for over/unders and side-by-sides with five lead shot chokes.

Cutts Compensator
The Cutts Compensator is one of the oldest variable choke devices available. Manufactured by Lyman Gunsight Corporation, it is available with a steel body. A series of vents allows gas to escape upward and downward. For the 12-ga. Comp body, six fixed-choke tubes are available: the Spreader—popular with Skeet shooters; Improved Cylinder; Modified; Full; Superfull, and Magnum Full. Full, Modified and Spreader tubes are available for 12 or 20, and an Adjustable Tube, giving Full through Improved Cylinder chokes, is offered in 12 and 20 gauges. Cutts Compensator, complete with wrench, adaptor and any single tube **$69.80**; with adjustable tube **$91.00**. All single choke tubes **$26.00** each; adjustable tube **$53.95**. No factory installation available.

Dayson Automatic Brake System
This system fits most single barrel shotguns threaded for choke tubes, and cuts away 30 grooves on the exterior of a standard one-piece wad as it exits the muzzle. This slows the wad, allowing shot and wad to separate faster, reducing shot distortion and tightening patterns. The A.B.S. Choke Tube is claimed to reduce recoil by about 25 percent, and with the Muzzle Brake up to 60 percent. Ventilated Choke Tubes available from .685" to .725", in .005" increments. Model I Ventilated Choke Tube for use with A.B.S. Muzzle Brake, **$49.95**; for use without Muzzle Brake, **$52.95**; A.B.S. Muzzle Brake, from **$69.95**. Contact Dayson Arms for more data.

Gentry Quiet Muzzle Brake
Developed by gunmaker David Gentry, the "Quiet Muzzle Brake" is said to reduce recoil by up to 85 percent with no loss of accuracy or velocity. There is no increase in noise level because the noise and gases are directed away from the shooter. The barrel is threaded for installation and the unit is blued to match the barrel finish. Price, installed, is **$150.00**. Add **$15.00** for stainless steel, **$25.00** for knurled cap to protect threads.

Intermountain Arms Recoil Brake
The Custom Compact Recoil Brake is said to reduce felt recoil by 50 percent in most calibers. Machined with an expansion chamber to maximize efficiency. There are 42 ports to direct gases away from the shooter. Individually machined, polished and blued to match each barrel. Adds 1 3/4" to the barrel. Blued or stainless steel, **$169.00**. From Intermountain Arms.

JP Muzzle Brake
Designed for single shot handguns, AR-15, Ruger Mini-14, Ruger Mini Thirty and other sporting rifles, the JP Muzzle Brake redirects high pressure gases against a large frontal surface which applies forward thrust to the gun. All gases are directed up, rearward and to the sides. Priced at **$49.95** (AR-15), **$69.95** (bull barrel and SKS, AK models), **$79.95** (Ruger Minis), Dual Chamber model **$74.95**. From JP Enterprises, Inc.

KDF Slim Line Muzzle Brake
This threaded muzzlebrake has 30 pressure ports that direct combustion gases in all directions to reduce felt recoil up to a claimed 80 percent without affecting accuracy or ballistics. It is said to reduce felt recoil of a 30-06 to that of a 243. Price, installed, is **$179.00**. From KDF, Inc.

Mag-Na-Port
Electrical Discharge Machining works on any firearm except those having non-conductive shrouded barrels. EDM is a metal erosion technique using carbon electrodes that control the area to be processed. The Mag-Na-Port venting process utilizes small trapezoidal openings to direct powder gases upward and outward to reduce recoil. No effect is had on bluing or nickeling outside the Mag-Na-Port area so no refinishing is needed. Rifle-style porting on single shot or large caliber handguns with barrels 7 1/2" or longer is **$95.00**; Dual Trapezoidal porting on most handguns with minimum barrel length of 3", **$95.00**; standard revolver porting, **$65.00**; porting through the slide and barrel for semi-autos, **$90.00**; traditional rifle porting, **$115.00**. Prices do not include shipping, handling and insurance. From Mag-Na-Port International.

Mag-Na-Brake
A screw-on brake under 2" long with progressive integrated exhaust chambers to neutralize expanding gases. Gases dissipate with an opposite twist to prevent the brake from unscrewing, and with a 5-degree forward angle to minimize sound pressure level. Available in blue, satin blue, bright or satin stainless. Standard and Light Contour installation cost **$159.00** for bolt-action rifles, many single action and single shot handguns. A knurled thread protector costs **$30.00**. Also available in Varmint style with exhaust chambers covering 220 degrees for prone-position shooters. From Mag-Na-Port International.

Poly-Choke
Marble Arms Corp., manufacturer of the Poly-Choke adjustable shotgun choke, now offers two models in 12-, 16-, 20-, and 28-gauge—the Ventilated and Standard style chokes. Each provides nine choke settings including Xtra-Full and Slug. The Ventilated model reduces 20 percent of a shotgun's recoil, the company claims, and is priced at **$92.00**. The Standard Model is **$85.00**. Postage not included. Contact Marble Arms for more data.

Reed-Choke
Reed-Choke is a system of interchangeable choke tubes that can be installed in any single or double-barreled shotgun, including over/unders. The existing chokes are bored out, the muzzles over-bored and threaded for the tubes. A choice of three Reed-Choke tubes are supplied—Skeet, Imp. Cyl., Mod., Imp. Mod., or Full. Flush fitting, no notches exposed. Designed for thin-walled barrels. Made from 174 stainless steel. Cost of the installation is **$179.95** for single-barrel guns, **$229.95** for doubles. Extra tubes cost **$40.00** each. Postage and handling charges are **$8.50**. From Clinton River Gun Service.

Pro-port
A compound ellipsoid muzzle venting process similar to Mag-Na-Porting, only exclusively applied to shotguns. Like Mag-Na-Porting, this system reduces felt recoil, muzzle jump, and shooter fatigue. Very helpful for trap doubles shooters. Pro-Port is a patented process and installation is available in both the U.S. and Canada. Cost for the Pro-Port process is **$110.00** for over/unders (both barrels); **$80.00** for only the top or bottom barrel; and **$69.00** for single-barrel shotguns. Optional pigeon porting costs **$25.00** extra per barrel. Prices do not include shipping and handling. From Pro-port Ltd.

SSK Arrestor Brake
This is a true muzzlebrake with an expansion chamber. It takes up about 1" of barrel and reduces velocity accordingly. Some Arrestors are added to a barrel, increasing its length. Said to reduce the felt recoil of a 458 to that approaching a 30-06. Can be set up to give zero muzzle rise in any caliber, and can be added to most guns. For handgun or rifle. Prices start at **$95.00**. Contact SSK Industries for full data.

Walker Choke Tubes
This interchangeable choke tube system uses an adaptor fitted to the barrel without swaging. Therefore, it can be fitted to any single-barreled gun. The choke tubes use the conical-parallel system as used on all factory-choked barrels. These tubes can be used in Winchester, Mossberg, Smith & Wesson, Weatherby, or similar barrels made for the standard screw-in choke system. Available for 10-, 12-, 16- and 20-gauge. Factory installation (single barrel) with standard Walker choke tube is **$95.00**, **$190.00** for double barrels with two choke tubes. A full range of constriction is available. Contact Walker Arms for more data.

Walker Full Thread Choke Tubes
An interchangeable choke tube system using fully threaded inserts. No swaging, adaptor or change in barrel exterior dimensions. Available in 12- or 20-gauge. Factory installation cost: **$95.00** with one tube; extra tubes **$20.00** each. Contact Walker Arms Co. for more data.

SCOPES & MOUNTS

Maker and Model	Magn.	Field at 100 Yds. (feet)	Eye Relief (in.)	Length (in.)	Tube Dia. (in.)	W&E Adjustments	Weight (ozs.)	Price	Other Data
AAL OPTICS									
Micro-Dot Scopes[1]									[1]Brightness-adjustable fiber optic red dot reticle. Waterproof, nitrogen-filled one-piece tube tube. Tinted see-through lens covers and battery included. [2]Parallax adjustable. [3]Ultra Dot sights include rings, battery, polarized filter, and 5-year warranty. All models available in black or satin finish. [4]Illuminated red dot has eleven brightness settings. Shock-proof aluminum tube. [5]Fiber optic red dot has five brightness settings. Shock-proof polymer tube. From AAL Optics.
1.5-4.5x20 Rifle	1.5-4.5	80-26	3	9.8	1	Int.	10.5	$287.00	
2-7x32	2-7	54-18	3	11.0	1	Int.	12.1	299.00	
3-9x40	3-9	40-14	3	12.2	1	Int.	13.3	319.00	
4x-12x56[2]	4-12	30-10	3	14.3	1	Int.	18.3	409.00	
Ultra-Dot Sights[3]									
Ultra-Dot 25[4]	1	—	—	5.1	1	Int.	3.9	139.00	
Ultra-Dot 30[4]	1	—	—	5.1	30mm	Int.	4.0	149.00	
Ultra Dot Patriot[5]	1	—	—	5.1	1	Int.	2.9	119.00	
ADCO									[1]Multi-Color Dot system changes from red to green. [2]For airguns, paintball, rimfires. Uses common lithium wafer battery. [3]Comes with standard dovetail mount. [4]3/8" dovetail mount; poly body; adj. intensity diode. All come with extension tube for mounting. Black or matte nickel finish. Optional 2x booster available. Five year warranty. From ADCO Sales.
MiRAGE Ranger 1"	0	—	—	5.2	1	Int.	4.5	159.00	
MiRAGE Ranger 30mm	0	—	—	5.5	30mm	Int.	5.5	169.00	
MiRAGE Sportsman[1]	0	—	—	5.2	1	Int.	4.5	219.00	
MiRAGE Competitor[1]	0	—	—	5.5	30mm	Int.	5.5	249.00	
IMP Sight[2]	0	—	—	4.5	—	Int.	2	19.95	
Square Shooter[3]	0	—	—	5.0	—	Int.	5	118.00	
MiRAGE Eclipse[1]	0	—	—	5.5	30mm	Int.	5.3	219.00	
MiRAGE Champ Red Dot	0	—	—	4.5	—	Int.	2	39.95	
AIMPOINT									Illuminates red dot in field of view. Noparallax (dot does not need to be centered). Unlimited field of view and eye relief. On/off, adj. intensity. Dot covers 3" @ 100 yds. Mounts avail. for all sights and scopes. [1]Comes with 30mm rings, battery, lens cloth. [2]Requires 1" rings. Black or stainless finish. 3x scope attachment (for rifles only), **$129.95**. [3]Projects red dot of visible laser light onto target. Black finish (LSR-2B) or stainless (LSR-2S); or comes with rings and accessories. Optional toggle switch, **$34.95**. Lithium battery life up to 15 hours. [4]Black finish (AP 5000-B) or stainless (AP 5000-S); avail. with regular 3-min. or 10-min. Mag Dot as B2 or S2. [5] For Beretta, Browning, Colt Gov't., Desert Eagle, Glock, Ruger, SIG-Sauer, S&W. [6]For Colt, S&W. From Aimpoint.
Comp	0	—	—	4.6	30mm	Int.	4.3	308.00	
Series 5000[4]	0	—	—	5.75	30mm	Int.	5.8	277.00	
Series 3000 Universal[2]	0	—	—	5.5	1	Int.	5.5	232.00	
Series 5000/2x[1]	2	—	—	7	30mm	Int.	9	367.00	
Laserdot[3]	—	—	—	3.5	1	Int.	4.0	319.95	
Autolaser[5]	—	—	—	3.75	1	Int.	4.3	351.00	
Revolver Laser[6]	—	—	—	3.5	1	Int.	3.6	339.00	
APPLIED LASER SYSTEMS									[1]Output power 5mW; also MA-35, power less than 3mW, **$350.00**; [2]for HK USP, 5mW; also HK USP 635nm (3mW), **$350.00**; [3]also SP 89/MP5 635nm (3mW), **$350.00**; [4]5mW power. Mounts avail. for Browning Hi-Power, S&W, Colt 1911, Beretta 92F, Glock, SIG-Sauer, Ruger P-85 MkII, Firestor. From Applied Laser Systems.
MiniAimer MA-3[1]	—	—	—	1.36	—	Int.	.88	246.00	
Custom MiniAimer[2]	—	—	—	1.74	—	Int.	1.6	298.00	
Custom MiniAimer[3]	—	—	—	2.08	—	Int.	1.2	298.00	
T2 Custom Aimer[4]	—	—	—	2.8	—	Int.	2.2	198.00	
AR-15 Custom Aimer[4]	—	—	—	2.0	—	Int.	3.0	279.00	
Custom Glock Mini Laser[4]	—	—	—	.75	—	Int.	.8	385.00	
ARMSON O.E.G.									Shows red dot aiming point. No batteries needed. Standard model fits 1" ring mounts (not incl.). Other models available for many popular shotguns, para-military rifles and carbines. [1]Daylight Only Sight with 3/8" dovetail mount for 22s. Does not contain tritium. From Trijicon, Inc.
Standard	0	—	—	5 1/8	1	Int.	4.3	175.00	
22 DOS[1]	0	—	—	3 3/4	—	Int.	3.0	104.00	
22 Day/Night	0	—	—	3 3/4	—	Int.	3.0	146.00	
M16/AR-15	0	—	—	5 1/8	—	Int.	5.5	209.00	
Colt Pistol	0	—	—	3 3/4	—	Int.	3.0	209.00	
BAUSCH & LOMB									[1]Adj. objective, sunshade. [2]Also in matte and silver finish, **$626.00**. [3]Also in matte finish, **$584.00**. [4]Also in matte finish, **$370.95**; silver finish, **$370.95**. [5]Also in matte finish, **$358.95**. [6]50mm objective; matte finish, **$449.95**. [7]Also in matte finish, **$430.95**. [8]Also in silver finish, **$318.95**. [9]Also in silver finish, **$428.95 Contact Bausch & Lomb Sports Optics Div. for details.**
Elite 4000									
40-6244A[1]	6-24	18-4.5	3	16.9	1	Int.	20.2	696.00	
40-2104G[2]	2.5-10	41.5-10.8	3	13.5	1	Int.	16	599.00	
40-1636G[3]	1.5-6	61.8-16.1	3	12.8	1	Int.	15.4	561.00	
40-1040	10	10.5	3.6	13.8	1	Int.	22.1	1,729.00	
Elite 3000									
30-4124A[1]	4-12	26.9-9	3	13.2	1	Int.	15.0	418.95	
30-3940G[4]	3-9	33.8-11.5	3	12.6	1	Int.	13.0	348.95	
30-2732G[5]	2-7	44.6-12.7	3	11.6	1	Int.	12.0	339.95	
30-3950G[6]	3-9	31.5-10.5	3	15.7	1	Int.	19	430.95	
30-1545G[7]	1.5-4.5	73-24	3.3	9.7	1	Int.	10	411.95	
30-3955E	3-9	31.5-10.5	3	15.6	30mm	Int.	22	628.95	
Elite 3000 Handgun									
30-2028G[8]	2	23	9-26	8.4	1	Int.	6.9	299.95	
30-2632G[9]	2-6	10-4	20	9.0	1	Int.	10.0	409.95	
BEEMAN									All scopes have 5-point reticle, all glass, fully coated lenses. [1]Includes mount. [2]Also as 66RL with lighted color reticle, **$355.00**. [3]Also as SS-2L 3x with color 4pt. reticle. Imported by Beeman
Blue Ribbon SS-3[1]	1.5-4	42-25	3	5.8	7/8	Int.	8.5	300.00	
Blue Ribbon 66R[2]	2-7	62-16	3	11.4	1	Int.	14.9	315.00	
Blue Ribbon SS-2[1,3]	4	25	3.5	7.0	1.4	Int.	13.7	305.00	
Blue Ribbon 25 Pistol	2	19	10-24	9.1	1	Int.	7.4	155.00	

CAUTION: PRICES SHOWN ARE SUPPLIED BY THE MANUFACTURER OR IMPORTER. CHECK YOUR LOCAL GUNSHOP.

HUNTING, TARGET & VARMINT SCOPES

Maker and Model	Magn.	Field at 100 Yds. (feet)	Eye Relief (in.)	Length (in.)	Tube Dia. (in.)	W&E Adjustments	Weight (ozs.)	Price	Other Data
B-SQUARE									[1]Blue finish; stainless, **$209.95**. T-slot mount; cord or integral switch. [2]Blue finish; stainless, **$259.95**. T-slot mount; cord or integral switch. Uses common A76 batteries. [3]High intensity 635 beam, **$349.95** (blue), **$359.95** (stainless). Dimensions 1.1"x1.1"x.6". From B-Square.
BSL-1[1]	—	—	—	2.75	.75	Int.	2.25	199.95	
Mini-Laser[2,3]	—	—	—	1.1	—	Int.	2.9	239.95	
BURRIS									All scopes avail. in Plex reticle. Steel-on-steel click adjustments. [1]Dot reticle on some models. [2]Post crosshair reticle extra. [3]Matte satin finish. [4]Available with parallax adjustment (standard on 10x, 12x, 4-12x, 6-12x, 6-18x, 6x HBR and 3-12x Signature). [5]Silver matte finish extra. [6]Target knobs extra, standard on silhouette models, LER and XER with P.A., 6x HBR. [7]Sunshade avail. [8]Avail. with Fine Plex reticle. [9]Available with Heavy Plex reticle. [10]Available with Posi-Lock. [11]Available with Peep Plex reticle. [12]Also avail. for rimfires, airguns.
Fullfield									
1x LER[3]	1	51	4.5-20	8.8	1	Int.	7.9	247.00	
1½x[9]	1.6	62	3.5-3.75	10¼	1	Int.	9.0	247.00	
2½x[9]	2.5	55	3.5-3.75	10¼	1	Int.	9.0	258.00	
4x[1,2,3]	3.75	36	3.5-3.75	11¼	1	Int.	11.5	277.00	
6x[1,3]	5.8	23	3.5-3.75	13	1	Int.	12.0	297.00	
12x[1,4,6,7,8]	11.8	10.5	3.5-3.75	15	1	Int.	15	374.00	
1-4x XER[3]	1.0-3.8	53-15	4.25-30	8.8	1	Int.	10.3	325.00	
1¾-5x[1,2,9,10]	1.7-4.6	66-25	3.5-3.75	10⅞	1	Int.	13	323.00	
2-7x[1,2,3]	2.5-6.8	47-18	3.5-3.75	12	1	Int.	14	348.00	
3-9x[1,2,3,10]	3.3-8.7	38-15	3.5-3.75	12⅝	1	Int.	15	332.00	
3.5-10x50mm[3,5,10]	3.7-9.7	29.5-11	3.5-3.75	14	1	Int.	19	429.00	
4-12x[1,4,8,11]	4.4-11.8	27-10	3.5-3.75	15	1	Int.	18	437.00	
6-18x[1,3,4,6,7,8]	6.5-17.6	16-7	3.5-3.75	15.8	1	Int.	18.5	455.00	
Compact Scopes									
4x[4,5]	3.6	24	3¾-5	8¼	1	Int.	7.8	223.00	
6x[1,4]	5.5	17	3¾-5	9	1	Int.	8.2	238.00	
6x HBR[1,5,8]	6.0	13	4.5	11¼	1	Int.	13.0	307.00	
2-7x	2.5-6.9	32-14	3¾-5	12	1	Int.	10.5	305.00	
3-9x[5]	3.6-8.8	25-11	3¾-5	12⅝	1	Int.	11.5	312.00	
4-12x[1,4,6]	4.5-11.6	19-8	3¾-4	15	1	Int.	15	413.00	
Signature Series									LER=Long Eye Relief; IER=Intermediate Eye Relief; XER=Extra Eye Relief. Partial listing shown, contact maker for complete data. From Burris.
1.5-6x[2,3,5,9,10]	1.7-5.8	70-20	3.5-4.0	10.8	1	Int.	13.0	413.00	
4x[3]	4.0	30	3.5-4.0	12⅛	1	Int.	14	336.00	
6x[3]	6.0	20	3.5-4.0	12⅛	1	Int.	14	353.00	
2-8x[3,5,11]	2.1-7.7	53-17	3.5-4.0	11.75	1	Int.	14	480.00	
3-9x[3,5,10]	3.3-8.8	36-14	3.5-4.0	12⅞	1	Int.	15.5	489.00	
2½-10x[3,5,10]	2.7-9.5	37-10.5	3.5-4.0	14	1	Int.	19.0	552.00	
3-12x[3,10]	3.3-11.7	34-9	3.5-4.0	14¼	1	Int.	21	612.00	
4-16x[1,3,5,6,8,10]	4.3-15.7	33-9	3.5-4.0	15.4	1	Int.	23.7	624.00	
6-24x[1,3,5,6,8,10]	6.6-23.8	17-6	3.5-4.0	16.0	1	Int.	22.7	638.00	
8-32x[8,10,12]	8.6-31.4	13-3.8	3.5-4.0	17	1	Int.	24	699.00	
Handgun									
1½-4x LER[1,5,10]	1.6-3.	16-11	11-25	10¼	1	Int.	11	342.00	
2-7x LER[3,4,5,10]	2-6.5	21-7	7-27	9.5	1	Int.	12.6	334.00	
3-9x LER[4,5,10]	3.4-8.4	12-5	22-14	11	1	Int.	14	376.00	
1x LER[1]	1.1	27	10-24	8¾	1	Int.	6.8	212.00	
2x LER[4,5,6]	1.7	21	10-24	8¾	1	Int.	6.8	219.00	
3x LER[4,6]	2.7	17	10-20	8⅞	1	Int.	6.8	236.00	
4x LER[1,4,5,6,10]	3.7	11	10-22	9⅝	1	Int.	9.0	245.00	
7x IER[1,4,5,6]	6.5	6.5	10-16	11¼	1	Int.	10	307.00	
10x IER[1,4,6]	9.5	4	8-12	13½	1	Int.	14	363.00	
Scout Scope									
1½x XER[3,9]	1.5	22	7-18	9	1	Int.	7.3	218.00	
2¾x XER[3,9]	2.7	15	7-14	9⅜	1	Int.	7.5	223.00	
BUSHNELL									[1]45mm objective. [2]Wide angle; silver or matte finish, **$195.95**. [3]Also silver finish, **$204.95**. [4]Also silver finish, **$257.95**. [5]56mm objective. [6]Selective red L.E.D. dot for low light hunting. [7]Also silver finish, **$68.95**. [8]Adj. obj. **Only selected models shown.** Contact Bausch & Lomb Sports Optics Div. for details.
Trophy									
73-0130[1]	1	61	—	5.25	30mm	Int.	5.5	280.95	
73-2545[1]	2.5-10	39-10	3	13.75	1	Int.	14	307.95	
73-1500[2]	1.75-5	68-23	3.5	10.8	1	Int.	12.3	257.95	
73-2733[2]	2-7	63-18	3	10	1	Int.	11.3	254.95	
73-4124[2]	4-12	32-11	3	12.5	1	Int.	16.1	286.95	
73-3940[2]	3-9	42-14	3	11.7	1	Int.	13.2	184.95	
73-6184	6-18	17.3-6	3	14.8	1	Int.	17.9	335.95	
Trophy Handgun									
73-0232[3]	2	20	9-26	8.7	1	Int.	7.7	189.95	
73-2632[4]	2-6	21-7	9-26	9.1	1	Int.	9.6	244.95	
Banner Standard									
71-2520	2.5	44	3.6	10	1	Int.	7.5	84.95	
71-3956[5]	3-9	37-12	3.5	13.7	1	Int.	17.3	286.95	
Lite-Site									
71-3940[6]	3-9	36-13	3.1	12.8	1	Int.	15.5	365.95	
Sportview									
79-0004	4	31	4	11.7	1	Int.	11.2	91.95	
79-0039	3-9	38-13	3.5	10.75	1	Int.	11.2	108.95	
79-0412[8]	4-12	27-9	3.2	13.1	1	Int.	14.6	131.95	
79-0640	6	20.5	3	12.25	1	Int.	10.4	91.95	
79-1393[7]	3-9	35-12	3.5	11.75	1	Int.	10	66.95	
79-1545	1.5-4.5	69-24	3	10.7	1	Int.	8.6	88.95	
79-2532	2.5	44	3.5	10.75	1	Int.	8	88.95	
79-3145	3.5-10	36-13	3	12.75	1	Int.	13.9	144.95	
79-1403	4	29	4	11.75	1	Int.	9.2	53.95	

HUNTING, TARGET & VARMINT SCOPES

Maker and Model	Magn.	Field at 100 Yds. (feet)	Eye Relief (in.)	Length (in.)	Tube Dia. (in.)	W&E Adjustments	Weight (ozs.)	Price	Other Data
Bushnell (cont.)									
79-3938	3-9	42-14	3	12.7	1	Int.	12.5	105.95	
79-3720	3-7	23-11	2.6	11.3	.75	Int.	5.7	40.95	
Turkey & Brush									
73-1420	1.75-4	73-30	3.5	10.8	32mm	Int.	10.9	263.95	
CHARLES DALY									Waterproof, fog-proof. [1]Shotgun scope. From Outdoor Sports Headquarters.
4x32	4	28	3.25	11.75	1	Int.	9.5	70.00	
4x32[1]	4	16	6	8.8	1	Int.	9.2	90.00	
4x40 WA	4	36	3.25	13	1	Int.	11.5	98.00	
2-7x32 WA	2-7	56-17	3	11.5	1	Int.	12	125.00	
3-9x40	3-9	35-14	3	12.5	1	Int.	11.25	110.00	
3-9x40 WA	3-9	36-13	3	12.75	1	Int.	12.5	125.00	
4-12x40 WA	4-12	30-11	3	13.75	1	Int.	14.5	133.00	
DOCTER OPTIC									Matte black and matte silver finish available. All lenses multi-coated. Illuminated reticle avail., choice of reticles. Rail mount, aspherical lenses avail. [1]Aspherical lens model, **$1,375.00**. Imported from Germany by Docter Optic Technologies, Inc.
Fixed Power									
4x32	4	31	3	10.7	26mm	Int.	10.0	898.00	
6x42	6	20	3	12.8	26mm	Int.	12.7	1,004.00	
8x56[1]	8	15	3	14.7	26mm	Int.	15.6	1,240.00	
Variables									
1-4x24	1-4	79.7-31.3	3	10.8	30mm	Int.	13	1,300.00	
1.2-5x32	1.2-5	65-25	3	11.6	30mm	Int.	15.4	1,345.00	
1.5-6x42	1.5-6	41.3-20.6	3	12.7	30mm	Int.	16.8	1,378.00	
2.5-10x48	2.5-10	36.6-12.4	3	13.7	30mm	Int.	18.6	1,378.00	
2-12x56	3-12	44.2-13.8	3	14.8	30mm	Int.	20.3	1,425.00	
FROM JENA									[1]Military scope with adjustable parallax. Fixed powers have 26mm tubes, variables have 30mm tubes. Some models avail. with steel tubes. All lenses multi-coated. Dust and water tight. From Jena, Europtik, Ltd.
4x36	4	39	3.5	11.6	26mm	Int.	14	695.00	
6x36	6	21	3.5	12	26mm	Int.	14	795.00	
6x42	6	21	3.5	13	26mm	Int.	15	860.00	
8x56	8	18	3.5	14.4	26mm	Int.	20	890.00	
1.5-6x42	1.5-6	61.7-23	3.5	12.6	30mm	Int.	17	975.00	
2-8x42	2-8	52-17	3.5	13.3	30mm	Int.	17	1,050.00	
2.5-10x56	2.5-10	40-13.6	3.5	15	30mm	Int.	21	1,195.00	
3-12x56	3-12	NA	NA	NA	30mm	Int.	NA	1,195.00	
4-16x56	4-16	NA	NA	NA	30mm	Int.	NA	1,225.00	
3-9x40	3-9	NA	NA	NA	1	Int.	NA	1,120.00	
2.5-10x46	2.5-10	NA	NA	NA	30mm	Int.	NA	1,150.00	
4-16x56[1]	4-16	NA	NA	NA	30mm	Int.	NA	1,490.00	
INTERAIMS									Intended for handguns. Comes with rings. Dot size less than 1½" @ 100 yds. Waterproof. Battery life 50-10,000 hours. Black or nickel finish. 2x booster, 1" or 30mm, **$139.00** Imported by Stoeger.
One V	0	—	—	4.5	1	Int.	4	159.95	
One V 30	0	—	—	4.5	30mm	Int.	4	176.95	
KAHLES									[1]Steel tube. [2]Ballistic cam system with military rangefinder. Waterproof, fogproof, nitrogen filled. Choice of reticles. Imported from Austria by Swarovski Optic NA.
K1.5-6x42-L	1.5-6	61-21	—	12.5	30mm	Int.	15.8	721.12	
K2.2-9x42-L	2.2-9	39.5-15	—	13.3	30mm	Int.	15.5	887.78	
K3-12x56-L	3-12	30-11	—	15.2	30mm	Int.	18	943.33	
KZF84-6[1,2]	6	23	—	12.5	1	Int.	17.6	1,245.00	
KZF84-10[1,2]	10	13	—	13.25	1	Int.	18	1,245.00	
KILHAM									Unlimited eye relief; internal click adjustments; crosshair reticle. Fits Thompson/Center rail mounts, for S&W K, N, Ruger Blackhawk, Super, Super Single-Six, Contender.
Hutson Handgunner II	1.7	8	—	5½	7/8	Int.	5.1	119.95	
Hutson Handgunner	3	8	10-12	6	7/8	Int.	5.3	119.95	
LASERAIM									[1]300-yd. range; 15-hr. batt. [2]Red dot laser; fits Weaver-style mounts; also LA2XM with Hotdot, **$269.95**. [3]300-yd. range; 2" dot at 100 yds.; rechargeable Nicad battery. [4]1.5-mile range; 1" dot at 100 yds.; 20+ hrs. batt. life. [5]1.5-mile range; 1" dot at 100 yds.; rechargeable Nicad battery (comes with in-field charger); [6]Black or satin finish. With mount, **$169.00**. [7]Fits any pistol magazine without bumper pad; Hotdot model (LA18), **$319.00**. [8]Laser mounts in revolver grip (included); Hotdot model (LA20), **$292.00**. [9]Rings included; 6-MOA dot, seven brightness settings. [10]Ext. tube, polarizing filter incl.; 4-MOA dot, seven brightness settings. [11]Auto. brightness control; 30mm lens; fits std. Weaver base, no rings required. [12]Fits std. Weaver base, no rings required; 6-MOA dot; seven brightness settings. All have w&e adj.; black or satin silver finish. From Emerging Technologies, Inc.
LA8[1]	—	—	—	2.94	.74	Int.	NA	139.00	
LA2X Dualdot[2]	—	—	—	NA	30mm	Int.	NA	319.00	
LA5[3]	—	—	—	2	.75	Int.	1.2	236.00	
LA10 Hotdot[4]	—	—	—	3.87	.75	Int.	NA	396.00	
LA11 Hotdot[5]	—	—	—	2.75	.75	Int.	NA	292.00	
LA14	—	—	—	NA	NA	Int.	NA	314.00	
LA16 Hotdot Mighty Sight[6]	—	—	—	1.5	NA	Int.	1.5	140.00	
LA17 Clip Sight[7]	—	—	—	1.5	NA	Int.	2.0	278.00	
LA19 Grip Sight[8]	—	—	—	1.5	NA	Int.	NA	244.00	
Red Dot Sights									
LA94 Illusion II[9]	—	—	—	6.0	30mm	Int.	6.0	111.00	
LA99 Illusion[10]	—	—	—	5.5	1	Int.	5.0	138.00	
LA930 Auto Illusion[11]	—	—	—	4.75	—	Int.	5.75	181.00	
LA9750 Grand Illusion[12]	—	—	—	5.5	50mm	Int.	7.0	236.00	
LASER DEVICES									Projects high intensity beam of laser light onto target as an aiming point. Adj. for w. & e. [1]Diode laser system. From Laser Devices, Inc.
He Ne FA-6	—	—	—	6.2	—	Int.	11	229.50	
He Ne FA-9	—	—	—	12	—	Int.	16	299.00	
He Ne FA-9P	—	—	—	9	—	Int.	14	299.00	
FA-4[1]	—	—	—	4.5	—	Int.	3.5	299.00	
LASERSIGHT									Projects a highly visible beam of concentrated laser light onto the target. Adjustable for w.& e. Visible up to 500 yds. at night. For handguns, rifles, shotguns. Uses two standard 9V batteries. From Imatronic Lasersight.
LS45	0	—	—	7.5	—	Int.	8.5	245.00	
LS25	0	—	—	6	3/4	Int.	3.5	270.00	
LS55	0	—	—	7	1	Int.	—	299.00	

CAUTION: PRICES SHOWN ARE SUPPLIED BY THE MANUFACTURER OR IMPORTER. CHECK YOUR LOCAL GUNSHOP.

HUNTING, TARGET & VARMINT SCOPES

Maker and Model	Magn.	Field at 100 Yds. (feet)	Eye Relief (in.)	Length (in.)	Tube Dia. (in.)	W&E Adjust-ments	Weight (ozs.)	Price	Other Data
LEATHERWOOD									
ART II	3.0-8.8	31-12	3.5	13.9	1	Int.	42	750.00	Compensates for bullet drop via external circular cam. Matte gray finish. Designed specifically for the M1A/M-14 rifle. Quick Detachable model for rifles with Weaver-type bases. From North American Specialties.
LEUPOLD									
Vari-X III 3.5x10 STD Tactical	3.5-10	29.5-10.7	3.6-4.6	12.5	1	Int.	13.5	687.50	Constantly centered reticles, choice of Duplex, tapered CPC, Leupold Dot, Crosshair and Dot. CPC and Dot reticles extra. [2]2x and 4x scopes have from 12"-24" of eye relief and are suitable for handguns, top ejection arms and muzzleloaders. [3]3x9 Compact, 6x Compact, 12x, 3x9, 3.5x10 and 6.5x20 come with adjustable objective. [3]Target scopes have 1-min. divisions with ¼-min. clicks, and adjustable objectives. 50-ft. Focus Adaptor available for indoor target ranges, $51.80. Sunshade available for all adjustable objective scopes, $19.60-37.50. [4]Also available in matte finish for about $22.00 extra. [5]Silver finish about $22.00 extra. [6]Matte finish. [7]Battery life 60 min.; dot size .625" @ 25 yds. Black matte finish Partial listing shown. **Contact Leupold for complete details.**
M8-2X EER[1]	1.7	21.2	12-24	7.9	1	Int.	6.0	264.30	
M8-2X EER Silver[1]	1.7	21.2	12-24	7.9	1	Int.	6.0	285.70	
M8-4X EER[1]	3.7	9	12-24	8.4	1	Int.	7.0	357.10	
M8-4X EER Silver[1]	3.7	9	12-24	8.4	1	Int.	7.0	357.10	
Vari-X 2.5-8 EER	2.5-8.0	13-4.3	11.7-12	9.7	1	Int.	10.9	514.30	
M8-4X Compact	3.6	25.5	4.5	9.2	1	Int.	7.5	326.80	
Vari-X 2-7x Compact	2.5-6.6	41.7-16.5	5-3.7	9.9	1	Int.	8.5	405.40	
Vari-X 3-9x Compact	3.2-8.6	34-13.5	4.0-3.0	11-11.3	1	Int.	11.0	419.60	
M8-4X[4]	4.0	24	4.0	10.7	1	Int.	9.3	326.80	
M8-6X[6]	5.9	17.7	4.3	11.4	1	Int.	10.0	348.20	
M8-6x 42mm	6.0	17	4.5	12	1	Int.	11.3	432.10	
M8-12x A.O. Varmint	11.6	9.1	4.2	13.0	1	Int.	13.5	558.90	
BR-24X[3]	24.0	4.7	3.2	13.8	1	Int.	15.3	869.60	
BR-36X[3]	36.0	3.2	3.4	14.1	1	Int.	15.6	910.70	
Vari-X 3-9x Compact EFR A.O.	3.8-8.6	34.0-13.5	4.0-3.0	11.0	1	Int.	11	475.00	
Vari-X-II 1x4	1.6-4.2	70.5-28.5	4.3-3.8	9.2	1	Int.	9.0	357.10	
Vari-X-II 2x7[4]	2.5-6.6	42.5-17.8	4.9-3.8	11.0	1	Int.	10.5	387.50	
Vari-X-II 3x9[1,4,5]	3.3-8.6	32.3-14.0	4.1-3.7	12.3	1	Int.	13.5	391.10	
Vari-X-II 3-9x50mm[4]	3.3-8.6	32.3-14	4.7-3.7	12	1	Int.	13.6	469.60	
Vari-X-II 4-12 A.O. Matte	4.4-11.6	22.8-11.0	5.0-3.3	12.3	1	Int.	13.5	530.40	
Vari-X-III 1.5x5	1.5-4.5	66.0-23.0	5.3-3.7	9.4	1	Int.	9.5	532.10	
Vari-X-III 1.75-6x 32	1.9-5.6	47-18	4.8-3.7	9.8	1	Int.	11	555.40	
Vari-X-III 2.5x8[4]	2.6-7.8	37.0-13.5	4.7-3.7	11.3	1	Int.	11.5	573.20	
Vari-X-III 3.5-10x50 A.O.	3.3-9.7	29.5-10.7	4.6-3.6	12.4	1	Int.	13.0	692.90	
Vari-X-III 3.5-10x50[2,4]	3.3-9.7	29.5-10.7	4.6-3.6	12.4	1	Int.	14.4	594.60	
Vari-X-III 4.5-14	4.7-13.7	20.8-7.4	5.0-3.7	12.4	1	Int.	14.5	689.30	
Vari-X-III 4.5-14x50	4.7-13.7	20.8-7.4	5.0-3.7	12.4	1	Int.	14.5	789.30	
Vari-X-III 6.5-20 A.O. Varmint	6.5-19.2	14.2-5.5	5.3-3.6	14.2	1	Int.	17.5	775.00	
Vari-X-III 6.5-20x Target EFR A.O.	6.5-19.2	—	5.3-3.6	14.2	1	Int.	16.5	766.10	
Mark 4 M3-6x	6	17.7	4.5	13.1	30mm	Int.	21	1,550.00	
Mark 4 M1-10x[6]	10	11.1	3.6	13 1/8	1	Int.	21	1,550.00	
Mark 4 M1-16x[6]	16	6.6	4.1	12 7/8	1	Int.	22	1,550.00	
Mark 4 M3-10x[6]	10	11.1	3.6	13 1/8	1	Int.	21	1,550.00	
Vari-X-III 6.5x20[2]	6.5-19.2	14.2-5.5	5.3-3.6	14.2	1	Int.	16.0	694.60	
Rimfire									
Vari-X-II 2-7x RF Special	3.6	25.5	4.5	9.2	1	Int.	7.5	405.40	
Shotgun									
M8 4x	3.7	9.0	12-24	8.4	1	Int.	6.0	348.20	
Vari-X-II 1x4	1.6-4.2	70.5-28.5	4.3-3.8	9.2	1	Int.	9.0	378.60	
Vari-X-II 2x7	2.5-6.6	42.5-17.8	4.9-3.8	11.0	1	Int.	9.0	408.90	
Laser									
LaserLight[7]	—	—	—	1.18	NA	Int.	.5	266.10	
LYMAN									
Super TargetSpot[1]	10,12,15,20, 25,30	5.5	2	24.3	.75	Int.	27.5	685.00	Made under license from Lyman to Lyman's orig. specs. Blue steel. Three-point suspension rear mount with ¼-min. click adj. Data listed are for 20x model. [1]Price approximate. Made in U.S. by Parsons Optical Mfg. Co.
McMILLAN									
Vision Master 2.5-10x	2.5-10	14.2-4.4	4.3-3.3	13.3	30mm	Int.	17.0	1,250.00	42mm obj. lens; ¼-MOA clicks; nitrogen filled, fogproof, waterproof; etched duplex-type reticle. [1]Tactical Scope with external adj. knobs, military reticle; 60+ min. adj.
Vision Master Model I[1]	2.5-10	14.2-4.4	4.3-3.3	13.3	30mm	Int.	17.0	1,250.00	
MILLET									
Red Dot 1 Inch	1	36.65	—	NA	1	Int.	NA	189.95	Full coated lenses; parallax-free; three lenses; 30mm has 10-min. dot, 1-Inch has 3-min. dot. Black or silver finish. From Millett Sights.
Red Dot 30mm	1	58	—	NA	30mm	Int.	NA	289.95	
MIRADOR									
RXW 4x40[1]	4	37	3.8	12.4	1	Int.	12	179.95	[1]Wide Angle scope. Multi-coated objective lens. Nitrogen filled; waterproof; shockproof. From Mirador Optical Corp.
RXW 1.5-5x20[1]	1.5-5	46-17.4	4.3	11.1	1	Int.	10	188.95	
RXW 3-9x40	3-9	43-14.5	3.1	12.9	1	Int.	13.4	251.95	
NIKON									
4x40[2]	4	26.7	3.5	11.7	1	Int.	11.7	284.00	Super multi-coated lenses and blackening of all internal metal parts for maximum light gathering capability; positive ¼-MOA; fogproof; waterproof; shockproof; luster and matte finish. [1]Also available in matte silver finish. [2]Available in silver matte finish. From Nikon, Inc.
1.5-4.5x20	1.5-4.5	67.8-22.5	3.7-3.2	10.1	1	Int.	9.5	358.00	
1.5-4.5x24 EER	1.5-4.4	13.7-5.8	24-18	8.9	1	Int.	9.3	352.00	
2-7x32	2-7	46.7-13.7	3.9-3.3	11.3	1	Int.	11.3	367.00	
3-9x40[1]	3-9	33.8-11.3	3.6-3.2	12.5	1	Int.	12.5	371.00	
3.5-10x50	3.5-10	25.5-8.9	3.9-3.8	13.7	1	Int.	15.5	489.00	
4-12x40 A.O.	4-12	25.7-8.6	3.6-3.2	14	1	Int.	16.6	476.00	
4-12x50 A.O.	4-12	25.4-8.5	3.6-3.5	14.0	1	Int.	18.3	578.00	
6.5-20x44	6.5-19.4	16.2-5.4	3.5-3.1	14.8	1	Int.	19.6	591.00	
2x20 EER	2	22	26.4	8.1	1	Int.	6.3	213.00	

HUNTING, TARGET & VARMINT SCOPES

Maker and Model	Magn.	Field at 100 Yds. (feet)	Eye Relief (in.)	Length (in.)	Tube Dia. (in.)	W&E Adjust-ments	Weight (ozs.)	Price	Other Data
PARSONS									Adjustable for parallax, focus. Micrometer rear mount with 1/4-min. click adjustments. Price is approximate. Made in U.S. by Parsons Optical Mfg. Co.
Parsons Long Scope	6	10	2	28-34+	3/4	Ext.	13	475.00-525.00	
PENTAX									[1]Glossy finish; matte finish, **$530.00**; satin chrome, **$550.00**. [2]Glossy finish; matte finish, **$560.00**; satin chrome **$580.00**. [3]Glossy finish; matte finish, **$580.00**; satin chrome, **$600.00**. [4]Glossy-XL finish; matte-XL finish, **$720.00**; satin chrome-XL, **$740.00**. [5]Glossy finish; matte finish, **$770.00**. [6]Glossy finish, Fine Plex; matte finish, Fine Plex, **$810.00**; dot reticle, add **$10.00**. [7]Glossy finish; matte finish, **$380.00**; satin chrome, **$380.00**. [8]Glossy finish; matte finish, **$420.00**; satin chrome **$440.00**. [9]Glossy finish; matte finish, **$360.00**. [10]Glossy finish; matte finish, **$560.00**. [11]Glossy finish; matte finish, **$360.00**. [12]Glossy finish; matte finish, **$440.00**. [13]Glossy finish; matte finish, **$310.00**; Mossy Oak, **$330.00**. [14]Glossy finish; satin chrome, **$260.00**. [15]Glossy finish; satin chrome, **$380.00**. [16]Glossy finish; satin chrome, **$390.00**. Imported by Pentax Corp.
Lightseeker 2-8x[1]	2-8	53-17	3-3.5	11.7	1	Int.	14.0	510.00	
Lightseeker 3-9x[2]	3-9	36-14	3-3.5	12.7	1	Int.	15.0	540.00	
Lightseeker 3.5-10x[3]	3.5-10	29.5-11	3-3.25	14.0	1	Int.	19.5	560.00	
Lightseeker 3-11x[4]	3-11	38.5-13	3-3.25	13.3	1	Int.	19	700.00	
Lightseeker 4-16x AO[5]	4-16	3-3.5	33-9	15.4	1	Int.	23.7	750.00	
Lightseeker 6-24 AO[6]	6-24	18-5.5	3-3.25	16	1	Int.	22.7	790.00	
1.5-5x[7]	1.5-5	66-25	3-3.25	11	1	Int.	13.0	340.00	
3-9x[8]	3-9	38-14.7	3-3.25	13.0	1	Int.	15.0	400.00	
Mini 3-9x[9]	3-9	25-11	3.75-5	10.4	1	Int.	13.0	340.00	
6-18x AO[10]	6-18	16-7	3-3.25	15.8	1	Int.	18.5	540.00	
Shotgun									
Lightseeker Zero-X SG Plus[11]	0	51	4.5-15	8.9	1	Int.	7.9	340.00	
Lightseeker Zero-X/V SG Plus[12]	0-4	53.8-15	3.5-7	8.9	1	Int.	10.3	420.00	
Lightseeker 2.5x SG Plus[13]	2.5	55	3.25	10.0	1	Int.	9.0	290.00	
Pistol									
2x[14]	2	21	10-24	8.8	1	Int.	6.8	230.00	
1.5-4x[15]	1.5-4	16-11	11-25, 11-18	10.0	1	Int.	11.0	350.00	
2.5-7x[16]	2.5-7	12-7.5	11-28, 9-14	12.0	1	Int.	12.5	370.00	
RWS									Air gun scopes. All have Dyna-Plex reticle. Model 800 is for air pistols. [1]M450, 3-9x40mm, **$200.00**. Imported from Japan by Dynamit Nobel-RWS.
300	4	—	8	12 3/4	1	Int.	11	170.00	
400[1]	2-7	—	8	12 3/4	1	Int.	12	190.00	
450	3-9	42-14	3.5	13	1	Int.	12	215.00	
500	4	38	3.5	13	1	Int.	12	225.00	
550	2-7	55-17	3.5	12	1	Int.	10.5	235.00	
600	3-9	44-15	3.5	12.5	1	Int.	12.5	260.00	
650EP	1.5-5	66-20	3.5	11.75	1	Int.	15.5	465.00	
700EP	3-9	44-15	3.5	13	1	Int.	18.75	495.00	
REDFIELD									*Accutrac feature avail. on these scopes at extra cost. Traditionals have round lenses. 4-Plex reticle is standard. [1]Magnum proof. Specially designed for magnum and auto pistols. Uses Double Dovetail mounts. Also in nickel-plated finish, 2x, **$239.95**, 4x, **$239.95**, 2 1/2-7x, **$322.95**, 2 1/2-7x matte black, **$322.95**. [2]With matte finish **$619.95**. [3]Also available with matte finish at extra cost. [4]All Golden Five Star scopes come with Butler Creek flip-up lens covers. [5]56mm adj. objective; European #4 or 4-Plex reticle; comes with 30mm steel rings with Rotary Dovetail System. 1/4-min. click adj. Also in matte finish, **$805.95**. [6]Also available nickel-plated **$363.95**. [7]With target knob, **$439.95**; black matte finish, **$493.95**; black matte with target knob, **$446.95**. [8]Black matte finish, **$400.95**. [9]Also avail. in black matte, **$246.95**. [10]Also avail. in black matte, **$462.95**; black matte with target knobs, **$480.95**; with Accu-Trac, black matte, **$512.95**. Selected models shown. **Contact Redfield for full data.**
Ultimate Illuminator 3-9x	3.4-9.1	27-9	3-3.5	15.1	30mm	Int.	20.5	705.95	
Ultimate Illuminator 3-12x[5]	2.9-11.7	27-10.5	3-3 1/2	15.4	30mm	Int.	23	805.95	
Widefield Illuminator 2-7x	2.0-6.8	56-17	3-3.5	11.7	1	Int.	13.5	539.95	
Widefield Illuminator 3-9x*[2]	2.9-8.7	38-13	3 1/2	12 3/4	1	Int.	17	609.95	
Widefield Illuminator 3-10x	3-10.1	29-10.5	3-3.5	14.75	1	Int.	18.0	681.95	
Tracker 4x[3]	3.9	28.9	3 1/2	11.02	1	Int.	9.8	187.95	
Tracker 6x[3]	6.2	18	3.5	12.4	1	Int.	11.1	217.95	
Tracker 8x	8.1	13.5	3.5	12.4	1	Int.	11.1	226.95	
Tracker 2-7x[3]	2.3-6.9	36.6-12.2	3 1/2	12.20	1	Int.	11.6	239.95	
Tracker 3-9x[3]	3.0-9.0	34.4-11.3	3 1/2	14.96	1	Int.	13.4	269.95	
Traditional 4x 3/4"	4	24 1/2	3 1/2	9 3/8	3/4	Int.	—	229.95	
Traditional 2 1/2x	2 1/2	43	3 1/2	10 1/4	1	Int.	8 1/2	161.95	
Golden Five Star 4x[4]	4	28.5	3.75	11.3	1	Int.	9.75	259.95	
Golden Five Star 6x[4]	6	18	3.75	12.2	1	Int.	11.5	282.95	
Golden Five Star 2-7x[4]	2.4-7.4	42-14	3-3.75	11.25	1	Int.	12	333.95	
Golden Five Star 3-9x[4,6]	3.0-9.1	34-11	3-3.75	12.50	1	Int.	13	409.95	
Golden Five Star 3-9x 50mm[4]	3.0-9.1	36.0-11.5	3-3.5	12.8	1	Int.	16	440.95	
Golden Five Star 4-12x A.O.*[4,10]	3.9-11.4	27-9	3-3.75	13.8	1	Int.	16	505.95	
Golden Five Star 6-18x A.O.*[4,7]	6.1-18.1	18.6	3-3.75	14.3	1	Int.	18	483.95	
I.E.R. 1-4x Shotgun	1.3-3.8	48-16	6	10.2	1	Int.	12	373.95	
Compact Scopes									
Golden Five Star Compact 2-7x	2.4-7.1	40-16	3-3.5	9.75	1	Int.	9.8	329.95	
Golden Five Star Compact 3-9x	3.3-9.1	32-11.25	3-3.5	10.7	1	Int.	10.5	346.95	
Golden Five Star Compact 4-12x	4.1-12.4	22.4-8.3	3-3.5	12	1	Int.	13	439.95	
Handgun Scopes									
Golden Five Star 2x	2	24	9.5-20	7.88	1	Int.	6	223.95	
Golden Five Star 4x	4	75	13-19	8.63	1	Int.	6.1	223.95	
Golden Five Star 2 1/2-7x	2 1/2-7	11-3.75	11-26	9.4	1	Int.	9.3	303.95	
Widefield Low Profile Compact									
Widefield 4xLP Compact	3.7	33	3.5	9.35	1	Int.	10	303.95	
Widefield 3-9x LP Compact	3.3-9	37.0-13.7	3-3.5	10.20	1	Int.	13	387.95	
Low Profile Scopes									
Widefield 2 3/4xLP	2 3/4	55 1/2	3 1/2	10 1/2	1	Int.	8	283.95	
Widefield 4xLP	3.6	37 1/2	3 1/2	11 1/2	1	Int.	10	317.95	
Widefield 6xLP	5.5	23	3 1/2	12 3/4	1	Int.	11	340.95	
Widefield 1 3/4x-5xLP[8]	1 3/4-5	70-27	3 1/2	10 3/4	1	Int.	11 1/2	389.95	

CAUTION: PRICES SHOWN ARE SUPPLIED BY THE MANUFACTURER OR IMPORTER. CHECK YOUR LOCAL GUNSHOP.

HUNTING, TARGET & VARMINT SCOPES

Maker and Model	Magn.	Field at 100 Yds. (feet)	Eye Relief (in.)	Length (in.)	Tube Dia. (in.)	W&E Adjustments	Weight (ozs.)	Price	Other Data
Redfield (cont.)									
Widefield 2x-7xLP*	2-7	49-19	3½	11¾	1	Int.	13	400.95	
Widefield 3x-9xLP*	3-9	39-15	3½	12½	1	Int.	14	445.95	
SCHMIDT & BENDER									All scopes have 30-yr. warranty, click adjustments, centered reticles, rotation indicators. [1]Glass reticle available. Available in aluminum with mounting rail. [2]Also available with aluminum tube. [3]Steel tube. Choice of two bullet drop compensators, two sunshades, three rangefinding reticles. From Schmidt & Bender, Inc.
Fixed									
4x36	4	30	3.25	11	1	Int.	14	680.00	
6x42	6	21	3.25	13	1	Int.	17	743.00	
8x56	8	16.5	3.25	14	1	Int.	22	857.00	
10x42	10	10.5	3.25	13	1	Int.	18	850.00	
Variables									
1.25-4x20[1,2]	1.25-4	96-16	3.25	10	30mm	Int.	15.5	919.00	
1.5-6x42[1,2]	1.5-6	60-19.5	3.25	12	30mm	Int.	19.7	997.00	
2.5-10x56[1,2]	2.5-10	37.5-12	3.25	14	30mm	Int.	24.6	1,228.00	
3-12x42	3-12	34.5-11.5	3.25	13.5	30mm	Int.	19.0	1,183.00	
3-12x50[1,2]	3-12	33.3-12.6	3.25	13.5	30mm	Int.	22.9	1,183.00	
Police/Marksman									
Fixed									
6x42[3]	6	21	3.25	13.0	1	Int.	17.0	985.00	
10x42[3]	10	10.5	3.25	13.0	1	Int.	18	1,060.00	
Variables									
3-12x42[3]	3-12	34.5-11.5	3.25	13.5	30mm	Int.	NA	1,650.00	
3-12x50[3]	3-12	33.3-12.6	3.25	13.5	30mm	Int.	NA	1,650.00	
1.5-6x42[3]	1.5-6	60-19.5	3.25	12.0	30mm	Int.	NA	1,650.00	
SHEPHERD									[1]Also avail. as 310-P, 310-PE, **$499.29**. [2]Also avail. as 310-P1, 310-P2, 310-P3, 310-Pla, 310-PE1, 310-P22, 310-P22 Mag., 310-PE, **$499.29**. All have patented Dual Reticle system with rangefinder bullet drop compensation; multi-coated lenses, waterproof, shockproof, nitrogen filled, matte finish. From Shepherd Scope, Ltd.
3940-E	3-9	43.5-15	3.3	13	1	Int.	17	657.00	
310-2[1,2]	3-10	35.3-11.6	3-3.75	12.8	1	Int.	18	499.29	
SIGHTRON									[1]Black finish; also stainless. [2]3 MOA dot; also with 5 or 10 MOA dot. [3]Variable 3, 5, 10 MOA dot; black finish; also stainless. [4]Satin black; also stainless. Electronic Red Dot scopes come with ring mounts, front and rear extension tubes, polarizing filter, battery, haze filter caps, wrench. Rifle, pistol, shotgun scopes have aluminum tubes, Exac Trak adjustments. Lifetime warranty. From Sightron, Inc.
Electronic Red Dot									
S33-3[1,2]	1	58	—	5.15	33mm	Int.	5.43	279.99	
S33-30[3]	1	58	—	5.74	33mm	Int.	6.27	369.99	
Riflescopes									
Variables									
SII 1.56x42	1.5-6	51-16	3.8-4.0	11.8	1	Int.	15.35	377.99	
SII 39x42[4]	3-9	34-12	3.6-4.2	12.34	1	Int.	13.22	358.99	
Fixed									
SII 4x42	4	31	4.0	12.48	1	Int.	12.34	289.99	
SII 6x42[4]	6	20	4.0	12.48	1	Int.	12.34	289.99	
SII 8x42[4]	8	16	4.0	12.48	1	Int.	12.34	289.99	
Target									
SII 24x44	24	4	4.33	13.26	1	Int.	15.87	406.99	
SII 416x42	4-16	27-7	3.5-3.6	13.74	1	Int.	16.0	426.99	
SII 624-42	6-24	16-5	3.7-3.8	14.7	1	Int.	18.7	449.99	
Compact									
SII 4x32	4	25	4.5	9.72	1	Int.	9.34	247.99	
Shotgun									
SII 2.5x20SG	2.5	41	4.3	10.23	1	Int.	8.46	232.99	
Pistol									
SII 1x28P[1]	1	30	9.0-24.0	9.44	1	Int.	8.46	197.99	
SII 2x28P[1]	2	16-10	9.0-24.0	9.56	1	Int.	8.28	196.99	
SIMMONS									[1]Matte; also polished finish. [2]Silver; also black matte or polished. [3]Black matte finish. [4]Granite finish; black polish **$216.95**; silver $218.95; also with 50mm obj., black granite **$336.95**. [5]Camouflage. [6]Black polish. [7]With ring mounts. [8]Black polished; also black or silve matte. [9]Lighted reticle, Black Granite finish. [10]50mm obj.; black matte. [11]Black or silver matte. [12]Realtree camo finish, with rings. [13]TV view. [14]75-yd. parallax; black or silver matte. [15]TV view. [16]Adj. obj. **Only selected models shown.** Contact Simmons Outdoor Corp. for complete details.
AETEC									
2100[8]	2.8-10	44-14	5	11.9	1	Int.	15.5	349.95	
44 Mag									
M-1044	3-10	36.2-10.5	3.4-3.3	13.1	1	Int.	16.3	259.95	
M-1045	4-12	27-9	3	12.6	1	Int.	19.5	279.95	
M-1047	6.5-20	14-.5	2.6-3.4	12.8	1	Int.	19.5	289.95	
Prohunter									
7700[1]	2-7	58-17	3.25	11.6	1	Int.	12.4	169.95	
7710[2]	3-9	40-15	3	12.6	1	Int.	13.4	179.95	
7716	4-12	29.6-10.0	3	13.6	1	Int.	20	199.95	
7720	6-18	38-13	2.5	12.5	1	Int.	13.5	224.95	
7740[3]	6	34.1	3	12.6	1	Int.	9.5	144.95	
Whitetail Classic									
WTC9[9]	3	11.5	11-20	9.0	1	Int.	9.2	329.95	
WTC11[4]	1.5-5	80-23.5	3.4-3.2	12.6	1	Int.	11.8	184.95	
WTC12[4]	2.5-8	46.5-14.5	3.2-3	12.6	1	Int.	12.8	199.95	
WTC13[4]	3.5-10	35-12	3.2-3	12.4	1	Int.	12.8	219.95	
WTC16	4	36.8	4	9.9	1	Int.	12	149.95	
WTC17	4-12	26-7.9	3	12.8	1	Int.	19.5	329.95	
Pro50									
8830[10]	2.5-10	30.5-11	3.2	12.75	1	Int.	13.0	169.95	
8800[10]	4-12	27-9	3.5	13.2	1	Int.	18.25	179.95	
8810[10]	6-18	17-5.8	3.6	13.2	1	Int.	18.25	199.95	

HUNTING, TARGET & VARMINT SCOPES

Maker and Model	Magn.	Field at 100 Yds. (feet)	Eye Relief (in.)	Length (in.)	Tube Dia. (in.)	W&E Adjustments	Weight (ozs.)	Price	Other Data
Simmons (cont.)									
Master Red Dot									
5100[11]	1	40	—	5.25	30mm	Int.	4.8	269.95	
Realtree									
2470[6,12]	4	26	3.3	12.0	1	Int.	9.9	129.95	
2470[5,12]	2.5	24	6	7.4	1	Int.	7.0	129.95	
2472[9,12,13]	3-9	32-11	3.3-2.9	12.6	1	Int.	12.5	169.95	
Deerfield									
21006	4	28	4	12.0	1	Int.	9.1	74.95	
21029	3-9	32-11	3.4	12.6	1	Int.	12.3	104.95	
21031	4-12	28-11	3-2.8	13.9	1	Int.	14.6	139.95	
Gold Medal Silhouette									
23000	12	8.7	3.1-3	14.5	1	Int.	18.3	469.95	
23001	24	4.3	3	14.5	1	Int.	18.3	479.95	
23002	6-20	17.4-5.4	3	14.5	1	Int.	18.3	529.95	
Gold Medal Handgun									
22002[6]	2.5-7	9.7-4.0	8.9-19.4	9.25	1	Int.	9.0	329.95	
22004[6]	2	3.9	8.6-19.5	7.3	1	Int.	7.4	229.95	
22006[6]	4	8.9	9.8-18.7	9	1	Int.	8.8	269.95	
Shotgun									
21005	2.5	29	4.6	7.1	1	Int.	7.2	99.95	
7789D	2	27	6	8.8	1	Int.	8.1	129.95	
7788	1	60	3.8	9.4	1	Int.	10.2	129.95	
7790D	4	16	5.5	8.8	1	Int.	9.2	139.95	
7791	1.5-5	75-23	3.4	9.3	1	Int.	9.7	139.95	
Rimfire									
1022[7]	4	36	3.5	11.5	¾	Int.	10	74.95	
Blackpowder									
BP2520M[14]	2.5	24	6	7.4	1	Int.	7.3	109.95	
BP420M[14]	4	19.5	4	7.5	1	Int.	8.3	109.95	
BP2732M[14]	2-7	57.7-16.6	3	11.6	1	Int.	12.4	129.95	
Fireview									
21507[15]	4	34	3.3	12.8	1	Int.	9	89.95	
21513[15]	3-9	40-13	3.5-2.6	12.8	1	Int.	11.7	99.95	
Competition Air Gun									
21612[16]	4-12	25-9	3.1-2.9	13.1	1	Int.	15.8	179.95	
21618[16]	6-18	18-7	2.9-2.7	13.8	1	Int.	18.2	189.95	
STEINER									
Penetrator									
4x24 STANAG[1]	4	30	2.4	9	30mm	Int.	12	1,699.00	Waterproof, fogproof, nitrogen filled, accordion-type eye cup. [1]Mount not included; uses STANAG 2324 post-type mounting system. From Pioneer Marketing & Research, Inc.
6x42	6	20.4	3.1	14.8	26mm	Int.	14	1,099.00	
8x56	8	15	3.1	14.8	26mm	Int.	17	1,299.00	
1.5x6x42	1.5-6	64-21	3.1	12.8	30mm	Int.	17	1,389.00	
3-12x56	3-12	29-10	3.1	14.8	30mm	Int.	21	1,699.00	
SWAROVSKI HABICHT									
PH Series									
1.25-4x24[1]	1.25-4	86-27	4.5	10.6	30mm	Int.	15.9	943.33	All models offered in either steel or lightweight alloy tubes. Weights shown are for lightweight versions. Choice of nine constantly centered reticles. Eyepiece recoil mechanism and rubber ring shield to protect face. American-style plex reticle available in 2.2-9x42 and 3-12x56 traditional European scopes. [1]Alloy weighs 12.3 oz. [2]Alloy weighs 15.9 oz. [3]Alloy weighs 14.8 oz. [4]Alloy weighs 18.3 oz. [5]Alloy weighs 16.6 oz. Imported by Swarovski Optik North America Ltd.
1.5-6x42[2]	1.5-6	65.4-21	3.75	13	30mm	Int.	20.5	1,043.33	
2.5-10x42[3]	2.5-10	39.6-12.3	3.75	13.2	30mm	Int.	19.4	1,216.67	
2.5-10x56[4]	2.5-10	39.6-12.3	3.75	14.7	30mm	Int.	24.3	1,276.67	
3-12x50[5]	3-12	33-10.5	3.75	14.3	30mm	Int.	22.0	1,265.66	
6x42	6	23	3.25	12.6	1	Int.	17.9	832.22	
8x50	8	17	3.25	14.4	30mm	Int.	19.9	865.00	
8x56	8	17	3¼	14.4	30mm	Int.	23	910.00	
AL Series									
4x32A	4	30	3.2	11.5	1	Int.	10.8	521.11	
6x36A	6	21	3.2	11.9	1	Int.	11.5	550.00	
1.5-4.5x20A	1.5-4.5	75-25.8	3.5	9.53	1	Int.	10.6	643.33	
3-9x36	3-9	39-13.5	3.3	11.9	1	Int.	13	665.56	
SWIFT									
600 4x15	4	16.2	2.4	11	¾	Int.	4.7	24.00	All Swift scopes, with the exception of the 4x15, have Quadraplex reticles and are fogproof and waterproof. The 4x15 has crosshair reticle and is non-waterproof. [1]Available in black or silver finish—same price. [2]Comes with ring mounts, wrench, lens caps, extension tubes, filter, battery. From Swift Instruments.
601 3-7x20	3-7	25-12	3-2.9	11	1	Int.	5.6	53.00	
649 4-12x50	4-12	30-10	3-2.8	13.2	1	Int.	14.6	216.00	
650 4x32	4	29	3.5	12	1	Int.	9	80.00	
653 4x40WA[1]	4	35.5	3.75	12.25	1	Int.	12	98.00	
654 3-9x32	3-9	35.75-12.75	3	12.75	1	Int.	13.75	95.00	
656 3-9x40WA[1]	3-9	42.5-13.5	2.75	12.75	1	Int.	14	103.00	
657 6x40	6	18	3.75	13	1	Int.	10	99.50	
660 4x20	4	25	4	11.8	1	Int.	9	80.00	
664 4-12x40[1]	4-12	27-9	3-2.8	13.3	1	Int.	14.8	143.00	
665 1.5-4.5x21	1.5-4.5	69-24.5	3.5-3	10.9	1	Int.	9.6	98.00	
666 Shotgun 1x20	1	113	3.2	7.5	1	Int.	9.6	102.00	
667 Fire-Fly[2]	1	—	—	5.3	30mm	Int.	5	215.00	
668 4x32	4	25	4	10	1	Int.	8.9	95.00	
Pistol Scopes									
661 4x32	4	90	10-22	9.2	1	Int.	9.5	115.00	
662 2.5x32	2.5	14.3	9-22	8.9	1	Int.	9.3	110.00	
663 2x20[1]	2	18.3	9-21	7.2	1	Int.	8.4	115.00	

CAUTION: PRICES SHOWN ARE SUPPLIED BY THE MANUFACTURER OR IMPORTER. CHECK YOUR LOCAL GUNSHOP.

HUNTING, TARGET & VARMINT SCOPES

Maker and Model	Magn.	Field at 100 Yds. (feet)	Eye Relief (in.)	Length (in.)	Tube Dia. (in.)	W&E Adjustments	Weight (ozs.)	Price	Other Data
TASCO									[1]Water, fog & shockproof; fully coated optics; 1/4-min. click stops; haze filter caps; 30-day/limited lifetime warranty. [2]30/30 range finding reticle. [3]World Class Wide Angle; Supercon multi-coated optics; Opti-Centered® 30/30 range finding reticle; lifetime warranty. [4]1/3 greater zoom range. [5]Trajectory compensating scopes, Opti-Centered® stadia reticle. [6]Anodized finish. [7]True one-power scope. [8]Coated optics; crosshair reticle; ring mounts included to fit most 22, 10mm receivers. [9]Fits Remington 870, 1100, 11-87. [10]Electronic dot reticle with rheostat; coated optics; adj. for windage and elevation; waterproof, shockproof, fogproof; Lithium battery; 3x power booster avail.; matte black or matte aluminum finish; dot or T-3 reticle. [11]TV view. [12]Also matte aluminum finish. [13]Also with crosshair reticle. [14]Also 30/30 reticle. [15]Dot size 1.5" at 100 yds.; waterproof. [16]Also in stainless finish. [17]Black matte or stainless finish. [18]Also with stainless finish. [19]Also in matte black. [20]Available with 5-min. or 10-min. dot. [21]Available with 10, 15, 20-min. dot. [22]20mm; also 32mm. [23]20mm; black matte; also stainless steel; also 32mm. **Contact Tasco for details on complete line.**
World Class									
WA4x40	4	36	3	13	1	Int.	11.5	161.00	
WA6x40	6	23	3	12.75	1	Int.	11.5	170.00	
WA13.5x20[1,3,10]	1-3.5	115-31	3.5	9.75	1	Int.	10.2	305.00	
WA1.75-5x20[1,3]	1.75-5	72-24	3	10 5/8	1	Int.	10.0	305.00	
WA2.58x40[18]	2.5-8	44-14	3	11.75	1	Int.	14.25	220.00	
WA27x32[1,3,9]	2-7	56-17	3.25	11.5	1	Int.	12	191.00	
WA39x40[1,3,6,11,18]	3-9	43.5-15	3	12.75	1	Int.	13.0	199.00	
World Class Airgun									
AG4x40WA	4	36	3	13	1	Int.	14	374.00	
AG39x50WA	3-9	41-14	3	15	1	Int.	17.5	509.00	
World Class Electronic									
ER39x40WA	3-9	41-14	3	12.75	1	Int.	16	679.00	
World Class Mag IV-44									
WC2510x44[6,19]	2.5-10	41-11	3.5	12.5	1	Int.	14.4	305.00	
World Class TS									
TS24x44	24	4.5	3	14	1	Int.	17.9	526.00	
TS36x44	36	3	3	14	1	Int.	17.9	560.00	
TS832x44	8-24	11-3.5	3	14	1	Int.	19.5	662.00	
TS624x44	6-24	15-4.5	3	14	1	Int.	18.5	611.00	
World Class TR									
TR39x40WA	3-9	41-14	3	13.0	1	Int.	12.5	340.00	
TR416x40	4-16	26-7	3.25	14.25	1	Int.	15.6	373.00	
TR624x40	6-24	17-4	3	15.25	1	Int.	16.8	407.00	
World Class Pistol									
PWC2x22[12]	2	25	11-20	8.75	1	Int.	7.3	288.00	
PWC4x28[12]	4	8	12-19	9.45	1	Int.	7.9	340.00	
P1.254x28	1.25-4	23-9	15-23	9.25	1	Int.	8.2	339.00	
Mag IV									
W312x40[1,2,4]	3-12	35-9	3	12.25	1	Int.	12	183.00	
W416x40[1,2,4,17]	4-16	26-7	3	14.25	1	Int.	15.6	229.00	
W624x40	6-24	17-4	3	15.25	1	Int.	16.8	290.00	
Golden Antler									
GA4x32TV	4	32	3	13	1	Int.	12.7	79.00	
GA2.510x44TV	2.5-10	35-9	3.5	12.5	1	Int.	14.4	305.00	
GA39x32TV[11]	3-9	39-13	3	—	1	Int.	12.2	102.00	
GA39x40TV	3-9	39-13	3	12.5	1	Int.	13	135.00	
GA39x40WA	3-9	41-15	3	12.75	1	Int.	13	128.00	
Silver Antler									
SA2.5x32	2.5	42	3 1/4	11	1	Int.	10	86.00	
SA4x40	4	32	3	12	1	Int.	12.5	99.00	
SA39x32WA	3-9	40-14	3	13.25	1	Int.	12.2	129.00	
SA39x40WA[12]	3-9	41-15	3	12.75	1	Int.	13	152.00	
SA39x40	3-9	39-13	3	12.5	1	Int.	13	135.00	
SA2.150x44	2.5-10	35-9	3.5	—	1	Int.	14.4	305.00	
SA4x32[12]	4	32	3	13	1	Int.	12.7	79.00	
Pronghorn									
PH2.5x20	2.5	43	3.75	10	1	Int.	7.1	76.00	
PH2.5x32	2.5	42	3.25	11	1	Int.	10	78.00	
PH4x32	4	32	3	12	1	Int.	12.5	73.00	
PH6x40	6	20	3	12.5	1	Int.	11.5	98.00	
PH39x32	3-9	39-13	3	12	1	Int.	11	91.00	
PH39x40	3-9	39-13	3	13	1	Int.	12.1	122.00	
High Country									
HC416x40	4-16	26-7	3.25	14.25	1	Int.	15.6	254.00	
HC624x10	6-24	17-4	3	15.25	1	Int.	16.8	280.00	
HC39x40	3-9	41-15	3	12.75	1	Int.	13.0	195.00	
HC3.510x40	3.5-10	30-10.5	3	11.75	1	Int.	14.25	220.00	
Rubber Armored									
RC39x40A	3-9	35-12	3.25	12.5	1	Int.	14.3	229.00	
TR Scopes									
TR39x40WA	3-9	41-14	3	13	1	Int.	12.5	339.00	
TR416x40	4-16	26-7	3	14.25	1	Int.	16.8	373.00	
TR624x40	6-24	17-4	3	15.5	1	Int.	17.5	407.00	
Bantam									
S1.5-45x20[22]	1.5-4.5	69.5-23	4	10.25	1	Int.	10	NA	
S2.5x20[23]	2.5	22	6	7.5	1	Int.	7.5	NA	
Airgun									
AG4x20	4	20	2.5	10.75	.75	Int.	5	40.00	
AG4x40WA	4	36	3	13.0	1	Int.	14	373.00	
AG4x32N	4	30	3	—	1	Int.	12.25	144.00	
AG27x32	2-7	48-17	3	12.25	1	Int.	14	178.00	
AG37x20	3-7	24-11	3	11.5	1	Int.	6.5	73.00	
AG39x50WA	3-9	41-14	3	15	1	Int.	17.5	475.00	
Rimfire									
RF4x15[8]	4	22.5	2.5	11	.75	Int.	4	17.00	
RF4x32	4	31	3	12.25	1	Int.	12.6	91.00	
RF37x20	3-7	24-11	2.5	11.5	.75	Int.	5.7	49.00	
P1.5x15	1.5	22.5	9.5-20.75	8.75	.75	Int.	3.25	37.00	
Propoint									
PDP2[10,12,20]	1	40	—	5	30mm	Int.	5	267.00	

CAUTION: PRICES SHOWN ARE SUPPLIED BY THE MANUFACTURER OR IMPORTER. CHECK YOUR LOCAL GUNSHOP.

HUNTING, TARGET & VARMINT SCOPES

Maker and Model	Magn.	Field at 100 Yds. (feet)	Eye Relief (in.)	Length (in.)	Tube Dia. (in.)	W&E Adjustments	Weight (ozs.)	Price	Other Data
Tasco (cont.)									
PDP3[10,12,20]	1	52	—	5	30mm	Int.	5	367.00	
PDP4[17,21]	1	82	—	—	45mm	Int.	6.1	458.00	
PB1[13]	3	35	3	5.5	30mm	Int.	6.0	183.00	
PB3	2	30	—	1.25	30mm	Int.	2.6	214.00	
World Class Plus									
WCP4x44	4	32	3¼	12.75	1	Int.	13.5	392.00	
WCP3.510x50	3.5-10	30-10.5	3¾	13	1	Int.	17.1	492.00	
WCP24x50	24	4.8	3.25	13.25	1	Int.	15.9	730.00	
WCP36x50	36	3	3.5	14	1	Int.	15.9	760.00	
WCP6x44	6	21	3.25	12.75	1	Int.	13.6	407.00	
WCP39x44[1]	3-9	39-14	3.5	12.75	1	Int.	15.8	407.00	
LaserPoint LP2[15]	—	—	—	2	5/8	Int.	.75	374.00	
THOMPSON/CENTER RECOIL PROOF PISTOL SCOPES									
Pistol Scopes									[1]Black finish; silver, **$224.00**. [2]Rail mount. [3]Black finish; silver, **$330.00**. [4]Black; silver, **$254.00**. [5]Lighted reticle, black, rail mount; std. mount, **$290.00**; silver, std., **$300**. [6]Lighted reticle, black. [7]Red dot scope. [8]lighted reticle. [9]Adj. obj. [10]Adj. obj. From Thompson/Center.
8356[1]	2	22.1	10.5-26.4	7⁴⁄₅	1	Int.	6.4	220.00	
8312[2]	2.5	15	9-21	7²⁄₅	1	Int.	6.6	210.00	
8315[3]	2.5-7	15-5	8-21, 8-11	9¼	1	Int.	9.2	300.00	
8352[4]	4	22.1	10.5-26.4	7⁴⁄₅	1	Int.	6.4	250.00	
8320[5]	2.5	15	9-21	7²⁄₅	1	Int.	8.2	300.00	
8326[6]	2.5-7	15-5	8-21, 8-11	9¼	1	Int.	10.5	360.00	
8650[7]	1	40	—	5¼	30mm	Int.	4.8	238.00	
Muzzleloader Scopes									
8626[8]	3-9	33-11	3	10¾	1	Int.	10.1	360.00	
8664[9]	6-18	18.8-6.2	3	14⅓	1	Int.	13.5	184.00	
8666[10]	4-12	26.7-9	3	12⁴⁄₅	1	Int.	19.5	230.00	
TRIJICON									[1]Also 24mm. [2]Also 20mm, **$495.00** to **$595.00**. [3]Advanced Combat Optical Gunsight for AR-15, M-16, with integral mount. From Trijicon, Inc.
Reflex	1	—	—	4.25	1.35	Int.	—	299.00	
1x16[1]	1	43.8	4.4	4.6	—	Int.	—	467.00	
1.5x16[1]	1.5	43.8	2.4	4.1	—	Int.	—	495.00-595.00	
2x16[2]	2	43.8	1.6	3.7	—	Int.	—	485.00-585.00	
2.5x20	2.5	43.8	1.4	4.2	—	Int.	—	519.00-619.00	
2.25x24	2.25	28.9	2	5.1	—	Int.	—	519.00-619.00	
3x24	3	28.9	1.4	4.8	—	Int.	—	519.00-619.00	
Variables									
2.5-10x42	2.5-10	7.4-2.3	4.3-3.3	13.4	—	Int.	—	1,080.00	
3-12x56	3-12	6.6-1.9	3.9-3.3	14.4	—	Int.	—	1,200.00	
8-24x56	8-24	—	—	—	—	Int.	—	1,480.00	
ACOG 3.5x35	3.5	29	2.4	8.0	—	Int.	14.0	1,295.00	
ACOG 4x32[3]	4	37	1.5	5.8	—	Int.	9.7	895.00	
UNERTL									[1]Dural ¼-MOA click mounts. Hard coated lenses. Non-rotating objective lens focusing. 2¼-MOA click mounts. [3]With target mounts. [4]With calibrated head. [5]Same as 1" Target but without objective lens focusing. [6]With new Posa mounts. [7]Range focus unit near rear of tube. Price is with Posa or standard mounts. Magnum clamp. From Unertl.
1" Target	6,8,10	16-10	2	21½	¾	Ext.	21	307.00	
1¼" Target[1]	8,10,12,14	12-16	2	25	¾	Ext.	21	399.00	
1½" Target	10,12,14,16,18,20	11.5-3.2	2¼	25½	¾	Ext.	31	416.00	
2" Target[2]	10,12,14,16,18,24,30,32,36	8	2¼	26¼	1	Ext.	44	549.00	
Varmint, 1¼"[3]	6,8,10,12	1-7	2½	19½	⅞	Ext.	26	395.00	
Ultra Varmint, 2"[4]	8,10,12,15	12.6-7	2½	24	1	Ext.	34	538.00	
Small Game[5]	3,4,6	25-17	2¼	18	¾	Ext.	16	243.00	
Programmer 200[7]	10,12,14,16,18,20,24,30,36	11.3-4	—	26½	1	Ext.	45	688.00	
BV-20[8]	20	8	4.4	17⅞	1	Ext.	21¼	508.00	
Tube Sight	—	—	—	17	—	Ext.	—	226.00	
U.S. OPTICS									Prices shown are estimates; scopes built as ordered, to order; choice of reticles; choice of front or rear focal plane; extra-heavy MIL-SPEC construction; extra-long turrets; individual w&e rebound springs; up to 88mm dia. objectives; up to 50mm tubes; all lenses multi-coated. Made in U.S. by U. S. Optics.
SN-1/TAR Fixed Power System									
9.6x	10	11.3	3.8	14.5	30mm	Int.	24	1,100.00	
16.2x	15	8.6	4.3	16.5	30mm	Int.	27	1,200.00	
22.4x	20	5.8	3.8	18.0	30mm	Int.	29	1,300.00	
26x	24	5.0	3.4	18.0	30mm	Int.	31	1,400.00	
31x	30	4.6	3.5	18.0	30mm	Int.	32	1,500.00	
37x	36	4.0	3.6	18.0	30mm	Int.	32	1,600.00	
42x	40	3.6	3.7	18.0	30mm	Int.	32	1,700.00	
48x	50	3.0	3.8	18.0	30mm	Int.	32	1,800.00	
Variables									
SN-2	4-22	26.8-5.8	5.4-3.8	18.0	30mm	Int.	24	1,256.00	
SN-3	1.6-8	—	4.4-4.8	18.4	30mm	Int.	36	1,010.00	
SN-4	1-4	116-31.2	4.6-4.9	18.0	30mm	Int.	35	680.00	
Fixed Power									
SN-6	4,6,8,10	—	4.2-4.8	9.2	30mm	Int.	18	655.00	
SN-8	4, 10, 20, 40	32	3.3	7.5	30mm	Int.	11.1	620.00	

CAUTION: PRICES SHOWN ARE SUPPLIED BY THE MANUFACTURER OR IMPORTER. CHECK YOUR LOCAL GUNSHOP.

HUNTING, TARGET & VARMINT SCOPES

Maker and Model	Magn.	Field at 100 Yds. (feet)	Eye Relief (in.)	Length (in.)	Tube Dia. (in.)	W&E Adjust-ments	Weight (ozs.)	Price	Other Data
WEAVER									Micro-Trac adjustment system with ¼-minute clicks on all models. All have Dual-X reticle. One-piece aluminum tube, satin finish, nitrogen filled, multi-coated lenses, waterproof. [1]Also available in matte finish: V3, **$190.56**; K4, **$157.71**; V9, **$205.33**; V10, **$218.47**. [2]Available with Dual-X, fine crosshair or ¼-min. dot reticles. [3]4 MOA red dot; also with 12 MOA dot; comes with Weaver q.d. rings. [4]Variable 4, 8, 12 MOA red dot; comes with Weaver q.d. rings. [5]4 MOA, 12 MOA, variable 4, 8, 12 MOA (**$364.86**). [6]Stainless finish, **$207.71**. [7]Stainless finish, **$218.64**. [8]Stainless finish, **$263.83**. From Weaver.
K2.5	2.5	35	3.7	9.5	1	Int.	7.3	138.47	
K4[1]	3.7	26.5	3.3	11.3	1	Int.	10	150.13	
K6	5.7	18.5	3.3	11.4	1	Int.	10	163.61	
V3[1]	1.1-2.8	88-32	3.9-3.7	9.2	1	Int.	8.5	181.49	
V9[1]	2.8-8.7	33-11	3.5-3.4	12.1	1	Int.	11.1	195.56	
V10[1]	2.2-9.6	38.5-9.5	3.4-3.3	12.2	1	Int.	11.2	207.96	
V16[2]	3.8-15.5	26.8-6.8	3.1	13.9	1	Int.	16.5	365.57	
KT15	14.6	7.5	3.2	12.9	1	Int.	14.7	325.94	
T-10	10	9.3	3.0	15.1	1	Int.	16.7	755.96	
T-16	16	6.5	3.0	15.1	1	Int.	16.7	761.90	
T-24	24	4.4	3.0	15.1	1	Int.	16.7	767.86	
T-36	36	3.0	3.0	15.1	1	Int.	16.7	773.81	
Qwik-Point									
QP30[3]	1	12.6	—	5.39	30mm	Int.	5.3	224.57	
QP33[4]	1	14.4	—	5.74	33mm	Int.	6.3	364.11	
QP45[5]	1	21.8	—	4.8	45mm	Int.	8.46	282.09	
Handgun									
2x28[6]	2	21	4-29	8.5	1	Int.	6.7	196.80	
4x28[7]	4	18	11.5-18	8.5	1	Int.	6.7	207.71	
1.5-4x20[8]	1.5-4	13.5-5.8	12-24, 10.5-17	8.6	1	Int.	8.1	252.91	
WILLIAMS									[1]Matte or glossy black finish. TNT models. From Williams Gunsight Co.
Twilight Crosshair TNT	1½-5	57¾-21	3½	10¾	1	Int.	10	221.37	
Twilight Crosshair TNT	2½	32	3¾	11¼	1	Int.	8½	156.66	
Twilight Crosshair TNT	4	29	3½	11¾	1	Int.	9½	163.79	
Twilight Crosshair TNT	2-6	45-17	3	11½	1	Int.	11½	221.37	
Twilight Crosshair TNT	3-9	36-13	3	12¾	1	Int.	13½	222.62	
Guideline II									
4x[1]	4	29	3.6	11¾	1	Int.	9½	237.81	
1.5-5x[1]	1.5-5	57¾-21	3.5	10¾	1	Int.	10	286.01	
2-6x[1]	2-6	45½-10¾	3	11½	1	Int.	11½	286.01	
3-9x[1]	3-9	36½-12¾	3.1-2.9	12¾	1	Int.	13½	317.08	
ZEISS									All scopes have ¼-minute click-stop adjustments. Choice of Z-Plex or fine crosshair reticles. Rubber armored objective bell, rubber eyepiece ring. Lenses have T-Star coating for highest light transmission. Z-Series scopes offered in non-rail tubes with duplex reticles only; 1" and 30mm. [1]Black matte finish. [2]Also in stainless matte finish. [3]Also with illuminated reticle, **$1,738.00**. Bullet Drop Compensator avail. for all Z-Series scopes. Imported from Germany by Carl Zeiss Optical, Inc.
Diatal Z 6x42	6	22.9	3.2	12.7	1.02 (26mm)	Int.	13.4	917.00	
Diatal Z 8x56	8	18	3.2	13.8	1.02 (26mm)	Int.	17.6	1,092.00	
Diavari 1.25-4x24	1.25-4	105-33	3.2	11.46	30mm	Int.	17.3	1,041.00	
Diavari Z 2.5x10x48[1,2]	2.5-10	33-11.7	3.2	14.5	30mm	Int.	24	1,407.00	
Diavari C 3-9x36	3-9	36-13	3.5	11.2	1	Int.	15.2	783.00	
Diavari Z 1.5-6x42[1,2]	1.5-6	65.5-22.9	3.2	12.4	1.18 (30mm)	Int.	18.5	1,190.00	
Diavari Z 3-12x56[1,2,3]	3-12	27.6-9.9	3.2	15.3	1.18 (30mm)	Int.	25.8	1,515.00	

Hunting scopes in general are furnished with a choice of reticle—crosshairs, post with crosshairs, tapered or blunt post, or dot crosshairs, etc. The great majority of target and varmint scopes have medium or fine crosshairs but post or dot reticles may be ordered. W—Windage E—Elevation MOA—Minute of angle or 1" (approx.) at 100 yards, etc.

Burris 1-4x XER Fullfield.

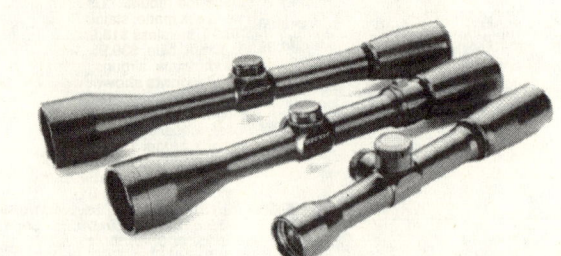

Sightron 39x42, 4x12, 2x28P.

Weaver Qwik-Point 1x 33mm.

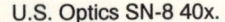

U.S. Optics SN-8 40x.

Bushnell Trophy 1.75-4x32 Turkey.

Simmons AETEC 2.8-10x.

SCOPE MOUNTS

Maker, Model, Type	Adjust.	Scopes	Price
AIMPOINT	No	1"	$49.95-89.95
Laser Mounts[1]	No	1", 30mm	51.95

Mounts/rings for all Aimpoint sights and 1" scopes. For many popular revolvers, auto pistols, shotguns, military-style rifles/carbines, sporting rifles. Most require no gunsmithing. [1]Mounts Aimpoint Laser-dot below barrel; many popular handguns, military-style rifles. Contact Aimpoint.

Maker, Model, Type	Adjust.	Scopes	Price
AIMTECH			
Handguns			
AMT Auto Mag II, III	No	1"	56.99-64.95
Auto Mag IV	No	1"	64.95
Astra revolvers	No	1"	63.25
Beretta/Taurus auto	No	1"	63.25
Browning Buck Mark/Challenger II	No	1"	56.99
Browning Hi-Power	No	1"	63.25
Glock 17, 17L, 19, 22, 23	No	1"	63.25
Govt. 45 Auto	No	1"	63.25
Rossi revolvers	No	1"	63.25
Ruger Mk I, Mk II	No	1"	49.95
S&W K,L,N frame	No	1"	63.25
S&W Model 41 Target	No	1"	63.25
S&W Model 52 Target	No	1"	63.25
S&W 45, 9mm autos	No	1"	56.99
S&W 422/622/2206	No	1"	56.99
Taurus revolvers	No	1"	63.25
TZ/CZ/P9 9mm	No	1"	63.25
Rifles			
AR-15	No	1"	21.95
Browning A-Bolt	No	1"	21.95
Knight MK85	No	1"	21.95
Remington 700	No	1"	21.95
Ruger 10/22	No	1"	21.95
Savage 110G	No	1"	21.95
Winchester 70	No	1"	21.95
Winchester 94	No	1"	21.95
Shotguns			
Benelli Super 90	No	1"	40.95
Ithaca 37	No	1"	40.95
Mossberg 500	No	1"	40.95
Mossberg 835 Ultimag	No	1"	40.95
Mossberg 5500	No	1"	40.95
Remington 870/1100	No	1"	40.95
Winchester 1300/1400	No	1"	40.95

Mount scopes, lasers, electronic sights using Weaver-style base. All mounts allow use of iron sights; no gunsmithing. Available in satin black or satin stainless finish. **Partial listing shown.** Contact maker for full details. From L&S Technologies, Inc.

Maker, Model, Type	Adjust.	Scopes	Price
A.R.M.S.			
M16A1/A2/AR-15	No	Weaver-type rail	59.95
Multibase	No	Weaver-type rail	59.95
M21/14 Mount	No	Weaver-type rail	155.00
#19 Weaver/STANAG Throw Lever Rail	No	Weaver-type rail	140.00
STANAG Rings	No	30mm	75.00
Ring Inserts	No	1", 30mm	29.00
#38 Std. Swan Sleeve[1]	No	—	150.00

[1]Avail in three lengths. From A.R.M.S., Inc.

Maker, Model, Type	Adjust.	Scopes	Price
ARMSON			
AR-15[1]	No	1"	45.00
Mini-14[2]	No	1"	66.00
H&K[3]	No	1"	82.00

[1]Fastens with one nut. [2]Models 181, 182, 183, 184, etc. [3]Claw mount. From Trijicon, Inc.

Maker, Model, Type	Adjust.	Scopes	Price
ARMSPORT			
100 Series[1]	No	1" rings. Low, med., high	10.75
104 22-cal.	No	1"	10.75
201 See-Thru	No	1"	13.00
1-Piece Base[2]	No	—	5.50
2-Piece Base[2]	No	—	2.75

[1]Weaver-type rings. [2]Weaver-type base; most popular rifles. Made in U.S. From Armsport.

Maker, Model, Type	Adjust.	Scopes	Price
B-SQUARE			
Pistols			
Beretta/Taurus 92/99[6]	—	1"	69.95
Browning Buck Mark[6]	No	1"	49.95
Colt 45 Auto	E only	1"	69.95
Colt Python/MkIV, 4",6",8"[1,6]	E	1"	59.95
Dan Wesson Clamp-On[2,6]	E	1"	59.95
Ruger 22 Auto Mono-Mount[3]	No	1"	59.95
Ruger Single-Six[4]	No	1"	59.95
Ruger Blackhawk, Super B'hwk[8]	W&E	1"	59.95
Ruger GP-100[9]	No	1"	59.95
Ruger Redhawk[8]	W&E	1"	59.95
S&W 422/2206[9]	No	1"	59.95
Taurus 66[9]	No	1"	59.95
S&W K, L, N frame[2,6]	No	1"	59.95
T/C Contender (Dovetail Base)	W&E	1"	39.95
Rifles			
Charter AR-7	No	1"	29.95
Mini-14 (dovetail/NATO Stanag)[5,6]	W&E	1"	59.95
M-94 Side Mount	W&E	1"	49.95
RWS, Beeman/FWB, Anschutz, Diana, Walther Air Rifles	E only	—	39.95
SMLE Side Mount with rings	W&E	1"	69.95
Military			
AK-47/AKS/SKS-56[10]	No	1"	59.95
AK-47, SKS-56[11]	No	1"	59.95
M1-A[7]	W&E	1"	99.95
AR-15/16[7]	W&E	1"	59.95
FN-LAR/FAL[6,7]	E only	1"	99.95
HK-91/93/94[6,7]	E only	1"	99.95
Shotguns[6]			
Ithaca 37[6]	No	1"	49.95
Mossberg 500, 712, 5500[6]	No	1"	49.95
Rem. 870/1100 (12 & 20 ga.)[6]	No	1"	49.95
Rem. 870, 1100 (and L.H.)[6]	No	1"	49.95
BSL Laser Mounts			
Scope Tube Clamp[12,13,16]	No	—	39.95
45 Auto[12,13,16]	No	—	39.95
SIG P226[12,13,16]	No	—	39.95
Beretta 92F/Taurus PT99[12,13,16]	No	—	39.95
Colt King Cobra, Python, MkV[12,13,16]	No	—	39.95
S&W L Frame[13,16]	No	—	39.95
Browning HP[12,13,16]	No	—	39.95
Glock	No	—	39.95
Star Firestar[12,13,16]	No	—	39.95
Rossi small frame revolver[12,13,16]	No	—	39.95
Taurus 85 revolver[12,13,16]	No	—	39.95
Interlock Rings			
Standard Dovetail[17]	No	1", 30mm	34.95
Vertical Split[18]	No	1", 30mm	12.95
High/View Thru[19]	No	1"	15.95
Tip-Off 3/8" Dovetail[20]	No	1", 30mm	29.95
Interlock Bases			
One-Piece[21]	No	Standard dovetail rings	9.95-10.95

[1]Clamp-on, blue finish; stainless finish **$59.95**. [2]Blue finish; stainless finish **$59.95**. [3]Clamp-on, blue; stainless finish **$59.95**. [4]Dovetail; stainless finish **$59.95**. [5]No gunsmithing, no sight removal; blue; stainless finish **$79.95**. [6]Weaver-style rings. Rings not included with Weaver-type bases; stainless finish add **$10**. [7]NATO Stanag dovetail model, **$99.50**. [8]Blue; stainless finish **$69.95**. [9]Blue; stainless finish **$69.95**. [10]Handguard mounts. [11]Receiver mounts. [12]Stainless finish add **$10**. [13]Under-barrel mount, no gunsmithing. [14]Ejector rod mount. [15]Guide rod mount. [16]Used with B-Square BSL-1 Laser Sight only. [17]With recoil key. Blue, black matte; stainless finish **$39.95**. [18]Blue; stainless finish, **$14.95**; 30mm, blue **$16.95**, stainless **$18.95**. [19]Blue; stainless finish, **$18.95**. [20]Blue; stainless finish, **$34.95**; 30mm, blue, **$39.95**, stainless **$44.95**. [21]Most popular sporting rifles. Mounts for many shotguns, airguns, military and law enforcement guns also available. **Partial listing of mounts shown here.** Contact B-Square for more data.

B-Square makes mounts for the following military rifles: AK47/AKS, Egyptian Hakim, French MAS 1936, M91 Argentine Mauser, Model 98 Brazilian and German Mausers, Model 93, Spanish Mauser (long and short), Model 1916 Mauser, Model 38 and 96 Swedish Mausers, Model 91 Russian (round and octagon receivers), Chinese SKS 56, SMLE No. 1, Mk. III, 1903 Springfield, U.S. 30-cal. Carbine, and others. Those following replace gun's rear sight: AK47/AKS, P14/1917 Enfield, FN49, M1 Garand, M1-A/M14 (no sight removal), SMLE No. 1, Mk III/No. 4 & 5, Mk. 1, 1903/1903-A3 Springfield, Beretta AR 70 (no sight removal).

Maker, Model, Type	Adjust.	Scopes	Price
BEEMAN			
Two-Piece, Med.	No	1"	29.00
Deluxe Two-Piece, High	No	1"	31.00
Deluxe Two-Piece	No	30mm	39.00
Deluxe One-Piece	No	1"	47.00
Dampamount	No	1"	99.00

All grooved receivers and scope bases on all known air rifles and 22-cal. rimfire rifles (1/2" to 5/8"—6mm to 15mm).

Maker, Model, Type	Adjust.	Scopes	Price
BOCK			
Swing ALK[1]	W&E	1", 26mm, 30mm	224.00
Safari KEMEL[2]	W&E	1", 26mm, 30mm	149.00
Claw KEMKA[3]	W&E	1", 26mm, 30mm	224.00

CAUTION: PRICES SHOWN ARE SUPPLIED BY THE MANUFACTURER OR IMPORTER. CHECK YOU LOCAL GUNSHOP.

SCOPE MOUNTS

Maker, Model, Type	Adjust.	Scopes	Price
Bock (cont.)			
ProHunter Fixed[4]	No	1", 26mm, 30mm	95.00

[1]Q.D.; pivots right for removal. For Steyr-Mannlicher, Win. 70, Rem. 700, Mauser 98, Dakota, Sako, Sauer 80, 90. Magnum has extra-wide rings, same price. [2]Heavy-duty claw-type; reversible for front or rear removal. For Steyr-Mannlicher rifles. [3]True claw mount for bolt-action rifles. Also in extended model. For Steyr-Mannlicher, Win. 70, Rem. 700. Also avail. as Gunsmith Bases—bases not drilled or contoured—same price. [4]Extra-wide rings. Imported from Germany by GSI, Inc.

Maker, Model, Type	Adjust.	Scopes	Price
BURRIS			
Supreme (SU) One Piece (T)[1]	W only	1" split rings, 3 heights	1 piece base—27.00-34.00
Trumount (TU) Two Piece (T)	W only	1" split rings, 3 heights	2 piece base—25.00-39.00
Trumount (TU) Two Piece Ext.	W only	1" split rings	31.00
Browning 22-cal. Auto Mount[2]	No	1" split rings	21.00
1" 22-cal. Ring Mounts[3]	No	1" split rings	1" rings—23.00-46.00
L.E.R. (LU) Mount Bases[4]	W only	1" split rings	25.00-66.00
L.E.R. No Drill-No Tap Bases[4,7,8]	W only	1" split rings	46.00-52.00
Extension Rings[5]	No	1" scopes	44.00-52.00
Ruger Ring Mount[6,9]	W only	1" split rings	52.00-74.00
Std. 1" Rings[9]	—	Low, medium, high heights	35.00-48.00
Zee Rings[9]		Fit Weaver bases; medium and high heights	33.00-46.00

[1]Most popular rifles. Universal rings, mounts fit Burris, Universal, Redfield, Leupold and Browning bases. Comparable prices. [2]Browning Standard 22 Auto rifle. [3]Grooved receivers. [4]Universal dovetail; accept Burris, Universal, Redfield, Leupold rings. For Dan Wesson, S&W, Virginian, Ruger Blackhawk, Win. 94. [5]Medium standard front, extension rear, per pair. Low standard front, extension rear, per pair. [6]Compact scopes, scopes with 2" bell, for M77R. [7]Selected rings and bases available with matte Safari or silver finish. [8]For S&W K,L,N frames, Colt Python, Dan Wesson with 6" or longer barrels. [9]Also in 30mm.

CAPE OUTFITTERS			
Quick Detachable	No	1" split rings, lever quick detachable	99.95

Double rifles; Rem. 700-721, Colt Sauer, Sauer 200, Kimber, Win. 61-63-07-100-70, Browning High Power, 22, BLR, BAR, BBR, A-Bolt; Wea. Mark V, Vanguard; Modern Muzzle Loading, Knight, Thompson/Center, CVA rifles, Dixie rifles. All steel; returns to zero. From Cape Outfitters.

CLEAR VIEW			
Universal Rings, Mod. 101[1]	No	1" split rings	21.95
Standard Model[2]	No	1" split rings	21.95
Broad View[3]	No	1"	21.95
22 Model[4]	No	3/4", 7/8", 1"	13.95
SM-94 Winchester[5]	No	1"	23.95
94 EJ[6]	No	1" split rings	21.95

[1]Most rifles by using Weaver-type base; allows use of iron sights. [2]Most popular rifles; allows use of iron sights. [3]Most popular rifles; low profile, wide field of view. [4]22 rifles with grooved receiver. [5]Side mount. [6]For Win. A.E. From Clear View Mfg.

CONETROL			
Huntur[1]	W only	1", 26mm, 26.5mm solid or split rings, 3 heights	59.88
Gunnur[2]	W only	1", 26mm, 26.5mm solid or split rings, 3 heights	79.92
Custum[3]	W only	1", 26mm, 26.5mm solid or split rings, 3 heights	99.96
One Piece Side Mount Base[4]	W only	1", 26mm, 26.5mm solid or split rings, 3 heights	—
DapTar Bases[5]	W only	1", 26mm, 26.5mm solid or split rings, 3 heights	—
Pistol Bases, 2 or 3-ring[6]	W only	1" scopes	—
Fluted Bases[7]	W only	Standard Conetrol rings	99.96
30mm Rings[8]	W only	30mm	49.98-69.96

[1]All popular rifles, including metric-drilled foreign guns. Price shown for base, two rings. Matte finish. [2]Gunnur grade has mirror-finished rings, satin-finish base. Price shown for base, two rings. [3]Custum grade has mirror-finished rings and mirror-finished, streamlined base. Price shown for base, two rings. [4]Win. 94, Krag, older split-bridge Mannlicher-Schoenauer, Mini-14, etc. Prices same as above. [5]For all popular guns with integral mounting provision, including Sako, BSA, Ithacagun, Ruger, Tikka, H&K, BRNO—**$29.94-$49.98**—and many others. Also for grooved receiver rimfires and air rifles. Prices same as above. [6]For XP-100, T/C Contender, Colt SAA, Ruger Blackhawk, S&W. [7]Sculptured two-piece bases as found on fine custom rifles. Price shown is for base alone. Also available unfinished—**$74.91**, or finished but unblued—**$87.45**. [8]30mm rings made in projectionless style, medium height only. Three-ring mount available for T/C Contender and other pistols in Conetrol's three grades.

Maker, Model, Type	Adjust.	Scopes	Price
EAW			
Quick-Loc Mount	W&E	1", 26mm	253.00
	W&E	30mm	270.00
Magnum Fixed Mount	W&E	1", 26mm	198.00
	W&E	30mm	214.00

Fit most popular rifles. Avail. in 4 heights, 4 extensions. Reliable return to zero. Stress-free mounting. Imported by New England Custom Gun Svc.

GENTRY			
Feather-Light Rings	No	1", 30mm	75.00

One-piece of stainless or chrome moly; matte blue or gray. From David Gentry.

GRACE			
Swan G-3	No	Weaver-type	259.95

For HK G-3 guns. All-steel; provides iron sight see-through. From Grace Tool, Inc.

GRIFFIN & HOWE			
Standard Double Lever (S)	No	1" or 26mm split rings	405.00

All popular models (Garand $255). All rings $105. Top ejection rings available. Price installed for side mount.

GUNS, GEAR & GADGETS, L.L.C.			
Swan G-3[1]	No	Weaver-type rail	225.00
FN FAL[2]	No	Weaver-type rail	139.00
Remington 700	No	Weaver base	85.00

[1]Universal top claw lock. [2]Paratrooper model, $149.00. From Guns, Gear & Gadgets.

IRONSIGHTER			
Wide Ironsighter™	No	1" split rings	32.95
Ironsighter Center Fire[1]	No	1" split rings	32.95
Ironsighter S-94	No	1" split rings	33.95
Ironsighter AR-15/M-16[8]	No	1", 30mm	$103.95
Ironsighter 22-Cal. Rimfire			
Model #500[2]	No	1" split rings	20.95
Model #600[3]	No	7/8" split rings also fits 3/4"	16.95
Series #700[5]	No	1" split rings	32.95
Ruger Base Mounts[6]	No	1" split rings	83.95
Ironsighter Handguns[4]	No	1" split rings	33.95-58.95
Blackpowder Mount[7]	No	1"	32.95-76.95

[1]Most popular rifles, including Ruger Mini-14, H&R M700, and muzzleloaders. Rings have oval holes to permit use of iron sights. [2]For 1" dia. scopes. [3]For 3/4" or 7/8" dia. scopes. [4]For 1" dia. extended eye relief scopes. [5]702—Browning A-Bolt; 709—Marlin 39A. [6]732—Ruger 77/22 R&RS, No. 1, Ranch Rifle; 778 fits Ruger 77R, RS. Both 733, 778 fit Ruger integral bases. [7]Fits most popular blackpowder rifles; one model for Holden Ironsighter mounts, one for Weaver rings. [8]Model 716 with 1" #540 rings; Model 717 with 30mm #530 rings. Adj. rear sight is integral. Some models in stainless finish. From Ironsighter Co.

K MOUNT By KENPATABLE			
Shotgun Mount	No	1", laser or red dot device	49.95
SKS	No	1"	39.95

Wrap-around design; no gunsmithing required. Models for Browning BPS, A-5 12-ga., Sweet 16, 20, Rem. 870/1100 (LTW L.H.) and S&W 916, Mossberg 500, Ithaca 37 & 51 12-ga., S&W 1000/3000, Win. 1400. [1]Requires simple modification to gun. From KenPatable Ent.

KRIS MOUNTS			
Side-Saddle[1]	No	1", 26mm split rings	12.98
Two Piece (T)[2]	No	1", 26mm split rings	8.98
One Piece (T)[3]	No	1", 26mm split rings	12.98

[1]One-piece mount for Win. 94. [2]Most popular rifles and Ruger. [3]Blackhawk revolver. Mounts have oval hole to permit use of iron sights.

KWIK-SITE			
KS-See-Thru[1]	No	1"	31.95
KS-22 See-Thru[2]	No	1"	23.95
KS-W94[3]	No	1"	39.95
Bench Rest	No	1"	31.95
KS-WEV	No	1"	31.95
KS-WEV-HIGH	No	1"	37.95
KS-T22 1"[4]	No	1"	23.95
KS-FL Flashlite[5]	No	Mini or C cell flashlight	49.95
KS-T88[6]	No	1"	11.95
KS-T89	No	30mm	14.95
KSN 22 See-Thru	No	1", 7/8"	20.95
KSN-T22	No	1", 7/8"	20.95
KSN-M16 See-Thru	No	1"	99.95
KSB Base Set	—	—	5.95
Combo Bases & Rings	No	1"	31.95

Bases interchangeable with Weaver bases. [1]Most rifles. Allows use of iron sights. [2]22-cal. rifles with grooved receivers. Allows use of iron sights. [3]Model 94, 94 Big Bore. No drilling or tapping. Also in adjustable model **$49.95**. [4]Non-see-through model for grooved receivers. [5]Allows Mag Lite or C or D, Mini Mag Lites to be mounted atop See-Thru mounts. [6]Fits any Redfield, Tasco, Weaver or universal-style Kwik-Site dovetail base. Bright blue, black matte or satin finish. Standard, high heights.

SCOPE MOUNTS

Maker, Model, Type	Adjust.	Scopes	Price
LASER AIM	No	Laser Aim	29.00-69.00
Mounts Laser Aim above or below barrel. Avail. for most popular handguns, rifles, shotguns, including militaries. From Emerging Technologies, Inc.			
LASERSIGHT	No	LS45 only	29.95-149.00
For the LS45 Lasersight. Allows LS45 to be mounted alongside any 1" scope. Universal adapter attaches to any full-length Weaver-type base. For most popular military-type rifles, Mossberg, Rem. shotguns, Python, Desert Eagle, S&W N frame, Colt 45ACP. From Imatronic Lasersight.			
LEUPOLD			
STD Bases[1]	W only	One- or two-piece bases	23.40
STD Rings[2]	—	1" super low, low, medium, high	31.00
STD Handgun mounts[3]	No	—	56.00
Dual Dovetail Bases[1,4]	No	—	23.40
Dual Dovetail Rings[9]	—	1", super low, low	31.00
Ring Mounts[5,6,7]	No	7/8", 1"	78.60
22 Rimfire[9]	No	7/8", 1"	58.20
Gunmaker Base[8]	W only	1"	16.30
Quick Release Rings	—	1", low, med., high	31.00-66.90
Quick Release Bases[10]	No	1", one- or two-piece	67.30
[1]Rev. front and rear combinations; matte finish **$22.90**. [2]Avail. polished, matte or silver (low, med. only) finish. [3]Base and two rings; Casull, Ruger, S&W, T/C; add $5.00 for silver finish. [4]Rem. 700, Win. 70-type actions. [5]For Ruger No. 1, 77, 77/22; interchangeable with Ruger units. [6]For dovetailed rimfire rifles. [7]Sako; high, medium, low. [8]Must be drilled, tapped for each action. [9]Most dovetail-receiver 22s. [10]BSA Monarch, Rem. 40X, 700, 721, 725, Ruger M77, S&W 1500, Weatherby Mark V, Vanguard, Win M70.			
LEATHERWOOD			
Bridge Bases[1]	No	ART II or all dovetail rings	15.00
M1A/M-14 Q.D.	No	ART II or all dovetail rings	105.00
AR-15/M-16 Base	No	ART II or all dovetail rings	25.00
FN-FAL Base	No	ART II or all dovetail rings	100.00
FN Para. Base	No	ART II or all dovetail rings	110.00
Steyr SSG Base	No	ART II or all dovetail rings	55.00
[1]Many popular bolt actions. Mounts accept Weaver or dovetail-type rings. From North American Specialties.			
MARLIN			
One Piece QD (T)	No	1" split rings	14.95
Most Marlin lever actions.			
MILLETT			
Black Onyx Smooth	—	1", low, medium, high	31.15
Chaparral Engraved	—	engraved	46.15
One-Piece Bases[6]	Yes	1"	23.95
Universal Two-Piece Bases			
700 Series	W only	Two-piece bases	25.15
FN Series	W only	Two-piece bases	25.15
70 Series[1]	W only	1", two-piece bases	25.15
Angle-Loc Rings[2]	W only	1", low, medium, high	32.20-47.20
Ruger 77 Rings[3]	—	1"	47.20
Shotgun Rings[4]	—	1"	28.29
Handgun Bases, Rings[5]	—	1"	34.60-69.15
30mm Rings[7]	—	30mm	37.75-42.95
Extension Rings[8]	—	1"	35.65
See-Thru Mounts[9]	No	1"	27.95-32.95
Shotgun Mounts[10]	No	1"	49.95
[1]Rem. 40X, 700, 722, 725, Ruger 77 (round top), Weatherby, FN Mauser, FN Brownings, Colt 57, Interarms Mark X, Parker-Hale, Sako (round receiver), many others. [2]Fits Win. M70, 70XTR, 670, Browning BBR, BAR, BLR, A-Bolt, Rem. 7400/7600, Four, Six, Marlin 336, Win. 94 A.E., Sav. 110. [3]To fit Weaver-type bases. [4]Engraved. Smooth **$34.60**. [5]For Rem. 870, 1100; smooth. [6]Two and three-ring sets for Colt Python, Trooper, Diamondback, Peacekeeper, Dan Wesson, Ruger Redhawk, Super Redhawk. [7]Turn-in bases and Weaver-style for most popular rifles and T/C Contender, XP-100 pistols. [8]Both Weaver and turn-in styles; three heights. [9]Med. or high; ext. front— std. rear, ext. rear— std. front, ext. front— ext. rear; **$40.90** for double extension. [10]Many popular rifles, Knight MK-85, T/C Hawken, Renegade, Mossberg 500 Slugster, 835 Slug. [11]For Rem. 870/1100, Win. 1200, 1300/1400, 1500, Mossberg 500. Some models available in nickel at extra cost. From Millett Sights.			
OAKSHORE			
Handguns			
Browning Buck Mark	No	1"	29.00
Colt Cobra, Diamondback, Python, 1911	No	1"	38.00-52.00
Ruger 22 Auto, GP100	No	1"	33.00-49.00
S&W N Frame	No	1"	45.00-60.00
S&W 422	No	1"	35.00-38.00
Rifles			
Colt AR-15	No	1"	26.00-34.00
H&K 91, 93, 94, MP-5, G-3	No	1"	56.00
Galil	No	1"	75.00
Marlin 336 & 1800 Series	No	1"	21.00
Win. 94	No	1"	39.00
Shotguns			
Mossberg 500	No	1"	40.00
Rem. 870, 1100	No	1"	33.00-52.00
Rings	—	1", med., high	5.20-9.80
See Through offered in some models. Black or silver finish; 1" rings also avail. for 3/8" grooved receivers (See Through). From Oakshore Electronic Sights, Inc.			
PEM'S			
22T Mount[1]	No	1"	17.95
The Mount[2]	Yes	1"	27.50
[1]Fit all 3/8" dovetail on rimfire rifles. [2]Base and ring set; for over 100 popular rifles; low, medium rings. From Pem's.			
RAM-LINE			
Mini-14 Mount	Yes	1"	24.97
No drilling or tapping. Use std. dovetail rings. Has built-in shell deflector. Made of solid black polymer. From Ram-Line, Inc.			
REDFIELD			
American Rings[6]	No	1", low, med., high	16.95
American Bases[6]	No	—	2.65-10.55
American Widefield See-Thru[7]	No	1"	16.95
JR-SR (T)[1]	W only	3/4", 1", 26mm, 30mm	JR—26.95-52.95 SR—20.95-22.95
Ring (T)[2]	No	3/4" and 1"	30.95-45.95
Three-Ring Pistol System SMP[3]	No	1" split rings (three)	56.95-62.95
Widefield See-Thru Mounts	No	1"	16.95
Ruger Rings[4]	No	1", med., high	36.95
Ruger 30mm[5]	No	1"	47.95
Midline Ext. Rings	No	1"	24.95
[1]Low, med. & high, split rings. Reversible extension front rings for 1". 2-piece bases for Sako, Colt Sauer bases **$39.95**. Med. Top Access JR rings nickel-plated, **$28.95**. SR two-piece mount nickel-plated, **$22.95**. [2]Split rings for grooved 22s; 30mm, black matte **$42.95**. [3]Used with MP scopes for: S&W K, L or N frame, XP-100, T/C Contender, Ruger receivers. [4]For Ruger Model 77 rifles, medium and high; medium only for M77/22. [5]For Model 77. Also in matte finish, **$45.95**. [6]Aluminum 22 groove mount **$14.95**; base and medium rings **$18.95**. [7]Fits American or Weaver-style base.			
S&K			
Insta-Mount (T) bases and rings[1]	W only	Use S&K rings only	47.00-117.00
Conventional rings and bases[2]	W only	1" split rings	From 65.00
Skulptured Bases, Rings[2]	W only	1", 26mm, 30mm	From 65.00
Smooth Kontoured Rings[3]	No	1", 26mm, 30mm	50.00-74.00
[1]1903, A3, M1 Carbine, Lee Enfield #1, Mk. III, #4, #5, M1917, M98 Mauser, AR-15, AR-180, M-14, M-1, Ger. K-43, Mini-14, M1-A, Krag, AKM, Win. 94, SKS Type 56, Daewoo, H&K. [2]Most popular rifles already drilled and tapped. [3]No projections; weigh 1/2-oz. each; matte or gloss finish. Horizontally and vertically split rings, matte or high gloss.			
SSK INDUSTRIES			
T'SOB	No	1"	65.00-145.00
Quick Detachable	No	1"	From 160.00
Custom installation using from two to four rings (included). For T/C Contender, most 22 auto pistols, Ruger and other S.A. revolvers, Ruger, Dan Wesson, S&W, Colt DA revolvers. Black or white finish. Uses Kimber rings in two- or three-ring sets. In blue or SSK Khrome. For T/C Contender or most popular revolvers. Standard, non-detachable model also available, from **$65.00**.			
SAKO			
QD Dovetail	W only	1" only	70.00-155.00
Sako, or any rifle using Sako action, 3 heights available. Stoeger, importer.			
SPRINGFIELD, INC.			
M1A Third Generation	No	1"	123.00
M1A Standard	No	1"	77.00
SAR-4800 Mount	No	—	96.60
M6 Scount Mount	No	—	29.00
From Springfield, Inc.			
TASCO			
World Class			
Universal "W" Ringmount[1]	No	1", 30mm	25.50-30.00
Ruger[2]	No	1", 30mm	31.00-73.00
Tasco (cont.)			
22, Air Rifle[3]	No	1", 30mm	18.00-82.00
Ringsets[4]	No	1", 26mm, 30mm	39.00-66.00
Tasco (cont.)			

CAUTION: PRICES SHOWN ARE SUPPLIED BY THE MANUFACTURER OR IMPORTER. CHECK YOU LOCAL GUNSHOP.

SCOPE MOUNTS

Maker, Model, Type	Adjust.	Scopes	Price
Handgun Revolver	No	1"	33.50-58.00
Handgun Competition	No	1"	103.00
Traditional Ringsets	No	1"	33.00-66.00
See-Thru	No	1"	19.00
Bases[5]	Yes	—	24.00-61.00

[1]Steel; low, high only; also high-profile see-through; fit Tasco, Weaver, other universal bases; black gloss or satin chrome. [2]Low, high only; for Redhawk and Super, No.1, Mini-14 & Thirty, 77, 77/22; blue or stainless. [3]Low, med., high; 3/8" grooved receivers; black or satin chrome. [4]Low, med., high; black gloss, matte satin chrome; also Traditional Ringsets $31.00 (1"), $42.00 (26mm), $53.00 (30mm). [5]For popular rifles and shotguns; one-piece, two-piece, Q.D., long and short action, extension. Handgun bases have w&e adj. From Tasco.

THOMPSON/CENTER

Maker, Model, Type	Adjust.	Scopes	Price
Contender 9741[1]	No	2½, 4 RP	17.00
Duo-Ring Mount[2]	No	1"	57.20
Weaver-Style Bases[3]	No	—	12.00
Weaver-Style Rings[4]	No	1"	25.00-37.00
Weaver-Style See-Through Rings[5]	No	1"	23.00
Quick Release System[6]	No	1"	Rings 48.00 Base 24.50

[1]T/C rail mount scopes; all Contenders except vent. rib. [2]Attaches directly to T/C Contender bbl., no drilling/tapping; also for T/C M/L rifles, needs base adapter; blue or stainless; for M/L guns, $59.80. [3]For T/C ThunderHawk, FireHawk rifles; blue; silver, $37.00. [4]Medium and high; blue or silver finish. [5]For T/C FireHawk, ThunderHawk; blue; silver, $25.00. [6]For Contender pistol, Carbine, Scout, all M/L long guns. From Thompson/Center.

UNERTL

Maker, Model, Type	Adjust.	Scopes	Price
¼ Click[1]	Yes	¾", 1" target scopes	Per set 165.00

[1]Unertl target or varmint scopes. Posa or standard mounts, less bases. From Unertl.

WARNE

Maker, Model, Type	Adjust.	Scopes	Price
Deluxe Series (all steel non-Q.D. rings)			
Standard	No	1", 3 heights	76.50
		30mm, 2 heights	88.50
Sako	No	1", 4 heights	76.50
		30mm, 3 heights	88.50
Deluxe Series Rings fit Premier Series Bases			
Premier Series (all-steel Q.D. rings)			
Adjustable Double Levers	No	1", 4 heights	99.50
		26mm, 2 heights	111.50
		30mm, 3 heights	111.50
Thumb Knob	No	1", 4 heights	79.50
		26mm, 2 heights	91.50
		30mm, 3 heights	91.50
Brno 19mm	No	1", 3 heights	99.50
		30mm, 2 heights	111.50
Brno 16mm		1" 2 heights	99.50
Ruger	No	1", 4 heights	99.50
		30mm, 3 heights	111.50
Ruger M77	No	1", 3 heights	99.50
		30mm, 2 heights	111.50
Sako Medium & Long Action	No	1", 4 heights	99.50
		30mm, 3 heights	111.50
Sako Short Action	No	1", 3 heights	99.50
All-Steel One-Piece Base, ea.			32.00
All-Steel Two-Piece Base, ea.			12.50
Maxima Series (Weaver-style Q.D. rings with Adjustable Double Levers)			
Aluminum	No	1", 3 heights	49.50
		30mm, 3 heights	55.50
Aluminum Two-Piece Base, ea.			5.00
All-Steel	No	1", 3 heights	59.50
		30mm, 3 heights	71.50
All-Steel Two-Piece Base, ea.			12.50

Vertically split rings with dovetail clamp, precise return to zero. Fit most popular rifles, handguns. Regular blue, matte blue, silver finish. From Warne Mfg. Co.

WEAVER

Maker, Model, Type	Adjust.	Scopes	Price
Detachable Mounts			
Top Mount[1]	No	7/8", 1"	25.00-38.00
Side Mount[2]	No	1", 1" Long	29.00-35.00
Pivot Mount[3]	No	1"	39.00
Tip-Off Mount[4]	No	7/8", 1"	21.00-27.00
See-Thru Mount			
Traditional[5]	No	1"	16.00-23.00
Tip-Off[4]	No	1", 7/8"	14.00-16.00
Pro View[5]	No	1"	14.00-16.00
Mount Base System[6]			
Blue Finish	No	1"	75.00
Stainless Finish	No	1"	105.00
Shotgun Converta-Mount System[7]	No	1"	75.00
Rifle Mount System[8]	No	1"	33.00
Paramount Mount Systems[9]			
Bases, pair	Yes	1"	26.00
Rings, pair	No	1"	34.00

[1]Nearly all modern rifles. Low, med., high. 1" extension $25.00. 1" low, med., high stainless steel $38.00. [2]Nearly all modern rifles, shotguns. [3]Most modern big bore rifles; std., high. [4]22s with 3/8" grooved receivers. [5]Most modern big bore rifles, some in stainless finish. $20.00-21.00. [6]No drilling, tapping. For Colt Python, Trooper, 357, Officer's Model, Ruger Blackhawk & Super, Mini-14, Security-Six, 22 auto pistols, Single-Six 22, Redhawk, Blackhawk SRM 357, S&W current K, L with adj. sights. [7]For Rem. 870, 1100, 11-87, Browning A-5, BPS, Ithaca 37, 87, Beretta A303, Beretta A-390, Winchester 1200-1500, Mossberg 500. [8]For some popular sporting rifles. [9]Dovetail design mount for Rem. 700, Win. 70, FN Mauser, low, med., high rings; std., extension bases. From Weaver.

WEIGAND

Maker, Model, Type	Adjust.	Scopes	Price
1911 PDP4[1]	No	40mm, PDP4	69.95
1911 General Purpose[2]	No	—	59.95
Ruger Mark II[3]	No	—	49.95
3rd Generation[4]	No	—	99.95
Pro Ringless[5]	No	30mm	99.95
Stabilizer I Ringless[6,7]	No	30mm	99.95
Revolver Mount[8]	No	—	35.50
Ruger 10/22[9]	No	—	39.95

[1]For Tasco PDP4 and similar 40mm sights. [2]Weaver rail; takes any standard rings. [3]No drilling, tapping. [4]For M1911; grooved top for Weaver-style rings; requires drilling, tapping. [5]Two-piece design; for M1911, P9/EA-9, CZ-75 copies; integral rings; silver alum. finish. [6]Three-piece design; fits M1911, P9/EA-9, TZ, CZ-75 copies; silver alum. finish. [7]Stabilizer II — more forward position; for M1911, McCormick frames. [8]Frame mount. [9]Barrel mount. From Weigand Combat Handguns, Inc.

WIDEVIEW

Maker, Model, Type	Adjust.	Scopes	Price
Premium 94 Angle Eject	No	1"	24.00
Premium See-Thru	No	1"	22.00
22 Premium See-Thru	No	¾", 1"	16.00
Universal Ring Angle Cut	No	1"	22.00
Universal Ring Straight Cut	No	1"	24.62
Solid Mounts			
Lo Ring Solid[1]	No	1"	16.00
Hi Ring Solid[1]	No	1"	16.00
SR Rings	—	1", 30mm	18.64
22 Grooved Receiver	No	1"	16.00
94 Side Mount	No	1"	26.00
Blackpowder Mounts[2]	No	1"	22.00-44.00

[1]For Weaver-type bases. Models for many popular rifles. Low ring, high ring and grooved receiver types. [2]No drilling, tapping; for T/C Renegade, Hawken, CVA, Knight Traditions guns. From Wideview Scope Mount Corp.

WILLIAMS

Maker, Model, Type	Adjust.	Scopes	Price
Sidemount with HCO Rings[1]	No	1", split or extension rings.	74.21
Sidemount, offset rings[2]	No	Same	61.08
Sight-Thru Mounts[3]	No	1", 7/8" sleeves	24.70
Streamline Mounts	No	1" (bases form rings).	25.70
Guideline Handgun[4]	No	1" split rings.	61.75

[1]Most rifles, Br. S.M.L.E. (round rec.) $14.41 extra. [2]Most rifles including Win. 94 Big Bore. [3]Many modern rifles, including CVA Apollo, others with 1" octagon barrels. [4]No drilling, tapping required; heat treated alloy. For Ruger MkII Bull Barrel ($61.75); Streamline Top Mount for T/C Contender ($41.15), Scout Rifle ($51.45), High Top Mount with sub-base ($51.45). From Williams Gunsight Co.

YORK

Maker, Model, Type	Adjust.	Scopes	Price
M-1 Garand	Yes	1"	39.95

Centers scope over the action. No drilling, tapping or gunsmithing. Uses standard dovetail rings. From York M-1 Conversions.

NOTES

(S)—Side Mount (T)—Top Mount; 22mm=.866"; 25.4mm=1.024"; 26.5mm=1.045"; 30mm=1.81".

SPOTTING SCOPES

BAUSCH & LOMB PREMIER HDR 60mm objective, 15-45x zoom. Straight or 45° eyepiece. Field at 1000 yds. 125 ft. (15x), 68 ft. (45x). Length 13.0"; weight 38 oz. Interchangeable bayonet-style eyepieces.
Price: Straight or angled, 15-45x ... **$549.95**
Price: 22x wide angle eyepiece ... **$81.95**
Price: 30x long eye relief eyepiece ... **$127.95**

BAUSCH & LOMB DISCOVERER 15x to 60x zoom, 60mm objective. Constant focus throughout range. Field at 1000 yds. 38 ft (60x), 150 ft. (15x). Comes with lens caps. Length 17$\frac{1}{2}$"; weight 48.5 oz.
Price: ... **$364.95**

BAUSCH & LOMB ELITE 15x to 45x zoom, 60mm objective. Field at 1000 yds., 119-62 ft. Length is 12.2"; weight, 26.5 oz. Waterproof, armored. Tripod mount. Comes with black case.
Price: ... **$713.95**

BAUSCH & LOMB 77MM ELITE 20x, 30x or 20-60x zoom, 77mm objective. Field of view at 1000 yds. 175 ft. (20x), 78 ft. (30x), 108-62 ft. (zoom). Weight 51 oz. (20x, 30x), 54 oz. (zoom); length 16.8". Interchangeable bayonet-style eyepieces. Built-in peep sight.
Price: ... **$750.00**
Price: With EDPrime Glass ... **$1,550.00**
Price: 20-60x zoom eyepiece ... **$386.95**
Price: 20x wide angle eyepiece ... **$276.95**
Price: 30x eyepiece ... **$273.95**

BURRIS 20x SPOTTER 20x, 50mm objective. Straight type. Field at 100 yds. 15 ft. Length 10"; weight 21 oz. Rubber armor coating, multi-coated lenses, 22mm eye relief. Recessed focus adjustment. Nitrogen filled. Retractable sunshade.
Price: 20x 50mm ... **$565.00**
Price: 24x 60mm ... **$583.00**
Price: 30x 60mm ... **$609.00**

BUSHNELL COMPACT TROPHY 50mm objective, 20-50x zoom. Field at 1000 yds. 84 ft. (20x), 48 ft. (50x). Length 11"; weight 16.5 oz. Black rubber armored, waterproof.
Price: ... **$303.95**

BUSHNELL BANNER SENTRY 18-36x zoom, 50mm objective. Field at 1000 yds. 115-78 ft. Length 14.5", weight 27 oz. Black rubber armored. Built-in peep sight. Comes with tripod.
Price: ... **$189.95**
Price: With 45° field eyepiece, includes tripod ... **$210.95**

BUSHNELL COMPACT COMPETITOR 20x, 40mm objective. Field at 1000 yds. 141 ft. Focuses down to 40 ft. for indoor use. Tripod mount. Length 10.5"; weight 14.5 oz. Comes with tripod.
Price: ... **$143.95**

BUSHNELL SPACEMASTER 15x-45x zoom. Rubber armored, prismatic. 60mm objective. Field at 1000 yds. 125-65 ft. Minimum focus 20 ft. Length with caps 11.6"; weight 38.4 oz.
Price: With tripod and carrying case. ... **$496.95**
Price: Interchangeable eyepieces 20x, 25x, 60x, each ... **$59.95**
Price: 22x Wide Angle ... **$93.95**
Price: 15-45x zoom eyepiece ... **$170.95**

BUSHNELL STALKER 10x to 30x zoom, 50mm objective. Field at 1000 yds. 142 ft. (10x) to 86 ft. (30x). Length 10.5"; weight 16 oz. Camo armored. Comes with tripod.
Price: ... **$412.95**

KOWA TSN-1-45° Offset-type. 77mm objective, 25x, fixed and zoom eyepieces; field at 1000 yds. 94 ft.; relative brightness 9.6; length 15.4"; weight 48.8 oz. Lens shade and caps. Straight-type (TSN-2) also available with similar specs and prices.
Price: Without eyepiece ... **$575.00**
Price: 20x-60x zoom eyepiece ... **$250.00**
Price: 20x eyepiece (wide angle) ... **$190.00**
Price: 25x, 40x eyepiece ... **$119.00, $132.00**
Price: 25x LER eyepiece ... **$178.00**
Price: 30x eyepiece (wide angle) ... **$220.00**
Price: 60x eyepiece ... **$190.00**
Price: 77x eyepiece ... **$195.00**
Price: TSN-2 (straight), no eyepiece ... **$545.00**

KOWA TS-601 45° off-set type. 60mm multi-coated objective, 25x fixed and zoom eyepieces; field at 1000 yds. 93 ft.; relative brightness 5.8; length 14.8"; weight 37 oz. Comes with lens shade and caps. Straight-type also available (TS-602).
Price: Without eyepiece ... **$425.00**
Price: 25x eyepiece ... **$95.00**
Price: 20x eyepiece (wide angle) ... **$114.00**
Price: 40x eyepiece ... **$99.00**
Price: 20x-60x zoom eyepiece ... **$205.00**
Price: 25x LER eyepiece ... **$175.00**

KOWA TS-610 SERIES SPOTTING SCOPES 60mm objective lens. Straight or angled, fixed (20x WA, 25x LER, 25x, 27x WA, 40x) or zoom (20x-60x) eyepieces. Partly rubber armored composite body. Field at 1000 yds. 102 ft. (25x), 162-56 ft. (20x-60x). Length 11.7"; weight 27.5 oz. Partial listing shown.
Price: TS-611, 45°, 20x-60x zoom ... **$725.00**
Price: TS-611, 40x, fixed ... **$619.00**
Price: TS-612, straight, 20x-60x zoom ... **$670.00**
Price: TS-612, 25x LER ... **$640.00**
Price: TS-613 ED, 45°, 20x-60x zoom ... **$1,215.00**
Price: TS-613 ED, 27x, Wide Angle ... **$1,180.00**
Price: TS-614 ED, straight, 20x-60x zoom ... **$1,140.00**
Price: TS-614 ED, 20x Wide Angle ... **$1,049.00**

KOWA TS-9C Straight-type. 50mm objective, 20x compact model; fixed power eyepieces; objective focusing down to 17 ft.; field at 1000 yds. 157 ft.; relative brightness 6.3; length 9.65"; weight 22.9 oz. Lens caps.
Price: With 20x eyepiece ... **$193.00**
Price: 15x, 20x eyepieces, each ... **$35.00, $33.00**
Price: 11x-33x zoom eyepiece ... **$111.00**
Price: As above, rubber armored, 20x (TS-9R) ... **$212.00**
Price: TS-9B (45° offset), 20x ... **$236.00**

LEUPOLD 12-40x60 VARIABLE 60mm objective, 12-40x. Field at 100 yds. 17.5-5.3 ft.; eye relief 1.2" (20x). Overall length 11.5", weight 32 oz. Rubber armored.
Price: ... **$1,026.80**

LEUPOLD 20x50 COMPACT 50mm objective, 20x. Field at 100 yards 11.5 ft.; eye relief 1"; length 9.4"; weight 20.5 oz.
Price: Armored model ... **$646.40**
Price: Packer Tripod ... **$87.50**

LEUPOLD 25x50 COMPACT 50mm objective, 25x. Field at 100 yds. 8.3 ft.; eye relief 1"; length overall 9.4"; weight 20.5 oz.
Price: Armored model ... **$646.40**
Price: Armored, with reticle ... **$689.30**
Price: Packer Tripod ... **$87.50**

LEUPOLD 30x60 COMPACT 60mm objective, 30x. Field at 100 yds. 6.4 ft.; eye relief 1"; length overall 12.9"; weight 26 oz.
Price: Armored model ... **$710.70**
Price: Packer Tripod ... **$87.50**

MIRADOR TTB SERIES Draw tube armored spotting scopes. Available with 75mm or 80mm objective. Zoom model (28x-62x, 80mm) is 11$\frac{7}{8}$" (closed), weighs 50 oz. Field at 1000 yds. 70-42 ft. Comes with lens covers.
Price: 28-62x80mm ... **$1,133.95**
Price: 32x80mm ... **$971.95**
Price: 26-58x75mm ... **$989.95**
Price: 30x75mm ... **$827.95**

MIRADOR SSD SPOTTING SCOPES 60mm objective, 15x, 20x, 22x, 25x, 40x, 60x, 20-60x; field at 1000 yds. 37 ft.; length 10$\frac{1}{4}$"; weight 33 oz.
Price: 25x ... **$575.95**
Price: 22x Wide Angle ... **$593.95**
Price: 20-60x Zoom ... **$746.95**
Price: As above, with tripod, case ... **$944.95**

MIRADOR SIA SPOTTING SCOPES Similar to the SSD scopes except with 45° eyepiece. Length 12$\frac{1}{4}$"; weight 39 oz.
Price: 25x ... **$809.95**
Price: 22x Wide Angle ... **$827.95**
Price: 20-60x Zoom ... **$980.95**

MIRADOR SSR SPOTTING SCOPES 50mm or 60mm objective. Similar to SSD except rubber armored in black or camouflage. Length 11$\frac{1}{8}$"; weight 31 oz.
Price: Black, 20x ... **$521.95**
Price: Black, 18x Wide Angle ... **$539.95**
Price: Black, 16-48x Zoom ... **$692.95**
Price: Black, 20x, 60mm, EER ... **$692.95**
Price: Black, 22x Wide Angle, 60mm ... **$701.95**
Price: Black, 20-60x Zoom ... **$854.95**

MIRADOR SSF FIELD SCOPES Fixed or variable power, choice of 50mm, 60mm, 75mm objective lens. Length 9$\frac{3}{4}$"; weight 20 oz. (15-32x50).
Price: 20x50mm ... **$359.95**
Price: 25x60mm ... **$440.95**
Price: 30x75mm ... **$584.95**
Price: 15-32x50mm Zoom ... **$548.95**
Price: 18-40x60mm Zoom ... **$629.95**
Price: 22-47x75mm Zoom ... **$773.95**

MIRADOR SRA MULTI ANGLE SCOPES Similar to SSF Series except eyepiece head rotates for viewing from any angle.
Price: 20x50mm ... **$503.95**
Price: 25x60mm ... **$647.95**
Price: 30x75mm ... **$764.95**

Price: 15-32x50mm Zoom $692.95
Price: 18-40x60mm Zoom $836.95
Price: 22-47x75mm Zoom $953.95

MIRADOR SIB FIELD SCOPES Short-tube, 45° scopes with porro prism design. 50mm and 60mm objective. Length 10¼"; weight 18.5 oz. (15-32x50mm); field at 1000 yds. 129-81 ft.

Price: 20x50mm $386.95
Price: 25x60mm $449.95
Price: 15-32x50mm Zoom $575.95
Price: 18-40x60mm Zoom $638.95

NIKON FIELDSCOPES 60mm and 78mm lens. Field at 1000 yds. 105 ft. (60mm, 20x), 126 ft. (78mm, 25x). Length 12.8" (straight 60mm), 12.6" (straight 78mm); weight 34.5-47.5 oz. Eyepieces available separately.

Price: 60mm straight body $610.00
Price: 60mm angled body $740.00
Price: 60mm straight ED body $1,090.00
Price: 60mm angled ED body $1,190.00
Price: 78mm straight ED body $1,860.00
Price: 78mm angled ED body $1,980.00
Price: Eyepieces (15x to 60x) .... $134.00 to $290.00
Price: 15-45x eyepiece (25-56x for 78mm) $281.00

NIKON SPOTTING SCOPE 60mm objective, 20x fixed power or 15-45x zoom. Field at 1000 yds. 145 ft. (20x). Gray rubber armored. Straight or angled eyepiece. Weighs 44.2 oz., length 12.1" (20x).

Price: 20x60 fixed $426.00
Price: 15-45x zoom $658.00

PENTAX 30x60 HG 60mm objective lens, 30x. Field of view 86 ft. at 1000 yds. Length 12.1"; weight 35 oz. Waterproof, rubber armor, multi-coated lenses. Comes with lens cap, case, neck strap.

Price: $450.00

REDFIELD WATERPROOF 20-45x SPOTTER 60mm objective, 20-45x. Field at 1000 yds. 45-63 ft. Length 12.5"; weight 23 oz. Black rubber armor coat. With vinyl carrying case.

Price: $557.95
Price: As above, with adjustable tripod, aluminum carrying case with shoulder strap $699.95

REDFIELD REGAL IV Conventional straight through viewing. Regal IV has 60mm objective and interchangeable 25x and 20x-60x zoom eyepieces. Field at 1000 yds. 94 ft. (25x). With tripod and aluminum carrying case.

Price: Regal IV with black rubber Armorcoat $925.95

REDFIELD REGAL VI 60mm objective, 25x fixed and 20x-60x interchangeable eyepieces. Has 45° angled eyepiece, front-mounted focus ring, 180° tube rotation. Field at 1000 yds. 94 ft. (25x); length 12¼"; weight 40 oz. Comes with tripod, aluminum carrying case.

Price: Regal VI $1,000.95

SIMMONS 1205 COMPACT 50mm objective, 12-36x zoom. Textured black finish. Ocular focus and variable power magnification.

Price: With tripod $239.95
Price: Model 25109 (Mossy Oak camo finish) $261.95
Price: Model 24109 (Realtree rubber) $249.95

SIMMONS 1207 COMPACT 50mm objective, 25x fixed power. Ocular focus. Green rubber-armored finish.

Price: With tripod $199.95
Price: Model 1206 (black rubber-armored finish) $199.95

SIMMONS 24108 COMPACT 50mm objective, 25x fixed power. Ocular focus. Realtree rubber camo.

Price: With tripod $229.95

SWAROVSKI CT EXTENDIBLE SCOPES 75mm or 85mm objective, 20-60x zoom, or fixed 15x, 22x, 30x, 32x eyepieces. Field at 1000 yds. 135 ft. (15x), 99 ft. (32x); 99 ft. (20x), 5.2 ft. (60x) for zoom. Length 12.4" (closed), 17.2" (open) for the CT75; 9.7"/17.2" for CT85. Weight 40.6 oz. (CT75), 49.4 oz. (CT85). Green rubber armored.

Price: CT75 body $883.33
Price: CT85 body $1,100.00
Price: 20-60x eyepiece $300.00
Price: 15x, 22x eyepiece $155.55
Price: 30x eyepiece $216.67

SWAROVSKI AT-80/ST-80 SPOTTING SCOPES 80mm objective, 20-60x zoom, or fixed 15x, 22x, 30x, 32x eyepieces. Field at 1000 yds. 135 ft. (15x), 99 ft. (32x); 99 ft. (20x), 52.5 ft. (60x) for zoom. Length 16" (AT-80), 15.6" (ST-80); weight 51.8 oz. Available with HD (high density) glass.

Price: AT-80 (angled) body $1,100.00
Price: ST-80 (straight) body $1,100.00
Price: With HD glass $1,438.00
Price: 20-60x eyepiece $300.00
Price: 15x, 22x eyepiece $155.00
Price: 30x eyepiece $216.67

SWIFT NIGHTHAWK M849U 80mm objective, 28-75x zoom, or fixed 25x, 31x, 50x, 75x eyepieces. Has rubber armored body, 1.8x optical finder, retractable lens hood, 45° eyepiece. Field at 1000 yds. 60 ft. (28x), 41 ft. (75x). Length 13.4 oz.,; weight 39 oz.

Price: Body only $850.00
Price: 28-75x eyepiece $285.00
Price: Fixed eyepieces .... $90.00 to $200.00
Price: Model 849 (straight) body $780.00

SWIFT NIGHTHAWK M850U 65mm objective, 22-60x zoom, or fixed 20x, 25x, 40x, 60x eyepieces. Rubber armored with a 1.8x optical finder, retractable lens hood. Field at 1000 yds. 83 ft. (22x), 52 ft. (60x). Length 12.3"; weight 30 oz. Has 45° eyepiece.

Price: Body only $630.00
Price: 22-60x eyepiece $285.00
Price: Fixed eyepieces .... $90.00 to $200.00
Price: Model 850 (straight) body $560.00

SWIFT LEOPARD M837 50mm objective, 25x. Length 9$^{11}/_{16}$" to 10½". Weight with tripod 28 oz. Rubber armored. Comes with tripod.

Price: $150.00

SWIFT TELEMASTER M841 60mm objective. 15x to 60x variable power. Field at 1000 yds. 160 feet (15x) to 40 feet (60x). Weight 3.25 lbs.; length 18" overall.

Price: $399.50

SWIFT M700R 10x-40x, 40mm objective. Field of 210 feet at 10x, 70 feet at 40x. Length 16.3", weight 21.4 oz. Has 45° eyepiece.

Price: $198.00

SWIFT SEARCHER M839 60mm objective, 20x, 40x. Field at 1000 yds. 118 ft. (30x), 59 ft. (40x). Length 12.6"; weight 3 lbs. Rotating eyepiece head for straight or 45° viewing.

Price: $460.00
Price: 30x, 50x eyepieces, each $65.00

TASCO MS2530 MINI-SPOTTER 30mm objective, 25x. Field at 100 yds 11 ft., 6 in. Weighs 10.3 oz.; length 7¼" overall. Comes with tripod, case.

Price: $40.00

TASCO WC26TZ SPOTTING SCOPE 60mm objective, 15-45x zoom. Field at 100 yds. 11.4 ft. (15x), 6.2 ft. (45x). Length 15" overall; weight 28 oz. Comes with tripod.

Price: $386.00
Price: WC27TZ (45° model) $386.00

TASCO 5001 COMPACT ZOOM 50mm objective, 12-36x zoom. Field at 100 yds. 16 ft., 9 in. Includes photo adapter tube, tripod with panhead lever, case.

Price: $288.00

TASCO 37ZB SPOTTING SCOPE 50mm objective. 18-36x zoom. Field at 100 yds. 12 ft., 6 in. to 7 ft., 9 in. Black rubber armored.

Price: $229.00
Price: Model 37ZBC (brown camo rubber) $229.00
Price: Model 3700 (black, with tripod, case) $271.00
Price: Model 3701 (as above, brown camo) $271.00

TASCO CW50TZB, CW50TZBC ZOOM SPOTTING SCOPES 50mm objective lens, 12-36x zoom. Field at 100 yds. 16-9 ft. Available in black or brown camo rubber armor. With panhead lever tripod.

Price: CW50TZB (brown) $289.00
Price: CW50TZBC (camo) $289.00

TASCO CW50TR COMPACT SPOTTING SCOPE 50mm objective lens, 25x fixed power. Field at 100 yds. 11 ft. Comes with panhead lever tripod.

Price: $226.00

TASCO 17EB SPOTTING SCOPE 60mm objective lens, 20-60x zoom with black metal tripod, micro-adjustable elevation control. Built-in sights.

Price: $214.00

TASCO 20EB SPOTTING SCOPE 50mm objective lens, 15-45x zoom. Field at 100 yds. 8-3.7 ft.; includes tripod with pan-head lever. Built-in sights.

Price: $115.00

TASCO 21EB ZOOM 50mm objective lens, 15-45x zoom. Field at 100 yds. 11 ft. (15x). Weight 22 oz.; length 18.3" overall. Comes with panhead lever tripod.

Price: $115.00

TASCO 22EB ZOOM 60mm objective lens, 20-60x zoom. Field at 100 yds. 7 ft., 2 in. (20x). Weight 28 oz.; length 21.5" overall. Comes with micro-adjustable tripod.

Price: $214.00

TASCO 35TZB COMPACT ZOOM 50mm objective lens, 10-25x zoom. Field at 100 yds. 22 ft. (10x) Weight 23.3 oz.; length 11" overall. Comes with panhead lever tripod.

Price: $238.00

TASCO MS2040 MINI SPOTTING SCOPE 40mm objective lens, 20x fixed power. Field at 100 yds. 7 ft., 8 in. Weight 12.4 oz.; length 8.5" overall. Comes with tripod with bendable legs.

Price: $122.00

TASCO 9002T WORLD CLASS SPOTTING SCOPE 60mm objective lens, 15-60x zoom. Field at 100 yds. 14.6 ft. (15x). Fully multi-coated optics, includes camera adaptor, camera case, tripod with pan-head lever.

Price: $682.00

UNERTL "FORTY-FIVE" 54mm objective. 20x (single fixed power). Field at 100 yds. 10',10"; eye relief 1"; focusing range infinity to 33 ft. Weight about 32 oz.; overall length 15¾". With lens covers.

Price: With multi-layer lens coating $496.00
Price: With mono-layer magnesium coating $414.00

UNERTL STRAIGHT PRISMATIC 63.5mm objective, 24x. Field at 100 yds., 7 ft. Relative brightness, 6.96. Eye relief ½". Weight 40 oz.; length closed 19". Push-pull and screw-focus eyepiece. 16x and 32x eyepieces **$100.00** each.

Price: $369.00

UNERTL 20x STRAIGHT PRISMATIC 54mm objective, 20x. Field at 100 yds. 8.5 ft. Relative brightness 6.1. Eye relief ½". Weight 36 oz.; length closed 13½". Complete with lens covers.

Price: $343.00

UNERTL TEAM SCOPE 100mm objective. 15x, 24x, 32x eyepieces. Field at 100 yds. 13 to 7.5 ft. Relative brightness, 39.06 to 9.79. Eye relief 2" to 1½". Weight 13 lbs.; length 29⅞" overall. Metal tripod, yoke and wood carrying case furnished (total weight 80 lbs.).

Price: $2,200.00

PERIODICAL PUBLICATIONS

The A.C.G.Q. Journal (M)
Write to Ian Skennerton, Journal Editor, P.O. Box 433, Ashmore City 4214, Queensland, Australia. Published monthly.

AAFTA News (M)
5911 Cherokee Ave., Tampa, FL 33604. Official newsletter of the American Airgun Field Target Assn.

Action Pursuit Games Magazine (M)
CFW Enterprises, Inc., 4201 W. Vanowen Pl., Burbank, CA 91505 818-845-2656. $2.95 single copy U.S., $3.50 Canada. Editor: Jessica Sparks, 818-845-2656. World's leading magazine of paintball sports.

Air Gunner Magazine
4 The Courtyard, Denmark St., Wokingham, Berkshire RG11 2AZ, England/011-44-734-771677. $U.S. $44 for 1 yr. Leading monthly airgun magazine in U.K.

Airgun Ads
Box 33, Hamilton, MT 59840/406-363-3805. $35 1 yr. (for first mailing; $20 for second mailing; $35 for Canada and foreign orders.) Monthly tabloid with extensive For Sale and Wanted airgun listings.

The Airgun Letter
Gapp, Inc., 4614 Woodland Rd., Ellicott City, MD 41042-6329/410-730-5496. $18 U.S., $21 Canada, $24 Mexico and $30 other foreign orders, 1 yr. Monthly newsletter for airgun users and collectors.

Airgun World
4 The Courtyard, Denmark St., Wokingham, Berkshire RG11 2AZ, England/011-44-734-771677. Call for subscription rates. Oldest monthly airgun magazine in the U.K., now a sister publication to *Air Gunner.*

Alaska Magazine
Alaska Publishing Properties Inc., 808 E St., Suite 200, Anchorage, AK 99501. $24.00 yr. Hunting, Fishing and Life on the Last Frontier articles of Alaska and western Canada. Outdoors Editor, Ken Marsh.

American Firearms Industry
Nat'l. Assn. of Federally Licensed Firearms Dealers, 2455 E. Sunrise Blvd., Suite 916, Ft. Lauderdale, FL 33304. $25.00 yr. For firearms retailers, distributors and manufacturers.

American Handgunner
591 Camino de la Reina, Suite 200, San Diego, CA 92108. $16.75 yr. Articles for handgun enthusiasts, competitors, police and hunters.

American Hunter (M)
National Rifle Assn., 11250 Waples Mill Rd., Fairfax, VA 22030 (Same address for both.) Publications Div. $35.00 yr. Wide scope of hunting articles.

American Rifleman (M)
National Rifle Assn., 11250 Waples Mill Rd., Fairfax, VA 22030 (Same address for both). Publications Div. $35.00 yr. Firearms articles of all kinds.

American Single Shot Rifle News* (M)
Membership Secy. Tim Mather, 1180 Easthill SE, N. Canton, Ohio. Annual dues $20 for 6 issues. Official journal of the American Single Shot Rifle Assn.

American Survival Guide
McMullen and Yee Publishing, Inc., 774 S. Placentia Ave., Placentia, CA 92670-6846. 12 issues $19.95/714-572-2255; FAX: 714-572-1864.

American West
American West Management Corp., 7000 E. Tanque Verde Rd., Suite #30, Tucson, AZ 85715. $15.00 yr.

Arms Collecting (Q)
Museum Restoration Service, P.O. Box 70, Alexandria Bay, NY 13607-0070. $22.00 yr.; $62.00 3 yrs.; $112.00 5 yrs.

Australian Shooters Journal
Sporting Shooters' Assn. of Australia, Inc., P.O. Box 2066, Kent Town SA 5071, Australia. $45.00 yr. locally; $55.00 yr. overseas surface mail only. Hunting and shooting articles.

The Backwoodsman Magazine
P.O. Box 627, Westcliffe, CO 81252. $15.00 for 6 issues per yr.; $28.00 for 2 yrs.; sample copy $2.50. Subjects include muzzle-loading, woodslore, primitive survival, trapping, homesteading, blackpowder cartridge guns, 19th century how-to.

Black Powder Times
P.O. Box 1131, Stanwood, WA 98292. $15.00 yr.; add $2 per year for Canada, $5 per year other foreign. Tabloid newspaper for blackpowder activities; test reports.

The Blade Magazine
700 East State St., Iola, WI 54990-0001. $19.95 for 12 issues. Foreign price $35.00. A magazine for all enthusiasts of the edged blade.

Caliber
GFI-Verlag, Theodor-Heuss Ring 62, 50668 K"ln, Germany. For hunters, target shooters and reloaders.

The Caller (Q) (M)
National Wild Turkey Federation, P.O. Box 530, Edgefield, SC 29824. Tabloid newspaper for members; 4 issues per yr.

Cartridge Journal (M)
Robert Mellichamp, 907 Shirkmere, Houston, TX 77008/713-869-0558. Dues $12 for U.S. and Canadian members (includes the newsletter); 6 issues.

The Cast Bullet*(M)
Official journal of The Cast Bullet Assn. Director of Membership, 4103 Foxcraft Dr., Traverse City, MI 49684. Annual membership dues $14, includes 6 issues.

COLTELLI, che Passione (Q)
Casella postale N.519, (-20101 Milano, Italy/Fax:02-48402857. $15 1 yr., $27 2 yrs. Covers all types of knives—collecting, combat, historical. Italian text.

Combat Handguns*
Harris Publications, Inc., 1115 Broadway, New York, NY 10010. Single copy $2.95 U.S.A.; $3.25 Canada.

The Custom Rifle Gazette (Q)
The Custom Rifle Gazette Inc., 926 Blue Stem Rd., Enid, OK 73703/405-237-8335; Fax:405-202-2508. $40 yr.; Canada and Mexico add $10 surface, $18 air; outside North America add $12 surface. For the custom rifle enthusiast.

The Derringer Peanut (M)
The National Association of Derringer Collectors, P.O. Box 20572, San Jose, CA 95160. A newsletter dedicated to developing the best derringer information. Write for details.

Deutsches Waffen Journal
Journal-Verlag Schwend GmbH, Postfach 100340, D-74523 Schwäbisch Hall, Germany/0791-404-500; FAX:0791-404-505 and 404-424. DM97. 7 yr. (interior); DM120.30 (abroad), postage included. Antique and modern arms and equipment. German text.

Double Gun Journal
5014 Rockery School Rd., East Jordan, MI 49727/616-536-7439. $35 for 4 issues.

Ducks Unlimited, Inc. (M)
1 Waterfowl Way, Memphis, TN 38120

The Engraver (M) (Q)
P.O. Box 4365, Estes Park, CO 80517. Mike Dubber, editor. The journal of firearms engraving.

The Field
King's Reach Tower, Stamford St., London SE1 9LS England. £35.00 sterling U.S. (approx. $70.00) yr. Hunting and shooting articles, and all country sports.

Field & Stream
Times Mirror Magazines, Two Park Ave., New York, NY 10016. $11.94 yr. Monthly shooting column. Articles on hunting and fishing.

FIRE
Euro-Editions, Boulevard Lambermont 140, B1030 Brussels, Belgium. Belg. Franc 2100 for 6 issues. Arms, shooting, ammunition. French text.

Fur-Fish-Game
A.R. Harding Pub. Co., 2878 E. Main St., Columbus, OH 43209. $15.95 yr. "Gun Rack" column by Don Zutz.

The Gottlieb-Tartaro Report
Second Amendment Foundation, James Madison Bldg., 12500 NE 10th Pl., Bellevue, WA 98005/206-454-7012;Fax:206-451-3959. $30 for 12 issues. An insiders guide for gun owners.

Gray's Sporting Journal
Gray's Sporting Journal, Inc., P.O. Box 1207, Augusta, GA 30903. $35.95 per yr. for 6 consecutive issues. Hunting and fishing journals. Expeditions and Guides Book (Annual Travel Guide).

Gun List
700 E. State St., Iola, WI 54990. $27.95 yr. (26 issues); $52.00 2 yrs. (52 issues). Indexed market publication for firearms collectors and active shooters; guns, supplies and services.

Gun News Digest (Q)
Second Amendment Fdn., P.O. Box 488, Station C, Buffalo, NY 14209/716-885-6408;Fax:716-884-4471. $10 U.S.; $20 foreign.

The Gun Report
World Wide Gun Report, Inc., Box 38, Aledo, IL 61231-0038. $33.00 yr. For the antique and collectable gun dealer and collector.

Gunmaker (M) (Q)
ACGG, P.O. Box 812, Burlington, IA 52601-0812. The journal of custom gunmaking.

The Gunrunner
Div. of Kexco Publ. Co. Ltd., Box 565G, Lethbridge, Alb., Canada T1J 3Z4. $23.00 yr. Monthly newspaper, listing everything from antiques to artillery.

Gun Show Calendar (Q)
700 E. State St., Iola, WI 54990. $12.95 yr. (4 issues). Gun shows listed.

Gun Tests
11 Commerce Blvd., Palm Coast, FL 32142. The consumer resource for the serious shooter. Write for information.

Gun Trade News
The Street, West Raynham, Falkenham NR21 7EZ, England/01328/838755;Fax:01328-838523. Britain's only "trade only" magazine exclusive to the gun trade.

Gun Week†
Second Amendment Foundation, P.O. Box 488, Station C, Buffalo, NY 14209. $32.00 yr. U.S. and possessions; $40.00 yr. other countries. Tabloid paper on guns, hunting, shooting and collecting (50 issues).

Gun Week's Gun and Ammo Guide
Second Amendment Foundation, James Madison Bldg., 12500 NE 10th Pl., Bellevue, WA 98005. $5.95 Annual (1st issue forthcoming).

Gun World
Gallant/Charger Publications, Inc., 34249 Camino Capistrano, Capistrano Beach, CA 92624. $20.00 yr. For the hunting, reloading and shooting enthusiast.

Guns & Ammo
Petersen Publishing Co., 6420 Wilshire Blvd., Los Angeles, CA 90048. $21.94 yr. Guns, shooting, and technical articles.

Guns
Guns Magazine, P.O. Box 85201, San Diego, CA 92138. $19.95 yr.; $34.95 2 yrs.; $46.95 3 yrs. In-depth articles on a wide range of guns, shooting equipment and related accessories for gun collectors, hunters and shooters.

Guns and Gear
Creative Arts, Inc., 4901 Northwest 17th Way, Fort Lauderdale, FL 33309/305-772-2788; FAX: 305-351-0484. Single copy $4.95. Covering all aspects of the shooting sports.

Guns Review
Ravenhill Publishing Co. Ltd., Box 35, Standard House, Bonhill St., London EC 2A 4DA, England. œ20.00 sterling (approx. U.S. $38 USA & Canada) yr. For collectors and shooters.

H.A.C.S. Newsletter (M)
Harry Moon, Pres., P.O. Box 50117, South Slope RPO, Burnaby BC, V5J 5G3, Canada/604-936-9141. $15 p. yr. Canada; $17.00 outside Canada. Official newsletter of The Historical Arms Collectors of B.C. (Canada).

Handgunning*
PJS Publications, News Plaza, P.O. Box 1790, Peoria, IL 61656. Cover price $3.95; subscriptions $19.98 for 6 issues. Premier journal for multi-sport handgunners: hunting, reloading, law enforcement, practical pistol and target shooting, and home defense.

Handgun Times
Creative Arts, Inc., 4901 NW 17th Way, Fort Lauderdale, FL 33309/305-772-2788; FAX: 305-351-0484. Single copy $4.95. Technical evaluations, detailed information and testing by handgun experts.

Handloader*
Wolfe Publishing Co., 6471 Airpark Dr., Prescott, AZ 86301. $22.00 yr. The journal of ammunition reloading.

Hunting Horizons
Wolfe Publishing Co., 6471 Airpark Dr., Prescott, AZ 86301. $6.95 Annual. Dedicated to the finest pursuit of the hunt.

The Insider Gun News
The Gunpress Publishing Co., 1347 Webster St. NE, Washington, DC 20017. Editor, John D. Aquilino. $50.00 yr. (12 issues). Newsletter by former NRA communications director.

INSIGHTS*
NRA, 11250 Waples Mill Rd., Fairfax, VA 22030. Editor, John E. Robbins. $15.00 yr., which includes NRA junior membership; $10.00 for adult subscriptions (12 issues). Plenty of details for the young hunter and target shooter; emphasizes gun safety, marksmanship training, hunting skills.

International Shooting Sport*/UIT Journal
International Shooting Union (UIT), Bavariaring 21, D-80336 Munich, Germany. Europe: (Deutsche Mark) DM44.00 yr., 2 yrs. DM83.00; outside Europe: DM50.00 yr., 2 yrs. DM95.00 (air mail postage included.) For international sport shooting.

Internationales Waffen-Magazin
Habegger-Verlag Zürich, Postfach 9230, CH-8036 Zürich, Switzerland. SF 102.00 (approx. U.S. $82.00) surface mail for 10 issues. Modern and antique arms, self-defense. German text; English summary of contents.

IPPA News (M)
International Paintball Players Assn., P.O. Box 26669, San Diego, CA 92196-0669/619-695-8882. Call or write for subscription rates. Newsletter for members of the IPPA.

The Journal of the Arms & Armour Society (M)
E.J.B. Greenwood (Hon. Sec.), Field House, Upper Dicker, Hailsham, East Sussex, BN27 3PY, England. £15.00 surface mail; £20.00 airmail sterling only yr. Articles for the historian and collector.

Journal of the Historical Breechloading Smallarms Assn.
Published annually. Imperial War Museum, Lambeth Road, London SE1 6HZ, England. $13.00 yr. Articles for the collector plus mailings of short articles on specific arms, reprints, newsletters, etc.; a surcharge is made for airmail.

Knife World
Knife World Publications, P.O. Box 3395, Knoxville, TN 37927. $15.00 yr.; $25.00 2 yrs. Published monthly for knife enthusiasts and collectors. Articles on custom and factory knives; other knife-related interests, monthly column on knife identification, military knives.

Law and Order
Law and Order Magazine, 1000 Skokie Blvd., Wilmette, IL 60091. $20.00 yr. Articles for law enforcement professionals.

PERIODICAL PUBLICATIONS

Machine Gun News
Lane Publishing, P.O. Box 459, Dept. GD, Lake Hamilton, AR 71951/501-525-7514;Fax:501-525-7519. $29.95 yr. (12 issues); $5.00 sample copy. The magazine for full-auto enthusiasts, full-auto news, how to solve functioning problems, machine gun shoots from around the country and a free classified per year for subscribers.

Man At Arms*
P.O. Box 460, Lincoln, RI 02865. $27.00 yr., $52.00 2 yrs. plus $8.00 for foreign subscribers. The N.R.A. magazine of arms collecting-investing, with excellent articles for the collector of antique arms and militaria.

MAN/MAGNUM
S.A. Man (Pty) Ltd., P.O. Box 35204, Northway, Durban 4065, Republic of South Africa. SA Rand 125.00 for 12 issues. Africa's only publication on hunting, shooting, firearms, bushcraft, knives, etc.

The Marlin Collector (M)
R.W. Paterson, 407 Lincoln Bldg., 44 Main St., Champaign, IL 61820.

Muzzle Blasts (M)
National Muzzle Loading Rifle Assn., P.O. Box 67, Friendship, IN 47021. $30.00 yr. annual membership. For the blackpowder shooter.

Muzzleloader Magazine*
Rebel Publishing Co., Inc., Dept. Gun, Route 5, Box 347-M, Texarkana, TX 75501. $16.00 U.S.; $19.00 U.S. for foreign subscribers a yr. The publication for blackpowder shooters.

National Defense (M)*
American Defense Preparedness Assn., Two Colonial Place, Suite 400, 2101 Wilson Blvd., Arlington, VA 22201-3061/703-522-1820; FAX: 703-522-1885. $35.00 yr. Articles on both military and civil defense field, including weapons, materials technology, management.

National Knife Magazine (M)
Natl. Knife Coll. Assn., 7201 Shallowford Rd., P.O. Box 21070, Chattanooga, TN 37424-0070. Membership $35 yr.; $64.00 International yr.

National Rifle Assn. Journal (British) (Q)
Natl. Rifle Assn. (BR.), Bisley Camp, Brookwood, Woking, Surrey, England. GU24, OPB. £22.00 Sterling including postage.

National Wildlife*
Natl. Wildlife Fed., 1400 16th St. NW, Washington, DC 20036, $16.00 yr. (6 issues.); *International Wildlife*, 6 issues, $16.00 yr. Both, $22.00 yr., includes all membership benefits. Write attn.: Membership Services Dept., for more information.

New Zealand GUNS*
Waitekauri Publishing, P.O. 45, Waikino 3060, New Zealand. $NZ90.00 (6 issues) yr. Covers the hunting and firearms scene in New Zealand.

New Zealand Wildlife (Q)
New Zealand Deerstalkers Assoc., Inc., P.O. Box 6514, Wellington, N.Z. $30.00 (N.Z.). Hunting, shooting and firearms/game research articles.

North American Hunter* (M)
P.O. Box 3401, Minnetonka, MN 55343. $18.00 yr. (7 issues). Articles on all types of North American hunting.

Outdoor Life
Times Mirror Magazines, Two Park Ave., New York, NY 10016. Special 1-yr. subscription, $11.97. Extensive coverage of hunting and shooting. Shooting column by Jim Carmichel.

La Passion des Courteaux (Q)
Phenix Editions, 25 rue Mademoiselle, 75015 Paris, France. French text.

Paintball Consumer Reports
14573-C Jefferson Davis Highway, Woodridge, VA 22191/703-491-6199. $19.95 1 yr. U.S., $27.95 foreign. Product testing for the paintball industry.

Paintball Games International Magazine
Aceville Publications, Castle House, 97 High St., Colchester, Essex, England CO1 1TH/011-44-206-564840. Write for subscription rates. Leading magazine in the U.K. covering competitive paintball activities.

Paintball Hotline†
American Paintball Media and Marketing, 15507 S. Normandie Ave. #487, Gardena, CA 90247/310-323-1021. $50 U.S. 1 yr. $75 Mexico and Canada, $125 other foreign orders. Weekly newsletter that tracks inside industry news.

Paintball News
PBN Publishing, P.O. Box 1608, 24 Henniker St., Hillsboro, NH 03244/603-464-6080. $35 U.S. 1 yr. Bi-weekly newspaper covering new product reviews and industry features.

Paintball Players Bible*
American Paintball Media and Marketing, 15507 S. Normandie Ave. #487, Gardena, Ca 90247/310-323-1021. $12.95 U.S. 1 yr., $19.95 foreign. Publications w. profiles of guns and accessories.

Paintball Sports (Q)
Paintball Publications, Inc., 540 Main St., Mount Kisco, NY 10549/941-241-7400. $24.75 U.S. 1 yr., $32.75 foreign. Covering the competitive paintball scene.

Petersen's HUNTING Magazine
Petersen Publishing Co., 6420 Wilshire Blvd., Los Angeles, CA 90048. $19.94 yr.; Canada $29.34 yr.; foreign countries $29.94 yr. Hunting articles for all game; test reports.

P.I. Magazine
America's Private Investigation Journal, 755 Bronx Dr., Toledo, OH 43609. Chuck Klein, firearms editor with column about handguns.

Pirsch
BLV Verlagsgesellschaft mbH, Postfach 400320, 80703 Munich, Germany/089-12704-0;Fax:089-12705-354. German text.

Point Blank
Citizens Committee for the Right to Keep and Bear Arms (sent to contributors), Liberty Park, 12500 NE 10th Pl., Bellevue, WA 98005

POINTBLANK (M)
Natl. Firearms Assn., Box 4384 Stn. C, Calgary, AB T2T 5N2, Canada. Official publication of the NFA.

The Police Marksman*
6000 E. Shirley Lane, Montgomery, AL 36117. $17.95 yr. For law enforcement personnel.

Police Times (M)
Membership Records, 3801 Biscayne Blvd., Miami, FL 33137/305-573-0070.

Popular Mechanics
Hearst Corp., 224 W. 57th St., New York, NY 10019. $15.94 yr. Firearms, camping, outdoor oriented articles.

Precision Shooting
Precision Shooting, Inc., 222 McKee St., Manchester, CT 06040. $29.00 yr. Journal of the International Benchrest Shooters, and target shooting in general. Also considerable coverage of varmint shooting, as well as big bore, small bore, schuetzen, lead bullet, wildcats and precision reloading.

Rifle*
Wolfe Publishing Co., 6471 Airpark Dr., Prescott, AZ 86301. $19.00 yr. The sporting firearms journal.

Rod & Rifle Magazine
Lithographic Serv. Ltd., P.O. Box 38-138, Wellington, New Zealand. $50.00 yr. (6 issues). Hunting, shooting and fishing articles.

Safari* (M)
Safari Magazine, 4800 W. Gates Pass Rd., Tucson, AZ 85745/602-620-1220. $30.00 (6 times). The journal of big game hunting, published by Safari Club International. Also publish *Safari Times*, a monthly newspaper, included in price of $30.00 field membership.

Second Amendment Reporter
Second Amendment Foundation, James Madison Bldg., 12500 NE 10th Pl., Bellevue, WA 98005. $15.00 yr. (non-contributors).

Shooter's News
23146 Lorain Rd., Box 349, North Olmsted, OH 44070/216-979-5258;Fax:216-979-5259. $29 U.S. 1 yr., $54 2 yrs.; $52 foreign. A journal dedicated to precision riflery.

Shooting Industry
Publisher's Dev. Corp., 591 Camino de la Reina, Suite 200, San Diego, CA 92108. $50.00 yr. To the trade $25.00.

Shooting Sports USA
National Rifle Assn. of America, 11250 Waples Mill Road, Fairfax, VA 22030. Annual subscriptions for NRA members are $5 for classified shooters and $10 for non-classified shooters. Non-NRA member subscriptions are $15. Covering events, techniques and personalities in competitive shooting.

The Shooting Times & Country Magazine (England)†
IPC Magazines Ltd., King's Reach Tower, Stamford St, 1 London SE1 9LS, England/0171-261-6180;Fax:0171-261-7179. £65 (approx. $98.00) yr.; £79 yr. overseas (52 issues). Game shooting, wild fowling, hunting, game fishing and firearms articles. Britain's best selling field sports magazine.

Shooting Times
PJS Publications, News Plaza, P.O. Box 1790, Peoria, IL 61656/309-682-6626. $21.98 yr. Guns, shooting, reloading; articles on every gun activity.

The Shotgun News‡
Snell Publishing Co., Box 669, Hastings, NE 68902. $22.00 yr.; all other countries $110.00 yr. Sample copy $4.00. Gun ads of all kinds.

SHOT Business
Flintlock Ridge Office Center, 11 Mile Hill Rd., Newtown, CT 06470-2359/203-426-1320; FAX: 203-426-1087. For the shooting, hunting and outdoor trade retailer.

Shotgun Sports
P.O. Box 6810, Auburn, CA 95604/916-889-2220; FAX:916-889-9106. $28.00 yr. Trapshooting how-to's, shotshell reloading, shotgun patterning, shotgun tests and evaluations, Sporting Clays action, waterfowl/upland hunting. Call 1-800-676-8920 for a free sample copy.

The Sixgunner (M)
Handgun Hunters International, P.O. Box 357, MAG, Bloomingdale, OH 43910

The Skeet Shooting Review
National Skeet Shooting Assn., 5931 Roft Rd., San Antonio, TX 78253. $15.00 yr. (Assn. membership of $20.00 includes mag.) Competition results, personality profiles of top Skeet shooters, how-to articles, technical, reloading information.

Soldier of Fortune
Subscription Dept., P.O. Box 348, Mt. Morris, IL 61054. $24.95 yr.; $34.95 Canada; $45.95 foreign.

SPG Lubricants/BP Cartridge (Q)
SPG Lubricant, P.O. Box 761, Livingston, MT 59047. $15 yr. For the blackpowder cartridge enthusiast.

Sporting Clays Magazine
5211 South Washington Ave., Titusville, FL 32780/407-268-5010; FAX: 407-267-7216. $29.95 yr. (12 issues).

Sporting Goods Business
Miller Freeman, Inc., 1515 Broadway, New York, NY 10036. Trade journal.

Sporting Goods Dealer
Two Park Ave., New York, NY 10016. $100.00 yr. Sporting goods trade journal.

Sporting Gun
Bretton Court, Bretton, Peterborough PE3 8DZ, England. £27.00 (approx. U.S. $36.00), airmail £35.50 yr. For the game and clay enthusiasts.

Sports Afield
The Hearst Corp., 250 W. 55th St., New York, NY 10019. $13.97 yr. Tom Gresham on firearms, ammunition; Grits Gresham on shooting and Thomas McIntyre on hunting.

The Squirrel Hunter
P.O. Box 368, Chireno, TX 75937. $14.00 yr. Articles about squirrel hunting.

TACARMI
Via E. De Amicis, 25; 20123 Milano, Italy. $100.00 yr. approx. Antique and modern guns. (Italian text.)

Trap & Field
1200 Waterway Blvd., Indianapolis, IN 46202. $25.00 yr. Official publ. Amateur Trapshooting Assn. Scores, averages, trapshooting articles.

Turkey Call* (M)
Natl. Wild Turkey Federation, Inc., P.O. Box 530, Edgefield, SC 29824. $20.00 with membership (6 issues per yr.)

The U.S. Handgunner* (M)
U.S. Revolver Assn., 40 Larchmont Ave., Taunton, MA 02780. $10.00 yr. General handgun and competition articles. Bi-monthly sent to members.

U.S. Airgun Magazine (Q)
2603 Rollingbrook, Benton, AR 72015/501-778-2615. Cover the sport from hunting, 10-meter, field target and collecting. Write for details.

The Varmint Hunter Magazine (Q)
The Varmint Hunters Assn., Box 759, Pierre, SD 57501/800-528-4868. $24.00 yr.

Waffenmarkt-Intern
GFI-Verlag, Theodor-Heuss Ring 62, 50668 Köln, Germany. Only for gunsmiths, licensed firearms dealers and their suppliers in Germany, Austria and Switzerland.

Wild Sheep (M) (Q)
Foundation for North American Wild Sheep, 720 Allen Ave., Cody, WY 82414. Official journal of the foundation.

Women & Guns
P.O. Box 488, Sta. C, Buffalo, NY 14209. $24.00 yr. U.S.; (12 issues). Only magazine edited by and for women gun owners.

World War II*
Empire Press, Inc., 602 King St., Suite 300, Leesburg, VA 22075. Annual subscriptions $16.95 U.S.; $22.95 Canada and overseas. The title says it—WWII; good articles, ads, etc.

---

*Published bi-monthly †Published weekly ‡Published three times per month. All others are published monthly.
M=Membership requirements; write for details. Q=Published Quarterly.

The ARMS LIBRARY

FOR COLLECTOR • HUNTER • SHOOTER • OUTDOORSMAN

IMPORTANT NOTICE TO BOOK BUYERS

Books listed here may be bought from Ray Riling Arms Books Co., 6844 Gorsten St., P.O. Box 18925, Philadelphia, PA 19119, phone 215/438-2456. Joe Riling is the researcher and compiler of "The Arms Library" and a seller of gun books for over 30 years.

The Riling stock includes books classic and modern, many hard-to-find items, and many not obtainable elsewhere. These pages list a portion of the current stock. They offer prompt, complete service, with delayed shipments occurring only on out-of-print or out-of-stock books.

NOTICE FOR ALL CUSTOMERS: Remittance in U.S. funds must accompany all orders. For U.S. add $2.00 per book for postage and insurance. Minimum order $10.00. For UPS add 50% to mailing costs.

All foreign countries add $5.00 per book. All foreign orders are shipped at the buyer's risk unless an additional $5 for insurance is included.

Payments in excess of order or for "Backorders" are credited or fully refunded at request. Books "As-Ordered" are not returnable except by permission and a handling charge on these of $2.00 per book is deducted from refund or credit. Only Pennsylvania customers must include current sales tax.

A full variety of arms books also available from Rutgers Book Center, 127 Raritan Ave., Highland Park, NJ 08904.

*New Book

BALLISTICS and HANDLOADING

ABC's of Reloading, 5th Edition, by Dean A. Grennell, DBI Books, Inc., Northbrook, IL, 1993. 288 pp., illus. Paper covers. $19.95.
The definitive guide to every facet of cartridge and shotshell reloading.
Ammunition Making, by George E. Frost, National Rifle Association of America, Washington, D.C., 1990. 160 pp., illus. Paper covers. $17.95.
Reflects the perspective of "an insider" with half a century's experience in successful management of ammunition manufacturing operations.
Basic Handloading, by George C. Nonte, Jr., Outdoor Life Books, New York, NY, 1982. 192 pp., illus. Paper covers. $6.95.
How to produce high-quality ammunition using the safest, most efficient methods.
Big Bore Rifles And Cartridges, Wolfe Publishing Co., Prescott, AZ, 1991. Paper covers. $26.00.
This book covers cartridges from 8mm to .600 Nitro with loading tables.
Black Powder Guide, 2nd Edition, by George C. Nonte, Jr., Stoeger Publishing Co., So. Hackensack, NJ, 1991. 288 pp., illus. Paper covers. $14.95.
How-to instructions for selection, repair and maintenance of muzzleloaders, making your own bullets, restoring and refinishing, shooting techniques.
*Blackpowder Loading Manual, 3rd Edition, edited by Sam Fadala, DBI Books, Inc., Northbrook, IL, 1995. 368 pp., illus. Paper covers. $19.95.
Revised and expanded edition of this landmark blackpowder loading book. Covers hundreds of loads for most of the popular blackpowder rifles, handguns and shotguns.
The Bullet Swage Manual. MDSU/I, by Ted Smith, Corbin Manufacturing and Supply Co., White City, OR, 1988. 45 pp., illus. Paper covers. $10.00.
A book that fills the need for information on bullet swaging.
Cartridge Case Measurements, by Dr. Arthur J. Mack, Amrex Enterprises, Vienna, VA, 1990. 300 pp., illus. Paper covers. $49.95.
Lists over 5000 cartridges of all kinds. Gives basic measurements (rim, head, shoulder, neck, length, plus bullet diameter) in both English and Metric. Hundreds of experimental and wildcats.
Cartridges of the World, 7th Edition, by Frank Barnes, edited by Mike Bussard, DBI Books, Inc., Northbrook, IL, 1993. 464 pp., illus. Paper covers. $23.95
Completely revised edition of the general purpose reference work for which collectors, police, scientists and laymen reach first for answers to cartridge identification questions.
Cast Bullets, by Col. E. H. Harrison, A publication of the National Rifle Association of America, Washington, DC, 1979. 144 pp., illus. Paper covers. $12.95.
An authoritative guide to bullet casting techniques and ballistics.
The Complete Handloader for Rifles, Handguns and Shotguns, by John Wootters, Stackpole Books, Harrisburg, PA, 1988. 214 pp., $29.95.
Loading-bench know-how.
Firearms Pressure Factors, by Dr. Lloyd Brownell, Wolfe Publishing Co., Prescott, AZ, 1990. 200 pp., illus. $14.00.

The only book available devoted entirely to firearms and pressure. Contains chapters on secondary explosion effect, modern pressure measuring techniques in revolvers and rifles, and Dr. Brownell's series on pressure factors.
Game Loads and Practical Ballistics for the American Hunter, by Bob Hagel, Wolfe Publishing Co., Prescott, AZ, 1992. 310 pp., illus. $27.90.
Hagel's knowledge gained as a hunter, guide and gun enthusiast is gathered in this informative text.
Gibbs' Cartridges and Front Ignition Loading Technique, by Roger Stowers, Wolfe Publishing Co., Prescott, AZ, 1991. 64 pp., illus. Paper covers. $14.95.
The story of this innovative gunsmith who designed his own wildcat cartridges known for their flat trajectories, high velocity and accuracy.
Handbook of Bullet Swaging No. 7, by David R. Corbin, Corbin Manufacturing and Supply Co., White City, OR, 1986. 199 pp., illus. Paper covers. $10.00.
This handbook explains the most precise method of making quality bullets.
Handbook for Shooters and Reloaders, by P.O. Ackley, Salt Lake City, UT, 1970, (Vol. I), 567 pp., illus. (Vol. II), a new printing with specific new material. 495 pp., illus. $17.00 each.
Handbook of Metallic Cartridge Reloading, by Edward Matunas, Winchester Press, Piscataway, NJ, 1981. 272 pp., illus. $19.95.
Up-to-date, comprehensive loading tables prepared by four major powder manufacturers.
Handgun Reloading, The Gun Digest Book of, by Dean A. Grennell and Wiley M. Clapp, DBI Books, Inc., Northbrook, IL, 1987. 256 pp., illus. Paper covers. $16.95.
Detailed discussions of all aspects of reloading for handguns, from basic to complex. New loading data.
*Handloader's Digest 1996, 15th Edition, edited by Bob Bell, DBI Books, Inc., Northbrook, IL, 1995. 480pp., illus. Paper covers. $23.95.
Top writers in the field contribute helpful information on techniques and components. Greatly expanded and fully indexed catalog of all currently available tools, accessories and components for metallic, blackpowder cartridge, shotshell reloading and swaging.
Handloader's Guide, by Stanley W. Trzoniec, Stoeger Publishing Co., So. Hackensack, NJ, 1985. 256 pp., illus. Paper covers. $14.95.
The complete step-by-step fully illustrated guide to handloading ammunition.
Handloader's Manual of Cartridge Conversions, by John J. Donnelly, Stoeger Publishing Co., So. Hackensack, NJ, 1986. Unpaginated. $49.95.
From 14 Jones to 70-150 Winchester in English and American cartridges, and from 4.85 U.K. to 15.2x28R Gevelot in metric cartridges. Over 900 cartridges described in detail.
Handloading, by Bill Davis, Jr., NRA Books, Wash., D.C., 1980. 400 pp., illus. Paper covers. $15.95.
A complete update and expansion of the NRA Handloader's Guide.
Handloading for Hunters, by Don Zutz, Winchester Press, Piscataway, NJ, 1977. 288 pp., illus. $30.00.
Precise mixes and loads for different types of game and for various hunting situations with rifle and shotgun.
Hatcher's Notebook, by S. Julian Hatcher, Stackpole Books, Harrisburg, PA, 1992. 488 pp., illus. $29.95.
A reference work for shooters, gunsmiths, ballisticians, historians, hunters and collectors.
*Hodgdon Data Manual No. 26, Hodgdon Powder Co., Shawnee Mission, KS, 1993. 797 pp. $22.95.
Includes Hercules, Winchester and Dupont powders; data on cartridge cases; loads; silhouette; shotshell; pyrodex and blackpowder; conversion factors; weight equivalents, etc.

50th EDITION, 1996 **531**

The Home Guide to Cartridge Conversions, by Maj. George C. Nonte Jr., The Gun Room Press, Highland Park, NJ, 1976. 404 pp., illus. $24.95.
Revised and updated version of Nonte's definitive work on the alteration of cartridge cases for use in guns for which they were not intended.
Hornady Handbook of Cartridge Reloading, 4th Edition, Vol. I and II, Hornady Mfg. Co., Grand Island, NE, 1991. 1200 pp., illus. $28.50.
New edition of this famous reloading handbook. Latest loads, ballistic information, etc.
Hornady Handbook of Cartridge Reloading, Abridged Edition, Hornady Mfg. Co., Grand Island, NE, 1991. $19.95.
Ballistic data for 25 of the most popular cartridges.
Hornady Load Notes, Hornady Mfg. Co., Grand Island, NE, 1991. $4.95.
Complete load data and ballistics for a single caliber. Eight pistol 9mm-45ACP; 16 rifle, 222-45-70.
The Ideal Handbook of Useful Information for Shooters, No. 15, originally published by Ideal Manufacturing Co., reprinted by Wolfe Publishing Co., Prescott, AZ, 1991. 142 pp., illus. Paper covers. $10.95.
A facsimile reprint of one of the early Ideal Handbooks.
*__The Illustrated Reference of Cartridge Dimensions,__ edited by Dave Scovill, Wolfe Publishing Co., Prescott, AZ, 1994. 343 pp., illus. Paper covers. $19.00
A comprehensive volume with over 300 cartridges. Standard and metric dimensions have been taken from SAAMI drawings and/or fired cartridges.
Loading the Black Powder Rifle Cartridge, by Paul A Matthews, Wolfe Publishing Co., Prescott, AZ, 1993. 121 pp., illus. Paper covers. $22.50.
Author Matthews brings the black powder cartridge shooter valuable information on the basics, including cartridge care, lubes and moulds, powder charges and developing and testing loads in his usual authoritative style.
Lyman Cast Bullet Handbook, 3rd Edition, edited by C. Kenneth Ramage, Lyman Publications, Middlefield, CT, 1980. 416 pp., illus. Paper covers. $19.95.
Information on more than 5000 tested cast bullet loads and 19 pages of trajectory and wind drift tables for cast bullets.
Lyman Black Powder Handbook, ed. by C. Kenneth Ramage, Lyman Products for Shooters, Middlefield, CT, 1975. 239 pp., illus. Paper covers. $14.95.
Comprehensive load information for the modern blackpowder shooter.
Lyman Pistol & Revolver Handbook, edited by C. Kenneth Ramage, Lyman Publications, Middlefield, CT, 1978. 280 pp., illus. Paper covers. $14.95.
An extensive reference of load and trajectory data for the handgun.
Lyman Reloading Handbook No. 47, edited by Edward A. Matunas, Lyman Publications, Middlefield, CT, 1992. 480 pp., illus. Paper covers. $23.00.
"The world's most comprehensive reloading manual." Complete "How to Reload" information. Expanded data section with all the newest rifle and pistol calibers.
Lyman Shotshell Handbook, 3rd Edition, edited by C. Kenneth Ramage, Lyman Publications, Middlefield, CT, 1984. 312 pp., illus. Paper covers. $19.95.
Has 2000 loads, including slugs and buckshot, plus feature articles and a full color I.D. section.
*__Lyman's Guide to Big Game Cartridges & Rifles,__ by Edward Matunas, Lyman Publishing Corporation, Middlefield, CT, 1994. 287 pp., illus. Paper covers. $17.95.
A selection guide to cartridges and rifles for big game—antelope to elephant.
Making Loading Dies and Bullet Molds, by Harold Hoffman, H&P Publishing, San Angelo, TX, 1993. 230 pp., illus. Paper covers. $22.95.
A good book for learning tool and die making.
Metallic Cartridge Reloading, 2nd Edition, by Edward A. Matunas, DBI Books, Inc., Northbrook, IL., 1988. 320 pp., illus. Paper covers. $18.95.
A true reloading manual with a wealth of invaluable technical data provided by a recognized expert.
Modern Handloading, by Maj. Geo. C. Nonte, Winchester Press, Piscataway, NJ, 1972. 416 pp., illus. $15.00.
Covers all aspects of metallic and shotshell ammunition loading, plus more loads than any book in print.
Modern Practical Ballistics, by Art Pejsa, Pejsa Ballistics, Minneapolis, MN, 1990. 150 pp., illus. $24.95.
Covers all aspects of ballistics and new, simplified methods. Clear examples illustrate new, easy but very accurate formulas.
Nosler Reloading Manual No. 3, edited by Gail Root, Nosler Bullets, Inc., Bend, OR, 1989. 516 pp., illus. $21.95.
All-new book. New format including featured articles and cartridge introductions by well-known shooters, gun writers and editors.
The Paper Jacket, by Paul Matthews, Wolfe Publishing Co., Prescott, AZ, 1991. Paper covers. $13.50.
Up-to-date and accurate information about paper-patched bullets.
Precision Handloading, by John Withers, Stoeger Publishing Co., So. Hackensack, NJ, 1985. 224 pp., illus. Paper covers. $14.95.
An entirely new approach to handloading ammunition.
Propellant Profiles New and Expanded, 3rd Edition, Wolfe Publishing Co., Prescott, AZ, 1991. Paper covers. $16.95.
Reloader's Guide, 3rd Edition, by R.A. Steindler, Stoeger Publishing Co., So. Hackensack, NJ, 1984. 224 pp., illus. Paper covers. $11.95.
Complete, fully illustrated step-by-step guide to handloading ammunition.
Reloading for Shotgunners, 3rd Edition, by Edward A. Matunas, DBI Books, Inc., Northbrook, IL, 1993. 288 pp., illus. Paper covers. $16.95.
Expanded reloading tables with over 2,000 loads. Bushing charts for every major press and component maker. All new presentation on all aspects of shotshell reloading by one of the top experts in the field.
Sierra Handgun Manual, 3rd Edition, edited by Kenneth Ramage, Sierra Bullets, Santa Fe Springs, CA, 1990. 704 pp., illus. 3-ring binder. $19.95.
New listings for XP-100 and Contender pistols and TCU cartridges...part of a new single shot section. Covers the latest loads for 10mm Auto, 455 Super Mag, and Accurate powders.
Sierra Rifle Manual, 3rd Edition, edited by Kenneth Ramage, Sierra Bullets, Santa Fe Springs, CA, 1990. 856 pp., illus. 3-ring binder. $24.95.
Updated load information with new powder listings and a wealth of inside tips.
Sixgun Cartridges and Loads, by Elmer Keith, The Gun Room Press, Highland Park, NJ, 1986. 151 pp., illus. $24.95.
A manual covering the selection, uses and loading of the most suitable and popular revolver cartridges. Originally published in 1936. Reprint.
Speer Reloading Manual Number 12, edited by members of the Speer research staff, Omark Industries, Lewiston, ID, 1987. 621 pp., illus. $18.95.
Reloading manual for rifles and pistols.
Why Not Load Your Own?, by Col. T. Whelen, A. S. Barnes, New York, 1957, 4th ed., rev. 237 pp., illus. $20.00.
A basic reference on handloading, describing each step, materials and equipment. Includes loads for popular cartridges.
Wildcat Cartridges, Volume I, Wolfe Publishing Company, Prescott, AZ, 1992. 125 pp. Soft cover. $16.95.
From *Handloader* magazine, the more popular and famous wildcats are profiled.
Wildcat Cartridges, Volume II, compiled from *Handloader* and *Rifle* magazine articles written by featured authors, Wolfe Publishing Co., Prescott, AZ, 1992. 971 pp., illus. Paper covers. $34.95.
This volume details rifle and handtgun cartridges from the 14-221 to the 460 Van Horn. A comprehensive work containing loading tables and commentary.
Yours Truly, Harvey Donaldson, by Harvey Donaldson, Wolfe Publ. Co., Inc., Prescott, AZ, 1980. 288 pp., illus. $19.50.
Reprint of the famous columns by Harvey Donaldson which appeared in "Handloader" from May 1966 through December 1972.

COLLECTORS

The American Cartridge, by Charles R. Suydam, Borden Publishing Co., Alhambra, CA, 1986. 184 pp., illus. $18.00.
An illustrated study of the rimfire cartridge in the United States.
American Military Shoulder Arms: Volume 1, Colonial and Revolutionary War Arms, by George D. Moller, University Press of Colorado, Niwot, CO, 1993. 538 pp., illus. $75.00.
A superb in-depth study of the shoulder arms of the United States. This volume covers the pre-colonial period to the end of the American Revolution.
American Military Shoulder Arms: Volume 2, From the 1790's to the End of the Flintlock Period, by George D. Moller, University Press of Colorado, Niwot, CO, 1994. 496 pp., illus. $75.00.
Describes the rifles, muskets, carbines and other shoulder arms used by the armed forces of the United States from the 1790s to the end of the flintlock period in the 1840s.
*__Antique Guns, the Collector's Guide, 2nd Edition,__ edited by John Traister, Stoeger Publishing Co., S. Hackensack, NJ, 1994. 320 pp., illus. Paper covers. $19.95.
Covers a vast spectrum of pre-1900 firearms: those manufactured by U.S. gunmakers as well as Canadian, French, German, Belgian, Spanish and other foreign firms.
Arms & Accoutrements of the Mounted Police 1873-1973, by Roger F. Phillips and Donald J. Klancher, Museum Restoration Service, Ont., Canada, 1982. 224 pp., illus. $49.95.
A definitive history of the revolvers, rifles, machine guns, cannons, ammunition, swords, etc. used by the NWMP, the RNWMP and the RCMP during the first 100 years of the Force.
Arms Makers of Maryland, by Daniel D. Hartzler, George Shumway, York, PA, 1975. 200 pp., illus. $50.00.
A thorough study of the gunsmiths of Maryland who worked during the late 18th and early 19th centuries.
Artistry in Arms: The Guns of Smith & Wesson, by Roy G. Jinks, Smith & Wesson, Springfield, MA, 1991. 85 pp., illus. Paper covers. $19.95.
Catalog of the Smith & Wesson International Museum Tour 1991-1995 organized by the Connecticut Valley Historical Museum and Springfield Library and Museum Association.
Astra Automatic Pistols, by Leonardo M. Antaris, FIRAC Publishing Co., Sterling, CO, 1989. 248 pp., illus. $45.00.
Charts, tables, serial ranges, etc. The definitive work on Astra pistols.
Basic Documents on U.S. Marital Arms, commentary by Col. B. R. Lewis, reissue by Ray Riling, Phila., PA, 1956 and 1960. *Rifle Musket Model 1855.* The first issue rifle of musket caliber, a muzzle loader equipped with the Maynard Primer, 32 pp. *Rifle Musket Model 1863.* The typical Union muzzle-loader of the Civil War, 26 pp. *Breech-Loading Rifle Musket Model 1866.* The first of our 50-caliber breechloading rifles, 12 pp. *Remington Navy Rifle Model 1870.* A commercial type breech-loader made at Springfield, 16 pp. *Lee Straight Pull Navy Rifle Model 1895.* A magazine cartridge arm of 6mm caliber. 23 pp. *Breech-Loading Arms* (five models) 27 pp. *Ward-Burton Rifle Musket 1871*-16 pp. Each $10.00.
Beretta Automatic Pistols, by J.B. Wood, Stackpole Books, Harrisburg, PA, 1985. 192 pp., illus. $24.95.
Only English-language book devoted to the Beretta line. Includes all important models.
Blacksmith Guide to Ruger Flat-top & Super Blackhawks, by H.W. Ross, Jr., Blacksmith Corp., Chino Valley, AZ, 1990. 96 pp., illus. Paper covers. $9.95.
A key source on the extensively collected Ruger Blackhawk revolvers.
*__The Blunderbuss 1500-1900,__ by James D. Forman, Museum Restoration Service, Bloomfield, Ont., Canada, 1995. 40 pp., illus. Paper covers. $4.95.
The guns that had no peer as an anti-personal weapon throughout the flintlock era.
Boarders Away, Volume II: Firearms of the Age of Fighting Sail, by William Gilkerson, Andrew Mowbray, Inc. Publishers, Lincoln, RI, 1993. 331 pp., illus. $65.00.
Covers the pistols, muskets, combustibles and small cannon used aboard American and European fighting ships, 1626-1826.
The Book of the Springfield, by Edward C. Crossman and Roy F. Dunlap, Wolfe Publishing Co., Prescott, AZ, 1990. 567 pp., illus. $36.00.
A textbook covering the military, sporting and target rifles chambered for the caliber 30 Model 1906 cartridge; their metallic and telescopic sights and ammunition used in them.
The Boxer Cartridge, by B.A. Temple, I.D.S.A. Books, Piqua, OH, 1977. 200 pp., over 80 illus/tables. $25.00
Breech-Loading Carbines of the United States Civil War Period, by Brig. Gen. John Pitman, Armory Publications, Tacoma, WA, 1987. 94 pp., illus. $29.95.
The first in a series of previously unpublished manuscripts originated by the late Brigadier General John Putnam. Exploded drawings showing parts actual size follow each sectioned illustration.
*__The Breech-Loading Single-Shot Rifle,__ by Major Ned H. Roberts and Kenneth L. Waters, Wolfe Publishing Co., Prescott, AZ, 1995. 333 pp., illus. $28.50.
A comprehensive and complete history of the evolution of the Schutzen and single-shot rifle.
*__British Military Firearms 1650-1850,__ by Howard L. Blackmore, Stackpole Books, Mechanicsburg, PA, 1994. 224 pp., illus. $50.00.
The definitive work on British military firearms.
British Service Rifles and Carbines 1888-1900, by Alan M. Petrillo, Excaliber Publications, Latham, NY, 1994. 72 pp., illus, Paper covers. $11.95.
A complete review of the Lee-Metford and Lee-Enfield rifles and carbines.
British Small Arms Ammunition, 1864-1938, by Peter Labett, Armory Publications, Oceanside, CA, 1994. 352 pp., illus. $75.00.
The military side of the story illustrating the rifles, carbines, machine guns, revolvers and automatic pistols and their ammunition, experimental and adopted, from 577 Snider to modern times.
*__The British Soldier's Firearms from Smoothbore to Rifled Arms, 1850-1864,__ by Dr. C.H. Roads, R&R Books, Livonia, NY, 1994. 332 pp., illus. $49.00.

A reprint of the classic text covering the development of British military hand and shoulder firearms in the crucial years between 1850 and 1864.

British Sporting Rifle Cartridges, by Bill Fleming, Armory Publications, Oceanside, CA, 1994. 302 pp., illus. $60.00.

An expanded study of volume three of *The History & Development of Small Arms Ammunition.* Includes pertinent trade catalog pages, etc.

Browning Dates of Manufacture, compiled by George Madis, Art and Reference House, Brownsboro, TX, 1989. 48 pp. $5.00.

Gives the date codes and product codes for all models from 1824 to the present.

*__Browning Sporting Arms of Distinction 1903-1992,__ by Matt Eastman, Matt Eastman Publications, Fitzgerald, GA, 1995. 450 pp., illus. $49.95.

The most recognized publication on Browning sporting arms ever written; covers all models.

Bullard Arms, by G. Scott Jamieson, The Boston Mills Press, Ontario, Canada, 1989. 244 pp., illus. $35.00.

The story of a mechanical genius whose rifles and cartridges were the equal to any made in America in the 1880s.

Burning Powder, compiled by Major D.B. Wesson, Wolfe Publishing Company, Prescott, AZ, 1992. 110 pp. Soft cover. $10.95.

A rare booklet from 1932 for Smith & Wesson collectors.

The Burnside Breech Loading Carbines, by Edward A. Hull, Andrew Mowbray, Inc., Lincoln, RI, 1986. 95 pp., illus. $16.00.

No. 1 in the "Man at Arms Monograph Series." A model-by-model historical/technical examination of one of the most widely used cavalry weapons of the American Civil War based upon important and previously unpublished research.

California Gunsmiths 1846-1900, by Lawrence P. Sheldon, Far Far West Publ., Fair Oaks, CA, 1977. 289 pp., illus. $29.65.

A study of early California gunsmiths and the firearms they made.

*__Canadian Military Handguns 1855-1985,__ by Clive M. Law, Museum Restoration Service, Bloomfield, Ont. Canada, 1994. 130pp., illus. $40.00.

A long-awaited and important history for arms historians and pistol collectors.

Carbines of the Civil War, by John D. McAulay, Pioneer Press, Union City, TN, 1981. 123 pp., illus. Paper covers. $7.95.

A guide for the student and collector of the colorful arms used by the Federal cavalry.

Cartridges for Breechloading Rifles, by A. Mattenheimer, Armory Publications, Oceanside, CA, 1989. 90 pp. with two 15"x19" color lithos containing 163 drawings of cartridges and firearms mechanisms. $29.95.

Reprinting of this German work on cartridges. Text in German and English.

Civil War Breech Loading Rifles, by John D. McAulay, Andrew Mowbray, Inc., Lincoln, RI, 1991. 144 pp., illus. Paper covers. $15.00.

All the major breech-loading rifles of the Civil War and most, if not all, of the obscure types are detailed, illustrated and set in their historical context.

Civil War Carbines Volume 2: The Early Years, by John D. McAulay, Andrew Mowbray, Inc., Lincoln, RI, 1991. 144 pp., illus. Paper covers. $15.00.

Covers the carbines made during the exciting years leading up to the outbreak of war and used by the North and South in the conflict.

Civil War Pistols, by John D. McAulay, Andrew Mowbray Inc., Lincoln, RI, 1992. 166 pp., illus. $38.50.

A survey of the handguns used during the American Civil War.

A Collector's Guide to United States Combat Shotguns, by Bruce N. Canfield, Andrew Mowbray Inc., Lincoln, RI, 1992. 184 pp., illus. Paper covers. $24.00

This book provides full coverage of combat shotguns, from the earliest examples right up to the Gulf War and beyond.

A Collector's Guide to Winchester in the Service, by Bruce N. Canfield, Andrew Mowbray, Inc., Lincoln, RI, 1991. 192 pp., illus. Paper covers. $22.00.

The firearms produced by Winchester for the national defense. From Hotchkiss to the M14, each firearm is examined and illustrated.

A Collector's Guide to the M1 Garand and the M1 Carbine, by Bruce N. Canfield, Andrew Mowbray, Inc., Publisher, Lincoln, RI, 1988. 144 pp., illus., paper covers. $22.00.

A comprehensive guide to the most important and ubiquitous American arms of WWII and Korea.

A Collector's Guide to the '03 Springfield, by Bruce N. Canfield, Andrew Mowbray Inc, Lincoln, RI, 1989. 160 pp., illus. Paper covers. $22.00.

A comprehensive guide follows the '03 through its unparalleled tenure of service. Covers all of the interesting variations, modifications and accessories of this highly collectible military rifle.

Collector's Illustrated Encyclopedia of the American Revolution, by George C. Neumann and Frank J. Kravic, Rebel Publishing Co., Inc., Texarkana, TX, 1989. 286 pp., illus. $29.95.

A showcase of more than 2,300 artifacts made, worn, and used by those who fought in the War for Independence.

Colonial Frontier Guns, by T.M. Hamilton, Pioneer Press, Union City, TN, 1988. 176 pp., illus. Paper covers. $13.95.

A complete study of early flint muskets of this country.

Colt 45 Service Pistol Models of 1911 and 1911A1, by Charles W. Clawson, Charles W. Clawson, Fort Wayne, IN, 1991. 429 pp., illus. $65.00.

Complete military history, development and production 1900 through 1945 plus foreign pistols, gallery pistols, revolvers, cartridge development, and much more.

Colt Heritage, by R.L. Wilson, Simon & Schuster, 1979. 358 pp., illus. $75.00.

The official history of Colt firearms 1836 to the present.

Colt Peacemaker British Model, by Keith Cochran, Cochran Publishing Co., Rapid City, SD, 1989. 160 pp., illus. $35.00.

Covers those revolvers Colt squeezed in while completing a large order of revolvers for the U.S. Cavalry in early 1874, to those magnificent cased target revolvers used in the pistol competitions at Bisley Commons in the 1890s.

Colt Peacemaker Encyclopedia, by Keith Cochran, Keith Cochran, Rapid City, SD, 1986. 434 pp., illus. $65.00.

A must book for the Peacemaker collector.

Colt Peacemaker Encyclopedia, Volume 2, by Keith Cochran, Cochran Publishing Co., SD, 1992. 416 pp., illus. $60.00.

Included in this volume are extensive notes on engraved, inscribed, historical and noted revolvers, as well as those revolvers used by outlaws, lawmen, movie and television stars.

*__Colt Percussion Accoutrements 1834-1873,__ by Robin Rapley, Robin Rapley, Newport Beach, CA, 1994. 432 pp., illus. Paper covers. $39.95.

The complete collector's guide to the identification of Colt percussion accoutrements; including Colt conversions and their values.

Colt Revolvers and the Tower of London, by Joseph G. Rosa, Royal Armouries of the Tower of London, London, England, 1988. 72 pp., illus. Soft covers. $15.00.

Details the story of Colt in London through the early cartridge period.

Colt Revolvers and the U.S. Navy 1865-1889, by C. Kenneth Moore, Dorrance and Co., Bryn Mawr, PA, 1987. 140 pp., illus. $29.95.

The Navy's use of all Colt handguns and other revolvers during this era of change.

Colt Single Action Army Revolvers and the London Agency, by C. Kenneth Moore, Andrew Mowbray Publishers, Lincoln, RI, 1990. 144 pp., illus. $35.00.

Drawing on vast documentary sources, this work chronicles the relationship between the London Agency and the Hartford home office.

The Colt U.S. General Officers' Pistols, by Horace Greeley IV, Andrew Mowbray Inc., Lincoln, RI, 1990. 199 pp., illus. $38.00.

These unique weapons, issued as a badge of rank to General Officers in the U.S. Army from WWII onward, remain highly personal artifacts of the military leaders who carried them. Includes serial numbers and dates of issue.

Colt's Dates of Manufacture 1837-1978, by R.L. Wilson, published by Maurie Albert, Coburg, Australia; N.A. distributor I.D.S.A. Books, Hamilton, OH, 1983. 61 pp. $10.00.

An invaluable pocket guide to the dates of manufacture of Colt firearms up to 1978.

Colt's 100th Anniversary Firearms Manual 1836-1936: A Century of Achievement, Wolfe Publishing Co., Prescott, AZ, 1992. 100 pp., illus. Paper covers. $12.95.

Originally published by the Colt Patent Firearms Co., this booklet covers the history, manufacturing procedures and the guns of the first 100 years of the genius of Samuel Colt.

The Colt Whitneyville-Walker Pistol, by Lt. Col. Robert D. Whittington, Brownlee Books, Hooks, TX, 1984. 96 pp., illus. Limited edition. $20.00.

A study of the pistol and associated characters 1846-1851.

*__The Complete Guide to U.S. Infantry Weapons of World War Two,__ by Bruce Canfield, Andrew Mowbray, Publisher, Lincoln, RI, 1995. 303 pp., illus. $35.00.

A definitive work on the weapons used by the United States Armed Forces in WWII.

Compliments of Col. Ruger: A Study of Factory Engraved Single Action Revolvers, by John C. Dougan, Taylor Publishing Co., El Paso, TX, 1992. 238 pp., illus. $46.50.

Clearly detailed black and white photographs and a precise text present an accurate istory of the Sturm, Ruger & Co. single-action revolver engraving project.

Confederate Revolvers, by William A. Gary, Taylor Publishing Co., Dallas, TX, 1987. 174 pp., illus. $49.95.

Comprehensive work on the rarest of Confederate weapons.

Coykendall's 2nd Sporting Collectible Price Guide, by Ralf Coykendall, Jr., Lyons & Burford Publlishers, New York, NY, 1992. 223 pp., illus. Paper covers. $16.95.

The all-new second volume with new sections on knives and sporting magazines.

Cowboy Collectibles and Western Memorabilia, by Bob Bell and Edward Vebell, Schiffer Publishing, Atglen, PA, 1992. 160 pp., illus. Paper covers. $29.95.

The exciting era of the cowboy and the wild west collectibles including rifles, pistols, gun rigs, etc.

The Deringer in America, Volume 1, The Percussion Period, by R.L. Wilson and L.D. Eberhart, Andrew Mowbray Inc., Lincoln, RI, 1985. 271 pp., illus. $48.00.

A long awaited book on the American percussion deringer.

The Deringer in America, Volume 2, The Cartridge Period, by L.D. Eberhart and R.L. Wilson, Andrew Mowbray Inc., Publishers, Lincoln, RI, 1993. 284 pp., illus. $65.00.

Comprehensive coverage of cartridge deringers organized alphabetically by maker. Includes all types of deringers known by the authors to have been offered to the American market.

Development of the Henry Cartridge and Self-Contained Cartridges for the Toggle-Link Winchesters, by R. Bruce McDowell, A.M.B., Metuchen, NJ, 1984. 69 pp., illus. Paper covers. $10.00.

From powder and ball to the self-contained metallic cartridge.

The Devil's Paintbrush: Sir Hiram Maxim's Gun, by Dolf Goldsmith, 2nd Edition, expanded and revised, Collector Grade Publications, Toronto, Canada, 1993. 384 pp., illus. $69.95

The classic work on the world's first true automatic machine gun.

Drums A'beating Trumpets Sounding, by William H. Guthman, The Connecticut Historical Society, Westport, CT, 1993. 232 pp., illus. $75.00.

Artistically carved powder horns in the provincial manner, 1746-1781.

The Eagle on U.S. Firearms, by John W. Jordan, Pioneer Press, Union City, TN, 1992. 140 pp., illus. Paper covers. $14.95.

Stylized eagles have been stamped on government owned or manufactured firearms in the U.S. since the beginning of our country. This book lists and illustrates these various eagles in an informative and refreshing manner.

Early Indian Trade Guns: 1625-1775, by T.M. Hamilton, Museum of the Great Plains, Lawton, OK, 1968. 34 pp., illus. Paper covers. $12.95.

Detailed descriptions of subject arms, compiled from early records and from the study of remnants found in Indian country.

Encyclopedia of Ruger Rimfire Semi-Automatic Pistols: 1949-1992, by Chad Hiddleson, Krause Publications, Iola, WI, 1993. 250 pp., illus. $29.95.

Covers all physical aspects of Ruger 22-caliber pistols including important features such as boxes, grips, muzzlebrakes, instruction manuals, serial numbers, etc.

*__Encyclopedia of Ruger Semi-Automatic Rimfire Pistols 1949-1992,__ by Chad Hiddleson, Krause Publications, Iola, WI, 1994. 304 pp., illus. $29.95.

This book is a compilation of years of research, outstanding photographs and technical data on Ruger.

English Pistols: The Armories of H.M. Tower of London Collection, by Howard L. Blackmore, Arms and Armour Press, London, England, 1985. 64 pp., illus. Soft covers. $14.95.

All the pistols described and pictured are from this famed collection.

European Firearms in Swedish Castles, by Kaa Wennberg, Bohuslaningens Boktryckeri AB, Uddevalla, Sweden, 1986. 156 pp., illus. $50.00.

The famous collection of Count Keller, the Ettersburg Castle collection, and others. English text.

Fifteen Years in the Hawken Lode, by John D. Baird, The Gun Room Press, Highland Park, NJ, 1976. 120 pp., illus. $24.95.

A collection of thoughts and observations gained from many years of intensive study of the guns from the shop of the Hawken brothers.

'51 Colt Navies, by Nathan L. Swayze, The Gun Room Press, Highland Park, NJ, 1993. 243 pp., illus. $59.95.

The Model 1851 Colt Navy, its variations and markings.

Firearms and Tackle Memorabilia, by John Delph, Schiffer Publishing, Ltd., West Chester, PA, 1991. 124 pp., illus. $39.95.

A collector's guide to signs and posters, calendars, trade cards, boxes, envelopes, and other highly sought after memorabilia. With a value guide.

Flayderman's Guide to Antique American Firearms...and Their Values, 6th Edition, by Norm Flayderman, DBI Books, Inc., Northbrook, IL, 1994. 624 pp., illus. Paper covers. $29.95.

Updated edition of this bible of the antique gun field.

The .45-70 Springfield, by Joe Poyer and Craig Riesch, North Cape Publications, Tustin, CA, 1991. 112 pp., illus. Soft covers. $14.95.

A definitive work on the 45-70 Springfield. Organized by serial number and date of production to aid the collector in identifying models and rifle parts.

Frank and George Freund and the Sharps Rifle, by Gerald O. Kelver, Gerald O. Kelver, Brighton, CO, 1986. 60 pp., illus. Paper covers. $12.00.

Pioneer gunmakers of Wyoming Territory and Colorado.

French Military Weapons, 1717-1938, Major James E. Hicks, N. Flayderman & Co., Publishers, New Milford, CT, 1973. 281 pp., illus. $24.95.

Firearms, swords, bayonets, ammunition, artillery, ordnance equipment of the French army.

From the Kingdom of Lilliput: The Miniature Firearms of David Kucer, by K. Corey Keeble and **The Making of Miniatures,** by David Kucer, Museum Restoration Service, Ontario, Canada, 1994. 51 pp., illus, $25.00.

An overview of the subject of miniatures in general combined with an outline by the artist himself on the way he makes a miniature firearm.

Game Guns & Rifles: Percussion to Hammerless Ejector in Britain, by Richard Akehurst, Trafalgar Square, N. Pomfret, VT, 1993. 192 pp., illus. $34.95.

Long considered a classic this important reprint covers the period of British gunmaking between 1830-1900.

George Schreyer, Sr. and Jr., Gunmakers of Hanover, Pennsylvania, by George Shumway, George Shumway Publishers, York, PA, 1990. 160pp., illus. $50.00.

This monograph is a detailed photographic study of almost all known surviving long rifles and smoothbore guns made by highly regarded gunsmiths George Schreyer, Sr. and Jr.

The German Assault Rifle 1935-1945, by Peter R. Senich, Paladin Press, Boulder, CO, 1987. 328 pp., illus. $49.95.

A complete review of machine carbines, machine pistols and assault rifles employed by Hitler's Wehrmacht during WWII.

The German K98k Rifle, 1934-1945: The Backbone of the Wehrmacht, by Richard D. Law, Collector Grade Publications, Inc., Toronto, Canada, 1993. 336 pp., illus. $69.95.

The most comprehensive study ever published on the 14,000,000 bolt-action K98k rifles produced in Germany between 1934 and 1945.

German Machineguns, by Daniel D. Musgrave, Revised edition, Ironside International Publishers, Inc. Alexandria, VA, 1992. 586 pp., 650 illus. $49.95.

The most definitive book ever written on German machineguns. Covers the introduction and development of machineguns in Germany from 1899 to the rearmament period after WWII.

German Military Rifles and Machine Pistols, 1871-1945, by Hans Dieter Gotz, Schiffer Publishing Co., West Chester, PA, 1990. 245 pp., illus. $35.00.

This book portrays in words and pictures the development of the modern German weapons and their ammunition including the scarcely known experimental types.

German Pistols and Holsters 1934-1945, Vol. 2, by Robert Whittington, Brownlee Books, Hooks, TX, 1990. 312 pp., illus. $55.00.

This volume addresses pistols only: military (Heer, Luftwaffe, Kriegsmarine & Waffen-SS), captured, commercial, police, NSDAP and government.

German 7.9mm Military Ammunition, by Daniel W. Kent, Daniel W. Kent, Ann Arbor, MI, 1991. 244 pp., illus. $35.00.

The long-awaited revised edition of a classic among books devoted to ammunition.

German Pistols and Holsters, 1934-1945, Volume 4, by Lt. Col. Robert D. Whittington, 3rd, U.S.A.R., Brownlee Books, Hooks, TX, 1991. 208 pp. $30.00.

Pistols and holsters issued in 412 selected armed forces, army and Waffen-SS units including information on personnel, other weapons and transportation.

*__The Golden Age of Remington,__ by Robert W.D. Ball, Krause publications, Iola, WI, 1995. 208 pp., illus. $29.95.

For Remington collectors or firearms historians, this book provides a pictorial history of Remington through World War I. Includes value guide.

Great British Gunmakers: The Mantons 1782-1878, by D.H.L. Back, Historical Firearms, Norwich, England, 1994. 218 pp., illus. Limited edition of 500 copies. $175.00.

Contains detailed descriptions of all the firearms made by members of this famous family.

Great Irish Gunmakers: Messrs. Rigby 1760-1869, by D.H.L. Back, Historical Firearms, Norwich, England, 1993. 196 pp., illus. $150.00.

The history of this famous firm of Irish gunmakers illustrated with a wide selection of Rigby arms.

A Guide to the Maynard Breechloader, by George J. Layman, George J. Layman, Ayer, MA, 1993. 125 pp., illus. Paper covers. $17.95.

The first book dedicated entirely to the Maynard family of breech-loading firearms. Coverage of the arms is given from the 1850s through the 1880s.

Guide to Ruger Single Action Revolvers Production Dates, 1953-73, by John C. Dougan, Blacksmith Corp., Chino Valley, AZ, 1991. 22 pp., illus. Paper covers. $9.95.

A unique pocket-sized handbook providing production information for the popular Ruger single-action revolvers manufactured during the first 20 years.

Gun Collecting, by Geoffrey Boothroyd, Sportsman's Press, London, 1989. 208 pp., illus. $29.95.

The most comprehensive list of 19th century British gunmakers and gunsmiths ever published.

Gun Collector's Digest, 5th Edition, edited by Joseph J. Schroeder, DBI Books, Inc., Northbrook, IL, 1989. 224 pp., illus. Paper covers. $16.95.

The latest edition of this sought-after series.

Gunmakers of London 1350-1850, by Howard L. Blackmore, George Shumway Publisher, York, PA, 1986. 222 pp., illus. $35.00.

A listing of all the known workmen of gun making in the first 500 years, plus a history of the guilds, cutlers, armourers, founders, blacksmiths, etc. 260 gunmarks are illustrated.

*__Gunsmiths of Illinois,__ by Curtis L. Johnson, George Shumway Publishers, York, PA, 1995. 160 pp., illus. $50.00.

Genealogical information is provided for nearly one thousand gunsmiths. Contains hundreds of illustrations of rifles and other guns, of handmade origin, from Illinois.

The Gunsmiths of Manhattan, 1625-1900: A Checklist of Tradesmen, by Michael H. Lewis, Museum Restoration Service, Bloomfield, Ont., Canada, 1991. 40 pp., illus. Paper covers. $4.95.

This listing of more than 700 men in the arms trade in New York City prior to about the end of the 19th century will provide a guide for identification and further research.

Gun Tools, Their History and Identification, by James B. Shaffer, Lee A. Rutledge and R. Stephen Dorsey, Collector's Library, Eugene, OR, 1992. 375 pp., illus. $32.00.

Written history of foreign and domestic gun tools from the flintlock period to WWII.

*__Gun Trader's Guide, 18th Edition,__ published by Stoeger Publishing Co., S. Hackensack, NJ, 1995. 575 pp., illus. Paper covers. $19.95.

Complete, fully illustrated guide to identification of modern firearms along with current market values.

*__Handbook of Military Rifle Marks 1870-1950,__ by Richard A. Hoffman and Noel P. Schott, Mapleleaf Militaria Publishing, St. Louis, MO, 1995. 42 pp., illus. Spiral bound. $15.00.

An illustrated guide to identifying military rifle and marks.

The Handgun, by Geoffrey Boothroyd, David and Charles, North Pomfret, VT, 1989. 566 pp., illus. $60.00.

Every chapter deals with an important period in handgun history from the 14th century to the present.

The Hawken Rifle: Its Place in History, by Charles E. Hanson, Jr., The Fur Press, Chadron, NE, 1979. 104 pp., illus. Paper covers. $10.00.

A definitive work on this famous rifle.

Hawken Rifles, The Mountain Man's Choice, by John D. Baird, The Gun Room Press, Highland Park, NJ, 1976. 95 pp., illus. $24.95.

Covers the rifles developed for the Western fur trade. Numerous specimens are described and shown in photographs.

High Standard: A Collector's Guide to the Hamden & Hartford Target Pistols, by Tom Dance, Andrew Mowbray, Inc., Lincoln, RI, 1991. 192 pp., illus. Paper covers. $24.00.

From Citation to Supermatic, all of the production models and specials made from 1951 to 1984 are covered according to model number or series.

Historic Pistols: The American Martial Flintlock 1760-1845, by Samuel E. Smith and Edwin W. Bitter, The Gun Room Press, Highland Park, NJ, 1986. 353 pp., illus. $45.00.

Covers over 70 makers and 163 models of American martial arms.

Historical Hartford Hardware, by William W. Dalrymple, Colt Collector Press, Rapid City, SD, 1976. 42 pp., illus. Paper covers. $10.00.

Historically associated Colt revolvers.

The History and Development of Small Arms Ammunition, Volume 1, by George A. Hoyem, Armory Publications, Oceanside, CA, 1991. 230 pp., illus. $60.00.

Military musket, rifle, carbine and primitive machine gun cartridges of the 18th and 19th centuries, together with the firearms that chambered them.

The History and Development of Small Arms Ammunition, Volume 2, by George A. Hoyem, Armory Publications, Oceanside, CA, 1991. 303 pp., illus. $60.00.

Covers the blackpowder military centerfire rifle, carbine, machine gun and volley gun ammunition used in 28 nations and dominions, together with the firearms that chambered them.

The History and Development of Small Arms Ammunition (British Sporting Rifle) Volume 3, by George A. Hoyem, Armory Publications, Oceanside, CA, 1991. 300 pp., illus. $60.00.

Concentrates on British sporting rifle cartridges that run from the 4-bore through the .600 Nitro to the .297/.230 Morris.

The History of Smith and Wesson, by Roy G. Jinks, Willowbrook Enterprises, Springfield, MA, 1988. 290 pp., illus. $27.95.

Revised 10th Anniversary edition of the definite book on S&W firearms.

The History of Winchester Firearms 1866-1992, sixth edition, updated, expanded, and revised by Thomas Henshaw, New Win Publishing, Clinton, NJ, 1993. 280 pp., illus. $24.95.

This classic is the standard reference for all collectors and others seeking the facts about any Winchester firearm, old or new.

History of Winchester Repeating Arms Company, by Herbert G. House, Krause Publications, Iola, WI, 1994. 800 pp., illus. $50.00.

The complete Winchester history from 1856-1981.

How to Buy and Sell Used Guns, by John Traister, Stoeger Publishing Co., So. Hackensack, NJ, 1984. 192 pp., illus. Paper covers. $10.95.

A new guide to buying and selling guns.

Identification Manual on the .303 British Service Cartridge, No. 1-Ball Ammunition, by B.A. Temple, I.D.S.A. Books, Piqua, OH, 1986. 84 pp., 57 illus. $12.50

Identification Manual on the .303 British Service Cartridge, No. 2-Blank Ammunition, by B.A. Temple, I.D.S.A. Books, Piqua, OH, 1986. 95 pp., 59 illus. $12.50

Identification Manual on the .303 British Service Cartridge, No. 3-Special Purpose Ammunition, by B.A. Temple, I.D.S.A. Books, Piqua, OH, 1987. 82 pp., 49 illus. $12.50

Identification Manual on the .303 British Service Cartridge, No. 4-Dummy Cartridges Henry 1869-c.1900, by B.A. Temple, I.D.S.A. Books, Piqua, OH, 1988. 84 pp., 70 illus. $12.50

Identification Manual on the .303 British Service Cartridge, No. 5-Dummy Cartridges (2), by B.A. Temple, I.D.S.A. Books, Piqua, OH, 1994. 78 pp. $12.50

Illustrations of United States Military Arms 1776-1903 and Their Inspector's Marks, compiled by Turner Kirkland, Pioneer Press, Union City, TN, 1988. 37 pp., illus. Paper covers. $4.95.

Reprinted from the 1949 Bannerman catalog. Valuable information for both the advanced and beginning collector.

Indian War Cartridge Pouches, Boxes and Carbine Boots, by R. Stephen Dorsey, Collector's Library, Eugene, OR, 1993. 156 pp., illus. Paper Covers. $25.00.

The key reference work to the cartridge pouches, boxes, carbine sockets and boots of the Indian War period 1865-1890.

An Introduction to the Civil War Small Arms, by Earl J. Coates and Dean S. Thomas, Thomas Publishing Co., Gettysburg, PA, 1990. 96 pp., illus. Paper covers. $10.00.

The small arms carried by the individual soldier during the Civil War.

Iver Johnson's Arms & Cycle Works Handguns, 1871-1964, by W.E. "Bill" Goforth, Blacksmith Corp., Chino Valley, AZ, 1991. 160 pp., illus. Paper covers. $14.95.

Covers all of the famous Iver Johnson handguns from the early solid-frame pistols and revolvers to optional accessories, special orders and patents.

*__Jaeger Rifles,__ by George Shumway, George Shumway Publisher, York, PA, 1994. 108 pp., illus. Paper covers. $25.00.

Thirty-six articles previously published in *Muzzle Blasts* are reproduced here. They deal with late-17th, and 18th century rifles from Vienna, Carlsbad, Bavaria, Saxony, Brandenburg, Suhl, North-Central Germany, and the Rhine Valley.

James Reid and His Catskill Knuckledusters, by Taylor Brown, Andrew Mowbray Publishers, Lincoln, RI, 1990. 288 pp., illus. $24.95.

A detailed history of James Reid, his factory in the picturesque Catskill Mountains, and the pistols which he manufactured there.

*__Jane's Infantry Weapons, 21st Edition, 1995-96,__ Jane's Information Group, Alexandria, VA, 1995. 750 pp., illus. $265.00.

Complete coverage on over 1,700 weapons and accessories from nearly 300 manufacturers in 69 countries. Completely revised and updated.

Japanese Handguns, by Frederick E. Leithe, Borden Publishing Co., Alhambra, CA, 1985. 160 pp., illus. $22.95.

An identification guide to all models and variations of Japanese handguns.

The Kentucky Rifle, by Captain John G.W. Dillin, George Shumway Publisher, York, PA, 1993. 221 pp., illus. $50.00.

This well-known book was the first attempt to tell the story of the American longrifle. This edition retains the original text and illustrations with supplemental footnotes provided by Dr. George Shumway.

Know Your Broomhandle Mausers, by R.J. Berger, Blacksmith Corp., Southport, CT, 1985. 96 pp., illus. Paper covers. $9.95.

An interesting story on the big Mauser pistol and its variations.

Krag Rifles, by William S. Brophy, The Gun Room Press, Highland Park, NJ, 1980. 200 pp., illus. $35.00.

The first comprehensive work detailing the evolution and various models, both military and civilian.

The Kriegboff Parabellum, by Randall Gibson, Midland, TX, 1988. 279 pp., illus. $40.00.

A comprehensive text pertaining to the Lugers manufactured by H. Krieghoff Waffenfabrik.

*__The Lee-Enfield Story,__ by Ian Skennerton, Ian Skennerton, Ashmore City, Australia, 1993. 503 pp., illus. $59.95.

The Lee-Metford, Lee-Enfield, S.M.L.E. and No. 4 series rifles and carbines from 1880 to the present.

Levine's Guide to Knives And Their Values, 3rd Edition, by Bernard Levine, DBI Books, Inc., Northbrook, IL, 1993. 480 pp., illus. Paper covers. $25.95

All the basic tools for identifying, valuing and collecting folding and fixed blade knives.

Longrifles of North Carolina, by John Bivens, George Shumway Publisher, York, PA, 1988. 256 pp., illus. $50.00.

Covers art and evolution of the rifle, immigration and trade movements. Committee of Safety gunsmiths, characteristics of the North Carolina rifle.

Longrifles of Pennsylvania, Volume 1, Jefferson, Clarion & Elk Counties, by Russel H. Harringer, George Shumway Publisher, York, PA, 1984. 200 pp., illus. $50.00.

First in series that will treat in great detail the longrifles and gunsmiths of Pennsylvania.

Lugers at Random, by Charles Kenyon, Jr., Handgun Press, Glenview, IL, 1990. 420 pp., illus. $49.95.

A new printing of this classic, comprehensive reference for all Luger collectors.

Marlin Firearms: A History of the Guns and the Company That Made Them, by Lt. Col. William S. Brophy, USAR, Ret., Stackpole Books, Harrisburg, PA, 1989. 672 pp., illus. $75.00.

The definitive book on the Marlin Firearms Co. and their products.

Massachusetts Military Shoulder Arms 1784-1877, by George D. Moller, Andrew Mowbray Publisher, Lincoln, RI, 1989. 250 pp., illus. $24.00.

A scholarly and heavily researched study of the military shoulder arms used by Massachusetts during the 90-year period following the Revolutionary War.

*__Matt Eastman's Guide to Browning Belgium Firearms 1903-1994,__ by Matt Eastman, Matt Eastman Publications, Fitzgerald, GA, 1995. 150 pp. Paper covers. $14.95.

Covers all Belgium models through 1994. Manufacturing production figures on the Auto-5 and Safari rifles.

Mauser Bolt Rifles, by Ludwig Olson, F. Brownell & Son, Inc., Montezuma, IA, 1976. 364 pp., illus. $47.50.

The most complete, detailed, authoritative and comprehensive work ever done on Mauser bolt rifles.

Mauser Rifles and Pistols, by Walter H.B. Smith, Wolfe Publishing Co., Prescott, AZ, 1990. 234 pp., illus. $30.00.

A handbook covering Mauser history and the amrs Mauser manufactured.

*__Military Handguns of France 1858-1958,__ by Eugene Medlin and Jean Huon, Excalibur Publications, Latham, NY, 1994. 124 pp., illus. Paper covers. $24.95.

The first book written in English that provides students of arms with a thorough history of French military handguns.

Military Pistols of Japan, by Fred L. Honeycutt, Jr., Julin Books, Palm Beach Gardens, FL, 1991. 168 pp., illus. $34.00.

Covers every aspect of military pistol production in Japan through WWII.

The Military Remington Rolling Block Rifle, by George Layman, Wolfe Publishing Company, Prescott, AZ, 1992. 250 pp., illus. Soft cover. $21.00.

A reference work for the collector, tracing the history of this military rifle and disclosing previously unpublished data.

Military Rifles of Japan, 4th Edition, by F.L. Honeycutt, Julin Books, Lake Park, FL, 1989. 208 pp., illus. $42.00.

A new revised and updated edition. Includes the early Murata-period markings, etc.

Military Small Arms of the 20th Century, 6th Edition, by Ian V. Hogg, DBI Books, Inc., Northbrook, IL, 1991. 352 pp., illus. Paper covers. $20.95.

Fully revised and updated edition of the standard reference in its field.

M1 Carbine, by Larry Ruth, Gunroom Press, Highland Park, NJ, 1987. 291 pp., illus. Paper $19.95.

The origin, development, manufacture and use of this famous carbine of World War II.

The M1 Garand: Post World War, by Scott A. Duff, Scott A. Duff, Export, PA, 1990. 139 pp., illus. Soft covers. $19.95.

A detailed account of the activities at Springfield Armory through this period. International Harvester, H&R, Korean War production and quantities delivered. Serial numbers.

The M1 Garand: World War 2, by Scott A. Duff, Scott A. Duff, Export, PA, 1993. 210 pp., illus. Paper covers. $39.95.

The most comprehensive study available to the collector and historian on the M1 Garand of World War II.

*__Modern Beretta Firearms,__ by Gene Gangarosa, Jr., Stoeger Publishing Co., S. Hackensack, NJ, 1994. 288 pp., illus. Paper covers. $16.95.

Traces all models of modern Beretta pistols, rifles, machine guns and combat shotguns.

*__Modern Guns Identification and Values, 10th Edition,__ by Steven and Russell Quertermous, Collector Books, Paducah, KY, 1994. 496 pp., illus. Paper covers. $12.95.

Over 2,500 models of rifles, handguns and shotguns from 1900 to the present are described and prices given for NRA excellent and very good.

Modern Gun Values, The Gun Digest Book of, 9th Edition, Edited by Jack Lewis, DBI Books, Inc., Northbrook, IL., illus. Paper covers. $20.95.

Updated and expanded edition of the book that has become the standard for valuing modern firearms.

*__Modern Small Arms,__ by Ian Hogg, Book Sales, Edison, NJ, 1995. 160 pp., illus. $17.98.

Encyclopedia coverage of more than 150 of the most sought after small arms produced today—rifles, pistols, machine guns and shotguns are covered.

More Single Shot Rifles, by James C. Grant, The Gun Room Press, Highland Park, NJ, 1976. 324 pp., illus. $29.95.

Details the guns made by Frank Wesson, Milt Farrow, Holden, Borchardt, Stevens, Remington, Winchester, Ballard and Peabody-Martini.

Mortimer, the Gunmakers, 1753-1923, by H. Lee Munson, Andrew Mowbray Inc., Lincoln, RI, 1992. 320 pp., illus. $65.00.

Seen through a single, dominant, English gunmaking dynasty this fascinating study provides a window into the classical era of firearms artistry.

The Muzzle-Loading Cap Lock Rifle, by Ned H. Roberts, reprinted by Wolfe Publishing Co., Prescott, AZ, 1991. 432 pp., illus. $30.00.

Originally published in 1940, this fascinating study of the muzzle-loading cap lock rifle covers rifles on the frontier to hunting rifles, including the famous Hawken.

The Navy Luger, by Joachim Gortz and John Walter, Handgun Press, Glenview, IL, 1988. 128 pp., illus. $24.95.

The 9mm Pistole 1904 and the Imperial German Navy. A concise illustrated history.

*__1996 Shooter's Bible, No. 87,__ edited by William S. Jarrett, Stoeger Publishing Co., S. Hackensack, NJ, 1995. 576 pp., illus. Paper covers. $21.95.

Contains specifications, photos and retail prices of handguns, rifles, shotguns and blackpowder arms currently manufactured by major U.S. and foreign gunmakers.

*__The Number 5 Jungle Carbine,__ by Alan M. Petrillo, Excalibur Publications, Latham, NY, 1994. 32 pp., illus. Paper covers. $7.95.

A comprehensive treatment of the rifle that collectors have come to call the "Jungle Carbine"—the Lee-Enfield Number 5, Mark 1.

*__The '03 Era: When Smokeless Revolutionized U.S. Riflery,__ by Clark S. Campbell, Collector Grade Publications, Inc., Ontario, Canada, 1994. 334 pp., illus. $44.50.

A much-expanded version of Campbell's *The '03 Springfields*, representing forty years of in-depth research into "all things '03."

The P-08 Parabellum Luger Automatic Pistol, edited by J. David McFarland, Desert Publications, Cornville, AZ, 1982. 20 pp., illus. Paper covers. $10.00.

Covers every facet of the Luger, plus a listing of all known Luger models.

Packing Iron, by Richard C. Rattenbury, Zon International Publishing, Millwood, NY, 1993. 216 pp., illus. $45.00.

The best book yet produced on pistol holsters and rifle scabbards. Over 300 variations of holster and scabbards are illustrated in large, clear plates.

Patents for Inventions, Class 119 (Small Arms), 1855-1930. British Patent Office, Armory Publications, Oceanside, CA, 1993. 7 volume set. $350.00.

Contains 7980 abridged patent descriptions and their sectioned line drawings, plus a 37-page alphabetical index of the patentees.

Paterson Colt Pistol Variations, by R.L. Wilson and R. Phillips, Jackson Arms Co., Dallas, TX, 1979. 250 pp., illus. $35.00.

A book about the different models and barrel lengths in the Paterson Colt story.

Pennsylvania Longrifles of Note, by George Shumway, George Shumway, Publisher, York, PA, 1977. 63 pp., illus. Paper covers. $15.00.

Illustrates and describes rifles from a number of Pennsylvania rifle-making schools.

Pistols of the World, 3rd Edition, by Ian Hogg and John Weeks, DBI Books, Inc., Northbrook, IL, 1992. 320 pp., illus. Paper covers. $20.95.

A totally revised edition of one of the leading studies of small arms.

The Pitman Notes on U.S. Martial Small Arms and Ammunition, 1776-1933, Volume 2, Revolvers and Automatic Pistols, by Brig. Gen. John Pitman, Thomas Publications, Gettysburg, PA, 1990. 192 pp., illus. $29.95.

A most important primary source of information on United States military small arms and ammunition.

The Plains Rifle, by Charles Hanson, Gun Room Press, Highland Park, NJ, 1989. 169 pp., illus. $29.95.

All rifles that were made with the plainsman in mind, including pistols.

The Powder Flask Book, by Ray Riling, R&R Books, Livonia, NY, 1993. 514 pp., illus. $70.00.

The complete book on flasks of the 19th century. Exactly scaled pictures of 1,600 flasks are illustrated.

The Rare and Valuable Antique Arms, by James E. Serven, Pioneer Press, Union City, TN, 1976. 106 pp., illus. Paper covers. $4.95.

A guide to the collector in deciding which direction his collecting should go, investment value, historic interest, mechanical ingenuity, high art or personal preference.

Reloading Tools, Sights and Telescopes for Single Shot Rifles, by Gerald O. Kelver, Brighton, CO, 1982. 163 pp., illus. Paper covers. $15.00.

A listing of most of the famous makers of reloading tools, sights and telescopes with a brief description of the products they manufactured.

*__The Remington-Lee Rifle,__ by Eugene F. Myszkowski, Excalibur Publications, Latham, NY, 1995. 100 pp., illus. Paper covers. $22.50.

Features detailed descriptions, including serial number ranges, of each model from the first Lee Magazine Rifle produced for the U.S. Navy to the last Remington-Lee Small Bores shipped to the Cuban Rural Guard.

Revolvers of the British Services 1854-1954, by W.H.J. Chamberlain and A.W.F. Taylerson, Museum Restoration Service, Ottawa, Canada, 1989. 80 pp., illus. $27.50.

Covers the types issued among many of the United Kingdom's naval, land or air services.

Rhode Island Arms Makers & Gunsmiths, by William O. Archibald, Andrew Mowbray, Inc., Lincoln, RI, 1990. 108 pp., illus. $16.50.

A serious and informative study of an important area of American arms making.

Rifles of the World, by John Walter, DBI Books, Inc., Northbrook, IL, 1993. 320 pp., illus. Paper covers. $20.95.

Compiled as a companion volume to *Pistols of the World*, this reference work covers all centerfire military and commercial rifles produced from the perfection of the metal-case cartridge in the 1870's to the present time.

The Rock Island '03, by C.S. Ferris, C.S. Ferris, Arvada, CO, 1993. 58 pp., illus. Paper covers. $12.50.

A monograph of interenst to the collector or historian concentrating on the U.S. M1903 rifle made by the less publicized of our two producing facilities.

Ruger, edited by Joseph Roberts, Jr., the National Rifle Association of America, Washington, D.C., 1991. 109 pp. illus. Paper covers. $14.95.

The story of Bill Ruger's indelible imprint in the history of sporting firearms.

Sam Colt's Own Record 1847, by John Parsons, Wolfe Publishing Co., Prescott, AZ, 1992. 167 pp., illus. $24.50.

Chronologically presented, the correspondence published here completes the account of the manufacture, in 1847, of the Walker Model Colt revolver.

*__Scottish Firearms,__ by Claude Blair and Robert Woosnam-Savage, Museum Restoration Service, Bloomfield, Ont., Canada, 1995. 52 pp., illus. Paper covers. $4.95.

This revision of the first book devoted entirely to Scottish firearms is supplemented by a register of surviving Scottish long guns.

Sharps Firearms, by Frank Seller, Frank M. Seller, Denver, CO, 1982. 358 pp., illus. $45.00.

Traces the development of Sharps firearms with full range of guns made including all martial variations.

Simeon North: First Official Pistol Maker of the United States, by S. North and R. North, The Gun Room Press, Highland Park, NJ, 1972. 207 pp., illus. $15.95.

Reprint of the rare first edition.

The SKS Type 45 Carbines, by Duncan Long, Desert Publications, El Dorado, AZ, 1992. 110 pp., illus. Paper covers.

Covers the history and practical aspects of operating, maintaining and modifying this abundantly available rifle.

Small Arms: Pistols & Rifles, by Ian V. Hogg, Greenhill Books, London, England, 1994. 160 pp., illus. $19.95.

An in-depth description of small arms, focusing on pistols and rifles, with detailed information about all small arms used by the world's armed forces.

*__Smith & Wesson Handguns,__ by Roy McHenry and Walter Roper, Wolfe Publishing Co., Prescott, AZ, 1994. 233 pp., illus. $32.00.

The bible on Smith & Wesson handguns.

Southern Derringers of the Mississippi Valley, by Turner Kirkland, Pioneer Press, Tenn., 1971. 80 pp., illus., paper covers. $10.00.

A guide for the collector, and a much-needed study.

Soviet Russian Postwar Military Pistols and Cartridges, by Fred A. Datig, Handgun Press, Glenview, IL, 1988. 152 pp., illus. $29.95.

Thoroughly researched, this definitive sourcebook covers the development and adoption of the Makarov, Stechkin and the new PSM pistols. Also included in this source book is coverage on Russian clandestine weapons and pistol cartridges.

Soviet Russian Tokarev "TT" Pistols and Cartridges 1929-1953, by Fred Datig, Graphic Publishers, Santa Ana, CA, 1993. 168 pp., illus. $39.95.
Details of rare arms and their accessories are shown in hundreds of photos. It also contains a complete bibliography and index.

***Spencer Firearms,** by Roy Marcot, R&R Books, Livonia, NY, 1995. 237 pp., illus. $60.00.
The definitive work on one of the most famous Civil War firearms.

Sporting Collectibles, by Jim and Vivian Karsnitz, Schiffer Publishing Ltd., West Chester, PA, 1992. 160 pp., illus. Paper covers. $29.95.
The fascinating world of hunting related collectibles presented in an informative text.

The Springfield 1903 Rifles, by Lt. Col. William S. Brophy, USAR, Ret., Stackpole Books Inc., Harrisburg, PA, 1985. 608 pp., illus. $49.95.
The illustrated, documented story of the design, development, and production of all the models, appendages, and accessories.

Springfield Shoulder Arms 1795-1865, by Claud E. Fuller, S. & S. Firearms, Glendale, NY, 1986. 76 pp., illus. Paper covers. $15.00.
Exact reprint of the scarce 1930 edition of one of the most definitive works on Springfield flintlock and percussion muskets ever published.

***Standard Catalog of Firearms, 5th Edition,** by Ned Schwing and Herbert Houze, Krause Publications, Iola, WI, 1995. 900 pp., illus. Paper covers. $27.95.
Over 12,000 antique and modern firearm prices and 3,000 photographs to help collectors in this volatile gun market.

Stevens Pistols & Pocket Rifles, by K.L. Cope, Museum Restoration Service, Alexandria Bay, NY, 1992. 114 pp., illus. $24.50.
This is the story of the guns and the man who designed them and the company which he founded to make them.

The Sumptuous Flaske, by Herbert G. Houze, Andrew Mowbray, Inc., Lincoln, RI, 1989. 158 pp., illus. Soft covers. $35.00.
Catalog of a recent show at the Buffalo Bill Historical Center bringing together some of the finest European and American powder flasks of the 16th to 19th centuries.

***System Mauser—2nd Edition: An Illustrated History of the 1896 Self-Loading Pistol,** by John W. Breathed, Jr. and Joseph J. Schrieder, Jr., Handgun Press, Glenview, IL, 1995. Illus. $49.95.
Newly revised and enlarged edition of the definitive work on this famous German handgun.

Textbook of Automatic Pistols, by R.K. Wilson, Wolfe Publishing Co., Prescott, AZ, 1990. 349 pp., illus. $54.00.
Reprint of the 1943 classic being a treatise on the history, development and functioning of modern military self-loading pistols.

The Trapdoor Springfield, by M.D. Waite and B.D. Ernst, The Gun Room Press, Highland Park, NJ, 1983. 250 pp., illus. $39.95.
The first comprehensive book on the famous standard military rifle of the 1873-92 period.

United States Martial Flintlocks, by Robert M. Reilly, Andrew Mowbray, Inc., Lincoln, RI, 1986. 263 pp., illus. $39.50.
A comprehensive illustrated history of the flintlock in America from the Revolution to the demise of the system.

U.S. Breech-Loading Rifles and Carbines, Cal. 45, by Gen. John Pitman, Thomas Publications, Gettysburg, PA, 1992. 192 pp., illus. $29.95.
The third volume in the Pitman Notes on U.S. Martial Small Arms and Ammunition, 1776-1933. This book centers on the "Trapdoor Springfield" models.

U.S. Military Arms Dates of Manufacture from 1795, by George Madis, David Madis, Dallas, TX, 1989. 64 pp. Soft covers. $5.00.
Lists all U.S. military arms of collector interest alphabetically, covering about 250 models.

U.S. Military Small Arms 1816-1865, by Robert M. Reilly, The Gun Room Press, Highland Park, NJ, 1983. 270 pp., illus. $39.95.
Covers every known type of primary and secondary martial firearms used by Federal forces.

***U.S. M1 Carbines: Wartime Production,** by Craig Riesch, North Cape Publications, Tustin, CA, 1994. 72 pp., illus. Paper covers. $15.95.
Presents only verifiable and accurate information. Each part of the M1 Carbine is discussed fully in its own section; including markings and finishes.

U.S. Naval Handguns, 1808-1911, by Fredrick R. Winter, Andrew Mowbray Publishers, Lincoln, RI, 1990. 128 pp., illus. $26.00.
The story of U.S. Naval Handguns spans an entire century—included are sections on each of the important naval handguns within the period.

Variations of the Smooth Bore H&R Handy Gun, by Eric M. Larson, Eric M. Larson, Takoma Park, MD, 1993. 63 pp., illus. Paper covers. $10.00.
A pocket guide to the identification of the variations of the H&R Handy Gun.

Walther Models PP and PPK, 1929-1945, by James L. Rankin, assisted by Gary Green, James L. Rankin, Coral Gables, FL, 1974. 142 pp., illus. $35.00.
Complete coverage on the subject as to finish, proofmarks and Nazi Party inscriptions.

Walther P-38 Pistol, by Maj. George Nonte, Desert Publications, Cornville, AZ, 1982. 100 pp., illus. Paper covers. $11.95.
Complete volume on one of the most famous handguns to come out of WWII. All models covered.

Walther Volume II, Engraved, Presentation and Standard Models, by James L. Rankin, J.L. Rankin, Coral Gables, FL, 1977. 112 pp., illus. $35.00.
The new Walther book on embellished versions and standard models. Has 88 photographs, including many color plates.

Walther, Volume III, 1908-1980, by James L. Rankin, Coral Gables, FL, 1981. 226 pp., illus. $35.00.
Covers all models of Walther handguns from 1908 to date, includes holsters, grips and magazines.

Webley Revolvers, by Gordon Bruce and Christien Reinhart, Stocker-Schmid, Zurich, Switzerland, 1988. 256 pp., illus. $69.50.
A revised edition of Dowell's "Webley Story."

***Weimar and Early Lugers,** by Jan C. Still, Jan C. Still, Douglas, AK, 1994. 312 pp., illus.
Volume 5 of the series *The Pistol of Germany and Here Allies in Two World Wars.*

The Whitney Firearms, by Claud Fuller, Standard Publications, Huntington, WV, 1946, 334 pp., many plates and drawings, $50.00.
An authoritative history of all Whitney arms and their maker. Highly recommended. An exclusive with Ray Riling Arms Books Co.

Winchester: An American Legend, by R.L. Wilson, Random House, New York, NY, 1991. 403 pp., illus. $65.00.
The official history of Winchester firearms from 1849 to the present.

The Winchester Book, by George Madis, David Madis Gun Book Distributor, Dallas, TX, 1986. 650 pp., illus. $47.00.
A new, revised 25th anniversary edition of this classic book on Winchester firearms. Complete serial ranges have been added.

Winchester Dates of Manufacture 1849-1984, by George Madis, Art & Reference House, Brownsboro, TX, 1984. 59 pp. $5.95.
A most useful work, compiled from records of the Winchester factory.

Winchester Engraving, by R.L. Wilson, Beinfeld Books, Springs, CA, 1989. 500 pp., illus. $125.00.
A classic reference work, of value to all arms collectors.

The Winchester Handbook, by George Madis, Art & Reference House, Lancaster, TX, 1982. 287 pp., illus. $19.95.
The complete line of Winchester guns, with dates of manufacture, serial numbers, etc.

***Winchester Lever Action Repeating Firearms, Vol. 1, The Models of 1866, 1873 and 1876,** by Arthur Pirkie, North Cape Publications, Tustin, CA, 1995. 112 pp., illus. Paper covers. $19.95.
Complete, part-by-part description, including dimensions, finishes, markings and variations throughout the production run of these fine, collectible guns.

The Winchester Model 94: The First 100 Years, by Robert C. Renneberg, Krause Publications, Iola, WI, 1991. 208 pp., illus. $34.95.
Covers the design and evolution from the early years up to the many different editions that exist today.

***Winchester 1928,** reprinted by Armory Publications, Oceanside, CA, 1995. 235 pp., illus. Paper covers. $60.00.
A reproduction of the 1928 catalog illustrating and describing the full line of Winchester products at the time.

***Winchester Shotguns and Shotshells,** by Ronald W. Stadt, Krause Publications, Iola, WI, 1995. 256 pp., illus. $34.95.
The definitive book on collectible Winchester shotguns and shotshells manufactured through 1961.

Winchester Slide-Action Rifles, Volume 1: Model 1890 & 1906, by Ned Schwing, Krause Publications, Iola, WI, 1992. 352 pp., illus. $39.95.
First book length treatment of models 1890 & 1906 with over 50 charts and tables showing significant new information about caliber style and rarity.

Winchester Slide-Action Rifles, Volume 2: Model 61 & Model 62, by Ned Schwing, Krause Publications, Iola, WI, 1993. 256 pp., illus. $34.95.
A complete historic look into the Model 61 and the Model 62. These favorite slide-action guns receive a thorough presentation which takes you to the factory to explore receivers, barrels, markings, stocks, stampings and engraving in complete detail.

Winchester's 30-30, Model 94, by Sam Fadala, Stackpole Books, Inc., Harrisburg, PA, 1986. 223 pp., illus. $24.95.
The story of the rifle America loves.

EDGED WEAPONS

A.G. Russell's Knife Trader's Guide, by A.G. Russell, Paul Wahl Corp., Bogata, NJ, 1991. 160 pp., illus. Paper covers. $10.00.
Recent sales prices of many popular collectible knives.

***The American Blade Collectors Association Price Guide to Antique Knives,** by J. Bruce Voyles, Krause Publications, Iola, WI, 1995. 480 pp., illus. Paper covers. $16.95.
In this complete guide to pocketknives there are 40,000 current values in six grades of condition for knives produced from 1800-1970.

The American Eagle Pommel Sword: The Early Years 1793-1830, by Andrew Mowbray, Publisher, Lincoln, RI, 1988. 224 pp., illus. $45.00.
Provides an historical outline, a collecting structure and a vast new source of information for this rapidly growing field.

American Indian Tomahawks, by Harold L. Peterson, The Gun Room Press, Highland Park, NJ, 1993. 142 pp., illus. $49.95.
The tomahawk of the American Indian, in all its forms, as a weapon and as a tool.

American Knives; The First History and Collector's Guide, by Harold L. Peterson, The Gun Room Press, Highland Park, NJ, 1980. 178 pp., illus. $24.95.
A reprint of this 1958 classic. Covers all types of American knives.

American Primitive Knives 1770-1870, by G.B. Minnes, Museum Restoration Service, Ottawa, Canada, 1983. 112 pp., illus. $24.95.
Origins of the knives, outstanding specimens, structural details, etc.

American Socket Bayonets and Scabbards, by Robert M. Reilly, Andrew Mowbray, Inc., Lincoln, RI, 1990. 209 pp., illus. $40.00.
A comprehensive illustrated history of socket bayonets, scabbards and frogs in America from the Colonial period through the Civil War period.

The American Sword, 1775-1945, by Harold L. Peterson, Ray Riling Arms Books, Co., Phila., PA, 1980. 286 pp. plus 60 pp. of illus. $45.00.
1977 reprint of a survey of swords worn by U.S. uniformed forces, plus the rare "American Silver Mounted Swords, (1700-1815)."

American Swords and Sword Makers, by Richard H. Bezdek, Paladin Press, Boulder, CO, 1994. 648 pp., illus. $79.95.
The long-awaited definitive reference volume to American swords, sword makers and sword dealers from Colonial times to the present.

***The Ames Sword Company, 1829-1935,** by John D. Hamilton, Andrew Mowbray Publisher, Linclon, RI, 1995. 255 pp., illus. $45.00.
An exhaustively researched and comprehensive history of America's foremost sword manufacturer and arms supplier during the Civil War.

The Arms and Armour of Arabia in the 18th-19th and 20th Centuries, by Robert Elgood, Scolar Press, Brookfield, VT, 1994. 190 pp., illus. $99.50.
An outstanding documentary on this aspect of Arab culture. Examines surviving weapons, identifies new centers of manufacture and questions the origin of "Damascus" swords.

Battle Blades: A Professional's Guide to Combat/Fighting Knives, by Greg Walker; Foreword by Al Mar, Paladin Press, Boulder, CO, 1993. 168 pp., illus. $30.00.
The author evaluates daggers, Bowies, switchblades and utility blades according to their design, performance, reliability and cost.

***Bayonets from Janzen's Notebook,** by Jerry L. Janzen, Cedar Ridge Publications, Broken Arrow, OK, 1994. 512 pp., illus. $30.00.
A very popular reference book covering bayonets of the World.

***Bayonets of the Remington Cartridge Period,** by Jerry L. Janzen, Cedar Ridge Publications, Broken Arrow, OK, 1994. 200 pp., illus. $39.95.
The story of the bayonets which accompanied the Remington Rolling Block and its many successors. Included are the rifles, the countries who used them, pictures of the bayonets in use and detailed descriptions of each bayonet.

The Book of the Sword, by Richard F. Burton, Dover Publications, New York, NY, 1987. 199 pp., illus. Paper covers. $10.00.

Traces the swords origin from its birth as a charged and sharpened stick through diverse stages of development.

Borders Away, Volume 1: With Steel, by William Gilkerson, Andrew Mowbray, Inc., Lincoln, RI, 1991. 184 pp., illus. $48.00.

A comprehensive study of naval armament under fighting sail. This first voume covers axes, pikes and fighting blades in use between 1626-1826.

The Bowie Knife, by Raymond Thorp, Phillips Publications, Wiliamstown, NJ, 1992. 167 pp., illus. $9.95.

After forty-five years, the classic work on the Bowie knife is once again available.

Bowie Knives, by Robert Abels, Sherwood International Corp., Northridge, CA, 1988. 30 pp., illus. Paper covers. $14.95.

Reprint of the classic work on Bowie knives.

British & Commonwealth Bayonets, by Ian D. Skennerton and Robert Richardson, I.D.S.A. Books, Piqua, OH, 1986. 404 pp., 1300 illus. $40.00.

Collecting the Edged Weapons of Imperial Germany, by Thomas M. Johnson and Thomas T. Wittmann, Johnson Reference Books, Fredricksburg, VA, 1989. 363 pp., illus. $39.50.

An in-depth study of the many ornate military, civilian, and government daggers and swords of the Imperial era.

Collector's Guide to Ames U.S. Contract Military Edged Weapons: 1832-1906, by Ron G. Hickox, Pioneer Press, Union City, IN, 1993. 70 pp., illus. Paper covers. $14.95.

While this book deals primarily with edged weapons made by the Ames Manufacturing Company, this guide refers to other manufactureres of United States swords.

Collector's Handbook of World War 2 German Daggers, by LtC. Thomas M. Johnson, Johnson Reference Books, Fredericksburg, VA, 2nd edition, 1991. 252 pp., illus. Paper covers. $25.00.

Concise pocket reference guide to Third Reich daggers and accoutrements in a convenient format. With value guide.

The Complete Bladesmith: Forging Your Way to Perfection, by Jim Hrisoulas, Paladin Press, Boulder, CO, 1987. 192 pp., illus. $25.00.

Novice as well as experienced bladesmith will benefit from this definitive guide to smithing world-class blades.

***The Complete Book of Pocketknife Repair**, by Ben Kelly, Jr., Krause Publications, Iola, WI, 1995. 130 pp., illus. Paper covers. $10.95.

Everything you need to know about repairing knives can be found in this step-by-step guide to knife repair.

***Confederate Edged Weapons**, by W.A. Albaugh, R&R Books, Lavonia, NY, 1994. 198 pp., illus. $30.00.

The master reference to edged weapons of the Confederate forces. Features precise line drawings and an extensive text.

The Craft of the Japanese Sword, by Leon and Hiroko Kapp, Yoshindo Yoshihara, Kodanska Interantional, Tokyo, Japan, 1990. 167 pp., illus. $39.00.

The first book in English devoted to contemporary sword manufacturing in Japan.

Custom Knifemaking, 55D, by Tim McCreight, Stackpole Books, Inc., Harrisburg, PA, 1985. 224 pp., illus. $15.95.

Ten projects from a master craftsman.

***Exploring the Dress Daggers of the German Army**, by Thomas T. Wittmann, Johnson Reference Books, Fredericksburg, VA, 1995. 350 pp., illus. $59.95.

The first in-depth analysis of the dress daggers worn by the German Army.

German Clamshells and Other Bayonets, by G. Walker and R.J. Weinard, Johnson Reference Books, Fredericksburg, VA, 1994. 157 pp., illus. $22.95.

Includes unusual bayonets, many of which are shown for the first time. Current market values are listed.

***German Military Fighting Knives 1914-1945**, by Gordon A. Hughes, Johnson Reference Books, Fredericksburg, VA, 1994. 64 pp., illus. Paper covers. $24.50.

Documents the different types of German military fighting knives used during WWI and WWII. Makers' proofmarks are shown as well as details of blade inscriptions, etc.

The Handbook of British Bayonets, by Ian D. Skennerton, I.D.S.A. Books, Piqua, OH. 64 pp. $4.95

***How to Make Folding Knives**, by Ron Lake, Frank Centofante and Wayne Clay, Krause Publications, Iola, WI, 1995. 193 pp., illus. Paper covers. $13.95.

With step-by-step instructions, learn how to make your own folding knife from three top custom makers.

***How to Make Knives**, by Richard W. Barney and Robert W. Loveless, Krause Publications, Iola, WI, 1995. 182 pp., illus. Paper covers. $13.95.

Complete instructions from two premier knife makers on making high-quality, handmade knives.

Kentucky Knife Traders Manual No. 6, by R.B. Ritchie, Hindman, KY, 1980. 217 pp., illus. Paper covers. $10.00.

Guide for dealers, collectors and traders listing pocket knives and razor values.

Knife and Tomakawk Throwing: The Art of the Experts, by Harry K. McEvoy, Charles E. Tuttle, Rutland, VT, 1989. 150 pp., illus. Soft covers. $8.95.

The first book to employ side-by-side the fascinating art and science of knives and tomahawks.

Knifemaking, The Gun Digest Book of, by Jack Lewis and Roger Combs, DBI Books, Inc., Northbrook, IL, 1989. 256 pp., illus. Paper covers. $16.95.

All the ins and outs from the world of knifemaking in a brand new book.

Knife Throwing a Practical Guide, by Harry K. McEvoy, Charles E. Tuttle Co., Rutland, VT, 1973. 108 pp., illus. Paper covers. $8.95.

If you want to learn to throw a knife this is the "bible."

Knives, 4th Edition, The Gun Digest Book of, by Jack Lewis and Roger Combs, DBI Books, Inc., Northbook, IL, 1992. 256 pp., illus. Paper covers. $16.95.

Covers practically every aspect of the knife world.

***Knives '96, 16th Edition**, edited by Ken Warner, DBI Books, Inc., Northbrook, IL, 1995. 304 pp., illus. Paper covers. $18.95.

Visual presentation of current factory and custom designs in straight and folding patterns, in swords, miniatures and commercial cutlery.

Levine's Guide to Knives And Their Values, 3rd Edition, by Bernard Levine, DBI Books, Inc., Northbrook, IL, 1989. 512 pp., illus. Paper covers. $25.95.

All the basic tools for identifying, valuing and collecting folding and fixed blade knives.

The Master Bladesmith: Advanced Studies in Steel, by Jim Hrisoulas, Paladin Press, Boulder, CO, 1990. 296 pp., illus. $45.00.

The author reveals the forging secrets that for centuries have been protected by guilds.

Military Swords of Japan 1868-1945, by Richard Fuller and Ron Gregory, Arms and Armour Press, London, England, 1986. 127 pp., illus. Paper covers. $18.95.

A wide-ranging survey of the swords and dirks worn by the armed forces of Japan until the end of World War II.

Modern Combat Blades, by Duncan Long, Paladin Press, Boulder, CO, 1993. 128 pp., illus. $25.00.

Long discusses the pros and cons of bowies, bayonets, commando daggers, kukris, switchblades, butterfly knives, belt-buckle blades and many more.

On Damascus Steel, by Dr. Leo S. Figiel,Atlantis Arts Press, Atlantis, FL, 1991. 145 pp., illus. $65.00.

The historic, technical and artistic aspects of Oriental and mechanical Damascus. Persian and Indian sword blades, from 1600-1800, which have never been published, are illustrated.

***The Pattern-Welded Blade: Artistry in Iron**, by Jim Hrisoulas, Paladin Press, Boulder, CO, 1994. 120 pp., illus. $35.00.

Reveals the secrets of this craft—from the welding of the starting billet to the final assembly of the complete blade.

Randall Made Knives: The History of the Man and the Blades, by Robert L. Gaddis, Paladin Press, Boulder, CO, 1993. 304 pp., illus. $50.00.

The authorized history of Bo Randall and his blades, told in his own words and those of the people who knew him best.

Rice's Trowel Bayonet, reprinted by Ray Riling Arms Books, Co., Phila., PA, 1968. 8 pp., illus. Paper covers. $3.00.

A facsimile reprint of a rare circular originally published by the U.S. government in 1875 for the information of U.S. troops.

The Samurai Sword, by John M. Yumoto, Charles E. Tuttle Co., Rutland, VT, 1958. 191 pp., illus. $21.95.

A must for anyone interested in Japanese blades, and the first book on this subject written in English.

Scottish Swords from the Battlefield at Culloden, by Lord Archibald Campbell, The Mowbray Co., Providence, RI, 1973. 63 pp., illus. $15.00.

A modern reprint of an exceedingly rare 1894 privately printed edition.

Secrets of the Samurai, by Oscar Ratti and Adele Westbrook, Charles E. Tuttle Co., Rutland, VT, 1983. 483 pp., illus. $35.00.

A survey of the martial arts of feudal Japan.

Small Arms Identification Series, No. 6-British Service Sword & Lance Patterns, by Ian Skennerton, I.D.S.A. Books, Piqua, OH, 1994. 48 pp. $9.50.

Small Arms Series, No. 2. The British Spike Bayonet, by Ian Skennerton, I.D.S.A. Books, Piqua, OH, 1982. 32 pp., 30 illus. $9.00.

Sure Defence, The Bowie Knife Book, by Kenneth J. Burton, I.D.S.A. Books, Piqua, OH, 1988. 100 pp., 115 illus. $37.50.

Sword of the Samurai, by George R. Parulski, Jr., Paladin Press, Boulder, CO, 1985. 144 pp., illus. $34.95.

The classical art of Japanese swordsmanship.

Swords for the Highland Regiments 1757-1784, by Anthony D. Darling, Andrew Mowbray, Inc., Publisher, Lincoln, RI, 1988. 62 pp., illus. $18.00.

The basket-hilted swords used by private highland regiments in the 18th century British army.

Swords from Public Collections in the Commonwealth of Pennsylvania, edited by Bruce S. Bazelon, Andrew Mowbray Inc., Lincoln, RI, 1987. 127 pp., illus. Paper covers. $12.00.

Contains new information regarding swordmakers of the Philadelphia area.

The Scottish Dirk, by James D. Forman, Museum Restoration Service, Bloomfield, Ont., Canada, 1991. 60 pp., illus. Paper covers. $4.95.

More than 100 dirks are illustrated with a text that sets the dirk and Sgian Dubh in their socio-historic content following design changes through more than 300 years of evolution.

Swords and Blades of the American Revolution, by George C. Neumann, Rebel Publishing Co., Inc., Texarkana, TX, 1991. 288 pp., illus. $35.95.

The encyclopedia of bladed weapons—swords, bayonets, spontoons, halberds, pikes, knives, daggers, axes—used by both sides, on land and sea, in America's struggle for independence.

Tomahawks Illustrated, by Robert Kuck, Robert Kuck, New Knoxville, OH, 1977. 112 pp., illus. Paper covers. $15.00.

A pictorial record to provide a reference in selecting and evaluating tomahawks.

***World of Dress Daggers, 1900-1945, Volume 1**, by Robert Berger, Robert Berger, CT, 1995. 296 pp., illus. $34.95.

The photographs and illustrations, in conjunction with the author's descriptive outline for each model, help to clearly identify these collectible daggers.

GENERAL

Advanced Muzzleloader's Guide, by Toby Bridges, Stoeger Publishing Co., So. Hackensack, NJ, 1985. 256 pp., illus. Paper covers. $14.95.

The complete guide to muzzle-loading rifles, pistols and shotguns—flintlock and percussion.

Air Gun Digest, 3rd Edition, by J.I. Galan, DBI Books, Inc., Northbrook, IL, 1995. 258 pp., illus. Paper covers. $18.95

Everything from A to Z on air gun history, trends and technology.

American Gunsmiths, by Frank M. Sellers, The Gun Room Press, Highland Park, NJ, 1983. 349 pp. $39.95.

A comprehensive listing of the American gun maker, patentee, gunsmith and entrepreneur.

American and Imported Arms, Ammunition and Shooting Accessories, Catalog No. 18 of the Shooter's Bible, Stoeger, Inc., reprinted by Fayette Arsenal, Fayetteville, NC, 1988. 142 pp., illus. Paper covers. $10.95.

A facsimile reprint of the 1932 Stoeger's Shooter's Bible.

America's Great Gunmakers, by Wayne van Zwoll, Stoeger Publishing Co., So. Hackensack, NJ, 1992. 288 pp., illus. Paper covers. $16.95.

This book traces in great detail the evolution of guns and ammunition in America and the men who formed the companies that produced them.

***Archer's Digest, 6th Edition**, by Roger Combs, DBI Books, Inc., Northbrook, IL, 1995. 256 pp., illus. $18.95.

Authoritative information on all facets of the archer's sport.

Armed and Female, by Paxton Quigley, E.P. Dutton, New York, NY, 1989. 237 pp., illus. $16.95.

The first complete book on one of the hottest subjects in the media today, the arming of the American woman.

***Arms for the Nation: Springfield Longarms**, edited by David C. Clark, Scott A. Duff, Export, PA, 1994. 73 pp., illus. Paper covers. $9.95.

A brief history of the Springfield Armory and the arms made there.

Arsenal of Freedom, The Springfield Armory, 1890-1948: A Year-by-Year Account Drawn from Official Records, compiled and edited by Lt. Col, William S. Brophy, USAR Ret., Andrew Mowbray, Inc., Lincoln, RI, 1991. 400 pp., illus. Soft covers. $29.95.

A "must buy" for all students of American military weapolns, equipment and accoutrements.

Assault Weapons, 3rd Edition, The Gun Digest Book of, edited by Jack Lewis, DBI Books, Inc., Northbrook, IL, 1993. 256 pp., illus. Paper covers. $18.95.

An in-depth look at the history and uses of these arms.

Assault Weapons, 4th Edition, The Gun Digest Book of, edited by Jack Lewis, DBI Books, Inc., Northbrook, IL. Paper covers. $18.95. (Available January 1996)
An in-depth look at the history and uses of these arms.

A Bibliography of American Sporting Books, compiled by John C. Phillips, James Cummins, Bookseller, New York, NY, 1991. 650 pp. Edition limited to 250 numbered copies. $75.00.
A reprinting of the very scarce 1930 edition originally published by the Boone & Crockett Club.

The Blackpowder Notebook, by Sam Fadala, Wolfe Publishing Co., Prescott, AZ, 1994. 212 pp., illus. $22.50.
For anyone interested in shooting muzzleloaders, this book will help improve scores and obtain accuracy and reliability.

***Blackpowder Loading Manual, 3rd Edition,** edited by Sam Fadala, DBI Books, Inc., Northbrook, IL, 1995. 368 pp., illus. Paper covers. $19.95.
Revised and expanded edition of this landmark blackpowder loading book. Covers hundreds of loads for most of the popular blackpowder rifles, handguns and shotguns.

***Bolt Action Rifles, 3rd Edition,** edited by Frank de Haas, DBI Books, Inc., Northbrook, IL, 1995. 576 pp., illus. Paper covers. $24.95.
A revised edition of the most definitive work on all major bolt-action rifle designs.

Bows and Arrows of the Native Americans, by Jim Hamm, Lyons & Burford Publishers, New York, NY, 1991. 156 pp., illus. $19.95.
A complete step-by-step guide to wooden bows, sinew-backed bows, composite bows, strings, arrows and quivers.

Bowhunter's Digest, 3rd Edition, by Chuck Adams, DBI Books, Inc., Northbrook, IL, 1990. 288 pp., illus. Soft covers. $16.95.
All-new edition covers all the necessary equipment and how to use it, plus the fine points on how to improve your skill.

British Small Arms of World War 2, by Ian D. Skennerton, I.D.S.A. Books, Piqua, OH, 1988. 110 pp., 37 illus. $25.00.

British Sniper, by Ian Skennerton, I.D.S.A. Books, Piqua, OH, 1983. 26 pp., over 375 illus. $40.00.

Cartridges of the World, 7th Edition, by Frank Barnes, edited by Mike Bussard, DBI Books, Inc., Northbrook, IL, 1993. 464 pp., illus. Paper covers. $23.95.
Completely revised edition of the general purpose reference work for which collectors, police, scientists and laymen reach first for answers to cartridge identification questions.

Civil War Chief of Sharpshooters Hiram Berdan, Military Commander and Firearms Inventor, by Roy M. Marcot, Northwood Heritage Press, Irvine, CA, 1990. 400 pp., illus. $59.95.
Details the life and career of Col. Hiram Berdan and his U.S. Sharpshooters.

Combat Handgunnery, 3rd Edition, The Gun Digest Book of, by Chuck Karwan, DBI Books, Inc., Northbrook, IL, 1992. 256 pp., illus. Paper covers. $16.95.
This edition looks at real world combat handgunnery from three different perspectives—military, police and civilian.

Competitive Shooting, by A.A. Yuryev, introduction by Gary L. Anderson, NRA Books, The National Rifle Assoc. of America, Wash., DC, 1985. 399 pp., illus. $29.95.
A unique encyclopedia of competitive rifle and pistol shooting.

The Complete Black Powder Handbook, Revised Edition, by Sam Fadala, DBI Books, Inc., Northbrook, IL, 1990. 320 pp., illus. Soft covers. $18.95.
Expanded and refreshed edition of the definitive book on the subject of blackpowder.

Complete Book of Shooting: Rifles, Shotguns, Handguns, by Jack O'Connor, Stackpole Books, Harrisburg, PA, 1983. 392 pp., illus. $24.95.
A thorough guide to each area of the sport, appealing to those with a new or ongoing interest in shooting.

The Complete Guide to Game Care and Cookery, 3rd Edition, by Sam Fadala, DBI Books, Inc., Northbrook, IL, 1994. 320 pp., illus. Paper covers. $18.95.
Over 500 photos illustrating the care of wild game in the field and at home with a separate recipe section providing over 400 tested recipes.

***Complete Guide to Guns & Shooting,** by John Malloy, DBI Books, Inc., Northbrook, IL, 1995. 256 pp., illus. Paper covers. $18.95.
What every shooter and gun owner should know about firearms, ammunition, shooting techniques, safety, collecting and much more.

***Cowboy Action Shooting,** by Charly Gullett, Wolfe Publishing Co., Prescott, AZ, 1995. 400 pp., illus. Paper covers. $24.50.
The fast growing of the shooting sports is comprehensively covered in this text—the guns, loads, tactics and the fun and flavor of this Old West era competition.

Crossbows, edited by Roger Combs, DBI Books, Inc., Northbrook, IL, 1986. 192 pp., illus. Paper covers. $15.95.
Complete, up-to-date coverage of the hottest bow going—and the most controversial.

Death from Above: The German FG42 Paratrooper Rifle, by Thomas B. Dugelby and R. Blake Stevens, Collector Grade Publications, Toronto, Canada, 1990. 147 pp., illus. $39.95.
The first comprehensive study of all seven models of the FG42.

Encyclopedia of Modern Firearms, Vol. 1, compiled and publ. by Bob Brownell, Montezuma, IA, 1959. 1057 pp. plus index, illus. $60.00. Dist. By Bob Brownell, Montezuma, IA 50171.
Massive accumulation of basic information of nearly all modern arms pertaining to "parts and assembly." Replete with arms photographs, exploded drawings, manufacturers' lists of parts, etc.

Firearms Engraving as Decorative Art, by Dr. Fredric A. Harris, Barbara R. Harris, Seattle, WA, 1989. 172 pp., illus. $115.00.
The origin of American firearms engraving motifs in the decorative art of the Middle East. Illustrated with magnificent color photographs.

***Firing Back,** by Clayton E. Cramer, Krause Publications, Iola, WI, 1995. 208 pp., Paper covers. $9.95.
Proposes answers and arguments to counter the popular anti-gun sentiments.

Flayderman's Guide to Antique American Firearms...and Their Values, 6th Edition, by Norm Flayderman, DBI Books, Inc., Northbrook, IL, 1994. 624 pp., illus. Paper covers. $29.95.
Updated edition of this bible of the antique gun field.

The Frontier Rifleman, by H.B. LaCrosse Jr., Pioneer Press, Union City, TN, 1989. 183 pp., illus. Soft covers. $14.95.
The Frontier rifleman's clothing and equipment during the era of the American Revolution, 1760-1800.

***Gatling: A Photographic Remembrance,** by E. Frank Stephenson, Jr., Meherrin River Press, Murfreesboro, NC, 1994. 140 pp., illus. Paper covers. $25.00.
A new book on Richard Gatling and his famous gun; featuring 145 photographs, many rare and never before published.

The Gatling Gun: 19th Century Machine Gun to 21st Century Vulcan, by Joseph Berk, Paladin Press, Boulder, CO, 1991. 136 pp., illus. $29.95.
Here is the fascinating on-going story of a truly timeless weapon, from its beginnings during the Civil War to its current role as a state-of-the-art modern combat system.

Good Friends, Good Guns, Good Whiskey: The Selected Works of Skeeter Skelton, by Skeeter Skelton, PJS Publications, Peoria, IL, 1989. 347 pp. $21.95.
A guidebook to the world of Skeeter Skelton.

***Good Guns Again,** by Stephen Bodio, Wilderness Adventures Press, Bozeman, MT, 1994. 183 pp., illus. $29.00.
A celebration of fine sporting arms.

***Grand Old Lady of No Man's Land: The Vickers Machine Gun,** by Dolf L. Goldsmith, Collector Grade Publications, Cobourg, Canada, 1994. 600 pp., illus. $79.95.
Goldsmith brings his years of experience as a U.S. Army armourer, machine gun collector and shooter to bear on the Vickers, in a book sure to become a classic in its field.

Great Shooters of the World, by Sam Fadala, Stoeger Publishing Co., So. Hackensack, NJ, 1991. 288 pp., illus. Paper covers. $18.95.
This book offers gun enthusiasts an overview of the men and women who have forged the history of firearms over the past 150 years.

Guerrilla Warfare Weapons, by Terry Gander, Sterling Publishing Co., Inc., 1990. 128 pp., illus. Paper covers. $9.95.
The latest and most sophisticated armaments of the modern underground fighter's armory.

***Gun Digest, 1996, 50th Anniversary Edition,** edited by Ken Warner, DBI Books, Inc., Northbrook, IL, 1995. 592 pp., illus. Paper covers. $24.95.
The *1996 Gun Digest* celebrates the 50th edition of the world's best-selling gun book. Features include 15 pages of four-color, showcasing all 50 *Gun Digest* covers plus a reprint of selected articles and catalog offerings from the very first 1944 *Gun Digest*. *Gun Digest* is the only one to make the *USA Today* list of best-selling sports books.

Gun Digest Treasury, 7th Edition, edited by Harold A. Murtz, DBI Books, Inc., Northbrook, IL, 1994. 320 pp., illus. Paper covers. $16.95.
A collection of some of the most interesting articles which have appeared in Gun Digest over its first 45 years.

***Gun Notes,** by Elmer Keith, Safari Press, Huntington Beach, CA, 1995. 280 pp., illus. $24.95.
A collection of Elmer Keith's most interesting columns and feature stories that appeared in *Guns and Ammo* magazine from 1961 to the late 1970s.

Gunshot Injuries: How They Are Inflicted, Their Complications and Treatment, by Col. Louis A. La Garde, 2nd revised edition, Lancer Militaria, Mt. Ida, AR, 1991. 480 pp., illus. $34.95.
A classic work which was the standard textbook on the subject at the time of WWI.

***Guns Illustrated 1996, 28th Edition,** edited by Harold A. Murtz, DBI Books, Inc., Northbrook, IL, 1996. 352 pp., illus. Paper covers. $19.95.
Truly the journal of Gun Buffs, this all new edition consists of articles of interest to every shooter as well as a complete catalog of all U.S. and imported firearms with latest specs and prices.

Guns of the Wild West, by George Markham, Sterling Publishing Co., New York, NY, 1993. 160 pp., illus. Paper covers. $19.95.
Firearms of the American Frontier, 1849-1917.

Gun Talk, edited by Dave Moreton, Winchester Press, Piscataway, NJ, 1973. 256 pp., illus. $9.95.
A treasury of original writing by the top gun writers and editors in America. Practical advice about every aspect of the shooting sports.

The Gun That Made the Twenties Roar, by Wm. J. Helmer, rev. and enlarged by George C. Nonte, Jr., The Gun Room Press, Highland Park, NJ, 1977. Over 300 pp., illus. $24.95.
Historical account of John T. Thompson and his invention, the infamous "Tommy Gun."

The Gunfighter, Man or Myth? by Joseph G. Rosa, Oklahoma Press, Norman, OK, 1969. 229 pp., illus. (including weapons). Paper covers. $14.95.
A well-documented work on gunfights and gunfighters of the West and elsewhere. Great treat for all gunfighter buffs.

Gunproof Your Children/Handgun Primer, by Massad Ayoob, Police Bookshelf, Concord, NH, 1989. Paper covers. $4.95.
Two books in one. The first, keeping children safe from unauthorized guns in their hands; the second, a compact introduction to handgun safety.

Guns & Shooting: A Selected Bibliography, by Ray Riling, Ray Riling Arms Books Co., Phila., PA, 1982. 434 pp., illus. Limited, numbered edition. $75.
A limited edition of this superb bibliographical work, the only modern listing of books devoted to guns and shooting.

Guns, Loads, and Hunting Tips, by Bob Hagel, Wolfe Publishing Co., Prescott, AZ, 1986. 509 pp., illus. $19.95.
A large hardcover book packed with shooting, hunting and handloading wisdom.

Guns of the First World War, Rifle, Handguns and Ammunition from the Text Book of Small Arms, 1909, edited by John Walter, Presidio Press, Novato, CA, 1991. $30.00.
Details of the Austro-Hung. Mann., French Lebels, German Mausers, U.S. Springfields, etc.

Gunshot Wounds, by Vincent J.M. DiMaio, M.D., Elsevier Science Publishing Co., New York, NY, 1985. 331 pp., illus. $90.00.
Practical aspects of firearms, ballistics, and forensic techniques.

Gun Writers of Yesteryear, compiled by James Foral, Wolfe Publishing Co., Prescott, AZ, 1993. 449 pp. $35.00.
Here, from the pre-American rifleman days of 1898-1920, are collected some 80 articles by 34 writers from eight magazines.

***Handgun Digest, 3rd Edition,** edited by Chris Christian, DBI Books, Inc., Northbrook, IL, 1995. 256 pp., illus. Paper covers. $18.95.
Full coverage of all aspects of handguns and handgunning from a highly readable and knowledgeable author.

***Handguns '96, 8th Edition,** edited by Ray Ordorica, DBI Books, Inc., Northbrook, IL, 1996. 352 pp., illus. Paper covers. $19.95.
Hal Surssett, Jeff Cooper, Neal Knox, Wiley Clapp, Bill Jordan, Paxton Quigley and other top handgun experts cover what's new in the world of handguns and handgunning.

***Handloader's Digest 1996, 15th Edition,** edited by Bob Bell, DBI Books, Inc., Northbrook, IL, 1995. 480 pp., illus. Paper covers. $23.95.
Top writers in the field contribute helpful information on techniques and components. Greatly expanded and fully indexed catalog of all currently available tools, accessories and components for metallic, blackpowder cartridge, shotshell reloading and swaging.

"Hell, I Was There!," by Elmer Keith, Petersen Publishing Co., Los Angeles, CA, 1979. 308 pp., illus. $24.95.
Adventures of a Montana cowboy who gained world fame as a big game hunter.

Il Grande Libro Delle Incision (Modern Engravings Real Book), by Marco E. Nobili, Editrice Il Volo, Milano, Italy, 1992. 399 pp., illus. $95.00.
The best existing expressions of engravings on guns, knives and other items. Text in English and Italian.

Jim Dougherty's Guide to Bowhunting Deer, by Jim Dougherty, DBI Books, Inc., Northbrook, IL, 1992. 256 pp., illus. Paper covers. $16.95.
Dougherty sets down some important guidelines for bowhunting and bowhunting equipment.

GENERAL (cont.)

Knives '96, 16th Edition, edited by Ken Warner, DBI Books, Inc., Northbrook, IL, 1995. 304 pp., illus. Paper covers. $18.95.
Visual presentation of current factory and custom designs in straight and folding patterns, in swords, miniatures and commercial cutlery.

Lasers and Night Vision Devices, by Duncan Long, Desert Publications, El Dorado, AZ, 1993. 150 pp., illus. Paper covers. $29.95.
A comprehensive look at the evolution of devices that allow firearms to be operated in low light conditions and at night.

The Last Book: Confessions of a Gun Editor, by Jack O'Connor, Amwell Press, Clinton, NJ, 1984. 247 pp., illus. $30.00.
Jack's last book. Semi-autobiographical.

The Lewis Gun, by J. David Truby, Paladin Press, Boulder, CO, 1988. 206 pp., illus. $39.95.
The development and employment of this weapon throughout early decades of this century.

The Long-Range War: Sniping in Vietnam, by Peter R. Senich, Paladin Press, Boulder, CO, 1994. 280 pp., illus. $39.95.
The most complete report on Vietnam-era sniping ever documented.

Manual for H&R Reising Submachine Gun and Semi-Auto Rifle, edited by George P. Dillman, Desert Publications, El Dorado, AZ, 1994. 81 pp., illus. Paper covers. $12.95.
A reprint of the Harrington & Richardson 1943 factory manual and the rare military manual on the H&R submachine gun and semi-auto rifle.

The Manufacture of Gunflints, by Sydney B.J. Skertchly, facsimile reprint with new introduction by Seymour de Lotbiniere, Museum Restoration Service, Ontario, Canada, 1984. 90 pp., illus. $24.50.
Limited edition reprinting of the very scarce London edition of 1879.

Master Tips, by J. Winokur, Potshot Press, Pacific Palisades, CA, 1985. 96 pp., illus. Paper covers. $11.95.
Basics of practical shooting.

Military Rifle & Machine Gun Cartridges, by Jean Huon, Paladin Press, Boulder, CO, 1990. 392 pp., illus. $34.95.
Describes the primary types of military cartridges and their principal loadings, as well as their characteristics, origin and use.

Military Small Arms of the 20th Century, 6th Edition, by Ian V. Hogg, DBI Books, Inc., Northbrook, IL, 1991. 352 pp., illus. Paper covers. $20.95.
Fully revised and updated edition of the standard reference in its field.

Modern Gun Values, The Gun Digest Book of, 9th Edition, edited by Jack Lewis, DBI Books, Inc., Northbrook, IL, illus. Paper covers. $20.95.
Updated and expanded edition of the book that has become the standard for valuing modern firearms.

Modern Law Enforcement Weapons & Tactics, 2nd Edition, by Tom Ferguson, DBI Books, Inc., Northbrook, IL, 1991. 256 pp., illus. Paper covers. $18.95.
An in-depth look at the weapons and equipment used by law enforcement agencies of today.

Modern Sporting Guns, by Christopher Austyn, Safari Press, Huntington Beach, CA, 1994. 128 pp., illus. $40.00.
A discussion of the "best" English guns; round action, over-and-under, boxlocks, hammer guns, bolt action and double rifles as well as accessories.

The More Complete Cannoneer, by M.C. Switlik, Museum & Collectors Specialties Co., Monroe, MI, 1990. 199 pp., illus. $19.95.
Compiled agreeably to the regulations for the U.S. War Department, 1861, and containing current observations on the use of antique cannon.

The MP-40 Machine Gun, Desert Publications, El Dorado, AZ, 1995. 32 pp., illus. Paper covers. $11.95.
A reprint of the hard-to-find operating and maintenance manual for one of the most famous machine guns of World War II.

L.D. Nimschke Firearms Engraver, by R.L. Wilson, R&R Books, Livonia, NY, 1992. 108 pp., illus. $100.00.
The personal work record of one of the 19th century America's foremost engravers. Augmented by a comprehensive text, photographs of deluxe-engraved firearms, and detailed indexes.

No Second Place Winner, by Wm. H. Jordan, publ. by the author, Shreveport, LA (Box 4072), 1962. 114 pp., illus. $15.95.
Guns and gear of the peace officer, ably discussed by a U.S. Border Patrolman for over 30 years, and a first-class shooter with handgun, rifle, etc.

The Owen Gun, by Wayne Wardman, Wayne Wardman, Curtain, Australia, 1991. 209 pp., illus. $42.50.
The story of the Owen gun and its rise to the pinnacle of success to be recognized as the world's best submachine gun of its time.

Pin Shooting: A Complete Guide, by Mitchell A. Ota, Wolfe Publishing Co., Prescott, AZ, 1992. 145 pp., illus. Paper covers. $14.95.
Traces the sport from its humble origins to today's thoroughly enjoyable social event, including the mammoth eight-day Second Chance Pin Shoot in Michigan.

E.C. Prudhomme, Master Gun Engraver, A Retrospective Exhibition: 1946-1973, intro. by John T. Amber, The R. W. Norton Art Gallery, Shreveport, LA, 1973. 32 pp., illus. Paper covers. $9.95.
Examples of master gun engravings by Jack Prudhomme.

A Rifleman Went to War, by H. W. McBride, Lancer Militaria, Mt. Ida, AR, 1987. 398 pp., illus. $24.95.
The classic account of practical marksmanship on the battlefields of World War I.

Second to None, edited by John Culler and Chuck Wechsler, Live Oak Press, Inc., Camden, SC, 1988. 227 pp., illus. $39.95.
The most popular articles from *Sporting Classics* magazine on great sporting firearms.

Sharpshooting for Sport and War, by W.W. Greener, Wolfe Publishing Co., Prescott, AZ, 1995. 192 pp., illus. $30.00.
This classic reprint explores the *first* expanding bullet; service rifles; shooting positions; trajectories; recoil; external ballistics; and other valuable information.

Shooter's Bible, 1940, Stoeger Arms Corp., Stoeger, Inc., So. Hackensack, NJ, 1990. 512 pp., illus. Soft covers. $16.95.
Reprint of the Stoeger Arms Corp. catalog No. 33 of 1940.

Shooting, by J.H. FitzGerald, Wolfe Publishing Co., Prescott, AZ, 1993. 421 pp., illus. $29.00.
A classic book and reference for anyone interested in pistol and revolver shooting.

Shooting, by Edward A. Matunas, Stackpole Books, Harrisburg, PA, 1986. 416 pp., illus. $31.95.
How to become an expert marksman with rifle, shotgun, handgun, muzzle loader and bow.

Shots Fired in Anger, by Lt. Col. John George, The National Rifle Association of America, Washington, D.C., 2nd printing, 1991. 535 pp., illus. $19.95.
A rifleman's view of the war in the Pacific, 1942-45.

Sniping in France, by Major H. Hesketh-Prichard, Lancer Militaria, Mt. Ida, AR, 1993. 224 pp., illus. $24.95.

The author was a well-known British adventurer and big game hunter. He was called upon in the early days of "The Great War" to develop a program to offset an initial German advantage in sniping. How the British forces came to overcome this advantage.

The SPIW: Deadliest Weapon that Never Was, by R. Blake Stevens, and Edward C. Ezell, Collector Grade Publications, Inc., Toronto, Canada, 1985. 138 pp., illus. $29.95.
The complete saga of the fantastic flechette-firing Special Purpose Individual Weapon.

The Sporting Craftsmen: A Complete Guide to Contemporary Makers of Custom-Built Sporting Equipment, by Art Carter, Countrysport Press, Traverse City, MI, 1994. 240 pp., illus. $49.50.
Profiles leading makers of centerfire rifles; muzzleloading rifles; bamboo fly rods; fly reels; flies; waterfowl calls; decoys; handmade knives; and traditional longbows and recurves.

The Street Smart Gun Book, by John Farnam, Police Bookshelf, Concord, NH, 1986. 45 pp., illus. Paper covers. $11.95.
Weapon selection, defensive shooting techniques, and gunfight-winning tactics from one of the world's leading authorities.

Stress Fire, Vol. 1: Stress Fighting for Police, by Massad Ayoob, Police Bookshelf, Concord, NH, 1984. 149 pp., illus. Paper covers. $9.95.
Gunfighting for police, advanced tactics and techniques.

Survival Guns, by Mel Tappan, Desert Publications, El Dorado, AZ, 1993. 456 pp., illus. Paper covers. $21.95.
Discusses in a frank and forthright manner which handguns, rifles and shotguns to buy for personal defense and securing food, and the ones to avoid.

Thompson Guns 1921-1945, Anubis Press, Houston, TX, 1980. 215 pp., illus. Paper covers. $11.95.
Facsimile reprinting of five complete manuals on the Thompson submachine gun.

Triggernometry, by Eugene Cunningham, Caxton Printers Ltd., Caldwell, ID, 1970. 441 pp., illus. $17.95.
A classic study of famous outlaws and lawmen of the West—their stature as human beings, their exploits and skills in handling firearms. A reprint.

The Ultimate Sniper, by Major John L. Plaster, Paladin Press, Boulder, CO, 1994. 464 pp., illus. Paper covers. $39.95.
An advanced training manual for military and police snipers.

U.S. Marine Corp Rifle and Pistol Marksmanship, 1935, reprinting of a government publication, Lancer Militaria, Mt. Ida, AR, 1991. 99 pp., illus. Paper covers. $11.95.
The old corps method of precision shooting.

U.S. Marine Corps Scout/Sniper Training Manual, Lancer Militaria, Mt. Ida, AR, 1989. Soft covers. $14.95.
Reprint of the original sniper training manual used by the Marksmanship Training Unit of the Marine Corps Development and Education Command in Quantico, Virginia.

U.S. Marine Corps Scout-Sniper, World War II and Korea, by Peter R. Senich, Paladin Press, Boulder, CO, 1994. 236 pp., illus. $39.95.
The most thorough and accurate account ever printed on the training, equipment and combat experiences of the U.S. Marine Corps Scout-Snipers.

U.S. Marine Corps Sniping, Lancer Militaria, Mt. Ida, AR, 1989. Irregular pagination. Soft covers. $14.95.
A reprint of the official Marine Corps FMFM1-3B.

Unrepentant Sinner, by Charles Askins, Tejano Publications, San Antonio, TX, 1985. 322 pp., illus. Soft covers. $19.95.
The autobiography of Colonel Charles Askins.

Weapons of the Waffen-SS, by Bruce Quarrie, Sterling Publishing Co., Inc., 1991. 168 pp., illus. $24.95.
An in-depth look at the weapons that made Hitler's Waffen-SS the fearsome fighting machine it was.

Weatherby: The Man, The Gun, The Legend, by Grits and Tom Gresham, Cane River Publishing Co., Natchitoches, LA, 1992. 290 pp., illus. $24.95.
A fascinating look at the life of the man who changed the course of firearms development in America.

The Winchester Era, by David Madis, Art & Reference House, Brownsville, TX, 1984. 100 pp., illus. $14.95.
Story of the Winchester company, management, employees, etc.

With British Snipers to the Reich, by Capt. C. Shore, Lander Militaria, Mt. Ida, AR, 1988. 420 pp., illus. $24.95.
One of the greatest books ever written on the art of combat sniping.

You Can't Miss, by John Shaw and Michael Bane, John Shaw, Memphis, TN, 1983. 152 pp., illus. Paper covers. $12.95.
The secrets of a successful combat shooter; how to better defensive shooting skills.

GUNSMITHING

Advanced Rebarreling of the Sporting Rifle, by Willis H. Fowler, Jr., Willis H. Fowler, Jr., Anchorage, AK, 1994. 127 pp., illus. Paper covers. $32.50.
A manual outlining a superior method of fitting barrels and doing chamber work on the sporting rifle.

The Art of Engraving, by James B. Meek, F. Brownell & Son, Montezuma, IA, 1973. 196 pp., illus. $33.95.
A complete, authoritative, imaginative and detailed study in training for gun engraving. The first book of its kind—and a great one.

Artistry in Arms, The R. W. Norton Gallery, Shreveport, LA, 1970. 42 pp., illus. Paper covers. $9.95.
The art of gunsmithing and engraving.

Barrels & Actions, by Harold Hoffman, H&P Publishers, San Angelo, TX, 1990. 309 pp., illus. Sprial bound. $25.95.
A manual on barrel making.

Black Powder Hobby Gunsmithing, by Sam Fadala and Dale Storey, DBI Books, Inc., Northbrook, IL., 1994. 256 pp., illus. Paper covers. $17.95.
A how-to guide for gunsmithing blackpowder pistols, rifles and shotguns from two men at the top of their respective fields.

Checkering and Carving of Gun Stocks, by Monte Kennedy, Stackpole Books, Harrisburg, PA, 1962. 175 pp., illus. $34.95.
Revised, enlarged cloth-bound edition of a much sought-after, dependable work.

The Colt .45 Automatic Shop Manual, by Jerry Kuhnhausen, VSP Publishers, McCall, ID, 1987. 200 pp., illus. Paper covers. $22.95.
Covers repairing, accurizing, trigger/sear work, action tuning, springs, bushings, rebarreling, and custom .45 modification.

GUNSMITHING (cont.)

The Colt Double Action Revolvers: A Shop Manual, Volume 1, by Jerry Kuhnhausen, VSP Publishers, McCall, ID, 1988. 224 pp., illus. Paper covers. $24.95.
  Covers D, E, and I frames.

The Colt Double Action Revolvers: A Shop Manual, Volume 2, by Jerry Kuhnhausen, VSP Publishers, McCall, ID, 1988. 156 pp., illus. Paper covers. $18.95.
  Covers J, V, and AA models.

The Complete Metal Finishing Book, by Harold Hoffman, H&P Publishers, San Angelo, TX, 1992. 364 pp., illus. Paper covers. $28.95.
  Instructions for the different metal finishing operations that the normal craftsman or shop will use. Primarily firearm related.

***Custom Gunstock Carving,** by Philip Eck, Stackpole Books, Mechanicsburg, PA, 1995. 232 pp., illus. $34.95.
  Featuring a gallery of more than 100 full-size patterns for buttstocks, grips, accents and borders that carvers can use for their own projects.

Exploded Handgun Drawings, The Gun Digest Book of, edited by Harold A. Murtz, DBI Books, Inc., Northbrook, IL. 1992. 512 pp., illus. Paper covers. $20.95.
  Exploded or isometric drawings for 494 of the most popular handguns.

Exploded Long Gun Drawings, The Gun Digest Book of, edited by Harold A. Murtz, DBI Books, Inc., Northbrook, IL. 512 pp., illus. Paper covers. $20.95.
  Containing almost 500 rifle and shotgun exploded drawings. An invaluable aid to both professionals and hobbyists.

***The Finishing of Gun Stocks,** by Harold Hoffman, H&P Publishers, San Angelo, TX, 1994. 98 pp., illus. Paper covers. $15.95.
  Covers different types of finishing methods and finishes.

Firearms Assembly/Disassembly, Part I: Automatic Pistols, Revised Edition, The Gun Digest Book of, by J.B. Wood, DBI Books, Inc., Northbrook, IL, 1990. 480 pp., illus. Paper covers. $18.95.
  Covers 58 popular autoloading pistols plus nearly 200 variants of those models integrated into the text and completely cross-referenced in the index.

Firearms Assembly/Disassembly Part II: Revolvers, Revised Edition, The Gun Digest Book of, by J.B. Wood, DBI Books, Inc., Northbrook, IL, 1990. 480 pp., illus. Paper covers. $18.95.
  Covers 49 popular revolvers plus 130 variants. The most comprehensive and professional presentation available to either hobbyist or gunsmith.

Firearms Assembly/Disassembly Part III: Rimfire Rifles, Revised Edition, The Gun Digest Book of, by J.B. Wood, DBI Books, Inc., Northbrook, IL., 1994. 480 pp., illus. Paper covers. $18.95.
  Greatly expanded edition covering 65 popular rimfire rifles plus over 100 variants all completely cross-referenced in the index.

Firearms Assembly/Disassembly Part IV: Centerfire Rifles, Revised Edition, The Gun Digest Book of, by J.B. Wood, DBI Books, Inc., Northbrook, IL, 1991. 480 pp., illus. Paper covers. $18.95.
  Covers 54 popular centerfire rifles plus 300 variants. The most comprehensive and professional presentation available to either hobbyist or gunsmith.

Firearms Assembly/Disassembly, Part V: Shotguns, Revised Edition, The Gun Digest Book of, by J.B. Wood, DBI Books, Inc., Northbrook, IL, 1992. 480 pp., illus. Paper covers. $18.95.
  Covers 46 popular shotguns plus over 250 variants with step-by-step instructions on how to dismantle and reassemble each. The most comprehensive and professional presentation available to either hobbyist or gunsmith.

Firearms Assembly/Disassembly Part VI: Law Enforcement Weapons, The Gun Digest Book of, by J.B. Wood, DBI Books, Inc., Northbrook, IL, 1981. 288 pp., illus. Paper covers. $16.95.
  Step-by-step instructions on how to completely dismantle and reassemble the most commonly used firearms found in law enforcement arsenals.

Firearms Assembly 3: The NRA Guide to Rifle and Shotguns, NRA Books, Wash., DC, 1980. 264 pp., illus. Paper covers. $13.95.
  Text and illustrations explaining the takedown of 125 rifles and shotguns, domestic and foreign.

Firearms Assembly 4: The NRA Guide to Pistols and Revolvers, NRA Books, Wash., DC, 1980. 253 pp., illus. Paper covers. $13.95.
  Text and illustrations explaining the takedown of 124 pistol and revolver models, domestic and foreign.

Firearms Bluing and Browning, By R.H. Angier, Stackpole Books, Harrisburg, PA. 151 pp., illus. $18.95.
  A world master gunsmith reveals his secrets of building, repairing and renewing a gun, quite literally, lock, stock and barrel. A useful, concise text on chemical coloring methods for the gunsmith and mechanic.

***Firearms Disassembly—With Exploded Views,** by John A. Karns & John E. Traister, Stoeger Publishing Co., S. Hackensack, NJ, 1995. 320 pp., illus. Paper covers. $19.95.
  Provides the do's and don'ts of firearms disassembly. Enables owners and gunsmiths to disassemble firearms in a professional manner.

First Book of Gunsmithing, by John E. Traister, Stackpole Books, Harrisburg, PA, 1981. 192 pp., illus. $18.95.
  Beginner's guide to gun care, repair and modification.

Guns and Gunmaking Tools of Southern Appalachia, by John Rice Irwin, Schiffer Publishing Ltd., 1983. 118 pp., illus. Paper covers. $9.95.
  The story of the Kentucky rifle.

Gunsmithing Tips and Projects, a collection of the best articles from the *Handloader* and *Rifle* magazines, by various authors, Wolfe Publishing Co., Prescott, AZ, 1992. 443 pp., illus. Paper covers. $25.00.
  Includes such subjects as shop, stocks, actions, tuning, triggers, barrels, customizing, etc.

Gunsmith Kinks, by F.R. (Bob) Brownell, F. Brownell & Son, Montezuma, IA, 1st ed., 1969. 496 pp., well illus. $18.95.
  A widely useful accumulation of shop kinks, short cuts, techniques and pertinent comments by practicing gunsmiths from all over the world.

Gunsmith Kinks 2, by Bob Brownell, F. Brownell & Son, Publishers, Montezuma, IA, 1983. 496 pp., illus. $18.95.
  A collection of gunsmithing knowledge, shop kinks, new and old techniques, shortcuts and general know-how straight from those who do them best—the gunsmiths.

Gunsmith Kinks 3, edited by Frank Brownell, Brownells Inc., Montezuma, IA, 1993. 504 pp., illus. $19.95.
  Tricks, knacks and "kinks" by professional gunsmiths and gun tinkerers. Hundreds of valuable ideas are given in this volume.

Gunsmithing, by Roy F. Dunlap, Stackpole Books, Harrisburg, PA, 1990. 742 pp., illus. $29.95.
  A manual of firearm design, construction, alteration and remodeling. For amateur and professional gunsmiths and users of modern firearms.

Gunsmithing at Home, by John E. Traister, Stoeger Publishing Co., So. Hackensack, NJ, 1985. 256 pp., illus. Paper covers. $14.95.
  Over 25 chapters of explicit information on every aspect of gunsmithing.

The Gunsmith's Manual, by J.P. Stelle and Wm. B. Harrison, The Gun Room Press, Highland Park, NJ, 1982. 376 pp., illus. $19.95.
  For the gunsmith in all branches of the trade.

***Home Gunsmithing the Colt Single Action Revolvers,** by Loren W. Smith, Ray Riling Arms Books, Co., Phila., PA, 1995. 119 pp., illus. $24.95.
  Affords the Colt Single Action owner detailed, pertinent information on the operating and servicing of this famous and historic handgun.

The Mauser M91 Through M98 Bolt Actions: A Shop Manual, by Jerry Kuhnhausen, VSP Books, McCall, ID, 1991. 224 pp., illus. Paper covers. $26.95.
  An essential book if you work on or plan to work on a Mauser action.

The NRA Gunsmithing Guide—Updated, by Ken Raynor and Brad Fenton, National Rifle Association, Wash., DC, 1984. 336 pp., illus. Paper covers. $15.95.
  Material includes chapters and articles on all facets of the gunsmithing art.

Pistolsmithing, The Gun Digest Book of, by Jack Mitchell, DBI Books, Inc., Northbrook, IL, 1980. 256 pp., illus. Paper covers. $15.95.
  An expert's guide to the operation of each of the handgun actions with all the major functions of pistolsmithing explained.

Pistolsmithing, by George C. Nonte, Jr., Stackpole Books, Harrisburg, PA, 1974. 560 pp., illus. $29.95.
  A single source reference to handgun maintenance, repair, and modification at home, unequaled in value.

Practical Gunsmithing, by Edward A. Matunas, Stackpole Books, Harrisburg, PA, 1989. 352 pp., illus. $31.95.
  A complete guide to maintaining, repairing, and improving firearms.

Recreating the American Longrifle, by William Buchele, et al., George Shumway, Publisher, York, PA, 1983. 175 pp., illus. $30.00.
  Includes full-scale plans for building a Kentucky rifle.

The Remington M870 and M1100/M11-87 Shotguns: A Shop Manual, by Jerry Kuhnhausen, VSP Publishers, McCall, ID, 1992. 226 pp., illus. Paper covers. $26.95.
  Covers everything about gunsmithing these most popular Remington shotguns from fitting a recoil pad to installing choke tubes, and everything in between.

Riflesmithing, The Gun Digest Book of, by Jack Mitchell, DBI Books, Inc., Northbrook, IL, 1982. 256 pp., illus. Paper covers. $15.95.
  The art and science of rifle gunsmithing. Covers tools, techniques, designs, finishing wood and metal, custom alterations.

Ruger Double Action Revolvers, Vol. 1, Shop Manual, by Jerry Kuhnhausen, VSP Publishers, McCall, ID, 1989. 176 pp., illus. Soft covers. $18.95.
  Covers the Ruger Six series of revolvers: Security-Six, Service-Six, and Speed-Six. Includes step-by-step function checks, disassembly, inspection, repairs, rebuilding, reassembly, and custom work.

The S&W Revolver: A Shop Manual, by Jerry Kuhnhausen, VSP Publishers, McCall, ID, 1987. 152 pp., illus. Paper covers.
  Covers accurizing, trigger jobs, action tuning, rebarreling, barrel setback, forcing cone angles, polishing and rebluing.

Shotgun Gunsmithing, The Gun Digest Book of, by Ralph Walker, DBI Books, Inc., Northbrook, IL, 1983. 256 pp., illus. Paper covers. $15.95.
  The principles and practices of repairing, individualizing and accurizing modern shotguns by one of the world's premier shotgun gunsmiths.

The Story of Pope's Barrels, by Ray M. Smith, R&R Books, Livonia, NY, 1993. 203 pp., illus. $39.00.
  A reissue of a 1960 book whose author knew Pope personally. It will be of special interest to Schuetzen rifle fans, since Pope's greatest days were at the height of the Schuetzen-era before WWI.

Survival Gunsmithing, by J.B. Wood, Desert Publications, Cornville, AZ, 1986. 92 pp., illus. Paper covers. $9.95.
  A guide to repair and maintenance of the most popular rifles, shotguns and handguns.

The Trade Rifle Sketchbook, by Charles E. Hanson, The Fur Press, Chadron, NE, 1979. 48 pp., illus. Paper covers. $9.95.
  Includes full-scale plans for 10 rifles made for Indian and mountain men; from 1790 to 1860, plus plans for building three pistols.

HANDGUNS

***Advanced Master Handgunning,** by Charles Stephens, Paladin Press, Boulder, CO., 1994. 72 pp., illus. Paper covers. $10.00.
  Secrets and surefire techniques for winning handgun competitions.

Black Powder Hobby Gunsmithing, by Sam Fadala and Dale Storey, DBI Books, Inc., Northbrook, IL., 1994. 256 pp., illus. Paper covers. $17.95.
  A how-to guide for gunsmithing blackpowder pistols, rifles and shotguns from two men at the top of their respective fields.

Blue Steel and Gun Leather, by John Bianchi, Beinfeld Publishing, Inc., No. Hollywood, CA, 1978. 200 pp., illus. $19.95.
  A complete and comprehensive review of holster uses plus an examination of available products on today's market.

Browning Hi-Power Pistols, Desert Publications, Cornville, AZ, 1982. 20 pp., illus. Paper covers. $9.95.
  Covers all facets of the various military and civilian models of the Browning Hi-Power pistol.

Colt Automatic Pistols, by Donald B. Bady, Borden Publ. Co., Alhambra, CA, 1974, 368 pp., illus. $19.95.
  The rev. and enlarged ed. of a key work on a fascinating subject. Complete information on every automatic marked with Colt's name.

The Colt .45 Auto Pistol, compiled from U.S. War Dept. Technical Manuals, and reprinted by Desert Publications, Cornville, AZ, 1978. 80 pp., illus. Paper covers. $9.95.
  Covers every facet of this famous pistol from mechanical training, manual of arms, disassembly, repair and replacement of parts.

Combat Handgunnery, 3nd Edition, The Gun Digest Book of, by Chuck Karwan, DBI Books, Inc., Northbrook, IL, 1992. 256 pp., illus. Paper covers. $16.95.
  This all-new edition looks at real world combat handgunnery from three different perspectives—military, police and civilian.

Combat Pistols, by Terry Gander, Sterling Publishing Co., Inc., 1991. Paper covers. $9.95.
  The world's finest and deadliest pistols are shown close-up, with detailed specifications, muzzle velocity, rate of fire, ammunition, etc.

***Combat Raceguns,** by J.M. Ramos, Paladin Press, Boulder, CO 1994. 168 pp., illus. Paper covers. $25.00.
  Learn how to put together precision combat raceguns with the best compensators, frames, controls, sights and custom accessories.

The Complete Book of Combat Handgunning, by Chuck Taylor, Desert Publications, Cornville, AZ, 1982. 168 pp., illus. Paper covers. $16.95.
Covers virtually every aspect of combat handgunning.

***The Custom Government Model Pistol,** by Layne Simpson, Wolfe Publishing Co., Prescott, AZ, 1994. 639 pp., illus. Paper covers. $24.50.
The book about one of the world's greatest firearms and the things pistolsmiths do to make it even greater.

The CZ-75 Family: The Ultimate Combat Handgun, by J.M. Ramos, Paladin Press, Boulder, CO, 1990. 100 pp., illus. Soft covers. $16.00.
An in-depth discussion of the early-and-late model CZ-75s, as well as the many newest additions to the Czech pistol family.

Experiments of a Handgunner, by Walter Roper, Wolfe Publishing Co., Prescott, AZ, 1989. 202 pp., illus. $37.00.
A limited edition reprint. A listing of experiments with functioning parts of handguns, with targets, stocks, rests, handloading, etc.

Exploded Handgun Drawings, The Gun Digest Book of, edited by Harold A. Murtz, DBI Books, Inc., Northbrook, IL. 1992. 512 pp., illus. Paper covers. $20.95.
Exploded or isometric drawings for 494 of the most popular handguns.

***The Farnam Method of Defensive Handgunning,** by John S. Farnam, DTI, Inc., Seattle, WA, 1994. 191 pp., illus. Paper covers. $13.95.
A book intended to not only educate the new shooter, but also to serve as a guide and textbook for his and his instructor's training courses.

Fast and Fancy Revolver Shooting, by Ed. McGivern, Anniversary Edition, Winchester Press, Piscataway, NJ, 1984. 484 pp., illus. $18.95.
A fascinating volume, packed with handgun lore and solid information by the acknowledged dean of revolver shooters.

Firearms Assembly/Disassembly, Part I: Automatic Pistols, Revised Edition, The Gun Digest Book of, by J.B. Wood, DBI Books, Inc., Northbrook, IL, 1990. 480 pp., illus. Soft covers. $18.95.
Covers 58 popular autoloading pistols plus nearly 200 variants of those models integrated into the text and completely cross-referenced in the index.

Firearms Assembly/Disassembly Part II: Revolvers, Revised Edition, The Gun Digest Book of, by J.B. Wood, DBI Books, Inc., Northbrook, IL, 1990. 480 pp., illus. Soft covers. $18.95.
Covers 49 popular revolvers plus 130 variants. The most comprehensive and professional presentation available to either hobbyist or gunsmith.

.45 ACP Super Guns, by J.M. Ramos, Paladin Press, Boulder, CO, 1991. 144 pp., illus. Paper covers. $24.00.
Modified .45 automatic pistols for competition, hunting and personal defense.

The .45, The Gun Digest Book of, by Dean A. Grennell, DBI Books, Inc., Northbrook, IL, 1989. 256 pp., illus. Paper covers. $16.95.
Definitive work on one of America's favorite calibers.

Glock: The New Wave in Combat Handguns, by Peter Alan Kasler, Paladin Press, Boulder, CO, 1993. 304 pp., illus. $25.00.
Kasler debunks the myths that surround what is the most innovative handgun to be introduced in some time.

Great Combat Handguns, by Leroy Thompson and Rene Smeets, Sterling Publishing Co., New York, NY, 1993. 256 pp., illus. $29.95.
Revised and newly designed edition of the successful classic in handgun use and reference.

Hand Cannons: The World's Most Powerful Handguns, by Duncan Long, Paladin Press, Boulder, CO, 1995. 208 pp., illus. Paper covers. $20.00.
Long describes and evaluates each powerful gun according to their features.

***Handgun Digest, 3rd Edition,** edited by Chris Christian, DBI Books, Inc., Northbrook, IL, 1995. 256 pp., illus. Paper covers. $18.95.
Full coverage of all aspects of handguns and handgunning from a highly readable and knowledgeable author.

Handgun Reloading, The Gun Digest Book of, by Dean A. Grennell and Wiley M. Clapp, DBI Books, Inc., Northbrook, IL, 1987. 256 pp., illus. Paper covers. $16.95.
Detailed discussions of all aspects of reloading for handguns, from basic to complex. New loading data.

***Handguns '96, 8th Edition,** edited by Ray Ordorica, DBI Books, Inc., Northbrook, IL, 1995. 352 pp., illus. Paper covers. $19.95.
Jeff Cooper, Neal Knox, Wiley Clapp, Bill Jordan, Paxton Quigley and other top handgun experts cover what's new in the world of handguns and handgunning.

High Standard Automatic Pistols 1932-1950, by Charles E. Petty, The Gunroom Press, Highland Park, NJ, 1989. 124 pp., illus. $19.95.
A definitive source of information for the collector of High Standard arms.

How to Become a Master Handgunner: The Mechanics of X-Count Shooting, by Charles Stephens, Paladin Press, Boulder, CO, 1993. 64 pp., illus. Paper covers. $10.00.
Offers a simple formula for success to the handgunner who strives to master the technique of shooting accurately.

Hunting for Handgunners, by Larry Kelly and J.D. Jones, DBI Books, Inc., Northbrook, IL, 1990. 256 pp., illus. Paper covers. $16.95.
Covers the entire spectrum of hunting with handguns in an amusing, easy-flowing manner that combines entertainment with solid information.

***Illustrated Encyclopedia of Handguns,** by A.B. Zhuk, Stackpole Books, Mechanicsburg, PA, 1994. 256 pp., illus. $49.95.
Identifies more than 2,000 military and commercial pistols and revolvers with details of more than 100 popular handgun cartridges.

Instinct Combat Shooting, by Chuck Klein, Chuck Klein, The Goose Creek, IN, 1989. 49 pp., illus. Paper covers. $12.00.
Defensive handgunning for police.

Know Your Czechoslovakian Pistols, by R.J. Berger, Blacksmith Corp., Chino Valley, AZ, 1989. 96 pp., illus. Soft covers. $9.95.
A comprehensive reference which presents the fascinating story of Czech pistols.

Know Your 45 Auto Pistols—Models 1911 & A1, by E.J. Hoffschmidt, Blacksmith Corp., Southport, CT, 1974. 58 pp., illus. Paper covers. $9.95.
A concise history of the gun with a wide variety of types and copies.

Know Your Walther P.38 Pistols, by E.J. Hoffschmidt, Blacksmith Corp., Southport, CT, 1974. 77 pp., illus. Paper covers. $9.95.
Covers the Walther models Armee, M.P., H.P., P.38—history and variations.

Know Your Walther PP & PPK Pistols, by E.J. Hoffschmidt, Blacksmith Corp., Southport, CT, 1975. 87 pp., illus. Paper covers. $9.95.
A concise history of the guns with a guide to the variety and types.

The Mauser Self-Loading Pistol, by Belford & Dunlap, Borden Publ. Co., Alhambra, CA. Over 200 pp., 300 illus., large format. $24.95.
The long-awaited book on the "Broom Handles," covering their inception in 1894 to the end of production. Complete and in detail: pocket pistols, Chinese and Spanish copies, etc.

Metallic Silhouette Shooting, 2nd Edition, The Gun Digest Book of, by Elgin Gates, DBI Books, Inc., Northbrook, IL, 1988. 256 pp., illus. Paper covers. $18.95.
All about the rapidly growing sport. With a history and rules of the International Handgun Metallic Silhouette Association.

Modern American Pistols and Revolvers, by A.C. Gould, Wolfe Publishing Co., Prescott, AZ, 1988. 222 pp., illus. $37.00.
A limited edition reprint. An account of the development of those arms as well as the manner of shooting them.

The Modern Technique of the Pistol, by Gregory Boyce Morrison, Gunsite Press, Paulden, AZ, 1991. 153 pp., illus. $45.00.
The theory of effective defensive use of modern handguns.

9mm Handguns, 2nd Edition, The Gun Digest Book of, edited by Steve Comus, DBI Books, Inc., Northbrook, IL, 1993. 256 pp., illus. Paper covers. $17.95.
Covers the 9mmP cartridge and the guns that have been made for it in greater depth than any other work available.

9mm Parabellum; The History & Developement of the World's 9mm Pistols & Ammunition, by Klaus-Peter Konig and Martin Hugo, Schiffer Publishing Ltd., Atglen, PA, 1993. 304 pp., illus. $39.95.
Detailed history of 9mm weapons from Belguim, Italy, Germany, Israel, France, USA, Czechoslovakia, Hungary, Poland, Brazil, Finland and Spain.

***The 100 Greatest Combat Pistols,** by Timothy J. Mullin, Paladin Press, Boulder, CO, 1994. 409 pp., illus. Paper covers. $40.00.
Hands-on tests and evaluations of handguns from around the world.

P-38 Automatic Pistol, by Gene Gangarosa, Jr., Stoeger Publishing Co., S. Hackensack, NJ, 1993. 272 pp., illus. Paper covers. $16.95
This book traces the origins and development of the P-38, including the momentous political forces of the World War II era that caused its near demise and, later, its rebirth.

Pistol & Revolver Guide, 3rd Ed., by George C. Nonte, Stoeger Publ. Co., So. Hackensack, NJ, 1975. 224 pp., illus. Paper covers. $11.95.
The standard reference work on military and sporting handguns.

Pistol Guide, by George C. Nonte, Jr., Stoeger Publishing Co., So. Hackensack, NJ, 1991. 280 pp., illus. Paper covers. $13.95.
Covers handling and marksmanship, care and maintenance, pistol ammunition, how to buy a used gun, military pistols, air pistols and repairs.

Pistols of the World, 3rd Edition, by Ian Hogg and John Weeks, DBI Books, Inc., Northbrook, IL, 1992. 320 pp., illus. Paper covers. $20.95.
A totally revised edition of one of the leading studies of small arms.

Pistolsmithing, The Gun Digest Book of, by Jack Mitchell, DBI Books, Inc., Northbrook, IL, 1980, 288 pp., illus. Paper covers. $15.95.
An expert's guide to the operation of each of the handgun actions with all the major functions of pistolsmithing explained.

Police Handgun Manual, by Bill Clede, Stackpole Books, Inc., Harrisburg, PA, 1985. 128 pp., illus. $18.95.
How to get street-smart survival habits.

Powerhouse Pistols—The Colt 1911 and Browning Hi-Power Source Book, by Duncan Long, Paladin Press, Boulder, CO, 1989. 152 pp., illus. Soft covers. $19.95.
The author discusses internal mechanisms, outward design, test-firing results, maintenance and accessories.

Report of Board on Tests of Revolvers and Automatic Pistols, From the Annual Report of the Chief of Ordnance, 1907. Reprinted by J.C. Tillinghast, Marlow, NH, 1969. 34 pp., 7 plates, paper covers. $9.95.
A comparison of handguns, including Luger, Savage, Colt, Webley-Fosbery and other makes.

Revolver Guide, by George C. Nonte, Jr., Stoeger Publishing Co., So. Hackensack, NJ, 1991. 288 pp., illus. Paper covers. $10.95.
A detailed and practical encyclopedia of the revolver, the most common handgun to be found.

Ruger Automatic Pistols and Single Action Revolvers, by Hugo A. Lueders, edited by Don Findley, Blacksmith Corp., Chino Valley, AZ, 1993. 79 pp., illus. Paper covers. $14.95.
The definitive work on Ruger automatic pistols and single action revolvers.

The Ruger "P" Family of Handguns, by Duncan Long, Desert Publications, El Dorado, AZ, 1993. 128 pp., illus. Paper covers. $14.95.
A full-fledged documentary on a remarkable series of Sturm Ruger handguns.

The Ruger .22 Automatic Pistol, Standard/Mark I/Mark II Series, by Duncan Long, Paladin Press, Boulder, CO, 1989. 168 pp., illus. Paper covers. $12.00.
The definitive book about the pistol that has served more than 1 million owners so well.

The Semiautomatic Pistols in Police Service and Self Defense, by Massad Ayoob, Police Bookshelf, Concord, NH, 1990. 25 pp., illus. Soft covers. $9.95.
First quantitative, documented look at actual police experience with 9mm and 45 police service automatics.

The Sharpshooter—How to Stand and Shoot Handgun Metallic Silhouettes, by Charles Stephens, Yucca Tree Press, Las Cruces, NM, 1993. 86 pp., illus. Paper covers. $10.00.
A narration of some of the author's early experiences in silhouette shooting, plus how-to information.

Shoot a Handgun, by Dave Arnold, PVA Books, Canyon County, CA, 1983. 144 pp., illus. Paper covers. $12.95.
A complete manual of simplified handgun instruction.

Shoot to Win, by John Shaw, Blacksmith Corp., Southport, CT, 1985. 160 pp., illus. Paper covers. $15.50.
The lessons taught here are of interest and value to all handgun shooters.

Shooting, by J.H. FitzGerald, Wolfe Publishing Co., Prescott, AZ, 1993. 421 pp., illus. $29.00
Exhaustive coverage of handguns and their use for target shooting, defense, trick shooting, and in police work by an noted firearms expert.

***Sig/Sauer Handguns,** by Duncan Long, Desert Publications, El Dorado, AZ, 1995. 150 pp., illus. Paper covers. $16.95.
The history of Sig/Sauer handguns, including Sig, Sig-Hammerli and Sig/Sauer variants.

Sixgun Cartridges and Loads, by Elmer Keith, reprint edition by The Gun Room Press, Highland Park, NJ, 1984. 151 pp., illus. $24.95.
A manual covering the selection, use and loading of the most suitable and popular revolver cartridges.

Sixguns, by Elmer Keith, Wolfe Publishing Company, Prescott, AZ, 1992. 336 pp. Hardcover. $34.95.
The history, selection, repair, care, loading, and use of this historic frontiersman's friend—the one-hand firearm.

Skeeter Skelton on Handguns, by Skeeter Skelton, PJS Publications, Peoria, IL, 1980. 122 pp., illus. Soft covers. $5.00.
A treasury of facts, fiction and fables.

***Smith & Wesson's Automatics,** by Larry Combs, Desert Publications, El Dorado, AZ, 1994. 143 pp., illus. Paper covers. $27.95.
A must for every S&W auto owner or prospective owner.

HANDGUNS (cont.)

Successful Pistol Shooting, by Frank and Paul Leatherdale, The Crowood Press, Ramsbury, England, 1988. 144 pp., illus. $34.95.
  Easy-to-follow instructions to help you achieve better results and gain more enjoyment from both leisure and competitive shooting.

The .380 Enfield No. 2 Revolver, by Mark Stamps and Ian Skennerton, I.D.S.A. Books, Piqua, OH, 1993. 124 pp., 80 illus. Paper covers. $19.95.

Webley & Scott Automatic Pistols, by Gordon Bruch, Stocker-Schmid Publishing Co., Dietikon, Switzerland, 1992. 256 pp., illus. $69.95.
  The fundamental representation of the history and development of all Webley & Scott automatic pistols.

World's Deadliest Rimfire Battleguns, by J.M. Ramos, Paladin Press, Boulder, CO, 1990. 184 pp., illus. Paper covers. $14.00.
  This heavily illustrated book shows international rimfire assault weapon innovations from World War II to the present.

HUNTING

NORTH AMERICA

Advanced Wild Turkey Hunting & World Records, by Dave Harbour, Winchester Press, Piscataway, NJ, 1983. 264 pp., illus. $19.95.
  The definitive book, written by an authority who has studied turkeys and turkey calling for over 40 years.

*****Aggressive Whitetail Hunting,** by Greg Miller, Krause Publications, Iola, WI, 1995. 208 pp., illus. Paper covers. $14.95.
  Learn how to hunt trophy bucks in public forests, private farmlands and exclusive hunting grounds from one of America's foremost hunters.

All About Bears, by Duncan Gilchrist, Stoneydale Press Publishing Co., Stevensville, MT, 1989. 176 pp., illus. $19.95.
  Covers all kinds of bears—black, grizzly, Alaskan brown, polar and leans on a lifetime of hunting and guiding experiences to explore proper hunting techniques.

All-American Deer Hunter's Guide, edited by Jim Zumbo and Robert Elman, Winchester Press, Piscataway, NJ, 1983. 320 pp., illus. $29.95.
  The most comprehensive, thorough book yet published on American deer hunting.

All Season Hunting, by Bob Gilsvik, Winchester Press, Piscataway, NJ, 1976. 256 pp., illus. $14.95.
  A guide to early-season, late-season and winter hunting in America.

American Duck Shooting, by George Bird Grinnell, Stackpole Books, Harrisburg, PA, 1991. 640 pp., illus. Paper covers. $17.95.
  First published in 1901 at the height of the author's career. Describes 50 species of waterfowl, and discusses hunting methods common at the turn of the century.

Awesome Antlers of North America, by Odie Sudbeck, HTW Publications, Seneca, KS, 1993. 150 pp., illus. $35.00.
  500 world-class bucks in color and black and white. This book starts up where the Boone & Crockett recordbook leaves off.

Bare November Days, by George Bird Evans et al, Countrysport Press, Traverse City, MI, 1992. 136 pp., illus. $39.50.
  A new, original anthology, a tribute to ruffed grouse, king of upland birds.

The Bear Hunter's Century, by Paul Schullery, Stackpole Books, Harrisburg, PA, 1989. 240 pp., illus. $19.95.
  Thrilling tales of the bygone days of wilderness hunting.

Bear in Their World, by Erwin Bauer, an Outdoor Life Book, New York, NY, 1985. 254 pp., illus. $32.95.
  Covers all North American bears; including grizzlies, browns, blacks, and polars.

*****Becoming a Great Moose Hunter,** by Richard Hackenburg, Frank Amato Publications, Portland, OR, 1994. 111 pp., illus. Paper covers. $10.95.
  Explains habits and habitat of moose and how to hunt them with rifle or bow. Includes moose calling techniques.

The Best of Babcock, by Havilah Babcock, selected and with an introduction by Hugh Grey, The Gunnerman Press, Auburn Hills, MI, 1985. 262 pp., illus. $19.95.
  A treasury of memorable pieces, 21of which have never before appeared in book form.

*****The Best of Field & Stream,** edited by J.I. Merritt, with Margaret G. Nichols and the editor of *Field & Stream,* Lyons & Burford, New York, NY, 1995. 352 pp., illus. $25.00.
  100 years of great writing from America's premier sporting magazine.

*****The Best of Jack O'Connor,** by Jack O'Connor, The Amwell Press, Clinton, NJ, 1994. 192 pp., illus. $26.95.
  Amwell Press presents 34 prime selections from the grand master of outdoor writers.

The Best of Nash Buckingham, by Nash Buckingham, selected, edited and annotated by George Bird Evans, Winchester Press, Piscataway, NJ, 1973. 320 pp., illus. $35.00.
  Thirty pieces that represent the very cream of Nash's output on his whole range of outdoor interests—upland shooting, duck hunting, even fishing.

The Best of Sheep Hunting, by John Batten, Amwell Press, Clinton, NJ, 1992. 616 pp., illus. $47.50.
  This "Memorial Edition" is a collection of 40 articles and appendices covering sheep hunting in the North American area of Canada, Alaska, the West and Midwest as well as Africa and Europe.

Big Game, Big Country, by Dr. Chauncey Guy Suits, Great Northwest Publishing and Distributing Co., Anchorage, AK, 1987. 224 pp., illus. $29.50.
  Chronicles more than a decade of high-quality wilderness hunting by one of this country's more distinguished big game hunters.

Big Game Trails in the Far North, by Col. Philip Neuweiler, Great Northwest Publishing and Distributing Co., Inc., Anchorage, AK, 1990. 320 pp., illus. $35.00.
  This book is the result of 50 years hunting big game in the Far North.

Birds on the Horizon, by Stuart Williams, Countrysport Press, Traverse City, MI, 1993. 288 pp., illus. $49.50.
  Wingshooting adventures around the world.

*****Blackpowder Loading Manual, 3rd Edition,** edited by Sam Fadala, DBI Books, Inc., Northbrook, IL, 1995. 368 pp., illus. Paper covers. $19.95.
  Revised and expanded edition of this landmark blackpowder loading book. Covers hundreds of loads for most of the popular blackpowder rifles, handguns and shotguns.

Blacktail Trophy Tactics, by Boyd Iverson, Stoneydale Press, Stevensville, MI, 1992. 166 pp., illus. Paper covers. $14.95.
  A comprehensive analysis of blacktail deer habits, describing a deer's and man's use of scents, still hunting, tree techniques, etc.

Boone & Crockett Club's 21st Big Game Awards, edited by Gary Sitton & Jack Reneau, Missoula, MT, 1992. 537 pp., illus. $39.95.
  A book of the Boone & Crockett Club containing tabulations of outstanding North American big game trophies accepted during the 21st awards entry period of 1989-1991.

Bowhunter's Digest, 3rd Edition, by Chuck Adams, DBI Books, Inc., Northbrook, IL, 1990. 288 pp., illus. Soft covers. $16.95.
  All-new edition covers all the necessary equipment and how to use it, plus the fine points on how to improve your skill.

Brown Feathers, by Steven J. Julak, Stackpole Books, Harrisburg, PA 1988. 224 pp., illus. $16.95.
  Waterfowling tales and upland dreams.

Bugling for Elk, by Dwight Schuh, Stoneydale Press Publishing Co., Stevensville, MT, 1983. 162 pp., illus. $18.95.
  A complete guide to early season elk hunting.

Call of the Quail: A Tribute to the Gentleman Game Bird, by Michael McIntosh, et al., Countrysport Press, Traverse City, MI, 1990. 175 pp., illus. $39.50.
  A new anthology on quail hunting.

Calling All Elk, by Jim Zumbo, Jim Zumbo, Cody, WY, 1989. 169 pp., illus. Paper covers. $14.95.
  The only book on the subject of elk hunting that covers every aspect of elk vocalization.

Campfires and Game Trails: Hunting North American Big Game, by Craig Boddington, Winchester Press, Piscataway, NJ, 1985. 295 pp., illus. $23.95.
  How to hunt North America's big game species.

Come October, by Gene Hill et al, Countrysport Press, Inc., Traverse City, MI, 1991. 176 pp., illus. $39.50.
  A new and all-original anthology on the woodcock and woodcock hunting.

*****The Complete Guide to Bird Dog Training,** by John R. Falk, Lyons & Burford, New York, NY, 1994. 288 pp., illus. $22.95.
  The latest on live-game field training techniques using released quail and recall pens. A new chapter on the services available for entering field trials and other bird dog competitions.

The Complete Guide to Bowhunting Deer, by Chuck Adams, DBI Books, Inc., Northbrook, IL, 1984. 256 pp., illus. Paper covers. $16.95.
  Plenty on equipment, bows, sights, quivers, arrows, clothes, lures and scents, stands and blinds, etc.

*****The Complete Guide to Game Care & Cookery, 3rd Edition,** by Sam Fadala, DBI Books, Inc., Northbrook, IL, 1994. 320 pp., illus. Paper covers. $18.95.
  Over 500 photos illustrating the care of wild game in the field and at home with a separate recipe section providing over 400 tested recipes.

The Complete Smoothbore Hunter, by Brook Elliot, Winchester Press, Piscataway, NJ, 1986. 240 pp., illus. $16.95.
  Advice and information on guns and gunning for all varieties of game.

Confessions of an Outdoor Maladroit, by Joel M. Vance, Amwell Press, Clinton, NJ, 1983. $20.00.
  Anthology of some of the wildest, irreverent, and zany hunting tales ever.

Covey Rises and Other Pleasures, by David H. Henderson, Amwell Press, Clinton, NJ, 1983. 155 pp., illus. $17.50.
  A collection of essays and stories concerned with field sports.

Coveys and Singles: The Handbook of Quail Hunting, by Robert Gooch, A.S. Barnes, San Diego, CA, 1981. 196 pp., illus. $11.95.
  The story of the quail in North America.

*****Coyote Hunting,** by Phil Simonski, Stoneydale Press, Stevensville, MT, 1994. 126 pp., illus. Paper covers. $12.95.
  Probably the most thorough "How-to-do-it" book on coyote hunting ever written.

Deer & Deer Hunting, by Al Hofacker, Krause Publications, Iola, WI, 1993. 208 pp., illus. $34.95.
  Coffee-table volume packed full of how-to-information that will guide hunts for years to come.

Deer and Deer Hunting: The Serious Hunter's Guide, by Dr. Robert Wegner, Stackpole Books, Harrisburg, PA, 1984. 384 pp., illus. Paper covers. $16.95.
  In-depth information from the editor of "Deer & Deer Hunting" magazine. Major bibliography of English language books on deer and deer hunting from 1838-1984.

Deer and Deer Hunting Book 2, by Dr. Robert Wegner, Stackpole Books, Harrisburg, PA, 1987. 400 pp., illus. Paper covers. $16.95.
  Strategies and tactics for the advanced hunter.

Deer and Deer Hunting, Book 3, by Dr. Robert Wegner, Stackpole Books, Harrisburg, PA, 1990. 368 pp., ilus. $29.95.
  This comprehensive volume covers natural history, deer hunting lore, profiles of deer hunters, and discussion of important issues facing deer hunters today.

The Deer Book, edited by Lamar Underwood, Amwell Press, Clinton, NJ, 1982. 480 pp., illus. $25.00.
  An anthology of the finest stories on North American deer ever assembled under one cover.

Deer Hunter's Guide to Guns, Ammunition, and Equipment, by Edward A. Matunas, an Outdoor Life Book, distributed by Stackpole Books, Harrisburg, PA, 1983. 352 pp., illus. $24.95.
  Where to hunt for North American deer. An authoritative guide that will help every deer hunter get maximum enjoyment and satisfaction from his sport.

Deer Hunting, by R. Smith, Stackpole Books, Harrisburg, PA, 1978. 224 pp., illus. Paper covers. $14.95.
  A professional guide leads the hunt for North America's most popular big game animal.

Deer Hunting Coast to Coast, by C. Boddington and R. Robb, Safari Press, Long Beach, CA, 1989. 248 pp., illus. $24.95.
  Join the authors as they hunt whitetail deer in eastern woodlot, southern swamps, midwestern prairies, and western river bottom; mule deer in badland, deserts, and high alpine basins; blacktails in oak grasslands and coastal jungles.

Doves and Dove Shooting, by Byron W. Dalrymple, New Win Publishing, Inc., Hampton, NJ, 1992. 256 pp., illus. $17.95.
  The author reveals in this classic book his penchant for observing, hunting, and photographing this elegantly fashioned bird.

Dove Hunting, by Charley Dickey, Galahad Books, NY, 1976. 112 pp., illus. $10.00.
  This indispensable guide for hunters deals with equipment, techniques, types of dove shooting, hunting dogs, etc.

*****Dreaming the Lion,** by Thomas McIntyre, Countrysport Press, Traverse City, MI, 1994. 309 pp., illus. $35.00.
  Reflections on hunting, fishing and a search for the wild. Twenty-three stories by *Sports Afield* editor, Tom McIntyre.

Drummer in the Woods, by Burton L. Spiller, Stackpole Books, Harrisburg, PA, 1990. 240 pp., illus. Soft covers. $16.95.
  Twenty-one wonderful stories on grouse shooting by "the Poet Laureate of Grouse."

Duck Decoys and How to Rig Them, by Ralf Coykendall, revised by Ralf Coykendall, Jr., Nick Lyons Books, New York, NY, 1990. 137 pp., illus. Paper covers. $14.95.
  Sage and practical advice on the art of decoying ducks and geese.

HUNTING (cont.)

The Duck Hunter's Handbook, by Bob Hinman, revised, expanded, updated edition, Winchester Press, Piscataway, NJ, 1985. 288 pp., illus. $15.95.
The duck hunting book that has it all.

Ducks of the Mississippi Flyway, ed. by John McKane, North Star Press, St. Cloud, MN, 1969. 54 pp., illus. Paper covers. $10.00.
A duck hunter's reference. Full color paintings of some 30 species, plus descriptive text.

Early American Waterfowling, 1700's-1930, by Stephen Miller, Winchester Press, Piscataway, NJ, 1986. 256 pp., illus. $27.95.
Two centuries of literature and art devoted to the nation's favorite hunting sport—waterfowling.

Eastern Upland Shooting, by Dr. Charles C. Norris, Countrysport Press, Traverse City, MI, 1990. 424 pp., illus. $29.50.
A new printing of this 1946 classic with a new, original Foreword by the author's friend and hunting companion, renowned author George Bird Evans.

The Education of Pretty Boy, by Havilah Babcock, The Gunnerman Press, Auburn Hills, MI, 1985. 160 pp., illus. $19.95.
Babcock's only novel, a heartwarming story of an orphan boy and a gun-shy setter.

Elk and Elk Hunting, by Hart Wixom, Stackpole Books, Harrisburg, PA, 1986. 288 pp., illus. $29.95.
Your practical guide to fundamentals and fine points of elk hunting.

Elk Hunting in the Northern Rockies, by Ed. Wolff, Stoneydale Press, Stevensville, MT, 1984. 162 pp., illus. $18.95.
Helpful information about hunting the premier elk country of the northern Rocky Mountain states—Wyoming, Montana and Idaho.

Elk Hunting with the Experts, by Bob Robb, Stoneydale Press, Stevensville, MT, 1992. 176 pp., illus. Paper covers. $15.95.
A complete guide to elk hunting in North America by America's top elk hunting expert.

Elk Rifles, Cartridges and Hunting Tactics, by Wayne van Zwoll, Larsen's Outdoor Publishing, Lakeland, FL, 1992. 414 pp., illus. $24.95.
The definitive work on which rifles and cartridges are proper for hunting elk plus the tactics for hunting them.

Encyclopedia of Deer, by G. Kenneth Whitehead, Safari Press, Huntington, CA, 1993. 704 pp., illus. $130.00.
This massive tome will be the reference work on deer for well into the next century.

Fair Chase, by Jim Rikhoff, Amwell Press, Clinton, NJ, 1984. 323 pp., illus. $25.00.
A collection of hunting experiences from the Arctic to Africa, Mongolia to Montana, taken from over 25 years of writing.

Field Dressing Big Game, by James Churchill, Stackpole Books, Harrisburg, PA, 1989. 88 pp., illus. Soft covers. $10.95.
Dressing, caping, skinning and butchering instructions.

Firelight, by Burton L. Spiller, Gunnerman Press, Auburn Hills, MI, 1990. 196 pp., illus. $19.95.
Enjoyable tales of the outdoors and stalwart companions.

The Formidable Game, by John H. Batten, Amwell Press, Clinton, NJ, 1983. 264 pp., illus. $40.00.
Big game hunting in India, Africa and North America by a world famous hunter.

Fresh Looks at Deer Hunting, by Byron W. Dalrymple, New Win Publishing, Inc., Hampton, NJ, 1993. 288 pp., illus. $24.95.
Tips and techniques abound throughout the pages of this latest work by Mr. Dalrymple whose name is synonymous with hunting proficiency.

*****From the Peace to the Fraser,** by Prentis N. Gray, Boone and Crockett Club, Missoula, MT, 1995. 400 pp., illus. $49.95.
Newly discovered North American hunting and exploration journals from 1900 to 1930.

Fur Trapping In North America, by Steven Geary, Winchester Press, Piscataway, NJ, 1985. 160 pp., illus. Paper covers. $19.95.
A comprehensive guide to techniques and equipment, together with fascinating facts about fur bearers.

A Gallery of Waterfowl and Upland Birds, by Gene Hill, with illustrations by David Maass, Petersen Prints, Los Angeles, CA, 1978. 132 pp., illus. $44.95.
Gene Hill at his best. Liberally illustrated with 51 full-color reproductions of David Maass' finest paintings.

Game in the Desert Revisited, by Jack O'Connor, Amwell Press, Clinton, NJ, 1984. 306 pp., illus. $27.50.
Reprint of a Derrydale Press classic on hunting in the Southwest

Getting the Most Out of Modern Waterfowling, by John O. Cartier, St. Martin's Press, NY, 1974. 396 pp., illus. $22.50.
The most comprehensive, up-to-date book on waterfowling imaginable.

Getting a Stand, by Miles Gilbert, Pioneer Press, Union City, TN, 1993. 204 pp., illus. Paper covers. $10.95.
An anthology of 18 short personal experiences by buffalo hunters of the late 1800s, specifically from 1870-1882.

*****Gordon MacQuarrie Trilogy: Stories of the Old Duck Hunters,** by Gordon MacQuarrie, Willow Creek Press, Minocqua, WI, 1994. $49.00.
A slip-cased three volume set of masterpieces by one of America's finest outdoor writers.

The Grand Passage: A Chronicle of North American Waterfowling, by Gene Hill, et al., Countrysport Press, Traverse City, MI, 1990. 175 pp., illus. $39.50.
A new original anthology by renowned sporting authors on our world of waterfowling.

The Grand Spring Hunt for America's Wild Turkey Gobbler, by Bart Jacob with Ben Conger, Winchester Press, Piscataway, NJ, 1985. 176 pp., illus. $15.95.
The turkey book for novice and expert alike.

Grizzlies Don't Come Easy, by Ralph Young, Winchester Press, Piscataway, NJ, 1981. 200 pp., illus. $15.95.
The life story of a great woodsman who guided famous hunters such as O'Connor, Keith, Fitz, Page and others.

Grizzly Country, by Andy Russell, A.A. Knopf, NYC, 1973, 302 pp., illus. $15.95.
Many-sided view of the grizzly bear by a noted guide, hunter and naturalist.

Grouse of North America, by Tom Huggler, NorthWord Press, Inc., Minocqua, WI, 1990. 160 pp., illus. $29.95.
A cross-continental hunting guide.

Grouse Hunter's Guide, by Dennis Walrod, Stackpole Books, Harrisburg, PA, 1985. 192 pp., illus. $16.95.
Solid facts, observations, and insights on how to hunt the ruffed grouse.

Gun Clubs & Decoys of Back Bay & Currituck Sound, by Archie Johnson and Bud Coppedge, CurBac Press, Virginia Beach, VA, 1991. 224 pp., illus. $40.00.
This book identifies and presents a photographic history of over 100 hunting clubs and lodges on Back Bay, VA and Currituck Sound, NC.

Gunning for Sea Ducks, by George Howard Gillelan, Tidewater Publishers, Centreville, MD, 1988. 144 pp., illus. $14.95.
A book that introduces you to a practically untouched arena of waterfowling.

Heartland Trophy Whitetails, by Odie Sudbeck, HTW Publications, Seneca, KS, 1992. 130 pp., illus. $35.00.
A completely revised and expanded edition which includes over 500 photos of Boone & Crockett class whitetail, major mulies and unusual racks.

Horns in the High Country, by Andy Russell, Alfred A. Knopf, NY, 1973. 259 pp., illus. Paper covers. $12.95.
A many-sided view of wild sheep and their natural world.

How to Hunt, by Dave Bowring, Winchester Press, Piscataway, NJ, 1982. 208 pp., illus. Paper covers. $10.95; cloth, $15.00.
A basic guide to hunting big game, small game, upland birds, and waterfowl.

The Hunters and the Hunted, by George Laycock, Outdoor Life Books, New York, NY, 1990. 280 pp., illus. $34.95.
The pursuit of game in America from Indian times to the present.

A Hunter's Fireside Book, by Gene Hill, Winchester Press, Piscataway, NJ, 1972. 192 pp., illus. $16.95.
An outdoor book that will appeal to every person who spends time in the field—or who wishes he could.

A Hunter's Road, by Jim Fergus, Henry Holt & Co., NY, 1992. 290 pp. $22.50
A journey with gun and dog across the American uplands.

Hunt High for Rocky Mountain Goats, Bighorn Sheep, Chamois & Tahr, by Duncan Gilchrist, Stoneydale Press, Stevensville, MT, 1992. 192 pp., illus. Paper covers. $19.95.
The source book for hunting mountain goats.

The Hunter's Shooting Guide, by Jack O'Connor, Outdoor Life Books, New York, NY, 1982. 176 pp., illus. Paper covers. $5.95.
A classic covering rifles, cartridges, shooting techniques for shotguns/rifles/handguns.

The Hunter's World, by Charles F. Waterman, Winchester Press, Piscataway, NJ, 1983. 250 pp., illus. $29.95.
A classic. One of the most beautiful hunting books that has ever been produced.

Hunting America's Game Animals and Birds, by Robert Elman and George Peper, Winchester Press, Piscataway, NJ, 1975. 368 pp., illus. $16.95.
A how-to, where-to, when-to guide—by 40 top experts—covering the continent's big, small, upland game and waterfowl.

Hunting Boar, Hogs & Javelinas, by Bob Gooch, Atlantic Publishing Co., Tabor City, NC, 1989. 204 pp., illus. Paper covers. $9.95.
Thorough in explaining where, when and how to hunt these elusive creatures, along with a state-by-state hunting guide and a list of recipes.

Hunting Ducks and Geese, by Steven Smith, Stackpole Books, Harrisburg, PA, 1984. 160 pp., illus. $17.95.
Hard facts, good bets, and serious advice from a duck hunter you can trust.

Hunting for Handgunners, by Larry Kelly and J.D. Jones, DBI Books, Inc., Northbrook, IL, 1990. 256 pp., illus. Soft covers. $16.95.
A definitive work on an increasingly popular sport.

Hunting in Many Lands, edited by Theodore Roosevelt and George Bird Grinnell, et al., Boone & Crockett Club, Dumphries, VA, 1990. 447 pp., illus. $40.00.
A limited edition reprinting of the original Boone & Crockett Club 1895 printing.

*****Hunting Mature Bucks,** by Larry L. Weishuhn, Krause Publications, Iola, WI, 1995. 256 pp., illus. Paper covers. $14.95.
One of North America's top white-tailed deer authorities shares his expertise on hunting those big, smart and elusive bucks.

Hunting North America's Big Game, by Bob Hagel, Stackpole Books, Harrisburg, PA, 1987. 220 pp., illus. $34.95.
Complete coverage on how to approach, track, and shoot game in different terrains.

Hunting Open-Country Mule Deer, by Dwight Schuh, Sage Press, Nampa, ID, 1989. 180 pp., illus. $18.95.
A guide taking Western bucks with rifle and bow.

Hunting Predators for Hides and Profits, by Wilf E. Pyle, Stoeger Publishing Co., So. Hackensack, NJ, 1985. 224 pp., illus. Paper covers. $11.95.
The author takes the hunter through every step of the hunting/marketing process.

Hunting the American Wild Turkey, by Dave Harbour, Stackpole Books, Harrisburg, PA, 1975. 256 pp., illus. $14.95.
The techniques and tactics of hunting North America's largest, and most popular, woodland game bird.

Hunting Trips in North America, by F.C. Selous, Wolfe Publishing Co., Prescott, AZ, 1988. 395 pp., illus. $52.00.
A limited edition reprint. Coverage of caribou, moose and other big game hunting in virgin wilds.

Hunting Trophy Whitetails, by David Morris, Stoneydale Press, Stevensville, MT, 1993. 483 pp., illus. $29.95.
This is one of the best whitetail books published in the last two decades. The author is the former editor of *North American Whitetail* magazine.

*****Hunting Western Deer,** by Jim and Wes Brown, Stoneydale Press, Stevensville, MT, 1994. 174 pp., illus. Paper covers. $14.95.
A pair of expert Oregon hunters provide insight into hunting mule deer and blacktail deer in the western states.

*****Hunting Wild Boar in California,** by Bob Robb, new revised edition, Larsen's Outdoor Publications, Lakeland, FL, 1994. 160 pp., illus. Paper covers. $14.95.
The most complete guide to hunting California's most popular big game animal on public and private land.

Hunting Wild Turkeys in the West, by John Higley, Stoneydale Press, Stevensville, MT, 1992. 154 pp., illus. Paper covers. $12.95.
Covers the basics of calling, locating and hunting turkeys in the western states.

Hunting with the Twenty-two, by Charles Singer Landis, R&R Books, Livonia, NY, 1994. 429 pp., illus. $45.00.
A miscellany of articles touching on the hunting and shooting of small game.

I Don't Want to Shoot an Elephant, by Havilah Babcock, The Gunnerman Press, Auburn Hills, MI, 1985. 184 pp., illus. $19.95.
Eighteen delightful stories that will enthrall the upland gunner for many pleasurable hours.

In Search of the Wild Turkey, by Bob Gooch, Greatlakes Living Press, Ltd., Waukegan, IL, 1978. 182 pp., illus. $9.95.
A state-by-state guide to wild turkey hot spots, with tips on gear and methods for bagging your bird.

Indian Hunts and Indian Hunters of the Old West, by Dr. Frank C. Hibben, Safari Press, Long Beach, CA, 1989. 228 pp., illus. $24.95.
Tales of some of the most famous American Indian hunters of the Old West as told to the author by an old Navajo hunter.

Jack O'Connor's Gun Book, by Jack O'Connor, Wolfe Publishing Company, Prescott, AZ, 1992. 208 pp. Hardcover. $26.00.
Jack O'Connor imparts a cross-section of his knowledge on guns and hunting. Brings back some of his writings that have here-to-fore been lost.

HUNTING (cont.)

Jaybirds Go to Hell on Friday, by Havilah Babcock, The Gunnerman Press, Auburn Hills, MI, 1985. 149 pp., illus. $19.95.
Sixteen jewels that reestablish the lost art of good old-fashioned yarn telling.
Jim Dougherty's Guide to Bowhunting Deer, by Jim Dougherty, DBI Books, Inc., Northbrook, IL, 1992. 256 pp., illus. Paper covers. $16.95.
Dougherty sets down some important guidelines for bowhunting and bowhunting equipment.
*****Last Casts and Stolen Hunts,** edited by Jim Casada and Chuck Wechsler, Countrysport Press, Traverse City, MI, 1994. 270 pp., illus. $29.95.
The world's best hunting and fishing stories by writers such as Zane Grey, Jim Corbett, Jack O'Connor, Archibald Rutledge and others.
A Listening Walk...and Other Stories, by Gene Hill, Winchester Press, Piscataway, NJ, 1985. 208 pp., illus. $15.95.
Vintage Hill. Over 60 stories.
Longbows in the Far North, by E. Donnall Thomas, Jr. Stackpole Books, Mechanicsburg, PA, 1994. 200 pp., illus. $16.95.
An archer's adventures in Alaska and Siberia.
Making Game: An Essay on Woodcock, by Guy De La Valdene, Willow Creek Press, Oshkosh, WI, 1985. 202 pp., illus. $35.00.
The most delightful book on woodcock yet published.
*****Mammoth Monarchs of North America,** by Odie Sudbeck, HTW Publications, Seneca, KA, 1995. 288 pp., illus. $35.00.
This book reveals eye-opening big buck secrets.
Matching the Gun to the Game, by Clair Rees, Winchester Press, Piscataway, NJ, 1982. 272 pp., illus. $17.95.
Covers selection and use of handguns, blackpowder firearms for hunting, matching rifle type to the hunter, calibers for multiple use, tailoring factory loads to the game.
Measuring and Scoring North American Big Game Trophies, by Wm. H. Nesbitt and Philip L. Wright, The Boone and Crockett Club, Alexandria, VA, 1986. 176 pp., illus. $15.00.
The Boone and Crockett Club official scoring system, with tips for trophy evaluation.
Mixed Bag, by Jim Rikhoff, National Rifle Association of America, Wash., DC, 1981. 284 pp., illus. Paper covers. $9.95.
Reminiscences of a master raconteur.
Modern Pheasant Hunting, by Steve Grooms, Stackpole Books, Harrisburg, PA, 1982. 224 pp., illus. Paper covers. $10.95.
New look at pheasants and hunters from an experienced hunter who respects this splendid gamebird.
Modern Waterfowl Guns and Gunning, by Don Zutz, Stoeger Publishing Co., So. Hackensack, NJ, 1985. 224 pp., illus. Paper covers. $11.95.
Up-to-date information on the fast-changing world of waterfowl guns and loads.
Montana—Land of Giant Rams, by Duncan Gilchrist, Stoneydale Press Publishing Co., Stevensville, MT, 1990. 208 pp., illus. $19.95.
Latest information on Montana bighorn sheep and why so many Montana bighorn rams are growing to trophy size.
Montana—Land of Giant Rams, Volume 2, by Duncan Gilchrist, Outdoor Expeditions and Books, Corvallis, MT, 1992. 208 pp., illus. $34.95.
The reader will find stories of how many of the top-scoring trophies were taken.
More and Better Pheasant Hunting, by Steve Smith, Winchester Press, Piscataway, NJ, 1986. 192 pp., illus. $15.95.
Complete, fully illustrated, expert coverage of the bird itself, the dogs, the hunt, the guns, and the best places to hunt.
More Grouse Feathers, by Burton L. Spiller, Crown Publ., NY, 1972. 238 pp., illus. $25.00.
Facsimile of the original Derrydale Press issue of 1938. Guns and dogs, the habits and shooting of grouse, woodcock, ducks, etc. Illus. by Lynn Bogue Hunt.
More Tracks: 78 Years of Mountains, People & Happinesss, by Howard Copenhaver, Stoney dale Press, Stevensville, MT, 1992. 150 pp., illus. $18.95.
A collection of stories by one of the back country's best storytellers about the people who shared with Howard his great adventure in the high places and wild Montana country.
Mostly Huntin', by Bill Jordan, Everett Publishing Co., Bossier City, LA, 1987. 254 pp., illus. $21.95.
Jordan's hunting adventures in North America, Africa, Australia, South America and Mexico.
Mostly Tailfeathers, by Gene Hill, Winchester Press, Piscataway, NJ, 1975. 192 pp., illus. $15.95.
An interesting, general book about bird hunting.
Movin' Along with Charley Dickey, by Charlie Dickey, Winchester Press, Piscataway, NJ, 1985. 224 pp., illus. $15.95.
More wisdom, wild tales, and wacky wit from the Sage of Tallahassee.
"Mr. Buck": The Autobiography of Nash Buckingham, by Nash Buckingham, Countrysport Press, Traverse City, MI, 1990. 288 pp., illus. $39.50.
A lifetime of shooting, hunting, dogs, guns, and Nash's reflections on the sporting life, along with previously unknown pictures and stories written especially for this book.
Murry Burnham's Hunting Secrets, by Murry Burnham with Russell Tinsley, Winchester Press, Piscataway, NJ, 1984. 244 pp., illus. $17.95.
One of the great hunters of our time gives the reasons for his success in the field.
My Health is Better in November, by Havilah Babcock, University of S. Carolina Press, Columbia, SC, 1985. 284 pp., illus. $19.95.
Adventures in the field set in the plantation country and backwater streams of SC.
North American Big Game Animals, by Byron W. Dalrymple and Erwin Bauer, Outdoor Life Books/Stackpole Books, Harrisburg, PA, 1985. 258 pp., illus. $29.95.
Complete illustrated natural histories. Habitat, movements, breeding, birth and development, signs, and hunting.
The North American Big Game Muzzleloading Record Book, published by the Longhunter Society of the National Muzzle Loading Rifle Association, Friendship, IN, 1992. 180 pp., illus. $35.00.
Over 400 entries in 27 categories, personal hunting stories and over 100 photos of trophy animals.
North American Elk: Ecology and Management, edited by Jack Ward Thomas and Dale E. Toweill, Stackpole Books, Harrisburg, PA, 1982. 576 pp., illus. $39.95.
The definitive, exhaustive, classic work on the North American elk.
The North American Waterfowler, by Paul S. Bernsen, Superior Publ. Co., Seattle, WA, 1972. 206 pp. Paper covers. $9.95.
The complete inside and outside story of duck and goose shooting. Big and colorful, illustrations by Les Kouba.
Of Bears and Man, by Mike Cramond, University of Oklahoma Press, Norman, OK, 1986. 433 pp., illus. $29.95.
The author's lifetime association with bears of North America. Interviews with survivors of bear attacks.
*****The Old Man and the Boy,** by Robert Ruark, Henry Holt & Co., New York, NY, 303 pp., illus. Paper covers. $12.95.

A timeless classic, telling the story of a remarkable friendship between a young boy and his grandfather as the hunt and fish together.
The Old Man's Boy Grows Older, by Robert Ruark, Henry Holt & Co., Inc., New York, NY, 1993. 300 pp., illus. Paper covers. $12.95.
The heartwarming sequel to the best-selling *The Old Man and the Boy*. A warm and rewarding book.
The Old Pro Turkey Hunter, by Gene Nunnery, Gene Nunnery, Meridian, MS, 1980. 144 pp., illus. $12.95.
True facts and old tales of turkey hunters.
The Only Good Bear is a Dead Bear, by Jeanette Hortick Prodgers, Falcon Press, Helena, MT, 1986. 204 pp. Paper covers. $12.50.
A collection of the West's best bear stories.
*****Outdoor Pastimes of an American Hunter,** by Theodore Roosevelt, Stackpole Books, Mechanicsburg, PA, 1994. 480 pp., illus. Paper covers. $16.95.
Stories of hunting big game in the West and notes about animal pursued and observed.
Outdoor Yarns & Outright Lies, by Gene Hill and Steve Smith, Stackpole Books, Harrisburg, PA, 1984. 168 pp., illus. $18.95.
Fifty or so stories by two good sports.
The Outlaw Gunner, by Harry M. Walsh, Tidewater Publishers, Cambridge, MD, 1973. 178 pp., illus. $15.95.
A colorful story of market gunning in both its legal and illegal phases.
*****Pheasant Days,** by Chris Dorsey, Voyageur Press, Stillwater, MN, 1992. 233 pp., illus. $24.95.
The definitive resource on ringnecks. Includes everything from basic hunting techniques to the life cycle of the bird.
Pheasant Hunter's Harvest, by Steve Grooms, Lyons & Burford Publishers, New York, NY, 1990. 180 pp. $18.95.
A celebration of pheasant, pheasant dogs and pheasant hunting. Practical advice from a passionate hunter.
*****Pheasants of the Mind,** by Datus Proper, Wilderness Adventures Press, Bozeman, MT, 1994. 154 pp., illus. $25.00.
No single title sums up the life of the solitary pheasant hunter like this masterful work.
Pinnell and Talifson: Last of the Great Brown Bear Men, by Marvin H. Clark, Jr., Great Northwest Publishing and Distributing Co., Spokane, WA, 19880. 224 pp., Illus. $39.95
The story of these famous Alaskan guides and some of the record bears taken by both of them.
Predator Caller's Companion, by Gerry Blair, Winchester Press, Piscataway, NJ, 1981. 280 pp., illus. $18.95.
Predator calling techniques and equipment for the hunter and trapper.
Quail Hunting in America, by Tom Huggler, Stackpole Books, Harrisburg, PA, 1987. 288 pp., illus. $19.95.
Tactics for finding and taking bobwhite, valleys, Gambel's Mountain, scaled-blue, and Mearn's quail by season and habitat.
*****Quest for Giant Bighorns,** by Duncan Gilchrist, Outdoor Expeditions and Books, Corvallis, MT, 1994. 224 pp., illus. Paper covers. $19.95.
How some of the most successful sheep hunters hunt and how some of the best bighorns were taken.
Radical Elk Hunting Strategies, by Mike Lapinski, Stoneydale Press Publishing Co., Stevensville, MT, 1988. 161 pp., illus. $18.95.
Secrets of calling elk in close.
Ranch Life and the Hunting Trail, by Theodore Roosevelt, Readex Microprint Corp., Dearborn, MI, 1966. 186 pp. With drawings by Frederic Remington. $22.50.
A facsimile reprint of the original 1899 Century Co. edition. One of the most fascinating books of the West of that day.
Records of North American Big Game 1932, by Prentis N. Grey, Boone and Crockett Club, Dumfries, VA, 1988. 178 pp., illus. $79.95.
A reprint of the book that started the Club's record keeping for native North American big game.
Records of North American Whitetailed Deer, by the editors of the Boone and Crockett Club, Dumfries, VA, 1987. 256 pp., illus. Flexible covers. $15.00.
Contains data on 1293 whitetail trophies over the all-time record book minimum, listed and ranked by state or province and divided into typical and non-typical categories.
Ridge Runners & Swamp Rats, by Charles F. Waterman, Amwell Press, Clinton, NJ, 1983. 347 pp., illus. $25.00.
Tales of hunting and fishing.
The Rifles, the Cartridges, and the Game, by Clay Harvey, Stackpole Books, Harrisburg, PA, 1991. 254 pp., illus. $32.95.
Engaging reading combines with exciting photos to present the hunt with an intense level of awareness and respect.
Ringneck! Pheasants & Pheasant Hunting, by Ted Janes, Crown Publ., NY, 1975. 120 pp., illus. $15.95.
A thorough study of one of our more popular game birds.
Ruffed Grouse, edited by Sally Atwater and Judith Schnell, Stackpole Books, Harrisburg, PA, 1989. 370 pp., illus. $59.95.
Everything you ever wanted to know about the ruffed grouse. More than 25 wildlife professionals provided in-depth information on every aspect of this popular game bird's life. Lavishly illustrated with over 300 full-color photos.
Shadows of the Tundra, by Tom Walker, Stackpole Books, Harrisburg, PA, 1990. 192 pp., illus. $19.95.
Alaskan tales of predator, prey, and man.
*****Sheep Hunting in Alaska—The Dall Sheep Hunter's Guide,** by Tony Russ, Outdoor Expeditions and Books, Corvallis, MT, 1994. 160 pp., illus. Paper covers. $19.95.
A how-to guide for the Dall sheep hunter.
Sheep & Sheep Hunting, by Jack O'Connor, Safari Press, Huntington Beach, CA, 1992. 308 pp., illus. $35.00.
A new printing of the definitive book on wild sheep.
Shorebirds: The Birds, The Hunters, The Decoys, by John M. Levinson & Somers G. Headley, Tidewater Publishers, Centreville, MD, 1991. 160 pp., illus. $49.95.
A thorough study of shorebirds and the decoys used to hunt them. Photographs of more than 200 of the decoys created by prominent carvers are shown.
Shots at Big Game, by Craig Boddington, Stackpole Books, Harrisburg, PA, 1989. 198 pp., illus. $24.95.
How to shoot a rifle accurately under hunting conditions.
Sport and Travel; East and West, by Frederick Courteney Selous, Wolfe Publishing Co., Prescott, AZ, 1988. 311 pp., illus. $29.00.
A limited edition reprint. One of the few books Selous wrote covering North American hunting. His daring in Africa is equalled here as he treks after unknown trails and wild game.

Spring Turkey Hunting, by John M. McDaniel, Stackpole Books, Harrisburg, PA, 1986. 224 pp., illus. $21.95.
The serious hunter's guide.

Squirrels and Squirrel Hunting, by Bob Gooch. Tidewater Publ., Cambridge, MD, 1973. 148 pp., illus. $12.95.
A complete book for the squirrel hunter, beginner or old hand. Details methods of hunting, squirrel habitat, management, proper clothing, care of the kill, cleaning and cooking.

Strayed Shots and Frayed Lines, edited by John E. Howard, Amwell Press, Clinton, NJ, 1982. 425 pp., illus. $25.00.
Anthology of some of the finest, funniest stories on hunting and fishing ever assembled.

Successful Goose Hunting, by Charles L. Cadieux, Stone Wall Press, Inc., Washington, DC, 1986. 223 pp., illus. $24.95.
Here is a complete book on modern goose hunting by a lifetime waterfowler and professional wildlifer.

Taking Big Bucks, by Ed Wolff, Stoneydale Press, Stevensville, MT, 1987. 169 pp., illus. $18.95.
Solving the whitetail riddle.

Taking More Birds, by Dan Carlisle and Dolph Adams, Lyons & Burford Publishers, New York, NY, 1993. 160 pp., illus. $19.95.
A practical handbook for success at Sporting Clays and wing shooting.

Tales of Alaska's Big Bears, by Jim Rearden, Wolfe Publishing Co., Prescott, AZ, 1989. 125 pp., illus. Soft covers. $12.95.
A collection of bear yarns covering nearly three-quarters of a century.

Tales of Quails 'n Such, by Havilah Babcock, University of S. Carolina Press, Columbia, SC, 1985. 237 pp. $19.95.
A group of hunting stories, told in informal style, on field experiences in the South in quest of small game.

They Left Their Tracks, by Howard Coperhaver, Stoneydale Press Publishing Co., Stevensville, MT, 1990. 190 pp., illus. $18.95.
Recollections of 60 years as an outfitter in the Bob Marshall Wilderness.

Timberdoodle, by Frank Woolner, Nick Lyons Books, N. Y., NY, 1987. 168 pp., illus. $18.95.
The classic guide to woodcock and woodcock hunting.

Track of the Kodiak, by Marvin H. Clark, Great Northwest Publishing and Distributing Co., Anchorage, AK, 1984. 224 pp., illus. $39.95.
A full perspective on Kodiak Island bear hunting.

Tracking Wounded Deer, by Richard P. Smith, Stackpole Books, Harrisburg, PA, 1988. 159 pp., illus. Paper covers. $15.95.
How to find and tag deer shot with bow or gun.

Trail and Campfire, edited by George Bird Grinnel and Theodore Roosevelt, The Boone and Crockett Club, Dumfries, VA, 1989. 357 pp., illus. $39.50.
Reprint of the Boone and Crockett Club's 3rd book published in 1897.

Trail of the Eagle, by Bud Conkle, as told to Jim Rearden, Great Northwest Publishing & Distributing Co., Anchorage, AK, 1991. 280 pp., illus. $29.50.
Hunting Alaska with master guide Bud Conkle.

*__Trap & Skeet Shooting, 3rd Edition,__ edited by Chris Christian, DBI Books, Inc., Northbrook, IL, 1994. 288 pp., illus. Paper covers. $17.95.
A detailed look at the contemporary world of trap, Skeet and Sporting Clays.

*__Trophy Mule Deer: Finding & Evaluating Your Trophy,__ by Lance Stapleton, Outdoor Experiences Unlimited, Salem, OR, 1993. 290 pp., illus. Paper covers. $24.95.
The most comprehensive reference book on mule deer.

The Turkey Hunter's Book, by John M. McDaniel, Amwell Press, Clinton, NJ, 1980. 147 pp., illus. Paper covers. $9.95.
One of the most original turkey hunting books to be published in many years.

*__Turkey Hunter's Digest, Revised Edition,__ by Dwain Bland, DBI Books, Inc., Northbrook, IL, 1994. 256 pp., illus. Paper covers. $17.95.
A no-nonsense approach to hunting all five sub-species of the North American wild turkey that make up the Royal Grand Slam.

Turkey Hunting with Gerry Blair, by Gerry Blair, Krause Publications, Iola, WI, 1993. 280 pp., illus. $19.95.
Novice and veteran turkey hunters alike will enjoy this complete examination of the varied wild turkey subspecies, their environments, equipment needed to pursue them and the tactics to outwit them.

The Upland Gunner's Book, edited by George Bird Evans, The Amwell Press, Clinton, NJ, 1985. 263 pp., illus. In slipcase. $27.50.
An anthology of the finest stories ever written on the sport of upland game hunting.

Varmint and Small Game Rifles and Cartridges, by various authors, Wolfe Publishing Co., Prescott, AZ, 1993. 228 pp., illus. Paper covers. $26.00.
This is a collection of reprints of articles originally appearing in Wolfe's *Rifle* and *Handloader* magazines from 1966 through 1990.

Wegner's Bibliography on Dear and Deer Hunting, by Robert Wegner, St. Hubert's Press, Deforest, WI, 1993. 333 pp., 16 full-page illustrations. $45.00.
A comprehensive annotated compilation of books in English pertaining to deer and their hunting 1413-1991.

Western Hunting Guide, by Mike Lapinski, Stoneydale Press Publishing Co., Stevensville, MT, 1989. 168 pp., illus. $18.95.
A complete where-to-go and how-to-do-it guide to Western hunting.

*__Whispering Wings of Autumn,__ by Gene Hill and Steve Smith, Wilderness Adventures Press, Bozeman, MT, 1994. 150 pp., illus. $29.00.
Hill and Smith, masters of hunting literature, treat the reader to the best stories of grouse and woodcock hunting.

*__Whitetail: The Ultimate Challenge,__ by Charles J. Alsheimer, Krause Publications, Iola, WI, 1995. 228 pp., illus. Paper covers. $14.95.
Learn deer hunting's most intriguing secrets—fooling deer using decoys, scents and calls—from America's premier authority.

The Wild Turkey Book, edited and with special commentary by J. Wayne Fears, Amwell Press, Clinton, NJ, 1982. 303 pp., illus. $22.50.
An anthology of the finest stories on wild turkey ever assembled under one cover.

*__The Wilderness Hunter,__ by Theodore Roosevelt, Wolfe Publishing Co., Prescott, AZ, 1994. 200 pp., illus. $25.00.
Reprint of a classic by one of America's most famous big game hunters.

Wilderness Hunting and Wildcraft, by Townsend Whelen, Wolfe Publishing Co., Prescott, AZ, 1988. 338 pp., illus. $39.00.
A limited edition reprint. Plentiful information on sheep and mountain hunting with horses and on life histories of big game animals.

The Wildfowler's Quest, by George Reiger, Lyons & Burford, Publishers, New York, NY, 1989. 320 pp., illus. $24.95.
A richly evocative look into one man's passionate pursuit of ducks, geese, turkey, woodcock, and other wildfowl all over the world.

Wind on the Water, as told to Jim Rearden, Great Northwest Publishing & Distributing Co., Anchorage, AK, 1991. 280 pp., illus. $19.95.
The true-life account of a pioneering couple, Bud and Lenora Conkle, in the wilds. Hunting stories as well as takes of the trapline, winter hardship and wilderness life in the far North.

Wings for the Heart, by Jerry A. Lewis, West River Press, Corvallis, MT, 1991. 324 pp., illus. Paper covers. $14.95.
A delightful book on hunting Montan's upland birds and waterfowl.

The Woodchuck Hunter, by Paul C. Estey, R&R Books, Livonia, NY, 1994. 135 pp., illus. $25.00.
This book contains information on woodchuck equipment, the rifle, telescopic sights and includes interesting stories.

Woodcock, by John Alden Knight, Gunnerman Press, Auburn Hills, MI, 1989. 160 pp., illus. $21.95.
A new printing of one of the finest books ever written on the subject.

Woodcock Shooting, by Steve Smith, Stackpole Books, Inc., Harrisburg, PA, 1988. 142 pp., illus. $16.95.
A definitive book on woodcock hunting and the characteristics of a good woodcock dog.

AFRICA/ASIA/ELSEWHERE

Aagaard's Africa: A Hunter Remembers, by Finn Aagaard, National Rifle Association, Washington, DC, 1991. 196 pp., illus. $16.95.
Tales of life and livelihood in Kenya in the twilight of its glory days is told by native Kenyan Finn Aagaard.

African Adventures, by J.F. Burger, Safari Press, Huntington Beach, CA, 1993. 222 pp., illus. $35.00.
The reader shares adventures on the trail of the lion, the elephant and buffalo.

The African Adventures: A Return to the Silent Places, by Peter Hathaway Capstick, St. Martin's Press, New York, NY, 1992. 220 pp., illus. $22.95.
This book brings to life four turn-of-the-century adventurers and the savage frontier they braved. Frederick Selous, Constatine "Iodine" Ionides, Johnny Boyes and Jim Sutherland.

African Camp-fire Nights, by J.E. Burger, Safari Press, Huntington Beach, CA, 1993. 192 pp., illus. $32.50.
In this book the author writes of the men who made hunting their life's profession.

African Hunter, by Baron Bror von Blixen-Finecke, St. Martin's Press, New York, NY, 1986. 284 pp., illus. $14.95.
Reprint of the scarce 1938 edition. An African hunting classic.

African Hunting and Adventure, by William Charles Baldwin, Books of Zimbabwe, Bulawayo, 1981. 451 pp., illus. $75.00.
Facsimile reprint of the scarce 1863 London edition. African hunting and adventure from Natal to the Zambezi.

African Jungle Memories, by J.F. Burger, Safari Press, Huntington Beach, CA, 1993. 192 pp., illus. $32.50.
A book of reminiscences in which the reader is taken on many exciting adventures on the trail of the buffalo, lion, elephant and leopard.

African Nature Notes and Reminiscences, by Frederick Courteney Selous, St. Martin's Press, New York, NY, 1993. 356 pp., illus. $22.95.
This classic reprint shows both sides of Selous, the fearless tracker of game who became a legend in his hunting prowess, and the avowed conservationist who recorded his vast personal reserves of Africa lore.

African Rifles & Cartridges, by John Taylor, The Gun Room Press, Highland Park, NJ, 1977. 431 pp., illus. $35.00.
Experiences and opinions of a professional ivory hunter in Africa describing his knowledge of numerous arms and cartridges for big game. A reprint.

The African Safari, by P. Jay Fetner, St. Martin's Press, Inc., N. Y., NY, 1987. 700 pp., illus. $70.00.
A lavish, superbly illustrated, definitive work that brings together the practical elements of planning a safari with a proper appreciation for the animals and their environment.

*__African Twilight,__ by Robert F. Jones, Wilderness Adventure Press, Bozeman, MT, 1994. 208 pp., illus. $36.00.
Details the hunt, danger and changing face of Africa over a span of three decades.

After Big Game in Central Africa, by Edouard Foa, St. Martin's Press, New York, NY, 1989. 400 pp., illus. $16.95.
Reprint of the scarce 1899 edition. This sportsman covered 7200 miles, mostly on foot—from Zambezi delta on the east coast to the mouth of the Congo on the west.

*__A Man Called Lion: The Life and Times of John Howar "Pondoro" Taylor,__ by P.H. Capstick, Safari Press, Huntington Beach, CA, 1994. 240 pp., illus. $24.95.
With the help of Brian Marsh, an old Taylor acquaintance, Peter Capstick has cumulated over ten years of research into the life of this mysterious man.

*__Argali: High-Mountain Hunting,__ by Ricardo Medem, Safari Press, Huntington Beach, CA, 1995. 304 pp., illus. Limited, signed edition. $150.00.
Medem describes hunting seven different countries in the pursuit of sheep and other mountain game.

Bell of Africa, compiled and edited by Townsend Whelen, Safari Press, Huntington Beach, CA, 1990. 236 pp., illus. $24.95.
The autobiography of W.D.M. Bell compiled and edited by his lifetime friend from Bell's own papers.

Big Game and Big Game Rifles, by John Taylor, Safari Press, Huntington Beach, CA, 1993. 215 pp., illus. $24.95.
A classic by the man who probably knew more about ammunition and rifles for African game than any other hunter.

Big Game Hunting and Collecting in East Africa 1903-1926, by Kalman Kittenberger, St. Martin's Press, New York, NY, 1989. 496 pp., illus. $16.95.
One of the most heart stopping, charming and funny accounts of adventure in the Kenya Colony ever penned.

Big Game Hunting Around the World, by Bert Klineburger and Vernon W. Hurst, Exposition Press, Jericho, NY, 1969. 376 pp., illus. $30.00.
The first book that takes you on a safari all over the world.

Big Game Hunting in Asia, Africa, and Elsewhere, by Jacques Vettier, Trophy Room Books, Agoura, CA, 1993. 400 pp., illus. Limited, numbered edition. $150.00.
The first English language edition of the book that set a new standard in big game hunting book literature.

Big Game Hunting in North-Eastern Rhodesia, by Owen Letcher, St. Martin's Press, New York, NY, 1986. 272 pp., illus. $15.95.
A classic reprint and one of the very few books to concentrate on this fascinating area, a region that today is still very much safari country.

Big Game Shooting in Cooch Behar, the Duars and Assam, by The Maharajah of Cooch Behar, Wolfe Publishing Co., Prescott, AZ, 1993. 461 pp., illus. $118.00.
A reprinting of the book that has become legendary. This is the Maharajah's personal diary of killing 365 tigers.

50th EDITION, 1996 545

The Book of the Lion, by Sir Alfred E. Pease, St. Martin's Press, New York, NY, 1986. 305 pp., illus. $15.95.

Reprint of the finest book ever published on the subject. The author describes all aspects of lion history and lion hunting, drawing heavily on his own experiences in British East Africa.

***Chui! A Guide to Hunting the African Leopard,** by Lou Hallamore and Bruce Woods, Trophy Room Books, Agoura, CA, 1994. 239 pp., illus. $75.00.

Tales of exciting leopard encounters by one of today's most respected pros.

Death in a Lonely Land, by Peter Capstick, St. Martin's Press, New York, NY, 1990. 284 pp., illus. $19.95.

Twenty-three stories of hunting as only the master can tell them.

Death in the Dark Continent, by Peter Capstick, St. Martin's Press, New York, NY, 1983. 238 pp., illus. $15.95.

A book that brings to life the suspense, fear and exhilaration of stalking ferocious killers under primitive, savage conditions, with the ever present threat of death.

Death in the Long Grass, by Peter Hathaway Capstick, St. Martin's Press, New York, NY, 1977. 297 pp., illus. $17.95.

A big game hunter's adventures in the African bush.

Death in the Silent Places, by Peter Capstick, St. Martin's Press, New York, NY, 1981. 243 pp., illus. $15.95.

The author recalls the extraordinary careers of legendary hunters such as Corbett, Karamojo Bell, Stigand and others.

***Duck Hunting in Australia,** by Dick Eussen, Australia Outdoor Publishers Pty Ltd., Victoria, Australia, 1994. 106 pp., illus. Paper covers. $17.95.

Covers the many aspects of duck hunting from hides to hunting methods.

East Africa and its Big Game, by Captain Sir John C. Willowghby, Wolfe Publishing Co., Prescott, AZ, 1990. 312 pp., illus. $52.00.

A deluxe limited edition reprint of the very scarce 1889 edition of a narrative of a sporting trip from Zanzibar to the borders of the Masai.

East of the Sun and West of the Moon, by Theodore and Kermit Roosevelt, Wolfe Publishing Co., Prescott, AZ, 1988. 284 pp., illus. $25.00.

A limited edition reprint. A classic on Marco Polo sheep hunting. A life experience unique to hunters of big game.

Elephant, by Commander David Enderby Blunt, The Holland Press, London, England, 1985. 260 pp., illus. $35.00.

A study of this phenomenal beast by a world-leading authority.

Elephant Hunting in East Equatorial Africa, by A. Neumann, St. Martin's Press, New York, NY, 1994. 455 pp., illus. $26.95.

This is a reprint of one of the rarest elephant hunting titles ever.

Elephant Hunting in Portuguese East Africa, by Jose Pardal, Safari Press, Huntington Beach, CA, 1990. 256 pp., illus. $60.00.

This book chronicles the hunting-life story of a nearly vanished breed of man—those who single-handedly hunted elephants for prolonged periods of time.

Elephants of Africa, by Dr. Anthony Hall-Martin, New Holland Publishers, London, England, 1987. 120 pp., illus. $75.00.

A superbly illustrated overview of the African elephant with reproductions of paintings by the internationally acclaimed wildlife artist Paul Bosman.

***Encounters with Lions,** by Jan Hemsing, Trophy Room books, Agoura, CA, 1995. 302 pp., illus. $75.00.

Some stories fierce, fatal, frightening and even humorous of when man and lion meet.

Ends of the Earth, by Roy Chapman Andrews, Wolfe Publishing Co., Prescott, AZ, 1988. 230 pp., illus. $27.00.

A limited edition reprint. Includes adventures in China and hunting in Mongolia. Andrews was a distinguished hunter and scout.

First Wheel, by Bunny Allen, Amwell Press, Clinton, NJ, 1984. Limited, signed and numbered edition in the NSFL "African Hunting Heritage Series." 292 pp., illus. $100.00.

A white hunter's diary, 1927-47.

***The Fomidable Game,** by John Batten, The Amwell Press, Clinton, NJ, 1994. 336 pp., illus. $40.00.

Batten and his wife cover the globe in search of the world's dangerous game. Includes a section on the development of the big bore rifle for formidable game.

***The Great Arc of the Wild Sheep,** by J.L. Clark, Safari Press, Huntington Beach, CA, 1994. 247 pp., illus. $24.95.

Perhaps the most complete work done on all the species and subspecies of the wild sheep of the world.

Gun and Camera in Southern Africa, by H. Anderson Bryden, Wolfe Publishing Co., Prescott, AZ, 1989. 201 pp., illus. $37.00.

A limited edition reprint. The year was 1893 and author Bryden wandered for a year in Bechuanaland and the Kalahari Desert hunting the white rhino, lechwe, eland, and more.

Horned Death, by John F. Burger, Safari Press, Huntington Beach, CA, 1992. 343 pp., illus. $35.00.

The classic work on hunting the African buffalo.

Horn of the Hunter, by Robert Ruark, Safari Press, Long Beach, CA, 1987. 315 pp., illus. $35.00.

Ruark's most sought-after title on African hunting, here in reprint.

***Hunting in Botswana,** by Tony Sanchez-Arino, Safari Press, Huntington Beach, CA, 1995. 416 pp., illus. Limited, signed and numbered edition. $135.00.

The finest selection of hunting stories ever compiled on hunting this great game country.

Hunting in Botswana, An Anthology, by Tony Sanchez-Arino, Safari Press, Huntington Beach, CA, 1994. 416 pp., illus. Limited, signed and numbered edition, in a slipcase. $135.00.

The finest selection of stories compiled on hunting in Botswana.

Hunting in Many Lands, by Theodore Roosevelt and George Bird Grinnel, The Boone and Crockett Club, Dumfries, VA, 1987. 447 pp., illus. $40.00.

Limited edition reprint of this 1895 classic work on hunting in Africa, India, Mongolia, etc.

Hunting in the Sudan, An Anthology, compiled by Tony Sanchez-Arino, Safari Press, Huntington Beach, CA, 1992. 350 pp., illus. Limited, signed and numbered edition in a slipcase. $125.00.

The finest selection of hunting stories ever compiled on hunting in this great game country.

Hunting in Tanzania, An Anthology, by Tony Sanchez-Arino, Safari Press, Huntington Beach, CA, 1991. 416 pp., illus. Limited, signed and numbered edition, in a slipcase. $125.00.

The finest selection of hunting stories ever compiled on that great East African game country, Tanzania.

Hunting in Zimbabwe, An Anthology, by Tony Sanchez-Arino, Safari Press, Huntington Beach, CA, 1992. 350 pp., illus. Limited, signed and numbered edition, in a slipcase. $125.00.

The finest selection of hunting stories ever compiled on hunting in this great game country.

Hunting the Elephant in Africa, by Captain C.H. Stigand, St. Martin's Press, New York, NY, 1986. 379 pp., illus. $14.95.

A reprint of the scarce 1913 edition; vintage Africana at its best.

Jaguar Hunting in the Mato Grosso and Bolivia, by T. Almedia, Safari Press, Long Beach, CA, 1989. 256 pp., illus. $35.00.

Not since Sacha Siemel has there been a book on jaguar hunting like this one.

The Jim Corbett Collection, by Jim Corbett. Safari Press, Huntington, CA, 1991. 1124 pp., illus., five volumes in slipcase. $105.00.

This slip-cased set of Jim Corbett's works includes: *Jungle Lore, The Man-Eating Leopard of Rudraprayag, My India, Man-Eaters of Kumaon, Tree Tops,* and *Temple Tiger*.

Jim Corbett's India, stories selected by R.E. Hawkins, Oxford University Press, New York, NY, 1993. 250 pp. $24.95.

Stories and extracts from Jim Corbett's writings on tiger hunting by his publisher and editor.

Karamojo Safari, by W.D.M. Ball, Safari Press, Huntington Beach, CA, 1990. 288 pp., illus. $24.95.

The story of Bell's caravan travels through Karamojo, his exciting elephant hunts, and his life among the uncivilized and uncorrupted natives.

King of the Wa-Kikuyu, by John Boyes, St. Martin Press, New York, NY, 1993. 240 pp., illus. $19.95.

In the 19th and 20th centuries, Africa drew to it a large number of great hunters, explorers, adventurers and rogues. Many have become legendary, but John Boyes (1874-1951) was the most legendary of them all.

Lake Ngami, by Charles Anderson, New Holland Press, London, England, 1987. 576 pp., illus. $35.00.

Originally published in 1856. Describes two expeditions into what is now Botswana, depicting every detail of landscape and wildlife.

Last Horizons: Hunting, Fishing and Shooting on Five Continents, by Peter Capstick, St. Martin's Press, New York, NY, 1989. 288 pp., illus. $19.95.

The first in a two volume collection of hunting, fishing and shooting tales from the selected pages of The American Hunter, Guns & Ammo and Outdoor Life.

The Last Ivory Hunter: The Saga of Wally Johnson, by Peter Capstick, St. Martin's Press, New York, NY, 1988. 220 pp., illus. $18.95.

A grand tale of African adventure by the foremost hunting author of our time. Wally Johnson spent half a century in Mozambique hunting white gold—ivory.

Last of the Ivory Hunters, by John Taylor, Safari Press, Long Beach, CA, 1990. 354 pp., illus. $29.95.

Reprint of the classic book "Pondoro" by one of the most famous elephant hunters of all time.

The Man-Eaters of Tsavo, by Lt. Col. J.H. Patterson, St. Martin's Press, New York, NY, 1986. 346 pp., illus. $14.95.

A reprint of the scarce original book on the man-eating lions of Tsavo.

Memories of an African Hunter, by Denis D. Lyell, St. Martin's Press, New York, NY, 1986. 288 pp., illus. $15.95.

A reprint of one of the truly great writers on African hunting. A gripping and highly readable account of Lyell's many years in the African bush.

***The Nature of the Game,** by Ben Hoskyns, Quiller Press, Ltd., London, England, 1994. 160 pp., illus. $37.50.

The first complete guide to British, European and North American game.

One Happy Hunter, by George Barrington, Safari Press, Huntington Beach, CA, 1994. 240 pp., illus. $40.00.

A candid, straightforward look at safari hunting.

Peter Capstick's Africa: A Return to the Long Grass, by Peter Hathaway Capstick, St. Martin's Press, N. Y., NY, 1987. 213 pp., illus. $29.95.

A first-person adventure in which the author returns to the long grass for his own dangerous and very personal excursion.

The Recollections of an Elephant Hunter 1864-1875, by William Finaughty, Books of Zimbabwe, Bulawayo, Zimbabwe, 1980. 244 pp., illus. $85.00.

Reprint of the scarce 1916 privately published edition. The early game hunting exploits of William Finaughty in Matabeleland and Nashonaland.

Robert Ruark's Africa, by Robert Ruark, Countrysport Press, Inc., Traverse City, MI, 1991. 256 pp., illus. $29.50.

A new release of previously uncollected stories of the wanderings through Africa of this giant in American sporting literature.

Safari: A Chronicle of Adventure, by Bartle Bull, Viking/Penguin, London, England, 1989. 383 pp., illus. $40.00.

The thrilling history of the African safari, highlighting some of Africa's best-known personalities.

Safari Rifles: Double, Magazine Rifles and Cartridges for African Hunting, by Craig Boddington, Safari Press, Huntington Beach, CA, 1990. 416 pp., illus. $37.50.

A wealth of knowledge on the safari rifle. Historical and present double-rifle makers, ballistics for the large bores, and much, much more.

Safari: The Last Adventure, by Peter Capstick, St. Martin's Press, New York, NY, 1984. 291 pp., illus. $15.95.

A modern comprehensive guide to the African Safari.

Sands of Silence, by Peter H. Capstick, Saint Martin's Press, New York, NY, 1991. 224 pp., illus. $35.00.

Join the author on safari in Nambia for his latest big-game hunting adventures.

***Shoot Straight and Stay Alive: A Lifetime of Hunting Experiences,** by Fred Bartlett, Trophy Room Books, Argoura, CA, 1994. 262 pp., illus. $85.00.

A book written by a man who has left his mark on the maps of Africa's great gamelands.

***Skyline Pursuits,** by John Batten, The Amwell Press, Clinton, NJ, 1994. 372 pp., illus. $40.00.

A chronicle of Batten's own hunting adventures in the high country on four continents since 1928, traces a sheep hunting career that has accounted for both North American and International Grand Slams.

***Solo Safari,** by T. Cacek, Safari Press, Huntington Beach, CA, 1995. 270 pp., illus. $40.00.

Here is the story of Terry Cacek who hunted elephant, buffalo, leopard and plains game in Zimbabwe and Botswana on his own.

South Pacific Trophy Hunter, by Murray Thomas, Safari Press, Long Beach, CA, 1988. 181 pp., illus. $37.50.

A record of a hunter's search for a trophy of each of the 15 major game species in the South Pacific region.

Sport on the Pamirs and Turkestan Steppes, by Major C.S. Cumberland, Moncrieff & Smith, Victoria, Autralia, 1992. 278 pp., illus. $45.00.

The first in a series of facsimile reprints of great trophy hunting books by Moncrieff & Smith.

Tales of the Big Game Hunters, selected and introduced by Kenneth Kemp, The Sportsman's Press, London, 1986. 209 pp., illus. $15.00.

Writings by some of the best known hunters and explorers, among them: Frederick Courteney Selous, R.G. Gordon Cumming, Sir Samuel Baker, and elephant hunters Neumann and Sutherland.

***Theodore Roosevelt Outdoorsman,** by R.L. Wilson, Trophy Room Books, Agoura, CA, 1994. 326 pp., illus. $85.00.

This book presents Theodore Roosevelt as a rancher, Rough Rider, Governor, President, naturalist and international big game hunter.

Those Were the Days, by Rudolf Sand, Safari Press, Huntington Beach, CA, 1993. 300 pp., illus. $100.00.
Travel with Rudolf Sand to the pinnacles of the world in his pursuit of wild sheep and goats.
***Through the Brazilian Wilderness**, by Theodore Roosevelt, Stackpole Books, Mechanicsburg, PA, 1994. 448 pp., illus. Paper covers. $16.95.
Adventure and drama in the South American jungle.
***Trophy Hunter in Africa**, by Elgin Gates, Safari Press, Huntington Beach, CA, 1994. 315 pp., illus. $29.95.
This is the story of one man's adventure in Africa's wildlife paradise.
***Trophy Hunter in Asia**, by Elgin Gates, Charger Productions, Inc., Capistrano Beach, CA, 1982. 272 pp., illus. $19.95.
Facinating high adventure with Elgin T. Gates one of America's top trophy hunters.
Uganda Safaris, by Brian Herne, Winchester Press, Piscataway, NJ, 1979. 236 pp., illus. $12.95.
The chronicle of a professional hunter's adventures in Africa.
Use Enough Gun, by Robert Ruark, Safari Press, Huntington Beach, CA, 1992. 333 pp., illus. $30.00.
A record of a lifetime's bag hunting big game.
The Wanderings of an Elephant Hunter, by W.D.M. Bell, Safari Press, Huntington Beach, CA, 1990. 187 pp., illus. $24.95.
The greatest of elephant books by the greatest-of-all elephant hunter.
A White Hunters Life, by Angus MacLagan, an African Heritage Book, published by Amwell Press, Clinton, NJ, 1983. 283 pp., illus. Limited, signed, and numbered deluxe edition, in slipcase. $100.00.
True to life, a sometimes harsh yet intriguing story.
Wild Sports of Southern Africa, by William Cornwallis Harris, New Holland Press, London, England, 1987. 376 pp., illus. $35.00.
Originally published in 1863, describes the author's travels in Southern Africa.

RIFLES

The Accurate Varmint Rifle, by Boyd Mace, Precision Shooting, Inc., Whitehall, NY, 1991. 184 pp., illus. $24.95.
A long overdue and long needed work on what factors go into the selection of components for and the susequent assembly of...the accurate varmint rifle.
The AK-47 Assault Rifle, Desert Publications, Cornville, AZ, 1981. 150 pp., illus. Paper covers. $10.00.
Complete and practical technical information on the only weapon in history to be produced in an estimated 30,000,000 units.
The AR-15/M16, A Practical Guide, by Duncan Long. Paladin Press, Boulder, CO, 1985. 168 pp., illus. Paper covers. $16.95.
The definitive book on the rifle that has been the inspiration for so many modern assault rifles.
Assault Weapons, 3rd Edition, The Gun Digest Book of, edited by Jack Lewis, DBI Books, Inc., Northbrook, IL, 1993. 256 pp., illus. Paper covers. $18.95
An in-depth look into the history and uses of these arms.
***Assault Weapons, 4th Edition**, by Jack Lewis, DBI Books, Inc., Northbrook, IL, 1996. 256 pp., illus. Paper covers. (Available January 1996)
An in-depth look at the history and uses of these arms.
Australian Military Rifles & Bayonets, 200 Years of, by Ian Skennerton, I.D.S.A. Books, Piqua, OH, 1988. 124 pp., 198 illus. Paper covers. $19.50.
Australian Service Machineguns, 100 Years of, by Ian Skennerton, I.D.S.A. Books, Piqua, OH, 1989. 122 pp., 150 illus. Paper covers. $19.50.
The Big-Bore Rifle, by Michael McIntosh, Countrysport Press, Traverse City, MI, 1990. 224 pp., illus. $39.95.
The book of fine magazine and double rifles 375 to 700 calibers.
The Big Game Rifle, by Jack O'Connor, Safari Press, Huntington Beach, CA, 1994. 370 pp., illus. $37.50.
An outstanding description of every detail of construction, purpose and use of the big game rifle.
Big Game Rifles and Cartridges, by Elmer Keith, reprint edition by The Gun Room Press, Highland Park, NJ, 1984. 161 pp., illus. $29.95.
Reprint of Elmer Keith's first book, a most original and accurate work on big game rifles and cartridges.
Black Powder Hobby Gunsmithing, by Sam Fadala and Dale Storey, DBI Books, Inc., Northbrook, IL, 1994. 256 pp., illus. Paper covers. $17.95.
A how-to guide for gunsmithing blackpowder pistols, rifles and shotguns from two men at the top of their respective fields.
The Black Rifle, M16 Retrospective, R. Blake Stevens and Edward C. Ezell, Collector Grade Publications, Toronto, Canada, 1987. 400 pp., illus. $59.95
The complete story of the M16 rifle and its development.
***Bolt Action Rifles, 3rd Edition**, edited by Frank de Haas, DBI Books, Inc., Northbrook, IL, 1995. 576 pp., illus. Paper covers. $24.95.
A revised edition of the most definitive work on all major bolt-action rifle designs.
The Book of the Garand, by Maj.-Gen. J.S. Hatcher, The Gun Room Press, Highland Park, NJ, 1977. 292 pp., illus. $26.95.
A new printing of the standard reference work on the U.S. Army M1 rifle.
The Book of the Twenty-Two: The All American Caliber, by Sam Fadala, Stoeger Publishing Co., So. Hackensack, NJ, 1989. 288 pp., illus. Soft covers. $16.95.
The All American Caliber from BB caps up to the powerful 226 Barnes. It's about ammo history, plinking, target shooting, and the quest for the one-hole group.
British Military Martini, Treatise on the, Vol. 1, by B.A. Temple and Ian Skennerton, I.D.S.A. Books, Piqua, OH, 1983. 256 pp., 114 illus. $40.00.
British Military Martini, Treatise on the, Vol. 2, by B.A. Temple and Ian Skennerton, I.D.S.A. Books, Piqua, OH, 1989. 213 pp., 135 illus. $40.00.
British .22RF Training Rifles, by Dennis Lewis and Robert Washburn, Excaliber Publications, Latham, NY, 1993. 64 pp., illus. Paper covers. $10.95.
The story of Britain's training rifles from the early Aiming Tube models to the post-WWII trainers.
Combat Rifles of the 21st Century, by Duncan Long, Paladin Press, Boulder, CO, 1991. 115 pp., illus. Paper covers. $16.50.
An inside look at the U.S. Army's program to develop a super advanced combat rifle to replace the M16.
The Complete AR15/M16 Sourcebook, by Duncan Long, Paladin Press, Boulder, CO, 1993. 232 pp., illus. Paper covers. $35.00.
The latest development of the AR15/M16 and the many spin-offs now available, selective-fire conversion systems for the 1990s, the vast selection of new accessories.
Exploded Long Gun Drawings, The Gun Digest Book of, edited by Harold A. Murtz, DBI Books, Inc., Northbrook, IL, 512 pp., illus. Paper covers. $20.95.
Containing almost 500 rifle and shotgun exploded drawings. An invaluable aid to both professionals and hobbyists.
***The FAL Rifle**, by R. Blake Stevens and Jean van Rutten, Collector Grade Publications, Cobourg, Canada, 1993. 848 pp., illus. $129.95.
Originally published in three volumes, this classic edition covers North American, UK and Commonwealth and the metric FAL's.
The Fighting Rifle, by Chuck Taylor, Paladin Press, Boulder, CO, 1983. 184 pp., illus. Paper covers. $20.00.
The difference between assault and battle rifles and auto and light machine guns.
Firearms Assembly/Disassembly Part III: Rimfire Rifles, Revised Edition, The Gun Digest Book of, by J. B. Wood, DBI Books, Inc., Northbrook, IL., 1994. 480 pp., illus. Paper covers. $18.95.
Covers 65 popular rimfires plus over 100 variants, all cross-referenced in the index.
Firearms Assembly/Disassembly Part IV: Centerfire Rifles, Revised Edition, The Gun Digest Book of,, by J.B. Wood, DBI Books, Inc., Northbrook, IL, 1991. 480 pp., illus. Paper covers. $18.95.
Covers 54 popular centerfire rifles plus 300 variants. The most comprehensive and professional presentation available to either hobbyist or gunsmith.
F.N.-F.A.L. Auto Rifles, Desert Publications, Cornville, AZ, 1981. 130 pp., illus. Paper covers. $13.95.
A definitive study of one of the free world's finest combat rifles.
***The Hammerless Double Rifle**, by Alexander Gray, Wolfe Publishing Co., Prescott, AZ, 1994. 154 pp., illus. $39.50.
The history, design, construction and maintenance are explored for a better understanding of these firearms.
***Gough Thomas's Gun Book**, by G.T. Garwood, Gunnerman Press, Auburn Hills, MI, 1995. 273 pp., illus. $34.95.
A compilation of pieces by the dean of British shotgunning experts, Gough Thomas.
***Hints and Advice on Rifle-Shooting**, by Private R. McVittie with new introductory material by W.S. Curtis, W.S. Curtis Publishers, Ltd., Clwyd, England, 1993. 32 pp. Paper covers. $10.00.
A reprint of the original 1886 London edition.
The History and Development of the M16 Rifle and Its Cartridge, by David R. Hughes, Armory Publications, Oceanside, CA, 1990. 294 pp., illus. $49.95.
Study of small caliber rifle development culminating in the M16 with encyclopedic coverage of the .223/5.56mm cartridge.
Illustrated Handbook of Rifle Shooting, by A.L. Russell, Museum Restoration Service, Alexandria Bay, NY, 1992. 194 pp., illus. $24.50.
A new printing of the 1869 edition by one of the leading military marksman of the day.
Keith's Rifles for Large Game, by Elmer Keith, The Gun Room Press, Highland Park, NJ, 1986. 406 pp., illus. $39.95.
Covers all aspects of selecting, equipping, use and care of high power rifles for hunting big game, especially African.
Know Your M1 Garand, by E. J. Hoffschmidt, Blacksmith Corp., Southport, CT, 1975, 84 pp., illus. Paper covers. $9.95.
Facts about America's most famous infantry weapon. Covers test and experimental models, Japanese and Italian copies, National Match models.
Know Your Ruger 10/22 Carbine, by William E. Workman, Blacksmith Corp., Chino Valley, AZ, 1991. 96 pp., illus. Paper covers. $9.95.
The story and facts about the most popular 22 autoloader ever made.
The Lee Enfield No. 1 Rifles, by Alan M. Petrillo, Excaliber Publications, Latham, NY, 1992. 64 pp., illus. Paper covers. $10.95.
Highlights the SMLE rifles from the Mark 1-VI.
The Lee Enfield Number 4 Rifles, by Alan M. Petrillo, Excalibur Publications, Latham, NY, 1992. 64 pp., illus. Paper covers. $10.95.
A pocket-sized, bare-bones reference devoted entirely to the .303 World War II and Korean War vintage service rifle.
The Lee Enfield Story, by Ian Skennerton, I.D.S.A. Books, Piqua, OH, 1993. 504 pp., nearly 1,000 illus. $59.95.
The Lee Enfield Story, Delux Presentation Edition by Ian Skennerton, I.D.S.A. Books, Piqua, OH, 1993. 504 pp., nearly 1,000 illus. Leather cover. $150.00.
Legendary Sporting Rifles, by Sam Fadala, Stoeger Publishing Co., So. Hackensack, NJ, 1992. 288 pp., illus. Paper covers. $16.95.
Covers a vast span of time and technology beginning with the Kentucky Long-rifle.
***M14/M14A1 Rifles and Rifle Markmanship**, Desert Publications, El Dorado, AZ, 1995. 236 pp., illus. Paper covers. $16.95.
Contains a detailed description of the M14 and M14A1 rifles and their general characteristics, procedures for disassembly and assembly, operating and functioning of the rifles, etc.
The M-14 Rifle, facsimile reprint of FM 23-8, Desert Publications, Cornville, AZ, 50 pp., illus. Paper $7.95.
Well illustrated and informative reprint covering the M-14 and M-14E2.
Military Bolt Action Rifles, 1841-1918, by Donald B. Webster, Museum Restoration Service, Alexander Bay, NY, 1993. 150 pp., illus. $34.50.
A photographic survey of the principal rifles and carbines of the European and Asiatic powers of the last half of the 19th century and the first years of the 20th century.
Military and Sporting Rifle Shooting, by Captain E.C. Crossman, Wolfe Publishing Co., Prescott, AZ, 1988. 449 pp., illus. $45.00.
A limited edition reprint. A complete and practical treatise covering the use of rifles.
The Mini-14, by Duncan Long, Paladin Press, Boulder, CO, 1987. 120 pp., illus. Paper covers. $12.00.
History of the Mini-14, the factory-produced models, specifications, accessories, suppliers, and much more.
M1 Carbine Owner's Manual, M1, M2 & M3 .30 Caliber Carbines, Firepower Publications, Cornville, AZ, 1984. 102 pp., illus. Paper covers. $10.95.
The complete book for the owner of an M1 Carbine.
The Muzzle-Loading Rifle...Then and Now, by Walter M. Cline, National Muzzle Loading Rifle Association, Friendship, IN, 1991. 161 pp., illus. $32.00.
This extensive compilation of the muzzleloading rifle exhibits accumulative preserved data concerning the development of the "hallowed old arms of the Southern highlands."
The No. 4 (T) Sniper Rifle: An Armourer's Perspective, by Peter Laidler with Ian Skennerton, I.D.S.A. Books, Piqua, OH, 1993. 125 pp., 75 illus. Paper covers. $19.95.

***Notes on Rifle-Shooting,** by Henry William Heaton, reprinted with a new introduction by W.S. Curtis, W.S. Curtis Publishers, Ltd., Clwyd, England, 1993. 89 pp. $19.95.

A reprint of the 1864 London edition. Captain Heaton was one of the great rifle shots from the earliest days of the Volunteer Movement.

The Pennsylvania Rifle, by Samuel E. Dyke, Sutter House, Lititz, PA, 1975. 61 pp., illus. Paper covers. $5.00.

History and development, from the hunting rifle of the Germans who settled the area. Contains a full listing of all known Lancaster, PA, gunsmiths from 1729 through 1815.

***Police Rifles,** by Richard Fairburn, Paladin Press, Boulder, CO, 1994. 248 pp., illus. Paper covers. $30.00.

Selecting the right rifle for street patrol and special tactical situations.

A Potpourri of Single Shot Rifles and Actions, by Frank de Haas, Mark de Haas, Ridgeway, MO, 1993. 153 pp., illus. Paper covers. $22.50.

The author's 6th book on non-bolt-action single shots. Covers more than 40 single-shot rifles in historical and technical detail.

The Remington 700, by John F. Lacy, Taylor Publishing Co., Dallas, TX, 1990. 208 pp., illus. $44.95.

Covers the different models, limited editions, chamberings, proofmarks, serial numbers, military models, and much more.

The Revolving Rifles, by Edsall James, Pioneer Press, Union City, TN, 1975. 23 pp., illus. Paper covers. $2.50.

Valuable information on revolving cylinder rifles, from the earliest matchlock forms to the latest models of Colt and Remington.

Rifle Guide, by Sam Fadala, Stoeger Publishing Co., S. Hackensack, NJ, 1993. 288 pp., illus. Paper covers. $16.95.

This comprehensive, fact-filled book beckons to both the seasoned rifleman as well as the novice shooter.

The Rifle in America, by Philip B. Sharpe, Wolfe Publishing Co., Prescott, AZ, 1988. 641 pp., illus. $59.00.

A limited edition reprint. A marvelous volume packed with information for the man who is interested in rifles, from the man whose life was guns.

The Rifle: Its Development for Big-Game Hunting, by S.R. Truesdell, Safari Press, Huntington Beach, CA, 1992. 274 pp., illus. $35.00.

The full story of the development of the big-game rifle from 1834-1946.

Rifleman's Handbook: A Shooter's Guide to Rifles, Reloading & Results, by Rick Jamison, NRA Publications, Washington, DC, 1990. 303 pp., illus. $21.95.

Helpful tips on precision reloading, how to squeeze incredible accuracy out of an "everyday" rifle, etc.

Riflesmithing, The Gun Digest Book of, by Jack Mitchell, DBI Books, Inc., Northbrook, IL, 1982. 256 pp., illus. Paper covers. $15.95.

Covers tools, techniques, designs, finishing wood and metal, custom alterations.

Rifles of the World, by John Walter, DBI Books, Inc., Northbrook, IL, 1993. 320 pp., illus. Paper covers. $20.95.

Compiled as a companion volume to *Pistols of the World*, this brand new reference work covers all centerfire military and commercial rifles produced from the perfection of the metal-case cartridge in the 1870's to the present time.

Ned H. Roberts and the Schuetzen Rifle, edited by Gerald O. Kelver, Brighton, CO, 1982. 99 pp., illus. $15.00.

A compilation of the writings of Major Ned H. Roberts which appeared in various gun magazines.

***The Ruger 10/22,** by William E. Workman, Krause Publications, Iola, WI, 1994. 304 pp., illus. Paper covers. $19.95.

Learn all about the most popular, best-selling and perhaps best-built 22 caliber semi-automatic rifles of all time.

Schuetzen Rifles, History and Loading, by Gerald O. Kelver, Gerald O. Kelver, Publisher, Brighton, CO, 1972. Illus. $15.00.

Reference work on these rifles, their bullets, loading, telescopic sights, accuracy, etc. A limited, numbered ed.

Semi-Auto Rifles: Data and Comment, edited by Robert W. Hunnicutt, The National Rifle Association, Washington, DC, 1988. 156 pp., illus. Paper covers. $15.95.

A book for those who find military-style self-loading rifles interesting for their history, intriguing for the engineering that goes into their design, and a pleasure to shoot.

***Shooting the Blackpowder Cartridge Rifle,** by Paul A. Matthews, Wolfe Publishing Co., Prescott, AZ, 1994. 129 pp., illus. Paper covers. $22.50.

A general discourse on shooting the blackpowder cartridge rifle and the procedure required to make a particular rifle perform.

Single-Shot Actions, Their Design and Construction, by Frank and Mark Delisse, de Haas Books, Orange City, IA 1991. 247 pp., illus. $35.00.

Covers the best single shot rifles of the past plus a potpourri of modern single shot rifle actions.

Single-Shot Rifle Finale, by James Grant, Wolfe Publishing Co., Prescott, AZ, 1992. 556 pp., illus. $36.00.

The master's 5th book on the subject and his best.

Single Shot Rifles and Actions, by Frank de Haas, Orange City, IA, 1990. 352 pp., illus. Soft covers. $25.00.

The definitive book on over 60 single shot rifles and actions.

Sixty Years of Rifles, by Paul A. Matthews, Wolfe Publishing Co., Prescott, AZ, 1991. 224 pp., illus. $19.50.

About rifles and the author's experience and love affair with shooting and hunting.

S.L.R.—Australia's F.N. F.A.L. by Ian Skennerton and David Balmer, I.D.S.A. Books, Piqua, OH, 1989. 124 pp., 100 illus. Paper covers. $19.50.

Small Arms Identification Series, No. 2—.303 Rifle, No. 4 Marks I, & I*, Marks 1/2, 1/3 & 2, by Ian Skennerton, I.D.S.A. Books, Piqua, OH, 1994. 48 pp. $9.50.

Small Arms Identification Series, No. 3—9mm Austen Mk I & 9mm Owen Mk I Sub-Machine Guns, by Ian Skennerton, I.D.S.A. Books, Piqua, OH, 1994. 48 pp. $9.50.

Small Arms Identification Series, No. 4—.303 Rifle, No. 5 Mk I, by Ian Skennerton, I.D.S.A. Books, Piqua, OH, 1994. 48 pp. $9.50.

Small Arms Identification Series, No. 5—.303-in. Bren Light Machine Gun, by Ian Skennerton, I.D.S.A. Books, Piqua, OH, 1994. 48 pp. $9.50.

Small Arms Series, No. 1 DeLisle's Commando Carbine, by Ian Skennerton, I.D.S.A. Books, Piqua, OH, 1981. 32 pp., 24 illus. $9.00.

Small Arms Identification Series, No. 1—.303 Rifle, No. 1 S.M.L.E. Marks III and III*, by Ian Skennerton, I.D.S.A. Books, Piqua, OH, 1981. 48 pp. $9.50.

The Springfield Rifle M1903, M1903A1, M1903A3, M1903A4, Desert Publications, Cornville, AZ, 1982. 100 pp., illus. Paper covers. $12.00.

Covers every aspect of disassembly and assembly, inspection, repair and maintenance.

The Sturm, Ruger 10/22 Rifle and .44 Magnum Carbine, by Duncan Long, Paladin Press, Boulder, CO, 1988. 108 pp., illus. Paper covers. $12.00.

An in-depth look at both weapons detailing the elegant simplicity of the Ruger design. Offers specifications, troubleshooting procedures and ammunition recommendations.

Successful Rifle Shooting, by David Parish, Trafalgar Square, N. Pomfret, VT, 1993. 250 pp., illus. $39.95.

For the beginner and advanced shooter as well. Each position and firing the shot are closely examined as is each stage of entry and participation in competition.

To the Dreams of Youth: The .22 Caliber Single Shot Winchester Rifle, by Herbert Houze, Krause Publications, Iola, WI, 1993. 208 pp., illus. $34.95.

A thoroughly researched history of the 22-caliber Winchester single shot rifle, including interesting photographs.

U.S. Marine Corps AR15/M16 A2 Manual, reprinted by Desert Publications, El Dorado, AZ, 1993. 262 pp., illus. Paper covers. $16.95.

A reprint of TM05538C-23&P/2, August, 1987. The A-2 manual for the Colt AR15/M16.

U.S. Rifle M14—From John Garand to the M21, by R. Blake Stevens, Collector Grade Publications, Inc., Toronto, Canada, revised second edition, 1991. 350 pp., illus. $49.50.

A classic, in-depth examination of the development, manufacture and fielding of the last wood-and-metal ("lock, stock, and barrel") battle rifle to be issued to U.S. troops.

War Baby!: The U.S. Caliber 30 Carbine, Volume I, by Larry Ruth, Collector Grade Publications, Toronto, Canada, 1992. 512 pp., illus. $69.95.

Volume 1 of the in-depth story of the phenomenally popular U.S. caliber 30 carbine. Concentrates on design and production of the military 30 carbine during World War II.

War Baby Comes Home: The U.S. Caliber 30 Carbine, Volume 2, by Larry Ruth, Collector Grade Pulications, Toronto, Canada, 1993. 386 pp., illus. $49.95.

The triumphant competion of Larry Ruth's two-volume in-depth series on the most popular U.S. military small arm in history.

The Winchester Model 94: The First 100 Years, by Robert C. Renneberg, Krause Publications, Iola, WI, 1991. 207 pp., illus. $34.95.

Covers the design and evolution from the early years up to today.

SHOTGUNS

Advanced Combat Shotgun: The Stress Fire Concept, by Massad Ayoob, Police Bookshelf, Concord, NH, 1993. 197 pp., illus. Paper covers. $9.95.

Advanced combat shotgun fighting for police.

The American Shotgun, by Charles Askins, Wolfe Publishing Co., Prescott, AZ, 1988. 321 pp., illus. $39.00.

A limited edition reprint. Askins covers shotguns and patterning extremely well.

The American Shotgun, by David F. Butler, edited by C. Kenneth Ramage, Lyman Publications, Middlefield, CT, 1973. 243 pp., illus. Paper covers. $14.95.

A comprehensive history of the American smoothbore's evolution from Colonial times to the present day.

American Shotgun Design and Performance, by L.R. Wallack, Winchester Press, Piscataway, NJ, 1977. 184 pp., illus. $16.95.

An expert lucidly recounts the history and development of American shotguns.

The American Single Barrel Trap Gun, by Frank F. Conley, Frank F. Conley, Carmel Valley, CA, 1989. 241 pp., illus. $39.95.

History, serial numbers, collecting and how they were made. Covers Baker, Fox, Ithaca, Levefer, Meriden, Parker, L.C. Smith, etc.

Best Guns, by Michael McIntosh, Countrysport, Inc., Traverse City, MI, 1989. 288 pp., illus. $39.50.

Devoted to the best shotguns ever made in the United States and the best presently being made in the world.

The Better Shot, by Ken Davies, Quiller Press, London, England, 1992. 136 pp., illus. $39.95.

Step-by-step shotgun technique with Holland and Holland.

Black Powder Hobby Gunsmithing, by Sam Fadala and Dale Storey, DBI Books, Inc., Northbrook, IL, 1994. 256 pp., illus. Paper covers. $17.95.

A how-to guide for gunsmithing blackpowder pistols, rifles and shotguns from two men at the top of their respective fields.

The British Shotgun, Volume 1, 1850-1870, by I.M. Crudington and D.J. Baker, Barrie & Jenkins, London, England, 1979. 256 pp., illus. $59.95.

An attempt to trace, as accurately as is now possible, the evolution of the shotgun during its formative years in Great Britain.

The British Shotgun, Volume 2, 1871-1890, by I.M. Crudginton and D.J. Baker, Ashford Press, Southampton, England, 1989. 250 pp., illus. $59.95.

The second volume of a definitive work on the evolution and manufacture of the British shotgun.

Clay Pigeon Shooting for Beginners and Enthusiasts, by John King, The Sportsman's Press, London, England, 1991. 94 pp., illus. $24.95.

John King has devised this splendid guide to clay pigeon shooting in the same direct style in which he teaches at his popular Barbury Shooting School near Swindon.

Clay Shooting, by Peter Croft, Ward Lock, London, England, 1990. 160 pp., illus, $29.95.

A complete guide to Skeet, trap and sporting shooting.

Clay Target Handbook by Jerry Meyer, Lyons & Buford, Publisher, New York, NY, 1993. 182 pp., illus. $22.95.

Contains in-depth, how-to-do-it information on trap, Skeet, sporting clays, international trap, international Skeet and clay target games played around the country.

Clay Target Shooting, by Paul Bentley, A&C Black, London, England, 1987. 144 pp., illus. $25.00.

Practical book on clay target shooting written by a very successful international competitor, providing valuable professional advice and instruction for shooters of all disciplines.

A Collector's Guide to United States Combat Shotguns, by Bruce N. Canfield, Andrew Mowbray Inc., Publishers, Lincoln, RI, 1993. 184 pp., illus. Paper covers. $24.00.

Full coverage of the combat shotgun, from the earliest examples to the Gulf War and beyond.

The Complete Clay Shot, by Mike Barnes, Trafalgar Square, N. Pomfret, VT, 1993. 192 pp., illus. $39.95.

The latest compendium on the clay sports by Mike Barnes, a well-known figure in shotgunning in the U.S. and England.

Cradock on Shotguns, by Chris Cradock, Banford Press, London, England, 1989. 200 pp., illus. $45.00.

A definitive work on the shotgun by a British expert on shotguns.

The Defensive Shotgun, by Louis Awerbuck, S.W.A.T. Publications, Cornville, AZ, 1989. 77 pp., illus. Soft covers. $12.95.

SHOTGUNS (cont.)

Cuts through the myths concerning the shotgun and its attendant ballistic effects.

The Double Shotgun, by Don Zutz, Winchester Press, Piscataway, NJ, 1985. 304 pp., illus. $20.95.

Revised, updated, expanded edition of the history and development of the world's classic sporting firearms.

Ed Scherer on Sporting Clays, by Ed Scherer, Ed Scherer, Elk Grove, WI, 1993. 200 pp., illus. Paper covers. $29.95.

Covers footwork, gun fit, master eye checks, recoil reduction, noise abatement, eye and ear protection, league shooting, shot sizes and chokes.

Exploded Long Gun Drawings, The Gun Digest Book of, edited by Harold A. Murtz, DBI Books, Inc., Northbrook, IL. 512 pp., illus. Paper covers. $20.95.

Containing almost 500 rifle and shotgun exploded drawings. An invaluable aid to both professionals and hobbyists.

Field, Cover and Trap Shooting, by Adam H. Bogardus, Wolfe Publishing Co., Prescott, AZ, 1988. 446 pp., illus. $45.00.

A limited edition reprint. Hints for skilled marksmen as well as young sportsmen. Includes haunts and habits of game birds and waterfowl.

Finding the Extra Target, by Coach John R. Linn & Stephen A. Blumenthal, Shotgun Sports, Inc., Auburn, CA, 1989. 126 pp., illus. Paper covers. $14.95.

The ultimate training guide for all the clay target sports.

Firearms Assembly/Disassembly, Part V: Shotguns, Revised Edition, The Gun Digest Book of, by J.B. Wood, DBI Books, Inc., Northbrook, IL, 1992. 480 pp., illus. Paper covers. $18.95.

Covers 46 popular shotguns plus over 250 variants. The most comprehensive and professional presentation available to either hobbyist or gunsmith.

*****A.H. Fox "The Finest Gun in the World",** revised and enlarged edition, by Michael McIntosh, Countrysport, Inc., New Albany, OH, 1995. 408 pp., illus. $49.00.

The first detailed history of one of America's finest shotguns.

Fucili D'Autore (The Best Guns), by Marco E. Nobili, London Guns, Ltd., Santa Barbara, CA, 1992. 845 pp., illus. $125.00.

An exhaustive study on Italian luxury-grade shotguns and their makers, with information on European makers as well. Text in English and Italian.

The Golden Age of Shotgunning, by Bob Hinman, Wolfe Publishing Co., Inc., Prescott, AZ, 1982. $17.95.

A valuable history of the late 1800s detailing that fabulous period of development in shotguns, shotshells and shotgunning.

Hartman on Skeet, By Barney Hartman, Stackpole Books, Harrisburg, PA, 1973. 143 pp., illus. $19.95.

A definitive book on Skeet shooting by a pro.

The Ithaca Gun Company From the Beginning, by Walter Claude Snyder, Cook & Uline Publishing Co., Spencerport, NY, 1991. 256 pp., illus. $59.95.

The entire family of Ithaca Gun Company products is described together with a photo gallery section containing many previously unpublished photographs of the gun makers.

L.C. Smith Shotguns, by Lt. Col. William S. Brophy, The Gun Room Press, Highland Park, NJ, 1979. 244 pp., illus. $35.00.

The first work on this very important American gun and manufacturing company.

*****The Little Trapshooting Book,** by Frank Little, Shotgun Sports Magazine, Auburn, CA, 1994. 168 pp., illus. Paper covers. $19.95.

Packed with know-how from one of the greatest trapshooters of all time.

A Manual of Clayshooting, by Chris Cradock, Hippocrene Books, Inc., New York, NY, 1983. 192 pp., illus. $39.95.

Covers everything from building a range to buying a shotgun, with lots of illus. & dia.

The Mysteries of Shotgun Patterns, by George G. Oberfell and Charles E. Thompson, Oklahoma State University Press, Stillwater, OK, 1982. 164 pp., illus. Paper covers. $25.00.

Shotgun ballistics for the hunter in non-technical language.

The Orvis Wing-Shooting Handbook, by Bruce Bowlen, Nick Lyons Books, New York, NY, 1985. 83 pp., illus. Paper covers. $10.95.

Proven techniques for better shotgunning.

Police Shotgun Manual, by Bill Clede, Stackpole Books, Harrisburg, PA, 1986. 128 pp., illus. $18.95.

Latest shotgun techniques for tough situations.

*****Positive Shooting,** by Michael Yardley, Safari Press, Huntington Beach, CA, 1994. 160 pp., illus. $30.00.

An authoritative guide in which the many aspects of good shooting are covered.

Purdey's, the Guns and the Family, by Richard Beaumont, David and Charles, Pomfert, VT, 1984. 248 pp., illus. $39.95.

Records the history of the Purdey family from 1814 to today, how the guns were and are built and daily functioning of the factory.

Reloading for Shotgunners, 3rd Edition, by Edward A. Matunas, DBI Books, Inc., Northbrook, IL, 1993. 288 pp., illus. Paper covers. $16.95.

Expanded reloading tables with over 2,000 loads. Bushing charts for every major press and component maker. All new presentation on all aspects of shotshell reloading by one of the top experts in the field.

Robert Churchill's Game Shooting, edited by MacDonald Hastings, Countrysport Press, Traverse City, MI, 1990. 252 pp., illus. $29.50.

A new revised edition of the definitive book on the Churchill method of instinctive wingshooting for game and Sporting Clays.

75 Years with the Shotgun, by C.T. (Buck) Buckman, Valley, Publ., Fresno, CA, 1974. 141 pp., illus. $10.00.

An expert hunter and trapshooter shares experiences of a lifetime.

Scherer on Skeet 2, by Ed Scherer, Ed. Scherer, Waukesha, WI, 1993. 121 pp., illus. Paper covers. $19.95.

A "teaching" book, featuring the eight Skeet stations plus shootoff doubles.

Shooting at Clays, by Alan Jarrett, Stanley Paul, London, England, 1991. 176 pp., illus. $34.95.

This book unravels the complexities of clay pigeon shooting.

The Shooting Field with Holland & Holland, by Peter King, Quiller Press, London, England, new & enlarged edition, 1990. 184 pp., illus. $49.95.

The story of a company which has produced excellence in all aspects of gunmaking.

The Shotgun in Combat, by Tony Lesce, Desert Publications, Cornville, AZ, 1979. 148 pp., illus. Paper covers. $10.00.

A history of the shotgun and its use in combat.

Shotgun Digest, 4th Edition, edited by Jack Lewis, DBI Books, Inc., Northbrook, IL, 1993. 256 pp., illus. Paper covers. $17.95.

The all-new edition looking at what's happening with shotguns and shotgunning today.

Shotgun Gunsmithing, The Gun Digest Book of, by Ralph Walker, DBI Books, Inc., Northbrook, IL, 1983. 256 pp., illus. Paper covers. $15.95.

The principles and practices of repairing, individualizing and accurizing modern shotguns by one of the world's premier shotgun gunsmiths.

Shotgun Stuff, by Don Zutz, Shotgun Sports, Inc., Auburn, CA, 1991. 172 pp., illus. Paper covers. $19.95.

This book gives shotgunners all the "stuff" they need to achieve better performance and get more enjoyment from their favorite smoothbore.

Shotgunner's Notebook: The Advice and Reflections of a Wingshooter, by Gene Hill, Countrysport Press, Traverse City, MI, 1990. 192 pp., illus. $24.50.

Covers the shooting, the guns and the miscellany of the sport.

Shotgunning: The Art and the Science, by Bob Brister, Winchester Press, Piscataway, NJ, 1976. 321 pp., illus. $18.95.

Hundreds of specific tips and truly novel techniques to improve the field and target shooting of every shotgunner.

Shotgunning Trends in Transition, by Don Zutz, Wolfe Publishing Co., Prescott, AZ, 1990. 314 pp., illus. $29.50.

This book updates American shotgunning from post WWII to present.

Shotguns and Cartridges for Game and Clays, by Gough Thomas, edited by Nigel Brown, A & C Black, Ltd., Cambs, England, 1989. 256 pp., illus. Soft covers. $24.95.

Gough Thomas' well-known and respected book for game and clay pigeon shooters in a thoroughly up-dated edition.

Sidelocks & Boxlocks, by Geoffrey Boothroyd, Sand Lake Press, Amity, OR, 1991. 271 pp., illus. $29.95.

The story of the classic British shotgun.

*****Spanish Best: The Fine Shotguns of Spain,** by Terry Wieland, Countrysport, Inc., Traverse City, MI, 1994. 264 pp., illus. $49.50.

A practical source of information for owners of Spanish shotguns and a guide for those considering buying a used shotgun.

The Sporting Clay Handbook, by Jerry Meyer, Lyons and Burford Publishers, New York, NY, 1990. 140 pp., illus. Soft covers. $15.95.

Introduction to the fastest growing, and most exciting, gun game in America.

Sporting Clays, The Gun Digest Book of, by Jack Lewis, DBI Books, Inc., Northbrook, IL, 1991. 224 pp., illus. Paper covers. $17.95.

A superb introduction to the fastest growing gun game in America.

Sporting Clays, by Michael Pearce, Stackpole Books, Harrisburg, PA, 1991. 192 pp., illus. $16.95.

Expert techniques for every kind of clays course.

The Story of the Sporting Gun, by Ranulf Rayner, Trafalgar Square, North Pomfret, VT, 1991. 96 pp., illustrated. $75.00.

This magnificent volume traces the story of game shooting from the early development of the shotgun to the present day.

*****Successful Clay Pigeon Shooting,** compiled by T. Hoare, Trafalgar Square, N. Pomfret, VT, 1993. 176 pp., illus. $39.95.

This comprehensive guide has been written by ten leading personalities for all aspiring clay pigeon shooters.

*****Taking More Birds,** by Dan Carlisle & Dolph Adams, Lyons & Burford, New York, NY, 1993. 120 pp., illus. $19.95.

A practical guide to greater success at sporting clays and wing shooting.

*****Trap & Skeet Shooting, 3rd Edition,** edited by Chris Christain, DBI Books, Inc., Northbrook, IL, 1994. 288 pp., illus. Paper covers. $17.95.

A detailed look at the contemporary world of trap, Skeet and Sporting Clays.

*****Turkey Hunter's Digest, Revised Edition,** by Dwain Bland, DBI Books, Inc., Northbrook, IL, 1994. 256 pp., illus. Paper covers. $17.95.

Presents no-nonsense approach to hunting all five sub-species of the North American wild turkey.

U.S. Shotguns, All Types, reprint of TM9-285, Desert Publications, Cornville, AZ, 1987. 257 pp., illus. Paper covers. $9.95.

Covers operation, assembly and disassembly of nine shotguns used by the U.S. armed forces.

U.S. Winchester Trench and Riot Guns and Other U.S. Military Combat Shotguns, by Joe Poyer, North Cape Publications, Tustin, CA, 1992. 124 pp., illus. Paper covers. $15.95.

A detailed history of the use of military shotguns, and the acquisition procedures used by the U.S. Army's Ordnance Department in both World Wars.

The Winchester Model Twelve, by George Madis, David Madis, Dallas, TX, 1984. 176 pp., illus. $19.95.

A definitive work on this famous American shotgun.

The Winchester Model 42, by Ned Schwing, Krause Pub., Iola, WI, 1990. 159 pp., illus. $39.95.

Behind-the-scenes story of the model 42's invention and its early development. Production totals and manufacturing dates; reference work.

Winchester's Finest, the Model 21, by Ned Schwing, Krause Publicatons, Inc., Iola, WI, 1990. 360 pp., illus. $49.95.

The classic beauty and the interesting history of the Model 21 Winchester shotgun.

The World's Fighting Shotguns, by Thomas F. Swearengen, T. B. N. Enterprises, Alexandria, VA, 1979. 500 pp., illus. $34.95.

The complete military and police reference work from the shotgun's inception to date, with up-to-date developments.

ARMS ASSOCIATIONS

UNITED STATES

ALABAMA
Alabama Gun Collectors Assn.
Secretary, P.O. Box 70965, Tuscaloosa, AL 35407

ALASKA
Alaska Gun Collectors Assn., Inc.
C.W. Floyd, Pres., 5240 Little Tree, Anchorage, AK 99507

ARIZONA
Arizona Arms Assn.
Don DeBusk, President, 4837 Bryce Ave., Glendale, AZ 85301

CALIFORNIA
California Cartridge Collectors Assn.
Rick Montgomery, 1729 Christina, Stockton, CA 95204
California Waterfowl Assn.
4630 Northgate Blvd., #150, Sacramento, CA 95834
Greater Calif. Arms & Collectors Assn.
Donald L. Bullock, 8291 Carburton St., Long Beach, CA 90808-3302
Los Angeles Gun Ctg. Collectors Assn.
F.H. Ruffra, 20810 Amie Ave., Apt. #9, Torrance, CA 90503
Stock Gun Players Assn.
6038 Appian Way, Long Beach, CA, 90803

COLORADO
Colorado Gun Collectors Assn.
L.E.(Bud) Greenwald, 2553 S. Quitman St., Denver, CO 80219/303-935-3850
Rocky Mountain Cartridge Collectors Assn.
George Blakslee, 15072 E. Mississippi Ave. #1, Aurora, CO 80012

CONNECTICUT
Ye Connecticut Gun Guild, Inc.
Dick Fraser, P.O. Box 425, Windsor, CT 06095

FLORIDA
Unified Sportsmen of Florida
P.O. Box 6565, Tallahassee, FL 32314

GEORGIA
Georgia Arms Collectors Assn., Inc.
Michael Kindberg, President, P.O. Box 277, Alpharetta, GA 30239-0277

ILLINOIS
Illinois State Rifle Assn.
P.O. Box 637, Chatsworth, IL 60921
Mississippi Valley Gun & Cartridge Coll. Assn.
Bob Filbert, P.O. Box 61, Port Byron, IL 61275/309-523-2593
Sauk Trail Gun Collectors
Gordell M. Matson, P.O. Box 1113, Milan, IL 61264
Wabash Valley Gun Collectors Assn., Inc.
Roger L. Dorsett, 2601 Willow Rd., Urbana, IL 61801/217-284-7302

INDIANA
Indiana State Rifle & Pistol Assn.
Thos. Glancy, P.O. Box 552, Chesterton, IN 46304
Southern Indiana Gun Collectors Assn., Inc.
Sheila McClary, 309 W. Monroe St., Boonville, IN 47601/812-897-3742

IOWA
Beaver Creek Plainsmen Inc.
Steve Murphy, Secy., P.O. Box 298, Bondurant, IA 50035
Central States Gun Collectors Assn.
Avery Giles, 1104 S. 1st Ave., Marshtown, IA 50158

KANSAS
Kansas Cartridge Collectors Assn.
Bob Linder, Box 84, Plainville, KS 67663

KENTUCKY
Kentuckiana Arms Collectors Assn.
Charles Billips, President, Box 1776, Louisville, KY 40201
Kentucky Gun Collectors Assn., Inc.
Ruth Johnson, Box 64, Owensboro, KY 42302/502-729-4197

LOUISIANA
Washitaw River Renegades
Sandra Rushing, P.O. Box 256, Main St., Grayson, LA 71435

MARYLAND
Baltimore Antique Arms Assn.
Mr. Cillo, 1034 Main St., Darlington, MD 21304

MASSACHUSETTS
Bay Colony Weapons Collectors, Inc.
John Brandt, Box 111, Hingham, MA 02043
Massachusetts Arms Collectors
Bruce E. Skinner, P.O. Box 31, No. Carver, MA 02355/508-866-5259

MICHIGAN
Association for the Study and Research of .22 Caliber Rimfire Cartridges
George Kass, 4512 Nakoma Dr., Okemos, MI 48864

MINNESOTA
Sioux Empire Cartridge Collectors Assn.
Bob Cameron, 14597 Glendale Ave. SE, Prior Lake, MN 55372

MISSISSIPPI
Mississippi Gun Collectors Assn.
Jack E. Swinney, P.O. Box 16323, Hattiesburg, MS 39402

MISSOURI
Greater St. Louis Cartridge Collectors Assn.
Don MacChesney, 145 East Maple, Kirkwood, MO 63122
Mineral Belt Gun Collectors Assn.
D.F. Saunders, 1110 Cleveland Ave., Monett, MO 65708
Missouri Valley Arms Collectors Assn., Inc.
L.P Brammer II, Membership Secy., P.O. Box 33033, Kansas City, MO 64114

MONTANA
Montana Arms Collectors Assn.
Lewis E. Yearout, 308 Riverview Dr. East, Great Falls, MT 59404

NEBRASKA
Nebraska Cartridge Collectors Club
Gary Muckel, 6531 Carlsbad Dr., Lincoln, NE 68510

NEW HAMPSHIRE
New Hampshire Arms Collectors, Inc.
Frank H. Galeucia, Rt. 28, Box 44, Windham, NH 03087

NEW JERSEY
Englishtown Benchrest Shooters Assn.
Michael Toth, 64 Cooke Ave., Carteret, NJ 07008
Jersey Shore Antique Arms Collectors
Joe Sisia, P.O. Box 100, Bayville, NJ 08721-1950
New Jersey Arms Collectors Club, Inc.
Angus Laidlaw, President, 230 Valley Rd., Montclair, NJ 07042/201-746-0939

NEW YORK
Iroquois Arms Collectors Assn.
Bonnie Robinson, Show Secy., P.O. Box 142, Ransomville, NY 14131/716-791-4096
Mid-State Arms Coll. & Shooters Club
Jack Ackerman, 24 S. Mountain Terr., Binghamton, NY 13903

NORTH CAROLINA
North Carolina Gun Collectors Assn.
Jerry Ledford, 3231-7th St. Dr. NE, Hickory, NC 28601

OHIO
Ohio Gun Collectors Assn.
P.O. Box 9007, Maumee, OH 43537-9007/419-897-0861;Fax:419-897-0860
Shotshell Historical and Collectors Society
Madeline Bruemmer, 3886 Dawley Club, Ravenna, OH 44266
The Stark Gun Collectors, Inc.
William I. Gann, 5666 Waynesburg Dr., Waynesburg, OH 44688

OKLAHOMA
Indian Territory Gun Collector's Assn.
P.O. Box 4491, Tulsa, OK 74159/918-745-9141

OREGON
Oregon Arms Collectors Assn., Inc.
Phil Bailey, P.O. Box 13000-A, Portland, OR 97213
Oregon Cartridge Collectors Assn.
Gale Stockton, 52 N.W. 2nd, Gresham, OR 97030

PENNSYLVANIA
Presque Isle Gun Collectors Assn.
James Welch, 156 E. 37 St., Erie, PA 16504

SOUTH CAROLINA
Belton Gun Club, Inc.
J.K. Phillips, 195 Phillips Dr., Belton, SC 29627
Gun Owners of South Carolina
Membership Div.: William Strozier, Secretary, P.O. Box 70, Johns Island, SC 29457-0070/803-762-3240;Fax:803-795-0711

SOUTH DAKOTA
Dakota Territory Gun Coll. Assn., Inc.
Curt Carter, Castlewood, SD 57223

TENNESSEE
Smoky Mountain Gun Coll. Assn., Inc.
Hugh W. Yabro, President, P.O. Box 23225, Knoxville, TN 37933
Tennessee Gun Collectors Assn., Inc.
M.H. Parks, 3556 Pleasant Valley Rd., Nashville, TN 37204-3419

TEXAS
Houston Gun Collectors Assn., Inc.
P.O. Box 741429, Houston, TX 77274-1429
Texas Cartridge Collectors Assn., Inc.
Robert Mellichamp, Memb. Contact, 907 Shirkmere, Houston, TX 77008/713-869-0558
Texas Gun Collectors Assn.
Bob Eder, Pres., P.O. Box 12067/915-584-8183
Texas State Rifle Assn.
4600 Greenville Ave., #292, Dallas, TX 75206

WASHINGTON
Association of Cartridge Collectors on the Pacific Northwest
Robert Jardin, 14214 Meadowlark Drive KPN, Gig Harbor, WA 98329
Washington Arms Collectors, Inc.
J. Dennis Cook, P.O. Box 7335, Tacoma, WA 98407/206-752-2268

WISCONSIN
Great Lakes Arms Collectors Assn., Inc.
Edward C. Warnke, 2913 Woodridge Lane, Waukesha, WI 53188
Wisconsin Gun Collectors Assn., Inc.
Lulita Zellmer, P.O. Box 181, Sussex, WI 53089

WYOMING
Wyoming Weapons Collectors
P.O. Box 284, Laramie, WY 82070/307-745-4652 or 745-9530

NATIONAL ORGANIZATIONS

Amateur Trapshooting Assn.
601 W. National Rd., Vandalia, OH 45377
American Airgun Field Target Assn.
5911 Cherokee Ave., Tampa, FL 33604
American Coon Hunters Assn.
Opal Johnston, P.O. Cadet, Route 1, Box 492, Old Mines, MO 63630
American Custom Gunmakers Guild
Jan Billeb, Exec. Director, P.O. Box 812, Burlington, IA 52601-0812/319-752-6114 (Phone or Fax)
American Defense Preparedness Assn.
Two Colonial Place, 2101 Wilson Blvd., Suite 400, Arlington, VA 22201-3061
American Paintball League
P.O. Box 3561, Johnson City, TN 37602/800-541-9169
American Pistolsmiths Guild
Alex B. Hamilton, Pres., 1449 Blue Crest Lane, San Antonio, TX 78232/210-494-3063

ARMS ASSOCIATIONS IN AMERICA AND ABROAD

American Police Pistol & Rifle Assn.
3801 Biscayne Blvd., Miami, FL 33137
American Single Shot Rifle Assn.
Gary Staup, Secy., 709 Carolyn Dr., Delphos, OH 45833/419-692-3866
American Society of Arms Collectors
George E. Weatherly, P.O. Box 2567, Waxahachie, TX 75165
American Tactical Shooting Assn.(A.T.S.A.)
c/o Charles A. Davis. P.O. Box 12265, Silver Spring, MD 20908/301-924-1373;Fax:301-924-3854
Association of Firearm and Toolmark Examiners
Eugenia A. Bell, Secy., 7857 Esterel Dr., LaJolla, CA 92037; Membership Secy., Andrew B. Hart, 80 Mountain View Ave., Rensselaer, NY 12144
Boone & Crockett Club
250 Station Dr., Missoula, MT 59801-2753
B.R.I.T. (British Research and Investigative Team)
Pete de Coux, 235 Oak St., Butler, PA 16001/412-282-3426
Browning Collectors Assn.
Bobbie Hamit, P.O. Box 526, Aurora, NE 68818/402-694-6602
The Cast Bullet Assn., Inc.
Ralland J. Fortier, Membership Director, 4103 Foxcraft Dr., Traverse City, MI 49684
Citizens Committee for the Right to Keep and Bear Arms
Natl. Hq., Liberty Park, 12500 NE Tenth Pl., Bellevue, WA 98005
Colt Collectors Assn.
25000 Highland Way, Los Gatos, CA 95030
Ducks Unlimited, Inc.
One Waterfowl Way, Memphis, TN 38120
Fifty Caliber Shooters Assn.
11469 Olive St. Rd., Suite 50, St. Louis, MO 63141/601-475-7545;Fax:601-475-0452
Firearms Coalition
Box 6537, Silver Spring, MD 20906/301-871-3006
Firearms Engravers Guild of America
Robert Evans, Secy., 332 Vine St., Oregon City, OR 97045
Foundation for North American Wild Sheep
720 Allen Ave., Cody, WY 82414
Garand Collectors Assn.
P.O. Box 181, Richmond, KY 40475
Golden Eagle Collectors Assn.
Chris Showler, 11144 Slate Creek Rd., Grass Valley, CA 95945
Gun Owners of America
8001 Forbes Place, Suite 102, Springfield, VA 22151/703-321-8585
Handgun Hunters International
J.D. Jones, Director, P.O. Box 357 MAG, Bloomingdale, OH 43910
Harrington & Richardson Gun Coll. Assn.
George L. Cardet, 330 S.W. 27th Ave., Suite 603, Miami, FL 33135
Hopkins & Allen Arms & Memorabilia Society (HAAMS)
1309 Pamela Circle, Delphos, OH 45833
International Ammunition Association, Inc.
8 Hillock Lane, Chadds Ford, PA 19317/610-358-1258;Fax:610-358-1560
International Benchrest Shooters
Joan Borden, RD 1, Box 244A, Tunkhannock, PA 18657
International Blackpowder Hunting Assn.
P.O. Box 1180, Glenrock, WY 82637/307-436-9817
IHMSA (Intl. Handgun Metallic Silhouette Assn.)
Frank Scotto, P.O. Box 5038, Meriden, CT 06450
International Handloader Assn.
6471 Airpark Dr., Prescott, AZ 86301
International Paintball Field Operators Assn.
15507 S. Normandie Ave. #487, Gardena, CA 90247/310-323-1021
IPPA (International Paintball Players Assn.)
P.O. Box 26669, San Diego, CA 92196-0669/619-695-8882;Fax:619-695-6909
Jews for the Preservation of Firearms Ownership (JPFO) 501(c)(3)
2872 S. Wentworth Ave., Milwaukee, WI 53207/414-769-0760;Fax:414-483-8435
The Mannlicher Collectors Assn.
Rev. Don L. Henry, Secy., P.O. Box 7144, Salem, OR 97303
Marlin Firearms Collectors Assn., Ltd.
Dick Paterson, Secy., 407 Lincoln Bldg., 44 Main St., Champaign, IL 61820
Miniature Arms Collectors/Makers Society, Ltd.
Ralph Koebbeman, Pres., 4910 Kilburn Ave., Rockford, IL 61101/815-964-2569
M1 Carbine Collectors Assn. (M1-CCA)
P.O. Box 4895, Stateline, NV 89449
National Association of Buckskinners (NAB)
Tim Pray, P.O. Box 29307, Thornton, CO 80229
The National Association of Derringer Collectors
P.O. Box 20572, San Jose, CA 95160
National Assn. of Federally Licensed Firearms Dealers
Andrew Molchan, 2455 E. Sunrise, Ft. Lauderdale, FL 33304
National Association to Keep and Bear Arms
P.O. Box 78336, Seattle, WA 98178
National Automatic Pistol Collectors Assn.
Tom Knox, P.O. Box 15738, Tower Grove Station, St. Louis, MO 63163

National Bench Rest Shooters Assn., Inc.
Pat Baggett, 2027 Buffalo, Levelland, TX 79336
National Firearms Assn.
P.O. Box 160038, Austin, TX 78716/403-439-1094; FAX: 403-439-4091
National Muzzle Loading Rifle Assn.
Box 67, Friendship, IN 47021
National Professional Paintball League (NPPL)
540 Main St., Mount Kisco, NY 10549/914-241-7400
National Reloading Manufacturers Assn.
One Centerpointe Dr., Suite 300, Lake Oswego, OR 97035
National Rifle Assn. of America
11250 Waples Mill Rd., Fairfax, VA 22030
National Shooting Sports Foundation, Inc.
Robert T. Delfay, President, Flintlock Ridge Office Center, 11 Mile Hill Rd., Newtown, CT 06470-2359/203-426-1320; FAX: 203-426-1087
National Skeet Shooting Assn.
Mike Hampton, Exec. Director, P.O. Box 680007, San Antonio, TX 78268-0007
National Sporting Clays Association
5931 Roft Road, San Antonio, TX 78253-9261/800-877-5338
National Wild Turkey Federation, Inc.
P.O. Box 530, Edgefield, SC 29824
North American Hunting Club
P.O. Box 3401, Minnetonka, MN 55343
North American Paintball Referees Association (NAPRA)
584 Cestaric Dr., Milpitas, CA 95035
North-South Skirmish Assn., Inc.
Stevan F. Meserve, Exec. Secretary, 507 N. Brighton Court, Sterling, VA 20164-3919
Remington Society of America
Leon W. Wier Jr., President, 8268 Lone Feather Ln., Las Vegas, NV 89123
Rocky Mountain Elk Foundation
P.O. Box 8249, Missoula, MT 59807-8249/406-523-4500;Fax:406-523-4581
Ruger Collector's Assn., Inc.
P.O. Box 240, Greens Farms, CT 06436
Safari Club International
Philip DeLone, Executive Dir., 4800 W. Gates Pass Rd., Tucson, AZ 85745/602-620-1220
Sako Collectors Assn., Inc.
Mims Reed, 1725 Woodhill Ln., Bedford, TX 76021
Second Amendment Foundation
James Madison Building, 12500 NE 10th Pl., Bellevue, WA 98005
Smith & Wesson Collectors Assn.
George Linne, 2711 Miami St., St. Louis, MO 63118
The Society of American Bayonet Collectors
P.O. Box 234, East Islip, NY 11730-0234
Southern California Schuetzen Society
Dean Lillard, 34657 Ave. E., Yucaipa, CA 92399
Sporting Arms & Ammunition Manufacturers Institute (SAAMI)
Flintlock Ridge Office Center, 11 Mile Hill Rd., Newtown, CT 06470-2359/203-426-1320; FAX: 203-426-1087
Sporting Clays of America (SCA)
Ellen McCormick, Director of Membership Services, 9 Mott Ave., Suite 103, Norwalk, CT 06850/203-831-8483; FAX: 203-831-8497
The Thompson/Center Assn.
Joe Wright, President, Box 792, Northboro, MA 01532/508-845-6960
U.S. Practical Shooting Assn./IPSC
Marilyn Stanford, P.O. Box 811, Sedro Woolley, WA 98284/360-855-2245
U.S. Revolver Assn.
Brian J. Barer, 40 Larchmont Ave., Taunton, MA 02780/508-824-4836
U.S. Shooting Team
U.S. Olympic Shooting Center, One Olympic Plaza, Colorado Springs, CO 80909/719-578-4670
The Varmint Hunters Assn., Inc.
Box 759, Pierre, SD 57501/Member Services 800-528-4868
Weatherby Collectors Assn., Inc.
P.O. Box 128, Moira, NY 12957
The Wildcatters
P.O. Box 170, Greenville, WI 54942
Winchester Arms Collectors Assn.
Richard Berg, Executive Secy., P.O. Box 6754, Great Falls, MT 59406
The Women's Shooting Sports Foundation (WSSF)
1505 Highway 6 South, Suite 101, Houston, TX 77077

ARGENTINA
Association Argentina de Colleccionistas de Armes y Municiones
Castilla de Correas No. 28, Succursal I B, 1401 Buenos Aires, Republica Argentina

AUSTRALIA
The Arms Collector's Guild of Queensland Inc.
Ian Skennerton, P.O. Box 433, Ashmore City 4214, Queensland, Australia
Australian Cartridge Collectors Assn., Inc.
Bob Bennett, 126 Landscape Dr., E. Doncaster 3109, Victoria, Australia

Sporting Shooters Assn. of Australia, Inc.
P.O. Box 2066, Kent Town, SA 5071, Australia

CANADA
ALBERTA
Canadian Historical Arms Society
P.O. Box 901, Edmonton, Alb., Canada T5J 2L8
National Firearms Assn.
Natl. Hq: P.O. Box 1779, Edmonton, Alb., Canada T5J 2P1

BRITISH COLUMBIA
The Historical Arms Collectors of B.C. (Canada)
Harry Moon, Pres., P.O. Box 50117, South Slope RPO, Burnaby, BC V5J 5G3, Canada/604-936-9141

ONTARIO
Association of Canadian Cartridge Collectors
Monica Wright, RR 1, Millgrove, ON, LOR IVO, Canada
Tri-County Antique Arms Fair
P.O. Box 122, RR #1, North Lancaster Ont., Canada K0C 1Z0

EUROPE
BELGIUM
European Cartridge Researchers Assn.
Graham Irving, 21 Rue Schaltin, 49 Spa, Belgium

CZECHOSLOVAKIA
Spolecnost Pro Studium Naboju
JUDr. Jaroslav Bubak, Sovetske Armady 1439, 26601 Beroun 2, Czechoslovakia

DENMARK
Aquila Patronsamler Club (Danish Cartridge Collectors Club)
Sten Elgaard Moler, Ulriksdalsvej 7, 4840 Nr. Alslev, Denmark

ENGLAND
Arms and Armour Society
E.J.B. Greenwood, Field House, Upper Dicker, Hailsham, East Sussex, BN27 3PY, England
Dutch Paintball Federation
Aceville Publ., Castle House 97 High Street, Colchester, Essex C01 1TH, England/011-44-206-564840
European Paintball Sports Foundation
c/o Aceville Publ., Castle House 97 High St., Colchester, Essex, C01 1TH, England
Historical Breechloading Smallarms Assn.
D.J. Penn M.A., Imperial War Museum, Lambeth Rd., London SE 1 6HZ, England.
Journal and newsletter are $13 a yr., plus surcharge for airmail.
National Rifle Assn.
(Great Britain) Bisley Camp, Brookwood, Woking Surrey GU24 OPB, England/01483.797777
United Kingdom Cartridge Club
Ian Southgate, 20 Millfield, Elmley Castle, Nr. Pershore, Worcestershire, WR10 3HR, England

FRANCE
Syndicat National de l'Arquebuserie du Commerce de l'Arme Historique
B.P. No. 3, 78110 Le Vesinet, France

GERMANY
Bund Deutscher Sportschützen e.v. (BDS)
Borsigallee 10, 53125 Bonn 1, Germany
Deutscher Schützenbund
Lahnstrasse 120, 65195 Wiesbaden, Germany

SPAIN
Asociacion Espanola de Colleccionistas de Cartuchos
Francisco Carreras Morate, Rio Tajuna 5 II B, Alcala de Henares, Madrid, Spain

SWEDEN
Scandinavian Ammunition Research Assn.
Box 107, 77622 Hedemora, Sweden

NEW ZEALAND
New Zealand Cartridge Collectors Club
Terry Castle, 70 Tiraumea Dr., Pakuranga, Auckland, New Zealand
New Zealand Deerstalkers Assn.
Michael Watt, P.O. Box 6514, Wellington, New Zealand

SOUTH AFRICA
Historical Firearms Soc. of South Africa
P.O. Box 145, 7725 Newlands, Republic of South Africa
Republic of South Africa Cartridge Collectors Assn.
Arno Klee, 20 Eugene St., Malanshof Randburg 2194, Republic of South Africa
SAGA (S.A. Gunowners' Assn.)
P.O. Box 35203, Northway 4065, Republic of South Africa

DIRECTORY OF THE ARMS TRADE

The **Product Directory** contains 53 product categories. Note that in the Product Directory, a black bullet preceeding a manufacturer's name indicates the availability of a Warranty Service Center address, which can be found on page 497.

The **Manufacturers' Directory** alphabetically lists the manufacturers with their addresses, phone numbers and FAX numbers, if available.

DIRECTORY OF THE ARMS TRADE INDEX

PRODUCT DIRECTORY 553-569

AMMUNITION, COMMERCIAL 553	GUNSMITHS, CUSTOM (See Custom Gunsmiths)
AMMUNITION, CUSTOM 553	GUNSMITHS, HANDGUN (See Pistolsmiths)
AMMUNITION, FOREIGN 553	GUNSMITH SCHOOLS 562
AMMUNITION COMPONENTS	GUNSMITH SUPPLIES, TOOLS, SERVICES 562
—BULLETS, POWDER, PRIMERS 553	HANDGUN ACCESSORIES 562
ANTIQUE ARMS DEALERS 554	HANDGUN GRIPS 563
APPRAISERS—GUNS, ETC. 554	HEARING PROTECTORS 563
AUCTIONEERS—GUNS, ETC 555	HOLSTERS AND LEATHER GOODS 563
BOOKS (Publishers and Dealers) 555	HUNTING AND CAMP GEAR, CLOTHING, ETC 563
BULLET AND CASE LUBRICANTS 555	KNIVES AND KNIFEMAKER'S SUPPLIES
BULLET SWAGE DIES AND TOOLS 555	—FACTORY AND MAIL ORDER 564
CARTRIDGES FOR COLLECTORS 555	LABELS, BOXES, CARTRIDGE HOLDERS 564
CASES, CABINETS, RACKS AND SAFES—GUN 555	LOAD TESTING AND PRODUCT TESTING
CHOKE DEVICES, RECOIL ABSORBERS	(Chronographing, Ballistic Studies) 564
AND RECOIL PADS 556	MISCELLANEOUS 564
CHRONOGRAPHS AND PRESSURE TOOLS 556	MUZZLE-LOADING GUNS, BARRELS AND EQUIP. ...565
CLEANING AND REFINISHING SUPPLIES 556	PISTOLSMITHS 565
COMPUTER SOFTWARE—BALLISTICS 556	REBORING AND RERIFLING 566
CUSTOM GUNSMITHS 557	RELOADING TOOLS AND ACCESSORIES 566
CUSTOM METALSMITHS 558	RESTS—BENCH, PORTABLE—AND ACCESSORIES .567
DECOYS 558	RIFLE BARREL MAKERS
ENGRAVERS, ENGRAVING TOOLS 558	(See also Muzzle-Loading Guns, Barrels, Equip.) ...567
GAME CALLS 559	SCOPES, MOUNTS, ACCESSORIES, OPTICAL
GUN PARTS, U.S. AND FOREIGN 559	EQUIPMENT 567
GUNS, AIR 559	SHOOTING/TRAINING SCHOOLS 568
GUNS, FOREIGN—IMPORTERS 560	SIGHTS, METALLIC 568
GUNS, FOREIGN—MANUFACTURERS 560	STOCKS (Commercial and Custom) 568
GUNS, U.S.-MADE 561	TARGETS, BULLET AND CLAYBIRD TRAPS 569
GUNS AND GUN PARTS,	TAXIDERMY 569
REPLICA AND ANTIQUE 561	TRAP AND SKEET SHOOTER'S EQUIPMENT 569
GUNS, SURPLUS—PARTS AND AMMUNITION 561	TRIGGERS, RELATED EQUIPMENT 569

MANUFACTURERS' DIRECTORY 570-592

PRODUCT DIRECTORY

AMMUNITION, COMMERCIAL

Ace Custom 45's
ACTIV Industries, Inc.
American Ammunition
Arms Corp. of the Philippines
A-Square Co., Inc.
Ballistic Products, Inc.
Beeline Custom Bullets
Black Hills Ammunition, Inc.
Blammo Ammo
Blount, Inc.
Brenneke KG, Wilhelm
BulletMakers Workshop, The
California Magnum
CBC
Cherokee Gun Accessories
Cor-Bon Bullet & Ammo Co.
C.W. Cartridge Co.
Daisy Mfg. Co.
Delta Frangible Ammunition, LLC
Denver Bullets, Inc.
Diana
DKT, Inc.
Dynamit Nobel-RWS, Inc.
Eley Ltd.
Elite Ammunition
Estate Cartridge, Inc.
Federal Cartridge Co.
Fiocchi of America, Inc.
FN Herstal
Gamo
Garrett Cartridges, Inc.
GDL Enterprises
Gibbs Rifle Co., Inc.
Glaser Safety Slug, Inc.
Goldcoast Reloaders, Inc.
Grand Falls Bullets, Inc.
Hansen & Co.
Hansen Cartridge Co.
Hart & Son, Inc., Robert W.
Hirtenberger Aktiengesellschaft
Hornady Mfg. Co.
ICI-America
IMI
Jones, J.D.
Keng's Firearms Specialty, Inc.
Kent Cartridge Mfg. Co. Ltd.
KJM Fabritek, Inc.
Lapua Ltd.
Lomont Precision Bullets
M&D Munitions Ltd.
Magnum Research, Inc.
MagSafe Ammo Co.
Maionchi-L.M.I.
Markell, Inc.
Men—Metallwerk Elisenhuette, GmbH
Milstor Corp.
Moreton/Fordyce Enterprises
Mullins Ammo
Naval Ordnance Works
NECO
Neutralizer Police Munitions
New England Ammunition Co.
Oklahoma Ammunition Co.
Old Western Scrounger, Inc.
Omark Industries
PMC/Eldorado Cartridge Corp.
Polywad, Inc.
Pony Express Reloaders
Precision Delta Corp.
Pro Load Ammunition, Inc.
Ravell Ltd.
Remington Arms Co., Inc.
Rocky Fork Enterprises
Rucker Ammunition Co.
RWS
Shooting Components Marketing
Southern Ammunition Co., Inc.
Speer Products
SSK Industries
Star Reloading Co., Inc.
Talon Mfg. Co., Inc.
Tapco, Inc.
3-D Ammunition & Bullets
USAC
Valor Corp.
Victory USA
Vihtavuori Oy/Kaltron-Pettibone
Voere-KGH m.b.H.
Vom Hoffe
Vortek Products
Weatherby, Inc.
Widener's Reloading & Shooting Supply, Inc.
Winchester Div., Olin Corp.
Yukon Arms Classic Ammunition
Zero Ammunition Co., Inc.

AMMUNITION, CUSTOM

Accuracy Unlimited (Littleton, CO)
AFSCO Ammunition
Allred Bullet Co.
American Derringer Corp.
A-Square Co., Inc.
Ballistica Maximus North
Bear Arms
Berger Bullets
Bertram Bullet Co.
Black Hills Ammunition, Inc.
Brynin, Milton
BulletMakers Workshop, The
CBC
CHAA, Ltd.
Champlin Firearms, Inc.
Christman Jr., David
Country Armourer, The
Cubic Shot Shell Co., Inc.
Custom Tackle and Ammo
C.W. Cartridge Co.
Dakota Arms, Inc.
Dead Eye's Sport Center
DKT, Inc.
Elite Ammunition
Elko Arms
Ellis Sport Shop, E.W.
Epps "Orillia" Ltd., Ellwood
Estate Cartridge, Inc.
Fitz Pistol Grip Co.
Freedom Arms, Inc.
Gammog, Gregory B. Gally
Gonzalez Guns, Ramon B.
"Gramps" Antique Cartridges
Grand Falls Bullets, Inc.
Granite Custom Bullets
Heidenstrom Bullets
Hirtenberger Aktiengesellschaft
Hoelscher, Virgil
Horizons Unlimited
Hornady Mfg. Co.
Jackalope Gun Shop
Jensen Bullets
Jensen's Custom Ammunition
Jensen's Firearms Academy
Jett & Co., Inc.
Jones, J.D.
Kaswer Custom, Inc.
Keeler, R.H.
Kent Cartridge Mfg. Co. Ltd.
KJM Fabritek, Inc.
Kortz, Dr. L.
KLA Enterprises
Lindsley Arms Cartridge Co.
Lomont Precision Bullets
MagSafe Ammo Co.
Marple & Associates, Dick
MAST Technology
McMurdo, Lynn
Men-Metallwerk Elisenhuette, GmbH
Monte Kristo Pistol Grip Co.
Moreton/Fordyce Enterprises
Mullins Ammo
Naval Ordnance Works
NECO
Northern Precision Custom Swaged Bullets
Old Western Scrounger, Inc.
Oklahoma Ammunition Company
Parts & Surplus
Personal Protection Systems
Precision Delta Corp.
Precision Munitions, Inc.
Professional Hunter Supplies
Sanders Custom Gun Service
Sandia Die & Cartridge Co.
Slings & Arrows
Specialty Gunsmithing
Spence, George W.
Spencer's Custom Guns
SSK Industries
Star Custom Bullets
State Arms Gun Co.
Stewart's Gunsmithing
Swift Bullet Co.
Talon Mfg. Co., Inc.
3-D Ammunition & Bullets
3-Ten Corp.
Vitt/Boos
Vom Hoffe
Vulpes Ventures, Inc.
Warren Muzzleloading Co., Inc.
Weaver Arms Corp.
Westley Richards & Co.
Worthy Products, Inc.
Wyoming Armory, Inc.

AMMUNITION, FOREIGN

AFSCO Ammunition
Ammunition Consulting Services, Inc.
Armscorp USA, Inc.
A-Square Co., Inc.
Bertram Bullet Co.
B-West Imports, Inc.
BulletMakers Workshop, The
CBC
Century International Arms, Inc.
Cubic Shot Shell Co., Inc.
Diana
DKT, Inc.
Dynamit Nobel-RWS, Inc.
Fiocchi of America, Inc.
First, Inc., Jack
Forgett Jr., Valmore J.
Gamo
Gibbs Rifle Co., Inc.
"Gramps" Antique Cartridges
Hirtenberger Aktiengesellschaft
Hornady Mfg. Co.
IMI
IMI Services USA, Inc.
Jackalope Gun Shop
JagerSport, Ltd.
Kassnar
K.B.I., Inc.
Magnum Research, Inc.
MAGTECH Recreational Products, Inc.
Maionchi-L.M.I.
MAST Technology
Merkuria Ltd.
Monte Kristo Pistol Grip Co.
New England Arms Co.
Oklahoma Ammunition Co.
Old Western Scrounger, Inc.
Paragon Sales & Services, Inc.
Precision Delta Corp.
Ravell Ltd.
R.E.T. Enterprises
Rocky Fork Enterprises
RWS
Southern Ammunition Co., Inc.
Spence, George W.
SwaroSports, Inc.
Talon Mfg. Co., Inc.
T.F.C. S.p.A.
USA Sporting Inc.
Vom Hoffe

AMMUNITION COMPONENTS—BULLETS, POWDER, PRIMERS, CASES

Acadian Ballistic Specialties
Accuracy Unlimited (Littleton, CO)
Accurate Arms Co., Inc.
Action Bullets, Inc.
ACTIV Industries, Inc.
Alaska Bullet Works
Allred Bullet Co.
Alpha LaFranck Enterprises
American Products Co.
Ames Metal Products Co.
Arco
Armfield Custom Bullets
Arms Corp. of the Philippines
A-Square Co., Inc.
Ballard Built
Ballistic Products, Inc.
Banaczkowski Bullets
Barnes Bullets, Inc.
Beartooth Bullets
Beeline Custom Bullets
Bell Reloading, Inc.
Berger Bullets
Bergman & Williams
Berry's Bullets
Bertram Bullet Co.
Big Bore Express Ltd.
Bitterroot Bullet Co.
Black Belt Bullets
Black Hills Shooters Supply
Black Mountain Bullets
Blackhawk East
Blount, Inc.
Blue Mountain Bullets
Brenneke KG, Wilhelm
Briese Bullet Co., Inc.
Brown Co., E. Arthur
Brownells, Inc.
BRP, Inc.
Bruno Shooters Supply
Buck Stix
Buckeye Custom Bullets
Buckskin Bullet Co.
Buffalo Arms
Buffalo Bullet Co., Inc.
Buffalo Rock Shooters Supply
Bullet, Inc.
Bullet Mills
Bullseye Bullets
Bull-X, Inc.
Butler Enterprises
Buzztail Brass
Calhoon Varmint Bullets, James
Canadian Custom Bullets
Canyon Cartridge Corp.
Carnahan Bullets
Cascade Bullet Co., Inc.
CCI
Champion's Choice, Inc.
Cheddite France, S.A.
CheVron Bullets
Circle M Custom Bullets
Clark Custom Guns, Inc.
Classic Brass
Competitor Corp., Inc.
Complete Handloader, The
Cook Engineering Service
Corbin, Inc.
Cor-Bon Bullet & Ammo Co.
Crawford Co., Inc., R.M.
Creative Cartridge Co.
Cummings Bullets
Curtis Gun Shop
Custom Bullets by Hoffman
Cutsinger Bench Rest Bullets
D&J Bullet Co. & Custom Gun Shop, Inc.

50th EDITION, 1996 553

DIRECTORY OF THE ARMS TRADE

Dakota Arms, Inc.
DKT, Inc.
Dohring Bullets
Double A Ltd.
DuPont
Eichelberger Bullets, Wm.
Elkhorn Bullets
Federal Cartridge Co.
Finch Custom Bullets
Fiocchi of America, Inc.
First, Inc., Jack
Forkin, Ben
Fowler Bullets
Foy Custom Bullets
Freedom Arms, Inc.
Fusilier Bullets
G&C Bullet Co., Inc.
Gehmann, Walter
GOEX, Inc.
Golden Bear Bullets
Gonic Bullet Works
Gonzalez Guns, Ramon B.
Gotz Bullets
"Gramps" Antique Cartridges
Granite Custom Bullets
Grayback Wildcats
Green Bay Bullets
Grier's Hard Cast Bullets
Grizzly Bullets
Group Tight Bullets
Gun City
Guns
Hammets VLD Bullets
Hardin Specialty Dist.
Harris Enterprises
Harrison Bullets
Hart & Son, Inc., Robert W.
Haselbauer Products, Jerry
Hawk Laboratories, Inc.
Heidenstrom Bullets
Hercules, Inc.
HH Engineering
Hirtenberger Aktiengesellschaft
Hobson Precision Mfg. Co.
Hodgdon Powder Co., Inc.
Hornady Mfg. Co.
HT Bullets
Huntington Die Specialties
IMI
IMI Services USA, Inc.
Imperial Magnum Corp.
IMR Powder Co.
J-4, Inc.
J&D Components
J&L Superior Bullets
Jensen Bullets
Jensen's Firearms Academy
Jester Bullets
JLK Bullets
Johnson's Lage Uniwad
Jones, J.D.
Ka Pu Kapili
Kasmarsik Bullets
Kaswer Custom, Inc.
Keith's Bullets
Ken's Kustom Kartridge
Kent Cartridge Mfg. Co. Ltd.
KJM Fabritek, Inc.
KLA Enterprises
Kodiak Custom Bullets
Lapua Ltd.
Lathrop's, Inc.
Legend Products Corp.
Liberty Shooting Supplies
Lightfield Ammunition Corp., The Slug Group
Lindsley Arms Cartridge Co.
Littleton, J.F.
Lomont Precision Bullets
M&D Munitions Ltd.
Magnus Bullets
Maine Custom Bullets
Maionchi-L.M.I.
Marchmon Bullets
MarMik Inc.
MAST Technology
Master Class Bullets
McMurdo, Lynn
MEC, Inc.
Men-Metallwerk Elisenhuette, GmbH
Merkuria Ltd.
Michael's Antiques
Miller Enterprises, Inc.
Miller Enterprises, Inc., R.P.
Mitchell Bullets, R.F.
MI-TE Bullets
MoLoc Bullets

Montana Precision Swaging
Mt. Baldy Bullet Co.
Mulhern, Rick
Murmur Corp.
Mushroom Express Bullet Co.
Nagel's Bullets
National Bullet Co.
Naval Ordnance Works
Necromancer Industries, Inc.
Norma
North American Shooting Systems
North Devon Firearms Services
Northern Precision Custom Swaged Bullets
Nosler, Inc.
Oklahoma Ammunition Co.
Old Wagon Bullets
Old Western Scrounger, Inc.
Omark Industries
Ordnance Works, The
Pace Marketing, Inc.
Page Custom Bullets
Paragon Sales & Services, Inc.
Patrick Bullets
Pattern Control
Petro-Explo, Inc.
Phillippi Custom Bullets, Justin
Pinetree Bullets
Polywad, Inc.
Pomeroy, Robert
Powder Valley Services
Precision Components
Precision Components and Guns
Precision Delta Corp.
Precision Munitions, Inc.
Prescott Projectile Co.
Price Bullets, Patrick W.
Professional Hunter Supplies
Rainier Ballistics Corp.
Ranger Products
Red Cedar Precision Mfg.
Redwood Bullet Works
Reloading Specialties, Inc.
Remington Arms Co., Inc.
Radical Concepts
Rifle Works & Armory
R.I.S. Co., Inc.
R.M. Precision, Inc.
Robinson H.V. Bullets
Rolston, Inc., Fred W.
Rubright Bullets
Rucker Ammunition Co.
Scharch Mfg., Inc.
Schmidtman Custom Ammunition
Schneider Bullets
Schroeder Bullets
Scot Powder
Shappy Bullets
Shooting Components Marketing
Shotgun Bullets Mfg.
SOS Products Co.
Specialty Gunsmithing
Speer Products
Spencer's Custom Guns
Stanley Bullets
Star Custom Bullets
Stark's Bullet Mfg.
Stewart's Gunsmithing
Talon Mfg. Co., Inc.
Taracorp Industries
TCCI
TCSR
T.F.C. S.p.A.
Thompson Precision
3-D Ammunition & Bullets
TMI Products
Trico Plastics
Trophy Bonded Bullets, Inc.
True Flight Bullet Co.
USAC
Vann Custom Bullets
Vihtavuori Oy
Vihtavuori Oy/Kaltron-Pettibone
Vincent's Shop
Vitt/Boos
Vom Hoffe
Walters, John
Watson Trophy Match Bullets
Western Nevada West Coast Bullets
Widener's Reloading & Shooting Supply
Williams Bullet Co., J.R.
Winchester Div., Olin Corp.
Windjammer Tournament Wads, Inc.
Winkle Bullets
Woodleigh
Worthy Products, Inc.

Wosenitz VHP, Inc.
Wyant Bullets
Wyoming Armory, Inc.

Wyoming Bonded Bullets
Wyoming Custom Bullets
Zero Ammunition Co., Inc.

ANTIQUE ARMS DEALERS

Ad Hominem
Ahlman Guns
Antique American Firearms
Antique Arms Co.
Aplan Antiques & Art, James O.
Arms, Jackson
Bear Mountain Gun & Tool
Boggs, Wm.
British Arms Co. Ltd.
Buckskin Machine Works
Buffalo Arms
Bustani Appraisers, Leo
Cannon's Guns
Cape Outfitters
Carlson, Douglas R.
Chadick's Ltd.
Champlin Firearms, Inc.
Chuck's Gun Shop
Classic Guns, Inc.
Cole's Gun Works
Cullity Restoration, Daniel
D&D Gunsmiths, Ltd.
Delhi Gun House
Dixon Muzzleloading Shop, Inc.
Dyson & Son Ltd., Peter
Ed's Gun House
Enguix Import-Export
Epps "Orillia" Ltd., Ellwood
Fagan & Co., William
First, Inc., Jack
Fish, Marshall F.
Flayderman & Co., N.
Forgett Jr., Valmore J.
Forty Five Ranch Enterprises
Frielich Police Equipment
Fulmer's Antique Firearms, Chet
Galazan Shotgun Mfg. Co.
Glass, Herb
Goergen's Gun Shop, Inc.
Golden Age Arms Co.
Goodwin, Fred
Gun Room, The
Gun Room Press, The
Gun Works, The
Guncraft Sports, Inc.
Hallowell & Co.

Hansen & Co.
Hunkeler, A.
Johns, Bill
Kelley's
Ledbetter Airguns, Riley
LeFever Arms Co., Inc.
Lever Arms Service Ltd.
Lock's Philadelphia Gun Exchange
Log Cabin Sport Shop
Martin's Gun Shop
Mathews & Son, Inc., George E.
McKee Publications
McKinney, R.P.
Mendez, John A.
Montana Outfitters
Mountain Bear Rifle Works, Inc.
Museum of Historical Arms, Inc.
Muzzleloaders Etcetera, Inc.
Navy Arms Co.
N.C. Ordnance Co.
New England Arms Co.
New Orleans Arms Co.
Pioneer Guns
Pony Express Sport Shop, Inc.
Pre-Winchester 92-90-62 Parts Co.
P.S.M.G. Gun Co.
Retting, Inc., Martin B.
Rigby & Co., John
S&S Firearms
Sarco, Inc.
Schuetzen Gun Service
Scott Fine Guns, Inc., Thad
Semmer, Charles
Silver Ridge Gun Shop
Starnes Gunmaker, Ken
Steves House of Guns
Stott's Creek Armory, Inc.
Strawbridge, Victor W.
Track of the Wolf, Inc.
Vic's Gun Refinishing
Vintage Arms, Inc.
Wiest, M.C.
Winchester Sutler, Inc., The
Wood, Frank
Yearout, Lewis E.

APPRAISERS—GUNS, ETC.

Accuracy Gun Shop
Ad Hominem
Ahlman Guns
Ammunition Consulting Services, Inc.
Amodei, Jim
Antique Arms Co.
Armoury, Inc., The
Arundel Arms & Ammunition, Inc., A.
Behlert Precision
Billings Gunsmiths, Inc.
Blue Book Publications, Inc.
Bustani Appraisers, Leo
Butterfield & Butterfield
Camilli, Lou
Cannon's Guns
Cape Outfitters
Chadick's Ltd.
Champlin Firearms, Inc.
Christie's East
Clark Custom Guns, Inc.
Clark Firearms Engraving
Classic Guns, Inc.
Clements' Custom Leathercraft, Chas
Cole's Gun Works
Colonial Repair
Corry, John
Cullity Restoration, Daniel
Custom Tackle and Ammo
D&D Gunsmiths, Ltd.
DGR Custom Rifles
Dixon Muzzleloading Shop, Inc.
D.O.C. Specialists, Inc.
Duane's Gun Repair
Ed's Gun House
Ellis Sport Shop, E.W.
Enguix Import-Export
Epps "Orillia" Ltd., Ellwood
Fagan & Co., William
First, Inc., Jack
Fish, Marshall F.
Flayderman & Co., Inc., N.
Forgett, Valmore J., Jr.

Forty Five Ranch Enterprises
Fredrick Gun Shop
Frontier Arms Co., Inc.
Goergen's Gun Shop, Inc.
Golden Age Arms Co.
Gonzalez Guns, Ramon B.
Goodwin, Fred
Greenwald, Leon E. "Bud"
Griffin & Howe, Inc.
Groenewold, John
Gun Room Press, The
Gun Shop, The
Gun Works, The
Guncraft Sports, Inc.
Guns
Hallowell & Co.
Hammans, Charles E.
HandiCrafts Unltd.
Hank's Gun Shop
Hansen & Co.
Hughes, Steven Dodd
Irwin, Campbell H.
Jaeger, Inc., Paul/Dunn's
Jensen's Custom Ammunition
Jonas Appraisers—Taxidermy Animals, Jack
Kelley's
Ledbetter Airguns, Riley
Lee's Red Ramps
LeFever Arms Co., Inc.
Lock's Philadelphia Gun Exchange
Mac's .45 Shop
Mack's Sport Shop
Madis, George
Marple & Associates, Dick
Martin's Gun Shop
Mathews & Son, Inc., George E.
McCann's Machine & Gun Shop
McGowen Rifle Barrels
Montana Outfitters
Mountain Bear Rifle Works, Inc.
Mowrey's Guns & Gunsmithing

PRODUCT DIRECTORY

Museum of Historical Arms, Inc.
Muzzleloaders Etcetera, Inc.
Navy Arms Co.
N.C. Ordnance Co.
Old Western Scrounger, Inc.
Orvis Co., The
Parke-Bernet
Pasadena Gun Center
Pentheny de Pentheny
Perazzi USA, Inc.
Peterson Gun Shop, Inc., A.W.
Pettinger Books, Gerald
Pioneer Guns
Pony Express Sport Shop, Inc.
Pre-Winchester 92-90-62 Parts Co.
P.S.M.G. Gun Co.
R.E.T. Enterprises
Retting, Inc., Martin B.
Richards, John
Richards Classic Oil Finish
Rigby & Co., John
S&S Firearms
Safari Outfitters Ltd.
Sarco, Inc.
Scott Fine Guns, Inc., Thad
Shell Shack
Silver Ridge Gun Shop
Sipes Gun Shop
S.K. Guns, Inc.
Sotheby's
Starnes Gunmaker, Ken
Steger, James R.
Stott's Creek Armory, Inc.
Stratco, Inc.
Strawbridge, Victor W.
Thurston Sports, Inc.
Tillinghast, James C.
Ulrich, Doc & Bud
Unick's Gunsmithing
Vic's Gun Refinishing
Vom Hoffe
Walker Arms Co., Inc.
Wayne Firearms for Collectors and Investors, James
Wells Custom Gunsmith, R.A.
Wessinger Custom Guns & Engraving
Whildin & Sons Ltd., E.H.
Whitestone Lumber Corp.
Wiest, M.C.
Williams Shootin' Iron Service
Winchester Sutler, Inc., The
Wood, Frank
Yankee Gunsmith
Yearout, Lewis E.

AUCTIONEERS—GUNS, ETC.

Ammunition Consulting Services, Inc.
Bourne Co., Inc., Richard A.
Butterfield & Butterfield
Christie's East
Enguix Import-Export
Fagan & Co., William
Kelley's
"Little John's" Antique Arms
Parke-Bernet
Sotheby's
Tillinghast, James C.

BOOKS (Publishers and Dealers)

American Handgunner Magazine
Armory Publications
Arms & Armour Press
Ballistic Products, Inc.
Barnes Bullets, Inc.
Blackhawk East
Blackhawk Mountain
Blackhawk West
Blacksmith Corp.
Blacktail Mountain Books
Blue Book Publications, Inc.
British Arms Co. Ltd.
Brown Co., E. Arthur
Brownell's, Inc.
Buffalo Arms
Calibre Press, Inc.
Cape Outfitters
Colonial Repair
Colorado Sutlers Arsenal
Corbin, Inc.
DBI Books, Inc.
Faith Associates, Inc.
Flores Publications, Inc., J.
Golden Age Arms Co.
"Gramps" Antique Cartridges
Gun City
Gun Hunter Books
Gun Parts Corp., The
Gun Room Press, The
Gun Works, The
Guncraft Sports, Inc.
Gunnerman Books
Guns, (Div. of D.C. Engineering, Inc.)
GUNS Magazine
Gunsite Training Center
H&P Publishing
Handgun Press
Harris Publications
Hodgdon Powder Co., Inc.
Home Shop Machinist, The
Hornady Mfg. Co.
Hungry Horse Books
Ironside International Publishers, Inc.
Krause Publications, Inc.
Lane Publishing
Lapua Ltd.
Lethal Force Institute
Lyman Products Corp.
Madis, David
Magma Engineering Co.
MarMik Inc.
Martin Bookseller, J.
McKee Publications
MI-TE Bullets
Mountain South
New Win Publishing, Inc.
Old Western Scrounger, Inc.
Outdoorsman's Bookstore, The
Pejsa Ballistics
Petersen Publishing Co.
Pettinger Books, Gerald
Police Bookshelf
Powell & Son (Gunmakers) Ltd., William
Precision Shooting, Inc.
Ravell Ltd.
Reloading Specialties, Inc.
R.G.-G., Inc.
Rutgers Book Center
S&S Firearms
Safari Press, Inc.
Saunders Gun & Machine Shop
Shootin' Accessories, Ltd.
Sinclair International, Inc.
Stackpole Books
Stoeger Publishing Co.
"Su-Press-On," Inc.
Tapco, Inc.
Thomas, Charles C.
Track of the Wolf, Inc.
Trafalgar Square
Trotman, Ken
Vom Hoffe
VSP Publishers
WAMCO—New Mexico
Wiest, M.C.
Wilderness Sound Products Ltd.
Williams Gun Sight Co.
Wolfe Publishing Co.
Wolf's Western Traders

BULLET AND CASE LUBRICANTS

Bear Reloaders
Blackhawk Mountain
Blackhawk West
Blount, Inc.
Brass-Tech Industries
Break-Free, Inc.
Brown Co., E. Arthur
Buffalo Arms
Camp-Cap Products
C-H Tool & Die Corp.
Chem-Pak, Inc.
Cooper-Woodward
Corbin, Inc.
Dillon Precision Prods., Inc.
Eezox, Inc.
Elkhorn Bullets
E-Z-Way Systems
Forster Products
4-D Custom Die Co.
GAR
Green Bay Bullets
Guardsman Products
HEBB Resources
Hollywood Engineering
Hornady Mfg. Co.
Imperial
Javelina Products
Lee Precision, Inc.
Lithi Bee Bullet Lube
M&N Bullet Lube
Magma Engineering Co.
Micro-Lube
MI-TE Bullets
Monte Kristo Pistol Grip Co.
NECO
Old Western Scrounger, Inc.
Paco's
RCBS
Reardon Products
Redding Reloading Equipment
Rooster Laboratories
Shay's Gunsmithing
Small Custom Mould & Bullet Co.
SPG Lubricants
Tamarack Products, Inc.
Vom Hoffe
Warren Muzzleloading Co., Inc.
Widener's Reloading & Shooting Supply, Inc.
Winchester Sutler, Inc., The
Young Country Arms

BULLET SWAGE DIES AND TOOLS

Berger Bullets
Blount, Inc.
Bruno Shooters Supply
Brynin, Milton
Bullet Swaging Supply, Inc.
Camdex, Inc.
C-H Tool & Die Corp.
Corbin, Inc.
4-D Custom Die Co.
Holland's
Hollywood Engineering
King & Co.
LAP Systems Groups, N.A.
Monte Kristo Pistol Grip Co.
Necromancer Industries, Inc.
Niemi Engineering, W.B.
North Devon Firearms Services
Rorschach Precision Products
Speer Products
Sport Flite Manufacturing Co.

CARTRIDGES FOR COLLECTORS

Ad Hominem
Alpha 1 Drop Zone
Ammunition Consulting Services, Inc.
Buck Stix
Cameron's
Campbell, Dick
Cole's Gun Works
Colonial Repair
Delhi Gun House
Duffy, Charles E.
Ed's Gun House
Eichelberger Bullets, Wm.
Enguix Import-Export
Epps "Orillia" Ltd., Ellwood
First, Inc., Jack
Forty Five Ranch Enterprises
Goergen's Gun Shop, Inc.
"Gramps" Antique Cartridges
Gun Parts Corp., The
Hank's Gun Shop
Idaho Ammunition Service
MAST Technology
Michael's Antiques
Montana Outfitters
Monte Kristo Pistol Grip Co.
Mountain Bear Rifle Works, Inc.
Old Western Scrounger, Inc.
Pasadena Gun Center
Rifle Works & Armory
San Francisco Gun Exchange
Samco Global Arms, Inc.
SOS Products Co.
Sportsmen's Exchange & Western Gun Traders, Inc.
Tillinghast, James C.
Vom Hoffe
Ward & Van Valkenburg
Weatherby, Inc.
Yearout, Lewis E.

CASES, CABINETS, RACKS AND SAFES—GUN

Abel Safe & File, Inc.
Alco Carrying Cases
All Rite Products, Inc.
Allen Co., Bob
Allen Co., Inc.
Allen Sportswear, Bob
Alumna Sport by Dee Zee
American Display Co.
American Security Products Co.
Americase
Ansen Enterprises
Arizona Custom Case
Arkfeld Mfg. & Dist. Co., Inc.
Armes de Chasse
Art Jewel Enterprises Ltd.
Ashby Turkey Calls
Aspen Outdoors, Inc.
Bagmaster Mfg., Inc.
Barramundi Corp.
Berry's Mfg. Inc.
Big Sky Racks, Inc.
Big Spring Enterprises "Bore Stores"
Bill's Custom Cases
Bison Studios
Black Sheep Brand
Boyt
Brauer Bros. Mfg. Co.
Browning Arms Co.
Brunsport, Inc.
Bucheimer, J.M.
Bushmaster Hunting & Fishing
Cannon Safe, Inc.
Cascade Fabrication
Chipmunk
Clark Custom Guns, Inc.
Cobalt Mfg., Inc.
D&L Industries
Dara-Nes, Inc.
Deepeeka Exports Pvt. Ltd.
Doskocil Mfg. Co., Inc.
DTM International, Inc.
E&L Mfg., Inc.
Elk River, Inc.
EMF Co., Inc.
English Inc., A.G.
Enhanced Presentations, Inc.
Epps "Orillia" Ltd., Ellwood
Eversull Co., Inc., K.
Fort Knox Security Products
Frontier Safe Co.
Galati Internationl
Galaxy Imports Ltd., Inc.
GAR
Granite Custom Bullets
Gun Locker
Gun-Alert
Gun-Ho Sports Cases
Gusdorf Corp.
Hafner Creations, Inc.
Hall Plastics, Inc., John
Harrison-Hurtz Enterprises, Inc.
Hastings Barrels
Homak Mfg. Co., Inc.
Hoppe's Div.
Huey Gun Cases, Marvin
Hugger Hooks Co.
Hunter Co., Inc.
Impact Case Co.
Johanssons Vapentillbehor, Bert
Johnston Bros.
Jumbo Sports Products
Kalispel Case Line
Kane Products, Inc.
KK Air International
Knock on Wood Antiques
Kolpin Mfg., Inc.
Lakewood Products, Inc.
Liberty Safe
Marsh, Mike
Master Products, Inc.
Maximum Security Corp.
McWelco Products
Morton Booth Co.
Mountain States Engraving

50th EDITION, 1996   555

DIRECTORY OF THE ARMS TRADE

MPC
MTM Molded Products Co., Inc.
National Security Safe Co., Inc.
Necessary Concepts, Inc.
Nesci Enterprises, Inc.
Nielsen Custom Cases
Noble Co., Jim
Outa-Site Gun Carriers
Outdoor Connection, Inc., The
Pachmayr Ltd.
Palmer Security Products
Penguin Industries, Inc.
Perazzi USA, Inc.
Pflumm Mfg. Co.
Poburka, Philip
Powell & Son (Gunmakers) Ltd., William
Protecto Plastics
Prototech Industries, Inc.
Quality Arms, Inc.
Ravell Ltd.
Savana Sports, Inc.
Schulz Industries
Sonderman, Robert
Southern Security
Sportsman's Communicators
SSK Co.
Sun Welding Safe Co.
Surecase Co., The
Sweet Home, Inc.
Tinks & Ben Lee Hunting Products
Waller & Son, Inc., W.
WAMCO, Inc.
Warren, Kenneth W.
Weather Shield Sports Equipment, Inc.
Weatherby, Inc.
Wilson Case, Inc.
Woodstream
Zanotti Armor
Ziegel Engineering

CHOKE DEVICES, RECOIL ABSORBERS AND RECOIL PADS

Accuright
Action Products, Inc.
Ahlman Guns
Allen Co., Bob
Allen Sportswear, Bob
American Import Co., The/Export Division
Answer Products Co.
Arms Ingenuity Co.
Armsport, Inc.
Baer Custom, Inc., Les
Baker, Stan
Bansner's Gunsmithing Specialties
Bartlett Engineering
Black Sheep Brand
Briley Mfg., Inc.
B-Square Co., Inc.
Bull Mountain Rifle Co.
Butler Creek Corp.
C&H Research
Cape Outfitters
Cation
Cellini, Inc., Vito Francesca
Chuck's Gun Shop
Clark Custom Guns, Inc.
Clearview Products
Colonial Arms, Inc.
Craig Custom Ltd.
Crane Sales Co., George S.
CRL, Inc.
Danuser Machine Co.
Dayson Arms Ltd.
Delta Vectors, Inc.
Dever Co., Jack
Elsen, Inc., Pete
Fabian Bros. Sporting Goods, Inc.
FAPA Corp.
Franchi S.p.A., Luigi
Galati International
Galazan Shotgun Mfg. Co.
Gentry Custom Gunmaker, David
Graybill's Gun Shop
Great 870 Co., The
Guns, (Div. of D.C. Engineering, Inc.)
Gunsite Training Center
Harper, William E.
Hart & Son, Inc., Robert W.
Hastings Barrels
Holland's
I.N.C., Inc.
Intermountain Arms & Tackle, Inc.
Jaeger, Inc., Paul/Dunn's
Jenkins Recoil Pads, Inc.
J.P. Enterprises, Inc.
KDF, Inc.
Kick Eez
LaRocca Gun Works, Inc.
London Guns Ltd.
Lyman Instant Targets, Inc.
Lyman Products Corp.
Mag-Na-Port International, Inc.
Marble Arms
Meadow Industries
Morrow, Bud
Nelson/Weather-rite, Inc.
Nowlin Custom Mfg.
One Of A Kind
Pace Marketing, Inc.
Pachmayr Ltd.
Palsa Outdoor Products
PAST Sporting Goods, Inc.
Powell & Son (Gunmakers) Ltd., William
Pro-Port Ltd.
Protektor Model
Que Industries
Shotguns Unlimited
S.K. Guns, Inc.
Spencer's Custom Guns
Starnes Gunmaker, Ken
Stone Enterprises Ltd.
Tecni-Mec
Trulock Tool
Wise Guns, Dale

CHRONOGRAPHS AND PRESSURE TOOLS

Brown Co., E. Arthur
Canons Delcour
Chronotech
Competition Electronics, Inc.
Custom Chronograph, Inc.
D&H Precision Tooling
Firearms Supplies Inc.
Hornady Mfg. Co.
Kent Cartridge Mfg. Co. Ltd.
Ravell Ltd.
Oehler Research, Inc.
Old Western Scrounger, Inc.
Pace Marketing, Inc.
P.A.C.T., Inc.
Shooting Chrony, Inc.
SKAN A.R.
Stratco, Inc.
Tepeco
Vom Hoffe

CLEANING AND REFINISHING SUPPLIES

AC Dyna-tite Corp.
Acculube II, Inc.
Accupro Gun Care
Accuracy Products, S.A.
ADCO International
American Gas & Chemical Co., Ltd.
American Import Co., The/Export Division
Answer Products Co.
Armoloy Co. of Ft. Worth
Atlantic Mills, Inc.
Barnes Bullets, Inc.
Belltown, Ltd.
Beretta, Dr. Franco
Bill's Gun Repair
Birchwood Laboratories, Inc.
Blount, Inc.
Blue and Gray Products, Inc.
Break-Free, Inc.
Bridgers Best
Brown Co., E. Arthur
Bruno Shooters Supply
Cape Outfitters
Carroll Bullets
Chem-Pak, Inc.
Chopie Mfg., Inc.
Clenzoil Corp.
Corbin, Inc.
Crane & Crane Ltd.
Creedmoor Sports, Inc.
CRL, Inc.
Custom Products
D&H Prods. Co., Inc.
Dangler, Homer L.
Dara-Nes, Inc.
Deepeeka Exports Pvt. Ltd.
Dever Co., Jack
Dewey Mfg. Co., Inc., J.
Du-Lite Corp.
Dutchman's Firearms, Inc., The
Dykstra, Doug
E&L Mfg., Inc.
Eezox, Inc.
Ekol Leather Care
Faith Associates, Inc.
Firearms Supplies Inc.
Flaig's
Flitz International Ltd.
Flouramics, Inc.
Forster Products
Frontier Products Co.
G96 Products Co., Inc.
G.B.C. Industries, Inc.
Goddard, Allen
Golden Age Arms Co.
Gozon Corp.
Guardsman Products
Gun Works, The
Heatbath Corp.
Hoppe's Div.
Hornady Mfg. Co.
Hydrosorbent Products
Iosso Products
Jackalope Gun Shop
Jantz Supply
J-B Bore Cleaner
Johnston Bros.
Jones Custom Products, Neil
Kent Cartridge Mfg. Co. Ltd.
Kesselring Gun Shop
Kleen-Bore, Inc.
Laurel Mountain Forge
Lawrence Brand Shot
Lee Supplies, Mark
LEM Gun Specialties, Inc.
List Precision Engineering
LPS Laboratories, Inc.
Marble Arms
Micro Sight Co.
Minute Man High Tech. Ind.
Mountain View Sports, Inc.
MTM Molded Products Co., Inc.
Muscle Products Corp.
Nesci Enterprises, Inc.
Old Western Scrounger, Inc.
Old World Oil Products
Omark Industries
Original Mink Oil, Inc.
Outers Laboratories, Div. of Blount

COMPUTER SOFTWARE—BALLISTICS

Action Target, Inc.
AmBr Software Group Ltd.
Arms, Peripheral Data Systems
Ballistic Engineering & Software, Inc.
Ballistic Program Co., Inc., The
Barnes Bullets, Inc.
Beartooth Bullets
Blackwell, W.
Blount, Inc.
Canons Delcour
Corbin, Inc.
Corbin Applied Technology
Country Armourer, The
Data Tech Software Systems
Exe, Inc.
FlashTek, Inc.
Ford, Jack
JBM Software
Jensen Bullets
J.I.T. Ltd.
JWH = Software
Kent Cartridge Mfg. Co. Ltd.
Load From A Disk
Magma Engineering Co.
Maionchi-L.M.I.
P.A.C.T., Inc.
PC Bullet/ADC, Inc.
Pejsa Ballistics
Starnes Gunmaker, Ken
Tioga Engineering Co., Inc.

CUSTOM GUNSMITHS

A&W Repair
Ace Custom 45's
Ad Hominem
Accuracy Gun Shop
Accuracy Unlimited (Glendale, AZ)
Accurate Plating & Weaponry, Inc.
Ackley Rifle Barrels, P.O.
Adair Custom Shop, Bill
Ahlman Guns
Ahrends, Kim
Aldis Gunsmithing & Shooting Supply
Alpine's Precision Gunsmithing & Indoor Shooting Range
Amrine's Gun Shop
Answer Products Co.
Antique Arms Co.
Armament Gunsmithing Co., Inc.
Arms Craft Gunsmithing
Arms Ingenuity Co.
Ox-Yoke Originals, Inc.
P&M Sales and Service
Pace Marketing, Inc.
Pachmayr Ltd.
Parker Gun Finishes
Pendleton Royal
Penguin Industries, Inc.
Powell & Son (Gunmakers) Ltd., William
Precision Reloading, Inc.
Prolix
Pro-Shot Products, Inc.
R&S Industries Corp.
Radiator Specialty Co.
Ravell Ltd.
Richards, John
Richards Classic Oil Finish
Rickard, Inc., Pete
RIG Products Co.
Rod Guide Co.
Rooster Laboratories
Rusteprufe Laboratories
Rusty Duck Premium Gun Care Products
Saunders Gun & Machine Shop
Sharp Shooter, Inc.
Shiloh Creek
Shooter's Choice
Shootin' Accessories, Ltd.
Sinclair International, Inc.
Speer Products
Spencer's Custom Guns
Starr Trading Co., Jedediah
Stoney Point Products, Inc.
Svon Corp.
Tag Distributors
Tapco, Inc.
TDP Industries, Inc.
Tetra Gun Lubricants
Texas Platers Supply Co.
T.F.C. S.p.A.
Track of the Wolf, Inc.
United States Products Co.
Valor Corp.
Van Gorden & Son, Inc., C.S.
Venco Industries, Inc.
Vom Hoffe
Warren Muzzleloading Co., Inc.
WD-40 Co.
Whitestone Lumber Corp.
Williams Shootin' Iron Service
Willow Bend
Winchester Sutler, Inc., The
World of Targets
Young Country Arms
Z-Coat Industrial Coatings, Inc.

Arnold Arms Co., Inc.
Aro-Tek, Ltd.
Arrieta, S.L.
Art's Gun & Sport Shop, Inc.
Arundel Arms & Ammunition, Inc., A.
AWC Systems Technology
Baelder, Harry
Baer Custom, Inc., Les
Bain & Davis, Inc.
Baity's Custom Gunworks
Baker, Stan
Bansner's Gunsmithing Specialties
Barnes Bullets, Inc.
Barta's Gunsmithing
Baumannize Custom
Bear Arms
Bear Mountain Gun & Tool
Beaver Lodge
Behlert Precision

556 THE GUN DIGEST

PRODUCT DIRECTORY

Beitzinger, George
Belding's Custom Gun Shop
Bellm Contenders
Benchmark Guns
Bengtson Arms Co., L.
Biesen, Al
Biesen, Roger
Billeb, Stephen L.
Billings Gunsmiths, Inc.
Blackstar Barrel Accurizing
Bolden's
Bond Custom Firearms
Borden's Accuracy
Borovnik KG, Ludwig
Bowerly, Kent
Brace, Larry D.
Brgoch, Frank
Brian, C.T.
Briese Bullet Co., Inc.
Briganti & Co., A.
Briley Mfg., Inc.
Broad Creek Rifle Works
Brockmans Custom Gunsmithing
Broken Gun Ranch
Broughton Rifle Barrels
Brown Precision, Inc.
Bruno Shooters Supply
Buckhorn Gun Works
Buckskin Machine Works
Budin, Dave
Bull Mountain Rifle Co.
Bullberry Barrel Works, Ltd.
Bullet Meister Bullets
Burgess & Son Gunsmiths, R.W.
Burkhart Gunsmithing, Don
Burres, Jack
C&J Enterprises, Inc.
Cache La Poudre Rifleworks
CAM Enterprises
Camilli, Lou
Campbell, Dick
Cannon's Guns
Carter's Gun Shop
Caywood, Shane J.
Champlin, R. MacDonald
Champlin Firearms, Inc.
Chicasaw Gun Works
Christman Jr., David
Chuck's Gun Shop
Clark Custom Guns, Inc.
Clark Firearms Engraving
Classic Arms Corp.
Classic Guns, Inc.
Cloward's Gun Shop
Cochran, Oliver
Coffin, Charles H.
Cogar's Gunsmithing
Cole's Gun Works
Coleman's Custom Repair
Colonial Repair
Colt's Mfg. Co., Inc.
Competitive Pistol Shop, The
Conrad, C.A.
Corkys Gun Clinic
Costa, David
Cox, C. Ed
Craig Custom Ltd.
Creekside Gun Shop, Inc.
CRL, Inc.
Cullity Restoration, Daniel
Cumberland Knife & Gun Works
Curtis Custom Shop
Curtis Gun Shop
Custom Checkering Service
Custom Firearms
Custom Gun Products
Custom Gun Stocks
Custom Gunsmiths
Custom Shop, The
Cylinder & Slide, Inc.
D&D Gunsmiths, Ltd.
D&J Bullet Co. & Custom Gun Shop, Inc.
Dangler, Homer L.
Darlington Gun Works, Inc.
Davis, Don
Davis Service Center, Bill
Dever Co., Jack
Devereaux, R.H. "Dick"
DGS, Inc.
DGR Custom Rifles
Dietz Gun Shop & Range, Inc.
Dilliott Gunsmithing, Inc.
Donnelly, C.P.
Dowtin Gunworks
Duane's Gun Repair
Duffy, Charles E.
Duncan's Gun Works, Inc.
Dyson & Son Ltd., Peter
Echols & Co., D'Arcy
Eckelman Gunsmithing
Eggleston, Jere D.
EGW Evolution Gun Works
EMF Co., Inc.
Erhardt, Dennis
Eskridge Rifles, Steven Eskridge
Eyster Heritage Gunsmiths, Inc., Ken
F.A.I.R. Techni-Mec s.n.c.
Fanzoj GmbH
Ferris Firearms
First, Inc., Jack
Fish, Marshall F.
Fisher, Jerry A.
Fisher Custom Firearms
Flaig's
Fleming Firearms
Flynn's Custom Guns
Forster, Kathy
Forster, Larry L.
Forthofer's Gunsmithing & Knifemaking
Francesca, Inc.
Francotte & Cie S.A., Auguste
Frank Custom Gun Service, Ron
Frazier Brothers Enterprises
Fredrick Gun Shop
Frontier Arms Co., Inc.
Gander Mountain, Inc.
Gator Guns & Repair
Genecco Gun Works, K.
Gentry Custom Gunmaker, David
Gillmann, Edwin
Gilman-Mayfield, Inc.
Giron, Robert E.
Goens, Dale W.
Goodling's Gunsmithing
Goodwin, Fred
Gordie's Gun Shop
Grace, Charles E.
Graybill's Gun Shop
Green, Roger M.
Greg Gunsmithing Repair
Griffin & Howe, Inc.
Gun Shop, The
Guns
Gunsite Gunsmithy
Gunsite Training Center
Gunsmithing Ltd.
Hagn Rifles & Actions, Martin
Hallberg Gunsmith, Fritz
Hallowell & Co.
Hamilton, Alex B.
Hammans, Charles E.
Hammond Custom Guns Ltd., Guy
Hank's Gun Shop
Hanson's Gun Center, Dick
Hardison, Charles
Harold's Custom Gun Shop, Inc.
Harris-McMillan Gunworks
Hart & Son, Inc., Robert W.
Hartmann & Weiss GmbH
Hecht, Hubert J.
Heilmann, Stephen
Heinie Specialty Products
Hendricks Gun Works
Hensler, Jerry
Hensley, Darwin
High Bridge Arms, Inc.
High Performance International
High Standard Mfg. Co., Inc.
Highline Machine Co.
Hill, Loring F.
Hiptmayer, Armurier
Hiptmayer, Klaus
Hoag, James W.
Hobbie Gunsmithing, Duane A.
Hodgson, Richard
Hoehn Sales, Inc.
Hoelscher, Virgil
Hoenig & Rodman
Hofer Jagdwaffen, P.
Holland, Dick
Holland's
Hollis Gun Shop
Horst, Alan K.
Huebner, Corey O.
Hughes, Steven Dodd
Hunkeler, Al
Hyper-Single, Inc.
Imperial Magnum Corp.
Intermountain Arms & Tackle, Inc.
Irwin, Campbell H.
Island Pond Gun Shop
Ivanoff, Thomas G.
J&S Heat Treat
Jackalope Gun Shop
Jaeger, Inc., Paul/Dunn's
Jarrett Rifles, Inc.
Jensen's Custom Ammunition
Jim's Gun Shop
Johnson Gunsmithing, Inc., Neal G.
Johnston, James
Jones, J.D.
J.P. Enterprises, Inc.
Juenke, Vern
Jurras, L.E.
K-D, Inc.
KDF, Inc.
Ken's Gun Specialties
Kilham & Co.
Kimball, Gary
King's Gun Works
KLA Enterprises
Klein Custom Guns, Don
Kleinendorst, K.W.
Kneiper Custom Guns, Jim
Knippel, Richard
KOGOT
Kopp, Terry K.
Korzinek Riflesmith, J.
LaFrance Specialties
Lair, Sam
LaRocca Gun Works, Inc.
Laughridge, William R.
Lawson Co., Harry
Lebeau-Courally
LeFever Arms Co., Inc.
Liberty Antique Gunworks
Lilja Precision Rifle Barrels
Lind Custom Guns, Al
Linebaugh Custom Sixguns & Rifle Works
List Precision Engineering
Lock's Philadelphia Gun Exchange
Mac's .45 Shop
Mag-Na-Port International, Inc.
Mahony, Philip Bruce
Makinson, Nicholas
Manley Shooting Supplies, Lowell
Marble Arms
Marquart Precision Co., Inc.
Martin's Gun Shop
Martz, John V.
Masker, Seely
Mathews & Son, Inc., George E.
Mazur Restoration, Pete
McBros Rifle Co.
McCament, Jay
McCann's Machine & Gun Shop
McCann's Muzzle-Gun Works
McCluskey Precision Rifles
McFarland, Stan
McGowen Rifle Barrels
McKinney, R.P.
McMillan Rifle Barrels
MCS, Inc.
Mercer Custom Stocks, R.M.
Michael's Antiques
Mid-America Recreation, Inc.
Middlebrooks Custom Shop
Miller Co., David
Miller Custom
Mills Jr., Hugh B.
Mo's Competitor Supplies
Moeller, Steve
Monell Custom Guns
Moreton/Fordyce Enterprises
Morrison Custom Rifles, J.W.
Morrow, Bud
Mountain Bear Rifle Works, Inc.
Mowrey's Guns & Gunsmithing
Mullis Guncraft
Mustra's Custom Guns, Inc., Carl
Nastoff's 45 Shop, Inc., Steve
Nelson, Stephen
Nettestad Gun Works
New England Custom Gun Service
Newman Gunshop
Nicholson Custom
Nickels, Paul R.
Nicklas, Ted
Norman Custom Gunstocks, Jim
Norrell Arms, John
North American Shooting Systems
North Fork Custom Gunsmithing
Nowlin Custom Mfg.
Nu-Line Guns, Inc.
Oakland Custom Arms, Inc.
Old World Gunsmithing
Olson, Vic
Orvis Co., The
Ottmar, Maurice
Ozark Gun Works
P&S Gun Service
Pace Marketing, Inc.
Pagel Gun Works, Inc.
Pasadena Gun Center
Paterson Gunsmithing
Pell, John T.
PEM's Mfg. Co.
Pence Precision Barrels
Penrod Precision
Pentheny de Pentheny
Peterson Gun Shop, Inc., A.W.
Power Custom, Inc.
Pro-Port Ltd.
Quality Firearms of Idaho, Inc.
R&J Gun Shop
Ravell Ltd.
Ray's Gunsmith Shop
Renfrew Guns & Supplies
Ridgetop Sporting Goods
Ries, Chuck
Rifles Inc.
Rigby & Co., John
R.M. Precision, Inc.
RMS Custom Gunsmithing
Robar Co.'s, Inc., The
Roberts, J.J.
Robinson, Don
Rocky Mountain Arms, Inc.
Rocky Mountain Rifle Works Ltd.
Rogers Gunsmithing, Bob
Romain's Custom Guns
Rupert's Gun Shop
Ryan, Chad L.
Sanders Custom Gun Service
Schiffman, Curt
Schiffman, Mike
Schiffman, Norman
Schuetzen Gun Service
Schumakers Gun Shop, William
Schwartz Custom Guns, Wayne E.
Scott Fine Guns, Inc., Thad
Scott, Dwight
Scott, McDougall & Associates
Shaw, Inc., E.R.
Shay's Gunsmithing
Shell Shack
Shockley, Harold H.
Shooten' Haus, The
Shooter Shop, The
Shooters Supply
Shootin' Shack, Inc.
Shooting Specialties
Shotgun Shop, The
Shotguns Unlimited
Silver Ridge Gun Shop
Singletary, Kent
Sipes Gun Shop
Siskiyou Gun Works
S.K. Guns, Inc.
Skeoch, Brian R.
Sklany, Steve
Slezak, Jerome F.
Small Arms Mfg. Co.
Smith, Art
Smith, Sharmon
Snapp's Gunshop
Speiser, Fred D.
Spencer's Custom Guns
Spencer Reblue Service
Sportsmen's Exchange & Western Gun Traders, Inc.
Spradlin's
Springfield, Inc.
SSK Industries
Starnes Gunmaker, Ken
Steelman's Gun Shop
Steffens, Ron
Steger, James R.
Stiles Custom Guns
Storey, Dale A.
Stott's Creek Armory, Inc.
Strawbridge, Victor W.
Sullivan, David S.
Swampfire Shop, The
Swann, D.J.
Swenson's 45 Shop, A.D.
Swift River Gunworks, Inc.
Szweda, Robert
Talmage, William G.
Tank's Rifle Shop
Taylor & Robbins
Tecni-Mec
Ten-Ring Precision, Inc.
Thompson, Randall
300 Gunsmith Service, Inc.

50th EDITION, 1996 **557**

DIRECTORY OF THE ARMS TRADE

Thurston Sports, Inc.
Time Precision, Inc.
Titus, Daniel
Tom's Gun Repair
Tom's Gunshop
Tooley Custom Rifles
Trevallion Gunstocks
T.S.W. Conversions, Inc.
Tucker, James C.
Upper Missouri Trading Co.
USA Sporting Inc.
Van Epps, Milton
Van Horn, Gil
Van Patten, J.W.
Varmintmasters
Vest, John
Vic's Gun Refinishing
Vintage Arms, Inc.
Volquartsen Custom Ltd.
Von Minden Gunsmithing Services
Vorhes, David
Waffen-Weber Custom Gunsmithing
Walker Arms Co., Inc.
Wardell Precision Handguns Ltd.
Weaver Arms Corp.
Weaver's Gun Shop
Weems, Cecil
Weigand Combat Handguns, Inc.
Wells, Fred F.
Wells Custom Gunsmith, R.A.
Welsh, Bud
Werth, T.W.
Wessinger Custom Guns & Engraving
West, Robert G.
Westley Richards & Co.
Westwind Rifles, Inc.
Wichita Arms, Inc.
Wiebe, Duane
Williams Gun Sight Co.
Williams Shootin' Iron Service
Williamson Precision Gunsmithing
Wilson's Gun Shop
Winter, Robert M.
Wise Guns, Dale
Wiseman and Co., Bill
Wisner's Gun Shop, Inc.
Wood, Frank
Wright's Hardwood Gunstock Blanks
Yankee Gunsmith
Zeeryp, Russ

Sanders Custom Gun Service
Schuetzen Gun Service
Shirley Co. Gun & Riflemakers Ltd., J.A.
Silver Ridge Gun Shop
Sipes Gun Shop
S.K. Guns, Inc.
Skeoch, Brian R.
Snapp's Gunshop
Spencer's Custom Guns
Sportsmatch Ltd.
Sportsmen's Exchange & Western Gun Traders, Inc.
Starnes Gunmaker, Ken
Steffens, Ron
Stiles Custom Guns
Stott's Creek Armory, Inc.
Strawbridge, Victor W.
Szweda, Robert
Taylor & Robbins
Ten-Ring Precision, Inc.
Thompson, Randall
Time Precision, Inc.
Tom's Gun Repair
T.S.W. Conversions, Inc.
Unick's Gunsmithing

Van Horn, Gil
Van Patten, J.W.
Vic's Gun Refinishing
Von Minden Gunsmithing Services
Vorhes, David
Waffen-Weber Custom Gunsmithing
Waldron, Herman
Wardell Precision Handguns Ltd.
Wells, Fred F.
Werth, T.W.
Wessinger Custom Guns & Engraving
West, Robert G.
Western Design
Westrom, John
White Rock Tool & Die
Wiebe, Duane
Williams Gun Sight Co.
Williams Shootin' Iron Service
Williamson Precision Gunsmithing
Wilson's Gun Shop
Winter, Robert M.
Wise Guns, Dale
Wisner's Gun Shop, Inc.
Wood, Frank

CUSTOM METALSMITHS

Adair Custom Shop, Bill
Ahlman Guns
Aldis Gunsmithing & Shooting Supply
Allen, Richard L.
Amrine's Gun Shop
Answer Products Co.
Arundel Arms & Ammunition, Inc., A.
Baer Custom, Inc., Les
Bansner's Gunsmithing Specialties
Baron Technology
Bear Mountain Gun & Tool
Behlert Precision
Beitzinger, George
Benchmark Guns
Bengtson Arms Co., L.
Biesen, Al
Billingsley & Brownell
Brace, Larry D.
Brian, C.T.
Briganti & Co., A.
Broad Creek Rifle Works
Brockmans Custom Gunsmithing
Broughton Rifle Barrels
Brown Precision, Inc.
Buckhorn Gun Works
Bull Mountain Rifle Co.
Bullberry Barrel Works, Ltd.
C&J Enterprises, Inc.
Campbell, Dick
Carter's Gun Shop
Checkmate Refinishing
Classic Guns, Inc.
Colonial Repair
Costa, David
Craftguard
Crandall Tool & Machine Co.
Cullity Restoration, Daniel
Custom Gun Products
Custom Gunsmiths
Custom Shop, The
D&D Gunsmiths, Ltd.
D&H Precision Tooling
Desert Industries, Inc.
Dever Co., Jack
Dietz Gun Shop & Range, Inc.
Duncan's Gunworks, Inc.
Erhardt, Dennis
First, Inc., Jack
Fisher, Jerry A.
Forster, Larry L.
Francesca, Inc.
Frank Custom Gun Service, Ron
Fullmer, Geo. M.
Gentry Custom Gunmaker, David
Goodwin, Fred
Gordie's Gun Shop
Graybill's Gun Shop
Green, Roger M.
Griffin & Howe, Inc.
Gun Shop, The
Guns
Gunsite Training Center
Gunsmithing Ltd.
Hagn Rifles & Actions, Martin
Hallberg Gunsmith, Fritz
Hallowell & Co.
Hamilton, Alex B.
Harold's Custom Gun Shop, Inc.
Hart & Son, Inc., Robert W.
Hecht, Hubert J.
Heilmann, Stephen
Heppler's Machining
Highline Machine Co.
Hiptmayer, Armurier
Hiptmayer, Klaus
Hoag, James W.
Hoelscher, Virgil
Holland's
Hollis Gun Shop
Hyper-Single, Inc.
Intermountain Arms & Tackle
Island Pond Gun Shop
Ivanoff, Thomas G.
J&S Heat Treat
Jaeger, Inc., Paul/Dunn's
Jamison's Forge Works
Jeffredo Gunsight
Johnston, James
Jones Custom Products, Neil
Ken's Gun Specialties
Kilham & Co.
Klein Custom Guns, Don
Kleinendorst, K.W.
Kopp, Terry K.
LaFrance Specialties
Lampert, Ron
Lawson Co., Harry
List Precision Engineering
Lock's Philadelphia Gun Exchange
Mac's .45 Shop
Mains Enterprises, Inc.
Makinson, Nicholas
Marek, George
Martin's Gun Shop
McCament, Jay
McCann's Machine & Gun Shop
McCormick's Custom Gun Bluing
McFarland, Stan
McKinney, R.P.
Mid-America Recreation, Inc.
Morrison Custom Rifles, J.W.
Morrow, Bud
Mullis Guncraft
Nettestad Gun Works
New England Custom Gun Service
Newman Gunshop
Nicholson Custom
Noreen, Peter H.
North American Shooting Systems
North Fork Custom Gunsmithing
Olson, Vic
Ozark Gun Works
Pace Marketing, Inc.
Pagel Gun Works, Inc.
Parker Gun Finishes
Pasadena Gun Center
Penrod Precision
Precision Metal Finishing
Precise Metalsmithing Enterprises
Precision Metal Finishing, John Westrom
Precision Specialties
Pre-Winchester 92-90-62 Parts Co.
Rice, Keith
Rigby & Co., John
R.M. Precision, Inc.
Robar Co.'s, Inc., The
Rocky Mountain Arms, Inc.

DECOYS

A&M Waterfowl, Inc.
Baekgaard Ltd.
Carry-Lite, Inc.
Deer Me Products Co.
Fair Game International
Farm Form Decoys, Inc.
Feather Flex Decoys
Flambeau Products Corp.
G&H Decoys, Inc.
Herter's Manufacturing, Inc.
Hiti-Schuch, Atelier Wilma
Klingler Woodcarving

Molin Industries
North Wind Decoy Co.
Penn's Woods Products, Inc.
Powell & Son (Gunmakers) Ltd., William
Quack Decoy & Sporting Clays
Ravell Ltd.
Sports Innovations, Inc.
Tanglefree Industries
Waterfield Sports, Inc.
Woods Wise Products

ENGRAVERS, ENGRAVING TOOLS

Adair Custom Shop, Bill
Adams, John J.
Adams Jr., John J.
Ahlman Guns
Alfano, Sam
Allard, Gary
Allen, Richard L.
Altamont Co.
American Pioneer Video
Anthony and George Ltd.
Baron Technology
Bates Engraving, Billy
Bell Originals, Inc., Sid
Bleile, C. Roger
Boessler, Erich
Bone Engraving, Ralph
Bratcher, Dan
Brgoch, Frank
Brooker, Dennis
Burgess, Byron
CAM Enterprises
Churchill, Winston
Clark, Frank
Clark Firearms Engraving
Collings, Ronald
Creek Side Metal & Woodcrafters
Cullity Restoration, Daniel
Cupp, Custom Engraver, Alana
Davidson, Jere
Delorge, Ed
Dixon Muzzleloading Shop, Inc.
Dolbare, Elizabeth
Drain, Mark
Dubber, Michael W.
Dyson & Son Ltd., Peter
EMF Co., Inc.
Engraving Artistry
Evans Engraving, Robert
Fanzoj GmbH
Firearms Engraver's Guild of America
Flannery Engraving Co., Jeff W.
Floatstone Mfg. Co.
Fountain Products
Francolini, Leonard
Frank Custom Gun Service, Ron
Frank Knives
French, J.R.
Gene's Custom Guns
George, Tim
Glimm, Jerome C.
Golden Age Arms Co.
Gournet, Geoffroy
Grant, Howard V.
Griffin & Howe, Inc.
GRS Corp., Glendo
Gun Room, The
Guns
Gurney, F.R.
Gwinnell, Bryson J.
Hale, Peter
Hand Engravers Supply Co.
Hands Engraving, Barry Lee
Harris Hand Engraving, Paul A.
Harris-McMillan Gunworks
Harwood, Jack O.
Hendricks, Frank E.
Herrett's Stocks, Inc.
Hiptmayer, Heidemarie
Horst, Alan K.
Ingle, Ralph W.
Jaeger, Inc., Paul/Dunn's
Johns, Bill
Kamyk Engraving Co., Steve
Kehr, Roger
Kelly, Lance
Klingler Woodcarving
Koevenig's Engraving Service
Kudlas, John M.
LaFrance Specialties
Lebeau-Courally
LeFever Arms Co., Inc.
Leibowitz, Leonard
Letschnig, Franz
Lindsay, Steve
Little Trees Ramble
Lutz Engraving, Ron
Mains Enterprises, Inc.
Marek, George
Master Engravers, Inc.
McCombs, Leo
McDonald, Dennis
McKenzie, Lynton
Mele, Frank
Mid-America Recreation, Inc.
Mittermeier, Inc., Frank
Montgomery Community College
Moschetti, Mitchell R.
Mountain States Engraving
Nelson, Gary K.
New England Custom Gun Service
New Orleans Arms Co.
New Orleans Jewelers Supply Co.
NgraveR Co., The
Oker's Engraving
Old Dominion Engravers
P&S Gun Service
Palmgren Steel Products

PRODUCT DIRECTORY

Pedersen, C.R.
Pedersen, Rex C.
Pilgrim Pewter, Inc.
Pilkington, Scott
Piquette, Paul R.
Potts, Wayne E.
Rabeno, Martin
Reed, Dave
Reno, Wayne
Riggs, Jim
Roberts, J.J.
Rohner, Hans
Rohner, John
Rosser, Bob
Rundell's Gun Shop
Runge, Robert P.
Sampson, Roger
Schiffman, Mike
Sheffield Knifemakers Supply
Sherwood, George
Sinclair, W.P.
Singletary, Kent

Skaggs, R.E.
Smith & Wesson
Smith, Mark A.
Smith, Ron
Smokey Valley Rifles
Theis, Terry
Thiewes, George W.
Thirion Hand Engraving, Denise
Valade, Robert B.
Vest, John
Viramontez, Ray
Vorhes, David
Waffen-Weber Custom Gunsmithing
Wagoner, Vernon G.
Wallace, Terry
Warenski, Julie
Warren, Kenneth W.
Welch, Sam
Wells, Rachel
Wessinger Custom Guns & Engraving
Willig Custom Engraving, Claus

GAME CALLS

Adventure Game Calls
Arkansas Mallard Duck Calls
Ashby Turkey Calls
Blakemore Game Calls, Jim
Bostick Wildlife Calls, Inc.
Carter's Wildlife Calls, Inc., Garth
Cedar Hill Game Calls, Inc.
Crawford Co., Inc., R.M.
D&H Prods. Co., Inc.
D-Boone Ent., Inc.
Deepeeka Exports Pvt. Ltd.
Dr. O's Products Ltd.
Duck Call Specialists
Faulhaber Wildlocker
Faulk's Game Call Co., Inc.
Flow-Rite of Tennessee, Inc.
Green Head Game Call Co.
Hally Caller
Haydel's Game Calls, Inc.
Herter's Manufacturing, Inc.
Hunter's Specialties, Inc.
Keowee Game Calls
Kingyon, Paul L.
Knight & Hale Game Calls
Lohman Mfg. Co., Inc.
Mallardtone Game Calls
Marsh, Johnny
Moss Double Tone, Inc.

Mountain Hollow Game Calls
Oakman Turkey Calls
Olt Co., Philip S.
Penn's Woods Products, Inc.
Powell & Son (Gunmakers) Ltd., William
Primos, Inc.
Quaker Boy, Inc.
Ravell Ltd.
Rickard, Inc., Pete
Robbins Scent, Inc.
Rocky Mountain Wildlife Products
Salter Calls, Inc., Eddie
Savana Sports, Inc.
Sceery Co., E.J.
Scobey Duck & Goose Calls, Glynn
Scotch Hunting Products Co., Inc.
Scruggs' Game Calls, Stanley
Sports Innovations, Inc.
Stewart Game Calls, Inc., Johnny
Sure-Shot Game Calls, Inc.
Tanglefree Industries
Tink's & Ben Lee Hunting Products
Tink's Safariland Hunting Corp.
Wellington Outdoors
Wilderness Sound Products Ltd.
Woods Wise Products
Wyant's Outdoor Products, Inc.

GUN PARTS, U.S. AND FOREIGN

ABS Co. Inc./Lothar Walther
Accuracy Gun Shop
Ad Hominem
Ahlman Guns
American Bullets
Amherst Arms
Armscorp USA, Inc.
Badger Shooters Supply, Inc.
Bear Mountain Gun & Tool
Beauchamp & Son, Inc.
Behlert Precision
Billings Gunsmiths, Inc.
Bob's Gun Shop
Boyds' Gunstock Industries, Inc.
Briese Bullet Co., Inc.
British Arms Co. Ltd.
Bushmaster Firearms
C&J Enterprises, Inc.
Cape Outfitters
Caspian Arms Ltd.
Century International Arms, Inc.
Clark Custom Guns, Inc.
Cole's Gun Works
Colonial Repair
Cylinder & Slide, Inc.
Defense Moulding Enterprises
Delta Arms Ltd.
DGR Custom Rifles
Dibble, Derek A.
Duane's Gun Repair
Duffy, Charles E.
Dyson & Son Ltd., Peter
Elliott Inc., G.W.
EMF Co., Inc.
Enguix Import-Export
Fabian Bros. Sporting Goods, Inc.
F.A.I.R. Techni-Mec s.n.c.
FAPA Corp.
First, Inc., Jack
Fleming Firearms
Flintlocks, Etc.

Forrest, Inc., Tom
Forster Products
Galati International
Goodwin, Fred
Groenewold, John
Gun Parts Corp., The
Gun Shop, The
Guns
Gun-Tec
Hart & Son, Inc., Robert W.
Hastings Barrels
High Performance International
High Standard Mfg. Co., Inc.
Irwin, Campbell H.
I.S.S.
Jaeger, Inc., Paul/Dunn's
Johnson Gunsmithing, Inc., Neal G.
K&T Co.
Kimber, Inc.
K.K. Arms Co.
Krico/Kriegeskorte GmbH, A.
Laughridge, William R.
Liberty Antique Gunworks
List Precision Engineering
Lodewick, Walter H.
Mac's .45 Shop
Markell, Inc.
Martin's Gun Shop
Martz, John V.
McCann's Machine & Gun Shop
McCormick Corp., Chip
McKee Publications
Merkuria Ltd.
Morrow, Bud
Mountain Bear Rifle Works, Inc.
Nu-Line Guns, Inc.
Olympic Arms
Pace Marketing, Inc.
Pachmayr Ltd.
Parts & Surplus
Peacemaker Specialists

Pennsylvania Gun Parts
Perazone, Brian
Perazzi USA, Inc.
Peterson Gun Shop, Inc., A.W.
Precision Small Arms
Pre-Winchester 92-90-62 Parts Co.
Quality Firearms of Idaho, Inc.
Quality Parts Co.
Ranch Products
Randco UK
Retting, Inc., Martin B.
R.M. Precision, Inc.
S&S Firearms
Sabatti S.R.L.
Sarco, Inc.
Scherer
Shockley, Harold H.
Silver Ridge Gun Shop
Sipes Gun Shop
Smires, C.L.
Smith & Wesson
Southern Ammunition Co., Inc.
Southern Armory, The
Sportsmen's Exchange & Western Gun Traders, Inc.

Springfield, Inc.
Springfield Sporters, Inc.
Starnes Gunmaker, Ken
"Su-Press-On," Inc.
Swampfire Shop, The
Tapco, Inc.
Tecni-Mec
Track of the Wolf, Inc.
Tradewinds, Inc.
T.S.W. Conversions, Inc.
Twin Pine Armory
USA Sporting Inc.
Vintage Arms, Inc.
Vintage Industries, Inc.
Volquartsen Custom Ltd.
Walker Arms Co., Inc.
Weaver's Gun Shop
Westfield Engineering
Wilson's Gun Shop
Winchester Sutler, Inc., The
Wise Guns, Dale
Wisner's Gun Shop, Inc.
Wolff Co., W.C.
Wood, Mel

GUNS, AIR

Air Arms
●Air Rifle Specialists
●Air Venture
Air Werks International
●Airgun Repair Centre
Airguns-R-Us
Airrow
●Anschutz GmbH
Arms Corp. of the Philippines
Armsport, Inc.
Baikal
●Beeman Precision Airguns
●Benjamin/Sheridan Co.
Brass Eagle, Inc.
Brocock Ltd.
●BSA Guns Ltd.
Champion's Choice, Inc.
Component Concepts, Inc.
Crawford Co., Inc., R.M.
Creedmoor Sports, Inc.
●Crosman Airguns
Crosman Products of Canada Ltd.
●Daisy Mfg. Co.
Daystate Arms
●Diana
●Dynamit Nobel-RWS, Inc.
E.A.A. Corp.
●FAS
Frankonia Jagd
●FWB
●Gamo
●GFR Corp.
Great Lakes Airguns
GZ Paintball Sports Products
Hebard Guns, Gil
Hofmann & Co.
Howa Machinery, Ltd.
Hy-Score Arms Co. Ltd.
●Interarms
Labanu, Inc.
List Precision Engineering
●Mac-1 Distributors
●Marksman Products
Maryland Paintball Supply

MCS, Inc.
Merkuria Ltd.
Mo's Competitor Supplies
National Survival Game, Inc.
Nationwide Airgun Repairs
P&S Gun Service
●Pardini Armi Srl
Park Rifle Co., Inc.
Penguin Industries, Inc.
Powell & Son (Gunmakers) Ltd., William
●Precision Airgun Sales, Inc.
●Precision Sales Int'l, Inc.
Ravell Ltd.
Ripley Rifles
●Rossi S.A., Amadeo
Ruko Products, Inc.
Rutten
●RWS
Savana Sports, Inc.
S.G.S. Sporting Guns Srl
Shanghai Airguns, Ltd.
SKAN A.R.
Smart Parts
Sportsman Airguns, Inc.
Sportsmatch Ltd.
●Steyr Mannlicher AG
Stone Enterprises Ltd.
●Swivel Machine Works, Inc.
Tapco, Inc.
Taurus, S.A., Forjas
Theoben Engineering
Tippman Pneumatics, Inc.
Trooper Walsh
UltraSport Arms, Inc.
Valor Corp.
Venom Arms Co.
●Walther GmbH, Carl
●Webley and Scott Ltd.
●Weihrauch KG, Hermann
Whiscombe
Wright's Hardwood Gunstock Blanks
World Class Airguns

GUNS, FOREIGN—IMPORTERS (Manufacturers)

●Air Rifle Specialists (BSA Guns Ltd.; Theoben Engineering)
●Air Venture (airguns)
Air Werks International (Air Arms; Baikal; Park Rifle Co., Ltd.; Rutten)
Airguns-R-Us (Brocock Ltd.; Falcon Pneumatic Systems)
●Alessandri & Son, Lou (Rizzini, Battista)
●American Arms, Inc. (Fausti Cav. Stefano & Figlie snc; Franchi S.p.A., Luigi; Grulla Armes; Uberti, Aldo; Zabala Hermanos S.A.; blackpowder arms)
American Bullets (GSS Scheller; Spezial Waffen)
Armas Kemen S.A. (USA Sporting Inc.)
●Armes de Chasse (Armas Azor, J.A.; AYA; Francotte & Cie S.A., Auguste)

Armoury, Inc., The (blackpowder)
●Armscorp USA, Inc.
Armsport, Inc. (airguns; Bernardelli S.p.A., Vincenzo; blackpowder arms)
●Autumn Sales, Inc. (Blaser Jagdwaffen GmbH)
●Beauchamp & Son, Inc. (Pedersoli, Davide & C.)
●Beeman Precision Airguns (Beeman Precision Airguns; Feinwerkbau; FWB; Webley & Scott Ltd.; Weihrauch KG, Hermann)
●Bell's Legendary Country Wear (Miroku, B.C./Daly, Charles; Powell & Son, Ltd., William)
●Beretta U.S.A. Corp. (Beretta Firearms, Pietro)
●Bohemia Arms Co. (BRNO)
British Arms Co. Ltd.

50th EDITION, 1996   559

DIRECTORY OF THE ARMS TRADE

British Sporting Arms
- Browning Arms Co. (Browning Arms Co.)
  B-West Imports, Inc.
- Cabela's (Pedersoli, Davide & C.; blackpowder arms)
- Cape Outfitters (Armi Sport; Bertuzzi; Gamba; Pedersoli, Davide & C.; San Marco; Societa Armi Bresciane Srl.; Uberti, Aldo; Westley Richards & Co.; blackpowder arms)
- Century International Arms, Inc. (Famas; FEG; Norinco)
  Champion's Choice (Lapua)
- Chapuis USA (Chapuis Armes)
  Christopher Firearms Co., Inc., E.
- Cimarron Arms (Uberti, Aldo; blackpowder arms)
  Continental Imports & Distribution (Laurona Armas Eibar, S.A.D.)
  County Arms (I.T.S.)
- CVA (blackpowder arms)
- Daisy Mfg. Co. (Daisy Mfg. Co.; Gamo)
- Dixie Gun Works, Inc. (Pedersoli, Davide & C.; Uberti, Aldo; blackpowder arms)
- Dynamit Nobel-RWS, Inc. (Brenneke KG, Wilhelm; Diana; Gamo; Norma Precision AB; RWS)
- E.A.A. Corp. (Astra-Sport, S.A.; Benelli Armi S.p.A.; Sabatti S.r.l.; Tanfoglio S.r.l., Fratelli; Weihrauch KG, Hermann)
  Eagle Imports, Inc. (Bersa S.A., Gonzales Castillo)
- Ellett Bros. (Churchill)
- EMF Co., Inc. (Dakota; Pedersoli, Davide & C.; San Marco; Uberti, Aldo; blackpowder arms)
  Euroarms of America, Inc. (blackpowder arms)
- Fiocchi of America, Inc. (Fiocchi Munizioni S.p.A.)
- Forgett Jr., Valmore J. (Navy Arms Co.; Uberti, Aldo)
- Galaxy Imports Ltd., Inc. (Laurona Armas Eibar, S.A.D.)
  Gamba, USA (Societa Armi Bresciane Srl.)
  Giacomo Sporting, Inc. (Gamba)
- Gibbs Rifle Co., Inc. (Mauser Werke)
- Glock, Inc. (Glock GmbH)
  Great Lakes Airguns (Sharp)
- GSI, Inc. (Merkel Freres; Steyr; Steyr-Mannlicher AG)
- G.U., Inc. (SKB Arms Co.)
  Gunsite Training Center (Accuracy International Precision Rifles)
- Hammerli USA (Hammerli Ltd.)
  Harris-McMillan Gunworks (Peters Stahl GmbH)
- Heckler & Koch, Inc. (Benelli Armi S.p.A.; Heckler & Koch, GmbH)
- Hi-Grade Imports (Arrieta, S.L.)
  Imperial Magnum Corp. (Imperial Magnum Corp.)
- Interarms (Helwan; Howa Machinery Ltd.; Interarms; Korth; Norinco; Rossi S.A., Amadeo Rua; Star Bonifacio Echeverria S.A.; Walther GmbH, Carl)
- Ithaca Acquisition Corp. (Fabarm S.p.A.)
- JägerSport, Ltd. (Voere-KGH m.b.H.)
- Jansma, Jack J. (Arrieta, S.L.)
- J.O. Arms Inc. (KSN Industries, Ltd.)
- K.B.I., Inc. (Baikal; FEG; Kassnar; K.B.I., Inc.)
- Keng's Firearms Specialty, Inc. (Lapua; Ultralux)
- Krieghoff International, Inc. (Krieghoff Gun Co., H.)
  K-Sports Imports, Inc.
  London Guns Ltd. (London Guns Ltd.)
  Mac-1 Distributors (Venom Arms Co.)
- Magnum Research, Inc. (CZ; IMI) MAGTECH Recreational Products, Inc. (CBC; Magtech)

- Mandall Shooting Supplies, Inc. (Arizaga; Bretton; Cabanas; Crucelegui, Hermanos; Erma Werke GmbH; Firearms Co. Ltd./Alpine; Hammerli Ltd.; Korth; Krico/Kriegeskorte GmbH, A.; Morini; SIG; Tanner; Ugartechea S.A., Ignacio; Zanoletti, Pietro; blackpowder arms)
- Marksman Products (Marksman Products)
- MCS, Inc. (Pardini Armi Srl)
- MEC-Gar U.S.A., Inc. (MEC-Gar s.r.l.)
  Merwin's Assoc. (Kongsberg)
- Mitchell Arms, Inc. (Mitchell Arms, Inc.; blackpowder arms)
- Moore & Co., Wm. Larkin (Bertuzzi; FERLIB; Garbi, Armas Urki; Piotti; Rizzini, F.LLI)
- Nationwide Sports Distributors, Inc. (Daewoo Precision Industries Ltd.)
- Navy Arms Co. (Pedersoli, Davide & C.; Pietta; Uberti, Aldo; blackpowder and cartridge arms)
- Nevada Cartridge Co. (Beretta, Dr. Franco)
- New England Arms Co. (Arrieta, S.L.; Bertuzzi; Bosis; Cosmi Americo & Figlio s.n.c.; FERLIB; Gamba; Lebeau-Courally; Rizzini, Battista; Rizzini, F.LLI)
  New England Custom Gun Service (EAW)
- Nygord Precision Products (FAS; Morini; Pardini Armi Srl; Steyr; TOZ; Unique/M.A.P.F.)
- Olympic Arms (Peters Stahl GmbH)
- Orvis Co., Inc., The (Arrieta, S.L.)
- Pachmayr Ltd. (FERLIB)
- Para-Ordnance, Inc. (Para-Ordnance Mfg., Inc.)
- Paul Co., The (Norma Precision AB; Sauer)
  Pelaire Products (Whiscombe)
- Perazzi USA, Inc. (Perazzi m.a.p. S.p.A.)
  Powell Agency, William, The (William Powell & Son [Gunmakers] Ltd.)
- Precision Sales International, Inc. (Anschutz GmbH; Erma Werke GmbH; Marocchi F.lli S.p.A.)
- Quality Arms, Inc. (Arrieta, S.L.)
- Ruko Products (Ruko)
  Sarco, Inc.
- SGS Importers International, Inc. (Llama Gabilondo Y Cia)
  Sheridan USA, Inc., Austin
- Sigarms, Inc. (SIG-Sauer)
- Sile Distributors (Benelli Armi S.p.A.; Marocchi F.lli S.p.A.)
- Specialty Shooters Supply, Inc. (JSL Ltd.)
  Sphinx USA Inc. (Sphinx Engineering SA)
  Sportsman Airguns, Inc. (QB air rifles; Shanghai Airguns, Ltd.)
- Springfield, Inc. (Springfield, Inc.)
- Stoeger Industries (IGA; Sako Ltd.; Tikka)
  Stone Enterprises Ltd. (airguns)
- Swarovski Optik North America Inc.
- Taurus Firearms, Inc. (Taurus International Firearms)
- Taylor's & Co., Inc. (Armi San Marco; Armi Sport; I.A.B.; Pedersoli, Davide & C.; Pietta; Uberti, Aldo; Tradewinds, Inc. (blackpowder arms)
- Trooper Walsh (Venom Arms Co.)
- Turkish Firearms Corp. (Turkish Firearms Corp.)
- Uberti USA, Inc. (blackpowder arms)
  USA Sporting Inc. (Armas Kemen S.A.) Vintage Arms, Inc.
- Weatherby, Inc. (Weatherby, Inc.)
  Winchester Sutler, Inc., The (R.O.A.)
  World Class Airguns (Air Arms)

Armas Azor, J.A. (Armes de Chasse)
Armas Kemen S.A. (USA Sporting Inc.)
Armi San Marco (Taylor's & Co., Inc.)
Armi Sport (Cape Outfitters; Taylor's & Co., Inc.)
Arms Corp. of the Philippines
- Arrieta, S.L. (Hi-Grade Imports; Jansma, Jack J.; New England Arms Co.; The Orvis Co., Inc.; Quality Arms, Inc.)
- Astra Sport, S.A. (E.A.A. Corp.)
- ATIS Armi S.A.S.
- AYA (Armes de Chasse)
- Baikal (Air Werks International; K.B.I., Inc.)
- Beeman Precision Airguns (Beeman Precision Airguns)
- Benelli Armi S.p.A. (E.A.A. Corp.; Heckler & Koch, Inc.; Sile Distributors)
- Beretta, Dr. Franco (Nevada Cartridge Co.)
- Beretta Firearms, Pietro (Beretta U.S.A. Corp.)
- Bernardelli S.p.A., Vincenzo (Armsport, Inc.)
  Bersa S.A., Gonzales Castillo (Eagle Imports, Inc.)
- Bertuzzi (Cape Outfitters; Moore & Co., Wm. Larkin; New England Arms Co.)
- Blaser Jagdwaffen GmbH (Autumn Sales, Inc.)
  Bondini Paolo (blackpowder arms)
  Borovnik KG, Ludwig
  Bosis (New England Arms Co.)
  Brenneke KG, Wilhelm (Dynamit Nobel-RWS, Inc.)
  Bretton (Mandall Shooting Supplies, Inc.)
- BRNO (Bohemia Arms Co.)
  Brocock Ltd. (Airguns-R-Us)
- Browning Arms Co. (Browning Arms Co.)
- BSA Guns Ltd.
- Cabanas (Mandall Shooting Supplies, Inc.)
- CBC (MAGTECH Recreational Products, Inc.)
- Chapuis Armes (Chapuis USA)
- Churchill (Ellett Bros.)
- Cosmi Americo & Figlio s.n.c. (New England Arms Co.)
- Crucelegui, Hermanos (Mandall Shooting Supplies, Inc.)
- CVA (blackpowder arms)
- CZ (Magnum Research, Inc.)
- Daewoo Precision Industries Ltd. (Nationwide Sports Distributors, Inc.)
- Dakota (EMF Co., Inc.)
- Daisy Mfg. Co. (Daisy Mfg. Co.)
- Diana (Dynamit Nobel-RWS, Inc.)
  Dumoulin, Ernest
  EAW (New England Custom Gun Service)
- Erma Werke GmbH (Mandall Shooting Supplies, Inc.; Precision Sales International, Inc.)
- Fabarm S.p.A. (Ithaca Acquisition Corp.)
  F.A.I.R. Techni-Mec s.n.c.
  Falcon Pneumatic Systems (Airguns-R-Us)
- Famas (Century International Arms, Inc.)
- FAS (Nygord Precision Products)
- Fausti Cav. Stefano & Figlie snc (American Arms, Inc.)
- FEG (Century International Arms, Inc.; K.B.I., Inc.)
- FERLIB (Moore & Co., Wm. Larkin; New England Arms Co.; Pachmayr Co.; Quality Arms, Inc.)
  Fiocchi Munizioni S.P.A. (Fiocchi of America)
- Firearms Co. Ltd./Alpine (Mandall Shooting Supplies, Inc.)
  FN Herstal
- Franchi S.p.A, Luigi (American Arms, Inc.)
- Francotte & Cie S.A., Auguste (Armes de Chasse)
- FWB (Beeman Precision Airguns)
- Gamba S.p.A.-Societa Armi Bresciane Srl., Renato (Cape Outfitters; Giacomo Sporting, Inc.; New England Arms Co.)

- Gamo (Daisy Mfg. Co.; Dynamit Nobel-RWS, Inc.)
- Garbi, Armas Urki (Moore & Co., Wm. Larkin)
  Gaucher Armes S.A.
- Glock GmbH (Glock, Inc.)
- Grulla Armes (American Arms, Inc.)
  GSS Scheller (American Bullets)
- Hammerli Ltd. (Hammerli USA)
- Heckler & Koch, GmbH (Heckler & Koch, Inc.)
- Helwan (Interarms)
- Heym GmbH & Co., Friedrich Wilh. Holland & Holland Ltd.
- Howa Machinery Ltd. (Interarms)
- I.A.B. (Taylor's & Co., Inc.)
- IGA (Stoeger Industries)
- IMI (Magnum Research, Inc.)
  Imperial Magnum Corp. (Imperial Magnum Corp.)
- Interarms (Interarms)
  I.T.S. (County Arms)
- J.O. Arms & Ammunition Co. (J.O. Arms & Ammunition Co.)
- JSL Ltd. (Specialty Shooters Supply, Inc.)
- Kassnar (K.B.I., Inc.)
- K.B.I., Inc. (K.B.I., Inc.)
  Kongsberg (Merwin's Assoc.)
- Korth (Interarms; Mandall Shooting Supplies, Inc.)
- Krico/Kriegeskorte GmbH, A. (Mandall Shooting Supplies, Inc.)
- Krieghoff Gun Co., H. (Krieghoff International, Inc.)
  KSN Industries, Ltd. (J.O. Arms Inc.)
- Lakefield Arms Ltd.
  Lanber Armas S.A.
  Lapua (Champion's Choice; Keng's Firearms Specialty, Inc.)
- Laurona Armas Eibar S.A.D. (Continental Imports & Distribution; Galaxy Imports Ltd., Inc.)
- Lebeau-Courally (New England Arms Co.)
- Llama Gabilondo Y Cia (SGS Importers International, Inc.)
  London Guns Ltd. (London Guns Ltd.)
  Magtech (Magtech Recreational Products, Inc.)
- Marksman Products (Marksman Products)
- Marocchi F.lli S.p.A. (Precision Sales International, Inc.; Sile Distributors, Inc.)
  Mauser Werke (Gibbs Rifle Co., Inc.)
- MEC-Gar s.r.l. (MEC-Gar U.S.A., Inc.)
- Merkel Freres (GSI, Inc.)
- Miroku, B.C./Daly, Charles (Bell's Legendary Country Wear)
- Mitchell Arms, Inc. (Mitchell Arms, Inc.)
- Morini (Mandall Shooting Supplies; Nygord Precision Products)
- Navy Arms Co. (Forgett Jr., Valmore J.; Navy Arms Co.)
  Norica, Avnda Otaola
- Norinco (Century International Arms, Inc.; Interarms)
  Norma Precision AB (Dynamit Nobel-RWS Inc.; The Paul Co., Inc.)
- Para-Ordnance Mfg., Inc. (Para-Ordnance, Inc.)
- Pardini Armi Srl. (MCS, Inc.; Nygord Precision Products)
  Park Rifle Co., Ltd. (Air Werks International)
- Pedersoli, Davide & C. (Beauchamp & Son, Inc.; Cabela's; Cape Outfitters; Dixie Gun Works, Inc.; EMF Co., Inc.; Navy Arms Co.; Taylor's & Co., Inc.)
- Perazzi m.a.p. S.p.A. (Perazzi USA, Inc.)
  Perugini-Visini & Co. s.r.l.
- Peters Stahl GmbH (Harris-McMillan Gunworks; Olympic Arms)
  Pietta (Navy Arms Co.; Taylor's & Co., Inc.)
- Piotti (Moore & Co., Wm. Larkin)
- Powell & Son Ltd., William (Powell Agency, The, William)

GUNS, FOREIGN—MANUFACTURERS (Importers)

Accuracy International Precision Rifles (Gunsite Training Center)
- Air Arms (Air Werks International; World Class Airguns)
- Anschutz GmbH (Precision Sales International, Inc.)
- Arizaga (Mandall Shooting Supplies, Inc.)

PRODUCT DIRECTORY

QB air rifles (Sportsman Airguns, Inc.)
- Rigby & Co., John
- Rizzini, Battista (Alessandri & Son, Lou; New England Arms Co.)
- Rizzini, F.LLI (Moore & Co., Wm. Larkin; New England Arms Co.)
- R.O.A. (Winchester Sutler, Inc., The)
- Rossi S.A., Amadeo Rua (Interarms)
- Rutten (Air Werks International)
- RWS (Dynamit Nobel-RWS, Inc.)
- Sabatti S.R.L. (E.A.A. Corp.)
- Sako Ltd. (Stoeger Industries)
- San Marco (Cape Outfitters; EMF Co., Inc.)
- Sardius Industries Ltd.
- S.A.R.L. G. Granger
- Sauer (Paul Co., The)
- Shanghai Airguns, Ltd. (Sportsman Airguns, Inc.)
- Sharp (Great Lakes Airguns)
- SIG (Mandall Shooting Supplies, Inc.)
- SIG-Sauer (Sigarms, Inc.)
- SKB Arms Co. (G.U., Inc.)
- Societa Armi Bresciane Srl. (Gamba, USA)
- Spezial Waffen (American Bullets)
- Sphinx Engineering SA (Sphinx USA Inc.)
- Springfield, Inc. (Springfield, Inc.)
- Star Bonifacio Echeverria S.A. (Interarms)
- Steyr (GSI, Inc.; Nygord Precision Products)
- Steyr-Mannlicher AG (GSI, Inc.)
- Tanfoglio S.r.l., Fratelli (E.A.A. Corp.)
- Tanner (Mandall Shooting Supplies, Inc.)
- Taurus International Firearms (Taurus Firearms, Inc.)
- T.F.C. S.p.A.
- Tikka (Stoeger Industries)
- TOZ (Nygord Precision Products)
- Turkish Firearms Corp. (Turkish Firearms Corp.)
- Uberti, Aldo (American Arms, Inc.; Cape Outfitters; Cimarron Arms; Dixie Gun Works, Inc.; EMF Co., Inc.; Forgett Jr., Valmore J.; Navy Arms Co.; Taylor's & Co., Inc.)
- Ugartechea S.A., Ignacio (Mandall Shooting Supplies, Inc.)
- Ultralux (Keng's Firearms Specialty, Inc.)
- Unique/M.A.P.F. (Nygord Precision Products)
- USA Sporting Inc. (Armas Kemen)
- Venom Arms Co. (Mac-1 Distributors; Trooper Walsh)
- Voere-KGH m.b.H. (JägerSport, Ltd.)
- Walther GmbH, Carl (Interarms)
- Weatherby, Inc. (Weatherby, Inc.)
- Webley & Scott Ltd. (Beeman Precision Airguns)
- Weihrauch KG, Hermann (Beeman Precision Airguns; E.A.A. Corp.)
- Westley Richards & Co. (Cape Outfitters)
- Whiscombe (Pelaire Products)
- Zabala, Hermanos S.A. (American Arms, Inc.)
- Zanoletti, Pietro (Mandall Shooting Supplies, Inc.)
- Zoli, Antonio

GUNS, U.S.-MADE

- Accu-Tek
- Airrow
- American Arms & Ordnance, Inc.
- American Arms, Inc.
- American Derringer Corp.
- AMT
- Armalite, Inc.
- A-Square Co., Inc.
- Auto-Ordnance Corp.
- Baer Custom, Inc., Les
- Barrett Firearms Mfg., Inc.
- Benton & Brown Firearms, Inc.
- Beretta U.S.A. Corp.
- Braverman, R.J.
- Brolin Arms
- Brown Co., E. Arthur
- Browning Arms Co. (Parts & Service)
- Bryco Arms
- Bushmaster Firearms
- Calico Light Weapon Systems
- Century Gun Dist., Inc.
- CHARCO
- Charter Arms
- Colt's Mfg. Co., Inc.
- Competitor Corp., Inc.
- Connecticut Valley Classics
- Connecticut Shotgun Mfg. Co.
- Coonan Arms
- Cooper Arms
- Cumberland Mountain Arms
- CVA
- Dakota Arms, Inc.
- Davis Industries
- Desert Industries, Inc.
- D-Max, Inc.
- Eagle Arms, Inc.
- Emerging Technologies, Inc.
- Essex Arms
- Feather Industries, Inc.
- Federal Engineering Corp.
- Freedom Arms, Inc.
- Gibbs Rifle Co., Inc.
- Gilbert Equipment Co., Inc.
- Gonic Arms, Inc.
- H&R 1871, Inc.
- Harris-McMillan Gunworks
- Hart & Son, Inc., Robert W.
- Hatfield Gun Co., Inc.
- Hawken Shop, The
- High Standard Mfg. Co., Inc.
- Hi-Point Firearms
- HJS Arms, Inc.
- Holston Ent. Inc.
- H-S Precision, Inc.
- Intratec
- Ithaca Aquisition Corp./Ithaca Gun
- Jennings Firearms Inc.
- Kahr Arms
- Kel-Tec CNC Industries, Inc.
- Kimber of America, Inc.
- Kimel Industries
- Knight's Mfg. Co.
- L.A.R. Manufacturing, Inc.
- Laseraim, Inc.
- Lorcin Engineering Co., Inc.
- Magnum Research, Inc.
- Marlin Firearms Co.
- Maverick Arms, Inc.
- McBros Rifle Co.
- Mitchell Arms, Inc.
- MKS Supply, Inc.
- M.O.A. Corp.
- Montana Armory, Inc.
- Mossberg & Sons, Inc., O.F.
- Mowrey Gun Works
- New Advantage Arms Corp.
- New England Firearms
- North American Arms, Inc.
- Olympic Arms, Inc.
- Phoenix Arms
- Prairie River Arms
- Precision Small Arms
- Quality Parts Co.
- Remington Arms Co., Inc.
- Rocky Mountain Arms, Inc.
- Savage Arms, Inc.
- Scattergun Technologies, Inc.
- Seecamp Co., Inc., L.W.
- Sharps Arms Co., Inc., C.
- Shiloh Rifle Mfg.
- Smith & Wesson
- Sporting Arms Mfg., Inc.
- Springfield, Inc.
- Sturm, Ruger & Co., Inc.
- Sundance Industries, Inc.
- Survival Arms, Inc.
- Swivel Machine Works, Inc.
- Tar-Hunt Custom Rifles, Inc.
- Taurus Firearms, Inc.
- Texas Armory
- Texas Longhorn Arms, Inc.
- Thompson/Center Arms
- Ultra Light Arms, Inc.
- U.S. Repeating Arms Co.
- Wesson Firearms Co., Inc.
- White Shooting Systems, Inc.
- Wichita Arms, Inc.
- Wildey, Inc.
- Wilkinson Arms
- Wyoming Armory, Inc.

GUNS AND GUN PARTS, REPLICA AND ANTIQUE

Ahlman Guns
Armi San Paolo
Bear Mountain Gun & Tool
Beauchamp & Son, Inc.
Bill's Gun Repair
Bob's Gun Shop
British Arms Co. Ltd.
Buckskin Machine Works
Buffalo Arms
Burgess & Son Gunsmiths, R.W.
C&J Enterprises, Inc.
Cache La Poudre Riflework
Campbell, Dick
Cape Outfitters
Century International Arms, Inc.
Cogar's Gunsmithing
Cole's Gun Works
Colonial Repair
Curly Maple Stock Blanks
Dangler, Homer L.
Day & Sons, Inc., Leonard
D.B.A. Flintlocks, Etc.
Delhi Gun House
Delta Arms Ltd.
Dilliott Gunsmithing, Inc.
Dixon Muzzleloading Shop, Inc.
Dyson & Son Ltd., Peter
Ed's Gun House
EMF Co., Inc.
Enguix Import-Export
F.A.I.R. Techni-Mec s.n.c.
First, Inc., Jack
Flintlocks, Etc.
Flintlocks, Inc.
Forgett, Valmore J., Jr.
Forster Products
Franchi S.p.A., Luigi
Frank Custom Gun Service, Ron
Golden Age Arms Co.
Goodwin, Fred
Groenewold, John
Gun Parts Corp., The
Gun Works, The
Guns
Gun-Tec
Hastings Barrels
Hunkeler, A.
Liberty Antique Gunworks
List Precision Engineering
Log Cabin Sport Shop
Lucas, Edw. E.
Martin's Gun Shop
McCann's Muzzle-Gun Works
McKee Publications
McKinney, R.P.
Mountain Bear Rifle Works, Inc.
Mountain State Muzzleloading Supplies
Mowrey Gun Works
Munsch Gunsmithing, Tommy
Museum of Historical Arms, Inc.
Neumann GmbH
Newman Gunshop
Parker Gun Finishes
Pasadena Gun Center
PEM's Mfg. Co.
P.M. Enterprises, Inc.
Pony Express Sport Shop, Inc.
Precise Metalsmithing Enterprises
Quality Firearms of Idaho, Inc.
Radical Concepts
Randco UK
Retting, Inc., Martin B.
S&S Firearms
Sarco, Inc.
Schuetzen Gun Service
Silver Ridge Gun Shop
Sipes Gun Shop
Sklany, Steve
Starr Trading Co., Jedediah
Stott's Creek Armory, Inc.
Taylor's & Co., Inc.
Tecni-Mec
Tiger-Hunt
Track of the Wolf, Inc.
Uberti USA, Inc.
Vintage Industries, Inc.
Weisz Parts
Wescombe
Winchester Sutler, Inc., The

GUNS, SURPLUS—PARTS AND AMMUNITION

Armscorp USA, Inc.
Arundel Arms & Ammunition, Inc., A.
Aztec International Ltd.
Badger Shooters Supply, Inc.
Ballistica Maximus North
Bohemia Arms Co.
Bondini Paolo
Braun, M.
British Arms Co. Ltd.
Century International Arms, Inc.
Chuck's Gun Shop
Cole's Gun Works
Combat Military Ordnance Ltd.
Delta Arms Ltd.
F.A.I.R. Techni-Mec s.n.c.
First, Inc., Jack
Fleming Firearms
Forgett, Valmore J., Jr.
Forrest, Inc., Tom
Fulton Armory
Garcia National Gun Traders, Inc.
Goodwin, Fred
"Gramps" Antique Cartridges
Gun Parts Corp., The
Hank's Gun Shop
Hart & Son, Inc., Robert W.
Interarms
KLA Enterprises
Lever Arms Service Ltd.
Mathews & Son, Inc., George E.
Moreton/Fordyce Enterprises
Mountain Bear Rifle Works, Inc.
Navy Arms Co.
Nevada Pistol Academy Inc.
Newman Gunshop
Nu-Line Guns, Inc.
Oil Rod and Gun Shop
Old Western Scrounger, Inc.
Paragon Sales & Services, Inc.
Parts & Surplus
Pasadena Gun Center
Quality Firearms of Idaho, Inc.
Randall Firearms Research
Retting, Inc., Martin B.
Samco Global Arms, Inc.
Sanders Custom Gun Service
Sarco, Inc.
Silver Ridge Gun Shop
Sipes Gun Shop
Southern Ammunition Co., Inc.
Southern Armory, The
Sportsmen's Exchange & Western Gun Traders, Inc.
Springfield Sporters, Inc.
Starnes Gunmaker, Ken
Tecni-Mec
T.F.C. S.p.A.
Thurston Sports, Inc.
Vom Hoffe
Westfield Engineering
Whitestone Lumber Corp.

GUNSMITHS, CUSTOM (see Custom Gunsmiths)

GUNSMITHS, HANDGUN (see Pistolsmiths)

GUNSMITH SCHOOLS

Bull Mountain Rifle Co.
Colorado School of Trades
Cylinder & Slide, Inc.
Lassen Community College, Gunsmithing Dept.
Laughridge, William R.
Modern Gun Repair School
Montgomery Community College
Murray State College
North American Correspondence Schools
Nowlin Custom Mfg.

50th EDITION, 1996

DIRECTORY OF THE ARMS TRADE

NRI Gunsmith School
Pennsylvania Gunsmith School
Piedmont Community College
Pine Technical College
Professional Gunsmiths of America, Inc.
Southeastern Community College
Spencer's Custom Guns
Trinidad State Junior College Gunsmithing Dept.
Weigand Combat Handguns, Inc.
Wessinger Custom Guns & Engraving

GUNSMITH SUPPLIES, TOOLS, SERVICES

Actions by "T"
Aldis Gunsmithing & Shooting Supply
Alley Supply Co.
Aro-Tek, Ltd.
Baer Custom, Inc., Les
Bald Eagle Precision Machine Co.
Bear Mountain Gun & Tool
Behlert Precision
Bengtson Arms Co., L.
Biesen, Al
Biesen, Roger
Billingsley & Brownell
Birchwood Laboratories, Inc.
Blue Ridge Machinery & Tools, Inc.
Bowen Classic Arms Corp.
Boyds' Gunstock Industries, Inc.
Break-Free, Inc.
Briley Mfg., Inc.
Brownells, Inc.
B-Square Co., Inc.
Bull Mountain Rifle Co.
Carbide Checkering Tools
Chapman Manufacturing Co.
Chem-Pak, Inc.
Choate Machine & Tool Co., Inc.
Chopie Mfg., Inc.
Chuck's Gun Shop
Clark Custom Guns, Inc.
Colonial Arms, Inc.
Conetrol Scope Mounts
Corbin, Inc.
Craig Custom Ltd.
Cumberland Arms
Custom Checkering Service
Custom Gun Products
D&J Bullet Co. & Custom Gun Shop, Inc.
Dakota Arms, Inc.
Dayton Traister
Decker Shooting Products
Dem-Bart Hand Checkering Tools, Inc.
Dilliott Gunsmithing, Inc.
Dremel Mfg. Co.
Duffy, Charles E.
Du-Lite Corp.
Dutchman's Firearms, Inc., The
Dyson & Son Ltd., Peter
Echols & Co., D'Arcy
EGW Evolution Gun Works
Eilan S.A.L.
F.A.I.R. Techni-Mec s.n.c.
Faith Associates, Inc.
First, Inc., Jack
Fisher, Jerry A.
Forgreens Tool Mfg., Inc.
Forster, Kathy
Forster Products
Frazier Brothers Enterprises
G.B.C. Industries, Inc.
Grace Metal Products, Inc.
Greider Precision
Gunline Tools
Guns
Gunsite Training Center
Gun-Tec
Half Moon Rifle Shop
Hart & Son, Inc., Robert W.
Hastings Barrels
Henriksen Tool Co., Inc.
Hoelscher, Virgil
Holland's
Iosso Products
Ivanoff, Thomas G.
Jacobson, Teddy
Jantz Supply
Jarvis Gunsmithing, Inc.
JBM Software
JGS Precision Tool Mfg.
Kasenit Co., Inc.
KenPatable Ent., Inc.
Kimball, Gary
Kleinendorst, K.W.
Kmount
Korzinek Riflesmith, J.
Kwik Mount Corp.
LaBounty Precision Reboring
LaRocca Gun Works, Inc.
Lea Mfg. Co.
Lee's Red Ramps
Lee Supplies, Mark
List Precision Engineering
Lortone, Inc.
Marsh, Mike
Menck, Thomas W.
Metalife Industries
Metaloy Inc.
Michael's Antiques
Millett Sights
MMC
Morrow, Bud
Mowreys Guns & Supplies
N&J Sales
Nitex, Inc.
Nowlin Custom Mfg.
Ole Frontier Gunsmith Shop
Pace Marketing, Inc.
Palmgren Steel Products
Palsa Outdoor Products
PanaVise Products, Inc.
PEM's Mfg. Co.
Perazone, Brian
Power Custom, Inc.
Practical Tools, Inc.
Precision Metal Finishing
Precision Specialties
Pre-Winchester 92-90-62 Parts Co.
Reardon Products
Rice, Keith
Roto Carve
Ruvel & Co., Inc.
Scott, McDougall & Associates
Sharp Shooter, Inc.
Shirley Co. Gun & Riflemakers Ltd.
Shooter's Choice
Sinclair International, Inc.
S.K. Guns, Inc.
Smith Abrasives, Inc.
Starrett Co., L.S.
Stoney Point Products, Inc.
Stuart Products, Inc.
Sullivan, David S.
Sure Shot of LA, Inc.
Talley, Dave
TDP Industries, Inc.
Tecni-Mec
Texas Platers Supply
Time Precision, Inc.
Tom's Gun Repair
Track of the Wolf, Inc.
Trulock Tool
Turnbull Restoration, Doug
Venco Industries, Inc.
Vintage Industries, Inc.
Washita Mountain Whetstone Co.
Weaver's Gun Shop
Weigand Combat Handguns, Inc.
Wessinger Custom Guns & Engraving
Westfield Engineering
Westrom, John
Westwind Rifles, Inc.
White Rock Tool & Die
Wilcox All-Pro Tools & Supply
Will-Burt Co.
Williams Gun Sight Co.
Willow Bend
Wilson's Gun Shop
Wise Guns, Dale
World of Targets
Wright's Hardwood Gunstock Blanks

HANDGUN ACCESSORIES

Ace Custom 45's
ADCO International
Adventurer's Outpost
Aimtech Mount Systems
Ajax Custom Grips, Inc.
American Derringer Corp.
Armite Laboratories
Aro-Tek, Ltd.
Astra Sport, S.A.
Auto-Ordnance Corp.
Baer Custom, Inc., Les
Bagmaster Mfg., Inc.
Bar-Sto Precision Machine
Baumannize Custom
Behlert Precision
Black Sheep Brand
Blue and Gray Products, Inc.
Bob's Gun Shop
Boonie Packer Products
Bowen Classic Arms Corp.
Broken Gun Ranch
Brown Products, Inc., Ed
Brownells, Inc.
Bucheimer, J.M.
Bushmaster Firearms
Butler Creek Corp.
C3 Systems
Centaur Systems, Inc.
Central Specialties Ltd.
Clark Custom Guns, Inc.
Cobra Gunskin
Conetrol Scope Mounts
Craig Custom Ltd.
CRL, Inc.
Dade Screw Machine Products
Delhi Gun House
Doskocil Mfg. Co., Inc
E.A.A. Corp.
EGW Evolution Gun Works
Faith Associates, Inc.
FAS
Feather Industries, Inc.
Feminine Protection, Inc.
Ferris Firearms
Fleming Firearms
Forgett Jr., Valmore J.
Frielich Police Equipment
Glock, Inc.
GML Products, Inc.
Greider Precision
Gremmel Enterprises
Gun Parts Corp., The
Gun-Alert
Guncraft Sports, Inc.
Gunfitters, The
Gun-Ho Sports Cases
Gunsite Training Center
Hart & Son, Inc., Robert W.
Haselbauer Products, Jerry
Hebard Guns, Gil
Heinie Specialty Products
Hill Speed Leather, Ernie
H.K.S. Products
Hoppe's Div.
Hunter Co., Inc.
Jarvis Gunsmithing, Inc.
Jeffredo Gunsight
Jett & Co., Inc.
John's Custom Leather
Jones, J.D.
J.P. Enterprises, Inc.
Jumbo Sports Products
K&K Ammo Wrist Band
KeeCo Impressions
Keller Co., The
King's Gun Works
L&S Technologies Inc.
Lakewood Products, Inc.
LaRocca Gun Works, Inc.
Lee's Red Ramps
Lem Sports, Inc.
Loch Leven Industries
Lohman Mfg. Co., Inc.
Mac's .45 Shop
Magnolia Sports, Inc.
Magnum Research, Inc.
Marble Arms
Markell Inc.
Masen Co., Inc., John
Master Products, Inc.
McCann's Machine & Gun Shop
McCormick Corp., Chip
MEC-Gar S.R.L.
Menck, Thomas W.
Merkuria Ltd.
Michaels of Oregon Co.
Millett Sights
MTM Molded Products Co., Inc.
Mustra's Custom Guns, Inc., Carl
Noble Co., Jim
North American Specialties
No-Sho Mfg. Co.
Nowlin Custom Mfg.
Owen, Harry
Ox-Yoke Originals, Inc.
Pace Marketing, Inc.
Pardini Armi Srl
PAST Sporting Goods, Inc.
Peacemaker Specialists
Pendleton Royal
Penguin Industries, Inc.
Power Custom, Inc.
Practical Tools, Inc.
Protector Mfg. Co., Inc., The
Protektor Model
Quality Parts Co.
Ram-Line, Inc.
Ranch Products
Ravell Ltd.
Round Edge, Inc.
Safariland Ltd., Inc.
Scott, McDougall & Associates
Sinclair International, Inc.
Slings 'N Things, Inc.
Smith & Wesson
Sonderman, Robert
Southwind Sanctions
Sport Specialties
SSK Industries
Starnes Gunmaker, Ken
"Su-Press-On," Inc.
TacTell, Inc.
Tapco, Inc.
Tarnham Supply
Taurus, S.A., Forjas
T.F.C. S.p.A.
Thompson/Center Arms
TMI Products
Trijicon, Inc.
Triple-K Mfg. Co.
Tyler Mfg.-Dist., Melvin
Uncle Mike's
Valor Corp.
Vintage Industries, Inc.
Volquartsen Custom Ltd.
Weigand Combat Handguns, Inc.
Wessinger Custom Guns & Engraving
Western Design
Whitestone Lumber Corp.
Wichita Arms, Inc.

HANDGUN GRIPS

Ace Custom 45's
Ahrends, Kim
Ajax Custom Grips, Inc.
Altamont Co.
American Derringer Corp.
American Gripcraft
Arms Corp. of the Philippines
Aro-Tek, Ltd.
Art Jewel Enterprises Ltd.
Baer Custom, Inc., Les
Barami Corp.
Bear Hug Grips, Inc.
Bell Originals, Inc., Sid
Bob's Gun Shop
Boone's Custom Ivory Grips, Inc.
Brooks Tactical Systems
Brown Products, Inc., Ed
CAM Enterprises
Clark Custom Guns, Inc.
Cobra Gunskin
Cole-Grip
Colonial Repair
Curtis Gun Shop
Custom Firearms
Dayson Arms Ltd.
Desert Industries, Inc.
E.A.A. Corp.
Eagle Mfg. & Engineering
EMF Co., Inc.
Eyears Insurance
Ferris Firearms
Fisher Custom Firearms
Fitz Pistol Grip Co.
Forrest, Inc., Tom
Gunsite Training Center
Herrett's Stocks, Inc.
Hogue Grips
J.P. Enterprises, Inc.
KeeCo Impressions
Lett Custom Grips
Linebaugh Custom Sixguns & Rifle Works

PRODUCT DIRECTORY

Mac's .45 Shop
Masen Co., Inc., John
McCann's Machine & Gun Shop
Michaels of Oregon Co.
Millett Sights
Monte Kristo Pistol Grip Co.
N.C. Ordnance Co.
Newell, Robert H.
North American Specialties
Pardini Armi Srl
Peacemaker Specialists
Pilgrim Pewter, Inc.
Ravell Ltd.
Reiswig, Wallace E.
Rosenberg & Sons, Jack A.
Roy's Custom Grips
Savana Sports, Inc.
Sile Distributors, Inc.
Smith & Wesson
Spegel, Craig
Taurus, S.A., Forjas
Taurus Firearms, Inc.
Tyler Mfg.-Dist., Melvin
Uncle Mike's
Valor Corp.
Vintage Industries, Inc.
Volquartsen Custom Ltd.
Wayland Precision Wood Products
Wichita Arms, Inc.

Safety Speed Holster, Inc.
Savana Sports, Inc.
Schulz Industries
Second Chance Body Armor
Shoemaker & Sons, Inc., Tex
Silhouette Leathers
Smith Saddlery, Jesse W.
Southwind Sanctions
Sparks, Milt
Stalker, Inc.
Strong Holster Co.
Stuart, V. Pat
Tabler Marketing
Texas Longhorn Arms, Inc.
Top-Line USA Inc.
Torel, Inc.
Triple-K Mfg. Co., Inc.
Tyler Mfg.-Dist., Melvin
Uncle Mike's
Valor Corp.
Venus Industries
Viking Leathercraft, Inc.
Walt's Custom Leather
Whinnery, Walt
Whitestone Lumber Corp.
Wild Bill's Originals

HEARING PROTECTORS

Blount, Inc.
Brown Co., E. Arthur
Browning Arms Co.
Clark Co., Inc., David
Clark Custom Guns, Inc.
Cobra Gunskin
CRL, Inc.
E-A-R, Inc.
Faith Associates, Inc.
Firearms Supplies Inc.
Fitz Pistol Grip Co.
Flents Products Co., Inc.
Gonzalez Guns, Ramon B.
Hart & Son, Inc., Robert W.
Hoppe's Div.
Kesselring Gun Shop
Marble Arms
North American Specialties
North Specialty Products
Paterson Gunsmithing
Peltor, Inc.
Penguin Industries, Inc.
Powell & Son (Gunmakers) Ltd., William
Ravell Ltd.
RCBS
R.E.T. Enterprises
Safesport Manufacturing Co.
Silencio/Safety Direct
Smith & Wesson
Tyler Mfg.-Dist., Melvin
Valor Corp.
Willson Safety Prods. Div.

HOLSTERS AND LEATHER GOODS

A&B Industries, Inc.
Action Products, Inc.
Aker Leather Products
Alessi Holsters, Inc.
Alley Supply Co.
American Import Co., The/Export Division
American Sales & Kirkpatrick
Arratoonian, Andy
Bagmaster Mfg., Inc.
Baker's Leather Goods, Roy
Bandcor Industries
Bang-Bang Boutique
Barami Corp.
Bear Hug Grips, Inc.
Bianchi International, Inc.
Black Sheep Brand
Blocker's Holsters, Inc., Ted
Brauer Bros. Mfg. Co.
Brown, H.R.
Browning Arms Co.
Bucheimer, J.M.
Bushmaster Hunting & Fishing
Bushwacker Backpack & Supply Co.
Carvajal Belts & Holsters
Cathey Enterprises, Inc.
Chace Leather Products
Cimarron Arms
Clark Custom Guns, Inc.
Clements' Custom Leathercraft, Chas
Cobra Gunskin
Cobra Sport
Colonial Repair
Counter Assault
CRDC Laser Systems Group
Crawford Co., Inc., R.M.
Creedmoor Sports, Inc.
Davis Leather Co., G. Wm.
Delhi Gun House
DeSantis Holster & Leather Goods, Inc.
Easy Pull Outlaw Products
Ekol Leather Care
El Dorado Leather
El Paso Saddlery Co.
EMF Co., Inc.
Epps "Orillia" Ltd., Ellwood
Eutaw Co., Inc., The
F&A Inc.
Faust, Inc., T.G.
Ferdinand, Inc.
Firearms Supplies Inc.
Flores Publications, Inc., J.
Fobus International Ltd.
Forgett Jr., Valmore J.
Fury Cutlery
Gage Manufacturing
Galati International
GALCO International Ltd.
Glock, Inc.
GML Products, Inc.
Gonzalez Guns, Ramon B.
Gould & Goodrich
Gun Leather Limited
Gun Works, The
Gunfitters, The
Gunsite Training Center
Gusty Winds Corp.
Gutmann Cutlery Co., Inc.
Hafner Creations, Inc.
HandiCrafts Unltd.
Hebard Guns, Gil
Hellweg Ltd.
Henigson & Associates, Steve
High North Products, Inc.
Hill Speed Leather, Ernie
Holster Shop, The
Horseshoe Leather Products
Hoyt Holster Co., Inc.
Hume, Don
Hunter Co., Inc.
John's Custom Leather
Joy Enterprises
Jumbo Sports Products
Kane Products, Inc.
Keller Co., The
Kirkpatrick Leather Co.
Kolpin Mfg., Inc.
Korth
Kramer Handgun Leather, Inc.
L.A.R. Manufacturing, Inc.
Law Concealment Systems, Inc.
Lawrence Leather Co.
Leather Arsenal
Lone Star Gunleather
Magnolia Sports, Inc.
Markell, Inc.
Michaels of Oregon Co.
Minute Man High Tech. Ind.
Mixson Corp.
Nelson Combat Leather, Bruce
Noble Co., Jim
No-Sho Mfg. Co.
Null Holsters Ltd., K.L.
Ojala Holsters, Arvo
Oklahoma Leather Products, Inc.
Old West Reproductions, Inc.
Pace Marketing, Inc.
Pathfinder Sports Leather
Powell & Son (Gunmakers) Ltd., William
Protektor Model
PWL Gunleather
Ravell Ltd.
Renegade
Ringler Custom Leather Co.
Rybka Custom Leather Equipment, Thad
Safariland Ltd., Inc.

HUNTING AND CAMP GEAR, CLOTHING, ETC.

Ace Sportswear, Inc.
Action Products, Inc.
Adventure 16, Inc.
American Import Co., The/Export Division
Armor
Atlanta Cutlery Corp.
Atsko/Sno-Seal, Inc.
Baekgaard Ltd.
Barbour, Inc.
Barteaux Machetes, Inc.
Bauer, Eddie
Bausch & Lomb, Inc.
Bear Archery
Beaver Park Products, Inc
Better Concepts Co.
Big Beam Emergency Systems, Inc.
Boss Manufacturing Co.
Brell Mar Products
Brown Manufacturing
Browning Arms Co.
Buck Stop Lure Co., Inc.
Bullet Meister Bullets
Bushmaster Hunting & Fishing
Cabela's
Camofare Co.
Camp-Cap Products
Carhartt, Inc.
Catoctin Cutlery
Chameleon Camouflage Systems
Chippewa Shoe Co.
Churchill Glove Co., James
Clarkfield Enterprises, Inc.
Clements' Custom Leathercraft, Chas
Cobra Gunskin
Coghlan's Ltd.
Coleman Co., Inc.
Coulston Products, Inc.
Crawford Co., Inc., R.M.
Creedmoor Sports, Inc.
D&H Prods. Co., Inc.
Dakota Corp.
Danner Shoe Mfg. Co.
DeckSlider of Florida
Deer Me Products
Dr. O's Products Ltd.
Dunham Co.
Duofold, Inc.
Duxbak, Inc.
Dynalite Products, Inc.
E-A-R, Inc.
Ekol Leather Care
Erickson's Mfg., Inc., C.W.
Eutaw Co., Inc., The
F&A Inc.
Fish-N-Hunt, Inc.
Flow-Rite of Tennessee, Inc.
Forrest Tool Co.
Fox River Mills, Inc.
Frankonia Jagd
G&H Decoys, Inc.
Game Winner, Inc.
Gander Mountain, Inc.
Gerber Legendary Blades
Glacier Glove
Hafner Creations, Inc.
HandiCrafts Unltd.
Hawken Shop, The
Hinman Outfitters, Bob
Hodgman, Inc.
Hofmann & Co.
Houtz & Barwick
Hunter's Specialties, Inc.
Innovision Enterprises
Just Brass, Inc.
K&M Industries, Inc.
Kamik Outdoor Footwear
Kolpin Mfg., Inc.
LaCrosse Footwear, Inc.
Langenberg Hat Co.
Lansky Sharpeners & Crock Stick
Leatherman Tool Group, Inc.
Lectro Science, Inc.
Liberty Trouser Co.
L.L. Bean
Mack's Sport Shop
MAG Instrument, Inc.
Marathon Rubber Prods. Co., Inc.
McCann's Machine & Gun Shop
Melton Shirt Co., Inc.
Michaels of Oregon Co.
Molin Industries
Mountain Hollow Game Calls
Nelson/Weather-Rite, Inc.
Noble Co., Jim
North Specialty Products
Northlake Outdoor Footwear
Original Mink Oil, Inc.
Orvis Co., The
Outdoor Connection, Inc., The
Palsa Outdoor Products
Partridge Sales Ltd., John
Pendleton Woolen Mills
Pointing Dog Journal
Porta Blind, Inc.
Powell & Son (Gunmakers) Ltd., William
Pro-Mark
Pyromid, Inc.
Randolph Engineering, Inc.
Ranger Mfg. Co., Inc.
Ranging, Inc.
Rattlers Brand
Ravell Ltd.
Red Ball
Refrigiwear, Inc.
Re-Heater, Inc.
Rocky, Shoes & Boots
Rocky Mountain High Sports Glasses
Ruvel & Co., Inc.
Safesport Manufacturing Co.
Savana Sports, Inc.
Scansport, Inc.
Schaefer Shooting Sports
Scotch Hunting Products Co., Inc.
Servus Footwear Co.
Silencio/Safety Direct
Slings 'N Things, Inc.
Sno-Seal, Inc.
Streamlight, Inc.
Swanndri New Zealand
Tapco, Inc.
10-X Products Group
Thompson, Norm
T.H.U. Enterprises, Inc.
Tink's Safariland Hunting Corp.
Torel, Inc.
TrailTimer Co.
Uncle Mike's
Venus Industries
Wakina by Pic
Walker Co., B.B.
Walls Industries
Wilderness Sound Products Ltd.
Willson Safety Prods. Div.
Wolverine Boots & Outdoor Footwear Division
Woolrich Woolen Mills
Wyoming Knife Corp.
Yellowstone Wilderness Supply

KNIVES AND KNIFEMAKER'S SUPPLIES FACTORY AND MAIL ORDER

Adventure 16, Inc.
African Import Co.
Aitor-Cuchilleria Del Norte, S.A.
All Rite Products, Inc.

50th EDITION, 1996   **563**

DIRECTORY OF THE ARMS TRADE

American Import Co., The/Export Division
American Target Knives
Aristocrat Knives
Art Jewel Enterprises Ltd.
Atlanta Cutlery Corp.
B&D Trading Co., Inc.
Barteaux Machetes, Inc.
Bell Originals, Inc., Sid
Benchmark Knives
Beretta U.S.A. Corp.
Blackjack Knives, Ltd.
Blue Ridge Knives
Boker USA, Inc.
Bowen Knife Co. Inc.
Browning Arms Co.
Buck Knives, Inc.
Buster's Custom Knives
CAM Enterprises
Camillus Cutlery Co.
Campbell, Dick
Case & Sons Cutlery Co., W.R.
Catoctin Cutlery
Chicago Cutlery Co.
Christopher Firearms Co., Inc., E.
Clements' Custom Leathercraft, Chas
Coast Cutlery Co.
Cold Steel, Inc.
Coleman Co., Inc.
Colonial Knife Co., Inc.
Compass Industries, Inc.
Crawford Co., Inc., R.M.
Creative Craftsman, Inc., The
Crosman Blades
Cutco Cutlery
Cutlery Shoppe
Damascus-U.S.A.
Dan's Whetstone Co., Inc.
Degen Inc.
Delhi Gun House
DeSantis Holster & Leather Goods, Inc.
Diamontd Machining Technology, Inc.
EdgeCraft Corp.
EK Knife Co.
Empire Cutlery Corp.
Eze-Lap Diamond Prods.
Fish-N-Hunt, Inc.
Forrest Tool Co.
Forthofer's Gunsmithing & Knifemaking
Fortune Products, Inc.
Frank Knives
Frost Cutlery Co.
Fury Cutlery
Galati International
Gerber Legendary Blades
Gibbs Rifle Co., Inc.
Golden Age Arms Co.
Gun Room, The
Gutmann Cutlery Co., Inc.
H&B Forge Co.
HandiCrafts Unltd.
Harrington Cutlery, Inc., Russell
Harris Publications
Hart & Son, Inc., Robert W.
Hawken Shop, The
Henckels Zwillingswerk, Inc., J.A.
High North Products, Inc.
Hoppe's Div.
Hubertus Schneidwarenfabrik
Hunter Co., Inc.
Hunting Classics
Hy-Score Arms Co. Ltd.
Ibberson (Sheffield) Ltd., George
Imperial Schrade Corp.
Iron Mountain Knife Co.
J.A. Blades, Inc.
Jantz Supply
Jenco Sales, Inc.
Johnson Wood Products
Joy Enterprises
KA-BAR Knives
Kasenit Co., Inc.
Kellogg's Professional Products
Ken's Finn Knives
Kershaw Knives
Knife Importers, Inc.
Koval Knives
Lamson & Goodnow Mfg. Co.
Leatherman Tool Group, Inc.
Linder Solingen Knives
L.L. Bean
Mar Knives, Inc., Al
Matthews Cutlery
Molin Industries
Monte Kristo Pistol Grip Co.
Murphy Co., Inc., R.
Normark Corp.
North American Specialties
Outdoor Edge Cutlery Corp.
Penguin Industries, Inc.
Pilgrim Pewter, Inc.
Plaza Cutlery, Inc.
Powell & Son (Gunmakers) Ltd., William
Precise International
Queen Cutlery Co.
R&C Knives & Such
Randall-Made Knives
Ravell Ltd.
Ruko Products, Inc.
Russell Knives, Inc., A.G.
Safesport Manufacturing Co.
Sanders Custom Gun Service
Scansport, Inc.
Schiffman, Mike
Schrimsher's Custom Knifemaker's Supply, Bob
Sheffield Knifemakers Supply
Smith Saddlery, Jesse W.
Soque River Knives
Spyderco, Inc.
Stone Enterprises Ltd.
Swiss Army Knives, Inc.
Tapco, Inc.
T.F.C. S.p.A.
Traditions, Inc.
Tru-Balance Knife Co.
United Cutlery Corp.
Utica Cutlery Co.
Valor Corp.
Venus Industries
Walt's Custom Leather
Washita Mountain Whetstone Co.
Weber Jr., Rudolf
Wenoka/Seastyle
Western Cutlery Co.
Whinnery, Walt
Wostenholm
Wright's Hardwood Gunstock Blanks
Wyoming Knife Corp.

LABELS, BOXES, CARTRIDGE HOLDERS

Accuracy Products, S.A.
Ballistic Products, Inc.
Berry's Mfg. Inc.
British Arms Co. Ltd.
Brown Co., E. Arthur
Cabinet Mountain Outfitters Scents & Lures
Corbin, Inc.
Crane & Crane Ltd.
Del Rey Products
DeSantis Holster & Leather Goods, Inc.
Dyson & Son Ltd., Peter
Fitz Pistol Grip Co.
Flambeau Products Corp.
Galati International
J&J Products Co.
King & Co.
Kolpin Mfg., Inc.
Lakewood Products, Inc.
Loadmaster
Michaels of Oregon Co.
Midway Arms, Inc.
Monte Kristo Pistol Grip Co.
MTM Molded Products Co., Inc.
Noble Co., Jim
Pendleton Royal
Powell & Son (Gunmakers) Ltd., William
Scharch Mfg., Inc.
Sinclair International, Inc.
Uncle Mike's

LOAD TESTING AND PRODUCT TESTING, (Chronographing, Ballistic Studies)

Ammunition Consulting Services, Inc.
Ballistic Research
Briese Bullet Co., Inc.
Bustani Appraisers, Leo
Clerke Co., J.A.
D&H Precision Tooling
Dead Eye's Sport Center
Defense Training International, Inc.
DGR Custom Rifles
Duane's Gun Repair
Farr Studio, Inc.
FSI, Firearms & Supplies Inc.
Hank's Gun Shop
Hensler, Jerry
High North Products, Inc.
High Performance International
Hoelscher, Virgil
Jackalope Gun Shop
Jensen Bullets
Jones, J.D.
Jurras, L.E.
Lomont Precision Bullets
Maionchi-L.M.I.
MAST Technology
Master Class Bullets

MISCELLANEOUS

Actions, Rifle
Hall Manufacturing
Accurizing, Rifle
Stoney Baroque Shooters Supply
Adapters, Cartridge
Alex, Inc.
Owen, Harry
Adapters, Shotshell
PC Co.
Airgun Accessories
BSA Guns Ltd.
Assault Rifle Accessories
Feather Industries, Inc.
Ram-Line, Inc.
Barrel Stress Relieving
Cryo
Bi-Pods
B.M.F. Activator, Inc.
Body Armor
A&B Industries, Inc.
Faust, Inc., T.G.
Second Chance Body Armor
Top-Line USA Inc.
Bore Illuminator
Flashette Co.
Bore Lights
N.C. Ordnance Co.
MDS, Inc.
Brass Catcher
Gage Manufacturing
M.A.M. Products, Inc.
Bullets, Rubber
CIDCO
Calendar, Gun Shows
Stott's Creek Printers
Cannons, Miniature Replicas
Furr Arms
R.G.-G., Inc.
Convert-A-Pell
Jett & Co., Inc.
Dehumidifiers
Buenger Enterprises
Hydrosorbent Products
Dryers
Peet Shoe Dryer, Inc.
E-Z Loader
Del Rey Products
Firearm Restoration
Adair Custom Shop, Bill
Johns, Bill
Liberty Antique Gunworks
Mazur Restoration, Pete
Moeller, Steve
Nicholson Custom
FFL Record Keeping
Basics Information Systems, Inc.
PFRB Co.
R.E.T. Enterprises
Hunting Trips
J/B Adventures & Safaris, Inc.
Professional Hunter Specialties
Safaris Plus
Hypodermic Rifles/Pistols
Multipropulseurs
Industrial Dessicants
WAMCO—New Mexico
Insert Barrels
MCA Sports
Multi-Caliber Adapters
Owen, Harry/Sport Specialties
Lettering Restoration System
Pranger, Ed G.
Locks, Gun
Brown Manufacturing
Master Lock Co.
Mats
Brigade Quartermasters
McMurdo, Lynn
Moreton/Fordyce Enterprises
Multiplex International
Neutralizer Police Munitions
Newman Gunshop
Nowlin Custom Mfg.
Oil Rod and Gun Shop
Ransom International Corp.
R.I.S. Co., Inc.
Rupert's Gun Shop
Spencer's Custom Guns
SSK Industries
Whildin & Sons Ltd., E.H.
White Laboratory, Inc., H.P.
Whitestone Lumber Corp.
X-Spand Target Systems

Military Equipment/Accessories
Alpha 1 Drop Zone
Amherst Arms
Photographers, Gun
Bilal, Mustafa
Hanusin, John
Macbean, Stan
Payne Photography, Robert
Semmer, Charles
Smith, Michael
Weyer International
White Pine Photographic Services
Power Tools, Rotary Flexible Shaft
Foredom Electric Co.
Saddle Rings, Studs
Silver Ridge Gun Shop
Safety Devices
P&M Sales and Service
Tarnham Supply
Safeties
Harper, William E./The Great 870 Co.
P.M. Enterprises, Inc.
Scents and Lures
Buck Stop Lure Co., Inc.
Cabinet Mountain Outfitters Scents & Lures
Dr. O's Products Ltd.
Flow-Rite of Tennessee, Inc.
Rickard, Inc., Pete
Robbins Scent, Inc.
Tink's Safariland Hunting Corp.
Tinks & Ben Lee Hunting Products
Wellington Outdoors
Wildlife Research Center, Inc.
Scrimshaw
Boone's Custom Ivory Grips, Inc.
Dolbare, Elizabeth
Marek, George
Reno, Wayne
Sherwood, George
Shooting Range Equipment
Caswell International Corp.
Passive Bullet Traps, Inc.
Silencers
AWC Systems Technology
Ciener, Jonathan Arthur
DLO Mfg.
Fleming Firearms
S&H Arms Mfg. Co.
S.C.R.C.
Sound Technology
Ward Machine
Slings and Swivels
Boonie Packer Products
DTM International, Inc.
High North Products, Inc.
Leather Arsenal
Palsa Outoor Products
Pathfinder Sports Leather
Schulz Industries
Torel, Inc.
Treestands and Steps
A&J Products
Amacker International, Inc.
Apache Products, Inc.
Dr. O's Products Ltd.
Silent Hunter
Summit Specialties, Inc.
Trax America, Inc.
Treemaster
Warren & Sweat Mfg. Co.
Trophies
Blackinton & Co., Inc., V.H.
Ventilation
ScanCo Environmental Systems
Video Tapes
American Pioneer Video

PRODUCT DIRECTORY

Calibre Press, Inc.
Eastman Products, R.T.
Foothills Video Productions, Inc.
New Historians Productions, The
Primos, Inc.
Rocky Mountain Wildlife Products
Trail Visions
Wilderness Sound Products Ltd.
Xythos-Miniature Revolver
Andres & Dworsky

MUZZLE-LOADING GUNS, BARRELS AND EQUIPMENT

ABS Co. Inc./Lothar Walther
Accuracy Unlimited (Littleton, CO)
Ackermann & Co.
Adkins, Luther
Allen Manufacturing
American Bullets
●Anderson Manufacturing Co., Inc.
Armi San Paolo
●Armoury, Inc., The
●Armsport, Inc.
Beauchamp & Son, Inc.
Beaver Lodge
Bentley, John
Birdsong & Associates, W.E.
Blackhawk East
Blackhawk Mountain
Blackhawk West
Blake Affiliates
●Blount, Inc.
Blue and Gray Products, Inc.
Boyds' Gunstock Industries, Inc.
Bridgers Best
Buckskin Machine Works
Buffalo Bullet Co., Inc.
Burgess & Son Gunsmiths, R.W.
Butler Creek Corp.
Cache La Poudre Rifleworks
California Sights
Camas Hot Springs Mfg.
●Cape Outfitters
Cash Manufacturing Co., Inc.
CenterMark
Chambers Flintlocks, Ltd., Jim
Chopie Mfg., Inc.
●Cimarron Arms
Cogar's Gunsmithing
Colonial Repair
●Colt Blackpowder Arms Co.
Cousin Bob's Mountain Products
●Cumberland Arms
●Cumberland Knife & Gun Works
Curly Maple Stock Blanks
●CVA
Dangler, Homer L.
Day & Sons, Inc., Leonard
●Dayton Traister
D.B.A. Flintlocks, Etc.
deHaas Barrels
Delhi Gun House
Dewey Mfg. Co., Inc., J.
DGS, Inc.
Dilliott Gunsmithing, Inc.
●Dixie Gun Works
Dyson & Son Ltd., Peter
Eades' Muzzleloader Builders' Supply, Don
●EMF Co., Inc.
●Euroarms of America, Inc.
Eutaw Co., Inc., The
Fautheree, Andy
Feken, Dennis
Fellowes, Ted
Flintlocks, Etc.
●Forster Products
Fort Hill Gunstocks
Frontier
GOEX, Inc.
Golden Age Arms Co.
●Gonic Arms, Inc.
Gun Works, The
Hart & Son, Inc., Robert W.
Hastings Barrels
●Hatfield Gun Co., Inc.
●Hawken Shop, The
Hege Jagd-u. Sporthandels, GmbH
Hoppe's Div.
●Hornady Mfg. Co.
House of Muskets, Inc., The
Hunkeler, A.
Jamison's Forge Works
Jones Co., Dale
●JSL (Hereford) Ltd.
K&M Industries, Inc.
Kennedy Firearms
L&R Lock Co.
Legend Products Corp.
Lite Tek International
●Log Cabin Sport Shop
Lutz Engraving, Ron
●Lyman
McCann's Muzzle-Gun Works
Michaels of Oregon Co.
MMP
●Modern MuzzleLoading, Inc.
●Montana Armory, Inc.
Montana Precision Swaging
●Mossberg & Sons, Inc., O.F.
●Mowrey Gun Works
MSC Industrial Supply Co.
Mt. Alto Outdoor Products
Mushroom Express Bullet Co.
Muzzleloaders Etcetera, Inc.
Navy Arms Co.
North Star West
October Country
Oklahoma Leather Products, Inc.
Olson, Myron
Orion Rifle Barrel Co.
Ox-Yoke Originals, Inc.
●Pedersoli, Davide & C.
Penguin Industries, Inc.
Phyl-Mac
●Pioneer Arms Co.
Ravell Ltd.
R.E. Davis
Rusty Duck Premium Gun Care Products
R.V.I.
S&B Industries
S&S Firearms
Selsi Co., Inc.
●Sharps Arms Co., Inc., C.
Shooter's Choice
●Sile Distributors
Single Shot, Inc.
Slings 'N Things, Inc.
Smokey Valley Rifles
South Bend Replicas, Inc.
Southern Bloomer Mfg. Co.
SPG Bullet Lubricant
Starr Trading Co., Jedediah
Stone Mountain Arms
Storey, Dale A.
●Sturm, Ruger & Co., Inc.
TDP Industries, Inc.
Tennessee Valley Mfg.
Thompson Bullet Lube Co.
Thompson/Center Arms
●Thunder Mountain Arms
Tiger-Hunt
Time Precision, Inc.
Track of the Wolf, Inc.
●Traditions, Inc.
Treso, Inc.
UFA, Inc.
●Uberti, Aldo
Upper Missouri Trading Co.
Venco Industries, Inc.
Warren Muzzleloading Co., Inc.
Wescombe
White Owl Enterprises
●White Shooting Systems, Inc.
Williams Gun Sight Co.
Woodworker's Supply
Wright's Hardwood Gunstock Blanks
Young Country Arms

PISTOLSMITHS

Accuracy Gun Shop
Accuracy Unlimited (Glendale, AZ)
Accurate Plating & Weaponry, Inc.
Ace Custom 45's
Ackley Rifle Barrels, P.O.
Actions by "T"
Adair Custom Shop, Bill
Ahlman Guns
Ahrends, Kim
Aldis Gunsmithing & Shooting Supply
Alpha Precision, Inc.
Alpine's Precision Gunsmithing & Indoor Shooting Range
Amodei, Jim
Armament Gunsmithing Co., Inc.
AWC Systems Technology
Baer Custom, Inc., Les
Bain & Davis, Inc.
Baity's Custom Gunworks
Banks, Ed
Bar-Sto Precision Machine
Bear Arms
Behlert Precision
Bellm Contenders
Bengtson Arms Co., L.
Bowen Classic Arms Corp.
Brian, C.T.
Broken Gun Ranch
Campbell, Dick
Cannon's Guns
Caraville Manufacturing
Cellini, Inc., Vito Francesca
Clark Custom Guns, Inc.
Colonial Repair
Corkys Gun Clinic
Costa, David
Craig Custom Ltd.
Curtis Custom Shop
Custom Firearms
Custom Gunsmiths
D&L Sports
Davis Service Center, Bill
D.O.C. Specialists, Inc.
Ellicott Arms, Inc./Woods Pistolsmithing
EMF Co., Inc.
Ferris Firearms
First, Inc., Jack
Fisher Custom Firearms
Francesca, Inc.
Frielich Police Equipment
Garthwaite, Jim
Giron, Robert E.
Greider Precision
Guncraft Sports, Inc.
Gunsite Gunsmithy
Gunsite Training Center
Gunsmithing Ltd.
Hamilton, Keith
Hank's Gun Shop
Hanson's Gun Center, Dick
Hardison, Charles
Harris-McMillan Gunworks
Hebard Guns, Gil
Heinie Specialty Products
High Bridge Arms, Inc.
Highline Machine Co.
Hoag, James W.
Intermountain Arms & Tackle, Inc.
Irwin, Campbell H.
Island Pond Gun Shop
Ivanoff, Thomas G.
Jacobson, Teddy
Jarvis Gunsmithing, Inc.
Jensen's Custom Ammunition
Johnston, James
Jones, J.D.
J.P. Enterprises, Inc.
Jungkind, Reeves C.
K-D, Inc.
Ken's Gun Specialties
Kilham & Co.
Kimball, Gary
Kleinendorst, K.W.
Kopp, Terry K.
La Clinique du .45
LaRocca Gun Works, Inc.
Lawson, John G.
Lee's Red Ramps
Leckie Professional Gunsmithing
Linebaugh Custom Sixguns & Rifle Works
List Precision Engineering
Lock's Philadelphia Gun Exchange
Long, George F.
Mac's .45 Shop
Mahony, Philip Bruce
Marent, Rudolf
Marvel, Alan
Mathews & Son, Inc., George E.
Maxi-Mount
McCann's Machine & Gun Shop
MCS, Inc.
Mid-America Recreation, Inc.
Middlebrooks Custom Shop
Miller Custom
Mitchell's Accuracy Shop
MJK Gunsmithing, Inc.
Mo's Competitor Supplies
Moran, Jerry
Mountain Bear Rifle Works, Inc.
Mullis Guncraft
Mustra's Custom Guns, Inc., Carl
Nastoff's 45 Shop, Inc., Steve
North Fork Custom Gunsmithing
Novak's Inc.
Nowlin Custom Mfg.
Oglesby & Oglesby Gunmakers, Inc.
Pace Marketing, Inc.
Pardini Armi Srl
Paris, Frank J.
Pasadena Gun Center
Peacemaker Specialists
PEM's Mfg. Co.
Performance Specialists
Peterson Gun Shop, Inc., A.W.
Pierce Pistols
Plaxco, J. Michael
Precision Specialties
Randco UK
Ries, Chuck
Rim Pac Sports, Inc.
Robar Co.'s, Inc., The
Rogers Gunsmithing, Bob
Sanders Custom Gun Service
Scott, McDougall & Associates
Seecamp Co., Inc., L.W.
Shell Shack
Shooter Shop, The
Shooters Supply
Sight Shop, The
Sipes Gun Shop
S.K. Guns, Inc.
Smith & Wesson
Spokhandguns, Inc.
Springfield, Inc.
SSK Industries
Starnes, Ken
Steger, James R.
Strawbridge, Victor W.
Swampfire Shop, The
Swenson's 45 Shop, A.D.
Thompson, Randall
300 Gunsmith Service, Inc.
Thurston Sports, Inc.
Tom's Gun Repair
T.S.W. Conversions, Inc.
Ulrich, Doc & Bud
Unick's Gunsmithing
Vic's Gun Refinishing
Volquartsen Custom Ltd.
Walker Arms Co., Inc.
Walters Industries
Wardell Precision Handguns Ltd.
Weigand Combat Handguns, Inc.
Wessinger Custom Guns & Engraving
Williams Gun Sight Co.
Williamson Precision Gunsmithing
Wilson's Gun Shop

REBORING AND RERIFLING

Ackley Rifle Barrels, P.O.
Bauska Barrels
Bellm Contenders
Blackstar Barrel Accurizing
Flaig's
H&S Liner Service
Ivanoff, Thomas G.
Jackalope Gun Shop
K-D, Inc.
Kopp, Terry K.
LaBounty Precision Reboring
Matco, Inc.
Mid-America Recreation, Inc.
Morrow, Bud
Pence Precision Barrels
Redman's Rifling & Reboring
Rice, Keith
Ridgetop Sporting Goods
Schumakers Gun Shop, William
Shaw, Inc., E.R.
Siegrist Gun Shop
Sonora Rifle Barrel Co.
Starnes Gunmaker, Ken
300 Gunsmith Service, Inc.
Tom's Gun Repair
Van Patten, J.W.
Wells, Fred F.
Wessinger Custom Guns & Engraving
West, Robert G.
White Rock Tool & Die

50th EDITION, 1996

DIRECTORY OF THE ARMS TRADE

RELOADING TOOLS AND ACCESSORIES

AC Dyna-tite Corp.
Acadian Ballistic Specialties
Accuracy Components Co.
Action Bullets, Inc.
Advance Car Mover Co., Rowell Div.
Alpha LaFranck Enterprises
American Products Co.
●Ammo Load, Inc.
Armfield Custom Bullets
Arms Corp. of the Philippines
Bald Eagle Precision Machine Co.
Ballard Built
Ballistic Products, Inc.
Ballisti-Cast, Inc.
Barlett, J.
Bear Reloaders
Beeline Custom Bullets
Belltown, Ltd.
Ben's Machines
Berry's Mfg. Inc.
Bitterroot Bullet Co.
Blackhawk East
●Blount, Inc.
Brass-Tech Industries
Break-Free, Inc.
Brobst, Jim
●Brown Co., E. Arthur
BRP, Inc. High Performance Cast Bullets
Brynin, Milton
B-Square Co., Inc.
Buck Stix
Buffalo Arms
Bull Mountain Rifle Co.
Bullet Mills
Bullet Swaging Supply, Inc.
Bullseye Bullets
C&D Special Products
●Camdex, Inc.
Canyon Cartridge Corp.
Carbide Die & Mfg. Co., Inc.
Carroll Bullets
Case Sorting System
CCI
●C-H Tool & Die Corp.
Chem-Pak, Inc.
CheVron Case Master
Clark Custom Guns, Inc.
Claybuster
Clymer Manufacturing Co., Inc.
Coats, Mrs. Lester
Colorado Shooter's Supply
●Competitor Corp., Inc.
CONKKO
Cook Engineering Service
●Corbin, Inc.
Crouse's Country Cover
Curtis Gun Shop
Davis, Don
Davis Products, Mike
D.C.C. Enterprises
●Denver Instrument Co.
Dever Co., Jack
Dewey Mfg. Co., Inc., J.
●Dillon Precision Prods., Inc.
Double A Ltd.
Dutchman's Firearms, Inc., The
E&L Mfg., Inc.
Eagan, Donald V.
Eezox, Inc.
Engineered Accessories
Essex Metals
F&A Inc.
Federal Cartridge Co.
Feken, Dennis
Ferguson, Bill
First, Inc., Jack
Fisher Enterprises
Fish-N-Hunt, Inc.
Fitz Pistol Grip Co.
Flambeau Products Corp.
Forgett Jr., Valmore J.
Forgreens Tool Mfg., Inc.
●Forster Products
●4-D Custom Die Co.
●Fremont Tool Works
Fusilier Bullets
G&C Bullet Co., Inc.
Gage Manufacturing
Gehmann, Walter
Goddard, Allen
GOEX, Inc.
Gonzalez Guns, Ramon B.
"Gramps" Antique Cartridges
Graphics Direct
Graves Co.
Green, Arthur S.
Greenwood Precision
Grizzly Bullets
Gun Works, The
Guns
Hanned Line, The
Hanned Precision
Hardin Specialty Dist.
Harrell's Precision
Harris Enterprises
Harrison Bullets
●Hart & Son, Inc., Robert W.
Haselbauer Products, Jerry
Haydon Shooters' Supply, Russ
Heidenstrom Bullets
Hensley & Gibbs
Hirtenberger Aktiengesellschaft
Hoch Custom Bullet Moulds
Hoehn Sales, Inc.
Hoelscher, Virgil
●Hollywood Engineering
Hondo Industries
●Hornady Mfg. Co.
Howell Machine
●Huntington Die Specialties
IMI Services USA, Inc.
Imperial Magnum Corp.
INTEC International, Inc.
Iosso Products
J&D Components
J&L Superior Bullets
Jantz Supply
Javelina Products
JGS Precision Tool Mfg.
JLK Bullets
Jonad Corp.
Jones Custom Products, Neil
Jones Moulds, Paul
●K&M Services
K&S Mfg. Inc.
Kapro Mfg. Co., Inc.
Kent Cartridge Mfg. Co. Ltd.
King & Co.
KLA Enterprises
LAP Systems Group, N.A.
Lathrop's, Inc.
Lawrence Brand Shot
LBT
●Lee Precision, Inc.
Legend Products Corp.
Liberty Metals
Liberty Shooting Supplies
Lindsley Arms Cartridge Co.
Littleton, J.F.
Lortone, Inc.
Loweth Firearms, Richard
Luch Metal Merchants, Barbara
Lyman Instant Targets, Inc.
●Lyman Products Corp.
MA Systems
●Magma Engineering Co.
Magnus Bullets
Mag-Pack Corp.
MarMik Inc.
Marquart Precision Co., Inc.
MAST Technology
Master Class Bullets
Match Prep
McKillen & Heyer, Inc.
MCRW Associates Shooting Supplies
●MCS, Inc.
●MEC, Inc.
Midway Arms, Inc.
Miller Engineering
MI-TE Bullets
MKL Service Co.
MMP
Mo's Competitor Supplies
MoLoc Bullets
Montana Precision Swaging
Monte Kristo Pistol Grip Co.
Mt. Baldy Bullet Co.
MTM Molded Products Co., Inc.
Multi-Scale Charge Ltd.
Naval Ordnance Works
Necromancer Industries, Inc.
NEI Handtools, Inc.
Niemi Engineering, W.B.
Noble Co., Jim
North American Shooting Systems
North Devon Firearms Services
October Country
OK Weber, Inc.
Old West Bullet Moulds
●Old Western Scrounger, Inc.
Omark Industries
Pace Marketing, Inc.
Paco's
Pattern Control
Pedersoli, Davide & C.
Peerless Alloy, Inc.
Pend Oreille Sport Shop
Petro-Explo, Inc.
Pinetree Bullets
Plum City Ballistic Range
Policlips North America
Polywad, Inc.
Pomeroy, Robert
●Ponsness/Warren
Powder Valley Services
Precision Castings & Equipment, Inc.
Precision Components
●Precision Reloading, Inc.
Prime Reloading
Prolix
Pro-Shot Products, Inc.
Protector Mfg. Co., Inc., The
Quinetics Corp.
R&D Engineering & Manufacturing
Ransom International Corp.
Rapine Bullet Mould Mfg. Co.
Ravell Ltd.
Raytech
●RCBS
R.D.P. Tool Co., Inc.
●Redding Reloading Equipment
●Redding Reloading, Inc.
R.E.I.
Reloading Specialties, Inc.
Rice, Keith
Riebe Co., W.J.
RIG Products
R.I.S. Co., Inc.
R.M. Precision, Inc.
Roberts Products
Rochester Lead Works, Inc.
Rolston, Inc., Fred W.
Rooster Laboratories
Rorschach Precision Products
Rosenthal, Brad and Sallie
Rucker Ammunition Co.
SAECO
Sandia Die & Cartridge Co.
Saunders Gun & Machine Shop
Saville Iron Co.
●Scharch Mfg., Inc.
Scot Powder Co. of Ohio, Inc.
Scott, Dwight
Shiloh Creek
Shooting Components Marketing
Sierra Bullets
Sierra Specialty Prod. Co.
Silver Eagle Machining
Simmons, Jerry
Sinclair International, Inc.
Skip's Machine
S.L.A.P. Industries
Small Custom Mould & Bullet Co.
SOS Products Co.
●Speer Products
Spencer's Custom Guns
Sport Flite Manufacturing Co.
Sportsman Supply Co.
●Stalwart Corp.
●Star Machine Works
Stillwell, Robert
Stoney Point Products, Inc.
Talon Mfg. Co., Inc.
Tamarack Products, Inc.
Taracorp Industries
TCSR
Tetra Gun Lubricants
Thompson Bullet Lube Co.
Timber Heirloom Products
Time Precision, Inc.
TMI Products
Trammco, Inc.
Trophy Bonded Bullets, Inc.
Tru-Square Metal Prods., Inc.
TTM
Tyler Scott, Inc.
Varner's Service
Vega Tool Co.
VibraShine, Inc.
Vibra-Tek Co.
Vihtavuori Oy
Vihtavuori Oy/Kaltron-Pettibone
Vitt/Boos
Vom Hoffe
Von Minden Gunsmithing Services
Walters, John
Webster Scale Mfg. Co.
Welsh, Bud
Werner, Carl
Westfield Engineering
White Rock Tool & Die
Whitestone Lumber Corp.
Whitetail Design & Engineering Ltd.
Widener's Reloading & Shooting Supply
●William's Gun Shop, Ben
Wilson, Inc., L.E.
Winchester Sutler, Inc., The
Wise Guns, Dale
Wolf's Western Traders
Woodleigh
Yesteryear Armory & Supply
Young Country Arms
Zero Ammunition Co., Inc.

RESTS—BENCH, PORTABLE—AND ACCESSORIES

Accuright
Adaptive Technology
Adventure 16, Inc.
Armor Metal Products
Aspen Outdoors, Inc.
Bald Eagle Precision Machine Co.
Bartlett Engineering
Blount, Inc.
Browning Arms Co.
B-Square Co., Inc.
Bull Mountain Rifle Co.
Chem-Pak, Inc.
Cherokee Gun Accessories
Clift Mfg., L.R.
Clift Welding Supply
Cravener's Gun Shop
Decker Shooting Products
Desert Mountain Mfg.
F&A Inc.
Greenwood Precision
Harris Engineering, Inc.
Hart & Son, Inc., Robert W.
Hidalgo, Tony
Hoehn Sales, Inc.
Hoelscher, Virgil
Hoppe's Div.
Kolpin Mfg., Inc.
Kramer Designs
Midway Arms, Inc.
Millett Sights
MJM Manufacturing
PAST Sporting Goods, Inc.
Pease Accuracy, Bob
Penguin Industries, Inc.
Portus, Robert
Protektor Model
Ransom International Corp
Saville Iron Co.
Sinclair International, Inc.
Spencer's Custom Guns
Stoney Point Products, Inc.
Sure Shot of LA, Inc.
Tapco, Inc.
Thompson Target Technology
T.H.U. Enterprises, Inc.
Time Precision, Inc.
Tonoloway Tack Drivers
Varner's Service
Wichita Arms, Inc.
Ziegel Engineering

RIFLE BARREL MAKERS (See also Muzzle-Loading Guns, Barrels and Equipment)

ABS Co. Inc./Lothar Walther
Ackley Rifle Barrels, P.O.
Airrow
American Bullets
Bauska Barrels
Bellm Contenders
BlackStar Barrel Accurizing
Border Barrels Ltd.
Broughton Rifle Barrels
Brown Co., E. Arthur
Bullberry Barrel Works, Ltd.
Bustani Appraisers, Leo
Camas Hot Springs Mfg.
Carter's Gun Shop
Cincinnati Swaging
Clerke Co., J.A.

PRODUCT DIRECTORY

Competition Limited
Cryo
D&J Bullet Co. & Custom Gun Shop, Inc.
deHaas Barrels
Dilliott Gunsmithing, Inc.
DKT, Inc.
Donnelly, C.P.
Douglas Barrels, Inc.
Gaillard Barrels
Gentry Custom Gunmaker, David
Getz Barrel Co.
Green Mountain Rifle Barrel Co., Inc.
Half Moon Rifle Shop
Harold's Custom Gun Shop, Inc.
Harris-McMillan Gunworks
Hart Rifle Barrels, Inc.
Hastings Barrels
Hoelscher, Virgil
H-S Precision, Inc.
Jackalope Gun Shop
Jarvis Gunsmithing, Inc.
K-D, Inc.
KOGOT
Kopp, Terry K.
Krieger Barrels, Inc.
LaBounty Precision Reboring
Lilja Precision Rifle Barrels
Mac's .45 Shop
Marquart Precision Co., Inc.
Matco, Inc.
McGowen Rifle Barrels

McMillan Rifle Barrels
Mid-America Recreation, Inc.
Obermeyer Rifled Barrels
Olympic Arms, Inc.
Pac-Nor Barreling
Pell, John T.
Pence Precision Barrels
Perazone, Brian
Pre-Winchester 92-90-62 Parts Co.
R.M. Precision, Inc.
Rocky Mountain Rifle Works Ltd.
Rosenthal, Brad and Sallie
Sabatti S.R.L.
Sanders Custom Gun Service
Schneider Rifle Barrels, Inc., Gary
Shaw, Inc., E.R.
Shilen Rifles, Inc.
Siskiyou Gun Works
Small Arms Mfg. Co.
Sonora Rifle Barrel Co.
Specialty Shooters Supply, Inc.
Springfield, Inc.
Steyr Mannlicher AG
Strutz Rifle Barrels, Inc., W.C.
Swivel Machine Works, Inc.
Unique/M.A.P.F.
Verney-Carron
Volquartsen Custom Ltd.
West, Robert G.
Wilson Arms Co., The
Wiseman and Co., Bill

SCOPES, MOUNTS, ACCESSORIES, OPTICAL EQUIPMENT

Accuracy Innovations, Inc.
Accura-Site
Ace Custom 45's
ADCO International
Adventurer's Outpost
•Aimpoint, Inc.
•Aimtech Mount Systems
•Air Venture
Ajax Custom Grips, Inc.
All's, The Jim J. Tembelis Co., Inc.
Alley Supply Co.
American Import Co. The/Export Division
•Anderson Manufacturing Co., Inc.
Apel GmbH, Ernst
Applied Laser Systems, Inc.
A.R.M.S., Inc.
•Armscorp USA, Inc.
Aro-Tek, Ltd.
Baer Custom, Inc., Les
•Barrett Firearms Mfg., Inc.
•Bausch & Lomb, Inc.
Beaver Park Products, Inc.
•Blount, Inc.
•Bohemia Arms Co.
•Brown Co., E. Arthur
Brownells, Inc.
•Browning Arms Co.
Brunton U.S.A.
•B-Square Co., Inc.
Bull Mountain Rifle Co.
Bullberry Barrel Works, Ltd.
•Burris
•Bushnell
Butler Creek Corp.
California Grip
Celestron International
Center Lock Scope Rings
Champion's Choice, Inc.
Clark Custom Guns, Inc.
Clearview Mfg. Co., Inc.
Combat Military Ordnance Ltd.
Compass Industries, Inc.
Concept Development Corp.
Conetrol Scope Mounts
CRDC Laser Systems Group
Creedmoor Sports, Inc.
Custom Quality Products, Inc.
D&H Prods. Co., Inc.
D.C.C. Enterprises
Del-Sports, Inc.
DHB Products
Doctor Optic Technologies, Inc.
Eagle International, Inc.
Eagle Mfg. & Engineering
Edmund Scientific Co.
Ednar, Inc.
Eggleston, Jere D.
Emerging Technologies, Inc.
•Europtik Ltd.
Excaliber Enterprises
Faith Associates, Inc.

Farr Studio, Inc.
Feather Industries, Inc.
Firearms Supplies Inc.
•Forster Products
From Jena
Fujinon, Inc.
Galati International
Gentry Custom Gunmaker, David
G.G. & G.
Gonzalez Guns, Ramon B.
Grace Tool, Inc.
•GSI, Inc.
Gun South, Inc.
Guns, (Div. of D.C. Engineering, Inc.)
Guns, Gear & Gadgets, L.L.C.
Gunsite Training Center
Hakko Co. Ltd.
•Hammerli USA
•Hart & Son, Inc., Robert W.
Hermann Leather Co., H.J.
Hertel & Reuss
Hiptmayer, Armurier
Holland's
House of Muskets, Inc., The
Ironsighter Co.
•Jackalope Gun Shop
•Jaeger, Inc., Paul/Dunn's
JagerSport, Ltd.
Jeffredo Gunsight
Jenco Sales, Inc.
Jewell, Arnold W.
Johnson Gunsmithing, Inc., Neal G.
Jones, J.D.
•JSL (Hereford) Ltd.
•Kahles USA
KDF, Inc.
Kelbly, Inc.
•Keng's Firearms Specialty, Inc.
KenPatable Ent., Inc.
•Kesselring Gun Shop
Kimber, Inc.
Kmount
•Kowa Optimed, Inc.
Kris Mounts
KVH Industries, Inc.
Kwik Mount Corp.
Kwik-Site Co.
•L&S Technologies, Inc.
LaFrance Specialties
•Laser Devices, Inc.
•Laseraim
LaserMax
Lectro Science, Inc.
Lee Co., T.K.
•Leica USA, Inc.
•Leupold & Stevens, Inc.
Lightforce USA
List Precision Engineering
Lite Tek International
Lohman Mfg. Co., Inc.
London Guns Ltd.

Mac's .45 Shop
Maxi-Mount
McCann's Machine & Gun Shop
McMillan Optical Gunsight Co.
MDS
Meier Works
Merit Corp.
Michaels of Oregon Co.
Military Armament Corp.
Millett Sights
•Mirador Optical Corp.
Muzzle-Nuzzle Co.
MWG Co.
New Democracy, Inc.
New England Custom Gun Service
•Nikon, Inc.
North American Specialties
Nowlin Custom Mfg.
Oakshore Electronic Sights, Inc.
•Old Western Scrounger, Inc.
Olympic Optical Co.
Optolyth-USA, Inc.
Orchard Park Enterprise
Outdoor Connection, Inc., The
Pace Marketing, Inc.
Parsons Optical Mfg. Co.
PECAR Herbert Schwarz, GmbH
Peltor, Inc.
PEM's Mfg. Co.
•Pentax Corp.
Pilkington Gun Co.
Powell & Son (Gunmakers) Ltd., William
Precise Metalsmithing Enterprises
•Precision Sport Optics
Premier Reticles
•Ram-Line, Inc.
Ranch Products
Randolph Engineering, Inc.
•Ranging, Inc.
Ravell Ltd.
•Redfield, Inc.
Rice, Keith
Rocky Mountain High Sports Glasses
S&K Mfg. Co.
•Sanders Custom Gun Service
Saunders Gun & Machine Shop
•Schmidt & Bender, Inc.
Scope Control Inc.
ScopLevel
Seattle Binocular & Scope Repair Co.
Selsi Co., Inc.

•Shepherd Scope Ltd.
Sightron, Inc.
Silencio/Safety Direct
•Simmons Enterprises, Ernie
•Simmons Outdoor Corp.
Sinclair International, Inc.
Six Enterprises
SKAN A.R.
SKB Shotguns
•Speer Products
Spencer's Custom Guns
Sportsmatch Ltd.
•Springfield, Inc.
SSK Industries
Steyr Mannlicher AG
Sure Shot of LA, Inc.
SwaroSports, Inc.
Swarovski Optik North America Ltd.
•Swift Instruments, Inc.
Talley, Dave
Tank's Rifle Shop
•Tapco, Inc.
•Tasco Sales, Inc.
Tele-Optics
•Thompson/Center Arms
Time Precision, Inc.
•Trijicon, Inc.
Uncle Mike's
•Unertl Optical Co., Inc., John
United Binocular Co.
United States Optics Technologies, Inc.
Valor Corp.
Volquartsen Custom Ltd.
Vom Hoffe
Warne Manufacturing Co.
Warren Muzzleloading Co., Inc.
WASP Shooting Systems
Weaver Products
•Weaver Scope Repair Service
Weigand Combat Handguns, Inc.
Wessinger Custom Guns & Engraving
Western Design
Westfield Engineering
White Rock Tool & Die
•White Shooting Systems, Inc.
Wichita Arms, Inc.
Wideview Scope Mount Corp.
•Williams Gun Sight Co.
York M-1 Conversions
•Zeiss Optical, Carl

SHOOTING/TRAINING SCHOOLS

Accuracy Gun Shop
Alpine Precision Gunsmithing & Indoor Shooting Range
American Small Arms Academy
Auto Arms
Bob's Tactical Indoor Shooting Range & Gun Shop
Chapman Academy of Practical Shooting
Chelsea Gun Club of New York City, Inc.
Clark Custom Guns, Inc.
CQB Training
Daisy Mfg. Co.
Defense Training International, Inc.
Dowtin Gunworks
Executive Protection Institute
Firearm Training Center, The
Firearms Academy of Seattle
G.H. Enterprises Ltd.
Gunfitters, The
Gunsite Training Center
InSights Training Center, Inc.
International Shootists, Inc.
Jensen's Custom Ammunition
Jensen's Firearms Acadamy

J.P. Enterprises, Inc.
McMurdo, Lynn
Mendez, John A.
Nevada Pistol Academy Inc.
North Mountain Pines Training Center
Pace Marketing, Inc.
Pacific Pistolcraft
Quigley's Personal Protection Strategies, Paxton
River Road Sporting Clays
Robar Co.'s, Inc., The
SAFE
Scott, McDougall & Associates
Shooter's World
Shooting Gallery, The
Shotgun Shop, The
Smith & Wesson
Specialty Gunsmithing
Spencer's Custom Guns
Starlight Training Center, Inc.
Tactical Defense Institute
300 Gunsmith Service, Inc.
Western Missouri Shooters Alliance
Yavapai Firearms Academy Ltd.

SIGHTS, METALLIC

Accura-Site
All's, The Jim J. Tembelis Co., Inc.
Alpec Team, Inc.
Andela Tool & Machine, Inc.
Aro-Tek, Ltd.
Baer Custom, Inc., Les
Bob's Gun Shop
Bo-Mar Tool & Mfg. Co.
Bond Custom Firearms
Bowen Classic Arms Corp.
Bradley Gunsight Co.
British Arms Co. Ltd.
Brown Co., E. Arthur

Buffalo Arms
Bullberry Barrel Works, Ltd.
California Sights
Cape Outfitters
Champion's Choice, Inc.
C-More Systems
Colonial Repair
CRL, Inc.
DHB Products
Engineered Accessories
Evans Gunsmithing
F.A.I.R. Techni-Mec s.n.c.
Fautheree, Andy

50th EDITION, 1996

DIRECTORY OF THE ARMS TRADE

Gun Doctor, The
Guns, (Div. of D.C. Engineering, Inc.)
Gunsite Training Center
Hart & Son, Inc., Robert W.
Heinie Specialty Products
Hesco-Meprolight
House of Muskets, Inc., The
Innovative Weaponry, Inc.
Innovision Enterprises
Jackalope Gun Shop
Jaeger, Inc., Paul/Dunn's
Kwik-Site Co.
Lee's Red Ramps
List Precision Engineering
Lofland, James W.
London Guns Ltd.
L.P.A. Snc
Lyman Instant Targets, Inc.
Lyman Products Corp.
Mac's .45 Shop
Mag-Na-Port International, Inc.
Marble Arms
MCS, Inc.
Meadow Industries
MEC-Gar S.R.L.
Meier Works
Meprolight
Merit Corp.
Mid-America Recreation, Inc.
Millett Sights
MMC
Mo's Competitor Supplies
Montana Vintage Arms
New England Custom Gun Service
North American Specialties
Novak's Inc.
Oakshore Electronic Sights, Inc.
Pace Marketing, Inc.
Pachmayr Ltd.
PEM's Mfg. Co.
P.M. Enterprises, Inc.
Ravell Ltd.
Robar Co.'s, Inc., The
RPM
Shepherd Scope Ltd.
Slug Site Co.
Starnes Gunmaker, Ken
Talley, Dave
Tank's Rifle Shop
Tapco, Inc.
Tecni-Mec
T.F.C. S.p.A.
Time Precision, Inc.
Trijicon, Inc.
WASP Shooting Systems
Wichita Arms, Inc.
Williams Gun Sight Co.
Hiptmayer, Armurier
Hiptmayer, Klaus
Hoelscher, Virgil
Hoenig & Rodman
H-S Precision, Inc.
Huebner, Corey O.
Hughes, Steven Dodd
Intermountain Arms & Tackle, Inc.
Island Pond Gun Shop
Ivanoff, Thomas G.
Jackalope Gun Shop
Jaeger, Inc., Paul/Dunn's
Jarrett Rifles, Inc.
Johnson Gunsmithing, Inc., Neal G.
J.P. Gunstocks, Inc.
KDF, Inc.
Keith's Custom Gunstocks
Ken's Rifle Blanks
Kilham & Co.
Klein Custom Guns, Don
Klingler Woodcarving
Knippel, Richard
Lawson Co., Harry
Lind Custom Guns, Al
Lock's Philadelphia Gun Exchange
Lynn's Custom Gunstocks
Mac's .45 Shop
Martin's Gun Shop
Masen Co., Inc., John
Mathews & Son, Inc., George E.
McCament, Jay
McCann's Muzzle-Gun Works
McCullough, Ken
McDonald, Dennis
McFarland, Stan
McGowen Rifle Barrels
McGuire, Bill
McKinney, R.P.
McMillan Fiberglass Stocks, Inc.
Mercer Custom Stocks, R.M.
Mid-America Recreation, Inc.
Morrison Custom Rifles, J.W.
Morrow, Bud
MPI Stocks
Nelson, Stephen
Nettestad Gun Works
New England Arms Co.
New England Custom Gun Service
Newman Gunshop
Nickels, Paul R.
Norman Custom Gunstocks, Jim
Oakland Custom Arms, Inc.
Oil Rod and Gun Shop
Old World Gunsmithing
One Of A Kind
Or-Ün
Orvis Co., The
Pagel Gun Works, Inc.
Paulsen Gunstocks
Pecatonica River Longrifle
PEM's Mfg. Co.
Pentheny de Pentheny
Perazone, Brian
Perazzi USA, Inc.
R&J Gun Shop
Ram-Line, Inc.
Reagent Chemical and Research, Inc.
Reiswig, Wallace E.
Richards Micro-Fit Stocks
Rigby & Co., John
Rimrock Rifle Stocks
RMS Custom Gunsmithing
Robar Co.'s, Inc., The
Robinson, Don
Robinson Firearms Mfg. Ltd.
Roto Carve
Royal Arms
Ryan, Chad L.
Sanders Custom Gun Service
Saville Iron Co.
Schiffman, Curt
Schiffman, Mike
Schuetzen Gun Service
Schwartz Custom Guns, David W.
Schwartz Custom Guns, Wayne E.
Shell Shack
Sile Distributors, Inc.
Six Enterprises
Smith, Sharmon
Snider Stocks, Walter S.
Speedfeed, Inc.
Speiser, Fred D.
Starnes Gunmaker, Ken
Steyr Mannlicher AG
Stiles Custom Guns
Storey, Dale A.
Stott's Creek Armory, Inc.
Strawbridge, Victor W.
Swan, D.J.
Szweda, Robert
Talmage, William G.
Tapco, Inc.
Taylor & Robbins
Tecni-Mec
Tecnolegno S.p.A.
Tennessee Valley Mfg.
T.F.C. S.p.A.
Tiger-Hunt
Tirelli
Tom's Gun Repair
Trevallion Gunstocks
Tucker, James C.
Turkish Firearms Corp.
Tuttle, Dale
Vest, John
Vic's Gun Refinishing
Vintage Industries, Inc.
Volquartsen Custom Ltd.
Von Minden Gunsmithing Services
Waffen-Weber Custom Gunsmithing
Walker Arms Co., Inc.
Walnut Factory, The
Weatherby, Inc.
Weems, Cecil
Wells Custom Gunsmith, R.A.
Wenig Custom Gunstocks, Inc.
Werth, T.W.
West, Robert G.
Western Gunstock Mfg. Co.
Williams Gun Sight Co.
Williamson Precision Gunsmithing
Windish, Jim
Winter, Robert M.
Wright's Hardwood Gunstock Blanks
Yee, Mike
York M-1 Conversions
Zeeryp, Russ

STOCKS (Commercial and Custom)

Accuracy Unlimited (Glendale, AZ)
Adair Custom Shop, Bill
Ahlman Guns
Ahrends, Kim
Ajax Custom Grips, Inc.
Amrine's Gun Shop
Arms Ingenuity Co.
Artistry In Wood
Balickie, Joe
Bansner's Gunsmithing Specialties
Barnes Bullets, Inc.
Bartlett, Don
Beitzinger, George
Belding's Custom Gun Shop
Bell & Carlson, Inc.
Benchmark Guns
Biesen, Al
Biesen, Roger
Billeb, Stephen L.
Billings Gunsmiths, Inc.
Bob's Gun Shop
Boltin, John M.
Bowerly, Kent
Boyds' Gunstock Industries, Inc.
Brace, Larry D.
Brgoch, Frank
Briganti & Co., A.
Brockmans Custom Gunsmithing
Brown Co., E. Arthur
Brown Precision, Inc.
Brownell Checkering Tools, W.E.
Buckhorn Gun Works
Bull Mountain Rifle Co.
Bullberry Barrel Works, Ltd.
Burkhart Gunsmithing, Don
Burres, Jack
Butler Creek Corp.
Cali'co Hardwoods, Inc.
Camilli, Lou
Campbell, Dick
Caywood, Shane J.
Cherokee Gun Accessories
Chicasaw Gun Works
Christman Jr., David
Churchill, Winston
Clark Custom Guns, Inc.
Clifton Arms, Inc.
Cloward's Gun Shop
Cochran, Oliver
Coffin, Charles H.
Coffin, Jim
Colonial Repair
Conrad, C.A.
Costa, David
Crane Sales Co., George S.
Creedmoor Sports, Inc.
Curly Maple Stock Blanks
Custom Checkering Service
Custom Firearms
Custom Gun Products
Custom Gun Stocks
Custom Shop, The
D&D Gunsmiths, Ltd.
D&G Presicion Duplicators
D&J Bullet Co. & Custom Gun Shop, Inc.
Dahl's Custom Stocks
Dangler, Homer L.
D.D. Custom Stocks
Desert Industries, Inc.
de Treville & Co., Stan
Dever Co., Jack
Devereaux, R.H. "Dick"
DGS, Inc.
Dillon, Ed
Dowtin Gunworks
Dressel Jr., Paul G.
Duane Custom Stocks, Randy
Duncan's Gunworks, Inc.
Echols & Co., D'Arcy
Eggleston, Jere D.
Erhardt, Dennis
Eversull Co., Inc., K.
Fajen, Inc., Reinhart
Farmer-Dressel, Sharon
Fiberpro/California
Fibron Products, Inc.
Fisher, Jerry A.
Flaig's
Folks, Donald E.
Forster, Kathy
Forster, Larry L.
Frank Custom Gun Service, Ron
Game Haven Gunstocks
Gene's Custom Guns
Gervais, Mike
Gilman-Mayfield, Inc.
Giron, Robert E.
Glaser Safety Slug, Inc.
Goens, Dale W.
Golden Age Arms Co.
Gordie's Gun Shop
Goudy Classic Stocks, Gary
Grace, Charles E.
Grace Tool, Inc.
Green, Roger M.
Greene, M.L.
Greenwood Precision
Griffin & Howe, Inc.
Gun Shop, The
Guns
Guns, (Div. of D.C. Engineering, Inc.)
Gunsmithing Ltd.
Hallberg Gunsmith, Fritz
Halstead, Rick
Hank's Gun Shop
Hanson's Gun Center, Dick
Harper's Custom Stocks
Harris-McMillan Gunworks
Hart & Son, Inc., Robert W.
Hartmann & Weiss GmbH
Hastings Barrels
Hecht, Hubert J.
Heilmann, Stephen
Hensley, Darwin
Heppler, Keith M.
Herrett's Stocks, Inc.
Heydenberk, Warren R.
High Tech Specialties, Inc.
Hillmer Custom Gunstocks, Paul D.

TARGETS, BULLET AND CLAYBIRD TRAPS

Action Target, Inc.
American Target
American Whitetail Target Systems
A-Tech Corp.
Barsotti, Bruce
Beomat of America Inc.
Birchwood Laboratories, Inc.
Blount, Inc.
Blue and Gray Products, Inc.
Caswell International Corp.
Champion Target Co.
Champion's Choice, Inc.
Cunningham Co., Eaton
Curtis Gun Shop
Dapkus Co., Inc., J.G.
Datumtech Corp.
Dayson Arms Ltd.
D.C.C. Enterprises
Detroit-Armor Corp.
Diamond Mfg. Co.
Enguix Import-Export
Epps "Orillia" Ltd., Ellwood
Federal Champion Target Co.
Freeman Animal Targets
G.H. Enterprises Ltd.
Gozon Corp.
Gun Parts Corp., The
Hiti-Schuch, Atelier Wilma
Hornady Mfg. Co.
Hunterjohn
Innovision Enterprises
Jackalope Gun Shop
JWH = Software
Kennebec Journal
Kleen-Bore, Inc.
Littler Sales Co.
Lyman Instant Targets, Inc.
Lyman Products Corp.
Marksman Products
MSR Targets
National Target Co.
N.B.B., Inc.
North American Shooting Systems
Nu-Teck
Outers Laboratories
Ox-Yoke Originals, Inc.
Parker Reproductions
Pease Accuracy, Bob

PRODUCT DIRECTORY

PlumFire Press, Inc.
Quack Decoy & Sporting Clays
Ravell Ltd.
Red Star Target Co.
Remington Arms Co., Inc.
River Road Sporting Clays
Rockwood Corp., Speedwell Div.
Rocky Mountain Target Co.
Schaefer Shooting Sports
Seligman Shooting Products
Shooters Supply
Shooting Arts Ltd
Shoot-N-C Inc.
Shotgun Shop, The
Stoney Baroque Shooters Supply
Thompson Target Technology
Trius Products, Inc.
White Flyer Targets
World of Targets
X-Spand Target Systems
Zriny's Metal Targets

TAXIDERMY

Jonas Appraisers—Taxidermy Animals, Jack
Kulis Freeze Dry Taxidermy
Parker, Mark D.
World Trek, Inc.

TRAP AND SKEET SHOOTER'S EQUIPMENT

Allen Co., Bob
Allen Sportswear, Bob
Bagmaster Mfg., Inc.
Baker, Stan
Ballistic Products, Inc.
Beomat of America Inc.
Blount, Inc.
Clymer Manufacturing Co., Inc.
Crane & Crane Ltd.
Dayson Arms Ltd.
F&A Inc.
Ganton Manufacturing Ltd.
G.H. Enterprises Ltd.
Great 870 Co., The
Harper, William E.
Hart & Son, Inc., Robert W.
Hastings Barrels
Hoppe's Div.
H-S Precision, Inc.
Hunter Co., Inc.
K&T Co.
Ljutic Industries, Inc.
Lynn's Custom Gunstocks
Maionchi-L.M.I.
Meadow Industries
Moneymaker Guncraft Corp.
MTM Molded Products Co., Inc.
Nielsen Custom Cases
Noble Co., Jim
Outers Laboratories
Pace Marketing, Inc.
PAST Sporting Goods, Inc.
Penguin Industries, Inc.
Perazzi USA, Inc.
Pro-Port Ltd.
Protektor Model
Quack Decoy & Sporting Clays
Ravell Ltd.
Remington Arms Co., Inc.
Rhodeside, Inc.
Shootin' Accessories, Ltd.
Shooting Specialties
Shotgun Shop, The
Speer Products
Tecni-Mec
Titus, Daniel
Trius Products, Inc.
Universal Clay Pigeon Traps
X-Spand Target Systems

TRIGGERS, RELATED EQUIPMENT

Actions by "T"
B&D Trading Co., Inc.
Baer Custom, Inc., Les
Bob's Gun Shop
Bond Custom Firearms
Boyds' Gunstock Industries, Inc.
Bull Mountain Rifle Co.
Canjar Co., M.H.
Cape Outfitters
Clark Custom Guns, Inc.
Cycle Dynamics, Inc.
Dayton Traister
Electronic Trigger Systems, Inc.
Eversull Co., Inc., K.
F.A.I.R. Techni-Mec s.n.c.
Gentry Custom Gunmaker, David
Grace Tool, Inc.
Guns, (Div. of D.C. Engineering, Inc.)
Hastings Barrels
Hoelscher, Virgil
Holland's
Jackalope Gun Shop
Jacobson, Teddy
Jaeger, Inc., Paul/Dunn's
Jewell, Arnold W.
Jones Custom Products, Neil
J.P. Enterprises, Inc.
List Precision Engineering
Mahony, Philip Bruce
Master Lock Co.
Mid-America Recreation, Inc.
Miller Single Trigger Mfg. Co.
Pace Marketing, Inc.
Pease Accuracy, Bob
PEM's Mfg. Co.
Penrod Precision
Perazone, Brian
Perazzi USA, Inc.
S&B Industries
Shilen Rifles, Inc.
Tarnham Supply
Tecni-Mec
Tennessee Valley Mfg.
Time Precision, Inc.
Timney Mfg., Inc.
Tyler Mfg.-Dist., Melvin

MANUFACTURERS' DIRECTORY

A

A&B Industries, Inc. (See Top-Line USA, Inc.)
A&J Products, Inc., 5791 Hall Rd., Muskegon, MI 49442-1964
A&M Waterfowl, Inc., P.O. Box 102, Ripley, TN 38063/901-635-4003; FAX: 901-635-2320
A&W Repair, 2930 Schneider Dr., Arnold, MO 63010/314-287-3725
A.A. Arms, Inc., 4811 Persimmont Ct., Monroe, NC 28110/704-289-5356; FAX: 704-289-5859
AAL Optics, Inc., 2316 NE 8th Rd., Ocala, FL 33470/904-629-3211; FAX: 904-629-1433
Abel Safe & File, Inc., 124 West Locust St., Fairbury, IL 61739/800-346-9280, 815-692-2131; FAX: 815-692-3350
A.B.S. III, 9238 St. Morritz Dr., Fern Creek, KY 40291
ABS Co. Inc./Lothar Walther (See American Bullets)
AC Dyna-tite Corp., 155 Kelly St., P.O. Box 0984, Elk Grove Village, IL 60007/708-593-5566; FAX: 708-593-1304
Acadian Ballistic Specialties, P.O. Box 61, Covington, LA 70434
Acculube II, Inc., 4366 Shackleford Rd., Norcross, GA 30093-2912
Accupro Gun Care, 15512-109 Ave., Surrey, BC U3R 7E8, CANADA/604-583-7807
Accuracy Components Co., P.O. Box 60034, Renton, WA 98058/206-255-4577
Accuracy Den, The, 25 Bitterbrush Rd., Reno, NV 89523/702-345-0225
Accuracy Gun Shop, 7818 Wilkerson Ct., San Diego, CA 92111/619-282-8500
Accuracy Innovations, Inc., P.O. Box 376, New Paris, PA 15554/814-839-4517; FAX: 814-839-2601
Accuracy International Precision Rifles (See U.S. importer—Gunsite Training Center)
Accuracy Products, S.A., 14 rue de Lawsanne, Brussels, 1060 BELGIUM/32-2-539-34-42; FAX: 32-2-539-39-60
Accuracy Unlimited, 7479 S. DePew St., Littleton, CO 80123
Accuracy Unlimited, 16036 N. 49 Ave., Glendale, AZ 85306/602-978-9089
Accura-Site (See All's, The Jim Tembellis Co., Inc.)
Accurate Arms Company, Inc., Rt. 1, Box 167, McEwen, TN 37101/615-729-4207, 800-416-3006; FAX 615-729-4217
Accurate Plating & Weaponry, Inc., 1937 Calumet St., Clearwater, FL 34625/813-449-9112
Accuright, RR 2 Box 99, Sebeka, MN 56477/218-472-3383
Accu-Tek, 4525 Carter Ct., Chino, CA 91710/909-627-2404; FAX: 909-627-7817
Ace Custom 45's, 1880 1/2 Upper Turtle Creek Rd., Kerrville, TX 78028/210-257-4290; FAX: 210-257-5724
Ace Sportswear, Inc., 700 Quality Rd., Fayetteville, NC 28306/919-323-1223; FAX: 919-323-5392
Ackerman & Co., 16 Cortez St., Westfield, MA 01085/413-568-8008
Ackerman, Bill, 10236 Woodway, El Paso, TX 79925/915-592-5338
Ackley Rifle Barrels, P.O. (See Bellm Contenders)
Action Bullets, Inc., 1811 W. 13th Ave., Denver, CO 80204/303-595-9636; FAX: 303-893-9161
Action Products, Inc., 22 N. Mulberry St., Hagerstown, MD 21740/301-797-1414; FAX: 301-733-2073
Action Target, Inc., P.O. Box 636, Provo, UT 84603/801-377-8033; FAX: 801-377-8096
Actions by "T", Teddy Jacobson, 16315 Redwood Forest Ct., Sugar Land, TX 77478/713-277-4008
ACTIV Industries, Inc., 1000 Zigor Rd., P.O. Box 339, Kearneysville, WV 25430/304-725-0451; FAX: 304-725-2080
Ad Hominem, RR 3, Orillia, Ont. L3V 6H3, CANADA/705-689-5303
Adair Custom Shop, Bill, 2886 Westridge, Carrollton, TX 75006
Adams, John J., 87 Acorn Rd., Dennis, MA 02638/508-385-7971
Adams Jr., John J. , 87 Acorn Rd., Dennis, MA 02638/508-385-7971
Adaptive Technology, 939 Barnum Ave, Bridgeport, CT 06609/800-643-6735; FAX: 800-643-6735
ADCO International, 10 Cedar St., Unit 17, Woburn, MA 01801/617-935-1799; FAX: 617-935-1011
Adkins, Luther, 1292 E. McKay Rd., Shelbyville, IN 46176-9353/317-392-3795
Advance Car Mover Co., Rowell Div., P.O. Box 1, 240 N. Depot St., Juneau, WI 53039/414-386-4464; FAX: 414-386-4416
Adventure 16, Inc., 4620 Alvarado Canyon Rd., San Diego, CA 92120/619-283-6314
Adventure Game Calls, R.D. 1, Leonard Rd., Spencer, NY 14883/607-589-4611
Adventurer's Outpost, P.O. Box 70, Cottonwood, AZ 86326/800-762-7471; FAX: 602-634-8781
African Import Co., 20 Braunecker Rd., Plymouth, MA 02360/508-746-8552
AFSCO Ammunition, 731 W. Third St., P.O. Box L, Owen, WI 54460/715-229-2516
Ahlman Guns, Rt. 1, Box 20, Morristown, MN 55052/507-685-4243; FAX: 507-685-4247
Ahrends, Kim, Custom Firearms, Box 203, Clarion, IA 50525/515-532-3449
Aimpoint, Inc., 580 Herndon Parkway, Suite 500, Herndon, VA 22070/703-471-6828; FAX: 703-689-0575
Aimtech Mount Systems, P.O. Box 223, 101 Inwood Acres, Thomasville, GA 31799/912-226-4313; FAX: 912-227-0222
Air Arms, Hailsham Industrial Park, Diplocks Way, Hailsham, E. Sussex, BN27 3JF ENGLAND/011-0323-845853 (U.S. importers—Air Werks International; World Class Airguns)
Air Rifle Specialists, 311 East Water St., Elmira, NY 14901/607-734-7340; FAX: 607-733-3261
Air Venture, 9752 E. Flower St., Bellflower, CA 90706/310-867-6355

Air Werks International, 403 W. 24th St., Norfolk, VA 23517-1204/800-247-9375
Airgun Repair Centre, 3227 Garden Meadows, Lawrenceburg, IN 47025/812-637-1463; FAX: 812-637-1463
Airguns-R-Us, 300 S. Campbell, Columbia, TN 38401
Airrow (See Swivel Machine Works, Inc.)
Aitor-Cuchilleria Del Norte, S.A., Izelaieta, 17, 48260 Ermua (Vizcaya), SPAIN/43-17-08-50; FAX: 43-17-00-01
Ajax Custom Grips, Inc., Div. of A. Jack Rosenberg & Sons, 9130 Viscount Row, Dallas, TX 75247/214-630-8890; FAX: 214-630-4942
Aker Leather Products, 2248 Main St., Suite 6, Chula Vista, CA 91911/619-423-5182; FAX: 619-423-1363
Alaska Bullet Works, P.O. Box 54, Douglas, AK 99824/907-789-3834
Alcas Cutlery Corp. (See Cutco Cutlery)
Alco Carrying Cases, 601 W. 26th St., New York, NY 10001/212-675-5820; FAX: 212-691-5935
Aldis Gunsmithing & Shooting Supply, 502 S. Montezuma St., Prescott, AZ 86303/602-445-6723; FAX: 602-445-6763
Alessandri and Son, Lou, 24 French St., Rehoboth, MA 02769/508-252-3436, 800-248-5652; FAX: 508-252-3436
Alessi Holsters, Inc., 2465 Niagara Falls Blvd., Amherst, NY 14228-3527/716-691-5615
Alex, Inc., Box 3034, Bozeman, MT 59772/406-282-7396; FAX: 406-282-7396
Alfano, Sam, 36180 Henry Gaines Rd., Pearl River, LA 70452/504-863-3364; FAX: 504-863-7715
All's, The Jim J. Tembelis Co., Inc., 280 E. Fernau Ave., Oshkosh, WI 54901/414-426-1080; FAX: 414-426-1080
All American Lead Shot Corp., P.O. Box 224566, Dallas, TX 75062
All Rite Products, Inc., 5752 N. Silverstone Circle, Mountain Green, UT 84050/801-876-3330; 801-876-2216
Allard, Gary, Creek Side Metal & Woodcrafters, Fishers Hill, VA 22626/703-465-3903
Allen Co., Bob, 214 SW Jackson, P.O. Box 477, Des Moines, IA 50315/515-283-2191; 800-685-7020; FAX: 515-283-0779
Allen Co., Inc., 525 Burbank St., Broomfield, CO 80020/303-469-1857, 800-876-8600; FAX: 303-466-7437
Allen Mfg., 6449 Hodgson Rd., Circle Pines, MN 55014/612-429-8231
Allen, Richard L., 339 Grove Ave., Prescott, AZ 86301/602-778-1237
Allen Sportswear, Bob (See Allen Co., Bob)
Alley Supply Co., P.O. Box 848, Gardnerville, NV 89410/702-782-3800
Allred Bullet Co., 932 Evergreen Drive, Logan, UT 84321/801-752-6983
Alpec Team, Inc., 201 Rickenbacker Cir., Livermore, CA 94550/510-606-8245; FAX: 510-606-4279
Alpha 1 Drop Zone, 2121 N. Tyler, Wichita, KS 67212/316-729-0800
Alpha LaFranck Enterprises, P.O. Box 81072, Lincoln, NE 68501/402-466-3193
Alpha Precision, Inc., 2765-B Preston Rd. NE, Good Hope, GA 30641/404-267-6163
Alpine's Precision Gunsmithing & Indoor Shooting Range, 2401 Government Way, Coeur d'Alene, ID 83814/208-765-3559; FAX: 208-765-3559
Altamont Co., 901 N. Church St., P.O. Box 309, Thomasboro, IL 61878/217-643-3125, 800-626-5774; FAX: 217-643-7973
Alumna Sport by Dee Zee, 1572 NE 58th Ave., P.O. Box 3090, Des Moines, IA 50316/800-798-9899
Amacker International, Inc., P.O. Box 548, Delhi, LA 71232-0548/318-878-9061; FAX: 318-878-5532
AmBr Software Group Ltd., The, P.O. Box 301, Reisterstown, MD 21136-0301/410-526-4106; FAX: 410-526-7212
American Ammunition, 3545 NW 71st St., Miami, FL 33147/305-835-7400; FAX: 305-694-0037
American Arms & Ordnance, Inc., P.O. Box 2691, 1303 S. College Ave., Bryan, TX 77805/409-822-4983
American Arms, Inc., 715 Armour Rd., N. Kansas City, MO 64116/816-474-3161; FAX: 816-474-1225
American Bullets, 2190 C. Coffee Rd., Lithonia, GA 30058/404-482-4253; FAX: 404-482-9344
American Derringer Corp., 127 N. Lacy Dr., Waco, TX 76705/800-642-7817, 817-799-9111; FAX: 817-799-7935
American Display Co., 55 Cromwell St., Providence, RI 02907/401-331-2464; FAX: 401-421-1264
American Gas & Chemical Co., Ltd., 220 Pegasus Ave., Northvale, NJ 07647/201-767-7300
American Gripcraft, 3230 S. Dodge 2, Tucson, AZ 85713/602-790-1222
American Handgunner Magazine, 591 Camino de la Reina, Suite 200, San Diego, CA 92108/619-297-5350; FAX: 619-297-5353
American Import Co., The/Export Division, 1453 Mission St., San Francisco, CA 94103/415-863-1506; FAX: 415-863-0939
American Pioneer Video, P.O. Box 50049, Bowling Green, KY 42102-2649/800-743-4675
American Products Co., 14729 Spring Valley Road, Morrison, IL 61270/815-772-3336; FAX: 815-772-7921
American Sales & Kirkpatrick, P.O. Box 677, Laredo, TX 78042/210-723-6893; FAX: 210-725-0672
American Security Products Co., 11925 Pacific Ave., Fontana, CA 92337/909-685-9680, 800-421-6142; FAX: 909-685-9685
American Small Arms Academy, P.O. Box 12111, Prescott, AZ 86304/602-778-5623
American Target, 1328 S. Jason St., Denver, CO 80223/303-733-0433; FAX: 303-777-0311

MANUFACTURERS' DIRECTORY

American Target Knives, 1030 Brownwood NW, Grand Rapids, MI 49504/616-453-1998
American Whitetail Target Systems, P.O. Box 41, 106 S. Church St., Tennyson, IN 47637/812-567-4527
Americase, P.O. Box 271, 1610 E. Main, Waxahachie, TX 75165/800-880-3629; FAX: 214-937-8373
Ames Metal Products Co., 4324 S. Western Blvd., Chicago, IL/312-523-3230; FAX: 312-523-3854
Amherst Arms, P.O. Box 1457, Englewood, FL 34295/813-475-2020
Ammo Load, Inc., 1560 E. Edinger, Suite G, Santa Ana, CA 92705/714-558-8858; FAX: 714-569-0319
Amm-O-Mart, Ltd., P.O. Box 125, Hawkesbury, Ont., K6A 2R8 CANADA/613-632-9300
Ammunition Consulting Services, Inc., P.O. Box 701084, San Antonio, TX 78270-1084/201-646-9624; FAX: 210-646-0141
Amodei, Jim (See D.O.C. Specialists, Inc.)
Amrine's Gun Shop, 937 La Luna, Ojai, CA 93023/805-646-2376
Amsec, 11925 Pacific Ave., Fontana, CA 92337
AMT, 6226 Santos Diaz St., Irwindale, CA 91702/818-334-6629; FAX: 818-969-5247
Analog Devices, Box 9106, Norwood, MA 02062
Andela Tool & Machine, Inc., RD3, Box 246, Richfield Springs, NY 13439
Anderson Manufacturing Co., Inc., P.O. Box 2640, 2741 N. Crosby Rd., Oak Harbor, WA 98277/360-675-7300; FAX: 360-675-3939
Andres & Dworsky, Bergstrasse 18, A-3822 Karlstein, Thaya, Austria, EUROPE, 0 28 44-285
Angelo & Little Custom Gun Stock Blanks, P.O. Box 240046, Dell, MT 59724-0046
Anschutz GmbH, Postfach 1128, D-89001 Ulm, Donau, GERMANY (U.S. importer—Precision Sales International, Inc.)
Ansen Enterprises, Inc., 1506 W. 228th St., Torrance, CA 90501-5105/310-534-1837; FAX: 310-534-3162
Answer Products Co., 1519 Westbury Drive, Davison, MI 48423/810-653-2911
Anthony and George Ltd., Rt. 1, P.O. Box 45, Evington, VA 24550/804-821-8117
Antique American Firearms (See Carlson, Douglas R.)
Antique Arms Co., 1110 Cleveland Ave., Monett, MO 65708/417-235-6501
AO Safety Products, Div. of American Optical Corp. (See E-A-R, Inc.)
Apache Products, Inc., 4224 Old Sterington Rd., Monroe, LA 71203/318-325-1761; FAX: 318-325-4873
Apel GmbH, Ernst, Am Kirschberg 3, D-97218 Gerbrunn, GERMANY/0 (931) 70 71 91
Aplan Antiques & Art, James O., HC 80, Box 793-25, Piedmont, SD 57769/605-347-5016
Applied Laser Systems, 2160 NW Vine St., Unit A, Grants Pass, OR 97526/503-479-0484; FAX: 503-476-5105
Applied Laser Systems, Inc., 2160 NW Vine St., Grants Pass, OR 97526/503-479-0484; FAX: 503-476-5105
Arcadia Machine & Tool, Inc. (See AMT)
Arco, 3590 S. State Rd. 7, Suite 31, Miramar, FL 33023/305-989-9782; FAX: 305-962-8377
Aristocrat Knives, 1800 N. Highland Ave. No. 600, Los Angeles, CA 90028/213-461-1065; FAX: 213-461-3598
Arizaga (See U.S. importer—Mandall Shooting Supplies, Inc.)
Arizona Custom Case, 1015 S. 23rd St., Phoenix, AZ 85034/602-273-0220
Arkansas Mallard Duck Calls, Rt. Box 182, England, AR 72046/501-842-3597
Arkfeld Mfg. & Dist. Co., Inc., P.O. Box 54, Norfolk, NE 68702-0054/402-371-9430; 800-533-0676
Armalite, Inc., P.O. Box 486, Coal Valley, IL 61240/309-799-5767; FAX: 309-799-5150
Armament Gunsmithing Co., Inc., 525 Rt. 22, Hillside, NJ 07205/908-686-0960
Armas Azor, J.A. (See U.S. importer—Armes de Chasse)
Armas Kemen S.A. (See U.S. importer—USA Sporting)
Armes de Chasse, P.O. Box 827, Chadds Ford, PA 19317/610-388-1146; FAX: 610-388-1147
Armfield Custom Bullets, 4775 Caroline Drive, San Diego, CA 92115/619-582-7188; FAX: 619-287-3238
Armi San Marco (See U.S. importer—Taylor's & Co., Inc.)
Armi San Paolo, via Europa 71-A, l-25062 Concesio, 030-2751725 (BS) ITALY
Armi Sport (See U.S. importers—Cape Outfitters; Taylor's & Co., Inc.)
Armite Laboratories, 1845 Randolph St., Los Angeles, CA 90001/213-587-7768; FAX: 213-587-5075
Armoloy Co. of Ft. Worth, 204 E. Daggett St., Fort Worth, TX 76104/817-332-5604; FAX: 817-335-6517
Armor (See Buck Stop Lure Co., Inc.)
Armor Metal Products, P.O. Box 4609, Helena, MT 59604/406-442-5560
Armory Publications, P.O. Box 4206, Oceanside, CA 92052-4206/619-757-3930; FAX: 619-722-4108
Armoury, Inc., The, Rt. 202, Box 2340, New Preston, CT 06777/203-868-0001
A.R.M.S., Inc., 230 W. Center St., West Bridgewater, MA 02379-1620/508-584-7816; FAX: 508-588-8045
Arms, Peripheral Data Systems, P.O. Box 1526, Lake Oswego, OR 97035/800-366-5559, 503-697-0533; FAX: 503-697-3337
Arms & Armour Press, Villiers House, 41-47 Strand, London WC2N 5JE ENGLAND/071-839-4900; FAX: 071-839-1804
Arms Corp. of the Philippines, Bo. Parang Marikina, Metro Manila, PHILIPPINES
Arms Craft Gunsmithing, 1106 Linda Dr., Arroyo Grande, CA 93420/805-481-2830
Arms Ingenuity Co., P.O. Box 1, 51 Canal St., Weatogue, CT 06089/203-658-5624
Armscor Precision, 225 Lindbergh St., San Mateo, CA 94401/415-347-9556; FAX: 415-347-7634
Armscorp USA, Inc., 4424 John Ave., Baltimore, MD 21227/410-247-6200; FAX: 410-247-6205
Armsport, Inc., 3950 NW 49th St., Miami, FL 33142/305-635-7850; FAX: 305-633-2877
Arnold Arms Co., Inc., P.O. Box 1011, Arlington, WA /206-435-1011
Aro-Tek, Ltd., 206 Frontage Rd. North, Suite C, Pacific, WA 98047/206-351-2984; FAX: 206-833-4483
Arratoonian, Andy (See Horseshoe Leather Products)
Arrieta, S.L., Morkaiko, 5, Elgoibar, E-20870, SPAIN/(43) 74 31 50; FAX: (43) 74 31 54 (U.S. importers—Hi-Grade Imports; Jansma, Jack J.; New England Arms Co.; The Orvis Co., Inc.; Quality Arms, Inc.)
Art Jewel Enterprises Ltd., Eagle Business Ctr., 460 Randy Rd., Carol Stream, IL 60188/708-260-0400
Art's Gun & Sport Shop, Inc., 6008 Hwy. Y, Hillsboro, MO 63050
Artistry in Leather (See Stuart, V. Pat)

Artistry in Wood, 134 Zimmerman Rd., Kalispell, MT 59901/406-257-9003
Arundel Arms & Ammunition, Inc., A., 24 Defense St., Annapolis, MD 21401/301-224-8683
Ashby Turkey Calls, HCR 5, Box 345, Houston, MO 65483/417-967-3787
Aspen Outdoors, Inc., 1059 W. Market St., York, PA 17404/717-846-0255, 800-677-4780; FAX: 717-845-7447
A-Square Co., Inc., One Industrial Park, Bedford, KY 40006-9667/502-255-7456; FAX: 502-255-7657
Astra Sport, S.A., Apartado 3, 48300 Guernica, Espagne, SPAIN/34-4-6250100; FAX: 34-4-6255186 (U.S. importer—E.A.A. Corp.)
A-Tech Corp., P.O. Box 1281, Cottage Grove, OR 97424
ATIS Armi S.A.S., via Gussalli 24, Zona Industriale-Loc. Fornaci, 25020 Brescia, ITALY
Atlanta Cutlery Corp., 2143 Gees Mill Rd., Box 839 CIS, Conyers, GA 30207/800-883-0300; FAX: 404-388-0246
Atlantic Mills, Inc., 1325 Washington Ave., Asbury Park, NJ 07712/800-242-7374
Atlantic Research Marketing Systems (See A.R.M.S., Inc.)
Atsko/Sno-Seal, Inc., 2530 Russell SE, Orangeburg, SC 29115/803-531-1820; FAX: 803-531-2139
Audette, Creighton, 19 Highland Circle, Springfield, VT 05156/802-885-2331
Austin's Calls, Bill, Box 284, Kaycee, WY 82639/307-738-2552
Auto Arms, 738 Clearview, San Antonio, TX 78228/512-434-5450
Automatic Equipment Sales, 627 E. Railroad Ave., Salesburg, MD 21801
Auto-Ordnance Corp., Williams Lane, West Hurley, NY 12491/914-679-4190; FAX: 914-679-2698
Autumn Sales, Inc. (Blaser), 1320 Lake St., Fort Worth, TX 76103/817-335-1634; FAX: 817-338-0119
Avtac, 489 Rt. 32, Highland Mills, NY 10930-0522/800-348-9127
AWC Systems Technology, P.O. Box 41938, Phoenix, AZ 85080-1938/602-780-1050
AYA (See U.S. importer—Armes de Chasse)
A Zone Bullets, 2039 Walter Rd., Billings, MT 59105/800-252-3111; 406-248-1961
Aztec International Ltd., P.O. Box 1384, Clarkesville, GA 30523/706-754-7263

B

B&D Trading Co., Inc., 3935 Fair Hill Rd., Fair Oaks, CA 95628/800-334-3790, 916-967-9366; FAX: 916-967-4873
B&G Bullets, P.O. Box 14313, Oklahoma City, OK 73114/405-840-2353
Badger Shooters Supply, Inc., 202 N. Harding, Owen, WI 54460/715-229-2101; FAX: 715-229-2332
Baekgaard Ltd., 1855 Janke Dr., Northbrook, IL 60062/708-498-3040; FAX: 708-493-3106
Baelder, Harry, Alte Goennebeker Strasse 5, 24635 Rickling, GERMANY/04328-722732; FAX: 04328-722732
Baer Custom, Inc., Les, 29601 34th Ave., Hillsdale, IL 61257/309-658-2716; FAX: 309-658-2610
Bagmaster Mfg., Inc., 2731 Sutton Ave., St. Louis, MO 63143/314-781-8002; FAX: 314-781-3363
Baikal (See U.S. importers—Air Werks International; K.B.I., Inc.)
Bain & Davis, Inc., 307 E. Valley Blvd., San Gabriel, CA 91776-3522/818-573-4241, 213-283-7449
Baity's Custom Gunworks, 414 2nd St., N. Wilkesboro, NC 28659/919-667-8785
Baker, Stan, 10,000 Lake City Way, Seattle, WA 98125/206-522-4575
Baker's Leather Goods, Roy, P.O. Box 893, Magnolia, AR 71753/501-234-0344
Balaance Co., 340-39 Ave. S.E. Box 505, Calgary, AB, T2G 1X6 CANADA
Bald Eagle Precision Machine Co., 101 Allison St., Lock Haven, PA 17745/717-748-6772; FAX: 717-748-4443
Balickie, Joe, 408 Trelawney Lane, Apex, NC 27502/919-362-5185
Ballard Built, P.O. Box 1443, Kingsville, TX 78364/512-592-0853
Ballard Industries, 10271 Lockwood Dr., Suite B, Cupertino, CA 95014/408-996-0957; FAX: 408-257-6828
Ballistic Engineering & Software, Inc., 185 N. Park Blvd., Suite 330, Lake Orion, MI 48362/313-391-1074
Ballistic Products, Inc., 20015 75th Ave. North, Corcoran, MN 55340-9456/612-494-9237; FAX: 612-494-9236
Ballistic Program Co., Inc., The, 2417 N. Patterson St., Thomasville, GA 31792/912-228-5739, 800-368-0835
Ballistic Research, 1108 W. May Ave., McHenry, IL 60050/815-385-0037
Ballistica Maximus North, 107 College Park Plaza, Johnstown, PA 15904/814-266-8380
Ballisti-Cast, Inc., Box 383, Parshall, ND 58770/701-862-3324; FAX: 701-862-3331
Banaczkowski Bullets, 56 Victoria Dr., Mount Barker, S.A. 5251 AUSTRALIA
Bandcor Industries, Div. of Man-Sew Corp., 6108 Sherwin Dr., Port Richey, FL 34668/813-848-0432
Bang-Bang Boutique (See Holster Shop, The)
Banks, Ed, 2762 Hwy. 41 N., Ft. Valley, GA 31030/912-987-4665
Bansner's Gunsmithing Specialties, 261 East Main St. Box VH, Adamstown, PA 19501/800-368-2379; FAX: 717-484-0523
Barami Corp., 6689 Orchard Lake Rd. No. 148, West Bloomfield, MI 48322/810-738-0462; FAX: 810-855-4084
Barbour, Inc., 55 Meadowbrook Dr., Milford, NH 03055/603-673-1313; FAX: 603-673-6510
Barlett, J., 6641 Kaiser Ave., Fontana, CA 92336-3265
Barnes Bullets, Inc., P.O. Box 215, American Fork, UT 84003/801-756-4222, 800-574-9200; FAX: 801-756-2465
Baron Technology, 62 Spring Hill Rd., Trumbull, CT 06611/203-452-0515; FAX: 203-452-0663
Barramundi Corp., P.O. Drawer 4259, Homosassa Springs, FL 32687/904-628-0200
Barrett Firearms Manufacturer, Inc., P.O. Box 1077, Murfreesboro, TN 37133/615-896-2938; FAX: 615-896-7313
Barsotti, Bruce (See River Road Sporting Clays)
Bar-Sto Precision Machine, 73377 Sullivan Rd., P.O. Box 1838, Twentynine Palms, CA 92277/619-367-2747; FAX: 619-367-2407
Barta's Gunsmithing, 10231 US Hwy. 10, Cato, WI 54206/414-732-4472
Barteaux Machete, 1916 SE 50th Ave., Portland, OR 97215-3238/503-233-5880
Bartlett, Don, 3704 E. Pine Needle Ave., Colbert, WA 99005/509-467-5009
Bartlett Engineering, 40 South 200 East, Smithfield, UT 84335-1645/801-563-5910; FAX: 801-563-8416
Basics Information Systems, Inc., 1141 Georgia Ave., Suite 515, Wheaton, MD 20902/301-949-1070; FAX: 301-949-5326

50th EDITION, 1996 **571**

DIRECTORY OF THE ARMS TRADE

Bates Engraving, Billy, 2302 Winthrop Dr., Decatur, AL 35603/205-355-3690
Bauer, Eddie, 15010 NE 36th St., Redmond, WA 98052
Baumannize Custom, 4784 Sunrise Hwy., Bohemia, NY 11716/800-472-4387; FAX: 516-567-0001
Baumgartner Bullets, 3011 S. Alane St., W. Valley City, UT 84120
Bausch & Lomb, Inc., 42 East Ave., Rochester, NY 14603/913-752-3433, 800-828-5423; FAX: 913-752-3489
Bausch & Lomb Sports Optics Div., 9200 Cody, Overland Park, KS 66214/913-752-3400, 800-423-3537; FAX: 913-752-3550
Bauska Barrels, 105 9th Ave. W., Kalispell, MT 59901/406-752-7706
Bear Archery, RR 4, 4600 Southwest 41st Blvd., Gainesville, FL 32601/904-376-2327
Bear Arms, 121 Rhodes St., Jackson, SC 29831/803-471-9859
Bear Hug Grips, Inc., 17230 County Rd. 338, Buena Vista, CO 81211/800-232-7710
Bear Mountain Gun & Tool, 120 N. Plymouth, New Plymouth, ID 83655/208-278-5221; FAX: 208-278-5221
Bear Reloaders, P.O. Box 1613, Akron, OH 44309-1613/216-920-1811
Beartooth Bullets, P.O. Box 491, Dept. HLD, Dover, ID 83825-0491/208-448-1865
Beauchamp & Son, Inc., 160 Rossiter Rd., Richmond, MA 01254/413-698-3822; FAX: 413-698-3866
Beaver Lodge (See Fellowes, Ted)
Beaver Park Products, Inc., 840 J St., Penrose, CO 81240/719-372-6744
Beeline Custom Bullets, P.O. Box 85, Yarmouth, Nova Scotia CANADA B5A 4B1/902-648-3494; FAX: 902-648-0253
Beeman Precision Airguns, 5454 Argosy Dr., Huntington Beach, CA 92649/714-890-4800; FAX: 714-890-4808
Behlert Precision, P.O. Box 288, 7067 Easton Rd., Pipersville, PA 18947/215-766-8681; FAX: 215-766-8681
Beitzinger, George, 116-20 Atlantic Ave., Richmond Hill, NY 11419/718-847-7661
Belding's Custom Gun Shop, 10691 Sayers Rd., Munith, MI 49259/517-596-2388
Bell & Carlson, Inc., Dodge City Industrial Park/101 Allen Rd., Dodge City, KS 67801/800-634-8586, 316-225-6688; FAX: 316-225-9095
Bell Originals, Inc., Sid, 7776 Shackham Rd., Tully, NY 13159-9333/607-842-6431
Bell Reloading, Inc., 1725 Harlin Lane Rd., Villa Rica, GA 30180
Bell's Gun & Sport Shop, 3309-19 Mannheim Rd, Franklin Park, IL 60131
Bell's Legendary Country Wear, 22 Circle Dr., Bellmore, NY 11710/516-679-1158
Bellm Contenders, P.O. Ackley Rifle Barrels, P.O. Box 459, Cleveland, UT 84518/801-653-2530
Belltown, Ltd., 11 Camps Rd., Kent, CT 06757/203-354-5750
Ben's Machines, 1151 S. Cedar Ridge, Duncanville, TX 75137/214-780-1807; FAX: 214-780-0316
Benchmark Guns, 12593 S. Ave. 5 East, Yuma, AZ 85365
Benchmark Knives (See Gerber Legendary Blades)
Benelli Armi, S.p.A., Via della Stazione, 61029 Urbino, ITALY/39-722-328633; FAX: 39-722-327427 (U.S. importers—E.A.A. Corp.; Heckler & Koch, Inc.; Sile Distributors)
Bengtson Arms Co., L., 6345-B E. Akron St., Mesa, AZ 85205/602-981-6375
Benjamin/Sheridan Co., Crossman, Rts. 5 and 20, E. Bloomfield, NY 14443/716-657-6161; FAX: 716-657-5405
Bentley, John, 128-D Watson Dr., Turtle Creek, PA 15145
Benton & Brown Firearms, 311 W. First, P.O. Box 326, Delhi, LA 71232-0326/318-878-2499; FAX: 817-284-9300
Beomat of America Inc., 300 Railway Ave., Campbell, CA 95008/408-379-4829
Beretta Firearms, Pietro, 25063 Gardone V.T., ITALY (U.S. importer—Beretta U.S.A. Corp.)
Beretta, Dr. Franco, via Rossa, 4, Concesio (BC), Italy I-25062/030-2751955; FAX: 030-218-0414 (U.S. importer—Nevada Cartridge Co.
Beretta U.S.A. Corp., 17601 Beretta Drive, Accokeek, MD 20607/301-283-2191; FAX: 301-283-0435
Berger Bullets, Ltd., 5342 W. Camelback Rd., Suite 500, Glendale, AZ 85301/602-842-4001; FAX: 602-934-9083
Bergman & Williams, 2450 Losee Rd., Suite F, Las Vegas, NV 89030/702-642-1901; FAX: 702-642-1540
Bernardelli S.p.A., Vincenzo, 125 Via Matteotti, P.O. Box 74, Gardone V.T., Brescia ITALY, 25063/39-30-8912851-2-3; FAX: 39-30-8910249 (U.S. importer—Armsport, Inc.)
Berry's Bullets, Div. of Berry's Mfg., Inc., 401 N. 3050 E., St. George, UT 84770-9004
Berry's Mfg., Inc., 401 North 3050 East St., St. George, UT 84770/801-634-1682; FAX: 801-634-1683
Bersa S.A., Gonzales Castillo 312, 1704 Ramos Mejia, ARGENTINA/541-656-2377; FAX: 541-656-2093 (U.S. importer—Eagle Imports, Inc.)
Bertram Bullet Co., P.O. Box 313, Seymour, Victoria 3660, AUSTRALIA/61-57-922912; FAX: 61-57-991650
Bertuzzi (See U.S. importers—Cape Outfitters; Moore & Co., Wm. Larkin; New England Arms Co.)
Better Concepts Co., 663 New Castle Rd., Butler, PA 16001/412-285-9000
Beverly, Mary, 3201 Horseshoe Trail, Tallahassee, FL 32312
Bianchi International, Inc., 100 Calle Cortez, Temecula, CA 92590/909-676-5621; FAX: 909-676-6777
Biesen, Al, 5021 Rosewood, Spokane, WA 99208/509-328-9340
Biesen, Roger, 5021 W. Rosewood, Spokane, WA 99208/509-328-9340
Big Beam Emergency Systems, Inc., 290 E. Prairie St., Crystal Lake, IL 60039
Big Bear Arms & Sporting Goods, Inc., 2714 Fairmount St., Dallas, TX 75201/214-871-7061, 800-400-BEAR; FAX: 214-754-0449
Big Sky Racks, Inc., P.O. Box 729, Bozeman, MT 59771-0729/406-586-9393; FAX: 406-585-7378
Big Spring Enterprises "Bore Stores", P.O. Box 1115, Big Spring, Rd./Yellville, AR 72687 501-449-5297; FAX: 501-449-4446
Bilal, Mustafa, 5429 Russell Ave. NW, Suite 202, Seattle, WA 98107/206-782-4164
Bill's Custom Cases, P.O. Box 2, Dunsmuir, CA 96025/916-235-0177; FAX: 916-235-4959
Bill's Gun Repair, 1007 Burlington St., Mendota, IL 61342/815-539-5786
Billeb, Stephen L., 1101 N. 7th St., Burlington, IA 52601/319-753-2110
Billings Gunsmiths, Inc., 1940 Grand Ave., Billings, MT 59102/406-652-3104
Billingsley & Brownell, P.O. Box 25, Dayton, WY 82830/307-655-9344
Birchwood Casey, 7900 Fuller Rd., Eden Prairie, MN 55344/800-328-6156, 612-937-7933; FAX: 612-937-7979
Birdsong & Assoc., W.E., 4832 Windermere, Jackson, MS 39206/601-366-8270

Bismuth Cartridge Co., 3500 Maple Ave., Suite 1650, Dallas, TX 75219/800-759-3333, 214-521-5880; FAX: 214-521-9035
Bison Studios (See Philip Poburka)
Bitterroot Bullet Co., Box 412, Lewiston, ID 83501-0412/208-743-5635
Black Belt Bullets, Big Bore Express Inc., 7154 W. State St., Suite 200, Boise, ID 83703
Black Hills Ammunition, Inc., P.O. Box 3090, Rapid City, SD 57709-3090/605-348-5150; FAX: 605-348-9827
Black Hills Shooters Supply, P.O. Box 4220, Rapid City, SD 57709/800-289-2506
Black Mountain Bullets, Rt. 7, Box 297, Warrenton, VA 22186/703-347-1199
Black Sheep Brand, 3220 W. Gentry Parkway, Tyler, TX 75702/903-592-3853; FAX: 903-590-0527
Blackhawk East, Box 2274, Loves Park, IL 61131
Blackhawk West, Box 285, Hiawatha, KS 66434
Blackinton & Co., Inc., V.H., 221 John L. Dietsch, Attleboro Falls, MA 02763-0300/508-699-4436; FAX: 508-695-5349
Blackjack Knives, Ltd., 1307 W. Wabash, Effingham, IL 62401/217-347-7700; FAX: 217-347-7737
Blacksmith Corp., 830 N. Road No. 1 E., P.O. Box 1752, Chino Valley, AZ 86323/602-636-4456; FAX: 602-636-4457
BlackStar Barrel Accurizing, 11609 N. Galayda St., Houston, TX 77086/713-448-5300; FAX: 713-448-7298
Blacktail Mountain Books, 42 First Ave. West, Kalispell, MT 59901/406-257-5573
Blackwell, W. (See Load From a Disk)
Blakemore Game Calls, Jim, Rt. 2, Box 544, Cape Girardeau, MO 63701
Blammo Ammo, P.O. Box 1677, Seneca, SC 29679/803-882-1768
Blaser Jagdwaffen GmbH, D-88316 Isny Im Allgau, GERMANY (U.S. importer—Autumn Sales, Inc.)
Bleile, C. Roger, 5040 Ralph Ave., Cincinnati, OH 45238/513-251-0249
Blocker's Holsters, Inc., Ted, 5360 NE 112, Portland, OR 97220/503-254-9950
Blount, Inc., Sporting Equipment Div., 2299 Snake River Ave., P.O. Box 856, Lewiston, ID 83501/800-627-3640, 208-746-2351; FAX: 208-746-2915
Blue and Gray Products, Inc. (See Ox-Yoke Originals, Inc.)
Blue Book Publications, Inc., One Appletree Square, Minneapolis, MN 55425/800-877-4867, 612-854-5229; FAX: 612-853-1486
Blue Mountain Bullets, HCR 77, P.O. Box 231, John Day, OR 97845/503-820-4594
Blue Ridge Knives, Rt. 6, Box 185, Marion, VA 24354/703-783-6143; FAX: 703-783-9298
Blue Ridge Machinery & Tools, Inc., P.O. Box 536-GD, Hurricane, WV 25526/800-872-6500; FAX: 304-562-5311
BMC Supply, Inc., 26051 - 179th Ave. S.E., Kent, WA 98042
B.M.F. Activator, Inc., 803 Mill Creek Run, Plantersville, TX 77363/409-894-2005, 800-527-2881
Bob's Gun Shop, P.O. Box 200, Royal, AR 71968/501-767-1970
Bob's Tactical Indoor Shooting Range & Gun Shop, 122 Lafayette Rd., Salisbury, MA 01952/508-465-5561
Boessler, Erich, Am Vogeltal 3, 97702 Munnerstadt, GERMANY/9733-9443
Boggs, Wm., 1816 Riverside Dr. C, Columbus, OH 43212/614-486-6965
Bohemia Arms Co., 17101 Los Modelos, Fountain Valley, CA 92708/619-442-7005; FAX: 619-442-7005
Boker USA, Inc., 14818 West 6th Ave., Suite 10A, Golden, CO 80401-5045/303-279-5997; FAX: 303-279-5919
Bolden's, P.O. Box 33178, Kerrville, TX 78029/210-634-2703
Boltin, John M., P.O. Box 644, Estill, SC 29918/803-625-2185
Bo-Mar Tool & Mfg. Co., Rt. 12, Box 405, Longview, TX 75605/903-759-4784; FAX: 903-759-9141
Bonanza (See Forster Products)
Bond Custom Firearms, 8954 N. Lewis Ln., Bloomington, IN 47408/812-332-4519
Bondini Paolo, Via Sorrento, 345, San Carlo di Cesena, ITALY I-47020/0547 663 240; FAX: 0547 663 780
Bone Engraving, Ralph, 718 N. Atlanta, Owasso, OK 74055/918-272-9745
Boone Trading Co., Inc., P.O. Box BB, Brinnan, WA 98320
Boone's Custom Ivory Grips, Inc., 562 Coyote Rd., Brinnon, WA 98320/206-796-4330
Boonie Packer Products, P.O. Box 12204, Salem, OR 97309/800-477-3244, 503-581-3244; FAX: 503-581-3191
Borden's Accuracy, RD 1, Box 250BC, Springville, PA 18844/717-965-2505; FAX: 717-965-2328
Border Barrels Ltd., Riccarton Farm, Newcastleton SCOTLAND U.K. TD9 0SN
Borovnik KG, Ludwig, 9170 Ferlach, Bahnhofstrasse 7, AUSTRIA/042 27 24 42; FAX: 042 26 43 49
Bosis (See U.S. importer—New England Arms Co.)
Boss Manufacturing Co., 221 W. First St., Kewanee, IL 61443/309-852-2131, 800-447-4581; FAX: 309-852-0848
Bostick Wildlife Calls, Inc., P.O. Box 728, Estill, SC 29918/803-625-2210, 803-625-4512
Bowen Classic Arms Corp., P.O. Box 67, Louisville, TN 37777/615-984-3583
Bowen Knife Co., Inc., P.O. Box 590, Blackshear, GA 31516/912-449-4794
Bowerly, Kent, HCR Box 1903, Camp Sherman, OR 97730/503-595-6028
Bowlin, Gene, Rt. 1, Box 890, Snyder, TX 79549
Boyds'Gunstock Industries, Inc., 3rd & Main, P.O. Box 305, Geddes, SD 57342/605-337-2125; FAX: 605-337-3363
Boyt, 509 Hamilton, P.O. Drawer 668, Iowa Falls, IA 50126/515-648-4626; FAX: 515-648-2385
Brace, Larry D., 771 Blackfoot Ave., Eugene, OR 97404/503-688-1278
Bradley Gunsight Co., P.O. Box 140, Plymouth, VT 05056/203-589-0531; FAX: 203-582-6294
Brass and Bullet Alloys, P.O. Box 1238, Sierra Vista, AZ 85636/602-458-5321; FAX: 602-458-9125
Brass Eagle, Inc., 7050A Bramalea Rd., Unit 19, Mississauga, Ont. L4Z 1C7, CANADA/416-848-4844
Brass-Tech Industries, P.O. Box 521-v, Wharton, NJ 07885/201-366-8540
Bratcher, Dan, 311 Belle Air Pl., Carthage, MO 64836/417-358-1518
Brauer Bros. Mfg. Co., 2020 Delman Blvd., St. Louis, MO 63103/314-231-2864; FAX: 314-249-4952
Braun, M., 32, rue Notre-Dame, 2440 LUXEMBURG
Braverman Corp., R.J., 88 Parade Rd., Meridith, NH 03293/800-736-4867
Break-Free, Inc., P.O. Box 25020, Santa Ana, CA 92799/714-953-1900; FAX: 714-953-0402
Brell Mar Products, Inc., 5701 Hwy. 80 West, Jackson, MS 39209

MANUFACTURERS' DIRECTORY

Brenneke KG, Wilhelm, Ilmenauweg 2, 30851 Langenhagen, GERMANY/0511/97262-0; FAX: 0511/97262-62 (U.S. importer—Dynamit Nobel-RWS, Inc.)
Bretton, 19, rue Victor Grignard, F-42026 St.-Etienne (Cedex 1) FRANCE/77-93-54-69; FAX: 77-93-57-98 (U.S. importer—Mandall Shooting Supplies, Inc.)
Brgoch, Frank, 1580 S. 1500 East, Bountiful, UT 84010/801-295-1885
Brian, C.T., Pistolsmith, P.O. Box 308, Rocky Ford, CO 81067/719-254-3849
Bridgers Best, P.O. Box 1410, Berthoud, CO 80513
Briese Bullet Co., Inc., RR1, Box 108, Tappen, ND 58487/701-327-4578; FAX: 701-327-4579
Brigade Quartermasters, 1025 Cobb International Blvd., Dept. VH, Kennesaw, GA 30144-4300/404-428-1248, 800-241-3125; FAX: 404-426-7726
Briganti & Co., A., 475 Rt. 32, Highland Mills, NY 10930/914-928-9573
Briley Mfg., Inc., 1230 Lumpkin, Houston, TX 77043/800-331-5718, 713-932-6995; FAX: 713-932-1043
British Arms Co. Ltd., P.O. Box 7, Latham, NY 12110/518-783-0773
British Sporting Arms, RR1, Box 130, Millbrook, NY 12545/914-677-8303
BRNO (See U.S. importers—Bohemia Arms Co.)
Broad Creek Rifle Works, 120 Horsey Ave., Laurel, DE 19956/302-875-5446
Brobst, Jim, 299 Poplar St., Hamburg, PA 19526/215-562-2103
Brockman's Custom Gunsmithing, P.O. Box 357, Gooding, ID 83330/208-934-5050
Brocock Ltd., 43 River Street, Digbeth, Birmingham, B5 5SA ENGLAND/011-021-773-1200 (U.S. importer—Airguns-R-Us)
Broken Gun Ranch, 10739 126 Rd., Spearville, KS 67876/316-385-2587; FAX: 316-385-2597
Brolin Arms, 2755 Thompson Creek Rd., Pomona, CA 91767/909-392-2345; FAX: 909-392-2354
Brooker, Dennis, Rt. 1, Box 12A, Derby, IA 50068/515-533-2103
Brooks Tactical Systems, 279-A Shorewood Ct., Fox Island, WA 98333/800-410-4747; FAX: 206-572-6797
Brown Co., E. Arthur, 3404 Pawnee Dr., Alexandria, MN 56308/612-762-8847
Brown, H.R. (See Silhouette Leathers)
Brown Manufacturing, P.O. Box 9219, Akron, OH 44305/800-837-GUNS
Brown Precision, Inc., 7786 Molinos Ave., Los Molinos, CA 96055/916-384-2506; FAX: 916-384-1638
Brown Products, Inc., Ed, Rt. 2, Box 2922, Perry, MO 63462/314-565-3261; FAX: 565-2791
Brownell Checkering Tools, W.E., 9390 Twin Mountain Circle, San Diego, CA 92126/619-695-2479; FAX: 619-695-2479
Brownells, Inc., 200 S. Front St., Montezuma, IA 50171/515-623-5401; FAX: 515-623-3896
Browning Arms Co.(Gen. Offices), One Browning Place, Morgan, UT 84050/801-876-2711; FAX: 801-876-3331
Browning Arms Co. (Parts & Service), 3005 Arnold Tenbrook Rd., Arnold, MO 63010-9406/314-287-6800; FAX: 314-287-9751
BRP, Inc. High Performance Cast Bullets, 1210 Alexander Rd., Colorado Springs, CO 80909/719-633-0658
Bruno Shooters Supply, 106 N. Wyoming St., Hazleton, PA 18201/717-455-2211; FAX: 717-455-2211
Brunswick, Inc., 1131 Bayview Dr., Quincy, IL 62301/217-223-8844; FAX: 217-223-8847
Brunton U.S.A., 620 E. Monroe Ave., Riverton, WY 82501/307-856-6559; FAX: 307-856-1840
Bryco Arms (See U.S. distributor—Jennings Firearms, Inc.)
Brynin, Milton, P.O. Box 383, Yonkers, NY 10710/914-779-4333
BSA Guns Ltd., Armoury Rd. Small Heath, Birmingham, ENGLAND B11 2PX/011-021-772-8543; FAX: 011-021-773-0845
B-Square Company, Inc., P.O. Box 11281, 2708 St. Louis Ave., Ft. Worth, TX 76110/817-923-0964, 800-433-2909; FAX: 817-926-7012
Bucheimer, J.M., Jumbo Sports Products, 721 N. 20th St., St. Louis, MO 63103/314-241-1020
Buck Knives, Inc., 1900 Weld Blvd., P.O. Box 1267, El Cajon, CA 92020/619-449-1100, 800-326-2825; FAX: 619-562-5774, 800-729-2825
Buck Stix—SOS Products Co., Box 3, Neenah, WI 54956
Buck Stop Lure Co., Inc., 3600 Grow Rd. NW, P.O. Box 636, Stanton, MI 48888/517-762-5091; FAX: 517-762-5124
Buckeye Custom Bullets, 6490 Stewart Rd., Elida, OH 45807/419-641-4463
Buckhorn Gun Works, 115 E. North St., Rapid City, SD 57701/605-341-2277
Buckskin Bullet Co., P.O. Box 245, Cedar City, UT 84721/801-586-3286
Buckskin Machine Works, A. Hunkeler, 3235 S. 358th St., Auburn, WA 98001/206-927-5412
Budin, Dave, Main St., Margaretville, NY 12455/914-568-4103; FAX: 914-586-4105
Buenger Enterprises/Goldenrod Dehumidifier, 3600 S. Harbor Blvd., Oxnard, CA 93035/800-451-6797; FAX: 805-985-1534
Buffalo Arms, 123 S. Third, Suite 6, Sandpoint, ID 83864/208-263-6953; FAX: 208-265-2096
Buffalo Bullet Co., Inc., 12637 Los Nietos Rd., Unit A, Santa Fe Springs, CA 90670/310-944-0322; FAX: 310-944-5054
Buffalo Rock Shooters Supply, R.R. 1, Ottawa, IL 61350/815-433-2471
Bull Mountain Rifle Co., 6327 Golden West Terrace, Billings, MT 59106/406-656-0778
Bullberry Barrel Works, Ltd., 2430 W. Bullberry Ln. 67-5, Hurricane, UT 84737/801-635-9866
Bullet, Inc., 3745 Hiram Alworth Rd., Dallas, GA 30132
Bullet Meister Bullets (See Gander Mountain)
Bullet Mills, P.O. Box 102, Port Carbon, PA 17965/717-622-0657
Bullet Swaging Supply, Inc., P.O. Box 1056, 303 McMillan Rd, West Monroe, LA 71291/318-387-7257; FAX: 318-387-7779
BulletMakers Workshop, The, RFD 1 Box 1755, Brooks, ME 04921
Bullseye Bullets, 1610 State Road 60, No. 12, Valrico, FL 33594/813-654-6563
Bull-X, Inc., P.O. Box 182, 520 N. Main., Farmer City, IL 61842/309-928-2574, 800-248-3845 orders only; FAX: 309-928-2130
Burgess, Byron, P.O. Box 6853, Los Osos, CA 93412/805-534-1304
Burgess & Son Gunsmiths, R.W., P.O. Box 3364, Warner Robins, GA 31099/912-328-7487
Burkhart Gunsmithing, Don, P.O. Box 852, Rawlins, WY 82301/307-324-6007
Burnham Bros., P.O. Box 1148, Menard, TX 78659/915-396-4572; FAX: 915-396-4574
Burres, Jack, 10333 San Fernando Rd., Pacoima, CA 91331/818-899-8000
Burris Co., Inc., P.O. Box 1747, 331 E. 8th St., Greeley, CO 80631/303-356-1670; FAX: 303-356-8702
Bushmann Hunters & Safaris, P.O. Box 293088, Lewisville, TX 75029/214-317-0768
Bushmaster Firearms (See Quality Parts Co./Bushmaster Firearms)
Bushmaster Hunting & Fishing, 451 Alliance Ave., Toronto, Ont. M6N 2J1 CANADA/416-763-4040; FAX: 416-763-0623
Bushnell (See Bausch & Lomb)
Bushwacker Backpack & Supply Co. (See Counter Assault)
Bustani Appraisers, Leo, P.O. Box 8125, W. Palm Beach, FL 33407/305-622-2710
Buster's Custom Knives, P.O. Box 214, Richfield, UT 84701/801-896-5319
Butler Creek Corp., 290 Arden Dr., Belgrade, MT 59714/800-423-8327, 406-388-1356; FAX: 388-7204
Butler Enterprises, 834 Oberting Rd., Lawrenceburg, IN 47025/812-537-3584
Butterfield & Butterfield, 220 San Bruno Ave., San Francisco, CA 94103/415-861-7500
Buzztail Brass, 5306 Bryant Ave., Klamath Falls, OR 97603-5020/503-884-1072
B-West Imports, Inc., 2425 N. Huachuca Dr., Tucson, AZ 85745-1201/602-628-1990; FAX: 602-628-3602

C

C3 Systems, 678 Killingly St., Johnston, RI 02919
C&D Special Products (Claybuster), 309 Sequoya Dr., Hopkinsville, KY 42240/800-922-6287, 800-284-1746, 502-885-8088; FAX: 502-885-1951
C&H Research, 115 Sunnyside Dr., Box 351, Lewis, KS 67552/316-324-5445
C&J Enterprises, Inc., 7101 Jurupa Ave., No. 12, Riverside, CA 92504/909-689-7758
Cabanas (See U.S. importer—Mandall Shooting Supplies, Inc.)
Cabela's, 812-13th Ave., Sidney, NE 69160/308-254-6644; FAX: 308-254-6669
Cabinet Mtn. Outfitters Scents & Lures, P.O. Box 766, Plains, MT 59859/406-826-3970
Cache La Poudre Rifleworks, 140 N. College, Ft. Collins, CO 80524/303-482-6913
Cadre Supply (See Parts & Surplus)
Calhoon Varmint Bullets, James, Shambo Rt., Box 304, Havre, MT 59501
Calibre Press, Inc., 666 Dundee Rd., Suite 1607, Northbrook, IL 60062-2760/800-323-0037; FAX: 708-498-6869
Cali'co Hardwoods, Inc., 3580 Westwind Blvd., Santa Rosa, CA 95403/707-546-4045; FAX: 707-546-4027
Calico Light Weapon Systems, 405 E. 19th St., Bakersfield, CA 93305/805-323-1327; FAX: 805-323-7844
California Grip, 1323 Miami Ave., Clovis, CA 93612/209-299-1316
California Magnum, 20746 Dearborn St., Chatsworth, CA 91313/818-341-7302; FAX: 818-341-7304
California Sight, P.O. Box 4607, Pagosa Springs, CO 81157/303-731-5003
CAM Enterprises, 5090 Iron Springs Rd., Box 2, Prescott, AZ 86301/602-776-9640
Camas Hot Springs Mfg., P.O. Box 639, Hot Springs, MT 59845/406-741-3756
Camdex, Inc., 2330 Alger, Troy, MI 48083/810-528-2300; FAX: 810-528-0989
Cameron's, 16690 W. 11th Ave., Golden, CO 80401/303-279-7365; FAX: 303-628-5413
Camilli, Lou, 4700 Oahu Dr. NE, Albuquerque, NM 87111/505-293-5259
Camillus Cutlery Co./Western Cutlery Co., 54 Main St., Camillus, NY 13031/315-672-8111; FAX: 315-672-8832
Campbell, Dick, 20,000 Silver Ranch Rd., Conifer, CO 80433/303-697-0150
Camp-Cap Products, P.O. Box 173, Chesterfield, MO 63006/314-532-4340
Canjar Co., M.H., 500 E. 45th Ave., Denver, CO 80216/303-295-2638
Cannon's Guns, Box 1036, 320 Main St., Polson, MT 59860/406-887-2048
Cannon Safe, Inc., 9358 Stephens St., Pico Rivera, CA 90660/310-692-0636, 800-242-1055; FAX: 310-692-7252
Canons Delcour, Rue J.B. Cools, B-4040 Herstal, BELGIUM 32.(0)41.40.13.40; FAX: 32(0)412.40.22.88
Canyon Cartridge Corp., P.O. Box 152, Albertson, NY 11507/FAX: 516-294-8946
Cape Outfitters, 599 County Rd. 206, Cape Girardeau, MO 63701/314-335-4103; FAX: 314-335-1555
Caraville Manufacturing, P.O. Box 4545, Thousand Oaks, CA 91359/805-499-1234
Carbide Checkering Tools, P.O. Box 77, 200 Lyons Hill Rd., Athol, MA 01331/508-249-9241
Carbide Die & Mfg. Co., Inc., 15615 E. Arrow Hwy., Irwindale, CA 91706/818-337-2518
Carhartt, Inc., P.O. Box 600, 3 Parklane Blvd., Dearborn, MI 48121/800-358-3825, 313-271-8460; FAX: 313-271-3455
Carlson, Douglas R., Antique American Firearms, P.O. Box 71035, Dept. GD, Des Moines, IA 50325/515-224-6552
Carnahan Bullets, 17645 110th Ave. SE, Renton, WA 98055
Carolina Precision Rifles, 1200 Old Jackson Hwy., Jackson, SC 29831/803-827-2069
Carrell's Precision Firearms, P.O. Box 232, 201 S. Park, Joliet, MT 59041/406-962-3593
Carroll Bullets (See Precision Reloading, Inc.)
Carry-Lite, Inc., 5203 W. Clinton Ave., Milwaukee, WI 53223/414-355-3520; FAX: 414-355-4775
Carter's Gun Shop, 225 G St., Penrose, CO 81240/719-372-6240
Carter's Wildlife Calls, Inc., Garth, P.O. Box 821, Cedar City, UT 84720/801-586-7639
Carvajal Belts & Holsters, 422 Chestnut, San Antonio, TX 78202/210-222-1634
Cascade Arms, Inc., 22457 S. Highway 211, Colton, Oregon 97017/503-824-4979
Cascade Bullet Co., Inc., 2355 South 6th St., Klamath Falls, OR 97601/503-884-9316
Cascade Fabrication, 1090 Bailey Hill Rd. Unit A, Eugene, OR 97402/503-485-3433; FAX: 503-485-3543
Cascade Shooters, 2155 N.W. 12th St., Redwood, OR 97756
Case & Sons Cutlery Co., W.R., Owens Way, Bradford, PA 16701/814-368-4123, 800-523-6350; FAX: 814-768-5369
Case Sorting System, 12695 Cobblestone Creek Rd., Poway, CA 92064/619-486-9340
Cash Mfg. Co., Inc., P.O. Box 130, 201 S. Klein Dr., Waunakee, WI 53597-0130/608-849-5664; FAX: 608-849-5664
Caspian Arms Ltd., 14 North Main St., Hardwick, VT 05843/802-472-6454; FAX: 802-472-6709
Caswell International Corp., 1221 Marshall St. NE, Minneapolis, MN 55413-1055/612-379-2000; FAX: 612-379-2367
Catco-Ambush, Inc., P.O. Box 300, Corte Madera, CA 94926
Cathey Enterprises, Inc., P.O. Box 2202, Brownwood, TX 76804/915-643-2553; FAX: 915-643-3653
Cation, 2341 Alger St., Troy, MI 48083/810-689-0658; FAX: 810-689-7558
Catoctin Cutlery, P.O. Box 188, 17 S. Main St., Smithsburg, MD 21783/301-824-7416; FAX: 301-824-6138
Caywood, Shane J., P.O. Box 321, Minocqua, WI 54548/715-277-3866 evenings

50th EDITION, 1996 **573**

DIRECTORY OF THE ARMS TRADE

CBC, Avenida Humberto de Campos, 3220, 09400-000 Ribeirao Pires-SP-BRAZIL/55-11-742-7500; FAX: 55-11-459-7385 (U.S. importer—MAGTECH Recreational Products, Inc.)
C.C.G. Enterprises, 5217 E. Belknap St., Halton City, TX 76117/817-834-9554
CCI, Div. of Blount, Inc., 2299 Snake River Ave., P.O. Box 856, Lewiston, ID 83501/800-627-3640, 208-746-2351; FAX: 208-746-2915
Cedar Hill Game Calls, Inc., Rt. 2 Box 236, Downsville, LA 71234/318-982-5632; FAX: 318-368-2245
Celestron International, P.O. Box 3578, 2835 Columbia St., Torrance, CA 90503/310-328-9560; FAX: 310-212-5835
Centaur Systems, Inc., 1602 Foothill Rd., Kalispell, MT 59901/406-755-8609; FAX: 406-755-8609
Center Lock Scope Rings, 9901 France Ct., Lakeville, MN 55044/612-461-2114
CenterMark, P.O. Box 4066, Parnassus Station, New Kensington, PA 15068/412-335-1319
Central Specialties Ltd., 1122 Silver Lake Road, Cary, IL 60013/708-639-3900; FAX: 708-639-3972
Century Gun Dist., Inc., 1467 Jason Rd., Greenfield, IN 46140/317-462-4524
Century International Arms, Inc., P.O. Box 714, St. Albans, VT 05478-0714/802-527-1252; FAX: 802-527-0470
CF Ventures, 509 Harvey Dr., Bloomington, IN 47403
C-H Tool & Die Corp. (See 4-D Custom Die Co.)
CHAA, Ltd., P.O. Box 565, Howell, MI 48844/800-677-8737; FAX: 313-894-6930
Chace Leather Products, 507 Alden St., Fall River, MA 02722/508-678-7556; FAX: 508-675-9666
Chadick's Ltd., P.O. Box 100, Terrell, TX 75160/214-563-7577
Chambers Flintlocks Ltd., Jim, Rt. 1, Box 513-A, Candler, NC 28715/704-667-8361
Chameleon Camouflage Systems, 15199 S. Maplelane Rd., Oregon City, OR 97045/503-657-2266
Champion Target Co., 232 Industrial Parkway, Richmond, IN 47374/800-441-4971
Champion's Choice, Inc., 201 International Blvd., LaVergne, TN 37086/615-793-4066; FAX: 615-793-4070
Champlin, R. MacDonald, P.O. Box 132, Candia, NH 03034
Champlin Firearms, Inc., P.O. Box 3191, Woodring Airport, Enid, OK 73701/405-237-7388; FAX: 405-242-6922
Chapman Academy of Practical Shooting, 4350 Academy Rd., Hallsville, MO 65255/314-696-5544; FAX: 314-696-2266
Chapman Manufacturing Co., 471 New Haven Rd., P.O. Box 250, Durham, CT 06422/203-349-9228; FAX: 203-349-0084
Chapuis Armes, 21 La Gravoux, BP15, 42380 St. Bonnet-le-Chateau, FRANCE/(33)77.50.06.96 (U.S. importer—Chapuis USA)
Chapuis USA, 416 Business Park, Bedford, KY 40006
CHARCO, 26 Beaver St., Ansonia, CT 06401/203-735-4686; 203-735-6569
Charter Arms (See CHARCO)
Checkmate Refinishing, 370 Champion Dr., Brooksville, FL 34601/904-799-5774
Cheddite France, S.A., 99, Route de Lyon, F-26500 Bourg-les-Valence, FRANCE/33-75-56-4545; FAX: 33-75-56-3587
Chelsea Gun Club of New York City, Inc., 237 Ovington Ave., Apt. D53, Brooklyn, NY 11209/718-836-9422, 718-833-2704
Chem-Pak, Inc., 11 Oates Ave., P.O. Box 1685, Winchester, VA 22604/800-336-9828, 703-667-1341; FAX: 703-722-3993
Cherokee Gun Accessories (See Glaser Safety Slug, Inc.)
Cherry's Fine Guns, P.O. Box 5307, Greensboro, NC 27435-0307/919-854-4182
Chesapeake Importing & Distributing Co. (See CIDCO)
CheVron Bullets, RR1, Ottawa, IL 61350/815-433-2471
CheVron Case Master (See CheVron Bullets)
Chicago Cutlery Co., 1536 Beech St., Terre Haute, IN 47804/800-457-2665
Chicasaw Gun Works (See Cochran, Oliver)
Chipmunk (See Oregon Arms, Inc.)
Chippewa Shoe Co., P.O. Box 2521, Ft. Worth, TX 76113/817-332-4385
Choate Machine & Tool Co., Inc., P.O. Box 218, 116 Lovers Ln., Bald Knob, AR 72010/501-724-6193, 800-972-6390; FAX: 501-724-5873
Chopie Mfg., Inc., 700 Copeland Ave., LaCrosse, WI 54603/608-784-0926
Christie's East, 219 E. 67th St., New York, NY 10021/212-606-0400
Christman Jr., David, 937 Lee Hedrick Rd., Colville, WA 99114/509-684-5686 days; 509-684-3314 evenings
Christopher Firearms Co., E., Inc., Route 128 & Ferry St., Miamitown, OH 45041/513-353-1321
Chronotech, 1655 Siamet Rd. Unit 6, Mississauga, Ont. L4W 1Z4 CANADA/905-625-5200; FAX: 905-625-5190
Chu Tani Ind., Inc., P.O. Box 2064, Cody, WY 82414-2064
Chuck's Gun Shop, P.O. Box 597, Waldo, FL 32694/904-468-2264
Churchill (See U.S. importer—Ellett Bros.)
Churchill, Winston, Twenty Mile Stream Rd., RFD P.O. Box 29B, Proctorsville, VT 05153/802-226-7772
Churchill Glove Co., James, P.O. Box 298, Centralia, WA 98531
CIDCO, 21480 Pacific Blvd., Sterling, VA 22170/703-444-5353
Ciener, Inc., Jonathan Arthur, 8700 Commerce St., Cape Canaveral, FL 32920/407-868-2200; FAX: 407-868-2201
Cimarron Arms, P.O. Box 906, Fredericksburg, TX 78624-0906/210-997-9090; FAX: 210-997-0802
Cincinnati Swaging, 2605 Marlington Ave., Cincinnati, OH 45208
Circle M Custom Bullets, 29 Avenida de Silva, Abilene, TX 79602-7509/915-698-3106
Clark Co., Inc., David, P.O. Box 15054, Worcester, MA 01615-0054/508-756-6216; FAX: 508-753-5827
Clark Custom Guns, Inc., P.O. Box 530, 11462 Keatchie Rd., Keithville, LA 71047/318-925-0836; FAX: 318-925-9425
Clark Firearms Engraving, P.O. Box 80746, San Marino, CA 91118/818-287-1652
Clarkfield Enterprises, Inc., 1032 10th Ave., Clarkfield, MN 56223/612-669-7140
Classic Arms Corp., P.O. Box 106, Dunsmuir, CA 96025-0106/916-235-2000
Classic Brass, 14 Grove St., Plympton, MA 02367/FAX: 617-585-5673
Classic Guns, Inc., Frank S. Wood, 3230 Medlock Bridge Rd., Suite 110, Norcross, GA 30092/404-242-7944
Clearview Mfg. Co., Inc., 413 S. Oakley St., Fordyce, AR 71742/501-352-8557; FAX: 501-352-8557
Clearview Products, 3021 N. Portland, Oklahoma City, OK 73107
Cleland's Gun Shop, Inc., 10306 Airport Hwy., Swanton, OH 43558/419-865-4713

Clements' Custom Leathercraft, Chas, 1741 Dallas St., Aurora, CO 80010-2018/303-364-0403
Clenzoil Corp., P.O. Box 80226, Sta. C, Canton, OH 44708-0226/216-833-9758
Clerke Co., J.A., P.O. Box 627, Pearblossom, CA 93553-0627/805-945-0713
Clift Mfg., L.R., 3821 Hammonton Rd., Marysville, CA 95901/916-755-3390; FAX: 916-755-3393
Clift Welding Supply & Cases, 1332-A Colusa Hwy., Yuba City, CA 95993/916-755-3390; FAX: 916-755-3393
Cloward's Gun Shop, 4023 Aurora Ave. N, Seattle, WA 98103/206-632-2072
Clymer Manufacturing Co., Inc., 1645 W. Hamlin Rd., Rochester Hills, MI 48309-1530/810-853-5555, 810-853-5627; FAX: 810-853-1530
C-More Systems, P.O. Box 1750, 7553 Gary Rd., Manassas, VA 22110/703-361-2663; FAX: 703-361-5881
Coast Cutlery Co., 609 SE Ankeny St., Portland, OR 97214/503-234-4545; FAX: 503-234-4422
Coats, Mrs. Lester, 300 Luman Rd., Space 125, Phoenix, OR 97535/503-535-1611
Cobalt Mfg., Inc., 1020 Shady Oak Dr., Denton, TX 76205/817-382-8986; FAX: 817-383-4281
Cobra Gunskin, 133-30 32nd Ave., Flushing, NY 11354/718-762-8181; FAX: 718-762-0890
Cobra Sport s.r.l., Via Caduti Nei Lager No. 1, 56020 San Romano, Montopoli v/Arno (Pi), ITALY/0039-571-450490; FAX: 0039-571-450492
Cochran, Oliver, Box 868, Shady Spring, WV 25918/304-763-3838
Coffin, Charles H., 3719 Scarlet Ave., Odessa, TX 79762/915-366-4729
Coffin, Jim, 250 Country Club Lane, Albany, OR 97321/503-928-4391
Cogar's Gunsmithing, P.O. Box 755, Houghton Lake, MI 48629/517-422-4591
Coghlan's Ltd., 121 Irene St., Winnipeg, Man., CANADA R3T 4C7/204-284-9550; FAX: 204-475-4127
Cold Steel, Inc., 2128-D Knoll Dr., Ventura, CA 93003/800-255-4716, 800-624-2363 (in CA); FAX: 805-642-9727
Cole's Gun Works, Old Bank Building, Rt. 4, Box 250, Moyock, NC 27958/919-435-2345
Cole-Grip, 16135 Cohasset St., Van Nuys, CA 91406/818-782-4424
Coleman Co., Inc., 250 N. St. Francis, Wichita, KS 67201
Coleman's Custom Repair, 4035 N. 20th Rd., Arlington, VA 22207/703-528-4486
Collings, Ronald, 1006 Cielta Linda, Vista, CA 92083
Colonial Arms, Inc., P.O. Box 636, Selma, AL 36702-0636/334-872-9455; FAX: 334-872-9540
Colonial Knife Co., Inc., P.O. Box 3327, Providence, RI 02909/401-421-1600; FAX: 401-421-2047
Colonial Repair, P.O. Box 372, Hyde Park, MA 02136-9998/617-469-4951
Colorado School of Trades, 1575 Hoyt St., Lakewood, CO 80215/800-234-4594; FAX: 303-233-4723
Colorado Shooter's Supply, 1163 W. Paradise Way, Fruita, CO 81521/303-858-9191
Colorado Sutlers Arsenal, 365 S. Moore, Lurewood, CO 80226/303-985-2983
Colt Blackpowder Arms Co., 5 Centre Market Place, New York, NY 10013/212-925-2159; FAX: 212-966-4986
Colt's Mfg. Co., Inc., P.O. Box 1868, Hartford, CT 06144-1868/800-962-COLT, 203-236-6311; FAX: 203-244-1449
Combat Military Ordnance Ltd., 3900 Hopkins St., Savannah, GA 31405/912-238-1900; FAX: 912-236-7570
Companhia Brasileira de Cartuchos (See CBC)
Compass Industries, Inc., 104 East 25th St., New York, NY 10010/212-473-2614, 800-221-9904; FAX: 212-353-0826
Competition Electronics, Inc., 3469 Precision Dr., Rockford, IL 61109/815-874-8001; FAX: 815-874-8181
Competitive Pistol Shop, The, 5233 Palmer Dr., Ft. Worth, TX 76117-2433/817-834-8479
Competitor Corp., Inc., P.O. Box 244, 293 Townsend Rd., West Groton, MA 01472/508-448-3521; FAX: 508-448-6691
Complete Handloader, The, P.O. Box 5264, Arvada, CO 80005/303-460-9489
Component Concepts, Inc., 10240 SW Nimbus Ave., Suite L-8, Portland, OR 97223/503-684-9262; FAX: 503-620-4285
Concept Development Corp., 14715 N. 78th Way, Suite 300, Scottsdale, AZ 85260/800-472-4405; FAX: 602-948-7560
Condon, Inc., David, 109 E. Washington St., Middleburg, VA 22117/703-687-5642
Conetrol Scope Mounts, 10225 Hwy. 123 south, Seguin, TX 78155/210-379-3030, 800-CONETROL
CONKKO, P.O. Box 40, Broomall, PA 19008/215-356-0711
Connecticut Shotgun Mfg. Co., P.O. Box 1692, 35 Woodland St., New Britain, CT 06051-1692/203-225-6581; FAX: 203-832-8707
Connecticut Valley Arms Co. (See CVA)
Connecticut Valley Classics, P.O. Box 2068, 12 Taylor Lane, Westport, CT 06880/203-435-4600; FAX: 203-256-1180
Conrad, C.A., 3964 Ebert St., Winston-Salem, NC 27127/919-788-5469
Continental Kite & Key (See CONKKO)
Cook Engineering Service, 891 Highbury Rd., Vermont VICT 3133 AUSTRALIA
Coonan Arms, 1465 Selby Ave., St. Paul, MN 55104/612-641-1263; FAX: 612-641-1173
Cooper Arms, P.O. Box 114, Stevensville, MT 59870/406-777-5534; FAX: 406-777-5228
Cooper-Woodward, 3800 Pelican Rd., Helena, MT 59601/406-458-3800
Corbin, Inc., 600 Industrial Circle, P.O. Box 2659, White City, OR 97503/503-826-5211; FAX: 503-826-8669
Cor-Bon Bullet & Ammo Co., 1311 Industry Rd., Sturgis, SD 57785/800-626-7266; FAX: 800-923-2666
Corkys Gun Clinic, 4401 Hot Springs Dr., Greeley, CO 80634/303-330-0516
Corry, John, 861 Princeton Ct., Neshanic Station, NJ 08853/908-369-8019
Cosmi Americo & Figlio s.n.c., Via Flaminia 307, Ancona, ITALY I-60020/071-888208; FAX: 071-887008 (U.S. importer—New England Arms Co.)
Costa, David, Island Pond Gun Shop, P.O. Box 428, Cross St., Island Pond, VT 05846/802-723-4546
Coulston Products, Inc., P.O. Box 30, 201 Ferry St., Suite 212, Easton, PA 18044-0030/215-253-0167, 800-445-9927; FAX: 215-252-1511
Counter Assault, Box 4721, Missoula, MT 59806/406-728-6241; FAX: 406-728-8800
Country Armourer, The, P.O. Box .308, Ashby, MA 01431-0308/508-386-7590; FAX: 508-386-7789

MANUFACTURERS' DIRECTORY

County Arms, 11020 Whitman Ln., Tamarac, FL 33321/305-720-2066; FAX: 305-722-6353
Cousin Bob's Mountain Products, 7119 Ohio River Blvd., Ben Avon, PA 15202/412-766-5114; FAX: 412-766-5114
Cox, C. Ed, RD 2, Box 192, Prosperity, PA 15329/412-228-4984
CP Specialties, 1814 Mearns Rd., Warminster, PA 18974
CQB Training, P.O. Box 1739, Manchester, MO 63011
Craftguard, 3624 Logan Ave., Waterloo, IA 50703/319-232-2959
Craig Custom Ltd., Research & Development, 629 E. 10th, Hutchinson, KS 67501/316-669-0601
Crandall Tool & Machine Co., 1545 N. Mitchell St., P.O. Box 569, Cadillac, MI 49601/616-775-5562
Crane & Crane Ltd., 105 N. Edison Way 6, Reno, NV 89502-2355/702-856-1516; FAX: 702-856-1616
Crane Sales Co., George S., P.O. Box 385, Van Nuys, CA 91408/818-505-8337
Crawford Co., R.M., Inc., P.O. Box 277, Everett, PA 15537/814-652-6536; FAX: 814-652-9526
CRDC Laser Systems Group, 3972 Barranca Parkway, Ste. J-484, Irvine, CA 92714/714-586-1295; FAX: 714-831-4823
Creative Cartridge Co., 56 Morgan Rd., Canton, CT 06019/203-693-2529
Creative Craftsman, Inc., The, 95 Highway 29 North, P.O. Box 331, Lawrenceville, GA 30246/404-963-2112; FAX: 404-513-9488
Creedmoor Sports, Inc., P.O. Box 1040, Oceanside, CA 92051/619-757-5529
Creek Side Metal & Woodcrafters (See Allard, Gary)
Creekside Gun Shop, Inc., Main St., Holcomb, NY 14469/716-657-6338; FAX: 716-657-7900
Crit'R Call, Box 999V, La Porte, CO 80535/303-484-2768
CRL, Inc., 420 Industrial Park, P.O. Box 111, Gladstone, MI 49837/906-428-3710; FAX: 906-428-3711
Crosman Airguns, Rts. 5 and 20, E. Bloomfield, NY 14443/716-657-6161; FAX: 716-657-5405
Crosman Blades (See Coleman Co., Inc.)
Crosman Products of Canada Ltd., 1173 N. Service Rd. West, Oakville, Ontario, L6M 2V9 CANADA/905-827-1822
Crouse's Country Cover, P.O. Box 160, Storrs, CT 06268/203-429-4715
Crucelegui Hermanos (See U.S. importer—Mandall Shooting Supplies, Inc.)
Cryo, 2121 S. Imboden Ct., Decatur, IL 62521/217-423-3070; FAX: 217-423-2756
Cubic Shot Shell Co., Inc., 98 Fatima Dr., Campbell, OH 44405/216-755-0349; FAX: 216-755-0349
Cullity Restoration, Daniel, 209 Old County Rd., East Sandwich, MA 02537/508-888-1147
Cumberland, Dave, Dept. MCA, 12924 Highway A-12, Montague, CA 96064/916-459-5445
Cumberland Arms, Rt. l, Box 1150 Shafer Rd., Blantons Chapel, Manchester, TN 37355/800-797-8414
Cumberland Knife & Gun Works, 5661 Bragg Blvd., Fayetteville, NC 28303/919-867-0009
Cummings Bullets, 1417 Esperanza Way, Escondido, CA 92027
Cunningham Co., Eaton, 607 Superior St., Kansas City, MO 64106/816-842-2600
Cupp, Alana , Custom Engraver, P.O. Box 207, Annabella, UT 84711/801-896-4834
Curly Maple Stock Blanks (See Tiger-Hunt)
Curtis Custom Shop, RR1, Box 193A, Wallingford, KY 41093/703-659-4265
Curtis Gun Shop, Dept. ST, 119 W. College, Bozeman, MT 59715/406-587-4934
Custom Barreling & Stocks, 937 Lee Hedrick Rd., Colville, WA 99114/509-684-5686 (days), 509-684-3314 (evenings)
Custom Bullets by Hoffman, 2604 Peconic Ave., Seaford, NY 11783
Custom Checkering Service, Kathy Forster, 2124 SE Yamhill St., Portland, OR 97214/503-236-5874
Custom Chronograph, Inc., 5305 Reese Hill Rd., Sumas, WA 98295/360-988-7801
Custom Firearms (See Ahrends, Kim)
Custom Gun Products, 5021 W. Rosewood, Spokane, WA 99208/509-328-9340
Custom Gun Stocks, Rt. 6, P.O. Box 177, McMinnville, TN 37110/615-668-3912
Custom Gunsmiths, 4303 Friar Lane, Colorado Springs, CO 80907/719-599-3366
Custom Hunting Ammo & Arms (See CHAA, Ltd.)
Custom Products (See Jones Custom Products, Neil)
Custom Quality Products, Inc., 345 W. Girard Ave., P.O. Box 71129, Madison Heights, MI 48071/810-585-1616; FAX: 810-585-0644
Custom Shop, The, 890 Cochrane Crescent, Peterborough, Ont. K9H 5N3 CANADA/705-742-6693
Custom Tackle and Ammo, P.O. Box 1886, Farmington, NM 87499/505-632-3539
Cutco Cutlery, P.O. Box 810, Olean, NY 14760/716-372-3111
Cutlery Shoppe, 5461 Kendall St., Boise, ID 83706-1248/800-231-1272
Cutsinger Bench Rest Bullets, RR 8, Box 161-A, Shelbyville, IN 46176/317-729-5360
CVA, 5988 Peachtree Corners East, Norcross, GA 30071/800-251-9412; FAX: 404-242-8546
C.W. Cartridge Co., 242 Highland Ave., Kearney, NJ 07032/201-998-1030
C.W. Cartridge Co., 71 Hackensack St., Wood Ridge, NJ 07075
Cycle Dynamics, Inc., 74 Garden St., Feeding Hills, MA 01030/413-786-0141
Cylinder & Slide, Inc., William R. Laughridge, 245 E. 4th St., Fremont, NE 68025/402-721-4277; FAX: 402-721-0263
CZ (See U.S. importer—Magnum Research, Inc.)

D

D&D Gunsmiths, Ltd., 363 E. Elmwood, Troy, MI 48083/313-583-1512
D&G Precision Duplicators, M.L. Greene Engineering Services, P.O. Box 1150, Golden, CO 80402-1150/303-279-2383
D&H Precision Tooling, 7522 Barnard Mill Rd., Ringwood, IL 60072/815-653-4011
D&H Prods. Co., Inc., 465 Denny Rd., Valencia, PA 16059/412-898-2840, 800-776-0281; FAX: 412-898-2013
D&J Bullet Co. & Custom Gun Shop, Inc., 426 Ferry St., Russell, KY 41169/606-836-2663; FAX: 606-836-2663
D&L Industries, 10602 Horton Ave., Downey, CA 90241/310-806-0891
D&L Sports, P.O. Box 651, Gillette, WY 82717/307-686-4008
D&R Distributing, 308 S.E. Valley St., Myrtle Creek, OR 97457/503-863-6850
Dade Screw Machine Products, 2319 NW 7th Ave., Miami, FL 33127/305-573-5050
Daewoo Precision Industries Ltd., 34-3 Yeoeuido-Dong, Yeongdeungpo-GU, 15th, Fl./Seoul, KOREA (U.S. importer—Nationwide Sports Distributors)

Dahl's Custom Stocks, N2863 Schofield Rd., Lake Geneva, WI 53147/414-248-2464
Daisy Mfg. Co., P.O. Box 220, Rogers, AR 72757/501-636-1200; FAX: 501-636-1601
Dakota (See U.S. importer—EMF Co., Inc.)
Dakota Arms, Inc., HC 55, Box 326, Sturgis, SD 57785/605-347-4686; FAX: 605-347-4459
Dakota Corp., 77 Wales St., P.O. Box 543, Rutland, VT 05701/802-775-6062, 800-451-4167; FAX: 802-773-3919
Daly, Charles (See B.C. Miroku/Charles Daly)
Damascus-U.S.A., RR 1, Box 206-A, Tyner, NC 27980/919-221-2010; FAX: 919-221-2009
Dan's Whetstone Co., Inc., 130 Timbs Place, Hot Springs, AR 71913/501-767-1616; FAX: 501-767-9598
Dangler, Homer L., Box 254, Addison, MI 49220/517-547-6745
Danner Shoe Mfg. Co., 12722 NE Airport Way, Portland, OR 97230/503-251-1100, 800-345-0430; FAX: 503-251-1119
Danuser Machine Co., 550 E. Third St., P.O. Box 368, Fulton, MO 65251/314-642-2246; FAX: 314-642-2240
Dapkus Co., Inc., J.G., P.O. Box 293, Durham, CT 06422
Dara-Nes, Inc. (See Nesci Enterprises, Inc.)
Darlington Gun Works, Inc., P.O. Box 698, 516 S. 52 Bypass, Darlington, SC 29532/803-393-3931
Data Tech Software Systems, 19312 East Eldorado Drive, Aurora, CO 80013
Datumtech Corp., 2275 Wehrle Dr., Buffalo, NY 14221
Davidson, Jere, RR. 1, Box 132, Rustburg, VA 24588/804-821-3637
Davis, Don, 1619 Heights, Katy, TX 77493/713-391-3090
Davis Co., R.E., 3450 Pleasantville NE, Pleasantville, OH 43148/614-654-9990
Davis Industries, 15150 Sierra Bonita Ln., Chino, CA 91710/909-597-4726; FAX: 909-393-9771
Davis Leather Co., G. Wm., 3990 Valley Blvd., Unit D, Walnut, CA 91789/909-598-5620
Davis Products, Mike, 643 Loop Dr., Moses Lake, WA 98837/509-765-6178, 509-766-7281 orders only
Davis Service Center, Bill, 7221 Florin Mall Dr., Sacramento, CA 95823/916-393-4867
Day & Sons, Inc., Leonard, P.O. Box 122, Flagg Hill Rd., Heath, MA 01346/413-337-8369
Dayson Arms Ltd., P.O. Box 532, Vincennes, IN 47591/812-882-8680; FAX: 812-882-8680
Daystate Arms, Newcastle Street, Stone, Staffs, ST 15 8UJ ENGLAND/011-0785-812473
Dayton Traister, 4778 N. Monkey Hill Rd., P.O. Box 593, Oak Harbor, WA 98277/206-679-4657; FAX:206-675-1114
DBASE Consultants (See Arms, Peripheral Data Systems)
DBI Books, Inc., 4092 Commercial Ave., Northbrook, IL 60062/708-272-6310; FAX: 708-272-2051
D-Boone Ent., Inc., 5900 Colwyn Dr., Harrisburg, PA 17109
D.C.C. Enterprises, 259 Wynburn Ave., Athens, GA 30601
D.D. Custom Stocks, R.H. "Dick" Devereaux, 5240 Mule Deer Dr., Colorado Springs, CO 80919/719-548-8468
de Treville & Co., Stan, 4129 Normal St., San Diego, CA 92103/619-298-3393
Dead Eye's Sport Center, RD 1, Box 147B, Shickshinny, PA 18655/717-256-7432
Decker Shooting Products, 1729 Laguna Ave., Schofield, WI 54476/715-359-5873
DeckSlider of Florida, 27641-2 Reahard Ct., Bonita Springs, FL 33923/800-782-1474
Deepeeka Exports Pvt. Ltd., D-78, Saket, Meerut-250-006, INDIA/011-91-121-512889, 011-91-121-545363; FAX: 011-91-121-542988, 011-91-121-511599
Deer Me Products Co., Box 34, 1208 Park St., Anoka, MN 55303/612-421-8971; FAX: 612-422-0526
Defense Moulding Enterprises, 16781 Daisey Ave., Fountain Valley, CA 92708/714-842-5062
Defense Training International, Inc., 749 S. Lemay, Ste. A3-337, Ft. Collins, CO 80524/303-482-2520; FAX: 303-482-0548
Degen Inc. (See Aristocrat Knives)
deHaas Barrels, RR 3, Box 77, Ridgeway, MO 64481/816-872-6308
Del Rey Products, P.O. Box 91561, Los Angeles, CA 90009/213-823-0494
Delhi Gun House, 1374 Kashmere Gate, Delhi, INDIA 110 006/(011)237375 239116; FAX: 91-11-2917344
Delorge, Ed, 2231 Hwy. 308, Thibodaux, LA 70301/504-447-1633
Del-Sports, Inc., Box 685, Main St., Margaretville, NY 12455/914-586-4103; FAX: 914-586-4105
Delta Arms Ltd., P.O. Box 1000, Delta, VT 84624-1000
Delta Co. Ammo Bunker, 1209 16th Place, Yuma, AZ 85364/602-783-4563
Delta Enterprises, 284 Hagemann Drive, Livermore, CA 94550
Delta Frangible Ammunition, LLC, 1111 Jefferson Davis Hwy., Suite 508, Arlington, VA 22202/703-416-4928; FAX: 703-416-4934
Dem-Bart Checkering Tools, Inc., 6807 Bickford Ave., Old Hwy. 2, Snohomish, WA 98290/206-568-7356; FAX: 206-568-3134
Denver Bullets, Inc., 1811 W. 13th Ave., Denver, CO 80204/303-893-3146; FAX: 303-893-9161
Denver Instrument Co., 6542 Fig St., Arvada, CO 80004/800-321-1135, 303-431-7255; FAX: 303-423-4831
DeSantis Holster & Leather Goods, Inc., P.O. Box 2039, 149 Denton Ave., New Hyde Park, NY 11040-0701/516-354-8000; FAX: 516-354-7501
Desert Industries, Inc., P.O. Box 93443, Las Vegas, NV 89193-3443/702-597-1066; FAX: 702-871-9452
Desert Mountain Mfg., P.O. Box 2767, Columbia Falls, MT 59912/800-477-0762, 406-892-7772
Detroit-Armor Corp., 720 Industrial Dr. No. 112, Cary, IL 60013/708-639-7666; FAX: 708-639-7694
Dever Co., Jack, 8590 NW 90, Oklahoma City, OK 73132/405-721-6393
Devereaux, R.H. "Dick" (See D.D. Custom Stocks)
Dewey Mfg. Co., Inc., J., P.O. Box 2014, Southbury, CT 06488/203-264-3064; FAX: 203-598-3119
DGR Custom Rifles, RR1, Box 8A, Tappen, ND 58487/701-327-8135
DGS, Inc., Dale A. Storey, 1117 E. 12th, Casper, WY 82601/307-237-2414
DHB Products, P.O. Box 3092, Alexandria, VA 22302/703-836-2648
Diamond Machining Techonology (See DMT—Diamond Machining Technology)
Diamond Mfg. Co., P.O. Box 174, Wyoming, PA 18644/800-233-9601
Diana (See U.S. importer—Dynamit Nobel-RWS, Inc.)
Dibble, Derek A., 555 John Downey Dr., New Britain, CT 06051/203-224-2630

DIRECTORY OF THE ARMS TRADE

Dietz Gun Shop & Range, Inc., 421 Range Rd., New Braunfels, TX 78132/210-885-4662
Dilliott Gunsmithing, Inc., 657 Scarlett Rd., Dandridge, TN 37725/615-397-9204
Dillon, Ed, 1035 War Eagle Dr. N., Colorado Springs, CO 80919/719-598-4929; FAX: 719-598-4929
Dillon Precision Products, Inc., 8009 East Dillon's Way, Scottsdale, AZ 85260/602-948-8009, 800-762-3845; FAX: 602-998-2786
Dina Arms Corp., P.O. Box 46, Royersford, PA 19468/215-287-0266
Division Lead Co., 7742 W. 61st Pl., Summit, IL 60502
Dixie Gun Works, Inc., Hwy. 51 South, Union City, TN 38261/901-885-0561, order 800-238-6785; FAX: 901-885-0440
Dixon Muzzleloading Shop, Inc., RD 1, Box 175, Kempton, PA 19529/610-756-6271
DKT, Inc., 14623 Vera Drive, Union, MI 49130-9744/616-641-7120; FAX: 616-641-2015
DLO Mfg., 415 Howe Ave., Shelton, CT 06484/203-924-2952
D-Max, Inc., RR1, Box 473, Bagley, MN 56621/218-785-2278
DMT—Diamond Machining Technology, Inc., 85 Hayes Memorial Dr., Marlborough, MA 01752/508-481-5944; FAX: 508-485-3924
D.O.C. Specialists, Inc.; Doc & Bud Ulrich, Jim Amodei, 2209 S. Central Ave., Cicero, IL 60650/708-652-3606; FAX: 708-652-2516
Doctor Optic Technologies, Inc., 4685 Boulder Highway, Suite A, Las Vegas, NV 89121/800-290-3634, 702-898-7161; FAX: 702-898-3737
Dogtown Varmint Supplies, 1048 Irvine Ave. No. 333, Newport Beach, CA 92660/714-642-3997
Dohring Bullets, 100 W. 8 Mile Rd., Ferndale, MI 48220
Dolbare, Elizabeth, 39 Dahlia, Casper, WY 82604/307-266-5924
Donnelly, C.P., 405 Kubli Rd., Grants Pass, OR 97527/503-846-6604
Doskocil Mfg. Co., Inc., P.O. Box 1246, 4209 Barnett, Arlington, TX 76017/817-467-5116; FAX: 817-472-9810
Double A Ltd., Dept. ST, Box 11306, Minneapolis, MN 55411
Douglas Barrels, Inc., 5504 Big Tyler Rd., Charleston, WV 25313-1398/304-776-1341; FAX: 304-776-8560
Dowtin Gunworks, Rt. 4, Box 930A, Flagstaff, AZ 86001/602-779-1898
Dr. O's Products Ltd., P.O. Box 111, Niverville, NY 12130/518-784-3333; FAX: 518-784-2800
Drain, Mark, SE 3211 Kamilche Point Rd., Shelton, WA 98584/206-426-5452
Dremel Mfg. Co., 4915-21st St., Racine, WI 53406
Dressel Jr., Paul G., 209 N. 92nd Ave., Yakima, WA 98908/509-966-9233; FAX: 509-966-3365
Dri-Slide, Inc., 411 N. Darling, Fremont, MI 49412/616-924-3950
Dropkick, 29 West Fourth St., Williamsport, PA 17701
DTM International, Inc., 40 Joslyn Rd., P.O. Box 5, Lake Orion, MI 48035/313-693-6670
Duane Custom Stocks, Randy, 110 W. North Ave., Winchester, VA 22601/703-667-9461; FAX: 703-722-3993
Duane's Gun Repair (See DGR Custom Rifles)
Dubber, Michael W., P.O. Box 312, Evansville, IN 47702/812-424-9000; FAX: 812-424-6551
Duck Call Specialists, P.O. Box 124, Jerseyville, IL 62052/618-498-9855
Duffy, Charles E., Williams Lane, West Hurley, NY 12491/914-679-2997
Du-Lite Corp., 171 River Rd., Middletown, CT 06457/203-347-2505; FAX: 203-347-9404
Dumoulin, Ernest, Rue Florent Boclinville 8-10, 13-4041 Votten, BELGIUM/41 27 78 92
Duncan's Gun Works, Inc., 1619 Grand Ave., San Marcos, CA 92069/619-727-0515
Dunham Co., P.O. Box 813, Brattleboro, VT 05301/802-254-2316
Dunphy, Ted, W. 5100 Winch Rd., Rathdrum, ID 83858/208-687-1399; FAX: 208-687-1399
Duofold, Inc., RD 3, 309 Valley Square Mall, Tamaqua, PA 18252/717-386-2666; FAX: 717-386-3652
DuPont (See IMR Powder Co.)
Dutchman's Firearms, The, 4143 Taylor Blvd., Louisville, KY 40215/502-366-0555
Duxbak, Inc., 903 Woods Rd., Cambridge, MD 21613/301-228-2990, 800-334-1845
Dybala Gun Shop, P.O. Box 1024, FM 3156, Bay City, TX 77414/409-245-0866
Dykstra, Doug, 411 N. Darling, Fremont, MI 49412/616-924-3950
Dynalite Products, Inc., 215 S. Washington St., Greenfield, OH 45123/513-981-2124
Dynamit Nobel-RWS, Inc., 81 Ruckman Rd., Closter, NJ 07624/201-767-7971; FAX: 201-767-1589
Dyson & Son Ltd., Peter, 29-31 Church St., Honley, Huddersfield, W. Yorkshire HDL7 2AH, ENGLAND/0484-661062; FAX: 0484 663709

E

E&L Mfg., Inc., 4177 Riddle by Pass Rd., Riddle, OR 97469/503-874-2137; FAX: 503-874-3107
E.A.A. Corp., P.O. Box 1299, Sharpes, FL 32959/407-639-4842, 800-536-4442; FAX: 407-639-7006
Eades' Muzzleloader Builders' Supply, Don, 201-J Beasley Dr., Franklin, TN 37064/615-791-1731
Eagan, Donald V., P.O. Box 196, Benton, PA 17814/717-925-6134
Eagle Arms, Inc., 128 E. 23rd Ave., Coal Valley, IL 61240/309-799-5619, 800-336-0184; FAX: 309-799-5150
Eagle Grips, Eagle Business Center, 460 Randy Rd., Carol Stream, IL 60188/800-323-6144, 708-260-0400; FAX: 708-260-0486
Eagle International, Inc., 5195 W. 58th Ave., Suite 300, Arvada, CO 80002/303-426-8100; FAX: 303-426-5475
Eagle Mfg. & Engineering, 2648 Keen Dr., San Diego, CA 92139/619-479-4402; FAX: 619-472-5585
Eagle Products Co., 1520 Adelia Ave., S. El Monte, CA 91733
E-A-R, Inc., Div. of Cabot Safety Corp., 5457 W. 79th St., Indianapolis, IN 46268/800-327-3431; FAX: 800-488-8007
Eastman Products, R.T., P.O. Box 1531, Jackson, WY 83001/307-733-3217, 800-624-4311
Easy Pull Outlaw Products, 316 1st St. East, Polson, MT 59860/406-883-6822
Echols & Co., D'Arcy, 164 W. 580 S., Providence, UT 84332/801-753-2367
Eckelman Gunsmithing, 3125 133rd St. SW, Fort Ripley, MN 56449/218-829-3176
Ed's Gun House, Rt. 1, Box 62, Minnesota City, MN 55959/507-689-2925
Edenpine, Inc. c/o Six Enterprises, Inc., 320 D Turtle Creek Ct., San Jose, CA 95125/408-999-0201; FAX: 408-999-0216
EdgeCraft Corp., P.O. Box 3000, Limestone and Southwood Rd., Avondale, PA 19311/215-268-0500, 800-342-3255; FAX: 215-268-3545

Edmisten Co., P.O. Box 1293, Boone, NC 28607
Edmund Scientific Co., 101 E. Gloucester Pike, Barrington, NJ 08033/609-543-6250
Ednar, Inc., 2-4-8 Kayabacho, Nihonbashi, Chuo-ku, Tokyo, JAPAN 103/81(Japan)-3-3667-1651; FAX: 81-3-3661-8113
Eezox, Inc., P.O. Box 772, Waterford, CT 06385-0772/203-447-8282, 800-462-3331; FAX: 203-447-3484
Eggleston, Jere D., 400 Saluda Ave., Columbia, SC 29205/803-799-3402
EGW Evolution Gun Works, 4050 B-8 Skyron Dr., Doylestown, PA 18901/215-348-9892; FAX: 215-348-1056
Eichelberger Bullets, Wm., 158 Crossfield Rd., King of Prussia, PA 19406
EK Knife Co., 601 N. Lombardy St., Richmond, VA 23220/804-257-7272
Ekol Leather Care, P.O. Box 2652, West Lafayette, IN 47906/317-463-2250; FAX: 317-463-7004
El Dorado Leather, P.O. Box 2603, Tucson, AZ 85702/602-623-0606; FAX: 602-623-0606
El Gavilan, 8633 N.W. 54th St., Miami, FL 33166
El Paso Saddlery Co., P.O. Box 27194, El Paso, TX 79926/915-544-2233; FAX: 915-544-2535
Eldorado Cartridge Corp. (See PMC/Eldorado Cartridge Corp.)
Electro Prismatic Collimators, Inc., 1441 Manatt St., Lincoln, NE 68521
Electronic Shooters Protection, Inc., 3575 South Sherman St. No. 2, Englewood, Colorado 80110/800-767-7791
Electronic Trigger Systems, Inc., P.O. Box 13, 230 Main St. S., Hector, MN 55342/612-848-2760
Eley Ltd., P.O. Box 705, Witton, Birmingham, B6 7UT, ENGLAND/021-356-8899; FAX: 021-331-4173
Elite Ammunition, P.O. Box 3251, Oakbrook, IL 60522/708-366-9006
Elk River, Inc., 1225 Paonia St., Colorado Springs, CO 80915/719-574-4407
Elkhorn Bullets, P.O. Box 5293, Central Point, OR 97502/503-826-7440
Elko Arms, Dr. L. Kortz, 28 rue Ecole Moderne, B-7060 Soignies, BELGIUM/(32)67-33-29-34
Ellett Bros., P.O. Box 128, 267 Columbia Ave., Columbia, SC 29036/803-345-3751, 800-845-3711; FAX: 803-345-1820
Ellicott Arms, Inc./Woods Pistolsmithing, 3840 Dahlgren Ct., Ellicott City, MD 21042/410-465-7979
Elliott Inc., G.W., 514 Burnside Ave., East Hartford, CT 06108/203-289-5741; FAX: 203-289-3137
Ellis Sport Shop, E.W., RD 1, Route 9N, P.O. Box 315, Corinth, NY 12822/518-654-6444
Elsen, Inc., Pete, 529 S. 113th St., West Allis, WI 53214
Emerging Technologies, Inc., 721 Main St., Little Rock, AR 72201/501-375-2227; FAX: 501-372-1445
EMF Co., Inc., 1900 E. Warner Ave. Suite 1-D, Santa Ana, CA 92705/714-261-6611; FAX: 714-756-0133
Empire Cutlery Corp., 12 Kruger Ct., Clifton, NJ 07013/201-472-5155; FAX: 201-779-0759
Engineered Accessories, 1307 W. Wabash Ave., Effingham, IL 62401/217-347-7700; FAX: 217-347-7737
English, Inc., A.G., 708 S. 12th St., Broken Arrow, OK 74012/918-251-3399
Englishtown Sporting Goods Co., Inc., David J. Maxham, 38 Main St., Englishtown, NJ 07726/201-446-7717
Engraving Artistry, 36 Alto Rd., RFD 2, Burlington, CT 06013/203-673-6837
Enguix Import-Export, Alpujarras 58, Alzira, Valencia, SPAIN 46600/(96) 241 43 95; FAX: (96) (241 43 95) 240 21 53
Enhanced Presentations, Inc., 5929 Market St., Wilmington, NC 28405/910-799-1622; FAX: 910-799-5004
Enlow, Charles, 895 Box, Beaver, OK 73932/405-625-4487
Ensign-Bickford Co., The, 660 Hopmeadow St., Simsbury, CT 06070
EPC, 1441 Manatt St., Lincoln, NE 68521/402-476-3946
Epps "Orillia" Ltd., Ellwood, RR 3, Hwy. 11 North, Orillia, Ont. L3V 6H3, CANADA/705-689-5333
Erhardt, Dennis, 3280 Green Meadow Dr., Helena, MT 59601/406-442-4533
Erickson's Mfg., Inc., C.W., 530 Garrison Ave. N.E., Buffalo, MN 55313/612-682-3665; FAX: 612-682-4328
Erma Werke GmbH, Johan Ziegler St., 13/15/FeldiglSt., D-8060 Dachau, GERMANY (U.S. importers—Mandall Shooting Supplies, Inc.; Precision Sales International, Inc.)
Eskridge Rifles, Steven Eskridge, 218 N. Emerson, Mart, TX 76664/817-876-3544
Essex Arms, P.O. Box 345, Island Pond, VT 05846/802-723-4313
Essex Metals, 1000 Brighton St., Union, NJ 07083/800-282-8369
Estate Cartridge, Inc., 2778 FM 830, Willis, TX 77078/409-856-7277; FAX: 409-856-5486
Euroarms of America, Inc., 208 E. Piccadilly St., Winchester, VA 22601/703-662-1863; FAX: 703-662-4464
European American Armory Corp. (See E.A.A. Corp.)
Europtik Ltd., P.O. Box 319, Dunmore, PA 18512/717-347-6049; FAX: 717-969-4330
Eutaw Co., Inc., The, P.O. Box 608, U.S. Hwy. 176 West, Holly Hill, SC 29059/803-496-3341
Evans Engraving, Robert, 332 Vine St., Oregon City, OR 97045/503-656-5693
Evans Gunsmithing, 47532 School St., Oakridge, OR 97463/503-782-4432
Eversull Co., Inc., K., 1 Tracemont, Boyce, LA 71409/318-793-8728; FAX: 318-793-5483
Excaliber Enterprises, P.O. Box 400, Fogelsville, PA 18051-0400/610-391-9106; FAX: 610-391-9223
Exe, Inc., 18830 Partridge Circle, Eden Prairie, MN 55346/612-944-7662
Executive Protection Institute, Rt. 2, Box 3645, Berryville, VA 22611/703-955-1128
Eyears Insurance, 4926 Annhurst Rd., Columbus, OH 43228-1341
Eyster Heritage Gunsmiths, Inc., Ken, 6441 Bishop Rd., Centerburg, OH 43011/614-625-6131
Eze-Lap Diamond Prods., P.O. Box 2229, 15164 Weststate St., Westminster, CA 92683/714-847-1555; FAX: 714-897-0280
E-Z-Way Systems, Box 4310, Newark, OH 43058-4310/614-345-6645, 800-848-2072; FAX: 614-345-6600

F

F&A Inc., 50 Elm St., Richfield Springs, NY 13439/315-858-1470; FAX: 315-858-2969
Fabarm S.p.A., Via Averolda 31, 25039 Travagliato, Brescia, ITALY/030-6863629; FAX: 030-6863684 (U.S. importer—Ithaca Acquisition Corp.)

MANUFACTURERS' DIRECTORY

Fabian Bros. Sporting Goods, Inc., 1510 Morena Blvd., Suite "G", San Diego, CA 92110/619-275-0816; FAX: 619-276-8733
Fagan & Co., William, 22952 15 Mile Rd., Mt. Clemens, MI 48043/313-465-4637; FAX: 313-792-6996
Fair Game International, P.O. Box 77234-34053, Houston, TX 77234/713-941-6269
F.A.I.R. Techni-Mec s.n.c. Di Isidoro Rizzini & C., Via Gitti 41, 25060 Marcheno (BS), ITALY/030/861162-8610344; FAX: 030/8610179
Faith Associates, Inc., 1139 S. Greenville Hwy., Hendersonville, NC 28739/704-692-1916; FAX: 704-697-6827
Fajen, Inc., Reinhart, 1000 Red Bud Dr., P.O. Box 338, Warsaw, MO 65355/816-438-5111; FAX: 816-438-5175
Falcon Pneumatic Systems (See U.S. importer—Airguns-R-Us)
Famas (See U.S. importer—Century International Arms, Inc.)
Fanzoj GmbH, Griesgasse 1, 9170 Ferlach, AUSTRIA 9170/(43) 04227-2283; FAX: (43) 04227-2867
FAPA Corp., P.O. Box 1439, New London, NH 03257/603-735-5652; FAX: 603-735-5154
Far North Outfitters, Box 1252, Bethel, AK 99559
Farm Form Decoys, Inc., 1602 Biovu, P.O. Box 748, Galveston, TX 77553/409-744-0762, 409-765-6361; FAX: 409-765-8513
Farmer-Dressel, Sharon, 209 N. 92nd Ave., Yakima, WA 98908/509-966-9233; FAX: 509-966-3365
Farr Studio, Inc., 1231 Robinhood Rd., Greeneville, TN 37743/615-638-8825
Farrar Tool Co., Inc., 12150 Bloomfield Ave., Suite E, Santa Fe Springs, CA 90670/310-863-4367; FAX: 310-863-5123
FAS, Via E. Fermi, 8, 20019 Settimo Milanese, Milano, ITALY/02-3285846; FAX: 02-33500196 (U.S. importer—Nygord Precision Products)
Faulhaber Wildlocker, Dipl.-Ing. Norbert Wittasek, Seilergasse 2, A-1010 Wien, EUROPE
Faulk's Game Call Co., Inc., 616 18th St., Lake Charles, LA 70601/318-436-9726
Faust, Inc., T.G., 544 Minor St., Reading, PA 19602/610-375-8549; FAX: 610-375-4488
Fausti Cav. Stefano & Figlie snc, Via Martiri Dell Indipendenza, 70, Marcheno, ITALY 25060 (U.S. importer—American Arms, Inc.)
Fautheree, Andy, P.O. Box 4607, Pagosa Springs, CO 81157/303-731-5003
Feather Flex Decoys, 1655 Swan Lake Rd., Bossier City, LA 71111/318-746-8596; FAX: 318-742-4815
Feather Industries, Inc., 37600 Liberty Dr., Trinidad, CO 81082/719-846-2699; FAX: 719-846-2644
Federal Cartridge Co., 900 Ehlen Dr., Anoka, MN 55303/612-323-2300; FAX: 612-323-2506
Federal Champion Target Co., 232 Industrial Parkway, Richmond, IN 47374/800-441-4971; FAX: 317-966-7747
Federal Engineering Corp., 1090 Bryn Mawr, Bensenville, IL 60106/708-860-1938; FAX: 708-860-2085
Federated-Fry, 6th Ave., 41st St., Altuna, PA 16602/814-946-1611
FEG, Budapest, Soroksariut 158, H-1095 HUNGARY (U.S. importers—Century International Arms, Inc.; K.B.I., Corp.)
Feinwerkbau Westinger & Altenburger GmbH (See FWB)
Feken, Dennis, Rt. 2 Box 124, Perry, OK 73077/405-336-5611
Fellowes, Ted, Beaver Lodge, 9245 16th Ave. SW, Seattle, WA 98106/206-763-1698
Feminine Protection, Inc., 10514 Shady Trail, Dallas, TX 75220/214-351-4500; FAX: 214-352-4686
Ferdinand, Inc., P.O. Box 5, 201 Main St., Harrison, ID 83833/208-689-3012, 800-522-6010 (U.S.A.), 800-258-5266 (Canada); FAX: 208-689-3142
Ferguson, Bill, P.O. Box 1238, Sierra Vista, AZ 85636/520-458-5321; FAX: 520-458-9125
FERLIB, Via Costa 46, 25063 Gardone V.T. (Brescia) ITALY/30 89 12 586; FAX: 30 89 12 586 (U.S. importers—Wm. Larkin Moore & Co.; New England Arms Co., Pachmayr Ltd.)
Ferris Firearms, 30115 U.S. Hwy. 281 North, Suite 158, Bulverde, TX 78163/210-980-4811
Fiberpro/California, P.O. Box 370944, San Diego, CA 92138/619-223-0425; FAX: 619-223-0425
Fibron Products, Inc., P.O. Box 430, Buffalo, NY 14209-0430/716-886-2378; FAX: 716-886-2394
Final Option Enterprises, P.O. Box 1128, Easthampton, MA 01027/413-548-8119
Finch Custom Bullets, 40204 La Rochelle, Prairieville, LA 70769
Fiocchi Munizioni s.p.a. (See U.S. importer—Fiocchi of America, Inc.)
Fiocchi of America, Inc., 5030 Fremont Rd., Ozark, MO 65721/417-725-4118, 800-721-2666; FAX: 417-725-1039
Firearm Training Center, The, 9555 Blandville Rd., West Paducah, KY 42086/502-554-5886
Firearms Academy of Seattle, P.O. Box 2814, Kirkland, WA 98083/206-820-4853
Firearms Co. Ltd./Alpine (See U.S. importer—Mandall Shooting Supplies, Inc.)
Firearms Safety Products, Inc. (See FSPI)
Firearms Supplies Inc., 514 Quincy St., Hancock, MI 49930/906-482-1673; FAX: 906-482-3822
First, Inc., Jack, 1201 Turbine Dr., Rapid City, SD 57701/605-343-9544; FAX: 605-343-9420
Fish, Marshall F., Rt. 22 N., P.O. Box 2439, Westport, NY 12993/518-962-4897
Fisher, Jerry A., 535 Crane Mt. Rd., Big Fork, MT 59911/406-837-2722
Fisher Custom Firearms, 2199 S. Kittredge Way, Aurora, CO 80013/303-755-3710
Fisher Enterprises, 655 Main St. 305, Edmonds, WA 98020/206-776-4365
Fish-N-Hunt, Inc., 5651 Beechnut St., Houston, TX 77096-1021/713-777-3285; FAX: 713-777-9884
Fitz Pistol Grip Co., P.O. Box 610, Douglas City, CA 96024/916-623-4019
Flaig's, 2200 Evergreen Rd., Millvale, PA 15209/412-821-1717
Flambeau Products Corp., 15981 Valplast Rd., Middlefield, OH 44062/216-632-1631; FAX: 216-632-1581
Flannery Engraving Co., Jeff W., 11034 Riddles Run Rd., Union, KY 41091/606-384-3127
Flashette Co., 4725 S. Kolin Ave., Chicago, IL 60632/312-927-1302; FAX: 312-927-3083
FlashTek, Inc., 714 Indian Hills Dr., Moscow, ID 83843/208-882-6892; FAX: 208-882-7275
Flayderman & Co., Inc., N., P.O. Box 2446, Ft. Lauderdale, FL 33303/305-761-8855
Fleming Firearms, 9525-J East 51st St., Tulsa, OK 74145/918-665-3624
Flents Products Co., Inc., P.O. Box 2109, Norwalk, CT 06852/203-866-2581; FAX: 203-854-9322
Flintlocks, Etc. (See Beauchamp & Son, Inc.)
Flitz International Ltd., 821 Mohr Ave., Waterford, WI 53185/414-534-5898; FAX: 414-534-2991
Floatstone Mfg. Co., 106 Powder Mill Rd., P.O. Box 765, Canton, CT 06019/203-693-1977
Flores Publications, Inc., J., P.O. Box 830131, Miami, FL 33283/305-559-4652
Flouramics, Inc., 18 Industrial Ave., Mahwah, NJ 07430/800-922-0075, 201-825-7035
Flow-Rite of Tennessee, Inc., 107 Allen St., P.O. Box 196, Bruceton, TN 38317/901-586-2271; FAX: 901-586-2300
Flynn's Custom Guns, P.O. Box 7461, Alexandria, LA 71306/318-455-7130
FN Herstal, Voie de Liege 33, Herstal 4040, BELGIUM/(32)41.40.82.83; FAX: (32)41.40.86.79
Fobus International Ltd., Kfar Hess, ISRAEL 40692/972-9-911716; FAX: 972-9-911716
Folks, Donald E., 205 W. Lincoln St., Pontiac, IL 61764/815-844-7901
Foothills Video Productions, Inc., P.O. Box 651, Spartanburg, SC 29304/803-573-7023, 800-782-5358
Ford, Jack, 1430 Elkwood, Missouri City, TX 77489/713-499-9984
Foredom Electric Co., Rt. 6, 16 Stony Hill Rd., Bethel, CT 06801/203-792-8622
Forgett Jr., Valmore J., 689 Bergen Blvd., Ridgefield, NJ 07657/201-945-2500; FAX: 201-945-6859
Forgreens Tool Mfg., Inc., P.O. Box 990, 723 Austin St., Robert Lee, TX 76945/915-453-2800
Forkin, Ben, 20 E. Tamarack St., Bozeman, MT 59715-2913
Forrest, Inc., Tom, P.O. Box 326, Lakeside, CA 92040/619-561-5800; FAX: 619-561-0227
Forrest Tool Co., P.O. Box 768, 44380 Gordon Lane, Mendocino, CA 95460/707-937-2141; FAX: 717-937-1817
Forster, Kathy (See Custom Checkering Service)
Forster, Larry L., P.O. Box 212, 220 First St. NE, Gwinner, ND 58040-0212/701-678-2475
Forster Products, 82 E. Lanark Ave., Lanark, IL 61046/815-493-6360; FAX: 815-493-2371
Fort Hill Gunstocks, 12807 Fort Hill Rd., Hillsboro, OH 45133/513-466-2763
Fort Knox Security Products, 1051 N. Industrial Park Rd., Orem, UT 84057/801-224-7233, 800-821-5216; FAX: 801-226-5493
Forthofer's Gunsmithing & Knifemaking, 5535 U.S. Hwy 93S, Whitefish, MT 59937-8411/406-862-2674
Fortune Products, Inc., HC04, Box 303, Marble Falls, TX 78654/210-693-6111; FAX: 210-693-6394
Forty Five Ranch Enterprises, Box 1080, Miami, OK 74355-1080/918-542-5875
Fouling Shot, The, 6465 Parfet St., Arvada, CO 80004
Fountain Products, 492 Prospect Ave., West Springfield, MA 01089/413-781-4651; FAX: 413-733-8217
4-D Custom Die Co., 711 N. Sandusky St., P.O. Box 889, Mt. Vernon, OH 43050-0889/614-397-7214; FAX: 614-397-6600
4W Ammunition, Rt. 1, P.O. Box 313, Tioga, TX 76271/817-437-2458; FAX: 817-437-2228
Fowler Bullets, 806 Dogwood Dr., Gastonia, NC 28054/704-867-3259
Fox River Mills, Inc., P.O. Box 298, 227 Poplar St., Osage, IA 50461/515-732-3798; FAX: 515-732-5128
Foy Custom Bullets, 104 Wells Ave., Daleville, AL 36322
Francesca, Inc., 3115 Old Ranch Rd., San Antonio, TX 78217/512-826-2584; FAX: 512-826-8211
Franchi S.p.A., Luigi, Via del Serpente, 12, 25020 Fornaci, ITALY (U.S. importer—American Arms, Inc.)
Francolini, Leonard, 106 Powder Mill Rd., P.O. Box 765, Canton, CT 06019/203-693-1977
Francotte & Cie S.A., Auguste, rue du Trois Juin 109, 4400 Herstal-Liege, BELGIUM/41-48.13.18; FAX: 41-48.11.79 (U.S. importer—Armes de Chasse)
Frank Custom Gun Service, Ron, 7131 Richland Rd., Ft. Worth, TX 76118/817-284-4426; FAX: 817-284-9300
Frank Knives, Box 984, Whitefish, MT 59937/406-862-2681; FAX: 406-862-2681
Frankonia Jagd, Hofmann & Co., D-97064 Wurzburg, GERMANY/09302-200; FAX: 09302-20200
Frazier Brothers Enterprises, 1118 N. Main St., Franklin, IN 46131/317-736-4000; FAX: 317-736-4000
Fredrick Gun Shop, 10 Elson Dr., Riverside, RI 02915/401-433-2805
Freedom Arms, Inc., P.O. Box 1776, Freedom, WY 83120/307-883-2468, 800-833-4432 (orders only); FAX: 307-883-2005
Freeman Animal Targets, 2559 W. Morris St., Plainsfield, IN 46168/317-271-5314; FAX: 317-271-9106
Fremont Tool Works, 1214 Prairie, Ford, KS 67842/316-369-2327
French, J.R., 1712 Creek Ridge Ct., Irving, TX 75060/214-254-2654
Frielich Police Equipment, 211 East 21st St., New York, NY 10010/212-254-3045
From Jena, Europtik Ltd., P.O. Box 319, Dunmore, PA 18512/717-347-6049, 800-873-5362; FAX: 717-969-4330
Frontier, 2910 San Bernardo, Laredo, TX 78040/512-723-5409
Frontier Arms Co., Inc., 401 W. Rio Santa Cruz, Green Valley, AZ 85614-3932
Frontier Products Co., 164 E. Longview Ave., Columbus, OH 43202/614-262-9357
Frontier Safe Co., 3201 S. Clinton St., Fort Wayne, IN 46806/219-744-7233; FAX: 219-744-6678
Frost Cutlery Co., P.O. Box 22636, Chattanooga, TN 37422/615-894-6079; FAX: 615-894-9576
FSPI, 5885 Glenridge Dr. Suite 220A, Atlanta, GA 30328/404-843-2881; FAX: 404-843-0271
Fujinon, Inc., 10 High Point Dr., Wayne, NJ 07470/201-633-5600; FAX: 201-633-5216
Fullmer, Geo. M., 2499 Mavis St., Oakland, CA 94601/510-533-4193
Fulmer's Antique Firearms, Chet, P.O. Box 792, Rt. 2 Buffalo Lake, Detroit Lakes, MN 56501/218-847-7712
Fulton Armory, 8725 Bollman Place No. 1, Savage, MD 20763/301-490-9485; FAX: 301-490-9547
Furr Arms, 91 N. 970 W., Orem, UT 84057/801-226-3877; FAX: 801-226-0085
Fury Cutlery, 801 Broad Ave., Ridgefield, NJ 07657/201-943-5920; FAX: 201-943-1579
Fusilier Bullets, 10010 N. 6000 W., Highland, UT 84003/801-756-6813

50th EDITION, 1996 **577**

DIRECTORY OF THE ARMS TRADE

FWB, Neckarstrasse 43, 78727 Oberndorf a. N., GERMANY/07423-814-0; FAX: 07423-814-89 (U.S. importer—Beeman Precision Airguns)

G

G3 & Co., 18 Old Northville Rd., New Milford, CT 06776/203-354-7500
G96 Products Co., Inc., River St. Station, P.O. Box 1684, Paterson, NJ 07544/201-684-4050; FAX: 201-684-3848
G&C Bullet Co., Inc., 8835 Thornton Rd., Stockton, CA 95209/209-477-6479; FAX: 209-477-2813
G&H Decoys, Inc., P.O. Box 1208, Hwy. 75 North, Henryetta, OK 74437/918-652-3314; FAX: 918-652-3400
Gage Manufacturing, 663 W. 7th St., San Pedro, CA 90731
Gaillard Barrels, P.O. Box 21, Pathlow, Sask., S0K 3B0 CANADA/306-752-3769; FAX: 306-752-5969
Galati International, P.O. Box 326, Catawissa, MO 63015/314-257-4837; FAX: 314-257-2268
Galaxy Imports Ltd., Inc., P.O. Box 3361, Victoria, TX 77903/512-573-4867; FAX: 512-576-9622
Galazan, Div. of Connecticut Shotgun Mfg. Co., P.O. Box 622, 35 Woodland St., New Britain, CT 06051-0622/203-225-6581; FAX: 203-832-8707
GALCO International Ltd., 2019 W. Quail Ave., Phoenix, AZ 85027/602-258-8295; FAX: 602-582-6854
Gamba, USA, P.O. Box 60452, Colorado Springs, CO 80960/719-578-1145; FAX: 719-444-0731
Gamba-Societa Armi Bresciane Srl., Renato, Via Artigiani, 93, 25063 Gardone Val Trompia (BS), ITALY/30-8911640, 30-8911648 (U.S. importers—Cape Outfitters; Giacomo Sporting, Inc.; New England Arms Co.)
Game Haven Gunstocks, 13750 Shire Rd., Wolverine, MI 49799/616-525-8257
Game Winner, Inc., 2625 Cumberland Parkway, Suite 220, Atlanta, GA 30339/404-434-9210; FAX: 404-434-9215
Gammog, Gregory B. Gally, 14608 Old Gunpowder Rd., Laurel, MD 20707-3131/301-725-3838
Gamo (See U.S. importers—Daisy Mfg. Co.; Dynamit Nobel-RWS, Inc.)
Gander Mountain, Inc., P.O. Box 128, Hwy. "W,", Wilmot, WI 53192/414-862-2331,Ext. 6425
Ganton Manufacturing Ltd., Depot Lane, Seamer Rd., Scarborough, North Yorkshire, Y012 4EB ENGLAND/0723-371910; FAX: 0723-501671
GAR, 139 Park Lane, Wayne, NJ 07470/201-256-7641
Garbi, Armas Urki, 12-14, 20.600 Eibar (Guipuzcoa) SPAIN/43-11 38 73 (U.S. importer—Moore & Co., Wm. Larkin)
Garcia National Gun Traders, Inc., 225 SW 22nd Ave., Miami, FL 33135/305-642-2355
Garrett Cartridges, Inc., P.O. Box 178, Chehalis, WA 98532/206-736-0702
Garthwaite, Jim, Rt. 2, Box 310, Watsontown, PA 17777/717-538-1566
Gator Guns & Repair, 6255 Spur Hwy., Kenai, AK 99611/907-283-7947
Gaucher Armes, S.A., 46, rue Desjoyaux, 42000 Saint-Etienne, FRANCE/77 33 38 92; FAX: 767 41 95 72
G.B.C. Industries, Inc., P.O. Box 1602, Spring, TX 77373/713-350-9690; FAX: 713-350-0601
G.C.C.T., 4455 Torrance Blvd., Ste. 453, Torrance, CA 90509-2806
GDL Enterprises, 409 Le Gardeur, Slidell, LA 70460/504-649-0693
Gehmann, Walter (See Huntington Die Specialties)
Genco, P.O. Box 5704, Asheville, NC 28803
Genecco Gun Works, K., 10512 Lower Sacramento Rd., Stockton, CA 95210/209-951-0706
General Lead, Inc., 1022 Grand Ave., Phoenix, AZ 85007
Gene's Custom Guns, P.O. Box 10534, White Bear Lake, MN 55110/612-429-5105
Gene's Gun Shop, Rt. 1 Box 890, Snyder, TX 79549/915-573-2323
Gentry Custom Gunmaker, David, 314 N. Hoffman, Belgrade, MT 59714/406-388-4867
George & Roy's, 2950 NW 29th, Portland, OR 97210/503-228-5424, 800-553-3022; FAX: 503-225-9409
George, Tim, Rt. 1, P.O. Box 45, Evington, VA 24550/804-821-8117
Gerber Legendary Blades, 14200 SW 72nd Ave., Portland, OR 97223/503-639-6161, 800-950-6161; FAX: 503-684-7008
Gervais, Mike, 3804 S. Cruise Dr., Salt Lake City, UT 84109/801-277-7729
Getz Barrel Co., P.O. Box 88, Beavertown, PA 17813/717-658-7263
GFR Corp., P.O. Box 430, Andover, NH 03216/603-735-5300
G.G. & G., 3602 E. 42nd Stravenue, Tucson, AZ 85713/602-748-7167; FAX: 602-748-7583
G.H. Enterprises Ltd., Bag 10, Okotoks, Alberta T0L 1T0 CANADA/403-938-6070
Giacomo Sporting, Inc., Delta Plaza, Rt. 26N, Rome, NY 13440
Gibbs Rifle Co., Inc., Cannon Hill Industrial Park, Rt. 2, Box 214 Hoffman, Rd./Martinsburg, WV 25401/304-274-0458; FAX: 304-274-0078
Gilbert Equipment Co., Inc., 960 Downtowner Rd., Mobile, AL 36609/205-344-3322
Gillmann, Edwin, 33 Valley View Dr., Hanover, PA 17331/717-632-1662
Gilman-Mayfield, Inc., 3279 E. Shields, Fresno, CA 93703/209-221-9415; FAX: 209-221-9419
Gilmore Sports Concepts, 5949 S. Garnett, Tulsa, OK 74146/918-250-4867; FAX: 918-250-3845
Giron, Robert E., 1328 Pocono St., Pittsburgh, PA 15218/412-731-6041
Glacier Glove, 4890 Aircenter Circle, Suite 210, Reno, NV 89502/702-825-8225; FAX: 702-825-6544
Glaser Safety Slug, Inc., P.O. Box 8223, Foster City, CA 94404/800-221-3489, 415-345-7677; FAX: 415-345-8217
Glass, Herb, P.O. Box 25, Bullville, NY 10915/914-361-3021
Glimm, Jerome C., 19 S. Maryland, Conrad, MT 59425/406-278-3574
Glock GmbH, P.O. Box 50, A-2232 Deutsch Wagram, AUSTRIA (U.S. importer—Glock, Inc.)
Glock, Inc., 6000 Highlands Parkway, Smyrna, GA 30082/404-432-1202: FAX: 404-433-8179
GML Products, Inc., 394 Laredo Dr., Birmingham, AL 35226/205-979-4867
Goddard, Allen, 716 Medford Ave., Hayward, CA 94541/510-276-6830
Goens, Dale W., P.O. Box 224, Cedar Crest, NM 87008/505-281-5419
Goergen's Gun Shop, Inc., Rt. 2, Box 182BB, Austin, MN 55912/507-433-9280
GOEX, Inc., 1002 Springbrook Ave., Moosic, PA 18507/717-457-6724; FAX: 717-457-1130

Goldcoast Reloaders, Inc., 2421 NE 4th Ave., Pompano Beach, FL 33064/305-783-4849
Golden Age Arms Co., 115 E. High St., Ashley, OH 43003/614-747-2488
Golden Bear Bullets, 3065 Fairfax Ave., San Jose, CA 95148/408-238-9515
Gonic Arms, Inc., 134 Flagg Rd., Gonic, NH 03839/603-332-8456, 603-332-8457
Gonic Bullet Works, P.O. Box 7365, Gonic, NH 03839
Gonzalez Guns, Ramon B., P.O. Box 370, Monticello, NY 12701/914-794-4515
Goodling's Gunsmithing, R.D. 1, Box 1097, Spring Grove, PA 17362/717-225-3350
Goodwin, Fred, Silver Ridge Gun Shop, Sherman Mills, ME 04776/207-365-4451
Gordie's Gun Shop, 1401 Fulton St., Streator, IL 61364/815-672-7202
Gotz Bullets, 7313 Rogers St., Rockford, IL 61111
Goudy Classic Stocks, Gary, 263 Hedge Rd., Menlo Park, CA 94025-1711/415-322-1338
Gould & Goodrich, P.O. Box 1479, Lillington, NC 27546/910-893-2071; FAX: 910-893-4742
Gournet, Geoffroy, 820 Paxinosa Ave., Easton, PA 18042/215-559-0710
Gozon Corp., U.S.A., P.O. Box 6278, 152 Bittercreek Dr., Folson, CA 95763/916-983-2020; FAX: 916-983-9500
Grace, Charles E., 6943 85.5 Rd., Trinchera, CO 81081/719-846-9435
Grace Metal Products, Inc., P.O. Box 67, Elk Rapids, MI 49629/616-264-8133
"Gramps" Antique Cartridges, Box 341, Washago, Ont. L0K 2B0 CANADA/705-689-5348
Grand Falls Bullets, Inc., P.O. Box 720, 803 Arnold Wallen Way, Stockton, MO 65785/816-229-0112
Granite Custom Bullets, Box 190, Philipsburg, MT 59858/406-859-3245
Grant, Howard V., Hiawatha 15, Woodruff, WI 54568/715-356-7146
Graphics Direct, P.O. Box 372421, Reseda, CA 91337-2421/818-344-9002
Graves Co., 1800 Andrews Av., Pompano Beach, FL 33069/800-327-9103; FAX: 305-960-0301
Grayback Wildcats, 5306 Bryant Ave., Klamath Falls, OR 97603/503-884-1072
Graybill's Gun Shop, 1035 Ironville Pike, Columbia, PA 17512/717-684-2739
Great 870 Co., The, P.O. Box 6309, El Monte, CA 91734
Great Lakes Airguns, 6175 S. Park Ave., Hamburg, NY 14075/716-648-6666; FAX: 716-648-5279
Green, Arthur S., 485 S. Robertson Blvd., Beverly Hills, CA 90211/310-274-1283
Green, Roger M., P.O. Box 984, 435 E. Birch, Glenrock, WY 82637/307-436-9804
Green Bay Bullets, 1638 Hazelwood Dr., Sobieski, WI 54171/414-826-7760
Green Genie, Box 114, Cusseta, GA 31805
Green Head Game Call Co., RR 1, Box 33, Lacon, IL 61540/309-246-2155
Green Mountain Rifle Barrel Co., Inc., RFD 2, Box 8 Center, Conway, NH 03813/603-356-2047; FAX: 603-356-2048
Greenwald, Leon E. "Bud", 2553 S. Quitman St., Denver, CO 80219/303-935-3850
Greenwood Precision, P.O. Box 468, Nixa, MO 65714-0468/417-725-2330
Greg Gunsmithing Repair, 3732 26th Ave. North, Robbinsdale, MN 55422/612-529-8103
Greg's Superior Products, P.O. Box 46219, Seattle, WA 98146
Greidler Precision, 431 Santa Marina Ct., Escondido, CA 92029/619-480-8892
Gremmel Enterprises, 271 Sterling Dr., Eugene, OR 97404/503-688-3319
Grier's Hard Cast Bullets, 1107 11th St., LaGrande, OR 97850/503-963-8796
Griffin & Howe, Inc., 33 Claremont Rd., Bernardsville, NJ 07924/908-766-2287; FAX: 908-766-1068
Griffin & Howe, Inc., 36 W. 44th St., Suite 1011, New York, NY 10036/212-921-0980
Grifon, Inc., 58 Guinan St., Waltham, MS 02154
Grip-Master, P.O. Box 32, Westbury, NY 11490/800-752-0164; FAX: 516-997-5142
Grizzly Bullets, 322 Green Mountain Rd., Trout Creek, MT 59874/406-847-2627
Groenewold, John, P.O. Box 830, Mundelein, IL 60060/708-566-2365
Group Tight Bullets, 482 Comerwood Court, San Francisco, CA 94080/415-583-1550
GRS Corp., Glendo, P.O. Box 1153, 900 Overlander St., Emporia, KS 66801/316-343-1084, 800-835-3519
Grulla Armes, Apartado 453, Avda Otaloa, 12, Eiber, SPAIN (U.S. importer—American Arms, Inc.)
GSI, Inc., 108 Morrow Ave., P.O. Box 129, Trussville, AL 35173/205-655-8299; FAX: 205-655-7078
GSS Scheller (See U.S. importer—American Bullets)
GTM, 15915B E. Main St., La Puente, CA 91744
G.U. Inc., 4325 S. 120th St., Omaha, NE 68137/402-330-4492; FAX: 402-330-8029
Guardsman Products, 411 N. Darling, Fremont, MI 49412/616-924-3950
Gun City, 212 W. Main Ave., Bismarck, ND 58501/701-223-2304
Gun Doctor, The, 435 East Maple, Roselle, IL 60172/708-894-0668
Gun Doctor, The, P.O. Box 39242, Downey, CA 90242/310-862-3158
Gun Hunter Books, Div. of Gun Hunter Trading Co., 5075 Heisig St., Beaumont, TX 77705/409-835-3006
Gun Leather Limited, 116 Lipscomb, Ft. Worth, TX 76104/817-334-0225; 800-247-0609
Gun List (See Krause Publications, Inc.)
Gun Locker, Div. of Airmold, W.R. Grace & Co.-Conn., Becker Farms Ind. Park,, P.O. Box 610/Roanoke Rapids, NC 27870/800-344-5716; FAX: 919-536-2201
Gun Parts Corp., The, 226 Williams Lane, West Hurley, NY 12491/914-679-2417; FAX: 914-679-5849
Gun Room, The, 1121 Burlington, Muncie, IN 47302/317-282-9073; FAX: 317-282-9073
Gun Room Press, The, 127 Raritan Ave., Highland Park, NJ 08904/908-545-4344; FAX: 908-545-6886
Gun Shop, The, 5550 S. 900 East, Salt Lake City, UT 84117/801-263-3633
Gun Shop, The, 62778 Spring Creek Rd., Montrose, CO 81401
Gun South, Inc. (See GSI, Inc.)
Gun Works, The, 236 Main St., Springfield, OR 97477/503-741-4118
Gun-Alert, Master Products, Inc., 1010 N. Maclay Ave., San Fernando, CA 91340/818-365-0864; FAX: 818-365-1308
Guncraft Books (See Guncraft Sports, Inc.)
Guncraft Sports, Inc., 10737 Dutchtown Rd., Knoxville, TN 37932/615-966-4545; FAX: 615-966-4500
Gunfitters, The, P.O. 426, Cambridge, WI 53523-0426/608-764-8128
Gun-Ho Sports Cases, 110 E. 10th St., St. Paul, MN 55101/612-224-9491
Gunline Tools, P.O. Box 478, Placentia, CA 92670/714-528-5252; FAX: 714-572-4128
Gunnerman Books, P.O. Box 214292, Auburn Hills, MI 48321/810-879-2779
Guns, 81 E. Streetsboro St., Hudson, OH 44236/216-650-4563
Guns, Div. of D.C. Engineering, Inc., 8633 Southfield Fwy., Detroit, MI 48228/313-271-7111, 800-886-7623 (orders only); FAX: 313-271-7112

578 GUN DIGEST

MANUFACTURERS' DIRECTORY

Guns, Gear & Gadgets, L.L.C., P.O. Box 35722, Tucson, AZ 85240-5222/602-747-9578; FAX: 602-747-9715
GUNS Magazine, 591 Camino de la Reina, Suite 200, San Diego, CA 92108/619-297-5350; FAX: 619-297-5353
Gunsight, The, 1712 North Placentia Ave., Fullerton, CA 92631
Gunsite Gunsmithy, P.O. Box 451, Paulden, AZ 86334/602-636-4565; FAX: 602-636-1236
Gunsite Training Center, P.O. Box 700, Paulden, AZ 86334/602-636-4565; FAX: 602-636-1236
Gunsmith in Elk River, The, 14021 Victoria Lane, Elk River, MN 55330/612-441-7761
Gunsmithing Ltd., 57 Unquowa Rd., Fairfield, CT 06430/203-254-0436
Gun-Tec, P.O. Box 8125, W. Palm Beach, FL 33407
Gurney, F.R., Box 13, Sooke, BC V0S 1N0 CANADA/604-642-5282
Gusdorf Corp., 11440 Lackland Rd., St. Louis, MO 63146/314-567-5249
Gusty Winds Corp., 2950 Bear St., Suite 120, Costa Mesa, CA 92626/714-536-3587
Gwinnell, Bryson J., P.O. Box 248C, Maple Hill Rd., Rochester, VT 05767/802-767-3664
GZ Paintball Sports Products, P.O. Box 430, Andover, NH 03216/603-735-5300; FAX: 603-735-5154

H

H&B Forge Co., Rt. 2 Geisinger Rd., Shiloh, OH 44878/419-895-1856
H&P Publishing, 7174 Hoffman Rd., San Angelo, TX 76905/915-655-5953
H&R 1871, Inc., 60 Industrial Rowe, Gardner, MA 01440/508-632-9393; FAX: 508-632-2300
H&S Liner Service, 515 E. 8th, Odessa, TX 79761/915-332-1021
Hafner Creations, Inc., P.O. Box 1987, Lake City, FL 32055/904-755-6481; FAX: 904-755-6595
Hagn Rifles & Actions, Martin, P.O. Box 444, Cranbrook, B.C. VIC 4H9, CANADA/604-489-4861
Hakko Co. Ltd., 5F Daini-Tsunemi Bldg., 1-13-12, Narimasu, Itabashiku Tokyo 175, JAPAN/03-5997-7870; FAX: 81-3-5997-7840
Hale, Peter, 800 E. Canyon Rd., Spanish Fork, UT 84660/801-798-8215
Half Moon Rifle Shop, 490 Halfmoon Rd., Columbia Falls, MT 59912/406-892-4409
Hall Manufacturing, 1801 Yellow Leaf Rd., Clanton, AL 35045/205-755-4094
Hall Plastics, John, Inc., P.O. Box 1526, Alvin, TX 77512/713-489-8709
Hallberg Gunsmith, Fritz, 33 S. Main, Payette, ID 83661
Hallowell & Co., 340 W. Putnam Ave., Greenwich, CT 06830/203-869-2190; FAX: 203-869-0692
Hally Caller, 443 Wells Rd., Doylestown, PA 18901/215-345-6354
Halstead, Rick, RR4, Box 272, Miami, OK 74354/918-540-0933
Hamilton, Alex B. (See Ten-Ring Precision, Inc.)
Hamilton, Keith, P.O. Box 871, Gridley, CA 95948/916-846-2316
Hammans, Charles E., P.O. Box 788, 2022 McCracken, Stuttgart, AR 72106/501-673-1388
Hammerli Ltd., Seonerstrasse 37, CH-5600 Lenzburg, SWITZERLAND/064-50 11 44; FAX: 064-51 38 27 (U.S. importer—Hammerli USA)
Hammerli USA, 19296 Oak Grove Circle, Groveland, CA 95321/209-962-5311; FAX: 209-962-5931
Hammets VLD Bullets, P.O. Box 479, Rayville, LA 71269/318-728-2019
Hammond Custom Guns Ltd., Guy, 619 S. Pandora, Gilbert, AZ 85234/602-892-3437
Hammonds Rifles, RD 4, Box 504, Red Lion, PA 17356/717-244-7879
Hand Engravers Supply Co., 601 Springfield Dr., Albany, GA 31707/912-432-9683
Handgun Press, P.O. Box 406, Glenview, IL 60025/708-657-6500; FAX: 708-724-8831
HandiCrafts Unltd. (See Clements' Custom Leathercraft, Chas)
Hands Engraving, Barry Lee, 26192 E. Shore Route, Bigfork, MT 59911/406-837-0035
Hank's Gun Shop, Box 370, 50 West 100 South, Monroe, UT 84754/801-527-4456
Hanned Line, The, P.O. Box 2387, Cupertino, CA 95015-2387
Hanned Precision (See Hanned Line, The)
Hansen & Co. (See Hansen Cartridge Co.)
Hansen Cartridge Co., 244-246 Old Post Rd., Southport, CT 06490/203-259-6222, 203-259-7337; FAX: 203-254-3832
Hanson's Gun Center, Dick, 233 Everett Dr., Colorado Springs, CO 80911
Hanusin, John, 3306 Commercial, Northbrook, IL 60062/708-564-2706
Hardin Specialty Dist., P.O. Box 338, Radcliff, KY 40159-0338/502-351-6649
Hardison, Charles, P.O. Box 356, 200 W. Baseline Rd., Lafayette, CO 80026-0356/303-666-5171
Harold's Custom Gun Shop, Inc., Broughton Rifle Barrels, Rt. 1, Box 447, Big Spring, TX 79720/915-394-4430
Harper, William E. (See Great 870 Co., The)
Harper's Custom Stocks, 928 Lombrano St., San Antonio, TX 78207/512-732-5780
Harrell's Precision, 5756 Hickory Dr., Salem, VA 24133/703-380-2683
Harrington & Richardson (See H&R 1871, Inc.)
Harrington Cutlery, Inc., Russell, Subs. of Hyde Mfg. Co., 44 River St., Southbridge, MA 01550/617-765-0201
Harris Engineering, Inc., Rt. 1, Barlow, KY 42024/502-334-3633; FAX: 502-334-3000
Harris Enterprises, P.O. Box 105, Bly, OR 97622/503-353-2625
Harris Hand Engraving, Paul A., 10630 Janet Lee, San Antonio, TX 78230/512-391-5121
Harris Publications, 1115 Broadway, New York, NY 10010/212-807-7100; FAX: 212-627-4678
Harris-McMillan Gunworks, 302 W. Melinda Lane, Phoenix, AZ 85027/602-582-9627; FAX: 602-582-5178
Harrison Bullets, 6437 E. Hobart St., Mesa, AZ 85205
Harrison-Hurtz Enterprises, Inc., P.O. Box 268, RR1, Wymore, NE 68466/402-645-3378; FAX: 402-645-3606
Hart & Son, Inc., Robert W., 401 Montgomery St., Nescopeck, PA 18635/717-752-3655, 800-368-3656; FAX: 717-752-1088
Hart Rifle Barrels, Inc., RD 2, Apulia Rd., P.O. Box 182, Lafayette, NY 13084/315-677-9841; FAX: 315-677-9610
Hartmann & Weiss GmbH, Rahlstedter Bahnhofstr. 47, 22143 Hamburg, GERMANY/(40) 677 55 85; FAX: (40) 677 55 92
Harwood, Jack O., 1191 S. Pendlebury Lane, Blackfoot, ID 83221/208-785-5368
Haselbauer Products, Jerry, P.O. Box 27629, Tucson, AZ 85726/602-792-1075
Hastings Barrels, 320 Court St., Clay Center, KS 67432/913-632-3169; FAX: 913-632-6554
Hatfield Gun Co., Inc., 224 N. 4th St., St. Joseph, MO 64501/816-279-8688; FAX: 816-279-2716
Hawk Laboratories, Inc., P.O. Box 1689, Glenrock, WY 82637/307-436-5561
Hawken Shop, The (See Dayton Traister)
Haydel's Game Calls, Inc., 5018 Hazel Jones Rd., Bossier City, LA 71111/318-746-3586, 800-HAYDELS; FAX: 318-746-3711
Haydon Shooters' Supply, Russ, 15018 Goodrich Dr. NW, Gig Harbor, WA 98329/206-857-7557
Heatbath Corp., P.O. Box 2978, Springfield, MA 01101/413-543-3381
Hebard Guns, Gil, 125-129 Public Square, Knoxville, IL 61448
HEBB Resources, P.O. Box 999, Mead, WA 99021-09996/509-466-1292
Hecht, Hubert J., Waffen-Hecht, P.O. Box 2635, Fair Oaks, CA 95628/916-966-1020
Heckler & Koch GmbH, Postfach 1329, D-7238 Oberndorf, Neckar, GERMANY (U.S. importer—Heckler & Koch, Inc.)
Heckler & Koch, Inc., 21480 Pacific Blvd., Sterling, VA 20166-8903/703-450-1900; FAX: 703-450-8160
Hege Jagd-u. Sporthandels, GmbH, P.O. Box 101461, W-7770 Ueberlingen a. Bodensee, GERMANY
Heidenstrom Bullets, Urds GT 1 Heroya, 3900 Porsgrunn, NORWAY
Heilmann, Stephen, P.O. Box 657, Grass Valley, CA 95945/916-272-8758
Heinie Specialty Products, 323 W. Franklin St., Havana, IL 62644/309-543-4535; FAX: 309-543-2521
Heintz, David, 800 N. Hwy. 17, Moffat, CO 81143/719-256-4194
Hellweg Ltd., 40356 Oak Park Way, Suite H, Oakhurst, CA 93644/209-683-3030; FAX: 209-683-3422
Helwan (See U.S. importer—Interarms)
Henckels Zwillingswerk, Inc., J.A., 9 Skyline Dr., Hawthorne, NY 10532/914-592-7370
Hendricks, Frank E., Master Engravers, Inc., HC03, Box 434, Dripping Springs, TX 78620/512-858-7828
Hendricks Gun Works, 1162 Gillionville Rd., Albany, GA 31707/912-439-2003
Henigson & Associates, Steve, 2049 Kerwood Ave., Los Angeles, CA 90025/213-305-8288
Henriksen Tool Co., Inc., 8515 Wagner Creek Rd., Talent, OR 97540/503-535-2309
Hensler, Jerry, 6614 Country Field, San Antonio, TX 78240/210-690-7491
Hensley & Gibbs, Box 10, Murphy, OR 97533/503-862-2341
Hensley, Darwin, P.O. Box 329, Brightwood, OR 97011/503-622-5411
Heppler, Keith M., Keith's Custom Gunstocks, 540 Banyan Circle, Walnut Creek, CA 94598/510-934-3509; FAX: 510-934-3143
Heppler's Machining, 2240 Calle Del Mundo, Santa Clara, CA 95054/408-748-9166; FAX: 408-988-7711
Hercules, Inc., Hercules Plaza, 1313 N Market St., Wilmington, DE 19894/800-276-9337, 302-594-5000; FAX: 302-594-5305
Heritage Firearms, 4600 NW 135th St., Opa Locka, FL 33054/305-685-5966; FAX: 305-687-6721
Hermann Leather Co., H.J., Rt. 1, P.O. Box 525, Skiatook, OK 74070/918-396-1226
Herrett's Stocks, Inc., P.O. Box 741, Twin Falls, ID 83303/208-733-1498
Hertel & Reuss, Werk f r Optik und Feinmechanik GmbH, Quellhofstrabe 67, 34 127 Kassel, GERMANY/0561-83006; FAX: 0561-893308
Herter's Manufacturing, Inc., 111 E. Burnett St., P.O. Box 518, Beaver Dam, WI 53916/414-887-1765; FAX: 414-887-8444
Hesco-Meprolight, 2821 Greenville Rd., LaGrange, GA 30240/706-884-7967; FAX: 706-882-4683
Heydenberk, Warren R., 1059 W. Sawmill Rd., Quakertown, PA 18951/215-538-2682
Heym GmbH & Co. KG, Friedrich Wilh, Coburger Str.8, D-97702 Muennerstadt, GERMANY
HH Engineering, Box 642, Dept. HD, Narberth, PA 19072-0642
Hickman, Jaclyn, Box 1900, Glenrock, WY 82637
Hidalgo, Tony, 12701 SW 9th Pl., Davie, FL 33325/305-476-7645
High Bridge Arms, Inc., 3185 Mission St., San Francisco, CA 94110/415-282-8358
High North Products, Inc., P.O. Box 2, Antigo, WI 54409/715-627-2331
High Performance International, 5734 W. Florist Ave., Milwaukee, WI 53218/414-466-9040
High Standard Mfg. Co., Inc., 264 Whitney St., Hartford, CT 06105-2270/203-586-8220; FAX: 203-231-0411
High Tech Specialties, Inc., P.O. Box 387R, Adamstown, PA 19501/215-484-0405, 800-231-9385
Highline Machine Co., 654 Lela Place, Grand Junction, CO 81504/303-434-4971
Hi-Grade Imports, 8655 Monterey Rd., Gilroy, CA 95021/408-842-9301; FAX: 408-842-2374
Hill, Loring F., 304 Cedar Rd., Elkins Park, PA 19117
Hill Speed Leather, Ernie, 4507 N. 195th Ave., Litchfield Park, AZ 85340/602-853-9222; FAX: 602-853-9235
Hillmer Custom Gunstocks, Paul D., 7251 Hudson Heights, Hudson, IA 50643/319-988-3941
Hinman Outfitters, Bob, 1217 W. Glen, Peoria, IL 61614/309-691-8132
Hi-Point Firearms, 5990 Philadelphia Dr., Dayton, OH 45415/513-275-4991; FAX: 513-275-4991
Hiptmayer, Armurier, RR 112 750, P.O. Box 136, Eastman, Quebec J0E 1P0, CANADA/514-297-2492
Hiptmayer, Heidemarie, RR 112 750, P.O. Box 136, Eastman, Quebec J0E 1P0, CANADA/514-297-2492
Hiptmayer, Klaus, RR 112 750, P.O. Box 136, Eastman, Quebec J0E 1P0, CANADA/514-297-2492
Hirtenberger Aktiengesellschaft, Leobersdorferstrasse 31, A-2552 Hirtenberg, AUSTRIA/43(0)2256 81184; FAX: 43(0)2256 81807
HiTek International, 484 El Camino Real, Redwood City, CA 94063/415-363-1404, 800-54-NIGHT; FAX: 415-363-1408
Hiti-Schuch, Atelier Wilma, A-8863 Predlitz, Pirming Y1 AUSTRIA/0353418278
HJS Arms, Inc., P.O. Box 3711, Brownsville, TX 78523-3711/800-453-2767, 210-542-2767
H.K.S. Products, 7841 Founion Dr., Florence, KY 41042/606-342-7841, 800-354-9814; FAX: 606-342-5685
Hoag, James W., 8523 Canoga Ave., Suite C, Canoga Park, CA 91304/818-998-1510
Hobbie Gunsmithing, Duane A., 2412 Pattie Ave., Wichita, KS 67216/316-264-8266
Hobson Precision Mfg. Co., Rt. 1, Box 220-C, Brent, AL 35034/205-926-4662
Hoch Custom Bullet Moulds (See Colorado Shooter's Supply)
Hodgdon Powder Co., Inc., P.O. Box 2932, 6231 Robinson, Shawnee Mission, KS 66202/913-362-9455; FAX: 913-362-1307

50th EDITION, 1996 **579**

DIRECTORY OF THE ARMS TRADE

Hodgman, Inc., 1750 Orchard Rd., Montgomery, IL 60538/708-897-7555; FAX: 708-897-7558
Hodgson, Richard, 9081 Tahoe Lane, Boulder, CO 80301
Hoehn Sales, Inc., 75 Greensburg Ct., St. Charles, MO 63304/314-441-4231
Hoelscher, Virgil, 11047 Pope Ave., Lynwood, CA 90262/310-631-8545
Hoenig & Rodman, 6521 Morton Dr., Boise, ID 83704/208-375-1116
Hofer Jagdwaffen, P., Buchsenmachermeister, Kirchgasse 24, A-9170 Ferlach, AUSTRIA/04227-3683
Hoffman New Ideas, 821 Northmoor Rd., Lake Forest, IL 60045/312-234-4075
Hogue Grips, P.O. Box 1138, Paso Robles, CA 93447/800-438-4747, 805-239-1440; FAX: 805-239-2553
Holland, Dick, 422 NE 6th St., Newport, OR 97365/503-265-7556
Holland's, Box 69, Powers, OR 97466/503-439-5155; FAX: 503-439-5155
Hollis Gun Shop, 917 Rex St., Carlsbad, NM 88220/505-885-3782
Hollywood Engineering, 10642 Arminta St., Sun Valley, CA 91352/818-842-8376
Holster Shop, The, 720 N. Flagler Dr., Ft. Lauderdale, FL 33304/305-463-7910; FAX: 305-761-1483
Holston Ent., Inc., P.O. Box 493, Piney Flats, TN 37686
Homak Mfg. Co., Inc., 3800 W. 45th St., Chicago, IL 60632/312-523-3100, FAX: 312-523-9455
Home Shop Machinist, The, Village Press Publications, P.O. Box 1810, Traverse City, MI 49685/800-447-7367; FAX: 616-946-3289
Hondo Ind., 510 S. 52nd St.,l04, Tempe, AZ 85281
Hoppe's Div., Penguin Industries, Inc., Airport Industrial Mall, Coatesville, PA 19320/610-384-6000
Horizons Unlimited, P.O. Box 426, Warm Springs, GA 31830/706-655-3603; FAX: 706-655-3603
Hornady Mfg. Co., P.O. Box 1848, Grand Island, NE 68802/800-338-3220, 308-382-1390; FAX: 308-382-5761
Horseshoe Leather Products, Andy Arratoonian, The Cottage Sharow, Ripon HG4 5BP ENGLAND/0765-605858
Horst, Alan K., 3221 2nd Ave. N., Great Falls, MT 59401/406-454-1831
Horton Dist. Co., Inc., Lew, 15 Walkup Dr., Westboro, MA 01581/508-366-7400; FAX: 508-366-5332
House of Muskets, Inc., The, P.O. Box 4640, Pagosa Springs, CO 81157/303-731-2295
Houtz & Barwick, P.O. Box 435, W. Church St., Elizabeth City, NC 27909/800-775-0337, 919-335-4191; FAX: 919-335-1152
Howa Machinery, Ltd., Sukagawa, Shinkawa-cho, Nishikasugai-gun, Aichi 452, JAPAN (U.S. importer—Interarms)
Howell Machine, 815 1/2 D St., Lewiston, ID 83501/208-743-7418
Hoyt Holster Co., Inc., P.O. Box 69, Coupeville, WA 98239-0069/360-678-6640; FAX: 360-678-6549
H-S Precision, Inc., 1301 Turbine Dr., Rapid City, SD 57701/605-341-3006; FAX: 605-342-8964
HT Bullets, 244 Belleville Rd., New Bedford, MA 02745/508-999-3338
Hubertus Schneidwarenfabrik, P.O. Box 180 106, D-42626 Solingen, GERMANY/01149-212-59-19-94; FAX: 01149-212-59-19-92
Huebner, Corey O., P.O. Box 2074, Missoula, MT 59806-2074/406-721-1658
Huey Gun Cases, Marvin, P.O. Box 22456, Kansas City, MO 64113/816-444-1637
Hugger Hooks Co., 3900 Easley Way, Golden, CO 80403/303-279-0600
Hughes, Steven Dodd, P.O. Box 11455, Eugene, OR 97440/503-485-8869
Hume, Don, P.O. Box 351, Miami, OK 74355/918-542-6604
Hungry Horse Books, 4605 Hwy. 93 South, Whitefish, MT 59937/406-862-7997
Hunkeler, A. (See Buckskin Machine Works)
Hunter Co., Inc., 3300 W. 71st Ave., Westminster, CO 80030/303-427-4626; FAX: 303-428-3980
Hunter's Specialties, Inc., 6000 Huntington Ct. NE, Cedar Rapids, IA 52402-1268/319-395-0321; FAX: 319-395-0326
Hunterjohn, P.O. Box 477, St. Louis, MO 63166/314-531-7250
Hunting Classics Ltd., P.O. Box 2089, Gastonia, NC 28053/704-867-1307; FAX: 704-867-0491
Huntington Die Specialties, 601 Oro Dam Blvd., Oroville, CA 95965/916-534-1210; FAX: 916-534-1212
Hydrosorbent Products, P.O. Box 437, Ashley Falls, MA 01222/413-229-2967; FAX: 413-229-8743
Hyper-Single, Inc., 520 E. Beaver, Jenks, OK 74037/918-299-2391

I

I.A.B. (See U.S. importer—Taylor's & Co., Inc.)
IAI, 6226 Santos Diaz St., Irwindale, CA 91702/818-334-1200
Ibberson (Sheffield) Ltd., George, 25-31 Allen St., Sheffield, S3 7AW ENGLAND/0114-2766123; FAX: 0114-2738465
ICI-America, P.O. Box 751, Wilmington, DE 19897/302-575-3000
Idaho Ammunition Service, 2816 Mayfair Dr., Lewiston, ID 83501/208-743-0270; FAX: 208-743-4930
IGA (See U.S. importer—Stoeger Industries)
Illinois Lead Shop, 7742 W. 61st Place, Summit, IL 60501
IMI, P.O. Box 1044, Ramat Hasharon 47100, ISRAEL/972-3-5485222 (U.S. importer—Magnum Research, Inc.)
IMI Services USA, Inc., 2 Wisconsin Circle, Suite 420, Chevy Chase, MD 20815/301-215-4800; FAX: 301-657-1446
Impact Case Co., P.O. Box 9912, Spokane, WA 99209-0912/800-262-3322, 509-467-3303; FAX: 509-326-5436
Imperial (See E-Z-Way Systems)
Imperial Magnum Corp., P.O. Box 249, Oroville, WA 98844/604-495-3131; FAX: 604-495-2816
Imperial Schrade Corp., 7 Schrade Ct., Box 7000, Ellenville, NY 12428/914-647-7601; FAX: 914-647-8701
IMR Powder Co., 1080 Military Turnpike, Suite 2, Plattsburgh, NY 12901/518-563-2253; FAX: 518-563-6916
I.N.C., Inc. (See Kick Eez)
Independent Machine & Gun Shop, 1416 N. Hayes, Pocatello, ID 83201
Info-Arm, P.O. Box 1262, Champlain, NY 12919
Ingle, Ralph W., 4 Missing Link, Rossville, GA 30741/404-866-5589
Innovative Weaponry, Inc., 337 Eubank NE, Albuquerque, NM 87123/800-334-3573, 505-296-4645; FAX: 505-271-2633

Innovision Enterprises, 728 Skinner Dr., Kalamazoo, MI 49001/616-382-1681; FAX: 616-382-1830
InSights Training Center, Inc., 240 NW Gilman Blvd., Issaquah, WA 98027/206-391-4834
INTEC International, Inc., P.O. Box 5708, Scottsdale, AZ 85261/602-483-1708
Interarms, 10 Prince St., Alexandria, VA 22314/703-548-1400; FAX: 703-549-7826
Intermountain Arms & Tackle, Inc., 105 E. Idaho St., Meridian, ID 83642/208-888-4911; FAX: 208-888-4381
International Shooters Service (See I.S.S.)
International Shootists, Inc., P.O. Box 5354, Mission Hills, CA 91345/818-891-1723
Intratec, 12405 SW 130th St., Miami, FL 33186/305-232-1821; FAX: 305-253-7207
Iosso Products, 1485 Lively Blvd., Elk Grove Village, IL 60007/708-437-8400; FAX: 708-437-8478
Iron Bench, 12619 Bailey Rd., Redding, CA 96003/916-241-4623
Iron Mountain Knife Co., P.O. Box 2146, Sparks, NV 89432-2146/702-356-3632; FAX: 702-359-2785
Ironside International Publishers, Inc., P.O. Box 55, 800 Slaters Lane, Alexandria, VA 22313/703-684-6111; FAX: 703-683-5486
Ironsighter Co., 5555 Treadwell St., Wayne, MI 48184/313-326-8731; FAX: 313-326-3378
Irwin, Campbell H., 140 Hartland Blvd., East Hartland, CT 06027/203-653-3901
Irwindale Arms, Inc. (See IAI)
Israel Military Industries Ltd. (See IMI)
I.S.S., P.O. Box 185234, Ft. Worth, TX 76181/817-595-2090
I.S.W., 106 E. Cairo Dr., Tempe, AZ 85282
Ithaca Aquisition Corp., Ithaca Gun; 891 Route 34B, King Ferry, NY 13081/315-364-7171; FAX: 315-364-5134
I.T.S. (See U.S. importer—County Arms)
Ivanoff, Thomas G. (See Tom's Gun Repair)

J

J-4, Inc., 1700 Via Burton, Anaheim, CA 92806/714-254-8315; FAX: 714-956-4421
J&D Components, 75 East 350 North, Orem, UT 84057-4719/801-225-7007
J&J Products, Inc., 9240 Whitmore, El Monte, CA 91731/818-571-5228, 800-927-8361; FAX: 818-571-8704
J&L Superior Bullets (See Huntington Die Specialties)
J&R Enterprises, 4550 Scotts Valley Rd., Lakeport, CA 95453
J&S Heat Treat, 803 S. 16th St., Blue Springs, MO 64015/816-229-2149; FAX: 816-228-1135
J.A. Blades, Inc. (See Christopher Firearms Co., Inc., E.)
Jackalope Gun Shop, 1048 S. 5th St., Douglas, WY 82633/307-358-3441
JACO Precision Co., 11803 Indian Head Dr., Austin, TX 78753/512-836-4418
Jaeger, Inc., Paul/Dunn's, P.O. Box 449, 1 Madison Ave., Grand Junction, TN 38039/901-764-6909; FAX: 901-764-6503
JagerSport, Ltd., One Wholesale Way, Cranston, RI 02920/800-962-4867, 401-944-9682; FAX: 401-946-2587
Jamison's Forge Works, 4527 Rd. 6.5 NE, Moses Lake, WA 98837/509-762-2659
Jansma, Jack J., 4320 Kalamazoo Ave., Grand Rapids, MI 49508/616-455-7810; FAX: 616-455-5212
Jantz Supply, P.O. Box 584-GD, Davis, OK 73030/405-369-2316; FAX: 405-369-3082
Jarrett Rifles, Inc., 383 Brown Rd., Jackson, SC 29831/803-471-3616
Jarvis Gunsmithing, Inc., 1123 Cherry Orchard Lane, Hamilton, MT 59840/406-961-4392
JAS, Inc., P.O. Box 0, Rosemount, MN 55068/612-890-7631
JASS (See Complete Handloader, The)
Javelina Products, P.O. Box 337, San Bernardino, CA 92402/714-882-5847; FAX: 714-434-6937
J/B Adventures & Safaris, Inc., 2275 E. Arapahoe Rd. Ste. 109, Littleton, CO 80122-1521/303-771-0977
J-B Bore Cleaner, 299 Poplar St., Hamburg, PA 19526/610-562-2103
JBM, P.O. Box 3648, University Park, NM 88003
Jeffredo Gunsight, P.O. Box 669, San Marcos, CA 92079/619-728-2695
Jenco Sales, Inc., P.O. Box 1000, Manchaca, TX 78652/800-531-5301; FAX: 800-263-2373
Jenkins Recoil Pads, Inc., RR 2, Box 471, Olney, IL 62450/618-395-3416
Jennings Firearms, Inc., 17692 Cowan, Irvine, CA 92714/714-252-7621; FAX: 714-252-7626
Jensen Bullets, 86 North, 400 West, Blackfoot, ID 83221/208-785-5590
Jensen's Custom Ammunition, 5146 E. Pima, Tucson, AZ 85712/602-325-3346; FAX: 602-322-5704
Jensen's Firearms Academy, 1280 W. Prince, Tucson, AZ 85705/602-293-8516
Jester Bullets, Rt. 1 Box 27, Orienta, OK 73737
Jett & Co., Inc., 104 W. Water St., Litchfield, IL 62056-2464/217-324-3779
Jewell, Arnold W., 1490 Whitewater Rd., New Braunfels, TX 78132/210-620-0971
J-Gar Co., 183 Turnpike Rd., Dept. 3, Petersham, MA 01366-9604
JGS Precision Tool Mfg., 1141 S. Summer Rd., Coos Bay, OR 97420/503-267-4331; FAX:503-267-5996
Jim's Gun Shop (See Spradlin's)
Jim's Precision, Jim Ketchum, 1725 Moclips Dr., Petaluma, CA 94952/707-762-3014
J.I.T., Ltd., P.O. Box 230, Freedom, WY 83120/708-494-0937
JLK Bullets, 414 Turner Rd., Dover, AR 72837/501-331-4194
J.O. Arms Inc., 5709 Hartsdale, Houston, TX 77036/713-789-0745; FAX: 713-789-7513
Johanssons Vapentillbehor, Bert, S-430 20 Veddige, SWEDEN
John's Custom Leather, 523 S. Liberty St., Blairsville, PA 15717/412-459-6802
Johns, Bill, 1412 Lisa Rae, Round Rock, TX 78664/512-255-8246
Johnson Wood Products, RR 1, Strawberry Point, IA 52076/319-933-4930
Johnson's Gunsmithing, Inc., Neal, 208 W. Buchanan St., Suite B, Colorado Springs, CO 80907/800-284-8671, 719-632-3795; FAX: 719-632-3493
Johnson's Lage Uniwad, P.O. Box 2302, Davenport, IA 52809/319-388-LAGE
Johnston, James (See North Fork Custom Gunsmithing)
Johnston Bros., 1889 Rt. 9, Unit 22, Toms River, NJ 08755/800-257-2595; FAX: 800-257-2534
Jonad Corp., 2091 Lakeland Ave., Lakewood, OH 44107/216-226-3161
Jonas Appraisals & Taxidermy, Jack, 1675 S. Birch, Suite 506, Denver, CO 80222/303-757-7347
Jones, J.D. (See SSK Industries)
Jones Co., Dale, 680 Hoffman Draw, Kila, MT 59920/406-755-4684

MANUFACTURERS' DIRECTORY

Jones Custom Products, Neil, RD 1, Box 483A, Saegertown, PA 16433/814-763-2769; FAX: 814-763-4228
Jones Moulds, Paul, 4901 Telegraph Rd., Los Angeles, CA 90022/213-262-1510
Joy Enterprises (See Fury Cutlery)
J.P. Enterprises, Inc., P.O. Box 26324, Shoreview, MN 55126/612-486-9064; FAX: 612-482-0970
J.P. Gunstocks, Inc., 4508 San Miguel Ave., North Las Vegas, NV 89030/702-645-0718
JP Sales, Box 307, Anderson, TX 77830
JRW, 2425 Taffy Ct., Nampa, ID 83687
JS Worldwide (See Coonan Arms)
JSL (Hereford) Ltd., 35 Church St., Hereford HR1 2LR ENGLAND/0432-355416; FAX: 0432-355242 (U.S. importer—Specialty Shooters Supply, Inc.)
Jumbo Sports Products (See Bucheimer, J.M.)
Jungkind, Reeves C., 5001 Buckskin Pass, Austin, TX 78745-2841/512-442-1094
Jurras, L.E., P.O. Box 680, Washington, IN 47501/812-254-7698
Just Brass, Inc., 121 Henry St., P.O. Box 112, Freeport, NY 11520/516-378-8588
JWH: Software, 6947 Haggerty Rd., Hillsboro, OH 45133/513-393-2402

K

K&K Ammo Wrist Band, R.D. 1, P.O. Box 448-CA18, Lewistown, PA 17044/717-242-2329
K&M Industries, Inc., Box 66, 510 S. Main, Troy, ID 83871/208-835-2281; FAX: 208-835-5211
K&M Services, 5430 Salmon Run Rd., Dover, PA 17315/717-764-1461
K&P Gun Co., 1024 Central Ave., New Rockford, ND 58356/701-947-2248
K&S Mfg., 2611 Hwy. 40 East, Inglis, FL 34449/904-447-3571
K&T Co., Div. of T&S Industries, Inc., 1027 Skyview Dr., W. Carrollton, OH 45449/513-859-8414
Ka Pu Kapili, P.O. Box 745, Honokaa, HI 96727/808-776-1644; FAX: 808-776-1731
KA-BAR Knives, 31100 Solon Rd., Solon, OH 44139/216-248-7000; 800-321-9316, ext. 329; FAX: 216-248-8651
Kahles U.S.A., P.O. Box 81071, Warwick, RI 02888/800-752-4537; FAX: 401-946-2587
Kahnke Gunworks, 206 West 11th St., Redwood Falls, MN 56283/507-637-2901
Kahr Arms, P.O. Box 220, 630 Route 303, Blauvelt, NY 10913/914-353-5996; FAX: 914-353-7833
Kalispel Case Line, P.O. Box 267, Cusick, WA 99119/509-445-1121
Kamik Outdoor Footwear, 554 Montee de Liesse, Montreal, Quebec, H4T 1P1 CANADA/514-341-3950; FAX: 514-341-1861
Kamyk Engraving Co., Steve, 9 Grandview Dr., Westfield, MA 01085-1810/413-568-0457
Kandel, P.O. Box 4529, Portland, OR 97208
Kane Products, Inc., 5572 Brecksville Rd., Cleveland, OH 44131/216-524-9962
Kapro Mfg. Co., Inc. (See R.E.I.)
Kasenit Co., Inc., 13 Park Ave., Highland Mills, NY 10930/914-928-9595; FAX: 914-928-7292
Kasmarsik Bullets, 152 Crstler Rd., Chehalis, WA 98532
Kassnar (See U.S. importer—K.B.I., Inc.)
Kaswer Custom, Inc., 13 Surrey Drive, Brookfield, CT 06804/203-775-0564; FAX: 203-775-6872
K.B.I., Inc., P.O. Box 5440, Harrisburg, PA 17110-0440/717-540-8518; FAX: 717-540-8567
K-D, Inc., Box 459, 585 N. Hwy. 155, Cleveland, UT 84518/801-653-2530
KDF, Inc., 2485 Hwy. 46 N., Seguin, TX 78155/210-379-8141; FAX: 210-379-5420
KeeCo Impressions, Inc., 346 Wood Ave., North Brunswick, NJ 08902/800-468-0546
Keeler, R.H., 817 "N" St., Port Angeles, WA 98362/206-457-4702
Kehr, Roger, 2131 Agate Ct. SE, Lacy, WA 98503/360-456-0831
Keith's Bullets, 942 Twisted Oak, Algonquin, IL 60102/708-658-3520
Keith's Custom Gunstocks (See Heppler, Keith M.)
Kelbly, Inc., 7222 Dalton Fox Lake Rd., North Lawrence, OH 44666/216-683-4674; FAX: 216-683-7349
Keller Co., The, 4215 McEwen Rd., Dallas, TX 75244/214-770-8585
Kelley's, P.O. Box 125, Woburn, MA 01801/617-935-3389
Kellogg's Professional Products, 325 Pearl St., Sandusky, OH 44870/419-625-6551; FAX: 419-625-6167
Kelly, Lance, 1723 Willow Oak Dr., Edgewater, FL 32132/904-423-4933
Kel-Tec CNC Industries, Inc., P.O. Box 3427, Cocoa, FL 32924/407-631-0068; FAX: 407-631-1169
Ken's Finn Knives, Rt. 1, Box 338, Republic, MI 49879/906-376-2132
Ken's Gun Specialties, Rt. 1, Box 147, Lakeview, AR 72642/501-431-5606
Ken's Kustom Kartridges, 331 Jacobs Rd., Hubbard, OH 44425/216-534-4595
Ken's Rifle Blanks, Ken McCullough, Rt. 2, P.O. Box 85B, Weston, OR 97886/503-566-3879
Keng's Firearms Specialty, Inc., 875 Wharton Dr. SW, Atlanta, GA 30336/404-691-7611; FAX: 404-505-8445
Kennebec Journal, 274 Western Ave., Augusta, ME 04330/207-622-6288
Kennedy Firearms, 10 N. Market St., Muncy, PA 17756/717-546-6695
KenPatable Ent., Inc., P.O. Box 19422, Louisville, KY 40259/502-239-5447
Kent Cartridge Mfg. Co. Ltd., Unit 16, Branbridges Industrial Estate, East, Peckham/Tonbridge, Kent, TN12 5HF ENGLAND/622-872255; FAX: 622-872645
Keowee Game Calls, 608 Hwy. 25 North, Travelers Rest, SC 29690/803-834-7204
Kershaw Knives, 25300 SW Parkway Ave., Wilsonville, OR 97070/503-682-1966, 800-325-2891; FAX: 503-682-7168
Kesselring Gun Shop, 400 Hwy. 99 North, Burlington, WA 98233/206-724-3113; FAX: 206-724-7003
Kick Eez, P.O. Box 12767, Wichita, KS 67277/316-721-9570; FAX: 316-721-5260
Kilham & Co., Main St., P.O. Box 37, Lyme, NH 03768/603-795-4112
Kimball, Gary, 1526 N. Circle Dr., Colorado Springs, CO 80909/719-634-1274
Kimber of America, Inc., 9039 SE Jannsen Rd., Clackamas, OR 97015/503-656-1704, 800-880-2418; FAX: 503-656-5357
Kimel Industries, 3800 Old Monroe Rd., P.O. Box 335, Matthews, NC 28105/800-438-9288; FAX: 704-821-6339
King & Co., P.O. Box 1242, Bloomington, IL 61701/309-473-3964
King's Gun Works, 1837 W. Glenoaks Blvd., Glendale, CA 91201/818-956-6010; FAX: 818-548-8606
Kingyon, Paul L., 607 N. 5th St., Burlington, IA 52601/319-752-4465
Kirk Game Calls, Inc., Dennis, RD1, Box 184, Laurens, NY 13796/607-433-2710; FAX: 607-433-2711
Kirkpatrick Leather Co., 1910 San Bernardo, Laredo, TX 78040/210-723-6631; FAX: 210-725-0672
KJM Fabritek, Inc., P.O. Box 162, Marietta, GA 30061/404-426-8251
KK Air International (See Impact Case Co.)
K.K. Arms Co., Star Route Box 671, Kerrville, TX 78028/210-257-4718; FAX: 210-257-4891
KLA Enterprises, P.O. Box 2028, Eaton Park, FL 33840/813-682-2829; FAX: 813-682-2829
Kleen-Bore, Inc., 16 Industrial Pkwy., Easthampton, MA 01027/413-527-0300; FAX: 413-527-2522
Klein Custom Guns, Don, 433 Murray Park Dr., Ripon, WI 54971/414-748-2931
Kleinendorst, K.W., RR 1, Box 1500, Hop Bottom, PA 18824/717-289-4687
Klingler Woodcarving, P.O. Box 141, Thistle Hill, Cabot, VT 05647/802-426-3811
Kmount, P.O. Box 19422, Louisville, KY 40259/502-239-5447
Kneiper Custom Guns, Jim, 99 N. River Rd., Snowmass, CO 81654-9037/303-963-9880
Knife Importers, Inc., P.O. Box 1000, Manchaca, TX 78652/512-282-6860
Knight & Hale Game Calls, Box 468 Industrial Park, Cadiz, KY 42211/502-924-1755; FAX: 502-924-1763
Knight's Mfg. Co., 7750 9th St. SW, Vero Beach, FL 32968/407-562-5697; FAX: 407-569-2955
Knippel, Richard, 5924 Carnwood, Riverbank, CA 95367/209-869-1469
Knock on Wood Antiques, 355 Post Rd., Darien, CT 06820/203-655-9031
Knoell, Doug, 9737 McCardle Way, Santee, CA 92071
Kodiak Custom Bullets, 8261 Henry Circle, Anchorage, AK 99507/907-349-2282
Koevenig's Engraving Service, Box 55 Rabbit Gulch, Hill City, SD 57745
KOGOT, 410 College, Trinidad, CO 81082/719-846-9406
Kokolus, Michael M., 7005 Herber Rd., New Tripoli, PA 18066/215-298-3013
Kolpin Mfg., Inc., P.O. Box 107, 205 Depot St., Fox Lake, WI 53933/414-928-3118; FAX: 414-928-3687
Kongsberg (See U.S. importer—Merwin's Assoc.)
Kopec Enterprises, John (See Peacemaker Specialists)
Kopp, Terry K., Route 1, Box 224F, Lexington, MO 64067/816-259-2636
Korth, Robert-Bosch-Str. 4, P.O. Box 1320, 23909 Ratzeburg, GERMANY/0451-4991497; FAX: 0451-4993230 (U.S. importer—Interarms; Mandall Shooting Supplies, Inc.)
Korzinek Riflesmith, J., RD 2, Box 73D, Canton, PA 17724/717-673-8512
Koval Knives, 5819 Zarley St., Suite A, New Albany, OH 43054/614-855-0777; FAX: 614-855-0945
Kowa Optimed, Inc., 20001 S. Vermont Ave., Torrance, CA 90502/310-327-1913; FAX: 310-327-4177
Kramer Designs, 302 Lump Gulch Rd., Clancy, MT 59634/406-933-8658; FAX: 406-933-8658
Kramer Handgun Leather, P.O. Box 112154, Tacoma, WA 98411/206-564-6652; FAX: 206-564-1214
Krause Publications, Inc., 700 E. State St., Iola, WI 54990/715-445-2214; FAX: 715-445-4087
Krico/Kriegeskorte GmbH, A., Nurnbergerstrasse 6, D-90602 Pyrbaum GERMANY/0911-796092; FAX: 0911-796074 (U.S. importer—Mandall Shooting Supplies, Inc.)
Krieger Barrels, Inc., N114 W18697 Clinton Dr., Germantown, WI 53022/414-255-9593; FAX: 414-255-9586
Kriegeskorte GmbH., A. (See Krico/Kriegeskorte GmbH., A.)
Krieghoff Gun Co., H., Boschstrasse 22, D-89079 Ulm, GERMANY/731-401820; FAX: 731-4018270 (U.S. importer—Krieghoff International, Inc.)
Krieghoff International, Inc., 7528 Easton Rd., Ottsville, PA 18942/610-847-5173; FAX: 610-847-8691
Kris Mounts, 108 Lehigh St., Johnstown, PA 15905/814-539-9751
KSN Industries, Ltd. (See U.S. importer—J.O. Arms Inc.)
K-Sports Imports, Inc., 2755 Thompson Creek Rd., Pomona, CA 91767/909-392-2345; FAX: 909-392-2354
Kudlas, John M., 622 14th St. SE, Rochester, MN 55904/507-288-5579
Kulis Freeze Dry Taxidermy, 725 Broadway Ave., Bedford, OH 44146/216-232-8352; FAX: 216-232-7305
KVH Industries, Inc., 110 Enterprise Center, Middletown, RI 02842/401-847-3327; FAX: 401-849-0045
Kwik Mount Corp., P.O. Box 19422, Louisville, KY 40259/502-239-5447
Kwik-Site Co., 5555 Treadwell, Wayne, MI 48184/313-326-1500; FAX: 313-326-4120

L

L&R Lock Co., 1137 Pocalla Rd., Sumter, SC 29150/803-775-6127
L&S Technologies, Inc. (See Aimtech Mount Systems)
La Clinique du .45, 1432 Rougemont, Chambly, Quebec, J3L 2L8 CANADA/514-658-1144
Labanu, Inc., 2201-F Fifth Ave., Ronkonkoma, NY 11779/516-467-6197; FAX: 516-981-4112
LaBounty Precision Reboring, P.O. Box 186, 7968 Silver Lk. Rd., Maple Falls, WA 98266/306-599-2047
LaCrosse Footwear, Inc., P.O. Box 1328, La Crosse, WI 54602/608-782-3020, 800-323-2668; FAX: 800-658-9444
Lady Clays, P.O. Box 457, Shawnee Mission, KS 66201/913-268-8006
LaFrance Specialties, P.O. Box 178211, San Diego, CA 92177-8211/619-293-3373
Lair, Sam, 520 E. Beaver, Jenks, OK 74037/918-299-2391
Lake Center, P.O. Box 38, St. Charles, MO 63302/314-946-7500
Lakefield Arms Ltd., 248 Water St., P.O. Box 129, Lakefield, Ont. K0L 2H0, CANADA/705-652-6735, 705-652-8000; FAX: 705-652-8431
Lakewood Products, Inc., 275 June St., P.O. Box 230, Berlin, WI 54923/800-US-BUILT; FAX: 414-361-5058
Lampert, Ron, Rt. 1, Box 177, Guthrie, MN 56461/218-854-7345
Lamson & Goodnow Mfg. Co., 45 Conway St., Shelburne Falls, MA 03170/413-625-6331
Lanber Armas, S.A., Zubiaurre 5, Zaldibar, SPAIN 48250/34-4-6827702; FAX: 34-4-6827999
Lane Bullets, Inc., 1011 S. 10th St., Kansas City, KS 66105/913-621-6113, 800-444-7468

50th EDITION, 1996 **581**

DIRECTORY OF THE ARMS TRADE

Lane Publishing, P.O. Box 759, Hot Springs, AR 71902/501-525-7514; FAX: 501-525-7519
Langenberg Hat Co., P.O. Box 1860, Washington, MO 63090/800-428-1860; FAX: 314-239-3151
Lanphert, Paul, P.O. Box 1985, Wenatchee, WA 98807
Lansky Sharpeners & Crock Stick, P.O. Box 800, Buffalo, NY 14072/716-877-7511; FAX: 716-877-6955
LAP Systems Groups, N.A., P.O. Box 162, Marietta, GA 30061
Lapua Ltd., P.O. Box 5, Lapua, FINLAND SF-62101/64-310111; FAX: 64-4388951 (U.S. importers—Champion's Choice; Keng's Firearms Specialty, Inc.
L.A.R. Mfg., Inc., 4133 W. Farm Rd., West Jordan, UT 84088/801-280-3505; FAX: 801-280-1972
LaRocca Gun Works, Inc., 51 Union Place, Worcester, MA 01608/508-754-2887; FAX: 508-754-2887
Laser Devices, Inc., 2 Harris Ct. A-4, Monterey, CA 93940/408-373-0701; FAX: 408-373-0903
Laseraim, Inc. (See Emerging Technologies, Inc.)
Laseraim Arms, Inc., P.O. Box 3548, Little Rock, AR 72203/501-375-2227; FAX: 501-372-1445
LaserMax, 3495 Winton Place, Bldg. B, Rochester, NY 14623/716-272-5420; FAX: 716-272-5427
Lassen Community College, Gunsmithing Dept., P.O. Box 3000, Hwy. 139, Susanville, CA 96130/916-257-6181 ext. 109 or 200; FAX: 916-257-8964
Lathrop's, Inc., 5146 E. Pima, Tucson, AZ 85712/602-881-0226, 800-875-4867
Laughridge, William R. (See Cylinder & Slide, Inc.)
Laurel Mountain Forge, P.O. Box 224, Romeo, MI 48065/810-749-5742
Laurona Armas Eibar, S.A.L., Avenida de Otaola 25, P.O. Box 260, 20600 Eibar, SPAIN/34-43-700600; FAX: 34-43-700616 (U.S. importers—Continental Imports & Distribution; Galaxy Imports Ltd., Inc.)
Law Concealment Systems, Inc., P.O. Box 3952, Wilmington, NC 28406/919-791-6656, 800-373-0116 orders
Lawrence Brand Shot (See Precision Reloading, Inc.)
Lawrence Leather Co., P.O. Box 1479, Lillington, NC 27546/910-893-2071; FAX: 910-893-4742
Lawson, John G. (See Sight Shop, The)
Lawson Co., Harry, 3328 N. Richey Blvd., Tucson, AZ 85716/520-326-1117
LBT, HCR 62, Box 145, Moyie Springs, ID 83845/208-267-3588
Lea Mfg. Co., 237 E. Aurora St., Waterbury, CT 06720/203-753-5116
Lead Bullets Technology (See LBT)
Leather Arsenal, 27549 Middleton Rd., Middleton, ID 83644/208-585-6212
Leatherman Tool Group, Inc., 12106 NE Ainsworth Cir., P.O. Box 20595, Portland, OR 97220/503-253-7826; FAX: 503-253-7830
Lebeau-Courally, Rue St. Gilles, 386, 4000 Liege, BELGIUM/041 52 48 43; FAX: 041 52 20 08 (U.S. importer—New England Arms Co.)
Leckie Professional Gunsmithing, 546 Quarry Rd., Ottsville, PA 18942/215-847-8594
Lectro Science, Inc., 6410 W. Ridge Rd., Erie, PA 16506/814-833-6487; FAX: 814-833-0447
Ledbetter Airguns, Riley, 1804 E. Sprague St., Winston Salem, NC 27107-3521/919-784-0676
Leding Loader, RR 1, Box 645, Ozark, AR 72949
Lee Co., T.K., One Independence Plaza, Suite 520, Birmingham, AL 35209/205-913-5222
Lee Precision, Inc., 4275 Hwy. U, Hartford, WI 53027/414-673-3075
Lee Supplies, Mark, 9901 France Ct., Lakeville, MN 55044/612-461-2114
Lee's Red Ramps, 4 Kristine Ln., Silver City, NM 88061/505-538-8529
LeFever Arms Co., Inc., 6234 Stokes, Lee Center Rd., Lee Center, NY 13363/315-337-6722; FAX: 315-337-1543
Legend Products Corp., 1555 E. Flamingo Rd., Suite 404, Las Vegas, NV 89119/702-228-1808, 702-796-5778; FAX: 702-228-7484
Leibowitz, Leonard, 1205 Murrayhill Ave., Pittsburgh, PA 15217/412-361-5455
Leica USA, Inc., 156 Ludlow Ave., Northvale, NJ 07647/201-767-7500; FAX: 201-767-8666
LEM Gun Specialties, Inc., P.O. Box 2855, Peachtree City, GA 30269-2024
Lem Sports, Inc., P.O. Box 2107, Aurora, IL 60506/815-286-7421, 800-688-8801 (orders only)
Lenahan Family Enterprise, P.O. Box 46, Manitou Springs, CO 80829
Lethal Force Institute (See Police Bookshelf)
Letschnig, Franz, RR 1, Martintown, Ont. K0C 1S0, CANADA/613-528-4843
Lett Custom Grips, 672 Currier Rd., Hopkinton, NH 03229
Leupold & Stevens, Inc., P.O. Box 688, Beaverton, OR 97075/503-646-9171; FAX: 503-526-1455
Lever Arms Service Ltd., 2131 Burrard St., Vancouver, B.C. V6J 3H7 CANADA/604-736-0004; FAX: 604-738-3503
Lewis, Ed, P.O. Box 875, Pico Rivera, CA 90660
Liberty Antique Gunworks, 19 Key St., P.O. Box 183, Eastport, ME 04631/207-853-4116
Liberty Metals, 2233 East 16th St., Los Angeles, CA 90021/213-581-9171; FAX: 213-581-9351
Liberty Safe, 1060 N. Spring Creek Pl., Springville, UT 84663/800-247-5625; FAX: 801-489-6409
Liberty Shooting Supplies, P.O. Box 357, Hillsboro, OR 97123/503-640-5518
Liberty Trouser Co., 3500 6 Ave S., Birmingham, AL 35222-2406/205-251-9143
Lightfield Ammunition Group, The Slug Group, P.O. Box 376, New Paris, PA 15554/814-839-4517; FAX: 814-839-2601
Lightforce U.S.A., Inc., P.O. Box 488, Vaughan, WA 98394/206-876-3225; FAX: 206-876-3249
Lilja Precision Rifle Barrels, P.O. Box 372, Plains, MT 59859/406-826-3084; FAX: 406-826-3083
Lincoln, Dean, Box 1886, Farmington, NM 87401
Lind Custom Guns, Al, 7821 76th Ave. SW, Tacoma, WA 98498/206-584-6361
Linder Solingen Knives, 4401 Sentry Dr., Tucker, GA 30084/404-939-6915; FAX: 404-939-6738
Lindsay, Steve, RR 2 Cedar Hills, Kearney, NE 68847/308-236-7885
Lindsley Arms Cartridge Co., P.O. Box 757, 20 College Hill Rd., Henniker, NH 03242/603-428-3127
Linebaugh Custom Sixguns, Route 2, Box 100, Maryville, MO 64468/816-562-3031
List Precision Engineering, Unit 1, Ingley Works, 13 River Road, Barking, Essex 1911 0HE/011-081-594-1686

Lite Tek International, 133-30 32nd Ave., Flushing, NY 11354/718-463-0650; FAX: 718-762-0890
Lithi Bee Bullet Lube, 1885 Dyson St., Muskegon, MI 49442/616-726-3400
"Little John's" Antique Arms, 1740 W. Laveta, Orange, CA 92668
Little Trees Ramble (See Scott Pilkington, Little Trees Ramble)
Littler Sales Co., 20815 W. Chicago, Detroit, MI 48228/313-273-6888; FAX: 313-273-1099
Littleton, J.F., 275 Pinedale Ave., Oroville, CA 95966/916-533-6084
Ljutic Industries, Inc., 732 N. 16th Ave., Suite 22, Yakima, WA 98902/509-248-0476; FAX: 509-576-8233
L.L. Bean, 386 Main St., Freeport, ME 04032/207-865-3111
Llama Gabilondo Y Cia, Apartado 290, E-01080, Victoria, SPAIN (U.S. importer—SGS Importers International, Inc.)
Load From A Disk, 9826 Sagedale, Houston, TX 77089/713-484-0935
Loadmaster, P.O. Box 1209, Warminster, Wilts. BA12 9XJ ENGLAND/01044 1985 218544; FAX: 01044 1985 214111
Loch Leven Industries, P.O. Box 2751, Santa Rosa, CA 95405/707-573-8735; FAX: 707-573-0369
Lock's Philadelphia Gun Exchange, 6700 Rowland Ave., Philadelphia, PA 19149/215-332-6225; FAX: 215-332-4800
Lodewick, Walter H., 2816 NE Halsey St., Portland, OR 97232/503-284-2554
Lofland, James W., 2275 Larkin Rd., Boothwyn, PA 19061/610-485-0391
Log Cabin Sport Shop, 8010 Lafayette Rd., Lodi, OH 44254/216-948-1082
Logan, Harry M., Box 745, Honokaa, HI 96727/808-776-1644
Lohman Mfg. Co., Inc., 4500 Doniphan Dr., P.O. Box 220, Neosho, MO 64850/417-451-4438; FAX: 417-451-2576
Lomont Precision Bullets, 4236 W. 700 South, Poneto, IN 46781/219-694-6792; FAX: 219-694-6797
London Guns Ltd., Box 3750, Santa Barbara, CA 93130/805-683-4141; FAX: 805-683-1712
Lone Star Gunleather, 1301 Brushy Bend Dr., Round Rock, TX 78681/512-255-1805
Lone Wolf Adventure Gear (See Fiberpro/California)
Long, George F., 1500 Rogue River Hwy., Ste. F, Grants Pass, OR 97527/503-476-7552
Lorcin Engineering Co., Inc., 10427 San Sevaine Way, Ste. A, Mira Loma, CA 91752/909-360-1406; FAX: 909-360-0623
Lortone, Inc., 2856 NW Market St., Seattle, WA 98107/206-789-3100
Lovestrand, Erik, 1211 Yorkshire St., Prattville, AL 36067-6821
Loweth, Richard, 29 Hedgegrow Lane, Kirby Muxloe, Leics. LE9 9BN ENGLAND
L.P.A. Snc, Via Alfieri 26, Gardone V.T., Brescia, ITALY 25063/30-891-14-81; FAX: 30-891-09-51
LPS Laboratories, Inc., 4647 Hugh Howell Rd., P.O. Box 3050, Tucker, GA 30084/404-934-7800
Lucas, Edward E., 32 Garfield Ave., East Brunswick, NJ 08816/201-251-5526
Lucas, Mike, 1631 Jessamine Rd., Lexington, SC 29073/803-356-0282
Luch Metal Merchants, Barbara, 48861 West Rd., Wixon, MI 48393/800-876-5337
Lutz Engraving, Ron, E. 1998 Smokey Valley Rd., Scandinavia, WI 54977/715-467-2674
Lyman Instant Targets, Inc. (See Lyman Products Corp.)
Lyman Products Corp., Rt. 147, Middlefield, CT 06455/203-349-3421, 800-22-LYMAN; FAX: 203-349-3586
Lynn's Custom Gunstocks, RR 1, Brandon, IA 52210/319-474-2453

M

M&D Munitions Ltd., 127 Verdi St., Farmingdale, NY 11735/800-878-2788, 516-752-1038; FAX: 516-752-1905
M&M Engineering (See Hollywood Engineering)
M&N Bullet Lube, P.O. Box 495, 151 NE Jefferson St., Madras, OR 97741/503-255-3750
MA Systems, P.O. Box 1143, Chouteau, OK 74337/918-479-6378
Mac's .45 Shop, P.O. Box 2028, Seal Beach, CA 90740/310-438-5046
Mac-1 Distributors, 13974 Van Ness Ave., Gardena, CA 90249/310-327-3582
Macbean, Stan, 754 North 1200 West, Orem, UT 84057/801-224-6446
Madis, David, 2453 West Five Mile Pkwy., Dallas, TX 75233/214-330-7168
Madis, George, P.O. Box 545, Brownsboro, TX 75756
MAG Instrument, Inc., 1635 S. Sacramento Ave., Ontario, CA 91761/909-947-1006; FAX: 909-947-3116
Mag-Na-Port International, Inc., 41302 Executive Dr., Harrison Twp., MI 48045-1306/810-469-6727; FAX: 810-469-0425
Mag-Pack Corp., P.O. Box 846, Chesterland, OH 44026
Magma Engineering Co., P.O. Box 161, 20955 E. Ocotillo Rd., Queen Creek, AZ 85242/602-987-9008; FAX: 602-987-0148
Magnolia Sports, Inc., 211 W. Main, Magnolia, AR 71753/501-234-8410, 800-530-7816; FAX: 501-234-8117
Magnum Grips, Box 801G, Payson, AZ 85547
Magnum Power Products, Inc., P.O. Box 17768, Fountain Hills, AZ 85268
Magnum Research, Inc., 7110 University Ave. NE, Minneapolis, MN 55432/612-574-1868; FAX: 612-574-0109
Magnus Bullets, P.O.Box 239, Toney, AL 35773/205-828-5089; FAX: 205-828-7756
MagSafe Ammo Co., 2725 Friendly Grove Rd NE, Olympia, WA 98506/206-357-6383
MAGTECH Recreational Products, Inc., 4737 College Park, Ste. 101, San Antonio, TX 78249/210-493-4427; FAX: 210-493-9534
Mahony, Philip Bruce, 67 White Hollow Rd., Lime Rock, CT 06039-2418/203-435-9341
Maine Custom Bullets, RFD 1, Box 1755, Brooks, ME 04921
Mains Enterprises, Inc., 3111 S. Valley View Blvd., Suite B120, Las Vegas, NV 89102-7790/702-876-6278; FAX: 702-876-1269
Maionchi-L.M.I., Via Di Coselli-Zona Industriale Di Guamo, Lucca, ITALY 55060/011 39-583 94291
Makinson, Nicholas, RR 3, Komoka, Ont. N0L 1R0 CANADA/519-471-5462
Malcolm Enterprises, 1023 E. Prien Lake Rd., Lake Charles, LA 70601
Mallardtone Game Calls, 2901 16th St., Moline, IL 61265/309-762-8089
M.A.M. Products, Inc., 153 B Cross Slope Court, Englishtown, NJ 07726/908-536-3604
Mandall Shooting Supplies, Inc., 3616 N. Scottsdale Rd., Scottsdale, AZ 85252/602-945-2553; FAX: 602-949-0734
Manley Shooting Supplies, Lowell, 3684 Pine St., Deckerville, MI 48427/313-376-3665
Manufacture D'Armes Des Pyrenees Francaises (See Unique/M.A.P.F.)

MANUFACTURERS' DIRECTORY

Mar Knives, Inc., Al, 5755 SW Jean Rd., Suite 101, Lake Oswego, OR 97035/503-635-9229; FAX: 503-223-0467
Marathon Rubber Prods. Co., Inc., 510 Sherman St., Wausau, WI 54401/715-845-6255
Marble Arms (See CRL, Inc.)
Marchmon Bullets, 8191 Woodland Shore Dr., Brighton, MI 48116
Marek, George, 55 Arnold St., Westfield, MA 01085/413-562-5673
Marent, Rudolf, 9711 Tiltree St., Houston, TX 77075/713-946-7028
Markell, Inc., 422 Larkfield Center 235, Santa Rosa, CA 95403/707-573-0792; FAX: 707-573-9867
Marksman Products, 5482 Argosy Dr., Huntington Beach, CA 92649/714-898-7535, 800-822-8005; FAX: 714-372-3041
Marlin Firearms Co., 100 Kenna Dr., New Haven, CT 06473/203-239-5621; FAX: 203-234-7991
MarMik Inc., 2116 S. Woodland Ave., Michigan City, IN 46361-7508/219-872-7231
Marocchi F.lli S.p.A., Via Galileo Galilei, I-25068 Zanano di Sarezzo, ITALY (U.S. importers—Precision Sales International, Inc.; Sile Distributors)
Marple & Associates, Dick, 21 Dartmouth St., Hooksett, NH 03106/603-627-1837; FAX: 603-641-4837
Marquart Precision Co., Inc., Rear 136 Grove Ave., Box 1740, Prescott, AZ 86302/602-445-5646
Marsh, Johnny, 1007 Drummond Dr., Nashville, TN 37211/615-833-3259
Marsh, Mike, Croft Cottage, Main St., Elton, Derbyshire DE4 2BY, ENGLAND/0629 650 669
Marshall Enterprises, 792 Canyon Rd., Redwood City, CA 94062
Martin Bookseller, J., P.O. Drawer AP, Beckley, WV 25802/304-255-4073; FAX: 304-255-4077
Martin's Gun Shop, 937 S. Sheridan Blvd., Lakewood, CO 80226/303-922-2184
Martz, John V., 8060 Lakeview Lane, Lincoln, CA 95648/916-645-2250
Marvel, Alan, 3922 Madonna Rd., Jarretsville, MD 21084/301-557-6545
Maryland Paintball Supply, 8507 Harford Rd., Parkville, MD 21234/410-882-5607
Masen Co., Inc., John, P.O. Box 5050, Suite 165, Lewisville, TX 75057/817-430-8732; FAX: 817-430-1715
Masker, Seely, 54 Woodshire S., Getzville, NY 14068/716-689-8894
MAST Technology, 4350 S. Arville, Suite 3, Las Vegas, NV 89103/702-362-5043; FAX: 702-362-9554
Master Class Bullets, 4209-D West 6th, Eugene, OR 97402/503-687-1263, 800-883-1263
Master Engravers, Inc. (See Hendricks, Frank E.)
Master Lock Co., 2600 N. 32nd St., Milwaukee, WI 53245/414-444-2800
Master Products, Inc. (See Gun-Alert/Master Products, Inc.)
Match Prep, P.O. Box 155, Tehachapi, CA 93581/805-822-5383
Matco, Inc., 1003-2nd St., N. Manchester, IN 46962/219-982-8282
Mathews & Son, Inc., George E., 10224 S. Paramount Blvd., Downey, CA 90241/310-862-6719; FAX: 310-862-6719
Matthews Cutlery, 4401 Sentry Dr., Tucker, GA 30084/404-939-6915; FAX: 404-939-6738
Mauser Werke Oberndorf Waffensysteme GmbH, Postfach 1349, 78722 Oberndorf/N. GERMANY (U.S. importer—Gibbs Rifle Co., Inc.)
Maverick Arms, Inc., 7 Grasso Ave., P.O. Box 497, North Haven, CT 06473/203-230-5300; FAX: 203-230-5420
Maxi-Mount, P.O. Box 291, Willoughby Hills, OH 44094-0291/216-585-1329
Maximum Security Corp., 32841 Calle Perfecto, San Juan Capistrano, CA 92675/714-493-3684; FAX: 714-496-7733
Mayville Engineering Co. (See MEC, Inc.)
Mazur Restoration, Pete, 13083 Drummer Way, Grass Valley, CA 95949/916-268-2412
MCA Sports, P.O. Box 8868, Palm Springs, CA 92263/619-770-2005
McBros Rifle Co., P.O. Box 86549, Phoenix, AZ 85080/602-780-2115; FAX: 602-581-3825
McCament, Jay, 1730-134th St. Ct. S., Tacoma, WA 98444/206-531-8832
McCann's Machine & Gun Shop, P.O. Box 641, Spanaway, WA 98387/206-537-6919; FAX: 206-537-6993
McCann's Muzzle-Gun Works, 14 Walton Dr., New Hope, PA 18938/215-862-2728
McCluskey Precision Rifles, 10502 14th Ave. NW, Seattle, WA 98177/206-781-2776
McCombs, Leo, 1862 White Cemetery Rd., Patriot, OH 45658/614-256-1714
McCormick Corp., Chip, 1825 Fortview Rd., Ste. 115, Austin, TX 78704/800-328-CHIP, 512-462-0004; FAX: 512-462-0009
McCullough, Ken (See Ken's Rifle Blanks)
McDonald, Dennis, 8359 Brady St., Peosta, IA 52068/319-556-7940
McFarland, Stan, 2221 Idella Ct., Grand Junction, CO 81505/303-243-4704
McGowen Rifle Barrels, 5961 Spruce Lane, St. Anne, IL 60964/815-937-9816; FAX: 815-937-4024
McGuire, Bill, 1600 N. Eastmont Ave., East Wenatchee, WA 98802/509-884-6021
McKee Publications, 121 Eatons Neck Rd., Northport, NY 11768/516-575-8850
McKenzie, Lynton, 6940 N. Alvernon Way, Tucson, AZ 85718/520-299-5090
McKillen & Heyer, Inc., 35535 Euclid Ave. Suite 11, Willoughby, OH 44094/216-942-2044
McKinney, R.P. (See Schuetzen Gun Service)
McMillan Fiberglass Stocks, Inc., 21421 N. 14th Ave., Phoenix, AZ 85027/602-582-9635; FAX: 602-581-3825
McMillan Optical Gunsight Co., 28638 N. 42nd St., Cave Creek, AZ 85331/602-585-7868; FAX: 602-585-7872
McMillan Rifle Barrels, P.O. Box 3427, Bryan, TX 77805/409-690-3456; FAX: 409-690-0156
McMurdo, Lynn (See Specialty Gunsmithing)
MCRW Associates Shooting Supplies, R.R. 1 Box 1425, Sweet Valley, PA 18656/717-864-3967; FAX: 717-864-2669
MCS, Inc., 34 Delmar Dr., Brookfield, CT 06804/203-775-1013; FAX: 203-775-9462
McWelco Products, 6730 Santa Fe Ave., Hesperia, CA 92345/619-244-8876; FAX: 619-244-9398
MDS, P.O. Box 1441, Brandon, FL 33509-1441/813-653-1180; FAX: 813-684-5953
Meadow Industries, P.O. Box 754, Locust Grove, VA 22508/703-972-2175; FAX: 703-972-2143
Measurement Group, Inc., Box 27777, Raleigh, NC 27611
MEC, Inc., 715 South St., Mayville, WI 53050/414-387-4500; FAX: 414-387-5802
MEC-Gar S.R.L., Via Madonnina 64, Gardone V.T., Brescia, ITALY 25063/39-30-8912687; FAX: 39-30-8910065 (U.S. importer—MEC-Gar U.S.A., Inc.)
MEC-Gar U.S.A., Inc., Box 112, 500B Monroe Turnpike, Monroe, CT 06468/203-635-8662; FAX: 203-635-8662

Meier Works, P.O. Box 423, Tijeras, NM 87059/505-281-3783
Mele, Frank, 201 S. Wellow Ave., Cookeville, TN 38501/615-526-4860
Melton Shirt Co., Inc., 56 Harvester Ave., Batavia, NY 14020/716-343-8750; FAX: 716-343-6887
Menck, Thomas W., 5703 S. 77th St., Ralston, NE 68127-4201
Mendez, John A., P.O. Box 620984, Orlando, FL 32862/407-282-2178
Men-Metallwerk Elisenhuette, GmbH, P.O. Box 1263, D-56372 Nassau/Lahn, GERMANY/2604-7819
Meprolight (See Hesco-Meprolight)
Mercer Custom Stocks, R.M., 216 S. Whitewater Ave., Jefferson, WI 53549/414-674-5130
Merit Corp., Box 9044, Schenectady, NY 12309/518-346-1420
Merkel Freres, Strasse 7 October, 10, Suhl, GERMANY (U.S. importer—GSI, Inc.)
Merkuria Ltd., Argentinska 38, 17005 Praha 7, CZECH REPUBLIC/422-875117; FAX: 422-809152
Merwin's Assoc., P.O. Box 252, Fairfield, CT 06430/203-259-0938; FAX: 203-259-2566
Metal Products Co. (See MPC)
Metalife Industries, Box 53 Mong Ave., Reno, PA 16343/814-436-7747; FAX: 814-676-5662
Metaloy Inc., Rt. 5, Box 595, Berryville, AR 72616/501-545-3611
Michael's Antiques, Box 591, Waldoboro, ME 04572
Michaels of Oregon Co., P.O. Box 13010, Portland, OR 97213/503-255-6890; FAX: 503-255-0746
Micro Sight Co., 242 Harbor Blvd., Belmont, CA 94002/415-591-0769; FAX: 415-591-7531
Microfusion Alfa S.A., Paseo San Andres N8, P.O. Box 271, Eibar, SPAIN 20600/34-43-11-89-16; FAX: 34-43-11-40-38
Micro-Lube, Rt. 2, P.O. Box 201, Deming, NM 88030/505-546-9116
Mid-America Recreation, Inc., 1328 5th Ave., Moline, IL 52807/309-764-5089; FAX: 309-764-2722
Middlebrooks Custom Shop, 7366 Colonial Trail East, Surry, VA 23883/804-357-0881; FAX: 804-365-0442
Midway Arms, Inc., 5875 W. Van Horn Tavern Rd., Columbia, MO 65203/800-243-3220, 314-445-6363; FAX: 314-446-1018
Midwest Gun Sport, 1108 Herbert Dr., Zebulon, NC 27597/919-269-5570
Midwest Sport Distributors, Box 129, Fayette, MO 65248
Military Armament Corp., P.O. Box 120, Mt. Zion Rd., Lingleville, TX 76461/817-965-3253
Miller Arms, Inc., P.O. Box 260 Purl St., St. Onge, SD 57779/605-642-5160; FAX: 605-642-5160
Miller Custom, 210 E. Julia, Clinton, IL 61727/217-935-9362
Miller Co., David, 3131 E. Greenlee Rd., Tucson, AZ 85716/602-326-3117
Miller Engineering, R&D Engineering & Manufacturing, P.O. Box 6342, Virginia Beach, VA 23456/804-468-1402
Miller Enterprises, Inc., R.P., 1557 E. Main St., P.O. Box 234, Brownsburg, IN 46112/317-852-8187
Miller Single Trigger Mfg. Co., Rt. 209 Box 1275, Millersburg, PA 17061/717-692-3704
Millett Sights, 16131 Gothard St., Huntington Beach, CA 92647/714-842-5575, 800-645-5388; FAX: 714-843-5707
Mills Jr., Hugh B., 3615 Canterbury Rd., New Bern, NC 28560/919-637-4631
Milstor Corp., 80-975 E. Valley Pkwy. C-7, Indio, CA 92201/619-775-9998; FAX: 619-772-4990
Miniature Machine Co. (See MMC)
Minute Man High Tech Industries, 3005B 6th Ave., Tacoma, WA 98406/800-233-2734
Mirador Optical Corp., P.O. Box 11614, Marina Del Rey, CA 90295-7614/310-821-5587; FAX: 310-305-0386
Miroku, B.C./Daly, Charles (See U.S. importer—Bell's Legendary Country Wear; U.S. distributor—Outdoor Sports Headquarters, Inc.)
Mitchell Arms, Inc., 3400-I W. MacArthur Blvd., Santa Ana, CA 92704/714-957-5711; FAX: 714-957-5732
Mitchell Bullets, R.F., 430 Walnut St., Westernport, MD 21562
Mitchell Leatherworks, 1220 Black Brook Rd., Dunbarton, NH 03045/603-774-6283
Mitchell's Accuracy Shop, 68 Greenridge Dr., Stafford, VA 22554/703-659-0165
MI-TE Bullets, R.R. 1 Box 230, Ellsworth, KS 67439/913-472-4575
Mittermeier, Inc., Frank, P.O. Box 2G, 3577 E. Tremont Ave., Bronx, NY 10465/718-828-3843
Mixson Corp., 7435 W. 19th Ct., Hialeah, FL 33014/305-821-5190, 800-327-0078; FAX: 305-558-9318
MJK Gunsmithing, Inc., 417 N. Huber Ct., E. Wenatchee, WA 98802/509-884-7683
MJM Mfg., 3283 Rocky Water Ln. Suite B, San Jose, CA 95148/408-270-4207
MKL Service Co., 610 S. Troy St., P.O. Box D, Royal Oak, MI 48068/810-548-5453
MKS Supply, Inc., 174 S. Mulberry St., Mansfield, OH 44902/419-522-8330; FAX: 513-522-8330
MMC, 606 Grace Ave., Ft. Worth, TX 76111/817-831-0837
MMP, Rt. 6, Box 384, Harrison, AR 72601/501-741-5019; FAX: 501-741-3104
M.O.A. Corp., 2451 Old Camden Pike, Eaton, OH 45320/513-456-3669
Modern Gun Repair School, 2538 N. 8th St., P.O. Box 5338, Dept. GNX96, Phoenix, AZ 85010/602-990-8346
Modern MuzzleLoading, Inc., 234 Airport Rd., P.O. Box 130, Centerville, IA 52544/515-856-2626; FAX: 515-856-2628
Moeller, Steve, 1213 4th St., Fulton, IL 61252/815-589-2300
Molin Industries, Tru-Nord Division, P.O. Box 365, 204 North 9th St., Brainerd, MN 56401/218-829-2870
Mo's Competitor Supplies (See MCS, Inc.)
MoLoc Bullets, P.O. Box 2810, Turlock, CA 95381-2810/209-632-1644
Monell Custom Guns, 228 Red Mills Rd., Pine Bush, NY 12566/914-744-3021
Moneymaker Guncraft Corp., 1420 Military Ave., Omaha, NE 68131/402-556-0226
Montana Armory, Inc., 100 Centennial Dr., Big Timber, MT 59011/406-932-4353
Montana Outfitters, Lewis E. Yearout, 308 Riverview Dr. E., Great Falls, MT 59404/406-761-0859
Montana Precision Swaging, P.O. Box 4746, Butte, MT 59702/406-782-7502
Montana Vintage Arms, 2354 Bear Canyon Rd., Bozeman, MT 59715
Monte Kristo Pistol Grip Co., P.O. Box 85, Whiskeytown, CA 96095/916-623-4019
Montgomery Community College, P.O. Box 787, Troy, NC 27371/919-572-3691
Moore & Co., Wm. Larkin, 31360 Via Colinas, Suite 109, Westlake Village, CA 91361/818-889-1986
Moreton/Fordyce Enterprises, P.O. Box 940, Saylorsburg, PA 18353/717-992-5742; FAX: 717-992-8775

DIRECTORY OF THE ARMS TRADE

Morini (See U.S. importers—Mandall Shooting Shpplies, Inc.; Nygord Precision Products)
Morrison Custom Rifles, J.W., 4015 W. Sharon, Phoenix, AZ 85029/602-978-3754
Morrow, Bud, 11 Hillside Lane, Sheridan, WY 82801-9729/307-674-8360
Morton Booth Co., P.O. Box 123, Joplin, MO 64802/417-673-1962; FAX: 417-673-3642
Moschetti, Mitchell R., P.O. Box 27065, Denver, CO 80227/303-733-9593
Moss Double Tone, Inc., P.O. Box 1112, 2101 S. Kentucky, Sedalia, MO 65301/816-827-0827
Mossberg & Sons, Inc., O.F, 7 Grasso Ave., North Haven, CT 06473/203-230-5361; FAX: 203-230-5420
Mountain Bear Rifle Works, Inc., 100 B Ruritan Rd., Sterling, VA 20164/703-430-0420; FAX: 703-430-7068
Mountain Hollow Game Calls, Box 121, Cascade, MD 21719/301-241-3282
Mountain South, P.O. Box 381, Barnwell, SC 29812/FAX: 803-259-3227
Mountain State Muzzleloading Supplies, Box 154-1, Rt. 2, Williamstown, WV 26187/304-375-7842; FAX: 304-375-3737
Mountain States Engraving, Kenneth W. Warren, P.O. Box 2842, Wenatchee, WA 98802/509-663-6123
Mountain View Sports, Inc., Box 188, Troy, NH 03465/603-357-9690; FAX: 603-357-9691
Mowrey Gun Works, P.O. Box 246, Waldron, IN 46182/317-525-6181; FAX: 317-525-6181
Mowrey's Guns & Gunsmithing, RR1, Box 82, Canajoharie, NY 13317/518-673-3483
MPC, P.O. Box 450, McMinnville, TN 37110-0450
MPI Fiberglass Stocks, 5655 NW St. Helens Rd., Portland, OR 97210/503-226-1215; FAX: 503-226-2661
MSC Industrial Supply Co., 151 Sunnyside Blvd., Plainview, NY 11803-9915/516-349-0330
MSR Targets, P.O. Box 1042, West Covina, CA 91793/818-331-7840
Mt. Alto Outdoor Products, Rt. 735, Howardsville, VA 24562
Mt. Baldy Bullet Co., 12981 Old Hill City Rd., Keystone, SD 57751-6623/605-666-4725
MTM Molded Products Co., Inc., 3370 Obco Ct., Dayton, OH 45414/513-890-7461; FAX: 513-890-1747
Mulhern, Rick, Rt. 5, Box 152, Rayville, LA 71269/318-728-2688
Mullins Ammo, Rt. 2, Box 304K, Clintwood, VA 24228/703-926-6772
Mullis Guncraft, 3523 Lawyers Road E., Monroe, NC 28110/704-283-6683
Multi-Caliber Adapters (See MCA Sports)
Multipax, 8086 S. Yale, Suite 286, Tulsa, OK 74136/918-496-1999; FAX: 918-492-7465
Multiplex International, 26 S. Main St., Concord, NH 03301/FAX: 603-796-2223
Multipropulseurs, La Bertrandiere, 42580 L'Etrat, FRANCE/77 74 01 30; FAX: 77 93 19 34
Multi-Scale Charge Ltd., 3269 Niagara Falls Blvd., N. Tonawanda, NY 14120/905-566-1255; FAX: 905-276-6295
Mundy, Thomas A., 69 Robbins Road, Somerville, NJ 08876/201-722-2199
Munsch Gunsmithing, Tommy, Rt. 2, P.O. Box 248, Little Falls, MN 56345/612-632-6695
Murmur Corp., 2823 N. Westmoreland Ave., Dallas, TX 75222/214-630-5400
Murphy Co., Inc., R., 13 Groton-Harvard Rd., P.O. Box 376, Ayer, MA 01432/617-772-3481
Murray State College, 100 Faculty Dr., Tishomingo, OK 73460/405-371-2371 ext. 238, 800-342-0698
Muscle Products Corp., 112 Fennell Dr., Butler, PA 16001/800-227-7049, 412-283-0567; FAX: 412-283-8310
Museum of Historical Arms Inc., 2750 Coral Way, Suite 204, Miami, FL 33145/305-444-9199
Mushroom Express Bullet Co., 601 W. 6th St., Greenfield, IN 46140/317-462-6362
Mustra's Custom Guns, Inc., Carl, 1002 Pennsylvania Ave., Palm Harbor, FL 34683/813-785-1403
Muzzleload Magnum Products (See MMP)
Muzzleloaders Etcetera, Inc., 9901 Lyndale Ave. S., Bloomington, MN 55420/612-884-1161
MWG Co., P.O. Box 971202, Miami, FL 33197/800-428-9394, 305-253-8393; FAX: 305-232-1247

N

N&J Sales, Lime Kiln Rd., Northford, CT 06472/203-484-0247
Nagel's Bullets, 9 Wilburn, Baytown, TX 77520
Nastoff's 45 Shop, Inc., Steve, 12288 Mahoning Ave., P.O. Box 446, North Jackson, OH 44451/216-538-2977
National Bullet Co., 1585 E. 361 St., Eastlake, OH 44095/216-951-1854; FAX: 216-951-7761
National Security Safe Co., Inc., P.O. Box 39, 620 S. 380 E., American Fork, UT 84003/801-756-7706, 800-544-3829; FAX: 801-756-8043
National Survival Game, Inc., P.O. Box 1439, New London, NH 03257/603-735-6165; FAX: 603-735-5154
National Target Co., 4690 Wyaconda Rd., Rockville, MD 20852/800-827-7060, 301-770-7060; FAX: 301-770-7892
Nationwide Airgun Repairs (See Airgun Repair Centre)
Nationwide Sports Distributors, Inc., 70 James Way, Southampton, PA 18966/215-322-2050, 800-355-3006; FAX: 702-358-2093
Naval Ordnance Works, Rt. 2, Box 919, Sheperdstown, WV 25443/304-876-0998
Navy Arms Co., 689 Bergen Blvd., Ridgefield, NJ 07657/201-945-2500; FAX: 201-945-6859
N.B.B., Inc., 24 Elliot Rd., Sterling, MA 01564/508-422-7538, 800-942-9444
N.C. Ordnance Co., P.O. Box 3254, Wilson, NC 27895/919-237-2440; FAX: 919-243-0927
NCP Products, Inc., 721 Maryland Ave. SW, Canton, OH 44710
Necessary Concepts, Inc., P.O. Box 571, Deer Park, NY 11729/516-667-8509; 800-671-8881
NECO, 1316-67th St., Emeryville, CA 94608/510-450-0420
Necromancer Industries, Inc., 14 Communications Way, West Newton, PA 15089/412-872-8722
NEI Handtools, Inc., 51583 Columbia River Hwy., Scappoose, OR 97056/503-543-6776; FAX: 503-543-6799
Nelson, Gary K., 975 Terrace Dr., Oakdale, CA 95361/209-847-4590
Nelson, Stephen, 7365 NW Spring Creek Dr., Corvallis, OR 97330/503-745-5232
Nelson Combat Leather, Bruce, P.O. Box 8691 CRB, Tucson, AZ 85738
Nelson/Weather-Rite, Inc., 14760 Santa Fe Trail Dr., Lenexa, KS 66215/913-492-3200; FAX: 913-492-8749
Nesci Enterprises, Inc., P.O. Box 119, Summit St., East Hampton, CT 06424/203-267-2588
Nesika Bay Precision, 22239 Big Valley Rd., Poulsbo, WA 98370/206-697-3830
Nettestad Gun Works, RR 1, Box 160, Pelican Rapids, MN 56572/218-863-4301
Neumann GmbH, Am Galgenberg 6, 90575 Langenzenn, GERMANY/09101/8258; FAX: 09101/6356
Neutralizer Police Munitions, 5029 Middle Rd., Horseheads, NY 14845-9568/607-739-8362; FAX: 607-594-3900
Nevada Cartridge Co., 44 Montgomery St., Suite 500, San Francisco, CA 94104/415-925-9394; FAX: 415-925-9396
Nevada Pistol Academy Inc., 4610 Blue Diamond Rd., Las Vegas, NV 89139/702-897-1100
New Advantage Arms Corp., 2843 N. Alvernon Way, Tucson, AZ 85712/602-881-7444; FAX: 602-323-0949
New Democracy, Inc., 751 W. Lamar Blvd., Suite 102, Arlington, TX 76012-2010
New England Ammunition Co., 1771 Post Rd. East, Suite 223, Westport, CT 06880/203-254-8048
New England Arms Co., Box 278, Lawrence Lane, Kittery Point, ME 03905/207-439-0593; FAX: 207-439-6726
New England Custom Gun Service, Brook Rd., RR2, Box 122W, W. Lebanon, NH 03784/603-469-3450; FAX: 603-469-3471
New England Firearms, 60 Industrial Rowe, Gardner, MA 01440/508-632-9393; FAX: 508-632-2300
New Historians Productions, The, 131 Oak St., Royal Oak, MI 48067/313-544-7544
New Orleans Arms Co., 5001 Treasure St., New Orleans, LA 70186/504-944-3371
New Orleans Jewelers Supply Co., 206 Charters St., New Orleans, LA 70130/504-523-3839; FAX: 504-523-3836
New Win Publishing, Inc., Box 5159, Clinton, NJ 08809/201-735-9701; FAX: 201-735-9703
Newark Electronics, 4801 N. Ravenswood Ave., Chicago, IL 60640
Newell, Robert H., 55 Coyote, Los Alamos, NM 87544/505-662-7135
Newman Gunshop, 119 Miller Rd., Agency, IA 52530/515-937-5775
NgraveR Co., The, 67 Wawecus Hill Rd., Bozrah, CT 06334/203-823-1533
Nicholson Custom, Rt. 1, Box 176-3, Sedalia, MO 65301/816-826-8746
Nickels, Paul R., 4789 Summerhill Rd., Las Vegas, NV 89121/702-435-5318
Nicklas, Ted, 5504 Hegel Rd., Goodrich, MI 48438/810-797-4493
Nielsen Custom Cases, P.O. Box 26297, Las Vegas, NV 89126/800-377-1341, 702-878-5611; FAX: 702-877-4433
Niemi Engineering, W.B., Box 126 Center Road, Greensboro, VT 05841/802-533-7180 days, 802-533-7141 evenings
Nikon, Inc., 1300 Walt Whitman Rd., Melville, NY 11747/516-547-8623; FAX: 516-547-0309
Nitex, Inc., P.O. Box 1706, Uvalde, TX 78801/512-278-8843
Noble Co., Jim, 1305 Columbia St., Vancouver, WA 98660/206-695-1309
Noreen, Peter H., 5075 Buena Vista Dr., Belgrade, MT 59714/406-586-7383
Norica, Avnda Otaola, 16, Apartado 68, 20600 Eibar, SPAIN
Norinco, 7A, Yun Tan N Beijing, CHINA (U.S. importers—Century International Arms, Inc.; Interarms)
Norma Precision AB (See U.S. importers—Dynamit Nobel-RWS Inc.; Paul Co. Inc., The)
Norman Custom Gunstocks, Jim, 14281 Cane Rd., Valley Center, CA 92082/619-749-6252
Normark Corp., 10395 Yellow Circle Dr., Minnetonka, MN 55343-9101/612-933-7060; FAX: 612-933-0046
Norrell Arms, John, 2608 Grist Mill Rd., Little Rock, AR 72207/501-225-7864
North American Arms, Inc., 2150 South 950 East, Provo, UT 84606-6285/800-821-5783, 801-374-9990; FAX: 801-374-9998
North American Correspondence Schools, The Gun Pro School, Oak & Pawney St., Scranton, PA 18515/717-342-7701
North American Shooting Systems, P.O. Box 306, Osoyoos, B.C. V0H 1V0 CANADA/604-495-3131; FAX: 604-495-2816
North American Specialties, P.O. Box 189, Baker City, OR 97814/503-523-6954
North Devon Firearms Services, 3 North St., Braunton, EX33 1AJ ENGLAND/01271 813624; FAX: 01271 813624
North Fork Custom Gunsmithing, James Johnston, 428 Del Rio Rd., Roseburg, OR 97470/503-673-4467
North Mountain Pine Training Center (See Executive Protection Institute)
North Specialty Products, 2664-B Saturn St., Brea, CA 92621/714-524-1665
North Star West, P.O. Box 488, Glencoe, CA 95232/209-293-7010
North Wind Decoy Co., 1005 N. Tower Rd., Fergus Falls, MN 56537/218-736-4378; FAX: 218-736-7060
Northern Precision Custom Swaged Bullets, 329 S. James St., Carthage, NY 13619/315-493-1711
Northlake Outdoor Footwear, P.O. Box 10, Franklin, TN 37065-0010/615-794-1556; FAX: 615-790-8005
No-Sho Mfg. Co., 10727 Glenfield Ct., Houston, TX 77096/713-723-5332
Nosler, Inc., P.O. Box 671, Bend, OR 97709/800-285-3701, 503-382-3921; FAX: 503-388-4667
Novak's, Inc., 1206 1/2 30th St., P.O. Box 4045, Parkersburg, WV 26101/304-485-9295; FAX: 304-428-6722
Nowlin Custom Mfg., Rt. 1, Box 308, Claremore, OK 74017/918-342-0689; FAX: 918-342-0624
NRI Gunsmith School, 4401 Connecticut Ave. NW, Washington, D.C. 20008
Nu-Line Guns, Inc., 1053 Caulks Hill Rd., Harvester, MO 63304/314-441-4500; FAX: 314-447-5018
Null Holsters Ltd., K.L., 161 School St. NW, Hill City Station, Resaca, GA 30735/706-625-5643; FAX: 706-625-9392
Numrich Arms Corp., 203 Broadway, W. Hurley, NY 12491
Nu-Teck, 30 Industrial Park Rd., Box 37, Centerbrook, CT 06409/203-767-3573; FAX: 203-767-9137

MANUFACTURERS' DIRECTORY

NW Sinker and Tackle, 380 Valley Dr., Myrtle Creek, OR 97457-9717
Nygord Precision Products, P.O. Box 8394, La Crescenta, CA 91224/818-352-3027; FAX: 818-352-3378

O

Oakland Custom Arms, Inc., 4690 W. Walton Blvd., Waterford, MI 48329/810-674-8261
Oakman Turkey Calls, RD 1, Box 825, Harrisonville, PA 17228/717-485-4620
Oakshore Electronic Sights, Inc., P.O. Box 4470, Ocala, FL 32678-4470/904-629-7112; FAX: 904-629-1433
Obermeyer Rifled Barrels, 23122 60th St., Bristol, WI 53104/414-843-3537; FAX: 414-843-2129
October Country, P.O. Box 969, Dept. GD, Hayden Lake, ID 83835/208-772-2068; FAX: 208-772-2068
Oehler Research, Inc., P.O. Box 9135, Austin, TX 78766/512-327-6900, 800-531-5125
Oglesby & Oglesby Gunmakers, Inc., RR 5, Springfield, IL 62707/217-487-7100
Oil Rod and Gun Shop, 69 Oak St., East Douglas, MA 01516/508-476-3687
Ojala Holsters, Arvo, P.O. Box 98, N. Hollywood, CA 91603/503-669-1404
OK Weber, Inc., P.O. Box 7485, Eugene, OR 97401/503-747-0458; FAX: 503-747-5927
Oker's Engraving, 365 Bell Rd., P.O. Box 126, Shawnee, CO 80475/303-838-6042
Oklahoma Ammunition Co., 4310 W. Rogers Blvd., Skiatook, OK 74070/918-396-3187; FAX: 918-396-4270
Oklahoma Leather Products, Inc., 500 26th NW, Miami, OK 74354/918-542-6651; FAX: 918-542-6653
Old Dominion Engravers, 100 Progress Drive, Lynchburg, VA 24502/804-237-4450
Old Wagon Bullets, 32 Old Wagon Rd., Wilton, CT 06897
Old West Bullet Moulds, P.O. Box 519, Flora Vista, NM 87415/505-334-6970
Old West Reproductions, Inc., 446 Florence S. Loop, Florence, MT 59833/406-273-2615
Old Western Scrounger, Inc., 12924 Hwy. A-l2, Montague, CA 96064/916-459-5445; FAX: 916-459-3944
Old World Gunsmithing, 2901 SE 122nd St., Portland, OR 97236/503-760-7681
Old World Oil Products, 3827 Queen Ave. N., Minneapolis, MN 55412/612-522-5037
Ole Frontier Gunsmith Shop, 2617 Hwy. 29 S., Cantonment, FL 32533/904-477-8074
Olsen Development Lab, 111 Lakeview Ave., Blackwood, NJ 08012
Olson, Myron, 989 W. Kemp, Watertown, SD 57201/605-886-9787
Olson, Vic, 5002 Countryside Dr., Imperial, MO 63052/314-296-8086
Olt Co., Philip S., P.O. Box 550, 12662 Fifth St., Pekin, IL 61554/309-348-3633; FAX: 309-348-3300
Olympic Arms, 620-626 Old Pacific Hwy. SE, Olympia, WA 98513/360-459-3471; FAX: 360-491-3447
Olympic Optical Co., P.O. Box 752377, Memphis, TN 38175-2377/901-794-3890, 800-238-7120; FAX: 901-794-0676, 800-748-1669
Omark Industries, Div. of Blount, Inc., 2299 Snake River Ave., P.O. Box 856, Lewiston, ID 83501/800-627-3640, 208-746-2351
Omnishock, 2219 Verde Oak Drive, Hollywood, CA 90068
One Of A Kind, 15610 Purple Sage, San Antonio, TX 78255/512-695-3364
Op-Tec, P.O. Box L632, Langhorn, PA 19047/215-757-5037
Orchard Park Enterprise, P.O. Box 563, Orchard Park, NY 14227/616-656-0356
Ordnance Works, The, 2969 Pidgeon Point Road, Eureka, CA 95501/707-443-3252
Original Mink Oil, Inc., 10652 NE Holman, Portland, OR 97220/503-255-2814, 800-547-5895; FAX: 503-255-2487
Orion Rifle Barrel Co., RR2, 137 Cobler Village, Kalispell, MT 59901/406-257-5649
Or-Ün, Tahtakale Menekse Han 18, Istanbul, TURKEY 34460/90212-522-5912; FAX: 90212-522-7973
Orvis Co., The, Rt. 7, Manchester, VT 05254/802-362-3622 ext. 283; FAX: 802-362-3525
Ottmar, Maurice, Box 657, 113 E. Fir, Coulee City, WA 99115/509-632-5717
Outa-Site Gun Carriers, 219 Market St., Laredo, TX 78040/210-722-4678, 800-880-9715; FAX: 210-726-4858
Outdoor Connection, Inc., The, 201 Cotton Dr., P.O. Box 7751, Waco, TX 76714-7751/800-533-6076; 817-772-5575; FAX: 817-776-3553
Outdoor Edge Cutlery Corp., 2888 Bluff St., Suite 130, Boulder, CO 80301/303-652-8212; FAX: 303-652-8238
Outdoor Enthusiast, 3784 W. Woodland, Springfield, MO 65807/417-883-9841
Outdoor Sports Headquarters, Inc., 967 Watertower Ln., West Carrollton, OH 45449/513-865-5855; FAX: 513-865-5962
Outdoorsman's Bookstore, The, Llangorse, Brecon, Powys LD3 7UE, U.K./44-1874-658-660; FAX: 44-1874-658-650
Outers Laboratories, Div. of Blount, Inc., Route 2, P.O. Box 39, Onalaska, WI 54650/608-781-5800; FAX: 608-781-0368
Owen, Harry, Sport Specialties, 100 N. Citrus Ave. 412, W. Covina, CA 91791-1614/818-968-5806
Ox-Yoke Originals, Inc., 34 Main St., Milo, ME 04463/800-231-8313, 207-943-7351; FAX: 207-943-2416
Ozark Gun Works, 11830 Cemetery Rd., Rogers, AR 72756/501-631-6944; FAX: 501-631-6944

P

P&M Sales and Service, 5724 Gainsborough Pl., Oak Forest, IL 60452/708-687-7149
P&S Gun Service, 2138 Old Shepardsville Rd., Louisvile, KY 40218/502-456-9346
Pace Marketing, Inc., P.O. Box 2039, Stuart, FL 34995/407-223-2189; FAX: 407-286-9547
Pachmayr, Ltd., 1875 S. Mountain Ave., Monrovia, CA 91016/818-357-7771, 800-423-9704; FAX: 818-358-7251
Pacific Pistolcraft, 1810 E. Columbia Ave., Tacoma, WA 98404/206-474-5465
Pacific Precision, 755 Antelope Rd., P.O. Box 2549, White City, OR 97503/503-826-5808; FAX: 503-826-5304
Pacific Tool Co., P.O. Box 2048, Ordnance Plant Rd., Grand Island, NE 68801
Pac-Nor Barreling, 99299 Overlook Rd., P.O. Box 6188, Brookings, OR 97415/503-469-7330; FAX: 503-469-7331
Paco's (See Small Custom Mould & Bullet Co.)
P.A.C.T., Inc., P.O. Box 531525, Grand Prairie, TX 75053/214-641-0049
Page Custom Bullets, P.O. Box 25, Port Moresby Papua, NEW GUINEA
Pagel Gun Works, Inc., 1407 4th St. NW, Grand Rapids, MN 55744/218-326-3003

Paintball Consumer Reports (International Paintball Pub. Inc.), 14573-C Jefferson Davis Highway, Woodridge, VA 22191/703-491-6199
Paintball Games International Magazine (Aceville Publications), Castle House, 97 High St./Colchester, Essex, CO1 1TH ENGLAND 011-44-206-564840
Paintball Sports Magazine, 540 Main St., Mt. Kisco, NY 10549/914-241-7400
Palmer Manufacturing Co., Inc., C., P.O. Box 220, West Newton, PA 15089/412-872-8200; FAX: 412-872-8302
Palmer Security Products, 2930 N. Campbell Ave., Chicago, IL 60618/800-788-7725; FAX: 312-267-8080
Palmgren Steel Products, 8383 S. Chicago Ave., Chicago, IL 60617/312-721-9675; FAX: 312-721-9739
Palsa Outdoor Products, P.O. Box 81336, Lincoln, NE 68501/402-488-5288, 800-456-9281; FAX: 402-488-2321
PanaVise Products, Inc., 1485 Southern Way, Sparks, NV 89431/702-353-2900; FAX: 702-353-2929
Paragon Sales & Services, Inc., P.O. Box 2022, Joliet, IL 60434/815-725-9212; FAX: 815-725-8974
Para-Ordnance Mfg., Inc., 3411 McNicoll Ave., Unit 14, Scarborough, Ont. M1V 2V6, CANADA/416-297-7855; FAX: 416-297-1289 (U.S. importer—Para-Ordnance, Inc.)
Para-Ordnance, Inc., 1919 NE 45th St., Ft. Lauderdale, FL 33308
Pardini Armi Srl, Via Italica 154, 55043 Lido Di Camaiore Lu, ITALY/584-90121; FAX: 584-90122 (U.S. importers—MCS, Inc.; Nygord Precision Products)
Paris, Frank J., 17417 Pershing St., Livonia, MI 48152-3822
The Park Rifle Co., Ltd., Unit 6a, Dartford Trade Park, Power Mill Lane, Dartford, Kent DA7 7NX/011-0322-222512 (U.S. importer—Air Werks International)
Parke-Bernet (See Sotheby's)
Parker, Mark D., 1240 Florida Ave. 7, Longmont, CO 80501/303-772-0214
Parker Div. Reageant Chemical (See Parker Reproductions)
Parker Gun Finishes, 9337 Smokey Row Rd., Strawberry Plains, TN 37871/615-933-3286
Parker Reproductions, 124 River Rd., Middlesex, NJ 08846/908-469-0100; FAX: 908-469-9692
Parsons Optical Mfg. Co., P.O. Box 192, Ross, OH 45061/513-867-0820; FAX: 513-867-8380
Partridge Sales Ltd., John, Trent Meadows, Rugeley, Staffordshire, WS15 2HS ENGLAND/0889-584438
Parts & Surplus, P.O. Box 22074, Memphis, TN 38122/901-683-4007
Pasadena Gun Center, 206 E. Shaw, Pasadena, TX 77506/713-472-0417; FAX: 713-472-1322
Passive Bullet Traps, Inc., 100 Springdale RD., Westfield, MA 01085/413-568-7001; FAX: 413-562-7764
PAST Sporting Goods, Inc., P.O. Box 1035, Columbia, MO 65205/314-445-9200; FAX: 314-446-6606
Paterson Gunsmithing, 438 Main St., Paterson, NJ 07502/201-345-4100
Pathfinder Sports Leather, 2920 E. Chambers St., Phoenix, AZ 85040/602-276-0016
Patrick Bullets, P.O. Box 172, Warwick QSLD 4370 AUSTRALIA
Pattern Control, 114 N. Third St., P.O. Box 462105, Garland, TX 75046/214-494-3551; FAX: 214-272-8447
Paul Co., The, 27385 Pressonville Rd., Wellsville, KS 66092/913-883-4444; FAX: 913-883-2525
Paulsen Gunstocks, Rt. 71, Box 11, Chinook, MT 59523/406-357-3403
Payne Photography, Robert, P.O. Box 141471, Austin, TX 78714/512-272-4554
PC Bullet/ADC, Inc., 32654 Coal Creek Rd., Scappoose, OR 97056-2601/503-543-5088; FAX: 503-543-5990
PC Co., 5942 Secor Rd., Toledo, OH 43623/419-472-6222
Peacemaker Specialists, P.O. Box 157, Whitmore, CA 96096/916-472-3438
Pease Accuracy, Bob, P.O. Box 310787, New Braunfels, TX 78131/210-625-1342
Peasley, David, P.O. Box 604, 2067 S. Hiway 17, Alamosa, CO 81101
PECAR Herbert Schwarz, GmbH, Kreuzbergstrasse 6, 10965 Berlin, GERMANY/004930-785-7383; FAX: 004930-785-1934
Pecatonica River Longrifle, 5205 Noddingham Dr., Rockford, IL 61111/815-968-1995; FAX: 815-968-1996
Pedersen, C.R., 2717 S. Pere Marquette Hwy., Ludington, MI 49431/616-843-2061
Pedersen, Rex C., 2717 S. Pere Marquette Hwy., Ludington, MI 49431/616-843-2061
Pedersoli Davide & C., Via Artigiani 57, Gardone V.T., Brescia, ITALY 25063/030-8912402; FAX: 030-8911019 (U.S. importers—Beauchamp & Son, Inc.; Cabela's; Cape Outfitters; Dixie Gun Works; EMF Co., Inc.; Navy Arms Co.; Taylor's & Co., Inc.)
Peerless Alloy, Inc., 1445 Osage St., Denver, CO 80204/303-825-6394, 800-253-1278
Peet Shoe Dryer, Inc., 130 S. 5th St., P.O. Box 618, St. Maries, ID 83861/208-245-2095, 800-222-PEET; FAX: 208-245-5441
Pejsa Ballistics, 2120 Kenwood Pkwy., Minneapolis, MN 55405/612-374-3337; FAX: 612-374-3337
Pelaire Products, 5346 Bonky Ct., W. Palm Beach, FL 33415/407-439-0691; FAX: 407-439-0691
Pell, John T., 410 College, Trinidad, CO 81082/719-846-9406
Peltor, Inc., 41 Commercial Way, E. Providence, RI 02914/401-438-4800; FAX: 401-434-1708, 800-EAR-FAX1
PEM's Mfg. Co., 5063 Waterloo Rd., Atwater, OH 44201/216-947-3721
Pence Precision Barrels, 7567 E. 900 S., S. Whitley, IN 46787/219-839-4745
Pend Oreille Sport Shop, 3100 Hwy. 200 East, Sandpoint, ID 83864/208-263-2412
Pendleton Royal, 4/7 Highgate St., Birmingham, ENGLAND B12 0X5/44 121 440 3060; FAX: 44 121 446 4165
Pendleton Woolen Mills, P.O. Box 3030, 220 N.W. Broadway, Portland, OR 97208/503-226-4801
Penguin Industries, Inc., Airport Industrial Mall, Coatesville, PA 19320/610-384-6000; FAX: 610-857-5980
Penn Bullets, P.O. Box 756, Indianola, PA 15051
Penn's Woods Products, Inc., 19 W. Pittsburgh St., Delmont, PA 15626/412-468-8311; FAX: 412-468-8975
Pennsylvania Gun Parts, 1701 Mud Run Rd., York Springs, PA 17372/717-259-8010
Pennsylvania Gunsmith School, 812 Ohio River Blvd., Avalon, Pittsburgh, PA 15202/412-766-1812
Penrod Precision, 312 College Ave., P.O. Box 307, N. Manchester, IN 46962/219-982-8385
Pentax Corp., 35 Inverness Dr. E., Englewood, CO 80112/303-799-8000; FAX: 303-790-1131

50th EDITION, 1996 **585**

DIRECTORY OF THE ARMS TRADE

Pentheny de Pentheny, 2352 Baggett Ct., Santa Rosa, CA 95401/707-573-1390; FAX: 707-573-1390
Perazone, Brian, Cold Spring Rd., Roxbury, NY 12474/607-326-4088
Perazzi m.a.p. S.P.A., Via Fontanelle 1/3, 1-25080 Botticino Mattina, ITALY (U.S. importer—Perazzi USA, Inc.)
Perazzi USA, Inc., 1207 S. Shamrock Ave., Monrovia, CA 91016/818-303-0068; FAX: 818-303-2081
Peregrine Sporting Arms, Inc., 14155 Brighton Rd., Brighton, CO 80601/303-654-0850
Performance Specialists, 308 Eanes School Rd., Austin, TX 78746/512-327-0119
Peripheral Data Systems (See Arms, Peripheral Data Systems)
Personal Protection Systems, RD 5, Box 5027-A, Moscow, PA 18444/717-842-1766
Perugini Visini & Co. s.r.l., Via Camprelle, 126, 25080 Nuvolera (Bs.), ITALY
Peters Stahl GmbH, Stettiner Strasse 42, D-33106 Paderborn, GERMANY/05251-750025; FAX: 05251-75611 (U.S. importers—Harris-McMillan Gunworks; Olympic Arms)
Petersen Publishing Co., 6420 Wilshire Blvd., Los Angeles, CA 90048/213-782-2000; FAX: 213-782-2867
Peterson Gun Shop, Inc., A.W., 4255 W. Old U.S. 441, Mt. Dora, FL 32757-3299/904-383-4258
Petro-Explo, Inc., 7650 U.S. Hwy. 287, Suite 100, Arlington, TX 76017/817-478-8888
Pettinger Books, Gerald, Rt. 2, Box 125, Russell, IA 50238/515-535-2239
Pflumm Mfg. Co., 10662 Widmer Rd., Lenexa, KS 66215/800-888-4867; FAX: 913-451-7857
PFRB Co., P.O. Box 1242, Bloomington, IL 61701/309-473-3964
Phil-Chem, Inc., 2950 NW 29th, Portland, OR 97210/800-553-3022
Phillippi Custom Bullets, Justin, P.O. Box 773, Ligonier, PA 15658/412-238-9671
Phillips, Jerry, P.O. Box L632, Langhorne, PA 19047/215-757-5037
Phoenix Arms, 1420 S. Archibald Ave., Ontario, CA 91761/909-947-4843; FAX: 909-947-6798
Photronic Systems Engineering Company, 6731 Via De La Reina, Bonsall, CA 92003/619-758-8000
Piedmont Community College, P.O. Box 1197, Roxboro, NC 27573/910-599-1181
Pierce Pistols, 2326 E. Hwy. 34, Newnan, GA 30263/404-253-8192
Pietta (See U.S. importers—Navy Arms Co.; Taylor's & Co., Inc.)
Pilgrim Pewter, Inc. (See Bell Originals, Inc., Sid)
Pilkington, Scott, Little Trees Ramble, P.O. Box 97, Monteagle, TN 37356/615-924-3475; FAX: 615-924-3489
Pilkington Gun Co., P.O. Box 1296, Muskogee, OK 74402/918-683-9418
Pine Technical College, 1100 4th St., Pine City, MN 55063/800-521-7463; FAX: 612-629-6766
Pinetree Bullets, 133 Skeena St., Kitimat BC, CANADA V8C 1Z1/604-632-3768; FAX: 604-632-3768
Pioneer Arms Co., 355 Lawrence Rd., Broomall, PA 19008/215-356-5203
Pioneer Guns, 5228 Montgomery Rd., Norwood, OH 45212/513-631-4871
Pioneer Research, Inc., 216 Haddon Ave., Suite 102, Westmont, NJ 08108/609-854-2424, 800-257-7742; FAX: 609-858-8695
Piotti (See U.S. importer—Moore & Co., Wm. Larkin)
Piquette, Paul R., 80 Bradford Dr., Feeding Hills, MA 01030/413-781-8300, Ext. 682
Plaxco, J. Michael, Rt. 1, P.O. Box 203, Roland, AR 72135/501-868-9787
Plaza Cutlery, Inc., 3333 Bristol, 161, South Coast Plaza, Costa Mesa, CA 92626/714-549-3932
Plum City Ballistic Range, N2162 80th St., Plum City, WI 54761-8622/715-647-2539
PlumFire Press, Inc., 30-A Grove Ave., Patchogue, NY 11772-4112/800-695-7246; FAX:516-758-4071
P.M. Enterprises, Inc., 146 Curtis Hill Rd., Chehalis, WA 98532/206-748-3743; FAX: 206-748-1802
PMC/Eldorado Cartridge Corp., P.O. Box 62508, 12801 U.S. Hwy. 95 S., Boulder City, NV 89005/702-294-0025; FAX: 702-294-0121
Poburka, Philip, 1409 South Commerce St., Las Vegas, NV 89102/702-388-2891
Pointing Dog Journal, Village Press Publications, P.O. Box 968, Dept. PGD, Traverse City, MI 49685/800-272-3246; FAX: 616-946-3289
Police Bookshelf, P.O. Box 122, Concord, NH 03301/603-224-6814; FAX: 603-226-3554
Policlips North America, 59 Douglas Crescent, Toronto, Ont. CANADA M4W 2E6/800-229-5089, 416-924-0383; FAX: 416-924-4375
Polywad, Inc., P.O. Box 7916, Macon, GA 31209/912-477-0669
Pomeroy, Robert, RR1, Box 50, E. Corinth, ME 04427/207-285-7721
Ponsness/Warren, P.O. Box 8, Rathdrum, ID 83858/208-687-2231; FAX: 208-687-2233
Pony Express Reloaders, 608 E. Co. Rd. D, Suite 3, St. Paul, MN 55117/612-483-9406; FAX: 612-483-9884
Pony Express Sport Shop, Inc., 16606 Schoenborn St., North Hills, CA 91343/818-895-1231
Porta Blind, Inc., 2700 Speedway, Wichita Falls, TX 76308/817-723-6620
Portus, Robert, 130 Ferry Rd., Grants Pass, OR 97526/503-476-4919
Potts, Wayne E., 912 Poplar St., Denver, CO 80220/303-355-5462
Powder Horn, Inc., The, P.O. Box 114 Patty Drive, Cusseta, GA 31805/404-989-3257
Powder Horn Antiques, P.O. Box 4196, Ft. Lauderdale, FL 33338/305-565-6060
Powder Valley Services, Rt. 1, Box 100, Dexter, KS 67038/316-876-5418
Powell & Son (Gunmakers) Ltd., William, 35-37 Carrs Lane, Birmingham B4 7SX ENGLAND/21-643-0689; FAX: 21-631-3504 (U.S. importer—The William Powell Agency)
Powell Agency, William, The, 22 Circle Dr., Bellmore, NY 11710/516-679-1158
Power Custom, Inc., RR 2, P.O. Box 756AB, Gravois Mills, MO 65307/314-372-5684
PPC Corp., 627 E. 24th St., Paterson, NJ 07514/201-278-5428
Practical Tools, Inc., Div. Behlert Precision, 7067 Easton Rd., P.O. Box 133, Pipersville, PA 18947/215-766-7301; FAX: 215-766-8681
Pragotrade, 307 Humberline Dr., Rexdale, Ontario, CANADA M9W 5V1/416-675-1322
Prairie River Arms, 1220 N. Sixth St., Princeton, IL 61356/815-875-1616; FAX: 815-875-1402
Pranger, Ed G., 1414 7th St., Anacortes, WA 98221/206-293-3488
Precise International, 15 Corporate Dr., Orangeburg, NY 10962/914-365-3500; FAX: 914-425-4700
Precise Metalsmithing Enterprises, 146 Curtis Hill Rd., Chehalis, WA 98532/206-748-3743; FAX: 206-748-8102
Precision, Jim, 1725 Moclip's Dr., Petaluma, CA 94952/707-762-3014
Precision Airgun Sales, Inc., 5139 Warrensville Center Rd., Maple Hts., OH 44137-1906/216-587-5005

Precision Bullet Co., 5200 A. Florence Loop, Dunsmuir, CA 96025/916-235-0565
Precision Cartridge, 176 Eastside Rd., Deer Lodge, MT 59722/800-397-3901, 406-846-3900
Precision Cast Bullets, 101 Mud Creek Lane, Ronan, MT 59864/406-676-5135
Precision Castings & Equipment, Inc., P.O. Box 326, Jasper, IN 47547-0135/812-634-9167
Precision Components, 3177 Sunrise Lake, Milford, PA 18337/717-686-4414
Precision Components and Guns, Rt. 55, P.O. Box 337, Pawling, NY 12564/914-855-3040
Precision Delta Corp., P.O. Box 128, Ruleville, MS 38771/601-756-2810; FAX: 601-756-2590
Precision Metal Finishing, John Westrom, P.O. Box 3186, Des Moines, IA 50316/515-288-8680; FAX: 515-244-3925
Precision Munitions, Inc., P.O. Box 8125, Jasper, IN 47547
Precision Ordnance, 1316 E. North St., Jackson, MI 49202
Precision Reloading, Inc., P.O. Box 122, Stafford Springs, CT 06076/203-684-7979; FAX: 203-684-6788
Precision Sales International, Inc., P.O. Box 1776, Westfield, MA 01086/413-562-5055; FAX: 413-562-5056
Precision Shooting, Inc., 222 McKee St., Manchester, CT 06040/203-645-8776; FAX: 203-643-8215
Precision Small Arms, 155 Carlton Rd., Charlottesville, VA 22902/804-293-6124; FAX: 804-295-0780
Precision Specialties, 131 Hendom Dr., Feeding Hills, MA 01030/413-786-3365; FAX: 413-786-3365
Precision Sport Optics, 15571 Producer Lane, Unit G, Huntington Beach, CA 92649/714-891-1309; FAX: 714-892-6920
Premier Reticles, 920 Breckinridge Lane, Winchester, VA 22601-6707
Prescott Projectile Co., 1808 Meadowbrook Road, Prescott, AZ 86303
Pre-Winchester 92-90-62 Parts Co., P.O. Box 8125, W. Palm Beach, FL 33407
Preslik's Gunstocks, 4245 Keith Ln., Chico, CA 95926/916-891-8236
Price Bullets, Patrick W., 16520 Worthley Drive, San Lorenzo, CA 94580/510-278-1547
Prime Reloading, 30 Chiswick End, Meldreth, Royston SG8 6LZ UK/0763-260636
Primos, Inc., P.O. Box 12785, Jackson, MS 39236-2785/601-366-1288; FAX: 601-362-3274
Pro Load Ammunition, Inc., 5180 E. Seltice Way, Post Falls, ID 83854/208-773-9444; FAX: 208-773-9441
Professional Firearms Record Book Co. (See PFRB Co.)
Professional Gunsmiths of America, Inc., Route 1, Box 224F, Lexington, MO 64067/816-259-2636
Professional Hunter Supplies (See Star Custom Bullets)
Prolix, P.O. Box 1348, Victorville, CA 92393/800-248-LUBE, 619-243-3129; FAX: 619-241-0148
Pro-Mark, Div. of Wells Lamont, 6640 W. Touhy, Chicago, IL 60648/312-647-8200
Pro-Port Ltd., 41302 Executive Dr., Harrison Twp., MI 48045-3448/810-469-7323; FAX: 810-469-0425
Pro-Shot Products, Inc., P.O. Box 763, Taylorville, IL 62568/217-824-9133; FAX: 217-824-8861
Protecto Plastics, Div. of Penguin Ind., Airport Industrial Mall, Coatesville, PA 19320/215-384-6000
Protector Mfg. Co., Inc., The, 443 Ashwood Place, Boca Raton, FL 33431/407-394-6011
Protektor Model, 1-11 Bridge St., Galeton, PA 16922/814-435-2442
Prototech Industries, Inc., Rt. 1, Box 81, Delia, KS 66418/913-771-3571; FAX: 913-771-2531
ProWare,Inc., 15847 NE Hancock St., Portland, OR 97230/503-239-0159
P.S.M.G. Gun Co., 10 Park Ave., Arlington, MA 02174/617-646-8845; FAX: 617-646-2133
PWL Gunleather, P.O. Box 450432, Atlanta, GA 31145/404-822-1640; FAX: 404-822-1704
Pyromid, Inc., 3292 S. Highway 97, Redmond, OR 97756/503-548-1041; FAX: 503-923-1004

Q

QB air rifles (See U.S. importer—Sportsman Airguns, Inc.)
Quack Decoy & Sporting Clays, 4 Ann & Hope Way, P.O. Box 98, Cumberland, RI 02864/401-723-8202; FAX: 401-722-5910
Quaker Boy, Inc., 5455 Webster Rd., Orchard Parks, NY 14127/716-662-3979; FAX: 716-662-9426
Quality Arms, Inc., Box 19477, Dept. GD, Houston, TX 77224/713-870-8377; FAX: 713-870-8524
Quality Firearms of Idaho, Inc., 114 13th Ave. S., Nampa, ID 83651/208-466-1631
Quality Parts Co./Bushmaster Firearms, 999 Roosevelt Trail, Bldg. 3, Windham, ME 04062/800-998-7928, 207-892-2005; FAX: 207-892-8068
Quartz-Lok, 13137 N. 21st Lane, Phoenix, AZ 85029
Que Industries, Inc., P.O. Box 2471, Dept. VH, Everett, WA 98203/800-769-6930, 206-347-9843; FAX: 206-514-3266
Queen Cutlery Co., P.O. Box 500, Franklinville, NY 14737/800-222-5233; FAX: 716-676-5535
Quigley's Personal Protection Strategies, Paxton, 9903 Santa Monica Blvd.,, 300/Beverly Hills, CA 90212 310-281-1762
Quinetics Corp., 5731 Kenwick, P.O. Box 13237, San Antonio, TX 78238/512-684-8561; FAX: 512-684-2912

R

R&C Knives & Such, P.O. Box 1047, Manteca, CA 95336/209-239-3722
R&J Gun Shop, 133 W. Main St., John Day, OR 97845/503-575-2130
R&S Industries Corp., 8255 Brentwood Industrial Dr., St. Louis, MO 63144/314-781-5400
Rabeno, Martin, 92 Spook Hole Rd., Ellenville, NY 12428/914-647-4567
Radiator Specialty Co., 1900 Wilkinson Blvd., P.O. Box 34689, Charlotte, NC 28234/800-438-6947; FAX: 800-421-9525
Radical Concepts, P.O. Box 1473, Lake Grove, OR 97035/503-636-6686
Rainier Ballistics Corp., 4500 15th St. East, Tacoma, WA 98424/800-638-8722, 206-922-7589; FAX: 206-922-7854

MANUFACTURERS' DIRECTORY

Ram-Line, Inc., 545 Thirty-One Rd., Grand Junction, CO 81504/303-434-4500; FAX: 303-434-4004
Ranch Products, P.O. Box 145, Malinta, OH 43535/313-277-3118; FAX: 313-565-8536
Randall-Made Knives, P.O. Box 1988, Orlando, FL 32802/407-855-8075
Randco UK, 286 Gipsy Rd., Welling, Kent DA16 1JJ, ENGLAND/44 81 303 4118
Randolph Engineering, Inc., 26 Thomas Patten Dr., Randolph, MA 02368/800-541-1405; FAX: 800-RANDOLPH
Ranger Mfg. Co., Inc., 1536 Crescent Dr., P.O. Box 14069, Augusta, GA 30919-0069/706-738-2023; FAX: 404-738-3608
Ranger Products, 2623 Grand Blvd., Suite 209, Holiday, FL 34609/813-942-4652, 800-407-7007; FAX: 813-942-6221
Ranger Shooting Glasses, 26 Thomas Patten Dr., Randolph, MA 02368/800-541-1405; FAX: 617-986-0337
Ranging, Inc., Routes 5 & 20, East Bloomfield, NY 14443/716-657-6161; FAX: 716-657-5405
Ransom International Corp., P.O. Box 3845, 1040-A Sandretto Dr., Prescott, AZ 86302/602-778-7899; FAX: 602-778-7993
Rapine Bullet Mould Mfg. Co., 9503 Landis Lane, East Greenville, PA 18041/215-679-5413; FAX: 215-679-9795
Rattlers Brand, P.O. Box 311, 115 E. Main St., Thomaston, GA 30286/706-647-7131, 800-825-7131; FAX: 706-647-6652
Ravell Ltd., 289 Diputacion St., 08009, Barcelona SPAIN
Ray's Gunsmith Shop, 3199 Elm Ave., Grand Junction, CO 81504/303-434-6162
Raytech, Div. of Lyman Products Corp., Rt. 32 Stafford Ind. Park, Box 6, Stafford Springs, CT 06076/203-684-4273; FAX: 203-684-7938
RCBS, Div. of Blount, Inc., 605 Oro Dam Blvd., Oroville, CA 95965/800-533-5000, 916-533-5191; FAX: 916-533-1647
R.D.P. Tool Co., Inc., 49162 McCoy Ave., East Liverpool, OH 43920/216-385-5129
Reagent Chemical & Research, Inc. (See Calico Hardwoods, Inc.)
Reardon Products, P.O. Box 126, Morrison, IL 61270/815-772-3155
Red Ball, 100 Factory St., Nashua, NH 03060/603-881-4420
Red Cedar Precision Mfg., P.O. Box 39, Sand Creek, WI 54765/715-658-1198
Red Diamond Dist. Co., 1304 Snowdon Dr., Knoxville, TN 37912
Red Star Target Co., 4519 Brisebois Dr. NW, Calgary AB T2L 2G3 CANADA/403-289-7939; FAX: 403-289-3275
Redding Reloading Equipment, 1089 Starr Rd., Cortland, NY 13045/607-753-3331; FAX: 607-756-8445
Redfield, Inc., 5800 E. Jewell Ave., Denver, CO 80227/303-757-6411; FAX: 303-756-2338
Redman's Rifling & Reboring, Rt. 3, Box 330A, Omak, WA 98841/509-826-5512
Redmist Rifles, 316 W. Olive, Fresno, CA 93728/209-266-6363; FAX: 209-266-4638
Redwood Bullet Works, 3559 Bay Rd., Redwood City, CA 94063/415-367-6741
Reed, Dave, Rt. 1, Box 374, Minnesota City, MN 55959/507-689-2944
Reedy & Assoc., C.L., 2485 Grassmere Dr., Melbourne, FL 32904
Refrigiwear, Inc., 71 Inip Dr., Inwood, Long Island, NY 11696
Re-Heater, Inc., 15828 S. Broadway, C, Gardena, CA 90248
R.E.I., P.O. Box 88, Tallevast, FL 34270/813-755-0085
Reiswig, Wallace E., Claro Walnut Gunstock Co., 1235 Stanley Ave., Chico, CA 95928/916-342-5188
Reloaders Equipment Co., 4680 High St., Ecorse, MI 48229
Reloading Specialties, Inc., Box 1130, Pine Island, MN 55463/507-356-8500; FAX: 507-356-8800
Remington Arms Co., Inc., Delle Donne Corp. Center, 1011 Centre Rd., 2nd, Floor, Wilmington, DE 19805-1270/800-537-2278, 302-993-8577; FAX: 302-993-8606
Renegade, P.O. Box 31546, Phoenix, AZ 85046/602-482-6777; FAX: 602-482-1952
Renfrew Guns & Supplies, R.R. 4, Renfrew, Ontario K7V 3Z7 CANADA/613-432-7080
Reno, Wayne, 2808 Stagestop Rd., Jefferson, CO 80456/719-836-3452
R.E.T. Enterprises, 2608 S. Chestnut, Broken Arrow, OK 74012/918-251-GUNS; FAX: 918-251-0587
Retting, Inc., Martin B., 11029 Washington, Culver City, CA 90232/213-837-2412
R.G.-G., Inc., P.O. Box 1261, Conifer, CO 80433-1261/303-697-4154; FAX: 303-697-4154
Rhodeside, Inc., 1704 Commerce Dr., Piqua, OH 45356/513-773-5781
Rice, Keith (See White Rock Tool & Die)
Richards, John, Richards Classic Oil Finish, Rt. 2, Box 325, Bedford, KY 40006/502-255-7222
Richards Micro-Fit Stocks, 8331 N. San Fernando Rd., P.O. Box 1066, Sun Valley, CA 91352/818-767-6097
Rickard, Inc., Pete, RD 1, Box 292, Cobleskill, NY 12043/800-282-5663; FAX: 518-234-2454
Ridgetop Sporting Goods, P.O. Box 306, 42907 Hilligoss Ln. East, Eatonville, WA 98328/206-832-6422
Riebe Co., W.J., 3434 Tucker Rd., Boise, ID 83703
Ries, Chuck, 415 Ridgecrest Dr., Grants Pass, OR 97527/503-476-5623
Rifle Works & Armory, 707 N 12 St., Cody, WY 82414/307-587-4914
Rifles Inc., 873 W. 5400 N., Cedar City, UT 84720/801-586-5996; FAX: 801-586-5996
RIG Products, 87 Coney Island Dr., Sparks, NV 89431-6334/702-331-5666; FAX: 702-331-5669
Rigby & Co., John, 66 Great Suffolk St., London SE1 0BU, ENGLAND
Riggs, Jim, 206 Azalea, Boerne, TX 78006/210-249-8567
Riling Arms Books Co., Ray, 6844 Gorsten St., P.O. Box 18925, Philadelphia, PA 19119/215-438-2456; FAX: 215-438-5395
Rim Pac Sports, Inc., 1034 N. Soldano Ave., Azusa, CA 91702-2135
Rimrock Rifle Stocks, P.O. Box 589, Vashon Island, WA 98070/206-463-5531
Ringler Custom Leather Co., P.O. Box 206, Cody, WY 82414/307-645-3255
Ripley Rifles, 42 Fletcher Street, Ripley, Derbyshire, DE5 3LP ENGLAND/011-0773-748353
R.I.S. Co., Inc., 718 Timberlake Circle, Richardson, TX 75080/214-235-0933
River Road Sporting Clays, Bruce Barsotti, P.O. Box 3016, Gonzales, CA 93926/408-675-2473
Rizzini, Battista, Via 2 Giugno, 7/7Bis-25060 Marcheno (Brescia), ITALY (U.S. importers—Alessandri & Son Lou; New England Arms Co.)
Rizzini, F.LLI (See U.S. importers—Moore & Co. Wm. Larkin; New England Arms Co.)
RLCM Enterprises, 110 Hill Crest Drive, Burleson, TX 76028
R.M. Precision, Inc., Attn. Greg F. Smith Marketing, P.O. Box 210, LaVerkin, UT 84745/801-635-4656; FAX: 801-635-4430
RMS Custom Gunsmithing, 4120 N. Bitterwell, Prescott Valley, AZ 86314/602-772-7626

R.O.A. (See U.S. importer—Winchester Sutler, Inc., The)
Robar Co.'s, Inc., The, 21438 N. 7th Ave., Suite B, Phoenix, AZ 85027/602-581-2648; FAX: 602-582-0059
Robbins Scent, Inc., P.O. Box 779, Connellsville, PA 15425/412-628-2529; FAX: 412-628-9598
Roberts, J.J., 7808 Lake Dr., Manassas, VA 22111/703-330-0448
Roberts Products, 25238 SE 32nd, Issaquah, WA 98027/206-392-8172
Robinett, R.G., P.O. Box 72, Madrid, IA 50156/515-795-2906
Robinson, Don, Pennsylvania Hse., 36 Fairfax Crescent, Southowram, Halifax, W. Yorkshire HX3 9SQ, ENGLAND/0422-364458
Robinson Firearms Mfg. Ltd., 1699 Blondeaux Crescent, Kelowna, B.C. CANADA V1Y 4J8/604-868-9596
Robinson H.V. Bullets, 3145 Church St., Zachary, LA 70791/504-654-4029
Rochester Lead Works, 76 Anderson Ave., Rochester, NY 14607/716-442-8500
Rockwood Corp., Speedwell Division, 136 Lincoln Blvd., Middlesex, NJ 08846/908-560-7171
Rocky Fork Enterprises, P.O. Box 427, 878 Battle Rd., Nolensville, TN 37135/615-941-1307
Rocky Mountain Arms, Inc., 600 S. Sunset, Unit C, Longmont, CO 80501/303-768-8522; FAX: 303-678-8766
Rocky Mountain High Sports Glasses, 8121 N. Central Park Ave., Skokie, IL 60076/708-679-1012; FAX: 708-679-0184
Rocky Mountain Rifle Works Ltd., 1707 14th St., Boulder, CO 80302/303-443-9189
Rocky Mountain Target Co., 3 Aloe Way, Leesburg, GA 34788/904-365-9598
Rocky Mountain Wildlife Products, P.O. Box 999, La Porte, CO 80535/303-484-2768; FAX: 303-223-9389
Rocky Shoes & Boots, 294 Harper St., Nelsonville, OH 45764/800-848-9452, 614-753-1951; FAX: 614-753-4024
Rod Guide Co., Box 1149, Forsyth, MO 65653/800-952-2774
Rogers Gunsmithing, Bob, P.O. Box 305, 344 S. Walnut St., Franklin Grove, IL 61031/815-456-2685; FAX: 815-288-7142
Rohner, Hans, 1148 Twin Sisters Ranch Rd., Nederland, CO 80466-9600
Rohner, John, 710 Sunshine Canyon, Boulder, CO 80302/303-444-3841
Rolston, Inc., Fred W., 210 E. Cummins St., Tecumseh, MI 49286/517-423-6002, 800-314-9061 (orders only); FAX: 517-423-6002
Romain's Custom Guns, RD 1, Whetstone Rd., Brockport, PA 15823/814-265-1948
Rooster Laboratories, P.O. Box 412514, Kansas City, MO 64141/816-474-1622; FAX: 816-474-1307
Rorschach Precision Products, P.O. Box 151613, Irving, TX 75015/214-790-3487
Rosenberg & Sons, Jack A., 12229 Cox Lane, Dallas, TX 75234/214-241-6302
Rosenthal, Brad and Sallie, 19303 Ossenfort Ct., St. Louis, MO 63038/314-273-5159; FAX: 314-273-5149
Ross & Webb (See Ross, Don)
Ross, Don, 12813 West 83 Terrace, Lenexa, KS 66215/913-492-6982
Rosser, Bob, 1824 29th Ave., Suite 24, Birmingham, AL 35209/205-870-4422
Rossi S.A., Amadeo, Rua: Amadeo Rossi, 143, Sao Leopoldo, RS, BRAZIL 93030-220/051-592-5566 (U.S. importer—Interarms)
Roto Carve, 2754 Garden Ave., Janesville, IA 50647
Round Edge, Inc., P.O. Box 723, Lansdale, PA 19446/215-361-0859
Rowe Engineering, Inc. (See R.E.I.)
Roy's Custom Grips, Rt. 3, Box 174-E, Lynchburg, VA 24504/804-993-3470
Royal Arms, 5126 3rd Ave. N., Great Falls, MT 59405/406-453-1149
RPM, 15481 N. Twin Lakes Dr., Tucson, AZ 85737/602-825-1233; FAX: 602-825-3333
Rubright Bullets, 1008 S. Quince Rd., Walnutport, PA 18088/215-767-1339
Rucker Ammunition Co., P.O. Box 479, Terrell, TX 75160
Rudnicky, Susan, 8714 Center St., Holland, NY 14080/716-941-3259
Ruger (See Sturm, Ruger & Co., Inc.)
Ruko Products, Inc., 2245 Kenmore Ave., No. 102, Buffalo, NY 14207/716-874-2707; FAX: 905-826-1353
Rundell's Gun Shop, 6198 Frances Rd., Clio, MI 48420/313-687-0559
Runge, Robert P., 94 Grove St., Ilion, NY 13357/315-894-3036
Rupert's Gun Shop, 2202 Dick Rd., Fenwick, MI 48834/517-248-3252
Russell Knives, Inc., A.G., 1705 Hwy. 71B North, Springdale, AR 72764/501-751-7341
Rusteprufe Laboratories, 1319 Jefferson Ave., Sparta, WI 54656/608-269-4144
Rusty Duck Premium Gun Care Products, 7785 Foundation Dr., Suite 6, Florence, KY 41042/606-342-5553; FAX: 606-342-5556
Rutgers Book Center, 127 Raritan Ave., Highland Park, NJ 08904/908-545-4344; FAX: 908-545-6686
Rutten (See U.S. importer—Air Werks International)
Ruvel & Co., Inc., 4128-30 W. Belmont Ave., Chicago, IL 60641/312-286-9494
R.V.I., P.O. Box 8019-56, Blaine, WA 98230/206-595-2933
RWS (See U.S. importer—Dynamit Nobel-RWS, Inc.)
Ryan, Chad L., RR 3, Box 72, Cresco, IA 52136/319-547-4384
Rybka Custom Leather Equipment, Thad, 134 Havilah Hill, Odenville, AL 35120

S

S&B Industries, 11238 McKinley Rd., Montrose, MI 48457/810-639-5491
S&H Arms Mfg. Co., Rt. 3, Box 689, Berryville, AR 72616/501-545-3511
S&K Mfg. Co., P.O. Box 247, Pittsfield, PA 16340/814-563-7808; FAX: 814-563-7808
S&S Firearms, 74-11 Myrtle Ave., Glendale, NY 11385/718-497-1100; FAX: 718-497-1105
Sabatti S.R.L., via Alessandro Volta 90, 25063 Gardone V.T., Brescia, ITALY/030-8912207-831312; FAX: 030-8912909 (U.S. importer—E.A.A. Corp.)
SAECO (See Redding Reloading Equipment)
Safari Outfitters Ltd., 71 Ethan Allan Hwy., Ridgefield, CT 06877/203-544-9505
Safari Plus, 218 Quinlan, Suite 322, Kerrville, TX 78028-5314/210-367-5209
Safari Press, Inc., 15621 Chemical Lane B, Huntington Beach, CA 92649/714-894-9080; FAX: 714-894-4949
Safariland Ltd., Inc., 3120 E. Mission Blvd., P.O. Box 51478, Ontario, CA 91761/909-923-7300; FAX: 909-923-7400
SAFE, P.O. Box 864, Post Falls, ID 83854/208-773-3624
Safesport Manufacturing Co., 1100 W. 45th Ave., Denver, CO 80211/303-433-6506, 800-433-6506; FAX: 303-433-4112
Safety Speed Holster, Inc., 910 S. Vail Ave., Montebello, CA 90640/213-723-4140; FAX: 213-726-6973
Sako Ltd., P.O. Box 149, SF-11101, Riihimaki, FINLAND (U.S. importer—Stoeger Industries)

DIRECTORY OF THE ARMS TRADE

Salter Calls, Inc., Eddie, Hwy. 31 South-Brewton Industrial Park, Brewton, AL 36426/205-867-2584; FAX: 206-867-9005
Samco Global Arms, Inc., 6995 NW 43rd St., Miami, FL 33166/305-593-9782
Sampson, Roger, 430 N. Grove, Mora, MN 55051/612-679-4868
San Francisco Gun Exchange, 124 Second St., San Francisco, CA 94105/415-982-6097
San Marco (See U.S. importers—Cape Outfitters; EMF Co., Inc.)
Sanders Custom Gun Service, 2358 Tyler Ln., Louisville, KY 40205/502-454-3338
Sanders Gun and Machine Shop, 145 Delhi Road, Manchester, IA 52057
Sandia Die & Cartridge Co., 37 Atancacio Rd. NE, Albuquerque, NM 87123/505-298-5729
Sarco, Inc., 323 Union St., Stirling, NJ 07980/908-647-3800
S.A.R.L. G. Granger, 66 cours Fauriel, 42100 Saint Etienne, FRANCE/04 77 25 14 73; FAX: 04 77 38 66 99
Sauer (See U.S. importer—Paul Co., The)
Saunders Gun & Machine Shop, R.R. 2, Delhi Road, Manchester, IA 52057
Savage Arms, Inc., 100 Springdale Rd., Westfield, MA 01085/413-568-7001; FAX: 413-562-7764
Savana Sports, Inc., 5763 Ferrier St., Montreal, Quebec, CANADA/514-739-1753; FAX: 514-739-1755
Saville Iron Co. (See Greenwood Precision)
Savino, Barbara J., P.O. Box 1104, Hardwick, VT 05843-1104
Scanco Environmental Systems, 5000 Highlands Parkway, Suite 180, Atlanta, GA 30082/404-431-0025; FAX: 404-431-0028
Scansport, Inc., P.O. Box 700, Enfield, NH 03748/603-632-7654
Scattergun Technologies, Inc., 518 3rd Ave. S., Nashville, TN 37202/615-254-1441; FAX: 615-254-1449
Sceery Co., E.J., 2308 Cedros Circle, Sante Fe, NM 87505/505-983-2125
Schaefer Shooting Sports, 1923 Grand Ave., Baldwin, NY 11510/516-379-4900; FAX: 516-379-6701
Scharch Mfg., Inc., 10325 Co. Rd. 120, Unit C, Salida, CO 81201/719-539-7242; FAX: 719-539-3021
Scherer, Box 250, Ewing, VA 24240/615-733-2615; FAX: 615-733-2073
Schiffman, Curt, 3017 Kevin Cr., Idaho Falls, ID 83402/208-524-4684
Schiffman, Mike, 8233 S. Crystal Springs, McCammon, ID 83250/208-254-9114
Schiffman, Norman, 3017 Kevin Cr., Idaho Falls, ID 83402/208-524-4684
Schmidpke, Karl, P.O. Box 51692, New Berlin, WI 53151
Schmidt & Bender, Inc., Brook Rd., P.O. Box 134, Meriden, NH 03770/603-469-3565, 800-468-3450; FAX: 603-469-3471
Schmidtman Custom Ammunition, 6 Gilbert Court, Cotati, CA 94931
Schneider Bullets, 3655 West 214th St., Fairview Park, OH 44126
Schneider Rifle Barrels, Inc., Gary, 12202 N. 62nd Pl., Scottsdale, AZ 85254/602-948-2525
School of Gunsmithing, The, 6065 Roswell Rd., Atlanta, GA 30328/800-223-4542
Schrimsher's Custom Knifemaker's Supply, Bob, P.O. Box 308, Emory, TX 75440/903-473-3330; FAX: 903-473-2235
Schroeder Bullets, 1421 Thermal Ave., San Diego, CA 92154/619-423-3523
Schuetzen Gun Service, 3717 S. Taft Hill Rd. No. 19, Fort Collins, CO 80526/303-223-3678
Schuetzen Pistol Works, 620-626 Old Pacific Hwy. SE, Olympia, WA 98513/360-459-3471; FAX: 360-491-3447
Schulz Industries, 16204 Minnesota Ave., Paramount, CA 90723/213-439-5903
Schumakers Gun Shop, William, 512 Prouty Corner Lp. A, Colville, WA 99114/509-684-4848
Schwartz Custom Guns, David W., 2505 Waller St., Eau Claire, WI 54703/715-832-1735
Schwartz Custom Guns, Wayne E., 970 E. Britton Rd., Morrice, MI 48857/517-625-4079
Scobey Duck & Goose Calls, Glynn, Rt. 3, Box 37, Newbern, TN 38059/901-643-6241
Scope Control, Inc., 5775 Co. Rd. 23 SE, Alexandria, MN 56308/612-762-7295
ScopLevel, 151 Lindbergh Ave., Suite H, Livermore, CA 94550/510-449-5052; FAX: 510-373-0861
Scot Powder, Rt.1 Box 167, McEwen, TN 37101/800-416-3006; FAX: 615-729-4211
Scott, Dwight, 23089 Englehardt St., Clair Shores, MI 48080/313-779-4735
Scott Fine Guns, Inc., Thad, P.O. Box 412, Indianola, MS 38751/601-887-5929
Scott, McDougall & Associates, 7950 Redwood Dr., Cotati, CA 94931/707-546-2264; FAX: 707-795-1911
S.C.R.C., P.O. Box 660, Katy, TX 77492-0660/FAX: 713-578-2124
Scruggs' Game Calls, Stanley, Rt. 1, Hwy. 661, Cullen, VA 23934/804-542-4241, 800-323-4828
Seattle Binocular & Scope Repair Co., P.O. Box 46094, Seattle, WA 98146/206-932-3733
Second Chance Body Armor, P.O. Box 578, Central Lake, MI 49622/616-544-5721; FAX: 616-544-9824
Security Awareness & Firearms Education (See SAFE)
Seebeck Assoc., R.E., P.O. Box 59752, Dallas, TX 75229
Seecamp Co., Inc., L.W., P.O. Box 255, New Haven, CT 06502/203-877-3429
Seligman Shooting Products, HC 1 33, Seligman, AZ 86337/602-422-3607
Selsi Co., Inc., 40 Veterans Blvd., Carlstadt, NJ 07072-0497/201-935-0388; FAX: 201-935-5851
Semmer, Charles, 7885 Cyd Dr., Denver, CO 80221/303-429-6947
Serva Arms Co., Inc., RD 1, Box 483A, Greene, NY 13778/607-656-4764
Service Armament, 689 Bergen Blvd., Ridgefield, NJ 07657
Servus Footwear Co., 1136 2nd St., Rock Island, IL 61204-3610/309-786-7741; FAX: 309-786-9808
SGS Importers International, Inc., 1750 Brielle Ave., Unit B1, Wanamassa, NJ 07712/908-493-0302; FAX: 908-493-0301
S.G.S. Sporting Guns Srl., Via Della Resistenza, 37, 20090 Buccinasco (MI) ITALY/2-45702446; FAX: 2-45702464
Shanghai Airguns, Ltd. (See U.S. importer—Sportsman Airguns, Inc.)
Shappy Bullets, 76 Milldale Ave., Plantsville, CT 06479/203-621-3704
Sharp (See U.S. importer—Great Lakes Airguns)
Sharp Shooter, Inc., P.O. Box 21362, St. Paul, MN 55121/612-452-4687
Sharps Arms Co., Inc., C. (See Montana Armory, Inc.)
Shaw, Inc., E.R. (See Small Arms Mfg. Co.)
Shay's Gunsmithing, 931 Marvin Ave., Lebanon, PA 17042
Sheffield Knifemakers Supply, P.O. Box 141, Deland, FL 32721/904-775-6453; FAX: 904-774-5754

Shell Shack, 113 E. Main, Laurel, MT 59044/406-628-8986
Shepherd Scope Ltd., Box 189, Waterloo, NE 68069/402-779-2424; FAX: 402-779-4010
Sheridan USA, Inc., Austin, P.O. Box 577, 36 Haddam Quarter Rd., Durham, CT 06422/203-349-1772; FAX: 203-349-1771
Sherwood, George, 46 N. River Dr., Roseburg, OR 97470/503-672-3159
Shilen Rifles, Inc., P.O. Box 1300, 205 Metro Park Blvd., Ennis, TX 75120/214-875-5318; FAX: 214-875-5402
Shiloh Creek, Box 357, Cottleville, MO 63338/314-447-2900; FAX: 314-447-2900
Shiloh Rifle Mfg., 201 Centennial Dr., Big Timber, MT 59011/406-932-4454; FAX: 406-932-5627
Shirley Co. Gun & Riflemakers Ltd., J.A., P.O. Box 368, High Wycombe, Bucks. HP13 6YN, ENGLAND/0494-446883; FAX: 0494-463685
Shockley, Harold H., 204 E. Farmington Rd., Hanna City, IL 61536/309-565-4524
Shoemaker & Sons, Inc., Tex, 714 W. Cienega Ave., San Dimas, CA 91750/714-592-2071; FAX: 714-592-2378
Shooten' Haus, The, 102 W. 13th, Kearney, NE 68847/308-236-7929
Shooter Shop, The, 221 N. Main, Butte, MT 59701/406-723-3842
Shooter's Choice, 16770 Hilltop Park Place, Chagrin Falls, OH 44023/216-543-8808; FAX: 216-543-8811
Shooter's Edge, Inc., P.O.Box 769, Trinidad, CO 81082
Shooter's Supply, RR1, Box 333B, Rt. 55, Poughquag, NY 12570/914-724-3088; FAX: 914-724-3454
Shooter's Supply, 1120 Tieton Dr., Yakima, WA 98902/509-452-1181
Shooter's World, 3828 N. 28th Ave., Phoenix, AZ 85017/602-266-0170
Shootin' Accessories, Ltd., P.O. Box 6810, Auburn, CA 95604/916-889-2220
Shootin' Shack, Inc., 1065 Silver Beach Rd., Riviera Beach, FL 33403/407-842-0990
Shooting Chrony, Inc., 3269 Niagara Falls Blvd., N. Tonawanda, NY 14120/905-276-6292; FAX: 416-276-6295
Shooting Components Marketing, P.O. Box 1069, Englewood, CO 80150/303-987-2543; FAX: 303-989-3508
Shooting Gallery, The, 8070 Southern Blvd., Boardman, OH 44512/216-726-7788
Shooting Specialties (See Titus, Daniel)
Shooting Star, 1825 Fortview Rd., Ste. 115, Austin, TX 78747/512-462-0009
Shoot-N-C Inc., 8951 Bonita Beach Rd., Bonita Springs, FL 33923/813-498-9221
Shotgun Bullets Mfg., Rt. 3, Box 41, Robinson, IL 62454/618-546-5043
Shotgun Shop, The, 14145 Proctor Ave., Suite 3, Industry, CA 91746/818-855-2737; FAX: 818-855-2735
Shotguns Unlimited, 2307 Fon Du Lac Rd., Richmond, VA 23229/804-752-7115
Siegrist Gun Shop, 8754 Turtle Road, Whittemore, MI 48770
Sierra Bullets, 1400 W. Henry St., Sedalia, MO 65301/816-827-6300; FAX: 816-827-6300
Sierra Specialty Prod. Co., 1344 Oakhurst Ave., Los Altos, CA 94024
SIG, CH-8212 Neuhausen, SWITZERLAND (U.S. importer—Mandall Shooting Supplies, Inc.)
Sigarms, Inc., Corporate Park, Exeter, NH 03833/603-772-2302; FAX: 603-772-9082
Sight Shop, The, John G. Lawson, 1802 E. Columbia Ave., Tacoma, WA 98404/206-474-5465
Sightron, Inc., 11701 NW 102nd Rd., Suite 21, Medley, FL 33178/305-863-6767; FAX: 305-863-6652
Signet Metal Corp., 551 Stewart Ave., Brooklyn, NY 11222/718-384-5400; FAX: 718-388-7488
SIG-Sauer (See U.S. importer—Sigarms, Inc.)
Sile Distributors, Inc., 7 Centre Market Pl., New York, NY 10013/212-925-4111; FAX: 212-925-3149
Silencio/Safety Direct, 56 Coney Island Dr., Sparks, NV 89431/800-648-1812, 702-354-4451; FAX: 702-359-1074
Silent Hunter, 1100 Newton Ave., W. Collingswood, NJ 08107/609-854-3276
Silhouette Leathers, P.O. Box 1161, Gunnison, CO 81230/A303-641-6639
Silver Eagle Machining, 18007 N. 69th Ave., Glendale, AZ 85308
Silver Ridge Gun Shop (See Goodwin, Fred)
Silver-Tip Corp., RR2, Box 184, Gloster, MS 39638-9520
Simmons, Jerry, 715 Middlebury St., Goshen, IN 46526/219-533-8546
Simmons Enterprises, Ernie, 709 East Elizabethtown Rd., Manheim, PA 17545/717-664-4040
Simmons Outdoor Corp., 2120 Killearney Way, Tallahassee, FL 32308-3402/904-878-5100; FAX: 904-878-0300
Sinclair, W.P., Box 1209, Warminster, Wiltshire BA12 9XJ, ENGLAND/01044-1985-218544; FAX: 01044-1985-214111
Sinclair International, Inc., 2330 Wayne Haven St., Fort Wayne, IN 46803/219-493-1858; FAX: 219-493-2530
Single Shot, Inc. (See Montana Armory, Inc.)
Singletary, Kent, 7516 W. Sells, Phoenix, AZ 85033/602-849-5917
Sipes Gun Shop, 7415 Asher Ave., Little Rock, AR 72204/501-565-8480
Siskiyou Gun Works (See Donnelly, C.P.)
Six Enterprises, 320-D Turtle Creek Ct., San Jose, CA 95125/408-999-0201; FAX: 408-999-0216
S.K. Guns, Inc., 3041A Main Ave., Fargo, ND 58103/701-293-4867; FAX: 701-232-0001
Skaggs, R.E., P.O. Box 555, Hamilton, IN 46742/219-488-3755
SKAN A.R., 4 St. Catherines Road, Long Melford, Suffolk, CO10 9JU ENGLAND/011-0787-312942
SKB Arms Co., C.P.O. Box 1401, Tokyo, JAPAN (U.S. importer—G.U., Inc.)
SKB Shotguns, 4325 S. 120th St., P.O. Box 37669, Omaha, NE 68137/800-752-2767; FAX: 402-330-8029
Skeoch, Brian R., P.O. Box 279, Glenrock, WY 82637/307-436-9655; FAX: 307-436-9034
Skip's Machine, 364 29 Road, Grand Junction, CO 81501/303-245-5417
Sklany, Steve, 566 Birch Grove Dr., Kalispell, MT 59901/406-755-4257
SKR Industries, POB 1382, San Angelo, TX 76902/915-658-3133
S.L.A.P. Industries, P.O. Box 1121, Parklands 2121, SOUTH AFRICA/27-11-788-0030; FAX: 27-11-788-0030
Slezak, Jerome F., 1290 Marlowe, Lakewood (Cleveland), OH 44107/216-221-1668
Slings 'N Things, Inc., 8909 Bedford Circle, Suite 11, Omaha, NE 68134/402-571-6954; FAX: 402-571-7082
Slug Group, The, P.O. Box 376, New Paris, PA 15554/814-839-4517; FAX: 814-839-2601
Slug Site Co., Ozark Wilds, Rt. 2, Box 158, Versailles, MO 65084/314-378-6430
Small Arms Mfg. Co., 5312 Thoms Run Rd., Bridgeville, PA 15017/412-221-4343; FAX: 412-221-4303

588 GUN DIGEST

MANUFACTURERS' DIRECTORY

Small Custom Mould & Bullet Co., Box 17211, Tucson, AZ 85731
Smart Parts, 1203 Spring St., Latrobe, PA 15650/412-539-2660; FAX: 412-539-2298
Smires, C.L., 28269 Old Schoolhouse Rd., Columbus, NJ 08022/609-298-3158
Smith & Wesson, 2100 Roosevelt Ave., Springfield, MA 01102/413-781-8300; FAX: 413-731-8980
Smith, Art, 230 Main St. S., Hector, MN 55342/612-848-2760
Smith, Mark A., P.O. Box 182, Sinclair, WY 82334/307-324-7929
Smith, Michael, 620 Nye Circle, Chattanooga, TN 37405/615-267-8341
Smith, Ron, 5869 Straley, Ft. Worth, TX 76114/817-732-6768
Smith, Sharmon, 4545 Speas Rd., Fruitland, ID 83619/208-452-6329
Smith Abrasives, Inc., 1700 Sleepy Valley Rd., P.O. Box 5095, Hot Springs, AR 71902-5095/501-321-2244; FAX: 501-321-9232
Smith Saddlery, Jesse W., 3601 E. Boone Ave., Spokane, WA 99202-4501/509-325-0622
Smokey Valley Rifles (See Lutz Engraving, Ron E.)
Snapp's Gunshop, 6911 E. Washington Rd., Clare, MI 48617/517-386-9226
Snider Stocks, Walter S., Rt. 2 P.O. Box 147, Denton, NC 27239
Sno-Seal (See Atsko/Sno-Seal)
Societa Armi Bresciane Srl. (See U.S. importer—Gamba, USA)
Sonderman, Robert, 735 Kenton Dr., Charleston, IL 61920/217-345-5429
Sonora Rifle Barrel Co., 14396 D. Tuolumne Rd., Sonora, CA 95370/209-532-4139
Soque River Knives, P.O. Box 880, Clarkesville, GA 30523/706-754-8500; FAX: 706-754-7263
SOS Products Co. (See Buck Stix—SOS Products Co.)
Sotheby's, 1334 York Ave. at 72nd St., New York, NY 10021
Sound Technology, P.O. Box 1132, Kodiak, AK 99615/907-486-8448
South Bend Replicas, Inc., 61650 Oak Rd., South Bend, IN 46614/219-289-4500
Southeastern Community College, 1015 S. Gear Ave., West Burlington, IA 52655/319-752-2731
Southern Ammunition Co., Inc., Rt. 1, Box 6B, Latta, SC 29565/803-752-7751; FAX: 803-752-2022
Southern Armory, The, Rt. 2, Box 134, Woodlawn, VA 24381/703-238-1343; FAX: 703-238-1453
Southern Bloomer Mfg. Co., P.O. Box 1621, Bristol, TN 37620/615-878-6660; FAX: 615-878-8761
Southern Security, 1700 Oak Hills Dr., Kingston, TN 37763/615-376-6297; 800-251-9992
Southwind Sanctions, P.O. Box 445, Aledo, TX 76008/817-441-8917
Sparks, Milt, 605 E. 44th St. No. 2, Boise, ID 83714-4800
Spartan-Realtree Products, Inc., 1390 Box Circle, Columbus, GA 31907/706-569-9101; FAX: 706-569-0042
Specialty Gunsmithing, Lynn McMurdo, P.O. Box 404, Afton, WY 83110/307-886-5535
Specialty Shooters Supply, Inc., 3325 Griffin Rd., Suite 9mm, Fort Lauderdale, FL 33317
Speedfeed, Inc., 3820 Industrial Way, Suite N, Belucia, CA 94510/707-746-1221; FAX: 707-746-1888
Speer Products, Div. of Blount, Inc., P.O. Box 856, Lewiston, ID 83501/208-746-2351; FAX: 208-746-2915
Spegel, Craig, P.O. Box 3108, Bay City, OR 97107/503-377-2697
Speiser, Fred D., 2229 Dearborn, Missoula, MT 59801/406-549-8133
Spence, George W., 115 Locust St., Steele, MO 63877/314-695-4926
Spencer Reblue Service, 1820 Tupelo Trail, Holt, MI 48842/517-694-7474
Spencer's Custom Guns, Rt. 1, Box 546, Scottsville, VA 24590/804-293-6836
Spezial Waffen (See U.S. importer—American Bullets)
SPG Lubricants, Box 761-H, Livingston, MT 59047
Sphinx Engineering SA, Ch. des Grandes-Vies 2, CH-2900 Porrentruy, SWITZERLAND/41 66 66 73 81; FAX: 41 66 66 30 90 (U.S. importer—Sphinx USA Inc.)
Sphinx USA Inc., 998 N. Colony, Meriden, CT 06450/203-238-1399; FAX: 203-238-1375
Spokhandguns, Inc., 1206 Fig St., Benton City, WA 99320/509-588-5255
Sport Flite Manufacturing Co., P.O. Box 1082, Bloomfield Hills, MI 48303/810-647-3747
Sport Specialties (See Owen, Harry)
Sporting Arms Mfg., Inc., 801 Hall Ave., Littlefield, TX 79339/806-385-5665; FAX: 806-385-3394
Sports Innovations, Inc., P.O. Box 5181, 8505 Jacksboro Hwy., Wichita Falls, TX 76307/817-723-6015
Sportsman Airguns, Inc., P.O. Box 4919, Cerritos, CA 90703/800-424-7486
Sportsman Safe Mfg. Co., 6309-6311 Paramount Blvd., Long Beach, CA 90805/800-266-7150, 310-984-5445
Sportsman Supply Co., 714 East Eastwood, P.O. Box 650, Marshall, MO 65340/816-886-9393
Sportsman's Communicators, 588 Radcliffe Ave., Pacific Palisades, CA 90272/800-538-3752
Sportsmatch Ltd., 16 Summer St., Leighton Buzzard, Bedfordshire, LU7 8HT ENGLAND/0525-381638; FAX: 0525-851236
Sportsmen's Exchange & Western Gun Traders, Inc., 560 S. "C" St., Oxnard, CA 93030/805-483-1917
Spradlin's, 113 Arthur St., Pueblo, CO 81004/719-543-9462
Springfield, Inc., 420 W. Main St., Geneseo, IL 61254/309-944-5631; FAX: 309-944-3676
Springfield Sporters, Inc., RD 1, Penn Run, PA 15765/412-254-2626; FAX: 412-254-9173
Spyderco, Inc., 4565 N. Hwy. 93, P.O. Box 800, Golden, CO 80403/303-279-8383, 800-525-7770; FAX: 303-278-2229
SSK Co., 220 N. Belvidere Ave., York, PA 17404/717-854-2897
SSK Industries, 721 Woodvue Lane, Wintersville, OH 43952/614-264-0176; FAX: 614-264-2257
Stackpole Books, 5067 Ritter Rd., Mechanicsburg, PA 17055-6921/717-234-5041; FAX: 717-234-1359
Stalker, Inc., P.O. Box 21, Fishermans Wharf Rd., Malakoff, TX 75148/903-489-1010
Stalwart Corporation, P.O. Box 357, Pocatello, ID 83204/208-232-7899; FAX: 208-232-0815
Stanley Bullets, 2085 Heatheridge Ln., Reno, NV 89509
Star Bonifacio Echeverria S.A., Torrekva 3, Eibar, SPAIN 20600/43-107340; FAX: 43-101524 (U.S. importer—Interarms)
Star Custom Bullets, P.O. Box 608, 468 Main St., Ferndale, CA 95536/707-786-9140; FAX: 707-786-9117
Star Machine Works, 418 10th Ave., San Diego, CA 92101/619-232-3216
Star Reloading Co., Inc., 5520 Rock Hampton Ct., Indianapolis, IN 46268/317-872-5840

Stark's Bullet Mfg., 2580 Monroe St., Eugene, OR 97405
Starkey Labs, 6700 Washington Ave. S., Eden Prairie, MN 55344
Starlight Training Center, Inc., Rt. 1, P.O. Box 88, Bronaugh, MO 64728/417-843-3555
Starline, 1300 W. Henry St., Sedalia, MO 65301/816-827-6640; FAX: 816-827-6650
Starnes Gunmaker, Ken, 32900 SW Laurelview Rd., Hillsboro, OR 97123/503-628-0705
Starr Trading Co., Jedediah, P.O. Box 2007, Farmington Hills, MI 48333/810-683-4343; FAX: 810-683-3282
Starrett Co., L.S., 121 Crescent St., Athol, MA 01331/617-249-3551
Starshot Holduxa, Bolognise 125, Miraflores, Lima PERU
State Arms Gun Co., 815 S. Division St., Waunakee, WI 53597/608-849-5800
Steel Reloading Components, Inc., P.O. Box 812, Washington, IN 47501/812-254-3775; FAX: 812-254-7269
Steelman's Gun Shop, 10465 Beers Rd., Swartz Creek, MI 48473/313-735-4884
Steffens, Ron, 18396 Mariposa Creek Rd., Willits, CA 95490/707-485-0873
Stegall, James B., 26 Forest Rd., Wallkill, NY 12589
Steger, James R., 1131 Dorsey Pl., Plainfield, NJ 07062
Steves House of Guns, Rt. 1, Minnesota City, MN 55959/507-689-2573
Stewart Game Calls, Johnny, Inc., P.O. Box 7954, 5100 Fort Ave., Waco, TX 76714/817-773-3261; FAX: 817-772-3670
Stewart's Gunsmithing, P.O. Box 5854, Pietersburg North 0750, Transvaal, SOUTH AFRICA/01521-89401
Steyr Mannlicher AG, Mannlicherstrasse 1, P.O.B. 1000, A-4400 Steyr, AUSTRIA/0043-7252-896-0; FAX: 0043-7252-68621 (U.S. importer—GSI, Inc.)
Stiles Custom Guns, RD3, Box 1605, Homer City, PA 15748/412-479-9945, 412-479-8666
Stillwell, Robert, 421 Judith Ann Dr., Schertz, TX 78154
Stoeger Industries, 5 Mansard Ct., Wayne, NJ 07470/201-872-9500, 800-631-0722; FAX: 201-872-0722
Stoeger Publishing Co. (See Stoeger Industries)
Stone Enterprises Ltd., Rt. 609, P.O. Box 335, Wicomico Church, VA 22579/804-580-5114; FAX: 804-580-8421
Stone Mountain Arms, 5988 Peachtree Corners E., Norcross, GA 30071/800-251-9412
Stoney Baroque Shooters Supply, John Richards, Rt. 2, Box 325, Bedford, KY 40006/502-255-7222
Stoney Point Products, Inc., 124 Stoney Point Rd., P.O. Box 5, Courtland, MN 56021-0005/507-354-3360; FAX: 507-354-7236
Storage Tech, 1254 Morris Ave., N. Huntington, PA 15642/800-437-9393
Storey, Dale A. (See DGS, Inc.)
Storm, Gary, P.O. Box 5211, Richardson, TX 75083/214-385-0862
Stott's Creek Armory, Inc., RR1, Box 70, Morgantown, IN 46160/317-878-5489
Stott's Creek Printers, RR1, Box 70, Morgantown, IN 46160/317-878-5489
Stratco, Inc., 200 E. Center St., Kalispell, MT 59901/406-755-4034; FAX: 406-257-4753
Strawbridge, Victor W., 6 Pineview Dr., Dover, NH 03820/603-742-0013
Streamlight, Inc., 1030 W. Germantown Pike, Norristown, PA 19403/215-631-0600; FAX: 610-631-0712
Strong Holster Co., 105 Maplewood Ave., Gloucester, MA 01930/508-281-3300; FAX: 508-281-6321
Strutz Rifle Barrels, Inc., W.C., P.O. Box 611, Eagle River, WI 54521/715-479-4766
Stuart, V. Pat, Rt.1, Box 447-S, Greenville, VA 24440/804-556-3845
Stuart Products, Inc., P.O. Box 1587, Easley, SC 29641/803-859-9360
Sturm, Ruger & Co., Inc., Lacey Place, Southport, CT 06490/203-259-4537; FAX: 203-259-2167
"Su-Press-On," Inc., P.O. Box 09161, Detroit, MI 48209/313-842-4222 7:30-11p.m. Mon-Thurs.
Sullivan, David S. (See Westwind Rifles, Inc.)
Summit Specialties, Inc., P.O. Box 786, Decatur, AL 35602/205-353-0634; FAX: 205-353-9818
Sun Jammer Products, Inc., 9600 N. IH-35, Austin, TX 78753/512-837-8696
Sun Welding Safe Co., 290 Easy St. No.3, Simi Valley, CA 93065/805-584-6678; FAX: 805-584-6169
Sundance Industries, Inc., 25163 W. Avenue Stanford, Valencia, CA 91355/805-257-4807
Sure Shot of LA, Inc., 103 Coachman Dr., Houma, LA 70360/504-876-6709
Surecase Co., The, 233 Wilshire Blvd., Ste. 900, Santa Monica, CA 90401/800-92ARMLOC
Sure-Shot Game Calls, Inc., P.O. Box 816, 6835 Capitol, Groves, TX 77619/409-962-1636; FAX: 409-962-5465
Survival Arms, Inc., 4500 Pine Cone Place, Cocoa, FL 32922/407-633-4880; FAX: 407-633-4975
Svon Corp., 280 Eliot St., Ashland, MA 01721/508-881-8852
Swampfire Shop, The (See Peterson Gun Shop, Inc., A.W.)
Swann, D.J., 5 Orsova Close, Eltham North, Vic. 3095, AUSTRALIA/03-431-0323
Swanndri New Zealand, 152 Elm Ave., Burlingame, CA 94010/415-347-6158
SwaroSports, Inc. (See JagerSport, Ltd.)
Swarovski Optik North America Ltd., One Wholesale Way, Cranston, RI 02920/401-942-3380, 800-426-3089; FAX: 401-946-2587
Sweet Home, Inc., P.O. Box 900, Orrville, OH 44667-0900
Swenson's 45 Shop, A.D., P.O. Box 606, Fallbrook, CA 92028
Swift Bullet Co., P.O. Box 27, 201 Main St., Quinter, KS 67752/913-754-3959; FAX: 913-754-2359
Swift Instruments, Inc., 952 Dorchester Ave., Boston, MA 02125/617-436-2960; FAX: 617-436-3232
Swift River Gunworks, Inc., 450 State St., Belchertown, MA 01007/413-323-4052
Swiss Army Knives, Inc., 151 Long Hill Crossroads, 37 Canal St., Shelton, CT 06484/800-243-4032
Swivel Machine Works, Inc., 167 Cherry St., Suite 286, Milford, CT 06460/203-926-1840; FAX: 203-874-9212
Szweda, Robert (See RMS Custom Gunsmithing)

T

Tabler Marketing, 2554 Lincoln Blvd., Suite 555, Marina Del Rey, CA 90291/818-755-4565; FAX: 818-831-3441
TacStar Industries, Inc., 211 Jennifer Ln., P.O. Box 70, Cottonwood, AZ 86326/602-639-0072, 800-762-7471; FAX: 602-634-8781
TacTell, Inc., P.O. Box 5654, Maryville, TN 37802/615-982-7855; FAX: 615-558-8294
Tactical Defense Institute, 574 Miami Bluff Ct., Loveland, OH 45140/513-677-8229
Tag Distributors, 1331 Penna. Ave., Emmaus, PA 18049/610-966-3839
Talley, Dave, P.O. Box 821, Glenrock, WY 82637/307-436-8724, 307-436-9315

50th EDITION, 1996 **589**

DIRECTORY OF THE ARMS TRADE

Talmage, William G., RR16, Box 102A, Brazil, IN 47834/812-442-0804
Talon Mfg. Co., Inc., 575 Bevans Industrial Ln., Paw Paw, WV 25434/304-947-7440; FAX: 304-947-7447
Tamarack Products, Inc., P.O. Box 625, Wauconda, IL 60084/708-526-9333; FAX: 708-526-9353
Tanfoglio S.r.l., Fratelli, via Valtrompia 39, 41, 25068 Gardone V.T., Brescia, ITALY/30-8910361; FAX: 30-8910183 (U.S. importer—E.A.A. Corp.)
Tanglefree Industries, 1261 Heavenly Dr., Martinez, CA 94553/800-982-4868; FAX: 510-825-3874
Tank's Rifle Shop, P.O. Box 474, Fremont, NE 68025/402-727-1317; FAX: 402-721-2573
Tanner (See U.S. importer—Mandall Shooting Supplies, Inc.)
Tapco, Inc., 3615 Kennesaw N. Ind. Pkwy., Kennesaw, GA 30144/800-554-1445 (orders); FAX: 404-425-1510
Taracorp Industries, Inc., 1200 Sixteenth St., Granite City, IL 62040/618-451-4400
Tar-Hunt Custom Rifles, Inc., RR3, P.O. Box 572, Bloomsburg, PA 17815-9351/717-784-6368; FAX: 717-784-6368
Tarnham Supply, 431 High St., Boscawen, NH 03303
Tasco Sales, Inc., 7600 NW 26th St., Miami, FL 33156/305-591-3670; FAX: 305-592-5895
Taurus Firearms, Inc., 16175 NW 49th Ave., Miami, FL 33014/305-624-1115; FAX: 305-623-7506
Taurus International Firearms (See U.S. importer—Taurus Firearms, Inc.)
Taurus S.A., Forjas, Avenida Do Forte 511, Porto Alegre, BRAZIL 91360/55-51-340-22-44; FAX: 55-51-340-49-81
Taylor & Robbins, P.O. Box 164, Rixford, PA 16745/814-966-3233
Taylor's & Co., Inc., 304 Lenoir Dr., Winchester, VA 22603/703-722-2017; FAX: 703-722-2018
TCCI, P.O. Box 302, Phoenix, AZ 85001/602-237-3823; FAX: 602-237-3858
TCSR, 3998 Hoffman Rd., White Bear Lake, MN 55110-4626/800-328-5323; FAX: 612-429-0526
TDP Industries, Inc., 603 Airport Blvd., Doylestown, PA 18901/215-345-8687; FAX: 215-345-6057
Techni-Mec, Via Gitti s.n., 25060 Marcheno (BS), ITALY
Tecnolegno S.p.A., Via A. Locatelli, 6, 10, 24019 Zogno, ITALY/0345-91114; FAX: 0345-93254
Tele-Optics, 5514 W. Lawrence Ave., Chicago, IL 60630/312-283-7757; FAX: 312-283-7757
Ten-Ring Precision, Inc., Alex B. Hamilton, 1449 Blue Crest Lane, San Antonio, TX 78232/210-494-3063; FAX: 210-494-3066
10-X Products Group, 2915 Lyndon B. Johnson Freeway, Suite 133, Dallas, TX 75234/214-243-4016, 800-433-2225; FAX: 214-243-4112
Tennessee Valley Mfg., P.O. Box 1175, Corinth, MS 38834/601-286-5014
Tepeco, P.O. Box 342, Friendswood, TX 77546/713-482-2702
Testing Systems, Inc., 220 Pegasus Ave., Northvale, NJ 07647
Teton Arms, Inc., P.O. Box 411, Wilson, WY 83014/307-733-3395
Tetra Gun Lubricants, 1812 Margaret Ave., Annapolis, MD 21401/410-268-6451; FAX: 410-268-8377 201 443-0004
Texas Armory, P.O. Box 154906, Waco, TX 76715/817-867-6972
Texas Longhorn Arms, Inc., 5959 W. Loop South, Suite 424, Bellaire, TX 77401/713-341-0775; FAX: 713-660-0493
Texas Platers Supply Co., 2453 W. Five Mile Parkway, Dallas, TX 75233/214-330-7168
T.F.C. S.p.A., Via G. Marconi 118, B, Villa Carcina, Brescia 25069, ITALY/030-881271; FAX: 030-881826
Theis, Terry, P.O. Box 535, Fredericksburg, TX 78624/210-997-6778
Theoben Engineering, Stephenson Road, St. Ives, Huntingdon, Cambs., PE17 4WJ ENGLAND/011-0480-461718
Thiewes, George W., 14329 W. Parada Dr., Sun City West, AZ 85375
Things Unlimited, 235 N. Kimbau, Casper, WY 82601/307-234-5277
Thirion Hand Engraving, Denise, P.O. Box 408, Graton, CA 95444/707-829-1876
Thomas, Charles C., 2600 S. First St., Springfield, IL 62794/217-789-8980; FAX: 217-789-9130
Thompson, Norm, 18905 NW Thurman St., Portland, OR 97209
Thompson, Randall (See Highline Machine Co.)
Thompson Bullet Lube Co., P.O. Box 472343, Garland, TX 75047-2343/214-271-8063; FAX: 214-840-6743
Thompson Precision, 110 Mary St., P.O. Box 251, Warren, IL 61087/815-745-3625
Thompson Target Technology, 618 Roslyn Ave., SW, Canton, OH 44710/216-453-7707; FAX: 216-478-4723
Thompson Tool Mount (See TTM)
Thompson/Center Arms, P.O. Box 5002, Rochester, NH 03867/603-332-2394; FAX: 603-332-5133
3-D Ammunition & Bullets, 112 W. Plum St., P.O. Box J, Doniphan, NE 68832/402-845-2285, 800-255-6712; FAX: 402-845-6546
300 Gunsmith Service, Inc., at Cherry Creek State Park Shooting Center, 12500 E. Belleview Ave./Englewood, CO 80111/303-690-3300
3-Ten Corp., P.O. Box 269, Feeding Hills, MA 01030/413-789-2086
T.H.U. Enterprises, Inc., P.O. Box 418, Lederach, PA 19450/215-256-1665; FAX: 215-256-9718
Thunder Mountain Arms, P.O. Box 593, Oak Harbor, WA 98277/206-679-4657; FAX: 206-675-1114
Thunderbird Cartridge Co., Inc. (See TCCI)
Thurston Sports, Inc., RD 3 Donovan Rd., Auburn, NY 13021/315-253-0966
Tiger-Hunt, Box 379, Beaverdale, PA 15921/814-472-5161
Tikka (See U.S. importer—Stoeger Industries)
Timber Heirloom Products, 618 Roslyn Ave. SW, Canton, OH 44710/216-453-7707; FAX: 216-478-4723
Time Precision, Inc., 640 Federal Rd., Brookfield, CT 06804/203-775-8343
Timney Mfg., Inc., 3065 W. Fairmont Ave., Phoenix, AZ 85017/602-274-2999; FAX: 602-241-0361
Tinks & Ben Lee Hunting Products (See Wellington Outdoors)
Tink's Safariland Hunting Corp., P.O. Box 244, 1140 Monticello Rd., Madison, GA 30650/706-342-4915; FAX: 706-342-7568
Tioga Engineering Co., Inc., P.O. Box 913, 13 Cone St., Wellsboro, PA 16901/717-724-3533, 717-662-3347
Tippman Pneumatics, Inc., 3518 Adams Center Rd., Fort Wayne, IN 46806/219-749-6022; FAX: 219-749-6619
Tirelli, Snc Di Tirelli Primo E.C., Via Matteotti No. 359, Gardone V.T., Brescia, ITALY 25063/030-8912819; FAX: 030-832240
Titus, Daniel, Shooting Specialties, 872 Penn St., Bryn Mawr, PA 19010/215-525-8829
TM Stockworks, 6355 Maplecrest Rd., Fort Wayne, IN 46835/219-485-5389
TMI Products, 930 S. Plumer Ave., Tucson, AZ 85719/602-792-1075; FAX: 602-792-0093
Tom's Gun Repair, Thomas G. Ivanoff, 76-6 Rt. Southfork Rd., Cody, WY 82414/307-587-6949
Tom's Gunshop, 3601 Central Ave., Hot Springs, AR 71913/501-624-3856
Tomboy, Inc., P.O. Box 846, Dallas, OR 97338/503-623-8405
Tonoloway Tack Drives, HCR 81, Box 100, Needmore, PA 17238
Tooley Custom Rifles, 516 Creek Meadow Dr., Gastonia, NC 28054/704-864-7525
Top-Line USA, Inc., 7920-28 Hamilton Ave., Cincinnati, OH 45231/513-522-2992, 800-346-6699; FAX: 513-522-0916
Torel, Inc., 1708 N. South St., P.O. Box 592, Yoakum, TX 77995/512-293-2341; FAX: 512-293-3413
Totally Dependable Products (See TDP Industries, Inc.)
TOZ (See Nygord Precision Products)
Track of the Wolf, Inc., P.O. Box 6, Osseo, MN 55369-0006/612-424-2500; FAX: 612-424-9860
Tradewinds, Inc., P.O. Box 1191, 2339-41 Tacoma Ave. S., Tacoma, WA 98401/206-272-4887
Traditions, Inc., P.O. Box 235, Deep River, CT 06417/203-526-9555; FAX: 203-526-4564
Trafalgar Square, P.O. Box 257, N. Pomfret, VT 05053/802-457-1911
Traft Gunshop, P.O. Box 1078, Buena Vista, CO 81211
Trail Visions, 5800 N. Ames Terrace, Glendale, WI 53209/414-228-1328
TrailTimer Co., 1992-A Suburban Ave., P.O. Box 19722, St. Paul, MN 55119/612-738-0925
Trammco, 839 Gold Run Rd., Boulder, CO 80302
Trappers Trading, P.O. Box 26946, Austin, TX 78755/800-788-9334
Trax America, Inc., P.O. Box 898, 1150 Eldridge, Forrest City, AR 72335/501-633-0410, 800-232-2327; FAX: 501-633-4788
Treadlok Gun Safe, Inc., 1764 Granby St. NE, Roanoke, VA 24012/800-729-8732, 703-982-6881; FAX: 703-982-1059
Treemaster, P.O. Box 247, Guntersville, AL 35976/205-878-3597
Treso, P.O. Box 4640, Pagosa Springs, CO 81157/303-731-2295
Trevallion Gunstocks, 9 Old Mountain Rd., Cape Neddick, ME 03902/207-361-1130
Trico Plastics, 590 S. Vincent Ave., Azusa, CA 91702
Trijicon, Inc., 49385 Shafer Ave., P.O. Box 6029, Wixom, MI 48393-6029/810-960-7700; FAX: 810-960-7725
Trinidad State Junior College, Gunsmithing Dept., 600 Prospect St., Trinidad, CO 81082/719-846-5631; FAX: 719-846-5667
Triple-K Mfg. Co., Inc., 2222 Commercial St., San Diego, CA 92113/619-232-2066; FAX: 619-232-7675
Trius Products, Inc., P.O. Box 25, 221 S. Miami Ave., Cleves, OH 45002/513-941-5682; FAX: 513-941-7970
Trooper Walsh, 2393 N. Edgewood St., Arlington, VA 22207
Trophy Bonded Bullets, Inc., 900 S. Loop W., Suite 190, Houston, TX 77054/713-645-4499; FAX: 713-741-6393
Trotman, Ken, 135 Ditton Walk, Unit 11, Cambridge CB5 8PY, ENGLAND/01223-211030; FAX: 01223-212317
Tru-Balance Knife Co., 2155 Tremont Blvd. NW, Grand Rapids, MI 49504/616-453-3679
True Flight Bullet Co., 5581 Roosevelt St., Whitehall, PA 18052/800-875-3625; FAX: 610-262-7806
Trulock Tool, Broad St., Whigham, GA 31797/912-762-4678
Tru-Square Metal Prods., Inc., 640 First St. SW, P.O. Box 585, Auburn, WA 98071/206-833-2310; FAX: 206-833-2349
T.S.W. Conversions, Inc., E. 115 Crain Rd., Paramus, NJ 07650-4017/201-265-1618
TTM, 1550 Solomon Rd., Santa Maria, CA 93455/805-934-1281
Tucker, James C., P.O. Box 15485, Sacramento, CA 95851/916-923-0571
Turkish Firearms Corp., 8487 Euclid Ave., Suite 1, Manassas Park, VA 22111/703-369-6848; FAX: 703-257-7709
Turnbull Restoration, Doug, 6426 County Rd. 30, Bloomfield, NY 14469/716-657-6338
Tuttle, Dale , 4046 Russell Rd., Muskegon, MI 49445/616-766-2250
Twin Pine Armory, P.O. Box 58, Hwy. 6, Adna, WA 98522/206-748-4590; FAX: 206-748-7011
Tyler Mfg.-Dist., Melvin, 1326 W. Britton Rd., Oklahoma City, OK 73114/405-842-8044
Tyler Scott, Inc., 313 Rugby Ave., Terrace Park, OH 45174/513-831-7603; FAX: 513-831-7417

U

Uberti, Aldo, Casella Postale 43, I-25063 Gardone V.T., ITALY (U.S. importers—American Arms, Inc.; Cape Outfitters; Cimarron Arms; Dixie Gun Works; EMF Co., Inc.; Forgett Jr., Valmore J.; Navy Arms Co; Taylor's & Co., Inc.)
Uberti USA, Inc., 362 Limerock Rd., P.O. Box 509, Lakeville, CT 06039/203-435-8068; FAX: 203-435-8146
UFA, Inc., 7655 East Evans Rd., Suite 2, Scottsdale, AZ 85260/602-998-3941, 800-616-2776; FAX: 602-922-0148
Ugartechea S.A., Ignacio, Chonta 26, Eibar, SPAIN 20600/43-121257; FAX: 43-121669 (U.S. importer—Mandall Shooting Supplies, Inc.)
Ulrich, Doc & Bud (See D.O.C. Specialists, Inc.)
Ultimate Accuracy, 121 John Shelton Rd., Jacksonville, AR 72076/501-985-2530
Ultra Light Arms, Inc., P.O. Box 1270, 214 Price St., Granville, WV 26505/304-599-5687; FAX: 304-599-5687
Ultralux (See U.S. importer—Keng's Firearms Specialty, Inc.)
UltraSport Arms, Inc., 1955 Norwood Ct., Racine, WI 53403/414-554-3237; FAX: 414-554-9731
Uncle Bud's, HCR 81, Box 100, Needmore, PA 17238/717-294-6000; FAX: 717-294-6005
Uncle Mike's (See Michaels of Oregon Co.)
Unertl Optical Co., Inc., John, 308 Clay Ave., P.O. Box 818, Mars, PA 16046-0818/412-625-3810
Unick's Gunsmithing, 5005 Center Rd., Lowellville, OH 44436/216-536-8015
Unique/M.A.P.F., 10, Les Allees, 64700 Hendaye, FRANCE 64700/33-59 20 71 93 (U.S. importer—Nygord Precision Products)
UniTec, 1250 Bedford SW, Canton, OH 44710/216-452-4017
United Binocular Co., 9043 S. Western Ave., Chicago, IL 60620

590 GUN DIGEST

MANUFACTURERS' DIRECTORY

United Cutlery Corp., 1425 United Blvd., Sevierville, TN 37876/615-428-2532, 800-548-0835; FAX: 615-428-2267
United States Ammunition Co. (See USAC)
United States Optics Technologies, Inc., 5900 Dale St., Buena Park, CA 90621/714-994-4901; FAX: 714-994-4904
United States Products Co., 518 Melwood Ave., Pittsburgh, PA 15213/412-621-2130
Universal Clay Pigeon Traps, Unit 5, Dalacre Industrial Estate, Wilbarston, ENGLAND LE16 8QL/011-44536771625; FAX: 011-44536771625
Upper Missouri Trading Co., 304 Harold St., Crofton, NE 68730/402-388-4844
U.S. General Technologies, Inc., 145 Mitchell Ave., South San Francisco, CA 94080/415-634-8440; FAX: 415-634-8452
U.S. Repeating Arms Co., Inc., 275 Winchester Ave., Morgan, UT 84050-9333/801-876-3440; FAX: 801-876-3737
U.S.A. Magazines, Inc!, P.O. Box 39115, Downey, CA 90241/800-872-2577
USA Sporting Inc., 1330 N. Glassell, Unit M, Orange, CA 92667/714-538-3109, 800-538-3109; FAX: 714-538-1334
USAC, 4500-15th St. East, Tacoma, WA 98424/206-922-7589
Utica Cutlery Co., 820 Noyes St., Utica, NY 13503/315-733-4663; FAX: 315-733-6602
Uvalde Machine & Tool, P.O. Box 1604, Uvalde, TX 78802

V

Valade Engraving, Robert, 931 3rd Ave., Seaside, OR 97138/503-738-7672
Valmet (See Tikka/U.S. importer—Stoeger Industries)
Valor Corp., 5555 NW 36th Ave., Miami, FL 33142/305-633-0127; FAX: 305-634-4536
Van Epps, Milton, Rt. 69-A, Parish, NY 13131/315-625-7251
Van Gorden & Son, Inc., C.S., 1815 Main St., Bloomer, WI 54724/715-568-2612
Van Horn, Gil, P.O. Box 207, Llano, CA 93544
Van Patten, J.W., P.O. Box 145, Foster Hill, Milford, PA 18337/717-296-7069
Vancini, Carl , 65 Glenbrook Rd., Apt. 8C, Stanford, CT 06902
Vann Custom Bullets, 330 Grandview Ave., Novato, CA 94947
Varmintmasters, P.O. Box 839, Arthur, Ont. N0G 1A0 CANADA/519-848-3374
Varner's Service, 102 Shaffer Rd., Antwerp, OH 45813/419-258-8631
Vega Tool Co., c/o T.R. Ross, 4865 Tanglewood Ct., Boulder, CO 80301/303-530-0174
Venco Industries, Inc. (See Shooter's Choice)
Venom Arms Co., Unit 1, Gun Garrel Industrial Centre, Hayseech, Cradley, Heath/West Midlands B64 7JZ ENGLAND/011-021-501-3794 (U.S. importers—Mac-1 Distributors, Trooper Walsh)
Venus Industries, P.O. Box 246, Sialkot-1, PAKISTAN/FAX: 92 432 85579
Verney-Carron, B.P. 72, 54 Boulevard Thiers, 42002 St. Etienne Cedex 1, FRANCE/33-77791500; FAX: 33-77790702
Vest, John, P.O. Box 1552, Susanville, CA 96130/916-257-7228
VibraShine, Inc., Rt. 1, Box 64, Mt. Olive, MS 39119/601-733-5614; FAX: 601-733-2226
Vibra-Tek Co., 1844 Arroya Rd., Colorado Springs, CO 80906/719-634-8611; FAX: 719-634-6886
Vic's Gun Refinishing, 6 Pineview Dr., Dover, NH 03820-6422/603-742-0013
Victory USA, P.O. Box 1021, Pine Bush, NY 12566/914-744-2060; FAX: 914-744-5181
Vihtavuori Oy, FIN-41330 Vihtavuori, FINLAND/358-41-3779211; FAX: 358-41-3771643
Vihtavuori Oy/Kaltron-Pettibone, 1241 Ellis St., Bensenville, IL 60106/708-350-1116; FAX: 708-350-1606
Viking Leathercraft, Inc., 1579A Jayken Way, Chula Vista, CA 91911/800-262-6666; FAX: 619-429-8268
Viking Video Productions, P.O. Box 251, Roseburg, OR 97470
Vincent's Shop, 210 Antoinette, Fairbanks, AK 99701
Vintage Arms, Inc., 6003 Saddle Horse, Fairfax, VA 22030/703-968-0779; FAX: 703-968-0780
Vintage Industries, Inc., 781 Big Tree Dr., Longwood, FL 32750/407-831-8949; FAX: 407-831-5346
VIP Products, 488 East 17th St., Ste. A-101, Costa Mesa, CA 92627/714-722-5986
Viramontez, Ray, 601 Springfield Dr., Albany, GA 31707/912-432-9683
Visible Impact Targets, Rts. 5 & 20, E. Bloomfield, NY 14443/716-657-6161; FAX: 716-657-5405
Vitt/Boos, 2178 Nichols Ave., Stratford, CT 06497/203-375-6859
Voere-KGH m.b.H., P.O. Box 416, A-6333 Kufstein, Tirol, AUSTRIA/0043-5372-62547; FAX: 0043-5372-65752 (U.S. importers—JagerSport, Ltd.)
Volquartsen Custom Ltd., RR 1, Box 33A, P.O. Box 271, Carroll, IA 51401/712-792-4238; FAX: 712-792-2542
Vom Hofe (See Old Western Scrounger, Inc., The)
Von Minden Gunsmithing Services, 2403 SW 39 Terrace, Cape Coral, FL 33914/813-542-8946
Vorhes, David, 3042 Beecham St., Napa, CA 94558/707-226-9116
Vortek Products, P.O. Box 871181, Canton, MI 48187
VSP Publishers, P.O. Box 887, McCall, ID 83638/208-634-4104
Vulpes Ventures, Inc., Fox Cartridge Division, P.O. Box 1363, Bolingbrook, IL 60440-7363/708-759-1229

W

Wagoner, Vernon G., 2325 E. Encanto, Mesa, AZ 85213/602-835-1307
Wakina by Pic, 24813 Alderbrook Dr., Santa Clarita, CA 91321/805-295-8194
Waldron, Herman, Box 475, 80 N. 17th St., Pomeroy, WA 99347/509-843-1404
Walker Arms Co., Inc., 499 County Rd. 820, Selma, AL 36701/334-872-6231
Walker Mfg., Inc., 8296 S. Channel, Harsen's Island, MI 48028
Walker Co., B.B., P.O. Box 1167, 414 E. Dixie Dr., Asheboro, NC 27203/910-625-1380; FAX: 910-625-8125
Wallace, Terry, 385 San Marino, Vallejo, CA 94589/707-642-7041
Waller & Son, Inc., W., 142 New Canaan Ave., Norwalk, CT 06850/203-838-4083
Walls Industries, Inc., P.O. Box 98, 1905 N. Main, Cleburne, TX 76031/817-645-4366; FAX: 817-645-7946
Walnut Factory, The, 235 West Rd. No. 1, Portsmouth, NH 03801/603-436-2225; FAX: 603-433-7003
Walt's Custom Leather, Walt Whinnery, 1947 Meadow Creek Dr., Louisville, KY 40218/502-458-4361
Walters, John, 500 N. Avery Dr., Moore, OK 73160/405-799-0376
Walters Industries, 6226 Park Lane, Dallas, TX 75225/214-691-6973

Walther GmbH, Carl, B.P. 4325, D-89081 Ulm, GERMANY (U.S. importer—Interarms)
WAMCO, Inc., Mingo Loop, P.O. Box 337, Oquossoc, ME 04964-0337/207-864-3344
WAMCO—New Mexico, P.O. Box 205, Peralta, NM 87042-0205/505-869-0826
Ward & Van Valkenburg, 114 32nd Ave. N., Fargo, ND 58102/701-232-2351
Ward Machine, 5620 Lexington Rd., Corpus Christi, TX 78412/512-992-1221
Wardell Precision Handguns Ltd., 48851 N. Fig Springs Rd., New River, AZ 85027-8513/602-465-7995
Warenski, Julie, 590 E. 500 N., Richfield, UT 84701/801-896-5319; FAX: 801-896-5319
Warne Manufacturing Co., 9039 SE Jannsen Rd., Clackamas, OR 97015/503-657-5590, 800-683-5590; FAX: 503-657-5695
Warren & Sweat Mfg. Co., P.O. Box 350440, Grand Island, FL 32784/904-669-3166; FAX: 904-669-7272
Warren, Kenneth W. (See Mountain States Engraving)
Warren Muzzleloading Co., Inc., Hwy. 21 North, P.O. Box 100, Ozone, AR 72854/501-292-3268
Washita Mountain Whetstone Co., P.O. Box 378, Lake Hamilton, AR 71951/501-525-3914
WASP Shooting Systems, Rt. 1, Box 147, Lakeview, AR 72642/501-431-5606
Waterfield Sports, Inc., 13611 Country Lane, Burnsville, MN 55337/612-435-8339
Watson Trophy Match Bullets, 2404 Wade Hampton Blvd., Greenville, SC 29615/803-244-7948
Watsontown Machine & Tool Co., 309 Dickson Ave., Watsontown, PA 17777/717-538-3533
Wayland Precision Wood Products, P.O. Box 1142, Mill Valley, CA 94942/415-381-3543; FAX: 415-389-1611
Wayne Firearms for Collectors and Investors, James, 2608 N. Laurent, Victoria, TX 77901/512-578-1258; FAX: 512-578-3559
Wayne Specialty Services, 260 Waterford Drive, Florissant, MO 63033/413-831-7083
WD-40 Co., 1061 Cudahy Pl., San Diego, CA 92110/619-275-1400; FAX: 619-275-5823
Weatherby, Inc., 3100 El Camino Real, Atascadero, CA 93422/805-466-1767, 800-227-2016, 800-334-4423 (Calif.); FAX: 805-466-2527
Weaver Arms Corp., P.O. Box 8, Dexter, MO 63841/314-568-3101
Weaver Products, Div. of Blount, Inc., P.O. Box 39, Onalaska, WI 54650/800-635-7656, 608-781-5800; FAX: 608-781-0368
Weaver Scope Repair Service, 1121 Larry Mahan Dr., Suite B, El Paso, TX 79925/915-593-1005
Weaver's Gun Shop, P.O. Box 8, Dexter, MO 63841/314-568-3101
Webb, Bill, 6504 North Bellefontaine, Kansas City, MO 64119/816-453-7431
Weber & Markin Custom Gunsmiths, 4-1691 Powick Rd., Kelowna, B.C. CANADA V1X 4L1/604-762-7575; FAX: 604-861-3655
Weber Jr., Rudolf, P.O. Box 160106, D-5650 Solingen, GERMANY/0212-592136
Webley and Scott Ltd., Frankley Industrial Park, Tay Rd., Rubery, Rednal, Birmingham B45 0PA, ENGLAND/011-021-453-1864; FAX: 021-457-7846 (U.S. importer—Beeman Precision Airguns)
Webster Scale Mfg. Co., P.O. Box 188, Sebring, FL 33870/813-385-6362
Weems, Cecil, P.O. Box 657, Mineral Wells, TX 76067/817-325-1462
Weigand Combat Handguns, Inc., P.O. Box 239, Crestwood Industrial Park, Mountain Top, PA 18707/717-474-9804; FAX: 717-474-9987
Weihrauch KG, Hermann, Industriestrasse 11, 8744 Mellrichstadt, GERMANY/09776-497-498 (U.S. importers—Beeman Precision Airguns; E.A.A. Corp.)
Weisz Parts, P.O. Box 20038, Columbus, OH 43220-0038/614-45-70-500; FAX: 614-846-8585
Welch, Sam, CVSR 2110, Moab, UT 84532/801-259-8131
Wellington Outdoors, P.O. Box 244, 1140 Monticello Rd., Madison, GA 30650/706-342-4915; FAX: 706-342-7568
Wells, Fred F., Wells Sport Store, 110 N. Summit St., Prescott, AZ 86301/602-445-3655
Wells, Rachel, 110 N. Summit St., Prescott, AZ 86301/602-445-3655
Wells Creek Knife & Gun Works, 32956 State Hwy. 38, Scottsburg, OR 97473/503-587-4202
Wells Custom Gunsmith, R.A., 3452 1st Ave., Racine, WI 53402/414-639-5223
Welsh, Bud, 80 New Road, E. Amherst, NY 14051/716-688-6344
Wenig Custom Gunstocks, Inc., 103 N. Market St., P.O. Box 249, Lincoln, MO 65338/816-547-3334; FAX: 816-547-2881
Wenoka/Seastyle, P.O. Box 10969, Riviera Beach, FL 33419/407-845-6155; FAX: 407-842-4247
Wentling Co., S.A., 546 W. Chocolate Ave., P.O. Box 355P, Hershey, PA 17033/717-533-2468; FAX: 717-534-1252
Werner, Carl, P.O. Box 492, Littleton, CO 80160
Werth, T.W., 1203 Woodlawn Rd., Lincoln, IL 62656/217-732-1300
Wescombe, P.O. Box 488, Glencoe, CA 95232/209-293-7010
Wessinger Custom Guns & Engraving, 268 Limestone Rd., Chapin, SC 29036/803-345-5677
Wesson Firearms Co., Inc., Maple Tree Industrial Center, Rt. 20, Wilbraham, Rd., Palmer, MA 01069/413-267-4081; FAX: 413-267-3601
West, Jack L., 1220 W. Fifth, P.O. Box 427, Arlington, OR 97812
West, Robert G., 3973 Pam St., Eugene, OR 97402/503-344-3700
Western Cutlery (See Camillus Cutlery Co.)
Western Design, 1629 Via Monserate, Fallbrook, CA 92028/619-723-9279
Western Gunstock Mfg. Co., 550 Valencia School Rd., Aptos, CA 95003/408-688-5884
Western Missouri Shooters Alliance, P.O. Box 11144, Kansas City, MO 64119/816-597-3950; FAX: 816-229-7350
Western Nevada West Coast Bullets, 2307 W. Washington St., Carson City, NV 89703/702-246-3941; FAX: 702-246-0836
Westfield Engineering, 6823 Watcher St., Commerce, CA 90040/FAX: 213-928-8270
Westley Richards & Co., 40 Grange Rd., Birmingham, ENGLAND B29 6AR/010-214722953 (U.S. importer—Cape Outfitters)
Westrom, John (See Precision Metal Finishing)
Westwind Rifles, Inc., David S. Sullivan, P.O. Box 261, 640 Briggs St., Erie, CO 80516/303-828-3823
Weyer International, 2740 Nebraska Ave., Toledo, OH 43607/419-534-2020; FAX: 419-534-2697
Whildin & Sons Ltd., E.H., RR2, Box 119, Tamaqua, PA 18252/717-668-6743; FAX: 717-668-6745
Whinnery, Walt (See Walt's Custom Leather)
Whiscombe (See U.S. importer—Pelaire Products)

50th EDITION, 1996 **591**

DIRECTORY OF THE ARMS TRADE

White Flyer Targets, 9139 W. Redfield Rd., Peoria, AZ 85381/800-647-2898, 417-673-5551, 602-972-7258 (export); FAX: 602-530-3360
White Flyer Targets, 124 River Rd., Middlesex, NJ 08846/908-469-0100; FAX: 908-469-9692
White Laboratory, H.P., Inc., 3114 Scarboro Rd., Street, MD 21154/410-838-6550; FAX: 410-838-2802
White Owl Enterprises, 2583 Flag Rd., Abilene, KS 67410/913-263-2613; FAX: 913-263-2613
White Pine Photographic Services, Hwy. 60, General Delivery, Wilno, Ontario K0J 2N0 CANADA/613-756-3452
White Rock Tool & Die, 6400 N. Brighton Ave., Kansas City, MO 64119/816-454-0478
White Shooting Systems, Inc., 25 E. Hwy. 40, Box 330-12, Roosevelt, UT 84066/801-722-3085; FAX: 801-722-3054
Whitehead, James D., 204 Cappucino Way, Sacramento, CA 95838
Whitestone Lumber Corp., 148-02 14th Ave., Whitestone, NY 11357/718-746-4400; FAX: 718-767-1748
Whitetail Design & Engineering Ltd., 9421 E. Mannsiding Rd., Clare, MI 48617/517-386-3932
Whits Shooting Stuff, Box 1340, Cody, WY 82414
Wichita Arms, Inc., 923 E. Gilbert, P.O. Box 11371, Wichita, KS 67211/316-265-0661; FAX: 316-265-0760
Wick, David E., 1504 Michigan Ave., Columbus, IN 47201/812-376-6960
Widener's Reloading & Shooting Supply, Inc., P.O. Box 3009 CRS, Johnson City, TN 37602/615-282-6786; FAX: 615-282-6651
Wideview Scope Mount Corp., 13535 S. Hwy. 16, Rapid City, SD 57701/605-341-3220; FAX: 605-341-9142
Wiebe, Duane, 3715 S. Browns Lake Dr. 103, Burlington, WI 53105-7931
Wiest, M.C., 10737 Dutchtown Rd., Knoxville, TN 37932/615-966-4545
Wilcox All-Pro Tools & Supply, RR 1, Montezuma, IA 50171/515-623-3138
Wild Bill's Originals, P.O. Box 13037, Burton, WA 98013/206-463-5738
Wilderness Sound Products Ltd., 4015 Main St. A, Springfield, OR 97478/503-741-0263, 800-437-0006; FAX: 503-741-7648
Wildey, Inc., P.O. Box 475, Brookfield, CT 06804/203-355-9000; FAX: 203-354-7759
Wildlife Research Center, Inc., 4345 157th Ave. NW, Anoka, MN 55304/612-427-3350, 800-USE-LURE; FAX: 612-427-8354
Wilkinson Arms, 26884 Pearl Rd., Parma, ID 83660/208-722-6771; FAX: 208-722-5197
Will-Burt Co., 169 S. Main, Orrville, OH 44667
William's Gun Shop, Ben, 1151 S. Cedar Ridge, Duncanville, TX 75137/214-780-1807
Williams Bullet Co., J.R., 2008 Tucker Rd., Perry, GA 31069/912-987-0274
Williams Gun Sight Co., 7389 Lapeer Rd., Box 329, Davison, MI 48423/810-653-2131, 800-530-9028; FAX: 810-658-2140
Williams Mfg. of Oregon, P.O. Box 98, 561 Upper Smith River Rd., Drain, OR 97435/503-836-7461; FAX: 503-836-7245
Williams Shootin' Iron Service, The Lynx-Line, 8857 Bennett Hill Rd., Central Lake, MI 49622/616-544-6615
Williamson Precision Gunsmithing, 117 W. Pipeline, Hurst, TX 76053/817-285-0064; FAX: 817-285-0064
Willig Custom Engraving, Claus, D-97422 Schweinfurt, Siedlerweg 17, GERMANY/01149-9721-41446; FAX: 01149-9721-44413
Willow Bend, P.O. Box 203, Chelmsford, MA 01824/508-256-8508; FAX: 508-256-9765
Willson Safety Prods. Div., P.O. Box 622, Reading, PA 19603-0622/610-376-6161; FAX: 610-371-7725
Wilson, Inc., L.E., Box 324, 404 Pioneer Ave., Cashmere, WA 98815/509-782-1328
Wilson Arms Co., The, 63 Leetes Island Rd., Branford, CT 06405/203-488-7297; FAX: 203-488-0135
Wilson Case, Inc., P.O. Box 1106, Hastings, NE 68902-1106/800-322-5493; FAX: 402-463-5276
Wilson's Gun Shop, Box 578, Rt. 3, Berryville, AR 72616/501-545-3618; FAX: 501-545-3310
Winchester (See U.S. Repeating Arms Co., Inc.)
Winchester Div., Olin Corp., 427 N. Shamrock, E. Alton, IL 62024/618-258-3566; FAX: 618-258-3599
Winchester Press (See New Win Publishing, Inc.)
Winchester Sutler, Inc., The, 270 Shadow Brook Lane, Winchester, VA 22603/703-888-3595
Windish, Jim, 2510 Dawn Dr., Alexandria, VA 22306/703-765-1994
Windjammer Tournament Wads, Inc., 750 W. Hampden Ave. Suite 170, Englewood, CO 80110/303-781-6329
Wingshooting Adventures, 4320 Kalamazoo Ave. SE, Grand Rapids, MI 49507/616-455-7810; FAX: 616-455-5212
Winkle Bullets, R.R. 1 Box 316, Heyworth, IL 61745
Winter, Robert M., P.O. Box 484, Menno, SD 57045/605-387-5322
Wise Guns, Dale, 333 W. Olmos Dr., San Antonio, TX 78212/210-828-3388
Wiseman and Co., Bill, P.O. Box 3427, Bryan, TX 77805/409-690-3456; FAX: 409-690-0156
Wisner's Gun Shop, Inc., 287 NW Chehalis Ave., Chehalis, WA 98532/206-748-8942; FAX: 206-748-7011
Wolf's Western Traders, 40 E. Works, No. 3F, Sheridan, WY 82801/307-674-5352
Wolfe Publishing Co., 6471 Airpark Dr., Prescott, AZ 86301/602-445-7810, 800-899-7810; FAX: 602-778-5124
W.C. Wolff Co., P.O. Box I, Newtown Square, PA 19073/610-359-9600, 800-545-0077
Wolverine Footwear Group, 9341 Courtland Dr. NE, Rockford, MI 49351/616-866-5500; FAX: 616-866-5658
Wood, Frank (See Classic Guns, Inc.)
Wood, Mel, P.O. Box 1255, Sierra Vista, AZ 85636/602-455-5541
Woodleigh (See Huntington Die Specialties)
Woods Wise Products, P.O. Box 681552, 2200 Bowman Rd., Franklin, TN 37068/800-735-8182; FAX: 615-726-2637
Woodstream, P.O. Box 327, Lititz, PA 17543/717-626-2125; FAX: 717-626-1912
Woodworker's Supply, 1108 North Glenn Rd., Casper, WY 82601/307-237-5354
Woolrich Inc., Mill St., Woolrich, PA 17701/800-995-1299; FAX: 717-769-6234/6259
World Class Airguns, 2736 Morningstar Dr., Indianapolis, IN 46229/317-897-5548
World of Targets (See Birchwood Casey)
World Trek, Inc., P.O. Box 11670, Pueblo, CO 81001-0670/719-546-2121; FAX: 719-543-6886
Worthy Products, Inc., RR 1, P.O. Box 213, Martville, NY 13111/315-324-5298
Wosenitz VHP, Inc., Box 741, Dania, FL 33004/305-923-3748; FAX: 305-925-2217
Wostenholm (See Ibberson [Sheffield] Ltd., George)
Wright's Hardwood Gunstock Blanks, 8540 SE Kane Rd., Gresham, OR 97080/503-666-1705
Wyant Bullets, Gen. Del., Swan Lake, MT 59911
Wyant's Outdoor Products, Inc., P.O. Box B, Broadway, VA 22815
Wyoming Armory, Inc., Box 28, Farson, WY 82932/307-273-5556
Wyoming Bonded Bullets, Box 91, Sheridan, WY 82801/307-674-8091
Wyoming Custom Bullets, 1626 21st St., Cody, WY 82414
Wyoming Knife Corp., 101 Commerce Dr., Ft. Collins, CO 80524/303-224-3454

X, Y

X-Spand Target Systems, 26-10th St. SE, Medicine Hat, AB T1A 1P7 CANADA/403-526-7997; FAX: 403-528-2362
Yankee Gunsmith, 2901 Deer Flat Dr., Copperas Cove, TX 76522/817-547-8433
Yavapai College, 1100 E. Sheldon St., Prescott, AZ 86301/602-776-2359; FAX: 602-776-2193
Yavapai Firearms Academy Ltd., P.O. Box 27290, Prescott Valley, AZ 86312/520-772-8262
Yearout, Lewis E. (See Montana Outfitters)
Yee, Mike, 29927 56 Pl. S., Auburn, WA 98001/206-839-3991
Yellowstone Wilderness Supply, P.O. Box 129, W. Yellowstone, MT 59758/406-646-7613
Yesteryear Armory & Supply, P.O. Box 408, Carthage, TN 37030
York M-1 Conversions, 803 Mill Creek Run, Plantersville, TX 77363/800-527-2881, 713-477-8442
Young, Paul A., RR 1 Box 694, Blowing Rock, NC 28605-9746
Young Country Arms, P.O. Box 3615, Simi Valley, CA 93093
Yukon Arms Classic Ammunition, 1916 Brooks, Suite 223, Missoula, MT 59801

Z

Zabala Hermanos S.A., P.O. Box 97, Eibar, SPAIN 20600/43-768085, 43-768076; FAX: 43-768201 (U.S. importer—American Arms, Inc.)
Zanoletti, Pietro, Via Monte Gugielpo, 4, I-25063 Gardone V.T., ITALY (U.S. importer—Mandall Shooting Supplies, Inc.)
Zanotti Armor, 123 W. Lone Tree Rd., Cedar Falls, IA 50613/319-232-9650
Z-Coat Industrial Coatings, Inc., 3375 U.S. Hwy. 98 S. No. A, Lakeland, FL 33803-8365/813-665-1734
Zeeryp, Russ, 1601 Foard Dr., Lynn Ross Manor, Morristown, TN 37814/615-586-2357
Zeiss Optical, Carl, 1015 Commerce St., Petersburg, VA 23803/804-861-0033; FAX: 804-733-4024
Zero Ammunition Co., Inc., 1601 22nd St. SE, P.O. Box 1188, Cullman, AL 35056-1188/800-545-9376; FAX: 205-739-4683
Ziegel Engineering, 2108 Lomina Ave., Long Beach, CA 90815/310-596-9481; FAX: 310-598-4734
Zim's Inc., 4370 S. 3rd West, Salt Lake City, UT 84107/801-268-2505
Zoli, Antonio, Via Zanardelli 39, Casier Postal 21, I-25063 Gardone V.T., ITALY
Zriny's Metal Targets, P.O. Box 78, South Newbury, NH 03272/603-428-3127
Zufall, Joseph F., P.O. Box 304, Golden, CO 80402-0304